NISSAN SENTRA AND PULSAR 1982-92 REPAIR MANUAL

CHILTON'S

Senior Vice President Ronald A. Hoxter

Publisher Kerry A. Freeman, S.A.E.
Editor-In-Chief Dean F. Morgantini, S.A.E.
Director of Manufacturing Mike D'Imperio
Production Manager W. Calvin Settle, Jr., S.A.E.
Senior Editor Richard J. Rivele, S.A.E.
Project Manager Martin J. Gunther
Editor James B. Steele

CHILTON BOOK COMPANY

*ONE OF THE **DIVERSIFIED PUBLISHING COMPANIES,***
*A PART OF **CAPITAL CITIES/ABC, INC.***

Manufactured in USA

Chilton Way, Radnor, PA 19089
ISBN 0-8019-8263-4
Library of Congress Catalog Card No. 91-058872
1234567890 1098765432

Contents

Contents

SAFETY NOTICE

Proper service and repair procedures are vital to the safe, reliable operation of all motor vehicles, as well as the personal safety of those performing repairs. This manual outlines procedures for servicing and repairing vehicles using safe, effective methods. The procedures contain many NOTES, CAUTIONS and WARNINGS which should be followed along with standard safety procedures to eliminate the possibility of personal injury or improper service which could damage the vehicle or compromise its safety.

It is important to note that the repair procedures and techniques, tools and parts for servicing motor vehicles, as well as the skill and experience of the individual performing the work vary widely. It is not possible to anticipate all of the conceivable ways or conditions under which vehicles may be serviced, or to provide cautions as to all of the possible hazards that may result. Standard and accepted safety precautions and equipment should be used when handling toxic or flammable fluids, and safety goggles or other protection should be used during cutting, grinding, chiseling, prying, or any other process that can caus material removal or projectiles.

Some procedures require the use of tools specially designed for a specific purpose. Before substituting another tool or procedure, you must be completely satisfied that neither your personal safety, nor the performance of the vehicle will be endangered.

Although information in this manual is based on industry sources and is complete as possible at the time of publication, the possibility exists that some car manufacturers made later changes which could not be included here. While striving for total accuracy, Chilton Book Company cannot assume responsibility for any errors, changes or omissions that may occur in the compilation of this data.

PART NUMBERS

Part numbers listed in this reference are not recommendations by Chilton for any product by brand name. They are references that can be used with interchange manuals and aftermarket supplier catalogs to locate each brand supplier's discrete part number.

SPECIAL TOOLS

Special tools are recommended by the vehicle manufacturer to perform their specific job. Use has been kept to a minimum, but where absolutely necessary, they are referred to in the text by the part number of the tool manufacturer. These tools can be purchased, under the appropriate part number, from your Nissan dealer or regional distributor, or an equivalent tool can be purchased locally from a tool supplier or parts outlet. Before substituting any tool for the one recommended, read the SAFETY NOTICE at the top of this page.

ACKNOWLEDGMENTS

The Chilton Book Company expresses appreciation to Nissan Motor Company for their generous assistance.

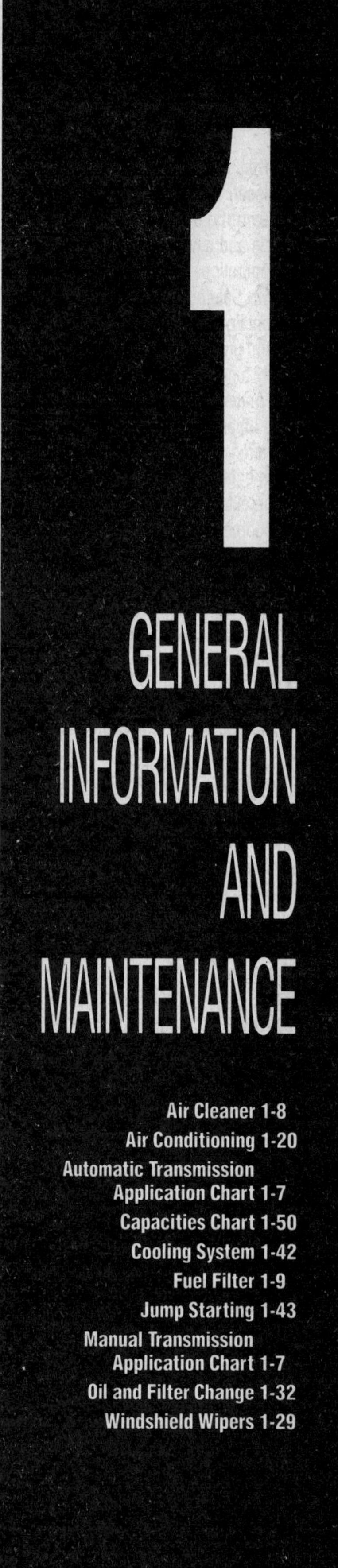
1
GENERAL
INFORMATION
AND
MAINTENANCE
Air Cleaner 1-8
Air Conditioning 1-20
Automatic Transmission
Application Chart 1-7
Capacities Chart 1-50
Cooling System 1-42
Fuel Filter 1-9
Jump Starting 1-43
Manual Transmission
Application Chart 1-7
Oil and Filter Change 1-32
Windshield Wipers 1-29

HOW TO USE THIS BOOK

Chilton's Total Car Care Manual for the 1982–92 Datsun/Nissan Sentra and Pulsar is intended to help you learn more about the inner workings of your vehicle and save you money on its upkeep and operation.

The first two Sections will be the most used, since they contain maintenance and tune-up information and procedures. Studies have shown that a properly tuned and maintained car can get at least 10% better gas mileage than an out-of-tune car. The other Sections deal with the more complex systems of your car. Operating systems from engine through brakes are covered to the extent that the average do-it-yourselfer becomes mechanically involved. This book will not explain such things as rebuilding the differential for the simple reason that the expertise required and the investment in special tools make this task uneconomical. It will give you detailed instructions to help you change your own brake pads and shoes, replace spark plugs, and do many more jobs that will save you money, give you personal satisfaction, and help you avoid expensive problems.

A secondary purpose of this book is a reference for owners who want to understand their car and/or their mechanics better. In this case, no tools at all are required.

Before removing any bolts, read through the entire procedure. This will give you the overall view of what tools and supplies will be required. There is nothing more frustrating than having to walk to the bus stop on Monday morning because you were short one bolt on Sunday afternoon. So read ahead and plan ahead. Each operation should be approached logically and all procedures thoroughly understood before attempting any work.

All Sections contain adjustments, maintenance, removal and installation procedures, and repair or overhaul procedures. When repair is not considered practical, we tell you how to remove the part and then how to install the new or rebuilt replacement. In this way, you at least save the labor costs. Backyard repair of such components as the alternator is just not practical.

Two basic mechanic's rules should be mentioned here. One, whenever the left side of the car or engine is referred to, it is meant to specify the driver's side of the car. Conversely, the right side of the car means the passenger's side. Secondly, most screws and bolt are removed by turning counterclockwise, and tightened by turning clockwise.

Safety is always the most important rule. Constantly be aware of the dangers involved in working on an automobile and take the proper precautions. (See the section in this Section Servicing Your Vehicle Safely and the SAFETY NOTICE on the acknowledgment page.)

Pay attention to the instructions provided. There are 3 common mistakes in mechanical work:

1. Incorrect order of assembly, disassembly or adjustment. When taking something apart or putting it together, doing things in the wrong order usually just costs you extra time; however, it CAN break something. Read the entire procedure before beginning disassembly. Do everything in the order in which the instructions say you should do it, even if you can't immediately see a reason for it. When you're taking apart something that is very intricate (for example, a carburetor), you might want to draw a picture of how it looks when assembled at one point in order to make sure you get everything back in its proper position. (We will supply exploded views whenever possible). When making adjustments, especially tune-up adjustments, do them in order; often, one adjustment affects another, and you cannot expect even satisfactory results unless each adjustment is made only when it cannot be changed by any order.

2. Overtorquing (or undertorquing). While it is more common for over-torquing to cause damage, undertorquing can cause a fastener to vibrate loose causing serious damage. Especially when dealing with aluminum parts, pay attention to torque specifications and utilize a torque wrench in assembly. If a torque figure is not available, remember that if you are using the right tool to do the job, you will probably not have to strain yourself to get a fastener tight enough. The pitch of most threads is so slight that the tension you put on the wrench will be multiplied many, many times in actual force on what you are tightening. A good example of how critical torque is can be seen in the case of spark plug installation, especially where you are putting the plug into an aluminum cylinder head. Too little torque can fail to crush the gasket, causing leakage of combustion gases and consequent overheating of the plug and engine parts. Too much torque can damage the threads, or distort the plug which changes the spark gap.

There are many commercial products available for ensuring that fasteners won't come loose, even if they are not torqued just right (a very common brand is Loctite®). If you're worried about getting something together tight enough to hold, but loose enough to avoid mechanical damage during assembly, one of these products might offer substantial insurance. Read the label on the package and make sure the products is compatible with the materials, fluids, etc. involved before choosing one.

3. Crossthreading. This occurs when a part such as a bolt is screwed into a nut or casting at the wrong angle and forced. Cross threading is more likely to occur if access is difficult. It helps to clean and lubricate fasteners, and to start threading with the part to be installed going straight in. Then, start the bolt, spark plug, etc. with your fingers. If you encounter resistance, unscrew the part and start over again at a different angle until it can be inserted and turned several turns without much effort. Keep in mind that many parts, especially spark plugs, used tapered threads so that gentle turning will automatically bring the part you're treading to the proper angle if you don't force it or resist a change in angle. Don't put a wrench on the part until its's been turned a couple of turns by hand. If you suddenly encounter resistance, and the part has not seated fully, don't force it. Pull it back out and make sure it's clean and threading properly.

Always take your time and be patient; once you have some experience, working on your car will become an enjoyable hobby.

TOOLS AND EQUIPMENT

The service procedures in this book presuppose a familiarity with hand tools and their proper use. However, it is possible that you may have a limited amount of experience with the sort of equipment needed to work on an automobile. This section is designed to help you assemble a basic set of tools that will handle most of the jobs you may undertake.

In addition to the normal assortment of

screwdrivers and pliers, automotive service work requires an investment in wrenches, sockets and the handles needed to drive them, plus various measuring tools such as torque wrenches and feeler gauges.

You will find that virtually every nut and bolt on your vehicle is metric. Therefore, despite a few close size similarities, standard inch-size tools will not fit and must not be used. You will need a set of metric wrenches as your most basic tool kit, ranging from about 6–22mm in size. High quality forged wrenches are available in three styles: open end, box end and combination open/box end. The combination tools are generally the most desirable as a starter set; the wrenches shown in the accompanying illustration are of the combination type.

The other set of tools inevitably required is a ratchet handle and socket set. This set should have the same size range as your wrench set. The ratchet, extensions and flex drives for the sockets are available in many sizes; it is advisable to choose a 3/8 in. drive set initially. One break in the inch/metric sizing war is that metric sized sockets sold in the U.S. have inch-sized drive (1/4 in., 3/8 in., 1/2 in. and etc.). Thus, if you already have an inch-sized socket set, you need only buy new metric sockets in the sizes needed. Sockets are available in 6- and 12-point versions; six point types are stronger and are a good choice for a first set. The choice of a drive handle for the sockets should be made with some care. If this is your first set, take the plunge and invest in a flex-head ratchet; it will get into many places otherwise accessible only through a long chain of universal joints, extensions and adapters. An alternative is a flex handle, which lacks the ratcheting feature but has a head which pivots 180°; such a tool is shown below the ratchet handle in the illustration. In addition to the range of sockets mentioned, a rubber lined spark plug socket should be purchased. The correct size for the plugs in your vehicle's engine is 13/16 in.

The most important thing to consider when purchasing hand tools is quality. Don't be misled by the low cost of bargain tools. Forged wrenches, tempered screwdriver blades and fine tooth ratchets are much better investments than their less expensive counterparts. The skinned knuckles and frustration inflicted by poor quality tools make any job an unhappy chore. Another consideration is that quality tools come with an unbeatable replacement guarantee; if the tool breaks, you get a new one, no questions asked.

Most jobs can be accomplished using the tools on the accompanying lists. There will be an occasional need for a special tool, such as snap ring pliers; that need will be mentioned in the text. It would not be wise to buy a large assortment of tools on the premise that someday they will be needed. Instead, the tools should be acquired one at a time, each for a specific job, both to avoid unnecessary expense and to be certain that you have the right tool.

The tools needed for basic maintenance jobs, in addition to the wrenches and sockets mentioned, include:

1. Jackstands, for support.
2. Oil filter wrench.
3. Oil filter spout or funnel.
4. Grease gun.
5. Battery post and clamp cleaner.
6. Container for draining oil.
7. Many rags for the inevitable spills.

In addition to these items there are several others which are not absolutely necessary but handy to have around. These include a transmission funnel and filler tube, a drop (trouble) light on a long cord, an adjustable (crescent) wrench and slip joint pliers.

A more advanced list of tools, suitable for tune-up work, can be drawn up easily. While the tools are slightly more sophisticated, they need not be outrageously expensive. The key to these purchases is to make them with an eye towards adaptability and wide range. A basic list of tune-up tools could include:

1. Tachometer/dwell meter.
2. Spark plug gauge and gapping tool.
3. Feeler gauges for valve adjustment.
4. Timing light.

Note that if your vehicle has electronic ignition, you will have no need for a dwell meter and of course a tachometer is provided on the instrument panel of the vehicle. You will need both the wire type (spark plugs) and the flat type (valves) feeler gauges. The choice of a timing light should be made carefully. A light which works on the DC current supplied by the vehicle battery is the best choice; it should have a xenon tube for brightness. Since most of the vehicles have electronic ignition or will have it in the future, the light should have an inductive pickup which clamps around the No. 1 spark plug cable (the timing light illustrated has one of these pickups).

In addition to these basic tools, there are several other tools and gauges which you may find useful. These include:

1. A compression gauge. The screw-in type is slower to use but eliminates the possibility of faulty reading due to escaping pressure.
2. A manifold vacuum gauge.
3. A test light.
4. A combination volt/ohmmeter.
5. An induction meter, used to determine whether or not there is current flowing in a wire, an extremely helpful tool for electrical troubleshooting.

Finally, you will find a torque wrench necessary for all but the most basic of work. The beam type models are perfectly adequate. The newer click type (breakaway) torque wrenches are more accurate but are much more expensive and must be periodically recalibrated.

Special Tools

Special tools are available from:

Kent-Moore Corporation
29784 Little Mack
Roseville, Michigan 48066
In Canada:
Kent-Moore of Canada, Ltd.,
2395 Cawthra
Mississauga, Ontario
Canada L5A 3P2

Fig. 74 Always use jackstands or ramps when working under the vehicle

SERVICING YOUR CAR SAFELY

It is virtually impossible to anticipate all of the hazards involved with automotive maintenance and service, but care and common sense will prevent most accidents.

The rules of safety for mechanics range from "don't smoke around gasoline," to "use the proper tool(s) for the job." The trick to avoiding injuries is to develop safe work habits and take every possible precaution.

Do's

• Do keep a fire extinguisher and first aid kit within easy reach.

• Do wear safety glasses or goggles when cutting, drilling, grinding or prying, even if you have 20–20 vision. If you wear glasses for the sake of vision, they should be made of hardened glass that can serve also as safety glasses or wear safety goggles over your regular glasses.

• Do shield your eyes whenever you work around the battery. Batteries contain sulphuric acid. In case of contact with the eyes or skin, flush the area with water or a mixture of water/baking soda and get medical attention immediately.

• Do use safety stands for any undercar service. Jacks are for raising vehicles; safety stands are for making sure the vehicle stays raised until you want to come down. Whenever the car is raised, block the wheels remaining on the ground and set the parking brake.

• Do use adequate ventilation when working with any chemicals or hazardous materials. Like carbon monoxide, the asbestos dust resulting from break lining wear can be poisonous in sufficient quantities.

• Do disconnect the negative battery cable when working on the electrical system. The secondary ignition system can contain up to 40,000 volts.

• Do follow manufacturer's directions whenever working with potentially hazardous materials. Both brake fluid and antifreeze are poisonous if taken internally.

• Do properly maintain your tools. Loose hammerheads, mushroomed punches and chisels, frayed or poorly grounded electrical cords, excessively worn screwdrivers, spread wrenches (open end), cracked sockets, slipping ratchets or faulty droplight sockets can cause accidents.

• Do use the proper size and type of tool for the job being done.

• Do, when possible, pull on a wrench handle rather than push on it and adjust your stance to prevent a fall.

• Do be sure the adjustable wrenches are tightly closed on the nut or bolt and pulled so that the face is on the side of the fixed jaw.

• Do select a wrench or socket that fits the nut or bolt. The wrench or socket should sit straight, not cocked.

• Do strike squarely with a hammer; avoid glancing blows.

• Do set the parking brake and block the drive wheels if the work requires the engine running.

Don'ts

• Don't run an engine in a garage or anywhere else without proper ventilation–EVER! Carbon monoxide is poisonous; it takes a long time to leave the human body and you can build up a deadly supply of it in your system by simply breathing in a little every day. You may not realize you are slowly poisoning yourself. Always use power vents, windows, fans or open the garage doors.

• Don't work around moving parts while wearing a necktie or other loose clothing. Short sleeves are much safer than long, loose sleeves; hard-toed shoes with neoprene soles protect your toes and give a better grip on slippery surfaces. Jewelry such as watches, fancy belt buckles, beads or body adornment of any kind is not safe working around a car. Long hair should be hidden under a hat or cap.

• Don't use pockets for toolboxes. A fall or bump can drive a screwdriver deep into your body. Even a wiping cloth hanging from the back pocket can wrap around a spinning shaft or fan.

• Don't smoke when working around gasoline, cleaning solvent or other flammable material.

• Don't smoke when working around the battery. When the battery is being charged, it gives off explosive hydrogen gas.

• Don't use gasoline to wash your hands; there are excellent soaps available. Gasoline may contain lead, which can enter the body through a cut, accumulating in the body until you are very ill. Gasoline also removes all the natural oils from the skin so that bone dry hands will suck up oil and grease.

• Don't service the air conditioning system unless you are equipped with the necessary tools and training. The refrigerant (R-12) is under pressure; when released into the air, it will instantly freeze any surface it contacts, including your eyes. Although the refrigerant is normally non-toxic, R-12 becomes a deadly poisonous gas in the presence of an open flame. One good whiff of the vapors from burning refrigerant can be fatal.

HISTORY

The first Datsun automobile was built in 1914, a small 10 horsepower car with motorcycle fenders. The original name of the company, D.A.T., was derived from the last initials of the company's three main financial backers. A sports-type two seater was produced in 1918 and called the "son of D.A.T.", which later evolved into Datsun. Throughout the 1920's and 1930's the Datsun automobile looked like the English Austin after which it was closely patterned, while the company also began to branch out into the truck market. The year 1933 saw the formation of Nissan Motor Company, and was also the first year Datsuns were exported.

Following the end of World War II (in which Nissan produced military vehicles and aircraft engines), the company managed to resume truck and passenger car production. It wasn't until 1960 that the first Datsun was imported into the United States; since then, Datsun has moved up into second place in imported car sales. The company's introduction of the Sentra model (under the Nissan badge) in 1982 moved Nissan into the forefront of the fuel mileage competition for gasoline-engined cars.

In 1982, Datsun Corporation merged with Nissan Corporation to become known as the Datsun/Nissan Corporation and in 1984, the Datsun name was dropped and the new company emerged as Nissan Corporation.

In 1983, a new sport model was introduced; known as the Pulsar, it uses an E16 or E16S carbureted engine, which is larger than the E15 engine. Only during 1984 did Nissan introduce into Canada the E15ET (EFI) engine, which is the turbo-charged version of the E15 engine. In 1987 the Pulsar E16i (fuel injected version of the E16S) and CA16DE were introduced. The CA16DE (1.6L) is a dual overhead camshaft, 16 valve engine. In 1988 the CA18DE (1.8L) replaced the CA16DE which is basically the same engine but larger. In 1991, the Pulsar was dropped and the Sentra NX Coupe was introduced.

SERIAL NUMBER IDENTIFICATION

Chassis

The chassis number is on the firewall under the hood on all models. All vehicles also have the chassis number (also known as the vehicle identification number) on a plate attached to the top of the instrument panel on the driver's side, visible through the windshield. The chassis serial number is preceded by the model designation. All models have an Emission Control information label on the firewall or on the underside of the hood.

The chassis serial number is stamped into the firewall. The chassis number is also located on a dashboard plate which is visible through the windshield. The vehicle identification number is broken down as follows:

- The first 3 digits are "JN1"—Nissan passenger vehicle; or "1N4"—U.S.A. produced passenger vehicle.
- The next letter refers to the type of engine in use. For example, "P" refers to the E16i gasoline engine and "S" refers to the CD17 diesel.
- The third letter refers to the model—for example, "B" refers to the Sentra.
- The fourth space is filled by a number referring to the model.
- The fifth space refers to the body type.
- Next comes the restraint system—"S" for Standard and "Y" for four wheel drive.
- The seventh space is occupied by a check digit (this keeps anyone from creating a fictitious serial number based on this basic information).
- Next comes the model year—for example, "J" for 1988.
- The ninth space contains a letter referring to the manufacturing plant.
- The final block contains the 6 digit sequential serial or "chassis" number for the actual vehicle.

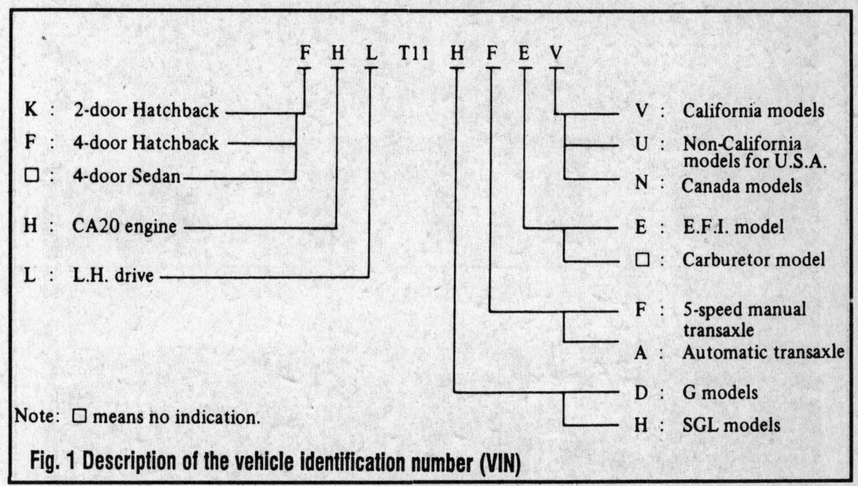
F H L T11 H F E V
K : 2-door Hatchback
F : 4-door Hatchback
□ : 4-door Sedan
H : CA20 engine
L : L.H. drive
V : California models
U : Non-California models for U.S.A.
N : Canada models
E : E.F.I. model
□ : Carburetor model
F : 5-speed manual transaxle
A : Automatic transaxle
D : G models
H : SGL models
Note: □ means no indication.

Fig. 1 Description of the vehicle identification number (VIN)

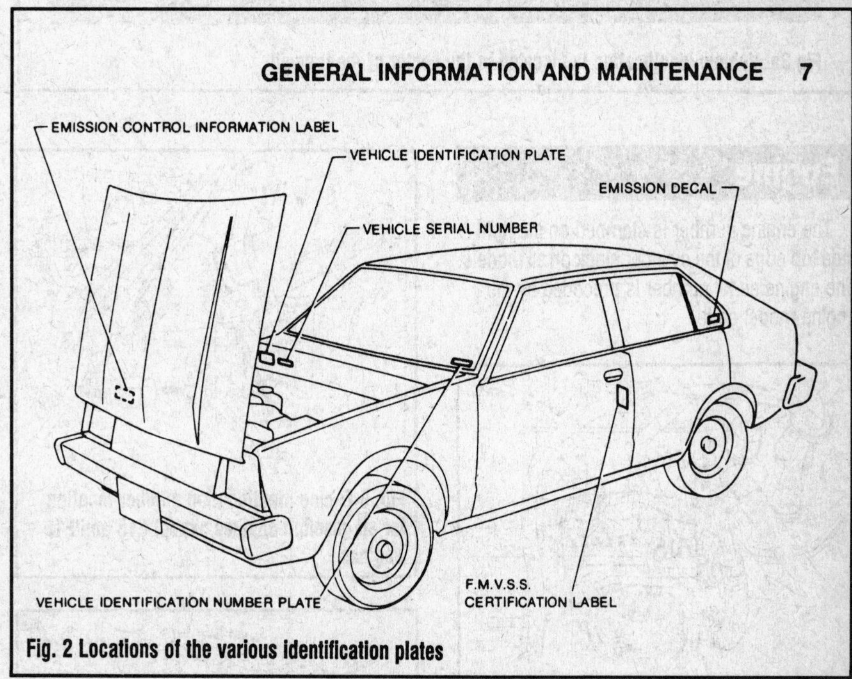
GENERAL INFORMATION AND MAINTENANCE 7
EMISSION CONTROL INFORMATION LABEL
VEHICLE IDENTIFICATION PLATE
EMISSION DECAL
VEHICLE SERIAL NUMBER
VEHICLE IDENTIFICATION NUMBER PLATE
F.M.V.S.S. CERTIFICATION LABEL

Fig. 2 Locations of the various identification plates

Vehicle Identification Plate

SEE FIGS. 1, 2, 3

The vehicle identification plate is attached to the right-side of the firewall. This plate gives the vehicle type, identification number, model, body color code, trim color code, engine model and displacement, transaxle model and axle model.

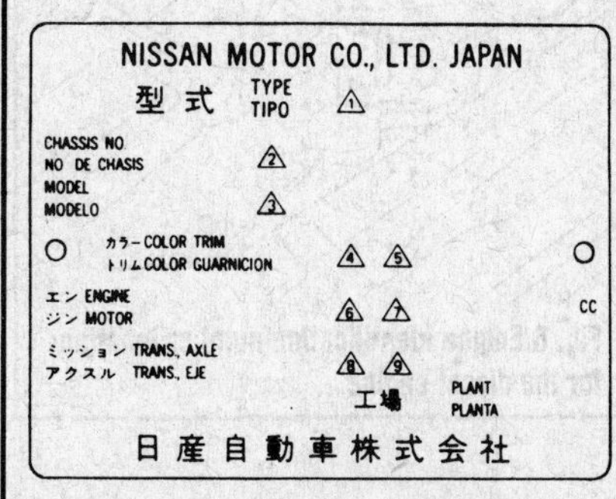
NISSAN MOTOR CO., LTD. JAPAN
型式 TYPE TIPO 1
CHASSIS NO. NO DE CHASIS 2
MODEL MODELO 3
カラー COLOR TRIM トリム COLOR GUARNICION 4 5
エンジン ENGINE MOTOR 6 7 CC
ミッション TRANS. AXLE アクスル TRANS. EJE 8 9
工場 PLANT PLANTA
日産自動車株式会社

1. Type
2. Vehicle identification number (chassis number)
3. Model
4. Body color code
5. Trim color code
6. Engine model
7. Engine displacement
8. Transaxle model
9. Axle model

Fig. 3 View of the identification plate located at the firewall

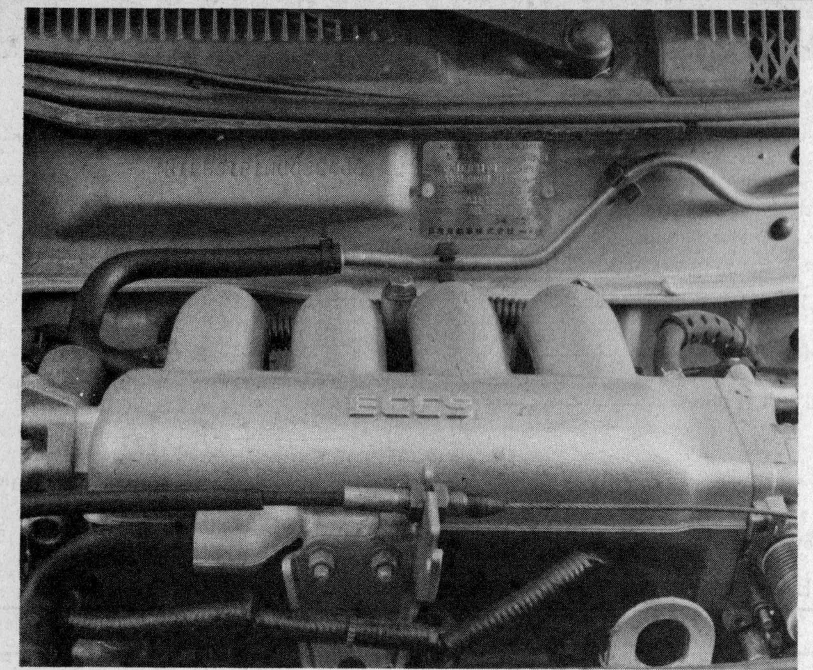

Fig 3a. Vehicle idenification tag located in the center of the firewall

Engine

The engine number is stamped on the right-side top edge of the cylinder block on all models. The engine serial number is preceded by the engine model code.

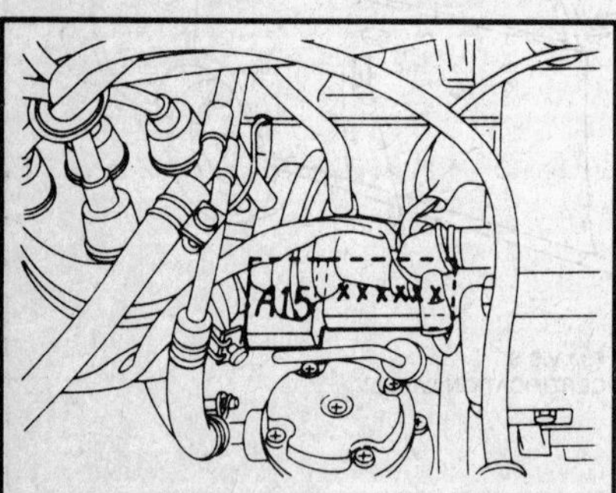
A15 XXXXXX

Fig. 4 Engine identification number location for E15 and E16 engines

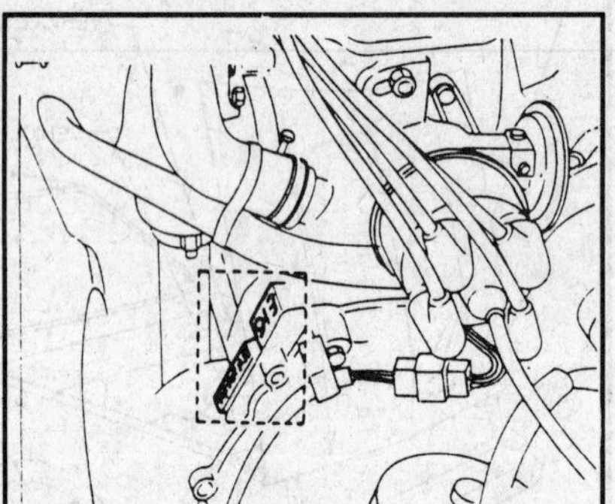

Fig. 5 Engine identification number location for all gasoline engines except E15 and E16 engines

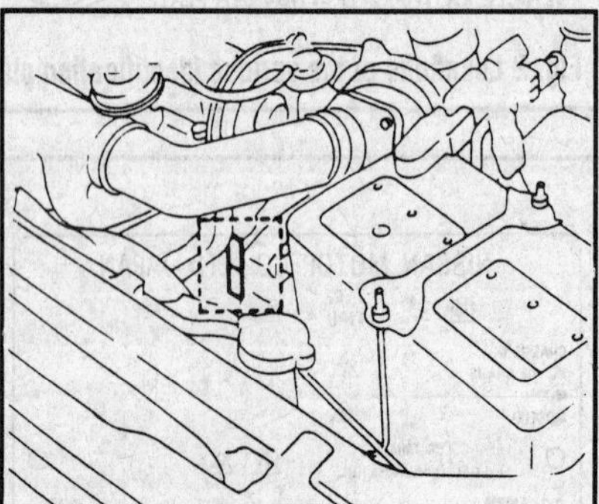

Fig. 6 Engine identification number location for the diesel engine

Transaxle

The transaxle number is stamped on the front upper face of the transaxle case for automatic or attached to the clutch withdrawal lever for manual transaxles.

Fig. 7 Manual transaxle number location

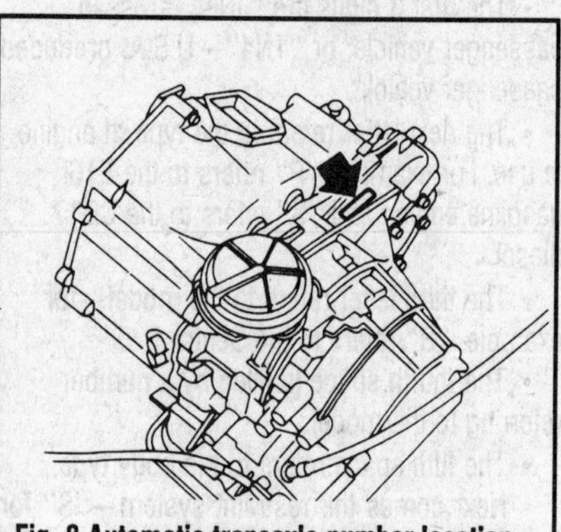

Fig. 8 Automatic transaxle number location

ENGINE IDENTIFICATION

Year	Model	Engine Displacement Liters (cc)	Engine Series (ID/VIN)	Fuel System	No. of Cylinders	Engine Type
1982	Sentra	1.5 (1488)	E15	2 bbl	4	SOHC
1983	Sentra	1.5 (1488)	E15	2 bbl	4	SOHC
	Sentra, Pulsar	1.6 (1597)	E16	2 bbl	4	SOHC
	Sentra	1.7 (1680)	CD17	Diesel	4	SOHC
1984	Pulsar	1.5 (1488)	E15ET	EFI-Turbo	4	SOHC
	Sentra, Pulsar	1.6 (1597)	E16, E16S	2 bbl	4	SOHC
	Sentra	1.7 (1680)	CD17	Diesel	4	SOHC
1985	Sentra, Pulsar	1.6 (1597)	E16, E16S	2 bbl	4	SOHC
	Sentra	1.7 (1680)	CD17	Diesel	4	SOHC
1986	Sentra, Pulsar	1.6 (1597)	E16, E16S	2 bbl	4	SOHC
	Sentra	1.7 (1680)	CD17	Diesel	4	SOHC
1987	Sentra, Pulsar	1.6 (1597)	E16S	2 bbl	4	SOHC
	Sentra, Pulsar	1.6 (1597)	E16I	EFI	4	SOHC
	Pulsar	1.6 (1598)	CA16DE	EFI	4	DOHC
	Sentra	1.7 (1680)	CD17	Diesel	4	SOHC
1988	Sentra, Pulsar	1.6 (1597)	E16I	EFI	4	SOHC
	Pulsar	1.8 (1809)	CA18DE	EFI	4	DOHC
1989	Sentra, Pulsar	1.6 (1597)	GA16I	EFI	4	SOHC
	Pulsar	1.8 (1809)	CA18DE	EFI	4	DOHC
1990	Sentra, Pulsar	1.6 (1597)	GA16I	EFI	4	SOHC
1991	Sentra	1.6 (1597)	GA16DE	EFI	4	DOHC
	Sentra	2.0 (1998)	SR20DE	EFI	4	DOHC
1992	Sentra	1.6 (1597)	GA16DE	EFI	4	DOHC
	Sentra	2.0 (1998)	SR20DE	EFI	4	DOHC

EFI—Electronic Fuel Injection
SOHC—Single Overhead Cam
DOHC—Double Overhead Cam

TRANSMISSION APPLICATION CHART

Year	Model	Transmission Identification	Transmission Type
1982	Sentra	RN3F01A	3-spd automatic
1982-86	Sentra	RN4F30A	4-spd manual
1982-87	Sentra, Pulsar	RS5F30A	5-spd manual
1983-92	Sentra, Pulsar	RL3F01A	3-spd automatic
1987-92	Sentra	RN4F31A	4-spd manual
1988-92	Sentra, Pulsar	RS5F31A	5-spd manual
1991-92	Sentra	RL4F03A	4-spd automatic
1991-92	Sentra	RL4F03V	4-spd automatic
1991-92	Sentra	RS5F32V	5-spd manual

ROUTINE MAINTENANCE

Air Cleaner

➧ SEE FIGS. 9, 10

REMOVAL & INSTALLATION

All vehicles covered in this guide are equipped with a disposable paper cartridge air cleaner element. At every tune-up or sooner, if the car is operated in a dusty area, remove the housing cover and remove the element. Check the element by holding a drop light or equivalent up to the filter if light can be seen through the filter then filter should be OK. Replace the filter if it is extremely dirty. Loose dust can sometimes be removed by striking the filter against a hard surface several times or by blowing through it with compressed air from the inside out. The filter should be replaced every 30,000 miles or 24 months. Before installing either the original or a replacement filter, wipe out the inside of the air cleaner housing with a clean rag or paper towel. Install the paper air cleaner filter, seat the top cover on the bottom housing and tighten the cover.

➡ **Carbureted engines use a round element and fuel injected engines use a panel type element. The panel (flat-rectangular) elements have the word UP** printed on them; be sure the side with **UP** on it, faces upward.

Fig. 9 Air cleaner replacement – Except Multi-port injected engines

Fig 10a. Removing the air cleaner assembly after releasing the snaps—fuel injected engines

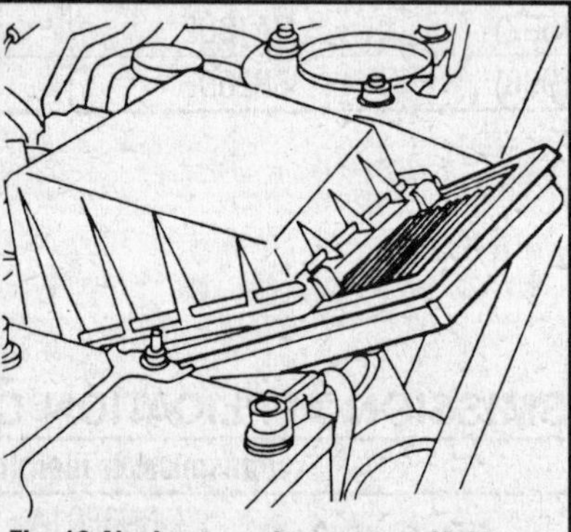

Fig. 10 Air cleaner replacement – Multi-port injected engines

Air Induction Valve Filter

REMOVAL & INSTALLATION

This filter is located in the air cleaner on both fuel injected and carburetor models. To replace it, remove the screws and the valve filter case. Install the new filter, paying attention to which direction the valve is facing so that exhaust gases will not flow backwards through the system.

➡ **Not all years and models use this filter.**

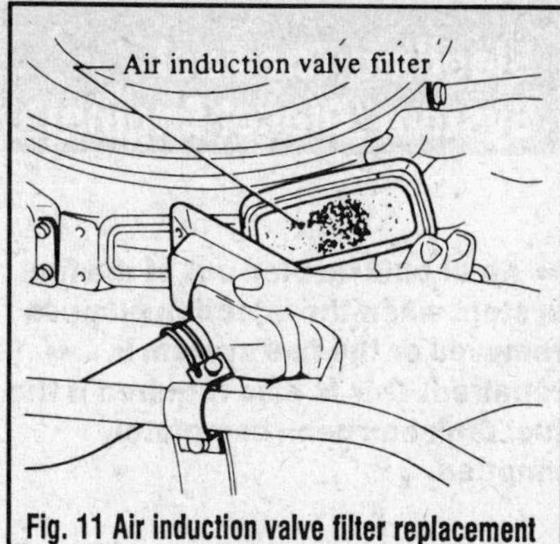
Air induction valve filter
Fig. 11 Air induction valve filter replacement

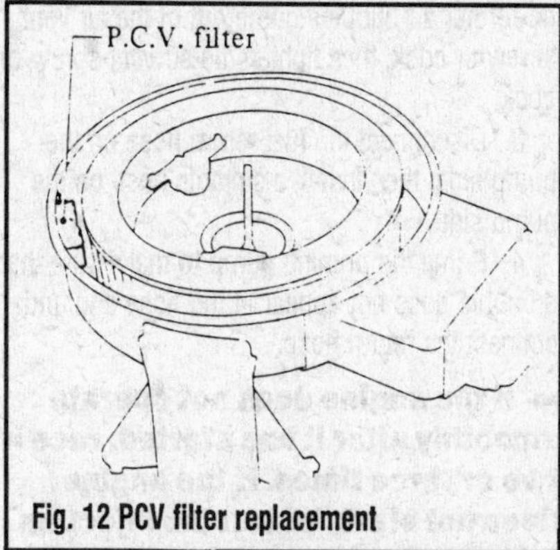
P.C.V. filter
Fig. 12 PCV filter replacement

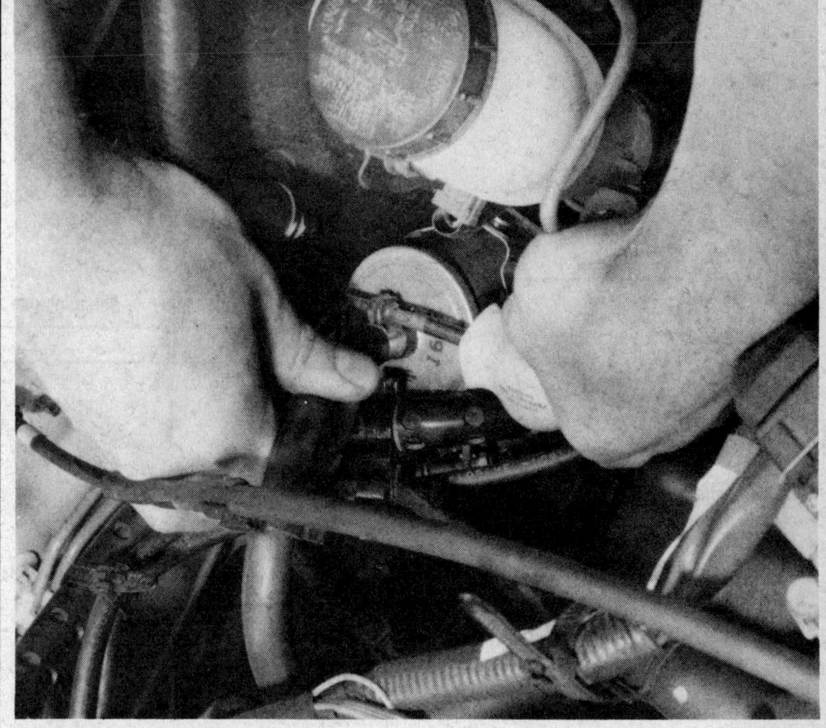
Fig 15a. Removing the fuel filter assembly—1991-92 Sentra EFI engine

PCV Filter

The PCV filter is located in the air cleaner assembly. Remove the filter from the assembly and clean in solvent. Thoroughly dry the element and reinstall. Check the hoses and clamps for deterioration and leakage. Replace the filter if it is damaged or worm out.

Fuel Filter

REMOVAL & INSTALLATION

The fuel filter on all models is a disposable plastic unit; located at the rear of the engine compartment. The filter should be replaced at least every 24,000 miles. A dirty filter will starve the engine and cause poor running.

CAUTION

If equipped with an Electronic Fuel Injected (EFI) engine, refer to the Fuel Pressure Release Procedure in this section and release the fuel pressure before removing filter.

1. Locate fuel filter on right-side of the engine compartment and place a container under the filter to catch the excess fuel.
2. Disconnect the inlet and outlet hoses from the fuel filter. Make certain that the inlet hose (bottom) doesn't fall below the fuel tank level or the gasoline will drain out.
3. Pry the fuel filter from its clip and replace the assembly.
4. Replace the inlet and outlet lines. Always replace the hose clamps. Tighten hose clamp so that clamp end is 3mm from the hose end.

➡ Ensure that the screw does not contact adjacent parts.

5. Start the engine and check for leaks.

FUEL PRESSURE RELEASE PROCEDURE

1. Start the engine.
2. On non-turbocharged engines, disconnect the (black) electrical harness connector, located under the passenger seat. On the turbocharged engines, disconnect the (green) electrical connector from the fuel pump relay, located on the fender at the front-left of the engine compartment. On 1989–1992 fuel injected vehicles, remove the fuel pump fuse from the fuse block.

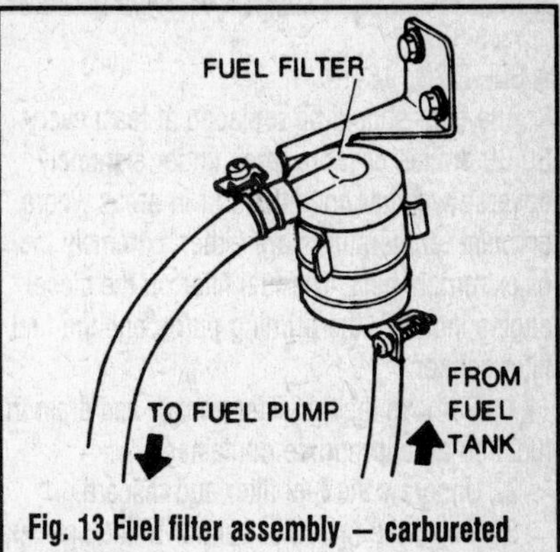
FUEL FILTER
TO FUEL PUMP
FROM FUEL TANK
Fig. 13 Fuel filter assembly – carbureted engines

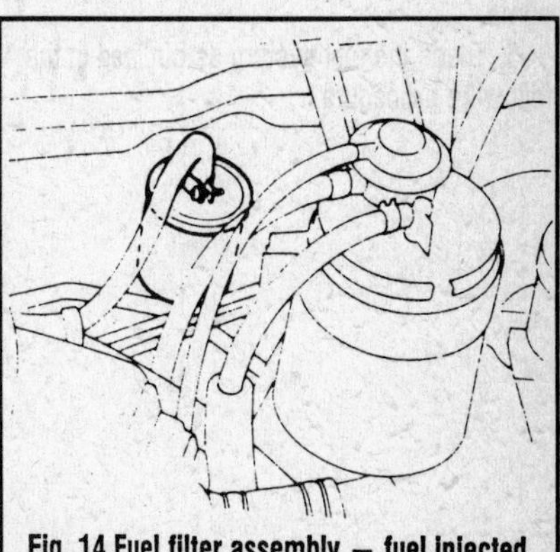
Fig. 14 Fuel filter assembly – fuel injected engines

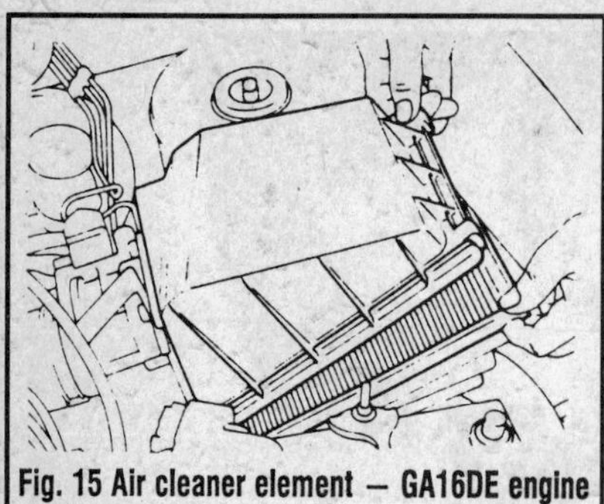
Fig. 15 Air cleaner element — GA16DE engine

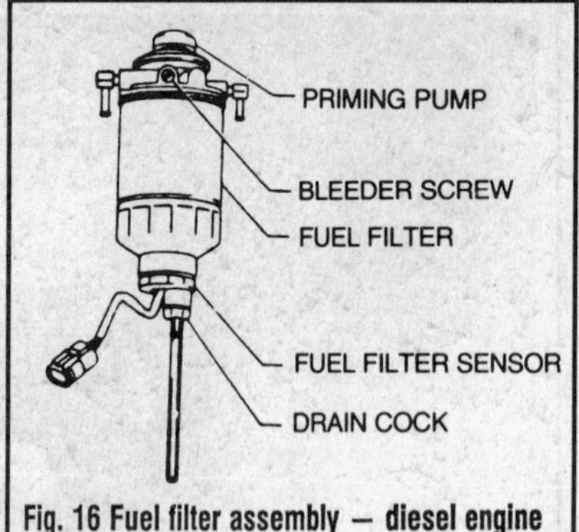
PRIMING PUMP
BLEEDER SCREW
FUEL FILTER
FUEL FILTER SENSOR
DRAIN COCK
Fig. 16 Fuel filter assembly — diesel engine

3. After the engine has stalled, crank it over 2–3 times.

4. Turn **OFF** the ignition switch and reconnect the electrical connector or install the fuse.

➡ **On all Pulsar and Sentra models that are fuel injected if the fuse box is equipped with a fuse for fuel pump, this fuse can be removed instead of disconnecting the electrical connector from the fuel pump or relay.**

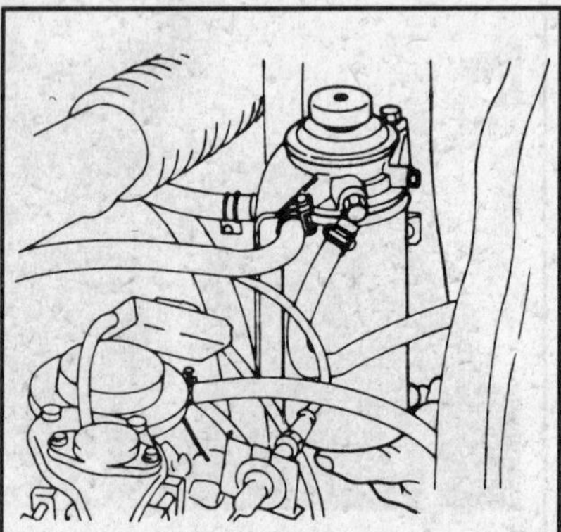
Fig. 17 Hand tighten the diesel fuel filter

Fuel/Water Separator (Diesel Engine)

♦ SEE FIGS. 16-19

The filter should be replaced at least every 30,000 miles or more often under extremely adverse weather conditions or in areas where ambient temperatures are either extremely low or extremely high. The fuel filter on the diesel engine includes the priming pump and the fuel filter sensor.

1. Remove the fuel filter sensor and drain the fuel into an appropriate container.
2. Unscrew the fuel filter and discard.
3. Install the fuel filter sensor to the new fuel filter.
4. Hand tighten the fuel filter to the priming pump.
5. Bleed the fuel system as outlined in the following procedure.

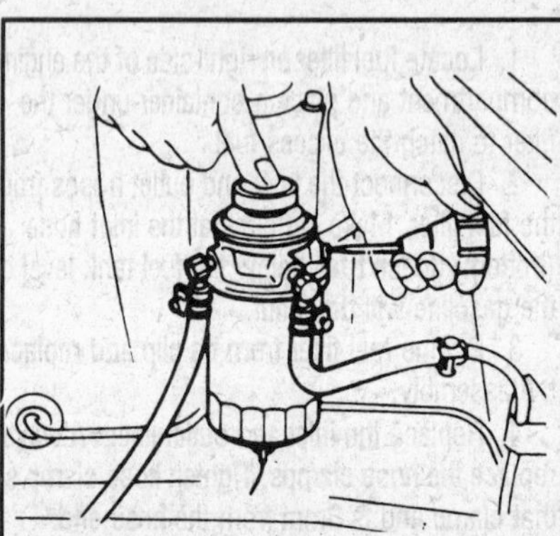
Fig. 18 Loosen the priming pump vent screw by turning counterclockwise with a suitable tool

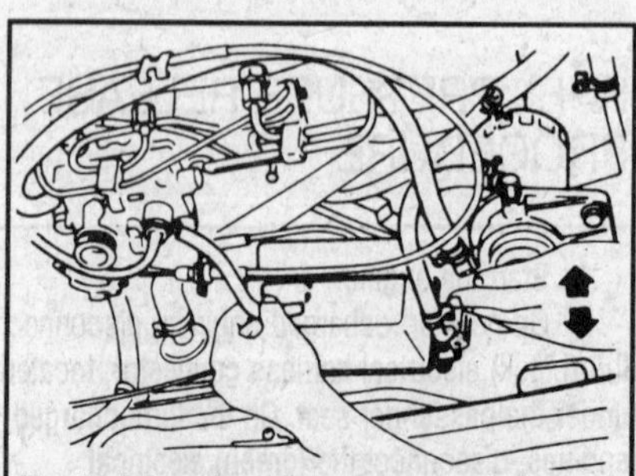
Fig. 19 Prime the priming pump and check for an air bubble at the hose end

Bleeding The Fuel System (Diesel Engine)

➡ **Air should be bled out of the fuel system when the injection pump is removed or the fuel system is repaired. This is also required if the fuel tank has been completely emptied.**

1. Loosen the air vent screw or cock.
2. Move the priming pump up and down until no further air bubbles come out of the air vent screw or cock, then tighten the air vent screw or cock.
3. Disconnect the fuel return hose on the pump side, then install a suitable hose on the pump side.
4. Prime the priming pump to make sure that a bubble does not appear at the hose end and connect the return hose.

➡ **If the engine does not operate smoothly after it has started, race it two or three times. If the engine does not start, loosen the injection tubes at the nozzle side and crank the engine until fuel overflows from the injection tubes. Tighten the injection tube flare nuts.**

Draining Water From The Diesel Fuel System

If the filter warning light illuminates and a chime sounds (on models so equipped) while the engine is running, drain any water that is in the fuel filter.

1. Disconnect the harness connector at the bottom of the fuel filter assembly.
2. Place a container under the fuel filter, then loosen the drain cock 4 or 5 turns to drain the water.

➡ **If the water does not drain sufficiently move the priming pump up and down.**

3. After draining the water completely, close the drain cock and reconnect the harness connector.
4. Bleed the air from the fuel system as outlined earlier.

Positive Crankcase Ventilation (PCV) Valve

REMOVAL & INSTALLATION

This valve feeds crankcase blow-by gases into the intake manifold to be burned with the normal air/fuel mixture. The PCV valve should be replaced every 24,000 miles. Make sure that all PCV connections are tight. Check that the connecting hoses are clear and not clogged. Replace any brittle or broken hoses.

To replace the valve, which is located in the intake manifold:

1. Squeeze the hose clamp with pliers and remove the hose.
2. Using a wrench, unscrew the PCV valve and remove the valve.
3. Disconnect the ventilation hoses and flush with solvent.
4. Install the new PCV valve, then replace the hoses and clamp.

➡ **To replace the PCV filter, remove the wing nut from the air cleaner lid and remove lid, gently lift out the filter which is mounted on the side of the air cleaner. This filter is usually about 4 in. (102mm) long.**

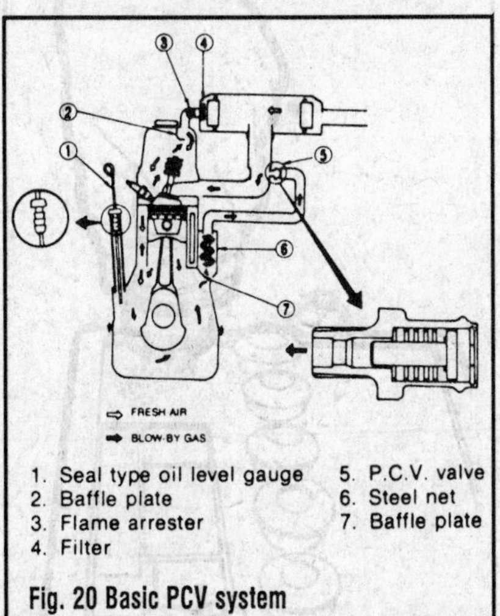
FRESH AIR
BLOW-BY GAS
1. Seal type oil level gauge
2. Baffle plate
3. Flame arrester
4. Filter
5. P.C.V. valve
6. Steel net
7. Baffle plate

Fig. 20 Basic PCV system

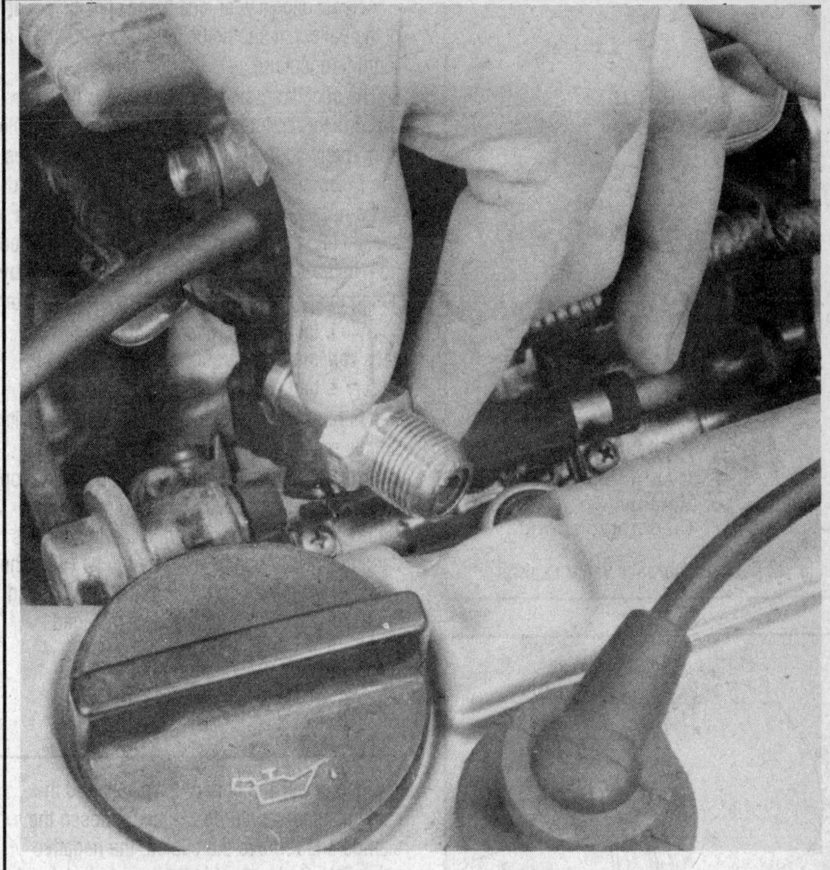

Fig 12a. Removing the PCV valve—GA16DE engine, others similar

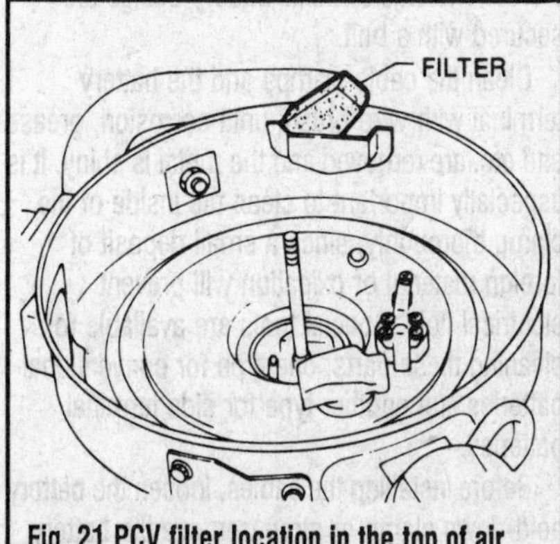
FILTER

Fig. 21 PCV filter location in the top of air cleaner

Evaporative Canister

SERVICING

A carbon filled canister stores fuel vapors until the engine is started and the vapors are drawn into the combustion chambers and burned. To check the operation of the carbon canister purge control valve, disconnect the rubber hose between the canister control valve and the T-fitting, at the T-fitting. Apply vacuum to the hose leading to the control valve. The vacuum condition should be maintained indefinitely. If the control valve leaks, remove the top cover of the valve and check for a dislocated or cracked diaphragm. If the diaphragm is damaged, a repair kit containing a new diaphragm, retainer and spring is available and should be installed.

The carbon canister has an air filter in the bottom of the canister. The filter element should be checked once a year or every 12,000 miles; more frequently if the car is operated in dust areas. Replace the filter by pulling it out of the bottom of the canister and installing a new one.

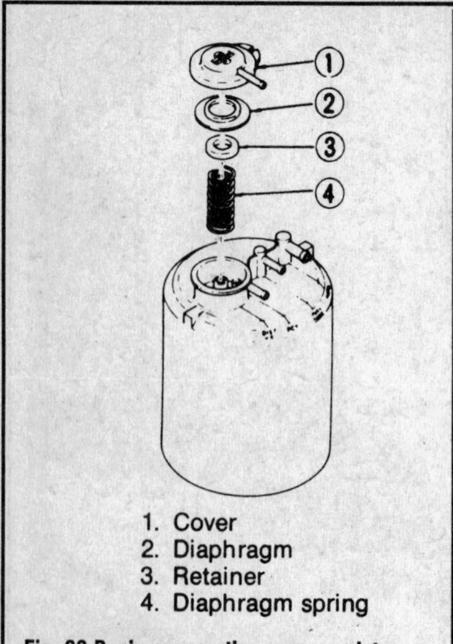
1
2
3
4
1. Cover
2. Diaphragm
3. Retainer
4. Diaphragm spring

Fig. 22 Basic evaporative vapor canister

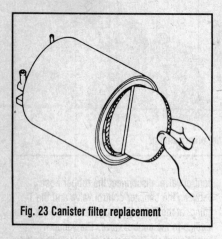

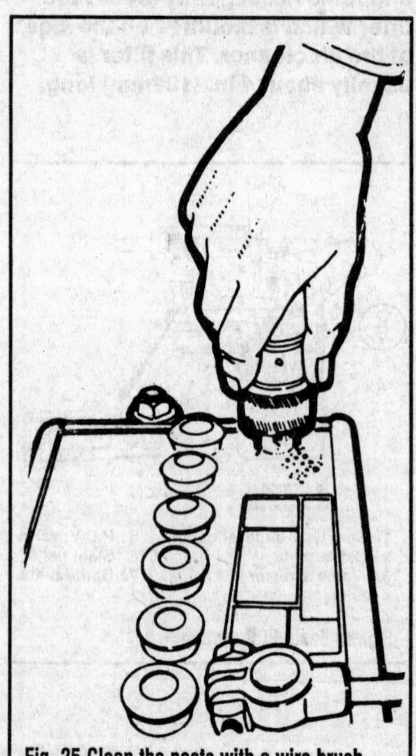

Fig. 23 Canister filter replacement

Battery

SPECIFIC GRAVITY (EXCEPT "MAINTENANCE FREE" BATTERIES)

✲✲ WARNING

Do not remove the caps on a sealed maintenance free battery. Damage to the battery and vehicle may result. If the fluid is low in this type of battery, an overcharging problem or a defective battery may be at fault.

At least once a year, check the specific gravity of the battery. It should be between 1.20–1.26 at room temperature.

The specific gravity can be checked with an hydrometer, an inexpensive instrument available from many sources, including auto parts stores. The hydrometer has a squeeze bulb at one end and a nozzle at the other. Battery electrolyte is sucked into the hydrometer until the float is lifted from its seat. The specific gravity is then read by noting the position of the float. Generally, if after charging, the specific gravity between any 2 cells varies more than 50 points (0.050), the battery is bad and should be replaced.

It is not possible to check the specific gravity (in this manner) on sealed , maintenance free batteries. Instead, the indicator built into the top of the case must be relied on to display any signs of battery deterioration. If the indicator is dark, the battery can be assumed to be OK. If the indicator is light, the specific gravity is low and the battery should be charged or replaced.

CABLES AND CLAMPS

Once a year the battery terminals and the cable clamps should be cleaned. Loosen the clamps and remove the cables, the negative cable first. On top post batteries, a special puller is used to remove the cable clamps; these are inexpensive and are available from the auto parts stores. The side terminal battery cables are secured with a bolt.

Clean the cable clamps and the battery terminal with wire brush, until corrosion, grease and etc. are removed and the metal is shiny. It is especially important to clean the inside of the clamp thoroughly, since a small deposit of foreign material or oxidation will prevent electrical flow. Special tools are available for cleaning these parts, one type for conventional batteries and another type for side terminal batteries.

Before installing the cables, loosen the battery hold-down clamp or strap, remove the battery and check the battery tray. Clear it of any debris and check it for soundness. Rust should be wire brushed away and the metal given a coat of anti-rust paint. Replace the battery and tighten the hold-down clamp or strap securely, but be careful not to overtighten, which will crack the battery case.

After the clamps and the terminals are clean, reinstall the cables, negative cable last; do not hammer on the clamps to install. Tighten the clamps securely but do not distort them. Give the clamps and the terminals a thin coat of petroleum jelly or equivalent after installation, to retard corrosion.

Check the cables at the same time that the terminals are cleaned. If the cable insulation is cracked, broken or if the ends are frayed, the cable should be replaced with a new cable of the same length and gauge.

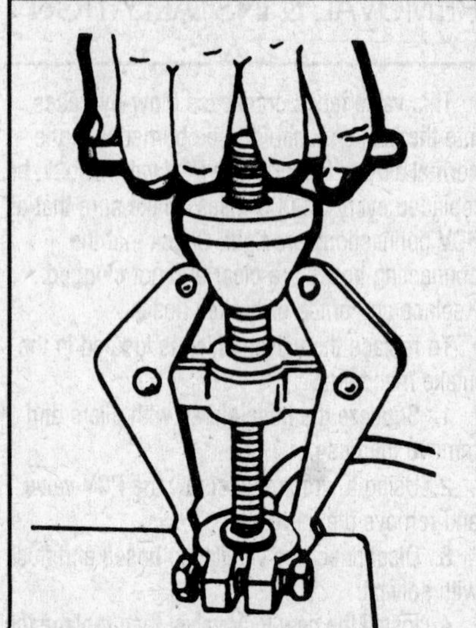

Fig. 24 Removing the battery cable clamp with a special puller. If this puller is not used, damage to the battery may result

Fig. 25 Clean the posts with a wire brush or a terminal cleaner made for this purpose

⁂ CAUTION

Keep flames or sparks away from the battery; it gives off explosive hydrogen gas. The electrolyte contains sulphuric acid. If you should splash any on your skin or in your eyes, flush the affected area with plenty of fresh water; if it gets into your eyes, get medical help immediately.

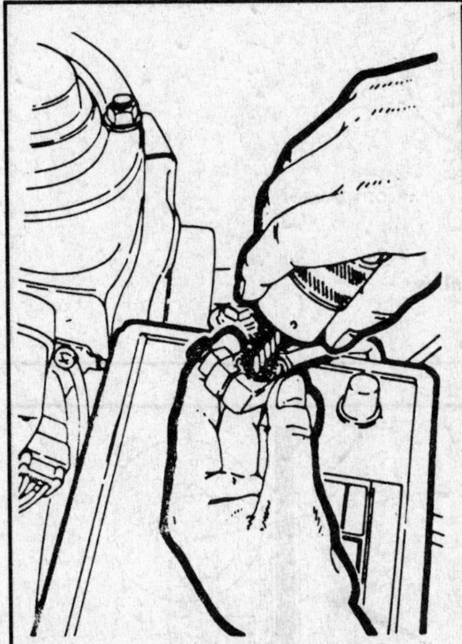

Fig. 26 Clean the inside of the clamps with a wire brush or the special tool

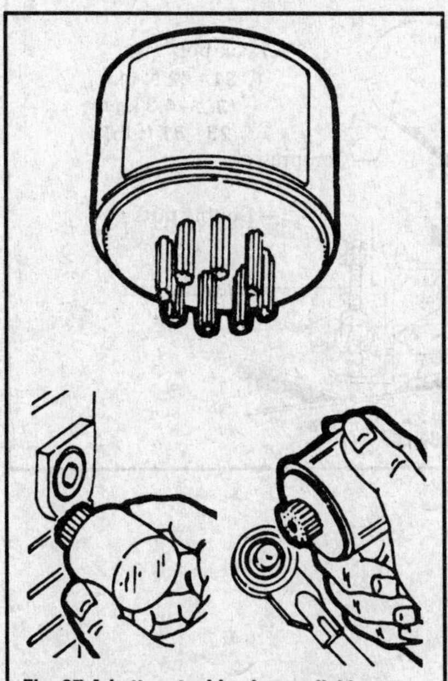

Fig. 27 A battery tool is also available for cleaning the posts and clamps on side terminal batteries

REPLACEMENT

When it becomes necessary to replace the battery, select one with a rating equal to or greater than the original. Deterioration, embrittlement or just plain aging of the battery cables, starter motor and associated wiring makes the batteries job harder in successive years. The slow increase in electrical resistance over time makes it prudent to install a new battery with a greater capacity than the old.

1. Raise the hood and support.
2. Remove the negative battery cable first and then the positive terminal.
3. Lubricate the hold-down with penetrating oil before loosening. Remove the battery clamp or hold-down.
4. Using an approved battery carrier, lift the battery out of the tray and away from the vehicle.
5. Clean the rust and corrosion from the battery tray with a wire brush.
6. Mix up a solution of baking soda and water to a thick paste. Paint the solution onto the corroded areas and allow to work for about one minute. Reapply another coat and repeat this step.
7. Rinse with warm water to remove baking soda.
8. Apply a coat of rust converter to the rusted areas and allow to dry. Apply another coat of rust converter after the first coat has dryed.
9. Apply two coats of high quality metal primer to the affected areas and allow to completely dry before going any further.
10. Apply a coat of undercoating to the battery tray area and allow to dry overnight if possible.
11. Clean the battery with soap and water.
12. Install the battery and tighten the hold-down bolt or clamp.
13. Apply a light coat of petroleum jelly or equivalent to the terminal posts.
14. Tighten the battery cable terminals to 10 ft. lbs. (15 Nm).
15. Clean the cable ends that connect to the body and starter motor if a problem still exits.
16. If a slow to no start problem still exists, the positive cable or starter motor may be defective.

➡ The 1982 and later engines do not use a heat control valve under the carburetor. Instead, these engines warm the fuel mixture by a coolant passage under the carburetor. No maintenance is required.

Belts

INSPECTION

Check the drive belts for cracks, fraying, wear and tension every 6,000 miles. It is recommended that the belts be replaced every 24 months or 24,000 miles. Belt deflection at the midpoint of the longest span between pulleys should not be more than $^7/_{16}$ in. (11mm) with 22 lbs. (10 kg) of pressure applied to the belt when engine is cold.

ADJUSTING

➡ An overtight belt will wear out the pulley bearings on the assorted components.

To adjust the tension on all components except the air conditioning compressor and power steering pump, loosen the pivot and mounting bolts of the component which the belt is driving, then, using a wooden lever or equivalent pry the component toward or away from the engine until the proper tension is achieved. Tighten the component mounting bolts securely. If a new belt is installed, recheck the tension after driving about 1,000 miles.

Belt tension adjustments for the factory installed air conditioning compressor are made at the idler pulley. The idler pulley is the smallest of the 3 pulleys. At the top of the slotted bracket holding the idler pulley there is a bolt which is used to either raise or lower the pulley. To free the bolt for adjustment, it is necessary to loosen the lock nut in the face of the idler pulley. After adjusting the belt tension, tighten the lock nut in the face of the idler pulley.

Belt tension adjustments for the power steering oil pump are made at the pump. Loosen the power steering oil pump adjusting lock bolt and its securing bolt. Adjust the adjusting bolt until the belt deflection is correct. Tighten the adjusting bolt lock bolt and oil pump securing bolt securely.

REMOVAL & INSTALLATION

➧ SEE FIGS. 28–32

To replace a drive belt loosen the pivot and mounting bolts of the component which the belt is driving, then, using a wooden lever or equivalent pry the component inward to relieve the tension on the drive belt, always be careful where you locate the pry bar not to damage the component. Slip the belt off the component pulley, match up the new belt with the old belt for length and width, these measurement must be the same or problems will occur when you go to adjust the new belt. After new belt is installed correctly adjust the tension of the new belt.

➡ When replacing more than one belt it is a good idea, to make note or mark what belt goes around what pulley. This will make installation fast and easy.

On air conditioning compressor and power steering pump belt replacements loosen the lock bolt for the adjusting bolt on idler pulley or power steering pump and then loosen the adjusting bolt. Pry pulley or pump inward to relieve the tension on the drive belt, always be careful where you locate the pry bar not to damage the component or pulley.

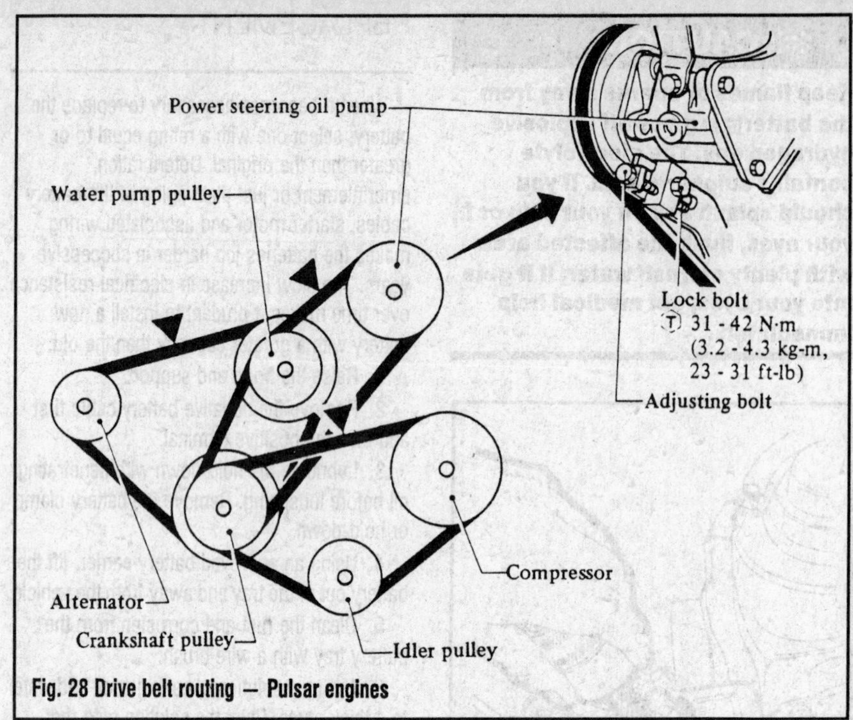
Power steering oil pump
Water pump pulley
Lock bolt
T 31 - 42 N·m
(3.2 - 4.3 kg-m,
23 - 31 ft-lb)
Adjusting bolt
Compressor
Alternator
Crankshaft pulley
Idler pulley

Fig. 28 Drive belt routing — Pulsar engines

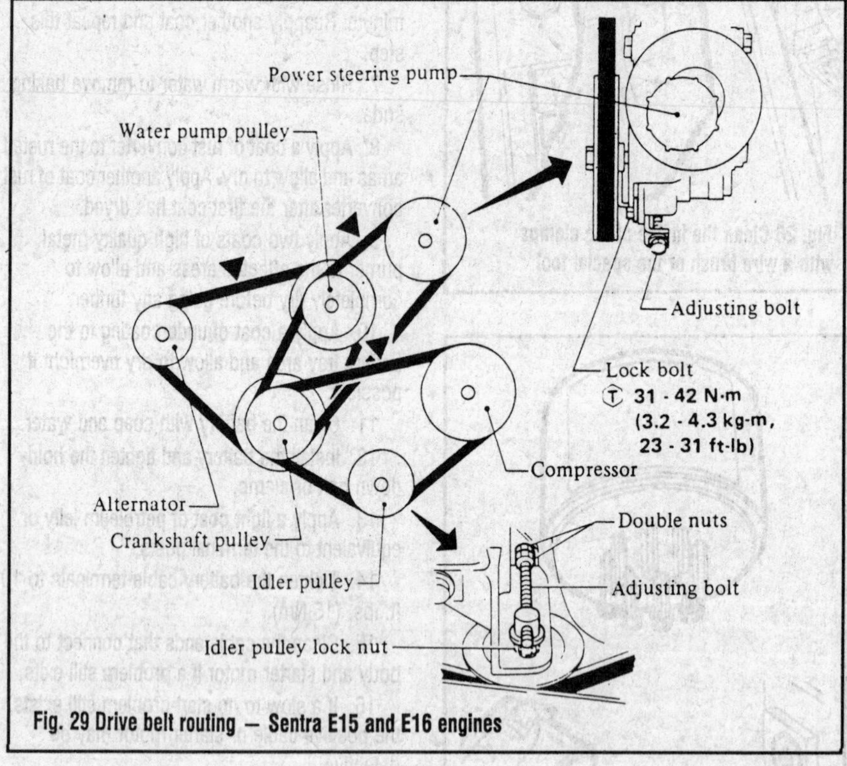
Power steering pump
Water pump pulley
Adjusting bolt
Lock bolt
T 31 - 42 N·m
(3.2 - 4.3 kg-m,
23 - 31 ft-lb)
Compressor
Alternator
Crankshaft pulley
Double nuts
Adjusting bolt
Idler pulley
Idler pulley lock nut

Fig. 29 Drive belt routing — Sentra E15 and E16 engines

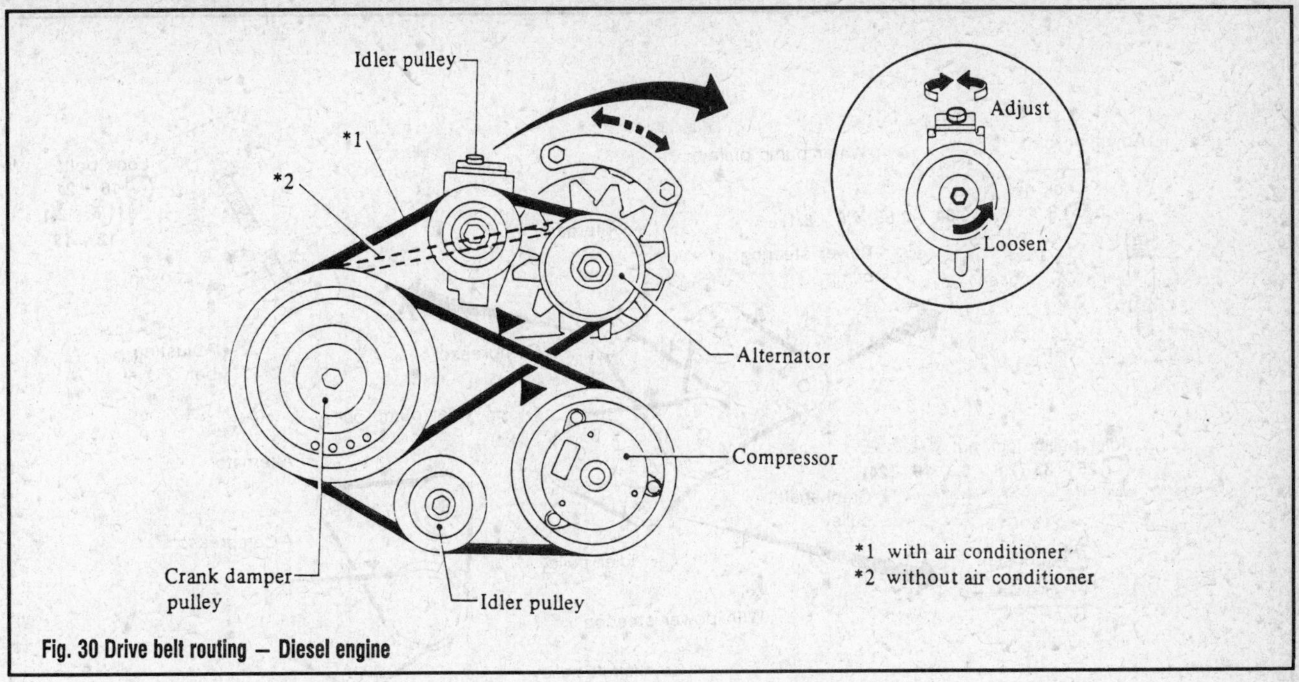
Idler pulley
*1
*2
Adjust
Loosen
Alternator
Compressor
Crank damper pulley
Idler pulley
*1 with air conditioner
*2 without air conditioner
Fig. 30 Drive belt routing — Diesel engine

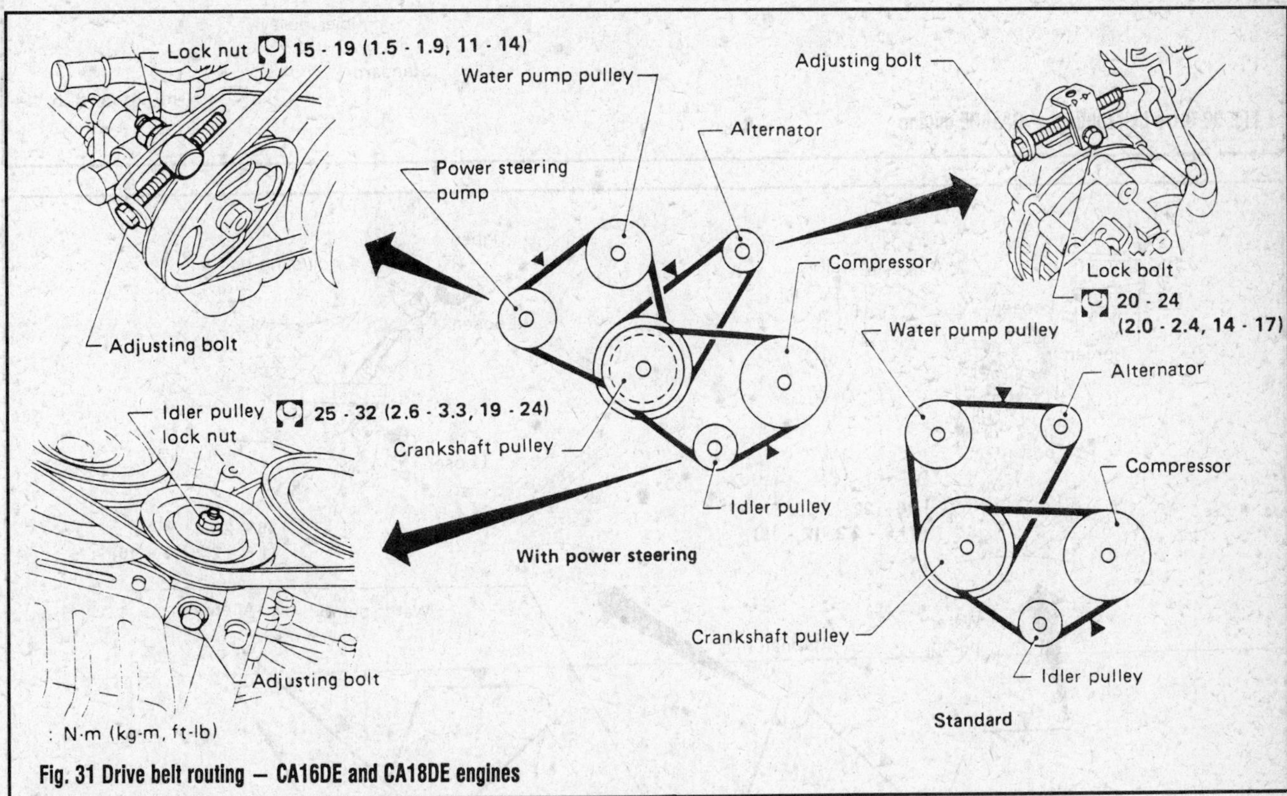
Lock nut 15 - 19 (1.5 - 1.9, 11 - 14)
Water pump pulley
Adjusting bolt
Alternator
Power steering pump
Compressor
Lock bolt
20 - 24
(2.0 - 2.4, 14 - 17)
Adjusting bolt
Water pump pulley
Alternator
Idler pulley lock nut 25 - 32 (2.6 - 3.3, 19 - 24)
Crankshaft pulley
Compressor
Idler pulley
With power steering
Crankshaft pulley
Adjusting bolt
Idler pulley
: N·m (kg-m, ft-lb)
Standard
Fig. 31 Drive belt routing — CA16DE and CA18DE engines

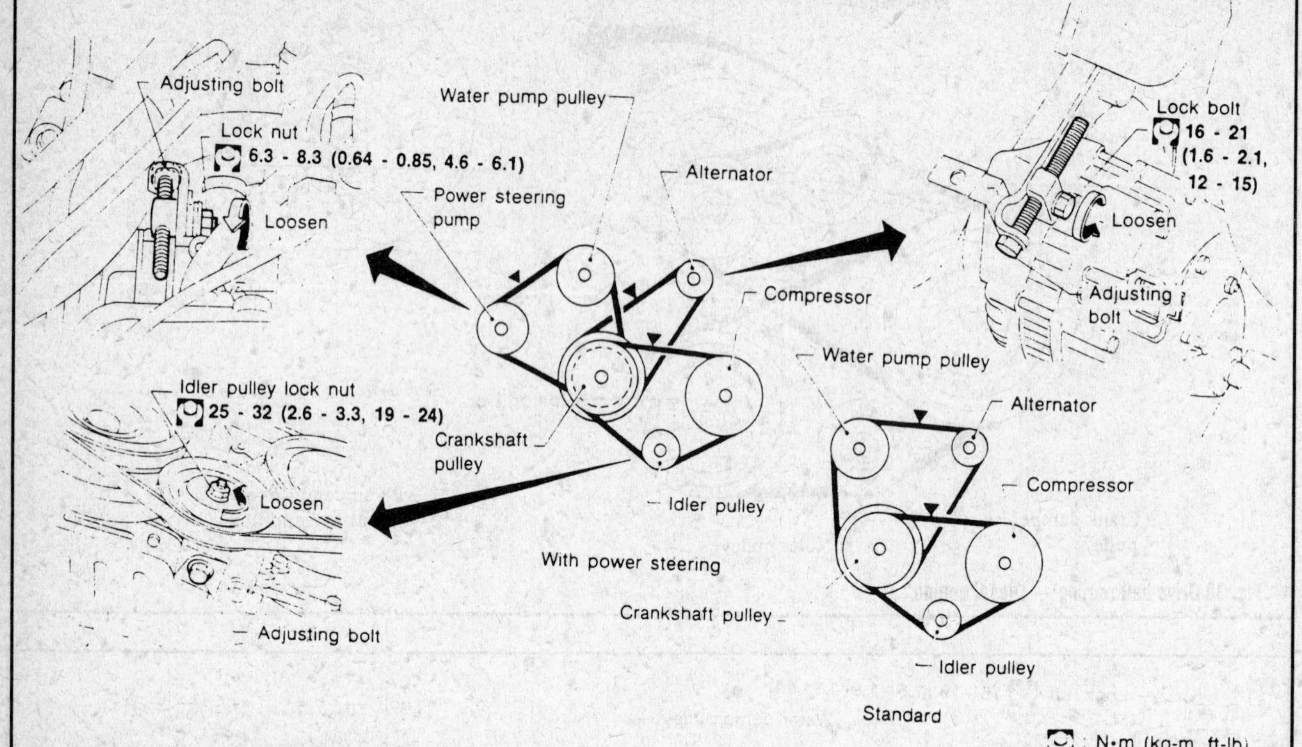

Adjusting bolt
Lock nut
6.3 - 8.3 (0.64 - 0.85, 4.6 - 6.1)
Loosen
Water pump pulley
Alternator
Power steering pump
Lock bolt
16 - 21 (1.6 - 2.1, 12 - 15)
Loosen
Adjusting bolt
Compressor
Idler pulley lock nut
25 - 32 (2.6 - 3.3, 19 - 24)
Loosen
Crankshaft pulley
Idler pulley
With power steering
Adjusting bolt
Water pump pulley
Alternator
Compressor
Crankshaft pulley
Idler pulley
Standard
: N•m (kg-m, ft-lb)

Fig. 32 Drive belt routing — GA16DE engine

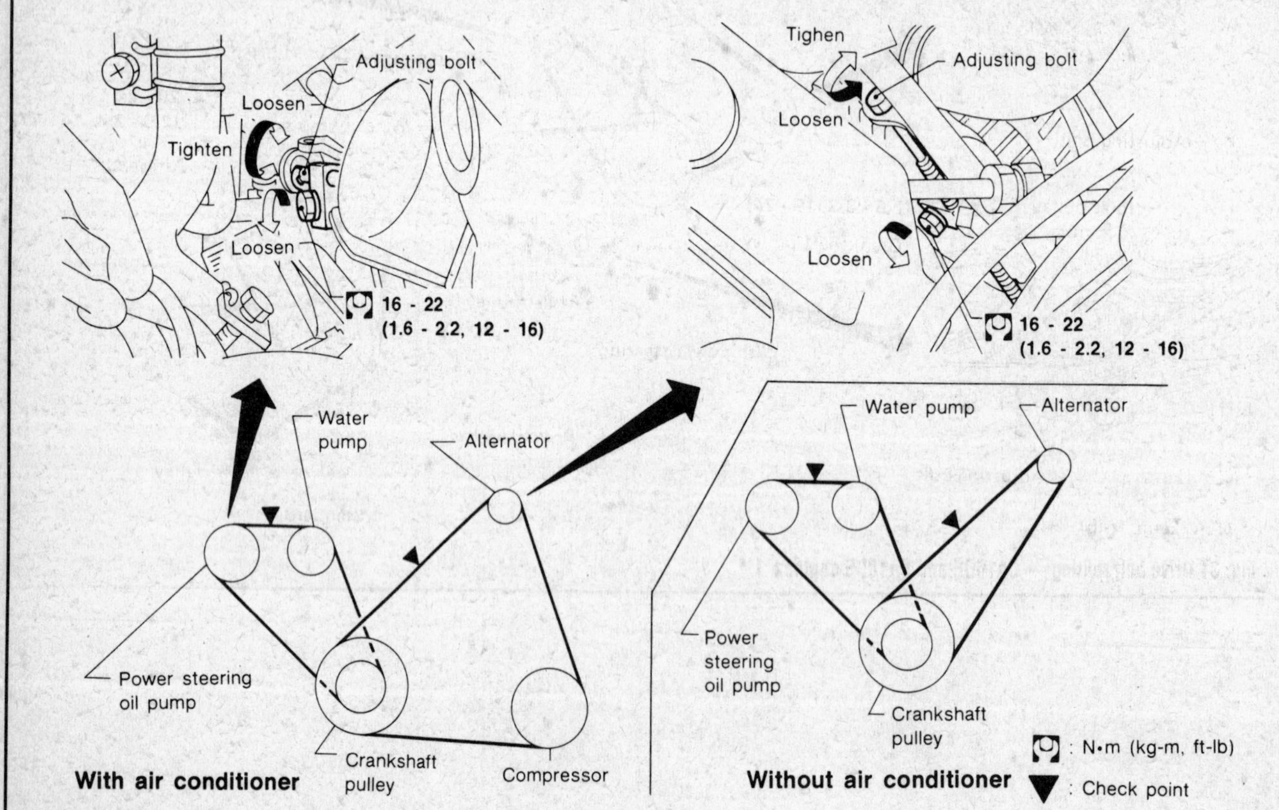

Adjusting bolt
Loosen
Tighten
Loosen
16 - 22 (1.6 - 2.2, 12 - 16)
Tighen
Adjusting bolt
Loosen
Loosen
16 - 22 (1.6 - 2.2, 12 - 16)
Water pump
Alternator
Power steering oil pump
Crankshaft pulley
Compressor
With air conditioner
Water pump
Alternator
Power steering oil pump
Crankshaft pulley
Without air conditioner
: N•m (kg-m, ft-lb)
: Check point

Fig. 32a Drive belt routing — SR20DE engine

HOW TO SPOT WORN V-BELTS

V–Belts are vital to efficient engine operation—they drive the fan, water pump and other accessories. They require little maintenance (occasional tightening) but they will not last forever. Slipping or failure of the V–belt will lead to overheating. If your V–belt looks like any of these, it should be replaced.

Cracking or Weathering

This belt has deep cracks, which cause it to flex. Too much flexing leads to heat build–up and premature failure. These cracks can be caused by using the belt on a pulley that is too small. Notched belts are available for small diameter pulleys.

Softening (Grease and Oil)

Oil and grease on a belt can cause the belt's rubber compounds to soften and separate from the reinforcing cords that hold the belt together. The belt will first slip, then finally fail altogether.

Glazing

Glazing is caused by a belt that is slipping. A slipping belt can cause a run-down battery, erratic power steering, overheating or poor accessory performance. The more the belt slips, the more glazing will be built up on the surface of the belt. The more the belt is glazed, the more it will slip. If the glazing is light, tighten the belt.

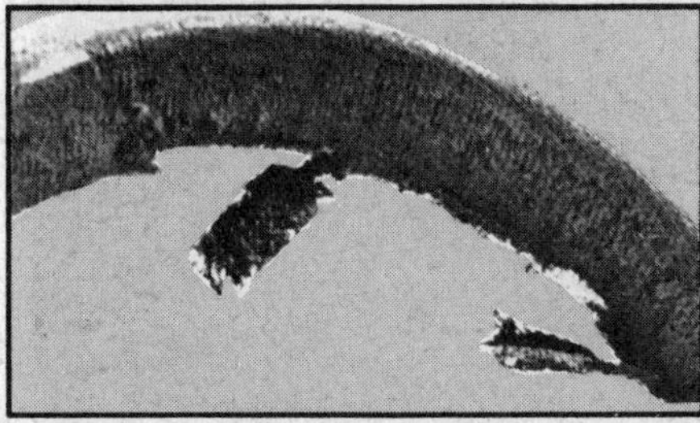

Worn Cover

The cover of this belt is worn off and is peeling away. The reinforcing cords will begin to wear and the belt will shortly break. When the belt cover wears in spots or has a rough jagged appearance, check the pulley grooves for roughness.

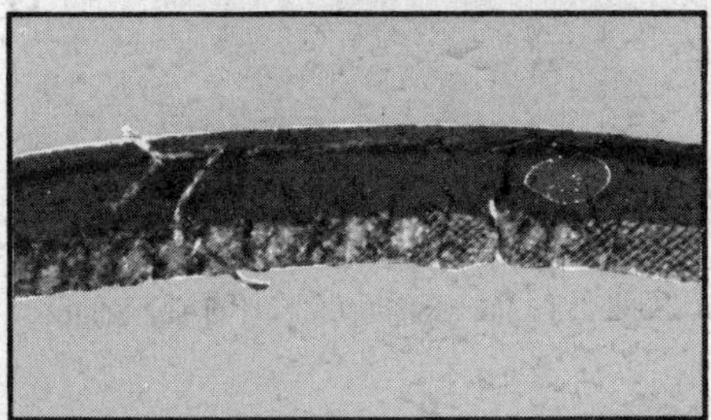

Separation

This belt is on the verge of breaking and leaving you stranded. The layers of the belt are separating and the reinforcing cords are exposed. It's just a matter of time before it breaks completely.

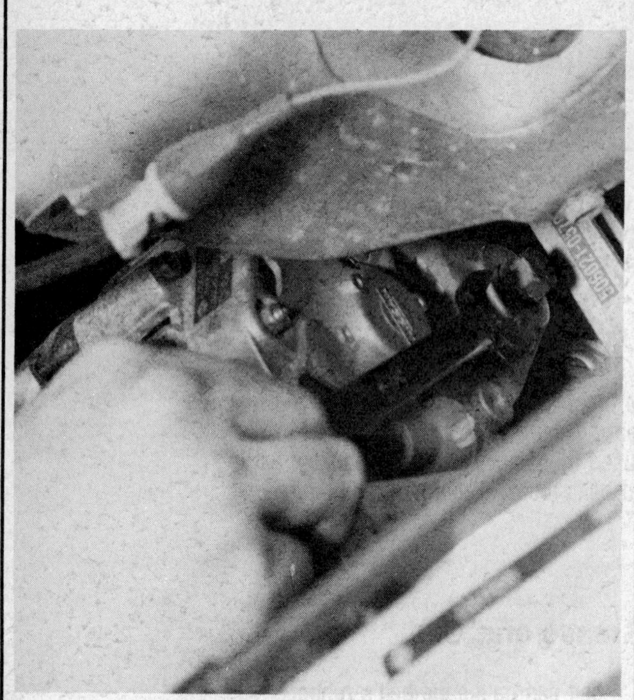

Fig 32b. Loosening the alternator retaining bolt for belt adjustment —1991-92 Sentra, others similar

Fig 32c. Adjusting the alternator belt using the adjusting bolt

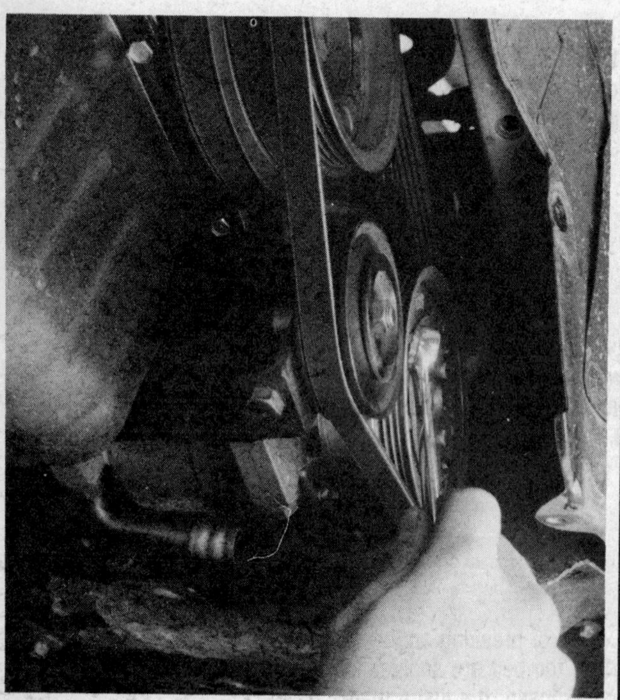

Fig 32d. Loosening the A/C belt idler pulley to adjust the belt —1991-92 Sentra

Fig 32e. Adjusting the A/C belt using the adjusting bolt—1991-92 Sentra

HOW TO SPOT BAD HOSES

Both the upper and lower radiator hoses are called upon to perform difficult jobs in an inhospitable environment. They are subject to nearly 18 psi at under hood temperatures often over 280°F, and must circulate nearly 7500 gallons of coolant an hour – 3 good reasons to have good hoses.

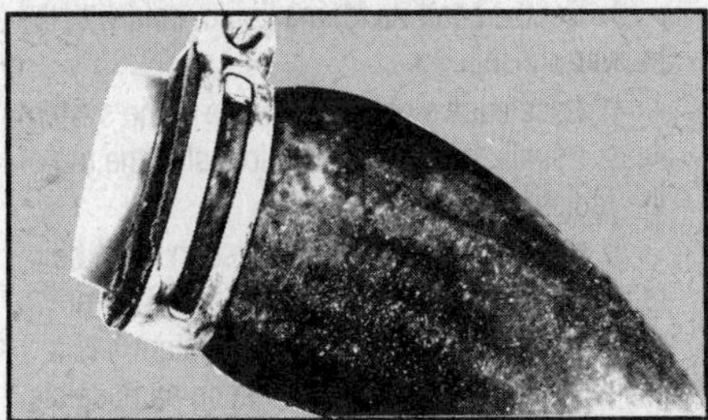

Swollen Hose

A good test for any hose is to feel it for soft or spongy spots. Frequently these will appear as swollen areas of the hose. The most likely cause is oil soaking. This hose could burst at any time, when hot or under pressure.

Cracked Hose

Cracked hoses can usually be seen but feel the hoses to be sure they have not hardened; a prime cause of cracking. This hose has cracked down to the reinforcing cords and could split at any of the cracks.

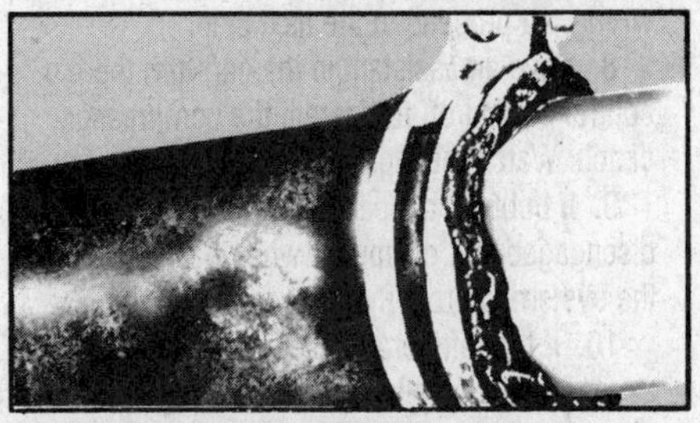

Frayed Hose End (Due to Weak Clamp)

Weakened clamps frequently are the cause of hose and cooling system failure. The connection between the pipe and hose has deteriorated enough to allow coolant to escape when the engine is hot.

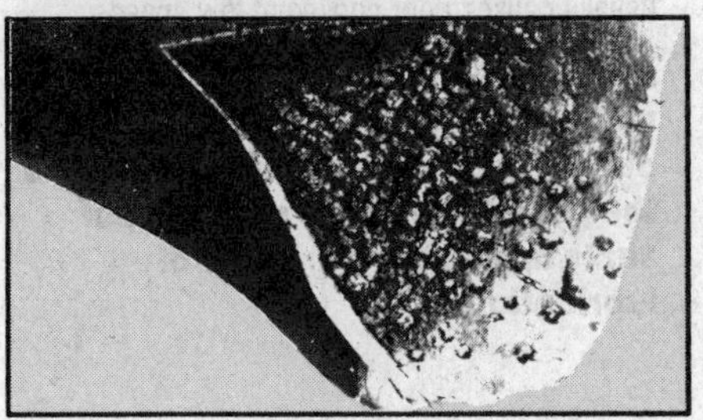

Debris in Cooling System

Debris, rust and scale in the cooling system can cause the inside of a hose to weaken. This can usually be felt on the outside of the hose as soft or thinner areas.

Hoses

REMOVAL & INSTALLATION

After engine is cold, remove the radiator cap and drain the radiator into a clean pan if you are going to reuse the old coolant. Remove the hose clamps and remove the hose by either cutting it off or twisting it to break its seal on the radiator and engine coolant inlets. When installing the new hose, do not overtighten the hose clamps or you might cut the hose or destroy the neck of the radiator. Refill the radiator with coolant, run the engine with the radiator cap on and then recheck the coolant level after engine has reached operating temperature which is about 5 minutes.

➡ It always is good idea, to replace hose clamps when replacing radiator hoses.

Air Conditioning

SAFTEY WARNINGS

Because of the importance of the necessary safety precautions that must be exercised when working with air conditioning systems and R-12 refrigerant, a recap of the safety precautions are outlined.

1. Avoid contact with a charged refrigeration system, even when working on another part of the air conditioning system or vehicle. If a heavy tool comes into contact with a section of copper tubing or a heat exchanger, it can easily cause the relatively soft material to rupture.
2. When it is necessary to apply force to a fitting which contains refrigerant, as when checking that all system couplings are securely tightened, use a wrench on both parts of the fitting involved, if possible. This will avoid putting torque on refrigerant tubing. (It is advisable, when possible, to use tube or line wrenches when tightening these flare nut fittings.)
3. Do not attempt to discharge the system by merely loosening a fitting, or removing the service valve caps and cracking these valves. Precise control is possibly only when using the service gauges. Place a rag under the open end of the center charging hose while discharging the system to catch any drops of liquid that might escape. Wear protective gloves when connecting or disconnecting service gauge hoses.
4. Discharge the system only in a well ventilated area, as high concentrations of the gas can exclude oxygen and act as an anesthesia. When leak testing or soldering, this is particularly important, as toxic gas is formed when R-12 contacts any flame.
5. Never start a system without first verifying that both service valves are backseated, if equipped, and that all fittings are throughout the system are snugly connected.
6. Avoid applying heat to any refrigerant line or storage vessel. Charging may be aided by using water heated to less than +125°F (+51°C) to warm the refrigerant container. Never allow a refrigerant storage container to sit out in the sun, or near any other source of heat, such as a radiator.
7. Always wear goggles when working on a system to protect the eyes. If refrigerant contacts the eye, it is advisable in all cases to see a physician as soon as possible.
8. Frostbite from liquid refrigerant should be treated by first gradually warming the area with cool water, and then gently applying petroleum jelly. A physician should be consulted.
9. Always keep refrigerant can fittings capped when not in use. Avoid sudden shock to the can which might occur from dropping it, or from banging a heavy tool against it. Never carry a can in the passenger compartment of a car.
10. Always completely discharge the system before painting the vehicle (if the paint is to be baked on), or before welding anywhere near the refrigerant lines.

SYSTEM INSPECTION

✲✲ CAUTION

The compressed refrigerant used in the air conditioning system expands into the atmosphere at a temperature of -2°F (-19°C) or lower. This will freeze any surface, including your eyes, that it contacts. In addition, the refrigerant decomposes into a poisonous gas in the presence of a flame. Do not open or disconnect any part of the air conditioning system.

Sight Glass Check

You can safely make a few simple checks to determine if your air conditioning system needs service. The tests work best if the temperature is warm — about 70°F (21°C).

➡ If your vehicle is equipped with an aftermarket air conditioner, the following system check may not apply. You should contact the manufacturer of the unit for instructions on systems checks.

1. Place the automatic transmission in **PARK** or the manual transaxle in **NEUTRAL**. Set the parking brake.
2. Run the engine at a fast idle (about 1,500 rpm) either with the help of a friend or by temporarily readjusting the idle speed screw.
3. Set the controls for maximum cold with the blower on High.
4. Locate the sight glass in one of the system lines. Usually it is on the left alongside the top of the radiator.
5. If you see bubbles, the system must be recharged. Very likely there is a leak at some point. If it is determined that the system has a leak, it should be corrected as soon as possible. Leaks may allow moisture to enter and cause a very expensive rust problem.
6. If there are no bubbles, there is either no refrigerant at all or the system is fully charged. Feel the 2 hoses going to the belt-driven compressor. If they are both at the same temperature, the system is empty and must be recharged.
7. If one hose (high-pressure) is warm and the other (low-pressure) is cold, the system may be all right. However, you are probably making these tests because you think there is something wrong, so proceed to the next step.
8. Have an assistant in the car, turn the fan control on and off to operate the compressor clutch. Watch the sight glass.
9. If bubbles appear when the clutch is disengaged and disappear when it is engaged, the system is properly charged.
10. If the refrigerant takes more than 45 seconds to bubble when the clutch is disengaged, the system is overcharged. This usually causes poor cooling at low speeds.

➡ Run the air conditioner for a few minutes, every 2 weeks or so, during the cold months. This avoids the possibility of the compressor seals drying out from lack of lubrication.

GAUGE SETS

Most of the service work performed in air conditioning requires the use of a set of 2 gauges, one for the high (head) pressure side of the system, the other for the low (suction) side.

The low side gauge records both pressure and vacuum. Vacuum readings are calibrated from 0 to 30 inches Hg and the pressure graduations read from 0 to no less than 60 psi.

The high side gauge measures pressure from 0 to at last 600 psi.

Both gauges are threaded into a manifold that contains two hand shut-off valves. Proper manipulation of these valves and the use of the attached test hoses allow the user to perform the following services:

1. Test high and low side pressures.
2. Remove air, moisture, and contaminated refrigerant.
3. Purge the system (of refrigerant).
4. Charge the system (with refrigerant).

The manifold valves are designed so that they have no direct effect on gauge readings, but serve only to provide for, or cut off, flow of refrigerant through the manifold. During all testing and hook-up operations, the valves are kept in a close position to avoid disturbing the refrigeration system. The valves are opened only to purge the system or refrigerant or to charge it.

DISCHARGING THE SYSTEM

R-12 refrigerant is a chlorofluorocarbon which, when released into the atmosphere, can contribute to the depletion of the ozone layer in the upper atmosphere. Ozone filters out harmful radiation from the sun. If possible, an approved R-12 Recovery/Recycling machine that meets SAE standards should be employed when discharging the system. Follow the operating instructions provided with the approved equipment exactly to properly discharge the system.

1. Close the high and low pressure valves of the manifold gauge fully.
2. Connect the 2 charging hoses of the manifold gauge to their respective service valves.
3. Open both manifold gauge valves and discharge the refrigerant from the system.

➡ Do not allow the refrigerant to rush out. Otherwise, compressor oil will be discharged along with the refrigerant.

EVACUATING THE SYSTEM

This procedure requires the use of a vacuum pump.

➡ An old refrigerator compressor (that works) can be an inexpensive alternative for a vacuum pump. Remove the compressor from the refrigerator and soldier a brass fitting that is the same size as the A/C system fittings to the suction pipe. The compressor oil will be lost if the vacuum pump is turned on without the manifold gauges hooked to the vacuum pump and the vehicle. A slight amount of refrigerant oil will be expelled from the discharge pipe of the vacuum pump. Before every use, squirt a few drops of refrigerant oil into the suction side of the vacuum pump.

1. Connect the manifold gauge set.
2. Discharge the system.
3. Connect the center service hose to the inlet fitting of the vacuum pump.
4. Turn both gauge set valves to the wide open position.
5. Start the pump and note the low side gauge reading.
6. Operate the pump for a minimum of 30 minutes after the lowest observed gauge reading.
7. Leak test the system. Close both gauge set valves. Turn off the pump and note the low side gauge reading. The needle should remain stationary at the point at which the pump was turned off. If the needle drops to 0 rapidly, there is a leak in the system which must be repaired.
8. If the needle remains stationary for 3 to 5 minutes, open the gauge set valves and run the pump for at least 30 minutes more.
9. Close both gauge set valves, stop the pump and disconnect the gauge set. The system is now ready for charging.

CHARGING THE SYSTEM

➧ SEE FIGS. 33–38, 75–79

1. Close (clockwise) both gauge set valves.
2. Connect the gauge set.
3. Connect the center hose to the refrigerant can opener valve.
4. Make sure the can opener valve is closed, that is, the needle is raised, and connect the valve to the can. Open the valve, puncturing the can with the needle.
5. Loosen the center hose fitting at the pressure gauge, allowing refrigerant to purge the hose of air.
6. Open the low side gauge set valve and the can valve.

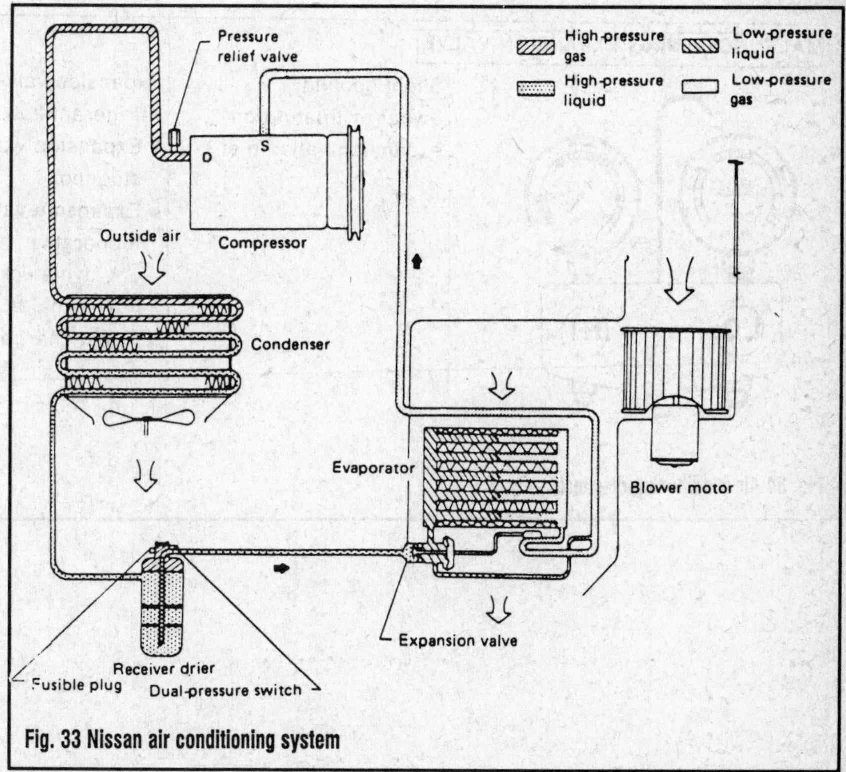
Pressure relief valve
High-pressure gas
Low-pressure liquid
High-pressure liquid
Low-pressure gas
S
D
Outside air
Compressor
Condenser
Evaporator
Blower motor
Expansion valve
Receiver drier
Fusible plug
Dual-pressure switch

Fig. 33 Nissan air conditioning system

Condition	Probable cause	Corrective action
INSUFFICIENT REFRIGERANT CHARGE 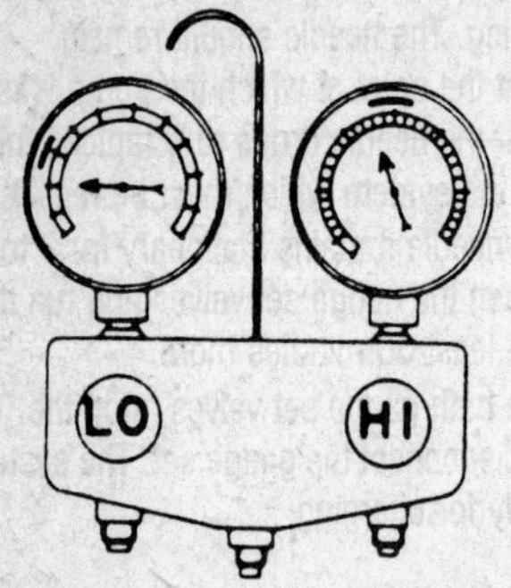 Insufficient cooling. Bubbles appear in sight glass.	Refrigerant is low, or leaking slightly.	1. Leak test. 2. Repair leak. 3. Charge system. **Evacuate, as necessary, and recharge system.**
ALMOST NO REFRIGERANT 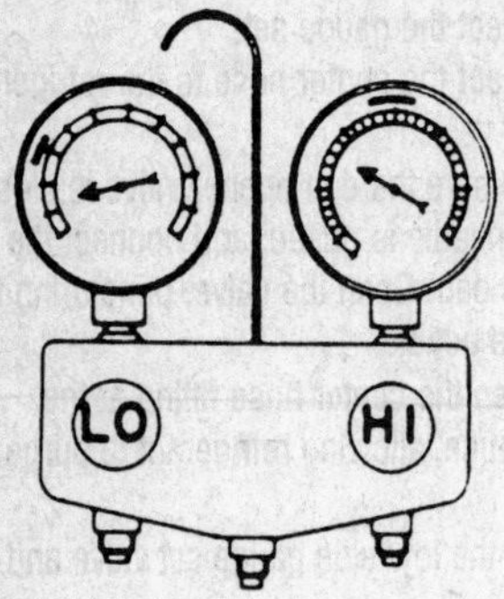 No cooling action. A lot of bubbles or something like mist appears in sight glass.	Serious refrigerant leak.	**Stop compressor immediately.** 1. Leak test. 2. Discharge system. 3. Repair leak(s). 4. Replace receiver drier if necessary. 5. Check oil level. 6. Evacuate and recharge system.
MALFUNCTIONING EXPANSION VALVE 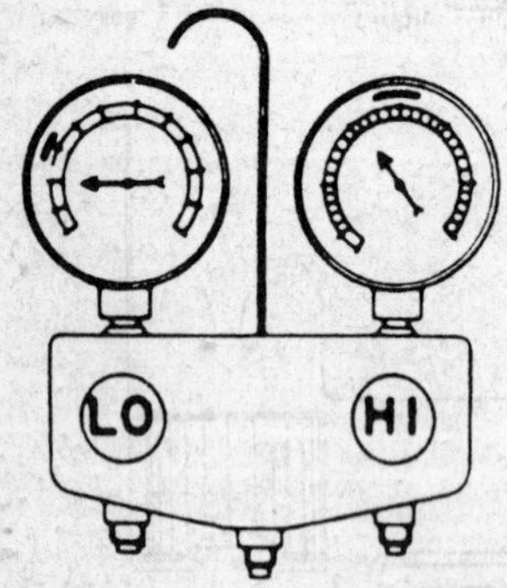 Slight cooling. Sweat or frosting on expansion valve inlet.	Expansion valve restricts refrigerant flow. • Expansion valve is clogged. • Expansion valve is inoperative. Valve stuck closed. Thermal bulb has lost charge.	If valve inlet reveals sweat or frost: 1. Discharge system. 2. Remove valve and clean it. Replace it if necessary. 3. Evacuate system. 4. Charge system. If valve does not operate: 1. Discharge system. 2. Replace valve. 3. Evacuate and charge system.

Fig. 34 Air conditioning diagnosis — part 1

Condition	Probable cause	Corrective action
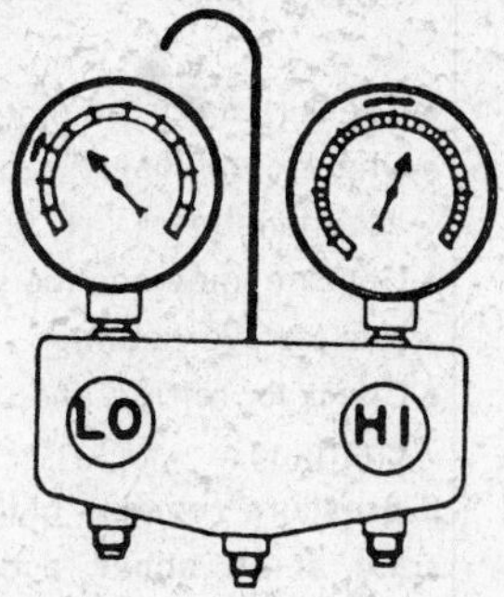 Insufficient cooling. Sweat on suction line.	Expansion valve allows too much refrigerant through evaporator.	Check valve for operation. If suction side does not show a pressure decrease, replace valve.
 No cooling. Sweat or frosting on suction line.	Malfunctioning expansion valve.	1. Discharge system. 2. Replace valve. 3. Evacuate and charge system.
AIR IN SYSTEM		
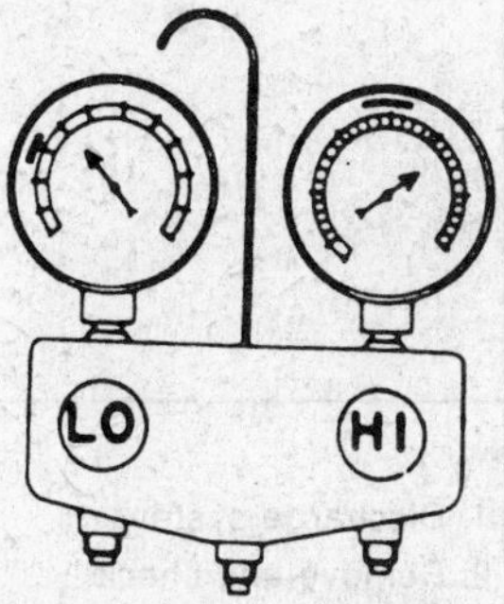 Insufficient cooling. Sight glass shows occasional bubbles.	Air mixed with refrigerant in system.	1. Discharge system. 2. Replace receiver drier. 3. Evacuate and charge system.
MOISTURE IN SYSTEM		
 After short operation, suction side may show vacuum pressure reading. During this condition, discharge air will be warm. As a warning of this, reading vibrates around 39 kPa (0.4 kg/cm^2. 6 psi).	Drier is saturated with moisture. Moisture has frozen in expansion valve. Refrigerant flow is restricted.	1. Discharge system. 2. Replace receiver drier (twice if necessary). 3. Evacuate system completely. (Repeat 30-minutes evacuating three times.) 4. Recharge system.

Fig. 35 Air conditioning diagnosis — part 2

Condition		Probable cause	Corrective action
MALFUNCTIONING CONDENSER 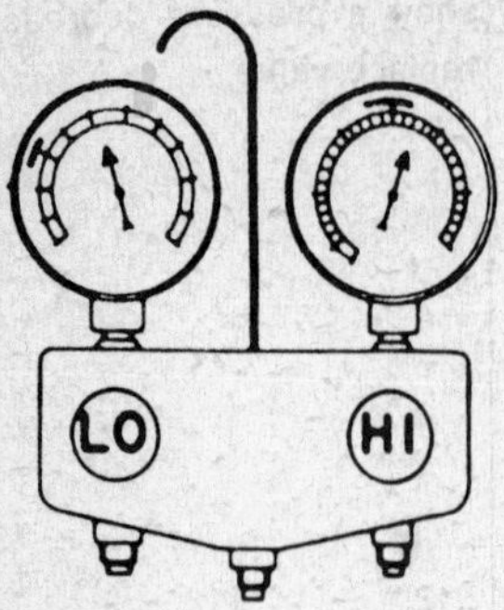	No cooling action: engine may overheat. Bubbles appear in sight glass of drier. Suction line is very hot.	Usually a malfunctioning condenser.	• Check radiator fan motors. • Check condenser for dirt accumulation. • Check engine cooling system for overheating. • Check for refrigerant overcharging. **If pressure remains high in spite of all above actions taken, remove and inspect the condenser for possible oil clogging.**
HIGH PRESSURE LINE BLOCKED 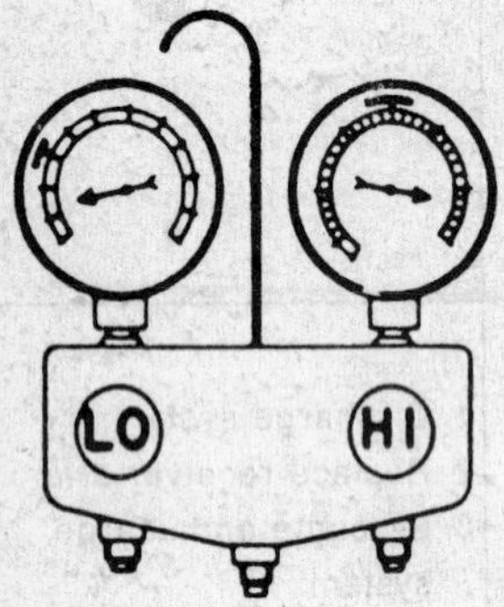	Insufficient cooling. Frosted high pressure liquid line.	Drier clogged, or restriction in high pressure line.	1. Discharge system. 2. Remove receiver drier or strainer and replace it. 3. Evacuate and charge system.
MALFUNCTIONING COMPRESSOR 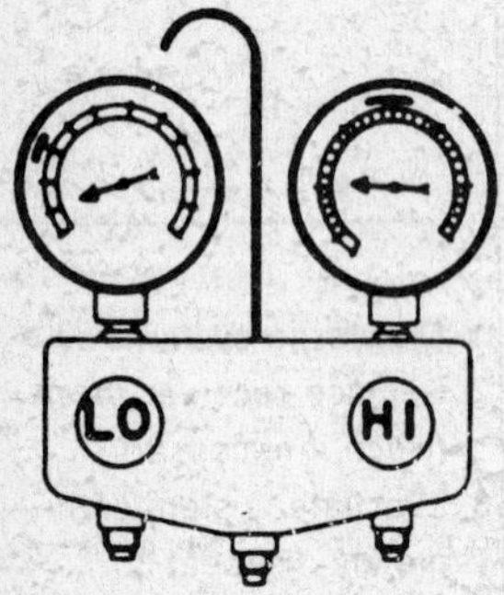	Insufficient cooling.	Internal problem in compressor, or damaged gasket and valve.	1. Discharge system. 2. Remove and check compressor. 3. Repair or replace compressor. 4. Check oil level. 5. Replace receiver drier. 6. Evacuate and charge system.

Fig. 36 Air conditioning diagnosis — part 3

Condition		Probable cause	Corrective action
TOO MUCH OIL IN SYSTEM (Excessive)			
	Insufficient cooling.	Too much oil circulates with refrigerant, causing the cooling capacity of the system to be reduced.	Refer to COMPRESSOR OIL for correcting oil level.

Fig. 37 Air conditioning diagnosis — part 4

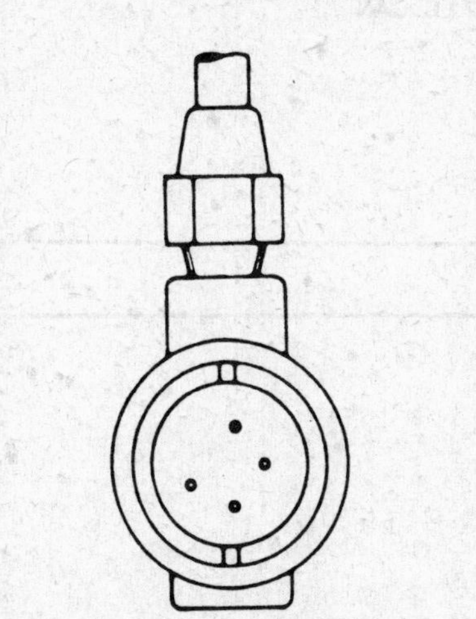

Fig. 38 Air conditioning sight glass. Here is how the sight glass will look if there are just a few bubbles

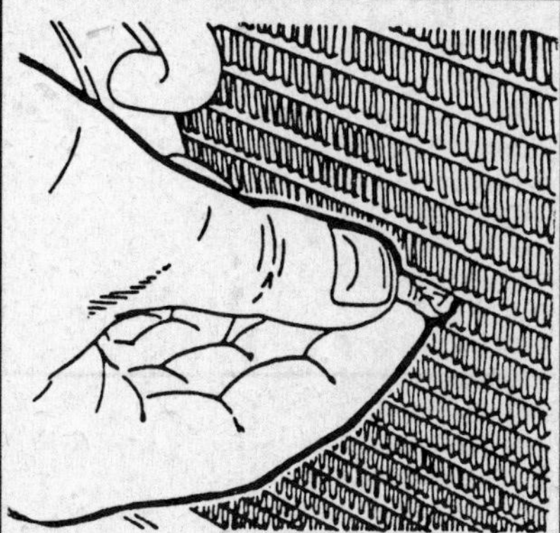

Fig. 75 Clean the radiator and condenser fins of debris

7. Start the engine and turn the air conditioner to the maximum cooling mode. The compressor will operate and pull refrigerant gas into the system.

➡ To help speed the process, the can may be placed, upright, in a pan of warm water, not exceeding +125°F (+51°C).

8. If more than one can of refrigerant is needed, close the can valve and gauge set low side valve when the can is empty and connect a new can to the opener. Repeat the charging process until the sight glass indicates a full charge.
9. When the charging process has been completed, close the gauge set valve and can valve. Run the system for at least 5 minutes to allow it to normalize.
10. Loosen both service hoses at the gauges to allow any refrigerant to escape. Remove the gauge set and install the dust caps on the service valves.

➡ Multi-can dispensers are available which allow a simultaneous hook-up of up to four 1 lb. (454 g) cans of R-12.

⁂ CAUTION

Never exceed the recommended maximum charge for the system!

The maximum R-12 charge for the A/C system is as follows. Remember that most 1 pound R-12 cans are either 12 or 14 ozs. (340 or 397 g)

- 1982–86 Sentra and Pulsar — 1.80–2.20 lbs. (0.8–1.0 kg)
- 1987 Sentra — 2.00–2.40 lbs. (0.9–1.1 kg)
- 1987–89 Pulsar — 1.87–2.09 lbs. (0.85–0.95 kg)
- 1988–90 Sentra — 1.87–2.09 lbs. (0.85–0.95 kg)
- 1991–92 Sentra NX — 1.43–1.65 lbs. (0.65–0.75 kg)

LEAK TESTING

Checking the A/C system for leaks can be a difficult procedure because of the engine compartment congestion. The recommended method is the use of an approved electronic refrigerant leak detector.

1. A R-12 charge of at least a half pound is needed for leak testing. Check all fitting connections and the front of the compressor for wetness and oil. A slight amount of oil in front of the compressor is normal
2. Apply some soapy water to the fittings in the engine compartment. Check for bubbles from the fittings.
3. If white smoke comes out of the A/C vents, this may indicate a leak in the evaporator or fittings inside the evaporator housing.

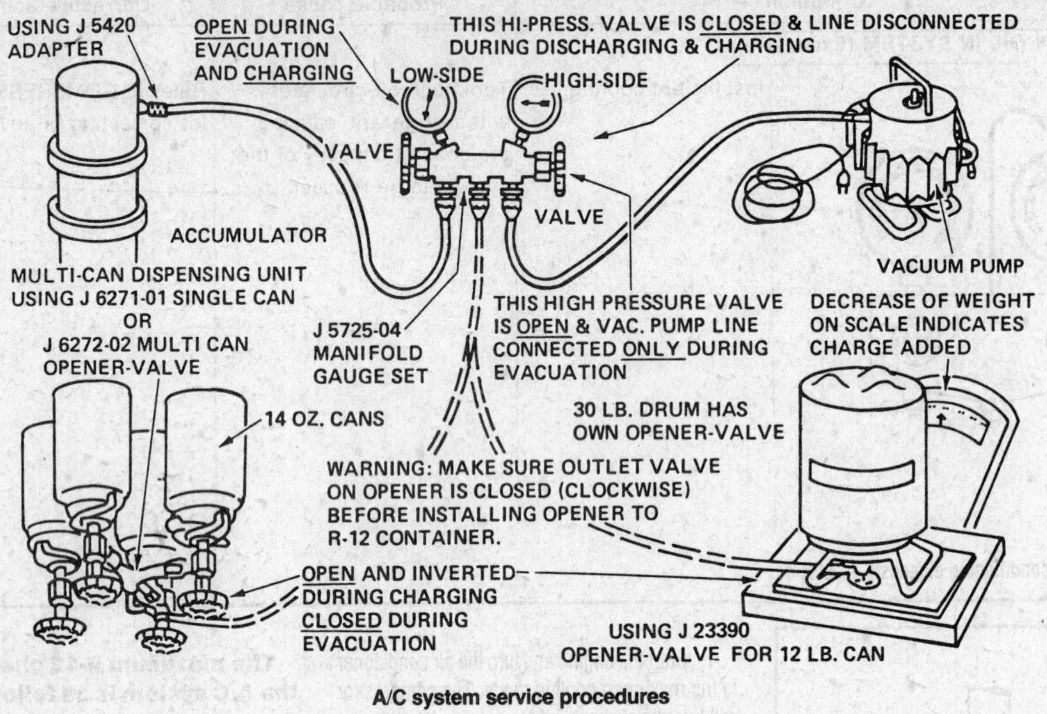

USING J 5420 ADAPTER
OPEN DURING EVACUATION AND CHARGING
THIS HI-PRESS. VALVE IS CLOSED & LINE DISCONNECTED DURING DISCHARGING & CHARGING
LOW-SIDE
HIGH-SIDE
VALVE
VALVE
ACCUMULATOR
VACUUM PUMP
MULTI-CAN DISPENSING UNIT USING J 6271-01 SINGLE CAN OR J 6272-02 MULTI CAN OPENER-VALVE
J 5725-04 MANIFOLD GAUGE SET
THIS HIGH PRESSURE VALVE IS OPEN & VAC. PUMP LINE CONNECTED ONLY DURING EVACUATION
DECREASE OF WEIGHT ON SCALE INDICATES CHARGE ADDED
14 OZ. CANS
30 LB. DRUM HAS OWN OPENER-VALVE
WARNING: MAKE SURE OUTLET VALVE ON OPENER IS CLOSED (CLOCKWISE) BEFORE INSTALLING OPENER TO R-12 CONTAINER.
OPEN AND INVERTED DURING CHARGING CLOSED DURING EVACUATION
USING J 23390 OPENER-VALVE FOR 12 LB. CAN

A/C system service procedures

Fig. 76 A/C system service procedures

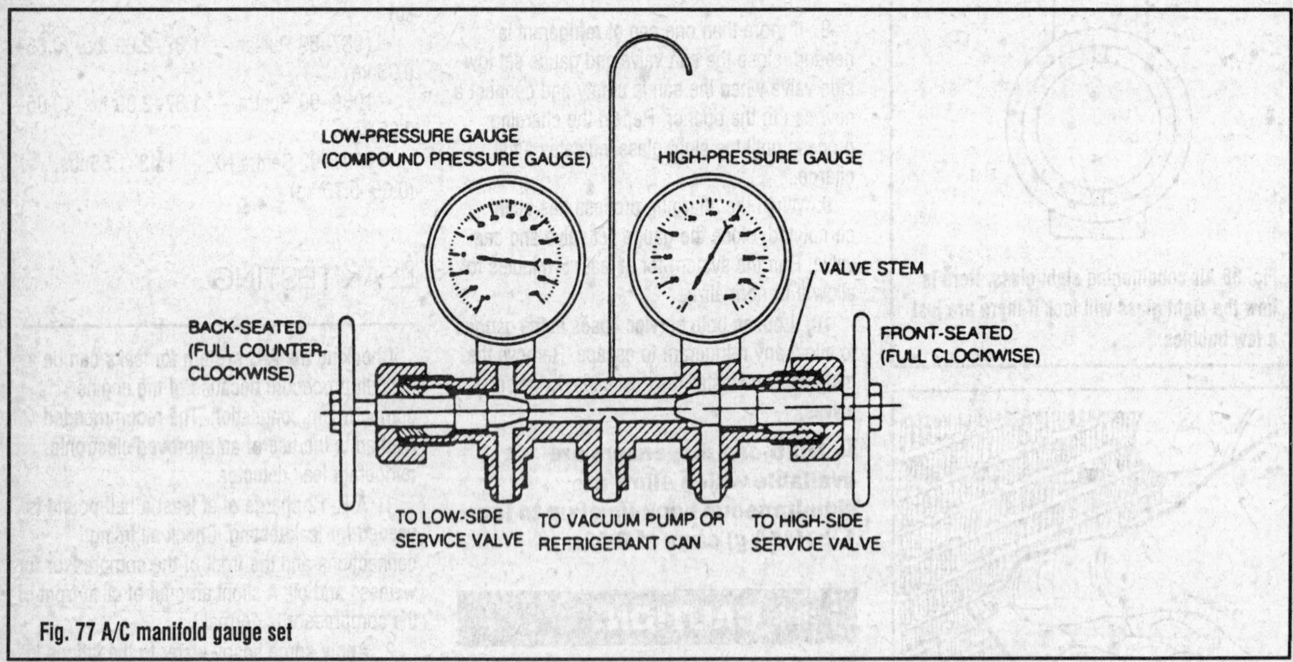
LOW-PRESSURE GAUGE
(COMPOUND PRESSURE GAUGE)
HIGH-PRESSURE GAUGE
VALVE STEM
BACK-SEATED
(FULL COUNTER-
CLOCKWISE)
FRONT-SEATED
(FULL CLOCKWISE)
TO LOW-SIDE
SERVICE VALVE
TO VACUUM PUMP OR
REFRIGERANT CAN
TO HIGH-SIDE
SERVICE VALVE

Fig. 77 A/C manifold gauge set

RELATIVE HUMIDITY (%)	AMBIENT AIR TEMP °F	AMBIENT AIR TEMP °C	LOW SIDE kPa	LOW SIDE PSIG	ENGINE SPEED (rpm)	CENTER DUCT AIR TEMPERATURE °F	CENTER DUCT AIR TEMPERATURE °C	HIGH SIDE kPa	HIGH SIDE PSIG
20	70	21	200	29	2000	40	4	1034	150
	80	27	200	29		44	7	1310	190
	90	32	207	30		48	9	1689	245
	100	38	214	31		57	14	2103	305
30	70	21	200	29	2000	42	6	1034	150
	80	27	207	30		47	8	1413	205
	90	32	214	31		51	11	1827	265
	100	38	221	32		61	16	2241	325
40	70	21	200	29	2000	45	7	1138	165
	80	27	207	30		49	9	1482	215
	90	32	221	32		55	13	1931	280
	100	38	269	39		65	18	2379	345
50	70	21	207	30	2000	47	8	1241	180
	80	27	221	32		53	12	1620	235
	90	32	234	34		59	15	2034	295
	100	38	276	40		69	21	2413	350
60	70	21	207	30	2000	48	9	1241	180
	80	27	228	33		56	13	1655	240
	90	32	249	36		63	17	2069	300
	100	38	296	43		73	23	2482	360
70	70	21	207	30	2000	50	10	1276	185
	80	27	234	34		58	14	1689	245
	90	32	262	38		65	18	2103	305
	100	38	303	44		75	24	2517	365
80	70	21	207	30	2000	50	10	1310	190
	80	27	234	34		59	15	1724	250
	90	32	269	39		67	19	2137	310
90	70	21	207	30	2000	50	10	1379	200
	80	27	249	36		62	17	1827	265
	90	32	290	42		71	22	2275	330

Fig. 78 A/C performance test chart

Check item / Amount of refrigerant	Almost no refrigerant	Insufficient	Suitable	Too much refrigerant
Temperature of high pressure and low pressure lines.	Almost no difference between high pressure and low pressure side temperature.	High pressure side is warm and low pressure side is fairly cold.	High pressure side is hot and low pressure side is cold.	High pressure side is abnormally hot.
State in sight glass	Bubbles flow continuously. Bubbles will disappear and something like mist will flow when refrigerant is nearly gone.	The bubbles are seen at intervals of 1 - 2 seconds.	Almost transparent. Bubbles may appear when engine speed is raised and lowered. No clear difference exists betwen these two conditions.	No bubbles can be seen.
Pressure of system.	High pressure side is abnormally low.	Both pressure on high and low pressure sides are slightly low.	Both pressures on high and low pressure sides are normal.	Both pressures on high and low pressure sides are abnormally high.
Repair.	Stop compressor immediately and conduct an overall check.	Check for gas leakage, repair as required, replenish and charge system.		Discharge refrigerant from service valve of low pressure side.

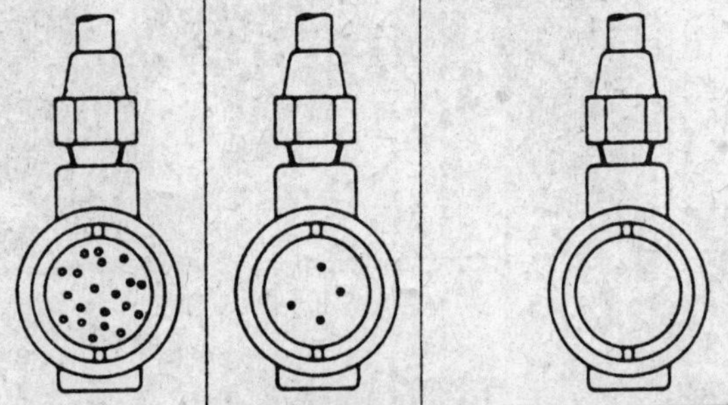

Fig. 79 Using a sight glass to determine the relative refrigerant charge

Fig 79a. A/C high and low gauge ports—1991-92 Sentra shown, others similar

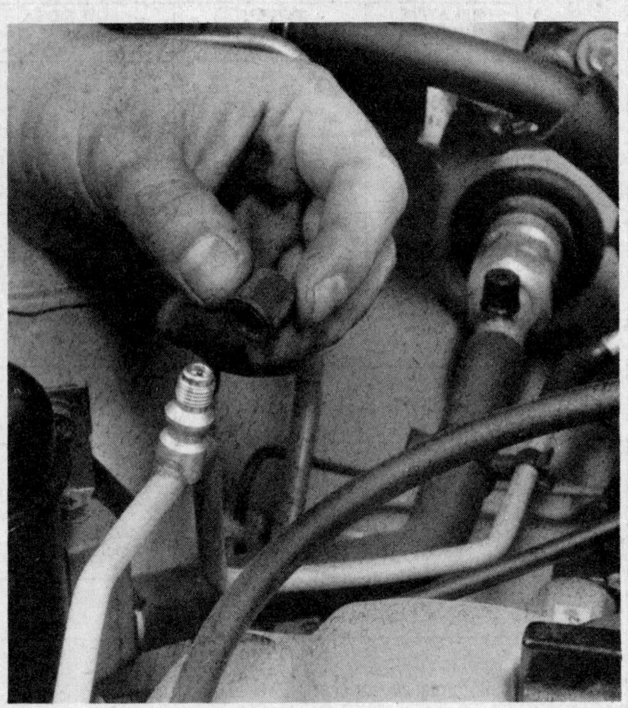

Fig 79b. A/C high side gauge port—1991-92 Sentra

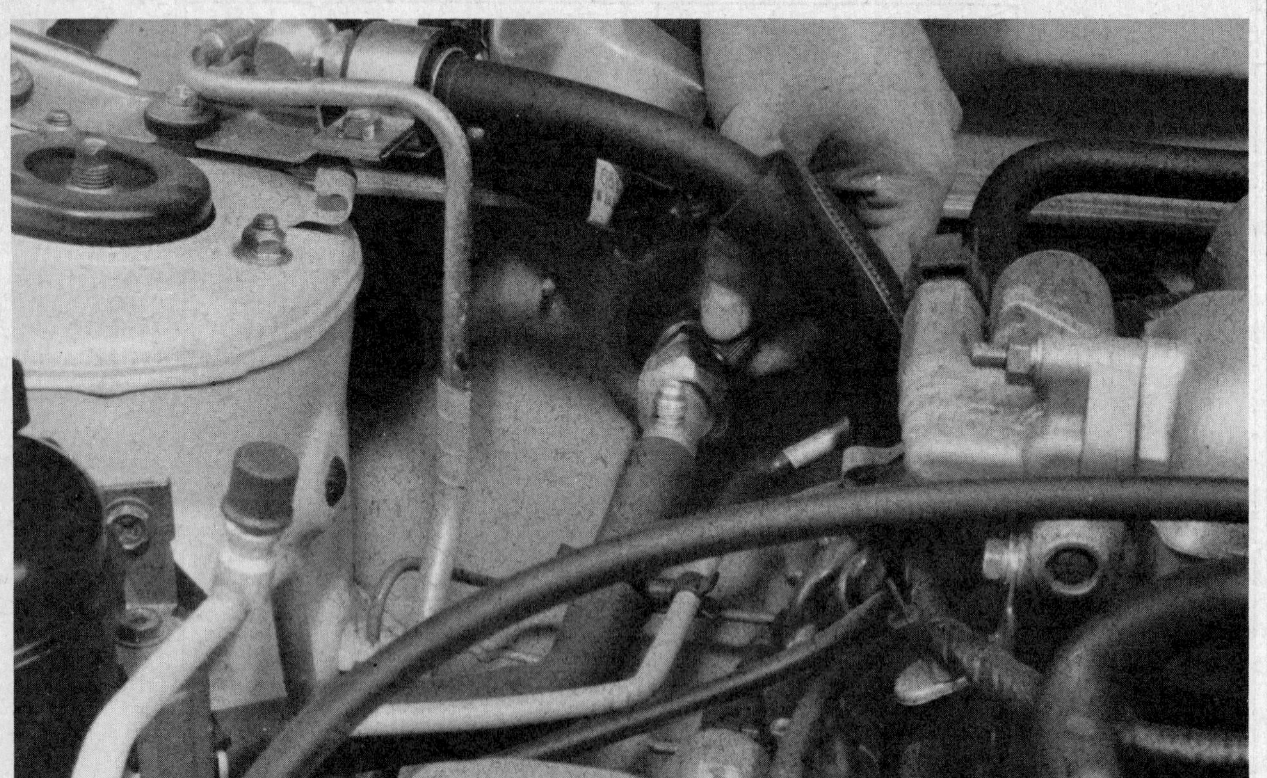

Fig 79c. A/C low side gauge port—1991-92 Sentra

4. Coat the compressor with a soap solution and check for bubbles around the compressor housing halves and fittings.

5. Check all rubber hoses for cracks and deterioration. A hose that looks OK, may be deteriorated and leaking slowly.

6. Check for a damaged condenser.

Windshield Wipers

For maximum effectiveness and longest element life, the windshield and wiper blades should be kept clean. Dirt, tree sap, road tar and so on will cause streaking, smearing and blade deterioration if left on the windshield. It is advisable to wash the windshield carefully with a commercial glass cleaner at least once a month. Wipe off the rubber blades with a wet rag afterwards. Do not attempt to move the wipers back and forth by hand; damage to the motor and drive mechanism will result.

If the blades are found to be cracked, broken or torn they should be replaced immediately. Replacement intervals will vary with usage, although ozone deterioration usually limits blade life to about 1 year. If the wiper pattern is smeared or streaked, or if the blade chatters across the glass, the blades should be replaced. It is easiest and most sensible to replace them in pairs.

There are basically 3 different types of wiper blade refills, which differ in their method of replacement. One type has 2 release buttons, approximately 1/3 of the way up from the ends of the blade frame. Pushing the buttons down releases a lock and allows the rubber blade to be removed from the frame. The new blade slides back into the frame and locks in place.

The second type of refill has 2 metal tabs which are unlocked by squeezing them together. The rubber blade can then be withdrawn from the frame jaws. A new one is installed by inserting it into the front frame jaws and sliding it rearward to engage the remaining frame jaws. There are usually 4 jaws; be certain when installing that the refill is engaged in all of them. At the end of its travel, the tabs will lock into place on the front jaws of the wiper blade frame.

The third type is a refill made from polycarbonate. The refill has a simple locking device at one end which flexes downward out of the groove into which the jaws of the holder fit, allowing easy release. By sliding the new refill through all the jaws and pushing through the slight resistance when it reaches the end of its travel, the refill will lock into position.

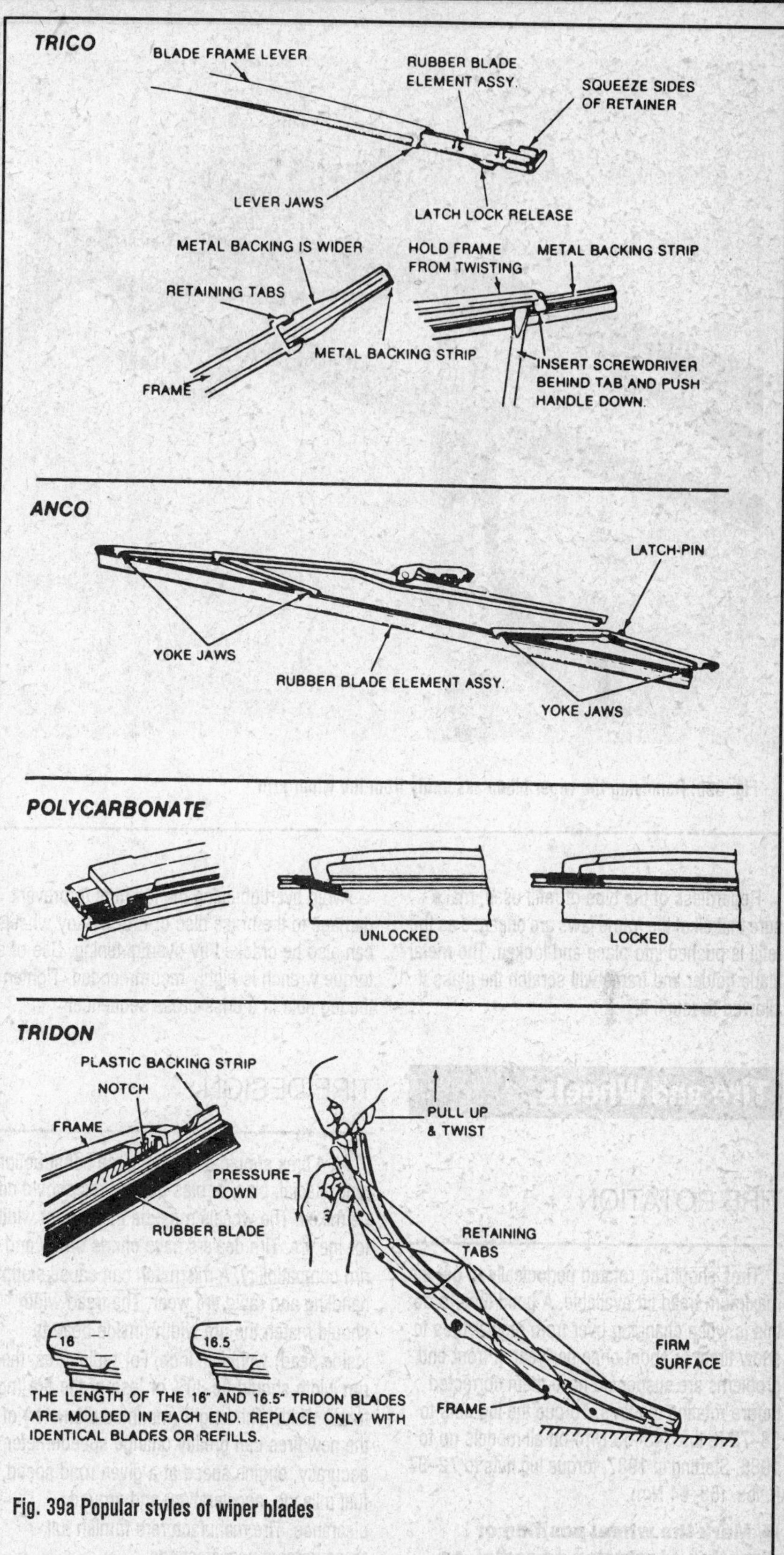
TRICO
BLADE FRAME LEVER
RUBBER BLADE ELEMENT ASSY.
SQUEEZE SIDES OF RETAINER
LEVER JAWS
LATCH LOCK RELEASE
METAL BACKING IS WIDER
HOLD FRAME FROM TWISTING
METAL BACKING STRIP
RETAINING TABS
METAL BACKING STRIP
INSERT SCREWDRIVER BEHIND TAB AND PUSH HANDLE DOWN.
FRAME
ANCO
LATCH-PIN
YOKE JAWS
RUBBER BLADE ELEMENT ASSY.
YOKE JAWS
POLYCARBONATE
UNLOCKED
LOCKED
TRIDON
PLASTIC BACKING STRIP
NOTCH
FRAME
PRESSURE DOWN
RUBBER BLADE
PULL UP & TWIST
RETAINING TABS
16
16.5
FIRM SURFACE
FRAME
THE LENGTH OF THE 16" AND 16.5" TRIDON BLADES ARE MOLDED IN EACH END. REPLACE ONLY WITH IDENTICAL BLADES OR REFILLS.
Fig. 39a Popular styles of wiper blades

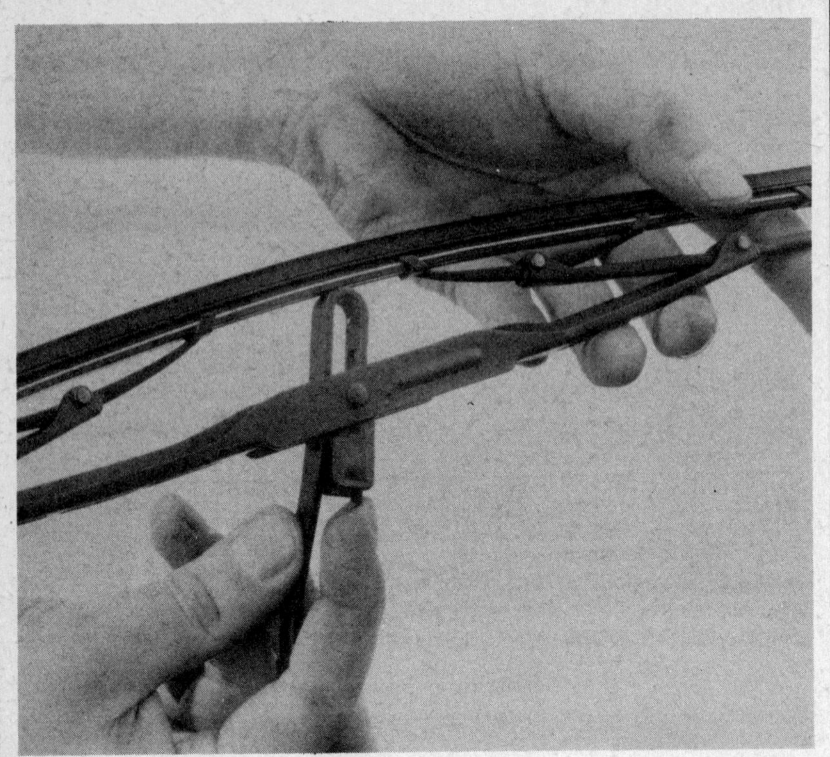

Fig. 39b. Removing the wiper blade assembly from the wiper arm

Regardless of the type of refill used, make sure that all of the frame jaws are engaged as the refill is pushed into place and locked. The metal blade holder and frame will scratch the glass if allowed to touch it.

Tire and Wheels

TIRE ROTATION

Tires should be rotated periodically to get the maximum tread lift available. A good time to do this is when changing over from regular tires to snow tires, or about once per year. If front end problems are suspected have them corrected before rotating the tires. Torque the lug nuts to 58–72 ft. lbs. (43–53 Nm) on all models up to 1986. Starting in 1987, torque lug nuts to 72–87 ft. lbs. (53–64 Nm).

➡ **Mark the wheel position or direction of rotation on radial, or studded snow tires before removing them.**

Avoid overtightening the lug nuts to prevent damage to the brake disc or drum. Alloy wheels can also be cracked by overtightening. Use of a torque wrench is highly recommended. Tighten the lug nuts in a criss-cross sequence.

TIRE DESIGN

All 4 tires should be of the same construction type. Radial, bias, or bias-belted tires should not be mixed. The wheels must be the correct width for the tire. Tire dealers have charts of tire and rim compatibility. A mismatch can cause sloppy handling and rapid tire wear. The tread width should match the rim width (inside bead to inside bead) within an inch. For radial tires, the rim width should be 80% or less of the tire (not tread) width. The height (mounted diameter) of the new tires can greatly change speedometer accuracy, engine speed at a given road speed, fuel mileage, acceleration, and ground clearance. Tire manufacturers furnish full measurement specifications.

TIRE INFLATION

The tires should be checked frequently for proper air pressure. Make sure that the tires are cool, as you will get a false reading when the tires are heated because air pressure increases with temperature. A chart in the glove compartment or on the driver's door pillar gives the recommended inflation pressure. Maximum fuel economy and tire life will result if pressure is maintained at the highest figure given on chart. When checking pressures, do not neglect the spare tire. The tires should be checked before driving since pressure can increase as much as 6 psi (41.4 kpa) due to heat buildup.

➡ **Some spare tires require pressures considerably higher than those used in other tires.**

While you are checking the tire pressure, take a look at the tread. The tread should be wearing evenly across the tire. Excessive wear in the center of the tread could indicate over-inflation. Excessive wear on the outer edges could indicate under inflation. An irregular wear pattern is usually a sign of incorrect front wheel alignment or wheel balance. A front end that is out of alignment will usually pull the car to one side of a flat road when the steering wheel is released. Incorrect wheel balance will produce vibration in the steering wheel, while unbalanced rear wheels will result in floor or trunk vibration.

It is a good idea to have your own accurate gauge, and to check pressures weekly. Not all gauges on service station air pumps can be trusted.

Tires should be replaced when a tread wear indicator appears as a solid band across the tread.

CARE OF SPECIAL WHEELS

Normal appearance maintenance of aluminum wheels includes frequent washing and waxing. However, you **must be careful to avoid the use of abrasive cleaners**. Failure to heed this warning will cause the protective coating to be damaged.

The special coating may be abraded by repeated washing of the car in an automatic car wash using certain types of brushes. Once the finish abrades, it will provide less protection and normal exposure to either caustic cleaners or road salt will cause the process to continue. If the wheel reaches the point where it requires refinishing, it must be specially prepared and then coated with an enamel clearcoat. This is an extremely lengthy process and every step must be performed in precisely the right way. Special protective gear must be worn to protect the person performing the refinishing operation from the solvents in the cleaners and coatings. We therefore suggest that you have a professional paint shop perform the work for best and safest results.

Aluminum wheels should be cleaned and waxed regularly. Do not use abrasive

cleaners, as they could damage the protective coating. Inspect wheel rims regularly for dents or corrosion, which may cause loss of pressure, damage the tire bead, or sudden wheel failure.

FLUIDS AND LUBRICANTS

Fuel Recommendations

All engines covered in this book have been designed to run on unleaded fuel. The minimum octane requirement for non-turbo and high performance engines is 91 RON (Research Octane Number) or 87 AKI (Anti-Knock Index). Turbo and high performance engine require an octane of 93 RON. All unleaded fuels sold in the U.S. are required to meet minimum octane ratings.

The use of a fuel too low in octane (a measurement of anti-knock quality) will result in spark knock. Since many factors such as altitude, terrain, air temperature and humidity affect the operating efficiency, knocking may result even though the recommended fuel is being used. If persistent knocking occurs, it may be necessary to switch to a higher grade of fuel. Continuous or heavy knocking may result in engine damage.

➡ Your engine's fuel requirement can change with time, mainly due to carbon buildup, which will in turn change the compression ratio. If your engine pings, knocks or runs on, switch to a higher grade of fuel. Sometimes just changing brands will cure the problem. If it becomes necessary to retard the timing from the specifications, don't change it more than a few degrees. Retarded timing will reduce power output and fuel mileage, in addition to increasing the engine temperature.

Engine Oil Recommendations

Oil must be selected with regard to the anticipated temperatures during the period before the next oil change. Using the chart, select the oil viscosity for the lowest expected temperature and you will be assured of easy cold starting and sufficient engine protection. The oil you pour into your engine should have the designation **SG** marked on the top of its container. Cheap engine oil is cheap engine protection. Is a few cents worth the engine in your vehicle?

SYNTHETIC OIL

There are many excellent synthetic and fuel-efficient oils currently available that can provide better gas mileage, longer service life, and in some cases better engine protection. These benefits do not come without a few hitches, however the main one being the price of synthetic oils, which is 3 or 4 times the price per quart of conventional oil.

Synthetic oil is not for every car and every type of driving, so you should consider your engine's condition and your type of driving. Also, check your car's warranty guidelines at the dealership that you purchased the car from, regarding the use of synthetic oils and your powertrain and or extended warranty.

Both brand new engines and older, high mileage engines are the wrong candidates for synthetic oil. The synthetic oils are so slippery that they can prevent the proper break-in of new engines; most manufacturers recommend that you wait until the engine is properly broken in (5,000 miles) until using synthetic oil. Older engines with wear have a different problem with synthetics: they use (consume during operation) more oil as they age. Slippery synthetic oils get past these worn parts easily. If your engine is using conventional oil, it will use synthetics much faster. Also, if your car is leaking oil past old seals you'll have a much greater leak problem with synthetics.

Cars used under harder circumstances, such as stop-and-go, city type driving, short trips, or extended idling, should be serviced more frequently. For the engines in these cars, the much greater cost of synthetic or fuel-efficient oils may not be worth the investment. Internal wear increases much quicker on these cars, causing greater oil consumption and leakage.

➡ The mixing of conventional and synthetic oils is not recommended. If you are using synthetic oil, it might be wise to carry 2 or 3 quarts with you no matter where you drive, as not all service stations carry this type of lubricant.

OIL LEVEL CHECK

The best time to check the engine oil is before operating the engine or after it has been sitting for at least 10 minutes in order to gain an accurate reading. This will allow the oil to drain back in the crankcase. To check the engine oil level, make sure that the vehicle is resting on a level surface, remove the oil dipstick, wipe it clean and reinsert the stick firmly for an accurate reading. The oil dipstick has two marks to indicate high and low oil level. If the oil is at or below the **low level** mark on the dipstick, oil should be added as necessary. The oil level should be maintained in the safety margin, neither going above the **high level** mark or below the **low level** mark.

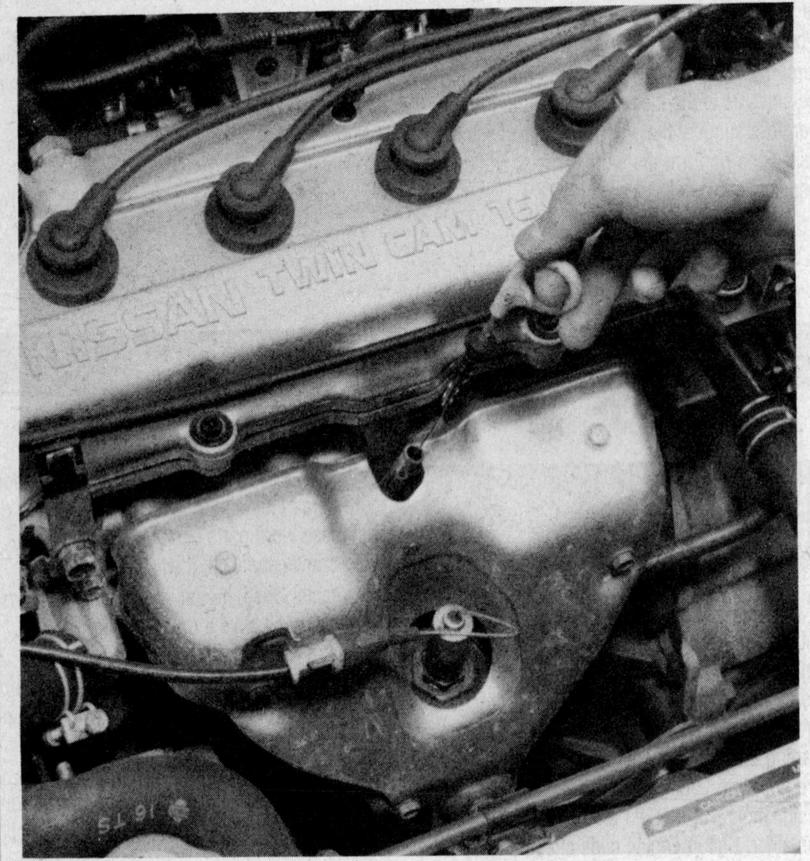
Fig. 40a. Check the engine oil level with the dipstick—1991-92 Sentra with a GA16DE engine

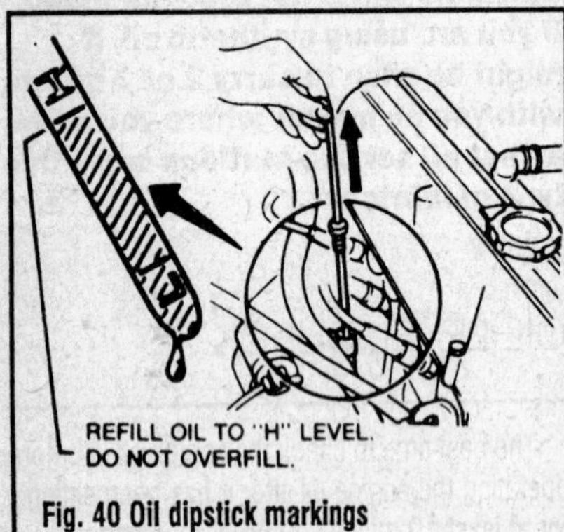
REFILL OIL TO "H" LEVEL.
DO NOT OVERFILL.
Fig. 40 Oil dipstick markings

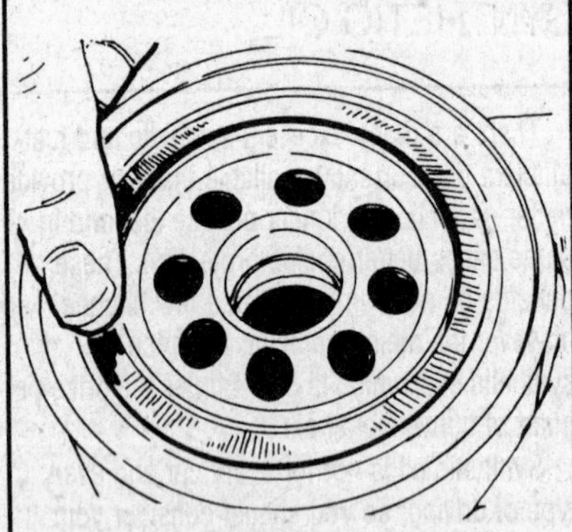
Fig. 42 Apply a light coat of oil to the filter gasket before installation

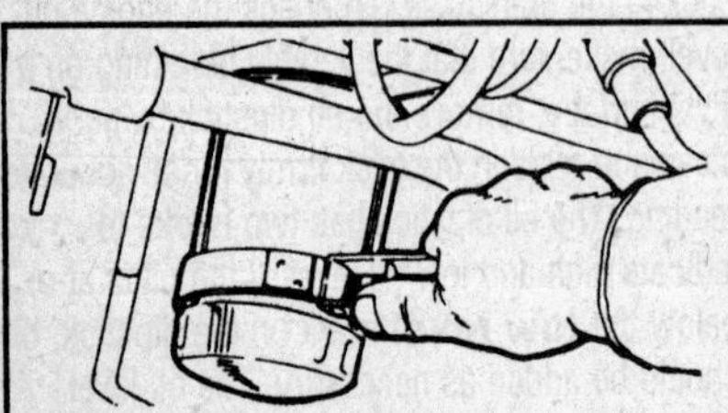
Fig. 41 Removing the oil filter with a strap wrench

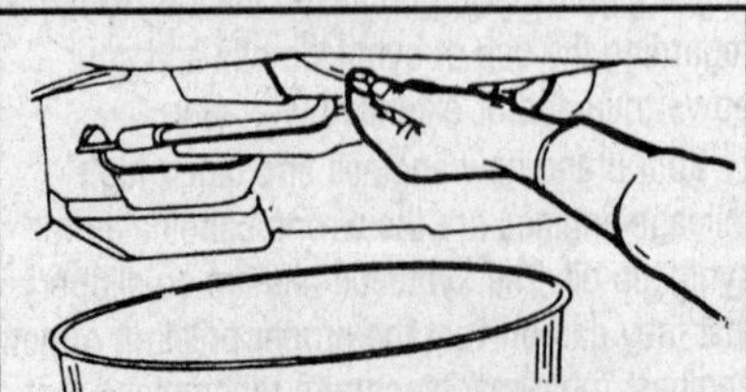
Fig. 43 By keeping inward pressure on the plug while unscrewing the filter, oil will not escape past the threads

OIL AND FILTER CHANGE

➡ **Datsun/Nissan factory maintenance intervals (every 7,500 miles) specify changing the oil filter at every second oil change after the initial service. We recommend replacing the oil filter with every oil change. For the small price of an oil filter, it's cheap insurance to replace the filter at every oil change. One of the larger filter manufacturers points out in its advertisements that not changing the filter leaves about 1 quart (0.95 L) of dirty oil in the engine. This claim is true and should be kept in mind when changing your oil.**

1. Run the engine until it reaches normal operating temperature.
2. Jack up the front of the car and support it on safety stands if necessary to gain access to the filter.
3. Slide a drain pan of at least 6 quarts (5.7 L) capacity under the oil pan.
4. Loosen the drain plug. Turn the plug out by hand. By keeping an inward pressure on the plug as you unscrew it, oil won't escape past the threads and you can remove it without being burned by hot oil.
5. Allow the oil to drain completely and then install the drain plug. Don't overtighten the plug or you'll be buying a new pan or a trick replacement plug for damaged threads.
6. Using a strap wrench, remove the oil filter. Keep in mind that it's holding about 1 quart (0.95 L) of dirty, hot oil.
7. Empty the old filter into the drain pan and dispose of the filter and old oil.

➡ **One ecologically desirable solution to the used oil disposal problem is to find a cooperative gas station owner who will allow you to dump your used oil into his tank or take the oil to a reclamation center (often at garages and gas stations.**

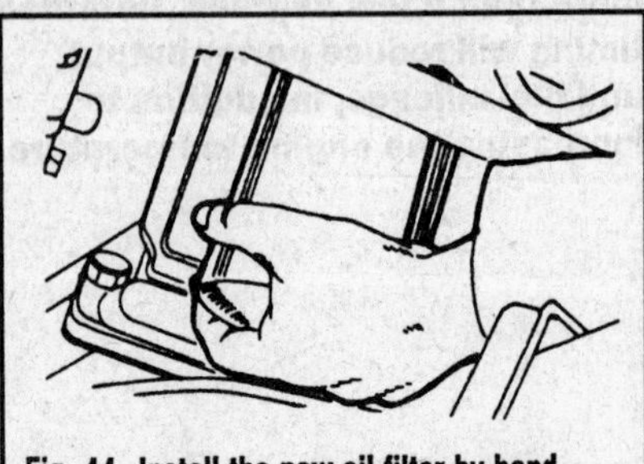
Fig. 44 Install the new oil filter by hand

Fig. 45a. Oil pan drain plug

FRAM
Extra
Guard
FRAM

Fig. 45b. Engine oil filter assembly

8. Using a clean rag, wipe off the filter adapter on the engine block. Be sure that the rag doesn't leave any lint which could clog an oil passage.

9. Coat the rubber gasket on the filter with fresh oil. Spin it onto the engine **by hand**; when the gasket touches the adapter surface give it another $\frac{1}{2}$–$\frac{3}{4}$ turn. No more or you'll squash the gasket and it will leak.

10. Refill the engine with the correct amount of fresh oil. See the Capacities chart.

11. Crank the engine over several times and then start it. If the oil pressure indicator light doesn't go out or the pressure gauge shows zero, shut the engine down and find out what's wrong.

12. If the oil pressure is OK and there are no leaks, shut the engine off and lower the car.

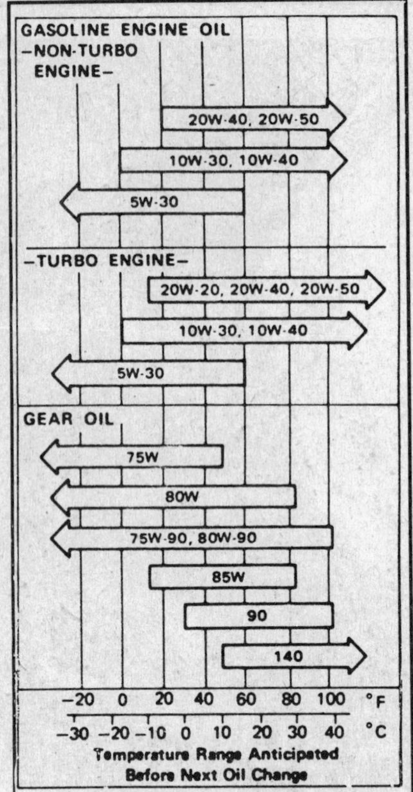
GASOLINE ENGINE OIL
–NON-TURBO ENGINE–
20W-40, 20W-50
10W-30, 10W-40
5W-30
–TURBO ENGINE–
20W-20, 20W-40, 20W-50
10W-30, 10W-40
5W-30
GEAR OIL
75W
80W
75W-90, 80W-90
85W
90
140
–20 0 20 40 60 80 100 °F
–30 –20 –10 0 10 20 30 40 °C
Temperature Range Anticipated Before Next Oil Change

Fig. 46 Manual transaxle and engine oil recommendations; automatic transaxle uses Dexron®II automatic transaxle fluid

Manual Transaxle

➧ SEE FIGS. 46–48

FLUID RECOMMENDATION

For manual transaxles, there are a variety of fluids available (depending upon the outside temperature); be sure to use fluid with an API GL-4 rating.

LEVEL CHECK

You should inspect the manual transaxle gear oil at 3,000 miles or once a month at this point you should correct the level or replace the oil as necessary. The lubricant level should be even with the bottom of the filler hole. Hold in on the filler plug when unscrewing it. When you are sure that all of the threads of the plug are free of the transaxle case, move the plug away from the case slightly. If lubricant begins to flow out of the transaxle, then you know it is full. If not, add gear oil as necessary

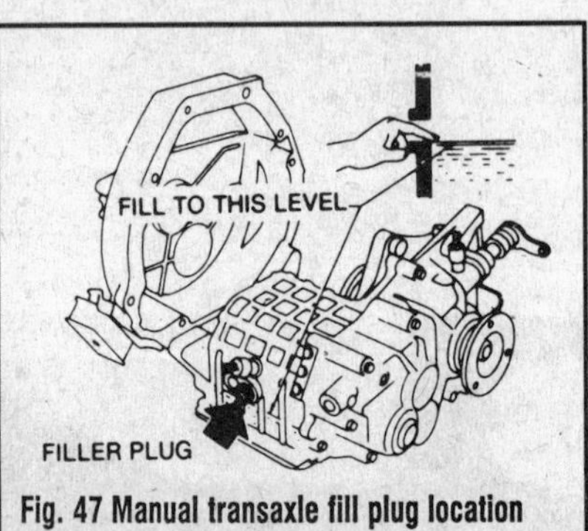
FILL TO THIS LEVEL
FILLER PLUG

Fig. 47 Manual transaxle fill plug location

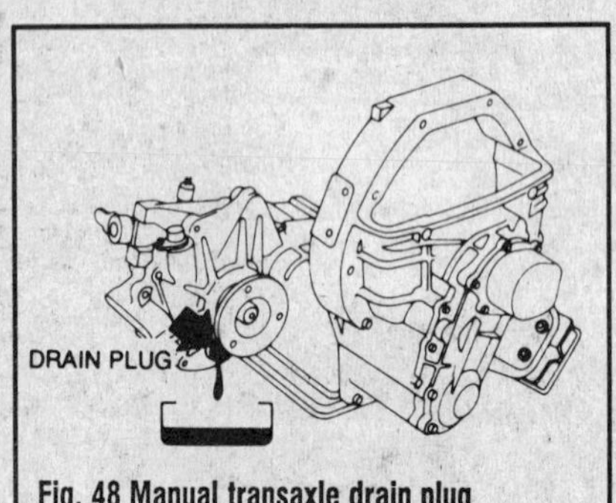
DRAIN PLUG

Fig. 48 Manual transaxle drain plug

DRAIN AND REFILL

➡ It is recommended that the manual transaxle fluid be changed every 30,000 miles. If the vehicle is normally used in severe service, the interval should be halved. You may also want to change it if you have bought your car used or if it has been driven in water deep enough to reach the transaxle case.

1. Run the engine until it reaches normal operating temperature then turn key to the **OFF** position.

2. Jack up the front of the car and support it on safety stands if necessary to gain access.

3. Remove the filler plug from the left-side of the transaxle to provide a vent.

4. The drain plug is located on the bottom of the transaxle case. Place a pan under the drain plug and remove it.

⁂ CAUTION

The oil will be HOT. Push up against the threads as you unscrew the plug to prevent leakage.

5. Allow the oil to drain completely. Clean off the plug and replace it. DO NOT OVERTIGHTEN PLUG!

6. Fill the transaxle with gear oil through the filler plug hole. Use API service GL-4 gear oil of the proper viscosity (see the "Viscosity Chart"). This oil usually comes in a squeeze bottle with a long nozzle. If the bottle isn't, use a plastic squeeze bottle (the type used in the kitchen). Auto supply stores sell inexpensive hand pumps for gear oil and other fluids. The pump screws into the top of the fluid container for easy installation. Refer to the "Capacities" chart for the amount of oil needed.

7. The oil level should come up to the edge of the filler hole. You can stick your finger in to verify this. Watch out for sharp threads.

8. Replace the filler plug. Lower the vehicle, dispose of the old oil in the same manner as old engine oil. Take a drive in the vehicle, stop and check for leaks.

Automatic Transaxle

FLUID RECOMMENDATION

All automatic transaxle, use Dexron®II ATF (automatic transaxle fluid)

LEVEL CHECK

You should inspect the automatic transaxle gear oil at 3,000 miles or once a month, at this point you should correct the level or replace the oil as necessary. There is a dipstick at the right rear of the engine. It has a scale on each side, one for **COLD** and the other for **HOT**. The transmission is considered hot after 15 miles of highway driving. Park the car on a level surface with the engine running. If the transaxle is not hot, shift into Drive, Low, then Park. Set the hand brake and block the wheels.

➡ **The fluid level should be checked when the engine is at normal operating temperature and engine running. The COLD range is used for reference only.**

Remove the dipstick, wipe it clean, then reinsert it firmly. Remove the dipstick and check the fluid level on the appropriate scale. The level should be at the Full mark. If the level is below the Full mark, add Dexron®II AFT (automatic transaxle fluid) as necessary, with the engine running, through the dipstick tube. Do not overfill, as this may cause the transaxle to malfunction and damage itself.

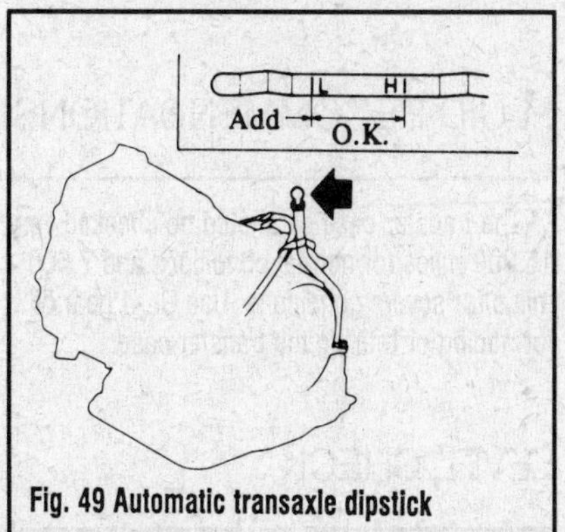
L
HI
Add
O.K.
Fig. 49 Automatic transaxle dipstick

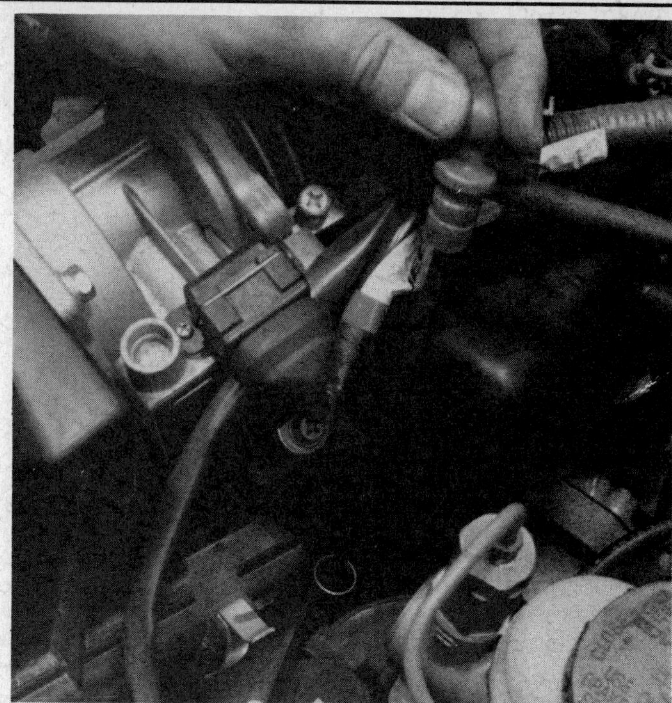
Fig. 49a. Checking the automatic transaxle fluid—1991-92 Sentra, others similar

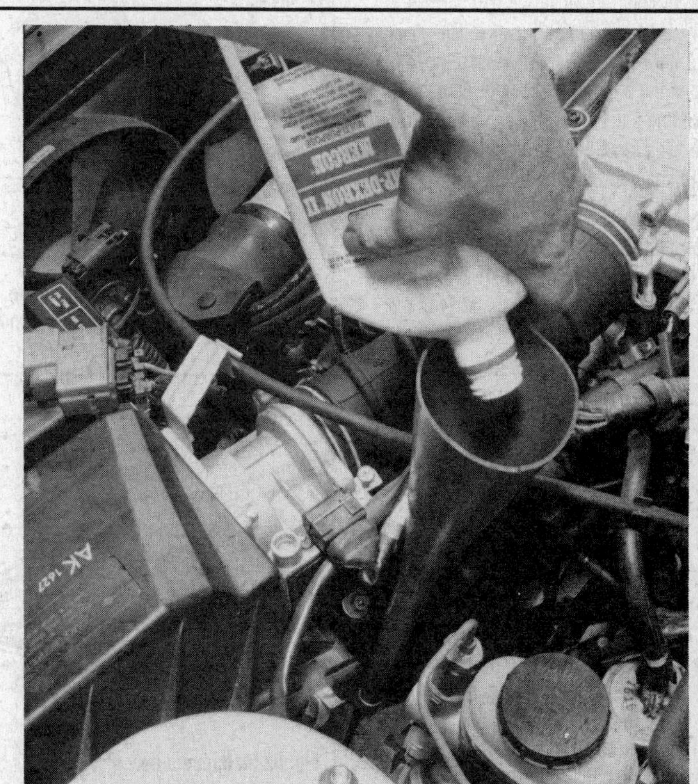
Fig. 49b. Adding automatic transaxle fluid using a long funnel

DRAIN AND REFILL

➡ It is recommended that the automatic transaxle fluid be changed every 30,000 miles. If the vehicle is normally used in severe service, the interval should be halved. You may also want to change it if you have bought your car used or if it has been driven in water deep enough to reach the transaxle case.

1. Run the engine until it reaches normal operating temperature then turn the key to the **OFF** position.
2. Jack up the front of the car and support it on safety stands if necessary to gain access.
3. If There is no drain plug, the fluid pan must be removed. On newer models, there is a hexagon drain plug near the oil pan, if so equipped remove the plug and then drain the transaxle, refill and road test.
4. If not partially remove the pan screws until the pan can be pulled down at one corner. Place a container under the transaxle, lower a rear corner of the pan and allow the fluid to drain.
5. After draining, remove the pan screws completely, then the pan and gasket. On RL4F031A and RL4F01A transaxles, remove the drain plug in the side of the case or oil pan.
6. Clean the pan thoroughly and allow it to air dry. If you wipe it out with a rag, be sure there is no lint left behind to clog the oil passages.

➡ It is very important to clean the old gasket from the oil pan, to prevent leaks upon installation, a razor blade does a excellent job at this.

7. Install the pan using a new gasket and a small bead of RTV sealant; be sure to apply sealant around the outside of the pan bolt holes. Tighten the pan screws evenly in rotation from the center outwards, to 36–60 inch lbs., then lower the vehicle.
8. It is a good idea to measure the amount of fluid drained to determine how much fresh fluid to add. This is because some part of the transaxle, such as the torque converter, will not drain completely and using the dry refill amount specified in the Capacities chart may lead to overfilling. Fluid is added through the dipstick tube. Make sure that the funnel, hose or whatever your are using is completely clean and dry before pouring transaxle fluid through it. Use Dexron®II automatic transaxle fluid.

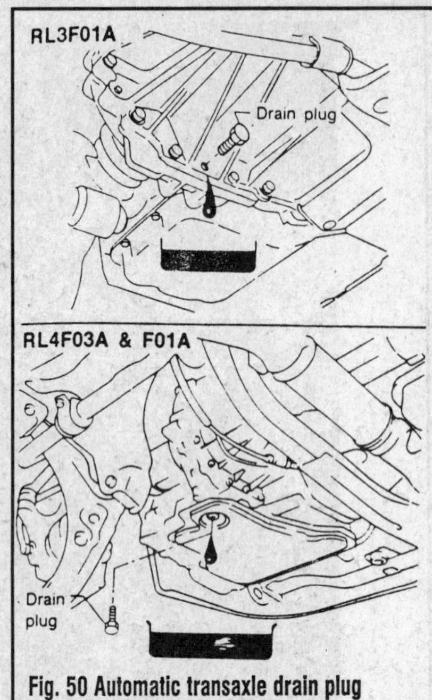
RL3F01A
Drain plug
RL4F03A & F01A
Drain plug

Fig. 50 Automatic transaxle drain plug — some early models do not have these plugs

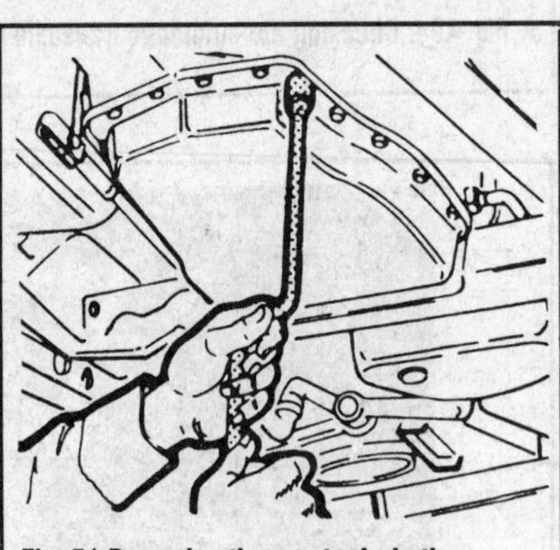

Fig. 51 Removing the pan to drain the automatic transaxle on models with no drain plug

Fig. 52 Installing a new pan gasket

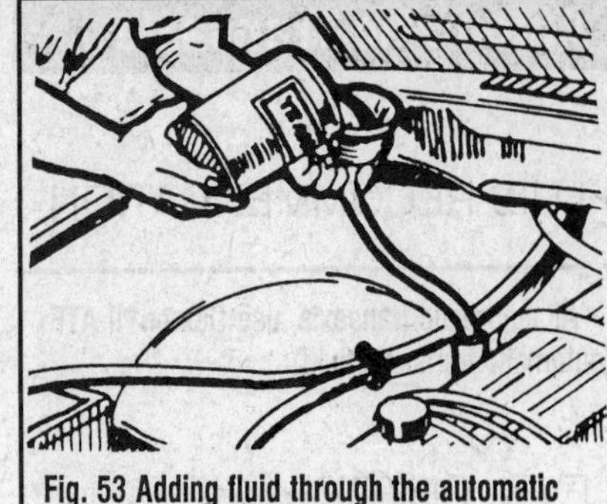

Fig. 53 Adding fluid through the automatic transaxle dipstick tube

9. Replace the dipstick after filling. Start the engine and allow it to idle. DO NOT race the engine.
10. After the engine has idled for a few minutes, shift the transaxle slowly through the gears, then return the lever to **PARK**. With the engine idling, check the fluid level on the dip stick. It should be between the **H** and **L** marks. If below **L**, add sufficient fluid to raise the level to between the marks.
11. Drive the car until the transaxle is at operating temperature. The fluid should be at the **H** mark. If not, add sufficient fluid until this is the case. Be careful not to overfill; overfilling causes slippage, overheating and seal damage.

➡ If the drained fluid is discolored (brown or black), thick or smells burnt, serious transaxle problems due to overheating should be suspected. Your car's transaxle should be inspected by a transaxle specialist to determine the cause.

4WD Transfer Case

FLUID RECOMMENDATIONS

The transfer case oil should be checked very 15,000 miles for normal conditions and 7,500 miles for severe conditions. Use GL-4 gear oil for adding or refilling the transfer case.

LEVEL CHECK

Never start the engine while check the oil level. Raise the vehicle and support safely. Remove the plug in the passenger side of the case. Fill with fluid until it reaches the bottom of the fill hole. Install the plug and torque to 13–18 ft. lbs. (18–25 Nm).

Fig. 54 Transfer case drain plug and center bearing check — 4WD Sentra

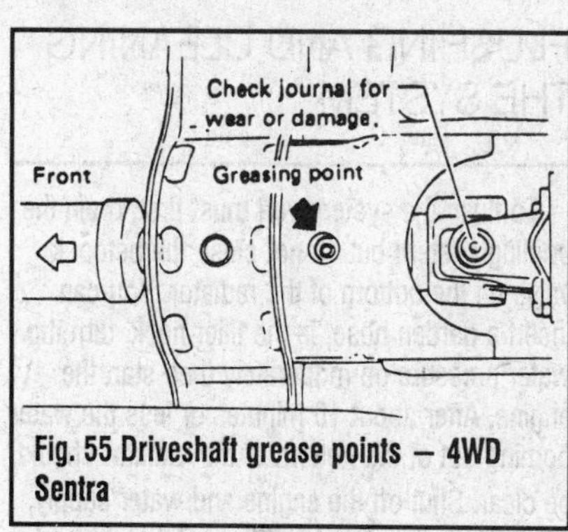
Check journal for wear or damage.
Front
Greasing point

Fig. 55 Driveshaft grease points — 4WD Sentra

DRAIN AND REFILL

1. Warm up the engine to temperature and turn OFF. Raise the vehicle and support safely.
2. Place a drain pan under the transfer case drain plug.
3. Remove the drain plug under the transfer case and allow to drain completely.
4. Install the drain plug and torque to 13–18 ft. lbs. (18–25 Nm).
5. Remove the fill plug on the side of the case. Using an approved pump, fill the transfer case with GL-4 gear oil until it reaches the bottom of the fill plug.
6. Install the fill plug and torque to 13–18 ft. lbs. (18–25 Nm).
7. Lower the vehicle and road test. Check for leaks after road test.

4WD Drive Axle

FLUID RECOMMENDATIONS

The rear drive axle oil should be checked very 15,000 miles for normal conditions and 7,500 miles for severe conditions. Use GL-4 gear oil for adding or refilling the transfer case.

LEVEL CHECK

Never start the engine while check the oil level. Raise the vehicle and support safely. Remove the plug in the rear housing. Fill with fluid until it reaches the bottom of the fill hole. Install the plug and torque to 13–18 ft. lbs. (18–25 Nm).

DRAIN AND REFILL

1. Drive the vehicle to warm up the drive axle to temperature. Raise the vehicle and support safely.
2. Place a drain pan under the drive axle drain plug. The case may not have a drain plug. The gear oil may have to be sucked out of the fill hole in the rear of the housing. If this is the case, use a suction pump to remove the gear oil.
3. If so equipped, remove the drain plug under the drive axle housing and allow to drain completely.
4. Install the drain plug and torque to 13–18 ft. lbs. (18–25 Nm).
5. Remove the fill plug on the side of the case. Using an approved pump, fill the drive axle with GL-4 gear oil until it reaches the bottom of the fill plug hole.
6. Install the fill plug and torque to 13–18 ft. lbs. (18–25 Nm).
7. Lower the vehicle and road test. Check for leaks after road test.

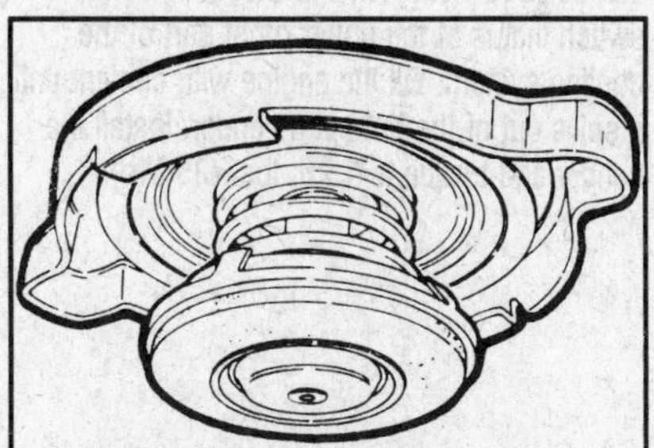

Fig. 56a Always check the gasket in the radiator cap when checking coolant level

Cooling System

FLUID RECOMMENDATION

The cooling fluid or antifreeze, should be changed every 30,000 miles or 24 months. When replacing the fluid, use a mixture of 50% water and 50% ethylene glycol antifreeze.

LEVEL CHECK

Check the coolant level every 3,000 miles or once a month. In hot weather operation, it may be a good idea to check the level once a week. Check for loose connections and signs of deterioration of the coolant hoses. Maintain the coolant level 3/4–1 1/4 in. (19–32mm) below the level of the filler neck when the engine is cold. If the engine is equipped with a coolant recovery bottle check the coolant level in the bottle when the engine is cold, the level should be up to the **MAX** mark. If the bottle is empty, check the level in the radiator and refill as necessary, then fill the bottle up to the MAX level.

CAUTION

Never remove the radiator cap when the vehicle is hot or overheated. Wait until it has cooled. Place a thick cloth over the radiator cap to shield yourself from the heat and turn the radiator cap, SLIGHTLY, until the sound of escaping pressure can be heard. DO NOT turn any more; allow the pressure to release gradually. When no more pressure can be heard escaping, remove the cap with the heavy cloth, CAUTIOUSLY!

➡ Never add cold water to an overheated engine while the engine is not running.

After filling the radiator, run the engine until it reaches normal operating temperature, to make sure that the thermostat has opened and all the air is bled from the system.

DRAIN AND REFILL

To drain the cooling system, allow the engine to cool down **BEFORE ATTEMPTING TO REMOVE THE RADIATOR CAP**. Then turn the cap until it hisses. Wait until all pressure is off the cap before removing it completely.

CAUTION

To avoid burns and scalding, always handle a warm radiator cap with a heavy rag.

1. At the dash, set the heater TEMP control lever to the fully HOT position.
2. With the radiator cap removed, drain the radiator by loosening the petcock at the bottom of the radiator.

➡ On the Sentra models, remove the heater inlet hose from the connector pipe at the left rear of the cylinder block to drain completely. After draining, reconnect the hose to the pipe.

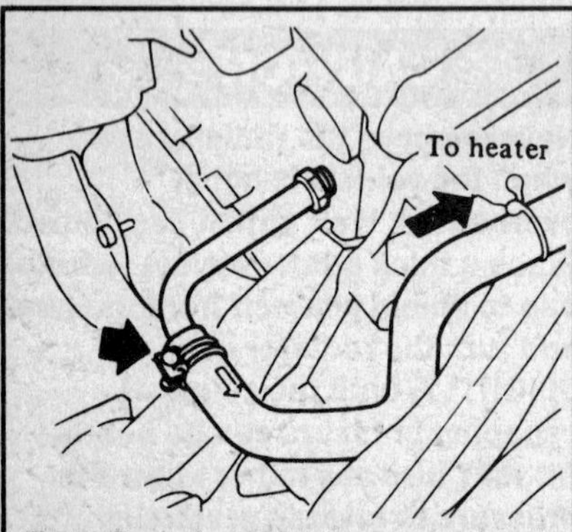
To heater
Fig. 57 Removing the inlet hose from the connector pipe

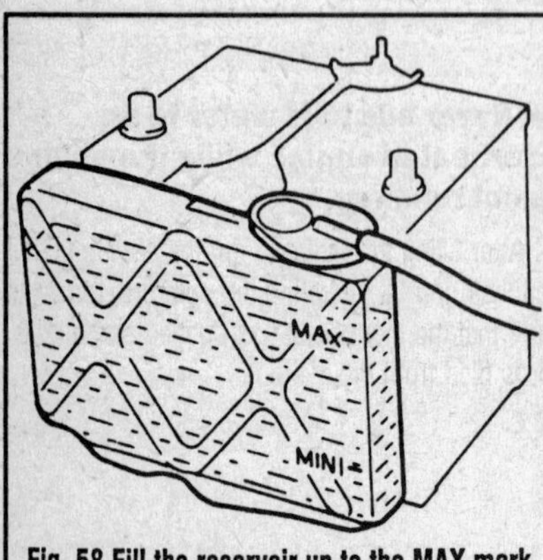
MAX
MINI
Fig. 58 Fill the reservoir up to the MAX mark

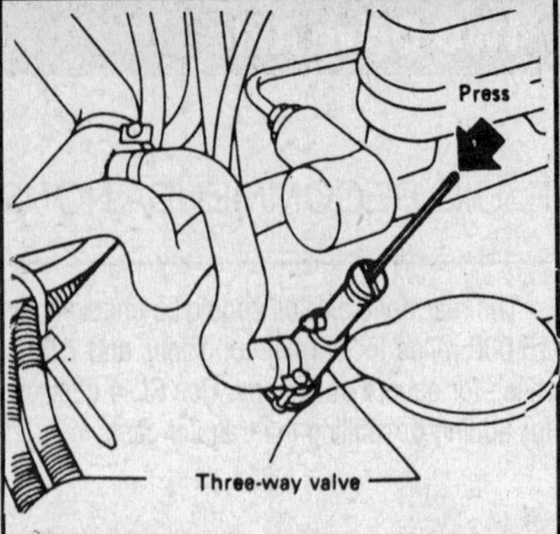
Press
Three-way valve
Fig. 59 Using the 3-way valve to bleed the cooling system

3. Close the petcock, then refill the system with a 50/50 mix of ethylene glycol antifreeze; fill the system to 3/4–1 1/4 in. (19–32mm) from the bottom of the filler neck. Reinstall the radiator cap.

➡ If equipped with a fluid reservoir tank, fill it up to the MAX level.

4. Operate the engine at 2,000 rpm for a few minutes and check the system for signs of leaks.

WARNING

If the cooling system is not bled, air can be trapped in the cylinder head and cause engine damage when the engine heats up. Always bleed the cooling system after draining. The air has to escape from the highest point in the cooling system.

If you have replaced or repaired any cooling system component, the system must be bled. Insert a 3mm pin into the 3-way valve, located at the firewall, and push it in as far as it will go for early model vehicles. While pushing in on the pin, fill the radiator up to the filler opening. Replace the radiator cap and fill the reservoir. Loosen the plug in the upper part of the cylinder head for later model vehicles. If no plug or valve can be accessed. Remove a cooling sender switch that is at the upper most part of the cooling system. Fill the engine with coolant until it spills out of the removed sender. Install the sender and torque to 15 ft. lbs. (25 Nm).

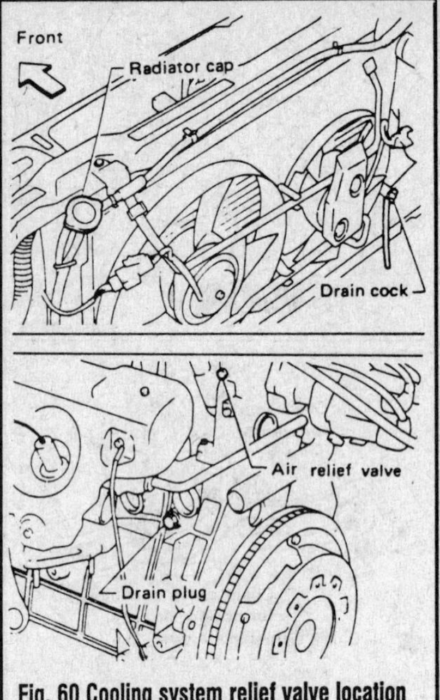
Front
Radiator cap
Drain cock
Air relief valve
Drain plug
Fig. 60 Cooling system relief valve location – GA16I engine, others similar

FLUSHING AND CLEANING THE SYSTEM

To flush the system you must first, drain the cooling system but do not close the petcock valve on the bottom of the radiator. You can insert a garden hose, in the filler neck, turn the water pressure on moderately then start the engine. After about 10 minutes or less the water coming out of the bottom of the radiator should be clear. Shut off the engine and water supply, allow the radiator to drain then refill and bleed the system as necessary.

➡ DO NOT allow the engine to overheat. The supply of water going in the top must be equal in amount to the water draining from the bottom, this way the radiator will always be full when the engine us running.

Usually flushing the radiator using water is all that is necessary to maintain the proper condition in the cooling system.

Radiator flush is the only cleaning agent that can be used to clean the internal portion of the radiator. Radiator flush can be purchased at any auto supply store. Follow the directions on the label.

Brake and Clutch Master Cylinder

FLUID RECOMMENDATION

When adding or changing the fluid in the systems, use a quality brake fluid of DOT 3 specifications.

➡ **Never reuse old brake fluid.**

LEVEL CHECK

Check the levels of brake fluid in the brake and clutch master cylinder reservoirs every 3,000 miles or once a month. The fluid level should be maintained to a level not below the bottom line on the reservoirs and not above the top line. Any sudden decrease in the level in either of the 3 reservoirs (2 for the brakes and 1 for the clutch) indicates a leak in that particular system and should be checked out. Gradual decreases in fluid level is normal due to brake pad wear.

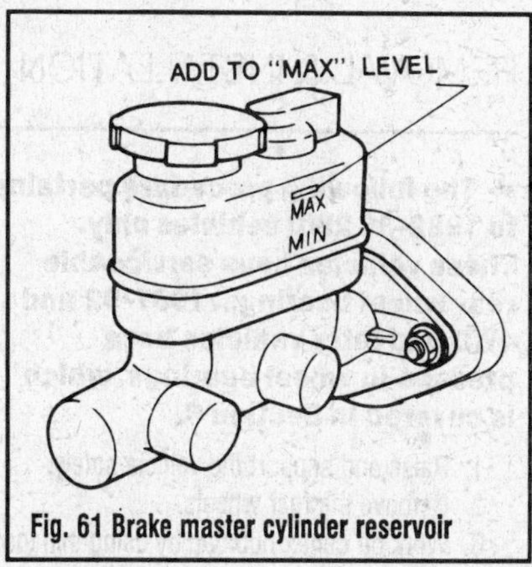
ADD TO "MAX" LEVEL
MAX
MIN
Fig. 61 Brake master cylinder reservoir

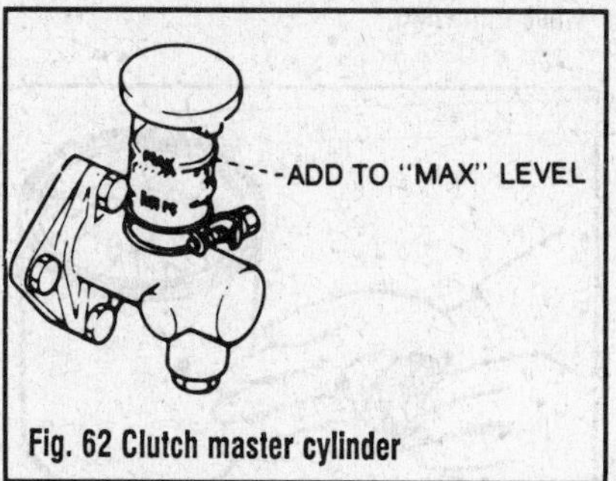
ADD TO "MAX" LEVEL
Fig. 62 Clutch master cylinder

Power Steering System

FLUID RECOMMENDATION

When adding or changing the power steering fluid, use Dexron®II ATF (Automatic Transmission Fluid); the system uses approximately 1 1/8 qts. (1.06 L) of fluid.

LEVEL CHECK

➡ **Like all other general maintenance items, check every 3,000 miles or once a month.**

Check the oil level in the reservoir by checking the side of the dipstick marked **HOT** after running the vehicle or the side marked **COLD** when the car has not been used. In each case, the fluid should reach the appropriate full line. See Section 8, "Suspension and Steering" for system bleeding procedures if necessary.

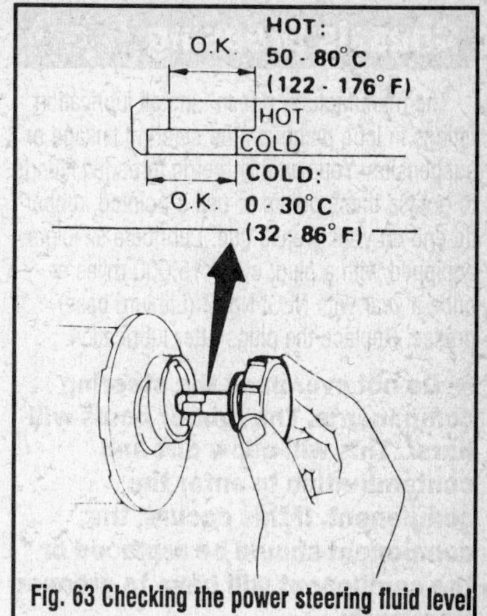
HOT:
O.K.
50 - 80°C
(122 - 176°F)
HOT
COLD
COLD:
O.K.
0 - 30°C
(32 - 86°F)
Fig. 63 Checking the power steering fluid level

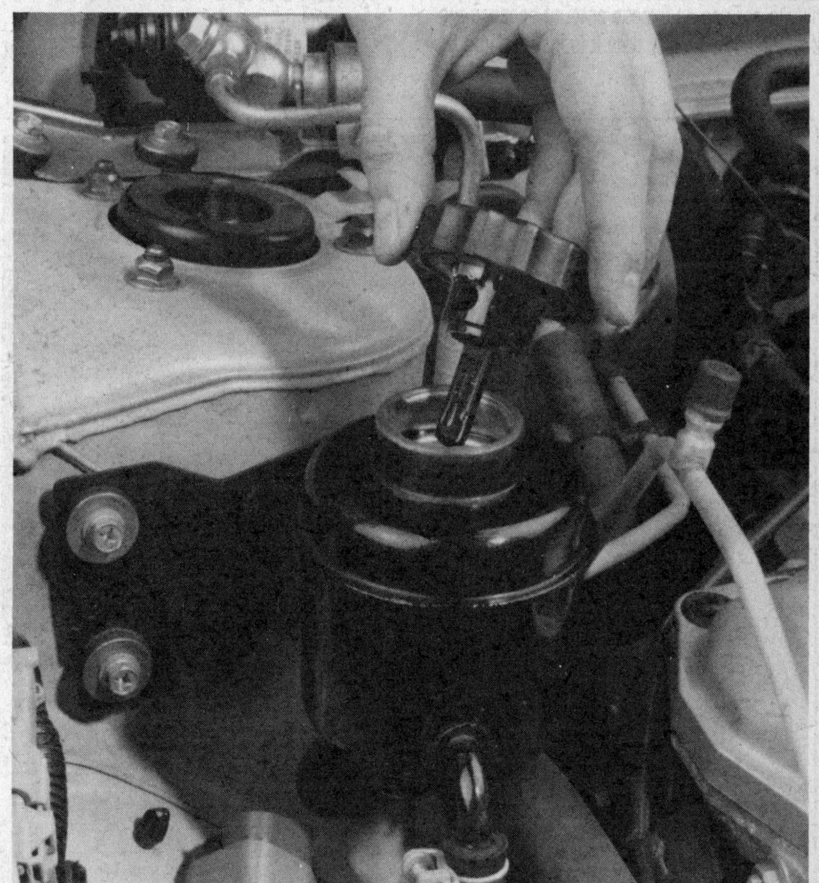
Fig. 62a. Checking the power steering fluid—1991-92 Sentra, others similar

Chassis Greasing

The manufacturer doesn't install lubrication fittings in lube points on the steering linkage or suspension. You can buy metric threaded fittings to grease these points or use a pointed, rubber tip end on your grease gun. Lubricate all joints equipped with a plug, every 15,000 miles or once a year with NLGI No. 2 (Lithium base) grease. Replace the plugs after lubrication.

➡ Do not over pack the steering components. The rubber boots will burst. This will allow dirt and contamination to enter the component. If this occurs, the component should be replaced or the component will have to greased frequently.

Body Lubrication

Lubricate all body hinges, latches and moving parts with high quality white lithium grease. Lubricate key locks with penetrating oil or motor oil. Do not use an excess amount because the key will be oily every time it is inserted into the lock. Lubricate rubber door seals with silicone spray. For best results, spray into a rag and wipe the seal with the rag.

Rear Wheel Bearings

For front wheel bearings and 1987–92 rear wheel bearings, refer to the procedures in Section 8.

REMOVAL, REPACKING, INSTALLATION, ADJUSTMENT

Before handling the bearings, there are a few things that you should remember to do and not to do.

Remember to DO the following:

- Remove all outside dirt from the housing before exposing the bearing.
- Treat a used bearing as gently as you would a new one.
- Work with clean tools in clean surroundings.
- Use clean, dry canvas gloves, or at least clean, dry hands.
- Clean solvents and flushing fluids are a must.
- Use clean paper when laying out the bearings to dry.
- Protect disassembled bearings from rust and dirt. Cover them up.
- Use clean rags to wipe bearings.
- Keep the bearings in oil-proof paper when they are to be stored or are not in use.
- Clean the inside of the housing before replacing the bearing.

Do NOT do the following:

- Don't work in dirty surroundings.
- Don't use dirty, chipped or damaged tools.
- Try not to work on wooden work benches or use wooden mallets.
- Don't handle bearings with dirty or moist hands.
- Do not use gasoline for cleaning; use a safe solvent.
- Do not spin-dry bearings with compressed air. They will be damaged.
- Do not spin dirty bearings.
- Avoid using cotton waste or dirty cloths to wipe bearings.
- Try not to scratch or nick bearing surfaces.
- Do not allow the bearing to come in contact with dirt or rust at any time.

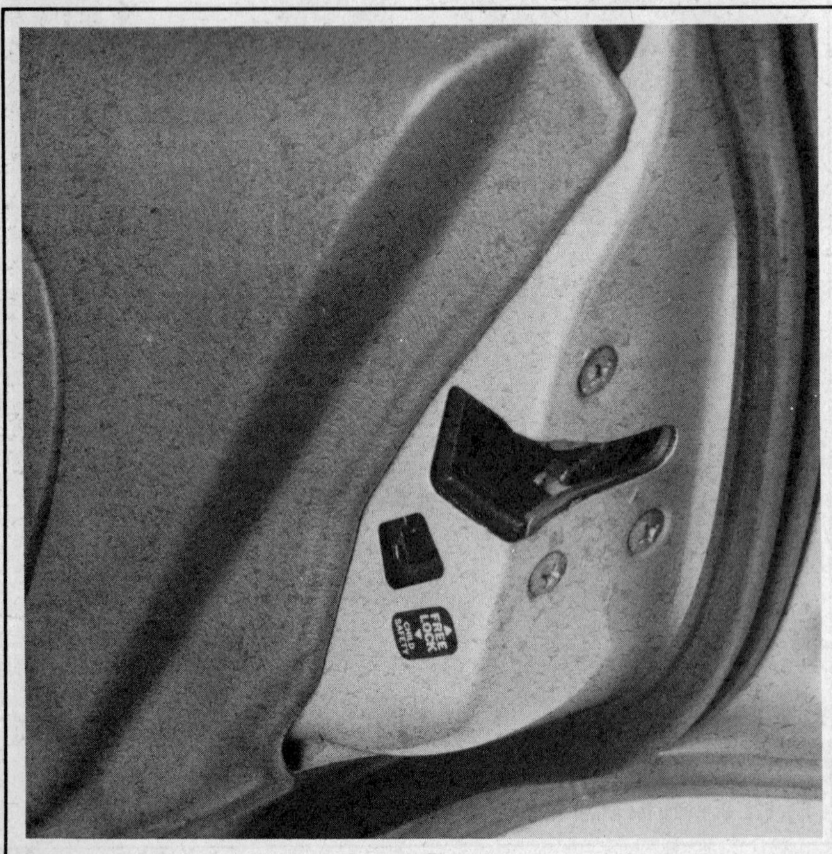
FREE
LOCK
CHILD SAFETY
Fig. 63a. Child safety locks located on the inside of the door frame on late model 4 door vehicles

REMOVAL & INSTALLATION

➡ The following procedure pertains to 1982–86 2WD vehicles only. These vehicles have serviceable rear wheel bearings. 1987–92 and 4WD and later vehicles have pressed-in wheel bearings, which is covered in Section 8.

1. Raise and support the vehicle safely.
2. Remove the rear wheels.
3. Work off center hub cap by using thin tool. If necessary tap around it with a soft hammer while removing.

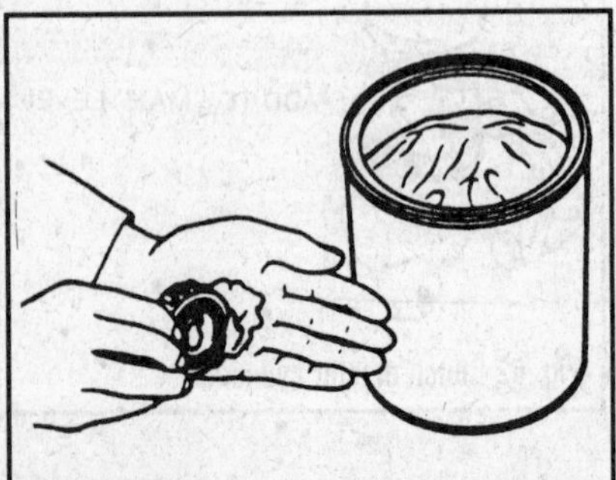
Fig. 65 Packing the wheel bearings with high temperature grease

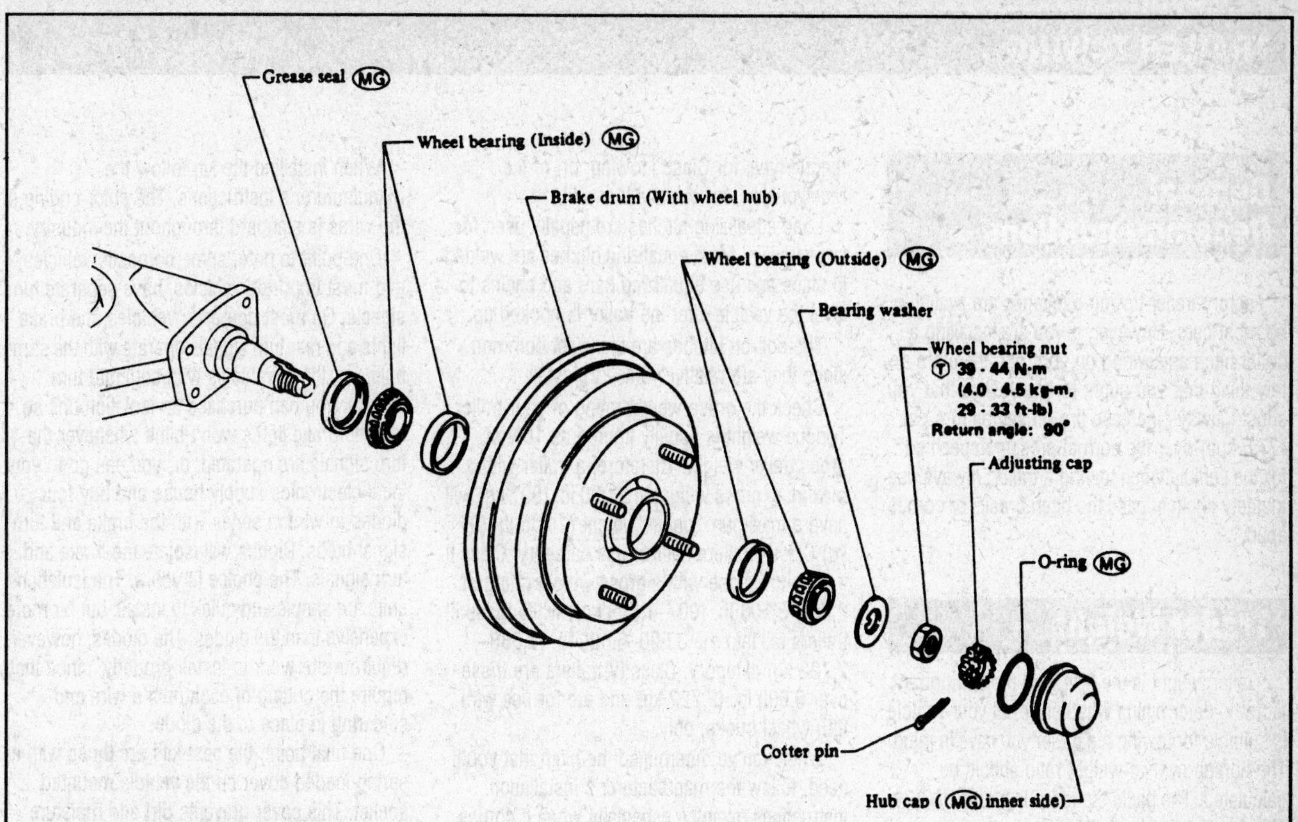

Grease seal (MG)
Wheel bearing (Inside) (MG)
Brake drum (With wheel hub)
Wheel bearing (Outside) (MG)
Bearing washer
Wheel bearing nut
(T) 39 - 44 N·m
(4.0 - 4.5 kg-m,
29 - 33 ft-lb)
Return angle: 90°
Adjusting cap
O-ring (MG)
Cotter pin
Hub cap ((MG) inner side)

Fig. 64 Wheel bearing installation

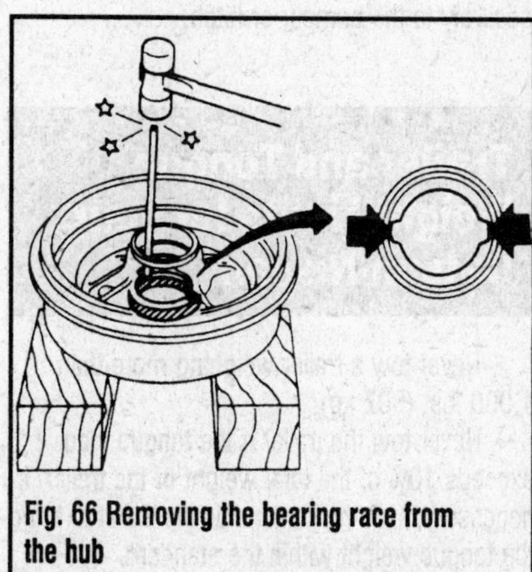

Fig. 66 Removing the bearing race from the hub

4. Pry off cotter pin and take out adjusting cap and wheel bearing lock nut.

➡ **During removal, be careful to avoid damaging O ring in dust cap.**

5. Remove the drum with bearing inside.

➡ **On Pulsar models, a circular clip holds inner wheel bearing in brake hub.**

6. Remove the bearing from drum using long brass drift pin or equivalent.

7. Install the inner bearing assembly in the brake drum and install the drum on the vehicle.

➡ **The rear wheel bearings must be adjusted after installation, if one piece bearing is used just the torque wheel bearing lock nut.**

8. Install the outer bearing assembly, wheel bearing lock nut, adjusting cap and cotter pin.

9. Install the center cap and the wheel assembly. To remove the wheel bearing races knock them out of the brake drum using a suitable brass punch.

ADJUSTMENT

1. Raise the rear of the vehicle and support it on jackstands.
2. Remove the wheel/tire assembly.
3. Remove the bearing dust cap with a pair of channel locks pliers.
4. Remove the cotter pin and retaining nut cap (if equipped), dispose of the cotter pin.
5. Tighten the wheel bearing nut to 29–33 ft. lbs.
6. Rotate the drum back and forth a few revolutions to snug down the bearing.
7. After turning the wheel, recheck the torque of the nut, then loosen it 90° from its position.
8. Install the retaining nut cap (if equipped). Align the cotter pin holes in the nut or nut cap with the hole in the spindle by turning the nut clockwise. Tighten the nut no more than 15° to align the holes.
9. Install the cotter pin, bend up its ends and install the dust cap.

TRAILER TOWING

General Recommendations

Factory trailer towing packages are available on most cars. However, if you are installing a trailer hitch and wiring on your car, there are a few thing that you ought to know. Note that you should always increase tire pressures to 4 psi (27.5 kpa) over the normal pressure specified for the vehicle when towing a trailer. Always use a safety chain in case the hitch breaks or comes apart.

Trailer Weight

Trailer weight is the first, and most important, factor in determining whether or not your vehicle is suitable for towing the trailer you have in mind. The horsepower-to-weight ratio should be calculated. The basic standard is a ratio of 35:1. That is, 35 pounds of GVW for every horsepower.

To calculate this ratio, multiply you engine's rated horsepower by 35, then subtract the weight of the vehicle, including passengers and luggage. The resulting figure is the ideal maximum trailer weight that you can tow. One point to consider: a numerically higher axle ratio can offset what appears to be a low trailer weight. If the weight of the trailer that you have in mind is somewhat higher than the weight you just calculated, you might consider changing your rear axle ratio to compensate.

Hitch Weight

There are three kinds of hitches: bumper mounted, frame mounted, and load equalizing.

Bumper mounted hitches are those which attach solely to the vehicle's bumper. Many states prohibit towing with this type of hitch, when it attaches to the vehicle's stock bumper, since it subjects the bumper to stresses for which it was not designed. Aftermarket rear step bumpers, designed for trailer towing, are acceptable for use with bumper mounted hitches.

Frame mounted hitches can be of the type which bolts to two or more points on the frame, plus the bumper, or just to several points on the frame. Frame mounted hitches can also be of the tongue type, for Class I towing, or, of the receiver type, for classes II and III.

Load equalizing hitches are usually used for large trailers. Most equalizing hitches are welded in place and use equalizing bars and chains to level the vehicle after the trailer is hooked up.

The bolt-on hitches are the most common, since they are relatively easy to install.

Check the gross weight rating of your trailer. Tongue weight is usually figured as 10% of gross trailer weight. Therefore, a trailer with a maximum gross weight of 2,000 lb. (907 kg) will have a maximum tongue weight of 200 lb. (91 kg) Class I trailers fall into this category. Class II trailers are those with a gross weight rating of 2,000–3,500 lb. (907–1,588 kg), while Class III trailers fall into the 3,500–6,000 lb. (1,588–2,722 kg) category. Class IV trailers are those over 6,000 lb. (2,722 kg) and are for use with fifth wheel trucks, only.

When you've determined the hitch that you'll need, follow the manufacturer's installation instructions, exactly, especially when it comes to fastener torques. The hitch will subjected to a lot of stress and good hitches come with hardened bolts. Never substitute an inferior bolt for a hardened bolt.

Wiring

Wiring the car for towing is fairly easy. There are a number of good wiring kits available and these should be used, rather than trying to design your own. All trailers will need brake lights and turn signals as well as tail lights and side marker lights. Most states require extra marker lights for overly wide trailers. Also, most states have recently required back-up lights for trailers, and most trailer manufacturers have been building trailers with back-up lights for several years.

Additionally, some Class I, most Class II and just about all Class III trailers will have electric brakes.

Add to this number an accessories wire, to operate trailer internal equipment or to charge the trailer's battery, and you can have as many as seven wires in the harness.

Determine the equipment on your trailer and buy the wiring kit necessary. The kit will contain all the wires needed, plus a plug adapter set which included the female plug, mounted on the bumper or hitch, and the male plug, wired into, or plugged into the trailer harness.

When installing the kit, follow the manufacturer's instructions. The color coding of the wires is standard throughout the industry.

One point to note, some domestic vehicles, and most imported vehicles, have separate turn signals. On most domestic vehicles, the brake lights and rear turn signals operate with the same bulb. For those vehicles with separate turn signals, you can purchase an isolation unit so that the brake lights won't blink whenever the turn signals are operated, or, you can go to your local electronics supply house and buy four diodes to wire in series with the brake and turn signal bulbs. Diodes will isolate the brake and turn signals. The choice is yours. The isolation units are simple and quick to install, but far more expensive than the diodes. The diodes, however, require more work to install properly, since they require the cutting of each bulb's wire and soldering in place of the diode.

One final point, the best kits are those with a spring loaded cover on the vehicle mounted socket. This cover prevents dirt and moisture from corroding the terminals. Never let the vehicle socket hang loosely. Always mount it securely to the bumper or hitch.

Trailer and Tongue Weight Limits for your Datsun/Nissan

- Never tow a trailer weighing more than 1,000 lbs. (907 kg).
- Never tow the trailer if the tongue load exceeds 10% of the total weight of the trailer. If necessary, shift the load inside the trailer to bring the tongue weight within the standard.
- Never allow the combined weight of vehicle and trailer to exceed the GVWR as listed on the F.M.V.S.S. Certification Label.

Cooling

ENGINE

One of the most common, if not THE most common, problems associated with trailer towing is engine overheating.

If you have a standard cooling system, without an expansion tank, you'll definitely need to get an aftermarket expansion tank kit, preferably one with at least a 2 quart (1.9 L) capacity. These kits are easily installed on the radiator's overflow hose, and come with a pressure cap designed for expansion tanks.

Another helpful accessory is a Flex Fan. These fan are large diameter units are designed to provide more airflow at low speeds, with blades that have deeply cupped surfaces. The blades then flex, or flatten out, at high speed, when less cooling air is needed. These fans are far lighter in weight than stock fans, requiring less horsepower to drive them. Also, they are far quieter than stock fans.

If you do decide to replace your stock fan with a flex fan, note that if your car has a fan clutch, a spacer between the flex fan and water pump hub will be needed.

Aftermarket engine oil coolers are helpful for prolonging engine oil life and reducing overall engine temperatures. Both of these factors increase engine life.

While not absolutely necessary in towing Class I and some Class II trailers, they are recommended for heavier Class II and all Class III towing.

Engine oil cooler systems consist of an adapter, screwed on in place of the oil filter, a remote filter mounting and a multi-tube, finned heat exchanger, which is mounted in front of the radiator or air conditioning condenser.

TRANSAXLE

An automatic transaxle is usually recommended for trailer towing. Modern automatics have proven reliable and, of course, easy to operate, in trailer towing.

The increased load of a trailer, however, causes an increase in the temperature of the automatic transaxle fluid. Heat is the worst enemy of an automatic transaxle. As the temperature of the fluid increases, the life of the fluid decreases.

It is essential, therefore, that you install an automatic transmission cooler.

The cooler, which consists of a multi-tube, finned heat exchanger, is usually installed in front of the radiator or air conditioning compressor, and hooked inline with the transaxle cooler tank inlet line. Follow the cooler manufacturer's installation instructions.

Select a cooler of at least adequate capacity, based upon the combined gross weights of the car and trailer.

Cooler manufacturers recommend that you use an aftermarket cooler in addition to, and not instead of, the present cooling tank in your radiator. If you do want to use it in place of the radiator cooling tank, get a cooler at least two sizes larger than normally necessary.

➡ **A transaxle cooler can, sometimes, cause slow or harsh shifting in the transmission during cold weather, until the fluid has a chance to come up to normal operating temperature. Some coolers can be purchased with or retrofitted with a temperature bypass valve which will allow fluid flow through the cooler only when the fluid has reached operating temperature, or above.**

Handling A Trailer

Towing a trailer with ease and safety requires a certain amount of experience. It's a good idea to learn the feel of a trailer by practicing turning, stopping and backing in an open area such as an empty parking lot.

PUSHING AND TOWING

All manual transaxle vehicles can be push started; automatic transaxles may not be push started. Check to make sure that the bumpers of both vehicles are aligned so neither will be damaged. Be sure that all electrical system components are turned OFF (headlights, heater blower and etc.). Turn **ON** the ignition switch. Place the shift lever in 3rd or 4th gear and push in the clutch pedal. At about 15 mph, signal the driver of the pushing vehicle to fall back, depress the accelerator pedal and release the clutch pedal slowly. The engine should start.

The manufacturer advises against trying to tow-start your vehicle for fear of ramming the tow vehicle when the engine starts.

Both types of transaxles may be towed for short distances and at speeds of no more than 20 mph (automatic) or 50 mph (manual). If the car must be towed a great distance, it should be done with the drive wheels off the ground.

JUMP STARTING

Jump starting is the favored method of starting a car with a dead battery. Make sure that the cables are properly connected, negative from the dead vehicle to engine ground of the jumper vehicle and positive-to-positive or you stand a chance of damaging the electrical systems of both vehicles.

JUMP STARTING A DEAD BATTERY

The chemical reaction in a battery produces explosive hydrogen gas. This is the safe way to jump start a dead battery, reducing the chances of an accidental spark that could cause an explosion.

Jump Starting Precautions

1. Be sure both batteries are of the same voltage.
2. Be sure both batteries are of the same polarity (have the same grounded terminal).
3. Be sure the vehicles are not touching.
4. Be sure the vent cap holes are not obstructed.
5. Do not smoke or allow sparks around the battery.
6. In cold weather, check for frozen electrolyte in the battery. Do not jump start a frozen battery.
7. Do not allow electrolyte on your skin or clothing.
8. Be sure the electrolyte is not frozen.

CAUTION: Make certin that the ignition key, in the vehicle with the dead battery, is in the OFF position. Connecting cables to vehicles with on-board computers will result in computer destruction if the key is not in the OFF position.

Jump Starting Procedure

1. Determine voltages of the two batteries; they must be the same.
2. Bring the starting vehicle close (they must not touch) so that the batteries can be reached easily.
3. Turn off all accessories and both engines. Put both vehicles in Neutral or Park and set the handbrake.
4. Cover the cell caps with a rag—do not cover terminals.
5. If the terminals on the run-down battery are heavily corroded, clean them.
6. Identify the positive and negative posts on both batteries and connect the cables in the order shown.
7. Start the engine of the starting vehicle and run it at fast idle. Try to start the car with the dead battery. Crank it for no more than 10 seconds at a time and let it cool for 20 seconds in between tries.
8. If it doesn't start in 3 tries, there is something else wrong.
9. Disconnect the cables in the reverse order.
10. Replace the cell covers and dispose of the rags.

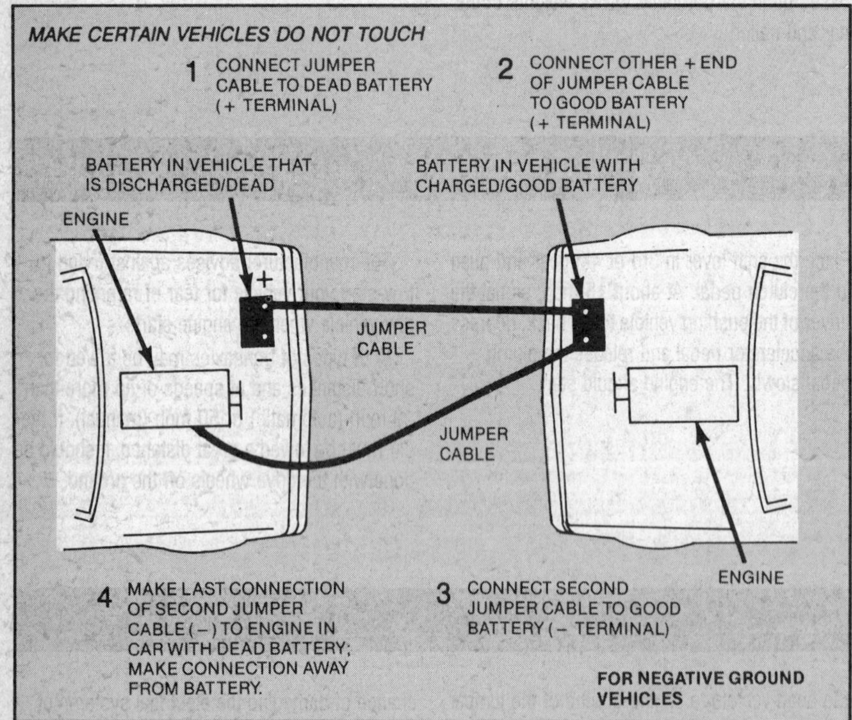

MAKE CERTAIN VEHICLES DO NOT TOUCH
1 CONNECT JUMPER CABLE TO DEAD BATTERY (+ TERMINAL)
2 CONNECT OTHER + END OF JUMPER CABLE TO GOOD BATTERY (+ TERMINAL)
BATTERY IN VEHICLE THAT IS DISCHARGED/DEAD
BATTERY IN VEHICLE WITH CHARGED/GOOD BATTERY
ENGINE
+
−
JUMPER CABLE
JUMPER CABLE
ENGINE
4 MAKE LAST CONNECTION OF SECOND JUMPER CABLE (−) TO ENGINE IN CAR WITH DEAD BATTERY; MAKE CONNECTION AWAY FROM BATTERY.
3 CONNECT SECOND JUMPER CABLE TO GOOD BATTERY (− TERMINAL)
FOR NEGATIVE GROUND VEHICLES

Side terminal batteries occasionally pose a problem when connecting jumper cables. There frequently isn't enough room to clamp the cables without touching sheet metal. Side terminal adaptors are available to alleviate this problem and should be removed after use

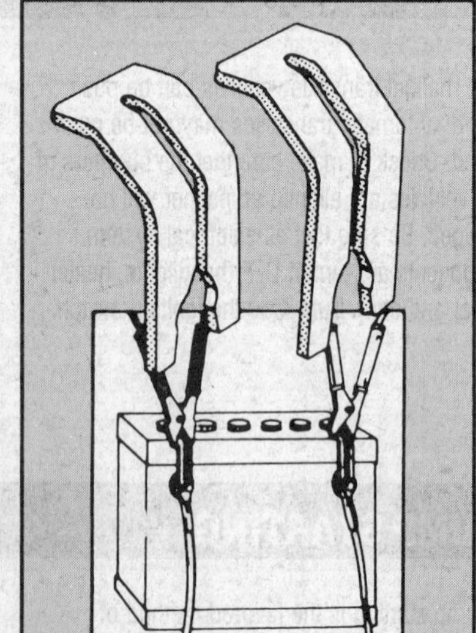

JACKING

Never use the tire changing jack for anything other than that. If you intend to use this tool to perform your own maintenance, a good scissors or small hydraulic jack and 2 sturdy jackstands would be a wise purchase. Always chock the wheels when changing a tire or working beneath the vehicle. It cannot be over-emphasized,

CLIMBING UNDER A CAR SUPPORTED BY JUST THE JACK IS EXTREMELY DANGEROUS!

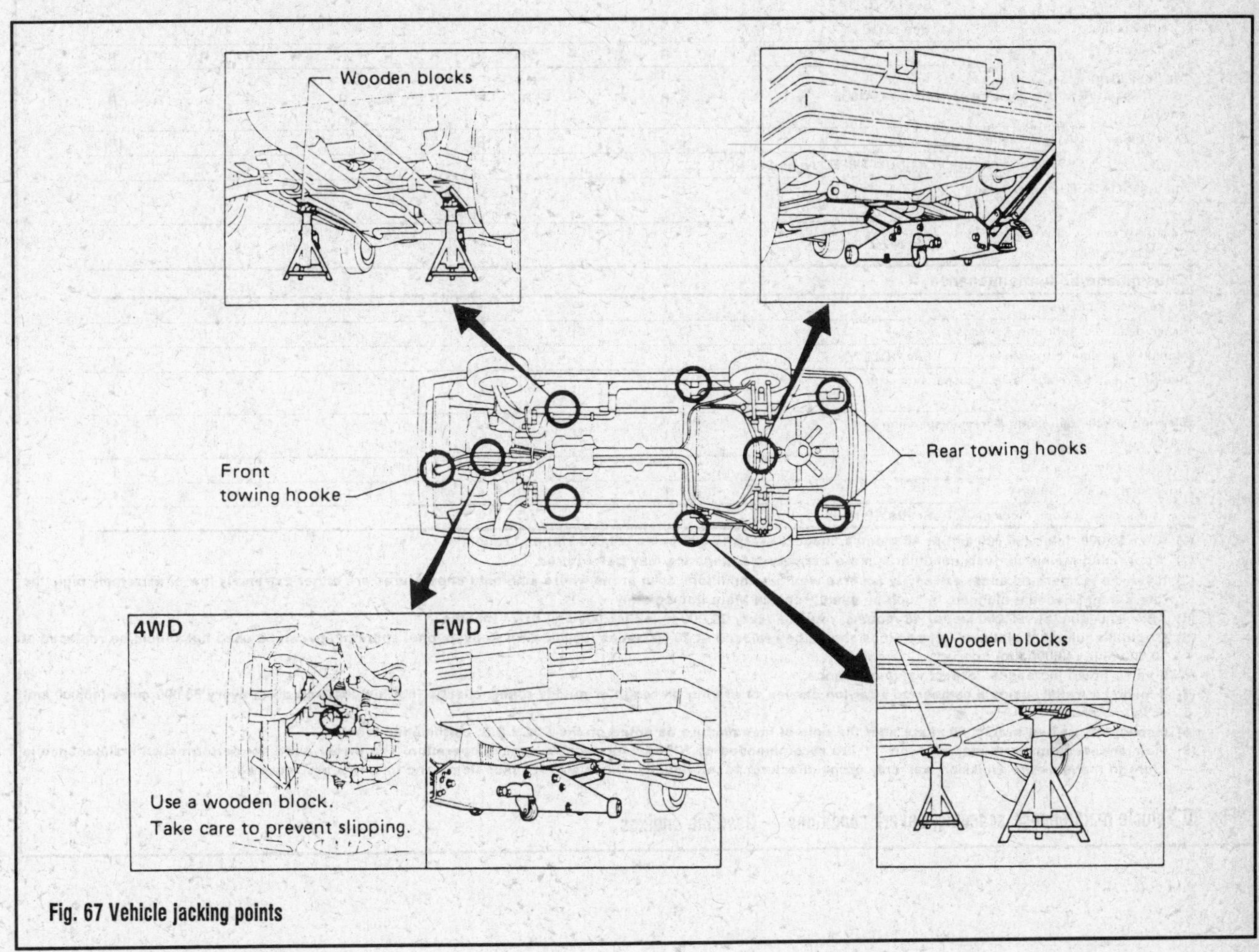
Wooden blocks
Front
towing hooke
Rear towing hooks
4WD
FWD
Use a wooden block.
Take care to prevent slipping.
Wooden blocks

Fig. 67 Vehicle jacking points

Abbreviations: R — Replace. I = Inspect. Correct or replace if necessary.

MAINTENANCE OPERATION	MAINTENANCE INTERVAL																
Perform at number of miles, kilometers or months, whichever comes first.	Miles x 1,000 (km x 1,000) Months	3.75 (6) 3	7.5 (12) 6	11.25 (18) 9	15 (24) 12	18.75 (30) 15	22.5 (36) 18	26.25 (42) 21	30 (48) 24	33.75 (54) 27	37.5 (60) 30	41.25 (66) 33	45 (72) 36	48.75 (78) 39	52.5 (84) 42	56.25 (90) 45	60 (96) 48
Emission control system maintenance																	
Drive belts	See NOTE (1).																I*
Air cleaner filter	See NOTE (2).								[R]								[R]
Vapor lines									I*								I*
Fuel lines									I*								I*
Fuel filter	See NOTE (3)*.																
Engine coolant	See NOTE (4).																R*
Engine oil		R	R	R	R	R	R	R	R	R	R	R	R	R	R	R	R
Engine oil filter (Use Nissan PREMIUM type or equivalent for GA16DE engine.)		R	R	R	R	R	R	R	R	R	R	R	R	R	R	R	R
Spark plugs	GA16DE engine								[R]								[R]
	SR20DE engine (Use PLATINUM-TIPPED type.) See NOTE (5).																[R]
Idle rpm (GA16DE engine)									I*								I*
Intake & exhaust valve clearance (GA16DE engine)	See NOTE (6)*																
Chassis and body maintenance																	
Brake lines & cables					I				I				I				I
Brake pads, discs, drums & linings			I		I		I		I		I		I		I		I
Manual & automatic transaxle oil	See NOTE (7).				I				I				I				I
Steering gear & linkage, axle & suspension parts			I		I		I		I		I		I		I		I
Steering linkage ball joints & front suspension ball joints			I		I		I		I		I		I		I		I
Exhaust system			I		I		I		I		I		I		I		I
Drive shaft boots			I		I		I		I		I		I		I		I
Air bag system (Coupe models)	See NOTE (8).																

NOTE:
(1) After 60,000 miles (96,000 km) or 48 months, inspect every 15,000 miles (24,000 km) or 12 months.
(2) If operating mainly in dusty conditions, more frequent maintenance may be required.
(3) If vehicle is operated under extremely adverse weather conditions or in areas where ambient temperatures are either extremely low or extremely high, the filters might become clogged. In such an event, replace them immediately.
(4) After 60,000 miles (96,000 km) or 48 months, replace every 30,000 miles (48,000 km) or 24 months.
(5) Original equipment platinum-tipped plugs should be replaced at 60,000 miles (96,000 km). Conventional spark plugs can be used but should be replaced at 30,000 mile (48,000 km) intervals.
(6) If valve noise increases, inspect valve clearance.
(7) If towing a trailer, using a camper or a car-top carrier, or driving on rough or muddy roads, change (not just inspect) oil at every 30,000 miles (48,000 km) or 24 months.
(8) Inspect the air bag system 10 years after the date of manufacture as noted on the F.M.V.S.S. certification label.
(9) Maintenance items and intervals with "*" are recommended by NISSAN for reliable vehicle operation. The owner need not perform such maintenance in order to maintain the emission warranty or manufacturer recall liability. Other maintenance items and intervals are required.

Fig. 70 Vehicle maintenance schedule, severe conditions — Gasoline engines

MAINTENANCE OPERATION		MAINTENANCE INTERVAL							
Perform at number of miles, kilometers or months, whichever comes first.	Miles x 1,000 (km x 1,000) Months	7.5 (12) 6	15 (24) 12	22.5 (36) 18	30 (48) 24	37.5 (60) 30	45 (72) 36	52.5 (84) 42	60 (96) 48
Emission control system maintenance									
Drive belts	See NOTE (1).								I*
Air cleaner filter					[R]				[R]
Vapor lines					I*				I*
Fuel lines					I*				I*
Fuel filter	See NOTE (2)*.								
Engine coolant	See NOTE (3).								R*
Engine oil		R	R	R	R	R	R	R	R
Engine oil filter (Use Nissan PREMIUM type or equivalent for GA16DE engine.)		R		R		R		R	
Spark plugs — GA16DE engine					[R]				[R]
Spark plugs — SR20DE engine (Use PLATINUM-TIPPED type.)	See NOTE (4).								[R]
Idle rpm (GA16DE engine)					I*				I*
Intake & exhaust valve clearance (GA16DE engine)	See NOTE (5)*.								
Chassis and body maintenance									
Brake lines & cables			I		I		I		I
Brake pads, discs, drums & linings			I		I		I		I
Manual & automatic transaxle oil			I		I		I		I
Steering gear linkage, axle & suspension parts					I				I
Exhaust system			I		I		I		I
Drive shaft boots			I		I		I		I
Air bag system (Coupe models)	See NOTE (6).								

NOTE: (1) After 60,000 miles (96,000 km) or 48 months, inspect every 15,000 miles (24,000 km) or 12 months.

(2) If vehicle is operated under extremely adverse weather conditions or in areas where ambient temperatures are either extremely low or extremely high, the filters might become clogged. In such an event, replace them immediately.

(3) After 60,000 miles (96,000 km) or 48 months, replace every 30,000 miles (48,000 km) or 24 months.

(4) Original equipment platinum-tipped plugs should be replaced at 60,000 miles (96,000 km). Conventional spark plugs can be used but should be replaced at 30,000 mile (48,000 km) intervals.

(5) If valve noise increases, inspect valve clearance.

(6) Inspect the air bag system 10 years after the date of manufacture as noted on the F.M.V.S.S. certification label.

(7) Maintenance items and intervals with "*" are recommended by NISSAN for reliable vehicle operation. The owner need not perform such maintenance in order to maintain the emission warranty or manufacturer recall liability. Other maintenance items and intervals are required.

Fig. 71 Vehicle maintenance schedule, normal conditions — Gasoline engines

Emission control system maintenance

MAINTENANCE OPERATION		MAINTENANCE INTERVAL				
Periodic maintenance should be performed at number of miles, kilometers or months, whichever comes first.	Miles x 1,000 (Kilometers x 1,000) Months	7.5 (12) 6	15 (24) 12	30 (48) 24	45 (72) 36	60 (96) 48
Drive belts			I	I	I	I
Air cleaner filter		Replace every 30,000 miles (48,000 km).				
Fuel lines (hoses, piping, connections, etc.)				I*		I*
Rubber hoses (water, air, fuel, blow-by, oil, etc.)				I		I
Fuel filter	See NOTE (1).			R		R
Engine coolant				R		R
Engine oil	See NOTE (2).	R	Then replace every 7,500 miles (12,000 km) or 6 months.			
Engine oil filter						
During the first 15,000 miles (24,000 km):		R	R			
After the first 15,000 miles (24,000 km):		Replace every 15,000 miles (24,000 km) or 12 months.				
Injection nozzle tips		Inspect every 15,000 miles (24,000 km).				
Intake & exhaust valve clearance			A	A	A	A
Idle rpm				I		I
Fuel injection timing		Inspect every 30,000 miles (48,000 km).				
Timing belts		Replace every 60,000 miles (96,000 km).				

Chassis and body maintenance

MAINTENANCE OPERATION		MAINTENANCE INTERVAL			
Periodic maintenance should be performed at number of miles, kilometers or months, whichever comes first.	Miles x 1,000 (Kilometers x 1,000) Months	15 (24) 12	30 (48) 24	45 (72) 36	60 (96) 48
Brake lines & hoses		I	I	I	I
Brake pads, discs, drums & linings		Inspect every 15,000 miles (24,000 km).			
Manual and automatic transaxle gear oil		Inspect every 15,000 miles (24,000 km).			
Power steering lines & hoses		I	I	I	I
Steering gear & linkage, axle & suspension parts & front drive shaft boots		I	I	I	I
Locks, hinges & hood latch		L	L	L	L
Front wheel bearing grease			I		I
Exhaust system		I	I	I	I
Seat belts, buckles, retractors, anchors & adjuster		I	I	I	I

NOTE:

(1) **If vehicle is operated under extremely adverse weather conditions or in areas where ambient temperatures are either extremely low or extremely high, the filters might become clogged. In such an event, replace them immediately.**

(2) **Old engine oil should be drained completely, then new oil added. Never mix new oil with old oil.**

(3) **Maintenance items and intervals with "*" are recommended by NISSAN. Other maintenance items and intervals are required.**

Abbreviations:
A = Adjust
R = Replace
L = Lubricate
I = Inspect. Correct or replace if necessary.

Fig. 72 Vehicle maintenance schedule — Canada diesel engines

Emission control system maintenance

MAINTENANCE OPERATION		MAINTENANCE INTERVAL				
Periodic maintenance should be performed at number of miles, kilometers or months, whichever comes first.	Miles x 1,000	5	15	30	45	60
	(Kilometers x 1,000)	(8)	(24)	(48)	(72)	(96)
	Months	6	12	24	36	48
Drive belts			I	I	I	I
Air cleaner filter		Replace every 30,000 miles (48,000 km).				
Fuel lines (hoses, piping, connections, etc.)				I*		I*
Rubber hoses (water, air, fuel, blow-by, oil etc.)				I		I
Fuel filter	See NOTE (1).			R		R
Engine coolant				R		R
Engine oil	See NOTE (2).	R	Then replace every 5,000 miles (8,000 km) or 6 months.			
Engine oil filter		Replace every 10,000 miles (16,000 km) or 12 months.				
Injection nozzle tips		Inspect every 15,000 miles (24,000 km).				
Intake & exhaust valve clearance			A	A	A	A
Idle rpm				I		I
Fuel injection timing		Inspect every 30,000 miles (48,000 km).				
Timing belts		Replace every 60,000 miles (96,000 km).				

Chassis and body maintenance

MAINTENANCE OPERATION		MAINTENANCE INTERVAL			
Periodic maintenance should be performed at number of miles, kilometers or months, whichever comes first.	Miles x 1,000	15	30	45	60
	(Kilometers x 1,000)	(24)	(48)	(72)	(96)
	Months	12	24	36	48
Brake lines & hoses		I	I	I	I
Brake pads, discs, drums & linings		Inspect every 15,000 miles (24,000 km).			
Manual and automatic transaxle gear oil		Inspect every 15,000 miles (24,000 km).			
Power steering lines & hoses		I	I	I	I
Steering gear & linkage, axle & suspension parts & front drive shaft boots		I	I	I	I
Locks, hinges & hood latch		L	L	L	L
Front wheel bearing grease			I		I
Exhaust system		I	I	I	I
Seat belts, buckles, retractors, anchors & adjuster		I	I	I	I

NOTE:

(1) If vehicle is operated under extremely adverse weather conditions or in areas where ambient temperatures are either extremely low or extremely high, the filters might become clogged. In such an event, replace them immediately.

(2) Old engine oil should be drained completely, then new oil added. Never mix new oil with old oil.

(3) Maintenance items and intervals with "*" are recommended by NISSAN. Other maintenance items and intervals are required.

Abbreviations: A = Adjust
R = Replace
L = Lubricate
I = Inspect. Correct or replace if necessary.

Fig. 73 Vehicle maintenance schedule — US diesel engines

CAPACITIES

Year	Model	Engine ID/VIN	Engine Displacement Liters (cc)	Engine Crankcase with Filter	Transmission (pts.) 4-Spd	5-Spd	Auto.	Drive Axle Rear (pts.)	Fuel Tank (gal.)	Cooling System (qts.)
1982	Sentra	E15	1.5 (1488)	4.1	4.9	5.8	13.0	—	13.3	5.5
1983	Sentra	E15	1.5 (1488)	4.1	4.9	5.8	13.0	—	13.3	5.5
	Sentra	E16	1.6 (1597)	3.5	4.9	5.8	13.0	—	13.3	5.5
	Pulsar	E16	1.6 (1597)	3.9	—	5.8	13.0	—	13.3	5.5
	Sentra	CD17	1.7 (1680)	4.3	4.9	5.8	13.0	—	13.3	7.5
1984	Pulsar	E15ET	1.5 (1488)	4.8	—	5.8	13.0	—	13.3	5.5
	Sentra	E16	1.6 (1597)	3.5	4.9	5.8	13.0	—	13.3	5.5
	Pulsar	E16	1.6 (1597)	3.9	—	5.8	13.0	—	13.3	5.5
	Sentra	CD17	1.7 (1680)	4.3	4.9	5.8	13.0	—	10.8	7.5
1985	Sentra, Pulsar	E16	1.6 (1597)	3.5	4.9	5.8	13.0	—	13.3	5.5
	Sentra	CD17	1.7 (1680)	4.3	4.9	5.8	13.0	—	10.8	7.5
1986	Sentra, Pulsar	E16	1.6 (1597)	3.5	4.9	5.8	13.0	—	13.3	5.5
	Sentra	CD17	1.7 (1680)	4.3	4.9	5.8	13.0	—	10.8	7.5
1987	Sentra, Pulsar	E16	1.6 (1597)	3.5	—	5.8	13.0	2.1	13.3 ④	⑥
	Pulsar	CA16DE	1.6 (1598)	3.8	—	5.8	—	—	13.3	5.9
	Sentra	CD17	1.7 (1680)	4.3	—	5.8	13.0	2.1	13.8	6.9
1988	Sentra, Pulsar	E16	1.6 (1597)	3.4	5.7	5.9	13.2	2.1	13.3 ⑤	⑥
	Pulsar	CA18DE	1.8 (1809)	3.7	—	10.0	14.4	—	13.3	⑦
1989	Sentra, Pulsar	GA16i	1.6 (1597)	3.4	5.8	5.9	13.2	2.1	13.3	5.6
	Pulsar	CA18DE	1.8 (1809)	3.7	—	10.0	7.3	—	13.3	5.9
1990	Sentra, Pulsar	GA16i	1.6 (1597)	3.5	5.8	5.9	6.6	1.2	13.3 ⑤	5.8 ⑧
	Pulsar	GA16i	1.6 (1597)	3.4	—	5.9	6.6	—	13.3	5.8 ⑧
1991	Sentra	GA16DE	1.6 (1597)	3.4	5.9	⑨	6.4	—	13.3	⑩
	Sentra	SR20DE	2.0 (1998)	3.6	5.9	⑨	7.4	—	13.3	⑦
1992	Sentra	GA16DE	1.6 (1597)	3.4	5.9	⑨	6.4	—	13.3	⑩
	Sentra	SR20DE	2.0 (1998)	3.6	5.9	⑨	7.4	—	13.3	⑦

① Pulsar
② Turbo
③ DOHC
④ 4WD—13.8 gal.
⑤ 4WD—12.4 gal.
⑥ MT—4.9, AT—5.5
⑦ MT—5.9, AT—6.1
⑧ 4WD and AT—6.3 qts.
⑨ RS5F31A—6.2 pts.
RS5F32V—7.8 pts.
⑩ MT—5.4, AT—5.7 qts.

Troubleshooting Basic Air Conditioning Problems

Problem	Cause	Solution
There's little or no air coming from the vents (and you're sure it's on)	• The A/C fuse is blown • Broken or loose wires or connections • The on/off switch is defective	• Check and/or replace fuse • Check and/or repair connections • Replace switch
The air coming from the vents is not cool enough	• Windows and air vent wings open • The compressor belt is slipping • Heater is on • Condenser is clogged with debris • Refrigerant has escaped through a leak in the system • Receiver/drier is plugged	• Close windows and vent wings • Tighten or replace compressor belt • Shut heater off • Clean the condenser • Check system • Service system
The air has an odor	• Vacuum system is disrupted • Odor producing substances on the evaporator case • Condensation has collected in the bottom of the evaporator housing	• Have the system checked/repaired • Clean the evaporator case • Clean the evaporator housing drains
System is noisy or vibrating	• Compressor belt or mountings loose • Air in the system	• Tighten or replace belt; tighten mounting bolts • Have the system serviced
Sight glass condition		
Constant bubbles, foam or oil streaks	• Undercharged system	• Charge the system
Clear sight glass, but no cold air	• No refrigerant at all	• Check and charge the system
Clear sight glass, but air is cold	• System is OK	
Clouded with milky fluid	• Receiver drier is leaking dessicant	• Have system checked
Large difference in temperature of lines	• System undercharged	• Charge and leak test the system
Compressor noise	• Broken valves • Overcharged • Incorrect oil level • Piston slap • Broken rings • Drive belt pulley bolts are loose	• Replace the valve plate • Discharge, evacuate and install the correct charge • Isolate the compressor and check the oil level. Correct as necessary. • Replace the compressor • Replace the compressor • Tighten with the correct torque specification
Excessive vibration	• Incorrect belt tension • Clutch loose • Overcharged • Pulley is misaligned	• Adjust the belt tension • Tighten the clutch • Discharge, evacuate and install the correct charge • Align the pulley
Condensation dripping in the passenger compartment	• Drain hose plugged or improperly positioned • Insulation removed or improperly installed	• Clean the drain hose and check for proper installation • Replace the insulation on the expansion valve and hoses

Troubleshooting Basic Air Conditioning Problems (cont.)

Problem	Cause	Solution
Frozen evaporator coil	• Faulty thermostat • Thermostat capillary tube improperly installed • Thermostat not adjusted properly	• Replace the thermostat • Install the capillary tube correctly • Adjust the thermostat
Low side low—high side low	• System refrigerant is low • Expansion valve is restricted	• Evacuate, leak test and charge the system • Replace the expansion valve
Low side high—high side low	• Internal leak in the compressor—worn	• Remove the compressor cylinder head and inspect the compressor. Replace the valve plate assembly if necessary. If the compressor pistons, rings or
Low side high—high side low (cont.)		cylinders are excessively worn or scored replace the compressor
	• Cylinder head gasket is leaking	• Install a replacement cylinder head gasket
	• Expansion valve is defective • Drive belt slipping	• Replace the expansion valve • Adjust the belt tension
Low side high—high side high	• Condenser fins obstructed • Air in the system • Expansion valve is defective • Loose or worn fan belts	• Clean the condenser fins • Evacuate, leak test and charge the system • Replace the expansion valve • Adjust or replace the belts as necessary
Low side low—high side high	• Expansion valve is defective • Restriction in the refrigerant hose	• Replace the expansion valve • Check the hose for kinks—replace if necessary
Low side low—high side high	• Restriction in the receiver/drier • Restriction in the condenser	• Replace the receiver/drier • Replace the condenser
Low side and high normal (inadequate cooling)	**• Air in the system** **• Moisture in the system**	**• Evacuate, leak test and charge the system** **• Evacuate, leak test and charge the system**

Troubleshooting Basic Wheel Problems

Problem	Cause	Solution
The car's front end vibrates at high speed	• The wheels are out of balance • Wheels are out of alignment	• Have wheels balanced • Have wheel alignment checked/adjusted
Car pulls to either side	• Wheels are out of alignment • Unequal tire pressure • Different size tires or wheels	• Have wheel alignment checked/adjusted • Check/adjust tire pressure • Change tires or wheels to same size
The car's wheel(s) wobbles	• Loose wheel lug nuts • Wheels out of balance • Damaged wheel • Wheels are out of alignment • Worn or damaged ball joint • Excessive play in the steering linkage (usually due to worn parts) • Defective shock absorber	• Tighten wheel lug nuts • Have tires balanced • Raise car and spin the wheel. If the wheel is bent, it should be replaced • Have wheel alignment checked/adjusted • Check ball joints • Check steering linkage • Check shock absorbers
Tires wear unevenly or prematurely	• Incorrect wheel size • Wheels are out of balance • Wheels are out of alignment	• Check if wheel and tire size are compatible • Have wheels balanced • Have wheel alignment checked/adjusted

Troubleshooting Basic Tire Problems

Problem	Cause	Solution
The car's front end vibrates at high speeds and the steering wheel shakes	• Wheels out of balance • Front end needs aligning	• Have wheels balanced • Have front end alignment checked
The car pulls to one side while cruising	• Unequal tire pressure (car will usually pull to the low side) • Mismatched tires • Front end needs aligning	• Check/adjust tire pressure • Be sure tires are of the same type and size • Have front end alignment checked
Abnormal, excessive or uneven tire wear See "How to Read Tire Wear"	• Infrequent tire rotation • Improper tire pressure • Sudden stops/starts or high speed on curves	• Rotate tires more frequently to equalize wear • Check/adjust pressure • Correct driving habits
Tire squeals	• Improper tire pressure • Front end needs aligning	• Check/adjust tire pressure • Have front end alignment checked

Tire Size Comparison Chart

"Letter" sizes			Inch Sizes	Metric-inch Sizes		
"60 Series"	"70 Series"	"78 Series"	1965–77	"60 Series"	"70 Series"	"80 Series"
			5.50-12, 5.60-12	165/60-12	165/70-12	155-12
		Y78-12	6.00-12			
		W78-13	5.20-13	165/60-13	145/70-13	135-13
		Y78-13	5.60-13	175/60-13	155/70-13	145-13
			6.15-13	185/60-13	165/70-13	155-13, P155/80-13
A60-13	A70-13	A78-13	6.40-13	195/60-13	175/70-13	165-13
B60-13	B70-13	B78-13	6.70-13	205/60-13	185/70-13	175-13
			6.90-13			
C60-13	C70-13	C78-13	7.00-13	215/60-13	195/70-13	185-13
D60-13	D70-13	D78-13	7.25-13			
E60-13	E70-13	E78-13	7.75-13			195-13
			5.20-14	165/60-14	145/70-14	135-14
			5.60-14	175/60-14	155/70-14	145-14
			5.90-14			
A60-14	A70-14	A78-14	6.15-14	185/60-14	165/70-14	155-14
	B70-14	B78-14	6.45-14	195/60-14	175/70-14	165-14
	C70-14	C78-14	6.95-14	205/60-14	185/70-14	175-14
D60-14	D70-14	D78-14				
E60-14	E70-14	E78-14	7.35-14	215/60-14	195/70-14	185-14
F60-14	F70-14	F78-14, F83-14	7.75-14	225/60-14	200/70-14	195-14
G60-14	G70-14	G77-14, G78-14	8.25-14	235/60-14	205/70-14	205-14
H60-14	H70-14	H78-14	8.55-14	245/60-14	215/70-14	215-14
J60-14	J70-14	J78-14	8.85-14	255/60-14	225/70-14	225-14
L60-14	L70-14		9.15-14	265/60-14	235/70-14	
	A70-15	A78-15	5.60-15	185/60-15	165/70-15	155-15
B60-15	B70-15	B78-15	6.35-15	195/60-15	175/70-15	165-15
C60-15	C70-15	C78-15	6.85-15	205/60-15	185/70-15	175-15
	D70-15	D78-15				
E60-15	E70-15	E78-15	7.35-15	215/60-15	195/70-15	185-15
F60-15	F70-15	F78-15	7.75-15	225/60-15	205/70-15	195-15
G60-15	G70-15	G78-15	8.15-15/8.25-15	235/60-15	215/70-15	205-15
H60-15	H70-15	H78-15	8.45-15/8.55-15	245/60-15	225/70-15	215-15
J60-15	J70-15	J78-15	8.85-15/8.90-15	255/60-15	235/70-15	225-15
	K70-15		9.00-15	265/60-15	245/70-15	230-15
L60-15	L70-15	L78-15, L84-15	9.15-15			235-15
	M70-15	M78-15				255-15
		N78-15				

NOTE: Every size tire is not listed and many size comaprisons are approximate, based on load ratings. Wider tires than those supplied new with the vehicle should always be checked for clearance

2
ENGINE PERFORMANCE AND TUNE-UP
Electronic Ignition 2-5
Firing Orders 2-5
Idle Speed and Mixture Adjustment 2-14
Ignition Timing 2-9
Tune-up Charts 2-2
Valve Lash Adjustment 2-13

GASOLINE ENGINE TUNE-UP SPECIFICATIONS

Year	Engine ID	Engine Displacement Liters (cc)	Spark Plugs Gap (in.)	Ignition Timing (deg.) MT	Ignition Timing (deg.) AT	Fuel Pump (psi)	Idle Speed (rpm) MT	Idle Speed (rpm) AT	Valve Clearance In.	Valve Clearance Ex.
1982	E15	1.5 (1488)	0.041	2A ①	6A	3.0–3.8	750	650	0.011	0.011
1983	E15	1.5 (1488)	0.041	2A	—	3.0–3.8	700	—	0.011	0.011
	E16	1.6 (1597)	0.041	5A	5A	3.0–3.8	750	650	0.011	0.011
1984	E16	1.6 (1597)	0.041	15B	15B	2.8–3.8	750	650	0.011	0.011
	E15ET	1.5 (1488)	0.041	15B ②	8B ②	30–37	800 ③	650	0.011	0.011
1985	E16	1.6 (1597)	0.041	15B ②	8B ②	2.8–3.8	800 ③	650	0.011	0.011
1986	E16	1.6 (1597)	0.041	10B ②	10B ②	2.8–3.8	800	650	0.011	0.011
1987	E16	1.6 (1597)	0.041	2A	2A	2.8–3.8	800	700	0.011	0.011
	E16i	1.6 (1597)	0.041	7B	7B	⑨	800	700	0.011	0.011
	CA16DE	1.6 (1597)	⑦	15B	—	36	800	—	Hyd.	Hyd.
1988	E16i	1.6 (1597)	0.041	7B	7B	⑨	800	700	0.011	0.011
	CA18DE	1.8 (1809)	⑦	15B	15B	36	800	700	Hyd.	Hyd.
1989	GA16i	1.6 (1597)	0.041	7B	7B	34	800	750	Hyd.	Hyd.
	CA18DE	1.8 (1809)	⑦	15B	15B	36	800	700	Hyd.	Hyd.
1990	GA16i	1.6 (1597)	0.041	7B	7B	34	800	900	Hyd.	Hyd.
1991	GA16DE	1.6 (1597)	0.041	10B	10B	36	650 ⑧	800	0.015	0.016
	SR20DE	2.0 (1998)	0.033	15B	15B	36	800	800	Hyd.	Hyd.
1992	GA16DE	1.6 (1597)	0.041	10B	10B	36	650 ⑧	800	0.015	0.016
	SR20DE	2.0 (1998)	0.033	15B	15B	36	800	800	Hyd.	Hyd.

NOTE: The lowest cylinder pressure should be within 75% of the highest cylinder pressure reading. For example, if the highest cylinder is 134 psi, the lowest should be 101. Engine should be at normal operating temperature with throttle valve in the wide open position.

The underhood specifications sticker often reflects tune-up specification changes in production. Sticker figures must be used if they disagree with those in this chart.

① Canada—4A
② California and Canada—5A
③ California and Canada—750
④ Turbo
⑤ EFI
⑥ DOHC
⑦ Do not adjust plug gap
⑧ Canada—750
⑨ 14 psi—2WD
37 psi—4WD

DIESEL ENGINE TUNE-UP SPECIFICATIONS

Year	Engine ID/VIN	Engine Displacement Liters (cc)	Valve Clearance Intake (in.)	Valve Clearance Exhaust (in.)	Intake Valve Opens (deg.)	Injection Pump Setting (deg.)	Injection Nozzle Pressure (psi) New	Injection Nozzle Pressure (psi) Used	Idle Speed (rpm)	Cranking Compression Pressure (psi)
1983	CD17	1.7 (1680)	0.008–0.012	0.016–0.020	NA	①	1920–2033	1778–1920	750	455 @ 200
1984	CD17	1.7 (1680)	0.008–0.012	0.016–0.020	NA	①	1920–2033	1778–1920	750	455 @ 200
1985	CD17	1.7 (1680)	0.008–0.012	0.016–0.020	NA	①	1920–2033	1778–1920	750	455 @ 200
1986	CD17	1.7 (1680)	0.008–0.012	0.016–0.020	NA	0.0370	1920–2033	1778–1920	②	448 @ 284
1987	CD17	1.7 (1680)	0.008–0.012	0.016–0.020	NA	0.0370	1920–2033	1778–1920	700	448 @ 284

① Plunger lift—See text
Low altitudes
M/T 0.0370 in.
A/T 0.0346 in.
High altitudes
M/T 0.0394 in.
A/T 0.0370 in.
② M/T—750
A/T—670 in. Drive

GASOLINE TUNE-UP PROCEDURES

The 1982 through 1992 vehicles, use a more durable spark plug in all models. The manufacturer recommends that the new plugs be replaced every 30,000 miles (48,300km) or 24 months, which ever comes first. On the engines with platinum-tipped spark plugs, replace every 60,000 miles (96,500km) or 48 months, which ever comes first. If conventional spark plugs are used (after first change) these should be replaced at 30,000 miles (48,300km) or 24 months. Certain 1980 Canadian vehicles still use the conventional 12 month, 12,000 mile (19,300km) spark plugs. All models have electronic ignition systems, so there are no breaker points and condenser to replace.

Even though the manufacturer suggests a 30,000 mile (48,300km), 24 month spark plug replacement span for 1982 and later models, it would be wise to remove the plugs and inspect them every 12,000 miles (19,300km) or once a year. Severe driving conditions; such as, stop and go driving, prolonged idling and hard acceleration facilitate changing the spark plugs about every 15,000–20,000 miles (24,000–32,000km).

It might be noted that the tune-up is a good time to take a look around the engine compartment for problems in the making, such as oil and fuel leaks, deteriorating radiator or heater hoses, loose and/or frayed fan belts and etc.

Spark Plugs

➡ **Blue rings on the ceramic portion indicate that the plugs are platinum-tipped type. Do not check and adjust the plug gap.**

A typical spark plug consists of a metal shell surrounding a ceramic insulator. A metal electrode extends downward through the center of the insulator and protrudes a small distance. Located at the end of the plug and attached to the side of the outer metal shell is the side electrode. The side electrode bends in at a 90° angle, so that its tip is even with and parallel to, the tip of the center electrode. The distance between these two electrodes (measured in thousandths of an inch) is called the spark plug gap. The spark plug in no way produces a spark but merely provides a gap across which the current can arc. The coil produces anywhere from 20,000–40,000 volts, which travels to the distributor where it is distributed through the spark plug wire to the spark plugs. The current passes along the center electrode, then jumps the gap to the side electrode and ignites the air/fuel mixture in the combustion chamber.

Spark plug life and efficiency depend upon the condition of the engine and the temperatures to which the plug is exposed. Combustion chamber temperatures are affected by many factors such as compression ratio of the engine, air/fuel mixtures, exhaust emission equipment and the type of driving you do. Spark plugs are designed and classified by number according to the heat range at which they will operate most efficiently.

➡ **A few of the most common reasons for plug fouling and a description of the plug's appearance, are listed in the Color Insert Section, which also offers solutions to the problem.**

HEAT RANGE

While the spark plug heat range has always seemed to be somewhat of a mystical subject for many people, in reality, the entire subject is quite simple. Basically, it boils down to this; the amount of heat the plug absorbs is determined by the length of the lower insulator. The longer the insulator (or the further it extends into the engine), the hotter the plug will operate; the shorter the insulator the cooler it will operate. A plug that absorbs little heat and remains too cool will quickly accumulate deposits of oil and carbon since it is not hot enough to burn them off. This leads to plug fouling and consequently to misfiring. A plug that absorbs too much heat will have no deposits but due to the excessive heat, the electrodes will burn away quickly and in some instances, preignition may result. Preignition takes place when plug tips get so hot that they glow sufficiently to ignite the fuel/air mixture before the actual spark occurs. This early ignition will usually cause a pinging during low speeds and heavy loads. In severe cases, the heat may become high enough to start the fuel/air mixture burning throughout the combustion chamber rather than just to the front of the plug as in normal operation. At this time, the piston is rising in the cylinder making its compression stroke. The burning mass is compressed and an explosion results, forcing the piston back down in the cylinder while it is still trying to go up. Obviously, something must go and it does: pistons are often damaged.

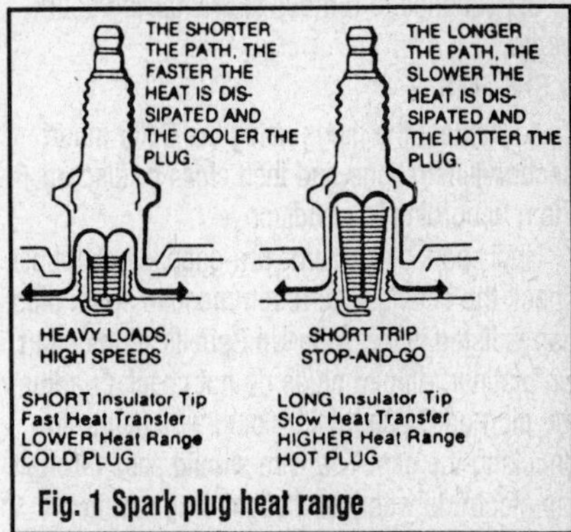
THE SHORTER THE PATH, THE FASTER THE HEAT IS DISSIPATED AND THE COOLER THE PLUG.
THE LONGER THE PATH, THE SLOWER THE HEAT IS DISSIPATED AND THE HOTTER THE PLUG.
HEAVY LOADS, HIGH SPEEDS
SHORT TRIP STOP-AND-GO
SHORT Insulator Tip
Fast Heat Transfer
LOWER Heat Range
COLD PLUG
LONG Insulator Tip
Slow Heat Transfer
HIGHER Heat Range
HOT PLUG
Fig. 1 Spark plug heat range

➧ SEE FIG. 1

The general rule of thumb for choosing the correct heat range when picking a spark plug is: if most of your driving is long distance, high speed travel, use a colder plug; if most of your driving is stop and go, use a hotter plug. Factory installed plugs are, of course, compromise plugs, since the factory has no way of knowing what sort of driving you do. It should be noted that most people never have the need to change their plugs from the factory recommended heat range.

REMOVAL & INSTALLATION

➡ **On Pulsar engines, CA16DE and CA18DE the ornament cover (8 screws) must be removed to gain access to the spark plugs.**

1. Grasp the spark plug boot and pull it straight out. Don't pull on the wire. If the boot(s) are cracked, replace them.
2. Place the spark plug socket firmly on the plug. Turn the spark plug out of the cylinder head in a counterclockwise direction.

➡ **The cylinder head is aluminum, which is easily stripped. Remove the plugs ONLY when the engine is cold. If removal is difficult, loosen the plug only slightly and drip penetrating oil onto the threads. Allow the oil time enough to work and then unscrew the plug. If removal is still difficult, retighten and loosen until the plug comes free. Proceeding in this manner will prevent damaging the cylinder head threads. Be sure to keep the socket straight to avoid breaking the ceramic insulator. During**

installation, coat the plug threads with anti-seize compound to ease future removal.

3. Continue to remove the remaining spark plugs.

➧ SEE FIGS. 2–6

4. Inspect the plugs using the Color Insert section illustrations and then clean or discard them according to condition.

New spark plugs come pre-gapped but double check the setting. The recommended spark plug gap is listed in the Tune-Up Specifications chart. On platinum-tipped plugs do not check or adjust the plug gap. Use a spark plug wire gauge for checking the gap. The wire should pass through the electrode with just a slight drag. Using the electrode bending tool on the end of the gauge, bend the side electrode to adjust the gap. Never attempt to adjust the center electrode. Lightly oil the threads of the replacement plug and install it hand-tight. It is a good practice to use a torque wrench to tighten the spark plugs on any vehicle, especially the aluminum head type. Torque the spark plugs to 14–22 ft. lbs. (18–26 Nm). Install the ignition wire boots firmly on the spark plugs.

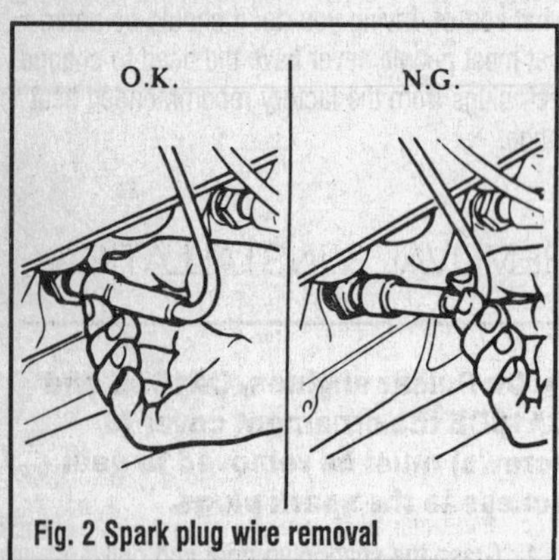
O.K.
N.G.

Fig. 2 Spark plug wire removal

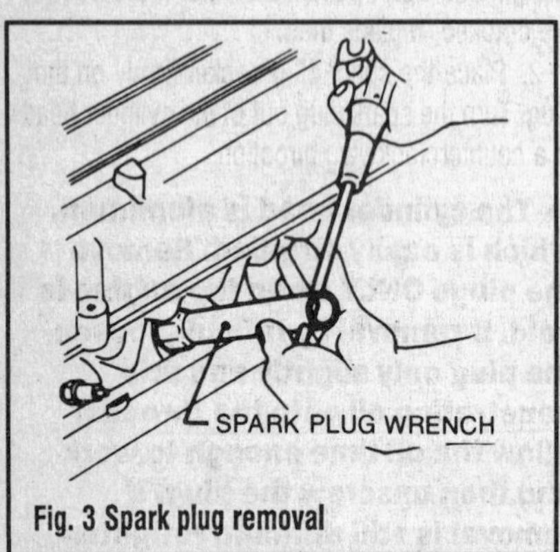
SPARK PLUG WRENCH

Fig. 3 Spark plug removal

➡ Always start threading the spark plugs by hand. Never use a tool to start threading a spark plug. Be careful not to crossthread the spark plug.

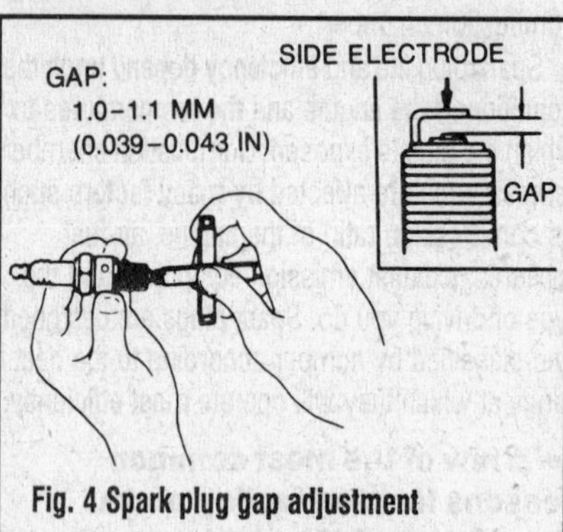
SIDE ELECTRODE
GAP:
1.0–1.1 MM
(0.039–0.043 IN)
GAP

Fig. 4 Spark plug gap adjustment

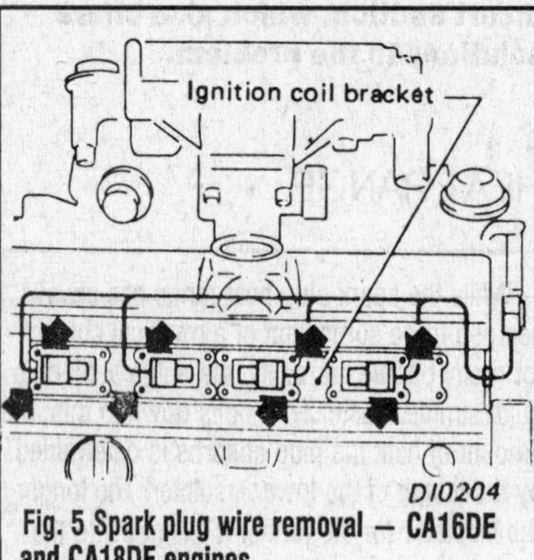
Ignition coil bracket
DI0204

Fig. 5 Spark plug wire removal — CA16DE and CA18DE engines

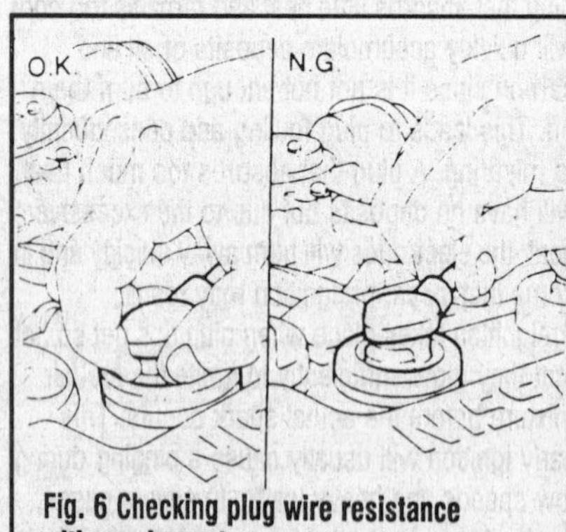
O.K.
N.G.

Fig. 6 Checking plug wire resistance with an ohmmeter

Spark Plug Wires

Visually inspect the spark plug cables for burns, cuts or breaks in the insulation. Check the spark plug boots and the nipples on the distributor cap and coil. Replace any damaged wiring. If no physical damage is obvious, the wires can be checked with an ohmmeter for excessive resistance. Remove the distributor cap and leave the wires connected to the cap. Connect one lead of the ohmmeter to the corresponding electrode inside the cap and the other lead to the spark plug terminal (remove it from the spark plug for the test). Replace any wire which shows over 50,000Ω. Generally speaking, however, resistance should run between 35,000–50,000Ω. Test the coil wire by connecting the ohmmeter between the center contact in the cap and either of the primary terminals at the coil. If the total resistance of the coil and the cable is more than 25,000Ω, remove the cable from the coil and check the resistance of the cable. If the resistance is higher than 15,000Ω, replace the cable. It should be remembered that wire resistance is a function of length and that the longer the cable, the greater the resistance. Thus, if the cables on your car are longer than the factory originals, resistance will be higher and quite possibly outside of these limits.

➧ SEE FIG.7

When installing a new set of spark plug cables, replace the cables one at a time so that you can match up the length of each old plug wire with the new ones and there will be no mix-up. Start by replacing the longest cable first. Install the boot firmly over the spark plug. Route the wire exactly the same as the original. Insert the nipple firmly into the tower on the distributor cap. Repeat the process for each cable.

➡ On the Pulsar engines, CA16DE and CA18DE no spark plug wires are used.

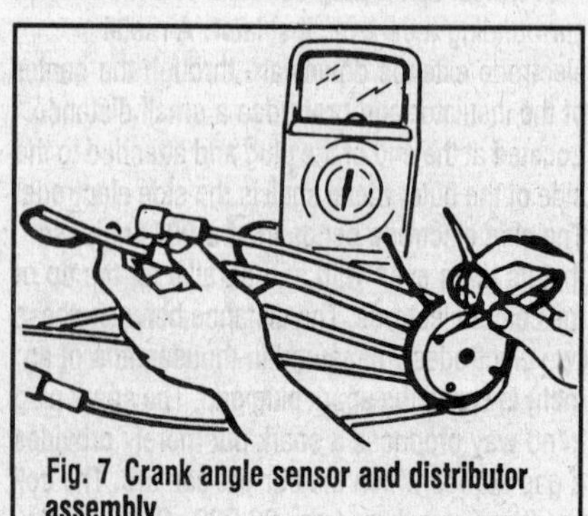

Fig. 7 Crank angle sensor and distributor assembly

FIRING ORDERS

➡ To avoid confusion, remove and tag the wires one at a time, for replacement.

➧ SEE FIG.8

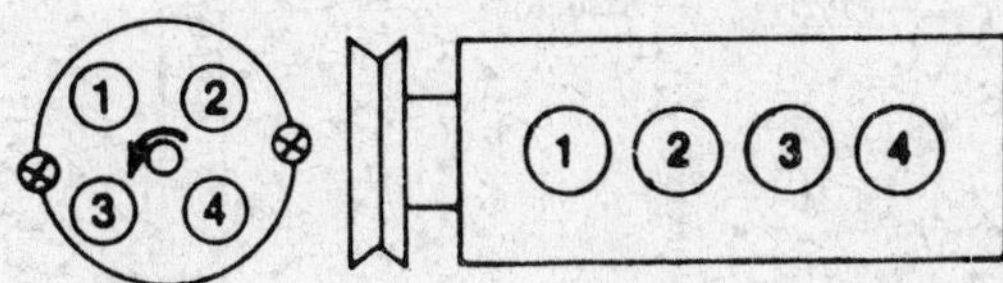
1
2
3
4
1
2
3
4

Fig. 8 Firing order: 1-3-4-2 — all engines

ELECTRONIC IGNITION

Except Direct Ignition

DESCRIPTION AND OPERATION

The electronic ignition system differs from the conventional breaker points system in form only; its function is exactly the same: to supply a spark to the spark plugs at precisely the right moment to ignite the compressed gas in the cylinders and create mechanical movement.

Located in the distributor, in addition to the rotor cap, is a spoked reluctor which fits on the distributor shaft where the breaker points cam is found on non-electronic ignitions. The reluctor revolves with the rotor head, as it passes a pickup coil inside the distributor body it breaks a high flux field, which occurs in the space between the reluctor and the pickup coil. The breaking of the field allows current to flow to the pickup coil. Primary ignition current is then cut off by the electronic ignition unit, allowing the magnetic field in the ignition coil to collapse, creating the spark which the distributor passes on to the spark plug.

There are 4 different types of distributors used with electronic ignition systems. A single post pickup coil with a transistor ignition unit, a ring type pickup coil with a IC ignition unit, IC ignition unit without a pick up coil and a crank angle sensor are the main differences in the distributors used for these systems.

➧ SEE FIGS. 9–12

Because no points or condenser are used, and because dwell is determined by the electronic unit, no adjustments are necessary. Ignition timing is generally checked in the usual way (be careful to check for slight variations depending on model and engine), but unless the distributor is disturbed it is not likely to ever change very much.

Service consists of inspection of the distributor cap, rotor, and ignition wires, replacing when necessary. These parts can be expected to last at least 40,000 miles (64,300km). In addition, the reluctor air gap should be checked periodically.

The 1983 Pulsar for the 49 states and the California and Canada models used no pickup coil for the electronic ignition system and the IC ignition unit is mounted on the inside of the distributor. The 1984–86 Pulsar for California and Canada models without a turbocharged engine uses no pickup coil for the electronic ignition system and the IC ignition unit is mounted on the inside of the distributor housing.

The 1984–88 (E16 engine only) for the 49 states, the 1987–88 California and Canada models (E16 engine only) and the turbocharged version of the Pulsar use a crank angle sensor. This sensor monitors engine speed and piston position and sends to the computer signals on which the controls of the fuel injection, ignition timing and other functions are based.

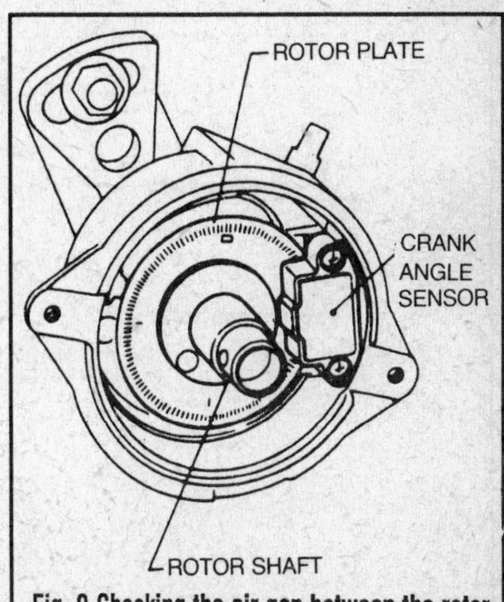
ROTOR PLATE
CRANK ANGLE SENSOR
ROTOR SHAFT

Fig. 9 Checking the air gap between the rotor and stator

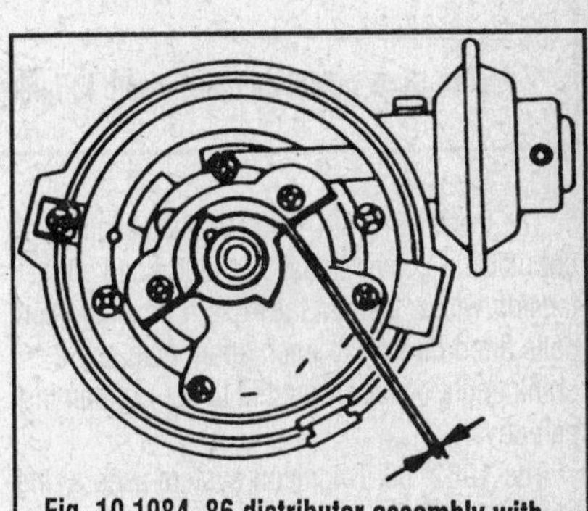

Fig. 10 1984–86 distributor assembly with IC igniter unit and pickup coil

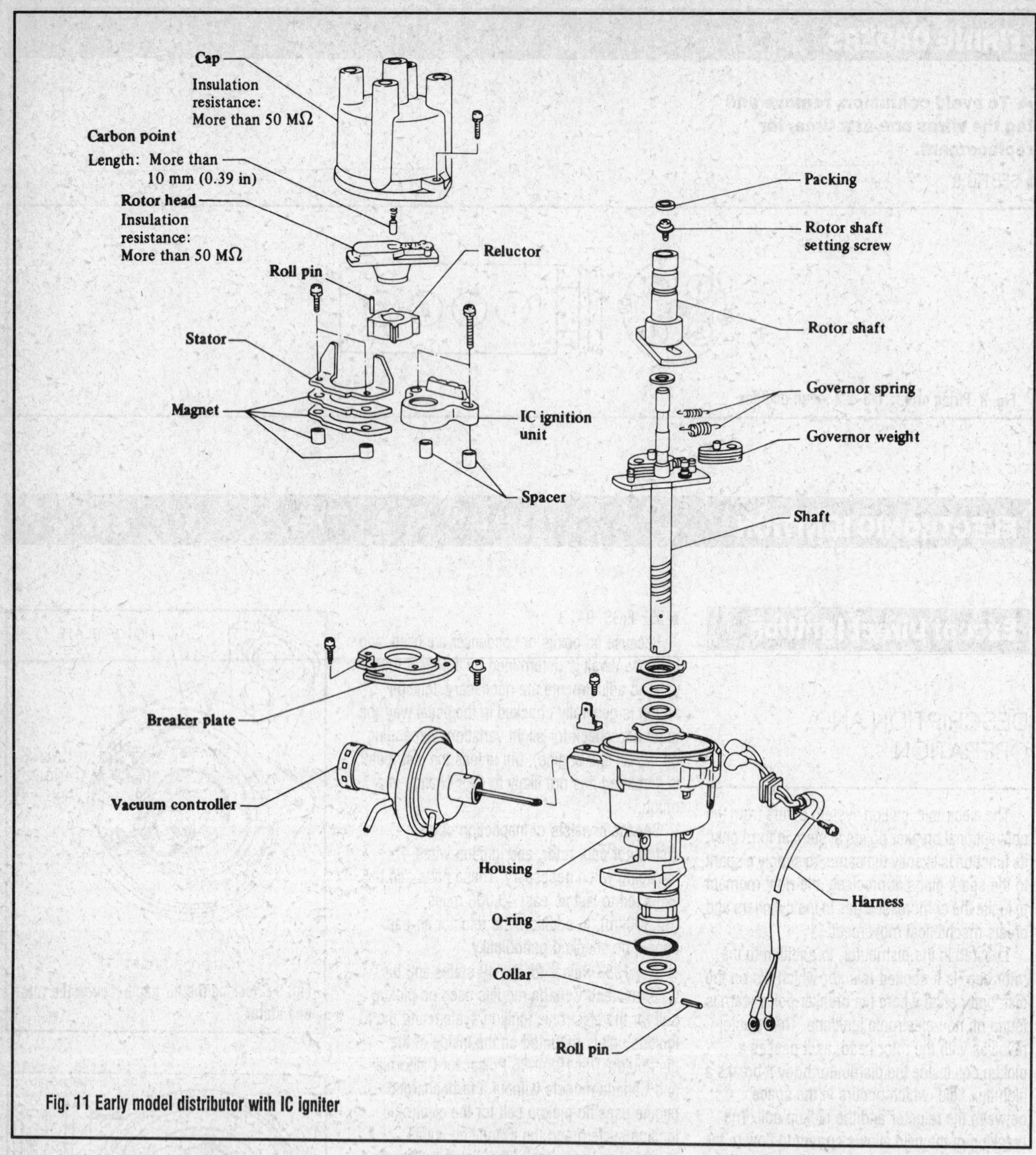

Cap
Insulation resistance: More than 50 MΩ
Carbon point
Length: More than 10 mm (0.39 in)
Rotor head
Insulation resistance: More than 50 MΩ
Roll pin
Reluctor
Stator
Magnet
IC ignition unit
Spacer
Packing
Rotor shaft setting screw
Rotor shaft
Governor spring
Governor weight
Shaft
Breaker plate
Vacuum controller
Housing
O-ring
Collar
Roll pin
Harness

Fig. 11 Early model distributor with IC igniter

The Pulsar CA16DE and CA18DE engines do not utilize a conventional distributor and high tension wires. Instead they use 4 small ignition coils fitted directly to each spark plug and a crank angle sensor mounted in the front timing belt cover.

The 1982–86 IC ignition system uses a ring-type pickup coil which surrounds the reluctor instead of the single post type pickup coil on earlier models.

1987–92 Sentra models are equipped with a different means of generating the distributor signal. The reluctor and pickup coil are replaced by a rotor plate and crank angle sensor. The rotor plate is machined with slits that break and then restore a beam of light (a light emitting diode is situated above the plate and a photo-sensitive diode is located underneath). There are 360 slits in the plate to generate an engine speed signal and 4 slits to generate 180° crank angle signals.

When the slits in the rotor plate break and then restore the beam of light, the photo diode generates rough pulses. Then, a wave forming circuit located in the base of the distributor converts these pulses to clear on-off pulses. The Electronic Control Unit, a microcomputer, then utilizes these signals, in combination with others, to generate the actual on-off signal that controls the ignition coil and fires the ignition.

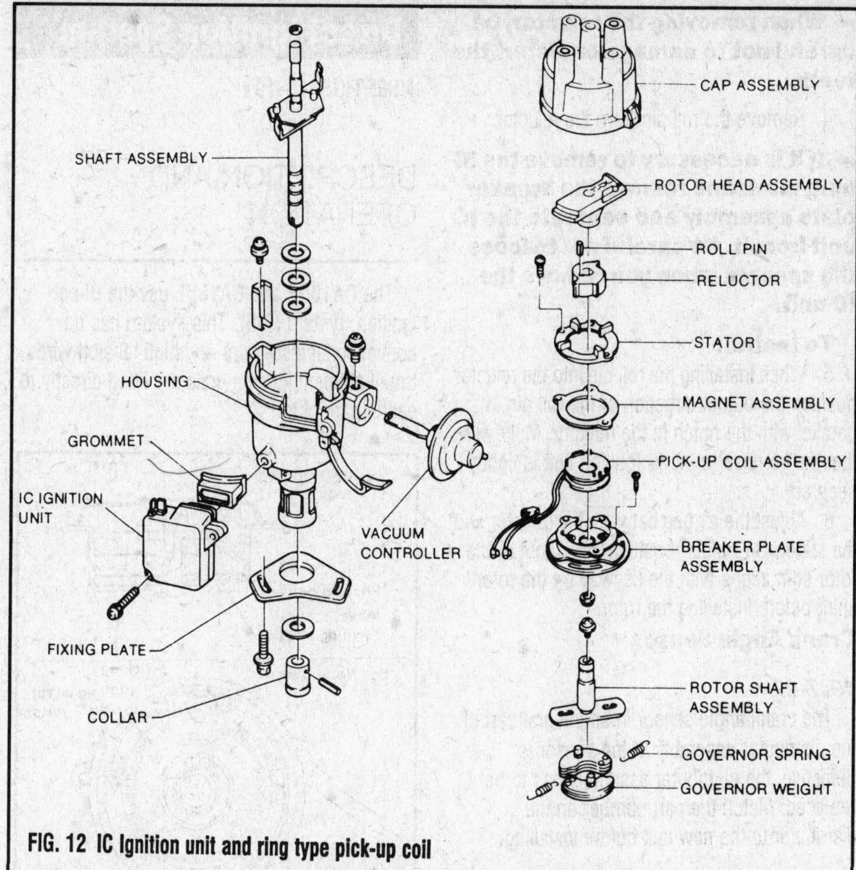
CAP ASSEMBLY
SHAFT ASSEMBLY
ROTOR HEAD ASSEMBLY
ROLL PIN
RELUCTOR
STATOR
HOUSING
MAGNET ASSEMBLY
GROMMET
PICK-UP COIL ASSEMBLY
IC IGNITION UNIT
VACUUM CONTROLLER
BREAKER PLATE ASSEMBLY
FIXING PLATE
ROTOR SHAFT ASSEMBLY
COLLAR
GOVERNOR SPRING
GOVERNOR WEIGHT

FIG. 12 IC Ignition unit and ring type pick-up coil

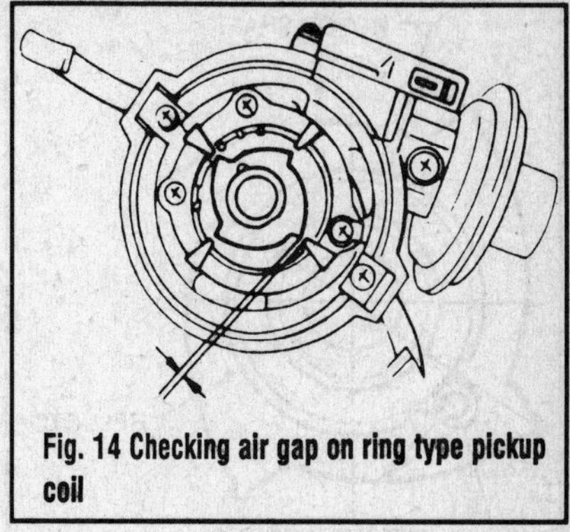

Fig. 14 Checking air gap on ring type pickup coil

Service on electronic ignition systems consist of inspection of the distributor cap, rotor and ignition wires replacing them when necessary. Check the ignition wires for cracking of exterior insulation and for proper fit on the distributor cap and spark plugs. These parts can be expected to last for at least 40,000 miles (64,300km) but you should inspect these parts every 2 years or 30,000 miles (48,300km). In addition, the reluctor air gap should be checked periodically if the system has no crank angle sensor.

DIAGNOSIS AND TESTING

1982–86 Models

IGNITION COIL

1. Using a spark tester, verify that no spark is present at a plug wire.

2. Check the coil resistance at the 2 terminals. The resistance should be 1.04–1.27Ω. Check the resistance between the negative terminal and the center tower. The resistance should be 7300–11000Ω. If not, replace the ignition coil.

1987–92

Diagnosis and testing of the electronic ignition system for 1987–92 vehicles is covered extensively in Section 4 under "Electronic Engine Controls."

ADJUSTMENT

Air Gap (1982–86)

1. The distributor cap is held on by 2 spring clips. Release them with a screwdriver and lift the cap straight up and off, with the wires attached.

2. Pull the rotor head (not the spoked reluctor) straight up to remove it.

3. Check the reluctor air gap by using a non-magnetic feeler gauge. Rotate the engine until a reluctor spoke is aligned with the single post pickup coil or stator depending on the type used on the vehicle. Bump the engine around with the starter or turn it with a wrench on the crankshaft pulley bolt. The gap should measure 0.012–0.020 in. (0.3–0.5mm). Adjustment, if necessary, is made by loosening the single post pickup coil mounting screws and shifting the coil either closer to or farther from the reluctor on early models. Measure the air gap between the reluctor and stator. If not within specifications, loosen stator retaining screws and adjust.

➧ SEE FIG. 14

PARTS REPLACEMENT

Reluctor and IC Ignition Unit

1982–86

➡ The engines of this period are equipped with a slightly different ignition system and do not utilize a pickup coil.

1. Remove the distributor cap and pull the rotor from the distributor shaft.

➡ The rotor on the Stanza is held to the distributor shaft by a retaining screw, which must be removed.

2. Remove the wiring harness and the vacuum controller from the housing.

➧ SEE FIGS. 15–17

3. Using 2 flat bladed screwdrivers, place one on each side of the reluctor and pry it from the distributor shaft.

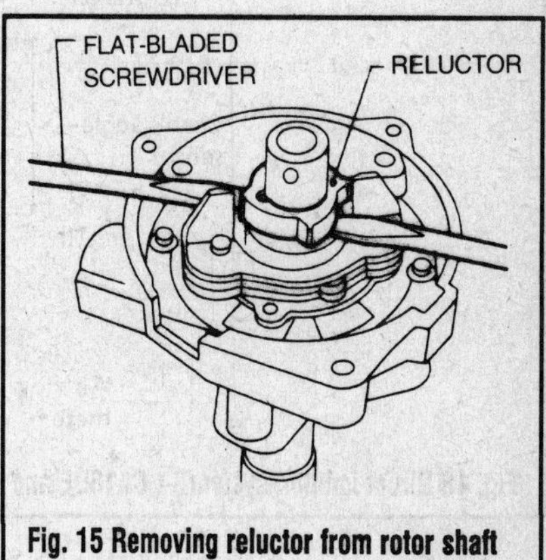
FLAT-BLADED SCREWDRIVER
RELUCTOR

Fig. 15 Removing reluctor from rotor shaft

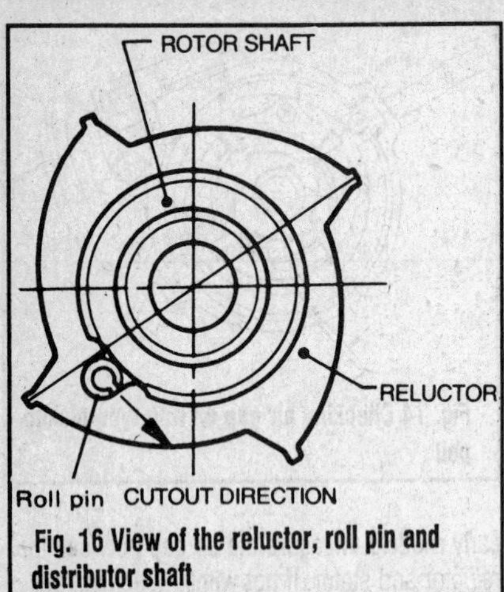
ROTOR SHAFT
RELUCTOR
Roll pin
CUTOUT DIRECTION
Fig. 16 View of the reluctor, roll pin and distributor shaft

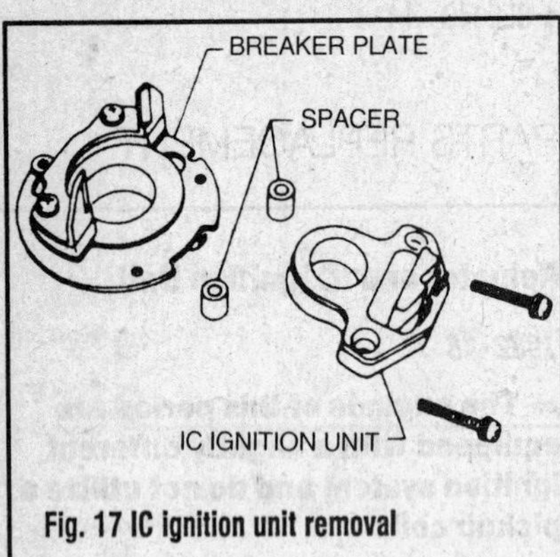
BREAKER PLATE
SPACER
IC IGNITION UNIT
Fig. 17 IC ignition unit removal

➡ **When removing the reluctor, be careful not to damage or distort the teeth.**

4. Remove the roll pin from the reluctor.

➡ **If it is necessary to remove the IC unit, mark and remove the breaker plate assembly and separate the IC unit from it. Be careful not to loose the spacers when you remove the IC unit.**

To install:

5. When installing the roll pin into the reluctor position the cutout direction of the roll pin in parallel with the notch in the reluctor. Make sure that the harness to the IC ignition unit is tightly secured.

6. Adjust the air gap between the reluctor and the stator. On Pulsar, position the cutout of the rotor so it aligns with the keyway on the rotor shaft before installing the rotor.

Crank Angle Sensor

1987–92

The crank angle sensor in an integral part of the distributor assembly. If the sensor is defective, the distributor assembly has to be replaced. Match the part number on the distributor to the new unit before installing.

Direct Ignition System

➧ SEE FIGS. 18–19

DESCRIPTION AND OPERATION

The CA16DE and CA18DE use the Direct Ignition System (DIS). This system has no conventional distributor and high tension wires. Small efficient ignition coils are fitted directly to each spark plug.

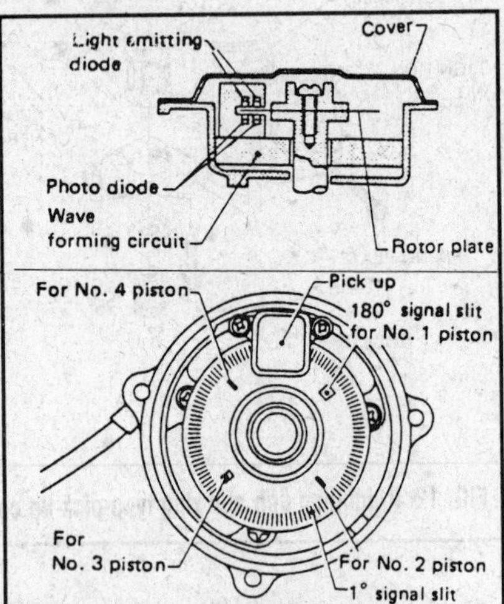
Light emitting diode
Cover
Photo diode
Wave forming circuit
Rotor plate
For No. 4 piston
Pick up
180° signal slit for No. 1 piston
For No. 3 piston
For No. 2 piston
1° signal slit
Fig. 19 Crank angle sensor inside the distributor — distributor is serviced as a complete unit

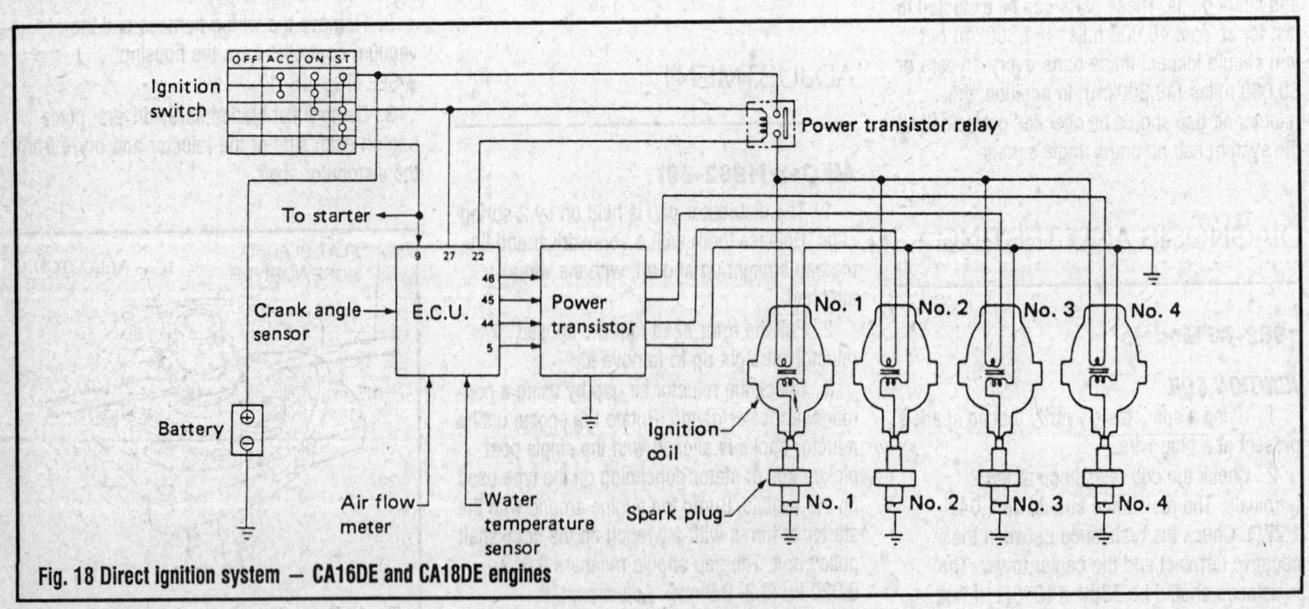
OFF
ACC
ON
ST
Ignition switch
Power transistor relay
To starter
9
27
22
46
45
44
5
Crank angle sensor
E.C.U.
Power transistor
No. 1
No. 2
No. 3
No. 4
Battery
Ignition coil
Air flow meter
Water temperature sensor
Spark plug
No. 1
No. 2
No. 3
No. 4
Fig. 18 Direct ignition system — CA16DE and CA18DE engines

The DIS system uses a crank angle sensor as does the late model conventional distributor. The sensor monitors engine speed and piston position. It sends signals to the ECU for control of fuel injection, ignition timing and other functions. The crank angle sensor has a rotor plate and a wave forming circuit. The rotor plate has 360 slits for one degree and 4 slits for 180 degrees. Light Emitting Diode (LED) and photo diodes are built into the wave forming circuit.

When the rotor plate passes the space between the LED and photo diode, the slits of the rotor plate continually cut the light which is sent to the photo diode. This causes rough shaped pulses. They are converted into on-off pulses by the wave forming circuit and then sent to the ECU.

➡ **Diagnosis and testing of the DIS system will be covered in Section 4, under "Electronic Engine Controls"**

IGNITION TIMING

** CAUTION

When performing this or any other operation with the engine running, be very careful of the alternator belt and pulleys. Make sure that your timing light wires don't interfere with the belt. Also, avoid touching the spark plug wires while the engine is running. Failure to follow this caution may cause severe personal injury.

Ignition timing is an important part of the tune-up. The 3 basic types of timing lights are available, the neon, the DC and the AC powered. Of the 3 the DC light is the most frequently used by professional mechanics. The bright flash put out by the DC light makes the timing marks stand out on even the brightest of days. Another advantage of the DC light is that you don't need to be near an electrical outlet. Neon lights are available for a few dollars but their weak flash makes it necessary to use them in a fairly dark work area. The 1 neon light lead is attached to the spark plug and the other to the plug wire. The DC light attaches to the spark plug and the wire with an adapter and 2 clips attach to the battery posts for power. The AC unit is similar, except that the power cable is plugged into a house outlet.

Ignition timing is the measurement, in degrees of crankshaft rotation, of the point at which the spark plugs fire in each of the cylinders. It is measured in degrees before or after Top Dead Center (TDC) of the compression stroke. Basic Ignition timing is controlled by turning the distributor body in the engine. Electronic spark timing is controlled by the Electronic Control Unit (ECU).

Ideally, the air/fuel mixture in the cylinder will be ignited by the spark plug just as the piston passes TDC of the compression stroke. If this happens, the piston will be beginning its downward motion of the power stroke just as the compressed and ignited air/fuel mixture starts to expand. The expansion of the air/fuel mixture then forces the piston down on the power stroke and turns the crankshaft.

Because it takes a fraction of a second for the spark plug to ignite the mixture in the cylinder, the spark plug must fire a little before the piston reaches TDC. Otherwise, the mixture will not be completely ignited as the piston passes TDC and the full power of the explosion will not be used by the engine.

The timing measurement is given in degrees of crankshaft rotation before or after the piston reaches TDC (ATDC) (BTDC). If the setting for the ignition timing is 5° BTDC, the spark plug must fire 5° before each piston reaches TDC. This only holds true, however, when the engine is at idle speed.

As the engine speed increases, the pistons go faster. The spark plugs have to ignite the fuel even sooner, if it is to be completely ignited when the piston reaches TDC. To do this, the distributor has a means to advance the timing of the spark as the engine speed increases. This is accomplished by centrifugal weights within the distributor and a vacuum diaphragm, mounted on the side of the distributor (vehicles without a crank angle sensor). It is necessary to disconnect the vacuum line from the diaphragm when the ignition timing is being set. 1987 or later vehicles are equipped with electronic spark timing to adjust timing as the engine rpm increases.

The timing is best checked with a timing light. This device is connected in series with the No. 1 spark plug. The current which fires the spark plug also causes the timing light to flash. The timing marks consist of a notch or cut out line on the crankshaft pulley and a numbered plate showing crankshaft rotation attached to the front cover. When the engine is running, the timing light is aimed at the marks on the crankshaft pulley and the pointer.

On 1987–88 models, the E.C.C.S. system controls the timing there is no mechanical or vacuum advance used in the distributor. Different sensors send signals to the E.C.U. (E.C.C.S. control unit) which controls the timing.

On the CA16DE and CA18DE engines do not utilize a conventional distributor and spark plug wires. Instead they use 4 small ignition coils fitted directly to each spark plug and a crank angle sensor mounted in the front timing belt.

ADJUSTMENT

All Engines Except CA16DE, CA18DE, GA16DE and SR20DE

➧ SEE FIGS. 20–24

1. If equipped with a point type distributor, set the dwell to the proper specification. If equipped with electronic ignition type distributor, check and/or adjust the reluctor air gap.
2. Locate the timing marks on the crankshaft pulley and the front of the engine.
3. Clean off the timing marks so that you can see them.
4. Use chalk or white paint to color the mark on the crankshaft pulley and the mark on the scale which will indicate the correct timing when aligned with the notch on the crankshaft pulley.
5. Attach a tachometer and a timing light to the engine, according to the manufacturer's instructions.
6. Disconnect and plug the vacuum line at the distributor vacuum diaphragm if so equipped. Distributors with a crank angle sensor do not have a vacuum diaphragm. Distributors with a crank angle sensor go to Step 7. The 1984–89 Pulsar (E16 engine only) for the 49 states, the 1987–89 California, Canada models (E16 engine only), the turbocharged version of the Pulsar and 1987–92 Sentra and NX Coupe use a crank angle sensor.

➡ On the Pulsar, E15ET (1984, Canadian Turbo) engines, disconnect the Idle Control (ICV) valve harness connector. On the Pulsar, E16 (1984 and later, except Calif. and Canada) engines, disconnect the Vacuum Control Modulator (VCM) valve harness connector to adjust the idle speed, then reconnect the harness and make sure that the idle speed is within the proper range.

➧ SEE FIGS. 20–24

7. Check to make sure that all of the wires clear the fan and then start the engine. Allow the engine to reach normal operating temperature.

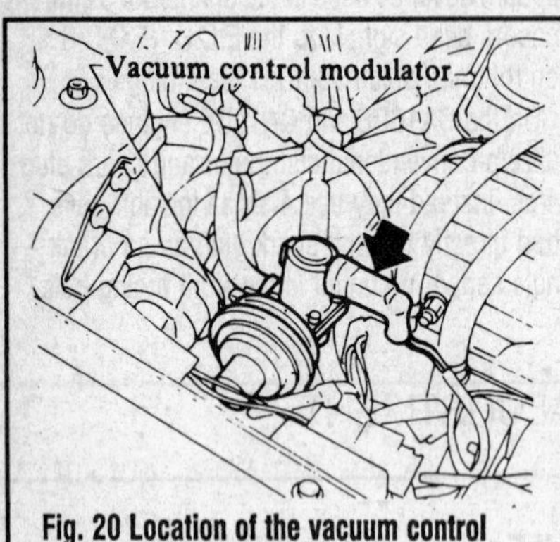
Vacuum control modulator

Fig. 20 Location of the vacuum control models — E16 engine

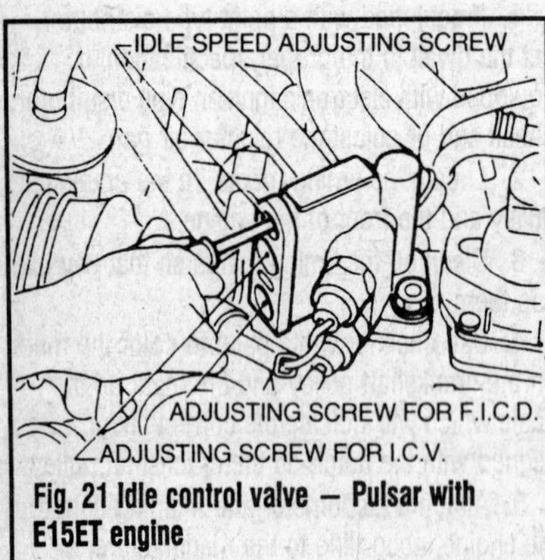
IDLE SPEED ADJUSTING SCREW
ADJUSTING SCREW FOR F.I.C.D.
ADJUSTING SCREW FOR I.C.V.

Fig. 21 Idle control valve — Pulsar with E15ET engine

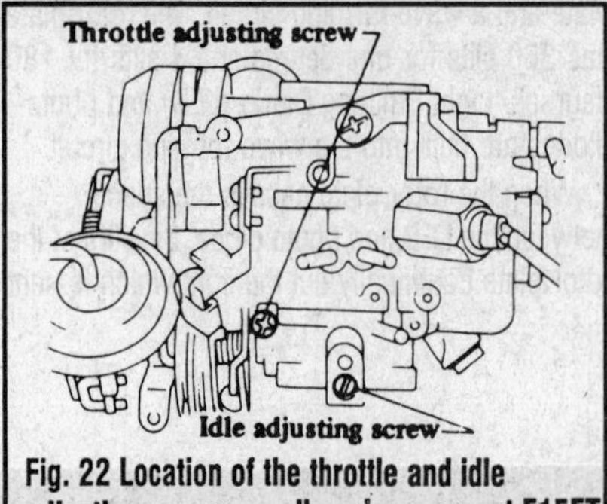
Throttle adjusting screw
Idle adjusting screw

Fig. 22 Location of the throttle and idle adjusting screws — all engines, except E15ET

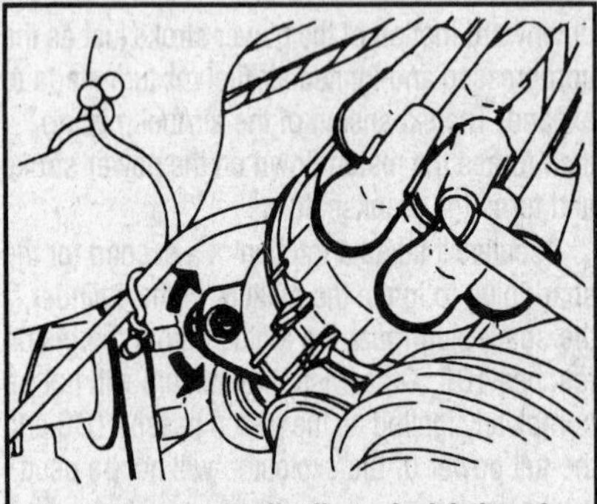

Fig. 23 Loosen the distributor lock bolt and turn the distributor slightly to advance or retard the timing. Advance will increase rpm

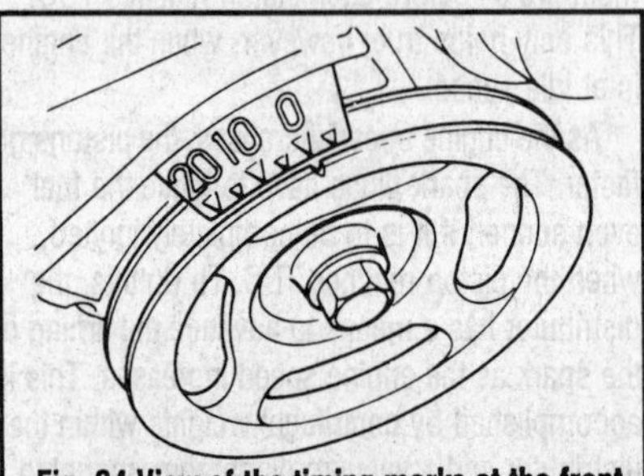
20
10
0

Fig. 24 View of the timing marks at the front of the engine

⁂ CAUTION

Be sure to block the wheels and set the parking brake; if equipped with an automatic transaxle, place the shift selector in the DRIVE position.

8. Adjust the idle to the correct setting.

➡ Before checking and/or adjusting the timing, make sure the electrical switches, such as: the headlights, the radiator cooling fan, the heater blower and the air conditioning are turned OFF; if equipped with power steering, make sure that the wheels are faced straight ahead.

9. Aim the timing light at the timing marks at the front of the engine cover. If the timing marks are aligned when the light flashes, the timing is correct. Turn off the engine, then remove the tachometer and the timing light.

10. If the timing marks are not aligned, proceed with the following steps:

a. Turn off the engine.

b. Loosen the distributor lock bolt, just enough, so that the distributor can be turned with a little effort.

c. Start the engine. Keep the wires of the timing light clear of the fan.

d. With the timing light aimed at the crankshaft pulley and the timing plate on the engine, turn the distributor in the direction of rotor rotation to retard the spark and in the opposite direction to advance the spark. Align the marks on the pulley and the engine scale with the flashes of the timing light.

e. Tighten the holddown bolt. Remove the tachometer and the timing light.

CA16DE And CA18DE Engines

➡ The CA16DE and CA18DE engines do not utilize a conventional distributor and high tension wires. Instead they use 4 small ignition coils fitted directly to each spark plug. The ECU controls the coils by means of a crank angle sensor. The crank angle sensor can be found attached to the upper front timing belt cover.

1. Run the engine until it reaches normal operating temperature.

2. Check that the idle speed is at specifications.

3. Disconnect the air duct and both air hoses at the throttle chamber.

4. Remove the ornament cover between the camshaft covers. It has 8 screws and says "Twin Cam".

5. Remove the ignition coil at the No. 1 cylinder.

6. Connect the No. 1 ignition coil to the No. 1 spark plug with a suitable high tension wire.

7. Use an inductive pick-up type timing light and clamp it to the wire connected in Step 6.

8. Reconnect the air duct and hoses and then start the engine.

9. Check the ignition timing. If not to specifications, turn off the engine and loosen the crank angle sensor mounting bolts slightly.

10. Restart the engine and adjust the timing by turning the sensor body slightly until the timing comes into specifications.

SEE FIGS. 25–29A

GA16DE and SR20DE Engines

1. Start the engine allow to warm to temperature.

2. Run the engine at 2000 rpm for 2 minutes and return to idle.

3. Turn the engine OFF and disconnect the throttle position sensor harness connector.

4. Start the engine and race the engine to 2000 rpm, 3 times.

5. Connect a timing light to the No. 1 spark plug wire and battery.

6. Loosen the distributor hold-down bolt and adjust the ignition timing to **10 degrees BTDC for the GA16DE and 15 degrees for the SR20DE engines.**

7. Turn the engine OFF and reconnect the throttle position sensor harness.

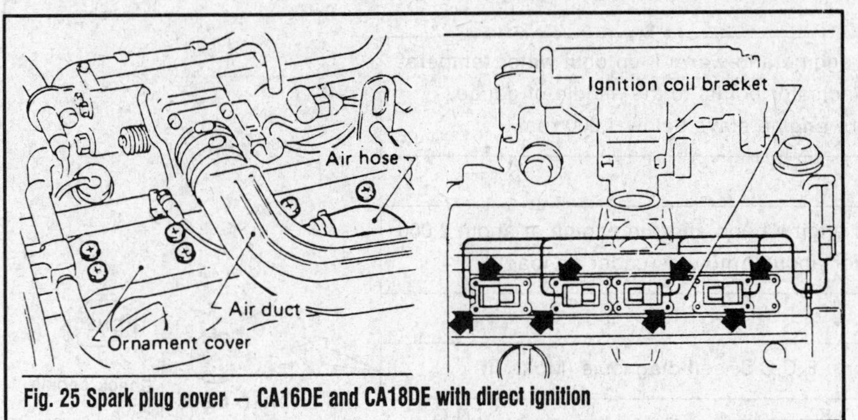
Air hose
Air duct
Ornament cover
Ignition coil bracket
Fig. 25 Spark plug cover — CA16DE and CA18DE with direct ignition

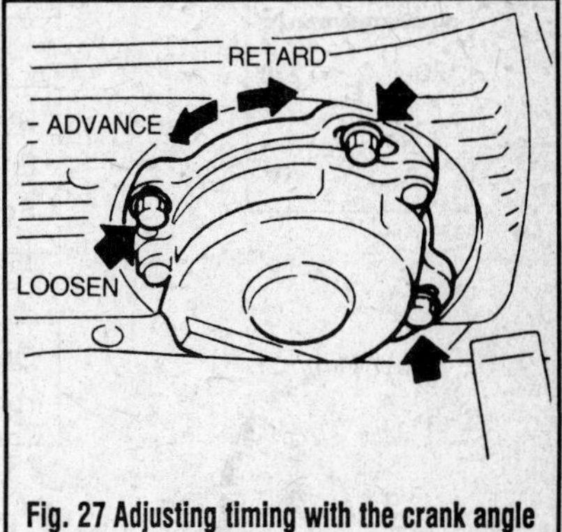
RETARD
ADVANCE
LOOSEN
Fig. 27 Adjusting timing with the crank angle sensor — CA16DE and CA18DE engines

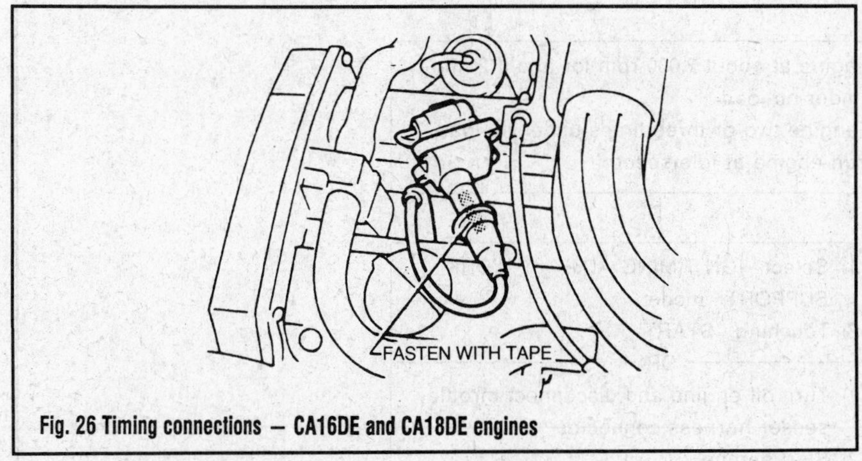
FASTEN WITH TAPE
Fig. 26 Timing connections — CA16DE and CA18DE engines

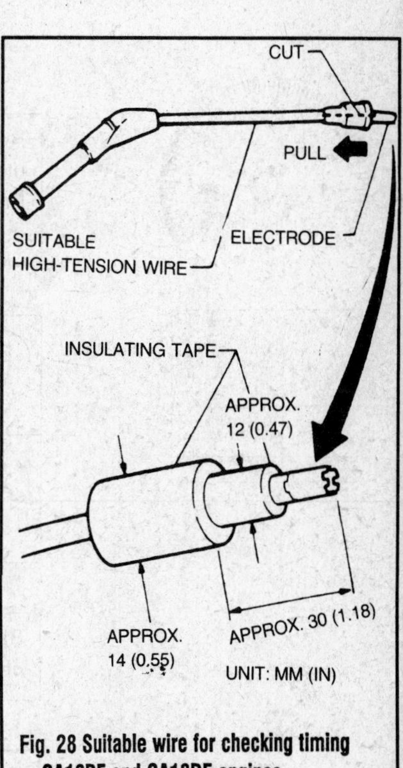
CUT
PULL
SUITABLE
HIGH-TENSION WIRE
ELECTRODE
INSULATING TAPE
APPROX.
12 (0.47)
APPROX.
14 (0.55)
APPROX. 30 (1.18)
UNIT: MM (IN)
Fig. 28 Suitable wire for checking timing — CA16DE and CA18DE engines

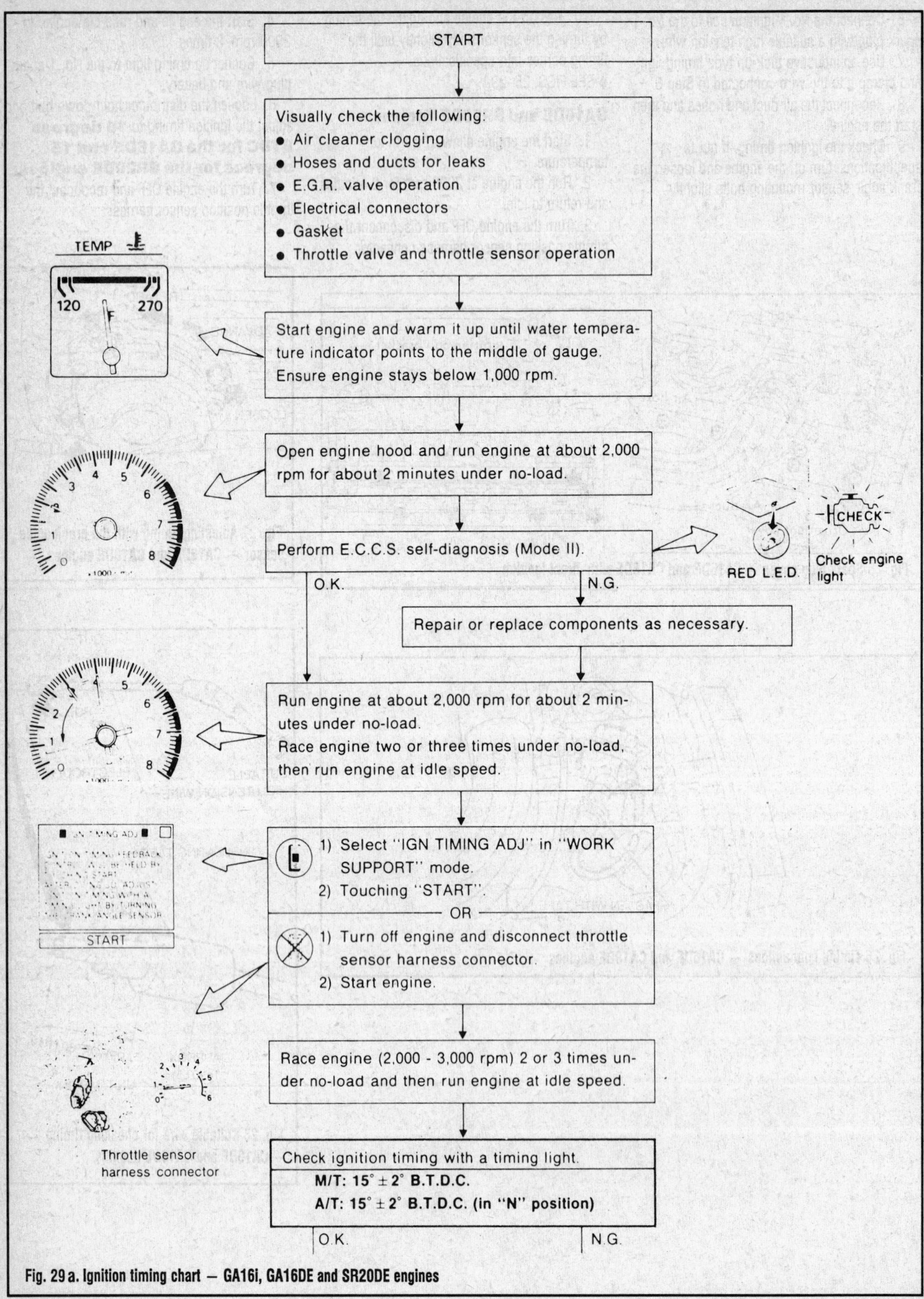
START
Visually check the following:
• Air cleaner clogging
• Hoses and ducts for leaks
• E.G.R. valve operation
• Electrical connectors
• Gasket
• Throttle valve and throttle sensor operation
TEMP
120
270
Start engine and warm it up until water temperature indicator points to the middle of gauge. Ensure engine stays below 1,000 rpm.
Open engine hood and run engine at about 2,000 rpm for about 2 minutes under no-load.
Perform E.C.C.S. self-diagnosis (Mode II).
CHECK
RED L.E.D.
Check engine light
O.K.
N.G.
Repair or replace components as necessary.
Run engine at about 2,000 rpm for about 2 minutes under no-load.
Race engine two or three times under no-load, then run engine at idle speed.
START
1) Select "IGN TIMING ADJ" in "WORK SUPPORT" mode.
2) Touching "START".
OR
1) Turn off engine and disconnect throttle sensor harness connector.
2) Start engine.
Race engine (2,000 - 3,000 rpm) 2 or 3 times under no-load and then run engine at idle speed.
Throttle sensor
harness connector
Check ignition timing with a timing light.
M/T: 15° ± 2° B.T.D.C.
A/T: 15° ± 2° B.T.D.C. (in "N" position)
O.K.
N.G.

Fig. 29 a. Ignition timing chart – GA16i, GA16DE and SR20DE engines

VALVE LASH

Valve adjustment determines how far the valves enter the cylinder and how long they stay open and closed.

If the valve clearance is too large, part of the lift of the camshaft will be used in removing the excessive clearance. Consequently, the valve will not be opening as far as it should. This condition has 2 effects:

a. The valve train components will emit a tapping sound as they take up the excessive clearance.

b. The engine will perform poorly for the valves will not open fully and allow the proper amount of gases to flow through the cylinders.

If the valve clearance is too small, the valves will open too far and not fully seat in the cylinder head when they close. When a valve seats itself in the cylinder head, it does 2 things:

a. It seals the combustion chamber so that none of the gases in the cylinder escape.

b. It cools itself by transferring some of the heat it absorbs from the combustion process, through the cylinder head into the engine's cooling system.

If the valve clearance is too small, the engine will run poorly because of the gases escaping from the combustion chamber. The valves will also become overheated and warped, since they cannot transfer heat unless they are touching the valve seat in the cylinder head.

➡ **While all valve adjustments must be made as accurately as possible, it is better to have the valve adjustment slightly loose than slightly tight, as a burned valve may result from overly tight adjustments.**

VALVE ADJUSTMENT

Except CD17 Diesel and GA16DE Engines

➡ **The GA16i, CA16DE, CA18DE and SR20DE engines use hydraulic lifters. No valve adjustment is necessary or possible. Datsun/Nissan recommends that valve adjustment all other models should be done every 12 months or 15,000 miles (24,000km).**

1. Run the engine until it reaches normal operating temperature. Oil temperature, not water temperature, is critical to valve adjustment. With this in mind, make sure the engine is fully warmed up since this is the only way to make sure the parts have reached their full expansion. Generally speaking, this takes around 15 minutes. After the engine has reached normal operating temperature, shut it off.

➧ SEE FIGS. 29–30

2. Purchase a new valve cover gasket before removing the valve cover. The new silicone gasket sealers are just as good or better if you can't find a gasket.

3. Note the location of any hoses or wires which may interfere with valve cover removal, disconnect and move them aside. Remove the bolts which hold the valve cover in place.

4. After the valve cover has been removed, the next step is to get the number one piston at TDC on the compression stroke. There are at least two ways to do this: Bump the engine over with the starter or turn it over by using a wrench on the front crankshaft pulley bolt. The easiest way to find TDC is to turn the engine over slowly with a wrench (after first removing No. 1 plug) until the piston is at the top of its stroke and the TDC timing mark on the crankshaft pulley is in alignment with the timing mark pointer. At this point, the valves for No. 1 cylinder should be closed.

➡ **Make sure both valves are closed with the valve springs up as high as they will go. An easy way to find the compression stroke is to remove the distributor cap and observe which spark plug lead the rotor is pointing to. If the rotor points to No. 1 spark plug lead, No. 1 cylinder is on its compression stroke. When the rotor points to the No. 2 spark plug lead, No. 2 cylinder is on its compression stroke.**

5. Set the No. 1 piston at TDC of the compression stroke, then check and/or adjust the valve clearance Nos. 1, 2, 3 and 6.

6. To adjust the clearance, loosen the locknut with a wrench and turn the adjuster with a screwdriver while holding the locknut. The correct size feeler gauge should pass with a slight drag between the rocker arm and the valve stem.

7. Turn the crankshaft one full revolution to position the No. 4 piston at TDC of the compression stroke. Check and/or adjust the valves (counting from the front to the rear) Nos. 4, 5, 7 and 8.

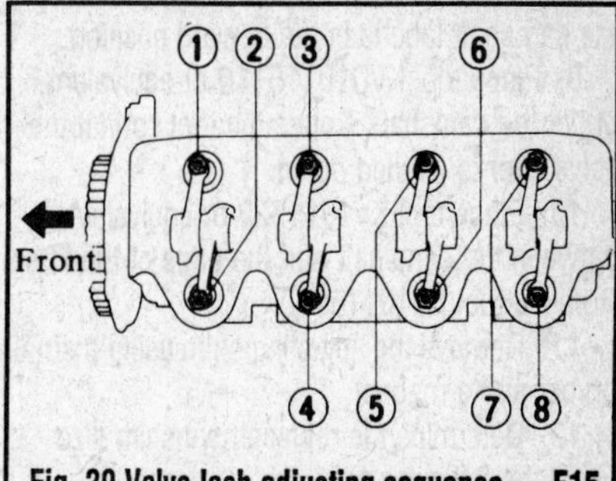
① ② ③
⑥
Front
④ ⑤
⑦ ⑧

Fig. 29 Valve lash adjusting sequence — E15 and E16 engines

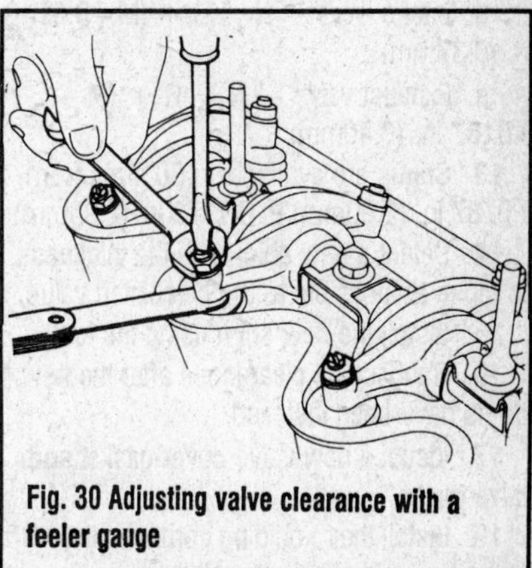

Fig. 30 Adjusting valve clearance with a feeler gauge

8. Replace the valve cover and torque the bolts on the valve cover down evenly.

GA16DE Engine

➧ SEE FIGS. 61–66

1. Warm up the engine to normal operating temperature and turn OFF. Disconnect the negative battery cable.

2. Remove the valve cover and spark plugs.

3. Set No. 1 cylinder to TDC of the compression stroke. Align the pointer with the TDC mark on the crankshaft pulley. Check that the valve lifters on No. 1 cylinder are loose and lifters for No. 4 cylinder are tight.

4. Check the valve clearance for intake valves of No. 1 and 2 cylinders. Check the clearance for exhaust valves of No. 1 and 3 cylinders.

5. Use a feeler gauge to measure the clearances:

Intake valves (hot) — 0.009–0.019 in. (0.21–0.49mm)

Exhaust valves (hot) — 0.012–0.023 in. (0.30–0.58mm)

6. Turn the crankshaft one revolution and align the TDC mark.

7. Check the valve clearance for intake valves of No. 3 and 4 cylinders. Check the clearance for exhaust valves of No. 2 and 4 cylinders.

8. To adjust the valves, turn the crankshaft so the camshaft lobe is in the upward position.

9. Place tool KVC10115110 or equivalent, under the camshaft. Rotate the tool so that the valve lifter is pushed down.

10. Place tool KV1011520 or equivalent, between the camshaft and the edge of the lifter. Remove tool KV10115110.

11. Remove the adjusting shim using a small prybar and a magnet.

12. Determine the replacement shim size using the following formula:

a. R = thickness of removed shim.

b. N = thickness of new shim.

c. M = measured valve clearance.

d. Intake valve — N = R + (M – 0.0146 in. (0.37mm)

e. Exhaust valve — N = R + (M – 0.0157 in. (0.40mm)

13. Shims are available in 50 sizes from 0.0787 in. (2.00mm) to 0.1173 in. (2.98mm).

14. Select a new shim with the thickness as close as possible to the calculated value.

15. Install the new shim using the tool.

16. Recheck all clearances after the new shims have been installed.

17. Install a new valve cover gasket and valve cover.

18. Install the remaining components, start the engine and check operation.

19. If the engine has an unusually rough idle, the valve clearance may be too tight. If this is the case, readjust the valve clearance before internal engine damage.

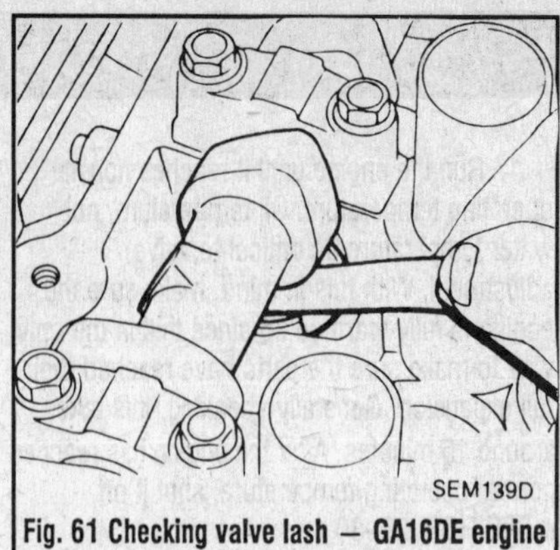
SEM139D
Fig. 61 Checking valve lash — GA16DE engine

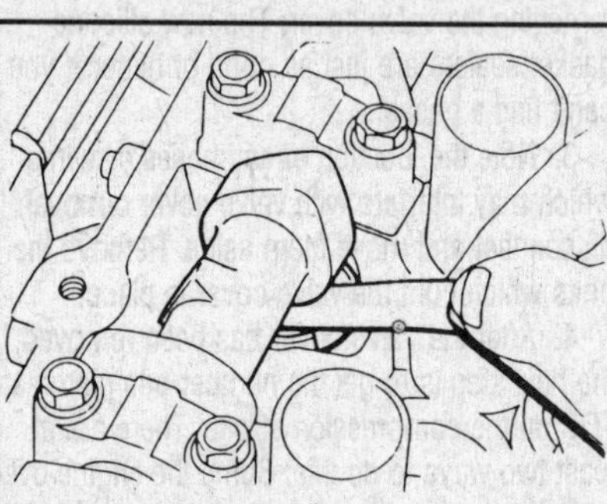
Fig. 62 Checking valve clearance with a feeler gauge — GA16DE engine

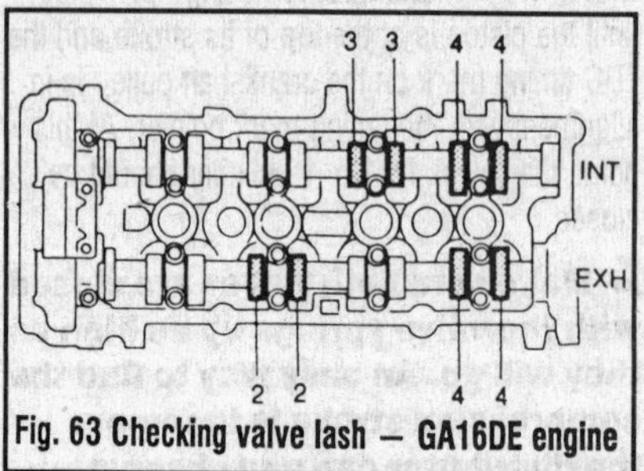
3 3
4 4
INT
EXH
2 2
4 4
Fig. 63 Checking valve lash — GA16DE engine

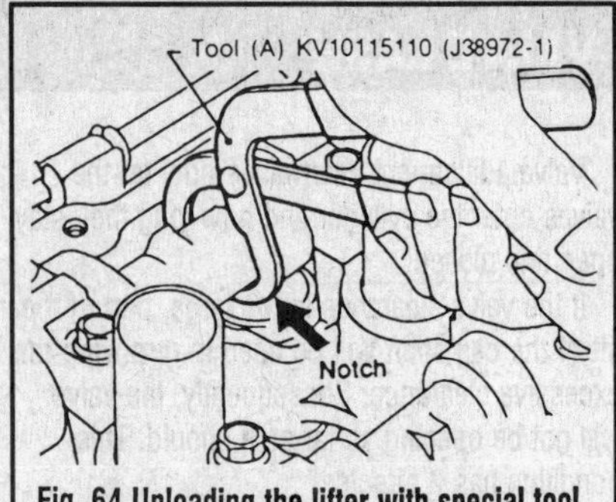
Tool (A) KV10115110 (J38972-1)
Notch
Fig. 64 Unloading the lifter with special tool — GA16DE engine

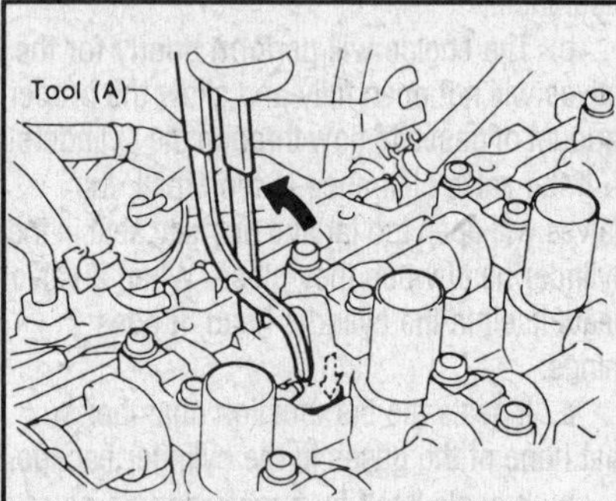
Tool (A)
Fig. 65 Unloading the lifter with special tool — GA16DE engine

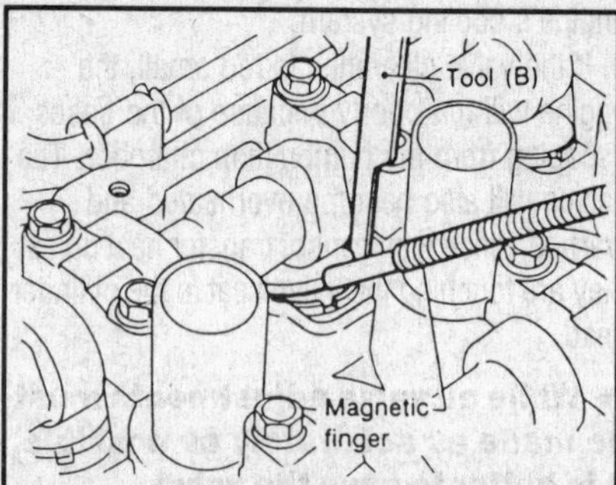
Tool (B)
Magnetic finger
Fig. 66 Removing the adjusting shim with a magnet — GA16DE engine

IDLE SPEED AND MIXTURE ADJUSTMENT

Idle Speed

CARBURETOR

✱✱ CAUTION

When checking the idle speed, set the parking brake and block the drive wheels.

E15 and E16 Engines

➧ SEE FIG. 39

1. Connect a tachometer to the engine according the manufacturer's instructions.

2. Start the engine and run it until it reaches normal operating temperatures.

3. Operate it at idle for 2 minutes under no-load, then race to 2,000–3,000 a few times and allow it to return to idle speed.

4. Turn **OFF** the engine.

➡ For U.S.A. models, disconnect the vacuum control modulator harness connector. For Canada models, disconnect and plug the air induction hose at the air filter; also, for Canada models (1984–86), disconnect and plug the throttle opener control valve vacuum hose at the throttle opener control valve side.

5. Start the engine and check the idle speed.

➡ If the cooling fan is operating, wait until it stops.

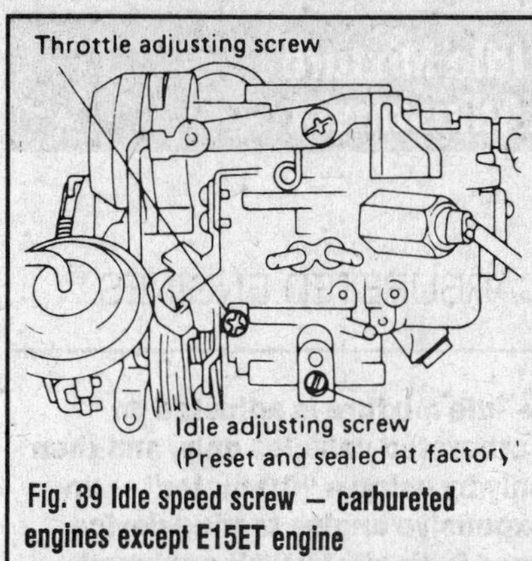
Throttle adjusting screw
Idle adjusting screw
(Preset and sealed at factory)
Fig. 39 Idle speed screw — carbureted engines except E15ET engine

6. If equipped with a manual transaxle, place the shift selector in **NEUTRAL**; if equipped with an automatic transaxle, place the shift selector in **DRIVE**.

7. If the idle speed is not correct, adjust the throttle adjusting screw at the carburetor.

8. When the idle speed is correct, stop the engine, reconnect the vacuum control modulator and the throttle opener control valve vacuum hose (if equipped), then disconnect the tachometer.

FUEL INJECTED

E16i Engine

1. Connect a tachometer to the engine, according to the manufacturer's instructions.

2. Start and operate the engine until it reaches normal operating temperatures. Operate the engine for 5 minutes under no load.

➡ Engage the parking brake and block the drive wheels. If equipped with a manual transaxle, place the shift selector in the NEUTRAL position. If equipped with an automatic transaxle, place the shift selector in the DRIVE position.

3. Check and/or adjust the engine speed. If necessary to adjust, turn the idle speed adjusting screw on the I.A.A. (Idle Air Adjusting) unit.

➧ SEE FIG. 40

4. With the idle speed adjusted, stop the engine and disconnect the tachometer.

Pulsar E15ET Engine

1. Connect a tachometer to the engine, according to the manufacturer's instructions.

2. Start and run the engine until it reaches normal operating temperatures. Operate the engine at 2,000 rpm, for 2 minutes under no-load.

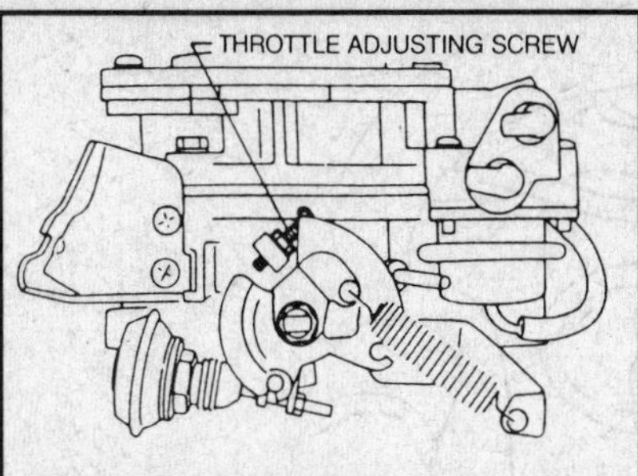
THROTTLE ADJUSTING SCREW
Fig. 40 Idle speed adjusting screw — E16i engine

3. Race the engine to 2,000–3,000 rpm a few times and allow it to go to idle speed.

➡ Engage the parking brake and block the drive wheels. If equipped with a manual transaxle, place the shift selector in the NEUTRAL position. If equipped with an automatic transaxle, place the shift selector in the DRIVE position.

4. Check and/or adjust the engine speed. If necessary to adjust, turn the throttle adjusting screw in the idle control valve.

➧ SEE FIG. 41

5. With the idle speed adjusted, stop the engine and disconnect the tachometer.

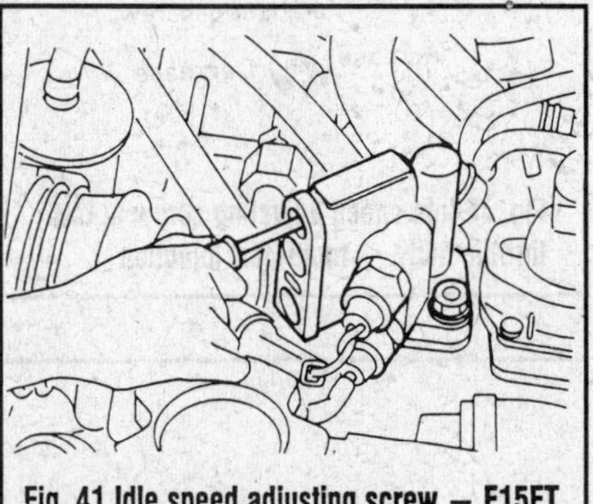
Fig. 41 Idle speed adjusting screw — E15ET engine

CA16DE and CA18DE Engines

1. Before adjusting the idle speed on these engines you must visually check the following items first: air cleaner for being clogged, hoses and ducts for leaks, EGR valve for proper operation, all electrical connectors, gaskets and the throttle valve, throttle valve switch on the CA16DE engine and idle switch on the CA18DE engine.

2. Start the engine and warm the engine so it reaches normal operating temperature. The water temperature indicator should be in the middle of the gauge.

3. Then race the engine to 2,000–3,000 rpm a few times under no load and then allow it to return to the idle speed.

4. Connect a voltage type tachometer to the engine by using a suitable type tool in the check connector for a lead outlet.

5. Check the idle speed on the manual transaxle model in **NEUTRAL** and on the automatic transaxle model check in **DRIVE**.

6. If the idle speed has to be adjusted you must disconnect the A.A.C. valve harness connector (Auxiliary Air Control).

7. Adjust the idle speed by turning the idle speed adjusting screw on the I.A.A. unit (Idle Air Adjusting).

➧ SEE FIGS. 42–44

8. Recheck the engine idle speed.

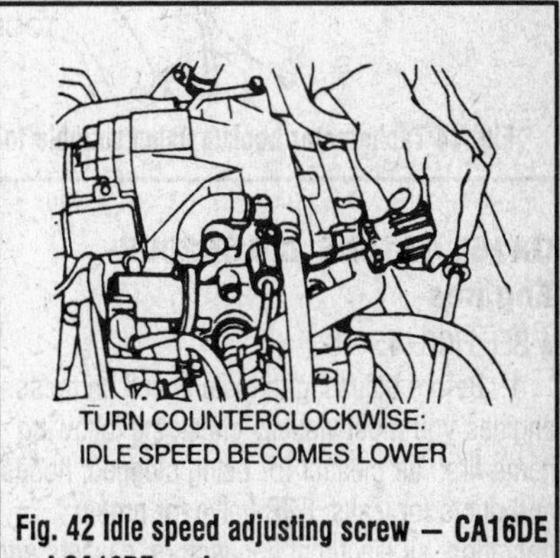
TURN COUNTERCLOCKWISE:
IDLE SPEED BECOMES LOWER
Fig. 42 Idle speed adjusting screw — CA16DE and CA18DE engines

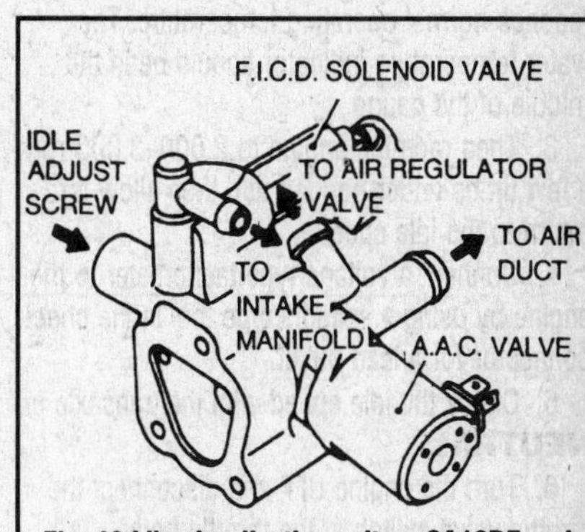
F.I.C.D. SOLENOID VALVE
IDLE ADJUST SCREW
TO AIR REGULATOR VALVE
TO AIR DUCT
TO INTAKE MANIFOLD
A.A.C. VALVE
Fig. 43 Idle air adjusting unit — CA16DE and CA18DE engine

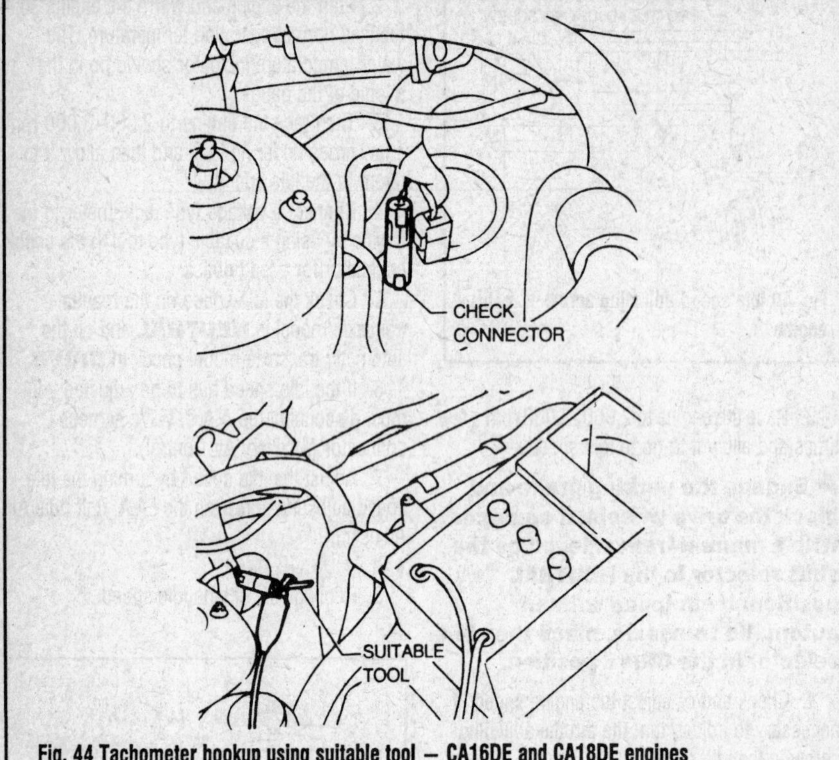
CHECK
CONNECTOR
SUITABLE
TOOL
Fig. 44 Tachometer hookup using suitable tool — CA16DE and CA18DE engines

GA16i, GA16DE and SR20DE Engines

➧ SEE FIGS. 45–46

1. Before adjusting the idle speed on these engines you must visually check the following items first: air cleaner for being clogged, hoses and ducts for leaks, EGR valve for proper operation, all electrical connectors, gaskets and the throttle valve and throttle valve switch.

2. Start the engine and warm the engine so it reaches normal operating temperature. The water temperature indicator should be in the middle of the gauge.

3. Then race the engine to 2,000–3,000 rpm a few times under no load and then allow it to return to the idle speed.

4. Connect a voltage type tachometer to the engine by using a suitable type tool in the check connector for a lead outlet.

5. Check the idle speed with the transaxle in **NEUTRAL**.

6. Turn the engine OFF and disconnect the throttle valve switch at the throttle body assembly.

7. Start the engine and check idle speed. If not within specifications, turn the idle adjusting screw at the throttle body until idle is within specifications. Race the engine to 2,000–3,000 rpm and recheck the idle speed.

8. Turn the engine OFF and reconnect the throttle valve switch.

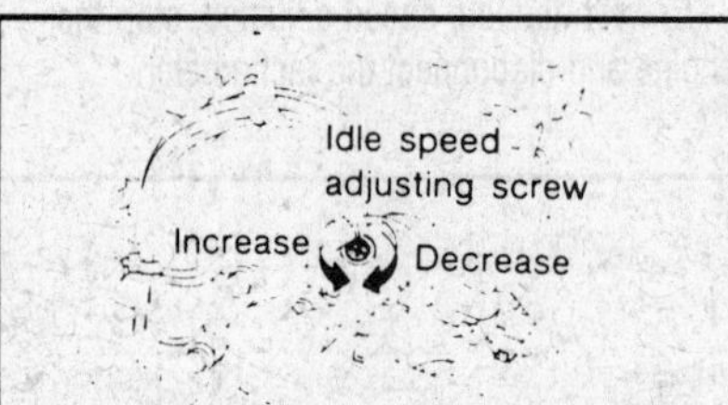
Idle speed
adjusting screw
Increase
Decrease
Fig. 45 Idle speed adjusting screw at the throttle body — multi-port injection

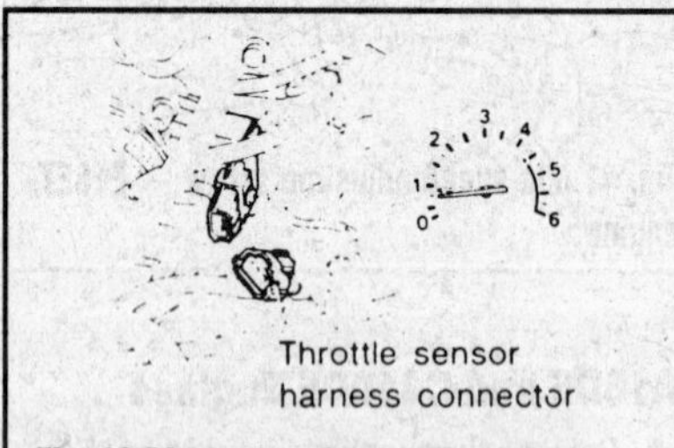
Throttle sensor
harness connector
Fig. 46 Disconnect the throttle sensor (throttle position sensor) harness when adjusting idle

Idle Mixture Adjustment

CARBURETED ENGINES

➡ Idle mixture is adjusted on carbureted vehicles only, and then only by using a "CO meter" — an expensive engine testing device used typically by well-equipped repair shops in the repair of emission system problems. Before attempting to adjust CO, make sure there are no vacuum system leaks, tuning problems (idle speed, ignition timing, spark plug condition or gap problems), or engine operating problems such as burned or misadjusted valves. It is possible that, if your car idles roughly in the absence of any of these problems, the cost of having the CO adjusted can be reduced by following the procedure given here.

1. Remove the carburetor from the engine as described in Section 5.

➧ SEE FIGS. 51–52

2. Locate the mixture adjustment plug located to the right of and below the idle speed screw. Find a drill that is **considerably smaller** than the diameter of the orifice in the carburetor casting into which the plug is mounted.

3. Drill **very cautiously** and slowly. Feel for the point where the drill **just** penetrates the inner end of the plug. **Don't drill farther, or the carburetor mixture screw will be damaged.**

4. Once you have drilled through the plug, use a less brittle metal object that will fit through the hole in the plug to pry it out of the carburetor orifice. Carefully clean all metal shavings out of the bore so the mixture screw threads will not be damaged.

5. Install the carburetor back onto the car. Make sure all vacuum lines are securely connected.

6. Have the person adjusting the CO with the required equipment follow these procedures:

a. Run the engine until it is hot. Then, shut it off.

b. Disconnect the air/fuel ratio solenoid harness connector. Disconnect the air induction hose from the air cleaner and plug or cap the hose.

c. Start the engine and race it three times to 2,500 rpm. Then, allow it to idle.

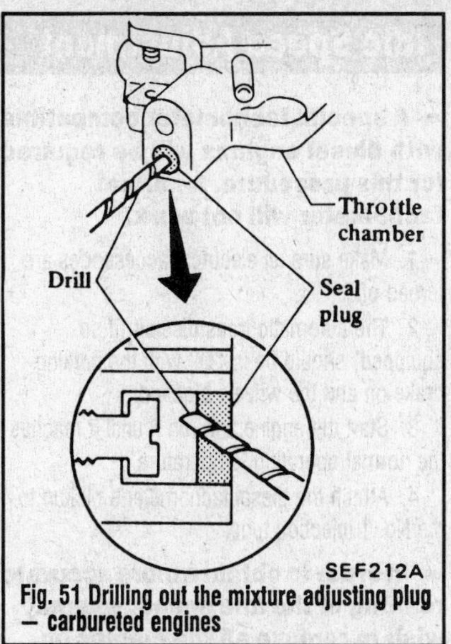
Throttle chamber
Drill
Seal plug
SEF212A
Fig. 51 Drilling out the mixture adjusting plug — carbureted engines

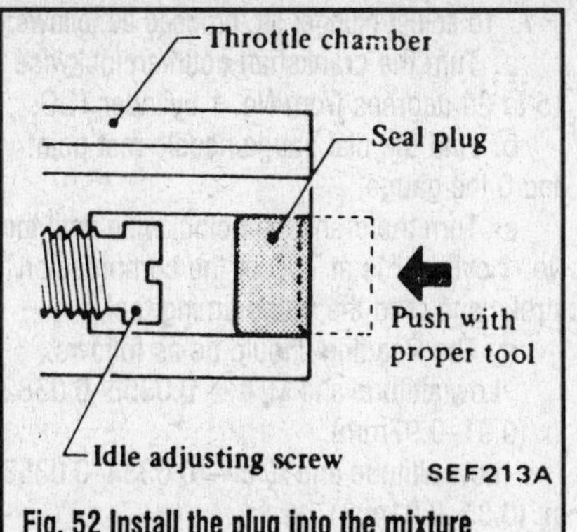
Throttle chamber
Seal plug
Push with proper tool
Idle adjusting screw
SEF213A
Fig. 52 Install the plug into the mixture adjusting screw orifice so it is just slightly inside the bore

d. Insert the CO meter probe 16 in. (41cm) into the tailpipe. Read the CO. If necessary, adjust the mixture screw to obtain 4–6% for California and Canadian cars and 2–4% for 49 States cars.

7. Tap a new seal plug squarely into the carburetor bore with an object with a perfectly flat front. The object should be just slightly smaller than the bore.

8. Restore all disconnected hoses and electrical connectors. Then, repeat the idle speed adjustment procedure above.

FUEL INJECTED ENGINES

Fuel injected engines fuel mixture is controlled by the Electronic Control Unit (ECU). No fuel mixture adjustment is necessary or possible.

DIESEL TUNE-UP PROCEDURES

Valve Lash

SEE FIGS. 31–33

1. Run the engine to normal operating temperature.
2. Shut off the engine and remove the valve cover.
3. Turn the crankshaft until #1 piston is at TDC of the compression stroke.
4. The following valves may now be adjusted:
   #1 intake and exhaust
   #2 intake
   #3 exhaust
5. Measure the clearance between the cam lobe and the lifter. Valve clearance should be adjusted one valve at a time. Adjustment is made by removing or adding shims in the lifter. Lifters are removed or added, not at TDC, nut 1/4 turn PAST TDC, in the normal direction of the rotation. A special tool, Nissan #KV11102600 is used. The tool should be inserted from the injector nozzle side of the head. The lifter has a cutout portion to aid in removing the shim. Turn the lifter so that this cutout is on the nozzle side. The shim should be stamped with their size, in millimeters. If, when you measure the clearance, you find that an adjustment is needed, remove the shim, note what size it is and determine what size you need to correct the gap.

   Intake: 0.008–0.012 in. (0.20–0.30mm)
   Exhaust: 0.016–0.020 in. (0.40–0.50mm)
6. Turn the crankshaft until #4 piston is at TDC compression. The following valves may now be adjusted:
   #2 exhaust
   #3 intake
   #4 intake and exhaust

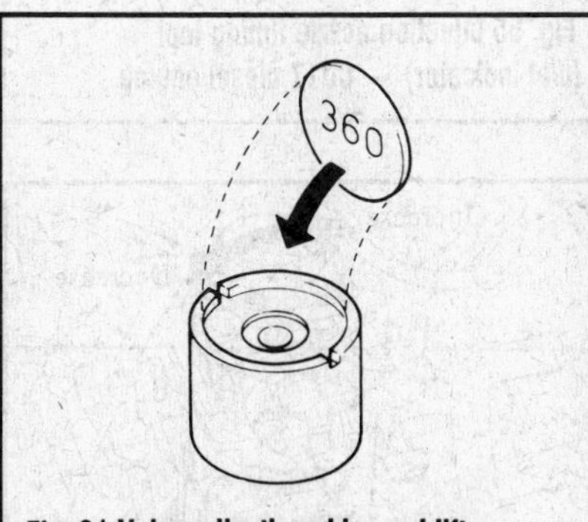
360
Fig. 31 Valve adjusting shim and lifter — CD17 diesel and GA16DE engines

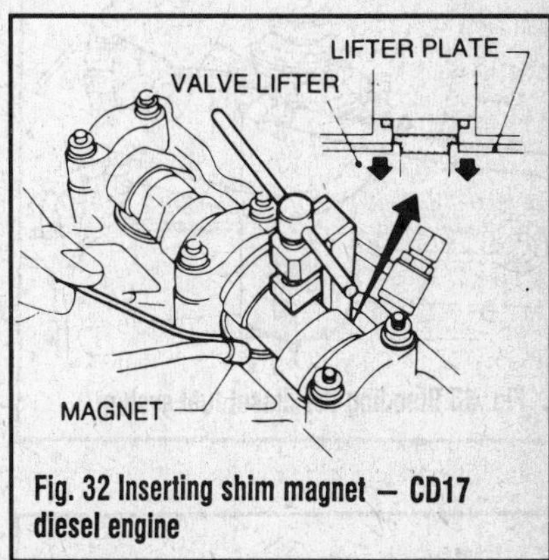
LIFTER PLATE
VALVE LIFTER
MAGNET
Fig. 32 Inserting shim magnet — CD17 diesel engine

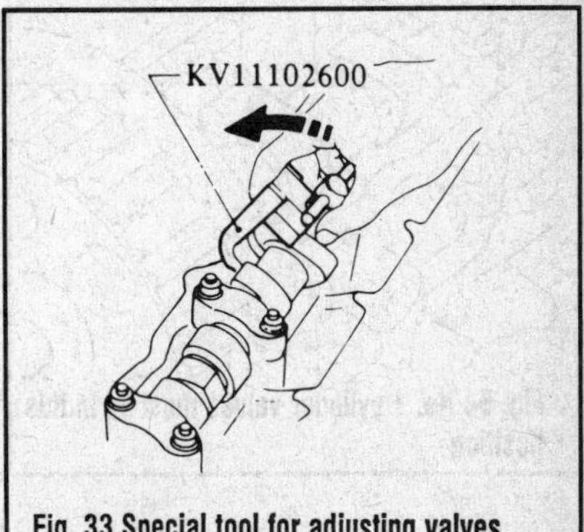
KV11102600
Fig. 33 Special tool for adjusting valves — CD17 diesel engine

Injection Pump Timing

SEE FIGS. 53–56

A special pump timing tool KV11229352, or equivalent is needed to adjust the injection pump timing. Do not attempt this procedure without this tool.

1. Set the No. 1 cylinder to TDC of the compression stroke and align the pointer on the engine block with the notch in the crankshaft pulley.
2. Make sure the No. 1 cylinder valves are in the closed position.
3. Remove all injection tubes.
4. Turn the cold start device to the free position by turning the linkage clockwise and set a block between the cold start device and linkage.
5. Remove the plug bolt from the rear side of the injection pump. Install the pump timing tool KV11229352 or equivalent, into the hole.
6. Loosen the pump mounting nuts and bracket bolt.
7. To adjust plunger lift, proceed as follows:
   a. Turn the crankshaft counterclockwise 15 to 20 degrees from No. 1 cylinder TDC.
   b. Find the dial gauge needle rest point and 0 the gauge.
   c. Turn the crankshaft clockwise until the No. 1 cylinder is at TDC of the compression stroke and read the pump timing tool.
   d. The Reading should be as follows:
      Low altitude and M/T — 0.0358–0.0382 in. (0.91–0.97mm)
      Low altitude and A/T — 0.0334–0.0358 in. (0.85–0.91mm)
      High altitude and M/T — 0.0382–0.0406 in. (0.97–1.03mm)
      High altitude and A/T — 0.0358–0.0382 in. (0.91–0.97mm)
8. If the timing in not within the range, turn the pump body until the reading is obtained.
9. Tighten the pump retaining bolts, remove the timing tool and install the plug. Remove the block from the cold start device. Torque all injector tubes to 40 ft. lbs. (55 Nm).
10. Start the engine and check operation.

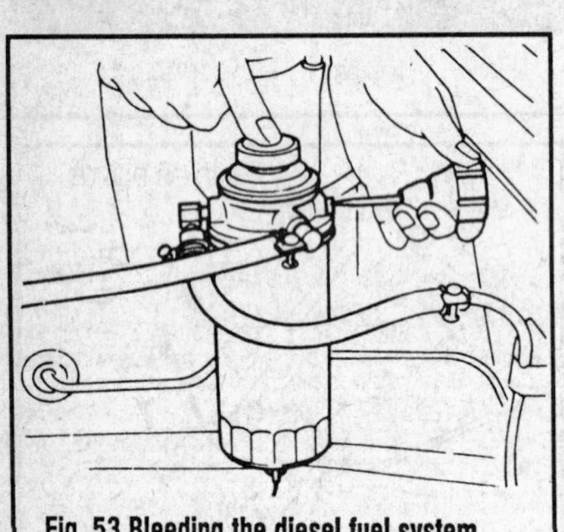
Fig. 53 Bleeding the diesel fuel system

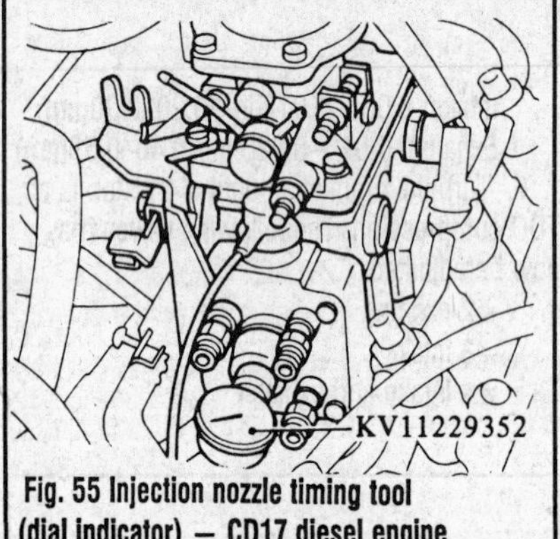
KV11229352
Fig. 55 Injection nozzle timing tool (dial indicator) — CD17 diesel engine

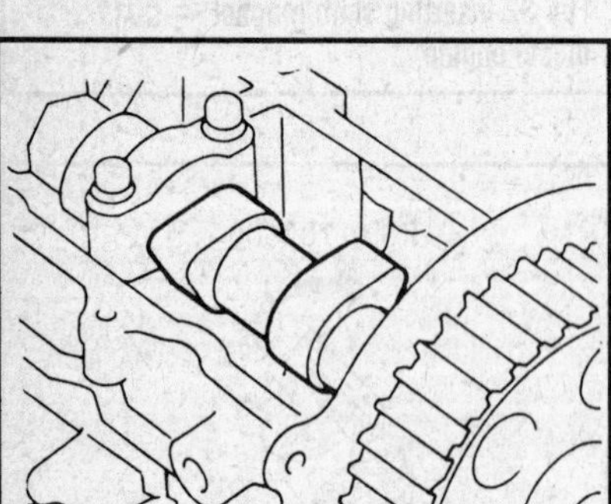
Fig. 54 No. 1 cylinder valves must be in this position

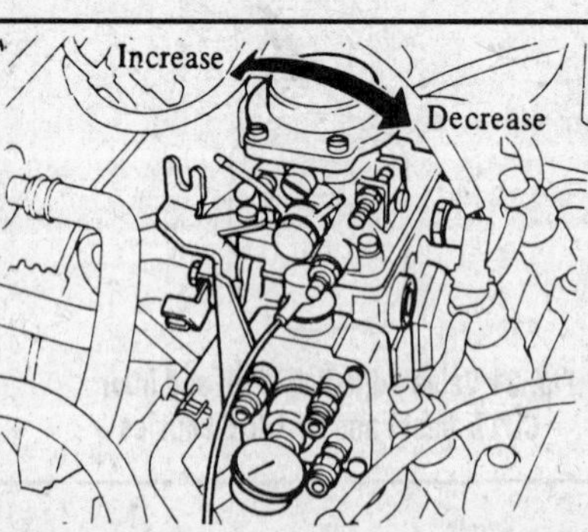
Increase
Decrease
Fig. 56 Turning the injection pump to change pump timing

Idle Speed Adjustment

A special tachometer compatible with diesel engines will be required for this procedure. A normal tachometer will not work.

1. Make sure all electrical accessories are turned off.
2. The automatic transmission (if so equipped) should be in "D" with the parking brake on and the wheels blocked.
3. Start the engine and run it until it reaches the normal operating temperature.
4. Attach the diesel tachometer's pickup to the No. 1 injection tube.

In order to obtain a more accurate reading of the idle speed, you may wish to remove all the clamps on the No. 1 injection tube.

5. Run the engine at about 2,000 rpm for two minutes under no-load conditions.
6. Slow the engine down to idle speed for about 1 min. and then check the idle.
7. If the engine is not idling at the proper speed, turn it off and disconnect the accelerator wire from the injection pump control lever.

It is not necessary to disconnect the accelerator wire on the CD17.

8. Move the control lever to the full acceleration side, and then loosen the idle screw lock nut while still holding the control lever.
9. Start the engine again and turn the adjusting screw until the proper idle is obtained. Stop the engine.
10. Tighten the idle adjusting screw locknut while still holding the control lever to the full acceleration side and then connect the accelerator wire.

SEE FIGS. 47–50

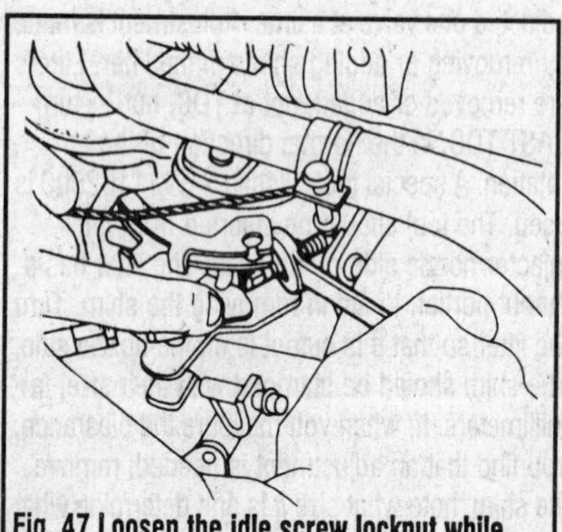
Fig. 47 Loosen the idle screw locknut while holding the control lever — CD17 diesel engine

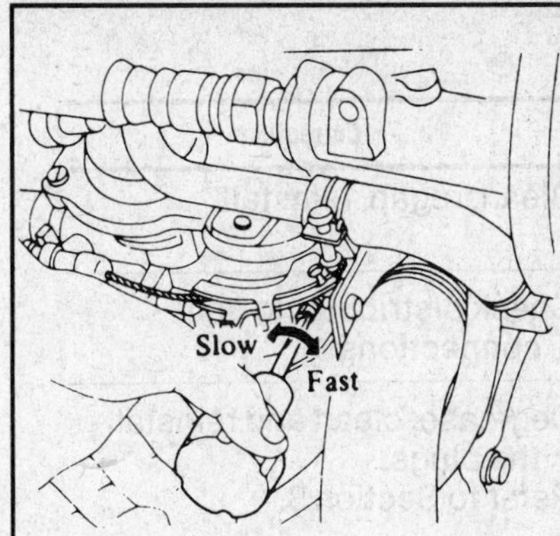
Slow
Fast
Fig. 48 Idle speed adjusting screw — CD17 diesel engine

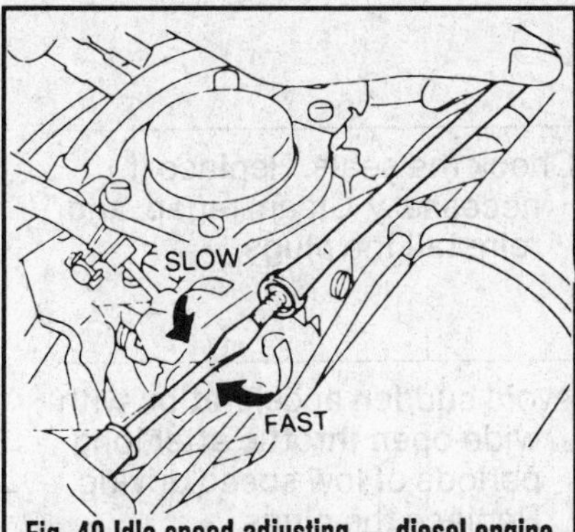
SLOW
FAST
Fig. 49 Idle speed adjusting — diesel engine, except 1987

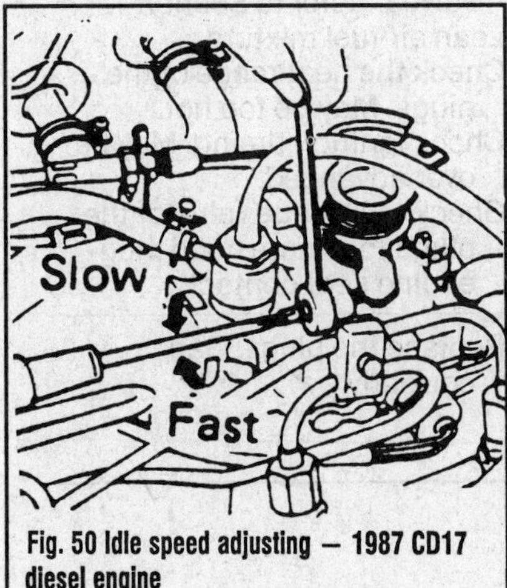
Slow
Fast
Fig. 50 Idle speed adjusting — 1987 CD17 diesel engine

Injector Nozzle Service

➧ SEE FIGS. 57–60

➡ Always replace the injector nozzle gaskets at the bottom of the bore when removing the injector nozzles for service. Make sure the gasket is installed correctly.

1. Remove the injection tubes on the nozzle side and loosen the tubes on the pump side.
2. Remove the spill tubes from the injector nozzles.
3. Remove the injector and gasket.
4. Clean the injector hole with a soft brush and carburetor cleaner.
5. Install new nozzle gaskets as shown in the figure.
6. Place the nozzle in a soft vise and nut while holding the body in the vise.
7. Arrange the parts in order of disassembly.
8. Clean all parts with clean diesel fuel or carburetor cleaner. Use special brushes and nozzle cleaning tools so no internal damage is done.
9. After removing all sludge and dirt, assemble the nozzle as disassembled.
10. Install the new gasket and nozzle. Torque the nozzle to 51 ft. lbs. (69 Nm). Install the injection tubes loosely. Do not tighten at this time.
11. Bleed the fuel system by loosening the priming pump vent screw and pump the plunger on top of the filter assembly.
12. Torque the injection tubes at the pump to 18 ft. lbs. (25 Nm).
13. Crank the engine until fuel comes out of all tube fittings.
15. Torque the tube fittings to 18 ft. lbs. (25 Nm).
16. Start the engine and check operation.

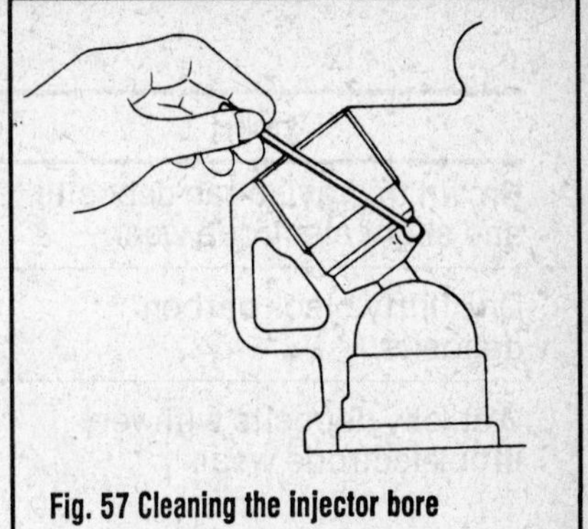
Fig. 57 Cleaning the injector bore

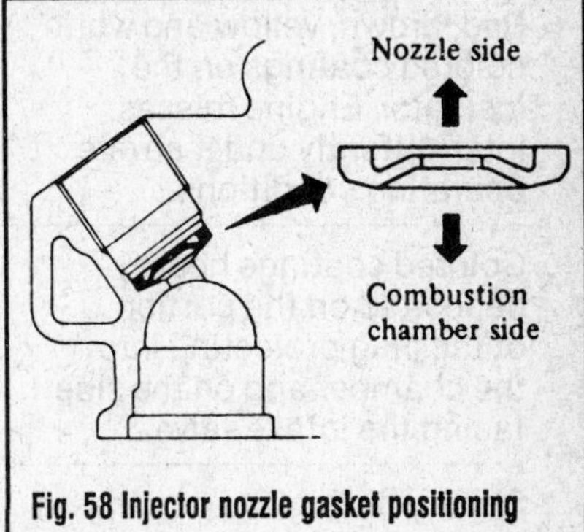
Nozzle side
Combustion
chamber side
Fig. 58 Injector nozzle gasket positioning

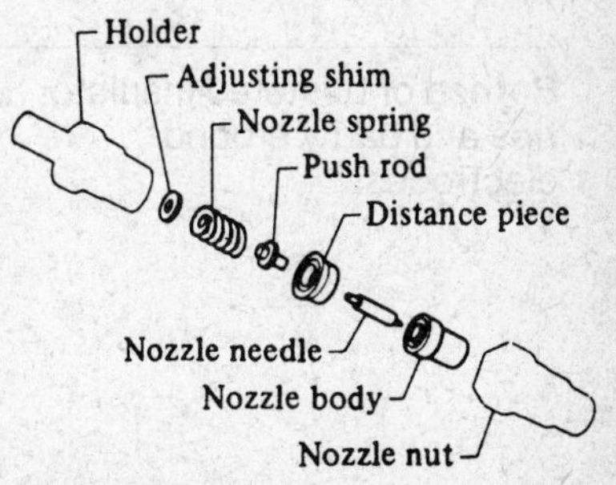

Holder
Adjusting shim
Nozzle spring
Push rod
Distance piece
Nozzle needle
Nozzle body
Nozzle nut

Fig. 59 Injector nozzle assembly — CD17 diesel engine

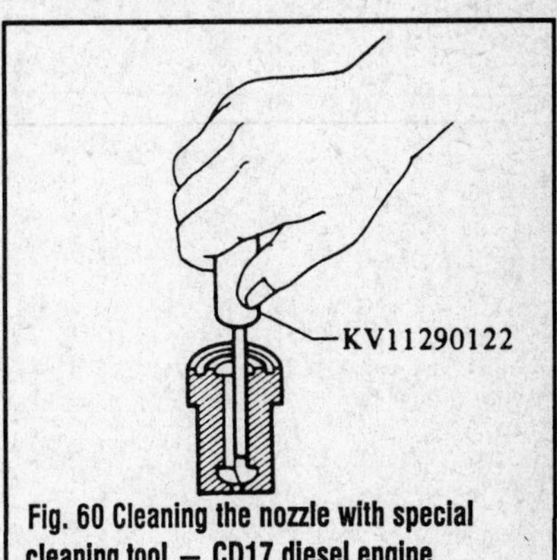
KV11290122
Fig. 60 Cleaning the nozzle with special cleaning tool — CD17 diesel engine

Diagnosis of Spark Plugs

Problem	Possible Cause	Correction
Brown to grayish-tan deposits and slight electrode wear.	• Normal wear.	• Clean, regap, reinstall.
Dry, fluffy black carbon deposits.	• Poor ignition output.	• Check distributor to coil connections.
Wet, oily deposits with very little electrode wear.	• "Break-in" of new or recently overhauled engine. • Excessive valve stem guide clearances. • Worn intake valve seals.	• Degrease, clean and reinstall the plugs. • Refer to Section 3. • Replace the seals.
Red, brown, yellow and white colored coatings on the insulator. Engine misses intermittently under severe operating conditions.	• By-products of combustion.	• Clean, regap, and reinstall. If heavily coated, replace.
Colored coatings heavily deposited on the portion of the plug projecting into the chamber and on the side facing the intake valve.	• Leaking seals if condition is found in only one or two cylinders.	• Check the seals. Replace if necessary. Clean, regap, and reinstall the plugs.
Shiny yellow glaze coating on the insulator.	• Melted by-products of combustion.	• Avoid sudden acceleration with wide-open throttle after long periods of low speed driving. Replace the plugs.
Burned or blistered insulator tips and badly eroded electrodes.	• Overheating.	• Check the cooling system. • Check for sticking heat riser valves. Refer to Section 1. • Lean air-fuel mixture. • Check the heat range of the plugs. May be too hot. • Check ignition timing. May be over-advanced. • Check the torque value of the plugs to ensure good plug-engine seat contact.
Broken or cracked insulator tips.	• Heat shock from sudden rise in tip temperature under severe operating conditions. Improper gapping of plugs.	• Replace the plugs. Gap correctly.

3

ENGINE AND ENGINE OVERHAUL

Troubleshooting the Cooling System

Problem	Cause	Solution
High temperature gauge indication—overheating	• Coolant level low	• Replenish coolant
	• Fan belt loose	• Adjust fan belt tension
	• Radiator hose(s) collapsed	• Replace hose(s)
	• Radiator airflow blocked	• Remove restriction (bug screen, fog lamps, etc.)
	• Faulty radiator cap	• Replace radiator cap
	• Ignition timing incorrect	• Adjust ignition timing
	• Idle speed low	• Adjust idle speed
	• Air trapped in cooling system	• Purge air
	• Heavy traffic driving	• Operate at fast idle in neutral intermittently to cool engine
	• Incorrect cooling system component(s) installed	• Install proper component(s)
	• Faulty thermostat	• Replace thermostat
	• Water pump shaft broken or impeller loose	• Replace water pump
	• Radiator tubes clogged	• Flush radiator
	• Cooling system clogged	• Flush system
	• Casting flash in cooling passages	• Repair or replace as necessary. Flash may be visible by removing cooling system components or removing core plugs.
	• Brakes dragging	• Repair brakes
	• Excessive engine friction	• Repair engine
	• Antifreeze concentration over 68%	• Lower antifreeze concentration percentage
	• Missing air seals	• Replace air seals
	• Faulty gauge or sending unit	• Repair or replace faulty component
	• Loss of coolant flow caused by leakage or foaming	• Repair or replace leaking component, replace coolant
	• Viscous fan drive failed	• Replace unit
Low temperature indication—undercooling	• Thermostat stuck open	• Replace thermostat
	• Faulty gauge or sending unit	• Repair or replace faulty component
Coolant loss—boilover	• Overfilled cooling system	• Reduce coolant level to proper specification
	• Quick shutdown after hard (hot) run	• Allow engine to run at fast idle prior to shutdown
	• Air in system resulting in occasional "burping" of coolant	• Purge system
	• Insufficient antifreeze allowing coolant boiling point to be too low	• Add antifreeze to raise boiling point
	• Antifreeze deteriorated because of age or contamination	• Replace coolant
	• Leaks due to loose hose clamps, loose nuts, bolts, drain plugs, faulty hoses, or defective radiator	• Pressure test system to locate source of leak(s) then repair as necessary

Troubleshooting the Cooling System (cont.)

Problem	Cause	Solution
Coolant loss—boilover	• Faulty head gasket • Cracked head, manifold, or block • Faulty radiator cap	• Replace head gasket • Replace as necessary • Replace cap
Coolant entry into crankcase or cylinder(s)	• Faulty head gasket • Crack in head, manifold or block	• Replace head gasket • Replace as necessary
Coolant recovery system inoperative	• Coolant level low • Leak in system • Pressure cap not tight or seal missing, or leaking • Pressure cap defective • Overflow tube clogged or leaking • Recovery bottle vent restricted	• Replenish coolant to FULL mark • Pressure test to isolate leak and repair as necessary • Repair as necessary • Replace cap • Repair as necessary • Remove restriction
Noise	• Fan contacting shroud • Loose water pump impeller • Glazed fan belt • Loose fan belt • Rough surface on drive pulley • Water pump bearing worn • Belt alignment	• Reposition shroud and inspect engine mounts • Replace pump • Apply silicone or replace belt • Adjust fan belt tension • Replace pulley • Remove belt to isolate. Replace pump. • Check pulley alignment. Repair as necessary.
No coolant flow through heater core	• Restricted return inlet in water pump • Heater hose collapsed or restricted • Restricted heater core • Restricted outlet in thermostat housing • Intake manifold bypass hole in cylinder head restricted • Faulty heater control valve • Intake manifold coolant passage restricted	• Remove restriction • Remove restriction or replace hose • Remove restriction or replace core • Remove flash or restriction • Remove restriction • Replace valve • Remove restriction or replace intake manifold

NOTE: *Immediately after shutdown, the engine enters a condition known as heat soak. This is caused by the cooling system being inoperative while engine temperature is still high. If coolant temperature rises above boiling point, expansion and pressure may push some coolant out of the radiator overflow tube. If this does not occur frequently it is considered normal.*

ENGINE ELECTRICAL

Understanding the Engine Electrical System

The engine electrical system can be broken down into three separate and distinct systems:

1. The starting system.
2. The charging system.
3. The ignition system.

BATTERY AND STARTING SYSTEM

Basic Operating Principles

The battery is the first link in the chain of mechanisms which work together to provide cranking of the automobile engine. In most modern cars, the battery is a lead/acid electrochemical device consisting of six 2v subsections connected in series so the unit is capable of producing approximately 12v of electrical pressure. Each subsection, or cell, consists of a series of positive and negative plates held a short distance apart in a solution of sulfuric acid and water. The two types of plates are of dissimilar metals. This causes a chemical reaction to be set up, and it is this reaction which produces current flow from the battery when its positive and negative terminals are connected to an electrical appliance such as a lamp or motor. The continued transfer of electrons would eventually convert the sulfuric acid in the electrolyte to water, and make the two plates identical in chemical composition. As electrical energy is removed from the battery, its voltage output tends to drop. Thus, measuring battery voltage and battery electrolyte composition are two ways of checking the ability of the unit to supply power. During the starting of the engine, electrical energy is removed from the battery. However, if the charging circuit is in good condition and the operating conditions are normal, the power removed from the battery will be replaced by the generator (or alternator) which will force electrons back through the battery, reversing the normal flow, and restoring the battery to its original chemical state.

The battery and starting motor are linked by very heavy electrical cables designed to minimize resistance to the flow of current. Generally, the major power supply cable that leaves the battery goes directly to the starter, while other electrical system needs are supplied by a smaller cable. During starter operation, power flows from the battery to the starter and is grounded through the car's frame and the battery's negative ground strap.

The starting motor is a specially designed, direct current electric motor capable of producing a very great amount of power for its size. One thing that allows the motor to produce a great deal of power is its tremendous rotating speed. It drives the engine through a tiny pinion gear (attached to the starter's armature), which drives the very large flywheel ring gear at a greatly reduced speed. Another factor allowing it to produce so much power is that only intermittent operation is required of it. This, little allowance for air circulation is required, and the windings can be built into a very small space.

The starter solenoid is a magnetic device which employs the small current supplied by the starting switch circuit of the ignition switch. This magnetic action moves a plunger which mechanically engages the starter and electrically closes the heavy switch which connects it to the battery. The starting switch circuit consists of the starting switch contained within the ignition switch, a transmission neutral safety switch or clutch pedal switch, and the wiring necessary to connect these in series with the starter solenoid or relay.

A pinion, which is a small gear, is mounted to a one-way drive clutch. This clutch is splined to the starter armature shaft. When the ignition switch is moved to the **start** position, the solenoid plunger slides the pinion toward the flywheel ring gear via a collar and spring. If the teeth on the pinion and flywheel match properly, the pinion will engage the flywheel immediately. If the gear teeth butt one another, the spring will be compressed and will force the gears to mesh as soon as the starter turns far enough to allow them to do so. As the solenoid plunger reaches the end of its travel, it closes the contacts that connect the battery and starter and then the engine is cranked.

As soon as the engine starts, the flywheel ring gear begins turning fast enough to drive the pinion at an extremely high rate of speed. At this point, the one-way clutch begins allowing the pinion to spin faster than the starter shaft so that the starter will not operate at excessive speed. When the ignition switch is released from the starter position, the solenoid is de-energized, and a spring contained within the solenoid assembly pulls the gear out of mesh and interrupts the current flow to the starter.

Some starter employ a separate relay, mounted away from the starter, to switch the motor and solenoid current on and off. The relay thus replaces the solenoid electrical switch, buy does not eliminate the need for a solenoid mounted on the starter used to mechanically engage the starter drive gears. The relay is used to reduce the amount of current the starting switch must carry.

THE CHARGING SYSTEM

Basic Operating Principles

The automobile charging system provides electrical power for operation of the vehicle's ignition and starting systems and all the electrical accessories. The battery services as an electrical surge or storage tank, storing (in chemical form) the energy originally produced by the engine driven generator. The system also provides a means of regulating generator output to protect the battery from being overcharged and to avoid excessive voltage to the accessories.

The storage battery is a chemical device incorporating parallel lead plates in a tank containing a sulfuric acid/water solution. Adjacent plates are slightly dissimilar, and the chemical reaction of the two dissimilar plates produces electrical energy when the battery is connected to a load such as the starter motor. The chemical reaction is reversible, so that when the generator is producing a voltage (electrical pressure) greater than that produced by the battery, electricity is forced into the battery, and the battery is returned to its fully charged state.

The vehicle's generator is driven mechanically, through V-belts, by the engine crankshaft. It consists of two coils of fine wire, one stationary (the stator), and one movable (the rotor). The rotor may also be known as the armature, and consists of fine wire wrapped around an iron core which is mounted on a shaft. The electricity which flows through the two coils of wire (provided initially by the battery in some cases) creates an intense magnetic field around both rotor and stator, and the interaction between the two fields creates voltage, allowing the generator to power the accessories and charge the battery.

There are two types of generators: the earlier is the direct current (DC) type. The current produced by the DC generator is generated in the armature and carried off the spinning armature by stationary brushes contacting the commutator. The commutator is a series of smooth metal contact plates on the end of the armature. The commutator is a series of smooth metal contact plates on the end of the armature. The commutator plates, which are separated from one another by a very short gap, are connected to the armature circuits so that current will flow in one directions only in the wires carrying the generator output. The generator stator consists of two stationary coils of wire which draw some of the output current of the generator to form a powerful magnetic field and create the interaction of fields which generates the voltage. The generator field is wired in series with the regulator.

Newer automobiles use alternating current generators or alternators, because they are more efficient, can be rotated at higher speeds, and have fewer brush problems. In an alternator, the field rotates while all the current produced passes only through the stator winding. The brushes bear against continuous slip rings rather than a commutator. This causes the current produced to periodically reverse the direction of its flow. Diodes (electrical one-way switches) block the flow of current from traveling in the wrong direction. A series of diodes is wired together to permit the alternating flow of the stator to be converted to a pulsating, but unidirectional flow at the alternator output. The alternator's field is wired in series with the voltage regulator.

The regulator consists of several circuits. Each circuit has a core, or magnetic coil of wire, which operates a switch. Each switch is connected to ground through one or more resistors. The coil of wire responds directly to system voltage. When the voltage reaches the required level, the magnetic field created by the winding of wire closes the switch and inserts a resistance into the generator field circuit, thus reducing the output. The contacts of the switch cycle open and close many times each second to precisely control voltage.

While alternators are self-limiting as far as maximum current is concerned, DC generators employ a current regulating circuit which responds directly to the total amount of current flowing through the generator circuit rather than to the output voltage. The current regulator is similar to the voltage regulator except that all system current must flow through the energizing coil on its way to the various accessories.

ENGINE ELECTRICAL

Ignition Coil

➧ SEE FIGS. 1 and 2

TESTING

Primary Resistance Check

With the ohmmeter set on the X1 range, the reading should be 1.04–1.27 ohms for 1982–86 models. For 1987–92 models, refer to the Ignition System diagnosis charts in Section 4. If the reading is more than specified, replace the ignition coil assembly.

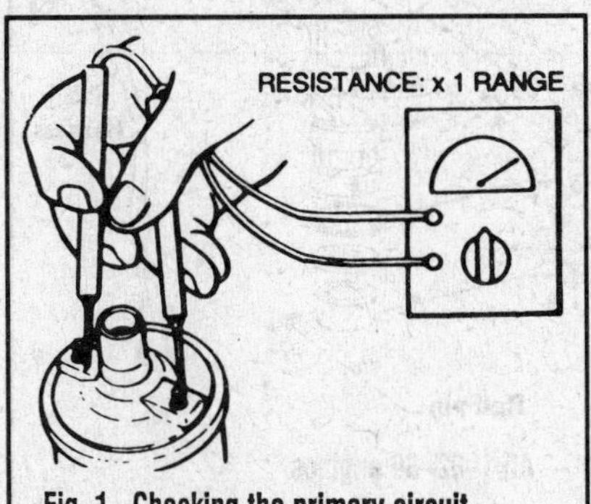
RESISTANCE: x 1 RANGE

Fig. 1. Checking the primary circuit resistance of the early model ignition coil

Secondary Resistance Check

Turn the ignition key **OFF**, then remove the high tension and a primary coil wire from the coil using an ohmmeter, set it on the X1000 scale. Touch one lead to a primary terminal and the other lead to the center terminal. The resistance should be 7,300–11,000 ohms for 310 1982–86 vehicles. For 1987–92 models, refer to the Ignition System diagnosis charts in Section 4. If the reading is not correct, replace the ignition coil.

➡ **On the Pulsar E16 1984–86 (49 states models), Pulsar E16 1987–88 (all models), a power transistor is used with the ignition coil. The ignition signal from the E.C.U. is amplified by the power transistor, which turns the ignition coil primary circuit on and off, inducing the proper high voltage in the secondary circuit. On these models the the ignition coil is a small molded type. Checking the ignition coils on the 1987–88 Pulsar (CA16DE and CA18DE) involves complicated diagnostic procedures. Refer to Ignition System diagnosis charts in Section 4.**

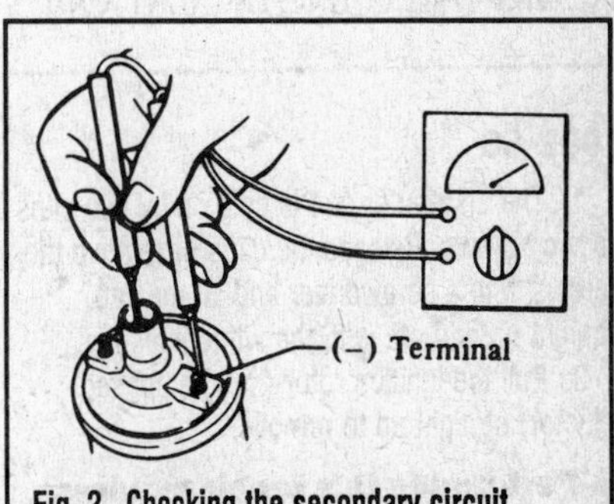
(–) Terminal

Fig. 2. Checking the secondary circuit resistance of the early model ignition coil

REMOVAL & INSTALLATION

On all models with the exception of the Pulsar CA16DE and CA18DE engines the coil is either mounted to the wall of the engine compartment or the engine. To remove disconnect and mark all electrical connections then transfer coil mounting bracket if so equipped to the new coil. When installing the new coil make sure that the coil wire and all other electrical connections are properly installed.

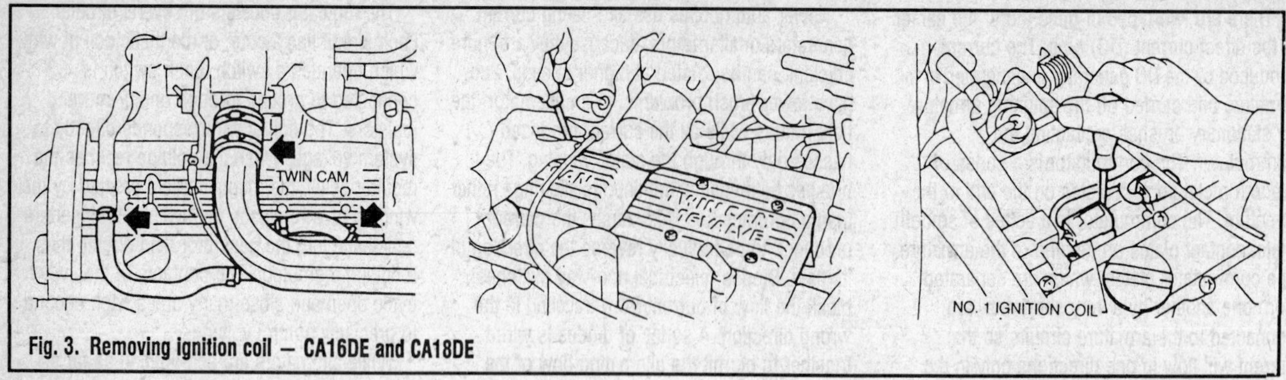
TWIN CAM
NO. 1 IGNITION COIL

Fig. 3. Removing ignition coil — CA16DE and CA18DE

On the Pulsar CA16DE and CA18DE engines 4 small ignition coil fit directly to each spark plug. The ECU controls the coils by means of a crank angle sensor. To remove disconnect the air duct and the air hoses then remove the ornament cover. Remove the holding down screws and careful remove the ignition coil from the spark plug.

Ignition Module

REMOVAL & INSTALLATION

1982–86

1. The distributor cap is held on by two clips or two screws. Release the clips or remove the screws with a screwdriver and lift the cap straight up and off, with the wires attached.
2. Pull the ignition rotor (not the spoked reluctor) straight up to remove.

➡ **Performing this repair requires working with small parts in a confined space. Look the job over. It may be better to remove the distributor, as described just below, in order to make it easier to complete the work without losing any parts.**

3. To replace the IC ignition unit on reluctor type distributors:
   a. First use two small, dull prying devices to work the reluctor off the distributor shaft. Pry evenly and simultaneously to do this. Make sure to catch the roll pin and save it with the reluctor.
   b. Note their routing and then unplug the two electrical connectors for the ignitor unit. Pull the grommet out of the side of the distributor for additional working space and to keep the wires out of the way.

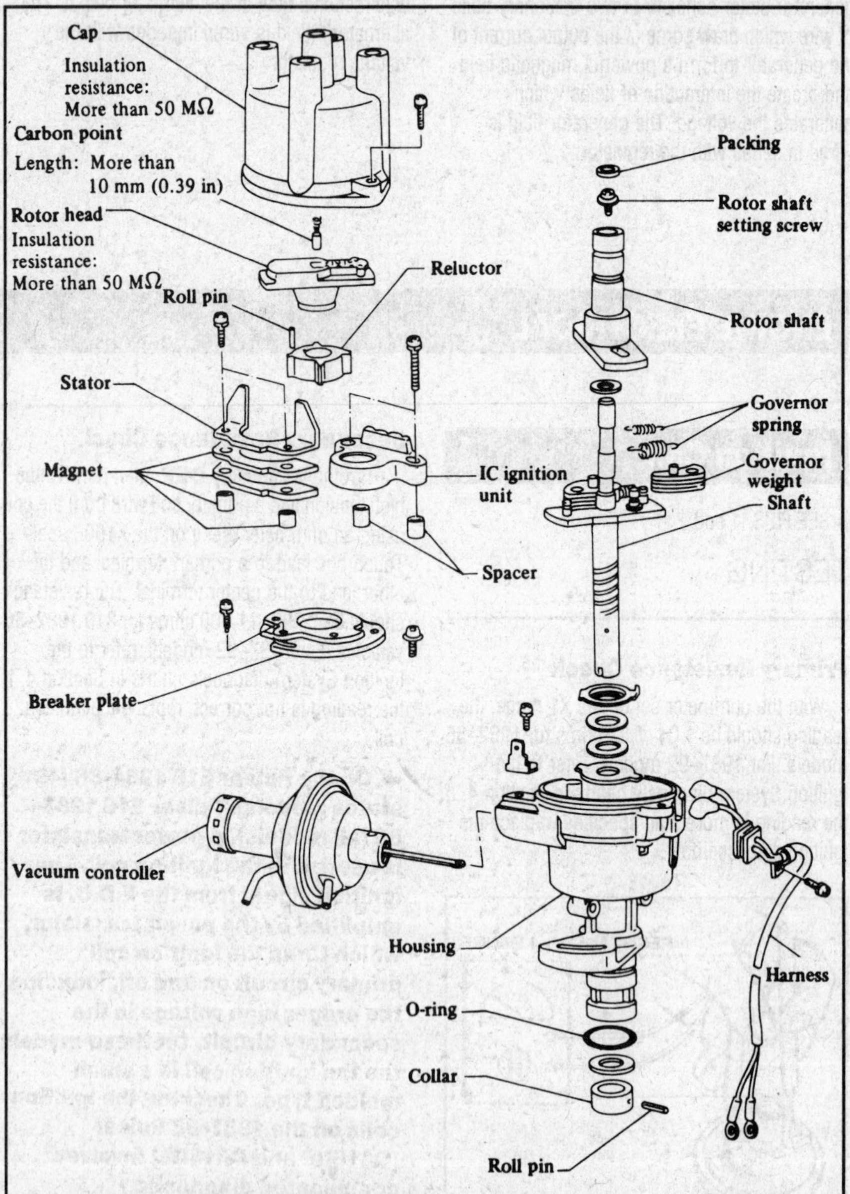

Fig. 4. Exploded view of the electronic distributor — All 1982–86 engines

c. Remove the mounting screws and remove the ignitor and the two spacers.

To install:

4. To install a new crank angle sensor:

a. First remove the sealing cover. Unplug the harness connector, if it has not already been unplugged in removing the distributor. Then, remove the two screws attaching the crank angle sensor to the electronic components underneath.

b. Slide the rotor plate and the sensor upward together. Once the plate clears the shaft and the sensor clears the edge of the distributor body, separate them. Install in reverse order. Make sure to install the reluctor roll pin so as to hold the reluctor in the proper position relative to the distributor shaft.

1987–92

➡ The 1987–92 ignition module (crank angle sensor) is an integral part of the distributor assembly. The components are not serviceable separately. If a component is found defective, replace the distributor assembly.

Distributor

REMOVAL & INSTALLATION

Engine Not Disturbed

➡ The Pulsar CA16DE and CA18DE engines do not utilize a conventional distributor. The CA16DE and CA18DE engines use a crank angle sensor in place of the distributor. Removal and installation is the same procedure.

1. Unfasten the retaining clips and lift the distributor cap straight up. It will be easier to install the distributor if the wiring is not disconnected from the cap. If the wires must be removed from the cap, mark their positions to aid in installations.
2. Disconnect the distributor wiring harness.
3. Disconnect the vacuum lines.
4. Note the position of the rotor in relation to the base. Scribe a mark on the base of the distributor and on the engine block to facilitate reinstallation. Align the marks with the direction the metal tip of the rotor is pointing.
5. Remove the bolt which hold the distributor to the engine.
6. Pull the distributor assembly from the engine.

To install:

7. Insert the distributor shaft and assembly into the engine. Line up the mark on the distributor and the one on the engine with the metal tip of the rotor. Make sure that the vacuum advance diaphragm is pointed in the same direction as it was pointed originally. This will be done automatically if the marks on the engine and the distributor are lined up with the rotor.
8. Install the distributor holddown bolt and clamp. Leave the screw loose so that you can move the distributor with heavy hand pressure.
9. Connect the primary wire to the coil. Install the distributor cap on the distributor housing. Secure the distributor cap with the spring clips.
10. Install the spark plug wires if removed. Make sure that the wires are pressed all the way into the top of the distributor cap and firmly onto the spark plug.
11. Set the ignition timing.

➡ If the crankshaft has been turned or the engine disturbed in any manner (disassembled and/or rebuilt) while the distributor was removed or if the marks were not drawn, it will be necessary to initially time the engine. Follow the procedure given below.

Installation With Engine Disturbed

➧ SEE FIGS. 5, 6, 7

1. It is necessary to place the No. 1 cylinder in the firing position to correctly install the distributor. To locate this position, the ignition timing marks on the crankshaft front pulley are used.
2. Remove the No. 1 cylinder spark plug. Turn the crankshaft until the piston in the No. 1 cylinder is moving up on the compression stroke. This can be determined by placing your thumb over the spark plug hole and feeling the air being forced out of the cylinder. Stop turning the crankshaft when the timing marks that are used to time the engine are aligned.
3. Oil the distributor housing lightly where the distributor bears on the cylinder block.
4. Install the distributor with the rotor, which is mounted on the shaft, pointing toward the No. 1 spark plug terminal on the distributor cap. Of course you won't be able to see the direction in which the rotor is pointing if the cap is on the distributor.

➡ Lay the cap on top of the distributor and make a mark on the side of the distributor housing just below the No. 1 spark plug terminal. Make sure that the rotor points toward that mark when you install the distributor.

5. When the distributor shaft has reached the bottom of the hole, move the rotor back and forth slightly until the driving lug on the end of the shaft enters the slots cut in the end of the oil pump shaft or camshaft and the distributor assembly slides down into place.
6. Install the distributor holddown bolt.
7. Install the spark plug.

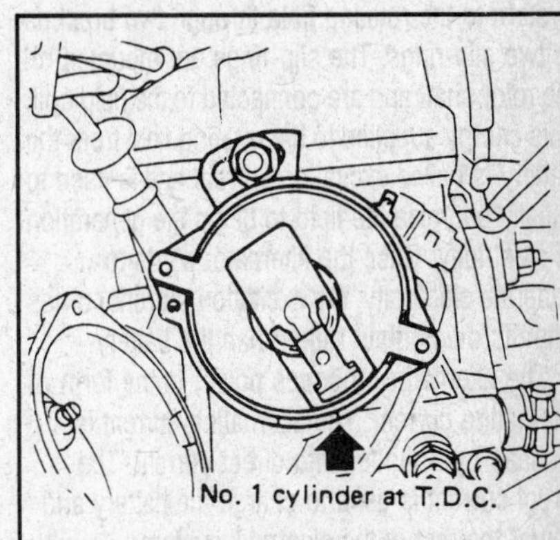
No. 1 cylinder at T.D.C.

Fig. 5. On the 1987–92 engines, if the engine crankshaft is turned to TDC, the rotor and the marks on the distributor body will align

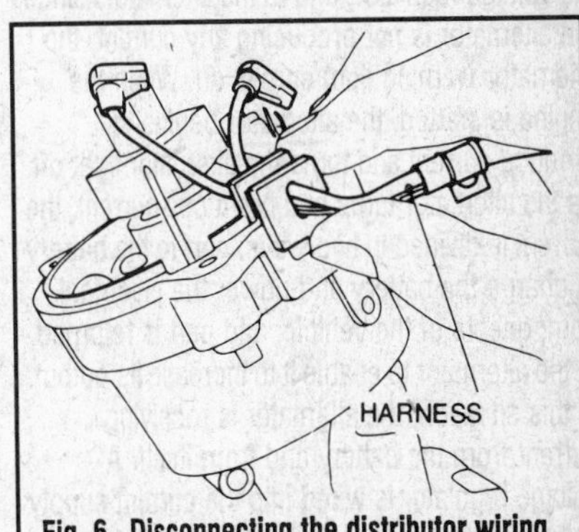
HARNESS

Fig. 6. Disconnecting the distributor wiring harness on distributors with a reluctor

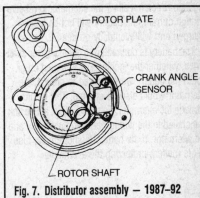

Fig. 7. Distributor assembly — 1987–92 engines

Alternator

The alternator charging system is a negative (–) ground system which consists of an alternator, a regulator, a charge indicator, a storage battery and wiring connecting the components, and fuse link wire.

The alternator is belt-driven from the engine. Energy is supplied from the alternator/regulator system to the rotating field through two brushes to two slip-rings. The slip-rings are mounted on the rotor shaft and are connected to the field coil. This energy supplied to the rotating field from the battery is called excitation current and is used to initially energize the field to begin the generation of electricity. Once the alternator starts to generate electricity, the excitation current comes from its own output rather than the battery.

The alternator produces power in the form of alternating current. The alternating current is rectified by 6 diodes into direct current. The direct current is used to charge the battery and power the rest of the electrical system.

When the ignition key is turned on, current flows from the battery, through the charging system indicator light on the instrument panel, to the voltage regulator, and to the alternator. Since the alternator is not producing any current, the alternator warning light comes on. When the engine is started, the alternator begins to produce current and turns the alternator light off. As the alternator turns and produces current, the current is divided in two ways: part to the battery to charge the battery and power the electrical components of the vehicle, and part is returned to the alternator to enable it to increase its output. In this situation, the alternator is receiving current from the battery and from itself. A voltage regulator is wired into the current supply to the alternator to prevent it from receiving too much current which would cause it to put out too much current. Conversely, if the voltage regulator does not allow the alternator to receive enough current, the battery will not be fully charged and will eventually go dead.

The battery is connected to the alternator at all times, whether the ignition key is turned on or not. If the battery were shorted to ground, the alternator would also be shorted. This would damage the alternator. To prevent this, a fuse link is installed in the wiring between the battery and the alternator. If the battery is shorted, the fuse link is melted, protecting the alternator.

ALTERNATOR PRECAUTIONS

To prevent damage to the alternator and regulator, the following precautionary measures must be taken when working with the electrical system.

1. Never reverse the battery connections.
2. Booster batteries for starting must be connected properly: positive-to-positive and negative-to-ground.
3. Disconnect the battery cables before using a fast charger; the charger has a tendency to force current through the diodes in the opposite direction for which they were designed. This burns out the diodes.
4. Never use a fast charger as a booster for starting the vehicle.
5. Never disconnect the voltage regulator while the engine is running.
6. Avoid long soldering times when replacing diodes or transistors. Prolonged heat is damaging to AC generators.
7. Do not use test lamps of more than 12 volts (V) for checking diode continuity.
8. Do not short across or ground any of the terminals on the AC generator.
9. The polarity of the battery, generator, and regulator must be matched and considered before making any electrical connections within the system.
10. Never operate the alternator on an open circuit. make sure that all connections within the circuit are clean and tight.
11. Disconnect the battery terminals when performing any service on the electrical system. This will eliminate the possibility of accidental reversal of polarity.
12. Disconnect the battery ground cable if arc welding is to be done on any part of the car.

CHARGING SYSTEM TROUBLESHOOTING

SEE FIGS. 8 and 9

The main reason for charging system problems is dirty, damaged or loose battery cables or alternator wiring. Always check these problems before going further. After eliminating these causes, a no charge condition usually is the fault of the IC regulator or worn brushes. The brushes have wear indicator lines. If the brush is near or at the indicator, the brush will not contact the rotor slip rings and cause a no charge condition.

REMOVAL & INSTALLATION

The alternators for Pulsar and Stanza have not changed much over the years. The 1987–88 alternators for Pulsar and Stanza have a different internal diode assembly.

1. Disconnect the negative battery terminal.
2. Disconnect the 2 lead wires and connector from the alternator.
3. Loosen the drive belt adjusting bolt and remove the belt.
4. Unscrew the alternator attaching bolts and remove the alternator from the vehicle.

To install:

5. Install the alternator and retaining bolts loosely.
6. Install the belt and wiring. Adjust the belt as outlined in Section 1. Torque the retaining bolts to 25 ft. lbs. (34 Nm).

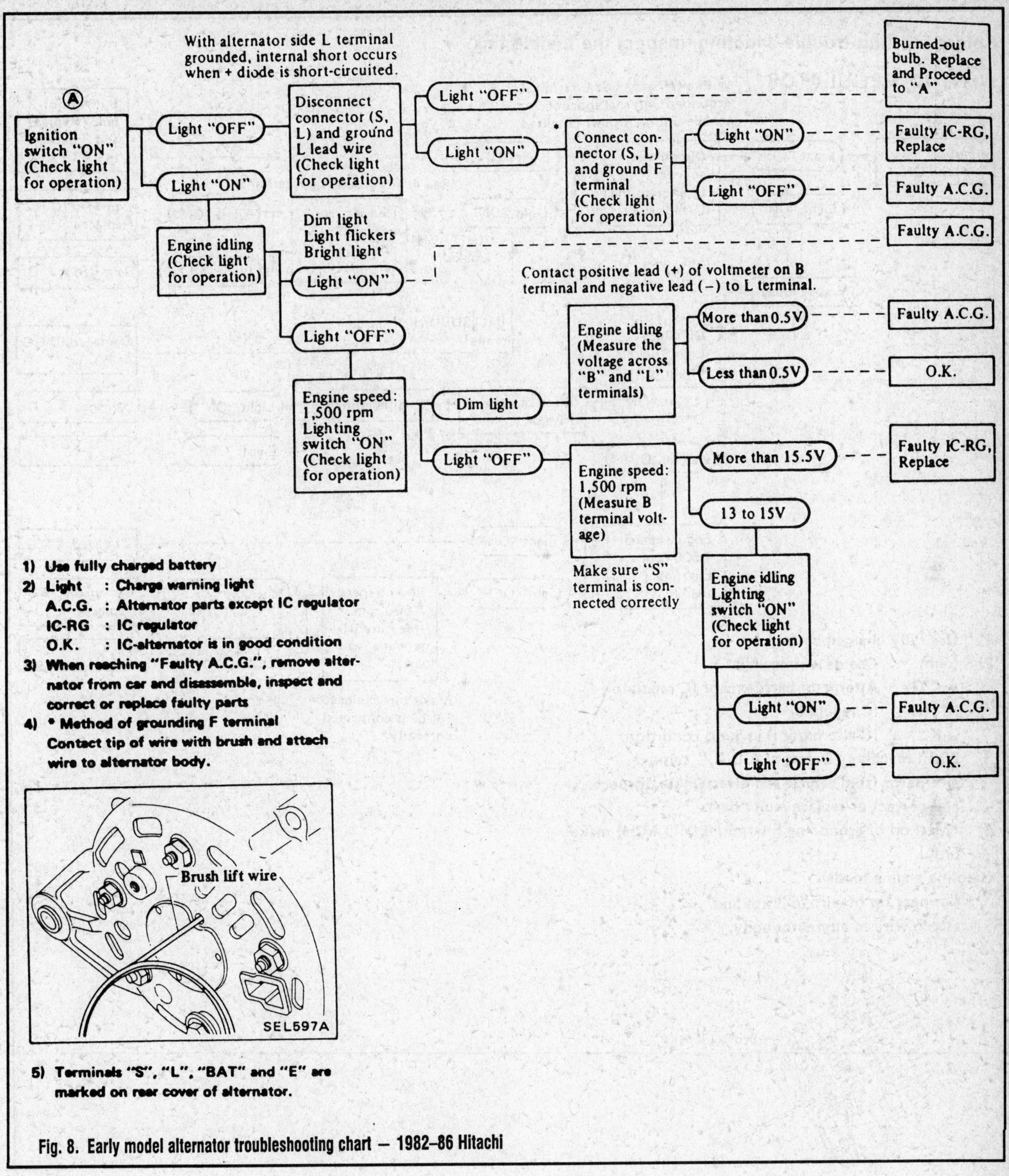

With alternator side L terminal grounded, internal short occurs when + diode is short-circuited.
A
Ignition switch "ON" (Check light for operation)
Light "OFF"
Light "ON"
Disconnect connector (S, L) and ground L lead wire (Check light for operation)
Light "OFF"
Burned-out bulb. Replace and Proceed to "A"
Light "ON"
*
Connect connector (S, L) and ground F terminal (Check light for operation)
Light "ON"
Faulty IC-RG, Replace
Light "OFF"
Faulty A.C.G.
Engine idling (Check light for operation)
Dim light
Light flickers
Bright light
Light "ON"
Faulty A.C.G.
Light "OFF"
Contact positive lead (+) of voltmeter on B terminal and negative lead (–) to L terminal.
Engine speed: 1,500 rpm Lighting switch "ON" (Check light for operation)
Dim light
Engine idling (Measure the voltage across "B" and "L" terminals)
More than 0.5V
Faulty A.C.G.
Less than 0.5V
O.K.
Light "OFF"
Engine speed: 1,500 rpm (Measure B terminal voltage)
Make sure "S" terminal is connected correctly
More than 15.5V
Faulty IC-RG, Replace
13 to 15V
Engine idling Lighting switch "ON" (Check light for operation)
Light "ON"
Faulty A.C.G.
Light "OFF"
O.K.
1) Use fully charged battery
2) Light : Charge warning light
A.C.G. : Alternator parts except IC regulator
IC-RG : IC regulator
O.K. : IC-alternator is in good condition
3) When reaching "Faulty A.C.G.", remove alternator from car and disassemble, inspect and correct or replace faulty parts
4) * Method of grounding F terminal
Contact tip of wire with brush and attach wire to alternator body.
Brush lift wire
SEL597A
5) Terminals "S", "L", "BAT" and "E" are marked on rear cover of alternator.

Fig. 8. Early model alternator troubleshooting chart — 1982–86 Hitachi

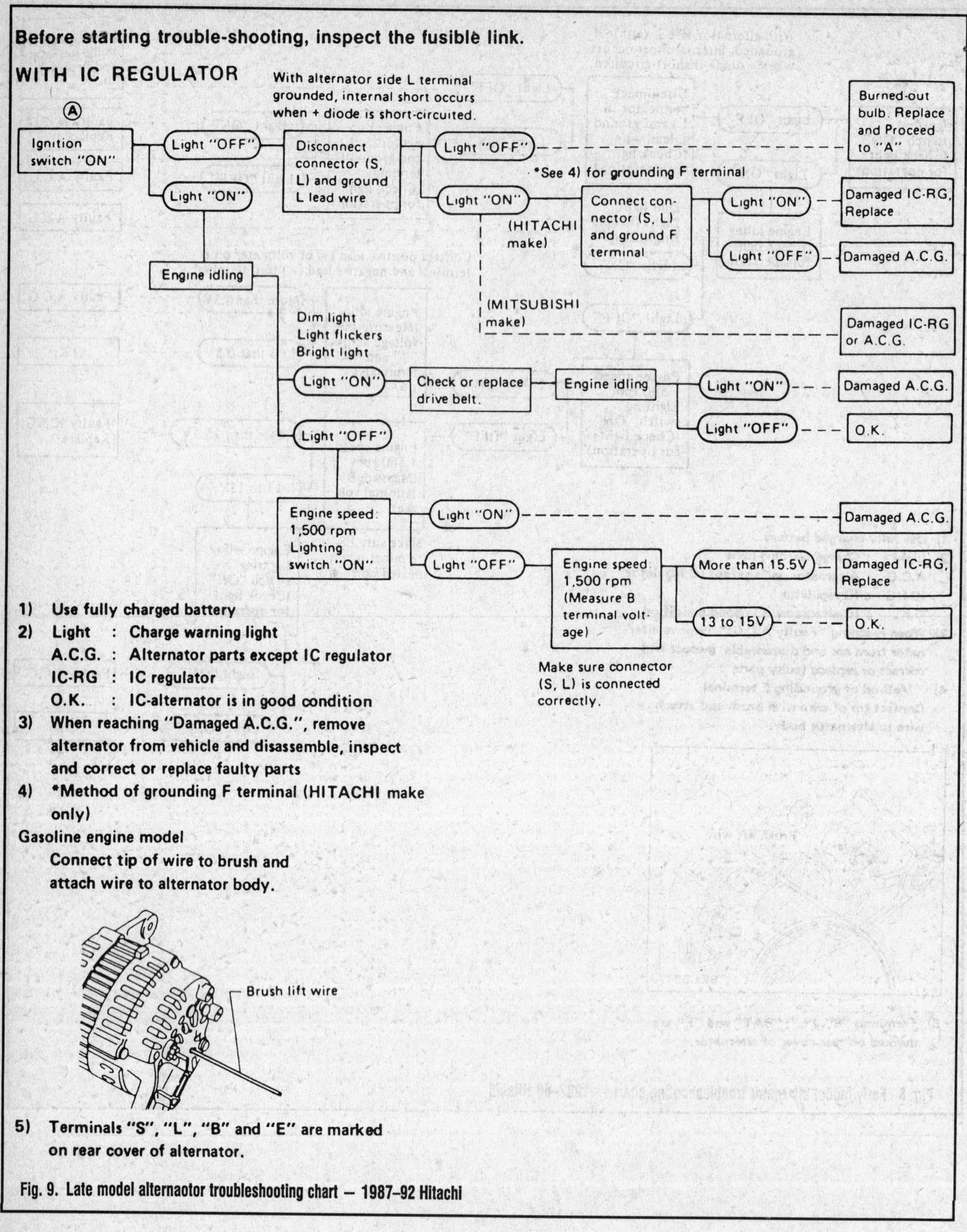

Before starting trouble-shooting, inspect the fusible link.
WITH IC REGULATOR
With alternator side L terminal grounded, internal short occurs when + diode is short-circuited.
Ⓐ
Ignition switch "ON"
Light "OFF"
Light "ON"
Disconnect connector (S, L) and ground L lead wire
Light "OFF"
Burned-out bulb. Replace and Proceed to "A"
*See 4) for grounding F terminal
Light "ON"
(HITACHI make)
Connect connector (S, L) and ground F terminal
Light "ON"
Damaged IC-RG, Replace
Light "OFF"
Damaged A.C.G.
(MITSUBISHI make)
Damaged IC-RG or A.C.G.
Engine idling
Dim light
Light flickers
Bright light
Light "ON"
Check or replace drive belt.
Engine idling
Light "ON"
Damaged A.C.G.
Light "OFF"
O.K.
Light "OFF"
Engine speed: 1,500 rpm Lighting switch "ON"
Light "ON"
Damaged A.C.G.
Light "OFF"
Engine speed: 1,500 rpm (Measure B terminal voltage)
More than 15.5V
Damaged IC-RG, Replace
13 to 15V
O.K.
Make sure connector (S, L) is connected correctly.
1) Use fully charged battery
2) Light : Charge warning light
A.C.G. : Alternator parts except IC regulator
IC-RG : IC regulator
O.K. : IC-alternator is in good condition
3) When reaching "Damaged A.C.G.", remove alternator from vehicle and disassemble, inspect and correct or replace faulty parts
4) *Method of grounding F terminal (HITACHI make only)
Gasoline engine model
Connect tip of wire to brush and attach wire to alternator body.
Brush lift wire
5) Terminals "S", "L", "B" and "E" are marked on rear cover of alternator.

Fig. 9. Late model alternaotor troubleshooting chart – 1987–92 Hitachi

IC Regulator and Brushes

SEE FIGS. 10–13

REMOVAL & INSTALLATION

All models are equipped with internal voltage regulator. Since the regulator is part of the alternator, no adjustments are possible or necessary.

1. Disconnect the negative battery cable.
2. Remove the alternator from the vehicle.
3. Carefully remove the 3 or 4 long through bolts. Be careful not to damage the bolt head. Place a matchmark on the 2 case halves before disassembly.
4. Lightly tap on the rear housing and separate the 2 housings. If the halves will not come apart. Heat the rear housing bearing boss with a 200 watt soldering iron. Do not use heat gun, internal components may be damaged.
5. Remove the diode and brush holder assembly nuts from the rear case. Label all nuts and insulators before removal.
6. Remove the IC regulator from the housing.
7. Remove the brushes from the brush holder. Some units have soldered brush wires. Using a 200 watt soldering iron, remove the brush wire from the brush holder.

To install:

8. Install the brush into the holder so the wire is through the hole.
9. Solder the wire and make sure the brush moves freely inside the brush holder.
10. Install the brush holder, IC regulator and diode assembly into the rear case. Install the retaining nuts and insulators. Torque the nuts to 36 inch lbs. (8 Nm).
11. Push the brushes into the holder and insert a wire through the rear housing into the brush holder to retain the brushes during installation.
12. Carefully install the 2 case halves together, making sure the brushes are held in place.
13. After the halves are together, install the through bolts and torque to 48 inch lbs. (9 Nm).
14. Remove the brush retaining wire and install the alternator to the vehicle.
15. Adjust belt tension and reconnect all wiring.
16. Start the engine and check operation.

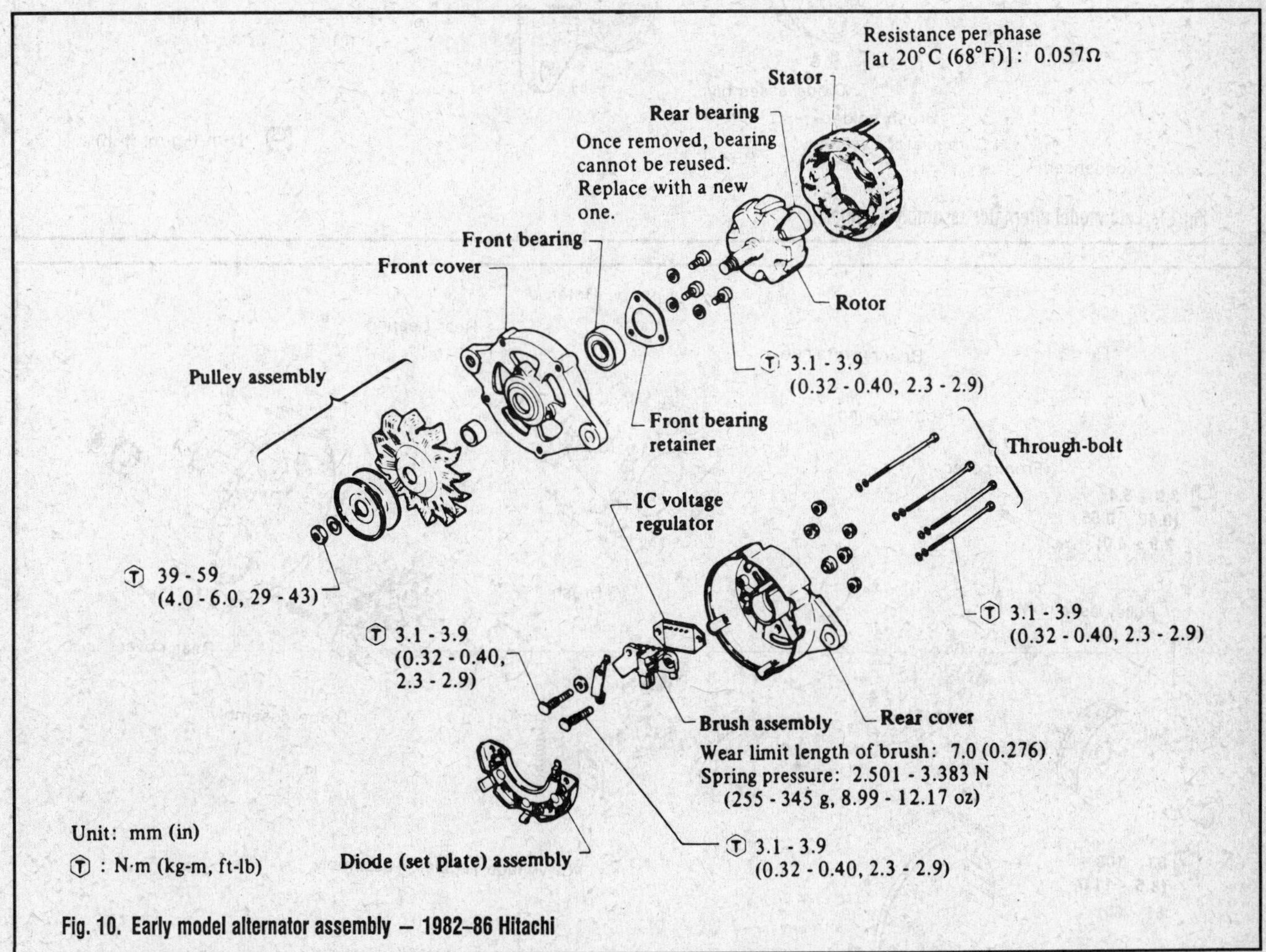
Resistance per phase
[at 20°C (68°F)]: 0.057Ω
Stator
Rear bearing
Once removed, bearing cannot be reused. Replace with a new one.
Front bearing
Front cover
Rotor
Pulley assembly
3.1 - 3.9
(0.32 - 0.40, 2.3 - 2.9)
Front bearing retainer
Through-bolt
IC voltage regulator
39 - 59
(4.0 - 6.0, 29 - 43)
3.1 - 3.9
(0.32 - 0.40, 2.3 - 2.9)
3.1 - 3.9
(0.32 - 0.40, 2.3 - 2.9)
Brush assembly
Rear cover
Wear limit length of brush: 7.0 (0.276)
Spring pressure: 2.501 - 3.383 N
(255 - 345 g, 8.99 - 12.17 oz)
Unit: mm (in)
: N·m (kg-m, ft-lb)
Diode (set plate) assembly
3.1 - 3.9
(0.32 - 0.40, 2.3 - 2.9)

Fig. 10. Early model alternator assembly — 1982–86 Hitachi

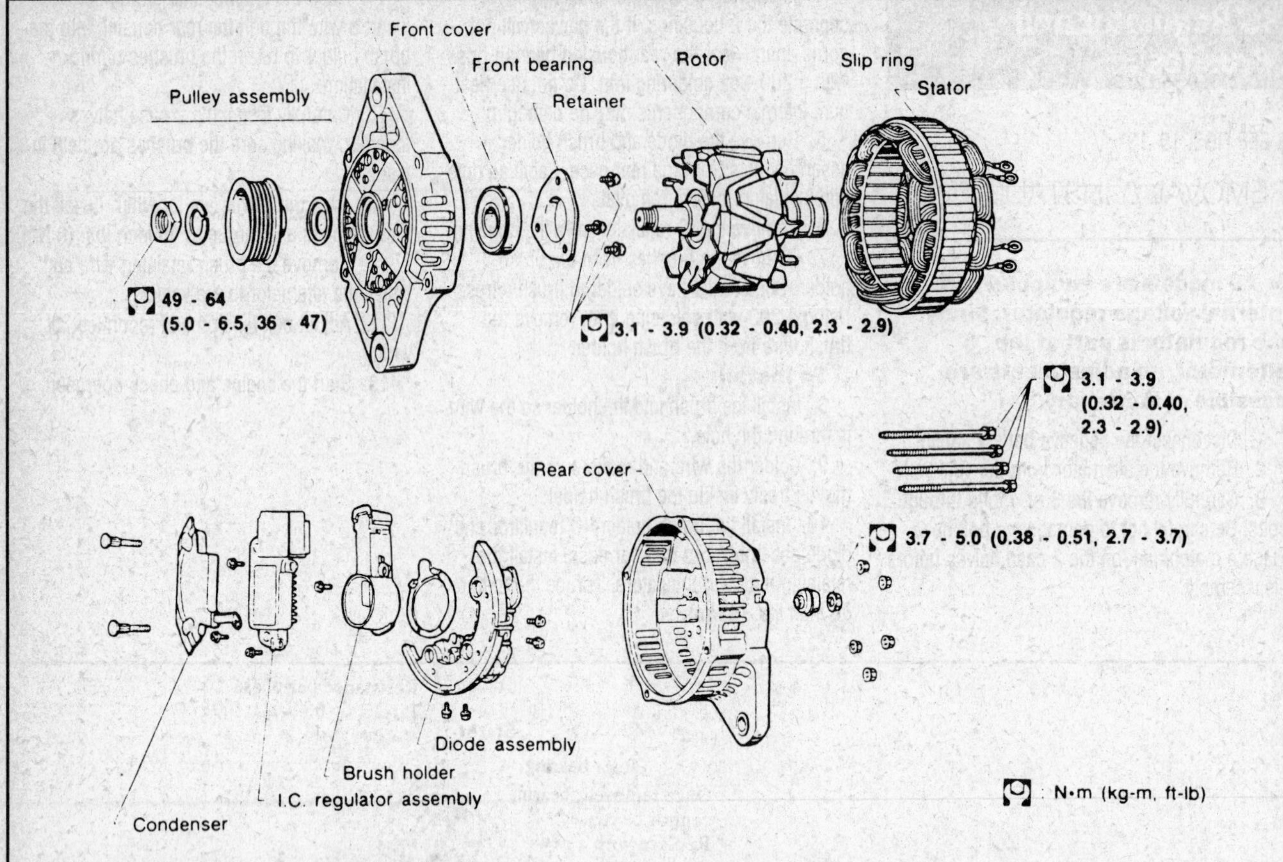

Front cover
Front bearing
Rotor
Slip ring
Pulley assembly
Retainer
Stator
49 - 64
(5.0 - 6.5, 36 - 47)
3.1 - 3.9 (0.32 - 0.40, 2.3 - 2.9)
3.1 - 3.9
(0.32 - 0.40,
2.3 - 2.9)
Rear cover
3.7 - 5.0 (0.38 - 0.51, 2.7 - 3.7)
Diode assembly
Brush holder
I.C. regulator assembly
Condenser
: N·m (kg-m, ft-lb)

Fig.11. Late model alternator assembly – Hitachi

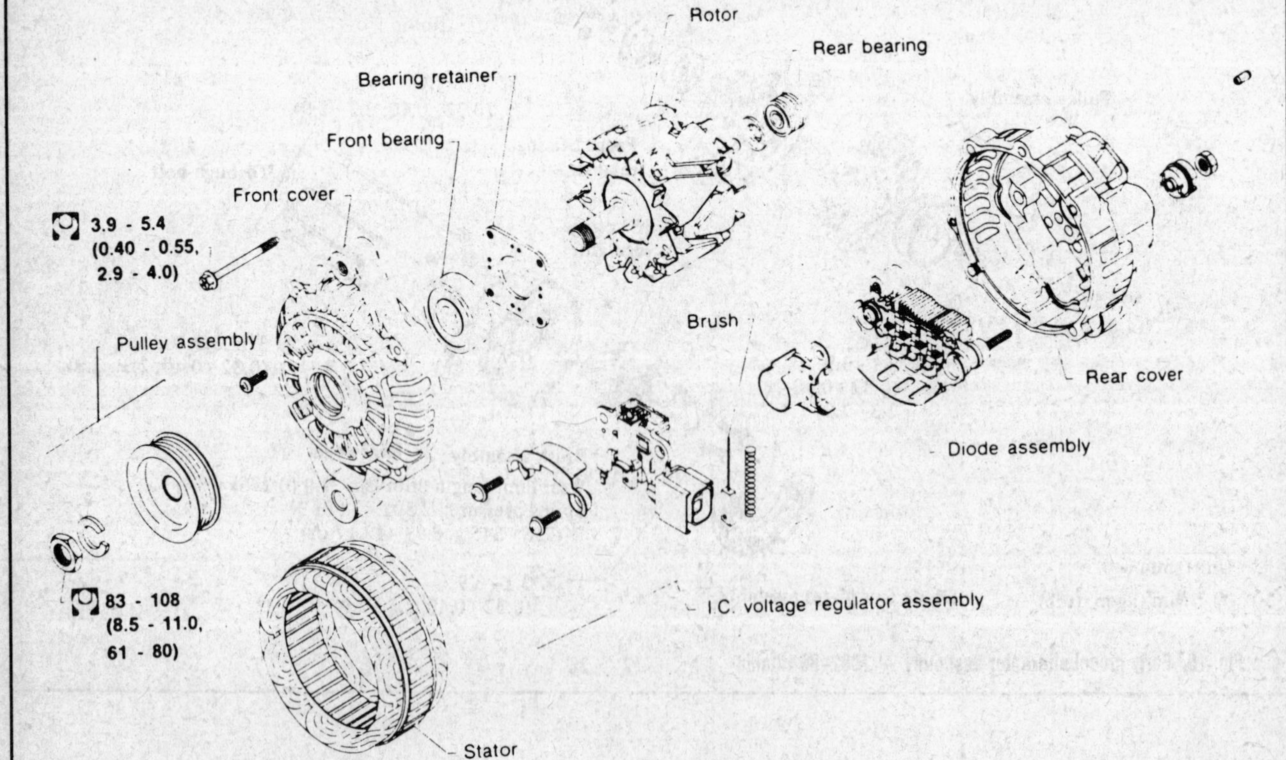

Rotor
Rear bearing
Bearing retainer
Front bearing
Front cover
3.9 - 5.4
(0.40 - 0.55,
2.9 - 4.0)
Pulley assembly
Brush
Rear cover
Diode assembly
83 - 108
(8.5 - 11.0,
61 - 80)
I.C. voltage regulator assembly
Stator

Fig. 12. Late model alternator assembly – Mitsubishi

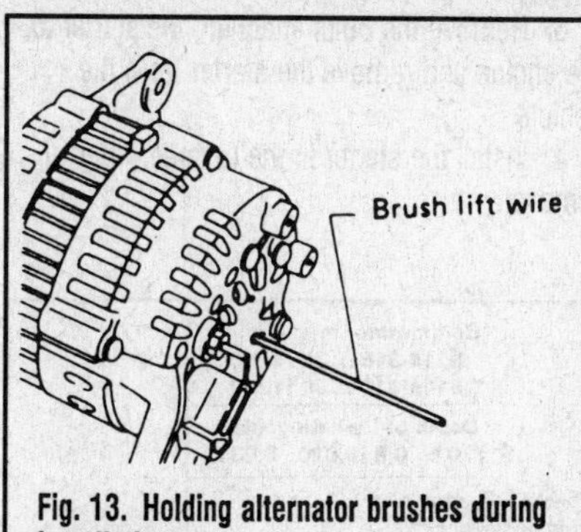
Brush lift wire

Fig. 13. Holding alternator brushes during installation

Battery

Refer to Section 1 for details on battery maintenance.

REMOVAL & INSTALLATION

1. Disconnect the negative (ground) cable from the terminal and then the positive cable. Special pullers are available to remove the cable clamps. To avoid sparks, always disconnect the ground cable first and connect it last.
2. Remove the battery holddown clamp.
3. Remove the battery, being careful not to spill the acid.

➡ **Spilled acid can be neutralized with a baking soda/water solution. If you somehow get acid into your eyes, flush it out with lots of water and get to a doctor.**

4. Clean the battery posts thoroughly before reinstalling or when installing a new battery.
5. Clean the cable clamps, using a wire brush, both inside and out.
6. Install the battery and the holddown clamp or strap. Connect the positive, and then the negative cable. DO NOT hammer them in place.

➡ **The terminals should be coated lightly (externally) with vasoline to prevent corrosion. There are also felt washers impregnated with an anti-corrosion substance which are slipped over the battery posts before installing the cables; these are available in auto parts stores. Make absolutely sure that the battery is connected properly before you turn on the ignition switch. Reversed polarity can burn out your alternator and regulator within a matter of a slit second.**

Starter

➧ SEE FIGS. 14–35

REMOVAL & INSTALLATION

In 1978, a gear reduction starter was introduced on some Canadian and United States models. The differences between the gear reduction and conventional starters are: the gear reduction starter has a set of ratio reduction gears while the conventional starter does not.

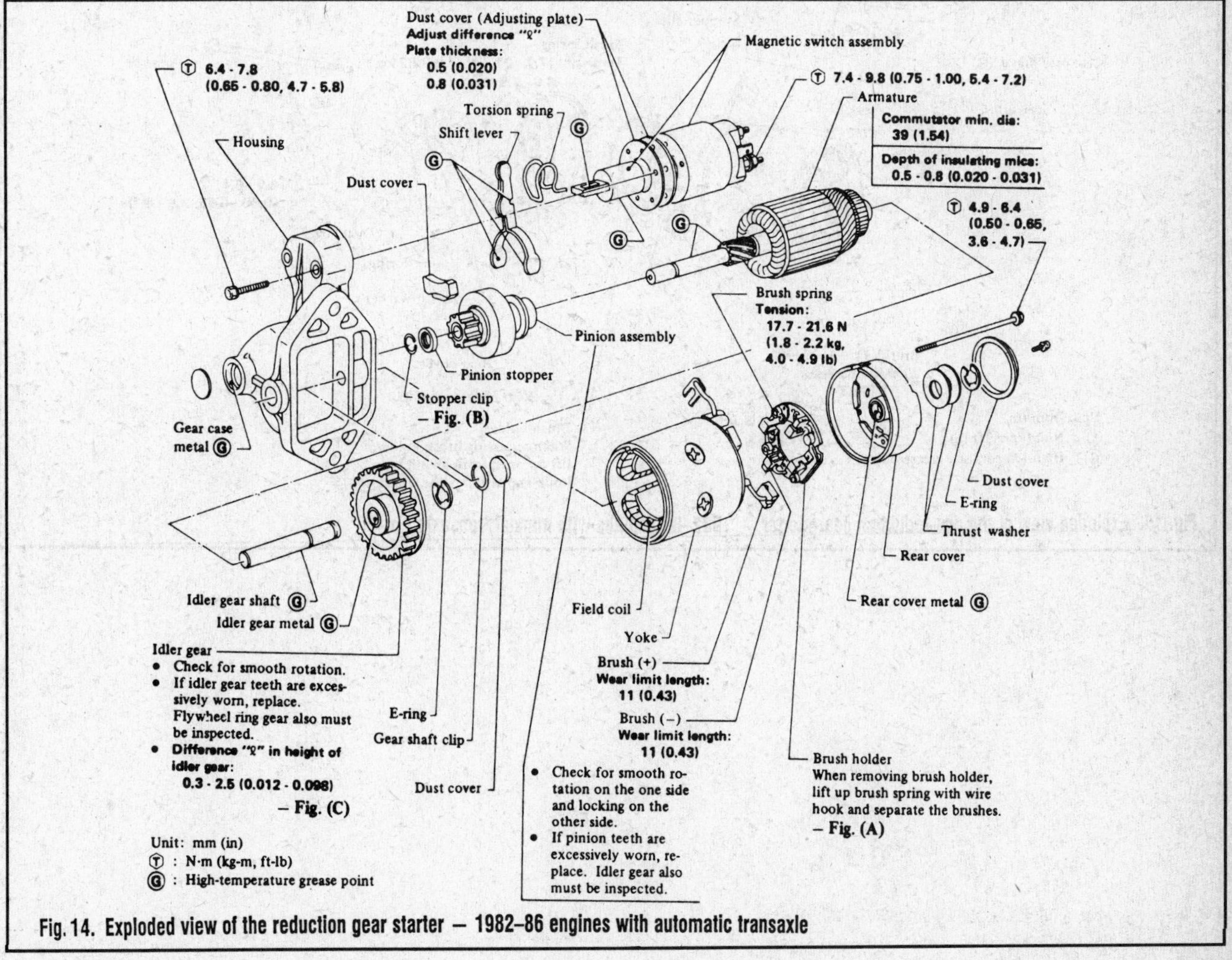

Fig. 14. Exploded view of the reduction gear starter — 1982–86 engines with automatic transaxle

The extra gears on the gear reduction starter make the starter pinion gear turn at about half the speed of the starter, giving the starter twice the turning power of a conventional starter.

1. Disconnect the negative battery cable from the battery.
2. Disconnect the starter wiring at the starter, taking note of the positions for correct reinstallation.
3. Remove the bolts attaching the starter to the engine and remove the starter from the vehicle.
4. Install the starter in the reverse order of removal.

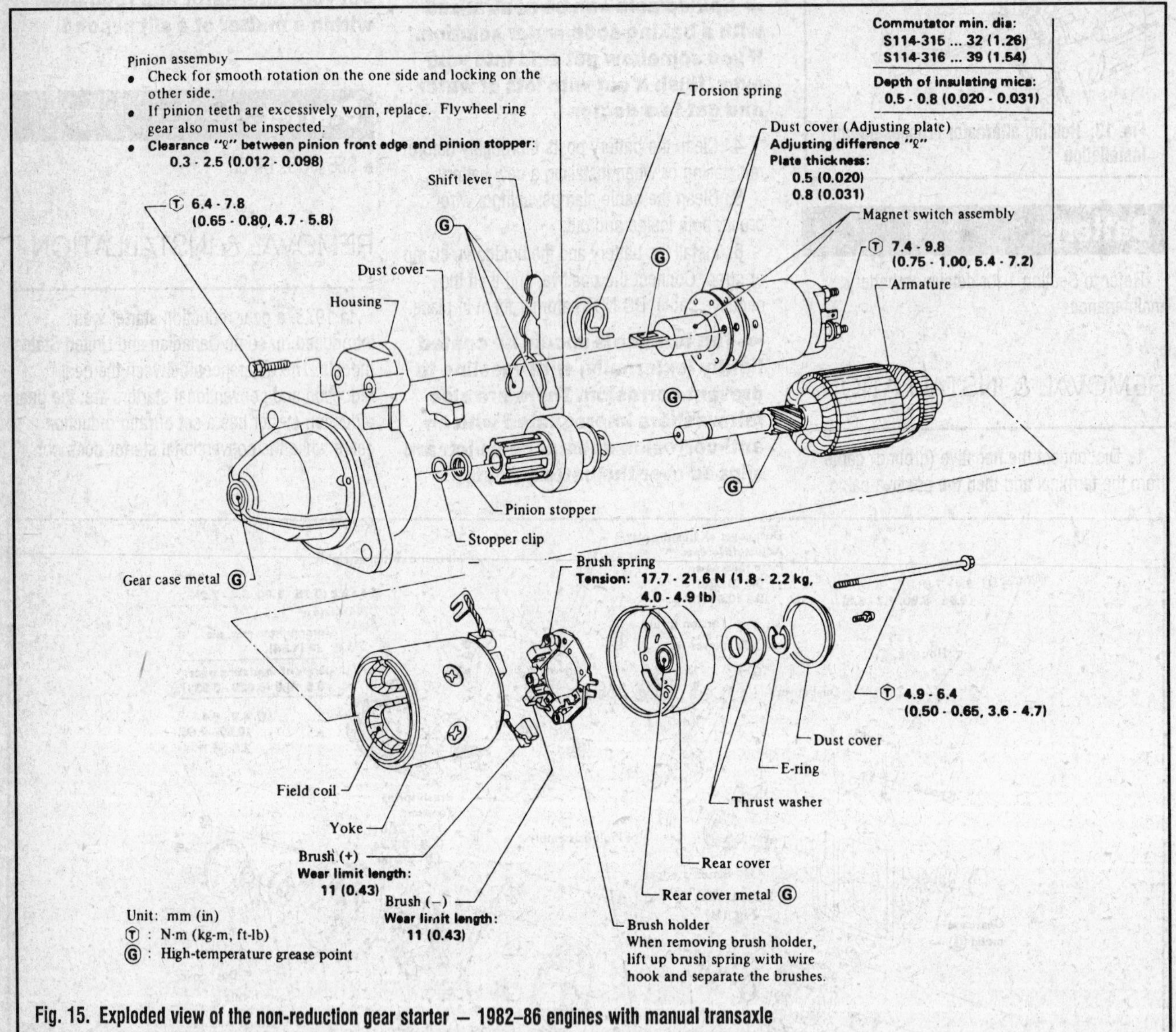
Commutator min. dia:
S114-315 ... 32 (1.26)
S114-316 ... 39 (1.54)
Depth of insulating mica:
0.5 - 0.8 (0.020 - 0.031)
Pinion assembly
• Check for smooth rotation on the one side and locking on the other side.
• If pinion teeth are excessively worn, replace. Flywheel ring gear also must be inspected.
• Clearance "ℓ" between pinion front edge and pinion stopper:
0.3 - 2.5 (0.012 - 0.098)
Torsion spring
Dust cover (Adjusting plate)
Adjusting difference "ℓ"
Plate thickness:
0.5 (0.020)
0.8 (0.031)
Shift lever
6.4 - 7.8
(0.65 - 0.80, 4.7 - 5.8)
Magnet switch assembly
7.4 - 9.8
(0.75 - 1.00, 5.4 - 7.2)
Dust cover
Armature
Housing
Pinion stopper
Stopper clip
Gear case metal
Brush spring
Tension: 17.7 - 21.6 N (1.8 - 2.2 kg, 4.0 - 4.9 lb)
4.9 - 6.4
(0.50 - 0.65, 3.6 - 4.7)
Dust cover
E-ring
Field coil
Thrust washer
Yoke
Brush (+)
Wear limit length:
11 (0.43)
Rear cover
Rear cover metal
Brush (−)
Wear limit length:
11 (0.43)
Unit: mm (in)
T : N·m (kg-m, ft-lb)
G : High-temperature grease point
Brush holder
When removing brush holder, lift up brush spring with wire hook and separate the brushes.

Fig. 15. Exploded view of the non-reduction gear starter — 1982–86 engines with manual transaxle

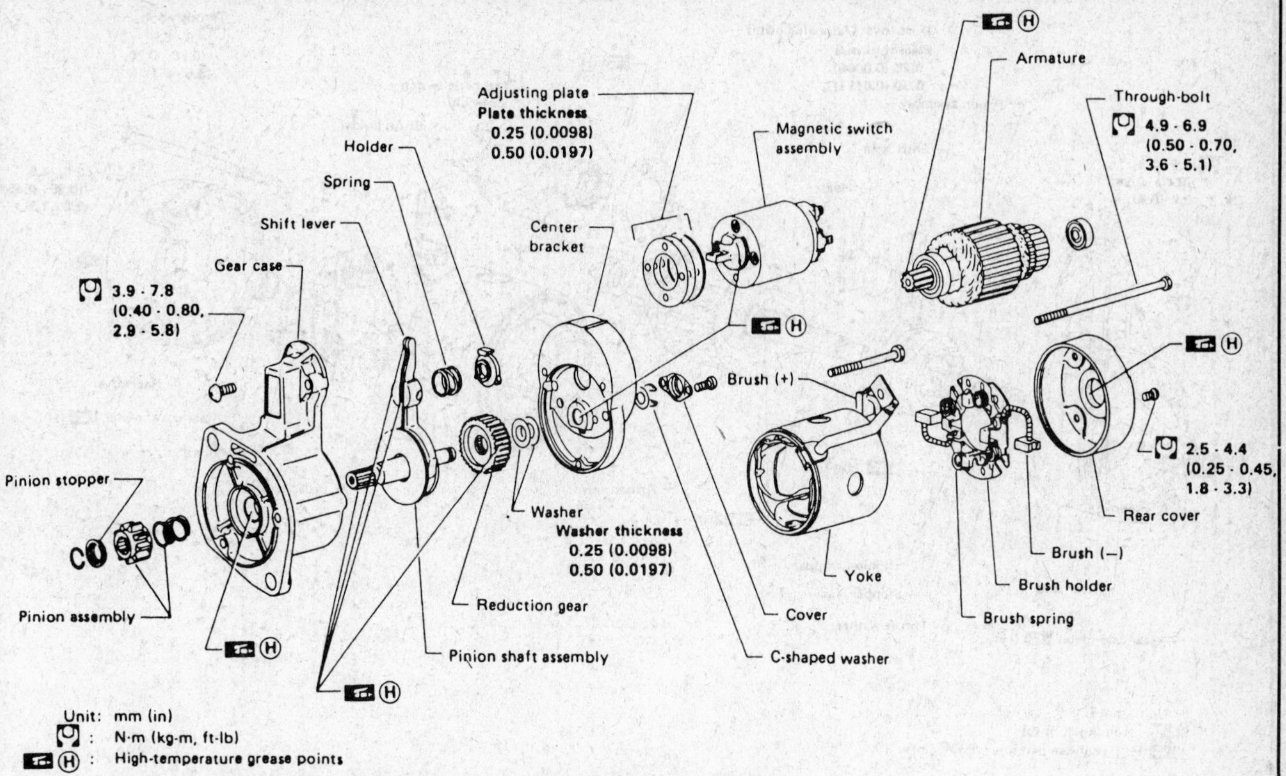

Armature
Through-bolt
4.9 - 6.9
(0.50 - 0.70,
3.6 - 5.1)
Adjusting plate
Plate thickness
0.25 (0.0098)
0.50 (0.0197)
Magnetic switch assembly
Holder
Spring
Shift lever
Center bracket
Gear case
3.9 - 7.8
(0.40 - 0.80,
2.9 - 5.8)
Brush (+)
2.5 - 4.4
(0.25 - 0.45,
1.8 - 3.3)
Pinion stopper
Washer
Washer thickness
0.25 (0.0098)
0.50 (0.0197)
Rear cover
Brush (−)
Yoke
Brush holder
Reduction gear
Pinion assembly
Cover
Brush spring
Pinion shaft assembly
C-shaped washer
Unit: mm (in)
: N·m (kg-m, ft-lb)
(H) : High-temperature grease points

Fig. 16. Exploded view of the reduction gear starter — 1987–89 engines with manual transaxle

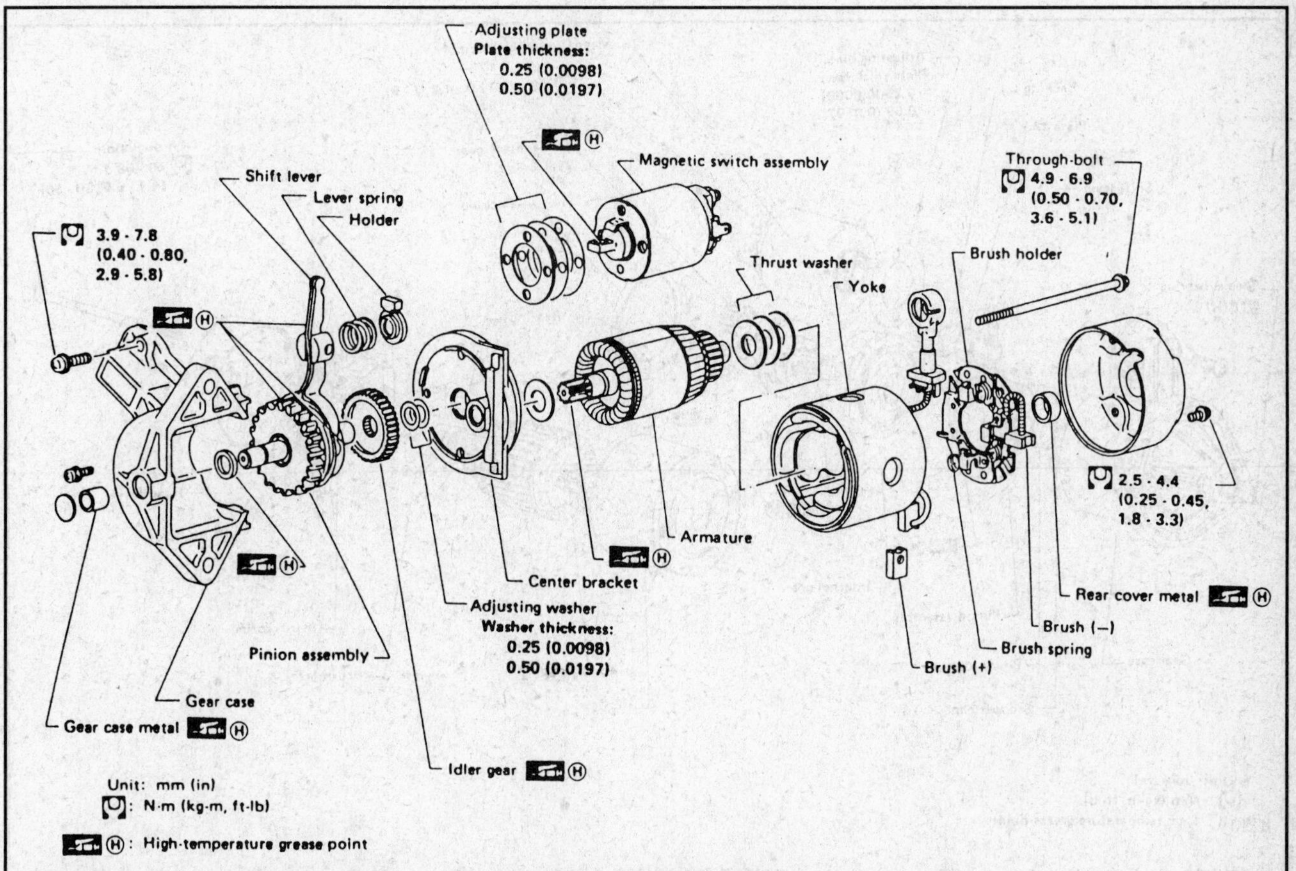

Adjusting plate
Plate thickness:
0.25 (0.0098)
0.50 (0.0197)
Magnetic switch assembly
Shift lever
Lever spring
Holder
Through-bolt
4.9 - 6.9
(0.50 - 0.70,
3.6 - 5.1)
3.9 - 7.8
(0.40 - 0.80,
2.9 - 5.8)
Brush holder
Thrust washer
Yoke
2.5 - 4.4
(0.25 - 0.45,
1.8 - 3.3)
Armature
Center bracket
Rear cover metal (H)
Adjusting washer
Washer thickness:
0.25 (0.0098)
0.50 (0.0197)
Brush (−)
Brush spring
Pinion assembly
Brush (+)
Gear case
Gear case metal (H)
Idler gear (H)
Unit: mm (in)
: N·m (kg-m, ft-lb)
(H) : High-temperature grease point

Fig. 17. Exploded view of the reduction gear starter — 1986–89 engines with automatic transaxle

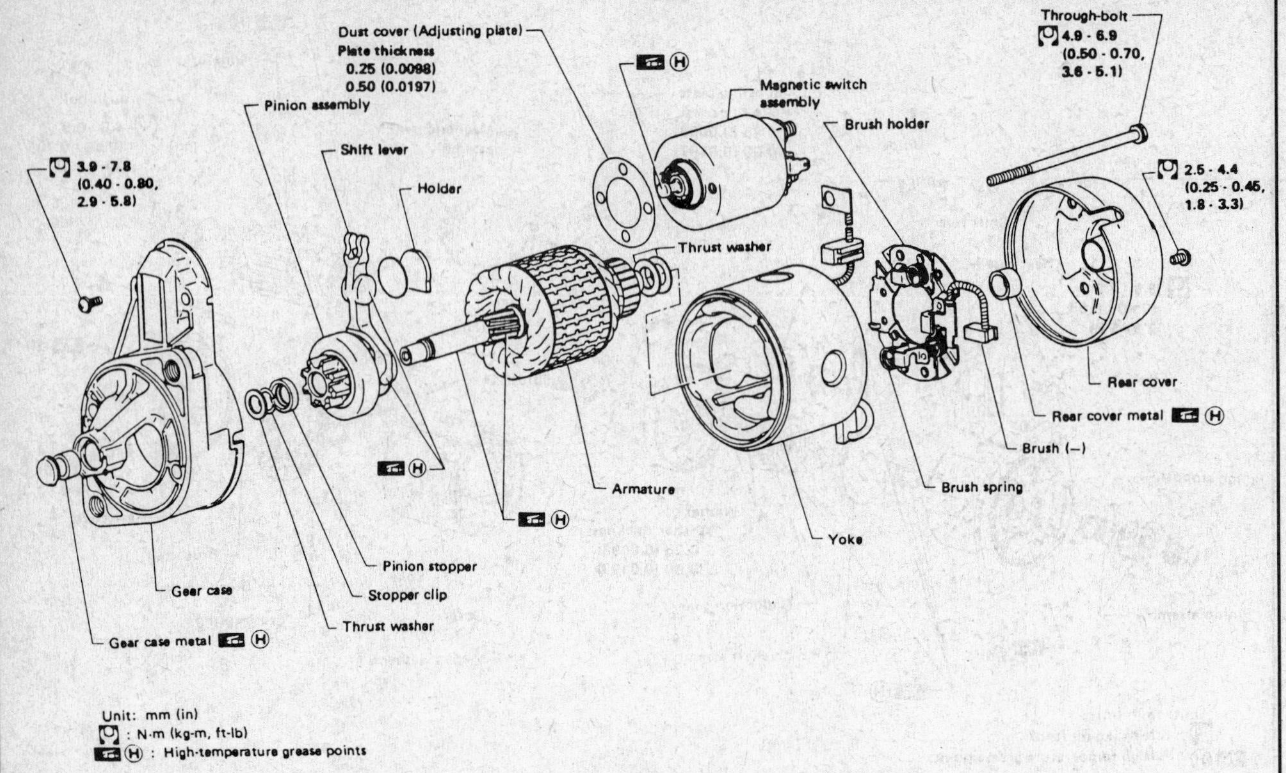

Fig. 18. Exploded view of the non-reduction gear starter — E16i (Calif. only) with automatic transaxle

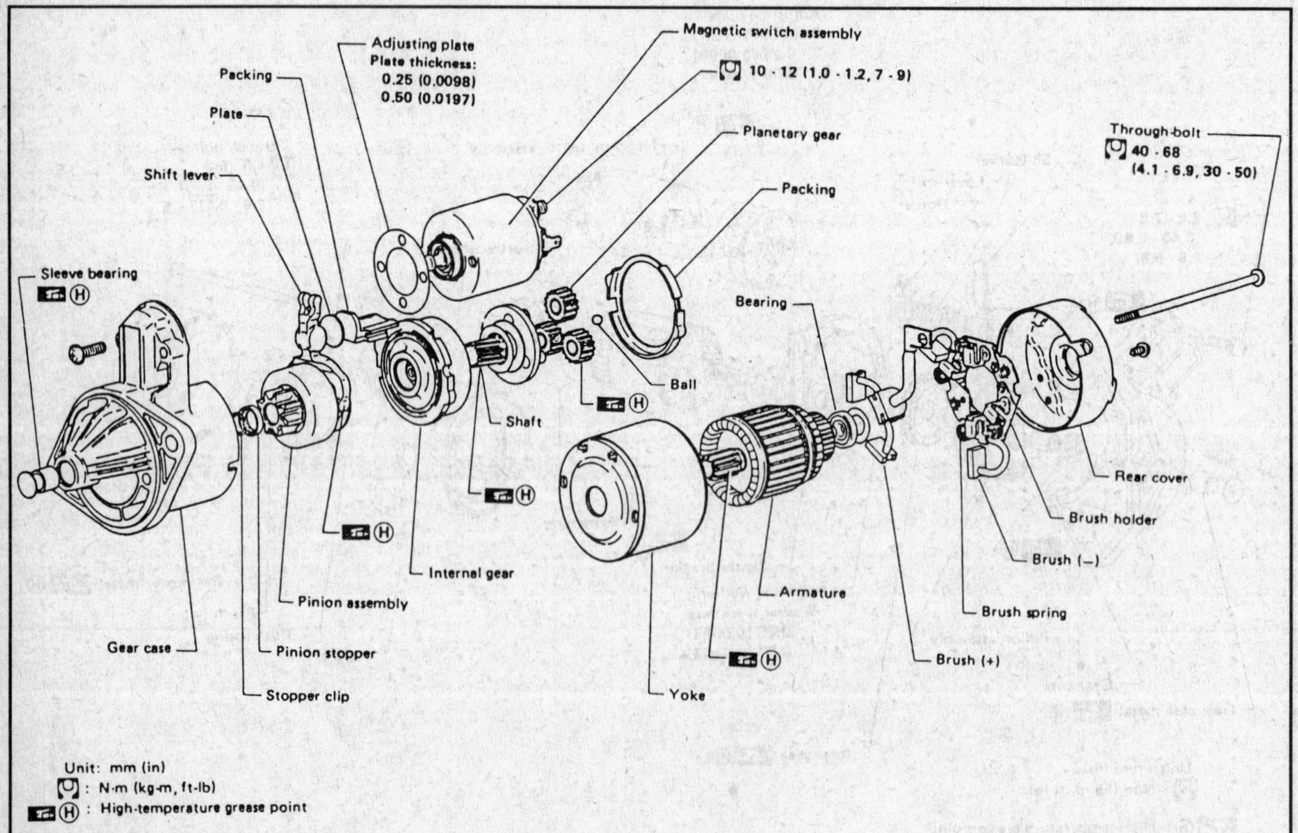

Fig. 19. Exploded view of the reduction gear starter — CA16DE and CA18DE engines

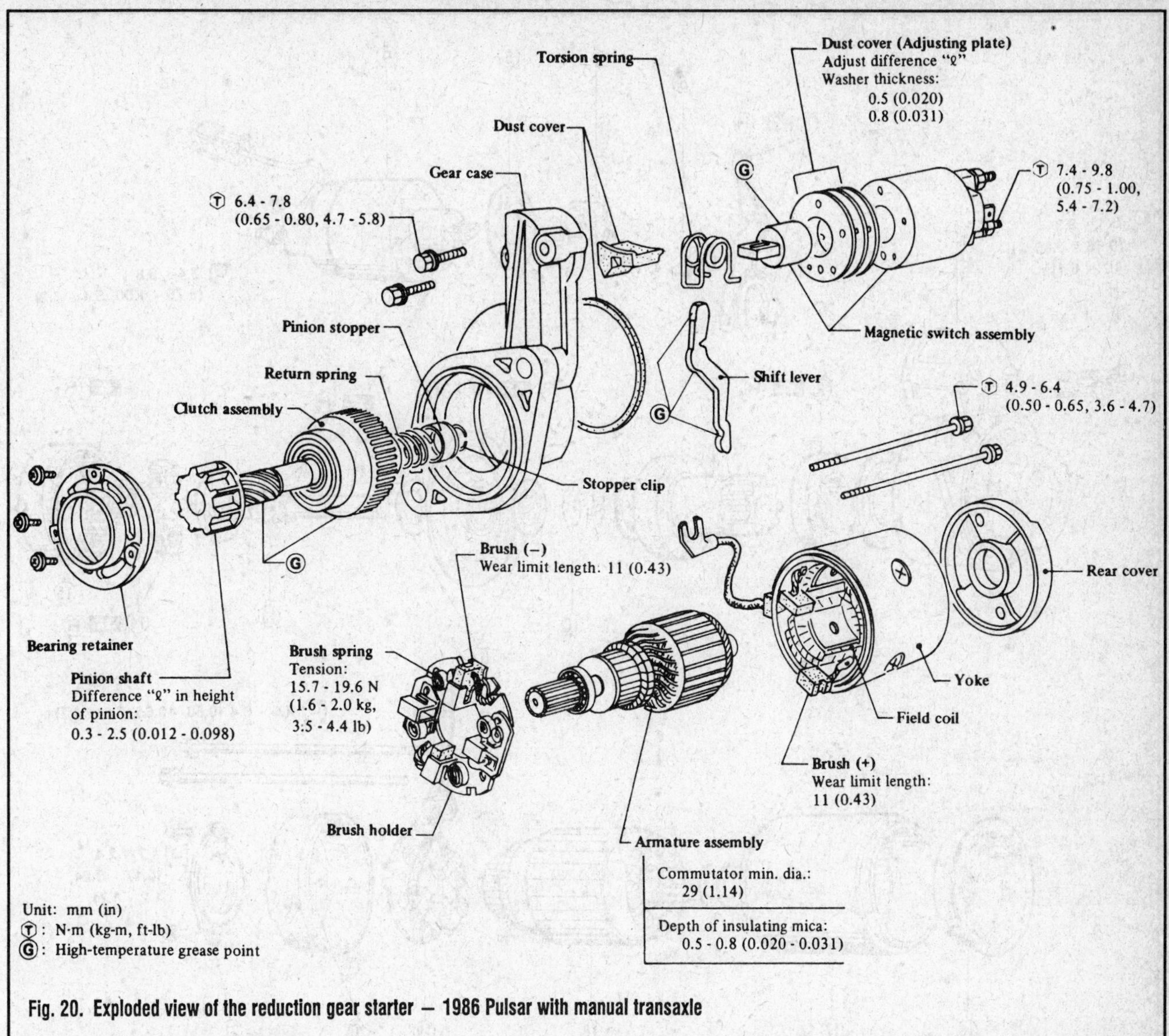
Torsion spring
Dust cover (Adjusting plate)
Adjust difference "ℓ"
Washer thickness:
0.5 (0.020)
0.8 (0.031)
Dust cover
Gear case
Ⓣ 6.4 - 7.8
(0.65 - 0.80, 4.7 - 5.8)
Ⓖ
Ⓣ 7.4 - 9.8
(0.75 - 1.00,
5.4 - 7.2)
Magnetic switch assembly
Pinion stopper
Return spring
Shift lever
Clutch assembly
Ⓣ 4.9 - 6.4
(0.50 - 0.65, 3.6 - 4.7)
Stopper clip
Brush (–)
Wear limit length: 11 (0.43)
Rear cover
Bearing retainer
Pinion shaft
Difference "ℓ" in height
of pinion:
0.3 - 2.5 (0.012 - 0.098)
Brush spring
Tension:
15.7 - 19.6 N
(1.6 - 2.0 kg,
3.5 - 4.4 lb)
Yoke
Field coil
Brush (+)
Wear limit length:
11 (0.43)
Brush holder
Armature assembly
Commutator min. dia.:
29 (1.14)
Depth of insulating mica:
0.5 - 0.8 (0.020 - 0.031)
Unit: mm (in)
Ⓣ: N·m (kg-m, ft-lb)
Ⓖ: High-temperature grease point

Fig. 20. Exploded view of the reduction gear starter — 1986 Pulsar with manual transaxle

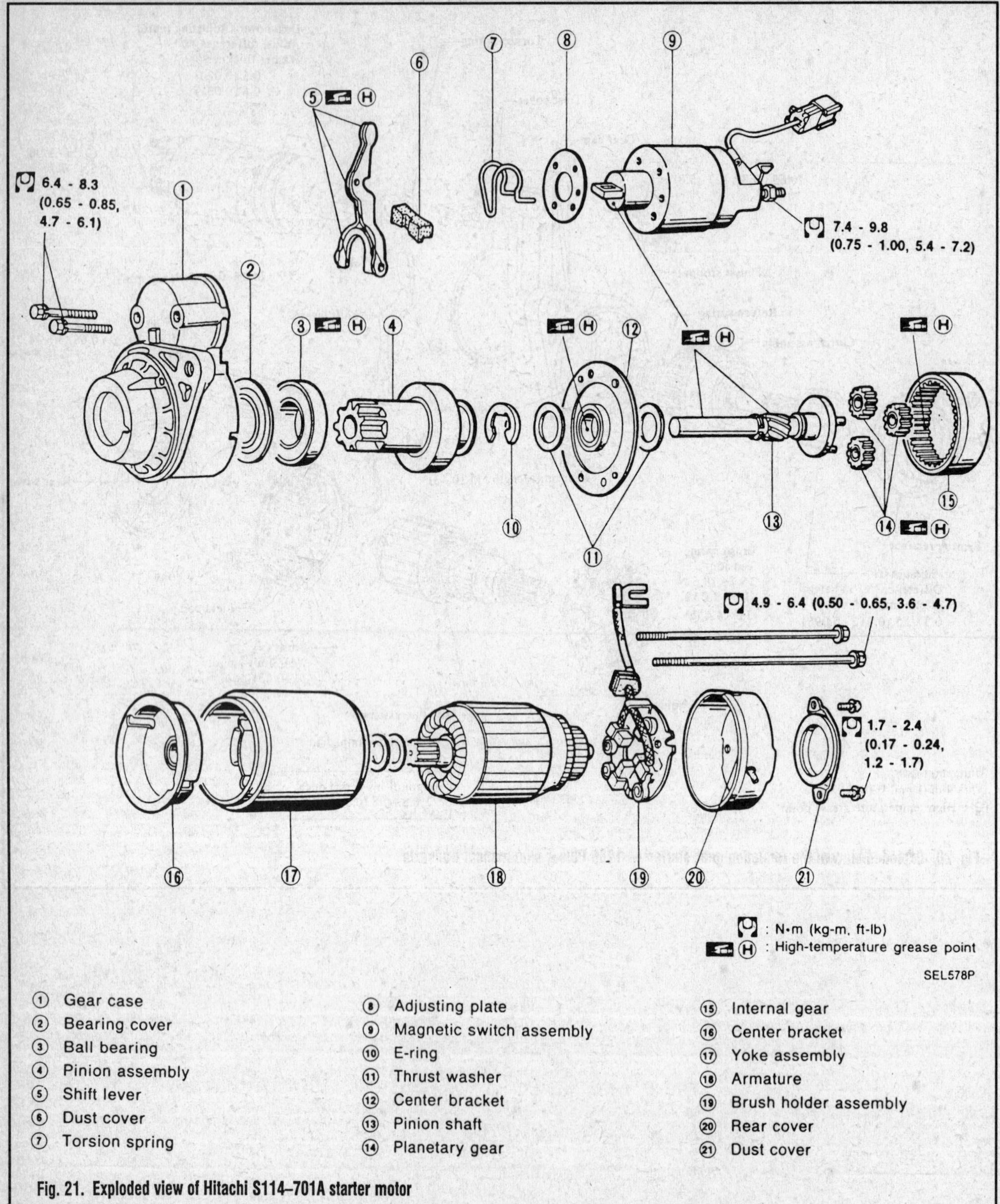
6.4 - 8.3
(0.65 - 0.85,
4.7 - 6.1)
7.4 - 9.8
(0.75 - 1.00, 5.4 - 7.2)
4.9 - 6.4 (0.50 - 0.65, 3.6 - 4.7)
1.7 - 2.4
(0.17 - 0.24,
1.2 - 1.7)
: N•m (kg-m, ft-lb)
: High-temperature grease point
SEL578P
① Gear case
② Bearing cover
③ Ball bearing
④ Pinion assembly
⑤ Shift lever
⑥ Dust cover
⑦ Torsion spring
⑧ Adjusting plate
⑨ Magnetic switch assembly
⑩ E-ring
⑪ Thrust washer
⑫ Center bracket
⑬ Pinion shaft
⑭ Planetary gear
⑮ Internal gear
⑯ Center bracket
⑰ Yoke assembly
⑱ Armature
⑲ Brush holder assembly
⑳ Rear cover
㉑ Dust cover

Fig. 21. Exploded view of Hitachi S114–701A starter motor

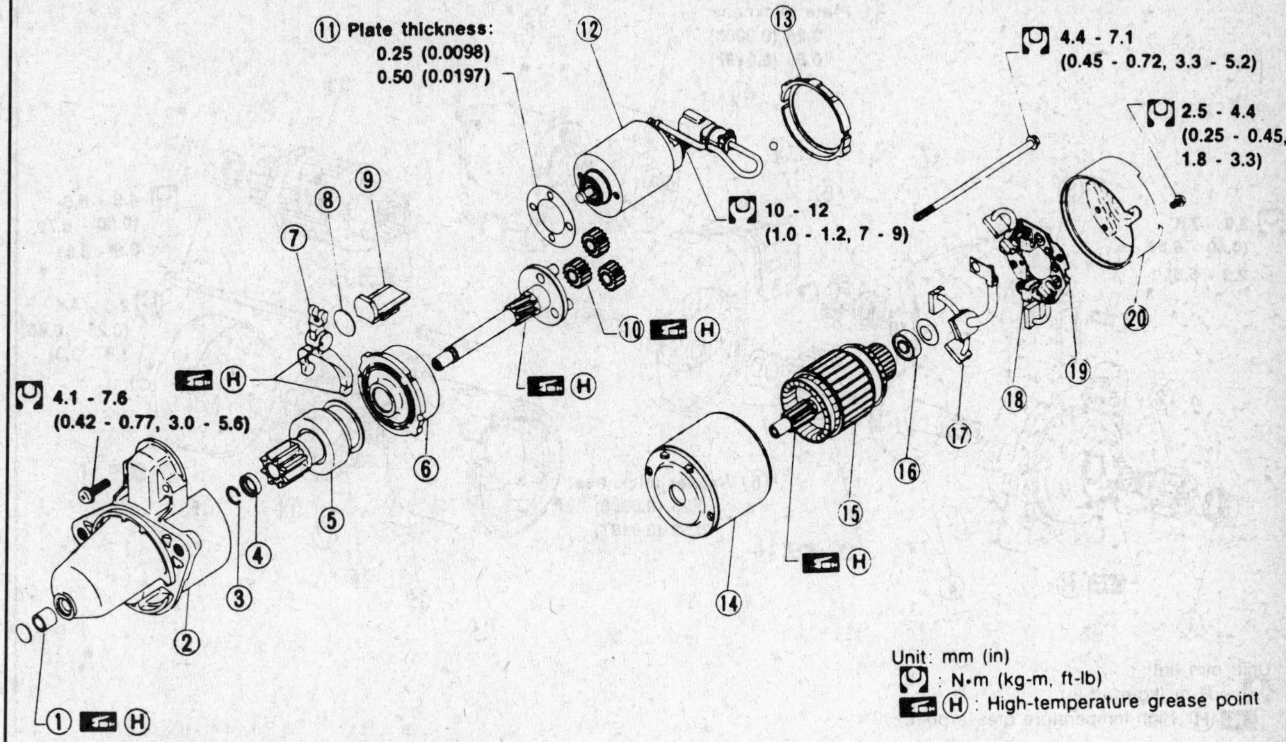

⑪ Plate thickness:
0.25 (0.0098)
0.50 (0.0197)

⑫ ⑬

4.4 - 7.1
(0.45 - 0.72, 3.3 - 5.2)

2.5 - 4.4
(0.25 - 0.45,
1.8 - 3.3)

10 - 12
(1.0 - 1.2, 7 - 9)

⑦ ⑧ ⑨ ⑩ H

4.1 - 7.6
(0.42 - 0.77, 3.0 - 5.6)

② ③ ④ ⑤ ⑥ ⑭ ⑮ ⑯ ⑰ ⑱ ⑲ ⑳

① H

Unit: mm (in)
: N•m (kg-m, ft-lb)
H : High-temperature grease point

Fig. 23. Exploded view of Hitachi S114–486 starter motor

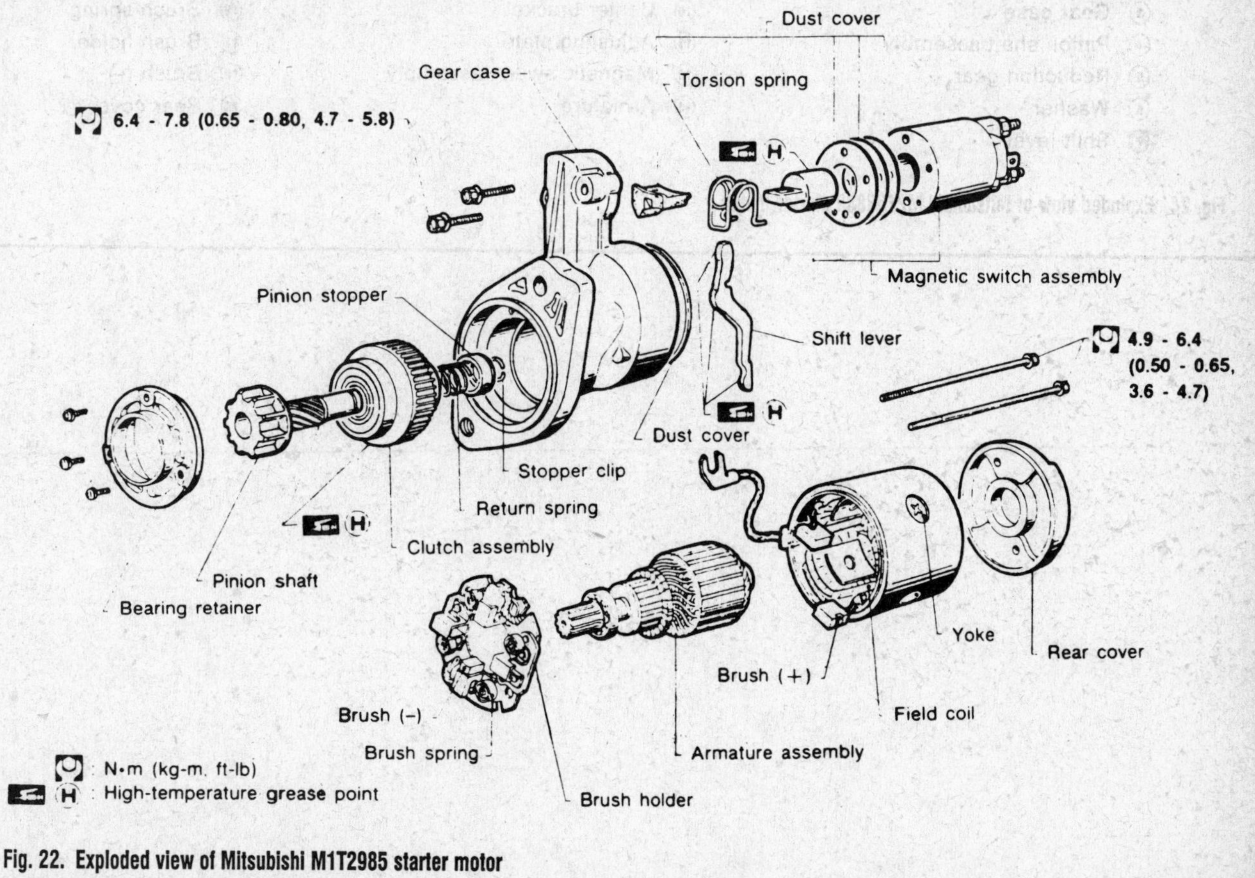

Dust cover
Gear case
Torsion spring
6.4 - 7.8 (0.65 - 0.80, 4.7 - 5.8)
Magnetic switch assembly
Pinion stopper
Shift lever
4.9 - 6.4
(0.50 - 0.65,
3.6 - 4.7)
Dust cover
Stopper clip
Return spring
Clutch assembly
Pinion shaft
Bearing retainer
Yoke
Rear cover
Brush (+)
Field coil
Brush (–)
Brush spring
Armature assembly
Brush holder

: N•m (kg-m, ft-lb)
H : High-temperature grease point

Fig. 22. Exploded view of Mitsubishi M1T2985 starter motor

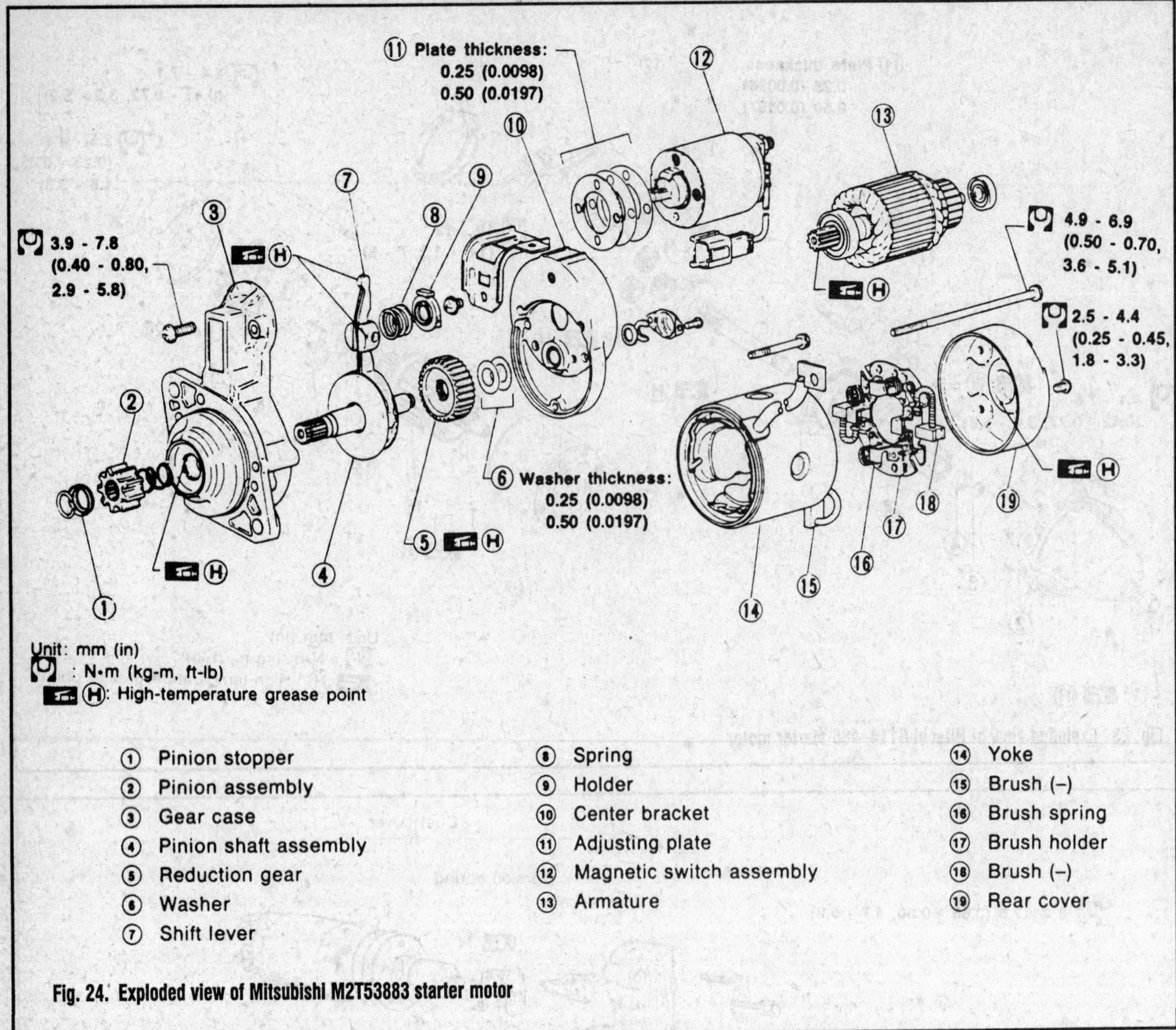

⑪ Plate thickness:
0.25 (0.0098)
0.50 (0.0197)
3.9 - 7.8
(0.40 - 0.80,
2.9 - 5.8)
4.9 - 6.9
(0.50 - 0.70,
3.6 - 5.1)
2.5 - 4.4
(0.25 - 0.45,
1.8 - 3.3)
⑥ Washer thickness:
0.25 (0.0098)
0.50 (0.0197)
Unit: mm (in)
: N•m (kg-m, ft-lb)
Ⓗ: High-temperature grease point

① Pinion stopper	⑧ Spring	⑭ Yoke
② Pinion assembly	⑨ Holder	⑮ Brush (–)
③ Gear case	⑩ Center bracket	⑯ Brush spring
④ Pinion shaft assembly	⑪ Adjusting plate	⑰ Brush holder
⑤ Reduction gear	⑫ Magnetic switch assembly	⑱ Brush (–)
⑥ Washer	⑬ Armature	⑲ Rear cover
⑦ Shift lever		

Fig. 24. Exploded view of Mitsubishi M2T53883 starter motor

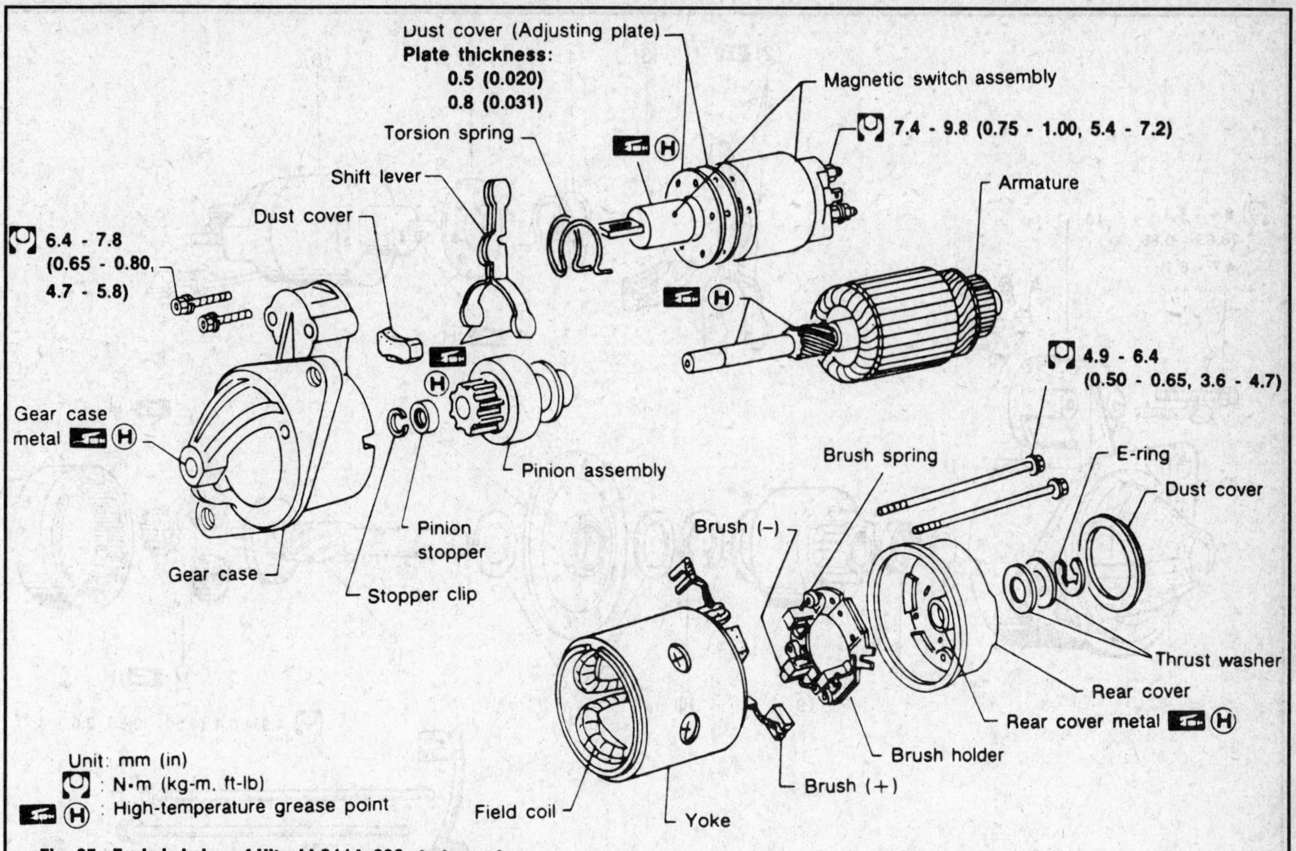

Dust cover (Adjusting plate)
Plate thickness:
0.5 (0.020)
0.8 (0.031)
Magnetic switch assembly
7.4 - 9.8 (0.75 - 1.00, 5.4 - 7.2)
Torsion spring
Shift lever
Armature
Dust cover
6.4 - 7.8
(0.65 - 0.80,
4.7 - 5.8)
4.9 - 6.4
(0.50 - 0.65, 3.6 - 4.7)
Gear case
metal
E-ring
Brush spring
Dust cover
Pinion assembly
Brush (−)
Pinion
stopper
Gear case
Stopper clip
Thrust washer
Rear cover
Rear cover metal
Brush holder
Unit: mm (in)
: N•m (kg-m, ft-lb)
: High-temperature grease point
Brush (+)
Field coil
Yoke

Fig. 25. Exploded view of Hitachi S114–630 starter motor

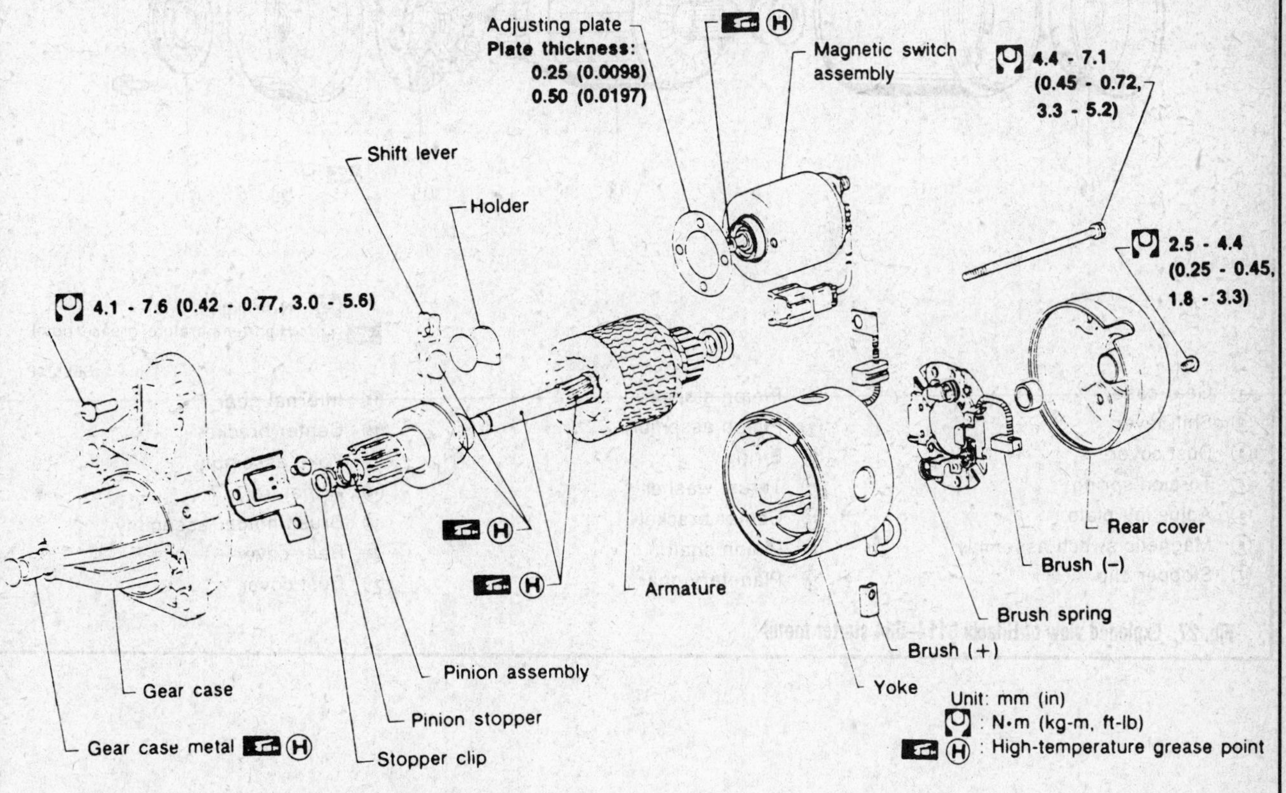

Adjusting plate
Plate thickness:
0.25 (0.0098)
0.50 (0.0197)
Magnetic switch
assembly
4.4 - 7.1
(0.45 - 0.72,
3.3 - 5.2)
Shift lever
Holder
2.5 - 4.4
(0.25 - 0.45,
1.8 - 3.3)
4.1 - 7.6 (0.42 - 0.77, 3.0 - 5.6)
Rear cover
Brush (−)
Armature
Brush spring
Brush (+)
Pinion assembly
Gear case
Yoke
Unit: mm (in)
Pinion stopper
: N•m (kg-m, ft-lb)
Gear case metal
: High-temperature grease point
Stopper clip

Fig. 26. Exploded view of Mitsubishi M3T37783 starter motor

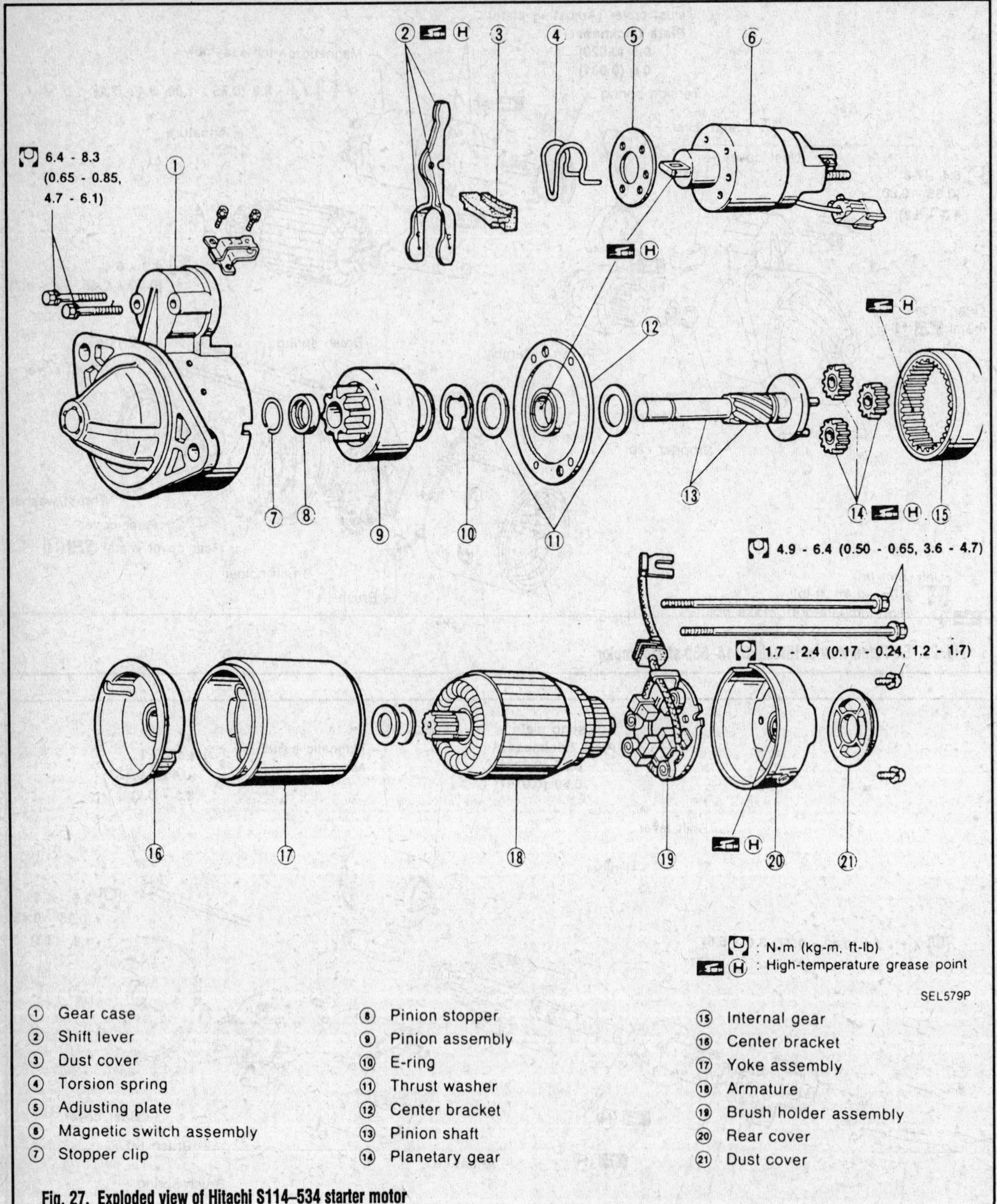
6.4 - 8.3
(0.65 - 0.85,
4.7 - 6.1)
H
4.9 - 6.4 (0.50 - 0.65, 3.6 - 4.7)
1.7 - 2.4 (0.17 - 0.24, 1.2 - 1.7)
: N•m (kg-m, ft-lb)
H : High-temperature grease point
SEL579P
① Gear case
② Shift lever
③ Dust cover
④ Torsion spring
⑤ Adjusting plate
⑥ Magnetic switch assembly
⑦ Stopper clip
⑧ Pinion stopper
⑨ Pinion assembly
⑩ E-ring
⑪ Thrust washer
⑫ Center bracket
⑬ Pinion shaft
⑭ Planetary gear
⑮ Internal gear
⑯ Center bracket
⑰ Yoke assembly
⑱ Armature
⑲ Brush holder assembly
⑳ Rear cover
㉑ Dust cover

Fig. 27. Exploded view of Hitachi S114–534 starter motor

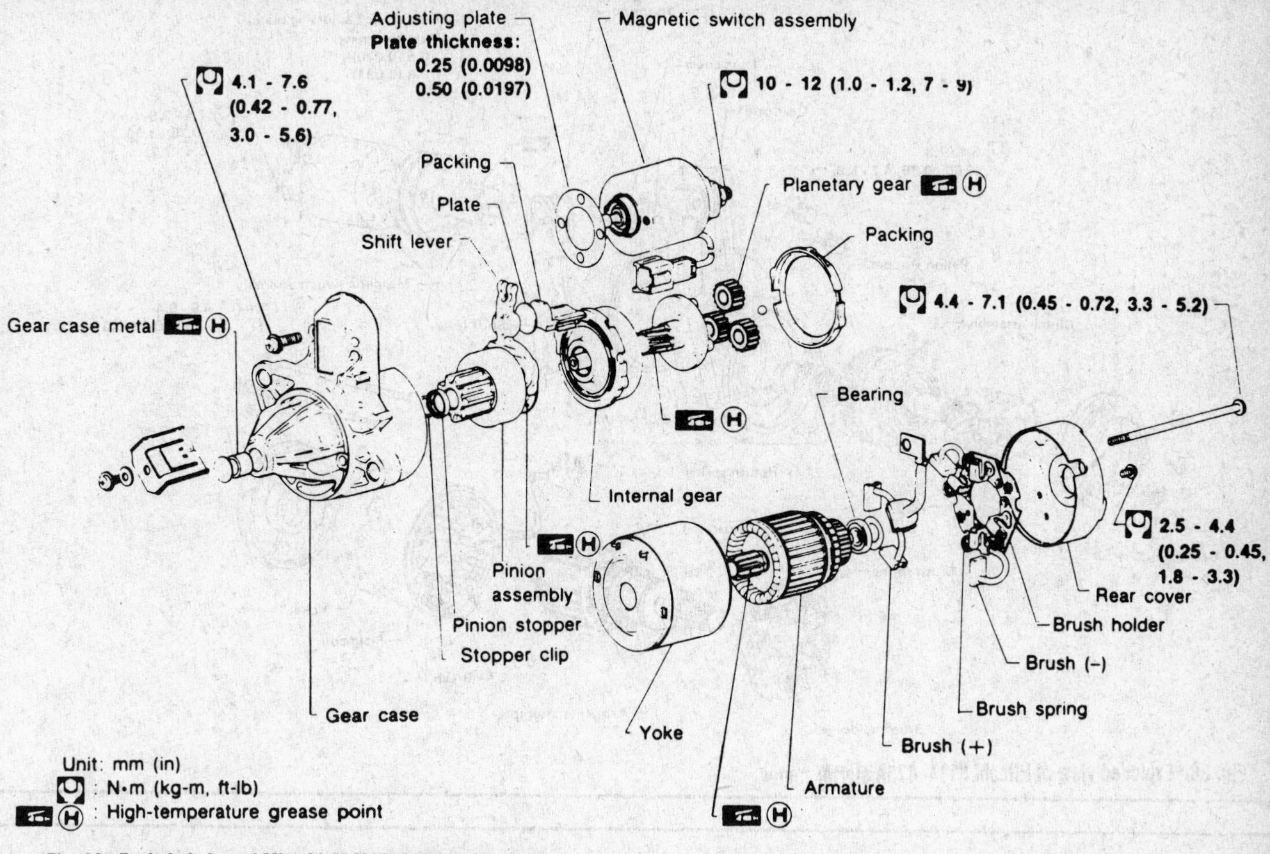

Adjusting plate
Plate thickness:
0.25 (0.0098)
0.50 (0.0197)
Magnetic switch assembly
4.1 - 7.6 (0.42 - 0.77, 3.0 - 5.6)
10 - 12 (1.0 - 1.2, 7 - 9)
Packing
Plate
Shift lever
Planetary gear H
Packing
Gear case metal H
4.4 - 7.1 (0.45 - 0.72, 3.3 - 5.2)
H
Bearing
Internal gear
H
2.5 - 4.4 (0.25 - 0.45, 1.8 - 3.3)
Pinion assembly
Rear cover
Pinion stopper
Brush holder
Stopper clip
Brush (–)
Brush spring
Gear case
Yoke
Brush (+)
Unit: mm (in)
: N·m (kg-m, ft-lb)
H : High-temperature grease point
Armature
H

Fig. 28. Exploded view of Mitsubishi M1T72088 starter motor

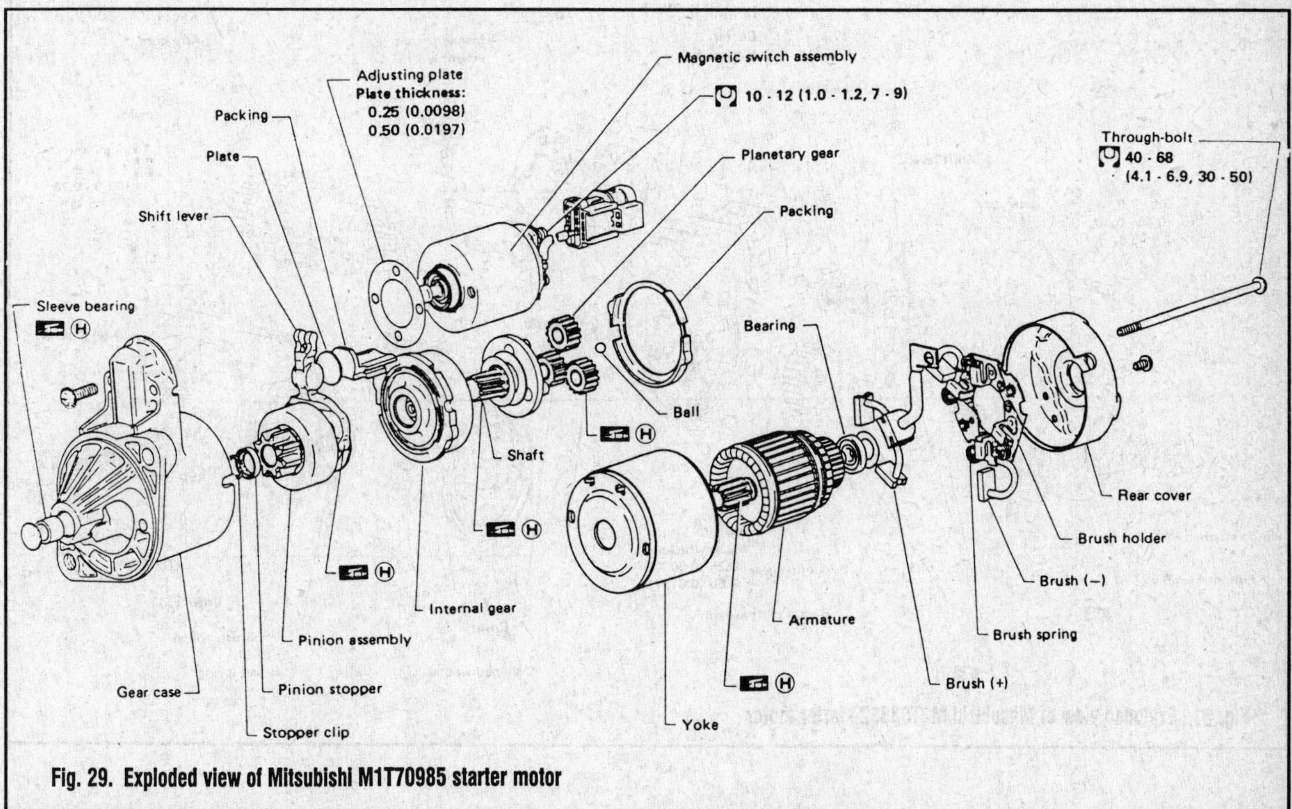
Magnetic switch assembly
Adjusting plate
Plate thickness:
0.25 (0.0098)
0.50 (0.0197)
10 - 12 (1.0 - 1.2, 7 - 9)
Packing
Plate
Through-bolt
40 - 68
(4.1 - 6.9, 30 - 50)
Planetary gear
Shift lever
Packing
Sleeve bearing
H
Bearing
Ball
H
Shaft
Rear cover
H
Brush holder
H
Brush (–)
Internal gear
Armature
Pinion assembly
Brush spring
H
Gear case
Pinion stopper
Brush (+)
Yoke
Stopper clip

Fig. 29. Exploded view of Mitsubishi M1T70985 starter motor

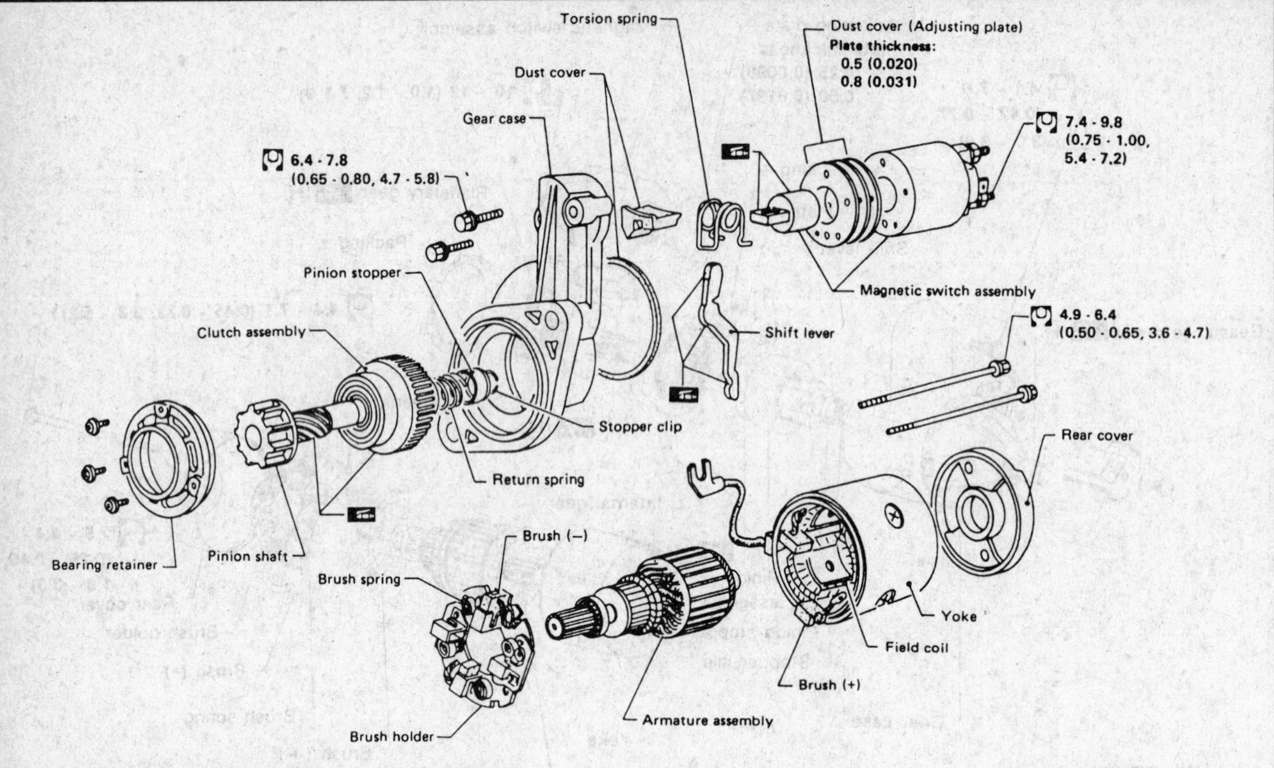

Torsion spring
Dust cover (Adjusting plate)
Plate thickness:
0.5 (0.020)
0.8 (0.031)
Dust cover
Gear case
7.4 - 9.8
(0.75 - 1.00,
5.4 - 7.2)
6.4 - 7.8
(0.65 - 0.80, 4.7 - 5.8)
Pinion stopper
Magnetic switch assembly
Clutch assembly
Shift lever
4.9 - 6.4
(0.50 - 0.65, 3.6 - 4.7)
Stopper clip
Rear cover
Return spring
Brush (–)
Bearing retainer
Pinion shaft
Brush spring
Yoke
Field coil
Brush (+)
Armature assembly
Brush holder

Fig. 30. Exploded view of Hitachi S114–475A starter motor

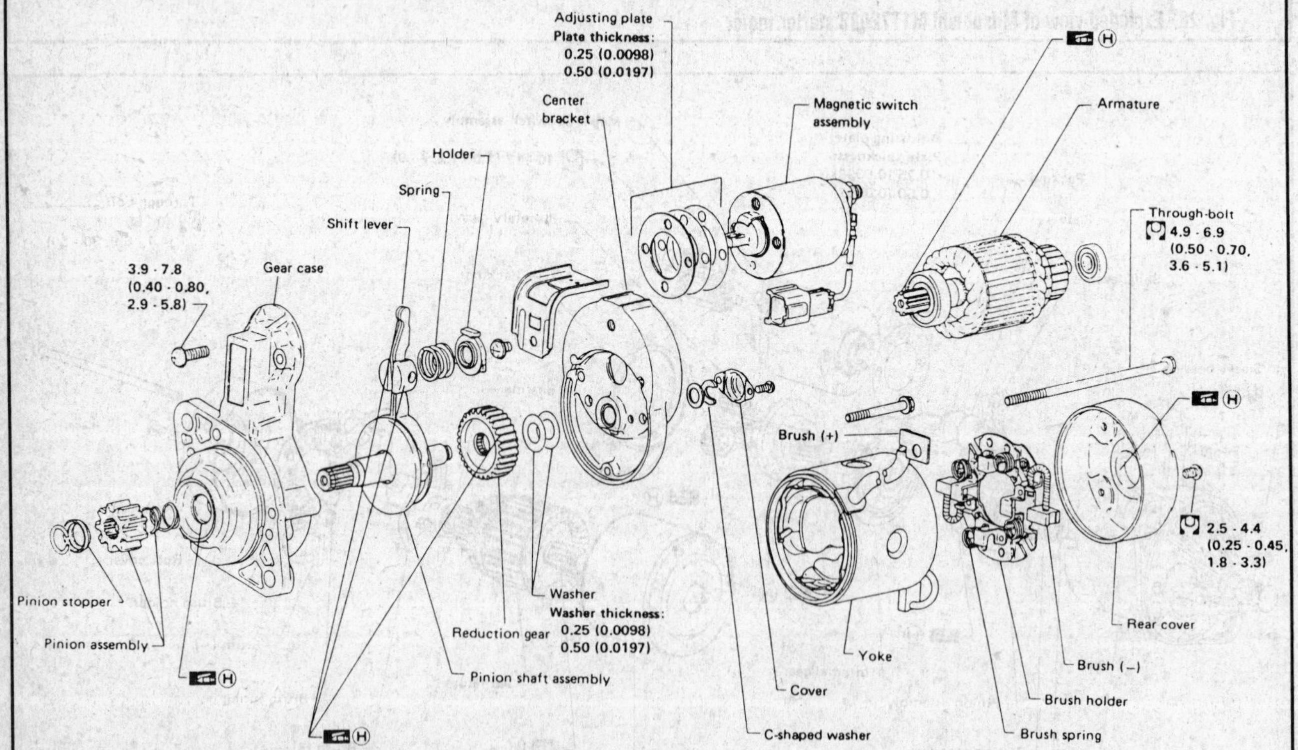

Adjusting plate
Plate thickness:
0.25 (0.0098)
0.50 (0.0197)
Center
bracket
Magnetic switch
assembly
Armature
H
Holder
Spring
Shift lever
Through-bolt
4.9 - 6.9
(0.50 - 0.70,
3.6 - 5.1)
3.9 - 7.8
(0.40 - 0.80,
2.9 - 5.8)
Gear case
H
Brush (+)
2.5 - 4.4
(0.25 - 0.45,
1.8 - 3.3)
Pinion stopper
Washer
Washer thickness:
0.25 (0.0098)
0.50 (0.0197)
Rear cover
Pinion assembly
Reduction gear
Yoke
Brush (–)
H
Pinion shaft assembly
Cover
Brush holder
H
C-shaped washer
Brush spring

Fig. 31. Exploded view of Mitsubishi M2T53882 starter motor

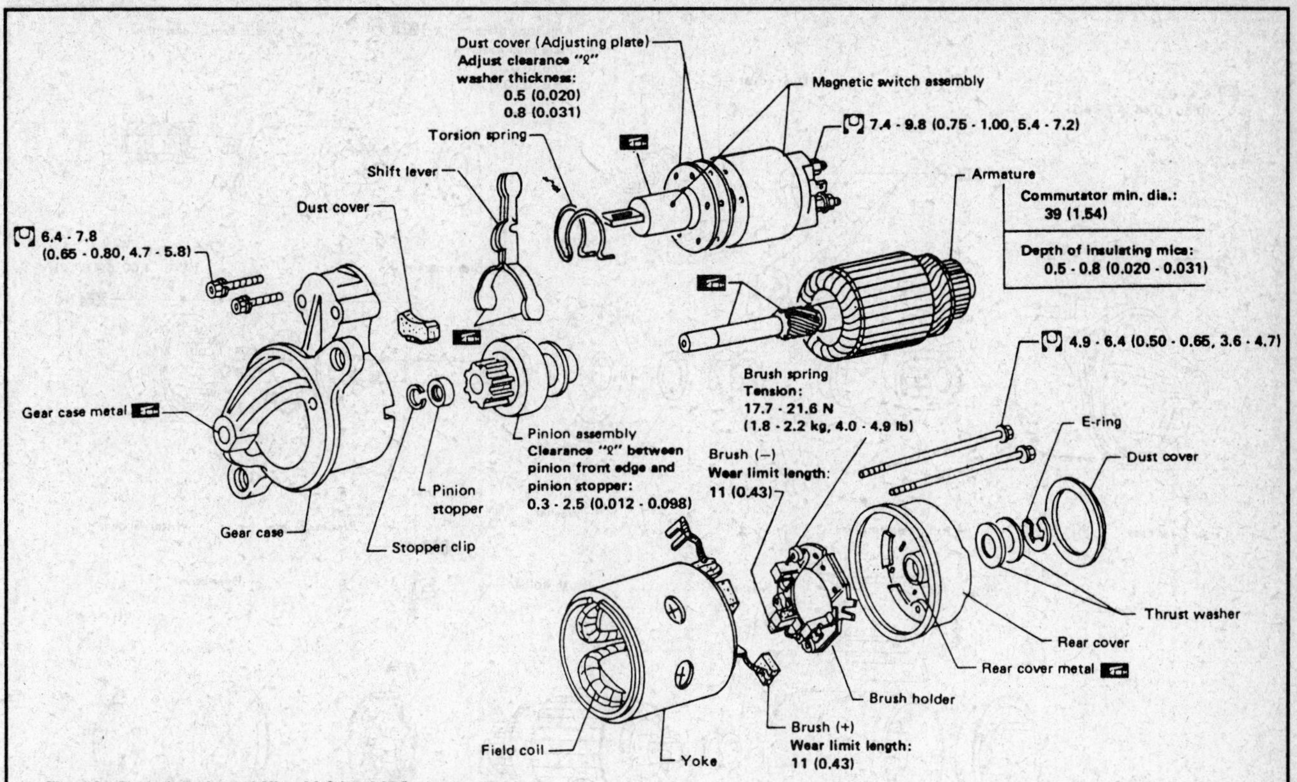

Dust cover (Adjusting plate)
Adjust clearance "ℓ"
washer thickness:
0.5 (0.020)
0.8 (0.031)
Magnetic switch assembly
7.4 - 9.8 (0.75 - 1.00, 5.4 - 7.2)
Torsion spring
Shift lever
Armature
Commutator min. dia.:
39 (1.54)
Depth of insulating mica:
0.5 - 0.8 (0.020 - 0.031)
Dust cover
6.4 - 7.8
(0.65 - 0.80, 4.7 - 5.8)
4.9 - 6.4 (0.50 - 0.65, 3.6 - 4.7)
Brush spring
Tension:
17.7 - 21.6 N
(1.8 - 2.2 kg, 4.0 - 4.9 lb)
Gear case metal
E-ring
Pinion assembly
Clearance "ℓ" between
pinion front edge and
pinion stopper:
0.3 - 2.5 (0.012 - 0.098)
Brush (−)
Wear limit length:
11 (0.43)
Dust cover
Pinion
stopper
Gear case
Stopper clip
Thrust washer
Rear cover
Rear cover metal
Brush holder
Brush (+)
Wear limit length:
11 (0.43)
Field coil
Yoke

Fig. 32. Exploded view of Hitachi S14–617A starter motor

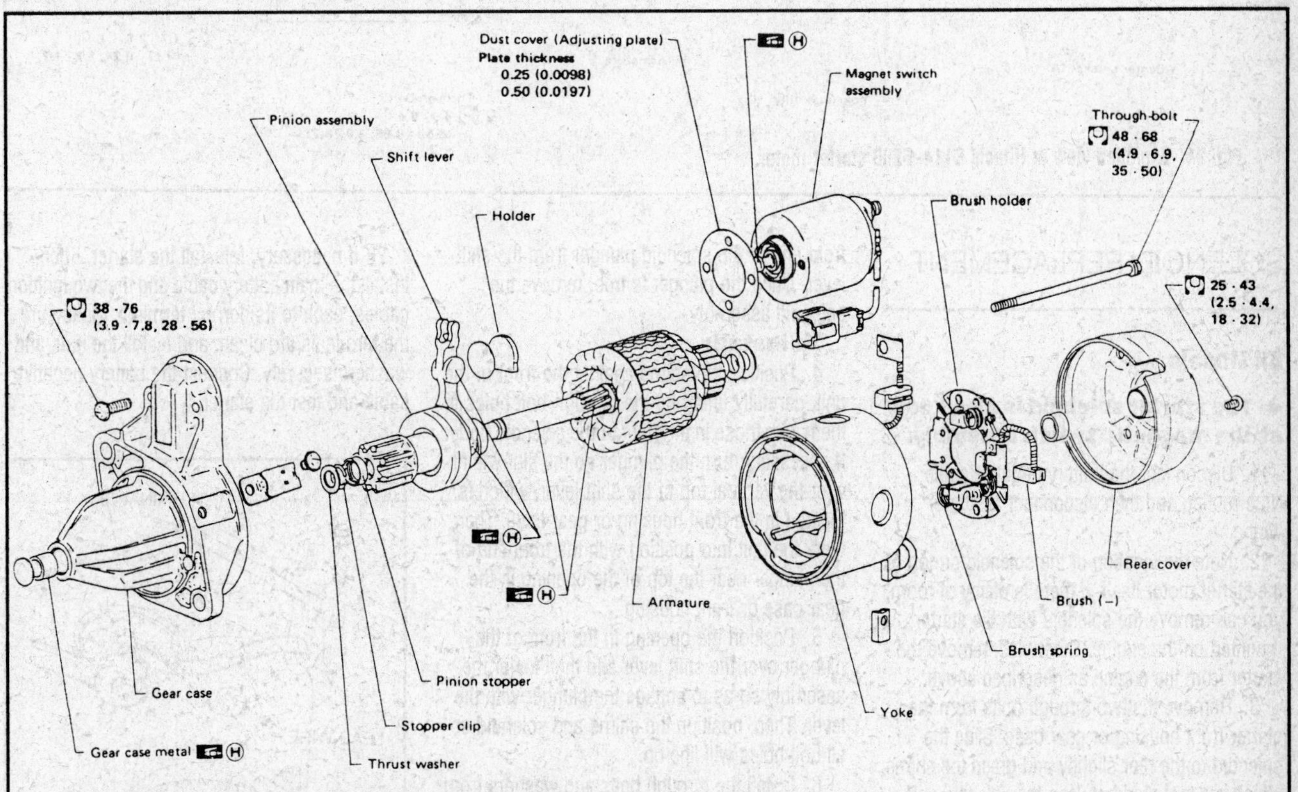

Dust cover (Adjusting plate)
Plate thickness
0.25 (0.0098)
0.50 (0.0197)
Magnet switch
assembly
Pinion assembly
Through-bolt
48 - 68
(4.9 - 6.9,
35 - 50)
Shift lever
Brush holder
Holder
38 - 76
(3.9 - 7.8, 28 - 56)
25 - 43
(2.5 - 4.4,
18 - 32)
Rear cover
Brush (−)
Armature
Brush spring
Pinion stopper
Gear case
Yoke
Stopper clip
Gear case metal
Thrust washer

Fig. 33. Exploded view of Mitsubishi M3T37782 starter motor

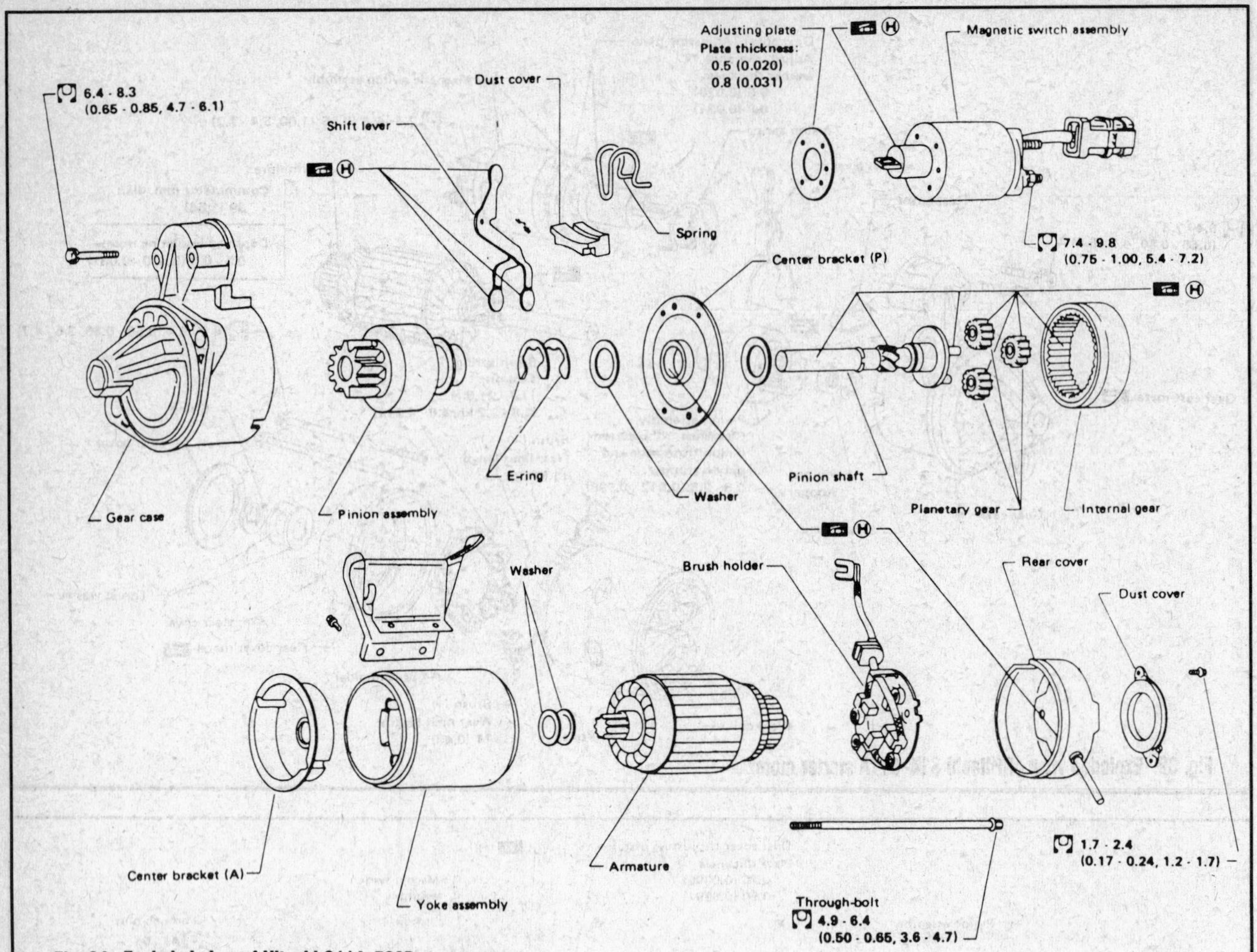

Fig. 34. Exploded view of Hitachi S114–520B starter motor

SOLENOID REPLACEMENT

All Models

➡ **The starter solenoid is also know as the magnetic switch assembly.**

1. Disconnect the battery negative cable. Note routing and then disconnect all starter wiring.
2. Note the location of the solenoid on top of the starter motor itself. If there is plenty of room, you can remove the solenoid with the starter mounted on the engine. Otherwise, remove the starter from the engine as described above.
3. Remove the two through bolts from the starter front housing or gear case. Slide the solenoid to the rear slightly and grasp the shims which are mounted between the solenoid and front housing or gear case to keep them with the assembly. Then, pull the solenoid assembly upward and to the rear so as to disengage the front end of the solenoid plunger from the shift lever. Once the plunger is free, remove the solenoid assembly.

To install:

4. Position the shims against the front of the unit, carefully lining up the through-bolt holes in them with those in the front of the solenoid body. If necessary, turn the plunger so the slot will fit over the vertical top of the shift lever, which is located in the front housing or gear case. Then, work the unit into position with the front end of the plunger near the top of the opening in the gear case or front housing.
5. Position the opening in the front of the plunger over the shift lever and then lower the assembly so as to engage the plunger with the lever. Then, position the shims and solenoid so all bolt holes will line up.
6. Install the through bolts and washers from in front of the gear case or front housing, if necessary turning the shims and solenoid assembly to line up the holes more perfectly. Torque the through bolts alternately and evenly to about 5 ft. lbs. (7 Nm).
7. If necessary, reinstall the starter. Then, install the main battery cable and the two ignition cables, each to its correct terminal. Make sure the terminals are clean, and install the nuts and washers securely. Connect the battery negative cable and test the starter.

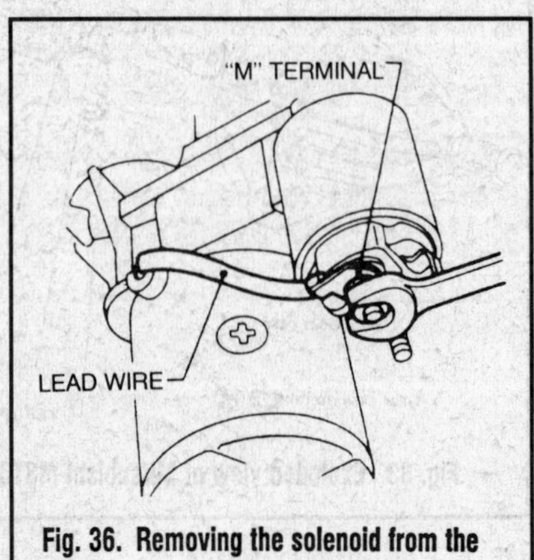
"M" TERMINAL
LEAD WIRE

Fig. 36. Removing the solenoid from the starter

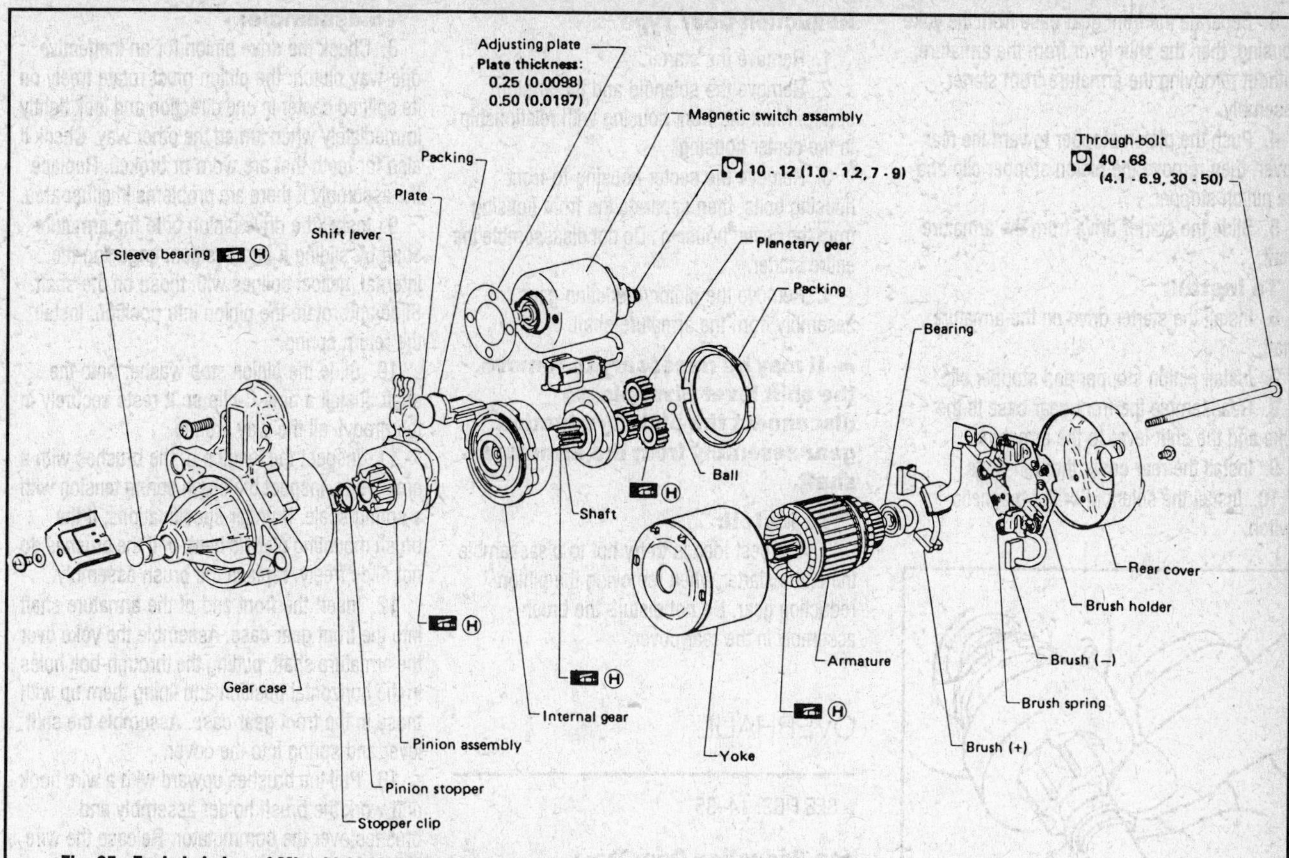

Adjusting plate
Plate thickness:
0.25 (0.0098)
0.50 (0.0197)
Magnetic switch assembly
Packing
10 - 12 (1.0 - 1.2, 7 - 9)
Through-bolt
40 - 68
(4.1 - 6.9, 30 - 50)
Plate
Shift lever
Sleeve bearing (H)
Planetary gear
Packing
Bearing
Ball
(H)
Shaft
Rear cover
Brush holder
(H)
Armature
Brush (−)
(H)
Brush spring
Gear case
Internal gear
(H)
Pinion assembly
Yoke
Brush (+)
Pinion stopper
Stopper clip

Fig. 35. Exploded view of Mitsubishi M1T72085 starter motor

BRUSH REPLACEMENT

Non-reduction Gear Type

1. With the starter out of the vehicle, remove the bolts holding the solenoid to the top of the starter and remove the solenoid.
2. To remove the brushes, remove the 2 through-bolts, the 2 rear cover attaching screws (some models) and the rear cover.

➡ **Remove the dust cover, E-ring and thrust washers from the armature shaft before the rear cover.**

3. Using a wire hook, lift the brush springs to separate the brushes from the commutator.
4. Install the brushes in the reverse order of removal and reassemble the rear cover to the starter.

Reduction Gear Type

1. Remove the starter, then the solenoid or magnetic switch.
2. Remove the dust cover, E-ring and thrust washers.
3. Remove the starter through-bolts and brush holder setscrews.

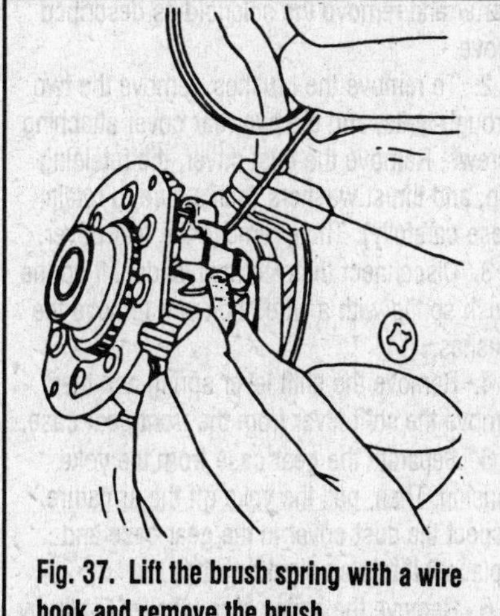

Fig. 37. Lift the brush spring with a wire hook and remove the brush

4. Remove the rear cover. The rear cover can be pried off with a screwdriver, be careful not to damage the O-ring or gasket if equipped.
5. Remove the starter housing, armature and brush holder from the center housing. They can be removed as an assembly.
6. Using a wire hook on the spring, lift the spring then remove the positive side brush from its holder. The positive brush is insulated from the brush holder and its lead wire is connected to the field coil.
7. Using a wire hook on the spring, lift the spring and remove the negative brush from the holder.
8. Replace all the brushes in the starter assembly.

To Install:

9. Insert the new brushes in the brush holder.
10. Install the starter housing, armature and brush holder to the center housing.
11. Install the brush holder setscrews, rear cover and starter through-bolts.
12. Install the thrust washers, E-ring and dust cover.
13. Install the solenoid or magnetic switch.

STARTER DRIVE REPLACEMENT

Non-reduction Gear Type

1. With the starter motor removed from the vehicle, remove the solenoid from the starter.
2. Remove the 2 through-bolts at the rear cover but do not disassemble the entire starter. Mark the front gear cover with relationship to the yoke housing.

3. Separate the front gear case from the yoke housing, then the shift lever from the armature, without removing the armature from starter assembly.

4. Push the pinion stopper toward the rear cover, then remove the pinion stopper clip and the pinion stopper.

5. Slide the starter drive from the armature shaft.

To install:

6. Install the starter drive on the armature shaft.

7. Install pinion stopper and stopper clip.

8. Reassemble the front gear case to the yoke and the shift lever to the armature.

9. Install the rear cover through-bolts.

10. Install the solenoid or the magnetic switch.

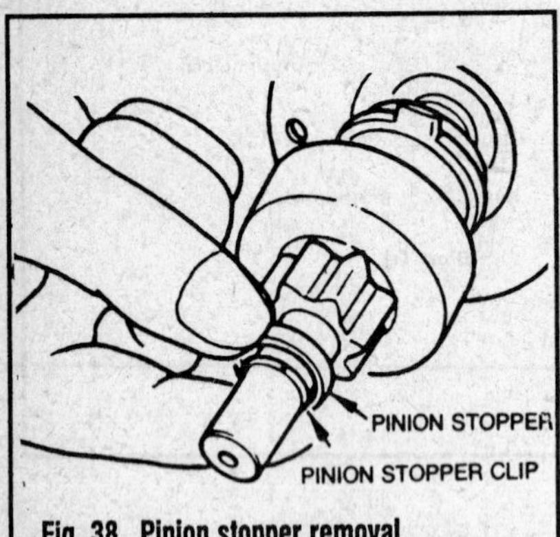
PINION STOPPER
PINION STOPPER CLIP
Fig. 38. Pinion stopper removal

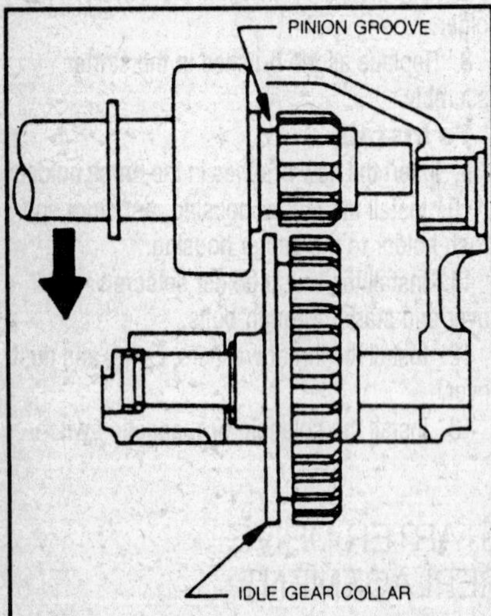
PINION GROOVE
IDLE GEAR COLLAR
Fig. 39. Align the flange or collar on the idler gear with the groove on the pinion gear when assembling the armature into the front gear case on the reduction gear starter

Reduction Gear Type

1. Remove the starter.

2. Remove the solenoid and the torsion spring. Mark the front housing with relationship to the center housing.

3. Remove the center housing-to-front housing bolts, then separate the front housing from the center housing . Do not disassemble the entire starter.

4. Remove the pinion/reduction gear assembly from the armature shaft.

➡ **It may be necessary to remove the shift lever pivot pin, to disconnect the pinion/reduction gear assembly from the armature shaft.**

To install:

5. The best idea is to try not to disassemble the entire starter when removing the pinion/ reduction gear. Do not disturb the brush assembly in the rear cover.

OVERHAUL

➧ SEE FIGS. 14–35

Non-Reduction Gear Type

1. With the starter out of the vehicle, remove the bolts holding the solenoid to the top of the starter and remove the solenoid as described above.

2. To remove the brushes, remove the two through-bolts, and the two rear cover attaching screws. Remove the dust cover, the retaining clip, and thrust washers (make sure to retain these carefully). Then, remove the rear cover.

3. Disconnect the electrical leads, lift up the brush spring with a wire hook and remove the brushes.

4. Remove the shift lever spring and then remove the shift lever from the front gear case.

5. Separate the gear case from the yoke housing. Then, pull the yoke off the armature. Inspect the dust cover in the gear case and replace it if it is cracked or brittle.

6. Remove the pinion stop washer C-clip by prying it out of the groove with a screwdriver and then sliding it off the shaft. Slide the return spring off the shaft. Slide the pinion stop washer off the shaft.

7. Slide the starter drive pinion off the armature shaft.

To assemble:

8. Check the drive pinion for an ineffective one-way clutch: the pinion must rotate freely on its splined center in one direction and lock tightly immediately when turned the other way. Check it also for teeth that are worn or broken. Replace the assembly if there are problems in either area.

9. Install the drive pinion onto the armature shaft by sliding it into position, engaging the internal, helical splines with those on the shaft. Slide and rotate the pinion into position. Install the return spring.

10. Slide the pinion stop washer onto the shaft. Install a new C-clip so it rests securely in the groove all the way around.

11. Inspect the lengths of the brushes with a small ruler. Inspect the brush spring tension with a spring scale. If under specifications, if the brush mounting plate is bent, or if the brushes do not slide freely, replace the brush assembly.

12. Insert the front end of the armature shaft into the front gear case. Assemble the yoke over the armature shaft, putting the through-bolt holes in the horizontal position and lining them up with those in the front gear case. Assemble the shift lever and spring into the cover.

13. Pull the brushes upward with a wire hook and work the brush holder assembly and brushes over the commutator. Release the wire hook and then connect the electrical connectors.

14. Install the rear cover over the armature shaft and yoke assembly, aligning all the bolt holes. Install the through bolts and cover bolts.

15. Install the thrust washers, E-clip and dust cover.

16. Install the solenoid as described above. Wire the primary connectors to the solenoid without connecting the large field connector. Then, energize the solenoid for a short time (30 seconds or less) while you measure the distance between the front of the pinion gear and the inside of the gear case. Clearance must be 0.30–2.5mm. If not, change the solenoid mounting shims to correct the clearance (thicker shims increase the clearance).

17. Install the starter as described above.

Reduction Gear Type

1. Remove the starter. Remove the solenoid.

2. Remove the dust cover. Pry the E-ring off with a small, blunt instrument. Remove the thrust washers. Remove the through bolts, brush holder setscrews, and the rear cover. The rear cover can be pried off with a small, blunt instrument, but be careful not to damage the O-ring.

3. Lift the brush spring and hold it against the side of the negative brush (at the top) to separate the brush from the commutator. The positive brush is insulated from the brush holder, and its lead wire is connected to the field coil in the yoke. Remove the positive brush from the brush holder by lifting the brush spring upward. Then, remove the brush holder from the commutator.

4. Remove the yoke from the armature and front gear case. Then, remove the armature and the shift lever from the front gear case.

5. Slide the pinion-retaining stop washer toward the rear. Then, carefully pry the C-clip out of the groove in the forward direction and work it off the shaft. Finally, slide the washer off the armature shaft followed by the pinion assembly.

6. Pry the E-clip off the idler gear shaft. Then, remove the dust cover and drive the idler gear shaft out of the gear housing toward the rear by gently tapping the end with a hammer and dull punch.

7. Inspect the commutator surface. It may be sanded very lightly with No. 500–600 sandpaper. If there is a great deal of wear or roughness, it should be taken to an electrical shop and machined. Ideally, the armature and field coils should be taken to an electrical shop and subjected to a number of continuity tests to verify that insulation and conductors are in good shape.

8. Inspect the length of each brush. Replace any that are worn beyond limits. The new brush must be soldered onto the field coil in the yoke. This work should be performed by a competent auto-electrical shop. Test the brush springs for tension and replace, if necessary.

9. Check the drive pinion for an ineffective one-way clutch: the pinion must rotate freely on its splined center in one direction and lock tightly immediately when turned the other way. Check it also for teeth that are worn or broken. Replace the assembly if there are problems in either area.

To assemble:

10. Apply multipurpose grease sparingly to the following parts:

- The frictional surface of the pinion.
- The wearing surfaces of the shift lever.
- The solenoid plunger where it slides mechanically.
- The armature bearing surfaces in the front gear case and rear cover.

11. Then, install the idler gear into the gear housing with the flange facing the rear. Insert the shaft with the E-clip groove facing to the rear and tap it into the housing from the rear. Install the E-clip onto the idler gear shaft. Install the dust cover.

12. Install the pinion gear onto the armature shaft, followed by the retaining washer. Work the C-clip onto the shaft and into the groove. Then, work the washer back over the C-clip.

13. Carefully position the armature into the front gear case with the flange on the idler gear fitting into the groove at the rear of the pinion gear.

14. Install the shift lever and dust cover. Install the yoke over the armature with the through-bolt holes aligned.

15. Install the brush holder around the commutator. Install the negative brush (at the top) so it rests against the commutator. Install the positive brush into the brush holder by lifting the brush spring upward.

16. Install the through bolts, brush holder setscrews, and the rear cover. Install the thrust washers and the E-ring. Install the dust cover.

17. Install the solenoid as described above. Energize the solenoid primary terminals by connecting them to the battery with a jumper wire and mark the position of the front of the idler gear. Then, measure the position of the front of the gear when it is pulled forward all the way by hand and its center rests against the housing. This dimension must be 0.3–2.5mm. If necessary, change the number/thickness of the shims under the solenoid to bring the dimension within specifications.

18. Install the starter into the car and reconnect the battery.

STARTER SPECIFICATION CHART

				No Load Test			Min.
Year	Vehicle	Model	Manuf.	Amps	Volts	RPM	Brush Length
1982–83 1988	Gas w/ M/T	S114-315	Hitachi	>60	11.5	<7000	0.43
1982–85	Gas w/ M/T (option)	S114-316	Hitachi	>60	11.5	<7000	0.43
1982	Gas w/ A/T (Canada)	S114-317	Hitachi	>60	11.5	<7000	0.43
1982–85	Gas w/ A/T	S114-318	Hitachi	>60	11.5	<6000	0.43
1983–85	Gas w/ A/T (Canada)	S114-345	Hitachi	>60	11.5	<2000	0.43
1983–86	Diesel	S144-357	Hitachi	>100	11.0	<3900	0.43
1984–85	Gas w/ A/T	S144-345A	Hitachi	>60	12.0	<2000	0.43
1984	Turbo w/ M/T	S114-377	Hitachi	>60	12.0	<2350	0.43
	Turbo w/ A/T	S114-378	Hitachi	>60	12.0	<2000	0.43
1986–88	Gas w/ M/T	S114-440	Hitachi	>100	12.0	<3900	0.43
	Sentra Gas w/ A/T	S114-441	Hitachi	>70	12.0	<1800	0.47
	Pulsar w/ A/T	M3T26685	Mitsubishi	>70	11.5	<1800	0.47
1987	Pulsar CA16DE	M1T71681	Mitsubishi	50–70	11.0	3000–4000	0.47

STARTER SPECIFICATION CHART

Year	Vehicle	Model	Manuf.	No Load Test Amps	Volts	RPM	Min. Brush Length
1987-88	Pulsar E16i	M2T53881	Mitsubishi	>100	11.0	<2900	0.45
1987	Diesel	S13-105	Hitachi	>140	11.0	<3900	0.35
1988	4WD w/ A/T	M3T26685	Mitsubishi	>70	11.5	<1800	0.45
1988-89	CA18DE	M1T70985	Mitsubishi	50-75	11.0	3000-4000	0.47
	M/T for Calif.	M3T27781D	Mitsubishi	>60	11.5	<6500	0.45
1989-90	GA16i w/ M/T	S1140475A	Hitachi	>100	11.0	<3900	0.43
	GA16i w/ M/T (Calif.)	S114-617A	Hitachi	>60	11.5	<7000	0.43
	GA16i w/ M/T	M2TS3882	Mitsubishi	>100	11.0	<2900	0.45
	GA16i w/ M/T (Calif.)	M3T37782	Mitsubishi	>60	11.5	<6500	0.45
	GA16i w/ A/T	S114-520B	Hitachi	>90	11.0	<2950	0.43
	GA16i w/ A/T	M1T72085	Mitsubishi	50-75	11.0	3000-4000	0.47
1991-92	SR20DE	S114-701A	Hitachi	>90	11.0	<2950	0.43
	GA16DE w/ M/T	S114-486	Hitachi	>100	11.0	<3900	0.43
	GA16DE w/ M/T (Calif.)	S114-630	Hitachi	>60	11.5	<7000	0.43
	GA16DE w/ A/T	S114-534	Hitachi	>90	11.0	<2950	0.43
	SR20DE	M1T72985	Mitsubishi	50-75	11.0	3000-4000	0.47
	GA1DE w/ M/T	M2T53883	Mitsubishi	>100	11.0	<2900	0.45
	GA16DE w/ M/T (Calif.)	M3T37783	Mitsubishi	>60	11.5	<6500	0.45
	GA16DE w/ A/T	M1T72088	Mitsubishi	50-75	11.0	3000-4000	0.47

> = greater than
< = less than

Sending Units and Sensors

The following components are not electronic engine control related. Refer to Section 4 for engine controls.

REMOVAL, INSTALLATION AND LOCATION

✲✲ CAUTION

When draining the coolant, keep in mind that cats and dogs are attracted by the ethylene glycol antifreeze, and are quite likely to drink any that is left in an uncovered container or in puddles on the ground. This will prove fatal in sufficient quantity. Always drain the coolant into a sealable container. Coolant should be reused unless it is contaminated or several years old.

Gasoline Engines

1. Anti-dieseling solenoid. Is located on the side of the carburetor. Remove the wire and remove from the carburetor. Install and torque to 10 ft. lbs. (15 Nm).
2. Air Temperature control air cleaner temperature sensor. Is located inside the air cleaner housing. Remove the air cleaner cover, disconnect the vacuum hoses and remove the sensor (carbureted engine).
3. Water temperature sender. Is located in water passage in intake manifold. Drain the engine coolant and remove the sensor from the manifold. Install and torque to 25 ft. lbs. (34 Nm).
4. Mixture heater. Is located under the carburetor. Remove the carburetor and remove the heater assembly. Install with new gaskets and torque the carburetor nuts to 25 ft. lbs. (34 Nm).

5. Cooling fan sensor. Is located in bottom hose tee of radiator. Drain the coolant from the radiator. Remove the hose tee and place in a vise. Remove the sensor from the tee. Apply thread sealing tape to the threads and torque to 15 ft. lbs. (20 Nm). Some late model vehicles have the sensor threaded into the radiator tank. Be careful not to damage the radiator threads when removing.

6. Neutral safety switch. Is located at the transaxle.

7. Clutch switch. Is located at the clutch pedal.

Diesel Engine

1. Cooling fan switch. Is located in the radiator side tank. Drain the coolant and remove the switch. Apply thread sealing tape and torque to 18 ft. lbs. (25 Nm).

2. Fuel cut solenoid. Is located in the side of the injection pump. It has 1 wire going to the top of the solenoid.

3. Water temperature sensor. Is located at the front of cylinder head.

4. Oil Pressure sender is located in the engine block oil passage.

ENGINE MECHANICAL

Engine Overhaul Tips

Most engine overhaul procedures are fairly standard. In addition to specific parts replacement procedures and complete specifications for your individual engine, this Section also is a guide to accept rebuilding procedures. Examples of standard rebuilding practice are shown and should be used along with specific details concerning your particular engine.

Competent and accurate machine shop services will ensure maximum performance, reliability and engine life.

In most instances it is more profitable for the do-it-yourself mechanic to remove, clean and inspect the component, buy the necessary parts and deliver these to a shop for actual machine work.

On the other hand, much of the rebuilding work (crankshaft, block, bearings, piston rods, and other components) is well within the scope of the do-it-yourself mechanic.

TOOLS

The tools required for an engine overhaul or parts replacement will depend on the depth of your involvement. With a few exceptions, they will be the tools found in a mechanic's tool kit (see Section 1). More in-depth work will require any or all of the following:

- a dial indicator (reading in thousandths) mounted on a universal base
- micrometers and telescope gauges
- jaw and screw-type pullers
- scraper
- valve spring compressor
- ring groove cleaner
- piston ring expander and compressor
- ridge reamer
- cylinder hone or glaze breaker
- Plastigage®
- engine stand

The use of most of these tools is illustrated in this Section. Many can be rented for a one-time use from a local parts jobber or tool supply house specializing in automotive work.

Occasionally, the use of special tools is called for. See the information on Special Tools and Safety Notice in the front of this book before substituting another tool.

INSPECTION TECHNIQUES

Procedures and specifications are given in this Section for inspecting, cleaning and assessing the wear limits of most major components. Other procedures such as Magnaflux® and Zyglo® can be used to locate material flaws and stress cracks. Magnaflux® is a magnetic process applicable only to ferrous materials. The Zyglo® process coats the material with a fluorescent dye penetrant and can be used on any material Check for suspected surface cracks can be more readily made using spot check dye. The dye is sprayed onto the suspected area, wiped off and the area sprayed with a developer. Cracks will show up brightly.

OVERHAUL TIPS

Aluminum has become extremely popular for use in engines, due to its low weight. Observe the following precautions when handling aluminum parts:

- Never hot tank aluminum parts (the caustic hot tank solution will eat the aluminum.
- Remove all aluminum parts (identification tag, etc.) from engine parts prior to the tanking.
- Always coat threads lightly with engine oil or anti-seize compounds before installation, to prevent seizure.
- Never overtorque bolts or spark plugs especially in aluminum threads.

Stripped threads in any component can be repaired using any of several commercial repair kits (Heli-Coil®, Microdot®, Keenserts®, etc.).

When assembling the engine, any parts that will be frictional contact must be prelubed to provide lubrication at initial start-up. Any product specifically formulated for this purpose can be used, but engine oil is not recommended as a prelube.

When semi-permanent (locked, but removable) installation of bolts or nuts is desired, threads should be cleaned and coated with Loctite® or other similar, commercial non-hardening sealant.

REPAIRING DAMAGED THREADS

Several methods of repairing damaged threads are available. Heli-Coil® (shown here), Keenserts® and Microdot® are among the most widely used. All involve basically the same principle — drilling out stripped threads, tapping the hole and installing a prewound insert — making welding, plugging and oversize fasteners unnecessary.

Two types of thread repair inserts are usually supplied: a standard type for most Inch Coarse, Inch Fine, Metric Course and Metric Fine thread sizes and a spark lug type to fit most spark plug port sizes. Consult the individual manufacturer's catalog to determine exact applications. Typical thread repair kits will contain a selection of prewound threaded inserts, a tap (corresponding to the outside diameter threads of the insert) and an installation tool. Spark plug inserts usually differ because they require a tap equipped with pilot threads and a combined reamer/tap section. Most manufacturers also supply blister-packed thread repair inserts separately in addition to a master kit containing a variety of taps and inserts plus installation tools.

Before effecting a repair to a threaded hole, remove any snapped, broken or damaged bolts or studs. Penetrating oil can be used to free frozen threads. The offending item can be removed with locking pliers or with a screw or stud extractor. After the hole is clear, the thread can be repaired, as shown in the series of accompanying illustrations.

Checking Engine Compression

A noticeable lack of engine power, excessive oil consumption and/or poor fuel mileage measured over an extended period are all indicators of internal engine war. Worn piston rings, scored or worn cylinder bores, blown head gaskets, sticking or burnt valves and worn valve seats are all possible culprits here. A check of each cylinder's compression will help you locate the problems.

As mentioned in the Tools and Equipment section of Section 1, a screw-in type compression gauge is more accurate that the type you simply hold against the spark plug hole, although it takes slightly longer to use. It's worth it to obtain a more accurate reading. Follow the procedures below.

Testing the compression on diesel engines requires the use of special adapters and pressure gauges. Consult a tool distributor or dealership for the proper tools.

Gasoline Engines

➧ SEE FIG. 40

1. Warm up the engine to normal operating temperature.
2. Remove all the spark plugs.
3. Disconnect the high tension lead from the ignition coil.
4. On fully open the throttle either by operating the carburetor throttle linkage by hand or by having an assistant floor the accelerator pedal.
5. Screw the compression gauge into the no.1 spark plug hole until the fitting is snug.

✲✲ WARNING

Be careful not to crossthread the plug hole. On aluminum cylinder heads use extra care, as the threads in these heads are easily ruined.

6. Ask an assistant to depress the accelerator pedal fully on both carbureted and fuel injected vehicles. Then, while you read the compression gauge, ask the assistant to crank the engine four in short bursts using the ignition switch.
7. Read the compression gauge at the end of each series of cranks, and record the highest of these readings. Repeat this procedure for each of the engine's cylinders. Compare the highest reading of each cylinder to the following compression pressures:
   a. E15, E16, E16S, E16i and GA16i — 181 psi (1248kpa)
   b. E15ET — 180 psi (1241kpa)
   c. CA16DE and CA18DE — 199 psi (1372kpa)
   d. SR20DE — 178 psi (1227kpa)
   e. GA16DE — 192 psi (1324kpa)

A cylinder's compression pressure is usually acceptable if it is not less than 80% of maximum. The difference between any two cylinders should be no more than 12–14 pounds.

8. If a cylinder is unusually low, pour a tablespoon of clean engine oil into the cylinder through the spark plug hole and repeat the compression test. If the compression comes up after adding the oil, it appears that the cylinder's piston rings or bore are damaged or worn. If the pressure remains low, the valves may not be seating properly (a valve job is needed), or the head gasket may be blown near that cylinder. If compression in any two adjacent cylinders is low, and if the addition of oil doesn't help the compression, there is leakage past the head gasket. Oil and coolant water in the combustion chamber can result from this problem. There may be evidence of water droplets on the engine dipstick when a head gasket has blown.

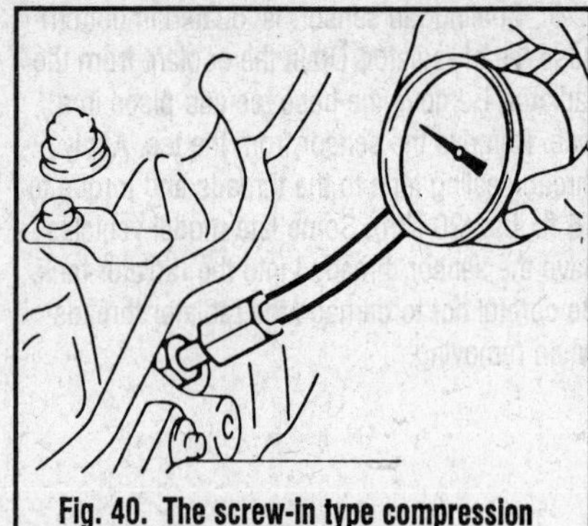

Fig. 40. The screw-in type compression gauge is more accurate

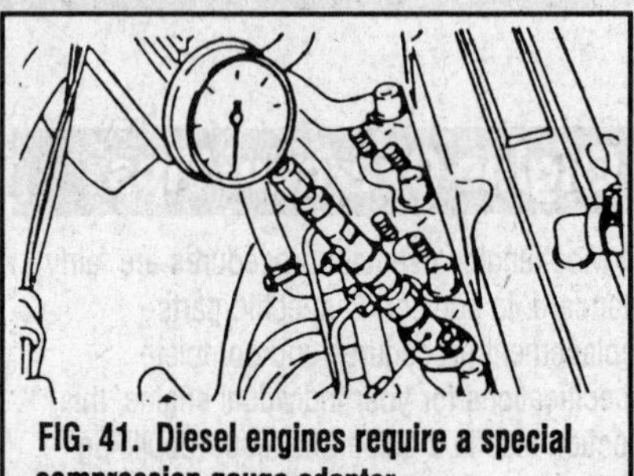

FIG. 41. Diesel engines require a special compression gauge adapter

Diesel Engines

➧ SEE FIG. 41

Checking cylinder compression on diesel engines is basically the same procedure as on gasoline engines except for the following:

1. A special compression gauge adaptor suitable for diesel engines (because these engines have much greater compression pressures) must be used.
2. Remove the injector tubes and remove the injectors from each cylinder.

➡ Don't forget to remove the washer underneath each injector; otherwise, it may get lost when the engine is cranked.

3. When fitting the compression gauge adaptor to the cylinder head, make sure the bleeder of the gauge (if equipped) is closed.
4. Crank the engine and read the gauge. The compression pressure should be 455 psi (minimum).
5. When reinstalling the injector assemblies, install new washers underneath each injector.

GENERAL ENGINE SPECIFICATIONS

Year	Engine ID/VIN	Engine Displacement Liters (cc)	Fuel System Type	Net Horsepower @ rpm	Net Torque @ rpm (ft. lbs.)	Bore × Stroke (in.)	Com-pression Ratio	Oil Pressure @ rpm
1982	E15	1.5 (1488)	2 bbl	67 @ 5200	85 @ 3200	2.92 × 3.23	9.0:1	43 @ 1700
1983	E15	1.5 (1488)	2 bbl	67 @ 5200	85 @ 3200	2.92 × 3.23	9.0:1	43 @ 1700
	E16	1.6 (1597)	2 bbl	69 @ 5200	93 @ 3200	2.99 × 3.46	9.4:1	43 @ 1700
	CD17	1.7 (1680)	Diesel	55 @ 4800	104 @ 2800	3.15 × 3.29	22.2:1	43 @ 1700
1984	E15ET	1.5 (1488)	EFI-Turbo	100 @ 5200	152 @ 3200	2.92 × 3.23	7.8:1	43 @ 1700
	E16	1.6 (1597)	2 bbl	69 @ 5200	93 @ 3200	2.99 × 3.46	9.4:1	43 @ 1700
	CD17	1.7 (1680)	Diesel	55 @ 4800	104 @ 2800	3.15 × 3.29	21.9:1	43 @ 1700
1985	E16	1.6 (1597)	2 bbl	69 @ 5200	93 @ 3200	2.99 × 3.46	9.4:1	43 @ 1700
	CD17	1.7 (1680)	Diesel	55 @ 4800	104 @ 2800	3.15 × 3.29	21.9:1	43 @ 1700
1986	E16	1.6 (1597)	2 bbl	69 @ 5200	93 @ 3200	2.99 × 3.46	9.4:1	43 @ 1700
	CD17	1.7 (1680)	Diesel	55 @ 4800	104 @ 2800	3.15 × 3.29	21.9:1	43 @ 1700
1987	E16	1.6 (1597)	2 bbl	69 @ 5200	93 @ 3200	2.99 × 3.46	9.4:1	43 @ 1700
	E16i	1.6 (1597)	EFI	70 @ 5000	94 @ 2800	2.99 × 3.46	9.4:1	43 @ 1700
	CA16DE	1.6 (1598)	EFI DOHC	113 @ 6400	99 @ 4800	3.07 × 3.29	10.0:1	67 @ 2000
	CD17	1.7 (1680)	Diesel	55 @ 4800	104 @ 2800	3.15 × 3.29	21.9:1	43 @ 1700
1988	E16i	1.6 (1597)	EFI	70 @ 5000	94 @ 2800	2.99 × 3.46	9.4:1	43 @ 1700
	CA18DE	1.8 (1809)	EFI DOHC	125 @ 6400	115 @ 4800	3.27 × 3.29	10.0:1	67 @ 2000
1989	GA16i	1.6 (1597)	EFI	90 @ 6000	96 @ 3200	2.99 × 3.46	9.4:1	43 @ 1700
	CA18DE	1.8 (1809)	EFI DOHC	96 @ 3200	115 @ 4800	3.27 × 3.29	9.5:1	43 @ 1700
1990	GA16i	1.6 (1597)	EFI	90 @ 6000	96 @ 3200	2.99 × 3.46	9.4:1	43 @ 1700
1991	GA16DE	1.6 (1597)	EFI DOHC	110 @ 6000	108 @ 4000	2.99 × 3.46	9.5:1	50–64 @ 3000
	SR20DE	2.0 (1998)	EFI DOHC	140 @ 6400	132 @ 4800	3.39 × 3.39	9.5:1	46–57 @ 3200
1992	GA16DE	1.6 (1597)	EFI DOHC	110 @ 6000	108 @ 4000	2.99 × 3.46	9.5:1	50–64 @ 3000
	SR20DE	2.0 (1998)	EFI DOHC	140 @ 6400	132 @ 4800	3.39 × 3.39	9.5:1	46–57 @ 3200

NOTE: Horsepower and torque are SAE net figures. They are measured at the rear of the transmission with all accessories installed and operating. Since the figures vary when a given engine is installed in different models, some are representative rather than exact.
EFI—Electronic Fuel Injection
DOHC—Double Overhead Cam

VALVE SPECIFICATIONS

Year	Engine ID/VIN	Engine Displacement Liters (cc)	Seat Angle (deg.)	Face Angle (deg.)	Spring Test Pressure (lbs. @ in.)	Spring Installed Height (in.)	Stem-to-Guide Clearance (in.)		Stem Diameter (in.)	
							Intake	Exhaust	Intake	Exhaust
1982	E15	1.5 (1488)	①	45.5	128 @ 1.20	1.543	0.0008–0.0020	0.0018–0.0030	0.2794–0.2750	0.2734–0.2740
1983	E15	1.5 (1488)	①	45.5	—	1.543	0.0008–0.0020	0.0018–0.0030	0.2744–0.2750	0.2734–0.2740
	E16	1.6 (1597)	①	45.5	—	1.543	0.0008–0.0020	0.0018–0.0030	0.2744–0.2750	0.2734–0.2740
	CD17	1.7 (1680)	45	45.5	—	②	0.0008–0.0021	0.0016–0.0029	0.2742–0.2748	0.2734–0.2740

VALVE SPECIFICATIONS

Year	Engine ID/VIN	Engine Displacement Liters (cc)	Seat Angle (deg.)	Face Angle (deg.)	Spring Test Pressure (lbs. @ in.)	Spring Installed Height (in.)	Stem-to-Guide Clearance (in.)		Stem Diameter (in.)	
							Intake	Exhaust	Intake	Exhaust
1984	E15ET ③	1.5 (1488)	④	⑤	127 @ 1.54	1.543	0.0008–0.0020	0.0018–0.0030	0.2744–0.2750	0.2734–0.2740
	E16	1.6 (1597)	①	45.5	—	1.543	0.0008–0.0020	0.0018–0.0030	0.2744–0.2750	0.2734–0.2740
	CD17	1.7 (1680)	45	45.5	—	②	0.0008–0.0021	0.0018–0.0030	0.2744–0.2750	0.2734–0.2740
1985	E16	1.6 (1597)	①	45.5	—	1.543	0.0008–0.0020	0.0018–0.0030	0.2744–0.2750	0.2734–0.2740
	CD17	1.7 (1680)	45	45.5	—	②	0.0008–0.0021	0.0016–0.0028	0.2742–0.2748	0.2734–0.2740
1986	E16	1.6 (1597)	①	45.5	—	1.543	0.0008–0.0020	0.0018–0.0030	0.2744–0.2750	0.2734–0.2740
	CD17	1.7 (1680)	45	45.5	—	②	0.0008–0.0021	0.0016–0.0028	0.2742–0.2748	0.2734–0.2740
1987	E16i	1.6 (1597)	①	45.5	—	1.543	0.0008–0.0020	0.0018–0.0030	0.2744–0.2750	0.2734–0.2740
	CA16DE ⑥	1.6 (1597)	⑦	45.5	—	—	0.0008–0.0021	0.0016–0.0029	0.2348–0.2354	0.2341–0.2346
	CD17	1.7 (1680)	45	45.5	—	②	0.0008–0.0021	0.0016–0.0028	0.2742–0.2748	0.2734–0.2740
1988	E16i	1.6 (1597)	①	45.5	—	1.543	0.0008–0.0020	0.0018–0.0030	0.2744–0.2750	0.2734–0.2740
	CA18DE ⑥	1.8 (1809)	⑧	45.5	—	—	0.0008–0.0021	0.0016–0.0029	0.2348–0.2354	0.2341–0.2346
1989	GA16i	1.6 (1597)	⑨	45.5	—	1.543	0.0008–0.0020	0.0012–0.0022	0.2348–0.2354	0.2582–0.2587
	CA18DE ⑥	1.8 (1809)	⑦	45.5	—	—	0.0008–0.0021	0.0016–0.0029	0.2348–0.2354	0.2341–0.2346
1990	GA16i	1.6 (1597)	⑨	45.5	—	1.543	0.0008–0.0020	0.0012–0.0022	0.2348–0.2354	0.2582–0.2587
1991	GA16DE ⑥	1.6 (1597)	⑩	45.5	77.4 @ 0.994	1.622	0.0008–0.0020	0.0016–0.0028	0.2152–0.2157	0.2144–0.2150
	SR20DE ⑥	2.0 (1998)	⑪	45.5	135 @ 1.18	1.943	0.0008–0.0021	0.0016–0.0029	0.2348–0.2354	0.2341–0.2346
1992	GA16DE ⑥	1.6 (1597)	⑩	45.5	77.4 @ 0.994	1.622	0.0008–0.0020	0.0016–0.0028	0.2152–0.2157	0.2144–0.2150
	SR20DE ⑥	2.0 (1998)	⑪	45.5	135 @ 1.18	1.943	0.0008–0.0021	0.0016–0.0029	0.2348–0.2354	0.2341–0.2346

① Intake—30°, 45°, 50°
Exhaust—45°, 50°
② Inner—1.417
Outer—1.555
③ Turbo engine
④ Intake—45°, 60°
Exhaust—45°
⑤ Intake—60.5°
Exhaust—45.5°
⑥ DOHC engine
⑦ Intake—30°, 45°, 60°
Exhaust—15°, 45°, 60°
⑧ Intake°10, 45°
Exhaust—15°, 45°
⑨ Intake—30°, 45°, 60°
Exhaust—10°, 45°
⑩ Intake—30°, 45°, 60°
Exhaust—10°, 45°, 60°
⑪ Intake—23°, 45°, 50°
Exhaust—45°, 50°

CAMSHAFT SPECIFICATIONS

All measurements given in inches.

Year	Engine ID/VIN	Engine Displacement Liters (cc)	Journal Diameter 1	2	3	4	5	Elevation In.	Ex.	Bearing Clearance	Camshaft End Play
1982	E15	1.5 (1488)	1.6515–1.6522	1.6498–1.6505	1.6515–1.6522	1.6498–1.6505	1.6515–1.6522	1.4128–1.4226	1.4031–1.4130	0.0014–0.0030	0.0160
1983	E15	1.5 (1488)	1.6515–1.6522	1.6498–1.6505	1.6515–1.6522	1.6498–1.6505	1.6515–1.6522	1.4128–1.4226	1.4031–1.4130	0.0014–0.0030	0.0160
	E16	1.6 (1597)	1.6515–1.6522	1.6498–1.6505	1.6515–1.6522	1.6498–1.6505	1.6515–1.6522	1.4128–1.4226	1.4031–1.4130	0.0014–0.0030	0.0160
	CD17	1.7 (1680)	1.1795–1.1803	1.1795–1.1803	1.1795–1.1803	1.1795–1.1803	1.1795–1.1803	1.7518–1.7520	1.7911–1.7913	0.0008–0.0024	0.0067
1984	E15ET	1.5 (1488)	1.6515–1.6522	1.6498–1.6505	1.6515–1.6522	1.6498–1.6505	1.6515–1.6522	1.4128–1.4226	1.4031–1.4130	0.0014–0.0030	0.0160
	E16	1.6 (1597)	1.6515–1.6522	1.6498–1.6505	1.6515–1.6522	1.6498–1.6505	1.6515–1.6522	1.4128–1.4226	1.4031–1.4130	0.0014–0.0030	0.0160
	CD17	1.7 (1680)	1.1795–1.1803	1.1795–1.1803	1.1795–1.1803	1.1795–1.1803	1.1795–1.1803	1.7518–1.7520	1.7911–1.7913	0.0008–0.0024	0.0067
1985	E16	1.6 (1597)	1.6515–1.6522	1.6498–1.6505	1.6515–1.6522	1.6498–1.6505	1.6515–1.6522	1.4128–1.4226	1.4031–1.4130	0.0014–0.0030	0.0160
	CD17	1.7 (1680)	1.1795–1.1803	1.1795–1.1803	1.1795–1.1803	1.1795–1.1803	1.1795–1.1803	1.7500–1.7520	1.7895–1.7913	0.0008–0.0024	0.0024–0.0067
1986	E16	1.6 (1597)	1.6515–1.6522	1.6498–1.6505	1.6515–1.6522	1.6498–1.6505	1.6515–1.6522	1.4128–1.4226	1.4031–1.4130	0.0014–0.0030	0.0160
	CD17	1.7 (1680)	1.1795–1.1803	1.1795–1.1803	1.1795–1.1803	1.1795–1.1803	1.1795–1.1803	1.7500–1.7520	1.7895–1.7913	0.0008–0.0024	0.0024–0.0067
1987	E16	1.6 (1597)	1.6515–1.6522	1.6498–1.6505	1.6515–1.6522	1.6498–1.6505	1.6515–1.6522	1.4128–1.4226	1.4031–1.4130	0.0014–0.0030	0.0160
	CA16DE	1.6 (1597)	1.0998–1.1006	1.0998–1.1006	1.0998–1.1006	1.0998–1.1006	1.0996–1.1006	0.335	0.335	0.0018–0.0035	0.0028–0.0059
	CD17	1.7 (1680)	1.1795–1.1803	1.1795–1.1803	1.1795–1.1803	1.1795–1.1803	1.1795–1.1803	1.7500–1.7520	1.7895–1.7913	0.0008–0.0024	0.0024–0.0067
1988	E16i	1.6 (1597)	1.6515–1.6522	1.6498–1.6505	1.6515–1.6522	1.6498–1.6505	1.6515–1.6522	1.4128–1.4226	1.4031–1.4130	0.0014–0.0030	0.0160
	CA18DE	1.8 (1809)	1.0998–1.1006	1.0998–1.1006	1.0998–1.1006	1.0998–1.1006	1.0996–1.1006	0.335	0.335	0.0018–0.0035	0.0028–0.0059
1989	GA16i	1.6 (1597)	1.6510–1.6518	1.6510–1.6518	1.6510–1.6518	1.6510–1.6518	1.6510–1.6518	1.4147–1.4222	1.4073–1.4148	0.0018–0.0035	0.0079
	CA18DE	1.8 (1809)	1.0998–1.1006	1.0998–1.1006	1.0998–1.1006	1.0998–1.1006	1.0996–1.1006	0.335	0.335	0.0018–0.0035	0.0028–0.0059
1990	GA16i	1.6 (1597)	1.6510–1.6518	1.6510–1.6518	1.6510–1.6518	1.6510–1.6518	1.6510–1.6518	1.4147–1.4222	1.4073–1.4148	0.0018–0.0035	0.0079
1991	GA16DE	1.6 (1597)	1.0998–1.1006	1.9423–1.9431	1.9423–1.9431	1.9423–1.9431	1.9423–1.9431	1.5984–1.6059	1.5701–1.5776	0.0018–0.0034	0.0079
	SR20DE	2.0 (1998)	1.0998–1.1006	1.0998–1.1006	1.0998–1.1006	1.0998–1.1006	1.0998–1.1006	0.394	0.362	0.0018–0.0034	0.0079
1992	GA16DE	1.6 (1597)	1.0998–1.1006	1.9423–1.9431	1.9423–1.9431	1.9423–1.9431	1.9423–1.9431	1.5984–1.6059	1.5701–1.5776	0.0018–0.0034	0.0079
	SR20DE	2.0 (1998)	1.0998–1.1006	1.0998–1.1006	1.0998–1.1006	1.0998–1.1006	1.0998–1.1006	0.394	0.362	0.0018–0.0034	0.0079

① Turbo
② DOHC engine

CRANKSHAFT AND CONNECTING ROD SPECIFICATIONS

All measurements are given in inches.

Year	Engine ID/VIN	Engine Displacement Liters (cc)	Crankshaft Main Brg. Journal Dia.	Crankshaft Main Brg. Oil Clearance	Crankshaft Shaft End-play	Crankshaft Thrust on No.	Connecting Rod Journal Diameter	Connecting Rod Oil Clearance	Connecting Rod Side Clearance
1982	E15	1.5 (1488)	1.9663–1.9671	①	0.0020–0.0071	3	1.5730–1.5738	0.0012–0.0024	0.0040–0.0146
1983	E15	1.5 (1488)	1.9663–1.9671	①	0.0020–0.0071	3	1.5730–1.5738	0.0012–0.0024	0.0040–0.0146
	E16	1.6 (1597)	1.9663–1.9671	②	0.0020–0.0071	3	1.5730–1.5738	0.0012–0.0024	0.0040–0.0146
	CD17	1.7 (1680)	2.0847–2.0852	0.0015–0.0026	0.0020–0.0071	Center	1.7701–1.7706	0.0009–0.0026	0.0080–0.0120
1984	E15ET	1.5 (1488)	1.9663–1.9671	②	0.0020–0.0071	3	1.5730–1.5738	0.0012–0.0024	0.0040–0.0146
	E16	1.6 (1597)	1.9663–1.9671	②	0.0020–0.0071	3	1.5730–1.5738	0.0012–0.0024	0.0040–0.0146
	CD17	1.7 (1680)	2.0847–2.0852	0.0015–0.0026	0.0020–0.0071	Center	1.5730–1.5738	0.0012–0.0024	0.0040–0.0146
1985	E16	1.6 (1597)	1.9663–1.9671	②	0.0020–0.0071	3	1.5730–1.5738	0.0012–0.0024	0.0040–0.0146
	CD17	1.7 (1680)	2.0847–2.0852	0.0015–0.0026	0.0020–0.0071	Center	1.7701–1.7706	0.0009–0.0026	0.0080–0.0120
1986	E16	1.6 (1597)	1.9663–1.9671	②	0.0020–0.0071	3	1.5730–1.5738	0.0004–0.0017	0.0040–0.0146
	CD17	1.7 (1680)	2.0847–2.0852	0.0015–0.0026	0.0020–0.0071	Center	1.7701–1.7706	0.0009–0.0026	0.0080–0.0120
1987	E16i	1.6 (1597)	1.9663–1.9671	②	0.0020–0.0071	3	1.5730–1.5738	0.0004–0.0017	0.0040–0.0146
	CA16DE	1.6 (1597)	2.0847–2.0856	0.0008–0.0019	0.0020–0.0071	3	1.7698–1.7706	0.0007–0.0018	0.0079–0.0138
	CD17	1.7 (1680)	③	0.0015–0.0026	0.0020–0.0071	3	1.7701–1.7706	0.0013–0.0026	0.0080–0.0120
1988	E16i	1.6 (1597)	1.9661–1.9671	②	0.0020–0.0065	3	1.5730–1.5738	0.0004–0.0017	0.0040–0.0146
	CA18DE	1.8 (1809)	2.0847–2.0856	0.0008–0.0019	0.0020–0.0071	3	1.7698–1.7706	0.0007–0.0018	0.0079–0.0138
1989	GA16i	1.6 (1597)	1.9661–1.9671	②	0.0020–0.0071	3	1.5730–1.5738	0.0004–0.0017	0.0040–0.0146
	CA18DE	1.8 (1809)	2.0847–2.0856	0.0008–0.0019	0.0020–0.0071	3	1.7698–1.7706	0.0007–0.0018	0.0079–0.0138
1990	GA16i	1.6 (1597)	1.9661–1.9671	0.0008–0.0017	0.0024–0.0071	3	1.5731–1.5738	0.0004–0.0014	0.0079–0.0185
1991	GA16DE	1.6 (1597)	1.9668–1.9671	0.0007–0.0017	0.0024–0.0071	3	1.5735–1.5738	0.0004–0.0014	0.0079–0.0185
	SR20DE	2.0 (1998)	2.1643–2.1646	0.0002–0.0009	0.0039–0.0102	3	1.8885–1.8887	0.0008–0.0018	0.0079–0.0138
1992	GA16DE	1.6 (1597)	1.9668–1.9671	0.0007–0.0017	0.0024–0.0071	3	1.5735–1.5738	0.0004–0.0014	0.0079–0.0185
	SR20DE	2.0 (1998)	2.1643–2.1646	0.0002–0.0009	0.0039–0.0102	3	1.8885–1.8887	0.0008–0.0018	0.0079–0.0138

① Except MPG model
1 and 5—0.0012–0.0030
2, 3, 4—0.0012–0.0036

MPG model
1, 3 and 5—0.0019–0.0030
2 and 4—0.0012–0.0036

② 1 and 5—0.0012–0.0030
2, 3, 4—0.0012–0.0036

③ Grade 0—2.0853–2.0856
Grade 1—2.0850–2.0853
Grade 2—2.0847–2.0856

PISTON AND RING SPECIFICATIONS

All measurements are given in inches.

Year	Engine ID/VIN	Engine Displacement Liters (cc)	Piston Clearance	Ring Gap Top Compression	Ring Gap Bottom Compression	Ring Gap Oil Control	Ring Side Clearance Top Compression	Ring Side Clearance Bottom Compression	Ring Side Clearance Oil Control
1982	E15	1.5 (1488)	0.0009–0.0017	0.0079–0.0138	0.0059–0.0118	0.0118–0.0354	0.0016–0.0029	0.0012–0.0025	0.0020–0.0057
1983	E15	1.5 (1488)	0.0009–0.0017	0.0079–0.0138	0.0059–0.0118	0.0118–0.0354	0.0016–0.0029	0.0012–0.0025	0.0020–0.0057
	E16	1.6 (1597)	0.0009–0.0017	0.0079–0.0138	0.0059–0.0118	0.0118–0.0354	0.0016–0.0029	0.0012–0.0025	0.0020–0.0057
	CD17	1.7 (1680)	0.0020–0.0028	0.0079–0.0138	0.0079–0.0138	0.0118–0.0177	0.0024–0.0039	0.0016–0.0031	0.0012–0.0028
1984	E15ET ①	1.5 (1488)	0.0016–0.0024	②	0.0059–0.0098	0.0079–0.0236	0.0016–0.0029	0.0012–0.0025	0.0020–0.0049
	E16	1.6 (1597)	0.0009–0.0017	0.0079–0.0138	0.0059–0.0118	0.0118–0.0354	0.0016–0.0029	0.0012–0.0025	0.0020–0.0057
	CD17	1.7 (1680)	0.0020–0.0028	0.0079–0.0138	0.0079–0.0138	0.0118–0.0177	0.0008–0.0024	0.0016–0.0031	0.0012–0.0028
1985	E16	1.6 (1597)	0.0009–0.0017	0.0079–0.0138	0.0059–0.0118	0.0118–0.0354	0.0016–0.0029	0.0012–0.0025	0.0020–0.0057
	CD17	1.7 (1680)	0.0020–0.0028	0.0079–0.0138	0.0079–0.0138	0.0118–0.0177	0.0008–0.0024	0.0016–0.0031	0.0012–0.0028
1986	E16	1.6 (1597)	0.0009–0.0017	0.0079–0.0138	0.0059–0.0118	0.0118–0.0354	0.0016–0.0029	0.0012–0.0025	0.0020–0.0057
	CD17	1.7 (1680)	0.0020–0.0028	0.0079–0.0138	0.0079–0.0138	0.0118–0.0177	0.0008–0.0024	0.0016–0.0031	0.0012–0.0028
1987	E16i	1.6 (1597)	0.0009–0.0017	0.0079–0.0138	0.0059–0.0118	0.0118–0.0354	0.0016–0.0029	0.0012–0.0025	0.0020–0.0057
	CA16DE ③	1.6 (1597)	0.0009–0.0017	0.0087–0.0154	0.0075–0.0177	0.0079–0.0236	0.0016–0.0029	0.0012–0.0025	0.0010–0.0033
	CD17	1.7 (1680)	0.0010–0.0018	④	④	⑤	0.0008–0.0024	0.0016–0.0031	0.0012–0.0028
1988	E16i	1.6 (1597)	0.0009–0.0017	0.0079–0.0118	0.0059–0.0098	0.0079–0.0236	0.0016–0.0029	0.0012–0.0025	0.0002–0.0070
	CA18DE ③	1.8 (1809)	0.0006–0.0014	0.0087–0.0154	0.0075–0.0177	0.0079–0.0299	0.0016–0.0029	0.0012–0.0025	0.0010–0.0033
1989	GA16i	1.6 (1597)	0.0006–0.0014	0.0079–0.0138	0.0146–0.0205	0.0079–0.0236	0.0016–0.0031	0.0012–0.0028	—
	CA18DE ③	1.8 (1809)	0.0006–0.0014	0.0087–0.0154	0.0075–0.0177	0.0079–0.0299	0.0016–0.0029	0.0012–0.0025	0.0010–0.0033
1990	GA16i	1.6 (1597)	0.0006–0.0014	0.0079–0.0138	0.0146–0.0205	0.0079–0.0236	0.0016–0.0031	0.0012–0.0028	—
1991	GA16DE ③	1.6 (1597)	0.0006–0.0014	0.0079–0.0138	0.0146–0.0205	0.0079–0.0236	0.0016–0.0031	0.0012–0.0028	—
	SR20DE ③	2.0 (1997)	0.0004–0.0012	0.0079–0.0118	0.0138–0.0197	0.0079–0.0236	0.0018–0.0031	0.0012–0.0026	—

PISTON AND RING SPECIFICATIONS

All measurements are given in inches.

Year	Engine ID/VIN	Engine Displacement Liters (cc)	Piston Clearance	Ring Gap: Top Compression	Ring Gap: Bottom Compression	Ring Gap: Oil Control	Ring Side Clearance: Top Compression	Ring Side Clearance: Bottom Compression	Ring Side Clearance: Oil Control
1992	GA16DE ③	1.6 (1597)	0.0006–0.0014	0.0079–0.0138	0.0146–0.0205	0.0079–0.0236	0.0016–0.0031	0.0012–0.0028	—
	SR20DE ③	2.0 (1998)	0.0004–0.0012	0.0079–0.0118	0.0138–0.0197	0.0079–0.0236	0.0018–0.0031	0.0012–0.0028	—

① Turbocharged
② Piston grades 1 and 2
0.0079–0.0102 (yellow)
Piston grades 3, 4 and 5
0.0055–0.0079
③ Electronic Fuel Injection—Double Overhead Cam
④ Grade 1—0.0079-0.0091
Grade 2—0.0091-0.0106
Grade 3—0.0106-0.0118
Grade 4—0.0118-0.0130
Grade 5—0.0130-0.0146
⑤ Grade 1—0.0118-0.0130
Grade 2—0.0130-0.0142
Grade 3—0.0142-0.0154
Grade 4—0.0154-0.0164
Grade 5—0.0164-0.0181

TORQUE SPECIFICATIONS

All readings in ft. lbs.

Year	Engine ID/VIN	Engine Displacement Liters (cc)	Cylinder Head Bolts	Main Bearing Bolts	Rod Bearing Bolts	Crankshaft Damper Bolts	Flywheel Bolts	Manifold: Intake	Manifold: Exhaust	Spark Plugs	Lug Nut
1982	E15	1.5 (1488)	①	36–43	23–27	108–145	58–65	11–14	11–14	14–22	60–75
1983	E15	1.5 (1488)	①	36–43	23–27	83–108	58–65	11–14	11–14	14–22	60–75
	E16	1.6 (1597)	①	36–43	23–27	83–108	58–65	11–14	11–14	14–22	60–75
	CD17	1.7 (1680)	72–80②	33–40	23–27	90–98	72–80	13–16	13–16	—	60–75
1984	E15ET	1.5 (1488)	51–54③	36–43	23–27	83–108	58–65	12–15	12–15	14–22	60–75
	E16	1.6 (1597)	③	36–43	23–27	83–108	58–65	12–15	12–15	14–22	60–75
	CD17	1.7 (1680)	72–80②	33–40	23–27	90–98	72–80	13–16	13–16	—	60–75
1985	E16	1.6 (1597)	③	36–43	23–27	83–108	58–65	12–15	12–15	14–22	60–75
	CD17	1.7 (1680)	72–80②	33–40	23–27	90–98	72–80	13–16	13–16	—	60–75
1986	E16	1.6 (1597)	③	36–43	23–27	80–94	58–65	12–15	12–15	14–22	60–75
	CD17	1.7 (1680)	72–80②	33–40	23–27	90–98	72–80	13–16	13–16	—	60–75
1987	E16	1.6 (1597)	③⑥	36–43	23–27	80–94	58–65	12–15	12–15	14–22	60–75
	CA16DE④	1.6 (1597)	⑤	33–40	30–33	105–112	61–69	14–19	27–35	14–22	60–75
	CD17	1.7 (1680)	72–80②	33–40	23–27	90–98	72–80	13–16	13–16	—	60–75
1988	E16i	1.6 (1597)	⑦	36–43	23–27	80–94	58–65⑧	12–15	12–15	14–22	60–75
	CA18DE④	1.8 (1809)	⑤	33–40	⑨	105–112	61–69	14–19	27–35	14–22	60–75
1989	GA16i	1.6 (1597)	⑫	34–38	⑨	132–152	69–76	12–15	12–15	14–22	60–75
	CA18DE④	1.8 (1809)	⑤	33–40	⑨	105–112	61–69	12–15	12–15	14–22	60–75
1990	GA16i	1.6 (1597)	⑫	34–38	⑨	132–152	69–76	12–15	12–15	14–22	60–75
1991	GA16DE④	1.6 (1597)	⑪	34–38	⑨	98–112	61–69⑧	12–15	16–21	14–22	60–75
	SR20DE④	2.0 (1998)	⑩	51–61	⑨	105–122	61–69	13–15	27–35	14–22	60–75

TORQUE SPECIFICATIONS

All readings in ft. lbs.

Year	Engine ID/VIN	Engine Displacement Liters (cc)	Cylinder Head Bolts	Main Bearing Bolts	Rod Bearing Bolts	Crankshaft Damper Bolts	Flywheel Bolts	Manifold Intake	Manifold Exhaust	Spark Plugs	Lug Nut
1992	GA16DE ④	1.6 (1597)	⑪	34–38	⑨	98–112	61–69 ⑧	12–15	16–21	14–22	60–75
	SR20DE ④	2.0 (1998)	⑩	51–61	⑨	105–122	61–69	13–15	27–35	14–22	60–75

① Torque in 2 steps:
1st step—33 ft. lbs.
2nd step—51-54 ft. lbs.

② Torque in 3 steps:
1st step—
2nd step—
3rd step—

③ Torque in 5 steps:
1st step—10 ft. lbs.
2nd step—20 ft. lbs.
3rd step—30 ft. lbs.
4th step—40 ft. lbs.
5th step—51-54 ft. lbs.

④ Double Overhead Cam

⑤ Set No. 1 cylinder to TDC
1st step—22 ft. lbs.
2nd step—76 ft. lbs.
3rd step—loosen all bolts completely
4th step—22 ft. lbs.
5th step—76 ft. lbs. plus an additional 85-90 degrees clockwise

⑥ Refer to note ⑦ for the E16i engine

⑦ Torque in 5 steps:
1st step—22 ft. lbs.
2nd step—51 ft. lbs.
3rd step—loosen all bolts completely
4th step—22 ft. lbs.
5th step—51-54 ft. lbs.

⑧ AT drive plate—69-76 ft. lbs.

⑨ Torque in 3 steps:
1st step—10-12 ft. lbs.
2nd step—28-33 ft. lbs.
3rd step—60-65 degrees clockwise

⑩ Torque in 6 steps:
1st step—29 ft. lbs.
2nd step—58 ft. lbs.
3rd step—loosen all bolts completely
4th step—25-33 ft. lbs.
5th step—Turn 90-100 degrees clockwise

⑪ Torque in 5 steps:
1st step—22 ft. lbs.
2nd step—43 ft. lbs.
3rd step—loosen all bolts completely
4th step—22 ft. lbs.
5th step—50-55 degrees clockwise

⑫ Torque in 6 steps:
1st step—22 ft. lbs.
2nd step—47 ft. lbs.
3rd step—loosen all bolts completely
4th step—22 ft. lbs.
5th step—Turn bolt (1) 80-85 degrees and bolts (2)-(10) 60-65 egrees clockwise
6th step—bolts (11)-(15) to 4.6-6.1 ft. lbs.

Gasoline Engine

➧ SEE FIGS. 42–56

REMOVAL & INSTALLATION

⁂ CAUTION

When draining the coolant, keep in mind that cats and dogs are attracted by the ethylene glycol antifreeze, and are quite likely to drink any that is left in an uncovered container or in puddles on the ground. This will prove fatal in sufficient quantity. Always drain the coolant into a sealable container. Coolant should be reused unless it is contaminated or several years old.

1982–87

⁂ CAUTION

On EFI equipped models, release the fuel pressure in the system (as outlined in Section 4) before disconnecting the fuel lines. Situate the vehicle on as flat and solid a surface as possible. Place chocks or equivalent at front and rear of rear wheels to stop vehicle from rolling.

➡ The engine and transaxle must be removed as a single unit. The engine and transaxle is removed from the top of the vehicle.

1. Mark the location of the hinges on the hood. Remove the hood by holding at both sides and unscrewing bolts. This requires 2 people.
2. Disconnect the battery cables and remove the battery.
3. Drain the coolant from the radiator, then remove the radiator and the heater hoses.
4. Remove the air cleaner-to-rocker cover hose and the air cleaner cover, then place a clean rag in the carburetor or throttle body opening to keep out the dirt or any foreign object.

➡ Disconnect and label all the necessary vacuum hoses and electrical connectors, for reinstallation purposes. A good rule of thumb when disconnecting the rather complex engine wiring of today's cars is to put a piece of masking tape on the wire and on the connection you removed the wire from, then mark both pieces of tape 1, 2, 3, etc. When replacing wiring, simply match the pieces of tape.

5. If equipped, disconnect the air pump cleaner and remove the carbon canister.
6. Remove the auxiliary fan, the washer tank and the radiator grille. Remove the radiator together with the fan motor assembly as a unit.
7. Remove the clutch control wire or cable from the transaxle. Remove the right and the left buffer rods but do not alter the length of these rods. Disconnect the speedometer cable from the transaxle and plug the hole with a clean rag.
8. If equipped with air conditioning, loosen the idler pulley nut and the adjusting bolt, then remove the compressor belt. Remove the compressor to one side and suspend on a wire. Do not disconnect the A/C hoses if at all possible. Remove the condenser and the receiver drier and place them on the right fender.

➡ **If equipped with AC, DO NOT ATTEMPT TO UNFASTEN ANY OF THE REFRIGERANT HOSES. See Section 1 for additional warnings. If equipped with power steering, loosen the idler pulley nut and adjusting bolt, then remove the drive belt and the power steering pulley.**

9. If equipped with a manual transaxle, disconnect the transaxle shifting rods by removing the securing bolts (1982 and later). If equipped with an automatic transaxle, disconnect the mounting bracket and the control wire from the transaxle.

10. Attach the engine sling, tool Nos. 10005M4900 and 10006M4900 (1976–81), 1000501M00 and 1000623M00 at each end of the engine block. Connect a chain or cable to the engine slingers.

11. Unbolt the exhaust pipe from the exhaust manifold. There are 3 bolts which attach the pipe to the manifold and bolts which attach the pipe support to the engine.

➡ **On the Pulsar and Sentra, remove the tie rod ends and the lower ball joints. Disconnect the right and left side drive shafts from their side flanges and remove the bolt holding the radius link support. When drawing out the halfshafts, it is necessary to loosen the strut head bolts also be careful not to damage the grease seals.**

12. On 1982 and later models, refer to Section 7, for the axle shaft, removal and installation procedures, then remove the axle shafts.

13. Remove the radius link support bolt, then lower the transaxle shift selector rods.

14. Unbolt the engine from the engine and the transaxle mounts.

15. Using an overhead lifting device, attach it to the engine lifting sling and slowly remove the engine and transaxle assembly from the vehicle.

➡ **When removing the engine, be careful not to knock it against the adjacent parts.**

16. Separate the engine from the transaxle if necessary.

To install:

17. Install the transaxle and torque the bolts to 35 ft. lbs. (48 Nm).

18. Install all the necessary parts on the engine before lowering it into the vehicle, such as, spark plugs, water pump etc.

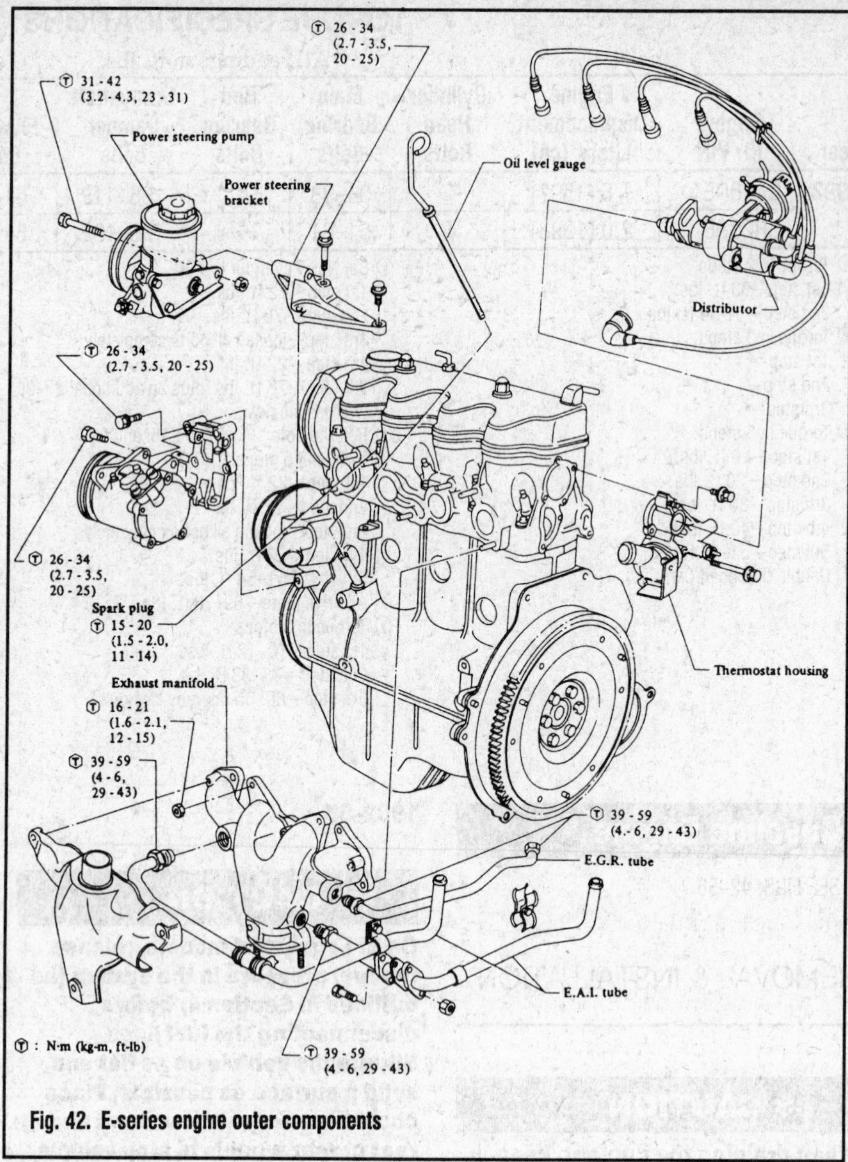

Ⓣ 26 - 34 (2.7 - 3.5, 20 - 25)
Ⓣ 31 - 42 (3.2 - 4.3, 23 - 31)
Power steering pump
Oil level gauge
Power steering bracket
Distributor
Ⓣ 26 - 34 (2.7 - 3.5, 20 - 25)
Ⓣ 26 - 34 (2.7 - 3.5, 20 - 25)
Spark plug
Ⓣ 15 - 20 (1.5 - 2.0, 11 - 14)
Thermostat housing
Exhaust manifold
Ⓣ 16 - 21 (1.6 - 2.1, 12 - 15)
Ⓣ 39 - 59 (4 - 6, 29 - 43)
Ⓣ 39 - 59 (4 - 6, 29 - 43)
E.G.R. tube
E.A.I. tube
Ⓣ : N·m (kg-m, ft-lb)
Ⓣ 39 - 59 (4 - 6, 29 - 43)

Fig. 42. E-series engine outer components

19. Lower the engine and transaxle as an assembly into the car and onto the frame, make sure to keep it as level as possible.

20. Check the clearance between the frame and clutch housing and make sure that the engine mount bolts are seated in the groove of the mounting bracket.

21. Install the motor mounts, remove the engine sling and install the buffer rods, tighten the engine mount bolts first, then apply a load to the mounting insulators before tightening the buffer rod and sub-mounting bolts.

22. If the buffer rod length has not been altered, they should still be correct. Shims are placed under the engine mounts, be sure to replace the exact ones in the correct places.

23. Install the transaxle shift selector rods or cable and attaching parts.

24. Install the axle shafts and the attaching parts.

25. Install the exhaust pipe to the manifold, it is a good idea to replace the gasket for the exhaust pipe at this time.

26. Install slave cylinder, clutch cable if so equipped and speedometer cable.

27. Install the condenser, receiver drier, air conditioning compressor, power steering pump and all drive belts.

28. Install the radiator with fan motor attached as assembly, radiator grille, washer tank and the auxiliary fan.

29. Install air pump cleaner, if so equipped and the carbon canister.

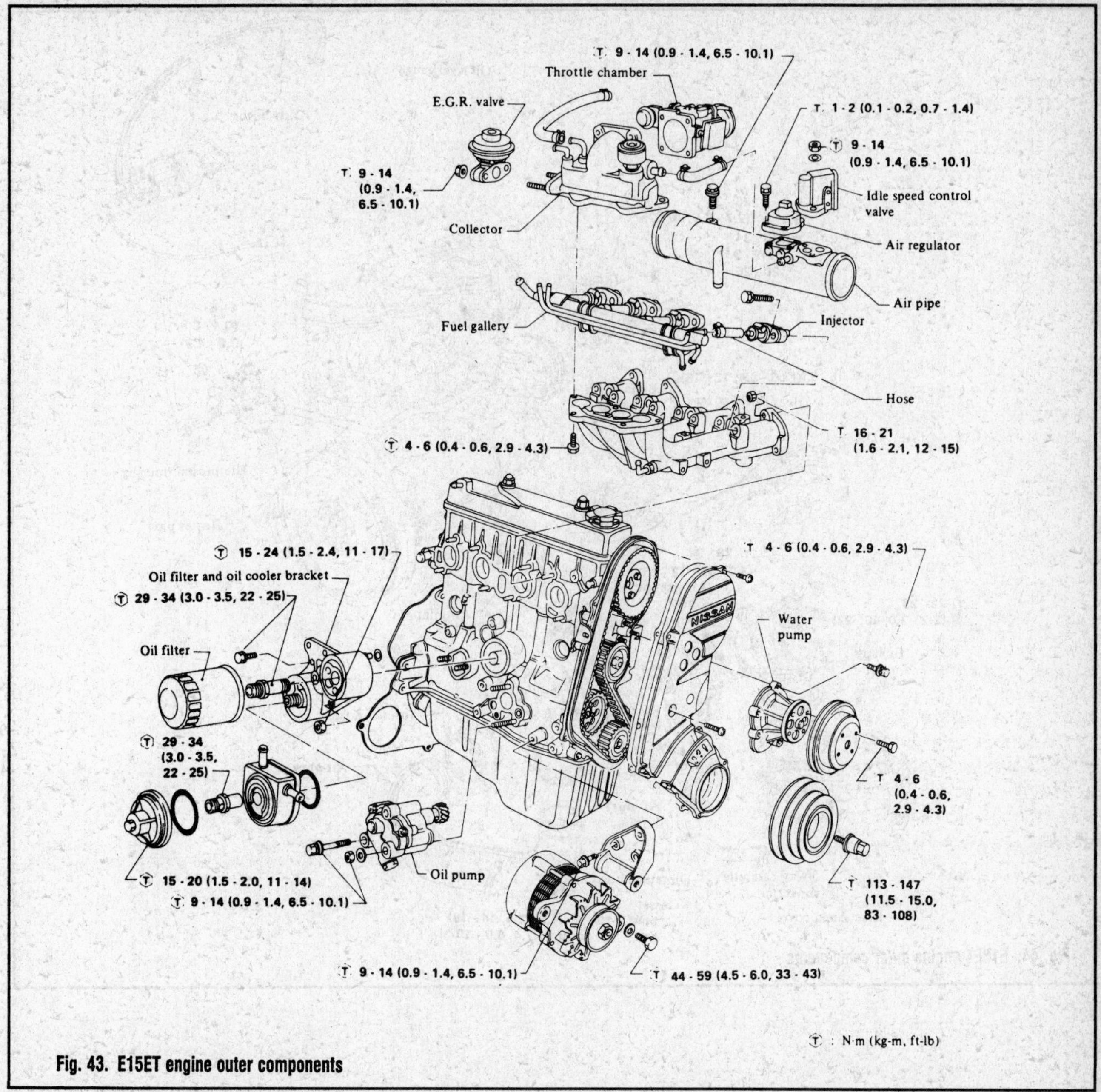
T 9 - 14 (0.9 - 1.4, 6.5 - 10.1)
Throttle chamber
E.G.R. valve
T 1 - 2 (0.1 - 0.2, 0.7 - 1.4)
T 9 - 14
(0.9 - 1.4, 6.5 - 10.1)
T 9 - 14
(0.9 - 1.4,
6.5 - 10.1)
Idle speed control
valve
Collector
Air regulator
Air pipe
Injector
Fuel gallery
Hose
T 16 - 21
(1.6 - 2.1, 12 - 15)
T 4 - 6 (0.4 - 0.6, 2.9 - 4.3)
T 15 - 24 (1.5 - 2.4, 11 - 17)
T 4 - 6 (0.4 - 0.6, 2.9 - 4.3)
Oil filter and oil cooler bracket
T 29 - 34 (3.0 - 3.5, 22 - 25)
Water
pump
Oil filter
T 29 - 34
(3.0 - 3.5,
22 - 25)
T 4 - 6
(0.4 - 0.6,
2.9 - 4.3)
Oil pump
T 15 - 20 (1.5 - 2.0, 11 - 14)
T 9 - 14 (0.9 - 1.4, 6.5 - 10.1)
T 113 - 147
(11.5 - 15.0,
83 - 108)
T 9 - 14 (0.9 - 1.4, 6.5 - 10.1)
T 44 - 59 (4.5 - 6.0, 33 - 43)
T : N·m (kg-m, ft-lb)

Fig. 43. E15ET engine outer components

30. Install all other attaching parts such as brackets etc. and the air cleaner that were removed and connect all the vacuum hoses and the electrical connectors.

31. Connect the radiator and heater hoses and refill the system with the correct amount of antifreeze.

32. Install the battery and reconnect the battery cables.

33. Install the hood in the same location as you removed it from.

34. Fill and check all fluids, start engine, let it warm up and check for leaks.

35. Road test vehicle after you are sure there are no leaks.

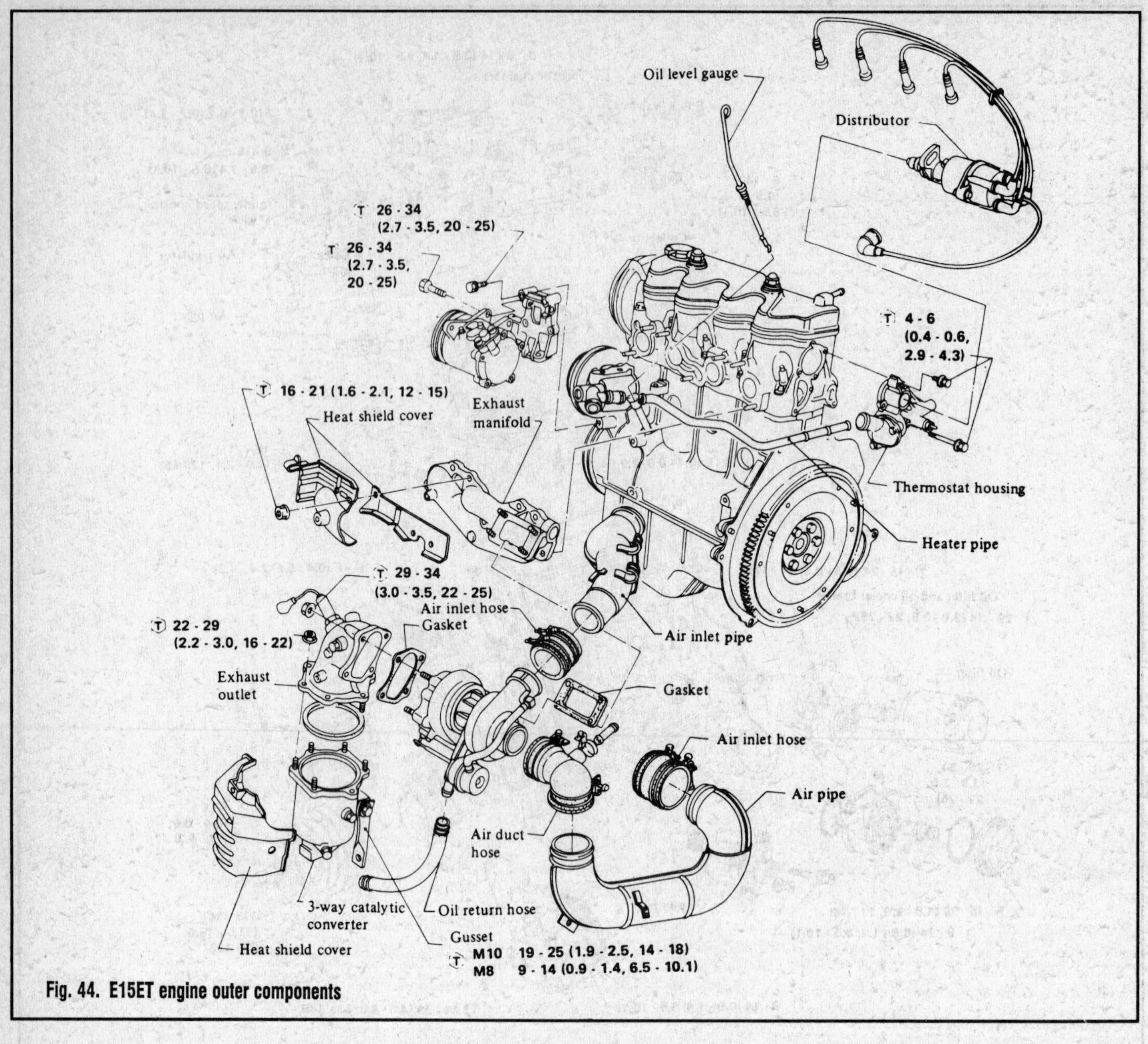

Oil level gauge
Distributor
T 26 - 34
(2.7 - 3.5, 20 - 25)
T 26 - 34
(2.7 - 3.5,
20 - 25)
T 4 - 6
(0.4 - 0.6,
2.9 - 4.3)
T 16 - 21 (1.6 - 2.1, 12 - 15)
Heat shield cover
Exhaust
manifold
Thermostat housing
Heater pipe
T 29 - 34
(3.0 - 3.5, 22 - 25)
Air inlet hose
Gasket
T 22 - 29
(2.2 - 3.0, 16 - 22)
Air inlet pipe
Exhaust
outlet
Gasket
Air inlet hose
Air pipe
Air duct
hose
3-way catalytic
converter
Oil return hose
Gusset
Heat shield cover
T M10 19 - 25 (1.9 - 2.5, 14 - 18)
M8 9 - 14 (0.9 - 1.4, 6.5 - 10.1)

Fig. 44. E15ET engine outer components

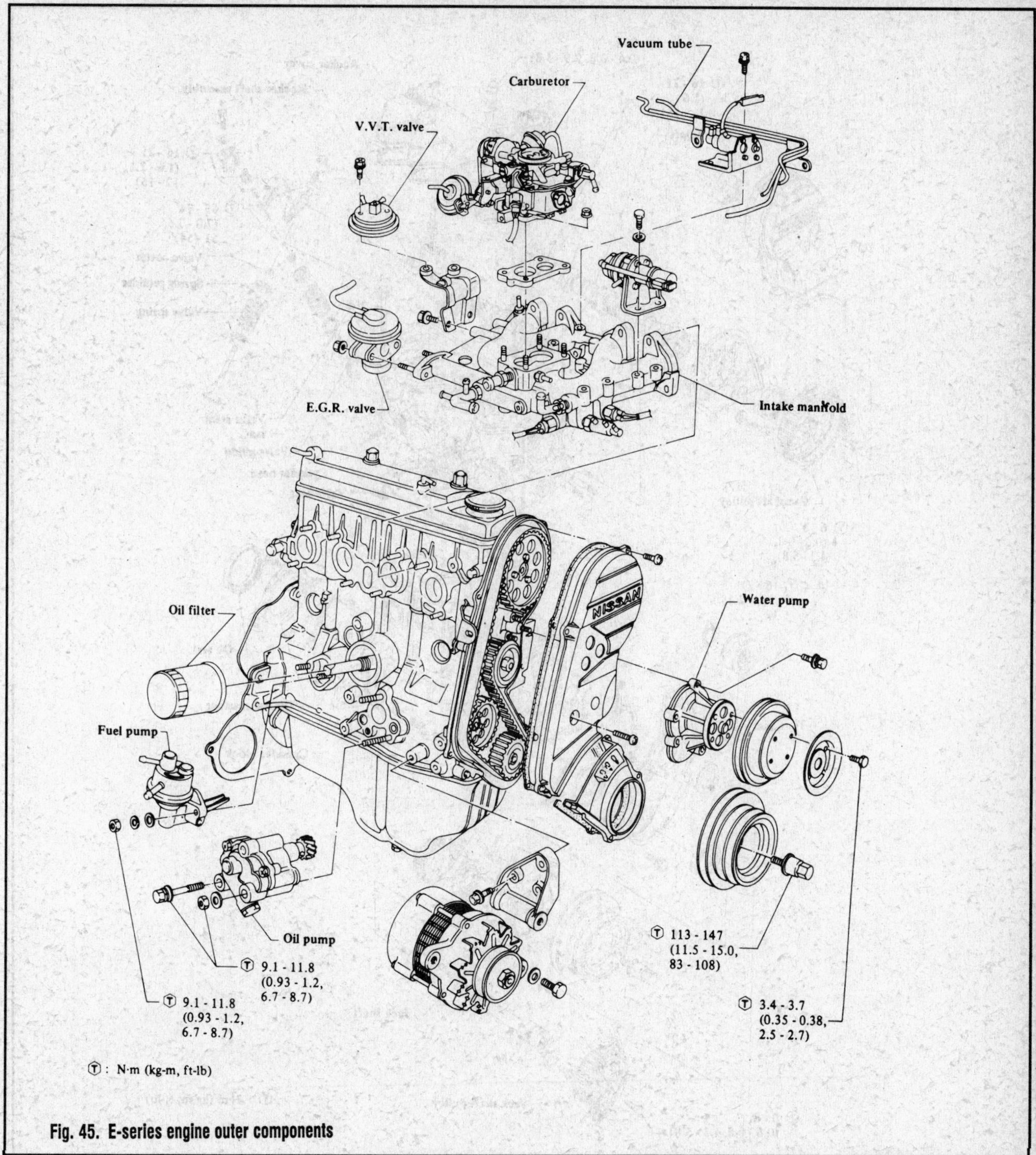
Vacuum tube
Carburetor
V.V.T. valve
E.G.R. valve
Intake manifold
Water pump
Oil filter
Fuel pump
Oil pump
Ⓣ 9.1 - 11.8
(0.93 - 1.2,
6.7 - 8.7)
Ⓣ 9.1 - 11.8
(0.93 - 1.2,
6.7 - 8.7)
Ⓣ 113 - 147
(11.5 - 15.0,
83 - 108)
Ⓣ 3.4 - 3.7
(0.35 - 0.38,
2.5 - 2.7)
Ⓣ : N·m (kg-m, ft-lb)

Fig. 45. E-series engine outer components

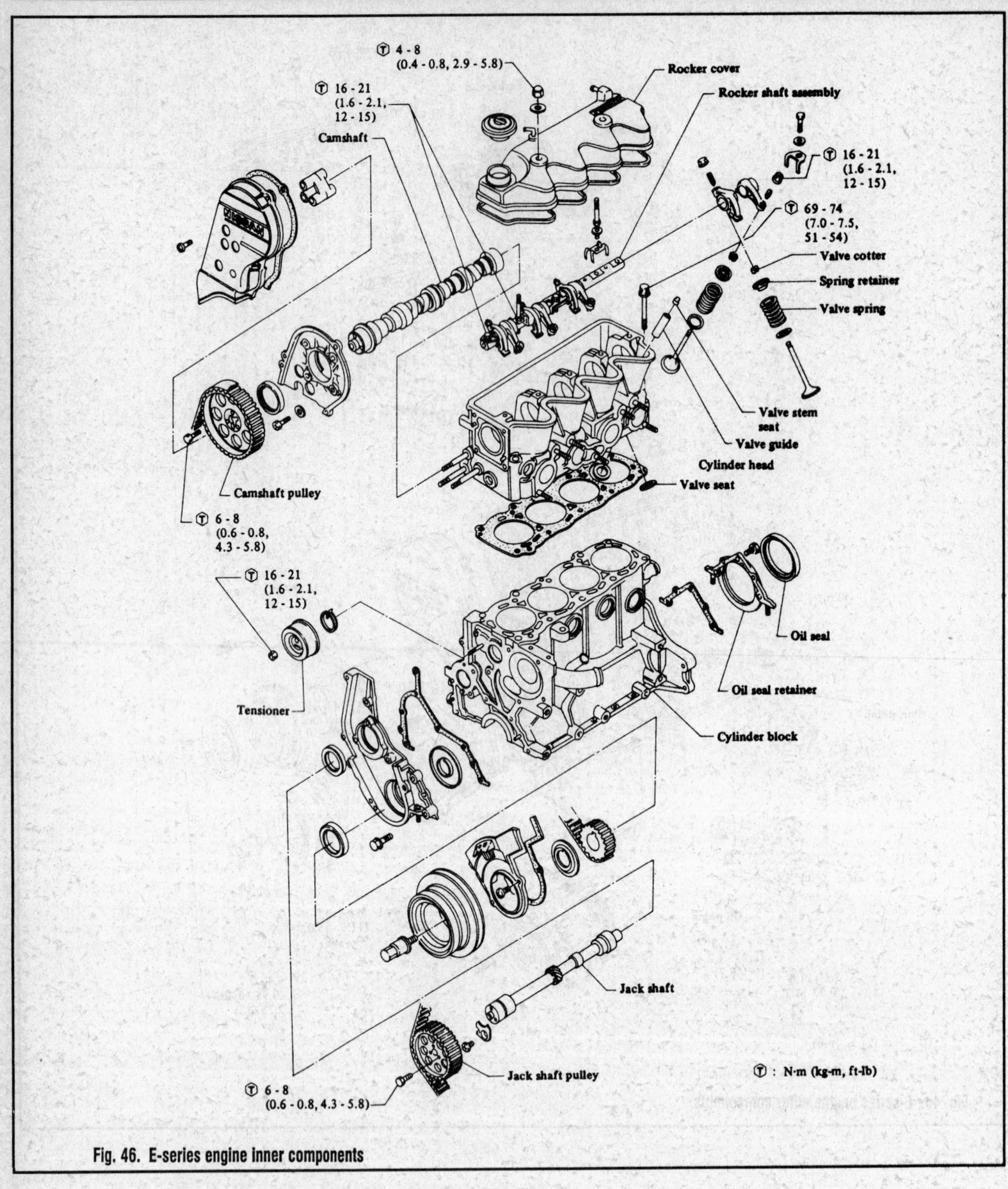
4 - 8
(0.4 - 0.8, 2.9 - 5.8)
Rocker cover
16 - 21
(1.6 - 2.1,
12 - 15)
Rocker shaft assembly
Camshaft
16 - 21
(1.6 - 2.1,
12 - 15)
69 - 74
(7.0 - 7.5,
51 - 54)
Valve cotter
Spring retainer
Valve spring
Valve stem
seat
Valve guide
Cylinder head
Valve seat
Camshaft pulley
6 - 8
(0.6 - 0.8,
4.3 - 5.8)
16 - 21
(1.6 - 2.1,
12 - 15)
Oil seal
Tensioner
Oil seal retainer
Cylinder block
Jack shaft
Jack shaft pulley
: N·m (kg-m, ft-lb)
6 - 8
(0.6 - 0.8, 4.3 - 5.8)
Fig. 46. E-series engine inner components

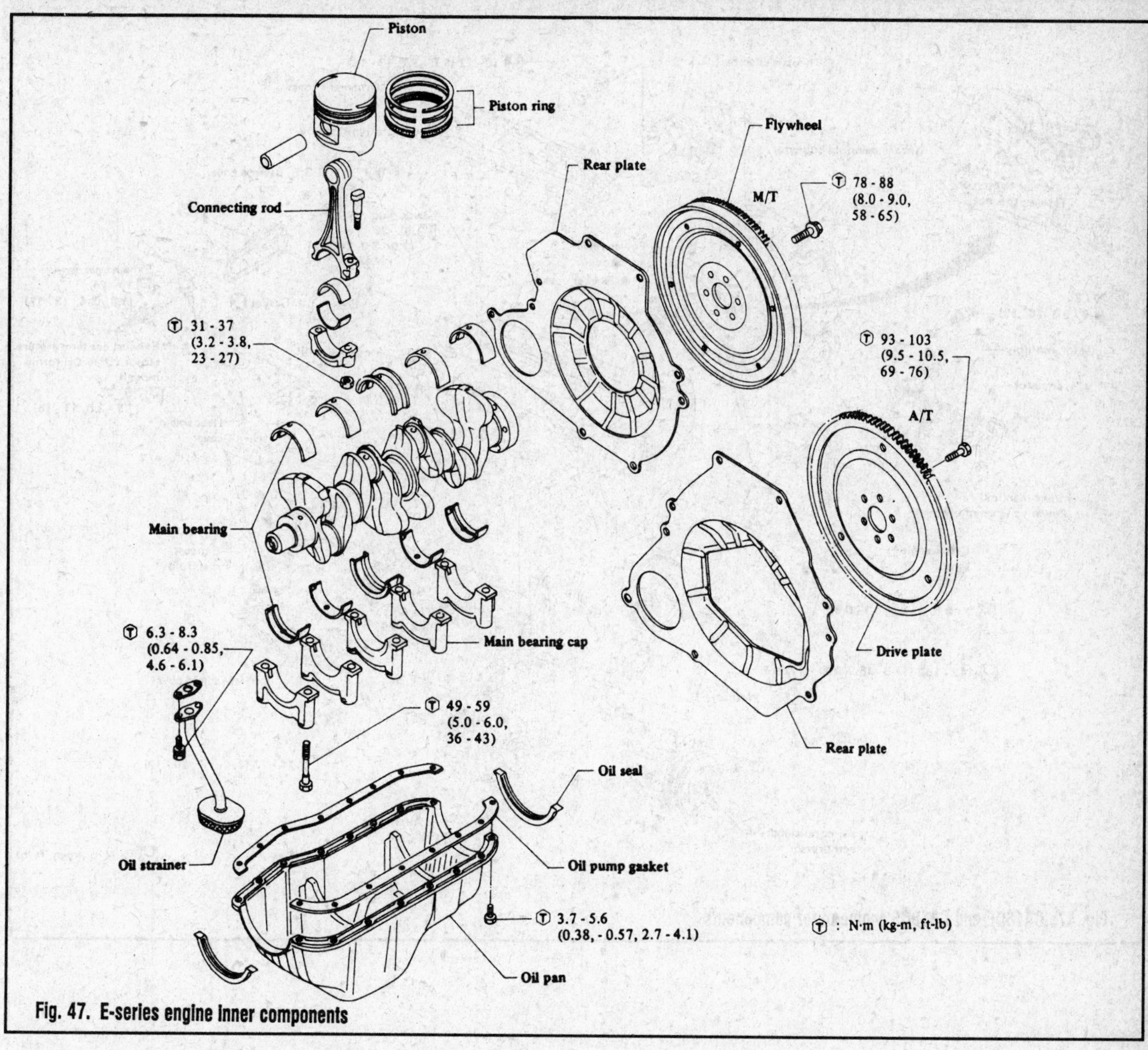
Piston
Piston ring
Flywheel
Rear plate
78 - 88
(8.0 - 9.0,
58 - 65)
M/T
Connecting rod
31 - 37
(3.2 - 3.8,
23 - 27)
93 - 103
(9.5 - 10.5,
69 - 76)
A/T
Main bearing
6.3 - 8.3
(0.64 - 0.85,
4.6 - 6.1)
Main bearing cap
Drive plate
49 - 59
(5.0 - 6.0,
36 - 43)
Rear plate
Oil seal
Oil strainer
Oil pump gasket
3.7 - 5.6
(0.38, - 0.57, 2.7 - 4.1)
: N·m (kg-m, ft-lb)
Oil pan
Fig. 47. E-series engine inner components

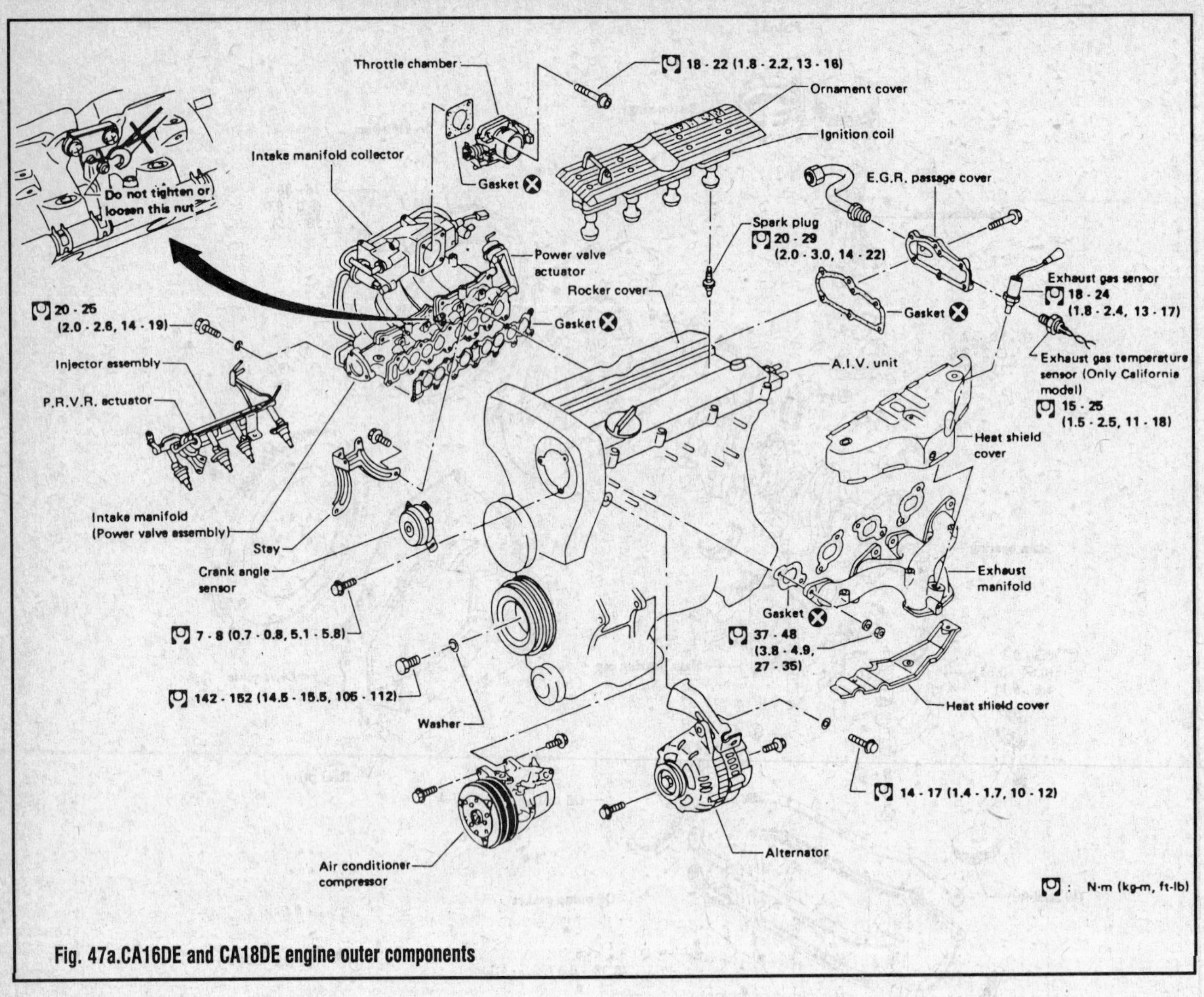
Throttle chamber
18 - 22 (1.8 - 2.2, 13 - 16)
Ornament cover
Ignition coil
Intake manifold collector
Gasket
E.G.R. passage cover
Do not tighten or loosen this nut
Spark plug
20 - 29
(2.0 - 3.0, 14 - 22)
Power valve actuator
Exhaust gas sensor
18 - 24
(1.8 - 2.4, 13 - 17)
Rocker cover
Gasket
Gasket
20 - 25
(2.0 - 2.6, 14 - 19)
Exhaust gas temperature sensor (Only California model)
Injector assembly
A.I.V. unit
15 - 25
(1.5 - 2.5, 11 - 18)
P.R.V.R. actuator
Heat shield cover
Intake manifold
(Power valve assembly)
Stay
Crank angle sensor
Exhaust manifold
Gasket
7 - 8 (0.7 - 0.8, 5.1 - 5.8)
37 - 48
(3.8 - 4.9,
27 - 35)
142 - 152 (14.5 - 15.5, 105 - 112)
Heat shield cover
Washer
14 - 17 (1.4 - 1.7, 10 - 12)
Alternator
Air conditioner compressor
: N·m (kg-m, ft-lb)

Fig. 47a.CA16DE and CA18DE engine outer components

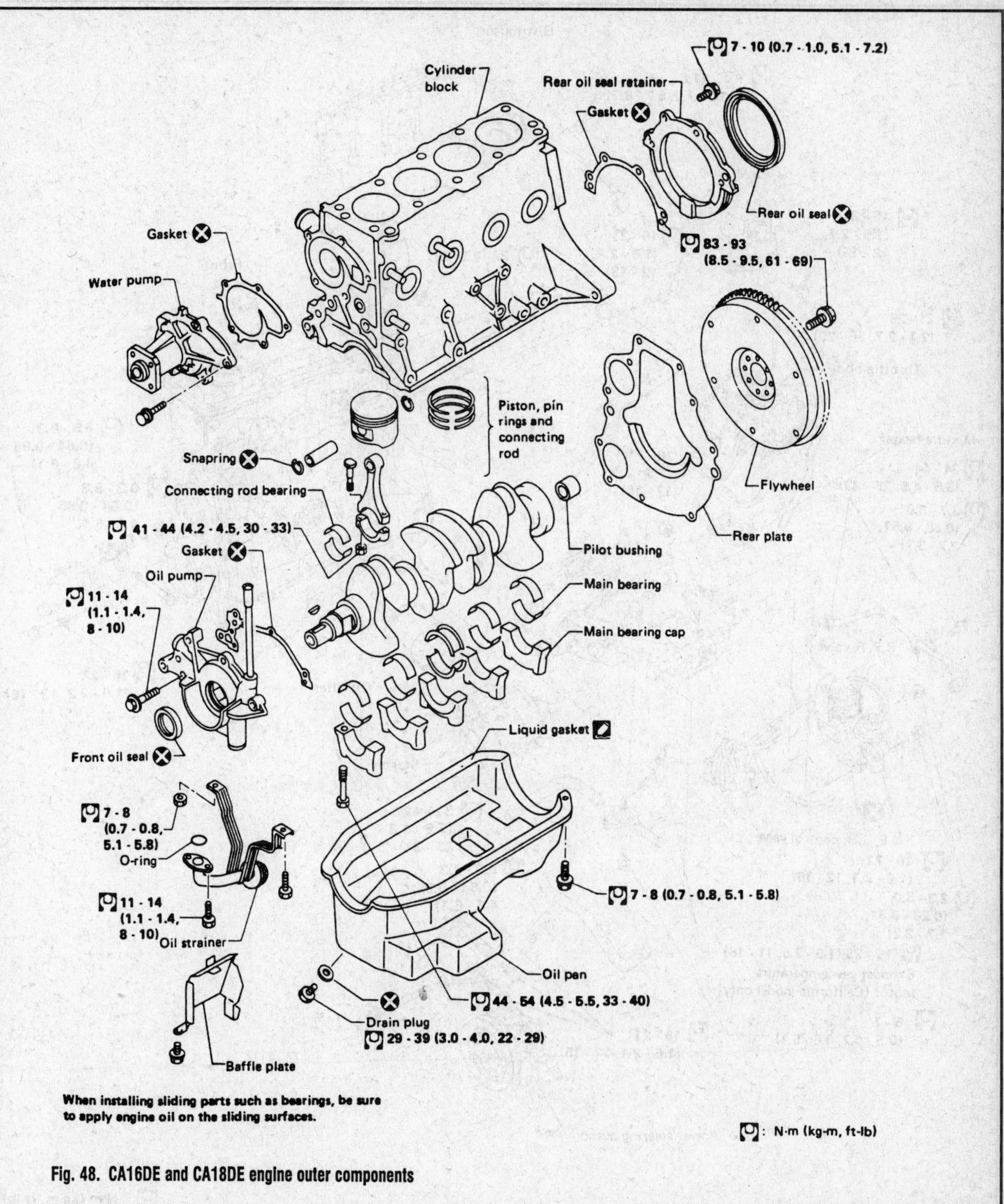

7 - 10 (0.7 - 1.0, 5.1 - 7.2)
Cylinder block
Rear oil seal retainer
Gasket
Rear oil seal
83 - 93 (8.5 - 9.5, 61 - 69)
Gasket
Water pump
Piston, pin rings and connecting rod
Snapring
Connecting rod bearing
Flywheel
41 - 44 (4.2 - 4.5, 30 - 33)
Rear plate
Gasket
Pilot bushing
Oil pump
Main bearing
11 - 14 (1.1 - 1.4, 8 - 10)
Main bearing cap
Front oil seal
Liquid gasket
7 - 8 (0.7 - 0.8, 5.1 - 5.8)
O-ring
7 - 8 (0.7 - 0.8, 5.1 - 5.8)
11 - 14 (1.1 - 1.4, 8 - 10)
Oil strainer
Oil pan
44 - 54 (4.5 - 5.5, 33 - 40)
Drain plug
29 - 39 (3.0 - 4.0, 22 - 29)
Baffle plate
When installing sliding parts such as bearings, be sure to apply engine oil on the sliding surfaces.
: N·m (kg-m, ft-lb)

Fig. 48. CA16DE and CA18DE engine outer components

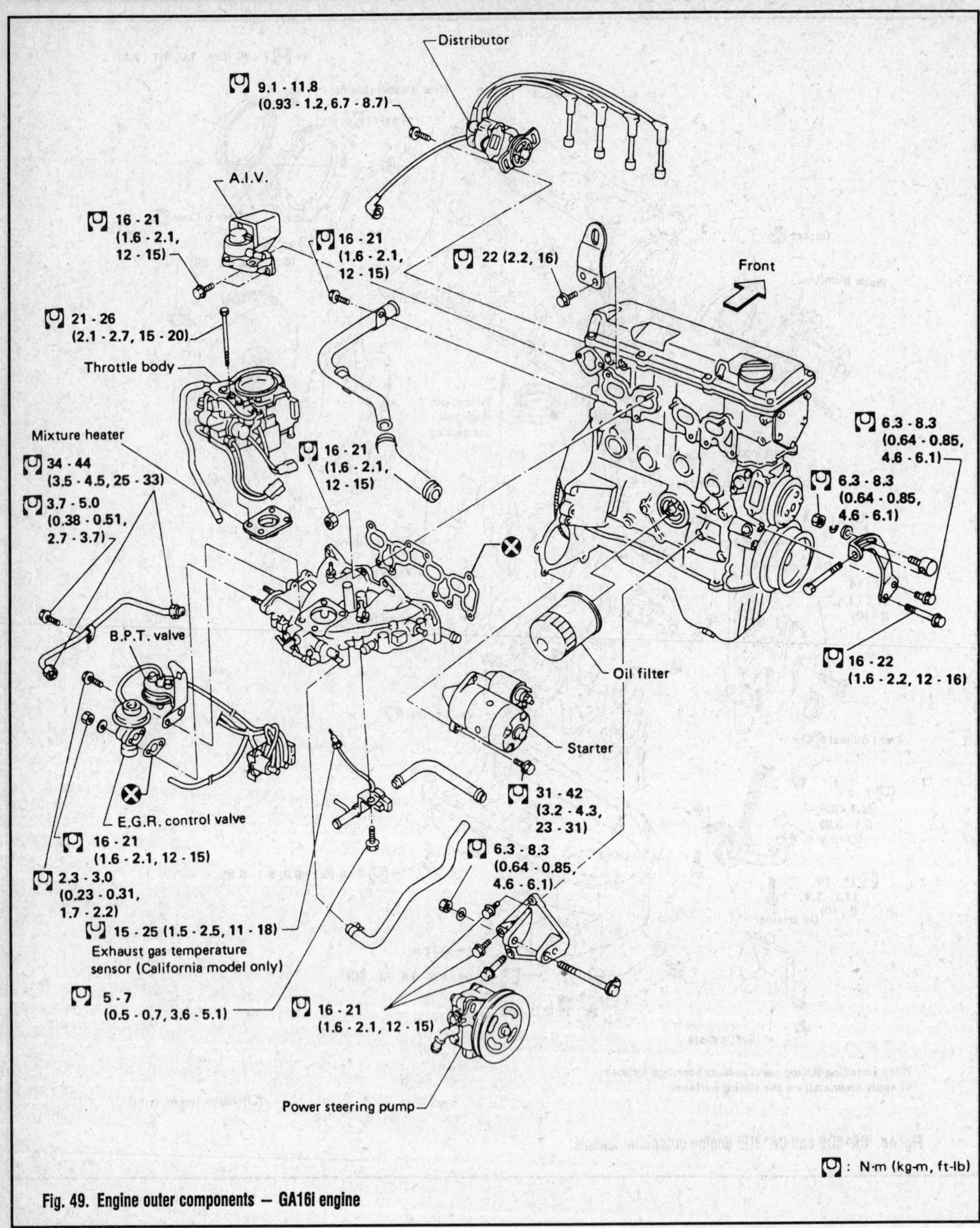
Distributor
9.1 - 11.8
(0.93 - 1.2, 6.7 - 8.7)
A.I.V.
16 - 21
(1.6 - 2.1,
12 - 15)
16 - 21
(1.6 - 2.1,
12 - 15)
22 (2.2, 16)
Front
21 - 26
(2.1 - 2.7, 15 - 20)
Throttle body
Mixture heater
34 - 44
(3.5 - 4.5, 25 - 33)
3.7 - 5.0
(0.38 - 0.51,
2.7 - 3.7)
16 - 21
(1.6 - 2.1,
12 - 15)
6.3 - 8.3
(0.64 - 0.85,
4.6 - 6.1)
6.3 - 8.3
(0.64 - 0.85,
4.6 - 6.1)
B.P.T. valve
Oil filter
16 - 22
(1.6 - 2.2, 12 - 16)
Starter
E.G.R. control valve
31 - 42
(3.2 - 4.3,
23 - 31)
16 - 21
(1.6 - 2.1, 12 - 15)
2.3 - 3.0
(0.23 - 0.31,
1.7 - 2.2)
6.3 - 8.3
(0.64 - 0.85,
4.6 - 6.1)
15 - 25 (1.5 - 2.5, 11 - 18)
Exhaust gas temperature
sensor (California model only)
5 - 7
(0.5 - 0.7, 3.6 - 5.1)
16 - 21
(1.6 - 2.1, 12 - 15)
Power steering pump
: N·m (kg-m, ft-lb)

Fig. 49. Engine outer components — GA16i engine

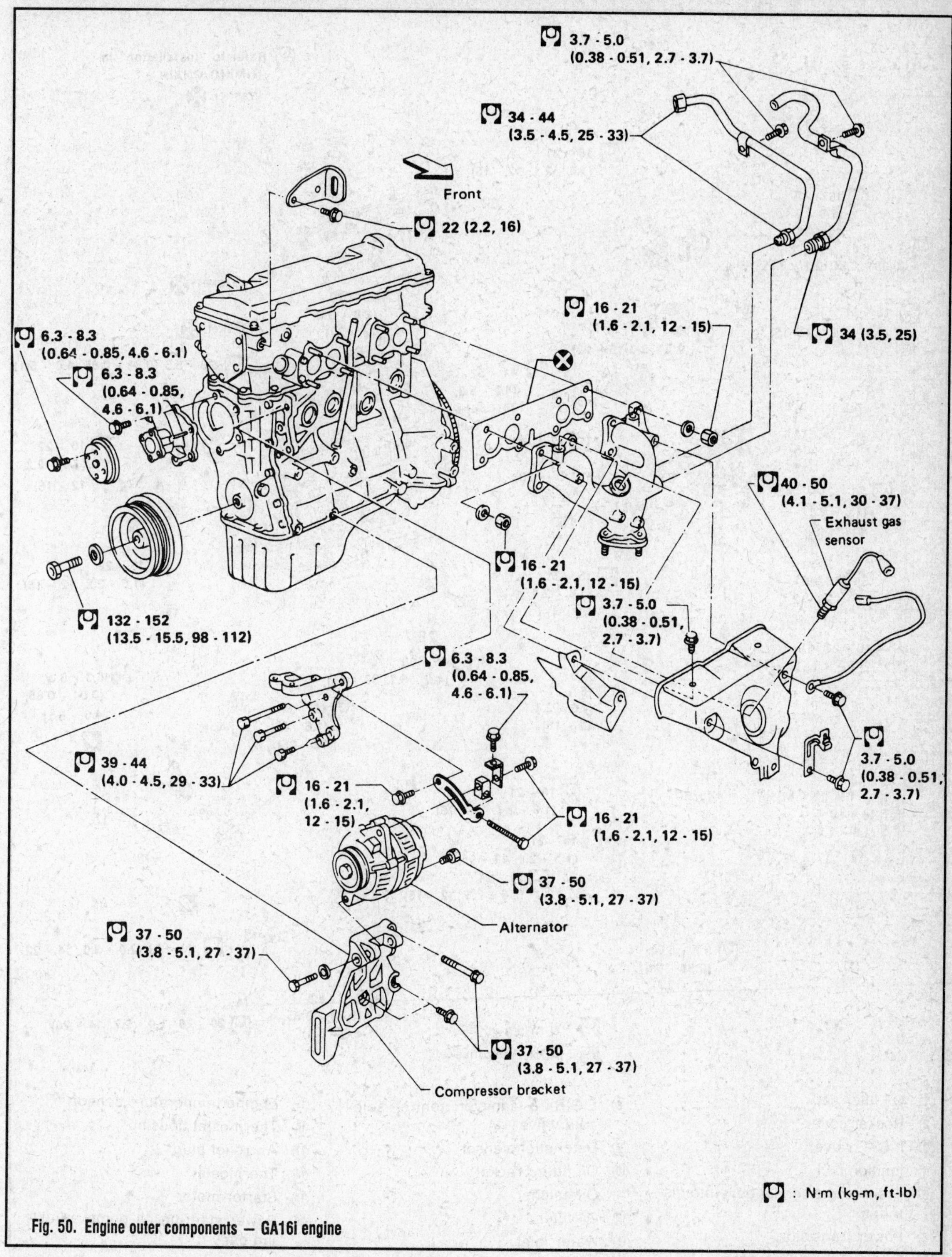
3.7 - 5.0
(0.38 - 0.51, 2.7 - 3.7)
34 - 44
(3.5 - 4.5, 25 - 33)
Front
22 (2.2, 16)
16 - 21
(1.6 - 2.1, 12 - 15)
34 (3.5, 25)
6.3 - 8.3
(0.64 - 0.85, 4.6 - 6.1)
6.3 - 8.3
(0.64 - 0.85,
4.6 - 6.1)
40 - 50
(4.1 - 5.1, 30 - 37)
Exhaust gas
sensor
16 - 21
(1.6 - 2.1, 12 - 15)
3.7 - 5.0
(0.38 - 0.51,
2.7 - 3.7)
132 - 152
(13.5 - 15.5, 98 - 112)
6.3 - 8.3
(0.64 - 0.85,
4.6 - 6.1)
39 - 44
(4.0 - 4.5, 29 - 33)
16 - 21
(1.6 - 2.1,
12 - 15)
16 - 21
(1.6 - 2.1, 12 - 15)
3.7 - 5.0
(0.38 - 0.51,
2.7 - 3.7)
37 - 50
(3.8 - 5.1, 27 - 37)
Alternator
37 - 50
(3.8 - 5.1, 27 - 37)
37 - 50
(3.8 - 5.1, 27 - 37)
Compressor bracket
: N·m (kg-m, ft-lb)

Fig. 50. Engine outer components — GA16i engine

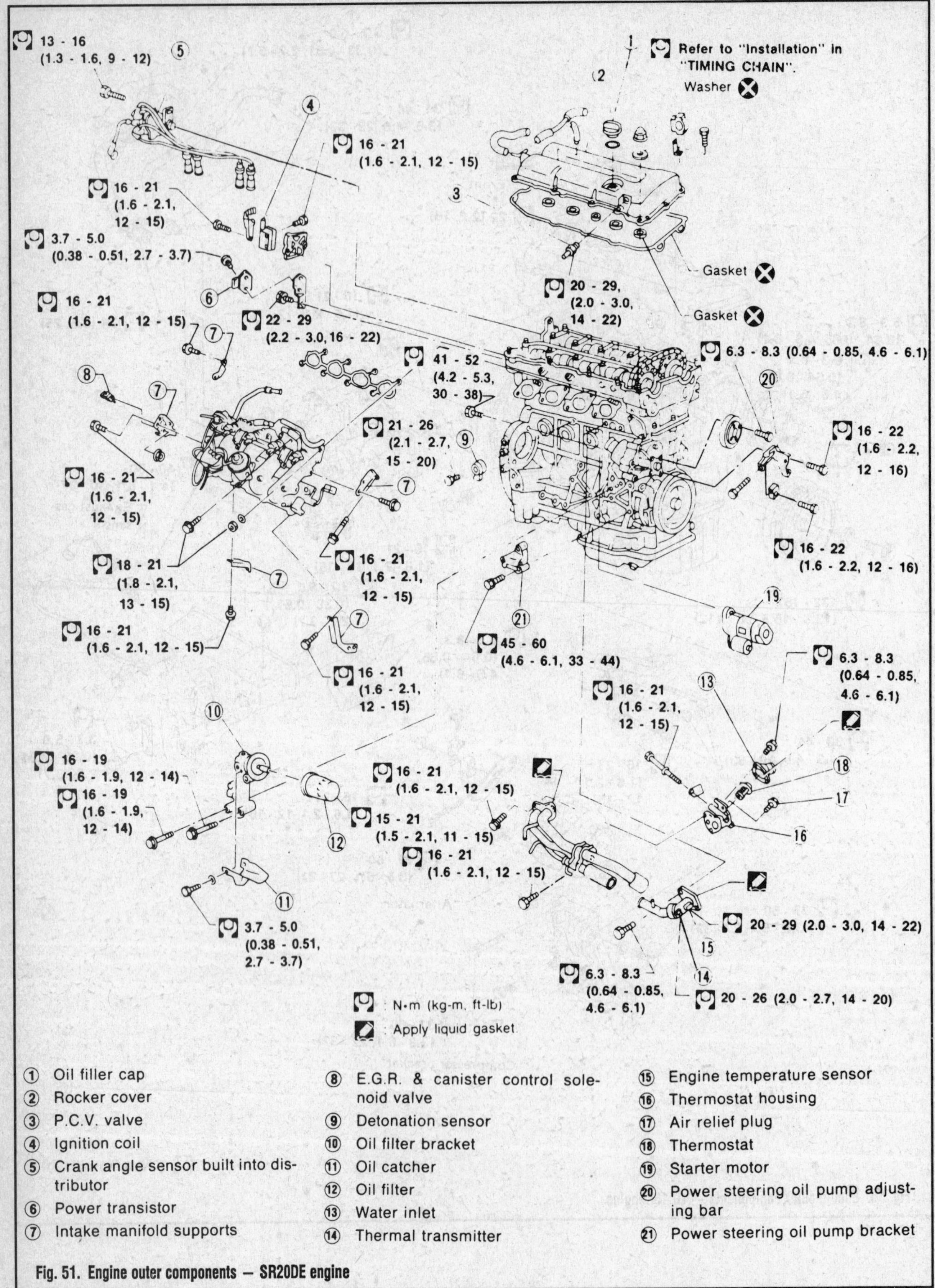

13 - 16 (1.3 - 1.6, 9 - 12)
Refer to "Installation" in "TIMING CHAIN".
Washer
16 - 21 (1.6 - 2.1, 12 - 15)
16 - 21 (1.6 - 2.1, 12 - 15)
3.7 - 5.0 (0.38 - 0.51, 2.7 - 3.7)
Gasket
20 - 29, (2.0 - 3.0, 14 - 22)
Gasket
16 - 21 (1.6 - 2.1, 12 - 15)
22 - 29 (2.2 - 3.0, 16 - 22)
6.3 - 8.3 (0.64 - 0.85, 4.6 - 6.1)
41 - 52 (4.2 - 5.3, 30 - 38)
21 - 26 (2.1 - 2.7, 15 - 20)
16 - 22 (1.6 - 2.2, 12 - 16)
16 - 21 (1.6 - 2.1, 12 - 15)
18 - 21 (1.8 - 2.1, 13 - 15)
16 - 21 (1.6 - 2.1, 12 - 15)
16 - 22 (1.6 - 2.2, 12 - 16)
16 - 21 (1.6 - 2.1, 12 - 15)
45 - 60 (4.6 - 6.1, 33 - 44)
6.3 - 8.3 (0.64 - 0.85, 4.6 - 6.1)
16 - 21 (1.6 - 2.1, 12 - 15)
16 - 21 (1.6 - 2.1, 12 - 15)
16 - 19 (1.6 - 1.9, 12 - 14)
16 - 19 (1.6 - 1.9, 12 - 14)
16 - 21 (1.6 - 2.1, 12 - 15)
15 - 21 (1.5 - 2.1, 11 - 15)
16 - 21 (1.6 - 2.1, 12 - 15)
3.7 - 5.0 (0.38 - 0.51, 2.7 - 3.7)
20 - 29 (2.0 - 3.0, 14 - 22)
6.3 - 8.3 (0.64 - 0.85, 4.6 - 6.1)
20 - 26 (2.0 - 2.7, 14 - 20)
: N•m (kg-m, ft-lb)
: Apply liquid gasket
① Oil filler cap
② Rocker cover
③ P.C.V. valve
④ Ignition coil
⑤ Crank angle sensor built into distributor
⑥ Power transistor
⑦ Intake manifold supports
⑧ E.G.R. & canister control solenoid valve
⑨ Detonation sensor
⑩ Oil filter bracket
⑪ Oil catcher
⑫ Oil filter
⑬ Water inlet
⑭ Thermal transmitter
⑮ Engine temperature sensor
⑯ Thermostat housing
⑰ Air relief plug
⑱ Thermostat
⑲ Starter motor
⑳ Power steering oil pump adjusting bar
㉑ Power steering oil pump bracket

Fig. 51. Engine outer components — SR20DE engine

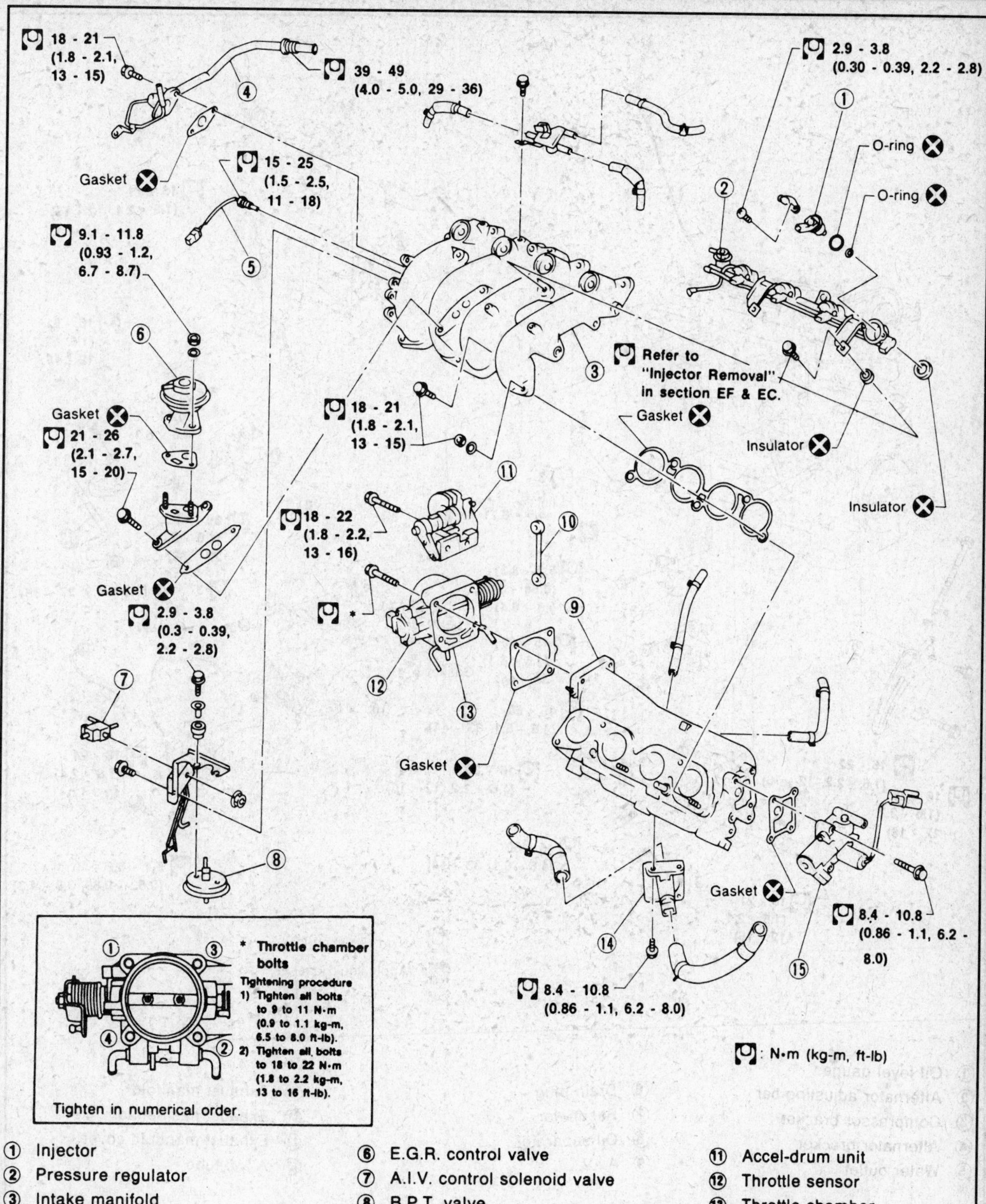
18 - 21
(1.8 - 2.1,
13 - 15)
39 - 49
(4.0 - 5.0, 29 - 36)
2.9 - 3.8
(0.30 - 0.39, 2.2 - 2.8)
O-ring
O-ring
Gasket
15 - 25
(1.5 - 2.5,
11 - 18)
9.1 - 11.8
(0.93 - 1.2,
6.7 - 8.7)
Refer to
"Injector Removal"
in section EF & EC.
Gasket
Gasket
21 - 26
(2.1 - 2.7,
15 - 20)
18 - 21
(1.8 - 2.1,
13 - 15)
Insulator
Insulator
18 - 22
(1.8 - 2.2,
13 - 16)
Gasket
*
2.9 - 3.8
(0.3 - 0.39,
2.2 - 2.8)
Gasket
Gasket
8.4 - 10.8
(0.86 - 1.1, 6.2 - 8.0)
8.4 - 10.8
(0.86 - 1.1, 6.2 - 8.0)
* Throttle chamber bolts
Tightening procedure
1) Tighten all bolts to 9 to 11 N·m (0.9 to 1.1 kg-m, 6.5 to 8.0 ft-lb).
2) Tighten all bolts to 18 to 22 N·m (1.8 to 2.2 kg-m, 13 to 16 ft-lb).
Tighten in numerical order.
: N·m (kg-m, ft-lb)

1. Injector
2. Pressure regulator
3. Intake manifold
4. E.G.R. tube
5. Exhaust gas temperature sensor
6. E.G.R. control valve
7. A.I.V. control solenoid valve
8. B.P.T. valve
9. Intake manifold collector
10. Rod
11. Accel-drum unit
12. Throttle sensor
13. Throttle chamber
14. Air regulator
15. A.A.C. valve

Fig. 52. Engine outer components — SR20DE engine

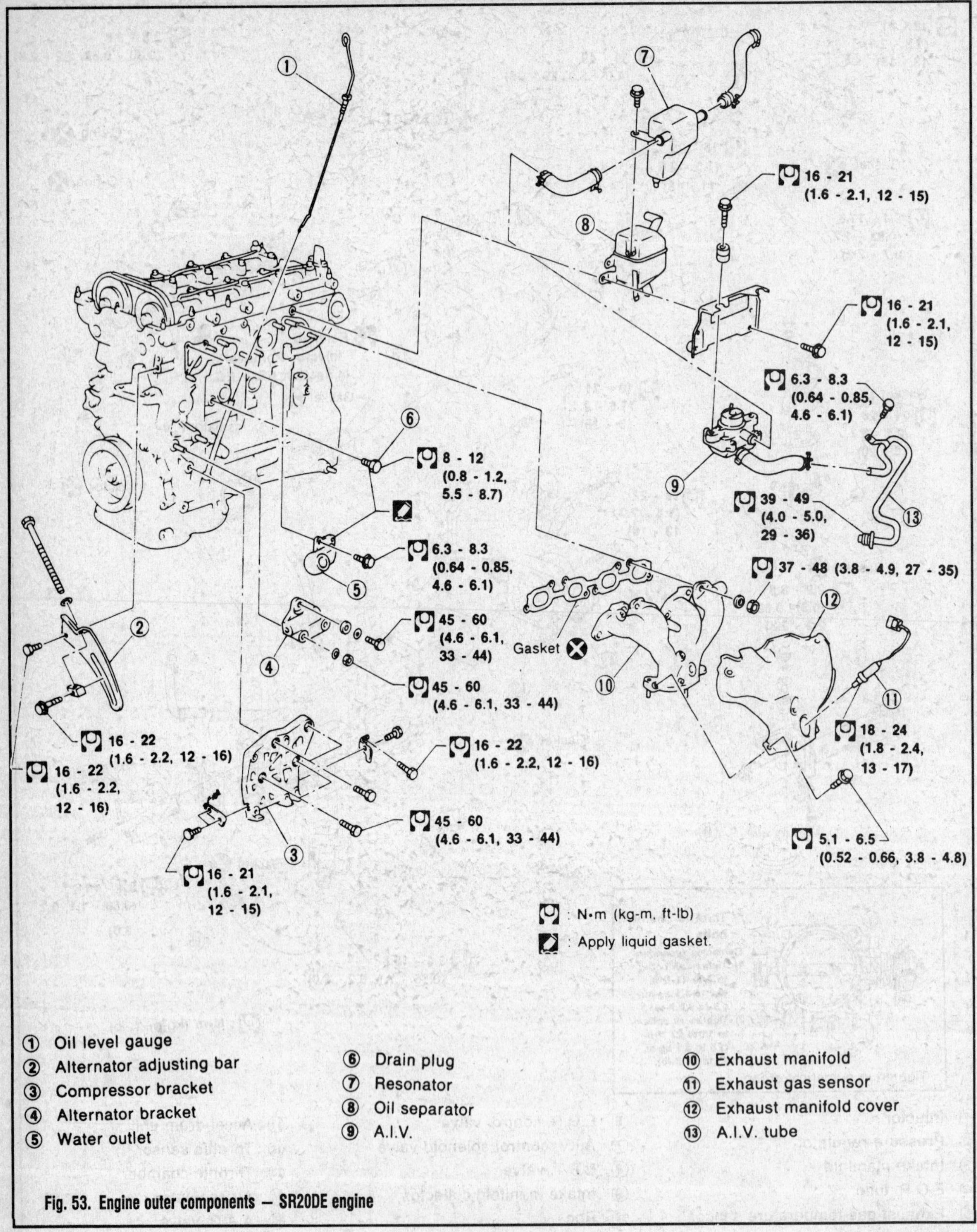
16 - 21
(1.6 - 2.1, 12 - 15)
16 - 21
(1.6 - 2.1,
12 - 15)
6.3 - 8.3
(0.64 - 0.85,
4.6 - 6.1)
8 - 12
(0.8 - 1.2,
5.5 - 8.7)
39 - 49
(4.0 - 5.0,
29 - 36)
6.3 - 8.3
(0.64 - 0.85,
4.6 - 6.1)
37 - 48 (3.8 - 4.9, 27 - 35)
45 - 60
(4.6 - 6.1,
33 - 44)
Gasket
45 - 60
(4.6 - 6.1, 33 - 44)
18 - 24
(1.8 - 2.4,
13 - 17)
16 - 22
(1.6 - 2.2, 12 - 16)
16 - 22
(1.6 - 2.2, 12 - 16)
16 - 22
(1.6 - 2.2,
12 - 16)
45 - 60
(4.6 - 6.1, 33 - 44)
5.1 - 6.5
(0.52 - 0.66, 3.8 - 4.8)
16 - 21
(1.6 - 2.1,
12 - 15)
: N•m (kg-m, ft-lb)
: Apply liquid gasket.
① Oil level gauge
② Alternator adjusting bar
③ Compressor bracket
④ Alternator bracket
⑤ Water outlet
⑥ Drain plug
⑦ Resonator
⑧ Oil separator
⑨ A.I.V.
⑩ Exhaust manifold
⑪ Exhaust gas sensor
⑫ Exhaust manifold cover
⑬ A.I.V. tube

Fig. 53. Engine outer components — SR20DE engine

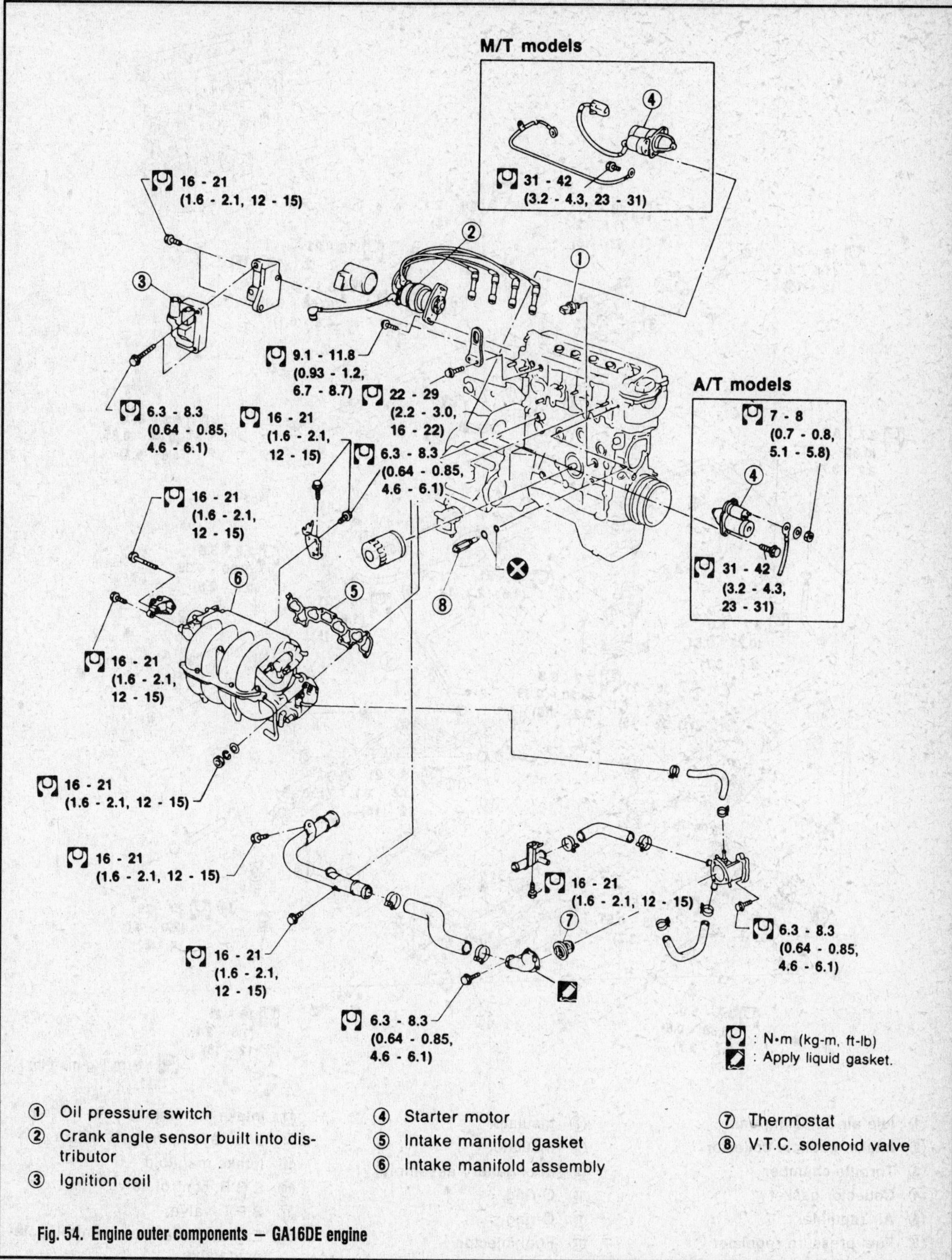
M/T models
31 - 42
(3.2 - 4.3, 23 - 31)
16 - 21
(1.6 - 2.1, 12 - 15)
9.1 - 11.8
(0.93 - 1.2,
6.7 - 8.7)
22 - 29
(2.2 - 3.0,
16 - 22)
6.3 - 8.3
(0.64 - 0.85,
4.6 - 6.1)
16 - 21
(1.6 - 2.1,
12 - 15)
6.3 - 8.3
(0.64 - 0.85,
4.6 - 6.1)
16 - 21
(1.6 - 2.1,
12 - 15)
A/T models
7 - 8
(0.7 - 0.8,
5.1 - 5.8)
31 - 42
(3.2 - 4.3,
23 - 31)
16 - 21
(1.6 - 2.1,
12 - 15)
16 - 21
(1.6 - 2.1, 12 - 15)
16 - 21
(1.6 - 2.1, 12 - 15)
16 - 21
(1.6 - 2.1, 12 - 15)
16 - 21
(1.6 - 2.1,
12 - 15)
6.3 - 8.3
(0.64 - 0.85,
4.6 - 6.1)
6.3 - 8.3
(0.64 - 0.85,
4.6 - 6.1)
: N•m (kg-m, ft-lb)
: Apply liquid gasket.
① Oil pressure switch
② Crank angle sensor built into distributor
③ Ignition coil
④ Starter motor
⑤ Intake manifold gasket
⑥ Intake manifold assembly
⑦ Thermostat
⑧ V.T.C. solenoid valve

Fig. 54. Engine outer components — GA16DE engine

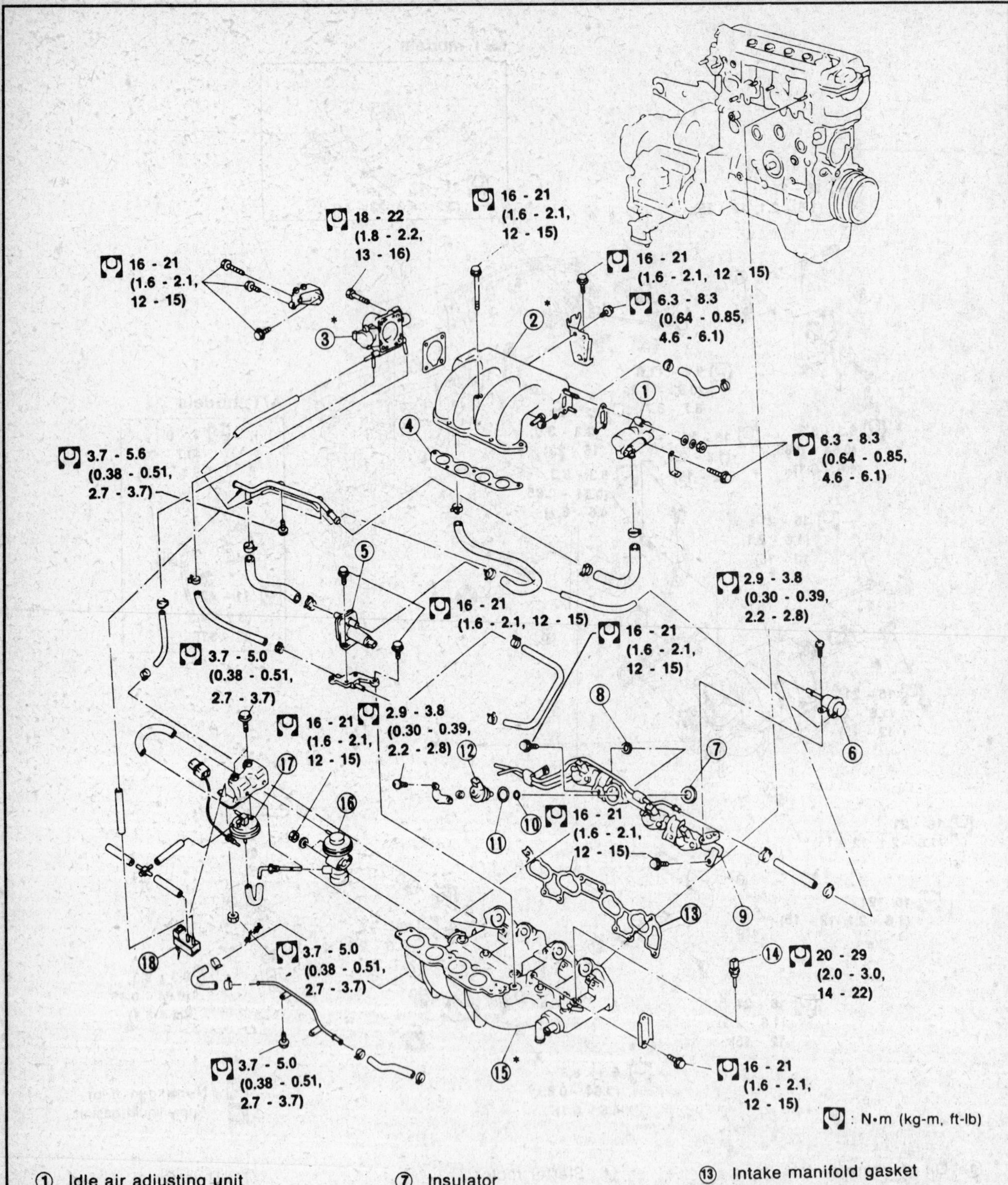
16 - 21
(1.6 - 2.1,
12 - 15)
18 - 22
(1.8 - 2.2,
13 - 16)
16 - 21
(1.6 - 2.1,
12 - 15)
16 - 21
(1.6 - 2.1, 12 - 15)
6.3 - 8.3
(0.64 - 0.85,
4.6 - 6.1)
6.3 - 8.3
(0.64 - 0.85,
4.6 - 6.1)
3.7 - 5.6
(0.38 - 0.51,
2.7 - 3.7)
2.9 - 3.8
(0.30 - 0.39,
2.2 - 2.8)
16 - 21
(1.6 - 2.1, 12 - 15)
16 - 21
(1.6 - 2.1,
12 - 15)
3.7 - 5.0
(0.38 - 0.51,
2.7 - 3.7)
16 - 21
(1.6 - 2.1,
12 - 15)
2.9 - 3.8
(0.30 - 0.39,
2.2 - 2.8)
16 - 21
(1.6 - 2.1,
12 - 15)
20 - 29
(2.0 - 3.0,
14 - 22)
3.7 - 5.0
(0.38 - 0.51,
2.7 - 3.7)
3.7 - 5.0
(0.38 - 0.51,
2.7 - 3.7)
16 - 21
(1.6 - 2.1,
12 - 15)
: N•m (kg-m, ft-lb)

1. Idle air adjusting unit
2. Intake manifold collector
3. Throttle chamber
4. Collector gasket
5. Air regulator
6. Fuel pressure regulator
7. Insulator
8. Insulator
9. Fuel gallery assembly
10. O-ring
11. O-ring
12. Fuel injector
13. Intake manifold gasket
14. Engine temperature sensor
15. Intake manifold
16. E.G.R. control valve
17. B.P.T. valve
18. E.G.R. & canister control solenoid valve

Fig. 55. Engine outer components — GA16DE engine

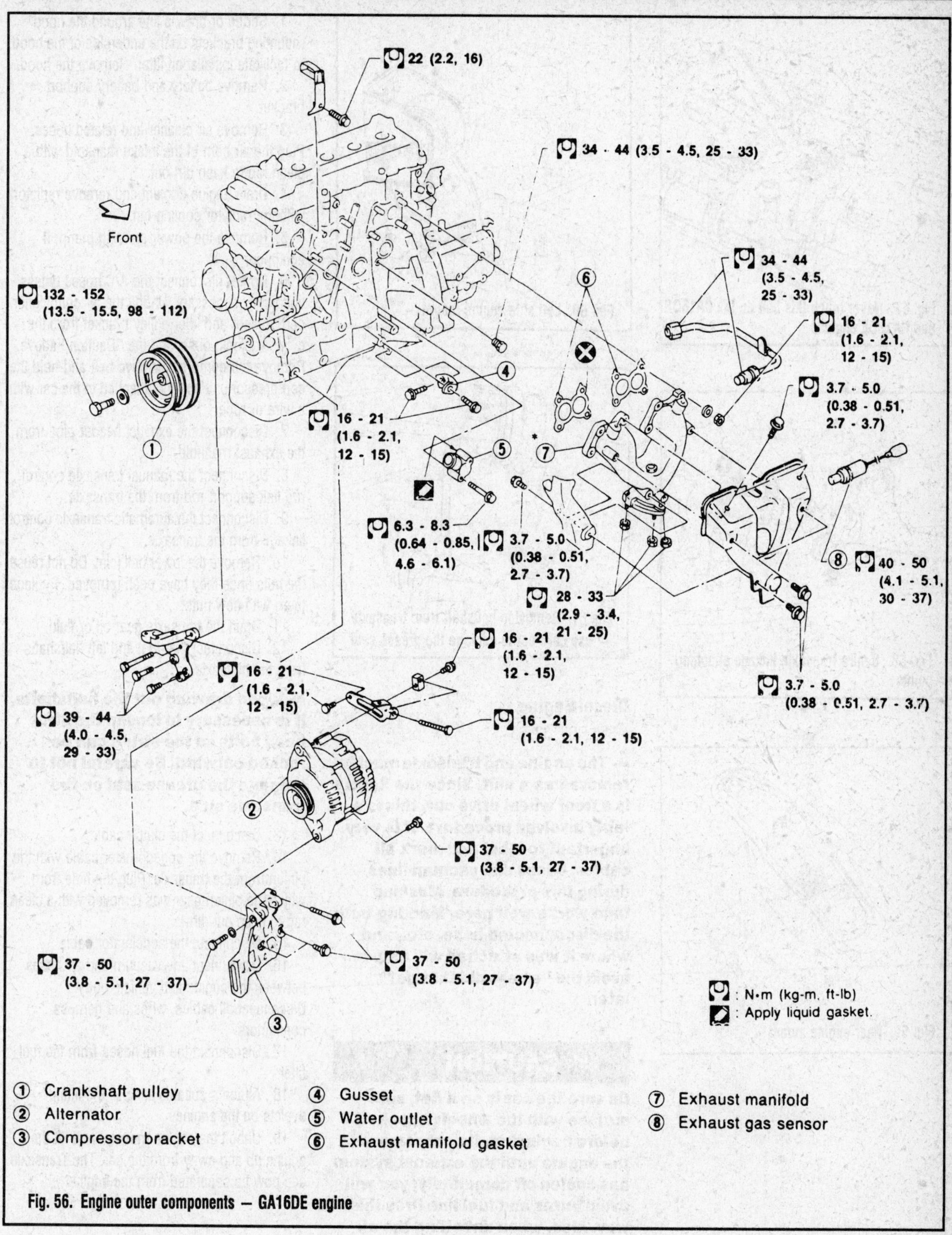
22 (2.2, 16)
34 - 44 (3.5 - 4.5, 25 - 33)
Front
132 - 152
(13.5 - 15.5, 98 - 112)
34 - 44
(3.5 - 4.5,
25 - 33)
16 - 21
(1.6 - 2.1,
12 - 15)
3.7 - 5.0
(0.38 - 0.51,
2.7 - 3.7)
16 - 21
(1.6 - 2.1,
12 - 15)
6.3 - 8.3
(0.64 - 0.85,
4.6 - 6.1)
3.7 - 5.0
(0.38 - 0.51,
2.7 - 3.7)
40 - 50
(4.1 - 5.1,
30 - 37)
28 - 33
(2.9 - 3.4,
21 - 25)
16 - 21
(1.6 - 2.1,
12 - 15)
3.7 - 5.0
(0.38 - 0.51, 2.7 - 3.7)
16 - 21
(1.6 - 2.1,
12 - 15)
16 - 21
(1.6 - 2.1, 12 - 15)
39 - 44
(4.0 - 4.5,
29 - 33)
37 - 50
(3.8 - 5.1, 27 - 37)
37 - 50
(3.8 - 5.1, 27 - 37)
37 - 50
(3.8 - 5.1, 27 - 37)
: N·m (kg-m, ft-lb)
: Apply liquid gasket.
① Crankshaft pulley
② Alternator
③ Compressor bracket
④ Gusset
⑤ Water outlet
⑥ Exhaust manifold gasket
⑦ Exhaust manifold
⑧ Exhaust gas sensor

Fig. 56. Engine outer components — GA16DE engine

Fig. 57. Never touch this bolt on the CA16DE and CA18DE engines

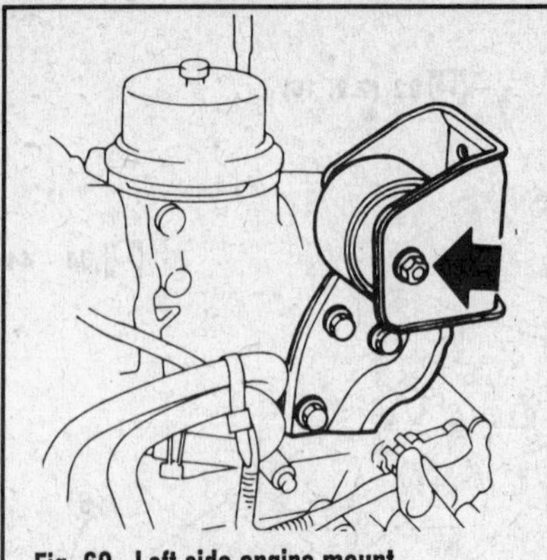
Fig. 60. Left side engine mount

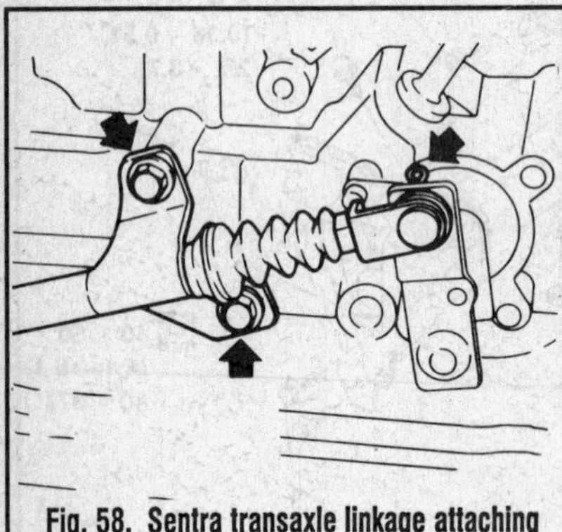
Fig. 58. Sentra transaxle linkage attaching points

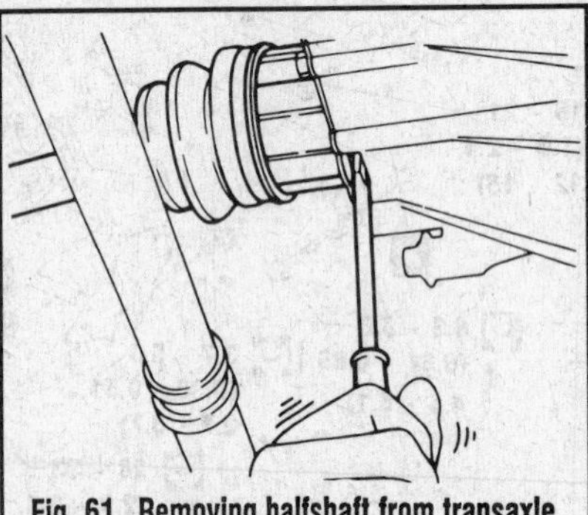
Fig. 61. Removing halfshaft from transaxle — use care not to damage the grease seal

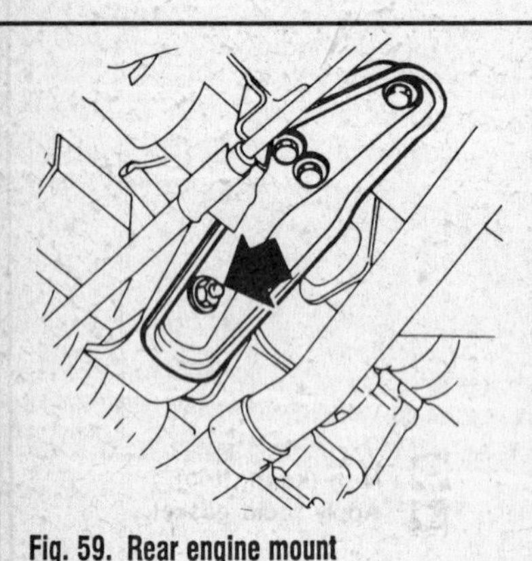
Fig. 59. Rear engine mount

Diesel Engine

SEE FIGS. 62, 63

➡ The engine and transaxle must be removed as a unit. Since the Sentra is a front wheel drive car, this is a fairly involved procedure. It is very important to label and mark all cables, hoses and vacuum lines during this procedure. Masking tape works well here. Marking both the disconnected hose, etc., and where it was attached will help to avoid the "where did that go?" later.

✻✻ CAUTION

Be sure the car is on a flat, solid surface with the wheels chocked before beginning. Do not remove the engine until the exhaust system has cooled off completely; you will avoid burns and fuel line fires this way. Also, when unbolting the air conditioner compressor and idler pulley mount, DO NOT disconnect any air conditioning fittings or hoses.

1. Scribe or draw a line around the hood mounting brackets on the underside of the hood, to facilitate installation later. Remove the hood.
2. Remove battery and battery support bracket.
3. Remove air cleaner and related hoses. Plug the air horn of the intake manifold with a clean rag to keep dirt out.
4. Drain engine coolant and remove radiator with the radiator cooling fan.
5. Remove the power steering pump, if equipped.
6. Do not disconnect the A/C hoses unless absolutely necessary. Unbolt the air conditioner compressor and idler pulley bracket from the cylinder block, observing the "Caution" above. Remove the compressor drive belt and hold the compressor unit upright, attached to the car with a wire or rope.
7. Disconnect the exhaust header pipe from the exhaust manifold.
8. Disconnect the manual transaxle control rod link support rod from the transaxle.
9. Disconnect the automatic transaxle control linkage from the transaxle.
10. Remove the lower ball joint. Do not reuse the nuts once they have been removed. Replace them with new nuts.
11. Drain the transaxle gear oil or fluid.
12. Disconnect the right and left halfshafts from the transaxle.

➡ When drawing out the halfshafts, it is necessary to loosen the strut head bolts so the struts can be rocked outward. Be careful not to damage the grease seal on the transaxle side.

13. Disconnect the clutch cable.
14. Remove the speedometer cable with the pinion from the transaxle. Plug the hole from which the pinion gear was removed with a clean rag to keep out dirt.
15. Disconnect the accelerator cable.
16. Disconnect any vacuum and air hoses between the engine and vehicle body. Disconnect all cables, wires and harness connectors.
17. Disconnect the fuel hoses from the fuel filter.
18. Attach a suitable sling to the lifting eyelets on the engine.
19. Unbolt the engine mounts, and lift the engine up and away from the car. The Transaxle can now be separated from the engine.

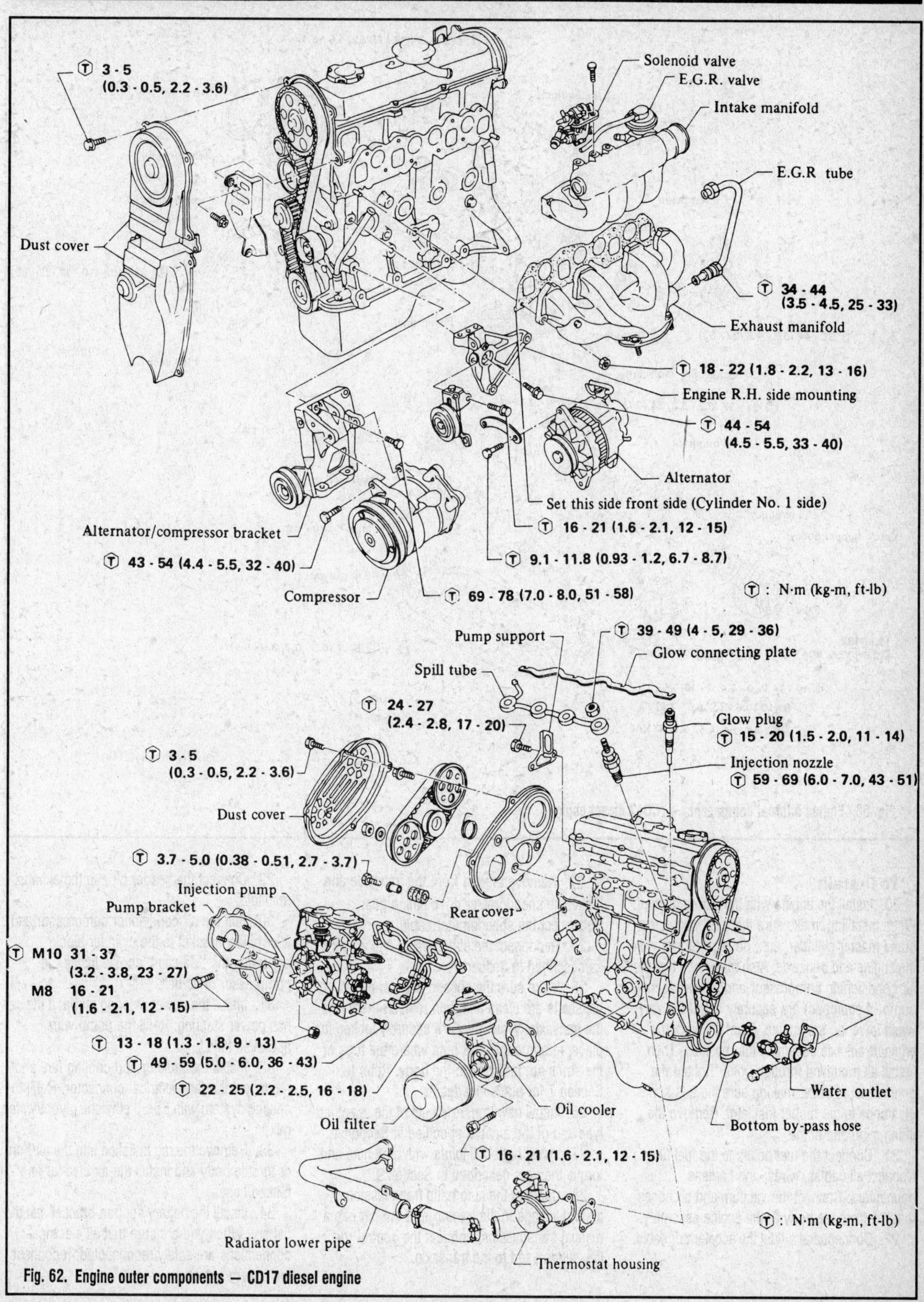

Ⓣ 3 - 5
(0.3 - 0.5, 2.2 - 3.6)
Solenoid valve
E.G.R. valve
Intake manifold
E.G.R tube
Dust cover
Ⓣ 34 - 44
(3.5 - 4.5, 25 - 33)
Exhaust manifold
Ⓣ 18 - 22 (1.8 - 2.2, 13 - 16)
Engine R.H. side mounting
Ⓣ 44 - 54
(4.5 - 5.5, 33 - 40)
Alternator
Set this side front side (Cylinder No. 1 side)
Ⓣ 16 - 21 (1.6 - 2.1, 12 - 15)
Alternator/compressor bracket
Ⓣ 43 - 54 (4.4 - 5.5, 32 - 40)
Ⓣ 9.1 - 11.8 (0.93 - 1.2, 6.7 - 8.7)
Compressor
Ⓣ 69 - 78 (7.0 - 8.0, 51 - 58)
Ⓣ : N·m (kg-m, ft-lb)
Pump support
Ⓣ 39 - 49 (4 - 5, 29 - 36)
Glow connecting plate
Spill tube
Ⓣ 24 - 27
(2.4 - 2.8, 17 - 20)
Glow plug
Ⓣ 15 - 20 (1.5 - 2.0, 11 - 14)
Ⓣ 3 - 5
(0.3 - 0.5, 2.2 - 3.6)
Injection nozzle
Ⓣ 59 - 69 (6.0 - 7.0, 43 - 51)
Dust cover
Ⓣ 3.7 - 5.0 (0.38 - 0.51, 2.7 - 3.7)
Injection pump
Pump bracket
Rear cover
Ⓣ M10 31 - 37
(3.2 - 3.8, 23 - 27)
M8 16 - 21
(1.6 - 2.1, 12 - 15)
Ⓣ 13 - 18 (1.3 - 1.8, 9 - 13)
Ⓣ 49 - 59 (5.0 - 6.0, 36 - 43)
Ⓣ 22 - 25 (2.2 - 2.5, 16 - 18)
Water outlet
Oil cooler
Oil filter
Bottom by-pass hose
Ⓣ 16 - 21 (1.6 - 2.1, 12 - 15)
Ⓣ : N·m (kg-m, ft-lb)
Radiator lower pipe
Thermostat housing

Fig. 62. Engine outer components — CD17 diesel engine

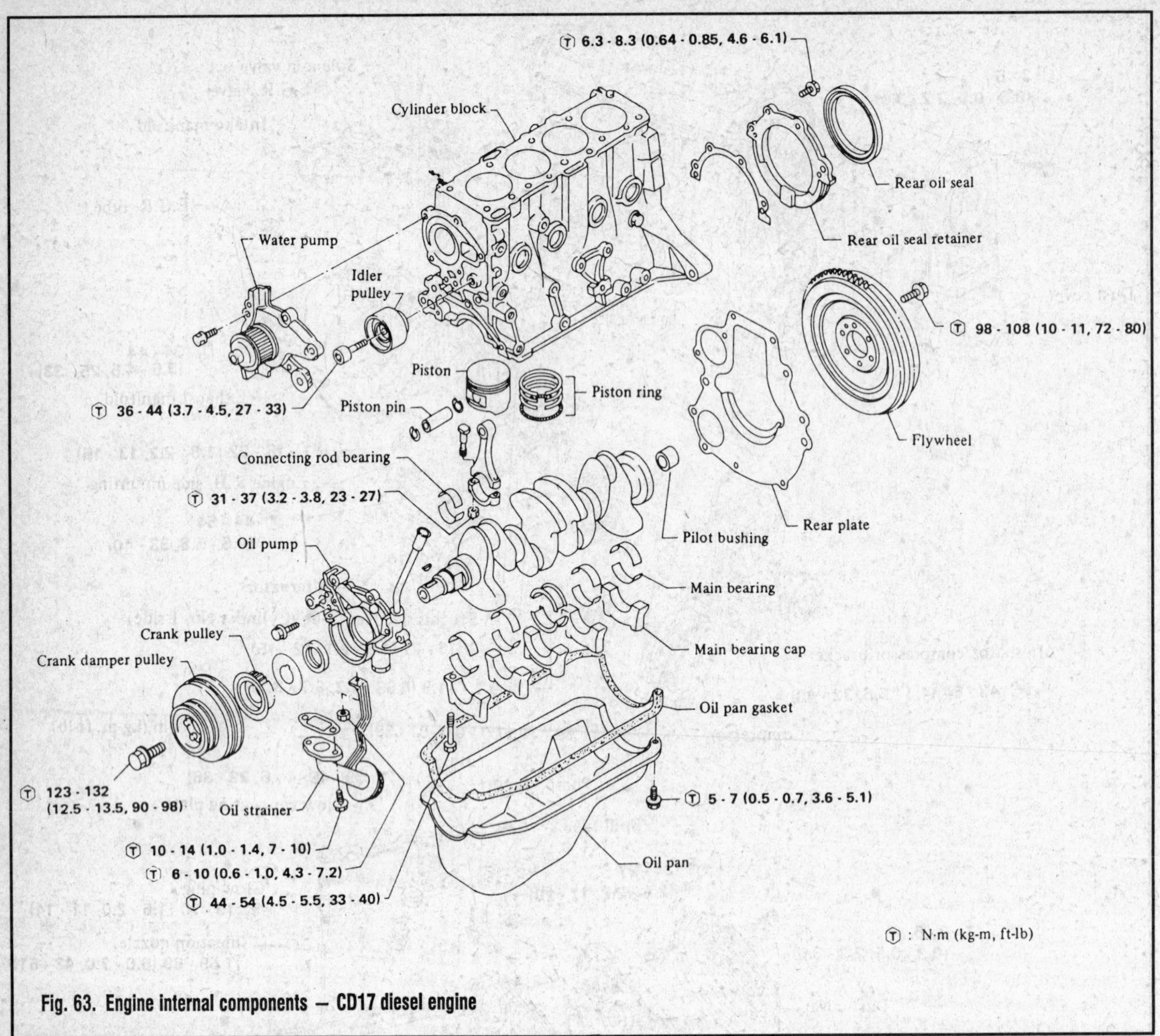
6.3 - 8.3 (0.64 - 0.85, 4.6 - 6.1)
Cylinder block
Rear oil seal
Rear oil seal retainer
Water pump
Idler pulley
98 - 108 (10 - 11, 72 - 80)
Piston
Piston ring
36 - 44 (3.7 - 4.5, 27 - 33)
Piston pin
Flywheel
Connecting rod bearing
31 - 37 (3.2 - 3.8, 23 - 27)
Rear plate
Pilot bushing
Oil pump
Main bearing
Crank pulley
Crank damper pulley
Main bearing cap
Oil pan gasket
123 - 132
(12.5 - 13.5, 90 - 98)
Oil strainer
5 - 7 (0.5 - 0.7, 3.6 - 5.1)
10 - 14 (1.0 - 1.4, 7 - 10)
6 - 10 (0.6 - 1.0, 4.3 - 7.2)
Oil pan
44 - 54 (4.5 - 5.5, 33 - 40)
: N·m (kg-m, ft-lb)

Fig. 63. Engine internal components — CD17 diesel engine

To install:

20. Install the engine with transaxle attached. When installing, make sure that the brake lines, brake master cylinder, etc., do not interfere with the engine and transaxle. Also make sure that the air conditioning compressor and power steering pump (if equipped) are securely out of the way when lowering the engine. Carefully work the engine/transaxle assembly into position. Then, install all mounting through bolts. Tighten the engine mount bolts, making sure there is some clearance in the rubber insulator. Remove the lifting sling and crane.

21. Connect the fuel hoses to the fuel filter. Connect all cables, wires, and harness connectors. Connect the vacuum and air hoses that run from the body to the engine assembly.

22. Connect and adjust the accelerator cable.

23. Remove the rag from the transaxle and install the speedometer drive pinion gear. Reconnect the speedometer cable.

24. Reconnect the clutch cable and adjust it as described in Section 7.

25. Make sure the splined ends of the halfshafts are clean and then reinsert them into the transaxle. When they are securely locked in place, retorque the strut nuts where the tops of the struts are fastened to the body. Refer to Section 7 for additional details.

26. Install new transaxle fluid of the specified type and of the amount specified in Section 1.

27. Install both ball joints with new nuts and torque them as described in Section 9.

28. Connect the automatic transmission control linkage to the transaxle. If the car has a manual transmission, connect the control rod link support rod to the transaxle.

29. Connect the header pipe to the exhaust manifold.

30. Bolt the air conditioner compressor and idler pulley bracket to the cylinder block, observing the "Caution" above. Install the compressor drive belt.

31. Install the power steering pump, if the car has power steering. Refill the pump with approved fluid.

32. Install the radiator and cooling fan, and reconnect the fan electrical connector. Refill the cooling system with 50/50 ethylene glycol/water mix.

33. Remove the rag installed into the air horn or throttle body and install the air cleaner and related hoses.

34. Install the battery support bracket and the battery. When you are sure that all electrical connections are safely reconnected, reconnect the battery cables.

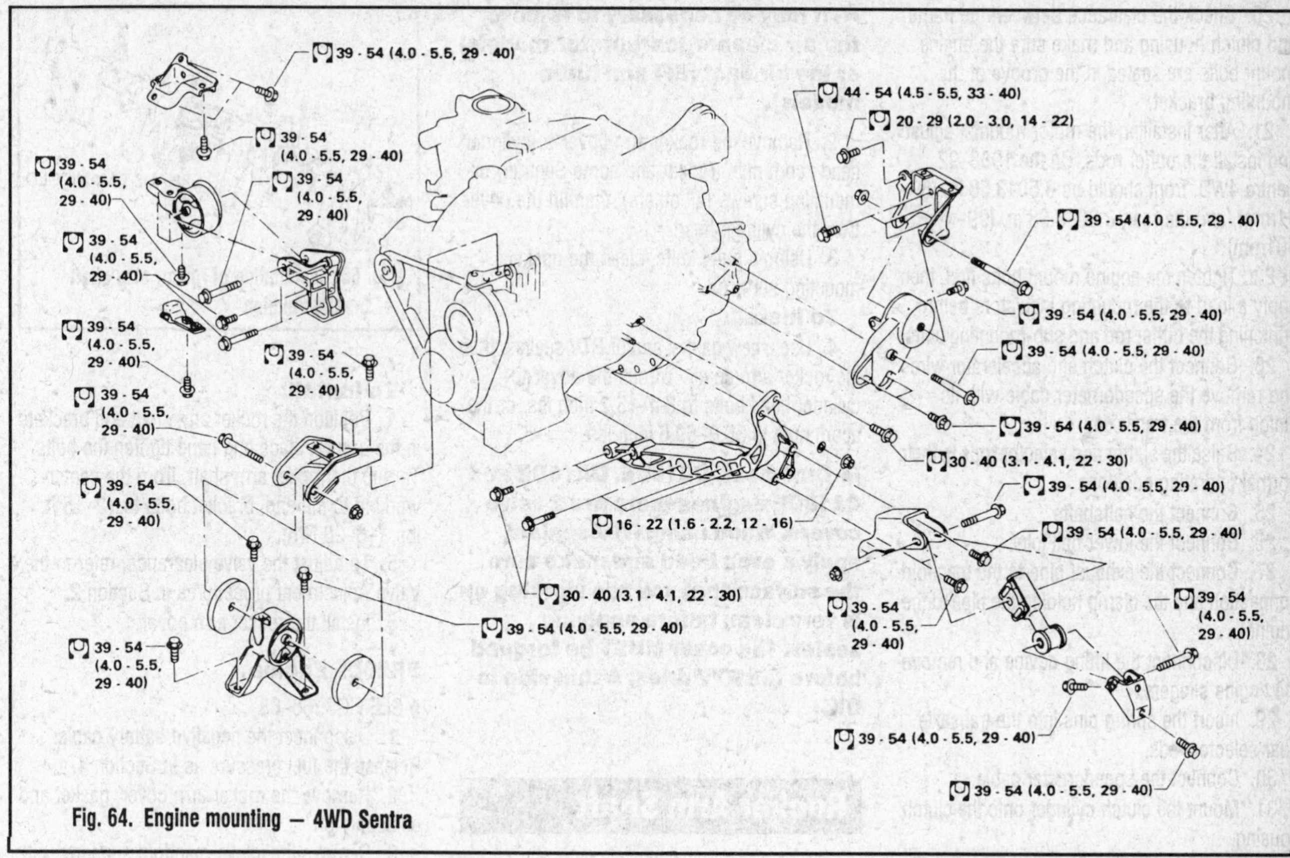
39 - 54 (4.0 - 5.5, 29 - 40)
44 - 54 (4.5 - 5.5, 33 - 40)
20 - 29 (2.0 - 3.0, 14 - 22)
30 - 40 (3.1 - 4.1, 22 - 30)
16 - 22 (1.6 - 2.2, 12 - 16)
Fig. 64. Engine mounting — 4WD Sentra

35. Install the hood with bolts loose. Align it with the marks made earlier and then torque the bolts to 15 ft. lbs. (20 Nm).

36. Bleed the fuel system as outlined in Section 2.

37. Start the engine, check for leaks, bleed the cooling system, and recheck and if necessary refill all fluid reservoirs.

4WD Sentra

It is recommended that the engine and transaxle be removed as a unit. If need be, the units may be separated after removal.

➡ **If equipped with 4WD, remove the engine, transaxle and transfer case together.**

1. Mark the hood hinge relationship and remove the hood.

2. Release the fuel system pressure, disconnect the negative battery cable and raise and support the vehicle safely.

3. Drain the cooling system and the oil pan.

4. Remove the air cleaner and disconnect the throttle cable.

5. Disconnect or remove the following:

- Drive belts
- Ignition wire from the coil to the distributor
- Ignition coil ground wire and the engine ground cable
- Block connector from the distributor
- Fusible links
- Engine harness connectors
- Fuel and fuel return hoses
- Upper and lower radiator hoses
- Heater inlet and outlet hoses
- Engine vacuum hoses
- Carbon canister hoses and the air pump air cleaner hose
- Any interfering engine accessory: power steering pump, air conditioning compressor or alternator
- Driveshaft from transfer case. Make sure to matchmark flanges

6. Remove the air pump air cleaner.

7. Remove the carbon canister.

8. Remove the auxiliary fan, washer tank, grille and radiator (with fan assembly).

9. Remove the clutch cylinder from the clutch housing for manual transaxles.

10. Remove both buffer rods without altering the length of the rods. Disconnect the speedometer cable.

11. Remove the spring pins from the transaxle gear selector rods.

12. Install engine slingers to the block and connect a suitable lifting device to the slingers. Do not tension the lifting device at this point.

13. Disconnect the exhaust pipe at both the manifold connection and the clamp holding the pipe to the engine.

14. Remove the lower ball joint.

15. Drain the transaxle gear oil.

16. Disconnect the right and left side halfshafts from their side flanges and remove the bolt holding the radius link support.

➡ **When drawing out the halfshafts, it is necessary to loosen the strut head bolts.**

17. Lower the shifter and selector rods and remove the bolts from the motor mount brackets. Remove the nuts holding the front and rear motor mounts to the frame. On the Sentra, Stanza and Pulsar, disconnect the clutch and accelerator wires and remove the speedometer cable with its pinion from the transaxle.

18. Lift the engine/transaxle assembly up and away from the vehicle.

To Install:

19. Lower the engine transaxle assembly into the vehicle. When lowering the engine onto the frame, make sure to keep it as level as possible.

20. Check the clearance between the frame and clutch housing and make sure the engine mount bolts are seated in the groove of the mounting bracket.

21. After installing the motor mounts, adjust and install the buffer rods. On the 1988–92 Sentra 4WD: front should be 3.50–3.58 in. (89–91mm), and the rear, 3.90–3.98 in. (99–101mm).

22. Tighten the engine mount bolts first, then apply a load to the mounting insulators before tightening the buffer rod and sub-mounting bolts.

23. Connect the clutch and accelerator wires and remove the speedometer cable with its pinion from the transaxle.

24. Raise the shifter and selector rods to their normal operating positions.

25. Connect the halfshafts.

26. Connect the lower ball joint.

27. Connect the exhaust pipe to the manifold connection and the clamp holding the pipe to the engine.

28. Disconnect the lifting device and remove the engine slingers.

29. Insert the spring pins into the transaxle gear selector rods.

30. Connect the speedometer cable.

31. Mount the clutch cylinder onto the clutch housing.

32. Install the auxiliary fan, washer tank, grille and radiator (with fan assembly).

33. Install the carbon canister.

34. Install the air pump air cleaner.

35. Install or connect all hoses, belts, harnesses, connectors and components that were necessary to remove the engine.

36. Connect the throttle cable and install the air cleaner.

37. Fill the transaxle and cooling system to the proper levels.

38. Install the hood and connect the negative battery cable.

39. Make all the necessary engine adjustments. Charge the air conditioning system. Road test the vehicle for proper operation.

Rocker Arm Cover

REMOVAL & INSTALLATION

1. Remove or disconnect any electrical lines, hoses or tubes which may interfere with the removal procedures.

➡ It may be necessary to remove the air cleaner (carburetor models) or the air duct (EFI and turbo models).

2. Remove the rocker arm cover-to-cylinder head acorn nuts (Pulsar and some Sentras) or mounting screws (all others), then lift the cover from the cylinder head.

3. Using a putty knife, clean the gasket mounting surfaces.

To install:

4. Use a new gasket and/or RTV sealant, then the rocker arm cover. Torque the cover-to-cylinder head bolts to 8.4–13.2 inch lbs. or the acorn nuts to 35.0–69.6 inch lbs.

➡ On Pulsar, CA16DE, GA16DE and CA18DE engines there are 2 valve covers. When using RTV sealant apply a even bead and make sure the surface that you are working on is very clean before applying sealer. The cover MUST be torqued before the RTV dries. A thin skin is OK.

Rocker Arm Shaft

REMOVAL & INSTALLATION

Except SR20DE Engine

➧ SEE FIG. 65

1. Refer the Rocker Arm Cover, Removal and Installation procedure in this section and remove the cover.

➡ The CA16DE, GA16DE, CA18DE and CD17 (diesel) engines do not use rocker arm shafts.

2. Loosen the valve rocker adjusting nuts, then turn the adjusting screws to separate them from the push rods.

3. Evenly, loosen the rocker shaft bolts, then remove the bolts and lift the rocker shafts from the cylinder head.

➡ If it is necessary to remove the rocker arms from the shafts, perform the following procedures: remove the shaft bolts and the spring clips, then slide the rocker arms from the shaft. Be sure to keep the parts in order for reassembly purposes.

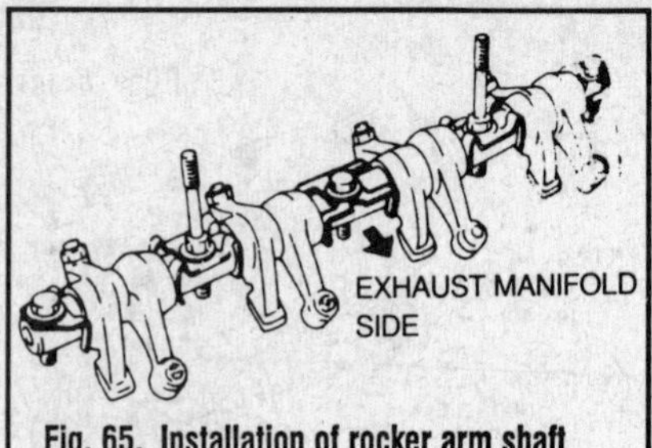
EXHAUST MANIFOLD SIDE

Fig. 65. Installation of rocker arm shaft — E-series engine

To install:

4. Position the rocker arm shaft and brackets in the correct place and hand tighten the bolts. Torque the rocker arm shaft, from the center working to the end, bracket bolts to 12–15 ft. lbs. (16–20 Nm).

5. To adjust the valve clearance, refer to the Valve Adjustment procedures in Section 2.

6. Install the rocker arm cover.

SR20DE Engine

➧ SEE FIGS. 66–68

1. Disconnect the negative battery cable. Release the fuel pressure as in Section 4.

2. Remove the rocker arm cover, gasket and oil separator.

3. Remove the intake manifold supports, oil filter bracket and power steering pump.

4. Set No. 1 cylinder at TDC on the compression stroke.

5. Remove the timing chain tensioner on the side of the head.

6. Matchmark and remove the distributor.

7. Remove the timing chain guide. Remove the camshaft sprockets while holding the camshaft stationary with a large wrench. Secure the timing chain with wire so the timing is not lost. The front cover will have to be removed if the chain timing is lost.

➡ When removing the camshafts, loosen the journal caps in the opposite sequence of tightening. Camshaft damage may result if this step is not followed.

8. Remove the camshafts, brackets, oil tubes and baffle plate. Label all components for proper installation.

9. Remove the rocker arms, shims, rocker arm guides and hydraulic lash adjusters. Label all components for proper installation.

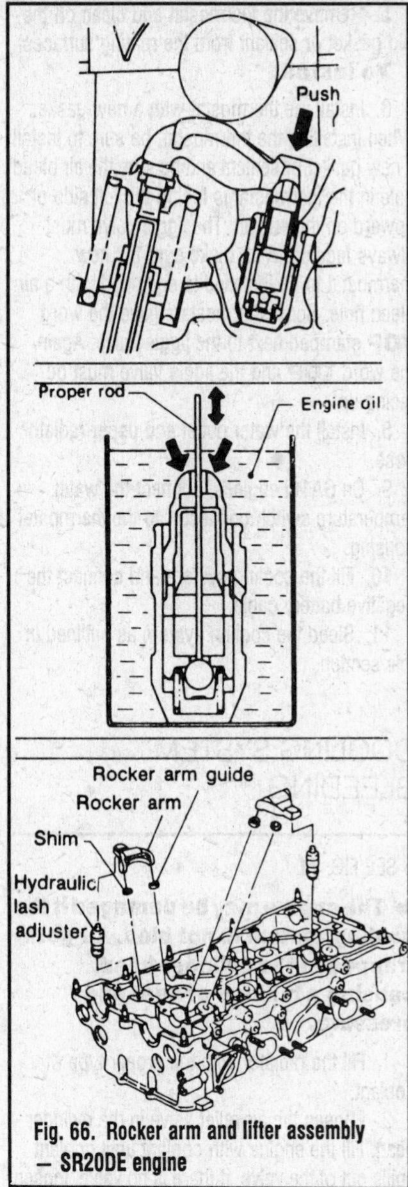
Push
Proper rod
Engine oil
Rocker arm guide
Rocker arm
Shim
Hydraulic lash adjuster

Fig. 66. Rocker arm and lifter assembly — SR20DE engine

To install:

10. Install the rocker arms, shims, rocker arm guides and hydraulic lash adjusters in the proper location.

11. Install the camshafts, brackets, oil tubes and baffle plate in the proper location. Torque the bolts in 3 steps in proper sequence. The 1st step to 17 inch lbs. (3.5 Nm), the 2nd step to 50 inch lbs. (9 Nm) and the 3rd step to 105 inch lbs. (11 Nm) for all caps, except the distributor cap. Torque the distributor cap to 230 inch lbs. (25 Nm).

12. Install the timing chain guide and camshaft sprockets while holding the camshaft stationary with a large wrench.

13. Install the distributor.

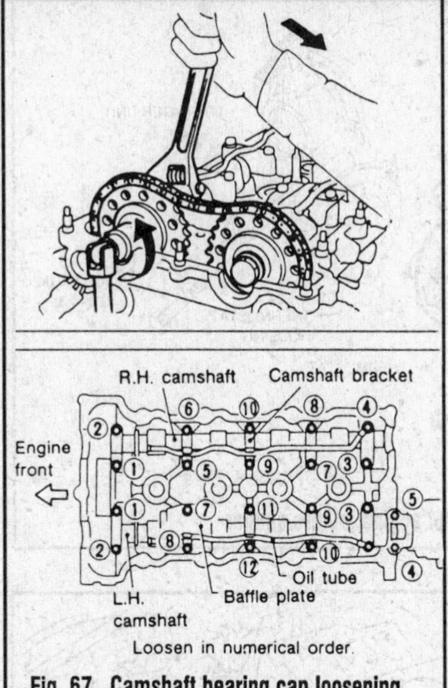
R.H. camshaft
Camshaft bracket
Engine front
Oil tube
L.H. camshaft
Baffle plate
Loosen in numerical order.

Fig. 67. Camshaft bearing cap loosening sequence — SR20DE engine

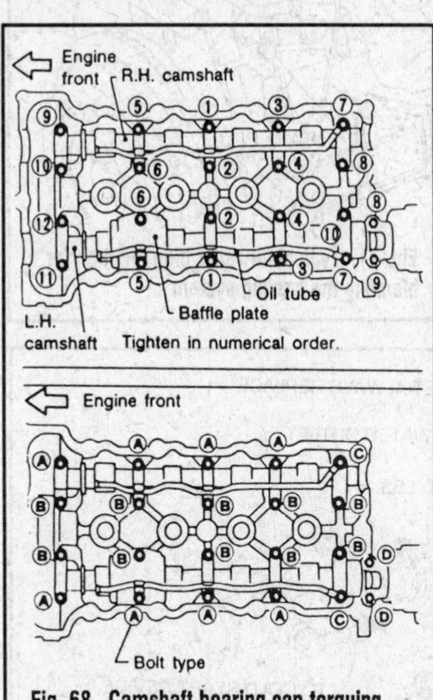
Engine front
R.H. camshaft
Oil tube
Baffle plate
L.H. camshaft
Tighten in numerical order.
Engine front
Bolt type

Fig. 68. Camshaft bearing cap torquing sequence — SR20DE engine

14. Install the timing chain tensioner on the side of the head.

15. Install the intake manifold supports, oil filter bracket and power steering pump.

16. Install the rocker arm cover, gasket and oil separator.

17. Connect the negative battery cable. Adjust the ignition timing as outlined in Section 2.

Thermostat

➧ SEE FIGS. 69, 70, 72

REMOVAL & INSTALLATION

✱✱ CAUTION

When draining the coolant, keep in mind that cats and dogs are attracted by the ethylene glycol antifreeze, and are quite likely to drink any that is left in an uncovered container or in puddles on the ground. This will prove fatal in sufficient quantity. Always drain the coolant into a sealable container. Coolant should be reused unless it is contaminated or several years old.

1982–87 Engines

➡ The engine thermostat is housed in the water outlet casting on the cylinder head.

1. Open the drain cock on the radiator and drain the coolant into a suitable drain pan.

2. Remove the upper radiator hose from the water outlet side and remove the bolts securing the water outlet to the cylinder head.

3. On E16 models, remove the exhaust air induction tube clamp bolts, then the water outlet bolts.

4. Remove the water outlet and thermostat.

To install:

5. Clean off the old gasket from the mating surfaces with a razor blade or equivalent.

6. When installing the thermostat, be sure to install a new gasket and be sure the air bleed hole in the thermostat is facing the left side (or upward) of the engine and that the spring is toward the inside of the engine. Also make sure that the new thermostat to be installed is equipped with a air bleed hole.

1988–92 Engines

1. Disconnect the negative battery cable and drain the coolant from the radiator and the left side drain cocks on the cylinder block.

2. On GA16i engines, disconnect the water temperature switch connector from the thermostat housing.

4. Remove the radiator hose from the water outlet side and remove the bolts securing the water outlet to the cylinder head.

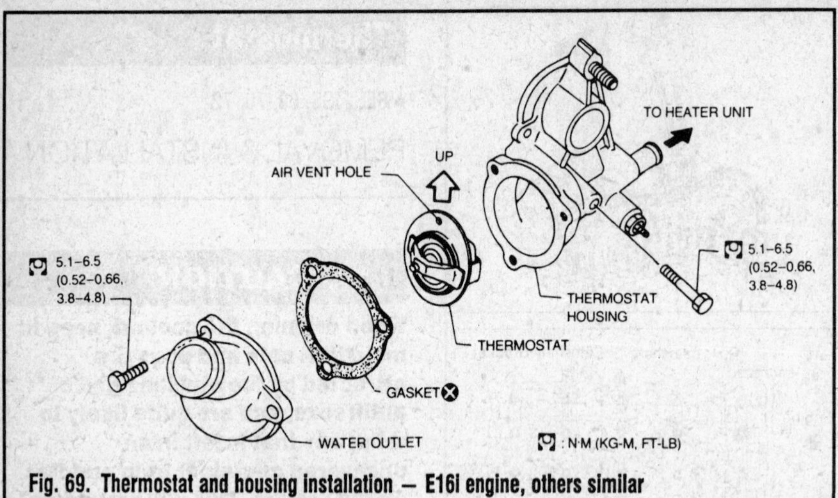
TO HEATER UNIT
UP
AIR VENT HOLE
5.1–6.5
(0.52–0.66,
3.8–4.8)
5.1–6.5
(0.52–0.66,
3.8–4.8)
THERMOSTAT
HOUSING
THERMOSTAT
GASKET
WATER OUTLET
: N·M (KG-M, FT-LB)
Fig. 69. Thermostat and housing installation — E16i engine, others similar

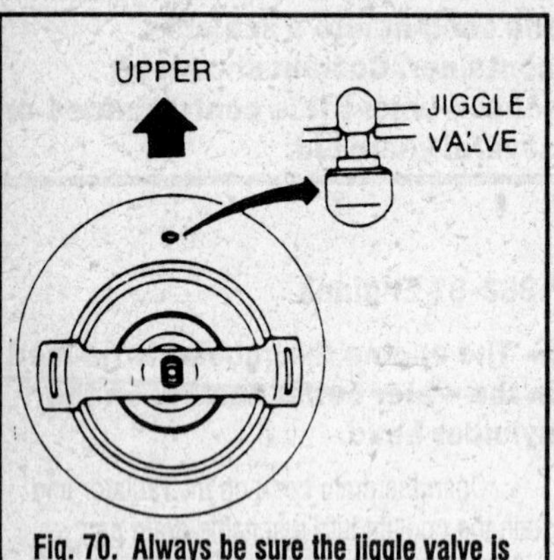
UPPER
JIGGLE
VALVE
Fig. 70. Always be sure the jiggle valve is facing upward when installing the thermostat

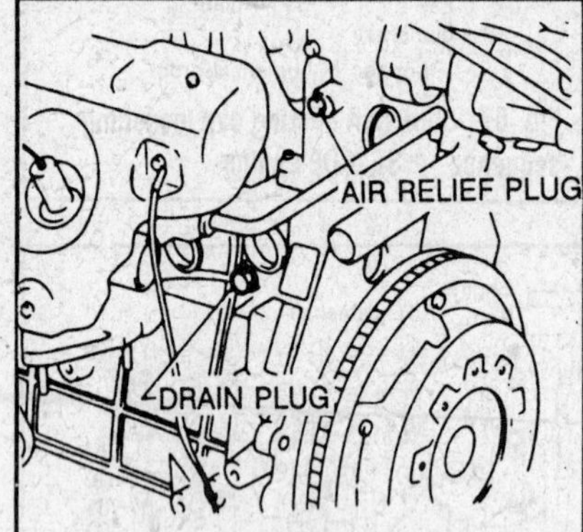
AIR RELIEF PLUG
DRAIN PLUG
Fig. 71. Typical air relief plug location for bleeding the cooling system

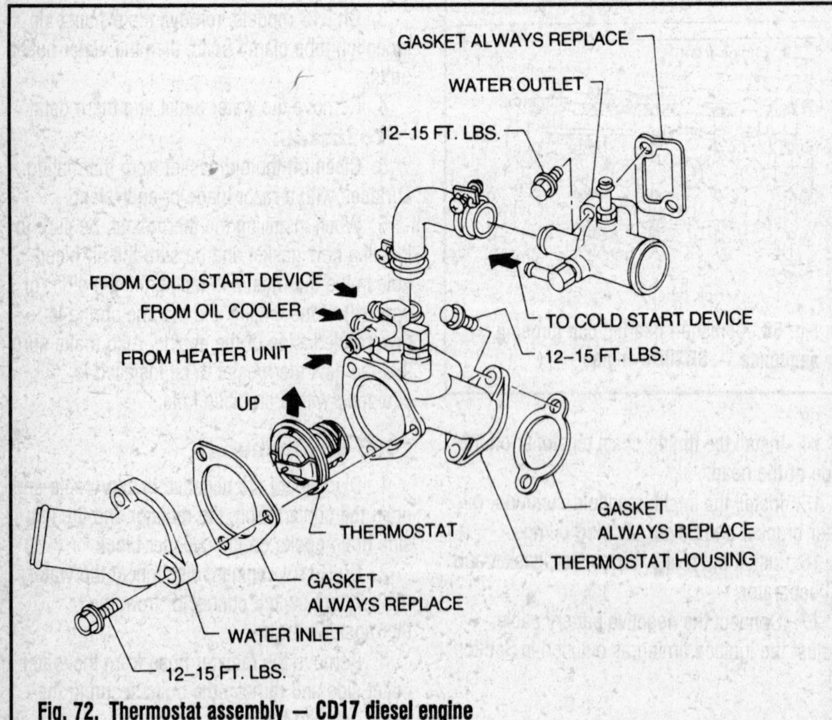
GASKET ALWAYS REPLACE
WATER OUTLET
12–15 FT. LBS.
FROM COLD START DEVICE
FROM OIL COOLER
FROM HEATER UNIT
TO COLD START DEVICE
12–15 FT. LBS.
UP
GASKET
ALWAYS REPLACE
THERMOSTAT
THERMOSTAT HOUSING
GASKET
ALWAYS REPLACE
WATER INLET
12–15 FT. LBS.
Fig. 72. Thermostat assembly — CD17 diesel engine

5. Remove the thermostat and clean off the old gasket or sealant from the mating surfaces.

To install:

6. Install the thermostat with a new gasket. When installing the thermostat, be sure to install a new gasket or sealant and be sure the air bleed hole in the thermostat is facing the left side or upward on the engine. The jiggle valve must always face up. Also make sure the new thermostat to be installed is equipped with a air bleed hole. Some thermostats have the word **TOP** stamped next to the jiggle valve. Again, the word **TOP** and the jiggle valve must be facing up.
8. Install the water outlet and upper radiator hose.
9. On GA16i engines, connect the water temperature switch connector to the thermostat housing.
10. Fill the cooling system and connect the negative battery cable.
11. Bleed the cooling system as outlined in this section.

COOLING SYSTEM BLEEDING

SEE FIG. 71

The engine may be damaged if the cooling system is not bled. Air gets trapped in the cylinder head, causing a buildup of heat and pressure.

1. Fill the radiator with the proper type of coolant.
2. Loosen the air relief valve in the cylinder head. Fill the engine with coolant until coolant spills out of the valve. If there is no valve, loosen a temperature sender that is nearest the top of the engine. Install the sender when coolant spills from the hole.
3. With the radiator cap off, start the engine and allow it to run and reach normal operating temperature.
4. Run the heater at full force and with the temperature lever in the hot position. Be sure that the heater control valve is functioning.
5. Shut the engine off and recheck the coolant level, refill as necessary.

Intake Manifold

REMOVAL & INSTALLATION

✲✲ CAUTION

When draining the coolant, keep in mind that cats and dogs are attracted by the ethylene glycol antifreeze, and are quite likely to drink any that is left in an uncovered container or in puddles on the ground. This will prove fatal in sufficient quantity. Always drain the coolant into a sealable container. Coolant should be reused unless it is contaminated or several years old.

Carbureted E-Series

1. Remove the air cleaner assembly together with all of the hoses.

➡ When unplugging wires and hoses, mark each hose and its connection with a piece of masking tape, then match code the 2 pieces of tape with the numbers 1, 2, 3, etc. When assembling, simply match up the pieces of tape.

2. Disconnect and label the throttle linkage, the fuel and the vacuum lines from the carburetor and the intake manifold components.

➡ The carburetor can be removed from the manifold at this point or can be removed as an assembly with the intake manifold.

3. Remove the intake manifold bolts or nuts and the manifold from the engine.
4. Using a putty knife, clean the gasket mounting surfaces.

To install:

5. Install the intake manifold and gasket on the engine. Always use a new gasket. Tighten the mounting bolts from the, center working to the end, in two or three stages. Torque the intake manifold bolts to 12–15 ft. lbs. (15–18 Nm).
6. Install throttle linkage, fuel and vacuum lines and the air cleaner assembly.
7. Start engine and check for leaks.

1984 Turbocharged E15ET Engine

➡ Refer to the Fuel Release Procedure in Section 5 and release the fuel pressure.

1. Disconnect the air intake duct between the air filter and the air pipe, then the air intake duct between the air pipe and the turbocharger. Remove the air inlet duct between the turbocharger and the throttle body. Remove the air pipe.
2. Disconnect and label all of the electrical connectors and the vacuum hoses to the throttle, the intake manifold assembly and the related components. Remove the high tension wires from the spark plugs.
3. Disconnect the EGR valve tube from the exhaust manifold and the fuel line(s) from the fuel injector assembly.

➡ For clearance purposes, it may be necessary to remove the throttle body and the collector chamber from the intake manifold; if the fuel injector assembly is in the way, remove it.

4. Remove the intake manifold mounting nuts and the intake manifold.

To install:

5. Using a putty knife, clean the gasket mounting surfaces.
6. Install the intake manifold and gasket on the engine. Always use a new gasket. Tighten the mounting bolts from the, center working to the end, in two or three stages. Torque the intake manifold-to-cylinder head nuts to 12–15 ft. lbs. (16–20 Nm), the intake manifold-to-collector chamber bolts to 2.9–4.3 ft. lbs. (16–20 Nm) and the air pipe bolt(s) to 6.5–10.1 ft. lbs. (9–14 Nm).
7. Install the throttle body and the collector chamber on the intake manifold if it was removed.
8. Connect the EGR valve tube to the exhaust manifold and the fuel line(s) to the fuel injector assembly.
9. Install the spark plug wires, electrical connectors and the vacuum hoses to the throttle, the intake manifold assembly and the related components.
10. Connect the air intake duct between the air filter and the air pipe, then connect the air intake duct between the air pipe and the turbocharger. Install the air inlet duct between the turbocharger and the throttle body. Connect the air pipe.
11. Start engine and check for leaks.

1987 and Later Fuel Injected Engines

➧ SEE FIGS. 75–77

➡ Refer to the Fuel Release Procedure in Section 5 and release the fuel pressure in the system.

1. Remove the air cleaner assembly together with all of the attending hoses.
2. Disconnect the throttle linkage and fuel and vacuum lines from the throttle body on the engines).
3. The throttle body can be removed from the manifold at this point or can be removed as an assembly with the intake manifold.
4. Remove the manifold support stay on the CA16DE and CA18DE.
5. Remove the EGR valve assembly, air regulator and F.I.C.D valve from the manifold on the CA16DE and CA18DE.
6. Loosen the intake manifold attaching nuts, working from the two ends toward the center, and then remove them.

➡ NEVER tighten or loosen the power valve adjusting screw on the CA16DE or CA18DE engines.

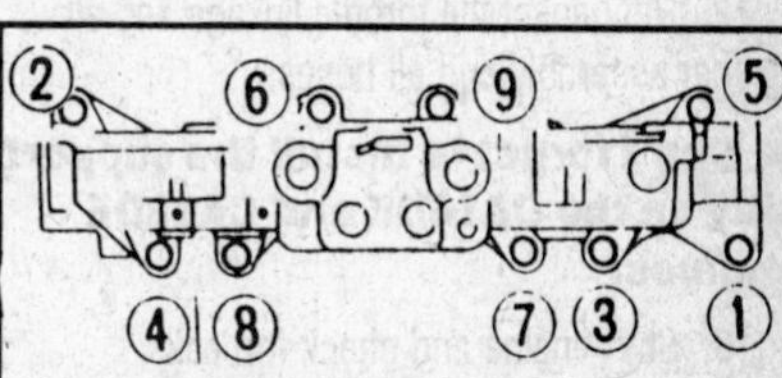
2
6
9
5
4
8
7
3
1

Fig. 75. Intake manifold loosening sequence – GA16i, GA16DE and SR20DE engines

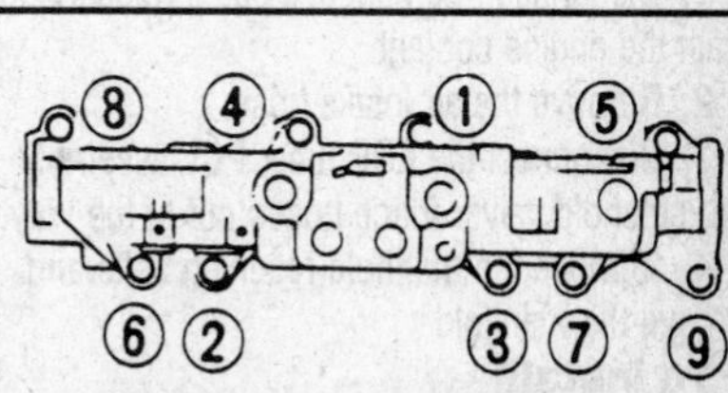
8
4
1
5
6
2
3
7
9

Fig. 76. Intake manifold tightening sequence – GA16i, GA16DE and SR20DE engines

7. Remove the intake manifold from the engine.
8. Install the intake manifold and gasket on the engine. Always use a new gasket. Tighten the intake manifold attaching nuts, working from the center toward the ends, in two or three stages. Torque the intake manifold to 12–15 ft. lbs. (15–18 Nm) on the E16i, GA16DE and SR20DE engines and 27–35 ft. lbs. (34–48 Nm) on the CA16DE and CA18DE engines.

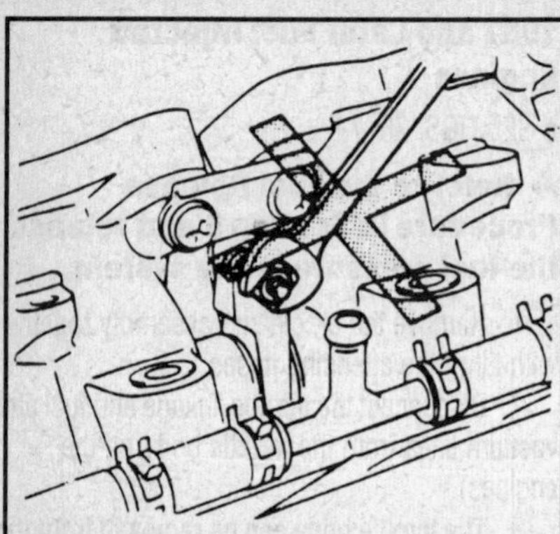

Fig. 77. Never touch this bolt on the CA16DE and CA18DE engines

9. Install the EGR valve assembly, air regulator and F.I.C.D valve on the manifold on the CA16DE, GA16DE, CA18DE and SR20DE, if so equipped.

10. Connect the manifold support stay on the CA16DE, GA16DE, CA18DE and SR20DE engines.

11. Install the throttle body if it was removed, then reconnect all fuel and vacuum lines and any related components.

12. Reconnect the throttle linkage and air cleaner assembly and all hoses.

➡ **Don't forget to install the support stay on the CA16DE and CA18DE engines.**

13. Start engine and check for leaks.

Diesel Engine

➧ SEE FIG. 73

1. Disconnect the negative battery cable and drain the engine coolant.
2. Remove the air intake hose.
3. Disconnect the EGR tube, PCV assembly and solenoid valve. Place hoses out of the way.
4. Remove the manifold retaining bolts and remove the manifold.

To install:

5. Clean the gasket mating surfaces.
6. Install a new gasket with the end tab facing the No. 1 cylinder.
7. Install the manifold and torque the bolts to 13–16 ft. lbs. (l8–22 Nm).
8. Install the remaining components. Apply anti-seize compound to the EGR tube and torque to 35 ft. lbs. (48 Nm).
9. Connect the negative battery cable and check operation.

This portion is No. 1 cylinder side.

Fig. 73. Intake manifold gasket positioning – CD17 diesel engine

Exhaust Manifold

➧ SEE FIG. 74

REMOVAL & INSTALLATION

All Engines, Except E15ET

➡ **If any fuel system components must be removed, make to relieve the fuel system pressure first.**

1. Disconnect the negative battery cable. Raise and support the vehicle safely.
2. Remove the undercover and dust covers, if equipped.
3. Remove the air cleaner or collector assembly, if necessary for access.
4. Remove the heat shield(s), if equipped.
5. Disconnect the exhaust pipe from the exhaust manifold.
6. Remove or disconnect the temperature sensors, oxygen sensors, air induction pipes, bracketry and other attachments from the manifold.
7. Disconnect the EAI and EGR tubes from their fittings if so equipped.
8. Loosen and remove the exhaust manifold attaching nuts and remove the manifold(s) from the block. Discard the exhaust manifold gaskets and replace with new.
9. Clean the gasket surfaces and check the manifold for cracks and warpage.

To install:

10. Install the exhaust manifold with a new gasket. Torque the manifold fasteners from the center outward in several stages to 13–16 ft. lbs. (16–18 Nm), all engines except CA16DE, CA18DE and SR20DE. Torque those engines to 27–35 ft. lbs. (34–48 Nm).
11. Connect the EAI and EGR tubes to the connections on the manifold as necessary.
12. Install or connect the temperature sensors, oxygen sensors, air induction pipes, bracketry and other attachments to the manifold.
13. Connect the exhaust pipe to the manifold or turbo outlet using a new gasket.
14. Install the heat shields.

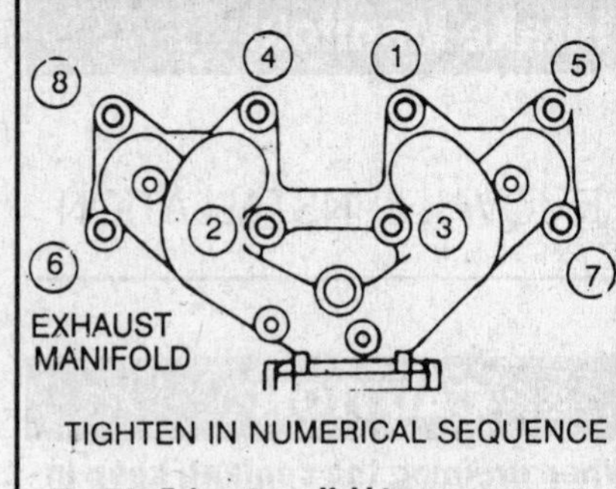
8
4
1
5
2
3
6
7
EXHAUST
MANIFOLD
TIGHTEN IN NUMERICAL SEQUENCE

Fig. 74. Exhaust manifold torque sequence – GA16i engine

15. Install the air cleaner or collector assembly.
16. Install the undercovers and dust covers.
17. Connect the negative battery cable.

1984 Turbocharged E15ET Engine

1. Refer to the Turbocharger, Removal and Installation procedure in this section and remove the turbocharger.
2. Remove the exhaust manifold's heat shields, the exhaust manifold from the cylinder head.
3. Using a putty knife, clean the gasket mounting surfaces.

To install:

4. Use new gaskets and install the manifold. Torque the exhaust manifold-to-cylinder head bolts to 12–15 ft. lbs. (15–18 Nm), the turbocharger-to-exhaust manifold nuts to 22–25 ft. lbs. (28–34 Nm), the exhaust outlet-to-turbo nuts to 22–25 ft. lbs. (28–34 Nm), the converter's mounting bracket bolt to 14–18 ft. lbs. (16–20 Nm) (10mm) or 6.5–10.1 ft. lbs. (10–14 Nm) (8mm), the oil pressure tube fitting-to-turbo to 14–22 ft. lbs. (17–30 Nm).
5. Install the remaining components.

Turbocharger

REMOVAL & INSTALLATION

1984 Pulsar w/E15ET Engine

1. Disconnect the negative battery cable. Disconnect the air inlet and the outlet pipes from the turbocharger.
2. Disconnect the oil pressure tube and the oil return hose from the turbocharger. Disconnect and mark the high tension wires from the spark plugs.
3. Remove the catalytic converter heat shield, then the converter's mounting bracket.

➡ Soak the exhaust pipe outlet bolts with penetrating oil if necessary to loosen them.

4. Remove the exhaust outlet-to-turbocharger mounting nuts and separate the outlet from the turbocharger.
5. Remove the turbocharger-to-exhaust manifold mounting nuts and lift the turbocharger from the exhaust manifold.
6. Using a putty knife, clean the gasket mounting surfaces.

To install:

7. Use new gaskets, install the turbocharger to the exhaust manifold. Observe the following torques:
   • Exhaust manifold-to-cylinder head bolts — 12–15 ft. lbs. (15–18 Nm)
   • Turbocharger-to-exhaust manifold nuts — 22–25 ft. lbs. (28–34 Nm)
   • Exhaust outlet-to-turbo nuts — 22–25 ft. lbs. (28–34 Nm)
   • Converter mounting bracket bolt — 14–18 ft. lbs. (16–20 Nm) (10mm) or 6.5–10.1 ft. lbs. (10–14 Nm) (8mm)
   • Oil pressure tube fitting-to-turbo — 14–22 ft. lbs. (17–30 Nm).
8. Install the remaining components. Connect the negative battery cable and check operation.

Air Conditioning Compressor

➧ SEE FIGS. 78–80

Refer to Section 1 for Charging and Discharging procedures.

REMOVAL & INSTALLATION

All Models

✲✲ CAUTION

The compressed refrigerant used in the air conditioning system expands into the atmosphere at a temperature of -2°F (-19°C) or lower. This will freeze any surface, including your eyes, that it contacts. In addition, the refrigerant decomposes into a poisonous gas in the presence of a flame. Do not open or disconnect any part of the air conditioning system until you have read the SAFETY WARNINGS section in Section 1.

1. Disconnect the negative battery cables.
2. Remove all the necessary equipment in order to gain access to the compressor mounting bolts.
3. Remove the compressor drive belt.

➡ To facilitate removal of the compressor belt, remove the idler pulley and bracket as an assembly beforehand from the underside of the car.

4. Discharge the air conditioning system.
5. Disconnect and plug the refrigerant lines with a clean shop towel.

➡ Be sure to use 2 wrenches (one to loosen fitting — one to hold fitting in place) when disconnecting the refrigerant lines.

6. Disconnect and tag all electrical connections.
7. Remove the compressor mounting bolts. Remove the compressor from the vehicle.

To install:

8. Install the compressor on the engine and evenly torque all the mounting bolts the same.
9. Connect all the electrical connections and unplug and reconnect all refrigerant lines.
10. Install all the necessary equipment in order to gain access to the compressor mounting bolts.
11. Install and adjust the drive belt.
12. Connect the negative battery cable.
13. Evacuate and charge the system as required. Make sure the oil level is correct for the compressor.

➡ Do not attempt to the leave the compressor on its side or upside down for more than a couple minutes, as the oil in the compressor will enter the low pressure chambers. Be sure to always replace the O-rings.

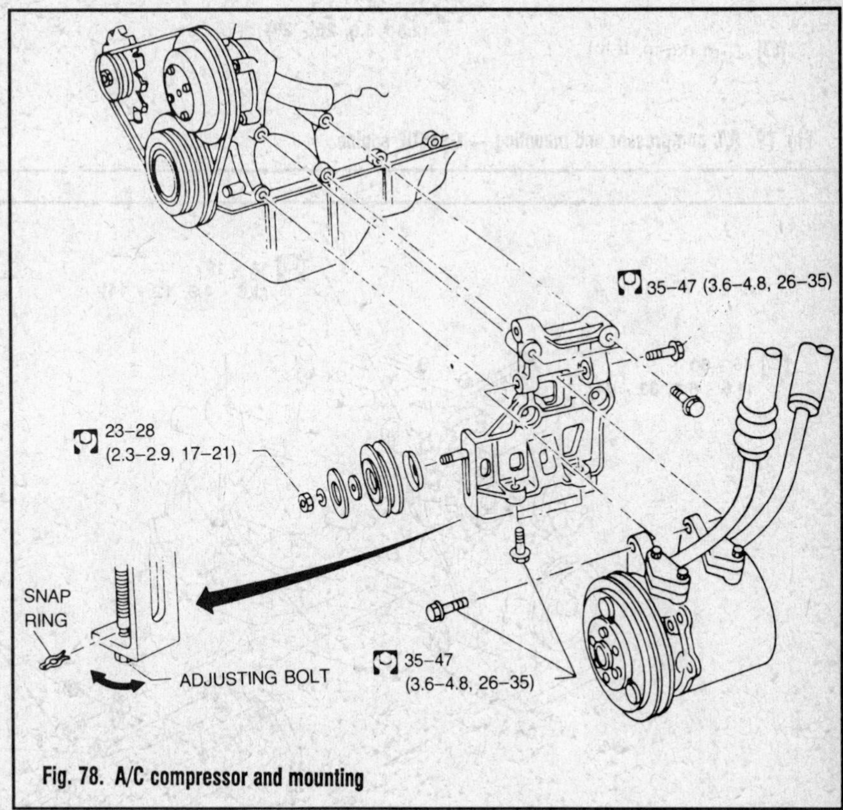
35–47 (3.6–4.8, 26–35)
23–28
(2.3–2.9, 17–21)
SNAP
RING
ADJUSTING BOLT
35–47
(3.6–4.8, 26–35)

Fig. 78. A/C compressor and mounting

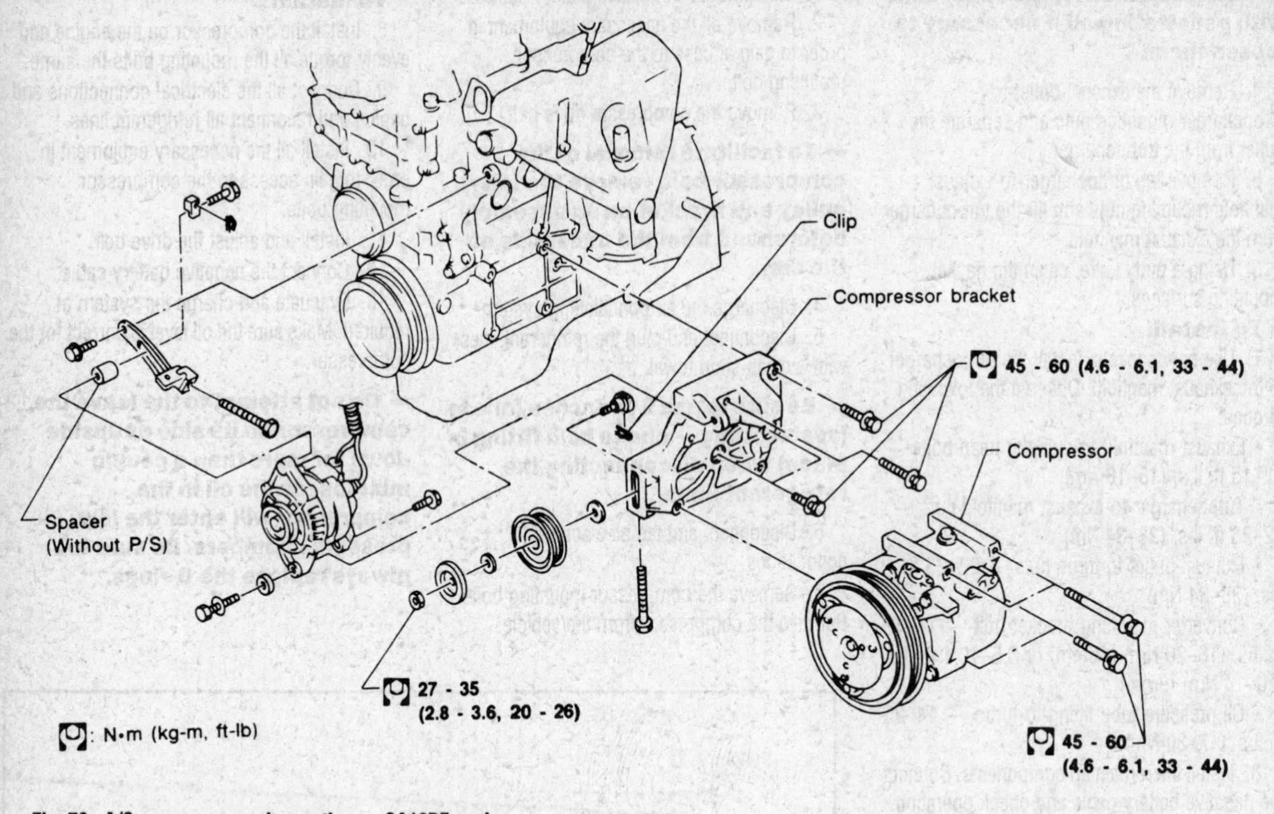

Clip
Compressor bracket
45 - 60 (4.6 - 6.1, 33 - 44)
Compressor
Spacer
(Without P/S)
27 - 35
(2.8 - 3.6, 20 - 26)
: N•m (kg-m, ft-lb)
45 - 60
(4.6 - 6.1, 33 - 44)

Fig. 79. A/C compressor and mounting — GA16DE engine

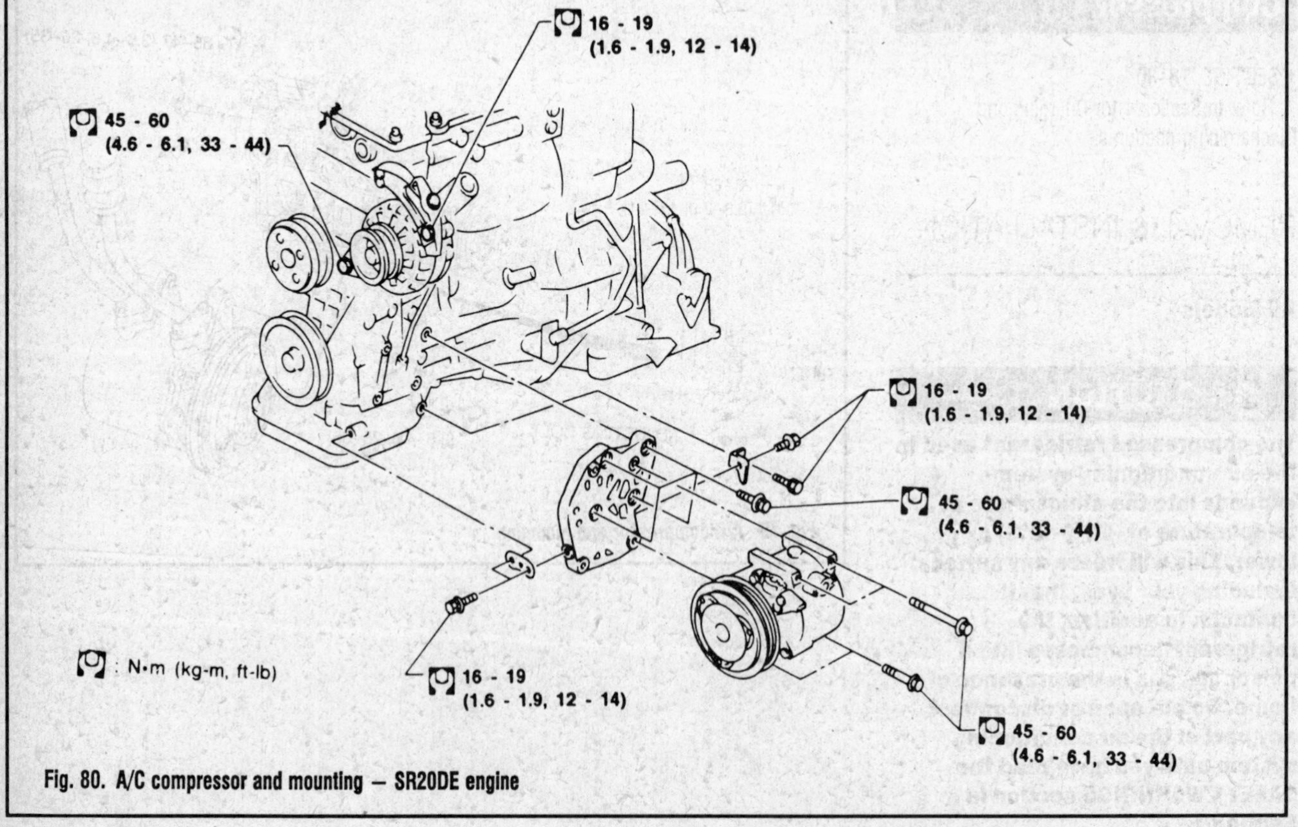

16 - 19
(1.6 - 1.9, 12 - 14)
45 - 60
(4.6 - 6.1, 33 - 44)
16 - 19
(1.6 - 1.9, 12 - 14)
45 - 60
(4.6 - 6.1, 33 - 44)
: N•m (kg-m, ft-lb)
16 - 19
(1.6 - 1.9, 12 - 14)
45 - 60
(4.6 - 6.1, 33 - 44)

Fig. 80. A/C compressor and mounting — SR20DE engine

Radiator and Cooling Fan

SEE FIGS. 81–85, 92

REMOVAL & INSTALLATION

1. Drain the cooling system.

CAUTION

When draining the coolant, keep in mind that cats and dogs are attracted by the ethylene glycol antifreeze, and are quite likely to drink any that is left in an uncovered container or in puddles on the ground. This will prove fatal in sufficient quantity. Always drain the coolant into a sealable container. Coolant should be reused unless it is contaminated or several years old.

2. Unbolt and set aside the power steering pump if necessary to gain access. DO NOT disconnect the power steering pressure hoses or drain the system.
3. Disconnect the upper and lower radiator hoses, reservoir hose.
4. If equipped with an automatic transaxle, disconnect and cap the cooling lines at the radiator. Disconnect the water temperature switch.
5. Disconnect the fan motor wires and remove the fan assembly. Remove the radiator and cooling fan assembly. Later model vehicles condenser cooling fans. It is the smaller of the 2. Remove the fan motor from the shroud if the motor is defective.

To install:

6. Install the fan motor and blade to the shroud and tighten the bolts.
7. Install the radiator on the vehicle and torque the mounting bolts evenly.
8. Install the fan assembly and connect the fan motor electrical connectors.
9. If equipped with an automatic transaxle, connect the cooling lines at the radiator and connect the upper and lower hoses to the radiator and the reservoir hose.
10. Install the power steering pump if removed. Connect the water temperature switch.
11. Refill the radiator and the automatic transaxle (if equipped). Operate the engine until warm and then check the water level, leaks and fan operation.

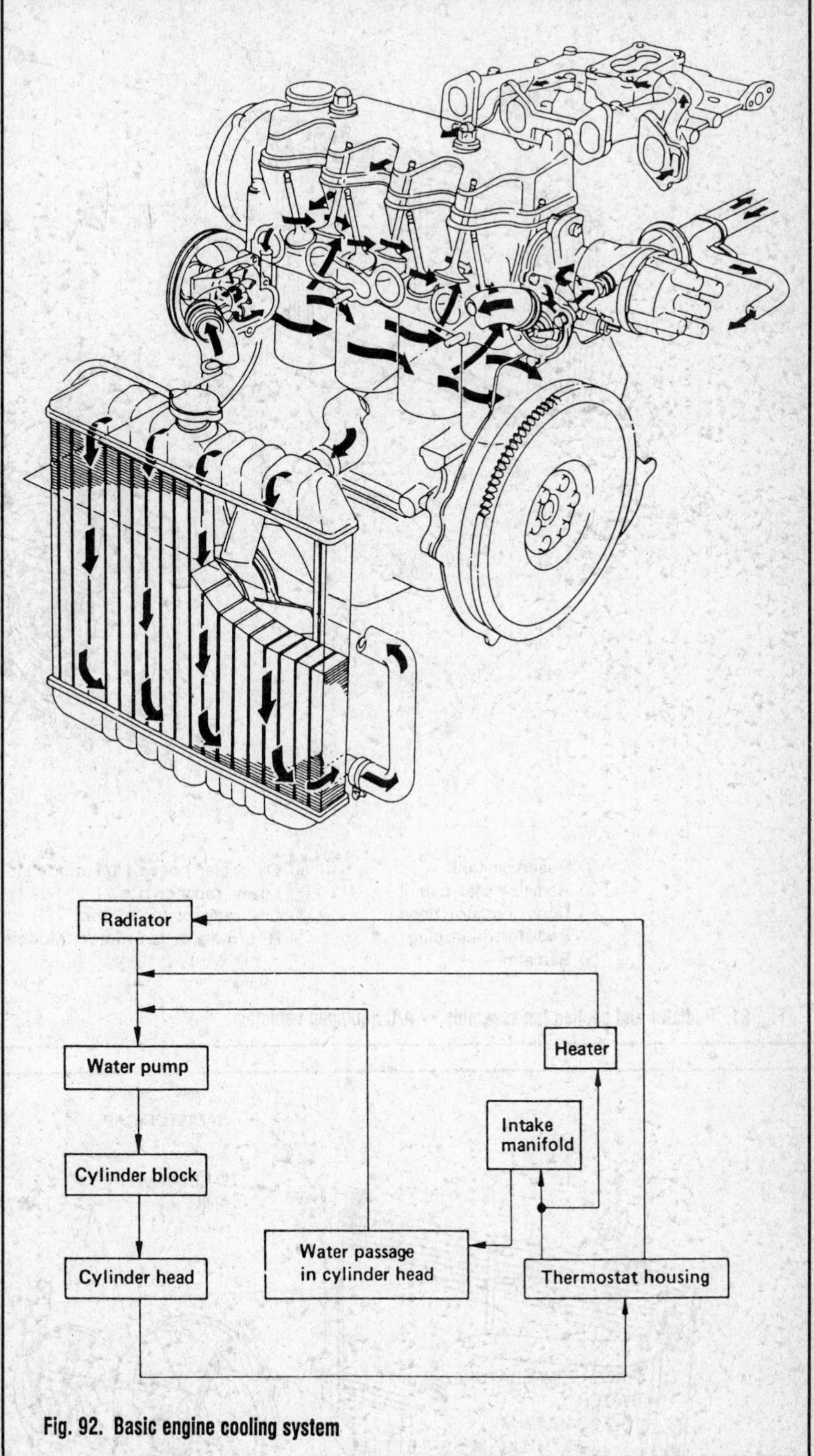
Radiator
Water pump
Cylinder block
Cylinder head
Heater
Intake manifold
Water passage in cylinder head
Thermostat housing

Fig. 92. Basic engine cooling system

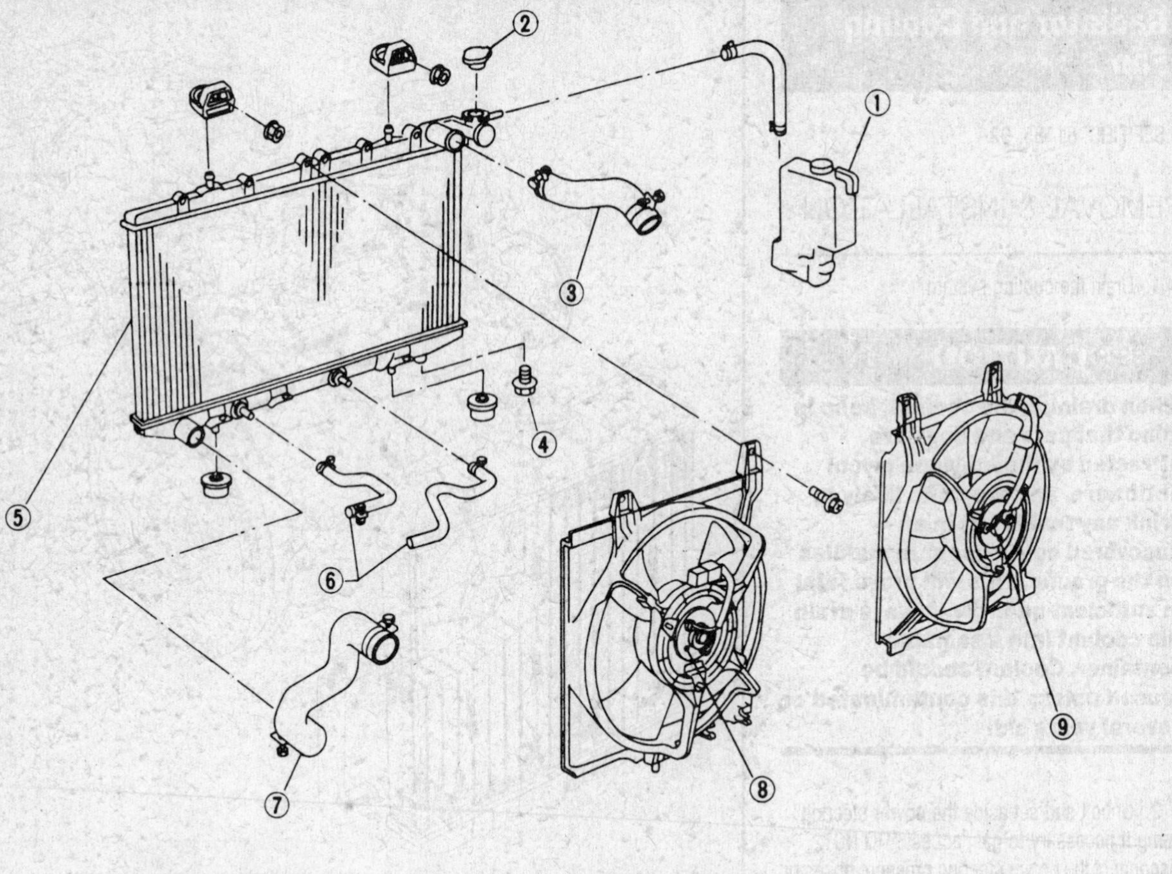

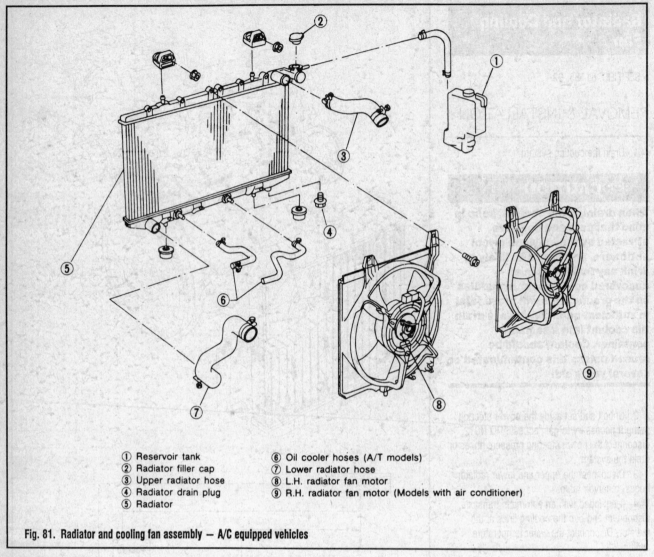

① Reservoir tank
② Radiator filler cap
③ Upper radiator hose
④ Radiator drain plug
⑤ Radiator
⑥ Oil cooler hoses (A/T models)
⑦ Lower radiator hose
⑧ L.H. radiator fan motor
⑨ R.H. radiator fan motor (Models with air conditioner)

Fig. 81. Radiator and cooling fan assembly – A/C equipped vehicles

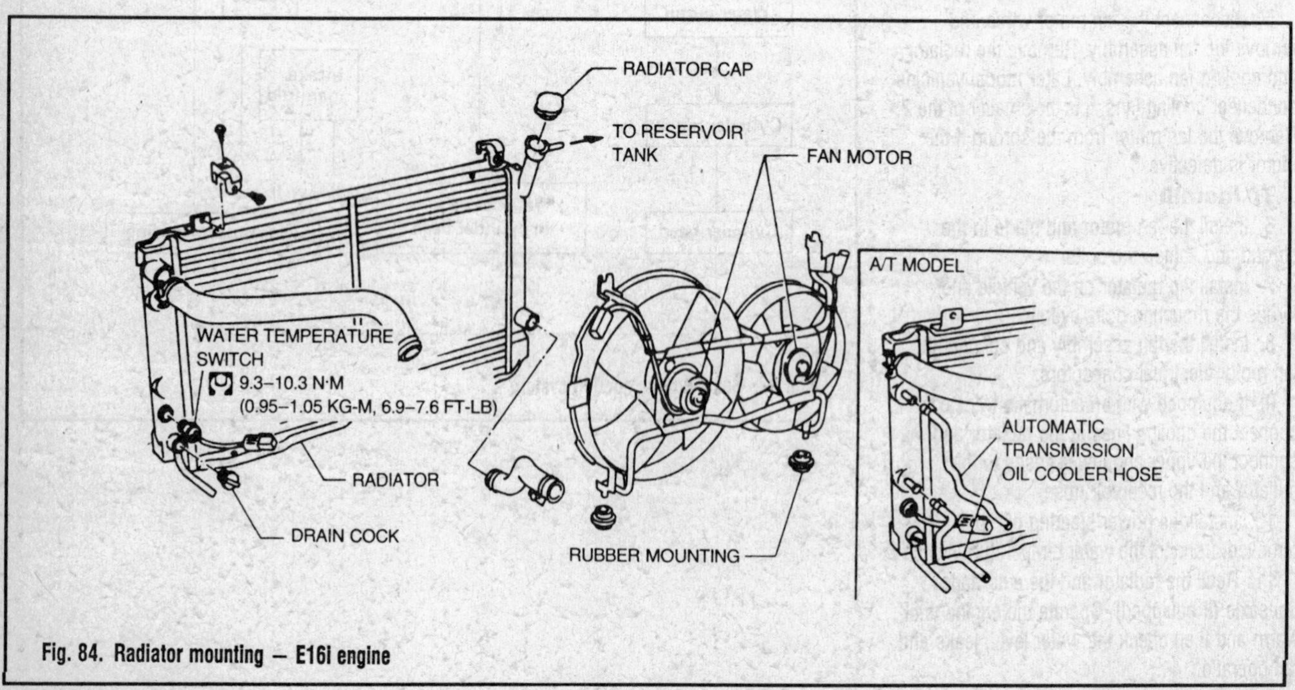
RADIATOR CAP
TO RESERVOIR TANK
FAN MOTOR
A/T MODEL
WATER TEMPERATURE SWITCH
9.3–10.3 N·M
(0.95–1.05 KG-M, 6.9–7.6 FT-LB)
AUTOMATIC TRANSMISSION OIL COOLER HOSE
RADIATOR
DRAIN COCK
RUBBER MOUNTING

Fig. 84. Radiator mounting – E16i engine

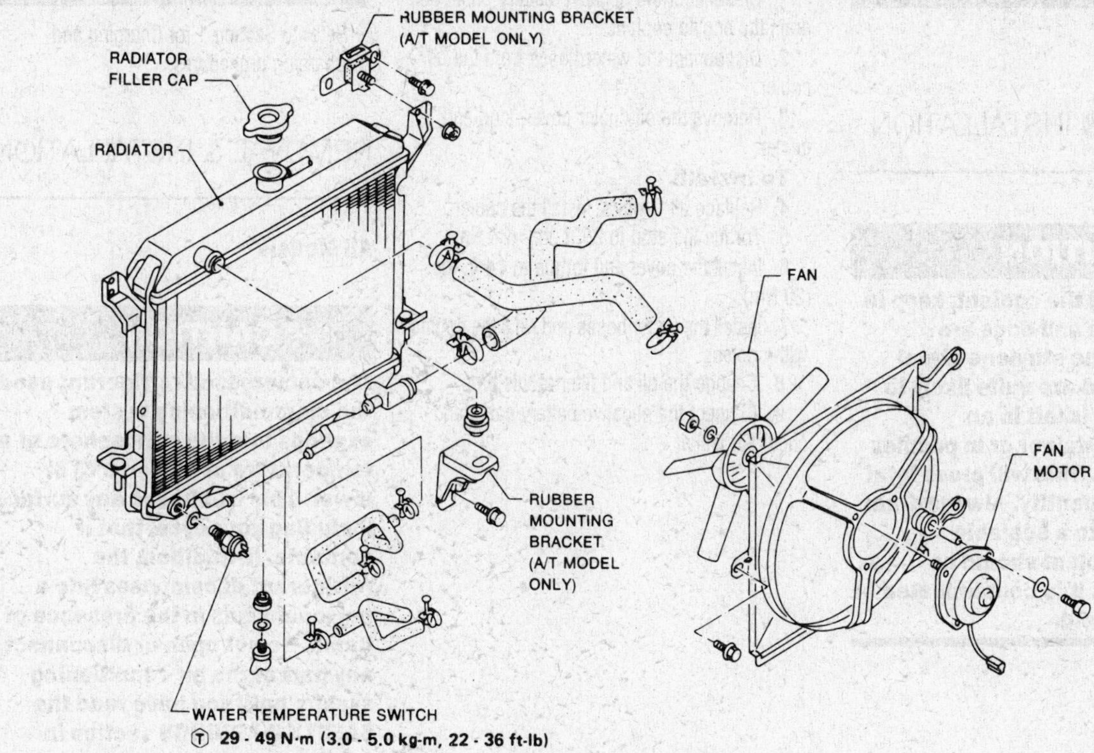

RUBBER MOUNTING BRACKET (A/T MODEL ONLY)
RADIATOR FILLER CAP
RADIATOR
FAN
FAN MOTOR
RUBBER MOUNTING BRACKET (A/T MODEL ONLY)
WATER TEMPERATURE SWITCH
29 - 49 N·m (3.0 - 5.0 kg-m, 22 - 36 ft-lb)

Fig. 82. Radiator and cooling fan assembly — all except, GA16DE and SR20DE engines

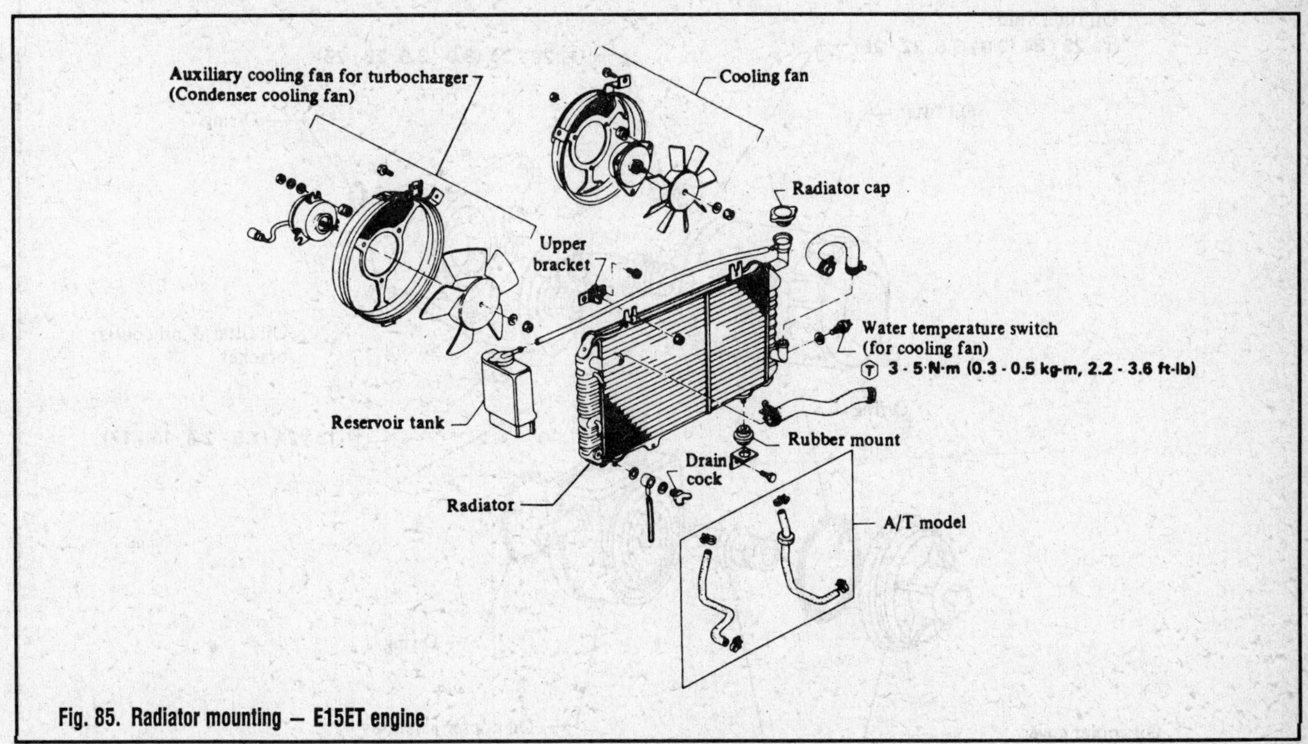
Auxiliary cooling fan for turbocharger
(Condenser cooling fan)
Cooling fan
Radiator cap
Upper bracket
Water temperature switch
(for cooling fan)
3 - 5 N·m (0.3 - 0.5 kg-m, 2.2 - 3.6 ft-lb)
Reservoir tank
Rubber mount
Drain cock
Radiator
A/T model

Fig. 85. Radiator mounting — E15ET engine

Engine Oil Cooler

SEE FIG. 83

REMOVAL & INSTALLATION

CAUTION

When draining the coolant, keep in mind that cats and dogs are attracted by the ethylene glycol antifreeze, and are quite likely to drink any that is left in an uncovered container or in puddles on the ground. This will prove fatal in sufficient quantity. Always drain the coolant into a sealable container. Coolant should be reused unless it is contaminated or several years old.

E15ET Turbocharged Engine

1. Disconnect the negative battery cable and drain the engine coolant.
2. Disconnect the water hoses from the oil cooler.
3. Remove the oil cooler cover, stud and cooler.

To install:

4. Replace all O-rings. Install the cooler.
5. Torque the stud to 25 ft. lbs. (34 Nm).
6. Install the cover and torque to 14 ft. lbs. (20 Nm).
7. Install the water hoses and refill the engine with coolant.
8. Change the oil and filter at this time.
9. Connect the negative battery cable and check for leaks.

A/C Condenser

Refer to Section 1 for Charging and Discharging procedures.

REMOVAL & INSTALLATION

All Models

CAUTION

The compressed refrigerant used in the air conditioning system expands into the atmosphere at a temperature of -2°F (-19°C) or lower. This will freeze any surface, including your eyes, that it contacts. In addition, the refrigerant decomposes into a poisonous gas in the presence of a flame. Do not open or disconnect any part of the air conditioning system until you have read the SAFETY WARNINGS section in Section 1.

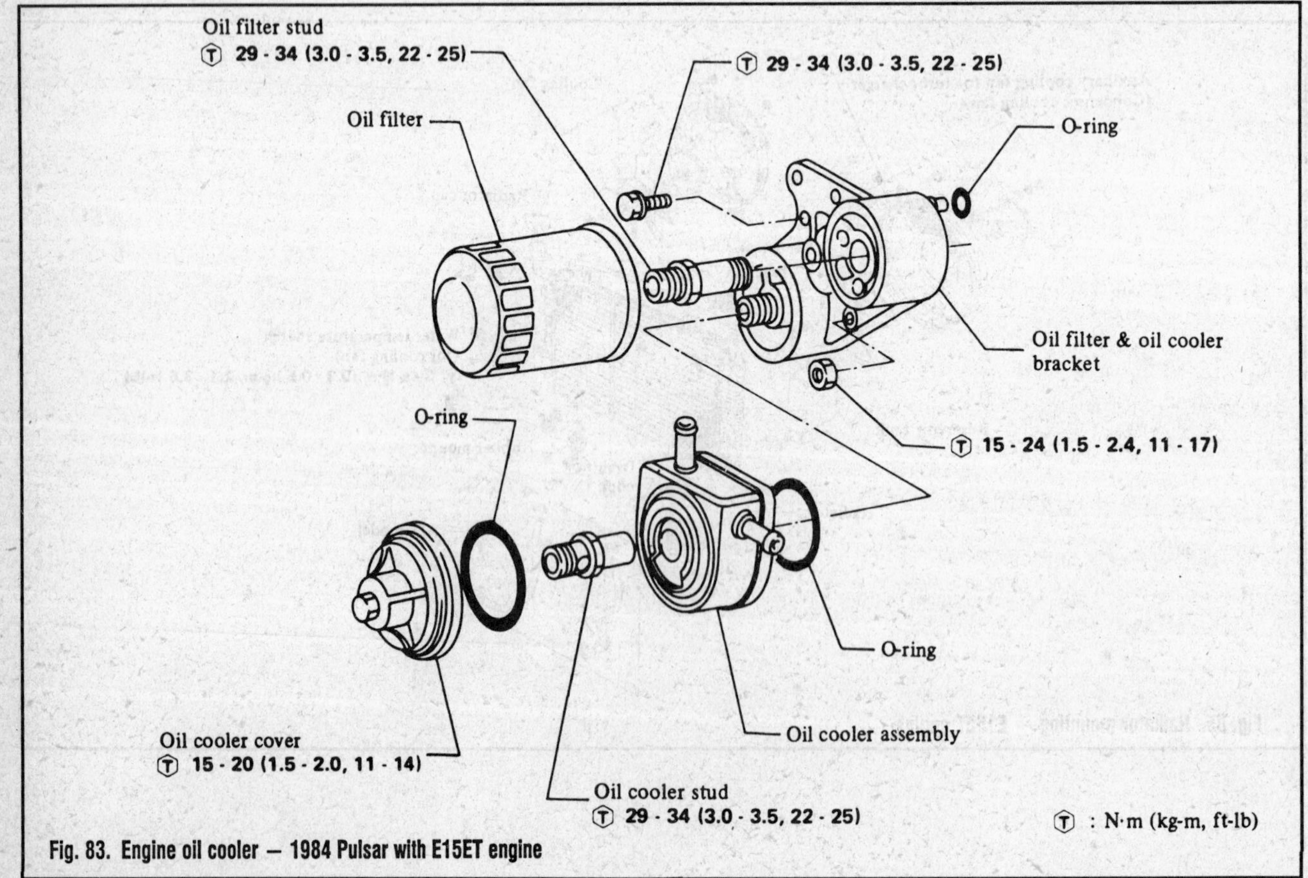

Oil filter stud
Ⓣ 29 - 34 (3.0 - 3.5, 22 - 25)
Ⓣ 29 - 34 (3.0 - 3.5, 22 - 25)
Oil filter
O-ring
Oil filter & oil cooler bracket
Ⓣ 15 - 24 (1.5 - 2.4, 11 - 17)
O-ring
O-ring
Oil cooler assembly
Oil cooler cover
Ⓣ 15 - 20 (1.5 - 2.0, 11 - 14)
Oil cooler stud
Ⓣ 29 - 34 (3.0 - 3.5, 22 - 25)
Ⓣ : N·m (kg-m, ft-lb)

Fig. 83. Engine oil cooler — 1984 Pulsar with E15ET engine

1. Disconnect the negative battery cables.
2. Remove the compressor drive belt.
3. Remove the necessary components in order to gain access to the condenser retaining bolts. If equipped, remove the condenser fan motor, as necessary.
4. Discharge the system. Remove the condenser refrigerant lines and plug them with a clean shop towel.
5. Remove the condenser retaining bolts. Remove the condenser from the vehicle.
6. Install the condenser in the vehicle and evenly torque all the mounting bolts the same.

➡ **Always use new O-rings in all refrigerant lines.**

7. Reconnect all the refrigerant lines.
8. Install all the necessary equipment in order to gain access to the condenser mounting bolts. If removed, install the condenser fan motor.
9. Install and adjust the drive belt.
10. Connect the negative battery cable.
11. Evacuate and charge the system as required.

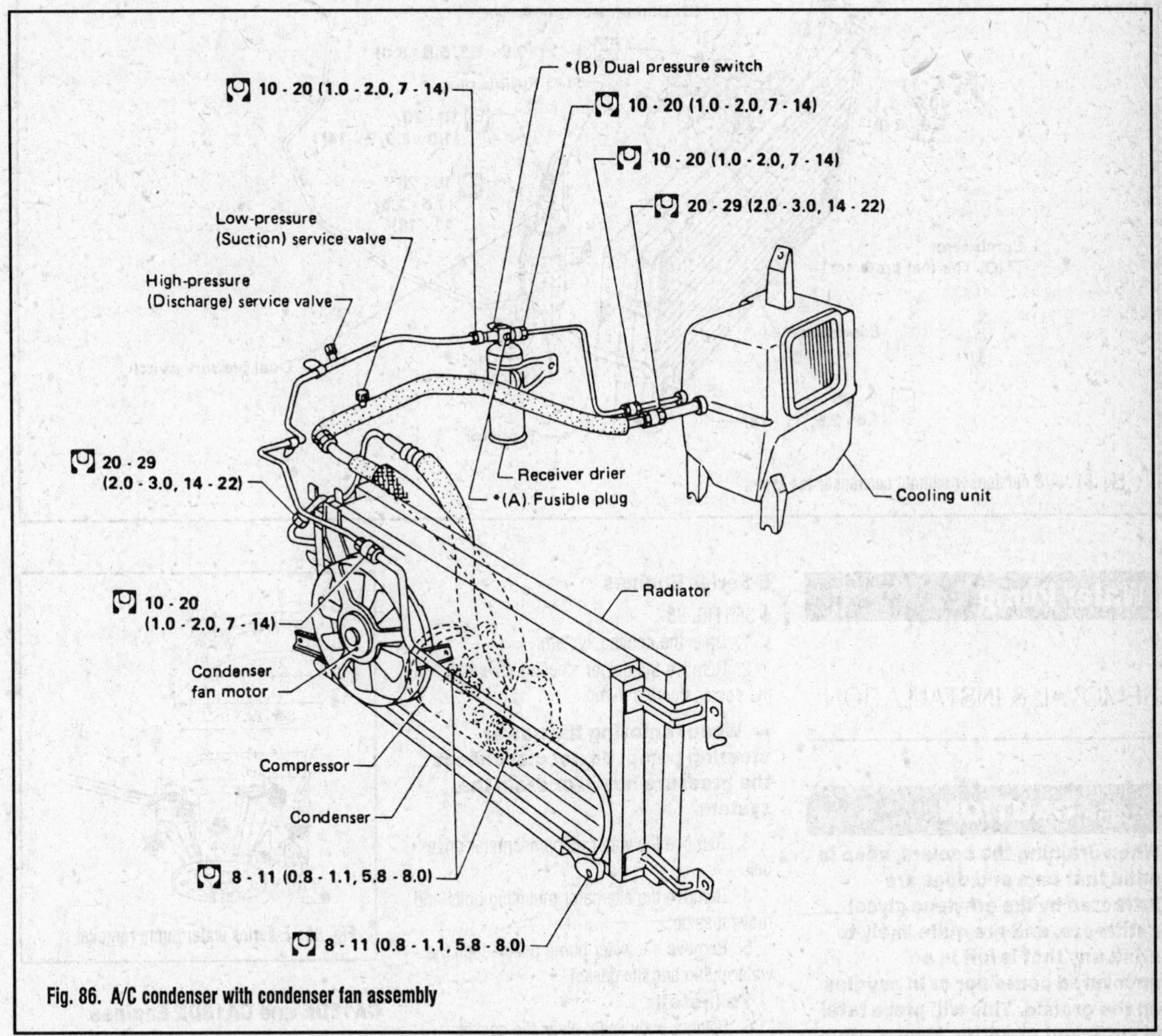
*(B) Dual pressure switch
10 - 20 (1.0 - 2.0, 7 - 14)
10 - 20 (1.0 - 2.0, 7 - 14)
10 - 20 (1.0 - 2.0, 7 - 14)
20 - 29 (2.0 - 3.0, 14 - 22)
Low-pressure
(Suction) service valve
High-pressure
(Discharge) service valve
20 - 29
(2.0 - 3.0, 14 - 22)
Receiver drier
*(A) Fusible plug
Cooling unit
Radiator
10 - 20
(1.0 - 2.0, 7 - 14)
Condenser
fan motor
Compressor
Condenser
8 - 11 (0.8 - 1.1, 5.8 - 8.0)
8 - 11 (0.8 - 1.1, 5.8 - 8.0)

Fig. 86. A/C condenser with condenser fan assembly

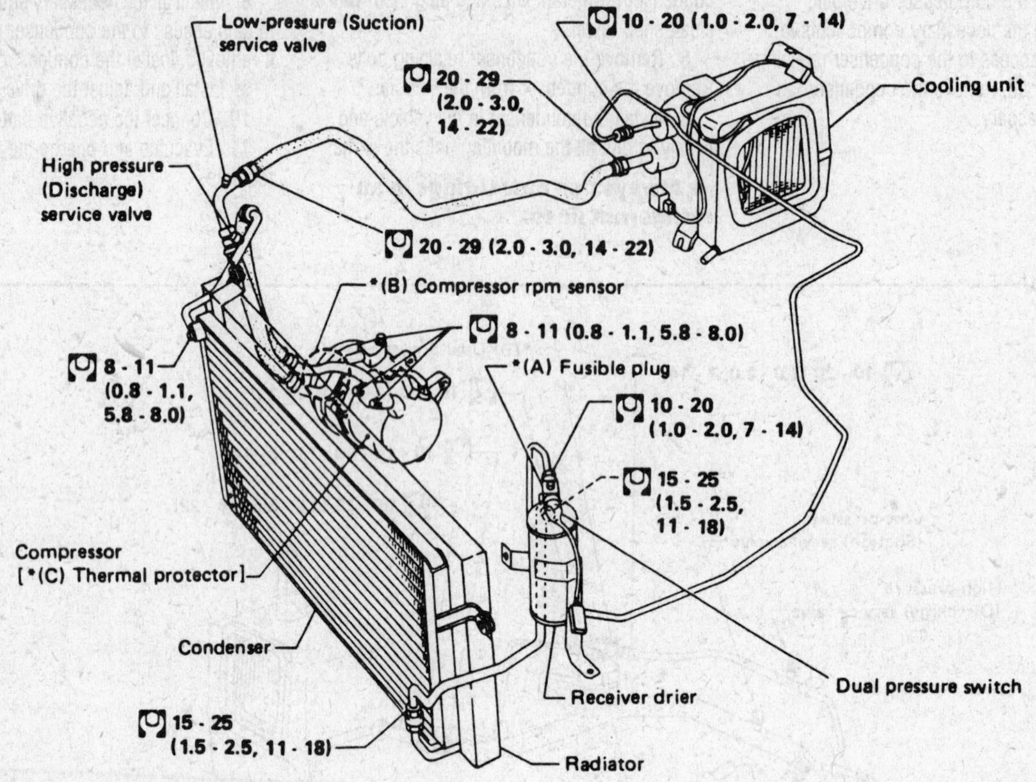

Fig. 87. A/C condenser without condenser fan motor

Water Pump

REMOVAL & INSTALLATION

✲✲ CAUTION

When draining the coolant, keep in mind that cats and dogs are attracted by the ethylene glycol antifreeze, and are quite likely to drink any that is left in an uncovered container or in puddles on the ground. This will prove fatal in sufficient quantity. Always drain the coolant into a sealable container. Coolant should be reused unless it is contaminated or several years old.

E-Series Engines

➧ SEE FIG. 88

1. Drain the cooling system.
2. Remove the power steering drive belt and the power steering pump.

➡ When removing the power steering pump, do not disconnect the pressure hoses or drain the system.

3. Remove the water pump/alternator drive belt.
4. Remove the alternator mounting bolts and move it aside.
5. Remove the water pump pulley, then the water pump and the gasket.

To install:

6. Using a putty knife, clean the gasket mounting surfaces.
7. Install the water pump on the engine, with a new gasket. Torque the water pump bolts evenly, to 6.5–10 ft. lbs. (9–13 Nm).
8. Install the water pump pulley, alternator and the power steering pump.
9. Adjust the drive belts and refill the cooling system. Start the engine and check for leaks.

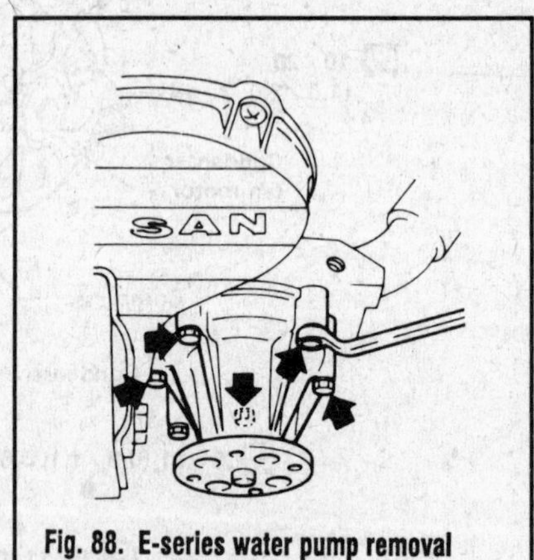

Fig. 88. E-series water pump removal

CA16DE and CA18DE Engines

➧ SEE FIG. 89

1. Drain the engine coolant.
2. Loosen the bolts retaining the fan shroud to the radiator and remove the shroud.
3. Loosen the belt, then remove the fan and pulley from the water pump hub.
4. Remove the bolts retaining the pump and remove the pump together with the gasket from the front cover.

To install:

5. Remove all traces of gasket material and install the pump in the reverse order. Use a new gasket and sealer. Tighten the bolts uniformly and torque to 12–14 ft. lbs. (16–18 Nm).

6. Install the pulley and fan onto the water pump hub.

7. Install and adjust the drive belt and radiator shroud.

8. Refill the cooling system and start the engine and check for leaks.

➡ The water pump cannot be disassembled and must be replaced as a unit. Be careful not to get coolant on the timing belt

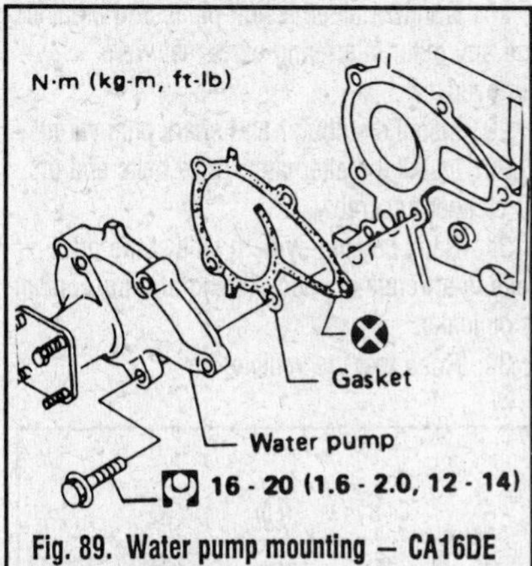
N·m (kg-m, ft-lb)
Gasket
Water pump
16 - 20 (1.6 - 2.0, 12 - 14)

Fig. 89. Water pump mounting — CA16DE and CA18DE engines

GA16i, GA16DE and SR20DE Engines

➧ SEE FIG. 90

1. Disconnect the negative battery cable.

2. Drain the coolant from the radiator and cylinder block.

3. Remove all the drive belts.

4. Unbolt the water pump pulley and the water pump attaching bolts.

5. Separate the water pump with the gasket, if installed, from the cylinder block.

6. Remove all gasket material or sealant from the water pump mating surfaces. All sealant must be removed from the groove in the water pump surface also.

To install:

7. Apply a continuous bead of high temperature liquid gasket to the water pump housing mating surface. The housing must be attached to the cylinder block within 5 minutes after the sealant is applied. After the pump housing is bolted to the block, wait at least 30 minutes for the sealant to cure before starting the engine.

8. Position the water pump (and gasket) onto the block and install the attaching bolts. Torque the small retaining bolts to about 5 ft. lbs. (10 Nm) and large retaining bolts 12–14 ft. lbs. (18–20 Nm).

9. Install the water pump pulley.

10. Install the drive belts and adjust the tension.

11. Fill the cooling system to the proper level.

12. Connect the negative battery cable.

CD17 Diesel Engine

1. Disconnect the negative battery cable. Drain the cooling system.

2. Remove the alternator and air conditioning compressor drive belts, if equipped.

3. Remove the front crankshaft pulley after first setting the No. 1 cylinder at TDC on the compression stroke.

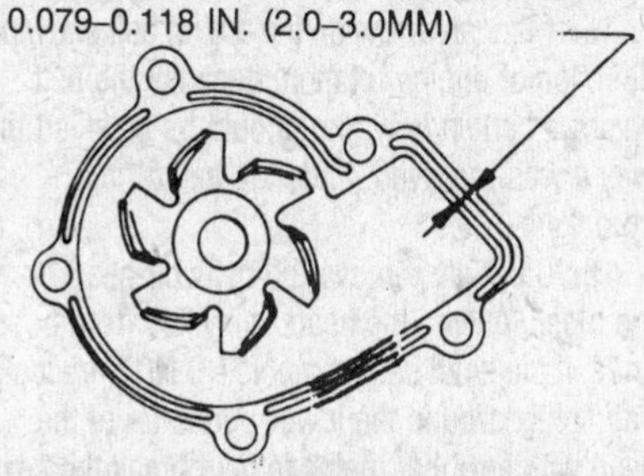

DIAMETER OF LIQUID GASKET BEAD: 0.079–0.118 IN. (2.0–3.0MM)

Fig. 90. Apply a continuous bead of RTV sealer to the water pump housing mating surface

4. Remove the front engine covers.

5. Remove the timing belt.

6. Loosen the mounting bolts and remove the water pump. Take note of the location and length of each bolt, as there are three different lengths.

To install:

7. Clean all gasket surfaces before reassembly. Install new gaskets, and install the pump. Torque the bolts, going around in several stages to 12–14 ft. lbs. (16–19 Nm).

8. Refer to "Timing Belt Removal and Installation" for the CD17 engine later in this Section, and install the timing belt and timing belt covers. Make sure to replace the timing belt if the pump has been leaking, as antifreeze will destroy timing belts.

9. The remaining steps of installation are the reverse of removal. **Make sure there is adequate clearance between the hose clamp and the timing cover** to avoid deforming the cover.

➡ The water pump cannot be disassembled and must be replaced as a unit. Inspect the timing belt for wear or damage and replace if necessary.

➧ SEE FIG. 91

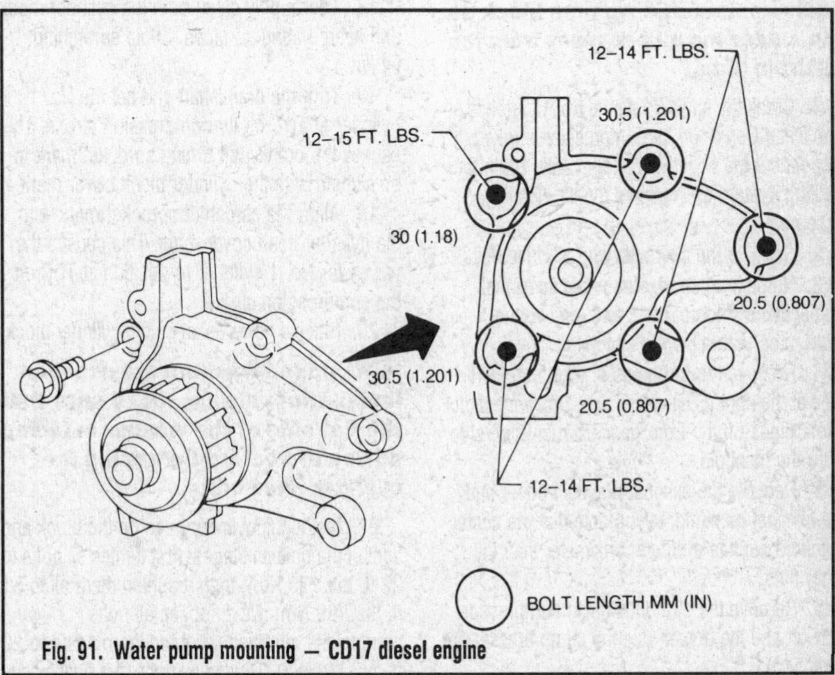
12–14 FT. LBS.
30.5 (1.201)
12–15 FT. LBS.
30 (1.18)
20.5 (0.807)
30.5 (1.201)
20.5 (0.807)
12–14 FT. LBS.
BOLT LENGTH MM (IN)

Fig. 91. Water pump mounting — CD17 diesel engine

Cylinder Head

➧ SEE FIGS. 93–111

REMOVAL & INSTALLATION

**** CAUTION**

When draining the coolant, keep in mind that cats and dogs are attracted by the ethylene glycol antifreeze, and are quite likely to drink any that is left in an uncovered container or in puddles on the ground. This will prove fatal in sufficient quantity. Always drain the coolant into a sealable container. Coolant should be reused unless it is contaminated or several years old.

➡ To prevent distortion or warping of the cylinder head, allow the engine to cool completely before removing the head bolts.

E-Series Engines, Except E16i

➡ If the engine mounting bracket must be removed. Support the engine by placing a jack or equivalent, with a wooden block on top, under the oil pan away from the oil drain plug.

1. Crank the engine until the No. 1 piston is at Top Dead Center on its compression stroke and disconnect the negative battery cable. Drain the cooling system and remove the air cleaner assembly.
2. Remove the alternator and all drive belts.
3. Number all spark plug wires as to their respective cylinders, mark and remove the distributor, with all wires attached.
4. Remove the EAI pipes bracket and EGR tube at the right (EGR valve) side. Disconnect the same pipes on the front (exhaust manifold) side from the manifold.
5. Remove the exhaust manifold cover and the exhaust manifold, taking note that the center manifold nut has a different diameter than the other nuts.
6. Remove the air conditioning compressor bracket and the power steering pump bracket (if equipped).
7. Label and disconnect the carburetor throttle linkage, fuel line, and all vacuum and electrical connections.
8. Remove the intake manifold with carburetor or throttle body.
9. Remove water pump pulley and the crankshaft pulley.
10. Remove the rocker (valve) cover.
11. Remove upper and lower dust cover on the camshaft timing belt shroud.
12. With the shroud removed, the cam sprocket, crankshaft sprocket, jackshaft sprocket, tensioner pulley, and toothed rubber timing belt are exposed.
13. Mark the relationship of the camshaft sprocket to the timing belt and the crankshaft sprocket to the timing belt with paint or a grease pencil. This will make setting everything up during reassembly much easier if the engine is disturbed during disassembly.
14. Remove the belt tensioner pulley.
15. Mark an arrow on the timing belt showing direction of engine rotation, because the belt wears a certain way and should be installed the way it was removed. Slide the belt off the sprockets.
16. Carefully remove the cylinder head from the block, pulling the head up evenly from both ends. If the head seems stuck, DO NOT pry it off. Tap lightly around the lower perimeter of the head with a rubber mallet to help break the seal. Label all head bolts with tape, as they must go back in their original positions. On some engines bolts are different size.

To install:

17. Thoroughly clean both the cylinder block and head mating surfaces. Avoid scratching either.
18. Turn the crankshaft and set the No. 1 cylinder at TDC on its compression stroke. This causes the crankshaft timing sprocket mark to be aligned with the cylinder block cover mark.
19. Align the camshaft sprocket mark with the cylinder head cover mark. This causes the valves for No. 1 cylinder to position at TDC on the compression stroke.
20. Place a new gasket on the cylinder block.

➡ If cupped washers are used for installation, always make sure that the flat side of the washer is facing downward before tightening the cylinder head bolts.

21. Install the cylinder head on the block and tighten the bolts in stages: first tighten all bolts to 22 ft. lbs. (30 Nm), then retighten them all to 51 ft. lbs. (69 Nm). Next, loosen all bolts completely, and then retighten them again to 22 ft. lbs. (30 Nm). Tighten all bolts to a final torque of 51–54 ft. lbs. (69–74 Nm).
22. Install the timing belt, tensioner, upper and lower dust cover. Make sure all timing marks are in proper alignment. Connect the engine mount bracket.
23. Install the valve cover, water pump drive belt and pulley. Install the crankshaft pulley.
24. Install the intake manifold with carburetor or throttle body.
25. Connect the carburetor throttle linkage, fuel line, and all vacuum and electrical connections.
26. Install the air conditioning compressor bracket and the power steering pump bracket (if equipped).
27. Install the exhaust manifold and the exhaust manifold cover.
28. Connect all emission pipes and brackets and any other interfering parts that were removed.
29. Install distributor and spark plug wires.
30. Install the alternator, drive belts and the air cleaner assembly.
31. Refill cooling system, adjust the drive belts, start engine, check timing and for coolant or oil leaks.
32. Road test the vehicle.

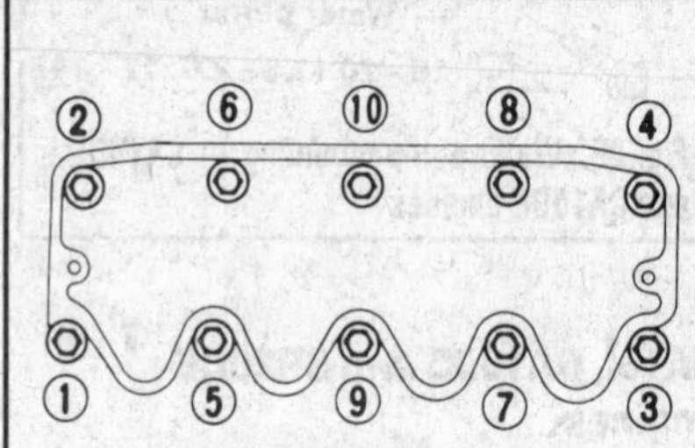
2
6
10
8
4
1
5
9
7
3

Fig. 93. E-series cylinder head bolt loosening sequence

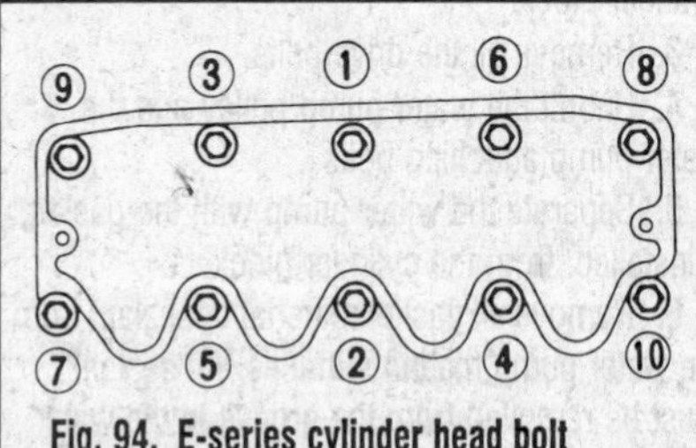
9
3
1
6
8
7
5
2
4
10

Fig. 94. E-series cylinder head bolt tightening sequence

CA16DE and CA18DE Double Overhead Camshaft Engines

1. Crank the engine until the No. 1 piston is at Top Dead Center on its compression stroke and disconnect the negative battery cable. Drain the cooling system and remove the air cleaner assembly and upper radiator hose.

2. Loosen the alternator and remove all drive belts. Remove the alternator. If necessary remove the right side under cover.

3. Disconnect the air duct at the throttle chamber.

4. Tag and disconnect all lines, hoses and wires which may interfere with cylinder head removal.

5. Remove the 8 screws and lift off the ornament cover.

6. Disconnect the O_2 sensor.

7. Remove the 2 exhaust heat shield covers.

8. Unbolt the exhaust manifold and wire the entire assembly out of the way.

9. Disconnect the EGR tube at the passage cover and then remove the passage cover and its gasket.

10. Disconnect and remove the crank angle sensor from the upper front cover.

➡ **Put aligning mark on crank angle sensor and timing belt cover.**

11. Remove the support stay from under the intake manifold assembly.

12. Unbolt the intake manifold and remove it along with the collector and throttle chamber.

13. Disconnect and remove the fuel injectors as an assembly.

14. Remove the upper and lower front covers.

➡ **Remove engine mount bracket but support engine under oil pan with wooden blocks or equivalent. Do not position the support near the drain plug.**

15. Remove the timing belt and camshaft sprockets.

➡ **When the timing belt has been removed, NEVER rotate the crankshaft and camshaft separately because the valves will hit the pistons!**

16. Remove the camshaft cover.

17. Remove the breather separator.

18. Gradually loosen the cylinder head bolts in several stages, in the sequence illustrated.

19. Carefully remove the cylinder head from the block, pulling the head up evenly from both ends. If the head seems stuck, DO NOT pry it off. Tap lightly around the lower perimeter of the head with a rubber mallet to help break the seal. Label all head bolts with tape or magic marker, as they must go back in their original positions.

To install:

20. Thoroughly clean both the cylinder block and head mating surfaces. Avoid scratching either.

21. Install the cylinder head with bolts on the block. When installing the bolts tighten the two center bolts temporarily to 15 ft. lbs. (20 Nm) and install the head bolts loosely. After the timing belt and front cover have been installed, torque all the head bolts in the torque sequence. Tighten all bolts to 22 ft. lbs. (30 Nm). Re-tighten all bolts to 76 ft. lbs. (103 Nm). Loosen all bolts completely and then re-tighten them once again to 22 ft. lbs. (30 Nm). Tighten all bolts to a final torque of 76 ft. lbs. ((103 Nm).

➡ **If cupped washers are used for installation, always make sure that the flat side of the washer is facing downward before tightening the cylinder head bolts.**

22. Install the camshaft sprocket, timing belt and front covers.

23. Reconnect the engine mount support.

24. Install the fuel injectors, intake manifold assembly with collector and throttle chamber attached.

25. Connect the support stay to the intake manifold.

26. Install the crank angle sensor. Align the sensor with mark that was made before removal.

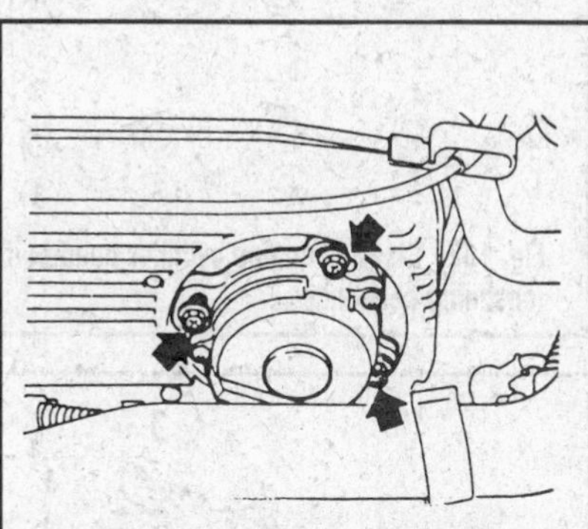

Fig. 95. Crank angle sensor location on timing cover — CA16DE and CA18DE engines

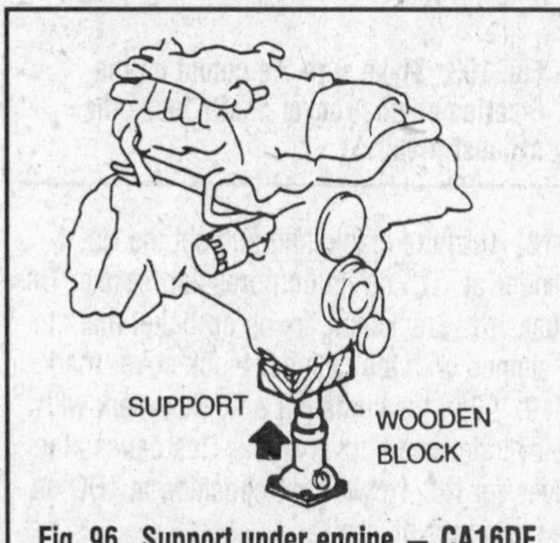
SUPPORT
WOODEN
BLOCK

Fig. 96. Support under engine — CA16DE and CA18DE engines

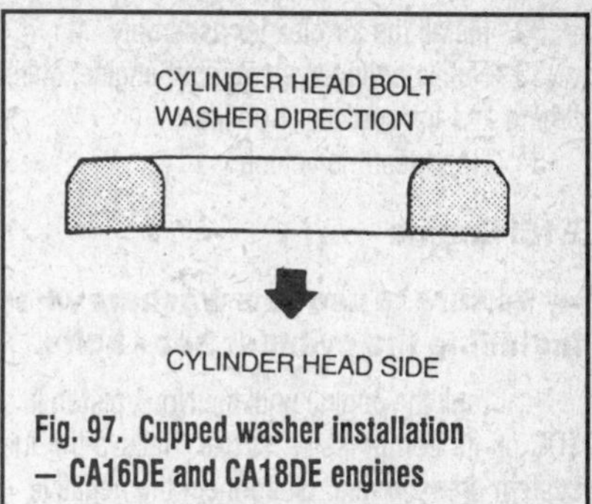
CYLINDER HEAD BOLT
WASHER DIRECTION
CYLINDER HEAD SIDE

Fig. 97. Cupped washer installation — CA16DE and CA18DE engines

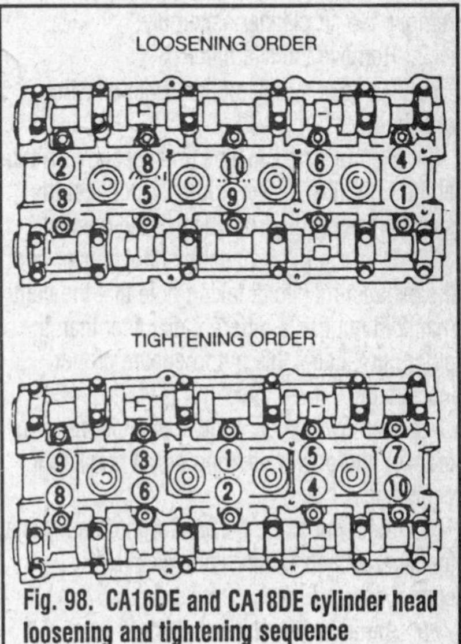
LOOSENING ORDER
2
8
10
6
4
3
5
9
7
1
TIGHTENING ORDER
9
3
1
5
7
8
6
2
4
10

Fig. 98. CA16DE and CA18DE cylinder head loosening and tightening sequence

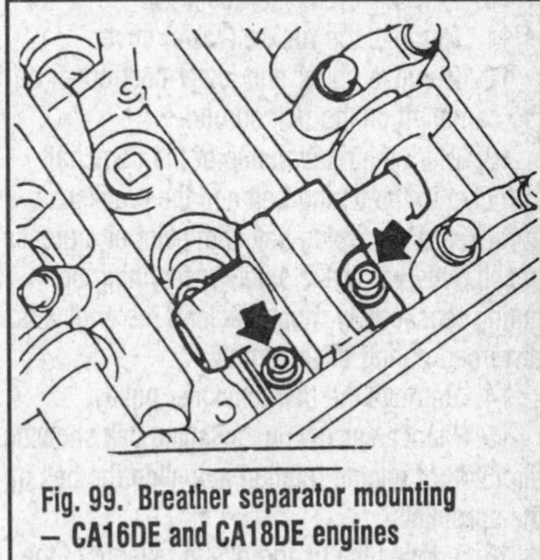

Fig. 99. Breather separator mounting — CA16DE and CA18DE engines

27. Connect EGR tube and passage cover with a new gasket.

28. Install the exhaust manifold assembly and heat shields.

29. Reconnect the O_2 sensor and ornament cover.

30. Reconnect the air duct at the throttle chamber. Connect all lines, hoses and wires that were removed.

31. Install the alternator and adjust all the drive belts.

32. Install the air cleaner assembly.

33. Refill cooling system, start engine, check timing and for coolant or oil leaks.

34. Road test the vehicle.

E16i Engine

➡ Be sure to use new washers when installing the cylinder head bolts.

1. Crank the engine until the No. 1 piston is at TDC on its compression stroke. Relieve the fuel system pressure and disconnect the negative battery cable. Drain the cooling system and remove the air cleaner assembly.

2. Remove the alternator.

3. Remove the distributor, with all wires attached.

4. Remove the EAI pipe bracket and EGR tube at the right (EGR valve) side. Disconnect the same pipes on the front side of the manifold.

5. Remove the exhaust manifold cover and the exhaust manifold, taking note that the center manifold nut has a different diameter than the other nuts. Label this nut to ensure proper installation.

6. Remove the air conditioning compressor bracket and power steering pump bracket, if equipped.

7. Disconnect the carburetor throttle linkage, fuel line, and all vacuum and electrical connections.

8. Remove the intake manifold.

9. Remove water pump drive belt and pulley.

10. Remove crankshaft pulley.

11. Remove the rocker (valve) cover.

12. Remove upper and lower dust cover on the camshaft timing belt shroud.

13. Mark the relationship of the camshaft sprocket to the timing belt and the crankshaft sprocket to the timing belt with paint or a grease pencil. This will make setting everything up during reassembly much easier if the engine is disturbed during disassembly.

14. Remove the belt tensioner pulley.

15. Mark an arrow on the timing belt showing direction of engine rotation and slide the belt off the sprockets.

16. Loosen the head bolts in reverse of the tightening sequence and carefully remove the cylinder head from the block, pulling the head up evenly from both ends. If the head seems stuck, do not pry it off. Tap lightly around the lower perimeter of the head with a rubber mallet to help break the seal. Label all head bolts with tape, as they must go back in their original positions.

To install:

17. Thoroughly clean both the cylinder block and head mating surfaces. Avoid scratching either.

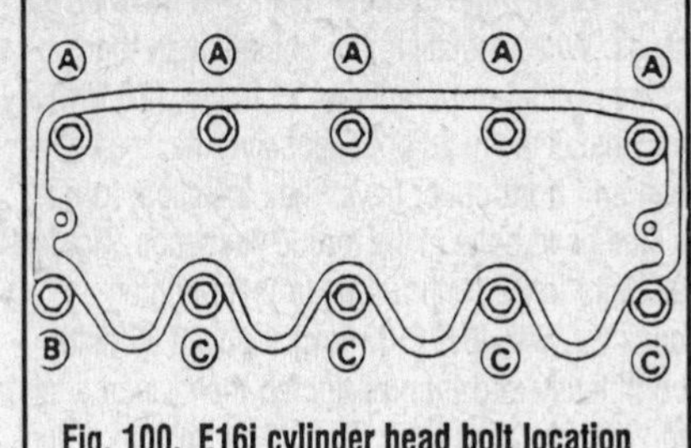
A
A
A
A
A
B
C
C
C
C

Fig. 100. E16i cylinder head bolt location

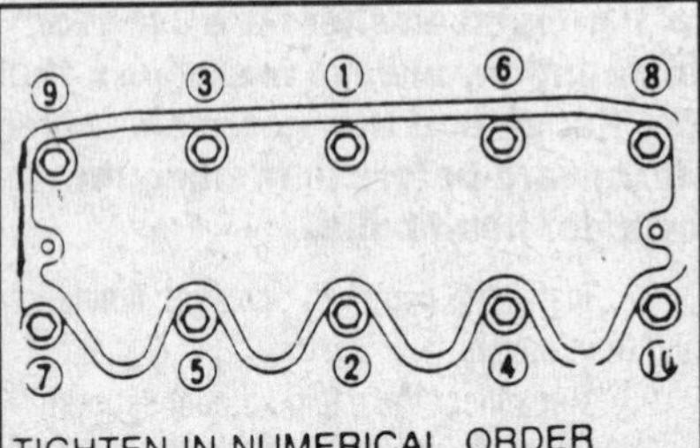
9
3
1
6
8
7
5
2
4
10
TIGHTEN IN NUMERICAL ORDER

Fig. 101. E16i cylinder head bolt tightening sequence

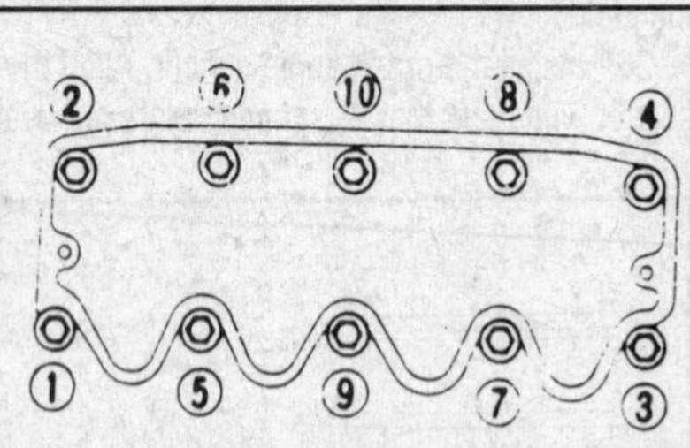
2
6
10
8
4
1
5
9
7
3

Fig. 102. E-series engine cylinder head bolt loosening sequence

EXHAUST MANIFOLD SIDE

Fig. 103. Make sure the cutout on the E-series engine rocker shafts faces the exhaust manifold

18. Turn the crankshaft and set the No. 1 cylinder at TDC on its compression stroke. This causes the crankshaft timing sprocket mark to be aligned with the cylinder block cover mark.

19. Align the camshaft sprocket mark with the cylinder head cover mark. This causes the valves for No. 1 cylinder to position at TDC on the compression stroke.

20. Place a new gasket on the cylinder block.

➡ There are 3 different size head bolts used on the E16i engine. Bolt (A) is 3.74 in. (95mm), bolt (B) is 4.33 in. (110mm) and bolt (C) is 3.15 in. (80mm). Measure the length of each bolt prior to installation and make sure they are installed in their proper locations on the head.

21. Install the cylinder head on the block and tighten the bolts as follows:

a. Tighten all bolts to 22 ft. lbs. (29 Nm), then retighten them all to 51 ft. lbs. (69 Nm).

b. Loosen all bolts completely, and then retighten them again to 22 ft. lbs. (29 Nm).

c. Tighten all bolts to a final torque of 51–54 ft. lbs. (69–74 Nm); or if an angle wrench is used, turn each bolt until they have achieved the specified number of degrees — bolts 1, 3, 6, 8 and 9: 45–50 degrees; bolt 7: 55–60 degrees and bolts 2, 4, 5 and 10: 40–45 degrees.

22. Install the timing belt.

23. Install the upper and lower dust covers on the camshaft timing belt shroud.

24. Install the rocker arm cover.

25. Install the crankshaft pulley, water pump pulley and drive belt.

26. Install the intake manifold.

27. Connect the throttle linkage, fuel line, and all vacuum and electrical connections.

28. Install the air conditioning compressor bracket and the power steering pump bracket, if equipped.

29. Install the exhaust manifold and exhaust manifold cover. Make sure the center manifold nut, which has a different diameter, is installed in the proper location.

30. Connect the EAI exhaust pipes and tubing.

31. Install the distributor and connect the spark plug wiring.

32. Install the alternator and air cleaner.

33. Fill the cooling system to the proper level and connect the negative battery cable.

34. Make all the necessary engine adjustments. Road test the vehicle for proper operation.

GA16i Engine

1. Disconnect the negative battery cable, drain the cooling system and relieve the fuel system pressure.

2. Disconnect the exhaust tube from the exhaust manifold.

3. Remove the intake manifold support bracket.

4. Remove the air cleaner assembly.

5. Disconnect the center wire from the distributor cap.

6. Remove the rocker arm cover.

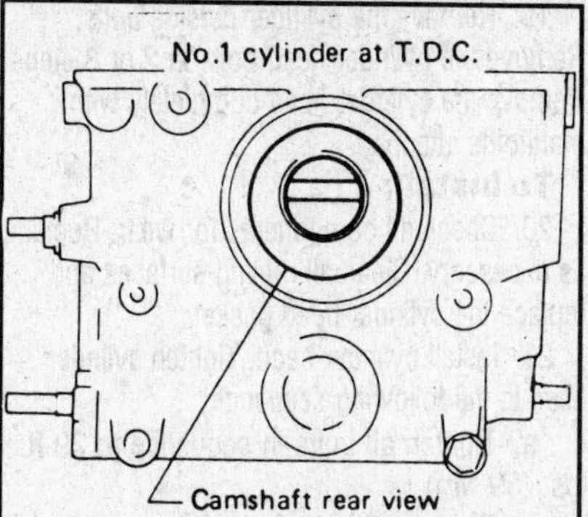
No.1 cylinder at T.D.C.
Camshaft rear view
Fig. 104. When the camshaft is aligned as shown, the No. 1 cylinder is at TDC — GA16i engine

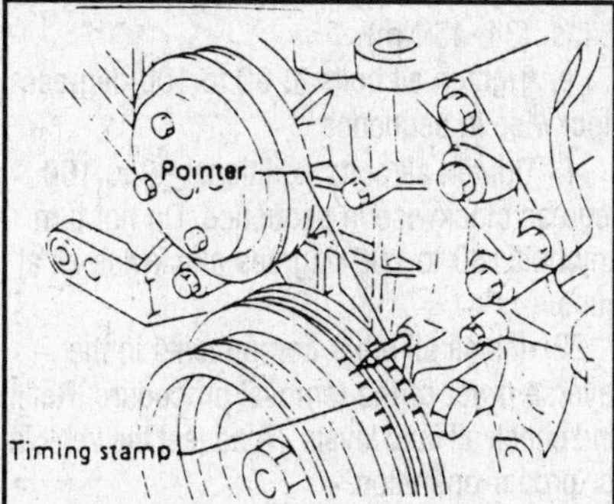
Pointer
Timing stamp
Fig. 105. When the crankshaft pulley marks are aligned as shown, the No. 1 cylinder is at TDC

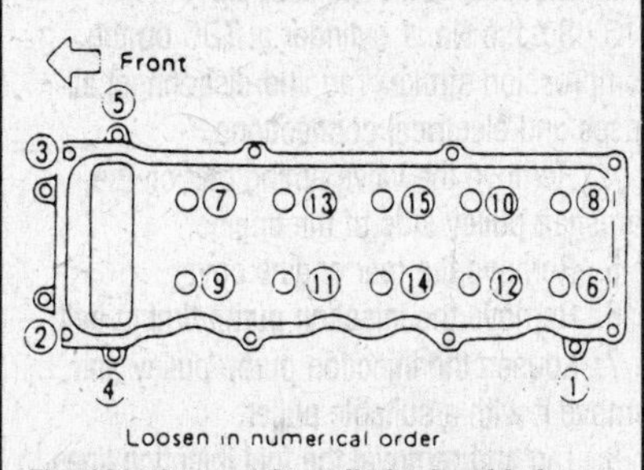
Front
Loosen in numerical order
Fig. 106. Loosen the cylinder head bolts in several stages — GA16i and GA16DE engines

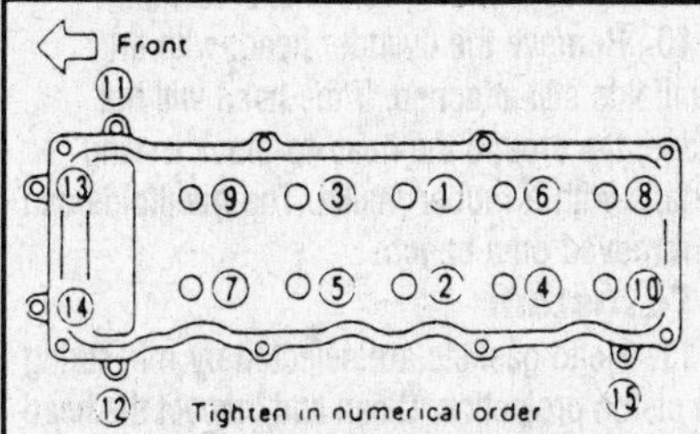
Front
Tighten in numerical order
Fig. 107. Cylinder head bolts tightening sequence — GA16i and GA16DE engines

7. Remove the distributor.
8. Remove the spark plugs.
9. Set the No. 1 cylinder at TDC of the compression stroke by rotating the engine until the cut out machined in the rear of the camshaft is horizontally aligned with the cylinder head.
10. Hold the camshaft sprocket stationary with the proper tool and loosen the sprocket bolt. Place highly visible and accurate paint or chalk alignment marks on the camshaft sprocket and the timing chain, then slide the sprocket from the camshaft and lift the timing chain from the sprocket. Remove the sprocket. The timing chain will not fall off the crankshaft sprocket unless the front cover is removed. This is due to the cast portion of the front cover located on the lower side of the crankshaft sprocket which acts a stopper mechanism. For this reason a chain stopper (wedge) is not required to remove the cylinder head.
11. Loosen the cylinder bolts in 2–3 stages to prevent warpage and cracking of the head. One of the cylinder head bolts is longer than the rest. Mark this bolt and make a note of its location.
12. Carefully remove the cylinder head from the block, pulling the head up evenly from both ends. If the head seems stuck, do not pry it off. Tap lightly around the lower perimeter of the head with a rubber mallet to help break the seal. The cylinder head and the intake and exhaust manifolds are removed together. Remove the cylinder head gasket.

To install:

13. Thoroughly clean both the cylinder block and head mating surfaces. Avoid scratching either.
14. Turn the crankshaft and set the No. 1 cylinder at TDC on its compression stroke. This is done by aligning the timing pointer with the appropriate timing mark on the pulley. To ensure that the No. 1 piston is at TDC, verify that the knock pin in the front of the camshaft is set at the top.
15. Place a new gasket on the block and lower the head onto the gasket.

➡ These engines use 2 different length cylinder head bolts. Bolt (1) is 5.24 in. (133mm) while bolts (2) thru (10) are 4.33 in. (110mm). Do not confuse the location of these bolts.

16. Coat the threads and the seating surface of the head bolts with clean engine oil and use a new set of washers. Install the cylinder head bolts in their proper locations and tighten as follows:

a. Tighten all the bolts in sequence to 22 ft. lbs. (30 Nm).
b. Tighten all bolts in sequence to 47 ft. lbs.(64 Nm).
c. Loosen all bolts in reverse of the tightening sequence.
d. Tighten all bolts again to 22 ft. lbs. (30 Nm).
e. If an angle torque wrench is not available, torque the bolts in sequence to 43–51 ft. lbs. (58–59 Nm). If using an angle torque wrench for this step, tighten bolt (1) 80–85 degrees clockwise and bolts (6) thru (10) 60–65 degrees clockwise.
f. Finally, tighten bolts (11) thru (15) to 4.6– 6.1 ft. lbs. (6.3–8.3 Nm).

17. Place the timing chain on the camshaft sprocket using the alignment marks. Slide the sprocket and timing chain onto the camshaft and install the center bolt.
18. At this point, check the hydraulic valve lifters for proper operation pushing hard on each lifter hard with fingertip pressure. Make sure the rocker arm arm is not on the cam lobe when making this check. If the valve lifter moves more than 0.04 in. (1mm), air may be inside it.
19. Install the spark plugs.
20. Install the distributor.
21. Install the rocker arm cover.
22. Connect the center wire to the distributor cap.
23. Install the air cleaner assembly.
24. Install the intake manifold support bracket.
25. Fill the cooling system to the proper level and connect the negative battery cable.
26. Make all the necessary engine adjustments. If there was air in the lifters, bleed the air by running the engine at 1000 rpm for 10 minutes. Road test the vehicle for proper operation.

GA16DE Engine

1. Disconnect the negative battery cable, drain the cooling system and relieve the fuel system pressure.
2. Remove all drive belts. Disconnect the exhaust tube from the exhaust manifold.
3. Remove the power steering bracket.
4. Remove the air duct to intake manifold collector.
5. Remove the front right side wheel, splash cover and front undercovers.
6. Remove the front exhaust pipe and engine front mounting bracket.
7. Remove the rocker arm cover.
8. Remove the distributor cap. Remove the spark plugs.

9. Set the No. 1 cylinder at TDC of the compression stroke.

10. Mark and remove the distributor assembly.

11. Remove the cam sprocket cover and gusset. Remove the water pump pulley. Remove the thermostat housing.

12. Remove the chain tensioner, chain guide. Loosen idler sprocket bolt.

13. Remove the camshaft sprocket bolts, camshaft sprocket, camshaft brackets and camshafts. Remove the idler sprocket bolt. These parts should be reassembled in their original position. Bolts should be loosen in 2 or 3 steps.

14. Loosen the cylinder bolts in 2–3 stages to prevent warpage and cracking of the head and note location of all head bolts.

15. Carefully remove the cylinder head from the block, pulling the head up evenly from both ends. If the head seems stuck, do not pry it off. Tap lightly around the lower perimeter of the head with a rubber mallet to help break the seal. The cylinder head and the intake and exhaust manifolds are removed together. Remove the cylinder head gasket.

To install:

16. Thoroughly clean both the cylinder block and head mating surfaces. Avoid scratching either.

17. Coat the threads and the seating surface of the head bolts with clean engine oil and use a new set of washers as necessary. Install the cylinder head assembly (always replace the head gasket). Install head bolts (with washers) in their proper locations and tighten as follows:

a. Tighten all the bolts in sequence to 22 ft. lbs. (29 Nm).

b. Tighten all bolts in sequence to 43 ft. lbs.(59 Nm).

c. Loosen all bolts in reverse of the tightening sequence.

d. Tighten all bolts again in sequence to 22 ft. lbs. (29 Nm).

e. Tighten bolts to 50–55 degrees clockwise in sequence or if angle wrench is not available, tighten bolts to 40–46 ft. lbs. (54–62 Nm) in sequence.

f. Finally, tighten bolts (11) thru (15) to 4.6–6.1 ft. lbs. (6.3–8.3 Nm).

18. Install the upper timing chain assembly.

19. Install all other components in the reverse order of the removal procedure. Refill and check all fluid levels. Road test the vehicle for proper operation.

SR20DE Engine

1. Release the fuel pressure. Disconnect the negative battery cable.

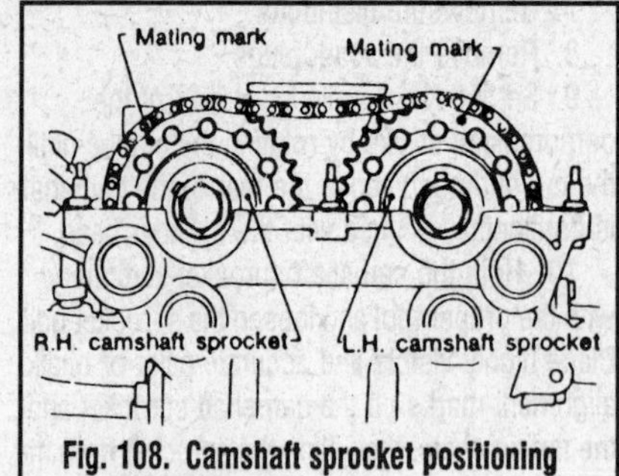
Mating mark
Mating mark
R.H. camshaft sprocket
L.H. camshaft sprocket

Fig. 108. Camshaft sprocket positioning – SR20DE engine

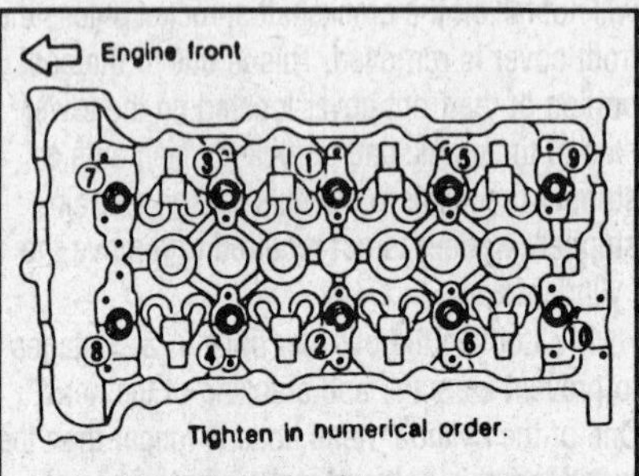
Engine front
Tighten in numerical order.

Fig. 109. Cylinder head torque sequence – SR20DE engine

2. Raise and safely support the vehicle. Remove the engine undercovers.

3. Remove the front right wheel and engine side cover.

4. Drain the cooling system. Remove the radiator assembly.

5. Remove the air duct to intake manifold.

6. Remove the drive belts and water pump pulley.

7. Remove the alternator and power steering pump.

8. Remove all vacuum hoses, fuel hoses, wires, electrical connections.

9. Remove all spark plugs.

10. Remove the A.I.V. valve and resonator.

11. Remove the rocker cover and oil separator.

12. Remove the intake manifold supports, oil filter bracket and power steering bracket.

13. Set No. 1 at TDC on the compression stroke. Rotate crankshaft until mating marks on camshaft sprockets are in the correct position.

14. Remove the timing chain tensioner.

15. Mark and remove the distributor assembly. Remove the timing chain guide and camshaft sprockets.

16. Remove the camshafts, camshaft brackets, oil tubes and baffle plate. Keep all parts in order for correct installation.

17. Remove the water hose from the cylinder block and water hose from the heater.

18. Remove the starter motor. Remove the water pipe bolt.

19. Remove the cylinder outside bolts. Remove the cylinder head bolts in 2 or 3 steps. Remove the cylinder head completely with manifolds attached.

To install:

20. Check all components for wear. Replace as necessary. Clean all mating surfaces and replace the cylinder head gasket.

21. Install cylinder head. Tighten cylinder head in the following sequence:

a. Tighten all bolts in sequence to 29 ft. lbs. (39 Nm).

b. Tighten all bolts in sequence to 58 ft. lbs. (79 Nm).

c. Loosen all bolts in sequence completely.

d. Tighten all bolts in sequence to 25–33 ft. lbs. (34–45 Nm).

e. Tighten all bolts to 90 to 100 degrees clockwise in sequence

f. Tighten all bolts additional 90 to 100 degrees clockwise in sequence. Do not turn any bolt 180 to 200 degrees clockwise all at once.

22. Install all other components in the reverse order of the removal procedure. Refill and check all fluid levels. Road test the vehicle for proper operation.

CD17 Diesel

1. Drain the coolant and disconnect the battery.

2. Disconnect the exhaust pipe.

3. Set the No. 1 cylinder at TDC on the compression stroke. Tag and disconnect all hoses and electrical connections.

4. Remove the valve timing belt on the camshaft pulley side of the engine.

5. Remove the rear engine cover.

6. Remove the injection pump timing belt.

7. Loosen the injection pump pulley and remove it with a suitable puller.

8. Tag and removal the fuel injection lines from the injectors.

9. Remove the camshaft (valve) cover and loosen the cylinder head bolts in the reverse of the torque sequence given in this section.

10. Remove the cylinder head, with the manifolds still attached. If the head will not budge, tap around the head-to-block mating surface with a rubber mallet. The manifolds can be removed on a bench.

To install:

11. Head gaskets are selected by measuring the piston projection. Clean and inspect the head as described in this section. Then, once the proper gasket has been selected, install the gasket and head.

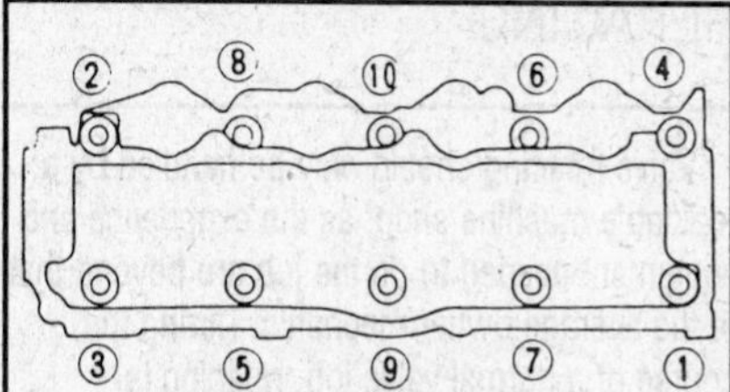

2
8
10
6
4
3
5
9
7
1

Fig. 110. Cylinder head loosening sequence – CD17 diesel engine

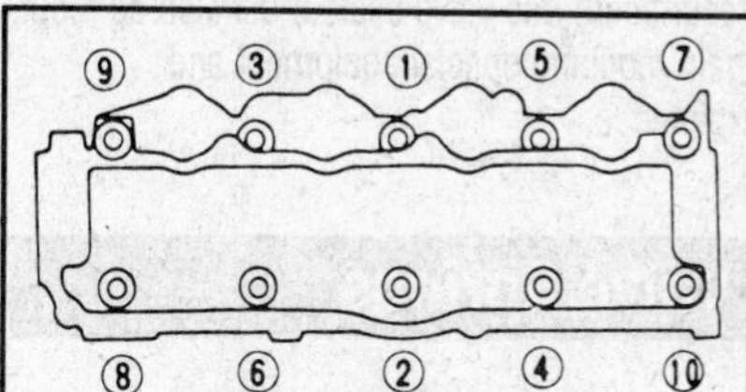

9
3
1
5
7
8
6
2
4
10

Fig. 111. Cylinder head tightening sequence – CD17 diesel engine

12. Lightly oil the head bolt threads and underside of the heads and install with washers. Torque the head bolts as follows:
   a. Torque all the bolts in the sequence shown to 29 ft. lbs. (39 Nm).
   b. Torque all the bolts in the sequence shown to 72–79 ft. lbs. (98–107 Nm).
   c. Loosen all the bolts completely.
   d. Torque all the bolts in the sequence shown to 29 ft. lbs. (39 Nm).
   e. If you do not have an angle type wrench, torque all the bolts in the sequence shown to 72–79 ft. lbs. (98–107 Nm). If you do have an angle wrench, turn each bolt, in the sequence shown, 82–87 degrees farther.
13. Adjust the valves as described in Section 2. Install the cam cover as described above.
14. Install the injection lines as described in Section 5.
15. Install the injection pump drive pulley. Then, install the pump timing belt as described later in this Section.
16. Install the rear timing belt cover.
17. Install the front engine timing belt and belt cover.
18. Connect all hoses and electrical connections according to the tags made earlier.
19. Connect the exhaust pipe. Refill the cooling system. Connect the battery. Start the engine and check for leaks.

CLEANING AND INSPECTION

Using a wire brush or equivalent, clean the carbon from the cylinder head, then check it for cracks and flaws. Make sure that the cylinder head and the block surfaces are clean. Check the cylinder head surface for flatness, using a straightedge and a feeler gauge. If the cylinder head and/or the block are warped more than 0.08mm, it must be trued by a machine shop; if this is not done, there will probably be a compression or water leak.

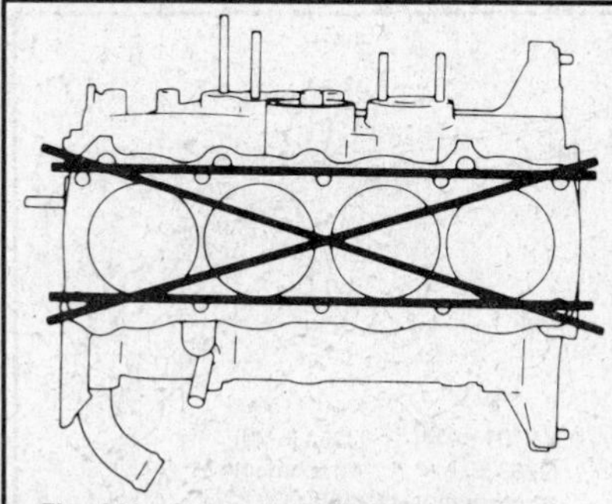
Fig. 112. Check the cylinder head for warpage – should not exceed 0.004 in. (0.101mm)

RESURFACING

Cylinder head resurfacing should be done only by a competent machine shop. If warpage exceeds the manufacturer's tolerance, the cylinder head must be replaced.

Valves and Springs

REMOVAL & INSTALLATION

➡ **If just removing the valve spring, the cylinder head does not have to be removed from the engine. Using a spark plug hole adapter, pressurize the cylinder with compressed air so the valve will not fall into the cylinder.**

1. Refer to the Cylinder Head, Removal and Installation procedures in this section and remove the cylinder head.
2. Loosen and back off the rocker arm adjusting screws, then remove the rocker arm assembly.

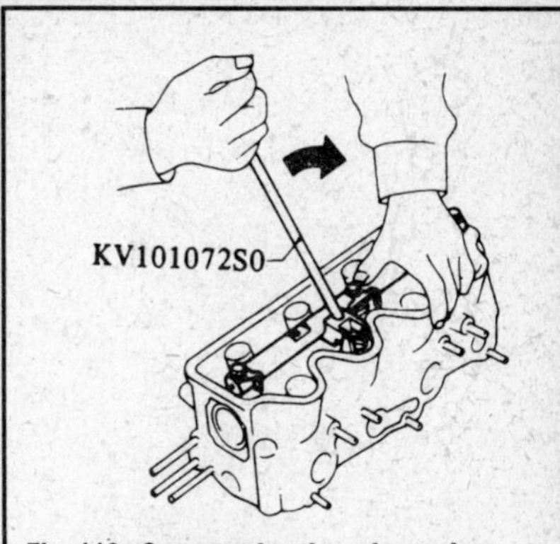

KV101072S0

Fig. 113. Compressing the valve spring – E-series engine

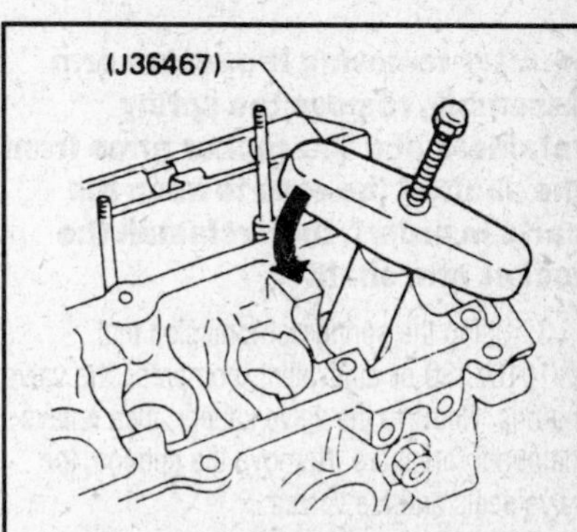

(J36467)

Fig. 114. Removing the valve oil seal – CA16DE and CA18DE shown, others similar

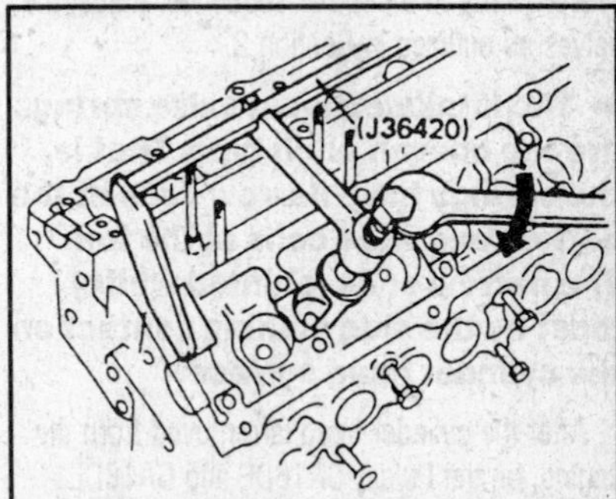

(J36420)

Fig. 115. Disassemble of valve mechanism – CA16DE and CA18DE shown, others similar

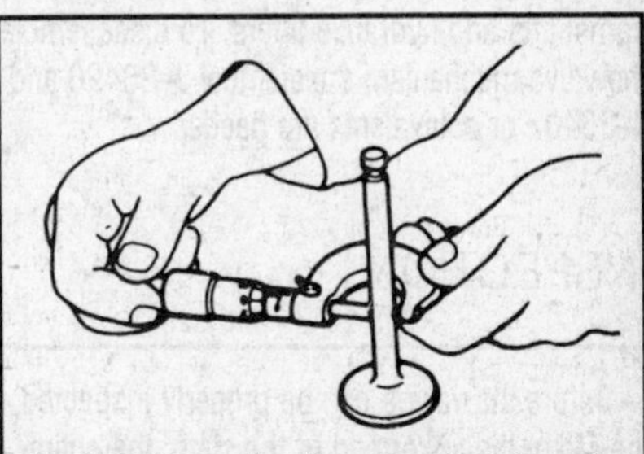
Fig. 116. Measuring the valve stem diameter

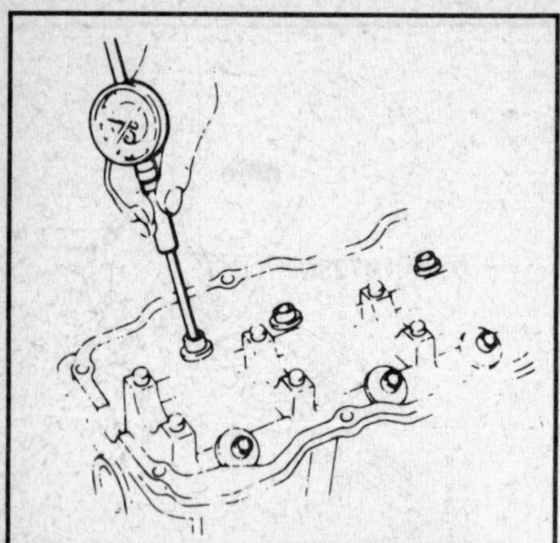

Fig. 117. Using an inside dial indicator to measure the valve guide inner diameter

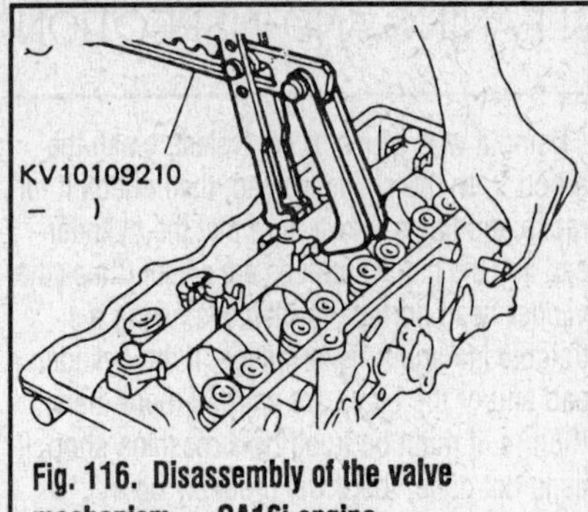
KV10109210
—)

Fig. 116. Disassembly of the valve mechanism — GA16i engine

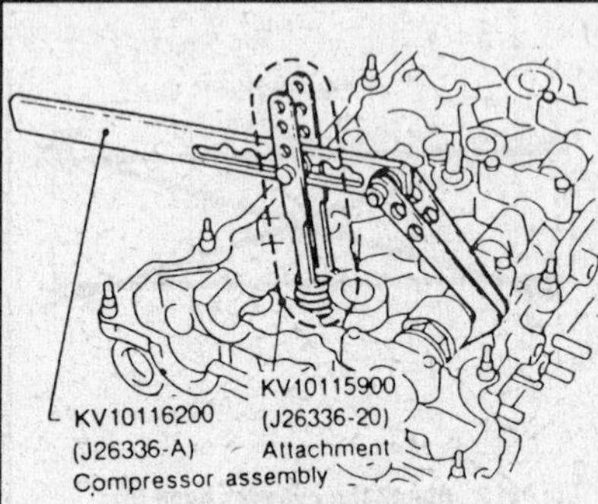
KV10116200
(J26336-A)
KV10115900
(J26336-20)
Attachment
Compressor assembly

Fig. 117. Disassembly of the valve mechanism — SR20DE and GA16DE engine

➡ After removing the rocker arm assembly, remove the spring retainers and the rocker arms from the shaft(s) (be sure to keep the parts in order), then reinstall the rocker arm shaft.

3. Using the spring compression tool KV101072S0 or equivalent, compress the valve springs. Remove the valve keeper, then relieve the spring pressure. Remove the springs, the valve seals and the valves.

To install:

4. Use new oil seals and check the valve guide for excessive side to side movement. Tighten the rocker shaft bolts to 14–18 ft. lbs. (19–24 Nm), in a circular sequence. Adjust the valves as outlined in Section 2.

➡ The intake/exhaust valve springs are the uneven pitch type. That is, the springs have narrow coils at the bottom and wide coils at the top. The narrow coils (painted white) must be the side making contact on the cylinder head surface.

After the cylinder head is removed from the engine, on the Pulsar CA16DE and CA18DE engines, remove the camhshaft sprockets, tensioner pulley and rear cover. Then remove the camshaft mounting bracket bolts gradually in two or three stages. Remove the front oil seals, camshafts and hydraulic lifters. To disassemble the valve mechanism special tool J-36420 and J-36467 or equivalents are needed.

INSPECTION

Before the valves can be properly inspected, the stem, the lower end of the stem, the entire valve face and head must be cleaned. An old valve works well for chipping carbon from the valve head, a wire brush, a gasket scraper or a putty knife can be used for cleaning the valve face and/or the area between the face and the lower stem. DO NOT scratch the valve face during cleaning. Clean the entire stem with a rag soaked in thinners to remove all of the varnish and gum.

Thorough inspection of the valves requires the use of a micrometer and a dial indicator. If these instruments are not available, the parts should be taken to a reputable machine shop for inspection. Refer to the Valve Specifications chart, for the valve stem and stem-to-guide specifications.

Using a dial indicator, measure the inside diameter of the valve guides at their bottom, midpoint and top positions, at 90° apart. Subtract the valve stem measurement; if the clearance exceeds that listed in the specifications chart under Stem-to-Guide Clearance, replace the valve(s).

Check the top of each valve for pitting and unusual wear due to improper rocker adjustment, etc. The stem tip can be ground flat if it is worn but no more that 0.50mm can be removed; if this limit must be exceeded to make the tip flat and square, then the valve must be replaced. If the valve stem tips are ground, make sure that the valve is fixed securely into the jig, so that the tip contacts the grinding wheel squarely at exactly 90°.

REFACING

Valve refacing should only be handled by a reputable machine shop, as the experience and equipment needed to do the job are beyond that of the average owner/mechanic. During the course of a normal valve job, refacing is necessary when simply lapping the valves into their seats will not correct the seat and face wear. When the valves are reground (resurfaced), the valve seats must also be recut, again requiring special equipment and experience.

Valve Springs

INSPECTION

1. Place the valve spring on a flat, clean surface, next to a square.
2. Measure the height of the spring and rotate it against the edge of the square to measure the distortion (out-of-roundness). If the spring height between springs varies or the distortion exceeds more than 1.6mm, replace the spring(s). The valve spring squareness should not exceed: 2.20mm (outer) or 1.90mm (inner).

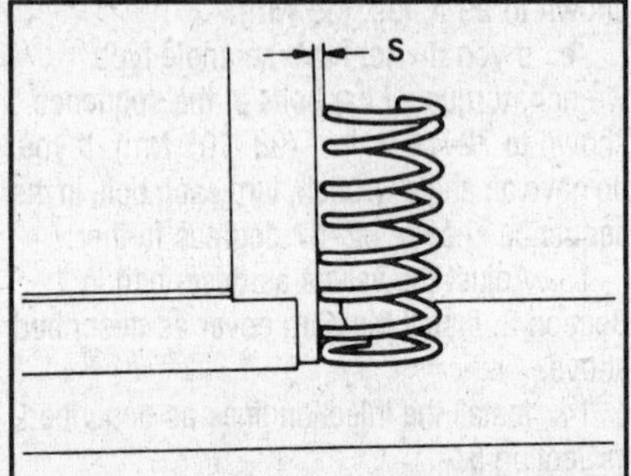
S

Fig. 120. Measuring the spring height and squareness. Make sure the closed coils face downward

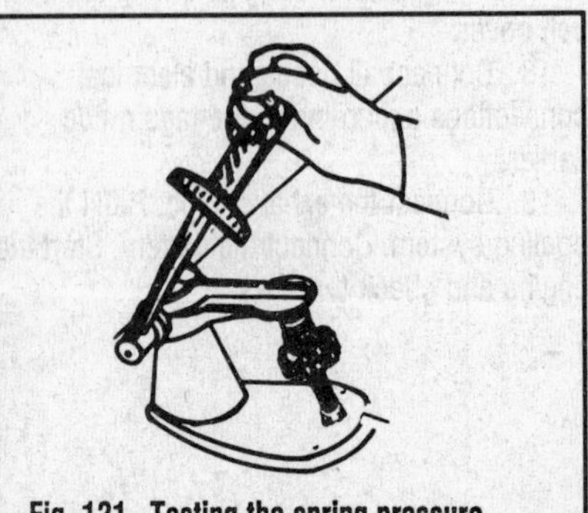

Fig. 121. Testing the spring pressure

3. A valve spring tester is needed to test the spring pressure. Compare the tested pressure with the pressures listed in the Valve Specifications chart in this section.

Valve Stem Seals

REMOVAL & INSTALLATION

Without Removing Cylinder Head

1. Remove the rocker arm (valve) cover as outlined in this Section.

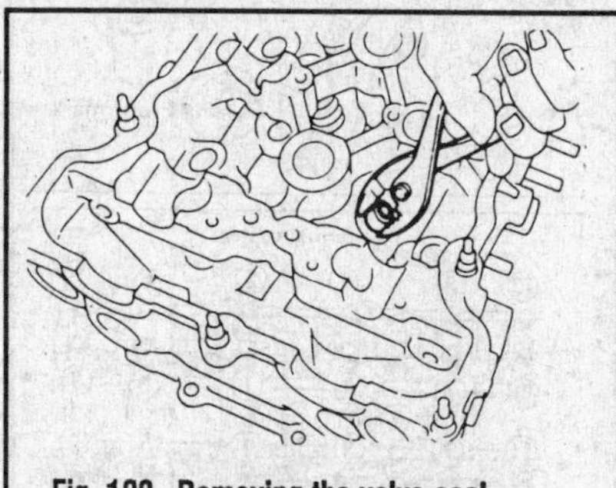

Fig. 122. Removing the valve seal

2. Remove the rocker arm assembly (engines with rocker arms). Remove the camshaft and valve lifters (engines without rocker arms).
3. Remove the spark plug of the affected cylinder.
4. Install a spark plug adapter and air chuck into the spark plug hole. Connect the air chuck to a compressed air source. This procedure fills the cylinder with compressed air so the valve does not fall into the cylinder when the valve spring is removed.
5. Using a valve spring compressor, remove the valve keepers, spring retainer and spring as outlined in this Section.
6. Remove the valve seal from the valve.

To install:

7. Lubricate the valve stem with engine oil and install the seal onto the valve guide. Make sure it is seated properly.
8. Install the spring or springs, spring retainer and compress the spring with the spring compressor as outlined in this Section.
9. Install the spring keepers and make sure they are properly seated before releasing the spring compressor.
10. Remove the air chuck and adapter.
11. Install the spark plug, camshaft or rocker arms.
12. Install the rocker arm shaft.
13. Install the remaining components, start the engine and check for proper operation and leaks.

With Cylinder Head Removed

1. Remove the cylinder head from the vehicle as outlined in this Section.
2. Remove the camshaft or rocker arm assembly.
3. Using a C-type spring compressor, remove the valve keepers, retainer and spring.
4. Remove the valve seal from the valve guide.

To install:

5. Lubricate the valve stem with engine oil and install the seal onto the valve guide. Make sure it is seated properly.
6. Install the spring or springs, spring retainer and compress the spring with the spring compressor as outlined in this Section.
7. Install the spring keepers and make sure they are properly seated before releasing the spring compressor.
8. Install the camshaft or rocker arms as outlined in this Section.
9. Install the cylinder head and remaining components.

Valve Seats

REMOVAL & INSTALLATION

➡ **To prevent damaging the other cylinder head components, completely disassemble the head.**

1. The old valve seat can be removed by machining it from the head or by heating the head in an 302–320°F (150–160°C) oil bath, then driving it from the head with a punch.

➡ **When removing the valve insert, be careful not to damage the cylinder head surface.**

2. Select a valve insert replacement and check the outside diameter, then ream the cylinder head recess at room temperature.
3. Heat the cylinder head to 302–320°F (150–160°C) in an oil bath, then press in the new valve seat, until it seats in the recess.

CUTTING THE SEATS

1. Allow the cylinder head to cool to room temperature. Using a valve seating tool kit, cut a new valve contact surface on the valve seat.

➡ **When repairing the valve seat, make sure that the valve and the guide are in good condition; if wear is evident, replace the valve and/or the guide, then correct the valve seat.**

2. To complete the operation, use valve grinding compound and lap the valve to the seat.
3. To install the removed components, reverse the removal procedures.

Valve Guides

REMOVAL & INSTALLATION

1. Using a 2-ton press or a hammer and a suitable driving tool, drive the old valve guide from the cylinder head, in the rocker cover to combustion chamber direction.

➡ **Heating the cylinder head to 302–392°F (150–200°C) will facilitate the operation.**

2. Using the Valve Guide Reamer tool KV11081000 (F10) or ST11081000 (all other models, ream the valve guide hole.
3. Using a new valve guide, press it into the cylinder head and ream the guide hole with the proper size reamer.
4. Using a valve seating tool kit, cut a new valve contact on the valve seat.
5. To install the removed components, reverse the removal procedures.

KNURLING

Valve guides which are not excessively worn or distorted may in some cases, be knurled rather than reamed. Knurling is a process in which metal inside the valve guide bores is displaced and raised (forming a very fine crosshatch pattern), thereby reducing clearance. Knurling also provides for excellent oil control. The possibility of knurling rather than reaming the guides should be discussed with a machinist.

Fig. 118. Lapping the valve seat and valve

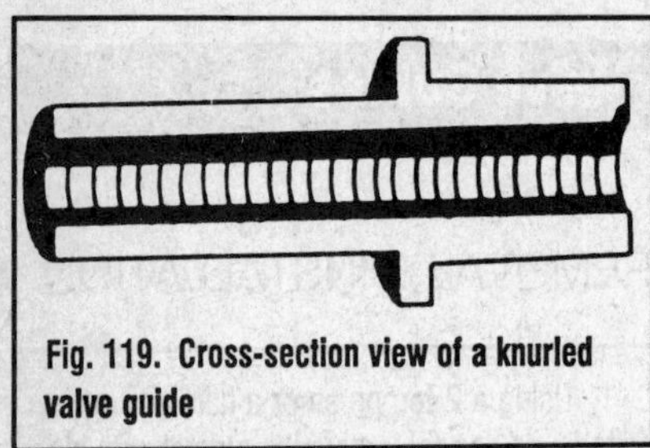
Fig. 119. Cross-section view of a knurled valve guide

Hydraulic Valve Lifters

REMOVAL & INSTALLATION

GA16i Engine

The hydraulic valve lifter is an integral part of the rocker arm assembly. The lifter is not serviced separately.

1. Remove the rocker arm cover and timing chain gear as outlined in this Section.
2. Slowly loosen the rocker arm shaft in 3 steps. Be careful not to bend the shaft.
3. Label all components before disassembling the rocker shaft.
4. Remove the retaining bolts and spacers.
5. Remove the rocker arm/lifter assembly from the shaft.
6. If reusing the rocker arm, soak the rocker arm in a pan of oil.

To install:

7. Install the rocker arm/lifters onto the shaft and install the entire assembly.
8. Torque the rocker shaft bolts to 27 ft. lbs. (37 Nm) in 3 steps.
9. Install the timing chain gear and rocker arm cover.
10. Install the remaining components.

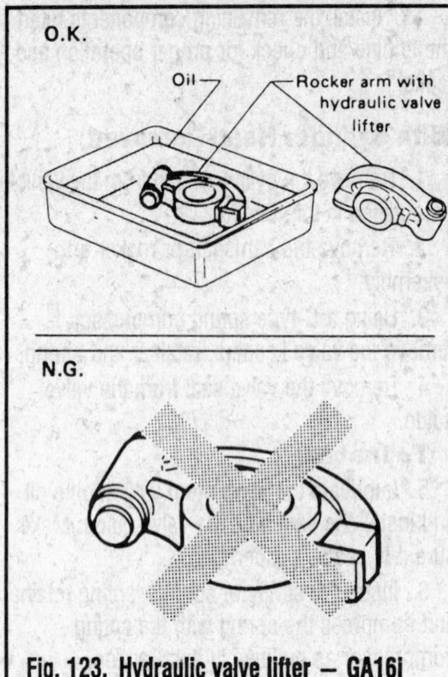
O.K.
Oil
Rocker arm with hydraulic valve lifter
N.G.
Fig. 123. Hydraulic valve lifter – GA16i engine

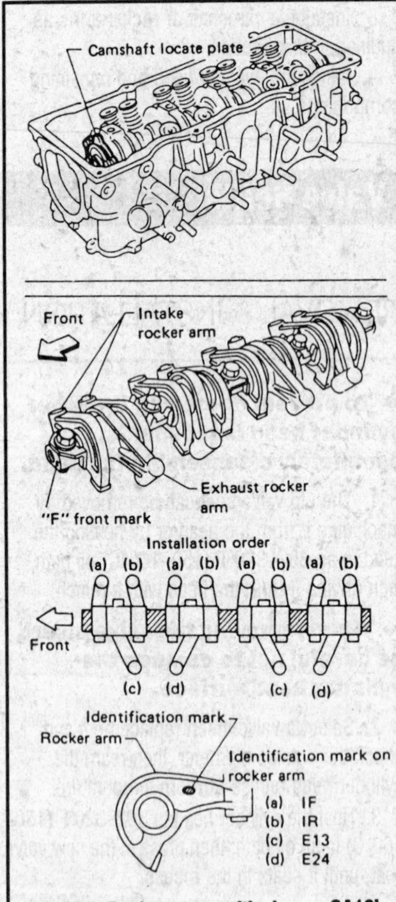
Camshaft locate plate
Front
Intake rocker arm
Exhaust rocker arm
"F" front mark
Installation order
(a) (b) (a) (b) (a) (b) (a) (b)
Front
(c) (d) (c) (d)
Identification mark
Rocker arm
Identification mark on rocker arm
(a) IF
(b) IR
(c) E13
(d) E24
Fig. 124. Rocker arm positioning – GA16i engine

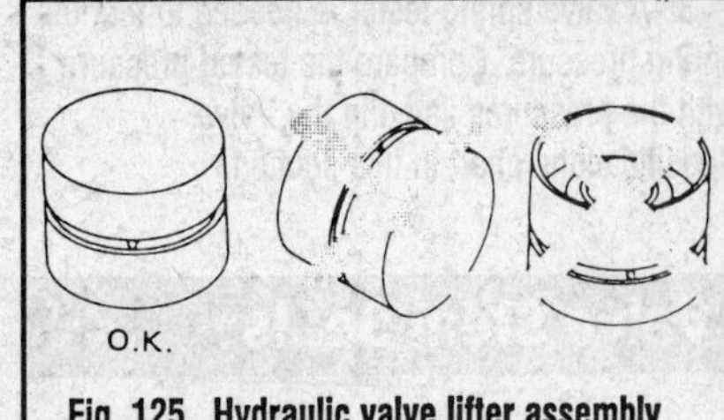
O.K.
Fig. 125. Hydraulic valve lifter assembly – CA18DE engine

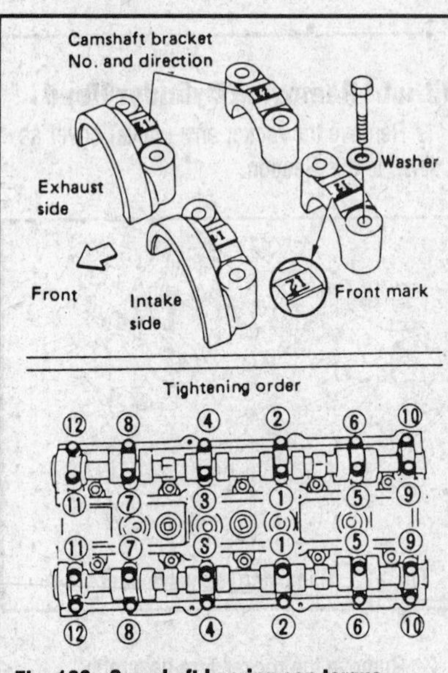
Camshaft bracket No. and direction
Washer
Exhaust side
Front
Intake side
Front mark
Tightening order
12 8 4 2 6 10
11 7 3 1 5 9
11 7 3 1 5 9
12 8 4 2 6 10
Fig. 126. Camshaft bearing cap torque sequence – CA16DE and CA18DE engine

11. Start the engine and allow to run with no load for 10 minutes to bleed the air out of the lifters.

CA16DE and CA18DE Engines

The hydraulic valve lifter is located under the camshaft lobe. Label all valve components for proper reinstallation. Mark the timing chain and sprocket locations to ensure correct valve timing.

1. Remove the camshaft cover as outlined in this Section.
2. Remove the timing chain sprockets and retain valve timing by hanging the sprocket with a piece of wire and wedge the chain with wood. These procedures are covered earlier in this Section.
3. Remove the camshaft bearing cap bolts in the opposite sequence of torquing. This is very important. Remove the camshaft.
4. Remove the valve lifter from the bore by turning and pulling upward.
5. Soak the removed lifters in a pan of clean engine oil before reassembly.

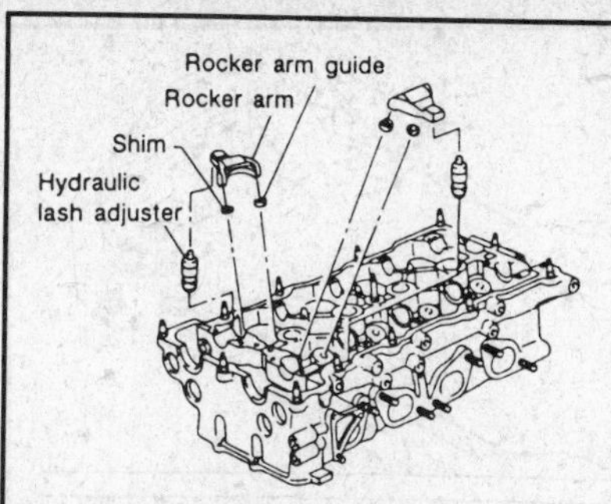
Rocker arm guide
Rocker arm
Shim
Hydraulic
lash adjuster

Fig. 127. Hydraulic valve lifter assembly – SR20DE engine

To Install:

6. Install the valve lifter into the bore.
7. Install the camshaft and bearing caps.
8. Torque the bolts in sequence to 7–9 ft. lbs. (10–12 Nm).
9. Install the timing chain gear and chain in the exact position as removed.
10. Turn the engine to make sure the camshaft is not binding.
11. Install the remaining components.
12. Start the engine and allow to run with no load for 10 minutes to bleed any air in the lifters.

SR20DE Engine

The hydraulic valve lifter is located under the rocker arm in the lifter bore. Label all valve components for exact reassembly. Mark the timing chain the gears for exact valve timing during reinstallation.

1. Remove the camshaft cover as outlined in this Section.
2. Remove the timing chain tensioner. Remove the timing chain sprockets and retain valve timing by hanging the sprocket with a piece of wire and wedge the chain with wood. These procedures are covered earlier in this Section.
3. Remove the camshaft bearing cap bolts in the opposite sequence of torquing. Refer to the Camshaft section of this Section. This is very important. Remove the camshaft, oil tubes and baffles.
4. Remove the valve rocker arm, shims, guides and hydraulic lifter from the bore. Document each part for reinstallation.
5. Soak the removed lifters in a pan of clean engine oil during the service procedure.

To Install:

6. Install the valve lifter into the bore. Install the guides, shims and rocker arms.
7. Install the camshaft, bearing caps, oil tubes and baffles.
8. Torque the bolts in sequence to the specification in the Camshaft section of this Section.

9. Install the timing chain gear and chain in the exact position as removed.
10. Turn the engine to make sure the camshaft is not binding.
11. Install the remaining components.
12. Start the engine and allow to run with no load for 10 minutes to bleed any air in the lifters.

Oil Pan

REMOVAL & INSTALLATION

✱✱ CAUTION

The EPA warns that prolonged contact with used engine oil may cause a number of skin disorders, including cancer! You should make every effort to minimize your exposure to used engine oil. Protective gloves should be worn when changing the oil. Wash your hands and any other exposed skin areas as soon as possible after exposure to used engine oil. Soap and water, or waterless hand cleaner should be used.

All Models except 1987–92 Engines

1. If the engine is in the vehicle, attach a lift, support the engine, and remove the engine mounting bolts.
2. Raise the engine slightly, watching to make sure that no hoses or wires are damaged.
3. Drain the engine oil.
4. Remove the oil pan bolts and slide the pan out to the rear.

To Install:

5. Use a new gasket, coated on both sides with sealer.
6. Apply a thin bead of silicone seal to the engine block at the junction of the block and front cover, and the junction of the block and rear main bearing cap. Then apply a thin coat of silicone seal to the new oil pan gasket, install the gasket to the block and install the pan.
7. Tighten the pan bolts in a circular pattern from the center to the ends, to 4–7 ft. lbs. (6–10 Nm). Overtightening will distort the pan lip, causing leakage.
8. Reinstall the engine mounting bolts.
9. Refill the oil pan to the specified level.

1987–92 Engines, Except SR20DE engine

1. Drain the engine oil.
2. Raise the vehicle and support it with safety stands.
3. Remove the right side splash cover. Remove the right side under cover.
4. Remove the center member.
5. Remove the forward section of the exhaust pipe.
6. Remove the front buffer rod and its bracket.
7. Remove the engine gussets.
8. Insert a seal cutter (SST KV10111100) between the oil pan and the cylinder block.

➡ **DO NOT use a screwdriver!**

9. Tapping the cutter with a hammer, slide it around the oil pan.
10. Remove the oil pan.

To Install:

11. Remove all old liquid gasket from the pan and block mating surfaces.
12. Apply a continuous bead (3.5–4.5mm) of liquid gasket around the oil pan. Apply the sealer to the **inner** surface around the bolt holes where there is no groove.
13. Install the pan within 5 minutes. Do not allow the sealer to dry. Tighten the pan bolts in a circular pattern from the center to the ends, to 4–7 ft. lbs. (6–10 Nm). Overtightening will distort the pan lip, causing leakage.
14. Install the engine gussets, buffer rod, exhaust pipe and center member.
15. Install the right side splash cover and the right side under cover.
16. Refill the oil pan to the specified level. Start engine and check for oil leaks.

SR20DE Engine

1. Drain the engine oil.
2. Raise the vehicle and support it with safety stands.
3. Remove the right side splash cover. Remove the right side under cover.
4. Remove the lower oil pan bolts and separate the pan using tool KV10111100.
5. Remove the baffle plate and front tube.
6. Place a transmission jack under the transaxle and raise.
7. Remove the center member and automatic transaxle shift control cable.
8. Remove the compressor gussets.
9. Remove the rear cover plate and aluminum oil pan bolts.
10. Remove the 2 engine-to-transaxle bolts and install them into the vacant holes. Tighten the bolts to release the oil pan from the cylinder block. The oil pan removing tool KV10111100 or equivalent, may have to be used to release the pan from the block.

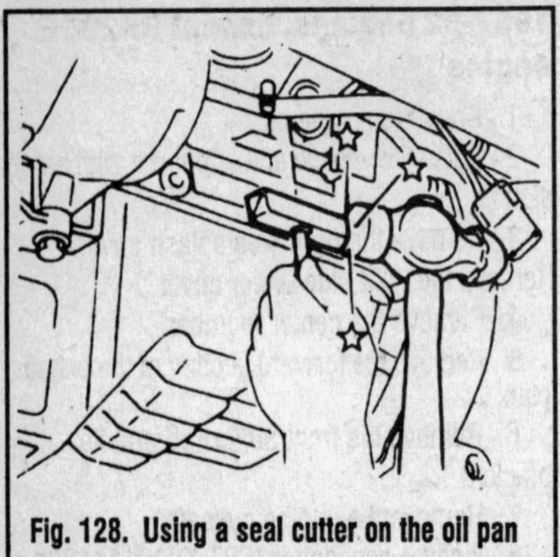
Fig. 128. Using a seal cutter on the oil pan

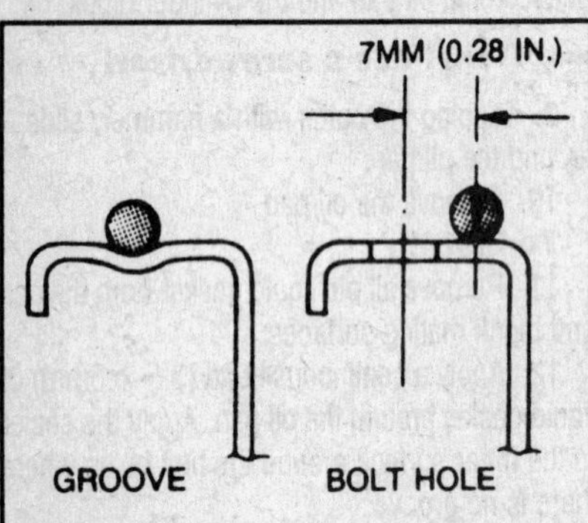

7MM (0.28 IN.)
GROOVE
BOLT HOLE

Fig. 129. Apply RTV sealer on the inside of the bolt holes

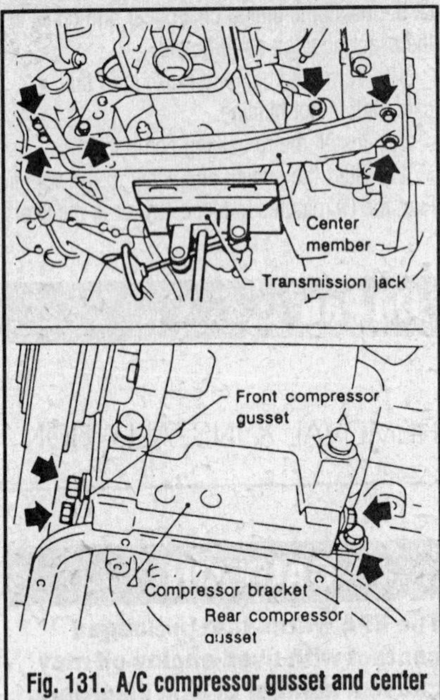

Center member
Transmission jack
Front compressor gusset
Compressor bracket
Rear compressor gusset

Fig. 131. A/C compressor gusset and center member removal — SR20DE engine

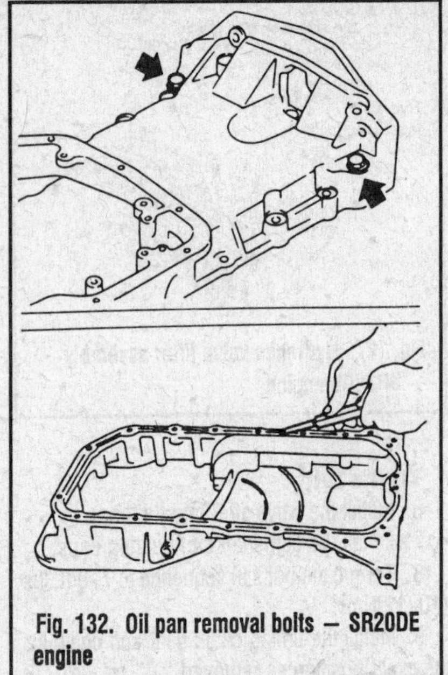
Fig. 132. Oil pan removal bolts — SR20DE engine

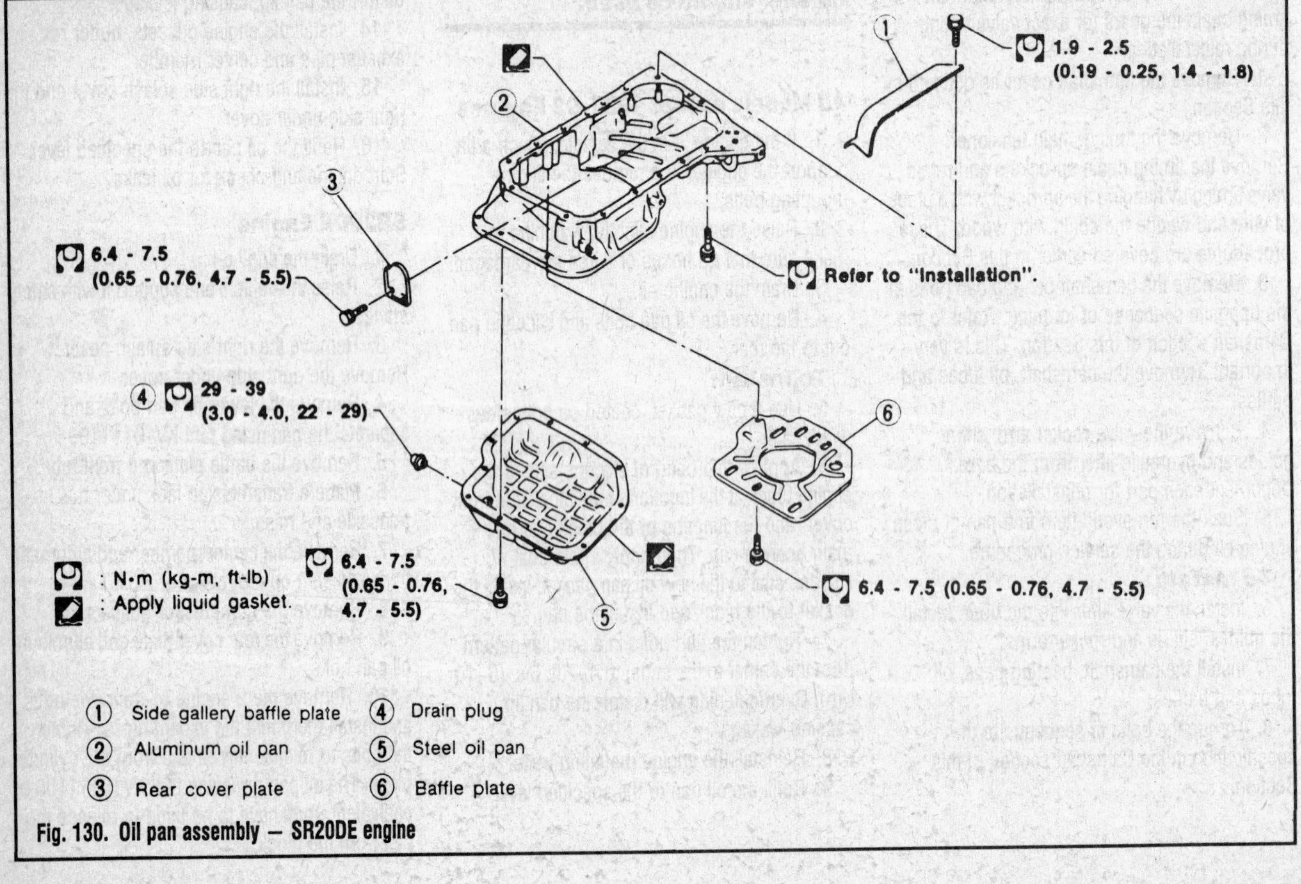

1.9 - 2.5 (0.19 - 0.25, 1.4 - 1.8)

Refer to "Installation".

6.4 - 7.5 (0.65 - 0.76, 4.7 - 5.5)

④ 29 - 39 (3.0 - 4.0, 22 - 29)

6.4 - 7.5 (0.65 - 0.76, 4.7 - 5.5)

6.4 - 7.5 (0.65 - 0.76, 4.7 - 5.5)

: N·m (kg-m, ft-lb)
: Apply liquid gasket.

①	Side gallery baffle plate	④	Drain plug
②	Aluminum oil pan	⑤	Steel oil pan
③	Rear cover plate	⑥	Baffle plate

Fig. 130. Oil pan assembly — SR20DE engine

To Install:

11. Remove all old liquid gasket from the pan and block mating surfaces.
12. Apply a continuous bead (3.5–4.5mm) of liquid gasket around the oil pan. Apply the sealer to the **inner** surface around the bolt holes where there is no groove.
13. Install the pan within 5 minutes. Tighten the pan bolts in a circular pattern from the center to the ends, to 4–7 ft. lbs. (6–8 Nm). Overtightening will distort the pan lip, causing leakage.
14. Install the 2 transaxle bolts.
15. Install the rear cover, compressor gussets, automatic shift cable, center member and lower the transaxle jack.
16. Install the front tube and baffle plate.
17. Remove all old liquid gasket from the lower pan and upper pan surfaces.
18. Apply a continuous bead (3.5–4.5mm) of liquid gasket around the oil pan. Apply the sealer to the **inner** surface around the bolt holes where there is no groove.
19. Install the pan within 5 minutes. Tighten the pan bolts in a circular pattern from the center to the ends, to 4–7 ft. lbs. (6–8 Nm). Overtightening will distort the pan lip, causing leakage.
20. Install the remaining components.
21. Wait at least 30 minutes before refilling with oil.
22. Refill the engine with oil. Start the engine and check for leaks.

Oil Pump

REMOVAL & INSTALLATION

CAUTION

The EPA warns that prolonged contact with used engine oil may cause a number of skin disorders, including cancer! You should make every effort to minimize your exposure to used engine oil. Protective gloves should be worn when changing the oil. Wash your hands and any other exposed skin areas as soon as possible after exposure to used engine oil. Soap and water, or waterless hand cleaner should be used.

E-Series Engine

1. Disconnect the negative battery cable. Drain the engine oil.
2. Loosen the alternator lower bolts.
3. Remove the alternator belt and adjusting bar bolt.
4. Move the alternator out of the way and support it safely.
5. Disconnect the oil pressure gauge harness.
6. Remove the oil filter.
7. Remove the pump assembly.

To Install:

8. Fill the pump with clean engine oil and rotate it several times or pack the pump housing with petroleum jelly.
9. Install the pump on the engine using a new gasket. Torque the pump mounting bolts to 7–9 ft. lbs. (10–14 Nm).
10. Install the oil filter and the oil pressure gauge harness connections.
11. Install the alternator, belt and bracket.
12. Start the engine and check for leaks.

CA16DE and CA18DE Engine

1. Disconnect the negative battery cable. Remove all accessory drive belts and the alternator.
2. Remove the timing (cam) belt covers and remove the timing belt.
3. Support the transaxle with a jack and remove the center member from the body. Remove the front crankshaft pulley.
4. Remove the oil pan.
5. Remove the oil pump assembly along with the oil strainer.

To Install:

6. If installing a new or rebuilt oil pump, first pack the pump cavity full of petroleum jelly to prevent the pump from cavitating when the engine is started. Apply RTV sealer to the front oil seal end of the pan prior to installation. Install the pump and the strainer as an assembly, torque the mounting bolts to 9–12 ft. lbs. (11–14 Nm).

➡ **Always use a new O-ring when installing the strainer to the pump body.**

7. Install the oil pan and bolt the engine in place.
8. Install the center member if it was removed.
9. Install the timing belt and covers. Install the crankshaft pulley.
10. Install the alternator and all drive belts. Reconnect the negative battery cable.
11. Start engine and check for leaks.

GA16i, GA16DE and SR20DE

The oil pump is located in the front timing cover.

1. Disconnect the negative battery cable. Drain the engine oil.
2. Remove the drive belts.
3. Remove the cylinder head and oil pans as outlined in this Section.
4. Remove the oil strainer and baffle plate, if so equipped.
5. Remove the front cover assembly.
6. Remove the oil pump retaining bolts and remove the pump gears.

To Install:

7. Install the pump gears and torque the cover bolts to 5–7 ft. lbs. (6–8 Nm).
8. Remove all traces of gasket material from all gasket mating surfaces.
9. Apply a continuous bead of RTV sealer to the front cover.
10. Within 5 minutes, install the front cover and torque the front cover bolts to 6 ft. lbs. (8 Nm).
11. Install the oil baffle and strainer.
12. Install the oil pans and cylinder head as outlined in this Section.
13. Install the drive belts.
14. Wait 30 minutes before adding engine oil.
15. Refill with engine oil, start the engine and check for leaks.

CD17 Diesel Engine

1. Remove the valve timing belt as described later in this Section.
2. Drain the oil and remove the oil pan.
3. The oil pump is bolted to the front of the engine block, at the front of the crankshaft. Loosen the mounting bolts and remove the oil pump assembly.

➡ **Remove the crankshaft key to avoid damage to the oil seal on the pump.**

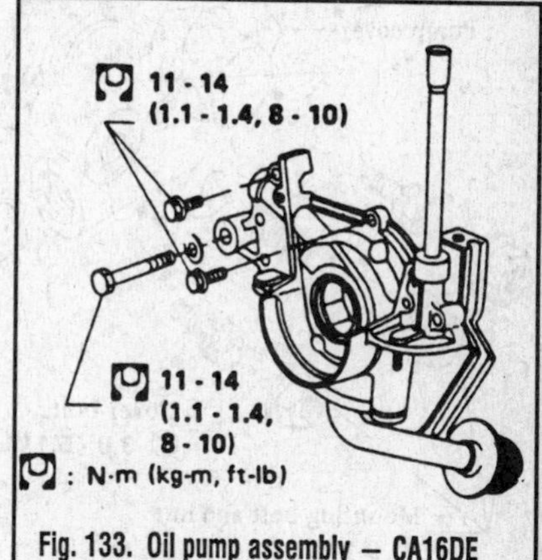
11 - 14
(1.1 - 1.4, 8 - 10)
11 - 14
(1.1 - 1.4,
8 - 10)
: N·m (kg-m, ft-lb)

Fig. 133. Oil pump assembly — CA16DE and CA18DE engines

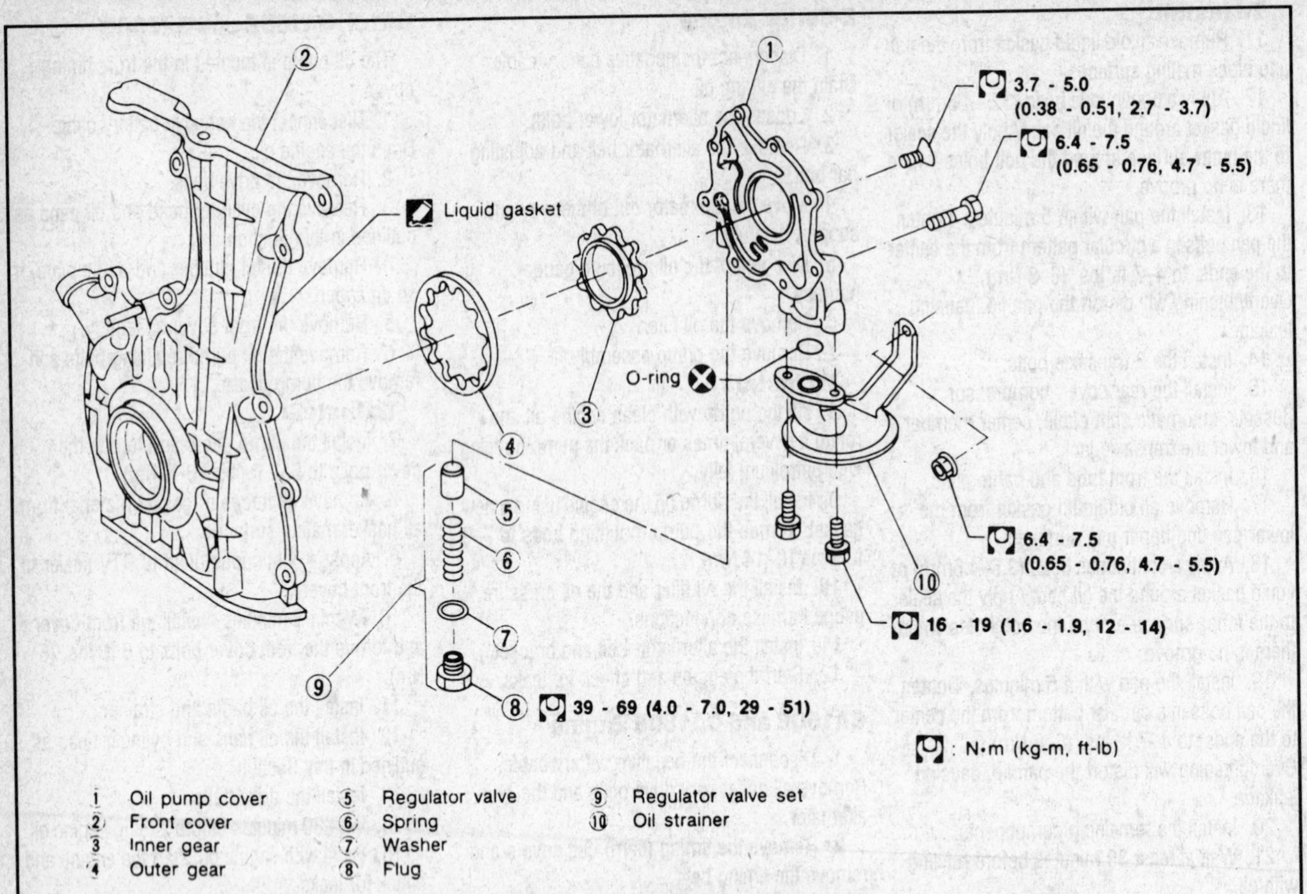

Liquid gasket

O-ring

3.7 - 5.0 (0.38 - 0.51, 2.7 - 3.7)

6.4 - 7.5 (0.65 - 0.76, 4.7 - 5.5)

6.4 - 7.5 (0.65 - 0.76, 4.7 - 5.5)

16 - 19 (1.6 - 1.9, 12 - 14)

39 - 69 (4.0 - 7.0, 29 - 51)

: N•m (kg-m, ft-lb)

1. Oil pump cover
2. Front cover
3. Inner gear
4. Outer gear
5. Regulator valve
6. Spring
7. Washer
8. Plug
9. Regulator valve set
10. Oil strainer

Fig. 134. Oil pump located in front cover — SR20DE shown, GA16i and GA16DE engines similar

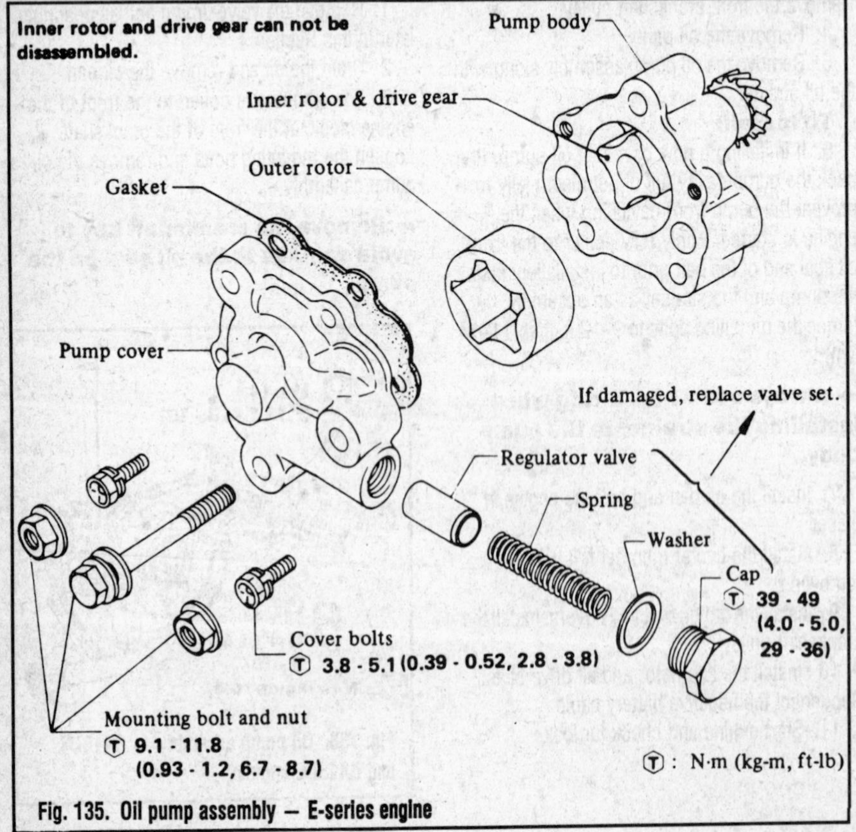

Inner rotor and drive gear can not be disassembled.
Pump body
Inner rotor & drive gear
Outer rotor
Gasket
Pump cover
If damaged, replace valve set.
Regulator valve
Spring
Washer
Cap
39 - 49
(4.0 - 5.0,
29 - 36)
Cover bolts
3.8 - 5.1 (0.39 - 0.52, 2.8 - 3.8)
Mounting bolt and nut
9.1 - 11.8
(0.93 - 1.2, 6.7 - 8.7)
: N·m (kg-m, ft-lb)

Fig. 135. Oil pump assembly — E-series engine

4. Remove the oil pump rear cover and check gear clearance using a feeler gauge. Body-to-outer gear clearance should be 0.1–0.2mm; outer gear-to-crescent clearance should be 0.2–0.3mm.

To Install:

5. Replace the oil seal in the pump by carefully prying it out. Coat the new seal liberally with clean engine oil before installation. Install the crankshaft key.

6. Install the pump to the block, using a new gasket and torquing the bolts to 9–12 ft. lbs. (12–16 Nm). Replace the oil pan, applying sealer to the four corners of the oil pan and use a new oil pan gasket. Install the drain plug and refill the pan with oil.

7. Replace the timing belt as described later. Start the engine and check for leaks.

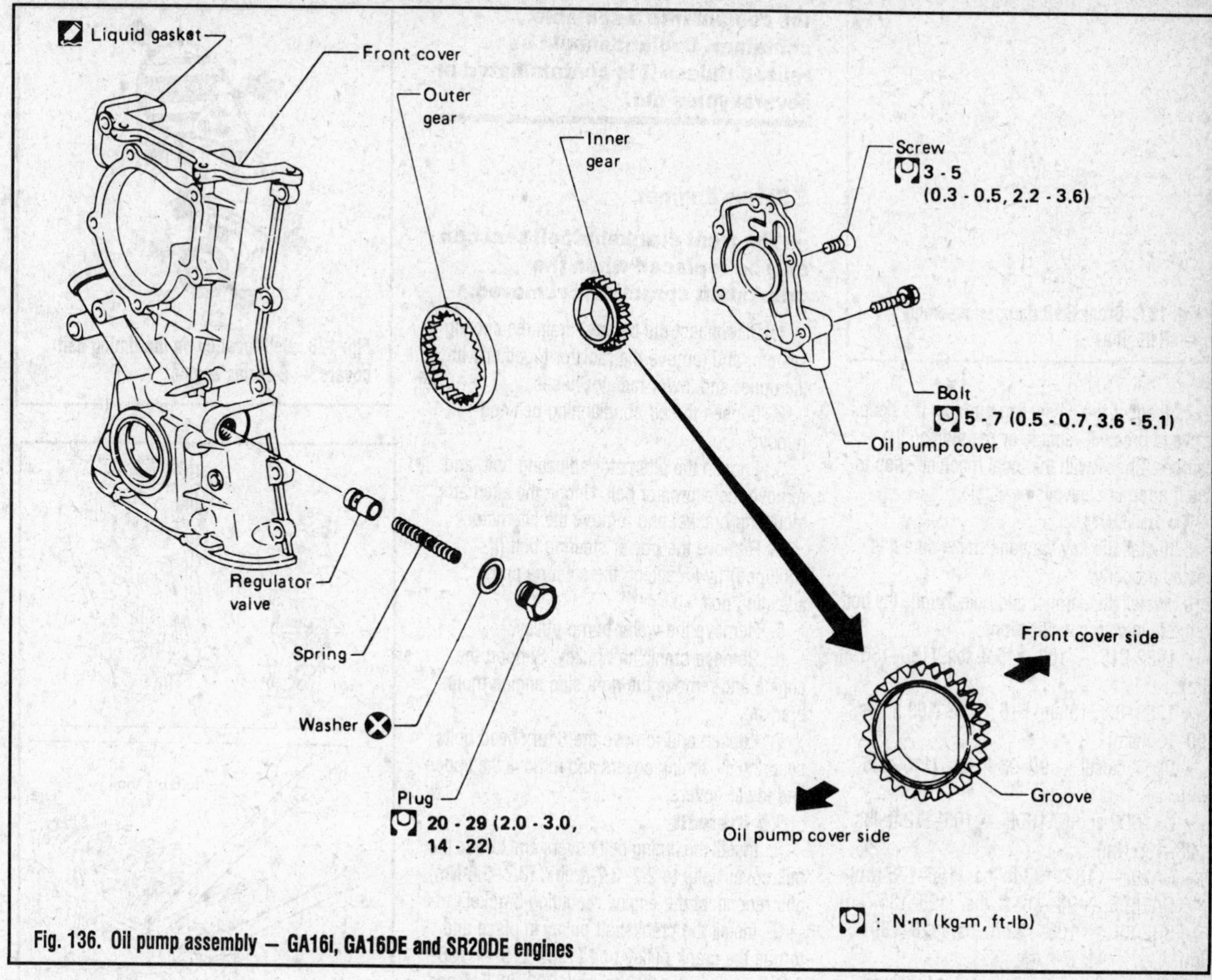
Liquid gasket
Front cover
Outer gear
Inner gear
Screw
3 - 5
(0.3 - 0.5, 2.2 - 3.6)
Bolt
5 - 7 (0.5 - 0.7, 3.6 - 5.1)
Oil pump cover
Regulator valve
Spring
Washer
Plug
20 - 29 (2.0 - 3.0, 14 - 22)
Front cover side
Groove
Oil pump cover side
: N·m (kg-m, ft-lb)

Fig. 136. Oil pump assembly — GA16i, GA16DE and SR20DE engines

INSPECTION

E-Series Engine

a. Check the pump body and cover for cracks or excessive wear.

b. Check the pump rotor for excessive wear.

c. Using a feeler gauge, check the rotor tip clearance. The clearance should be less than 0.0047 in. (0.12mm).

d. Using a feeler gauge, check the outer rotor to body clearance. The clearance should be 0.0059–0.0083 in. (0.15–0.21mm).

e. Using a straight edge, check the rotor to straight edge clearance. The clearance should be less than 0.0020 in. (0.05mm).

f. Using a straight edge, check the pump body to straight edge clearance. The clearance should be less than 0.0008 in. (0.02mm).

GA16i, GA16DE and SR20DE Engines

a. Check the pump body and cover for cracks or excessive wear.

b. Check the pump rotor for excessive wear.

c. Using a feeler gauge, check the pump to outer gear clearance. The clearance should be 0.0047–0.0078 in. (0.12–0.20mm).

d. Check the inner gear to crescent clearance. The clearance should be 0.0085–0.0129 in. (0.22–0.33mm).

e. Check the outer gear to crescent clearance. The clearance should be 0.0085–0.0129 in. (0.22–0.33mm).

f. Check the body to inner gear clearance. The clearance should be 0.0020–0.0035 in. (0.05–0.09mm).

g. Check the body to outer gear clearance. The clearance should be 0.0020–0.0043 in. (0.05–0.11mm).

h. Check the inner gear to brazed portion of housing clearance. The clearance should be 0.0018–0.0036 in. (0.05–0.09mm).

Crankshaft Damper

➧ SEE FIG. 137

REMOVAL & INSTALLATION

1. Disconnect the negative battery cable.
2. Loosen and remove the accessory drive belts.
3. Remove the belt pulleys from the damper, if so equipped.
4. Remove the large center bolt.
5. Using a crankshaft damper puller or equivalent, remove the damper from the crankshaft. Do not use a jaw puller on the damper. The outer ring will be pulled from the inner portion. Replace the damper if this the case.
6. Remove the key way if loose. Be careful not to damage the oil seal.

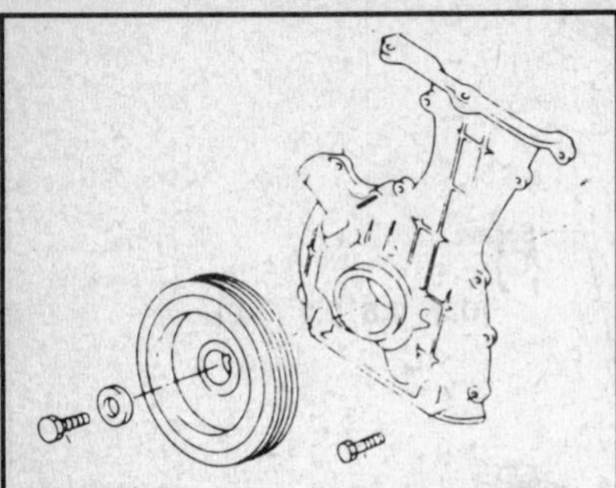

Fig. 137. Crankshaft damper assembly — all engines

7. Inspect the oil sealing surface. If a deep grove is present, replace or recondition the damper. Check with the local machine shop to see if a repair sleeve is available.

To install:

8. Install the key way and make sure it is seated properly.

9. Install the damper and bolt. Torque the bolt to the following specifications:

- 1982 E15 — 108–145 ft. lbs. (130–160 Nm)
- 1983–88 E15 and E16 — 83–108 ft. lbs. (99–120 Nm)
- CD17 diesel — 90–98 ft. lbs. (110–125 Nm)
- CA16DE and CA18DE — 105–112 ft. lbs. (128–135 Nm)
- GA16i — 132–152 ft. lbs. (150–175 Nm)
- GA16DE — 98–112 ft. lbs. (125–135 Nm)
- SR20DE — 105–122 ft. lbs. (128–139 Nm)

10. Install the belt pulleys, drive belts and connect the battery cable.

11. Start the engine and check for leaks.

Timing Chain/Belt Cover

REMOVAL & INSTALLATION

CAUTION

When draining the coolant, keep in mind that cats and dogs are attracted by the ethylene glycol antifreeze, and are quite likely to drink any that is left in an uncovered container or in puddles on the ground. This will prove fatal in sufficient quantity. Always drain the coolant into a sealable container. Coolant should be reused unless it is contaminated or several years old.

E-Series Engines

➡ The front crankshaft oil seal can only be replaced when the crankshaft sprocket is removed.

1. Disconnect the battery, drain the cooling system, and remove the radiator together with the upper and lower radiator hoses.

2. Loosen the air conditioning belt and remove.

3. Loosen the alternator adjusting bolt, and remove the alternator belt. Unbolt the alternator mounting bracket and remove the alternator.

4. Remove the power steering belt (if equipped) by loosening the steering pump adjusting bolt.

5. Remove the water pump pulley.

6. Remove crankshaft pulley. Support the engine and remove the right side engine mount bracket.

7. Loosen and remove the 8 torx head bolts securing the timing covers and remove the upper and lower covers.

To install:

8. Install the timing belt covers and torque the belt cover bolts to 2.7–3.7 ft. lbs. (3.7–5.0 Nm) and reconnect the engine mounting bracket.

9. Install the crankshaft pulley in place and torque the crank pulley bolt (1982 E15 — 108–145 ft. lbs. (130–160 Nm) or (1983–88 E15 and E16 — 83–108 ft. lbs. (99–120 Nm).

10. Install the water pump pulley.

11. Install the alternator and all the drive belts.

12. Install the radiator and all cooling hoses. Refill the cooling system.

13. Connect the battery cable and start engine.

CA16DE and CA18DE Engines

For removal and installation of the timing belt upper and lower covers refer to the timing belt procedures.

GA16i Engine

1. Disconnect the negative battery cable and drain the engine coolant.

2. Remove the oil pan as outlined in this Section.

3. Remove all drive belts and power steering pump bracket, if so equipped.

4. Remove the air cleaner.

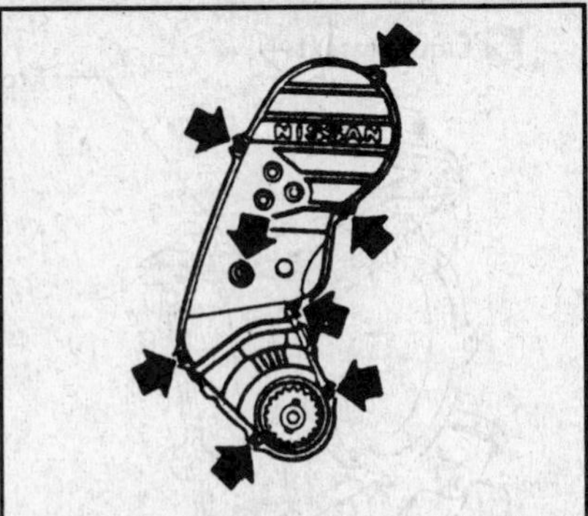

Fig. 138. Bolt location on the timing belt covers — E-series engine

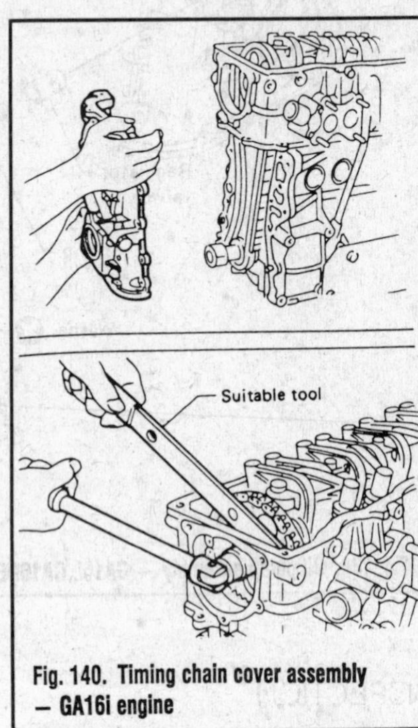
Suitable tool

Fig. 140. Timing chain cover assembly — GA16i engine

5. Install an engine lifting device to the front side of the engine. Remove the engine mounting bracket.

6. Remove the water pump as outlined in this Section.

7. Remove the timing chain tensioner from the front cover.

8. Remove the rocker arm cover and all spark plugs.

9. Set the No. 1 cylinder to TDC of the compression stroke and remove the crankshaft pulley.

10. Remove the front cover.

To install:

11. Apply RTV sealer to the front cover and install within 5 minutes. Torque the bolts to 5–7 ft. lbs. (7–10 Nm).

12. Install the crankshaft pulley and torque the bolt to 69–76 ft. lbs. (81–97 Nm).

13. Install the rocker arm cover and all spark plugs.
14. Install the timing chain tensioner to the front cover.
15. Install the water pump as outlined in this Section.
16. Install the engine mounting bracket.
17. Install the air cleaner.
18. Install all drive belts and power steering pump bracket, if so equipped.
19. Install the oil pan as outlined in this Section.
20. Connect the negative battery cable and refill the engine coolant.

GA16DE and SR20DE Engine

For removal and installation of the timing chain covers refer to the timing chain procedures.

CD17 Diesel Engine

This procedure includes oil seal removal and installation. If not removing the seal, only use steps 1–5, 9–13.

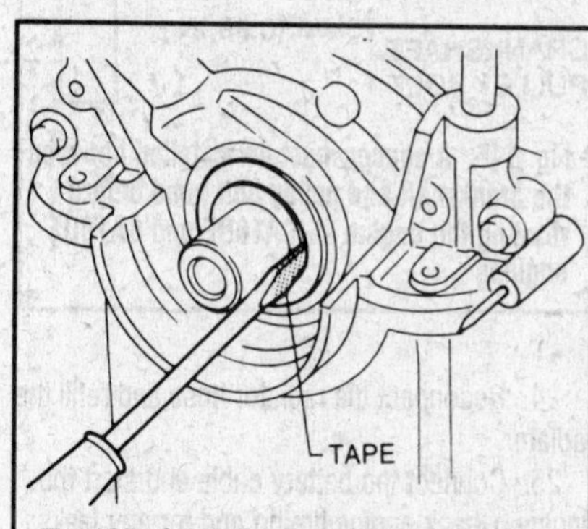
TAPE

Fig. 139. Carefully pry out the front oil seal

1. Disconnect the negative battery cable. Drain the cooling system and then remove the radiator together with the upper and lower radiator hoses.
2. Remove the fan, fan coupling and fan pulley. Using a gear puller, remove the crankshaft damper pulley.
3. Remove the power steering pump, bracket and idler pulley.
4. Support the engine securely with a jack and block of wood under the oil pan. Then, unbolt the mount that sits in front of the timing belt cover. Unbolt and remove the bracket that interferes with timing belt cover removal.
5. Remove the front belt cover. Remove the valve timing belt (see "Timing Belt and Camshaft" removal in this Section).
6. Remove the front oil seal by taping the end of a thin prybar or old prybar, and carefully pry the old seal out from around the end of the crankshaft. Do not scratch the shaft with the prybar.

To install:

7. Coat a new seal with clean engine oil. Slide it onto the crankshaft end and back into place in the front of the block. Use a small drift to evenly drive the seal back until it seats in position.
8. Follow the "Timing Belt and Camshaft" removal and installation procedure and install the timing belt.
9. Install front timing belt cover and install all attaching bolts.
10. Install the engine mounting bracket. Reconnect the engine mount. Remove the jack and block of wood from under the oil pan.
11. Install the power steering pump as described in Section 8.
12. Install the crankshaft damper pulley.Install the fan, fan coupling and fan pulley.
13. Install the radiator and hoses. Refill the cooling system. Connect the battery.

Timing Belt and/or Chain and Seal

REMOVAL & INSTALLATION

CAUTION

When draining the coolant, keep in mind that cats and dogs are attracted by the ethylene glycol antifreeze, and are quite likely to drink any that is left in an uncovered container or in puddles on the ground. This will prove fatal in sufficient quantity. Always drain the coolant into a sealable container. Coolant should be reused unless it is contaminated or several years old.

The manufacturer recommends that the timing belt be replaced every 60,000 miles (96,000 km). Broken timing belts may cause severe engine damage.

E-Series Overhead Camshaft Engines

1. Refer to the Timing Belt Cover, Removal and Installation procedures, in this section and remove the timing cover.
2. If necessary, remove the spark plug, then turn the crankshaft to position the No. 1 piston at TDC of the compression stroke.

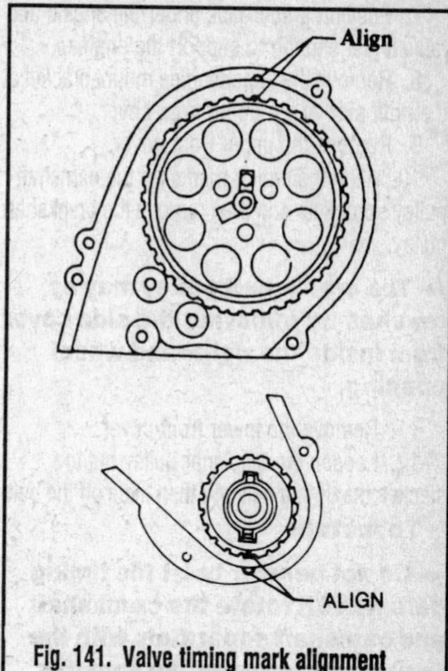
Align
ALIGN

Fig. 141. Valve timing mark alignment – E-series engine

Note the position of the timing marks on the camshaft sprocket, the timing belt and the crankshaft sprocket (see illustrations).

3. Loosen and/or remove the timing belt tensioner. Mark the rotation direction of the timing belt, then remove it from the sprockets.
4. To remove the front oil seal, pull off the crankshaft sprocket, then pry out the oil seal with a small pry bar (be careful not to scratch the crankshaft).

To install:

5. Clean the oil seal mounting surface.
6. Install a new oil seal, the timing belt and tensioner. Torque the tensioner pulley bolts to 13–16 ft. lbs. (17–22 Nm), the timing cover bolts to 2.5–4.0 ft. lbs. (3.4–5.4 Nm), the crankshaft pulley bolt to 83–108 ft. lbs. (113–147 Nm).
7. Install the timing belt covers.
8. Start engine and check timing.

CA16DE and CA18DE Engines

1. Disconnect the negative battery cable. Drain the cooling system.
2. Disconnect the upper radiator hose at the elbow and then position it out of the way.
3. Remove the right side engine undercover.
4. Loosen the power steering pump and the air conditioning compressor and then remove the drive belts.
5. Remove the water pump pulley.
6. Matchmark the crank angle sensor to the upper front cover and the remove it. Carefully position it out of the way.

7. Position a floor jack under the engine and raise it just enough to support the engine.
8. Remove the upper engine mount bracket at the right side of the upper front cover.
9. Remove the upper front cover.
10. Align the timing marks on the camshaft pulley sprockets and then remove the crankshaft pulley.

➡ The crankshaft pulley may be reached by removing the side cover from inside the righthand wheel opening.

11. Remove the lower front cover.
12. Loosen the tensioner pulley nut to slacken the timing belt and then slide off the belt.

To install:

➡ Do not bend or twist the timing belt. NEVER rotate the crankshaft and camshaft separately with the timing belt removed. Be sure the timing belt is free of any oil, water or debris.

13. Install the crankshaft sprocket with the sprocket plates.
14. Before installing the timing belt, ensure that the No. 1 piston is at TDC of the compression stroke (all sprocket timing marks will be in alignment with the marks on the case).

When the timing belt is on and in position, there should be 39 cogs between the timing mark on each of the camshaft sprocket and 48 cogs between the mark on the right camshaft sprocket and the mark on the crankshaft sprocket.

15. Loosen the timing belt tensioner pulley nut.
16. Temporarily install the crankshaft pulley bolt and then rotate the engine two complete revolutions.

➡ Fabricate and install a suitable 25mm thick spacer between the end of the crankshaft and the head of the crankshaft pulley bolt to prevent bolt damage.

17. Tighten the tensioner pulley bolt to 16–22 ft. lbs. (21–30 Nm).
18. Install the upper and lower front covers.
19. Install the crankshaft pulley with its washer and tighten it to 105–112 ft. lbs. (143–152 Nm).
20. Install the engine mount bracket.
21. Install the water pump pulley. Install the crank angle sensor so that the matchmarks made previously line up and tighten the bolts to 5.1–5.8 ft. lbs. (7.0–9.0 Nm).
22. Install all drive belts and adjust.
23. Install the right side engine undercover.

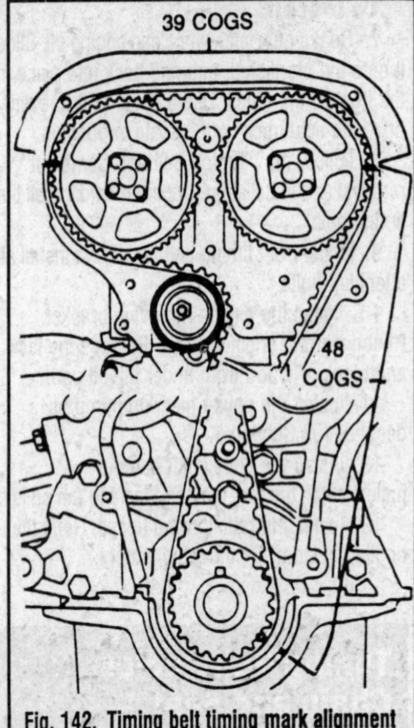
39 COGS
48
COGS
Fig. 142. Timing belt timing mark alignment – CA16DE and CA18DE engines

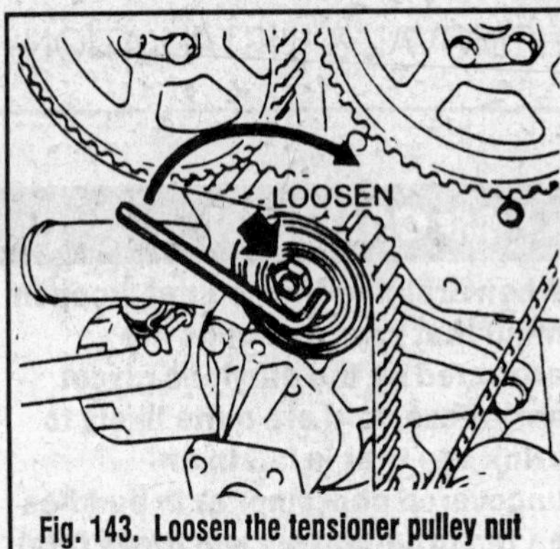
LOOSEN
Fig. 143. Loosen the tensioner pulley nut – CA16DE and CA18DE engines

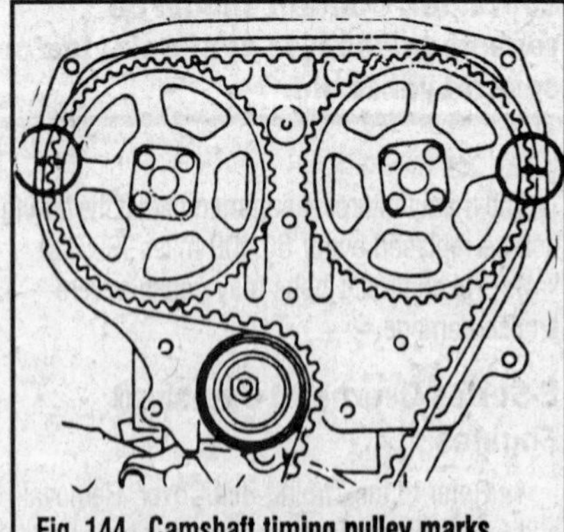
Fig. 144. Camshaft timing pulley marks – CA16DE and CA18DE engines

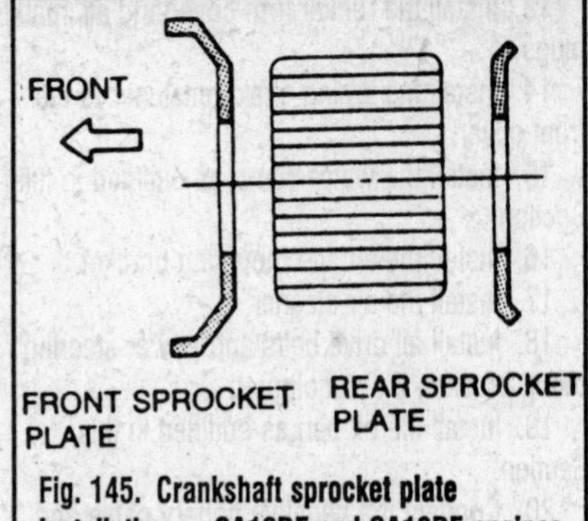
FRONT
FRONT SPROCKET PLATE
REAR SPROCKET PLATE
Fig. 145. Crankshaft sprocket plate installation – CA16DE and CA18DE engines

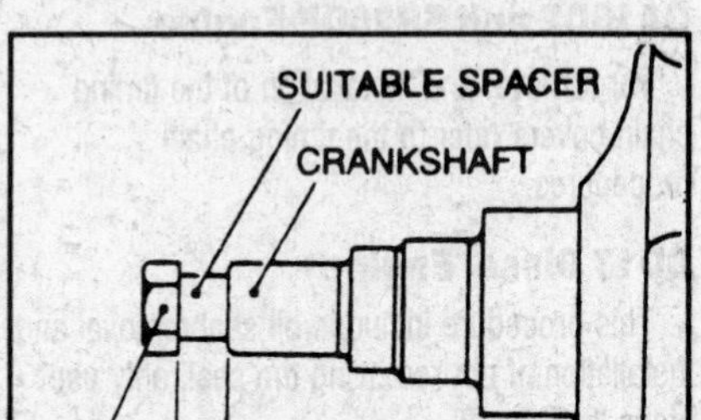
SUITABLE SPACER
CRANKSHAFT
ABOUT 25MM (0.98 IN.)
CRANKSHAFT PULLEY BOLT
Fig. 146. A spacer must be installed between the crankshaft and pulley bolt head before rotating the engine – CA16DE and CA18DE engines

24. Reconnect the radiator hose and refill the radiator.
25. Connect the battery cable and start the engine. Check engine timing and for any leaks. Road test.

GA16i Engine

1. Disconnect the negative battery cable.
2. Set the No. 1 piston at TDC of the compression stroke.
3. Remove the front cover.
4. If necessary, define the timing marks with chalk or paint to ensure proper alignment.
5. Hold the camshaft sprocket stationary with a spanner wrench or similar tool and remove the camshaft sprocket bolt.
6. Remove the chain guides.
7. Remove the camshaft sprocket.
8. Remove the oil pump spacer.
9. Remove the crankshaft sprocket and timing chain.

To install:

10. Verify that the No. 1 piston is at TDC of the compression stroke. The crankshaft keyways should be at the 12 o'clock position.

Fig. 147. Timing chain front cover oil seal installation

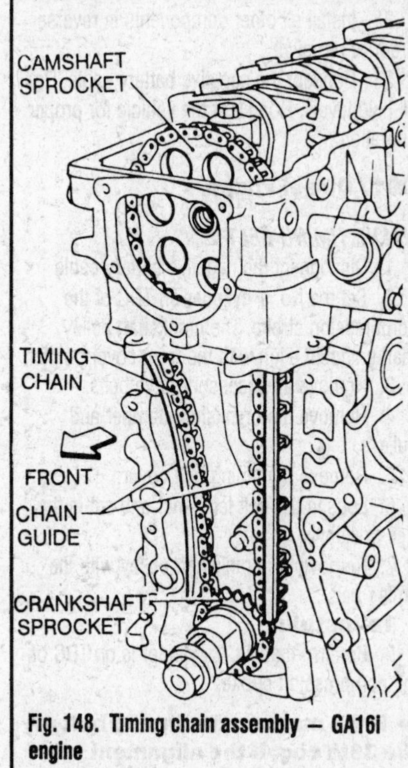
CAMSHAFT SPROCKET
TIMING CHAIN
FRONT
CHAIN GUIDE
CRANKSHAFT SPROCKET

Fig. 148. Timing chain assembly — GA16i engine

11. Install the camshaft sprocket, bolt and washer. The alignment mark must face towards the front. When installing the washer, place the non-chamfered side of the washer towards the face of camshaft sprocket. Tighten the bolt just enough to hold the sprocket in place.

12. Install the crankshaft sprocket making sure the alignment mark is facing the front.

13. Install the timing chain by aligning the silver links at the 12 o'clock and 6 o'clock positions on the chain with the timing marks on the crankshaft and camshaft sprockets. The number of links between the 2 silver links are the same for the left and the right sides of the chain, so either side of the chain may be used to align the sprocket timing marks.

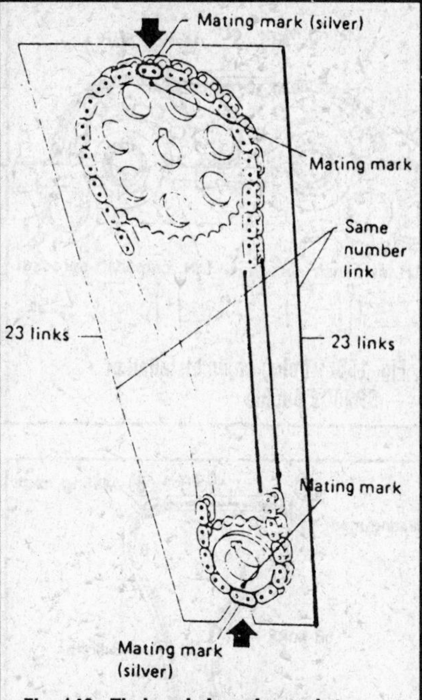
Mating mark (silver)
Mating mark
Same number link
23 links
23 links
Mating mark
Mating mark (silver)

Fig. 149. Timing chain and sprocket alignment marks — GA16i engine

14. Torque the camshaft sprocket bolt to 72–94 ft. lbs. (98–128 Nm) once the chain is in place and aligned.

15. Install the chain guides and tensioner. Use a new tensioner gasket and torque the tensioner and chain guide bolts to 9–14 ft. lbs. (13–19 Nm). When installing the chain guide, move the guide in the direction that applies tension to the chain.

16. Install the front cover.

17. Connect the negative battery cable. Road test the vehicle for proper operation.

GA16DE Engine

1. Disconnect the negative battery cable. Relieve the fuel pressure.
2. Remove the cylinder head assembly.
3. Remove the idle sprocket shaft from the rear side.
4. Remove the upper timing chain assembly.
5. Remove the center member.
6. Remove the oil pan assembly, oil strainer and crankshaft pulley.
7. Support engine and remove the engine front mounting bracket.
8. Remove the front cover. One retaining bolt for the front cover assembly is located on the water pump.
9. Remove the idler sprocket.
10. Remove the lower timing chain assembly, oil pump drive spacer, chain guide, crankshaft sprocket.

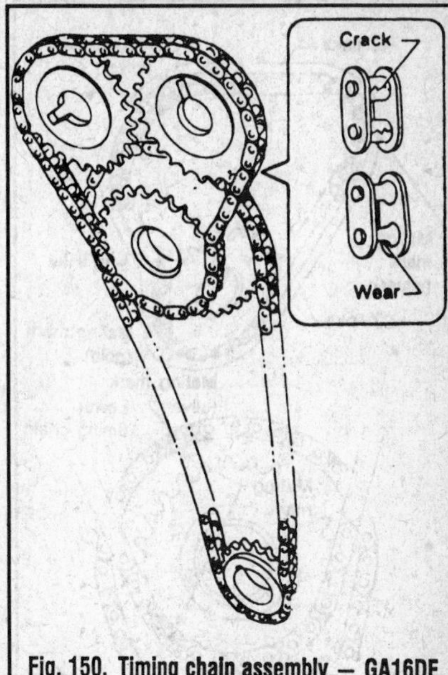
Crack
Wear

Fig. 150. Timing chain assembly — GA16DE engine

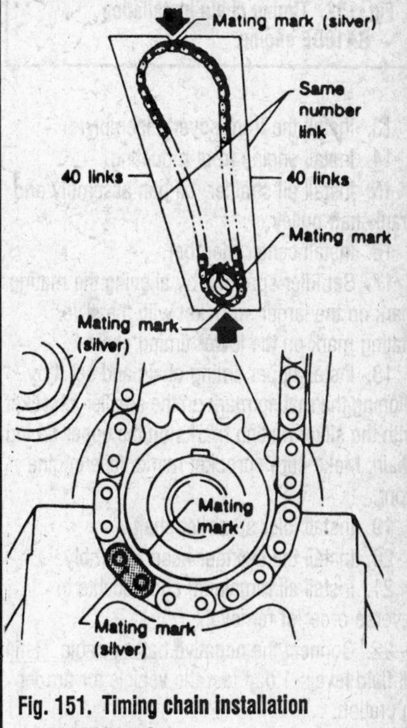
Mating mark (silver)
Same number link
40 links
40 links
Mating mark
Mating mark (silver)
Mating mark
Mating mark (silver)

Fig. 151. Timing chain installation — GA16DE engine

To Install:

11. Confirm that No. 1 piston is set at TDC on compression stroke. Install the chain guide.

12. Install crankshaft sprocket and lower timing chain. Set timing chain by aligning its mating mark with the one on the crankshaft sprocket. Make sure sprocket's mating mark faces engine front. The number of links between the alignment marks are the same for the left and right side.

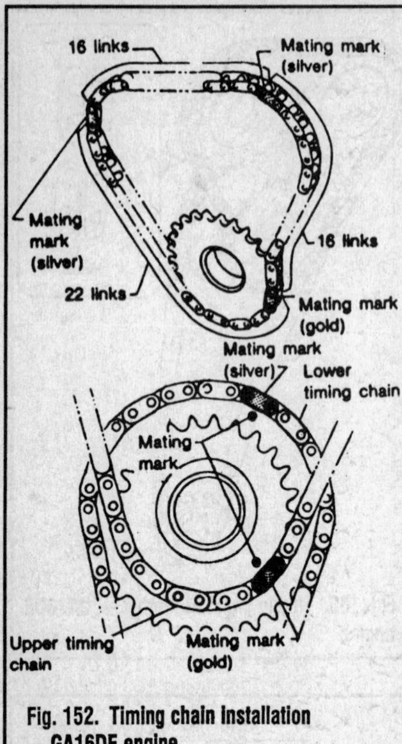
16 links
Mating mark (silver)
Mating mark (silver)
16 links
22 links
Mating mark (gold)
Mating mark (silver)
Lower timing chain
Mating mark
Upper timing chain
Mating mark (gold)

Fig. 152. Timing chain installation – GA16DE engine

13. Install the front cover assembly.

14. Install engine front mounting.

15. Install oil strainer, oil pan assembly and crankshaft pulley.

16. Install center member.

17. Set idler sprocket by aligning the mating mark on the larger sprocket with the silver mating mark on the lower timing chain.

18. Install upper timing chain and set it by aligning the mating mark on the smaller sprocket with the silver mating marks on the upper timing chain. Make sure sprocket marks face engine front.

19. Install idler sprocket shaft.

20. Install the cylinder head assembly.

21. Install all remaining components in reverse order of removal.

22. Connect the negative battery cable. Refill all fluid levels. Road test the vehicle for proper operation.

SR20DE Engine

1. Relieve the fuel system pressure and remove the negative battery cable.

2. Drain the coolant from the radiator and engine block. Remove the radiator.

3. Remove the right front wheel and engine side cover.

4. Remove the drive belts, water pump pulley, alternator and power steering pump.

5. Label and remove the vacuum hoses, fuel hoses and wire harness connectors.

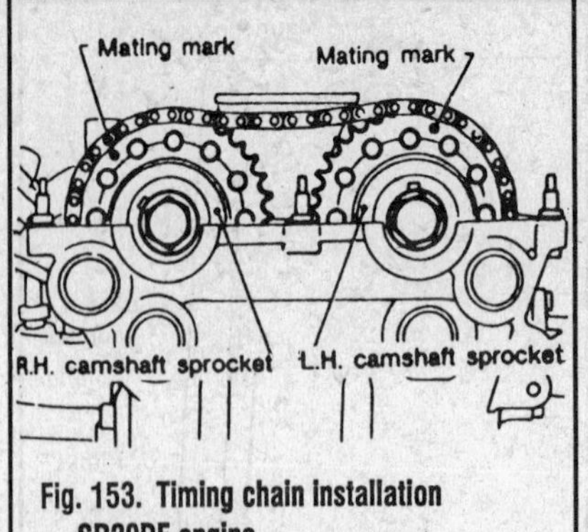
Mating mark
Mating mark
R.H. camshaft sprocket
L.H. camshaft sprocket

Fig. 153. Timing chain installation – SR20DE engine

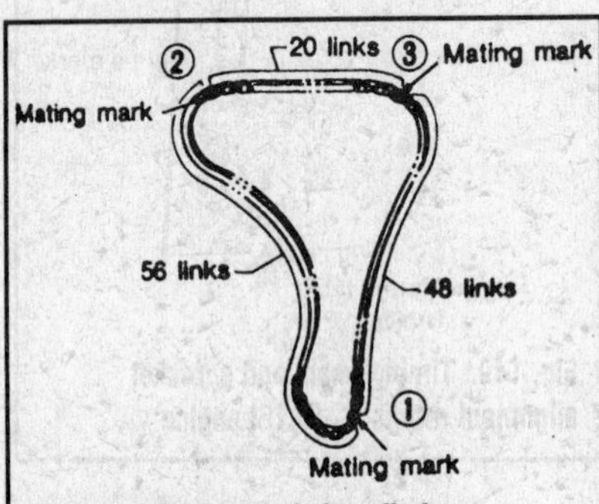
20 links
②
③
Mating mark
Mating mark
56 links
48 links
①
Mating mark

Fig. 154. Timing chain installation – SR20DE engine

6. Remove the cylinder head.

7. Raise and support the vehicle safely.

8. Remove the oil pan.

9. Remove the crankshaft pulley using a suitable puller.

10. Remove the engine front mount.

11. Remove the front cover.

12. Remove the timing chain guides and timing chain. Check the timing chain for excessive wear at the roller links. Replace the chain if necessary.

To install:

13. Install the crankshaft sprocket. Position the crankshaft so that No.1 piston is set at TDC (keyway at 12 o'clock, mating mark at 4 o'clock) fit timing chain to crankshaft sprocket so that mating mark is in line with mating mark on crankshaft sprocket. The mating marks on timing chain for the camshaft sprockets should be silver. The mating mark on the timing chain for the crankshaft sprocket should be gold.

14. Install the timing chain and timing chain guides.

15. Install front engine mount.

16. Install the crankshaft pulley and set No.1 piston at TDC on the compression stroke.

17. Install the oil strainer, baffle plate and oil pan.

18. Install the cylinder head, camshafts, oil tubes and baffles. Position the left camshaft key at 12 o'clock and the right camshaft key at 10 o'clock.

19. Install the camshaft sprockets by lining up the mating marks on the timing chain with the mating marks on the camshaft sprockets. Tighten the camshaft bolts to 101–116 ft. lbs. (137–157 Nm).

20. Install the timing chain guide and distributor. Ensure rotor is at 5 o'clock position.

21. Install the chain tensioner. Press the cam stopper down and the press-in sleeve until the hook can be engaged on the pin. When tensioner is bolted in position the hook will release automatically. Ensure the arrow on the outside faces the front of the engine.

22. Install all other components in reverse order of removal.

23. Connect the negative battery cable. Refill all fluid levels. Road test the vehicle for proper operation.

CD17 Diesel Engine

VALVE TIMING BELT

1. Disconnect the negative battery cable.

2. Set the No. 1 cylinder on TDC of the compression stroke. The crankshaft pulley marks should align with the front cover pointer.

3. Remove all accessory drive belts.

4. Remove the crankshaft damper and pulleys.

5. Remove the timing belt cover.

6. Loosen the belt tensioner and set in the free position.

7. Remove the crankshaft pulley with the timing belt.

To install:

8. Confirm that No. 1 cylinder is on TDC of the compression stroke.

➡ Put a mark on the timing belt at the 39th cog, if the alignment marks on the belt are worn away.

9. Align each mark and install the timing belt.

10. Install the crank pulley plate with the bezel facing the engine.

11. Loosen the tensioner bolt and turn crankshaft 2 times in the clockwise direction.

12. Turn the tensioner while holding it. If the tensioner turns while tightening, it may cause timing belt to be overloaded.

13. Torque the tensioner bolt to 90 ft. lbs. (123 Nm).

14. Install the front timing cover and crankshaft damper pulley. Torque the pulley bolt to 90–98 ft. lbs. (123–132 Nm).

15. Install the remaining components and start engine.

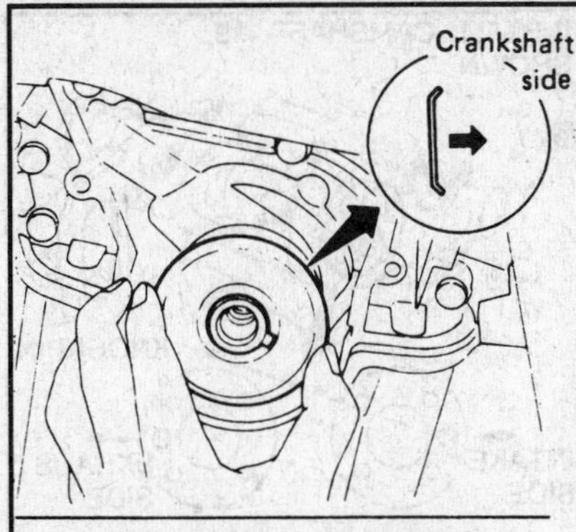
Crankshaft side

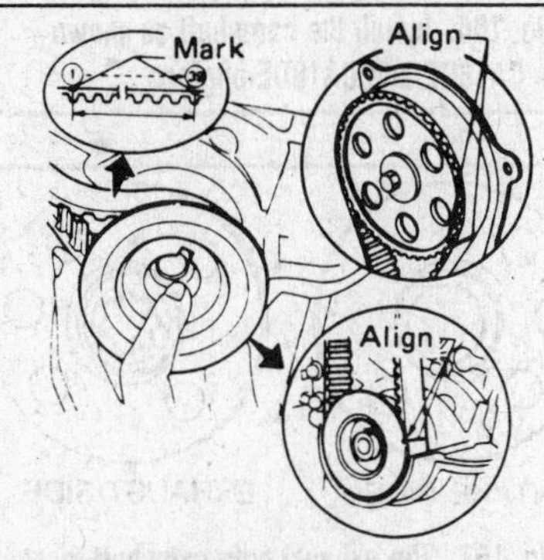
Mark
Align
Align

Fig. 156. Timing belt alignment marks — CD17 diesel engine

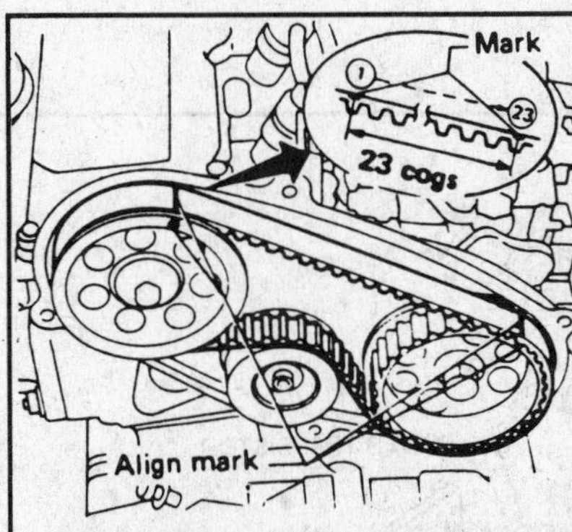
Mark
23 cogs
Align mark

Fig. 155. Aligning the timing marks for the injection pump drive belt — CD17 diesel engine

INJECTION TIMING BELT

1. Disconnect the negative battery cable.
2. Set the No. 1 cylinder on TDC of the compression stroke. The crankshaft pulley marks should align with the front cover pointer.
3. Remove the timing belt cover.
4. Loosen the belt tensioner and set to the free position.
5. Remove the belt from the pulleys.

To install:

6. Confirm that No. 1 cylinder is at TDC of the compression stroke.

➡ Put a mark on the timing belt at the 23rd cog, if the alignment marks on the belt are worn away.

7. Align each mark and install the timing belt.
8. Loosen the tensioner bolt and turn crankshaft 2 times in the normal direction.
9. Turn the tensioner while holding it. If the tensioner turns while tightening, it may cause timing belt to be overloaded.
10. Torque the tensioner bolt to 15 ft. lbs. (21 Nm).
11. Install the timing cover.
12. Install the remaining components and start engine.

Camshaft Sprocket

REMOVAL & INSTALLATION

1. Refer to the "Timing Belt/Chain, Removal and Installation" procedures, in this section and remove the timing chain/belt.
2. Remove the sprocket retaining bolt and remove the sprocket from the camshaft. On engines with a timing chain the chain and sprocket are removed at the same time.
3. To install, use new gaskets and reverse the removal procedures.

Camshaft and Bearings

➧ SEE FIGS. 162–180

REMOVAL & INSTALLATION

⁂ CAUTION

When draining the coolant, keep in mind that cats and dogs are attracted by the ethylene glycol antifreeze, and are quite likely to drink any that is left in an uncovered container or in puddles on the ground. This will prove fatal in sufficient quantity. Always drain the coolant into a sealable container. Coolant should be reused unless it is contaminated or several years old.

CA16DE and CA18DE Engines

➡ Since these engines DO NOT use replaceable camshaft bearings, overhaul is performed by replacement of the camshaft or the cylinder head. Check the camshaft bearing surfaces (in the cylinder head) with an internal micrometer and the bearing surfaces (of the camshaft) with a micrometer.

1. Remove the timing belt.
2. Remove the camshaft cover.
3. Remove the breather separator.
4. Remove the cylinder head.
5. While holding the camshaft sprockets, remove the 4 mounting bolts and then remove the sprockets themselves.
6. Remove the timing belt tensioner pulley. Remove the rear timing belt cover.
7. Loosen the camshaft bearing caps in several stages, in the order shown. Remove the bearing caps, but be sure to keep them in order.
8. Remove the front oil seals and then lift out the camshafts.
9. Check the camshaft runout, endplay, wear and journal clearance. Refer to the camshaft specification chart.

To install:

10. Position the camshafts in the cylinder head so the knockpin on each is on the outboard side.

➡ The exhaust side camshaft has splines to accept the crank angle sensor.

11. Position the camshaft bearing caps and finger tighten them. Each cap has an ID mark and a directional arrow stamped into its top surface.
12. Coat a NEW oil seal with engine oil (on the lip) and install it on each camshaft end.
13. Tighten the camshaft bearing cap bolts to 7–9 ft. lbs. (10–14 Nm) in sequence shown.
14. Install the rear timing cover.
15. Install the timing belt tensioner and tighten it to 16–22 ft. lbs. (21–30 Nm).
16. Install the camshaft sprockets and tighten the bolts to 10–14 ft. lbs. (14–20 Nm) while holding the camshaft in place.
17. Install the timing belt and the cylinder head.
18. Start engine, check timing and road test.

E-Series Engines

1. Remove the cylinder head.
2. Remove the rocker shaft along with the rocker arms. Loosen the bolts gradually, in two or three stages.
3. Carefully slide the camshaft out the front of the cylinder head.

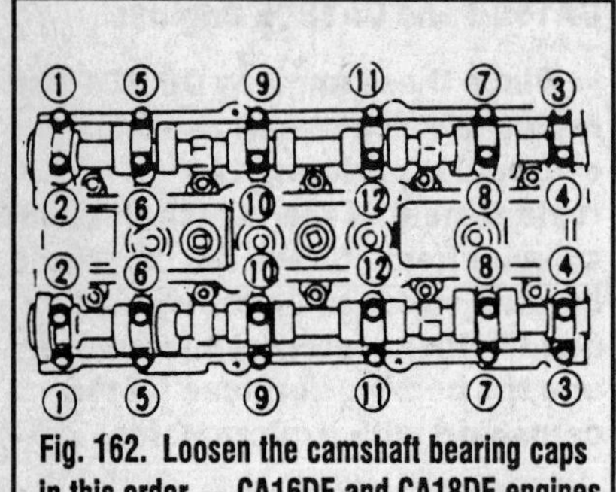
Fig. 162. Loosen the camshaft bearing caps in this order — CA16DE and CA18DE engines

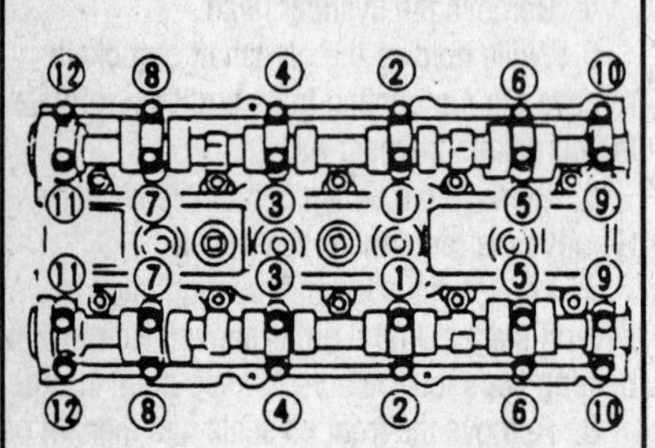
Fig. 163. Tighten the camshaft bearing caps in this order — CA16DE and CA18DE engines

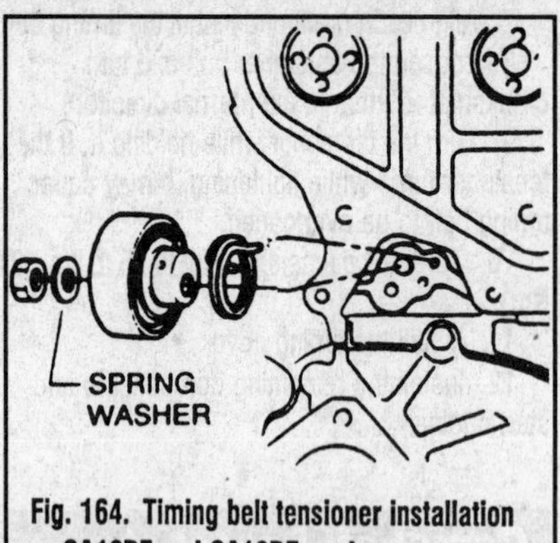
SPRING
WASHER
Fig. 164. Timing belt tensioner installation — CA16DE and CA18DE engines

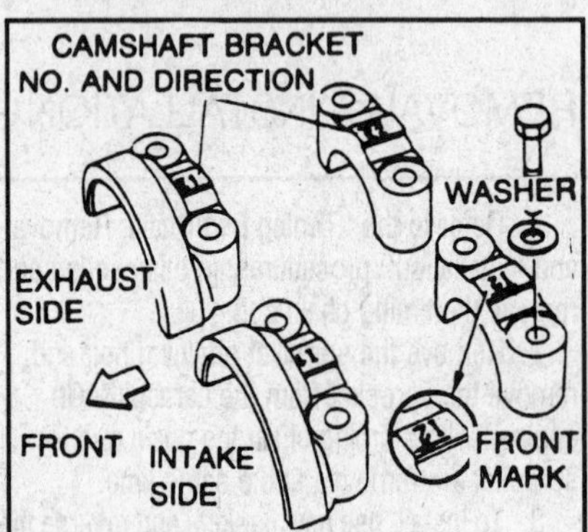
CAMSHAFT BRACKET
NO. AND DIRECTION
WASHER
EXHAUST
SIDE
FRONT
INTAKE
SIDE
FRONT
MARK
Fig. 165. Camshaft bearing cap positioning — CA16DE and CA18DE engines

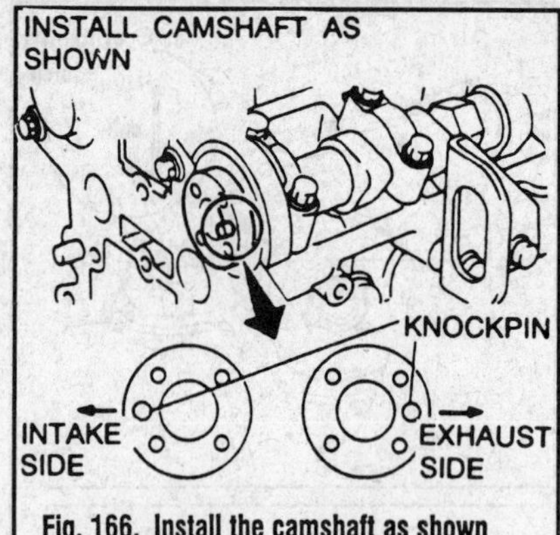
INSTALL CAMSHAFT AS
SHOWN
KNOCKPIN
INTAKE
SIDE
EXHAUST
SIDE
Fig. 166. Install the camshaft as shown — CA16DE and CA18DE engines

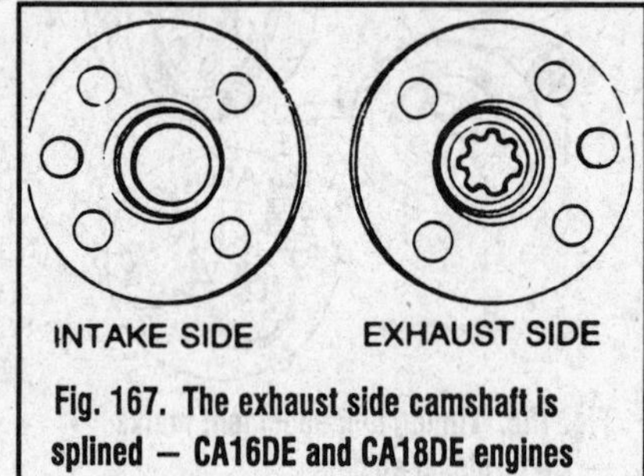
INTAKE SIDE
EXHAUST SIDE
Fig. 167. The exhaust side camshaft is splined — CA16DE and CA18DE engines

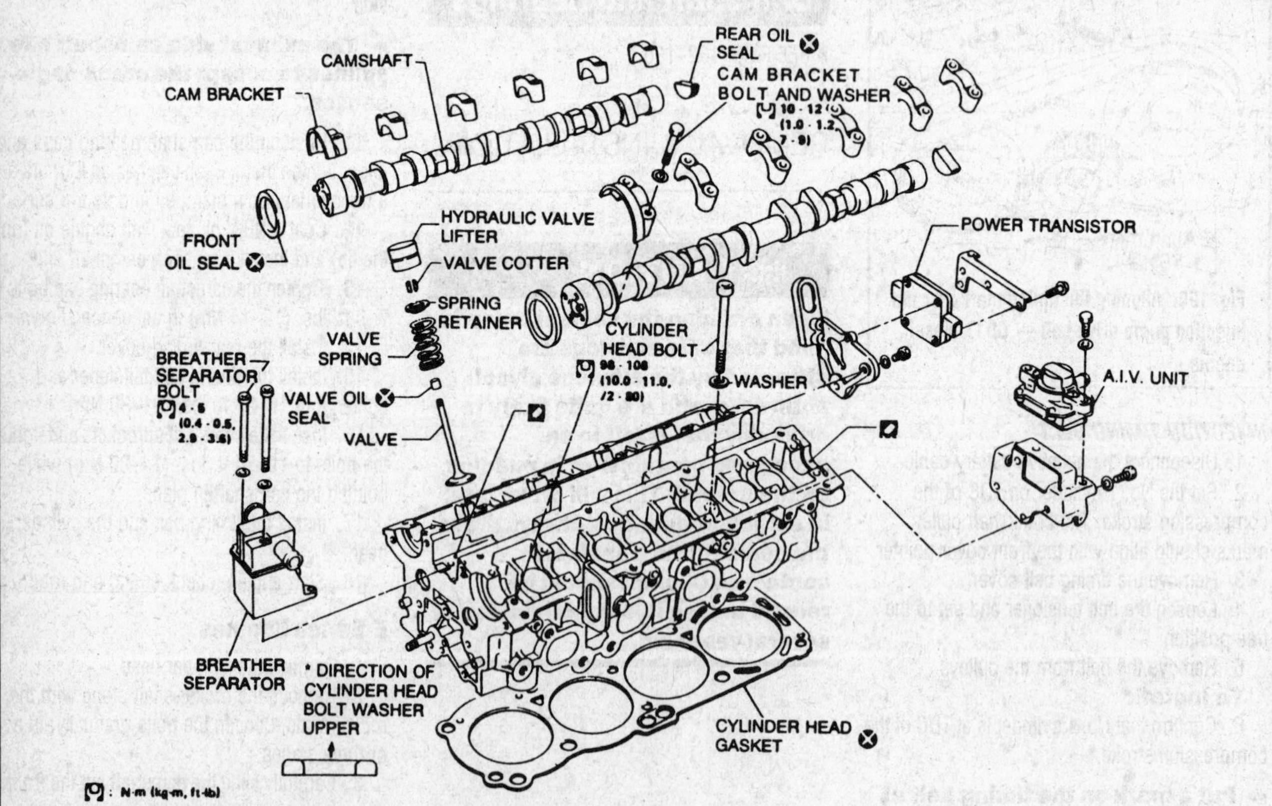

REAR OIL
SEAL
CAMSHAFT
CAM BRACKET
CAM BRACKET
BOLT AND WASHER
10 - 12 (1.0 - 1.2, 7 - 9)
FRONT
OIL SEAL
HYDRAULIC VALVE
LIFTER
VALVE COTTER
POWER TRANSISTOR
SPRING
RETAINER
VALVE
SPRING
CYLINDER
HEAD BOLT
98 - 108 (10.0 - 11.0, 72 - 80)
BREATHER
SEPARATOR
BOLT
4 - 5 (0.4 - 0.5, 2.9 - 3.6)
VALVE OIL
SEAL
VALVE
WASHER
A.I.V. UNIT
BREATHER
SEPARATOR
* DIRECTION OF
CYLINDER HEAD
BOLT WASHER
UPPER
CYLINDER HEAD
GASKET
: N·m (kg-m, ft-lb)
Fig. 168. Exploded view of the cylinder head — CA16DE and CA18DE engines

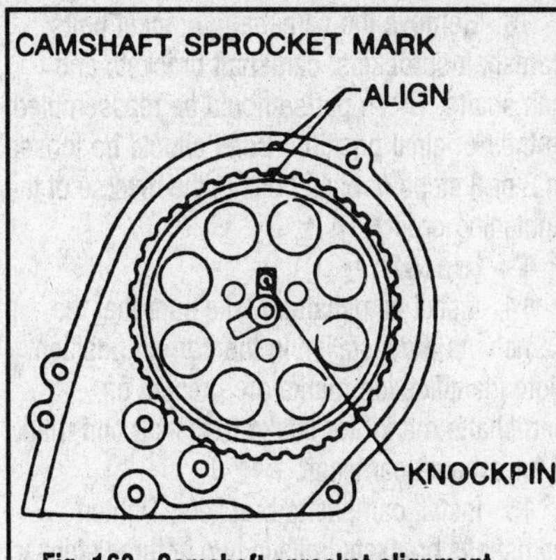
CAMSHAFT SPROCKET MARK
ALIGN
KNOCKPIN
Fig. 169. Camshaft sprocket alignment — E-series engine

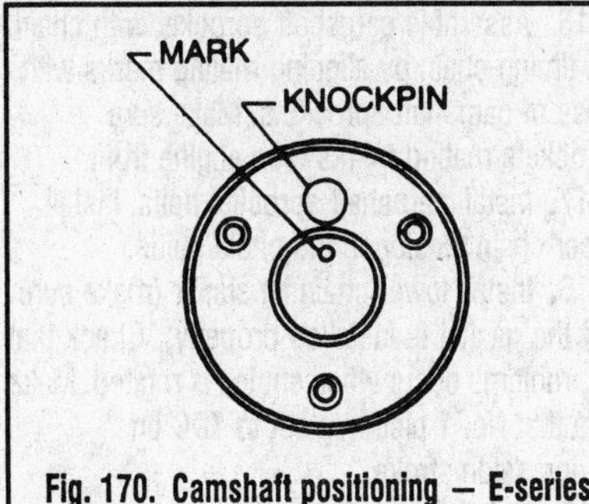
MARK
KNOCKPIN
Fig. 170. Camshaft positioning — E-series engine

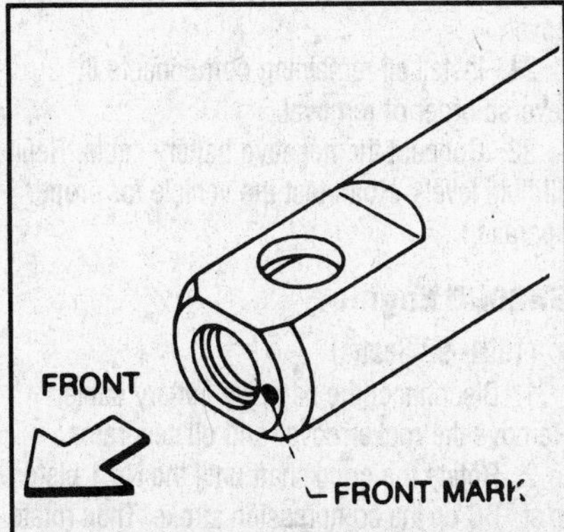
FRONT
FRONT MARK
Fig. 171. The punch mark on the rocker arm shaft should face forward — E-series engine

4. Check the camshaft runout, endplay, wear and journal clearance. Refer to the camshaft specifications chart.

To install:

5. Slide the camshaft into the cylinder head carefully and then install a NEW oil seal.
6. Install the cylinder head and rear timing belt cover.
7. Set the camshaft so that the knockpin faces upward and then install the camshaft sprocket so its timing mark aligns with the one on the rear timing cover.

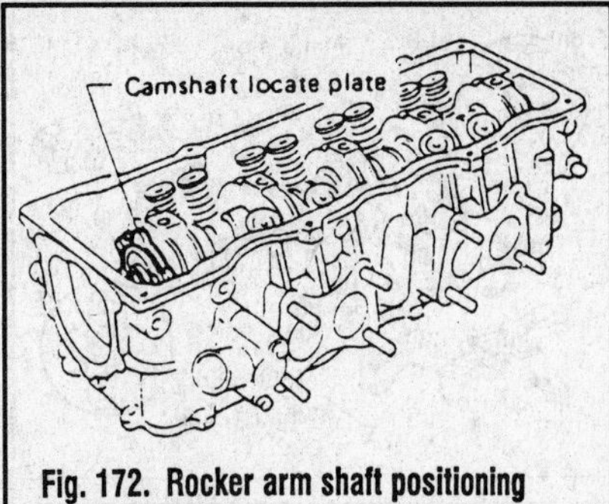
Camshaft locate plate
Fig. 172. Rocker arm shaft positioning — GA16i engine

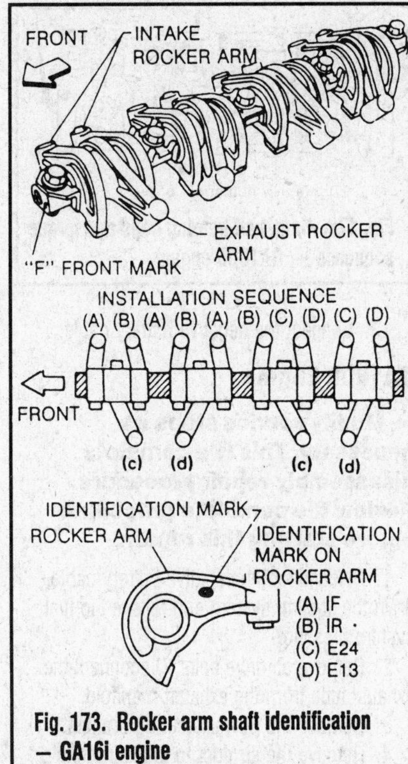
FRONT
INTAKE
ROCKER ARM
EXHAUST ROCKER
ARM
"F" FRONT MARK
INSTALLATION SEQUENCE
(A) (B) (A) (B) (A) (B) (C) (D) (C) (D)
FRONT
(c) (d) (c) (d)
IDENTIFICATION MARK
ROCKER ARM
IDENTIFICATION
MARK ON
ROCKER ARM
(A) IF
(B) IR
(C) E24
(D) E13
Fig. 173. Rocker arm shaft identification — GA16i engine

8. Install the timing belt.
9. Coat the rocker shaft and the interior of the rocker arm with engine oil. Install them so the punchmark on the shaft faces forward and the oil holes in the shaft face down. The cut-out in the center retainer on the shaft should face the exhaust manifold side of the engine.
10. Make sure the valve adjusting screws are loosened and then tighten the shaft bolts to 13–15 ft. lbs. (16–18 Nm) in several stages, from the center out. The first and last mounting bolts should have a new bolt stopper installed.
11. Adjust the valves and refill all fluid levels.
12. Start engine, check timing and road test.

GA16i Engine

1. Disconnect the negative battery cable.
2. Remove the timing chain.

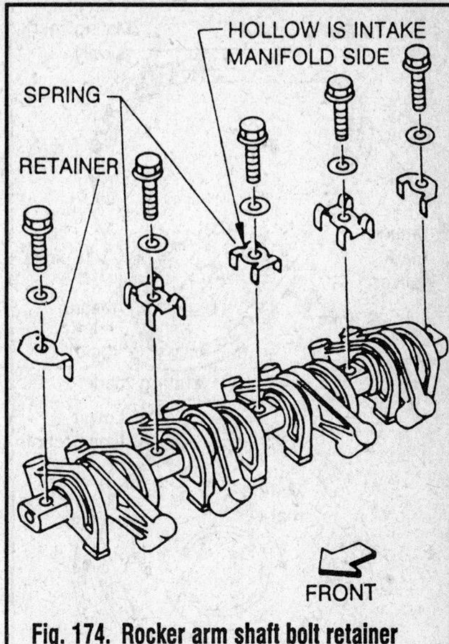
HOLLOW IS INTAKE
MANIFOLD SIDE
SPRING
RETAINER
FRONT
Fig. 174. Rocker arm shaft bolt retainer positioning — GA16i engine

3. Remove the cylinder head with manifolds attached.
4. Remove the intake and exhaust manifolds from the cylinder head. Loosen the bolts in 2–3 stages in the proper sequence.
5. Loosen the rocker arm shaft bolts in 2–3 stages and lift the rocker arm/shaft assembly from the cylinder head. The rocker arm shaft is marked with an **F** to indicate that it faces towards the front of the engine. Place a similar mark on the cylinder head for your own reference.
6. Loosen the thrust plate retaining bolt.
7. Withdraw the camshaft and the thrust plate from the front of the cylinder head. The thrust plate is located to the camshaft with a key. Retain this key.

To install:

8. Clean all cylinder head, intake and exhaust manifold gasket surfaces. Lubricate the camshaft and rocker arm/shaft assemblies with a liberal coating of clean engine oil. Then, slide the camshaft and thrust plate into the front of the cylinder head. Don't forget to install the thrust plate key.
9. Install the rocker shafts and rocker arms making sure the **F** on the rocker shaft points toward the front of the engine. Install the rocker shaft retaining bolts, spring clips and washers. The center spring clip has a recess cut into one side. When installing the center clip point this recess toward the intake manifold side of the head. Snug the bolts gradually in 2–3 stages starting from the center and working out. Attach the intake and exhaust manifold to the head with new gaskets.

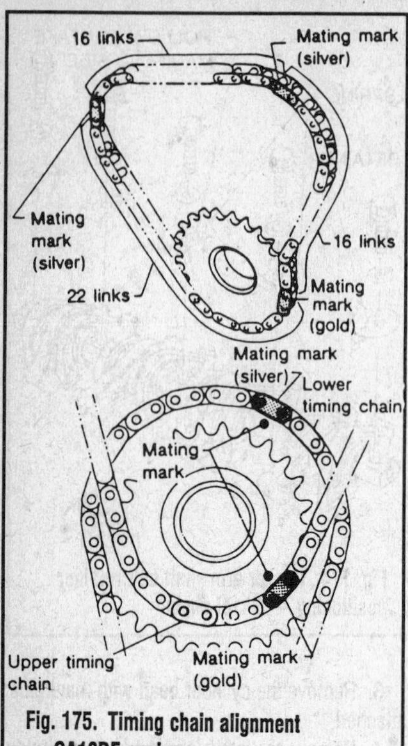
16 links
Mating mark (silver)
Mating mark (silver)
16 links
22 links
Mating mark (gold)
Mating mark (silver)
Lower timing chain
Mating mark
Upper timing chain
Mating mark (gold)
Fig. 175. Timing chain alignment – GA16DE engine

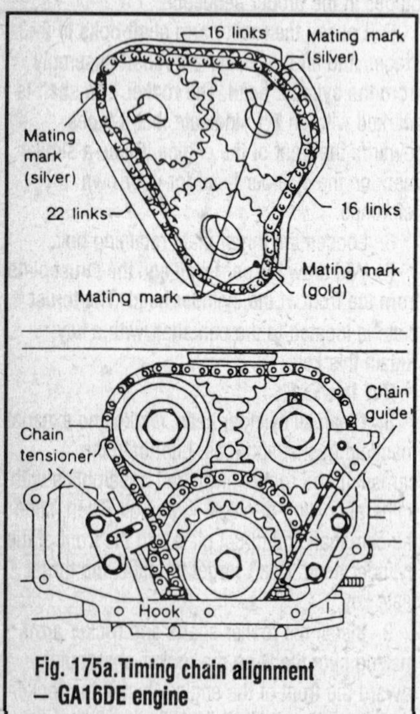
16 links
Mating mark (silver)
Mating mark (silver)
22 links
16 links
Mating mark (gold)
Mating mark
Chain guide
Chain tensioner
Hook
Fig. 175a. Timing chain alignment – GA16DE engine

10. Install the cylinder head and timing chain.

11. After the timing chain is in place, set the No. 1 cylinder to TDC of the compression stroke.

12. Torque the No. 1 and No. 2 rocker shaft bolts to 27–30 ft. lbs. (37–41 Nm). Then, set the No. 4 cylinder to TDC and torque the No. 3 and No. 4 rocker shaft bolts to 27–30 ft. lbs. (37–41 Nm).

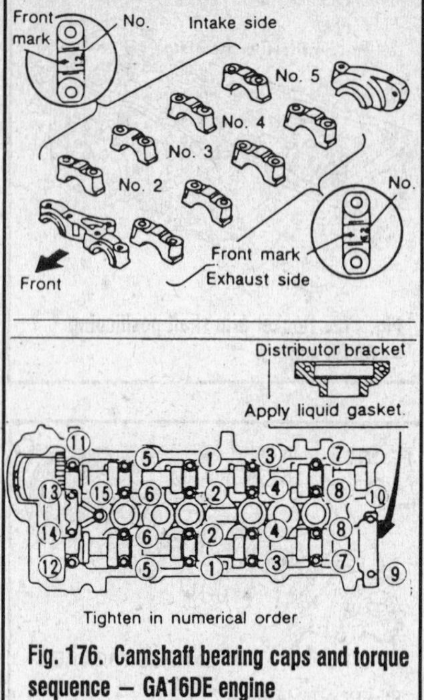
Front mark
No.
Intake side
No. 5
No. 4
No. 3
No. 2
No.
Front mark
Front
Exhaust side
Distributor bracket
Apply liquid gasket.
Tighten in numerical order
Fig. 176. Camshaft bearing caps and torque sequence – GA16DE engine

13. Connect the negative battery cable.

GA16DE Engine

➡ Modify service steps as necessary. This is a complete disassembly repair procedure. Review the complete procedure before starting this repair.

1. Disconnect the negative battery cable, drain the cooling system and relieve the fuel system pressure.

2. Remove all drive belts. Disconnect the exhaust tube from the exhaust manifold.

3. Remove the power steering bracket.

4. Remove the air duct to intake manifold collector.

5. Remove the front right side wheel, splash cover and front undercovers.

6. Remove the front exhaust pipe and engine front mounting bracket.

7. Remove the rocker arm cover.

8. Remove the distributor cap. Remove the spark plugs.

9. Set the No. 1 cylinder at TDC of the compression stroke.

10. Mark and remove the distributor assembly.

11. Remove the cam sprocket cover and gusset. Remove the water pump pulley. Remove the thermostat housing.

12. Remove the chain tensioner, chain guide. Loosen idler sprocket bolt.

13. Remove the camshaft sprocket bolts, camshaft sprockets, camshaft brackets and camshafts. These parts should be reassembled in their original position. Bolts should be loosen in 2 or 3 steps (loosen bolts in the reverse of the tightening order).

To install:

14. Install camshafts. Make sure that the camshafts are installed in the correct position. Note identification marks are present on camshafts mark I for intake camshaft and mark E for exhaust camshaft.

15. Install camshafts brackets. Tighten camshafts brackets bolts in two or three steps to 7–9 ft. lbs. (9–12 Nm) in the correct sequence. After completing assembly check valve clearance.

16. Assemble camshaft sprocket with chain. Set timing chain by aligning mating marks with those of camshaft sprockets. Make sure sprockets mating marks face engine front.

17. Install camshaft sprocket bolts. Install upper chain tensioner and chain guide.

18. Install lower chain tensioner (make sure that the gasket is installed properly). Check that no problems occur when engine is rotated. Make sure that No. 1 piston is set to TDC on compression stroke.

19. Install thermostat housing, water pump pulley. Install the distributor assembly.

20. Install cam sprocket cover and rocker cover.

21. Install all remaining components in reverse order of removal.

22. Connect the negative battery cable. Refill all fluid levels. Road test the vehicle for proper operation.

SR20DE Engine

(1991–92 Sentra)

1. Disconnect the negative battery cable. Remove the rocker cover and oil separator.

2. Rotate the crankshaft until the No.1 piston is at TDC on the compression stroke. Then rotate the crankshaft until the mating marks on the camshaft sprockets line up with the mating marks on the timing chain.

3. Remove the timing chain tensioner.

4. Remove the distributor.

5. Remove the timing chain guide.

6. Remove the camshaft sprockets. Use a wrench to hold the camshaft while loosening the sprocket bolt.

7. Loosen the camshaft bracket bolts in the opposite order of the torquing sequence.

8. Remove the camshaft.

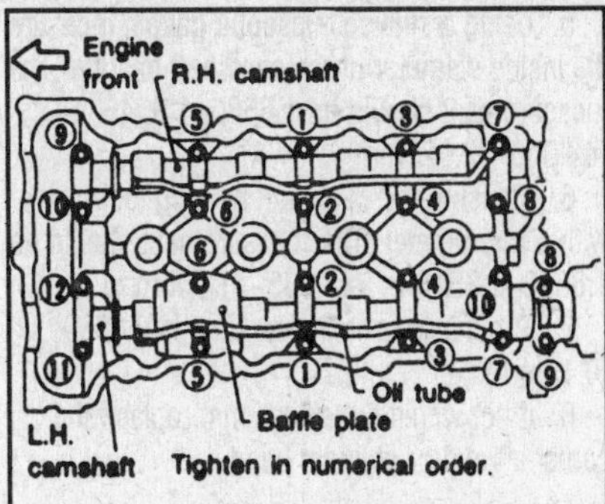
Engine front
R.H. camshaft
Oil tube
Baffle plate
L.H. camshaft
Tighten in numerical order.
Fig. 177. Camshaft bracket torque sequence – SR20DE engine

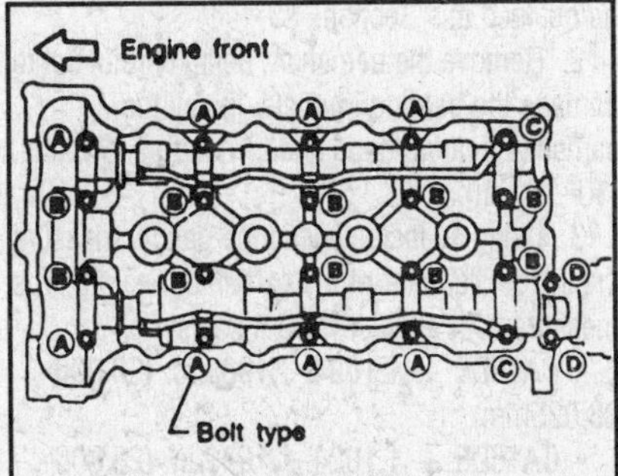
Engine front
Bolt type
Fig. 178. Camshaft bolt location – SR20DE engine

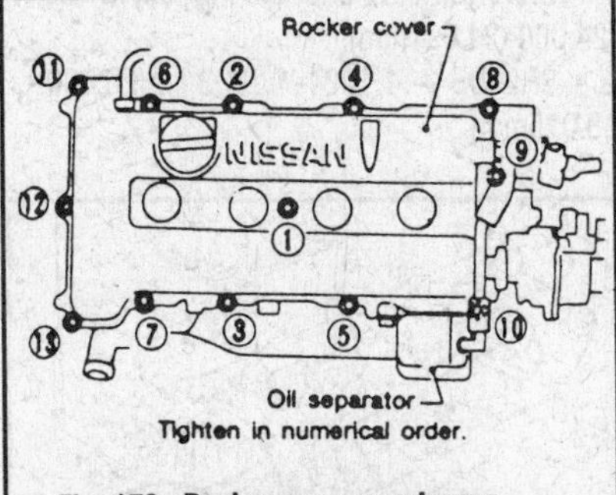
Rocker cover
NISSAN
Oil separator
Tighten in numerical order.
Fig. 179. Rocker arm cover torque sequence – SR20DE engine

To Install:

9. Clean the left hand camshaft end bracket and coat the mating surface with liquid gasket. Install the camshafts, camshaft brackets, oil tubes and baffle plate. Ensure the left camshaft key is at 12 o'clock and the right camshaft key is at 10 o'clock.

10. The procedure for tightening camshaft bolts must be followed exactly to prevent camshaft damage. Tighten bolts as follows:

a. Tighten right camshaft bolts 9 and 10 (in that order) to 1.5 ft. lbs. (2 Nm) then tighten bolts 1–8 (in that order) to the same specification.

b. Tighten left camshaft bolts 11 and 12 (in that order) to 1.5 ft. lbs. (2 Nm) then tighten bolts 1–10 (in that order) to the same specification.

c. Tighten all bolts in sequence to 4.5 ft. lbs. (6 Nm).

d. Tighten all bolts in sequence to 6.5–8.5 ft. lbs. (9–12 Nm) for type A, B and C bolts, and 13–19 ft. lbs. (18–25 Nm) for type D bolts.

11. Line up the mating marks on the timing chain and camshaft sprockets and install the sprockets. Tighten sprocket bolts to 101–116 ft. lbs. (137–157 Nm).

12. Install the timing chain guide, distributor (ensure that rotor head is at 5 o'clock position) and chain tensioner.

13. Clean the rocker cover and mating surfaces and apply a continuous bead of liquid gasket to the mating surface.

14. Install the rocker cover and oil separator. Tighten the rocker cover bolts as follows:

a. Tighten nuts 1, 10, 11, and 8 in that order to 3 ft. lbs. (4 Nm).

b. Tighten nuts 1–13 as indicated in the figure to 6–7 ft. lbs. (8–10 Nm).

15. Connect the negative battery cable. Refill all fluid levels. Road test the vehicle for proper operation.

CD17 Diesel Engine

➡ **The camshaft is normally removed with the cylinder head removed from the engine. Follow the procedure below for timing belt removal, then follow the "Cylinder Head Removal" procedure earlier in this section; the camshaft removal procedure follows timing belt removal. The injection pump has its own belt drive and is covered later in this section.**

1. Support the engine with a jack and remove the right side engine mount, then jack the engine up to allow working clearance.

2. Set the No. 1 cylinder at TDC on its compression stroke.

3. Remove the alternator and air conditioning compressor (if equipped) drive belts.

4. Using a puller, remove the crankshaft damper pulley.

5. Loosen the tensioner pulley and set it to the "free" position. Remove the idler pulley.

6. Remove the crankshaft pulley with the timing belt. Remove the injection pump timing belt as described below.

7. Check the belt for damage, missing teeth, wear or saturation with oil or grease. If damage is evident or if you are in doubt as to the belt's condition, replace the belt.

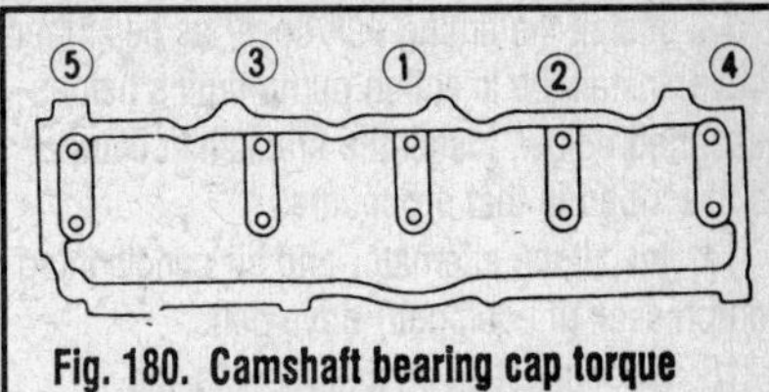
Fig. 180. Camshaft bearing cap torque sequence – CD17 diesel engine

➡ **Do not bend, twist or turn the timing belt inside out. Do not allow the belt to come into contact with any grease, oil or solvents.**

8. Remove the cylinder head and manifolds.

9. Remove the camshaft bearing caps and check the clearance with Plastigage®. Do not turn the camshaft. If the bearing clearance exceeds 0.1mm replace the bearing caps, camshaft or cylinder head.

10. After checking clearances, remove the bearing caps and remove the camshaft with both oil seals. Have the camshaft runout and lobe height checked; if worn beyond specification, replace the camshaft.

➡ **There are two different diameter seals used on the camshaft front and rear. Be sure to use the correct seal when installing. (The front seal has an arrow on the outer edge facing clockwise; the rear seal arrow points counterclockwise). If you are replacing the oil seals without removing the camshaft, remove the pulleys and carefully pry the seals out using a small pry bar or an old screwdriver covered with tape. Use care not to scratch the camshaft, cylinder head or bearing cap.**

To Install:

11. To install the camshaft, first lubricate all bearing surfaces with clean engine oil. Install the camshaft bearing caps and torque, in the sequence illustrated, to 13–16 ft. lbs. (19–22 Nm). Before installing the oil seals, lubricate with clean engine oil. Reinstall the cylinder head and check valve clearances; adjust if necessary.

12. Install the crankshaft and camshaft timing sprockets. Torque the camshaft timing sprocket bolt to 68–75 ft. lbs. (92–102 Nm). Install the timing belt assembly in the reverse order of removal. Align the marks on the timing belt with those on the camshaft and crankshaft pulleys. When tensioning the belt, loosen the tensioner bolt and turn the crankshaft two times in its normal rotating direction, then tighten the tensioner while holding it. Do not allow the tensioner to rotate when tightening, and NEVER turn the engine against its normal rotating direction.

13. Install the timing belt cover as described above. Install the injection pump timing belt as described below. Install the crankshaft damper as described in that procedure.

14. Install the alternator and air conditioning compressor (if equipped) drive belts.

15. Reconnect all engine mounts and mounting brackets securely and remove the supporting jack.

INSPECTION

➡ Since these engines DO NOT use replaceable camshaft bearings, overhaul is performed by replacement of the camshaft or the cylinder head. Check the camshaft bearing surfaces (in the cylinder head) with an internal micrometer and the bearing surfaces (of the camshaft) with a micrometer.

E-series Engine

1. Remove the cylinder head from the vehicle as outlined this Section.

2. Remove the camshaft sprocket and front cover assembly.

3. Remove the rocker arm assembly as outlined in this Section.

4. Remove the camshaft, being careful not to damage the bearing journals.

5. Using an inside telescope gauge, measure the inside diameter of the camshaft bearing. The measurement should be 1.6535–1.6545 in. (42.000–42.025mm).

6. Measure the camshaft bearing journals with a micrometer. The measurement should be 1.6515–1.6522 in. (41.949–41.965mm) for journals 1, 3 and 5. The measurement should be 1.6498–1.6505 in. (41.906–41.922mm) for journals 2 and 4.

7. The maximum oil clearance for 1, 3 and 5 should be 0.0059 (0.15mm) and 0.0079 in. (0.20mm) for 2 and 4.

8. If not within specifications, replace the camshaft and/or cylinder head.

GA16i Engine

1. Remove the cylinder head from the vehicle as outlined this Section.

2. Remove the camshaft sprocket and front cover assembly.

3. Remove the rocker arm assembly as outlined in this Section.

4. Remove the camshaft, being careful not to damage the bearing journals.

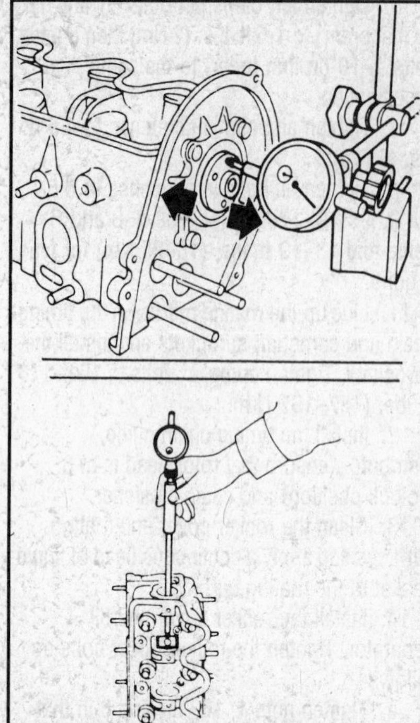

Fig. 157. Camshaft endplay and oil clearance inspection — E-series engine

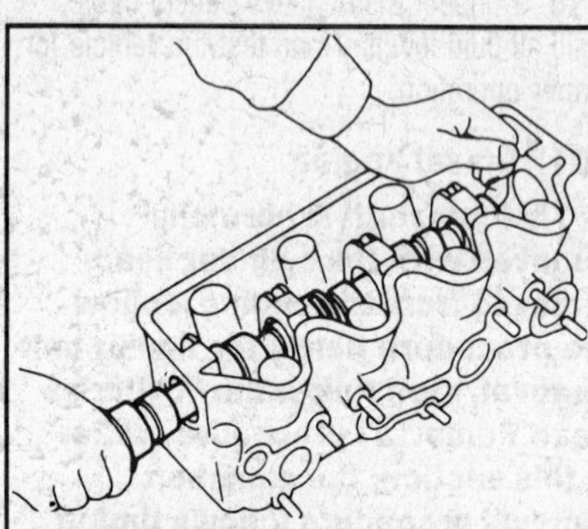

Fig. 158. Use care in removing camshaft from head — E-series engine

Fig. 159. Front camshaft retainer screws — E-series engine

5. Using an inside telescope gauge, measure the inside diameter of the camshaft bearing. The measurement should be 1.6535–1.6545 in. (42.000–42.025mm).

6. Measure the camshaft bearing journals with a micrometer. The measurement should be 1.6510–1.6518 in. (41.935–41.955mm).

7. The maximum oil clearance is 0.0059 (0.15mm).

8. If not within specifications, replace the camshaft and/or cylinder head.

CA16DE, GA16DE, CA18DE and SR20DE Engines

1. Remove the cylinder head from the vehicle as outlined this Section.

2. Remove the camshaft, being careful not to damage the bearing journals. Install the camshaft bearing caps and torque to 7–9 ft. lbs. (10–12 Nm).

3. Using an inside telescope gauge, measure the inside diameter of the camshaft bearing. The measurement should be as follows:

- CA18DE — 1.1024–1.1033 in. (28.000–28.025mm)
- CA16DE — 1.1024–1.1033 in. (28.000–28.025mm)
- GA16DE No. 1 journal — 1.1024–1.1032 in. (28.000–28.021mm)
- GA16DE No. 2–5 — 0.9449–09.457 in. (24.000–24.021mm)
- SR20DE — 1.1024–1.1033 in. (28.000–28.025mm)

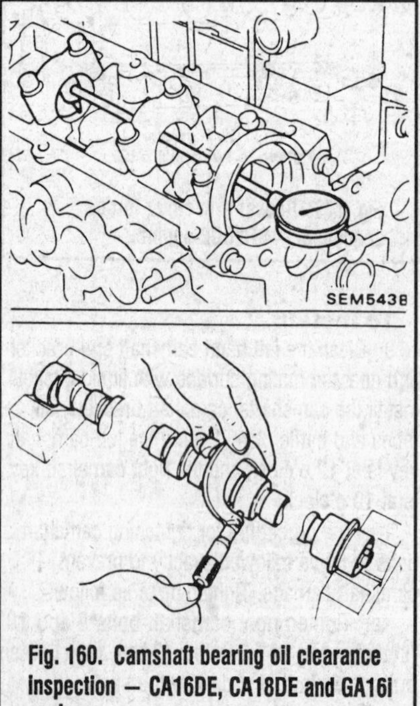
SEM543B

Fig. 160. Camshaft bearing oil clearance inspection — CA16DE, CA18DE and GA16i engines

4. Measure the camshaft bearing journals with a micrometer. The measurement should be as follows:

• CA18DE — 1.0998–1.1006 in. (27.935–27.955mm)
• CA16DE — 1.0998–1.1006 in. (27.935–27.955mm)
• GA16DE No. 1 journal — 1.0998–1.1006 in. (27.935–27.955mm)
• GA16DE No. 2–5 — 0.9423–0.9431 in. (23.935–23.955mm)
• SR20DE — 1.0998–1.1006 in. (27.935–27.955mm)

5. The maximum oil clearance is 0.0059 (0.15mm).
6. If not within specifications, replace the camshaft and/or cylinder head.

CD17 Diesel Engine

1. Remove the camshaft as outlined in this Section.
2. Clean all oil and dirt from the camshaft journal and bearing surface.
3. Place a piece of Plastigage® on the journal and install the bearing caps.
4. Torque the bearing cap to 13–16 ft. lbs. (18–22 Nm). Do not turn the camshaft.
5. Remove the bearing caps and measure the width of the Plastigage® at its widest point.
6. The oil clearance should be 0.0008–0.0040 in. (0.02–0.10mm).
7. If the clearance is not within specifications, replace the camshaft and/or cylinder head.

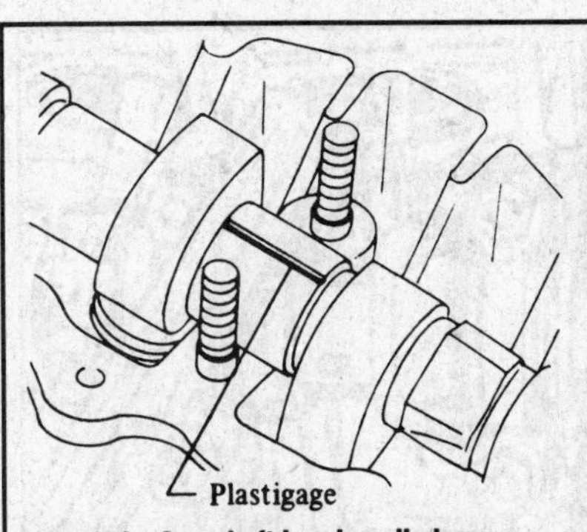
Plastigage

Fig. 161. Camshaft bearing oil clearance inspection — CD17 diesel engine

CHECKING CAMSHAFT RUNOUT

Place the camshaft on a set of V-blocks, supported by the outermost bearing surfaces. Place a dial micrometer, with it's finger resting on the center bearing surface, then turn the camshaft to check the runout; the runout should not exceed 0.004 in. (0.010mm), if it does exceed the limit, replace the camshaft.

Check the camshaft bearing surfaces (in the engine) with an internal micrometer and the bearing surfaces (of the camshaft) with a micrometer.

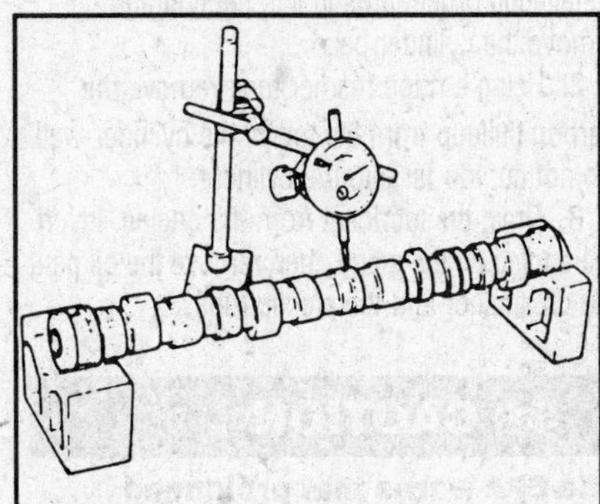

Fig. 181. Camshaft positioning — E-series engine

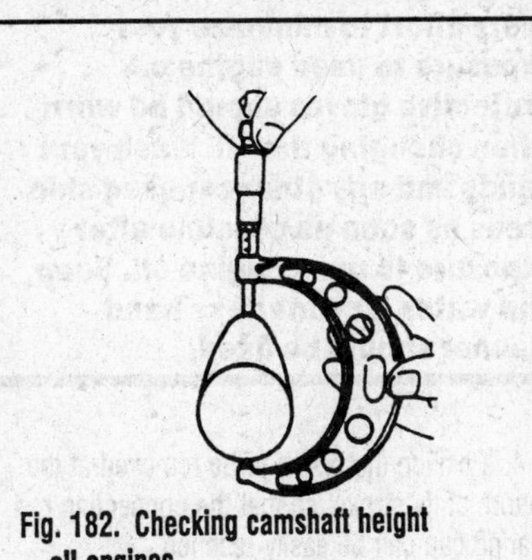

Fig. 182. Checking camshaft height — all engines

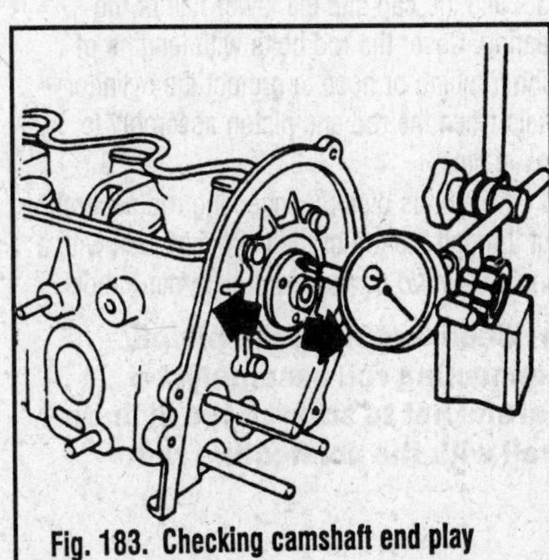

Fig. 183. Checking camshaft end play

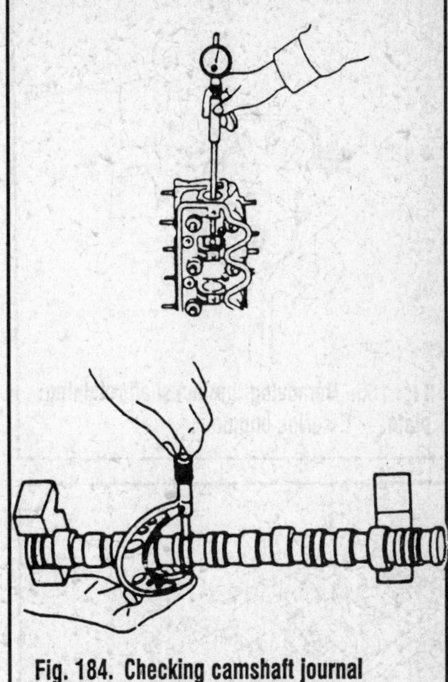

Fig. 184. Checking camshaft journal clearance — inside and outside measurement. Torque the bearing caps to specification

Auxiliary (Jack) Shaft

➧ SEE FIGS. 185–187

REMOVAL & INSTALLATION

1. Refer to the Timing Belt and/or Chain, Removal and Installation procedures in this section and remove the timing belt.
2. Pull the crankshaft sprocket from the crankshaft. Remove the jackshaft sprocket bolts, then separate the sprocket from the jackshaft.
3. Remove the lower locating plate from the cylinder block. Remove the jackshaft and the crankshaft oil seals from the locating plate.
4. Remove the jackshaft retaining plate, then pull the shaft out through the front of the cylinder block. Be careful not to damage the bearings.

To install:

5. Check the jackshaft bearing diameters (in the cylinder block) with an internal micrometer and the bearing diameters (of the jackshaft) with a micrometer; the clearance should not exceed 0.15mm, if it does exceed the limit, replace the jackshaft bearings.
6. Use a hammer and a brass drift, to remove and install the jackshaft bearings in the cylinder block.

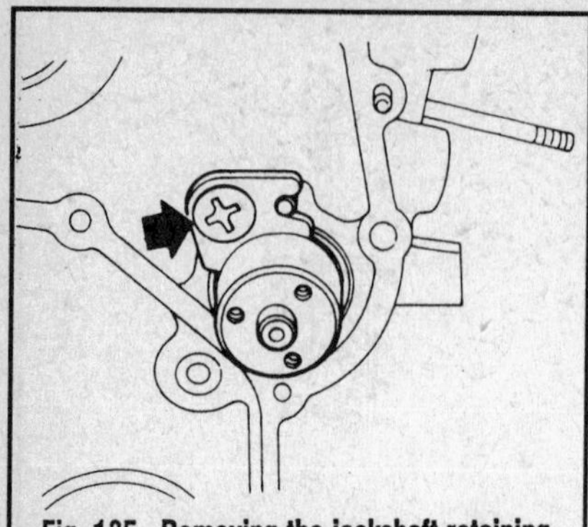
Fig. 185. Removing the jackshaft retaining plate — E-series engine

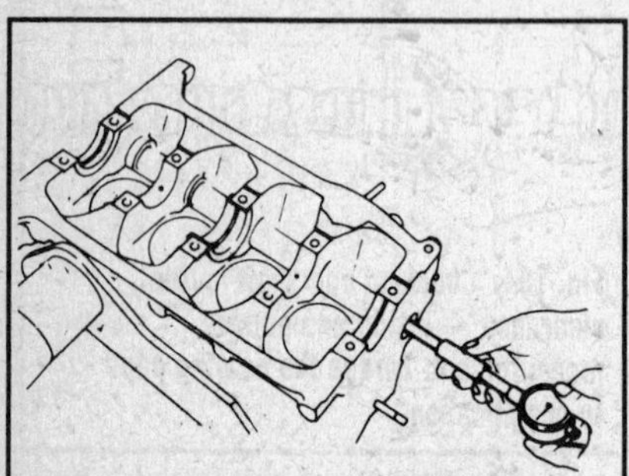
Fig. 186. Checking the jackshaft bearing diameters with an inside micrometer

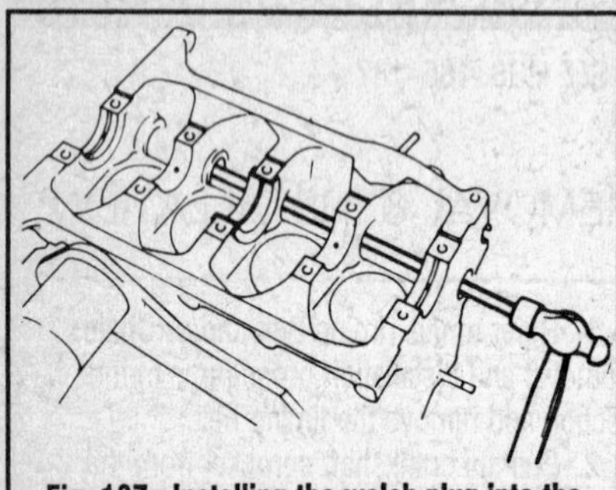
Fig. 187. Installing the welch plug into the cylinder block

➡ **Be sure to align the oil hole in the bearing with the hole in the cylinder block. After installation, check the bearing clearances. Using sealant, install a new welch plug into the cylinder block.**

7. Install the jackshaft in the cylinder block with the retaining plate. Torque the jackshaft sprocket bolts to 6.5–9.0 ft. lbs. (8.8–12.2 Nm), the oil pump bolts to 5.8–7.2 ft. lbs. (8.0–9.8 Nm), the tensioner pulley bolts to 12–15 ft. lbs. (15–20 Nm), the timing cover bolts to 2.5–4.0 ft. lbs. (3.4–6.0 Nm), the crankshaft pulley bolt to 83–108 ft. lbs. (113–147 Nm).
8. Install the lower locating plate on cylinder block with oil new seals.
9. Install both sprockets and the timing belt.
10. Start engine, check timing and road test.

Pistons and Connecting Rods

➧ SEE FIGS. 188–190

REMOVAL & INSTALLATION

It is recommended that the engine be removed from the vehicle and mount it on an engine stand, before removing the pistons and connecting rods from the engine.

1. Refer to the Cylinder Head, Removal and Installation procedures in this section and remove the cylinder head.
2. Using a ridge reamer tool, remove the carbon buildup from the top of the cylinder wall. Do not cut too far into the cylinder.
3. Drain the lubricant from the engine. Invert the engine on the stand, then remove the oil pan, the oil strainer and the pickup tube.

✻✻ CAUTION

The EPA warns that prolonged contact with used engine oil may cause a number of skin disorders, including cancer! You should make every effort to minimize your exposure to used engine oil. Protective gloves should be worn when changing the oil. Wash your hands and any other exposed skin areas as soon as possible after exposure to used engine oil. Soap and water, or waterless hand cleaner should be used.

4. Position the piston to be removed at the bottom of its stroke, so that the connecting rod bearing cap can be easily reached.
5. Remove the connecting rod bearing cap nuts and the cap and the lower half of the bearing. Cover the rod bolts with lengths of rubber tubing or hose to protect the cylinder walls when the rod and piston assembly is driven out.
6. Push the piston/connecting rod assembly, out through the top of the cylinder block with a length of wood or a wooden hammer handle.

➡ **When removing the piston/connecting rod assembly, be careful not to scratch the cylinder wall with the connecting rod.**

USE A SHORT
PIECE OF 3/8"
HOSE AS A
GUIDE
Fig. 188. Use lengths of vacuum hose or rubber tubing to protect the crankshaft journals and cylinder walls during piston installation

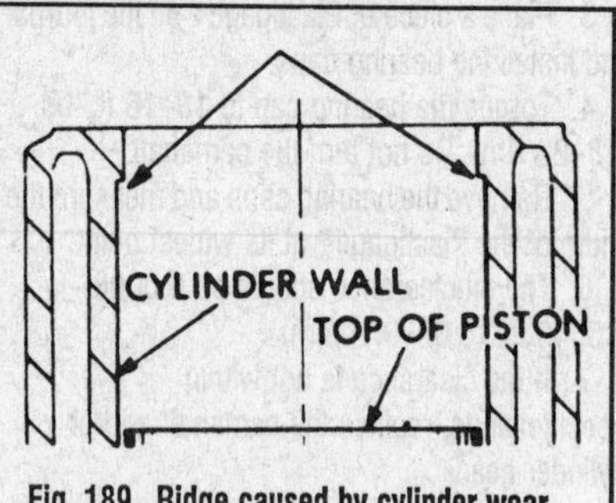
CYLINDER WALL
TOP OF PISTON
Fig. 189. Ridge caused by cylinder wear

Fig. 190. Driving out the piston assemblies with a wooden hammer handle. Note the tubing covering the rod bolts (arrow)

To install:

7. Keep all of the components from each cylinder together and install them in the cylinder from which they were removed.

8. Lubricate all of the piston/connecting rod components with engine oil, including the bearing face of the connecting rod and the outer face of the pistons with engine oil.

➡ **See the illustrations for the correct positioning of the piston rings.**

9. Turn the crankshaft until the rod journal of the particular cylinder you are working on is brought to the TDC position.

10. Clamp the piston/ring assembly into a ring compressor, the notched mark or number (on the piston head) must face the front of the engine and the oil hole (on the side of the connecting rod) must face the right side of the engine; push the piston/connecting rod assembly into the cylinder bore until the big bearing end of the connecting rod seats on the rod journal of the crankshaft.

➡ **Use care not to scratch the cylinder wall with the connecting rod.**

11. Push down on the piston/connecting rod assembly, while turning the crankshaft (the connecting rod rides around on the crankshaft rod journal), until the crankshaft rod journal is at the BDC (bottom dead center).

12. Align the mark on the connecting rod bearing cap with that on the connecting rod and torque the connecting rod bearing cap bolts to 24–27 ft. lbs. (33–37 Nm).

13. Install the oil strainer, pickup tube and oil pan.

14. Install the cylinder head.

15. Install engine assembly in vehicle.

16. Check all fluid levels and road test.

IDENTIFICATION AND POSITIONING

The pistons are marked with a notch or a number stamped on the piston head. When installed in the engine the notch or number markings must be facing the front of the engine.

The connecting rods are installed in the engine with the oil hole facing the right side of the engine.

➡ **It is advisable to number the pistons, connecting rods and bearing caps in some manner so that they can be reinstalled in the same cylinder, facing in the same direction from which they are removed.**

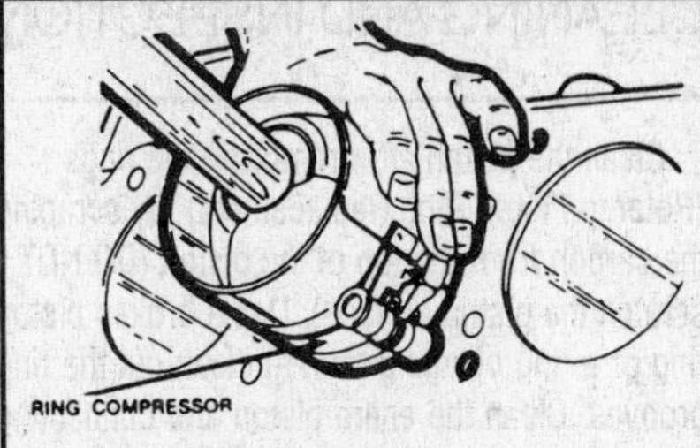
RING COMPRESSOR

Fig. 191. Lubricate the components, compress the rings and drive the piston into the bore

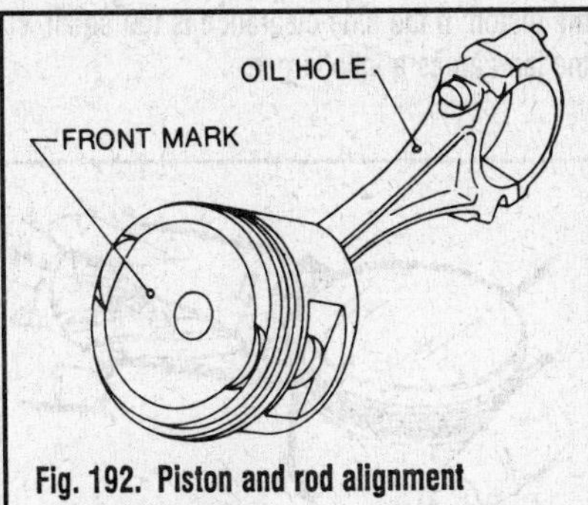
OIL HOLE
FRONT MARK

Fig. 192. Piston and rod alignment – E-series engine

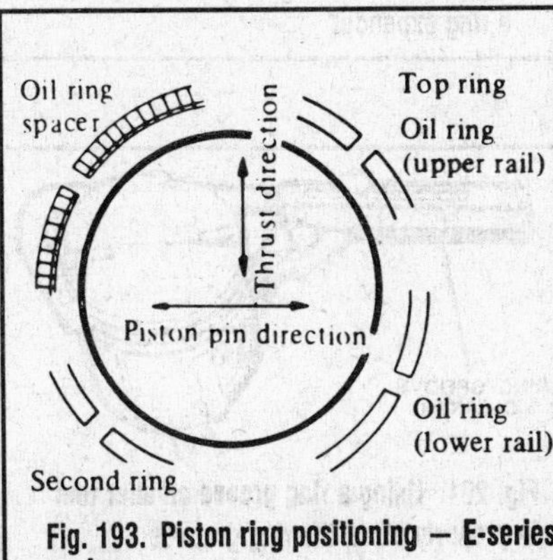
Oil ring spacer
Top ring
Oil ring (upper rail)
Thrust direction
Piston pin direction
Oil ring (lower rail)
Second ring

Fig. 193. Piston ring positioning – E-series engine

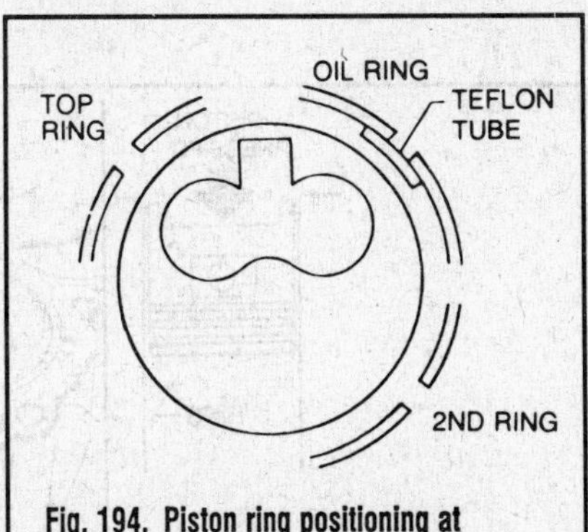
OIL RING
TOP RING
TEFLON TUBE
2ND RING

Fig. 194. Piston ring positioning at 120° apart – CD17 diesel engine

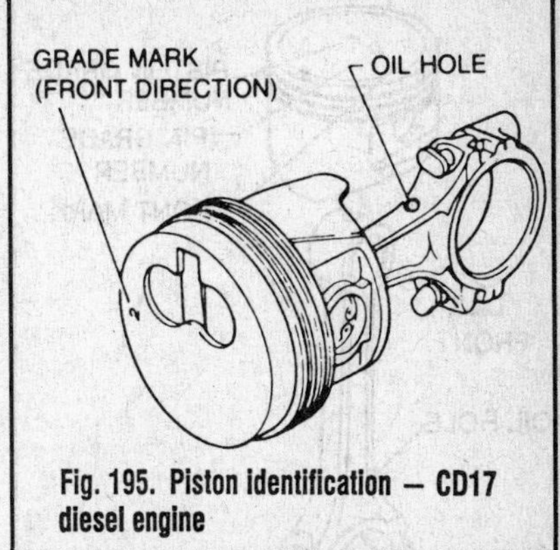
GRADE MARK (FRONT DIRECTION)
OIL HOLE

Fig. 195. Piston identification – CD17 diesel engine

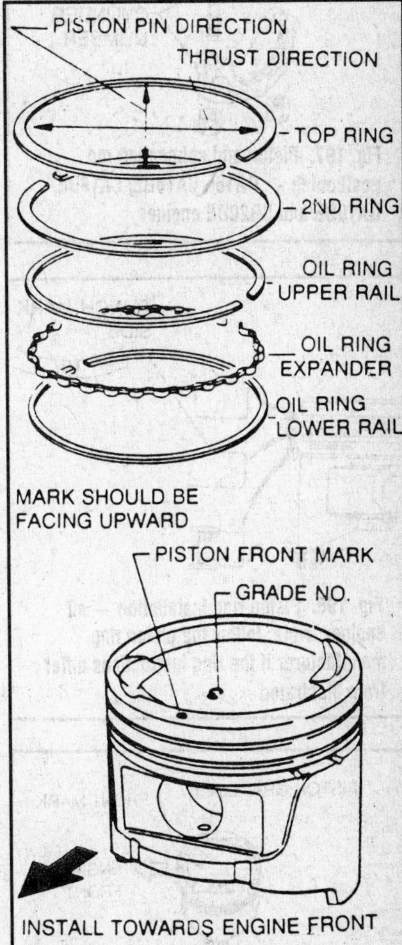
PISTON PIN DIRECTION
THRUST DIRECTION
TOP RING
2ND RING
OIL RING UPPER RAIL
OIL RING EXPANDER
OIL RING LOWER RAIL
MARK SHOULD BE FACING UPWARD
PISTON FRONT MARK
GRADE NO.
INSTALL TOWARDS ENGINE FRONT

Fig. 196. Piston ring identification and positioning – all engines

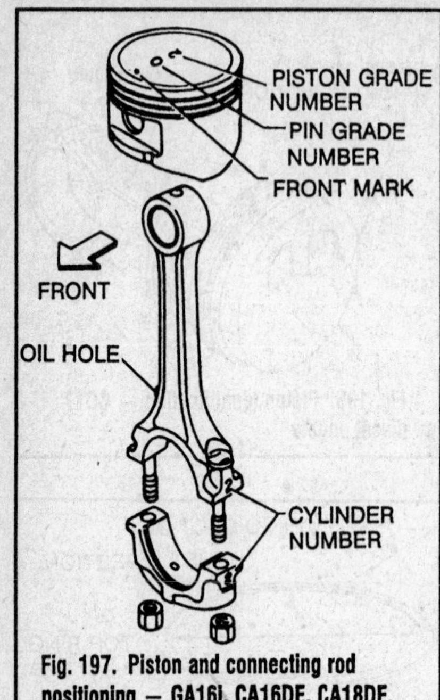
PISTON GRADE NUMBER
PIN GRADE NUMBER
FRONT MARK
FRONT
OIL HOLE
CYLINDER NUMBER
Fig. 197. Piston and connecting rod positioning — GA16i, CA16DE, CA18DE, GA16DE and SR20DE engines

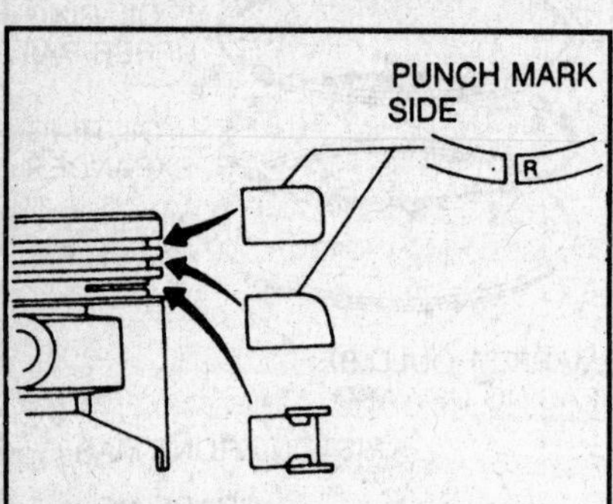
PUNCH MARK SIDE
R
Fig. 198. Piston ring installation — all engines. Note: follow the piston ring manufacturer if the ring instructions differ from illustrated

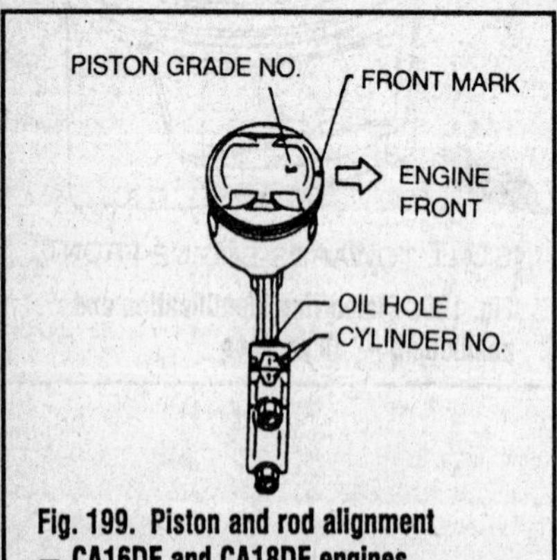
PISTON GRADE NO.
FRONT MARK
ENGINE FRONT
OIL HOLE
CYLINDER NO.
Fig. 199. Piston and rod alignment — CA16DE and CA18DE engines

CLEANING AND INSPECTION

Clean the piston after removing the rings (Refer to Piston Ring Replacement), by scraping the carbon from the top of the piston (DO NOT scratch the piston surface). Use a broken piston ring or a ring cleaning tool, to clean out the ring grooves. Clean the entire piston and connecting rod with solvent and a brush (NOT a wire brush).

With the piston thoroughly cleaned, place both compression rings on each piston. Using a feeler gauge, check the side clearance of the piston rings. If the side clearance is too large, replace the piston; if the side clearance is too small, cut the land areas a little larger.

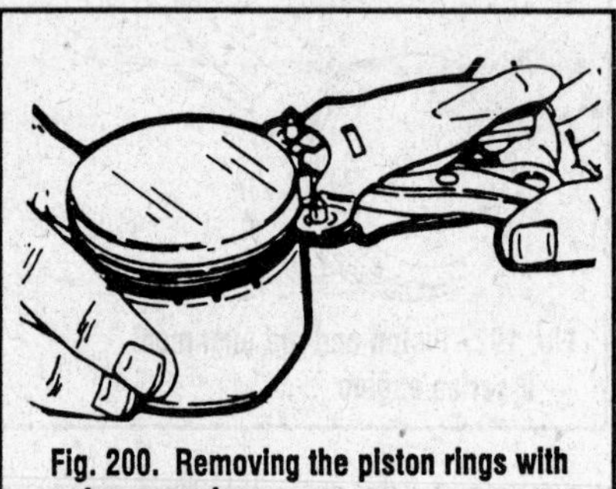
Fig. 200. Removing the piston rings with a ring expander

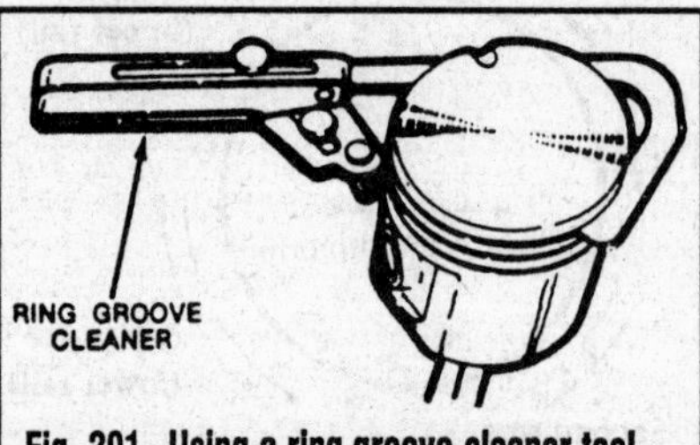
RING GROOVE CLEANER
Fig. 201. Using a ring groove cleaner tool to properly clean the ring grooves

Using a feeler gauge to check the ring end gap, lubricate the cylinder wall, then (using an inverted piston) drive the new ring(s) approximately 1–2 in. (25–51mm) below the top of the cylinder bore. If the ring gap is too small, carefully remove the rings and file the ends until the proper gap is required.

PISTON PIN REPLACEMENT

The piston pin, the piston and the connecting rod are held together as an assembly, by pressing piston pin into the connecting rod. An arbor press and a special pin removing stand tool No. KV10107400 or equivalent are used for removing and installing the piston pin.

PISTON RING REPLACEMENT

➧ SEE FIGS. 204

A piston ring expander is necessary for removing and installing the piston rings (to avoid damaging them). When the rings are removed, clean the ring grooves using an appropriate ring groove cleaning tool, using care not to cut too deeply. Use solvent to thoroughly remove all of the carbon and varnish deposits.

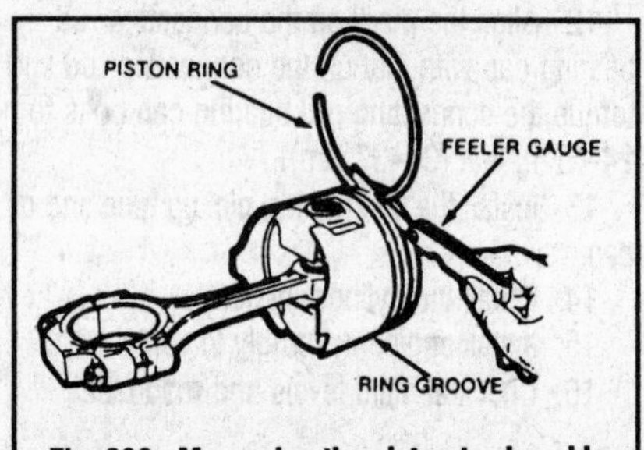
PISTON RING
FEELER GAUGE
RING GROOVE
Fig. 202. Measuring the piston-to-ring side clearance

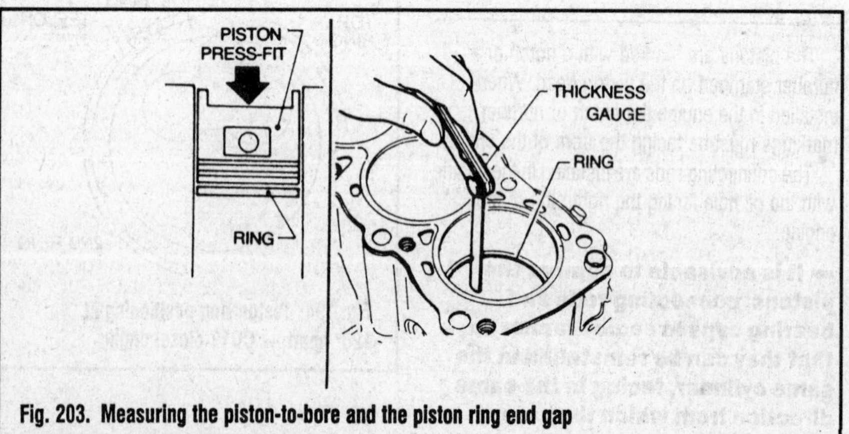
PISTON PRESS-FIT
RING
THICKNESS GAUGE
RING
Fig. 203. Measuring the piston-to-bore and the piston ring end gap

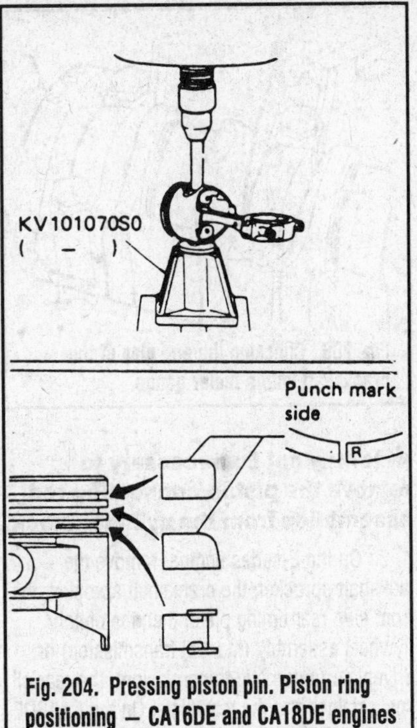
KV101070S0
(—)
Punch mark
side
R
Fig. 204. Pressing piston pin. Piston ring positioning — CA16DE and CA18DE engines

When installing the rings, make sure that the stamped mark on the ring is facing upwards. Install the bottom rings first, then the upper ones last. Be sure to use a ring expander, to keep from breaking the rings.

ROD BEARING REPLACEMENT

➧ SEE FIGS. 207–208

The connecting rod side clearance and the big-end bearing inspection should be performed while the rods are still installed in the engine. Determine the clearance between the connecting rod sides and the crankshaft, using a feeler gauge. If the side clearance is below the minimum tolerance — 0.0040–0.0197 in. (0.10–0.50mm) — have a machine shop correct the tolerance; if the clearance is excessive, substitute an unworn rod and recheck the clearance.

To check the connecting rod big-end bearing clearances, remove the rod bearing caps one at a time. Using a clean, dry shop rag, thoroughly clean all of the oil from the crank journal and the bearing insert in the cap.

➡ The Plastigage® gauging material you will be using to check the clearances with, is soluble in oil; therefore any oil on the journal or bearing could result in an incorrect reading.

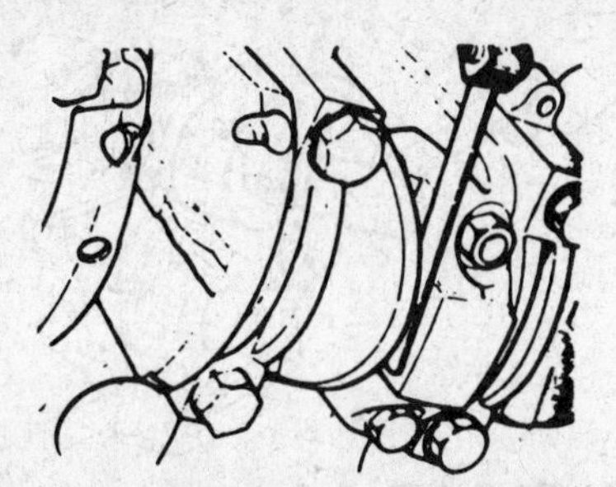
Fig. 207. Checking the connecting rod side clearance. Make sure that the feeler gauge is between the shoulder of the crankshaft journal and the side of the rod

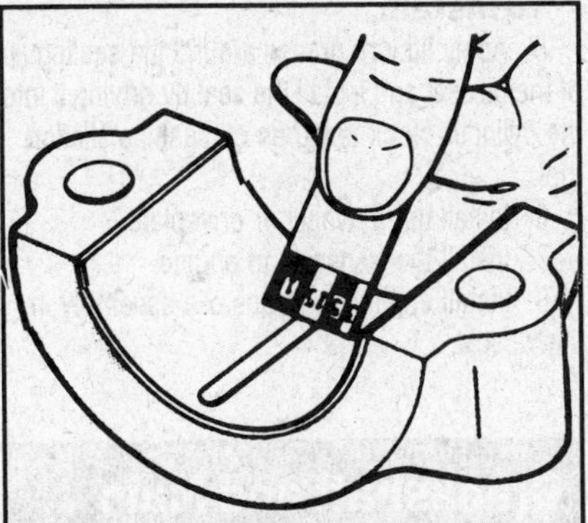
Fig. 208. Checking the connecting rod bearing with Plastigage®

Lay a strip of Plastigage® across the bearing insert. Reinsert the bearing cap and retorque to specifications.

Remove the rod cap and determine the bearing clearance by comparing the width of the now flattened Plastigage® to the scale on the Plastigage® envelope. The journal taper is determined by comparing the width of the strip near its ends. Rotate the crankshaft 90° and retest, to determine the journal eccentricity.

➡ DO NOT rotate the crankshaft with Plastigage® installed, for an incorrect reading will result.

If the clearances are not within the tolerances, the bearing inserts must be replaced with ones of the correct oversize or undersize and/or the crankshaft must be ground. If installing new bearing inserts, make sure that the tabs fit correctly into the notch of the bearing cap and rod. Lubricate the face of each insert before installing them onto the crankshaft.

➡ Install the upper connecting rod bearing with the oil hole aligned with the hole in the connecting rod. Align the bearing wedge with the cutout in the notch in the connecting rod. Make sure all dirt and carbon is removed from the bearing bore before installing.

PISTON AND CONNECTING ROD INSTALLATION

1. Place the crankshaft journal at the bottom of the travel. Install short pieces of rubber hose onto the connecting rod bolts to protect the cylinder walls.
2. Dip the piston assembly in clean engine oil. Lubricate the connecting rod bearing with assembly lube.
3. Using a approved piston ring compressor, compress the piston rings.
4. Place the assembly into the cylinder with the alignment mark on the piston facing the front of the engine.
5. Using a wooden hammer handle, tap the piston assembly into the cylinder. Make sure the connecting rod engages the crankshaft.
6. Install the bearing cap and torque the nuts to specifications. Check the bearing clearance with Plastigage® as outlined in this Section.

Freeze Plugs

REMOVAL & INSTALLATION

✻✻ CAUTION

When draining the coolant, keep in mind that cats and dogs are attracted by the ethylene glycol antifreeze, and are quite likely to drink any that is left in an uncovered container or in puddles on the ground. This will prove fatal in sufficient quantity. Always drain the coolant into a sealable container. Coolant should be reused unless it is contaminated or several years old.

The freeze plugs are located on the sides of the engine block. The freeze plugs serve 2 functions. The first function is to fill the hole where the casting sand is removed during the manufacturing process. The second function is to release internal pressure if the engine coolant freezes. The plug is supposed to pop out when the coolant freezes, reducing the chance of engine damage.

1. Drain the engine coolant.
2. Remove all components that are in the way.
3. If accessible, drill a hole in the plug and remove it with a dent puller. If not accessible, drive a chisel into the plug and pry out of the block.
4. Clean the block sealing surface with sandpaper.

➡ **Expandable rubber plugs are made for tight places were the standard freeze plug can not be installed. Consult the local parts warehouse for the rubber plugs**

5. Use a ratchet socket that fits into the freeze plug to install. Coat the sealing surface with RTV sealer.
6. Install the plug far enough to make a good seal.

Rear Main Oil Seal

➧ SEE FIG. 209

REMOVAL & INSTALLATION

1. Remove the engine and transaxle assembly from the vehicle.
2. Remove the transaxle from the engine.
3. Remove the clutch/flywheel assembly (manual transmission) or the driveplate (automatic transmission) from the crankshaft.

Fig. 209. Installing the rear oil seal using an installing tool

4. Using a small pry bar, pry the rear main oil seal from around the crankshaft.

To install:

5. Apply lithium grease around the sealing lip of the oil seal and install the seal by driving it into the cylinder block using an oil seal installation tool.
6. Install the flywheel or driveplate.
7. Install the transaxle to engine.
8. Install engine and transaxle assembly in the vehicle.

Crankshaft and Main Bearing

➧ SEE FIGS. 205–206

REMOVAL & INSTALLATION

E-series, CA16DE and CA18DE Engines

1. Refer to the Piston and Connecting Rod, Removal and Installation procedures, in this section and remove the connecting rod bearings from the crankshaft.

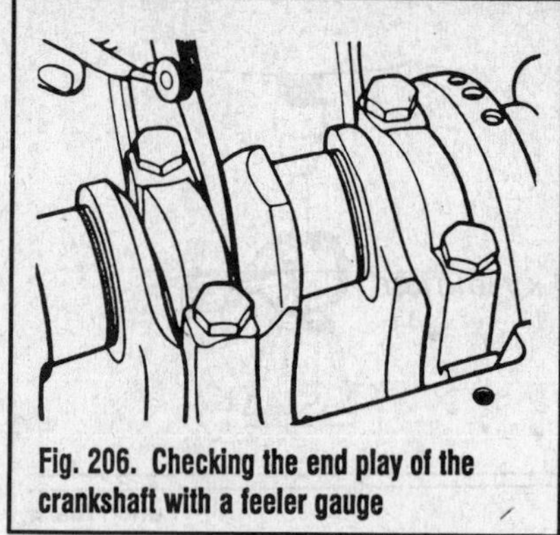

Fig. 206. Checking the end play of the crankshaft with a feeler gauge

➡ **It may not be necessary to remove the piston/connecting rod assemblies from the cylinder block.**

2. On the E-series engine, remove the jackshaft sprocket, the crankshaft sprocket, the front side rear timing plate, then the clutch/flywheel assembly (manual transmission) or driveplate (automatic transmission), the rear oil seal retainer and the rear plate. On the CA16DE and CA18DE engines, remove the water pump.
3. Check the crankshaft thrust clearance (end play) before removing the crankshaft from the engine block. Using a pry bar, pry the crankshaft forward to the extent of its travel and measure the clearance at the No. 3 main bearing. Pry the crankshaft rearward to the extent of its travel and measure the clearance on the other side of the bearing.

➡ **If the clearance is greater than specified, the thrust bearing must be replaced. When removing the crankshaft bearing caps, be sure to keep the bearing together with the caps, unless new bearings are going to be installed.**

4. Remove the crankshaft bearing caps, the cap bearings and the crankshaft from the engine.

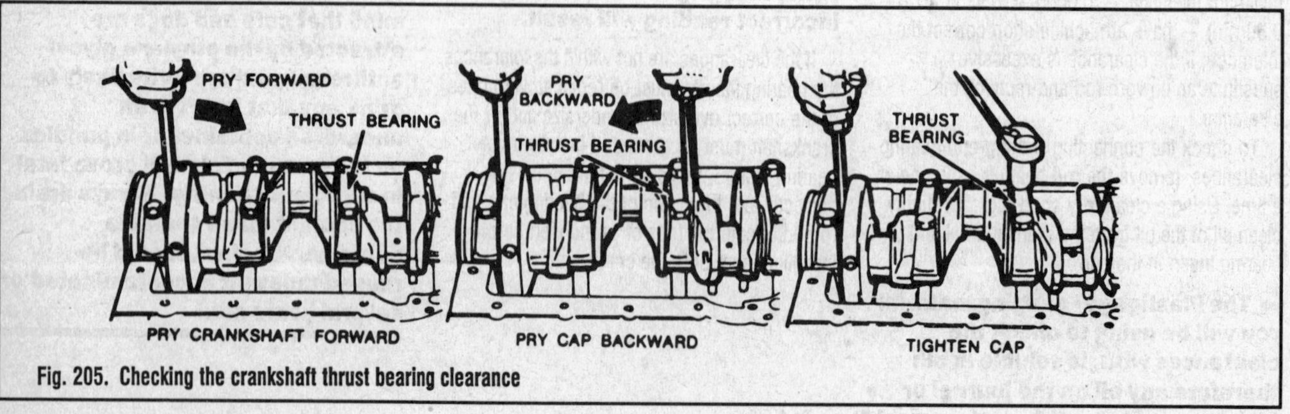
PRY FORWARD
THRUST BEARING
PRY CRANKSHAFT FORWARD
PRY BACKWARD
THRUST BEARING
PRY CAP BACKWARD
THRUST BEARING
TIGHTEN CAP

Fig. 205. Checking the crankshaft thrust bearing clearance

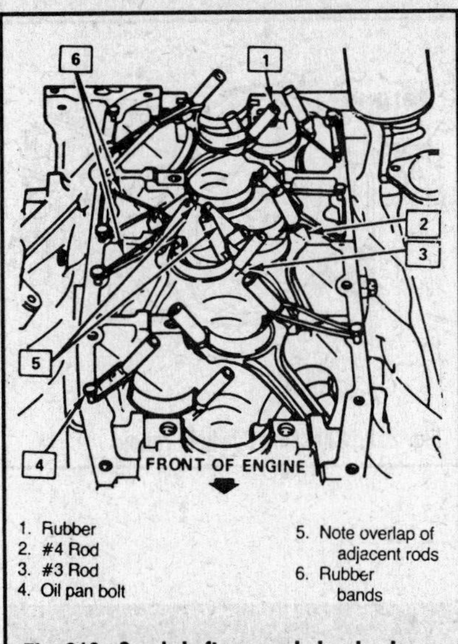
6
1
2
3
5
4
FRONT OF ENGINE
1. Rubber
2. #4 Rod
3. #3 Rod
4. Oil pan bolt
5. Note overlap of adjacent rods
6. Rubber bands

Fig. 210. Crankshaft removal showing hose lengths and rubber bands

5. To install, check the clearances with the Plastigage® method, then replace the bearings if necessary. Torque the crankshaft bearing cap bolts to specifications.
6. Reassemble the engine.

➡ **When torquing the main bearing caps, start with the center bearing and work towards both ends at the same time.**

All Other Engines

1. Disconnect the negative battery cable.
2. Remove the engine from the vehicle and separate from the transaxle.
3. Place the engine in a suitable workstand.
4. Remove the flywheel or converter plate from the crankshaft.
5. Remove the front timing cover.
6. Remove the oil pan.
7. Remove the crankshaft bearing caps.
8. Remove the connecting rod bearing caps and place rubber hoses over the connecting rod bolts to protect the crankshaft journals.
9. Remove the rear seal carrier.
10. Push the connecting rods into the cylinder.
11. Carefully lift the crankshaft out of the engine, turning slightly to disengage the connecting rods.

To install:

12. Install oil pan bolts adjacent to the connecting rods. Place rubber bands around the connecting rod bolt to hold the rod in place during crankshaft installation.
13. Lubricate all bearing surfaces with assembly lube. Make sure all bearings are in place before assembly.
14. Install the crankshaft with the help of an assistant.
15. Install the crankshaft bearing caps and torque to specifications.
16. Install the connecting rod bearing caps and torque to specifications.
17. Install the remaining components, install the engine and check for oil pressure.

CLEANING AND INSPECTION

The crankshaft inspection and servicing should be handled exclusively by a reputable machinist, for most necessary procedures require a dial indicator, fixing jigs and a large micrometer; also machine tools, such as: crankshaft grinder. The crankshaft should be thoroughly cleaned (especially the oil passages), Magnafluxed (to check for cracks) and the following checks made: Main journal diameter, crank pin (connecting rod journal) diameter, taper, out-of-round and run-out. Wear, beyond the specification limits, in any of these areas means the crankshaft must be reground or replaced.

MAIN BEARING CLEARANCE CHECK AND REPLACEMENT

Checking the main bearing clearances is done in the same manner as checking the connecting rod big-end clearances.

1. With the crankshaft installed, remove the main bearing cap. Clean all of the oil from the bearing insert (in the cap and the crankshaft journal), for the Plastigage® material is oil-soluble.
2. Lay a strip of Plastigage® across the full width of the bearing cap and install the bearing cap, then torque the cap to specifications.

➡ **DO NOT rotate the crankshaft with the Plastigage® installed.**

3. Remove the bearing cap and compare the scale on the Plastigage® envelope with the flattened Plastigage® material in the bearing. The journal taper is determined by comparing the width of both ends of the Plastigage® material. Rotate the crankshaft 90° and retest, to determine eccentricity.
4. Repeat the procedure for the remaining bearings. If the bearing journal and insert appear to be in good shape (with no unusual wear visible) and are within tolerances, no further main bearing service is required. If unusual wear is evident and/or the clearances are outside specifications, the bearings must be replaced and the cause of their wear determined.

BEARING REPLACEMENT

➧ SEE FIG. 211

Engine Installed in Vehicle

1. Remove the oil pan as outlined in this Section.
2. Remove the crankshaft bearing cap.
3. Bend over a cotter pin on the same angle as the oil hole in the crankshaft bearing journal.
4. Place the cotter pin into the oil hole.
5. Turn the crankshaft slowly until the cotter pin rotates the bearing shell out of the engine block.

To Install:

6. Lubricate the bearing with assembly lube.
7. Turn the new bearing into the block with the cotter pin.
8. Remove the cotter pin and install the bearing cap.
9. Torque the bearing cap to specifications.
10. Install the remaining components. Start the engine and check oil pressure.

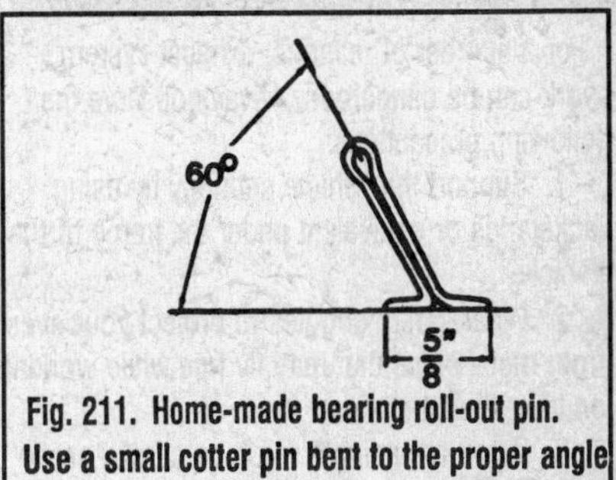
60°
5"/8

Fig. 211. Home-made bearing roll-out pin. Use a small cotter pin bent to the proper angle

Flywheel and Ring Gear

REMOVAL & INSTALLATION

1. If equipped with a manual transaxle, refer to the Clutch, Removal and Installation procedures in Section 7, then remove the transaxle and the clutch assembly. If equipped with an automatic transaxle, refer to the Automatic Transaxle, Removal and Installation procedures in Section 7, then remove the transaxle and the torque converter.
2. For manual transaxles, remove the flywheel-to-crankshaft bolts and the flywheel. For automatic transaxles, remove the drive plate-to-crankshaft bolts and the drive plate.
3. To install, reverse the removal procedures. Torque the flywheel-to-crankshaft bolts to specifications.

RING GEAR REPLACEMENT

➧ SEE FIGS. 212

Manual Transaxle Only

➡ **Ring gear replacement is best left to the engine machine shop or qualified personnel.**

1. Using a die grinder, cut the ring gear from the flywheel.
2. Heat the entire ring gear to cherry red with a torch.
3. Place the ring gear onto the flywheel and allow to cool. Do not cool with water. This will harden the gear. The gear will break when the starter drive makes contact.
4. Install the flywheel to the engine and torque the bolts to specifications in a star pattern.

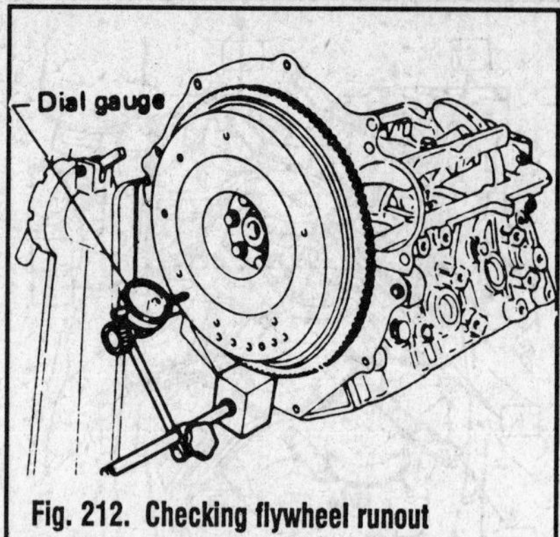
Dial gauge

Fig. 212. Checking flywheel runout

EXHAUST SYSTEM

➧ SEE FIGS. 214–221

Safety Precautions

For a number of reasons, exhaust system work can be dangerous. Always observe the following precautions:

1. Support the vehicle securely by using jackstands or equivalent under the frame of the vehicle.
2. Wear safety goggles to protect your eyes from metal chips that may fly free while working on the exhaust system.
3. If you are using a torch be careful not to come close to any fuel lines.
4. Always use the proper tool for the job.

Special Tools

A number of special exhaust tools can be rented or bought from a local auto parts store. It may also be quite helpful to use solvents designed to loosen rusted nuts or bolts. Remember that these products are often flammable, apply only to parts after they are cool.

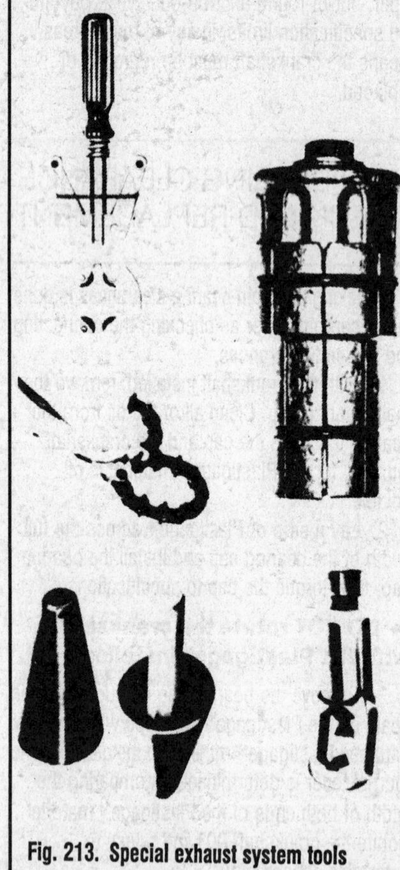

Fig. 213. Special exhaust system tools

Front Pipe

REMOVAL & INSTALLATION

Sentra Models with 2-Piece Front Pipe

1. Raise the car and support it securely. Make sure the engine has been turned off for an hour or more so all pipes are cool. Disconnect the negative battery cable.
2. Remove the bolts fastening the clamps to the head shields. Remove the two bolts fastening the two halves of the heat shield together at the rear. Remove the upper and lower halves of the heat shield.
3. Remove the three attaching nuts from underneath the flange fastening the pipe to the manifold. Then, remove the nuts and bolts from the flange at the rear of the pipe. Then, pull the pipe down at the front and out at the rear. Remove gaskets and any gasketing material left on sealing flanges.

To install:

4. Install a new gasket onto the front of the pipe. Install the pipe by inserting it into the muffler pipe (at its rear) and then inserting the front up into the exhaust manifold.
5. Install the bolts and nuts at the rear, torquing until the spring located between the flanges is fully compressed and the bolts reach 12–15 ft. lbs. (15–20 Nm). Torque the nuts at the front to 14–19 ft. lbs. (19–26 Nm).
6. Install the heat shield in reverse order, torquing the bolts to 36–72 inch lbs. (4–7 Nm).

Sentra and Pulsar with 1-piece Front Pipe

1. Support the vehicle securely by using jackstands or equivalent under the frame of the vehicle.
2. Remove the exhaust pipe clamps and any front exhaust pipe shield.
3. Soak the exhaust manifold or catalytic converter front pipe mounting studs with penetrating oil. Remove attaching nuts and gasket from the manifold or converter. Pulsar models have 2 catalytic converters.

➡ If these studs snap off, while removing the front pipe the manifold or catalytic converter will have to be removed and the stud will have to be drill out and the hole tapped.

4. Remove any exhaust pipe mounting hanger or bracket.
5. Remove front pipe from the catalytic converter.

To install:

6. Install the front pipe on the manifold or catalytic converter with seal if so equipped.
7. Install the pipe on the catalytic converter. Assemble all parts loosely and position pipe to insure proper clearance from body of vehicle.
8. Tighten mounting studs, bracket bolts exhaust clamps.
9. Install exhaust pipe shield.
10. Start engine and check for exhaust leaks.

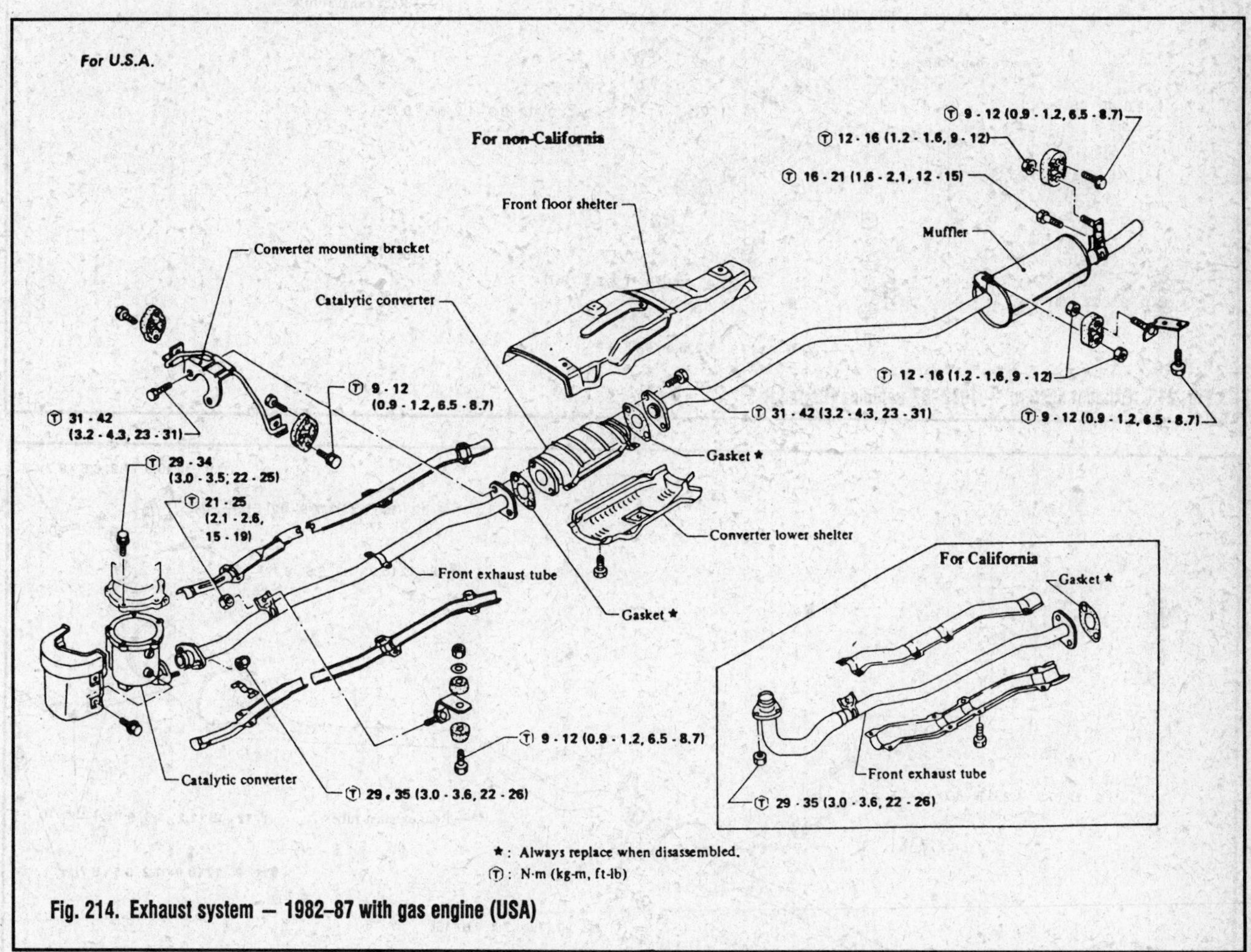
For U.S.A.
For non-California
Ⓣ 9 - 12 (0.9 - 1.2, 6.5 - 8.7)
Ⓣ 12 - 16 (1.2 - 1.6, 9 - 12)
Ⓣ 16 - 21 (1.6 - 2.1, 12 - 15)
Front floor shelter
Muffler
Converter mounting bracket
Catalytic converter
Ⓣ 9 - 12 (0.9 - 1.2, 6.5 - 8.7)
Ⓣ 31 - 42 (3.2 - 4.3, 23 - 31)
Ⓣ 12 - 16 (1.2 - 1.6, 9 - 12)
Ⓣ 31 - 42 (3.2 - 4.3, 23 - 31)
Ⓣ 9 - 12 (0.9 - 1.2, 6.5 - 8.7)
Ⓣ 29 - 34 (3.0 - 3.5, 22 - 25)
Gasket ★
Ⓣ 21 - 25 (2.1 - 2.6, 15 - 19)
Converter lower shelter
Front exhaust tube
Gasket ★
For California
Gasket ★
Ⓣ 9 - 12 (0.9 - 1.2, 6.5 - 8.7)
Front exhaust tube
Catalytic converter
Ⓣ 29 - 35 (3.0 - 3.6, 22 - 26)
Ⓣ 29 - 35 (3.0 - 3.6, 22 - 26)
★ : Always replace when disassembled.
Ⓣ : N·m (kg-m, ft-lb)

Fig. 214. Exhaust system — 1982–87 with gas engine (USA)

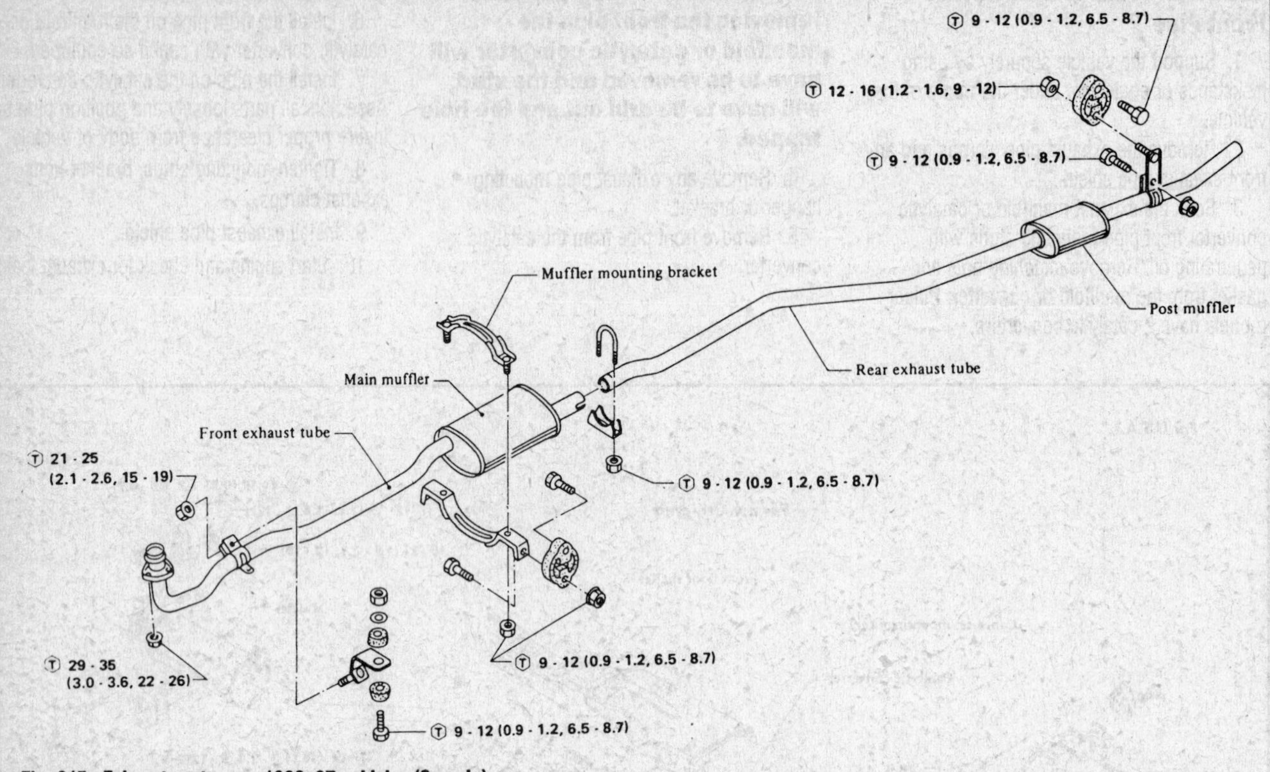

Ⓣ 9 - 12 (0.9 - 1.2, 6.5 - 8.7)
Ⓣ 12 - 16 (1.2 - 1.6, 9 - 12)
Ⓣ 9 - 12 (0.9 - 1.2, 6.5 - 8.7)
Muffler mounting bracket
Post muffler
Rear exhaust tube
Main muffler
Front exhaust tube
Ⓣ 21 - 25 (2.1 - 2.6, 15 - 19)
Ⓣ 9 - 12 (0.9 - 1.2, 6.5 - 8.7)
Ⓣ 29 - 35 (3.0 - 3.6, 22 - 26)
Ⓣ 9 - 12 (0.9 - 1.2, 6.5 - 8.7)
Ⓣ 9 - 12 (0.9 - 1.2, 6.5 - 8.7)

Fig. 215. Exhaust system — 1982–87 vehicles (Canada)

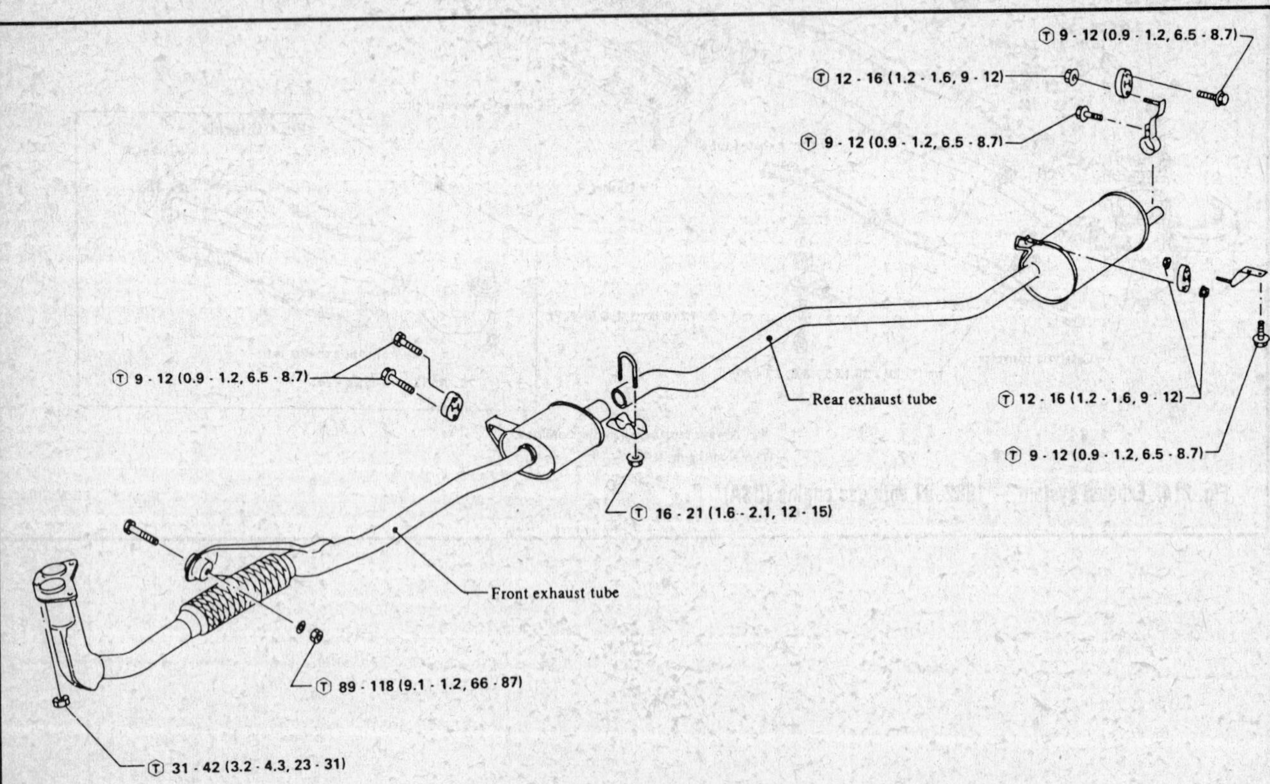

Ⓣ 9 - 12 (0.9 - 1.2, 6.5 - 8.7)
Ⓣ 12 - 16 (1.2 - 1.6, 9 - 12)
Ⓣ 9 - 12 (0.9 - 1.2, 6.5 - 8.7)
Ⓣ 9 - 12 (0.9 - 1.2, 6.5 - 8.7)
Rear exhaust tube
Ⓣ 12 - 16 (1.2 - 1.6, 9 - 12)
Ⓣ 9 - 12 (0.9 - 1.2, 6.5 - 8.7)
Ⓣ 16 - 21 (1.6 - 2.1, 12 - 15)
Front exhaust tube
Ⓣ 89 - 118 (9.1 - 1.2, 66 - 87)
Ⓣ 31 - 42 (3.2 - 4.3, 23 - 31)

Fig. 216. Exhaust system — Sentra diesel

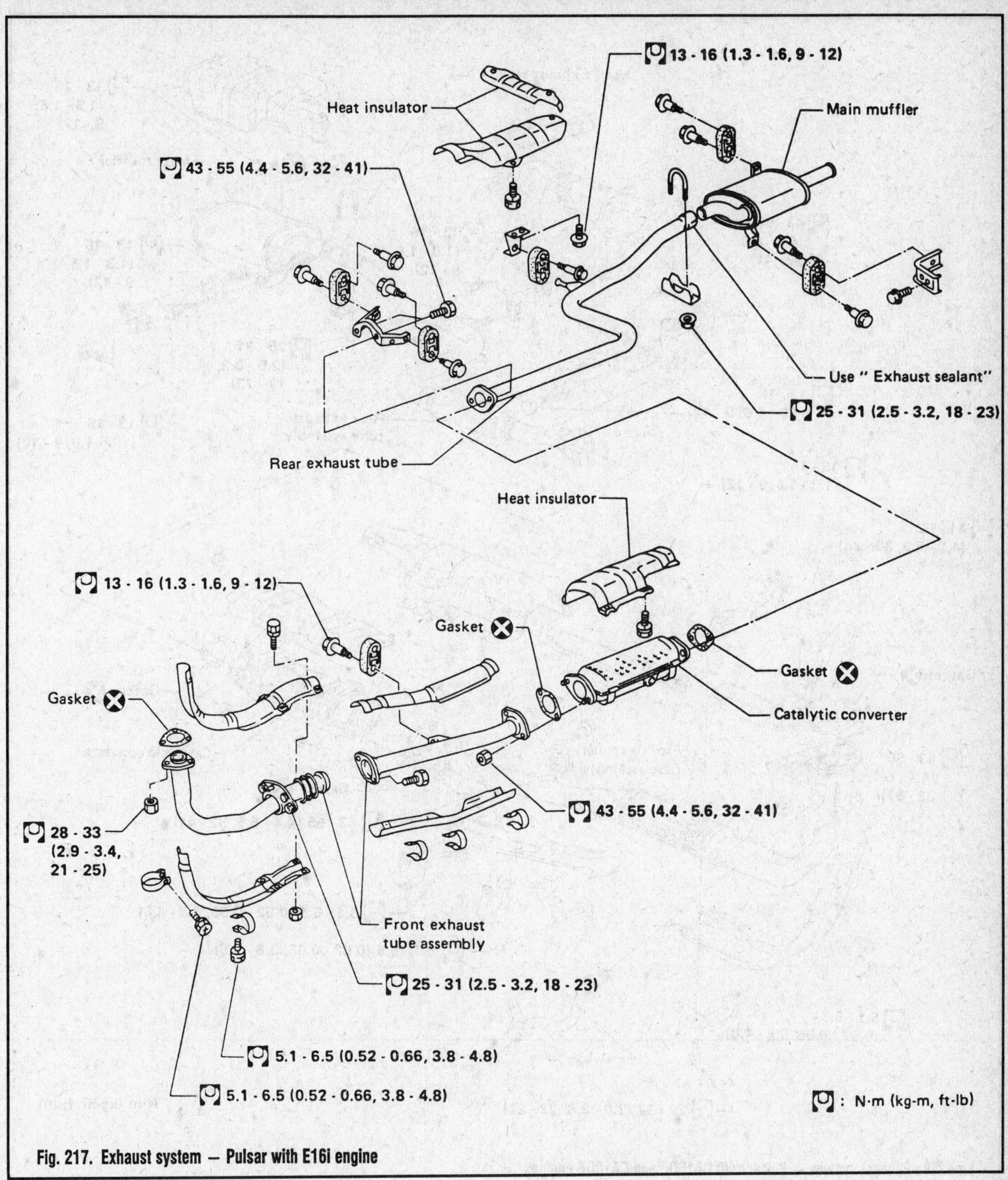
13 - 16 (1.3 - 1.6, 9 - 12)
Heat insulator
Main muffler
43 - 55 (4.4 - 5.6, 32 - 41)
Use " Exhaust sealant"
25 - 31 (2.5 - 3.2, 18 - 23)
Rear exhaust tube
Heat insulator
13 - 16 (1.3 - 1.6, 9 - 12)
Gasket
Gasket
Gasket
Catalytic converter
43 - 55 (4.4 - 5.6, 32 - 41)
28 - 33
(2.9 - 3.4,
21 - 25)
Front exhaust
tube assembly
25 - 31 (2.5 - 3.2, 18 - 23)
5.1 - 6.5 (0.52 - 0.66, 3.8 - 4.8)
5.1 - 6.5 (0.52 - 0.66, 3.8 - 4.8)
: N·m (kg-m, ft-lb)

Fig. 217. Exhaust system — Pulsar with E16i engine

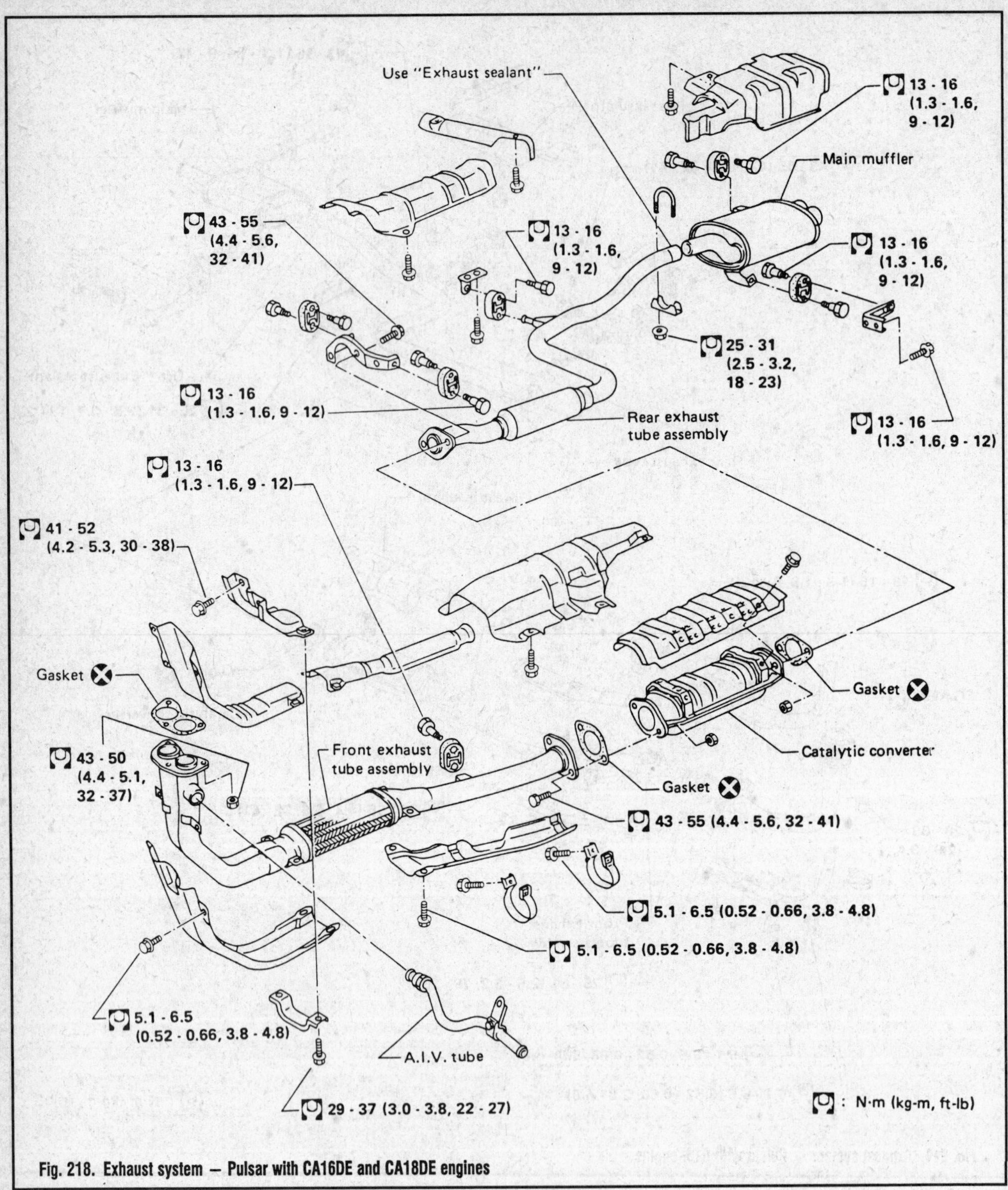

Use "Exhaust sealant"
13 - 16 (1.3 - 1.6, 9 - 12)
Main muffler
43 - 55 (4.4 - 5.6, 32 - 41)
13 - 16 (1.3 - 1.6, 9 - 12)
13 - 16 (1.3 - 1.6, 9 - 12)
25 - 31 (2.5 - 3.2, 18 - 23)
13 - 16 (1.3 - 1.6, 9 - 12)
Rear exhaust tube assembly
13 - 16 (1.3 - 1.6, 9 - 12)
13 - 16 (1.3 - 1.6, 9 - 12)
41 - 52 (4.2 - 5.3, 30 - 38)
Gasket
Gasket
43 - 50 (4.4 - 5.1, 32 - 37)
Front exhaust tube assembly
Catalytic converter
Gasket
43 - 55 (4.4 - 5.6, 32 - 41)
5.1 - 6.5 (0.52 - 0.66, 3.8 - 4.8)
5.1 - 6.5 (0.52 - 0.66, 3.8 - 4.8)
5.1 - 6.5 (0.52 - 0.66, 3.8 - 4.8)
A.I.V. tube
29 - 37 (3.0 - 3.8, 22 - 27)
: N·m (kg-m, ft-lb)

Fig. 218. Exhaust system — Pulsar with CA16DE and CA18DE engines

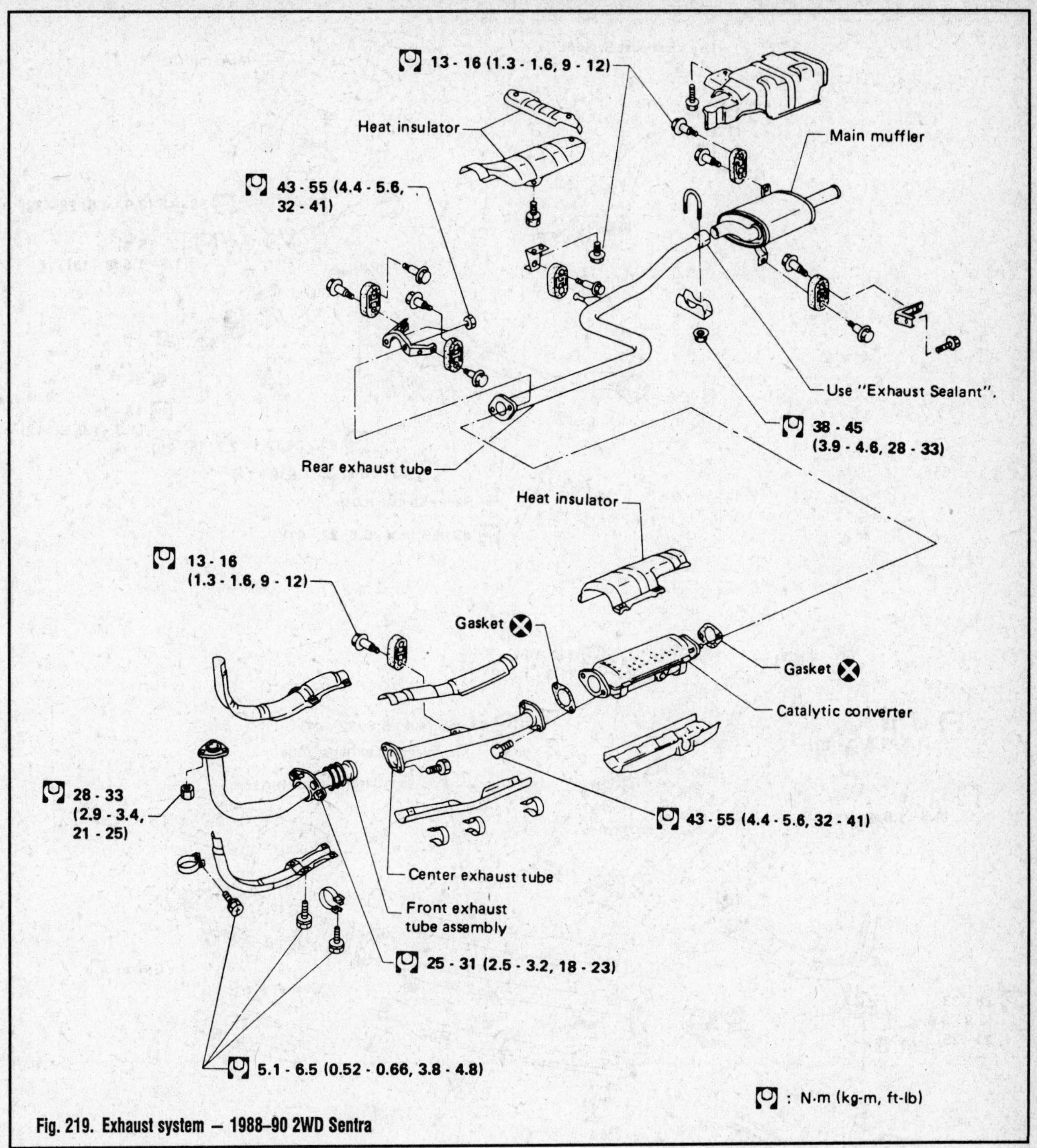
13 - 16 (1.3 - 1.6, 9 - 12)
Heat insulator
Main muffler
43 - 55 (4.4 - 5.6, 32 - 41)
Use "Exhaust Sealant".
38 - 45 (3.9 - 4.6, 28 - 33)
Rear exhaust tube
Heat insulator
13 - 16 (1.3 - 1.6, 9 - 12)
Gasket
Gasket
Catalytic converter
28 - 33 (2.9 - 3.4, 21 - 25)
43 - 55 (4.4 - 5.6, 32 - 41)
Center exhaust tube
Front exhaust tube assembly
25 - 31 (2.5 - 3.2, 18 - 23)
5.1 - 6.5 (0.52 - 0.66, 3.8 - 4.8)
: N·m (kg-m, ft-lb)
Fig. 219. Exhaust system — 1988–90 2WD Sentra

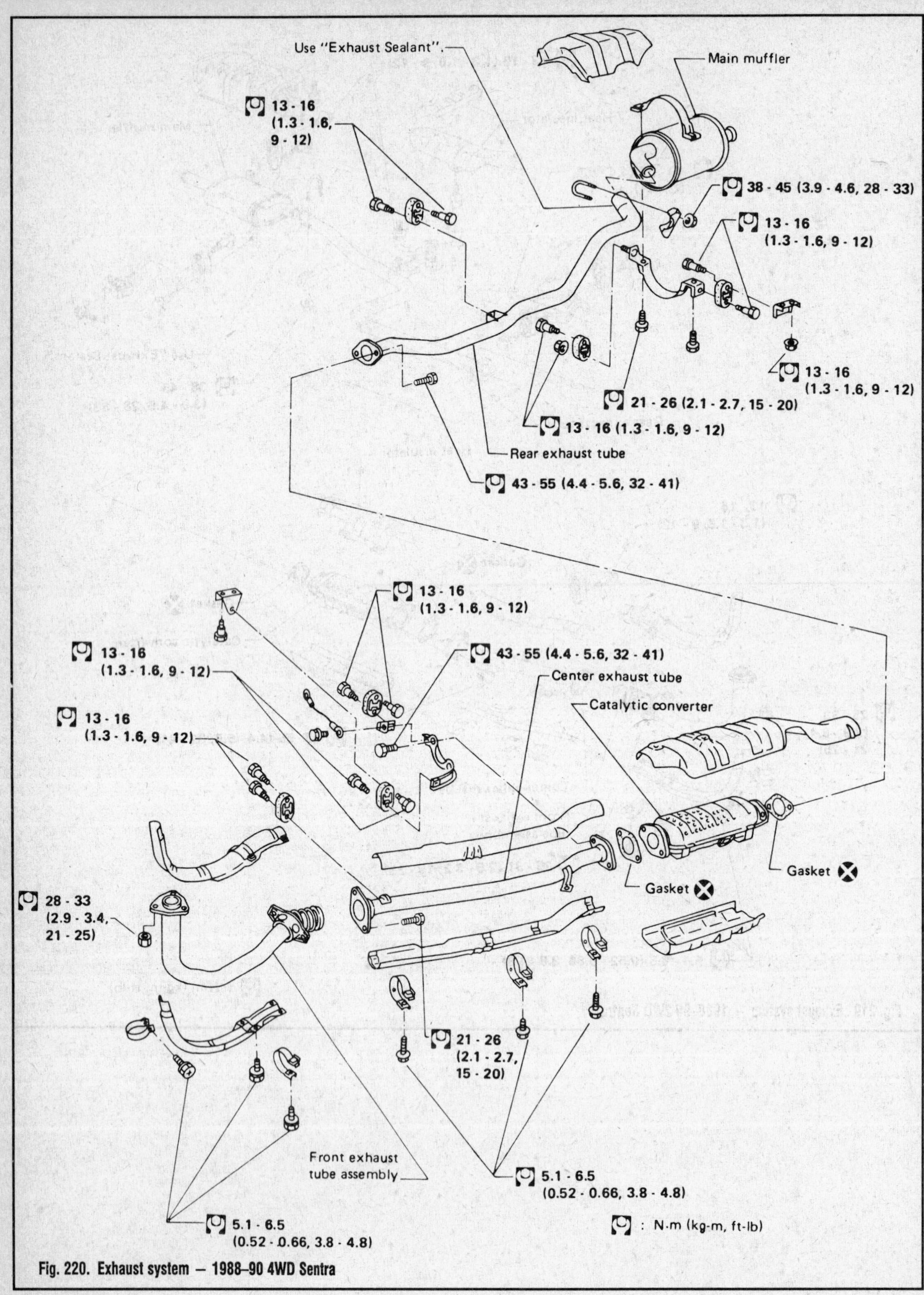
Use "Exhaust Sealant".
Main muffler
13 - 16 (1.3 - 1.6, 9 - 12)
38 - 45 (3.9 - 4.6, 28 - 33)
13 - 16 (1.3 - 1.6, 9 - 12)
13 - 16 (1.3 - 1.6, 9 - 12)
21 - 26 (2.1 - 2.7, 15 - 20)
13 - 16 (1.3 - 1.6, 9 - 12)
Rear exhaust tube
43 - 55 (4.4 - 5.6, 32 - 41)
13 - 16 (1.3 - 1.6, 9 - 12)
13 - 16 (1.3 - 1.6, 9 - 12)
43 - 55 (4.4 - 5.6, 32 - 41)
Center exhaust tube
Catalytic converter
13 - 16 (1.3 - 1.6, 9 - 12)
Gasket
Gasket
28 - 33 (2.9 - 3.4, 21 - 25)
21 - 26 (2.1 - 2.7, 15 - 20)
Front exhaust tube assembly
5.1 - 6.5 (0.52 - 0.66, 3.8 - 4.8)
5.1 - 6.5 (0.52 - 0.66, 3.8 - 4.8)
: N·m (kg-m, ft-lb)
Fig. 220. Exhaust system — 1988–90 4WD Sentra

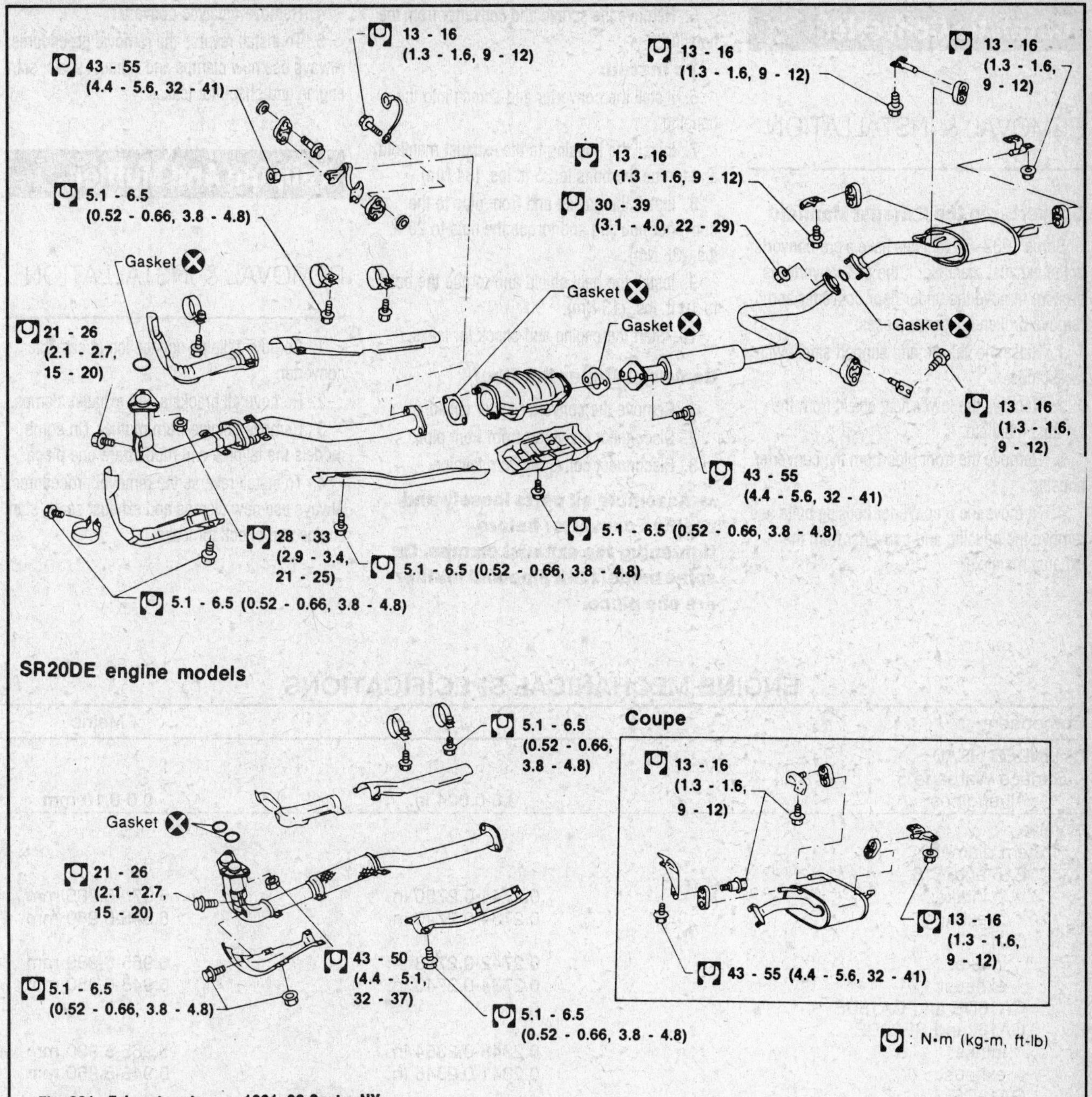
13 - 16
(1.3 - 1.6, 9 - 12)
43 - 55
(4.4 - 5.6, 32 - 41)
13 - 16
(1.3 - 1.6, 9 - 12)
13 - 16
(1.3 - 1.6,
9 - 12)
13 - 16
(1.3 - 1.6, 9 - 12)
5.1 - 6.5
(0.52 - 0.66, 3.8 - 4.8)
30 - 39
(3.1 - 4.0, 22 - 29)
Gasket
Gasket
Gasket
Gasket
21 - 26
(2.1 - 2.7,
15 - 20)
13 - 16
(1.3 - 1.6,
9 - 12)
43 - 55
(4.4 - 5.6, 32 - 41)
5.1 - 6.5 (0.52 - 0.66, 3.8 - 4.8)
28 - 33
(2.9 - 3.4,
21 - 25)
5.1 - 6.5 (0.52 - 0.66, 3.8 - 4.8)
5.1 - 6.5 (0.52 - 0.66, 3.8 - 4.8)
SR20DE engine models
5.1 - 6.5
(0.52 - 0.66,
3.8 - 4.8)
Coupe
13 - 16
(1.3 - 1.6,
9 - 12)
Gasket
21 - 26
(2.1 - 2.7,
15 - 20)
13 - 16
(1.3 - 1.6,
9 - 12)
43 - 50
(4.4 - 5.1,
32 - 37)
5.1 - 6.5
(0.52 - 0.66, 3.8 - 4.8)
43 - 55 (4.4 - 5.6, 32 - 41)
5.1 - 6.5
(0.52 - 0.66, 3.8 - 4.8)
: N•m (kg-m, ft-lb)

Fig. 221. Exhaust system — 1991–92 Sentra NX

Catalytic Converter

REMOVAL & INSTALLATION

Converter in the Exhaust Manifold

Some 1982–87 vehicles have a pre-converter in the exhaust manifold. If the pre-converter is broken, remove the under floor converter and remove broken converter pieces.

1. Raise the vehicle and support safely with jackstands.
2. Remove the lower heat shield from the exhaust manifold.
3. Remove the front pipe from the converter housing.
4. Remove the 5 converter housing bolts and remove the housing and converter from the exhaust manifold.
5. Remove the screen and converter from the housing.

To install:

6. Install the converter and screen into the housing.
7. Install the housing to the exhaust manifold and torque the bolts to 25 ft. lbs. (34 Nm).
8. Install the gasket and front pipe to the converter housing and torque the nuts to 26 ft. lbs. (36 Nm).
9. Install the heat shield and torque the bolts to 10 ft. lbs. (13 Nm).
10. Start the engine and check for leaks.

Converter Under the Floor

1. Remove the converter lower shield.
2. Disconnect converter from front pipe.
3. Disconnect converter from tailpipe.

➡ **Assemble all parts loosely and position converter before tightening the exhaust clamps. On some models tail pipe and muffler are one piece.**

4. Remove catalytic converter.
5. To install reverse the removal procedures. Always use new clamps and exhaust seals, start engine and check for leaks.

Tailpipe And Muffler

REMOVAL & INSTALLATION

1. Remove tailpipe connection at catalytic converter.
2. Remove all brackets and exhaust clamps.
3. Remove tailpipe from muffler. On some models the tailpipe and muffler are one piece.
4. To install reverse the removal procedures. Always use new clamps and exhaust seals, start engine and check for leaks.

ENGINE MECHANICAL SPECIFICATIONS

Component	U.S.	Metric
CYLINDER HEAD		
Surface Warpage		
All engines	0.0-0.004 in.	0.0-0.10 mm
Valve		
Stem diameter		
E15 and E16		
intake:	0.2744-0.2750 in.	6.970-6.985 mm
exhaust:	0.2734-0.2740 in.	6.945-6.960 mm
CD17		
intake:	0.2742-0.2748 in.	6.965-6.980 mm
exhaust:	0.2734-0.2740 in.	6.945-6.950 mm
CA16DE and CA18DE		
GA16i and SR20DE		
intake:	0.2348-0.2354 in.	5.965-5.980 mm
exhaust:	0.2341-0.2346 in.	5.945-5.960 mm
GA16DE		
intake:	0.2152-0.2157 in.	5.465-5.480 mm
exhaust:	0.2144-0.2150 in.	5.445-5.460 mm
Face angle		
E15 and E16	45 degrees 30min.	
CD17	45 degrees 30 min.	
CA16DE and CA18DE	45 degrees 30 min.	
GA16i	45 degrees 30 min.	
GA16DE and SR20DE	45 degrees 30 min.	
Valve margin		
E15, E16, GA16i	0.020 in.	0.50 mm
CD17 and SR20DE	0.020 in.	0.50 mm
CA16DE and CA18DE		
intake:	0.051 in.	1.30 mm
exhaust:	0.059 in.	1.50 mm
GA16DE	0.035-0.043 in.	0.90-1.10 mm

ENGINE MECHANICAL SPECIFICATIONS

Component	U.S.	Metric
Valve		
Valve tip removal limit		
E15 and E16	0.008 in.	0.20 mm
CD17	0.020 in.	0.50 mm
CA16DE and CA18DE	0.020 in.	0.50 mm
GA16i	0.020 in.	0.50 mm
GA16DE and SR20DE	0.008 in.	0.20 mm
Valve Spring		
Free height		
E15 and E16	1.8386 in.	46.70 mm
CD17		
outer:	1.8268 in.	46.40 mm
inner:	1.7009 in.	43.20 mm
CA16DE and CA18DE	1.6970 in.	43.10 mm
GA16i and GA16DE		
intake:	2.0709 in.	52.60 mm
exhaust:	2.1543 in.	54.72 mm
SR20DE	1.9433 in.	49.36 mm
Assembled height		
E15 and E16	1.543 in.@51.66 lb.	39.2mm@229.78N
CD17		
outer:	1.555 in.@33.70 lb.	39.5mm@150.00N
inner:	1.417 in.@19.20 lb.	36.0mm@85.00N
CA16DE and CA18DE	162.00 in.	28.4 mm
GA16i		
intake:	1.634 in.@49.70 lb.	41.7mm@221.05N
exhaust:	1.705 in.@54.00 lb.	43.4mm@240.17N
GA16DE		
intake:	1.331 in.@110.00 lb.	33.8mm@489.40N
exhaust:	1.346 in.@122.60 lb.	34.2mm@545.30N
SR20DE	1.181 in.@135.25 lb.	30.0mm@625.00N
Out of square		
E15 and E16	0.079 in.	2.00 mm
CD17	0.083 in.	2.10 mm
CA16DE and CA18DE	0.071 in.	1.80 mm
GA16i and GA16DE		
intake:	0.091 in.	2.30 mm
exhaust:	0.094 in.	2.40 mm
SR20DE	0.087 in.	2.20 mm
Valve Guide		
Outer diameter		
E15 and E16	0.4825-0.4832 in.	12.256-12.274 mm
CD17	0.4418-0.4423 in.	11.223-11.234 mm
CA16DE, CA18DE and SR20DE	0.3946-0.3950 in.	10.023-10.034 mm
GA16i		
intake:	0.3946-0.3950 in.	10.023-10.034 mm
exhaust:	0.4182-0.4187 in.	10.623-10.634 mm
GA16DE	0.3749-0.3754 in.	9.523-9.534 mm
Inner diameter		
E15 and E16	0.2758-0.2764 in.	7.005-7.020 mm
CD17	0.2756-0.2762 in.	7.000-7.015 mm
CA16DE, CA18DE and SR20DE	0.2362-0.2369 in.	6.000-6.018 mm
GA16i		
intake:	0.2362-0.2368 in.	6.000-6.015 mm
exhaust:	0.2598-0.2604 in.	6.600-6.615 mm
GA16DE	0.2165-0.2175 in.	5.500-5.515 mm

ENGINE MECHANICAL SPECIFICATIONS

Component	U.S.	Metric
Valve Guide		
Stem-to-guide clearance		
E15 and E16		
intake:	0.0008-0.0040 in.	0.020-0.l00 mm
exhaust:	0.0018-0.0040 in.	0.045-0.100 mm
CD17		
intake:	0.0008-0.0040 in.	0.020-0.100 mm
exhaust:	0.0016-0.0040 in.	0.040-0.100 mm
CA16DE and CA18DE		
intake:	0.0008-0.0021 in.	0.020-0.053 mm
exhaust:	0.0016-0.0029 in.	0.040-0.074 mm
GA16i		
intake:	0.0008-0.0020 in.	0.020-0.050 mm
exhaust:	0.0012-0.0022 in.	0.030-0.057 mm
GA16DE and SR20DE		
intake:	0.0008-0.0020 in.	0.020-0.050 mm
exhaust:	0.0016-0.0028 in.	0.040-0.070 mm
Deflection limit		
E15 and E16	0.008 in.	0.20 mm
CD17	0.004 in.	0.10 mm
GA16i, GA16DE and SR20DE	0.008 in.	0.20 mm
Valve seat		
Angle		
E15 and E16		
intake:	30, 45, 50 degrees	
exhaust:	45, 50 degrees	
CD17 45 degrees		
CA16DE and CA18DE		
intake:	30, 45, 60 degrees	
exhaust:	15, 45, 60 degrees	
GA16i		
intake:	30, 45, 60 degrees	
exhaust:	10, 45 degrees	
GA16DE		
intake:	30, 45, 60 degrees	
exhaust:	10, 45, 60 degrees	
SR20DE	44 deg. 53 min. -45 deg. 07 min.	
Camshaft and Bearings		
Bearing clearance		
E15 and E16		
No. 1,3,5	0.0014-0.0059 in.	0.035-0.150 mm
No. 2,4	0.0031-0.0079 in.	0.079-0.200 mm
CD17	0.0008-0.0040 in.	0.020-0.100 mm
CA16DE, CA18DE, GA16i, GA16DE	0.0018-0.0059 in.	0.045-0.150 mm
SR20DE	0.0018-0.0047 in.	0.045-0.120 mm
Journal diameter		
E15 and E16		
No. 1,3,5	1.6515-1.6522 in.	41.949-41.965 mm
No. 2,4	1.6498-1.6505 in.	41.906-41.922 mm
CD17	1.1795-1.1803 in.	29.960-29.980 mm
CA16DE and CA18DE	1.0998-1.1006 in.	27.935-27.955 mm
GA16i	1.6510-1.6518 in.	41.935-41.955 mm
GA16DE		
No. 1:	1.0998-1.1006 in.	27.935-27.955 mm
No. 2-5:	0.9423-0.9431 in.	23.935-23.955 mm
SR20DE	1.0998-1.1006 in.	27.935-27.955 mm
Camshaft out of round		
E15 and E16	0.0040 in. max.	0.10 mm
CD17	0.0020 in. max.	0.05 mm
CA16DE and CA18DE	0.0020 in. max.	0.05 mm
GA16i, GA16DE and SR20DE	0.0040 in. max.	0.10 mm

ENGINE MECHANICAL SPECIFICATIONS

Component	U.S.	Metric
Camshaft and Bearings		
Endplay		
E15 and E16	0.0160 max. in.	0.40 mm
CD17	0.0024-0.0067 in.	0.06-0.17 mm
CA16DE and CA18DE	0.0028-0.0059 in.	0.07-0.15 mm
GA16i	0.0012-0.0079 in.	0.03-0.20 mm
GA16DE	0.0045-0.0079 in.	0.115-0.200 mm
SR20DE	0.0022-0.0079 in.	0.055-0.200 mm
Lobe height		
E15 and E16		
intake:	1.4128-1.4226 in.	35.884-36.134 mm
exhaust:	1.4031-1.4130 in.	35.640-35.890 mm
CD17		
intake:	1.7500-1.7520 in.	44.450-44.500 mm
exhaust:	1.7894-1.7913 in.	45.450-45.500 mm
CA16DE and CA18DE	1.5931-1.5951 in.	40.485-40.515 mm
GA16i		
intake:	1.4147-1.4222 in.	35.933-36.123 mm
exhaust:	1.4073-1.4148 in.	35.746-35.936 mm
GA16DE		
intake:	1.5984-1.6059 in.	40.600-40.790 mm
exhaust:	1.5701-1.5776 in.	39.880-40.070 mm
SR20DE		
intake:	1.5121-1.5196 in.	38.408-38.598 mm
exhaust:	1.4921-1.5004 in.	37.920-38.110 mm
Lobe wear limit		
E15 and E16	0.0079 max. in.	0.20 mm
CD17		
intake:	1.7441 max. in.	44.300 mm
exhaust:	1.7835 max. in.	45.300 mm
CA16DE, CA18DE and SR20DE	0.0080 max. in.	0.20 mm
GA16i and GA16DE	0.0079 max. in.	0.20 mm
JACK SHAFT AND BEARING		
Journal clearance		
E15 and E16	0.0008-0.0059 in.	0.020-0.150 mm
End play		
E15 and E16	0.0018-0.0041 in.	0.045-0.105 mm
Fuel pump lobe height		
E15 and E16	1.094-1.098 in.	27.80-27.90 mm
ENGINE BLOCK		
Deck Warpage		
All engines	0.0059 max. in.	0.150 mm
Cylinder out of round		
E15 and E16	0.0006 max. in.	0.015 mm
CD17	0.0080 max. in.	0.200 mm
CA16DE, CA18DE, GA16i, GA16DE and SR20DE	0.0006 max. in.	0.015 mm
Cylinder taper		
E15 and E16	0.0008 max. in.	0.020 mm
CD17	0.0080 max. in.	0.200 mm
CA16DE, CA18DE, GA16i, GA16DE and SR20DE	0.0004 max. in.	0.010 mm
Piston to cylinder clearance		
E15 and E16	0.0009-0.0017 in.	0.023-0.043 mm
CD17	0.0020-0.0028 in.	0.050-0.070 mm
CA16DE, CA18DE, GA16i and GA16DE	0.0006-0.0014 in.	0.015-0.035 mm
SR20DE	0.0004-0.0012 in.	0.010-0.030 mm

ENGINE MECHANICAL SPECIFICATIONS

Component	U.S.	Metric
PISTON AND RINGS		
Piston pin hole diameter		
E15 and E16	0.7481-0.7485 in.	19.003-19.012 mm
CD17	0.9445-0.9448 in.	23.991-23.999 mm
CA16DE and CA18DE	0.7869-0.7874 in.	19.987-19.999 mm
GA16i and GA16DE	0.7475-0.7480 in.	18.987-18.999 mm
SR20DE	0.8656-0.8661 in.	21.987-21.999 mm
Ring side clearance		
E15 and E16		
top	0.0016-0.0080 in.	0.040-0.200 mm
2nd	0.0012-0.0080 in.	0.030-0.200 mm
oil	0.0020-0.0057 in.	0.050-0.145 mm
CD17		
top	0.0008-0.0080 in.	0.020-0.200 mm
2nd	0.0016-0.0059 in.	0.040-0.150 mm
oil	0.0012-0.0040 in.	0.030-0.100 mm
CA16DE and CA18DE		
top	0.0016-0.0400 in.	0.040-0.100 mm
2nd	0.0012-0.0400 in.	0.030-0.100 mm
oil	0.0010-0.0400 in.	0.025-0.100 mm
GA16i and GA16DE		
top	0.0016-0.0080 in.	0.040-0.200 mm
2nd	0.0012-0.0080 in.	0.030-0.200 mm
oil	snug	snug
SR20DE		
top	0.0018-0.0080 in.	0.045-0.200 mm
2nd	0.0012-0.0080 in.	0.030-0.200 mm
oil	snug	snug
Ring gap		
E15 and E16		
top	0.0079-0.0138 in.	0.200-0.350 mm
2nd	0.0059-0.0118 in.	0.150-0.300 mm
oil	0.0118-0.0354 in.	0.300-0.900 mm
CD17		
top	0.0079-0.0390 in.	0.200-1.000 mm
2nd	0.0079-0.0280 in.	0.200-0.700 mm
oil	0.0118-0.0240 in.	0.300-0.600 mm
CA16DE and CA18DE		
top	0.0087-0.0390 in.	0.220-1.000 mm
2nd	0.0075-0.0390 in.	0.190-1.000 mm
oil	0.0079-0.0390 in.	0.200-1.000 mm
GA16i and GA16DE		
top	0.0079-0.0390 in.	0.200-1.000 mm
2nd	0.0146-0.0390 in.	0.370-1.000 mm
oil	0.0079-0.0390 in.	0.200-1.000 mm
SR20DE		
top	0.0079-0.0390 in.	0.200-1.000 mm
2nd	0.0138-0.0390 in.	0.350-1.000 mm
oil	0.0079-0.0390 in.	0.200-1.000 mm
Piston pin diameter		
E15 and E16	0.7478-0.7480 in.	18.995-19.000 mm
CD17	0.9446-0.9449 in.	23.994-24.000 mm
CA16DE and CA18DE	0.7870-0.7874 in.	19.989-20.001 mm
GA16i and GA16DE	0.7476-0.7481 in.	18.989-19.001 mm
SR20DE	0.8656-0.8661 in.	21.987-21.999 mm
Piston pin clearance		
E15 and E16	0.0003-0.0005 in.	0.008-0.012 mm
CD17 and GA16DE	0.0000-0.0002 in.	0.000-0.004 mm
CA16DE, CA18DE and GA16i	0.0002-0.0007 in.	0.005-0.017 mm
SR20DE	0.0002-0.0009 in.	0.005-0.023 mm

ENGINE MECHANICAL SPECIFICATIONS

Component	U.S.	Metric
CONNECTING ROD		
Rod bend		
E15 and E16	0.0020 max. in.	0.050 mm
CD17, GA16i and GA16DE	0.0059 max. in.	0.150 mm
CA16DE and CA18DE	0.0040 max. in.	0.100 mm
SR20DE	0.0059 max. in.	0.150 mm
Big end play		
E15 and E16	0.020 max. in.	0.50 mm
CD17	0.012 max. in.	0.30 mm
CA16DE and CA18DE	0.016 max. in.	0.40 mm
CRANKSHAFT		
Main journal diameter		
E15 and E16	1.9663-1.9671 in.	49.943-49.964 mm
CD17	2.0847-2.0852 in.	52.951-52.964 mm
CA16DE and CA18DE	2.0847-2.0856 in.	52.951-52.975 mm
GA16i and GA16DE		
grade 0:	1.9668-1.9671 in.	49.956-49.964 mm
grade 1:	1.9665-1.9668 in.	49.948-49.956 mm
grade 2:	1.9661-1.9665 in.	49.940-49.948 mm
SR20DE		
grade 0:	2.1643-2.1646 in.	54.974-54.980 mm
grade 1:	2.1641-2.1643 in.	54.968-54.974 mm
grade 2:	2.1639-2.1641 in.	54.962-54.968 mm
grade 3:	2.1636-2.1639 in.	54.956-54.962 mm
Rod journal diameter		
E15 and E16	1.5730-1.5738 in.	39.954-39.974 mm
CD17	1.7701-1.7706 in.	44.961-44.974 mm
CA16DE and CA18DE	1.7698-1.7706 in.	44.954-44.974 mm
GA16i	1.5731-1.5738 in.	39.956-39.974 mm
GA16DE		
grade 0:	1.5735-1.5738 in.	39.968-39.974 mm
grade 1:	1.5733-1.5735 in.	39.962-39.968 mm
grade 2:	1.5731-1.5733 in.	39.956-39.962 mm
SR20DE		
grade 0:	1.8885-1.8887 in.	47.968-47.974 mm
grade 1:	1.8883-1.8885 in.	47.962-47.968 mm
grade 2:	1.8880-1.8883 in.	47.956-47.962 mm
Journal out of round		
E15, E16, CD17	0.0012 max. in.	0.030 mm
CA16DE, CA18DE, GA16i, GA16DE and SR20DE	0.0002 max. in.	0.005 mm
Crankshaft end play		
E15, E16, CD17 and SR20DE	0.0118 max. in.	0.300 mm
CA16DE, CA18DE, GA16i and GA16DE	0.0120 max. in.	0.300 mm
Main bearing clearance		
E15 and E16		
No. 1,5	0.0012-0.0039 in.	0.031-0.100 mm
No. 2,3,4	0.0012-0.0039 in.	0.031-0.100 mm
CD17	0.0015-0.0047 in.	0.039-0.120 mm
CA16DE, CA18DE and GA16i	0.0008-0.0040 in.	0.021-0.100 mm
GA16DE	0.0007-0.0040 in.	0.018-0.100 mm
SR20DE	0.0002-0.0020 in.	0.004-0.050 mm
Rod bearing clearance		
E15 and E16	0.0012-0.0039 in.	0.031-0.100 mm
CD17	0.0009-0.0047 in.	0.024-0.120 mm
CA16DE and CA18DE	0.0007-0.0040 in.	0.018-0.100 mm
GA16i and GA16DE	0.0004-0.0040 in.	0.010-0.100 mm
SR20DE	0.0008-0.0035 in.	0.020-0.090 mm

TORQUE SPECIFICATIONS

Component	U.S.	Metric
Belt/Chain Tensioner		
E15 and E16	12-15 ft. lbs.	14-20 Nm
CA16DE and CA18DE	23-31 ft. lbs.	31-42 Nm
GA16i	9-14 ft. lbs.	13-19 Nm
GA16DE	4-9 ft. lbs.	6-12 Nm
SR20DE	5-6 ft. lbs.	6-8 Nm
CD17	27-34 ft. lbs.	36-44 Nm
Camshaft Bearing Cap		
CA16DE and CA18DE	7-9 ft. lbs.	10-12 Nm
GA16DE	7-9 ft. lbs.	10-12 Nm
SR20DE		
1st step:	1.4 ft. lbs.	2 Nm
2nd step:	4.3 ft. lbs.	6 Nm
3rd step:		
bolts A,B,C:	7-9 ft. lbs.	9-12 Nm
bolt D:	13-19 ft. lbs.	18-25 Nm
CD17	13-16 ft. lbs.	18-22 Nm
Camshaft Pulley		
E15 and E16	4-6 ft. lbs.	5-8 Nm
CA16DE and CA18DE	4-6 ft. lbs.	5-8 Nm
GA16i	72-94 ft. lbs.	98-127 Nm
GA16DE		
upper:	72-94 ft. lbs.	98-127 Nm
lower:	32-43 ft. lbs.	43-58 Nm
SR20DE	101-116 ft. lbs.	137-157 Nm
CD17	68-75 ft. lbs.	92-102 Nm
Cylinder Head		
1982-83 E15 and E16		
1st step:	33 ft. lbs.	44 Nm
2nd step:	51-54 ft. lbs.	69-74 Nm
1984-86 E15ET and E16		
1st step:	10 ft. lbs.	14 Nm
2nd step:	20 ft. lbs.	28 Nm
3rd step:	30 ft. lbs.	41 Nm
4th step:	40 ft. lbs.	52 Nm
5th step:	51-54 ft. lbs.	69-74 Nm
1987-88 E16i		
1st step:	22 ft. lbs.	30 Nm
2nd step:	51 ft. lbs.	69 Nm
3rd step:	loosen all bolts completely	
4th step:	22 ft. lbs.	30 Nm
5th step:	51-54 ft. lbs.	69-74 Nm
CA16DE and CA18DE		
1st step:	22 ft. lbs.	30 Nm
2nd step:	76 ft. lbs.	103 Nm
3rd step:	loosen all bolts completely	
4th step:	22 ft. lbs.	30 Nm
5th step:	76 ft. lbs.	103 Nm
6th step:	plus an additional 85-90 degrees	
GA16i		
1st step:	22 ft. lbs.	30 Nm
2nd step:	47 ft. lbs.	64 Nm
3rd step:	loosen all bolts completely	
4th step:	22 ft. lbs.	30 Nm
5th step:	turn bolts (1) 80-85 degrees and (2-10) 60-65 degrees	
6th step:	turn bolts (11-15) to 4.6-6.1 ft. lbs.	
GA16DE		
1st step:	22 ft. lbs.	30 Nm
2nd step:	43 ft. lbs.	60 Nm
3rd step:	loosen all bolts completely	
4th step:	22 ft. lbs.	30 Nm
5th step:	plus an additional 50-55 degrees	

TORQUE SPECIFICATIONS

Component	U.S.	Metric
Cylinder Head		
SR20DE		
1st step:	29 ft. lbs.	39 Nm
2nd step:	58 ft. lbs.	79 Nm
3rd step:	loosen all bolts completely	
4th step:	25-33 ft. lbs.	35-45 Nm
5th step:	turn bolts 90-100 degrees	
6th step:	turn bolts 90-100 degrees	
CD17		
1st step:	29 ft. lbs.	39 Nm
2nd step:	58 ft. lbs.	79 Nm
3rd step:	72-80 ft. lbs.	98-108 Nm
Connecting Rod		
E15, E16, CD17	23-27 ft. lbs.	31-37 Nm
CA16DE	30-33 ft. lbs.	41-48 Nm
CA18DE, GA16i, GA16DE, SR20DE		
1st step:	10-12 ft. lbs.	14-16 Nm
2nd step:	28-33 ft. lbs.	38-45 Nm
3rd step:	turn bolts 60-65 degrees clockwise	
Crankshaft Bearing Cap		
E15 and E16	36-43 ft. lbs.	49-59 Nm
CA16DE, CA18DE, CD17	33-40 ft. lbs.	44-54 Nm
GA16i and GA16DE	34-38 ft. lbs.	46-53 Nm
SR20DE	51-61 ft. lbs.	69-83 Nm
Crankshaft Damper		
E15	108-145 ft. lbs.	147-197 Nm
1983-87 E15ET and E16	83-108 ft. lbs.	113-147 Nm
1988-89 E16	80-94 ft. lbs.	109-128 Nm
CA16DE and CA18DE	105-112 ft. lbs.	145-152 Nm
GA16i	132-152 ft. lbs.	179-207 Nm
GA16DE	98-112 ft. lbs.	133-152 Nm
SR20DE	105-122 ft. lbs.	145-166 Nm
CD17	90-98 ft. lbs.	122-133 Nm
Flywheel		
1982-87 E15 and E16	58-65 ft. lbs.	78-88 Nm
1988-89 E16		
M/T:	58-65 ft. lbs.	78-88 Nm
A/T:	69-76 ft. lbs.	94-103 Nm
CA16DE, CA18DE and SR20DE	61-69 ft. lbs.	83-94 Nm
GA16i	69-76 ft. lbs.	94-103 Nm
GA16DE		
M/T:	61-69 ft. lbs.	83-94 Nm
A/T:	69-76 ft. lbs.	94-103 Nm
CD17	90-98 ft. lbs.	122-133 Nm
Intake Manifold		
1982-83 E15 and E16	11-14 ft. lbs.	14-20 Nm
1984-91 E16, GA16i and GA16DE	12-15 ft. lbs.	16-22 Nm
CA16DE and CA18DE	14-19 ft. lbs.	19-26 Nm
SR20DE	13-15 ft. lbs.	18-22 Nm
CD17	13-16 ft. lbs.	18-24 Nm
Intake Plenum		
All EFI engines	13-15 ft. lbs.	18-22 Nm
Exhaust Manifold		
All engines, except	12-15 ft. lbs.	16-22 Nm
CA16DE, CA18DE and SR20DE	27-35 ft. lbs.	34-48 Nm
GA16DE	16-21 ft. lbs.	22-25 Nm
Exhaust Manifold-to-Pipe		
All engines	14-31 ft. lbs.	20-43 Nm

TORQUE SPECIFICATIONS

Component	U.S.	Metric
Oil Pump Bolts		
E15 and E16	7-9 ft. lbs.	10-12 Nm
CA16DE and CA18DE	5-6 ft. lbs.	7-8 Nm
GA16i	5-6 ft. lbs.	7-8 Nm
GA16DE	5-6 ft. lbs.	7-8 Nm
SR20DE	5-6 ft. lbs.	7-8 Nm
CD17	4-5 ft. lbs.	5-7 Nm
Spark Plug		
All engines	11-14 ft. lbs.	15-20 Nm
Water Pump		
E15 and E16	7-10 ft. lbs.	10-14 Nm
CA16DE and CA18DE	8-12 ft. lbs.	11-15 Nm
GA16i	5-6 ft. lbs.	6-8 Nm
GA16DE	6-8 ft. lbs.	8-10 Nm
SR20DE	5-6 ft. lbs.	6-8 Nm
CD17	12-14 ft. lbs.	16-20 Nm
Water Pump Pulley		
E15, E16, CA16DE and CA18DE	3-4 ft. lbs.	4-5 Nm
GA16i	6-8 ft. lbs.	8-10 Nm
GA16DE	6-8 ft. lbs.	8-10 Nm
SR20DE	5-6 ft. lbs.	6-8 Nm
CD17	6-8 ft. lbs.	8-10 Nm
Thermostat Housing		
E15 and E16	3-4 ft. lbs.	4-5 Nm
CA16DE and CA18DE	5-6 ft. lbs.	7-8 Nm
GA16i	6-8 ft. lbs.	8-10 Nm
GA16DE	6-8 ft. lbs.	8-10 Nm
SR20DE	6-8 ft. lbs.	8-10 Nm
CD17	6-8 ft. lbs.	8-10 Nm
Front Cover		
E15 and E16	3-4 ft. lbs.	4-5 Nm
CA16DE and CA18DE	4-5 ft. lbs.	6-7 Nm
GA16i	5-6 ft. lbs.	6-8 Nm
GA16DE	5-6 ft. lbs.	6-8 Nm
SR20DE	5-6 ft. lbs.	6-8 Nm
CD17	5-6 ft. lbs.	6-8 Nm
Jack Shaft Pulley		
E15 and E16	4-6 ft. lbs.	5-8 Nm
Oil Pan		
E15 and E16	3-4 ft. lbs.	4-5 Nm
CA16DE and CA18DE	5-6 ft. lbs.	6-8 Nm
GA16i	5-6 ft. lbs.	6-8 Nm
GA16DE	5-6 ft. lbs.	6-8 Nm
SR20DE	5-6 ft. lbs.	6-8 Nm
CD17	5-6 ft. lbs.	6-8 Nm
Rocker Arm Shaft		
E15 and E16	12-15 ft. lbs.	14-20 Nm
GA16i	27-30 ft. lbs.	37-41 Nm

Troubleshooting Basic Charging System Problems

Problem	Cause	Solution
Noisy alternator	• Loose mountings • Loose drive pulley • Worn bearings • Brush noise • Internal circuits shorted (High pitched whine)	• Tighten mounting bolts • Tighten pulley • Replace alternator • Replace alternator • Replace alternator
Squeal when starting engine or accelerating	• Glazed or loose belt	• Replace or adjust belt
Indicator light remains on or ammeter indicates discharge (engine running)	• Broken fan belt • Broken or disconnected wires • Internal alternator problems • Defective voltage regulator	• Install belt • Repair or connect wiring • Replace alternator • Replace voltage regulator
Car light bulbs continually burn out—battery needs water continually	• Alternator/regulator overcharging	• Replace voltage regulator/alternator
Car lights flare on acceleration	• Battery low • Internal alternator/regulator problems	• Charge or replace battery • Replace alternator/regulator
Low voltage output (alternator light flickers continually or ammeter needle wanders)	• Loose or worn belt • Dirty or corroded connections • Internal alternator/regulator problems	• Replace or adjust belt • Clean or replace connections • Replace alternator or regulator

Troubleshooting Basic Starting System Problems

Problem	Cause	Solution
Starter motor rotates engine slowly	• Battery charge low or battery defective • Defective circuit between battery and starter motor • Low load current • High load current	• Charge or replace battery • Clean and tighten, or replace cables • Bench-test starter motor. Inspect for worn brushes and weak brush springs. • Bench-test starter motor. Check engine for friction, drag or coolant in cylinders. Check ring gear-to-pinion gear clearance.
Starter motor will not rotate engine	• Battery charge low or battery defective • Faulty solenoid • Damage drive pinion gear or ring gear • Starter motor engagement weak • Starter motor rotates slowly with high load current • Engine seized	• Charge or replace battery • Check solenoid ground. Repair or replace as necessary. • Replace damaged gear(s) • Bench-test starter motor • Inspect drive yoke pull-down and point gap, check for worn end bushings, check ring gear clearance • Repair engine
Starter motor drive will not engage (solenoid known to be good)	• Defective contact point assembly • Inadequate contact point assembly ground • Defective hold-in coil	• Repair or replace contact point assembly • Repair connection at ground screw • Replace field winding assembly
Starter motor drive will not disengage	• Starter motor loose on flywheel housing • Worn drive end busing • Damaged ring gear teeth • Drive yoke return spring broken or missing	• Tighten mounting bolts • Replace bushing • Replace ring gear or driveplate • Replace spring
Starter motor drive disengages prematurely	• Weak drive assembly thrust spring • Hold-in coil defective	• Replace drive mechanism • Replace field winding assembly
Low load current	• Worn brushes • Weak brush springs	• Replace brushes • Replace springs

Troubleshooting Engine Mechanical Problems

Problem	Cause	Solution
External oil leaks	• Fuel pump gasket broken or improperly seated	• Replace gasket
	• Cylinder head cover RTV sealant broken or improperly seated	• Replace sealant; inspect cylinder head cover sealant flange and cylinder head sealant surface for distortion and cracks
	• Oil filler cap leaking or missing	• Replace cap
External oil leaks	• Oil filter gasket broken or improperly seated	• Replace oil filter
	• Oil pan side gasket broken, improperly seated or opening in RTV sealant	• Replace gasket or repair opening in sealant; inspect oil pan gasket flange for distortion
	• Oil pan front oil seal broken or improperly seated	• Replace seal; inspect timing case cover and oil pan seal flange for distortion
	• Oil pan rear oil seal broken or improperly seated	• Replace seal; inspect oil pan rear oil seal flange; inspect rear main bearing cap for cracks, plugged oil return channels, or distortion in seal groove
	• Timing case cover oil seal broken or improperly seated	• Replace seal
	• Excess oil pressure because of restricted PCV valve	• Replace PCV valve
	• Oil pan drain plug loose or has stripped threads	• Repair as necessary and tighten
	• Rear oil gallery plug loose	• Use appropriate sealant on gallery plug and tighten
	• Rear camshaft plug loose or improperly seated	• Seat camshaft plug or replace and seal, as necessary
	• Distributor base gasket damaged	• Replace gasket
Excessive oil consumption	• Oil level too high	• Drain oil to specified level
	• Oil with wrong viscosity being used	• Replace with specified oil
	• PCV valve stuck closed	• Replace PCV valve
	• Valve stem oil deflectors (or seals) are damaged, missing, or incorrect type	• Replace valve stem oil deflectors
	• Valve stems or valve guides worn	• Measure stem-to-guide clearance and repair as necessary
	• Poorly fitted or missing valve cover baffles	• Replace valve cover
	• Piston rings broken or missing	• Replace broken or missing rings
	• Scuffed piston	• Replace piston
	• Incorrect piston ring gap	• Measure ring gap, repair as necessary
	• Piston rings sticking or excessively loose in grooves	• Measure ring side clearance, repair as necessary
	• Compression rings installed upside down	• Repair as necessary
	• Cylinder walls worn, scored, or glazed	• Repair as necessary

Troubleshooting Engine Mechanical Problems (cont.)

Problem	Cause	Solution
	• Piston ring gaps not properly staggered	• Repair as necessary
	• Excessive main or connecting rod bearing clearance	• Measure bearing clearance, repair as necessary
No oil pressure	• Low oil level	• Add oil to correct level
	• Oil pressure gauge, warning lamp or sending unit inaccurate	• Replace oil pressure gauge or warning lamp
	• Oil pump malfunction	• Replace oil pump
	• Oil pressure relief valve sticking	• Remove and inspect oil pressure relief valve assembly
	• Oil passages on pressure side of pump obstructed	• Inspect oil passages for obstruction
	• Oil pickup screen or tube obstructed	• Inspect oil pickup for obstruction
	• Loose oil inlet tube	• Tighten or seal inlet tube
Low oil pressure	• Low oil level	• Add oil to correct level
	• Inaccurate gauge, warning lamp or sending unit	• Replace oil pressure gauge or warning lamp
	• Oil excessively thin because of dilution, poor quality, or improper grade	• Drain and refill crankcase with recommended oil
	• Excessive oil temperature	• Correct cause of overheating engine
	• Oil pressure relief spring weak or sticking	• Remove and inspect oil pressure relief valve assembly
	• Oil inlet tube and screen assembly has restriction or air leak	• Remove and inspect oil inlet tube and screen assembly. (Fill inlet tube with lacquer thinner to locate leaks.)
	• Excessive oil pump clearance	• Measure clearances
	• Excessive main, rod, or camshaft bearing clearance	• Measure bearing clearances, repair as necessary
High oil pressure	• Improper oil viscosity	• Drain and refill crankcase with correct viscosity oil
	• Oil pressure gauge or sending unit inaccurate	• Replace oil pressure gauge
	• Oil pressure relief valve sticking closed	• Remove and inspect oil pressure relief valve assembly
Main bearing noise	• Insufficient oil supply	• Inspect for low oil level and low oil pressure
	• Main bearing clearance excessive	• Measure main bearing clearance, repair as necessary
	• Bearing insert missing	• Replace missing insert
	• Crankshaft end play excessive	• Measure end play, repair as necessary
	• Improperly tightened main bearing cap bolts	• Tighten bolts with specified torque
	• Loose flywheel or drive plate	• Tighten flywheel or drive plate attaching bolts
	• Loose or damaged vibration damper	• Repair as necessary

Troubleshooting Engine Mechanical Problems (cont.)

Problem	Cause	Solution
Connecting rod bearing noise	• Insufficient oil supply	• Inspect for low oil level and low oil pressure
	• Carbon build-up on piston	• Remove carbon from piston crown
	• Bearing clearance excessive or bearing missing	• Measure clearance, repair as necessary
	• Crankshaft connecting rod journal out-of-round	• Measure journal dimensions, repair or replace as necessary
	• Misaligned connecting rod or cap	• Repair as necessary
	• Connecting rod bolts tightened improperly	• Tighten bolts with specified torque
Piston noise	• Piston-to-cylinder wall clearance excessive (scuffed piston)	• Measure clearance and examine piston
	• Cylinder walls excessively tapered or out-of-round	• Measure cylinder wall dimensions, rebore cylinder
	• Piston ring broken	• Replace all rings on piston
	• Loose or seized piston pin	• Measure piston-to-pin clearance, repair as necessary
	• Connecting rods misaligned	• Measure rod alignment, straighten or replace
	• Piston ring side clearance excessively loose or tight	• Measure ring side clearance, repair as necessary
	• Carbon build-up on piston is excessive	• Remove carbon from piston
Valve actuating component noise	• Insufficient oil supply	• Check for: (a) Low oil level (b) Low oil pressure (c) Plugged push rods (d) Wrong hydraulic tappets (e) Restricted oil gallery (f) Excessive tappet to bore clearance
	• Push rods worn or bent	• Replace worn or bent push rods
	• Rocker arms or pivots worn	• Replace worn rocker arms or pivots
	• Foreign objects or chips in hydraulic tappets	• Clean tappets
	• Excessive tappet leak-down	• Replace valve tappet
	• Tappet face worn	• Replace tappet; inspect corresponding cam lobe for wear
	• Broken or cocked valve springs	• Properly seat cocked springs; replace broken springs
	• Stem-to-guide clearance excessive	• Measure stem-to-guide clearance, repair as required
	• Valve bent	• Replace valve
	• Loose rocker arms	• Tighten bolts with specified torque
	• Valve seat runout excessive	• Regrind valve seat/valves
	• Missing valve lock	• Install valve lock
	• Push rod rubbing or contacting cylinder head	• Remove cylinder head and remove obstruction in head
	• Excessive engine oil (four-cylinder engine)	• Correct oil level

Troubleshooting the Cooling System

Problem	Cause	Solution
High temperature gauge indication—overheating	• Coolant level low	• Replenish coolant
	• Fan belt loose	• Adjust fan belt tension
	• Radiator hose(s) collapsed	• Replace hose(s)
	• Radiator airflow blocked	• Remove restriction (bug screen, fog lamps, etc.)
	• Faulty radiator cap	• Replace radiator cap
	• Ignition timing incorrect	• Adjust ignition timing
	• Idle speed low	• Adjust idle speed
	• Air trapped in cooling system	• Purge air
	• Heavy traffic driving	• Operate at fast idle in neutral intermittently to cool engine
	• Incorrect cooling system component(s) installed	• Install proper component(s)
	• Faulty thermostat	• Replace thermostat
	• Water pump shaft broken or impeller loose	• Replace water pump
	• Radiator tubes clogged	• Flush radiator
	• Cooling system clogged	• Flush system
	• Casting flash in cooling passages	• Repair or replace as necessary. Flash may be visible by removing cooling system components or removing core plugs.
	• Brakes dragging	• Repair brakes
	• Excessive engine friction	• Repair engine
	• Antifreeze concentration over 68%	• Lower antifreeze concentration percentage
	• Missing air seals	• Replace air seals
	• Faulty gauge or sending unit	• Repair or replace faulty component
	• Loss of coolant flow caused by leakage or foaming	• Repair or replace leaking component, replace coolant
	• Viscous fan drive failed	• Replace unit
Low temperature indication—undercooling	• Thermostat stuck open	• Replace thermostat
	• Faulty gauge or sending unit	• Repair or replace faulty component
Coolant loss—boilover	• Overfilled cooling system	• Reduce coolant level to proper specification
	• Quick shutdown after hard (hot) run	• Allow engine to run at fast idle prior to shutdown
	• Air in system resulting in occasional "burping" of coolant	• Purge system
	• Insufficient antifreeze allowing coolant boiling point to be too low	• Add antifreeze to raise boiling point
	• Antifreeze deteriorated because of age or contamination	• Replace coolant
	• Leaks due to loose hose clamps, loose nuts, bolts, drain plugs, faulty hoses, or defective radiator	• Pressure test system to locate source of leak(s) then repair as necessary

Troubleshooting the Cooling System (cont.)

Problem	Cause	Solution
Coolant loss—boilover	• Faulty head gasket • Cracked head, manifold, or block • Faulty radiator cap	• Replace head gasket • Replace as necessary • Replace cap
Coolant entry into crankcase or cylinder(s)	• Faulty head gasket • Crack in head, manifold or block	• Replace head gasket • Replace as necessary
Coolant recovery system inoperative	• Coolant level low • Leak in system • Pressure cap not tight or seal missing, or leaking • Pressure cap defective • Overflow tube clogged or leaking • Recovery bottle vent restricted	• Replenish coolant to FULL mark • Pressure test to isolate leak and repair as necessary • Repair as necessary • Replace cap • Repair as necessary • Remove restriction
Noise	• Fan contacting shroud • Loose water pump impeller • Glazed fan belt • Loose fan belt • Rough surface on drive pulley • Water pump bearing worn • Belt alignment	• Reposition shroud and inspect engine mounts • Replace pump • Apply silicone or replace belt • Adjust fan belt tension • Replace pulley • Remove belt to isolate. Replace pump. • Check pulley alignment. Repair as necessary.
No coolant flow through heater core	• Restricted return inlet in water pump • Heater hose collapsed or restricted • Restricted heater core • Restricted outlet in thermostat housing • Intake manifold bypass hole in cylinder head restricted • Faulty heater control valve • Intake manifold coolant passage restricted	• Remove restriction • Remove restriction or replace hose • Remove restriction or replace core • Remove flash or restriction • Remove restriction • Replace valve • Remove restriction or replace intake manifold

NOTE: *Immediately after shutdown, the engine enters a condition known as heat soak. This is caused by the cooling system being inoperative while engine temperature is still high. If coolant temperature rises above boiling point, expansion and pressure may push some coolant out of the radiator overflow tube. If this does not occur frequently it is considered normal.*

Troubleshooting the Serpentine Drive Belt

Problem	Cause	Solution
Tension sheeting fabric failure (woven fabric on outside circumference of belt has cracked or separated from body of belt)	• Grooved or backside idler pulley diameters are less than minimum recommended	• Replace pulley(s) not conforming to specification
	• Tension sheeting contacting (rubbing) stationary object	• Correct rubbing condition
	• Excessive heat causing woven fabric to age	• Replace belt
	• Tension sheeting splice has fractured	• Replace belt
Noise (objectional squeal, squeak, or rumble is heard or felt while drive belt is in operation)	• Belt slippage	• Adjust belt
	• Bearing noise	• Locate and repair
	• Belt misalignment	• Align belt/pulley(s)
	• Belt-to-pulley mismatch	• Install correct belt
	• Driven component inducing vibration	• Locate defective driven component and repair
	• System resonant frequency inducing vibration	• Vary belt tension within specifications. Replace belt.
Rib chunking (one or more ribs has separated from belt body)	• Foreign objects imbedded in pulley grooves	• Remove foreign objects from pulley grooves
	• Installation damage	• Replace belt
	• Drive loads in excess of design specifications	• Adjust belt tension
	• Insufficient internal belt adhesion	• Replace belt
Rib or belt wear (belt ribs contact bottom of pulley grooves)	• Pulley(s) misaligned	• Align pulley(s)
	• Mismatch of belt and pulley groove widths	• Replace belt
	• Abrasive environment	• Replace belt
	• Rusted pulley(s)	• Clean rust from pulley(s)
	• Sharp or jagged pulley groove tips	• Replace pulley
	• Rubber deteriorated	• Replace belt
Longitudinal belt cracking (cracks between two ribs)	• Belt has mistracked from pulley groove	• Replace belt
	• Pulley groove tip has worn away rubber-to-tensile member	• Replace belt
Belt slips	• Belt slipping because of insufficient tension	• Adjust tension
	• Belt or pulley subjected to substance (belt dressing, oil, ethylene glycol) that has reduced friction	• Replace belt and clean pulleys
	• Driven component bearing failure	• Replace faulty component bearing
	• Belt glazed and hardened from heat and excessive slippage	• Replace belt
"Groove jumping" (belt does not maintain correct position on pulley, or turns over and/or runs off pulleys)	• Insufficient belt tension	• Adjust belt tension
	• Pulley(s) not within design tolerance	• Replace pulley(s)
	• Foreign object(s) in grooves	• Remove foreign objects from grooves

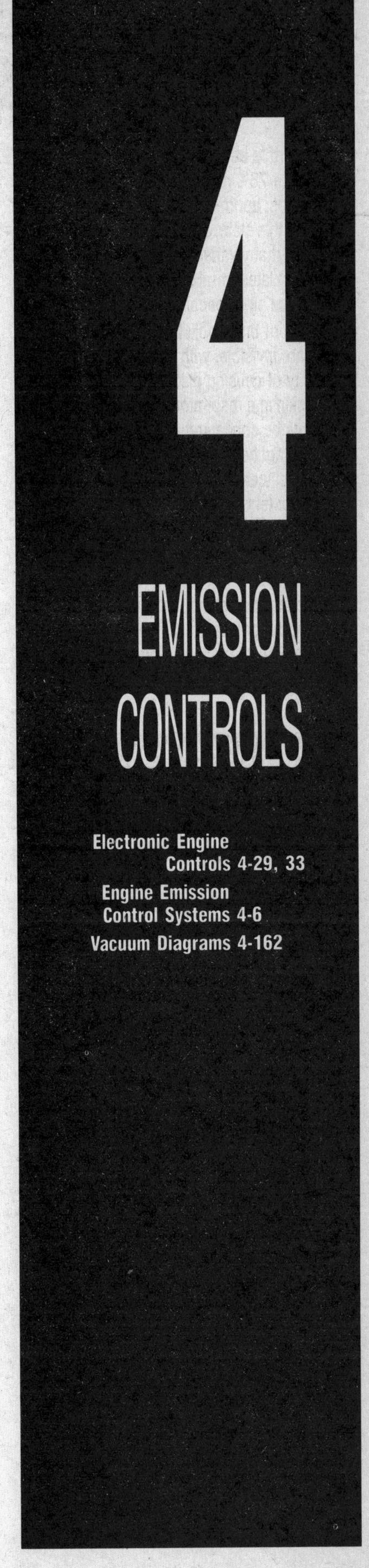

4 EMISSION CONTROLS

AIR POLLUTION

The earth's atmosphere, at or near sea level, consists of 78% nitrogen, 21% oxygen and 1% other gases, approximately. If it were possible to remain in this state, 100% clean air would result. However, many varied causes allow other gases and particulates to mix with the clean air, causing the air to become unclean or polluted.

Certain of these pollutants are visible while others are invisible, with each having the capability of causing distress to the eyes, ears, throat, skin and respiratory system. Should these pollutants be concentrated in a specific area and under the right conditions, death could result due to the displacement or chemical change of the oxygen content in the air. These pollutants can cause much damage to the environment and to the many man made objects that are exposed to the elements.

To better understand the causes of air pollution, the pollutants can be categorized into 3 separate types, natural, industrial and automotive.

Natural Pollutants

Natural pollution has been present on earth before man appeared and is still a factor to be considered when discussing air pollution, although it causes only a small percentage of the present overall pollution problem existing in our country. It is the direct result of decaying organic matter, wind born smoke and particulates from such natural events as plains and forest fires (ignited by heat or lightning), volcanic ash, sand and dust which can spread over a large area of the countryside.

Such a phenomenon of natural pollution has been recent volcanic eruptions, with the resulting plume of smoke, steam and volcanic ash blotting out the sun's rays as it spreads and rises higher into the atmosphere, where the upper air currents catch and carry the smoke and ash, while condensing the steam back into water vapor. As the water vapor, smoke and ash traveled on their journey, the smoke dissipates into the atmosphere while the ash and moisture settle back to earth in a trail hundred of miles long. In many cases, lives are lost and millions of dollars of property damage result, and ironically, man can only stand by and watch it happen.

Industrial Pollution

Industrial pollution is caused primarily by industrial processes, the burning of coal, oil and natural gas, which in turn produces smoke and fumes. Because the burning fuels contain much sulfur, the principal ingredients of smoke and fumes are sulfur dioxide (SO_2) and particulate matter. This type of pollutant occurs most severely during still, damp and cool weather, such as at night. Even in its less severe form, this pollutant is not confined to just cities. Because of air movements, the pollutants move for miles over the surrounding countryside, leaving in its path a barren and unhealthy environment for all living things.

Working with Federal, State and Local mandated rules, regulations and by carefully monitoring the emissions, industries have greatly reduced the amount of pollutant emitted from their industrial sources, striving to obtain an acceptable level. Because of the mandated industrial emission clean up, many land areas and streams in and around the cities that were formerly barren of vegetation and life, have now begun to move back in the direction of nature's intended balance.

Automotive Pollutants

The third major source of air pollution is the automotive emissions. The emissions from the internal combustion engine were not an appreciable problem years ago because of the small number of registered vehicles and the nation's small highway system. However, during the early 1950's, the trend of the American people was to move from the cities to the surrounding suburbs. This caused an immediate problem in the transportation areas because the majority of the suburbs were not afforded mass transit conveniences. This lack of transportation created an attractive market for the automobile manufacturers, which resulted in a dramatic increase in the number of vehicles produced and sold, along with a marked increase in highway construction between cities and the suburbs. Multi-vehicle families emerged with much emphasis placed on the individual vehicle per family member. As the increase in vehicle ownership and usage occurred, so did the pollutant levels in and around the cities, as the suburbanites drove daily to their businesses and employment in the city and its fringe area, returning at the end of the day to their homes in the suburbs.

It was noted that a fog and smoke type haze was being formed and at times, remained in suspension over the cities and did not quickly dissipate. At first this "smog", derived from the words "smoke" and "fog", was thought to result from industrial pollution but it was determined that the automobile emissions were largely to blame. It was discovered that as normal automobile emissions were exposed to sunlight for a period of time, complex chemical reactions would take place.

It was found the smog was a photo chemical layer and was developed when certain oxides of nitrogen (NOx) and unburned hydrocarbons (HC) from the automobile emissions were exposed to sunlight and was more severe when the smog would remain stagnant over an area in which a warm layer of air would settle over the top of a cooler air mass at ground level, trapping and holding the automobile emissions, instead of the emissions being dispersed and diluted through normal air flows. This type of air stagnation was given the name "Temperature Inversion".

Temperature Inversion

In normal weather situations, the surface air is warmed by the heat radiating from the earth's surface and the sun's rays and will rise upward, into the atmosphere, to be cooled through a convection type heat expands with the cooler upper air. As the warm air rises, the surface pollutants are carried upward and dissipated into the atmosphere.

When a temperature inversion occurs, we find the higher air is no longer cooler but warmer than the surface air, causing the cooler surface air to become trapped and unable to move. This warm air blanket can extend from above ground level to a few hundred or even a few thousand feet into the air. As the surface air is trapped, so are the pollutants, causing a severe smog condition. Should this stagnant air mass extend to a few thousand feet high, enough air movement with the inversion takes place to allow the smog layer to rise above ground level but the pollutants still cannot dissipate. This inversion can remain for days over an area, with only the smog level rising or lowering from ground level to a few hundred feet high. Meanwhile, the pollutant levels increases, causing eye irritation, respirator problems, reduced visibility, plant damage and in some cases, cancer type diseases.

This inversion phenomenon was first noted in the Los Angeles, California area. The city lies in a basin type of terrain and during certain weather conditions, a cold air mass is held in the basin while a warmer air mass covers it like a lid.

Because this type of condition was first documented as prevalent in the Los Angeles area, this type of smog was named Los Angeles Smog, although it occurs in other areas where a large concentration of automobiles are used and the air remains stagnant for any length of time.

Internal Combustion Engine Pollutants

Consider the internal combustion engine as a machine in which raw materials must be placed so a finished product comes out. As in any machine operation, a certain amount of wasted material is formed. When we relate this to the internal combustion engine, we find that by putting in air and fuel, we obtain power from this mixture during the combustion process to drive the vehicle. The by-product or waste of this power is, in part, heat and exhaust gases with which we must concern ourselves.

HEAT TRANSFER

The heat from the combustion process can rise to over 4000°F (2204°C). The dissipation of this heat is controlled by a ram air effect, the use of cooling fans to cause air flow and having a liquid coolant solution surrounding the combustion area and transferring the heat of combustion through the cylinder walls and into the coolant. The coolant is then directed to a thin-finned, multi-tubed radiator, from which the excess heat is transferred to the outside air by 1 or all of the 3 heat transfer methods, conduction, convection or radiation.

The cooling of the combustion area is an important part in the control of exhaust emissions. To understand the behavior of the combustion and transfer of its heat, consider the air/fuel charge. It is ignited and the flame front burns progressively across the combustion chamber until the burning charge reaches the cylinder walls. Some of the fuel in contact with the walls is not hot enough to burn, thereby snuffing out or Quenching the combustion process. This leaves unburned fuel in the combustion chamber. This unburned fuel is then forced out of the cylinder along with the exhaust gases and into the exhaust system.

Many attempts have been made to minimize the amount of unburned fuel in the combustion chambers due to the snuffing out or "Quenching", by increasing the coolant temperature and lessening the contact area of the coolant around the combustion area. Design limitations within the combustion chambers prevent the complete burning of the air/fuel charge, so a certain amount of the unburned fuel is still expelled into the exhaust system, regardless of modifications to the engine.

EXHAUST EMISSIONS

Composition Of The Exhaust Gases

The exhaust gases emitted into the atmosphere are a combination of burned and unburned fuel. To understand the exhaust emission and its composition review some basic chemistry.

When the air/fuel mixture is introduced into the engine, we are mixing air, composed of nitrogen (78%), oxygen (21%) and other gases (1%) with the fuel, which is 100% hydrocarbons (HC), in a semi-controlled ratio. As the combustion process is accomplished, power is produced to move the vehicle while the heat of combustion is transferred to the cooling system. The exhaust gases are then composed of nitrogen, a diatomic gas (N_2), the same as was introduced in the engine, carbon dioxide (CO2), the same gas that is used in beverage carbonation and water vapor (H_2O). The nitrogen (N_2), for the most part passes through the engine unchanged, while the oxygen (O_2) reacts (burns) with the hydrocarbons (HC) and produces the carbon dioxide (CO_2) and the water vapors (H_2O). If this chemical process would be the only process to take place, the exhaust emissions would be harmless. However, during the combustion process, other pollutants are formed and are considered dangerous. These pollutants are carbon monoxide (CO), hydrocarbons (HC), oxides of nitrogen (NOx) oxides of sulfur (SOx) and engine particulates.

Lead (Pb), is considered 1 of the particulates and is present in the exhaust gases whenever leaded fuels are used. Lead (Pb) does not dissipate easily. Levels can be high along roadways when it is emitted from vehicles and can pose a health threat. Since the increased usage of unleaded gasoline and the phasing out of leaded gasoline for fuel, this pollutant is gradually diminishing. While not considered a major threat lead is still considered a dangerous pollutant.

HYDROCARBONS

Hydrocarbons (HC) are essentially unburned fuel that have not been successfully burned during the combustion process or have escaped into the atmosphere through fuel evaporation. The main sources of incomplete combustion are rich air/fuel mixtures, low engine temperatures and improper spark timing. The main sources of hydrocarbon emission through fuel evaporation come from the vehicle's fuel tank and carburetor bowl.

To reduce combustion hydrocarbon emission, engine modifications were made to minimize dead space and surface area in the combustion chamber. In addition the air/fuel mixture was made more lean through improved carburetion, fuel injection and by the addition of external controls to aid in further combustion of the hydrocarbons outside the engine. Two such methods were the addition of an air injection system, to inject fresh air into the exhaust manifolds and the installation of a catalytic converter, a unit that is able to burn traces of hydrocarbons without affecting the internal combustion process or fuel economy.

To control hydrocarbon emissions through fuel evaporation, modifications were made to the fuel tank and carburetor bowl to allow storage of the fuel vapors during periods of engine shut-down, and at specific times during engine operation, to purge and burn these same vapors by blending them with the air/fuel mixture.

CARBON MONOXIDE

Carbon monoxide is formed when not enough oxygen is present during the combustion process to convert carbon (C) to carbon dioxide (CO_2). An increase in the carbon monoxide (CO) emission is normally accompanied by an increase in the hydrocarbon (HC) emission because of the lack of oxygen to completely burn all of the fuel mixture.

Carbon monoxide (CO) also increases the rate at which the photo chemical smog is formed by speeding up the conversion of nitric oxide (NO) to nitrogen dioxide (NO_2). To accomplish this, carbon monoxide (CO) combines with oxygen (O_2) and nitrogen dioxide (NO_2) to produce carbon dioxide (CO_2) and nitrogen dioxide (NO_2). ($CO + O_2 + NO = CO_2 + NO_2$).

The dangers of carbon monoxide, which is an odorless, colorless toxic gas are many. When carbon monoxide is inhaled into the lungs and passed into the blood stream, oxygen is replaced by the carbon monoxide in the red blood cells, causing a reduction in the amount of oxygen being supplied to the many parts of the body. This lack of oxygen causes headaches, lack of coordination, reduced mental alertness and should the carbon monoxide concentration be high enough, death could result.

NITROGEN

Normally, nitrogen is an inert gas. When heated to approximately 2500°F (1371°C) through the combustion process, this gas becomes active and causes an increase in the nitric oxide (NOx) emission.

Oxides of nitrogen (NOx) are composed of approximately 97–98% nitric oxide (NO2). Nitric oxide is a colorless gas but when it is passed into the atmosphere, it combines with oxygen and forms nitrogen dioxide (NO2). The nitrogen dioxide then combines with chemically active hydrocarbons (HC) and when in the presence of sunlight, causes the formation of photo chemical smog.

OZONE

To further complicate matters, some of the nitrogen dioxide (NO_2) is broken apart by the sunlight to form nitric oxide and oxygen. (NO_2 + sunlight = NO + O). This single atom of oxygen then combines with diatomic (meaning 2 atoms) oxygen (O_2) to form ozone (O_3). Ozone is 1 of the smells associated with smog. It has a pungent and offensive odor, irritates the eyes and lung tissues, affects the growth of plant life and causes rapid deterioration of rubber products. Ozone can be formed by sunlight as well as electrical discharge into the air.

The most common discharge area on the automobile engine is the secondary ignition electrical system, especially when inferior quality spark plug cables are used. As the surge of high voltage is routed through the secondary cable, the circuit builds up an electrical field around the wire, acting upon the oxygen in the surrounding air to form the ozone. The faint glow along the cable with the engine running that may be visible on a dark night, is called the "corona discharge." It is the result of the electrical field passing from a high along the cable, to a low in the surrounding air, which forms the ozone gas. The combination of corona and ozone has been a major cause of cable deterioration. Recently, different types and better quality insulating materials have lengthened the life of the electrical cables.

Although ozone at ground level can be harmful, ozone is beneficial to the earth's inhabitants. By having a concentrated ozone layer called the 'ozonosphere', between 10 and 20 miles (16–32km) up in the atmosphere much of the ultra violet radiation from the sun's rays are absorbed and screened. If this ozone layer were not present, much of the earth's surface would be burned, dried and unfit for human life.

There is much discussion concerning the ozone layer and its density. A feeling exists that this protective layer of ozone is slowly diminishing and corrective action must be directed to this problem. Much experimenting is presently being conducted to determine if a problem exists and if so, the short and long term effects of the problem and how it can be remedied.

OXIDES OF SULFUR

Oxides of sulfur (SOx) were initially ignored in the exhaust system emissions, since the sulfur content of gasoline as a fuel is less than $\frac{1}{10}$ of 1%. Because of this small amount, it was felt that it contributed very little to the overall pollution problem. However, because of the difficulty in solving the sulfur emissions in industrial pollutions and the introduction of catalytic converter to the automobile exhaust systems, a change was mandated. The automobile exhaust system, when equipped with a catalytic converter, changes the sulfur dioxide (SO_2) into the sulfur trioxide (SO_3).

When this combines with water vapors (H_2O), a sulfuric acid mist (H_2SO_4) is formed and is a very difficult pollutant to handle and is extremely corrosive. This sulfuric acid mist that is formed, is the same mist that rises from the vents of an automobile storage battery when an active chemical reaction takes place within the battery cells.

When a large concentration of vehicles equipped with catalytic converters are operating in an area, this acid mist will rise and be distributed over a large ground area causing land, plant, crop, paints and building damage.

PARTICULATE MATTER

A certain amount of particulate matter is present in the burning of any fuel, with carbon constituting the largest percentage of the particulates. In gasoline, the remaining percentage of particulates is the burned remains of the various other compounds used in its manufacture. When a gasoline engine is in good internal condition, the particulate emissions are low but as the engine wears internally, the particulate emissions increase. By visually inspecting the tail pipe emissions, a determination can be made as to where an engine defect may exist. An engine with light gray smoke emitting from the tail pipe normally indicates an increase in the oil consumption through burning due to internal engine wear. Black smoke would indicate a defective fuel delivery system, causing the engine to operate in a rich mode. Regardless of the color of the smoke, the internal part of the engine or the fuel delivery system should be repaired to a "like new" condition to prevent excess particulate emissions.

Diesel and turbine engines emit a darkened plume of smoke from the exhaust system because of the type of fuel used. Emission control regulations are mandated for this type of emission and more stringent measures are being used to prevent excess emission of the particulate matter. Electronic components are being introduced to control the injection of the fuel at precisely the proper time of piston travel, to achieve the optimum in fuel ignition and fuel usage. Other particulate after-burning components are being tested to achieve a cleaner particular emission.

Good grades of engine lubricating oils should be used, meeting the manufacturers specification. "Cut-rate" oils can contribute to the particulate emission problem because of their low "flash" or ignition temperature point. Such oils burn prematurely during the combustion process causing emissions of particulate matter.

The cooling system is an important factor in the reduction of particulate matter. With the cooling system operating at a temperature specified by the manufacturer, the optimum of combustion will occur. The cooling system must be maintained in the same manner as the engine oiling system, as each system is required to perform properly in order for the engine to operate efficiently for a long time.

Other Automobile Emission Sources

Before emission controls were mandated on the internal combustion engines, other sources of engine pollutants were discovered, along with the exhaust emission. It was determined the engine combustion exhaust produced 60% of the total emission pollutants, fuel evaporation from the fuel tank and carburetor vents produced 20%, with the another 20% being produced through the crankcase as a by-product of the combustion process.

CRANKCASE EMISSIONS

Crankcase emissions are made up of water, acids, unburned fuel, oil fumes and particulates. The emissions are classified as hydrocarbons (HC) and are formed by the small amount of unburned, compressed air/fuel mixture entering the crankcase from the combustion area during the compression and power strokes, between the cylinder walls and piston rings. The head of the compression and combustion help to form the remaining crankcase emissions.

Since the first engines, crankcase emissions were allowed to go into the air through a road draft tube, mounted on the lower side of the engine block. Fresh air came in through an open oil filler cap or breather. The air passed through the crankcase mixing with blow-by gases. The motion of the vehicle and the air blowing past the open end of the road draft tube caused a low pressure area at the end of the tube. Crankcase emissions were simply drawn out of the road draft tube into the air.

To control the crankcase emission, the road draft tube was deleted. A hose and/or tubing was routed from the crankcase to the intake manifold so the blow-by emission could be burned with the air/fuel mixture. However, it was found that intake manifold vacuum, used to draw the crankcase emissions into the manifold, would vary in strength at the wrong time and not allow the proper emission flow. A regulating type valve was needed to control the flow of air through the crankcase.

Testing, showed the removal of the blow-by gases from the crankcase as quickly as possible, was most important to the longevity of the engine. Should large accumulations of blow-by gases remain and condense, dilution of the engine oil would occur to form water, soots, resins, acids and lead salts, resulting in the formation of sludge and varnishes. This condensation of the blow-by gases occur more frequently on vehicles used in numerous starting and stopping conditions, excessive idling and when the engine is not allowed to attain normal operating temperature through short runs. The crankcase purge control or PCV system will be described in detail later in this section.

FUEL EVAPORATIVE EMISSIONS

Gasoline fuel is a major source of pollution, before and after it is burned in the automobile engine. From the time the fuel is refined, stored, pumped and transported, again stored until it is pumped into the fuel tank of the vehicle, the gasoline gives off unburned hydrocarbons (HC) into the atmosphere. Through redesigning of the storage areas and venting systems, the pollution factor has been diminished but not eliminated, from the refinery standpoint. However, the automobile still remained the primary source of vaporized, unburned hydrocarbon (HC) emissions.

Fuel pumped form an underground storage tank is cool but when exposed to a warner ambient temperature, will expand. Before controls were mandated, an owner would fill the fuel tank with fuel from an underground storage tank and park the vehicle for some time in warm area, such as a parking lot. As the fuel would warm, it would expand and should no provisions or area be provided for the expansion, the fuel would spill out the filler neck and onto the ground, causing hydrocarbon (HC) pollution and creating a severe fire hazard. To correct this condition, the vehicle manufacturers added overflow plumbing and/or gasoline tanks with built in expansion areas or domes.

However, this did not control the fuel vapor emission from the fuel tank and the carburetor bowl. It was determined that most of the fuel evaporation occurred when the vehicle was stationary and the engine not operating. Most vehicles carry 5–25 gallons (19–95 liters) of gasoline. Should a large concentration of vehicles be parked in one area, such as a large parking lot, excessive fuel vapor emissions would take place, increasing as the temperature increases.

To prevent the vapor emission from escaping into the atmosphere, the fuel system is designed to trap the fuel vapors while the vehicle is stationary, by sealing the fuel system from the atmosphere. A storage system is used to collect and hold the fuel vapors from the carburetor and the fuel tank when the engine is not operating. When the engine is started, the storage system is then purged of the fuel vapors, which are drawn into the engine and burned with the air/fuel mixture.

The components of the fuel evaporative system will be described in detail later in this section.

EMISSION CONTROL SYSTEMS

There are three types of automotive pollutants: crankcase fumes, exhaust gases and gasoline evaporation. The equipment that is used to limit these pollutants is commonly called emission control equipment.

Crankcase Ventilation System

➧ SEE FIGS. 1–3

The crankcase emission control equipment consists of a positive crankcase ventilation valve (PCV), an oil filler cap (sealed) and hoses (connected to the equipment). The CA16DE, CA18DE and SR20DE engines use an external oil separator (in the PCV line) to keep excess oil in the crankcase, away from the PCV valve.

OPERATION

When the engine is running, a small portion of the gases which are formed in the combustion chamber during combustion, leak by the piston rings and enter the crankcase. Since these gases are under pressure they tend to escape from the crankcase and enter into the atmosphere. If these gases were allowed to remain in the crankcase for any length of time, they would contaminate the engine oil and cause sludge to build up. If the gases are allowed to escape into the atmosphere, they would pollute the air, for they contain unburned hydrocarbons. The crankcase emission control equipment recycles these gases back into the engine combustion chamber where they are burned.

Crankcase gases are recycled in the following manner: when the engine is running, clean filtered air (from the carburetor air filter) is drawn into the crankcase or the rocker cover, through a hose. As the air passes through the crankcase it mixes with combustion gases, then carries them (out of the crankcase) through the PCV valve and into the intake manifold. After they enter the intake manifold they are drawn into the combustion chamber and burned.

The most critical component in the system is the PCV valve. This vacuum controlled valve regulates the amount of gases which are recycled into the combustion chamber. At low engine speeds, the valve is partially closed, limiting the flow of gases into the intake manifold. At increased engine speeds, the valve opens to admit greater quantities of the gases

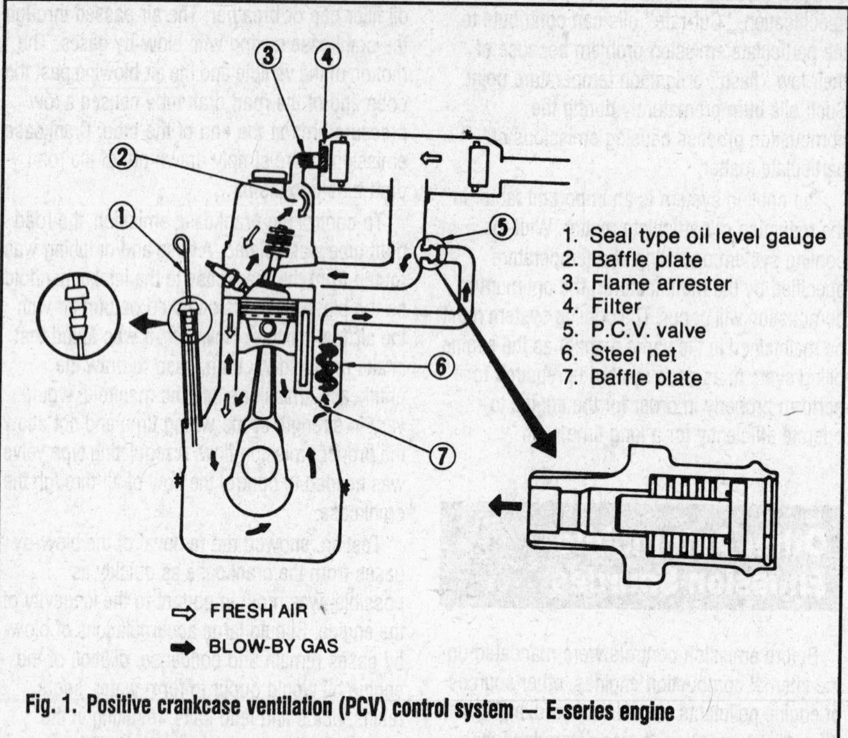
1. Seal type oil level gauge
2. Baffle plate
3. Flame arrester
4. Filter
5. P.C.V. valve
6. Steel net
7. Baffle plate
FRESH AIR
BLOW-BY GAS

Fig. 1. Positive crankcase ventilation (PCV) control system — E-series engine

into the intake manifold. If the valve should become blocked or plugged, the gases will be prevented from escaping from the crankcase by the normal route. Since these gases are under pressure, they will find their own way out of the crankcase. This alternate route is usually a weak oil seal or gasket in the engine. As the gas escapes by the gasket, it also creates an oil leak. Besides causing oil leaks, a clogged PCV valve also allows these gases to remain in the crankcase for an extended period of time, promoting the formation of sludge in the engine.

TESTING AND SERVICE

To check the PCV system, inspect the PCV valve, the air filter(s), the hoses, the connections and the oil separator (SR20DE, CA16DE and CA18DE engines); check for leaks, plugged valve(s) and/or filters, then replace or tighten, as necessary.

To check the PCV valve, remove it and blow through both of its ends. When blowing from the intake manifold side, very little air should pass through it. When blowing from the crankcase or valve cover side, air should pass through freely.

➡ If the valve fails to function as outlined, replace it with a new one; DO NOT attempt to clean or adjust it.

To check the hoses, use compressed air to free them or replace them. If the air filters are dirty, replace them.

REMOVAL & INSTALLATION

PCV Valve

To remove the PCV valve, simply loosen the hose clamp and remove the valve from the manifold-to-crankcase hose. Then, unscrew it from the intake manifold. Install the PCV valve in the reverse order of removal. Tighten the valve gently—it will seal completely with a slight amount of torque.

PCV Filter

Replace the PCV filter inside the air cleaner when you replace the PCV valve, or more frequently if operating in dusty or smoggy conditions.

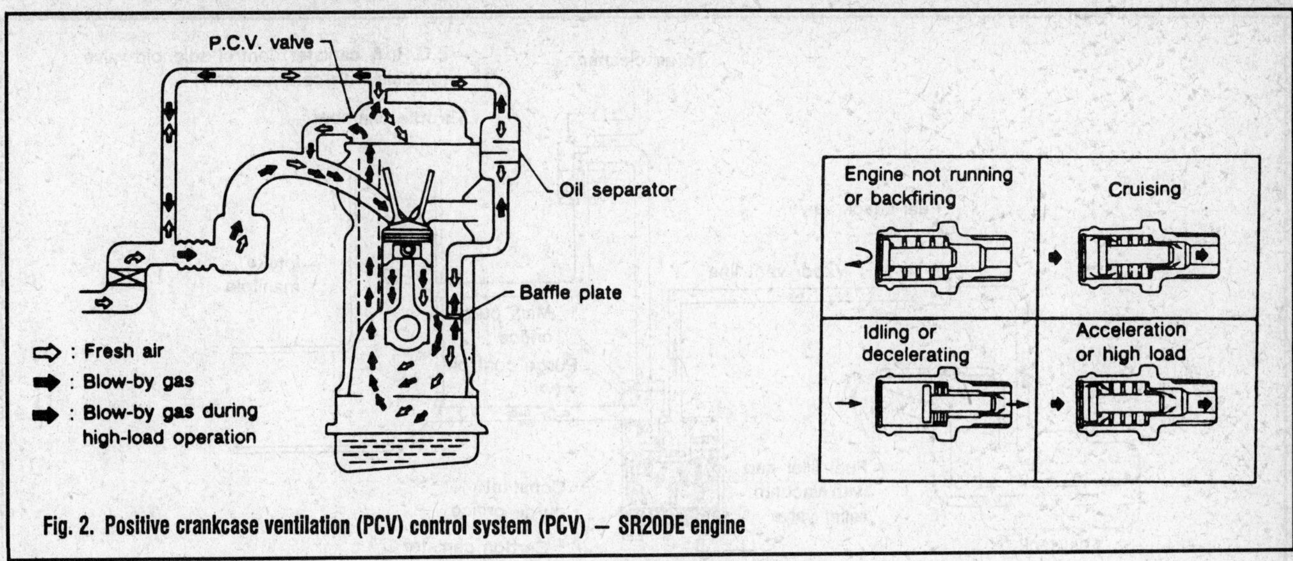
P.C.V. valve
Oil separator
Baffle plate
: Fresh air
: Blow-by gas
: Blow-by gas during high-load operation
Engine not running or backfiring
Cruising
Idling or decelerating
Acceleration or high load

Fig. 2. Positive crankcase ventilation (PCV) control system (PCV) – SR20DE engine

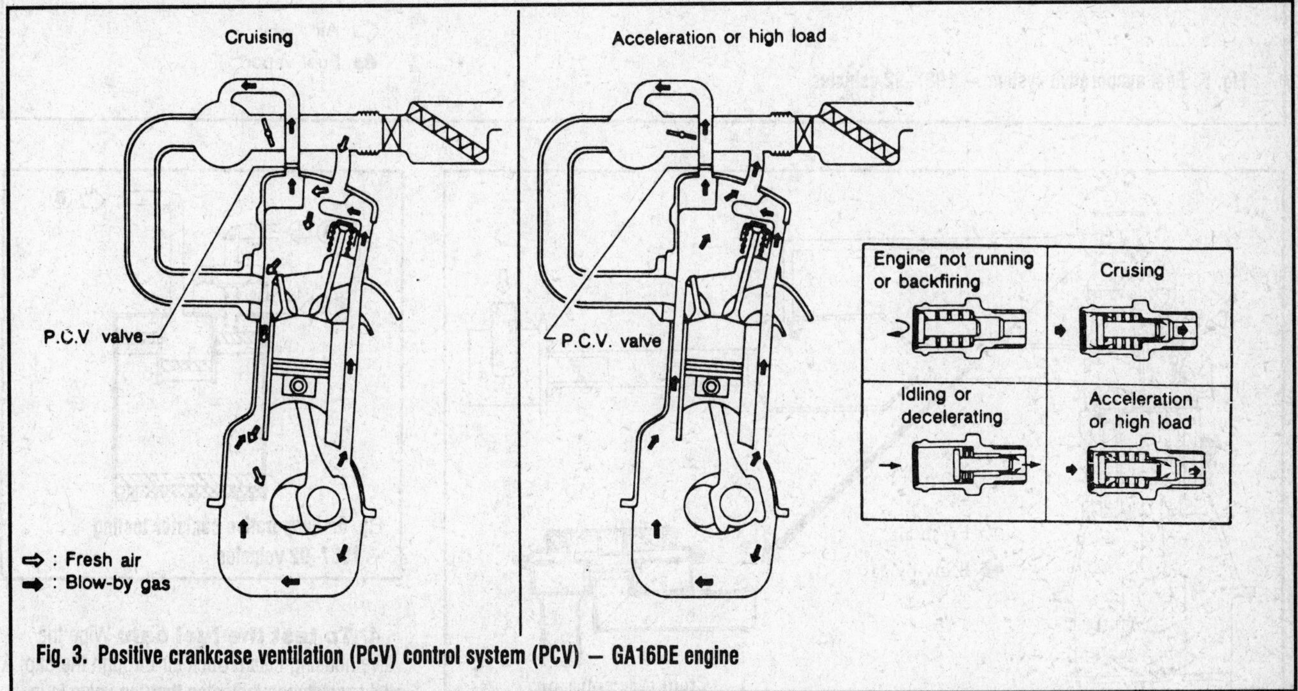
Cruising
Acceleration or high load
P.C.V valve
P.C.V. valve
: Fresh air
: Blow-by gas
Engine not running or backfiring
Crusing
Idling or decelerating
Acceleration or high load

Fig. 3. Positive crankcase ventilation (PCV) control system (PCV) – GA16DE engine

Evaporative Emission Controls

The system consists of sealed fuel tank, vapor/liquid separator (certain models only), vapor vent line, carbon canister, vacuum signal line, a canister purge line and a float bowl vent line (E-series, 1982 and later).

OPERATION

In operation, fuel vapors and/or liquid are routed to the liquid/vapor separator or check valve, where liquid fuel is directed back into the fuel tank as fuel vapors flow into the charcoal filled canister. The charcoal absorbs and stores the fuel vapors when the engine is not running or at idle. When the throttle valves are opened, vacuum from above the throttle valves is routed through a vacuum signal line to the purge control valve on the canister. The control valve opens, the fuel vapors move from the canister through a purge line, into the intake manifold and the combustion chambers.

INSPECTION AND SERVICE

Check the hoses for proper connections and damage. Replace as necessary. Check the vapor separator tank for fuel leaks, distortion and dents, then replace as necessary.

Carbon Canister and Purge Control Valve

1982–86

To check the operation of the carbon canister purge control valve, disconnect the rubber hose between the canister control valve and the T-fitting, at the T-fitting. Apply vacuum to the hose

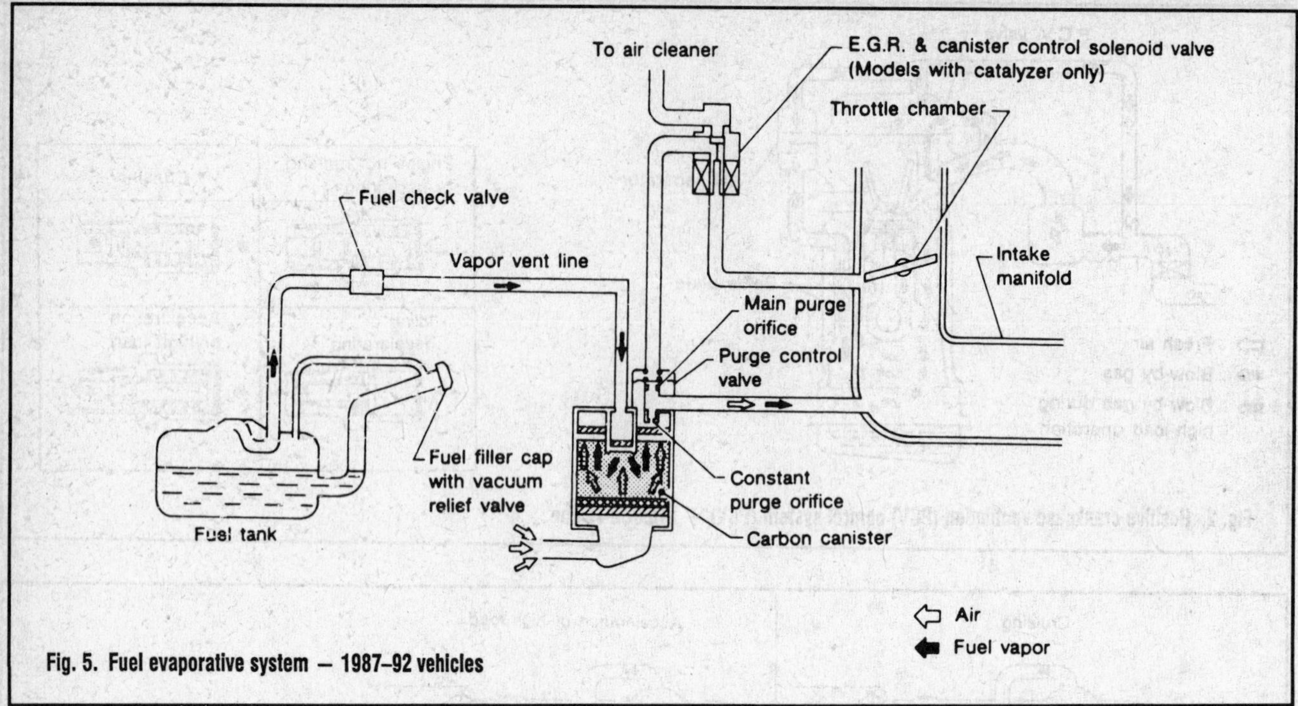
To air cleaner
E.G.R. & canister control solenoid valve (Models with catalyzer only)
Throttle chamber
Fuel check valve
Vapor vent line
Intake manifold
Main purge orifice
Purge control valve
Fuel filler cap with vacuum relief valve
Constant purge orifice
Fuel tank
Carbon canister
Air
Fuel vapor
Fig. 5. Fuel evaporative system — 1987–92 vehicles

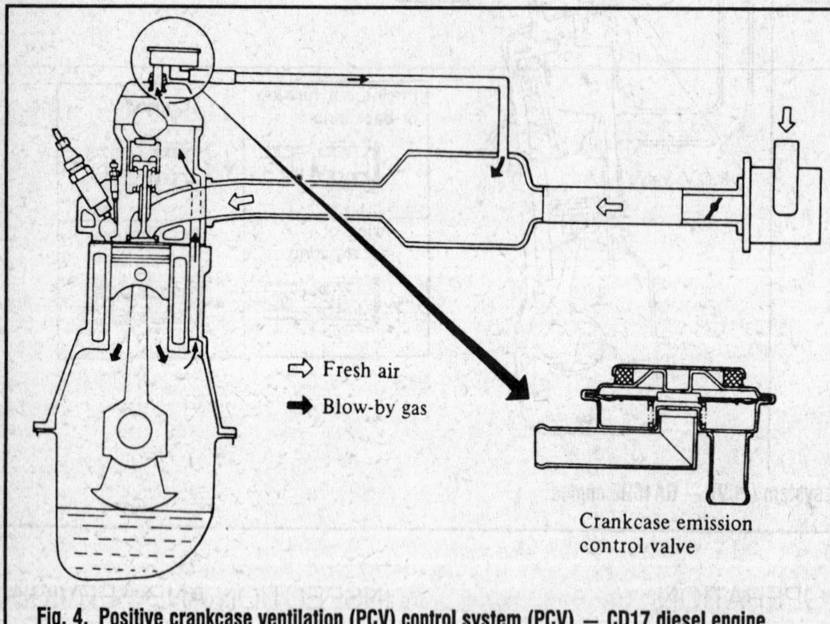
Fresh air
Blow-by gas
Crankcase emission control valve
Fig. 4. Positive crankcase ventilation (PCV) control system (PCV) — CD17 diesel engine

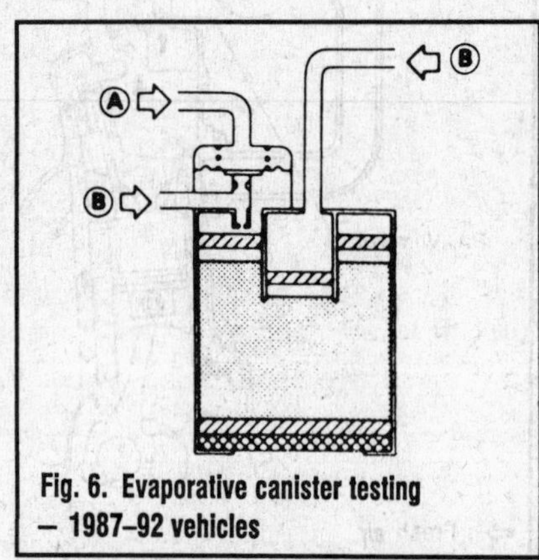
B
A
B
Fig. 6. Evaporative canister testing — 1987–92 vehicles

leading to the control valve. The vacuum condition should be maintained indefinitely. If the control valve leaks, remove the top cover of the valve and check for a dislocated or cracked diaphragm. If the diaphragm is damaged, a repair kit containing a new diaphragm, retainer and spring is available, replace it.

The carbon canister has an air filter in the bottom of the canister. The filter element should be checked once a year or every 12,000 miles; more frequently if the car is operated in dusty areas. Replace the filter by pulling it out of the bottom of the canister and installing a new one.

1987–92

1. **To test the canister:** Disconnect the canister and remove if necessary.

2. Blow air into port **A** and ensure that there is no leakage.

3. Blow air into ports **B** and ensure that there is leakage.

4. **To test the fuel cap:** Wipe the valve housing clean. Suck air through the cap. A slight resistance indicates that the valve is in good condition. Resistance should disappear when the valve clicks. If the valve is clogged or if no resistance is felt, replace the fuel cap.

5. **To check the fuel check valve:** Blow air through the connector on the tank side. A considerable resistance should be felt and a portion of air flow should be directed toward the canister.

6. Blow air through the connector on the canister side. Air flow should be smoothly directed toward the fuel tank.

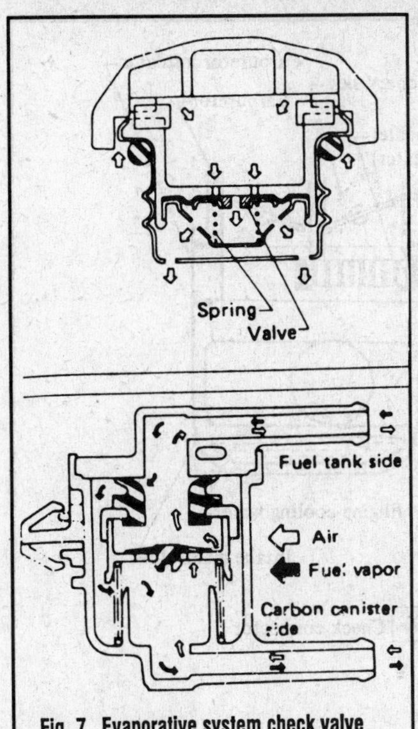
Spring
Valve
Fuel tank side
Air
Fuel vapor
Carbon canister side

Fig. 7. Evaporative system check valve and fuel cap check

REMOVAL & INSTALLATION

Removal and installation of the various evaporative emission control system components consists of disconnecting the hoses, loosening retaining screws and removing the part which is to be replaced or checked. Install in the reverse order. When replacing hose, make sure that it is fuel and vapor resistant.

Fuel Mixture Heating System

The system's purpose is to heat the air/fuel mixture when the engine is below normal operating temperature. E-series use an electric grid style heater under the carburetor or throttle body.

When the engine starts, the heater energizes and the air/fuel mixture is heated as it passes through the heater grid. When engine warm-up is complete, the current is cut off by the ECU or mixture heater relay.

INSPECTION

1982–86 E-series with Carburetor

1. Check the continuity between the heater terminals. If the resistance if too high, replace the carburetor insulator.

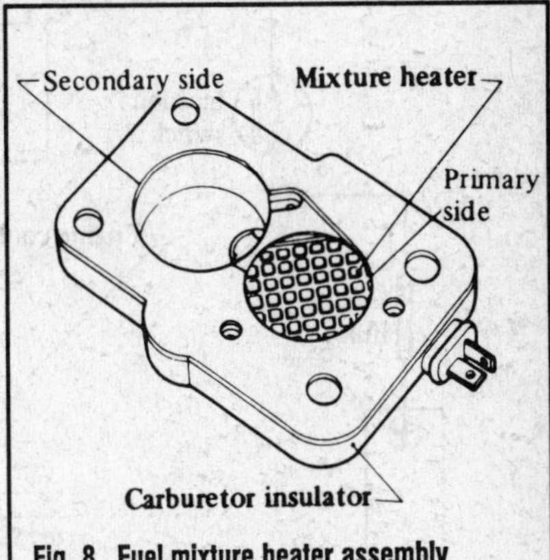
Secondary side
Mixture heater
Primary side
Carburetor insulator

Fig. 8. Fuel mixture heater assembly – carbureted engines

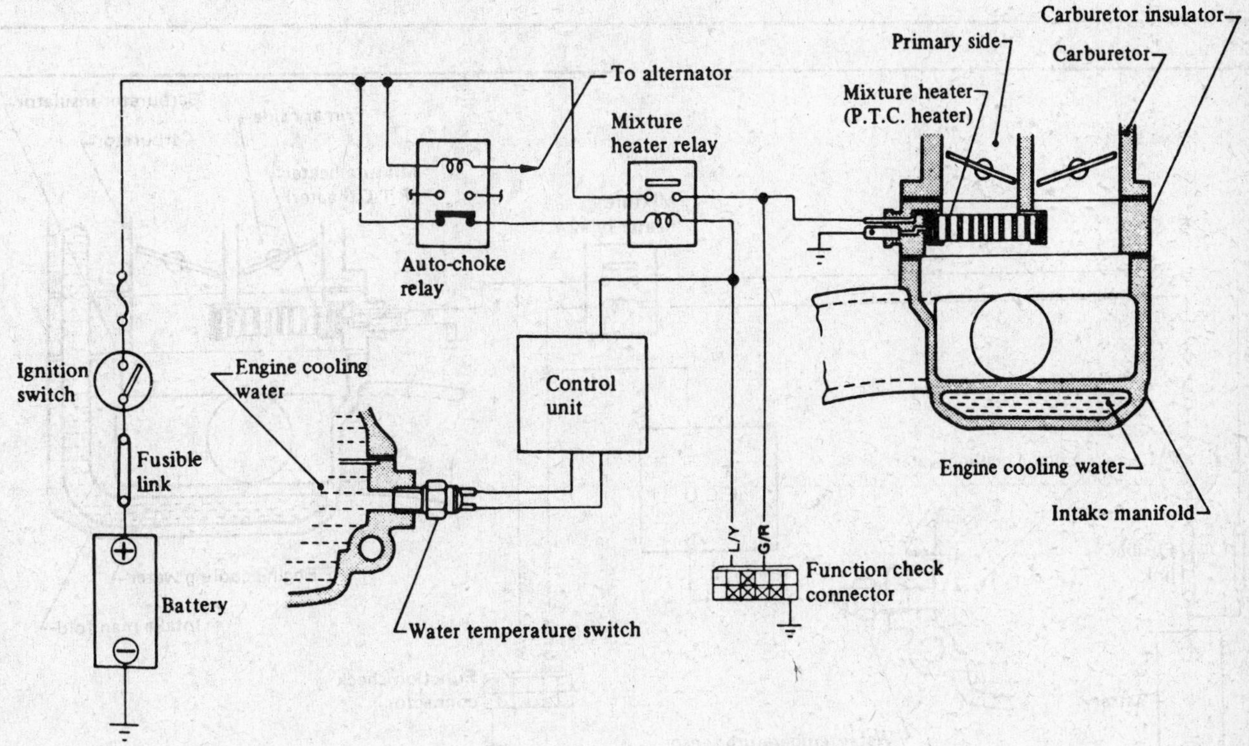

To alternator
Mixture heater relay
Auto-choke relay
Carburetor insulator
Primary side
Carburetor
Mixture heater (P.T.C. heater)
Ignition switch
Engine cooling water
Control unit
Fusible link
Battery
Water temperature switch
L/Y
G/R
Function check connector
Engine cooling water
Intake manifold

Fig. 10. Fuel mixture heater system – 1982–85 Sentra (Calif.)

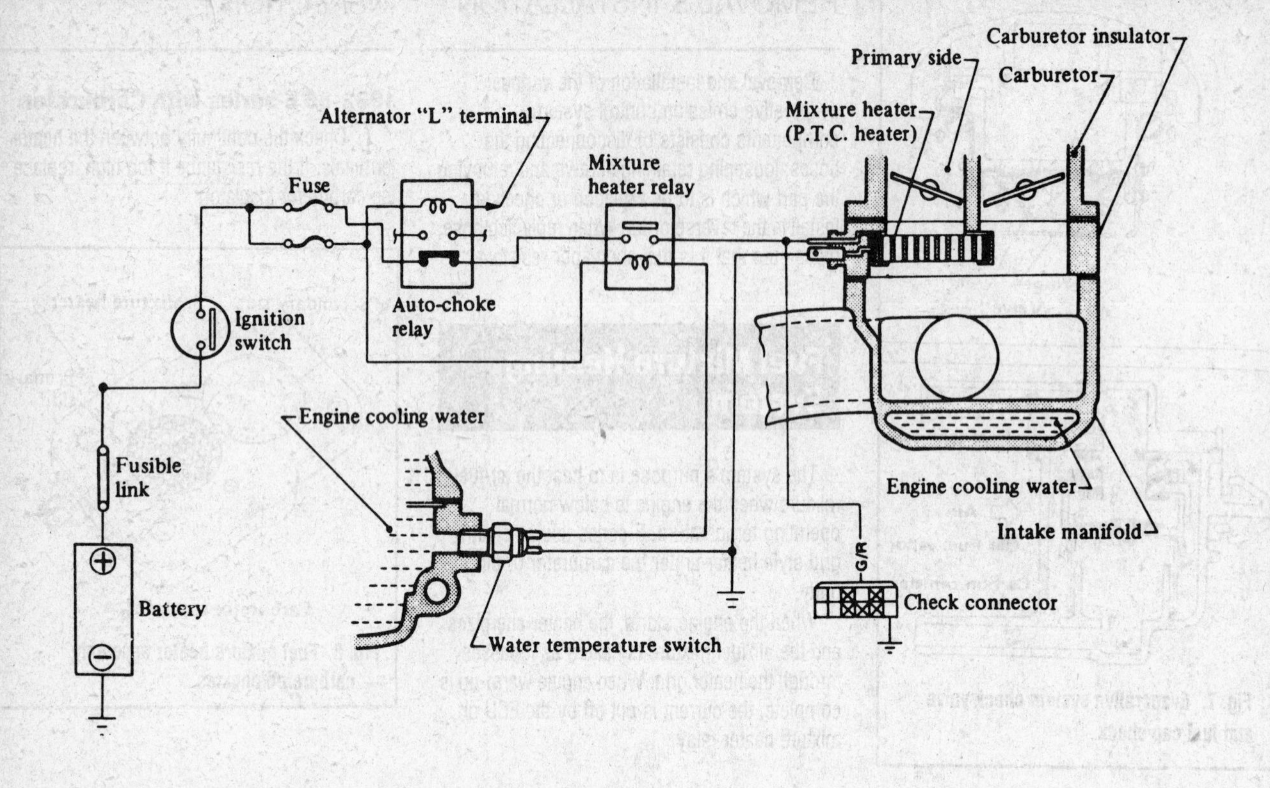

Carburetor insulator
Primary side
Carburetor
Mixture heater
(P.T.C. heater)
Alternator "L" terminal
Mixture
heater relay
Fuse
Auto-choke
relay
Ignition
switch
Engine cooling water
Fusible
link
Battery
G/R
Check connector
Water temperature switch
Engine cooling water
Intake manifold

Fig. 10a. Fuel mixture heater system – 1982–85 Sentra (US and Canada)

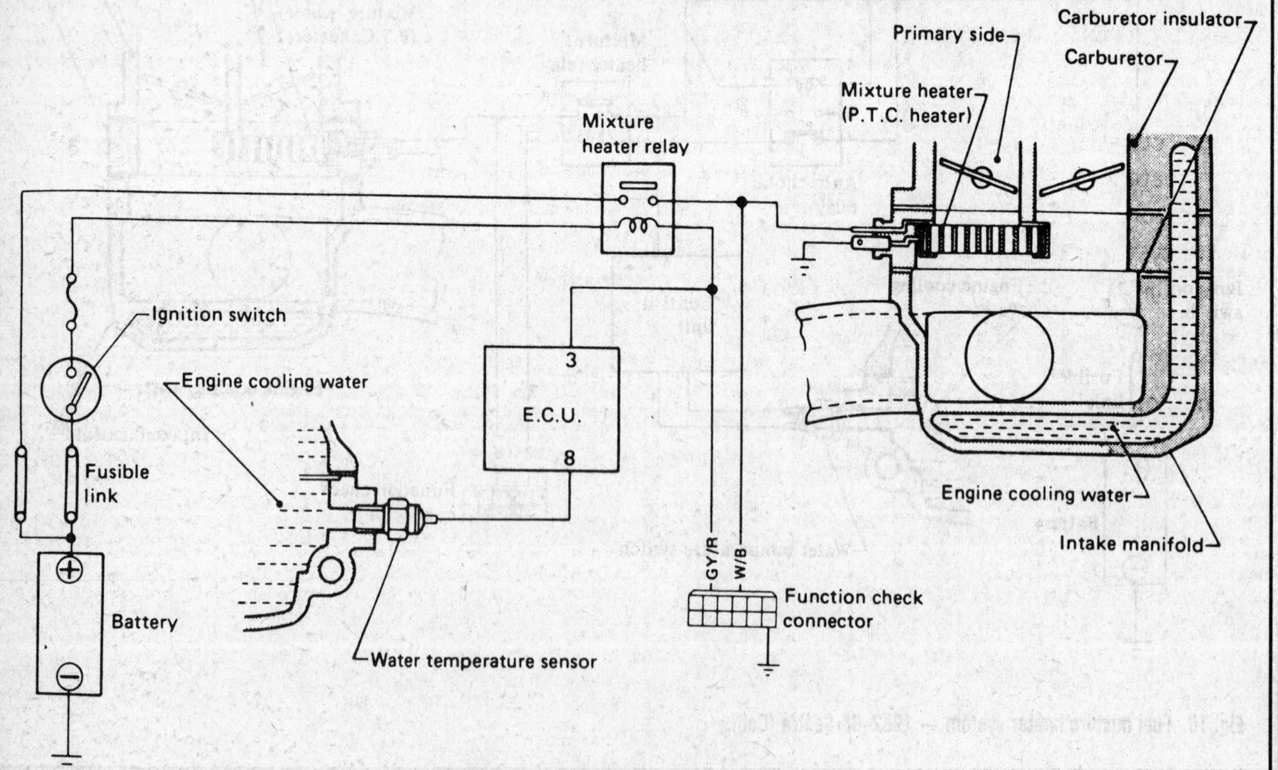

Carburetor insulator
Primary side
Carburetor
Mixture heater
(P.T.C. heater)
Mixture
heater relay
Ignition switch
Engine cooling water
3
E.C.U.
8
Fusible
link
Battery
GY/R
W/B
Function check
connector
Water temperature sensor
Engine cooling water
Intake manifold

Fig. 11. Fuel mixture heater system – 1986 E16S engine

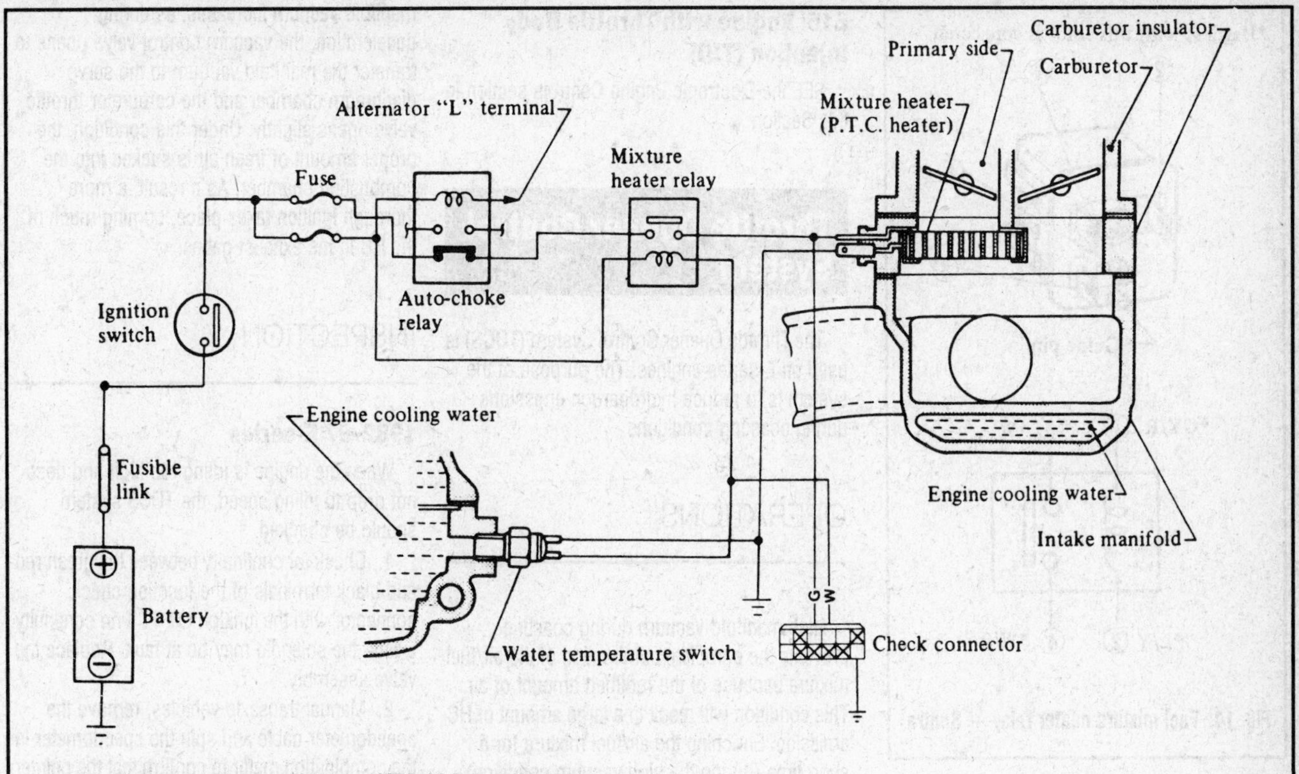

Carburetor insulator
Primary side
Carburetor
Alternator "L" terminal
Mixture heater
(P.T.C. heater)
Mixture
heater relay
Fuse
Auto-choke
relay
Ignition
switch
Engine cooling water
Fusible
link
Battery
Water temperature switch
Check connector
Engine cooling water
Intake manifold

Fig. 12. Fuel mixture heater system — 1983–86 Pulsar (Canada)

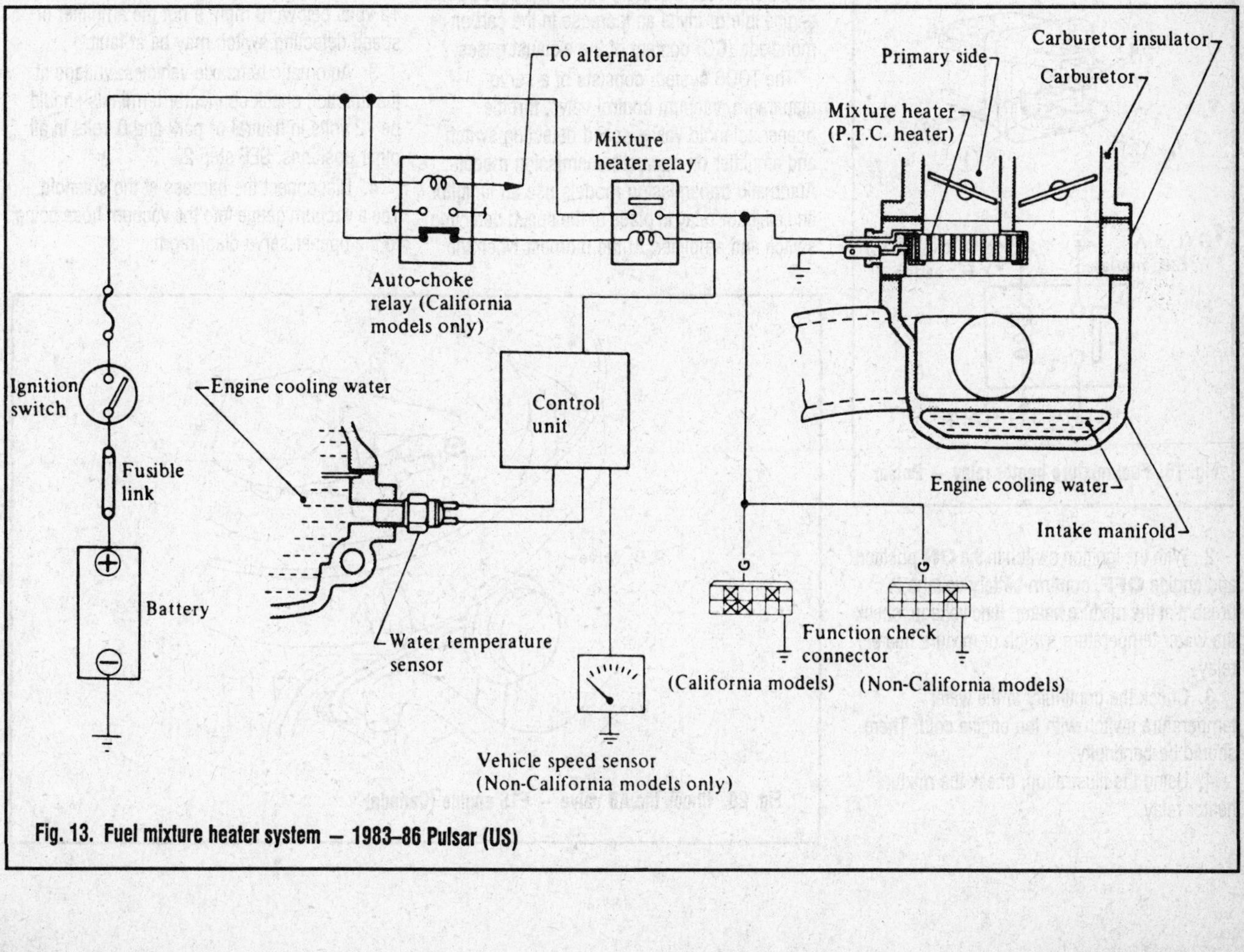

To alternator
Carburetor insulator
Primary side
Carburetor
Mixture heater
(P.T.C. heater)
Mixture
heater relay
Auto-choke
relay (California
models only)
Control
unit
Ignition
switch
Engine cooling water
Fusible
link
Battery
Water temperature
sensor
Function check
connector
(California models)
(Non-California models)
Engine cooling water
Intake manifold
Vehicle speed sensor
(Non-California models only)

Fig. 13. Fuel mixture heater system — 1983–86 Pulsar (US)

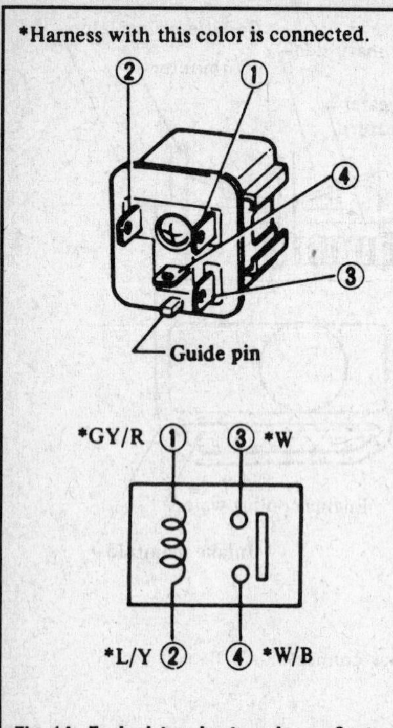
*Harness with this color is connected.
Guide pin
*GY/R ① ③ *W
*L/Y ② ④ *W/B

Fig. 14. Fuel mixture heater relay — Sentra

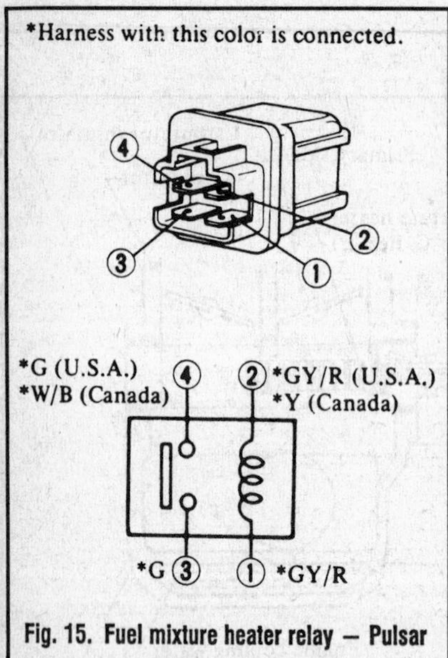
*Harness with this color is connected.
*G (U.S.A.)
*W/B (Canada)
*GY/R (U.S.A.)
*Y (Canada)
*G ③ ① *GY/R

Fig. 15. Fuel mixture heater relay — Pulsar

2. With the ignition switch in the **ON** position and engine **OFF**, confirm battery voltage is present at the mixture heater. If no voltage, check the water temperature switch or mixture heater relay.

3. Check the continuity at the water temperature switch with the engine cold. There should be continuity.

4. Using the illustration, check the mixture heater relay.

E16i Engine with Throttle Body Injection (TBI)

SEE the Electronic Engine Controls section in this Section.

Throttle Opener Control System

The Throttle Opener Control System (TOCS) is used on E-series engines. The purpose of the system is to reduce hydrocarbon emissions during coasting conditions.

OPERATIONS

High manifold vacuum during coasting prevents the complete combustion of the air/fuel mixture because of the reduced amount of air. This condition will result in a large amount of HC emission. Enriching the air/fuel mixture for a short time (during the high vacuum condition) will reduce the emission of the HC.

However, enriching the air/fuel mixture with only the mixture adjusting screw will cause poor engine idle or invite an increase in the carbon monoxide (CO) content of the exhaust gases.

The TOCS system consists of a servo diaphragm, vacuum control valve, throttle opener solenoid valve, speed detecting switch and amplifier on manual transmission models. Automatic transmission models use an inhibitor and inhibitor relay in place of the speed detecting switch and amplifier. At the moment when the manifold vacuum increases, as during deceleration, the vacuum control valve opens to transfer the manifold vacuum to the servo diaphragm chamber and the carburetor throttle valve opens slightly. Under this condition, the proper amount of fresh air is sucked into the combustion chamber. As a result, a more thorough ignition takes place, burning much of the HC in the exhaust gases.

INSPECTION

1982–87 E-series

When the engine is idling too high and does not drop to idling speed, the TOCS system should be checked.

1. Check for continuity between the green/red and black terminals of the function check connector with the ignition **OFF**. If no continuity exists, the solenoid may be at fault. Replace the valve assembly.

2. Manual transaxle vehicles: remove the speedometer cable and spin the speedometer in the combination meter to confirm that the pointer indicates more than 10 mph. The voltage at the function check connector green/red and black terminals should read 0 volts above 10 mph and 12 volts below 10 mph. If not the amplifier or speed detecting switch may be at fault.

3. Automatic transaxle vehicles: voltage at the function check connector terminals should be 12 volts in neutral or park and 0 volts in all other positions. SEE step 2.

4. Disconnect the harness at the solenoid. Tee a vacuum gauge into the vacuum hose going to the opener servo diaphragm.

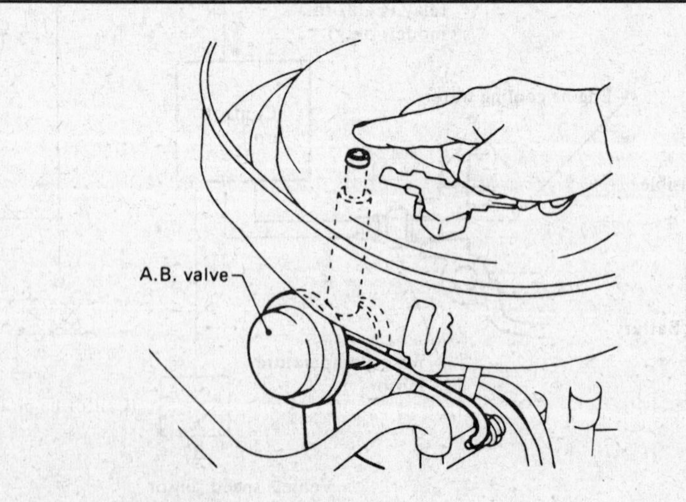
A.B. valve

Fig. 20. Check the AB valve — E16 engine (Canada)

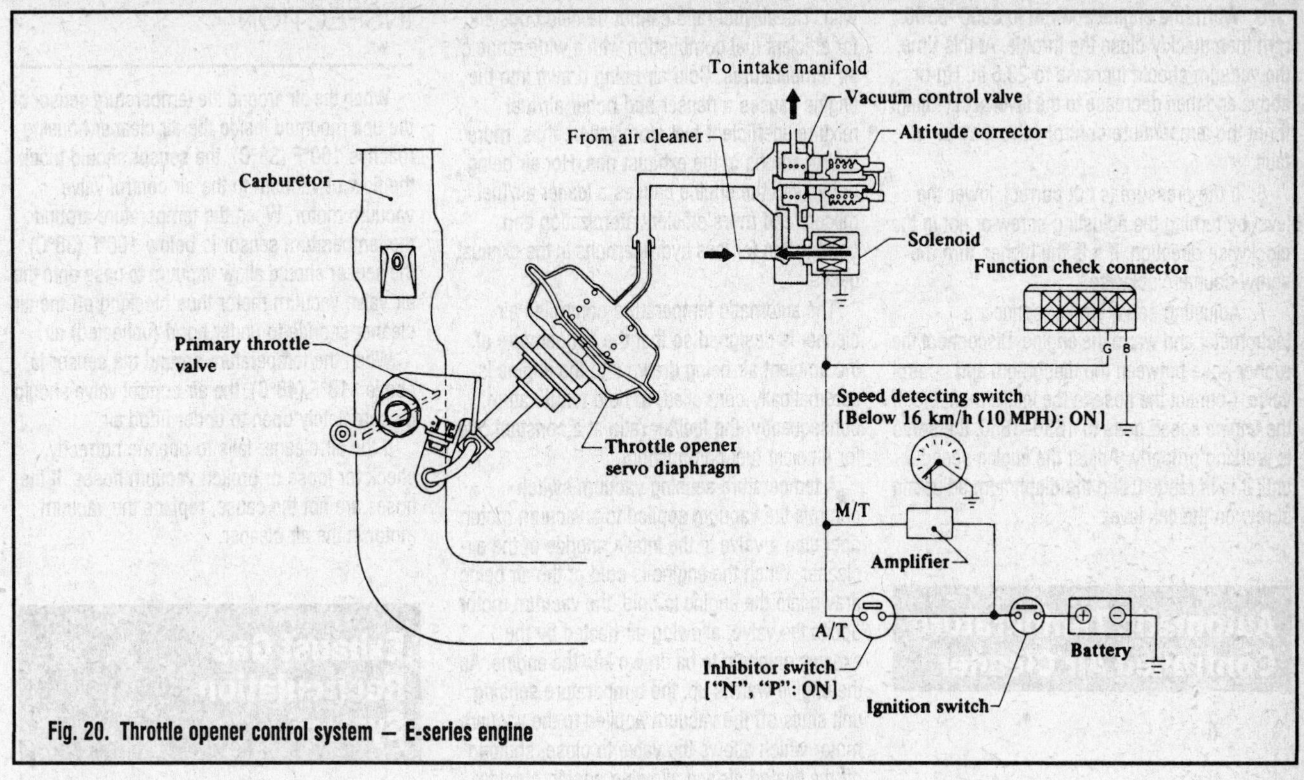
To intake manifold
Vacuum control valve
From air cleaner
Altitude corrector
Carburetor
Solenoid
Function check connector
G B
Primary throttle valve
Speed detecting switch
[Below 16 km/h (10 MPH): ON]
Throttle opener servo diaphragm
M/T
Amplifier
A/T
Battery
Inhibitor switch
["N", "P": ON]
Ignition switch

Fig. 20. Throttle opener control system — E-series engine

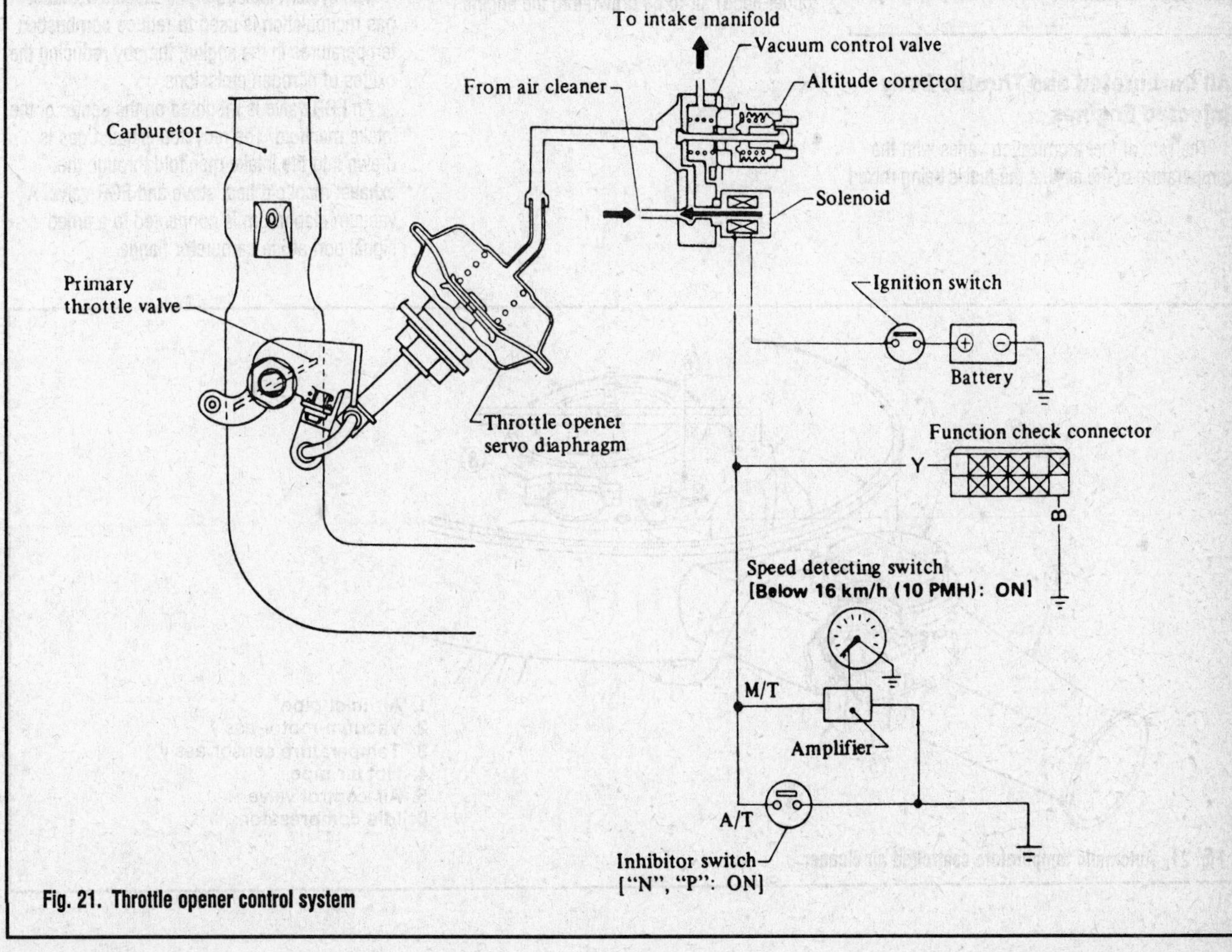

To intake manifold
Vacuum control valve
From air cleaner
Altitude corrector
Carburetor
Solenoid
Ignition switch
Primary throttle valve
Battery
Throttle opener servo diaphragm
Function check connector
Y
B
Speed detecting switch
[Below 16 km/h (10 PMH): ON]
M/T
Amplifier
A/T
Inhibitor switch
["N", "P": ON]

Fig. 21. Throttle opener control system

5. Warm the engine and run to 3000–3500 rpm then quickly close the throttle. At this time, the vacuum should increase to 23.6 in. Hg or above and then decrease to the level set at idling. If not the temperature control valve may be at fault.

6. If the pressure is not correct, lower the level by turning the adjusting screw or not in the clockwise direction. If it is the higher, turn the screw counterclockwise.

7. Adjusting servo stroke: connect a tachometer and warm the engine. Disconnect the rubber hose between the diaphragm and control valve. Connect the hose to the intake manifold. If the engine speed goes to 1650–1850, the servo is working properly. Adjust the engine speed until it is in range using the diaphragm adjusting screw on the link lever.

Automatic Temperature Controlled Air Cleaner

OPERATION

All Carbureted and Throttle Body Injected Engines

The rate of fuel atomization varies with the temperature of the air that the fuel is being mixed with. The air/fuel ratio cannot be held constant for efficient fuel combustion with a wide range of air temperatures. Cold air being drawn into the engine causes a denser and richer air/fuel mixture, inefficient fuel atomization, thus, more hydrocarbons in the exhaust gas. Hot air being drawn into the engine causes a leaner air/fuel mixture and more efficient atomization and combustion for less hydrocarbons in the exhaust gases.

The automatic temperature controlled air cleaner is designed so that the temperature of the ambient air being drawn into the engine is automatically controlled, to hold temperature, consequently, the fuel/air ratio at a constant rate for efficient fuel combustion.

A temperature sensing vacuum switch controls the vacuum applied to a vacuum motor, operating a valve in the intake snorkle of the air cleaner. When the engine is cold or the air being drawn into the engine is cold, the vacuum motor opens the valve, allowing air heated by the exhaust manifold to be drawn into the engine. As the engine warms up, the temperature sensing unit shuts off the vacuum applied to the vacuum motor which allows the valve to close, shutting off the heated air and allowing cooler, outside (under hood) air to be drawn into the engine.

INSPECTION

When the air around the temperature sensor of the unit mounted inside the air cleaner housing reaches 100°F (38°C), the sensor should block the flow of vacuum to the air control valve vacuum motor. When the temperature around the temperature sensor is below 100°F (38°C), the sensor should allow vacuum to pass onto the air valve vacuum motor thus blocking off the air cleaner snorkle to under hood (unheated) air.

When the temperature around the sensor is above 118°F (48°C), the air control valve should be completely open to under hood air.

If the air cleaner fails to operate correctly, check for loose or broken vacuum hoses. If the hoses are not the cause, replace the vacuum motor in the air cleaner.

Exhaust Gas Recirculation System

The system is used on all models. Exhaust gas recirculation is used to reduce combustion temperatures in the engine, thereby reducing the oxides of nitrogen emissions.

An EGR valve is mounted on the center of the intake manifold. The recycled exhaust gas is drawn into the intake manifold through the exhaust manifold heat stove and EGR valve. A vacuum diaphragm is connected to a timed signal port at the carburetor flange.

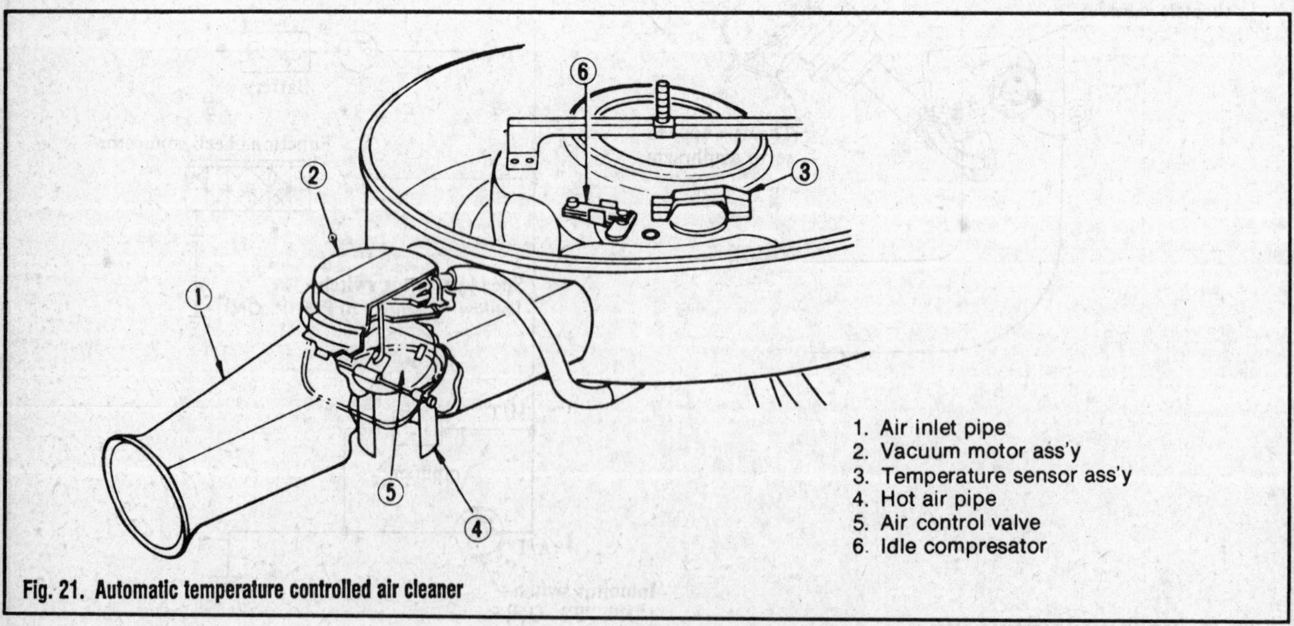
6
2
3
1
5
4
1. Air inlet pipe
2. Vacuum motor ass'y
3. Temperature sensor ass'y
4. Hot air pipe
5. Air control valve
6. Idle compresator

Fig. 21. Automatic temperature controlled air cleaner

OPERATIONS

As the throttle valve is opened, vacuum is applied to the EGR valve vacuum diaphragm. When the vacuum reaches about 2 in.Hg, the diaphragm moves against spring pressure and is in a fully up position at 8 in.Hg of vacuum. As the diaphragm moves up, it opens the exhaust gas metering valve which allows exhaust gas to be pulled into the engine intake manifold. The system does not operate when the engine is idling because the exhaust gas recirculation would cause a rough idle.

A thermal vacuum valve inserted in the engine thermostat housing controls the application of the vacuum to the EGR valve. When the engine coolant reaches a predetermined temperature, the thermal vacuum valve opens and allows vacuum to be routed to the EGR valve. Below the predetermined temperature, the thermal vacuum valve closes and blocks vacuum to the EGR valve.

Some models have a Back Pressure Transducer (BPT) valve installed between the EGR valve and the thermal vacuum valve. The BPT valve has a diaphragm which is raised or lowered by exhaust back pressure. The diaphragm opens or closes an air bleed, which is connected into the EGR vacuum line. High pressure results in higher levels of EGR, because the diaphragm is raised, closing off the air bleed, which allows more vacuum to reach and open the EGR valve. Thus, the amount of recirculated exhaust gas varies with exhaust pressure.

Some models use a Venturi Vacuum Transducer (VVT) valve. The VVT valve monitors exhaust pressure and carburetor vacuum in order to activate the diaphragm which controls the throttle vacuum applied to the EGR control valve. This system expands the operating range of the EGR unit, as well as increasing the EGR flow rate.

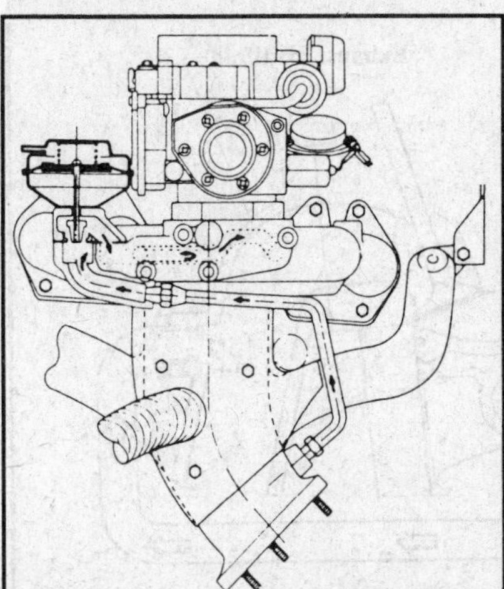

Fig. 22. Exhaust gas recirculation (EGR) system

Many vehicles are equipped with an EGR warning system which signals via a light in the dashboard that the EGR system may need service. The EGR warning light should come on every time the starter is engaged as a test to make sure the bulb is not blown. The system uses a counter which works in conjunction with the odometer and lights the warning signal after the vehicle has traveled a predetermined number of miles.

To reset the counter, which is mounted in the engine compartment, remove the grommet installed in the side of the counter, insert the tip of a small screwdriver into the hole and press down on the knob inside the hole, then reinstall the grommet.

TESTING

1. Remove the EGR valve and apply enough vacuum to the diaphragm to open the valve.
2. The valve should remain open for over 30 seconds after the vacuum is removed.
3. Check the valve for damage, such as warpage, cracks and excessive wear around the valve and seat.
4. Clean the seat with a brush and compressed air, then remove any deposits from around the valve and port (seat).
5. To check the operation of the thermal vacuum valve, remove the valve from the engine and apply vacuum to the valve ports; it should not allow vacuum to pass.
6. Place the valve in a container of water with a thermometer and heat the water. When the temperature of the water reaches 134–145°F (57–63°C), remove the valve and apply vacuum to the ports; the valve should allow vacuum to pass.
7. To test the BPT valve, disconnect the two vacuum hoses from the valve. Plug one of the ports. While applying pressure to the bottom of the valve, apply vacuum to the unplugged port and check for leakage. If any exists, replace the valve.
8. To check the VVT valve, disconnect the top and bottom center hoses and apply a vacuum to the top hose. Check for leaks. If a leak is present, replace the valve.

Mixture Ratio Rich/Lean and EGR Large/Small Exchange System ('82 Calif. Engines)

This system controls the air/fuel mixture ratio and the amount of recirculated exhaust gas (manual transmission models only) in accordance with the engine coolant temperature and car speed. The system consists of a vacuum switching valve, a power valve, a speed detecting switch located in the speedometer, a speed detecting switch amplifier and a water temperature switch.

When the coolant temperature is above 122°F (50°C) and the car is traveling at least 40 mph, the vacuum switching valve is on and acts to lean down the fuel mixture; a small amount of EGR is being burned. When the coolant temperature is above 122°F (50°C) but the vehicle is traveling less than 40 mph, the vacuum switching valve is off and allows the mixture to enrichen; a large amount of EGR is being burned. When coolant temperature is below 122°F (50°C), the vacuum switching valve is always on and acts to lean down the fuel mixture.

TESTING

Warm up the engine and raise the drive wheels off the ground; support the raised end of the vehicle with jack stands and block the wheels still on the ground. Start the engine, shift the transmission into TOP speed and maintain a speedometer speed higher than 50 MPH. Pinch off the vacuum switching valve-to-air cleaner hose, then see if the engine speed decreases and operates erratically. Shift the transmission into 3rd speed and run the vehicle at a speed lower than 30 MPH. Disconnect the vacuum switching valve-to-power valve hose, at the power valve and plug the open end with your finger. The engine should operate erratically. If the expected engine reaction in both of these tests does not happen, check all of the wiring connections and hoses for breaks and/or blockage.

Air Induction (Injection) System

OPERATION

1982–87 Carbureted Engines

➧ SEE FIGS. 23–27

The air induction system is used to send fresh secondary air to the exhaust manifold by utilizing vacuum created by the exhaust pulsation in the manifold. The system consists of a dual or single set of reed valves connected to the air filter housing, with tube(s) leading to the exhaust manifold.

Later model engines with ECU controlled carburetors use the system only when the engine is cold and idling.

OPERATION

The exhaust pressure usually pulsates in response to the opening and closing of the exhaust valve and it periodically decreases below atmospheric pressure. If a secondary air intake pipe is opened to the atmosphere under a vacuum condition, secondary air can then be drawn into the exhaust manifold in proportion of the vacuum. Because of this, the air induction system is able to reduce the CO and HC content in the exhaust gases. The system consists of two air induction valves, a filter, hoses and EAI tubes.

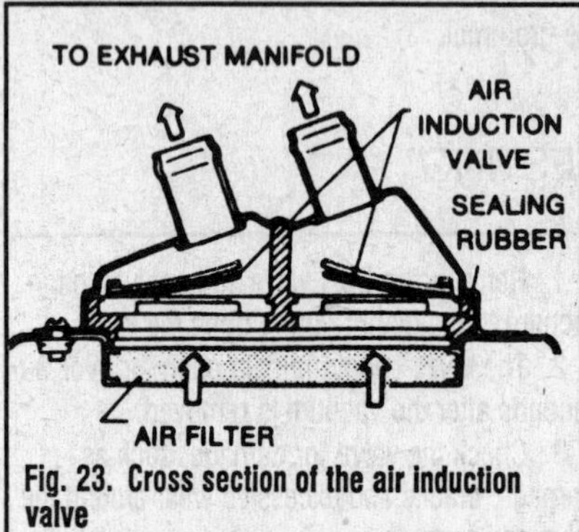
TO EXHAUST MANIFOLD
AIR INDUCTION VALVE
SEALING RUBBER
AIR FILTER

Fig. 23. Cross section of the air induction valve

TESTING

1. Models without control valves. Disconnect the air induction tube from the tube leading to the exhaust manifold. Place the tube to your mouth, then suck on the tube (air should move freely through the valve); try to blow through the tube (air should not flow through it). If the valve does not respond correctly, replace it.

2. Models with control valves. Disconnect the injection hose at the pipe side. Suck or blow into the hose and make sure that air flow does not exist.

3. Connect a vacuum pump to the air injection control valve located at the bottom of the valve case. Suck or blow air into the hose and make sure that air flows only on the air injection pipe side while control valve is operated.

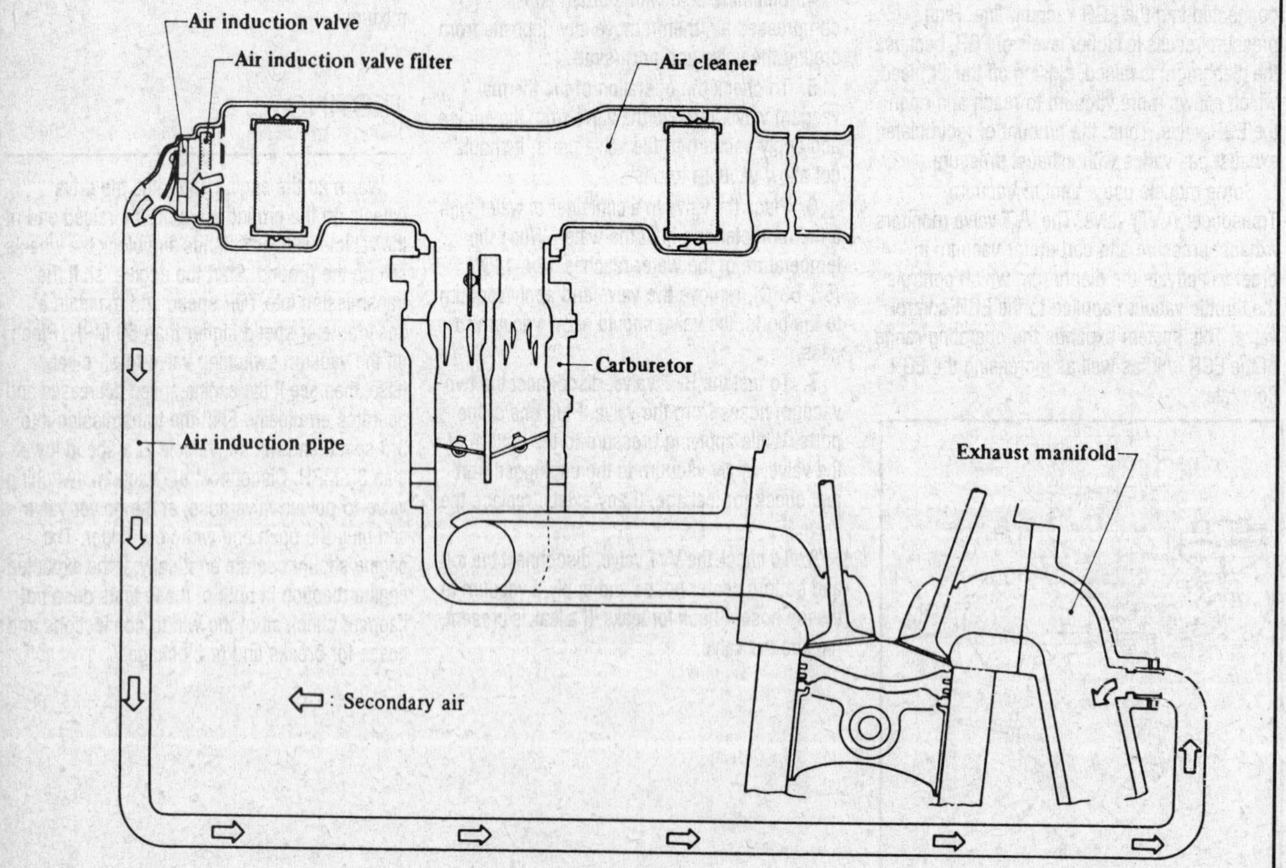

Fig. 23. Air induction system — 1982–86 E-series engine (Federal)

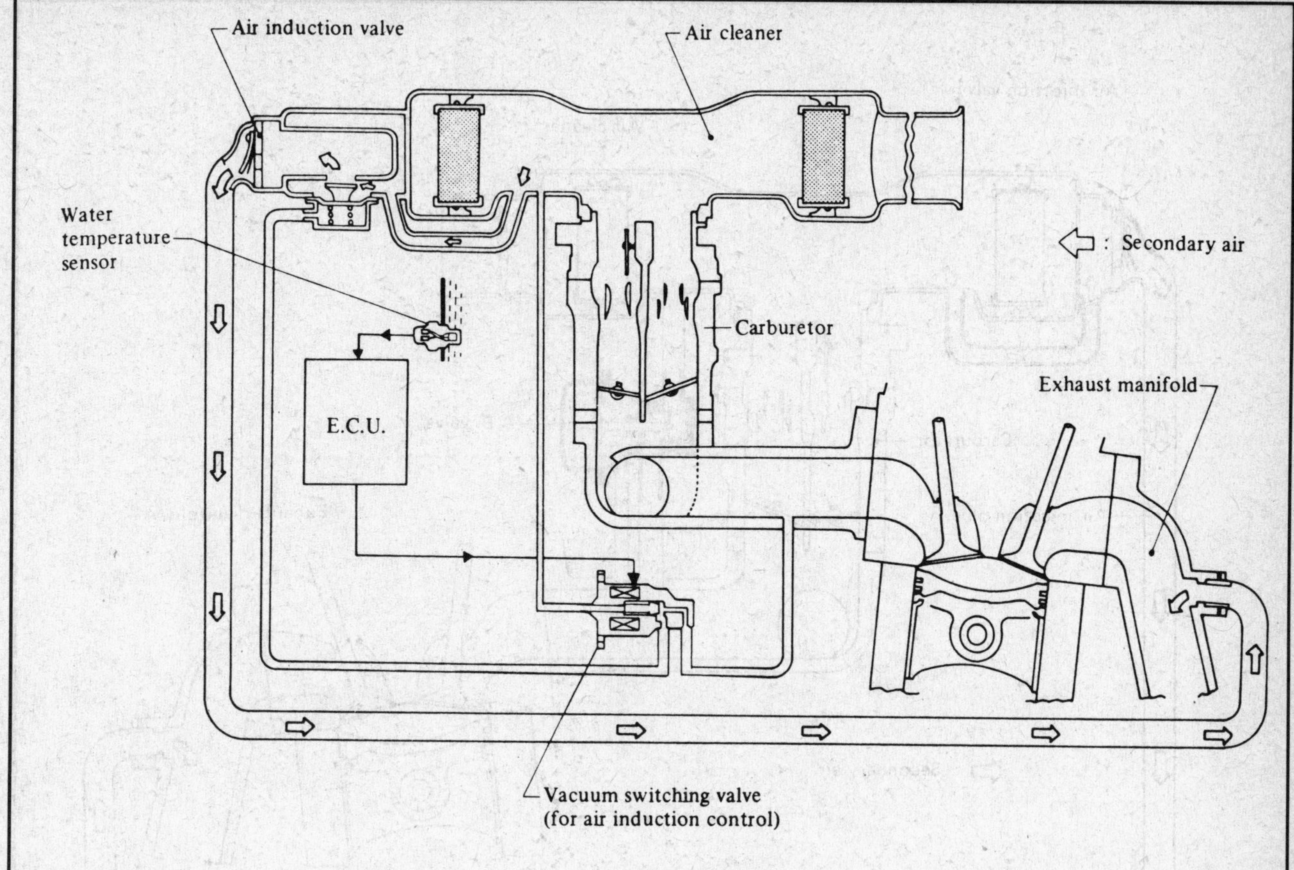
Air induction valve
Air cleaner
Water temperature sensor
: Secondary air
Carburetor
E.C.U.
Exhaust manifold
Vacuum switching valve (for air induction control)

Operation

Water temperature °C (°F)	Vacuum switching valve for air induction control	Air induction control valve	Air induction control system
Below 50 (122)	ON	Open	Operated
Above 50 (122)	OFF	Closed	Not operated

Fig. 24. Air induction system — 1982–86 E-series engine (Calif.)

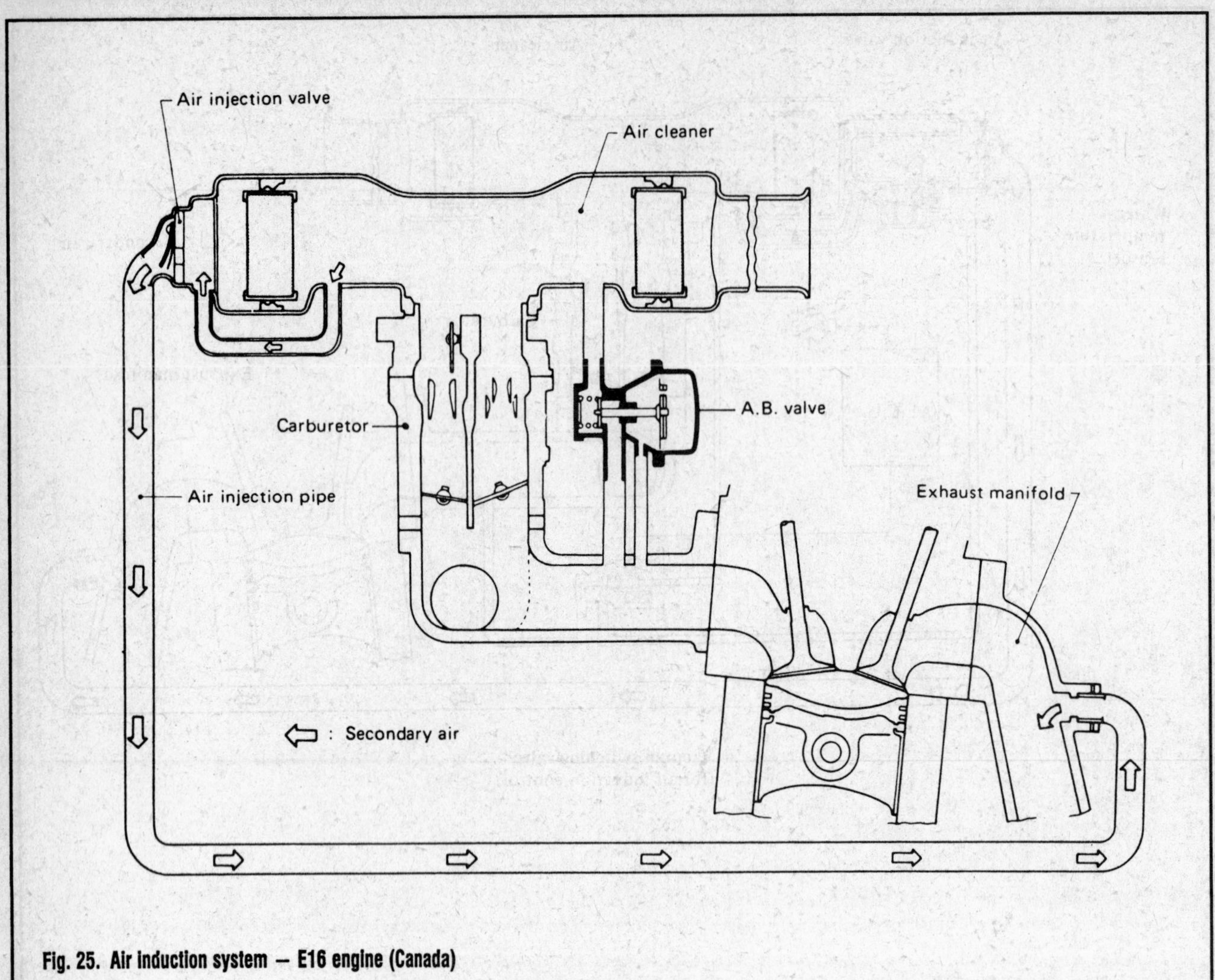
Air injection valve
Air cleaner
A.B. valve
Carburetor
Air injection pipe
Exhaust manifold
: Secondary air

Fig. 25. Air induction system — E16 engine (Canada)

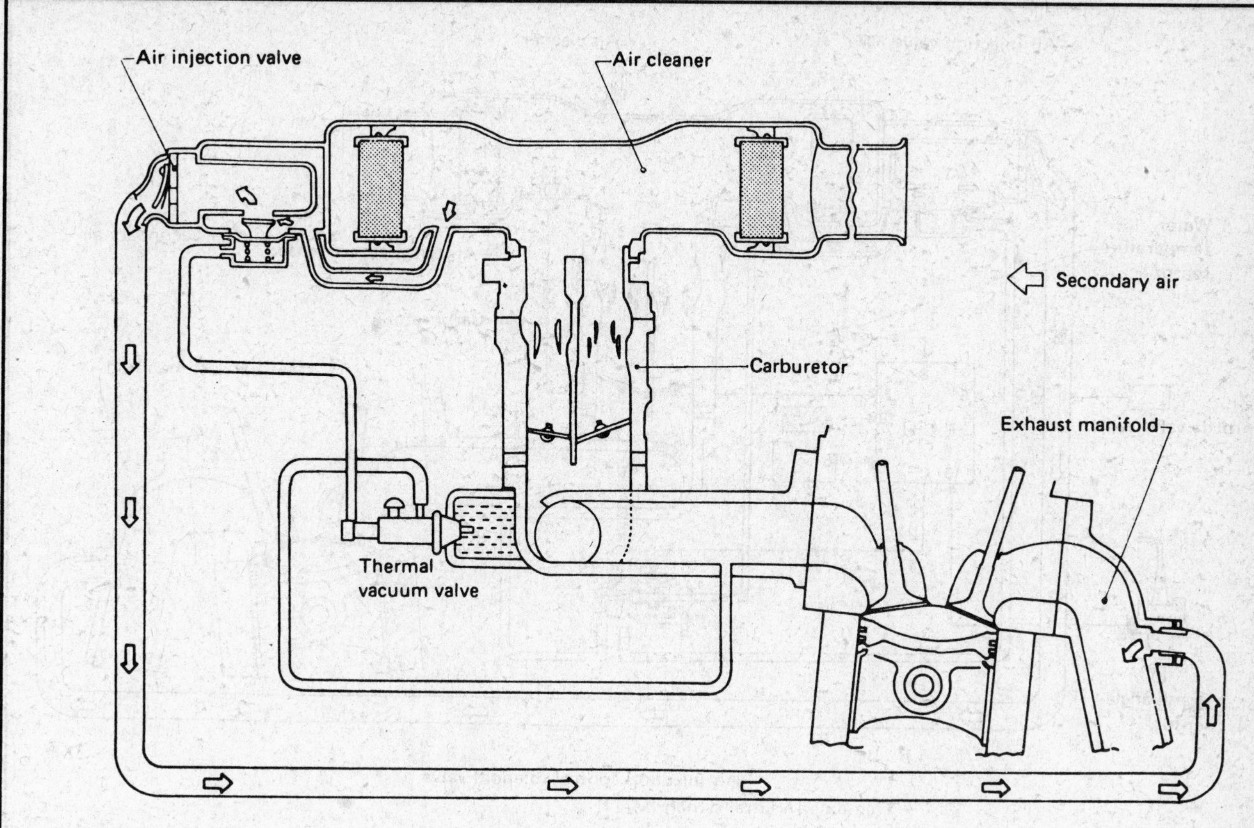
Air injection valve
Air cleaner
Secondary air
Carburetor
Exhaust manifold
Thermal
vacuum valve

OPERATION

Water temperature °C (°F)	Thermal vacuum valve	Air injection control valve	Air injection system
Between 15 (59) and 60 (140)	Open*	Open	Operated
Below 15 (59), above 60 (140)	Closed*	Closed	Not operated

*To intake manifold vacuum

Fig. 26. Air induction system — 1986 E16 engine (Calif.)

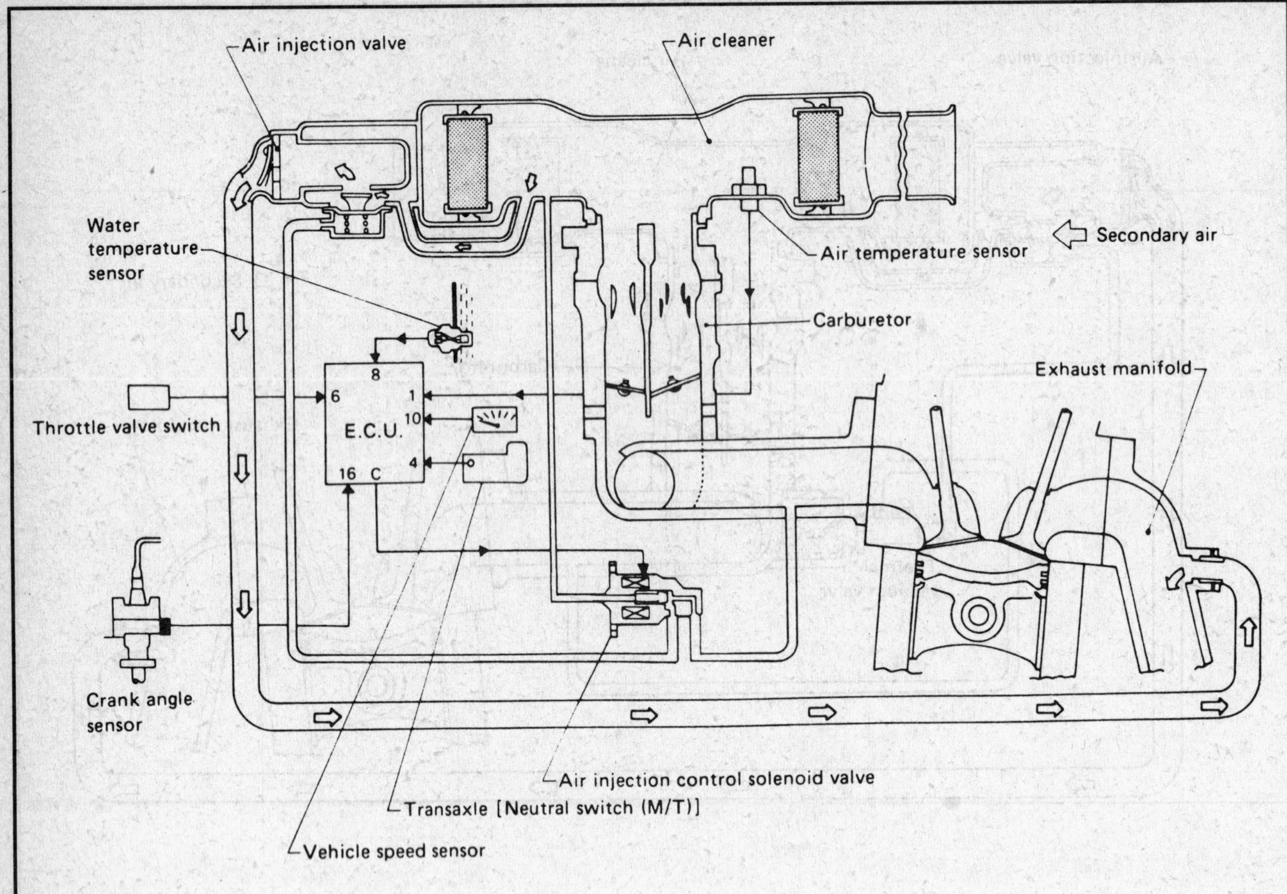
Air injection valve
Air cleaner
Water temperature sensor
Secondary air
Air temperature sensor
Carburetor
Exhaust manifold
Throttle valve switch
E.C.U.
8
6
1
10
4
16 C
Crank angle sensor
Air injection control solenoid valve
Transaxle [Neutral switch (M/T)]
Vehicle speed sensor

OPERATION

i) Cold condition

Water temperature °C (°F)	Air temperature °C (°F)	Air injection control solenoid valve	Air injection control valve	Air injection system
Between 15 (59) and 70 (158)	Above 15 (59)	ON	Open	Operated
	Below 15 (59)	OFF	Closed	Not operated
Below 15 (59), above 70 (158)	Above 15 (59)			
	Below 15 (59)			

Fig. 27. Air induction system — 1986 engines (Federal)

4. Check the air valve and control valve for binding or damage.

5. To check the AB valve for Canada vehicle. Warm the engine and disconnect the hose from the air cleaner. Place a finger near the outlet. Run the engine at about 3000 rpm under no load, then return to idle. A suction should be felt. If no vacuum is felt, replace the AB valve.

Fuel Shut-Off System

➡ **The 1982 and later, carburetor models, utilize the Electronic Control Unit (ECU) to control the operation of the anti-dieseling solenoid.**

OPERATION

The system is operated by an anti-dieseling solenoid valve in the carburetor which is controlled by a vacuum switch or ECU on later ECCS vehicles. When the intake manifold vacuum increases to an extremely high level (which it does during deceleration), the fuel flow

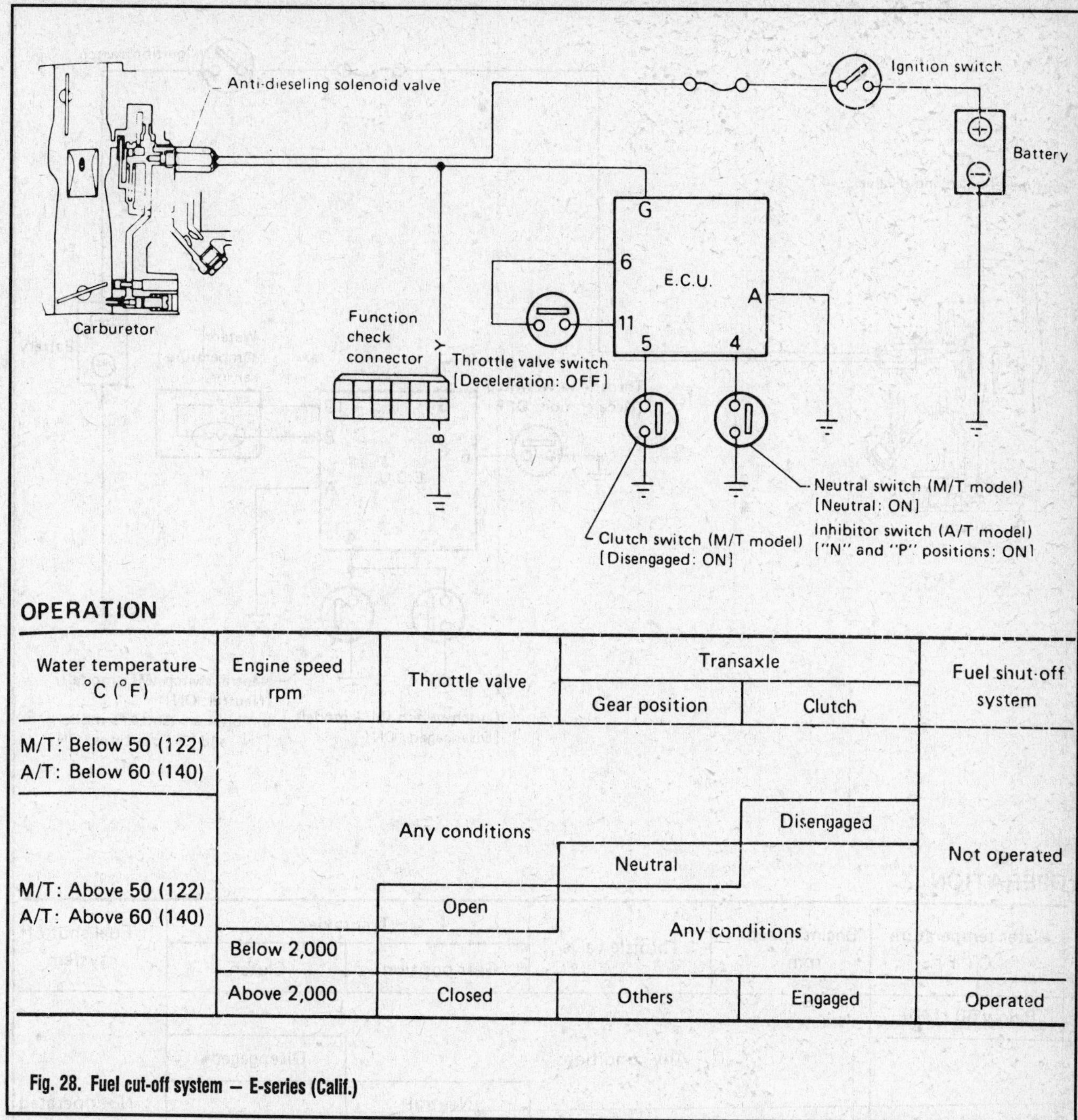
Anti-dieseling solenoid valve
Ignition switch
Battery
G
6
E.C.U.
A
11
5
4
Carburetor
Function
check
connector
Throttle valve switch
[Deceleration: OFF]
B
Neutral switch (M/T model)
[Neutral: ON]
Inhibitor switch (A/T model)
["N" and "P" positions: ON]
Clutch switch (M/T model)
[Disengaged: ON]

OPERATION

Water temperature °C (°F)	Engine speed rpm	Throttle valve	Transaxle: Gear position	Transaxle: Clutch	Fuel shut-off system
M/T: Below 50 (122) A/T: Below 60 (140)	Any conditions				Not operated
M/T: Above 50 (122) A/T: Above 60 (140)				Disengaged	
			Neutral		
		Open			
	Below 2,000		Any conditions		
	Above 2,000	Closed	Others	Engaged	Operated

Fig. 28. Fuel cut-off system – E-series (Calif.)

of the slow system is shut off by the anti-dieseling solenoid valve. When the intake manifold vacuum drops to a low level, the fuel flow of the slow system is resupplied. The solenoid is engaged when the clutch pedal is depressed or the vehicle is placed in neutral.

The fuel shut-off system is further controlled by the clutch switch and gear position switches such as the neutral switch (manual transmission) and the inhibitor switch (automatic transmission) to ensure that fuel cannot be shut off even it the manifold vacuum is high enough to trigger the normal fuel shut-off operation.

TESTING AND INSPECTION

1. ECU controlled systems. Check the clutch and neutral switches for continuity.

2. Turn the ignition switch **OFF** and disconnect the ECU connector, if so equipped. Turn the ignition **ON** and check for continuity at terminals 4 and 5 to ground. There should be continuity. If not, check the harness.

3. Non ECU controlled systems. Disconnect the fuel shut-off relay at the relay center and turn the ignition **ON**. Check for voltage at the green/red and black terminals. Should be 12 volts with the clutch disengaged and 0 volts with the clutch engaged (free).

4. Disconnect the vacuum hose from the vacuum switch. Apply vacuum with a vacuum pump and check continuity through the vacuum switch.

5. All systems: Disconnect the solenoid electrical connector and vacuum connector. The engine should stall. If not, replace the solenoid.

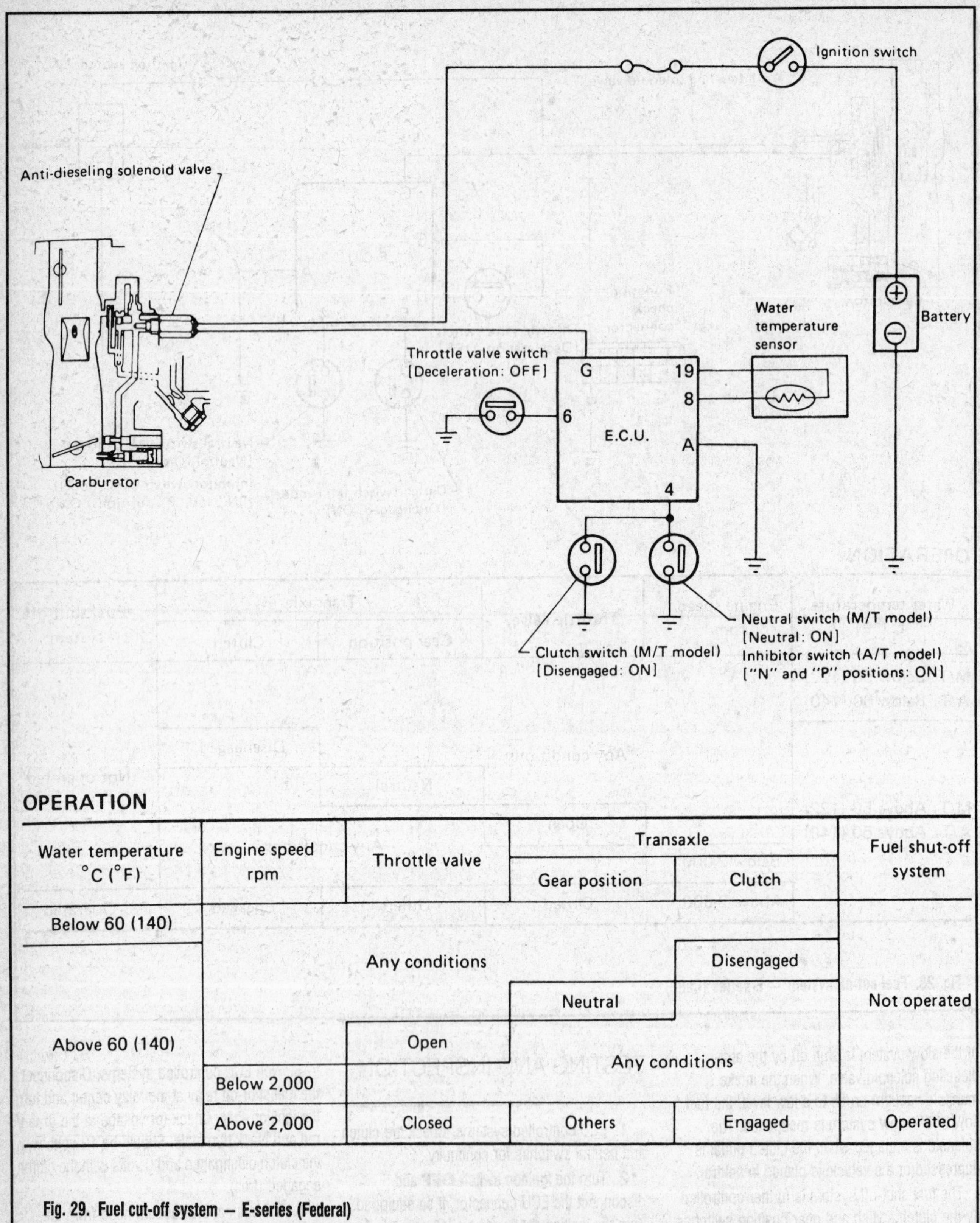
Ignition switch
Anti-dieseling solenoid valve
Water temperature sensor
Battery
Throttle valve switch [Deceleration: OFF]
G
19
8
6
E.C.U.
A
4
Carburetor
Neutral switch (M/T model) [Neutral: ON]
Inhibitor switch (A/T model) ["N" and "P" positions: ON]
Clutch switch (M/T model) [Disengaged: ON]

OPERATION

Water temperature °C (°F)	Engine speed rpm	Throttle valve	Transaxle: Gear position	Transaxle: Clutch	Fuel shut-off system
Below 60 (140)	Any conditions	Any conditions	Any conditions	Any conditions	Not operated
Above 60 (140)	Any conditions	Any conditions	Any conditions	Disengaged	Not operated
Above 60 (140)	Any conditions	Any conditions	Neutral	Any conditions	Not operated
Above 60 (140)	Below 2,000	Open	Any conditions	Any conditions	Not operated
Above 60 (140)	Above 2,000	Closed	Others	Engaged	Operated

Fig. 29. Fuel cut-off system – E-series (Federal)

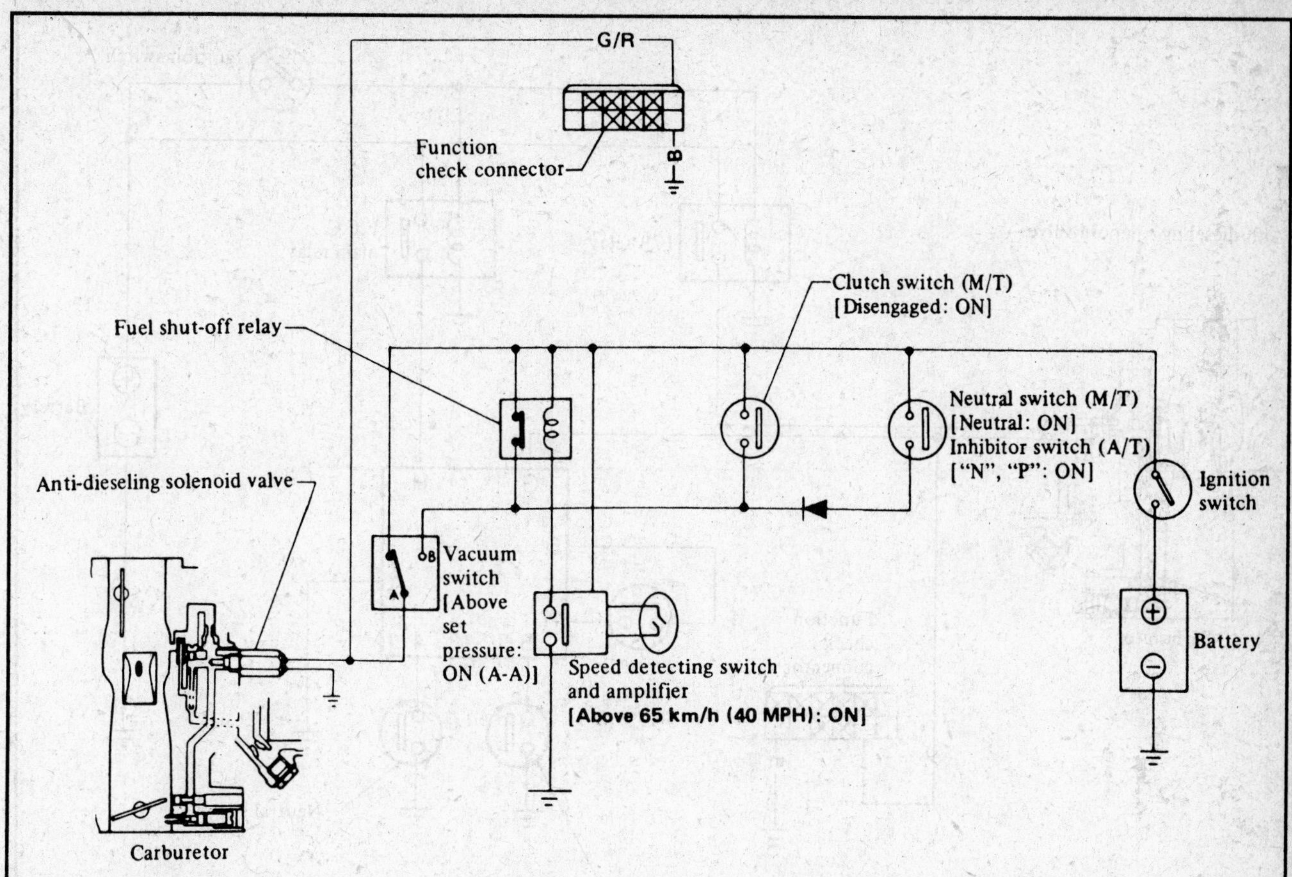
G/R
Function
check connector
B
Clutch switch (M/T)
[Disengaged: ON]
Fuel shut-off relay
Neutral switch (M/T)
[Neutral: ON]
Inhibitor switch (A/T)
["N", "P": ON]
Anti-dieseling solenoid valve
Ignition
switch
B
A
Vacuum
switch
[Above
set
pressure:
ON (A-A)]
Battery
Speed detecting switch
and amplifier
[Above 65 km/h (40 MPH): ON]
Carburetor

OPERATION

<table>
<tr><th rowspan="2">Ignition key</th><th rowspan="2">Intake vacuum
–kPa
(–mmHg, –inHg)</th><th rowspan="2">Car speed
km/h
(MPH)</th><th colspan="2">Transaxle</th><th rowspan="2">Fuel shut-off system</th></tr>
<tr><th>Gear position</th><th>Clutch</th></tr>
<tr><td>OFF</td><td colspan="4"></td><td rowspan="5">Not operated</td></tr>
<tr><td rowspan="5">ON</td><td>Below 77.3
(580, 22.83)
(during acceleration)</td><td colspan="3">Any conditions</td></tr>
<tr><td rowspan="4">Above 77.3
(580, 22.83)
(during deceleration)</td><td>Below
65 (40)</td><td colspan="2"></td></tr>
<tr><td rowspan="3">Above
65 (40)</td><td>Neutral</td><td>Any position</td></tr>
<tr><td rowspan="2">Others</td><td>Disengage</td></tr>
<tr><td>Engage</td><td>Operated</td></tr>
</table>

Fig. 30. Fuel cut-off system — 1982–85 engines (Federal)

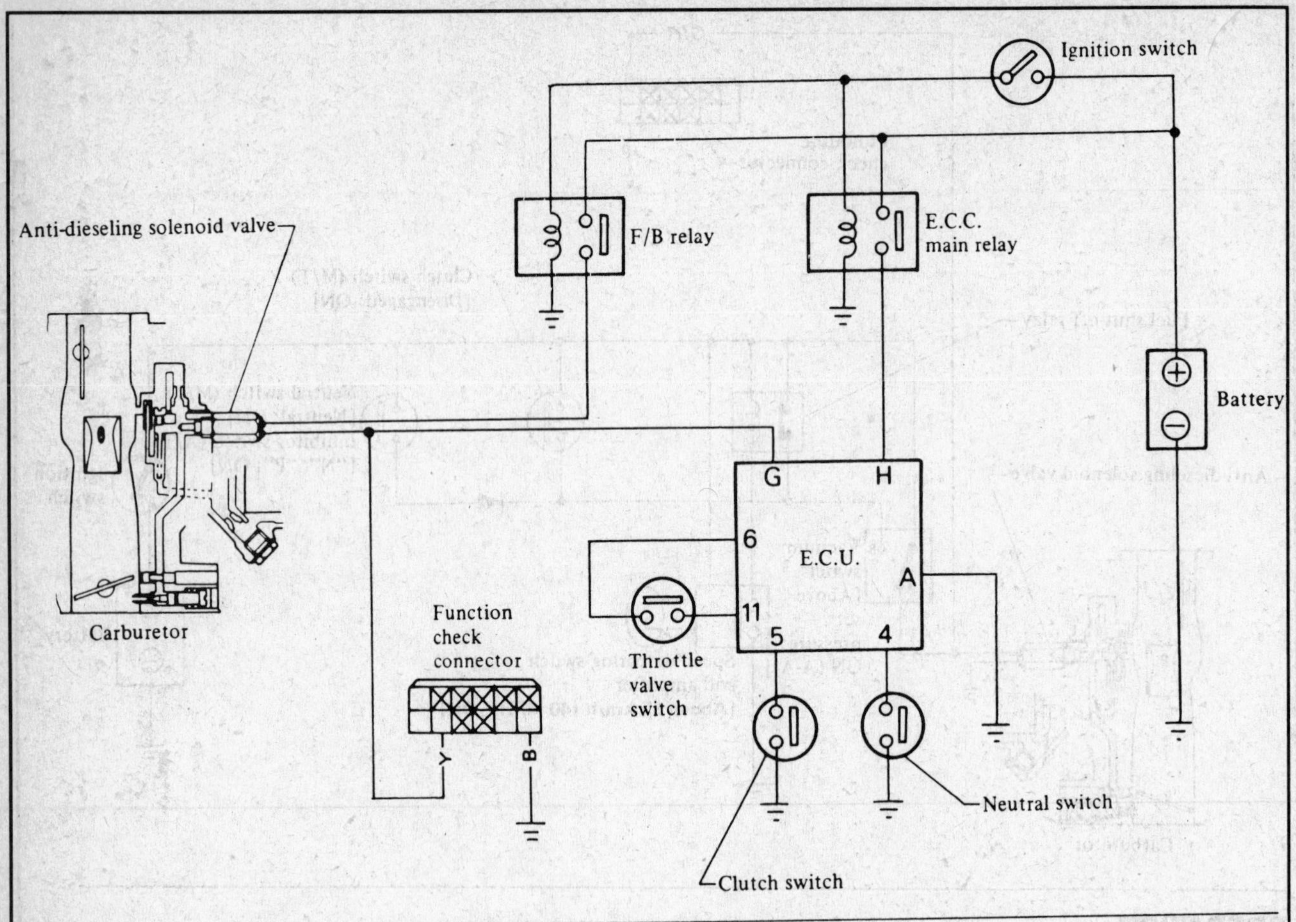
Ignition switch
Anti-dieseling solenoid valve
F/B relay
E.C.C.
main relay
Battery
G
H
6
E.C.U.
A
11
5
4
Function
check
connector
Throttle
valve
switch
Carburetor
Y
B
Neutral switch
Clutch switch

OPERATION

Water temperature °C (°F)	Engine speed rpm	Throttle valve	Transaxle: Gear position	Transaxle: Clutch	Fuel shut-off system
Below 50 (122)	Any conditions				Not operated
Above 50 (122)				Disengaged	
			Neutral		
		Open	Any conditions		
	Below 2,150				
	Above 2,150	Closed	Others	Engaged	Operated

Fig. 31. Fuel cut-off system — E16 engine with MPG system

Electric Choke

The purpose of the electric choke, is to shorten the time the choke is in operation after the engine is started, thus shortening the time of high HC output.

An electric heater warms the bimetal spring which controls the opening and closing of the choke valve. The heater starts to heat as soon as the engine starts.

Catalyst Warm-up System

OPERATION

This system was used on 1982–85 vehicles with carburetors. The MPG models are controlled by the ECU.

The catalyst warm-up system increases engine speed during warm-up periods to raise the temperature of the catalyst, thereby decreasing exhaust emissions.

The system consists of a vacuum switching valve, temperature sensor, neutral switch and vacuum delay valve. This system uses the throttle opener servo diaphragm as described earlier in this Section.

TESTING AND INSPECTION

1. Start the engine and warm to 59–104°F (15–40°C).
2. Shift gears to make sure that engine speed increases when gear is in neutral.
3. Warm the engine above 104°F (40°C) and make sure the engine rpm decreases and does not change when the gear is shifted to neutral. If the engine speed does not vary at all, disconnect the vacuum switching valve.
4. With the engine running, apply 12 volts to the valve and make sure the engine speed increases and ignition timing retards. If no change, check the vacuum switch, opener servo, distributor and vacuum hoses.

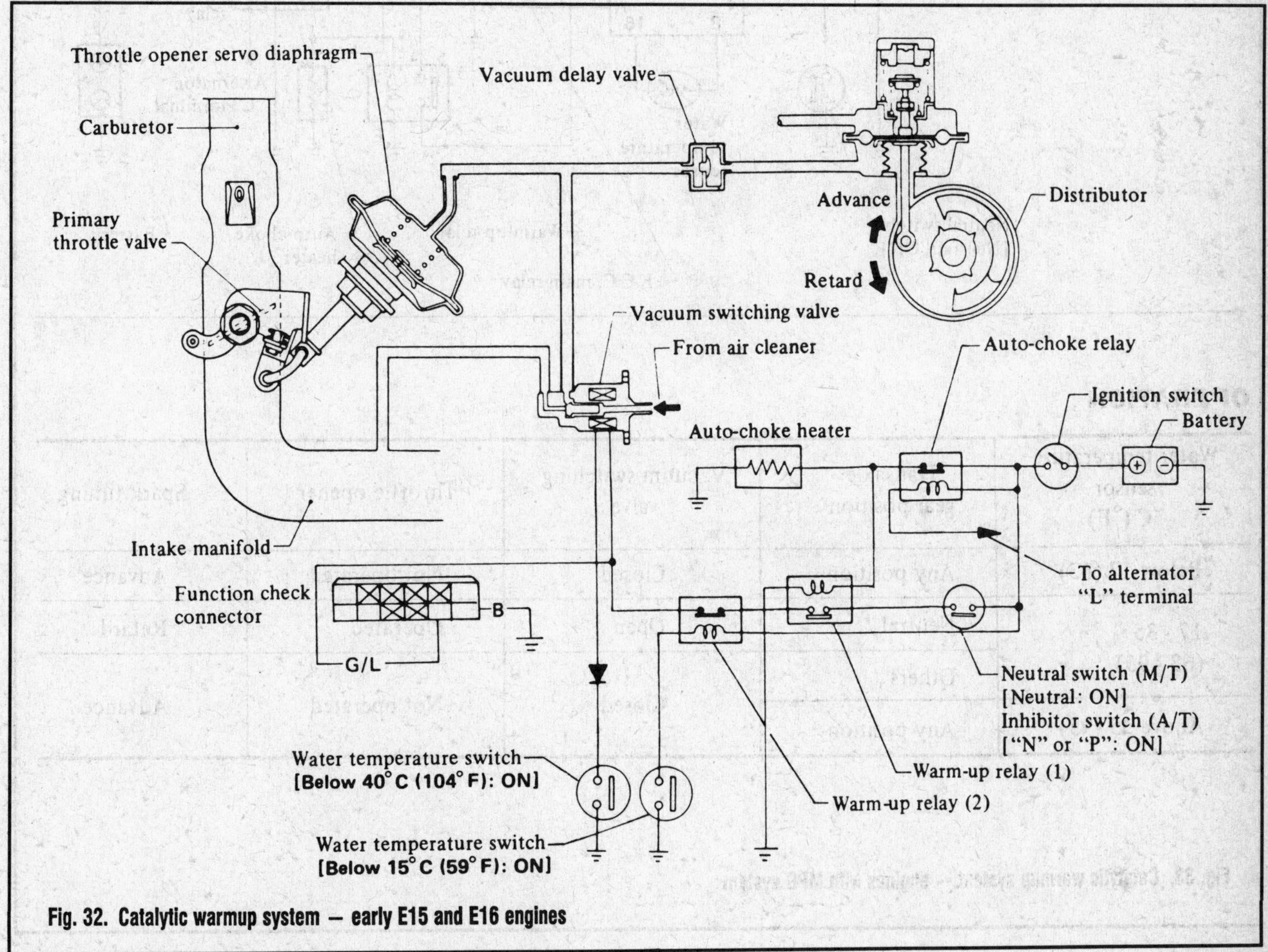
Throttle opener servo diaphragm
Vacuum delay valve
Carburetor
Primary throttle valve
Advance
Distributor
Retard
Vacuum switching valve
From air cleaner
Auto-choke relay
Ignition switch
Battery
Auto-choke heater
Intake manifold
To alternator "L" terminal
Function check connector
B
G/L
Neutral switch (M/T)
[Neutral: ON]
Inhibitor switch (A/T)
["N" or "P": ON]
Water temperature switch
[Below 40° C (104° F): ON]
Warm-up relay (1)
Warm-up relay (2)
Water temperature switch
[Below 15° C (59° F): ON]

Fig. 32. Catalytic warmup system — early E15 and E16 engines

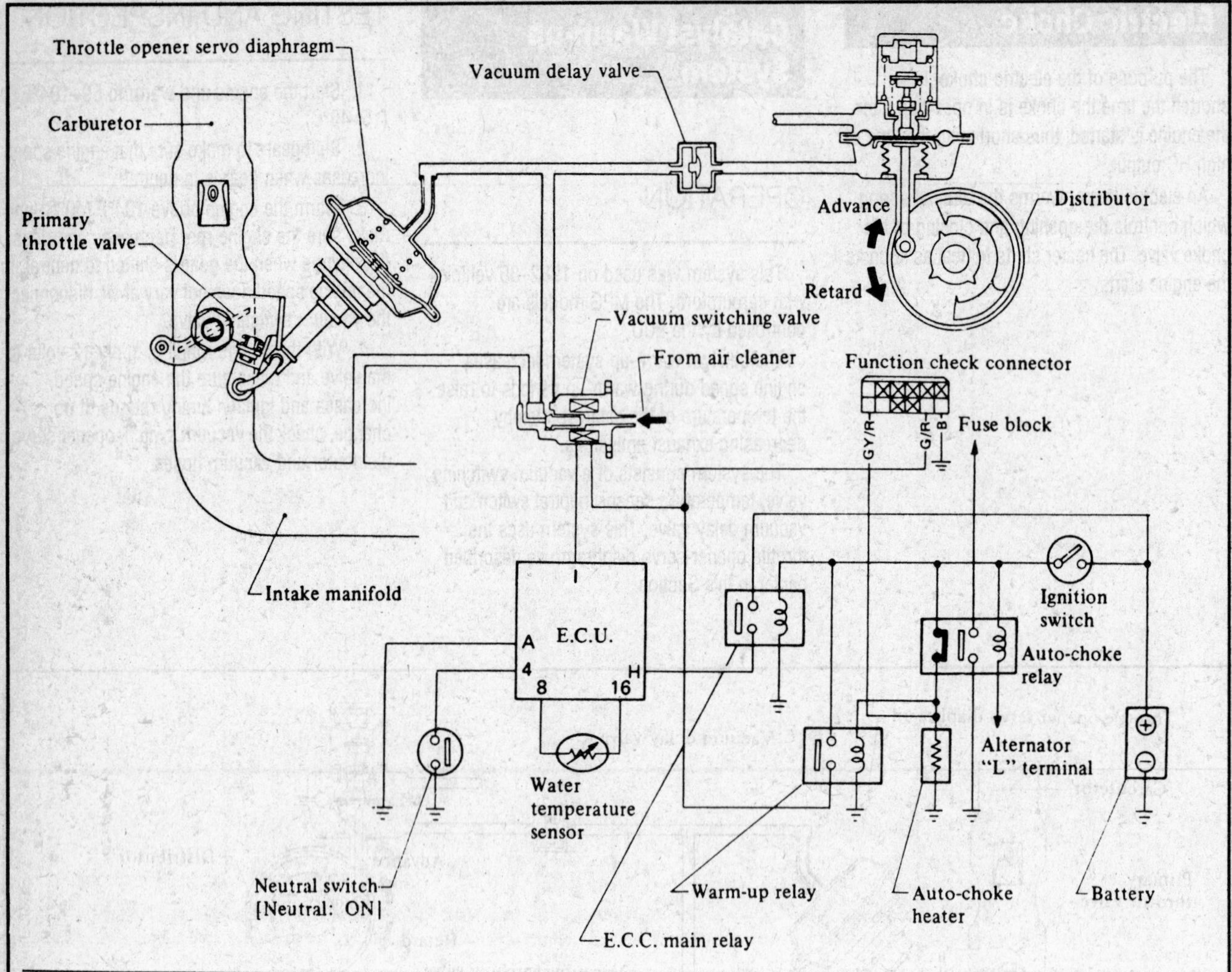

Throttle opener servo diaphragm
Vacuum delay valve
Carburetor
Primary throttle valve
Advance
Distributor
Retard
Vacuum switching valve
From air cleaner
Function check connector
GY/R
G/R
B
Fuse block
Intake manifold
E.C.U.
A
4
8
16
H
I
Ignition switch
Auto-choke relay
Alternator "L" terminal
Water temperature sensor
Neutral switch [Neutral: ON]
Warm-up relay
Auto-choke heater
Battery
E.C.C. main relay

OPERATION

Water temperature sensor ˚C (˚F)	Transaxle gear position	Vacuum switching valve	Throttle opener	Spark timing
Below 17 (63)	Any position	Closed	Not operated	Advance
17 - 35 (63 - 95)	Neutral	Open	Operated	Retard
	Others	Closed	Not operated	Advance
Above 35 (95)	Any position			

Fig. 33. Catalytic warmup system – engines with MPG system

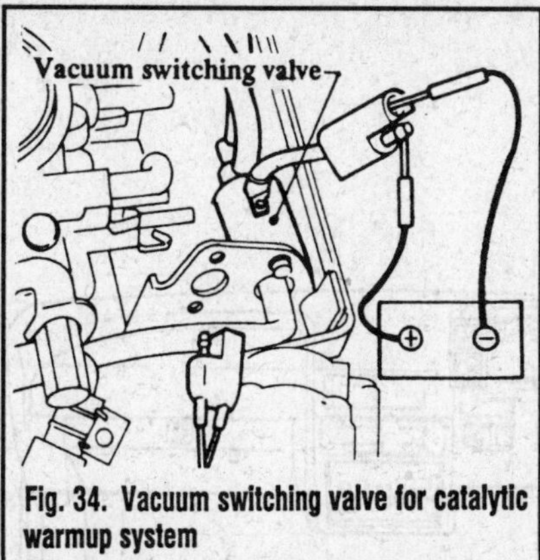
Vacuum switching valve

Fig. 34. Vacuum switching valve for catalytic warmup system

Spark Timing Control System

OPERATION

The spark timing control system is designed to control the distributor vacuum advance under various driving conditions in order to reduce HC and NOx emissions. With the water temperature below 59°F (15°C) and above 122° (50°C) the thermal vacuum valve is closed and the spark timing control system is activated. When the temperature is between the 2 temperatures, the valve is open and the system is not activated. Some early models are equipped with a vacuum delay valve, but all systems are basically the same.

TESTING AND INSPECTION

1. Ensure that the vacuum hoses are properly connected and the distributor vacuum controller and linkage functions properly.
2. Connect a timing light and start the engine when it is cold.
3. Check the spark timing when the system is activated. With the water temperature below 59°F (15°C) and above 122° (50°C) the thermal vacuum valve is closed and the spark timing control system is activated. When the temperature is between the 2 temperatures, the valve is open and the system is not activated.
4. If the timing does not change, check the thermal vacuum valve.

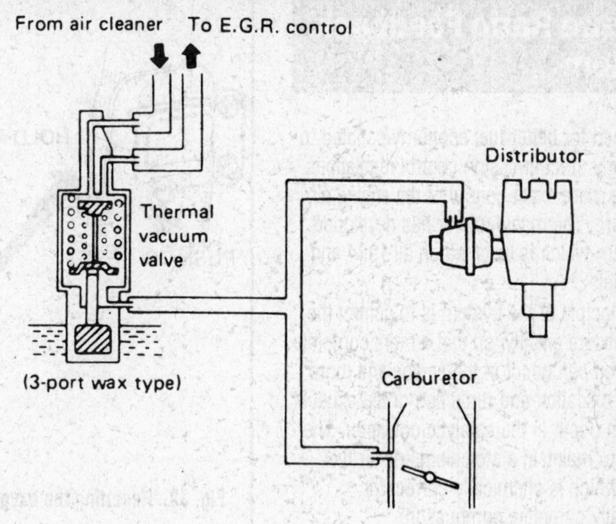
From air cleaner
To E.G.R. control
Thermal vacuum valve
(3-port wax type)
Distributor
Carburetor

OPERATION

Water temperature °C (°F)	Thermal vacuum valve	Spark timing control system
Below 15 (59)	Closed	Actuated
15 - 50 (59 - 122)	Open	Not actuated
Above 50 (122)	Closed	Actuated

Fig. 35. Spark timing control system — late model engine with carburetor

Catalytic Converter

This system is used on all models, except 1982–86 Canada models. The catalytic converter is a muffler-like container built into the exhaust system. The catalyst element consists of individual pellets or a honeycomb monolithic substrate coated with a noble metal such as platinum, palladium, rhodium or a combination. When the exhaust gases come into contact with the catalyst, it changes residual HC, CO and NOx in the exhaust gas into CO_2, H_2O and N, before the exhaust gas is discharged into the atmosphere.

All models equipped with an air pump use an emergency air relief valve as a catalyst protection device. When the temperature of the catalyst goes above maximum operating temperature, the temperature sensor signals the switching module to activate the emergency air relief valve. This stops air injection into the exhaust manifold and lowers the temperature of the catalyst.

1982–87 models with the 3-way converter have an oxygen sensor warning light on the dashboard, which illuminates at the first 30,000 mile internal signaling the need for oxygen sensor replacement. The oxygen sensor is part of the Mixture Ratio Feedback System.

Regular maintenance is required for the catalytic converter system, except for periodic replacement of the Air Induction System filter (if equipped). The Air Induction System (non-MPI engines) is used to supply the converter with fresh air; oxygen present in the air is used in the oxidation process.

Precautions

1. Use ONLY unleaded fuel.
2. Avoid prolonged idling; the engine should run no longer than 20 min. at curb idle and not longer than 10 min. at fast idle.
3. Do not disconnect any of the spark plug leads while the engine is running.
4. Make engine compression checks as quickly as possible.

Mixture Ratio Feedback System

The need for better fuel economy coupled to increasingly strict emission control regulations dictates a more exact control of the engine air/fuel mixture. The manufacturer has developed this system which is installed on all 1984 and later models.

The principle of the system is to control the air/fuel mixture exactly, so that a more complete combustion can occur in the engine and more thorough oxidation and reduction of the exhaust gases can occur in the catalytic converter. The object is to maintain a stoichiometric air/fuel mixture, which is chemically correct for theoretically complete combustion.

The components used in the system include an oxygen sensor, installed in the exhaust manifold upstream of the converter, a catalytic converter, an electronic control unit and the fuel injection system.

It should be noted that proper operation of the system is entirely dependent on the oxygen sensor. Thus, if the sensor is not replaced at the correct interval or if the sensor fails during normal operation, the engine fuel mixture will be incorrect, resulting in poor fuel economy, starting problems or stumbling and stalling of the engine when warm.

Maintenance Reminder Lights

RESETTING

Most 1982–86 Nissan models utilize an oxygen sensor. After 30,000 miles of operation, the sensor light in the dash will come on. This light indicates that the sensor should be inspected or replaced.

On models with a sensor relay, reset the relay by pushing or inserting a small screwdriver into the reset hole. Reset relay at 30,000 and 60,000 miles. At 90,000 miles, locate and disconnect warning light wire connector.

On models without sensor light relay locate and disconnect the single warning light harness connector. The reminder light will no longer function.

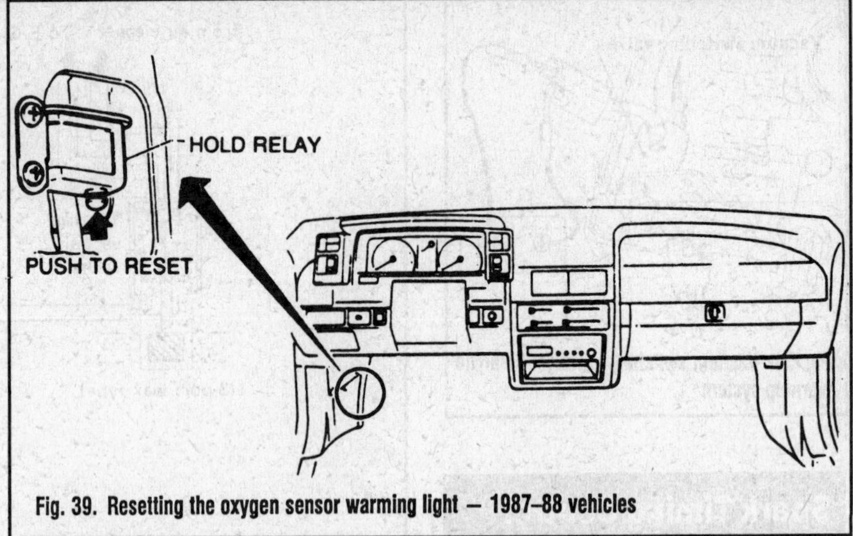
HOLD RELAY
PUSH TO RESET
Fig. 39. Resetting the oxygen sensor warming light – 1987–88 vehicles

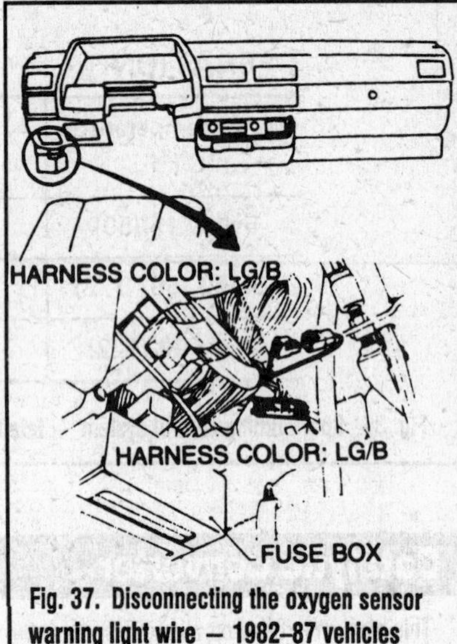
HARNESS COLOR: LG/B
HARNESS COLOR: LG/B
FUSE BOX
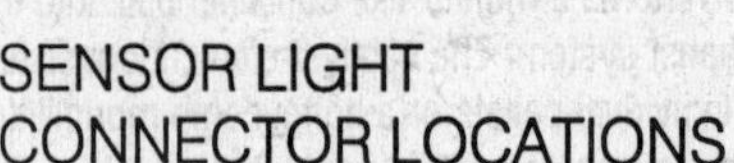
Fig. 37. Disconnecting the oxygen sensor warning light wire – 1982–87 vehicles

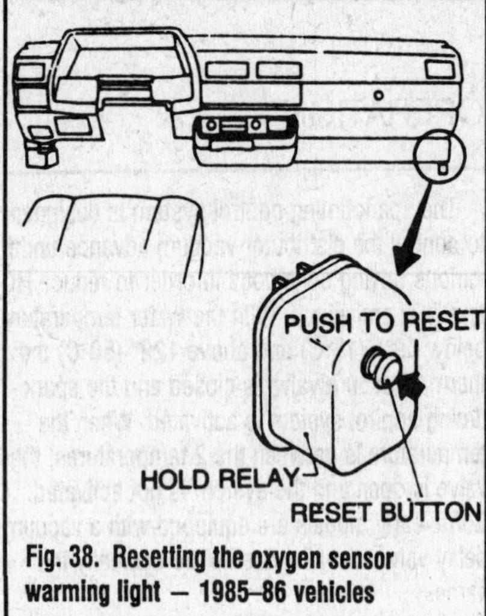
PUSH TO RESET
HOLD RELAY
RESET BUTTON
Fig. 38. Resetting the oxygen sensor warming light – 1985–86 vehicles

SENSOR LIGHT CONNECTOR LOCATIONS

1. 1983–86 – LIGHT GREEN/BLACK-LIGHT GREEN, above fuse box
2. 1987 – RED/BLACK-RED/BLUE, above fuse box

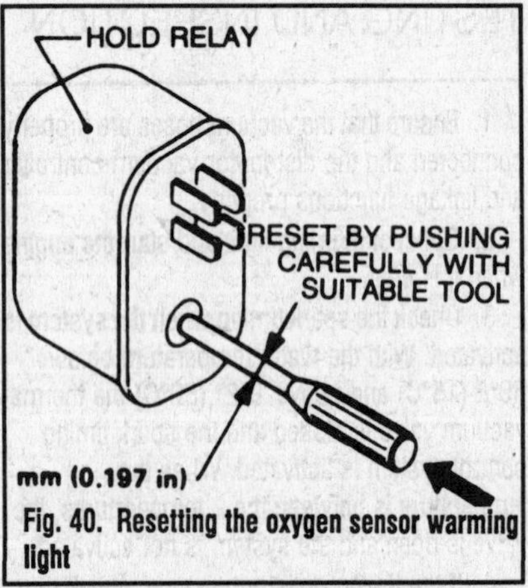
HOLD RELAY
RESET BY PUSHING CAREFULLY WITH SUITABLE TOOL
mm (0.197 in)
Fig. 40. Resetting the oxygen sensor warming light

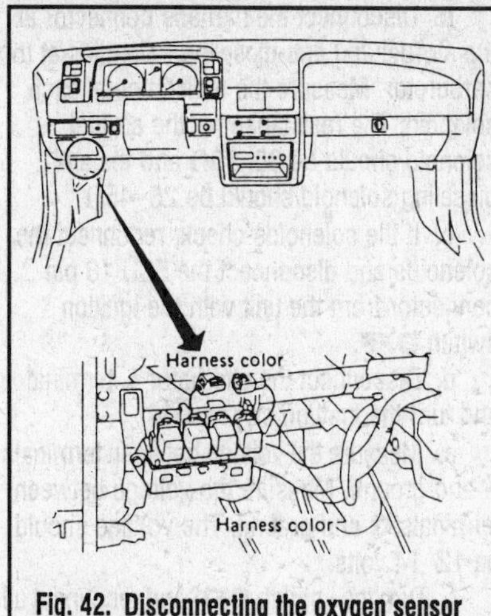
Harness color
Harness color

Fig. 42. Disconnecting the oxygen sensor wiring harness

Oxygen Sensor

The oxygen sensor monitors the density of the oxygen in the exhaust gas. The sensor consists of a closed-end tube made of ceramic zirconia and other components. Porous platinum electrodes cover the tubes inner and outer surfaces. The tubes outer surface is exposed to the exhaust gases in the exhaust manifold, while its inner surface is exposed to normal air.

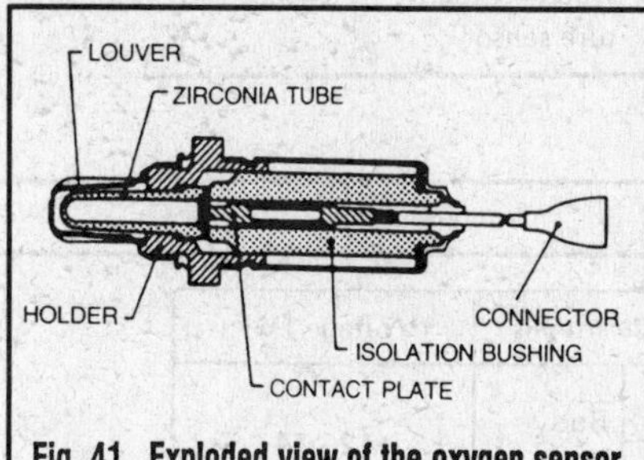
LOUVER
ZIRCONIA TUBE
HOLDER
CONNECTOR
ISOLATION BUSHING
CONTACT PLATE

Fig. 41. Exploded view of the oxygen sensor

REMOVAL & INSTALLATION

The oxygen sensor is installed in the exhaust manifold and is removed in the same manner as a spark plug. Always remove electrical connection before trying to remove the sensor. Exercise care when handling the sensor do not drop or handle the sensor roughly; the electrical connector and louvered end must be kept free of grease and dirt. If a anti-seize compound is used in installation, make sure to coat just the threads of the sensor and care should be used not to get compound on the sensor itself. You should disconnect the negative battery cable when servicing the oxygen sensor and torque the sensor to 13–17 ft. lbs. (18–27 Nm).

ELECTRONIC ENGINE CONTROLS

Electronic Controlled Carburetor (ECC) System

GENERAL INFORMATION

The self-diagnostic system determines malfunctions of signal systems such as sensors, actuators, and wire harnesses based on the status of the input signals received by the EFI control unit. A malfunction is displayed by both the red and green LED's (Light Emitting Diodes), if so equipped.

SELF-DIAGNOSIS

Preliminary Testing

➡ Do not condemn the electronic engine controls before fully checking the basics. Many electronic parts are replaced only to find out it is something simple. Electronic parts are usually not returnable. Make sure the component is defective before purchasing.

1. Check the engine for air and vacuum leaks. Most engines should draw about 15–20 inch Hg. at idle. The needle should be steady.
2. Check the air filter for clogging.
3. Inspect the dipstick, AB valve hose, air induction hose, intake manifold gasket, valve cover gasket, EGR gasket and oil filler cap for leaks.
4. Check the EGR valve seat and operation. A malfunction EGR can cause no or abnormal idle.
5. Check the fuel supply to the carburetor and make sure the fuel is at the proper octane. Old fuel can cause driveability problems that are difficult to diagnose.
6. Check the fuel filter for clogging.
7. With the engine idling, check the fuel level through the glass window on the carburetor bowl. The level should be at the middle dot. If not correct, remove the top of the carburetor and adjust the float level as outlined in Section 5.
8. Perform ignition tests with an oscilloscope. All firing voltages should be in the same range. Check the secondary ignition system with a spark tester.
9. Check and adjust the ignition to the proper specification in Section 2.
10. Check all engine related electrical harness connectors, including the ECU. Loose or corroded terminals can cause many driveability problems.

Testing

➡ Make sure the ignition switch is OFF before disconnecting any harness connectors. Disconnect the negative battery cable before disconnecting the ECU harness connector. Voltage spikes can damage the electronic components. Make sure the ECU (Electronic Control Unit) connector is fully seated during inspection.

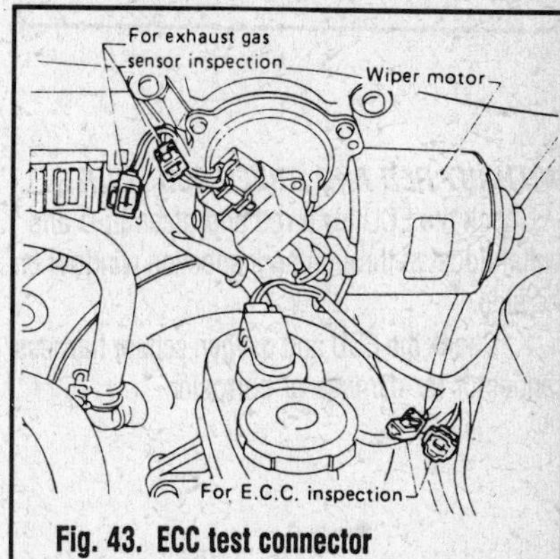
For exhaust gas sensor inspection
Wiper motor
For E.C.C. inspection

Fig. 43. ECC test connector

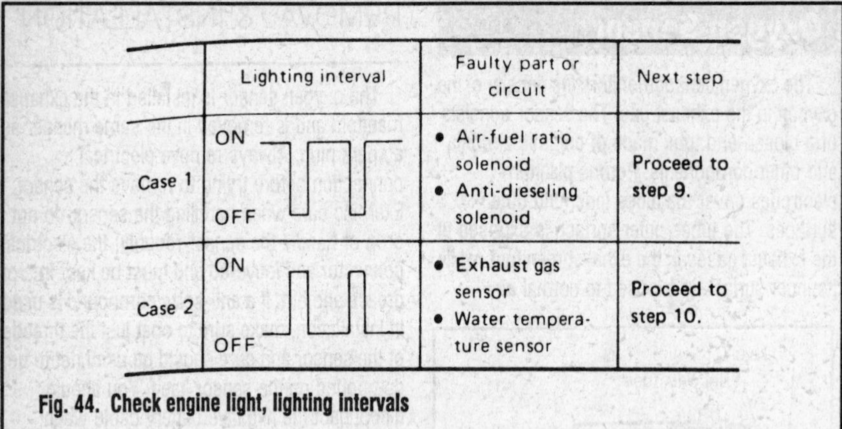

	Lighting interval	Faulty part or circuit	Next step
Case 1	ON / OFF	• Air-fuel ratio solenoid • Anti-dieseling solenoid	Proceed to step 9.
Case 2	ON / OFF	• Exhaust gas sensor • Water temperature sensor	Proceed to step 10.

Fig. 44. Check engine light, lighting intervals

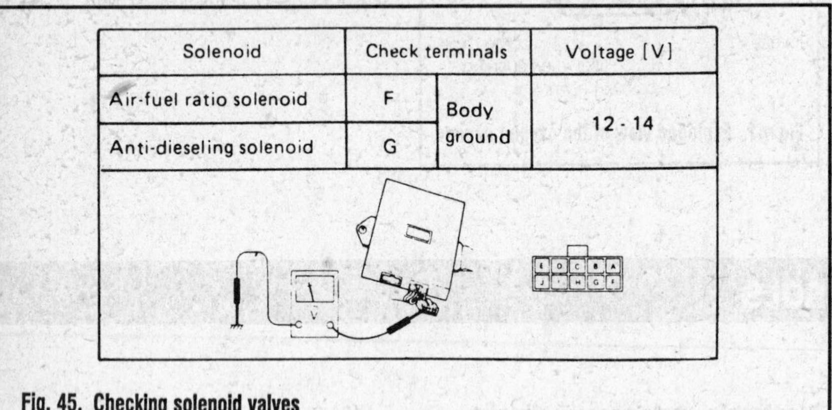

Solenoid	Check terminals		Voltage [V]
Air-fuel ratio solenoid	F	Body ground	12 - 14
Anti-dieseling solenoid	G	Body ground	12 - 14

Fig. 45. Checking solenoid valves

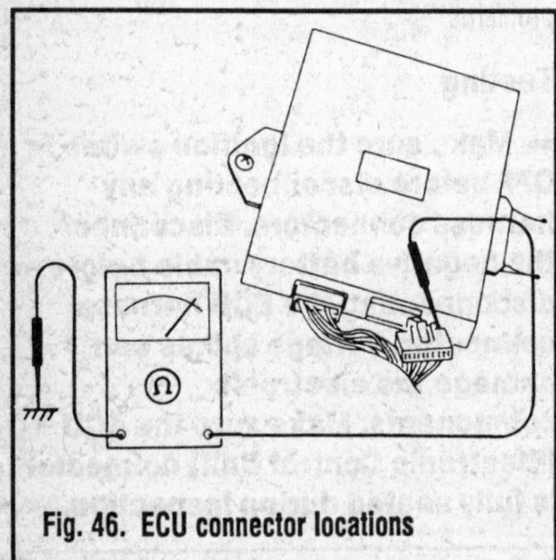

Fig. 46. ECU connector locations

WITHOUT RED AND GREEN ECU LIGHTS

Check the ECU for a red and green LED and switch located through an inspection window on the side.

1. Check the ECU and oxygen sensor harness connector for damage or corrosion.

2. Turn the ignition switch **ON** and check the CHECK ENGINE light on the instrument panel. If the bulb does not light, replace the bulb or repair wiring.

3. If the light stays **ON**, start the engine and warm.

4. Run the engine to 2000 rpm, for about 5 minutes. If the light goes **OFF**, there is no trouble.

5. If the light stays **ON**, turn the engine **OFF** and connect the ECC (Electronic Controlled Carburetor) test connector near the wiper motor.

6. Run the engine at idle to receive lighting intervals. If no light exists, check for an opening in the oxygen sensor circuit.

7. If the light comes **ON**, check the lighting intervals as illustrated in this section.

8. Check the air/fuel ratio solenoid as follows:

a. Turn the ignition **OFF** and check each harness for proper connection.

b. Disconnect the harness connector at the air/fuel and anti-dieseling solenoids at the carburetor. Measure the resistance at each solenoid. The resistance for the air/fuel solenoid should be 30–50Ω and the anti-dieseling solenoid should be 25–45Ω.

c. If the solenoids check, reconnect the solenoids and disconnect the ECU 10 pin connector from the unit with the ignition switch **OFF**.

d. Disconnect the alternator **L** terminal and turn the ignition switch **ON**.

e. Measure the voltage between terminals **F** and ground. Measure the voltage between terminals **G** and ground. The voltage should be 12–14 volts.

f. Turn the ignition **OFF** and reconnect all harness connectors. Disconnect the ECU 20 pin and oxygen sensor connectors. Ground the ECU end with a jumper wire.

g. Check the continuity between terminals **2** and ground of the 20 pin connector. If continuity exists, replace the oxygen sensor. If continuity does not exist, repair or replace the ECU.

h. Measure the coolant temperature sensor resistance between ECU terminal **8 and 16** of the 20 pin connector. The resistance should be below 2.9kΩ above 68°F (20°C) and above 2.1kΩ above the same temperature.

WITH RED AND GREEN ECU LIGHTS

➧ SEE FIGS. 47–52

Check the ECU for a red and green LED and switch located through an inspection window on the side.

1. Position the ECU so the red and green LED's can be easily seen.

2. Start the engine and warm. Verify that the diagnostic start switch on the ECU is **OFF**.

3. Run the engine at 2000 rpm for about 5 minutes. Keep the engine speed at 2000 rpm and check that the green LED goes ON and OFF during 10 seconds. If the LED does, check the oxygen sensor circuit.

4. To check the oxygen sensor circuit:

a. Turn the ignition **OFF** and reconnect all harness connectors. Disconnect the ECU 20 pin and oxygen sensor connectors. Ground the ECU end with a jumper wire.

b. Check the continuity between terminals **2** and ground of the 20 pin connector. If continuity exists, replace the oxygen sensor. If continuity does not exist, repair or replace the ECU.

	Red L.E.D.	Green L.E.D.	Faulty part or circuit
Case 1	ON	ON OFF	• Vacuum sensor • Barometric pressure sensor • Water temperature sensor • Air temperature sensor
Case 2	ON	ON OFF	• Mixture heater relay • Air-fuel ratio solenoid • Richer solenoid • Anti-dieseling solenoid • Air injection solenoid • Idle speed control solenoid
Case 3	OFF	ON	No problem

Fig. 48. Trouble code chart

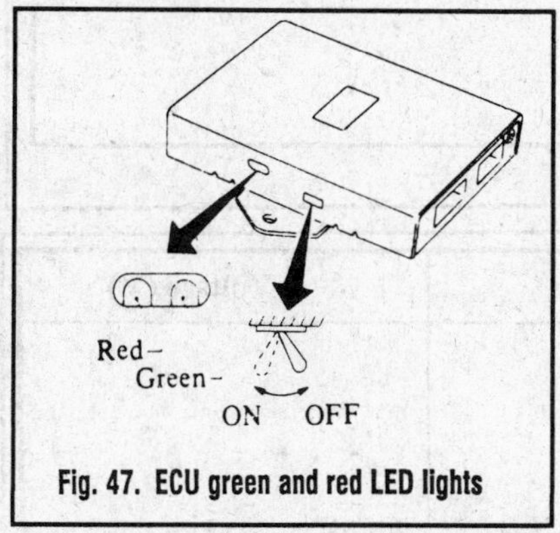
Red–
Green–
ON
OFF
Fig. 47. ECU green and red LED lights

Fig. 49. Checking the vacuum (MAP) sensor

Fig. 50. Vacuum (MAP) sensor terminals

5. Turn the ignition **OFF** and turn the ECU diagnostic switch **ON** and check the lighting intervals.

6. SEE the illustration. Check each sensor as follows. Check all connectors before continuing.

7. Disconnect the ECU 20 pin connector and connect the ECU and harness connector terminals 19 and 20 with suitable wire.

8. Disconnect the vacuum (MAP) sensor and connect the sensor terminals to battery and ground. Connect a voltmeter to the remaining terminal. Check the voltage as illustrated in the sensor values illustration.

9. Measure the resistance of the coolant temperature sensor with an ohmmeter. Check the wiring harness, if OK replace the ECU.

10. If every thing checks, reconnect all disconnected harnesses.

11. Turn the ignition **OFF** and check all solenoid harnesses.

12. Disconnect each harness and measure the resistance of each solenoid. SEE the illustration for values.

13. Reconnect all harness connectors.

14. Disconnect the ECU connectors. Turn the ignition switch **ON** and measure the voltages between each terminal and ground as illustrated in the solenoid voltage values.

Sensor	Circuit tester	Check terminals +	Check terminals −	Condition	Standard value
Vacuum sensor	V	9	19	0 kPa (0 mmHg, 0 inHg)	4.0V
				−88.0 kPa (−660 mmHg, −25.98 inHg)	0.5V
Water temperature sensor	Ω	8		20°C (68°F) or above	Below 2.9 kΩ
				Below 20°C (68°F)	2.1 kΩ or above
Air temperature sensor		1		20°C (68°F) or above	Below 2.9 kΩ
				Below 20°C (68°F)	2.1 kΩ or above

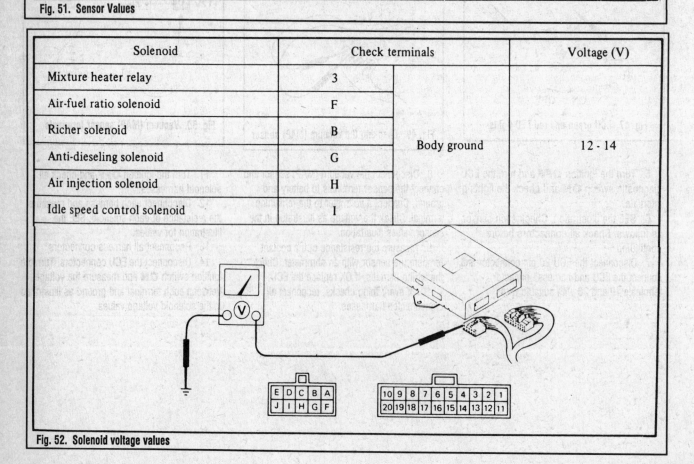

Fig. 51. Sensor Values

Solenoid	Check terminals		Voltage (V)
Mixture heater relay	3	Body ground	12 - 14
Air-fuel ratio solenoid	F		
Richer solenoid	B		
Anti-dieseling solenoid	G		
Air injection solenoid	H		
Idle speed control solenoid	I		

Fig. 52. Solenoid voltage values

Electronic Concentrated Control System (ECCS) with Electronic Fuel Injection

SELF-DIAGNOSTIC SYSTEM

Description

Nissan models have a self-diagnosis function as part of the Electronic Concentrated Control System (ECCS). The self-diagnostic system is useful in diagnosing malfunctions in major sensors, actuators and wire harnesses based on the status of the input signals received by the EFI/ECCS control unit.

The self-diagnostic function monitors the input signals whenever power is furnished to the ECU. When an abnormality is detected, the ECU stores the information in memory. The results are displayed only when the diagnostic mode selector, located on the side of the control unit, is turned **ON**. When activated, the malfunction is indicated by flashing a red and green Light Emitting Diode (LED) attached to the Electronic Control Unit (ECU). The flashes indicate a 2-digit code which identifies the malfunctioning part(s) group. The red LED flashes first, followed by the green LED. The red LED sees to the code's multiple of 10-digit and the green LED Sees to the single digit. For example, when the red LED flashes once and the green LED flashes twice this means that code number 12, showing the air flow meter signal, is malfunctioning.

Basically, self-diagnosis is always performed when the power is furnished to the EFI control unit. The self-diagnosis results are retained in the memory chip of the EFI control unit and are displayed only when the diagnosis mode selector (located on the side of the control unit) is turned ON.

The self-diagnostic system is provided with functions which display malfunctions being checked as well as those which are stored in the memory. In this sense, it is very effective in determining an "intermittent" malfunction. The results which is or was stored in the memory can be erased by following the steps specified.

A malfunctioning area is determined by the number of blinks of both the red and green LED's. First, the red LED blinks and then the green blinks. The red LED Sees to the tenth digit while the green one Sees to the unit digit. For example, when the red LED blinks three times and the green LED blinks twice, this implies number "32". In this way, all problems are classified by code numbers.

The self-diagnostic system is provided with functions which display malfunctions being checked currently as well as those stored in the memory. In this sense, it is very effective in determining an "intermittent" malfunction. For this reason, it is important not to clear the ECU memory before beginning diagnosis of the system. When the codes have been noted and/or repairs made, the memory can be cleared following specified steps.

If the system goes unserviced, codes will remain stored in the ECU memory until the starter has been operated 50 times; the codes will then be canceled automatically. If the malfunction which has been stored in memory occurs again, before the starter has been operated 50 times, the 2nd occurrence will replace the previous one. The new code will be stored in memory until the starter has been operated 50 times more.

Items Displayed All The Time

When performing the self-diagnosis, the items listed below are displayed by the EFI control unit as a malfunction even though they are working. Therefore, whenever performing the self-diagnosis, enter the appropriate signals for the items.

INPUT PROCEDURE

1. Throttle Valve Switch (Idle Switch) Circuit And Air Conditioner Switch Circuit — After the ignition switch is turned ON and "ON-OFF" signal from each switch are entered.

2. Start Signal — After the engine has started and when start signal "ON" and then "OFF" are entered.

3. Load Signal — After load signal is turned "ON", a signal is entered.

Items Retained In Memory

The following items will be retained in the memory from the time of detection until erased:

- Air Flow Meter Circuit — When the air flow meter produces an abnormally high output voltage with the engine off or low output voltage with the engine running
- Water Temperature Sensor Circuit — When the circuit is shorted or open
- Ignition Signal — When an ignition signal is not produced on the primary winding of the ignition coil after the engine has started
- Fuel Pump Circuit — When current flowing through the control unit to drive the fuel pump is too small or too large while the engine is operating
- Air Temperature Sensor Circuit — When the circuit is shorted or open

TESTING PRECAUTIONS

1. Before connecting or disconnecting control unit ECU harness connectors, make sure the ignition switch is OFF and the negative battery cable is disconnected to avoid the possibility of damage to the control unit.

2. When performing ECU input/output signal diagnosis, remove the pin terminal retainer from the 20 and 16–pin connectors to make it easier to insert tester probes into the connector.

3. When connecting or disconnecting pin connectors from the ECU, take care not to bend or break any pin terminals. Check that there are no bends or breaks on ECU pin terminals before attempting any connections.

Solenoid	Resistance (Ω)
Mixture heater relay	60 - 85
Air-fuel ratio solenoid	30 - 50
Richer solenoid	20 - 40
Anti-dieseling solenoid	25 - 45
Air injection solenoid	
Idle speed control solenoid	

Fig. 53. Solenoid ohm values

Mode	LED	Engine stopped	Engine running			
			Open loop condition	Closed loop condition		
Mode I (Monitor A)	Green	ON	OFF	• OFF: rich condition • ON: lean condition • Maintains conditions just before clamping		
	Red	ON	OFF	OFF		
Mode II (Monitor B)	Green	ON	OFF	• OFF: rich condition • ON: lean condition • Maintains conditions just before clamping		
	Red	OFF	OFF	Compensating mixture ratio		
				More than 5% rich	Between 5% lean and 5% rich	More than 5% lean
				OFF	Synchronized with green LED	ON

Fig. 54. Mixture ratio feedback control monitors — mode I and II, 1987–88 engines

4. Before replacing any ECU, perform the ECU input/output signal diagnosis to make sure the ECU is functioning properly or not.

5. After performing the Electronic Control System Inspection, perform the EFI self-diagnosis and driving test.

6. When measuring supply voltage of ECU controlled components with a circuit tester, separate one tester probe from another. If the two tester probes accidentally make contact with each other during measurement, a short circuit will result and damage the power transistor in the ECU.

ENTERING DIAGNOSTICS

See the diagnostic charts for entering, reading and erasing diagnostics and codes. Do not skip steps while going through the charts. And remember, always check the basics (low charging, loose or corroded wiring, mechanical problems) before condemning the electronic engine control systems.

COMPONENT LOCATION FOR ECCS SYSTEM – 1984 E15ET ENGINE

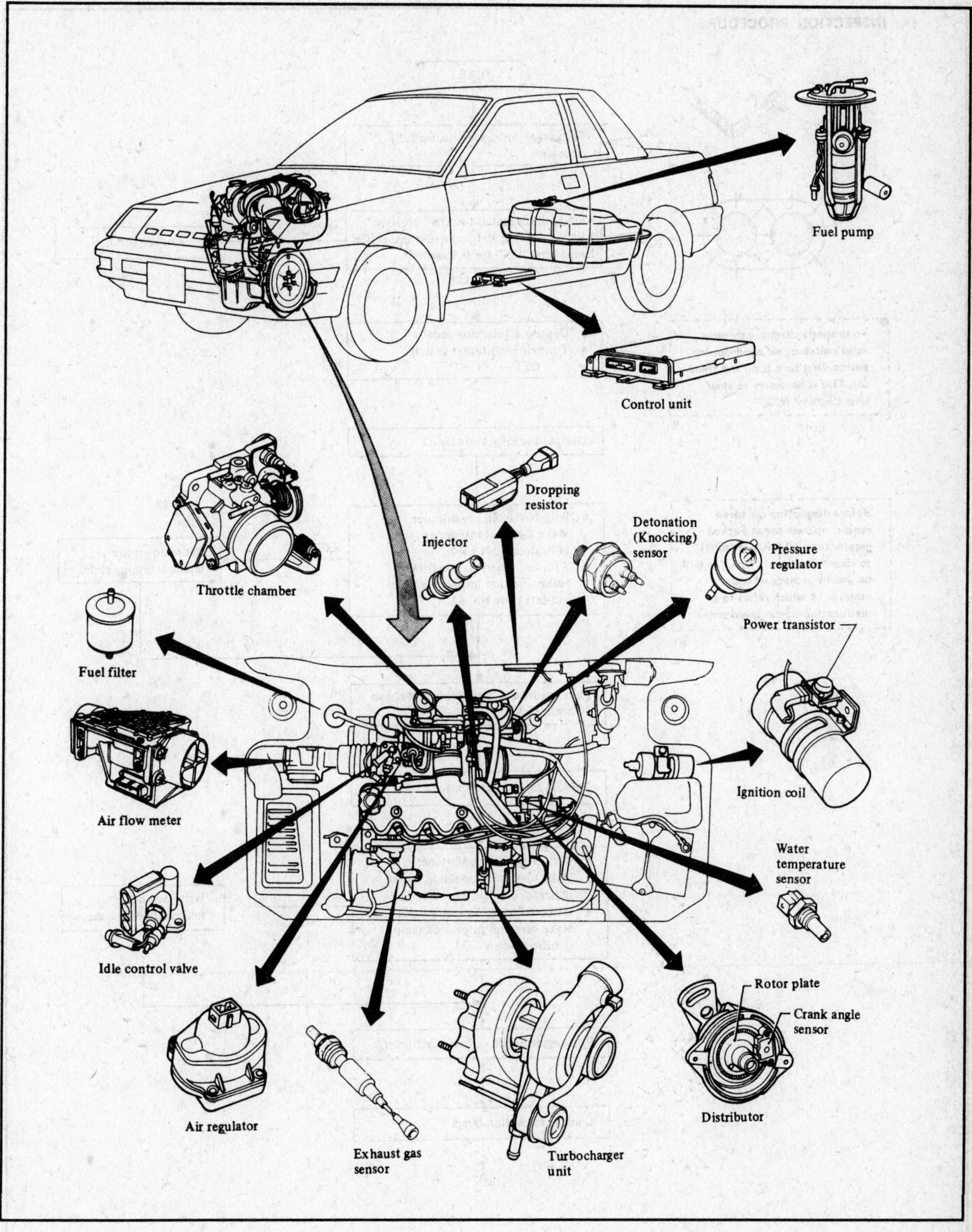
Fuel pump
Control unit
Throttle chamber
Dropping resistor
Injector
Detonation (Knocking) sensor
Pressure regulator
Power transistor
Fuel filter
Air flow meter
Ignition coil
Water temperature sensor
Idle control valve
Rotor plate
Crank angle sensor
Air regulator
Distributor
Exhaust gas sensor
Turbocharger unit

DIAGNOSTIC INSPECTION PROCEDURE — 1984 E15ET ENGINE, PART 1

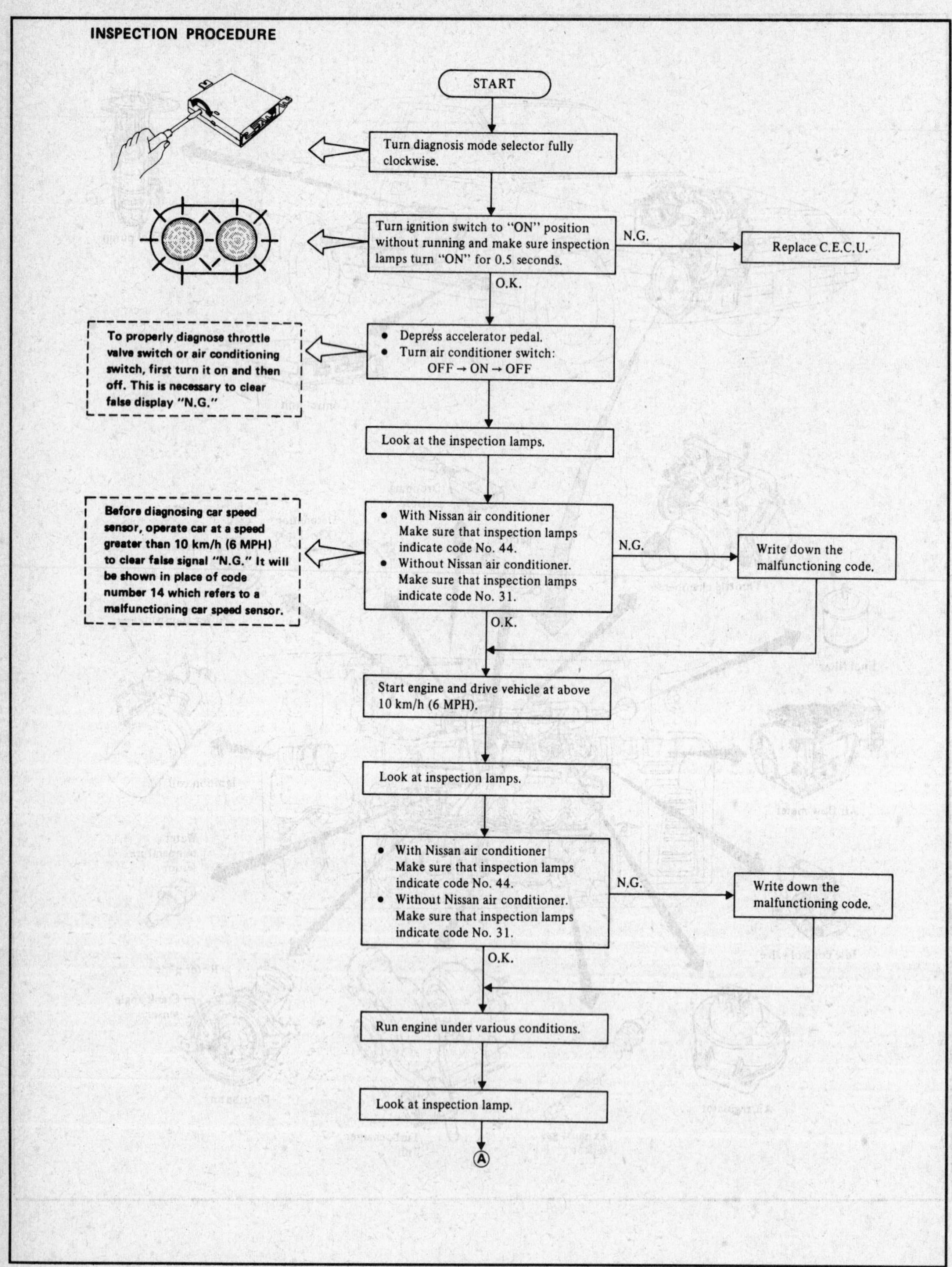
INSPECTION PROCEDURE
START
Turn diagnosis mode selector fully clockwise.
Turn ignition switch to "ON" position without running and make sure inspection lamps turn "ON" for 0.5 seconds.
N.G.
Replace C.E.C.U.
O.K.
To properly diagnose throttle valve switch or air conditioning switch, first turn it on and then off. This is necessary to clear false display "N.G."
• Depress accelerator pedal.
• Turn air conditioner switch: OFF → ON → OFF
Look at the inspection lamps.
Before diagnosing car speed sensor, operate car at a speed greater than 10 km/h (6 MPH) to clear false signal "N.G." It will be shown in place of code number 14 which refers to a malfunctioning car speed sensor.
• With Nissan air conditioner Make sure that inspection lamps indicate code No. 44.
• Without Nissan air conditioner. Make sure that inspection lamps indicate code No. 31.
N.G.
Write down the malfunctioning code.
O.K.
Start engine and drive vehicle at above 10 km/h (6 MPH).
Look at inspection lamps.
• With Nissan air conditioner Make sure that inspection lamps indicate code No. 44.
• Without Nissan air conditioner. Make sure that inspection lamps indicate code No. 31.
N.G.
Write down the malfunctioning code.
O.K.
Run engine under various conditions.
Look at inspection lamp.
A

DIAGNOSTIC INSPECIONN PROCEDURE – 1984 E15ET ENGINE, PART 2

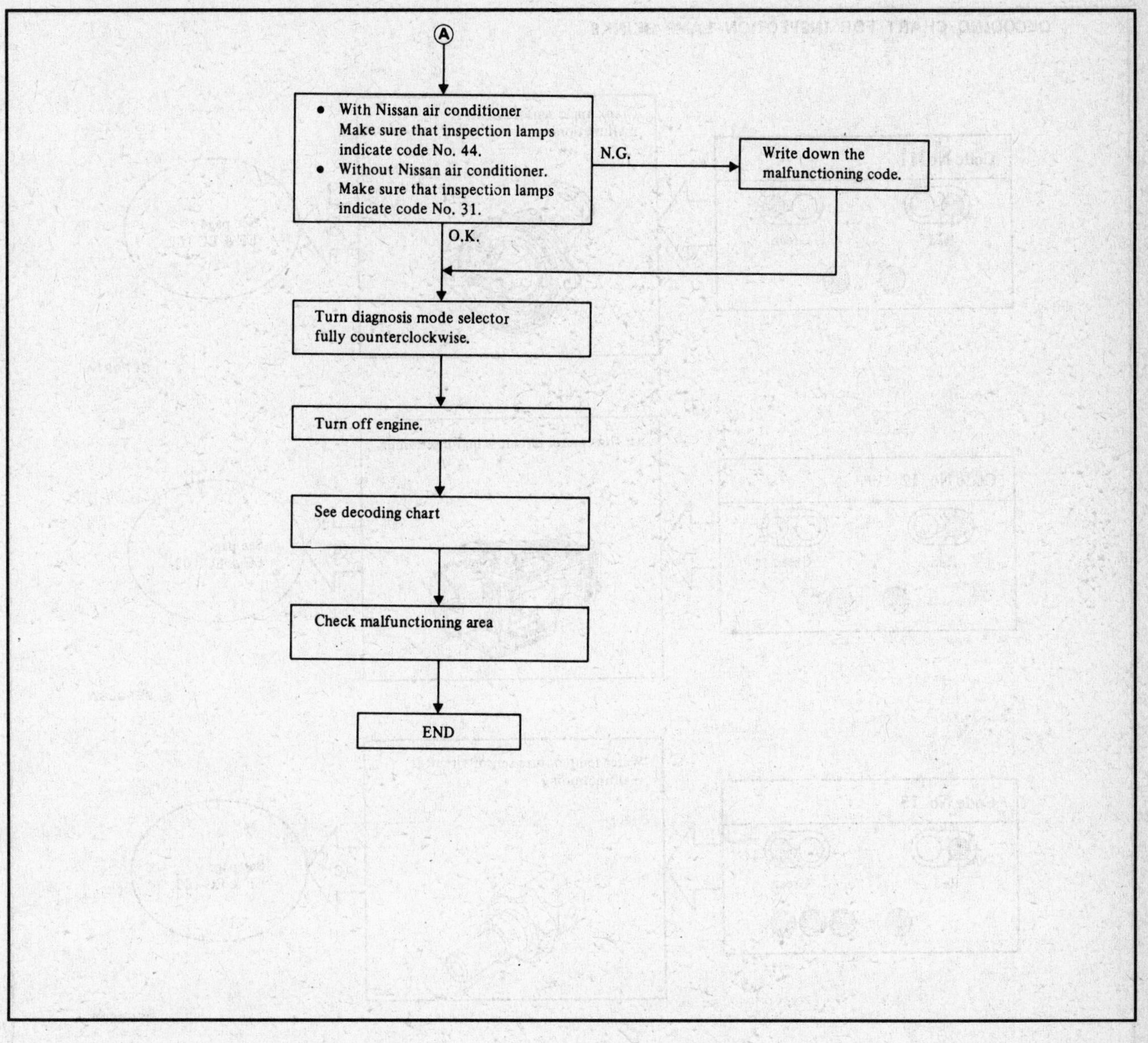
A
• With Nissan air conditioner Make sure that inspection lamps indicate code No. 44.
• Without Nissan air conditioner. Make sure that inspection lamps indicate code No. 31.
N.G.
Write down the malfunctioning code.
O.K.
Turn diagnosis mode selector fully counterclockwise.
Turn off engine.
See decoding chart
Check malfunctioning area
END

TROUBLE CODE DECODING CHART — 1984 E15ET ENGINE, PART 1

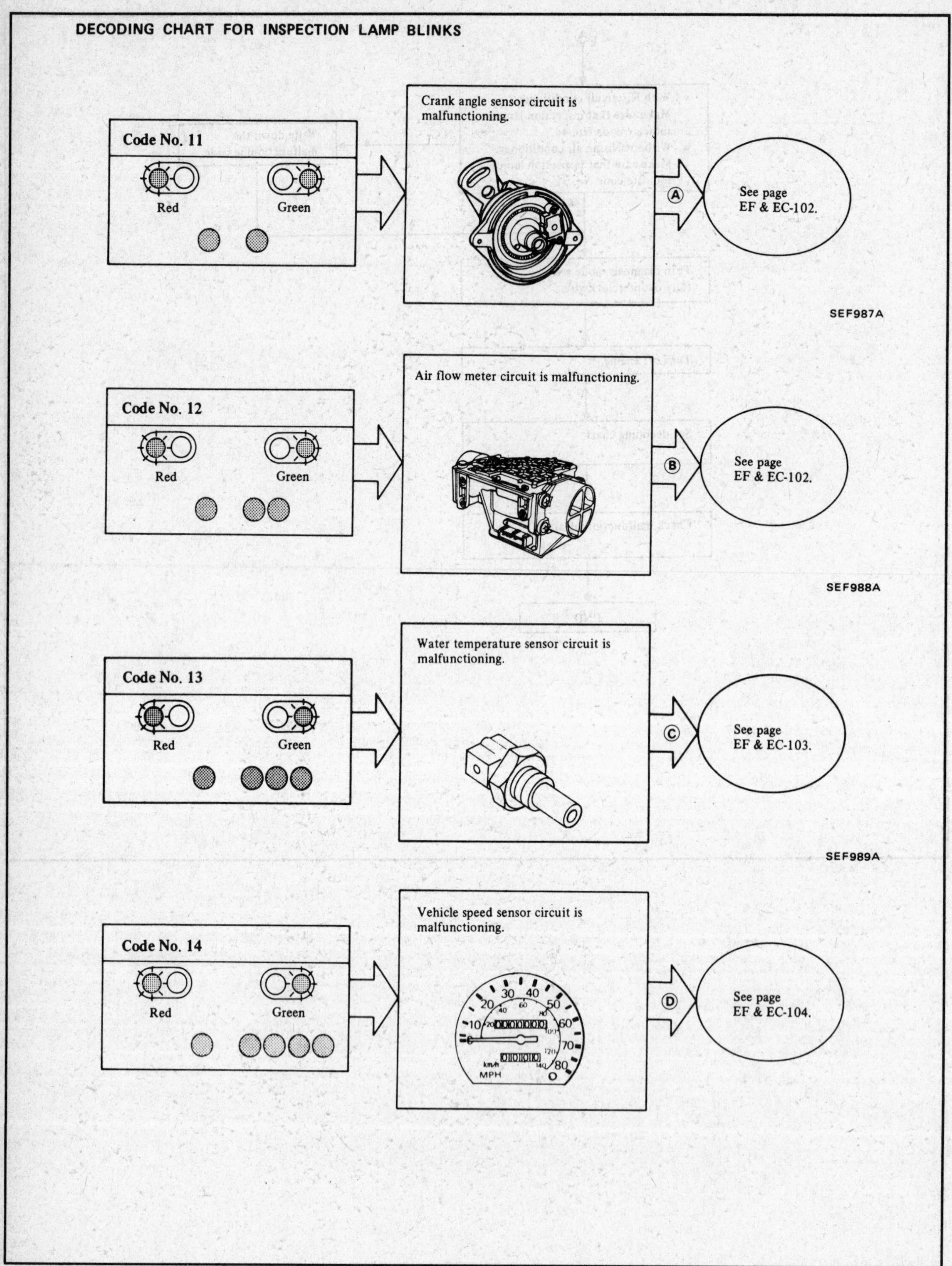
DECODING CHART FOR INSPECTION LAMP BLINKS
Code No. 11
Red
Green
Crank angle sensor circuit is malfunctioning.
A
See page EF & EC-102.
SEF987A
Code No. 12
Red
Green
Air flow meter circuit is malfunctioning.
B
See page EF & EC-102.
SEF988A
Code No. 13
Red
Green
Water temperature sensor circuit is malfunctioning.
C
See page EF & EC-103.
SEF989A
Code No. 14
Red
Green
Vehicle speed sensor circuit is malfunctioning.
D
See page EF & EC-104.

TROUBLE CODE DECODING CHART – 1984 E15ET ENGINE, PART 2

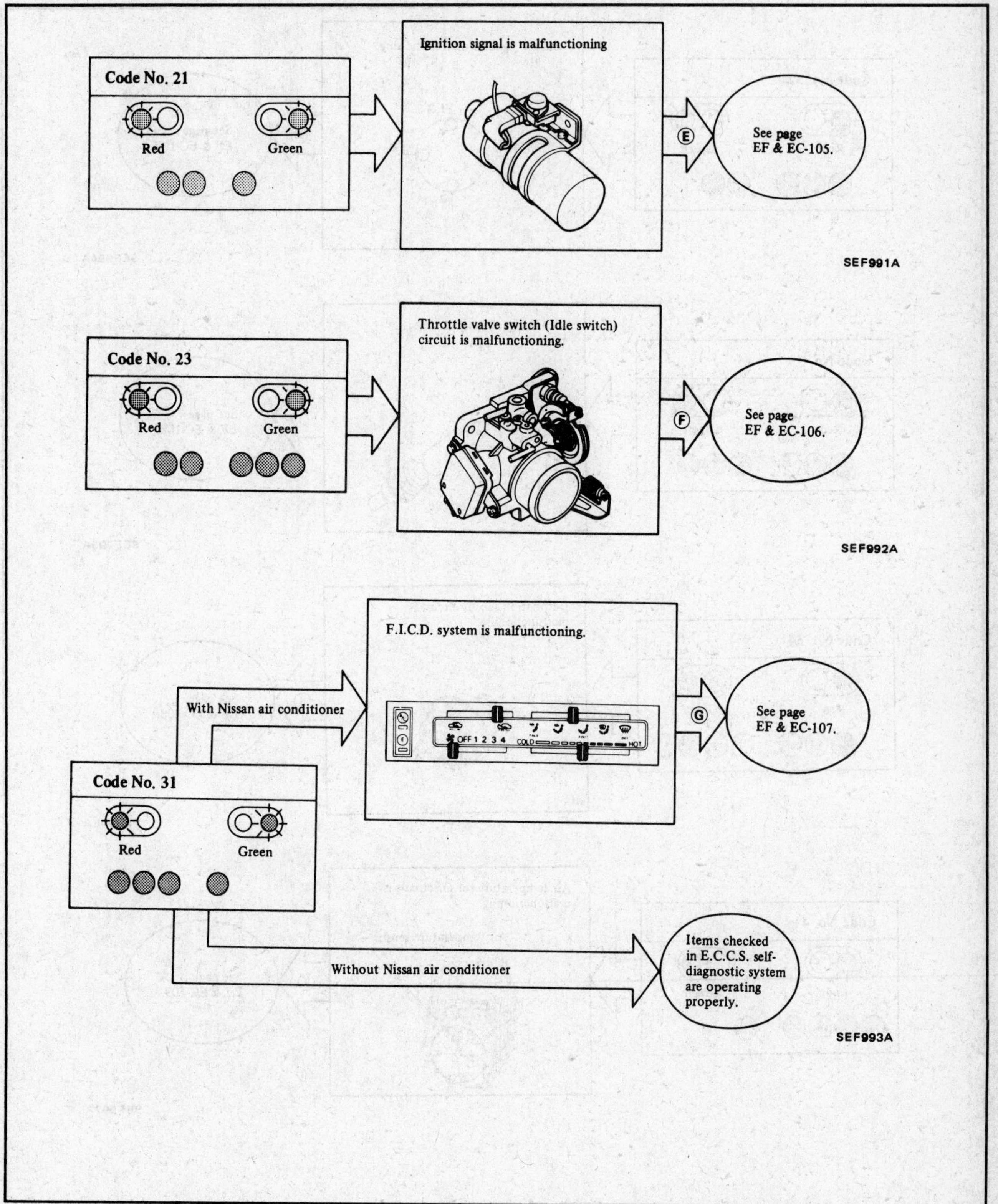
Code No. 21
Red
Green
Ignition signal is malfunctioning
E
See page
EF & EC-105.
SEF991A
Code No. 23
Red
Green
Throttle valve switch (Idle switch)
circuit is malfunctioning.
F
See page
EF & EC-106.
SEF992A
F.I.C.D. system is malfunctioning.
With Nissan air conditioner
OFF 1 2 3 4
COLD
HOT
G
See page
EF & EC-107.
Code No. 31
Red
Green
Without Nissan air conditioner
Items checked
in E.C.C.S. self-
diagnostic system
are operating
properly.
SEF993A

TROUBLE CODE DECODING CHART — 1984 E15ET ENGINE, PART 3

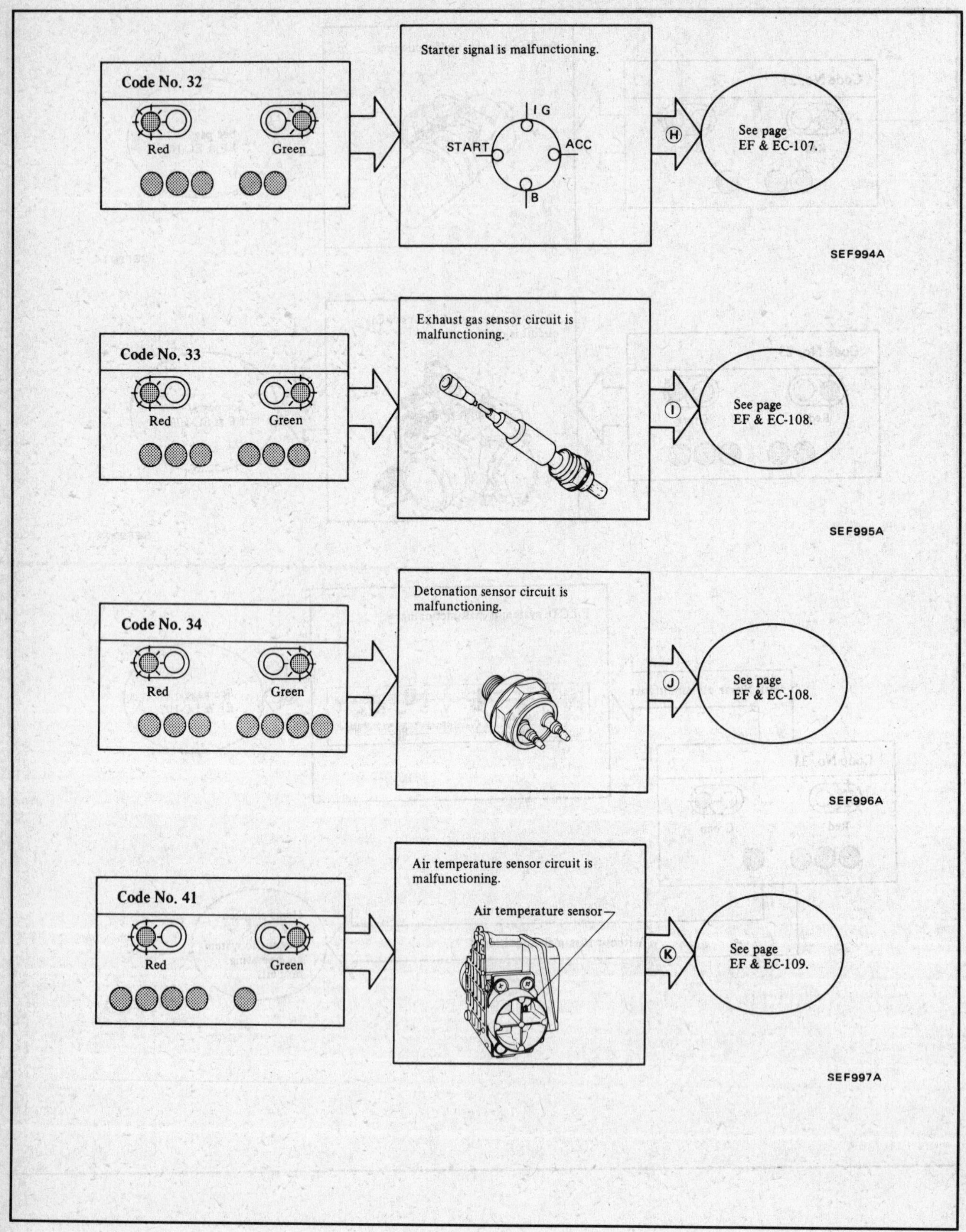
Code No. 32
Red
Green
Starter signal is malfunctioning.
I G
START
ACC
B
H
See page
EF & EC-107.
SEF994A
Code No. 33
Red
Green
Exhaust gas sensor circuit is
malfunctioning.
I
See page
EF & EC-108.
SEF995A
Code No. 34
Red
Green
Detonation sensor circuit is
malfunctioning.
J
See page
EF & EC-108.
SEF996A
Code No. 41
Red
Green
Air temperature sensor circuit is
malfunctioning.
Air temperature sensor
K
See page
EF & EC-109.
SEF997A

TROUBLE CODE DECODING CHART — 1984 E15ET ENGINE, PART 4

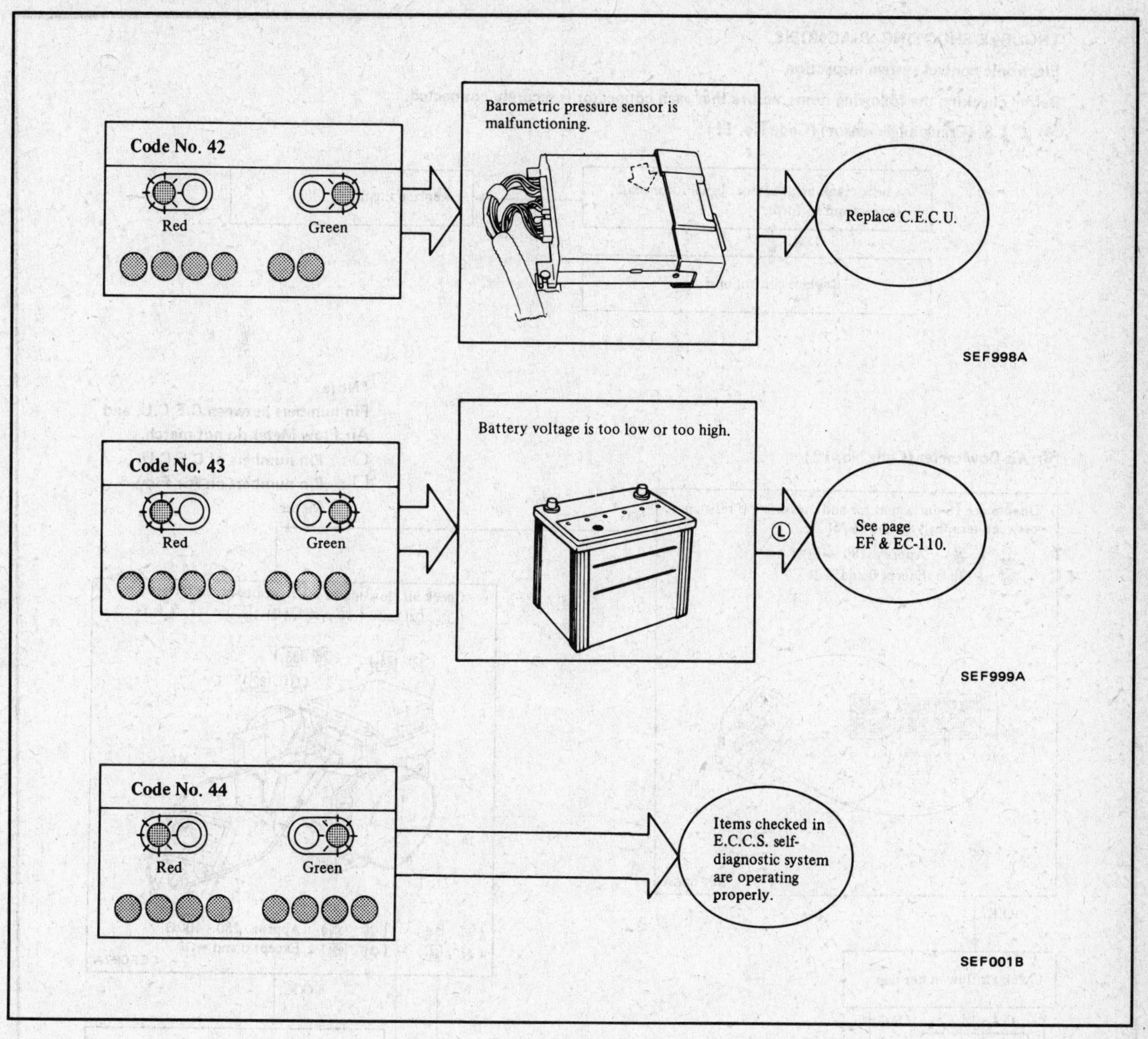
Code No. 42
Red
Green
Barometric pressure sensor is malfunctioning.
Replace C.E.C.U.
SEF998A
Code No. 43
Red
Green
Battery voltage is too low or too high.
L
See page EF & EC-110.
SEF999A
Code No. 44
Red
Green
Items checked in E.C.C.S. self-diagnostic system are operating properly.
SEF001B

CODE 12 (AIR FLOW SENSOR) – 1984 E15ET ENGINE

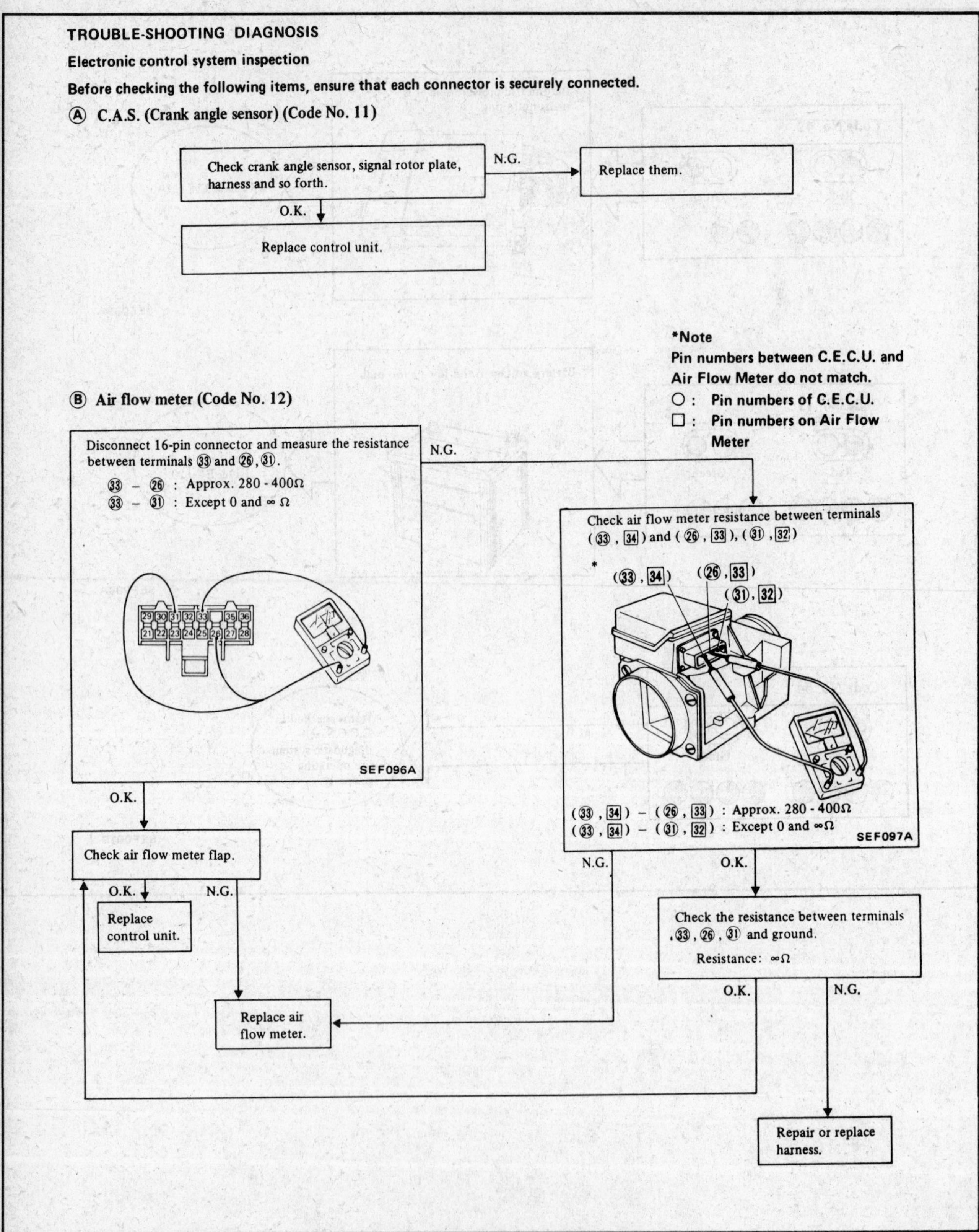
TROUBLE-SHOOTING DIAGNOSIS
Electronic control system inspection
Before checking the following items, ensure that each connector is securely connected.
Ⓐ C.A.S. (Crank angle sensor) (Code No. 11)
Check crank angle sensor, signal rotor plate, harness and so forth.
N.G.
Replace them.
O.K.
Replace control unit.
*Note
Pin numbers between C.E.C.U. and Air Flow Meter do not match.
○ : Pin numbers of C.E.C.U.
□ : Pin numbers on Air Flow Meter
Ⓑ Air flow meter (Code No. 12)
Disconnect 16-pin connector and measure the resistance between terminals ㉝ and ㉖, ㉛.
㉝ – ㉖ : Approx. 280 - 400Ω
㉝ – ㉛ : Except 0 and ∞ Ω
29 30 31 32 33 35 36
21 22 23 24 25 26 27 28
SEF096A
N.G.
Check air flow meter resistance between terminals (㉝, 34) and (㉖, 33), (㉛, 32)
*
(㉝, 34)
(㉖, 33)
(㉛, 32)
(㉝, 34) – (㉖, 33) : Approx. 280 - 400Ω
(㉝, 34) – (㉛, 32) : Except 0 and ∞Ω
SEF097A
O.K.
Check air flow meter flap.
O.K.
N.G.
Replace control unit.
N.G.
O.K.
Check the resistance between terminals ㉝, ㉖, ㉛ and ground.
Resistance: ∞Ω
O.K.
N.G.
Replace air flow meter.
Repair or replace harness.

CODE 13 (WATER TEMPERATURE SENSOR) – 1984 E15ET ENGINE

Ⓒ Water temperature sensor (Code No. 13)

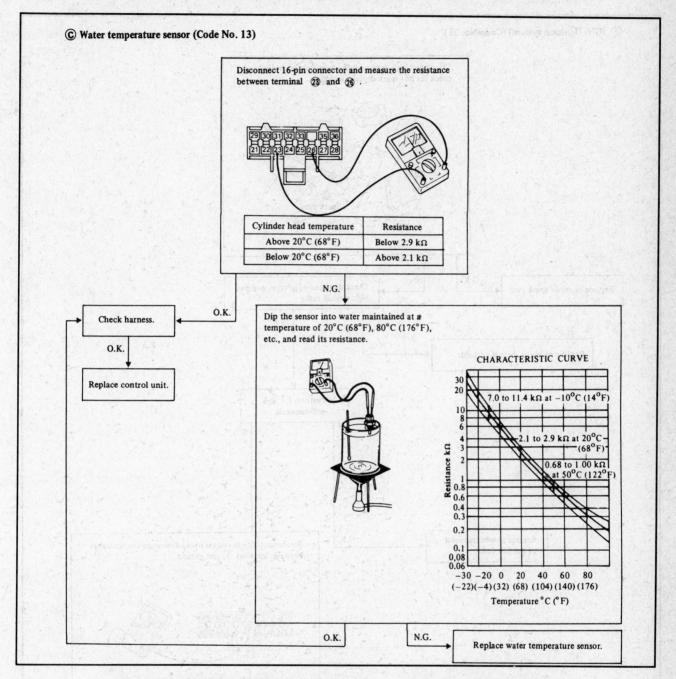

Disconnect 16-pin connector and measure the resistance between terminal ㉓ and ㉖.

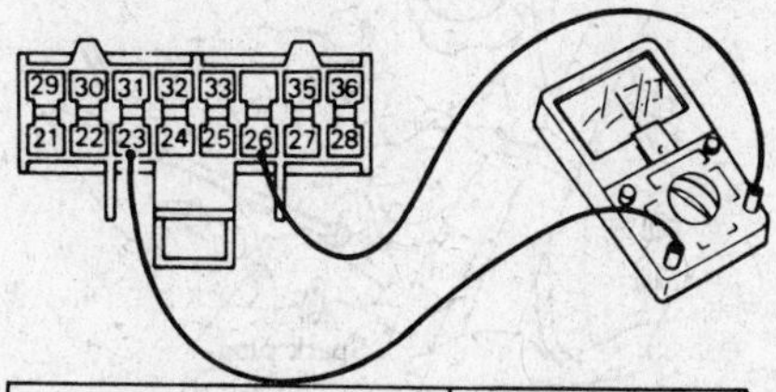

29 30 31 32 33 35 36
21 22 23 24 25 26 27 28

Cylinder head temperature	Resistance
Above 20°C (68°F)	Below 2.9 kΩ
Below 20°C (68°F)	Above 2.1 kΩ

O.K. → Check harness.

O.K. → Replace control unit.

N.G. → Dip the sensor into water maintained at a temperature of 20°C (68°F), 80°C (176°F), etc., and read its resistance.

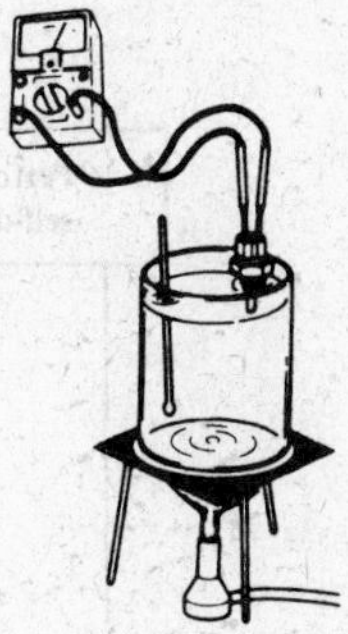

CHARACTERISTIC CURVE

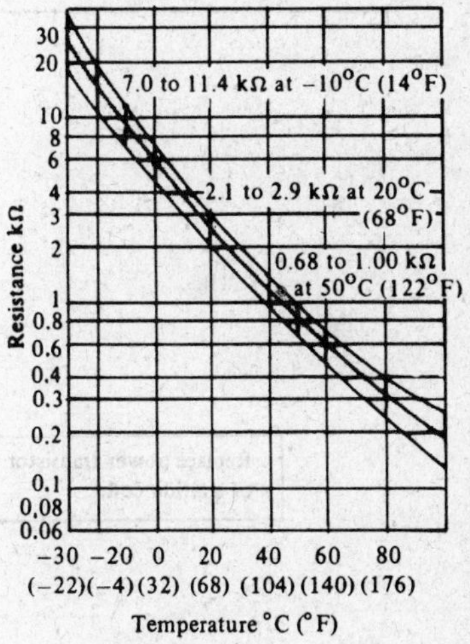

7.0 to 11.4 kΩ at −10°C (14°F)

2.1 to 2.9 kΩ at 20°C (68°F)

0.68 to 1.00 kΩ at 50°C (122°F)

Resistance kΩ: 30, 20, 10, 8, 6, 4, 3, 2, 1, 0.8, 0.6, 0.4, 0.3, 0.2, 0.1, 0,08, 0.06

−30 −20 0 20 40 60 80
(−22)(−4)(32) (68) (104) (140) (176)

Temperature °C (°F)

O.K. → Check harness.

N.G. → Replace water temperature sensor.

CODE 14 (VEHICLE SPEED SENSOR) – 1984 E15ET ENGINE

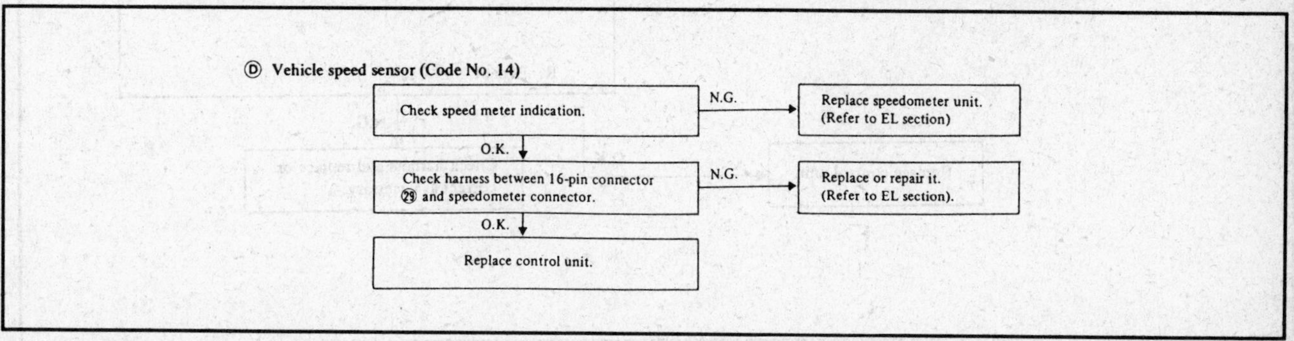
Ⓓ Vehicle speed sensor (Code No. 14)
Check speed meter indication.
N.G.
Replace speedometer unit. (Refer to EL section)
O.K.
Check harness between 16-pin connector ㉙ and speedometer connector.
N.G.
Replace or repair it. (Refer to EL section).
O.K.
Replace control unit.

CODE 21 (IGNITION SYSTEM) — 1984 E15ET ENGINE

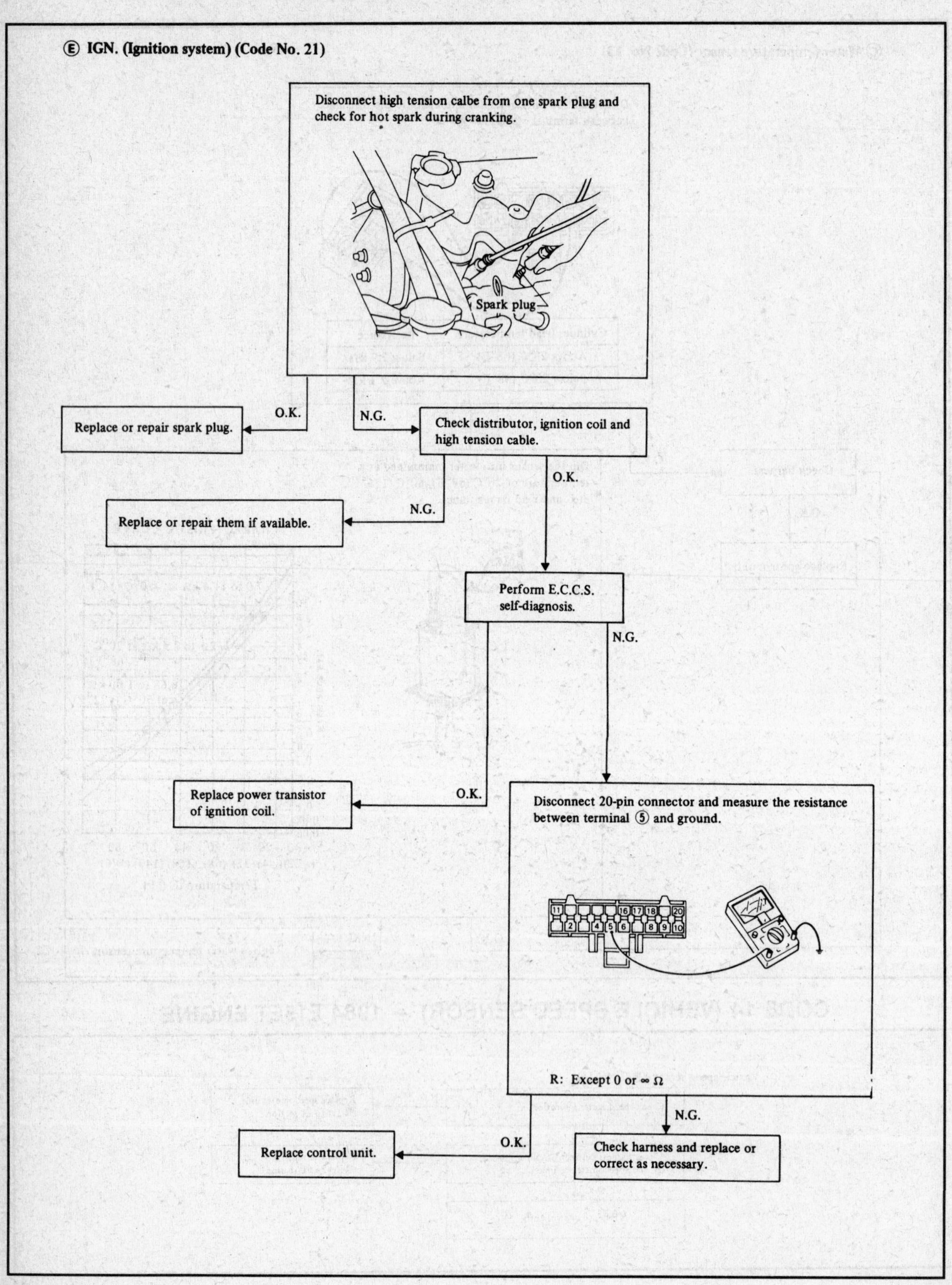
Ⓔ IGN. (Ignition system) (Code No. 21)
Disconnect high tension calbe from one spark plug and check for hot spark during cranking.
Spark plug
O.K.
Replace or repair spark plug.
N.G.
Check distributor, ignition coil and high tension cable.
N.G.
Replace or repair them if available.
O.K.
Perform E.C.C.S. self-diagnosis.
O.K.
Replace power transistor of ignition coil.
N.G.
Disconnect 20-pin connector and measure the resistance between terminal ⑤ and ground.
11
16 17 18 20
2 4 5 6 8 9 10
R: Except 0 or ∞ Ω
O.K.
Replace control unit.
N.G.
Check harness and replace or correct as necessary.

CODE 23 (THROTTLE SWITCH) — 1984 E15ET ENGINE

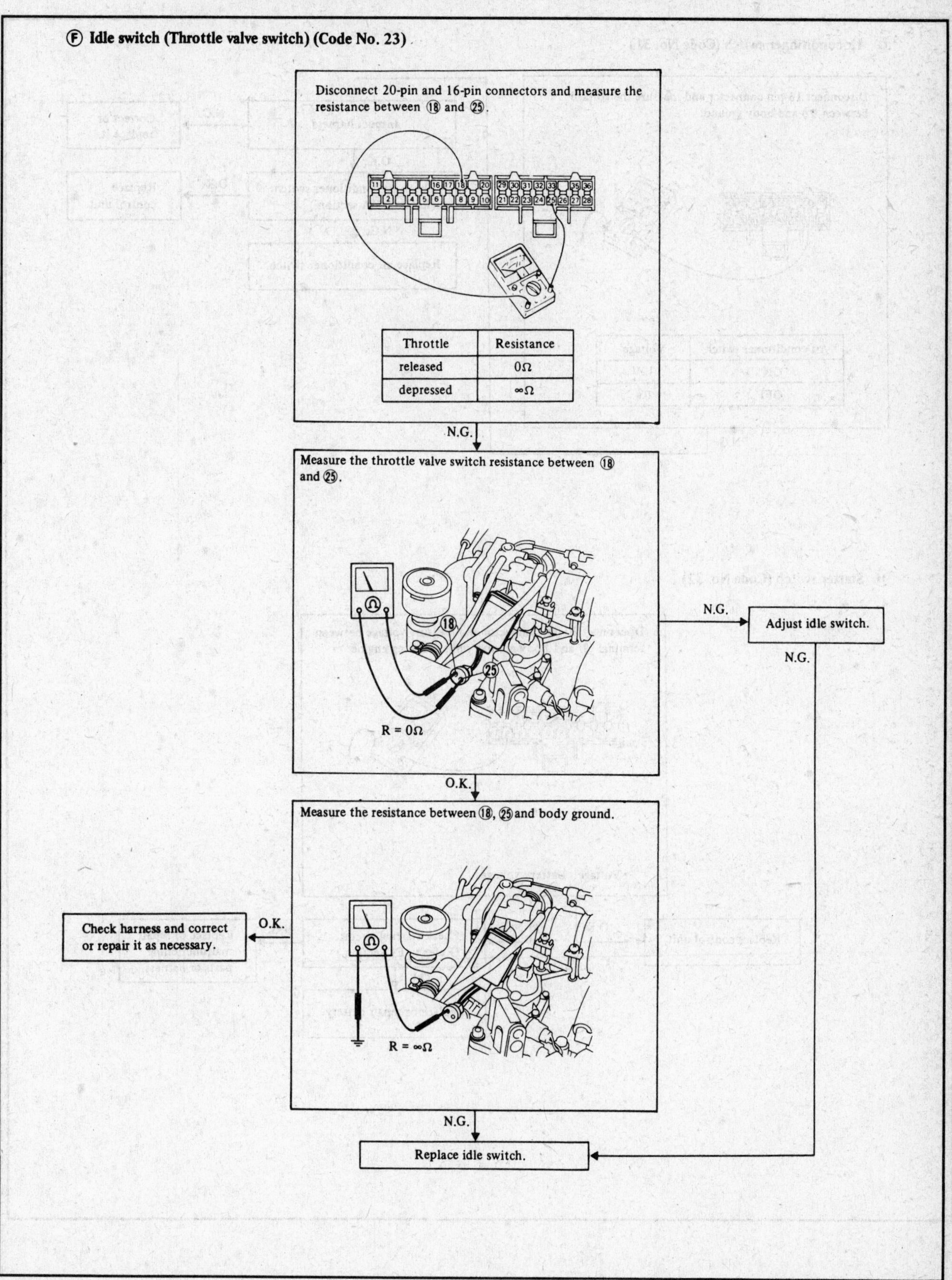
Ⓕ Idle switch (Throttle valve switch) (Code No. 23)
Disconnect 20-pin and 16-pin connectors and measure the resistance between ⑱ and ㉕.
Throttle | Resistance
released | 0Ω
depressed | ∞Ω
N.G.
Measure the throttle valve switch resistance between ⑱ and ㉕.
⑱
㉕
R = 0Ω
N.G.
Adjust idle switch.
N.G.
O.K.
Measure the resistance between ⑱, ㉕ and body ground.
R = ∞Ω
O.K.
Check harness and correct or repair it as necessary.
N.G.
Replace idle switch.

CODE 31 (A/C SWITCH) – 1984 E15ET ENGINE

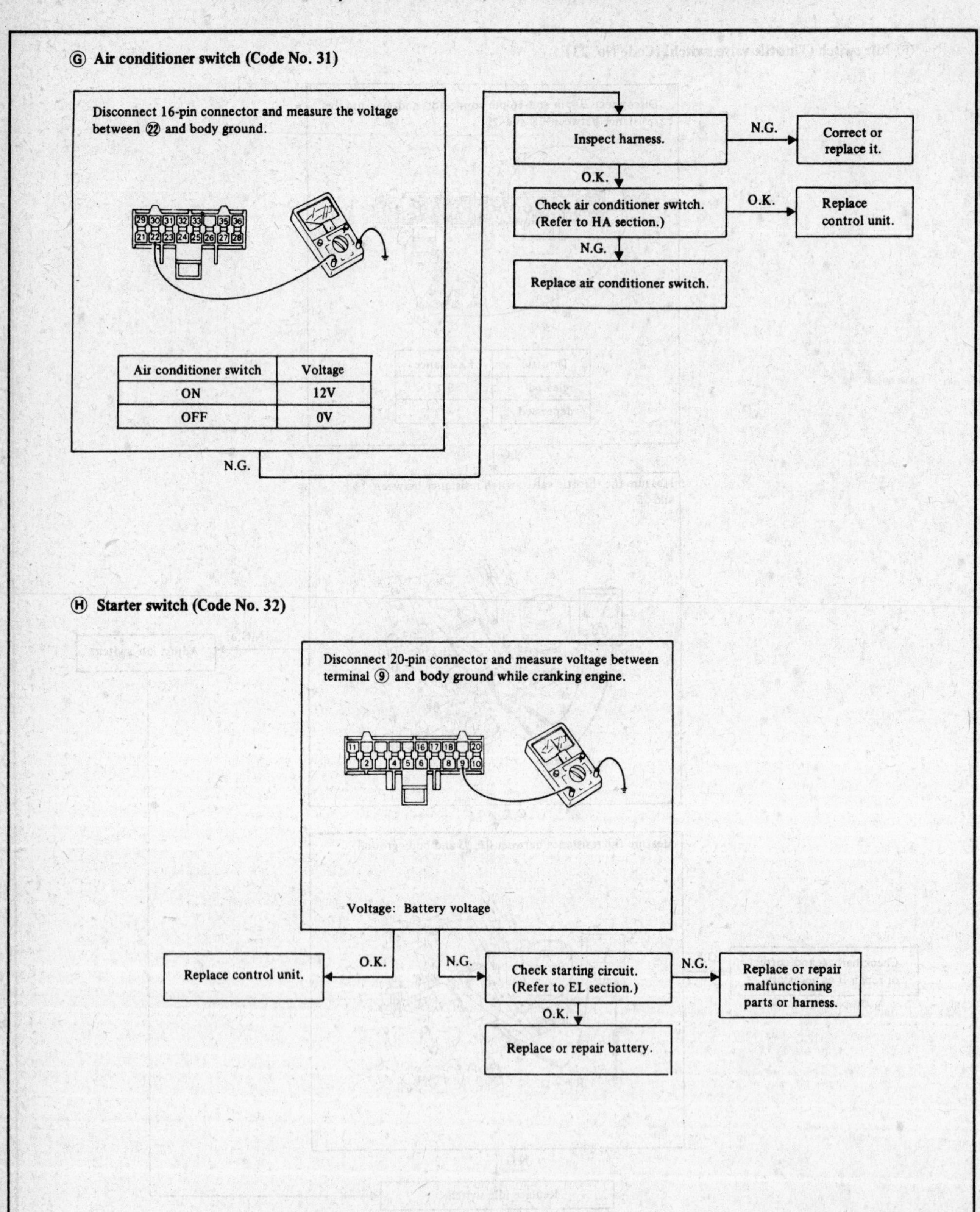
Ⓖ Air conditioner switch (Code No. 31)
Disconnect 16-pin connector and measure the voltage between ㉒ and body ground.
29 30 31 32 33 35 36
21 22 23 24 25 26 27 28
Air conditioner switch | Voltage
ON | 12V
OFF | 0V
N.G.
Inspect harness.
N.G.
Correct or replace it.
O.K.
Check air conditioner switch. (Refer to HA section.)
O.K.
Replace control unit.
N.G.
Replace air conditioner switch.
Ⓗ Starter switch (Code No. 32)
Disconnect 20-pin connector and measure voltage between terminal ⑨ and body ground while cranking engine.
11 16 17 18 20
2 4 5 6 8 9 10
Voltage: Battery voltage
O.K.
Replace control unit.
N.G.
Check starting circuit. (Refer to EL section.)
N.G.
Replace or repair malfunctioning parts or harness.
O.K.
Replace or repair battery.

CODE 33 (OXYGEN SENSOR) — 1984 E15ET ENGINE

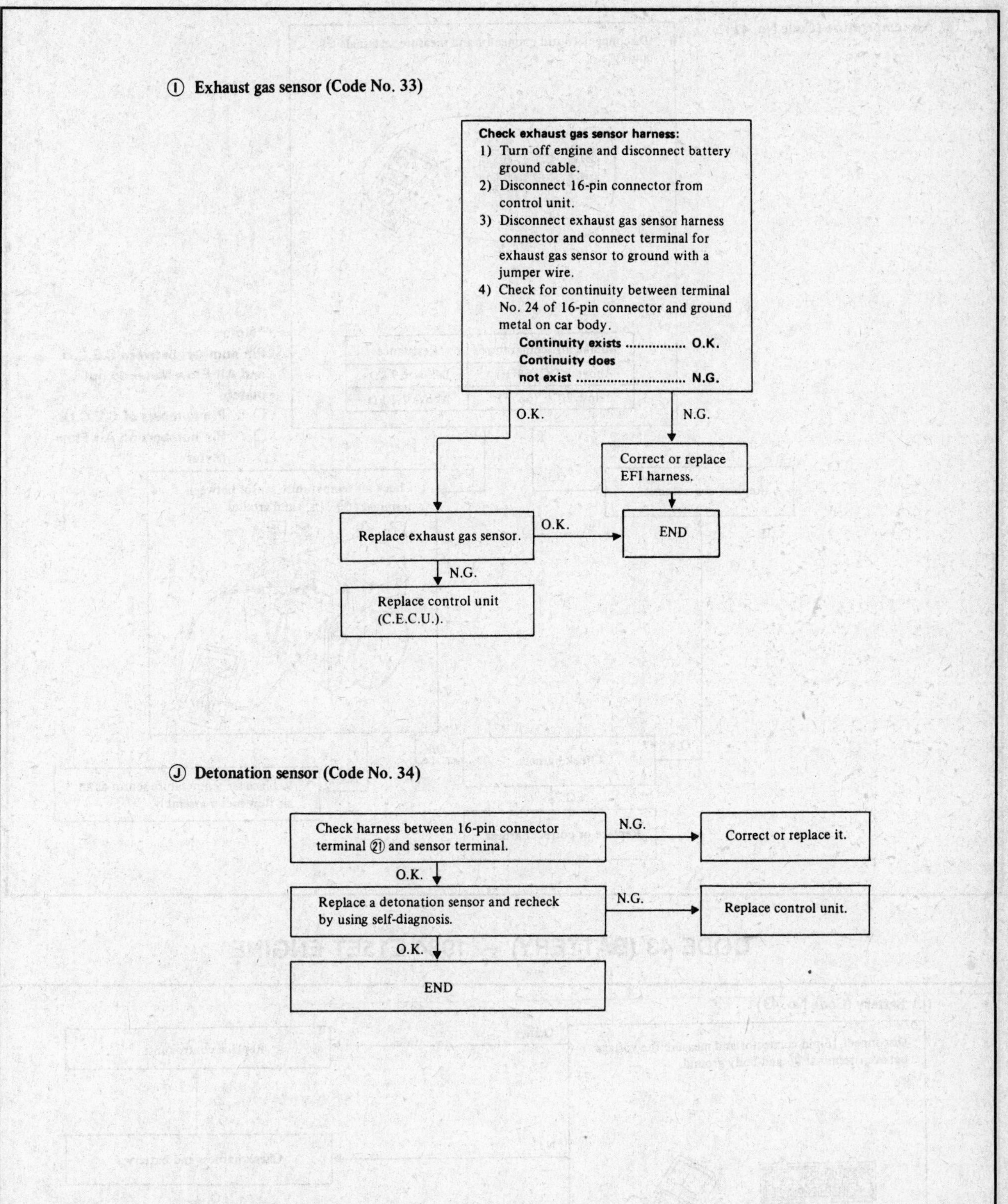

Ⓘ Exhaust gas sensor (Code No. 33)
Check exhaust gas sensor harness:
1) Turn off engine and disconnect battery ground cable.
2) Disconnect 16-pin connector from control unit.
3) Disconnect exhaust gas sensor harness connector and connect terminal for exhaust gas sensor to ground with a jumper wire.
4) Check for continuity between terminal No. 24 of 16-pin connector and ground metal on car body.
Continuity exists .... O.K.
Continuity does not exist .... N.G.
O.K.
N.G.
Correct or replace EFI harness.
Replace exhaust gas sensor.
O.K.
END
N.G.
Replace control unit (C.E.C.U.).
Ⓙ Detonation sensor (Code No. 34)
Check harness between 16-pin connector terminal ㉑ and sensor terminal.
N.G.
Correct or replace it.
O.K.
Replace a detonation sensor and recheck by using self-diagnosis.
N.G.
Replace control unit.
O.K.
END

CODE 41 (AIR TEMPERATURE SENSOR) – 1984 E15ET ENGINE

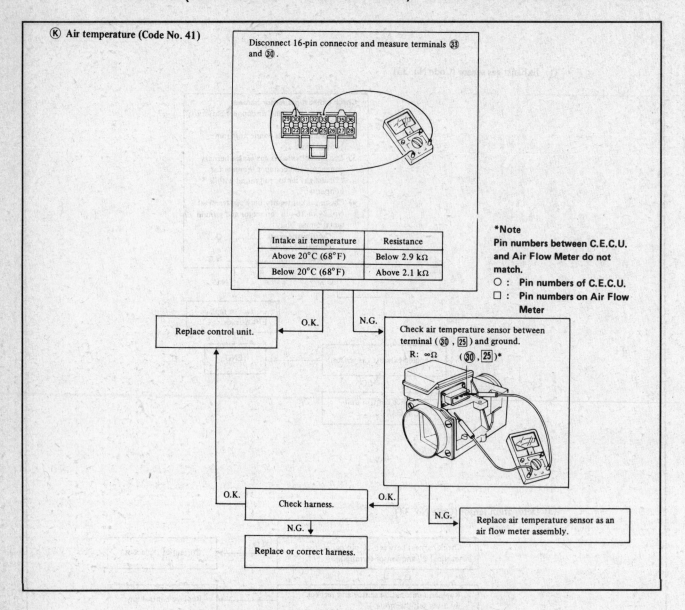

Ⓚ Air temperature (Code No. 41)

Disconnect 16-pin connector and measure terminals ㉝ and ㉚.

29 30 31 32 33 35 36
21 22 23 24 25 26 27 28

Intake air temperature	Resistance
Above 20°C (68°F)	Below 2.9 kΩ
Below 20°C (68°F)	Above 2.1 kΩ

O.K. → Replace control unit.

N.G. → Check air temperature sensor between terminal (㉚, [25]) and ground.
R: ∞Ω (㉚, [25])*

*Note
Pin numbers between C.E.C.U. and Air Flow Meter do not match.
○ : Pin numbers of C.E.C.U.
□ : Pin numbers on Air Flow Meter

O.K. → Check harness.
- O.K. → Replace control unit.
- N.G. → Replace or correct harness.

N.G. → Replace air temperature sensor as an air flow meter assembly.

CODE 43 (BATTERY) – 1984 E15ET ENGINE

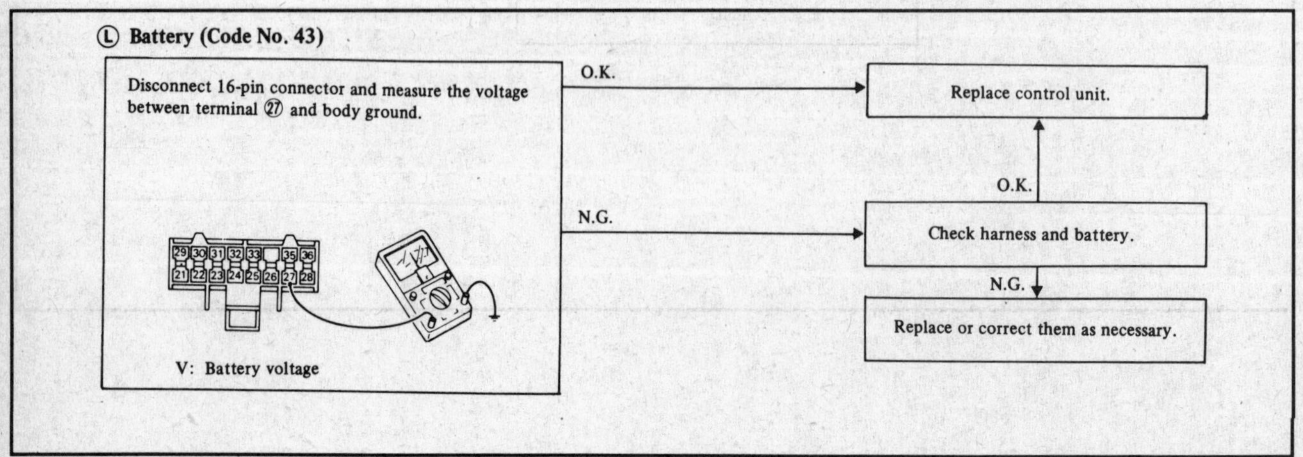
Ⓛ Battery (Code No. 43)
Disconnect 16-pin connector and measure the voltage between terminal ㉗ and body ground.
29 30 31 32 33 35 36
21 22 23 24 25 26 27 28
V: Battery voltage
O.K.
Replace control unit.
N.G.
Check harness and battery.
O.K.
N.G.
Replace or correct them as necessary.

MODE III, SELF-DIAGNOSTIC SYSTEM PROCEDURE – E16i ENGINE

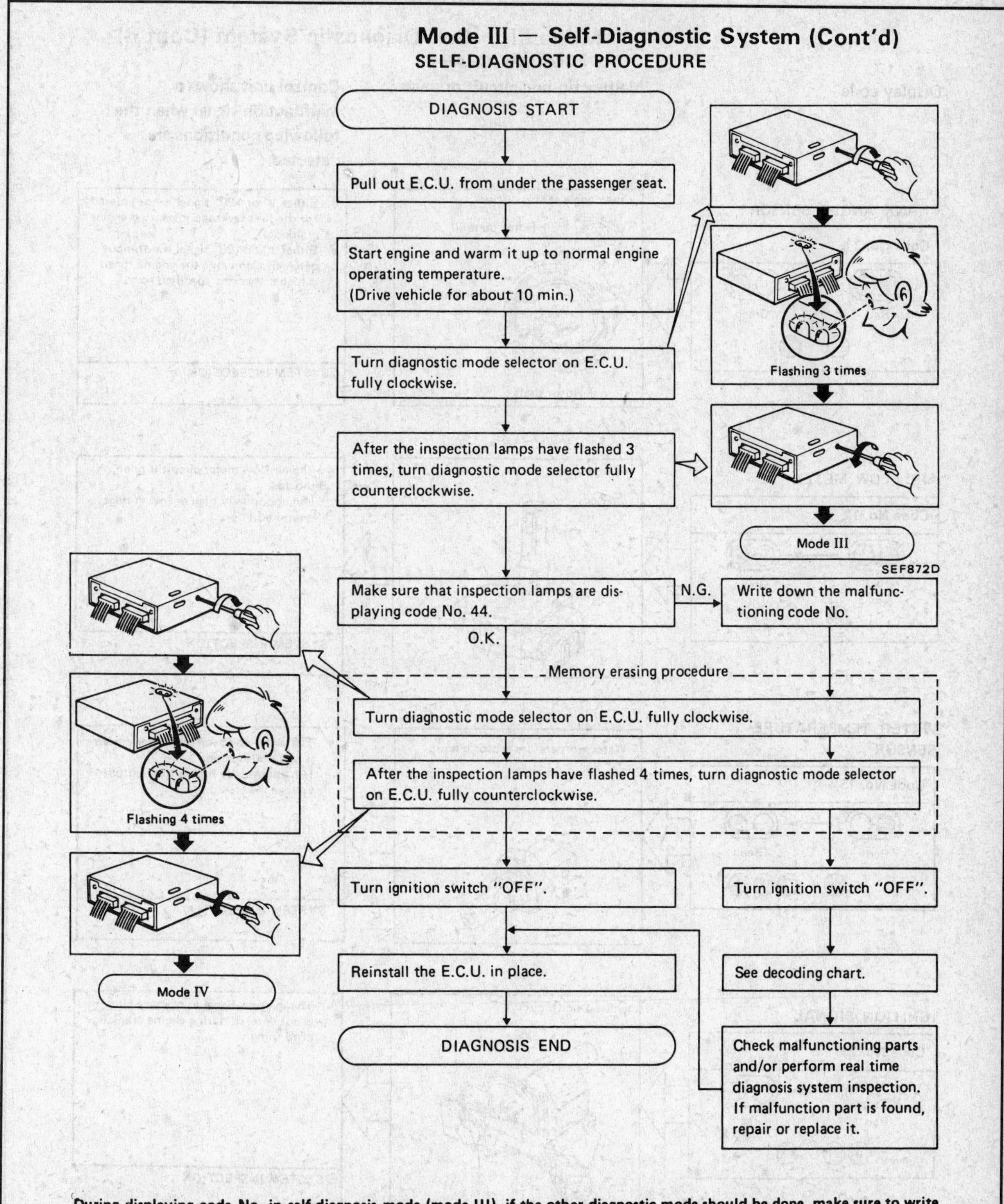

Mode III — Self-Diagnostic System (Cont'd)
SELF-DIAGNOSTIC PROCEDURE
DIAGNOSIS START
Pull out E.C.U. from under the passenger seat.
Start engine and warm it up to normal engine operating temperature. (Drive vehicle for about 10 min.)
Turn diagnostic mode selector on E.C.U. fully clockwise.
Flashing 3 times
After the inspection lamps have flashed 3 times, turn diagnostic mode selector fully counterclockwise.
Mode III
SEF872D
Make sure that inspection lamps are displaying code No. 44.
N.G.
Write down the malfunctioning code No.
O.K.
Memory erasing procedure
Turn diagnostic mode selector on E.C.U. fully clockwise.
After the inspection lamps have flashed 4 times, turn diagnostic mode selector on E.C.U. fully counterclockwise.
Flashing 4 times
Mode IV
Turn ignition switch "OFF".
Turn ignition switch "OFF".
Reinstall the E.C.U. in place.
See decoding chart.
DIAGNOSIS END
Check malfunctioning parts and/or perform real time diagnosis system inspection. If malfunction part is found, repair or replace it.

During displaying code No. in self-diagnosis mode (mode III), if the other diagnostic mode should be done, make sure to write down the malfunctioning code No. before turning diagnostic mode selector on E.C.U. fully clockwise, or select the diagnostic mode after turning switch "OFF". Otherwise self-diagnosis information stored in E.C.U. memory until now would be lost.

TROUBLE CODE DECODING CHART — E16i ENGINE, PART 1

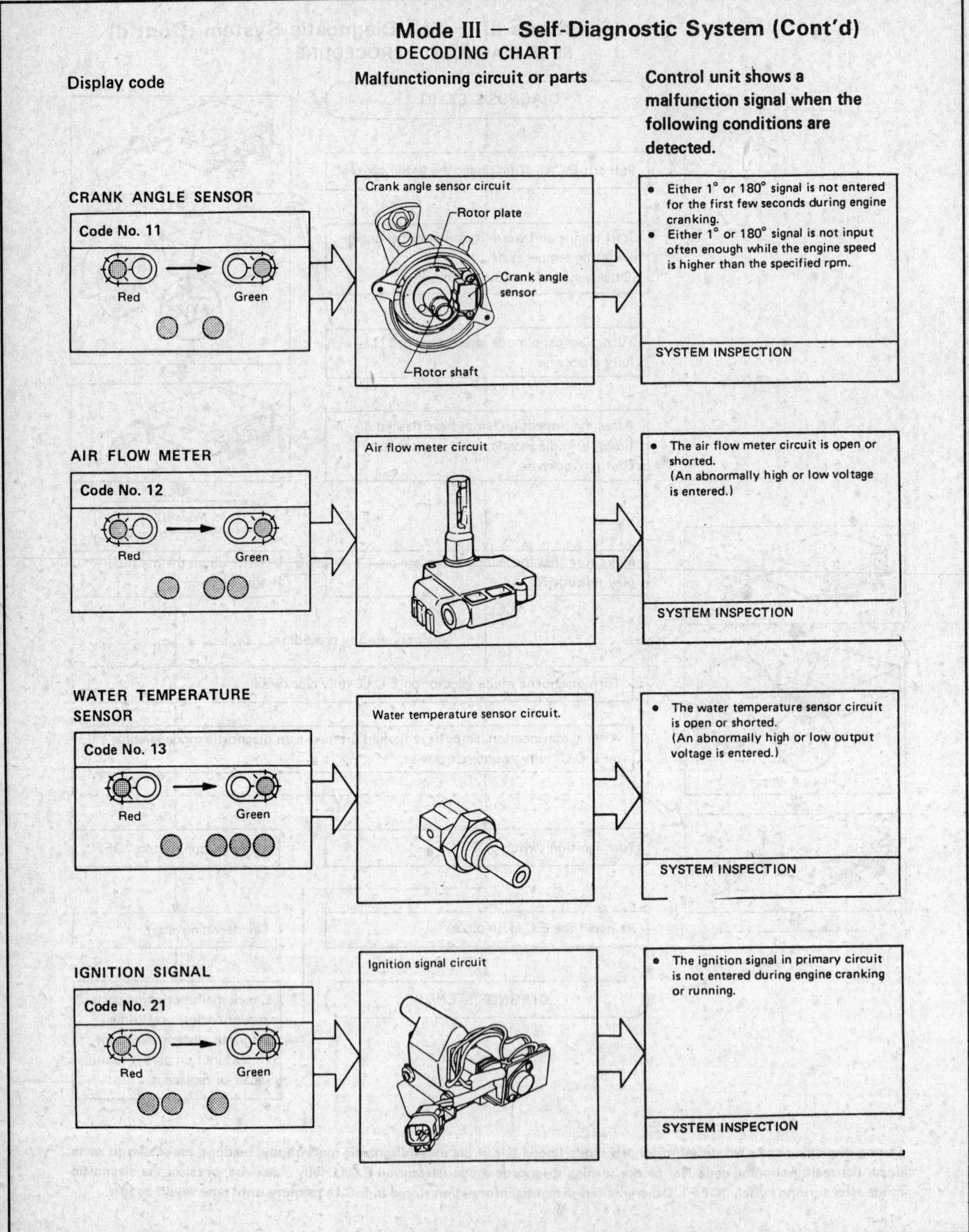
Mode III — Self-Diagnostic System (Cont'd)
DECODING CHART
Display code
Malfunctioning circuit or parts
Control unit shows a malfunction signal when the following conditions are detected.
CRANK ANGLE SENSOR
Code No. 11
Red
Green
Crank angle sensor circuit
Rotor plate
Crank angle sensor
Rotor shaft
• Either 1° or 180° signal is not entered for the first few seconds during engine cranking.
• Either 1° or 180° signal is not input often enough while the engine speed is higher than the specified rpm.
SYSTEM INSPECTION
AIR FLOW METER
Code No. 12
Red
Green
Air flow meter circuit
• The air flow meter circuit is open or shorted.
(An abnormally high or low voltage is entered.)
SYSTEM INSPECTION
WATER TEMPERATURE SENSOR
Code No. 13
Red
Green
Water temperature sensor circuit.
• The water temperature sensor circuit is open or shorted.
(An abnormally high or low output voltage is entered.)
SYSTEM INSPECTION
IGNITION SIGNAL
Code No. 21
Red
Green
Ignition signal circuit
• The ignition signal in primary circuit is not entered during engine cranking or running.
SYSTEM INSPECTION

TROUBLE CODE DECODING CHART – E16i ENGINE, PART 2

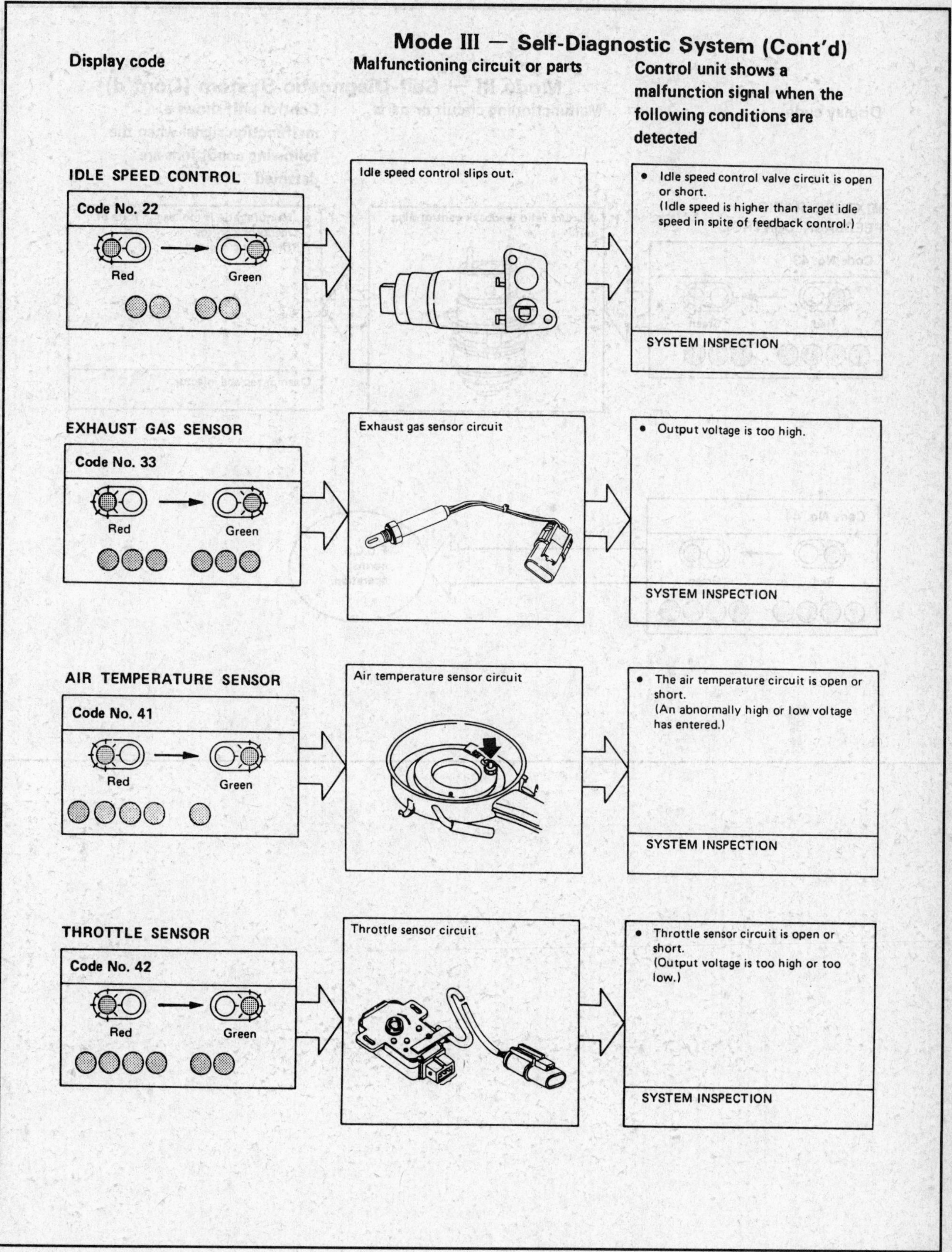
Mode III — Self-Diagnostic System (Cont'd)
Display code
Malfunctioning circuit or parts
Control unit shows a malfunction signal when the following conditions are detected
IDLE SPEED CONTROL
Code No. 22
Red
Green
Idle speed control slips out.
• Idle speed control valve circuit is open or short.
(Idle speed is higher than target idle speed in spite of feedback control.)
SYSTEM INSPECTION
EXHAUST GAS SENSOR
Code No. 33
Red
Green
Exhaust gas sensor circuit
• Output voltage is too high.
SYSTEM INSPECTION
AIR TEMPERATURE SENSOR
Code No. 41
Red
Green
Air temperature sensor circuit
• The air temperature circuit is open or short.
(An abnormally high or low voltage has entered.)
SYSTEM INSPECTION
THROTTLE SENSOR
Code No. 42
Red
Green
Throttle sensor circuit
• Throttle sensor circuit is open or short.
(Output voltage is too high or too low.)
SYSTEM INSPECTION

TROUBLE CODE DECODING CHART — E16i ENGINE, PART 3

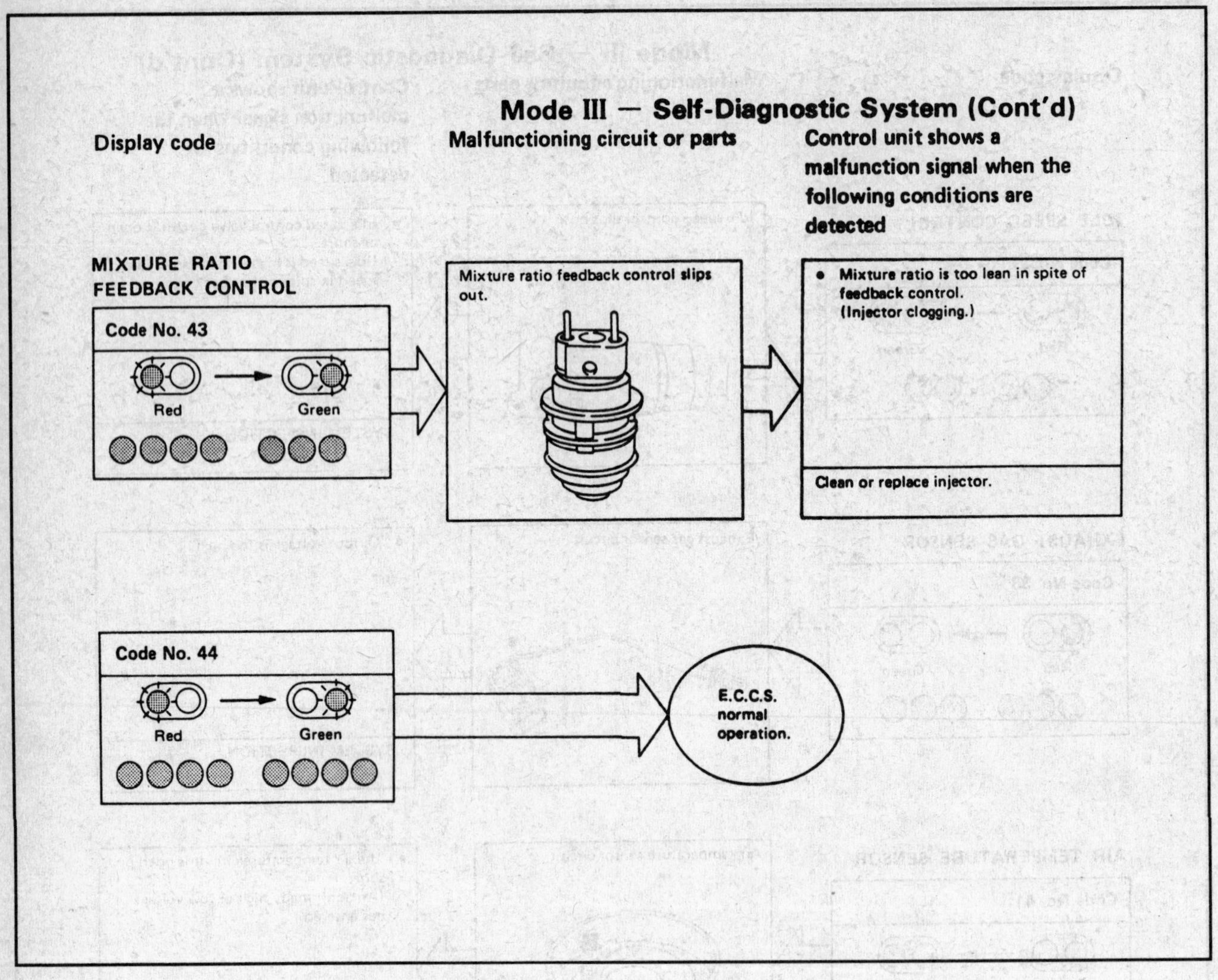
Mode III — Self-Diagnostic System (Cont'd)
Display code
Malfunctioning circuit or parts
Control unit shows a malfunction signal when the following conditions are detected
MIXTURE RATIO FEEDBACK CONTROL
Code No. 43
Red
Green
Mixture ratio feedback control slips out.
Mixture ratio is too lean in spite of feedback control. (Injector clogging.)
Clean or replace injector.
Code No. 44
Red
Green
E.C.C.S. normal operation.

MODE IV, SWITCHES ON/OFF DIAGNOSTIC SYSTEM – E16i ENGINE

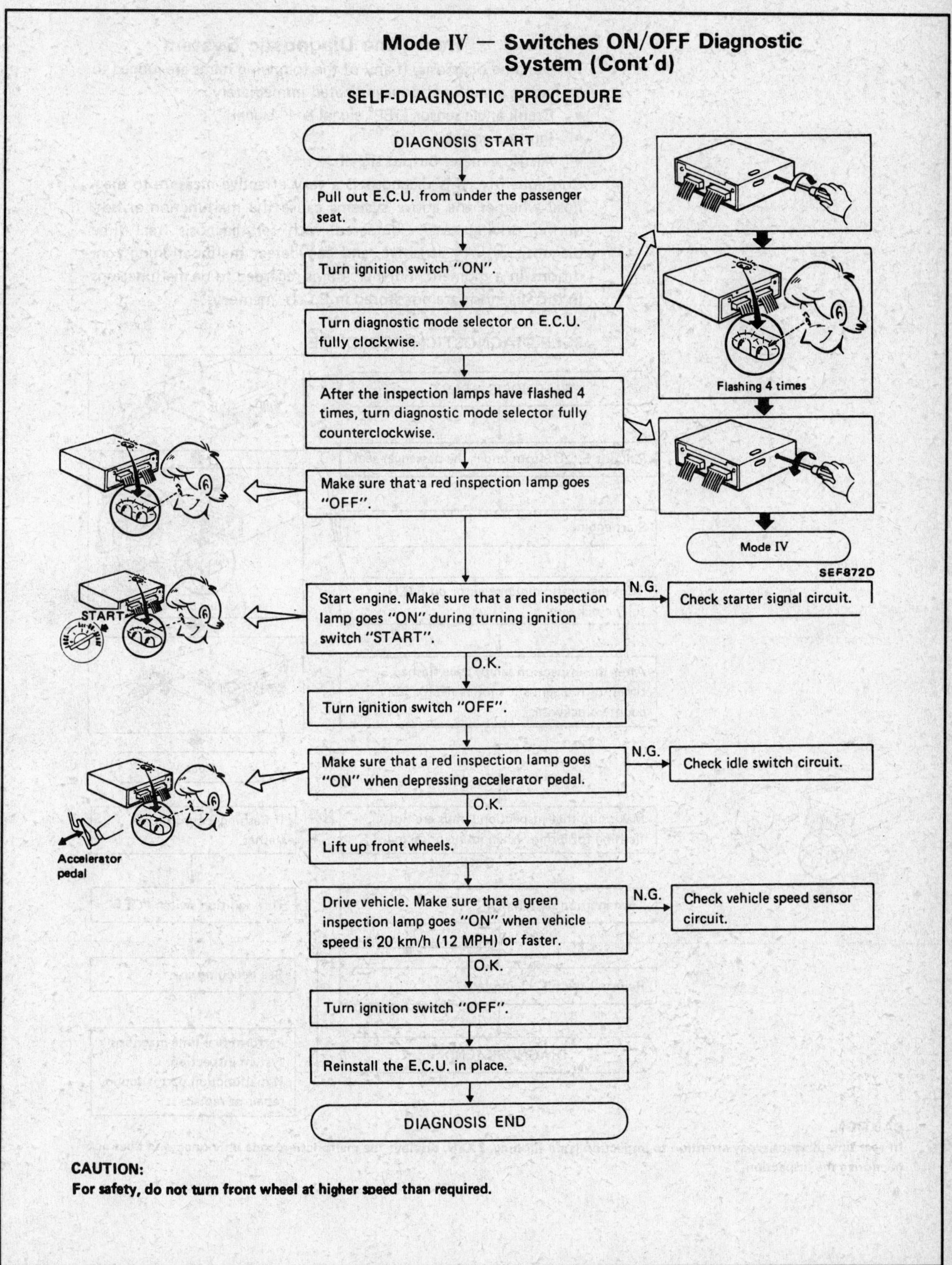
Mode IV — Switches ON/OFF Diagnostic System (Cont'd)
SELF-DIAGNOSTIC PROCEDURE
DIAGNOSIS START
Pull out E.C.U. from under the passenger seat.
Turn ignition switch "ON".
Turn diagnostic mode selector on E.C.U. fully clockwise.
After the inspection lamps have flashed 4 times, turn diagnostic mode selector fully counterclockwise.
Flashing 4 times
Mode IV
SEF872D
Make sure that a red inspection lamp goes "OFF".
Start engine. Make sure that a red inspection lamp goes "ON" during turning ignition switch "START".
START
N.G.
Check starter signal circuit.
O.K.
Turn ignition switch "OFF".
Make sure that a red inspection lamp goes "ON" when depressing accelerator pedal.
N.G.
Check idle switch circuit.
O.K.
Accelerator pedal
Lift up front wheels.
Drive vehicle. Make sure that a green inspection lamp goes "ON" when vehicle speed is 20 km/h (12 MPH) or faster.
N.G.
Check vehicle speed sensor circuit.
O.K.
Turn ignition switch "OFF".
Reinstall the E.C.U. in place.
DIAGNOSIS END
CAUTION:
For safety, do not turn front wheel at higher speed than required.

MODE V, REAL TIME DIAGNOSTIC SYSTEM – E16i ENGINE

Mode V — Real Time Diagnostic System

In real time diagnosis, if any of the following items are judged to be faulty, a malfunction is indicated immediately.

- Crank angle sensor (180° signal & 1° signal)
- Ignition signal
- Air flow meter output signal

Consequently, this diagnosis is a very effective measure to diagnose whether the above systems cause the malfunction or not, during driving test. Compared with self-diagnosis, real time diagnosis is very sensitive, and can detect malfunctioning conditions in a moment. Further, items regarded to be malfunctions in this diagnosis are not stored in E.C.U. memory.

SELF-DIAGNOSTIC PROCEDURE

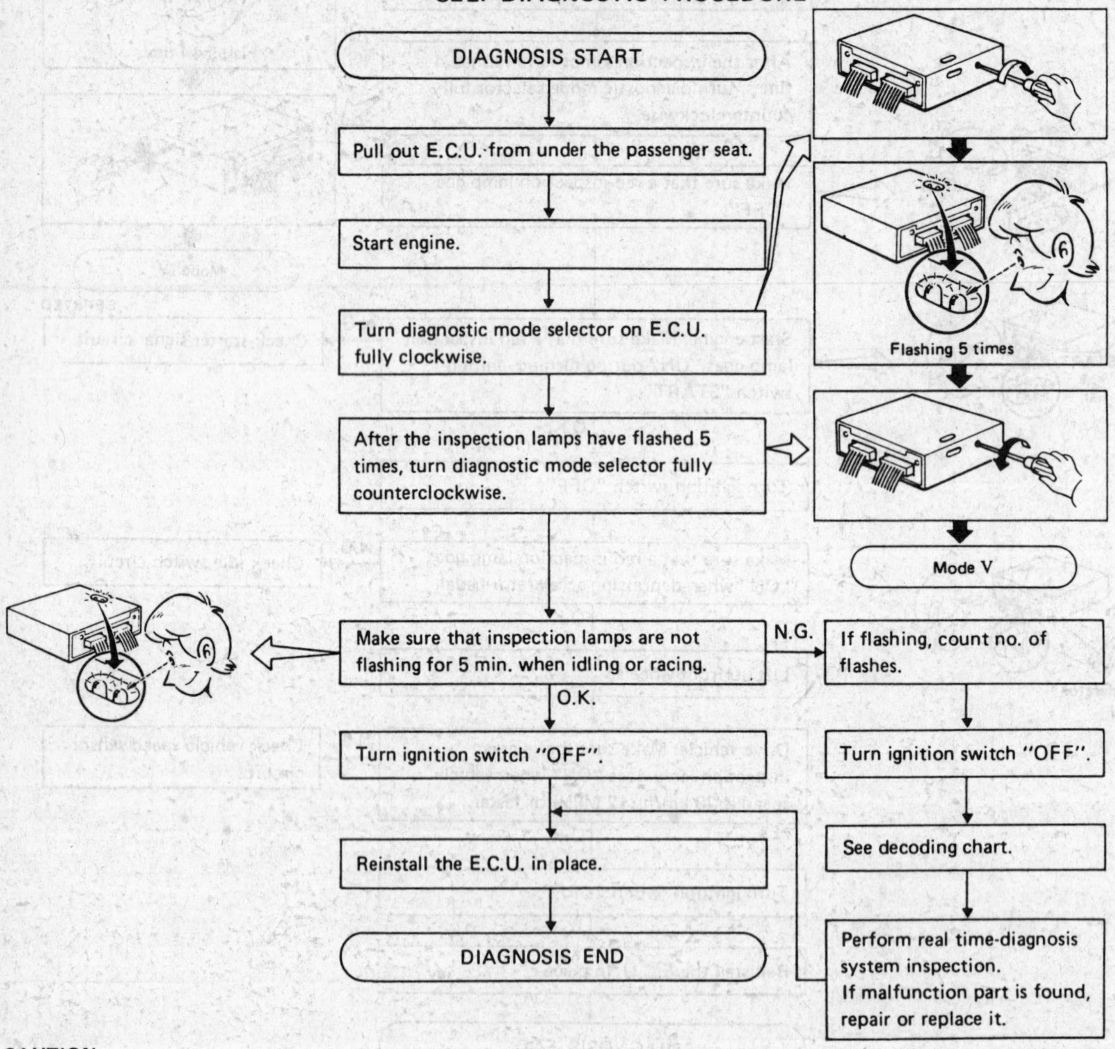
DIAGNOSIS START
Pull out E.C.U. from under the passenger seat.
Start engine.
Turn diagnostic mode selector on E.C.U. fully clockwise.
Flashing 5 times
After the inspection lamps have flashed 5 times, turn diagnostic mode selector fully counterclockwise.
Mode V
Make sure that inspection lamps are not flashing for 5 min. when idling or racing.
N.G.
If flashing, count no. of flashes.
O.K.
Turn ignition switch "OFF".
Turn ignition switch "OFF".
See decoding chart.
Reinstall the E.C.U. in place.
Perform real time-diagnosis system inspection.
If malfunction part is found, repair or replace it.
DIAGNOSIS END

CAUTION:
In real time diagnosis, pay attention to inspection lamp flashing. E.C.U. displays the malfunction code only once, and does not memorize the inspection.

MODE V TROUBLE CODE DECODING CHART – E16i ENGINE

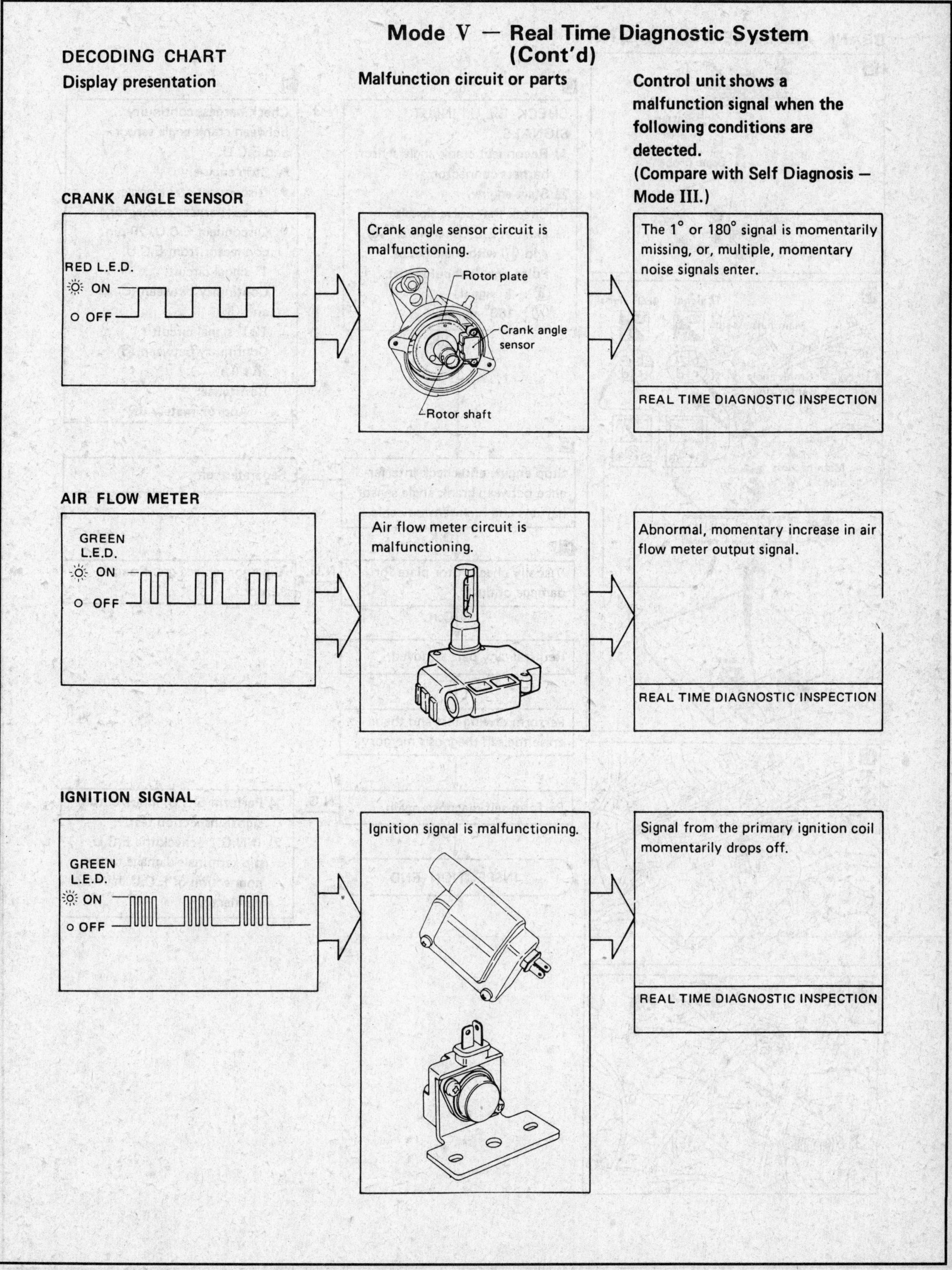
Mode V — Real Time Diagnostic System (Cont'd)
DECODING CHART
Display presentation
Malfunction circuit or parts
Control unit shows a malfunction signal when the following conditions are detected.
(Compare with Self Diagnosis – Mode III.)
CRANK ANGLE SENSOR
RED L.E.D.
ON
OFF
Crank angle sensor circuit is malfunctioning.
Rotor plate
Crank angle sensor
Rotor shaft
The 1° or 180° signal is momentarily missing, or, multiple, momentary noise signals enter.
REAL TIME DIAGNOSTIC INSPECTION
AIR FLOW METER
GREEN L.E.D.
ON
OFF
Air flow meter circuit is malfunctioning.
Abnormal, momentary increase in air flow meter output signal.
REAL TIME DIAGNOSTIC INSPECTION
IGNITION SIGNAL
GREEN L.E.D.
ON
OFF
Ignition signal is malfunctioning.
Signal from the primary ignition coil momentarily drops off.
REAL TIME DIAGNOSTIC INSPECTION

CODE 11 (CRANK ANGLE SENSOR) – E16i ENGINE

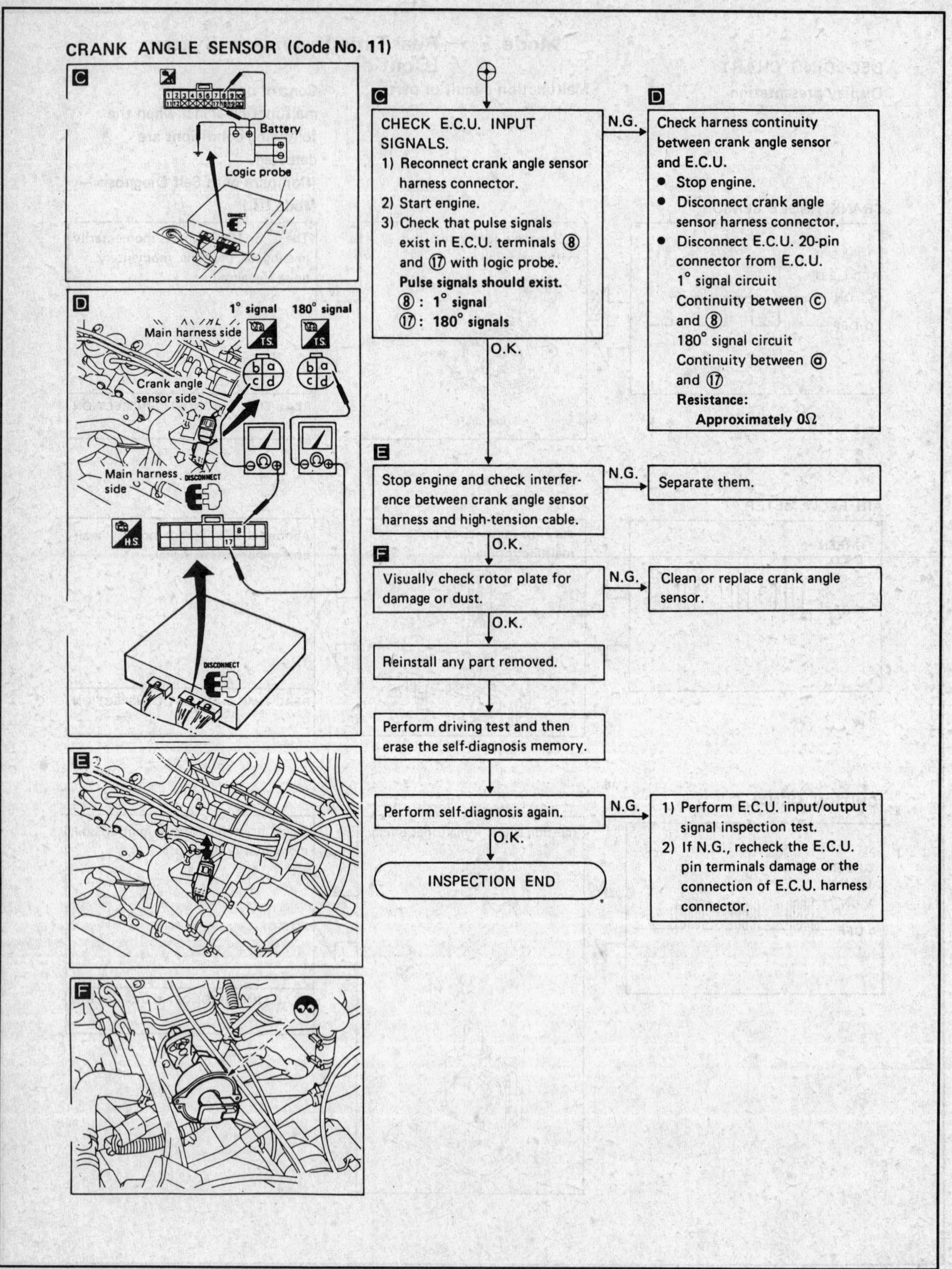

CRANK ANGLE SENSOR (Code No. 11)
C
Battery
Logic probe
D
1° signal
180° signal
Main harness side
Crank angle sensor side
Main harness side
T.S.
H.S.
DISCONNECT
8
17
E
F
C
CHECK E.C.U. INPUT SIGNALS.
1) Reconnect crank angle sensor harness connector.
2) Start engine.
3) Check that pulse signals exist in E.C.U. terminals ⑧ and ⑰ with logic probe.
Pulse signals should exist.
⑧ : 1° signal
⑰ : 180° signals
N.G.
D
Check harness continuity between crank angle sensor and E.C.U.
• Stop engine.
• Disconnect crank angle sensor harness connector.
• Disconnect E.C.U. 20-pin connector from E.C.U.
1° signal circuit
Continuity between ⓒ and ⑧
180° signal circuit
Continuity between ⓐ and ⑰
Resistance:
Approximately 0Ω
O.K.
E
Stop engine and check interference between crank angle sensor harness and high-tension cable.
N.G.
Separate them.
O.K.
F
Visually check rotor plate for damage or dust.
N.G.
Clean or replace crank angle sensor.
O.K.
Reinstall any part removed.
Perform driving test and then erase the self-diagnosis memory.
Perform self-diagnosis again.
N.G.
1) Perform E.C.U. input/output signal inspection test.
2) If N.G., recheck the E.C.U. pin terminals damage or the connection of E.C.U. harness connector.
O.K.
INSPECTION END

CODE 12 (AIR FLOW METER) – E16i ENGINE, PART 1

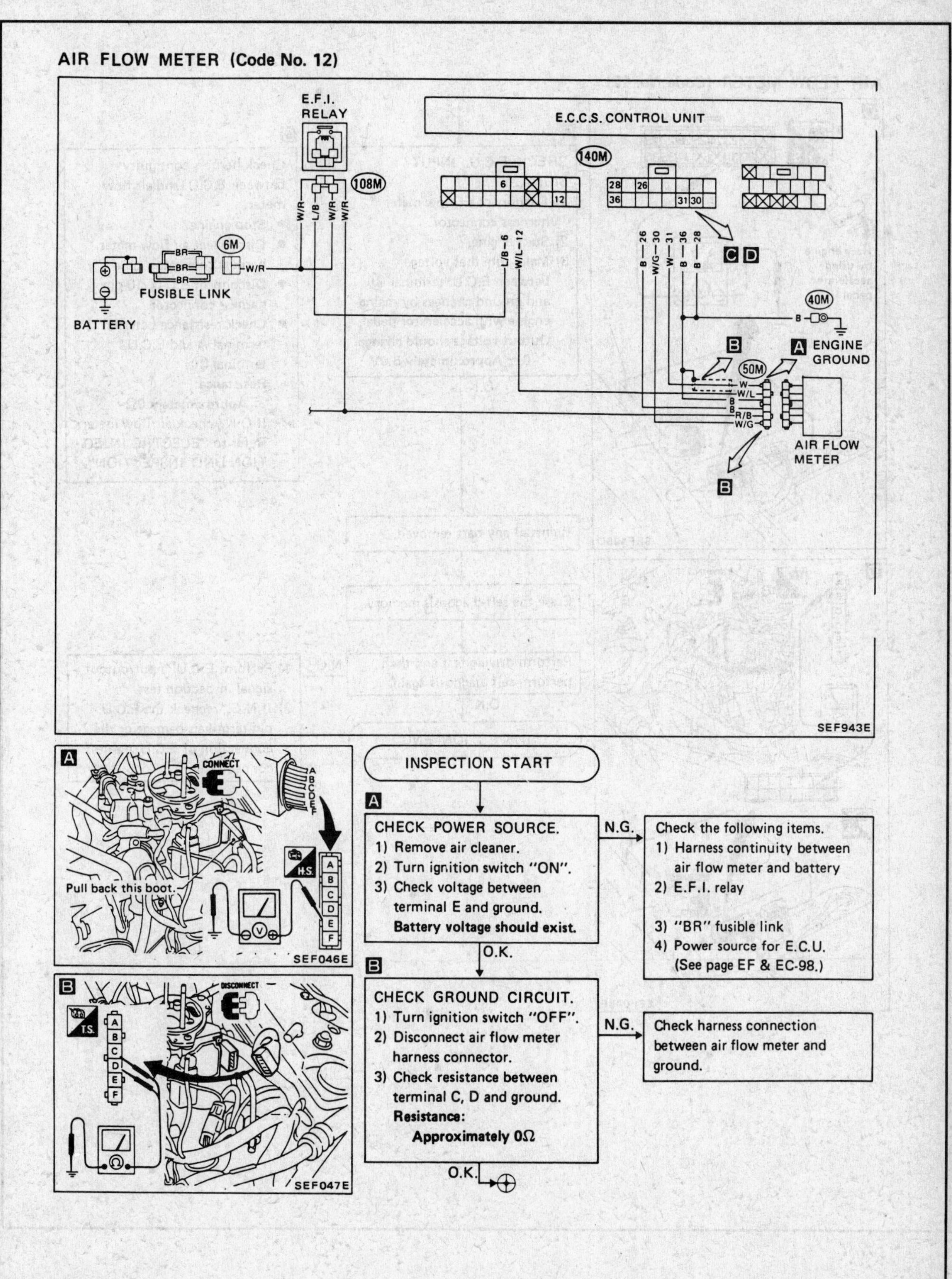
AIR FLOW METER (Code No. 12)
E.F.I. RELAY
E.C.C.S. CONTROL UNIT
140M
108M
6M
40M
50M
BATTERY
FUSIBLE LINK
ENGINE GROUND
AIR FLOW METER
SEF943E
Pull back this boot.
CONNECT
SEF046E
DISCONNECT
SEF047E
INSPECTION START
CHECK POWER SOURCE.
1) Remove air cleaner.
2) Turn ignition switch "ON".
3) Check voltage between terminal E and ground.
Battery voltage should exist.
N.G.
Check the following items.
1) Harness continuity between air flow meter and battery
2) E.F.I. relay
3) "BR" fusible link
4) Power source for E.C.U. (See page EF & EC-98.)
O.K.
CHECK GROUND CIRCUIT.
1) Turn ignition switch "OFF".
2) Disconnect air flow meter harness connector.
3) Check resistance between terminal C, D and ground.
Resistance:
Approximately 0Ω
N.G.
Check harness connection between air flow meter and ground.
O.K.

CODE 12 (AIR FLOW METER) – E16i ENGINE, PART 2

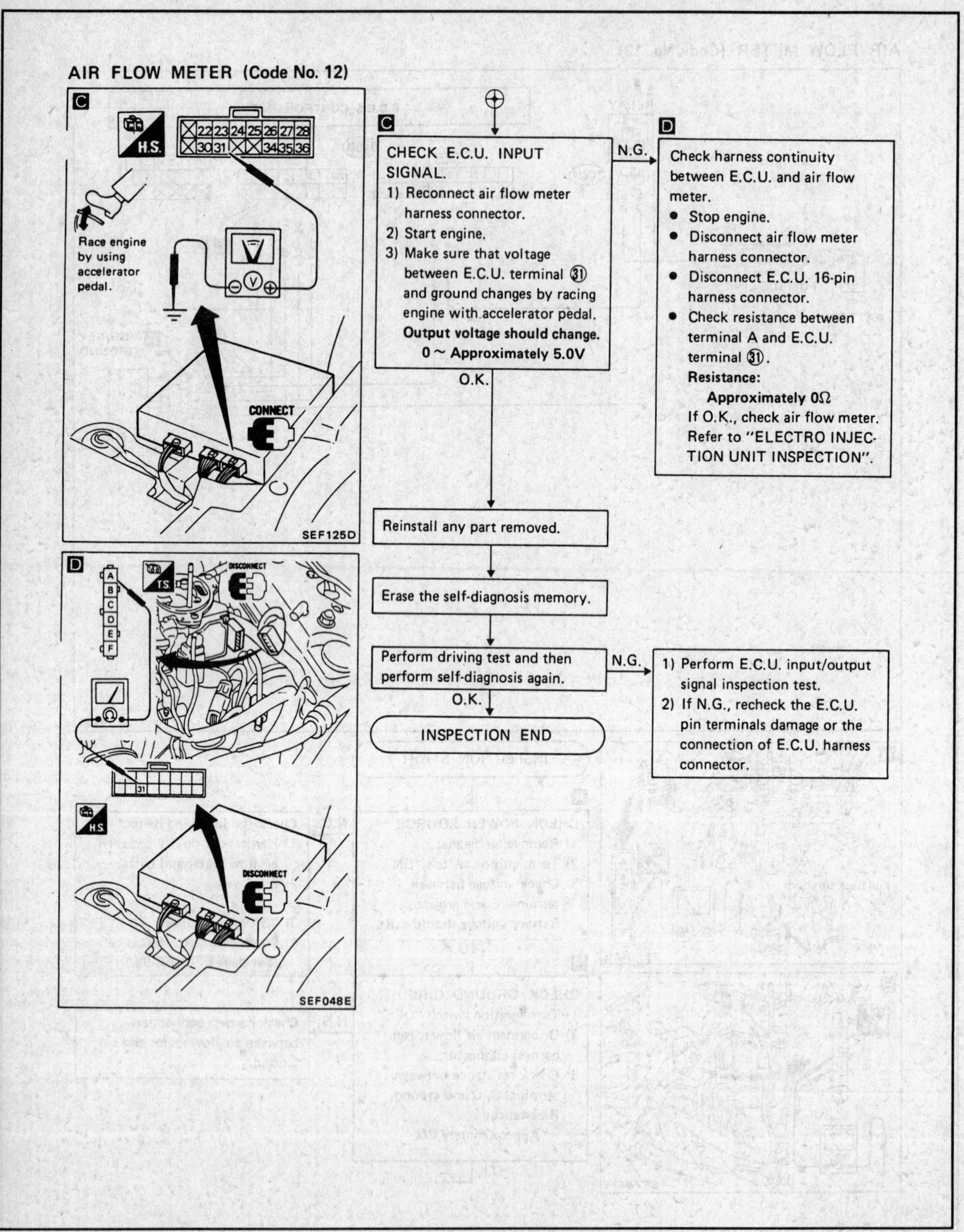
AIR FLOW METER (Code No. 12)
C
H.S.
22 23 24 25 26 27 28
30 31 34 35 36
Race engine by using accelerator pedal.
CONNECT
SEF125D
C
CHECK E.C.U. INPUT SIGNAL.
1) Reconnect air flow meter harness connector.
2) Start engine.
3) Make sure that voltage between E.C.U. terminal ㉛ and ground changes by racing engine with accelerator pedal.
Output voltage should change.
0 ~ Approximately 5.0V
N.G.
D
Check harness continuity between E.C.U. and air flow meter.
• Stop engine.
• Disconnect air flow meter harness connector.
• Disconnect E.C.U. 16-pin harness connector.
• Check resistance between terminal A and E.C.U. terminal ㉛.
Resistance:
Approximately 0Ω
If O.K., check air flow meter. Refer to "ELECTRO INJECTION UNIT INSPECTION".
O.K.
Reinstall any part removed.
Erase the self-diagnosis memory.
Perform driving test and then perform self-diagnosis again.
N.G.
1) Perform E.C.U. input/output signal inspection test.
2) If N.G., recheck the E.C.U. pin terminals damage or the connection of E.C.U. harness connector.
O.K.
INSPECTION END
D
A
B
C
D
E
F
T.S.
DISCONNECT
31
H.S.
DISCONNECT
SEF048E

CODE 13 (WATER TEMPERATURE SENSOR) – E16i ENGINE, PART 1

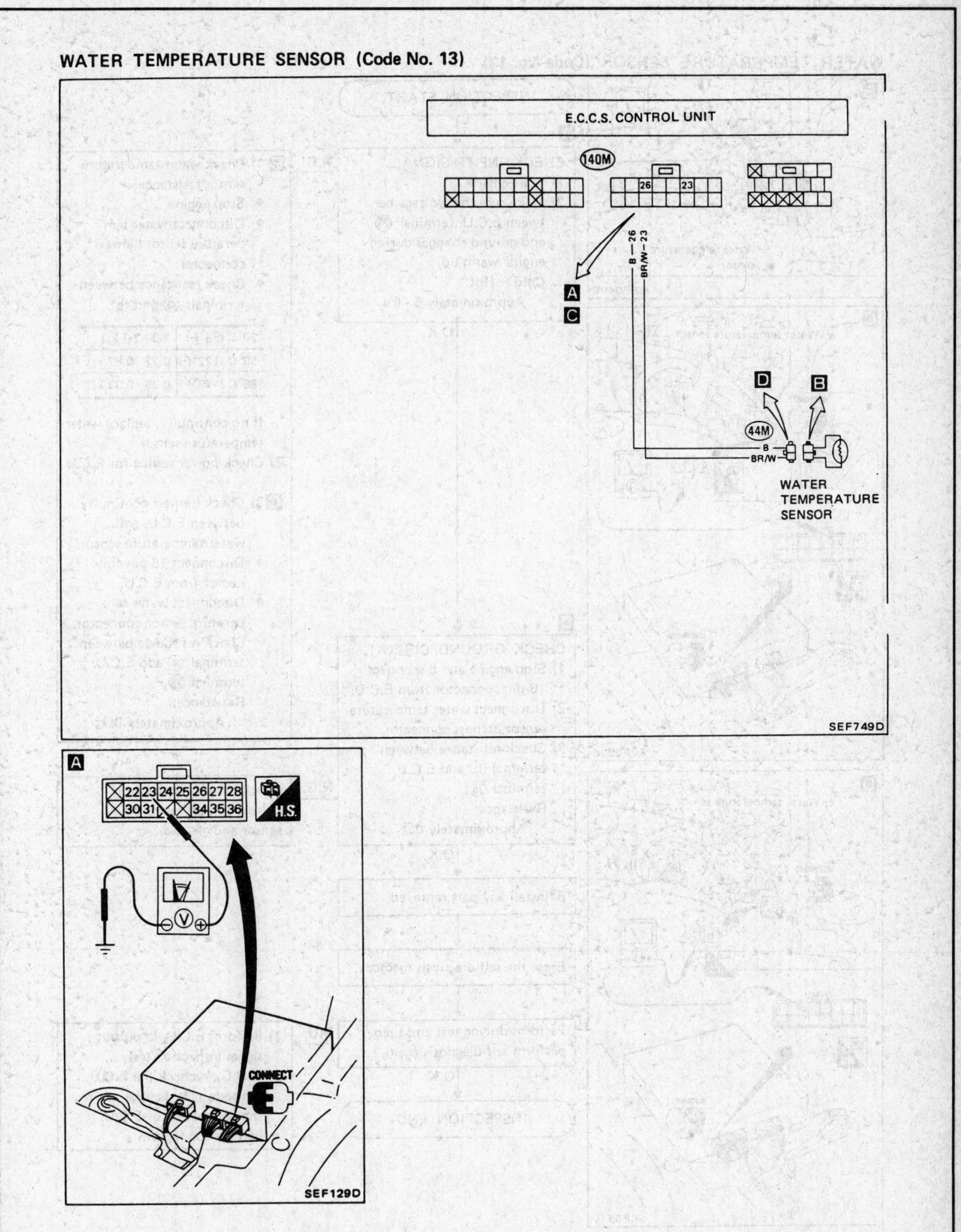
WATER TEMPERATURE SENSOR (Code No. 13)
E.C.C.S. CONTROL UNIT
140M
26
23
B – 26
BR/W – 23
A
C
D
B
44M
B
BR/W
WATER
TEMPERATURE
SENSOR
SEF749D
A
22 23 24 25 26 27 28
30 31 34 35 36
H.S.
CONNECT
SEF129D

CODE 13 (WATER TEMPERATURE SENSOR) – E16i ENGINE, PART 2

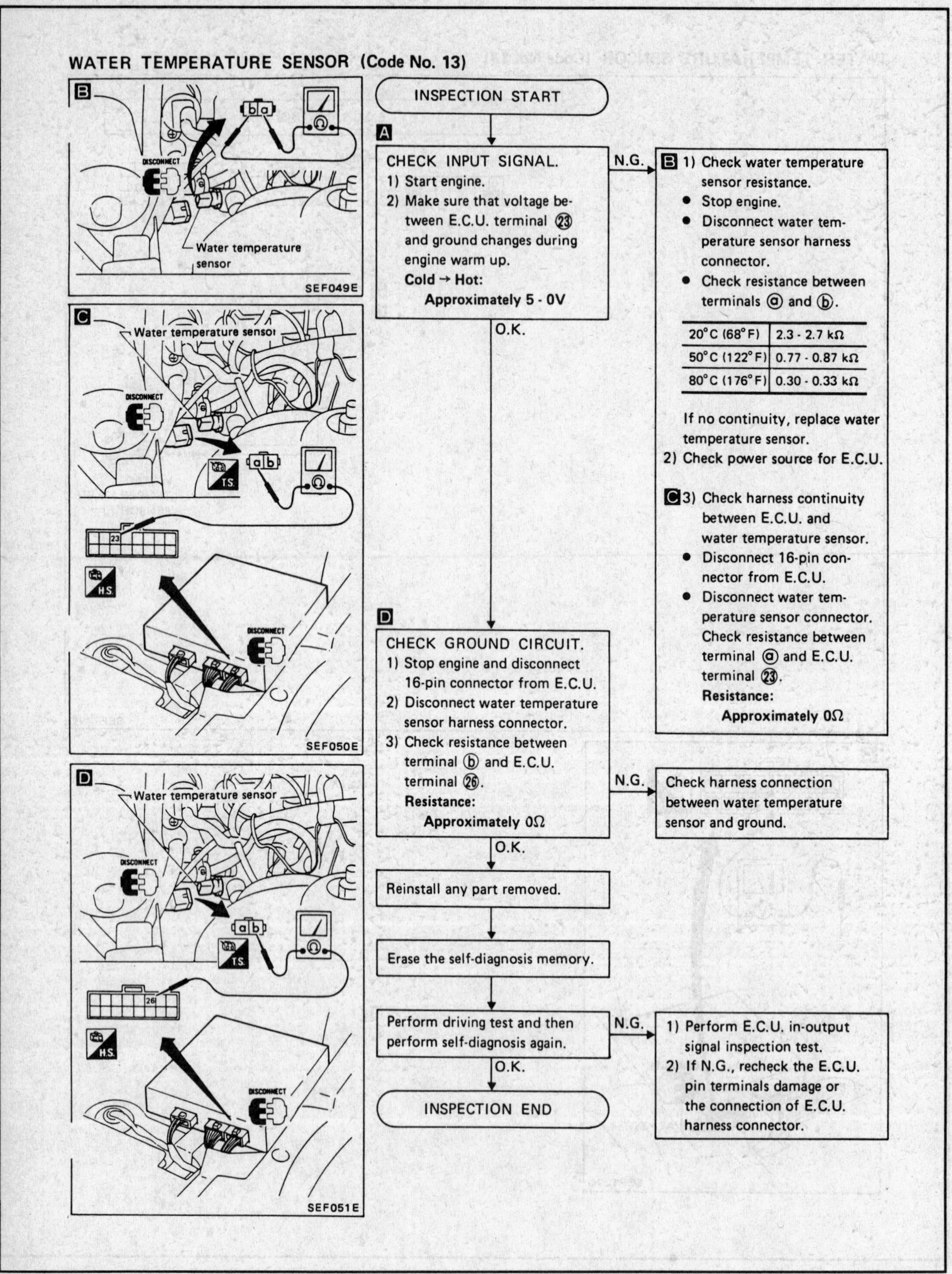

WATER TEMPERATURE SENSOR (Code No. 13)
B
DISCONNECT
Water temperature sensor
SEF049E
C
Water temperature sensor
DISCONNECT
T.S.
23
H.S.
SEF050E
D
Water temperature sensor
DISCONNECT
T.S.
26
H.S.
SEF051E
INSPECTION START
A
CHECK INPUT SIGNAL.
1) Start engine.
2) Make sure that voltage between E.C.U. terminal ㉓ and ground changes during engine warm up.
Cold → Hot:
Approximately 5 - 0V
N.G.
B 1) Check water temperature sensor resistance.
• Stop engine.
• Disconnect water temperature sensor harness connector.
• Check resistance between terminals ⓐ and ⓑ.
20°C (68°F) 2.3 - 2.7 kΩ
50°C (122°F) 0.77 - 0.87 kΩ
80°C (176°F) 0.30 - 0.33 kΩ
If no continuity, replace water temperature sensor.
2) Check power source for E.C.U.
C 3) Check harness continuity between E.C.U. and water temperature sensor.
• Disconnect 16-pin connector from E.C.U.
• Disconnect water temperature sensor connector.
Check resistance between terminal ⓐ and E.C.U. terminal ㉓.
Resistance:
Approximately 0Ω
O.K.
D
CHECK GROUND CIRCUIT.
1) Stop engine and disconnect 16-pin connector from E.C.U.
2) Disconnect water temperature sensor harness connector.
3) Check resistance between terminal ⓑ and E.C.U. terminal ㉖.
Resistance:
Approximately 0Ω
N.G.
Check harness connection between water temperature sensor and ground.
O.K.
Reinstall any part removed.
Erase the self-diagnosis memory.
Perform driving test and then perform self-diagnosis again.
N.G.
1) Perform E.C.U. in-output signal inspection test.
2) If N.G., recheck the E.C.U. pin terminals damage or the connection of E.C.U. harness connector.
O.K.
INSPECTION END

CODE 21 (IGNITION SIGNAL) – E16i ENGINE, PART 1

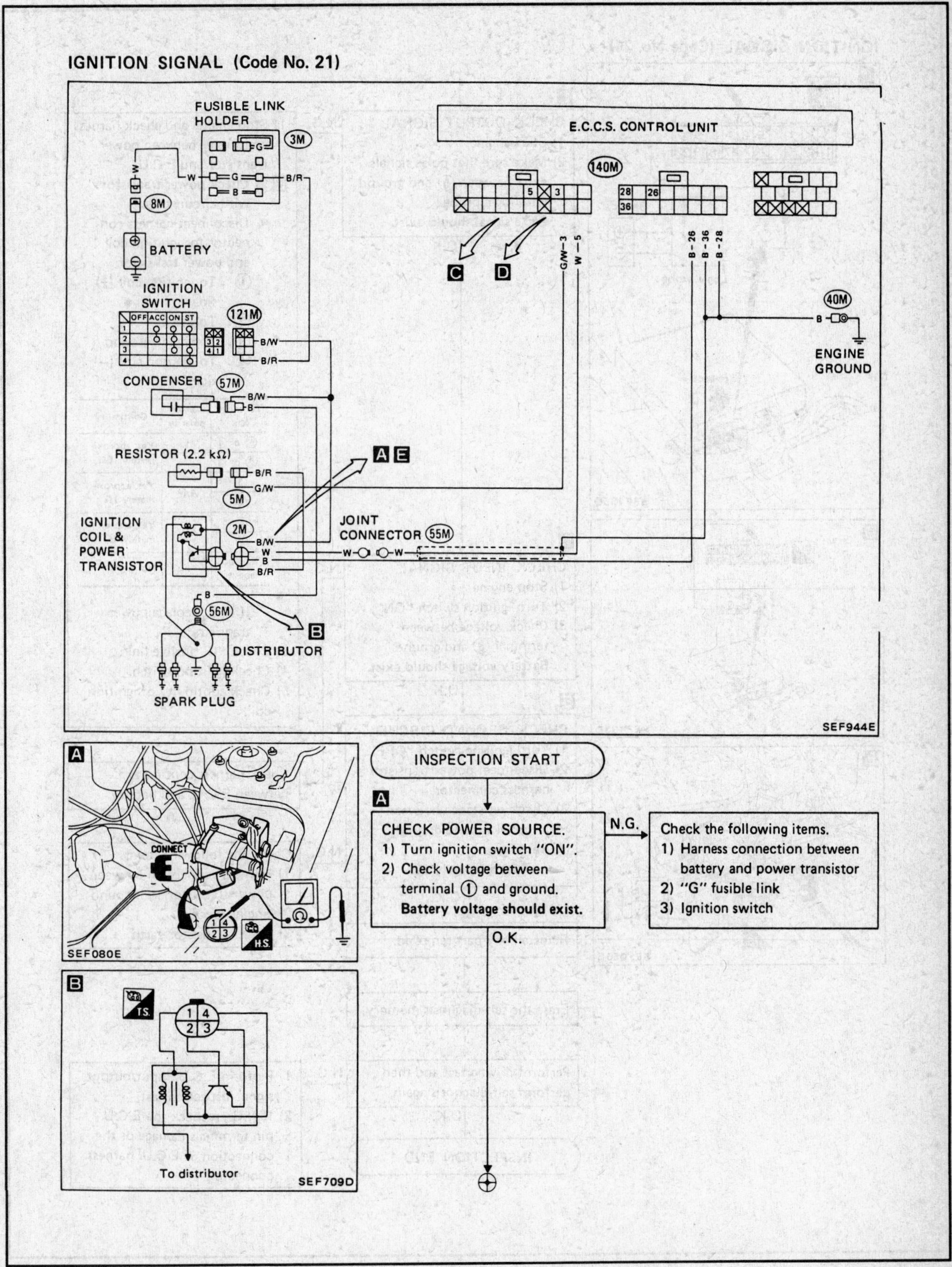
IGNITION SIGNAL (Code No. 21)
FUSIBLE LINK HOLDER
3M
8M
BATTERY
IGNITION SWITCH
121M
CONDENSER
57M
RESISTOR (2.2 kΩ)
5M
IGNITION COIL & POWER TRANSISTOR
2M
JOINT CONNECTOR 55M
56M
DISTRIBUTOR
SPARK PLUG
E.C.C.S. CONTROL UNIT
140M
40M
ENGINE GROUND
SEF944E
CONNECT
SEF080E
To distributor
SEF709D
INSPECTION START
CHECK POWER SOURCE.
1) Turn ignition switch "ON".
2) Check voltage between terminal ① and ground.
Battery voltage should exist.
N.G.
Check the following items.
1) Harness connection between battery and power transistor
2) "G" fusible link
3) Ignition switch
O.K.

CODE 21 (IGNITION SIGNAL) — E16i ENGINE, PART 2

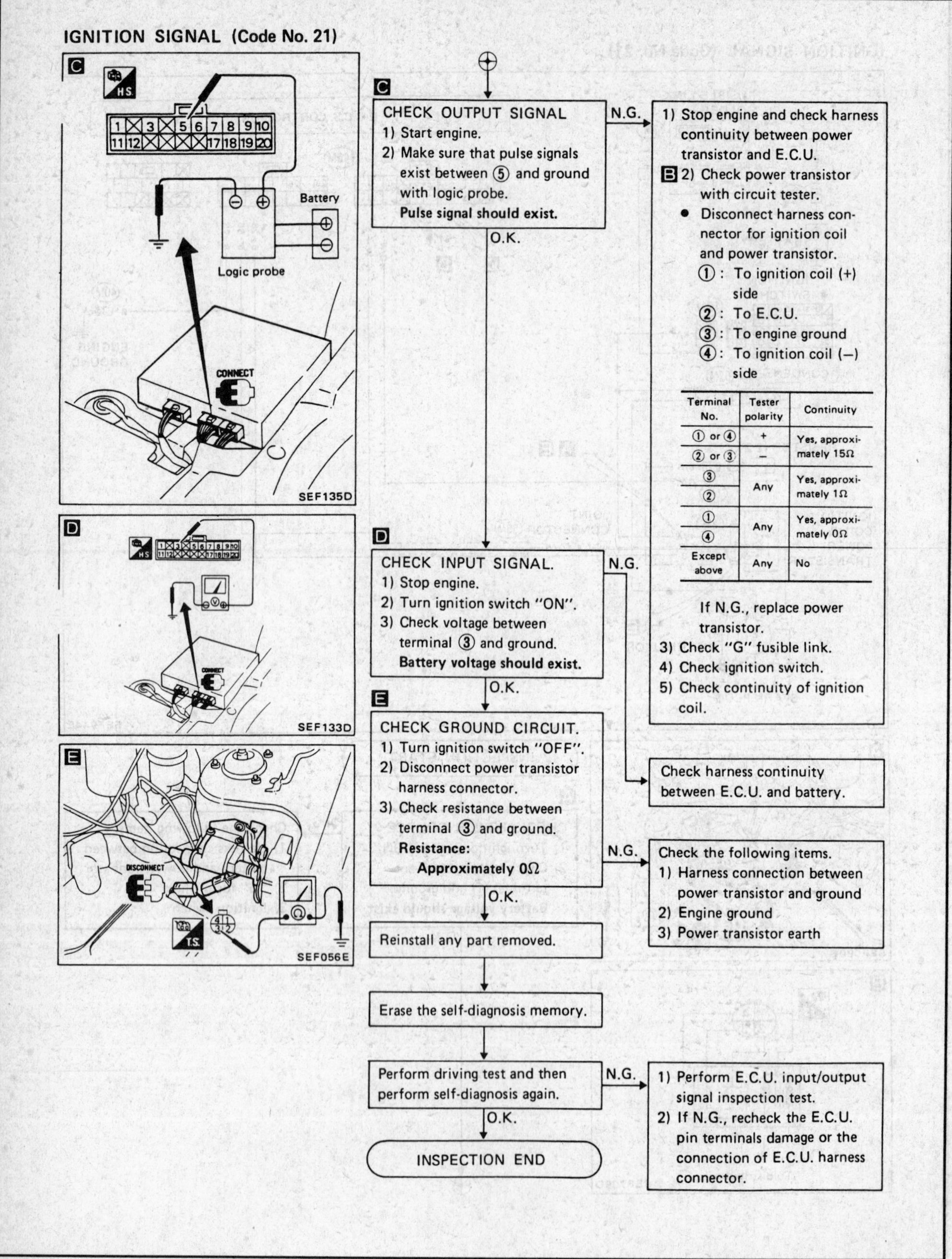
IGNITION SIGNAL (Code No. 21)
C
Battery
Logic probe
CONNECT
SEF135D
D
CONNECT
SEF133D
E
DISCONNECT
T.S.
SEF056E
C
CHECK OUTPUT SIGNAL
1) Start engine.
2) Make sure that pulse signals exist between ⑤ and ground with logic probe.
Pulse signal should exist.
N.G.
1) Stop engine and check harness continuity between power transistor and E.C.U.
B 2) Check power transistor with circuit tester.
• Disconnect harness connector for ignition coil and power transistor.
①: To ignition coil (+) side
②: To E.C.U.
③: To engine ground
④: To ignition coil (−) side
Terminal No. | Tester polarity | Continuity
① or ④ | + | Yes, approximately 15Ω
② or ③ | −
③ ② | Any | Yes, approximately 1Ω
① ④ | Any | Yes, approximately 0Ω
Except above | Any | No
If N.G., replace power transistor.
3) Check "G" fusible link.
4) Check ignition switch.
5) Check continuity of ignition coil.
O.K.
D
CHECK INPUT SIGNAL.
1) Stop engine.
2) Turn ignition switch "ON".
3) Check voltage between terminal ③ and ground.
Battery voltage should exist.
N.G.
Check harness continuity between E.C.U. and battery.
O.K.
E
CHECK GROUND CIRCUIT.
1) Turn ignition switch "OFF".
2) Disconnect power transistor harness connector.
3) Check resistance between terminal ③ and ground.
Resistance:
Approximately 0Ω
N.G.
Check the following items.
1) Harness connection between power transistor and ground
2) Engine ground
3) Power transistor earth
O.K.
Reinstall any part removed.
Erase the self-diagnosis memory.
Perform driving test and then perform self-diagnosis again.
N.G.
1) Perform E.C.U. input/output signal inspection test.
2) If N.G., recheck the E.C.U. pin terminals damage or the connection of E.C.U. harness connector.
O.K.
INSPECTION END

CODE 22 (IDLE SPEED CONTROL VALVE) – E16i ENGINE, PART 1

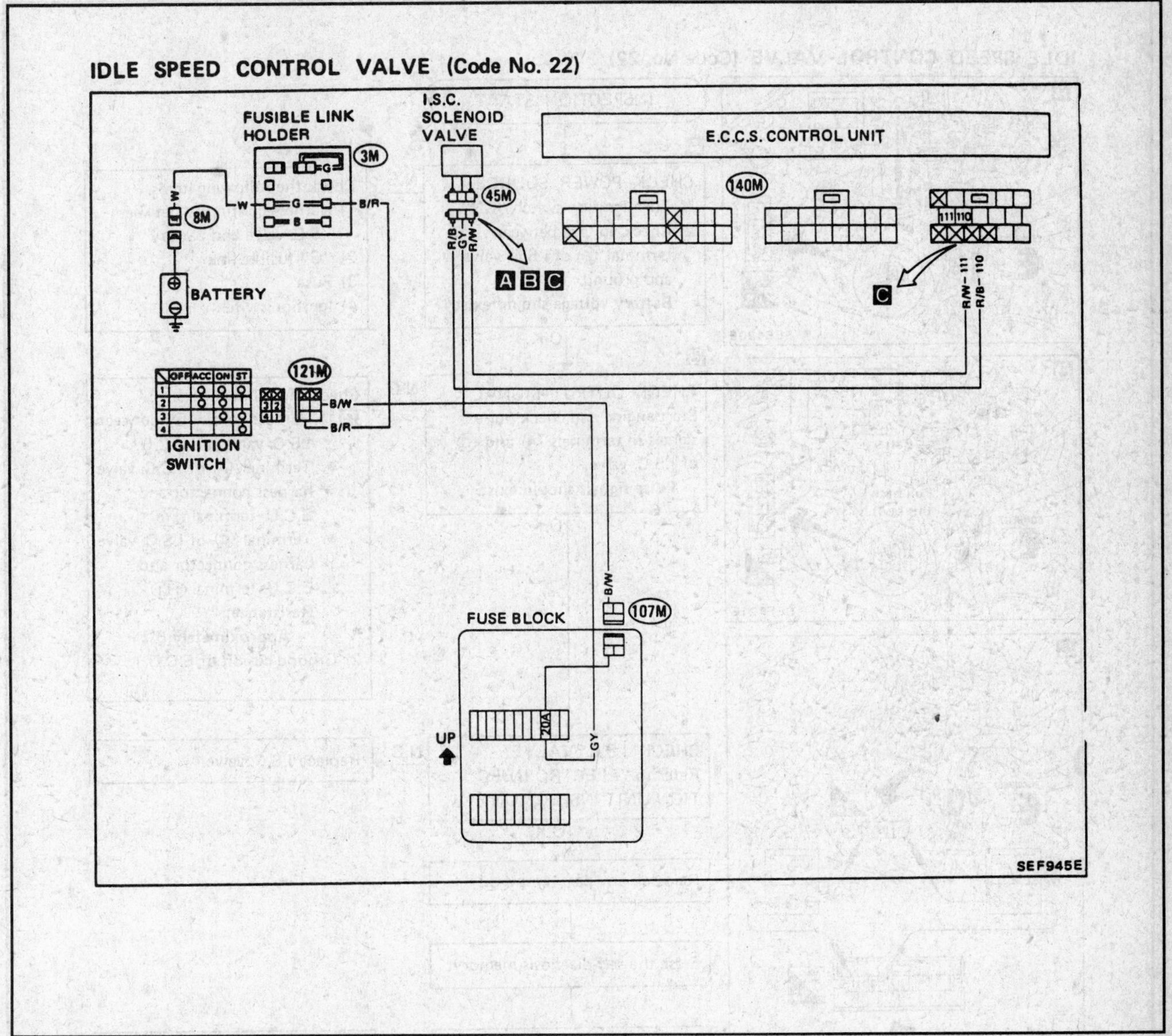
IDLE SPEED CONTROL VALVE (Code No. 22)
FUSIBLE LINK HOLDER
3M
I.S.C. SOLENOID VALVE
E.C.C.S. CONTROL UNIT
140M
45M
8M
W
G
B
B/R
R/B
GY
R/W
A B C
C
111 110
R/W - 111
R/B - 110
BATTERY
121M
OFF ACC ON ST
B/W
B/R
IGNITION SWITCH
B/W
107M
FUSE BLOCK
20A
GY
UP
SEF945E

CODE 22 (IDLE SPEED CONTROL VALVE) – E16i ENGINE, PART 2

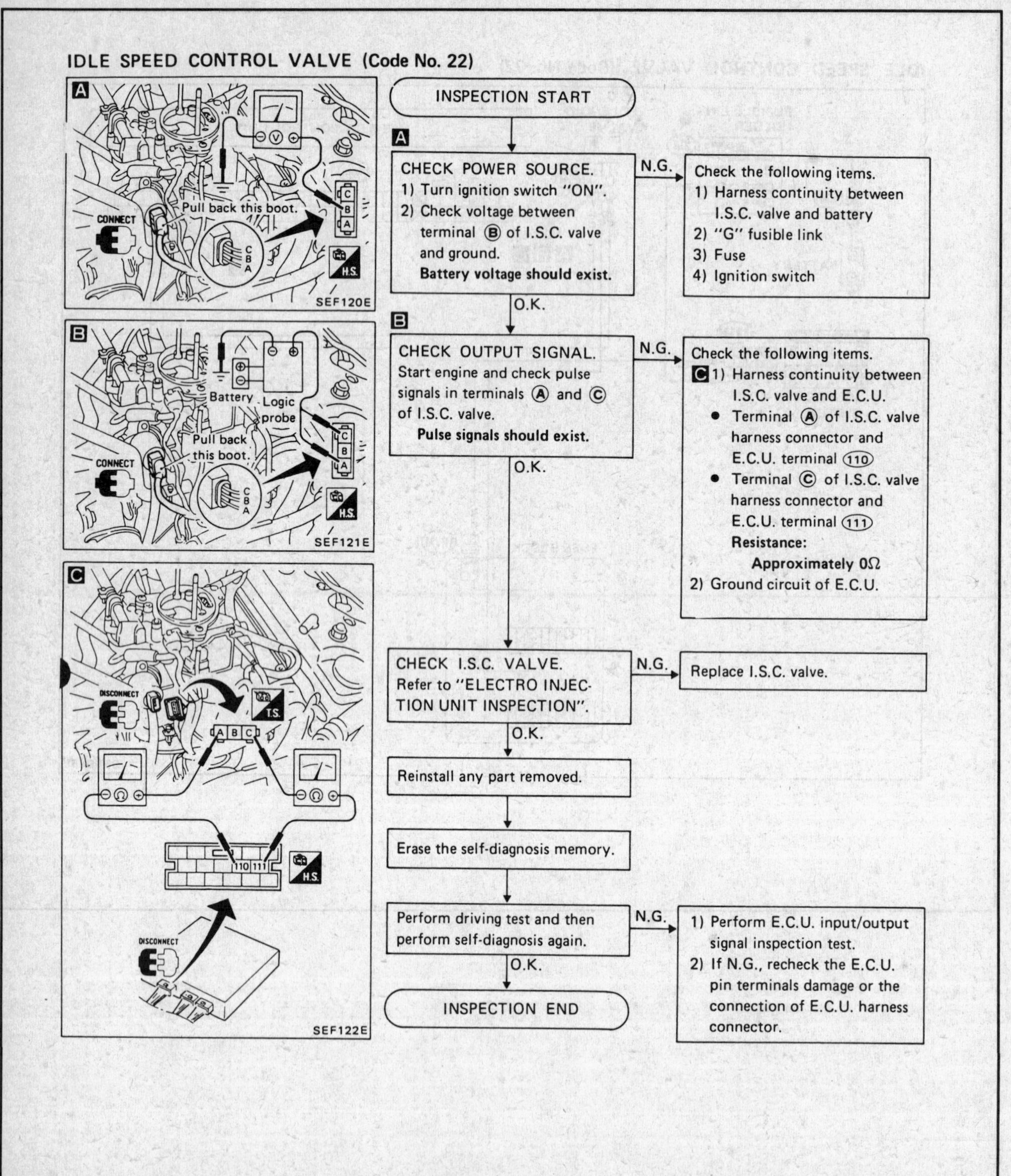

IDLE SPEED CONTROL VALVE (Code No. 22)
A
Pull back this boot.
CONNECT
C
B
A
H.S.
SEF120E
B
Battery
Logic probe
Pull back this boot.
CONNECT
H.S.
SEF121E
C
DISCONNECT
T.S.
A B C
110 111
H.S.
DISCONNECT
SEF122E
INSPECTION START
A
CHECK POWER SOURCE.
1) Turn ignition switch "ON".
2) Check voltage between terminal Ⓑ of I.S.C. valve and ground.
Battery voltage should exist.
N.G.
Check the following items.
1) Harness continuity between I.S.C. valve and battery
2) "G" fusible link
3) Fuse
4) Ignition switch
O.K.
B
CHECK OUTPUT SIGNAL.
Start engine and check pulse signals in terminals Ⓐ and Ⓒ of I.S.C. valve.
Pulse signals should exist.
N.G.
Check the following items.
C 1) Harness continuity between I.S.C. valve and E.C.U.
• Terminal Ⓐ of I.S.C. valve harness connector and E.C.U. terminal (110)
• Terminal Ⓒ of I.S.C. valve harness connector and E.C.U. terminal (111)
Resistance: Approximately 0Ω
2) Ground circuit of E.C.U.
O.K.
CHECK I.S.C. VALVE.
Refer to "ELECTRO INJECTION UNIT INSPECTION".
N.G.
Replace I.S.C. valve.
O.K.
Reinstall any part removed.
Erase the self-diagnosis memory.
Perform driving test and then perform self-diagnosis again.
N.G.
1) Perform E.C.U. input/output signal inspection test.
2) If N.G., recheck the E.C.U. pin terminals damage or the connection of E.C.U. harness connector.
O.K.
INSPECTION END

CODE 33 (OXYGEN SENSOR) – E16i ENGINE, PART 1

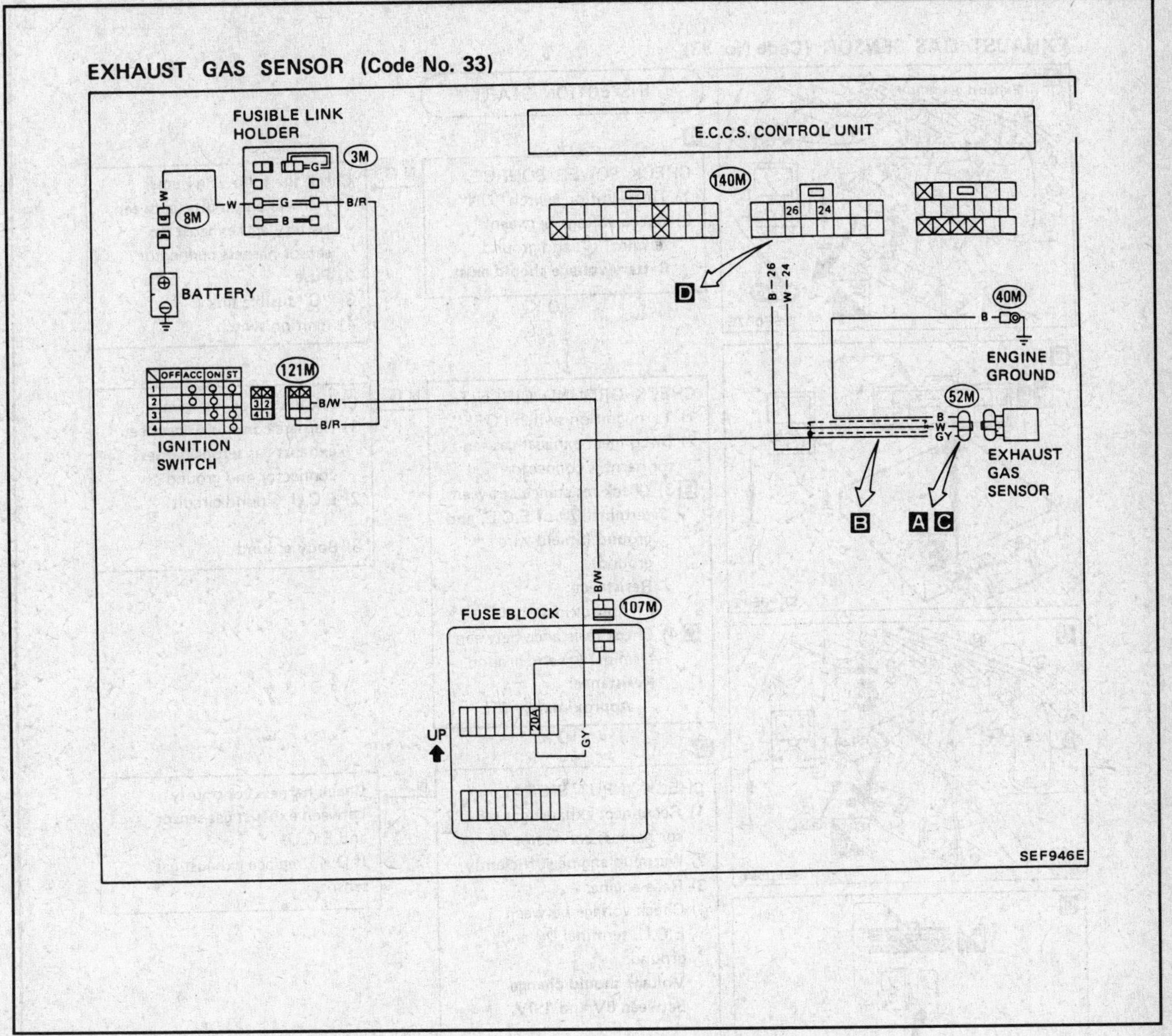
EXHAUST GAS SENSOR (Code No. 33)
FUSIBLE LINK HOLDER
3M
8M
BATTERY
E.C.C.S. CONTROL UNIT
140M
26
24
B – 26
W – 24
D
40M
ENGINE GROUND
52M
EXHAUST GAS SENSOR
B
A
C
121M
IGNITION SWITCH
OFF
ACC
ON
ST
B/W
B/R
FUSE BLOCK
107M
20A
GY
UP
SEF946E

CODE 33 (OXYGEN SENSOR) – E16i ENGINE, PART 2

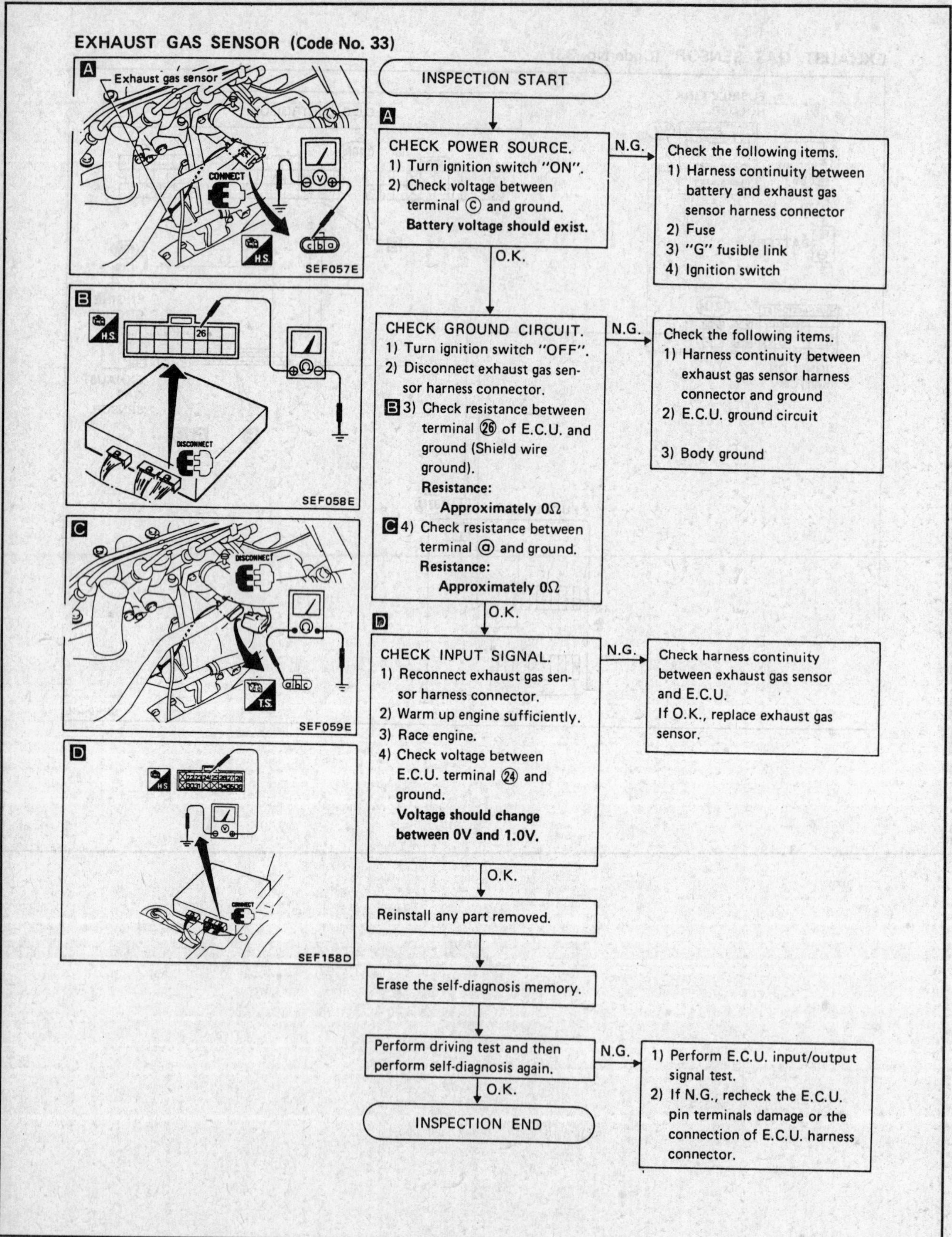
EXHAUST GAS SENSOR (Code No. 33)
A
Exhaust gas sensor
CONNECT
H.S.
c b a
SEF057E
B
H.S.
26
DISCONNECT
SEF058E
C
DISCONNECT
a b c
T.S.
SEF059E
D
H.S.
CONNECT
SEF158D
INSPECTION START
A
CHECK POWER SOURCE.
1) Turn ignition switch "ON".
2) Check voltage between terminal ⓒ and ground.
Battery voltage should exist.
N.G.
Check the following items.
1) Harness continuity between battery and exhaust gas sensor harness connector
2) Fuse
3) "G" fusible link
4) Ignition switch
O.K.
CHECK GROUND CIRCUIT.
1) Turn ignition switch "OFF".
2) Disconnect exhaust gas sensor harness connector.
B 3) Check resistance between terminal ㉖ of E.C.U. and ground (Shield wire ground).
Resistance:
Approximately 0Ω
C 4) Check resistance between terminal ⓐ and ground.
Resistance:
Approximately 0Ω
N.G.
Check the following items.
1) Harness continuity between exhaust gas sensor harness connector and ground
2) E.C.U. ground circuit
3) Body ground
O.K.
D
CHECK INPUT SIGNAL.
1) Reconnect exhaust gas sensor harness connector.
2) Warm up engine sufficiently.
3) Race engine.
4) Check voltage between E.C.U. terminal ㉔ and ground.
Voltage should change between 0V and 1.0V.
N.G.
Check harness continuity between exhaust gas sensor and E.C.U.
If O.K., replace exhaust gas sensor.
O.K.
Reinstall any part removed.
Erase the self-diagnosis memory.
Perform driving test and then perform self-diagnosis again.
N.G.
1) Perform E.C.U. input/output signal test.
2) If N.G., recheck the E.C.U. pin terminals damage or the connection of E.C.U. harness connector.
O.K.
INSPECTION END

CODE 41 (AIR TEMPERATURE SENSOR) – E16i ENGINE, PART 1

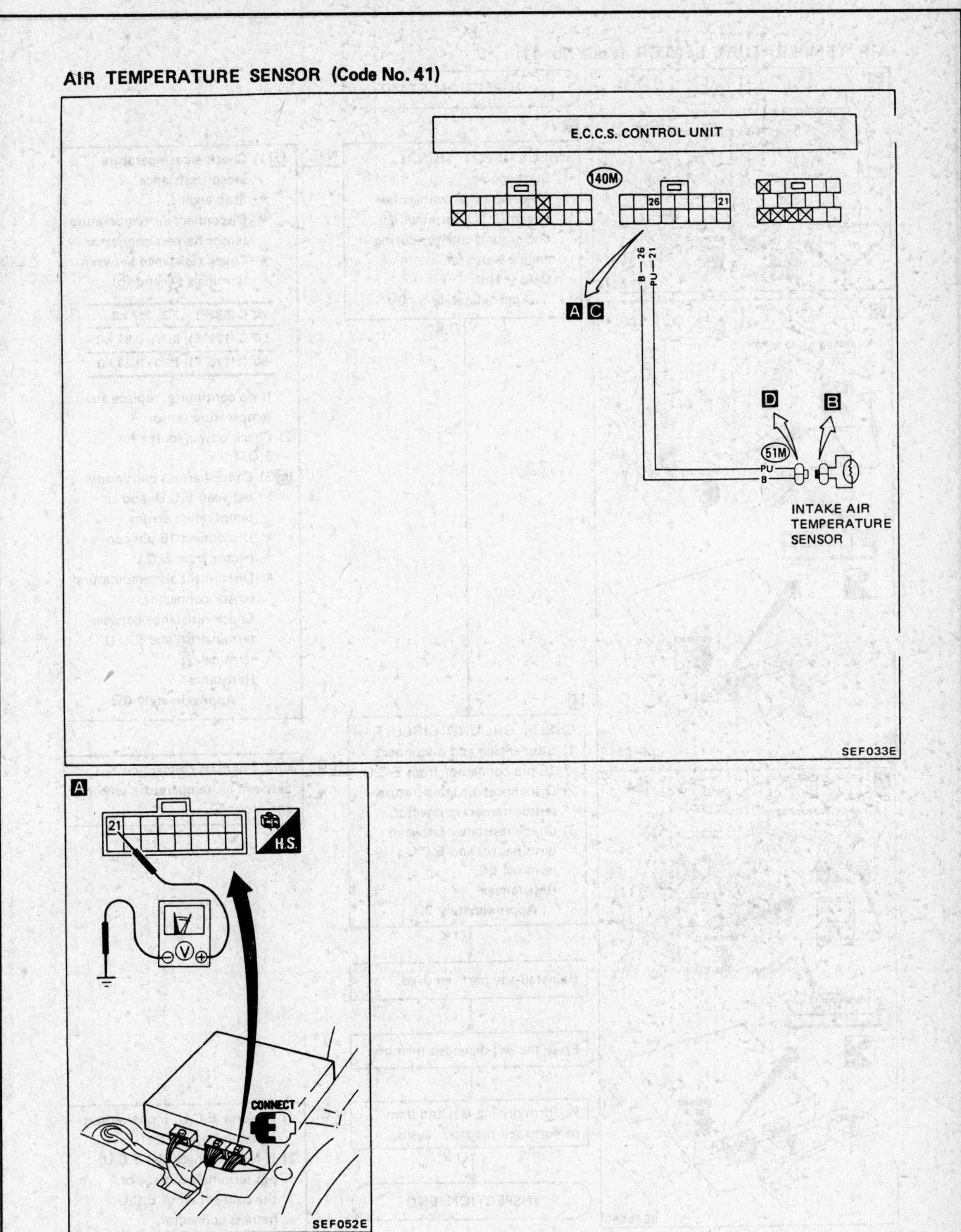
AIR TEMPERATURE SENSOR (Code No. 41)
E.C.C.S. CONTROL UNIT
140M
26
21
B — 26
PU — 21
A C
D
B
51M
PU
B
INTAKE AIR
TEMPERATURE
SENSOR
SEF033E
A
21
H.S.
CONNECT
SEF052E

CODE 41 (AIR TEMPERATURE SENSOR) – E16i ENGINE, PART 2

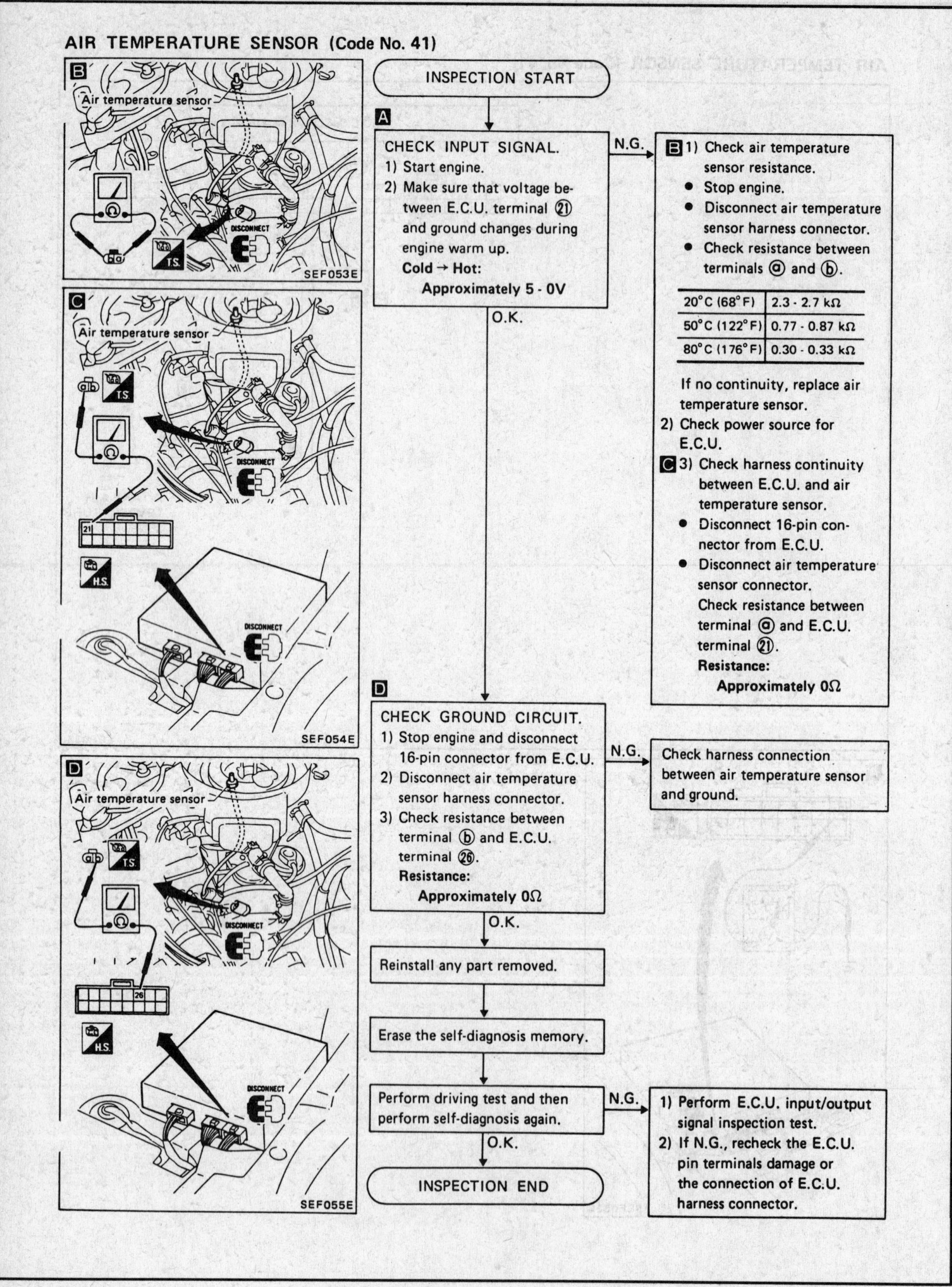
AIR TEMPERATURE SENSOR (Code No. 41)
B
Air temperature sensor
DISCONNECT
T.S.
SEF053E
C
Air temperature sensor
T.S.
DISCONNECT
21
H.S.
DISCONNECT
SEF054E
D
Air temperature sensor
T.S.
DISCONNECT
26
H.S.
DISCONNECT
SEF055E
INSPECTION START
A
CHECK INPUT SIGNAL.
1) Start engine.
2) Make sure that voltage between E.C.U. terminal ㉑ and ground changes during engine warm up.
Cold → Hot:
Approximately 5 - 0V
N.G.
B 1) Check air temperature sensor resistance.
• Stop engine.
• Disconnect air temperature sensor harness connector.
• Check resistance between terminals ⓐ and ⓑ.
20°C (68°F) | 2.3 - 2.7 kΩ
50°C (122°F) | 0.77 - 0.87 kΩ
80°C (176°F) | 0.30 - 0.33 kΩ
If no continuity, replace air temperature sensor.
2) Check power source for E.C.U.
C 3) Check harness continuity between E.C.U. and air temperature sensor.
• Disconnect 16-pin connector from E.C.U.
• Disconnect air temperature sensor connector.
Check resistance between terminal ⓐ and E.C.U. terminal ㉑.
Resistance:
Approximately 0Ω
O.K.
D
CHECK GROUND CIRCUIT.
1) Stop engine and disconnect 16-pin connector from E.C.U.
2) Disconnect air temperature sensor harness connector.
3) Check resistance between terminal ⓑ and E.C.U. terminal ㉖.
Resistance:
Approximately 0Ω
N.G.
Check harness connection between air temperature sensor and ground.
O.K.
Reinstall any part removed.
Erase the self-diagnosis memory.
Perform driving test and then perform self-diagnosis again.
N.G.
1) Perform E.C.U. input/output signal inspection test.
2) If N.G., recheck the E.C.U. pin terminals damage or the connection of E.C.U. harness connector.
O.K.
INSPECTION END

CODE 42 (THROTTLE SWITCH) – E16i ENGINE, PART 1

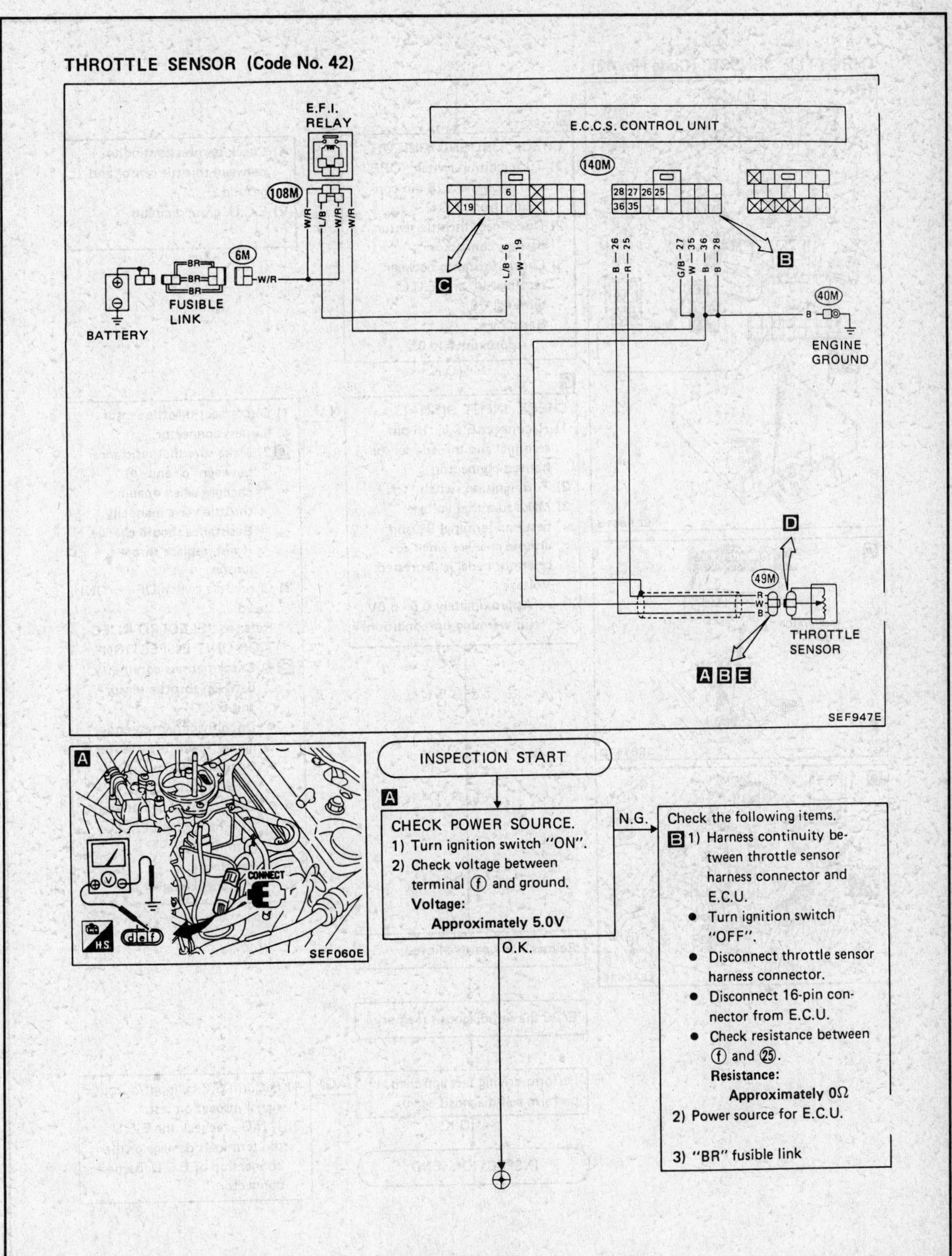
THROTTLE SENSOR (Code No. 42)
E.F.I. RELAY
E.C.C.S. CONTROL UNIT
140M
108M
6M
40M
49M
BATTERY
FUSIBLE LINK
W/R
L/B
BR
L/B – 6
W – 19
B – 26
R – 25
G/B – 27
W – 35
B – 36
B – 28
B
ENGINE GROUND
R
W
B
THROTTLE SENSOR
C
B
D
A B E
SEF947E
A
CONNECT
H.S.
d e f
SEF060E
INSPECTION START
A
CHECK POWER SOURCE.
1) Turn ignition switch "ON".
2) Check voltage between terminal ⓕ and ground.
Voltage:
Approximately 5.0V
N.G.
Check the following items.
B 1) Harness continuity between throttle sensor harness connector and E.C.U.
• Turn ignition switch "OFF".
• Disconnect throttle sensor harness connector.
• Disconnect 16-pin connector from E.C.U.
• Check resistance between ⓕ and ㉕.
Resistance:
Approximately 0Ω
2) Power source for E.C.U.
3) "BR" fusible link
O.K.

CODE 42 (THROTTLE SWITCH) – E16i ENGINE, PART 2

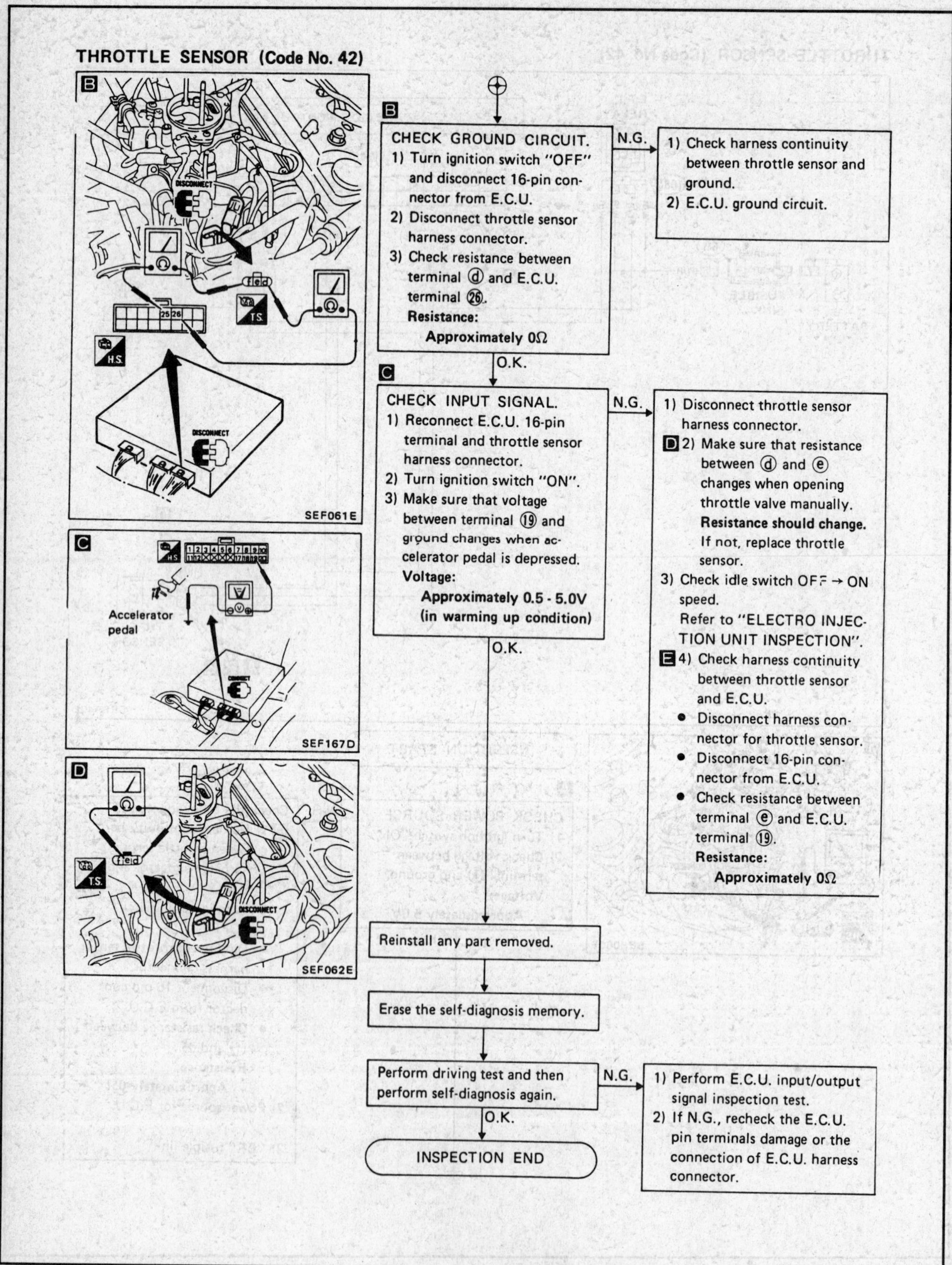
THROTTLE SENSOR (Code No. 42)
B
DISCONNECT
T.S.
H.S.
DISCONNECT
SEF061E
C
H.S.
Accelerator pedal
CONNECT
SEF167D
D
T.S.
DISCONNECT
SEF062E
B
CHECK GROUND CIRCUIT.
1) Turn ignition switch "OFF" and disconnect 16-pin connector from E.C.U.
2) Disconnect throttle sensor harness connector.
3) Check resistance between terminal ⓓ and E.C.U. terminal ㉖.
Resistance:
Approximately 0Ω
N.G.
1) Check harness continuity between throttle sensor and ground.
2) E.C.U. ground circuit.
O.K.
C
CHECK INPUT SIGNAL.
1) Reconnect E.C.U. 16-pin terminal and throttle sensor harness connector.
2) Turn ignition switch "ON".
3) Make sure that voltage between terminal ⑲ and ground changes when accelerator pedal is depressed.
Voltage:
Approximately 0.5 - 5.0V
(in warming up condition)
N.G.
1) Disconnect throttle sensor harness connector.
D 2) Make sure that resistance between ⓓ and ⓔ changes when opening throttle valve manually.
Resistance should change.
If not, replace throttle sensor.
3) Check idle switch OFF → ON speed.
Refer to "ELECTRO INJECTION UNIT INSPECTION".
E 4) Check harness continuity between throttle sensor and E.C.U.
• Disconnect harness connector for throttle sensor.
• Disconnect 16-pin connector from E.C.U.
• Check resistance between terminal ⓔ and E.C.U. terminal ⑲.
Resistance:
Approximately 0Ω
O.K.
Reinstall any part removed.
Erase the self-diagnosis memory.
Perform driving test and then perform self-diagnosis again.
N.G.
1) Perform E.C.U. input/output signal inspection test.
2) If N.G., recheck the E.C.U. pin terminals damage or the connection of E.C.U. harness connector.
O.K.
INSPECTION END

CODE 42 (THROTTLE SWITCH) – E16i ENGINE, PART 3

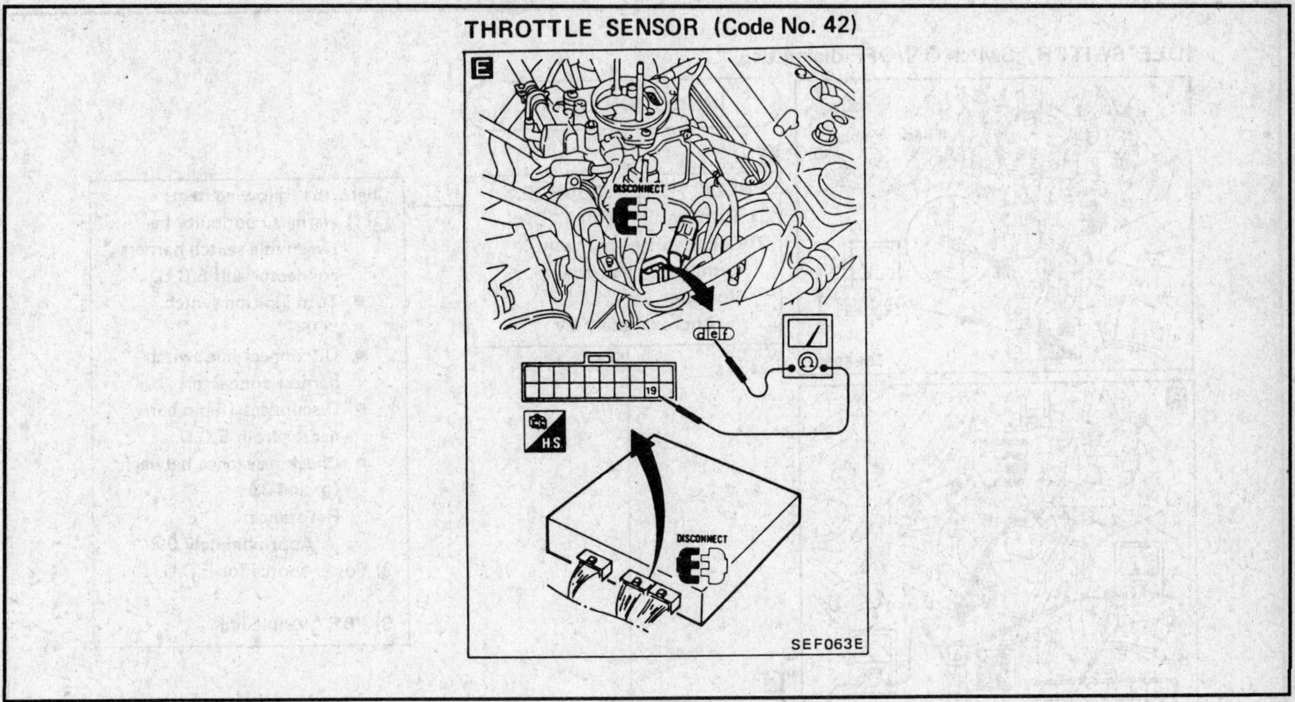
THROTTLE SENSOR (Code No. 42)
E
DISCONNECT
19
H.S.
DISCONNECT
SEF063E

ON/OFF DIAGNOSIS (IDLE SWITCH) – E16i ENGINE, PART 1

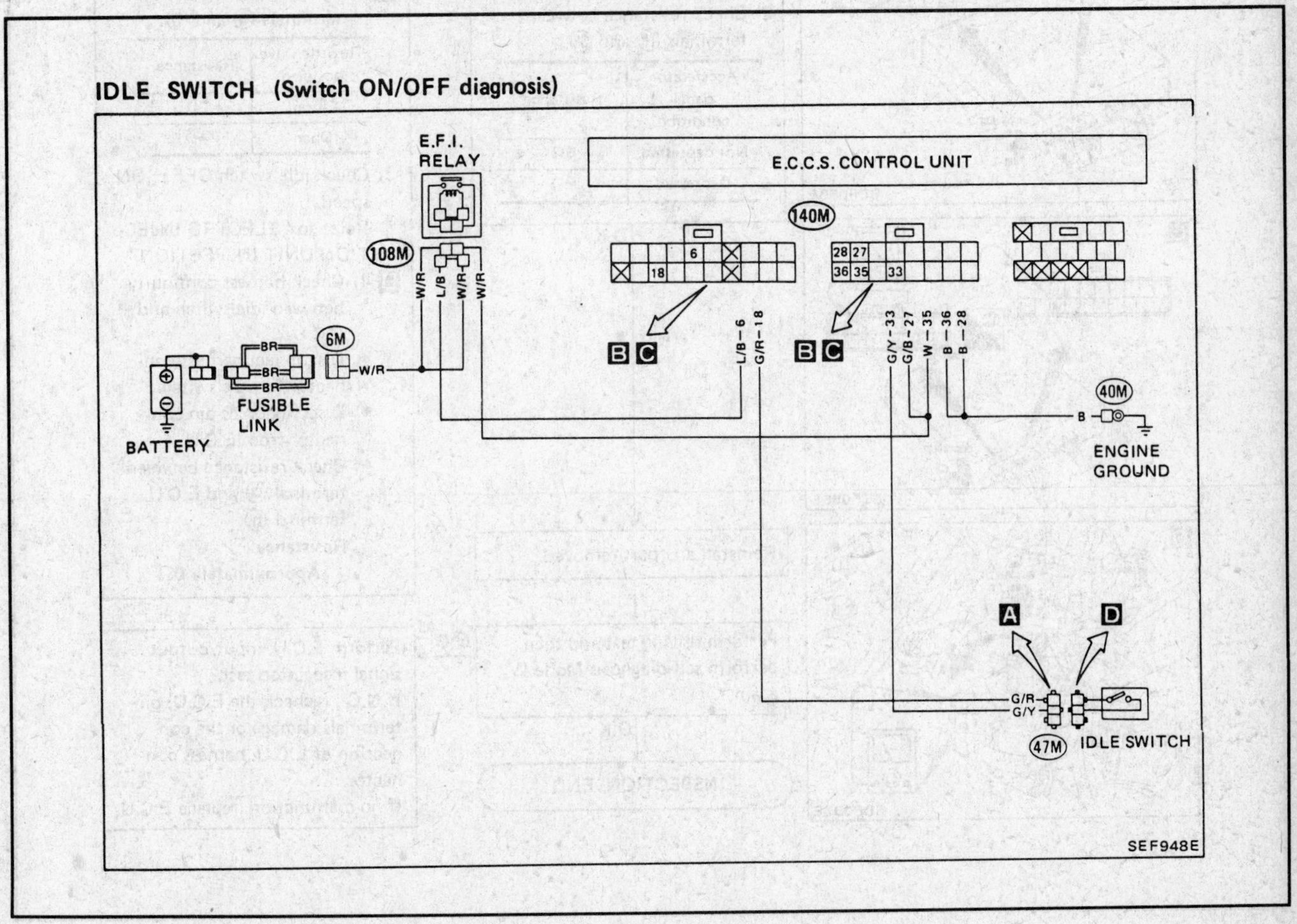

IDLE SWITCH (Switch ON/OFF diagnosis)

E.F.I. RELAY
108M
W/R L/B W/R W/R
E.C.C.S. CONTROL UNIT
140M
6 18
28 27 36 35 33
B C
L/B – 6
G/R – 18
B C
G/Y – 33
G/B – 27
W – 35
B – 36
B – 28
6M
W/R
BR
BR
BR
FUSIBLE LINK
BATTERY
40M
B
ENGINE GROUND
A
D
G/R
G/Y
47M
IDLE SWITCH
SEF948E

ON/OFF DIAGNOSIS (IDLE SWITCH) – E16i ENGINE, PART 2

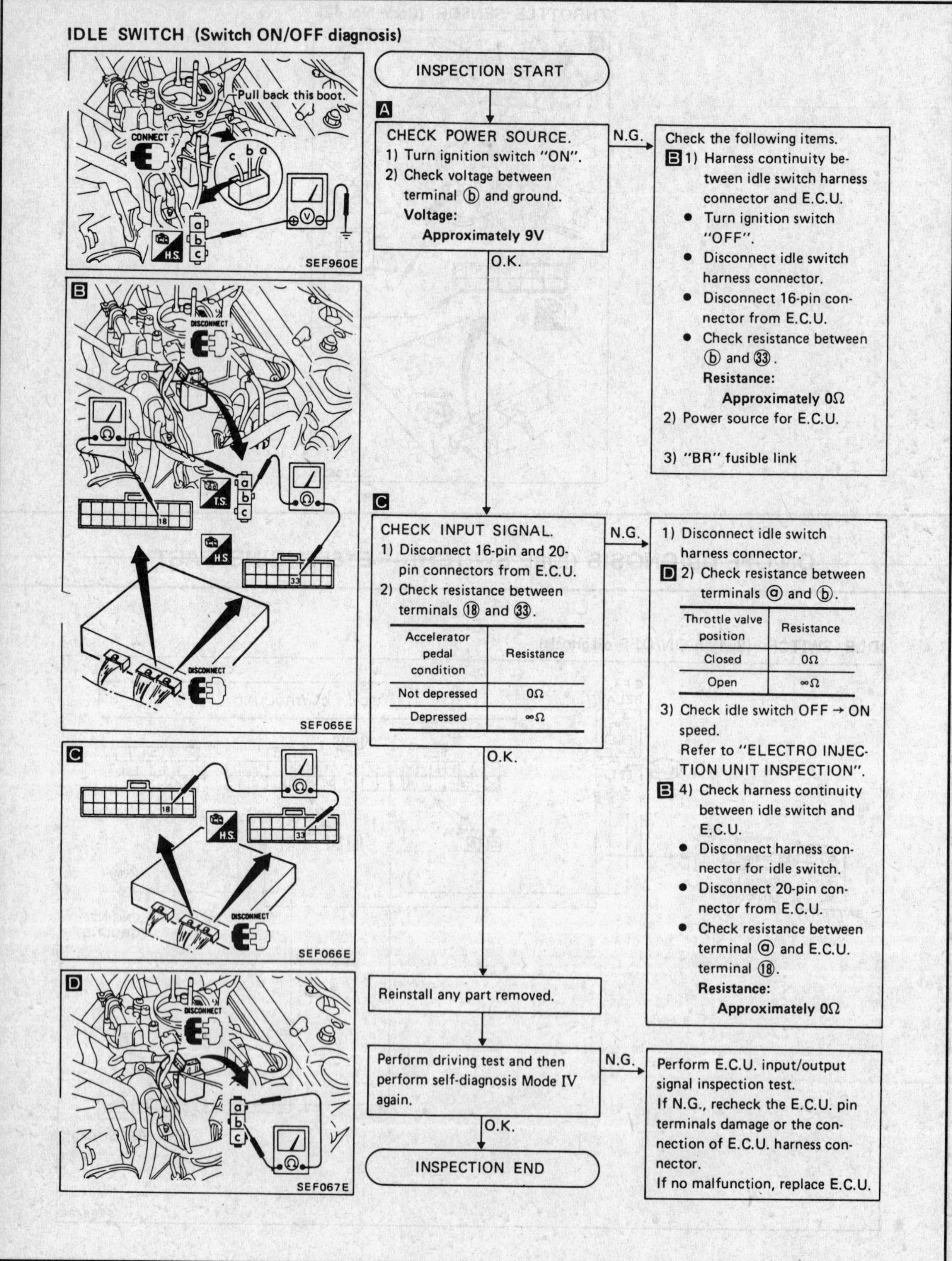
IDLE SWITCH (Switch ON/OFF diagnosis)
Pull back this boot.
CONNECT
c b a
H.S.
a
b
c
SEF960E
INSPECTION START
A
CHECK POWER SOURCE.
1) Turn ignition switch "ON".
2) Check voltage between terminal ⓑ and ground.
Voltage:
Approximately 9V
N.G.
Check the following items.
B 1) Harness continuity between idle switch harness connector and E.C.U.
• Turn ignition switch "OFF".
• Disconnect idle switch harness connector.
• Disconnect 16-pin connector from E.C.U.
• Check resistance between ⓑ and ㉝.
Resistance:
Approximately 0Ω
2) Power source for E.C.U.
3) "BR" fusible link
O.K.
B
DISCONNECT
T.S.
18
H.S.
33
DISCONNECT
SEF065E
C
CHECK INPUT SIGNAL.
1) Disconnect 16-pin and 20-pin connectors from E.C.U.
2) Check resistance between terminals ⑱ and ㉝.
Accelerator pedal condition
Resistance
Not depressed
0Ω
Depressed
∞Ω
N.G.
1) Disconnect idle switch harness connector.
D 2) Check resistance between terminals ⓐ and ⓑ.
Throttle valve position
Resistance
Closed
0Ω
Open
∞Ω
3) Check idle switch OFF → ON speed.
Refer to "ELECTRO INJECTION UNIT INSPECTION".
B 4) Check harness continuity between idle switch and E.C.U.
• Disconnect harness connector for idle switch.
• Disconnect 20-pin connector from E.C.U.
• Check resistance between terminal ⓐ and E.C.U. terminal ⑱.
Resistance:
Approximately 0Ω
O.K.
C
18
H.S.
33
DISCONNECT
SEF066E
D
DISCONNECT
a
b
c
SEF067E
Reinstall any part removed.
Perform driving test and then perform self-diagnosis Mode IV again.
N.G.
Perform E.C.U. input/output signal inspection test.
If N.G., recheck the E.C.U. pin terminals damage or the connection of E.C.U. harness connector.
If no malfunction, replace E.C.U.
O.K.
INSPECTION END

ON/OFF DIAGNOSIS (START SIGNAL) – E16i ENGINE

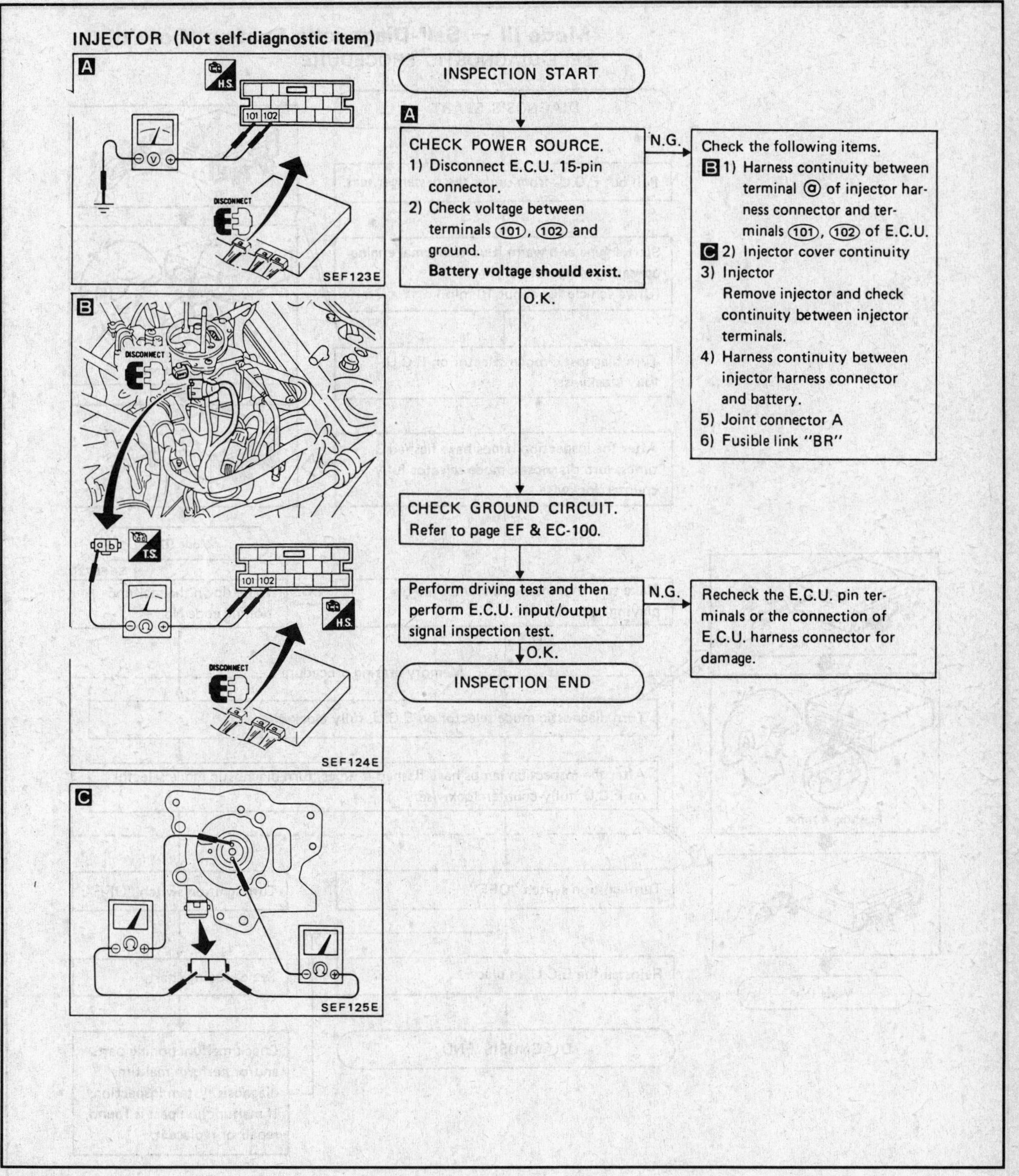
INJECTOR (Not self-diagnostic item)
A
H.S.
101 102
DISCONNECT
SEF123E
B
DISCONNECT
a b
T.S.
101 102
H.S.
DISCONNECT
SEF124E
C
SEF125E
INSPECTION START
A
CHECK POWER SOURCE.
1) Disconnect E.C.U. 15-pin connector.
2) Check voltage between terminals (101), (102) and ground.
Battery voltage should exist.
N.G.
Check the following items.
B 1) Harness continuity between terminal (a) of injector harness connector and terminals (101), (102) of E.C.U.
C 2) Injector cover continuity
3) Injector
Remove injector and check continuity between injector terminals.
4) Harness continuity between injector harness connector and battery.
5) Joint connector A
6) Fusible link "BR"
O.K.
CHECK GROUND CIRCUIT.
Refer to page EF & EC-100.
Perform driving test and then perform E.C.U. input/output signal inspection test.
N.G.
Recheck the E.C.U. pin terminals or the connection of E.C.U. harness connector for damage.
O.K.
INSPECTION END

MODE III, SELF-DIAGNOSTIC SYSTEM PROCEDURE CA16DE AND CA18DE ENGINES

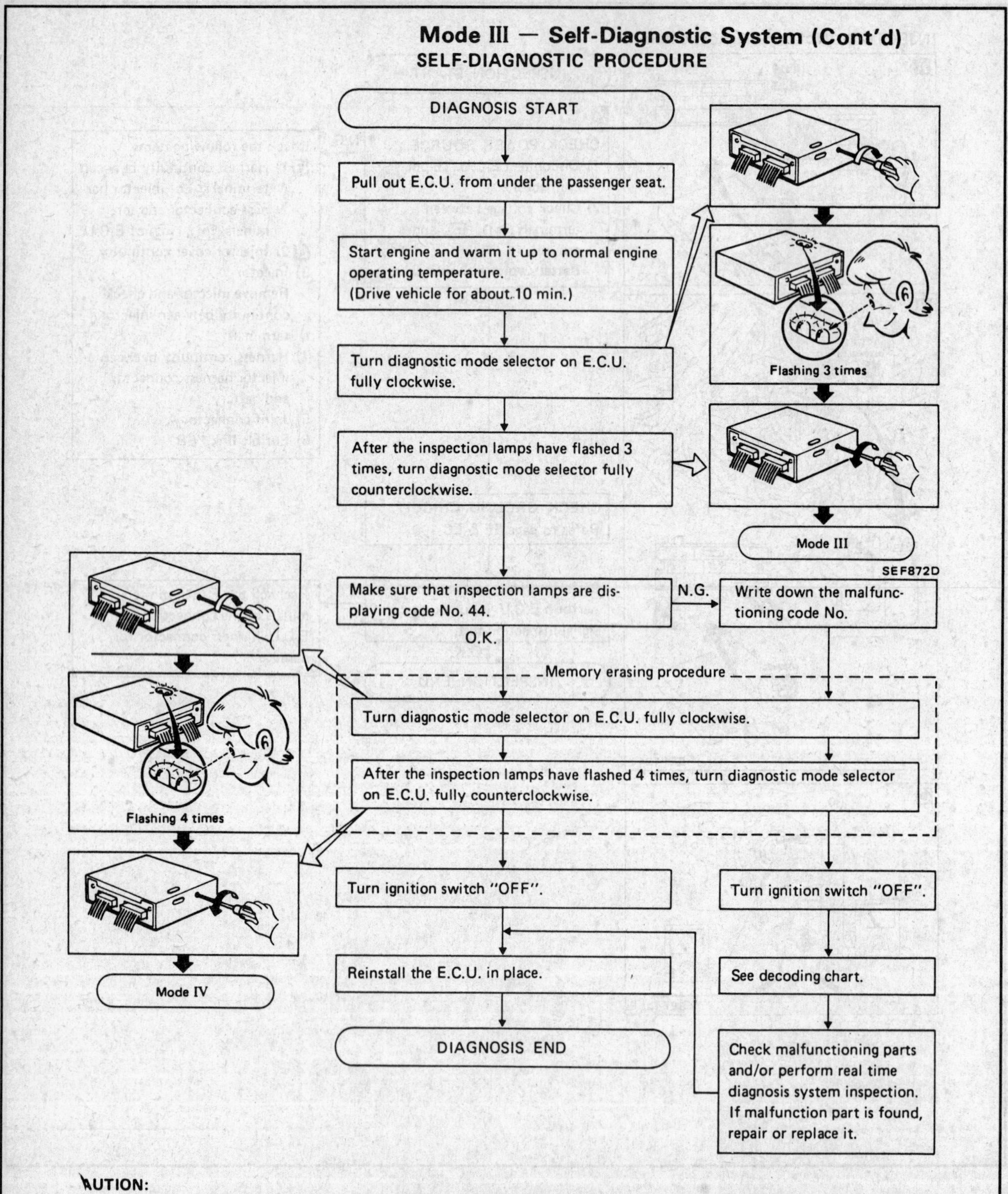
Mode III — Self-Diagnostic System (Cont'd)
SELF-DIAGNOSTIC PROCEDURE
DIAGNOSIS START
Pull out E.C.U. from under the passenger seat.
Start engine and warm it up to normal engine operating temperature. (Drive vehicle for about 10 min.)
Turn diagnostic mode selector on E.C.U. fully clockwise.
Flashing 3 times
After the inspection lamps have flashed 3 times, turn diagnostic mode selector fully counterclockwise.
Mode III
SEF872D
Make sure that inspection lamps are displaying code No. 44.
N.G.
Write down the malfunctioning code No.
O.K.
Memory erasing procedure
Turn diagnostic mode selector on E.C.U. fully clockwise.
After the inspection lamps have flashed 4 times, turn diagnostic mode selector on E.C.U. fully counterclockwise.
Flashing 4 times
Mode IV
Turn ignition switch "OFF".
Turn ignition switch "OFF".
Reinstall the E.C.U. in place.
See decoding chart.
DIAGNOSIS END
Check malfunctioning parts and/or perform real time diagnosis system inspection. If malfunction part is found, repair or replace it.

CAUTION:

During displaying code No. in self-diagnosis mode (mode III), if the other diagnostic mode should be done, make sure to write down the malfunctioning code No. before turning diagnostic mode selector on E.C.U. fully clockwise, or select the diagnostic mode after turning switch "OFF". Otherwise self-diagnosis information stored in E.C.U. memory until now would be lost.

TROUBLE CODE DECODING CHART – CA16DE AND CA18DE ENGINES

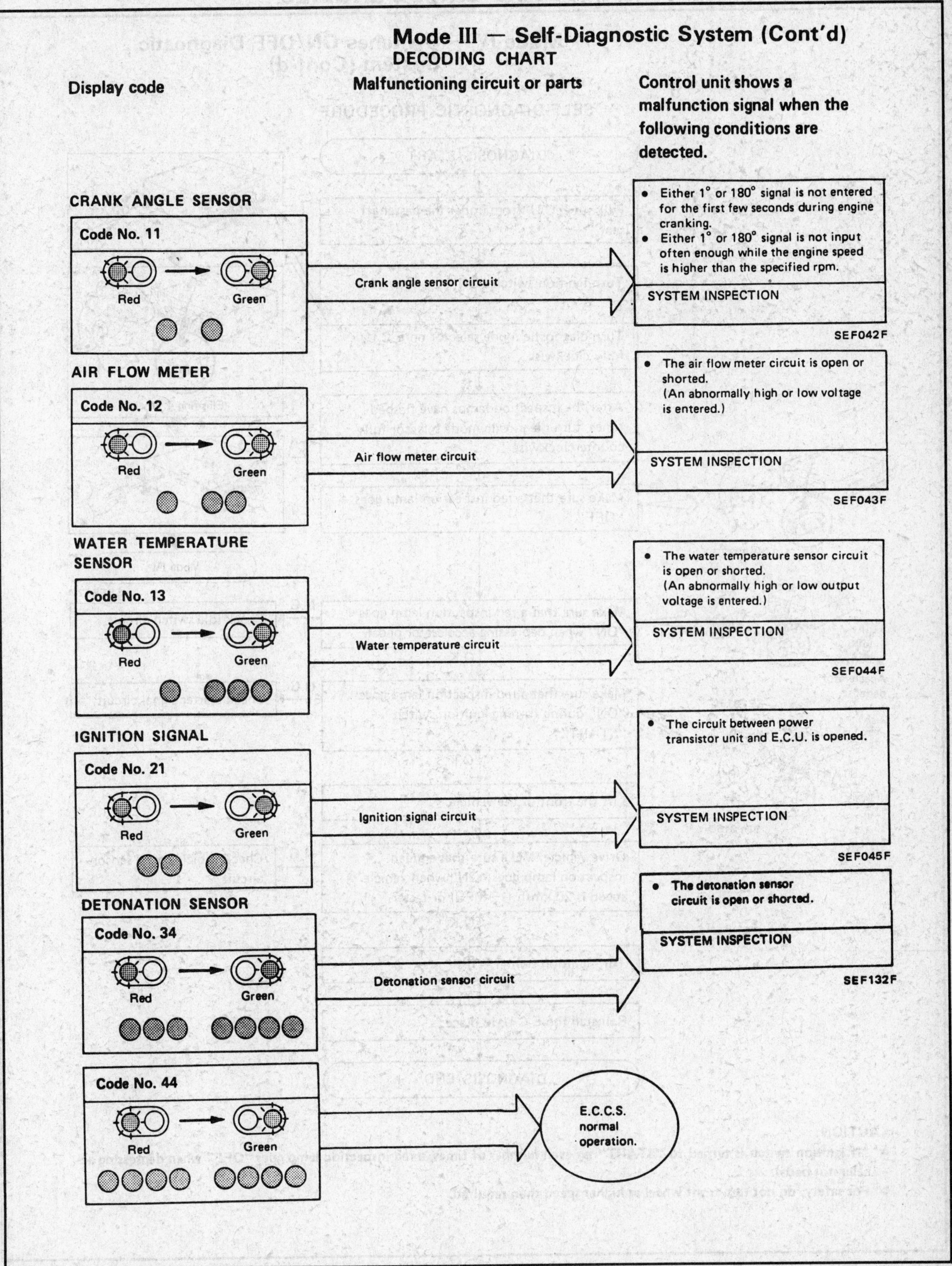
Mode III — Self-Diagnostic System (Cont'd)
DECODING CHART
Display code
Malfunctioning circuit or parts
Control unit shows a malfunction signal when the following conditions are detected.
CRANK ANGLE SENSOR
Code No. 11
Red
Green
Crank angle sensor circuit
• Either 1° or 180° signal is not entered for the first few seconds during engine cranking.
• Either 1° or 180° signal is not input often enough while the engine speed is higher than the specified rpm.
SYSTEM INSPECTION
SEF042F
AIR FLOW METER
Code No. 12
Red
Green
Air flow meter circuit
• The air flow meter circuit is open or shorted.
(An abnormally high or low voltage is entered.)
SYSTEM INSPECTION
SEF043F
WATER TEMPERATURE SENSOR
Code No. 13
Red
Green
Water temperature circuit
• The water temperature sensor circuit is open or shorted.
(An abnormally high or low output voltage is entered.)
SYSTEM INSPECTION
SEF044F
IGNITION SIGNAL
Code No. 21
Red
Green
Ignition signal circuit
• The circuit between power transistor unit and E.C.U. is opened.
SYSTEM INSPECTION
SEF045F
DETONATION SENSOR
Code No. 34
Red
Green
Detonation sensor circuit
• The detonation sensor circuit is open or shorted.
SYSTEM INSPECTION
SEF132F
Code No. 44
Red
Green
E.C.C.S. normal operation.

MODE IV, SWITCHES ON/OFF DIAGNOSTIC SYSTEM CA16DE AND CA18DE ENGINES

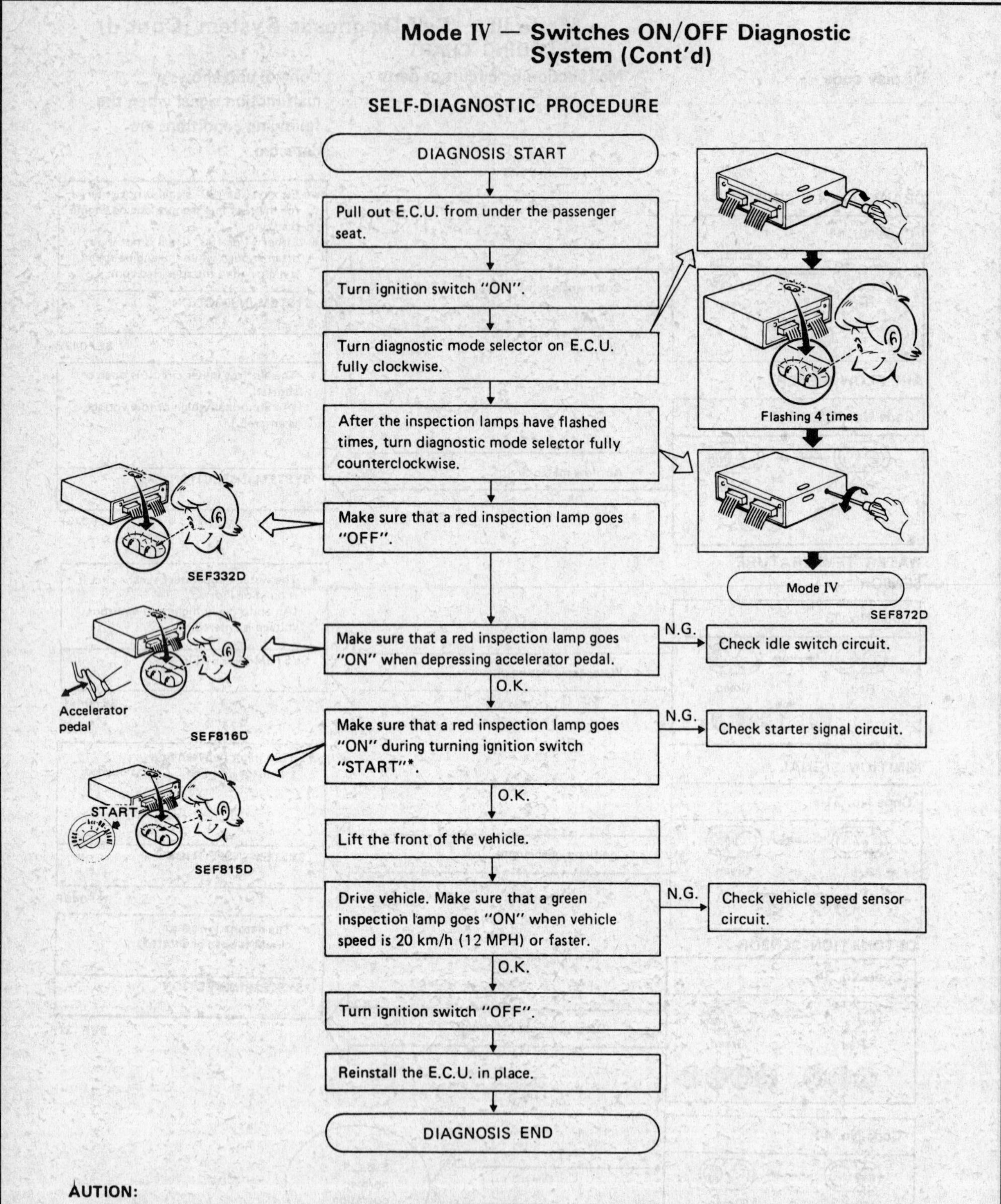
Mode IV — Switches ON/OFF Diagnostic System (Cont'd)
SELF-DIAGNOSTIC PROCEDURE
DIAGNOSIS START
Pull out E.C.U. from under the passenger seat.
Turn ignition switch "ON".
Turn diagnostic mode selector on E.C.U. fully clockwise.
After the inspection lamps have flashed times, turn diagnostic mode selector fully counterclockwise.
Make sure that a red inspection lamp goes "OFF".
Make sure that a red inspection lamp goes "ON" when depressing accelerator pedal.
N.G.
Check idle switch circuit.
O.K.
Make sure that a red inspection lamp goes "ON" during turning ignition switch "START"*.
N.G.
Check starter signal circuit.
O.K.
Lift the front of the vehicle.
Drive vehicle. Make sure that a green inspection lamp goes "ON" when vehicle speed is 20 km/h (12 MPH) or faster.
N.G.
Check vehicle speed sensor circuit.
O.K.
Turn ignition switch "OFF".
Reinstall the E.C.U. in place.
DIAGNOSIS END
Flashing 4 times
Mode IV
SEF872D
SEF332D
Accelerator pedal
SEF816D
START
SEF815D

AUTION:

- ***If ignition switch is turned to "START" an even number of times, a red inspection lamp goes "OFF" when depressing accelerator pedal.**
- **For safety, do not turn front wheel at higher speed than required.**

MODE V, REAL TIME DIAGNOSTIC SYSTEM — CA16DE AND CA18DE ENGINES

Mode V — Real Time Diagnostic System

In real time diagnosis, if any of the following items are judged to be faulty, a malfunction is indicated immediately.

- Crank angle sensor (180° signal & 1° signal)
- Ignition signal
- Air flow meter output signal

Consequently, this diagnosis is a very effective measure to diagnose whether the above systems cause the malfunction or not, during driving test. Compared with self-diagnosis, real time diagnosis is very sensitive, and can detect malfunctioning conditions in a moment. Further, items regarded to be malfunctions in this diagnosis are not stored in E.C.U. memory.

SELF-DIAGNOSITC PROCEDURE

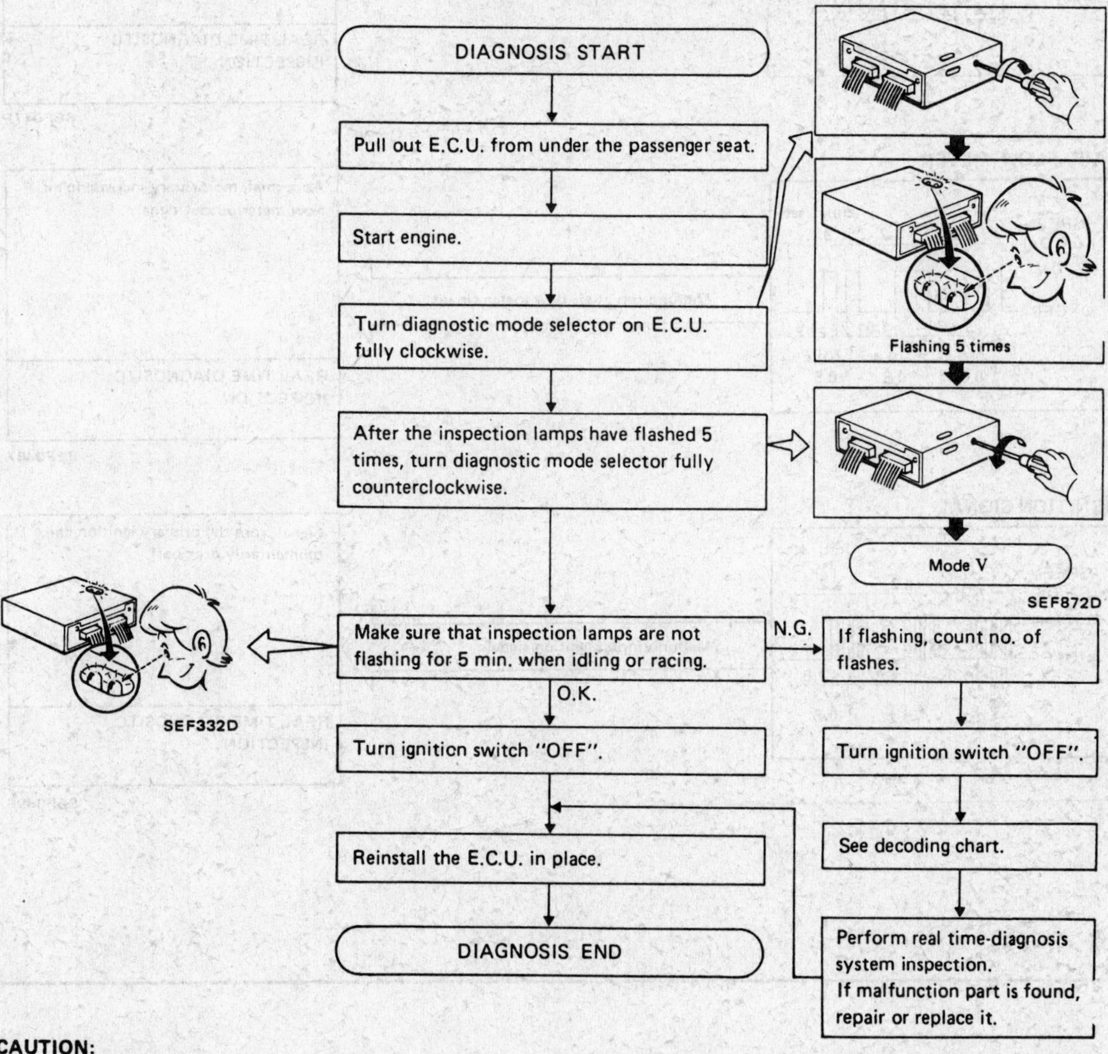
DIAGNOSIS START
Pull out E.C.U. from under the passenger seat.
Start engine.
Turn diagnostic mode selector on E.C.U. fully clockwise.
After the inspection lamps have flashed 5 times, turn diagnostic mode selector fully counterclockwise.
Flashing 5 times
Mode V
SEF872D
Make sure that inspection lamps are not flashing for 5 min. when idling or racing.
SEF332D
N.G.
If flashing, count no. of flashes.
O.K.
Turn ignition switch "OFF".
Turn ignition switch "OFF".
See decoding chart.
Reinstall the E.C.U. in place.
Perform real time-diagnosis system inspection.
If malfunction part is found, repair or replace it.
DIAGNOSIS END

CAUTION:

In real time diagnosis, pay attention to inspection lamp flashing. E.C.U. displays the malfunction code only once, and does not memorize the inspection.

MODE V TROUBLE CODE DECODING CHART – CA16DE AND CA18DE ENGINES

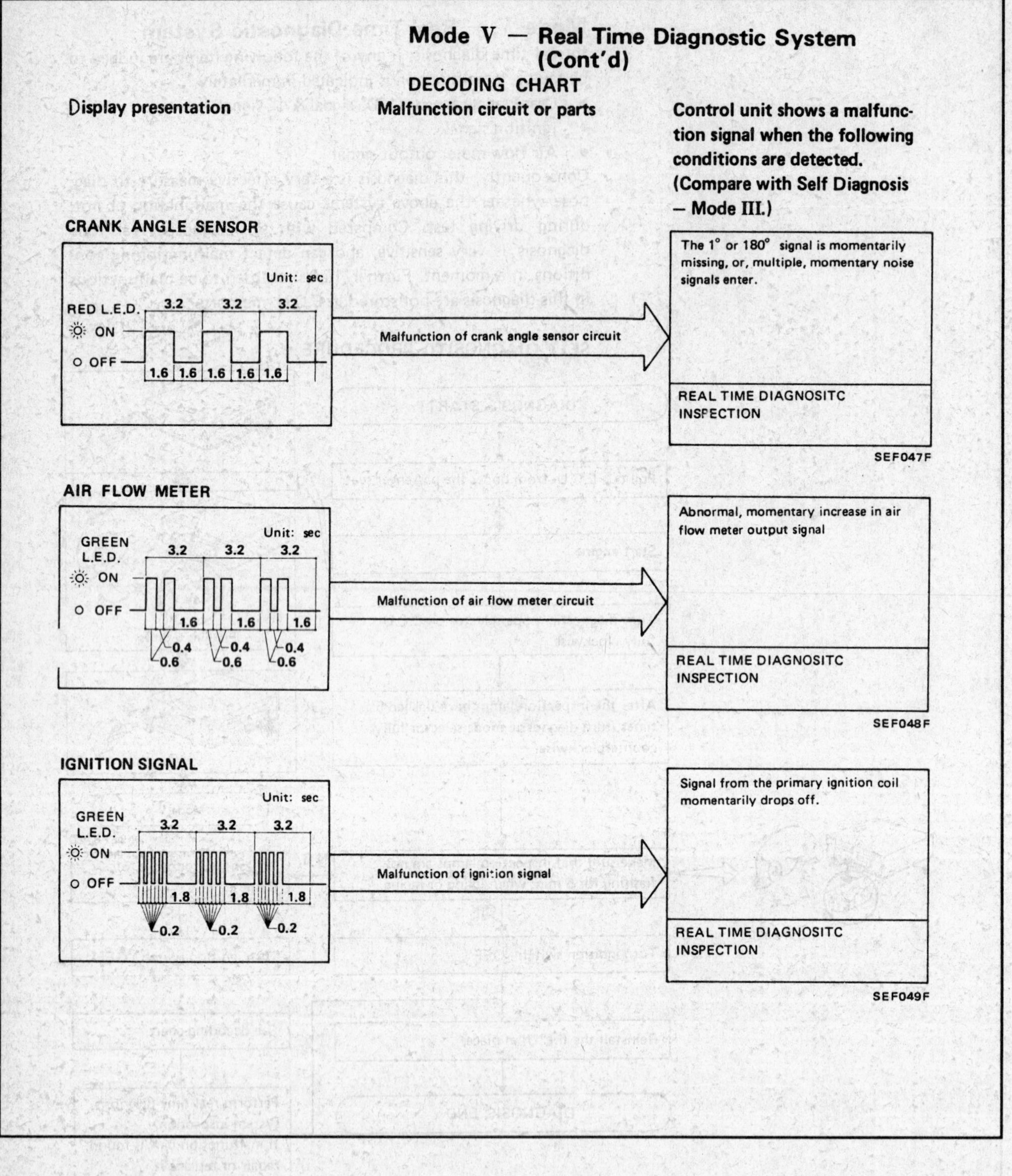
Mode V — Real Time Diagnostic System
(Cont'd)
DECODING CHART
Display presentation
Malfunction circuit or parts
Control unit shows a malfunction signal when the following conditions are detected. (Compare with Self Diagnosis – Mode III.)
CRANK ANGLE SENSOR
Unit: sec
RED L.E.D.
ON
OFF
3.2
1.6
Malfunction of crank angle sensor circuit
The 1° or 180° signal is momentarily missing, or, multiple, momentary noise signals enter.
REAL TIME DIAGNOSITC INSPECTION
SEF047F
AIR FLOW METER
GREEN L.E.D.
0.4
0.6
Malfunction of air flow meter circuit
Abnormal, momentary increase in air flow meter output signal
SEF048F
IGNITION SIGNAL
1.8
0.2
Malfunction of ignition signal
Signal from the primary ignition coil momentarily drops off.
SEF049F

ECU POWER SOURCE AND GROUND CIRCUIT CHART CA16DE AND CA18DE ENGINES, PART 1

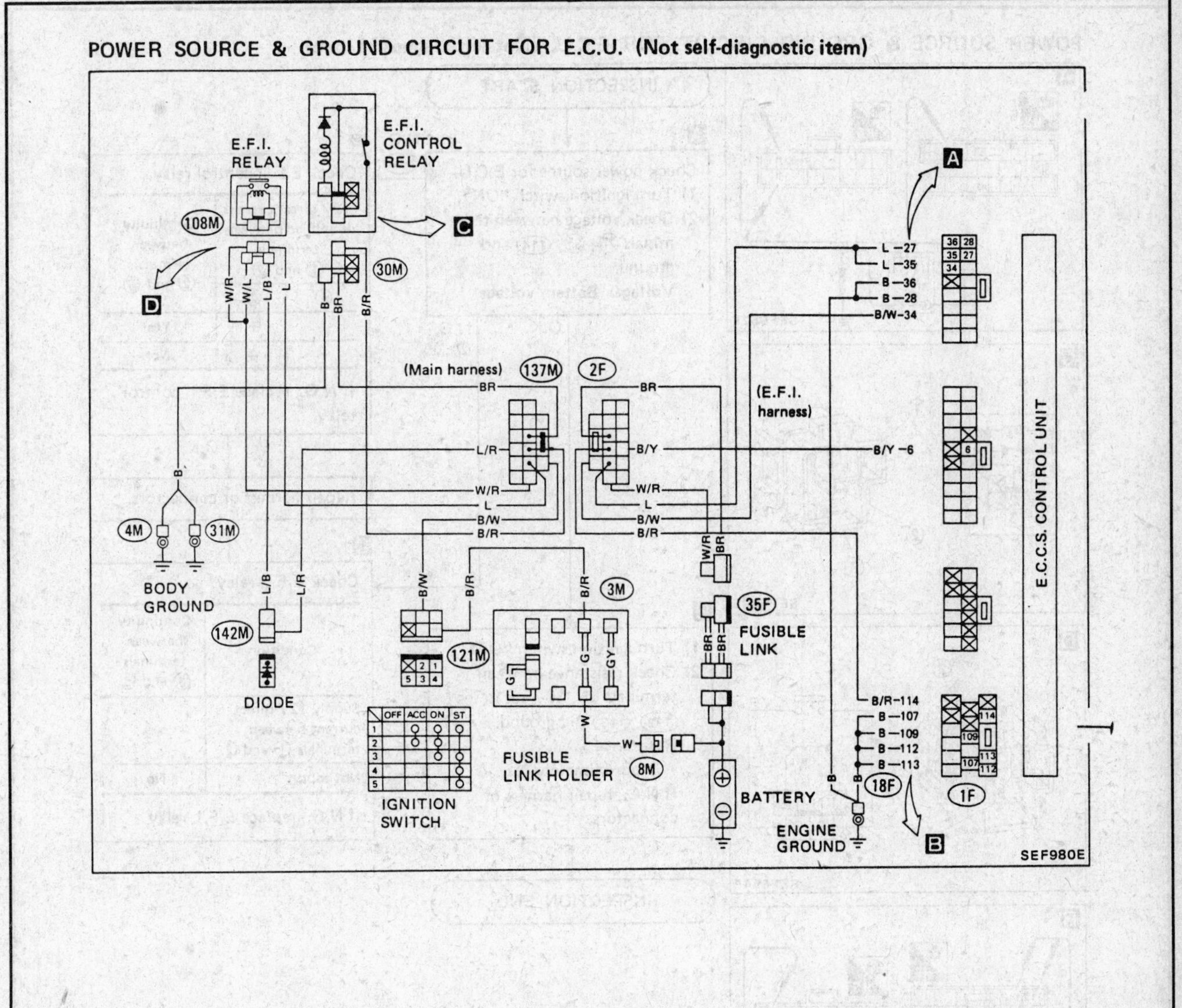
POWER SOURCE & GROUND CIRCUIT FOR E.C.U. (Not self-diagnostic item)
E.F.I. RELAY
E.F.I. CONTROL RELAY
108M
30M
C
D
A
B
(Main harness)
137M
2F
(E.F.I. harness)
4M
31M
BODY GROUND
142M
DIODE
121M
3M
FUSIBLE LINK HOLDER
8M
IGNITION SWITCH
OFF ACC ON ST
35F
FUSIBLE LINK
BATTERY
ENGINE GROUND
18F
1F
E.C.C.S. CONTROL UNIT
L-27
L-35
B-36
B-28
B/W-34
B/Y-6
B/R-114
B-107
B-109
B-112
B-113
SEF980E

ECU POWER SOURCE AND GROUND CIRCUIT CHART CA16DE AND CA18DE ENGINES, PART 2

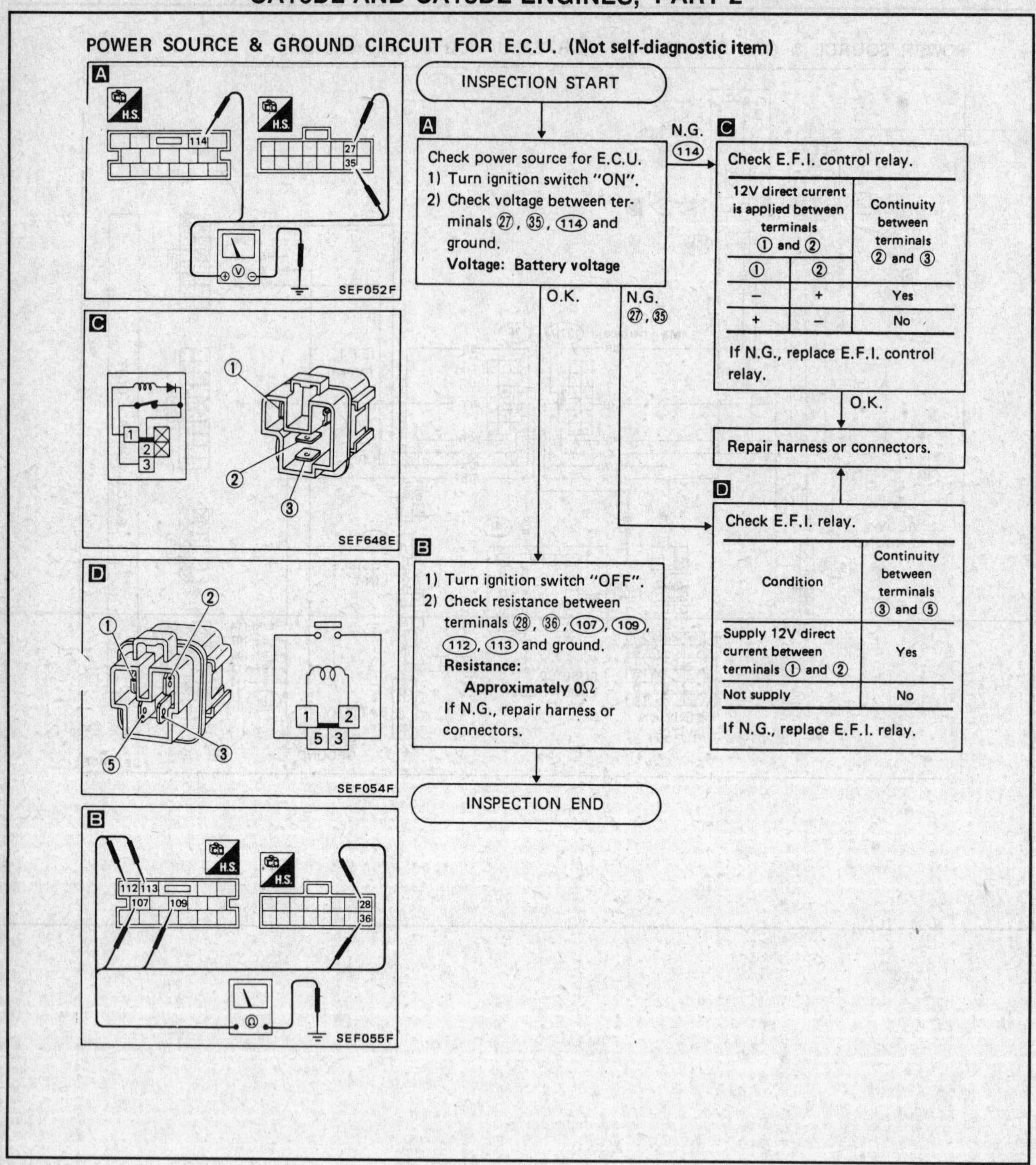
POWER SOURCE & GROUND CIRCUIT FOR E.C.U. (Not self-diagnostic item)
INSPECTION START
A
Check power source for E.C.U.
1) Turn ignition switch "ON".
2) Check voltage between terminals ㉗, ㉟, (114) and ground.
Voltage: Battery voltage
N.G. (114)
C
Check E.F.I. control relay.
12V direct current is applied between terminals ① and ②
Continuity between terminals ② and ③
① ②
– + Yes
+ – No
If N.G., replace E.F.I. control relay.
O.K.
Repair harness or connectors.
O.K.
N.G. ㉗, ㉟
D
Check E.F.I. relay.
Condition
Continuity between terminals ③ and ⑤
Supply 12V direct current between terminals ① and ②
Yes
Not supply
No
If N.G., replace E.F.I. relay.
B
1) Turn ignition switch "OFF".
2) Check resistance between terminals ㉘, ㊱, (107), (109), (112), (113) and ground.
Resistance:
Approximately 0Ω
If N.G., repair harness or connectors.
INSPECTION END
H.S.
114
27
35
SEF052F
SEF648E
SEF054F
112
113
107
109
28
36
SEF055F

CODE 11 (CRANK ANGLE SENSOR) – CA16DE AND CA18DE ENGINES, PART 1

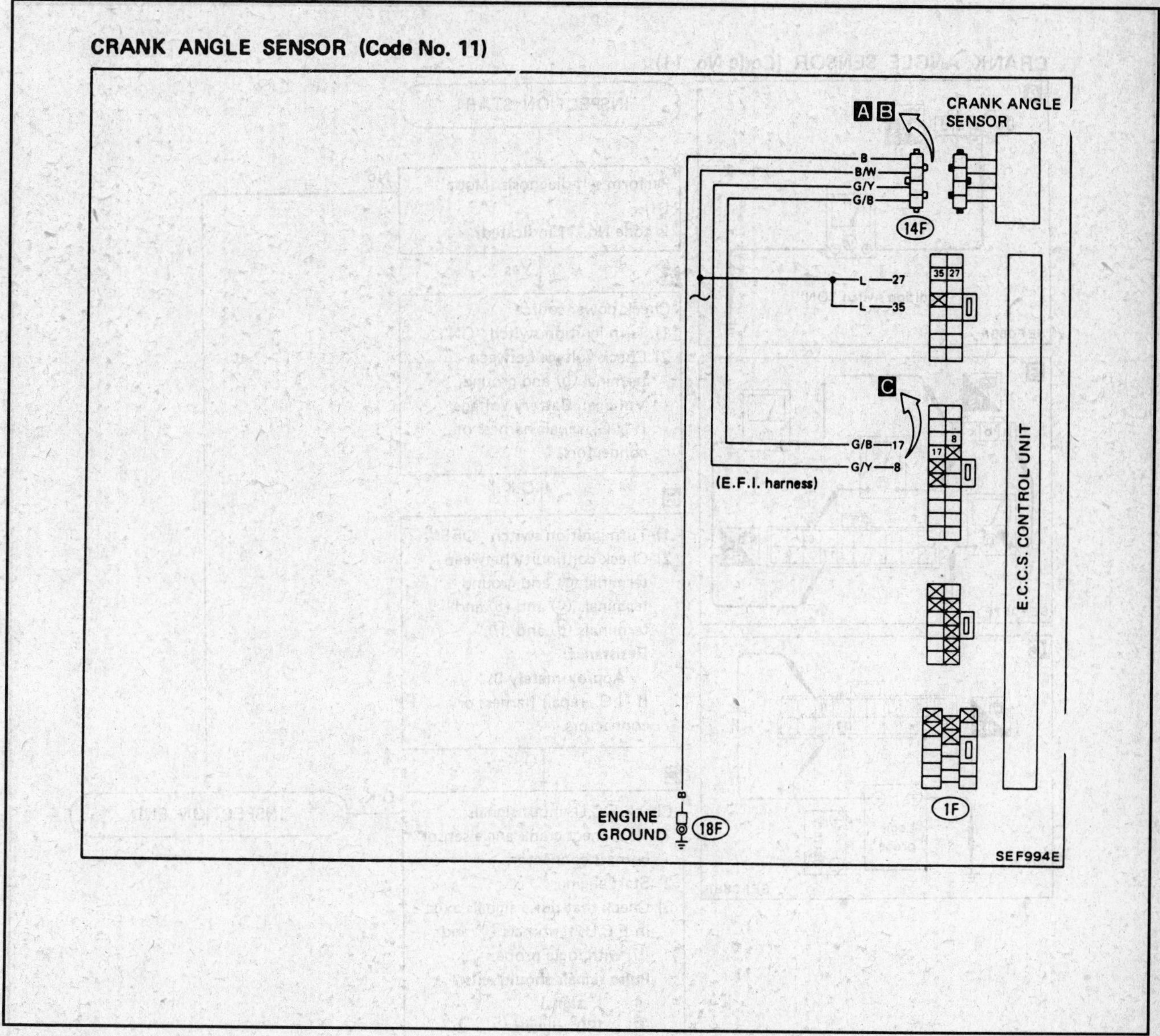
CRANK ANGLE SENSOR (Code No. 11)
A B
CRANK ANGLE SENSOR
B
B/W
G/Y
G/B
14F
L — 27
L — 35
35 27
C
G/B — 17
G/Y — 8
8
17
(E.F.I. harness)
E.C.C.S. CONTROL UNIT
B
ENGINE GROUND
18F
1F
SEF994E

CODE 11 (CRANK ANGLE SENSOR) – CA16DE AND CA18DE ENGINES, PART 2

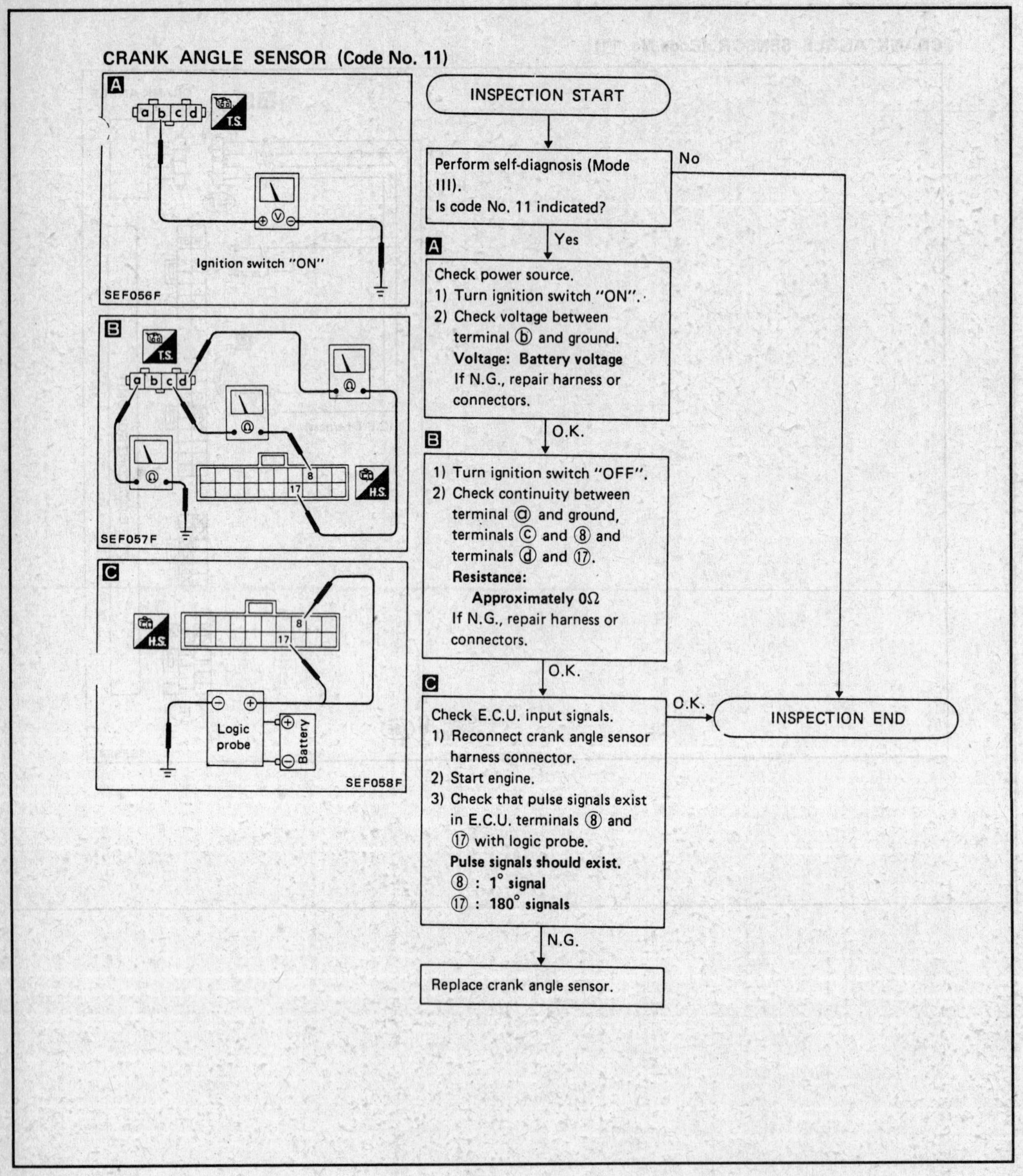
CRANK ANGLE SENSOR (Code No. 11)
A
a b c d
T.S.
Ignition switch "ON"
SEF056F
B
T.S.
a b c d
8
17
H.S.
SEF057F
C
H.S.
8
17
Logic probe
Battery
SEF058F
INSPECTION START
Perform self-diagnosis (Mode III).
Is code No. 11 indicated?
No
Yes
A
Check power source.
1) Turn ignition switch "ON".
2) Check voltage between terminal ⓑ and ground.
Voltage: Battery voltage
If N.G., repair harness or connectors.
O.K.
B
1) Turn ignition switch "OFF".
2) Check continuity between terminal ⓐ and ground, terminals ⓒ and ⑧ and terminals ⓓ and ⑰.
Resistance:
Approximately 0Ω
If N.G., repair harness or connectors.
O.K.
C
Check E.C.U. input signals.
1) Reconnect crank angle sensor harness connector.
2) Start engine.
3) Check that pulse signals exist in E.C.U. terminals ⑧ and ⑰ with logic probe.
Pulse signals should exist.
⑧ : 1° signal
⑰ : 180° signals
O.K.
INSPECTION END
N.G.
Replace crank angle sensor.

CODE 12 (AIR FLOW METER) – CA16DE AND CA18DE ENGINES

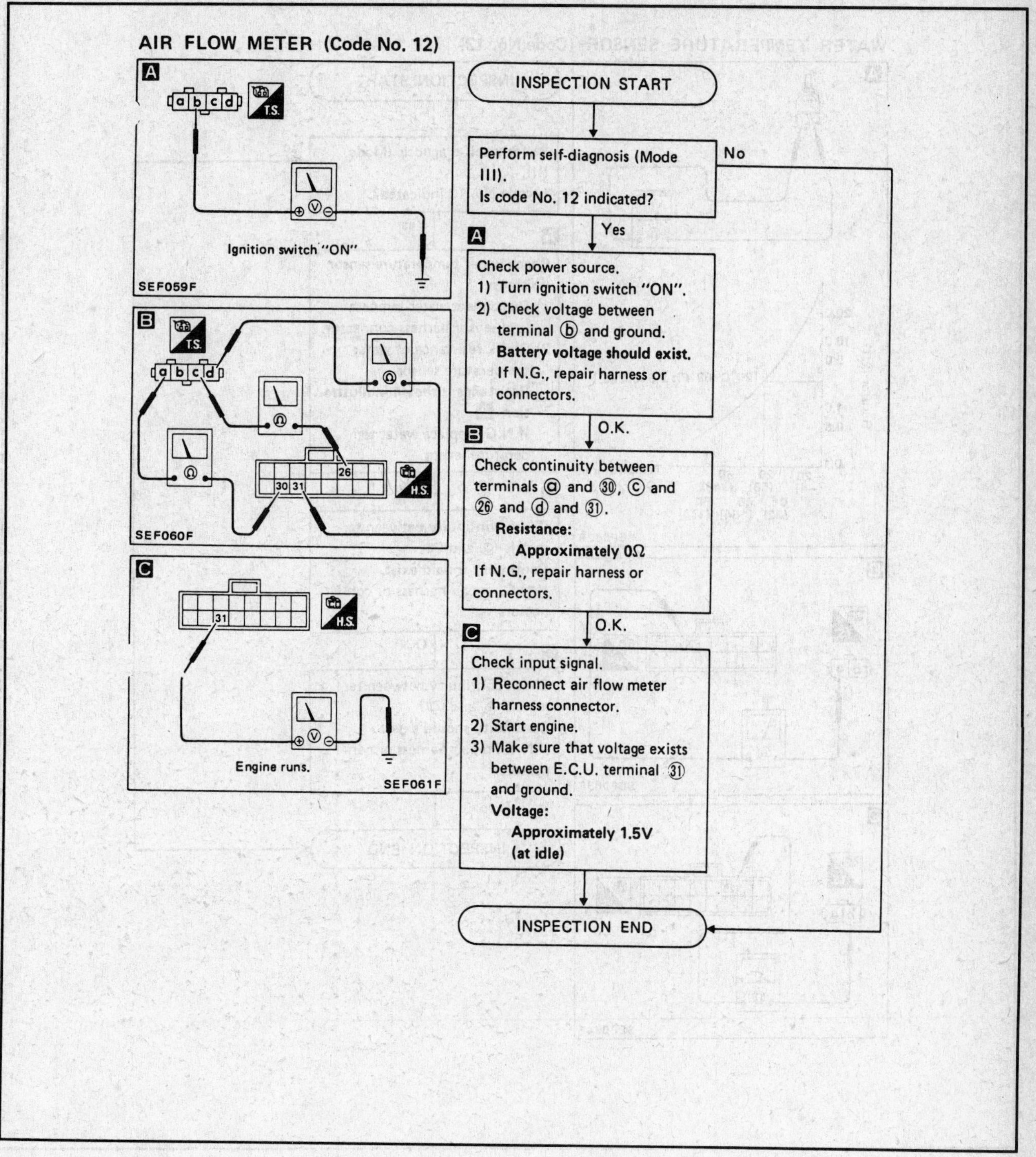
AIR FLOW METER (Code No. 12)
A
a b c d
T.S.
Ignition switch "ON"
SEF059F
B
T.S.
a b c d
26
30 31
H.S.
SEF060F
C
31
H.S.
Engine runs.
SEF061F
INSPECTION START
Perform self-diagnosis (Mode III).
Is code No. 12 indicated?
No
Yes
A
Check power source.
1) Turn ignition switch "ON".
2) Check voltage between terminal ⓑ and ground.
Battery voltage should exist.
If N.G., repair harness or connectors.
O.K.
B
Check continuity between terminals ⓐ and ㉚, ⓒ and ㉖ and ⓓ and ㉛.
Resistance:
Approximately 0Ω
If N.G., repair harness or connectors.
O.K.
C
Check input signal.
1) Reconnect air flow meter harness connector.
2) Start engine.
3) Make sure that voltage exists between E.C.U. terminal ㉛ and ground.
Voltage:
Approximately 1.5V
(at idle)
INSPECTION END

CODE 13 (WATER TEMPERATURE SENSOR) — CA16DE AND CA18DE ENGINES

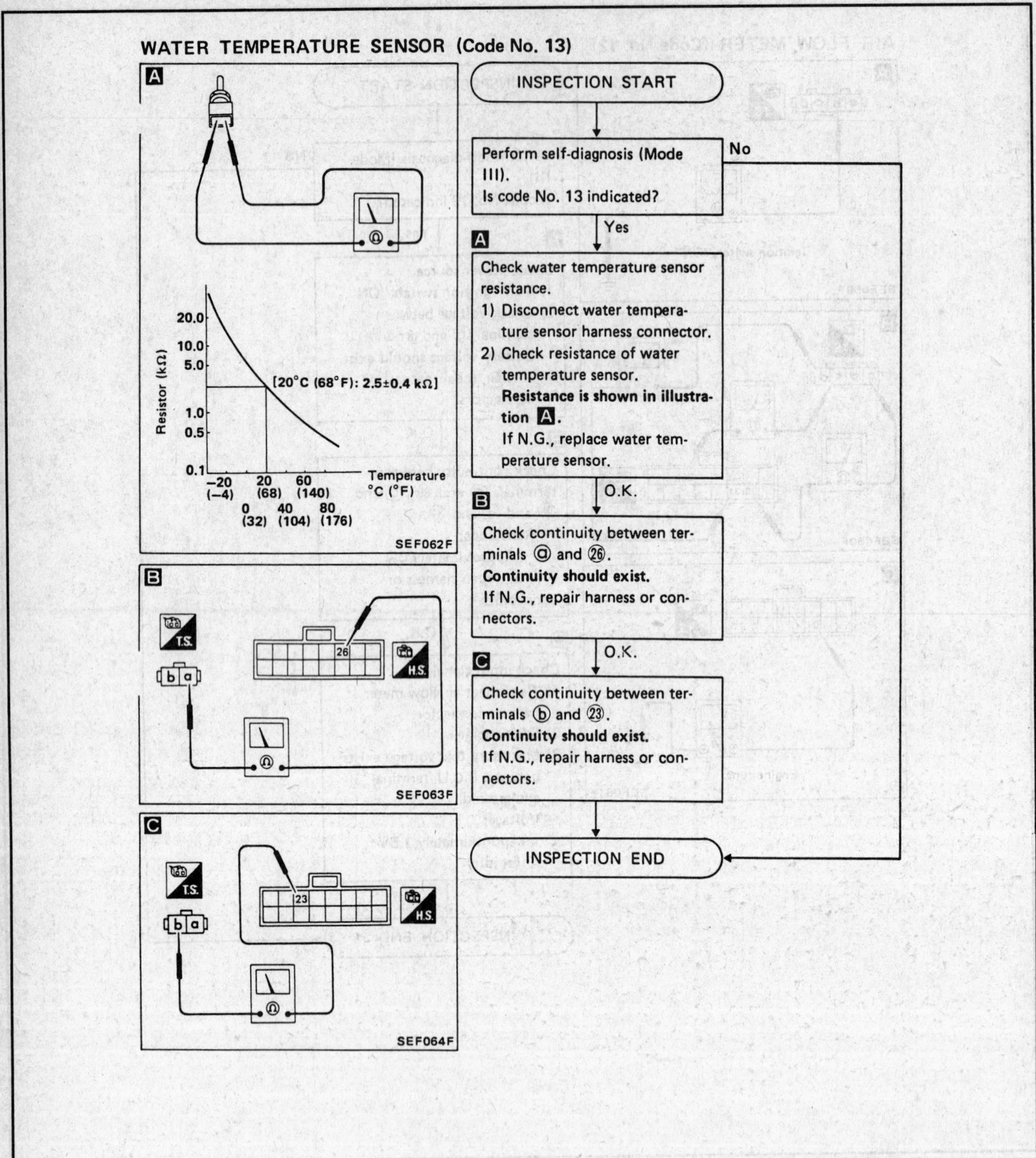
WATER TEMPERATURE SENSOR (Code No. 13)
A
20.0
10.0
5.0
Resistor (kΩ)
[20°C (68°F): 2.5±0.4 kΩ]
1.0
0.5
0.1
−20 (−4)
20 (68)
60 (140)
0 (32)
40 (104)
80 (176)
Temperature °C (°F)
SEF062F
B
T.S.
b a
26
H.S.
SEF063F
C
T.S.
b a
23
H.S.
SEF064F
INSPECTION START
Perform self-diagnosis (Mode III).
Is code No. 13 indicated?
No
Yes
A
Check water temperature sensor resistance.
1) Disconnect water temperature sensor harness connector.
2) Check resistance of water temperature sensor.
Resistance is shown in illustration A.
If N.G., replace water temperature sensor.
O.K.
B
Check continuity between terminals ⓐ and ㉖.
Continuity should exist.
If N.G., repair harness or connectors.
O.K.
C
Check continuity between terminals ⓑ and ㉓.
Continuity should exist.
If N.G., repair harness or connectors.
INSPECTION END

CODE 21 (IGNITION SIGNAL) – CA16DE AND CA18DE ENGINES, PART 1

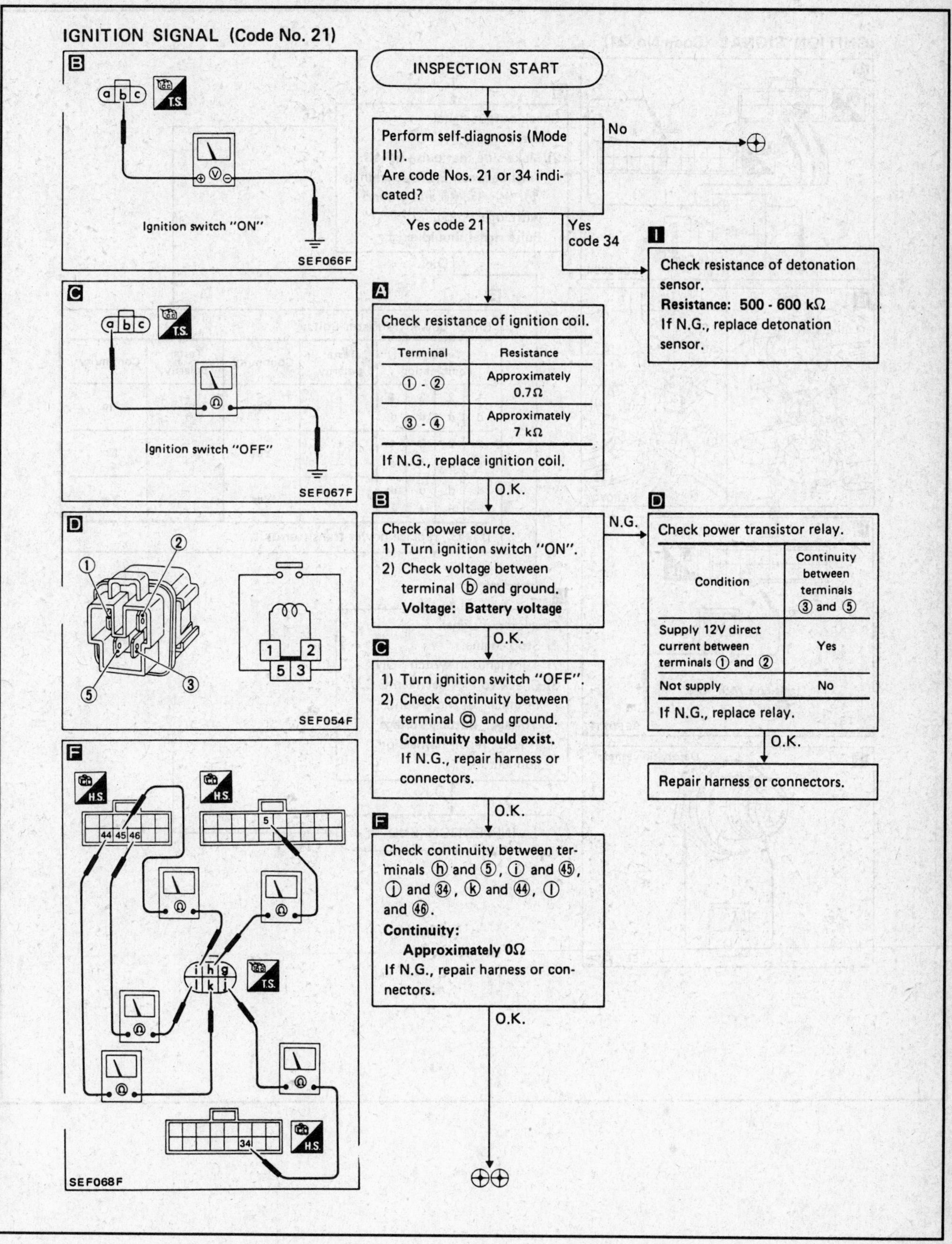
IGNITION SIGNAL (Code No. 21)
B
Ignition switch "ON"
SEF066F
C
Ignition switch "OFF"
SEF067F
D
SEF054F
F
SEF068F
INSPECTION START
Perform self-diagnosis (Mode III).
Are code Nos. 21 or 34 indicated?
No
Yes code 21
Yes code 34
I
Check resistance of detonation sensor.
Resistance: 500 - 600 kΩ
If N.G., replace detonation sensor.
A
Check resistance of ignition coil.
Terminal | Resistance
① - ② | Approximately 0.7Ω
③ - ④ | Approximately 7 kΩ
If N.G., replace ignition coil.
O.K.
B
Check power source.
1) Turn ignition switch "ON".
2) Check voltage between terminal ⓑ and ground.
Voltage: Battery voltage
N.G.
D
Check power transistor relay.
Condition | Continuity between terminals ③ and ⑤
Supply 12V direct current between terminals ① and ② | Yes
Not supply | No
If N.G., replace relay.
O.K.
Repair harness or connectors.
O.K.
C
1) Turn ignition switch "OFF".
2) Check continuity between terminal ⓐ and ground.
Continuity should exist.
If N.G., repair harness or connectors.
O.K.
F
Check continuity between terminals ⓗ and ⑤, ⓘ and ㊺, ⓙ and ㉞, ⓚ and ㊹, ⓛ and ㊻.
Continuity:
Approximately 0Ω
If N.G., repair harness or connectors.
O.K.

CODE 21 (IGNITION SIGNAL) – CA16DE AND CA18DE ENGINES, PART 2

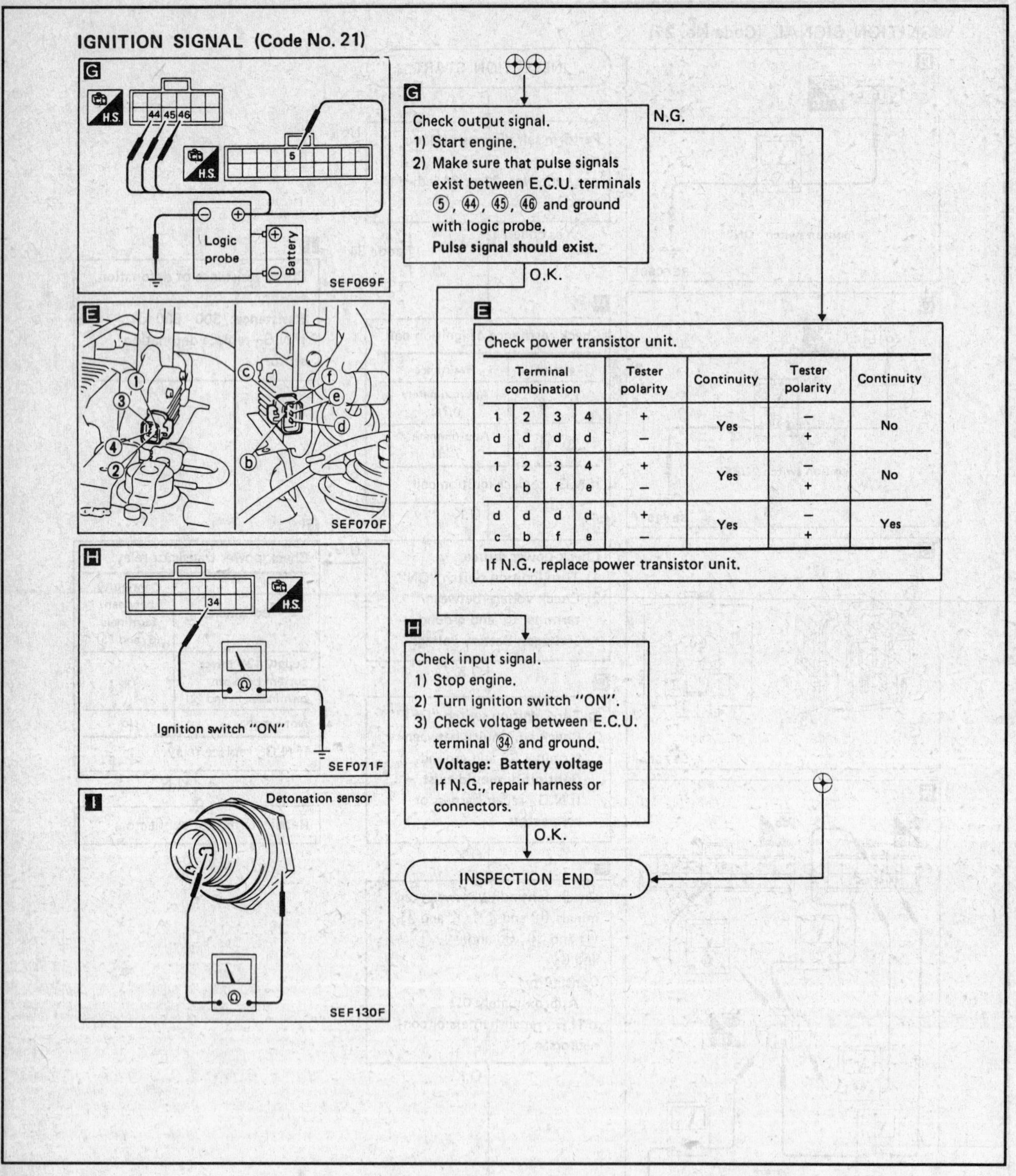
IGNITION SIGNAL (Code No. 21)
G
H.S.
44 45 46
5
H.S.
Logic probe
Battery
SEF069F
E
SEF070F
H
34
H.S.
Ignition switch "ON"
SEF071F
I
Detonation sensor
SEF130F
G
Check output signal.
1) Start engine.
2) Make sure that pulse signals exist between E.C.U. terminals ⑤, ㊹, ㊺, ㊻ and ground with logic probe.
Pulse signal should exist.
N.G.
O.K.
E
Check power transistor unit.

Terminal combination				Tester polarity	Continuity	Tester polarity	Continuity
1 d	2 d	3 d	4 d	+ –	Yes	– +	No
1 c	2 b	3 f	4 e	+ –	Yes	– +	No
d c	d b	d f	d e	+ –	Yes	– +	Yes

If N.G., replace power transistor unit.
H
Check input signal.
1) Stop engine.
2) Turn ignition switch "ON".
3) Check voltage between E.C.U. terminal ㉞ and ground.
Voltage: Battery voltage
If N.G., repair harness or connectors.
O.K.
INSPECTION END

ON/OFF DIAGNOSIS (THROTTLE VALVE SWITCH) – CA16DE AND CA18DE ENGINES

THROTTLE VALVE SWITCH (Switch ON/OFF diagnosis)

A
Throttle switch
ⓐ Idle switch
ⓑ ⊕
ⓒ Full switch
SEF077F

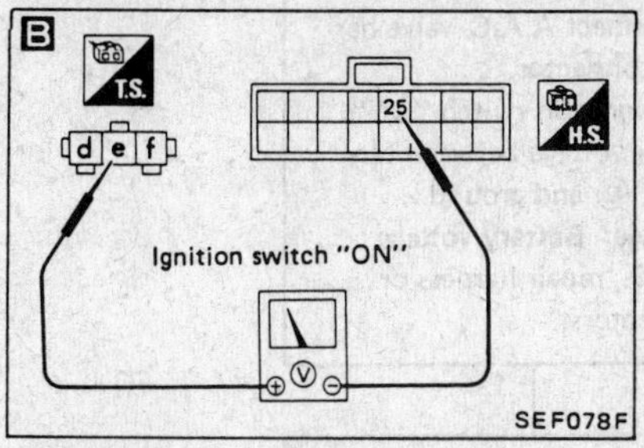

B
T.S.
H.S.
d e f
25
Ignition switch "ON"
SEF078F

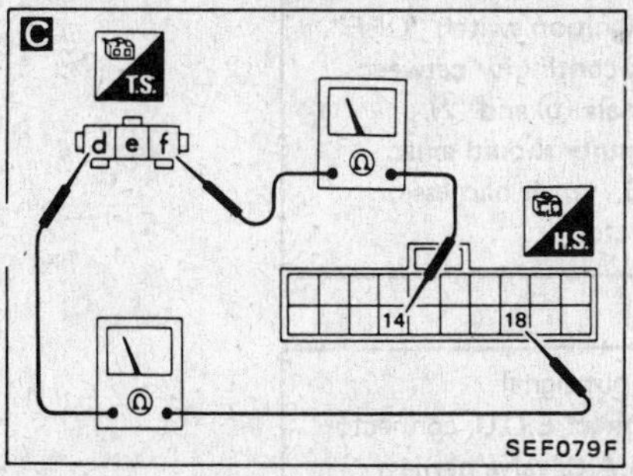

C
T.S.
H.S.
d e f
14
18
SEF079F

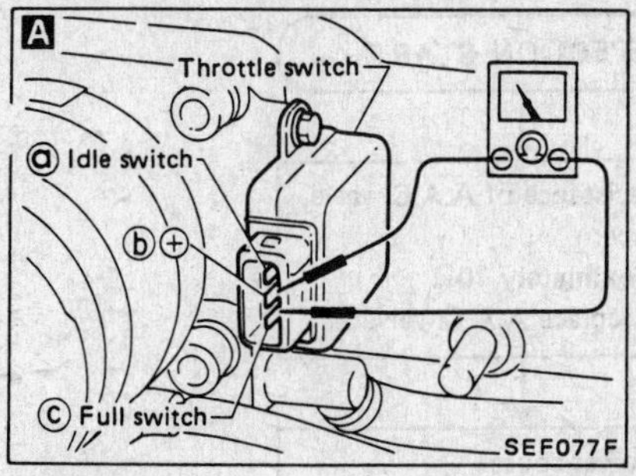

INSPECTION START

A

Check throttle valve switch (idle switch and full switch).

Accelerator pedal position	Continuity
Released	ⓐ - ⓑ
Depressed	ⓑ - ⓒ

If N.G., replace throttle valve switch.

O.K.

B

Check power source.
1) Turn ignition switch "ON".
2) Check voltage between terminals ⓔ and ㉕.
Voltage: 9 - 10V
If N.G., repair harness or connectors.

O.K.

C

1) Turn ignition switch "OFF".
2) Check continuity between terminals ⓓ and ⑱, ⓕ and ⑭.
Continuity should exist.
If N.G., repair harness or connectors.

INSPECTION END

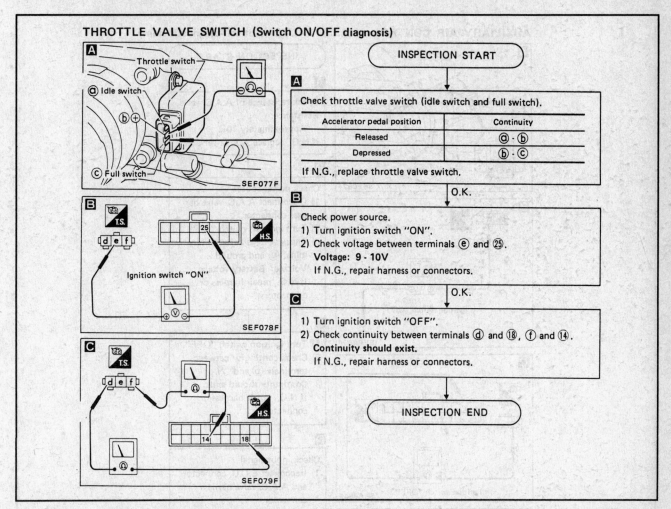

ON/OFF DIAGNOSIS (VEHICLE SPEED SENSOR) – CA16DE AND CA18DE ENGINES

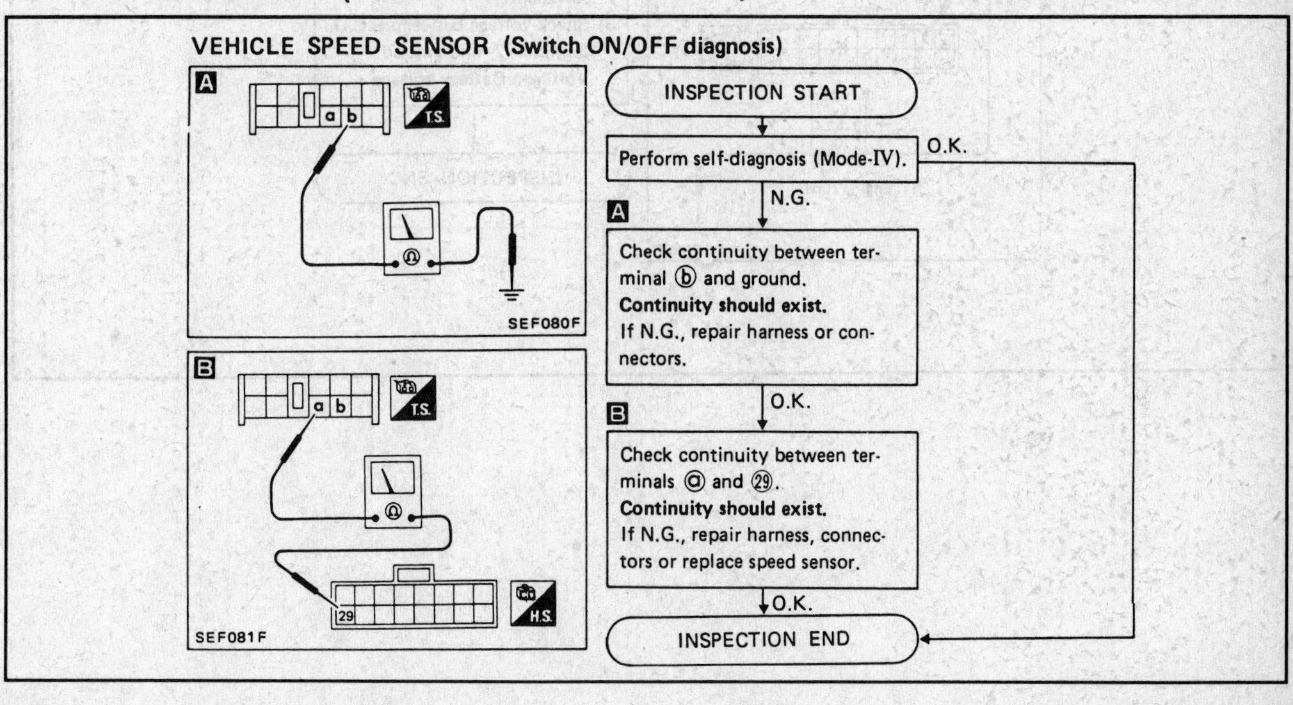
VEHICLE SPEED SENSOR (Switch ON/OFF diagnosis)
A
a b
T.S.
SEF080F
B
a b
T.S.
29
H.S.
SEF081F
INSPECTION START
Perform self-diagnosis (Mode-IV).
O.K.
N.G.
A
Check continuity between terminal ⓑ and ground.
Continuity should exist.
If N.G., repair harness or connectors.
O.K.
B
Check continuity between terminals ⓐ and ㉙.
Continuity should exist.
If N.G., repair harness, connectors or replace speed sensor.
O.K.
INSPECTION END

AUXILIARY AIR CONTROL VALVE DIAGNOSIS — CA16DE AND CA18DE ENGINES

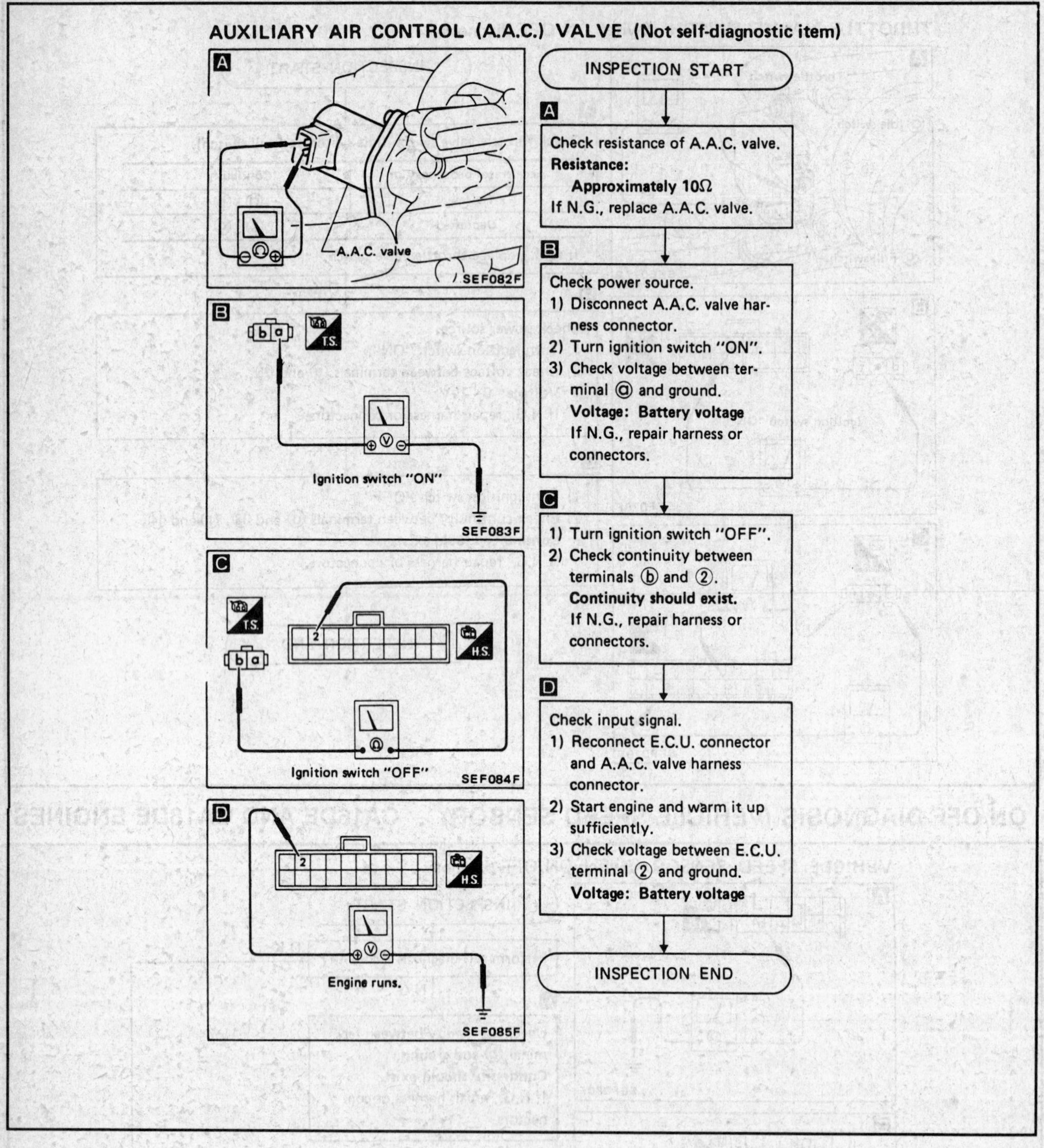
AUXILIARY AIR CONTROL (A.A.C.) VALVE (Not self-diagnostic item)
A
A.A.C. valve
SEF082F
B
T.S.
Ignition switch "ON"
SEF083F
C
T.S.
H.S.
Ignition switch "OFF"
SEF084F
D
H.S.
Engine runs.
SEF085F
INSPECTION START
A
Check resistance of A.A.C. valve.
Resistance:
Approximately 10Ω
If N.G., replace A.A.C. valve.
B
Check power source.
1) Disconnect A.A.C. valve harness connector.
2) Turn ignition switch "ON".
3) Check voltage between terminal ⓐ and ground.
Voltage: Battery voltage
If N.G., repair harness or connectors.
C
1) Turn ignition switch "OFF".
2) Check continuity between terminals ⓑ and ②.
Continuity should exist.
If N.G., repair harness or connectors.
D
Check input signal.
1) Reconnect E.C.U. connector and A.A.C. valve harness connector.
2) Start engine and warm it up sufficiently.
3) Check voltage between E.C.U. terminal ② and ground.
Voltage: Battery voltage
INSPECTION END

IAA CONTROL DIAGNOSIS – CA16DE AND CA18DE ENGINES

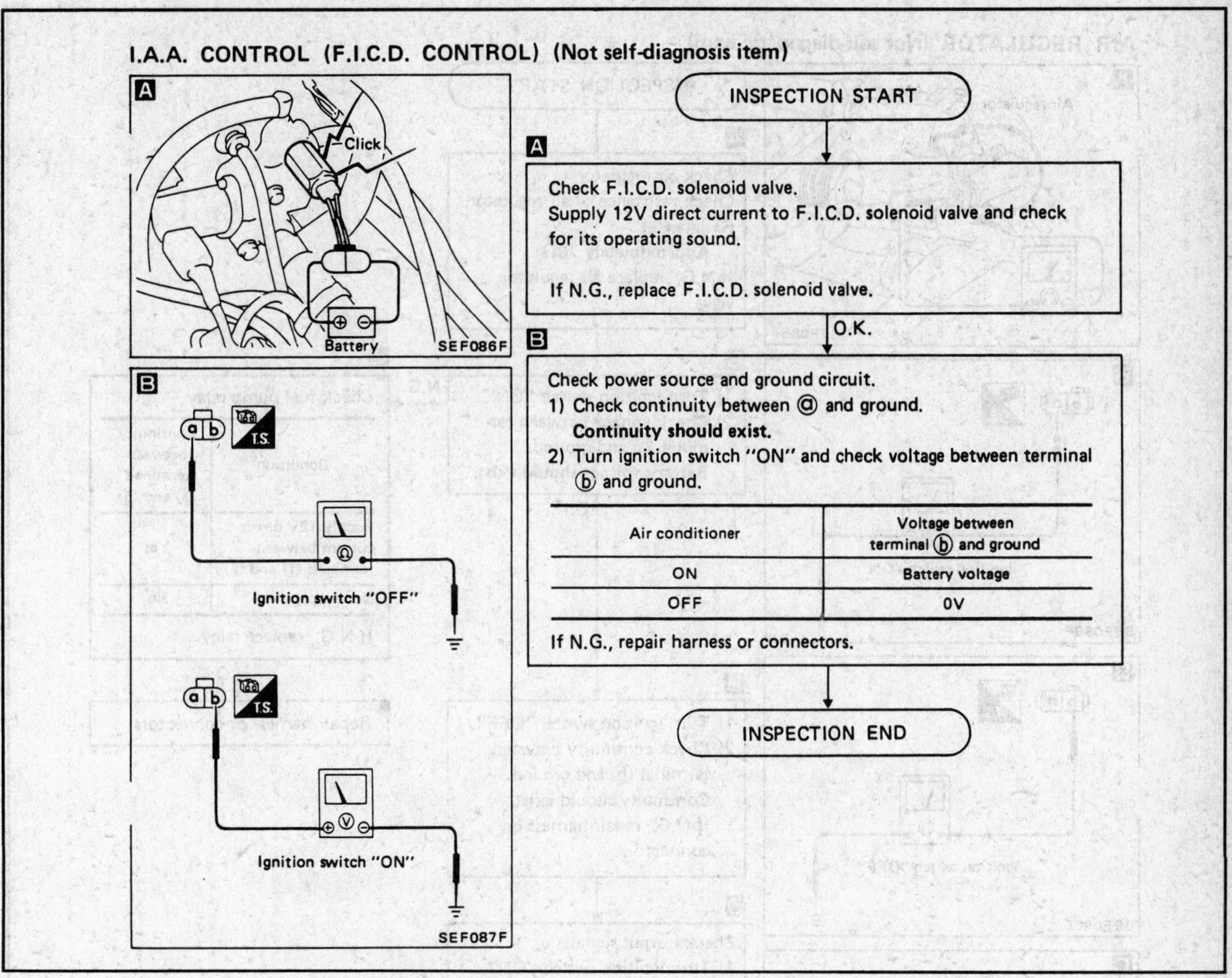
I.A.A. CONTROL (F.I.C.D. CONTROL) (Not self-diagnosis item)
A
Click
Battery
SEF086F
B
T.S.
Ignition switch "OFF"
Ignition switch "ON"
SEF087F
INSPECTION START
A
Check F.I.C.D. solenoid valve.
Supply 12V direct current to F.I.C.D. solenoid valve and check for its operating sound.
If N.G., replace F.I.C.D. solenoid valve.
O.K.
B
Check power source and ground circuit.
1) Check continuity between ⓐ and ground.
Continuity should exist.
2) Turn ignition switch "ON" and check voltage between terminal ⓑ and ground.
Air conditioner | Voltage between terminal ⓑ and ground
ON | Battery voltage
OFF | 0V
If N.G., repair harness or connectors.
INSPECTION END

AIR REGULATOR DIAGNOSIS – CA16DE AND CA18DE ENGINES

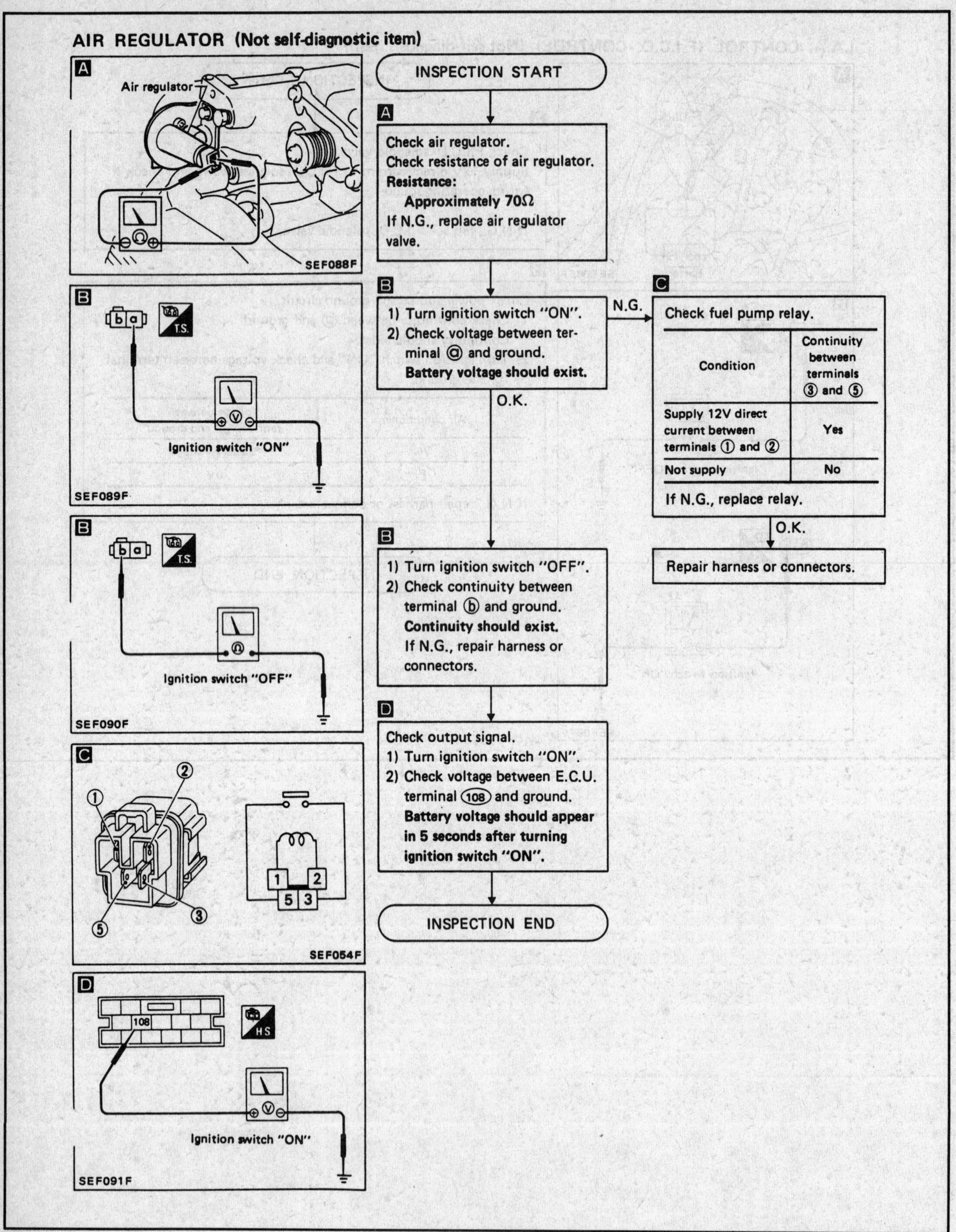
AIR REGULATOR (Not self-diagnostic item)
A
Air regulator
SEF088F
B
b a
T.S.
Ignition switch "ON"
SEF089F
B
b a
T.S.
Ignition switch "OFF"
SEF090F
C
①
②
③
⑤
1 2
5 3
SEF054F
D
108
H.S
Ignition switch "ON"
SEF091F
INSPECTION START
A
Check air regulator.
Check resistance of air regulator.
Resistance:
Approximately 70Ω
If N.G., replace air regulator valve.
B
1) Turn ignition switch "ON".
2) Check voltage between terminal ⓐ and ground.
Battery voltage should exist.
N.G.
C
Check fuel pump relay.
Condition
Continuity between terminals ③ and ⑤
Supply 12V direct current between terminals ① and ②
Yes
Not supply
No
If N.G., replace relay.
O.K.
Repair harness or connectors.
O.K.
B
1) Turn ignition switch "OFF".
2) Check continuity between terminal ⓑ and ground.
Continuity should exist.
If N.G., repair harness or connectors.
D
Check output signal.
1) Turn ignition switch "ON".
2) Check voltage between E.C.U. terminal (108) and ground.
Battery voltage should appear in 5 seconds after turning ignition switch "ON".
INSPECTION END

FUEL INJECTOR DIAGNOSIS – CA16DE AND CA18DE ENGINES

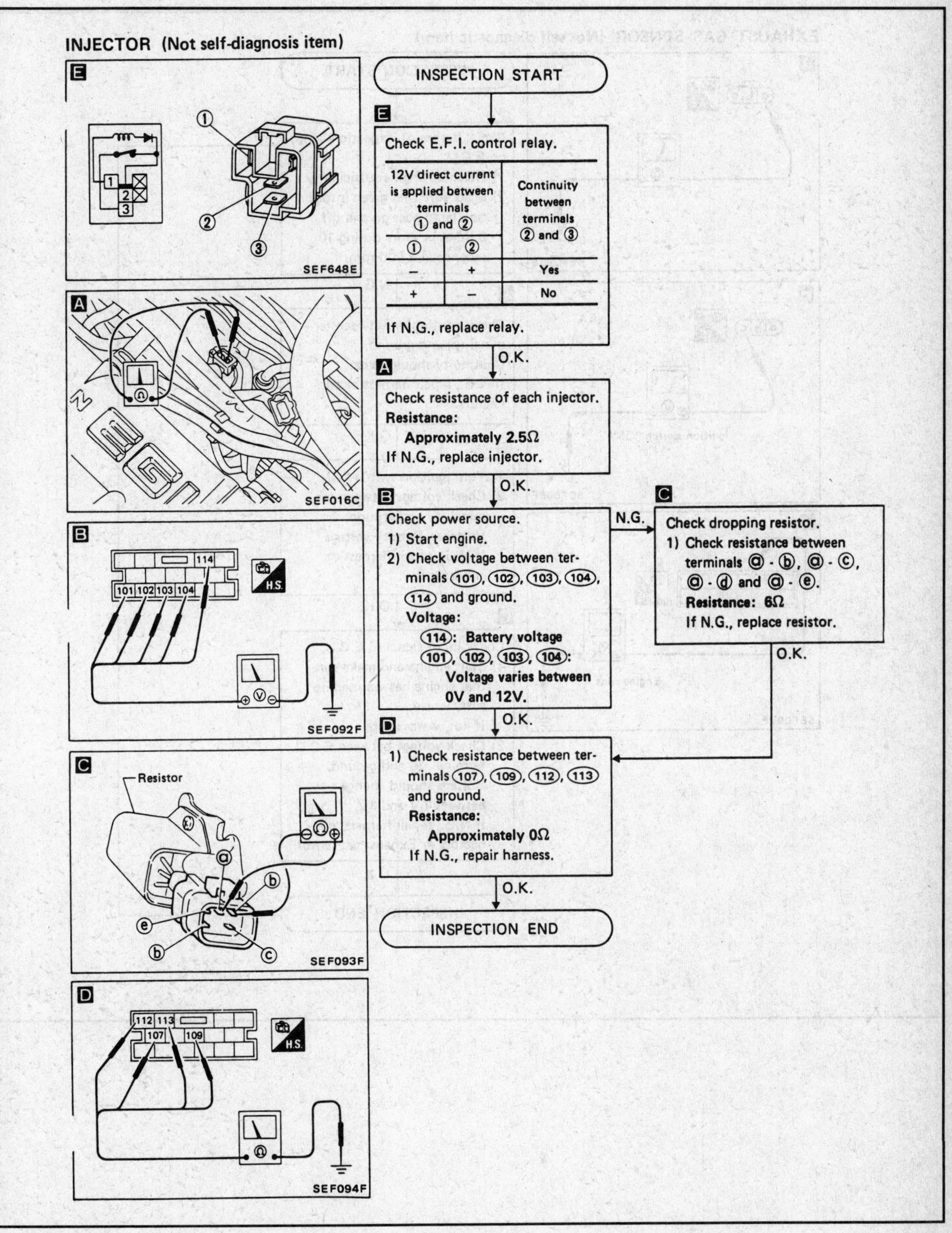
INJECTOR (Not self-diagnosis item)
E
SEF648E
A
SEF016C
B
101 102 103 104 114
H.S.
SEF092F
C
Resistor
SEF093F
D
112 113 107 109
H.S.
SEF094F
INSPECTION START
E
Check E.F.I. control relay.
12V direct current is applied between terminals ① and ②
Continuity between terminals ② and ③
① ②
– + Yes
+ – No
If N.G., replace relay.
O.K.
A
Check resistance of each injector.
Resistance:
Approximately 2.5Ω
If N.G., replace injector.
O.K.
B
Check power source.
1) Start engine.
2) Check voltage between terminals (101), (102), (103), (104), (114) and ground.
Voltage:
(114): Battery voltage
(101), (102), (103), (104): Voltage varies between 0V and 12V.
N.G.
C
Check dropping resistor.
1) Check resistance between terminals ⓐ - ⓑ, ⓐ - ⓒ, ⓐ - ⓓ and ⓐ - ⓔ.
Resistance: 6Ω
If N.G., replace resistor.
O.K.
O.K.
D
1) Check resistance between terminals (107), (109), (112), (113) and ground.
Resistance:
Approximately 0Ω
If N.G., repair harness.
O.K.
INSPECTION END

OXYGEN SENSOR DIAGNOSIS — CA16DE AND CA18DE ENGINES

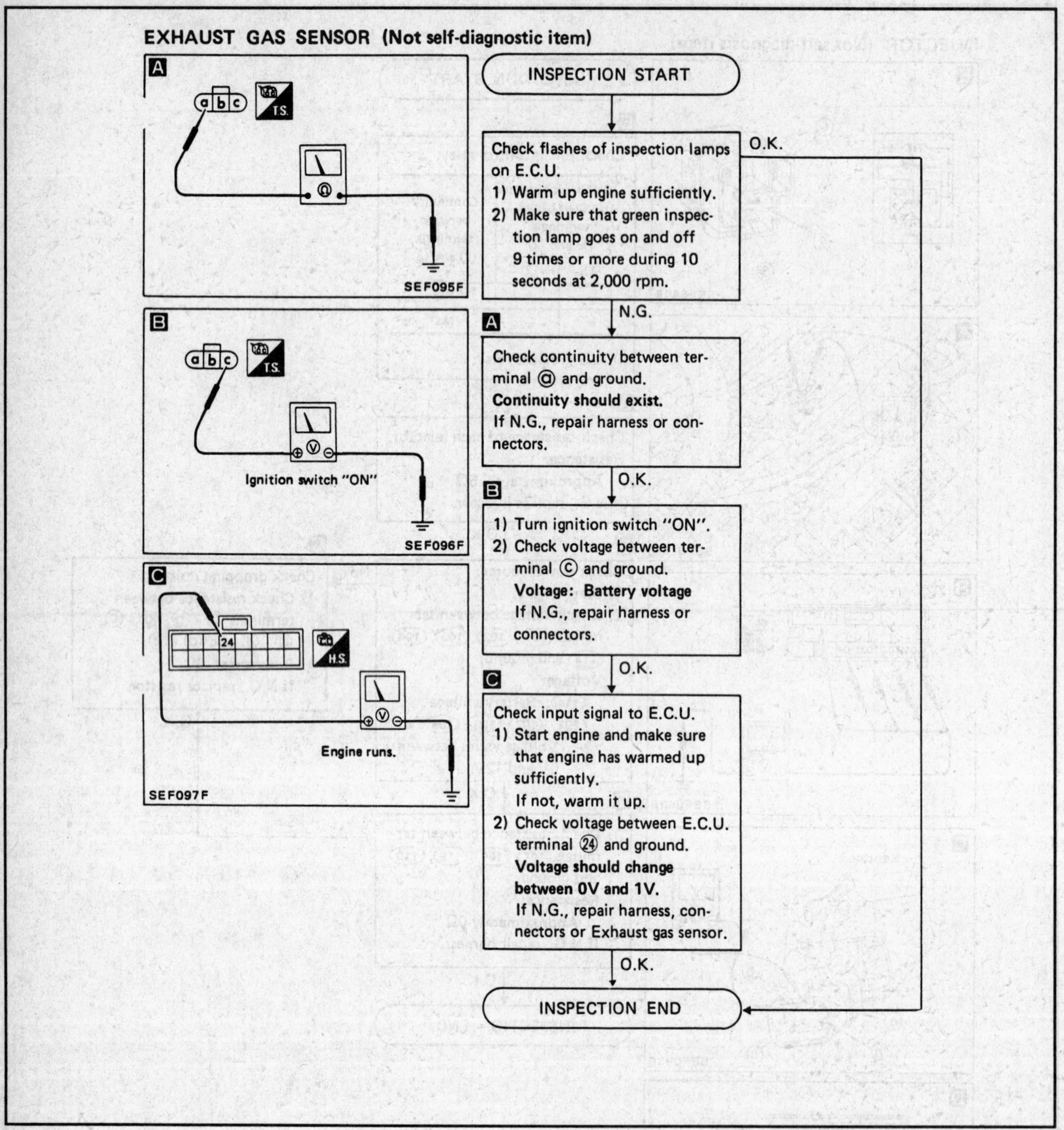

EXHAUST GAS SENSOR (Not self-diagnostic item)
A
a b c
T.S.
SEF095F
B
a b c
T.S.
Ignition switch "ON"
SEF096F
C
24
H.S.
Engine runs.
SEF097F
INSPECTION START
Check flashes of inspection lamps on E.C.U.
1) Warm up engine sufficiently.
2) Make sure that green inspection lamp goes on and off 9 times or more during 10 seconds at 2,000 rpm.
O.K.
N.G.
A
Check continuity between terminal ⓐ and ground.
Continuity should exist.
If N.G., repair harness or connectors.
O.K.
B
1) Turn ignition switch "ON".
2) Check voltage between terminal ⓒ and ground.
Voltage: Battery voltage
If N.G., repair harness or connectors.
O.K.
C
Check input signal to E.C.U.
1) Start engine and make sure that engine has warmed up sufficiently.
If not, warm it up.
2) Check voltage between E.C.U. terminal ㉔ and ground.
Voltage should change between 0V and 1V.
If N.G., repair harness, connectors or Exhaust gas sensor.
O.K.
INSPECTION END

AIR INJECTION VALVE DIAGNOSIS – CA16DE AND CA18DE ENGINES

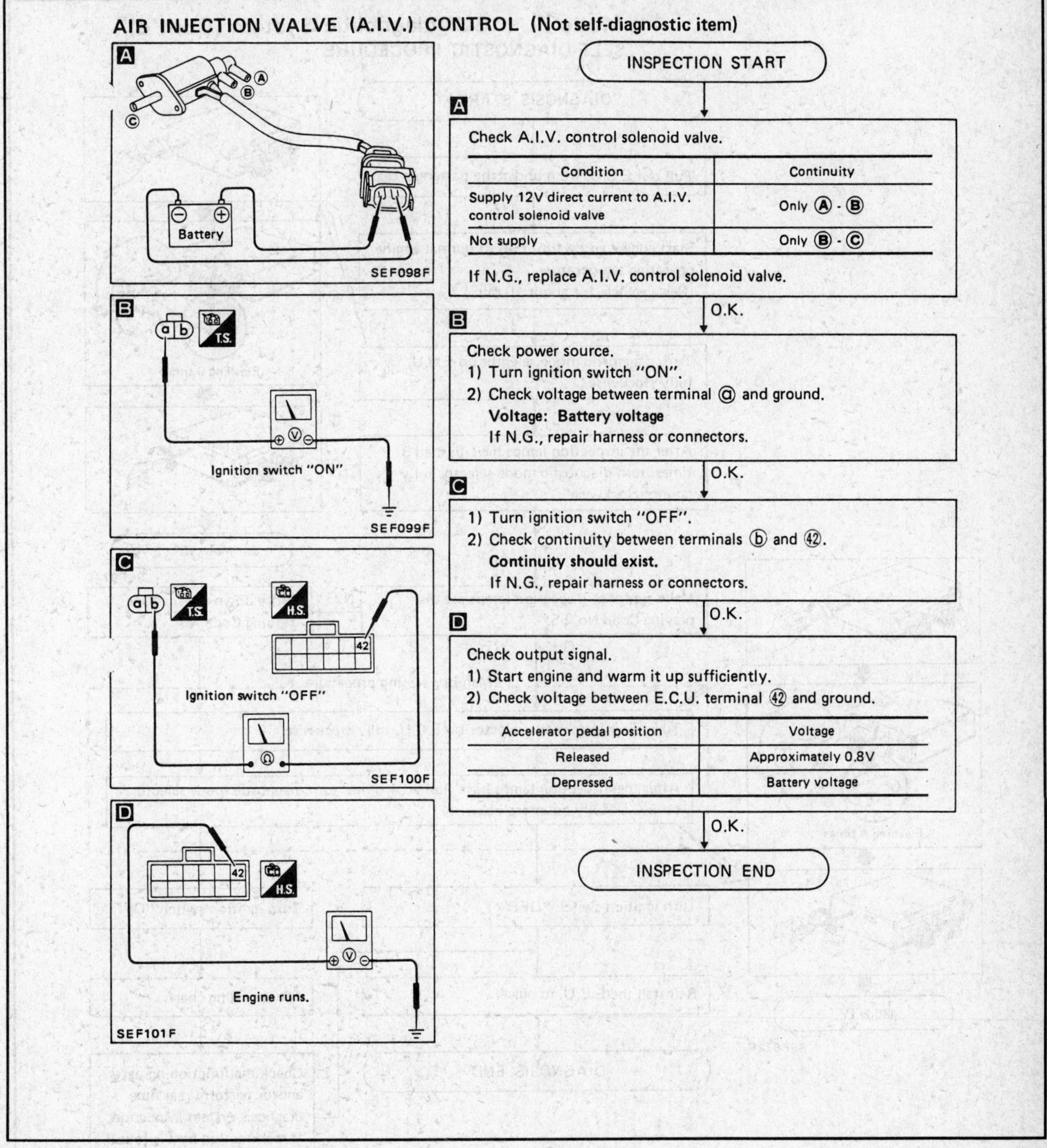
AIR INJECTION VALVE (A.I.V.) CONTROL (Not self-diagnostic item)
A
Ⓐ
Ⓑ
Ⓒ
Battery
SEF098F
B
a b
T.S.
Ignition switch "ON"
SEF099F
C
a b
T.S.
H.S.
42
Ignition switch "OFF"
SEF100F
D
42
H.S.
Engine runs.
SEF101F
INSPECTION START
A
Check A.I.V. control solenoid valve.
Condition
Continuity
Supply 12V direct current to A.I.V. control solenoid valve
Only Ⓐ - Ⓑ
Not supply
Only Ⓑ - Ⓒ
If N.G., replace A.I.V. control solenoid valve.
O.K.
B
Check power source.
1) Turn ignition switch "ON".
2) Check voltage between terminal ⓐ and ground.
Voltage: Battery voltage
If N.G., repair harness or connectors.
O.K.
C
1) Turn ignition switch "OFF".
2) Check continuity between terminals ⓑ and ㊷.
Continuity should exist.
If N.G., repair harness or connectors.
O.K.
D
Check output signal.
1) Start engine and warm it up sufficiently.
2) Check voltage between E.C.U. terminal ㊷ and ground.
Accelerator pedal position
Voltage
Released
Approximately 0.8V
Depressed
Battery voltage
O.K.
INSPECTION END

MODE III, SELF-DIAGNOSTIC SYSTEM PROCEDURE – GA16i ENGINE

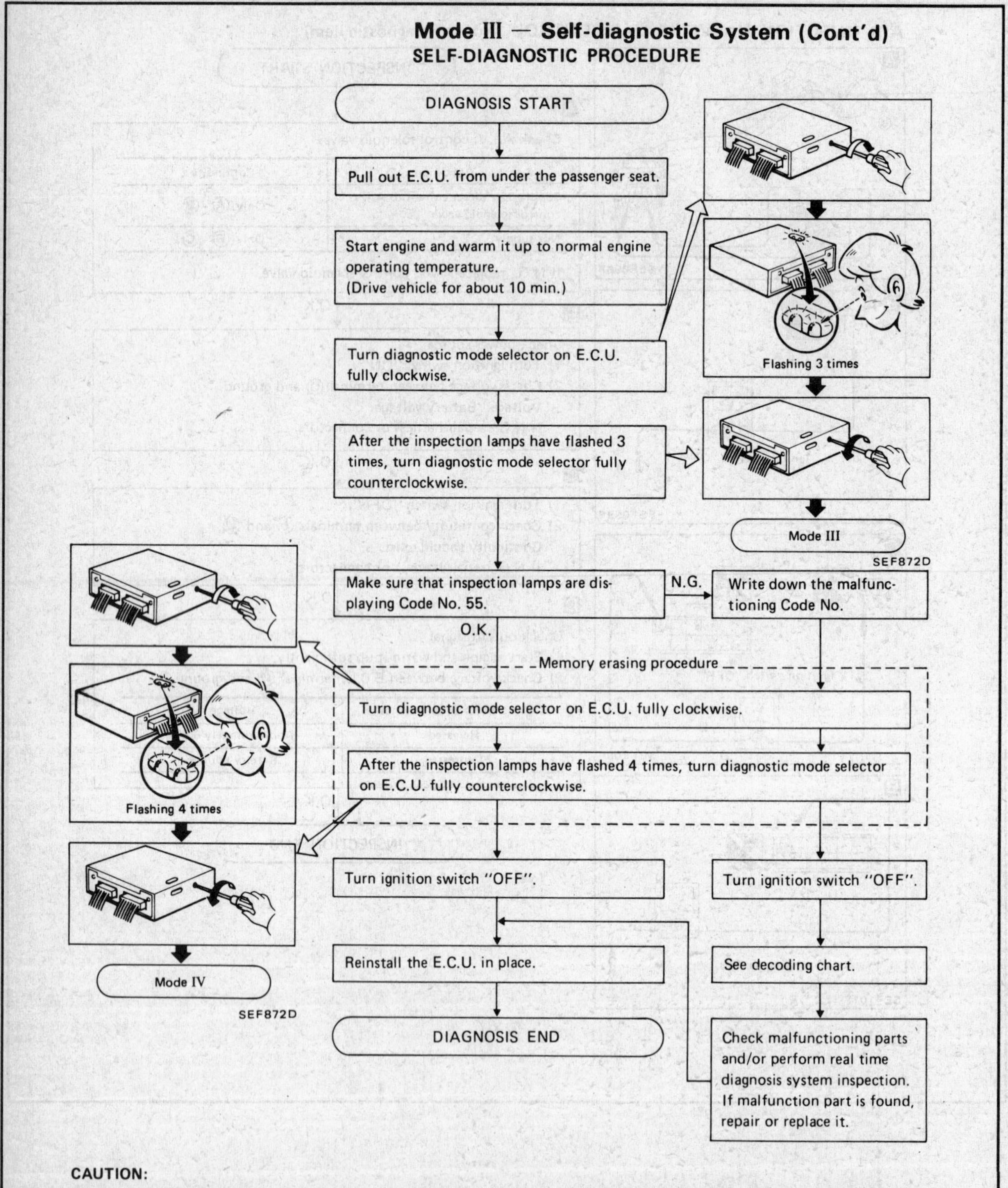

Mode III — Self-diagnostic System (Cont'd)
SELF-DIAGNOSTIC PROCEDURE
DIAGNOSIS START
Pull out E.C.U. from under the passenger seat.
Start engine and warm it up to normal engine operating temperature. (Drive vehicle for about 10 min.)
Turn diagnostic mode selector on E.C.U. fully clockwise.
Flashing 3 times
After the inspection lamps have flashed 3 times, turn diagnostic mode selector fully counterclockwise.
Mode III
SEF872D
Make sure that inspection lamps are displaying Code No. 55.
N.G.
Write down the malfunctioning Code No.
O.K.
Memory erasing procedure
Turn diagnostic mode selector on E.C.U. fully clockwise.
After the inspection lamps have flashed 4 times, turn diagnostic mode selector on E.C.U. fully counterclockwise.
Flashing 4 times
Turn ignition switch "OFF".
Turn ignition switch "OFF".
Reinstall the E.C.U. in place.
See decoding chart.
Mode IV
SEF872D
DIAGNOSIS END
Check malfunctioning parts and/or perform real time diagnosis system inspection. If malfunction part is found, repair or replace it.

CAUTION:
During displaying Code No. in self-diagnosis mode (Mode III), if the other diagnostic mode should be done, make sure to write down the malfunctioning Code No. before turning diagnostic mode selector on E.C.U. fully clockwise, or select the diagnostic mode after turning switch "OFF". Otherwise self-diagnosis information stored in E.C.U. memory until now would be lost.

TROUBLE CODE DECODING CHART – GA16i ENGINE, PART 1

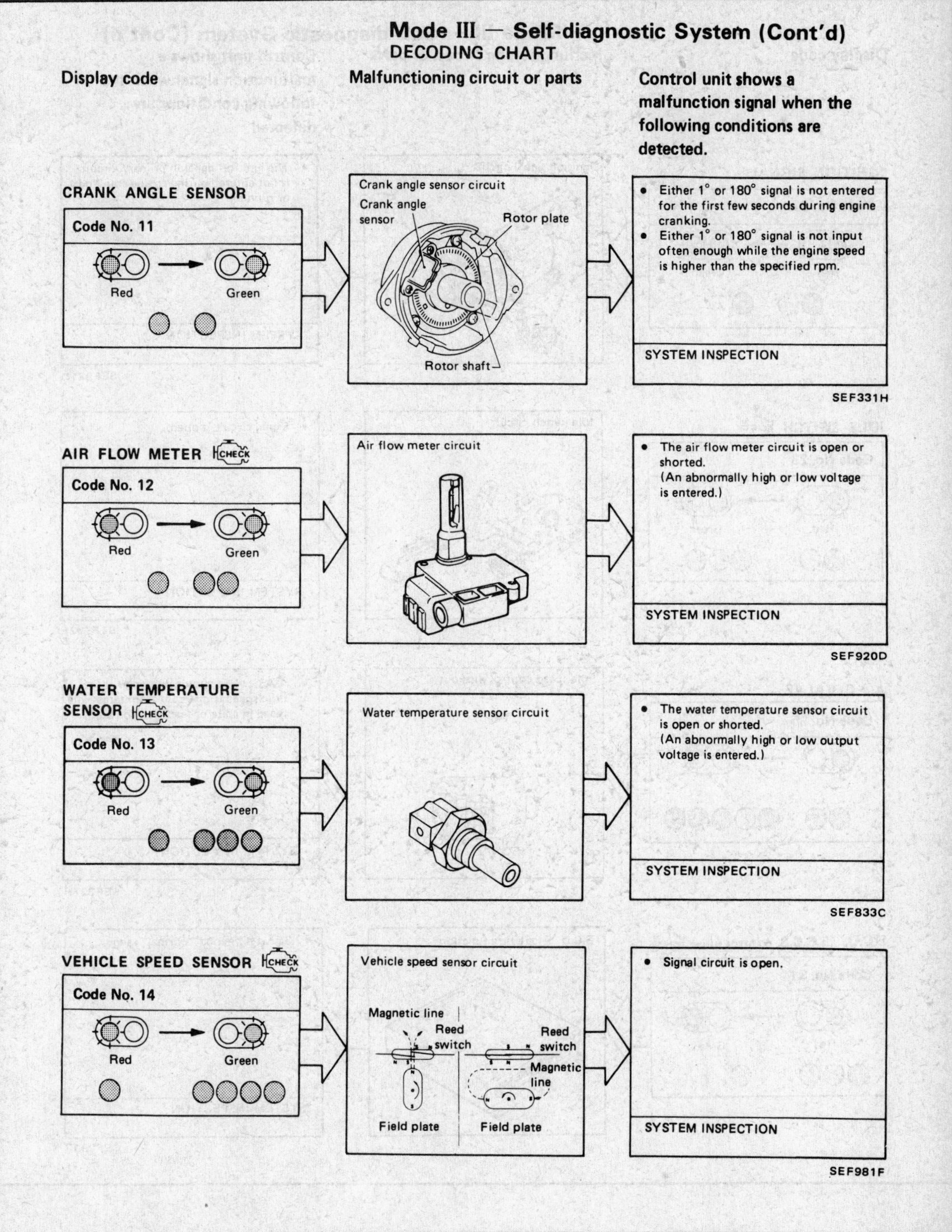
Mode III — Self-diagnostic System (Cont'd)
DECODING CHART
Display code
Malfunctioning circuit or parts
Control unit shows a malfunction signal when the following conditions are detected.
CRANK ANGLE SENSOR
Code No. 11
Red
Green
Crank angle sensor circuit
Crank angle sensor
Rotor plate
Rotor shaft
Either 1° or 180° signal is not entered for the first few seconds during engine cranking.
Either 1° or 180° signal is not input often enough while the engine speed is higher than the specified rpm.
SYSTEM INSPECTION
SEF331H
AIR FLOW METER CHECK
Code No. 12
Red
Green
Air flow meter circuit
The air flow meter circuit is open or shorted.
(An abnormally high or low voltage is entered.)
SYSTEM INSPECTION
SEF920D
WATER TEMPERATURE SENSOR CHECK
Code No. 13
Red
Green
Water temperature sensor circuit
The water temperature sensor circuit is open or shorted.
(An abnormally high or low output voltage is entered.)
SYSTEM INSPECTION
SEF833C
VEHICLE SPEED SENSOR CHECK
Code No. 14
Red
Green
Vehicle speed sensor circuit
Magnetic line
Reed switch
Reed switch
Magnetic line
Field plate
Field plate
Signal circuit is open.
SYSTEM INSPECTION
SEF981F

TROUBLE CODE DECODING CHART – GA16i ENGINE, PART 2

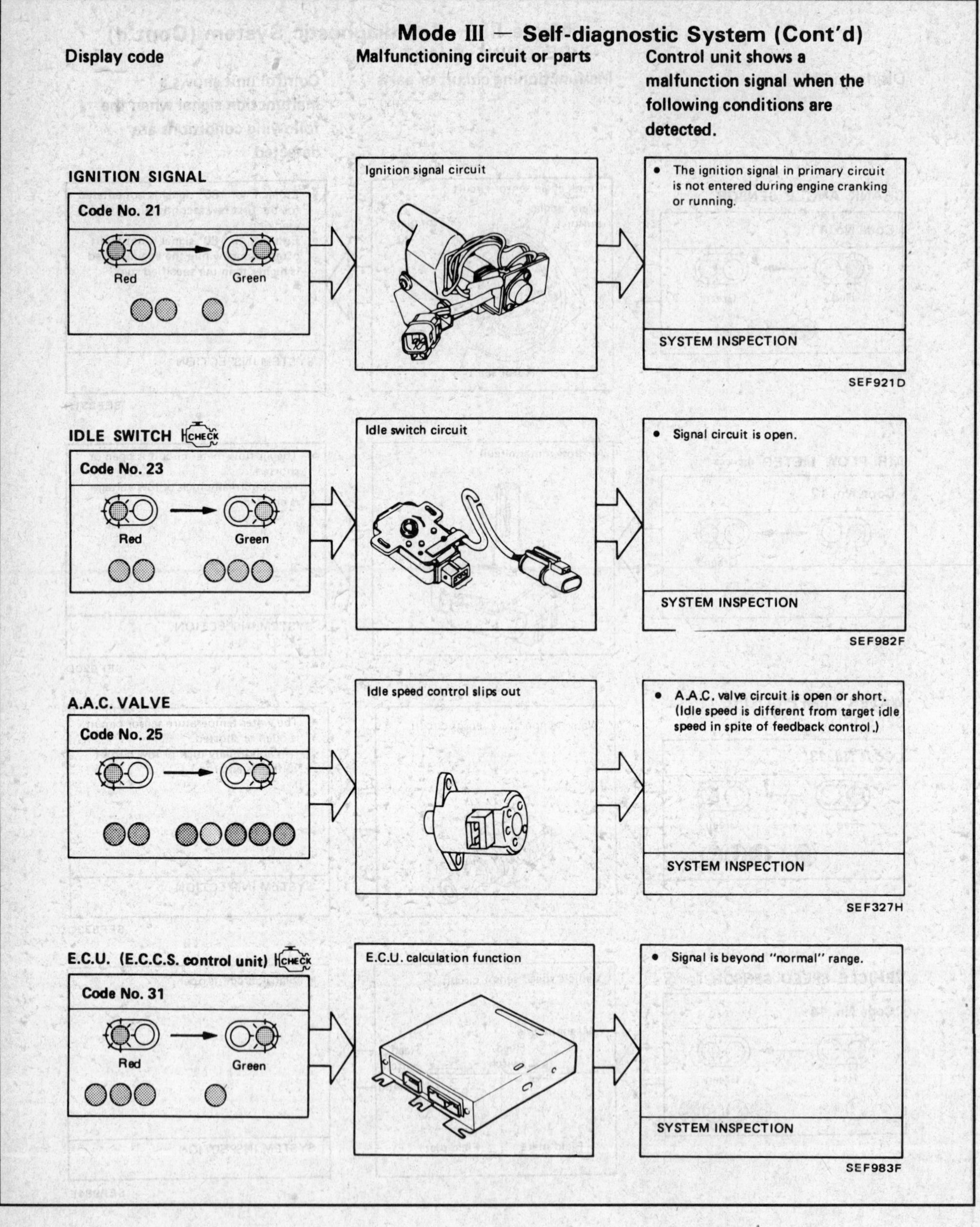
Mode III — Self-diagnostic System (Cont'd)
Display code
Malfunctioning circuit or parts
Control unit shows a malfunction signal when the following conditions are detected.
IGNITION SIGNAL
Code No. 21
Red
Green
Ignition signal circuit
• The ignition signal in primary circuit is not entered during engine cranking or running.
SYSTEM INSPECTION
SEF921D
IDLE SWITCH
CHECK
Code No. 23
Red
Green
Idle switch circuit
• Signal circuit is open.
SYSTEM INSPECTION
SEF982F
A.A.C. VALVE
Code No. 25
Idle speed control slips out
• A.A.C. valve circuit is open or short. (Idle speed is different from target idle speed in spite of feedback control.)
SYSTEM INSPECTION
SEF327H
E.C.U. (E.C.C.S. control unit)
CHECK
Code No. 31
Red
Green
E.C.U. calculation function
• Signal is beyond "normal" range.
SYSTEM INSPECTION
SEF983F

TROUBLE CODE DECODING CHART — GA16i ENGINE, PART 3

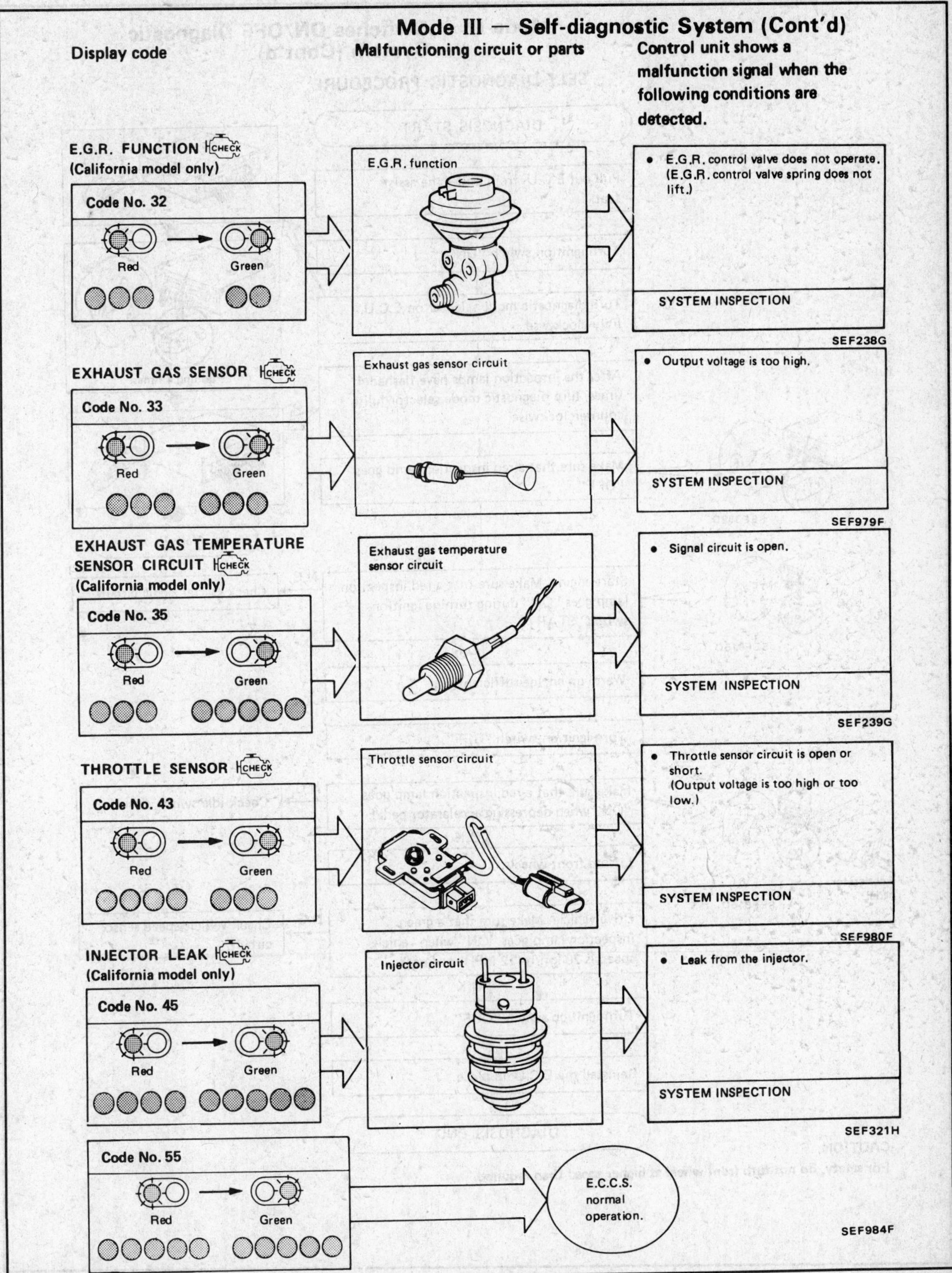
Mode III — Self-diagnostic System (Cont'd)
Display code
Malfunctioning circuit or parts
Control unit shows a malfunction signal when the following conditions are detected.
E.G.R. FUNCTION CHECK
(California model only)
Code No. 32
Red
Green
E.G.R. function
• E.G.R. control valve does not operate. (E.G.R. control valve spring does not lift.)
SYSTEM INSPECTION
SEF238G
EXHAUST GAS SENSOR CHECK
Code No. 33
Red
Green
Exhaust gas sensor circuit
• Output voltage is too high.
SYSTEM INSPECTION
SEF979F
EXHAUST GAS TEMPERATURE SENSOR CIRCUIT CHECK
(California model only)
Code No. 35
Red
Green
Exhaust gas temperature sensor circuit
• Signal circuit is open.
SYSTEM INSPECTION
SEF239G
THROTTLE SENSOR CHECK
Code No. 43
Red
Green
Throttle sensor circuit
• Throttle sensor circuit is open or short. (Output voltage is too high or too low.)
SYSTEM INSPECTION
SEF980F
INJECTOR LEAK CHECK
(California model only)
Code No. 45
Red
Green
Injector circuit
• Leak from the injector.
SYSTEM INSPECTION
SEF321H
Code No. 55
Red
Green
E.C.C.S. normal operation.
SEF984F

MODE IV, SWITCHES ON/OFF DIAGNOSTIC SYSTEM – GA16i ENGINE

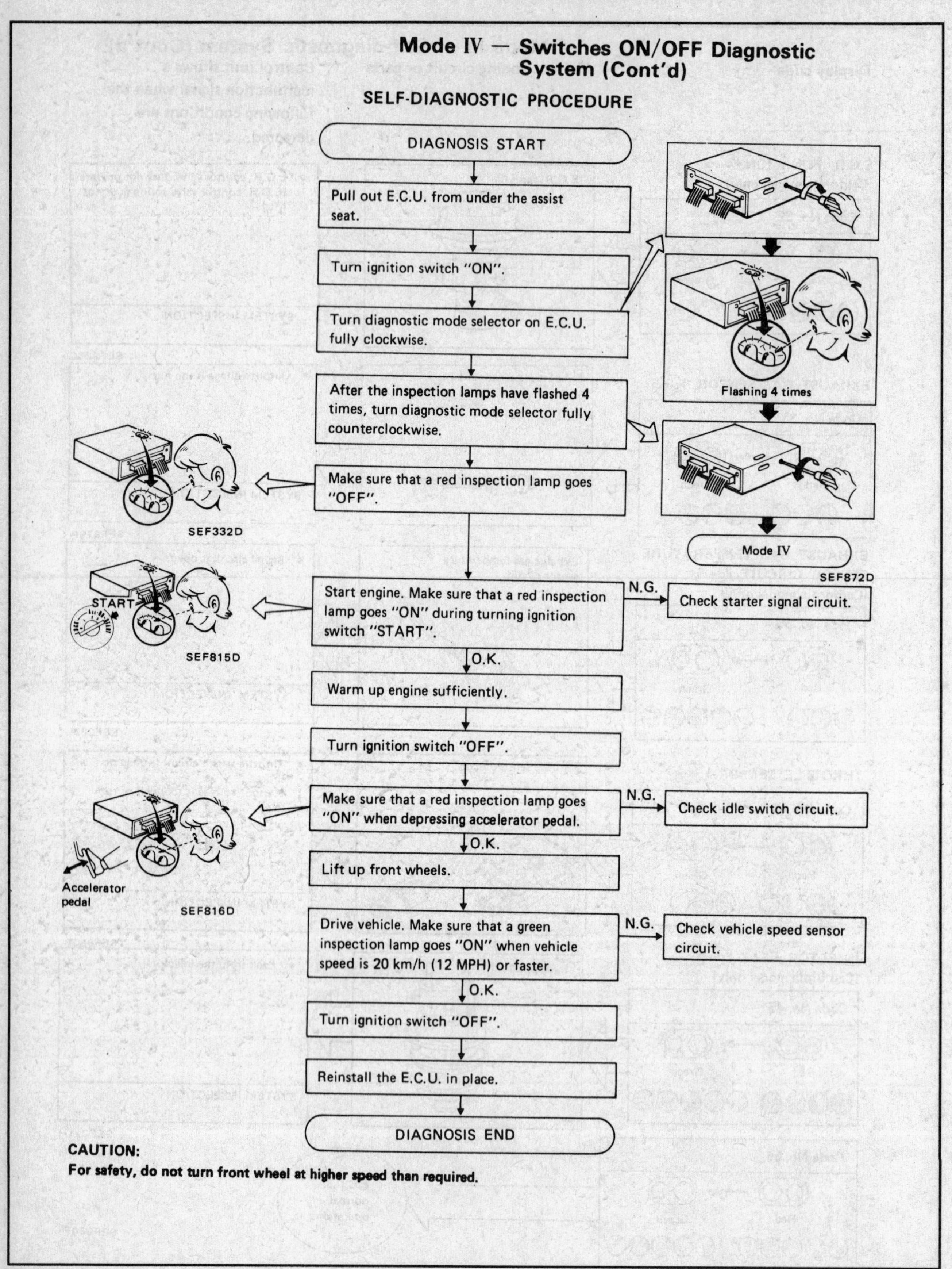

Mode IV — Switches ON/OFF Diagnostic System (Cont'd)
SELF-DIAGNOSTIC PROCEDURE
DIAGNOSIS START
Pull out E.C.U. from under the assist seat.
Turn ignition switch "ON".
Turn diagnostic mode selector on E.C.U. fully clockwise.
After the inspection lamps have flashed 4 times, turn diagnostic mode selector fully counterclockwise.
Flashing 4 times
Mode IV
SEF872D
Make sure that a red inspection lamp goes "OFF".
SEF332D
Start engine. Make sure that a red inspection lamp goes "ON" during turning ignition switch "START".
START
SEF815D
N.G.
Check starter signal circuit.
O.K.
Warm up engine sufficiently.
Turn ignition switch "OFF".
Make sure that a red inspection lamp goes "ON" when depressing accelerator pedal.
N.G.
Check idle switch circuit.
Accelerator pedal
SEF816D
O.K.
Lift up front wheels.
Drive vehicle. Make sure that a green inspection lamp goes "ON" when vehicle speed is 20 km/h (12 MPH) or faster.
N.G.
Check vehicle speed sensor circuit.
O.K.
Turn ignition switch "OFF".
Reinstall the E.C.U. in place.
DIAGNOSIS END

CAUTION:
For safety, do not turn front wheel at higher speed than required.

MODE V, REAL TIME DIAGNOSTIC SYSTEM – GA16i ENGINE

Mode V – Real Time Diagnostic System

In real time diagnosis, if any of the following items are judged to be faulty, a malfunction is indicated immediately.

- Crank angle sensor (180° signal & 1° signal)
- Ignition signal
- Air flow meter output signal

Consequently, this diagnosis is a very effective measure to diagnose whether the above systems cause the malfunction or not, during driving test. Compared with self-diagnosis, real time diagnosis is very sensitive, and can detect malfunctioning conditions in a moment. Further, items regarded to be malfunctions in this diagnosis are not stored in E.C.U. memory.

SELF-DIAGNOSTIC PROCEDURE

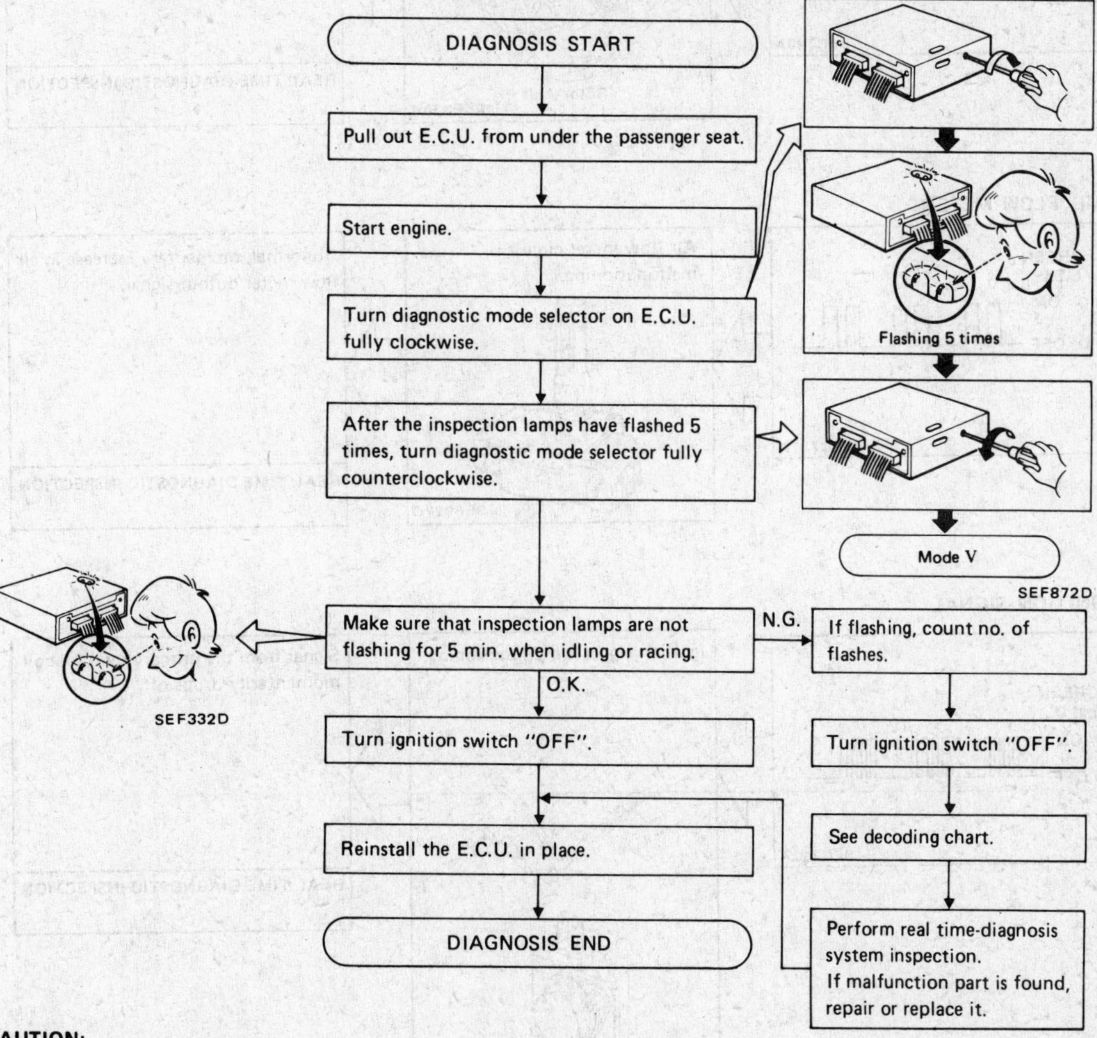
DIAGNOSIS START
Pull out E.C.U. from under the passenger seat.
Start engine.
Turn diagnostic mode selector on E.C.U. fully clockwise.
After the inspection lamps have flashed 5 times, turn diagnostic mode selector fully counterclockwise.
Flashing 5 times
Mode V
SEF872D
Make sure that inspection lamps are not flashing for 5 min. when idling or racing.
N.G.
O.K.
If flashing, count no. of flashes.
SEF332D
Turn ignition switch "OFF".
Turn ignition switch "OFF".
See decoding chart.
Reinstall the E.C.U. in place.
DIAGNOSIS END
Perform real time-diagnosis system inspection.
If malfunction part is found, repair or replace it.

CAUTION:
In real time diagnosis, pay attention to inspection lamp flashing. E.C.U. displays the malfunction code only once, and does not memorize the inspection.

MODE V TROUBLE CODE DECODING CHART — GA16i ENGINE

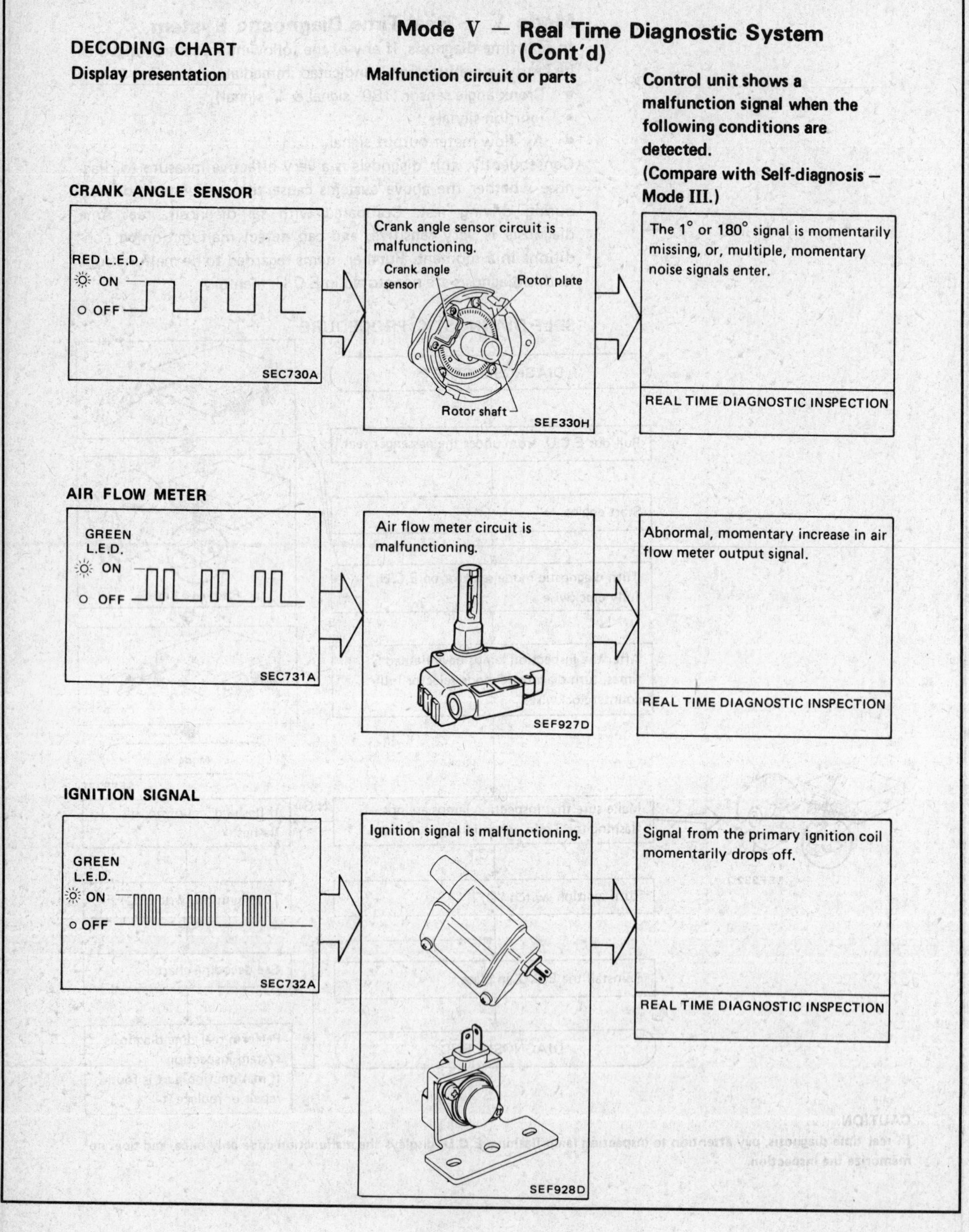
Mode V — Real Time Diagnostic System (Cont'd)
DECODING CHART
Display presentation
Malfunction circuit or parts
Control unit shows a malfunction signal when the following conditions are detected.
(Compare with Self-diagnosis — Mode III.)
CRANK ANGLE SENSOR
RED L.E.D.
ON
OFF
SEC730A
Crank angle sensor circuit is malfunctioning.
Crank angle sensor
Rotor plate
Rotor shaft
SEF330H
The 1° or 180° signal is momentarily missing, or, multiple, momentary noise signals enter.
REAL TIME DIAGNOSTIC INSPECTION
AIR FLOW METER
GREEN L.E.D.
ON
OFF
SEC731A
Air flow meter circuit is malfunctioning.
SEF927D
Abnormal, momentary increase in air flow meter output signal.
REAL TIME DIAGNOSTIC INSPECTION
IGNITION SIGNAL
GREEN L.E.D.
ON
OFF
SEC732A
Ignition signal is malfunctioning.
SEF928D
Signal from the primary ignition coil momentarily drops off.
REAL TIME DIAGNOSTIC INSPECTION

ECU POWER SOURCE AND GROUND CIRCUIT CHART — GA16i ENGINE

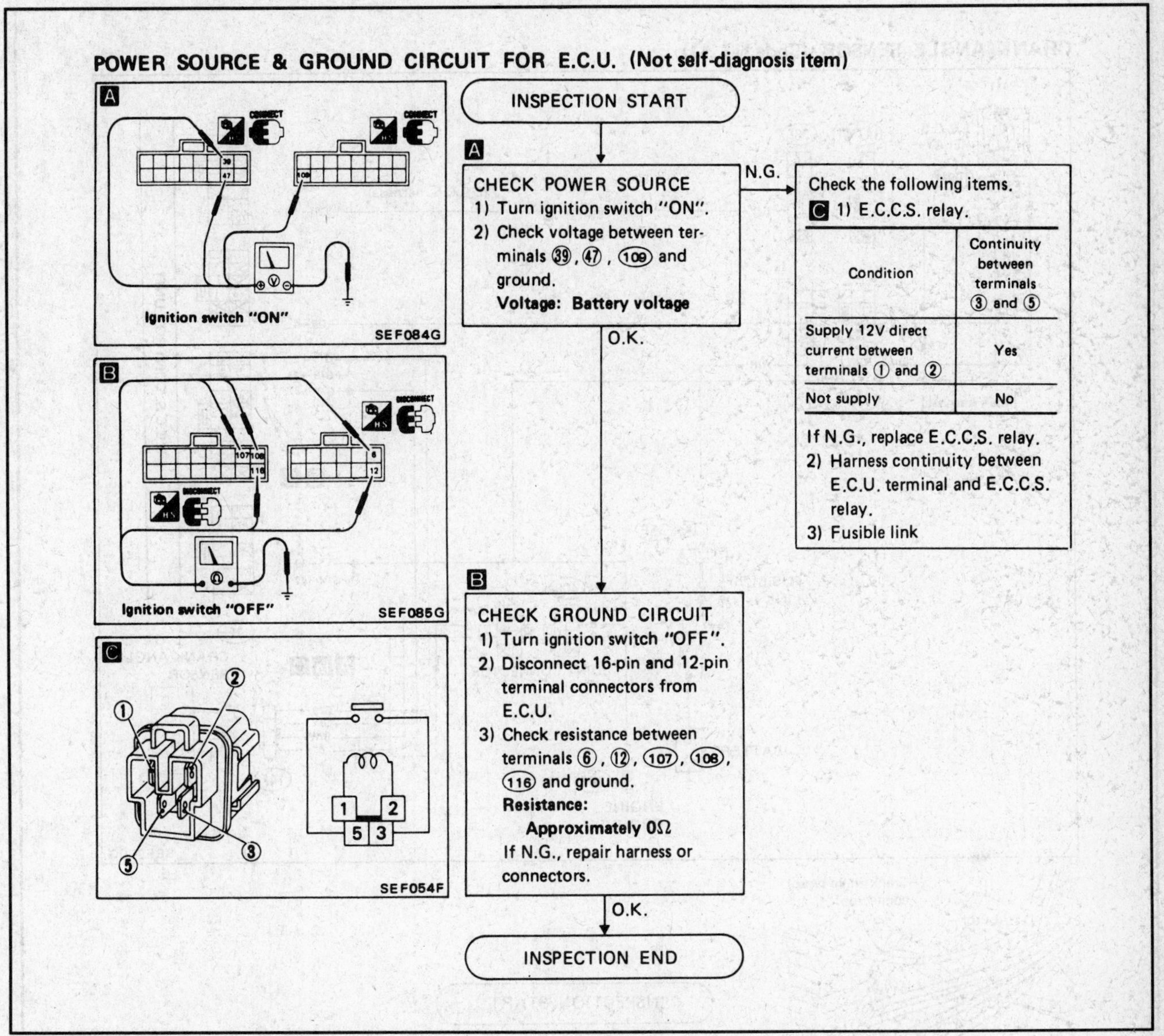
POWER SOURCE & GROUND CIRCUIT FOR E.C.U. (Not self-diagnosis item)
A
CONNECT
39
47
109
Ignition switch "ON"
SEF084G
B
DISCONNECT
107
108
116
6
12
Ignition switch "OFF"
SEF085G
C
① ② ③ ⑤
1 2 5 3
SEF054F
INSPECTION START
A
CHECK POWER SOURCE
1) Turn ignition switch "ON".
2) Check voltage between terminals (39), (47), (109) and ground.
Voltage: Battery voltage
N.G.
Check the following items.
C 1) E.C.C.S. relay.
Condition | Continuity between terminals ③ and ⑤
Supply 12V direct current between terminals ① and ② | Yes
Not supply | No
If N.G., replace E.C.C.S. relay.
2) Harness continuity between E.C.U. terminal and E.C.C.S. relay.
3) Fusible link
O.K.
B
CHECK GROUND CIRCUIT
1) Turn ignition switch "OFF".
2) Disconnect 16-pin and 12-pin terminal connectors from E.C.U.
3) Check resistance between terminals ⑥, ⑫, (107), (108), (116) and ground.
Resistance:
Approximately 0Ω
If N.G., repair harness or connectors.
O.K.
INSPECTION END

CODE 11 (CRANK ANGLE SENSOR) — GA16i ENGINE, PART 1

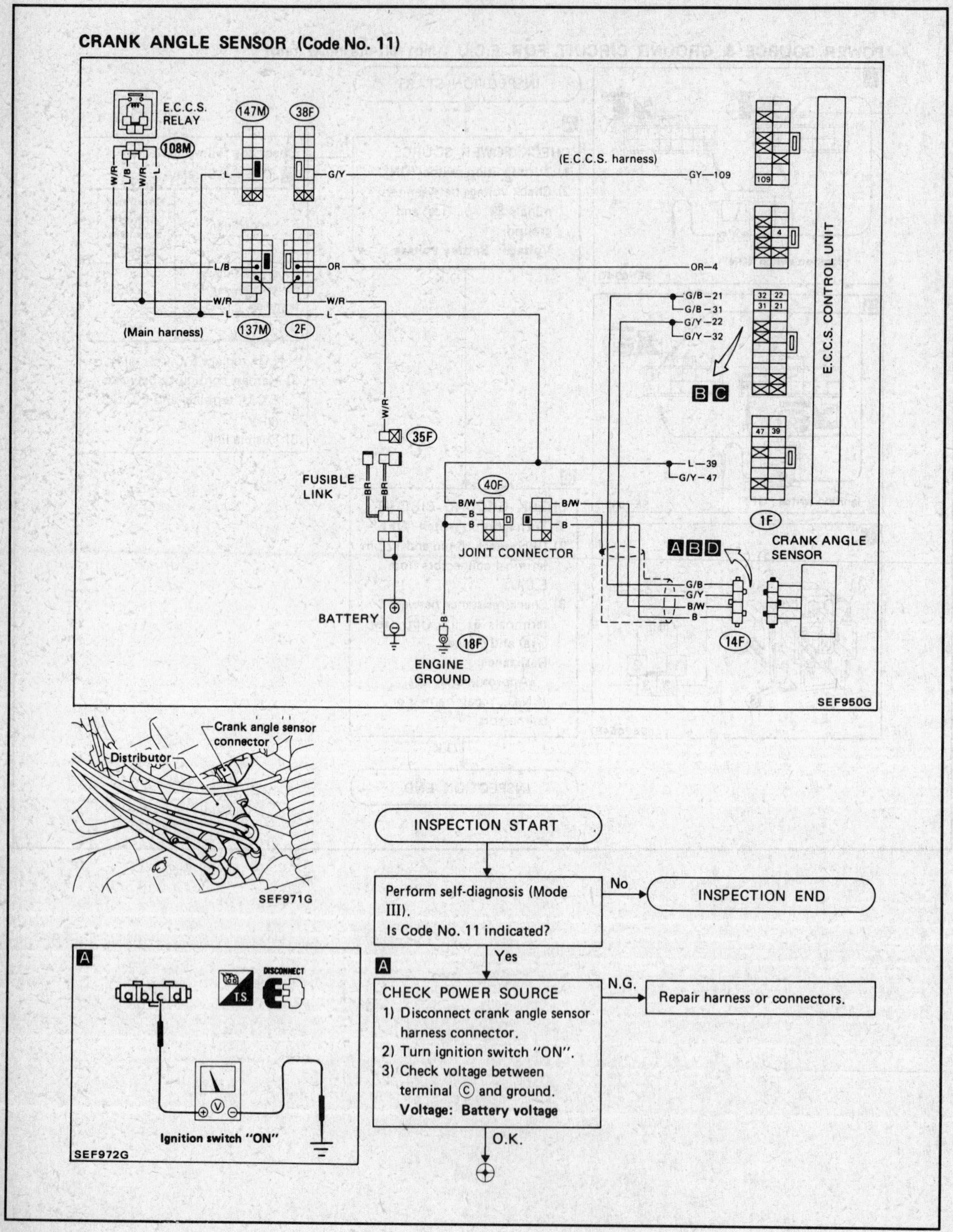
CRANK ANGLE SENSOR (Code No. 11)
E.C.C.S. RELAY
108M
147M
38F
137M
2F
(Main harness)
(E.C.C.S. harness)
GY—109
OR—4
G/B—21
G/B—31
G/Y—22
G/Y—32
L—39
G/Y—47
B C
E.C.C.S. CONTROL UNIT
35F
FUSIBLE LINK
40F
JOINT CONNECTOR
1F
A B D
CRANK ANGLE SENSOR
14F
BATTERY
18F
ENGINE GROUND
SEF950G
Crank angle sensor connector
Distributor
SEF971G
A
Ignition switch "ON"
SEF972G
INSPECTION START
Perform self-diagnosis (Mode III).
Is Code No. 11 indicated?
No
INSPECTION END
Yes
A
CHECK POWER SOURCE
1) Disconnect crank angle sensor harness connector.
2) Turn ignition switch "ON".
3) Check voltage between terminal ⓒ and ground.
Voltage: Battery voltage
N.G.
Repair harness or connectors.
O.K.

CODE 11 (CRANK ANGLE SENSOR) – GA16i ENGINE, PART 2

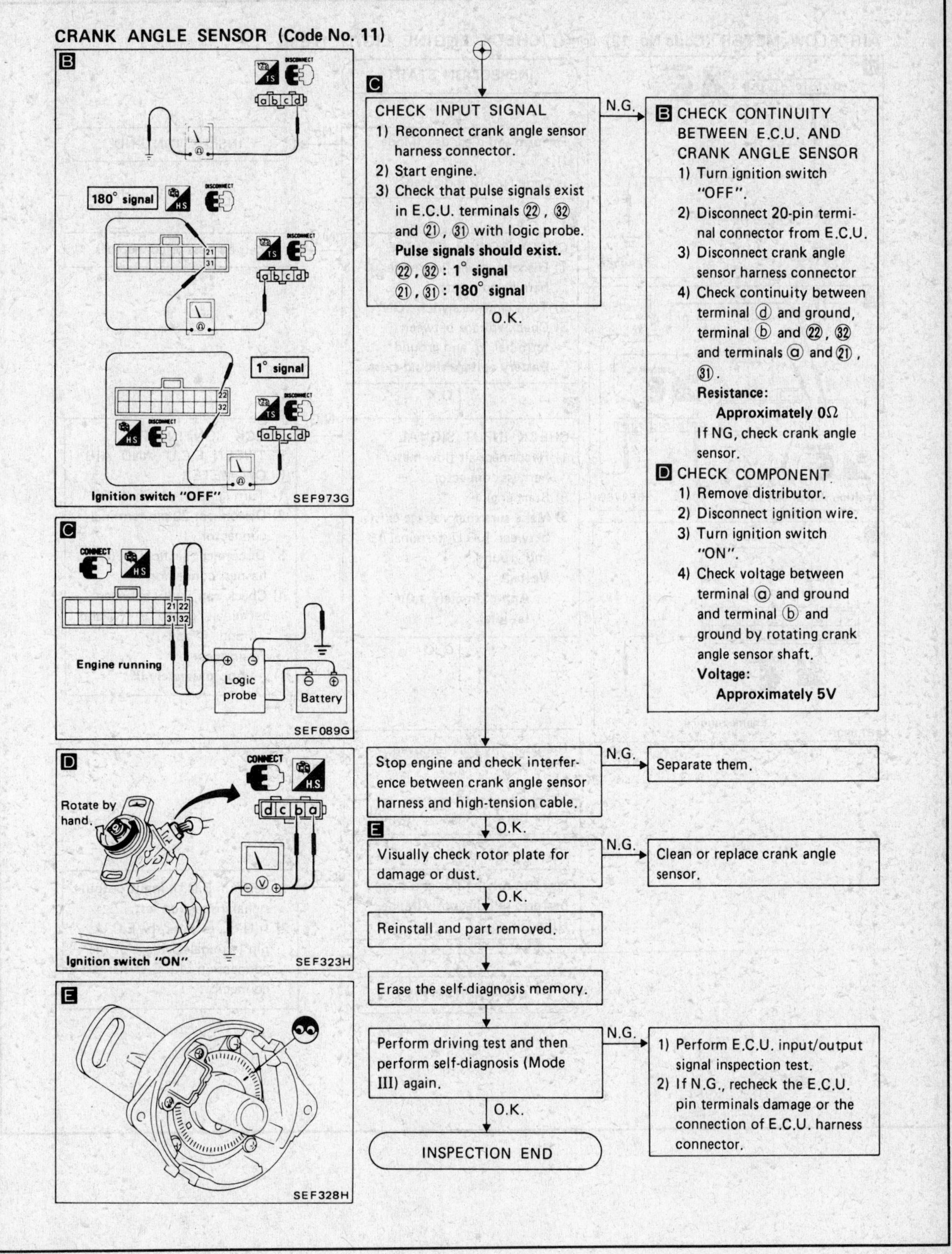
CRANK ANGLE SENSOR (Code No. 11)
B
DISCONNECT
TS
a b c d
180° signal
HS
21
31
1° signal
22
32
Ignition switch "OFF"
SEF973G
C
CONNECT
HS
21 22
31 32
Engine running
Logic probe
Battery
SEF089G
D
Rotate by hand.
CONNECT
H.S.
d c b a
Ignition switch "ON"
SEF323H
E
SEF328H
C
CHECK INPUT SIGNAL
1) Reconnect crank angle sensor harness connector.
2) Start engine.
3) Check that pulse signals exist in E.C.U. terminals ㉒, ㉜ and ㉑, ㉛ with logic probe.
Pulse signals should exist.
㉒, ㉜ : 1° signal
㉑, ㉛ : 180° signal
N.G.
B CHECK CONTINUITY BETWEEN E.C.U. AND CRANK ANGLE SENSOR
1) Turn ignition switch "OFF".
2) Disconnect 20-pin terminal connector from E.C.U.
3) Disconnect crank angle sensor harness connector
4) Check continuity between terminal ⓓ and ground, terminal ⓑ and ㉒, ㉜ and terminals ⓐ and ㉑, ㉛.
Resistance:
Approximately 0Ω
If NG, check crank angle sensor.
D CHECK COMPONENT
1) Remove distributor.
2) Disconnect ignition wire.
3) Turn ignition switch "ON".
4) Check voltage between terminal ⓐ and ground and terminal ⓑ and ground by rotating crank angle sensor shaft.
Voltage:
Approximately 5V
O.K.
Stop engine and check interference between crank angle sensor harness and high-tension cable.
N.G.
Separate them.
O.K.
E
Visually check rotor plate for damage or dust.
N.G.
Clean or replace crank angle sensor.
O.K.
Reinstall and part removed.
Erase the self-diagnosis memory.
Perform driving test and then perform self-diagnosis (Mode III) again.
N.G.
1) Perform E.C.U. input/output signal inspection test.
2) If N.G., recheck the E.C.U. pin terminals damage or the connection of E.C.U. harness connector.
O.K.
INSPECTION END

CODE 12 (AIR FLOW METER) – GA16i ENGINE

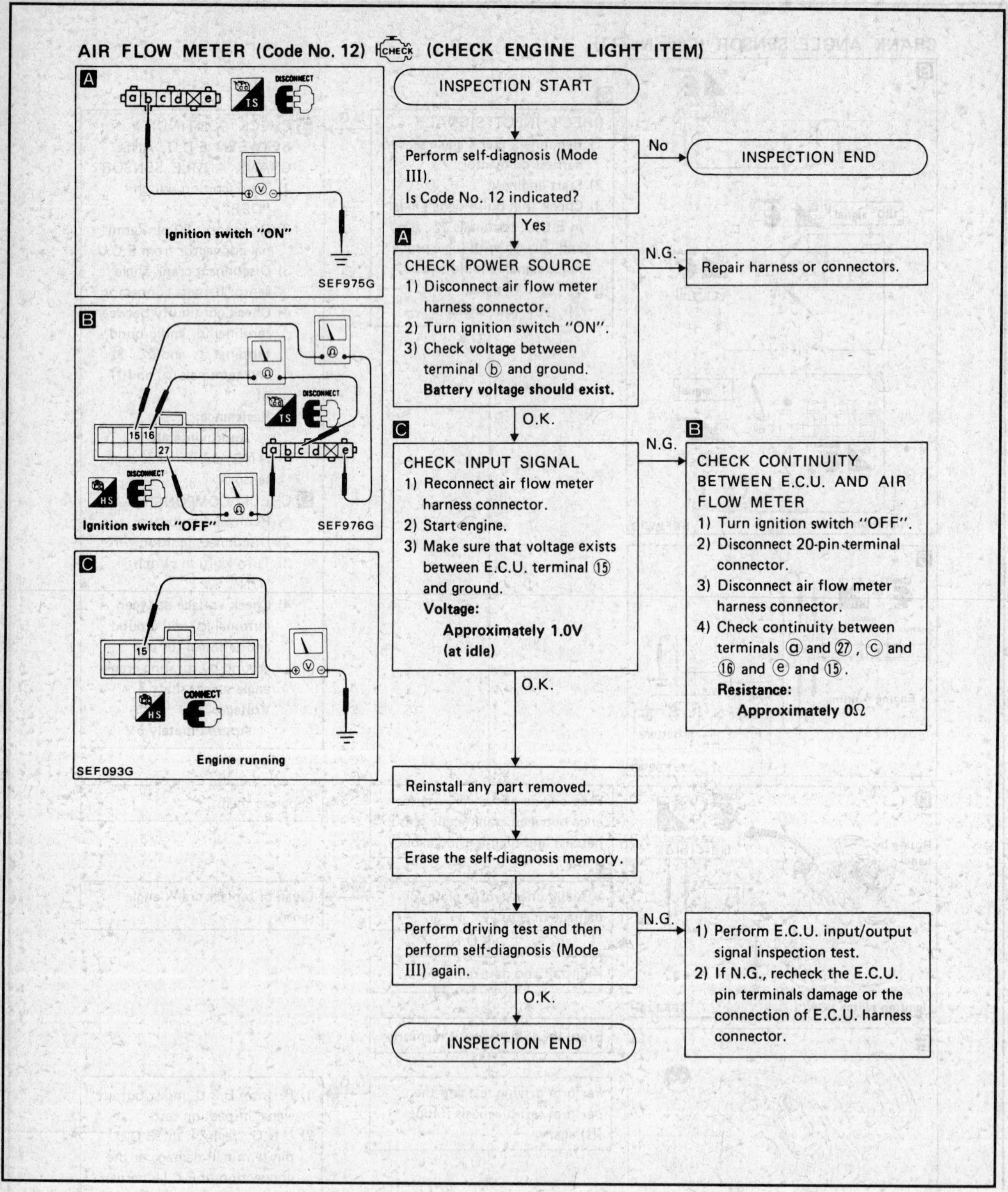
AIR FLOW METER (Code No. 12) CHECK (CHECK ENGINE LIGHT ITEM)
A
a b c d e
DISCONNECT
TS
Ignition switch "ON"
SEF975G
B
15 16
27
DISCONNECT
TS
a b c d e
DISCONNECT
HS
Ignition switch "OFF"
SEF976G
C
15
HS
CONNECT
Engine running
SEF093G
INSPECTION START
Perform self-diagnosis (Mode III).
Is Code No. 12 indicated?
No
INSPECTION END
Yes
A
CHECK POWER SOURCE
1) Disconnect air flow meter harness connector.
2) Turn ignition switch "ON".
3) Check voltage between terminal ⓑ and ground.
Battery voltage should exist.
N.G.
Repair harness or connectors.
O.K.
C
CHECK INPUT SIGNAL
1) Reconnect air flow meter harness connector.
2) Start engine.
3) Make sure that voltage exists between E.C.U. terminal ⑮ and ground.
Voltage:
Approximately 1.0V (at idle)
N.G.
B
CHECK CONTINUITY BETWEEN E.C.U. AND AIR FLOW METER
1) Turn ignition switch "OFF".
2) Disconnect 20-pin terminal connector.
3) Disconnect air flow meter harness connector.
4) Check continuity between terminals ⓐ and ㉗, ⓒ and ⑯ and ⓔ and ⑮.
Resistance:
Approximately 0Ω
O.K.
Reinstall any part removed.
Erase the self-diagnosis memory.
Perform driving test and then perform self-diagnosis (Mode III) again.
N.G.
1) Perform E.C.U. input/output signal inspection test.
2) If N.G., recheck the E.C.U. pin terminals damage or the connection of E.C.U. harness connector.
O.K.
INSPECTION END

CODE 13 (WATER TEMPERATURE SENSOR) – GA16i ENGINE

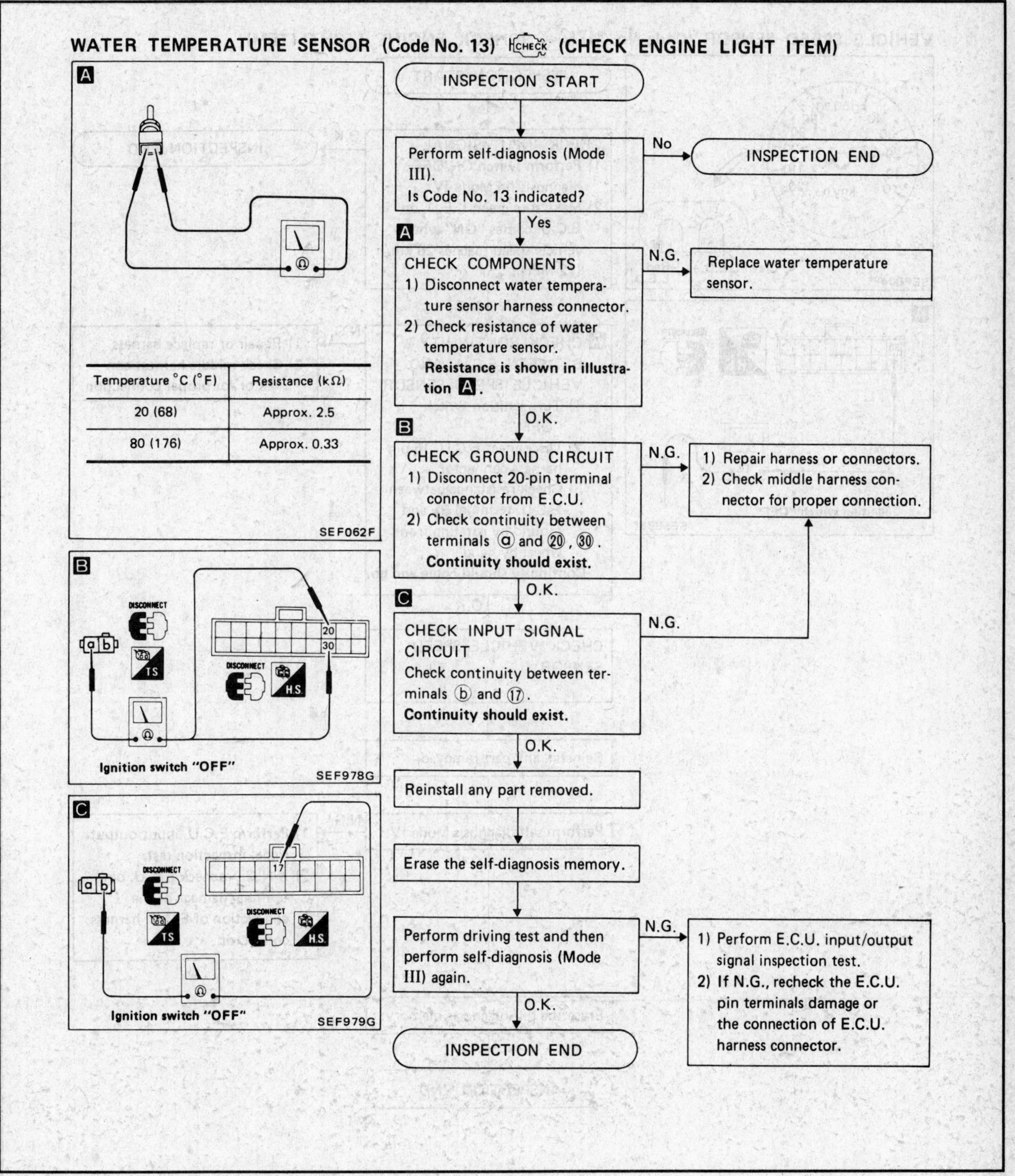
WATER TEMPERATURE SENSOR (Code No. 13) CHECK (CHECK ENGINE LIGHT ITEM)
A
Temperature °C (°F) | Resistance (kΩ)
20 (68) | Approx. 2.5
80 (176) | Approx. 0.33
SEF062F
B
DISCONNECT
TS
H.S
20
30
a b
Ignition switch "OFF"
SEF978G
C
DISCONNECT
TS
H.S.
17
a b
Ignition switch "OFF"
SEF979G
INSPECTION START
Perform self-diagnosis (Mode III).
Is Code No. 13 indicated?
No
INSPECTION END
Yes
A
CHECK COMPONENTS
1) Disconnect water temperature sensor harness connector.
2) Check resistance of water temperature sensor.
Resistance is shown in illustration A.
N.G.
Replace water temperature sensor.
O.K.
B
CHECK GROUND CIRCUIT
1) Disconnect 20-pin terminal connector from E.C.U.
2) Check continuity between terminals ⓐ and ⑳, ㉚.
Continuity should exist.
N.G.
1) Repair harness or connectors.
2) Check middle harness connector for proper connection.
O.K.
C
CHECK INPUT SIGNAL CIRCUIT
Check continuity between terminals ⓑ and ⑰.
Continuity should exist.
N.G.
O.K.
Reinstall any part removed.
Erase the self-diagnosis memory.
Perform driving test and then perform self-diagnosis (Mode III) again.
N.G.
1) Perform E.C.U. input/output signal inspection test.
2) If N.G., recheck the E.C.U. pin terminals damage or the connection of E.C.U. harness connector.
O.K.
INSPECTION END

CODE 14 (VEHICLE SPEED SENSOR – GA16i ENGINE

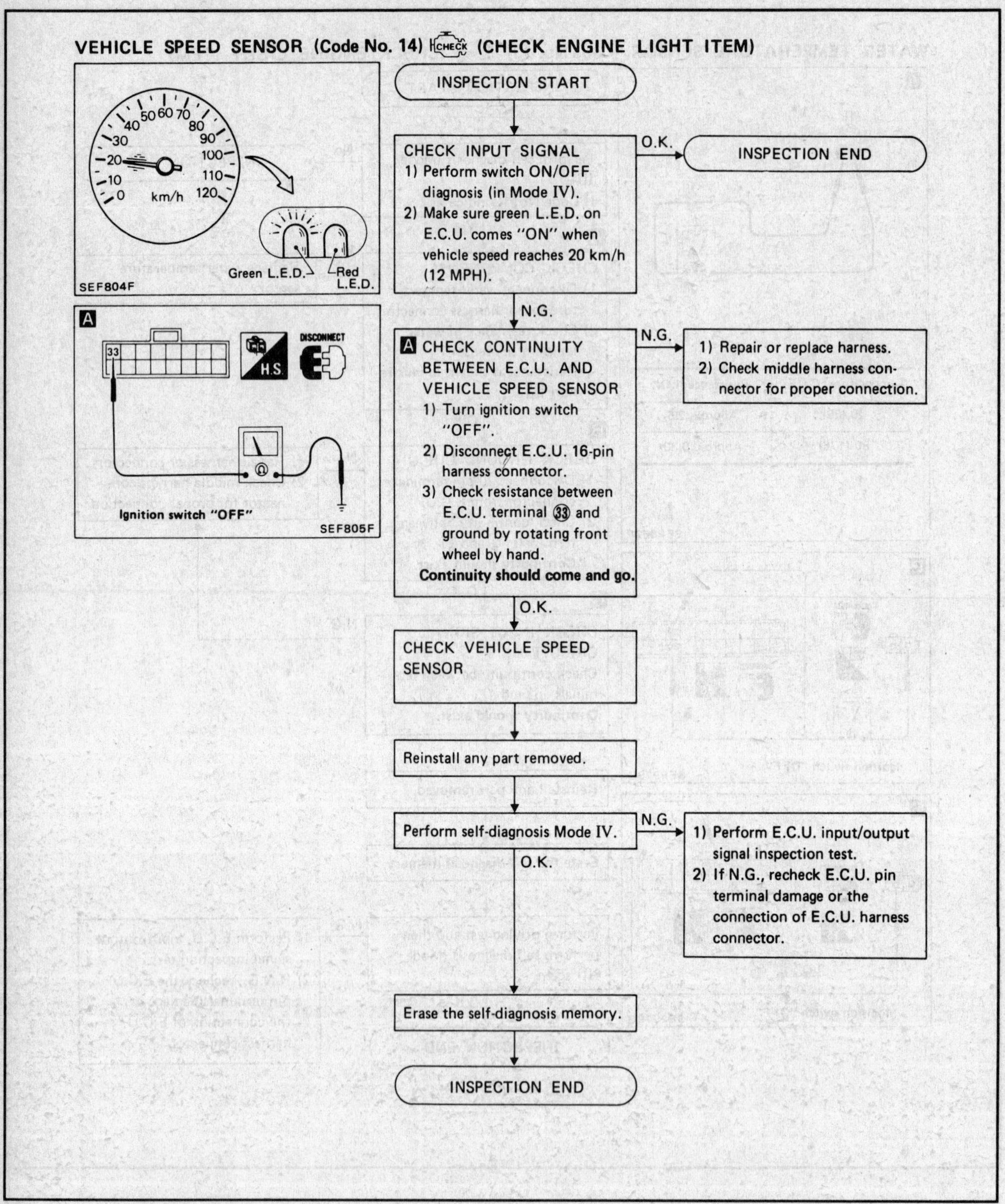

VEHICLE SPEED SENSOR (Code No. 14) CHECK (CHECK ENGINE LIGHT ITEM)
40 50 60 70 80
30 90
20 100
10 110
0 km/h 120
Green L.E.D.
Red L.E.D.
SEF804F
A
33
H.S.
DISCONNECT
Ignition switch "OFF"
SEF805F
INSPECTION START
CHECK INPUT SIGNAL
1) Perform switch ON/OFF diagnosis (in Mode IV).
2) Make sure green L.E.D. on E.C.U. comes "ON" when vehicle speed reaches 20 km/h (12 MPH).
O.K.
INSPECTION END
N.G.
A CHECK CONTINUITY BETWEEN E.C.U. AND VEHICLE SPEED SENSOR
1) Turn ignition switch "OFF".
2) Disconnect E.C.U. 16-pin harness connector.
3) Check resistance between E.C.U. terminal 33 and ground by rotating front wheel by hand.
Continuity should come and go.
N.G.
1) Repair or replace harness.
2) Check middle harness connector for proper connection.
O.K.
CHECK VEHICLE SPEED SENSOR
Reinstall any part removed.
Perform self-diagnosis Mode IV.
N.G.
1) Perform E.C.U. input/output signal inspection test.
2) If N.G., recheck E.C.U. pin terminal damage or the connection of E.C.U. harness connector.
O.K.
Erase the self-diagnosis memory.
INSPECTION END

CODE 21 (IGNITION SIGNAL) – GA16i ENGINE

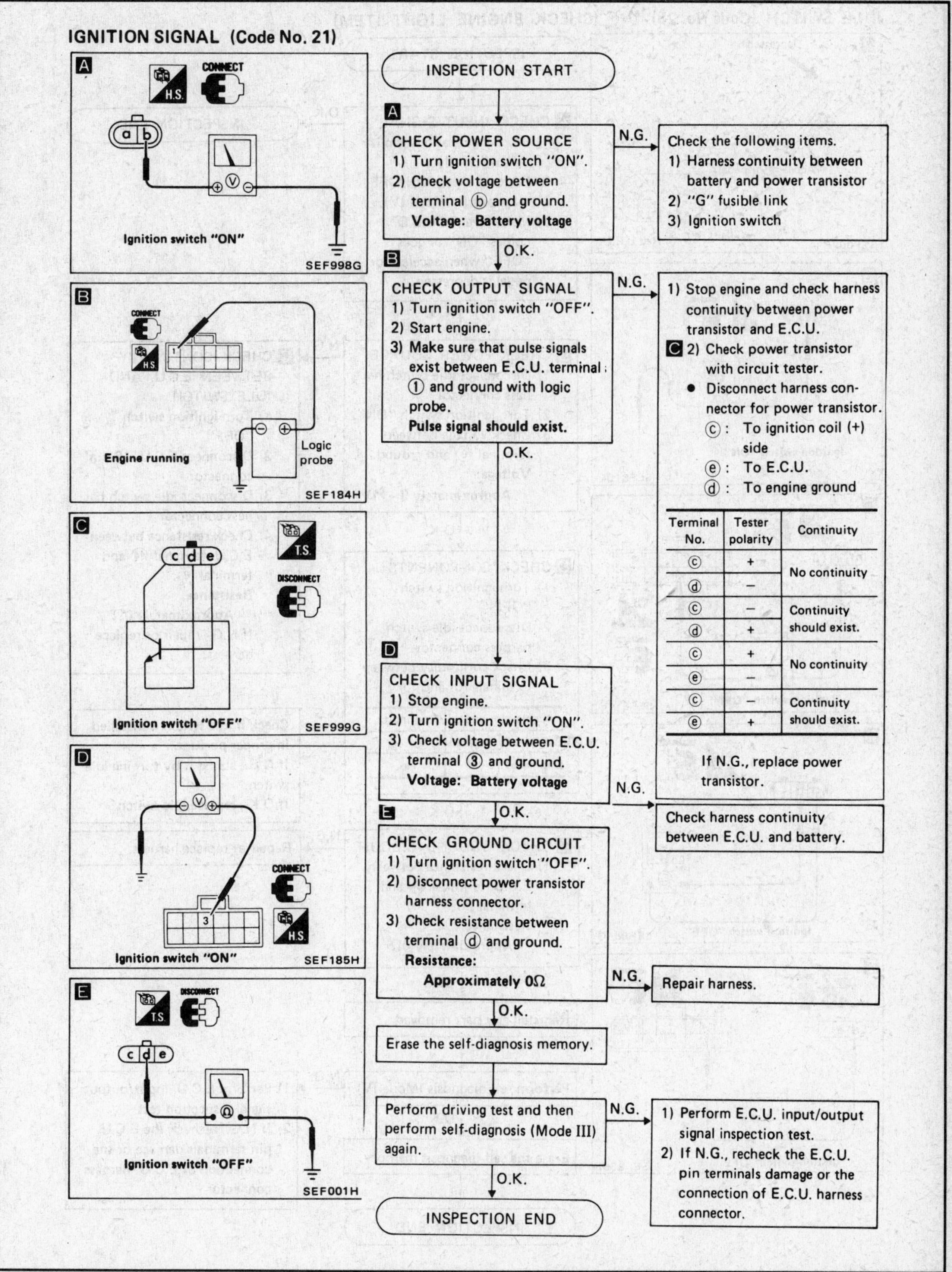
IGNITION SIGNAL (Code No. 21)
A
CONNECT
H.S.
a b
Ignition switch "ON"
SEF998G
B
CONNECT
H.S.
1
Engine running
Logic probe
SEF184H
C
T.S.
DISCONNECT
c d e
Ignition switch "OFF"
SEF999G
D
CONNECT
H.S.
3
Ignition switch "ON"
SEF185H
E
DISCONNECT
T.S.
c d e
Ignition switch "OFF"
SEF001H
INSPECTION START
A
CHECK POWER SOURCE
1) Turn ignition switch "ON".
2) Check voltage between terminal ⓑ and ground.
Voltage: Battery voltage
N.G.
Check the following items.
1) Harness continuity between battery and power transistor
2) "G" fusible link
3) Ignition switch
O.K.
B
CHECK OUTPUT SIGNAL
1) Turn ignition switch "OFF".
2) Start engine.
3) Make sure that pulse signals exist between E.C.U. terminal ① and ground with logic probe.
Pulse signal should exist.
N.G.
1) Stop engine and check harness continuity between power transistor and E.C.U.
C 2) Check power transistor with circuit tester.
• Disconnect harness connector for power transistor.
ⓒ : To ignition coil (+) side
ⓔ : To E.C.U.
ⓓ : To engine ground
Terminal No. | Tester polarity | Continuity
ⓒ | + | No continuity
ⓓ | − |
ⓒ | − | Continuity should exist.
ⓓ | + |
ⓒ | + | No continuity
ⓔ | − |
ⓒ | − | Continuity should exist.
ⓔ | + |
If N.G., replace power transistor.
O.K.
D
CHECK INPUT SIGNAL
1) Stop engine.
2) Turn ignition switch "ON".
3) Check voltage between E.C.U. terminal ③ and ground.
Voltage: Battery voltage
N.G.
Check harness continuity between E.C.U. and battery.
O.K.
E
CHECK GROUND CIRCUIT
1) Turn ignition switch "OFF".
2) Disconnect power transistor harness connector.
3) Check resistance between terminal ⓓ and ground.
Resistance: Approximately 0Ω
N.G.
Repair harness.
O.K.
Erase the self-diagnosis memory.
Perform driving test and then perform self-diagnosis (Mode III) again.
N.G.
1) Perform E.C.U. input/output signal inspection test.
2) If N.G., recheck the E.C.U. pin terminals damage or the connection of E.C.U. harness connector.
O.K.
INSPECTION END

CODE 23 (IDLE SWITCH) – GA16i ENGINE

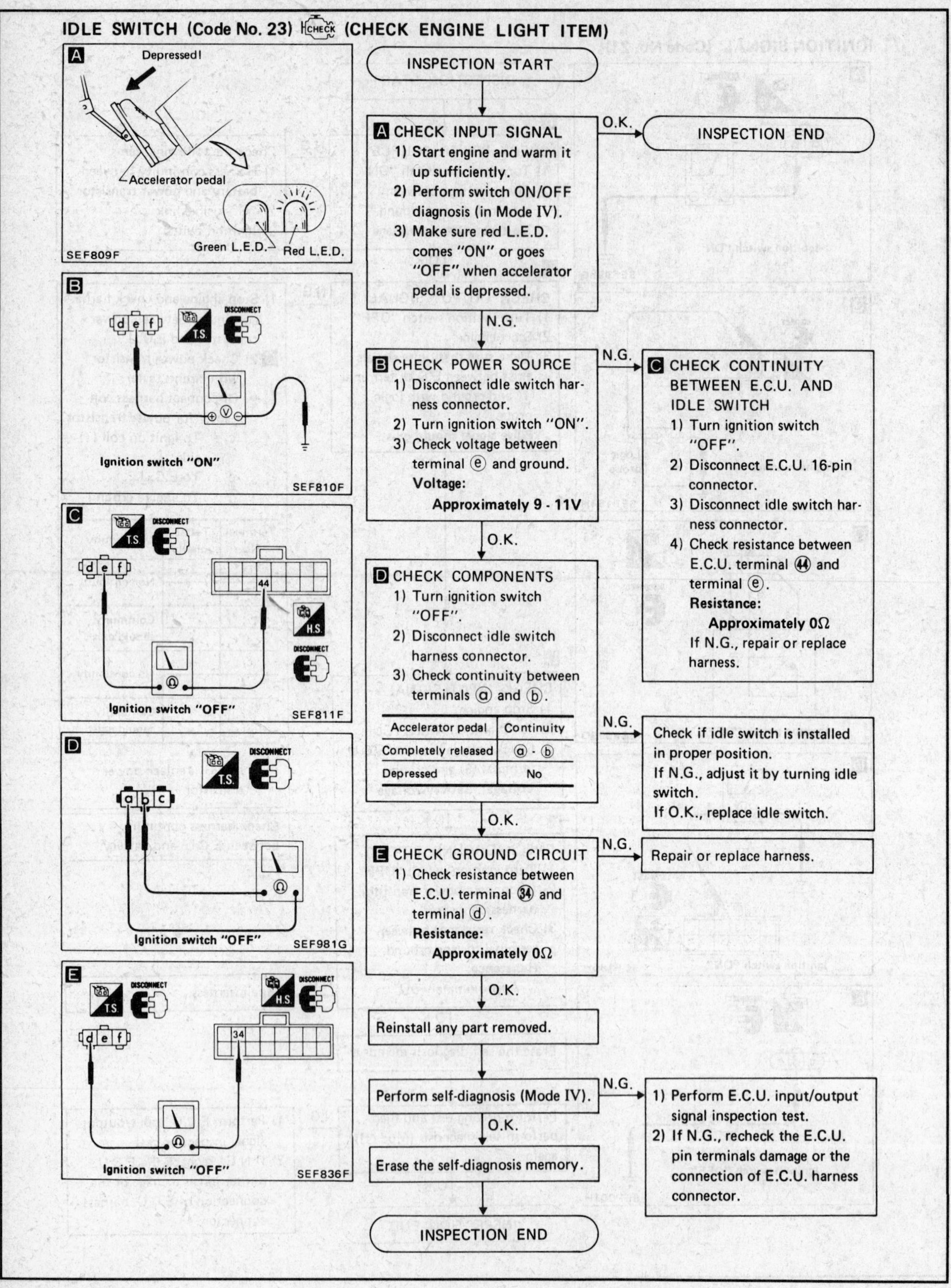
IDLE SWITCH (Code No. 23) CHECK (CHECK ENGINE LIGHT ITEM)
A
Depressed!
Accelerator pedal
Green L.E.D.
Red L.E.D.
SEF809F
B
d e f
T.S.
DISCONNECT
Ignition switch "ON"
SEF810F
C
T.S.
DISCONNECT
d e f
44
H.S.
DISCONNECT
Ignition switch "OFF"
SEF811F
D
T.S.
DISCONNECT
a b c
Ignition switch "OFF"
SEF981G
E
T.S.
DISCONNECT
H.S.
DISCONNECT
d e f
34
Ignition switch "OFF"
SEF836F
INSPECTION START
A CHECK INPUT SIGNAL
1) Start engine and warm it up sufficiently.
2) Perform switch ON/OFF diagnosis (in Mode IV).
3) Make sure red L.E.D. comes "ON" or goes "OFF" when accelerator pedal is depressed.
O.K.
INSPECTION END
N.G.
B CHECK POWER SOURCE
1) Disconnect idle switch harness connector.
2) Turn ignition switch "ON".
3) Check voltage between terminal ⓔ and ground.
Voltage:
Approximately 9 - 11V
N.G.
C CHECK CONTINUITY BETWEEN E.C.U. AND IDLE SWITCH
1) Turn ignition switch "OFF".
2) Disconnect E.C.U. 16-pin connector.
3) Disconnect idle switch harness connector.
4) Check resistance between E.C.U. terminal ㊹ and terminal ⓔ.
Resistance:
Approximately 0Ω
If N.G., repair or replace harness.
O.K.
D CHECK COMPONENTS
1) Turn ignition switch "OFF".
2) Disconnect idle switch harness connector.
3) Check continuity between terminals ⓐ and ⓑ.
Accelerator pedal | Continuity
Completely released | ⓐ - ⓑ
Depressed | No
N.G.
Check if idle switch is installed in proper position.
If N.G., adjust it by turning idle switch.
If O.K., replace idle switch.
O.K.
E CHECK GROUND CIRCUIT
1) Check resistance between E.C.U. terminal ㉞ and terminal ⓓ.
Resistance:
Approximately 0Ω
N.G.
Repair or replace harness.
O.K.
Reinstall any part removed.
Perform self-diagnosis (Mode IV).
N.G.
1) Perform E.C.U. input/output signal inspection test.
2) If N.G., recheck the E.C.U. pin terminals damage or the connection of E.C.U. harness connector.
O.K.
Erase the self-diagnosis memory.
INSPECTION END

CODE 25 (AUXILIARY AIR CONTROL VALVE) – GA16i ENGINE

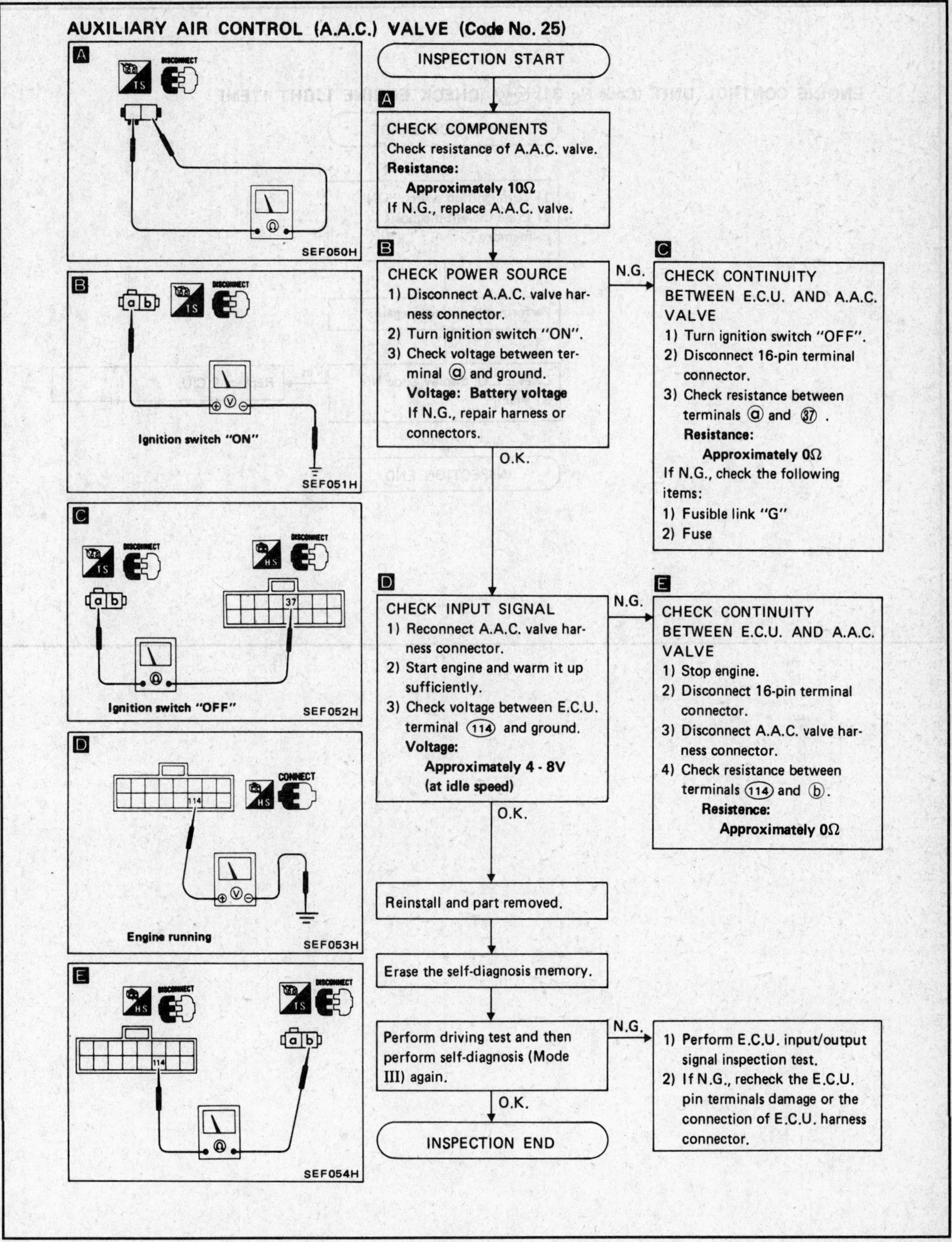
AUXILIARY AIR CONTROL (A.A.C.) VALVE (Code No. 25)
A
DISCONNECT
TS
SEF050H
B
DISCONNECT
TS
Ignition switch "ON"
SEF051H
C
DISCONNECT
TS
HS
37
Ignition switch "OFF"
SEF052H
D
CONNECT
HS
114
Engine running
SEF053H
E
DISCONNECT
HS
TS
114
SEF054H
INSPECTION START
A
CHECK COMPONENTS
Check resistance of A.A.C. valve.
Resistance:
Approximately 10Ω
If N.G., replace A.A.C. valve.
B
CHECK POWER SOURCE
1) Disconnect A.A.C. valve harness connector.
2) Turn ignition switch "ON".
3) Check voltage between terminal ⓐ and ground.
Voltage: Battery voltage
If N.G., repair harness or connectors.
N.G.
C
CHECK CONTINUITY BETWEEN E.C.U. AND A.A.C. VALVE
1) Turn ignition switch "OFF".
2) Disconnect 16-pin terminal connector.
3) Check resistance between terminals ⓐ and ㊲.
Resistance:
Approximately 0Ω
If N.G., check the following items:
1) Fusible link "G"
2) Fuse
O.K.
D
CHECK INPUT SIGNAL
1) Reconnect A.A.C. valve harness connector.
2) Start engine and warm it up sufficiently.
3) Check voltage between E.C.U. terminal (114) and ground.
Voltage:
Approximately 4 - 8V
(at idle speed)
N.G.
E
CHECK CONTINUITY BETWEEN E.C.U. AND A.A.C. VALVE
1) Stop engine.
2) Disconnect 16-pin terminal connector.
3) Disconnect A.A.C. valve harness connector.
4) Check resistance between terminals (114) and ⓑ.
Resistence:
Approximately 0Ω
O.K.
Reinstall and part removed.
Erase the self-diagnosis memory.
Perform driving test and then perform self-diagnosis (Mode III) again.
N.G.
1) Perform E.C.U. input/output signal inspection test.
2) If N.G., recheck the E.C.U. pin terminals damage or the connection of E.C.U. harness connector.
O.K.
INSPECTION END

CODE 31 (ECU) – GA16i ENGINE

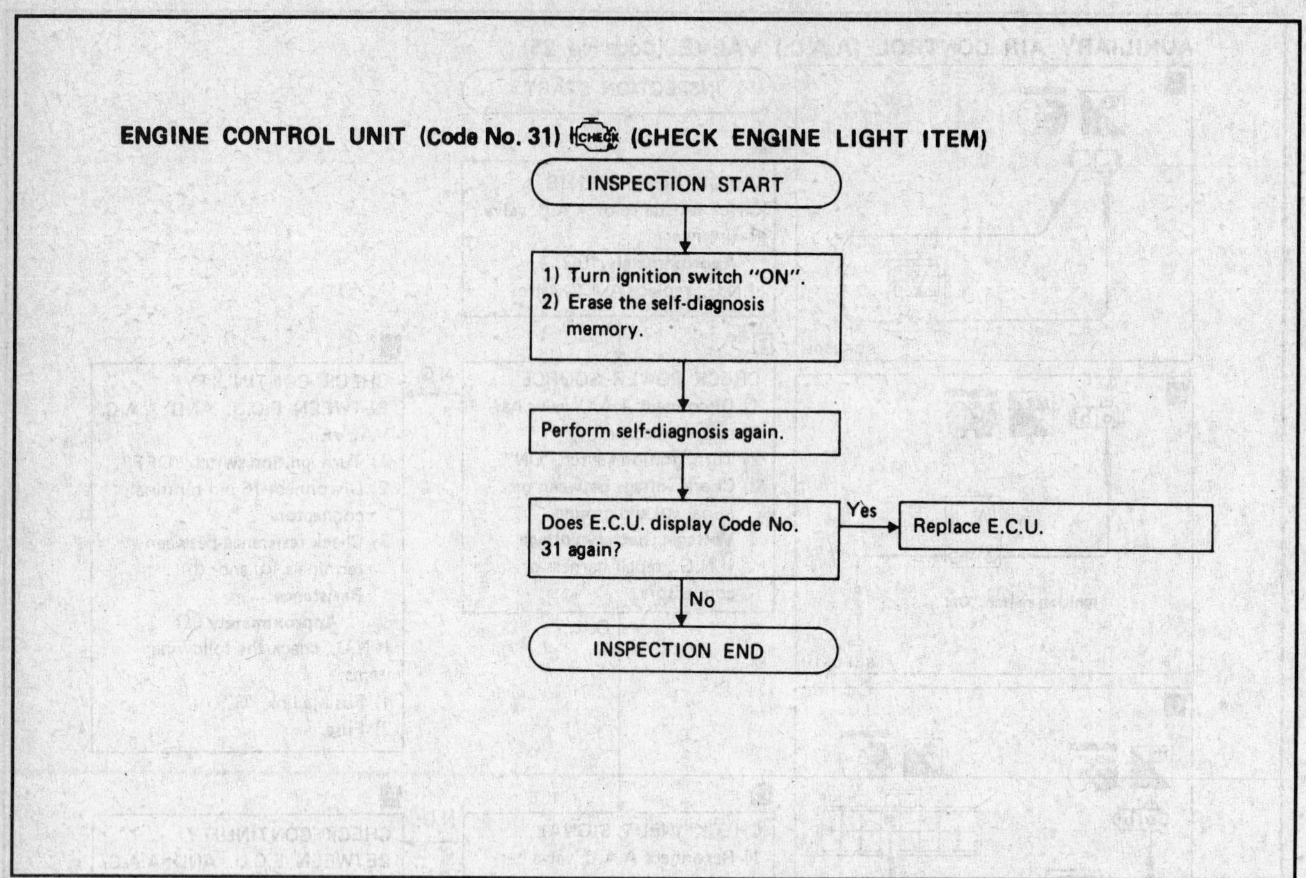
ENGINE CONTROL UNIT (Code No. 31) CHECK (CHECK ENGINE LIGHT ITEM)
INSPECTION START
1) Turn ignition switch "ON".
2) Erase the self-diagnosis memory.
Perform self-diagnosis again.
Does E.C.U. display Code No. 31 again?
Yes
Replace E.C.U.
No
INSPECTION END

CODE 32 (EGR FUNCTION) – GA16i CALIFORNIA ENGINE, PART 1

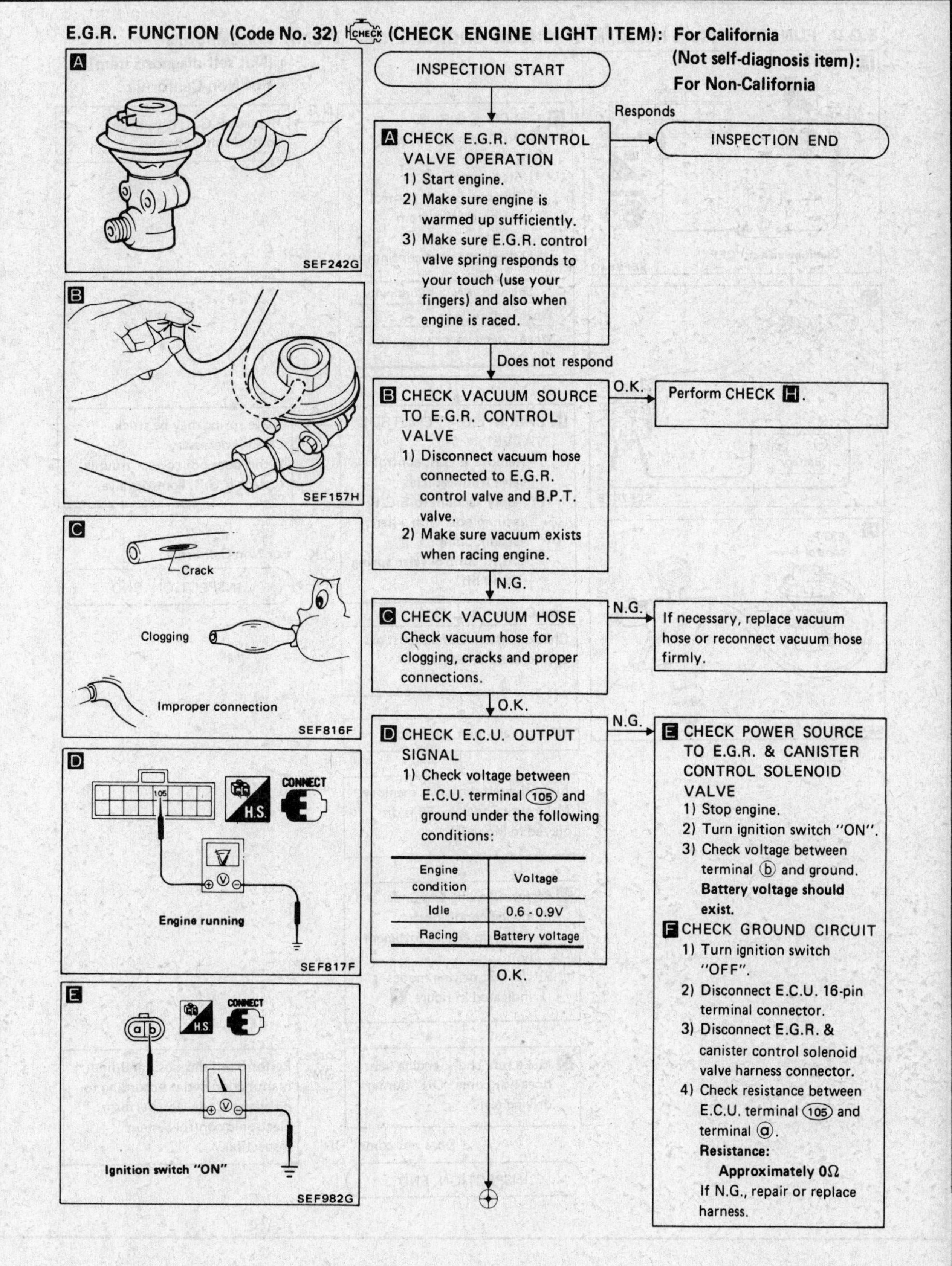
E.G.R. FUNCTION (Code No. 32) CHECK (CHECK ENGINE LIGHT ITEM): For California
(Not self-diagnosis item): For Non-California
INSPECTION START
A CHECK E.G.R. CONTROL VALVE OPERATION
1) Start engine.
2) Make sure engine is warmed up sufficiently.
3) Make sure E.G.R. control valve spring responds to your touch (use your fingers) and also when engine is raced.
Responds
INSPECTION END
Does not respond
B CHECK VACUUM SOURCE TO E.G.R. CONTROL VALVE
1) Disconnect vacuum hose connected to E.G.R. control valve and B.P.T. valve.
2) Make sure vacuum exists when racing engine.
O.K.
Perform CHECK H.
N.G.
C CHECK VACUUM HOSE
Check vacuum hose for clogging, cracks and proper connections.
N.G.
If necessary, replace vacuum hose or reconnect vacuum hose firmly.
O.K.
D CHECK E.C.U. OUTPUT SIGNAL
1) Check voltage between E.C.U. terminal (105) and ground under the following conditions:
Engine condition | Voltage
Idle | 0.6 - 0.9V
Racing | Battery voltage
N.G.
E CHECK POWER SOURCE TO E.G.R. & CANISTER CONTROL SOLENOID VALVE
1) Stop engine.
2) Turn ignition switch "ON".
3) Check voltage between terminal (b) and ground.
Battery voltage should exist.
F CHECK GROUND CIRCUIT
1) Turn ignition switch "OFF".
2) Disconnect E.C.U. 16-pin terminal connector.
3) Disconnect E.G.R. & canister control solenoid valve harness connector.
4) Check resistance between E.C.U. terminal (105) and terminal (a).
Resistance:
Approximately 0Ω
If N.G., repair or replace harness.
O.K.
A
SEF242G
B
SEF157H
C
Crack
Clogging
Improper connection
SEF816F
D
105
H.S.
CONNECT
Engine running
SEF817F
E
a b
H.S.
CONNECT
Ignition switch "ON"
SEF982G

CODE 32 (EGR FUNCTION) – GA16i CALIFORNIA ENGINE, PART 2

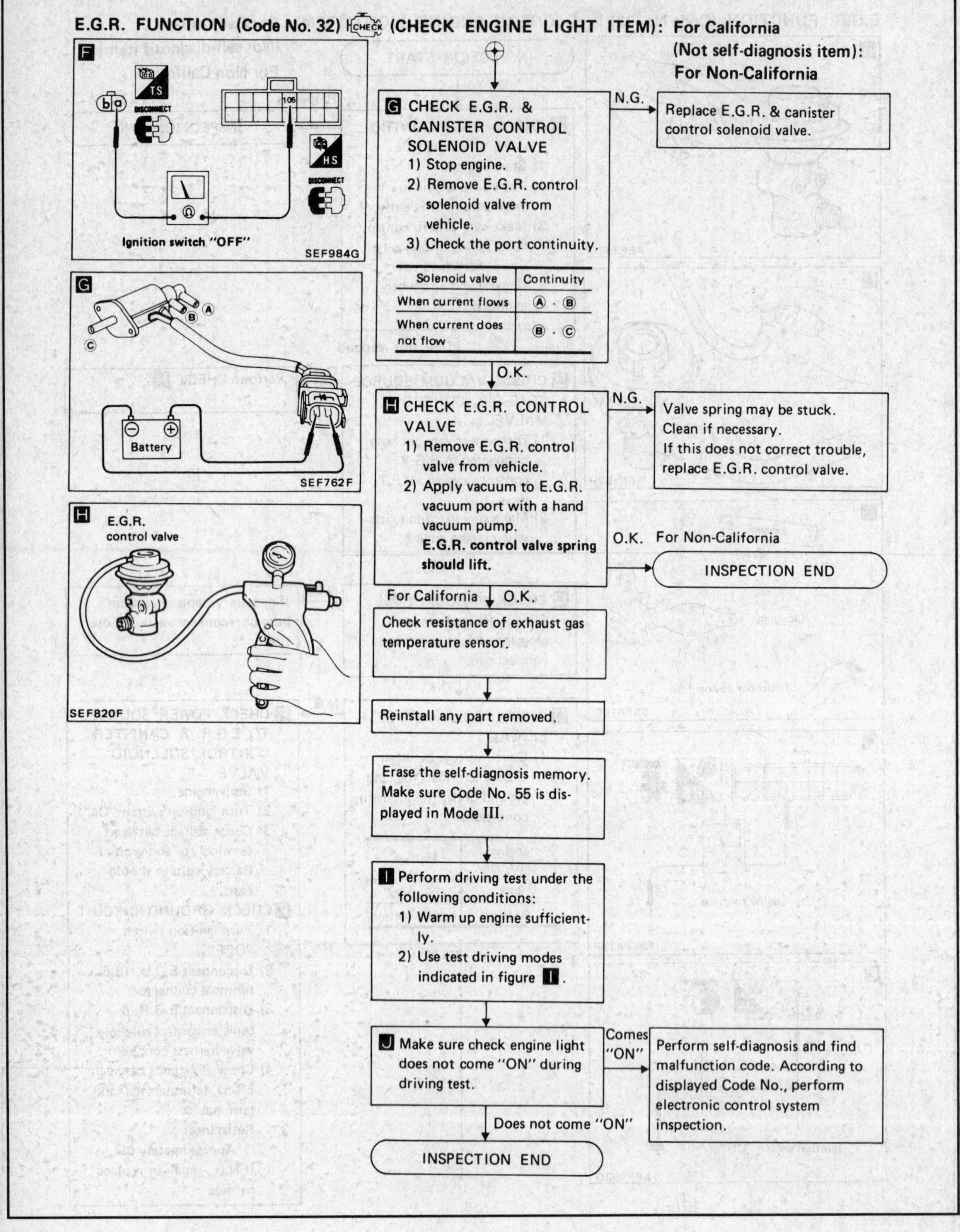
E.G.R. FUNCTION (Code No. 32) CHECK (CHECK ENGINE LIGHT ITEM): For California
(Not self-diagnosis item):
For Non-California
F
TS
DISCONNECT
105
HS
DISCONNECT
Ignition switch "OFF"
SEF984G
G
A
B
C
Battery
SEF762F
H
E.G.R.
control valve
SEF820F
G CHECK E.G.R. & CANISTER CONTROL SOLENOID VALVE
1) Stop engine.
2) Remove E.G.R. control solenoid valve from vehicle.
3) Check the port continuity.
Solenoid valve | Continuity
When current flows | Ⓐ - Ⓑ
When current does not flow | Ⓑ - Ⓒ
N.G.
Replace E.G.R. & canister control solenoid valve.
O.K.
H CHECK E.G.R. CONTROL VALVE
1) Remove E.G.R. control valve from vehicle.
2) Apply vacuum to E.G.R. vacuum port with a hand vacuum pump.
E.G.R. control valve spring should lift.
N.G.
Valve spring may be stuck. Clean if necessary.
If this does not correct trouble, replace E.G.R. control valve.
O.K. For Non-California
INSPECTION END
For California O.K.
Check resistance of exhaust gas temperature sensor.
Reinstall any part removed.
Erase the self-diagnosis memory. Make sure Code No. 55 is displayed in Mode III.
I Perform driving test under the following conditions:
1) Warm up engine sufficiently.
2) Use test driving modes indicated in figure I.
J Make sure check engine light does not come "ON" during driving test.
Comes "ON"
Perform self-diagnosis and find malfunction code. According to displayed Code No., perform electronic control system inspection.
Does not come "ON"
INSPECTION END

CODE 32 (EGR FUNCTION) — GA16i CALIFORNIA ENGINE, PART 3

E.G.R. FUNCTION (Code No. 32) (CHECK ENGINE LIGHT ITEM): For California
(Not self-diagnosis item): For Non-California

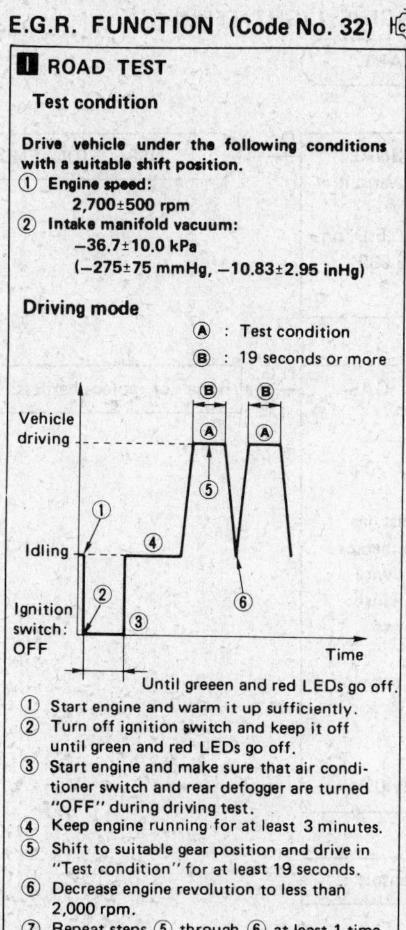

I ROAD TEST
Test condition
Drive vehicle under the following conditions with a suitable shift position.
① Engine speed: 2,700±500 rpm
② Intake manifold vacuum: −36.7±10.0 kPa (−275±75 mmHg, −10.83±2.95 inHg)
Driving mode
Ⓐ : Test condition
Ⓑ : 19 seconds or more
Vehicle driving
Idling
Ignition switch: OFF
Time
Until greeen and red LEDs go off.
① Start engine and warm it up sufficiently.
② Turn off ignition switch and keep it off until green and red LEDs go off.
③ Start engine and make sure that air conditioner switch and rear defogger are turned "OFF" during driving test.
④ Keep engine running for at least 3 minutes.
⑤ Shift to suitable gear position and drive in "Test condition" for at least 19 seconds.
⑥ Decrease engine revolution to less than 2,000 rpm.
⑦ Repeat steps ⑤ through ⑥ at least 1 time.
SEF302H

J
CHECK
CHECK ENGINE LIGHT
SEF924F

CODE 33 (OXYGEN SENSOR) — GA16i ENGINE

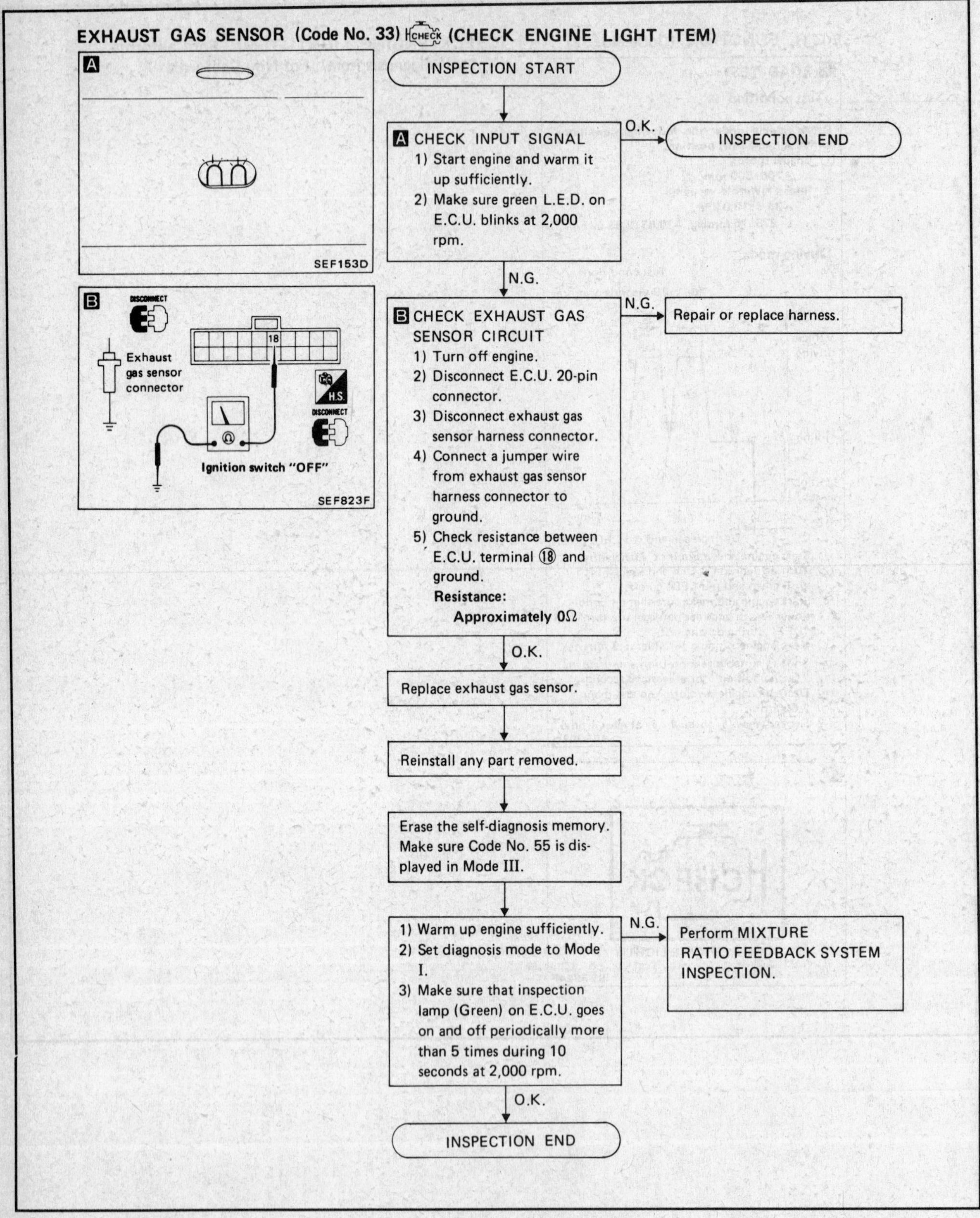
EXHAUST GAS SENSOR (Code No. 33) CHECK (CHECK ENGINE LIGHT ITEM)
A
SEF153D
B
DISCONNECT
18
Exhaust gas sensor connector
H.S.
DISCONNECT
Ignition switch "OFF"
SEF823F
INSPECTION START
A CHECK INPUT SIGNAL
1) Start engine and warm it up sufficiently.
2) Make sure green L.E.D. on E.C.U. blinks at 2,000 rpm.
O.K.
INSPECTION END
N.G.
B CHECK EXHAUST GAS SENSOR CIRCUIT
1) Turn off engine.
2) Disconnect E.C.U. 20-pin connector.
3) Disconnect exhaust gas sensor harness connector.
4) Connect a jumper wire from exhaust gas sensor harness connector to ground.
5) Check resistance between E.C.U. terminal ⑱ and ground.
Resistance:
Approximately 0Ω
N.G.
Repair or replace harness.
O.K.
Replace exhaust gas sensor.
Reinstall any part removed.
Erase the self-diagnosis memory. Make sure Code No. 55 is displayed in Mode III.
1) Warm up engine sufficiently.
2) Set diagnosis mode to Mode I.
3) Make sure that inspection lamp (Green) on E.C.U. goes on and off periodically more than 5 times during 10 seconds at 2,000 rpm.
N.G.
Perform MIXTURE RATIO FEEDBACK SYSTEM INSPECTION.
O.K.
INSPECTION END

CODE 35 (OXYGEN SENSOR TEMPERATURE SENSOR) GA16i CALIFORNIA ENGINE, PART 1

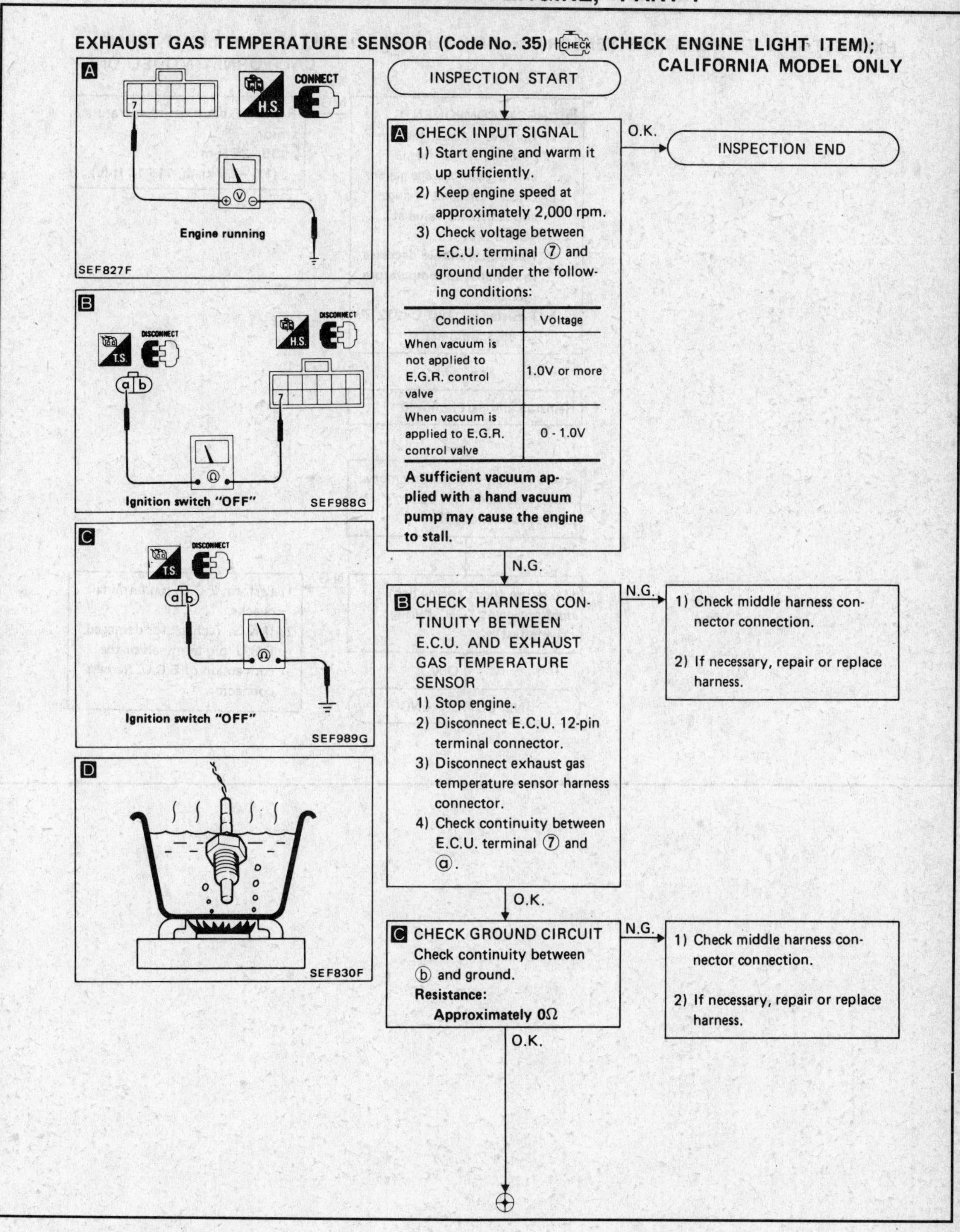
EXHAUST GAS TEMPERATURE SENSOR (Code No. 35) CHECK (CHECK ENGINE LIGHT ITEM);
CALIFORNIA MODEL ONLY
A
CONNECT
H.S.
7
Engine running
SEF827F
B
DISCONNECT
T.S.
a b
DISCONNECT
H.S.
7
Ignition switch "OFF"
SEF988G
C
DISCONNECT
T.S.
a b
Ignition switch "OFF"
SEF989G
D
SEF830F
INSPECTION START
A CHECK INPUT SIGNAL
1) Start engine and warm it up sufficiently.
2) Keep engine speed at approximately 2,000 rpm.
3) Check voltage between E.C.U. terminal ⑦ and ground under the following conditions:
Condition | Voltage
When vacuum is not applied to E.G.R. control valve | 1.0V or more
When vacuum is applied to E.G.R. control valve | 0 - 1.0V
A sufficient vacuum applied with a hand vacuum pump may cause the engine to stall.
O.K.
INSPECTION END
N.G.
B CHECK HARNESS CONTINUITY BETWEEN E.C.U. AND EXHAUST GAS TEMPERATURE SENSOR
1) Stop engine.
2) Disconnect E.C.U. 12-pin terminal connector.
3) Disconnect exhaust gas temperature sensor harness connector.
4) Check continuity between E.C.U. terminal ⑦ and ⓐ.
N.G.
1) Check middle harness connector connection.
2) If necessary, repair or replace harness.
O.K.
C CHECK GROUND CIRCUIT
Check continuity between ⓑ and ground.
Resistance:
Approximately 0Ω
N.G.
1) Check middle harness connector connection.
2) If necessary, repair or replace harness.
O.K.

CODE 35 (OXYGEN SENSOR TEMPERATURE SENSOR GA16i CALIFORNIA ENGINE, PART 2

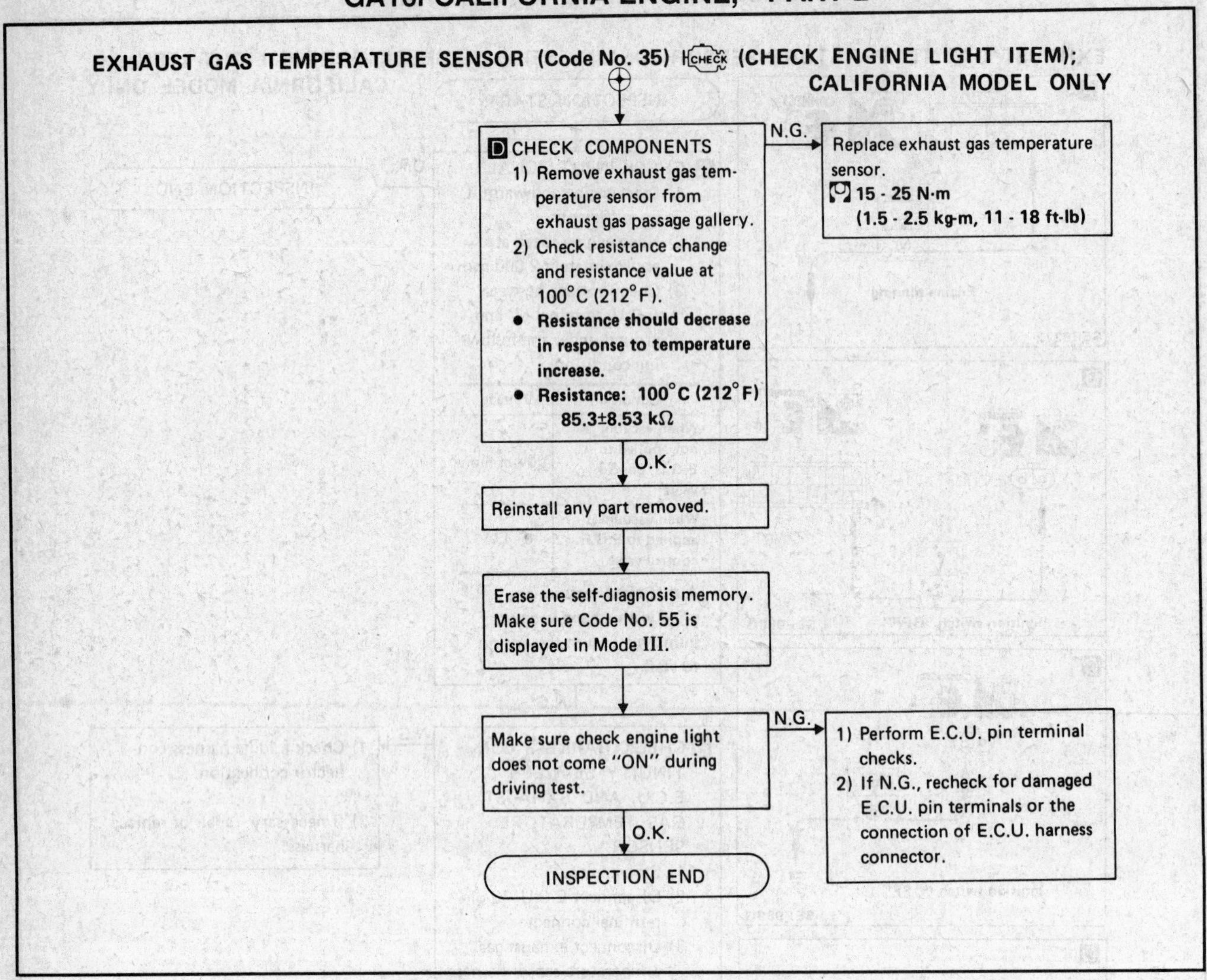
EXHAUST GAS TEMPERATURE SENSOR (Code No. 35) CHECK (CHECK ENGINE LIGHT ITEM); CALIFORNIA MODEL ONLY
D CHECK COMPONENTS
1) Remove exhaust gas temperature sensor from exhaust gas passage gallery.
2) Check resistance change and resistance value at 100°C (212°F).
• Resistance should decrease in response to temperature increase.
• Resistance: 100°C (212°F) 85.3±8.53 kΩ
N.G.
Replace exhaust gas temperature sensor.
15 - 25 N·m (1.5 - 2.5 kg-m, 11 - 18 ft-lb)
O.K.
Reinstall any part removed.
Erase the self-diagnosis memory. Make sure Code No. 55 is displayed in Mode III.
Make sure check engine light does not come "ON" during driving test.
N.G.
1) Perform E.C.U. pin terminal checks.
2) If N.G., recheck for damaged E.C.U. pin terminals or the connection of E.C.U. harness connector.
O.K.
INSPECTION END

CODE 43 (THROTTLE SENSOR) – GA16i ENGINE, PART 1

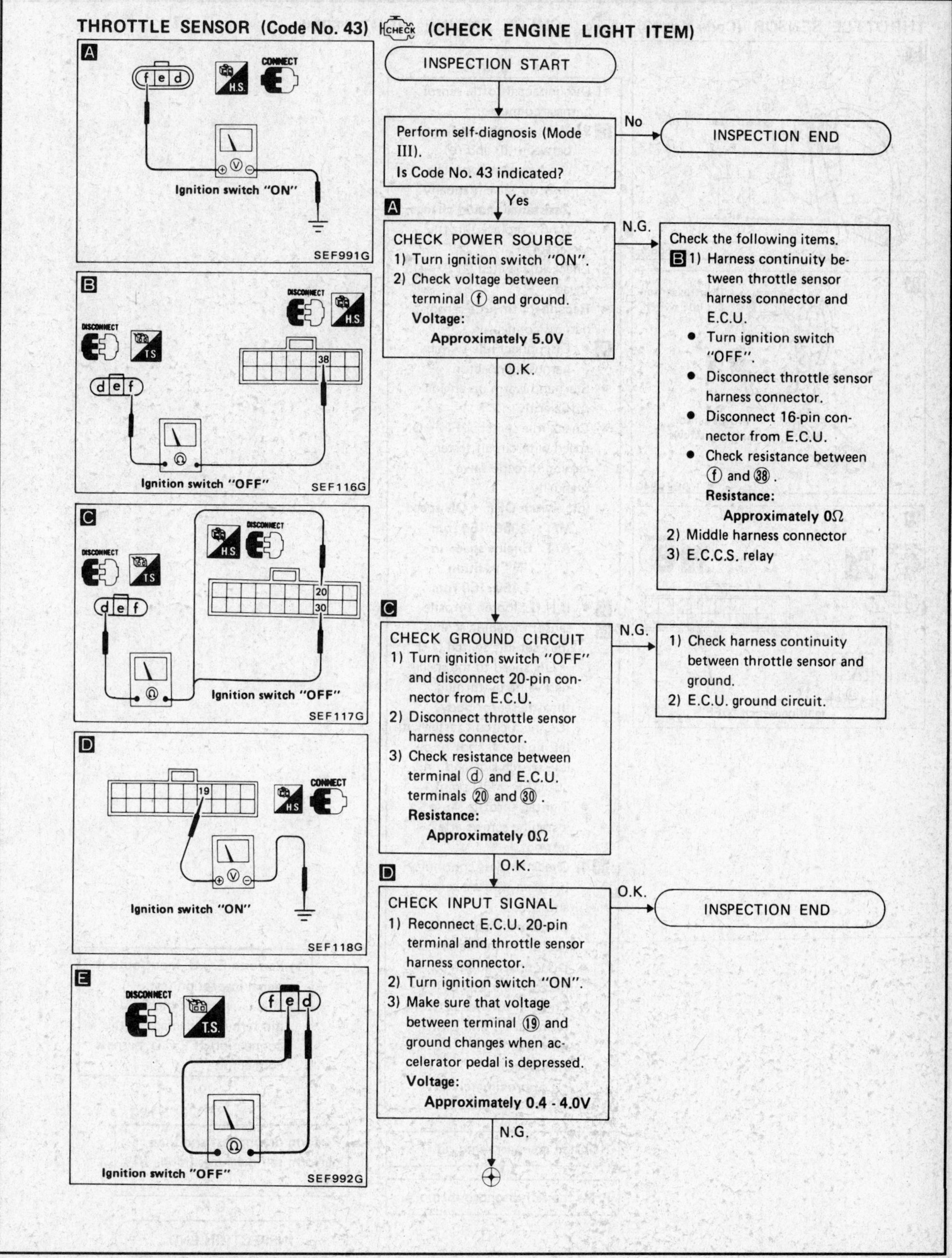
THROTTLE SENSOR (Code No. 43) CHECK (CHECK ENGINE LIGHT ITEM)
A
CONNECT
f e d
H.S.
Ignition switch "ON"
SEF991G
B
DISCONNECT
H.S.
T.S
38
d e f
Ignition switch "OFF"
SEF116G
C
DISCONNECT
H.S.
T.S
20
30
d e f
Ignition switch "OFF"
SEF117G
D
19
CONNECT
H.S
Ignition switch "ON"
SEF118G
E
DISCONNECT
T.S.
f e d
Ignition switch "OFF"
SEF992G
INSPECTION START
Perform self-diagnosis (Mode III).
Is Code No. 43 indicated?
No
INSPECTION END
Yes
A
CHECK POWER SOURCE
1) Turn ignition switch "ON".
2) Check voltage between terminal (f) and ground.
Voltage:
Approximately 5.0V
N.G.
Check the following items.
B 1) Harness continuity between throttle sensor harness connector and E.C.U.
• Turn ignition switch "OFF".
• Disconnect throttle sensor harness connector.
• Disconnect 16-pin connector from E.C.U.
• Check resistance between (f) and (38).
Resistance:
Approximately 0Ω
2) Middle harness connector
3) E.C.C.S. relay
O.K.
C
CHECK GROUND CIRCUIT
1) Turn ignition switch "OFF" and disconnect 20-pin connector from E.C.U.
2) Disconnect throttle sensor harness connector.
3) Check resistance between terminal (d) and E.C.U. terminals (20) and (30).
Resistance:
Approximately 0Ω
N.G.
1) Check harness continuity between throttle sensor and ground.
2) E.C.U. ground circuit.
O.K.
D
CHECK INPUT SIGNAL
1) Reconnect E.C.U. 20-pin terminal and throttle sensor harness connector.
2) Turn ignition switch "ON".
3) Make sure that voltage between terminal (19) and ground changes when accelerator pedal is depressed.
Voltage:
Approximately 0.4 - 4.0V
O.K.
INSPECTION END
N.G.

CODE 43 (THROTTLE SENSOR) — GA16i ENGINE, PART 2

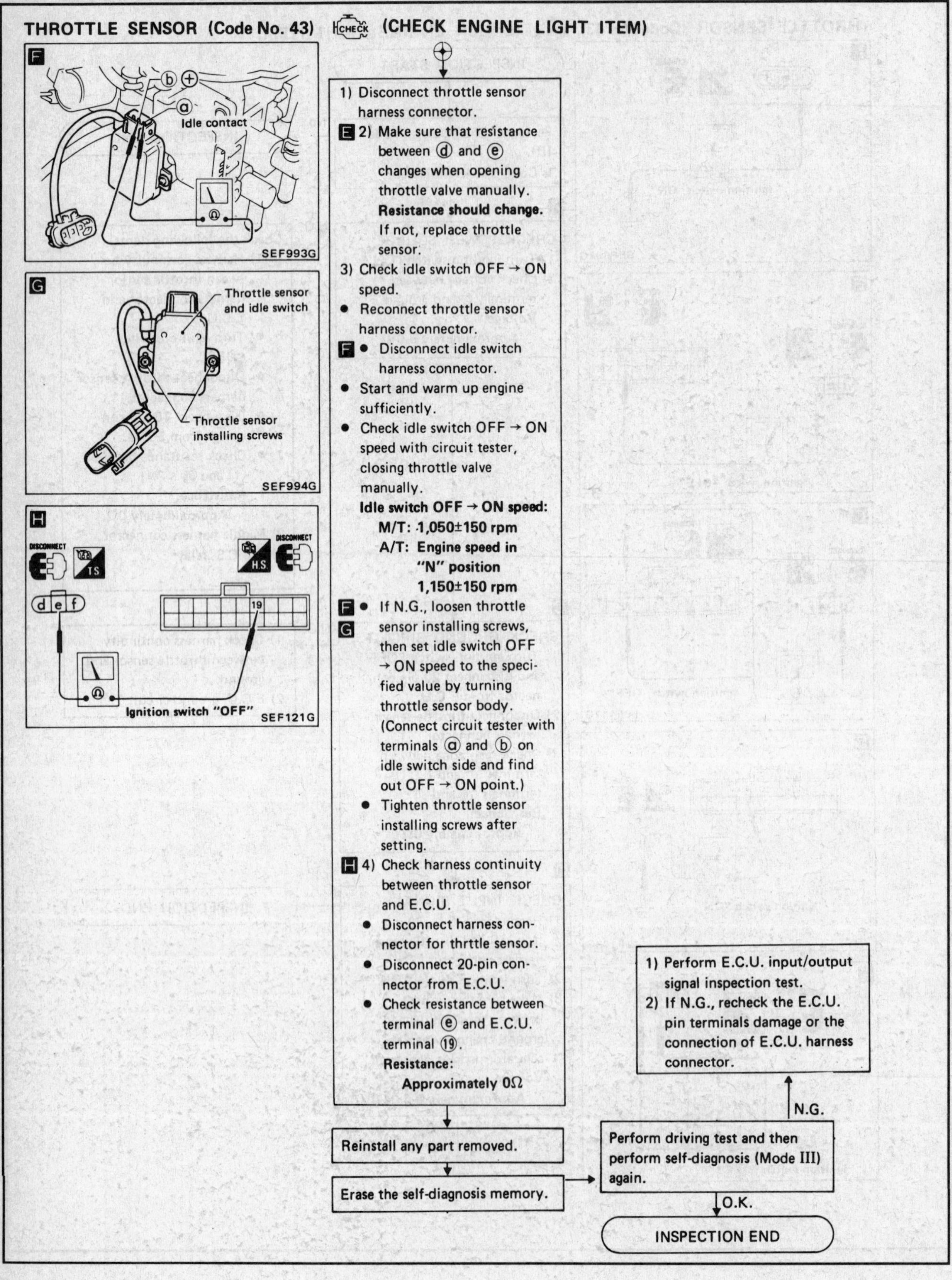
THROTTLE SENSOR (Code No. 43)
CHECK
(CHECK ENGINE LIGHT ITEM)
F
b
a
Idle contact
SEF993G
G
Throttle sensor and idle switch
Throttle sensor installing screws
SEF994G
H
DISCONNECT
TS
H.S.
d e f
19
Ignition switch "OFF"
SEF121G
1) Disconnect throttle sensor harness connector.
E 2) Make sure that resistance between ⓓ and ⓔ changes when opening throttle valve manually.
Resistance should change.
If not, replace throttle sensor.
3) Check idle switch OFF → ON speed.
● Reconnect throttle sensor harness connector.
F ● Disconnect idle switch harness connector.
● Start and warm up engine sufficiently.
● Check idle switch OFF → ON speed with circuit tester, closing throttle valve manually.
Idle switch OFF → ON speed:
M/T: 1,050±150 rpm
A/T: Engine speed in "N" position
1,150±150 rpm
F G ● If N.G., loosen throttle sensor installing screws, then set idle switch OFF → ON speed to the specified value by turning throttle sensor body.
(Connect circuit tester with terminals ⓐ and ⓑ on idle switch side and find out OFF → ON point.)
● Tighten throttle sensor installing screws after setting.
H 4) Check harness continuity between throttle sensor and E.C.U.
● Disconnect harness connector for thrttle sensor.
● Disconnect 20-pin connector from E.C.U.
● Check resistance between terminal ⓔ and E.C.U. terminal ⑲.
Resistance:
Approximately 0Ω
Reinstall any part removed.
Erase the self-diagnosis memory.
Perform driving test and then perform self-diagnosis (Mode III) again.
N.G.
1) Perform E.C.U. input/output signal inspection test.
2) If N.G., recheck the E.C.U. pin terminals damage or the connection of E.C.U. harness connector.
O.K.
INSPECTION END

CODE 45 (INJECTOR LEAK) — GA16i ENGINE

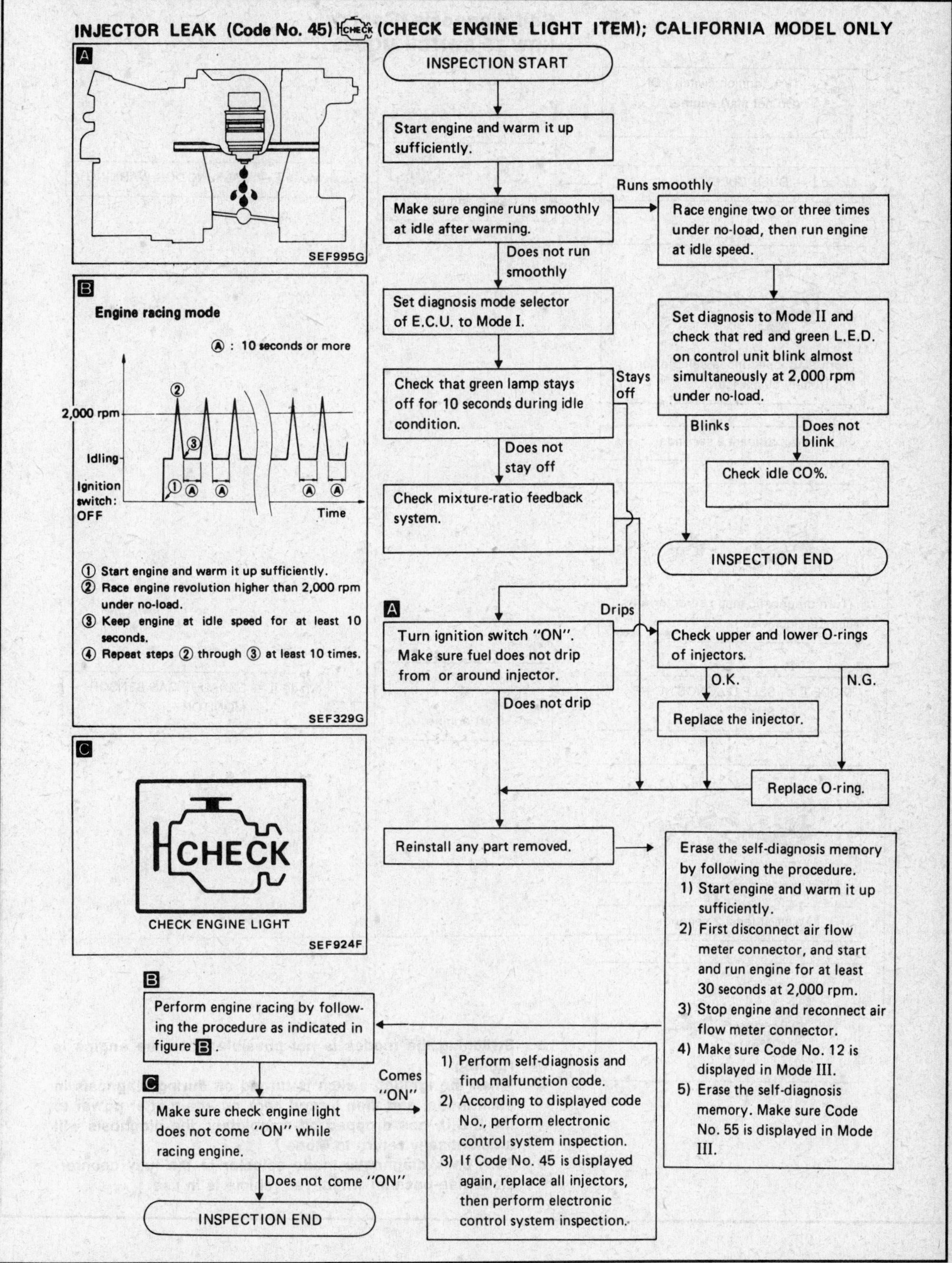
INJECTOR LEAK (Code No. 45) CHECK (CHECK ENGINE LIGHT ITEM); CALIFORNIA MODEL ONLY
A
SEF995G
B
Engine racing mode
Ⓐ : 10 seconds or more
2,000 rpm
Idling
Ignition switch: OFF
Time
① Start engine and warm it up sufficiently.
② Race engine revolution higher than 2,000 rpm under no-load.
③ Keep engine at idle speed for at least 10 seconds.
④ Repeat steps ② through ③ at least 10 times.
SEF329G
C
CHECK
CHECK ENGINE LIGHT
SEF924F
INSPECTION START
Start engine and warm it up sufficiently.
Make sure engine runs smoothly at idle after warming.
Runs smoothly
Race engine two or three times under no-load, then run engine at idle speed.
Does not run smoothly
Set diagnosis mode selector of E.C.U. to Mode I.
Set diagnosis to Mode II and check that red and green L.E.D. on control unit blink almost simultaneously at 2,000 rpm under no-load.
Check that green lamp stays off for 10 seconds during idle condition.
Stays off
Blinks
Does not blink
Does not stay off
Check idle CO%.
Check mixture-ratio feedback system.
INSPECTION END
A
Drips
Turn ignition switch "ON". Make sure fuel does not drip from or around injector.
Check upper and lower O-rings of injectors.
O.K.
N.G.
Does not drip
Replace the injector.
Replace O-ring.
Reinstall any part removed.
Erase the self-diagnosis memory by following the procedure.
1) Start engine and warm it up sufficiently.
2) First disconnect air flow meter connector, and start and run engine for at least 30 seconds at 2,000 rpm.
3) Stop engine and reconnect air flow meter connector.
4) Make sure Code No. 12 is displayed in Mode III.
5) Erase the self-diagnosis memory. Make sure Code No. 55 is displayed in Mode III.
B
Perform engine racing by following the procedure as indicated in figure B.
C
Make sure check engine light does not come "ON" while racing engine.
Comes "ON"
1) Perform self-diagnosis and find malfunction code.
2) According to displayed code No., perform electronic control system inspection.
3) If Code No. 45 is displayed again, replace all injectors, then perform electronic control system inspection.
Does not come "ON"
INSPECTION END

ENTERING SELF-DIAGNOSIS – GA16DE AND SR20DE ENGINES

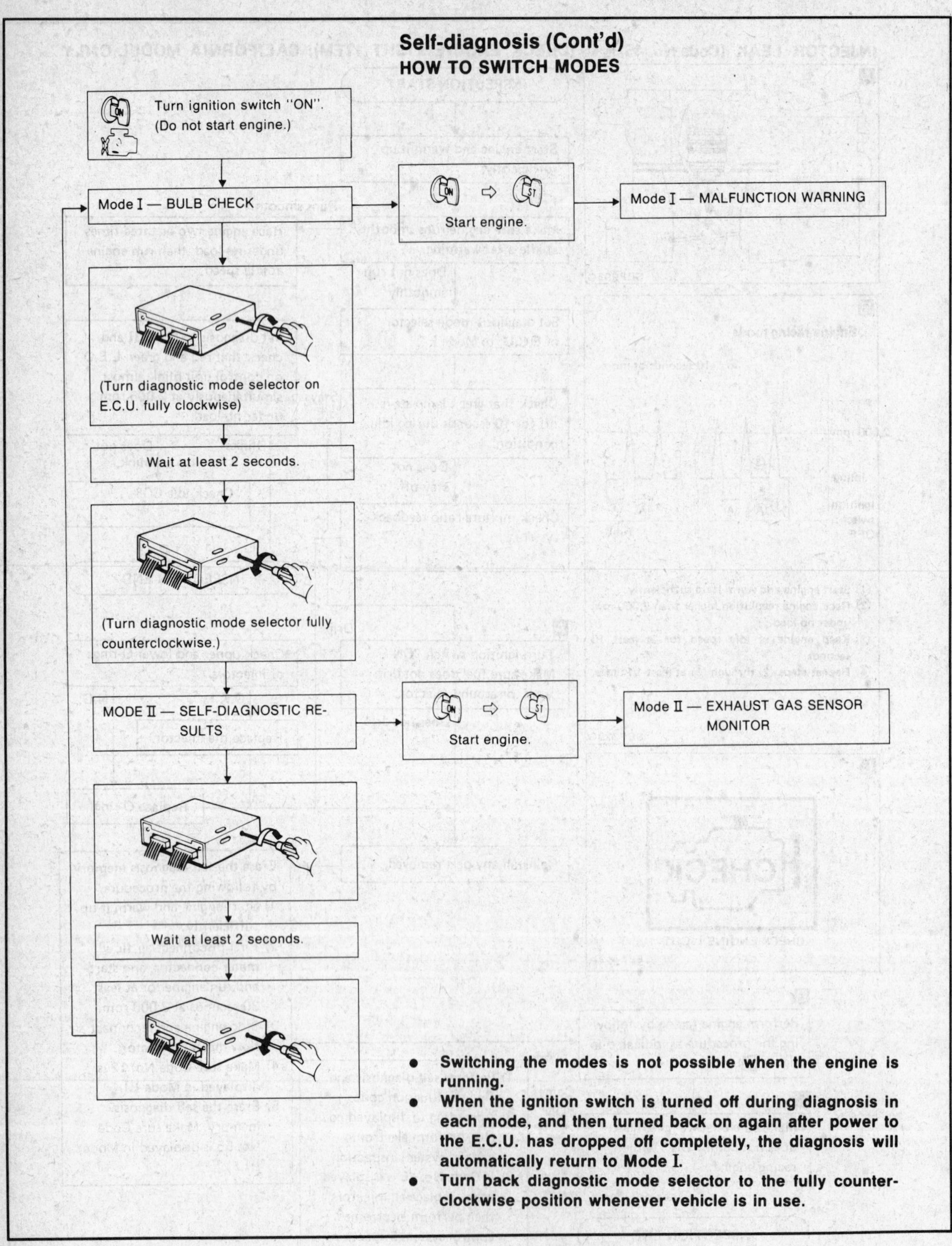
Self-diagnosis (Cont'd)
HOW TO SWITCH MODES
Turn ignition switch "ON".
(Do not start engine.)
Mode I — BULB CHECK
Start engine.
Mode I — MALFUNCTION WARNING
(Turn diagnostic mode selector on E.C.U. fully clockwise)
Wait at least 2 seconds.
(Turn diagnostic mode selector fully counterclockwise.)
MODE II — SELF-DIAGNOSTIC RESULTS
Start engine.
Mode II — EXHAUST GAS SENSOR MONITOR
Wait at least 2 seconds.
Switching the modes is not possible when the engine is running.
When the ignition switch is turned off during diagnosis in each mode, and then turned back on again after power to the E.C.U. has dropped off completely, the diagnosis will automatically return to Mode I.
Turn back diagnostic mode selector to the fully counter-clockwise position whenever vehicle is in use.

MAIN POWER SOURCE AND GROUND CIRCUIT GA16DE AND SR20DE ENGINES, PART 1

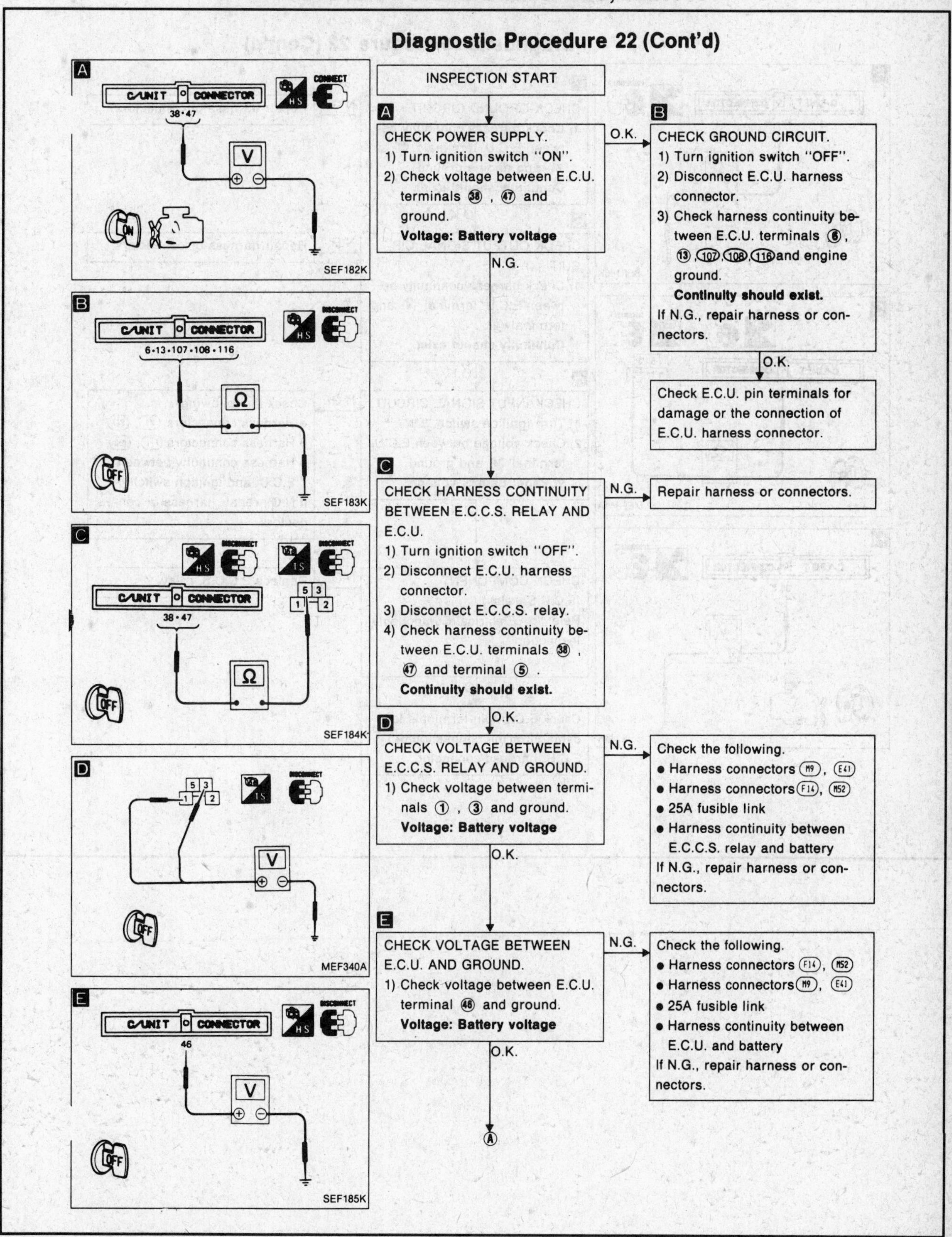

Diagnostic Procedure 22 (Cont'd)
A
C/UNIT CONNECTOR
38 · 47
HS
CONNECT
SEF182K
B
C/UNIT CONNECTOR
6 · 13 · 107 · 108 · 116
HS
DISCONNECT
SEF183K
C
C/UNIT CONNECTOR
38 · 47
HS
TS
DISCONNECT
SEF184K
D
TS
DISCONNECT
MEF340A
E
C/UNIT CONNECTOR
46
HS
DISCONNECT
SEF185K
INSPECTION START
A
CHECK POWER SUPPLY.
1) Turn ignition switch "ON".
2) Check voltage between E.C.U. terminals ㊳, ㊼ and ground.
Voltage: Battery voltage
O.K.
B
CHECK GROUND CIRCUIT.
1) Turn ignition switch "OFF".
2) Disconnect E.C.U. harness connector.
3) Check harness continuity between E.C.U. terminals ⑥, ⑬, 107, 108, 116 and engine ground.
Continuity should exist.
If N.G., repair harness or connectors.
O.K.
Check E.C.U. pin terminals for damage or the connection of E.C.U. harness connector.
N.G.
C
CHECK HARNESS CONTINUITY BETWEEN E.C.C.S. RELAY AND E.C.U.
1) Turn ignition switch "OFF".
2) Disconnect E.C.U. harness connector.
3) Disconnect E.C.C.S. relay.
4) Check harness continuity between E.C.U. terminals ㊳, ㊼ and terminal ⑤.
Continuity should exist.
N.G.
Repair harness or connectors.
O.K.
D
CHECK VOLTAGE BETWEEN E.C.C.S. RELAY AND GROUND.
1) Check voltage between terminals ①, ③ and ground.
Voltage: Battery voltage
N.G.
Check the following.
• Harness connectors M9, E41
• Harness connectors F14, M52
• 25A fusible link
• Harness continuity between E.C.C.S. relay and battery
If N.G., repair harness or connectors.
O.K.
E
CHECK VOLTAGE BETWEEN E.C.U. AND GROUND.
1) Check voltage between E.C.U. terminal ㊻ and ground.
Voltage: Battery voltage
N.G.
Check the following.
• Harness connectors F14, M52
• Harness connectors M9, E41
• 25A fusible link
• Harness continuity between E.C.U. and battery
If N.G., repair harness or connectors.
O.K.
Ⓐ

MAIN POWER SOURCE AND GROUND CIRCUIT GA16DE AND SR20DE ENGINES, PART 2

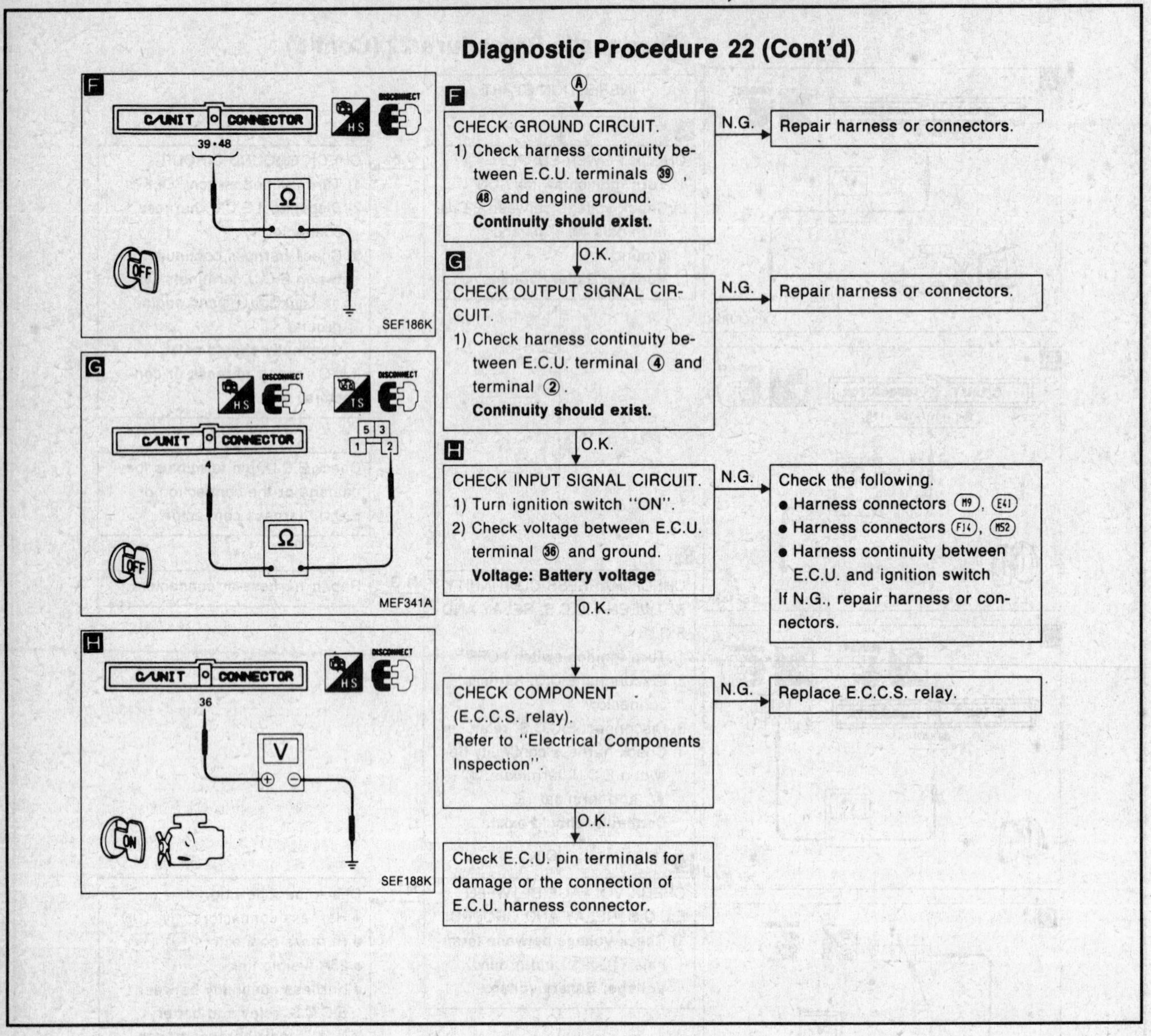
Diagnostic Procedure 22 (Cont'd)
F
C/UNIT CONNECTOR
DISCONNECT
HS
39 • 48
Ω
OFF
SEF186K
G
C/UNIT CONNECTOR
DISCONNECT
HS
TS
5 3
1 2
4
Ω
OFF
MEF341A
H
C/UNIT CONNECTOR
DISCONNECT
HS
36
V
ON
SEF188K
A
F
CHECK GROUND CIRCUIT.
1) Check harness continuity between E.C.U. terminals 39, 48 and engine ground.
Continuity should exist.
N.G.
Repair harness or connectors.
O.K.
G
CHECK OUTPUT SIGNAL CIRCUIT.
1) Check harness continuity between E.C.U. terminal 4 and terminal 2.
Continuity should exist.
N.G.
Repair harness or connectors.
O.K.
H
CHECK INPUT SIGNAL CIRCUIT.
1) Turn ignition switch "ON".
2) Check voltage between E.C.U. terminal 36 and ground.
Voltage: Battery voltage
N.G.
Check the following.
• Harness connectors M9, E41
• Harness connectors F14, M52
• Harness continuity between E.C.U. and ignition switch
If N.G., repair harness or connectors.
O.K.
CHECK COMPONENT (E.C.C.S. relay).
Refer to "Electrical Components Inspection".
N.G.
Replace E.C.C.S. relay.
O.K.
Check E.C.U. pin terminals for damage or the connection of E.C.U. harness connector.

CODE 11 (CRANK ANGLE SENSOR) – GA16DE AND SR20DE ENGINES

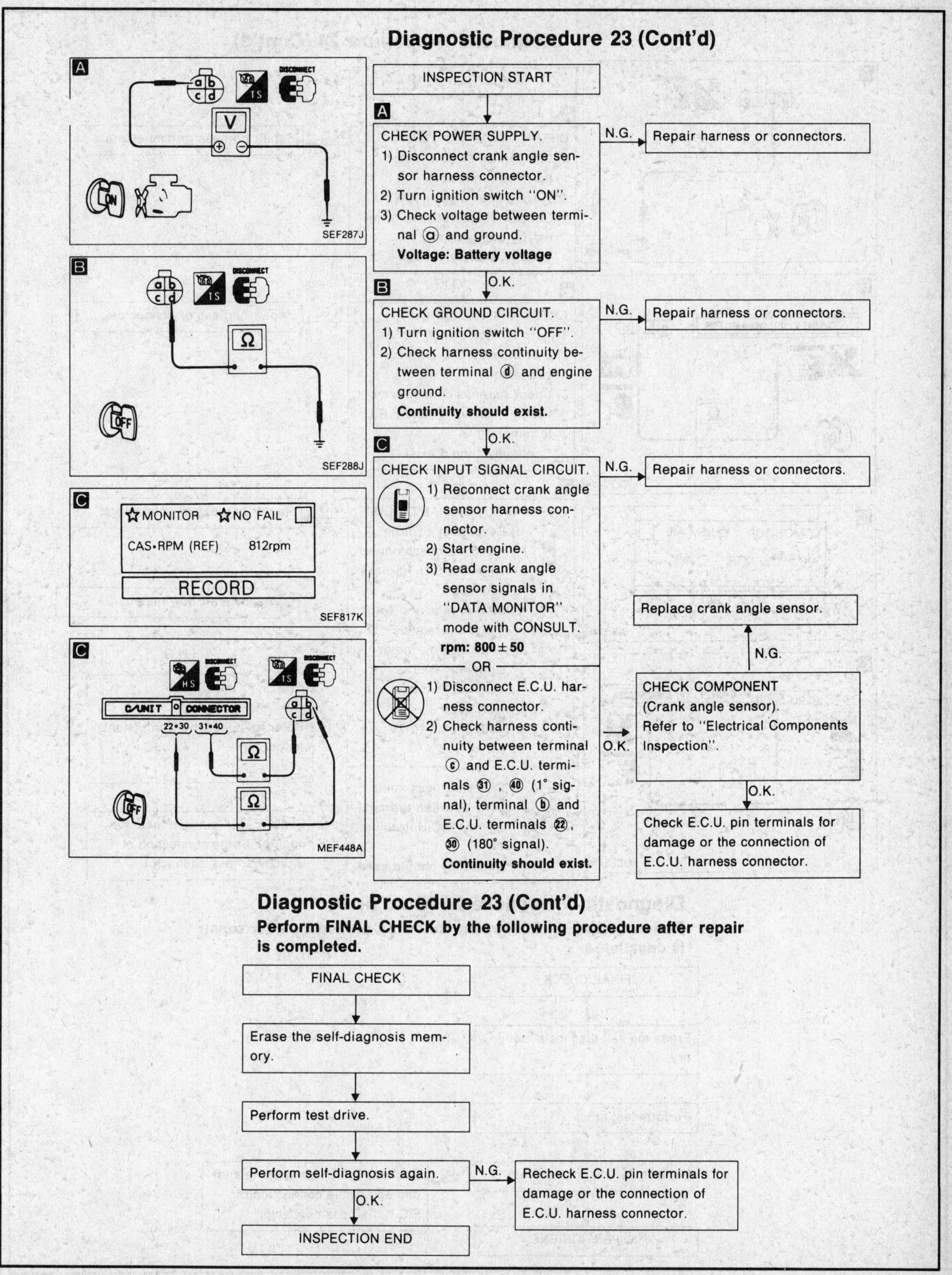
Diagnostic Procedure 23 (Cont'd)
A
DISCONNECT
TS
V
ON
SEF287J
B
DISCONNECT
TS
Ω
OFF
SEF288J
C
☆MONITOR ☆NO FAIL
CAS•RPM (REF) 812rpm
RECORD
SEF817K
C
DISCONNECT
HS
TS
C/UNIT CONNECTOR
22•30 31•40
Ω
Ω
OFF
MEF448A
INSPECTION START
A
CHECK POWER SUPPLY.
1) Disconnect crank angle sensor harness connector.
2) Turn ignition switch "ON".
3) Check voltage between terminal ⓐ and ground.
Voltage: Battery voltage
N.G.
Repair harness or connectors.
O.K.
B
CHECK GROUND CIRCUIT.
1) Turn ignition switch "OFF".
2) Check harness continuity between terminal ⓓ and engine ground.
Continuity should exist.
N.G.
Repair harness or connectors.
O.K.
C
CHECK INPUT SIGNAL CIRCUIT.
1) Reconnect crank angle sensor harness connector.
2) Start engine.
3) Read crank angle sensor signals in "DATA MONITOR" mode with CONSULT.
rpm: 800 ± 50
OR
1) Disconnect E.C.U. harness connector.
2) Check harness continuity between terminal ⓒ and E.C.U. terminals ㉛, ㊵ (1° signal), terminal ⓑ and E.C.U. terminals ㉒, ㉚ (180° signal).
Continuity should exist.
N.G.
Repair harness or connectors.
O.K.
CHECK COMPONENT
(Crank angle sensor).
Refer to "Electrical Components Inspection".
N.G.
Replace crank angle sensor.
O.K.
Check E.C.U. pin terminals for damage or the connection of E.C.U. harness connector.
Diagnostic Procedure 23 (Cont'd)
Perform FINAL CHECK by the following procedure after repair is completed.
FINAL CHECK
Erase the self-diagnosis memory.
Perform test drive.
Perform self-diagnosis again.
N.G.
Recheck E.C.U. pin terminals for damage or the connection of E.C.U. harness connector.
O.K.
INSPECTION END

CODE 12 (AIR FLOW METER) – GA16DE AND SR20DE ENGINES

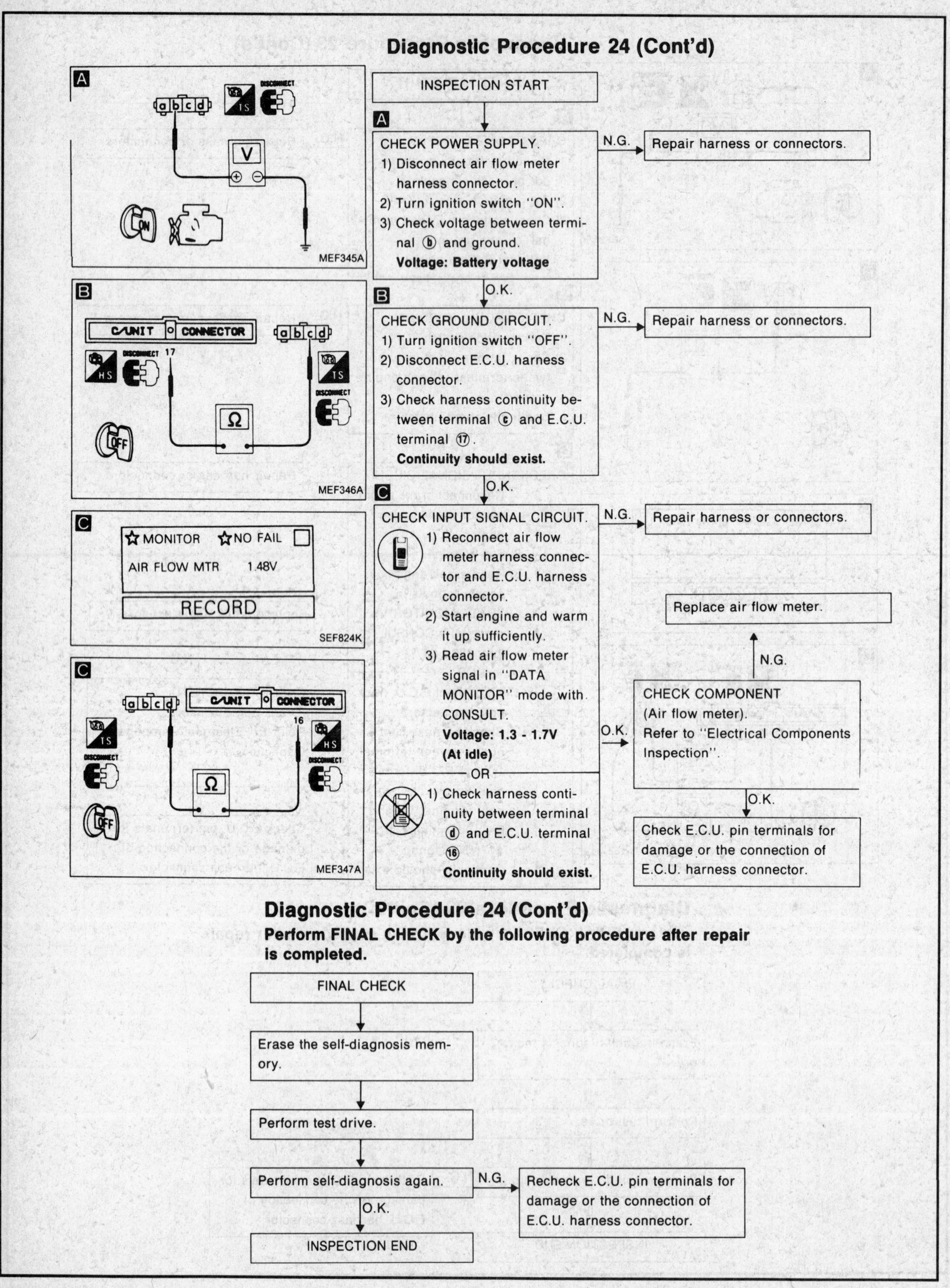
Diagnostic Procedure 24 (Cont'd)
INSPECTION START
A
CHECK POWER SUPPLY.
1) Disconnect air flow meter harness connector.
2) Turn ignition switch "ON".
3) Check voltage between terminal ⓑ and ground.
Voltage: Battery voltage
N.G.
Repair harness or connectors.
O.K.
B
CHECK GROUND CIRCUIT.
1) Turn ignition switch "OFF".
2) Disconnect E.C.U. harness connector.
3) Check harness continuity between terminal ⓒ and E.C.U. terminal ⑰.
Continuity should exist.
N.G.
Repair harness or connectors.
O.K.
C
CHECK INPUT SIGNAL CIRCUIT.
1) Reconnect air flow meter harness connector and E.C.U. harness connector.
2) Start engine and warm it up sufficiently.
3) Read air flow meter signal in "DATA MONITOR" mode with CONSULT.
Voltage: 1.3 - 1.7V (At idle)
OR
1) Check harness continuity between terminal ⓓ and E.C.U. terminal ⑯
Continuity should exist.
N.G.
Repair harness or connectors.
O.K.
CHECK COMPONENT (Air flow meter). Refer to "Electrical Components Inspection".
N.G.
Replace air flow meter.
O.K.
Check E.C.U. pin terminals for damage or the connection of E.C.U. harness connector.
A
a b c d
DISCONNECT
TS
V
ON
MEF345A
B
C/UNIT CONNECTOR
a b c d
HS
TS
DISCONNECT
17
Ω
OFF
MEF346A
C
MONITOR
NO FAIL
AIR FLOW MTR 1.48V
RECORD
SEF824K
C
a b c d
C/UNIT CONNECTOR
16
TS
HS
DISCONNECT
Ω
OFF
MEF347A
Diagnostic Procedure 24 (Cont'd)
Perform FINAL CHECK by the following procedure after repair is completed.
FINAL CHECK
Erase the self-diagnosis memory.
Perform test drive.
Perform self-diagnosis again.
N.G.
Recheck E.C.U. pin terminals for damage or the connection of E.C.U. harness connector.
O.K.
INSPECTION END

CODE 13 (WATER TEMPERATURE SENSOR) – GA16DE AND SR20DE ENGINES

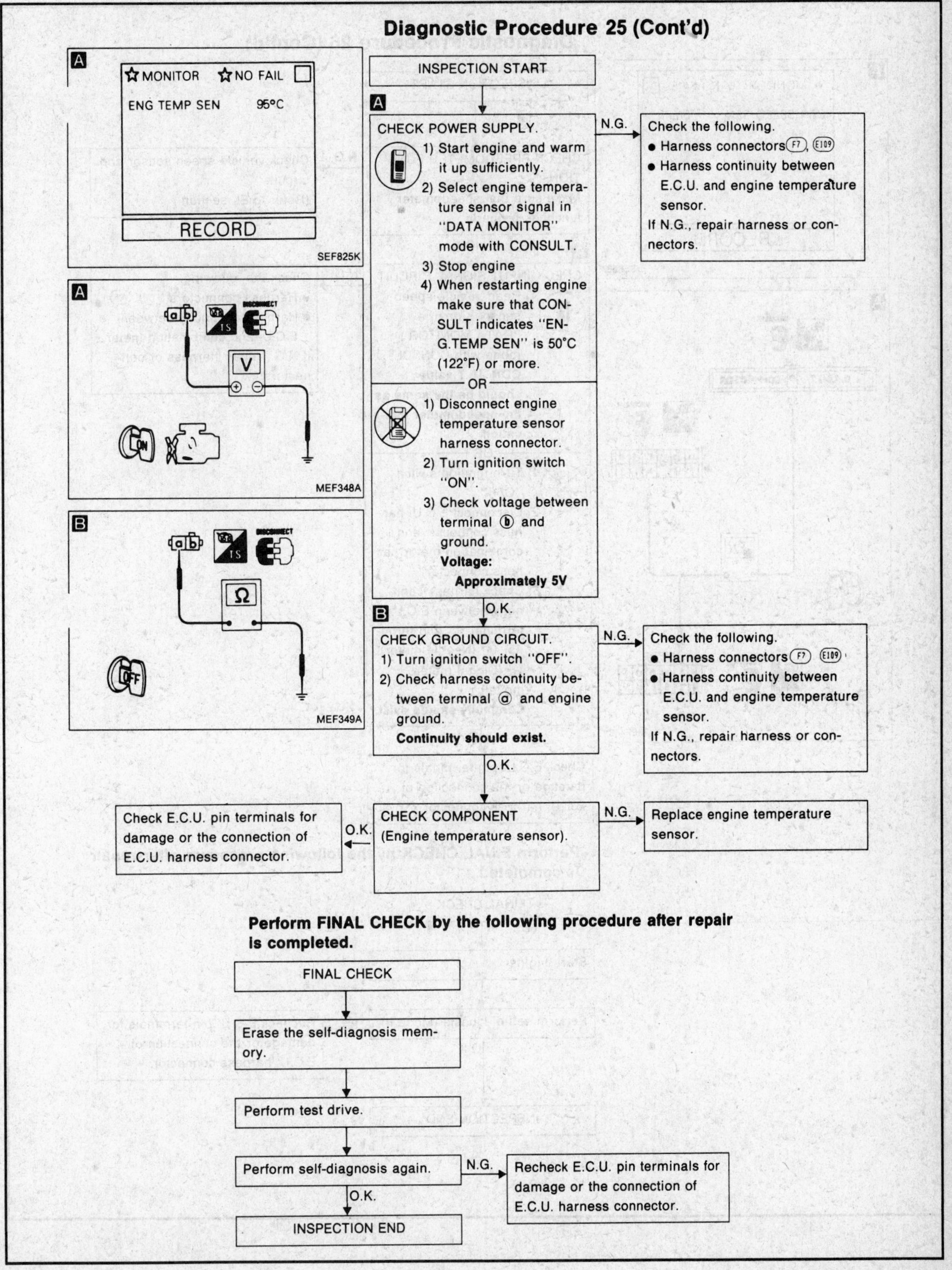

Diagnostic Procedure 25 (Cont'd)
A
☆MONITOR ☆NO FAIL
ENG TEMP SEN 95°C
RECORD
SEF825K
A
DISCONNECT
V
ON
MEF348A
B
DISCONNECT
Ω
OFF
MEF349A
INSPECTION START
A
CHECK POWER SUPPLY.
1) Start engine and warm it up sufficiently.
2) Select engine temperature sensor signal in "DATA MONITOR" mode with CONSULT.
3) Stop engine
4) When restarting engine make sure that CONSULT indicates "ENG.TEMP SEN" is 50°C (122°F) or more.
OR
1) Disconnect engine temperature sensor harness connector.
2) Turn ignition switch "ON".
3) Check voltage between terminal ⓑ and ground.
Voltage:
Approximately 5V
N.G.
Check the following.
• Harness connectors (F7), (E109)
• Harness continuity between E.C.U. and engine temperature sensor.
If N.G., repair harness or connectors.
O.K.
B
CHECK GROUND CIRCUIT.
1) Turn ignition switch "OFF".
2) Check harness continuity between terminal ⓐ and engine ground.
Continuity should exist.
N.G.
Check the following.
• Harness connectors (F7) (E109)
• Harness continuity between E.C.U. and engine temperature sensor.
If N.G., repair harness or connectors.
O.K.
CHECK COMPONENT
(Engine temperature sensor).
N.G.
Replace engine temperature sensor.
O.K.
Check E.C.U. pin terminals for damage or the connection of E.C.U. harness connector.
Perform FINAL CHECK by the following procedure after repair is completed.
FINAL CHECK
Erase the self-diagnosis memory.
Perform test drive.
Perform self-diagnosis again.
N.G.
Recheck E.C.U. pin terminals for damage or the connection of E.C.U. harness connector.
O.K.
INSPECTION END

CODE 14 (VEHICLE SPEED SENSOR) – GA16DE AND SR20DE ENGINES

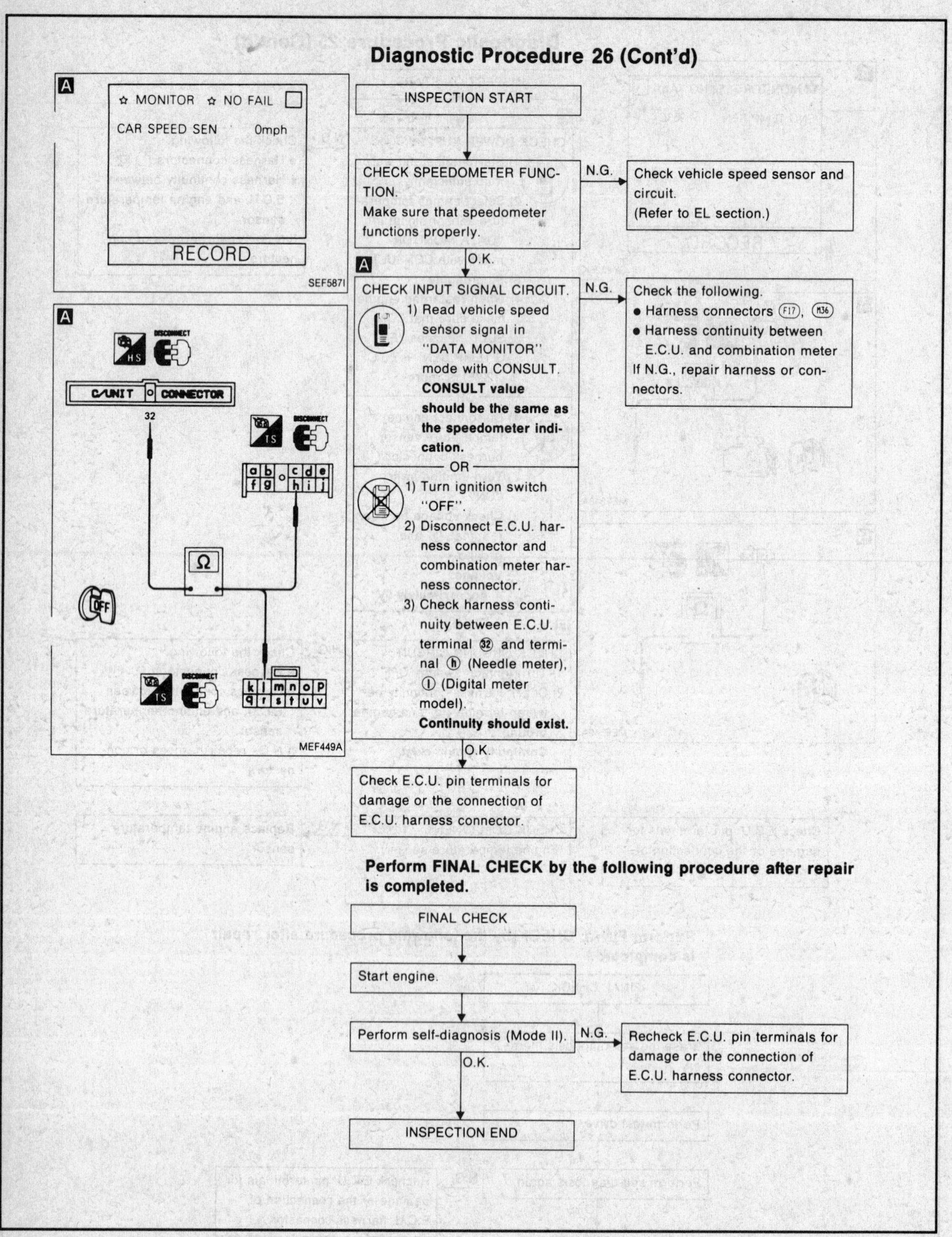
Diagnostic Procedure 26 (Cont'd)
A
☆ MONITOR ☆ NO FAIL
CAR SPEED SEN 0mph
RECORD
SEF587I
A
DISCONNECT
HS
C/UNIT CONNECTOR
32
TS
a b c d e
f g h i j
Ω
OFF
k l m n o p
q r s t u v
MEF449A
INSPECTION START
CHECK SPEEDOMETER FUNCTION.
Make sure that speedometer functions properly.
N.G.
Check vehicle speed sensor and circuit.
(Refer to EL section.)
O.K.
A
CHECK INPUT SIGNAL CIRCUIT.
1) Read vehicle speed sensor signal in "DATA MONITOR" mode with CONSULT.
CONSULT value should be the same as the speedometer indication.
OR
1) Turn ignition switch "OFF".
2) Disconnect E.C.U. harness connector and combination meter harness connector.
3) Check harness continuity between E.C.U. terminal ㉜ and terminal ⓗ (Needle meter), ⓘ (Digital meter model).
Continuity should exist.
N.G.
Check the following.
• Harness connectors F17, M36
• Harness continuity between E.C.U. and combination meter
If N.G., repair harness or connectors.
O.K.
Check E.C.U. pin terminals for damage or the connection of E.C.U. harness connector.
Perform FINAL CHECK by the following procedure after repair is completed.
FINAL CHECK
Start engine.
Perform self-diagnosis (Mode II).
N.G.
Recheck E.C.U. pin terminals for damage or the connection of E.C.U. harness connector.
O.K.
INSPECTION END

CODE 21 (IGNITION SIGNAL) – GA16DE AND SR20DE ENGINES, PART 1

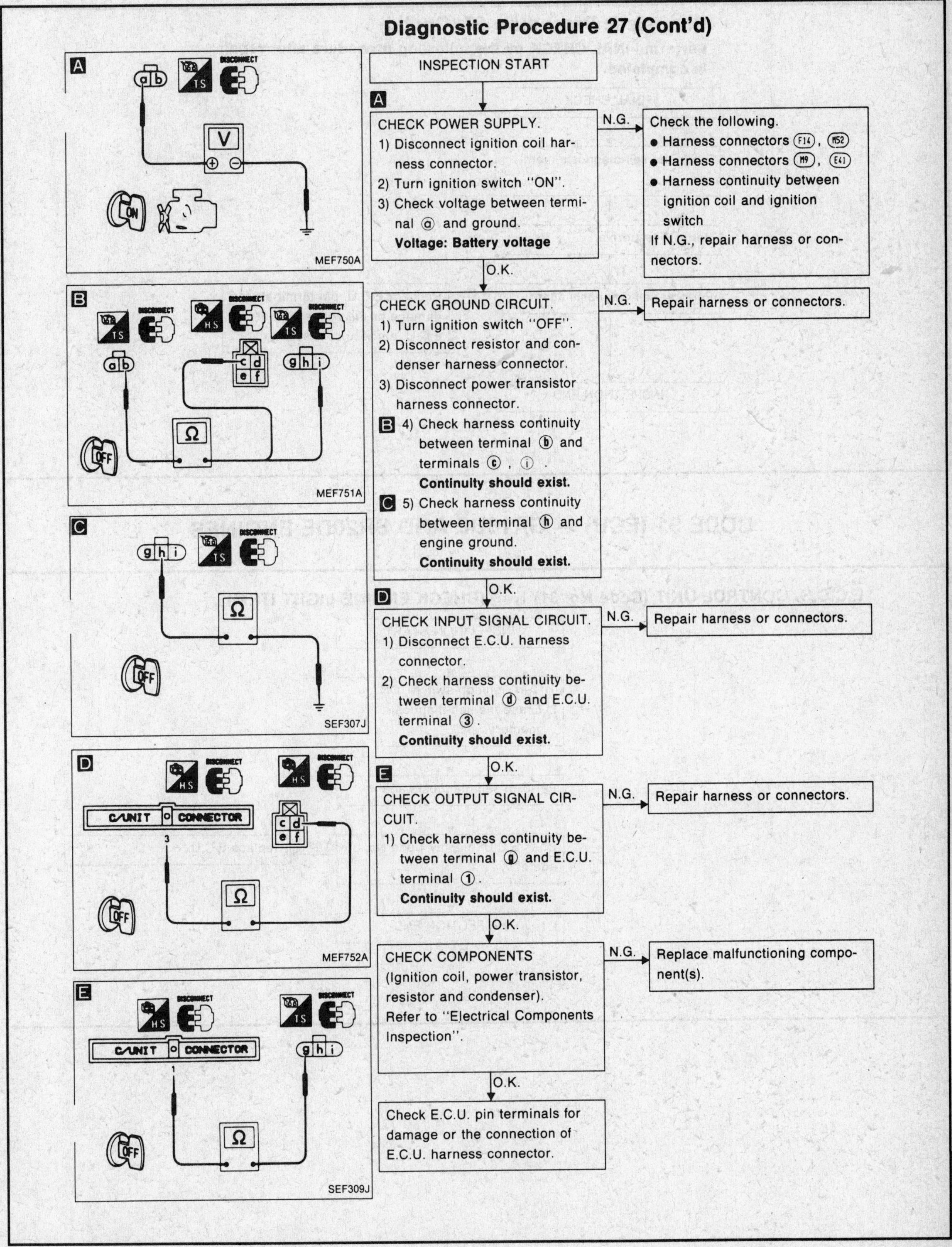
Diagnostic Procedure 27 (Cont'd)
A
DISCONNECT
TS
a b
V
ON
MEF750A
B
DISCONNECT
TS
HS
a b
c d
e f
g h i
OFF
MEF751A
C
DISCONNECT
TS
g h i
OFF
SEF307J
D
DISCONNECT
HS
C/UNIT CONNECTOR
3
c d
e f
OFF
MEF752A
E
DISCONNECT
HS
TS
C/UNIT CONNECTOR
1
g h i
OFF
SEF309J
INSPECTION START
A
CHECK POWER SUPPLY.
1) Disconnect ignition coil harness connector.
2) Turn ignition switch "ON".
3) Check voltage between terminal (a) and ground.
Voltage: Battery voltage
N.G.
Check the following.
• Harness connectors (F14), (M52)
• Harness connectors (M9), (E41)
• Harness continuity between ignition coil and ignition switch
If N.G., repair harness or connectors.
O.K.
CHECK GROUND CIRCUIT.
1) Turn ignition switch "OFF".
2) Disconnect resistor and condenser harness connector.
3) Disconnect power transistor harness connector.
B 4) Check harness continuity between terminal (b) and terminals (c), (i).
Continuity should exist.
C 5) Check harness continuity between terminal (h) and engine ground.
Continuity should exist.
N.G.
Repair harness or connectors.
O.K.
D
CHECK INPUT SIGNAL CIRCUIT.
1) Disconnect E.C.U. harness connector.
2) Check harness continuity between terminal (d) and E.C.U. terminal (3).
Continuity should exist.
N.G.
Repair harness or connectors.
O.K.
E
CHECK OUTPUT SIGNAL CIRCUIT.
1) Check harness continuity between terminal (g) and E.C.U. terminal (1).
Continuity should exist.
N.G.
Repair harness or connectors.
O.K.
CHECK COMPONENTS (Ignition coil, power transistor, resistor and condenser). Refer to "Electrical Components Inspection".
N.G.
Replace malfunctioning component(s).
O.K.
Check E.C.U. pin terminals for damage or the connection of E.C.U. harness connector.

CODE 21 (IGNITION SIGNAL) – GA16DE AND SR20DE ENGINES, PART 2

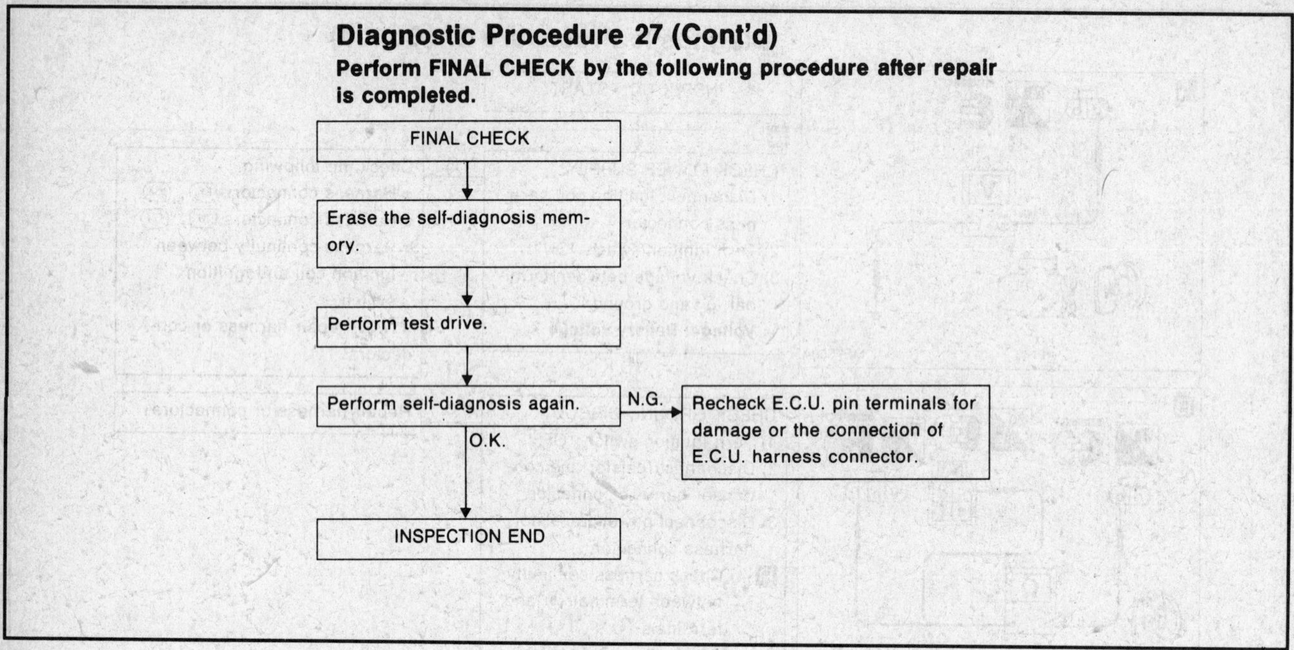
Diagnostic Procedure 27 (Cont'd)
Perform FINAL CHECK by the following procedure after repair is completed.
FINAL CHECK
Erase the self-diagnosis memory.
Perform test drive.
Perform self-diagnosis again.
N.G.
Recheck E.C.U. pin terminals for damage or the connection of E.C.U. harness connector.
O.K.
INSPECTION END

CODE 31 (ECU) – GA16DE AND SR20DE ENGINES

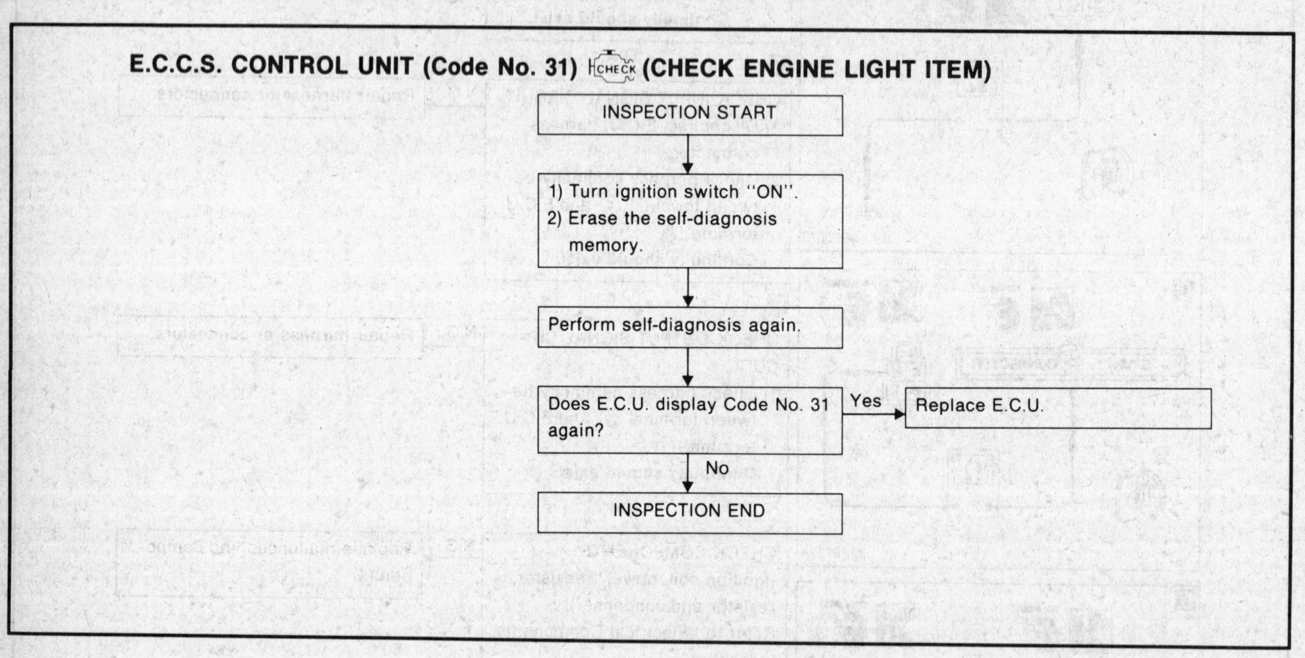
E.C.C.S. CONTROL UNIT (Code No. 31) CHECK (CHECK ENGINE LIGHT ITEM)
INSPECTION START
1) Turn ignition switch "ON".
2) Erase the self-diagnosis memory.
Perform self-diagnosis again.
Does E.C.U. display Code No. 31 again?
Yes
Replace E.C.U.
No
INSPECTION END

CODE 32 (EGR FUNCTION) – GA16DE AND SR20DE CALIFORNIA ENGINES, PART 1

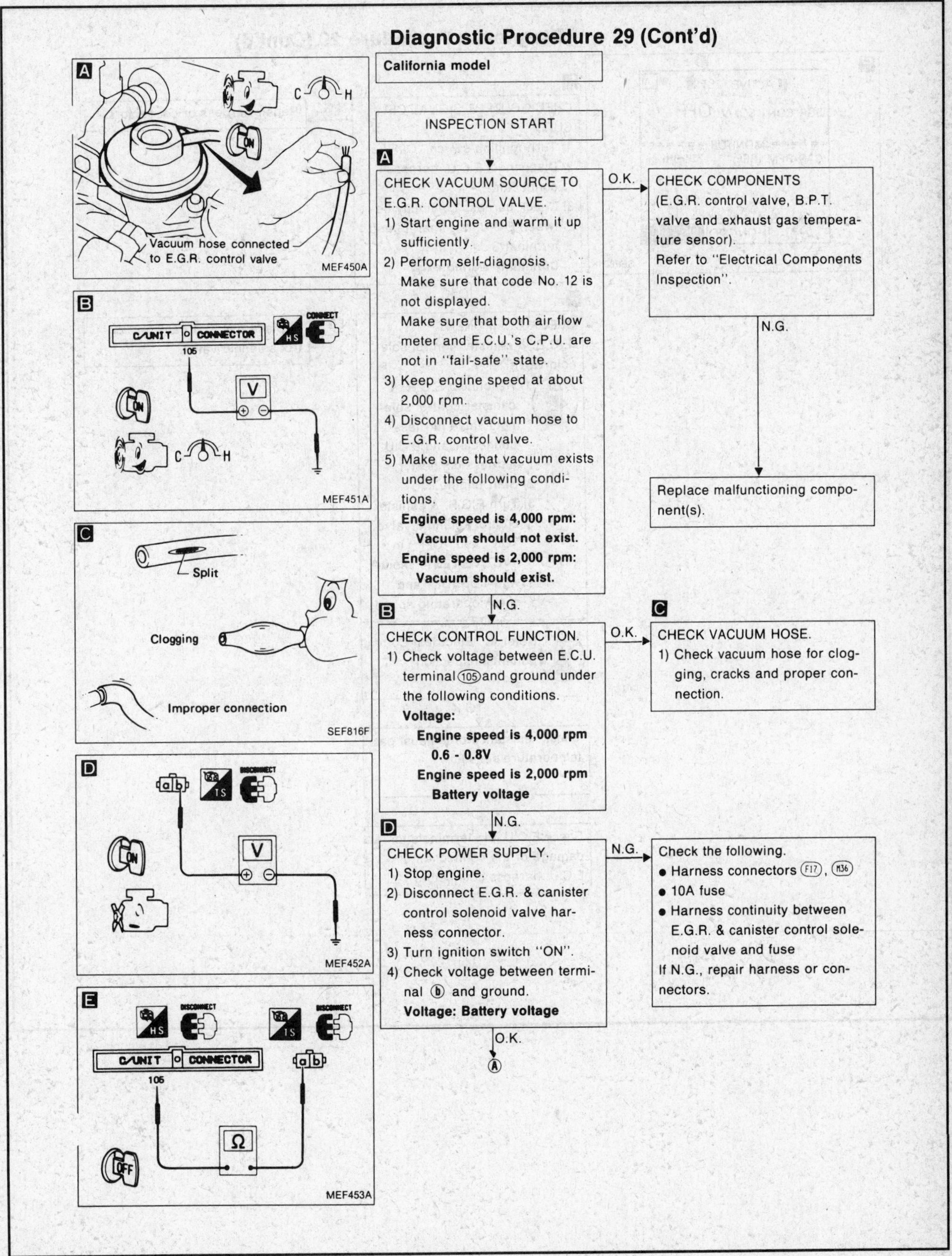
Diagnostic Procedure 29 (Cont'd)
California model
INSPECTION START
A
CHECK VACUUM SOURCE TO E.G.R. CONTROL VALVE.
1) Start engine and warm it up sufficiently.
2) Perform self-diagnosis. Make sure that code No. 12 is not displayed. Make sure that both air flow meter and E.C.U.'s C.P.U. are not in "fail-safe" state.
3) Keep engine speed at about 2,000 rpm.
4) Disconnect vacuum hose to E.G.R. control valve.
5) Make sure that vacuum exists under the following conditions.
Engine speed is 4,000 rpm: Vacuum should not exist.
Engine speed is 2,000 rpm: Vacuum should exist.
O.K.
CHECK COMPONENTS (E.G.R. control valve, B.P.T. valve and exhaust gas temperature sensor). Refer to "Electrical Components Inspection".
N.G.
Replace malfunctioning component(s).
N.G.
B
CHECK CONTROL FUNCTION.
1) Check voltage between E.C.U. terminal (105) and ground under the following conditions.
Voltage:
Engine speed is 4,000 rpm 0.6 - 0.8V
Engine speed is 2,000 rpm Battery voltage
O.K.
C
CHECK VACUUM HOSE.
1) Check vacuum hose for clogging, cracks and proper connection.
N.G.
D
CHECK POWER SUPPLY.
1) Stop engine.
2) Disconnect E.G.R. & canister control solenoid valve harness connector.
3) Turn ignition switch "ON".
4) Check voltage between terminal ⓑ and ground.
Voltage: Battery voltage
N.G.
Check the following.
• Harness connectors (F17), (M36)
• 10A fuse
• Harness continuity between E.G.R. & canister control solenoid valve and fuse
If N.G., repair harness or connectors.
O.K.
Ⓐ
A
C H
ON
Vacuum hose connected to E.G.R. control valve
MEF450A
B
C/UNIT CONNECTOR
105
CONNECT
HS
V
ON
C H
MEF451A
C
Split
Clogging
Improper connection
SEF816F
D
a b
TS
DISCONNECT
V
ON
MEF452A
E
HS
DISCONNECT
TS
DISCONNECT
C/UNIT CONNECTOR
105
a b
Ω
OFF
MEF453A

CODE 32 (EGR FUNCTION) – GA16DE AND SR20DE CALIFORNIA ENGINES, PART 2

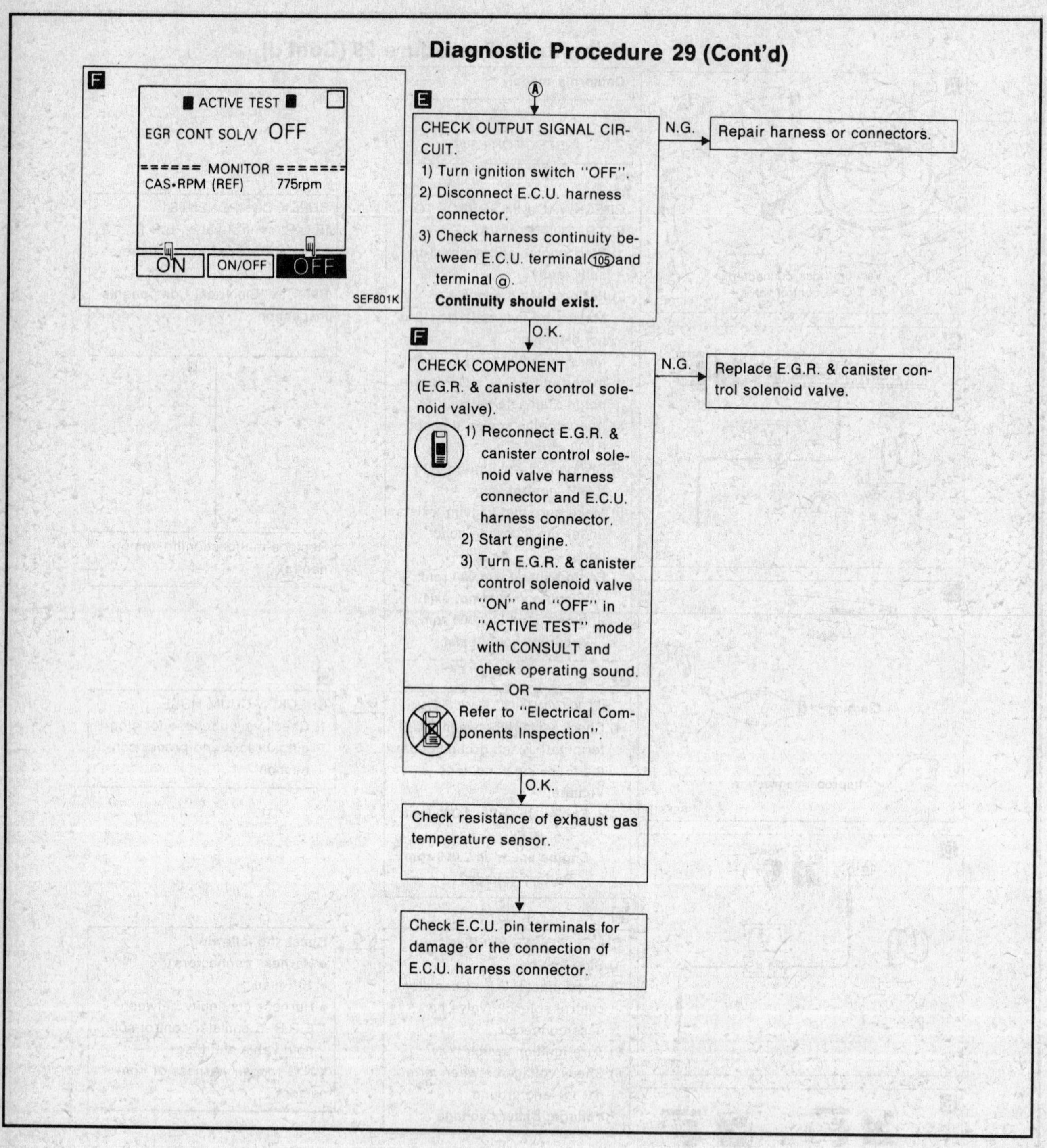
Diagnostic Procedure 29 (Cont'd)
F
ACTIVE TEST
EGR CONT SOL/V OFF
====== MONITOR ======
CAS•RPM (REF) 775rpm
ON
ON/OFF
OFF
SEF801K
A
E
CHECK OUTPUT SIGNAL CIRCUIT.
1) Turn ignition switch "OFF".
2) Disconnect E.C.U. harness connector.
3) Check harness continuity between E.C.U. terminal 105 and terminal a.
Continuity should exist.
N.G.
Repair harness or connectors.
O.K.
F
CHECK COMPONENT (E.G.R. & canister control solenoid valve).
1) Reconnect E.G.R. & canister control solenoid valve harness connector and E.C.U. harness connector.
2) Start engine.
3) Turn E.G.R. & canister control solenoid valve "ON" and "OFF" in "ACTIVE TEST" mode with CONSULT and check operating sound.
OR
Refer to "Electrical Components Inspection".
N.G.
Replace E.G.R. & canister control solenoid valve.
O.K.
Check resistance of exhaust gas temperature sensor.
Check E.C.U. pin terminals for damage or the connection of E.C.U. harness connector.

CODE 32 (EGR FUNCTION) – GA16DE AND SR20DE CALIFORNIA ENGINES, PART 3

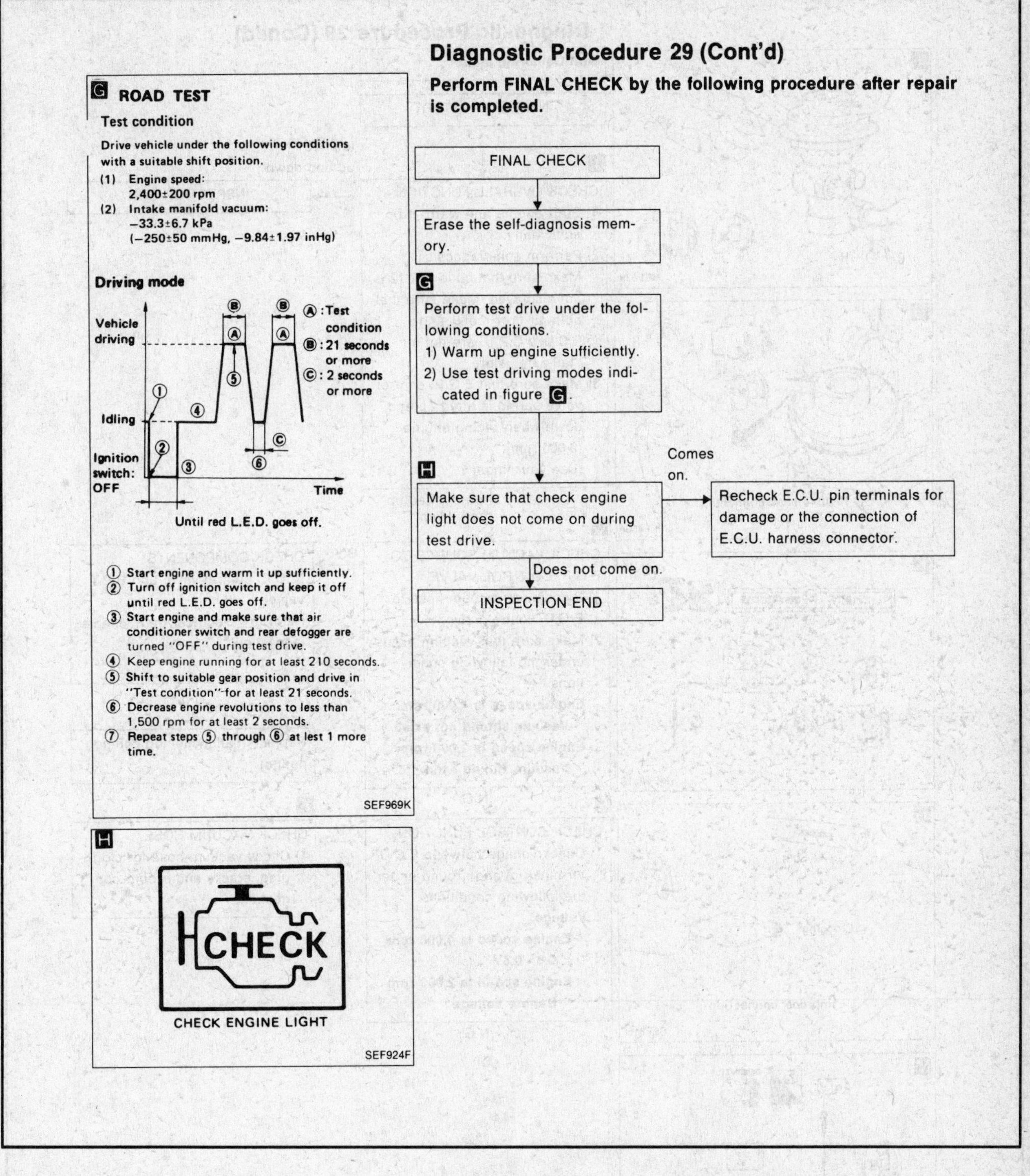

Diagnostic Procedure 29 (Cont'd)

Perform FINAL CHECK by the following procedure after repair is completed.

FINAL CHECK

↓

Erase the self-diagnosis memory.

↓ G

Perform test drive under the following conditions.
1) Warm up engine sufficiently.
2) Use test driving modes indicated in figure G.

↓ H

Make sure that check engine light does not come on during test drive.

- Comes on. → Recheck E.C.U. pin terminals for damage or the connection of E.C.U. harness connector.
- Does not come on. → INSPECTION END

G ROAD TEST

Test condition

Drive vehicle under the following conditions with a suitable shift position.

(1) Engine speed: 2,400±200 rpm
(2) Intake manifold vacuum: −33.3±6.7 kPa (−250±50 mmHg, −9.84±1.97 inHg)

Driving mode

Vehicle driving
Idling
Ignition switch: OFF
Time
Ⓐ: Test condition
Ⓑ: 21 seconds or more
Ⓒ: 2 seconds or more
Until red L.E.D. goes off.

① Start engine and warm it up sufficiently.
② Turn off ignition switch and keep it off until red L.E.D. goes off.
③ Start engine and make sure that air conditioner switch and rear defogger are turned "OFF" during test drive.
④ Keep engine running for at least 210 seconds.
⑤ Shift to suitable gear position and drive in "Test condition" for at least 21 seconds.
⑥ Decrease engine revolutions to less than 1,500 rpm for at least 2 seconds.
⑦ Repeat steps ⑤ through ⑥ at lest 1 more time.

SEF969K

H

CHECK

CHECK ENGINE LIGHT

SEF924F

EGR DIAGNOSTIC CHART – GA16DE AND SR20DE FEDERAL ENGINES, PART 1

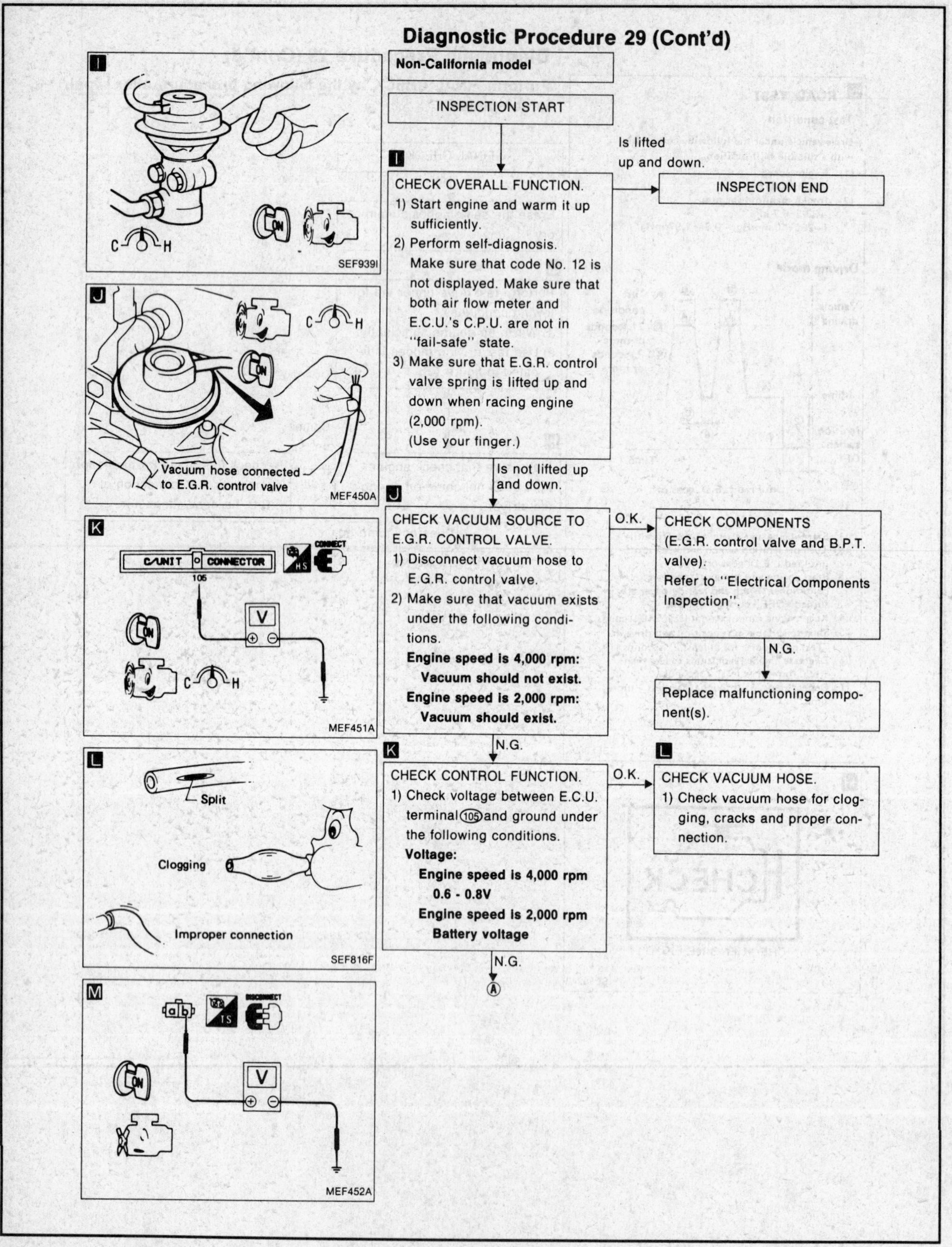

Diagnostic Procedure 29 (Cont'd)
Non-California model
INSPECTION START
I
CHECK OVERALL FUNCTION.
1) Start engine and warm it up sufficiently.
2) Perform self-diagnosis. Make sure that code No. 12 is not displayed. Make sure that both air flow meter and E.C.U.'s C.P.U. are not in "fail-safe" state.
3) Make sure that E.G.R. control valve spring is lifted up and down when racing engine (2,000 rpm). (Use your finger.)
Is lifted up and down.
INSPECTION END
Is not lifted up and down.
J
CHECK VACUUM SOURCE TO E.G.R. CONTROL VALVE.
1) Disconnect vacuum hose to E.G.R. control valve.
2) Make sure that vacuum exists under the following conditions.
Engine speed is 4,000 rpm: Vacuum should not exist.
Engine speed is 2,000 rpm: Vacuum should exist.
O.K.
CHECK COMPONENTS (E.G.R. control valve and B.P.T. valve). Refer to "Electrical Components Inspection".
N.G.
Replace malfunctioning component(s).
N.G.
K
CHECK CONTROL FUNCTION.
1) Check voltage between E.C.U. terminal 105 and ground under the following conditions.
Voltage:
Engine speed is 4,000 rpm 0.6 - 0.8V
Engine speed is 2,000 rpm Battery voltage
O.K.
L
CHECK VACUUM HOSE.
1) Check vacuum hose for clogging, cracks and proper connection.
N.G.
A
I
C H
SEF939I
J
C H
Vacuum hose connected to E.G.R. control valve
MEF450A
K
C/UNIT CONNECTOR
105
CONNECT
V
C H
MEF451A
L
Split
Clogging
Improper connection
SEF816F
M
a b
DISCONNECT
V
MEF452A

EGR DIAGNOSTIC CHART – GA16DE AND SR20DE FEDERAL ENGINES, PART 2

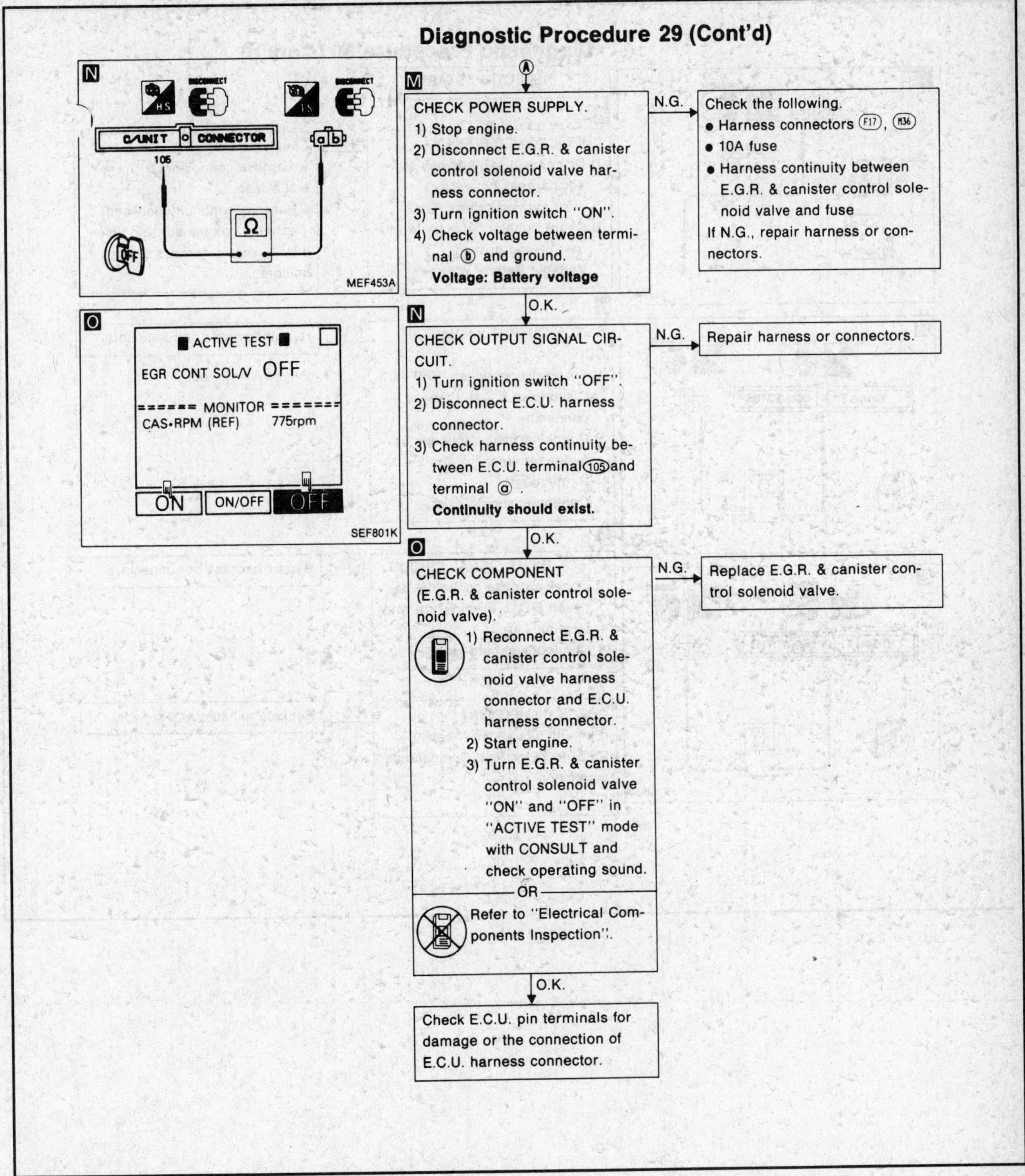
Diagnostic Procedure 29 (Cont'd)
N
DISCONNECT
DISCONNECT
C/UNIT
CONNECTOR
105
a b
Ω
OFF
MEF453A
M
Ⓐ
CHECK POWER SUPPLY.
1) Stop engine.
2) Disconnect E.G.R. & canister control solenoid valve harness connector.
3) Turn ignition switch "ON".
4) Check voltage between terminal ⓑ and ground.
Voltage: Battery voltage
N.G.
Check the following.
• Harness connectors (F17), (M36)
• 10A fuse
• Harness continuity between E.G.R. & canister control solenoid valve and fuse
If N.G., repair harness or connectors.
O.K.
O
ACTIVE TEST
EGR CONT SOL/V OFF
MONITOR
CAS•RPM (REF) 775rpm
ON
ON/OFF
OFF
SEF801K
N
CHECK OUTPUT SIGNAL CIRCUIT.
1) Turn ignition switch "OFF".
2) Disconnect E.C.U. harness connector.
3) Check harness continuity between E.C.U. terminal (105) and terminal ⓐ.
Continuity should exist.
N.G.
Repair harness or connectors.
O.K.
O
CHECK COMPONENT
(E.G.R. & canister control solenoid valve).
1) Reconnect E.G.R. & canister control solenoid valve harness connector and E.C.U. harness connector.
2) Start engine.
3) Turn E.G.R. & canister control solenoid valve "ON" and "OFF" in "ACTIVE TEST" mode with CONSULT and check operating sound.
OR
Refer to "Electrical Components Inspection".
N.G.
Replace E.G.R. & canister control solenoid valve.
O.K.
Check E.C.U. pin terminals for damage or the connection of E.C.U. harness connector.

CODE 33 (OXYGEN SENSOR) – GA16DE AND SR20DE ENGINES, PART 1

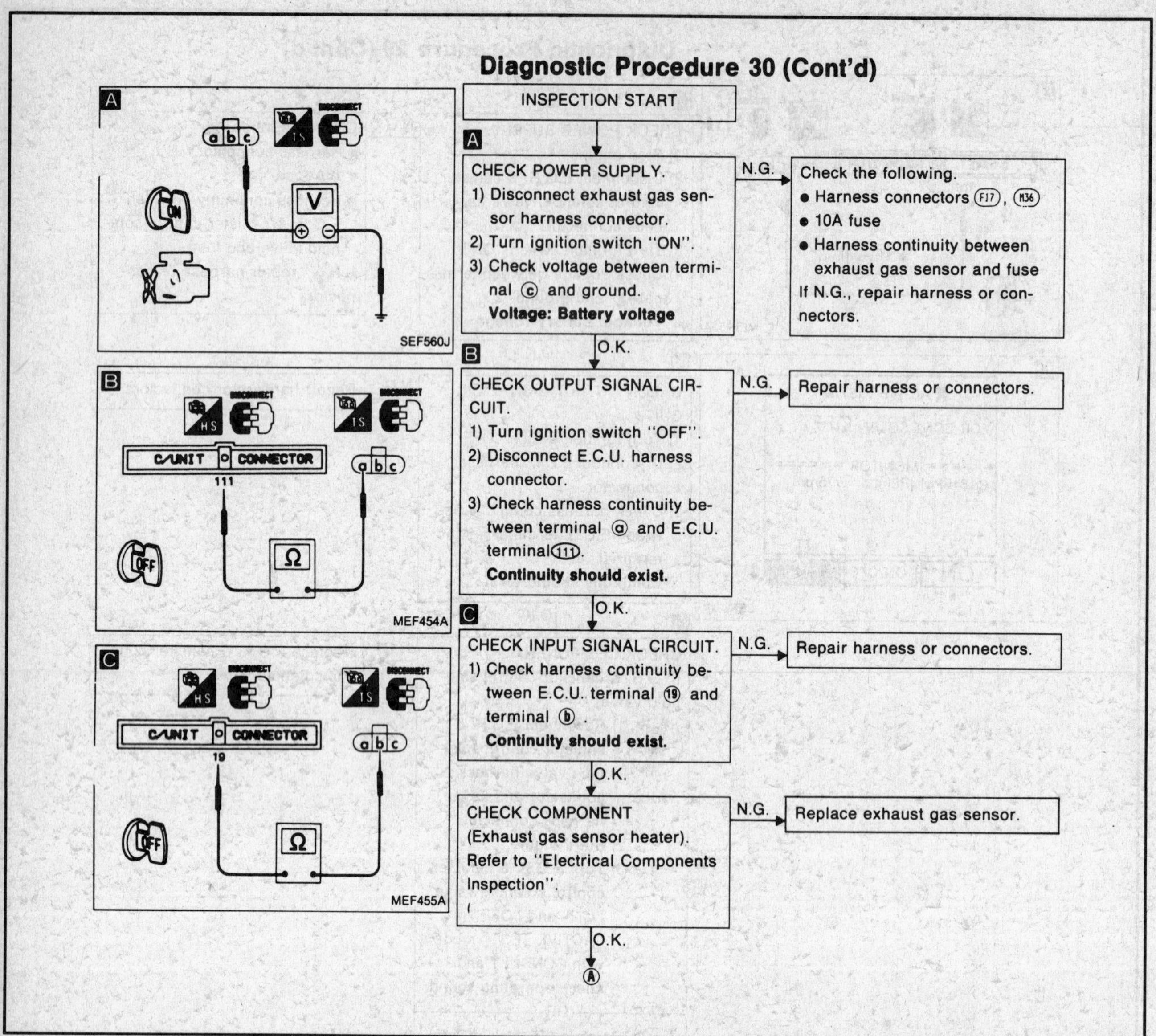

Diagnostic Procedure 30 (Cont'd)
INSPECTION START
A
CHECK POWER SUPPLY.
1) Disconnect exhaust gas sensor harness connector.
2) Turn ignition switch "ON".
3) Check voltage between terminal ⓒ and ground.
Voltage: Battery voltage
N.G.
Check the following.
● Harness connectors F17, M36
● 10A fuse
● Harness continuity between exhaust gas sensor and fuse
If N.G., repair harness or connectors.
O.K.
B
CHECK OUTPUT SIGNAL CIRCUIT.
1) Turn ignition switch "OFF".
2) Disconnect E.C.U. harness connector.
3) Check harness continuity between terminal ⓐ and E.C.U. terminal 111.
Continuity should exist.
N.G.
Repair harness or connectors.
O.K.
C
CHECK INPUT SIGNAL CIRCUIT.
1) Check harness continuity between E.C.U. terminal ⑲ and terminal ⓑ.
Continuity should exist.
N.G.
Repair harness or connectors.
O.K.
CHECK COMPONENT
(Exhaust gas sensor heater).
Refer to "Electrical Components Inspection".
N.G.
Replace exhaust gas sensor.
O.K.
Ⓐ
A
a b c
DISCONNECT
V
SEF560J
B
DISCONNECT
C/UNIT CONNECTOR
111
a b c
Ω
MEF454A
C
DISCONNECT
C/UNIT CONNECTOR
19
a b c
Ω
MEF455A

CODE 33 (OXYGEN SENSOR) – GA16DE AND SR20DE ENGINES, PART 2

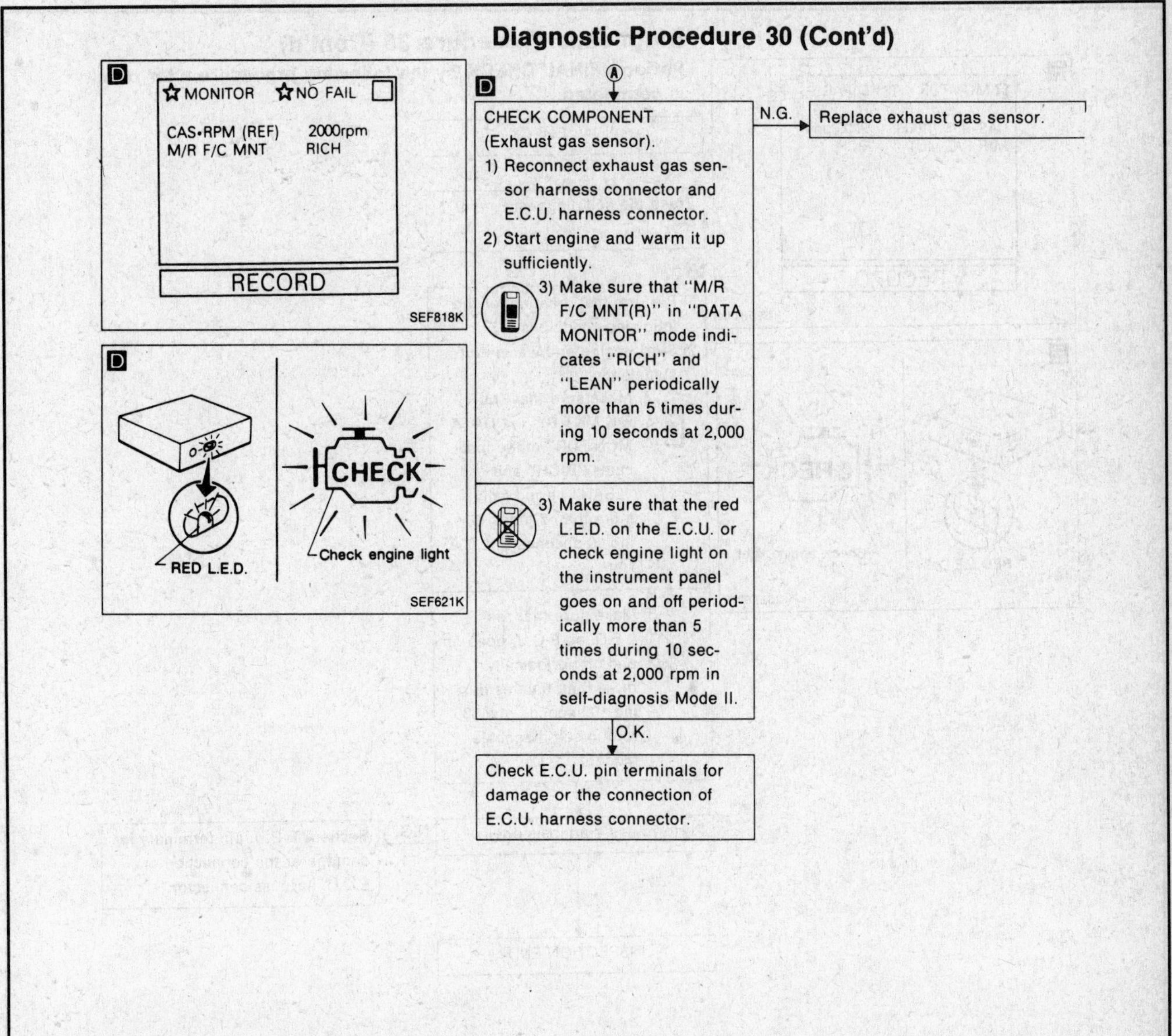
Diagnostic Procedure 30 (Cont'd)
D
☆MONITOR ☆NO FAIL
CAS•RPM (REF) 2000rpm
M/R F/C MNT RICH
RECORD
SEF818K
D
RED L.E.D.
CHECK
Check engine light
SEF621K
A
D
CHECK COMPONENT
(Exhaust gas sensor).
1) Reconnect exhaust gas sensor harness connector and E.C.U. harness connector.
2) Start engine and warm it up sufficiently.
3) Make sure that "M/R F/C MNT(R)" in "DATA MONITOR" mode indicates "RICH" and "LEAN" periodically more than 5 times during 10 seconds at 2,000 rpm.
3) Make sure that the red L.E.D. on the E.C.U. or check engine light on the instrument panel goes on and off periodically more than 5 times during 10 seconds at 2,000 rpm in self-diagnosis Mode II.
N.G.
Replace exhaust gas sensor.
O.K.
Check E.C.U. pin terminals for damage or the connection of E.C.U. harness connector.

CODE 33 (OXYGEN SENSOR) – GA16DE AND SR20DE ENGINES, PART 3

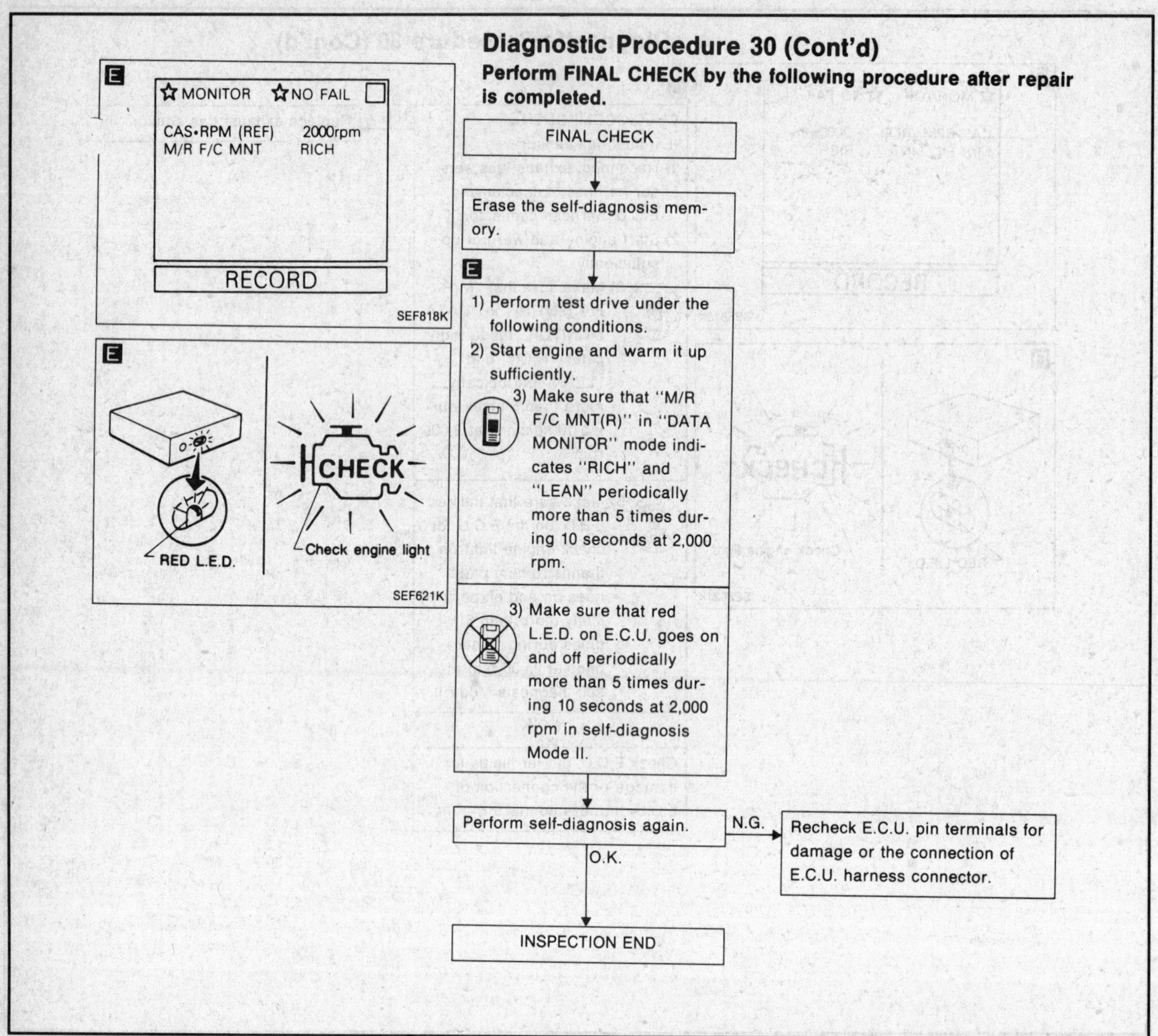
Diagnostic Procedure 30 (Cont'd)
Perform FINAL CHECK by the following procedure after repair is completed.
MONITOR
NO FAIL
CAS•RPM (REF) 2000rpm
M/R F/C MNT RICH
RECORD
SEF818K
CHECK
RED L.E.D.
Check engine light
SEF621K
FINAL CHECK
Erase the self-diagnosis memory.
1) Perform test drive under the following conditions.
2) Start engine and warm it up sufficiently.
3) Make sure that "M/R F/C MNT(R)" in "DATA MONITOR" mode indicates "RICH" and "LEAN" periodically more than 5 times during 10 seconds at 2,000 rpm.
3) Make sure that red L.E.D. on E.C.U. goes on and off periodically more than 5 times during 10 seconds at 2,000 rpm in self-diagnosis Mode II.
Perform self-diagnosis again.
N.G.
Recheck E.C.U. pin terminals for damage or the connection of E.C.U. harness connector.
O.K.
INSPECTION END

CODE 34 (DETONATION SENSOR) – GA16DE AND SR20DE ENGINES

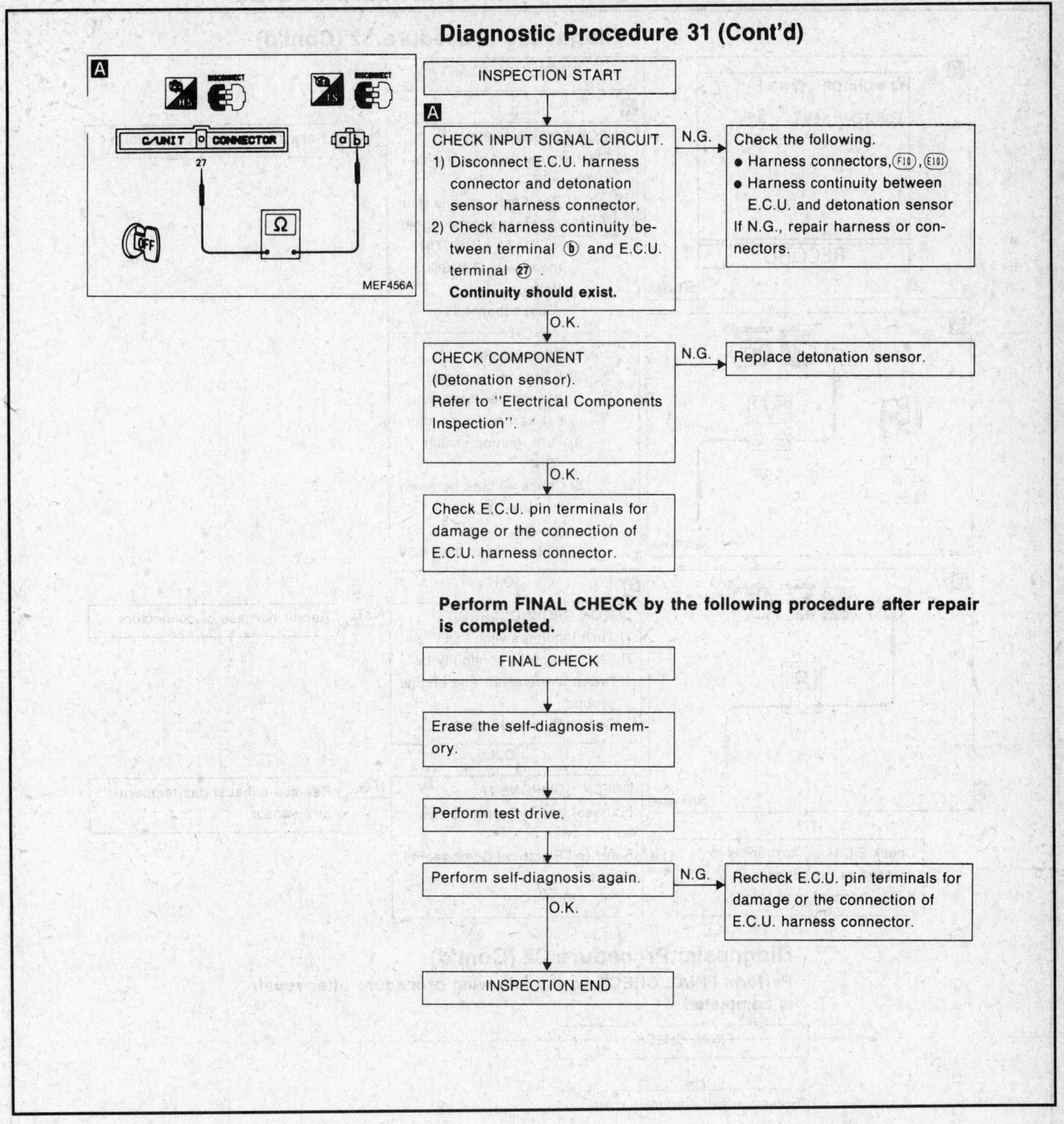
Diagnostic Procedure 31 (Cont'd)
A
C/UNIT CONNECTOR
27
Ω
OFF
MEF456A
INSPECTION START
A
CHECK INPUT SIGNAL CIRCUIT.
1) Disconnect E.C.U. harness connector and detonation sensor harness connector.
2) Check harness continuity between terminal ⓑ and E.C.U. terminal ㉗ .
Continuity should exist.
N.G.
Check the following.
● Harness connectors, F10, E101
● Harness continuity between E.C.U. and detonation sensor
If N.G., repair harness or connectors.
O.K.
CHECK COMPONENT (Detonation sensor).
Refer to "Electrical Components Inspection".
N.G.
Replace detonation sensor.
O.K.
Check E.C.U. pin terminals for damage or the connection of E.C.U. harness connector.
Perform FINAL CHECK by the following procedure after repair is completed.
FINAL CHECK
Erase the self-diagnosis memory.
Perform test drive.
Perform self-diagnosis again.
N.G.
Recheck E.C.U. pin terminals for damage or the connection of E.C.U. harness connector.
O.K.
INSPECTION END

CODE 35 (OXYGEN SENSOR TEMPERATURE SENSOR) GA16DE AND SR20DE CALIFORNIA ENGINES

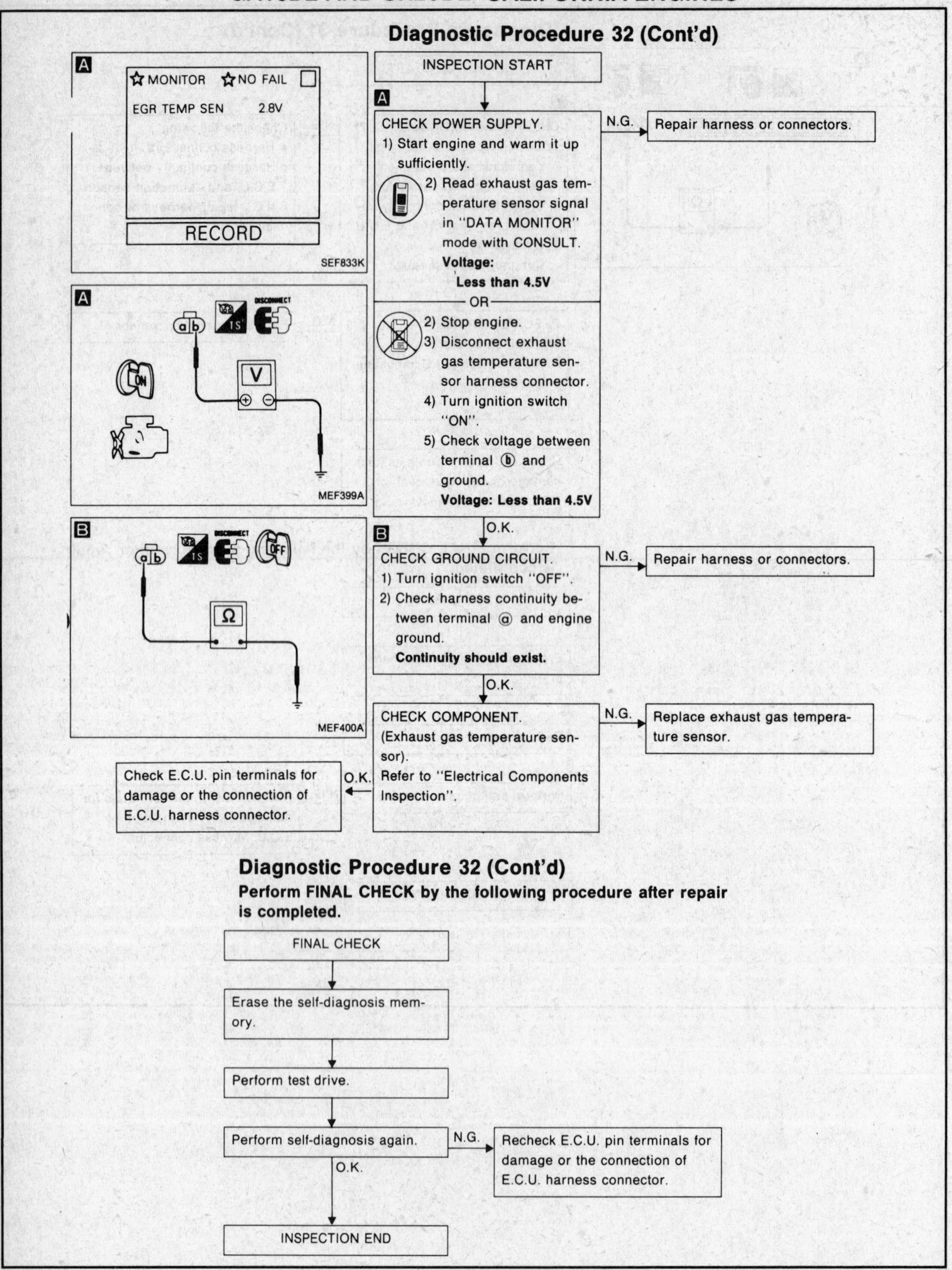

Diagnostic Procedure 32 (Cont'd)
A
☆MONITOR ☆NO FAIL
EGR TEMP SEN 2.8V
RECORD
SEF833K
A
DISCONNECT
V
ON
MEF399A
B
DISCONNECT
OFF
Ω
MEF400A
INSPECTION START
A
CHECK POWER SUPPLY.
1) Start engine and warm it up sufficiently.
2) Read exhaust gas temperature sensor signal in "DATA MONITOR" mode with CONSULT.
Voltage:
Less than 4.5V
OR
2) Stop engine.
3) Disconnect exhaust gas temperature sensor harness connector.
4) Turn ignition switch "ON".
5) Check voltage between terminal ⓑ and ground.
Voltage: Less than 4.5V
N.G.
Repair harness or connectors.
O.K.
B
CHECK GROUND CIRCUIT.
1) Turn ignition switch "OFF".
2) Check harness continuity between terminal ⓐ and engine ground.
Continuity should exist.
N.G.
Repair harness or connectors.
O.K.
CHECK COMPONENT.
(Exhaust gas temperature sensor).
Refer to "Electrical Components Inspection".
N.G.
Replace exhaust gas temperature sensor.
O.K.
Check E.C.U. pin terminals for damage or the connection of E.C.U. harness connector.
Diagnostic Procedure 32 (Cont'd)
Perform FINAL CHECK by the following procedure after repair is completed.
FINAL CHECK
Erase the self-diagnosis memory.
Perform test drive.
Perform self-diagnosis again.
N.G.
Recheck E.C.U. pin terminals for damage or the connection of E.C.U. harness connector.
O.K.
INSPECTION END

CODE 43 (THROTTLE SENSOR) — GA16DE AND SR20DE ENGINES

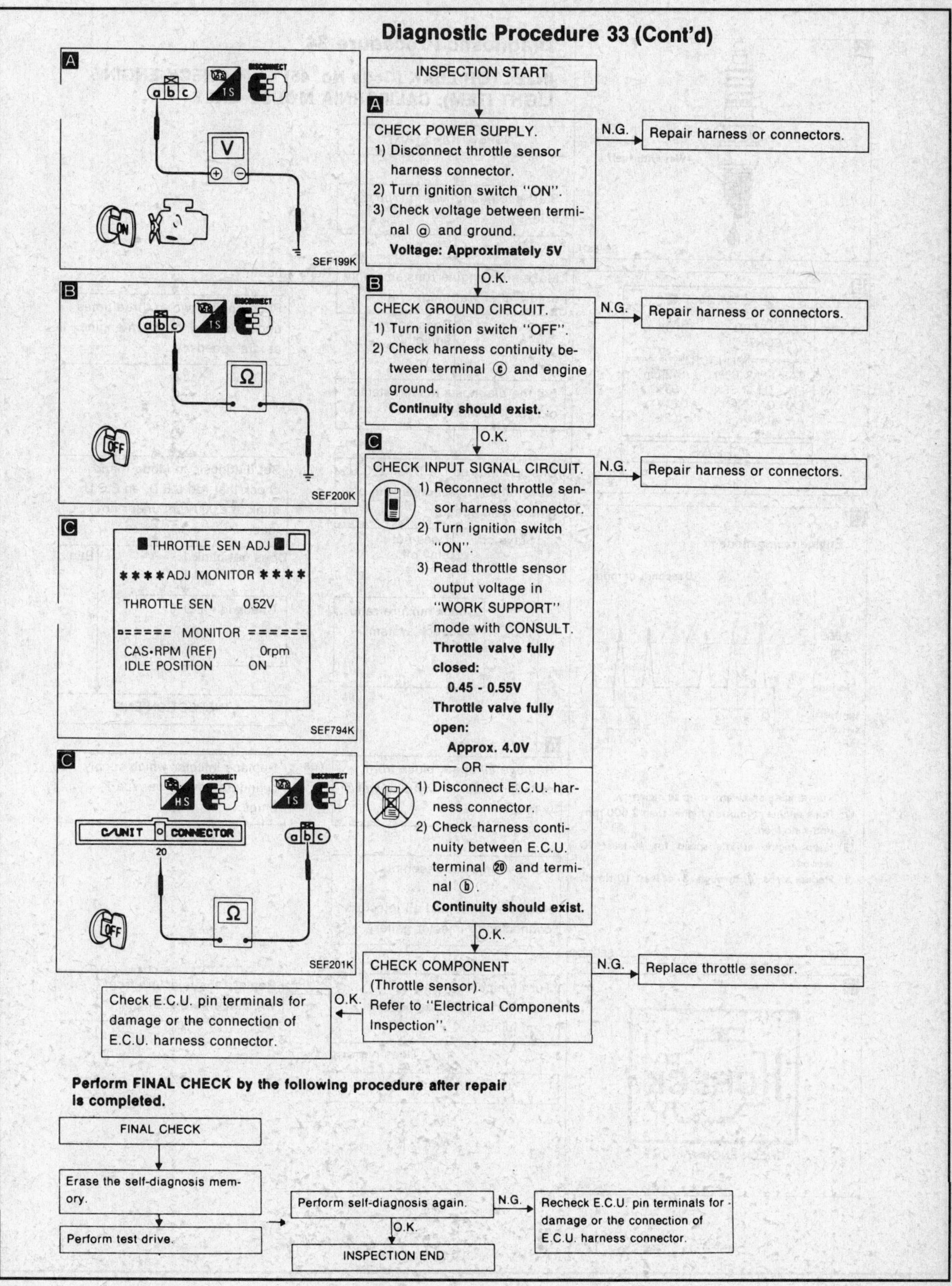

Diagnostic Procedure 33 (Cont'd)
A
abc
TS
DISCONNECT
V
ON
SEF199K
INSPECTION START
A
CHECK POWER SUPPLY.
1) Disconnect throttle sensor harness connector.
2) Turn ignition switch "ON".
3) Check voltage between terminal ⓐ and ground.
Voltage: Approximately 5V
N.G.
Repair harness or connectors.
O.K.
B
abc
TS
DISCONNECT
Ω
OFF
SEF200K
B
CHECK GROUND CIRCUIT.
1) Turn ignition switch "OFF".
2) Check harness continuity between terminal ⓒ and engine ground.
Continuity should exist.
N.G.
Repair harness or connectors.
O.K.
C
THROTTLE SEN ADJ
**** ADJ MONITOR ****
THROTTLE SEN 0.52V
====== MONITOR ======
CAS•RPM (REF) 0rpm
IDLE POSITION ON
SEF794K
C
CHECK INPUT SIGNAL CIRCUIT.
1) Reconnect throttle sensor harness connector.
2) Turn ignition switch "ON".
3) Read throttle sensor output voltage in "WORK SUPPORT" mode with CONSULT.
Throttle valve fully closed:
0.45 - 0.55V
Throttle valve fully open:
Approx. 4.0V
N.G.
Repair harness or connectors.
OR
C
HS
TS
DISCONNECT
C/UNIT CONNECTOR
20
abc
Ω
OFF
SEF201K
1) Disconnect E.C.U. harness connector.
2) Check harness continuity between E.C.U. terminal ⑳ and terminal ⓑ.
Continuity should exist.
O.K.
CHECK COMPONENT (Throttle sensor).
Refer to "Electrical Components Inspection".
N.G.
Replace throttle sensor.
O.K.
Check E.C.U. pin terminals for damage or the connection of E.C.U. harness connector.
Perform FINAL CHECK by the following procedure after repair is completed.
FINAL CHECK
Erase the self-diagnosis memory.
Perform test drive.
Perform self-diagnosis again.
N.G.
Recheck E.C.U. pin terminals for damage or the connection of E.C.U. harness connector.
O.K.
INSPECTION END

CODE 45 (FUEL INJECTOR LEAK) – GA16DE AND SR20DE ENGINES, PART 1

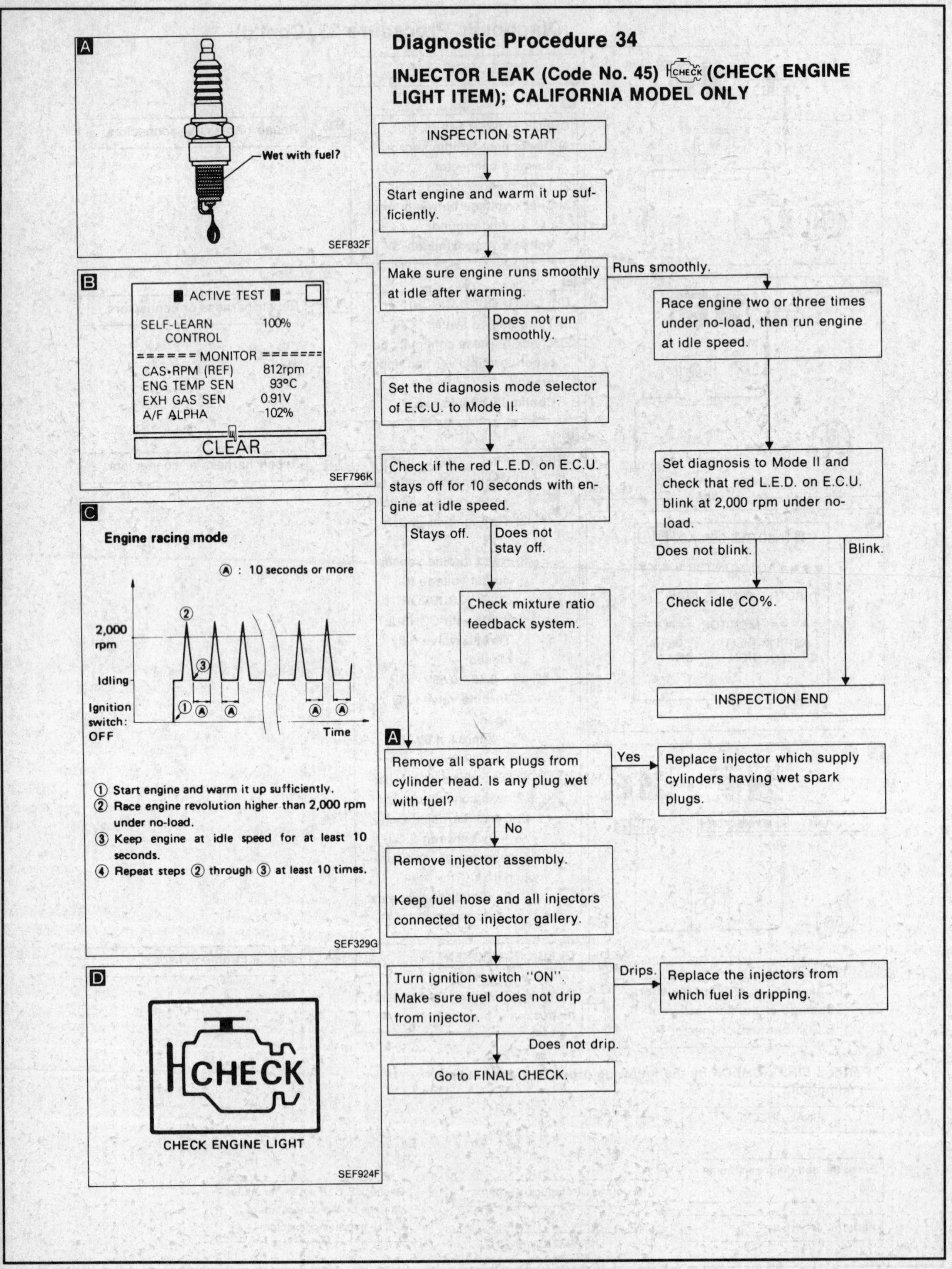
A
Wet with fuel?
SEF832F
B
ACTIVE TEST
SELF-LEARN CONTROL 100%
MONITOR
CAS•RPM (REF) 812rpm
ENG TEMP SEN 93°C
EXH GAS SEN 0.91V
A/F ALPHA 102%
CLEAR
SEF796K
C
Engine racing mode
Ⓐ : 10 seconds or more
2,000 rpm
Idling
Ignition switch: OFF
Time
① Start engine and warm it up sufficiently.
② Race engine revolution higher than 2,000 rpm under no-load.
③ Keep engine at idle speed for at least 10 seconds.
④ Repeat steps ② through ③ at least 10 times.
SEF329G
D
CHECK
CHECK ENGINE LIGHT
SEF924F
Diagnostic Procedure 34
INJECTOR LEAK (Code No. 45) CHECK (CHECK ENGINE LIGHT ITEM); CALIFORNIA MODEL ONLY
INSPECTION START
Start engine and warm it up sufficiently.
Make sure engine runs smoothly at idle after warming.
Runs smoothly.
Race engine two or three times under no-load, then run engine at idle speed.
Does not run smoothly.
Set the diagnosis mode selector of E.C.U. to Mode II.
Set diagnosis to Mode II and check that red L.E.D. on E.C.U. blink at 2,000 rpm under no-load.
Check if the red L.E.D. on E.C.U. stays off for 10 seconds with engine at idle speed.
Stays off.
Does not stay off.
Does not blink.
Blink.
Check mixture ratio feedback system.
Check idle CO%.
INSPECTION END
A
Remove all spark plugs from cylinder head. Is any plug wet with fuel?
Yes
Replace injector which supply cylinders having wet spark plugs.
No
Remove injector assembly.
Keep fuel hose and all injectors connected to injector gallery.
Turn ignition switch "ON". Make sure fuel does not drip from injector.
Drips.
Replace the injectors from which fuel is dripping.
Does not drip.
Go to FINAL CHECK.

CODE 45 (FUEL INJECTOR LEAK) – GA16DE AND SR20DE ENGINES, PART 2

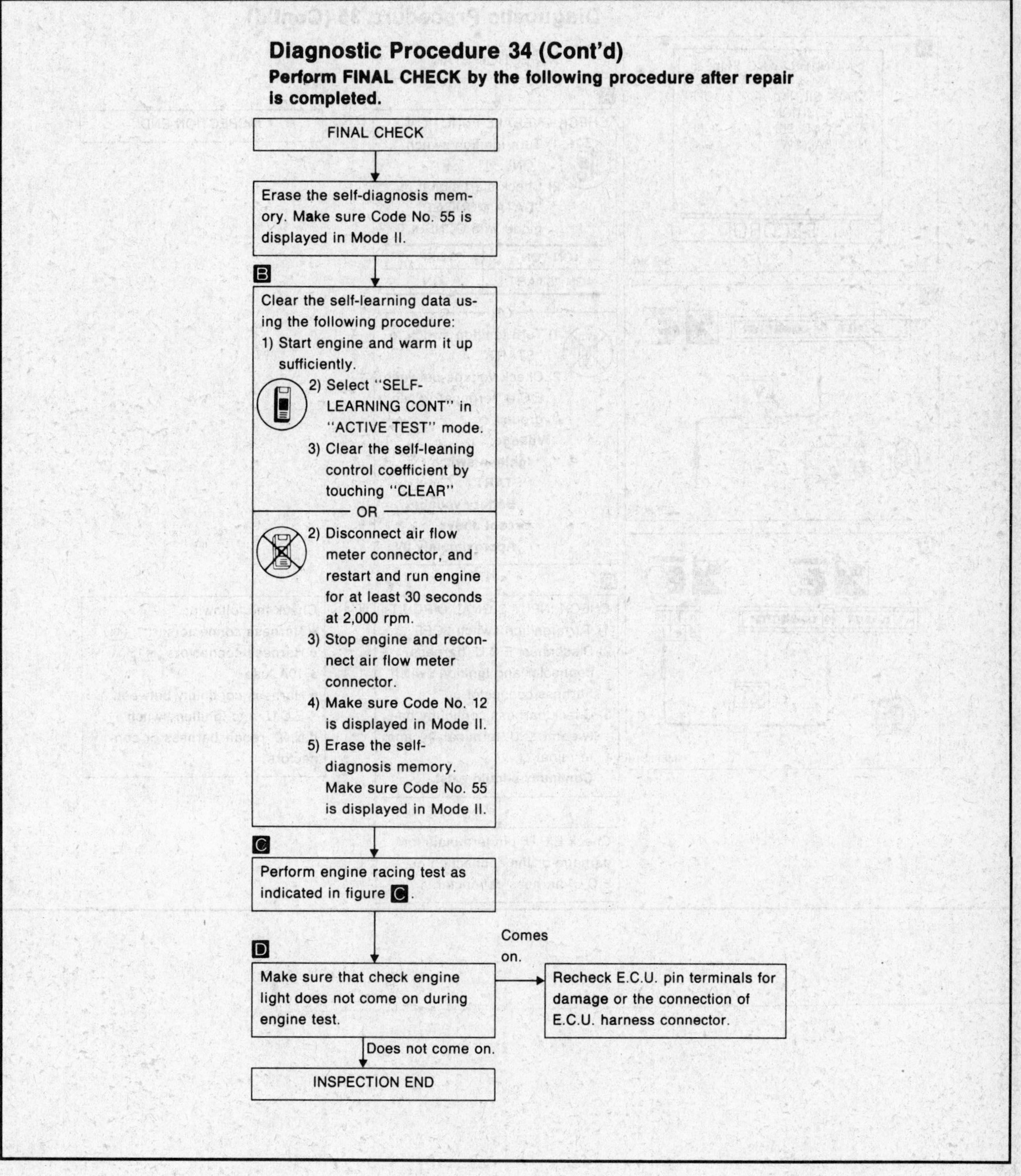
Diagnostic Procedure 34 (Cont'd)
Perform FINAL CHECK by the following procedure after repair is completed.
FINAL CHECK
Erase the self-diagnosis memory. Make sure Code No. 55 is displayed in Mode II.
B
Clear the self-learning data using the following procedure:
1) Start engine and warm it up sufficiently.
2) Select "SELF-LEARNING CONT" in "ACTIVE TEST" mode.
3) Clear the self-leaning control coefficient by touching "CLEAR"
OR
2) Disconnect air flow meter connector, and restart and run engine for at least 30 seconds at 2,000 rpm.
3) Stop engine and reconnect air flow meter connector.
4) Make sure Code No. 12 is displayed in Mode II.
5) Erase the self-diagnosis memory. Make sure Code No. 55 is displayed in Mode II.
C
Perform engine racing test as indicated in figure C.
D
Make sure that check engine light does not come on during engine test.
Comes on.
Recheck E.C.U. pin terminals for damage or the connection of E.C.U. harness connector.
Does not come on.
INSPECTION END

START SIGNAL DIAGNOSTIC CHART – GA16DE AND SR20DE ENGINES

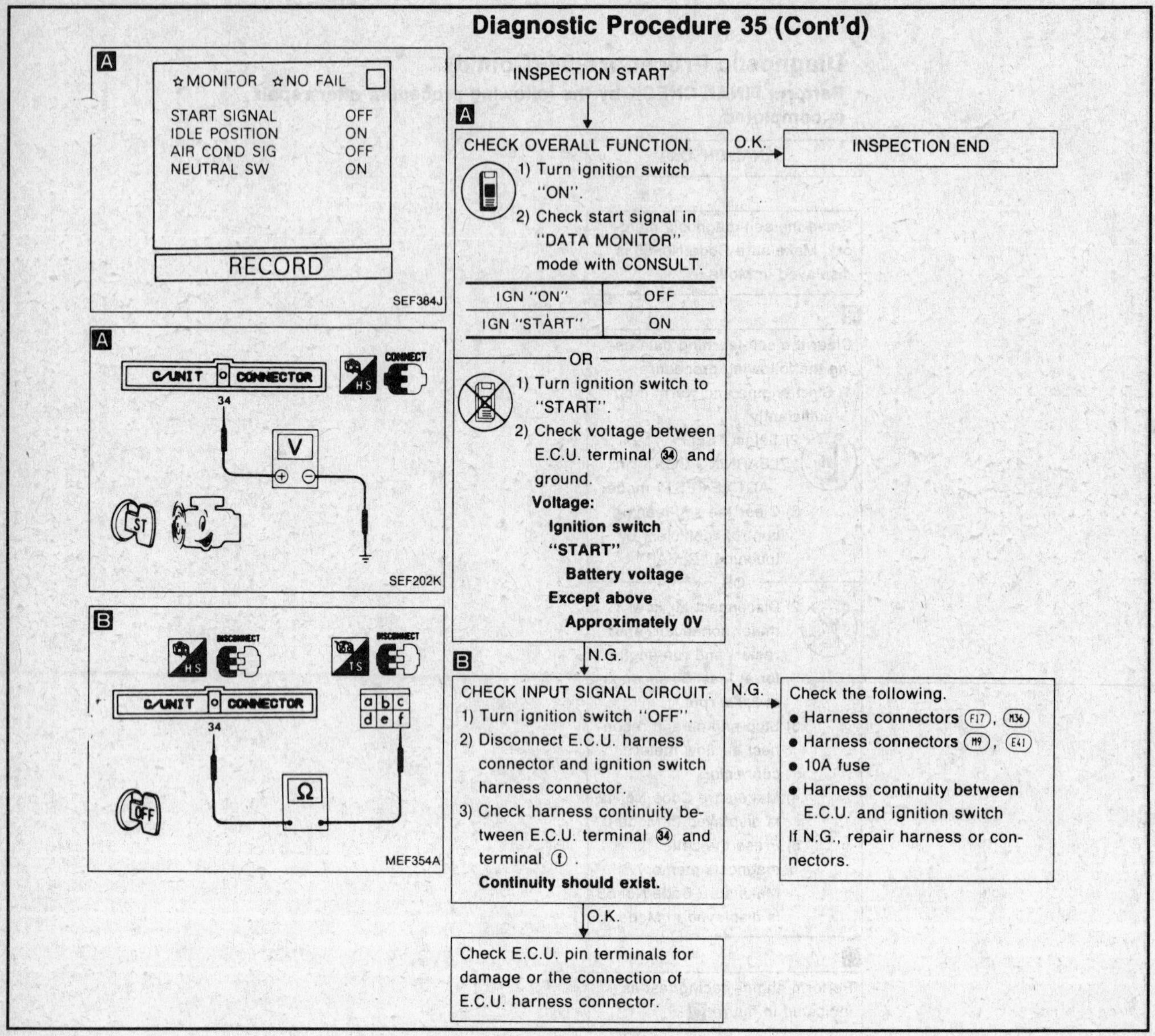
Diagnostic Procedure 35 (Cont'd)
A
☆MONITOR ☆NO FAIL
START SIGNAL OFF
IDLE POSITION ON
AIR COND SIG OFF
NEUTRAL SW ON
RECORD
SEF384J
A
C/UNIT CONNECTOR
CONNECT
34
V
ST
SEF202K
B
DISCONNECT
C/UNIT CONNECTOR
34
a b c
d e f
Ω
OFF
MEF354A
INSPECTION START
A
CHECK OVERALL FUNCTION.
1) Turn ignition switch "ON".
2) Check start signal in "DATA MONITOR" mode with CONSULT.
IGN "ON" OFF
IGN "START" ON
OR
1) Turn ignition switch to "START".
2) Check voltage between E.C.U. terminal ㉞ and ground.
Voltage:
Ignition switch "START"
Battery voltage
Except above
Approximately 0V
O.K.
INSPECTION END
N.G.
B
CHECK INPUT SIGNAL CIRCUIT.
1) Turn ignition switch "OFF".
2) Disconnect E.C.U. harness connector and ignition switch harness connector.
3) Check harness continuity between E.C.U. terminal ㉞ and terminal ⓕ.
Continuity should exist.
N.G.
Check the following.
• Harness connectors (F17), (M36)
• Harness connectors (M9), (E41)
• 10A fuse
• Harness continuity between E.C.U. and ignition switch
If N.G., repair harness or connectors.
O.K.
Check E.C.U. pin terminals for damage or the connection of E.C.U. harness connector.

AIR INJECTION VALVE DIAGNOSTIC CHART GA16DE AND SR20DE ENGINES, PART 1

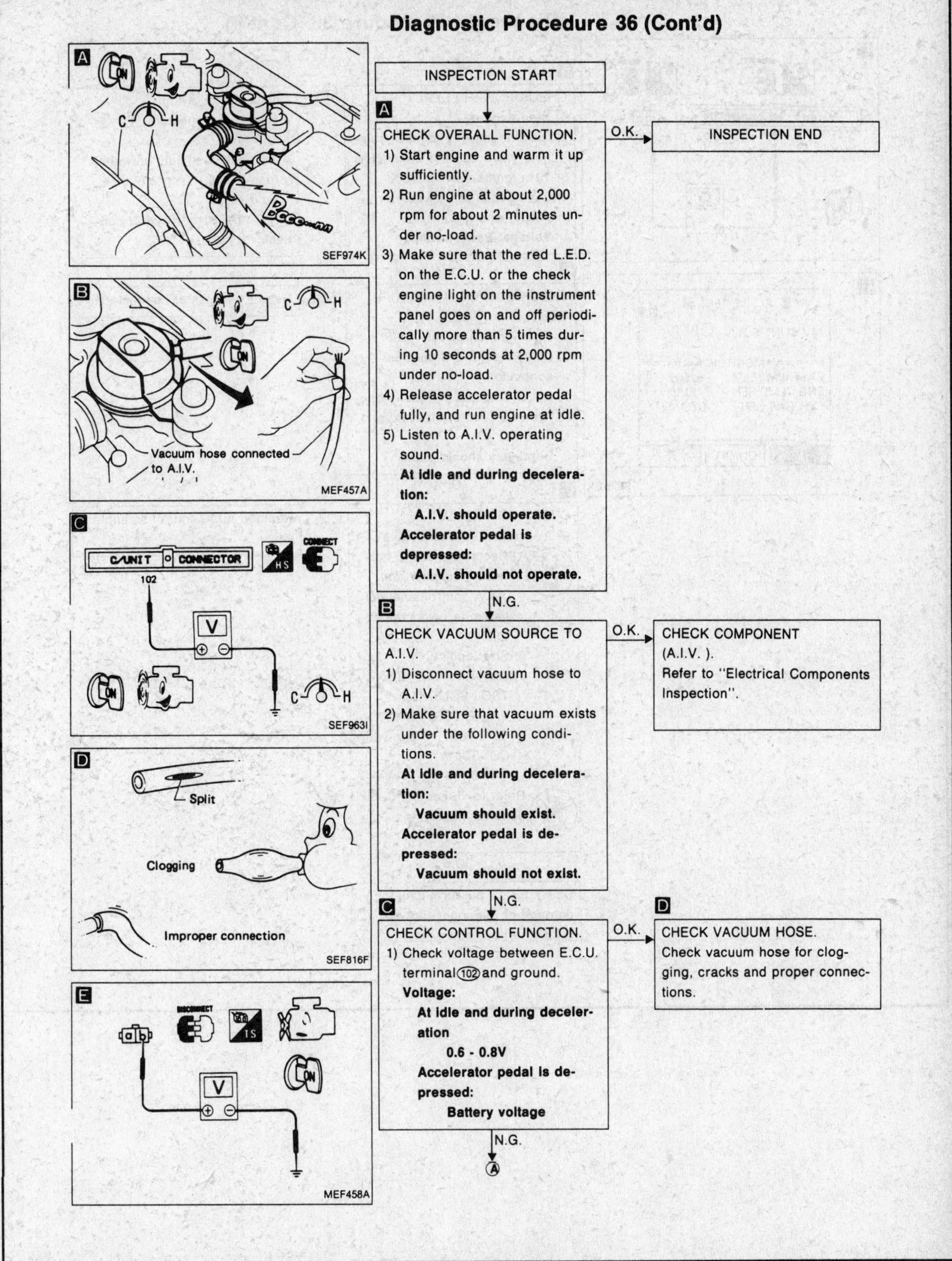
Diagnostic Procedure 36 (Cont'd)
A
C H
Bccco...nn
SEF974K
B
C H
Vacuum hose connected to A.I.V.
MEF457A
C
C/UNIT
CONNECTOR
HS
CONNECT
102
V
C H
SEF963I
D
Split
Clogging
Improper connection
SEF816F
E
DISCONNECT
TS
V
MEF458A
INSPECTION START
A
CHECK OVERALL FUNCTION.
1) Start engine and warm it up sufficiently.
2) Run engine at about 2,000 rpm for about 2 minutes under no-load.
3) Make sure that the red L.E.D. on the E.C.U. or the check engine light on the instrument panel goes on and off periodically more than 5 times during 10 seconds at 2,000 rpm under no-load.
4) Release accelerator pedal fully, and run engine at idle.
5) Listen to A.I.V. operating sound.
At idle and during deceleration:
A.I.V. should operate.
Accelerator pedal is depressed:
A.I.V. should not operate.
O.K.
INSPECTION END
N.G.
B
CHECK VACUUM SOURCE TO A.I.V.
1) Disconnect vacuum hose to A.I.V.
2) Make sure that vacuum exists under the following conditions.
At idle and during deceleration:
Vacuum should exist.
Accelerator pedal is depressed:
Vacuum should not exist.
O.K.
CHECK COMPONENT (A.I.V.).
Refer to "Electrical Components Inspection".
N.G.
C
CHECK CONTROL FUNCTION.
1) Check voltage between E.C.U. terminal (102) and ground.
Voltage:
At idle and during deceleration
0.6 - 0.8V
Accelerator pedal is depressed:
Battery voltage
O.K.
D
CHECK VACUUM HOSE.
Check vacuum hose for clogging, cracks and proper connections.
N.G.
A

AIR INJECTION VALVE DIAGNOSTIC CHART
GA16DE AND SR20DE ENGINES, PART 2

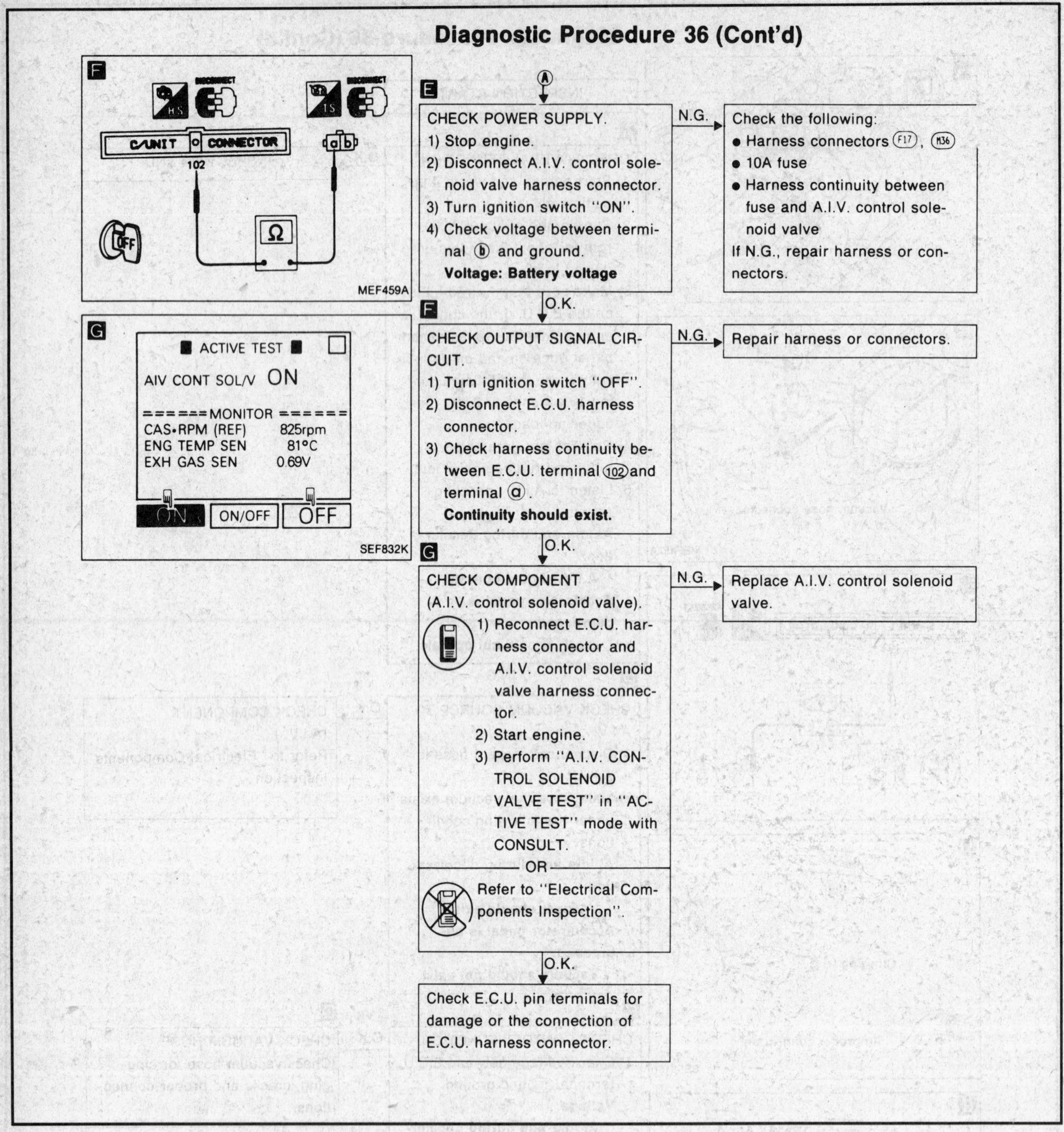
Diagnostic Procedure 36 (Cont'd)
F
C/UNIT CONNECTOR
102
MEF459A
G
ACTIVE TEST
AIV CONT SOL/V ON
======MONITOR======
CAS•RPM (REF) 825rpm
ENG TEMP SEN 81°C
EXH GAS SEN 0.69V
ON
ON/OFF
OFF
SEF832K
A
E
CHECK POWER SUPPLY.
1) Stop engine.
2) Disconnect A.I.V. control solenoid valve harness connector.
3) Turn ignition switch "ON".
4) Check voltage between terminal ⓑ and ground.
Voltage: Battery voltage
N.G.
Check the following:
● Harness connectors F17, M36
● 10A fuse
● Harness continuity between fuse and A.I.V. control solenoid valve
If N.G., repair harness or connectors.
O.K.
F
CHECK OUTPUT SIGNAL CIRCUIT.
1) Turn ignition switch "OFF".
2) Disconnect E.C.U. harness connector.
3) Check harness continuity between E.C.U. terminal 102 and terminal ⓐ.
Continuity should exist.
N.G.
Repair harness or connectors.
O.K.
G
CHECK COMPONENT
(A.I.V. control solenoid valve).
1) Reconnect E.C.U. harness connector and A.I.V. control solenoid valve harness connector.
2) Start engine.
3) Perform "A.I.V. CONTROL SOLENOID VALVE TEST" in "ACTIVE TEST" mode with CONSULT.
OR
Refer to "Electrical Components Inspection".
N.G.
Replace A.I.V. control solenoid valve.
O.K.
Check E.C.U. pin terminals for damage or the connection of E.C.U. harness connector.

FUEL INJECTOR DIAGNOSTIC CHART — GA16DE AND SR20DE ENGINES

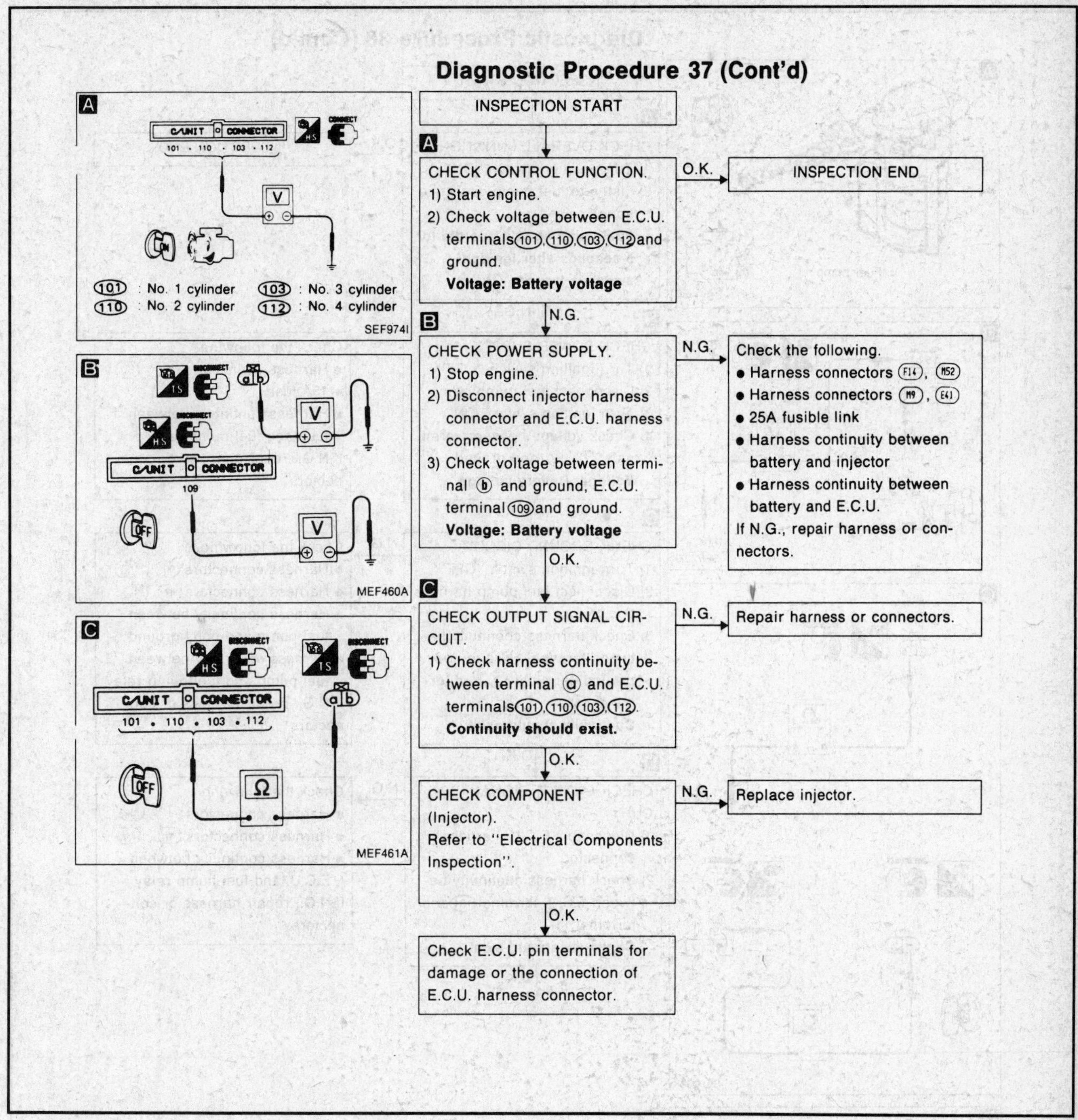
Diagnostic Procedure 37 (Cont'd)
A
C/UNIT CONNECTOR
101 · 110 · 103 · 112
CONNECT
HS
V
ON
101 : No. 1 cylinder
110 : No. 2 cylinder
103 : No. 3 cylinder
112 : No. 4 cylinder
SEF974I
B
TS
DISCONNECT
HS
DISCONNECT
a b
V
C/UNIT CONNECTOR
109
OFF
V
MEF460A
C
HS
DISCONNECT
TS
DISCONNECT
C/UNIT CONNECTOR
101 · 110 · 103 · 112
a b
OFF
Ω
MEF461A
INSPECTION START
A
CHECK CONTROL FUNCTION.
1) Start engine.
2) Check voltage between E.C.U. terminals 101, 110, 103, 112 and ground.
Voltage: Battery voltage
O.K.
INSPECTION END
N.G.
B
CHECK POWER SUPPLY.
1) Stop engine.
2) Disconnect injector harness connector and E.C.U. harness connector.
3) Check voltage between terminal b and ground, E.C.U. terminal 109 and ground.
Voltage: Battery voltage
N.G.
Check the following.
• Harness connectors F14, M52
• Harness connectors M9, E41
• 25A fusible link
• Harness continuity between battery and injector
• Harness continuity between battery and E.C.U.
If N.G., repair harness or connectors.
O.K.
C
CHECK OUTPUT SIGNAL CIRCUIT.
1) Check harness continuity between terminal a and E.C.U. terminals 101, 110, 103, 112.
Continuity should exist.
N.G.
Repair harness or connectors.
O.K.
CHECK COMPONENT (Injector).
Refer to "Electrical Components Inspection".
N.G.
Replace injector.
O.K.
Check E.C.U. pin terminals for damage or the connection of E.C.U. harness connector.

FUEL PUMP DIAGNOSTIC CHART – GA16DE AND SR20DE ENGINES, PART 1

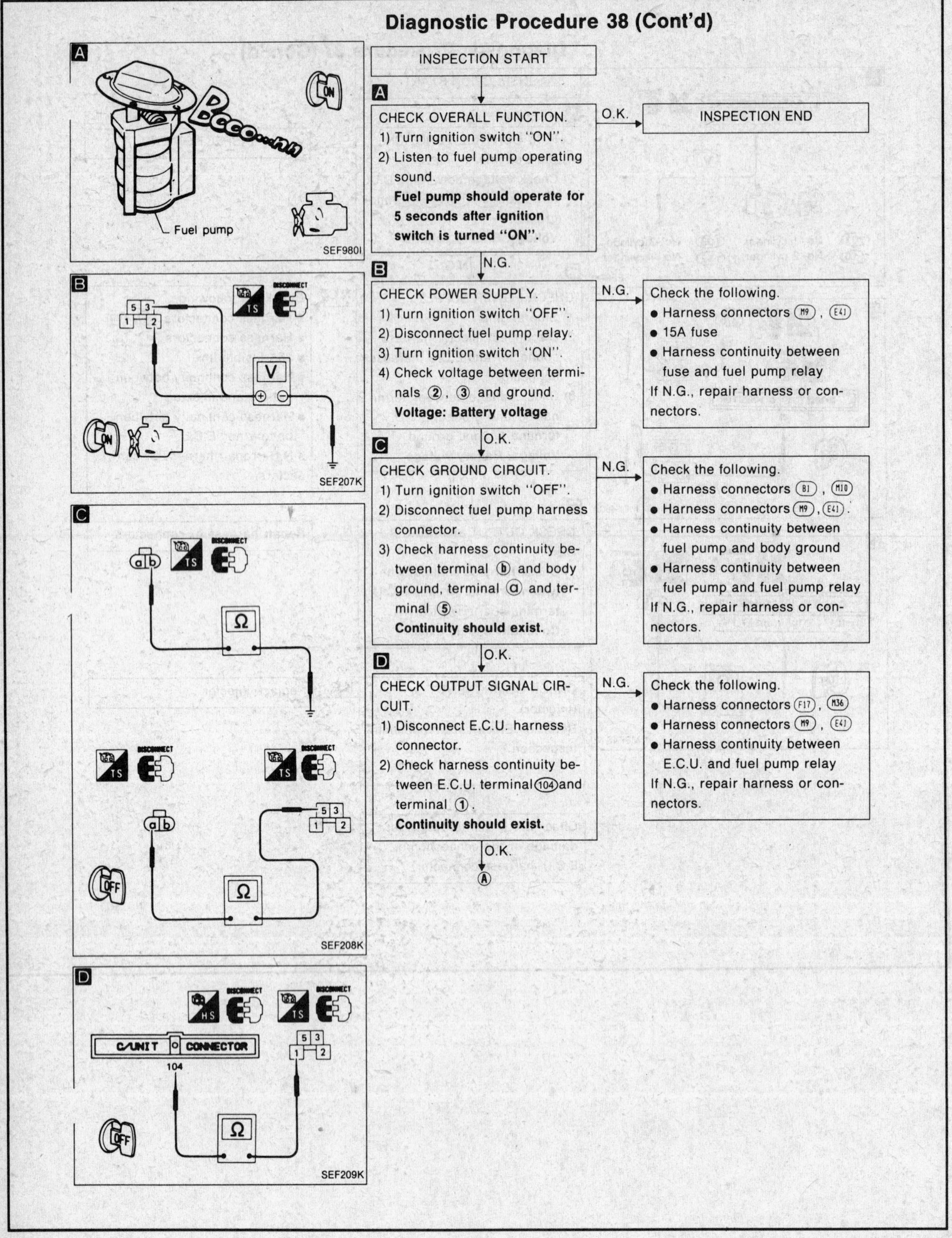
Diagnostic Procedure 38 (Cont'd)
A
Fuel pump
SEF980I
B
SEF207K
C
SEF208K
D
C/UNIT CONNECTOR
104
SEF209K
INSPECTION START
A
CHECK OVERALL FUNCTION.
1) Turn ignition switch "ON".
2) Listen to fuel pump operating sound.
Fuel pump should operate for 5 seconds after ignition switch is turned "ON".
O.K.
INSPECTION END
N.G.
B
CHECK POWER SUPPLY.
1) Turn ignition switch "OFF".
2) Disconnect fuel pump relay.
3) Turn ignition switch "ON".
4) Check voltage between terminals ②, ③ and ground.
Voltage: Battery voltage
N.G.
Check the following.
• Harness connectors (M9), (E41)
• 15A fuse
• Harness continuity between fuse and fuel pump relay
If N.G., repair harness or connectors.
O.K.
C
CHECK GROUND CIRCUIT.
1) Turn ignition switch "OFF".
2) Disconnect fuel pump harness connector.
3) Check harness continuity between terminal ⓑ and body ground, terminal ⓐ and terminal ⑤.
Continuity should exist.
N.G.
Check the following.
• Harness connectors (B1), (M10)
• Harness connectors (M9), (E41).
• Harness continuity between fuel pump and body ground
• Harness continuity between fuel pump and fuel pump relay
If N.G., repair harness or connectors.
O.K.
D
CHECK OUTPUT SIGNAL CIRCUIT.
1) Disconnect E.C.U. harness connector.
2) Check harness continuity between E.C.U. terminal (104) and terminal ①.
Continuity should exist.
N.G.
Check the following.
• Harness connectors (F17), (M36)
• Harness connectors (M9), (E41)
• Harness continuity between E.C.U. and fuel pump relay
If N.G., repair harness or connectors.
O.K.
Ⓐ

FUEL PUMP DIAGNOSTIC CHART – GA16DE AND SR20DE ENGINES, PART 2

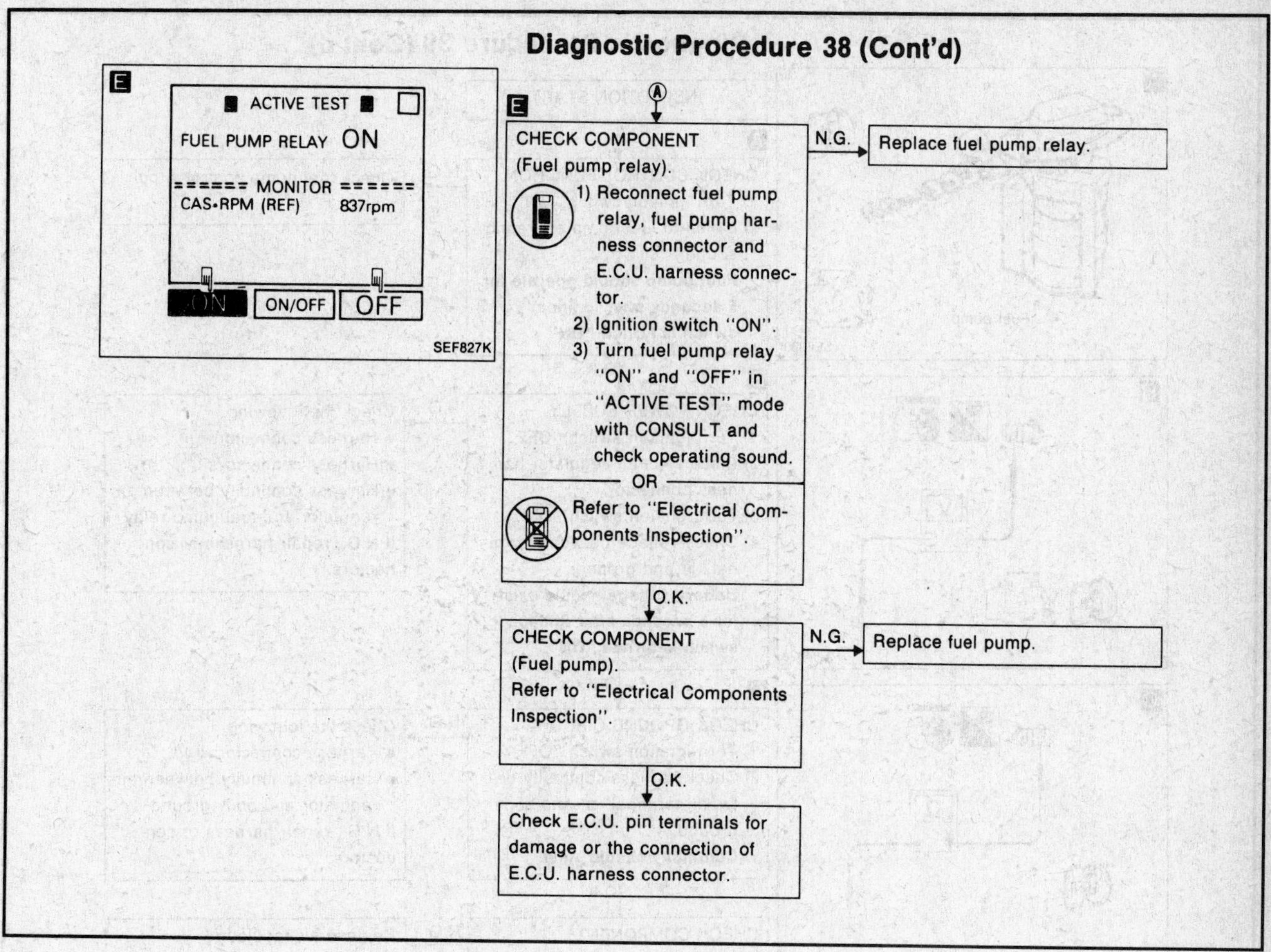

Diagnostic Procedure 38 (Cont'd)
E
ACTIVE TEST
FUEL PUMP RELAY ON
====== MONITOR ======
CAS•RPM (REF) 837rpm
ON
ON/OFF
OFF
SEF827K
A
E
CHECK COMPONENT
(Fuel pump relay).
1) Reconnect fuel pump relay, fuel pump harness connector and E.C.U. harness connector.
2) Ignition switch "ON".
3) Turn fuel pump relay "ON" and "OFF" in "ACTIVE TEST" mode with CONSULT and check operating sound.
OR
Refer to "Electrical Components Inspection".
N.G.
Replace fuel pump relay.
O.K.
CHECK COMPONENT
(Fuel pump).
Refer to "Electrical Components Inspection".
N.G.
Replace fuel pump.
O.K.
Check E.C.U. pin terminals for damage or the connection of E.C.U. harness connector.

AIR REGULATOR DIAGNOSTIC CHART – GA16DE AND SR20DE ENGINES

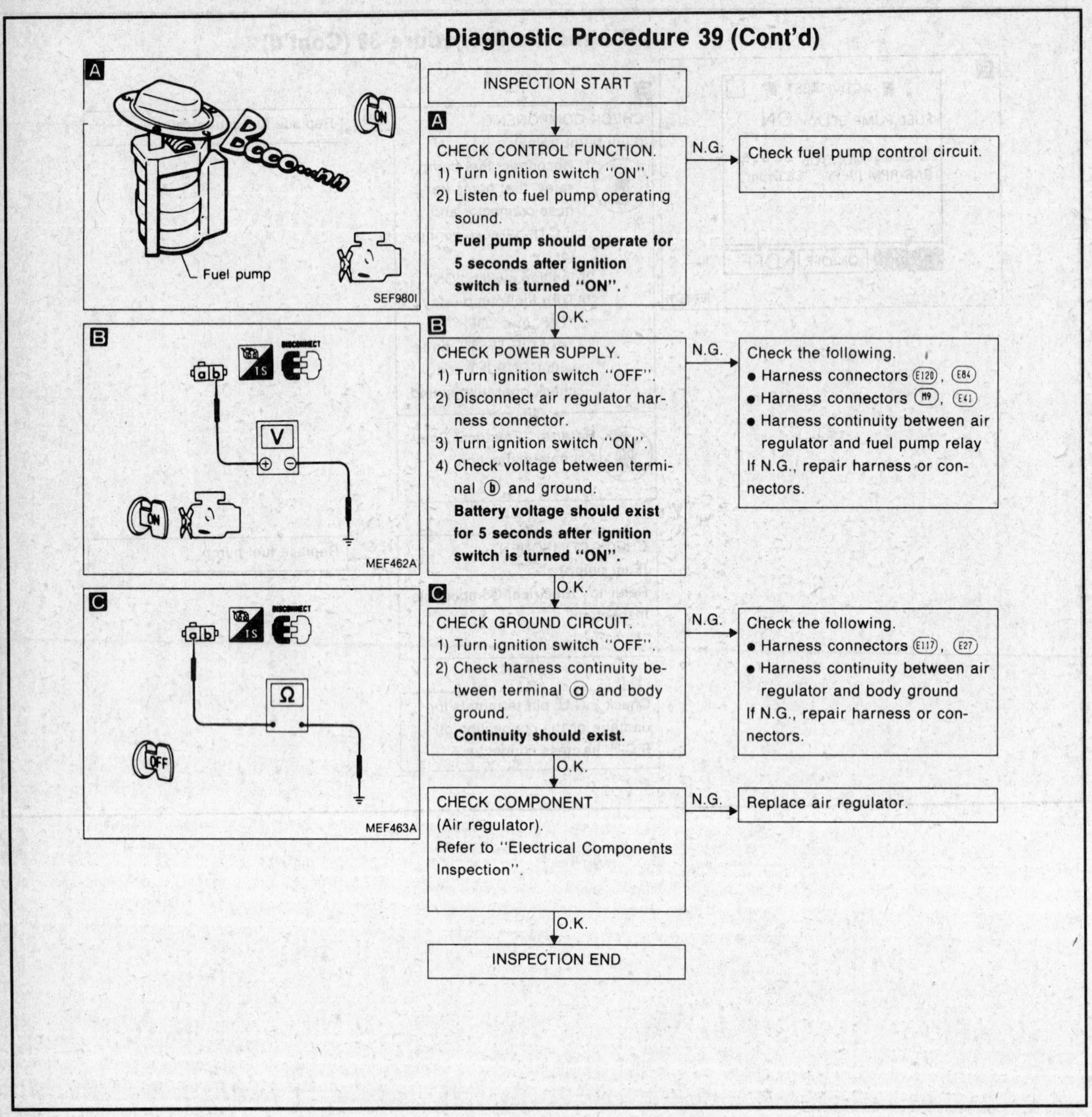
Diagnostic Procedure 39 (Cont'd)
A
Fuel pump
SEF980I
B
a b
V
MEF462A
C
a b
Ω
MEF463A
INSPECTION START
A
CHECK CONTROL FUNCTION.
1) Turn ignition switch "ON".
2) Listen to fuel pump operating sound.
Fuel pump should operate for 5 seconds after ignition switch is turned "ON".
N.G.
Check fuel pump control circuit.
O.K.
B
CHECK POWER SUPPLY.
1) Turn ignition switch "OFF".
2) Disconnect air regulator harness connector.
3) Turn ignition switch "ON".
4) Check voltage between terminal ⓑ and ground.
Battery voltage should exist for 5 seconds after ignition switch is turned "ON".
N.G.
Check the following.
• Harness connectors E120, E84
• Harness connectors M9, E41
• Harness continuity between air regulator and fuel pump relay
If N.G., repair harness or connectors.
O.K.
C
CHECK GROUND CIRCUIT.
1) Turn ignition switch "OFF".
2) Check harness continuity between terminal ⓐ and body ground.
Continuity should exist.
N.G.
Check the following.
• Harness connectors E117, E27
• Harness continuity between air regulator and body ground
If N.G., repair harness or connectors.
O.K.
CHECK COMPONENT
(Air regulator).
Refer to "Electrical Components Inspection".
N.G.
Replace air regulator.
O.K.
INSPECTION END

AAC VALVE DIAGNOSTIC CHART – GA16DE AND SR20DE ENGINES

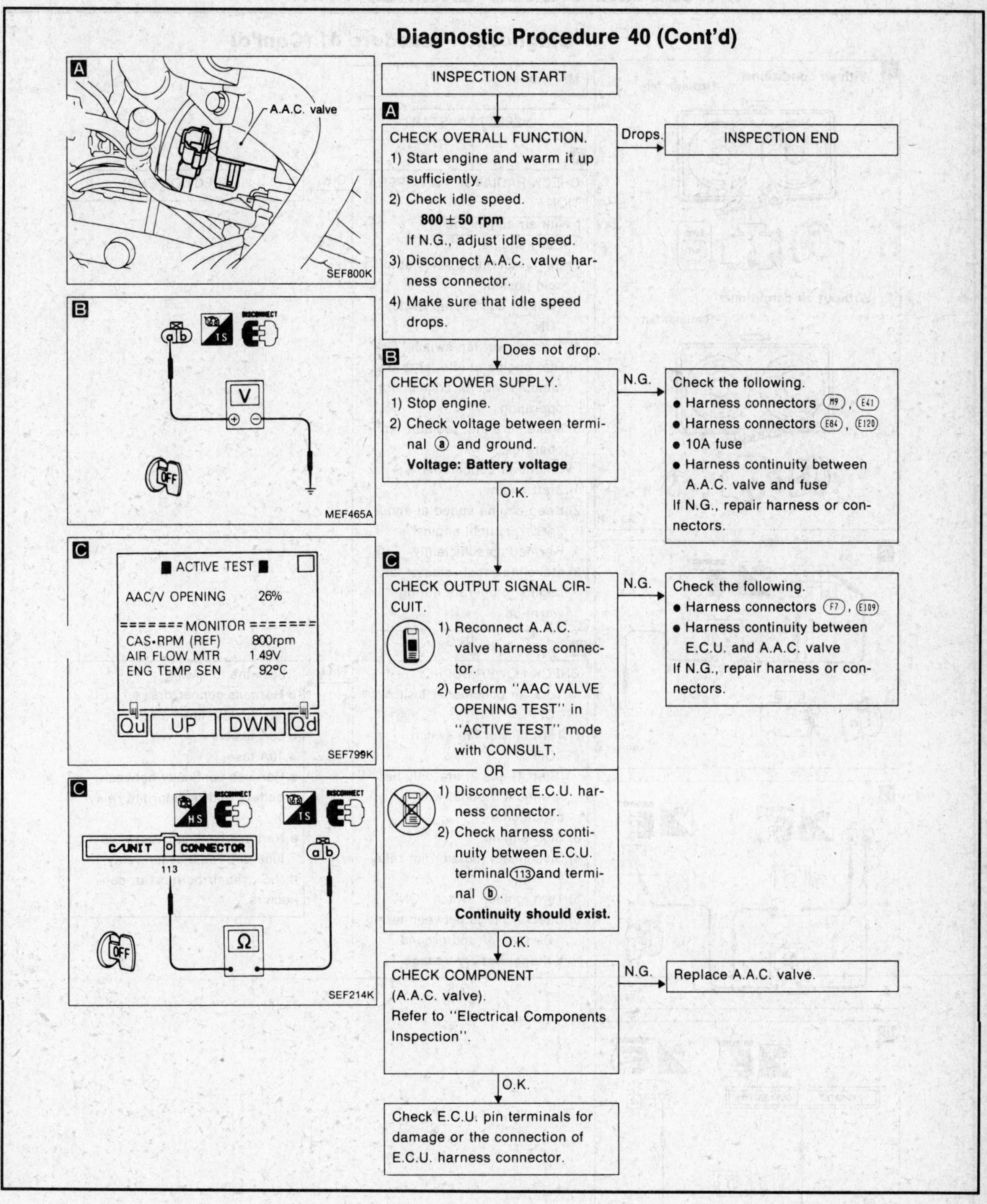
Diagnostic Procedure 40 (Cont'd)
A
A.A.C. valve
SEF800K
B
DISCONNECT
TS
V
OFF
MEF465A
C
ACTIVE TEST
AAC/V OPENING 26%
MONITOR
CAS•RPM (REF) 800rpm
AIR FLOW MTR 1.49V
ENG TEMP SEN 92°C
Qu UP DWN Qd
SEF799K
C
HS
DISCONNECT
TS
DISCONNECT
C/UNIT CONNECTOR
113
Ω
OFF
SEF214K
INSPECTION START
A
CHECK OVERALL FUNCTION.
1) Start engine and warm it up sufficiently.
2) Check idle speed.
800 ± 50 rpm
If N.G., adjust idle speed.
3) Disconnect A.A.C. valve harness connector.
4) Make sure that idle speed drops.
Drops.
INSPECTION END
Does not drop.
B
CHECK POWER SUPPLY.
1) Stop engine.
2) Check voltage between terminal ⓐ and ground.
Voltage: Battery voltage
N.G.
Check the following.
• Harness connectors M9, E41
• Harness connectors E84, E120
• 10A fuse
• Harness continuity between A.A.C. valve and fuse
If N.G., repair harness or connectors.
O.K.
C
CHECK OUTPUT SIGNAL CIRCUIT.
1) Reconnect A.A.C. valve harness connector.
2) Perform "AAC VALVE OPENING TEST" in "ACTIVE TEST" mode with CONSULT.
OR
1) Disconnect E.C.U. harness connector.
2) Check harness continuity between E.C.U. terminal 113 and terminal ⓑ.
Continuity should exist.
N.G.
Check the following.
• Harness connectors F7, E109
• Harness continuity between E.C.U. and A.A.C. valve
If N.G., repair harness or connectors.
O.K.
CHECK COMPONENT (A.A.C. valve).
Refer to "Electrical Components Inspection".
N.G.
Replace A.A.C. valve.
O.K.
Check E.C.U. pin terminals for damage or the connection of E.C.U. harness connector.

RADIATOR COOLING FAN CONTROL DIAGNOSTIC CHART
GA16DE AND SR20DE ENGINES, PART 1

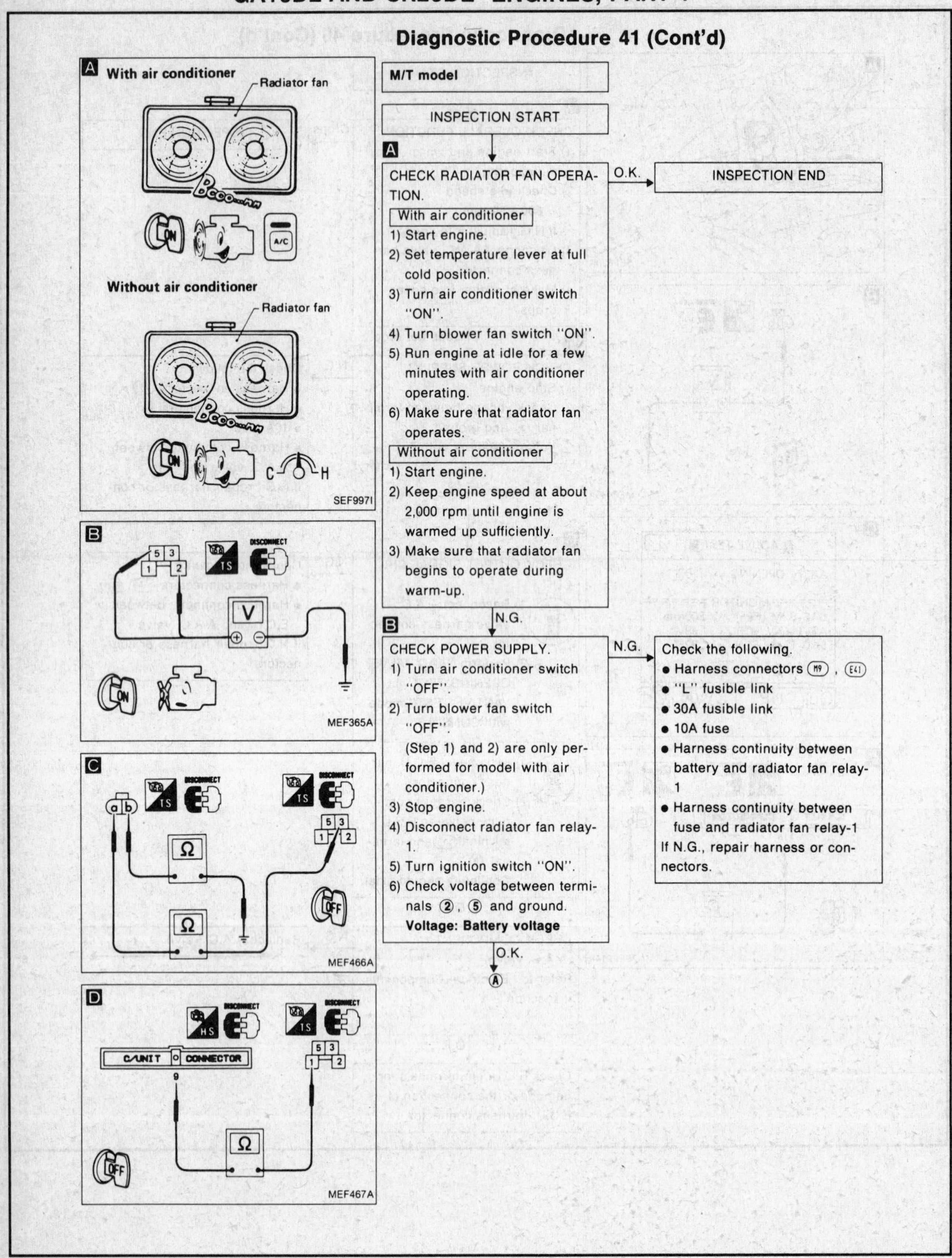
Diagnostic Procedure 41 (Cont'd)
A
With air conditioner
Radiator fan
Bcoo...nn
ON
A/C
Without air conditioner
Radiator fan
Bcoo...nn
ON
C
H
SEF997I
B
5 3
1 2
TS
DISCONNECT
V
ON
MEF365A
C
a b
TS
DISCONNECT
Ω
Ω
5 3
1 2
OFF
MEF466A
D
HS
DISCONNECT
TS
DISCONNECT
C/UNIT
CONNECTOR
9
5 3
1 2
Ω
OFF
MEF467A
M/T model
INSPECTION START
A
CHECK RADIATOR FAN OPERATION.
With air conditioner
1) Start engine.
2) Set temperature lever at full cold position.
3) Turn air conditioner switch "ON".
4) Turn blower fan switch "ON".
5) Run engine at idle for a few minutes with air conditioner operating.
6) Make sure that radiator fan operates.
Without air conditioner
1) Start engine.
2) Keep engine speed at about 2,000 rpm until engine is warmed up sufficiently.
3) Make sure that radiator fan begins to operate during warm-up.
O.K.
INSPECTION END
N.G.
B
CHECK POWER SUPPLY.
1) Turn air conditioner switch "OFF".
2) Turn blower fan switch "OFF".
(Step 1) and 2) are only performed for model with air conditioner.)
3) Stop engine.
4) Disconnect radiator fan relay-1.
5) Turn ignition switch "ON".
6) Check voltage between terminals ②, ⑤ and ground.
Voltage: Battery voltage
N.G.
Check the following.
● Harness connectors (M9), (E41)
● "L" fusible link
● 30A fusible link
● 10A fuse
● Harness continuity between battery and radiator fan relay-1
● Harness continuity between fuse and radiator fan relay-1
If N.G., repair harness or connectors.
O.K.
Ⓐ

RADIATOR COOLING FAN CONTROL DIAGNOSTIC CHART GA16DE AND SR20DE ENGINES, PART 2

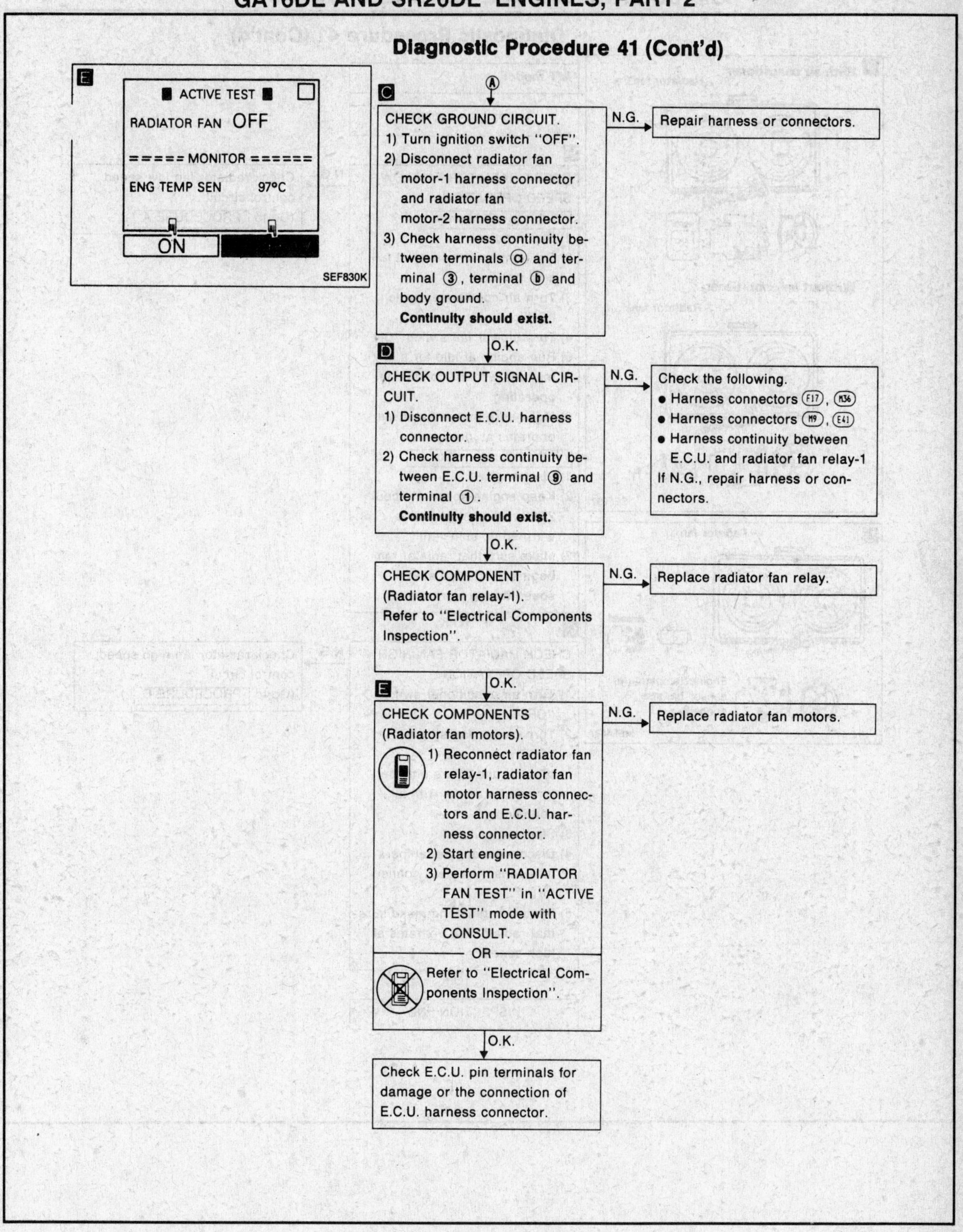
Diagnostic Procedure 41 (Cont'd)
E
ACTIVE TEST
RADIATOR FAN OFF
===== MONITOR ======
ENG TEMP SEN 97°C
ON
SEF830K
A
C
CHECK GROUND CIRCUIT.
1) Turn ignition switch "OFF".
2) Disconnect radiator fan motor-1 harness connector and radiator fan motor-2 harness connector.
3) Check harness continuity between terminals ⓐ and terminal ③, terminal ⓑ and body ground.
Continuity should exist.
N.G.
Repair harness or connectors.
O.K.
D
CHECK OUTPUT SIGNAL CIRCUIT.
1) Disconnect E.C.U. harness connector.
2) Check harness continuity between E.C.U. terminal ⑨ and terminal ①.
Continuity should exist.
N.G.
Check the following.
• Harness connectors (F17), (M36)
• Harness connectors (M9), (E41)
• Harness continuity between E.C.U. and radiator fan relay-1
If N.G., repair harness or connectors.
O.K.
CHECK COMPONENT (Radiator fan relay-1).
Refer to "Electrical Components Inspection".
N.G.
Replace radiator fan relay.
O.K.
E
CHECK COMPONENTS (Radiator fan motors).
1) Reconnect radiator fan relay-1, radiator fan motor harness connectors and E.C.U. harness connector.
2) Start engine.
3) Perform "RADIATOR FAN TEST" in "ACTIVE TEST" mode with CONSULT.
OR
Refer to "Electrical Components Inspection".
N.G.
Replace radiator fan motors.
O.K.
Check E.C.U. pin terminals for damage or the connection of E.C.U. harness connector.

RADIATOR COOLING FAN CONTROL DIAGNOSTIC CHART GA16DE AND SR20DE ENGINES, PART 3

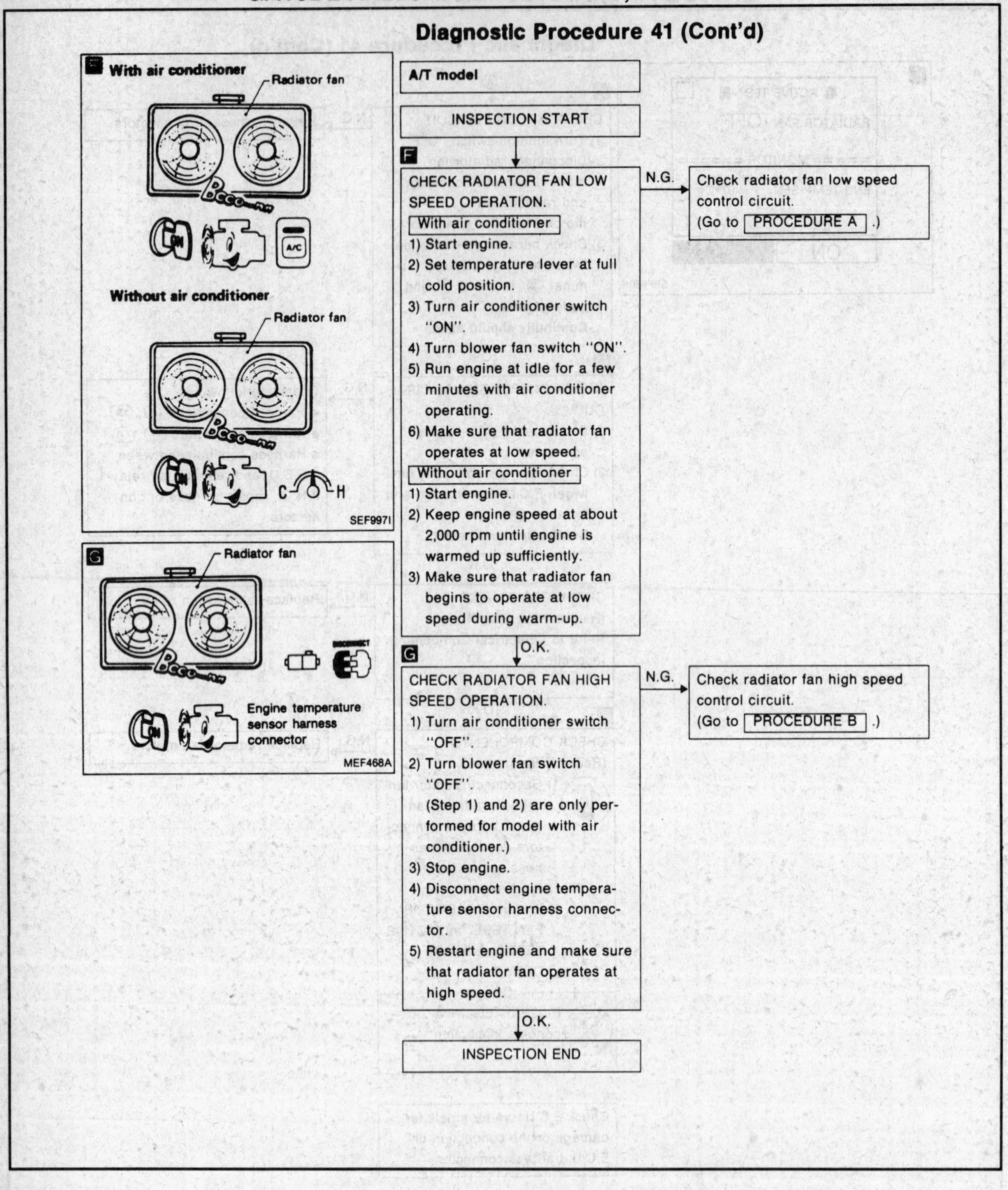
Diagnostic Procedure 41 (Cont'd)
F
With air conditioner
Radiator fan
A/C
Without air conditioner
Radiator fan
C
H
SEF997I
G
Radiator fan
DISCONNECT
Engine temperature sensor harness connector
MEF468A
A/T model
INSPECTION START
F
CHECK RADIATOR FAN LOW SPEED OPERATION.
With air conditioner
1) Start engine.
2) Set temperature lever at full cold position.
3) Turn air conditioner switch "ON".
4) Turn blower fan switch "ON".
5) Run engine at idle for a few minutes with air conditioner operating.
6) Make sure that radiator fan operates at low speed.
Without air conditioner
1) Start engine.
2) Keep engine speed at about 2,000 rpm until engine is warmed up sufficiently.
3) Make sure that radiator fan begins to operate at low speed during warm-up.
N.G.
Check radiator fan low speed control circuit.
(Go to PROCEDURE A .)
O.K.
G
CHECK RADIATOR FAN HIGH SPEED OPERATION.
1) Turn air conditioner switch "OFF".
2) Turn blower fan switch "OFF".
(Step 1) and 2) are only performed for model with air conditioner.)
3) Stop engine.
4) Disconnect engine temperature sensor harness connector.
5) Restart engine and make sure that radiator fan operates at high speed.
N.G.
Check radiator fan high speed control circuit.
(Go to PROCEDURE B .)
O.K.
INSPECTION END

RADIATOR COOLING FAN CONTROL DIAGNOSTIC CHART GA16DE AND SR20DE ENGINES, PART 4

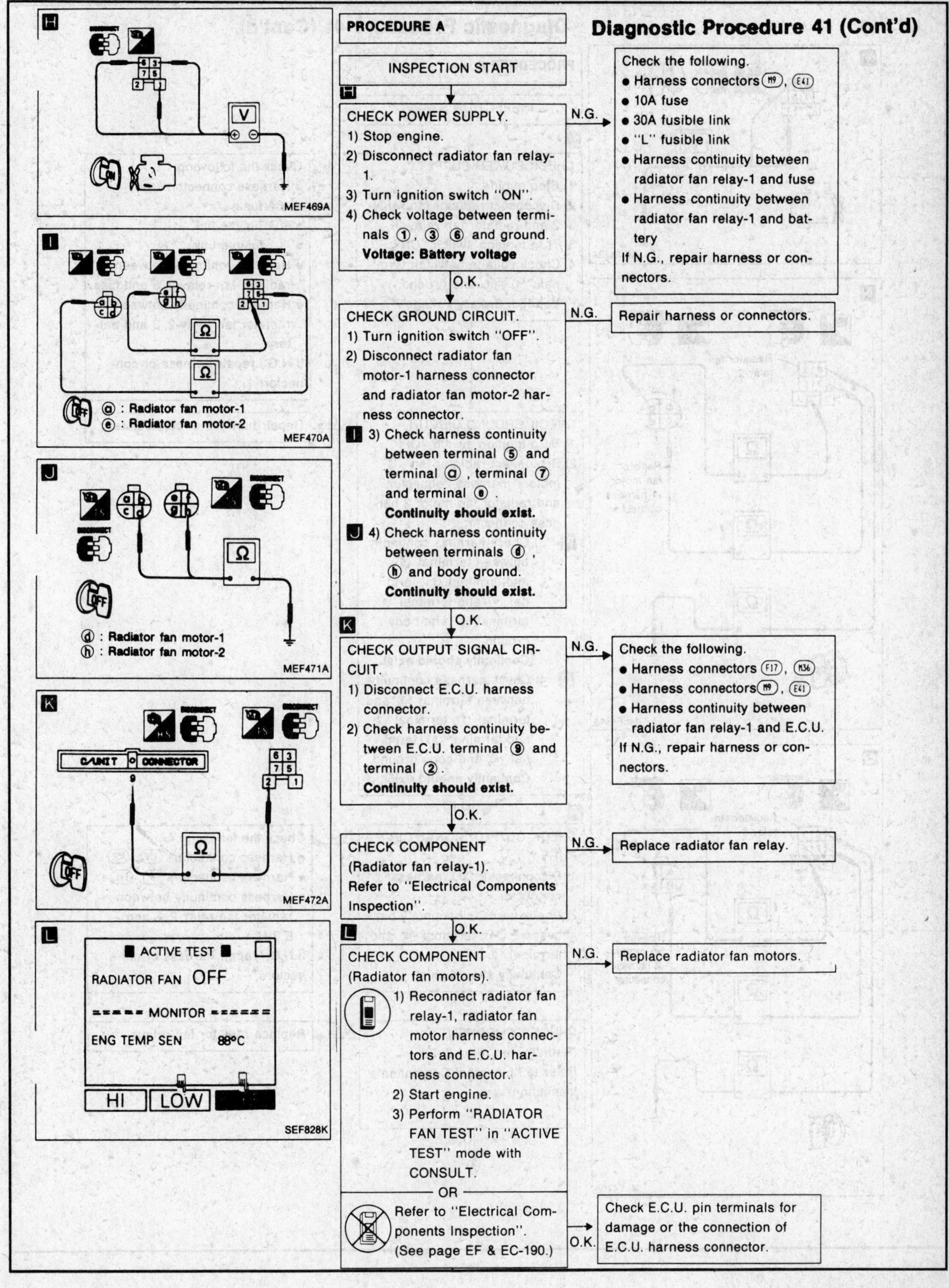

H
MEF469A
I
ⓐ : Radiator fan motor-1
ⓔ : Radiator fan motor-2
MEF470A
J
ⓓ : Radiator fan motor-1
ⓗ : Radiator fan motor-2
MEF471A
K
C/UNIT CONNECTOR
MEF472A
L
ACTIVE TEST
RADIATOR FAN OFF
MONITOR
ENG TEMP SEN 88°C
HI
LOW
SEF828K
PROCEDURE A
Diagnostic Procedure 41 (Cont'd)
INSPECTION START
H
CHECK POWER SUPPLY.
1) Stop engine.
2) Disconnect radiator fan relay-1.
3) Turn ignition switch "ON".
4) Check voltage between terminals ①, ③ ⑥ and ground.
Voltage: Battery voltage
N.G.
Check the following.
● Harness connectors (M9), (E41)
● 10A fuse
● 30A fusible link
● "L" fusible link
● Harness continuity between radiator fan relay-1 and fuse
● Harness continuity between radiator fan relay-1 and battery
If N.G., repair harness or connectors.
O.K.
CHECK GROUND CIRCUIT.
1) Turn ignition switch "OFF".
2) Disconnect radiator fan motor-1 harness connector and radiator fan motor-2 harness connector.
I 3) Check harness continuity between terminal ⑤ and terminal ⓐ, terminal ⑦ and terminal ⓔ.
Continuity should exist.
J 4) Check harness continuity between terminals ⓓ, ⓗ and body ground.
Continuity should exist.
N.G.
Repair harness or connectors.
O.K.
K
CHECK OUTPUT SIGNAL CIRCUIT.
1) Disconnect E.C.U. harness connector.
2) Check harness continuity between E.C.U. terminal ⑨ and terminal ②.
Continuity should exist.
N.G.
Check the following.
● Harness connectors (F17), (M36)
● Harness connectors (M9), (E41)
● Harness continuity between radiator fan relay-1 and E.C.U.
If N.G., repair harness or connectors.
O.K.
CHECK COMPONENT
(Radiator fan relay-1).
Refer to "Electrical Components Inspection".
N.G.
Replace radiator fan relay.
O.K.
L
CHECK COMPONENT
(Radiator fan motors).
1) Reconnect radiator fan relay-1, radiator fan motor harness connectors and E.C.U. harness connector.
2) Start engine.
3) Perform "RADIATOR FAN TEST" in "ACTIVE TEST" mode with CONSULT.
OR
Refer to "Electrical Components Inspection".
(See page EF & EC-190.)
N.G.
Replace radiator fan motors.
O.K.
Check E.C.U. pin terminals for damage or the connection of E.C.U. harness connector.

RADIATOR COOLING FAN CONTROL DIAGNOSTIC CHART
GA16DE AND SR20DE ENGINES, PART 5

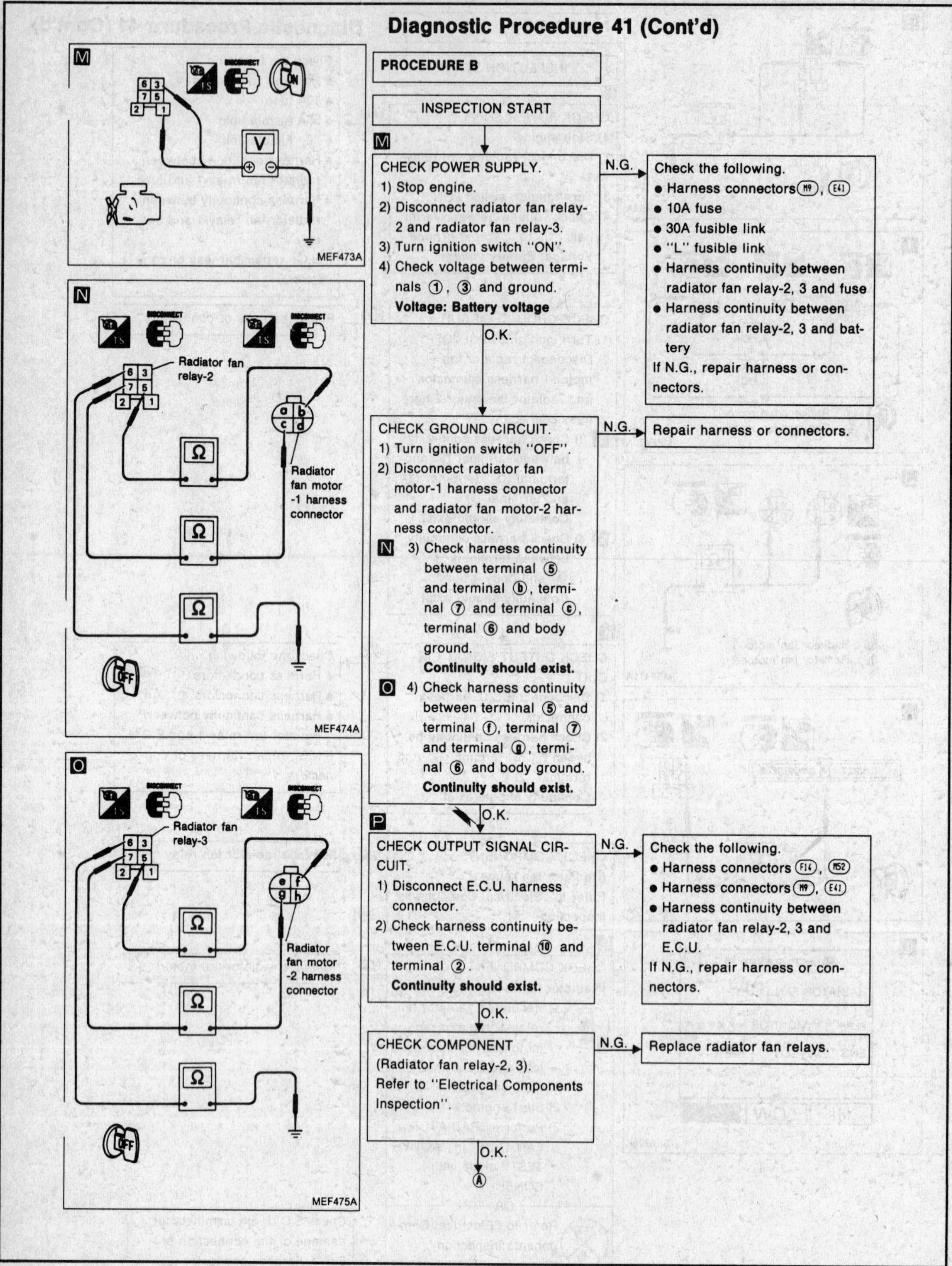
Diagnostic Procedure 41 (Cont'd)
M
DISCONNECT
ON
6 3
7 5
2 1
V
MEF473A
PROCEDURE B
INSPECTION START
M
CHECK POWER SUPPLY.
1) Stop engine.
2) Disconnect radiator fan relay-2 and radiator fan relay-3.
3) Turn ignition switch "ON".
4) Check voltage between terminals ①, ③ and ground.
Voltage: Battery voltage
N.G.
Check the following.
• Harness connectors (M9), (E41)
• 10A fuse
• 30A fusible link
• "L" fusible link
• Harness continuity between radiator fan relay-2, 3 and fuse
• Harness continuity between radiator fan relay-2, 3 and battery
If N.G., repair harness or connectors.
O.K.
N
DISCONNECT
Radiator fan relay-2
a b
c d
Radiator fan motor -1 harness connector
OFF
MEF474A
CHECK GROUND CIRCUIT.
1) Turn ignition switch "OFF".
2) Disconnect radiator fan motor-1 harness connector and radiator fan motor-2 harness connector.
N 3) Check harness continuity between terminal ⑤ and terminal ⓑ, terminal ⑦ and terminal ⓒ, terminal ⑥ and body ground.
Continuity should exist.
O 4) Check harness continuity between terminal ⑤ and terminal ⓕ, terminal ⑦ and terminal ⓖ, terminal ⑥ and body ground.
Continuity should exist.
N.G.
Repair harness or connectors.
O.K.
O
DISCONNECT
Radiator fan relay-3
e f
g h
Radiator fan motor -2 harness connector
OFF
MEF475A
P
CHECK OUTPUT SIGNAL CIRCUIT.
1) Disconnect E.C.U. harness connector.
2) Check harness continuity between E.C.U. terminal ⑩ and terminal ②.
Continuity should exist.
N.G.
Check the following.
• Harness connectors (F16), (M52)
• Harness connectors (M9), (E41)
• Harness continuity between radiator fan relay-2, 3 and E.C.U.
If N.G., repair harness or connectors.
O.K.
CHECK COMPONENT
(Radiator fan relay-2, 3).
Refer to "Electrical Components Inspection".
N.G.
Replace radiator fan relays.
O.K.
Ⓐ

RADIATOR COOLING FAN CONTROL DIAGNOSTIC CHART GA16DE AND SR20DE ENGINES PART 6

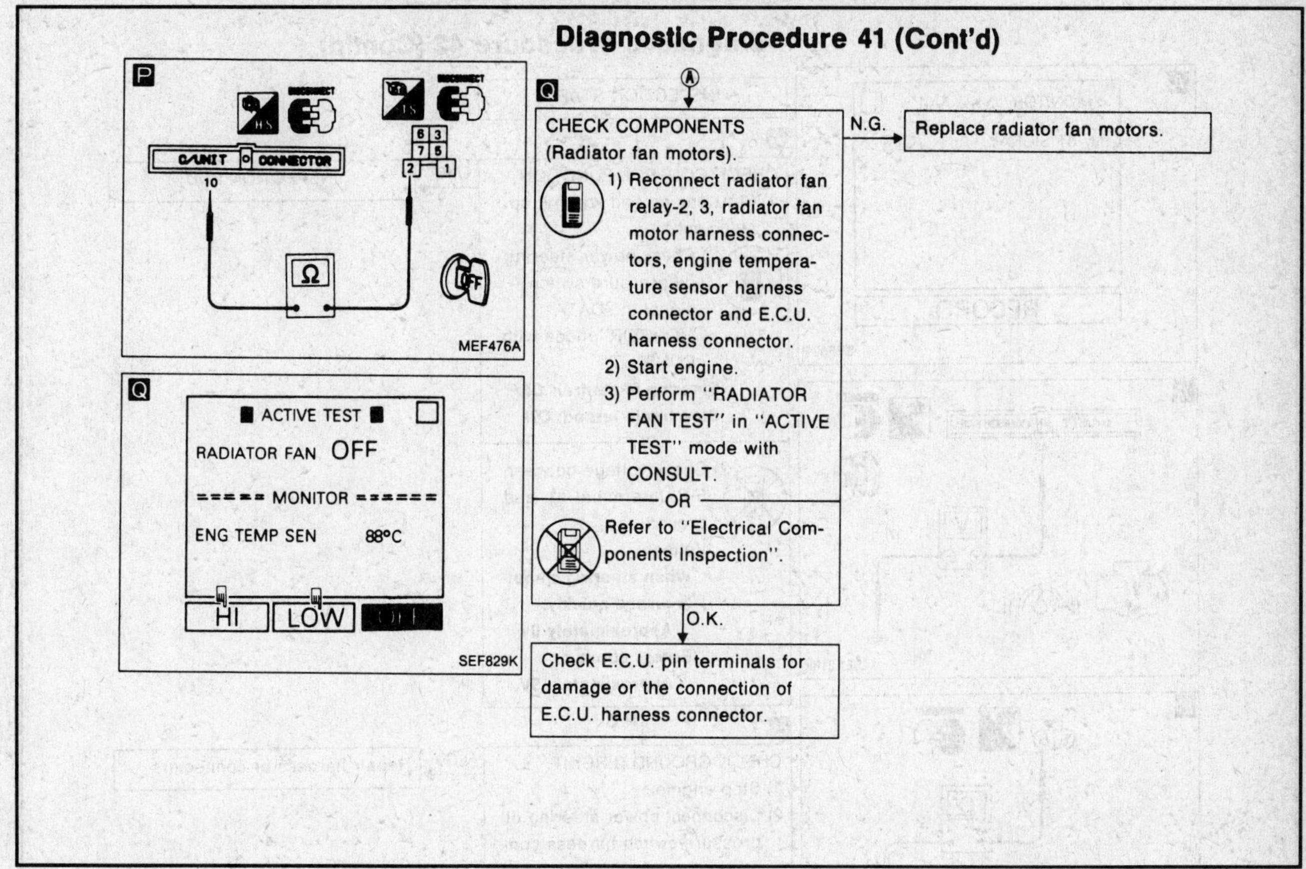
Diagnostic Procedure 41 (Cont'd)
P
C/UNIT CONNECTOR
10
6 3
7 5
2 1
Ω
OFF
MEF476A
Q
ACTIVE TEST
RADIATOR FAN OFF
MONITOR
ENG TEMP SEN 88°C
HI
LOW
OFF
SEF829K
Q
A
CHECK COMPONENTS
(Radiator fan motors).
1) Reconnect radiator fan relay-2, 3, radiator fan motor harness connectors, engine temperature sensor harness connector and E.C.U. harness connector.
2) Start engine.
3) Perform "RADIATOR FAN TEST" in "ACTIVE TEST" mode with CONSULT.
OR
Refer to "Electrical Components Inspection".
N.G.
Replace radiator fan motors.
O.K.
Check E.C.U. pin terminals for damage or the connection of E.C.U. harness connector.

POWER STEERING PRESSURE SWITCH DIAGNOSTIC CHART GA16DE AND SR20DE ENGINES

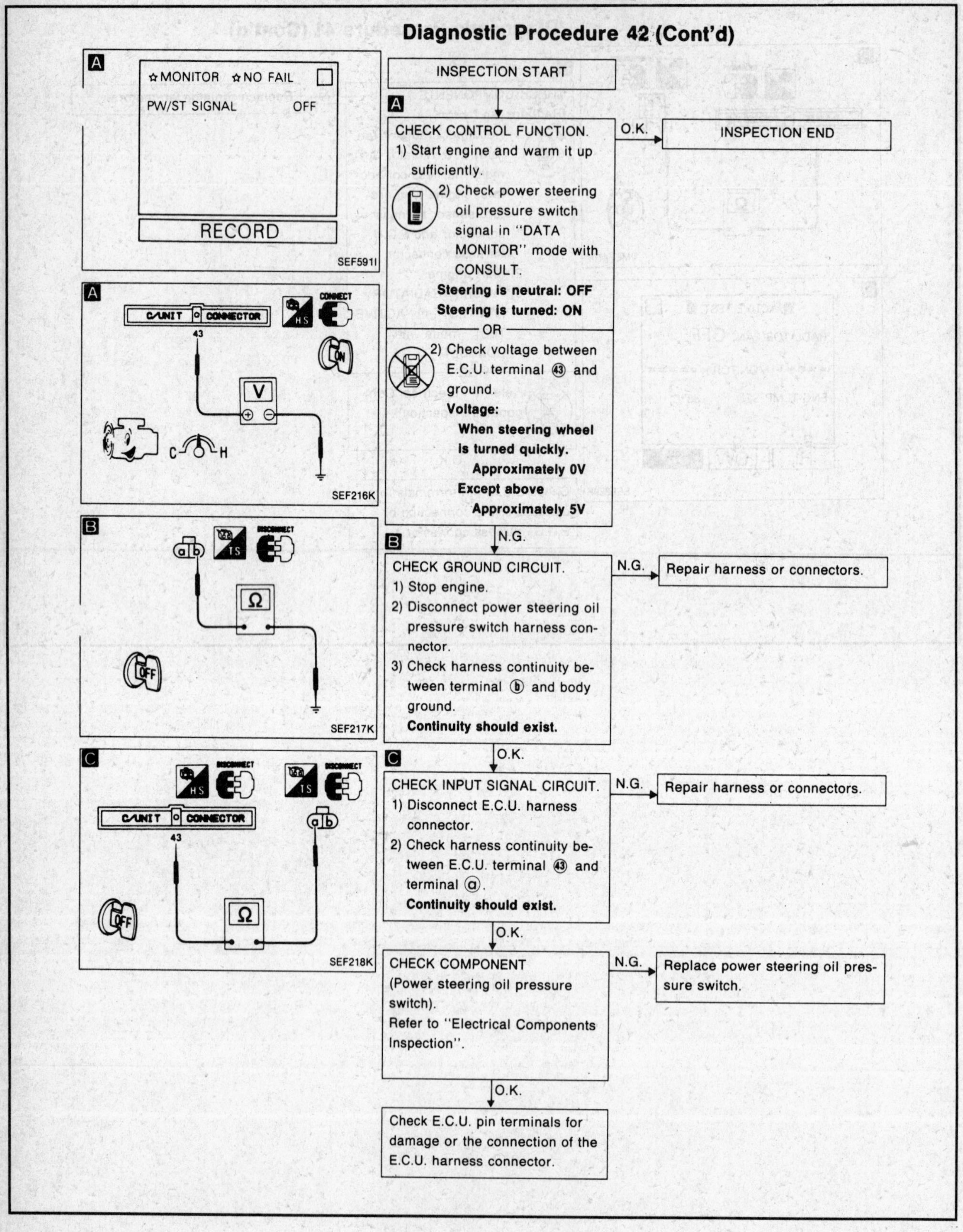
Diagnostic Procedure 42 (Cont'd)
A
☆MONITOR ☆NO FAIL
PW/ST SIGNAL OFF
RECORD
SEF591I
A
C/UNIT CONNECTOR
43
CONNECT
V
C H
SEF216K
B
DISCONNECT
Ω
OFF
SEF217K
C
DISCONNECT
DISCONNECT
C/UNIT CONNECTOR
43
Ω
OFF
SEF218K
INSPECTION START
A
CHECK CONTROL FUNCTION.
1) Start engine and warm it up sufficiently.
2) Check power steering oil pressure switch signal in "DATA MONITOR" mode with CONSULT.
Steering is neutral: OFF
Steering is turned: ON
OR
2) Check voltage between E.C.U. terminal 43 and ground.
Voltage:
When steering wheel is turned quickly.
Approximately 0V
Except above
Approximately 5V
O.K.
INSPECTION END
N.G.
B
CHECK GROUND CIRCUIT.
1) Stop engine.
2) Disconnect power steering oil pressure switch harness connector.
3) Check harness continuity between terminal b and body ground.
Continuity should exist.
N.G.
Repair harness or connectors.
O.K.
C
CHECK INPUT SIGNAL CIRCUIT.
1) Disconnect E.C.U. harness connector.
2) Check harness continuity between E.C.U. terminal 43 and terminal a.
Continuity should exist.
N.G.
Repair harness or connectors.
O.K.
CHECK COMPONENT
(Power steering oil pressure switch).
Refer to "Electrical Components Inspection".
N.G.
Replace power steering oil pressure switch.
O.K.
Check E.C.U. pin terminals for damage or the connection of the E.C.U. harness connector.

NEUTRAL INHIBITOR SWITCH DIAGNOSTIC CHART GA16DE AND SR20DE ENGINES, PART 1

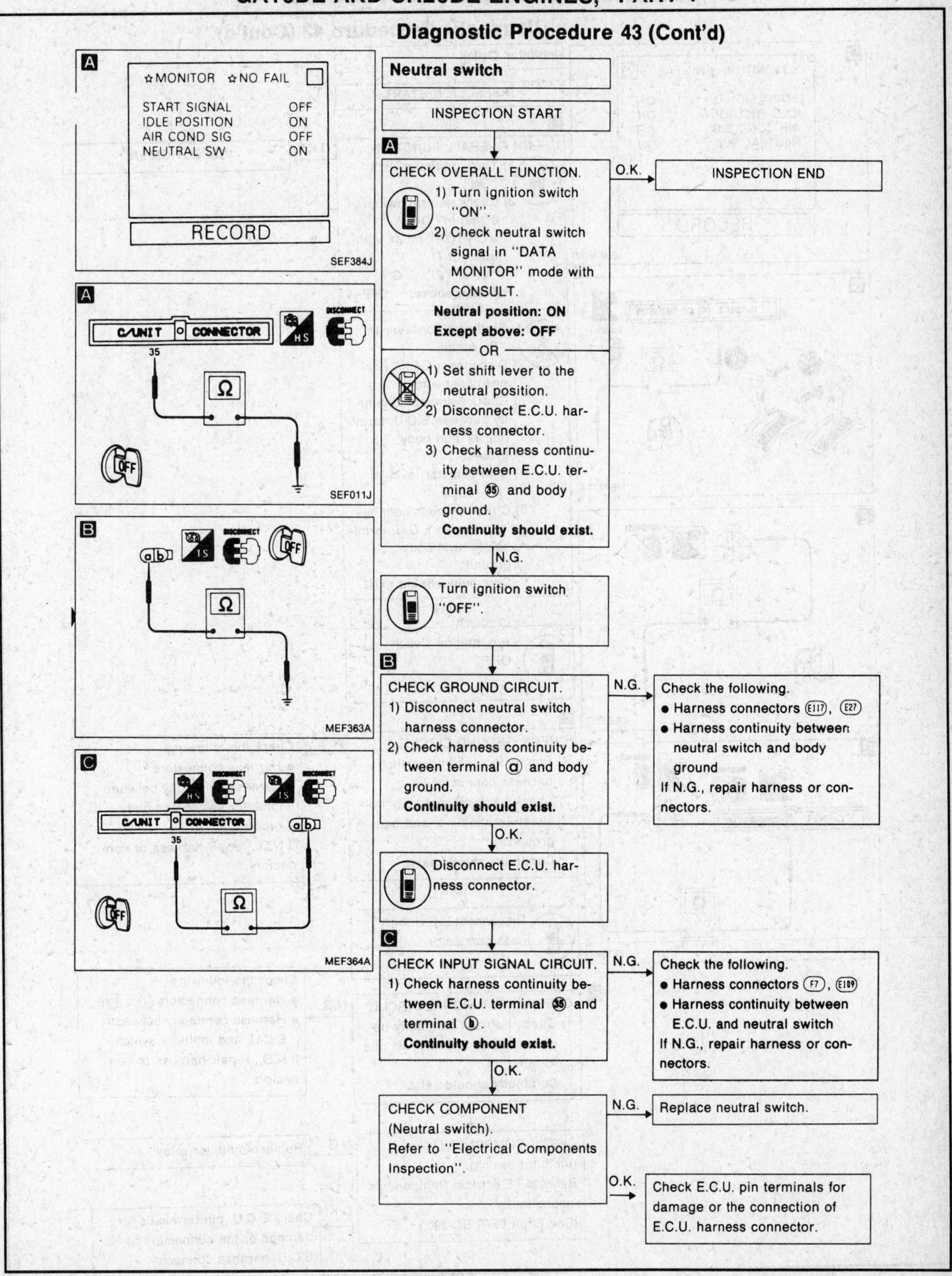
Diagnostic Procedure 43 (Cont'd)
A
☆MONITOR ☆NO FAIL
START SIGNAL OFF
IDLE POSITION ON
AIR COND SIG OFF
NEUTRAL SW ON
RECORD
SEF384J
A
C/UNIT CONNECTOR
DISCONNECT
35
OFF
SEF011J
B
DISCONNECT
OFF
MEF363A
C
DISCONNECT
C/UNIT CONNECTOR
35
OFF
MEF364A
Neutral switch
INSPECTION START
A
CHECK OVERALL FUNCTION.
1) Turn ignition switch "ON".
2) Check neutral switch signal in "DATA MONITOR" mode with CONSULT.
Neutral position: ON
Except above: OFF
OR
1) Set shift lever to the neutral position.
2) Disconnect E.C.U. harness connector.
3) Check harness continuity between E.C.U. terminal ㉟ and body ground.
Continuity should exist.
O.K.
INSPECTION END
N.G.
Turn ignition switch "OFF".
B
CHECK GROUND CIRCUIT.
1) Disconnect neutral switch harness connector.
2) Check harness continuity between terminal ⓐ and body ground.
Continuity should exist.
N.G.
Check the following.
● Harness connectors E117, E27
● Harness continuity between neutral switch and body ground
If N.G., repair harness or connectors.
O.K.
Disconnect E.C.U. harness connector.
C
CHECK INPUT SIGNAL CIRCUIT.
1) Check harness continuity between E.C.U. terminal ㉟ and terminal ⓑ.
Continuity should exist.
N.G.
Check the following.
● Harness connectors F7, E109
● Harness continuity between E.C.U. and neutral switch
If N.G., repair harness or connectors.
O.K.
CHECK COMPONENT
(Neutral switch).
Refer to "Electrical Components Inspection".
N.G.
Replace neutral switch.
O.K.
Check E.C.U. pin terminals for damage or the connection of E.C.U. harness connector.

NEUTRAL INHIBITOR SWITCH DIAGNOSTIC CHART GA16DE AND SR20DE ENGINES, PART 2

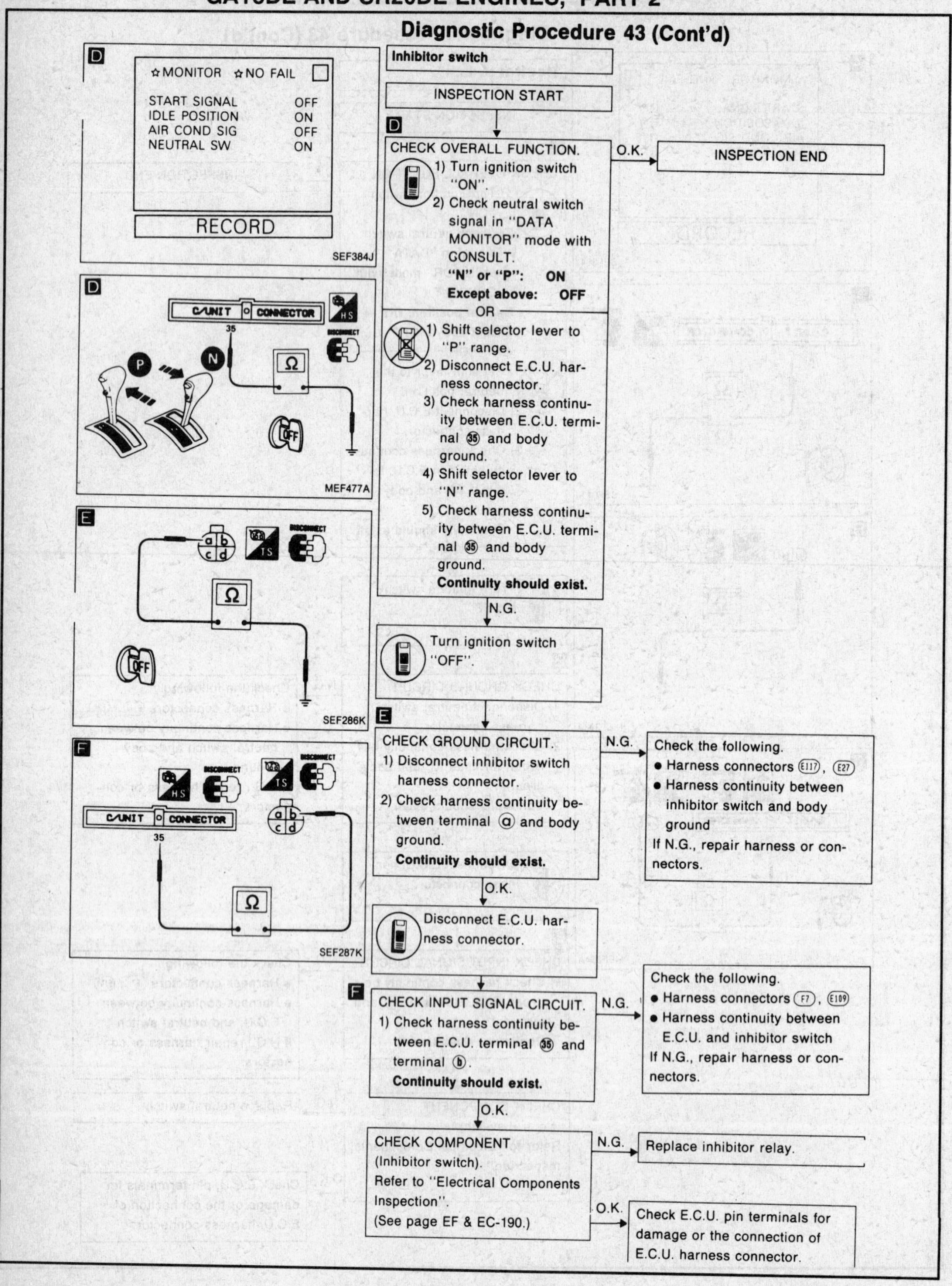

Diagnostic Procedure 43 (Cont'd)
D
☆MONITOR ☆NO FAIL
START SIGNAL OFF
IDLE POSITION ON
AIR COND SIG OFF
NEUTRAL SW ON
RECORD
SEF384J
D
C/UNIT CONNECTOR
35
P
N
DISCONNECT
HS
OFF
MEF477A
E
a b
c d
TS
DISCONNECT
OFF
SEF286K
F
HS
DISCONNECT
TS
DISCONNECT
C/UNIT CONNECTOR
35
a b
c d
SEF287K
Inhibitor switch
INSPECTION START
D
CHECK OVERALL FUNCTION.
1) Turn ignition switch "ON".
2) Check neutral switch signal in "DATA MONITOR" mode with CONSULT.
"N" or "P": ON
Except above: OFF
OR
1) Shift selector lever to "P" range.
2) Disconnect E.C.U. harness connector.
3) Check harness continuity between E.C.U. terminal 35 and body ground.
4) Shift selector lever to "N" range.
5) Check harness continuity between E.C.U. terminal 35 and body ground.
Continuity should exist.
O.K.
INSPECTION END
N.G.
Turn ignition switch "OFF".
E
CHECK GROUND CIRCUIT.
1) Disconnect inhibitor switch harness connector.
2) Check harness continuity between terminal a and body ground.
Continuity should exist.
N.G.
Check the following.
● Harness connectors E117, E27
● Harness continuity between inhibitor switch and body ground
If N.G., repair harness or connectors.
O.K.
Disconnect E.C.U. harness connector.
F
CHECK INPUT SIGNAL CIRCUIT.
1) Check harness continuity between E.C.U. terminal 35 and terminal b.
Continuity should exist.
N.G.
Check the following.
● Harness connectors F7, E109
● Harness continuity between E.C.U. and inhibitor switch
If N.G., repair harness or connectors.
O.K.
CHECK COMPONENT (Inhibitor switch).
Refer to "Electrical Components Inspection".
(See page EF & EC-190.)
N.G.
Replace inhibitor relay.
O.K.
Check E.C.U. pin terminals for damage or the connection of E.C.U. harness connector.

DIESEL EMISSION CONTROLS

Crankcase Ventilation System

OPERATION

The closed-type crankcase emission control system prevents blow-by gas from entering the atmosphere and keeps the internal crankcase pressure constant.

During engine operation, the blow-by gas is fed into the intake manifold by the crankcase emission control (PCV) valve. When the intake air flow is restricted by the throttle chamber, the internal rocker cover pressure decreases. The PCV valve keeps the engine pressure constant so that air or dust is not sucked in around the crankshaft seals.

SERVICE

Remove the valve from the top of the rocker cover and suck on the pipe to make sure that air flows on the intake manifold side. Close the rocker cover side and suck on the pipe to make sure that the diaphragm makes a clicking sound

To check the hoses, use compressed air to free them or replace them. If the hoses are damaged or dirty, replace them.

Exhaust Gas Recirculation (EGR) System

SEE FIG. 16

OPERATION

The EGR flow rate is controlled in 3 stages in accordance with the engine speed, load and altitude. Stage 1 is high EGR and is obtained with the throttle closed and EGR valve open. Stage 2 is low EGR and is obtained with the throttle valve and EGR open. Stage 3 is zero EGR and is obtained with the throttle open the the EGR valve closed.

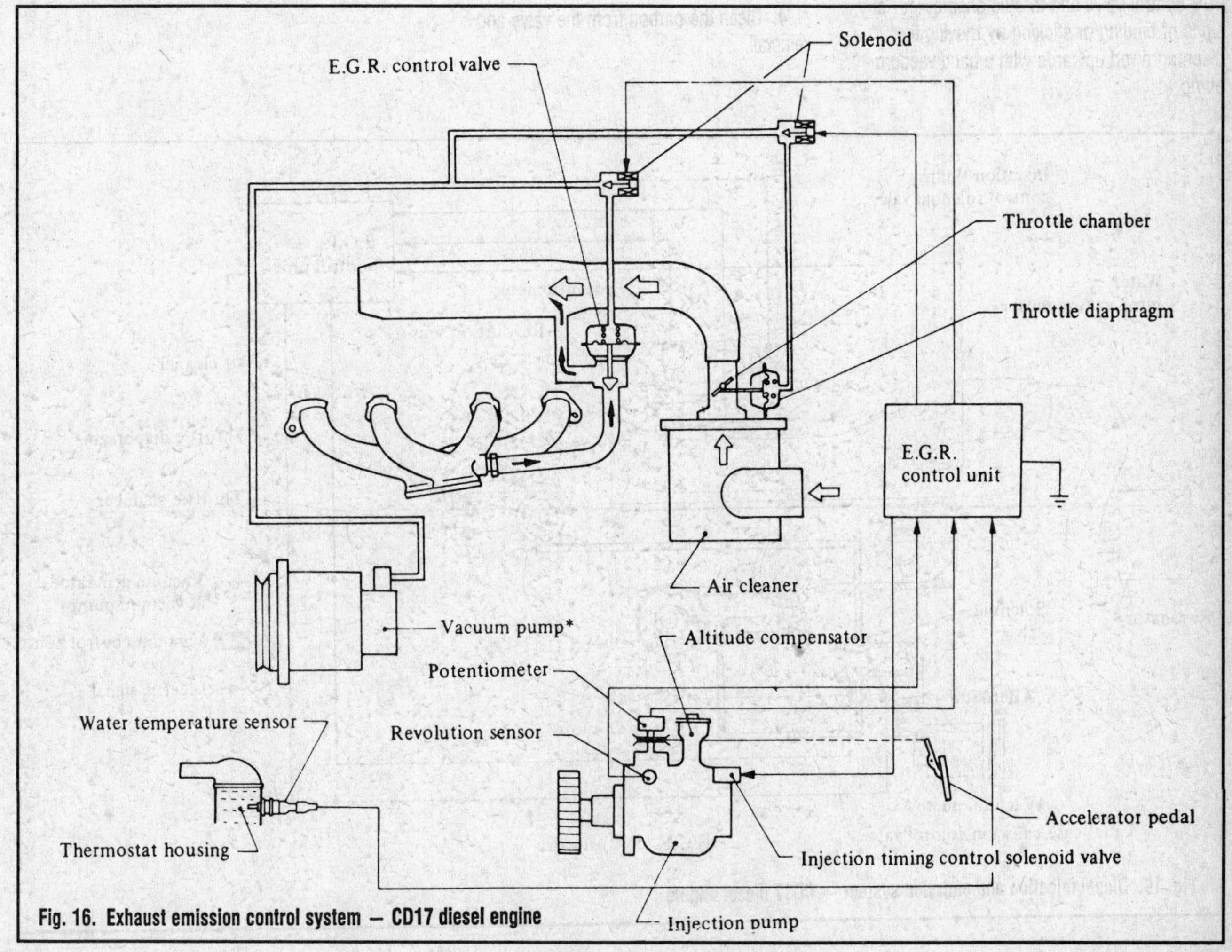
Solenoid
E.G.R. control valve
Throttle chamber
Throttle diaphragm
E.G.R. control unit
Air cleaner
Vacuum pump*
Altitude compensator
Potentiometer
Water temperature sensor
Revolution sensor
Accelerator pedal
Thermostat housing
Injection timing control solenoid valve
Injection pump

Fig. 16. Exhaust emission control system — CD17 diesel engine

The engine load signal is picked up by the potentiometer installed on the injection pump control lever. The engine speed signal is by the electromagnetic revolution sensor on the injection pump. The throttle diaphragm and EGR valve is activated by the vacuum generated at the belt driven vacuum pump. Solenoid valves are used to convert electric signals from the control unit to the vacuum signal.

The EGR system is not energized under the conditions that the water temperature is low. This is for good driveability and prevent unsafe cold engine conditions. A temperature sensor is used to indicate engine temperature to the EGR control unit.

TESTING

➧ SEE FIGS. 17–19

Entire System

1. Make a thorough check of The EGR control system and make sure all connections are connected properly.
2. With the engine not running, inspect the EGR control valve and throttle chamber for any signs of binding or sticking by moving the diaphragm rod upwards with a hand vacuum pump.
3. With the engine running, inspect the EGR control valve and throttle valve for normal operation. Place a finger on the EGR valve diaphragm to ensure that the valve is functioning.
4. When the water temperature is below 104°F (40°C). The EGR valve should not be operating.
5. After the engine is to normal operating temperature, the EGR valve should be closed until the throttle valve is opened.
6. If the EGR valve operates and throttle valve is closed before the engine is warm, check the temperature sensor. If the sensor checks, replace the EGR control unit under the left seat.
7. If the EGR valve and throttle valve does not operate when the engine is warm. Run the engine at idle and disconnect the harness to the solenoid valve. Apply 12 volts to the solenoid and check that the EGR valve operates with the throttle closed.

EGR Control Valve

1. Remove the EGR valve from the engine.
2. Apply vacuum to the valve. If the valve moves to the full position, it is normal.
3. The valve should remain open for at least 30 seconds.
4. Clean the carbon from the valve and reinstall.

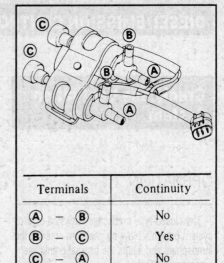

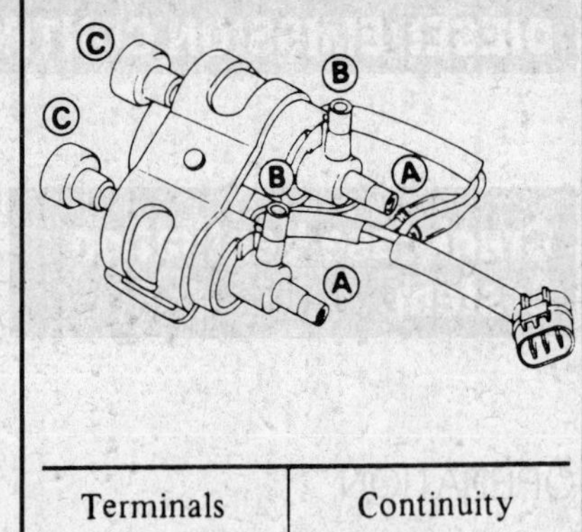

Terminals	Continuity
Ⓐ – Ⓑ	No
Ⓑ – Ⓒ	Yes
Ⓒ – Ⓐ	No

Fig. 17. Solenoid valves for CD17 diesel engine

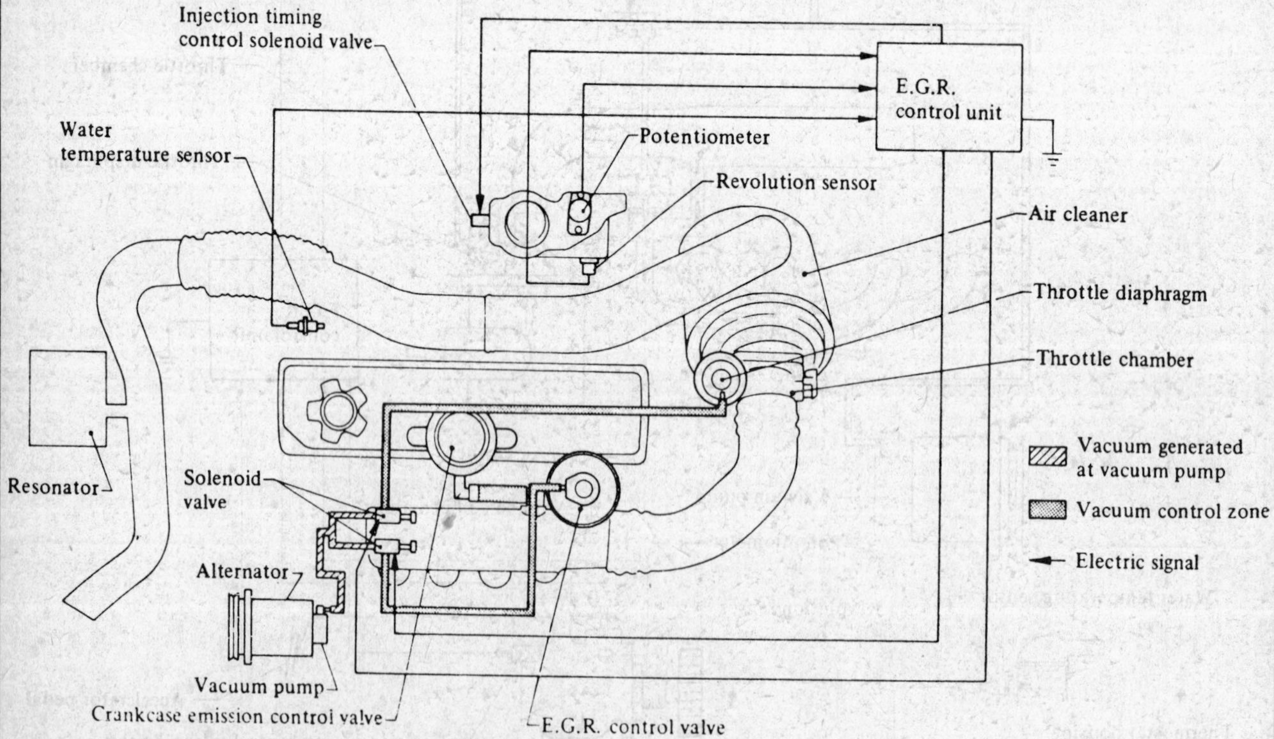

Fig. 19. Diesel injection and emission system — CD17 diesel engine

Fig. 18. Checking solenoid valves — CD17 diesel engine

Solenoid Valves

1. Remove the solenoid valves from the engine.
2. Check the continuity of the air passage by sucking or blowing into the valve ports. When blowing into ports **A and B** and **A and C**, there should be no air passing through the ports. When blowing into ports **B and C**, there should be air passing through.
3. Apply battery voltage to the solenoid valves. Check the continuity of the air passage by blowing into the valve ports. When blowing into ports **A and C** and **B and C**, there should be no air passing through the ports. When blowing into ports **A and B**, there should be air passing through.

Revolution Sensor

Disconnect the revolution sensor and connect an ohmmeter between the terminals. There should be continuity.

Potentiometer

Disconnect the potentiometer at the top of the injection pump. Connect an ohmmeter between the left and center terminals with the connector snap facing upward. The resistance should change with the opening angle of the control lever.

Temperature Sensor

Drain the cooling system. Remove the sensor from the cooling system. Place the sensor in a pan of water and check the resistance with the water at 66–70°F (19–21°C). The resistance should be 2.1–2.9kΩ.

High Altitude Emission Control and Injection Timing Control System

OPERATION

The high altitude emission control system is designed to control CO (carbon monoxide) and HC (hydrocarbons) and improve driveability in high altitude.

The altitude compensator is located on top of the injection pump with a pin connected to the control lever. The higher the altitude, the lower the atmospheric pressure. Due to this, the pressure inside the aneroid is higher than atmospheric pressure causing the aneroid to expand like a balloon. When this happens, the aneroid shaft is lower and the shaft and pin's contact surface is changed to decrease fuel. The system controls fuel in proportion to altitude.

The injection timing control solenoid (non–California) is installed on the top of the overflow connector of the injection pump and is connected to the bypass passage leading to the inlet connector. The solenoid valve controls the bypass passage in response to the electric signal from the EGR control unit which has a barometer built in. The valve is located below the altitude compensator.

1. At high altitude (above 26.57 in.Hg/90.00 kPa), the solenoid valve is ON, orifice is closed, fuel circulating in the injection pump increases, fuel pressure increases and injection timing is advanced 1.5°.
2. At low altitude (below 26.57 in.Hg/90.00 kPa), the solenoid valve is OFF, orifice is open, fuel circulating in the injection pump decreases, fuel pressure decreases and injection timing is not advanced.

VACUUM DIAGRAMS

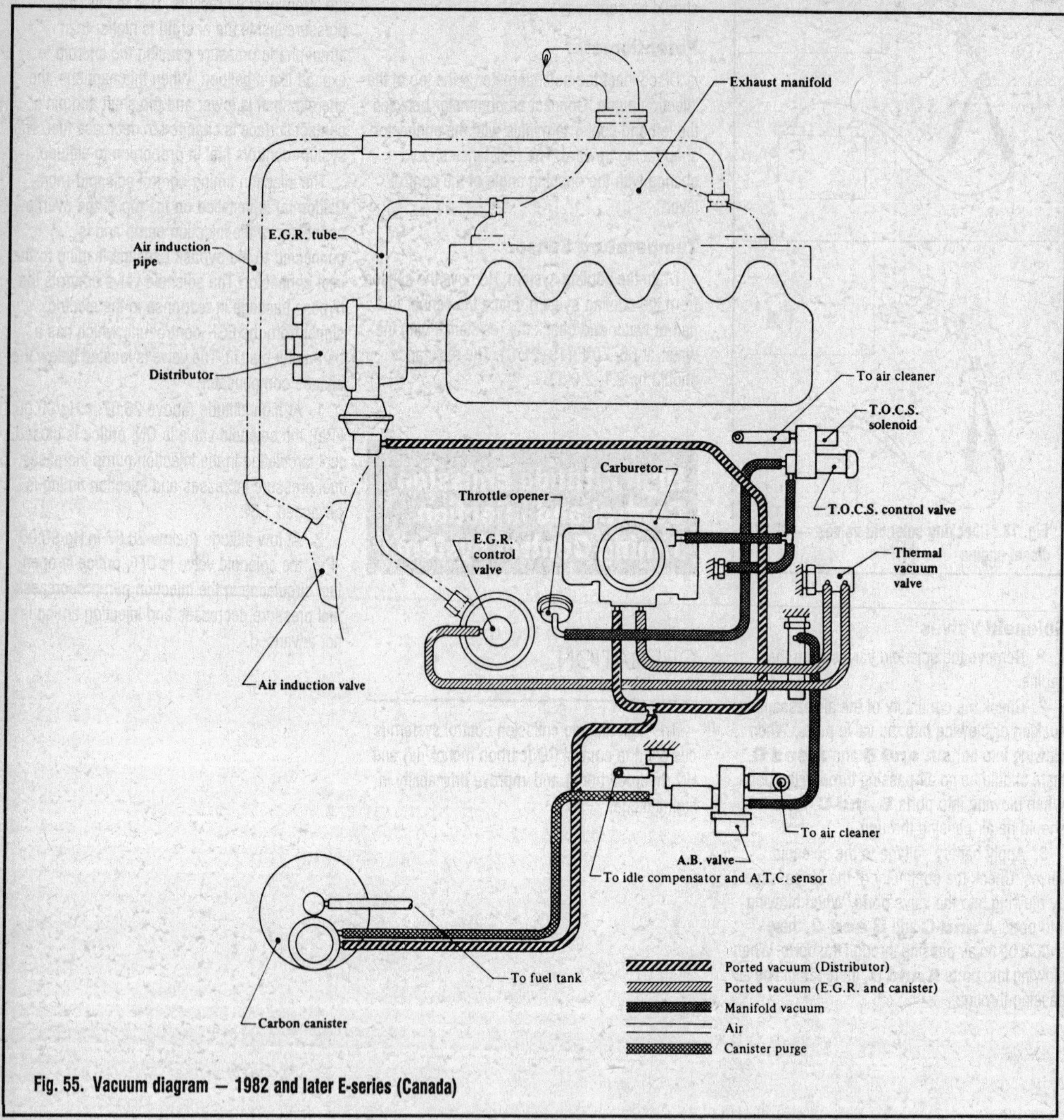
Exhaust manifold
E.G.R. tube
Air induction pipe
Distributor
To air cleaner
T.O.C.S. solenoid
Carburetor
Throttle opener
T.O.C.S. control valve
E.G.R. control valve
Thermal vacuum valve
Air induction valve
To air cleaner
A.B. valve
To idle compensator and A.T.C. sensor
To fuel tank
Carbon canister
Ported vacuum (Distributor)
Ported vacuum (E.G.R. and canister)
Manifold vacuum
Air
Canister purge

Fig. 55. Vacuum diagram — 1982 and later E-series (Canada)

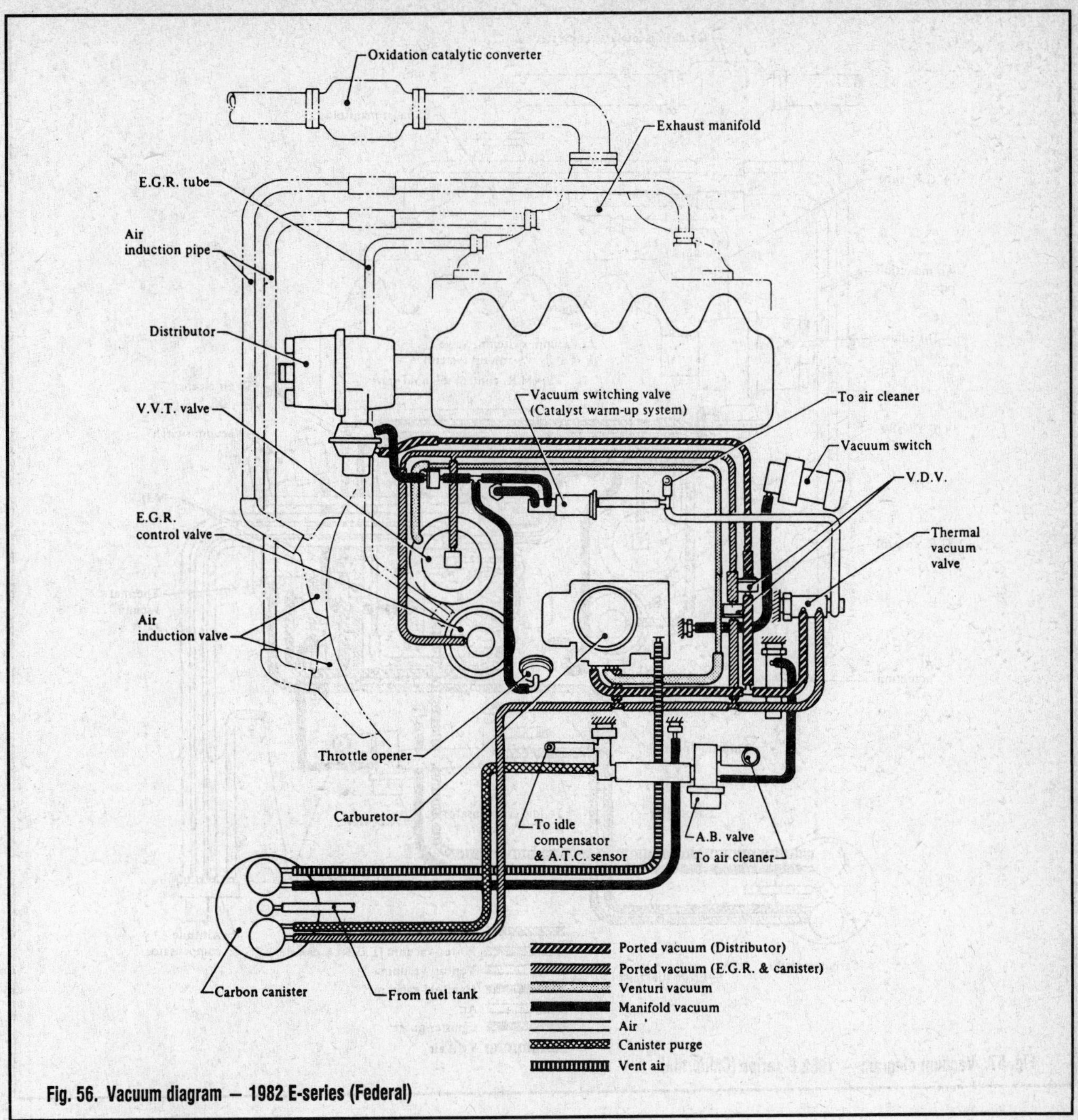

Oxidation catalytic converter
Exhaust manifold
E.G.R. tube
Air induction pipe
Distributor
V.V.T. valve
Vacuum switching valve (Catalyst warm-up system)
To air cleaner
Vacuum switch
V.D.V.
Thermal vacuum valve
E.G.R. control valve
Air induction valve
Throttle opener
Carburetor
To idle compensator & A.T.C. sensor
A.B. valve
To air cleaner
Carbon canister
From fuel tank
Ported vacuum (Distributor)
Ported vacuum (E.G.R. & canister)
Venturi vacuum
Manifold vacuum
Air
Canister purge
Vent air

Fig. 56. Vacuum diagram — 1982 E-series (Federal)

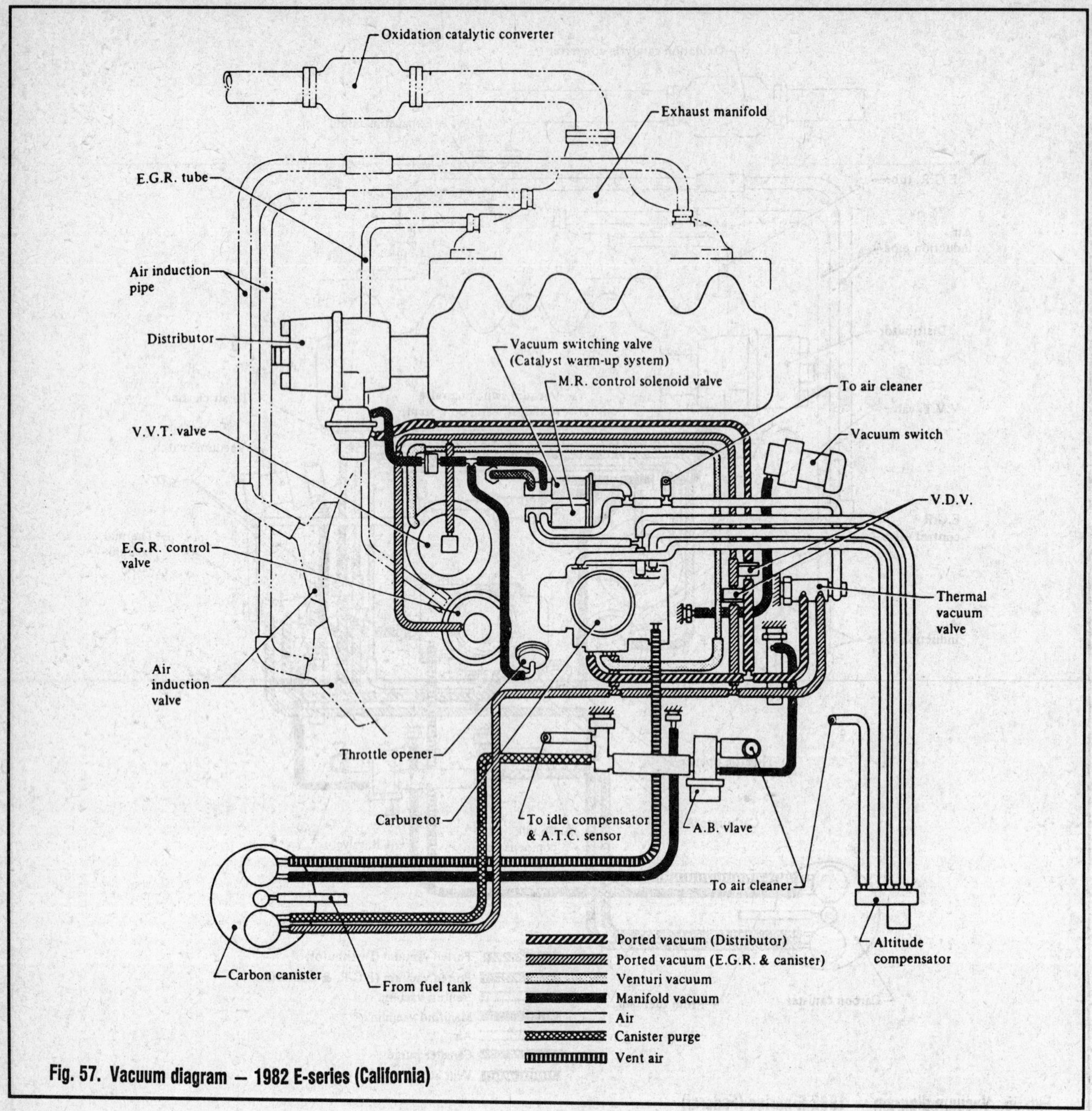
Oxidation catalytic converter
Exhaust manifold
E.G.R. tube
Air induction pipe
Distributor
Vacuum switching valve (Catalyst warm-up system)
M.R. control solenoid valve
To air cleaner
V.V.T. valve
Vacuum switch
V.D.V.
E.G.R. control valve
Thermal vacuum valve
Air induction valve
Throttle opener
Carburetor
To idle compensator & A.T.C. sensor
A.B. vlave
To air cleaner
Carbon canister
From fuel tank
Altitude compensator
Ported vacuum (Distributor)
Ported vacuum (E.G.R. & canister)
Venturi vacuum
Manifold vacuum
Air
Canister purge
Vent air

Fig. 57. Vacuum diagram — 1982 E-series (California)

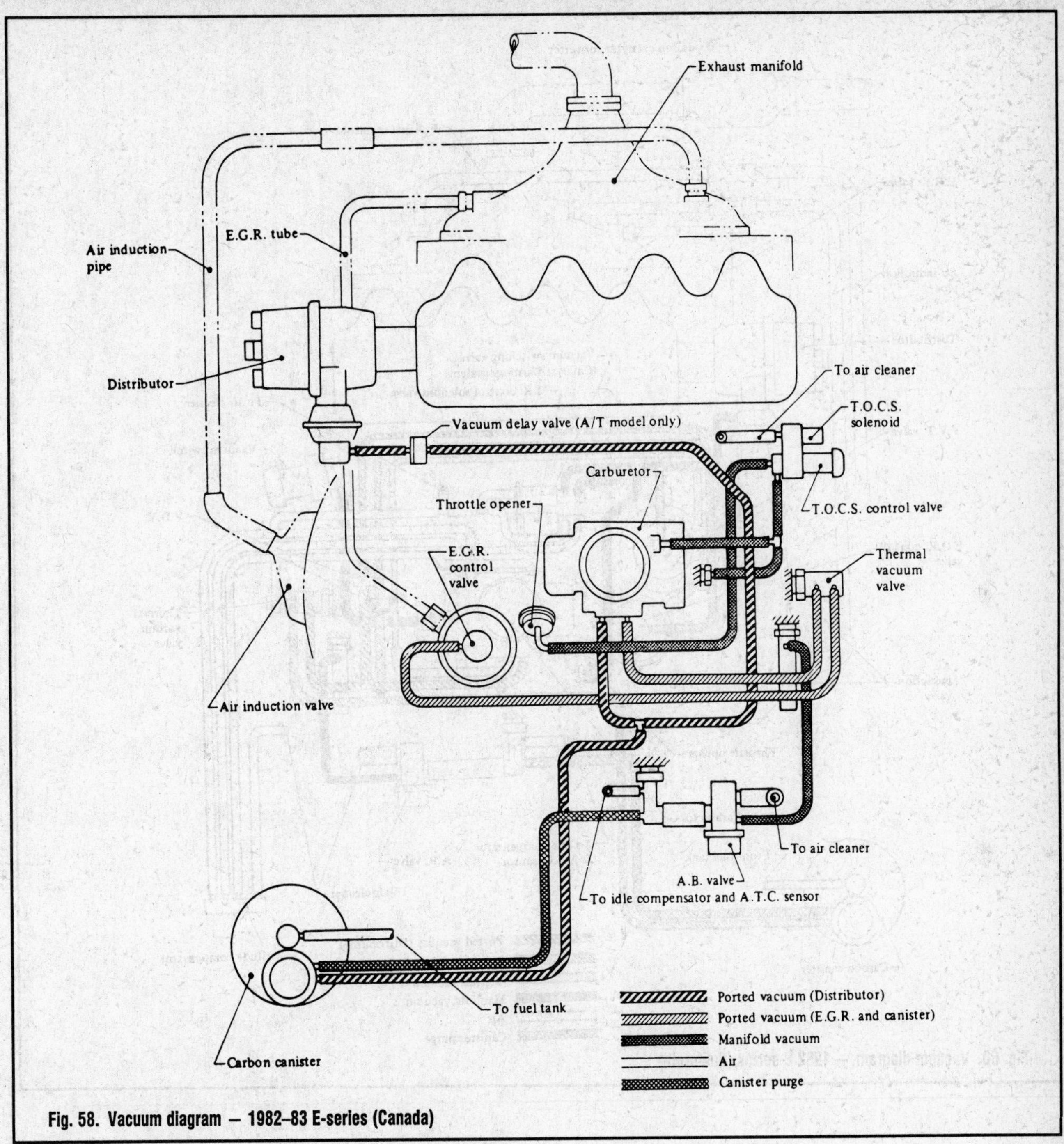
Exhaust manifold
E.G.R. tube
Air induction pipe
Distributor
To air cleaner
T.O.C.S. solenoid
Vacuum delay valve (A/T model only)
Carburetor
T.O.C.S. control valve
Throttle opener
E.G.R. control valve
Thermal vacuum valve
Air induction valve
To air cleaner
A.B. valve
To idle compensator and A.T.C. sensor
To fuel tank
Carbon canister
Ported vacuum (Distributor)
Ported vacuum (E.G.R. and canister)
Manifold vacuum
Air
Canister purge

Fig. 58. Vacuum diagram — 1982–83 E-series (Canada)

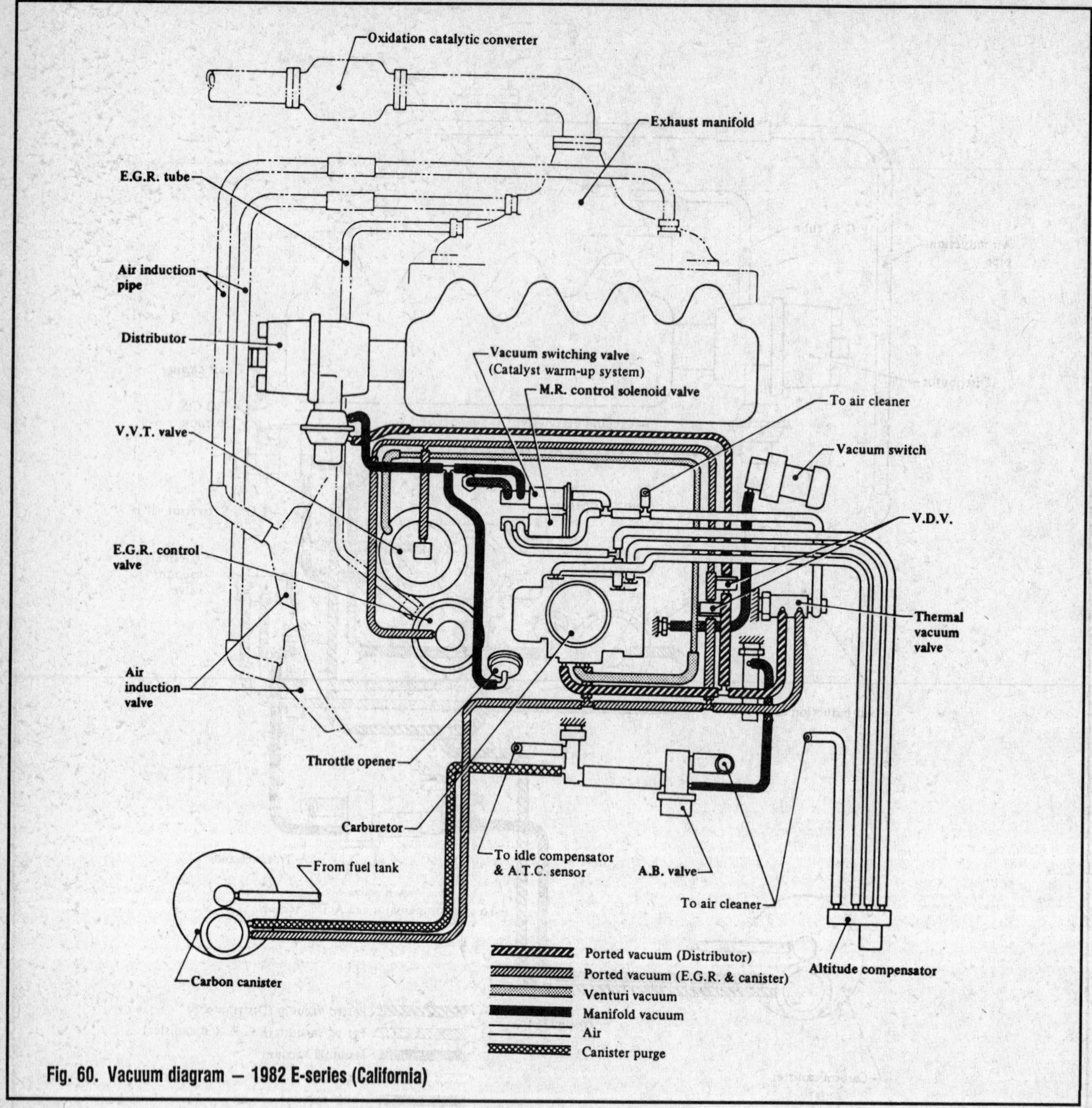

Oxidation catalytic converter
Exhaust manifold
E.G.R. tube
Air induction pipe
Distributor
Vacuum switching valve (Catalyst warm-up system)
M.R. control solenoid valve
To air cleaner
Vacuum switch
V.V.T. valve
V.D.V.
E.G.R. control valve
Thermal vacuum valve
Air induction valve
Throttle opener
Carburetor
To idle compensator & A.T.C. sensor
A.B. valve
From fuel tank
To air cleaner
Ported vacuum (Distributor)
Ported vacuum (E.G.R. & canister)
Venturi vacuum
Manifold vacuum
Air
Canister purge
Altitude compensator
Carbon canister

Fig. 60. Vacuum diagram — 1982 E-series (California)

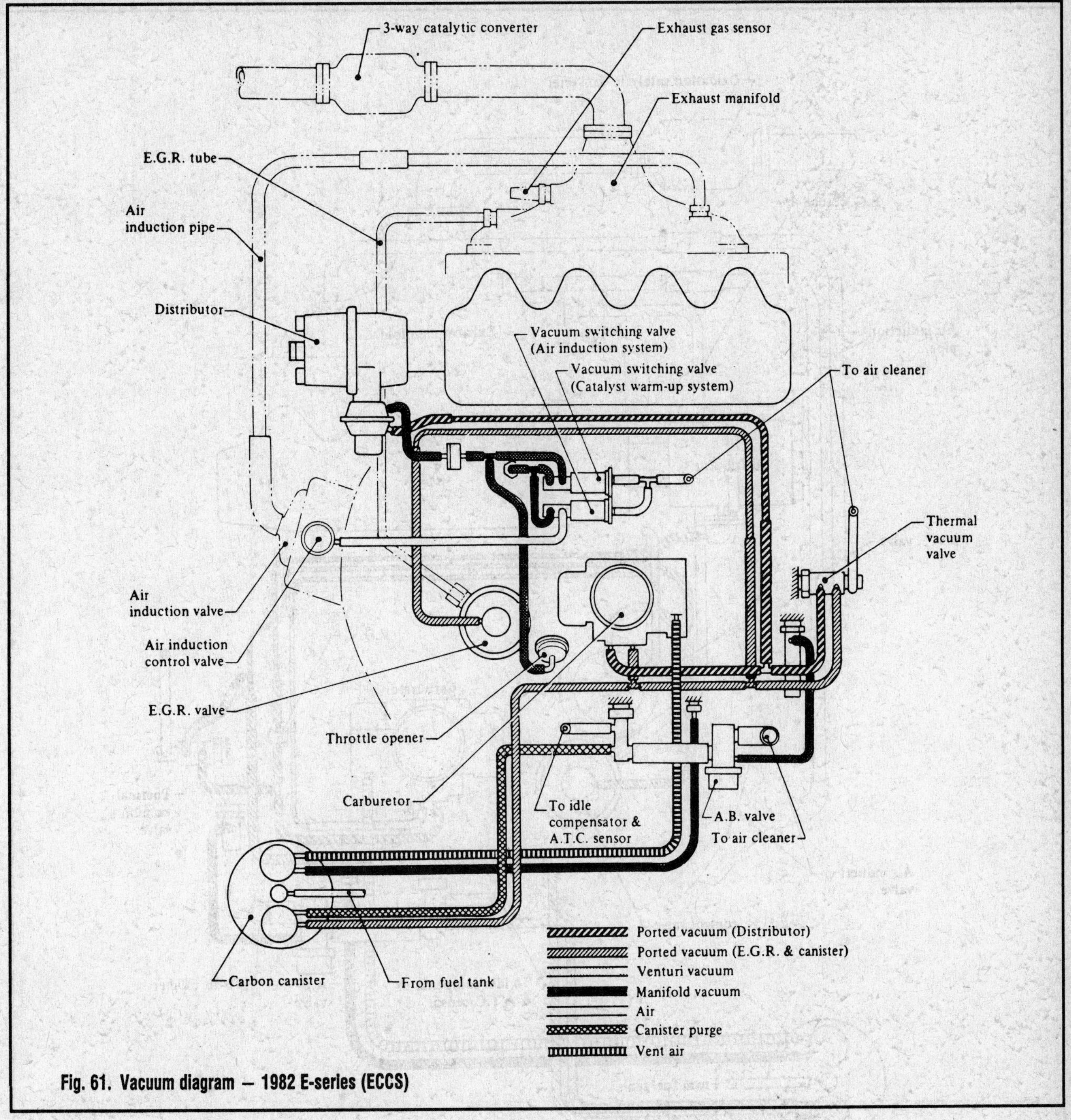
3-way catalytic converter
Exhaust gas sensor
Exhaust manifold
E.G.R. tube
Air
induction pipe
Distributor
Vacuum switching valve
(Air induction system)
Vacuum switching valve
(Catalyst warm-up system)
To air cleaner
Thermal
vacuum
valve
Air
induction valve
Air induction
control valve
E.G.R. valve
Throttle opener
Carburetor
To idle
compensator &
A.T.C. sensor
A.B. valve
To air cleaner
Carbon canister
From fuel tank
Ported vacuum (Distributor)
Ported vacuum (E.G.R. & canister)
Venturi vacuum
Manifold vacuum
Air
Canister purge
Vent air

Fig. 61. Vacuum diagram — 1982 E-series (ECCS)

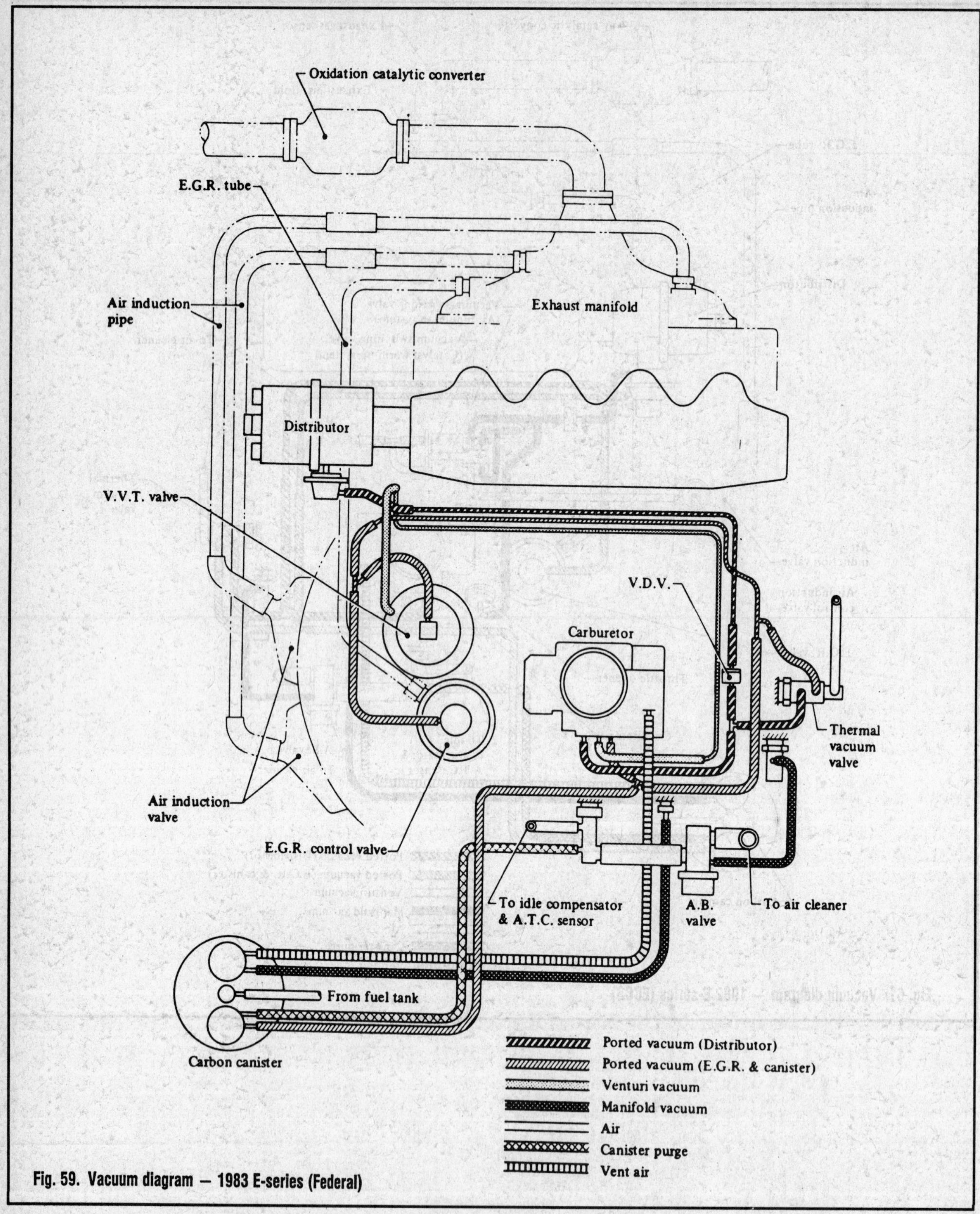
Oxidation catalytic converter
E.G.R. tube
Air induction pipe
Exhaust manifold
Distributor
V.V.T. valve
V.D.V.
Carburetor
Thermal vacuum valve
Air induction valve
E.G.R. control valve
To idle compensator & A.T.C. sensor
A.B. valve
To air cleaner
From fuel tank
Carbon canister
Ported vacuum (Distributor)
Ported vacuum (E.G.R. & canister)
Venturi vacuum
Manifold vacuum
Air
Canister purge
Vent air

Fig. 59. Vacuum diagram – 1983 E-series (Federal)

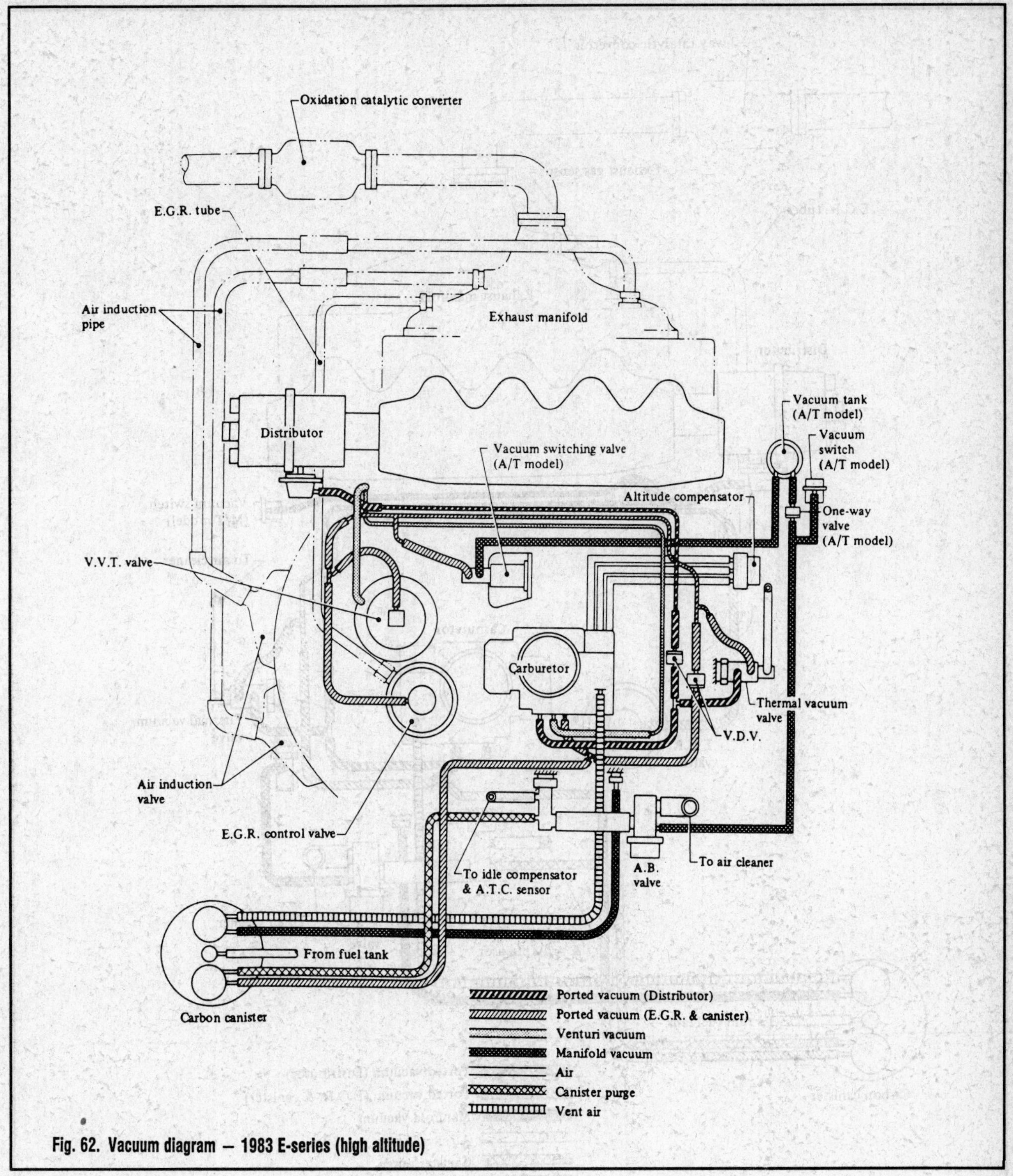
Oxidation catalytic converter
E.G.R. tube
Air induction pipe
Exhaust manifold
Distributor
Vacuum switching valve (A/T model)
Vacuum tank (A/T model)
Vacuum switch (A/T model)
Altitude compensator
One-way valve (A/T model)
V.V.T. valve
Carburetor
Thermal vacuum valve
V.D.V.
Air induction valve
E.G.R. control valve
To idle compensator & A.T.C. sensor
A.B. valve
To air cleaner
From fuel tank
Carbon canister
Ported vacuum (Distributor)
Ported vacuum (E.G.R. & canister)
Venturi vacuum
Manifold vacuum
Air
Canister purge
Vent air

Fig. 62. Vacuum diagram — 1983 E-series (high altitude)

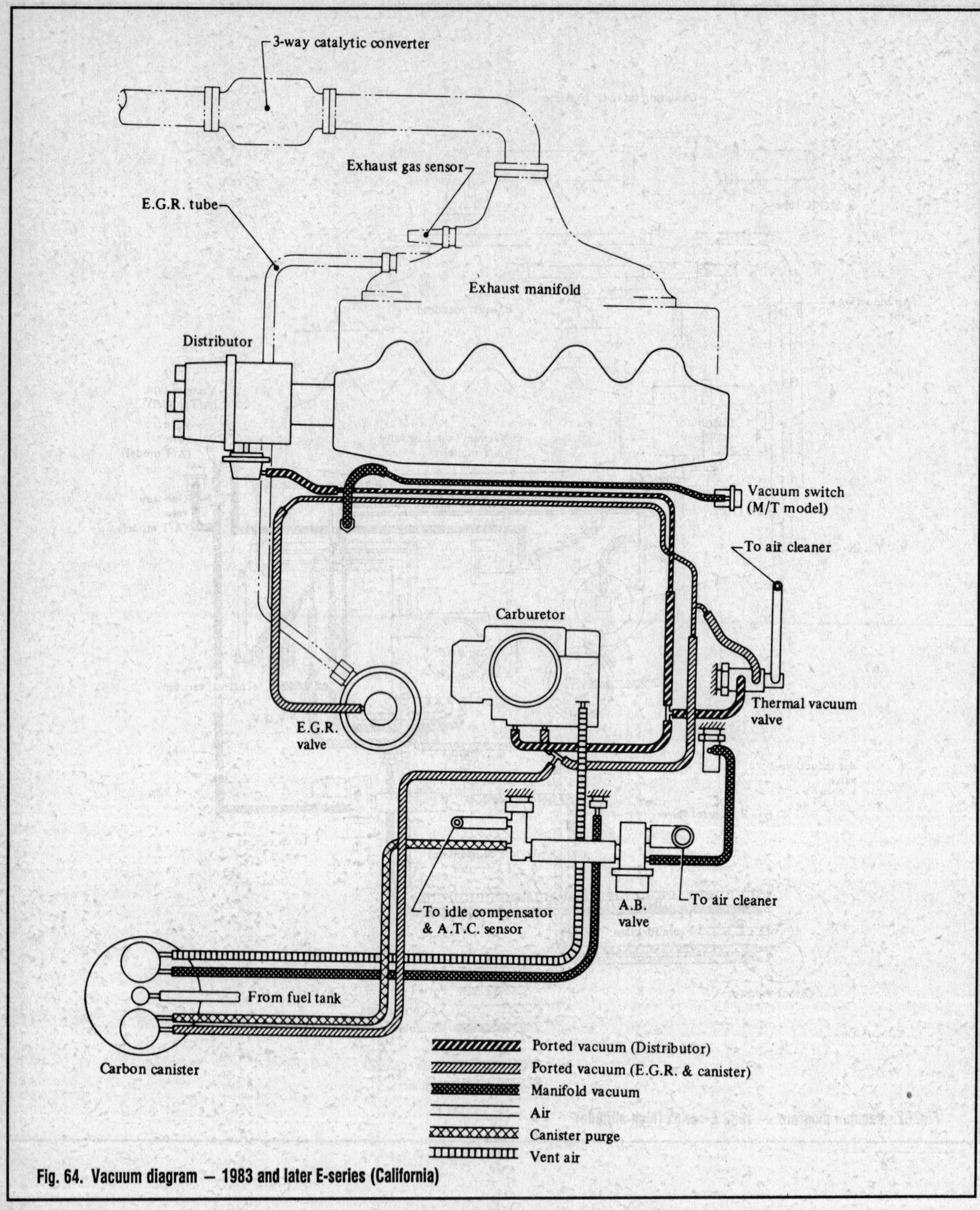
3-way catalytic converter
Exhaust gas sensor
E.G.R. tube
Exhaust manifold
Distributor
Vacuum switch
(M/T model)
To air cleaner
Carburetor
Thermal vacuum
valve
E.G.R.
valve
To idle compensator
& A.T.C. sensor
A.B.
valve
To air cleaner
From fuel tank
Carbon canister
Ported vacuum (Distributor)
Ported vacuum (E.G.R. & canister)
Manifold vacuum
Air
Canister purge
Vent air

Fig. 64. Vacuum diagram — 1983 and later E-series (California)

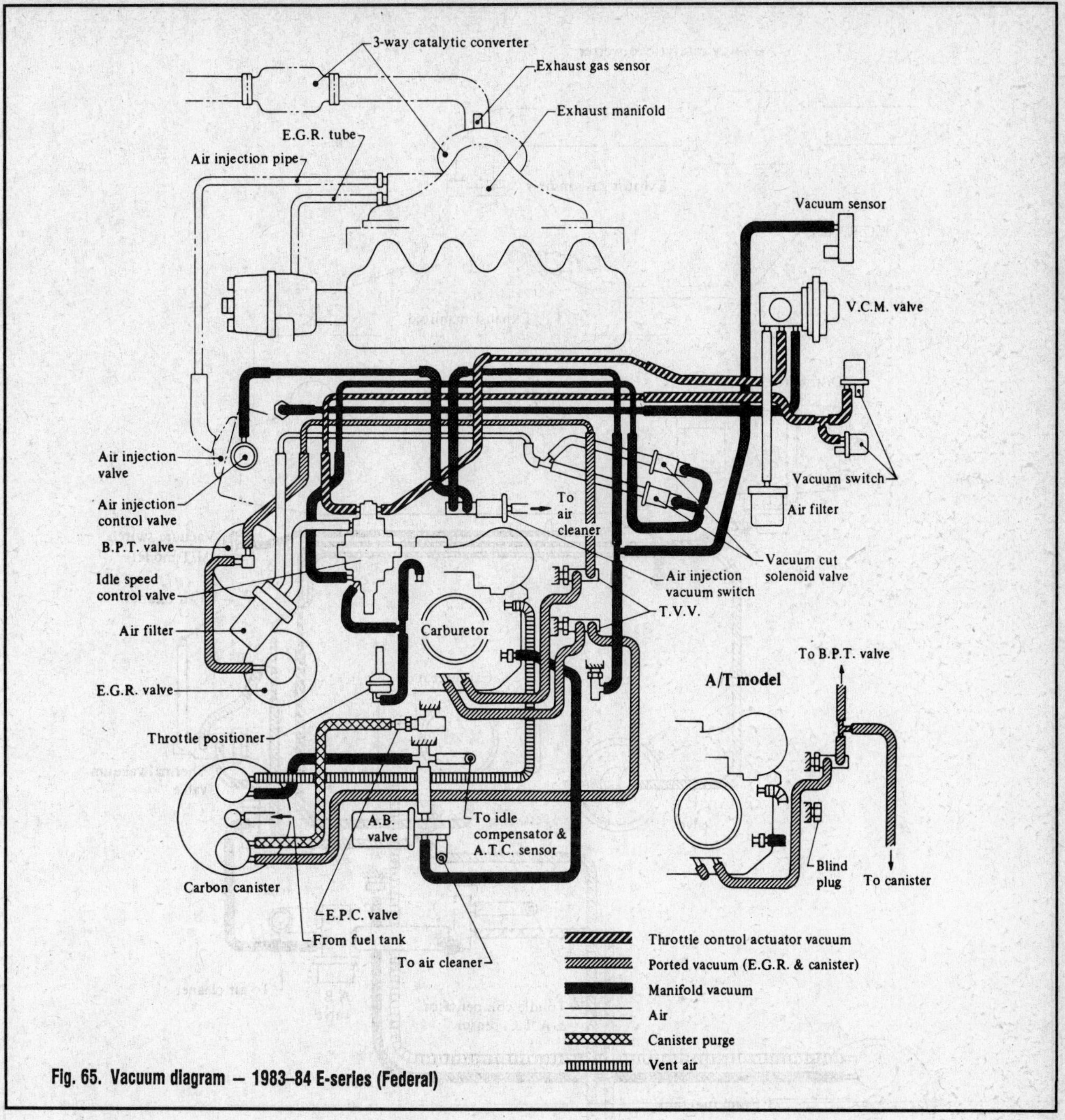
3-way catalytic converter
Exhaust gas sensor
Exhaust manifold
E.G.R. tube
Air injection pipe
Vacuum sensor
V.C.M. valve
Air injection valve
Vacuum switch
Air filter
Air injection control valve
To air cleaner
B.P.T. valve
Vacuum cut solenoid valve
Idle speed control valve
Air injection vacuum switch
T.V.V.
Air filter
Carburetor
To B.P.T. valve
E.G.R. valve
A/T model
Throttle positioner
A.B. valve
To idle compensator & A.T.C. sensor
Blind plug
To canister
Carbon canister
E.P.C. valve
From fuel tank
To air cleaner
Throttle control actuator vacuum
Ported vacuum (E.G.R. & canister)
Manifold vacuum
Air
Canister purge
Vent air

Fig. 65. Vacuum diagram — 1983–84 E-series (Federal)

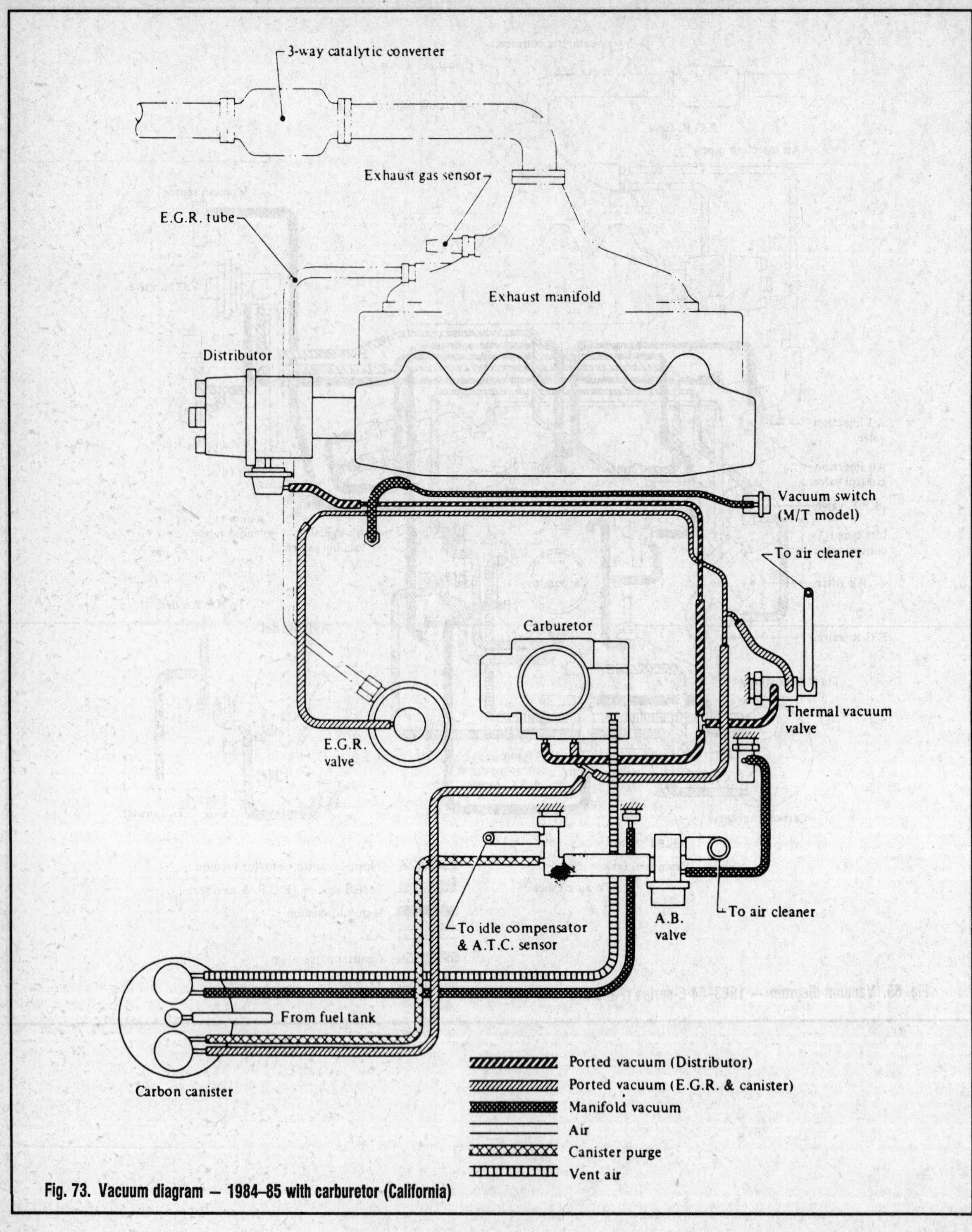
3-way catalytic converter
Exhaust gas sensor
E.G.R. tube
Exhaust manifold
Distributor
Vacuum switch
(M/T model)
To air cleaner
Carburetor
Thermal vacuum
valve
E.G.R.
valve
To idle compensator
& A.T.C. sensor
A.B.
valve
To air cleaner
From fuel tank
Carbon canister
Ported vacuum (Distributor)
Ported vacuum (E.G.R. & canister)
Manifold vacuum
Air
Canister purge
Vent air

Fig. 73. Vacuum diagram — 1984–85 with carburetor (California)

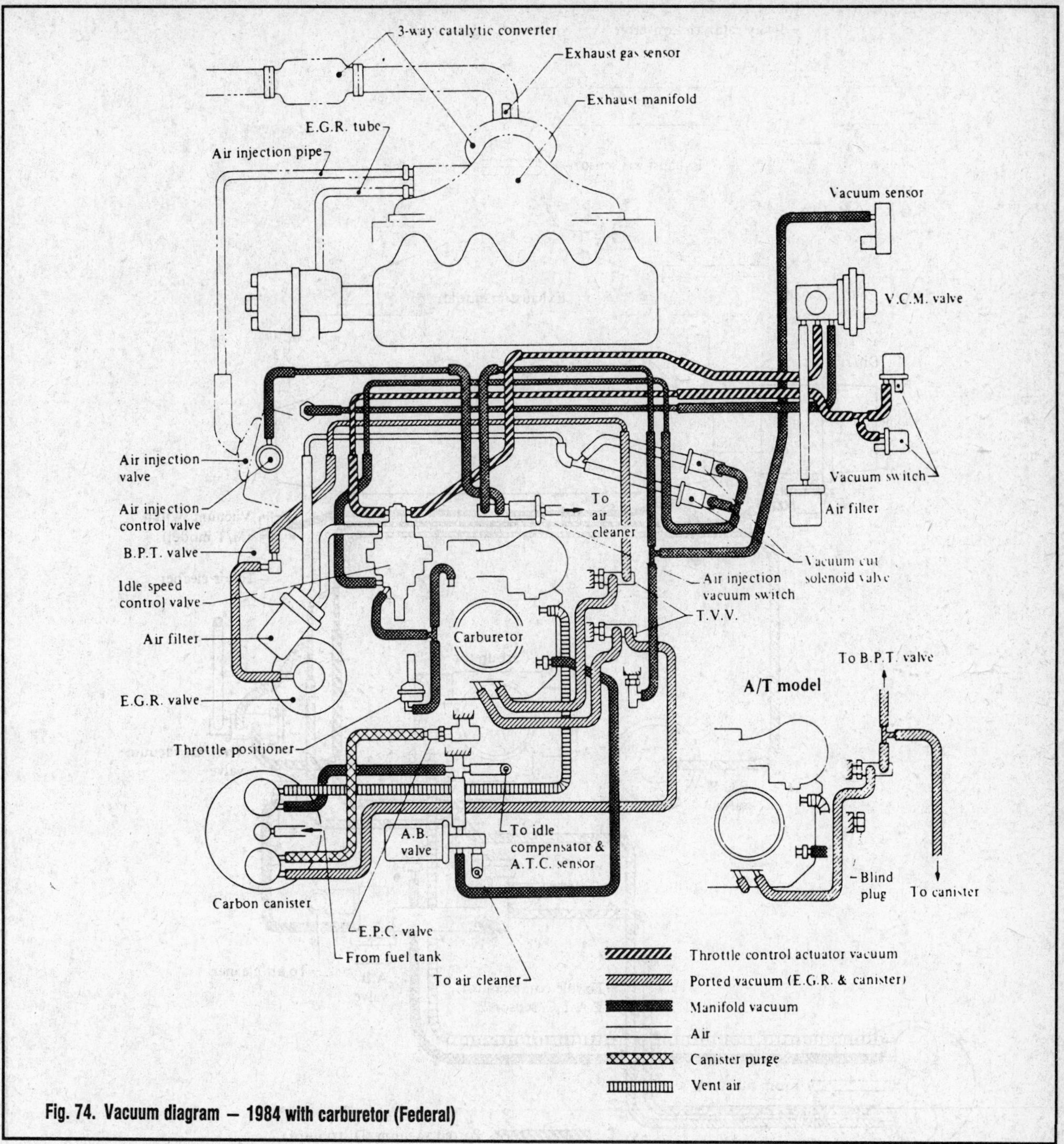
3-way catalytic converter
Exhaust gas sensor
Exhaust manifold
E.G.R. tube
Air injection pipe
Vacuum sensor
V.C.M. valve
Air injection valve
Vacuum switch
Air injection control valve
To air cleaner
Air filter
B.P.T. valve
Vacuum cut solenoid valve
Idle speed control valve
Air injection vacuum switch
T.V.V.
Air filter
Carburetor
To B.P.T. valve
E.G.R. valve
A/T model
Throttle positioner
A.B. valve
To idle compensator & A.T.C. sensor
Blind plug
To canister
Carbon canister
E.P.C. valve
From fuel tank
To air cleaner
Throttle control actuator vacuum
Ported vacuum (E.G.R. & canister)
Manifold vacuum
Air
Canister purge
Vent air

Fig. 74. Vacuum diagram — 1984 with carburetor (Federal)

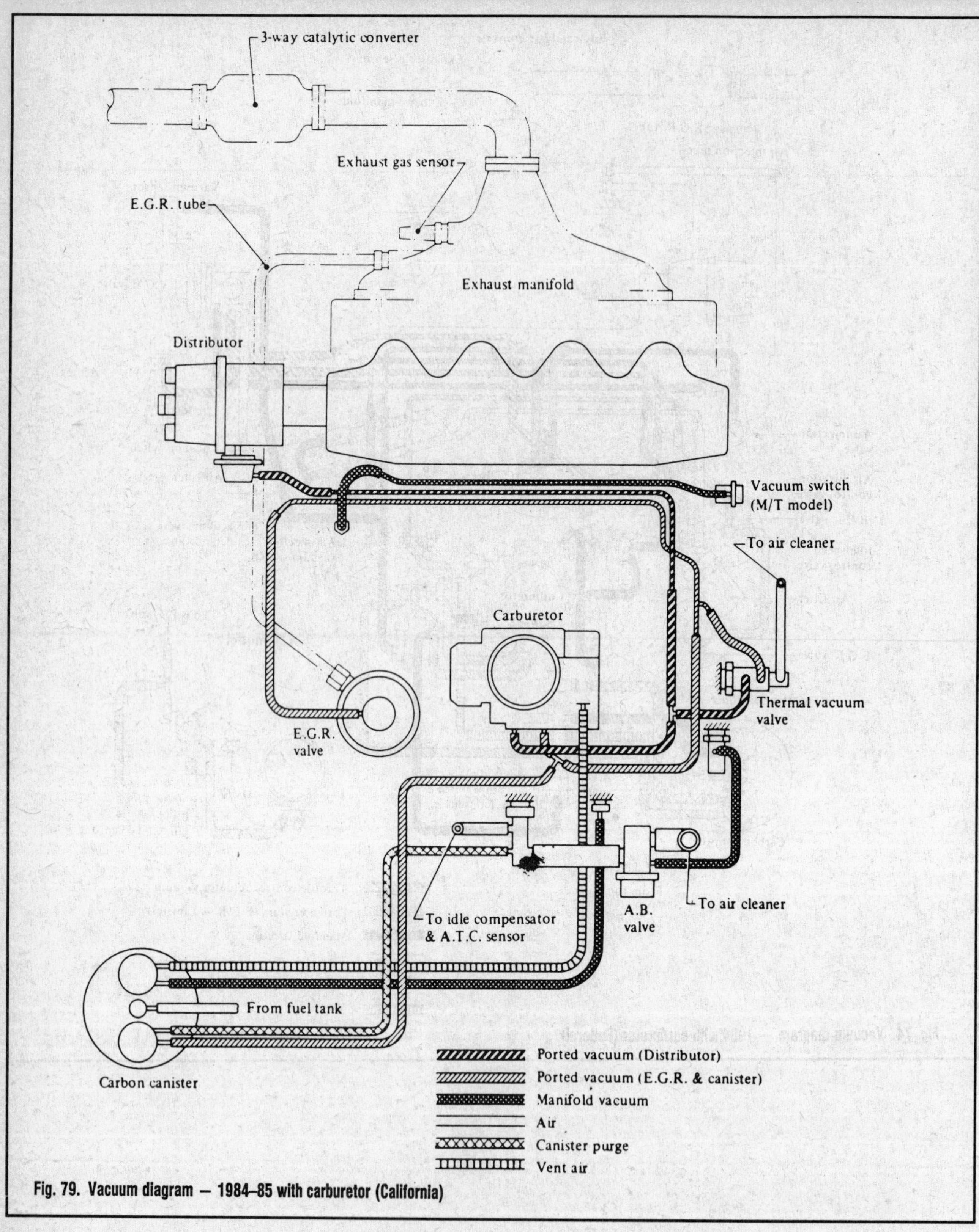
3-way catalytic converter
Exhaust gas sensor
E.G.R. tube
Exhaust manifold
Distributor
Vacuum switch
(M/T model)
To air cleaner
Carburetor
Thermal vacuum
valve
E.G.R.
valve
To air cleaner
A.B.
valve
To idle compensator
& A.T.C. sensor
From fuel tank
Carbon canister
Ported vacuum (Distributor)
Ported vacuum (E.G.R. & canister)
Manifold vacuum
Air
Canister purge
Vent air

Fig. 79. Vacuum diagram — 1984–85 with carburetor (California)

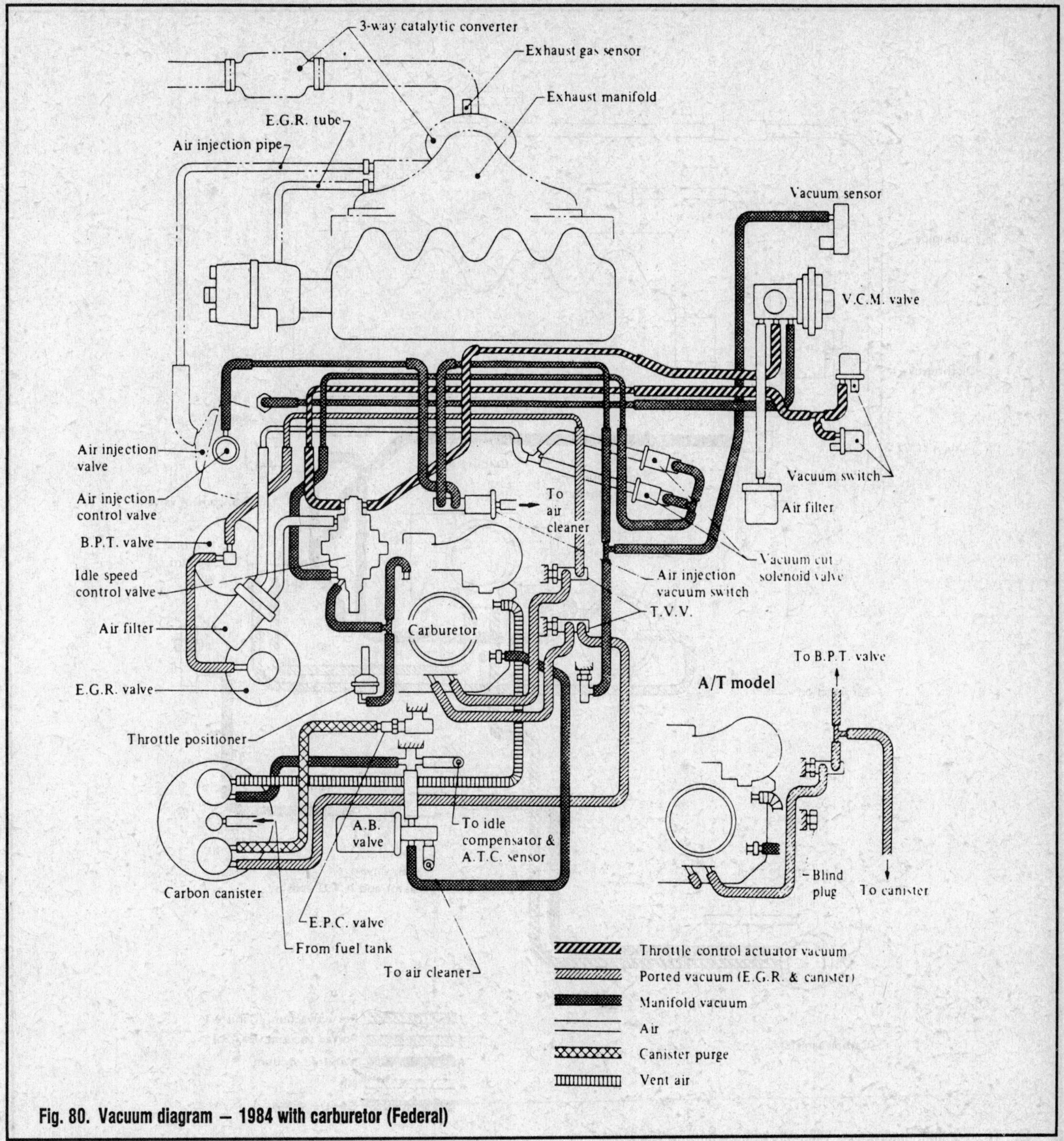
3-way catalytic converter
Exhaust gas sensor
Exhaust manifold
E.G.R. tube
Air injection pipe
Vacuum sensor
V.C.M. valve
Air injection valve
Air injection control valve
B.P.T. valve
Idle speed control valve
Air filter
E.G.R. valve
Throttle positioner
Carbon canister
To air cleaner
Vacuum switch
Air filter
Vacuum cut solenoid valve
Air injection vacuum switch
T.V.V.
Carburetor
A.B. valve
To idle compensator & A.T.C. sensor
E.P.C. valve
From fuel tank
To air cleaner
To B.P.T. valve
A/T model
Blind plug
To canister
Throttle control actuator vacuum
Ported vacuum (E.G.R. & canister)
Manifold vacuum
Air
Canister purge
Vent air

Fig. 80. Vacuum diagram — 1984 with carburetor (Federal)

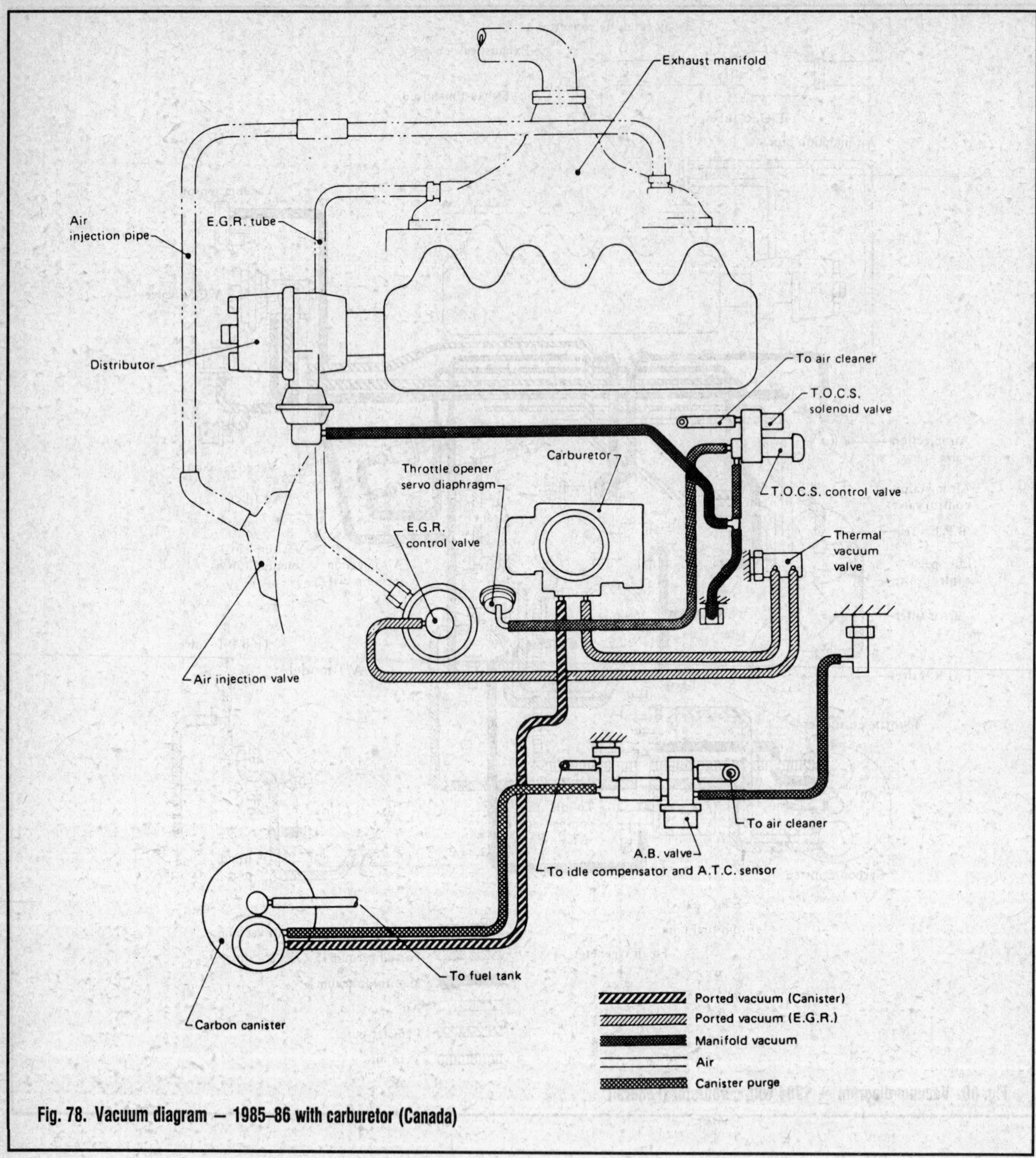
Exhaust manifold
Air
injection pipe
E.G.R. tube
Distributor
To air cleaner
T.O.C.S.
solenoid valve
Carburetor
Throttle opener
servo diaphragm
T.O.C.S. control valve
E.G.R.
control valve
Thermal
vacuum
valve
Air injection valve
To air cleaner
A.B. valve
To idle compensator and A.T.C. sensor
To fuel tank
Carbon canister
Ported vacuum (Canister)
Ported vacuum (E.G.R.)
Manifold vacuum
Air
Canister purge

Fig. 78. Vacuum diagram — 1985–86 with carburetor (Canada)

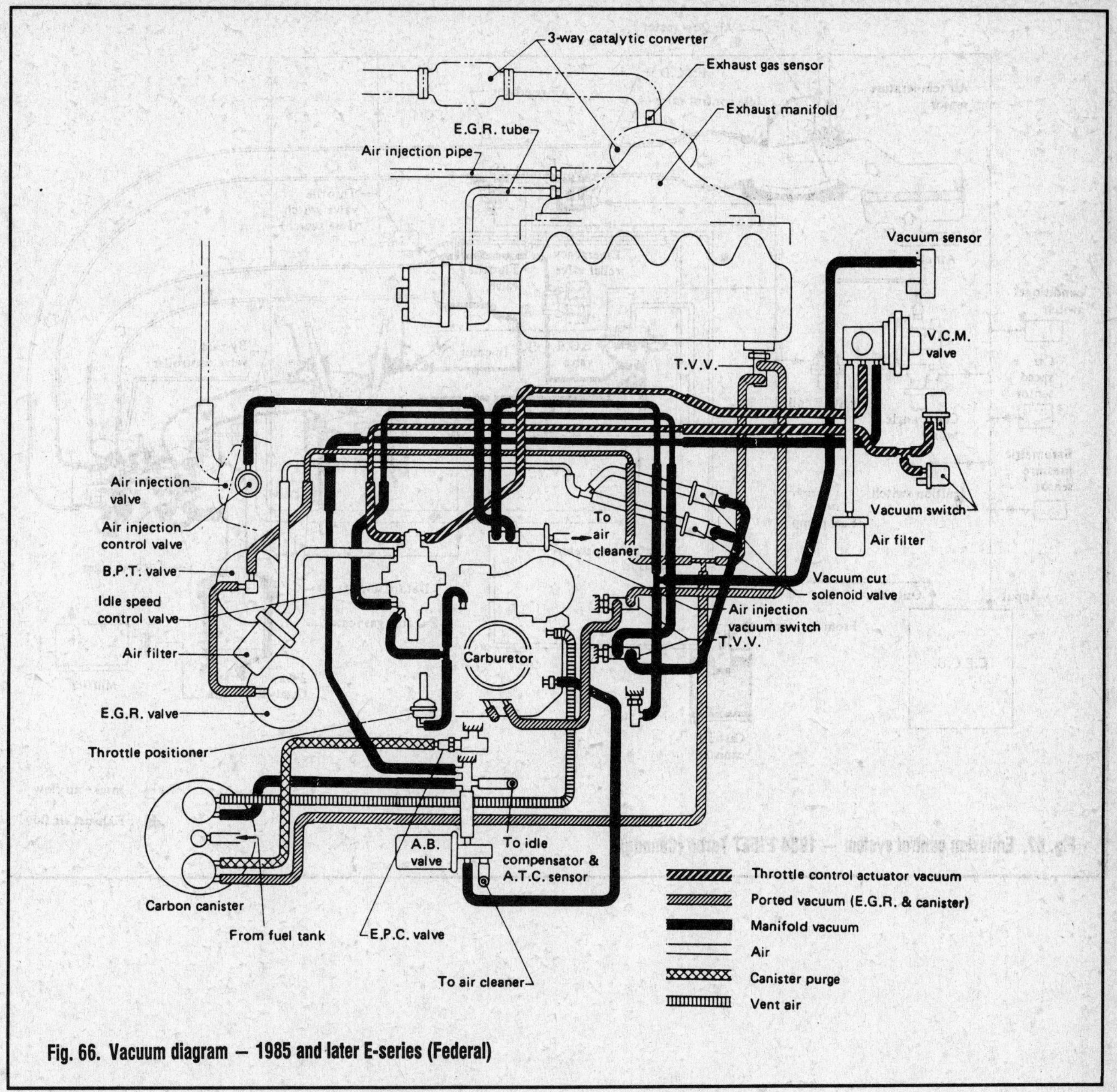
3-way catalytic converter
Exhaust gas sensor
Exhaust manifold
E.G.R. tube
Air injection pipe
Vacuum sensor
V.C.M. valve
T.V.V.
Air injection valve
Air injection control valve
B.P.T. valve
Idle speed control valve
Air filter
E.G.R. valve
Throttle positioner
To air cleaner
Carburetor
Vacuum switch
Air filter
Vacuum cut solenoid valve
Air injection vacuum switch
T.V.V.
A.B. valve
To idle compensator & A.T.C. sensor
Carbon canister
From fuel tank
E.P.C. valve
To air cleaner
Throttle control actuator vacuum
Ported vacuum (E.G.R. & canister)
Manifold vacuum
Air
Canister purge
Vent air

Fig. 66. Vacuum diagram — 1985 and later E-series (Federal)

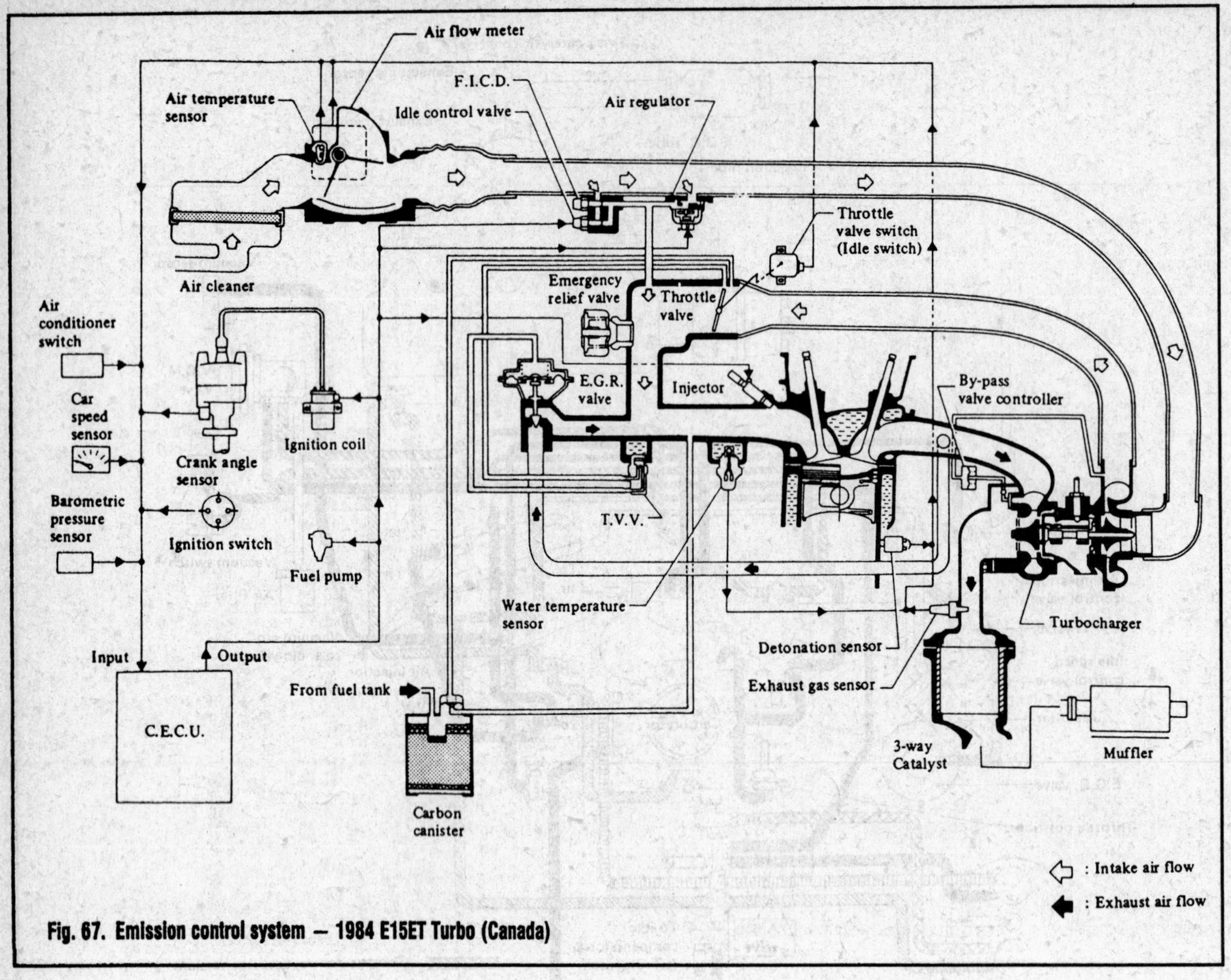
Air flow meter
F.I.C.D.
Air temperature sensor
Idle control valve
Air regulator
Throttle valve switch (Idle switch)
Air cleaner
Air conditioner switch
Emergency relief valve
Throttle valve
Car speed sensor
E.G.R. valve
Injector
By-pass valve controller
Ignition coil
Crank angle sensor
Barometric pressure sensor
T.V.V.
Ignition switch
Fuel pump
Water temperature sensor
Turbocharger
Detonation sensor
Input
Output
From fuel tank
Exhaust gas sensor
C.E.C.U.
3-way Catalyst
Muffler
Carbon canister
: Intake air flow
: Exhaust air flow

Fig. 67. Emission control system — 1984 E15ET Turbo (Canada)

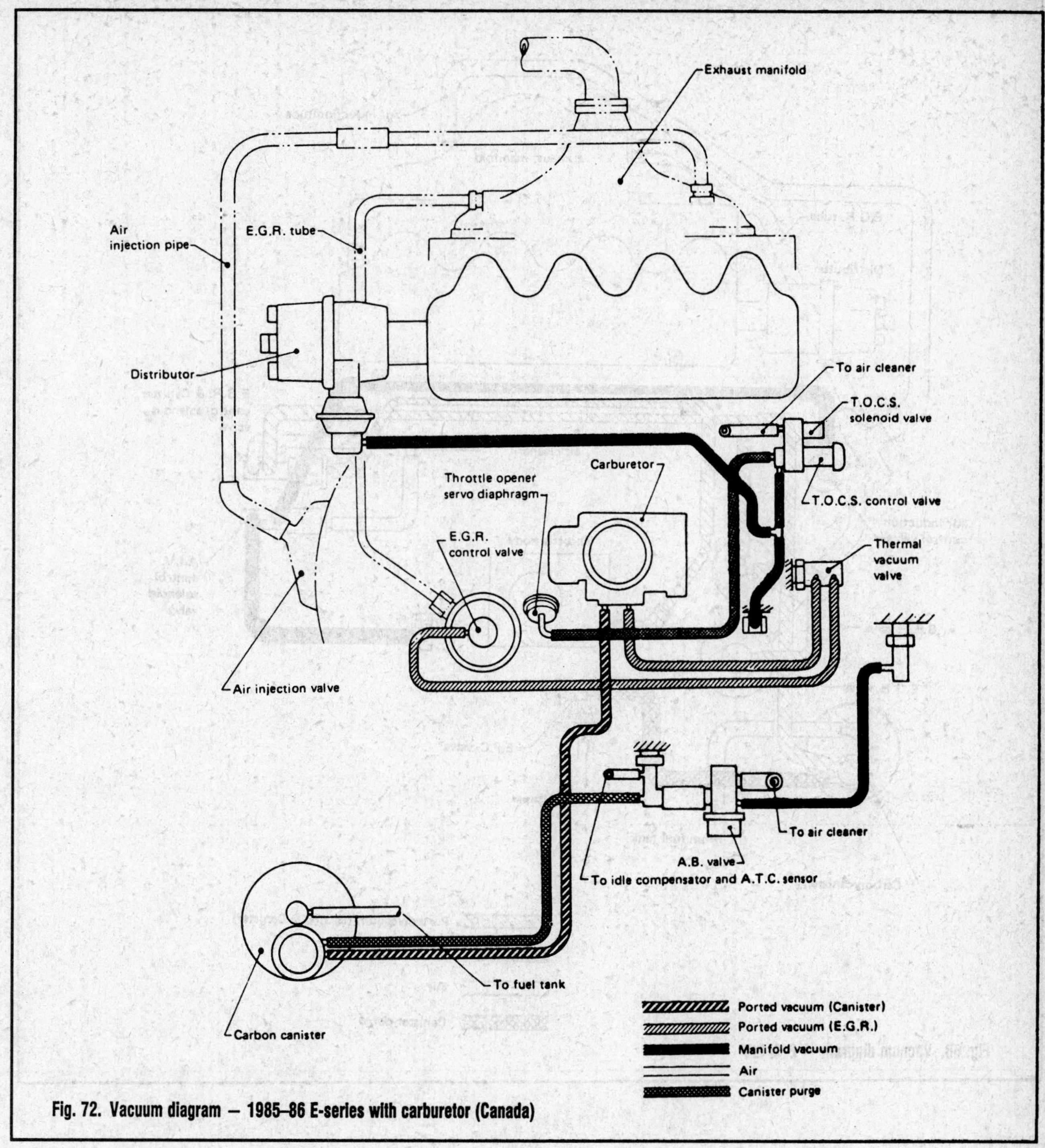

Exhaust manifold
Air injection pipe
E.G.R. tube
Distributor
To air cleaner
T.O.C.S. solenoid valve
Carburetor
Throttle opener servo diaphragm
T.O.C.S. control valve
E.G.R. control valve
Thermal vacuum valve
Air injection valve
To air cleaner
A.B. valve
To idle compensator and A.T.C. sensor
To fuel tank
Carbon canister
Ported vacuum (Canister)
Ported vacuum (E.G.R.)
Manifold vacuum
Air
Canister purge

Fig. 72. Vacuum diagram — 1985–86 E-series with carburetor (Canada)

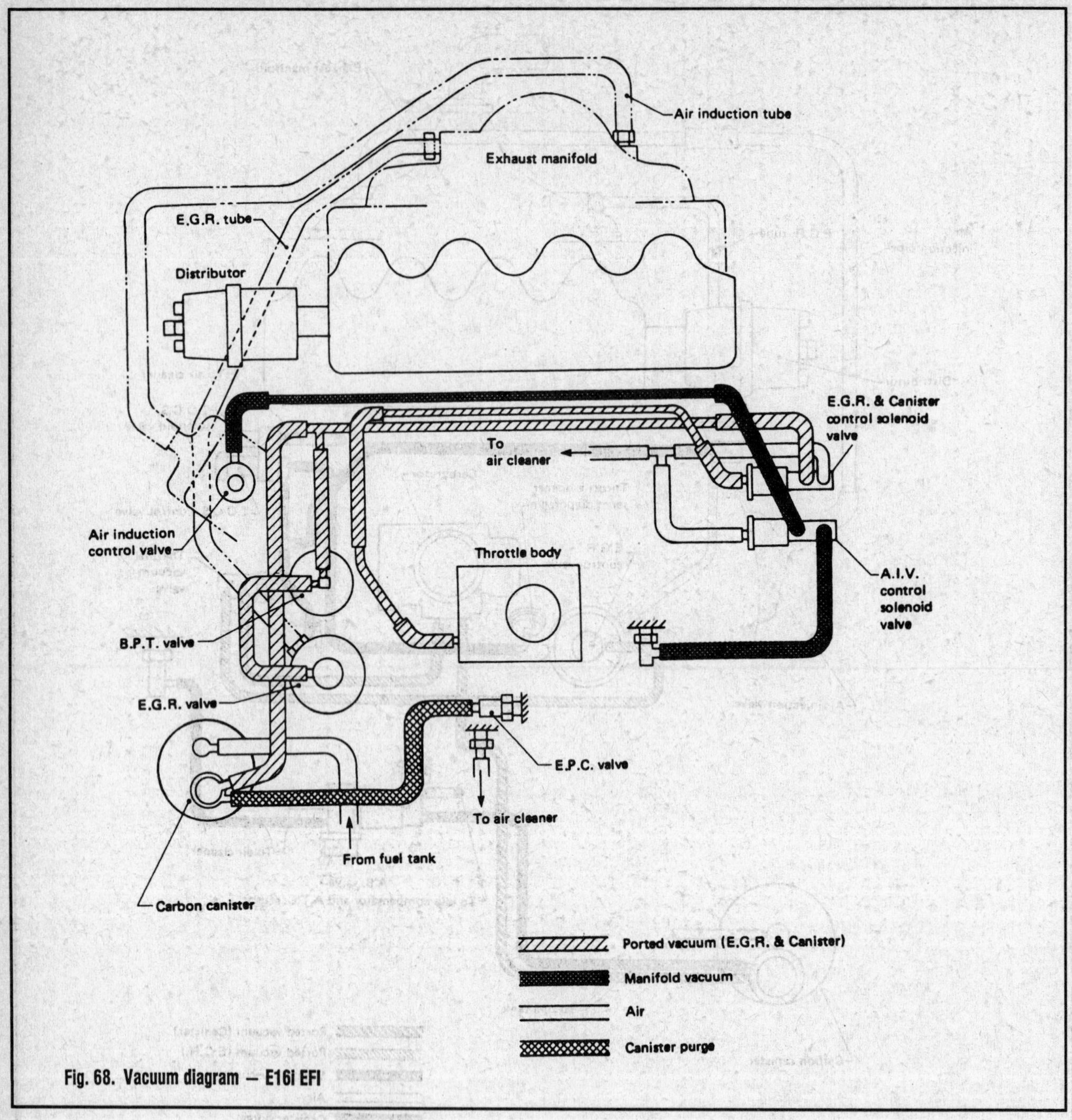
Air induction tube
Exhaust manifold
E.G.R. tube
Distributor
E.G.R. & Canister control solenoid valve
To air cleaner
Air induction control valve
Throttle body
A.I.V. control solenoid valve
B.P.T. valve
E.G.R. valve
E.P.C. valve
To air cleaner
From fuel tank
Carbon canister
Ported vacuum (E.G.R. & Canister)
Manifold vacuum
Air
Canister purge

Fig. 68. Vacuum diagram — E16i EFI

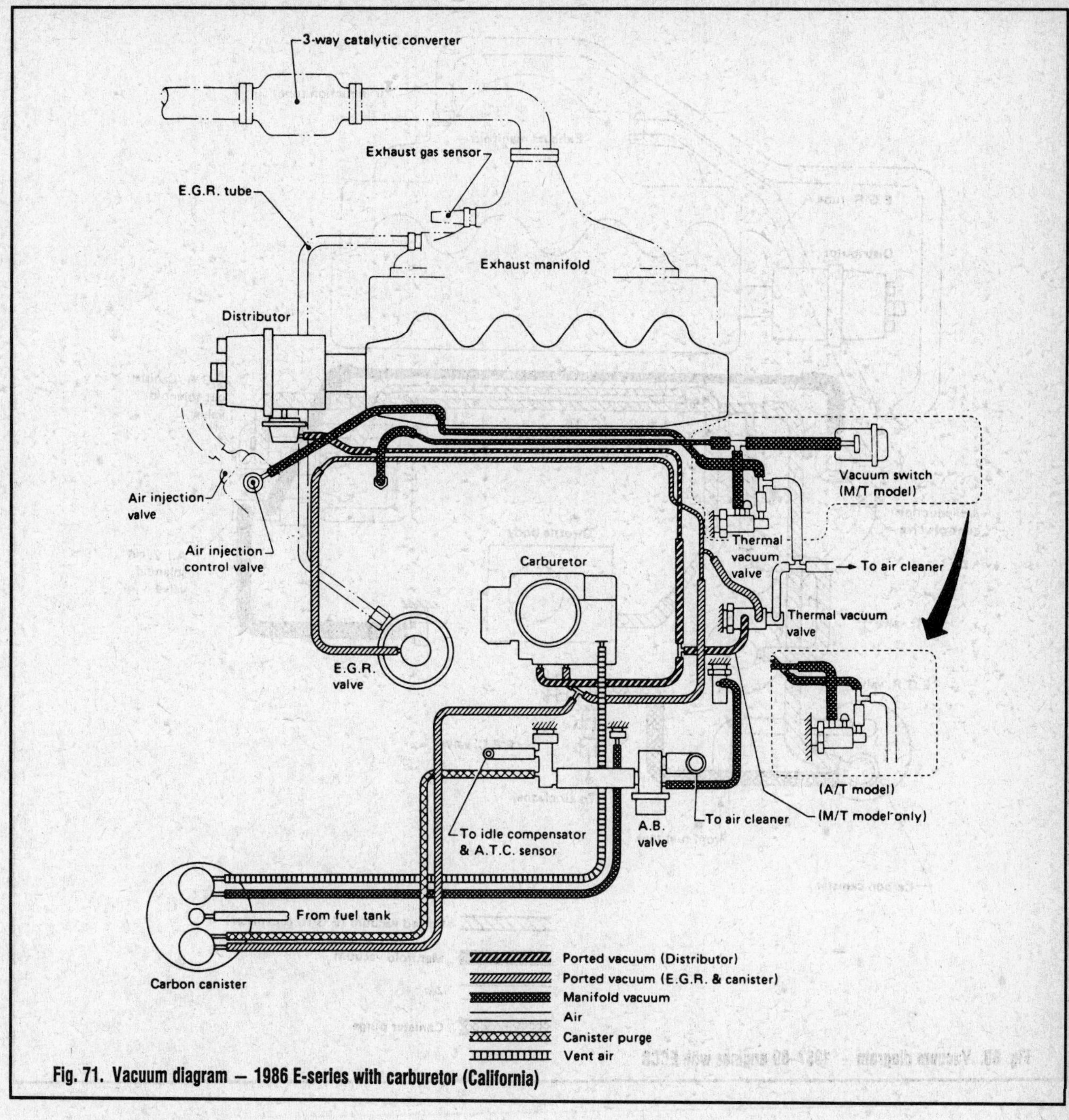
3-way catalytic converter
Exhaust gas sensor
E.G.R. tube
Exhaust manifold
Distributor
Air injection valve
Air injection control valve
Carburetor
Vacuum switch (M/T model)
Thermal vacuum valve
To air cleaner
Thermal vacuum valve
E.G.R. valve
(A/T model)
(M/T model only)
To air cleaner
A.B. valve
To idle compensator & A.T.C. sensor
From fuel tank
Carbon canister
Ported vacuum (Distributor)
Ported vacuum (E.G.R. & canister)
Manifold vacuum
Air
Canister purge
Vent air
Fig. 71. Vacuum diagram — 1986 E-series with carburetor (California)

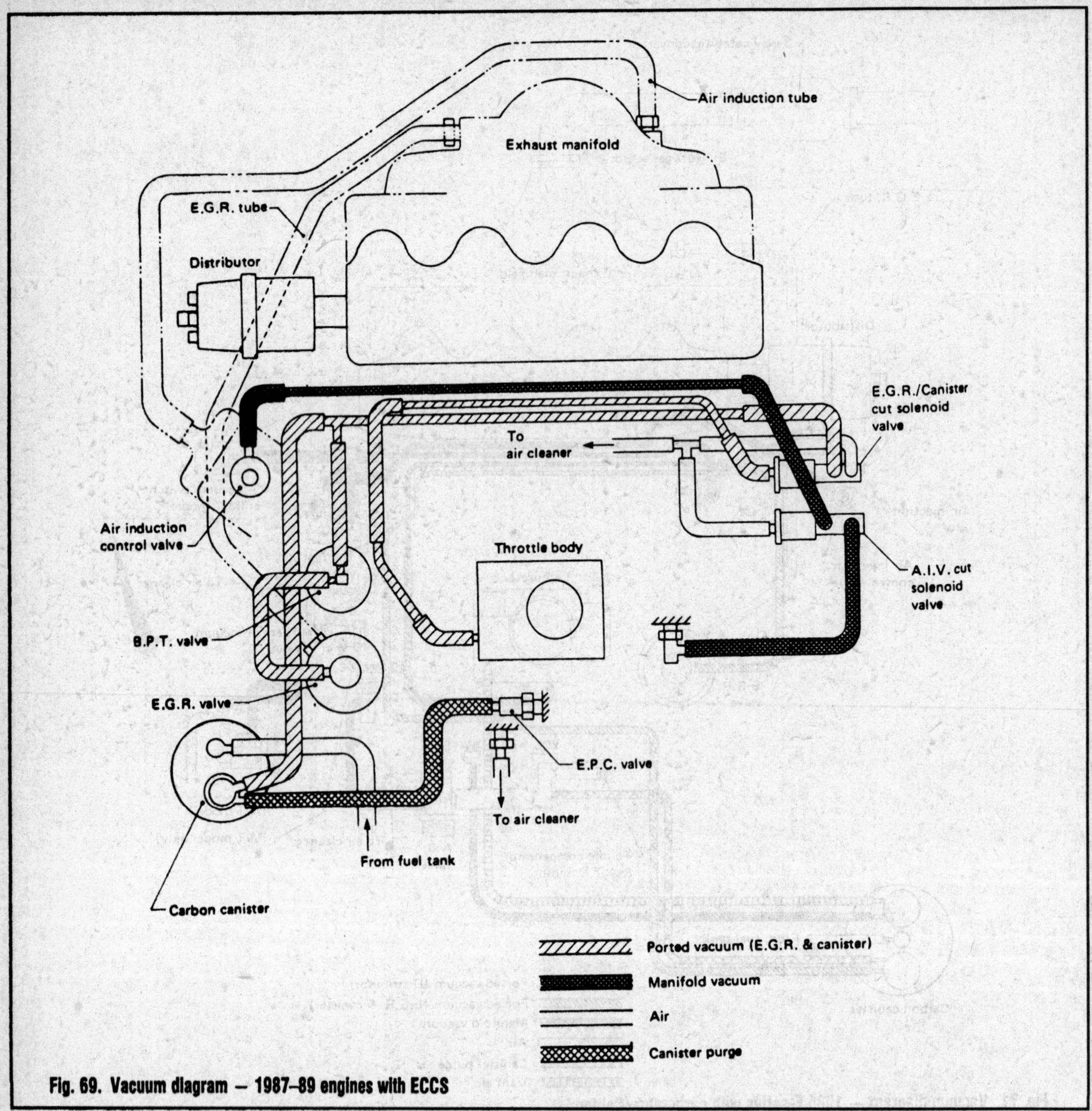
Air induction tube
Exhaust manifold
E.G.R. tube
Distributor
E.G.R./Canister cut solenoid valve
To air cleaner
Air induction control valve
Throttle body
A.I.V. cut solenoid valve
B.P.T. valve
E.G.R. valve
E.P.C. valve
To air cleaner
From fuel tank
Carbon canister
Ported vacuum (E.G.R. & canister)
Manifold vacuum
Air
Canister purge

Fig. 69. Vacuum diagram — 1987–89 engines with ECCS

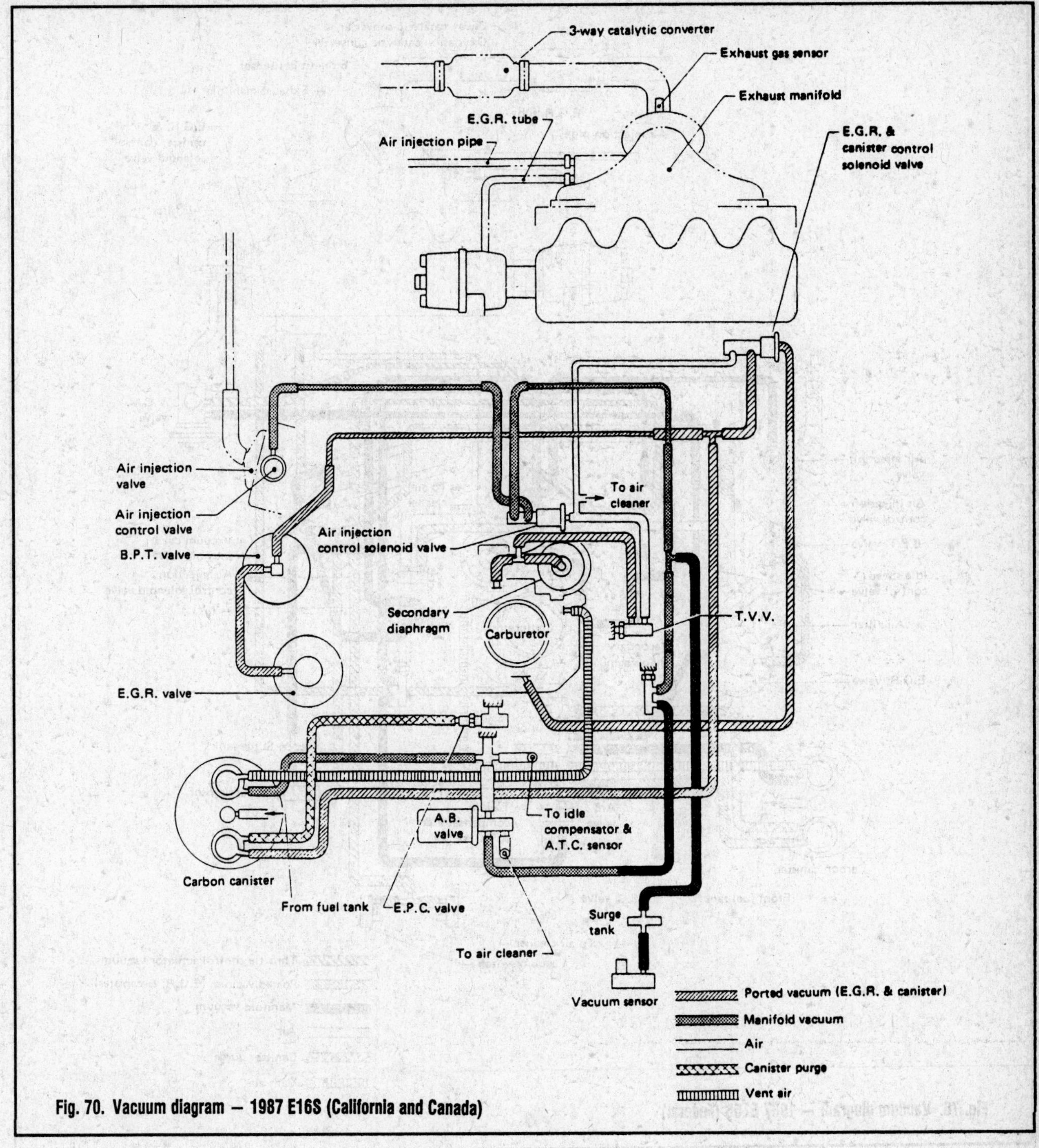
3-way catalytic converter
Exhaust gas sensor
Exhaust manifold
E.G.R. tube
Air injection pipe
E.G.R. & canister control solenoid valve
Air injection valve
Air injection control valve
To air cleaner
B.P.T. valve
Air injection control solenoid valve
Secondary diaphragm
T.V.V.
Carburetor
E.G.R. valve
To idle compensator & A.T.C. sensor
A.B. valve
Carbon canister
From fuel tank
E.P.C. valve
Surge tank
To air cleaner
Vacuum sensor
Ported vacuum (E.G.R. & canister)
Manifold vacuum
Air
Canister purge
Vent air

Fig. 70. Vacuum diagram — 1987 E16S (California and Canada)

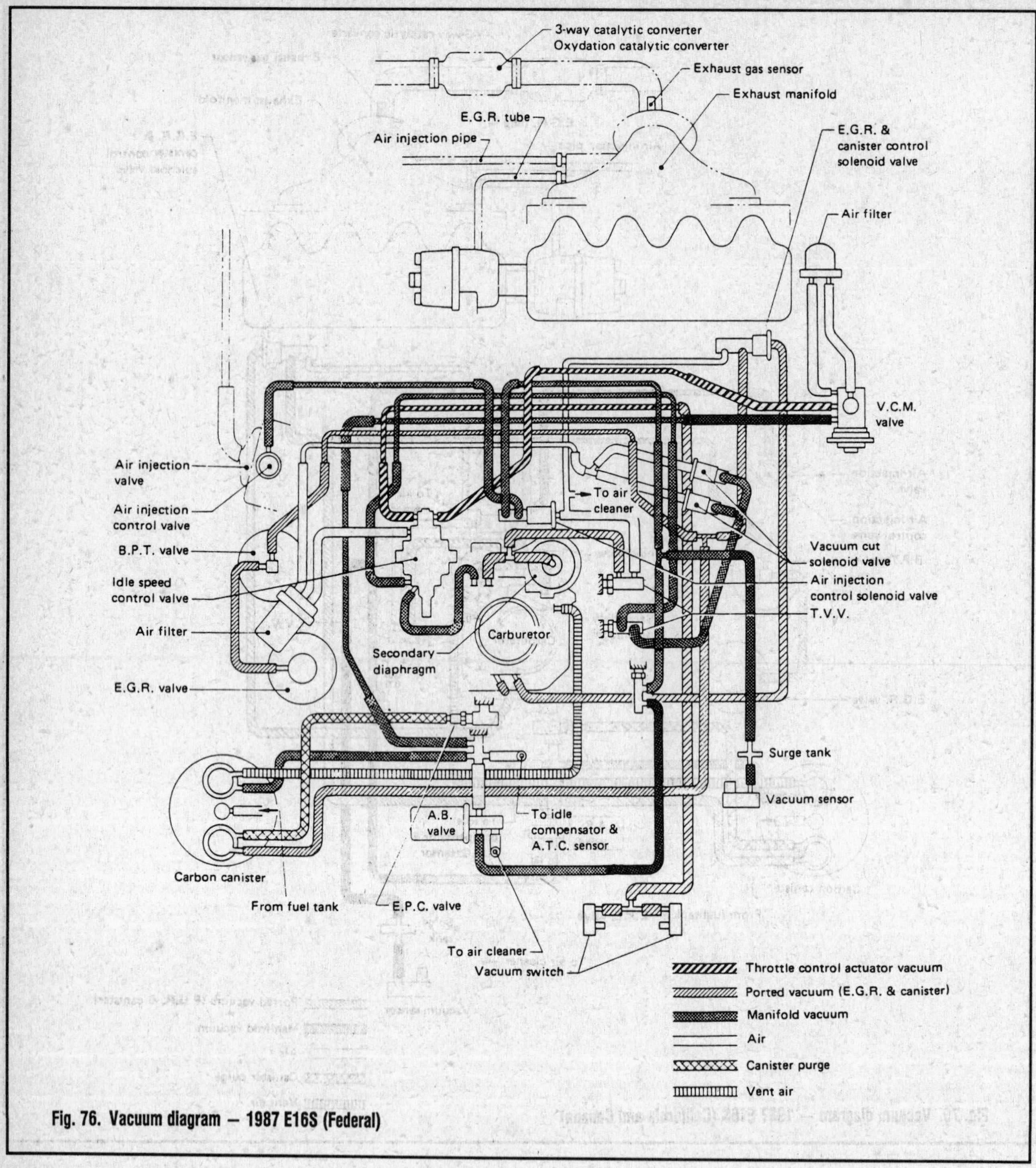
3-way catalytic converter
Oxydation catalytic converter
Exhaust gas sensor
Exhaust manifold
E.G.R. tube
Air injection pipe
E.G.R. & canister control solenoid valve
Air filter
V.C.M. valve
Air injection valve
Air injection control valve
To air cleaner
B.P.T. valve
Idle speed control valve
Vacuum cut solenoid valve
Air injection control solenoid valve
T.V.V.
Air filter
Carburetor
Secondary diaphragm
E.G.R. valve
Surge tank
Vacuum sensor
A.B. valve
To idle compensator & A.T.C. sensor
Carbon canister
From fuel tank
E.P.C. valve
To air cleaner
Vacuum switch
Throttle control actuator vacuum
Ported vacuum (E.G.R. & canister)
Manifold vacuum
Air
Canister purge
Vent air

Fig. 76. Vacuum diagram — 1987 E16S (Federal)

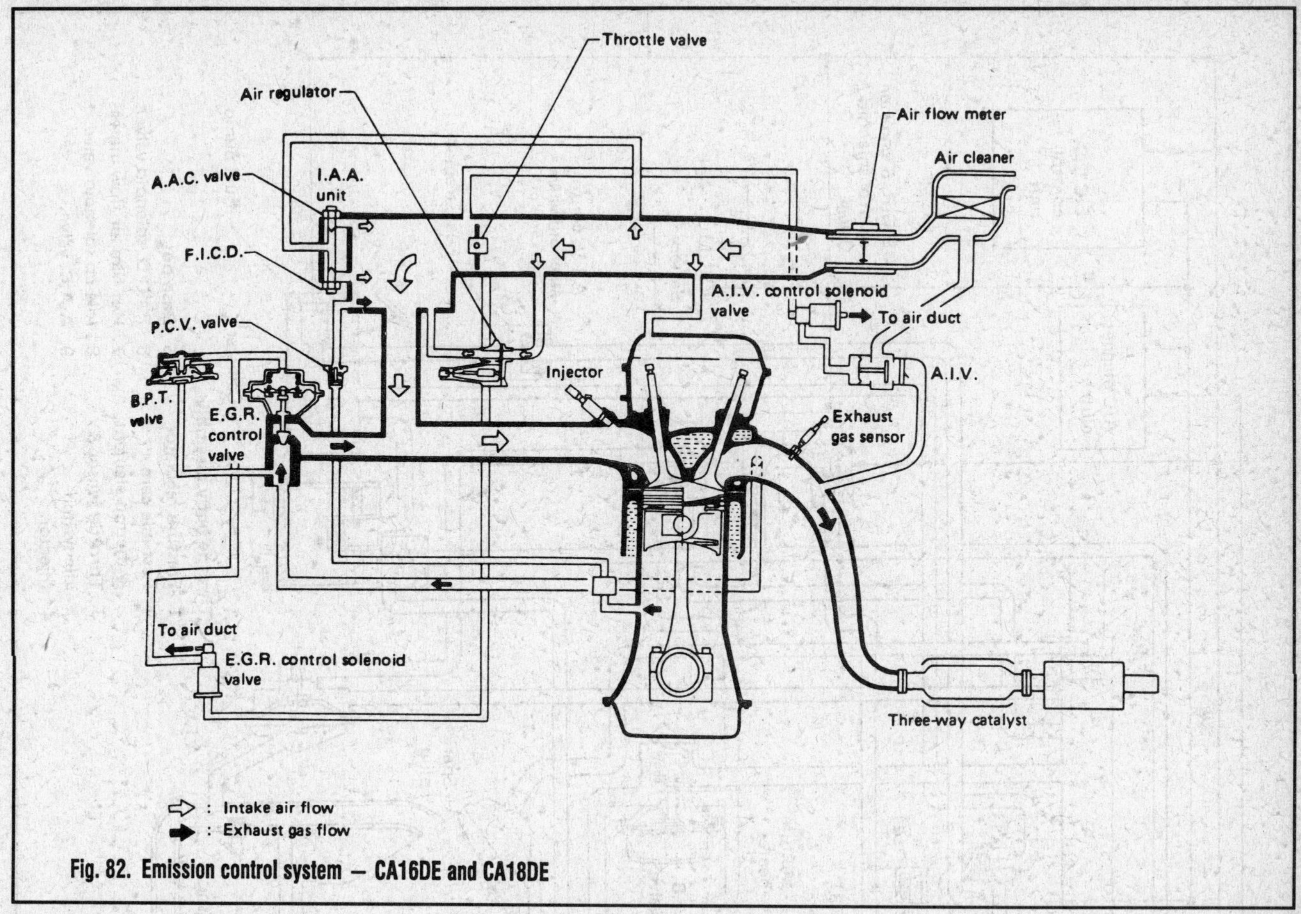
Throttle valve
Air regulator
Air flow meter
Air cleaner
A.A.C. valve
I.A.A. unit
F.I.C.D.
A.I.V. control solenoid valve
To air duct
P.C.V. valve
Injector
A.I.V.
B.P.T. valve
E.G.R. control valve
Exhaust gas sensor
To air duct
E.G.R. control solenoid valve
Three-way catalyst
: Intake air flow
: Exhaust gas flow

Fig. 82. Emission control system — CA16DE and CA18DE

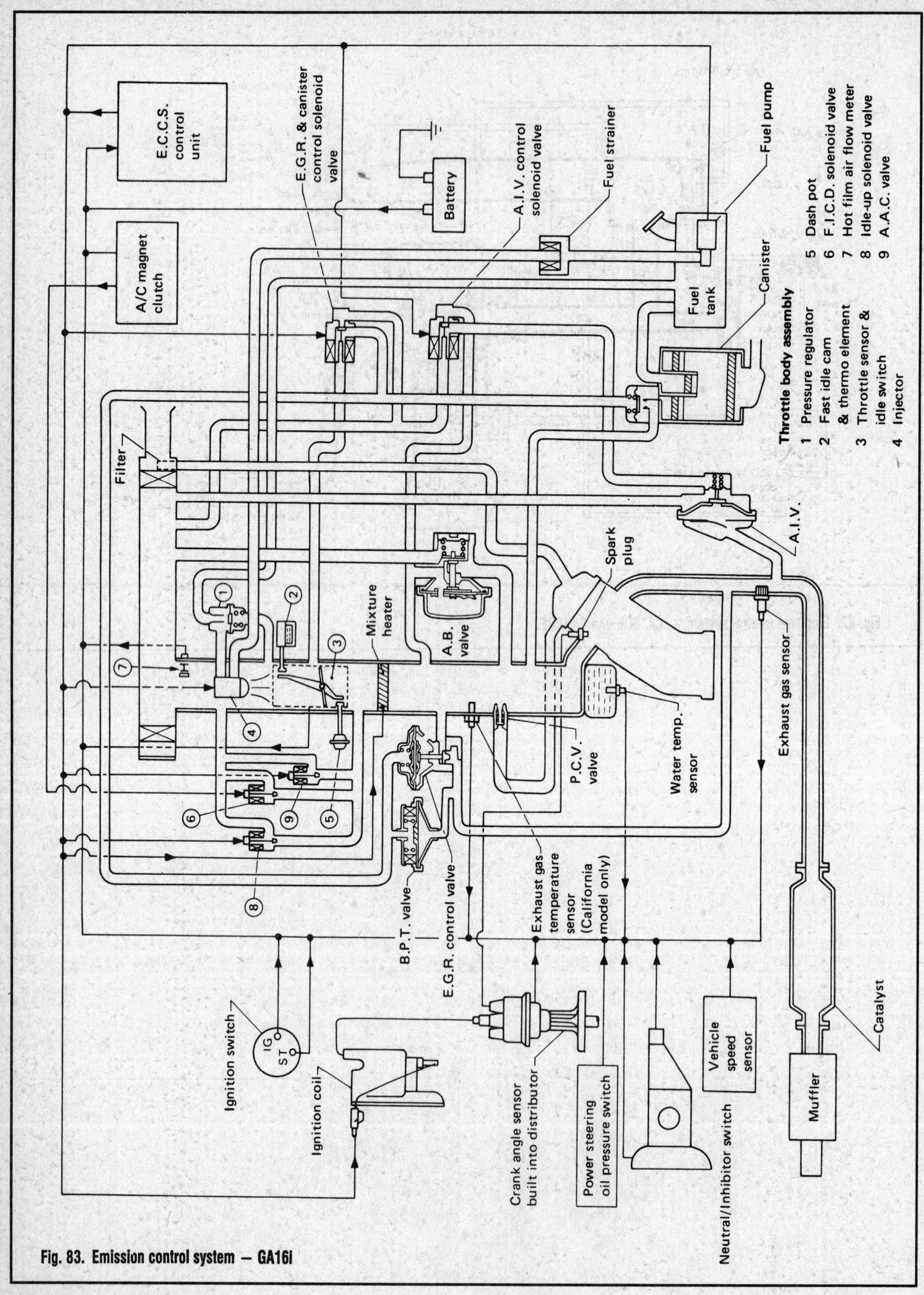

E.C.C.S. control unit
A/C magnet clutch
E.G.R. & canister control solenoid valve
Battery
A.I.V. control solenoid valve
Fuel strainer
Fuel pump
Fuel tank
Canister
Filter
Throttle body assembly
1 Pressure regulator
2 Fast idle cam & thermo element
3 Throttle sensor & idle switch
4 Injector
5 Dash pot
6 F.I.C.D. solenoid valve
7 Hot film air flow meter
8 Idle-up solenoid valve
9 A.A.C. valve
A.I.V.
Spark plug
Mixture heater
A.B. valve
Exhaust gas sensor
Water temp. sensor
P.C.V. valve
B.P.T. valve
E.G.R. control valve
Exhaust gas temperature sensor (California model only)
Ignition switch
IG
ST
Ignition coil
Crank angle sensor built into distributor
Power steering oil pressure switch
Neutral/Inhibitor switch
Vehicle speed sensor
Catalyst
Muffler

Fig. 83. Emission control system — GA16i

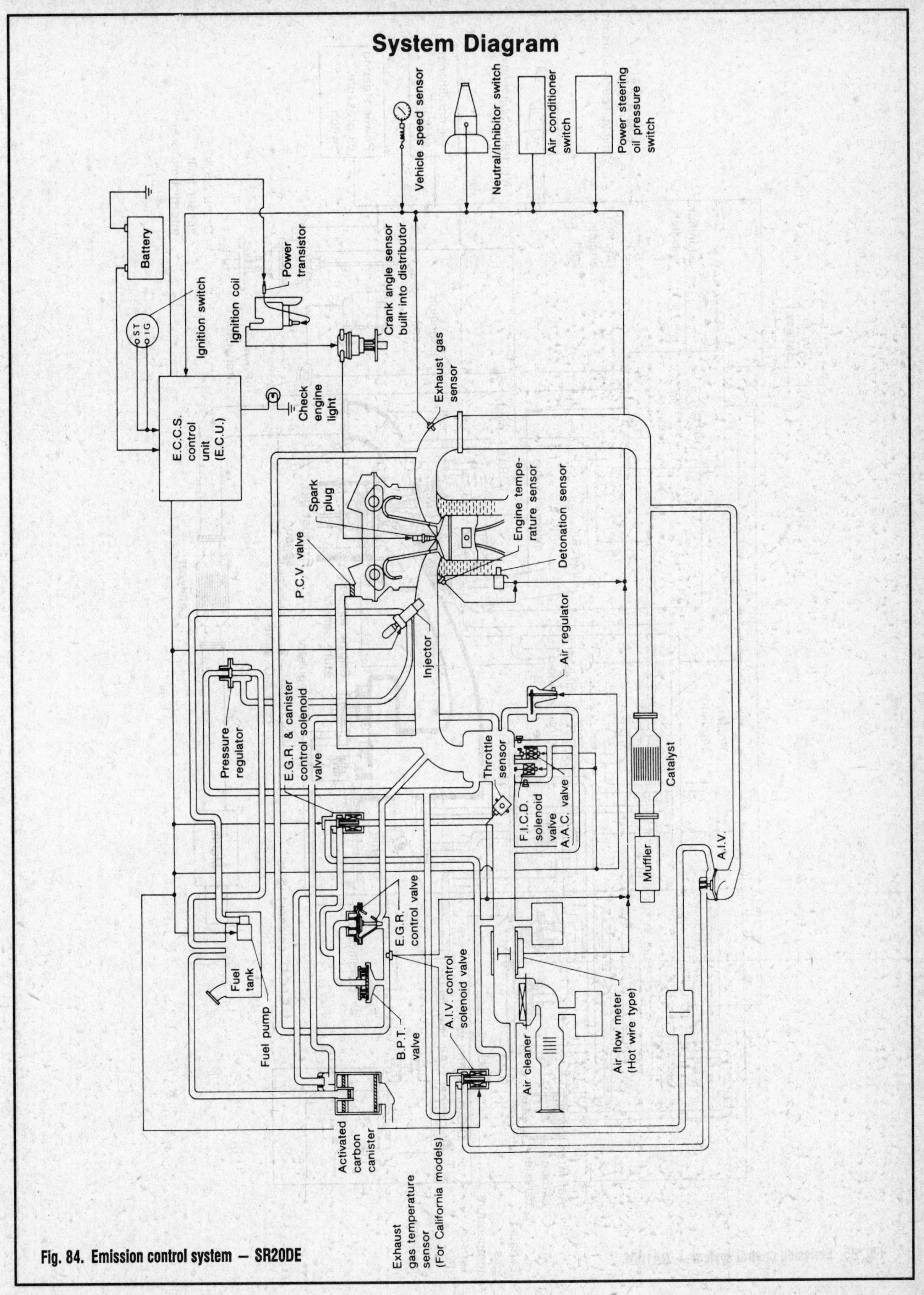
System Diagram
Vehicle speed sensor
Neutral/Inhibitor switch
Air conditioner switch
Power steering oil pressure switch
Battery
Power transistor
Ignition switch
ST
IG
Ignition coil
Crank angle sensor built into distributor
Exhaust gas sensor
Check engine light
E.C.C.S. control unit (E.C.U.)
Spark plug
Engine temperature sensor
Detonation sensor
P.C.V. valve
Injector
Air regulator
Pressure regulator
E.G.R. & canister control solenoid valve
Throttle sensor
Catalyst
F.I.C.D. solenoid valve
A.A.C. valve
Muffler
A.I.V.
E.G.R. control valve
Fuel tank
Fuel pump
B.P.T. valve
A.I.V. control solenoid valve
Air cleaner
Air flow meter (Hot wire type)
Activated carbon canister
Exhaust gas temperature sensor (For California models)

Fig. 84. Emission control system — SR20DE

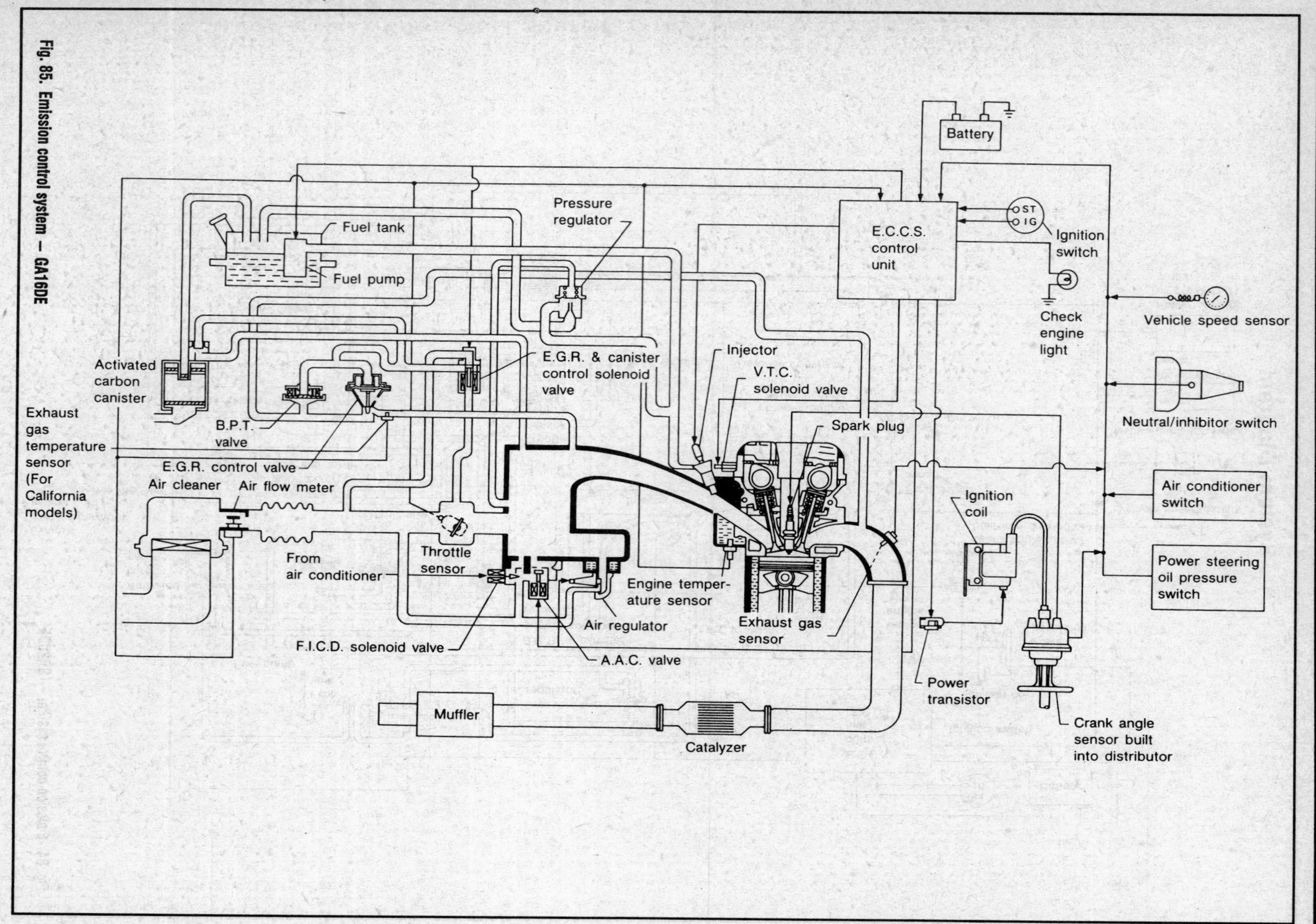
Battery
E.C.C.S. control unit
ST
IG
Ignition switch
Check engine light
Vehicle speed sensor
Neutral/inhibitor switch
Air conditioner switch
Power steering oil pressure switch
Crank angle sensor built into distributor
Ignition coil
Power transistor
Spark plug
V.T.C. solenoid valve
Injector
Exhaust gas sensor
Catalyzer
Muffler
Engine temperature sensor
Air regulator
A.A.C. valve
F.I.C.D. solenoid valve
Throttle sensor
From air conditioner
Pressure regulator
E.G.R. & canister control solenoid valve
Fuel tank
Fuel pump
Activated carbon canister
B.P.T. valve
E.G.R. control valve
Exhaust gas temperature sensor (For California models)
Air cleaner
Air flow meter

Fig. 85. Emission control system — GA16DE

5

FUEL SYSTEM

CARBURETED FUEL SYSTEMS

➡ This Section pertains to the removal, installation and adjustment of fuel system related components. For comprehensive diagnostic and testing of the emission and fuel systems, refer to Section 4.

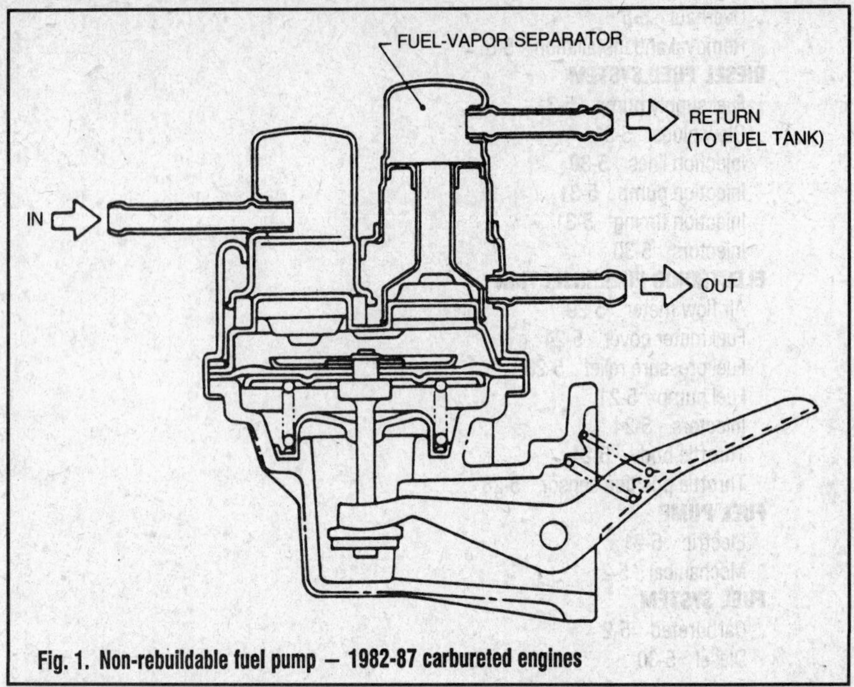
FUEL-VAPOR SEPARATOR
RETURN
(TO FUEL TANK)
IN
OUT

Fig. 1. Non-rebuildable fuel pump — 1982-87 carbureted engines

Mechanical Fuel Pump

The fuel pump is a mechanically operated, diaphragm type driven by the fuel pump eccentric on the camshaft. The pump is located on the lower right side.

The pump cannot be disassembled. If it fails either the pressure or the volume test, replace the unit.

REMOVAL & INSTALLATION

CAUTION

Never smoke when working around gasoline! Avoid all sources of sparks or ignition. Gasoline vapors are EXTREMELY volatile!

1. Disconnect the fuel lines from the fuel pump. Be sure to keep the line leading from the fuel tank up high to prevent the excess loss of fuel.
2. Remove the two fuel pump mounting nuts and the fuel pump assembly from the right side of the engine.
3. To install, use a new gasket, sealant and reverse the removal procedures. Torque the fuel pump bolts to 7–9 ft. lbs. (10–13 Nm).

TESTING

Static Pressure

CAUTION

Never smoke when working around gasoline! Avoid all sources of sparks or ignition. Gasoline vapors are EXTREMELY volatile!

1. Disconnect the fuel line at the carburetor. Using a T-connector, connect two rubber hoses to the connector, then install it between the fuel line and the carburetor fitting.

➡ When disconnecting the fuel line, be sure to place a container under the line to catch the excess fuel which will be present.

2. Connect a fuel pump pressure gauge to the T-connector and secure it with a clamp.
3. Start the engine and check the pressure at various speeds. The pressure should be 3.0–3.8 psi (20.7–26.2kpa) for 1982–83 or 2.8–3.8 psi (19.3–26.2kpa) 1984 and later. There is usually enough gas in the float bowl to perform this test.
4. If the pressure is OK, perform a capacity test. Remove the gauge and the T-connector assembly, then reinstall the fuel line to the carburetor.

Capacity Test

1. Disconnect the fuel line from the carburetor and place the line in a graduated container.
2. Fill the carburetor float bowl with gas.
3. Start the engine and run it for one minute at about 600 rpm. The pump should deliver 44.0 oz. (1300 mL) per minute.

Carburetor

The carburetor used is a 2-barrel down-draft type with a low speed (primary) side and a high speed (secondary) side.

All models have an electrically operated anti-dieseling solenoid. As the ignition switch is turned off, the valve is energized and shuts off the supply of fuel to the idle circuit of the carburetor.

All 1984 and later U.S.A. carbureted models are equipped with the E.C.C. System (Electronic Controlled Carburetor). The E.C.C control unit consists of a microcomputer, connectors for signal input and output and power supply, and an exhaust gas sensor monitor lamp. The control unit senses and controls various carburetor operations.

On all non-California models instead of the choke valve and fast idle cam of a conventional carburetor, this system utilizes a duty-controlled solenoid valve for fuel enrichment and an idle speed control actuator (ISCA) for the basic controls. These devices are controlled according to the engine speed , amount of intake air, and objective engine speed. Also, the air-fuel ratio and ignition timing are controlled according to the engine water temperature, atmospheric pressure, vehicle speed and transaxle gear position. In addition, this system controls the ignition timing and the idle speed according to applied electric loads such as a cooler, thereby achieving better emission control, fuel economy etc.

On California models the carburetor is equipped with an air-fuel ratio control on-off valve instead of a power valve. This on-off valve opens or closes the compensating air bleed and main jet to compensate for rich/lean air-fuel ratio, depending on varying conditions, such as acceleration, deceleration, low coolant temperature, low voltage, etc. These varying conditions are detected by various sensors which transmit corresponding signals to provide air-fuel ratio compensation.

ADJUSTMENTS

Throttle Linkage Adjustment

1. Disconnect the negative battery cable.
2. Remove the air cleaner.
3. Open the automatic choke valve by hand, while turning the throttle valve by pulling the throttle lever, then set the choke valve in the open position.

➡ If equipped with a vacuum controlled throttle positioner, use a vacuum hand pump to retract the the throttle positioner rod.

4. Adjust the throttle cable at the carburetor bracket, so that a 1.0–2.0mm of free pedal play exists.

Dashpot Adjustment

A dashpot is used on carburetors with automatic transaxles and some manual transaxles. The dashpot slowly closes the throttle on automatic transmissions to prevent stalling and serves as an emission control device on all late model vehicles.

The dashpot should be adjusted to contact the throttle lever on deceleration at approximately 2,300–2,500 rpm (E15) engines, 1,900–2,100 rpm (E16, automatic transmission) or 2,250–2,450 (E16, manual transmission).

➡ Before attempting to adjust the dashpot, make sure the idle speed, timing and mixture adjustments are correct.

1. Loosen the locknut (turn the dashpot, if necessary) and make sure the engine speed drops smoothly from 2,000 rpm to 1,000 rpm in 3 seconds.

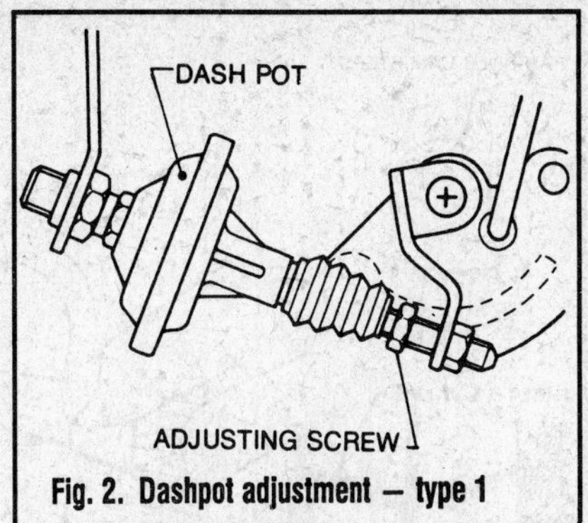
DASH POT
ADJUSTING SCREW
Fig. 2. Dashpot adjustment – type 1

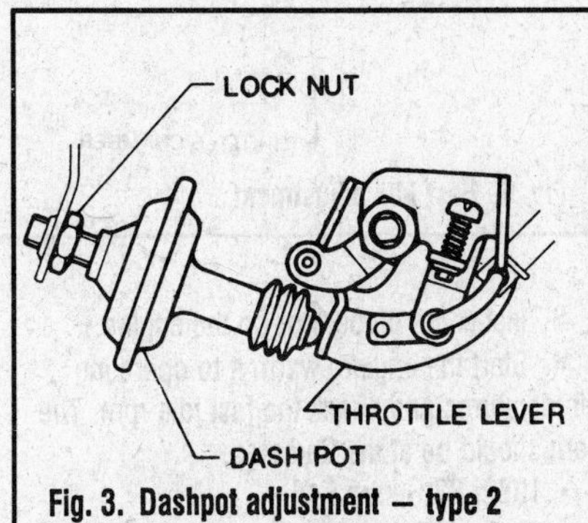
LOCK NUT
THROTTLE LEVER
DASH POT
Fig. 3. Dashpot adjustment – type 2

2. If the dashpot has been removed from the carburetor, it must be adjusted when installed. Adjust the gap between the primary throttle valve and the inner carburetor wall, when the dashpot stem comes in contact with the throttle arm. The dashpot gap is 0.66–0.86mm (manual transmission) or 0.49–0.69mm (automatic transmission).

Secondary Throttle Linkage Adjustment

All carburetors discussed in this book are two stage type carburetors. On this type of carburetor, the engine runs on the primary barrel most of the time, with the secondary barrel being used for acceleration purposes. When the throttle valve on the primary side opens to an angle of approximately 50° (from its fully closed position), the secondary throttle valve is pulled open by the connecting linkage. The 50° angle of throttle valve opening works out to a clearance measurement of 5.7–6.9mm between the throttle valve and the carburetor body. The easiest way to measure this is to use a drill bit. Drill bits from sizes H to P (standard letter size drill bits) should fit. Check the appendix in the back of the book for the exact size of the various drill bits. If an adjustment is necessary, bend the connecting link between the two linkage assemblies.

➡ The carburetor is equipped with a tang on the adjusting link, bend the tang to adjust the clearance.

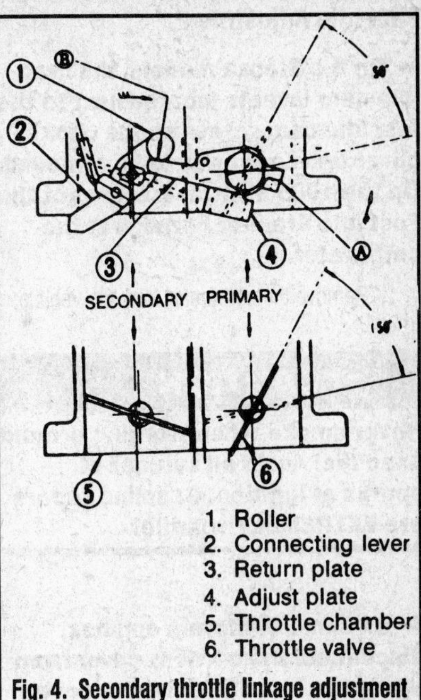
1
B
2
3
4
A
SECONDARY
PRIMARY
5
6
1. Roller
2. Connecting lever
3. Return plate
4. Adjust plate
5. Throttle chamber
6. Throttle valve
Fig. 4. Secondary throttle linkage adjustment

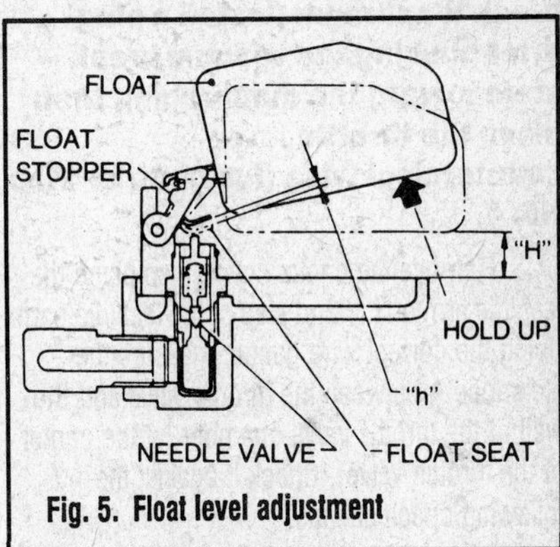
FLOAT
FLOAT STOPPER
"H"
HOLD UP
"h"
NEEDLE VALVE
FLOAT SEAT
Fig. 5. Float level adjustment

Float Level Adjustment

The fuel level is normal if it is within the lines or dot on the window glass of the float chamber (or the sight glass) when the vehicle is resting on level ground and the engine is off.

If the fuel level is outside the lines, remove the float housing cover. Have an absorbent cloth under the cover to catch the fuel from the fuel bowl. Adjust the float level by bending the needle seat on the float.

The needle valve should have an effective stroke of about 1.5mm. When necessary, the needle valve stroke can be adjusted by bending the float stopper.

➡ Be careful not to bend the needle valve rod when installing the float and baffle plate, if removed.

Fast Idle Adjustment

➡ On the Stanza models, the fast idle cam lever is located next to the fast idle cam screw, so the choke cover does not have to be removed. On the 1985 Stanza, disconnect the Fast Idle Breaker harness at the carburetor.

1. Remove the carburetor from the vehicle.

✱✱ CAUTION

Never smoke when working around gasoline! Avoid all sources of sparks or ignition. Gasoline vapors are EXTREMELY volatile!

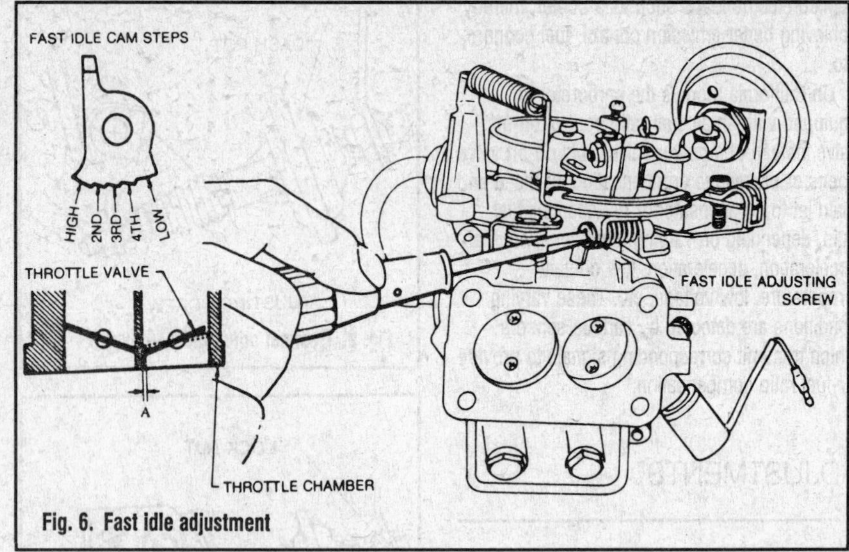
FAST IDLE CAM STEPS
HIGH
2ND
3RD
4TH
LOW
THROTTLE VALVE
A
THROTTLE CHAMBER
FAST IDLE ADJUSTING SCREW

Fig. 6. Fast idle adjustment

➡ On some California engines, disconnect the harness cover from the automatic choke heater cover, the vacuum hose from the vacuum break diaphragm (install a plug after pushing the vacuum break stem toward the diaphragm), then move the throttle lever counterclockwise (fully). Go to Step No. 4.

2. Remove the choke cover, then place the fast idle arm on the 2nd step of the fast idle cam. Using the correct wire gauge, measure the clearance A between the throttle valve and the wall of the throttle valve chamber (at the center of the throttle valve). Check it against the following specifications:

- 1982–88 Sentra: 0.80–0.87mm MT 1.07–1.14mm AT
- 1983 Pulsar: 0.79–0.93mm USA MT 1.08–1.22mm USA AT 0.65–0.79mm Canada MT 0.93–1.07mm Canada AT
- 1984–87 Pulsar: 0.76–0.96mm USA MT 1.05–1.25mm USA AT 0.54–0.82mm Canada MT 0.90–1.10mm Canada AT

➡ The first step of the fast idle adjustment procedure is not absolutely necessary.

3. Install the carburetor on the engine.
4. Start the engine, warm it to operating temperatures and check the fast idle rpm. The cam should be at the 2nd step.

- 1982–83 Sentra E15
  Federal: 2,400–3,200 rpm
  Calif.: 2,300–3,100 rpm
  Canada MT: 1,900–2,700 rpm
  Canada AT: 2,400–3,200 rpm
- 1984–87 Sentra E16
  Federal: Not adjustable
  Calif. MT: 2,600–3,400 rpm
  Calif. AT: 2,900–3,700 rpm
  Canada MT: 1,900–2,700 rpm
  Canada AT: 2,400–3,200 rpm
- 1983 Pulsar:
  Federal MT: 2,400–3,200 rpm
  Federal AT: 2,700–3,500 rpm
  Calif. MT: 2,600–3,400 rpm
  Calif. AT: 2,900–3,700 rpm
  Canada MT: 1,900–2,700 rpm
  Canada AT: 2,400–3,200 rpm
- 1984–87 Pulsar:
  Calif. MT: 2,600–3,400 rpm
  Calif. AT: 2,900–3,700 rpm
  Canada MT: 1,900–2,700 rpm
  Canada AT: 2,400–3,200 rpm

5. To adjust the fast idle speed, turn the fast idle adjusting screw counterclockwise to increase the fast idle speed and clockwise to decrease the fast idle speed.

Primary And Secondary Throttle Valve Interlock Opening Adjustment

With the carburetor removed from the engine, turn the throttle arm until the adjusting plate comes in contact with the lock lever at point "A" and Check clearance "G". Clearance should be 6.3mm.

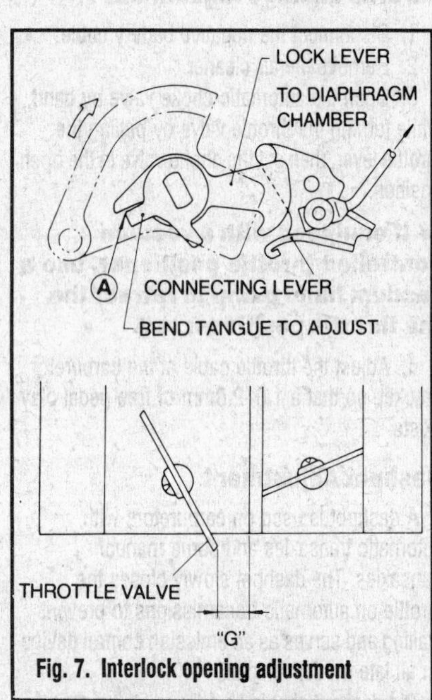
LOCK LEVER
TO DIAPHRAGM CHAMBER
A
CONNECTING LEVER
BEND TANGUE TO ADJUST
THROTTLE VALVE
"G"

Fig. 7. Interlock opening adjustment

Choke Unloader Adjustment

➡ The choke must be cold for this adjustment. This adjustment does not apply to 1984 and later non-California U.S.A. models, nor to 1987 California/Canada models.

1. Close the choke valve completely.
2. Hold the choke valve closed by stretching a rubber band between the choke piston lever and a stationary part of the carburetor.
3. Open the throttle lever fully.

➡ On all vehicles (except Stanza), the unloader cam is located next to the choke plate adjusting lever. On the Stanza, the unloader adjusting lever is connected to the primary throttle plate shaft, an intermediate cam is connected to the choke lever by a choke rod.

4. Adjustment is made by bending the unloader tongue. Gauge the gap between the choke plate and the carburetor body to:

- Pulsar: 2.96mm
- 1982–83 E-series engines: 2.36mm
- 1984–87 E-series engines: 3.00mm

Vacuum Break Adjustment

1. With the engine cold, close the choke completely.
2. Pull the vacuum break stem straight up as far as it will go.
3. Check the clearance between the choke plate and the carburetor wall.
   Clearance should be:
   - 1.33–1.73mm (below 63°F)
   - 2.40–2.80mm (above 75°F)
4. Adjustment is made by bending the tang at the choke plate lever assembly.

➡ Remove the choke cover, then connect a rubber band to the choke lever to hold it shut.

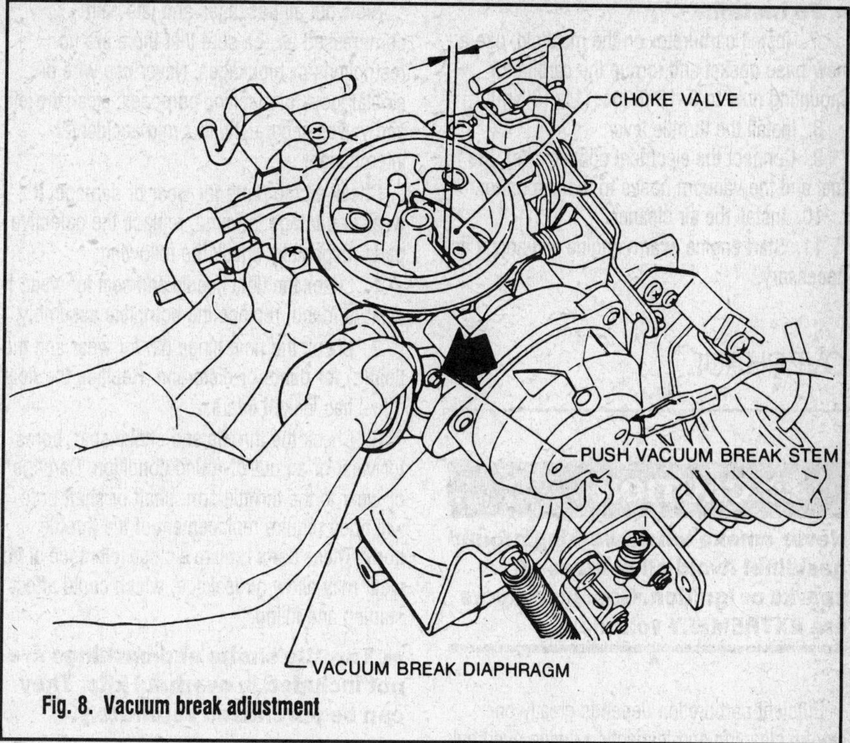
CHOKE VALVE
PUSH VACUUM BREAK STEM
VACUUM BREAK DIAPHRAGM

Fig. 8. Vacuum break adjustment

Accelerator Pump Adjustment

If a smooth constant stream of fuel is not injected into the carburetor bore when the throttle is opened, the accelerator pump needs adjustment.

1. Remove the carburetor from the engine.
2. Check the gap between the primary throttle valve and the inner wall of the carburetor when the pump lever comes in contact with the piston pin. This is the stroke limiter gap. It should be 1.3mm. If not, bend the stroke limiter.
3. Fill the carburetor bowl with fuel.
4. Fully open the choke.
5. Place a calibrated container under the throttle bore. Slowly open and close the throttle (full open to full closed) ten times keeping the throttle open 3 seconds each time. Measure the amount of fuel in the container. The amount should be 0.3–0.5 ml. If not, and the stroke limiter gap is correct, replace the accelerator pump unit.

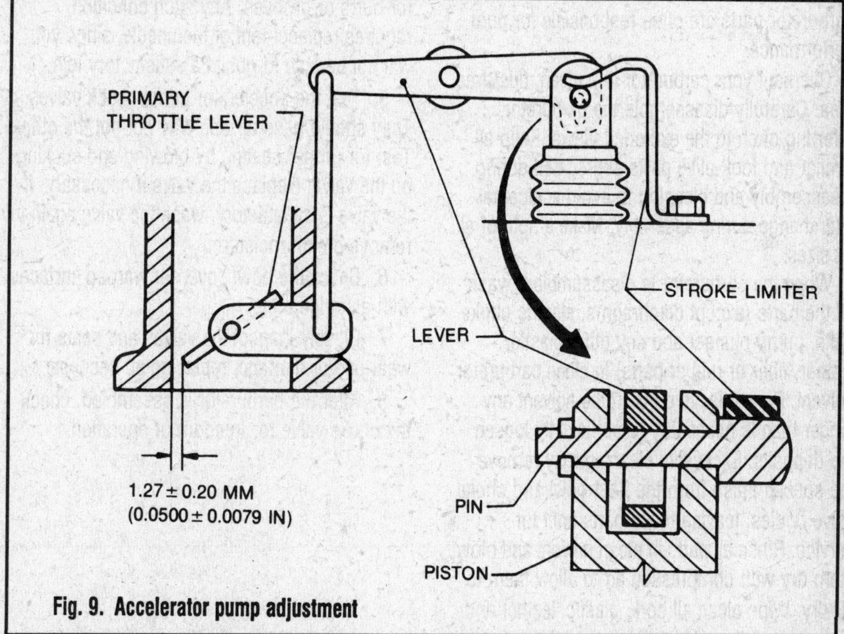
PRIMARY
THROTTLE LEVER
STROKE LIMITER
LEVER
1.27 ± 0.20 MM
(0.0500 ± 0.0079 IN)
PIN
PISTON

Fig. 9. Accelerator pump adjustment

Anti-Dieseling Solenoid

Check this valve if the engine continues to run after the key has been turned off.

1. Run the engine at idle speed and disconnect the lead wire at the anti-dieseling solenoid. The engine should stop.
2. If the engine does not stop, check the harness for current at the solenoid. If current is present, replace the solenoid. Installation torque for the solenoid is 13–16 ft. lbs. (18–22 Nm).

REMOVAL & INSTALLATION

1. Remove the air cleaner.
2. Disconnect the electrical connector(s), the fuel and the vacuum hoses from the carburetor.
3. Remove the throttle lever.
4. Remove the four nuts and washers retaining the carburetor to the manifold.
5. Lift the carburetor from the manifold.
6. Remove and discard the gasket used between the carburetor and the manifold.

To Install:

7. Install carburetor on the manifold, use a new base gasket and torque the carburetor mounting nuts to 9–13 ft. lbs. (11–18 Nm).
8. Install the throttle lever.
9. Connect the electrical connector(s), the fuel and the vacuum hoses to the carburetor.
10. Install the air cleaner.
11. Start engine, warm engine and adjust as necessary.

OVERHAUL

⁂ CAUTION

Never smoke when working around gasoline! Avoid all sources of sparks or ignition. Gasoline vapors are EXTREMELY volatile!

Efficient carburetion depends greatly on careful cleaning and inspection during overhaul, since dirt, gum, water and/or varnish in or on the carburetor parts are often responsible for poor performance.

Overhaul your carburetor in a clean, dust free area. Carefully disassemble the carburetor, referring often to the exploded views. Keep all similar and look-alike parts segregated during disassembly and cleaning to avoid accidental interchange during assembly. Make a note of all jet sizes.

When the carburetor is disassembled, wash all the parts (except diaphragms, electric choke units, pump plunger and any other plastic, leather, fiber or rubber parts) in clean carburetor solvent. Do not leave parts in the solvent any longer than is necessary to sufficiently loosen the deposits. Excessive cleaning may remove the special finish from the float bowl and choke valve bodies, leaving these parts unfit for service. Rinse all parts in clean solvent and blow them dry with compressed air to allow them to air dry. Wipe clean all cork, plastic, leather and fiber parts with a clean, lint-free cloth.

Blow out all passages and jets with compressed air, be sure that there are no restrictions or blockages. Never use wire or similar tools for cleaning purposes; clean the jets and valves separately, to avoid accidental interchange.

Check all the parts for wear or damage. If wear or damage is found, replace the defective parts. Especially check the following:

1. Check the float needle and seat for wear. If wear is found, replace the complete assembly.
2. Check the float hinge pin for wear and the float(s) for dents or distortion. Replace the float if fuel has leaked into it.
3. Check the throttle and choke shaft bores for wear or an out-of-round condition. Damage or wear to the throttle arm, shaft or shaft bore will often require replacement of the throttle body. These parts require a close tolerance of fit; wear may allow air leakage, which could affect starting and idling.

➡ Throttle shafts and bushings are not included in overhaul kits. They can be purchased separately.

4. Inspect the idle mixture adjusting needles for burrs or grooves. Any such condition requires replacement of the needle, since you will not be able to obtain a satisfactory idle.
5. Test the accelerator pump check valves. They should pass air one way but not the other. Test for proper seating by blowing and sucking on the valve. Replace the valve if necessary. If the valve is satisfactory, wash the valve again to remove breath moisture.
6. Check the bowl cover for warped surfaces with a straightedge.
7. Closely inspect the valves and seats for wear and/or damage, replacing as necessary.
8. After the carburetor is assembled, check the choke valve for freedom of operation.

Carburetor overhaul kits are recommended for each overhaul. These kits contain all gaskets and new parts to replace those that deteriorate most rapidly. Failure to replace all parts supplied with the kit (especially gaskets) can result in poor performance later.

Some carburetor manufacturers supply overhaul kits of three basic types: minor repair, major repair and gasket kits. Basically, they contain the following:

Minor Repair Kits:

- All gaskets
- Float needle valve
- Volume control screw
- All diaphragms
- Spring for the pump diaphragm

Major Repair Kits:

- All jets and gaskets
- All diaphragms
- Float needle valve
- Volume control screw
- Pump ball valve
- Main jet carrier
- Float

Gasket Kits:

- All gaskets

After cleaning and checking all components, reassemble the carburetor, using new parts and referring to the exploded view. When reassembling, make sure that all screws and jets are tight in their seats but do not overtighten as the tips will be distorted. Tighten all screws gradually in rotation. Do not tighten needle valves into their seats; uneven jetting will result. Always use new gaskets. Be sure to adjust the float level when reassembling.

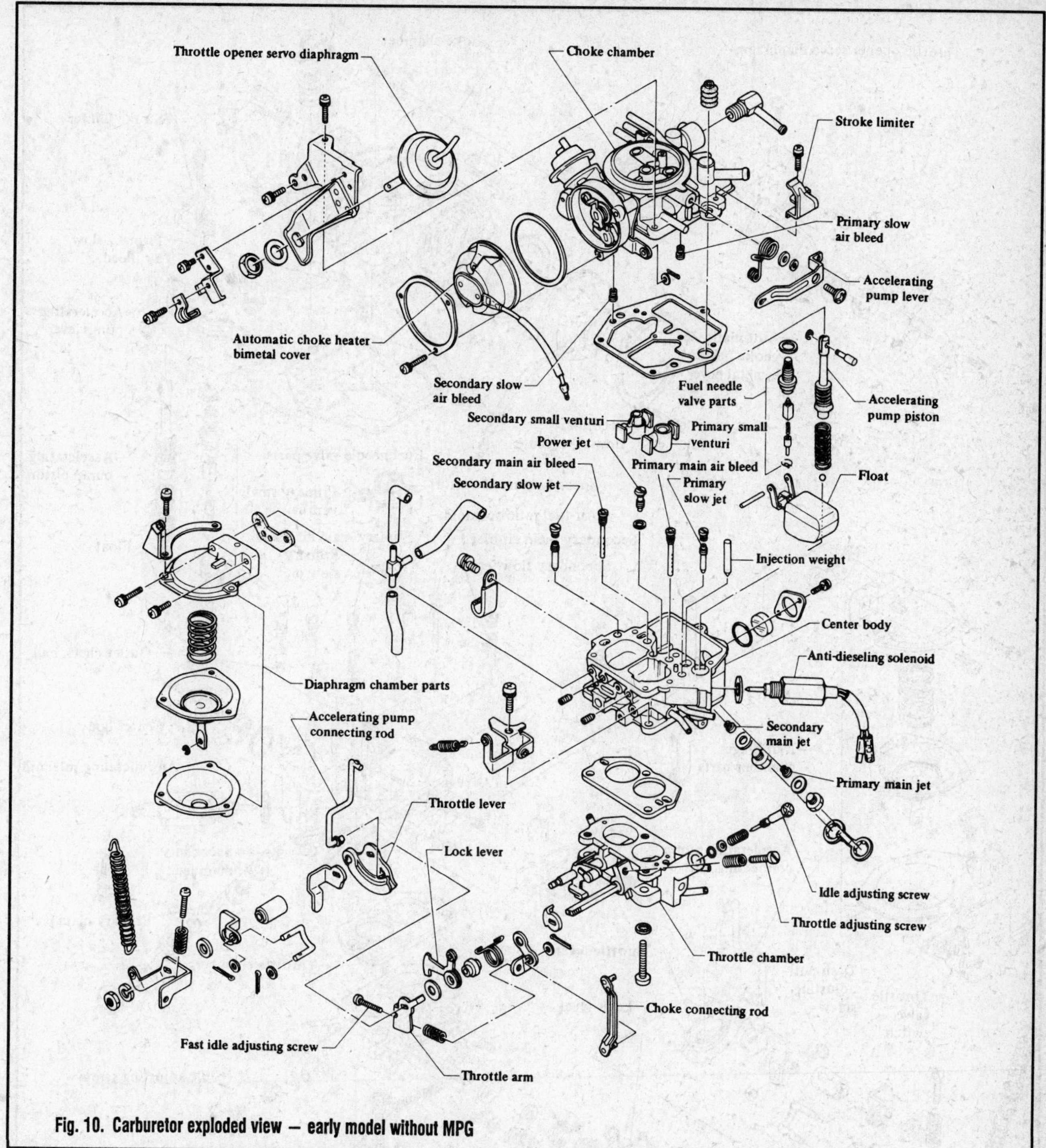
Throttle opener servo diaphragm
Choke chamber
Stroke limiter
Primary slow
air bleed
Accelerating
pump lever
Automatic choke heater
bimetal cover
Secondary slow
air bleed
Fuel needle
valve parts
Accelerating
pump piston
Secondary small venturi
Primary small
venturi
Power jet
Secondary main air bleed
Primary main air bleed
Float
Secondary slow jet
Primary
slow jet
Injection weight
Center body
Anti-dieseling solenoid
Diaphragm chamber parts
Accelerating pump
connecting rod
Secondary
main jet
Primary main jet
Throttle lever
Lock lever
Idle adjusting screw
Throttle adjusting screw
Throttle chamber
Choke connecting rod
Fast idle adjusting screw
Throttle arm

Fig. 10. Carburetor exploded view – early model without MPG

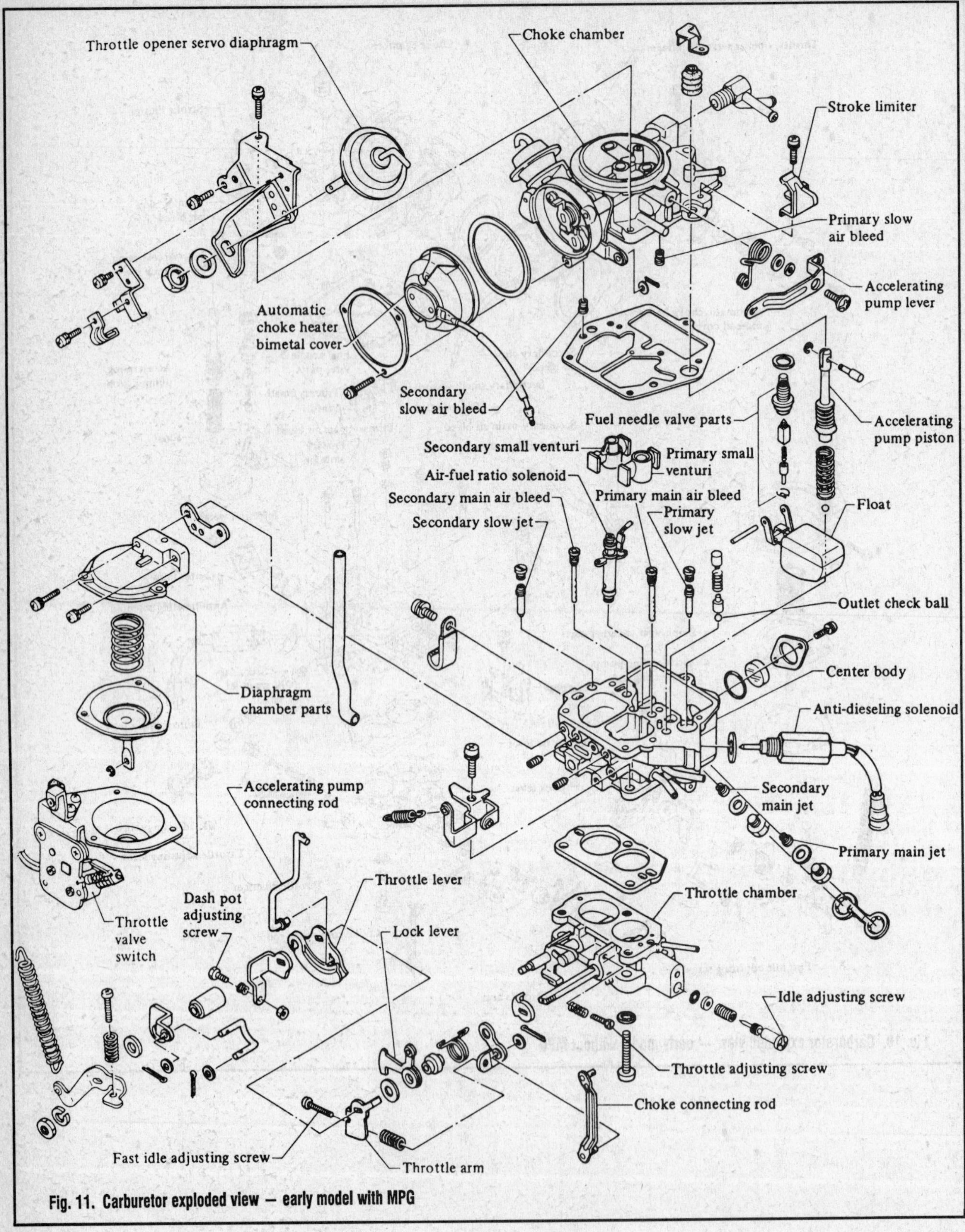
Throttle opener servo diaphragm
Choke chamber
Stroke limiter
Primary slow air bleed
Accelerating pump lever
Automatic choke heater bimetal cover
Secondary slow air bleed
Fuel needle valve parts
Accelerating pump piston
Secondary small venturi
Primary small venturi
Air-fuel ratio solenoid
Secondary main air bleed
Primary main air bleed
Primary slow jet
Secondary slow jet
Float
Outlet check ball
Center body
Anti-dieseling solenoid
Diaphragm chamber parts
Accelerating pump connecting rod
Secondary main jet
Primary main jet
Throttle lever
Throttle chamber
Dash pot adjusting screw
Throttle valve switch
Lock lever
Idle adjusting screw
Throttle adjusting screw
Choke connecting rod
Fast idle adjusting screw
Throttle arm

Fig. 11. Carburetor exploded view — early model with MPG

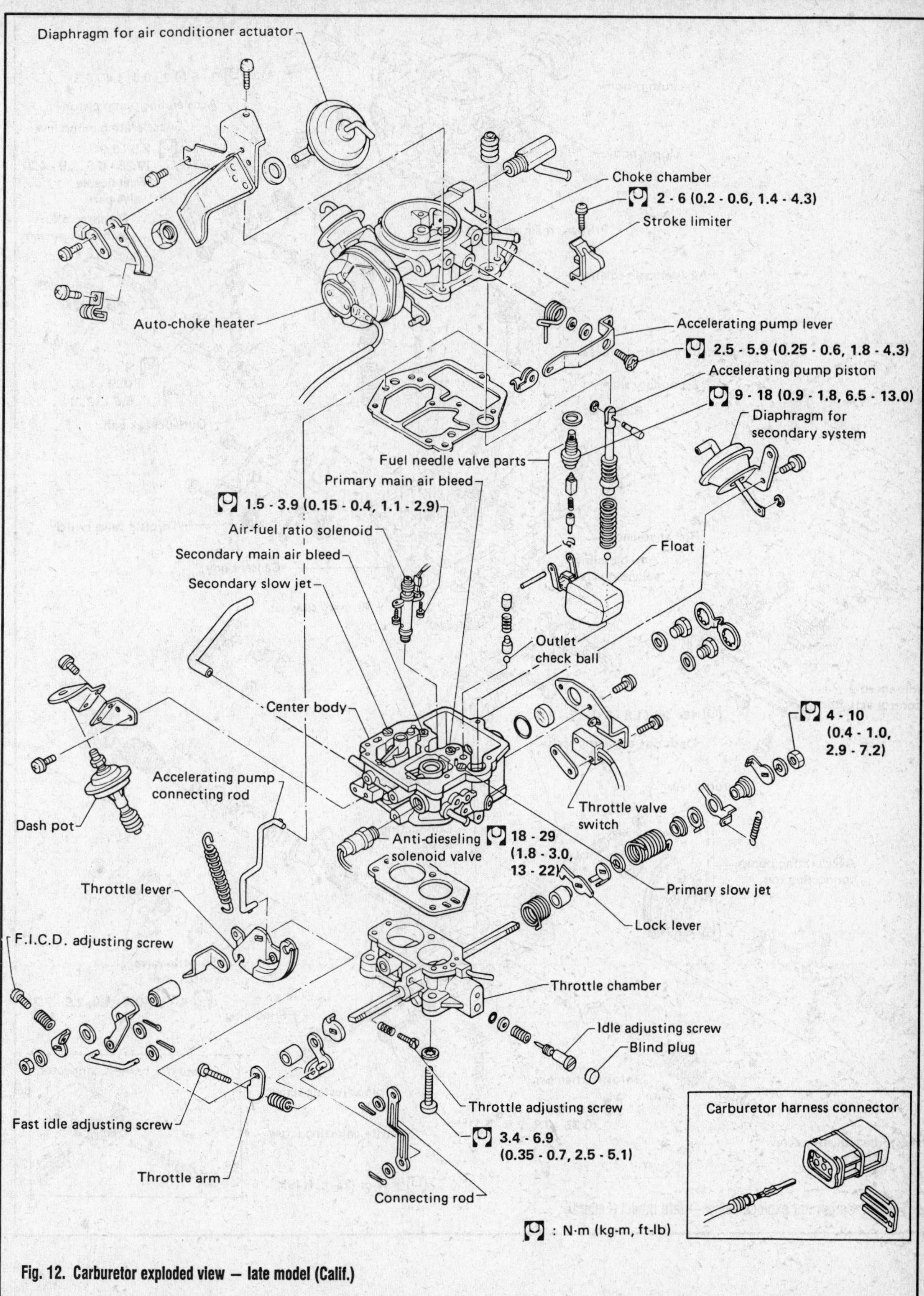
Diaphragm for air conditioner actuator
Choke chamber
2 - 6 (0.2 - 0.6, 1.4 - 4.3)
Stroke limiter
Auto-choke heater
Accelerating pump lever
2.5 - 5.9 (0.25 - 0.6, 1.8 - 4.3)
Accelerating pump piston
9 - 18 (0.9 - 1.8, 6.5 - 13.0)
Diaphragm for secondary system
Fuel needle valve parts
Primary main air bleed
1.5 - 3.9 (0.15 - 0.4, 1.1 - 2.9)
Air-fuel ratio solenoid
Secondary main air bleed
Secondary slow jet
Float
Outlet check ball
Center body
4 - 10 (0.4 - 1.0, 2.9 - 7.2)
Accelerating pump connecting rod
Dash pot
Throttle valve switch
Anti-dieseling solenoid valve
18 - 29 (1.8 - 3.0, 13 - 22)
Primary slow jet
Throttle lever
Lock lever
F.I.C.D. adjusting screw
Throttle chamber
Idle adjusting screw
Blind plug
Throttle adjusting screw
Carburetor harness connector
Fast idle adjusting screw
3.4 - 6.9 (0.35 - 0.7, 2.5 - 5.1)
Throttle arm
Connecting rod
: N·m (kg-m, ft-lb)

Fig. 12. Carburetor exploded view — late model (Calif.)

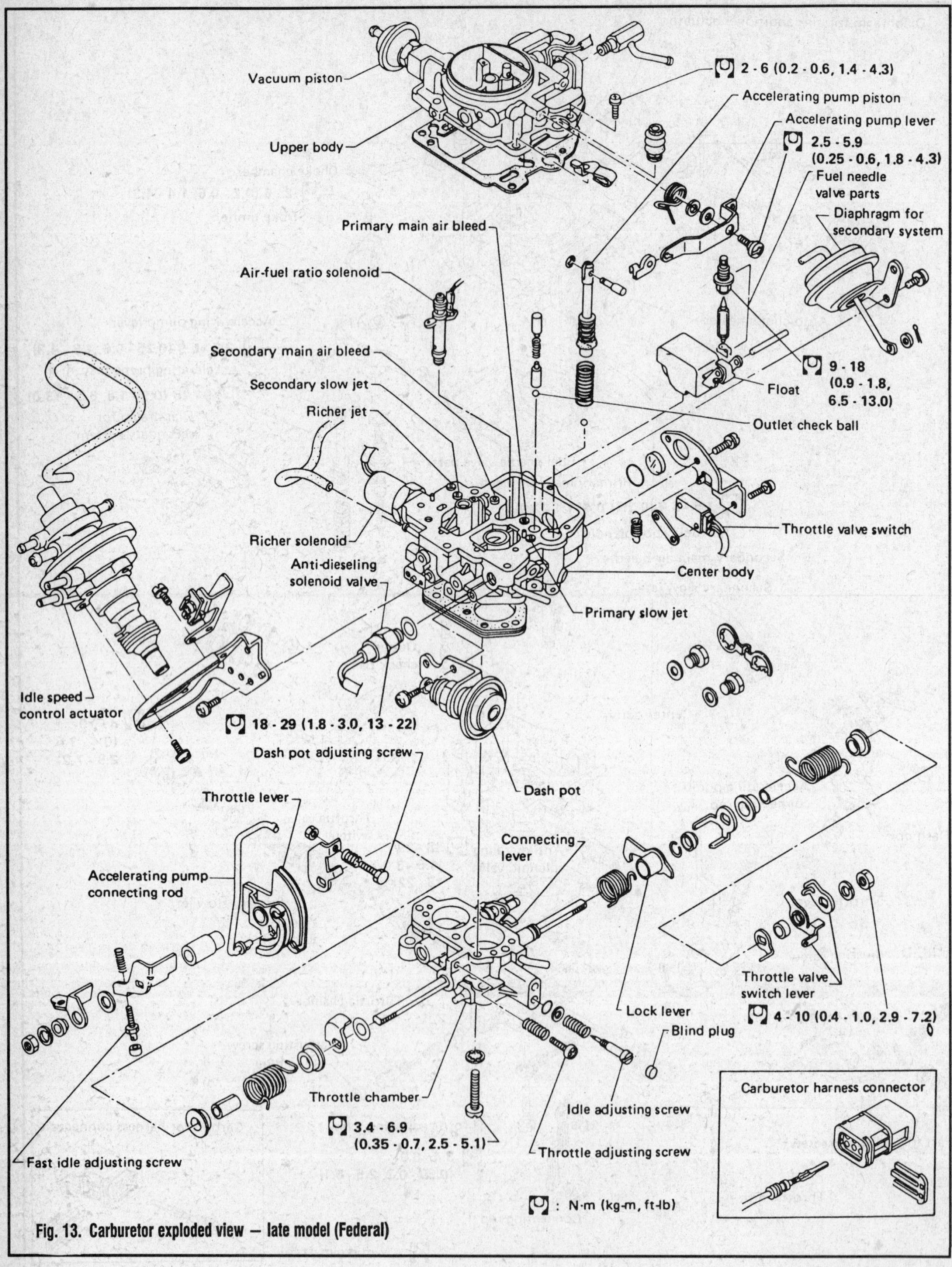

Vacuum piston
Upper body
2 - 6 (0.2 - 0.6, 1.4 - 4.3)
Accelerating pump piston
Accelerating pump lever
2.5 - 5.9
(0.25 - 0.6, 1.8 - 4.3)
Fuel needle valve parts
Diaphragm for secondary system
Primary main air bleed
Air-fuel ratio solenoid
Secondary main air bleed
Secondary slow jet
Richer jet
9 - 18
(0.9 - 1.8,
6.5 - 13.0)
Float
Outlet check ball
Throttle valve switch
Richer solenoid
Anti-dieseling solenoid valve
Center body
Primary slow jet
Idle speed control actuator
18 - 29 (1.8 - 3.0, 13 - 22)
Dash pot adjusting screw
Dash pot
Throttle lever
Connecting lever
Accelerating pump connecting rod
Throttle valve switch lever
Lock lever
4 - 10 (0.4 - 1.0, 2.9 - 7.2)
Blind plug
Carburetor harness connector
Throttle chamber
Idle adjusting screw
3.4 - 6.9
(0.35 - 0.7, 2.5 - 5.1)
Throttle adjusting screw
Fast idle adjusting screw
: N·m (kg-m, ft-lb)

Fig. 13. Carburetor exploded view — late model (Federal)

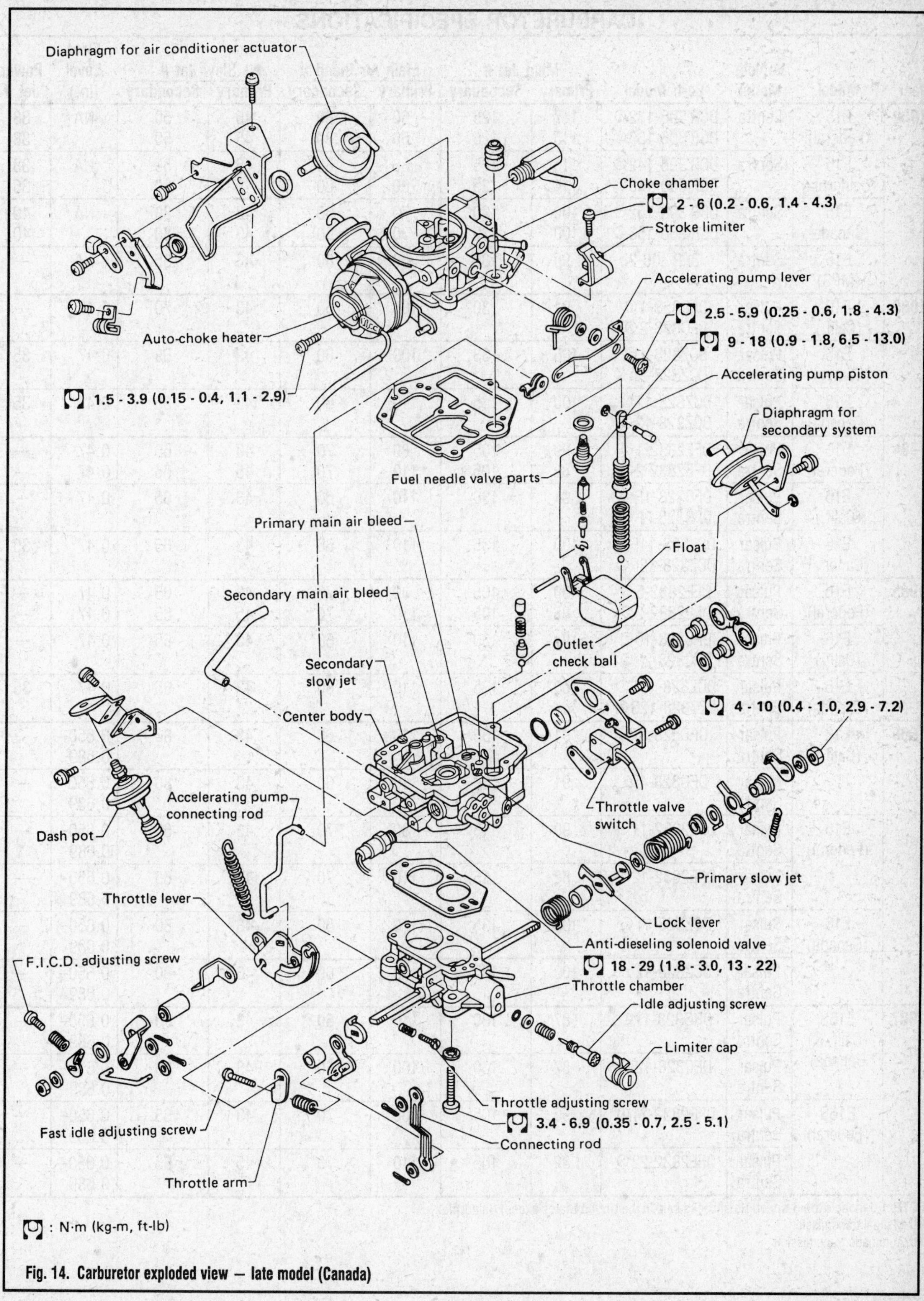
Diaphragm for air conditioner actuator
Choke chamber
2 - 6 (0.2 - 0.6, 1.4 - 4.3)
Stroke limiter
Accelerating pump lever
2.5 - 5.9 (0.25 - 0.6, 1.8 - 4.3)
9 - 18 (0.9 - 1.8, 6.5 - 13.0)
Auto-choke heater
Accelerating pump piston
1.5 - 3.9 (0.15 - 0.4, 1.1 - 2.9)
Diaphragm for secondary system
Fuel needle valve parts
Primary main air bleed
Float
Secondary main air bleed
Outlet check ball
Secondary slow jet
4 - 10 (0.4 - 1.0, 2.9 - 7.2)
Center body
Accelerating pump connecting rod
Throttle valve switch
Dash pot
Primary slow jet
Throttle lever
Lock lever
Anti-dieseling solenoid valve
F.I.C.D. adjusting screw
18 - 29 (1.8 - 3.0, 13 - 22)
Throttle chamber
Idle adjusting screw
Limiter cap
Throttle adjusting screw
3.4 - 6.9 (0.35 - 0.7, 2.5 - 5.1)
Fast idle adjusting screw
Connecting rod
Throttle arm
: N·m (kg-m, ft-lb)

Fig. 14. Carburetor exploded view — late model (Canada)

CARBURETOR SPECIFICATIONS

Year	Model	Vehicle Model	Carb Model	Main Jet # Primary	Main Jet # Secondary	Main Air Bleed # Primary	Main Air Bleed # Secondary	Slow Jet # Primary	Slow Jet # Secondary	Float Level (in.)	Power Jet #
1982	E15 (Federal)	Sentra	DCR 306-132 ①	117	125	60	80	45	50	NA	38
			DCR 306-133 ②	115	125	60	80	45	50		38
	E15 (California)	Sentra	DCR 306-142 ①	115	125	80	80	45	50	NA	38
			DCR 306-143 ②	114	125	80	80	45	50		35
	E15 (Canada)	Sentra	DCR 306-152 ①	100	130	70	60	43	80	NA	40
			DCR 306-153 ②	100	130	70	60	43	80		40
	E15 (MPG)	Sentra	DFP 306-2	98	135	60	80	43	55	NA	—
1983	E16 (Calif.)	Pulsar Sentra	DFC328-1 ① DFC328-2 ②	91	130	105	60	43	70	0.47	—
	E16 (Federal)	Pulsar Sentra	DCZ328-1 ① DCZ328-2 ②	106	133	100	60	43	55	0.47	35
	E16 (Canada)	Pulsar Sentra	DCZ328-11 ① DCZ328-12 ②	100	135	110	60	43	65	0.47	35
1984	E16 (Federal)	Pulsar	DFE2832-1 ①	90	105	80	70	43	65	0.47	—
		Sentra	DFE2832-2 ②	82	105	110	70	45	65	0.47	—
	E16 (Calif.)	Pulsar Sentra	DFC328-1F ② DFC328-2F ②	91	130	110	60	43	65	0.47	—
	E16 (Canada)	Pulsar Sentra	DCZ328-11F ① DCZ328-12F ②	100	135	110	60	43	65	0.47	35
1985	E16 (Federal)	Pulsar	DFE2832-5 ①	90	105	80	70	43	65	0.47	—
		Sentra	DFE2832-2 ②	82	105	110	70	45	65	0.47	—
	E16 (Calif.)	Pulsar Sentra	DFC328-1F ② DFC328-2F ②	91	130	110	60	43	65	0.47	—
	E16 (Canada)	Pulsar Sentra	DCZ328-11F ① DCZ328-12G ②	100	135	110	60	43	65	0.47	35
1986	E16 (Calif.)	Pulsar Sentra	DFC328-3 ①	91	130	110	60	43	80	0.650–0.689	—
		Pulsar Sentra	DFC328-4 ②	91	130	110	60	43	80	0.650–0.689	—
	E16 (Federal)	Pulsar Sentra	DFE2832-11 ①	90	115	80	70	43	65	0.650–0.689	—
		Pulsar Sentra	DFE2832-12 ②	82	115	110	70	45	65	0.650–0.689	—
	E16 (Canada)	Pulsar Sentra	DCZ328-11 ①	100	135	110	60	43	80	0.650–0.689	—
		Pulsar Sentra	DCZ328-12 ②	100	135	110	60	43	80	0.650–0.689	—
1987	E16S (Calif. & Canada)	Pulsar Sentra	DRC328-11 ①	87	130	110	60	43	80	0.650–0.689	—
		Pulsar Sentra	DFC328-12 ②	87	130	100	60	43	80	0.650–0.689	—
	E16S (Federal)	Pulsar Sentra	DFE2832-21 ①	90	105	80	70	43	65	0.650–0.689	—
		Pulsar Sentra	DFE2832-22 ②	82	105	110	70	45	65	0.650–0.689	—

NOTE: FU models are 5-speed Hatchbacks sold in the United States except California.
① Manual transmission
② Automatic transmission

GASOLINE FUEL INJECTION SYSTEM

➡ This Section pertains to the removal, installation and adjustment of fuel system related components. For comprehensive diagnostic and testing of the emission and fuel systems, refer to Section 4.

The electronic fuel injection (EFI) system is an electronic type using various types of sensors to convert engine operating conditions into electronic signals. The generated information is fed to an electronic control unit (ECU), where it is analyzed, then calculated electrical signals are sent to the various equipment, to control the idle speed, the timing and amount of fuel being injected into the engine.

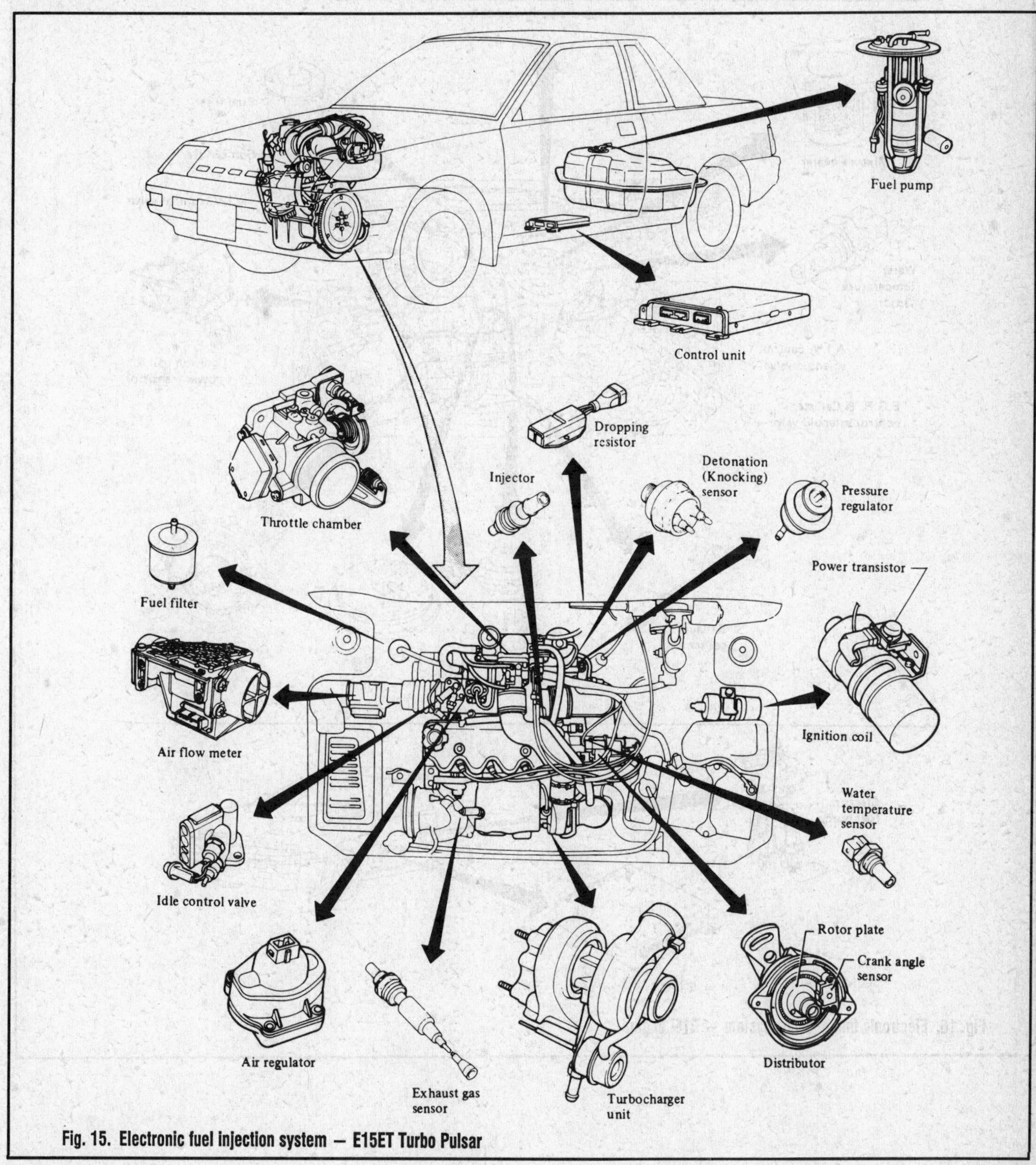
Fuel pump
Control unit
Dropping resistor
Injector
Detonation (Knocking) sensor
Pressure regulator
Throttle chamber
Fuel filter
Power transistor
Air flow meter
Ignition coil
Water temperature sensor
Idle control valve
Rotor plate
Crank angle sensor
Air regulator
Distributor
Exhaust gas sensor
Turbocharger unit

Fig. 15. Electronic fuel injection system – E15ET Turbo Pulsar

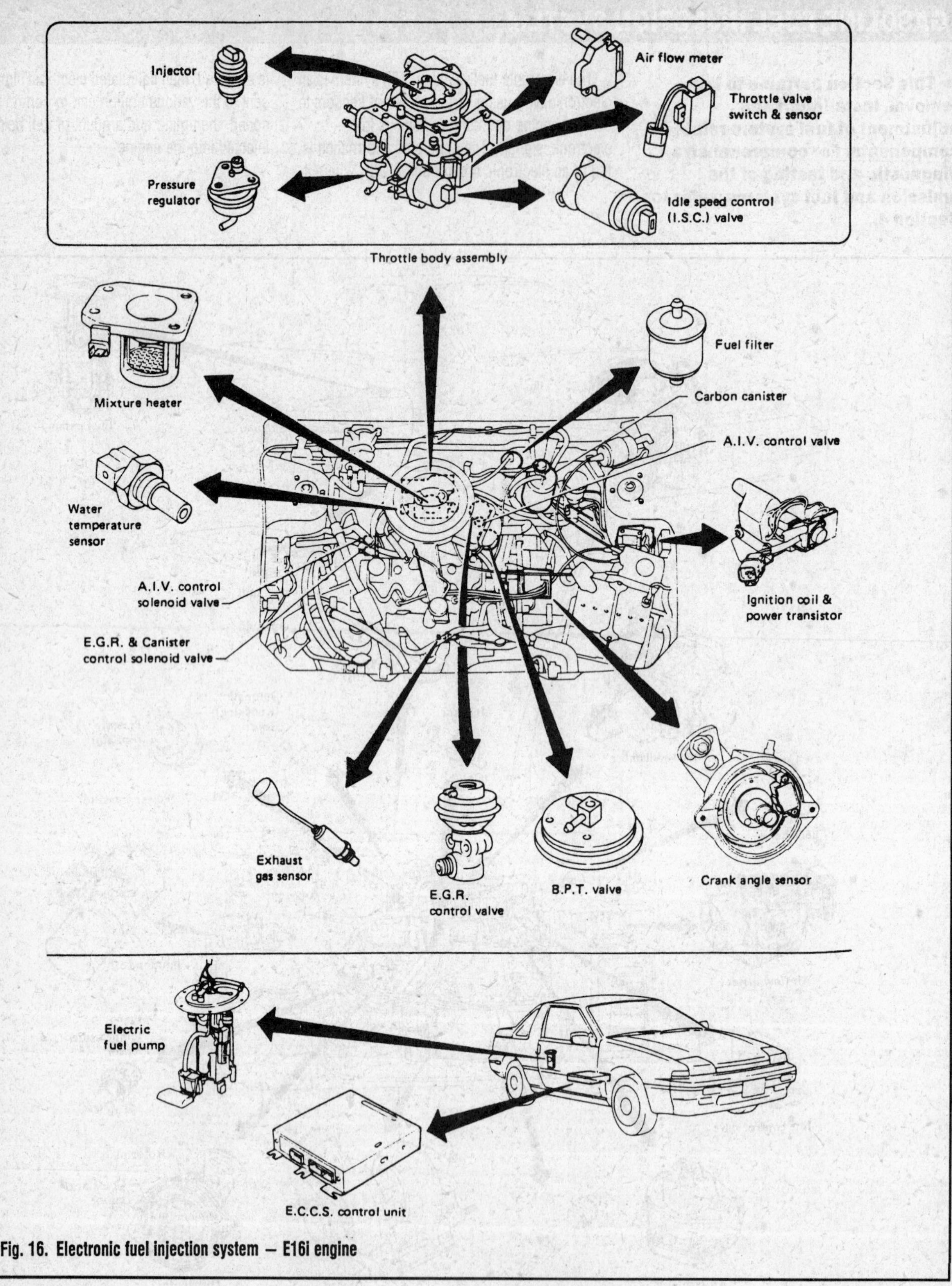
Injector
Air flow meter
Throttle valve switch & sensor
Pressure regulator
Idle speed control (I.S.C.) valve
Throttle body assembly
Mixture heater
Fuel filter
Carbon canister
A.I.V. control valve
Water temperature sensor
Ignition coil & power transistor
A.I.V. control solenoid valve
E.G.R. & Canister control solenoid valve
Exhaust gas sensor
E.G.R. control valve
B.P.T. valve
Crank angle sensor
Electric fuel pump
E.C.C.S. control unit

Fig. 16. Electronic fuel injection system – E16i engine

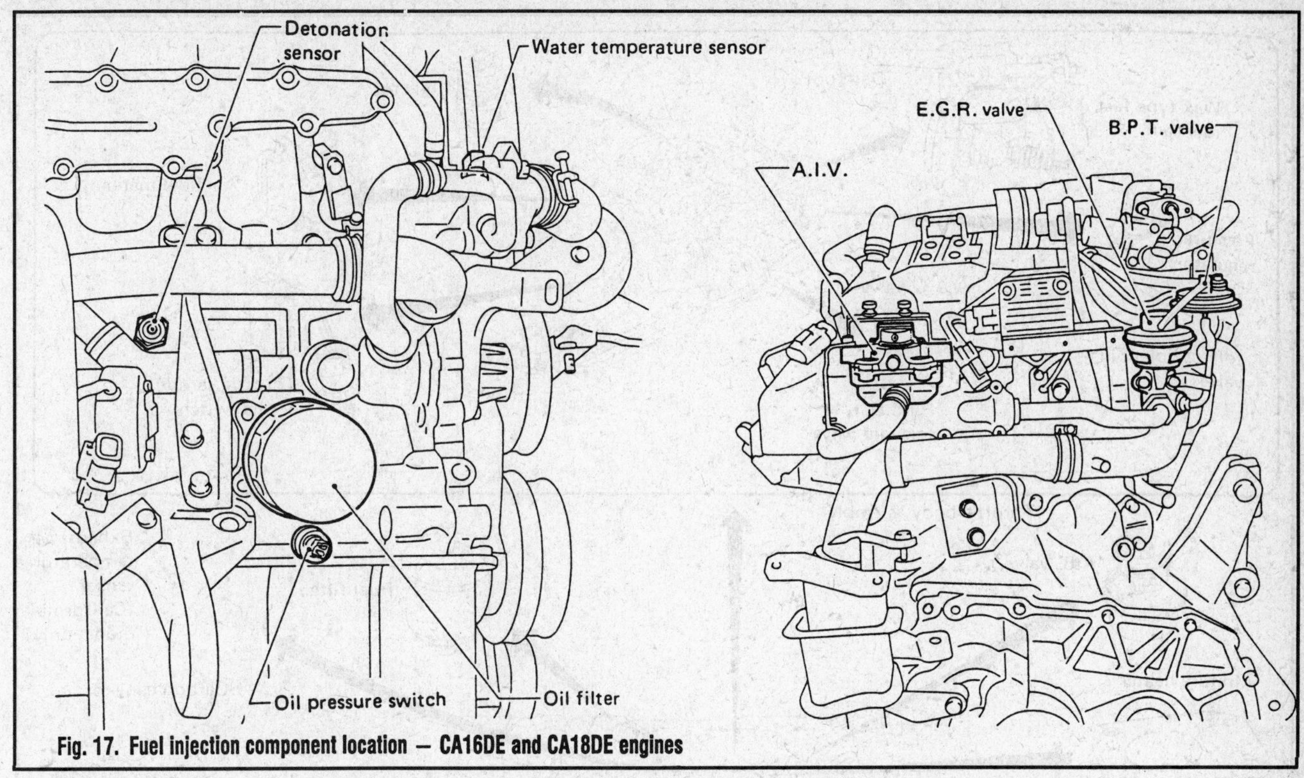
Detonation sensor
Water temperature sensor
E.G.R. valve
B.P.T. valve
A.I.V.
Oil pressure switch
Oil filter

Fig. 17. Fuel injection component location – CA16DE and CA18DE engines

Air regulator valve
Fuel pressure regulator valve
A.A.C. valve
Injector
Resistor (For injector)
F.I.C.D. solenoid valve
Vacuum tank (For power valve)
Altitude switch
E.F.I. control relay
Air flow meter
Power transistor
Exhaust gas sensor
Throttle switch
Crank angle sensor
Power valve actuator

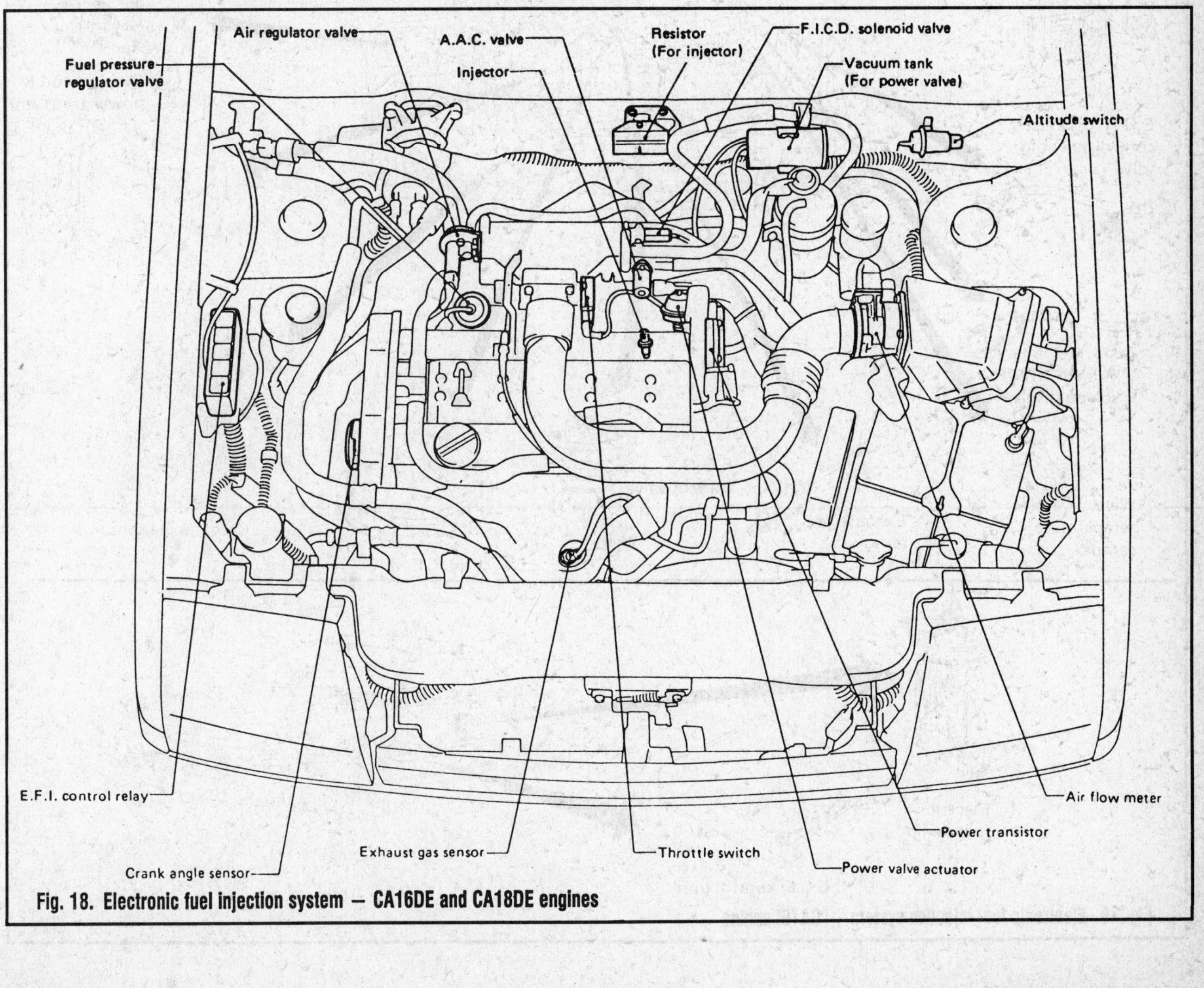

Fig. 18. Electronic fuel injection system – CA16DE and CA18DE engines

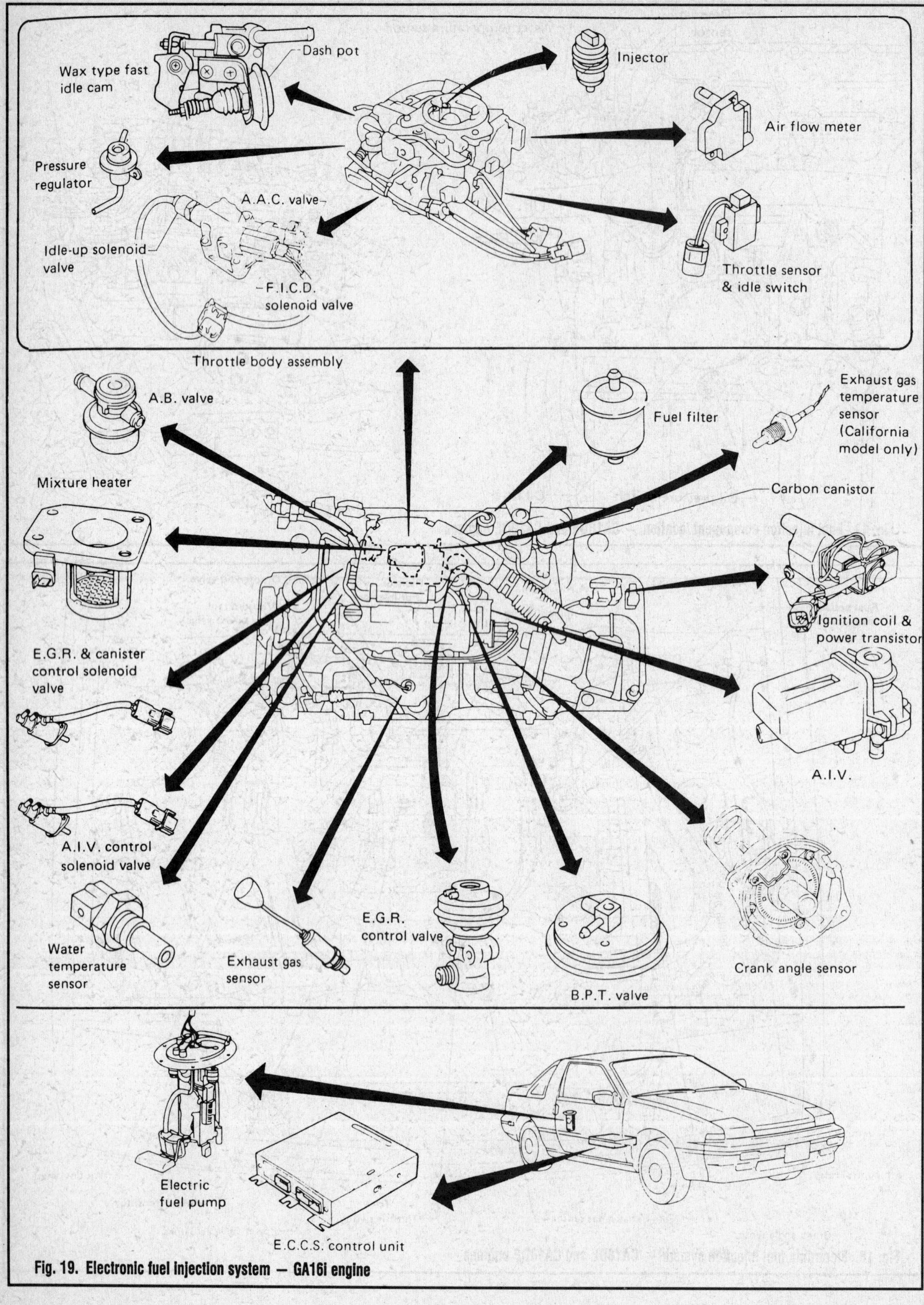
Dash pot
Wax type fast idle cam
Injector
Air flow meter
Pressure regulator
A.A.C. valve
Idle-up solenoid valve
F.I.C.D. solenoid valve
Throttle sensor & idle switch
Throttle body assembly
A.B. valve
Fuel filter
Exhaust gas temperature sensor (California model only)
Mixture heater
Carbon canister
Ignition coil & power transistor
E.G.R. & canister control solenoid valve
A.I.V.
A.I.V. control solenoid valve
Water temperature sensor
Exhaust gas sensor
E.G.R. control valve
B.P.T. valve
Crank angle sensor
Electric fuel pump
E.C.C.S. control unit

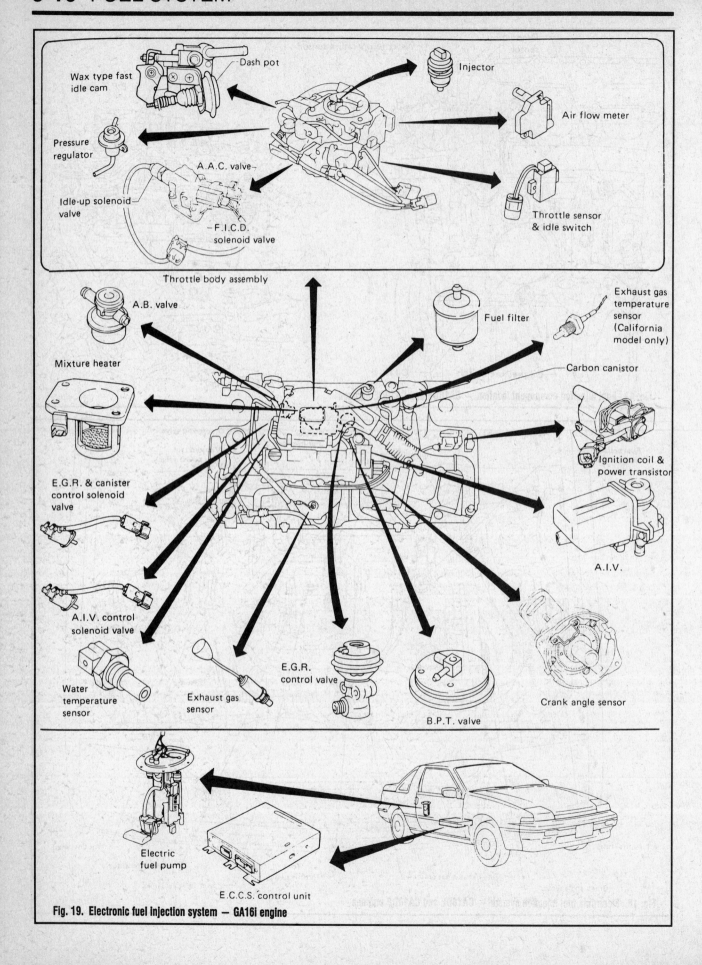

Fig. 19. Electronic fuel injection system — GA16i engine

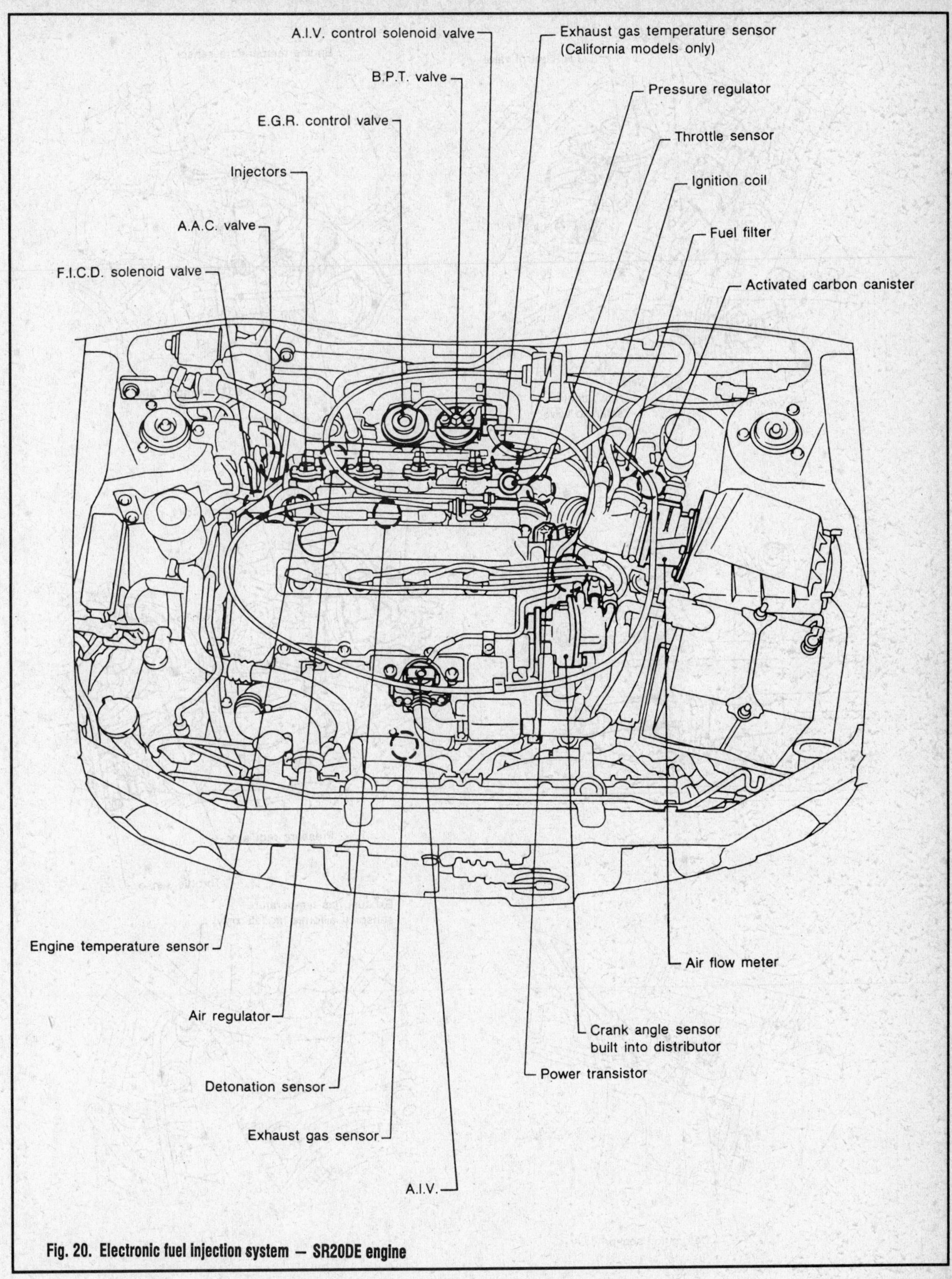
A.I.V. control solenoid valve
Exhaust gas temperature sensor
(California models only)
B.P.T. valve
Pressure regulator
E.G.R. control valve
Throttle sensor
Injectors
Ignition coil
A.A.C. valve
Fuel filter
F.I.C.D. solenoid valve
Activated carbon canister
Engine temperature sensor
Air flow meter
Air regulator
Crank angle sensor
built into distributor
Power transistor
Detonation sensor
Exhaust gas sensor
A.I.V.

Fig. 20. Electronic fuel injection system — SR20DE engine

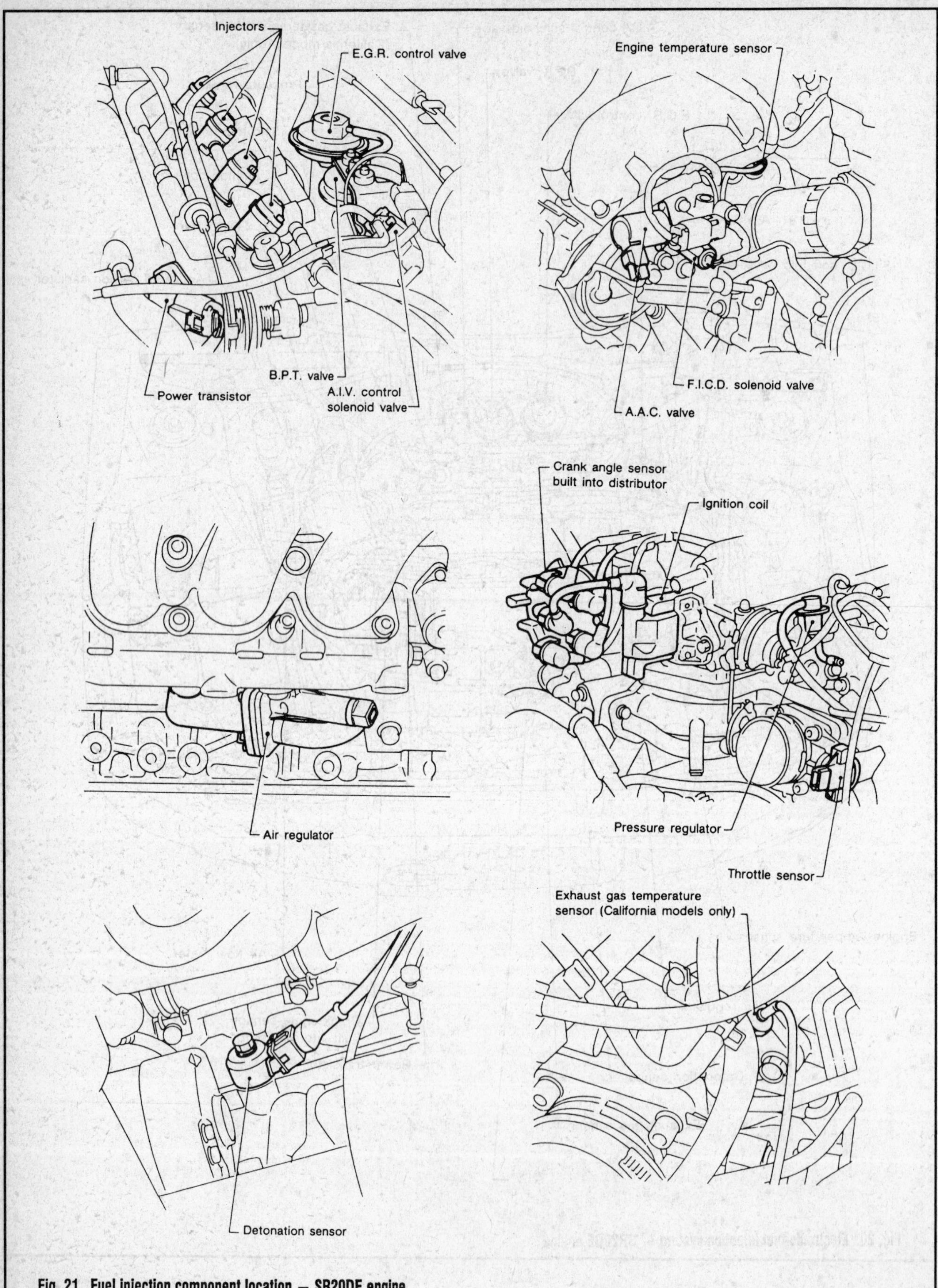
Injectors
E.G.R. control valve
B.P.T. valve
Power transistor
A.I.V. control solenoid valve
Engine temperature sensor
F.I.C.D. solenoid valve
A.A.C. valve
Crank angle sensor built into distributor
Ignition coil
Air regulator
Pressure regulator
Throttle sensor
Exhaust gas temperature sensor (California models only)
Detonation sensor

Fig. 21. Fuel injection component location – SR20DE engine

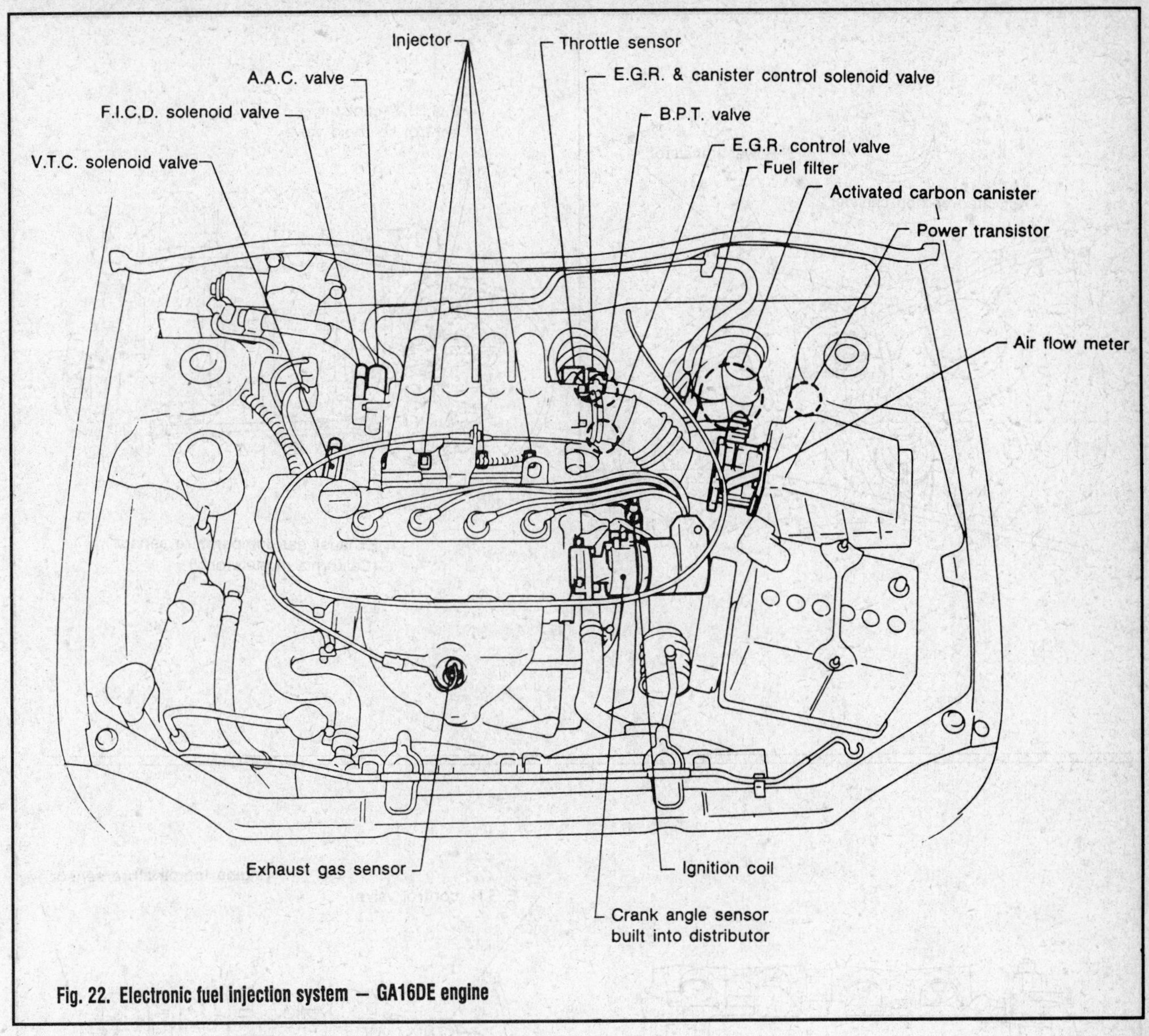
Injector
Throttle sensor
A.A.C. valve
E.G.R. & canister control solenoid valve
F.I.C.D. solenoid valve
B.P.T. valve
E.G.R. control valve
V.T.C. solenoid valve
Fuel filter
Activated carbon canister
Power transistor
Air flow meter
Exhaust gas sensor
Ignition coil
Crank angle sensor
built into distributor

Fig. 22. Electronic fuel injection system — GA16DE engine

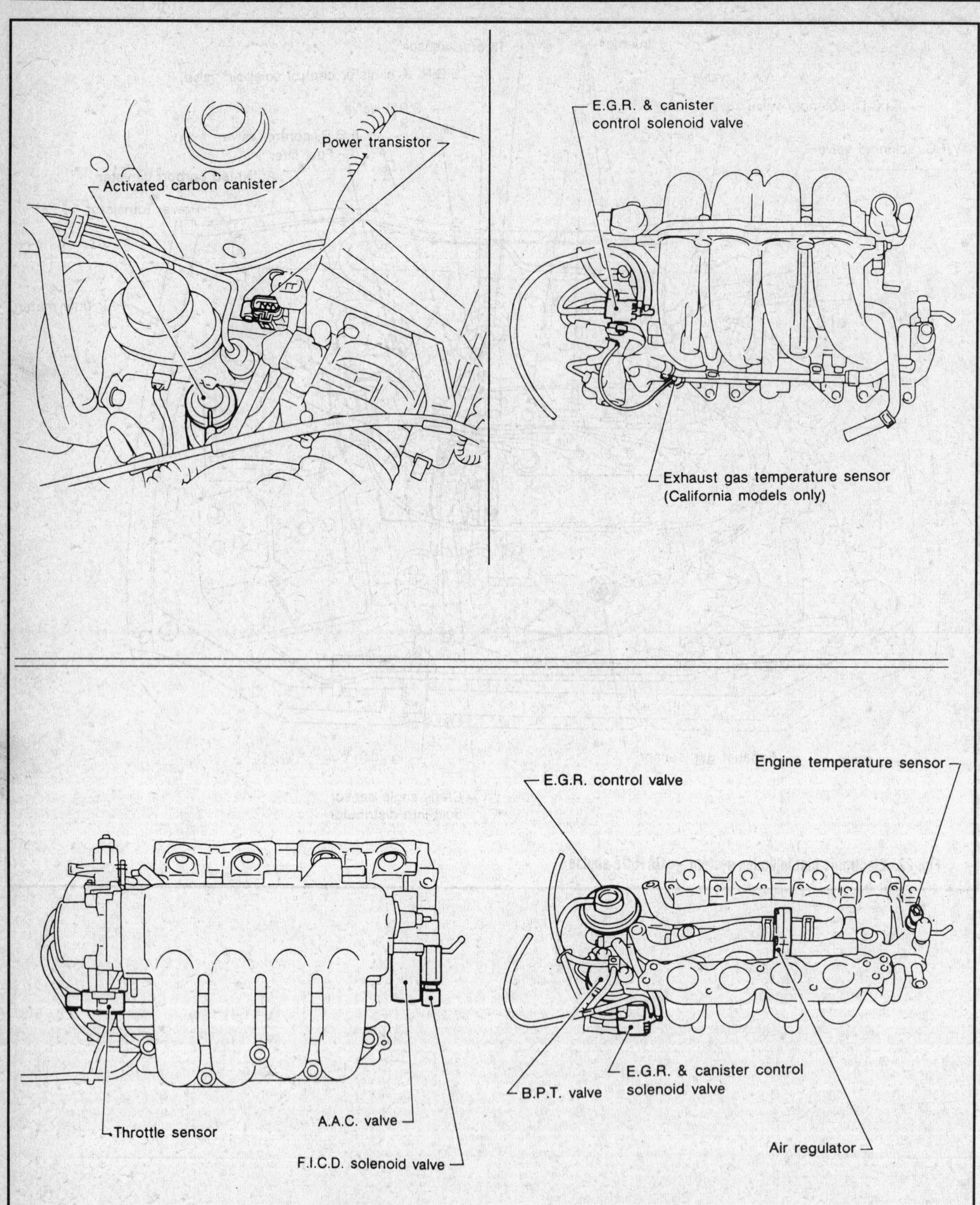
Power transistor
Activated carbon canister
E.G.R. & canister control solenoid valve
Exhaust gas temperature sensor (California models only)
Engine temperature sensor
E.G.R. control valve
Throttle sensor
A.A.C. valve
F.I.C.D. solenoid valve
E.G.R. & canister control solenoid valve
B.P.T. valve
Air regulator

Fig. 23. Fuel injection component location — GA16DE engine

Electrical Fuel Pump

All fuel injected models use an in-tank type pump. The fuel pumps are of a wet type, where the vane rollers are directly coupled to the motor, which is filled with fuel. A relief valve in the pump is designed to open, should a malfunction arise in the system.

➡ Before disconnecting the fuel lines or any of the fuel system components, refer to Fuel Pressure Release procedures, in this section and release the fuel pressure.

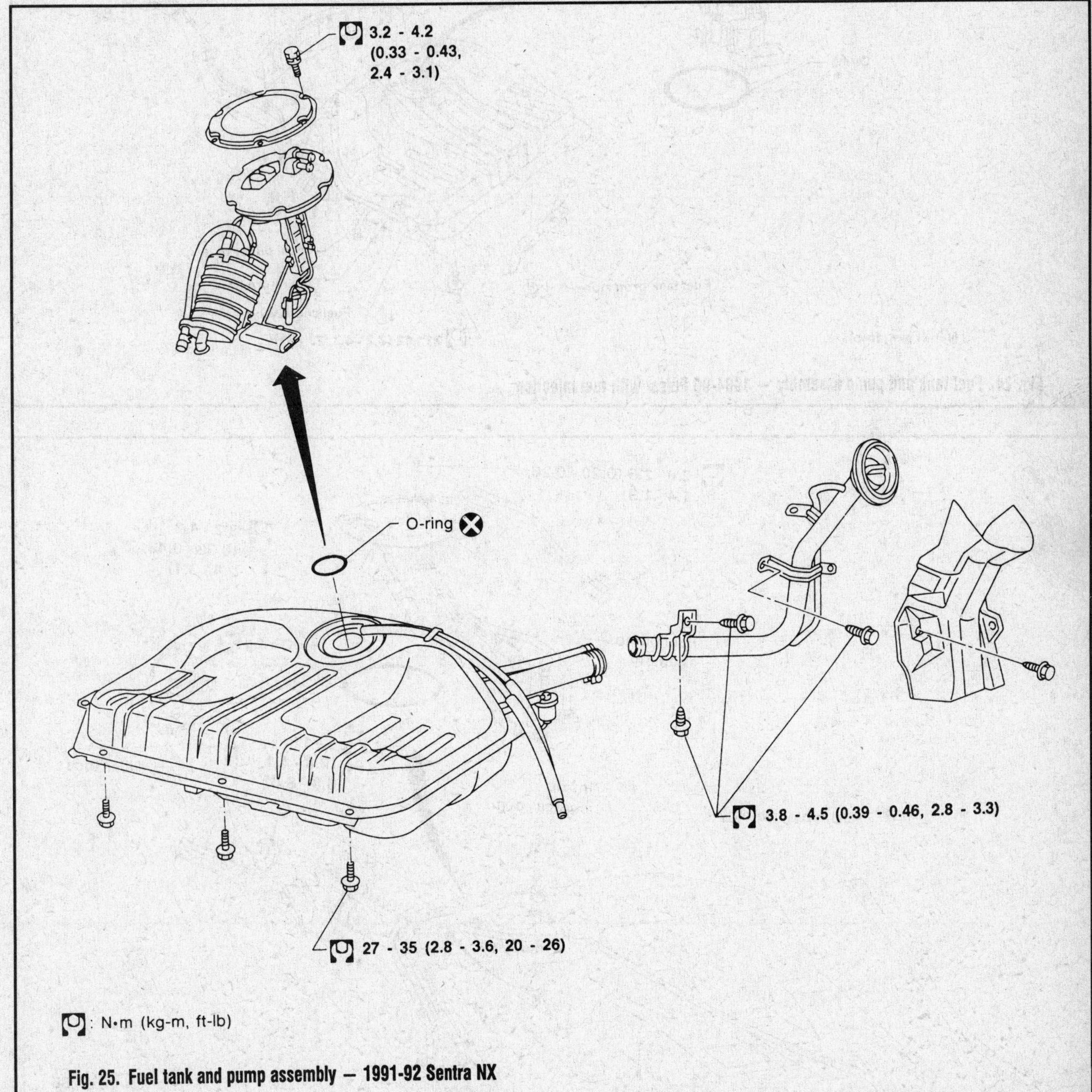

3.2 - 4.2
(0.33 - 0.43,
2.4 - 3.1)
O-ring
3.8 - 4.5 (0.39 - 0.46, 2.8 - 3.3)
27 - 35 (2.8 - 3.6, 20 - 26)
: N•m (kg-m, ft-lb)

Fig. 25. Fuel tank and pump assembly — 1991-92 Sentra NX

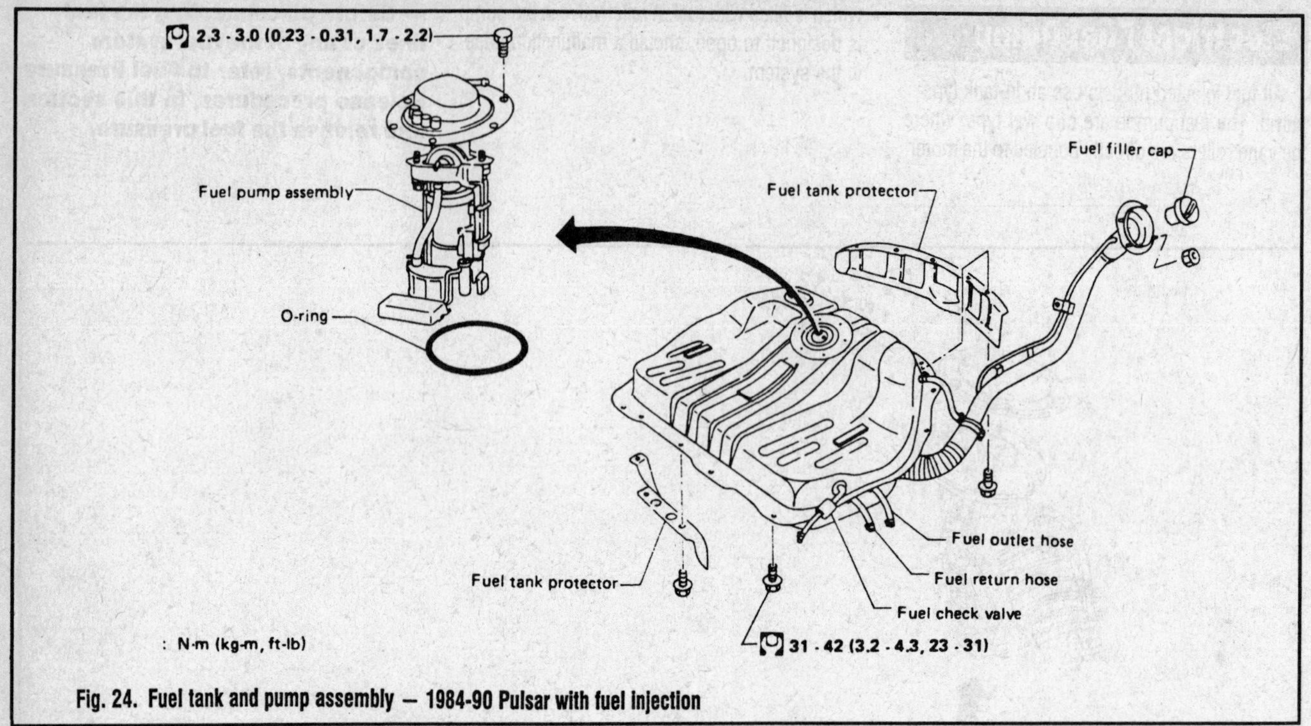
2.3 - 3.0 (0.23 - 0.31, 1.7 - 2.2)
Fuel pump assembly
O-ring
Fuel tank protector
Fuel filler cap
Fuel outlet hose
Fuel return hose
Fuel check valve
Fuel tank protector
31 - 42 (3.2 - 4.3, 23 - 31)
: N·m (kg-m, ft-lb)

Fig. 24. Fuel tank and pump assembly — 1984-90 Pulsar with fuel injection

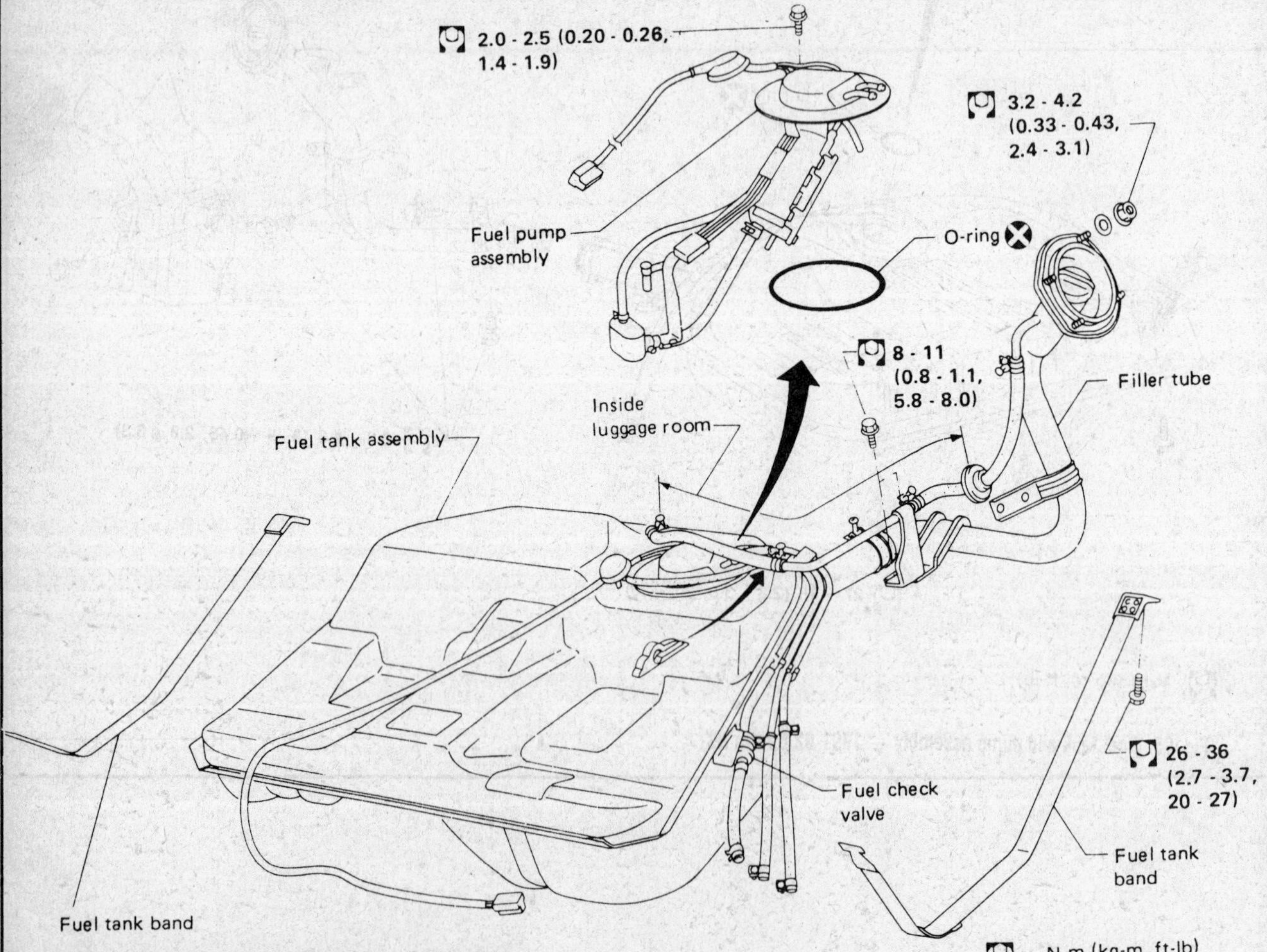

2.0 - 2.5 (0.20 - 0.26, 1.4 - 1.9)

3.2 - 4.2 (0.33 - 0.43, 2.4 - 3.1)

Fuel pump assembly

O-ring

8 - 11 (0.8 - 1.1, 5.8 - 8.0)

Filler tube

Inside luggage room

Fuel tank assembly

26 - 36 (2.7 - 3.7, 20 - 27)

Fuel check valve

Fuel tank band

Fuel tank band

: N·m (kg-m, ft-lb)

Fig. 29. Fuel tank and pump assembly — Sentra 4WD

Relieving Fuel System Pressure

CAUTION

Never smoke when working around gasoline! Avoid all sources of sparks or ignition. Gasoline vapors are EXTREMELY volatile! Any time the fuel system is being worked on, disconnect the negative battery cable, except for those tests where battery voltage is required and always keep a dry chemical (Class B) fire extinguisher near the work area.

1. Remove the fuel pump fuse from the fuse block, fuel pump relay or disconnect the harness connector at the tank while engine is running.
2. It should run and then stall when the fuel in the lines is exhausted. When the engine stops, crank the starter for about 3 seconds to make sure all pressure in the fuel lines is released.
3. Install the fuel pump fuse, relay or harness connector after repair is made.

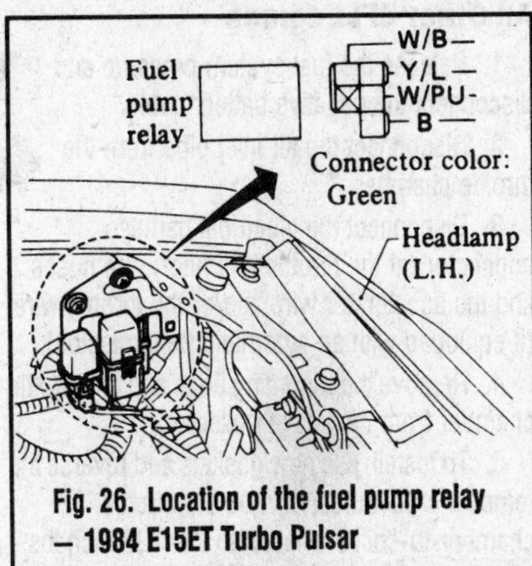
Fuel pump relay
W/B
Y/L
W/PU
B
Connector color: Green
Headlamp (L.H.)
Fig. 26. Location of the fuel pump relay – 1984 E15ET Turbo Pulsar

REMOVAL & INSTALLATION

CAUTION

Never smoke when working around gasoline! Avoid all sources of sparks or ignition. Gasoline vapors are EXTREMELY volatile!

1984–90 Vehicles

1. Disconnect the negative battery cable.
2. Open the trunk lid, disconnect the fuel gauge electrical connector and remove the fuel tank inspection cover.

➡ If vehicle has no fuel tank inspection cover the fuel tank must be removed.

3. Disconnect the fuel outlet and the return hoses.
4. Using a large brass drift pin and a hammer, drive the fuel tank locking ring in the counterclockwise direction.
5. Remove the locking ring and the O-ring, then lift the fuel pump assembly from the fuel tank. Plug the opening with a clean rag to prevent dirt from entering the system.

➡ When removing the fuel tank gauge unit, be careful not to damage or deform it. Install a new O-ring.

To install:

6. Install fuel pump assembly in tank. With a new O-ring install the fuel tank locking ring in place.
7. Reconnect the fuel lines and the electrical connection.
8. Install the fuel tank inspection cover.
9. Connect battery cable, start engine and check for leaks.

1991-92 Vehicles

➡ This procedure should be done with a half tank or less. Fuel may spill out of the fuel pump/sender opening when removed.

1. Disconnect the negative battery cable and relieve the fuel pressure.
2. Remove the rear seat and inspection hole cover located beneath the rear seat.
3. Disconnect the fuel pipe connections and wiring harness.
4. Remove the 6 retaining screws and lift the assembly from the tank.
5. Remove the fuel pump from the assembly.

To install:

6. Install the fuel pump into the assembly.
7. Install the 6 retaining screws and torque to 26–35 inch lbs. (3.2–4.2 Nm).
8. Connect the fuel pipe connections and wiring harness.
9. Install the inspection hole cover located beneath the rear seat and seat.
10. Connect the negative battery cable, turn the ignition **ON** and check for leaks.

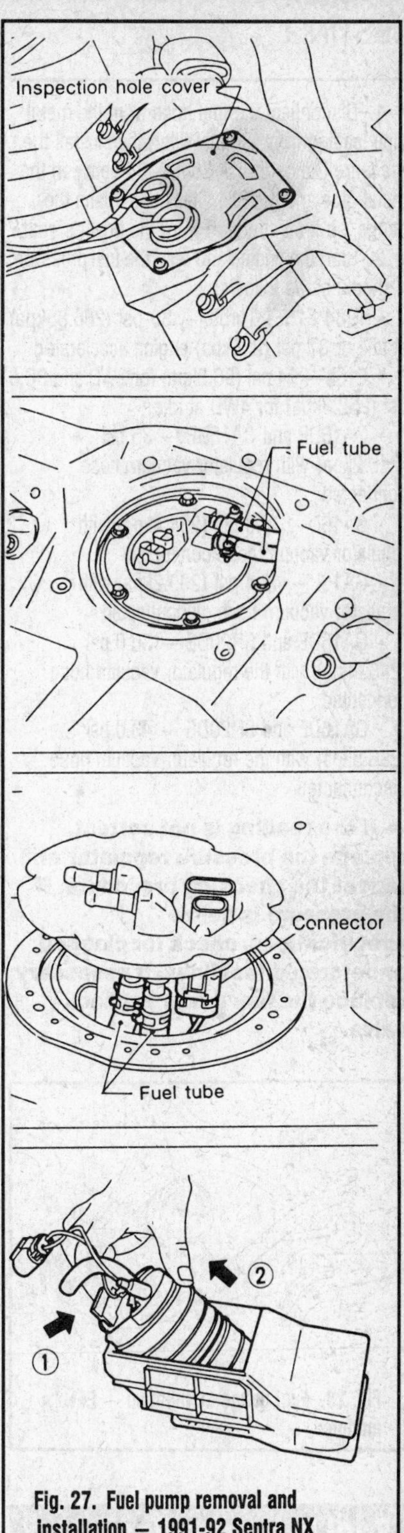
Inspection hole cover
Fuel tube
Connector
Fuel tube
①
②
Fig. 27. Fuel pump removal and installation – 1991-92 Sentra NX

TESTING

1. Disconnect the fuel hose from the metal pipe leading from the fuel filter, then install the Pressure Gauge tool J–25400–34 between the metal pipe and the fuel filter hose. Place the gauge, so it can be read from the driver's seat.
2. Start the engine and read the fuel pressure, it should be as follows:
   - 1984 E15ET Turbo — 30 psi (206.85kpa) at idle or 37 psi (255kpa) engine accelerated
   - E16i — 14 psi (96.5kpa) for 2WD and 36.6 psi (252.3kpa) for 4WD at idle
   - CA16DE and CA18DE — 36 psi (248.2kpa) with regulator vacuum hose connected
   - GA16i — 34.0 psi (234.4kpa) with regulator vacuum hose connected
   - GA16i — 43.4 psi (299.2kpa) with regulator vacuum hose disconnected
   - GA16DE and SR20DE — 36.0 psi (248.2kpa) with the regulator vacuum hose connected
   - GA16DE and SR20DE — 43.0 psi (296.5kpa) with the regulator vacuum hose disconnected

➡ If the reading is not correct, replace the pressure regulator and repeat the checking procedure. If the pressure is below specifications, check for clogged or deformed fuel lines; if necessary, replace the fuel pump or check valve.

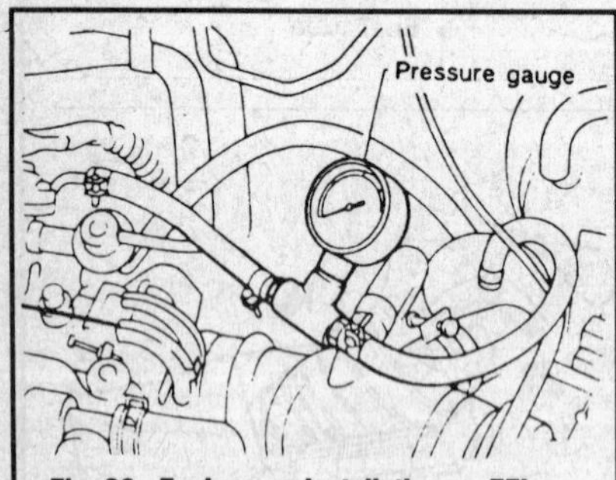
Pressure gauge
Fig. 28. Fuel gauge installation — EFI engines

Fuel Pressure Regulator

The pressure regulator is located on the fuel return side of the fuel injection rail and under the throttle body assembly on Throttle Body Injected (TBI models).

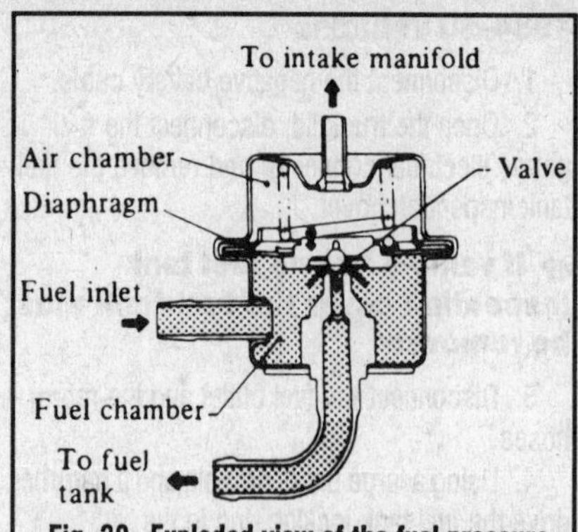
To intake manifold
Air chamber
Valve
Diaphragm
Fuel inlet
Fuel chamber
To fuel tank
Fig. 30. Exploded view of the fuel pressure regulator

REMOVAL & INSTALLATION

✲✲ CAUTION

Never smoke when working around gasoline! Avoid all sources of sparks or ignition. Gasoline vapors are EXTREMELY volatile!

E15ET Turbo Engine

To replace it, release fuel pressure, remove the fuel line clamps, the hoses and the mounting bracket. To install, use new hose clamps and reverse the removal procedures.

E16i and GA16i Engines

To replace it, release fuel pressure, remove the fuel line clamps, the hoses and the mounting screws from the throttle body assembly. To install, use new hose clamps and reverse the removal procedures.

All other EFI Engines

Release the fuel system pressure and disconnect the vacuum hose. Remove the regulator retainers and regulator. To install, use new hose clamps and O-rings, if so equipped.

Throttle Body/Chamber

REMOVAL & INSTALLATION

✲✲ CAUTION

Never smoke when working around gasoline! Avoid all sources of sparks or ignition. Gasoline vapors are EXTREMELY volatile!

E16i and GA16i Engines

1. Release the fuel pump pressure and disconnect the negative battery cable.
2. Disconnect the vacuum hoses, fuel line and the electrical connections from the throttle body. Disconnect the accelerator cable from the throttle body.
3. Remove the mounting bolts and the throttle body from the intake manifold.
4. To install, use a new gasket and reverse the removal procedures. Torque the throttle chamber bolts to 15–20 ft. lbs. (20–27 Nm). Adjust the throttle cable if necessary.

All Other EFI Engines

1. Release the fuel system pressure and disconnect the negative battery cable.
2. Disconnect the air inlet pipe from the throttle chamber.
3. Disconnect the electrical harness connector (at the throttle chamber), the hoses and the accelerator wire and/or the throttle wire (if equipped with an automatic transmission).
4. Remove the mounting bolts and the throttle chamber from the intake collector.
5. To install, use new gaskets and reverse the removal procedures. Torque the throttle chamber-to-collector bolts to 78–120 inch lbs. (9–14 Nm).

INJECTOR REPLACEMENT

✲✲ CAUTION

Never smoke when working around gasoline! Avoid all sources of sparks or ignition. Gasoline vapors are EXTREMELY volatile!

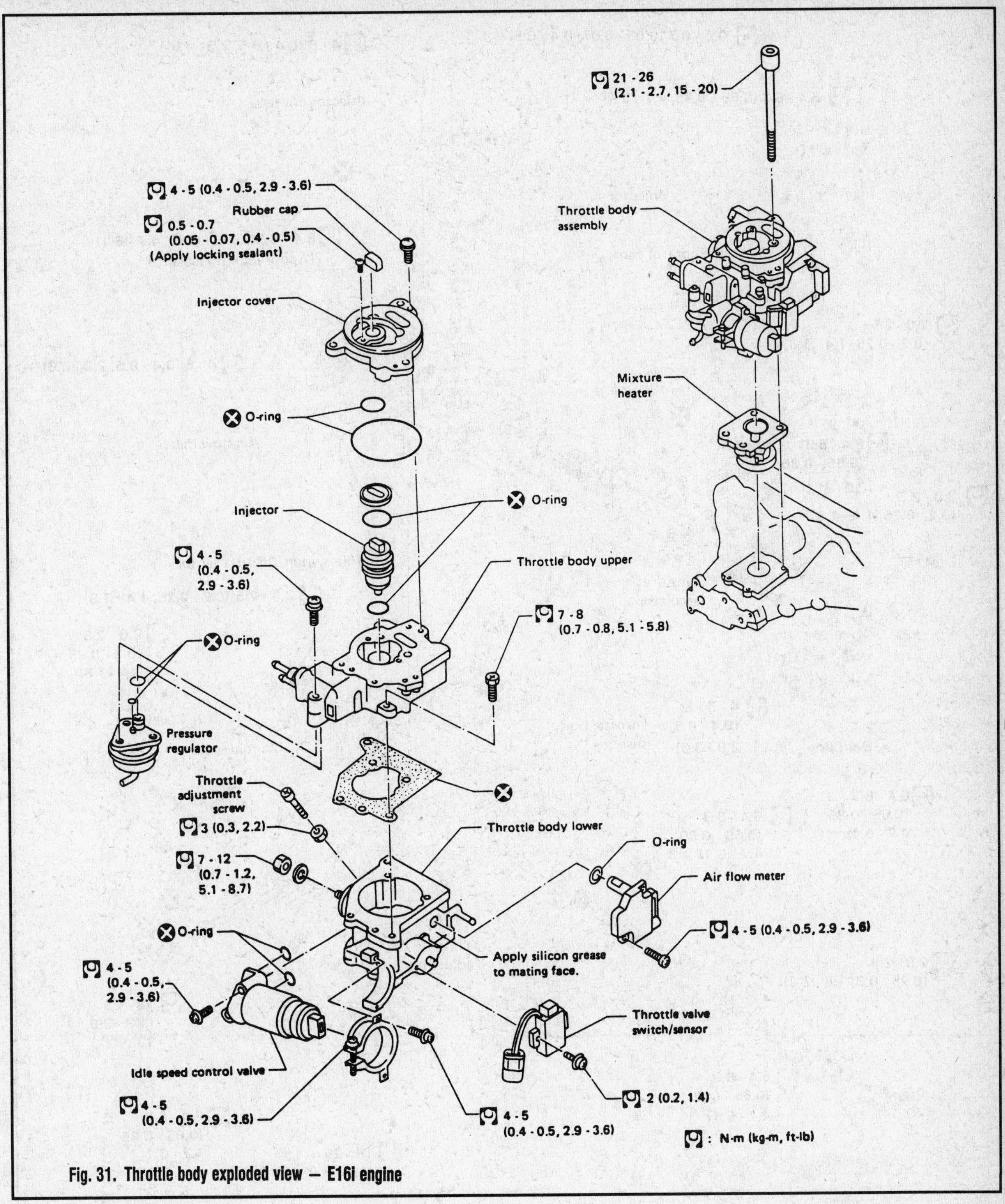

21 - 26
(2.1 - 2.7, 15 - 20)
4 - 5 (0.4 - 0.5, 2.9 - 3.6)
Rubber cap
0.5 - 0.7
(0.05 - 0.07, 0.4 - 0.5)
(Apply locking sealant)
Throttle body
assembly
Injector cover
Mixture
heater
O-ring
Injector
O-ring
4 - 5
(0.4 - 0.5,
2.9 - 3.6)
Throttle body upper
7 - 8
(0.7 - 0.8, 5.1 - 5.8)
O-ring
Pressure
regulator
Throttle
adjustment
screw
3 (0.3, 2.2)
Throttle body lower
O-ring
7 - 12
(0.7 - 1.2,
5.1 - 8.7)
Air flow meter
4 - 5 (0.4 - 0.5, 2.9 - 3.6)
O-ring
Apply silicon grease
to mating face.
4 - 5
(0.4 - 0.5,
2.9 - 3.6)
Throttle valve
switch/sensor
Idle speed control valve
2 (0.2, 1.4)
4 - 5
(0.4 - 0.5, 2.9 - 3.6)
4 - 5
(0.4 - 0.5, 2.9 - 3.6)
: N-m (kg-m, ft-lb)

Fig. 31. Throttle body exploded view — E16i engine

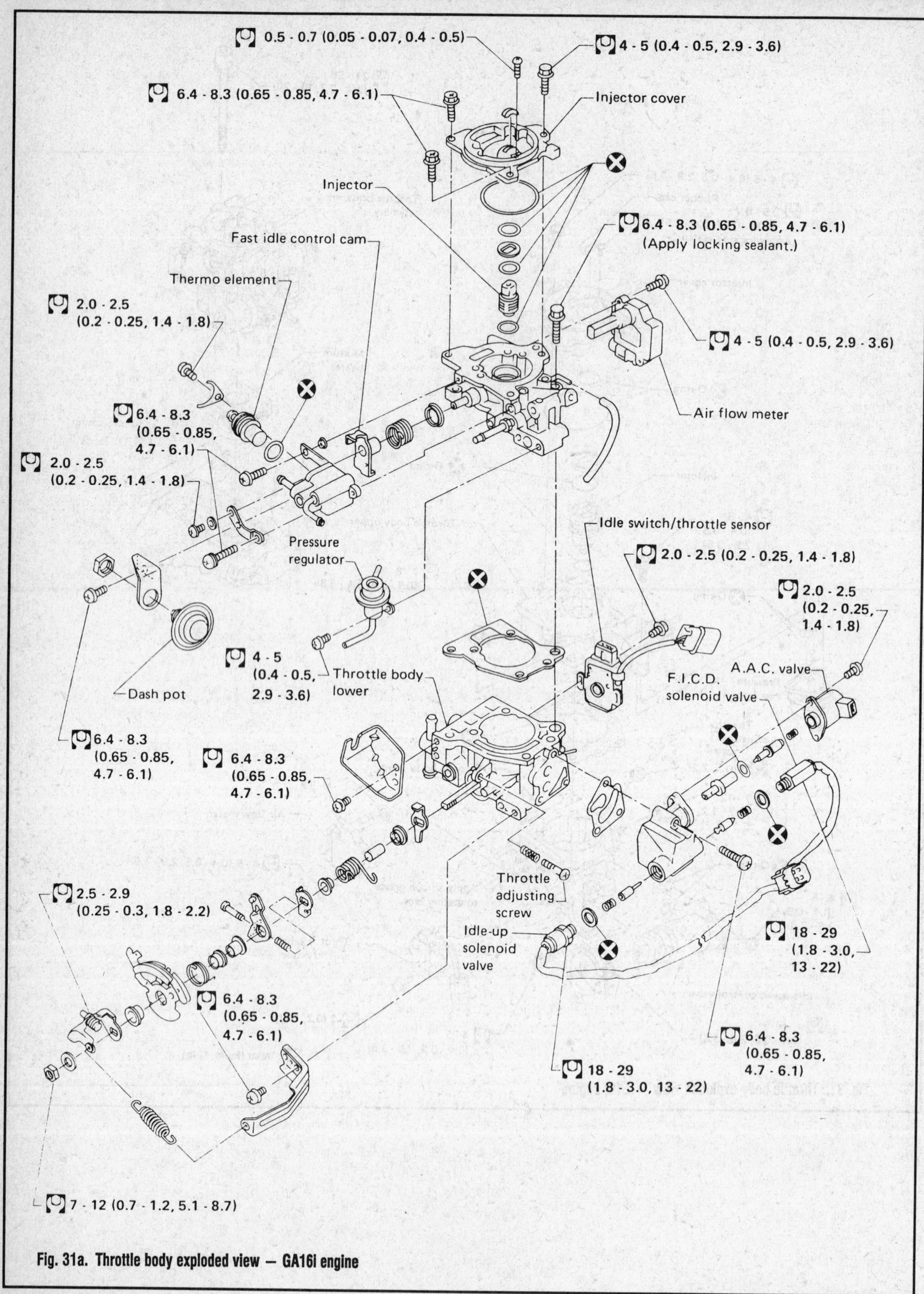

0.5 - 0.7 (0.05 - 0.07, 0.4 - 0.5)
4 - 5 (0.4 - 0.5, 2.9 - 3.6)
6.4 - 8.3 (0.65 - 0.85, 4.7 - 6.1)
Injector cover
Injector
6.4 - 8.3 (0.65 - 0.85, 4.7 - 6.1)
(Apply locking sealant.)
Fast idle control cam
Thermo element
2.0 - 2.5
(0.2 - 0.25, 1.4 - 1.8)
4 - 5 (0.4 - 0.5, 2.9 - 3.6)
6.4 - 8.3
(0.65 - 0.85,
4.7 - 6.1)
Air flow meter
2.0 - 2.5
(0.2 - 0.25, 1.4 - 1.8)
Idle switch/throttle sensor
Pressure
regulator
2.0 - 2.5 (0.2 - 0.25, 1.4 - 1.8)
2.0 - 2.5
(0.2 - 0.25,
1.4 - 1.8)
4 - 5
(0.4 - 0.5,
2.9 - 3.6)
Throttle body
lower
Dash pot
A.A.C. valve
F.I.C.D.
solenoid valve
6.4 - 8.3
(0.65 - 0.85,
4.7 - 6.1)
6.4 - 8.3
(0.65 - 0.85,
4.7 - 6.1)
2.5 - 2.9
(0.25 - 0.3, 1.8 - 2.2)
Throttle
adjusting
screw
Idle-up
solenoid
valve
18 - 29
(1.8 - 3.0,
13 - 22)
6.4 - 8.3
(0.65 - 0.85,
4.7 - 6.1)
6.4 - 8.3
(0.65 - 0.85,
4.7 - 6.1)
18 - 29
(1.8 - 3.0, 13 - 22)
7 - 12 (0.7 - 1.2, 5.1 - 8.7)

Fig. 31a. Throttle body exploded view — GA16i engine

E16i and GA16i Engines

1. Release fuel pressure.
2. Remove injector cover and pull out injector straight upward. Take care not to break or bend injector terminal.
3. Install a new lower injector O-ring in the throttle body.
4. Install the fuel injector and push it down using a suitable tool. Align the direction of the injector terminals. Take care not to break or bend injector terminal.
5. Install a new upper injector O-ring in the throttle body.
6. Install upper plate and injector cover with rubber plug removed.
7. Make sure that two O-rings (small one and big one) are installed in the injector cover.
8. Check for proper connection between injector terminal and injector cover terminal, then install rubber plug.
9. Start engine and check for fuel leaks.

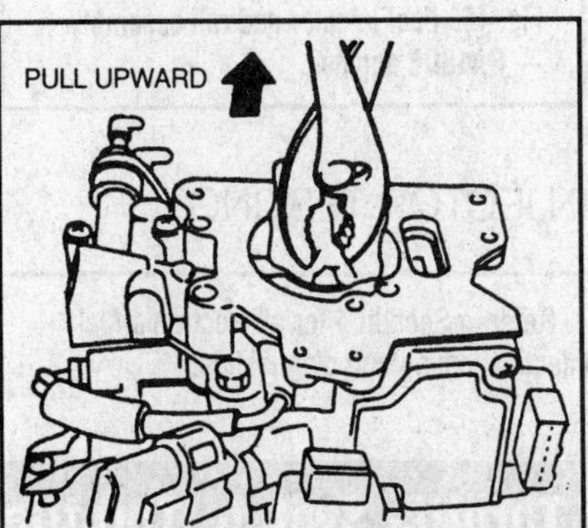
PULL UPWARD

Fig. 32. Fuel injector removal — E16i and GA16i engines

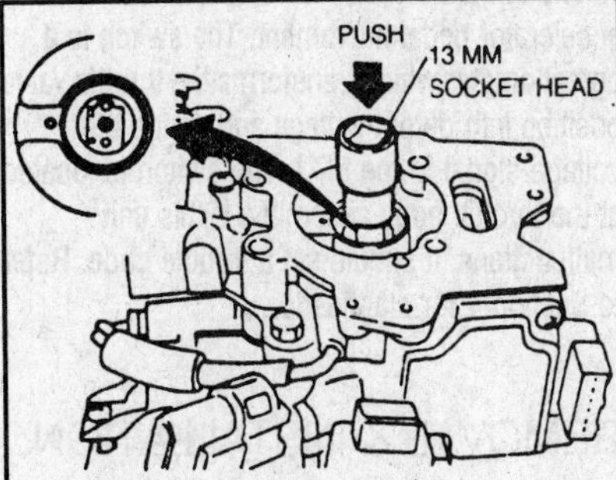
PUSH
13 MM
SOCKET HEAD

Fig. 33. Fuel injector installation — E16i and GA16i engines

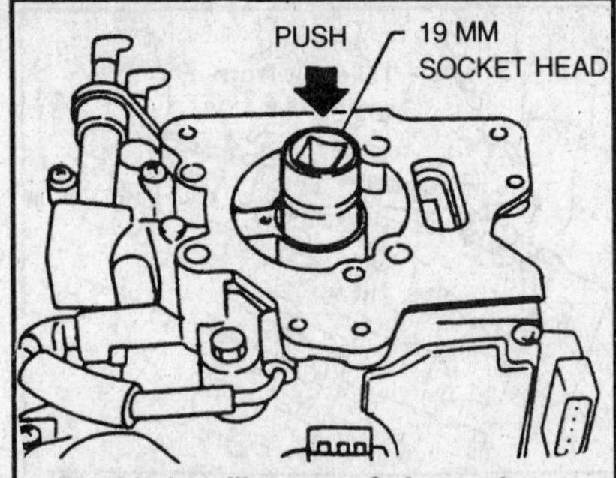
PUSH
19 MM
SOCKET HEAD

Fig. 34. Installing upper O-ring on the throttle body — E16i and GA16i engines

Fuel Injectors and Fuel Rail Assembly

REMOVAL & INSTALLATION

E15ET Turbo Engine

1. Refer to the Fuel Pressure Release procedure, in this section and lower the fuel pressure to zero.
2. Remove the air inlet pipe and the hose.
3. Disconnect the accelerator wire and (if equipped with an automatic transmission) the throttle wire.
4. Disconnect the throttle valve switch electrical harness connector, the mounting bolts and the throttle chamber.
5. Remove the PCV valve and the hose.
6. Loosen the clamps at both ends of the air pipe.
7. Disconnect the IVC and the air regulator harness connectors.
8. Remove the air pipe.
9. Disconnect the harness connectors from the injectors. Remove the fuel hoses. Remove the fuel rail mounting bolts and the fuel injector mounting screws.
10. Remove the fuel rail assembly by pulling out the fuel rail and the injectors.
11. Unfasten the fuel injector-to-fuel rail hose clamp and pull the injector from the fuel rail.

➡ When disconnecting the fuel injector from the fuel rail, place a rag under it to prevent fuel splash.

12. To remove the fuel hose from the injector, use a hot soldering iron, then cut (melt) a line in the fuel hose (to the braided reinforcement), starting at the injector socket to 19mm long (up the hose). Remove the hose from the injector, by hand.

➡ DO NOT allow the soldering iron to cut all the way through the hose, nor touch the injector seat or damage the plastic socket connector.

To install:

13. To install a new fuel hose, clean the injector tail section, wet the inside of the new hose with fuel, push the hose into the fuel injector hose socket (as far as it will go). Assemble the injector(s) onto the fuel rail.
14. Install injectors on fuel rail.
15. Install fuel rail to engine. Always use new O-rings on injectors.
16. Install fuel lines to fuel rail and electrical connections to injectors.
17. Install the air pipe.
18. Reconnect the IVC and the air regulator harness connectors.
19. Install PCV valve and hose.
20. Install the throttle chamber and attaching parts.
21. Install the air inlet pipe and hose.
22. Start engine and check for fuel leaks.

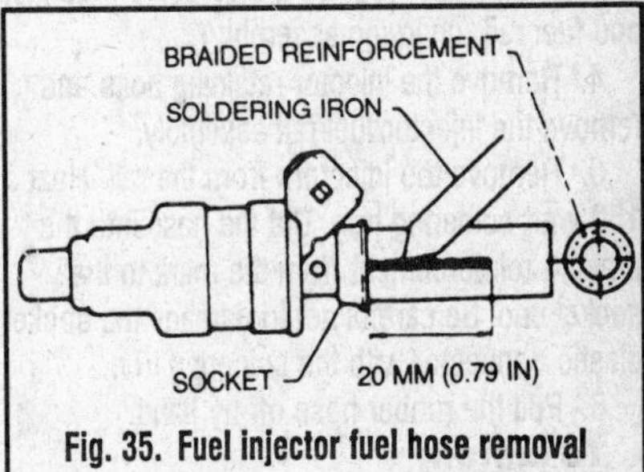
BRAIDED REINFORCEMENT
SOLDERING IRON
SOCKET
20 MM (0.79 IN)

Fig. 35. Fuel injector fuel hose removal

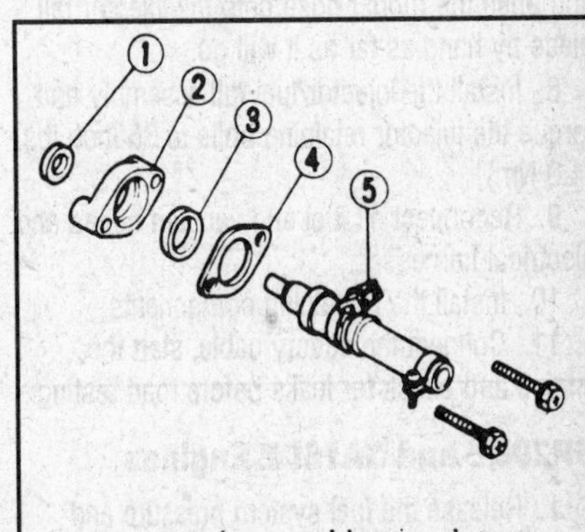
1
2
3
4
5

1 Injector lower rubber insulator
2 Injector lower holder
3 Injector upper rubber insulator
4 Injector upper holder
5 Injector

Fig. 36. Fuel injector assembly — E15ET shown, others similar

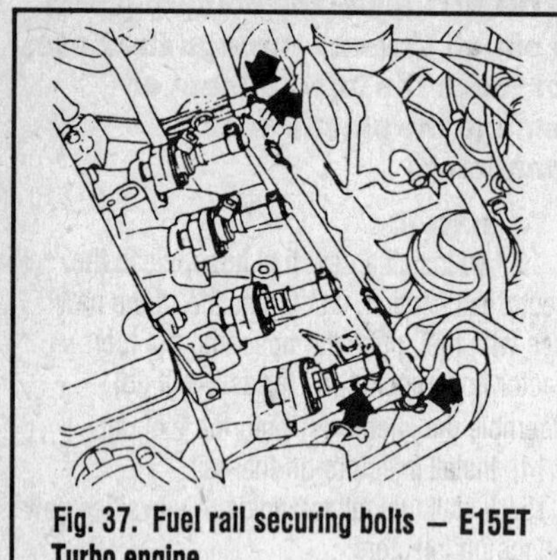

Fig. 37. Fuel rail securing bolts — E15ET Turbo engine

CA16DE and CA18DE Engines

1. Release the fuel system pressure and disconnect the negative battery cable.
2. Remove the throttle chamber, intake manifold stay, IAA unit and intake side rocker cover.
3. Disconnect all fuel and vacuum hoses and electrical harnesses from the pressure regulator and fuel rail (charging assembly).
4. Remove the injector retaining bolts and remove the injector/fuel rail assembly.
5. Remove the injectors from the rail. Heat a 150 watt soldering iron. Cut the hose into the braided reinforcement from the mark to the socket end. Be careful not to damage the socket plastic connector with the soldering iron.
6. Pull the rubber hose off by hand.

To install:

7. Wet the new injector hose with clean fuel and push the rubber hose onto the injector tail piece by hand as far as it will go.
8. Install the injector/fuel rail assembly and torque the injector retaining bolts to 35 inch lbs. (4.0 Nm).
9. Reconnect all fuel and vacuum hoses and electrical harnesses.
10. Install the remaining components.
11. Connect the battery cable, start the engine and check for leaks before road testing.

SR20DE and GA16DE Engines

1. Release the fuel system pressure and disconnect the negative battery cable.
2. Disconnect all fuel and vacuum hoses and electrical harnesses from the pressure regulator and fuel rail (charging assembly).
3. Remove the injector/fuel rail assembly.
4. Push out the injector from the fuel rail assembly. DO NOT remove by pinching the connector.

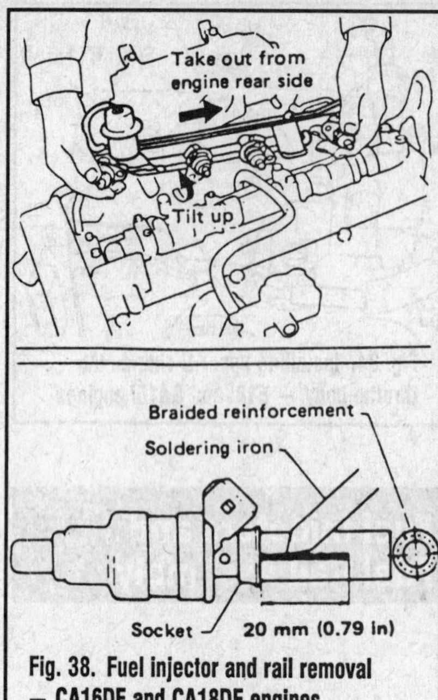
Take out from engine rear side
Tilt up
Braided reinforcement
Soldering iron
Socket
20 mm (0.79 in)

Fig. 38. Fuel injector and rail removal — CA16DE and CA18DE engines

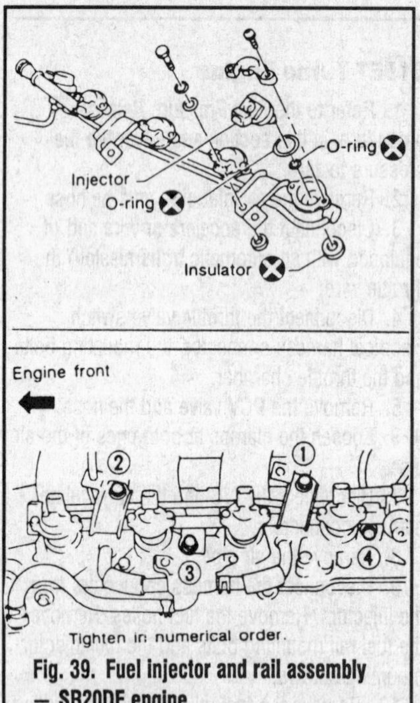
O-ring
Injector
O-ring
Insulator
Engine front
Tighten in numerical order.

Fig. 39. Fuel injector and rail assembly — SR20DE engine

To install:

5. Always replace the O-rings and insulators with new. Lubricate the O-rings with silicone oil (CRC®).
6. Install the injectors to the fuel rail and install the rail onto intake manifold.
7. Torque the fuel rail bolts to 8 ft. lbs. (11 Nm).
8. Install the remaining components.
9. Connect the battery cable, start the engine and check for leaks before road testing.

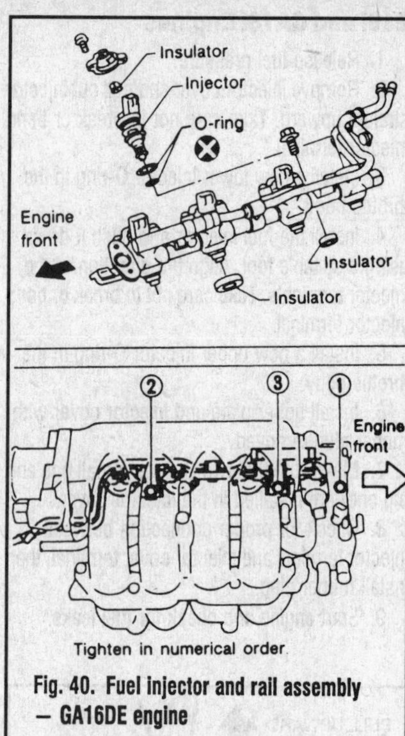
Insulator
Injector
O-ring
Engine front
Insulator
Insulator
Engine front
Tighten in numerical order.

Fig. 40. Fuel injector and rail assembly — GA16DE engine

INJECTOR TESTING

Refer to Section 4 for all electronic fuel injection testing and diagnostics.

Throttle Switch (Throttle Position Sensor)

The throttle switch responds to the accelerator pedal movement. The switch is a potentiometer which transforms the throttle valve position into output voltage and sends the voltage signal to the ECU. The switch is located at the throttle body assembly. If this unit malfunctions, it should set a trouble code. Refer to Section 4 for diagnostic.

REMOVAL & INSTALLATION

E16i and GA16i Engines

1. Disconnect the battery cable and remove the air cleaner.
2. Disconnect the switch connector and remove the retaining screws.

To Install:

3. Install the switch and leave the screws loose.

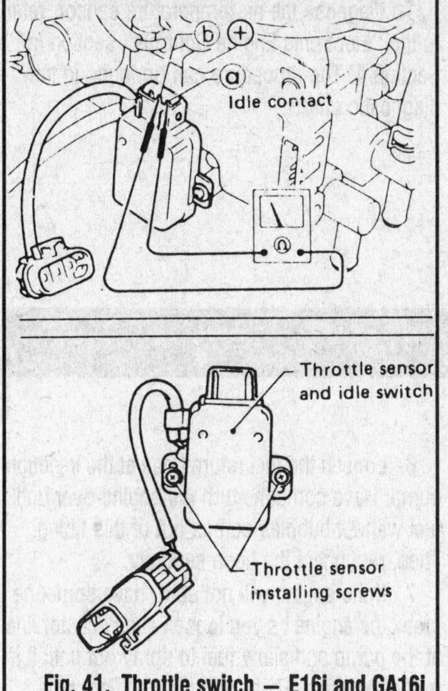
b
a
Idle contact
Throttle sensor and idle switch
Throttle sensor installing screws

Fig. 41. Throttle switch — E16i and GA16i engines

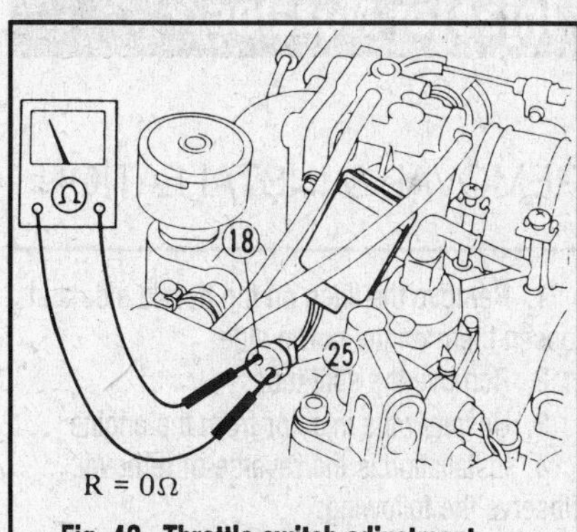
18
25
R = 0Ω

Fig. 42. Throttle switch adjustment — E15ET Turbo engine

4. Adjust the switch as follows:

a. Connect an approved tachometer and warm up the engine.

b. Disconnect the throttle switch connector. Check idle speed and adjust to specification in the Tune-up specifications chart in Section 2.

c. Manually open the throttle to about 2000 rpm, lower the engine speed slowly and read the engine speed at which the idle contact turns ON and OFF. The ON/OFF rpm should be 1050 ± 150 rpm.

d. If not within specifications, turn the throttle switch until the correct ON/OFF rpm is reached.

5. Tighten the switch screws and install the air cleaner.

E15ET Turbo Engine

1. Disconnect the battery cable and remove the air cleaner tube.

2. Disconnect the switch connector and remove the retaining screws.

To Install:

3. Install the switch and leave the screws loose.

4. Adjust the switch as follows:

a. Connect an approved tachometer and warm up the engine.

b. Disconnect the throttle switch connector. Check idle speed and adjust to specification in the Tune-up specifications chart in Section 2.

c. Connect an ohmmeter between terminals **18 and 25** and make sure continuity exists.

d. Manually open the throttle to about 2000 rpm, lower the engine speed slowly and read the engine speed at which the idle contact turns the switch ON and OFF. The ON/OFF rpm should be about 1100 rpm.

e. If not within specifications, turn the throttle switch until the continuity changes from ON to OFF at 1100 rpm with no load.

5. Tighten the switch screws and install the air cleaner tube.

All Other Engines

To diagnose and adjust the throttle switch (sensor), refer to the "Electronic Engine Controls" section in Section 4. The procedure can be found in the diagnostic charts.

Air Flow Meter

The air flow meter measures the quantity of intake air and sends a signal to the ECU so that the base injector pulse width can be determined. The air meter is provided with a flap in the air passage. As the air flows through the passage, the flap rotates and its angle of rotation signals the ECU. The sensor is located between the air cleaner and intake manifold for multi-port injected and at the throttle body for throttle body injected engines.

To diagnose the air flow sensor, refer to the "Electronic Engine Controls" section in Section 4. The procedure can be found in the diagnostic charts.

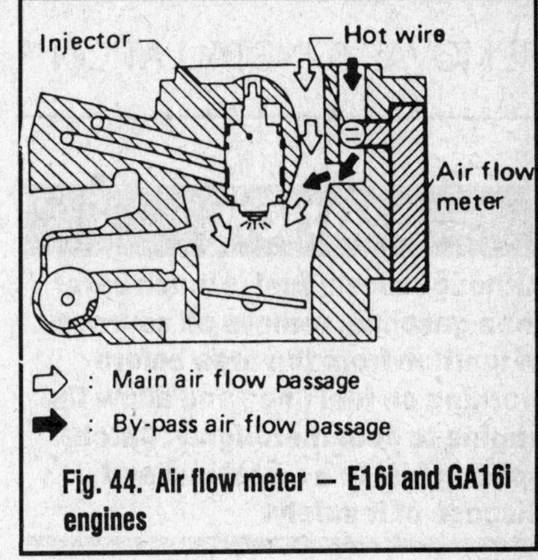
Injector
Hot wire
Air flow meter
: Main air flow passage
: By-pass air flow passage

Fig. 44. Air flow meter — E16i and GA16i engines

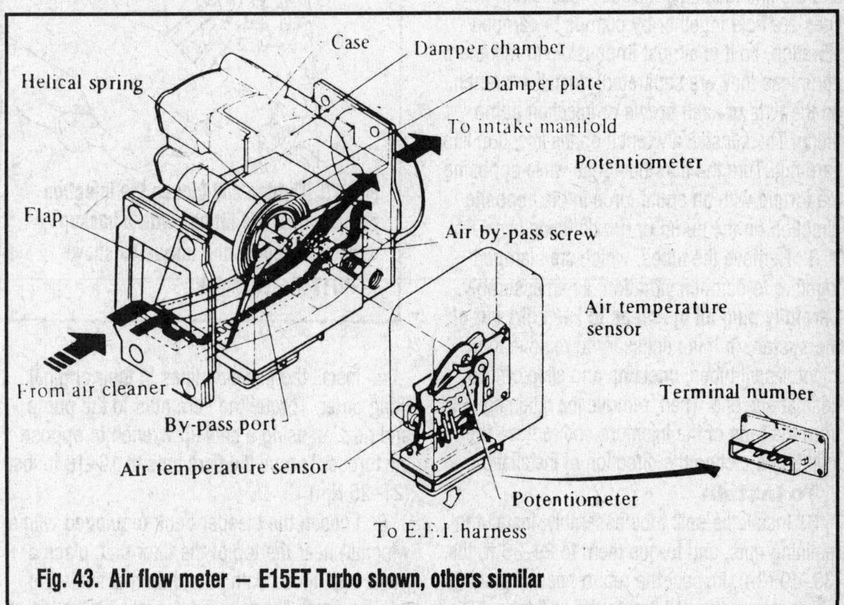
Case
Damper chamber
Helical spring
Damper plate
To intake manifold
Potentiometer
Flap
Air by-pass screw
Air temperature sensor
Terminal number
From air cleaner
By-pass port
Air temperature sensor
Potentiometer
To E.F.I. harness

Fig. 43. Air flow meter — E15ET Turbo shown, others similar

Air Temperature Sensor (E15ET Turbo)

The air temperature sensor is built into the air flow meter. It monitors changes in the intake air temperature and transmits a signal for the fuel enrichment to change the injector pulse duration. The resistance of the thermistor decreases in response to air temperature rise.

To diagnose the air temperature sensor, refer to the "Electronic Engine Controls" section in Section 4. The procedure can be found in the diagnostic charts.

DIESEL FUEL SYSTEM

Injection Lines

REMOVAL & INSTALLATION

CAUTION

Although diesel fuel is much safer than gasoline, remove all sources of ignition from the area before working on fuel lines and allow the engine to cool thoroughly. Catch spilling fuel in a metal cup and dispose of it safely.

1. Note the firing order of the injection pump and the line locations for easy reassembly (the lines are held together by clamps to dampen vibration, so it is almost impossible to mix them up unless they are separated). Install a wrench on the flats of each nozzle or injection pump fitting. Then, install a wrench on the injection line flare nut. Turn the flare nut loose while opposing the torque with an equal force in the opposite direction on the pump or nozzle fitting.
2. Remove the tubes, which are clamped together to dampen vibration, as an assembly. **Carefully plug all openings to keep dirt out of the system.** If it is necessary to remove the injector spill tubes, unclamp and slide off the hose at one end. Then, remove the retaining nuts from the tops of the injectors and remove the spill tubes, noting the direction of installation.

To install:

3. Install the spill tube assembly, install the retaining nuts, and torque them to 29–36 ft. lbs. (39–49 Nm). Inspect the return hose, replacing it if necessary. Install it onto the spill tube assembly and clamp it tightly.

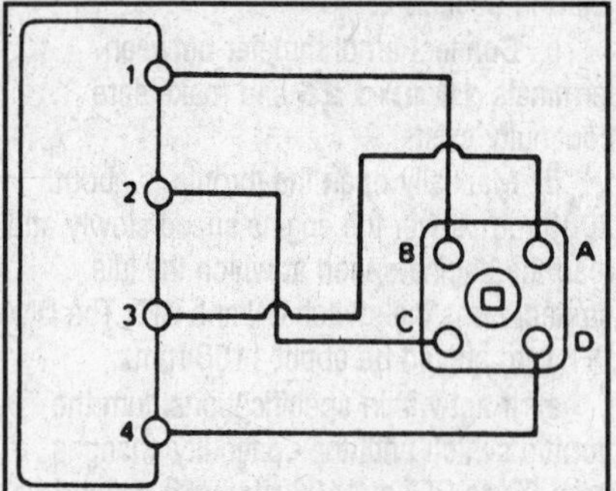
1
2
3
4
A
B
C
D
Fig. 45. Diesel engine injector line connections — CD17 diesel engine

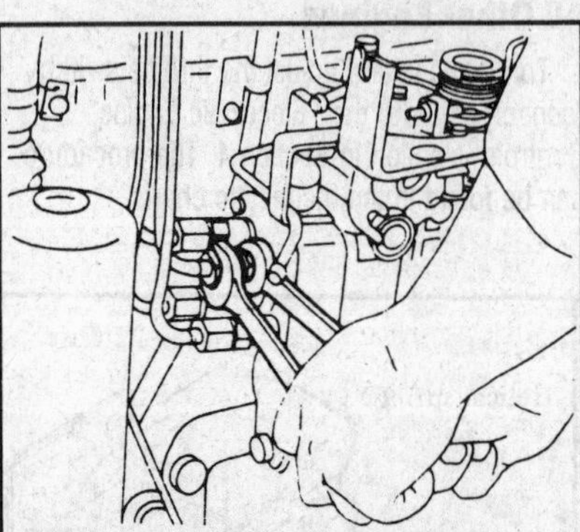
Fig. 47. Tighten and loosen the injection pump and nozzle fittings with a backup wrench to oppose the torque as shown — CD17 diesel engine

4. Install the injection lines in their original firing order. Torque the flare nuts to the pump and nozzles using a backup wrench to oppose the torque. Torque the flare nuts to 16–18 ft. lbs. (21–25 Nm).
5. Loosen the bleeder cock (equipped with a wingnut) near the top of the filter unit, place a metal cup underneath it, and then activate the priming pump by repeated depressing the top of the unit. When fuel without bubbles comes out, close the cock.
6. Loosen the fuel return hose at the injection pump. Have someone turn the engine over until fuel without bubbles comes out of this fitting. Then, reconnect the hose securely.
7. If the engine will not start, have someone crank the engine as you loosen each injector line at the pump and allow fuel to spray out until it is free of bubbles. Then, retorque the flare nuts.

Injector Nozzles

REMOVAL & INSTALLATION

1. Remove the lines on the nozzle side and loosen them on the pump side.
2. Remove the spill tube.
3. Unscrew the injector from the engine.
4. Installation is the reverse of removal. Observe the following:
   a. Always use a new injector gasket. Install the gasket in the proper direction.
   b. Torque the injectors to 43–51 ft. lbs. (58–68 Nm).
   c. Torque the lines to 16–18 ft. lbs. (21–25 Nm).
   d. Torque the spill tube to 29–36 ft. lbs. (39–48 Nm).

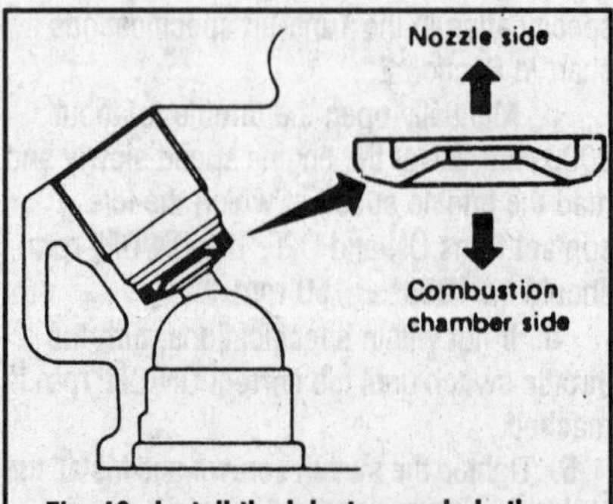
Nozzle side
Combustion chamber side
Fig. 46. Install the injector nozzle in the direction shown — CD17 diesel engine

Injection Pump

REMOVAL & INSTALLATION

1. Disconnect the battery ground.
2. Drain the coolant.

CAUTION

When draining the coolant, keep in mind that cats and dogs are attracted by the ethylene glycol antifreeze, and are quite likely to drink any that is left in an uncovered container or in puddles on the ground. This will prove fatal in sufficient quantity. Always drain the coolant into a sealable container. Coolant should be reused unless it is contaminated or several years old.

3. Disconnect and tag the wires and hoses attached to the pump or in the way of pump removal.
4. Remove the pump drive belt.
5. Remove the pump puiley.
6. Disconnect the injection lines at the pump.
7. Unbolt and remove the pump.

To install:

8. Observe the following points:
   a. Make sure that the engine is at TDC of #1 piston's compression stroke.
   b. Adjust the injection timing.
   c. Connect the injection lines in a 4–3–2–1 order.
   d. Bleed the fuel system.
9. Torque the injection pump nut to 9–13 ft. lbs. (13–19 Nm); the pump-to-rear bracket bolts to 17–23 ft. lbs. (23–31 Nm); the injection line nuts to 16–18 ft. lbs. (21–28 Nm).

INJECTION TIMING ADJUSTMENT

➡ Timing adjustment is necessary only if the injection pump or timing belt have been removed.

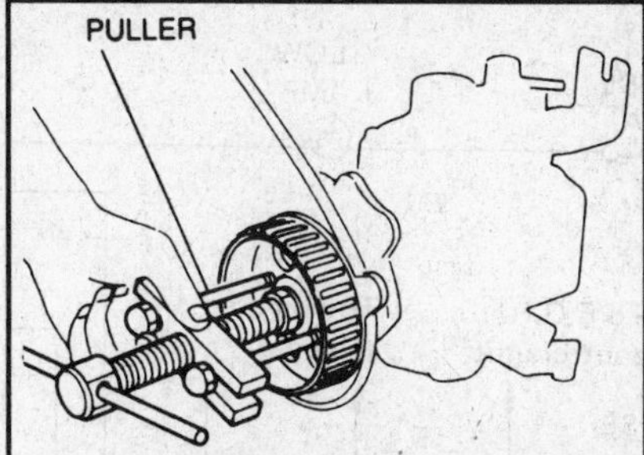
PULLER
Fig. 48. Injection pump pulley removal, use an approved puller — CD17 diesel engine

Fig. 48a. Move the injection pump belt tensioner to the free position — CD17 diesel engine

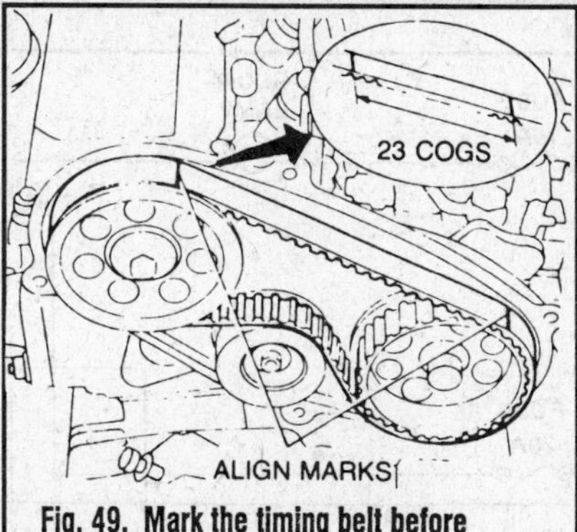
23 COGS
ALIGN MARKS
Fig. 49. Mark the timing belt before removal — CD17 diesel engine

1. Remove the air cleaner and duct.
2. Make sure that the #1 piston is at TDC of the compression stroke.
3. If the timing belt is still in position, remove it by freeing the tensioner.
4. If the injection pump was off the engine, install it at this time.
5. Clean the timing belt thoroughly and inspect it for cracks or wear. If any sign of wear exists, replace it.
6. On the outside of the belt, make a paint mark directly over one of the cogs. Count to your right, 23 cogs from the one with the paint mark, and place another paint mark directly over the 23rd cog.
7. If the engine is at TDC of #1 compression, the timing mark on the camshaft pulley should be roughly at the 1 o'clock position. Turn the injection pump pulley so that its timing mark is in roughly the same position. Install the timing belt so that the paint marks align with the timing marks on the pulleys. Some turning of the pulleys might be required.
8. When the timing marks are aligned, tighten the tensioner. Turn the engine over by hand, two complete revolutions in the normal direction of rotation and make sure that the timing marks are still aligned.

Glow Plug System

GENERAL DESCRIPTION

The auto glow system provides the pre-glow (fast glow) operation before the engine starts as well as after-glow operation after the engine has started. The system consists of a water temperature sensor, glow plug relays, dropping resistor and glow control unit.

The system incorporates a glow plug light on the instrument cluster. The length of time that the light is on is controlled by the temperature of the engine.

Pre-glow

The pre-glow system operates for about 6 seconds when the engine temperature is below 122°F (50°C). After the engine starts, the pre-glow system turns OFF.

After-glow

The after-glow system operates for a specified length of time after the ignition switch is turned from OFF or ST to ON when the engine temperature is below 122°F (50°C). The length of time is from 5 to 32 seconds. After pre-glow, the after-glow system turns OFF when the terminal voltage of the glow plug is higher than 7 volts. When the ignition switch is in the ST position, the after-glow system is energized.

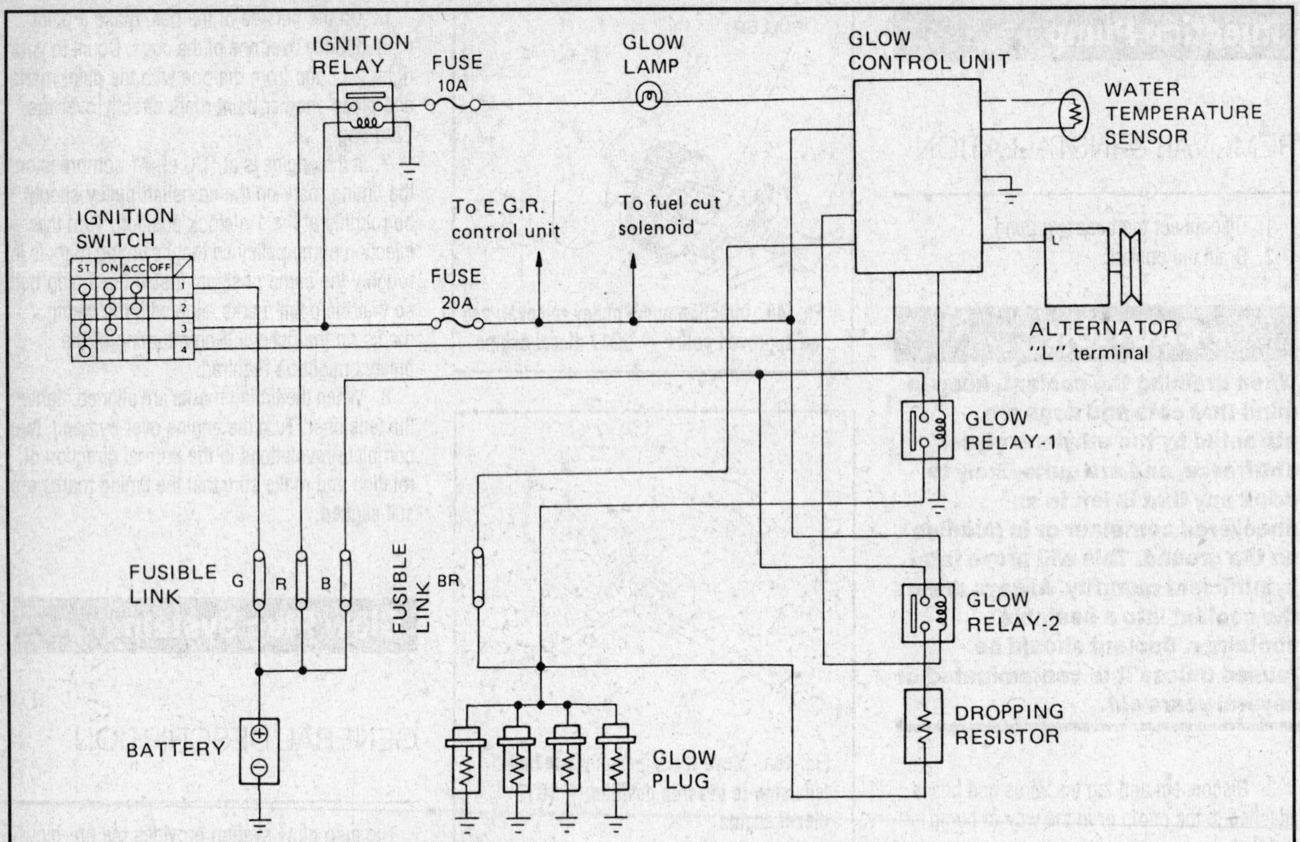

IGNITION RELAY
FUSE 10A
GLOW LAMP
GLOW CONTROL UNIT
WATER TEMPERATURE SENSOR
IGNITION SWITCH
ST ON ACC OFF
1
2
3
4
To E.G.R. control unit
To fuel cut solenoid
FUSE 20A
L
ALTERNATOR "L" terminal
GLOW RELAY-1
FUSIBLE LINK
G R B
FUSIBLE LINK
BR
GLOW RELAY-2
DROPPING RESISTOR
BATTERY
GLOW PLUG

Fig. 50. Glow plug system — 1982-85 Sentra diesel

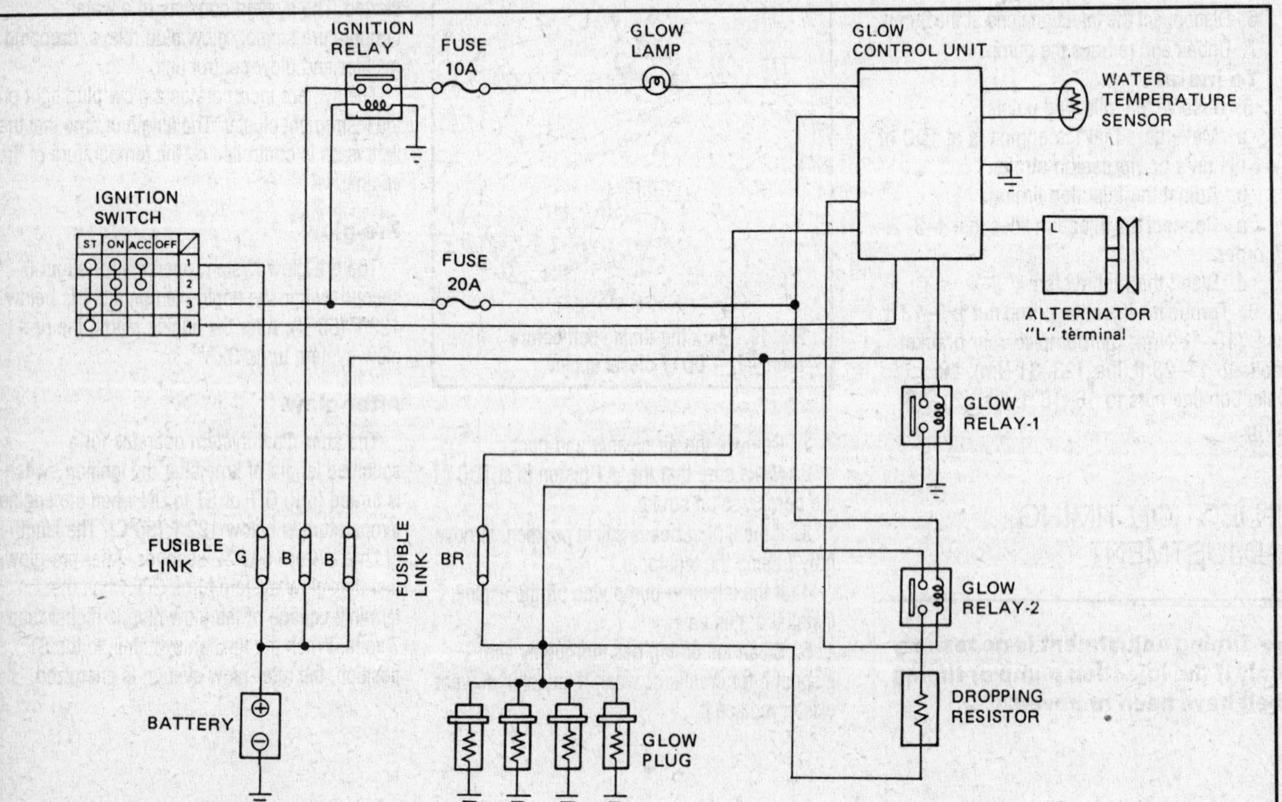

IGNITION RELAY
FUSE 10A
GLOW LAMP
GLOW CONTROL UNIT
WATER TEMPERATURE SENSOR
IGNITION SWITCH
ST ON ACC OFF
1
2
3
4
L
FUSE 20A
ALTERNATOR "L" terminal
GLOW RELAY-1
FUSIBLE LINK
G B B
FUSIBLE LINK
BR
GLOW RELAY-2
DROPPING RESISTOR
BATTERY
GLOW PLUG

Fig. 51. Glow plug system — 1986-87 Sentra diesel

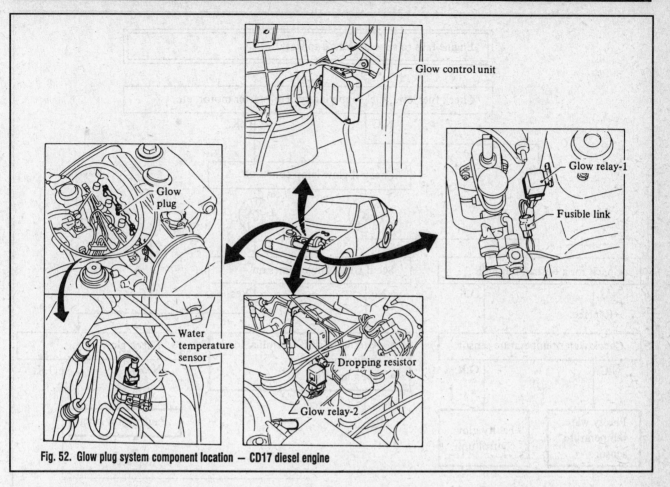

Fig. 52. Glow plug system component location — CD17 diesel engine

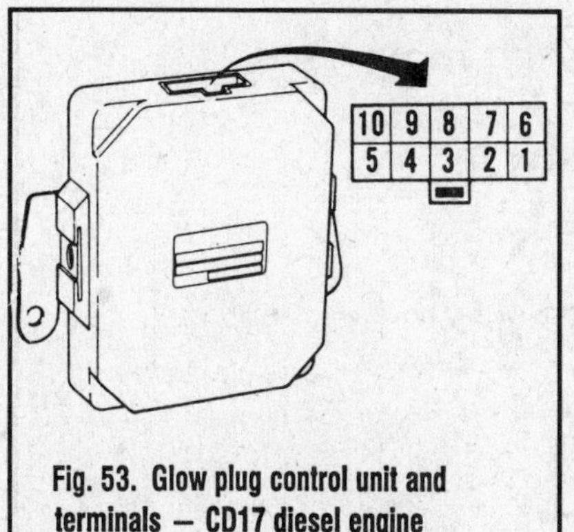
10 9 8 7 6
5 4 3 2 1

Fig. 53. Glow plug control unit and terminals — CD17 diesel engine

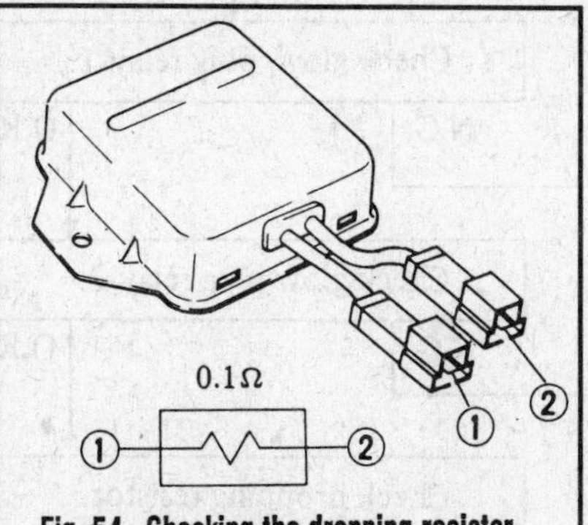
0.1Ω
①
②

Fig. 54. Checking the dropping resistor — CD17 diesel engine

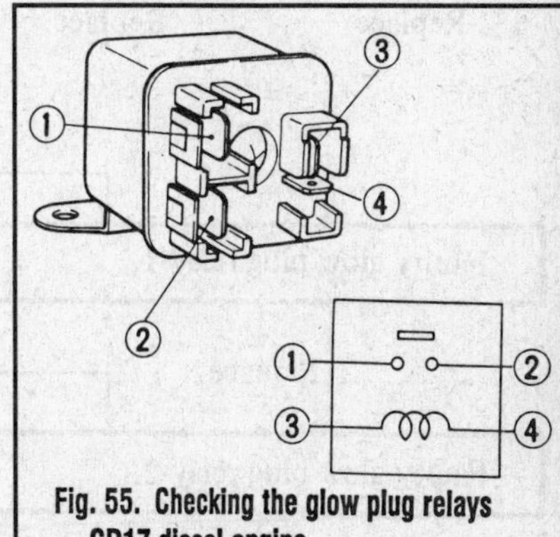
①
②
③
④

Fig. 55. Checking the glow plug relays — CD17 diesel engine

Glow Control Unit Terminals

- Terminal 1 — Measured voltage to the glow plug.
- Terminal 2 — Control unit power source.
- Terminal 3 — Control unit ground source.
- Terminal 4 — ON/OFF operation of glow relay 1.
- Terminal 5 — Water temperature sensor power terminal.
- Terminal 6 — Ignition switch START position.
- Terminal 7 — ON/OFF operation of glow relay 2.
- Terminal 8 — Water temperature sensor ground terminal.
- Terminal 9 — Glow light power source.
- Terminal 10 — Used to determine engine has started.

TESTING

Water Temperature Sensor

1. Remove the sensor from the engine and place in a pan of water.
2. Measure the resistance with an ohmmeter at varying temperatures.

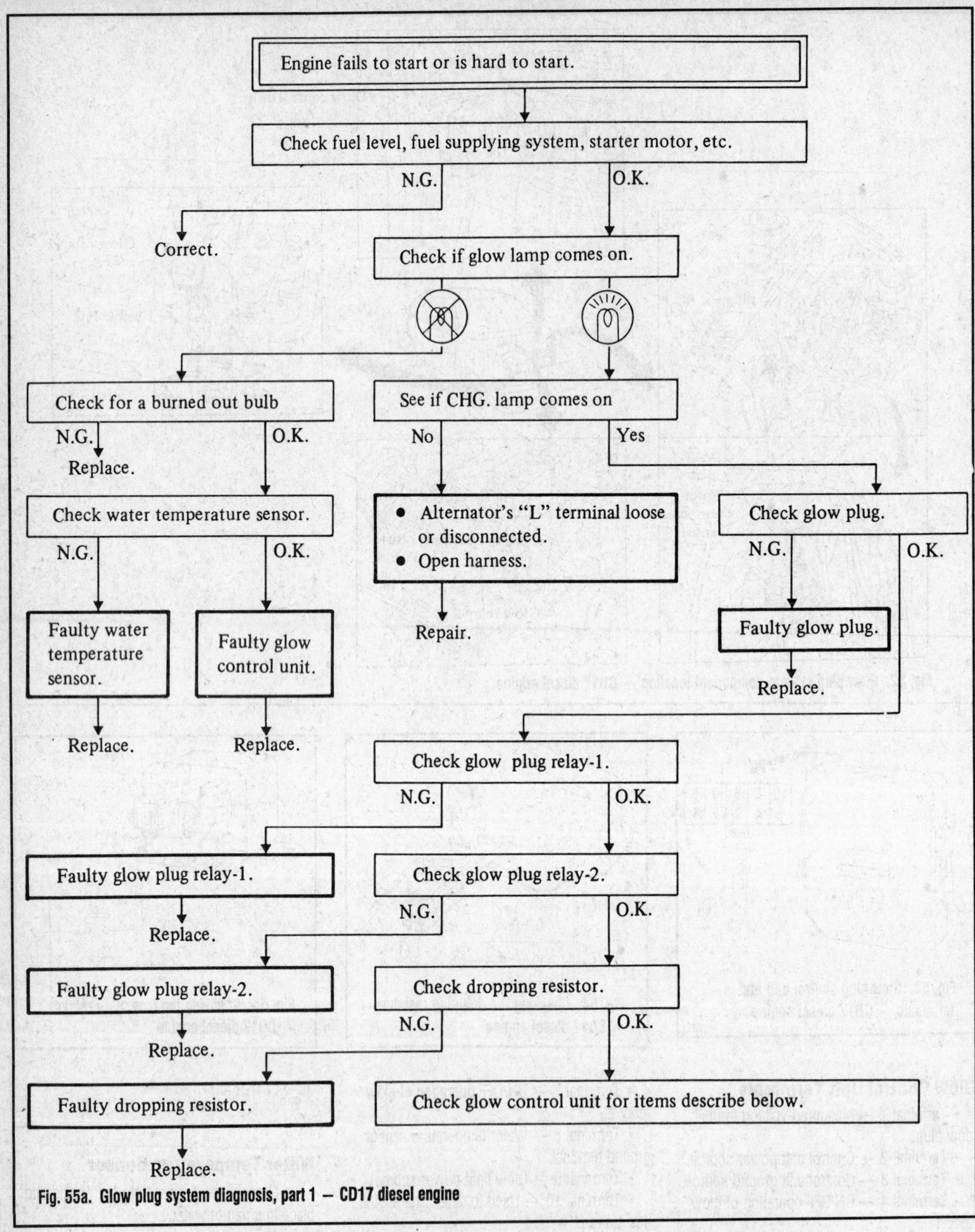

Engine fails to start or is hard to start.
Check fuel level, fuel supplying system, starter motor, etc.
N.G.
O.K.
Correct.
Check if glow lamp comes on.
Check for a burned out bulb
N.G.
O.K.
Replace.
See if CHG. lamp comes on
No
Yes
Check water temperature sensor.
N.G.
O.K.
● Alternator's "L" terminal loose or disconnected.
● Open harness.
Check glow plug.
N.G.
O.K.
Faulty water temperature sensor.
Faulty glow control unit.
Repair.
Faulty glow plug.
Replace.
Replace.
Replace.
Check glow plug relay-1.
N.G.
O.K.
Faulty glow plug relay-1.
Check glow plug relay-2.
Replace.
N.G.
O.K.
Faulty glow plug relay-2.
Check dropping resistor.
Replace.
N.G.
O.K.
Faulty dropping resistor.
Check glow control unit for items describe below.
Replace.

Fig. 55a. Glow plug system diagnosis, part 1 — CD17 diesel engine

3. Compare the readings to the following values:

- 50°F (10°C) – 3.7kΩ
- 68°F (20°C) – 2.5kΩ
- 122°F (50°C) – 0.85kΩ
- 176°F (80°C) – 0.33kΩ

4. Replace the sensor if found defective.

Glow Plug

Remove the glow plug from the engine. Using an ohmmeter, check that there is continuity in the plug. If not, replace the glow plug and torque to 25 ft. lbs. (34 Nm)

Dropping Resistor

Disconnect the resistor and measure the resistance between the 2 terminals. The resistance should be about 0.1Ω. If not, replace the dropping resistor.

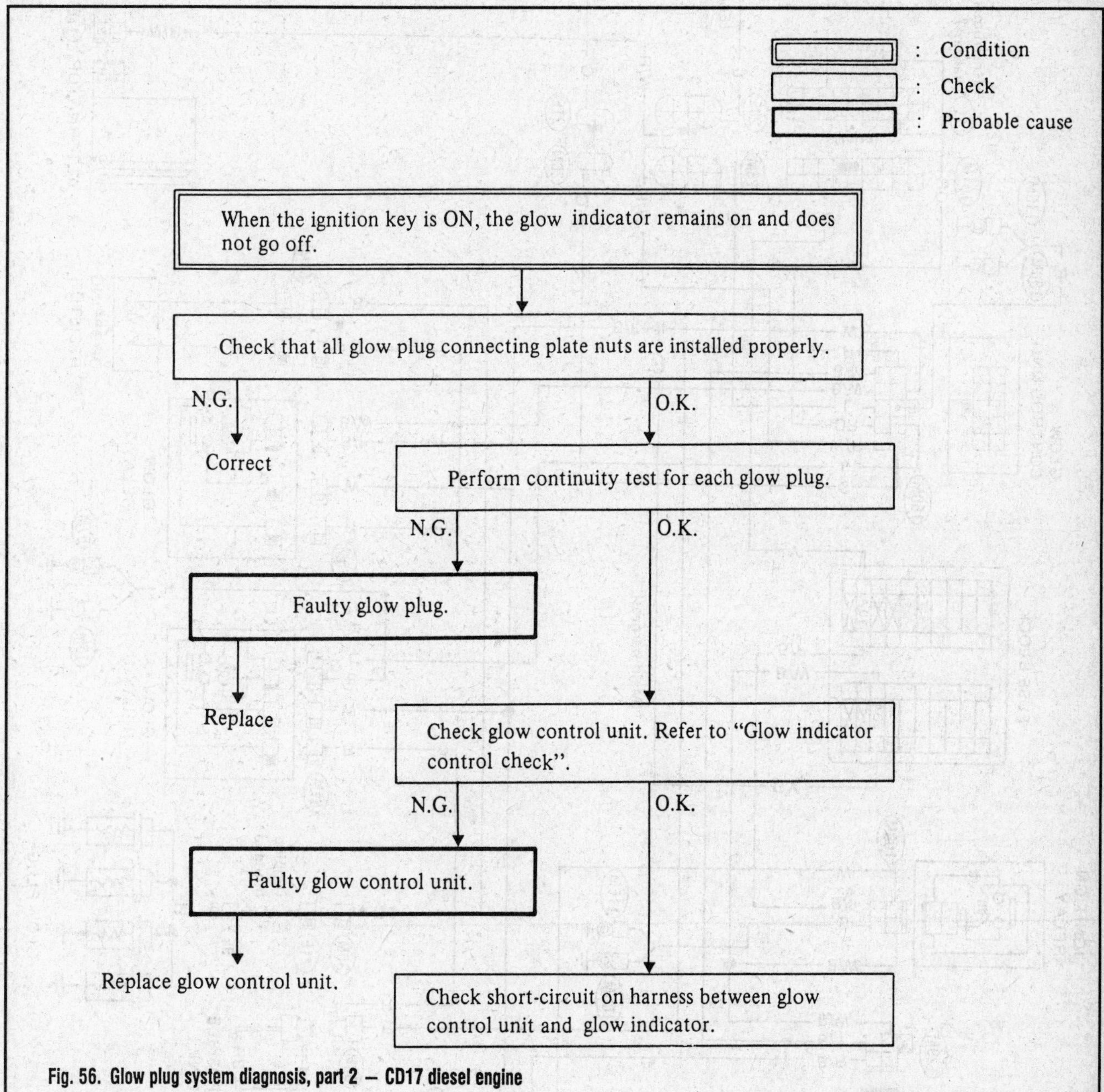
: Condition
: Check
: Probable cause
When the ignition key is ON, the glow indicator remains on and does not go off.
Check that all glow plug connecting plate nuts are installed properly.
N.G.
Correct
O.K.
Perform continuity test for each glow plug.
N.G.
Faulty glow plug.
Replace
O.K.
Check glow control unit. Refer to "Glow indicator control check".
N.G.
Faulty glow control unit.
Replace glow control unit.
O.K.
Check short-circuit on harness between glow control unit and glow indicator.

Fig. 56. Glow plug system diagnosis, part 2 – CD17 diesel engine

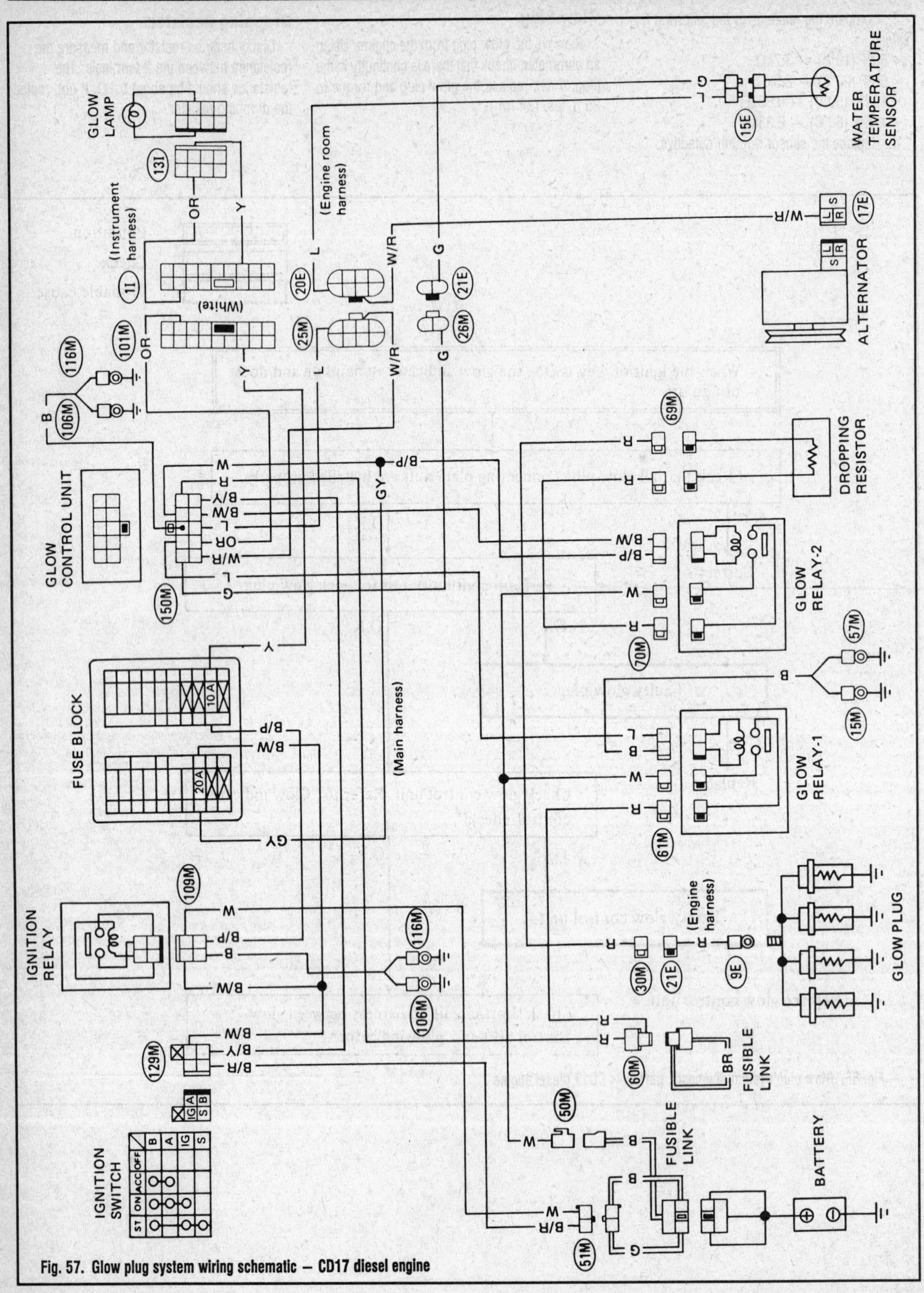
GLOW LAMP
13I
(Instrument harness)
OR
Y
1I
(White)
101M
116M
106M
B
(Engine room harness)
L
W/R
G
20E
25M
21E
26M
15E
WATER TEMPERATURE SENSOR
17E
ALTERNATOR
GLOW CONTROL UNIT
150M
B/P
GY
B/Y
B/W
R
69M
DROPPING RESISTOR
GLOW RELAY-2
70M
57M
15M
GLOW RELAY-1
61M
FUSE BLOCK
10A
20A
(Main harness)
IGNITION RELAY
109M
116M
106M
129M
B/R
IGNITION SWITCH
ST ON ACC OFF
B A IG S
(Engine harness)
30M
21E
9E
GLOW PLUG
60M
BR
FUSIBLE LINK
50M
51M
BATTERY

Fig. 57. Glow plug system wiring schematic — CD17 diesel engine

FUEL TANK

REMOVAL & INSTALLATION

⁂ CAUTION

Never smoke when working around gasoline! Avoid all sources of sparks or ignition. Gasoline vapors are EXTREMELY volatile!

1983-90 Pulsar
1991-92 Sentra NX

1. Drain the fuel tank.
2. Remove the rear seat cushion.
3. Remove the inspection cover.
4. Disconnect the fuel gauge electrical harness connector.
5. Disconnect the fuel filler and the ventilation hoses. Disconnect the fuel outlet, return and evaporation hoses, at the front of the tank. Plug open fuel lines.

➡ Remove the tank protector, if so equipped.

6. Remove the fuel tank mounting bolts and the tank from the vehicle.

To install:

7. Install the fuel tank to vehicle and torque the mounting bolts to 20–27 ft. lbs. (27–37 Nm).
8. Reconnect all fuel lines, ventilation hoses and the electrical connection.
9. Install the inspection cover and rear seat cushion.
10. Start engine and check for fuel leaks.

1982-90 Sentra (Except 4WD)

⁂ CAUTION

Remove all sources of ignition from the area of the car. Make sure the area is well ventilated to remove any fuel fumes that may collect. Make suer you have a safe, enclosed container for the fuel that is drained from the tank.

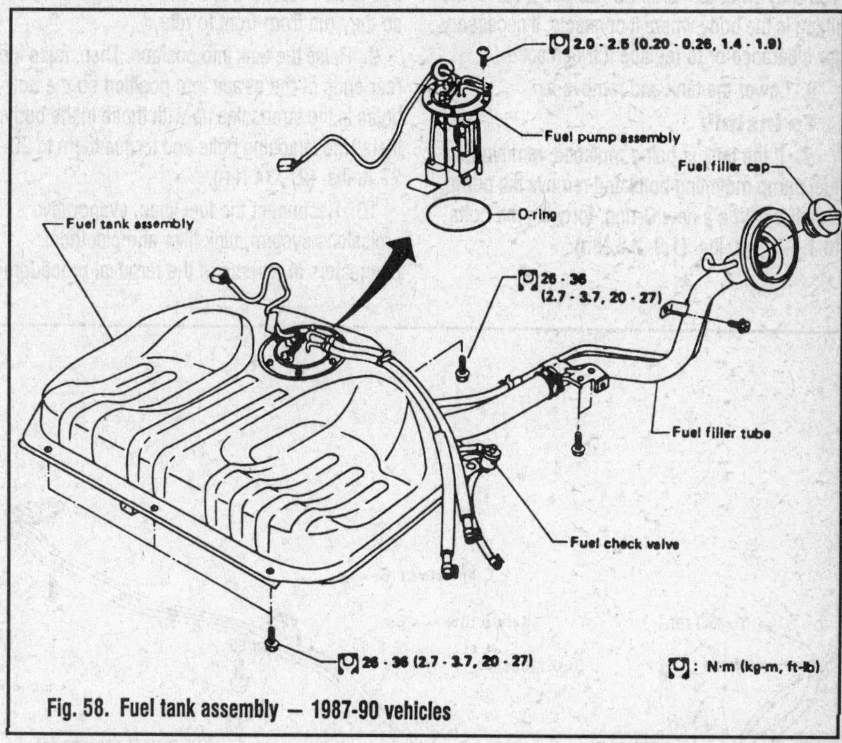
2.0 - 2.5 (0.20 - 0.26, 1.4 - 1.9)
Fuel pump assembly
Fuel filler cap
O-ring
Fuel tank assembly
26 - 36 (2.7 - 3.7, 20 - 27)
Fuel filler tube
Fuel check valve
26 - 36 (2.7 - 3.7, 20 - 27)
: N·m (kg-m, ft-lb)

Fig. 58. Fuel tank assembly — 1987-90 vehicles

1. Disconnect the negative battery cable. Drain fuel into a safe, enclosed, metal container.
2. Remove inspection cover and disconnect fuel tank gauge unit harness connector.
3. Disconnect fuel filler and ventilation tubes.

➡ Plug hose and pipe openings to prevent entry of dust and dirt.

4. Disconnect fuel outlet, return and evaporation hoses.
5. Place a suitable jack under the tank to support. Remove 6 bolts attaching fuel tank flange to the body and then lower the fuel tank.

To install:

6. Raise the tank and install the 6 bolts attaching fuel tank flange to the body. Torque the bolts to 20–27 ft. lbs. (27–34 Nm).
7. Connect fuel outlet, return and evaporation hoses.
8. Connect fuel filler and ventilation tubes.
9. Connect the fuel gauge and pump harness connectors. Install inspection cover.
10. Refill the fuel tank and check for leaks. Connect the negative battery cable, start the engine and check for leaks.

Sentra with 4WD

⁂ CAUTION

Remove all sources of ignition from the area of the car. Make sure the area is well ventilated to remove any fuel fumes that may collect. Make suer you have a safe, enclosed container for the fuel that is drained from the tank.

1. Disconnect the negative battery cable. Drain fuel into a safe, enclosed, metal container.
2. Remove inspection cover and disconnect fuel tank gauge unit harness connector.
3. Disconnect fuel filler and ventilation tubes.

➡ Plug hose and pipe openings to prevent entry of dust and dirt.

4. Disconnect the fuel outlet, return and evaporation hoses.

5. Raise the car and support it securely. Support the tank securely from underneath. Remove the bolt from the rear end of the support strap on either side (the bolts screw in upward). You may twist the strap 90° an pull it out of the fitting in the body where it connects, if necessary for clearance or to replace it if damaged.

6. Lower the tank and remove it.

To Install:

7. If the tank is being replaced, remove the fuel pump mounting bolts and remove the pump. Install it with a a new O-ring, torquing the bolts to 1.4–1.9 ft. lbs. (1.9–2.6 Nm).

8. Inspect the straps and, if they are bent or show cracks anywhere along their length, replace them. They can be installed by inserting the inner end into the body fitting with the outer end turned outboard and then turning them 90° so they run from front to rear.

9. Raise the tank into position. Then, raise the rear ends of the straps into position so the bolt holes in the straps line up with those in the body. Install the attaching bolts and torque them to 20–27 ft. lbs. (27–34 Nm).

10. Reconnect the fuel lines, evaporative emissions system, tank filler and electrical connectors in reverse of the removal procedure.

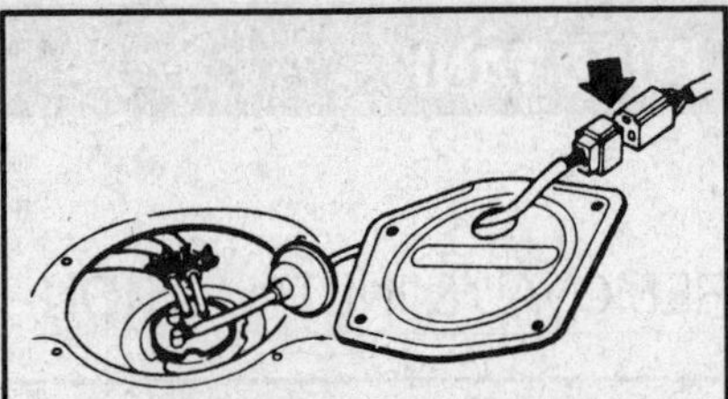

Fig. 60. Removing the fuel tank gauge unit and harness connector

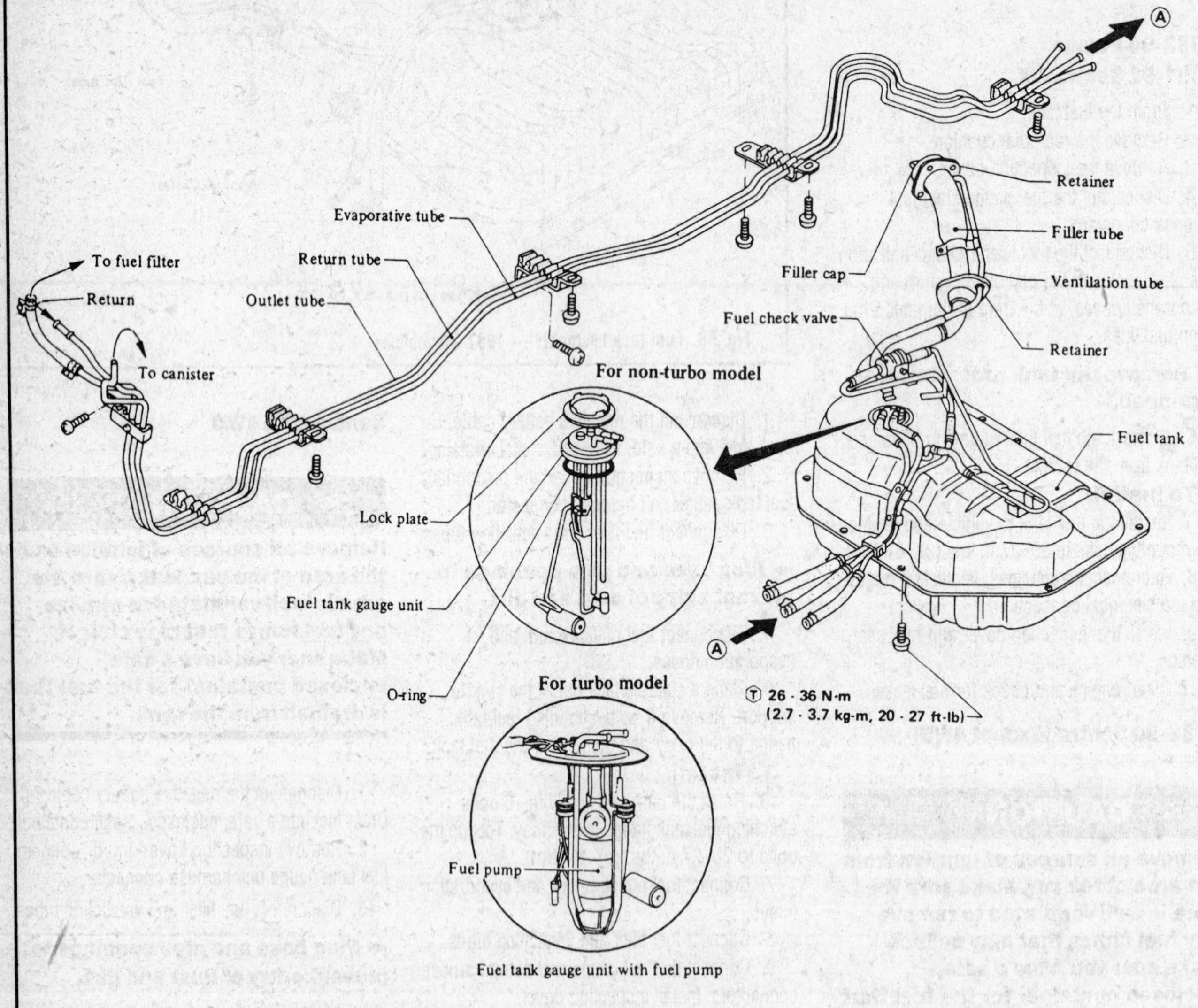

Ⓐ
Evaporative tube
To fuel filter
Return tube
Return
Outlet tube
To canister
Retainer
Filler tube
Filler cap
Ventilation tube
Fuel check valve
Retainer
For non-turbo model
Fuel tank
Lock plate
Fuel tank gauge unit
Ⓐ
For turbo model
O-ring
Ⓣ 26 - 36 N·m
(2.7 - 3.7 kg-m, 20 - 27 ft-lb)
Fuel pump
Fuel tank gauge unit with fuel pump

Fig. 59. Fuel tank assembly – 1983-86 Pulsar

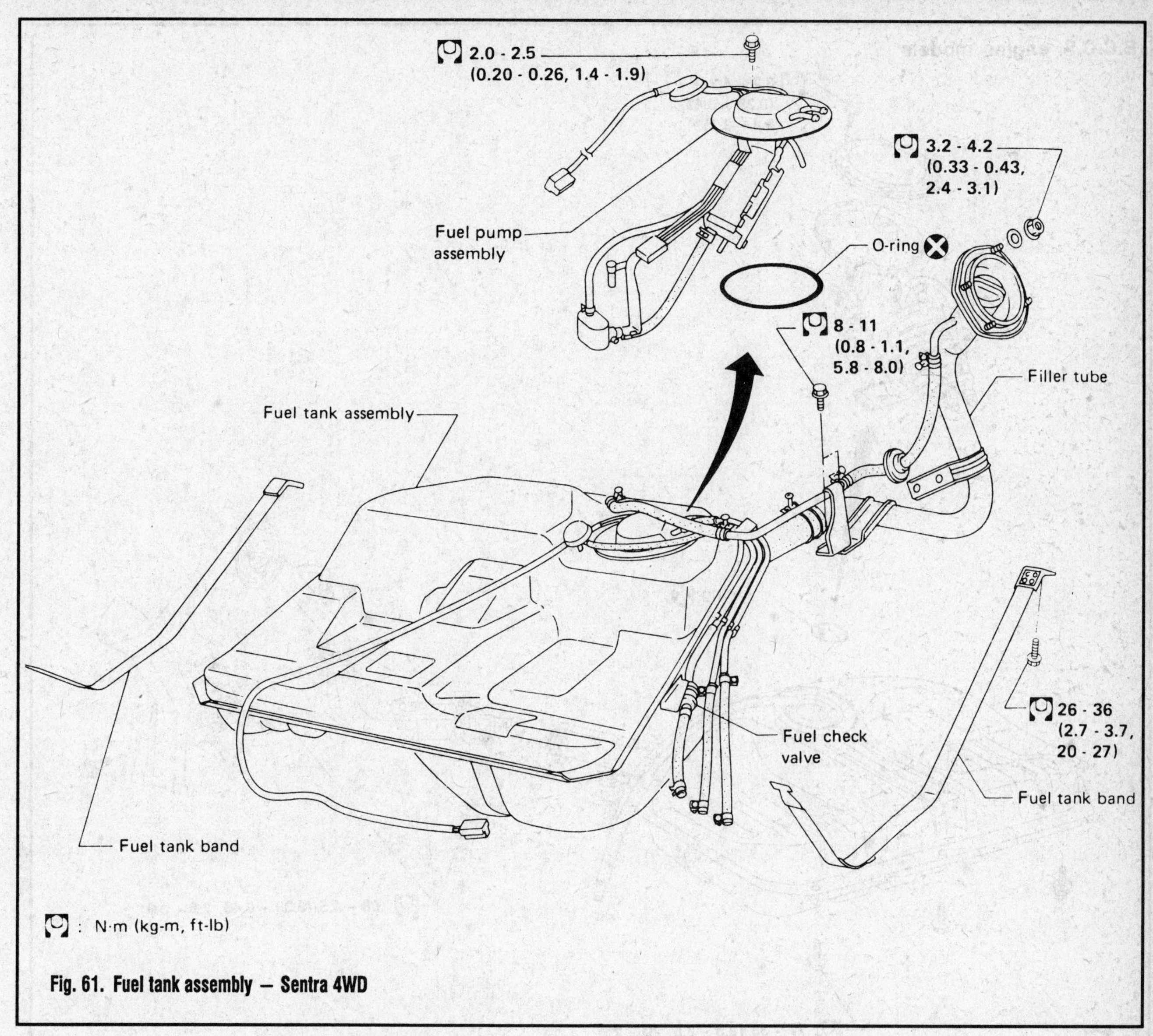
2.0 - 2.5
(0.20 - 0.26, 1.4 - 1.9)
3.2 - 4.2
(0.33 - 0.43,
2.4 - 3.1)
Fuel pump
assembly
O-ring
8 - 11
(0.8 - 1.1,
5.8 - 8.0)
Filler tube
Fuel tank assembly
26 - 36
(2.7 - 3.7,
20 - 27)
Fuel check
valve
Fuel tank band
Fuel tank band
: N·m (kg-m, ft-lb)

Fig. 61. Fuel tank assembly — Sentra 4WD

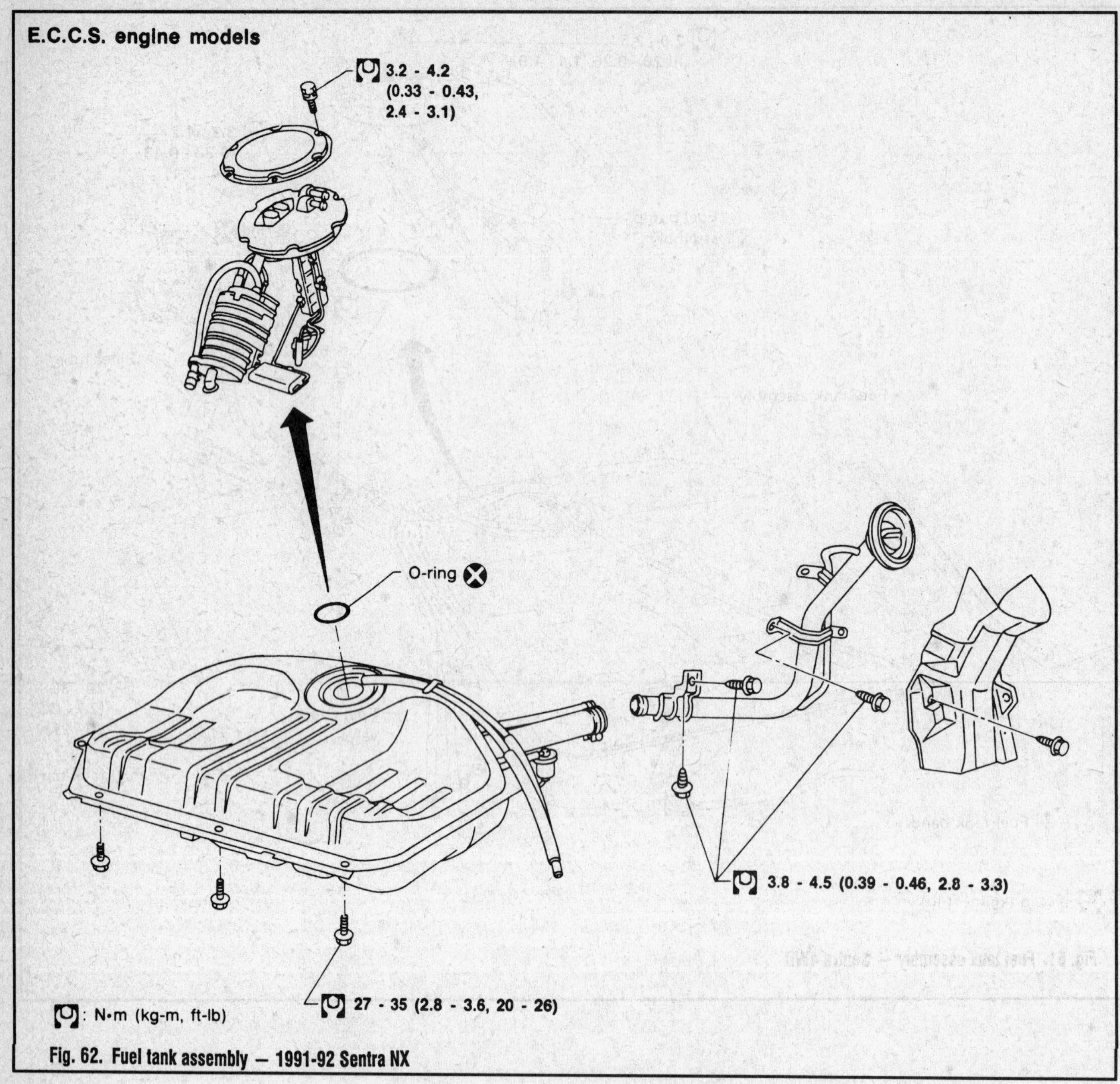
E.C.C.S. engine models
3.2 - 4.2 (0.33 - 0.43, 2.4 - 3.1)
O-ring
3.8 - 4.5 (0.39 - 0.46, 2.8 - 3.3)
: N•m (kg-m, ft-lb)
27 - 35 (2.8 - 3.6, 20 - 26)

Fig. 62. Fuel tank assembly — 1991-92 Sentra NX

TORQUE SPECIFICATIONS

Component	U.S.	Metric
Mechanical fuel pump	7-9 ft. lbs.	10-13 Nm
Anti-dieseling solenoid	13-16 ft. lbs.	18-22 Nm
Carburetor-to-manifold	9-13 ft. lbs.	11-18 Nm
Electric fuel pump-to-tank	26-35 inch lbs.	3.2-4.2 Nm
Throttle body bolts	15-20 ft. lbs.	20-27 Nm
Throttle body-to-collector	78-120 inch lbs.	9-14 Nm
Injector retaining bolts	35 inch lbs.	4.0 Nm
Fuel rail-to-manifold	8 ft. lbs.	11 Nm
Diesel injectors	43-51 ft. lbs.	58-68 Nm
Diesel injector lines	16-18 ft. lbs.	21-25 Nm
Diesel spill tubes	29-36 ft. lbs.	39-48 Nm
Diesel injector pump nut	9-13 ft. lbs.	13-19 Nm
Diesel pump-to-rear bracket	17-23 ft. lbs.	23-31 Nm
Diesel glow plug	25 ft. lbs.	34 Nm
Fuel tank-to-body bolts	20-27 ft. lbs.	27-37 Nm

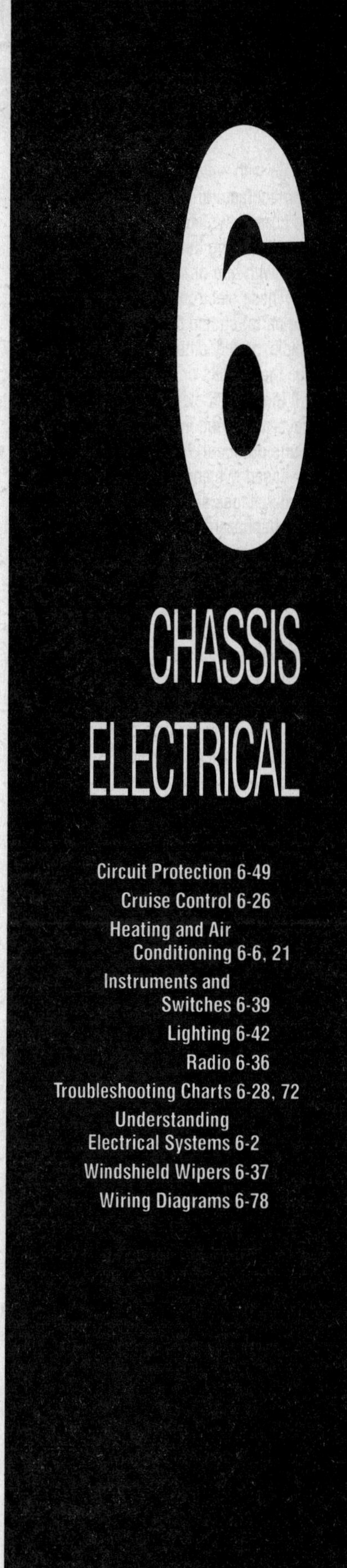

6 CHASSIS ELECTRICAL

ELECTRICAL SYSTEMS

At the rate with which both import and domestic manufacturers are incorporating electronic control systems into their production lines, it won't be long before every new vehicle is equipped with one or more on-board computer. These electronic components (with no moving parts) should theoretically last the life of the vehicle, provided nothing external happens to damage the circuits or memory chips.

While it is true that electronic components should never wear out, in the real world malfunctions do occur. It is also true that any computer-based system is extremely sensitive to electrical voltages and cannot tolerate careless or haphazard testing or service procedures. An inexperienced individual can literally do major damage looking for a minor problem by using the wrong kind of test equipment or connecting test leads or connectors with the ignition switch ON. When selecting test equipment, make sure the manufacturers instructions state that the tester is compatible with whatever type of electronic control system is being serviced. Read all instructions carefully and double check all test points before installing probes or making any test connections.

The following section outlines basic diagnosis techniques for dealing with computerized automotive control systems. Along with a general explanation of the various types of test equipment available to aid in servicing modern electronic automotive systems, basic repair techniques for wiring harnesses and connectors is given. Read the basic information before attempting any repairs or testing on any computerized system, to provide the background of information necessary to avoid the most common and obvious mistakes that can cost both time and money. Although the replacement and testing procedures are simple in themselves, the systems are not, and unless one has a thorough understanding of all components and their function within a particular computerized control system, the logical test sequence these systems demand cannot be followed. Minor malfunctions can make a big difference, so it is important to know how each component affects the operation of the overall electronic system to find the ultimate cause of a problem without replacing good components unnecessarily. It is not enough to use the correct test equipment; the test equipment must be used correctly.

Safety Precautions

** CAUTION

Whenever working on or around any computer based microprocessor control system, always observe these general precautions to prevent the possibility of personal injury or damage to electronic components.

- Never install or remove battery cables with the key ON or the engine running. Jumper cables should be connected with the key OFF to avoid power surges that can damage electronic control units. Engines equipped with computer controlled systems should avoid both giving and getting jump starts due to the possibility of serious damage to components from arcing in the engine compartment when connections are made with the ignition ON.
- Always remove the battery cables before charging the battery. Never use a high output charger on an installed battery or attempt to use any type of "hot shot" (24 volt) starting aid.
- Exercise care when inserting test probes into connectors to insure good connections without damaging the connector or spreading the pins. Always probe connectors from the rear (wire) side, NOT the pin side, to avoid accidental shorting of terminals during test procedures.
- Never remove or attach wiring harness connectors with the ignition switch ON, especially to an electronic control unit.
- Do not drop any components during service procedures and never apply 12 volts directly to any component (like a solenoid or relay) unless instructed specifically to do so. Some component electrical windings are designed to safely handle only 4 or 5 volts and can be destroyed in seconds if 12 volts are applied directly to the connector.
- Remove the electronic control unit if the vehicle is to be placed in an environment where temperatures exceed approximately 176°F (80°C), such as a paint spray booth or when arc or gas welding near the control unit location in the car.

ORGANIZED TROUBLESHOOTING

When diagnosing a specific problem, organized troubleshooting is a must. The complexity of a modern automobile demands that you approach any problem in a logical, organized manner. There are certain troubleshooting techniques that are standard:

1. Establish when the problem occurs. Does the problem appear only under certain conditions? Were there any noises, odors, or other unusual symptoms?
2. Isolate the problem area. To do this, make some simple tests and observations; then eliminate the systems that are working properly. Check for obvious problems such as broken wires, dirty connections or split or disconnected vacuum hoses. Always check the obvious before assuming something complicated is the cause.
3. Test for problems systematically to determine the cause once the problem area is isolated. Are all the components functioning properly? Is there power going to electrical switches and motors? Is there vacuum at vacuum switches and/or actuators? Is there a mechanical problem such as bent linkage or loose mounting screws? Doing careful, systematic checks will often turn up most causes on the first inspection without wasting time checking components that have little or no relationship to the problem.
4. Test all repairs after the work is done to make sure that the problem is fixed. Some causes can be traced to more than one component, so a careful verification of repair work is important to pick up additional malfunctions that may cause a problem to reappear or a different problem to arise. A blown fuse, for example, is a simple problem that may require more than another fuse to repair. If you don't look for a problem that caused a fuse to blow, for example, a shorted wire may go undetected.

TEST EQUIPMENT

Jumper Wires

Jumper wires are simple, yet extremely valuable, pieces of test equipment. Jumper wires are merely wires that are used to bypass sections of a circuit. The simplest type of jumper wire is merely a length of multistrand wire with an alligator clip at each end. Jumper wires are usually fabricated from lengths of standard automotive wire and whatever type of connector (alligator clip, spade connector or pin connector) that is required for the particular vehicle being tested. The well equipped tool box will have several different styles of jumper wires in several different lengths. Some jumper wires are made with three or more terminals coming from a common splice for special purpose testing. In cramped, hard-to-reach areas it is advisable to have insulated boots over the jumper wire terminals in order to prevent accidental grounding, sparks, and possible fire, especially when testing fuel system components.

Jumper wires are used primarily to locate open electrical circuits, on either the ground (–) side of the circuit or on the hot (+) side. If an electrical component fails to operate, connect the jumper wire between the component and a good ground. If the component operates only with the jumper installed, the ground circuit is open. If the ground circuit is good, but the component does not operate, the circuit between the power feed and component is open. You can sometimes connect the jumper wire directly from the battery to the hot terminal of the component, but first make sure the component uses 12 volts in operation. Some electrical components, such as fuel injectors, are designed to operate on about 4 volts and running 12 volts directly to the injector terminals can burn out the wiring. By inserting an inline fuse holder between a set of test leads, a fused jumper wire can be used for bypassing open circuits. Use a 5 amp fuse to provide protection against voltage spikes. When in doubt, use a voltmeter to check the voltage input to the component and measure how much voltage is being applied normally. By moving the jumper wire successively back from the lamp toward the power source, you can isolate the area of the circuit where the open is located. When the component stops functioning, or the power is cut off, the open is in the segment of wire between the jumper and the point previously tested.

➡ Never use jumpers made from wire that is of lighter gauge than used in the circuit under test. If the jumper wire is of too small gauge, it may overheat and possibly melt. Never use jumpers to bypass high resistance loads (such as motors) in a circuit. Bypassing resistances, in effect, creates a short circuit which may, in turn, cause damage and fire. Never use a jumper for anything other than temporary bypassing of components in a circuit.

12 Volt Test Light

The 12 volt test light is used to check circuits and components while electrical current is flowing through them. It is used for voltage and ground tests. Twelve volt test lights come in different styles but all have three main parts; a ground clip, a probe, and a light. The most commonly used 12 volt test lights have pick-type probes. To use a 12 volt test light, connect the ground clip to a good ground and probe wherever necessary with the pick. The pick should be sharp so that it can penetrate wire insulation to make contact with the wire, without making a large hole in the insulation. The wrap-around light is handy in hard to reach areas or where it is difficult to support a wire to push a probe pick into it. To use the wrap around light, hook the wire to probed with the hook and pull the trigger. A small pick will be forced through the wire insulation into the wire core.

➡ Do not use a test light to probe electronic ignition spark plug or coil wires. Never use a pick-type test light to probe wiring on computer controlled systems unless specifically instructed to do so. Any wire insulation that is pierced by the test light probe should be taped and sealed with silicone after testing.

Like the jumper wire, the 12 volt test light is used to isolate opens in circuits. But, whereas the jumper wire is used to bypass the open to operate the load, the 12 volt test light is used to locate the presence of voltage in a circuit. If the test light glows, you know that there is power up to that point; if the 12 volt test light does not glow when its probe is inserted into the wire or connector, you know that there is an open circuit (no power). Move the test light in successive steps back toward the power source until the light in the handle does glow. When it does glow, the open is between the probe and point previously probed.

➡ The test light does not detect that 12 volts (or any particular amount of voltage) is present; it only detects that some voltage is present. It is advisable before using the test light to touch its terminals across the battery posts to make sure the light is operating properly.

Self-Powered Test Light

The self-powered test light usually contains a 1.5 volt pen light battery. One type of self-powered test light is similar in design to the 12 volt test light. This type has both the battery and the light in the handle and pick-type probe tip. The second type has the light toward the open tip, so that the light illuminates the contact point. The self-powered test light is dual purpose piece of test equipment. It can be used to test for either open or short circuits when power is isolated from the circuit (continuity test). A powered test light should not be used on any computer controlled system or component unless specifically instructed to do so. Many engine sensors can be destroyed by even this small amount of voltage applied directly to the terminals.

Open Circuit Testing

To use the self-powered test light to check for open circuits, first isolate the circuit from the vehicle's 12 volt power source by disconnecting the battery or wiring harness connector. Connect the test light ground clip to a good ground and probe sections of the circuit sequentially with the test light. (start from either end of the circuit). If the light is out, the open is between the probe and the circuit ground. If the light is on, the open is between the probe and end of the circuit toward the power source.

Short Circuit Testing

By isolating the circuit both from power and from ground, and using a self-powered test light, you can check for shorts to ground in the circuit. Isolate the circuit from power and ground. Connect the test light ground clip to a good ground and probe any easy-to-reach test point in the circuit. If the light comes on, there is a short somewhere in the circuit. To isolate the short, probe a test point at either end of the isolated circuit (the light should be on). Leave the test light probe connected and open connectors, switches, remove parts, etc., sequentially, until the light goes out. When the light goes out, the short is between the last circuit component opened and the previous circuit opened.

➡ The 1.5 volt battery in the test light does not provide much current. A weak battery may not provide enough power to illuminate the test light even when a complete circuit is made (especially if there are high resistances in the circuit). Always make sure that the test battery is strong. To check the battery, briefly touch the ground clip to the probe; if the light glows brightly the battery is strong enough for testing. Never use a self-powered test light to perform checks for opens or shorts when power is applied to the electrical system under test. The 12 volt vehicle power will quickly burn out the 1.5 volt light bulb in the test light.

Voltmeter

A voltmeter is used to measure voltage at any point in a circuit, or to measure the voltage drop across any part of a circuit. It can also be used to check continuity in a wire or circuit by indicating current flow from one end to the other. Voltmeters usually have various scales on the meter dial and a selector switch to allow the selection of different voltages. The voltmeter has a positive and a negative lead. To avoid damage to the meter, always connect the negative lead to the negative (–) side of circuit (to ground or nearest the ground side of the circuit) and connect the positive lead to the positive (+) side of the circuit (to the power source or the nearest power source). Note that the negative voltmeter lead will always be black and that the positive voltmeter will always be some color other than black (usually red). Depending on how the voltmeter is connected into the circuit, it has several uses.

A voltmeter can be connected either in parallel or in series with a circuit and it has a very high resistance to current flow. When connected in parallel, only a small amount of current will flow through the voltmeter current path; the rest will flow through the normal circuit current path and the circuit will work normally. When the voltmeter is connected in series with a circuit, only a small amount of current can flow through the circuit. The circuit will not work properly, but the voltmeter reading will show if the circuit is complete or not.

Available Voltage Measurement

Set the voltmeter selector switch to the 20V position and connect the meter negative lead to the negative post of the battery. Connect the positive meter lead to the positive post of the battery and turn the ignition switch ON to provide a load. Read the voltage on the meter or digital display. A well charged battery should register over 12 volts. If the meter reads below 11.5 volts, the battery power may be insufficient to operate the electrical system properly. This test determines voltage available from the battery and should be the first step in any electrical trouble diagnosis procedure. Many electrical problems, especially on computer controlled systems, can be caused by a low state of charge in the battery. Excessive corrosion at the battery cable terminals can cause a poor contact that will prevent proper charging and full battery current flow.

Normal battery voltage is 12 volts when fully charged. When the battery is supplying current to one or more circuits it is said to be "under load". When everything is off the electrical system is under a "no-load" condition. A fully charged battery may show about 12.5 volts at no load; will drop to 12 volts under medium load; and will drop even lower under heavy load. If the battery is partially discharged the voltage decrease under heavy load may be excessive, even though the battery shows 12 volts or more at no load. When allowed to discharge further, the battery's available voltage under load will decrease more severely. For this reason, it is important that the battery be fully charged during all testing procedures to avoid errors in diagnosis and incorrect test results.

Voltage Drop

When current flows through a resistance, the voltage beyond the resistance is reduced (the larger the current, the greater the reduction in voltage). When no current is flowing, there is no voltage drop because there is no current flow. All points in the circuit which are connected to the power source are at the same voltage as the power source. The total voltage drop always equals the total source voltage. In a long circuit with many connectors, a series of small, unwanted voltage drops due to corrosion at the connectors can add up to a total loss of voltage which impairs the operation of the normal loads in the circuit.

INDIRECT COMPUTATION OF VOLTAGE DROPS

1. Set the voltmeter selector switch to the 20 volt position.
2. Connect the meter negative lead to a good ground.
3. Probe all resistances in the circuit with the positive meter lead.
4. Operate the circuit in all modes and observe the voltage readings.

DIRECT MEASUREMENT OF VOLTAGE DROPS

1. Set the voltmeter switch to the 20 volt position.
2. Connect the voltmeter negative lead to the ground side of the resistance load to be measured.
3. Connect the positive lead to the positive side of the resistance or load to be measured.
4. Read the voltage drop directly on the 20 volt scale.

Too high a voltage indicates too high a resistance. If, for example, a blower motor runs too slowly, you can determine if there is too high a resistance in the resistor pack. By taking voltage drop readings in all parts of the circuit, you can isolate the problem. Too low a voltage drop indicates too low a resistance. If, for example, a blower motor runs too fast in the MED and/or LOW position, the problem can be isolated in the resistor pack by taking voltage drop readings in all parts of the circuit to locate a possibly shorted resistor. The maximum allowable voltage drop under load is critical, especially if there is more than one high resistance problem in a circuit because all voltage drops are cumulative. A small drop is normal due to the resistance of the conductors.

HIGH RESISTANCE TESTING

1. Set the voltmeter selector switch to the 4 volt position.
2. Connect the voltmeter positive lead to the positive post of the battery.
3. Turn on the headlights and heater blower to provide a load.
4. Probe various points in the circuit with the negative voltmeter lead.
5. Read the voltage drop on the 4 volt scale. Some average maximum allowable voltage drops are:
   - FUSE PANEL — 7 volts
   - IGNITION SWITCH — 5 volts
   - HEADLIGHT SWITCH — 7 volts
   - IGNITION COIL (+) — 5 volts
   - ANY OTHER LOAD — 1.3 volts

➡ Voltage drops are all measured while a load is operating; without current flow, there will be no voltage drop.

Ohmmeter

The ohmmeter is designed to read resistance (ohms) in a circuit or component. Although there are several different styles of ohmmeters, all will usually have a selector switch which permits the measurement of different ranges of resistance (usually the selector switch allows the multiplication of the meter reading by 10, 100, 1,000, and 10,000). A calibration knob allows the meter to be set at zero for accurate measurement. Since all ohmmeters are powered by an internal battery (usually 9 volts), the ohmmeter can be used as a self-powered test light. When the ohmmeter is connected, current from the ohmmeter flows through the circuit or component being tested. Since the ohmmeter's internal resistance and voltage are known values, the amount of current flow through the meter depends on the resistance of the circuit or component being tested.

The ohmmeter can be used to perform continuity test for opens or shorts (either by observation of the meter needle or as a self-powered test light), and to read actual resistance in a circuit. It should be noted that the ohmmeter is used to check the resistance of a component or wire while there is no voltage applied to the circuit. Current flow from an outside voltage source (such as the vehicle battery) can damage the ohmmeter, so the circuit or component should be isolated from the vehicle electrical system before any testing is done. Since the ohmmeter uses its own voltage source, either lead can be connected to any test point.

➡ **When checking diodes or other solid state components, the ohmmeter leads can only be connected one way in order to measure current flow in a single direction. Make sure the positive (+) and negative (-) terminal connections are as described in the test procedures to verify the one-way diode operation.**

In using the meter for making continuity checks, do not be concerned with the actual resistance readings. Zero resistance, or any resistance readings, indicate continuity in the circuit. Infinite resistance indicates an open in the circuit. A high resistance reading where there should be none indicates a problem in the circuit. Checks for short circuits are made in the same manner as checks for open circuits except that the circuit must be isolated from both power and normal ground. Infinite resistance indicates no continuity to ground, while zero resistance indicates a dead short to ground.

RESISTANCE MEASUREMENT

The batteries in an ohmmeter will weaken with age and temperature, so the ohmmeter must be calibrated or "zeroed" before taking measurements. To zero the meter, place the selector switch in its lowest range and touch the two ohmmeter leads together. Turn the calibration knob until the meter needle is exactly on zero.

➡ **All analog (needle) type ohmmeters must be zeroed before use, but some digital ohmmeter models are automatically calibrated when the switch is turned on. Self-calibrating digital ohmmeters do not have an adjusting knob, but its a good idea to check for a zero readout before use by touching the leads together. All computer controlled systems require the use of a digital ohmmeter with at least 10 megohms impedance for testing. Before any test procedures are attempted, make sure the ohmmeter used is compatible with the electrical system or damage to the on-board computer could result.**

To measure resistance, first isolate the circuit from the vehicle power source by disconnecting the battery cables or the harness connector. Make sure the key is OFF when disconnecting any components or the battery. Where necessary, also isolate at least one side of the circuit to be checked to avoid reading parallel resistances. Parallel circuit resistances will always give a lower reading than the actual resistance of either of the branches. When measuring the resistance of parallel circuits, the total resistance will always be lower than the smallest resistance in the circuit. Connect the meter leads to both sides of the circuit (wire or component) and read the actual measured ohms on the meter scale. Make sure the selector switch is set to the proper ohm scale for the circuit being tested to avoid misreading the ohmmeter test value.

➡ **Never use an ohmmeter with power applied to the circuit. Like the self-powered test light, the ohmmeter is designed to operate on its own power supply. The normal 12 volt automotive electrical system current could damage the meter!**

Ammeters

An ammeter measures the amount of current flowing through a circuit in units called amperes or amps. Amperes are units of electron flow which indicate how fast the electrons are flowing through the circuit. Since Ohms Law dictates that current flow in a circuit is equal to the circuit voltage divided by the total circuit resistance, increasing voltage also increases the current level (amps). Likewise, any decrease in resistance will increase the amount of amps in a circuit. At normal operating voltage, most circuits have a characteristic amount of amperes, called "current draw" which can be measured using an ammeter. By referring to a specified current draw rating, measuring the amperes, and comparing the two values, one can determine what is happening within the circuit to aid in diagnosis. An open circuit, for example, will not allow any current to flow so the ammeter reading will be zero. More current flows through a heavily loaded circuit or when the charging system is operating.

An ammeter is always connected in series with the circuit being tested. All of the current that normally flows through the circuit must also flow through the ammeter; if there is any other path for the current to follow, the ammeter reading will not be accurate. The ammeter itself has very little resistance to current flow and therefore will not affect the circuit, but it will measure current draw only when the circuit is closed and electricity is flowing. Excessive current draw can blow fuses and drain the battery, while a reduced current draw can cause motors to run slowly, lights to dim and other components to not operate properly. The ammeter can help diagnose these conditions by locating the cause of the high or low reading.

Multimeters

Different combinations of test meters can be built into a single unit designed for specific tests. Some of the more common combination test devices are known as Volt/Amp testers, Tach/Dwell meters, or Digital Multimeters. The Volt/Amp tester is used for charging system, starting system or battery tests and consists of a voltmeter, an ammeter and a variable resistance carbon pile. The voltmeter will usually have at least two ranges for use with 6, 12 and 24 volt systems. The ammeter also has more than one range for testing various levels of battery loads and starter current draw and the carbon pile can be adjusted to offer different amounts of resistance. The Volt/Amp tester has heavy leads to carry large amounts of current and many later models have an inductive ammeter pickup that clamps around the wire to simplify test connections. On some models, the ammeter also has a zero-center scale to allow testing of charging and starting systems without switching leads or polarity. A digital multimeter is a voltmeter, ammeter and ohmmeter combined in an instrument which gives a digital readout. These are often used when testing solid state circuits because of their high input impedance (usually 10 megohms or more).

The tach/dwell meter combines a tachometer and a dwell (cam angle) meter and is a specialized kind of voltmeter. The tachometer scale is marked to show engine speed in rpm and the dwell scale is marked to show degrees of distributor shaft rotation. In most electronic ignition systems, dwell is determined by the control unit, but the dwell meter can also be used to check the duty cycle (operation) of some electronic engine control systems. Some tach/dwell meters are powered by an internal battery, while others take their power from the car battery in use. The battery powered testers usually require calibration much like an ohmmeter before testing.

Special Test Equipment

A variety of diagnostic tools are available to help troubleshoot and repair computerized engine control systems. The most sophisticated of these devices are the console type engine analyzers that usually occupy a garage service bay, but there are several types of aftermarket electronic testers available that will allow quick circuit tests of the engine control system by plugging directly into a special connector located in the engine compartment or under the dashboard. Several tool and equipment manufacturers offer simple, hand held testers that measure various circuit voltage levels on command to check all system components for proper operation. Although these testers usually cost about $300–500, consider that the average computer control unit (or ECM) can cost just as much and the money saved by not replacing perfectly good sensors or components in an attempt to correct a problem could justify the purchase price of a special diagnostic tester the first time it's used.

These computerized testers can allow quick and easy test measurements while the engine is operating or while the car is being driven. In addition, the on-board computer memory can be read to access any stored trouble codes; in effect allowing the computer to tell you where it hurts and aid trouble diagnosis by pinpointing exactly which circuit or component is malfunctioning. In the same manner, repairs can be tested to make sure the problem has been corrected. The biggest advantage these special testers have is their relatively easy hookups that minimize or eliminate the chances of making the wrong connections and getting false voltage readings or damaging the computer accidentally.

➡ It should be remembered that these testers check voltage levels in circuits; they don't detect mechanical problems or failed components if the circuit voltage falls within the preprogrammed limits stored in the tester PROM unit. Also, most of the hand held testes are designed to work only on one or two systems made by a specific manufacturer.

A variety of aftermarket testers are available to help diagnose different computerized control systems. Owatonna Tool Company (OTC), for example, markets a device called the OTC Monitor which plugs directly into the assembly line diagnostic link (ALDL). The OTC tester makes diagnosis a simple matter of pressing the correct buttons and, by changing the internal PROM or inserting a different diagnosis cartridge, it will work on any model from full size to subcompact, over a wide range of years. An adapter is supplied with the tester to allow connection to all types of ALDL links, regardless of the number of pin terminals used. By inserting an updated PROM into the OTC tester, it can be easily updated to diagnose any new modifications of computerized control systems.

Wiring Harnesses

The average automobile contains about 1/2 mile of wiring, with hundreds of individual connections. To protect the many wires from damage and to keep them from becoming a confusing tangle, they are organized into bundles, enclosed in plastic or taped together and called wire harnesses. Different wiring harnesses serve different parts of the vehicle. Individual wires are color coded to help trace them through a harness where sections are hidden from view.

A loose or corroded connection or a replacement wire that is too small for the circuit will add extra resistance and an additional voltage drop to the circuit. A ten percent voltage drop can result in slow or erratic motor operation, for example, even though the circuit is complete. Automotive wiring or circuit conductors can be in any one of three forms:

1. Single strand wire
2. Multistrand wire
3. Printed circuitry

Single strand wire has a solid metal core and is usually used inside such components as alternators, motors, relays and other devices. Multistrand wire has a core made of many small strands of wire twisted together into a single conductor. Most of the wiring in an automotive electrical system is made up of multistrand wire, either as a single conductor or grouped together in a harness. All wiring is color coded on the insulator, either as a solid color or as a colored wire with an identification stripe. A printed circuit is a thin film of copper or other conductor that is printed on an insulator backing. Occasionally, a printed circuit is sandwiched between two sheets of plastic for more protection and flexibility. A complete printed circuit, consisting of conductors, insulating material and connectors for lamps or other components is called a printed circuit board. Printed circuitry is used in place of individual wires or harnesses in places where space is limited, such as behind instrument panels.

Wire Gauge

Since computer controlled automotive electrical systems are very sensitive to changes in resistance, the selection of properly sized wires is critical when systems are repaired. The wire gauge number is an expression of the cross section area of the conductor. The most common system for expressing wire size is the American Wire Gauge (AWG) system.

Wire cross section area is measured in circular mils. A mil is 1/1000″ (0.001″); a circular mil is the area of a circle one mil in diameter. For example, a conductor 1/4″ in diameter is 0.250 in. or 250 mils. The circular mil cross section area of the wire is 250 squared (2506)or 62,500 circular mils. Imported car models usually use metric wire gauge designations, which is simply the cross section area of the conductor in square millimeters (mm6).

Gauge numbers are assigned to conductors of various cross section areas. As gauge number increases, area decreases and the conductor becomes smaller. A 5 gauge conductor is smaller than a 1 gauge conductor and a 10 gauge is smaller than a 5 gauge. As the cross section area of a conductor decreases, resistance increases and so does the gauge number. A conductor with a higher gauge number will carry less current than a conductor with a lower gauge number.

➡ Gauge wire size refers to the size of the conductor, not the size of the complete wire. It is possible to have two wires of the same gauge with different diameters because one may have thicker insulation than the other.

12 volt automotive electrical systems generally use 10, 12, 14, 16 and 18 gauge wire. Main power distribution circuits and larger accessories usually use 10 and 12 gauge wire. Battery cables are usually 4 or 6 gauge, although 1 and 2 gauge wires are occasionally used. Wire length must also be considered when making repairs to a circuit. As conductor length increases, so does resistance. An 18 gauge wire, for example, can carry a 10 amp load for 10 feet without excessive voltage drop; however if a 15 foot wire is required for the same 10 amp load, it must be a 16 gauge wire.

An electrical schematic shows the electrical current paths when a circuit is operating properly. It is essential to understand how a circuit works before trying to figure out why it doesn't. Schematics break the entire electrical system down into individual circuits and show only one particular circuit. In a schematic, no attempt is made to represent wiring and components as they physically appear on the vehicle; switches and other components are shown as simply as possible. Face views of harness connectors show the cavity or terminal locations in all multi-pin connectors to help locate test points.

If you need to backprobe a connector while it is on the component, the order of the terminals must be mentally reversed. The wire color code can help in this situation, as well as a keyway, lock tab or other reference mark.

➡ Wiring diagrams are not included in this book. As trucks have become more complex and available with longer option lists, wiring diagrams have grown in size and complexity. It has become almost impossible to provide a readable reproduction of a wiring diagram in a book this size. Information on ordering wiring diagrams from the vehicle manufacturer can be found in the owner's manual.

WIRING REPAIR

Soldering is a quick, efficient method of joining metals permanently. Everyone who has the occasion to make wiring repairs should know how to solder. Electrical connections that are soldered are far less likely to come apart and will conduct electricity much better than connections that are only "pig-tailed" together. The most popular (and preferred) method of soldering is with an electrical soldering gun. Soldering irons are available in many sizes and wattage ratings. Irons with higher wattage ratings deliver higher temperatures and recover lost heat faster. A small soldering iron rated for no more than 50 watts is recommended, especially on electrical systems where excess heat can damage the components being soldered.

There are three ingredients necessary for successful soldering; proper flux, good solder and sufficient heat. A soldering flux is necessary to clean the metal of tarnish, prepare it for soldering and to enable the solder to spread into tiny crevices. When soldering, always use a resin flux or resin core solder which is non-corrosive and will not attract moisture once the job is finished. Other types of flux (acid core) will leave a residue that will attract moisture and cause the wires to corrode. Tin is a unique metal with a low melting point. In a molten state, it dissolves and alloys easily with many metals. Solder is made by mixing tin with lead. The most common proportions are 40/60, 50/50 and 60/40, with the percentage of tin listed first. Low priced solders usually contain less tin, making them very difficult for a beginner to use because more heat is required to melt the solder. A common solder is 40/60 which is well suited for all-around general use, but 60/40 melts easier, has more tin for a better joint and is preferred for electrical work.

Soldering Techniques

Successful soldering requires that the metals to be joined be heated to a temperature that will melt the solder—usually 360–460°F (182–238°C). Contrary to popular belief, the purpose of the soldering iron is not to melt the solder itself, but to heat the parts being soldered to a temperature high enough to melt the solder when it is touched to the work. Melting flux-cored solder on the soldering iron will usually destroy the effectiveness of the flux.

➡ Soldering tips are made of copper for good heat conductivity, but must be "tinned" regularly for quick transference of heat to the project and to prevent the solder from sticking to the iron. To "tin" the iron, simply heat it and touch the flux-cored solder to the tip; the solder will flow over the hot tip. Wipe the excess off with a clean rag, but be careful as the iron will be hot.

After some use, the tip may become pitted. If so, simply dress the tip smooth with a smooth file and "tin" the tip again. An old saying holds that "metals well cleaned are half soldered." Flux-cored solder will remove oxides but rust, bits of insulation and oil or grease must be removed with a wire brush or emery cloth. For maximum strength in soldered parts, the joint must start off clean and tight. Weak joints will result in gaps too wide for the solder to bridge.

If a separate soldering flux is used, it should be brushed or swabbed on only those areas that are to be soldered. Most solders contain a core of flux and separate fluxing is unnecessary. Hold the work to be soldered firmly. It is best to solder on a wooden board, because a metal vise will only rob the piece to be soldered of heat and make it difficult to melt the solder. Hold the soldering tip with the broadest face against the work to be soldered. Apply solder under the tip close to the work, using enough solder to give a heavy film between the iron and the piece being soldered, while moving slowly and making sure the solder melts properly. Keep the work level or the solder will run to the lowest part and favor the thicker parts, because these require more heat to melt the solder. If the soldering tip overheats (the solder coating on the face of the tip burns up), it should be retinned. Once the soldering is completed, let the soldered joint stand until cool. Tape and seal all soldered wire splices after the repair has cooled.

Wire Harness and Connectors

The on-board computer (ECM) wire harness electrically connects the control unit to the various solenoids, switches and sensors used by the control system. Most connectors in the engine compartment or otherwise exposed to the elements are protected against moisture and dirt which could create oxidation and deposits on the terminals. This protection is important because of the very low voltage and current levels used by the computer and sensors. All connectors have a lock which secures the male and female terminals together, with a secondary lock holding the seal and terminal into the connector. Both terminal locks must be released when disconnecting ECM connectors.

These special connectors are weather-proof and all repairs require the use of a special terminal and the tool required to service it. This tool is used to remove the pin and sleeve terminals. If removal is attempted with an ordinary pick, there is a good chance that the terminal will be bent or deformed. Unlike standard blade type terminals, these terminals cannot be straightened once they are bent. Make certain that the connectors are properly seated and all of the sealing rings in place when connecting leads. On some models, a hinge-type flap provides a backup or secondary locking feature for the terminals. Most secondary locks are used to improve the connector reliability by retaining the terminals if the small terminal lock tangs are not positioned properly.

Molded-on connectors require complete replacement of the connection. This means splicing a new connector assembly into the harness. All splices in on-board computer systems should be soldered to insure proper contact. Use care when probing the connections or replacing terminals in them as it is possible to short between opposite terminals. If this happens to the wrong terminal pair, it is possible to damage certain components. Always use jumper wires between connectors for circuit checking and never probe through weatherproof seals.

Open circuits are often difficult to locate by sight because corrosion or terminal misalignment are hidden by the connectors. Merely wiggling a connector on a sensor or in the wiring harness may correct the open circuit condition. This should always be considered when an open circuit or a failed sensor is indicated. Intermittent problems may also be caused by oxidized or loose connections. When using a circuit tester for diagnosis, always probe connections from the wire side. Be careful not to damage sealed connectors with test probes.

All wiring harnesses should be replaced with identical parts, using the same gauge wire and connectors. When signal wires are spliced into a harness, use wire with high temperature insulation only. With the low voltage and current levels found in the system, it is important that the best possible connection at all wire splices be made by soldering the splices together. It is seldom necessary to replace a complete harness. If replacement is necessary, pay close attention to insure proper harness routing.

Secure the harness with suitable plastic wire clamps to prevent vibrations from causing the harness to wear in spots or contact any hot components.

➡ Weatherproof connectors cannot be replaced with standard connectors. Instructions are provided with replacement connector and terminal packages. Some wire harnesses have mounting indicators (usually pieces of colored tape) to mark where the harness is to be secured.

In making wiring repairs, it's important that you always replace damaged wires with wires that are the same gauge as the wire being replaced. The heavier the wire, the smaller the gauge number. Wires are color-coded to aid in identification and whenever possible the same color coded wire should be used for replacement. A wire stripping and crimping tool is necessary to install solderless terminal connectors. Test all crimps by pulling on the wires; it should not be possible to pull the wires out of a good crimp.

Wires which are open, exposed or otherwise damaged are repaired by simple splicing. Where possible, if the wiring harness is accessible and the damaged place in the wire can be located, it is best to open the harness and check for all possible damage. In an inaccessible harness, the wire must be bypassed with a new insert, usually taped to the outside of the old harness.

When replacing fusible links, be sure to use fusible link wire, NOT ordinary automotive wire. Make sure the fusible segment is of the same gauge and construction as the one being replaced and double the stripped end when crimping the terminal connector for a good contact. The melted (open) fusible link segment of the wiring harness should be cut off as close to the harness as possible, then a new segment spliced in as described. In the case of a damaged fusible link that feeds two harness wires, the harness connections should be replaced with two fusible link wires so that each circuit will have its own separate protection.

➡ Most of the problems caused in the wiring harness are due to bad ground connections. Always check all vehicle ground connections for corrosion or looseness before performing any power feed checks to eliminate the chance of a bad ground affecting the circuit.

Repairing Hard Shell Connectors

Unlike molded connectors, the terminal contacts in hard shell connectors can be replaced. Weatherproof hard-shell connectors with the leads molded into the shell have non-replaceable terminal ends. Replacement usually involves the use of a special terminal removal tool that depress the locking tangs (barbs) on the connector terminal and allow the connector to be removed from the rear of the shell. The connector shell should be replaced if it shows any evidence of burning, melting, cracks, or breaks. Replace individual terminals that are burnt, corroded, distorted or loose.

➡ The insulation crimp must be tight to prevent the insulation from sliding back on the wire when the wire is pulled. The insulation must be visibly compressed under the crimp tabs, and the ends of the crimp should be turned in for a firm grip on the insulation.

The wire crimp must be made with all wire strands inside the crimp. The terminal must be fully compressed on the wire strands with the ends of the crimp tabs turned in to make a firm grip on the wire. Check all connections with an ohmmeter to insure a good contact. There should be no measurable resistance between the wire and the terminal when connected.

Mechanical Test Equipment

Vacuum Gauge

Most gauges are graduated in inches of mercury (in.Hg), although a device called a manometer reads vacuum in inches of water (in. H_2O). The normal vacuum reading usually varies between 18 and 22 in.Hg at sea level. To test engine vacuum, the vacuum gauge must be connected to a source of manifold vacuum. Many engines have a plug in the intake manifold which can be removed and replaced with an adapter fitting. Connect the vacuum gauge to the fitting with a suitable rubber hose or, if no manifold plug is available, connect the vacuum gauge to any device using manifold vacuum, such as EGR valves, etc. The vacuum gauge can be used to determine if enough vacuum is reaching a component to allow its actuation.

Hand Vacuum Pump

Small, hand-held vacuum pumps come in a variety of designs. Most have a built-in vacuum gauge and allow the component to be tested without removing it from the vehicle. Operate the pump lever or plunger to apply the correct amount of vacuum required for the test specified in the diagnosis routines. The level of vacuum in inches of Mercury (in.Hg) is indicated on the pump gauge. For some testing, an additional vacuum gauge may be necessary.

Intake manifold vacuum is used to operate various systems and devices on late model vehicles. To correctly diagnose and solve problems in vacuum control systems, a vacuum source is necessary for testing. In some cases, vacuum can be taken from the intake manifold when the engine is running, but vacuum is normally provided by a hand vacuum pump. These hand vacuum pumps have a built-in vacuum gauge that allow testing while the device is still attached to the component. For some tests, an additional vacuum gauge may be necessary.

HEATER

Heater Assembly

REMOVAL & INSTALLATION

CAUTION

When draining the coolant, keep in mind that cats and dogs are attracted by the ethylene glycol antifreeze, and are quite likely to drink any that is left in an uncovered container or in puddles on the ground. This will prove fatal in sufficient quantity. Always drain the coolant into a sealable container. Coolant should be reused unless it is contaminated or several years old.

1983–90 Pulsar

Since the air conditioning evaporator is located between the blower motor and the heater core, the heater core can be removed without disturbing the air conditioning evaporator.

1. Set the TEMP lever to the maximum HOT position and drain the engine coolant.
2. Disconnect the heater assembly hoses in the engine compartment.
3. Remove the instrument panel assembly as outlined in section 10.
4. Remove the heater control assembly.
5. Remove the heater unit assembly.

To Install:

6. Install the heater unit in the vehicle.
7. Install the control assembly and instrument panel as outlined in section 10.
8. Reconnect the heater hoses and refill the cooling system.
9. Start engine and check system for proper operation.

1982–86 Sentra

1. Disconnect the negative battery cable. Set "TEMP" lever to maximum "HOT" position and drain engine coolant.
2. Disconnect the heater hoses at the engine compartment.
3. Remove the instrument panel assembly as follows:
   a. Disconnect the choke control cable, harness connectors, hood latch control cable, speedometer cable, and radio aerial cable.
   b. Remove the two screws from the lower side of the instrument hood and remove it.
   c. Remove the two screws from the top of the instrument cluster, pull it out to disconnect the electrical connectors, and remove it.
   d. Slide the ash tray out and then unscrew and remove the ash tray slider bracket.
   e. Remove the radio knobs and bezel. Disconnect the antenna and power cable, remove the attaching bolts, and remove the radio.

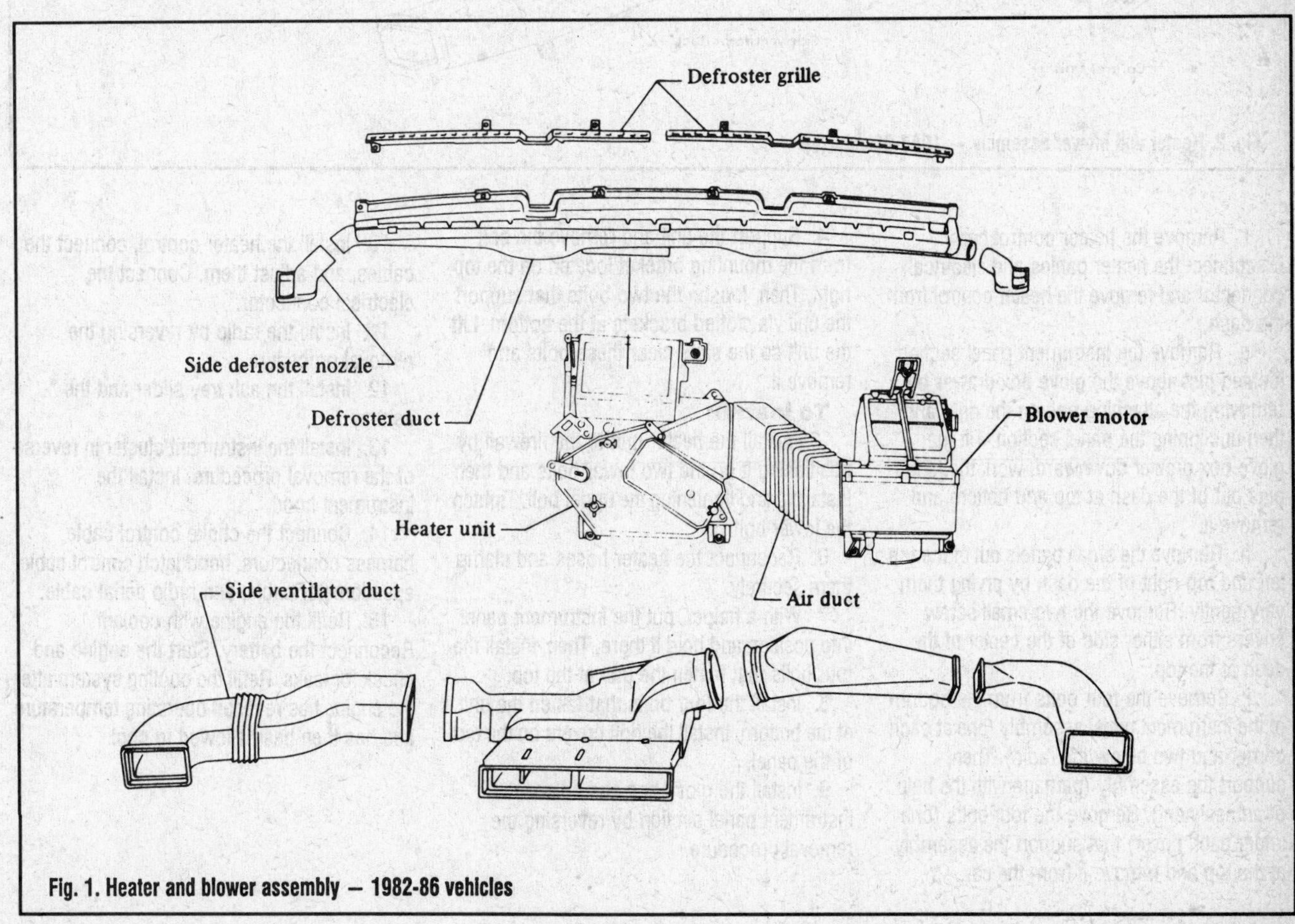
Defroster grille
Side defroster nozzle
Defroster duct
Blower motor
Heater unit
Side ventilator duct
Air duct

Fig. 1. Heater and blower assembly — 1982-86 vehicles

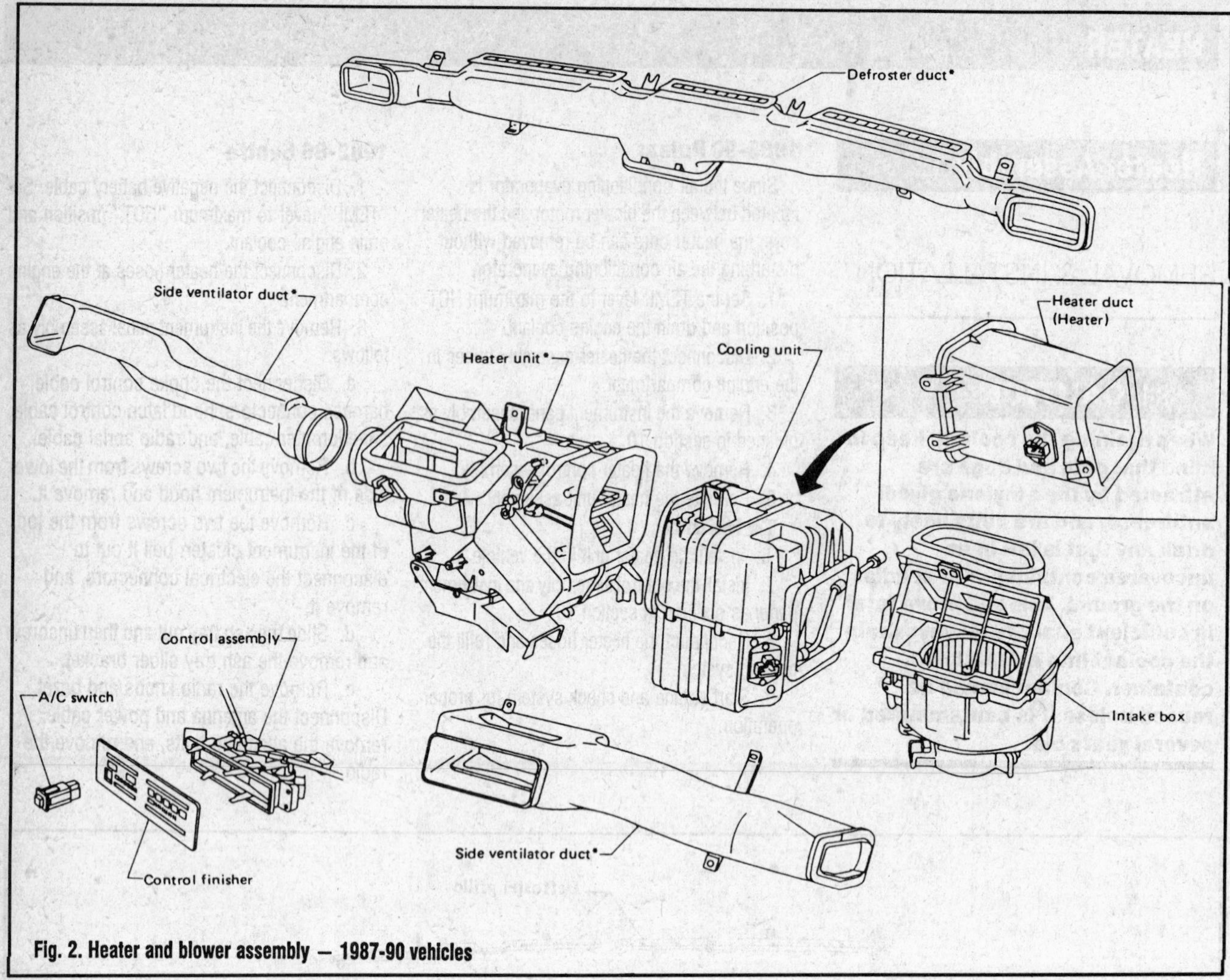
Defroster duct*
Heater duct
(Heater)
Side ventilator duct*
Heater unit*
Cooling unit
Control assembly
A/C switch
Intake box
Side ventilator duct*
Control finisher

Fig. 2. Heater and blower assembly — 1987-90 vehicles

f. Remove the heater control bezel. Disconnect the heater cables and electrical connector and remove the heater control from the dash.

g. Remove the instrument panel section located just above the glove box drawer by removing the attaching bolt on the right and then unclipping the panel section. Tilt the glove box drawer downward, work the hinge pins out of the dash at top and bottom and remove it.

h. Remove the small panels out of the top left and top right of the dash by prying them very gently. Remove the two small screw covers from either side of the center of the dash at the top.

i. Remove the four bolts from the bottom of the instrument panel assembly (one at each corner and two below the radio). Then, support the assembly (perhaps with the help of an assistant). Remove the four bolts (one under each cover) that support the assembly at the top and remove it from the car.

4. Support the unit and remove the bolt from the mounting bracket located on the top right. Then, loosen the two bolts that support the unit via slotted brackets at the bottom. Lift the unit so the slots clear these bolts and remove it.

To Install:

5. Install the heater unit to the firewall by positioning it on the two lower bolts and then installing and tightening the upper bolt. Tighten the lower bolt.

6. Reconnect the heater hoses and clamp them securely.

7. With a helper, put the instrument panel into position and hold it there. Then, install the four bolts that fasten the unit at the top.

8. Install the four bolts that fasten the unit at the bottom. Install the bolt covers on the top of the panel.

9. Install the glove box and adjacent instrument panel section by reversing the removal procedure.

10. Install the heater control, connect the cables, and adjust them. Connect the electrical connector.

11. Install the radio by reversing the removal procedure.

12. Install the ash tray slider and the ashtray.

13. Install the instrument cluster in reverse of the removal procedure. Install the instrument hood.

14. Connect the choke control cable, harness connectors, hood latch control cable, speedometer cable, and radio aerial cable.

15. Refill the engine with coolant. Reconnect the battery. Start the engine and check for leaks. Refill the cooling system after the engine has reached operating temperature and has then been allowed to cool.

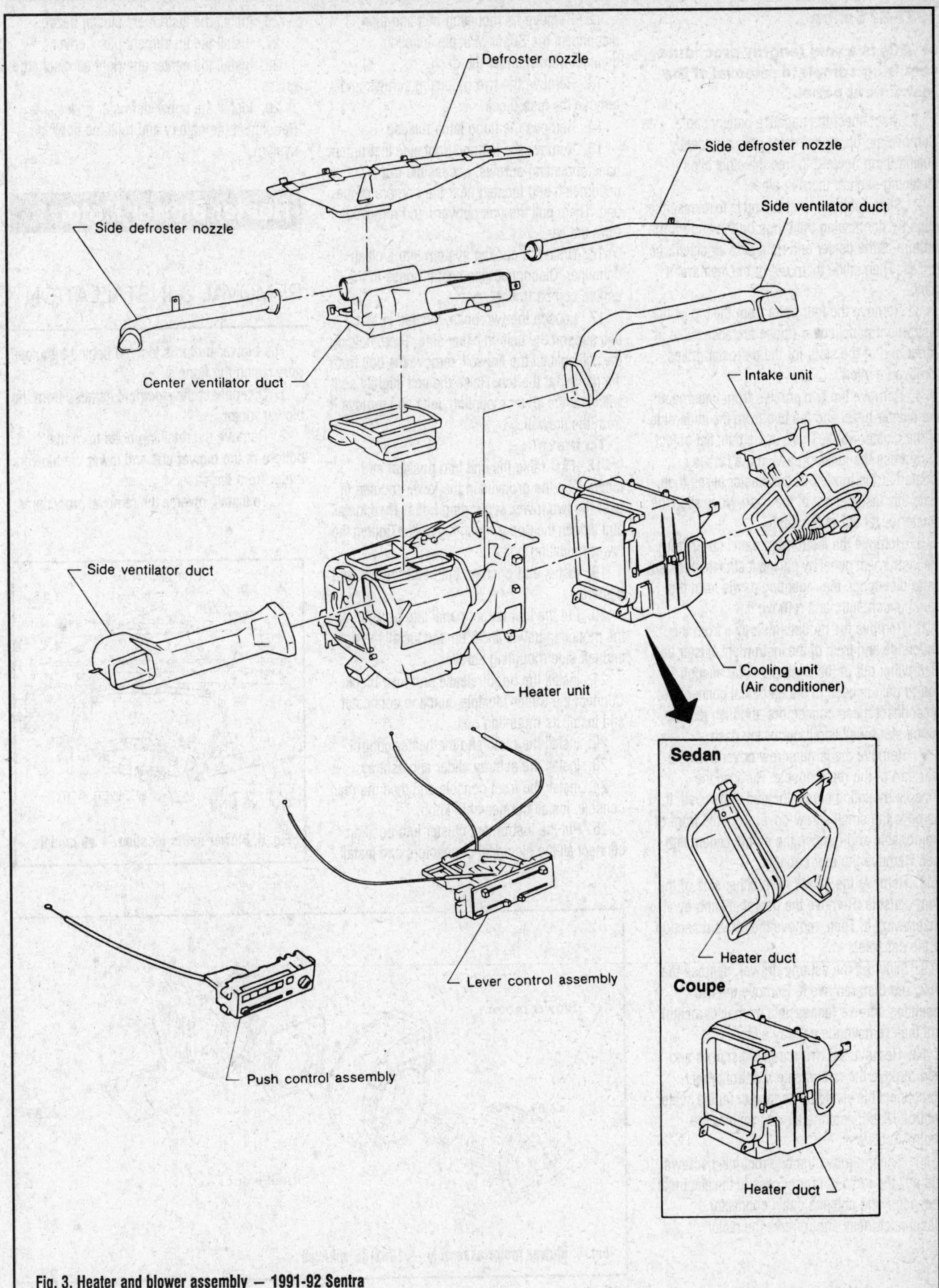
Defroster nozzle
Side defroster nozzle
Side ventilator duct
Side defroster nozzle
Center ventilator duct
Intake unit
Side ventilator duct
Cooling unit
(Air conditioner)
Heater unit
Sedan
Heater duct
Lever control assembly
Coupe
Push control assembly
Heater duct

Fig. 3. Heater and blower assembly — 1991-92 Sentra

1987-92 Sentra

➡ This is a very lengthy procedure, requiring complete removal of the instrument panel.

1. Disconnect the negative battery cable. Remove the upper defroster grilles by gently pulling them upward to free the eight clips fastening each of them in place.
2. Slide a thin, flat instrument in to release the clips by depressing the tangs on top and on the bottom of the center and right side air discharge grilles. Then, slide them out of the instrument panel.
3. Remove the four bolts from the top of the instrument panel cover (these are accessible at either end of the slots for the defroster grilles, removed earlier).
4. Remove the two screws from underneath the cluster bezel and the two from the underside of the cluster hood. Then, use a thin, flat object to depress the locking pawl in the fastener located at the top left of the cluster bezel; then, slide this fastener out of the dash. Now, slide the cluster bezel out of the dash.
5. Remove the instrument panel cover from the instrument panel by pulling it straight back so as to disengage the mounting pawls from the panel underneath, and remove it.
6. Remove the mounting screws from the underside and front of the instrument cluster and then pull it out of the dash panel far enough for you to gain access to the electrical connectors. Disconnect these connectors and then remove the cluster by sliding it out of the dash.
7. Remove the large screw cover from the rear part of the rear console. Remove the console mounting screw located underneath it. Remove the small screw cover from the front of the console and remove the screw underneath that. Remove the rear console.
8. Remove the screw from either side of the front console. Remove the gearshift knob by unscrewing it. Then, remove the forward section of the console.
9. Slide out the ashtray drawer, depress the lock, and then remove it. Remove the two mounting screws (accessible from underneath) and then remove the ashtray slider.
10. Remove the two mounting screws and then remove the radio/heater control bezel. Disconnect the electrical connector for the heater control. Disconnect the air door cables the control actuates.
11. Then, remove the two mounting screws and pull the radio out for access to the electrical connector and antenna cable connector. Disconnect these and remove the radio.
12. Remove its mounting bolt and then disconnect the Super Multiple Junction connector from under the dash.
13. Remove the two mounting screws and remove the fuse block.
14. Remove the hood latch release.
15. Remove the left and right side instrument panel mounting screws, accessible from underneath and located near the corners of the unit. Then, pull the unit outward and remove it from the car.
16. Drain the cooling system into a clean container. Disconnect the heater hoses in the engine compartment.
17. Loosen the two bolts, located in slots, that support the unit on either side. Then, holding the unit against the firewall, remove the bolt from the hanger at the top. Raise the unit slightly so it will clear the lower mounting bolts and remove it from the firewall.

To install:

18. First raise the unit into position and locate it so the grooves in the lower mounts fit over the two lower supporting bolts. Then install and tighten the upper mounting bolts. Tighten the lower mounting bolts.
19. Install and connect the heater hoses and clamps.
20. Put the instrument panel into position so the mounting pawls line it up and install the right and left side mounting screws.
21. Install the hood release and fuse block. Connect the Super Multiple Junction connector and install its mounting bolt.
22. Install the radio and the heater control.
23. Install the ashtray slider and ashtray.
24. Install the front console and then the rear console. Install the gearshift knob.
25. Put the instrument cluster into position, connect all the electrical connectors and install it.
26. Install the instrument cluster bezel.
27. Install the instrument panel cover.
28. Install the center and right air discharge grilles.
29. Install the upper defroster grilles. Reconnect the battery and refill the cooling system.

Heater Blower Motor

REMOVAL & INSTALLATION

The blower motor is located behind the glove box, facing the floor.

1. Disconnect the electrical harness from the blower motor.
2. Remove the retaining bolts from the bottom of the blower unit and lower the blower motor from the case.
3. To install, reverse the removal procedures.

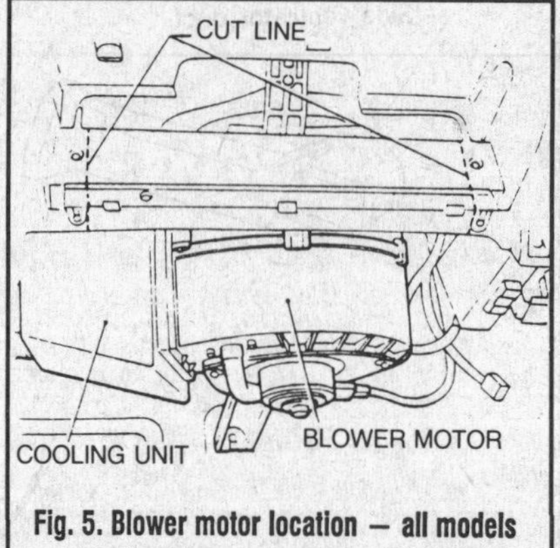
CUT LINE
COOLING UNIT
BLOWER MOTOR
Fig. 5. Blower motor location — all models

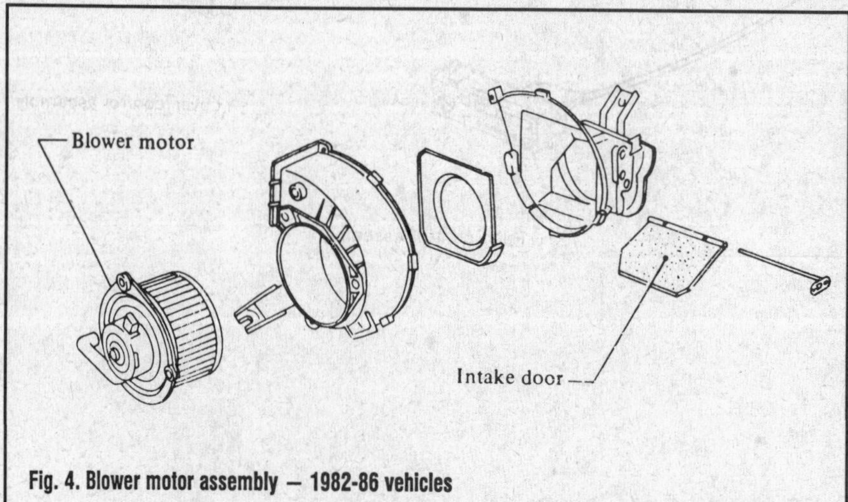
Blower motor
Intake door
Fig. 4. Blower motor assembly — 1982-86 vehicles

Heater Core

REMOVAL & INSTALLATION

1. Refer to the Heater Assembly, Removal and Installation procedures, in the section and remove the heater assembly from the vehicle.
2. Remove the heater assembly case bolts and separate the cases, then pull the heater core from the case.
3. To install, reverse the removal procedures. Refill the cooling system.

Heater Control Head

REMOVAL & INSTALLATION

Except 1991–92 Sentra

1. Disconnect the negative battery cable.
2. Remove control cables by unfastening clamps at door levers.
3. Remove the center finish panel screws and pull bezel out. Later models also have metal retaining clips. Refer to the "instrument panel" in section 10.
4. Disconnect electrical connector and remove heater control head assembly mounting bolts. Remove ground wire from intake box, if so equipped.
5. Remove heater control head assembly.

To install:

6. Install the heater control and reconnect the control cables and electrical connectors.
7. Install the center finish panel and check operation.

1991–92 Sentra

1. Disconnect the negative battery cable.
2. Remove the center trim panel and shift cover.
3. Disconnect the temperature control cable at the heater unit side.

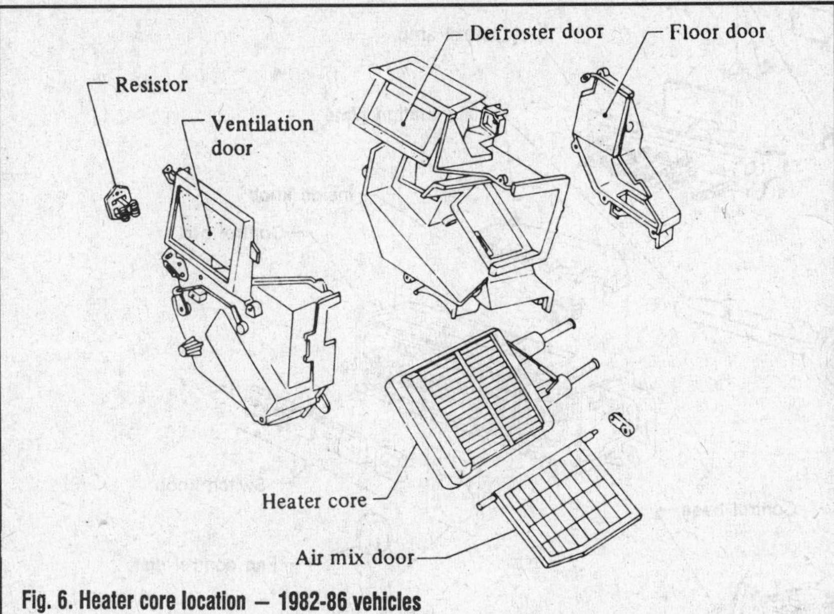
Defroster door
Floor door
Resistor
Ventilation door
Heater core
Air mix door

Fig. 6. Heater core location — 1982-86 vehicles

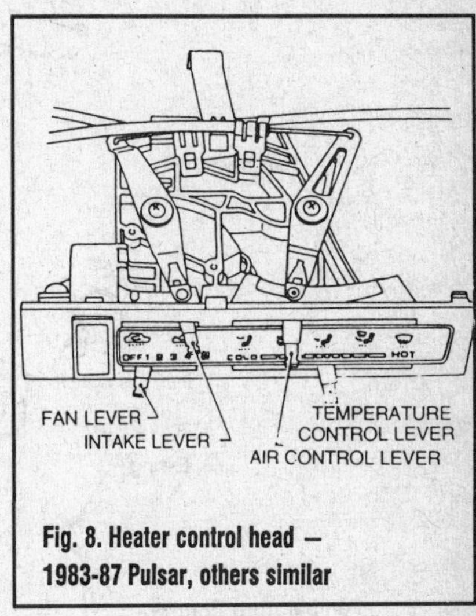
OFF 1 2 3 4
COLD
HOT
FAN LEVER
INTAKE LEVER
TEMPERATURE CONTROL LEVER
AIR CONTROL LEVER

Fig. 8. Heater control head — 1983-87 Pulsar, others similar

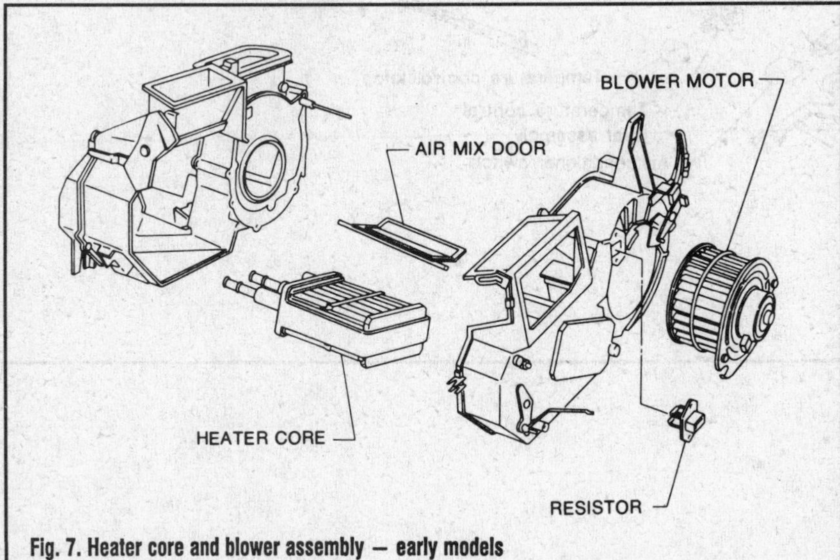
BLOWER MOTOR
AIR MIX DOOR
HEATER CORE
RESISTOR

Fig. 7. Heater core and blower assembly — early models

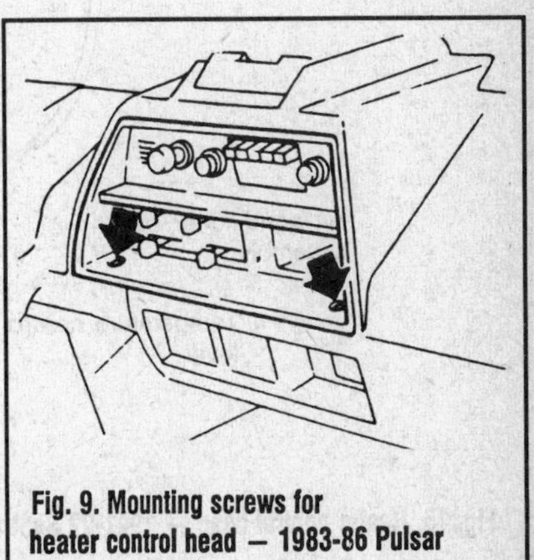

Fig. 9. Mounting screws for heater control head — 1983-86 Pulsar

4. Disconnect the fresh vent control cable at the heater unit side.
5. Remove the 6 bracket screws.
6. Pull the control assembly out and disconnect control harness and remove.

To install:

7. Install the control assembly and reconnect the harnesses.
8. Disconnect all cables and harnesses.
9. Adjust the temperature control cable by moving the control lever to MAX. hot and set the air door in the full hot mode. Pull the outer cable until all slack is taken out. Test the operation before going further.
10. Install the trim panel and shift cover.
11. Connect the battery cable and check operation.

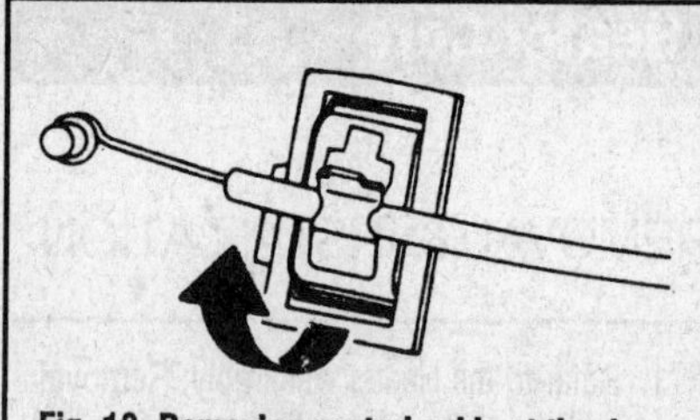

Fig. 10. Removing control cable at the door levers

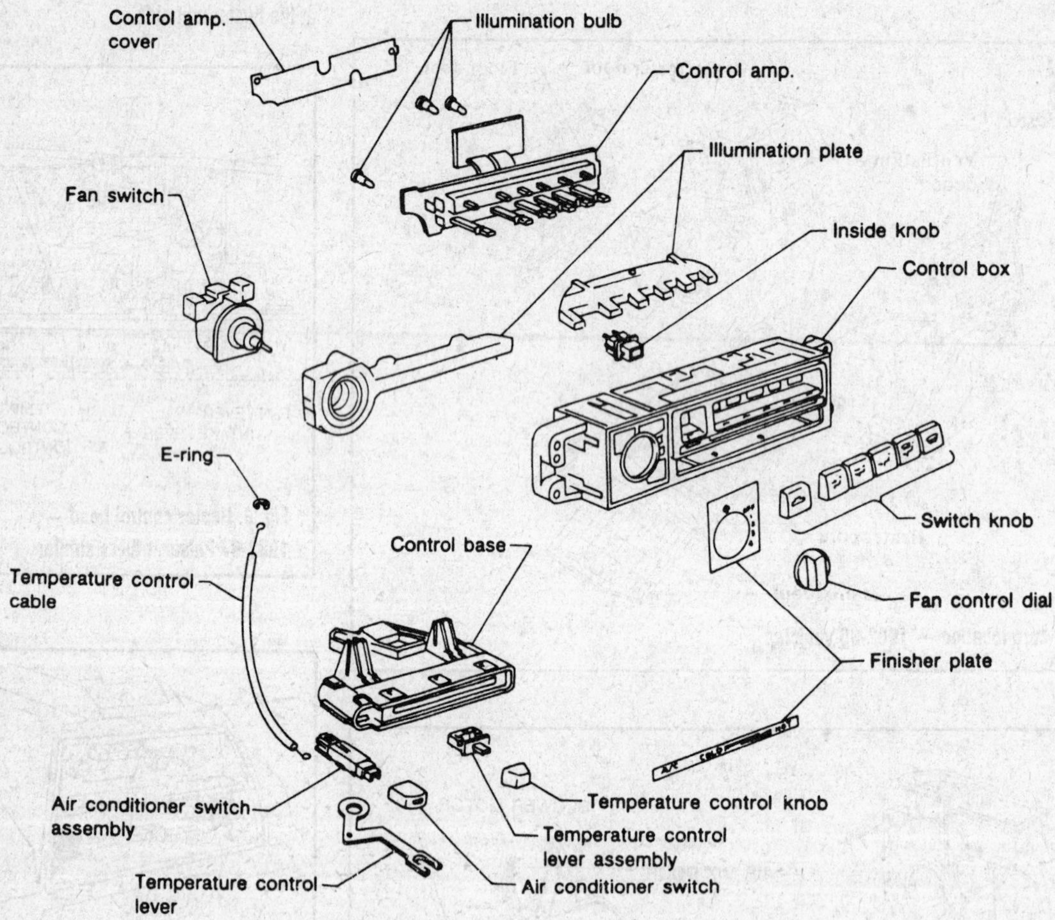

Control amp. cover
Illumination bulb
Control amp.
Illumination plate
Fan switch
Inside knob
Control box
E-ring
Switch knob
Control base
Temperature control cable
Fan control dial
Finisher plate
Temperature control knob
Air conditioner switch assembly
Temperature control lever assembly
Temperature control lever
Air conditioner switch

Fig. 16. Heater control head — 1991-92 Sentra

AIR CONDITIONER

➧ SEE FIGS. 17–22

Refer to section 1 for discharging, etc. of the air conditioning system

Special Precautions

1. All refrigerant service work must be done with the proper recycling equipment. Carefully follow the manufacturer's instructions for use of that equipment. Do not allow the freon to discharge to the air.

2. Any amount of water will make the system less effective. When any part of the system has been removed, plug or cap the lines to prevent moisture from the air entering the system. When installing a new component, do not uncap the fittings until ready to attach the lines.

3. When assembling a fitting, always use a new O-ring and lightly lubricate the fitting with compressor oil.

4. When a compressor is removed, do not leave it on its side or upside down for more than 10 minutes. The oil may leak into the low pressure chamber.

5. The proper amount of oil must be maintained in the system to prevent compressor damage and to maintain system efficiency. Be sure to measure and adjust the amount of oil removed or added to the system, especially when replacing the compressor.

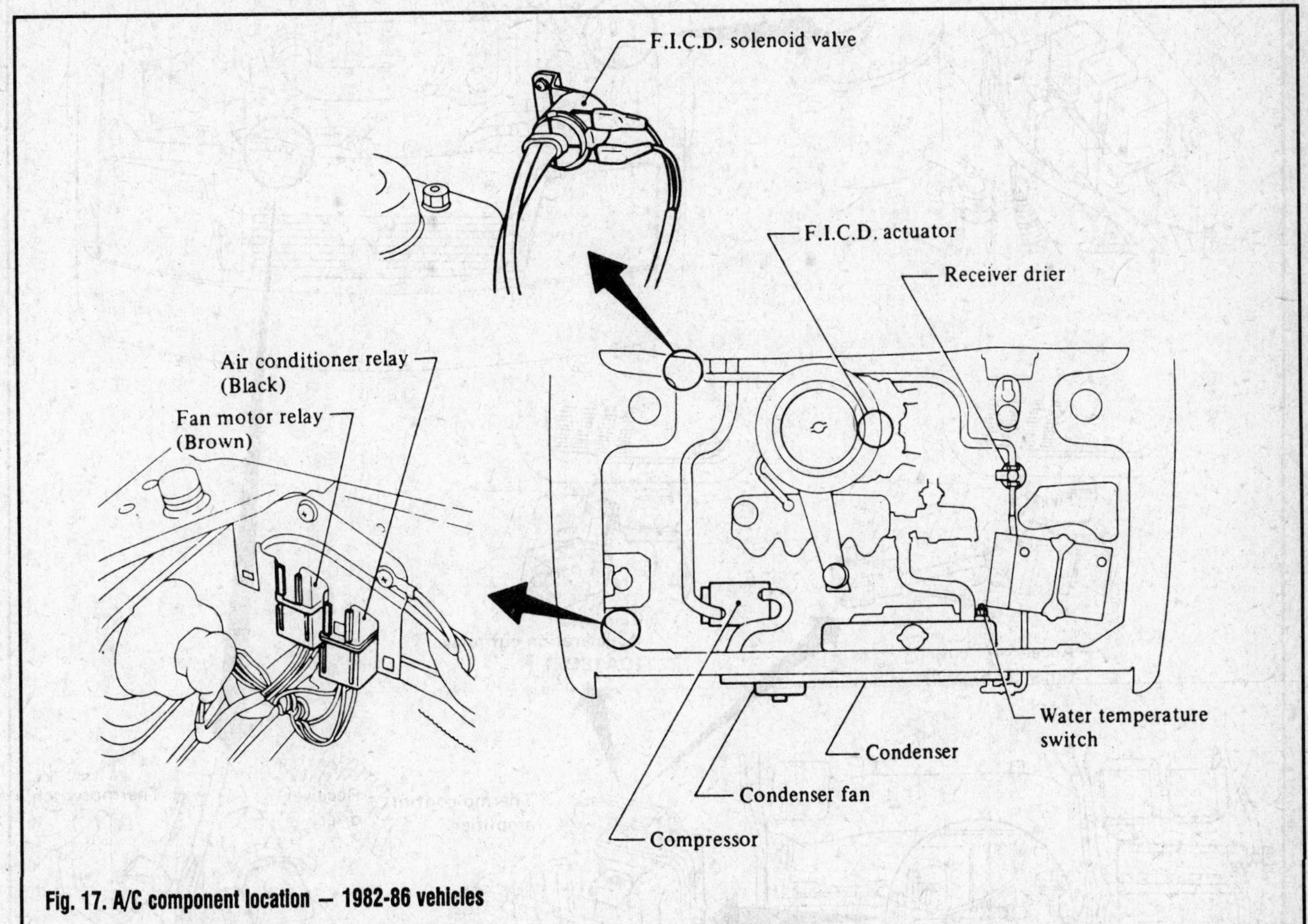
F.I.C.D. solenoid valve
F.I.C.D. actuator
Receiver drier
Air conditioner relay
(Black)
Fan motor relay
(Brown)
Water temperature
switch
Condenser
Condenser fan
Compressor

Fig. 17. A/C component location — 1982-86 vehicles

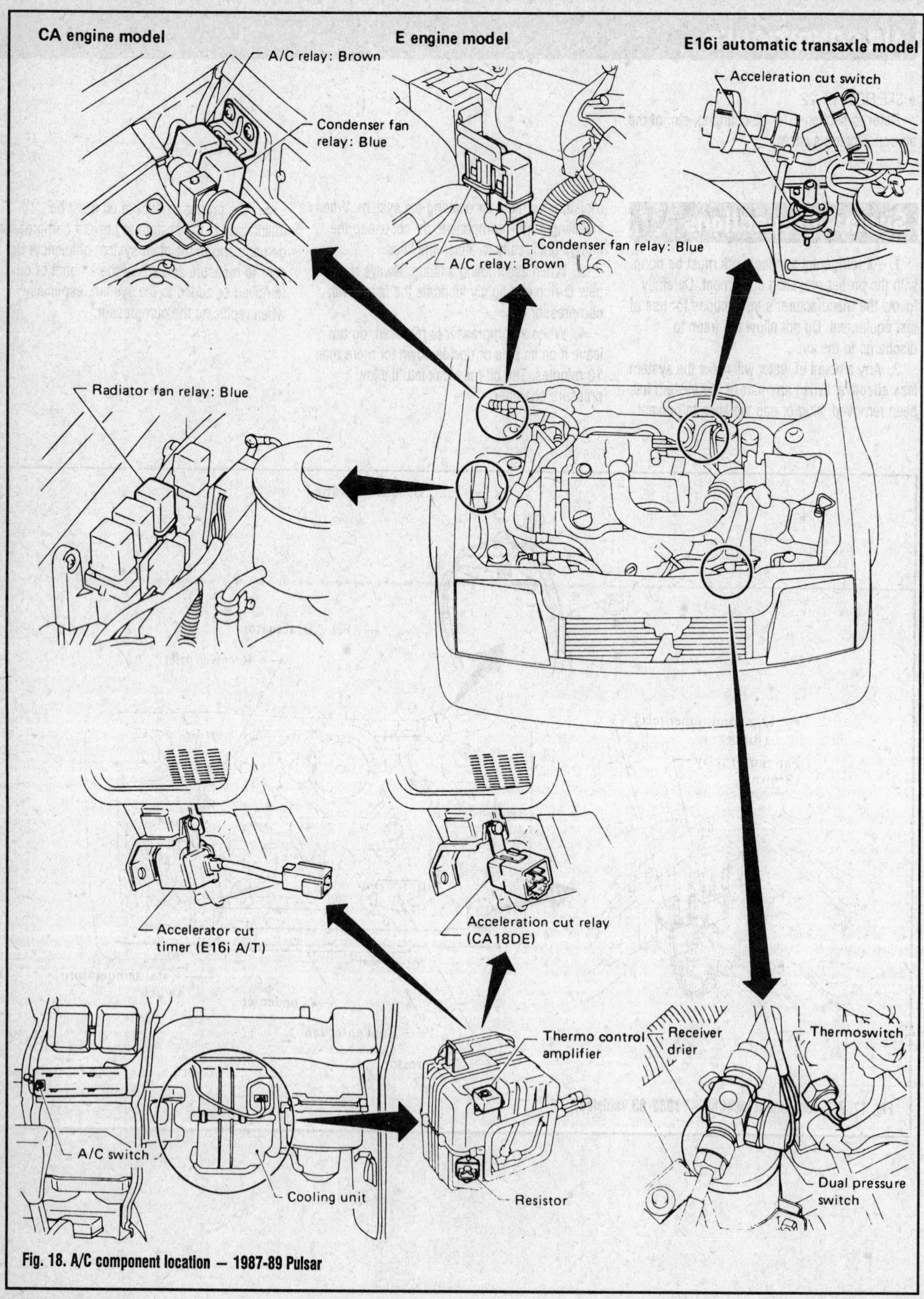
CA engine model
A/C relay: Brown
Condenser fan relay: Blue
E engine model
Condenser fan relay: Blue
A/C relay: Brown
E16i automatic transaxle model
Acceleration cut switch
Radiator fan relay: Blue
Accelerator cut timer (E16i A/T)
Acceleration cut relay (CA18DE)
Thermo control amplifier
Receiver drier
Thermoswitch
A/C switch
Cooling unit
Resistor
Dual pressure switch

Fig. 18. A/C component location — 1987-89 Pulsar

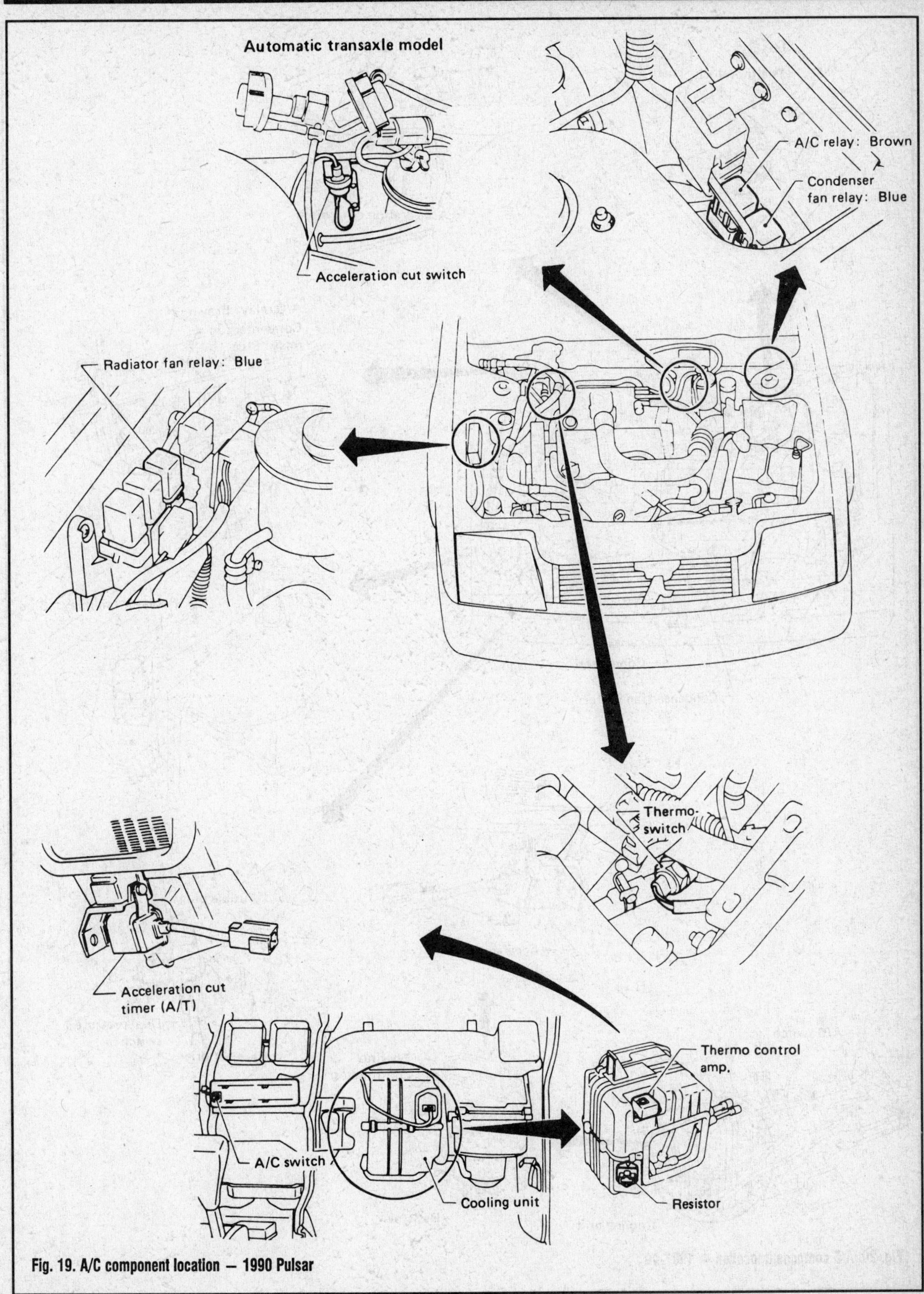
Automatic transaxle model
A/C relay: Brown
Condenser
fan relay: Blue
Acceleration cut switch
Radiator fan relay: Blue
Thermo-
switch
Acceleration cut
timer (A/T)
Thermo control
amp.
A/C switch
Cooling unit
Resistor

Fig. 19. A/C component location — 1990 Pulsar

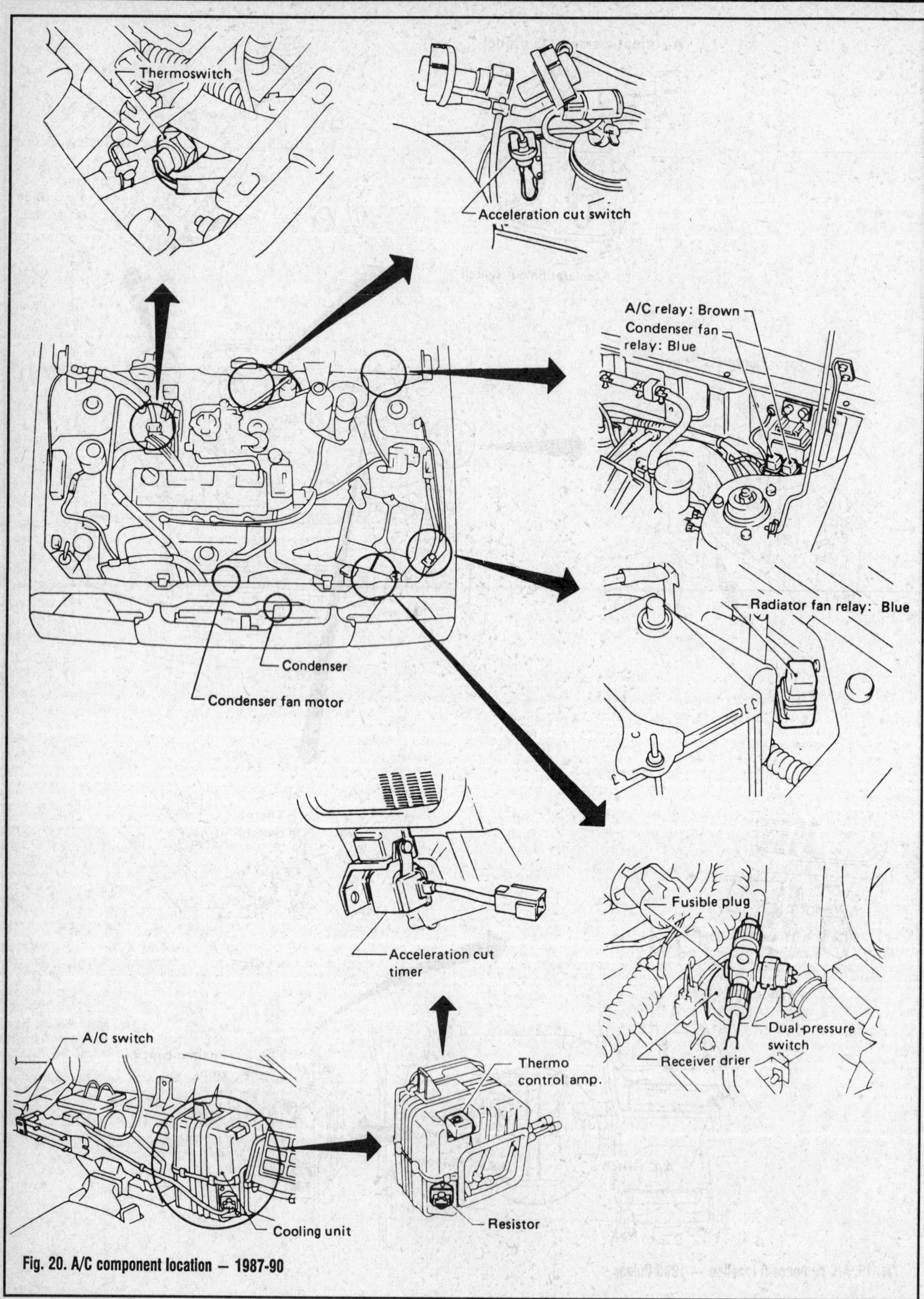
Thermoswitch
Acceleration cut switch
A/C relay: Brown
Condenser fan relay: Blue
Radiator fan relay: Blue
Condenser
Condenser fan motor
Fusible plug
Acceleration cut timer
Dual-pressure switch
Receiver drier
A/C switch
Thermo control amp.
Cooling unit
Resistor

Fig. 20. A/C component location — 1987-90

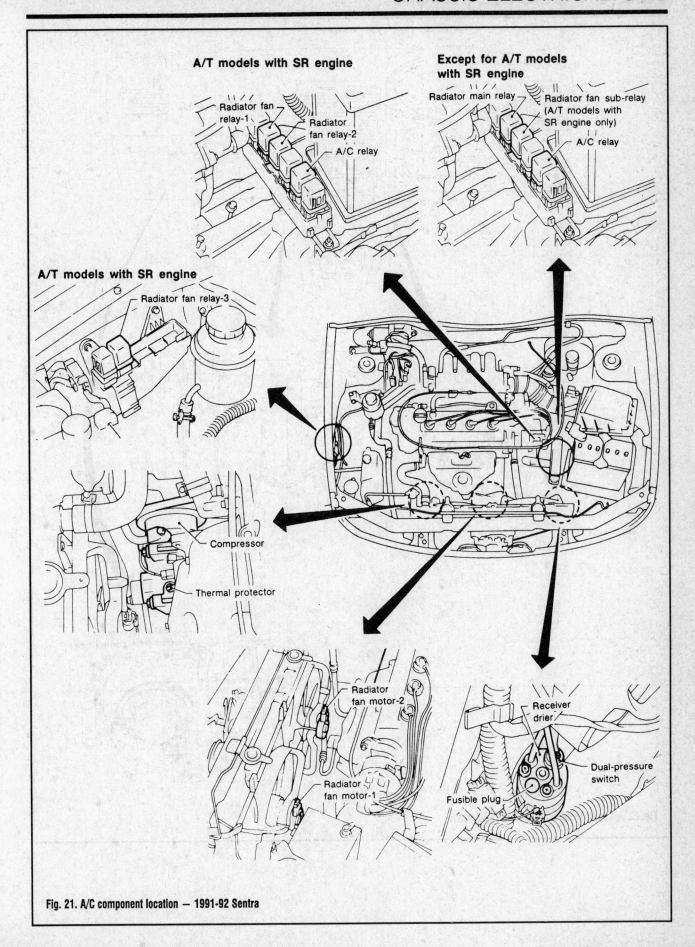

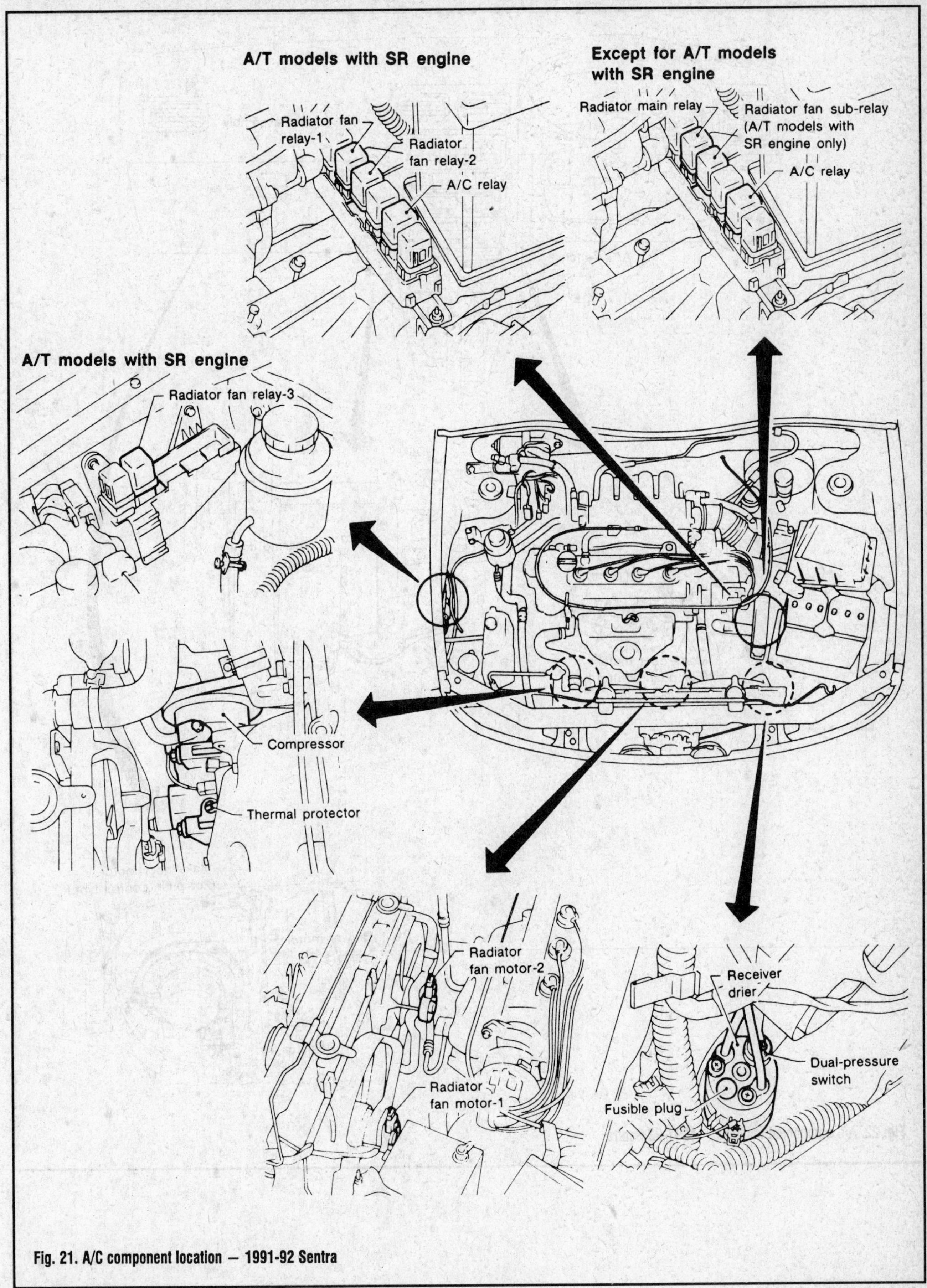
A/T models with SR engine
Radiator fan relay-1
Radiator fan relay-2
A/C relay
Except for A/T models with SR engine
Radiator main relay
Radiator fan sub-relay (A/T models with SR engine only)
A/C relay
A/T models with SR engine
Radiator fan relay-3
Compressor
Thermal protector
Radiator fan motor-2
Radiator fan motor-1
Receiver drier
Dual-pressure switch
Fusible plug

Fig. 21. A/C component location — 1991-92 Sentra

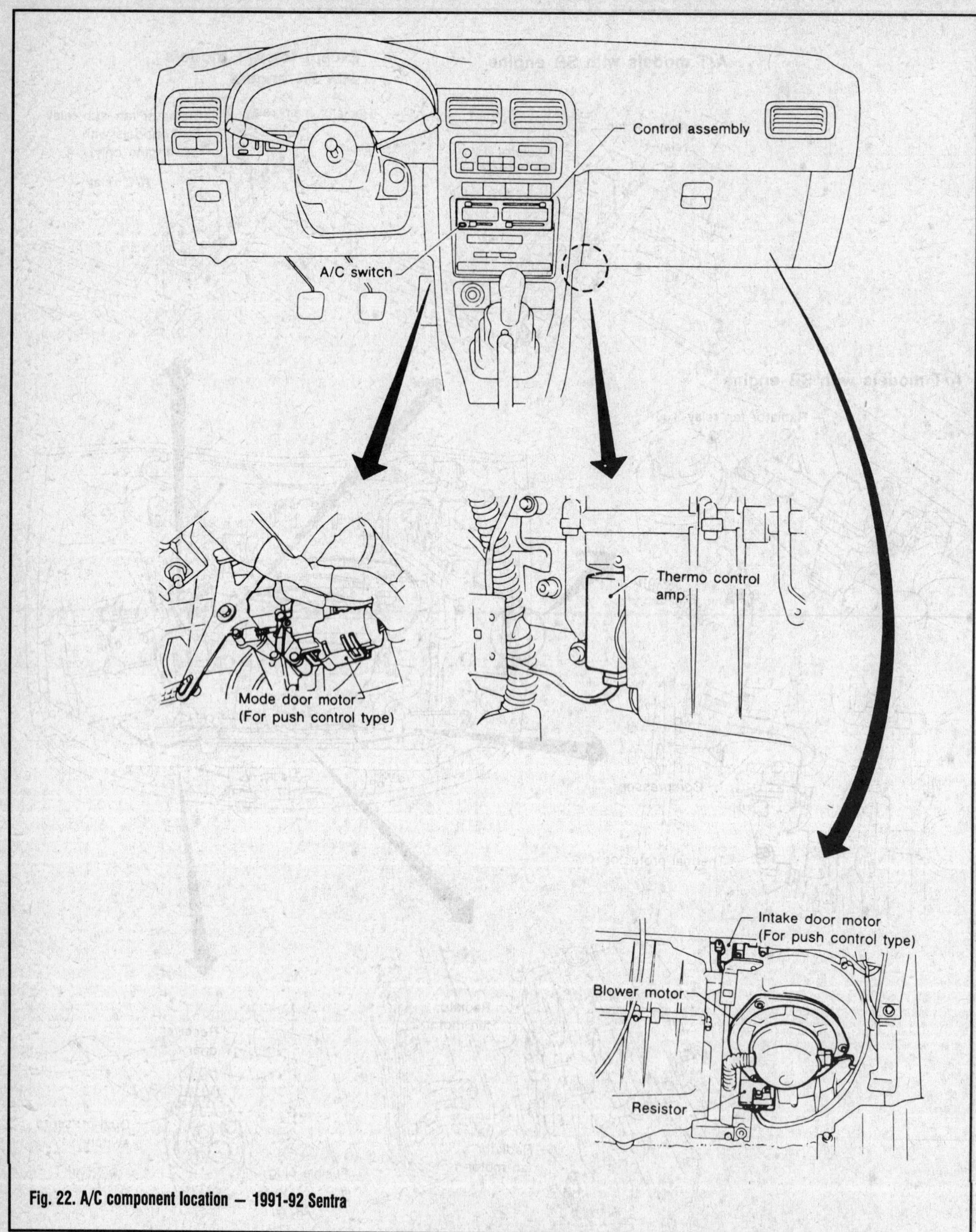
Control assembly
A/C switch
Thermo control amp.
Mode door motor (For push control type)
Intake door motor (For push control type)
Blower motor
Resistor

Fig. 22. A/C component location – 1991-92 Sentra

Air Conditioning Compressor

REMOVAL & INSTALLATION

All Models

✱✱ CAUTION

The compressed refrigerant used in the air conditioning system expands into the atmosphere at a temperature of -2°F or lower. This will freeze any surface, including your eyes, that it contacts. In addition, the refrigerant decomposes into a poisonous gas in the presence of a flame. Do not open or disconnect any part of the air conditioning system until you have read the SAFETY WARNINGS section in Section 1.

1. Disconnect the negative battery cables.
2. Remove all the necessary equipment in order to gain access to the compressor mounting bolts.
3. Remove the compressor drive belt.

➡ To facilitate removal of the compressor belt, remove the idler pulley and bracket as an assembly beforehand from the underside of the car.

4. Discharge the air conditioning system.
5. Disconnect and plug the refrigerant lines with a clean shop towel.

➡ Be sure to use 2 wrenches (one to loosen fitting — one to hold fitting in place) when disconnecting the refrigerant lines.

6. Disconnect and tag all electrical connections.
7. Remove the compressor mounting bolts. Remove the compressor from the vehicle.

To install:

8. Install the compressor on the engine and evenly torque all the mounting bolts the same.
9. Connect all the electrical connections and unplug and reconnect all refrigerant lines.
10. Install all the necessary equipment in order to gain access to the compressor mounting bolts.
11. Install and adjust the drive belt.
12. Connect the negative battery cable.
13. Evacuate and charge the system as required. Make sure the oil level is correct for the compressor.

➡ Do not attempt to the leave the compressor on its side or upside down for more than a couple minutes, as the oil in the compressor will enter the low pressure chambers. Be sure to always replace the O-rings.

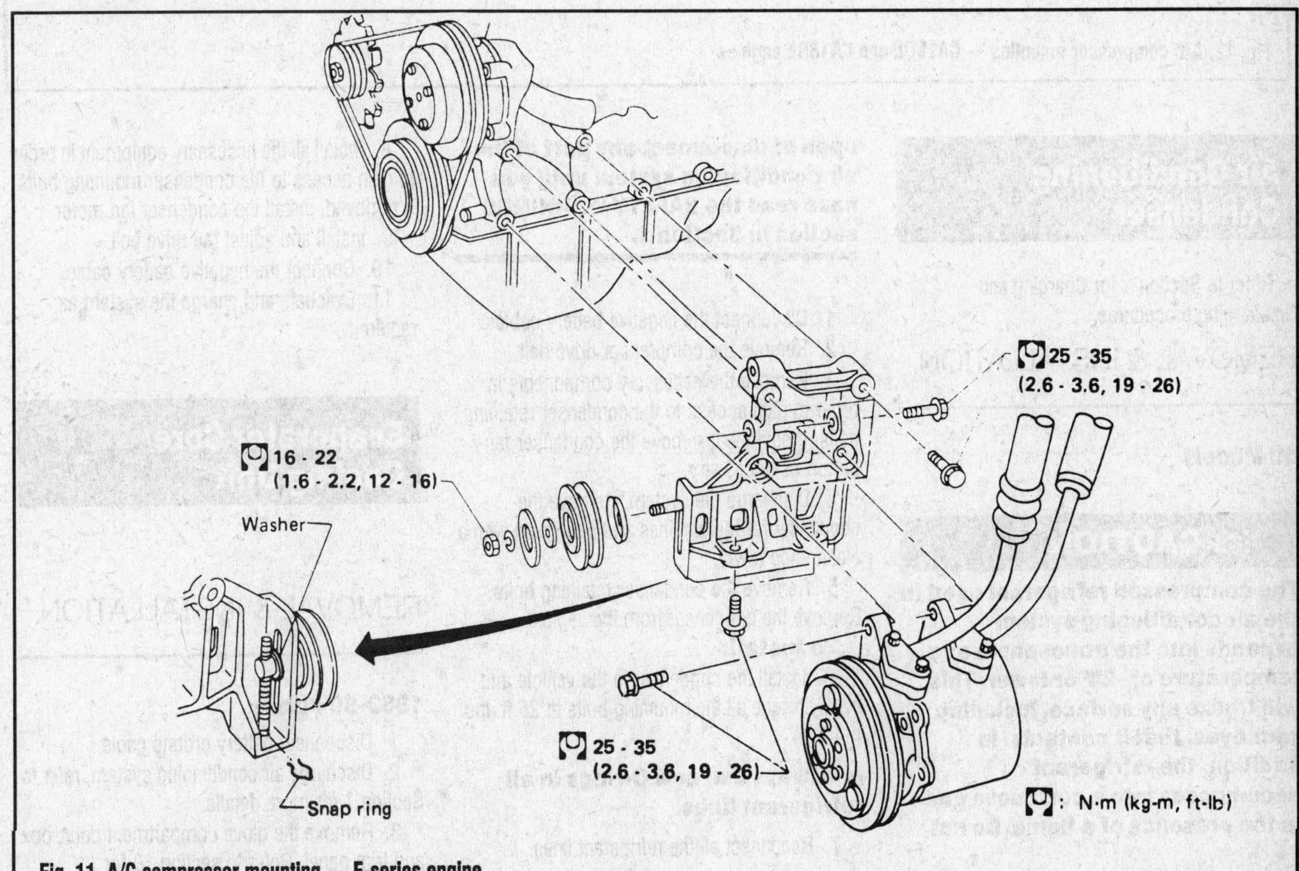
25 - 35
(2.6 - 3.6, 19 - 26)
16 - 22
(1.6 - 2.2, 12 - 16)
Washer
Snap ring
25 - 35
(2.6 - 3.6, 19 - 26)
: N·m (kg-m, ft-lb)

Fig. 11. A/C compressor mounting — E-series engine

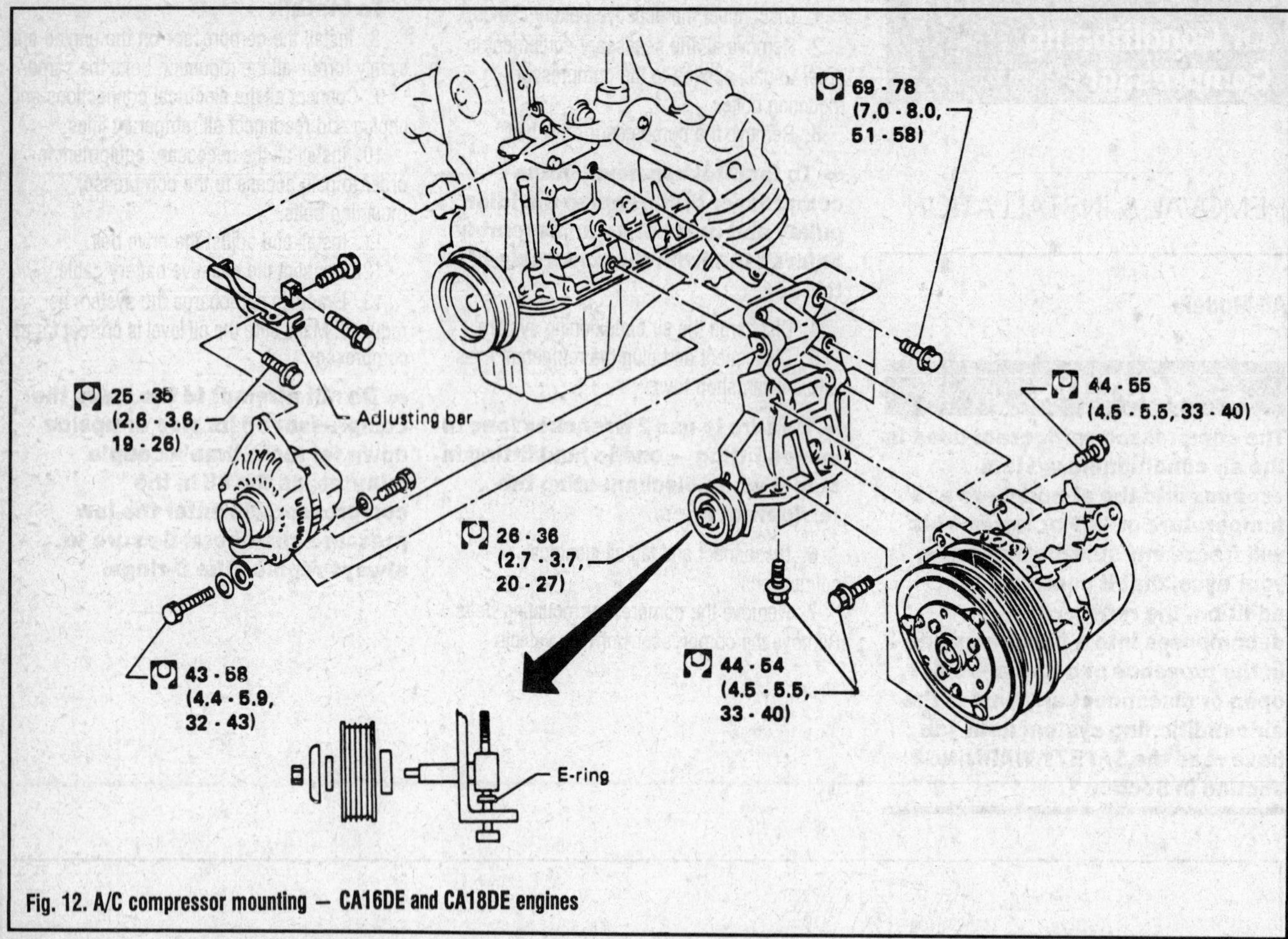
69 - 78
(7.0 - 8.0,
51 - 58)
44 - 55
(4.5 - 5.5, 33 - 40)
25 - 35
(2.6 - 3.6,
19 - 26)
Adjusting bar
26 - 36
(2.7 - 3.7,
20 - 27)
44 - 54
(4.5 - 5.5,
33 - 40)
43 - 58
(4.4 - 5.9,
32 - 43)
E-ring
Fig. 12. A/C compressor mounting — CA16DE and CA18DE engines

Air Conditioning Condenser

Refer to Section 1 for Charging and Discharging procedures.

REMOVAL & INSTALLATION

All Models

CAUTION

The compressed refrigerant used in the air conditioning system expands into the atmosphere at a temperature of -2°F or lower. This will freeze any surface, including your eyes, that it contacts. In addition, the refrigerant decomposes into a poisonous gas in the presence of a flame. Do not open or disconnect any part of the air conditioning system until you have read the SAFETY WARNINGS section in Section 1.

1. Disconnect the negative battery cables.
2. Remove the compressor drive belt.
3. Remove the necessary components in order to gain access to the condenser retaining bolts. If equipped, remove the condenser fan motor, as necessary.
4. Discharge the system. Remove the condenser refrigerant lines and plug them with a clean shop towel.
5. Remove the condenser retaining bolts. Remove the condenser from the vehicle.

To install:

6. Install the condenser in the vehicle and evenly torque all the mounting bolts to 25 ft. lbs. (34 Nm).

➡ Always use new O-rings in all refrigerant lines.

7. Reconnect all the refrigerant lines.
8. Install all the necessary equipment in order to gain access to the condenser mounting bolts. If removed, install the condenser fan motor.
9. Install and adjust the drive belt.
10. Connect the negative battery cable.
11. Evacuate and charge the system as required.

Evaporator Core/ Cooling Unit

REMOVAL & INSTALLATION

1983–90 Pulsar

1. Disconnect battery ground cable.
2. Discharge air conditioning system, refer to Section 1 for more details.
3. Remove the glove compartment door, box and trim panel. Refer to section 10 for instrument panel procedures.

4. Disconnect all electrical connectors from cooling unit. Disconnect the air conditioning pipes from the evaporator housing using a backup wrench.

➡ **For vehicles with factory installed air conditioning, cut instrument panel and discard. Before cutting, cover blower motor vent holes with tape. After cutting, brush shavings away from the area around blower motor and remove tape. This procedure may not be necessary on 1987-92 vehicles. check the clearance before cutting the instrument panel support.**

4. Remove cooling unit fixing bolts.
5. Remove cooling unit from vehicle.

To install:

6. Install the cooling unit and mounting bolts in the vehicle.
7. Connect all electrical connectors to the cooling unit.
8. Connect battery cable and charge the air conditioning system.
9. Check system for proper operation.

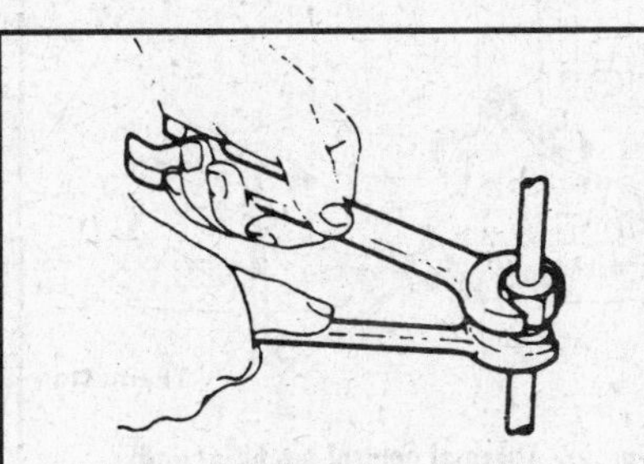

Fig. 13. Using 2 wrenches to remove or install A/C fittings

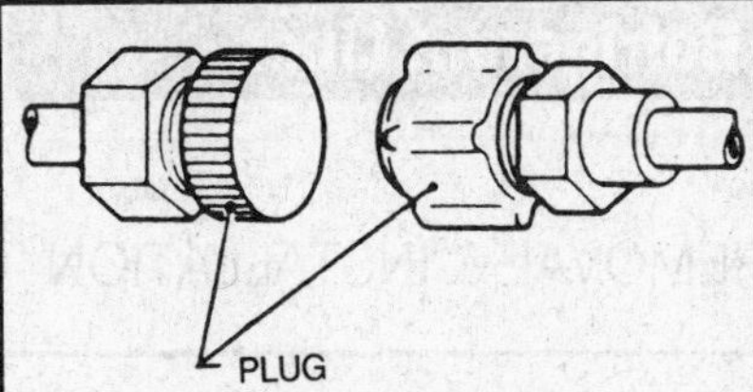
PLUG

Fig. 14. Always plug A/C lines after disconnecting to prevent moisture from entering the system

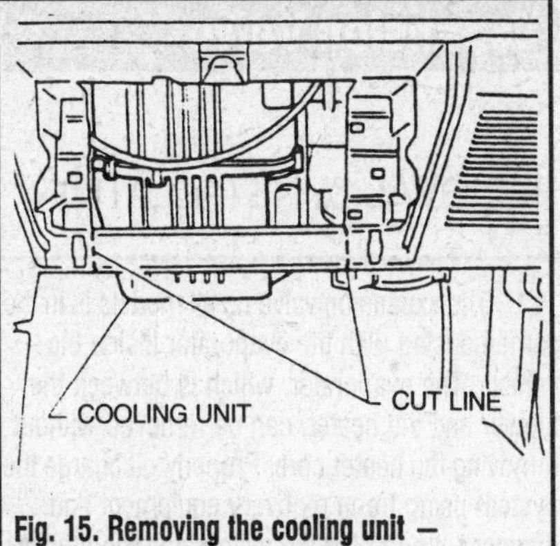
COOLING UNIT
CUT LINE

Fig. 15. Removing the cooling unit — 1983-90 Pulsar, Sentra similar

1982-86 Sentra

1. Discharge the refrigerant from the system as described in Section 1. Disconnect the battery ground cable.
2. Using a backup wrench, disconnect the refrigerant lines running to the evaporator on the engine compartment side of the firewall. Immediately tape or cap the openings. Remove the piping grommet and cover.
3. Remove the lower instrument panel cover from the passenger's side of the dash panel. Remove the glove box.
4. Cover the blower motor vent holes with tape. Then, cut out the section of the lower instrument panel brace between two bolt holes that will block removal of the blower and evaporator.
5. Clean all shavings away from the blower motor. Remove the blower motor. Remove the tape covering the blower motor cooling holes. Disconnect the electrical connector for the thermostat.
6. Unbolt the evaporator case from the firewall and remove it.
7. Cut the seals where upper and lower halves of the case fit together, using a knife. Then, remove the clips fastening the case halves together and separate the case halves.

To install:

8. Remove the evaporator coil. Install the evaporator back into the case and assemble it in reverse of disassembly. Use a sealer at the joints formed by cutting the seal earlier.
9. Begin installing the unit by guiding the tubes through the firewall. Then, situate it against the firewall with the bolt holes in the brackets and firewall lined up. Install and tighten the mounting bolts.
10. Connect the electrical connectors for the thermostat.
11. Install the blower motor.

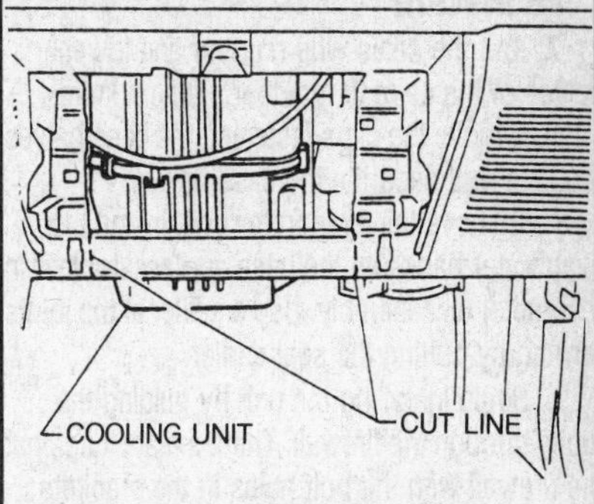
COOLING UNIT
CUT LINE

Fig. 23. If there is not enough clearance, cut out the section of instrument panel between the 2 lines using a hacksaw — all models

12. Install a replacement plate for the dash panel.
13. Install the glove box and lower instrument panel pad. Remove tape or plugs, coat the sealing surfaces of the flare fittings with clean refrigerant oil and tighten both, using a backup wrench.
14. Have the refrigerant system evacuated with a vacuum pump. Reconnect the battery. Have the system charged, or charge it with refrigerant yourself as described in Section 1. Check the system for proper operation and for leaks.

1987-92 Sentra

1. Discharge the refrigerant from the system as described in Section 1. Disconnect the battery ground cable.
2. Using a backup wrench, disconnect the refrigerant lines running to the evaporator on the engine compartment side of the firewall. Immediately tape or cap the openings. Remove the piping grommet and cover.
3. Remove the lower instrument panel cover from the passenger's side of the dash panel. Remove the glove box.
4. Cut out the section of the lower instrument panel brace located between the two marks in the illustration that will block removal of the evaporator.

➡ **This procedure may not have to be performed on the 1991-92 Sentra. Check the clearance between the instrument panel brace and evaporator housing before cutting.**

5. Disconnect the electrical connector for the thermostat.
6. Unbolt the evaporator case from the firewall and remove it.

To install:

7. Cut the seals where upper and lower halves of the case fit together, using a knife. Then, remove the clips fastening the case halves together and separate the case halves.

8. Remove the evaporator coil. Install the evaporator back into the case and assemble it in reverse of disassembly. Use a sealer at the joints formed by cutting the seal earlier.

9. Begin installing the unit by guiding the tubes through the firewall. Then, situate it against the firewall with the bolt holes in the brackets and firewall lined up. Install and tighten the mounting bolts.

10. Connect the electrical connectors for the thermostat.

11. Install the glove box and lower instrument panel pad. Remove tape or plugs, coat the sealing surfaces of the flare fittings with clean refrigerant oil and tighten both, using a backup wrench.

12. Have the refrigerant system evacuated with a vacuum pump. Reconnect the battery. Have the system charged, or charge it with refrigerant yourself as described in Section 1. Check the system for proper operation and for leaks.

Receiver/Drier

REMOVAL & INSTALLATION

The receiver/drier is a round soup can looking unit. It is located next to the condenser. The receiver/drier removes moisture from the air conditioning system. If the system has been exposed to atmosphere for a period of time, replace the receiver/drier. The unit will only hold a specific amount of moisture.

The receiver/drier is equipped with a fusible plug located at the top of the assembly. The plug will melt at 221°F (105°C), discharging the refrigerant to atmosphere. If the plug is melted or opened, check for an overheating condition and replace the receiver/drier.

1. On all models, the receiver/drier is on or near the condenser. Properly discharge the system into freon recovery equipment.

2. Disconnect the pressure switch.

3. Disconnect the freon lines and cap them to prevent moisture from entering the system.

4. Unbolt and remove the receiver/drier.

5. Installation is the reverse of removal. Be sure to use new O-rings and gaskets. Always evacuate, recharge and leak test as outlined in section 1.

Expansion Valve

REMOVAL & INSTALLATION

1. The expansion valve on all models is in the same housing with the evaporator inside the vehicle. The evaporator, which is between the blower and the heater, can be removed without removing the heater core. Properly discharge the system using freon recovery equipment and disconnect and plug the evaporator line fittings at the firewall.

2. The blower motor and its' housing must be removed first. Removing the glove compartment makes this easier. On some vehicles, the expansion valve can be accessed once the blower housing is removed.

3. It may be necessary to cut a section from the dash board behind the glove compartment to remove the evaporator. This piece cannot be reinstalled.

4. Installation is the reverse of removal. Make sure the seals between the housings are in good condition, replace as necessary. Always use new O-rings on the freon line fittings.

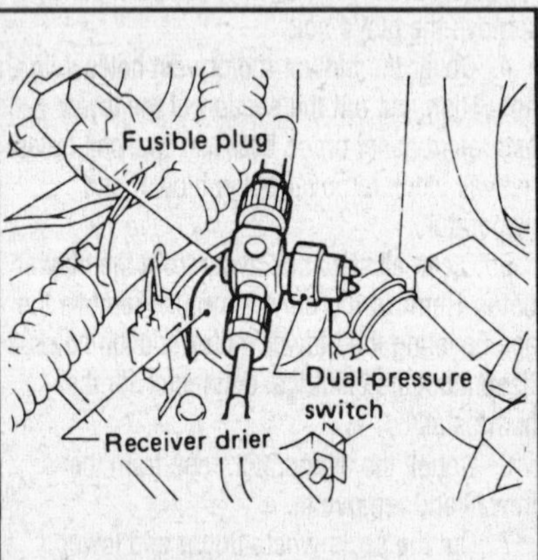
Fusible plug
Dual-pressure switch
Receiver drier

Fig. 24. Receiver/drier assembly — all models

Thermal Control Amplifier and Thermistor

The compressor cycles ON and OFF to maintain the evaporator temperature within a specified range. When the evaporator temperature falls below the specified temperature, the thermal control amplifier interrupts the compressor operation. When the temperature rises, the amplifier turn the compressor ON.

REMOVAL & INSTALLATION

Automatic Temperature Control

Remove the screws securing the thermistor retainer at the front of the cooling unit. The cooling unit does not have to be removed for these procedures.

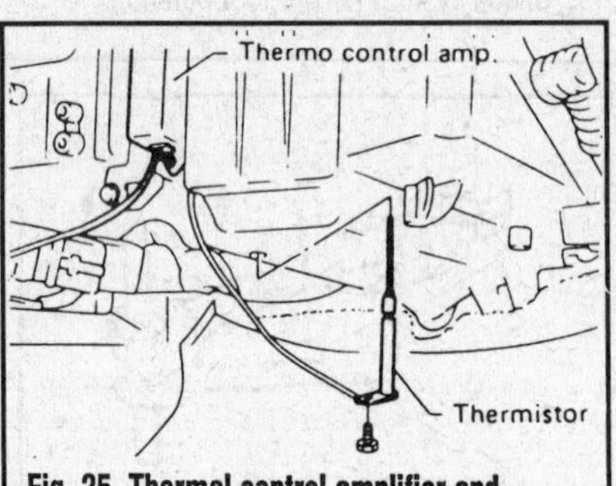
Thermo control amp.
Thermistor

Fig. 25. Thermal control amplifier and thermistor — automatic temperature control vehicles

Refrigerant Lines

REMOVAL & INSTALLATION

➡ Make sure all refrigerant is discharged into the recycling equipment and the pressure in the system is less than atmospheric pressure. Then gradually loosen the discharge side hose fitting and remove it.

When installing air conditioning components in the vehicle, the refrigerant pipes must be connected as the final stage of the operation. Remove the seal caps just before connecting the pipe to the air conditioning component.

1. Use a flare nut and backup wrench to loosen the air conditioning pipe fittings. If the fitting does not loosen on the first attempt, soak the area with refrigerant oil and let stand for 15 minutes. Slowly loosen the fitting. If the fitting binds, retighten. Go back and forth while lubricating until the fitting loosens.
2. Remove the refrigerant pipe from the vehicle.

➡ Always plug all open refrigerant pipes to prevent moisture from entering the system. An air tight system is good, moisture in the system is BAD.

To install:

3. Install the pipe with new O-rings lubricated with refrigerant oil only. Do not any other type of oil. This will contaminate the air conditioning system.
4. After inserting the tube into the union until the O-ring is no longer visible, torque the large fittings to 18–25 ft. lbs. (25–34 Nm) and the small fittings to 7–14 ft. lbs. (10–20 Nm).
5. After the system has been serviced: evacuate, recharge and leak test the air conditioning system as outlined in section 1.

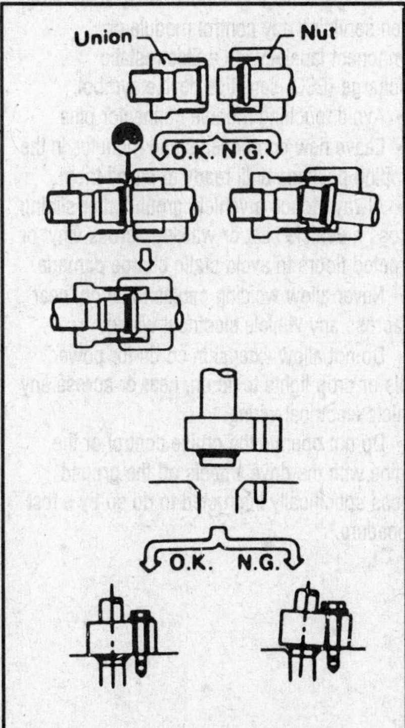
Union
Nut
O.K. N.G.
O.K. N.G.

Fig. 26. A/C refrigerant pipe fittings

Dual Pressure Switch

The dual pressure switch has 2 functions. The first is to turn the air conditioning compressor OFF when the refrigerant level is low. The second is to turn the compressor OFF when the refrigerant high side pressure is too high. Either condition can cause damage to the system. The switch is located in the pipe between the condenser and evaporator outlet on some early models. The switch is located on top of the receiver/drier.

The pressure switch will turn the compressor OFF if the cooling fan is defective.

REMOVAL & INSTALLATION

Discharge the air conditioning system as outlined in section 1. Disconnect the electrical connector and remove the switch from the high side pipe or receiver/drier. Use a wrench to prevent the component from twisting. To install, apply thread sealing tape to the pressure switch and torque to 20 ft. lbs. (28 Nm).

Pressure Relief Valve

The air conditioning system is protected by a pressure relief valve, located on the end of the high side hose near the compressor. When the refrigerant pressure reaches an abnormal level of 540 psi (3727 kPa), the release port automatically opens and releases refrigerant to the atmosphere.

Push Button Control Cables and Actuators

ADJUSTMENTS

Mode Door Motor

The mode door determines the air flow through the air distribution system depending on the mode selected (vent, defrost, etc.). The door linkage is located on the left side of the housing and is controlled by a motor. The motor has a built-in position sensor and will stop at the position called for by the controls. The adjustment procedure starts with the motor removed from the housing.

1. With the motor removed from the housing, connect the motor wiring and set the controls to the **VENT** mode.
2. Turn the ignition switch **ON**, let the motor go to its vent position, then turn the ignition **OFF**.
3. Manually move the linkage on the housing to the vent position, install the motor and attach the linkage.
4. With the ignition switch **ON**, cycle the system through all the modes and check the operation of the linkage.

Air Intake Door

1. With the door motor removed but wiring connected, turn the ignition switch **ON** and set the controls to recirculate by pushing the **REC** button.
2. Install the motor onto the blower housing.
3. Hold the door in the recirculate position and attach the linkage. Turn the **REC** button **ON** and **OFF** to check operation of the door.

Temperature Control Cable

This cable operates the air mix door inside the air distribution system. A control rod connects the air mix door lever and the water valve link lever on the heater core. The control rod should be adjusted first.

1. To adjust the control rod, disconnect the temperature control cable from the door lever.
2. The valve end of the rod is attached to the valve with a wire loop. With the rod loose at the air mix door end, move the air mix door lever and the valve lever all the way in the direction that would pull the rod away from the valve lever.
3. Gently pull the rod so there is about 0.80 in. (2mm) gap between the rod and valve lever and secure the rod at the door lever.
4. When attaching the temperature control lever, adjust the cable housing so the full cold lever position will completely shut off the heat.

Slide Lever Control Cables and Actuators

ADJUSTMENT

If the linkage has been disassembled, it should be adjusted as an assembly rather than trying to adjust only one part. First adjust the rods and levers, then connect and adjust the cables to the linkage.

Ventilator Door Control Rod

1. Viewed from the driver's side, rotate the side link fully clockwise.
2. With the upper and lower door levers pushed down, connect the lower rod first, then the upper rod.

Defroster Door Control Rod

1. Rotate the side link fully counterclockwise.
2. Push the defroster door lever towards the firewall and connect the rod.

Air Control Cable

1. Rotate the side link fully clockwise.
2. With the control lever in the **DEFROST** position, hook the cable to the side link.
3. Take up the slack in the cable housing by pushing it gently away from the firewall and secure the housing.

Water Valve Control Rod

1. To adjust the control rod, disconnect the temperature control cable from the door lever.
2. The valve end of the rod is attached to the valve with a wire loop. With the rod loose at the air mix door end, move the air mix door lever and the valve link lever all the way in the direction that would pull the rod away from the valve lever.
3. Gently pull the rod so there is about 0.080 in. (2mm) gap between the rod and valve lever and secure the rod at the door lever.

Temperature Control Cable

1. Move the control levers to the full **COLD** position.
2. Rotate the air mix door linkage towards the full cold position.
3. Attach the cable and take up the slack in the cable housing before securing it with the clip.

Intake Door Control Cable

1. Move the control lever to the **RECIRCULATE** position.
2. Move the intake door lever fully towards the cable housing clip.
3. Attach the cable and take up the slack in the housing before securing it with the clip.

CRUISE CONTROL

➧ SEE FIGS. 81-90

General Description

Nissan refers to their cruise control as the Automatic Speed Control Device (ASCD) system. The ASCD system maintains a desired speed of the vehicle under normal driving conditions. The cruise control system's main parts are the control switches, control unit, actuator, speed sensor, vacuum pump, vacuum pump relay, vacuum switch, vacuum tank, electrical release switches and electrical harness.

➡ The use of the speed control is not recommended when driving conditions do not permit maintaining a constant speed, such as in heavy traffic or on roads that are winding, icy, snow covered or slippery.

Diagnosis and Testing

SERVICE PRECAUTIONS

CAUTION

If equipped with an air bag system, the system must be fully disabled before performing repairs, following all safety precautions. Failure to disarm the system could result in personal injury and/or property damage.

- Never disconnect any electrical connection with the ignition switch **ON** unless instructed to do so in a test.
- Always wear a grounded wrist static strap when servicing any control module or component labeled with a Electrostatic Discharge (ESD) sensitive device symbol.
- Avoid touching module connector pins.
- Leave new components and modules in the shipping package until ready to install them.
- Always touch a vehicle ground after sliding across a vehicle seat or walking across vinyl or carpeted floors to avoid static charge damage.
- Never allow welding cables to lie on, near or across any vehicle electrical wiring.
- Do not allow extension cords for power tools or drop lights to lie on, near or across any vehicle electrical wiring.
- Do not operate the cruise control or the engine with the drive wheels off the ground unless specifically instructed to do so by a test procedure.

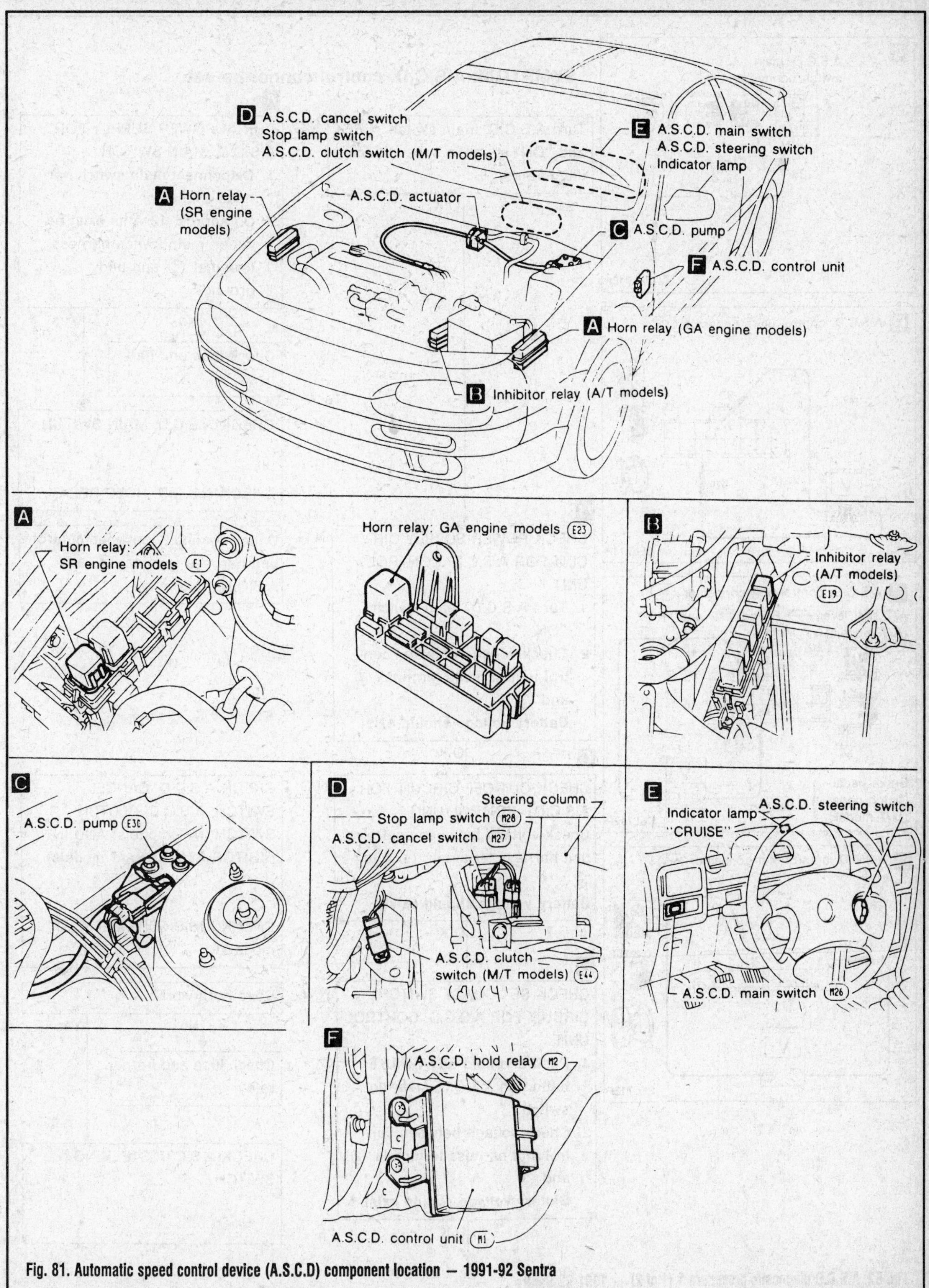

D A.S.C.D. cancel switch
Stop lamp switch
A.S.C.D. clutch switch (M/T models)
E A.S.C.D. main switch
A.S.C.D. steering switch
Indicator lamp
A Horn relay (SR engine models)
A.S.C.D. actuator
C A.S.C.D. pump
F A.S.C.D. control unit
A Horn relay (GA engine models)
B Inhibitor relay (A/T models)
A
Horn relay: SR engine models E1
Horn relay: GA engine models E23
B
Inhibitor relay (A/T models) E19
C
A.S.C.D. pump E30
D
Steering column
Stop lamp switch M28
A.S.C.D. cancel switch M27
A.S.C.D. clutch switch (M/T models) E44
E
Indicator lamp "CRUISE"
A.S.C.D. steering switch
A.S.C.D. main switch M26
F
A.S.C.D. hold relay M2
A.S.C.D. control unit M1

Fig. 81. Automatic speed control device (A.S.C.D) component location — 1991-92 Sentra

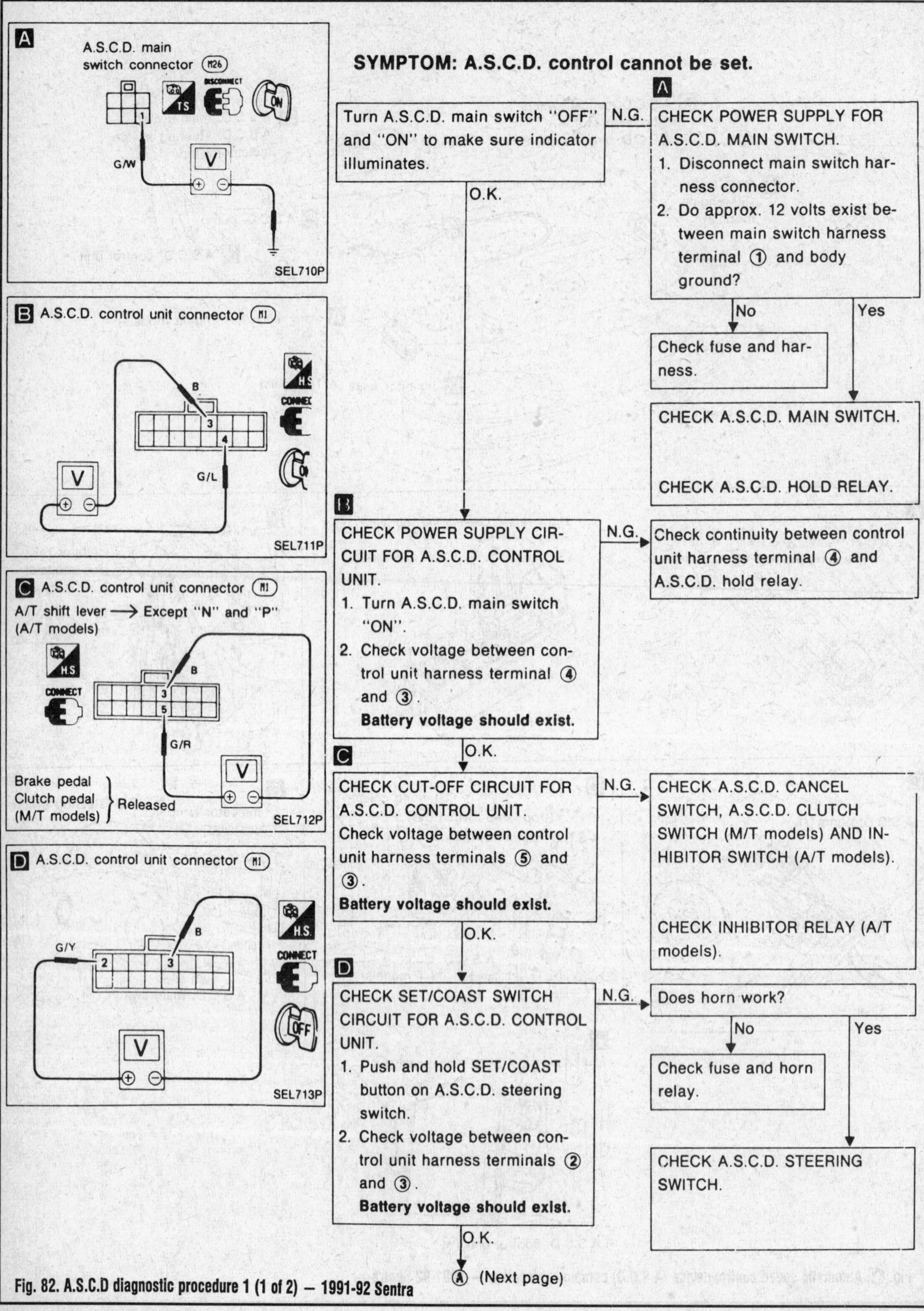
A
A.S.C.D. main switch connector (M26)
G/W
V
SEL710P
B A.S.C.D. control unit connector (M1)
B
G/L
V
SEL711P
C A.S.C.D. control unit connector (M1)
A/T shift lever → Except "N" and "P" (A/T models)
B
G/R
V
Brake pedal
Clutch pedal
(M/T models)
Released
SEL712P
D A.S.C.D. control unit connector (M1)
G/Y
B
V
SEL713P
SYMPTOM: A.S.C.D. control cannot be set.
Turn A.S.C.D. main switch "OFF" and "ON" to make sure indicator illuminates.
N.G.
A
CHECK POWER SUPPLY FOR A.S.C.D. MAIN SWITCH.
1. Disconnect main switch harness connector.
2. Do approx. 12 volts exist between main switch harness terminal ① and body ground?
No
Yes
Check fuse and harness.
CHECK A.S.C.D. MAIN SWITCH.
CHECK A.S.C.D. HOLD RELAY.
O.K.
B
CHECK POWER SUPPLY CIRCUIT FOR A.S.C.D. CONTROL UNIT.
1. Turn A.S.C.D. main switch "ON".
2. Check voltage between control unit harness terminal ④ and ③.
Battery voltage should exist.
N.G.
Check continuity between control unit harness terminal ④ and A.S.C.D. hold relay.
O.K.
C
CHECK CUT-OFF CIRCUIT FOR A.S.C.D. CONTROL UNIT.
Check voltage between control unit harness terminals ⑤ and ③.
Battery voltage should exist.
N.G.
CHECK A.S.C.D. CANCEL SWITCH, A.S.C.D. CLUTCH SWITCH (M/T models) AND INHIBITOR SWITCH (A/T models).
CHECK INHIBITOR RELAY (A/T models).
O.K.
D
CHECK SET/COAST SWITCH CIRCUIT FOR A.S.C.D. CONTROL UNIT.
1. Push and hold SET/COAST button on A.S.C.D. steering switch.
2. Check voltage between control unit harness terminals ② and ③.
Battery voltage should exist.
N.G.
Does horn work?
No
Yes
Check fuse and horn relay.
CHECK A.S.C.D. STEERING SWITCH.
O.K.
Ⓐ (Next page)

Fig. 82. A.S.C.D diagnostic procedure 1 (1 of 2) — 1991-92 Sentra

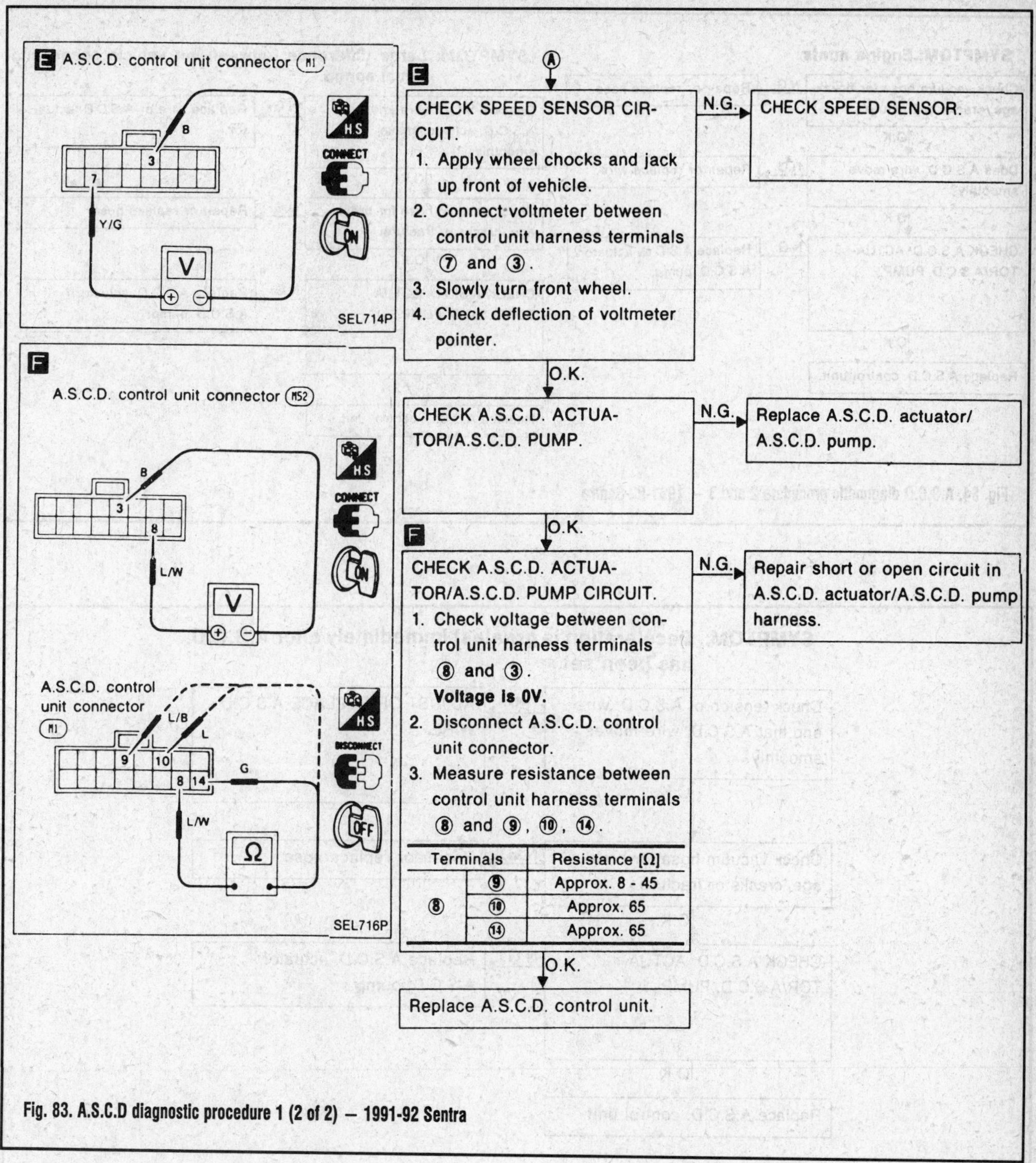
E A.S.C.D. control unit connector M1
B
3
7
Y/G
V
SEL714P
F
A.S.C.D. control unit connector M52
B
3
8
L/W
V
A.S.C.D. control unit connector M1
L/B
L
9
10
8
14
G
L/W
Ω
SEL716P
HS
CONNECT
ON
DISCONNECT
OFF
A
E
CHECK SPEED SENSOR CIRCUIT.
1. Apply wheel chocks and jack up front of vehicle.
2. Connect voltmeter between control unit harness terminals ⑦ and ③.
3. Slowly turn front wheel.
4. Check deflection of voltmeter pointer.
N.G.
CHECK SPEED SENSOR.
O.K.
CHECK A.S.C.D. ACTUATOR/A.S.C.D. PUMP.
N.G.
Replace A.S.C.D. actuator/A.S.C.D. pump.
O.K.
F
CHECK A.S.C.D. ACTUATOR/A.S.C.D. PUMP CIRCUIT.
1. Check voltage between control unit harness terminals ⑧ and ③.
Voltage is 0V.
2. Disconnect A.S.C.D. control unit connector.
3. Measure resistance between control unit harness terminals ⑧ and ⑨, ⑩, ⑭.
Terminals
Resistance [Ω]
⑧
⑨
Approx. 8 - 45
⑩
Approx. 65
⑭
Approx. 65
N.G.
Repair short or open circuit in A.S.C.D. actuator/A.S.C.D. pump harness.
O.K.
Replace A.S.C.D. control unit.

Fig. 83. A.S.C.D diagnostic procedure 1 (2 of 2) — 1991-92 Sentra

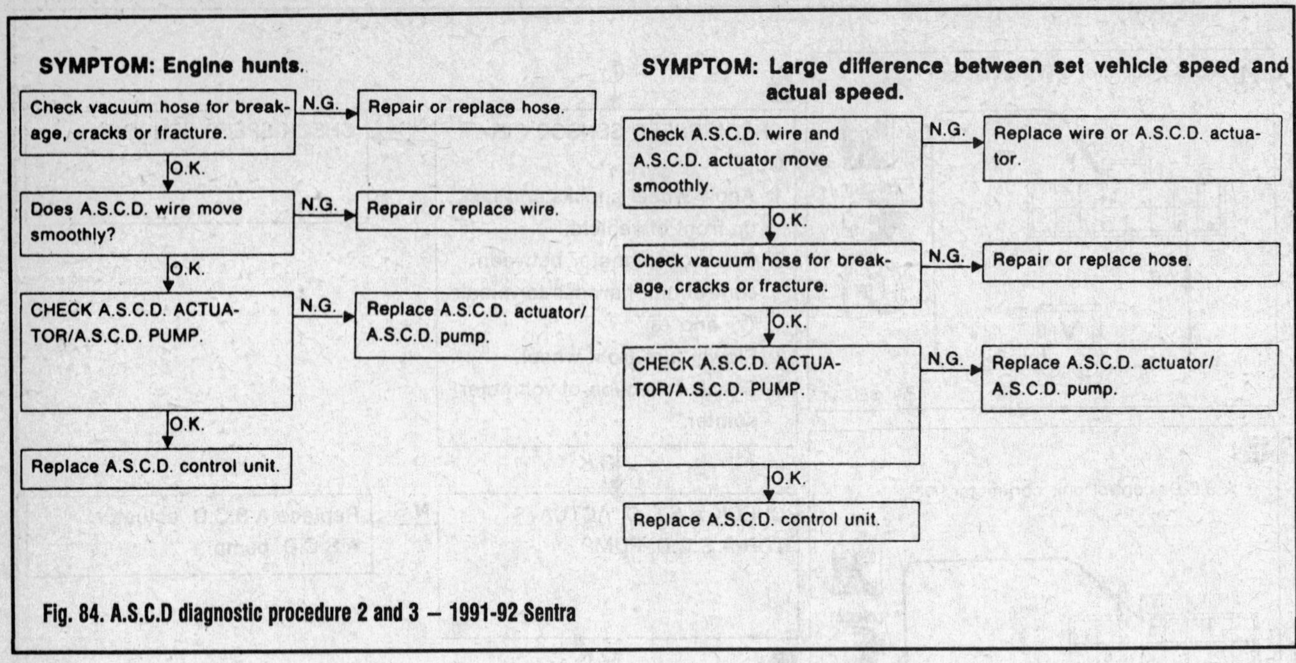
SYMPTOM: Engine hunts.
Check vacuum hose for breakage, cracks or fracture.
N.G.
Repair or replace hose.
O.K.
Does A.S.C.D. wire move smoothly?
N.G.
Repair or replace wire.
O.K.
CHECK A.S.C.D. ACTUATOR/A.S.C.D. PUMP.
N.G.
Replace A.S.C.D. actuator/ A.S.C.D. pump.
O.K.
Replace A.S.C.D. control unit.
SYMPTOM: Large difference between set vehicle speed and actual speed.
Check A.S.C.D. wire and A.S.C.D. actuator move smoothly.
N.G.
Replace wire or A.S.C.D. actuator.
O.K.
Check vacuum hose for breakage, cracks or fracture.
N.G.
Repair or replace hose.
O.K.
CHECK A.S.C.D. ACTUATOR/A.S.C.D. PUMP.
N.G.
Replace A.S.C.D. actuator/ A.S.C.D. pump.
O.K.
Replace A.S.C.D. control unit.

Fig. 84. A.S.C.D diagnostic procedure 2 and 3 – 1991-92 Sentra

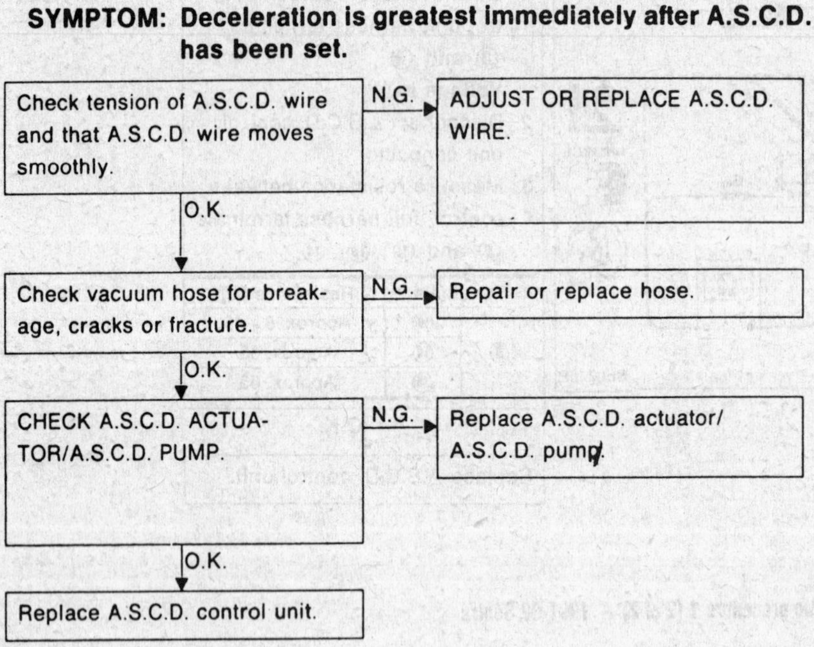

SYMPTOM: Deceleration is greatest immediately after A.S.C.D. has been set.

Check tension of A.S.C.D. wire and that A.S.C.D. wire moves smoothly. — N.G. → ADJUST OR REPLACE A.S.C.D. WIRE.

O.K. ↓

Check vacuum hose for breakage, cracks or fracture. — N.G. → Repair or replace hose.

O.K. ↓

CHECK A.S.C.D. ACTUATOR/A.S.C.D. PUMP. — N.G. → Replace A.S.C.D. actuator/ A.S.C.D. pump.

O.K. ↓

Replace A.S.C.D. control unit.

Fig. 85. A.S.C.D diagnostic procedure 4 – 1991-92 Sentra

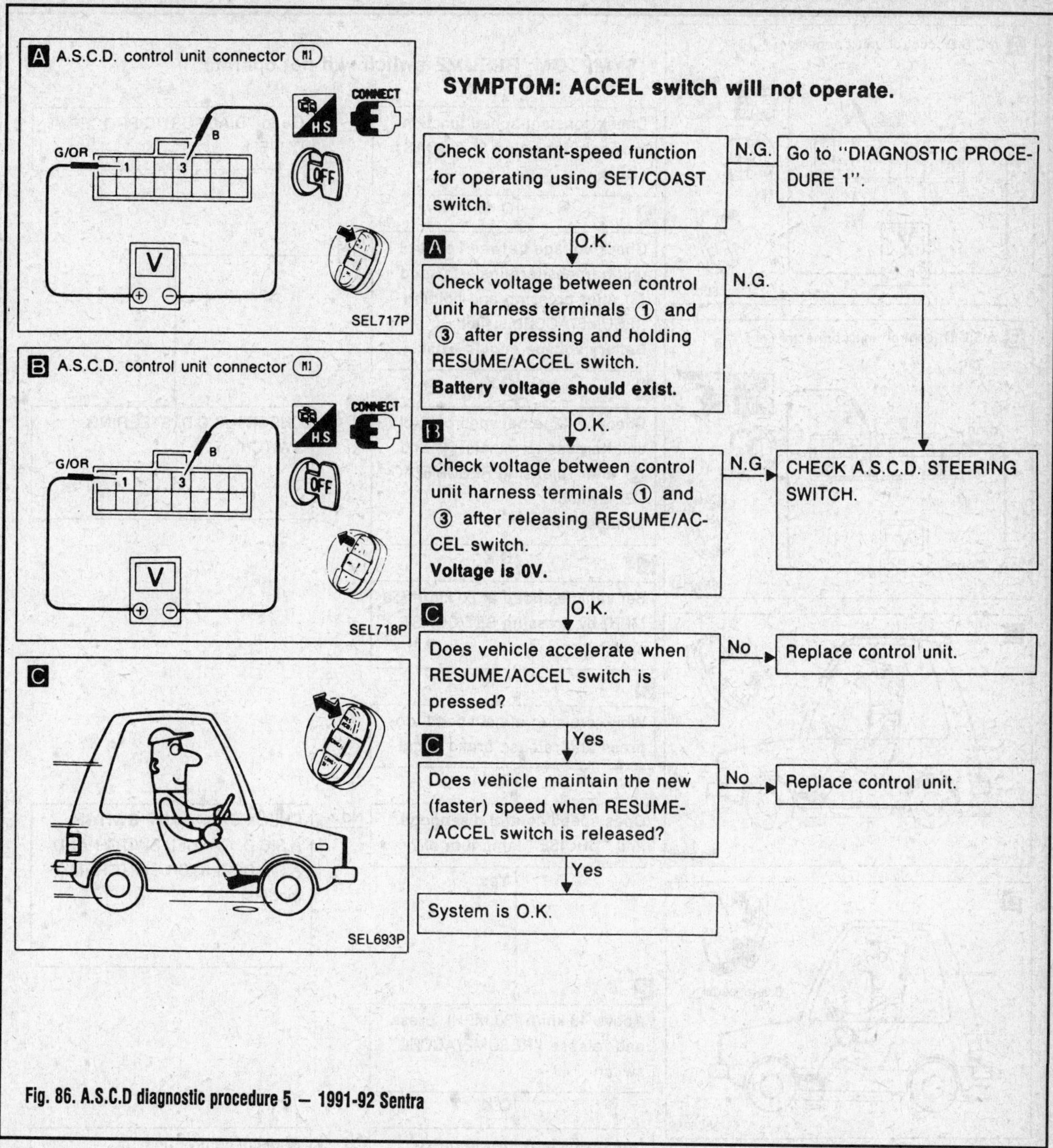
A A.S.C.D. control unit connector M1
CONNECT
H.S.
OFF
G/OR
B
1
3
V
SEL717P
B A.S.C.D. control unit connector M1
CONNECT
H.S.
OFF
G/OR
B
1
3
V
SEL718P
C
SEL693P
SYMPTOM: ACCEL switch will not operate.
Check constant-speed function for operating using SET/COAST switch.
N.G.
Go to "DIAGNOSTIC PROCEDURE 1".
O.K.
A
Check voltage between control unit harness terminals ① and ③ after pressing and holding RESUME/ACCEL switch.
Battery voltage should exist.
N.G.
O.K.
B
Check voltage between control unit harness terminals ① and ③ after releasing RESUME/ACCEL switch.
Voltage is 0V.
N.G
CHECK A.S.C.D. STEERING SWITCH.
O.K.
C
Does vehicle accelerate when RESUME/ACCEL switch is pressed?
No
Replace control unit.
Yes
C
Does vehicle maintain the new (faster) speed when RESUME-/ACCEL switch is released?
No
Replace control unit.
Yes
System is O.K.

Fig. 86. A.S.C.D diagnostic procedure 5 – 1991-92 Sentra

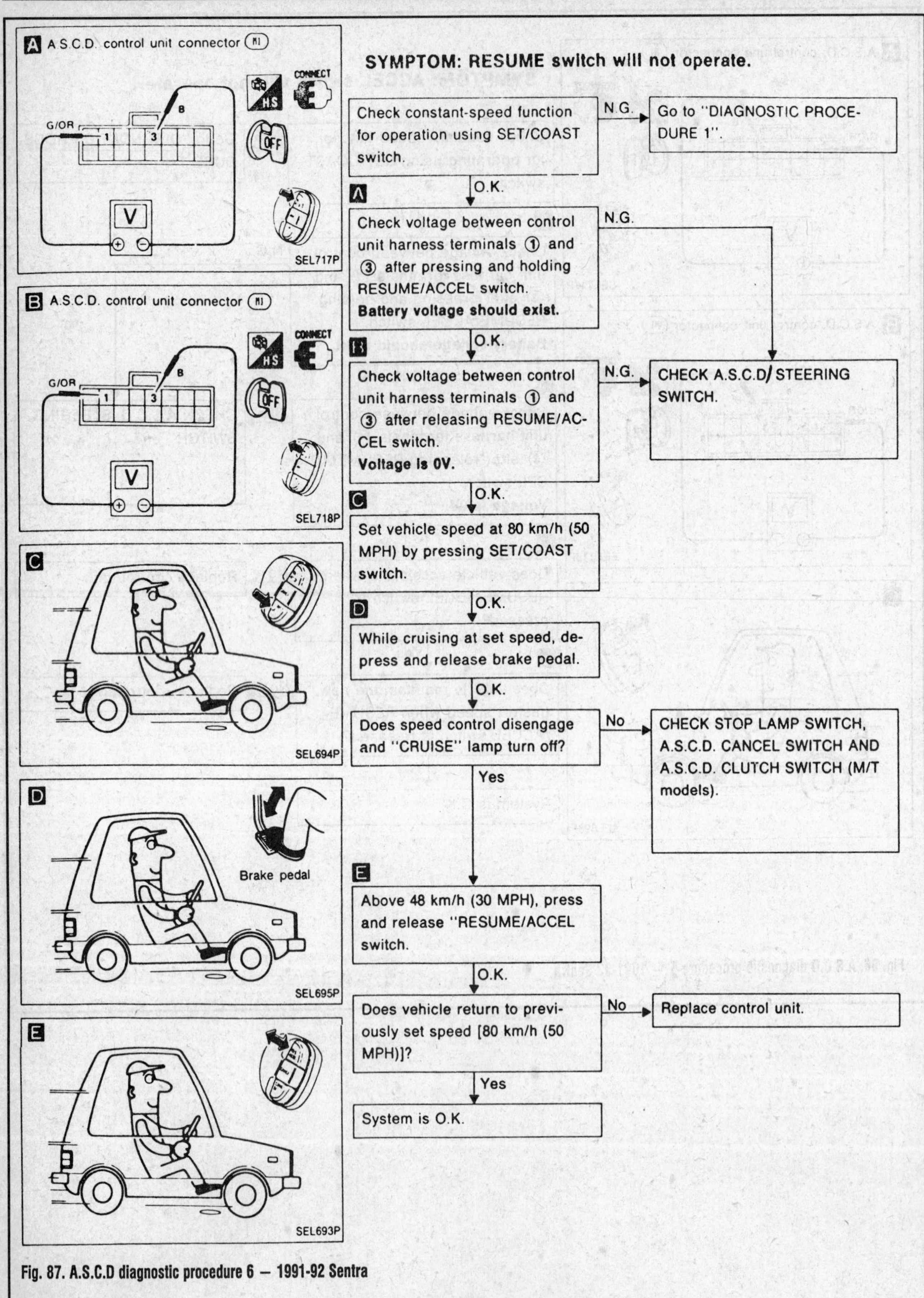
A A.S.C.D. control unit connector (M1)
G/OR
B
1
3
V
CONNECT
HS
OFF
SEL717P
B A.S.C.D. control unit connector (M1)
G/OR
B
1
3
V
CONNECT
HS
OFF
SEL718P
C
SEL694P
D
Brake pedal
SEL695P
E
SEL693P
SYMPTOM: RESUME switch will not operate.
Check constant-speed function for operation using SET/COAST switch.
N.G.
Go to "DIAGNOSTIC PROCEDURE 1".
O.K.
A
Check voltage between control unit harness terminals ① and ③ after pressing and holding RESUME/ACCEL switch.
Battery voltage should exist.
N.G.
O.K.
B
Check voltage between control unit harness terminals ① and ③ after releasing RESUME/ACCEL switch.
Voltage is 0V.
N.G.
CHECK A.S.C.D/ STEERING SWITCH.
O.K.
C
Set vehicle speed at 80 km/h (50 MPH) by pressing SET/COAST switch.
O.K.
D
While cruising at set speed, depress and release brake pedal.
O.K.
Does speed control disengage and "CRUISE" lamp turn off?
No
CHECK STOP LAMP SWITCH, A.S.C.D. CANCEL SWITCH AND A.S.C.D. CLUTCH SWITCH (M/T models).
Yes
E
Above 48 km/h (30 MPH), press and release "RESUME/ACCEL switch.
O.K.
Does vehicle return to previously set speed [80 km/h (50 MPH)]?
No
Replace control unit.
Yes
System is O.K.

Fig. 87. A.S.C.D diagnostic procedure 6 – 1991-92 Sentra

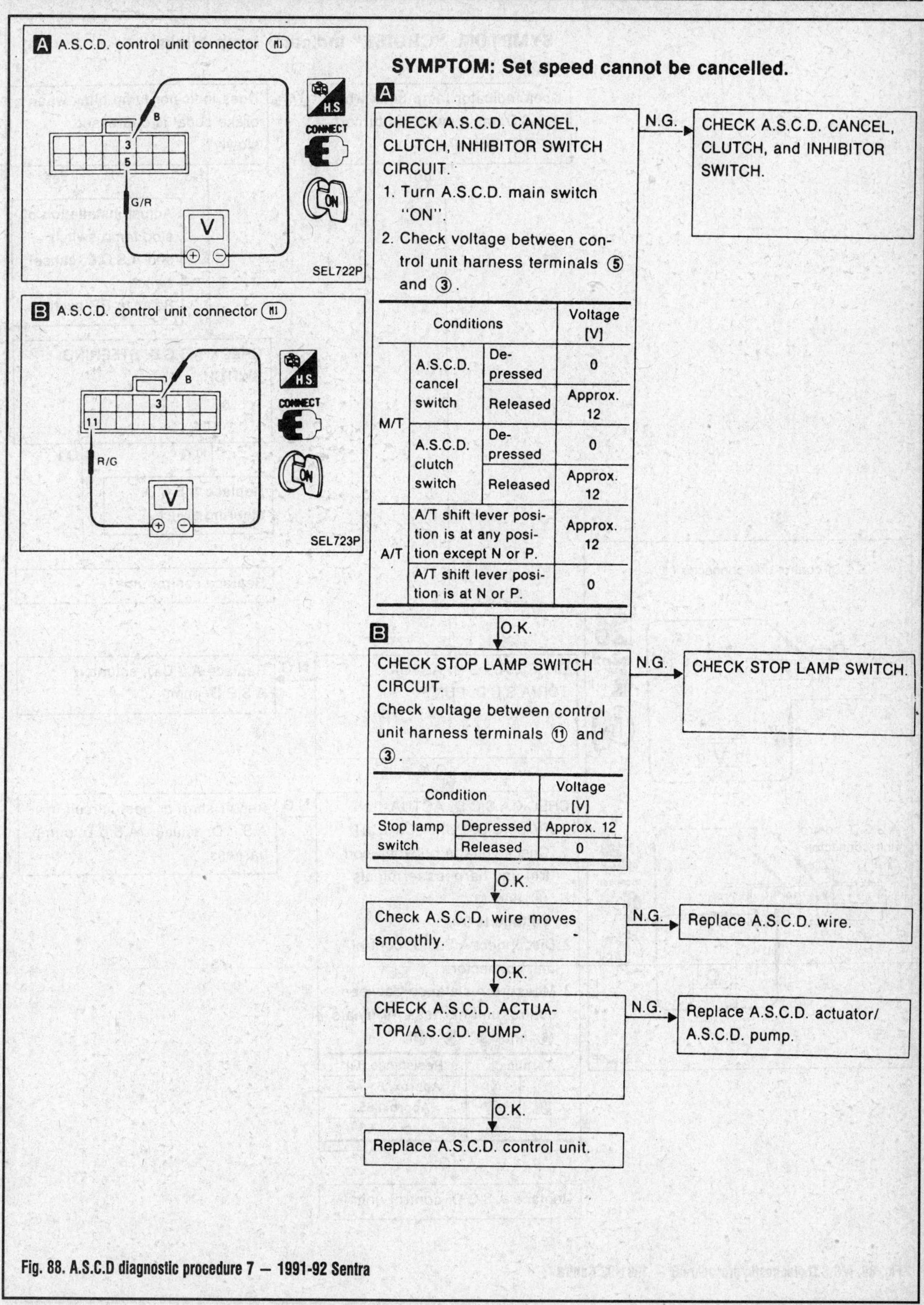
A A.S.C.D. control unit connector (M1)
B
3
5
G/R
V
H.S.
CONNECT
ON
SEL722P
B A.S.C.D. control unit connector (M1)
B
3
11
R/G
V
H.S.
CONNECT
ON
SEL723P
SYMPTOM: Set speed cannot be cancelled.
A
CHECK A.S.C.D. CANCEL, CLUTCH, INHIBITOR SWITCH CIRCUIT.
1. Turn A.S.C.D. main switch "ON".
2. Check voltage between control unit harness terminals ⑤ and ③.
N.G.
CHECK A.S.C.D. CANCEL, CLUTCH, and INHIBITOR SWITCH.
O.K.
B
CHECK STOP LAMP SWITCH CIRCUIT.
Check voltage between control unit harness terminals ⑪ and ③.
N.G.
CHECK STOP LAMP SWITCH.
O.K.
Check A.S.C.D. wire moves smoothly.
N.G.
Replace A.S.C.D. wire.
O.K.
CHECK A.S.C.D. ACTUATOR/A.S.C.D. PUMP.
N.G.
Replace A.S.C.D. actuator/ A.S.C.D. pump.
O.K.
Replace A.S.C.D. control unit.

Conditions			Voltage [V]
M/T	A.S.C.D. cancel switch	Depressed	0
		Released	Approx. 12
	A.S.C.D. clutch switch	Depressed	0
		Released	Approx. 12
A/T	A/T shift lever position is at any position except N or P.		Approx. 12
	A/T shift lever position is at N or P.		0

Condition		Voltage [V]
Stop lamp switch	Depressed	Approx. 12
	Released	0

Fig. 88. A.S.C.D diagnostic procedure 7 — 1991-92 Sentra

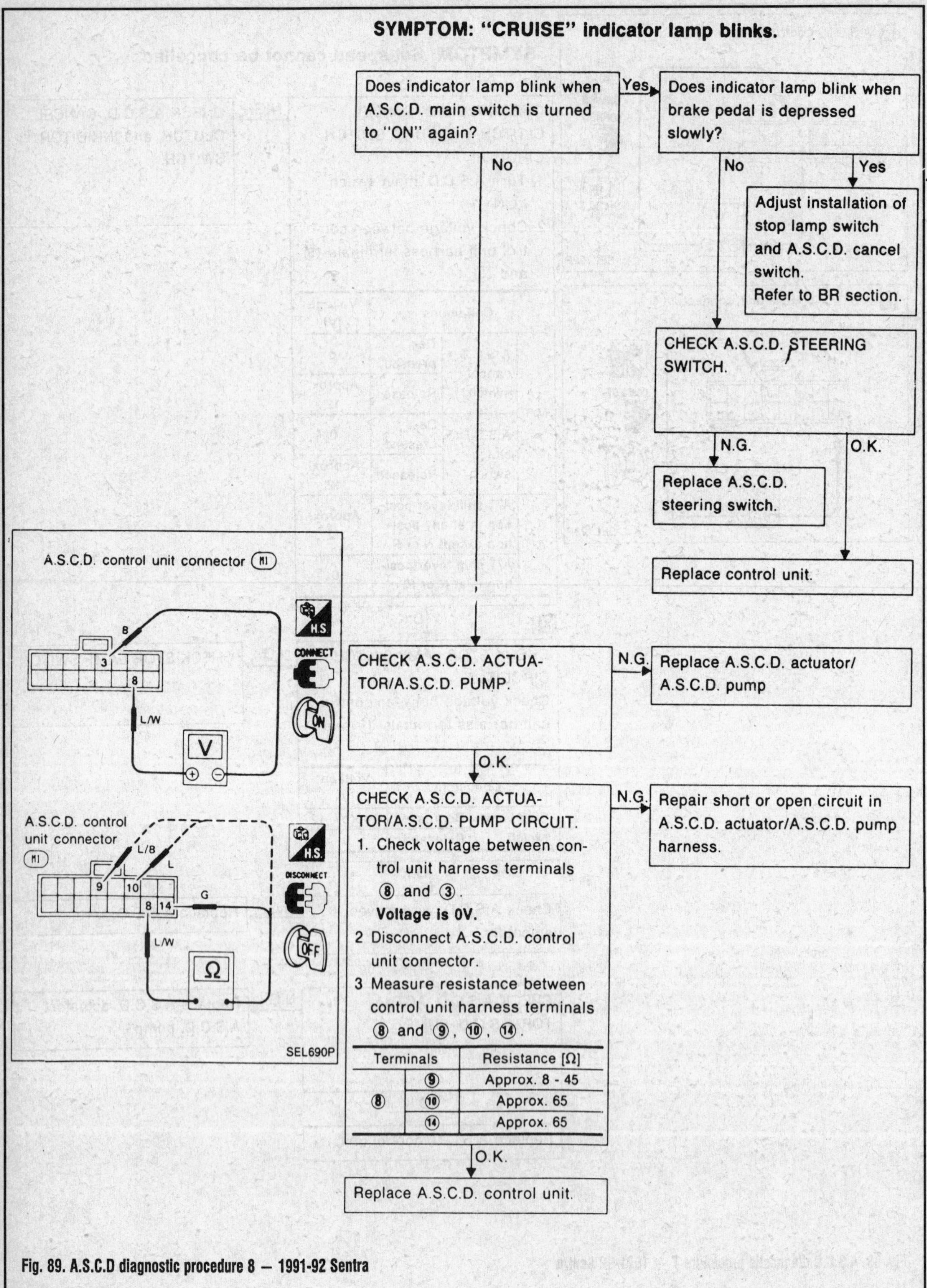
SYMPTOM: "CRUISE" indicator lamp blinks.
Does indicator lamp blink when A.S.C.D. main switch is turned to "ON" again?
Yes
Does indicator lamp blink when brake pedal is depressed slowly?
No
Yes
Adjust installation of stop lamp switch and A.S.C.D. cancel switch. Refer to BR section.
CHECK A.S.C.D. STEERING SWITCH.
N.G.
O.K.
Replace A.S.C.D. steering switch.
Replace control unit.
No
A.S.C.D. control unit connector M1
B
3
8
L/W
V
H.S.
CONNECT
ON
CHECK A.S.C.D. ACTUATOR/A.S.C.D. PUMP.
N.G.
Replace A.S.C.D. actuator/ A.S.C.D. pump
O.K.
A.S.C.D. control unit connector M1
L/B
L
9
10
8
14
G
L/W
Ω
H.S.
DISCONNECT
OFF
SEL690P
CHECK A.S.C.D. ACTUATOR/A.S.C.D. PUMP CIRCUIT.
1. Check voltage between control unit harness terminals ⑧ and ③.
Voltage is 0V.
2 Disconnect A.S.C.D. control unit connector.
3 Measure resistance between control unit harness terminals ⑧ and ⑨, ⑩, ⑭.
N.G.
Repair short or open circuit in A.S.C.D. actuator/A.S.C.D. pump harness.
O.K.
Replace A.S.C.D. control unit.

Terminals		Resistance [Ω]
⑧	⑨	Approx. 8 - 45
	⑩	Approx. 65
	⑭	Approx. 65

Fig. 89. A.S.C.D diagnostic procedure 8 — 1991-92 Sentra

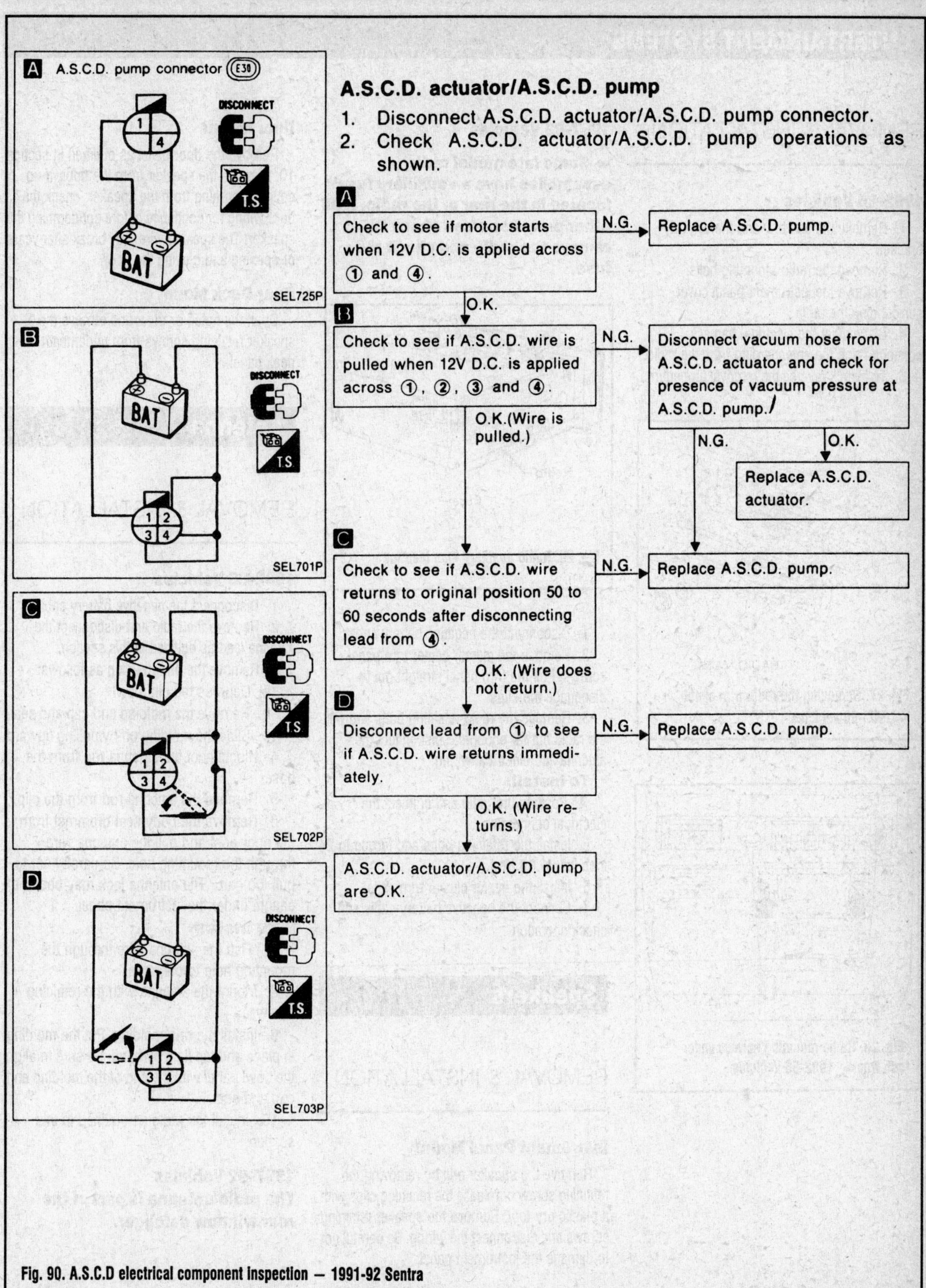
A A.S.C.D. pump connector E30
DISCONNECT
T.S.
BAT
SEL725P
B
SEL701P
C
SEL702P
D
SEL703P
A.S.C.D. actuator/A.S.C.D. pump
1. Disconnect A.S.C.D. actuator/A.S.C.D. pump connector.
2. Check A.S.C.D. actuator/A.S.C.D. pump operations as shown.
A
Check to see if motor starts when 12V D.C. is applied across ① and ④.
N.G.
Replace A.S.C.D. pump.
O.K.
B
Check to see if A.S.C.D. wire is pulled when 12V D.C. is applied across ①, ②, ③ and ④.
N.G.
Disconnect vacuum hose from A.S.C.D. actuator and check for presence of vacuum pressure at A.S.C.D. pump.
N.G.
O.K.
Replace A.S.C.D. actuator.
O.K. (Wire is pulled.)
C
Check to see if A.S.C.D. wire returns to original position 50 to 60 seconds after disconnecting lead from ④.
N.G.
Replace A.S.C.D. pump.
O.K. (Wire does not return.)
D
Disconnect lead from ① to see if A.S.C.D. wire returns immediately.
N.G.
Replace A.S.C.D. pump.
O.K. (Wire returns.)
A.S.C.D. actuator/A.S.C.D. pump are O.K.

Fig. 90. A.S.C.D electrical component inspection — 1991-92 Sentra

ENTERTAINMENT SYSTEMS

REMOVAL & INSTALLATION

1982–86 Vehicles

1. Remove the ash tray and the ash tray bracket.
2. Remove the radio mounting bolts.
3. Remove the instrument panel cover surrounding the radio.
4. Disconnect the electrical harness connector and the antenna plug from the radio.
5. To install, reverse the removal procedures.

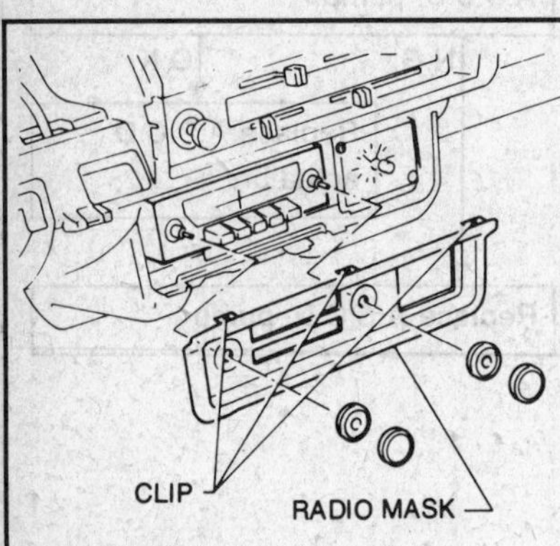
CLIP
RADIO MASK

Fig. 27. Removing the radio trim panel — 1982-86 vehicles

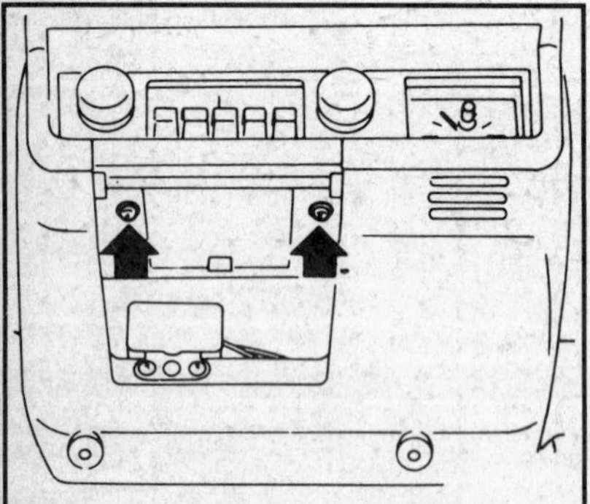

Fig. 28. Radio mounting screws under ash tray — 1982-86 vehicles

1987–92 Vehicles

➡ Some late model radio assemblies have an auxiliary fuse located in the rear of the radio. If all other power sources check OK, remove the radio and check the fuse.

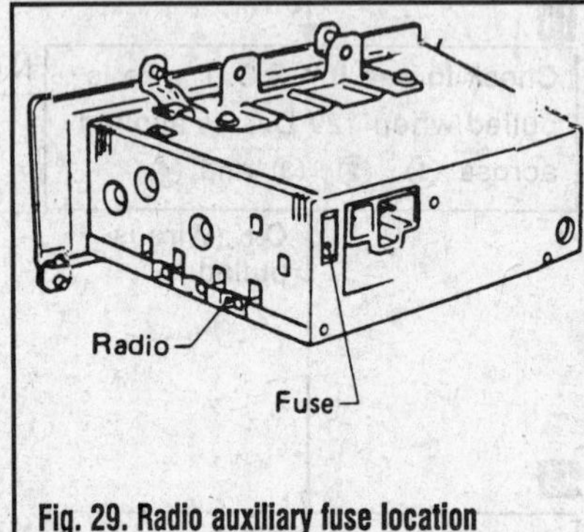
Radio
Fuse

Fig. 29. Radio auxiliary fuse location

1. Disconnect the negative battery cable.
2. Remove the cluster center trim panel screws. Pull the trim panel straight out to disengage the clips.
3. Remove the radio retaining bolts and pull the radio out far enough to disconnect the antenna and electrical wiring.

To install:

4. Position the radio and connect the electrical connectors.
5. Install the retaining bolts and torque to 24 inch lbs. (1.36 Nm).
6. Install the center cluster trim panel.
7. Connect the negative battery cable and check operation.

Speakers

REMOVAL & INSTALLATION

Instrument Panel Mount

Remove the speaker grill by removing the retaining screw or release the retaining clips with a plastic pry tool. Remove the speaker retaining screws and disconnect the wiring. Be careful not to damage the instrument panel.

Door Mount

Remove the door panel as outlined in section 10. Remove the speaker from the door. If no sound is coming from the speaker, check the door wiring for continuity before condemning the speaker. The speaker wire may break after years of opening and closing the door.

Rear Deck Mount

Open the hatch or trunk and remove the speaker retaining screws from underneath the deck panel.

Antenna

REMOVAL & INSTALLATION

1982–86 Vehicles

1. Disconnect the negative battery cable.
2. Remove the radio and disconnect the antenna lead as outlined in this section.
3. Remove the drip molding as follows:
   a. Depress the clip pawl.
   b. Remove the molding end cap and seal.
   c. Slide the molding off by pulling upward
4. Disconnect the antenna rod from the base.
5. Remove the antenna rod from the clip.
6. Remove the body seal grommet from the door post and pull the antenna wire through the mounting hole. Be careful not to pull too hard. The antenna jack may become caught under the instrument panel.

To install:

7. Fish the antenna wire through the mounting hole to the radio.
8. Mount the antenna with the retaining screws.
9. Install the drip molding. Put the molding in place and tap light by hand. Be sure to align the cowl panel with the end of the molding end cap and seal.
10. Install the radio as outlined in this section.

1987–92 Vehicles

The radio antenna is part of the rear window defogger.

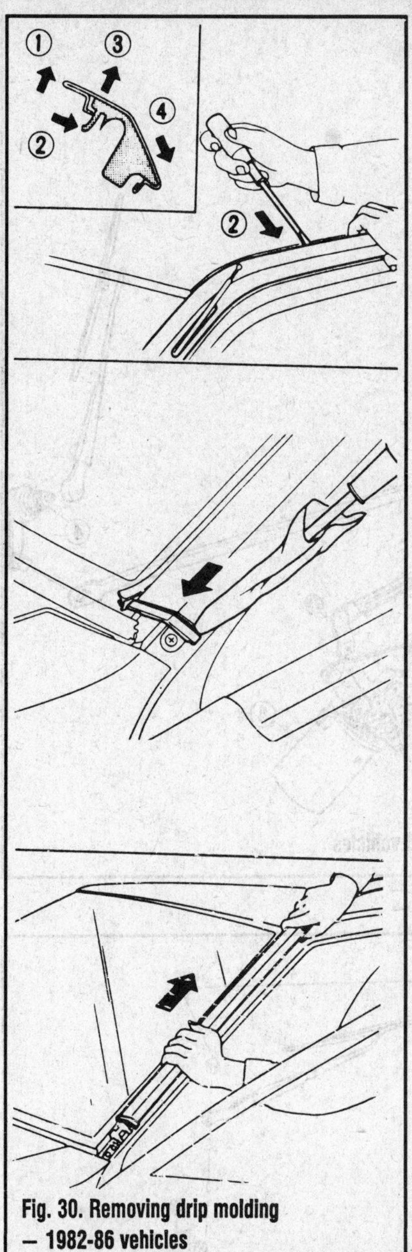

Fig. 30. Removing drip molding — 1982-86 vehicles

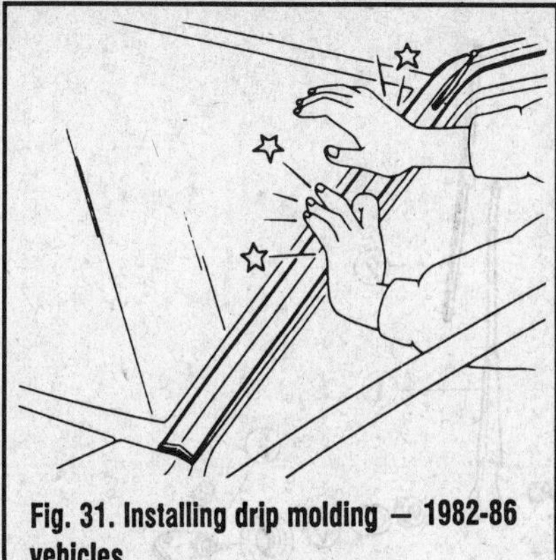

Fig. 31. Installing drip molding — 1982-86 vehicles

ELEMENT CHECK

1. Using an ohmmeter, check for continuity at the antenna terminals on both sides. If the element is broken, no continuity will exist.
2. To locate the broken point, move the ohmmeter probe to the left and right along the element until the meter shows continuity.
3. Repair the antenna element as follows:
   a. Wipe the broken wire and surrounding area with alcohol.
   b. Apply a small amount of conductive silver composition (Dupont® No. 4817 or equivalent) to the tip of drawing pen.
   c. Place a ruler on the glass along the broken line. Deposit the conductive silver on the break with the pen. Slightly overlap onto the ends of the wire.

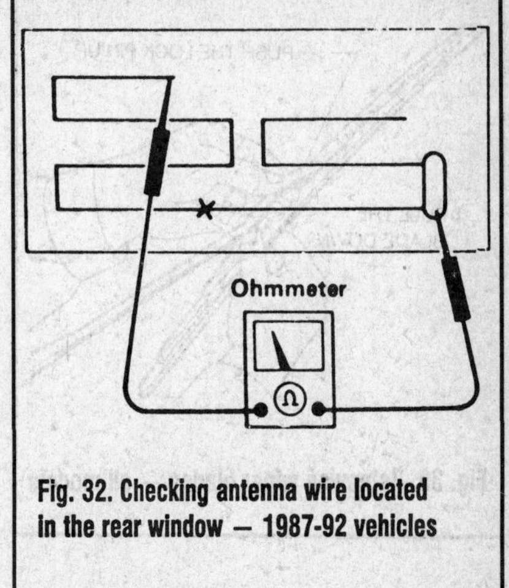
Ohmmeter

Fig. 32. Checking antenna wire located in the rear window — 1987-92 vehicles

   d. After the repair, allow the conductive silver to dry for at least 15 minutes. Check for continuity with the ohmmeter.
   d. If continuity exists, apply heat from a heat gun or hair dryer for approximately 20 minutes. If heat is not used, allow the area to dry for at least 24 hours.

WINDSHIELD WIPER AND WASHERS

Blade and Arm

REMOVAL & INSTALLATION

All Models

1. Some models have covers that are hinged to the arm. Pull these upward at the end of the arm opposite the blade. Other models have covers that fit over the end of the linkage shaft and the arm; simply pull these off. If necessary, turn the ignition switch on and turn the wipers on and then off again to bring them to the full park position.
2. Hold the wiper arm against the torque and loosen the nut which attaches the arm to the linkage shaft with a socket wrench. Remove the nut.
3. Note or measure the distance between the blade and the lower edge of the windshield (this is usually about 1"). The blade is usually parallel with the bottom of the windshield. Then, turn the arm outward on its hinges so its spring pressure is removed from the lower end. Pull the lower end of the arm straight off the splines on the shaft.

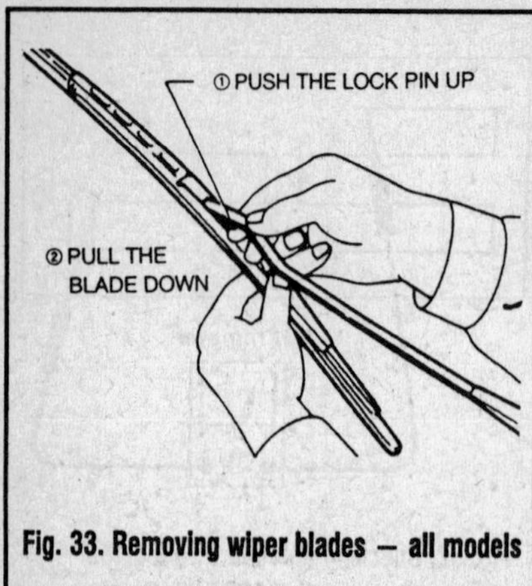
① PUSH THE LOCK PIN UP
② PULL THE BLADE DOWN
Fig. 33. Removing wiper blades — all models

To Install:

4. First line up the wiper blade with the bottom of the windshield at the proper clearance. Then, install the end of the arm over the end of the shaft, turning it slightly, if necessary, in either direction so the splines will engage.

5. Install the attaching nut. Hold the arm to minimize torque on the driveshaft and torque the nut to 9–13 ft. lbs. (12–18 Nm). Install decorative caps or covers in reverse of removal.

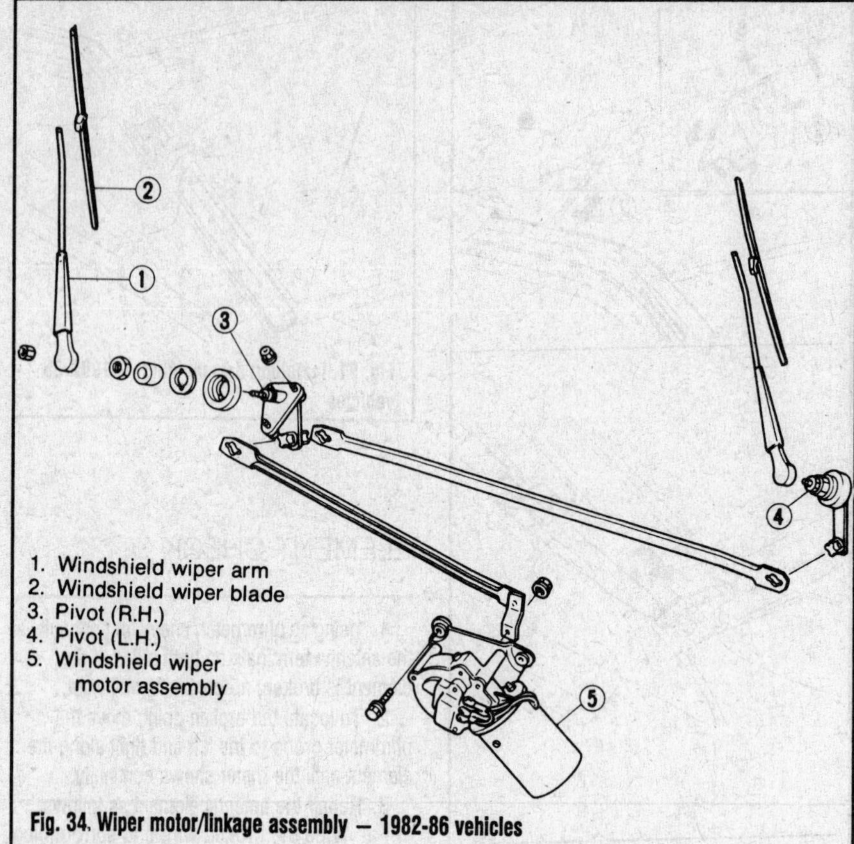
1. Windshield wiper arm
2. Windshield wiper blade
3. Pivot (R.H.)
4. Pivot (L.H.)
5. Windshield wiper motor assembly
Fig. 34. Wiper motor/linkage assembly — 1982-86 vehicles

Wiper Motor and Linkage

REMOVAL & INSTALLATION

1983–90 Pulsar

1. Disconnect the negative battery terminal and remove the motor wiring connection.
2. Unbolt the motor from the body.
3. Disconnect the wiper linkage from the motor and remove the motor.
4. Disconnect linkage from the pivot.
5. To install, reverse the removal procedures.

1982–90 Sentra

The wiper motor is on the firewall under the hood. The operating linkage is on the firewall inside the car.

1. Disconnect the negative battery cable. Detach the motor wiring plug.

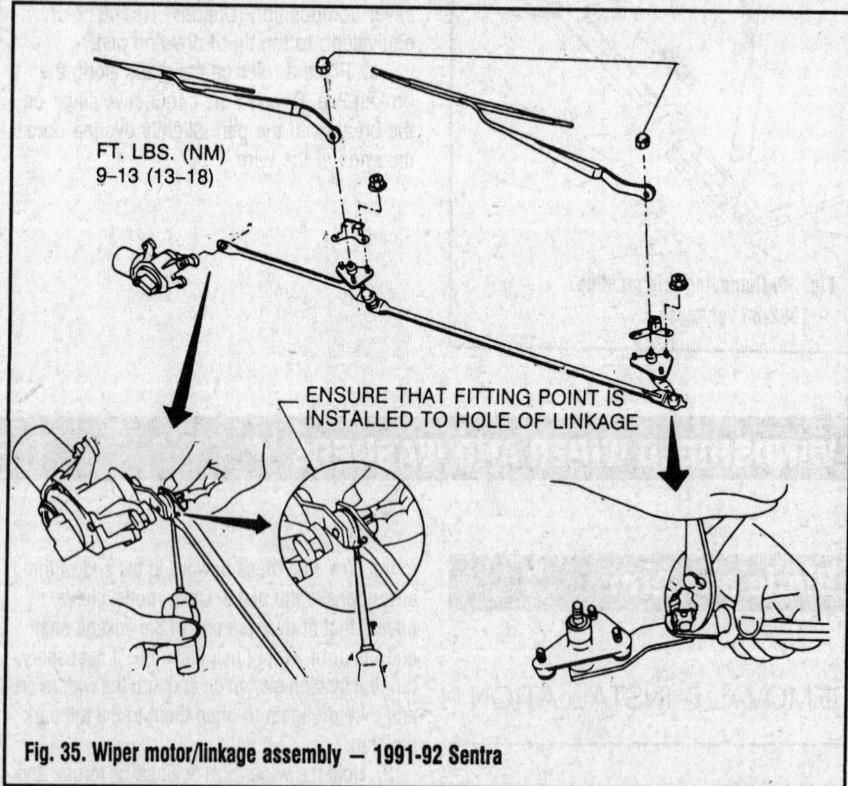
FT. LBS. (NM)
9–13 (13–18)
ENSURE THAT FITTING POINT IS INSTALLED TO HOLE OF LINKAGE
Fig. 35. Wiper motor/linkage assembly — 1991-92 Sentra

2. Inside the car, remove the nut connecting the linkage to the wiper shaft. Slide the linkage off the shaft. If there is a lot of resistance, use a small puller or force the linkage lever off the shaft with a pair of pliers. **Don't tap on the motor shaft with a hammer!**

3. Unbolt and remove the wiper motor from the firewall.

4. Remove the nut that attaches each wiper arm driveshaft unit to the cowl. Then, work the shaft downward and into the cowl interior.

5. Work the linkage out of the access holes and remove it from the vehicle.

To install:

6. Work the linkage into the access holes.

7. Install the nut that attaches each wiper arm driveshaft unit to the cowl. Torque the nuts to 10 ft. lbs. (13 Nm).

8. Install the wiper motor to the firewall.

9. Inside the car, install the nut connecting the linkage to the wiper shaft. Torque the nut to 60 inch lbs. (7 Nm). **Don't tap on the motor shaft with a hammer!**

10. Connect the negative battery cable. Attach the motor wiring plug.

1991–92 Sentra

The wiper motor is on the firewall under the hood. The operating linkage is on the firewall inside the vehicle.

1. Disconnect negative battery cable. Detach the motor wiring plug.

2. Working from inside the vehicle, remove the nut connecting the linkage to the wiper shaft.

3. Unbolt and remove the wiper motor from the firewall.

To install:

4. To reduce wiper arm looseness, prior to connecting the wiper arm, make sure the motor spline shaft and pivot area is completely free of debris and corrosion. Wire brush as necessary.

Rear Wiper Motor

REMOVAL & INSTALLATION

➡ To perform this procedure, you will need a soft material used to seal the plastic water shields used in vehicle doors and tailgates.

1. Disconnect the negative battery cable. Bend the wiper arm to raise the wiper blade off the rear window glass. Then, remove the attaching bolt or nut and washers and work the wiper arm off the motor shaft.

2. Remove the attaching screws and remove the tailgate inner finish panel. Carefully peel the plastic water shield off the sealer.

3. Disconnect the electrical connector at the motor. Remove the motor mounting bolts and remove the motor.

4. Install the motor in reverse of the removal procedure. Before installing the water shield, run a fresh ring of sealer around the outer edge.

Windshield Washer Fluid Reservoir

REMOVAL & INSTALLATION

Front and Rear

1. Disconnect the negative battery cable and reservoir electrical connector.

2. Disconnect the fluid tube from the washer motor. If the tube is too tight to remove, do not force. Heat the tube with a heat gun if the tube has no extra slack or cut the tube at the motor end.

3. Remove the reservoir retaining bolts and slide out of the bracket.

4. Installation is the reverse of removal. Apply petroleum jelly to the motor nipple before installing the washer tube.

Windshield Washer Motor

REMOVAL & INSTALLATION

Front and Rear

Remove the washer reservoir/motor assembly from the vehicle and drain into a suitable container. Pull the motor from the rubber grommet. If having difficulty, lubricate the grommet with penetrating oil and try again. Apply petroleum jelly to install the motor.

INSTRUMENTS AND SWITCHES

✻✻ CAUTION

To avoid rendering the SRS (Supplemental Restraint System) inoperative, which could lead to personal injury or death in the event of a severe frontal collision, extreme caution must be taken when servicing the electrical related systems. All SRS electrical wiring harnesses and connectors are covered with YELLOW outer insulation. Do not use electrical test equipment on any circuit related to the SRS (air bag).

Air Bag

DISARMING

On vehicles equipped with an air bag, turn the ignition switch to OFF position. The negative battery cable must be disconnected and wait 10 minutes after the cable is disconnected before working on the system. SRS sensors must always be installed with the arrow marks facing the front of the vehicle.

Instrument Cluster

REMOVAL & INSTALLATION

1983–90 Pulsar

1. Disconnect the negative battery terminal.
2. Loosen the tilt adjusting lever and completely lower the steering column.
3. Remove the steering column cover.
4. Remove the mounting screws and the instrument cluster hood.
5. Remove the instrument cluster screws, pull the cluster forward, then disconnect the speedometer cable and the harness connectors.
6. Remove the instrument cluster from the vehicle.

To install:

7. Install the instrument cluster and attaching screws.
8. Reconnect all electrical connections and speedometer cable.
9. Reconnect steering column and cover.
10. Connect the battery cable.
11. Start engine and check for proper operation of all components.

1982–86 Sentra

1. Disconnect the battery negative cable. Remove the two screws from the lower side of the instrument hood and remove it.
2. Remove the two screws from the top of the instrument cluster, pull it out to disconnect the electrical connectors, and remove it.
3. Install the cluster in reverse of the removal procedure.

1987–88 Sentra

1. Disconnect the battery negative cable. Remove the two screws from underneath the cluster bezel and the two from the underside of the cluster hood. Then, use a thin, flat object to depress the locking pawl in the fastener located at the top left of the cluster bezel; then, slide this fastener out of the dash. Now, slide the cluster bezel out of the dash.
2. Remove the mounting screws from the underside and front of the instrument cluster and then pull it out of the dash panel far enough for you to gain access to the electrical connectors. Disconnect these connectors and then remove the cluster by sliding it out of the dash.
3. Install the cluster by reversing the removal procedure.

1991–92 Sentra

1. Disconnect the negative battery cable.

✻✻ CAUTION

To avoid rendering the SRS (Supplemental Restraint System) inoperative, which could lead to personal injury or death in the event of a severe frontal collision, extreme caution must be taken when servicing the electrical related systems. All SRS electrical wiring harnesses and connectors are covered with YELLOW outer insulation. Do not use electrical test equipment on any circuit related to the SRS (air bag).

2. Remove the steering wheel and the steering column covers as outlined in section 8.
3. Remove the instrument cluster lid by removing its screws.
4. Remove the instrument cluster screws.
5. Gently withdraw the cluster from the instrument pad and disconnect all wiring and speedometer cable. Make sure the wires are marked clearly to avoid confusion during installation. Be careful not to damage the printed circuit.
6. Remove the cluster.

To install:

7. Install the cluster and connect all wiring and speedometer cable.
8. Install the instrument cluster screws.
9. Install the instrument cluster lid and its screws.
10. Install the steering wheel and the steering column covers.
11. Connect the negative battery cable and check operation.

Speedometer

➡ If equipped with a digital speedometer, the entire cluster assembly must be replaced if the speedometer is faulty.

REMOVAL & INSTALLATION

Analog (Needle Type) Speedometers

1. Disconnect the negative battery cable.
2. Remove the cluster.
3. Disconnect the speedometer cable and remove the speedometer fasteners.
4. Carefully remove the speedometer from the cluster. Be careful not to damage the printed circuit board.
5. Installation is the reverse of the removal procedure.

Speedometer Cable

REPLACEMENT

1. Remove any lower dash covers that may be in the way and disconnect the speedometer cable from the back of the speedometer.

➡ On some models it may be easier to remove the instrument cluster to gain access to the cable. On the Stanza and Pulsar, the cable connector-to-instrument cluster has a snap release; simply press on the connector tab to release it.

2. Pull the cable from the cable housing. If the cable is broken, the other half of the cable will have to be removed from the transaxle end. Unscrew the retaining knob at the transaxle and remove the cable from the transaxle extension housing.
3. Lubricate the cable with graphite powder (sold as speedometer cable lubricant) and feed the cable into the housing. It is best to start at the speedometer end and feed the cable down towards the transaxle.

➡ It is usually necessary to unscrew the transaxle connection and install the cable end to the gear, then reconnect the housing to the transaxle. Slip the cable end into the speedometer and reconnect the cable housing.

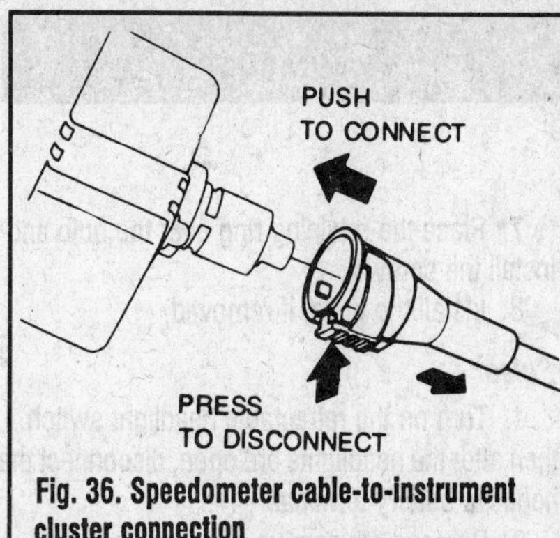
PUSH
TO CONNECT
PRESS
TO DISCONNECT
Fig. 36. Speedometer cable-to-instrument cluster connection

Windshield Wiper Switch

REMOVAL & INSTALLATION

1982-83 Vehicles

1. Remove the steering wheel and the steering column cover as outlined in section 8.
2. Disconnect all of the combination switch wires.
3. Loosen the retaining screw and remove the combination switch wires.
4. To install, reverse the removal procedures.

1984-92 Vehicles

The wiper switch can be removed without removing the combination switch from the steering column.

1. Remove the steering column cover.
2. Disconnect the wiper switch electrical connector.
3. Remove the wiper switch to combination switch retaining screws.
4. To install, reverse the removal procedures.

➡ On the 1987-88 Pulsar models the wiper switch is located in the dash. To remove this switch disconnect the electrical connector and remove the retaining screw.

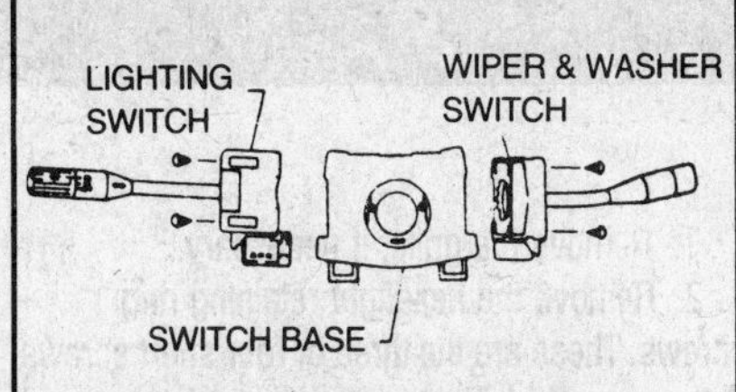
LIGHTING
SWITCH
WIPER & WASHER
SWITCH
SWITCH BASE
Fig. 37. Removing wiper switch from the combination switch — 1984-92 vehicles

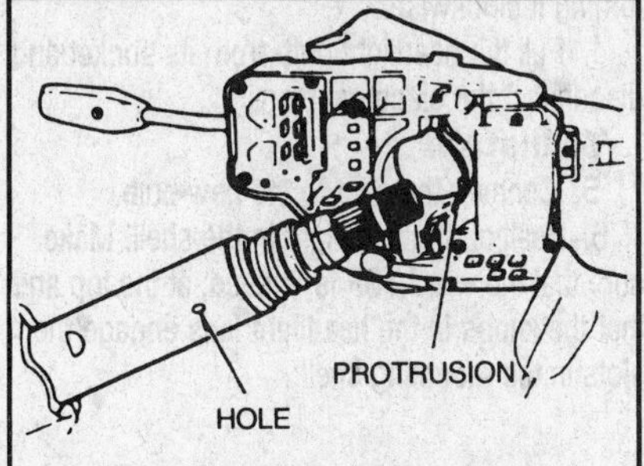
PROTRUSION
HOLE
Fig. 38. Removing combination switch from the steering column — all vehicles

Rear Window Wiper Switch

REMOVAL & INSTALLATION

1. Remove the instrument cluster.
2. Remove the nut that attaches the combination switch to the dash.
3. Disconnect the electrical connectors from the rear of the switch, then remove it.
4. Installation is the reverse of the removal procedure.

Headlight Switch

REMOVAL & INSTALLATION

1982-86 Sentra and 1983 Pulsar

1. Place the ignition switch in the **OFF** position and disconnect the negative battery terminal.
2. Remove the steering wheel and the steering column cover.
3. Disconnect the wiring harness from the combination switch.
4. Loosen the retaining screws and remove the combination switch.
5. To install, reverse the removal procedures.

1984-92 Vehicles

The headlight switch can be removed without removing the combination switch from the steering column.

1. Remove the steering column cover.
2. Disconnect the headlight switch electrical connector.
3. Remove the headlight switch to combination switch retaining screws.
4. To install, reverse the removal procedures.

➡ On the 1987-90 Pulsar models the headlight switch is located in the dash. To remove this switch disconnect the electrical connector and remove the retaining screw.

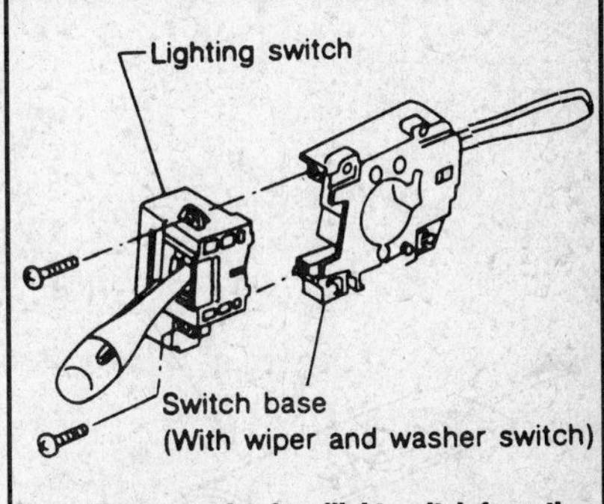
Lighting switch
Switch base
(With wiper and washer switch)
Fig. 39. Removing headlight switch from the combination switch — 1984-92 vehicles

Ignition Switch

Ignition switch removal and installation procedures are covered in section 8; Suspension and Steering.

LIGHTING

Headlights

REMOVAL & INSTALLATION

Sealed Beam Type

SENTRA

➡ Many vehicles have radiator grilles which are unit constructed to also serve as headlight frames. In this case, it will be necessary to remove the grille to gain access to the headlights.

1. Remove the grille, if necessary.
2. Remove the headlight retaining ring screws. These are the three or four short screws in the assembly. There are also two longer screws at the top and side of the headlight which are used to aim the headlight. Do not tamper with these or the headlight will have to be re-aimed.
3. Remove the ring on round headlights by turning it clockwise.
4. Pull the headlight bulb from its socket and disconnect the electrical plug.

To install:

5. Connect the plug to the new bulb.
6. Position the headlight in the shell. Make sure that the word TOP is, indeed, at the top and that the knobs in the headlight lens engage the slots in the mounting shell.
7. Place the retaining ring over the bulb and install the screws.
8. Install the grille, if removed.

Pulsar

1. Turn on the retractable headlight switch, then after the headlights are open, disconnect the negative battery terminal.
2. Remove the screws and the clip, then headlight cover.
3. Remove the retaining ring cover.
4. Pull out the headlight, remove the rubber cap and the wiring connector. Remove the headlight.
5. To install, reverse the removal procedures.

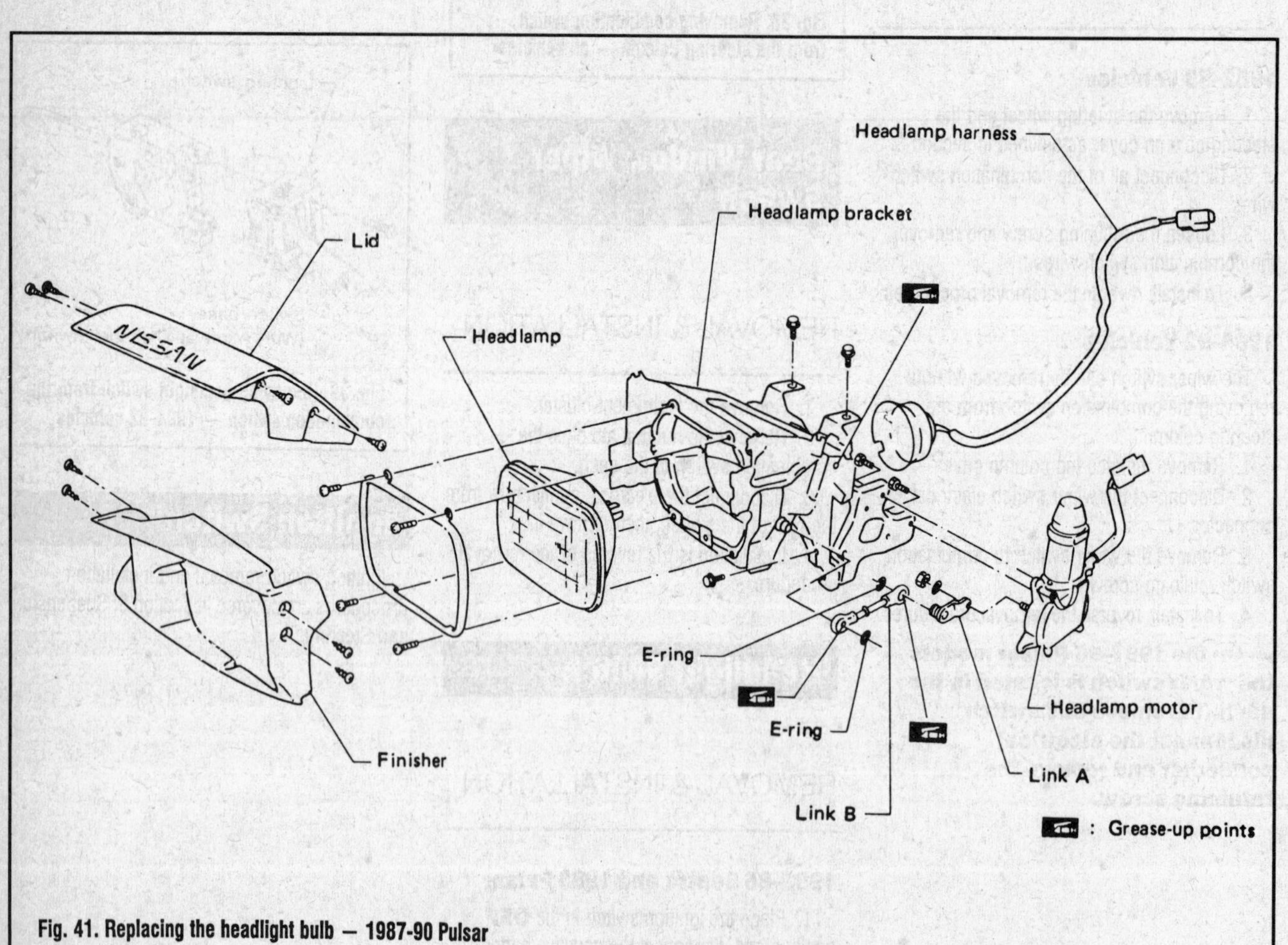
Headlamp harness
Headlamp bracket
Lid
NISSAN
Headlamp
E-ring
E-ring
Headlamp motor
Link A
Link B
Finisher
: Grease-up points

Fig. 41. Replacing the headlight bulb — 1987-90 Pulsar

Composite Type Headlight

SENTRA

➡ **Grasp only the plastic base when handling the bulb. Never touch the glass portion of the bulb. When the bulb is ON, the finger oil can cause the bulb to burst.**

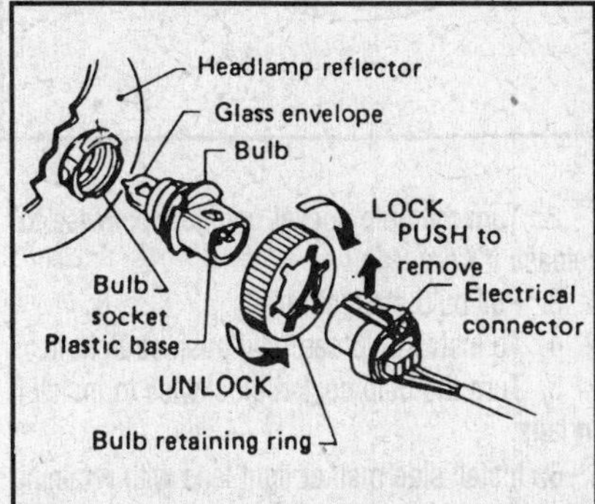

Headlamp reflector
Glass envelope
Bulb
LOCK
PUSH to remove
Bulb socket
Electrical connector
Plastic base
UNLOCK
Bulb retaining ring

Fig. 40. Composite type headlight bulb removal

1. Open the engine hood.
2. Turn the bulb retaining ring counterclockwise until it is free from the headlight reflector.
3. Disconnect the wiring harness from the backside of the bulb.
4. Remove the bulb from the retainer carefully.

To install:

5. Install the bulb into the retainer.
6. Apply electrical conductive grease to the harness connector and install the assembly.
7. Install the bulb into the reflector and turn clockwise until it stops.
8. Close the hood and check operation.

HEADLIGHT AIMING

➧ SEE FIGS. 42-46

1. Raise the headlight doors on 1983–90 Pulsar.
2. Turn the low beam ON.
3. Use the adjusting screws to perform aiming adjustment. The screw on the side is for side to side adjustment and the screw on the bottom is for up and down adjustment.
4. Park the vehicle in front of bare wall. Refer to the illustration.

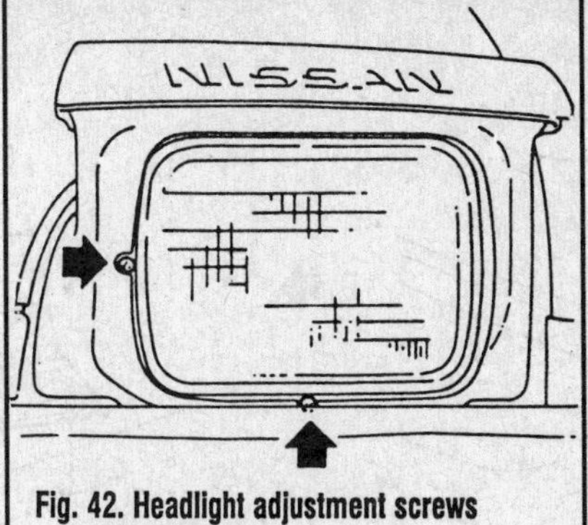
Fig. 42. Headlight adjustment screws — sealed beam type

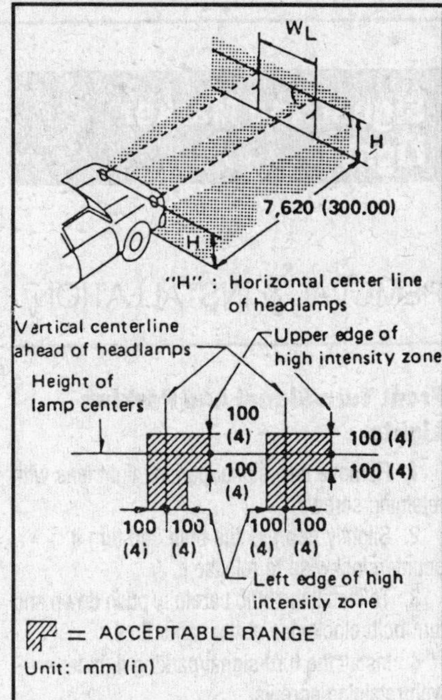

W L
H
7,620 (300.00)
H
"H" : Horizontal center line of headlamps
Vertical centerline ahead of headlamps
Upper edge of high intensity zone
Height of lamp centers
100 (4)
100 (4)
100 (4)
100 (4)
100 (4)
100 (4)
100 (4)
100 (4)
Left edge of high intensity zone
= ACCEPTABLE RANGE
Unit: mm (in)

Fig. 43. Headlight aiming illustration — early model vehicles, refer to text for procedures

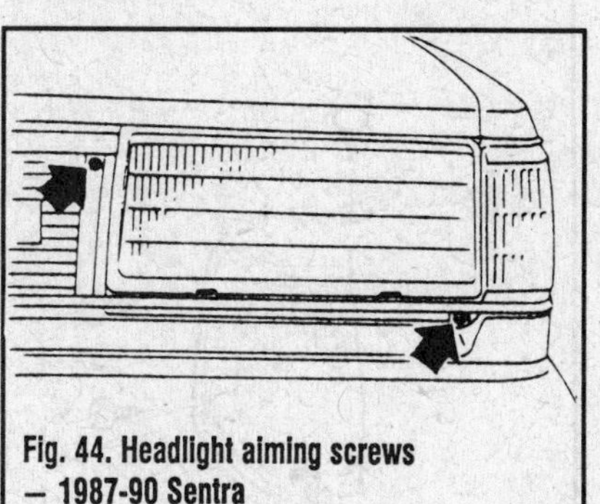
Fig. 44. Headlight aiming screws — 1987-90 Sentra

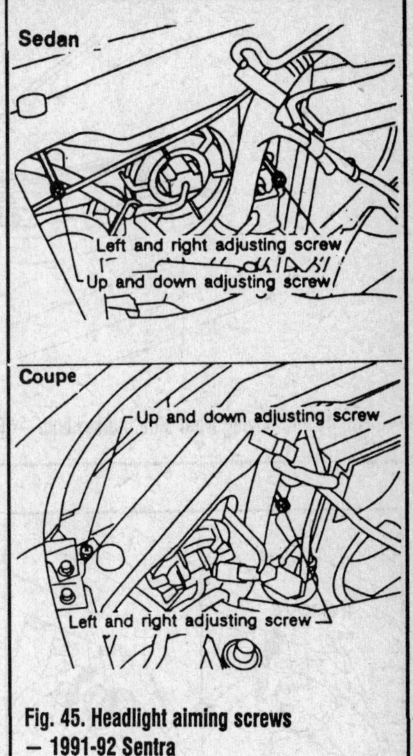

Sedan
Left and right adjusting screw
Up and down adjusting screw
Coupe
Up and down adjusting screw
Left and right adjusting screw

Fig. 45. Headlight aiming screws — 1991-92 Sentra

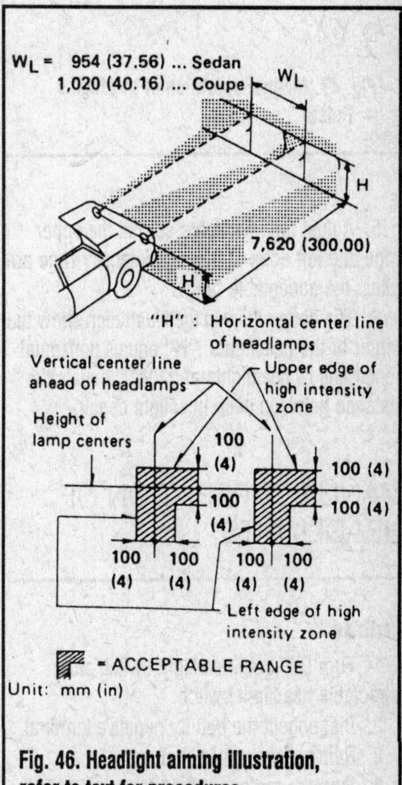

W L = 954 (37.56) ... Sedan
1,020 (40.16) ... Coupe
W L
H
7,620 (300.00)
H
"H" : Horizontal center line of headlamps
Vertical center line ahead of headlamps
Upper edge of high intensity zone
Height of lamp centers
100 (4)
100 (4)
100 (4)
100 (4)
100 (4)
100 (4)
100 (4)
100 (4)
Left edge of high intensity zone
- ACCEPTABLE RANGE
Unit: mm (in)

Fig. 46. Headlight aiming illustration, refer to text for procedures

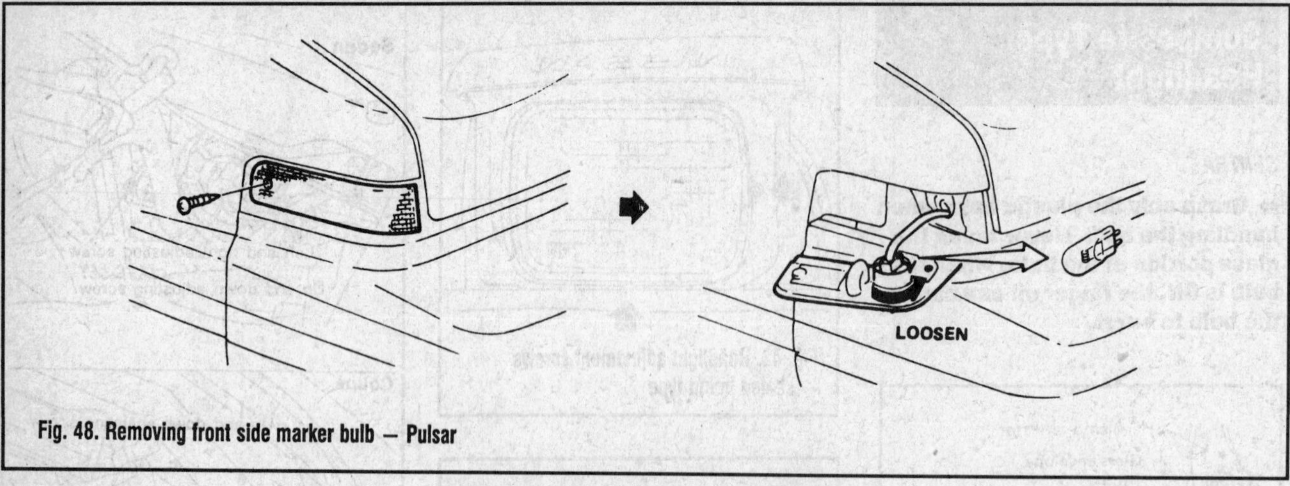
LOOSEN
Fig. 48. Removing front side marker bulb — Pulsar

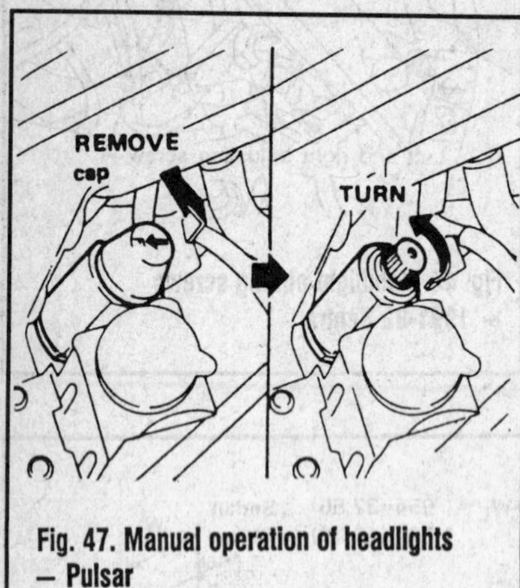
REMOVE
cap
TURN
Fig. 47. Manual operation of headlights — Pulsar

5. Adjust the headlights so that the upper edge and left edge of the high intensity zone are within the acceptable range.

6. The dotted lines in the illustration show the center of the headlights. "H" equals horizontal center line of headlights and "WL" equals the distance between each headlight center.

MANUAL OPERATION OF HEADLIGHTS

Pulsar

1. Turn OFF both headlight switch and retractable headlight switch.
2. Disconnect the battery negative terminal.
3. Remove the motor shaft cap.
4. Turn the motor shaft counterclockwise by hand until the headlights are opened or closed.
5. Reinstall the motor shaft cap and connect the battery cable.

Signal And Marker Lights

REMOVAL & INSTALLATION

Front Turn Signal And Parking Lights

1. Remove turn signal/parking light lens with retaining screws.
2. Slightly depress the bulb and turn it counterclockwise to release it.
3. To install the bulb carefully push down and turn bulb clockwise at the same time.
4. Install the turn signal/parking light lens with retaining screws.

Side Marker Lights

1. Remove side marker light lens with retaining screws.
2. Turn the bulb socket counterclockwise to release it from lens.
3. Pull bulb straight out.
4. To install bulb carefully push straight in.
5. Turn the bulb socket clockwise to install it in lens.
6. Install side marker light lens with retaining screws.

Rear Turn Signal, Brake And Parking Lights

1. Remove rear trim panel in rear of vehicle to gain access to the bulb socket.
2. Slightly depress the bulb and turn it counterclockwise to release it.
3. To install the bulb carefully push down and turn bulb clockwise at the same time.
4. Install trim panel.

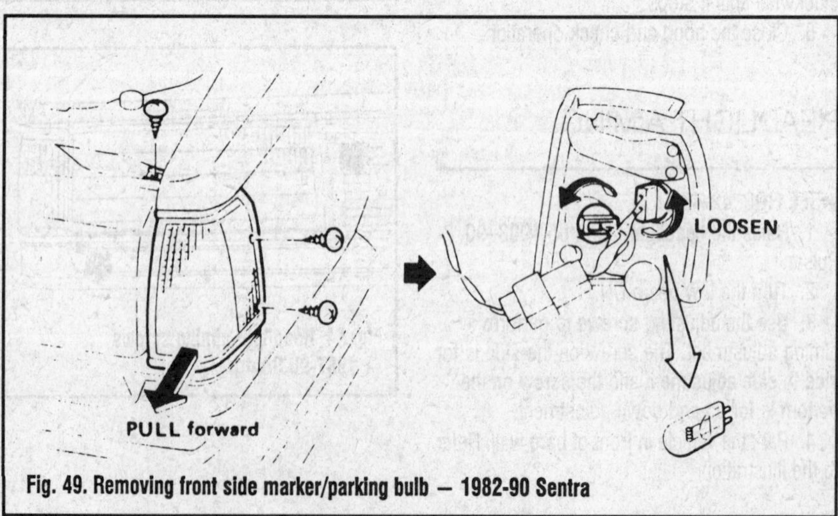
LOOSEN
PULL forward
Fig. 49. Removing front side marker/parking bulb — 1982-90 Sentra

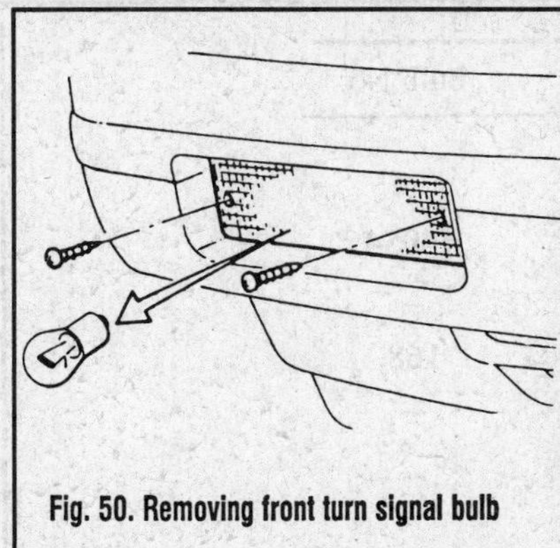

Fig. 50. Removing front turn signal bulb

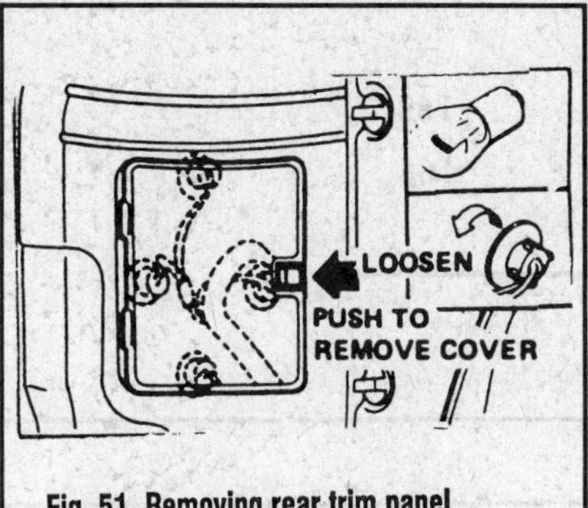
LOOSEN
PUSH TO
REMOVE COVER

Fig. 51. Removing rear trim panel — Sentra wagon, others similar

Item	Wattage (W)	SAE trade number
Headlamp (sealed beam) High/Low	65/55	–
Headlamp (Sealed beam halogen) High/Low	65/35	H6054
Front turn signal lamp	27	1156
Front side marker lamp	3.4	158
Clearance lamp	8	67
License plate lamp	10 8	– 67
Rear combination lamps		
Turn signal	27	1156
Back-up	27	1156
Stop/Tail	27/8	1157
Rear side marker lamp	3.4	158
Luggage compartment lamp	5	–
Interior lamp	10	–

Fig. 52. Light bulb application chart — 1982-84 Sentra

Item	Wattage (W)	Bulb No.
Headlamp (semi-sealed beam halogen) High/Low	65/45	9004
Front turn signal lamp	27	1156
Front side marker lamp	3.4	158
Clearance lamp	5	–
License plate lamp	10 8	– 67
Rear combination lamps		
Turn signal	27	1156
Back-up	27	1156
Stop/Tail	27/8	1157
Rear side marker lamp	3.4	158
Luggage compartment lamp	5	–
Interior lamp	10	–

Fig. 53. Light bulb application chart — 1985-86 Sentra

Item	Wattage (W)	Bulb No.
Headlamp (Sealed beam halogen)		
High/Low	65/35	H6054
Front turn signal lamp	23	–
Front side marker lamp	5	168
Clearance lamp	8	–
License plate lamp	10	–
Rear combination lamps		
Turn signal	23	–
Back-up	23	–
Stop/Tail	23/8	–
Rear side marker lamp	5	168
Luggage compartment lamp	5	168
Interior lamp	10	–

Fig. 54. Light bulb application chart — 1983-86 Pulsar

HEADLAMPS

Item	Wattage (W)	Bulb No.
Sealed beam (halogen)	65/35	H6054

OTHER LAMPS

Item	Wattage (W)	Bulb No.
Front side marker	3.8	194
Front turn signal lamp/Clearance	27/8	1157
License plate lamp	10, 8	–, 67*
Rear combination lamp		
Tail & Stop	27/8	1157
Turn signal	27	1156
Back-up	27	1156
High-mounted stop lamp (Interior)	27	1156
(Rear hatch)	27	1156
Rear side marker lamp	3.8	194
Interior lamp	10	–
Luggage compartment lamp	5	194

*For 8 (W) bulb

Fig. 55. Light bulb application chart — 1987-90 Pulsar

HEADLAMPS

Item	Wattage (W)	Bulb No.
Halogen bulb	65/45	9004

OTHER LAMPS

Sedan

Item	Wattage (W)	Bulb No.
Front turn signal lamp	27/8	1157NA
Front side marker lamp	3.8	194
Rear combination lamp		
Turn signal	27	1156
Stop/Tail	27/8	1157
Back-up	27	1156
Rear side marker	3.8	194
License plate lamp	5	
High-mounted stop lamp	13	
Interior lamp	10	
Trunk lamp	3.4	158

Coupe

Item	Wattage (W)	Bulb No.
Front clearance lamp	3.8	194
Front turn signal lamp	27	1156
Front side marker lamp	3.8	194
Front fog lamp	55	
Rear combination lamp		
Turn signal	27	1156
Stop/Tail	27/8	1157
Back-up	27	1156
Rear side marker lamp	3.8	194
License plate lamp	7.5	
High-mounted stop lamp	18	921
Interior lamp	10	
Luggage compartment lamp	5	

Fig. 57. Light bulb application chart — 1991-92 Sentra

HEADLAMPS

Item	Wattage (W)	Bulb No.
Halogen bulb	65/45	9004

OTHER LAMPS

Item	Wattage (W)	Bulb No.
Side combination lamp		
Clearance	3.8	194
Front side marker	3.8	194
Front turn signal lamp	27	1156
License plate lamp		
Sedan, Wagon	10	–
Coupe	5	–
Hatchback	7.5	–
Rear combination lamp		
Tail & Stop	27/8	1157
Turn signal	27	1156
Back-up	27	1156
High-mounted stop lamp		
Sedan, Wagon, Hatchback	27	1156
Coupe	12	1003
Rear side marker lamp	3.8	194
Interior lamp	10	–
Trunk room lamp	3.4	158
Luggage compartment lamp	5	194

Fig. 56. Light bulb application chart — 1987-90 Sentra

TRAILER WIRING

Wiring the car for towing is fairly easy. There are a number of good wiring kits available and these should be used, rather than trying to design your own. All trailers will need brake lights and turn signals as well as tail lights and side marker lights. Most states require extra marker lights for over wide trailers. Also, most states have recently required back-up lights for trailers, and most trailer manufacturers have been building trailers with back-up lights for several years.

Additionally, some Class I, most Class II and just about all Class III trailers will have electric brakes.

Add to this number an accessories wire, to operate trailer internal equipment or to charge the trailer's battery, and you can have as many as seven wires in the harness.

Determine the equipment on your trailer and buy the wiring kit necessary. The kit will contain all the wires needed, plus a plug adapter set which included the female plug, mounted on the bumper or hitch, and the male plug, wired into, or plugged into the trailer harness.

When installing the kit, follow the manufacturer's instructions. The color coding of the wires is standard throughout the industry.

One point to note, most imported vehicles, have separate turn signals. The signals operate with the same bulb. For those vehicles with separate turn signals, you can purchase an isolation unit so that the brake lights won't blink whenever the turn signals are operated, or, you can go to your local electronics supply house and buy four diodes to wire in series with the brake and turn signal bulbs. Diodes will isolate the brake and turn signals. The choice is yours. The isolation units are simple and quick to install, but far more expensive than the diodes. The diodes, however, require more work to install properly, since they require the cutting of each bulb's wire and soldering in place of the diode.

One final point, the best kits are those with a spring loaded cover on the vehicle mounted socket. This cover prevents dirt and moisture from corroding the terminals. Never let the vehicle socket hang loosely. Always mount it securely to the bumper or hitch.

CIRCUIT PROTECTION

Fuses

On all vehicles, the fuse block is located under the left side of the instrument panel. Later model vehicles have auxiliary fuse and relay boxes located in the engine compartment

REMOVAL & INSTALLATION

The fuses can be easily inspected to see if they are blown. Simply pull the fuse from the block, inspect it and replace it with a new one, if necessary.

➡ **When replacing a blown fuse, be certain to replace it with one of the correct amperage.**

Fusible Links

A fusible link(s) is a protective device used in an electrical circuit. When current increases beyond a certain amperage, the fusible metal wire of the link melts, thus breaking the electrical circuit and preventing further damage to the other components and wiring. Whenever a fusible link is melted because of a short circuit, correct the cause before installing a new link.

All fusible links are the plug in kind. To replace them, simply unplug the bad link and insert the new one.

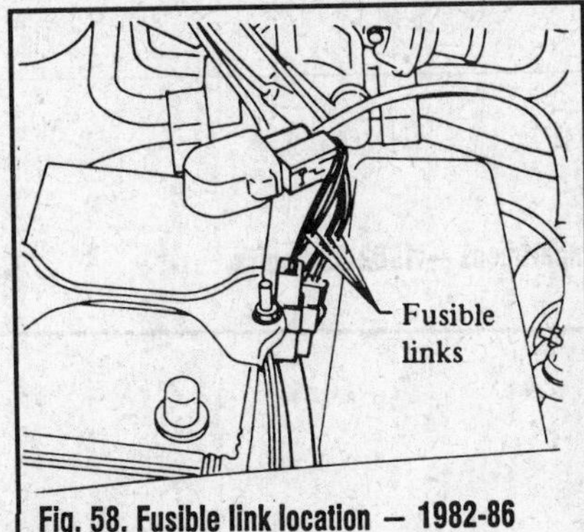
Fusible
links

Fig. 58. Fusible link location — 1982-86 vehicles

Circuit Breakers

Circuit breakers are also located in the fuse block. A circuit breaker is an electrical switch which breaks the circuit during an electrical overload. The circuit breaker will remain open until the short or overload condition in the circuit is corrected.

Flasher

To replace the flasher carefully pull it from the electrical connector. If necessary remove any component that restricts removal.

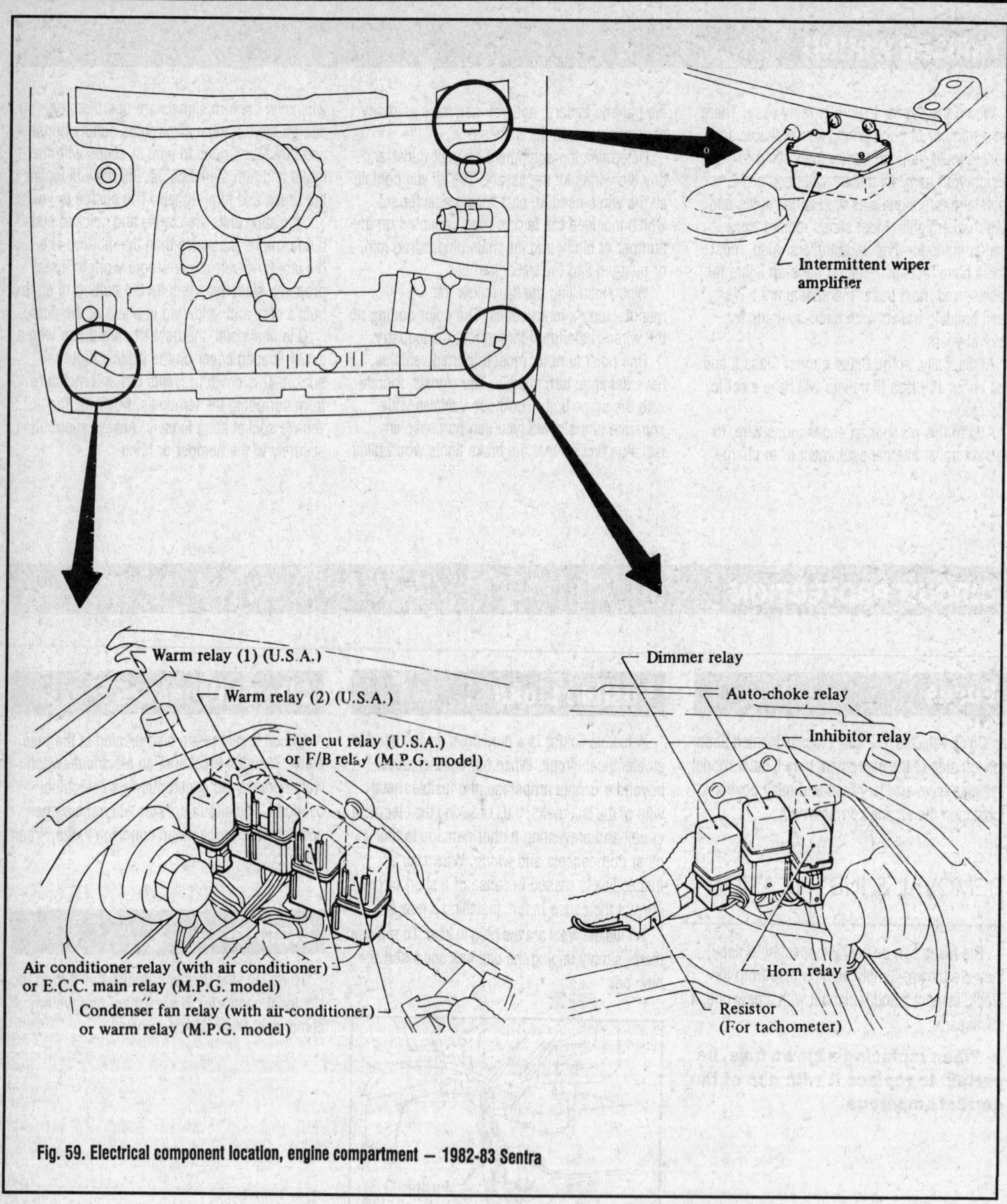
Intermittent wiper amplifier
Warm relay (1) (U.S.A.)
Warm relay (2) (U.S.A.)
Fuel cut relay (U.S.A.) or F/B relay (M.P.G. model)
Air conditioner relay (with air conditioner) or E.C.C. main relay (M.P.G. model)
Condenser fan relay (with air-conditioner) or warm relay (M.P.G. model)
Dimmer relay
Auto-choke relay
Inhibitor relay
Horn relay
Resistor (For tachometer)

Fig. 59. Electrical component location, engine compartment — 1982-83 Sentra

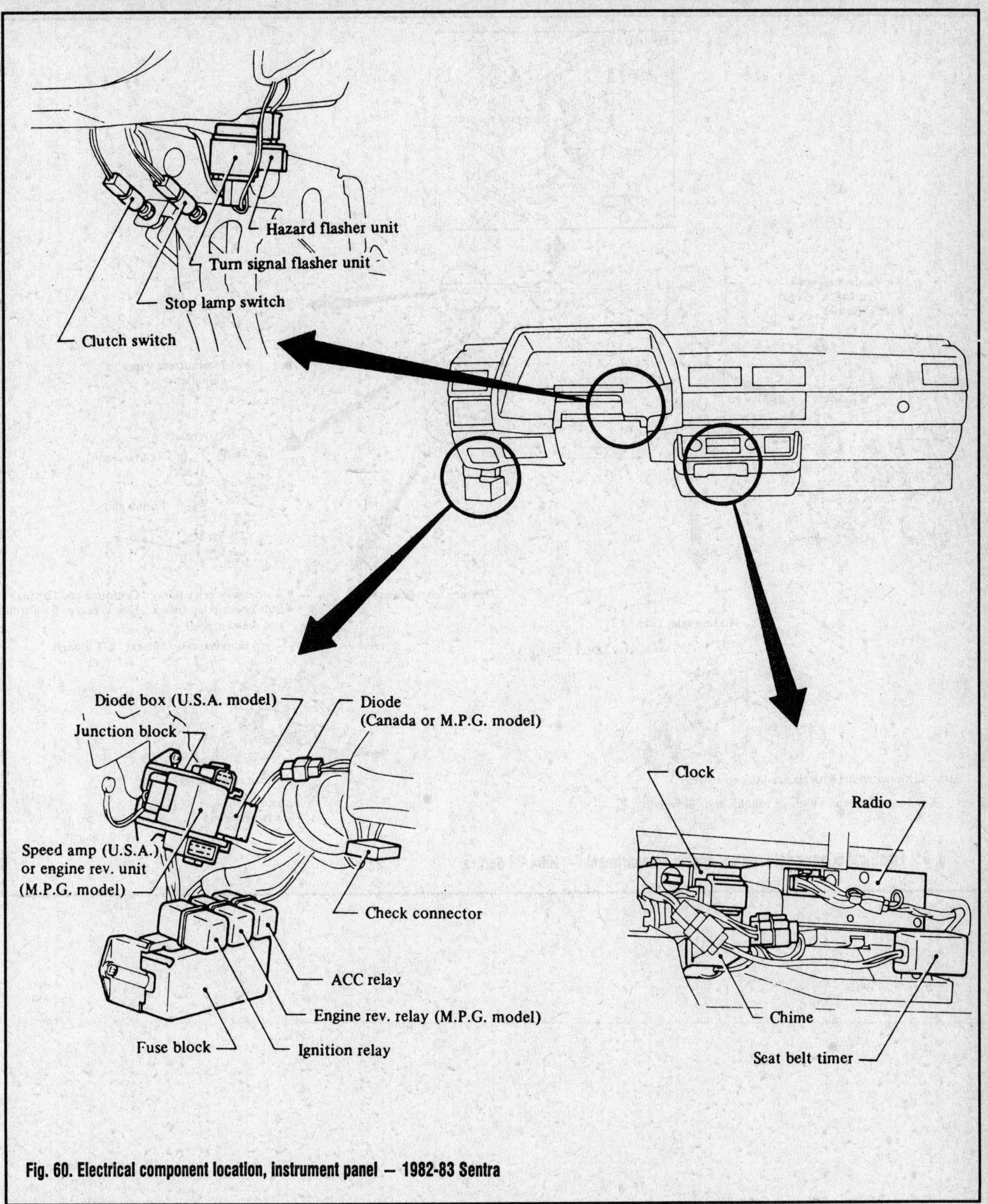
Hazard flasher unit
Turn signal flasher unit
Stop lamp switch
Clutch switch
Diode box (U.S.A. model)
Junction block
Diode
(Canada or M.P.G. model)
Speed amp (U.S.A.)
or engine rev. unit
(M.P.G. model)
Check connector
ACC relay
Engine rev. relay (M.P.G. model)
Fuse block
Ignition relay
Clock
Radio
Chime
Seat belt timer

Fig. 60. Electrical component location, instrument panel — 1982-83 Sentra

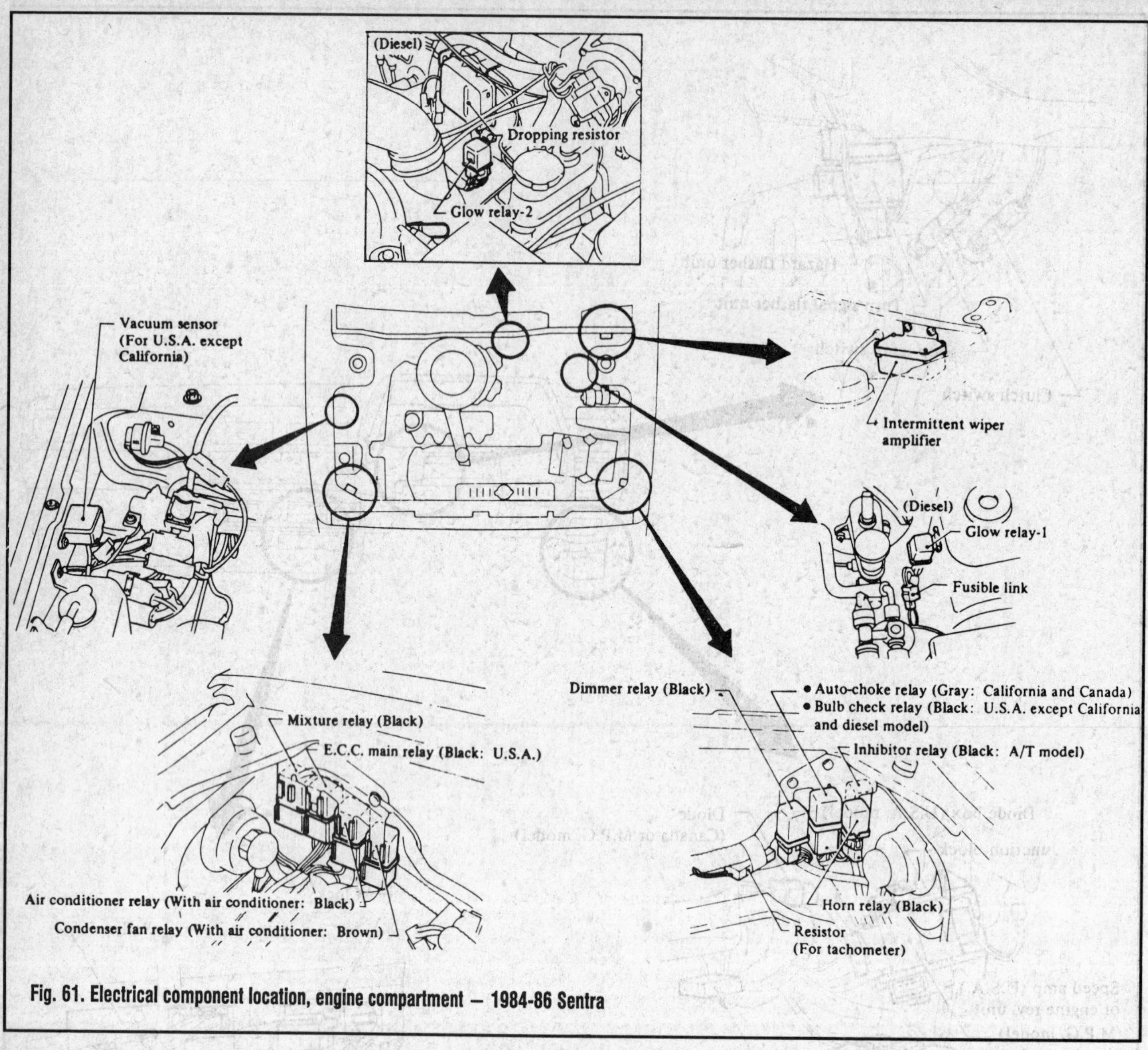
(Diesel)
Dropping resistor
Glow relay-2
Vacuum sensor
(For U.S.A. except
California)
Intermittent wiper
amplifier
(Diesel)
Glow relay-1
Fusible link
Dimmer relay (Black)
• Auto-choke relay (Gray: California and Canada)
• Bulb check relay (Black: U.S.A. except California
and diesel model)
Inhibitor relay (Black: A/T model)
Mixture relay (Black)
E.C.C. main relay (Black: U.S.A.)
Air conditioner relay (With air conditioner: Black)
Condenser fan relay (With air conditioner: Brown)
Horn relay (Black)
Resistor
(For tachometer)

Fig. 61. Electrical component location, engine compartment — 1984-86 Sentra

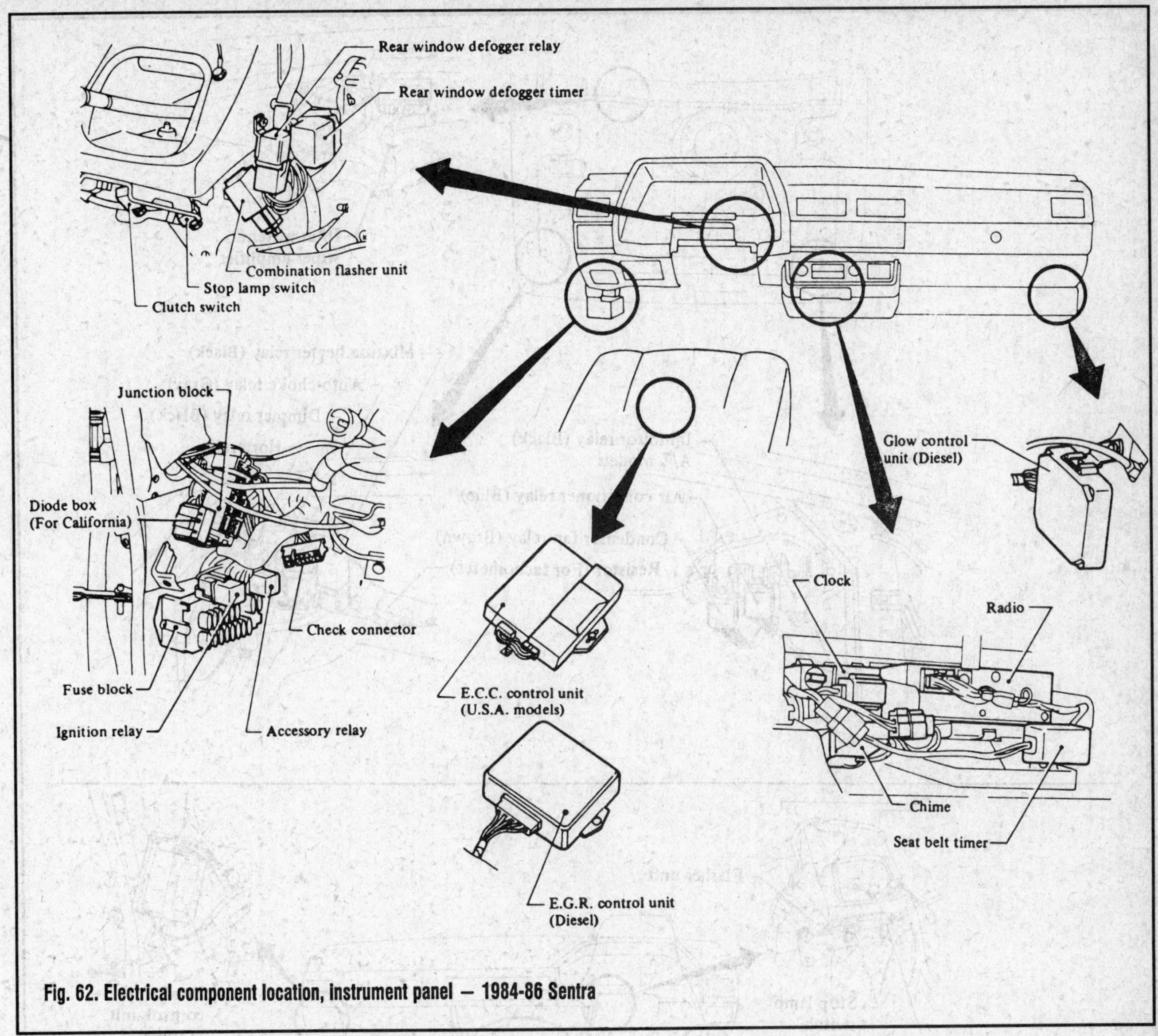
Rear window defogger relay
Rear window defogger timer
Combination flasher unit
Stop lamp switch
Clutch switch
Junction block
Diode box
(For California)
Check connector
Fuse block
Ignition relay
Accessory relay
E.C.C. control unit
(U.S.A. models)
E.G.R. control unit
(Diesel)
Glow control
unit (Diesel)
Clock
Radio
Chime
Seat belt timer

Fig. 62. Electrical component location, instrument panel — 1984-86 Sentra

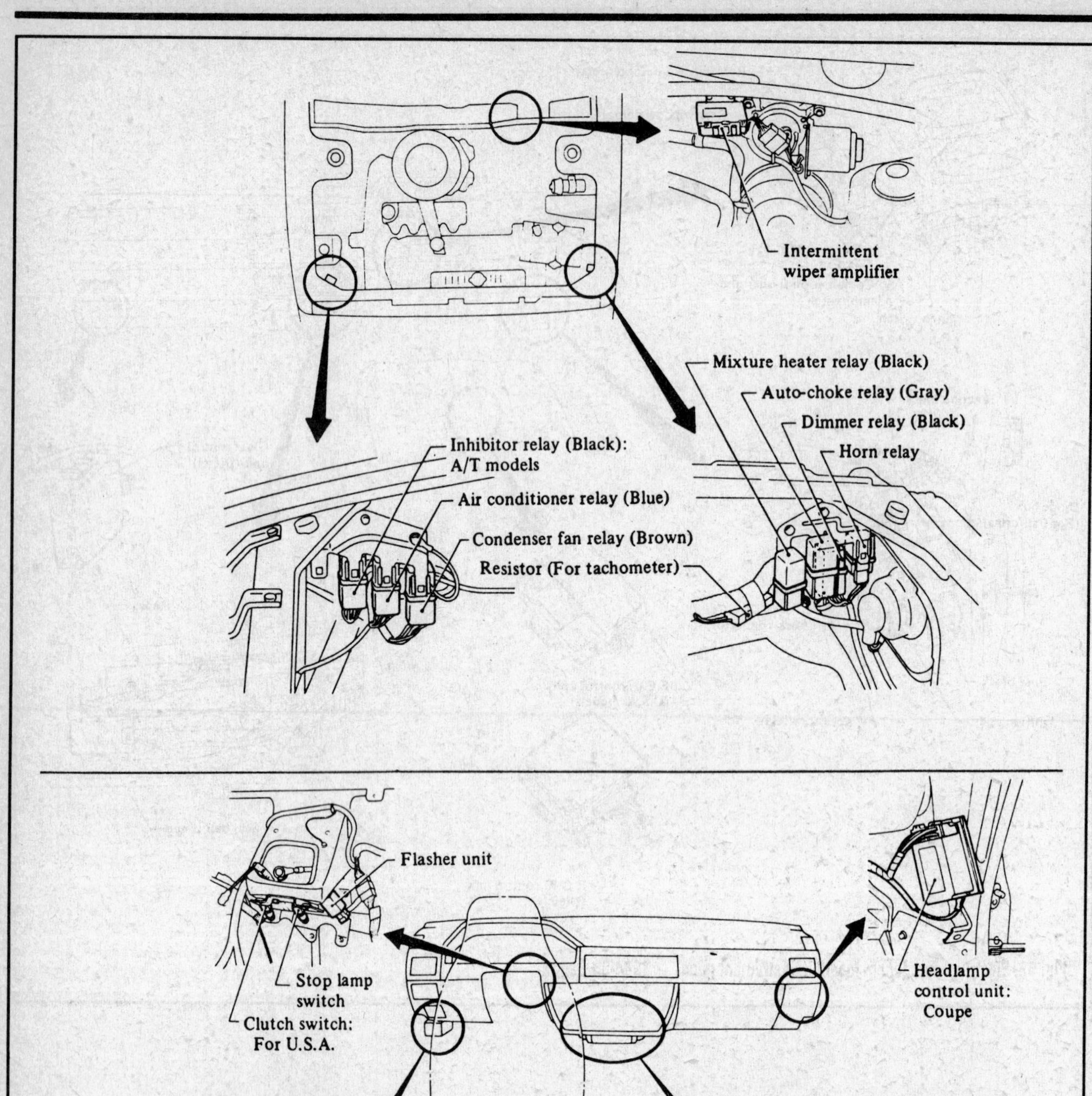
Intermittent wiper amplifier
Mixture heater relay (Black)
Auto-choke relay (Gray)
Dimmer relay (Black)
Horn relay
Inhibitor relay (Black): A/T models
Air conditioner relay (Blue)
Condenser fan relay (Brown)
Resistor (For tachometer)
Flasher unit
Stop lamp switch
Clutch switch: For U.S.A.
Headlamp control unit: Coupe
Engine revolution unit: U.S.A. except for California
10 km/h amplifier: For Canada
Seat belt timer
Check connector
Fuse block
Accessory relay (Black)
Ignition relay (Black)
E.C.C. control unit: For California
Warning chime

Fig. 63. Electrical component location — 1983-84 Pulsar

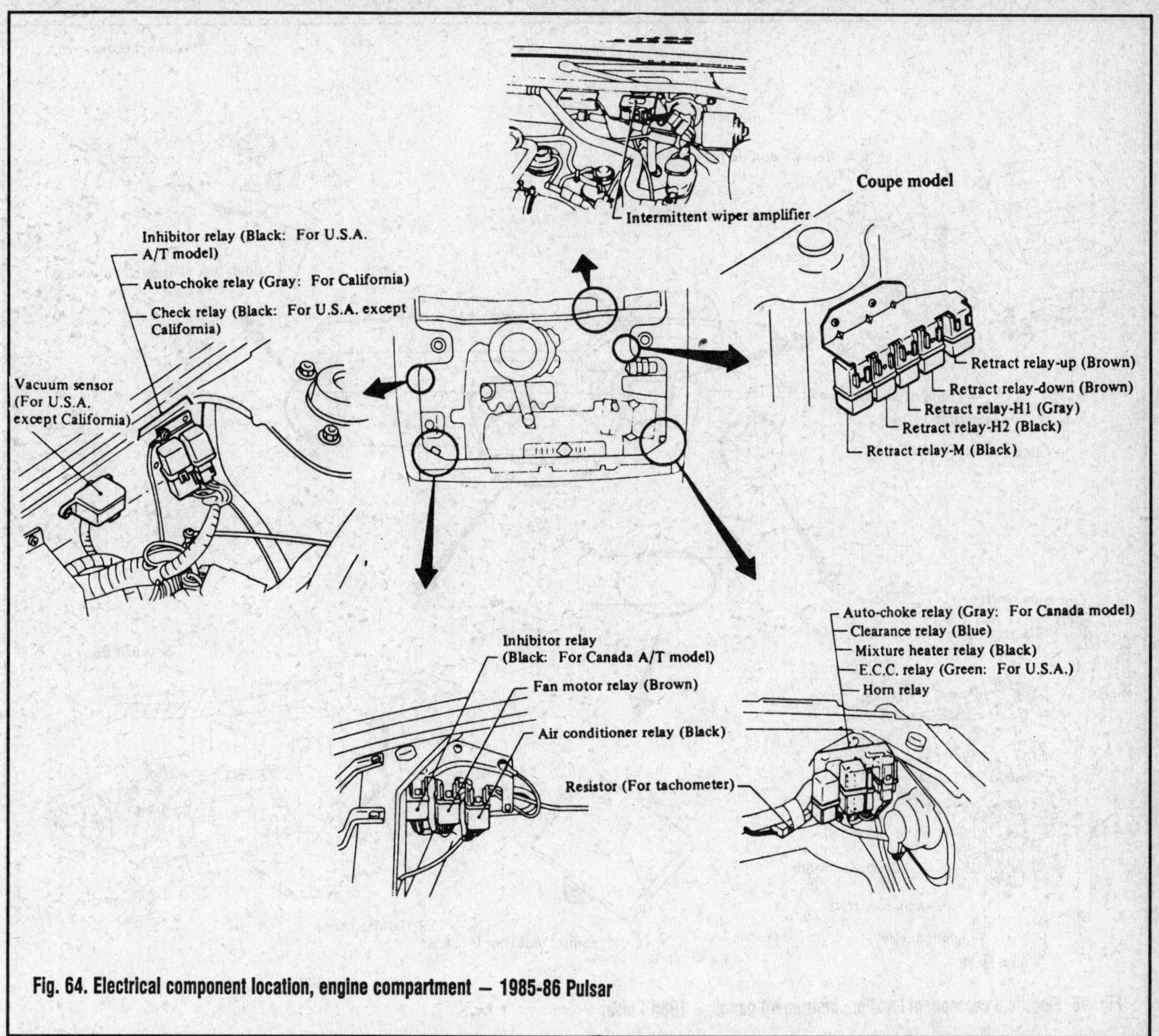
Coupe model
Intermittent wiper amplifier
Inhibitor relay (Black: For U.S.A. A/T model)
Auto-choke relay (Gray: For California)
Check relay (Black: For U.S.A. except California)
Vacuum sensor (For U.S.A. except California)
Retract relay-up (Brown)
Retract relay-down (Brown)
Retract relay-H1 (Gray)
Retract relay-H2 (Black)
Retract relay-M (Black)
Auto-choke relay (Gray: For Canada model)
Clearance relay (Blue)
Mixture heater relay (Black)
E.C.C. relay (Green: For U.S.A.)
Horn relay
Inhibitor relay (Black: For Canada A/T model)
Fan motor relay (Brown)
Air conditioner relay (Black)
Resistor (For tachometer)

Fig. 64. Electrical component location, engine compartment — 1985-86 Pulsar

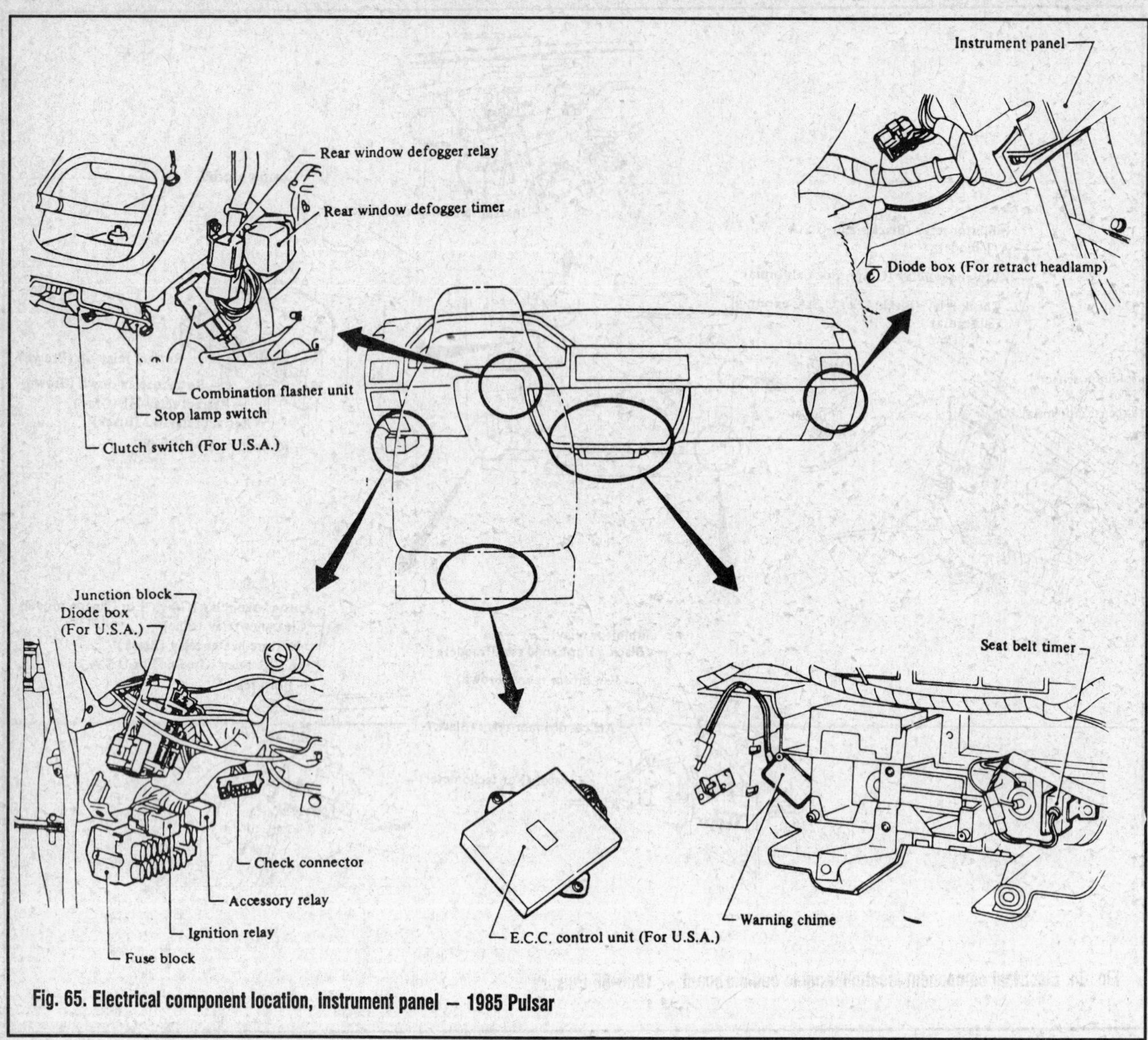
Instrument panel
Rear window defogger relay
Rear window defogger timer
Diode box (For retract headlamp)
Combination flasher unit
Stop lamp switch
Clutch switch (For U.S.A.)
Junction block
Diode box
(For U.S.A.)
Seat belt timer
Check connector
Accessory relay
Ignition relay
Fuse block
Warning chime
E.C.C. control unit (For U.S.A.)

Fig. 65. Electrical component location, instrument panel – 1985 Pulsar

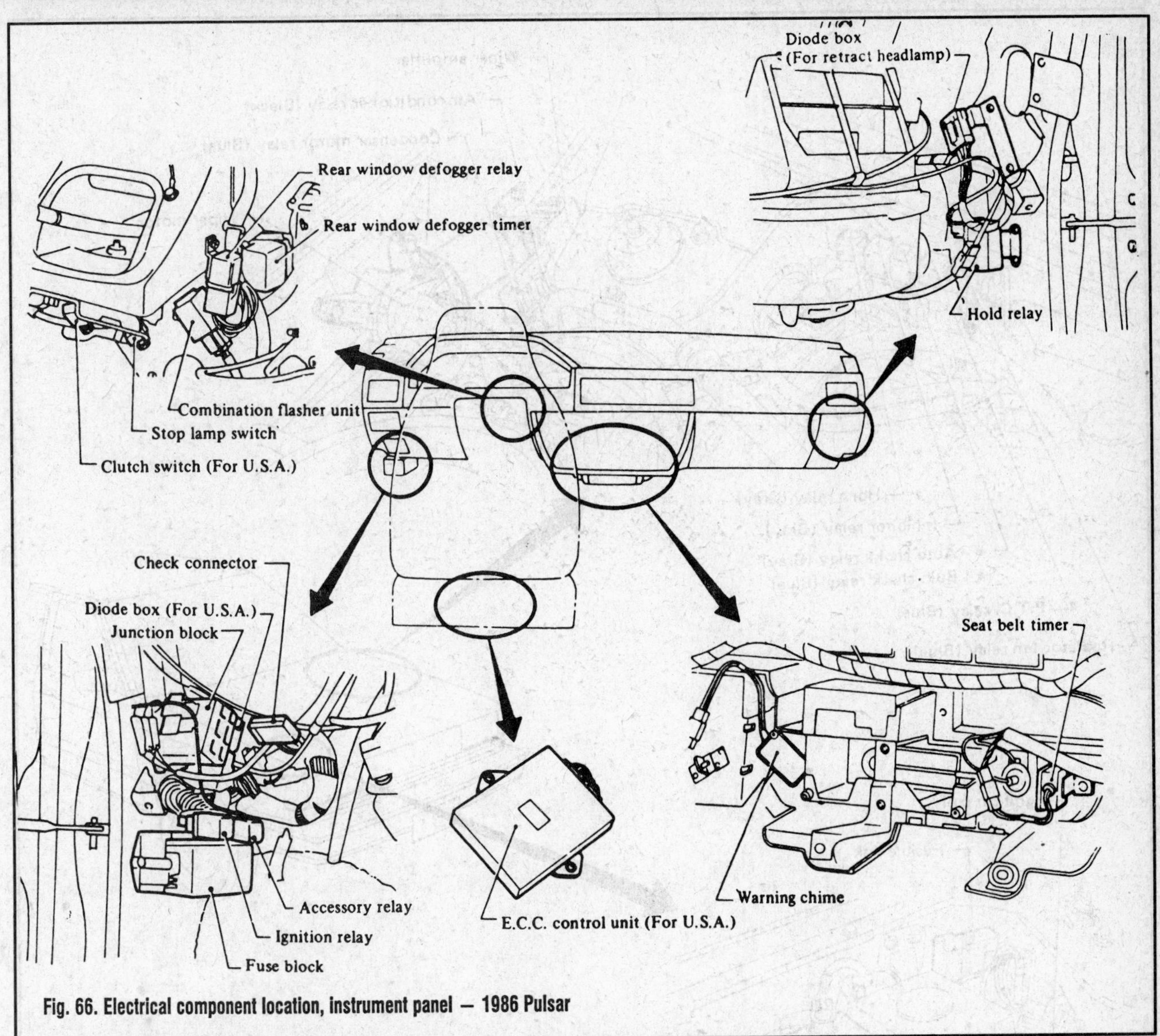
Diode box
(For retract headlamp)
Hold relay
Rear window defogger relay
Rear window defogger timer
Combination flasher unit
Stop lamp switch
Clutch switch (For U.S.A.)
Check connector
Diode box (For U.S.A.)
Junction block
Seat belt timer
Accessory relay
Ignition relay
Fuse block
E.C.C. control unit (For U.S.A.)
Warning chime

Fig. 66. Electrical component location, instrument panel — 1986 Pulsar

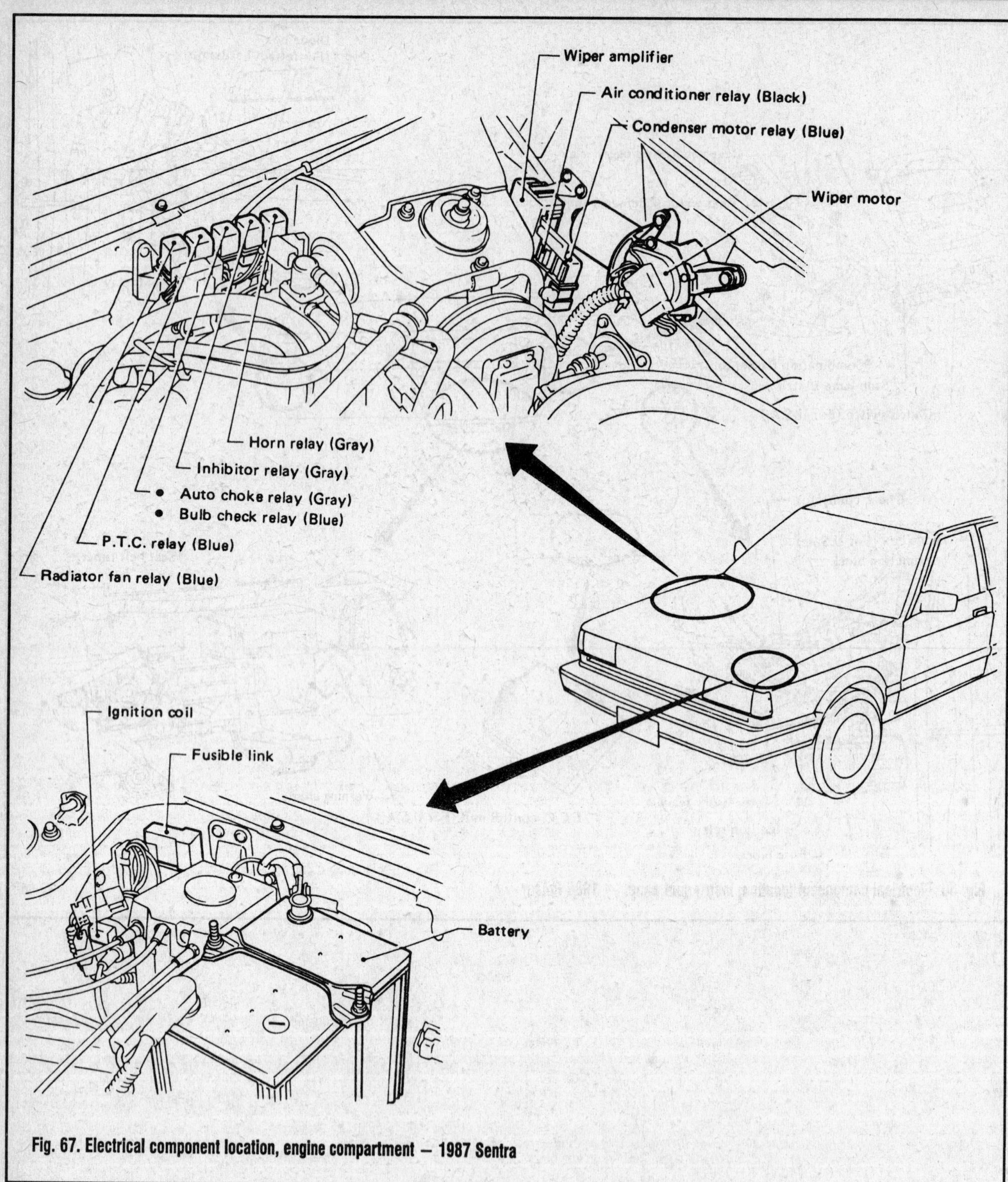
Wiper amplifier
Air conditioner relay (Black)
Condenser motor relay (Blue)
Wiper motor
Horn relay (Gray)
Inhibitor relay (Gray)
• Auto choke relay (Gray)
• Bulb check relay (Blue)
P.T.C. relay (Blue)
Radiator fan relay (Blue)
Ignition coil
Fusible link
Battery

Fig. 67. Electrical component location, engine compartment — 1987 Sentra

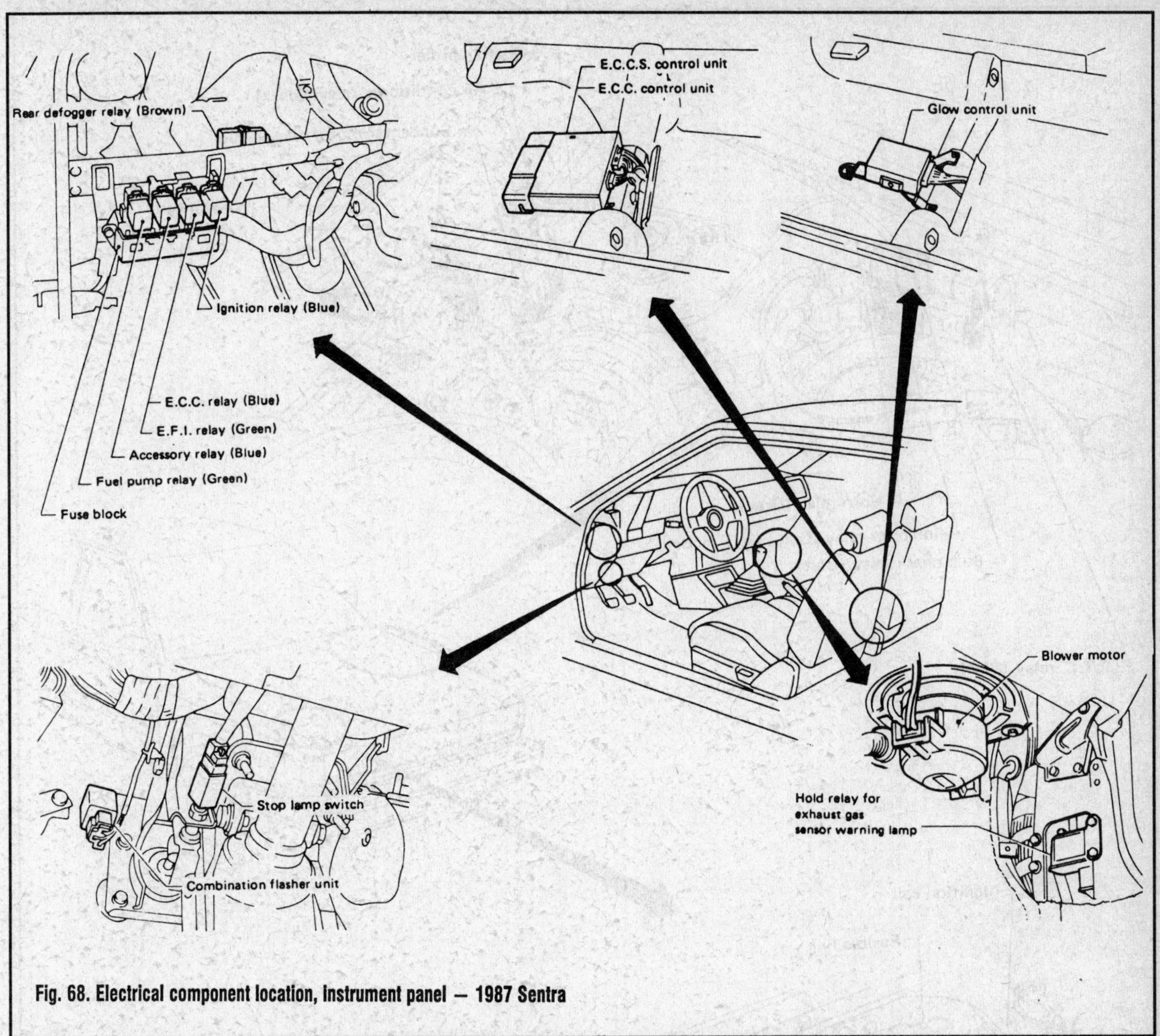
E.C.C.S. control unit
E.C.C. control unit
Glow control unit
Rear defogger relay (Brown)
Ignition relay (Blue)
E.C.C. relay (Blue)
E.F.I. relay (Green)
Accessory relay (Blue)
Fuel pump relay (Green)
Fuse block
Blower motor
Stop lamp switch
Combination flasher unit
Hold relay for
exhaust gas
sensor warning lamp

Fig. 68. Electrical component location, instrument panel — 1987 Sentra

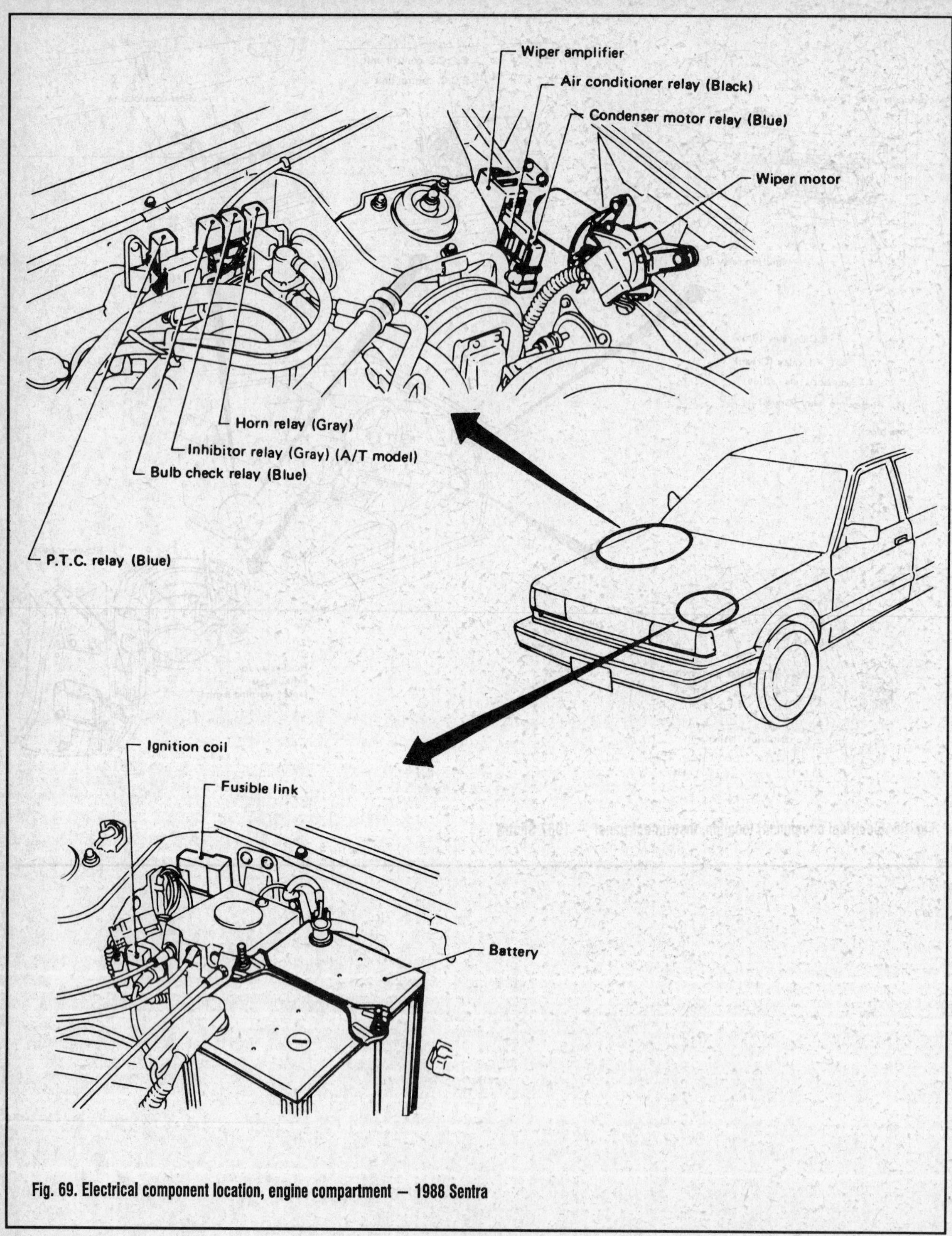
Wiper amplifier
Air conditioner relay (Black)
Condenser motor relay (Blue)
Wiper motor
Horn relay (Gray)
Inhibitor relay (Gray) (A/T model)
Bulb check relay (Blue)
P.T.C. relay (Blue)
Ignition coil
Fusible link
Battery

Fig. 69. Electrical component location, engine compartment – 1988 Sentra

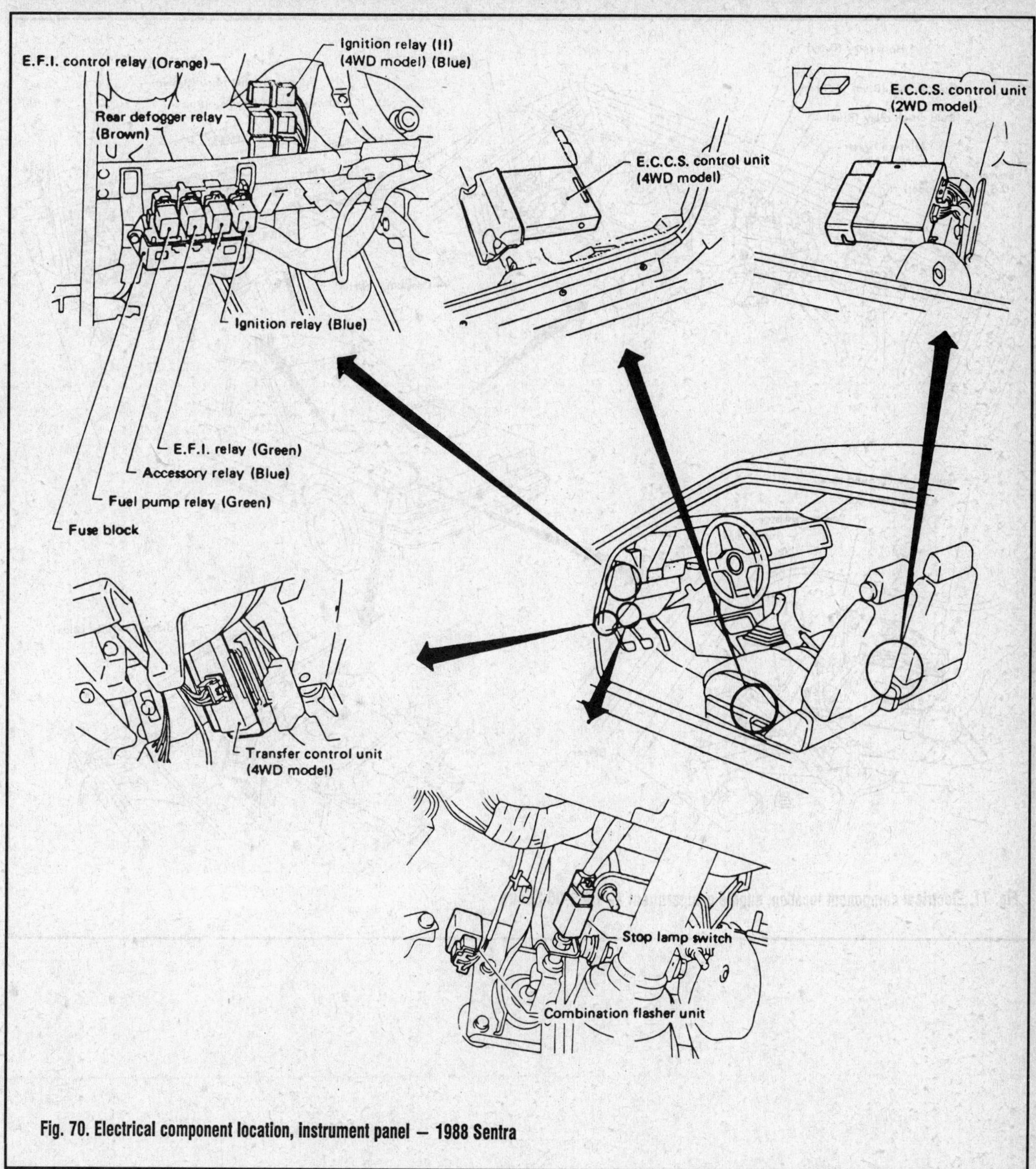
Ignition relay (II)
(4WD model) (Blue)
E.F.I. control relay (Orange)
Rear defogger relay
(Brown)
Ignition relay (Blue)
E.F.I. relay (Green)
Accessory relay (Blue)
Fuel pump relay (Green)
Fuse block
E.C.C.S. control unit
(4WD model)
E.C.C.S. control unit
(2WD model)
Transfer control unit
(4WD model)
Stop lamp switch
Combination flasher unit

Fig. 70. Electrical component location, instrument panel – 1988 Sentra

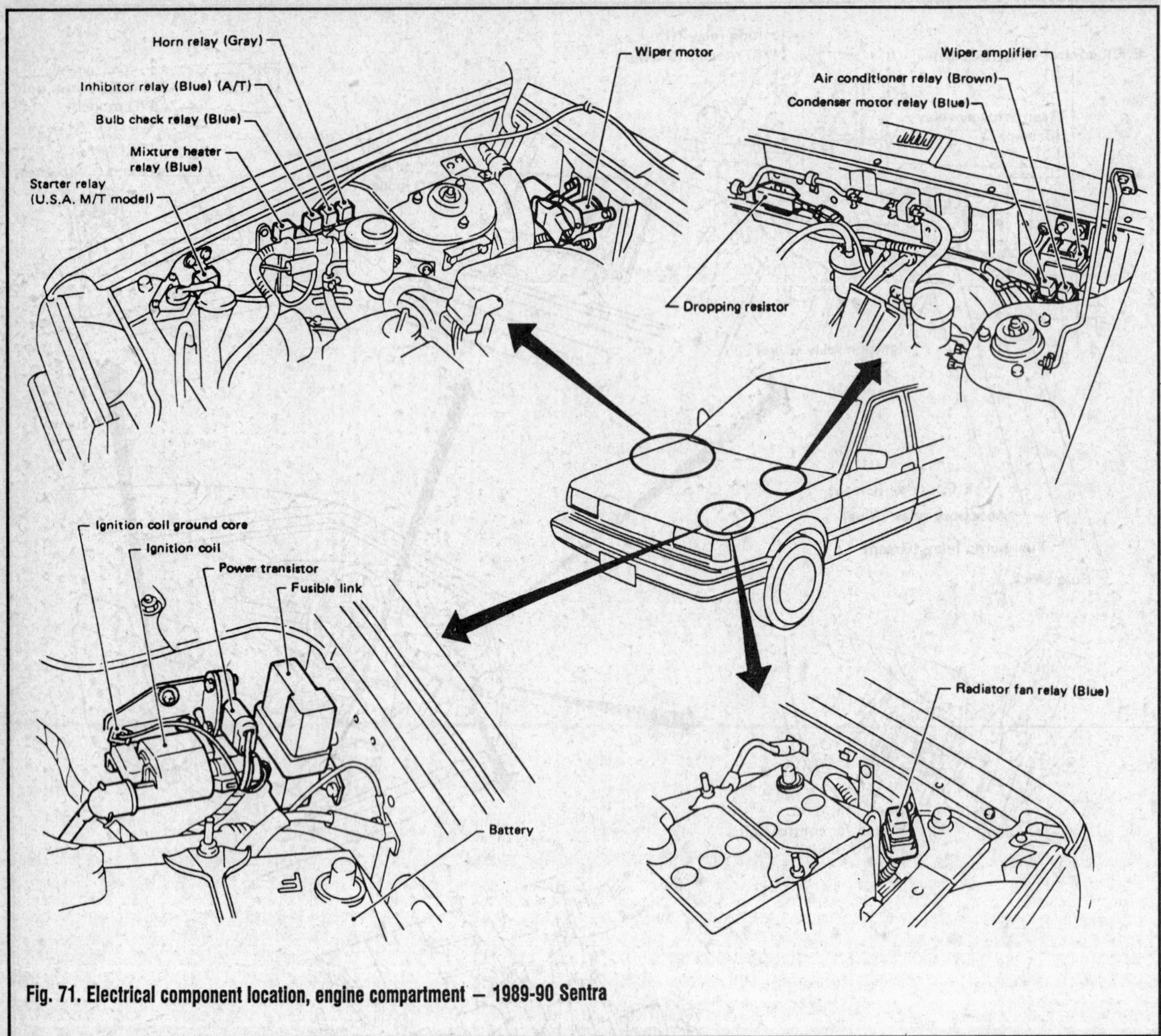
Horn relay (Gray)
Inhibitor relay (Blue) (A/T)
Bulb check relay (Blue)
Mixture heater relay (Blue)
Starter relay (U.S.A. M/T model)
Wiper motor
Wiper amplifier
Air conditioner relay (Brown)
Condenser motor relay (Blue)
Dropping resistor
Ignition coil ground core
Ignition coil
Power transistor
Fusible link
Battery
Radiator fan relay (Blue)

Fig. 71. Electrical component location, engine compartment – 1989-90 Sentra

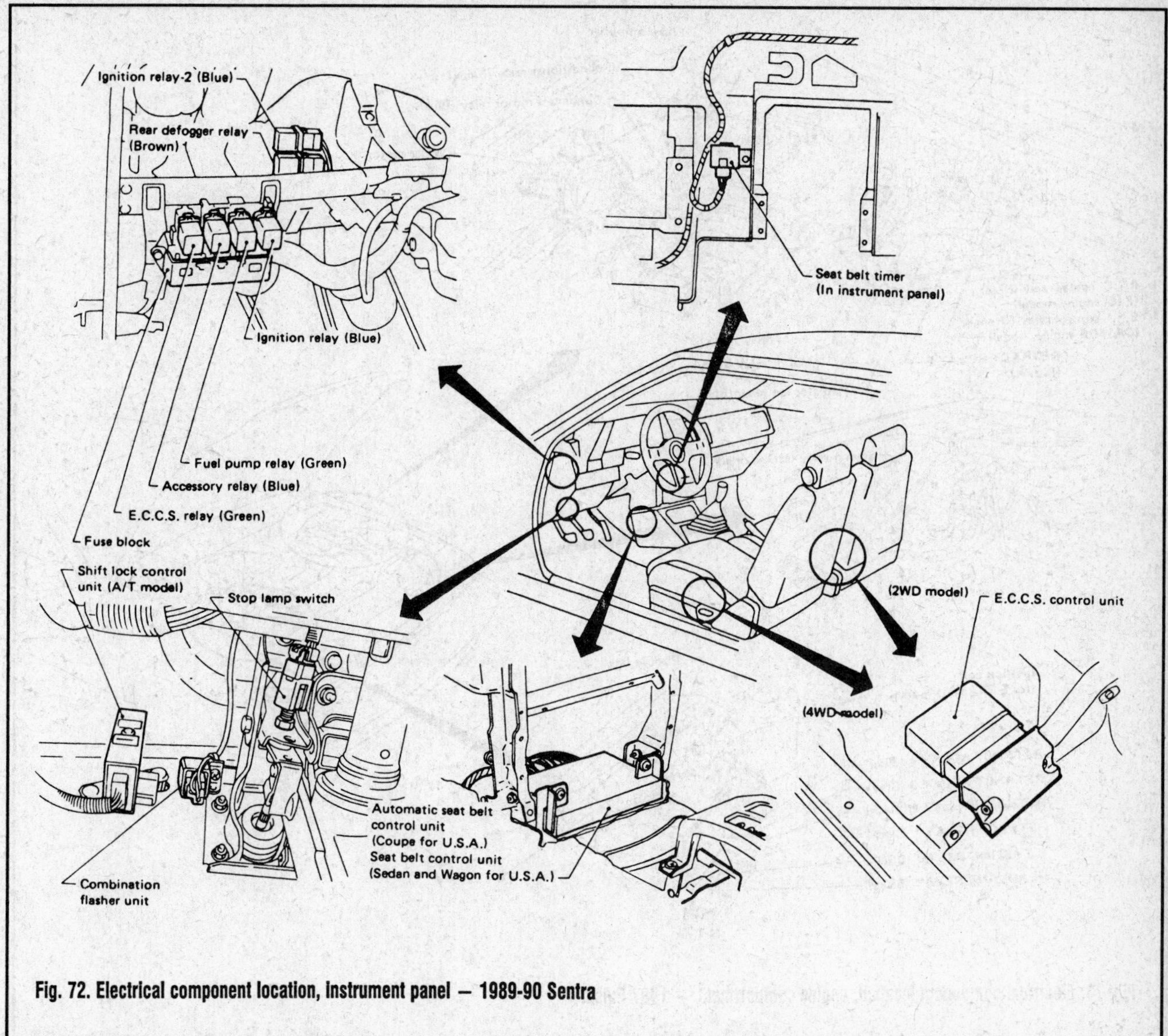
Ignition relay-2 (Blue)
Rear defogger relay (Brown)
Ignition relay (Blue)
Fuel pump relay (Green)
Accessory relay (Blue)
E.C.C.S. relay (Green)
Fuse block
Shift lock control unit (A/T model)
Stop lamp switch
Combination flasher unit
Automatic seat belt control unit (Coupe for U.S.A.)
Seat belt control unit (Sedan and Wagon for U.S.A.)
Seat belt timer (In instrument panel)
(2WD model)
E.C.C.S. control unit
(4WD model)

Fig. 72. Electrical component location, instrument panel — 1989-90 Sentra

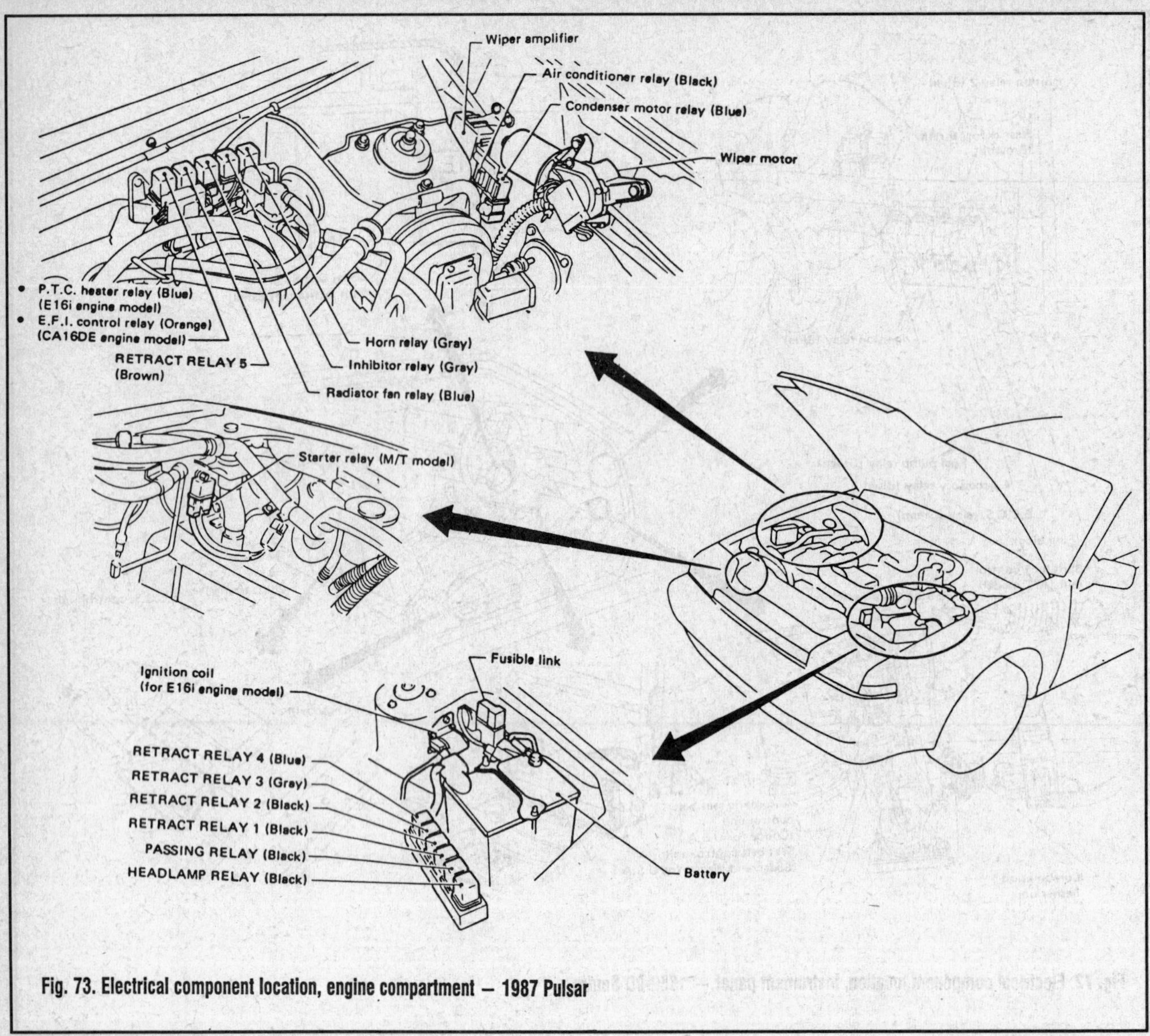
Wiper amplifier
Air conditioner relay (Black)
Condenser motor relay (Blue)
Wiper motor
• P.T.C. heater relay (Blue)
(E16i engine model)
• E.F.I. control relay (Orange)
(CA16DE engine model)
RETRACT RELAY 5
(Brown)
Horn relay (Gray)
Inhibitor relay (Gray)
Radiator fan relay (Blue)
Starter relay (M/T model)
Ignition coil
(for E16i engine model)
Fusible link
RETRACT RELAY 4 (Blue)
RETRACT RELAY 3 (Gray)
RETRACT RELAY 2 (Black)
RETRACT RELAY 1 (Black)
PASSING RELAY (Black)
HEADLAMP RELAY (Black)
Battery

Fig. 73. Electrical component location, engine compartment — 1987 Pulsar

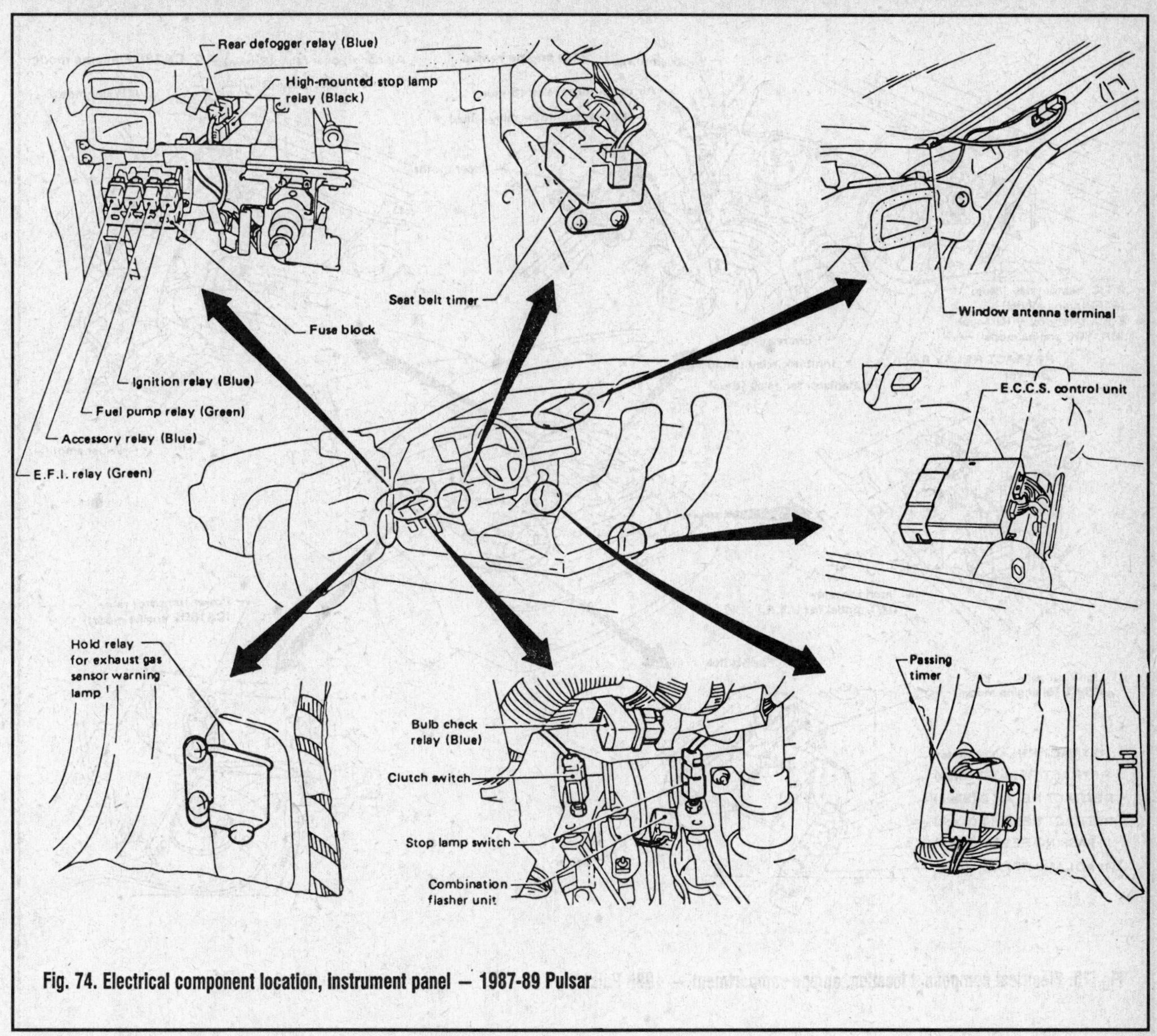
Rear defogger relay (Blue)
High-mounted stop lamp relay (Black)
Seat belt timer
Window antenna terminal
Fuse block
Ignition relay (Blue)
Fuel pump relay (Green)
Accessory relay (Blue)
E.F.I. relay (Green)
E.C.C.S. control unit
Hold relay for exhaust gas sensor warning lamp
Bulb check relay (Blue)
Clutch switch
Stop lamp switch
Combination flasher unit
Passing timer

Fig. 74. Electrical component location, instrument panel — 1987-89 Pulsar

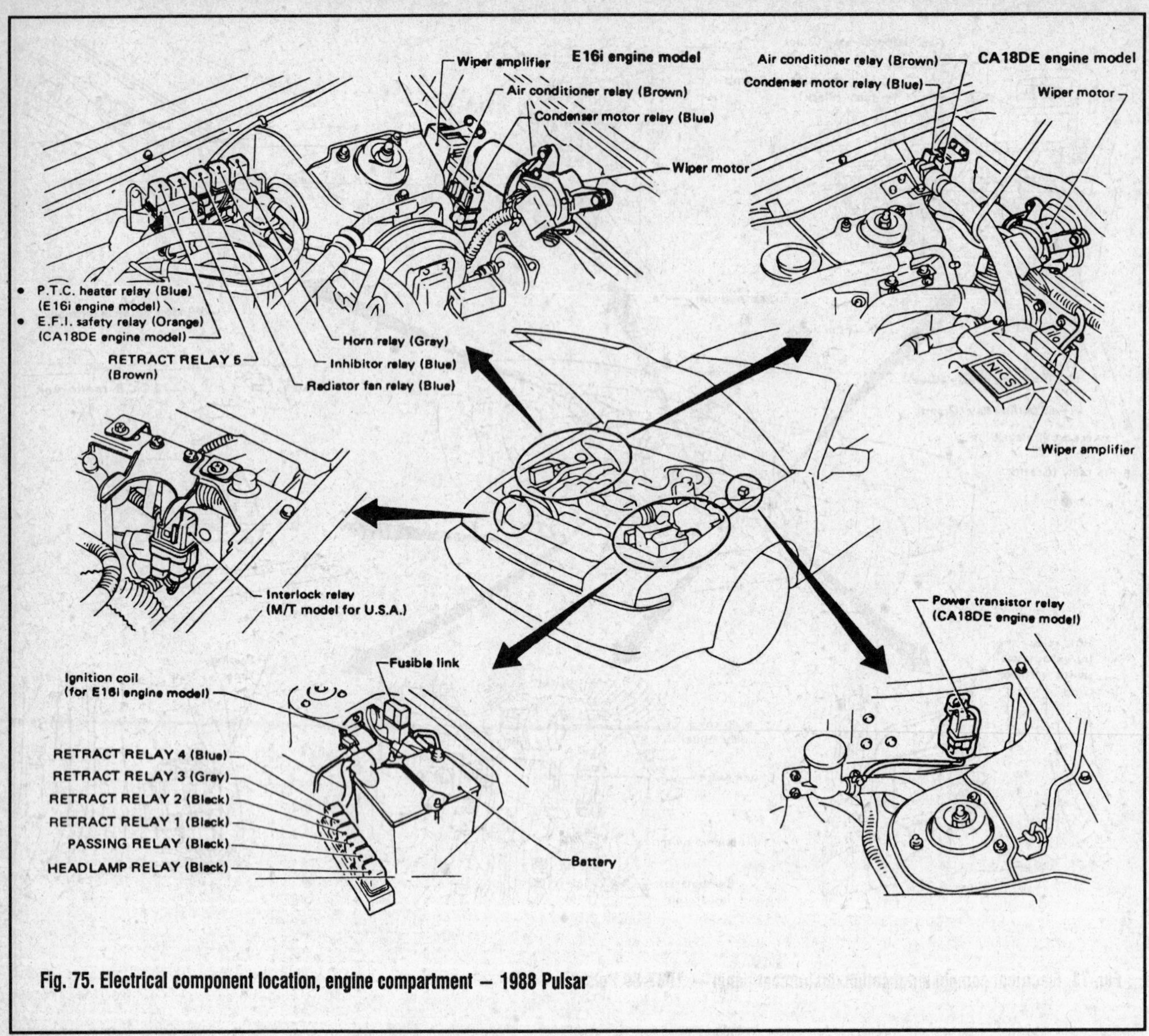
E16i engine model
Wiper amplifier
Air conditioner relay (Brown)
Condenser motor relay (Blue)
Wiper motor
P.T.C. heater relay (Blue)
(E16i engine model)
E.F.I. safety relay (Orange)
(CA18DE engine model)
RETRACT RELAY 5
(Brown)
Horn relay (Gray)
Inhibitor relay (Blue)
Radiator fan relay (Blue)
CA18DE engine model
Air conditioner relay (Brown)
Condenser motor relay (Blue)
Wiper motor
Wiper amplifier
NICS
Interlock relay
(M/T model for U.S.A.)
Power transistor relay
(CA18DE engine model)
Fusible link
Ignition coil
(for E16i engine model)
RETRACT RELAY 4 (Blue)
RETRACT RELAY 3 (Gray)
RETRACT RELAY 2 (Black)
RETRACT RELAY 1 (Black)
PASSING RELAY (Black)
HEADLAMP RELAY (Black)
Battery

Fig. 75. Electrical component location, engine compartment — 1988 Pulsar

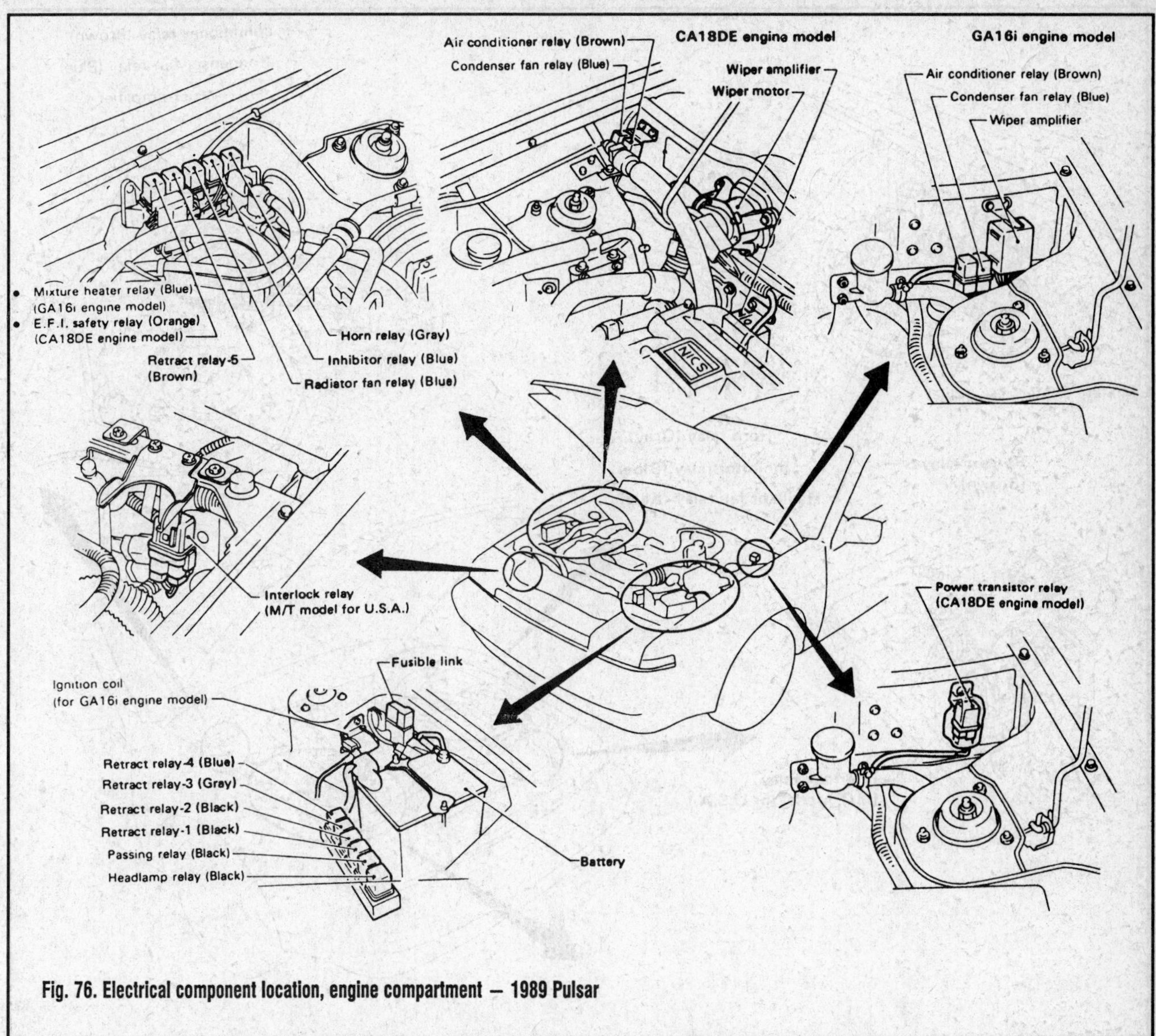
Air conditioner relay (Brown)
Condenser fan relay (Blue)
CA18DE engine model
Wiper amplifier
Wiper motor
GA16i engine model
Air conditioner relay (Brown)
Condenser fan relay (Blue)
Wiper amplifier
• Mixture heater relay (Blue)
(GA16i engine model)
• E.F.I. safety relay (Orange)
(CA18DE engine model)
Horn relay (Gray)
Retract relay-5
(Brown)
Inhibitor relay (Blue)
Radiator fan relay (Blue)
Interlock relay
(M/T model for U.S.A.)
Power transistor relay
(CA18DE engine model)
Fusible link
Ignition coil
(for GA16i engine model)
Retract relay-4 (Blue)
Retract relay-3 (Gray)
Retract relay-2 (Black)
Retract relay-1 (Black)
Passing relay (Black)
Headlamp relay (Black)
Battery

Fig. 76. Electrical component location, engine compartment — 1989 Pulsar

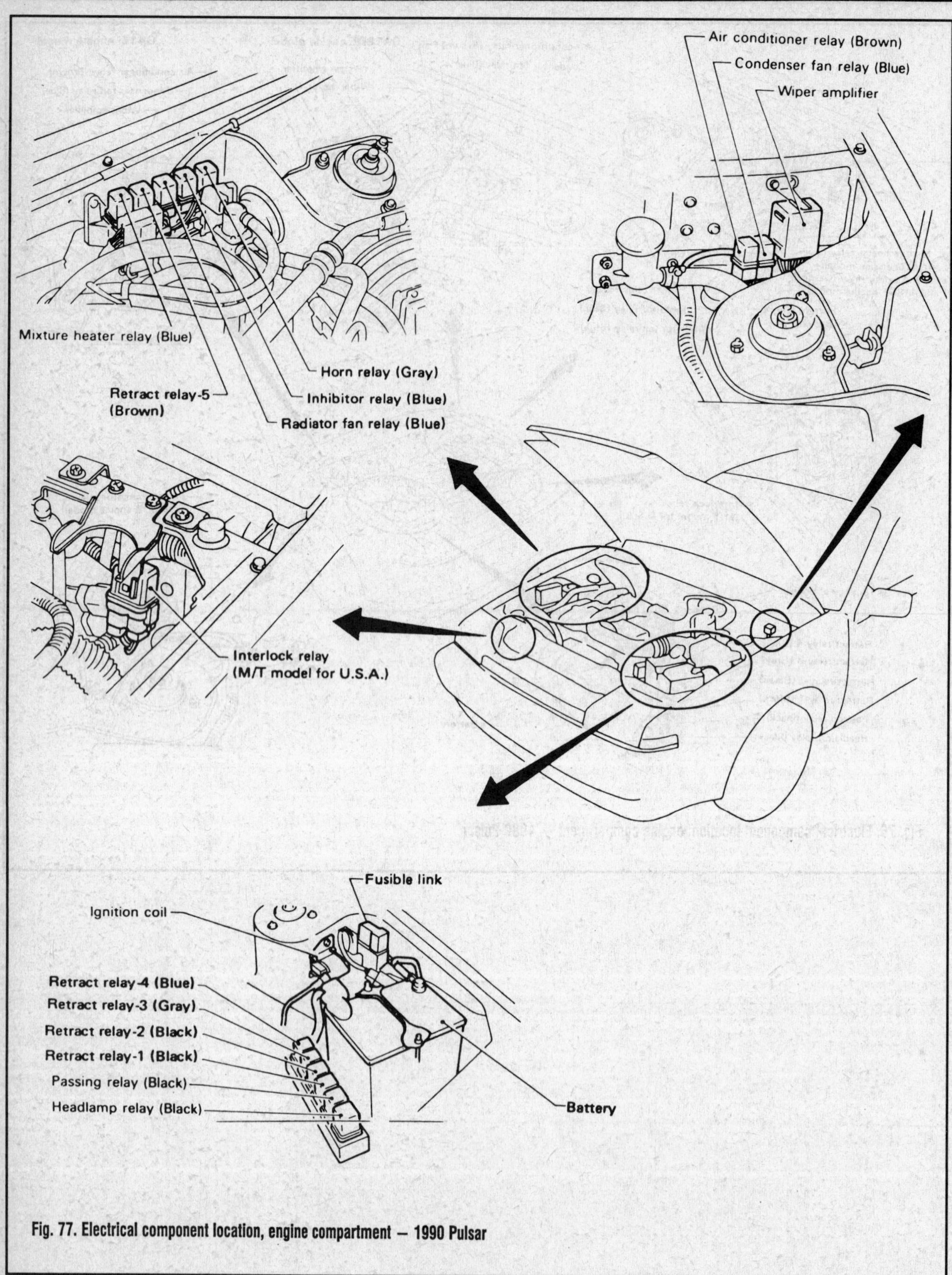

Air conditioner relay (Brown)
Condenser fan relay (Blue)
Wiper amplifier
Mixture heater relay (Blue)
Horn relay (Gray)
Retract relay-5 (Brown)
Inhibitor relay (Blue)
Radiator fan relay (Blue)
Interlock relay (M/T model for U.S.A.)
Fusible link
Ignition coil
Retract relay-4 (Blue)
Retract relay-3 (Gray)
Retract relay-2 (Black)
Retract relay-1 (Black)
Passing relay (Black)
Headlamp relay (Black)
Battery

Fig. 77. Electrical component location, engine compartment — 1990 Pulsar

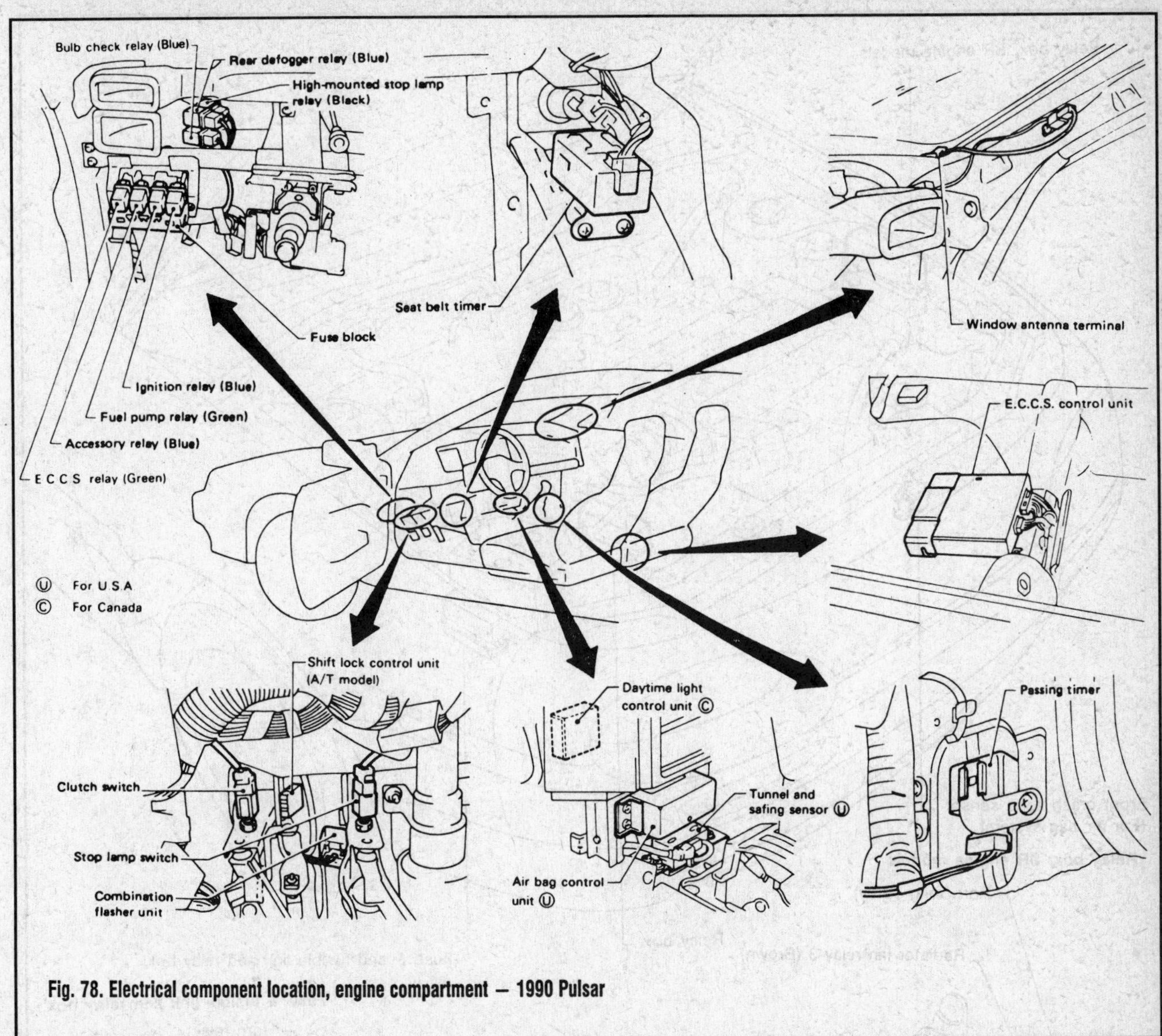
Bulb check relay (Blue)
Rear defogger relay (Blue)
High-mounted stop lamp relay (Black)
Seat belt timer
Window antenna terminal
Fuse block
Ignition relay (Blue)
Fuel pump relay (Green)
Accessory relay (Blue)
E C C S relay (Green)
E.C.C.S. control unit
Ⓤ For U.S.A
Ⓒ For Canada
Shift lock control unit (A/T model)
Daytime light control unit Ⓒ
Passing timer
Clutch switch
Tunnel and safing sensor Ⓤ
Stop lamp switch
Combination flasher unit
Air bag control unit Ⓤ

Fig. 78. Electrical component location, engine compartment — 1990 Pulsar

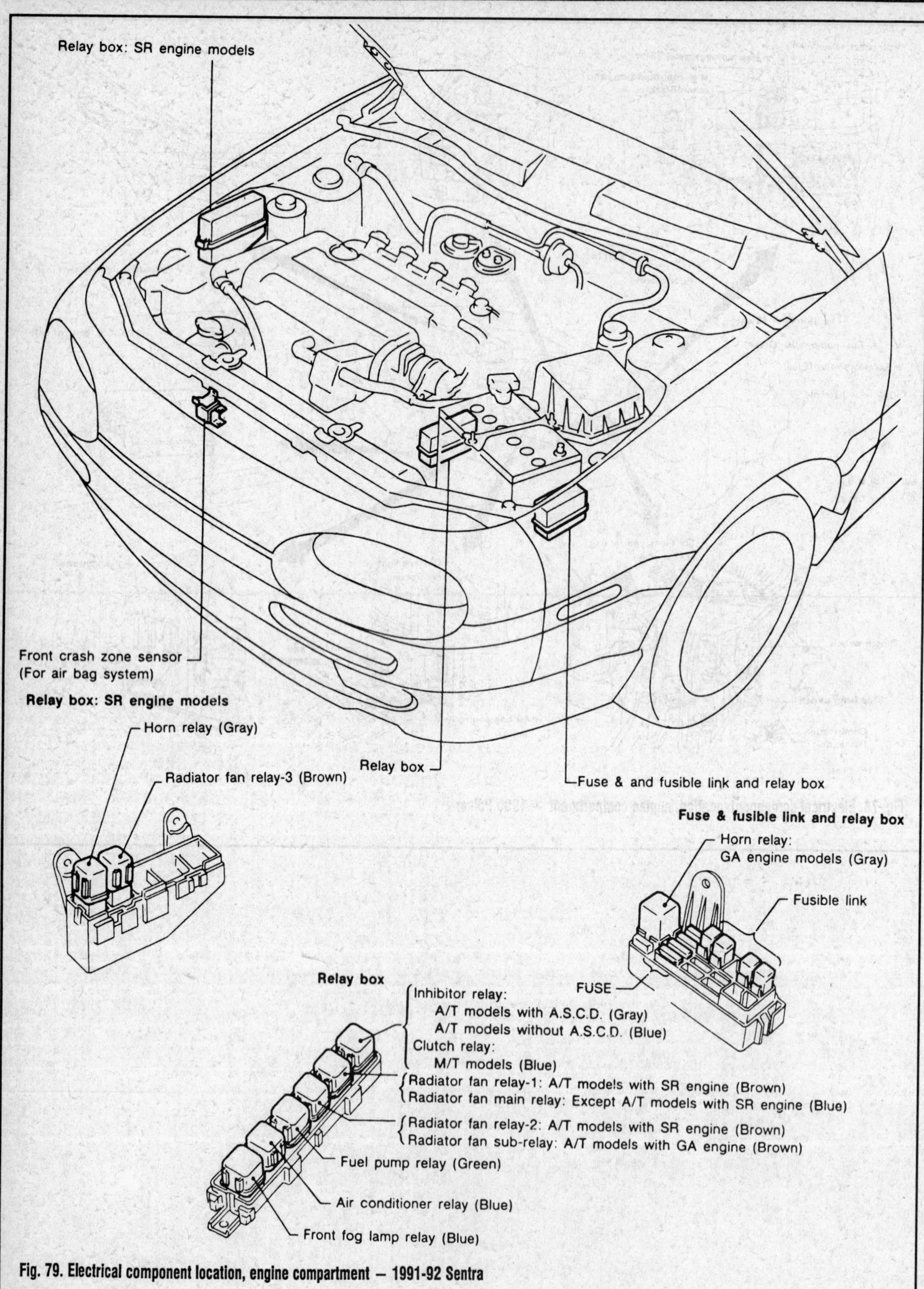

Relay box: SR engine models
Front crash zone sensor
(For air bag system)
Relay box: SR engine models
Horn relay (Gray)
Radiator fan relay-3 (Brown)
Relay box
Fuse & and fusible link and relay box
Fuse & fusible link and relay box
Horn relay:
GA engine models (Gray)
Fusible link
FUSE
Relay box
Inhibitor relay:
A/T models with A.S.C.D. (Gray)
A/T models without A.S.C.D. (Blue)
Clutch relay:
M/T models (Blue)
Radiator fan relay-1: A/T models with SR engine (Brown)
Radiator fan main relay: Except A/T models with SR engine (Blue)
Radiator fan relay-2: A/T models with SR engine (Brown)
Radiator fan sub-relay: A/T models with GA engine (Brown)
Fuel pump relay (Green)
Air conditioner relay (Blue)
Front fog lamp relay (Blue)

Fig. 79. Electrical component location, engine compartment – 1991-92 Sentra

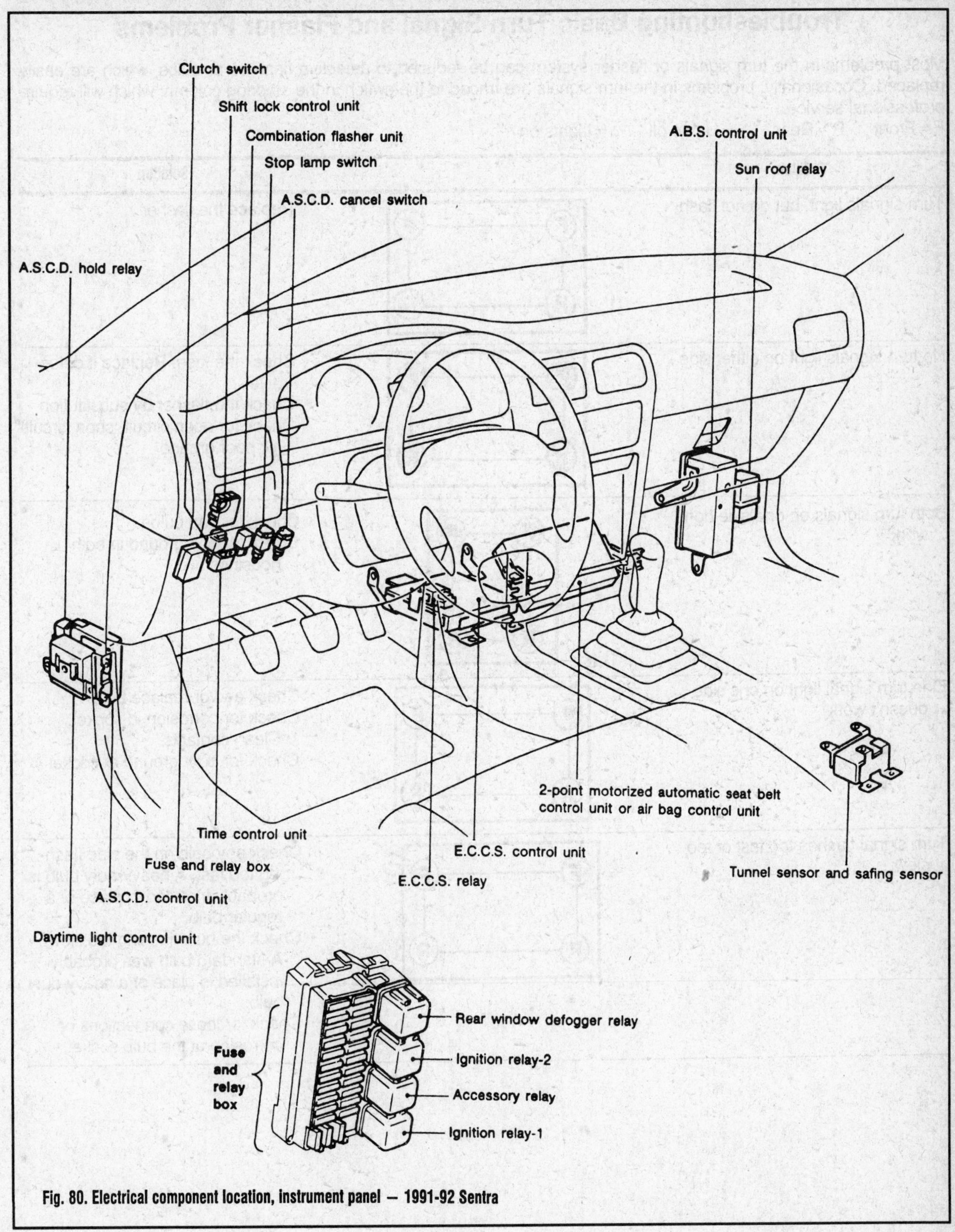
Clutch switch
Shift lock control unit
Combination flasher unit
Stop lamp switch
A.S.C.D. cancel switch
A.S.C.D. hold relay
A.B.S. control unit
Sun roof relay
2-point motorized automatic seat belt control unit or air bag control unit
Time control unit
Fuse and relay box
A.S.C.D. control unit
Daytime light control unit
E.C.C.S. control unit
E.C.C.S. relay
Tunnel sensor and safing sensor
Fuse and relay box
Rear window defogger relay
Ignition relay-2
Accessory relay
Ignition relay-1

Fig. 80. Electrical component location, instrument panel — 1991-92 Sentra

Troubleshooting Basic Turn Signal and Flasher Problems

Most problems in the turn signals or flasher system can be reduced to defective flashers or bulbs, which are easily replaced. Occasionally, problems in the turn signals are traced to the switch in the steering column, which will require professional service.

F = Front R = Rear ● = Lights off o = Lights on

Problem		Solution
Turn signals light, but do not flash	F F / R R (all lights on)	• Replace the flasher
No turn signals light on either side	F F / R R (all lights off)	• Check the fuse. Replace if defective. • Check the flasher by substitution • Check for open circuit, short circuit or poor ground
Both turn signals on one side don't work	F F / R R (left front and left rear off)	• Check for bad bulbs • Check for bad ground in both housings
One turn signal light on one side doesn't work	F F / R R (left front off)	• Check and/or replace bulb • Check for corrosion in socket. Clean contacts. • Check for poor ground at socket
Turn signal flashes too fast or too slow	F F / R R (right front flashing)	• Check any bulb on the side flashing too fast. A heavy-duty bulb is probably installed in place of a regular bulb. • Check the bulb flashing too slow. A standard bulb was probably installed in place of a heavy-duty bulb. • Check for loose connections or corrosion at the bulb socket

Troubleshooting Basic Turn Signal and Flasher Problems

Most problems in the turn signals or flasher system can be reduced to defective flashers or bulbs, which are easily replaced. Occasionally, problems in the turn signals are traced to the switch in the steering column, which will require professional service.

F = Front R = Rear ● = Lights off ○ = Lights on

Problem		Solution
Indicator lights don't work in either direction		• Check if the turn signals are working • Check the dash indicator lights • Check the flasher by substitution
One indicator light doesn't light		• On systems with 1 dash indicator: See if the lights work on the same side. Often the filaments have been reversed in systems combining stoplights with taillights and turn signals. Check the flasher by substitution • On systems with 2 indicators: Check the bulbs on the same side Check the indicator light bulb Check the flasher by substitution

Troubleshooting Basic Lighting Problems

Problem	Cause	Solution
Lights		
One or more lights don't work, but others do	• Defective bulb(s) • Blown fuse(s) • Dirty fuse clips or light sockets • Poor ground circuit	• Replace bulb(s) • Replace fuse(s) • Clean connections • Run ground wire from light socket housing to car frame
Lights burn out quickly	• Incorrect voltage regulator setting or defective regulator • Poor battery/alternator connections	• Replace voltage regulator • Check battery/alternator connections

Troubleshooting Basic Lighting Problems

Problem	Cause	Solution
Lights go dim	• Low/discharged battery • Alternator not charging • Corroded sockets or connections • Low voltage output	• Check battery • Check drive belt tension; repair or replace alternator • Clean bulb and socket contacts and connections • Replace voltage regulator
Lights flicker	• Loose connection • Poor ground • Circuit breaker operating (short circuit)	• Tighten all connections • Run ground wire from light housing to car frame • Check connections and look for bare wires
Lights "flare"—Some flare is normal on acceleration—if excessive, see "Lights Burn Out Quickly"	• High voltage setting	• Replace voltage regulator
Lights glare—approaching drivers are blinded	• Lights adjusted too high • Rear springs or shocks sagging • Rear tires soft	• Have headlights aimed • Check rear springs/shocks • Check/correct rear tire pressure
Turn Signals		
Turn signals don't work in either direction	• Blown fuse • Defective flasher • Loose connection	• Replace fuse • Replace flasher • Check/tighten all connections
Right (or left) turn signal only won't work	• Bulb burned out • Right (or left) indicator bulb burned out • Short circuit	• Replace bulb • Check/replace indicator bulb • Check/repair wiring
Flasher rate too slow or too fast	• Incorrect wattage bulb • Incorrect flasher	• Flasher bulb • Replace flasher (use a variable load flasher if you pull a trailer)
Indicator lights do not flash (burn steadily)	• Burned out bulb • Defective flasher	• Replace bulb • Replace flasher
Indicator lights do not light at all	• Burned out indicator bulb • Defective flasher	• Replace indicator bulb • Replace flasher

Troubleshooting Basic Dash Gauge Problems

Problem	Cause	Solution
Coolant Temperature Gauge		
Gauge reads erratically or not at all	• Loose or dirty connections • Defective sending unit	• Clean/tighten connections • Bi-metal gauge: remove the wire from the sending unit. Ground the wire for an instant. If the gauge registers, replace the sending unit.

Troubleshooting Basic Dash Gauge Problems

Problem	Cause	Solution
Gauge reads erratically or not at all	• Defective gauge	• Magnetic gauge: disconnect the wire at the sending unit. With ignition ON gauge should register COLD. Ground the wire; gauge should register HOT.
Ammeter Gauge—Turn Headlights ON (do not start engine). Note reaction		
Ammeter shows charge	• Connections reversed on gauge	• Reinstall connections
Ammeter shows discharge	• Ammeter is OK	• Nothing
Ammeter does not move	• Loose connections or faulty wiring	• Check/correct wiring
	• Defective gauge	• Replace gauge
Oil Pressure Gauge		
Gauge does not register or is inaccurate	• On mechanical gauge, Bourdon tube may be bent or kinked	• Check tube for kinks or bends preventing oil from reaching the gauge
	• Low oil pressure	• Remove sending unit. Idle the engine briefly. If no oil flows from sending unit hole, problem is in engine.
	• Defective gauge	• Remove the wire from the sending unit and ground it for an instant with the ignition ON. A good gauge will go to the top of the scale.
	• Defective wiring	• Check the wiring to the gauge. If it's OK and the gauge doesn't register when grounded, replace the gauge.
	• Defective sending unit	• If the wiring is OK and the gauge functions when grounded, replace the sending unit
All Gauges		
All gauges do not operate	• Blown fuse	• Replace fuse
	• Defective instrument regulator	• Replace instrument voltage regulator
All gauges read low or erratically	• Defective or dirty instrument voltage regulator	• Clean contacts or replace
All gauges pegged	• Loss of ground between instrument voltage regulator and car	• Check ground
	• Defective instrument regulator	• Replace regulator

Troubleshooting Basic Dash Gauge Problems

Problem	Cause	Solution
Warning Lights		
Light(s) do not come on when ignition is ON, but engine is not started	• Defective bulb • Defective wire • Defective sending unit	• Replace bulb • Check wire from light to sending unit • Disconnect the wire from the sending unit and ground it. Replace the sending unit if the light comes on with the ignition ON.
Light comes on with engine running	• Problem in individual system • Defective sending unit	• Check system • Check sending unit (see above)

Troubleshooting the Heater

Problem	Cause	Solution
Blower motor will not turn at any speed	• Blown fuse • Loose connection • Defective ground • Faulty switch • Faulty motor • Faulty resistor	• Replace fuse • Inspect and tighten • Clean and tighten • Replace switch • Replace motor • Replace resistor
Blower motor turns at one speed only	• Faulty switch • Faulty resistor	• Replace switch • Replace resistor
Blower motor turns but does not circulate air	• Intake blocked • Fan not secured to the motor shaft	• Clean intake • Tighten security
Heater will not heat	• Coolant does not reach proper temperature • Heater core blocked internally • Heater core air-bound • Blend-air door not in proper position	• Check and replace thermostat if necessary • Flush or replace core if necessary • Purge air from core • Adjust cable
Heater will not defrost	• Control cable adjustment incorrect • Defroster hose damaged	• Adjust control cable • Replace defroster hose

Troubleshooting Basic Windshield Wiper Problems

Problem	Cause	Solution
Electric Wipers		
Wipers do not operate— Wiper motor heats up or hums	• Internal motor defect • Bent or damaged linkage • Arms improperly installed on linking pivots	• Replace motor • Repair or replace linkage • Position linkage in park and reinstall wiper arms
Electric Wipers		
Wipers do not operate— No current to motor	• Fuse or circuit breaker blown • Loose, open or broken wiring • Defective switch • Defective or corroded terminals • No ground circuit for motor or switch	• Replace fuse or circuit breaker • Repair wiring and connections • Replace switch • Replace or clean terminals • Repair ground circuits
Wipers do not operate— Motor runs	• Linkage disconnected or broken	• Connect wiper linkage or replace broken linkage
Vacuum Wipers		
Wipers do not operate	• Control switch or cable inoperative • Loss of engine vacuum to wiper motor (broken hoses, low engine vacuum, defective vacuum/fuel pump) • Linkage broken or disconnected • Defective wiper motor	• Repair or replace switch or cable • Check vacuum lines, engine vacuum and fuel pump • Repair linkage • Replace wiper motor
Wipers stop on engine acceleration	• Leaking vacuum hoses • Dry windshield • Oversize wiper blades • Defective vacuum/fuel pump	• Repair or replace hoses • Wet windshield with washers • Replace with proper size wiper blades • Replace pump

NISSAN SENTRA
ENGINE HARNESS (M.P.G. MODELS)

NO.	FROM	TO
100	ENGINE ELECTRICAL SYSTEM	
100	MAIN H	ALTERNATOR
105	ALTERNATOR	100
108	MAIN H	ALTERNATOR
109	MAIN H	100
114	MAIN H	ST MO
161	MAIN H	CARB H
300	METER, GAUGES AND WARNING SYSTEM	
335	MAIN H	OIL PRESS
400	SIGNAL SYSTEM	
451	MAIN H	BACK-UP L SW
452	MAIN H	BACK-UP L SW
700	SUPPLEMENTAL NUMBERS	
702	CHECK TERMINAL	CARB H
703	MAIN H	CHECK TERMINAL
704	MAIN H	CARB H
705	CARB H	703
706	MAIN H	CARB H
714	MAIN H	NEUTRAL SW
721	MAIN H	WATER TEMP SENSOR
732	MAIN H	WATER TEMP SENSOR
735	MAIN H	WARM SOL
736	MAIN H	WARM SOL
737	MAIN H	EAI SOL
738	MAIN H	EAI SOL
900	GROUND	
913	ENG GROUND	BODY GROUND
914	913	NEUTRAL SW

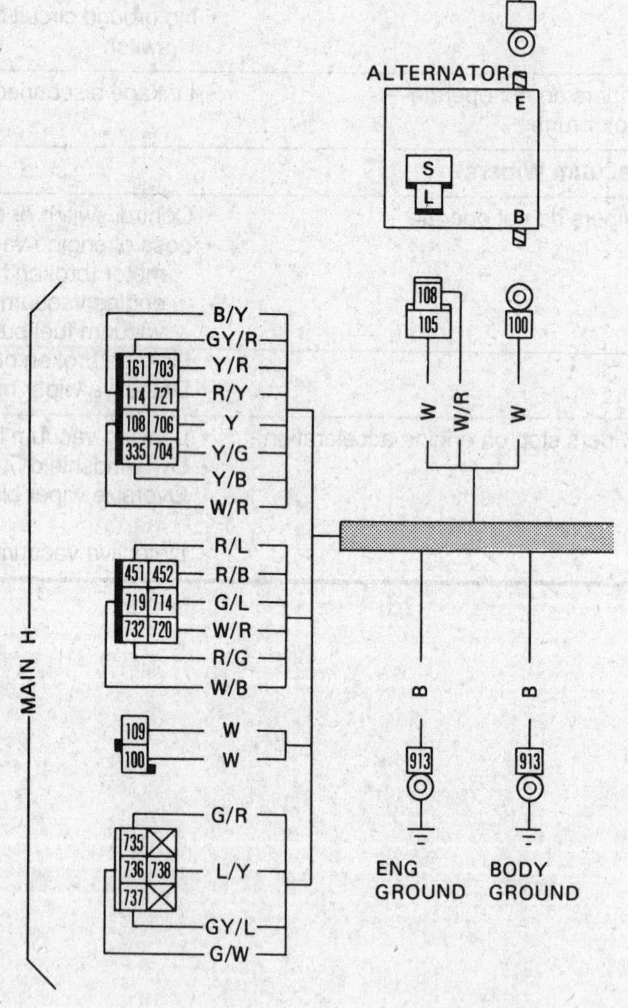
ALTERNATOR
E
S
L
B
108
105
100
W
W/R
W
B/Y
GY/R
161 703
Y/R
114 721
R/Y
108 706
Y
335 704
Y/G
Y/B
W/R
R/L
451 452
R/B
719 714
G/L
732 720
W/R
R/G
W/B
MAIN H
109
W
100
W
G/R
735
736 738
L/Y
737
GY/L
G/W
B
B
913
913
ENG GROUND
BODY GROUND

Fig. 1. Engine wiring diagram — 1982 Sentra (MPG models)

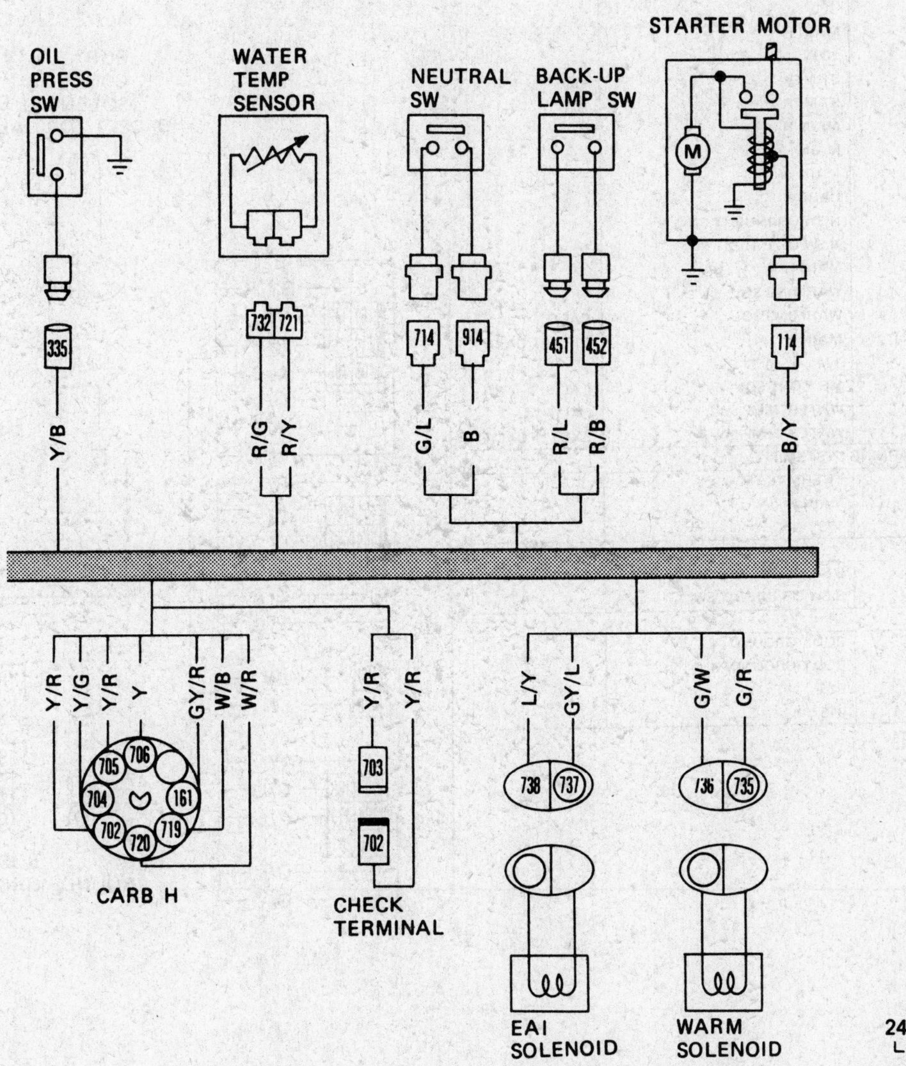
OIL
PRESS
SW
WATER
TEMP
SENSOR
NEUTRAL
SW
BACK-UP
LAMP SW
STARTER MOTOR
M
335
732
721
714
914
451
452
114
Y/B
R/G
R/Y
G/L
B
R/L
R/B
B/Y
Y/R
Y/G
Y/R
Y
GY/R
W/B
W/R
706
705
704
161
702
720
719
CARB H
Y/R
Y/R
703
702
CHECK
TERMINAL
L/Y
GY/L
738
737
G/W
G/R
736
735
EAI
SOLENOID
WARM
SOLENOID
24075 10A00 5
└24075 09A00

Fig. 1. Engine wiring diagram — 1982 Sentra (MPG models)

NISSAN SENTRA

ENGINE HARNESS (FOR U.S.A. EXCEPT M.P.G. MODELS)

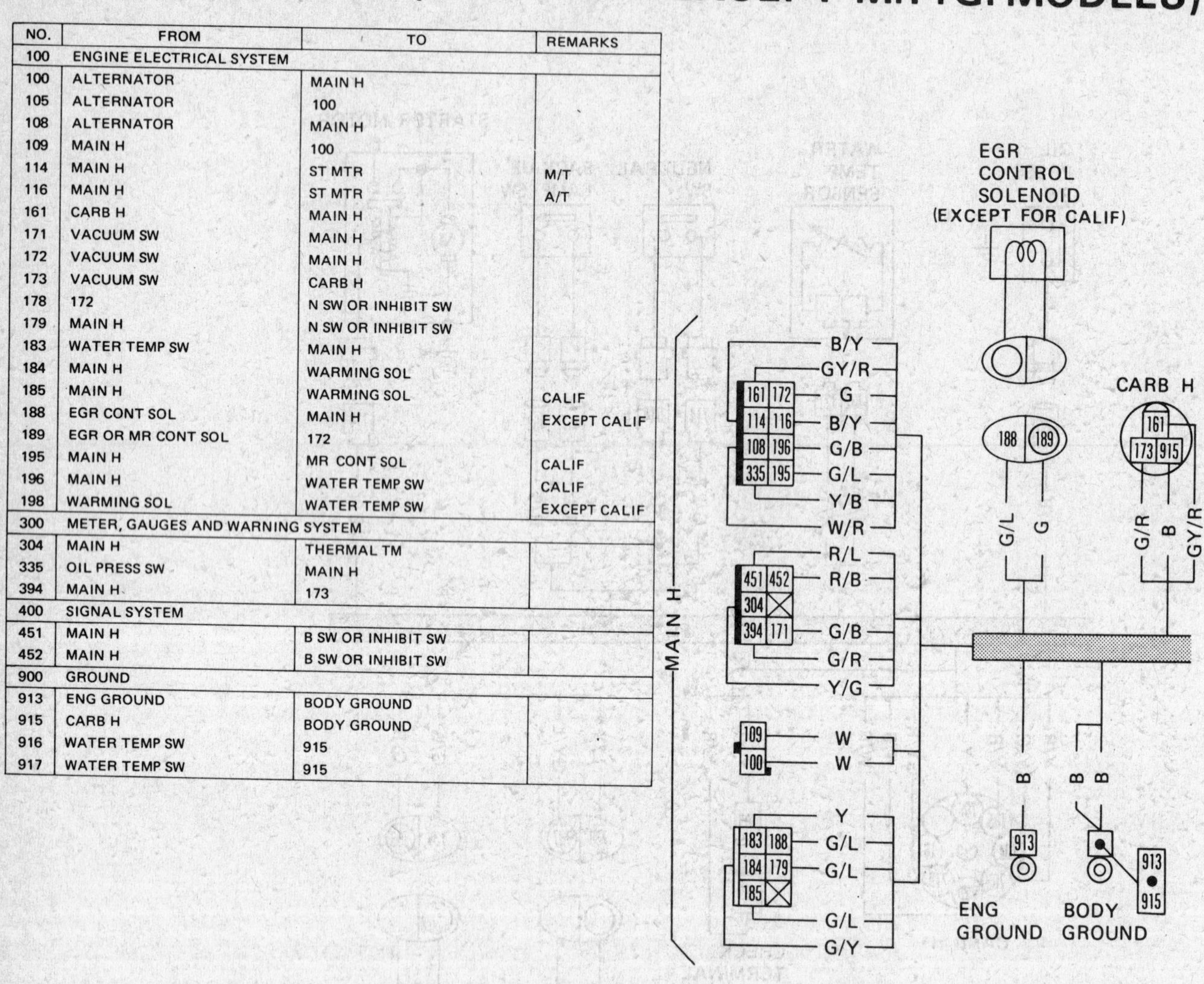

NO.	FROM	TO	REMARKS
100	ENGINE ELECTRICAL SYSTEM		
100	ALTERNATOR	MAIN H	
105	ALTERNATOR	100	
108	ALTERNATOR	MAIN H	
109	MAIN H	100	
114	MAIN H	ST MTR	M/T
116	MAIN H	ST MTR	A/T
161	CARB H	MAIN H	
171	VACUUM SW	MAIN H	
172	VACUUM SW	MAIN H	
173	VACUUM SW	CARB H	
178	172	N SW OR INHIBIT SW	
179	MAIN H	N SW OR INHIBIT SW	
183	WATER TEMP SW	MAIN H	
184	MAIN H	WARMING SOL	
185	MAIN H	WARMING SOL	CALIF
188	EGR CONT SOL	MAIN H	EXCEPT CALIF
189	EGR OR MR CONT SOL	172	
195	MAIN H	MR CONT SOL	CALIF
196	MAIN H	WATER TEMP SW	CALIF
198	WARMING SOL	WATER TEMP SW	EXCEPT CALIF
300	METER, GAUGES AND WARNING SYSTEM		
304	MAIN H	THERMAL TM	
335	OIL PRESS SW	MAIN H	
394	MAIN H	173	
400	SIGNAL SYSTEM		
451	MAIN H	B SW OR INHIBIT SW	
452	MAIN H	B SW OR INHIBIT SW	
900	GROUND		
913	ENG GROUND	BODY GROUND	
915	CARB H	BODY GROUND	
916	WATER TEMP SW	915	
917	WATER TEMP SW	915	

EGR
CONTROL
SOLENOID
(EXCEPT FOR CALIF)
CARB H
188 189
161
173 915
G/L G
G/R B GY/R
MAIN H
161 172
114 116
108 196
335 195
B/Y
GY/R
G
B/Y
G/B
G/L
Y/B
W/R
451 452
304
394 171
R/L
R/B
G/B
G/R
Y/G
109
100
W
W
183 188
184 179
185
Y
G/L
G/L
G/L
G/Y
B
B B
913
913
915
ENG
GROUND
BODY
GROUND

Fig. 2. Engine wiring diagram — 1982 Sentra (except MPG)

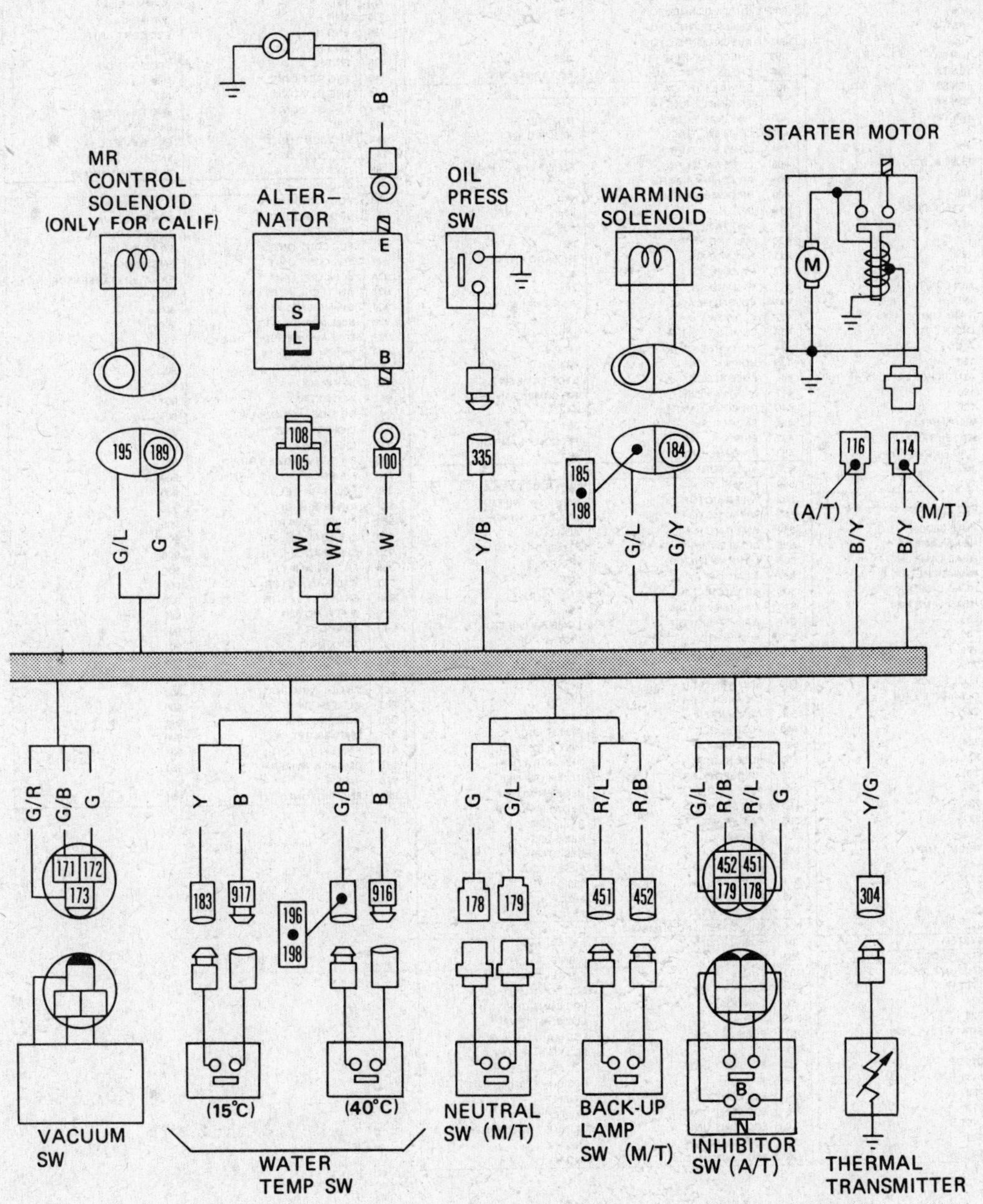
MR
CONTROL
SOLENOID
(ONLY FOR CALIF)
ALTER-
NATOR
OIL
PRESS
SW
WARMING
SOLENOID
STARTER MOTOR
E
S
L
B
M
195
189
108
105
100
335
185
198
184
116
114
(A/T)
(M/T)
G/L
G
W
W/R
W
Y/B
G/L
G/Y
B/Y
B/Y
G/R
G/B
G
Y
B
G/B
B
G
G/L
R/L
R/B
G/L
R/B
R/L
G
Y/G
171
172
173
183
917
196
198
916
178
179
451
452
452
451
179
178
304
VACUUM
SW
(15°C)
(40°C)
WATER
TEMP SW
NEUTRAL
SW (M/T)
BACK-UP
LAMP
SW (M/T)
B
N
INHIBITOR
SW (A/T)
THERMAL
TRANSMITTER
24075 04A00 4
24075 04A00
24075 04A10
24075 04A70

Fig. 2. Engine wiring diagram — 1982 Sentra (except MPG)

NISSAN SENTRA
MAIN HARNESS (M.P.G. MODELS)

NO.	FROM	TO
100	ENGINE ELECTRICAL SYSTEM	
100	ENG H	FUSIBLE LINK
106	FUSE BLOCK	100
107	FUSE BLOCK	106
108	ENG H	INST H
109	ENG H	100
110	FUSIBLE LINK	IGN SW
111	FUSE BLOCK	IGN SW
112	FUSE BLOCK	IGN SW
114	ENG H	IGN SW
117	111	IGN COIL (+)
118	IG RELAY	111
119	IG RELAY	106
120	IG RELAY	FUSE BLOCK
121	ACC RELAY	112
122	ACC RELAY	106
123	ACC RELAY	FUSE BLOCK
124	FUSE BLOCK	123
125	FUSE BLOCK	111
126	FUSE BLOCK	120
127	FUSE BLOCK	112
131	RESISTER	IGN COIL (–)
132	RESISTER	INST H
148	FUSE BLOCK	TANK UNIT
158	INST H	DIODE
159	324	DIODE
160	AUTO CHOKE RELAY	165
161	ENG H	AUTO CHOKE RELAY
162	AUTO CHOKE RELAY	190
163	AUTO CHOKE RELAY	108
165	FUSE BLOCK	WARM RELAY
190	FUSE BLOCK	WATER TEMP SW
191	WATER TEMP SW	RAD FAN MOTOR
192	AIR CON H (B)	190
193	AIR CON H (B)	191
200	LIGHTING SYSTEM	
200	COMB SW (LIGHT)	FUSE BLOCK
201	COMB SW (LIGHT)	FUSE BLOCK
202	COMB SW (LIGHT)	HEAD LAMP RH
203	COMB SW (LIGHT)	HEAD LAMP LH
204	COMB SW (LIGHT)	DIMMER RELAY
205	DIMMER RELAY	HEAD LAMP RH
206	DIMMER RELAY	HEAD LAMP RH
207	HEAD LAMP LH	205
208	HEAD LAMP LH	206
209	INST H	202
210	INST H	205
220	COMB SW (LIGHT)	FUSE BLOCK
222	COMB SW (LIGHT)	CLEARNCE L RH
223	CLEARANCE L LH	222
224	RR COMB LAMP RH	222
225	RR COMB LAMP LH	224
226	LICENSE LAMP	224
227	LICENSE LAMP	226
234	INST H	222
238	FAN SW	234
239	FAN SW	237
251	ROOM LAMP H	545
252	DOOR SW LH	ROOM LAMP H
256	LUGGAGE ROOM LAMP	545
271	SIDE MARKER LAMP RH	222
272	SIDE MARKER LAMP LH	223
273	RR SIDE MARKER RH	226
274	RR SIDE MARKER LH	226
300	METER, GAUGES AND WARNING SYSTEM	
301	INST H	FUSE BLOCK
304	INST H	THERMAL TRANS
305	TANK UNIT	INST H
320	INST H	324
322	PARKING BRAKE SW	323
323	INST H	BRAKE LEVEL SW
324	AUTO CHOKE RELAY	DIODE
325	323	DIODE
327	TANK UNIT	INST H
329	INST H	252
330	DOOR SW RH	252
335	ENG H	INST H
345	KEY SW	545
346	DOOR SW LH	KEY SW
347	DOOR SW LH	INST H
355	SEAT BELT SW	INST H
356	SEAT BELT SW	INST H
390	CHECK CONNECTOR	301
391	CHECK CONNECTOR	161
392	CHECK CONNECTOR	706
393	CHECK CONNECTOR	735
396	CHECK TERMINAL	ECC CONT UNIT
400	SIGNAL SYSTEM	
401	T/SIGNAL F/UNIT	301
402	T/SIGNAL F/UNIT	HAZARD SW
403	COMB SW (TURN)	HAZARD SW
404	COMB SW (TURN)	FR T/S LAMP RH
405	COMB SW (TURN)	FR T/S LAMP LH
408	RR COMB LAMP RH	404
409	RR COMB LAMP LH	405
410	INST H	404
411	INST H	405
420	HAZARD F/UNIT	431
421	HAZARD SW	HAZARD F/UNIT
422	HAZARD SW	404
423	HAZARD SW	405
431	FUSE BLOCK	HORN RELAY
432	COMB SW	HORN RELAY
433	COMB SW	432
434	HORN RELAY	HORN
435	HORN	434
441	FUSE BLOCK	STOP LAMP SW
442	STOP LAMP SW	RR COMB LAMP RH
443	RR COMB LAMP LH	442
451	ENG H	301
452	ENG H	RR COMB LAMP RH
453	RR COMB LAMP LH	452
500	ACCESSORY SYSTEM	
500	FUSE BLOCK	WIPER MOTOR
502	WIPER MOTOR	COMB SW (WIPER)
503	WIPER MOTOR	COMB SW (WIPER)
504	WIPER MOTOR	ADAPTOR
505	COMB SW (WIPER)	ADAPTOR
506	COMB SW (WIPER)	ADAPTOR
507	ADAPTOR	500
508	ADAPTOR	511
510	WASHER MOTOR	500
511	WASHER MOTOR	COMB SW (WIPER)
520	FUSE BLOCK	INST H
524	SPEAKER H RH	INST H
525	SPEAKER H RH	INST H
526	SPEAKER H LH	INST H
527	SPEAKER H LH	INST H
530	CONDENSER	117
540	FUSE BLOCK	INST H (CIG)
545	FUSE BLOCK	INST H (CLOCK)
550	FUSE BLOCK	INST H (RR DEF)
552	RR DEFOGGER	INST H (RR DEF)
560	FUSE BLOCK	BLOWER MOTOR
562	FAN SW (H)	BLOWER MOTOR
563	FAN SW (M)	RESISTOR
564	FAN SW (L)	RESISTOR
565	562	RESISTOR
570	AIR CON H (A)	FUSE BLOCK
571	AIR CON H (A)	560
575	AIR CON H (A)	FICD
582	AIR CON H (A)	FAN SW
700	SUPPLEMENTAL NUMBERS	
701	FUSIBLE LINK	F/B RELAY
702	111	F/B RELAY
703	ENG H	F/B RELAY
704	ENG H	ECC CONT UNIT
705	CHECK TERMINAL	ECC CONT UNIT
706	ENG H	ECC CONT UNIT
707	FUSIBLE LINK	ECC MAIN RELAY
708	702	ECC MAIN RELAY
709	ECC CONT UNIT	ECC MAIN RELAY
712	131	ECC CONT UNIT
714	ECC CONT UNIT	ENG H
716	ECC CONT UNIT	CLUTCH SW
718	ECC CONT UNIT	EXHAUST GAS SENSOR
719	ECC CONT UNIT	ENG H
720	ECC CONT UNIT	ENG H
721	ECC CONT UNIT	ENG H
732	ECC CONT UNIT	ENG H
733	161	WARM RELAY
735	ENG H	WARM RELAY
736	ENG H	ECC CONT UNIT
737	ENG H	165
738	ENG H	ECC CONT UNIT
740	ENG REV UNIT	165
741	ENG REV UNIT	132
742	ENG REV UNIT	ENG REV RELAY
743	740	ENG REV RELAY
744	ECC CONT UNIT	ENG REV RELAY
745	ECC CONT UNIT	ENG REV RELAY
755	INST H	CHECK TERMINAL
900	GROUND	
900	BODY GROUND	BODY GROUND
901	BODY GROUND	BODY GROUND
910	INST H	BODY GROUND
920	ECC CONT UNIT	ENG GROUND
921	ECC CONT UNIT	ENG GROUND
924	ECC CONT UNIT	EXHAUST GAS SENSOR
933	AUTO CHOKE RELAY	900
934	DIMMER RELAY	900
936	SIDE MARKER RH	900
937	SIDE MARKER LH	900
938	CHECK CONN	900
939	ROOM LAMP H	901
940	IG RELAY	901
941	ACC RELAY	901
943	RR SIDE MARKER LH	901
946	LICENSE LAMP	901
947	LICENSE LAMP	901
948	RR SIDE MARKER RH	901
949	F/B RELAY	900
950	ECC MAIN RELAY	900
951	AIR CON H (B)	900
953	FR T/S LAMP RH	900
954	CLEARANCE L RH	900
955	CLEARANCE L LH	900
956	FR T/S LAMP LH	900
957	RAD FAN MOTOR	900
958	BRAKE LEVEL SW	900
959	WIPER MOTOR	900
960	ADAPTOR	900
962	TANK UNIT	901
963	RR COMB LAMP LH	901
965	WARM RELAY	900
966	CHECK TERMINAL	900
967	CLUTCH SW	900
968	RR COMB LAMP RH	901
971	DIMMER RELAY	900
972	FAN SW	901
973	COMB SW (WIPER)	901
975	INST H	901
980	ENG REV UNIT	901

Fig. 3. Complete circuit wiring diagram — 1982 Sentra (MPG models)

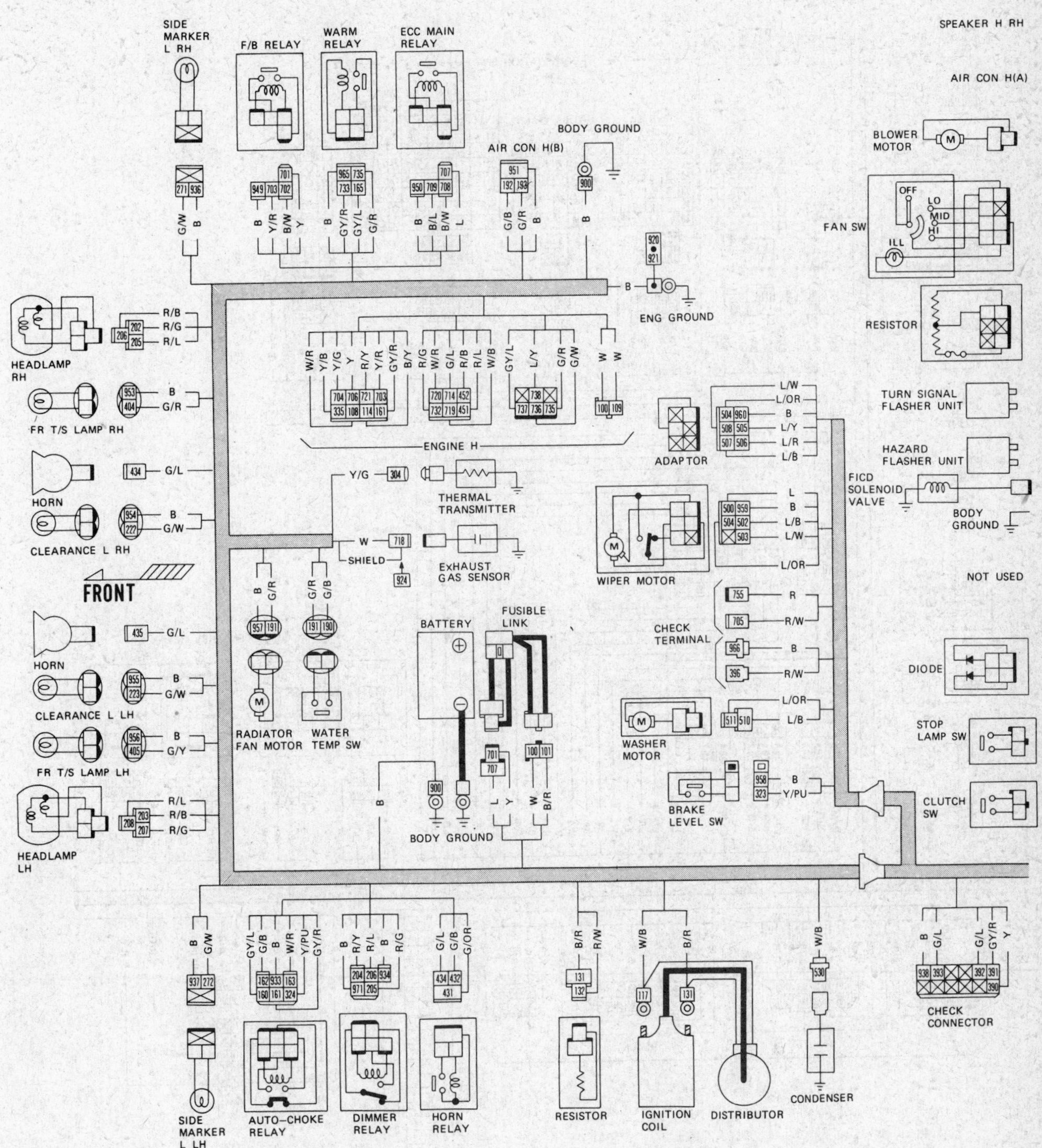
SIDE MARKER L RH
F/B RELAY
WARM RELAY
ECC MAIN RELAY
BODY GROUND
AIR CON H(B)
SPEAKER H RH
AIR CON H(A)
BLOWER MOTOR
FAN SW
OFF
LO
MID
HI
ILL
ENG GROUND
RESISTOR
HEADLAMP RH
FR T/S LAMP RH
ENGINE H
TURN SIGNAL FLASHER UNIT
HAZARD FLASHER UNIT
ADAPTOR
FICD SOLENOID VALVE
HORN
THERMAL TRANSMITTER
BODY GROUND
CLEARANCE L RH
SHIELD
EXHAUST GAS SENSOR
WIPER MOTOR
NOT USED
FRONT
FUSIBLE LINK
BATTERY
CHECK TERMINAL
HORN
DIODE
CLEARANCE L LH
STOP LAMP SW
FR T/S LAMP LH
RADIATOR FAN MOTOR
WATER TEMP SW
WASHER MOTOR
HEADLAMP LH
BODY GROUND
BRAKE LEVEL SW
CLUTCH SW
CHECK CONNECTOR
SIDE MARKER L LH
AUTO-CHOKE RELAY
DIMMER RELAY
HORN RELAY
RESISTOR
IGNITION COIL
DISTRIBUTOR
CONDENSER

Fig. 3. Complete circuit wiring diagram — 1982 Sentra (MPG models)

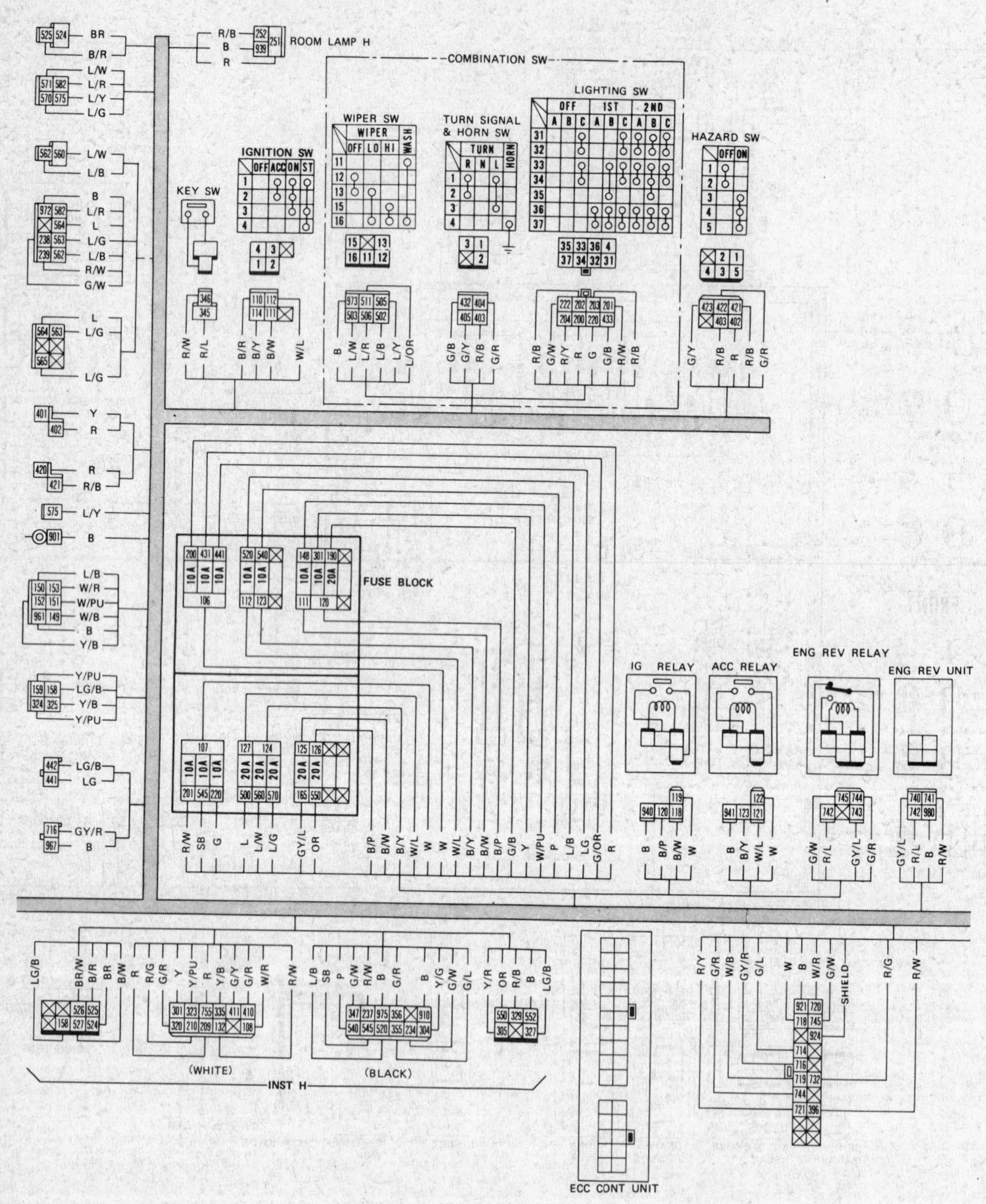
ROOM LAMP H
COMBINATION SW
LIGHTING SW
WIPER SW
TURN SIGNAL & HORN SW
HAZARD SW
IGNITION SW
KEY SW
FUSE BLOCK
IG RELAY
ACC RELAY
ENG REV RELAY
ENG REV UNIT
(WHITE)
(BLACK)
INST H
ECC CONT UNIT

Fig. 3. Complete circuit wiring diagram — 1982 Sentra (MPG models)

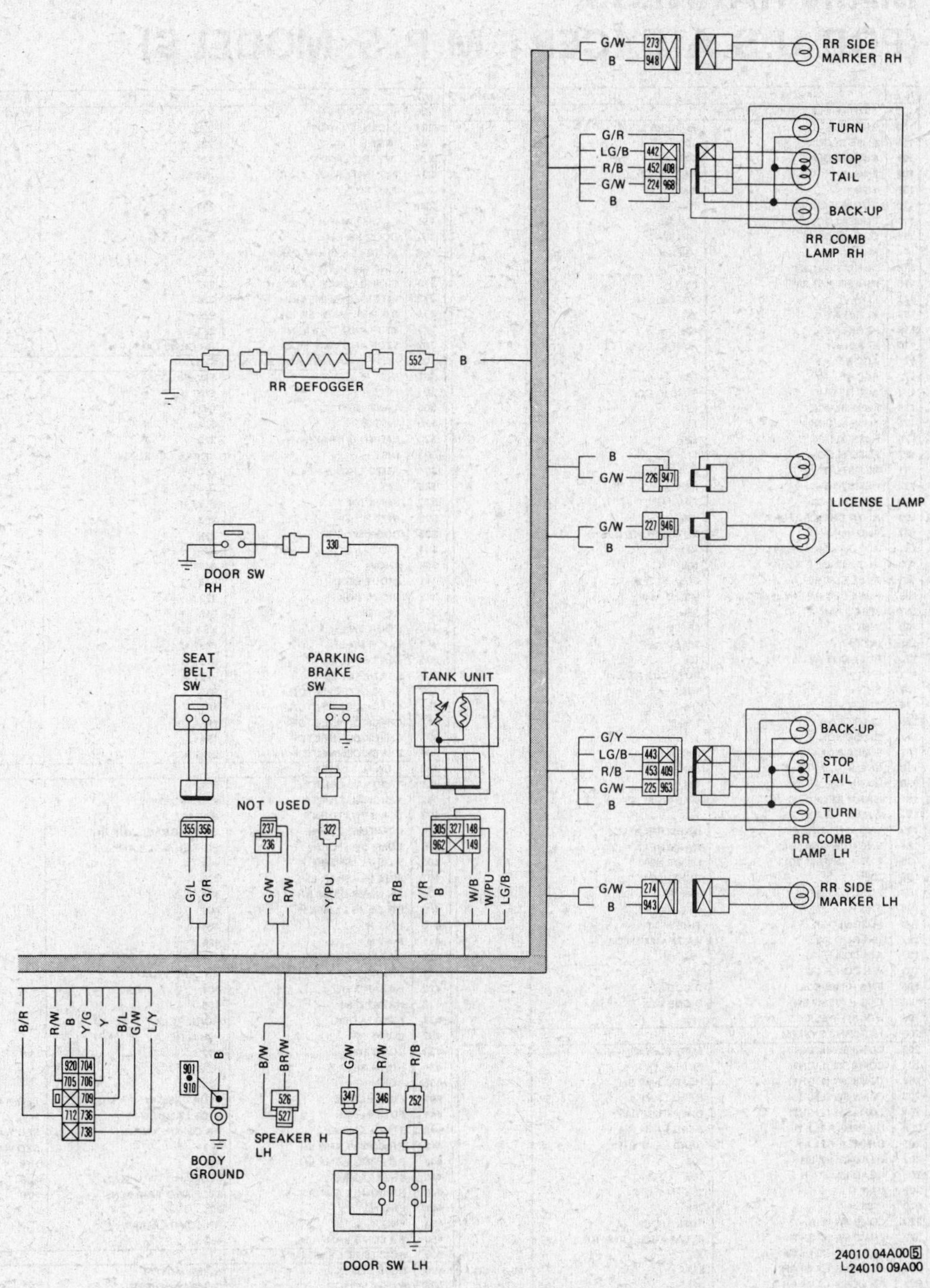
RR SIDE MARKER RH
TURN
STOP
TAIL
BACK-UP
RR COMB LAMP RH
RR DEFOGGER
LICENSE LAMP
DOOR SW RH
SEAT BELT SW
PARKING BRAKE SW
TANK UNIT
NOT USED
BACK-UP
STOP
TAIL
TURN
RR COMB LAMP LH
RR SIDE MARKER LH
BODY GROUND
SPEAKER H LH
DOOR SW LH
24010 04A00
24010 09A00

Fig. 3. Complete circuit wiring diagram — 1982 Sentra (MPG models)

NISSAN SENTRA
MAIN HARNESS (FOR U.S.A. EXCEPT M.P.G. MODELS)

NO.	FROM	TO	REMARKS
100	ENGINE ELECTRICAL SYSTEM		
100	ENG H	FUSIBLE LINK	
106	FUSE BLOCK	100	
107	FUSE BLOCK	106	
108	ENG H	INST H	
109	ENG H	100	
110	FUSIBLE LINK	IGN SW	
111	FUSE BLOCK	IGN SW	
112	FUSE BLOCK	IGN SW	
114	ENG H	IGN SW	
115	INHIBIT RELAY	114	
116	INHIBIT RELAY	ENG H	
117	111	IGN COIL (+)	
118	IG RELAY	111	
119	IG RELAY	106	
120	IG RELAY	FUSE BLOCK	
121	ACC RELAY	112	
122	ACC RELAY	106	
123	ACC RELAY	FUSE BLOCK	
124	FUSE BLOCK	123	
125	FUSE BLOCK	111	
126	FUSE BLOCK	120	
127	FUSE BLOCK	112	
131	RESISTOR	IGN COIL (−)	
132	RESISTOR	INST H	
148	FUSE BLOCK	TANK UNIT	
160	AUTO CHOKE RELAY	165	
161	ENG H	AUTO CHOKE RELAY	
162	AUTO CHOKE RELAY	190	
163	AUTO CHOKE RELAY	108	
165	FUEL CUT RELAY	FUSE BLOCK	
166	FUEL CUT RELAY	SPEED AMP	
167	SPEED AMP	165	
168	INST H	SPEED AMP	
169	INST H	SPEED AMP	
170	FUEL CUT RELAY	165	
171	ENG H	FUEL CUT RELAY	
172	ENG H	165	
174	CLUTCH SW	165	
175	CLUTCH SW	176	
176	DIODE BOX	171	
177	DIODE BOX	WARM RELAY (1)	
179	ENG H	177	
180	WARM RELAY (1)	161	
181	WARM RELAY (1)	WARM RELAY (2)	
182	WARM RELAY (2)	165	
183	ENG H (TEMP SW)	WARM RELAY (2)	
184	ENG H (WARM SOL)	WARM RELAY (2)	
185	ENG H (WARM SOL)	DIODE BOX	
186	196	DIODE BOX	
187	FUEL CUT RELAY	195	
188	ENG H	VACUUM SW	
190	FUSE BLOCK	THERMO SW	
191	THERMO SW	RAD FAN MOTOR	
192	AIR CON H (B)	190	
193	AIR CON H (B)	191	
195	ENG H (MR SOL)	DIODE BOX	
196	ENG H (TEMP SW)	DIODE BOX	
197	INHIBIT RELAY	177	
200	LIGHTING SYSTEM		
200	COMB SW (LIGHT)	FUSE BLOCK	
201	COMB SW (LIGHT)	FUSE BLOCK	
202	COMB SW (LIGHT)	HEAD LAMP RH	
203	COMB SW (LIGHT)	HEAD LAMP LH	
204	COMB SW (LIGHT)	DIMMER RELAY	
205	DIMMER RELAY	HEAD LAMP RH	
206	DIMMER RELAY	HEAD LAMP RH	
207	HEAD LAMP LH	205	
208	HEAD LAMP LH	206	
209	INST H	202	
210	INST H	206	
220	COMB SW (LIGHT)	FUSE BLOCK	
222	COMB SW (LIGHT)	CLEARANCE LAMP RH	
223	CLEARANCE LAMP LH	222	
224	RR COMB LAMP RH	222	SED WAG
225	RR COMB LAMP LH	224	SED WAG
225	RR COMB LAMP LH	282	H/B
226	LICENSE LAMP	224	SED
226	LICENSE LAMP	281	H/B

NO.	FROM	TO	REMARKS
226	BACK DOOR H	224	WAG
227	LICENSE LAMP	226	
234	INST H	222	
236	A/T IND LAMP	234	
237	A/T IND LAMP	INST H	
238	FAN SW	234	
239	FAN SW	237	
251	ROOM LAMP H	545	
252	DOOR SW LH	ROOM LAMP H	
256	LUGGAGE ROOM LAMP	545	
271	SIDE MARKER LAMP RH	222	
272	SIDE MARKER LAMP LH	223	
273	RR SIDE MARKER RH	226	
274	RR SIDE MARKER LH	226	
281	STOP AND TAIL SENS	222	H/B
282	STOP AND TAIL SENS	RR COMB LAMP RH	H/B
300	METER, GAUGES AND WARNING SYSTEM		
301	INST H	FUSE BLOCK	
304	INST H	ENG H	
305	TANK UNIT	INST H	
320	INST H	324	
322	PARKING BRAKE SW	323	
323	INST H	BRAKE LEVEL SW	
324	AUTO CHOKE RELAY	DIODE	
325	323	DIODE	
327	TANK UNIT	INST H	
329	INST H	252	
330	DOOR SW RH	252	
334	STOP AND TAIL SENS	INST H	H/B
335	ENG H	INST H	
341	DIODE BOX	346	H/B
342	DIODE BOX	222	H/B
345	KEY SW	545	
346	DOOR SW LH	KEY SW	
347	DOOR SW LH	INST H	
355	SEAT BELT SW	INST H	
356	SEAT BELT SW	INST H	
390	CHECK CONNECTOR	301	
391	CHECK CONNECTOR	161	
392	CHECK CONNECTOR	195	
393	CHECK CONNECTOR	184	
394	CHECK CONNECTOR	ENG H	
400	SIGNAL SYSTEM		
401	T/SIGNAL F/UNIT	301	
402	T/SIGNAL F/UNIT	HAZARD SW	
403	COMB SW (TURN)	HAZARD SW	
404	COMB SW (TURN)	FR T/SIGNAL LAMP RH	
405	COMB SW (TURN)	FR T/SIGNAL LAMP LH	
406	SIDE FLASHER L	404	
407	SIDE FLASHER L	405	
408	RR COMB LAMP RH	404	
409	RR COMB LAMP LH	405	
410	INST H	404	
411	INST H	405	
420	HAZARD F/UNIT	431	
421	HAZARD SW	HAZARD F/UNIT	
422	HAZARD SW	404	
423	HAZARD SW	405	
431	FUSE BLOCK	HORN RELAY	
432	COMB SW	HORN RELAY	
433	COMB SW	432	
434	HORN RELAY	HORN	
435	HORN	434	
441	FUSE BLOCK	STOP LAMP SW	SED WAG
441	FUSE BLOCK	STOP LAMP SW	H/B
442	STOP LAMP SW	RR COMB LAMP RH	SED WAG
443	RR COMB LAMP LH	442	SED WAG
443	RR COMB LAMP LH	446	H/B
445	STOP LAMP SW	STOP AND TAIL SENS	H/B
446	RR COMB LAMP RH	STOP AND TAIL SENS	H/B
451	ENG H	301	
452	ENG H	RR COMB LAMP RH	
453	RR COMB LAMP LH	452	
500	ACCESSORY SYSTEM		
500	FUSE BLOCK	WIPER MOTOR	
502	WIPER MOTOR	COMB SW (WIPER)	
503	WIPER MOTOR	COMB SW (WIPER)	
504	WIPER AMP	WIPER MOTOR	H/B
505	WIPER AMP	COMB SW (WIPER)	H/B

Fig. 4. Complete circuit wiring diagram — 1982 Sentra (except MPG)

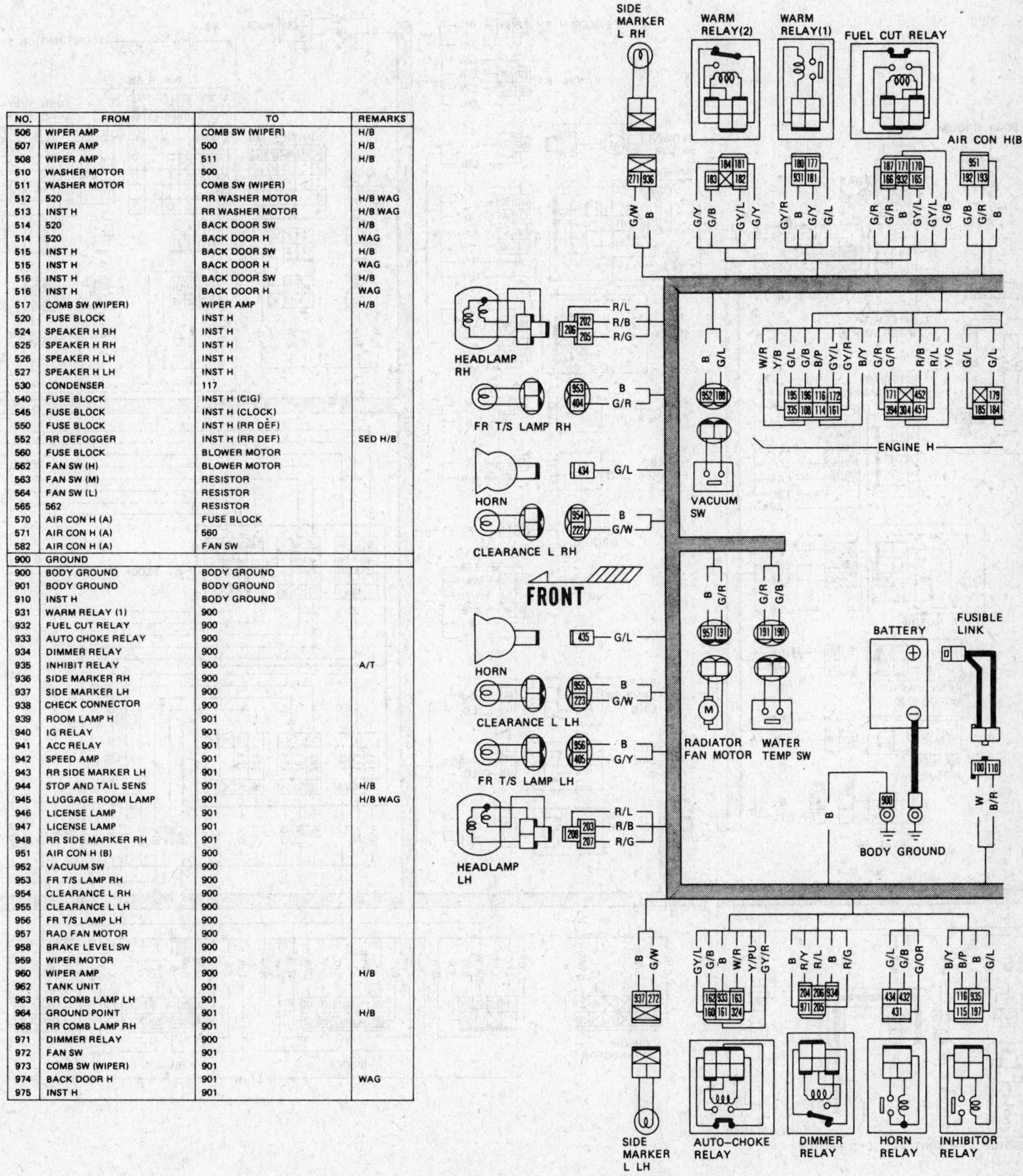

NO.	FROM	TO	REMARKS
506	WIPER AMP	COMB SW (WIPER)	H/B
507	WIPER AMP	500	H/B
508	WIPER AMP	511	H/B
510	WASHER MOTOR	500	
511	WASHER MOTOR	COMB SW (WIPER)	
512	520	RR WASHER MOTOR	H/B WAG
513	INST H	RR WASHER MOTOR	H/B WAG
514	520	BACK DOOR SW	H/B
514	520	BACK DOOR H	WAG
515	INST H	BACK DOOR SW	H/B
515	INST H	BACK DOOR H	WAG
516	INST H	BACK DOOR SW	H/B
516	INST H	BACK DOOR H	WAG
517	COMB SW (WIPER)	WIPER AMP	H/B
520	FUSE BLOCK	INST H	
524	SPEAKER H RH	INST H	
525	SPEAKER H RH	INST H	
526	SPEAKER H LH	INST H	
527	SPEAKER H LH	INST H	
530	CONDENSER	117	
540	FUSE BLOCK	INST H (CIG)	
545	FUSE BLOCK	INST H (CLOCK)	
550	FUSE BLOCK	INST H (RR DÈF)	
552	RR DEFOGGER	INST H (RR DEF)	SED H/B
560	FUSE BLOCK	BLOWER MOTOR	
562	FAN SW (H)	BLOWER MOTOR	
563	FAN SW (M)	RESISTOR	
564	FAN SW (L)	RESISTOR	
565	562	RESISTOR	
570	AIR CON H (A)	FUSE BLOCK	
571	AIR CON H (A)	560	
582	AIR CON H (A)	FAN SW	
900	GROUND		
900	BODY GROUND	BODY GROUND	
901	BODY GROUND	BODY GROUND	
910	INST H	BODY GROUND	
931	WARM RELAY (1)	900	
932	FUEL CUT RELAY	900	
933	AUTO CHOKE RELAY	900	
934	DIMMER RELAY	900	
935	INHIBIT RELAY	900	A/T
936	SIDE MARKER RH	900	
937	SIDE MARKER LH	900	
938	CHECK CONNECTOR	900	
939	ROOM LAMP H	901	
940	IG RELAY	901	
941	ACC RELAY	901	
942	SPEED AMP	901	
943	RR SIDE MARKER LH	901	
944	STOP AND TAIL SENS	901	H/B
945	LUGGAGE ROOM LAMP	901	H/B WAG
946	LICENSE LAMP	901	
947	LICENSE LAMP	901	
948	RR SIDE MARKER RH	901	
951	AIR CON H (B)	900	
952	VACUUM SW	900	
953	FR T/S LAMP RH	900	
954	CLEARANCE L RH	900	
955	CLEARANCE L LH	900	
956	FR T/S LAMP LH	900	
957	RAD FAN MOTOR	900	
958	BRAKE LEVEL SW	900	
959	WIPER MOTOR	900	
960	WIPER AMP	900	H/B
962	TANK UNIT	901	
963	RR COMB LAMP LH	901	
964	GROUND POINT	901	H/B
968	RR COMB LAMP RH	901	
971	DIMMER RELAY	900	
972	FAN SW	901	
973	COMB SW (WIPER)	901	
974	BACK DOOR H	901	WAG
975	INST H	901	

SIDE MARKER L RH
WARM RELAY(2)
WARM RELAY(1)
FUEL CUT RELAY
AIR CON H(B)
HEADLAMP RH
FR T/S LAMP RH
HORN
VACUUM SW
CLEARANCE L RH
ENGINE H
FRONT
HORN
BATTERY
FUSIBLE LINK
CLEARANCE L LH
RADIATOR FAN MOTOR
WATER TEMP SW
FR T/S LAMP LH
HEADLAMP LH
BODY GROUND
SIDE MARKER L LH
AUTO-CHOKE RELAY
DIMMER RELAY
HORN RELAY
INHIBITOR RELAY

Fig. 4. Complete circuit wiring diagram — 1982 Sentra (except MPG)

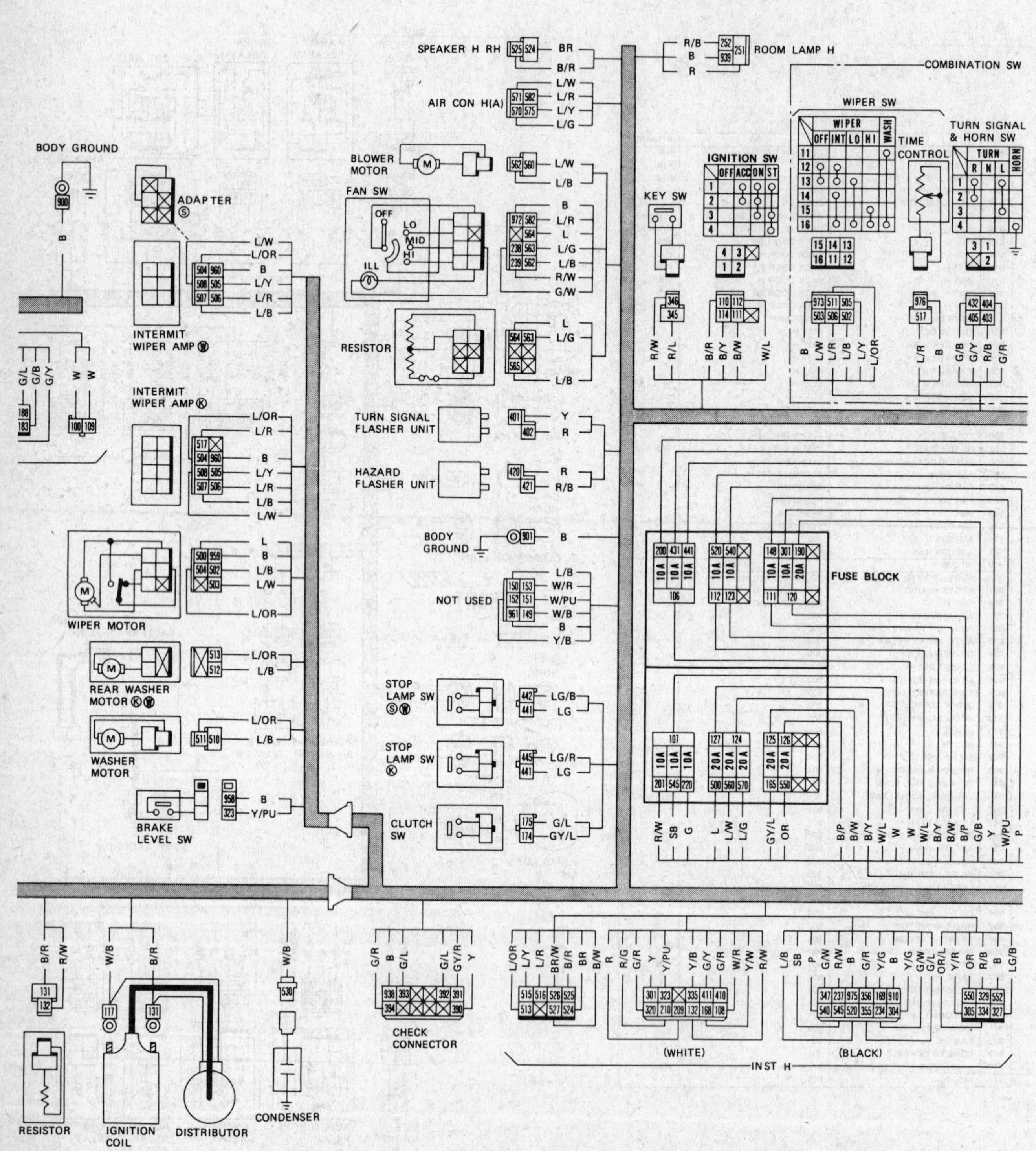
SPEAKER H RH
ROOM LAMP H
COMBINATION SW
AIR CON H(A)
WIPER SW
TURN SIGNAL & HORN SW
BODY GROUND
BLOWER MOTOR
IGNITION SW
TIME CONTROL
ADAPTER
FAN SW
KEY SW
INTERMIT WIPER AMP
RESISTOR
TURN SIGNAL FLASHER UNIT
HAZARD FLASHER UNIT
BODY GROUND
FUSE BLOCK
NOT USED
WIPER MOTOR
REAR WASHER MOTOR
STOP LAMP SW
WASHER MOTOR
BRAKE LEVEL SW
CLUTCH SW
CHECK CONNECTOR
(WHITE)
(BLACK)
INST H
RESISTOR
IGNITION COIL
DISTRIBUTOR
CONDENSER

Fig. 4. Complete circuit wiring diagram — 1982 Sentra (except MPG)

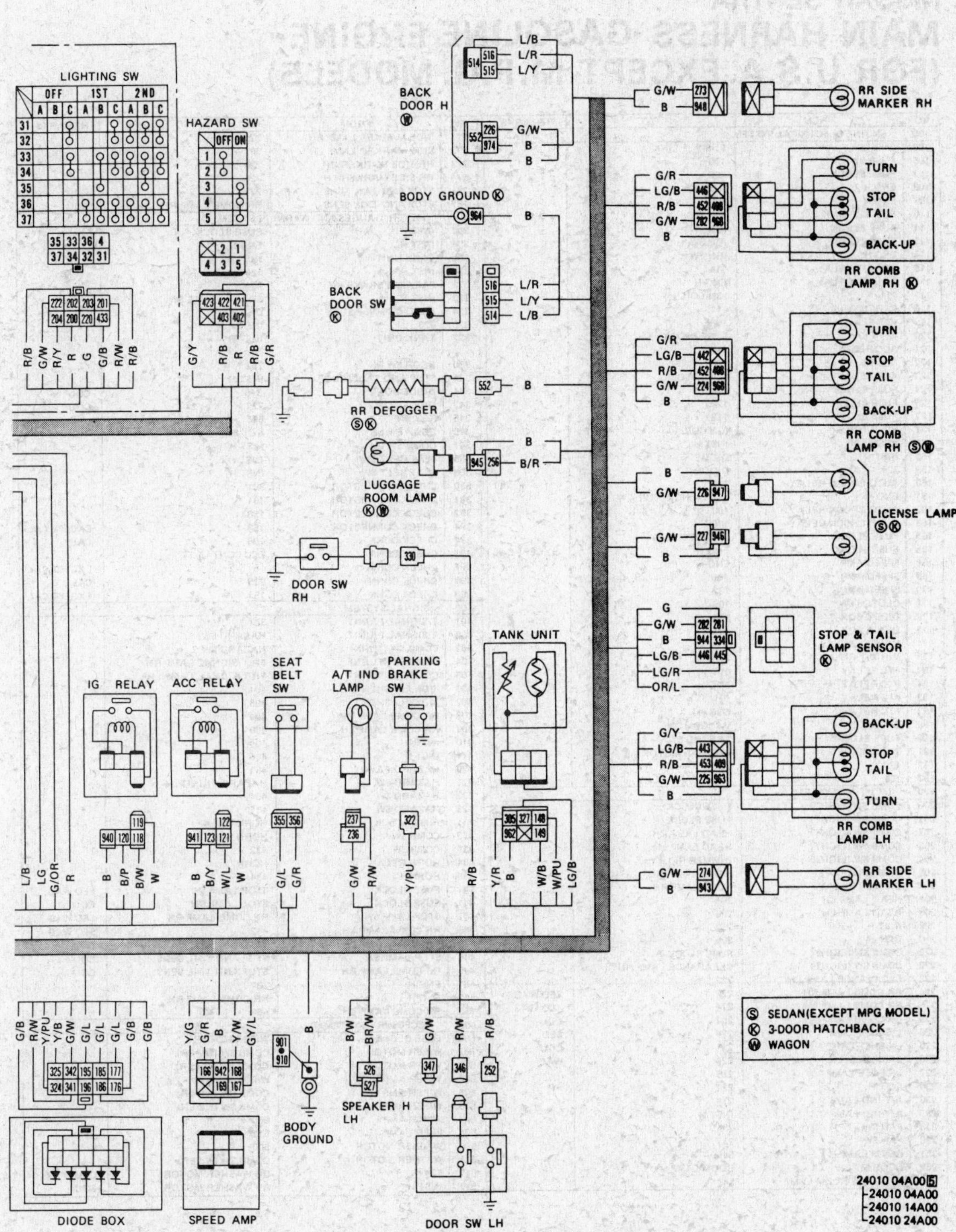
LIGHTING SW
HAZARD SW
BACK DOOR H
BODY GROUND
BACK DOOR SW
RR DEFOGGER
LUGGAGE ROOM LAMP
DOOR SW RH
IG RELAY
ACC RELAY
SEAT BELT SW
A/T IND LAMP
PARKING BRAKE SW
TANK UNIT
RR SIDE MARKER RH
TURN
STOP
TAIL
BACK-UP
RR COMB LAMP RH
LICENSE LAMP
STOP & TAIL LAMP SENSOR
RR COMB LAMP LH
RR SIDE MARKER LH
DIODE BOX
SPEED AMP
BODY GROUND
SPEAKER H LH
DOOR SW LH
Ⓢ SEDAN(EXCEPT MPG MODEL)
Ⓚ 3-DOOR HATCHBACK
Ⓦ WAGON
24010 04A00
24010 04A00
24010 14A00
24010 24A00

Fig. 4. Complete circuit wiring diagram — 1982 Sentra (except MPG)

NISSAN SENTRA
MAIN HARNESS -GASOLINE ENGINE- (FOR U.S.A. EXCEPT M.P.G. MODELS)

NO.	FROM	TO	REMARKS
100	ENGINE ELECTRICAL SYSTEM		
100	ENG H	FUSIBLE LINK	
106	FUSE BLOCK	100	
107	FUSE BLOCK	106	
108	ENG H	INST H	
109	ENG H	100	
110	FUSIBLE LINK	IGN SW	
111	FUSE BLOCK	IGN SW	
112	FUSE BLOCK	IGN SW	
114	ENG H	IGN SW	
115	INHIBIT RELAY	114	
116	INHIBIT RELAY	ENG H	
117	111	IGN COIL (+)	
118	IG RELAY	111	
119	IG RELAY	106	
120	IG RELAY	FUSE BLOCK	
121	ACC RELAY	112	
122	ACC RELAY	106	
123	ACC RELAY	FUSE BLOCK	
124	FUSE BLOCK	123	
126	FUSE BLOCK	120	
127	FUSE BLOCK	112	
131	RESISTOR	IGN COIL (-)	
132	RESISTOR	INST H	
158	INST H	DIODE	
159	324	DIODE	
160	AUTO CHOKE RELAY	165	
161	ENG H	AUTO CHOKE RELAY	
162	AUTO CHOCK RELAY	190	
163	AUTO CHOCK RELAY	108	
165	FUSE BLOCK	INHIBIT RELAY	
165	FUSE BLOCK	ENG H	EXCEPT CAL
168	SPEED AMP	ENG H	
169	SPEED AMP	165	
170	SPEED AMP	132	
171	CLUTCH SW	168	
172	DIODE BOX	168	
173	DIODE BOX	175	
174	INHIBIT RELAY	165	
175	INHIBIT RELAY	ENG H	
180	PTC RELAY	100	
181	PTC RELAY	ENG H	
182	PTC RELAY	161	
183	PTC RELAY	ENG H	
188	ENG H	VACUUM SW	
190	FUSE BLOCK	THERMO SW	
191	THERMO SW	RAD FAN MOTOR	
192	190	COND FAN RELAY	
193	191	COND FAN RELAY	
200	LIGHTING SYSTEM		
200	COMB SW (LIGHT)	FUSE BLOCK	
201	COMB SW (LIGHT)	FUSE BLOCK	
202	COMB SW (LIGHT)	HEAD LAMP RH	
203	COMB SW (LIGHT)	HEAD LAMP LH	
204	COMB SW (LIGHT)	DIMMER RELAY	
205	DIMMER RELAY	HEAD LAMP RH	
206	DIMMER RELAY	HEAD LAMP RH	
207	HEAD LAMP LH	205	
208	HEAD LAMP LH	206	
209	INST H	202	
210	INST H	205	
220	COMB SW (LIGHT)	FUSE BLOCK	
222	COMB SW (LIGHT)	CLEARANCE LAMP RH	
223	CLEARANCE LAMP LH	222	
224	RR COMB LAMP RH	222	SED WAG
225	RR COMB LAMP LH	224	SED WAG
225	RR COMB LAMP LH	282	COU
226	LICENSE LAMP	224	SED
226	LICENSE LAMP	281	COU
226	BACK DOOR H	224	WAG
227	LICENSE LAMP	226	
234	INST H	222	
236	A/T IND LAMP	234	
237	A/T IND LAMP	INST H	
238	FAN SW	234	
239	FAN SW	237	
251	ROOM LAMP H	545	
252	DOOR SW LH	ROOM LAMP H	
256	LUGGAGE ROOM LAMP	545	
271	SIDE MARKER LAMP RH	222	
272	SIDE MARKER LAMP LH	223	
273	RR SIDE MARKER RH	226	
274	RR SIDE MARKER LH	226	
281	STOP AND TAIL SENS	222	COU
282	STOP AND TAIL SENS	RR COMB LAMP RH	COU
300	METER, GAUGES AND WARNING SYTEM		
301	INST H	FUSE BLOCK	
304	INST H	ENG H	
305	TANK UNIT	INST H	
320	INST H	324	
322	PARKING BRAKE SW	323	
323	INST H	BRAKE LEVEL SW	
324	AUTO CHOCK RELAY	DIODE	
325	323	DIODE	
327	TANK UNIT	INST H	
330	DOOR SW RH	252	
334	STOP AND TAIL SENS	INST H	
341	DIODE BOX	346	COU
342	DIODE BOX	222	COU
345	KEY SW	545	
346	DOOR SW LH	KEY SW	
347	DOOR SW LH	INST H	
355	SEAT BELT SW	INST H	
356	SEAT BELT SW	INST H	
390	CHECK CONNECTOR	301	
391	CHECK CONNECTOR	161	
392	CHECK CONNECTOR	188	
394	CHECK CONNECTOR	168	EXCEPT CAL
394	CHECK CONN	706	CAL
396	CHECK CONN	ECC CONT UNIT	
397	CHECK CONN	181	EXCEPT CAL
398	CHECK CONN	738	CAL
398	CHECK CONN	183	EXCEPT CAL
400	SIGNAL SYSTEM		
401	T/SIGNAL F/UNIT	301	
402	T/SIGNAL F/UNIT	HAZARD SW	
403	COMB SW (TURN)	HAZARD SW	
404	COMB SW (TURN)	FR T/SIGNAL LAMP RH	
405	COMB SW (TURN)	FR T/SIGNAL LAMP LH	
406	SIDE FLASHER L	404	
407	SIDE FLASHER L	405	
408	RR COMB LAMP RH	404	
409	RR COMB LAMP LH	405	
410	INST H	404	
411	INST H	405	
420	HAZARD F/UNIT	431	
421	HAZARD SW	HAZARD F/UNIT	
422	HAZARD SW	404	
423	HAZARD SW	405	
431	FUSE BLOCK	HORN RELAY	
432	COMB SW	HORN RELAY	
433	COMB SW	432	
434	HORN RELAY	HORN	
435	HORN	434	
441	FUSE BLOCK	STOP LAMP SW	SED WAG
441	FUSE BLOCK	STOP LAMP SW	COU
442	STOP LAMP SW	RR COMB LAMP RH	SED WAG
443	RR COMB LAMP LH	442	SED WAG
443	RR COMB LAMP LH	446	COU
445	STOP LAMP SW	STOP AND TAIL SENS	COU
446	RR COMB LAMP RH	STOP AND TAIL SENS	COU
451	ENG H	301	
452	ENG H	RR COMB LAMP RH	
453	RR COMB LAMP LH	452	
500	ACCESSORY SYSTEM		
500	FUSE BLOCK	WIPER MOTOR	
502	WIPER MOTOR	COMB SW (WIPER)	
503	WIPER MOTOR	COMB SW (WIPER)	
504	WIPER AMP	WIPER MOTOR	
505	WIPER AMP	COMB SW (WIPER)	
506	WIPER AMP	COMB SW (WIPER)	
507	WIPER AMP	500	
508	WIPER AMP	511	
510	WASHER MOTOR	500	
511	WASHER MOTOR	COMB SW (WIPER)	
512	520	RR WASHER MOTOR	COU
513	INST H	RR WASHER MOTOR	COU

Fig. 5. Complete circuit wiring diagram — 1983 Sentra (except MPG)

NO.	FROM	TO	REMARKS
514	520	BACK DOOR SW	COU
514	520	BACK DOOR H	WAG
515	INST H	BACK DOOR H	WAG
515	INST H	BACK DOOR SW	COU
516	INST H	BACK DOOR SW	COU
516	INST H	BACK DOOR H	WAG
519	COMB SW	WIPER AMP	
520	FUSE BLOCK	INST H	
524	SPEAKER H RH	INST H	
525	SPEAKER H RH	INST H	
526	SPEAKER H LH	INST H	
527	SPEAKER H LH	INST H	
530	CONDENSER	117	
540	FUSE BLOCK	INST H (CIG)	
545	FUSE BLOCK	INST H (CLOCK)	
550	FUSE BLOCK	INST H (RR DEF)	
552	RR DEFOGGER	INST H (RR DEF)	
560	FUSE BLOCK	BLOWER MOTOR	
562	FAN SW (H)	BLOWER MOTOR	
563	FAN SW (M)	RESISTOR	
564	FAN SW (L)	RESISTOR	
565	562	RESISTOR	
570	FUSE BLOCK	A/C RELAY	
571	PRESSURE SW	A/C RELAY	
572	THERMO AMP	A/C RELAY	
573	THEMO AMP	A/C SW	
574	RESISTOR	FAN SW	
575	578	FAN SW	
576	A/C SW	THERMO AMP	
577	A/C SW	570	
578	A/C SW	THERMO AMP	
580	PRESSURE SW	COND FAN RELAY	
581	570	COND FAN RELAY	
582	COND FAN MOTOR	COND FAN RELAY	
583	580	COMPRESSOR	
584	580	FISD SOLENOID	
585	573	A/C RELAY	
586	THERMO AMP	A/C SW	
700	SUPPLEMENTAL NUMBERS		
701	FUSIBLE LINK	F/B RELAY	
702	111	F/B RELAY	
703	ENG H	F/B RELAY	
704	ENG H	ECC CONT UNIT	
705	INST H	CHECK CONNECTOR	
706	ENG H	ECC CONT UNIT	
707	FUSIBLE LINK	ECC MAIN RELAY	
708	702	ECC MAIN RELAY	
709	ECC CONT UNIT	ECC MAIN RELAY	
712	131	ECC CONT UNIT	
714	DIODE BOX	ENG H	
715	DIODE BOX	ECC CONT UNIT	
716	ECC CONT UNIT	CLUTCH SW	
718	ECC CONT UNIT	O2 SENSER	
719	ECC CONT UNIT	ENG H	
720	ECC CONT UNIT	ENG H	
721	ECC CONT UNIT	ENG H	
732	ECC CONT UNIT	ENG H	
733	161	MIXTURE RELAY	
734	100	MIXTURE RELAY	
735	ENG H	MIXTURE RELAY	
738	MIXTURE RELAY	ECC CONT UNIT	
740	DIODE BOX	INHIBIT RELAY	
741	DIODE BOX	714	
742	ECC CONT UNIT	VACUUM SW	
743	ECC CONT UNIT	VACUUM SW	
755	CHECK CONNECTOR	ECC CONT UNIT	
790	RESISTER	165	
791	RESISTER	108	
900	GROUND		
900	BODY GROUND	BODY GROUND	
901	BODY GROUND	BODY GROUND	
910	INST H	BODY GROUND	
920	ECC CONT UNIT	ENG GROUND	
921	ECC CONT UNIT	ENG GROUND	
924	ECC CONT UNIT	O2 SENSOR	
931	WARM RELAY (1)	900	
932	FUEL CUT RELAY	900	
933	AUTO CHOKE RELAY	900	
934	DIMMER RELAY	900	

NO.	FROM	TO	REMARKS
935	INHIBIT RELAY	900	A/T
936	SIDE MARKER RH	900	
937	SIDE MARKER LH	900	
938	CHECK CONNECTOR	900	
939	ROOM LAMP H	901	
940	IG RELAY	901	
941	ACC RELAY	901	
942	SPEED AMP	901	
943	RR SIDE MARKER LH	901	
944	STOP AND TAIL SENS	901	COU
945	LUGGAGE ROOM LAMP	901	COUWAG
946	LICENSE LAMP	901	
947	LICENSE LAMP	901	
948	RR SIDE MARKER RH	901	
951	AIR CON H (B)	900	
952	VACUUM SW	900	
953	FR T/S LAMP RH	900	
954	CLEARANCE L RH	900	
955	CLEARANCE L LH	900	
956	FR T/S LAMP LH	900	
957	RAD FAN MOTOR	900	
958	BRAKE LEVEL SW	900	
959	WIPER MOTOR	900	
960	WIPER AMP	900	COU
962	TANK UNIT	901	
963	RR COMB LAMP LH	901	
964	GROUND POINT	901	COU
968	RR COMB LAMP RH	901	
971	DIMMER RELAY	900	
972	FAN SW	901	
973	COMB SW (WIPER)	901	
974	BACK DOOR H	901	WAG
975	INST H	901	
976	CONDENSER FAN MOTOR	900	
977	F/B RELAY	900	
978	FICD SOLENOID	900	
979	ECC MAIN RELAY	900	
980	CONDENSER FAN RELAY	900	
981	FAN SW	901	
982	CHECK TERMINAL	900	
983	ENG REV UNIT	901	
984	TANK UNIT	901	

Fig. 5. Complete circuit wiring diagram — 1983 Sentra (except MPG)

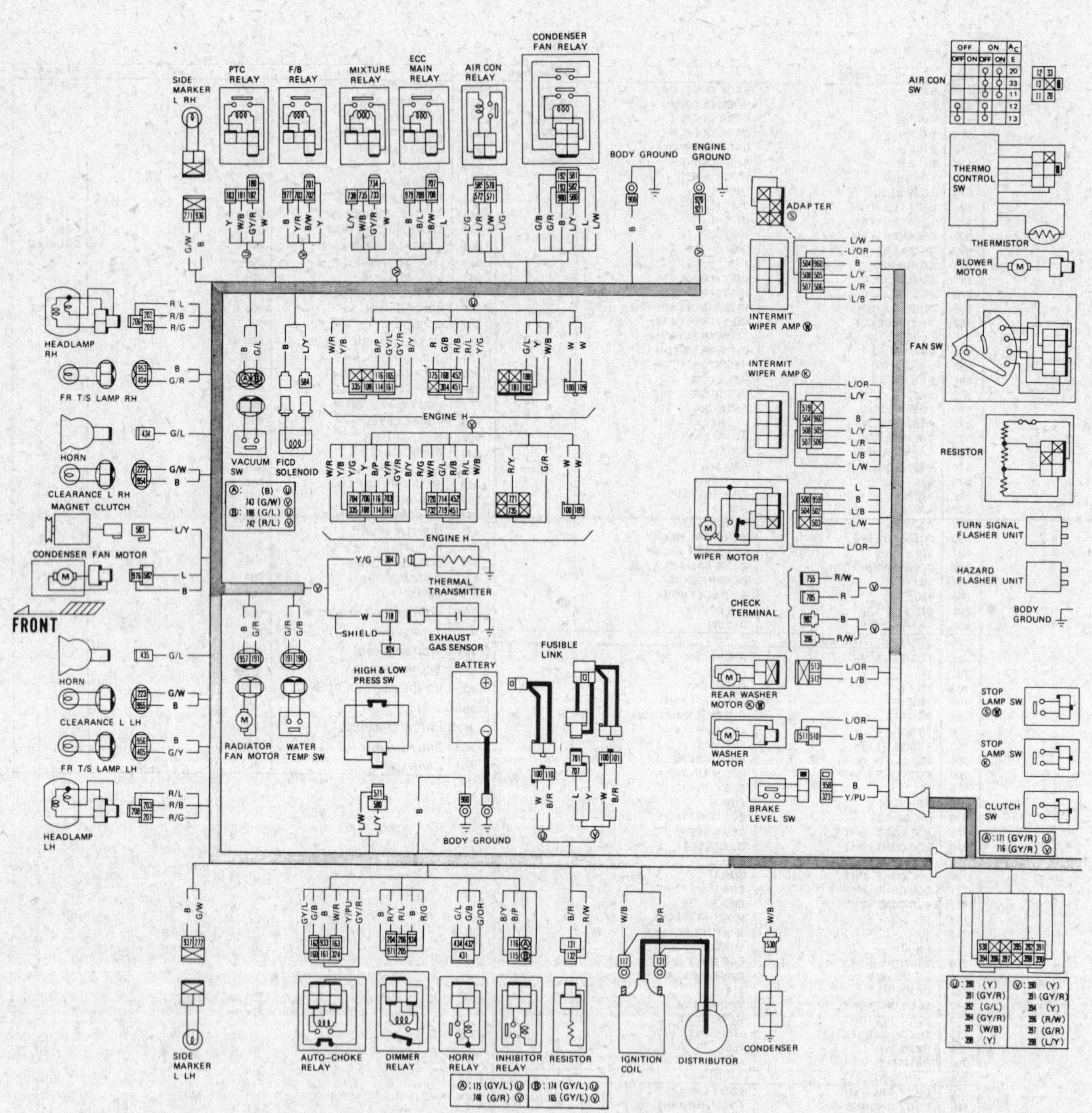
SIDE MARKER L RH
PTC RELAY
F/B RELAY
MIXTURE RELAY
ECC MAIN RELAY
AIR CON RELAY
CONDENSER FAN RELAY
BODY GROUND
ENGINE GROUND
ADAPTER
AIR CON SW
THERMO CONTROL SW
THERMISTOR
BLOWER MOTOR
INTERMIT WIPER AMP
FAN SW
HEADLAMP RH
FR T/S LAMP RH
HORN
CLEARANCE L RH
MAGNET CLUTCH
CONDENSER FAN MOTOR
FRONT
VACUUM SW
FICD SOLENOID
ENGINE H
RESISTOR
WIPER MOTOR
TURN SIGNAL FLASHER UNIT
HAZARD FLASHER UNIT
THERMAL TRANSMITTER
SHIELD
EXHAUST GAS SENSOR
CHECK TERMINAL
BODY GROUND
HORN
CLEARANCE L LH
FR T/S LAMP LH
HEADLAMP LH
HIGH & LOW PRESS SW
BATTERY
FUSIBLE LINK
REAR WASHER MOTOR
WASHER MOTOR
STOP LAMP SW
CLUTCH SW
RADIATOR FAN MOTOR
WATER TEMP SW
BRAKE LEVEL SW
BODY GROUND
SIDE MARKER L LH
AUTO-CHOKE RELAY
DIMMER RELAY
HORN RELAY
INHIBITOR RELAY
RESISTOR
IGNITION COIL
DISTRIBUTOR
CONDENSER

Fig. 5. Complete circuit wiring diagram — 1983 Sentra (except MPG)

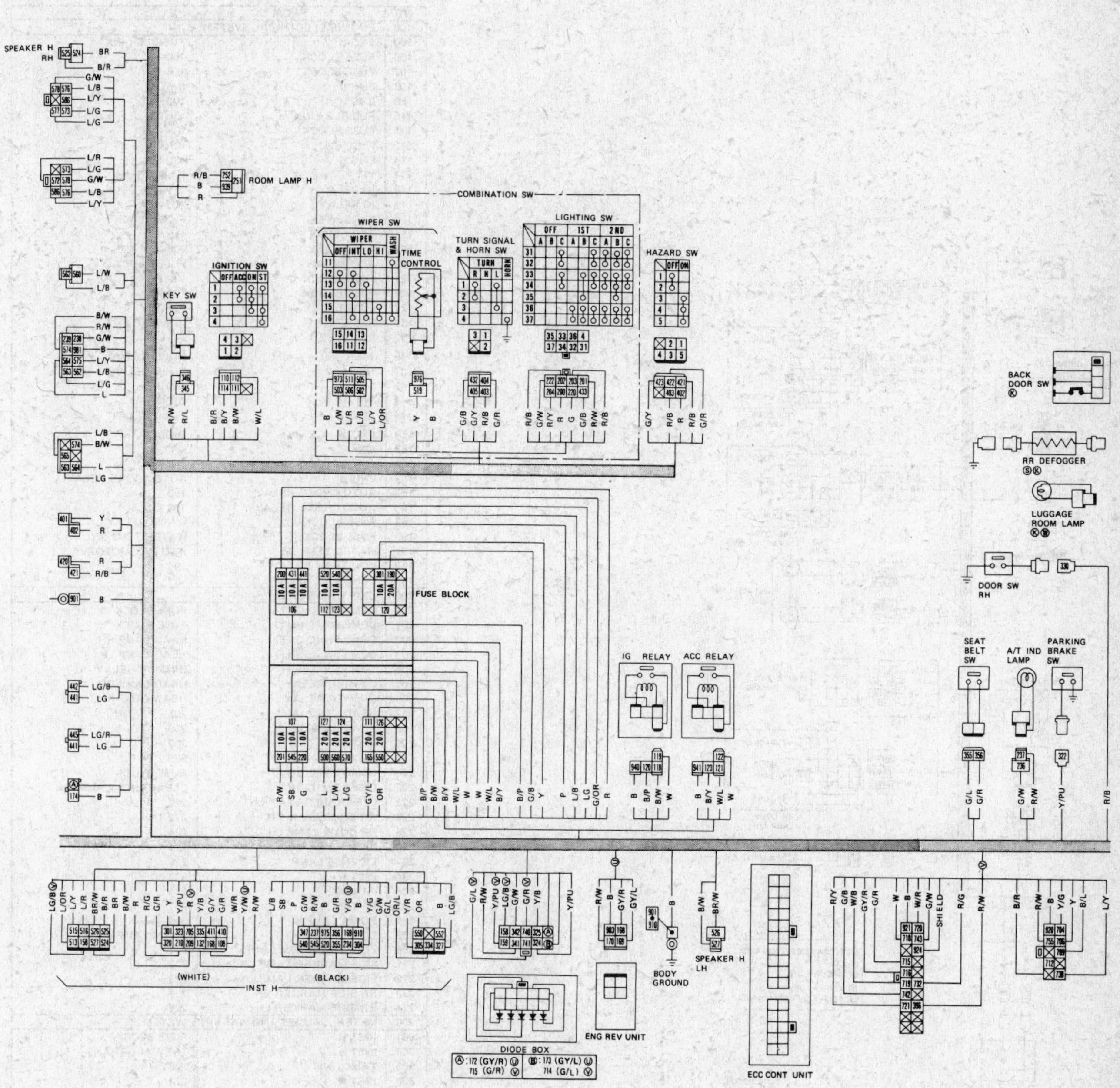
SPEAKER H RH
ROOM LAMP H
COMBINATION SW
WIPER SW
TIME CONTROL
TURN SIGNAL & HORN SW
LIGHTING SW
HAZARD SW
IGNITION SW
KEY SW
FUSE BLOCK
IG RELAY
ACC RELAY
BACK DOOR SW
RR DEFOGGER
LUGGAGE ROOM LAMP
DOOR SW RH
SEAT BELT SW
A/T IND LAMP
PARKING BRAKE SW
(WHITE)
(BLACK)
INST H
DIODE BOX
ENG REV UNIT
BODY GROUND
SPEAKER H LH
ECC CONT UNIT

Fig. 5. Complete circuit wiring diagram — 1983 Sentra (except MPG)

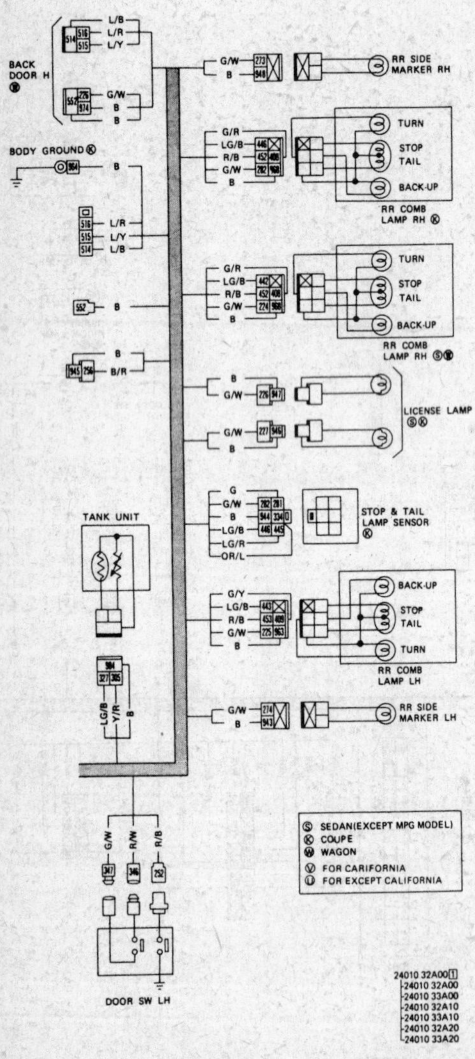

Fig. 5. Complete circuit wiring diagram — 1983 Sentra (except MPG)

MAIN HARNESS - GASOLINE ENGINE - (M.P.G. MODELS)

NO.	FROM	TO
100	ENGINE ELECTRICAL SYSTEM	
100	ENG H	FUSIBLE LINK
106	FUSE BLOCK	100
107	FUSE BLOCK	106
108	ENG H	INST H
109	ENG H	100
110	FUSIBLE LINK	IGN SW
111	FUSE BLOCK	IGN SW
112	FUSE BLOCK	IGN SW
114	ENG H	IGN SW
117	111	IGN COIL (+)
118	IG RELAY	111
119	IG RELAY	106
120	IG RELAY	FUSE BLOCK
121	ACC RELAY	112
122	ACC RELAY	106
123	ACC RELAY	FUSE BLOCK
124	FUSE BLOCK	123
126	FUSE BLOCK	120
127	FUSE BLOCK	112
131	RESISTER	IGN COIL (−)
132	RESISTER	INST H
140	165	HOLD RELAY
141	INST H	HOLD RELAY
142	141	DIODE
143	324	DIODE
144	INST H	HOLD RELAY
158	INST H	DIODE
159	324	DIODE
160	AUTO CHOKE RELAY	165
161	ENG H	AUTO CHOKE RELAY
162	AUTO CHOKE RELAY	190
163	AUTO CHOKE RELAY	108
165	FUSE BLOCK	WARM RELAY
190	FUSE BLOCK	WATER TEMP SW
191	WATER TEMP SW	RAD FAN MOTOR
192	COND FAN RELAY	190
193	COND FAN RELAY	191
200	LIGHTING SYSTEM	
200	COMB SW (LIGHT)	FUSE BLOCK
201	COMB SW (LIGHT)	FUSE BLOCK
202	COMB SW (LIGHT)	HEAD LAMP RH
203	COMB SW (LIGHT)	HEAD LAMP LH
204	COMB SW (LIGHT)	DIMMER RELAY
205	DIMMER RELAY	HEAD LAMP RH
206	DIMMER RELAY	HEAD LAMP RH
207	HEAD LAMP LH	205
208	HEAD LAMP LH	206
209	INST H	202
210	INST H	205
220	COMB SW (LIGHT)	FUSE BLOCK
222	COMB SW (LIGHT)	CLEARANCE LAMP RH
223	CLEARANCE LAMP LH	222
224	RR COMB LAMP RH	222
225	RR COMB LAMP LH	224
226	LICENSE LAMP	224
227	LICENSE LAMP	226
234	INST H	222
238	FAN SW	234
239	FAN SW	237
251	ROOM LAMP H	545
252	DOOR SW LH	ROOM LAMP H
256	LUGGAGE ROOM LAMP	545
271	SIDE MARKER LAMP RH	222
272	SIDE MARKER LAMP LH	223
273	RR SIDE MARKER RH	226
274	RR SIDE MARKER LH	226
300	METER, GAUGES AND WARNING SYSTEM	
301	INST H	FUSE BLOCK
304	INST H	THERMAL TRANS
305	TANK UNIT	INST H
320	INST H	324
322	PARKING BRAKE SW	323
323	INST H	BRAKE LEVEL SW
324	AUTO CHOKE RELAY	DIODE
325	323	DIODE
327	TANK UNIT	INST H
329	INST H	252
330	DOOR SW RH	252
335	ENG H	INST H
345	KEY SW	545
346	DOOR SW LH	KEY SW
347	DOOR SW LH	INST H
355	SEAT BELT SW	INST H

Fig. 6. Complete circuit wiring diagram — 1983 Sentra (MPG models)

NO.	FROM	TO
356	SEAT BELT SW	INST H
390	CHECK CONNECTOR	301
391	CHECK CONNECTOR	161
394	CHECK CONNECTOR	706
396	CHECK TERMINAL	ECC CONT UNIT
398	CHECK CONNECTOR	738
400	SIGNAL SYSTEM	
401	T/SIGNAL F/UNIT	301
402	T/SIGNAL F/UNIT	HAZARD SW
403	COMB SW (TURN)	HAZARD SW
404	COMB SW (TURN)	FR T/S LAMP RH
405	COMB SW (TURN)	FR T/S LAMP LH
408	RR COMB LAMP RH	404
409	RR COMB LAMP LH	405
410	INST H	404
411	INST H	405
420	HAZARD F/UNIT	431
421	HAZARD SW	HAZARD F/UNIT
422	HAZARD SW	404
423	HAZARD SW	405
431	FUSE BLOCK	HORN RELAY
432	COMB SW	HORN RELAY
433	COMB SW	432
434	HORN RELAY	HORN
441	FUSE BLOCK	STOP LAMP SW
442	STOP LAMP SW	RR COMB LAMP RH
443	RR COMB LAMP LH	442
451	ENG H	301
452	ENG H	RR COMB LAMP RH
453	RR COMB LAMP LH	452
500	ACCESSORY SYSTEM	
500	FUSE BLOCK	WIPER MOTOR
502	WIPER MOTOR	COMB SW (WIPER)
503	WIPER MOTOR	COMB SW (WIPER)
504	WIPER MOTOR	ADAPTOR
505	COMB SW (WIPER)	ADAPTOR
506	COMB SW (WIPER)	ADAPTOR
507	ADAPTOR	500
508	ADAPTOR	511
510	WASHER MOTOR	500
511	WASHER MOTOR	COMB SW (WIPER)
520	FUSE BLOCK	INST H
524	SPEAKER H RH	INST H
525	SPEAKER H RH	INST H
526	SPEAKER H LH	INST H
527	SPEAKER H LH	INST H
530	CONDENSER	117
540	FUSE BLOCK	INST H (CIG)
545	FUSE BLOCK	INST H (CLOCK)
550	FUSE BLOCK	INST H (RR DEF)
552	RR DEFOGGER	INST H (RR DEF)
560	FUSE BLOCK	BLOWER MOTOR
562	FAN SW (H)	BLOWER MOTOR
563	FAN SW (M)	RESISTOR
564	FAN SW (L)	RESISTOR
565	562	RESISTOR
570	AIR CON RELAY	FUSE BLOCK
571	H&L PRESS SW	AIR CON RELAY
572	THERMO CONT SW	AIR CON RELAY
573	THERMO CONT SW	AIR CON SW
574	RESISTOR	FAN SW
575	578	FAN SW
576	AIR CON SW	THERMO CONT SW
577	AIR CON SW	570
578	AIR CON SW	THERMO CONT SW
580	H&L PRESS SW	COND FAN RELAY
581	570	COND FAN RELAY
582	COND FAN MOTOR	COND FAN RELAY
583	580	MAGNET CLUTCH
585	573	AIR CON RELAY
586	THERMO CONT SW	AIR CON SW
587	580	FICD
700	SUPPLEMENTAL NUMBERS	
701	FUSIBLE LINK	F/B RELAY
702	111	F/B RELAY
703	ENG H	F/B RELAY
704	ENG H	ECC CONT UNIT
705	CHECK TERMINAL	INST H
706	ENG H	ECC CONT UNIT

NO.	FROM	TO
707	FUSIBLE LINK	ECC MAIN RELAY
708	702	ECC MAIN RELAY
709	ECC CONT UNIT	ECC MAIN RELAY
712	131	ECC CONT UNIT
714	ECC CONT UNIT	ENG H
716	ECC CONT UNIT	CLUTCH SW
718	ECC CONT UNIT	EXHAUST GAS SENSOR
719	ECC CONT UNIT	ENG H
720	ECC CONT UNIT	ENG H
721	ECC CONT UNIT	ENG H
732	ECC CONT UNIT	ENG H
733	161	WARM RELAY
735	ENG H	WARM RELAY
736	ENG H	ECC CONT UNIT
737	ENG H	165
738	ENG H	ECC CONT UNIT
740	ENG REV UNIT	165
741	ENG REV UNIT	132
742	ENG REV UNIT	ENG REV RELAY
743	740	ENG REV RELAY
744	ECC CONT UNIT	ENG REV RELAY
745	ECC CONT UNIT	ENG REV RELAY
755	ECC CONT UNIT	CHECK TERMINAL
900	GROUND	
900	BODY GROUND	BODY GROUND
901	BODY GROUND	BODY GROUND
910	INST H	BODY GROUND
920	ECC CONT UNIT	ENG GROUND
921	ECC CONT UNIT	ENG GROUND
924	ECC CONT UNIT	EXHAUST GAS SENSOR
933	AUTO CHOKE RELAY	900
934	DIMMER RELAY	900
936	SIDE MARKER RH	900
937	SIDE MARKER LH	900
938	CHECK CONN	900
939	ROOM LAMP H	901
940	IG RELAY	901
941	ACC RELAY	901
943	RR SIDE MARKER LH	901
946	LICENSE LAMP	901
947	LICENSE LAMP	901
948	RR SIDE MARKER RH	901
949	F/B RELAY	900
950	ECC MAIN RELAY	900
951	AIR CON H (B)	900
953	FR T/S LAMP RH	900
954	CLEARANCE L RH	900
955	CLEARANCE L LH	900
956	FR T/S LAMP LH	900
957	RAD FAN MOTOR	900
958	BRAKE LEVEL SW	900
959	WIPER MOTOR	900
960	ADAPTOR	900
962	TANK UNIT	901
963	RR COMB LAMP LH	901
965	WARM RELAY	900
966	CHECK TERMINAL	900
967	CLUTCH SW	900
968	RR COMB LAMP RH	901
971	DIMMER RELAY	900
972	FAN SW	901
973	COMB SW (WIPER)	901
975	INST H	901
980	ENG REV UNIT	901
981	CONDENSER FAN RELAY	900
982	CONDENSER FAN MOTOR	900
983	FAN SW	901
984	TANK UNIT	901
985	FAN SW	901

Fig. 6. Complete circuit wiring diagram — 1983 Sentra (MPG models)

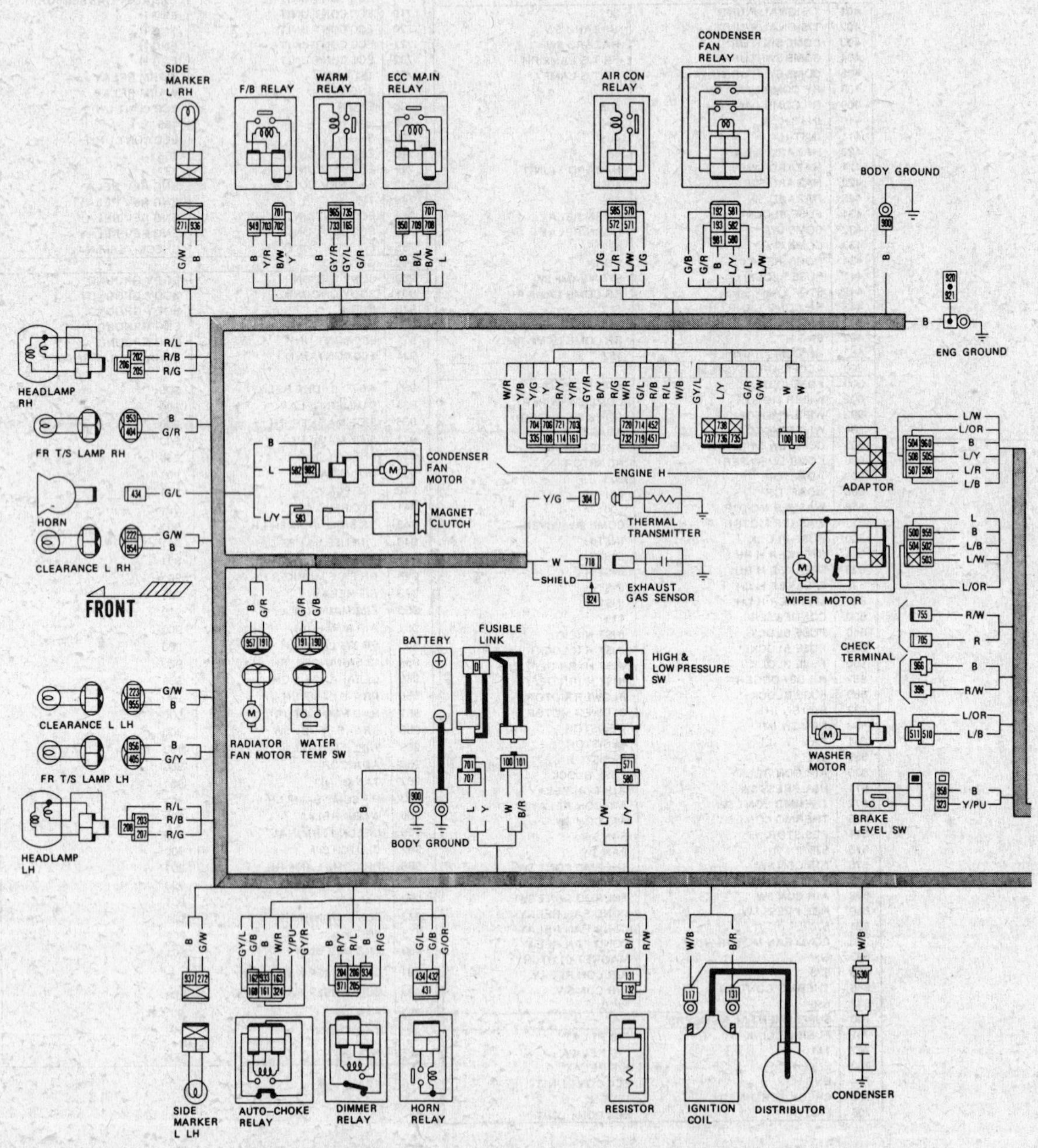
SIDE MARKER L RH
F/B RELAY
WARM RELAY
ECC MAIN RELAY
AIR CON RELAY
CONDENSER FAN RELAY
BODY GROUND
ENG GROUND
HEADLAMP RH
FR T/S LAMP RH
CONDENSER FAN MOTOR
MAGNET CLUTCH
ENGINE H
ADAPTOR
HORN
CLEARANCE L RH
THERMAL TRANSMITTER
EXHAUST GAS SENSOR
SHIELD
WIPER MOTOR
FRONT
BATTERY
FUSIBLE LINK
HIGH & LOW PRESSURE SW
CHECK TERMINAL
CLEARANCE L LH
FR T/S LAMP LH
RADIATOR FAN MOTOR
WATER TEMP SW
WASHER MOTOR
HEADLAMP LH
BODY GROUND
BRAKE LEVEL SW
SIDE MARKER L LH
AUTO-CHOKE RELAY
DIMMER RELAY
HORN RELAY
RESISTOR
IGNITION COIL
DISTRIBUTOR
CONDENSER

Fig. 6. Complete circuit wiring diagram — 1983 Sentra (MPG models)

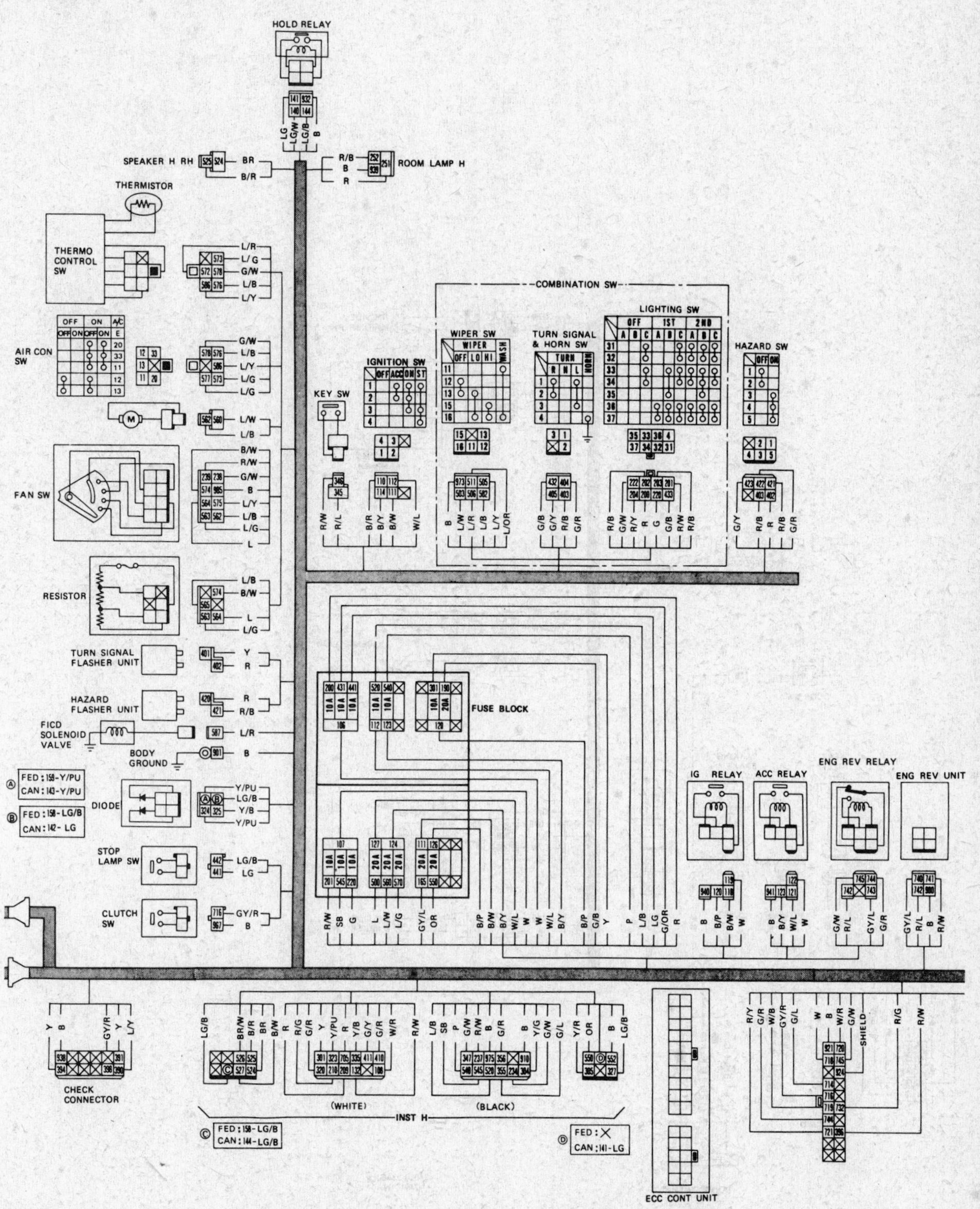
HOLD RELAY
SPEAKER H RH
ROOM LAMP H
THERMISTOR
THERMO CONTROL SW
AIR CON SW
FAN SW
RESISTOR
TURN SIGNAL FLASHER UNIT
HAZARD FLASHER UNIT
FICD SOLENOID VALVE
BODY GROUND
FED: 159-Y/PU CAN: 143-Y/PU
FED: 158-LG/B CAN: 142-LG
DIODE
STOP LAMP SW
CLUTCH SW
COMBINATION SW
LIGHTING SW
WIPER SW
TURN SIGNAL & HORN SW
IGNITION SW
KEY SW
HAZARD SW
FUSE BLOCK
IG RELAY
ACC RELAY
ENG REV RELAY
ENG REV UNIT
CHECK CONNECTOR
(WHITE)
(BLACK)
INST H
FED: 158-LG/B CAN: 144-LG/B
FED: X CAN: 141-LG
SHIELD
ECC CONT UNIT

Fig. 6. Complete circuit wiring diagram — 1983 Sentra (MPG models)

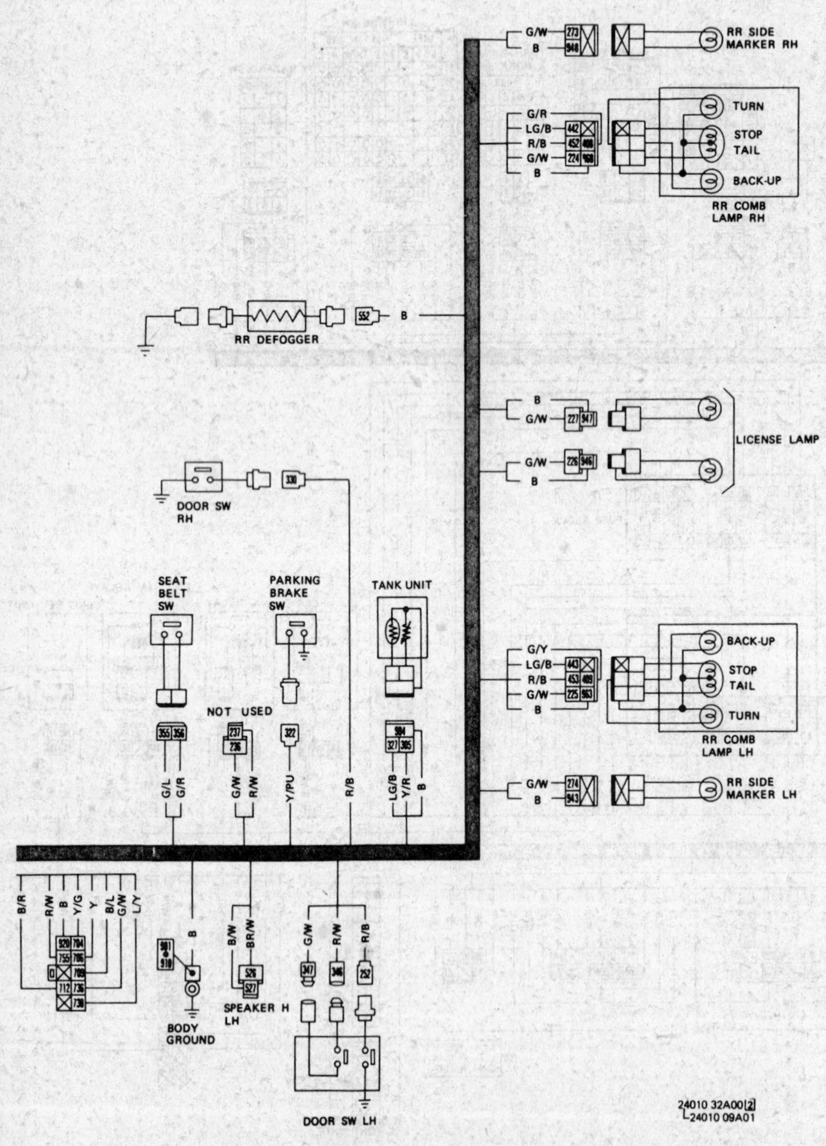
RR SIDE MARKER RH
TURN
STOP TAIL
BACK-UP
RR COMB LAMP RH
RR DEFOGGER
LICENSE LAMP
DOOR SW RH
SEAT BELT SW
PARKING BRAKE SW
TANK UNIT
NOT USED
BACK-UP
STOP TAIL
TURN
RR COMB LAMP LH
RR SIDE MARKER LH
BODY GROUND
SPEAKER H LH
DOOR SW LH
24010 32A00[2]
24010 09A01

Fig. 6. Complete circuit wiring diagram — 1983 Sentra (MPG models)

NISSAN SENTRA
INSTRUMENT HARNESS-GASOLINE ENGINE-

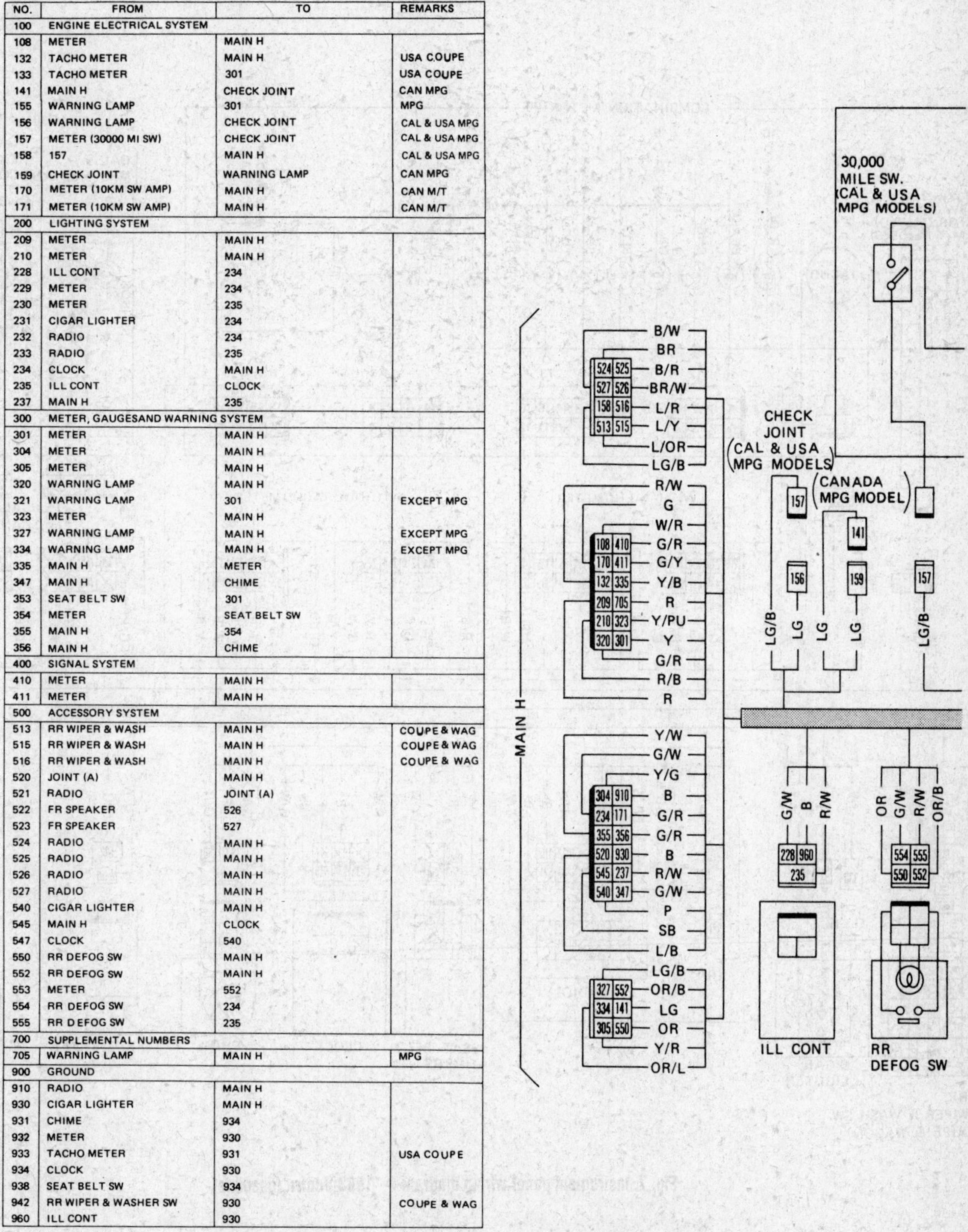

NO.	FROM	TO	REMARKS
100	ENGINE ELECTRICAL SYSTEM		
108	METER	MAIN H	
132	TACHO METER	MAIN H	USA COUPE
133	TACHO METER	301	USA COUPE
141	MAIN H	CHECK JOINT	CAN MPG
155	WARNING LAMP	301	MPG
156	WARNING LAMP	CHECK JOINT	CAL & USA MPG
157	METER (30000 MI SW)	CHECK JOINT	CAL & USA MPG
158	157	MAIN H	CAL & USA MPG
159	CHECK JOINT	WARNING LAMP	CAN MPG
170	METER (10KM SW AMP)	MAIN H	CAN M/T
171	METER (10KM SW AMP)	MAIN H	CAN M/T
200	LIGHTING SYSTEM		
209	METER	MAIN H	
210	METER	MAIN H	
228	ILL CONT	234	
229	METER	234	
230	METER	235	
231	CIGAR LIGHTER	234	
232	RADIO	234	
233	RADIO	235	
234	CLOCK	MAIN H	
235	ILL CONT	CLOCK	
237	MAIN H	235	
300	METER, GAUGESAND WARNING SYSTEM		
301	METER	MAIN H	
304	METER	MAIN H	
305	METER	MAIN H	
320	WARNING LAMP	MAIN H	
321	WARNING LAMP	301	EXCEPT MPG
323	METER	MAIN H	
327	WARNING LAMP	MAIN H	EXCEPT MPG
334	WARNING LAMP	MAIN H	EXCEPT MPG
335	MAIN H	METER	
347	MAIN H	CHIME	
353	SEAT BELT SW	301	
354	METER	SEAT BELT SW	
355	MAIN H	354	
356	MAIN H	CHIME	
400	SIGNAL SYSTEM		
410	METER	MAIN H	
411	METER	MAIN H	
500	ACCESSORY SYSTEM		
513	RR WIPER & WASH	MAIN H	COUPE & WAG
515	RR WIPER & WASH	MAIN H	COUPE & WAG
516	RR WIPER & WASH	MAIN H	COUPE & WAG
520	JOINT (A)	MAIN H	
521	RADIO	JOINT (A)	
522	FR SPEAKER	526	
523	FR SPEAKER	527	
524	RADIO	MAIN H	
525	RADIO	MAIN H	
526	RADIO	MAIN H	
527	RADIO	MAIN H	
540	CIGAR LIGHTER	MAIN H	
545	MAIN H	CLOCK	
547	CLOCK	540	
550	RR DEFOG SW	MAIN H	
552	RR DEFOG SW	MAIN H	
553	METER	552	
554	RR DEFOG SW	234	
555	RR DEFOG SW	235	
700	SUPPLEMENTAL NUMBERS		
705	WARNING LAMP	MAIN H	MPG
900	GROUND		
910	RADIO	MAIN H	
930	CIGAR LIGHTER	MAIN H	
931	CHIME	934	
932	METER	930	
933	TACHO METER	931	USA COUPE
934	CLOCK	930	
938	SEAT BELT SW	934	
942	RR WIPER & WASHER SW	930	COUPE & WAG
960	ILL CONT	930	

30,000
MILE SW.
(CAL & USA
MPG MODELS)
CHECK
JOINT
(CAL & USA
MPG MODELS)
(CANADA
MPG MODEL)
MAIN H
B/W
BR
B/R
BR/W
L/R
L/Y
L/OR
LG/B
R/W
G
W/R
G/R
G/Y
Y/B
R
Y/PU
Y
G/R
R/B
R
Y/W
G/W
Y/G
B
G/R
G/R
B
R/W
G/W
P
SB
L/B
LG/B
OR/B
LG
OR
Y/R
OR/L
ILL CONT
RR
DEFOG SW

Fig. 7. Instrument panel wiring diagram — 1983 Sentra (gasoline)

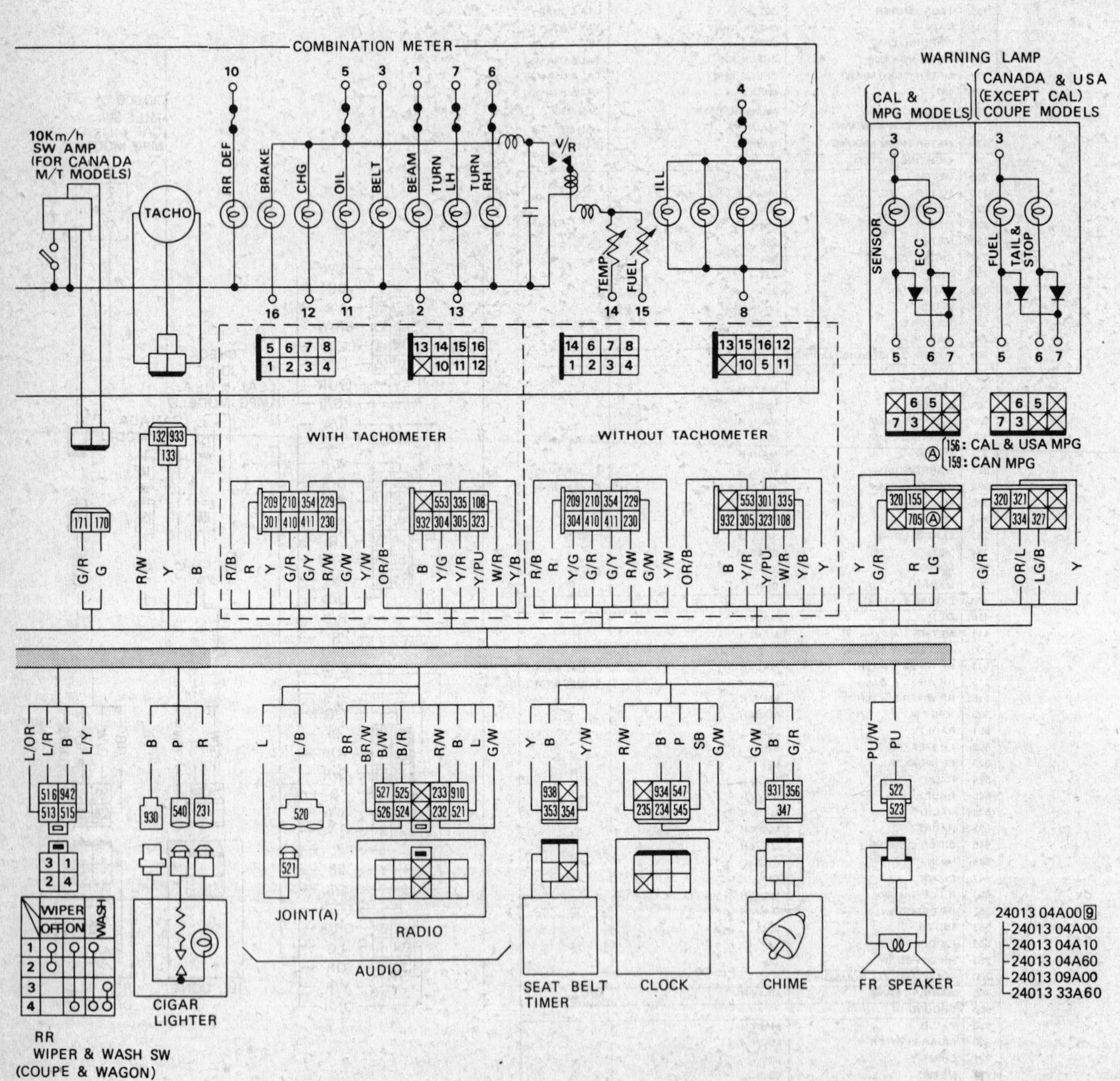
COMBINATION METER
10Km/h
SW AMP
(FOR CANADA
M/T MODELS)
TACHO
RR DEF
BRAKE
CHG
OIL
BELT
BEAM
TURN LH
TURN RH
V/R
TEMP
FUEL
ILL
WARNING LAMP
CAL & MPG MODELS
CANADA & USA (EXCEPT CAL) COUPE MODELS
SENSOR
ECC
FUEL
TAIL & STOP
WITH TACHOMETER
WITHOUT TACHOMETER
156: CAL & USA MPG
159: CAN MPG
WIPER
OFF ON
WASH
CIGAR
LIGHTER
RR
WIPER & WASH SW
(COUPE & WAGON)
JOINT(A)
RADIO
AUDIO
SEAT BELT
TIMER
CLOCK
CHIME
FR SPEAKER
24013 04A00 9
24013 04A00
24013 04A10
24013 04A60
24013 09A00
24013 33A60

Fig. 7. Instrument panel wiring diagram — 1983 Sentra (gasoline)

NISSAN SENTRA
ENGINE HARNESS-GASOLINE ENGINE-(EXCEPT M.P.G.)

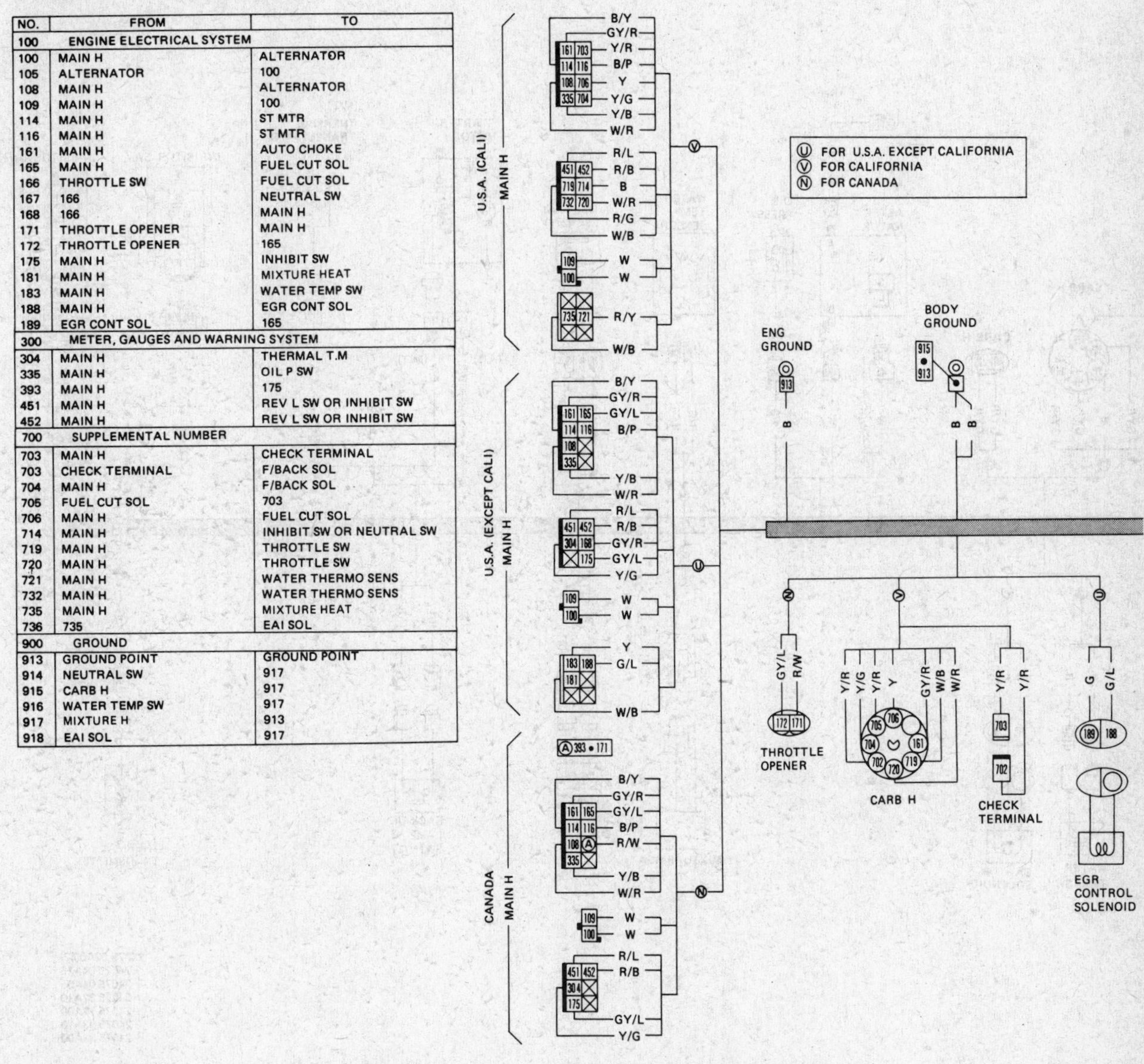

NO.	FROM	TO
100	ENGINE ELECTRICAL SYSTEM	
100	MAIN H	ALTERNATOR
105	ALTERNATOR	100
108	MAIN H	ALTERNATOR
109	MAIN H	100
114	MAIN H	ST MTR
116	MAIN H	ST MTR
161	MAIN H	AUTO CHOKE
165	MAIN H	FUEL CUT SOL
166	THROTTLE SW	FUEL CUT SOL
167	166	NEUTRAL SW
168	166	MAIN H
171	THROTTLE OPENER	MAIN H
172	THROTTLE OPENER	165
175	MAIN H	INHIBIT SW
181	MAIN H	MIXTURE HEAT
183	MAIN H	WATER TEMP SW
188	MAIN H	EGR CONT SOL
189	EGR CONT SOL	165
300	METER, GAUGES AND WARNING SYSTEM	
304	MAIN H	THERMAL T.M
335	MAIN H	OIL P SW
393	MAIN H	175
451	MAIN H	REV L SW OR INHIBIT SW
452	MAIN H	REV L SW OR INHIBIT SW
700	SUPPLEMENTAL NUMBER	
703	MAIN H	CHECK TERMINAL
703	CHECK TERMINAL	F/BACK SOL
704	MAIN H	F/BACK SOL
705	FUEL CUT SOL	703
706	MAIN H	FUEL CUT SOL
714	MAIN H	INHIBIT SW OR NEUTRAL SW
719	MAIN H	THROTTLE SW
720	MAIN H	THROTTLE SW
721	MAIN H	WATER THERMO SENS
732	MAIN H	WATER THERMO SENS
735	MAIN H	MIXTURE HEAT
736	735	EAI SOL
900	GROUND	
913	GROUND POINT	GROUND POINT
914	NEUTRAL SW	917
915	CARB H	917
916	WATER TEMP SW	917
917	MIXTURE H	913
918	EAI SOL	917

U.S.A. (CALI) — MAIN H
U.S.A. (EXCEPT CALI) — MAIN H
CANADA — MAIN H
Ⓤ FOR U.S.A. EXCEPT CALIFORNIA
Ⓥ FOR CALIFORNIA
Ⓝ FOR CANADA
ENG GROUND
BODY GROUND
THROTTLE OPENER
CARB H
CHECK TERMINAL
EGR CONTROL SOLENOID

Fig. 8. Engine wiring diagram — 1983 Sentra (except MPG)

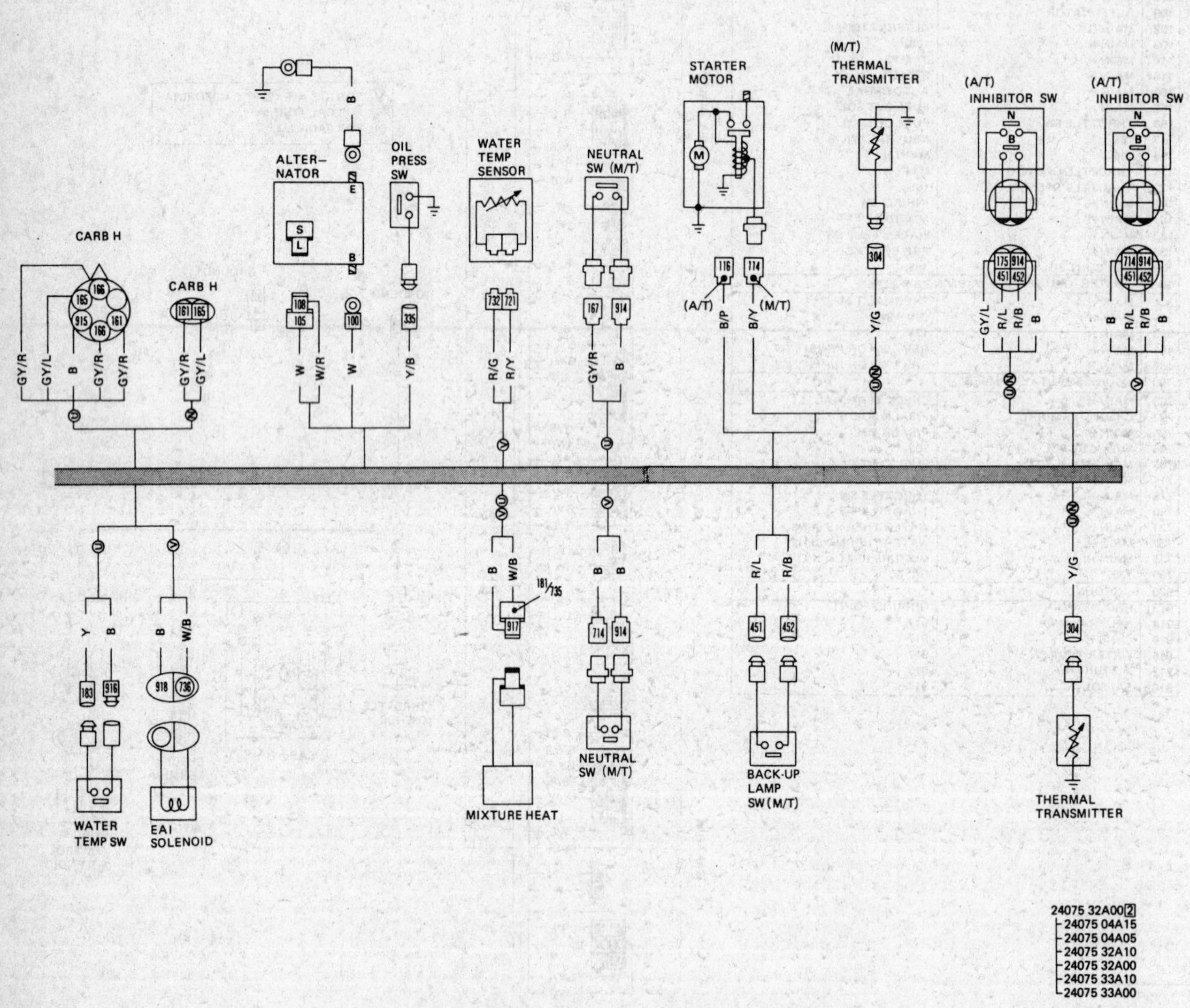

CARB H
CARB H
ALTER-
NATOR
OIL
PRESS
SW
WATER
TEMP
SENSOR
NEUTRAL
SW (M/T)
STARTER
MOTOR
(M/T)
THERMAL
TRANSMITTER
(A/T)
INHIBITOR SW
(A/T)
INHIBITOR SW
WATER
TEMP SW
EAI
SOLENOID
MIXTURE HEAT
NEUTRAL
SW (M/T)
BACK-UP
LAMP
SW (M/T)
THERMAL
TRANSMITTER
24075 32A00
24075 04A15
24075 04A05
24075 32A10
24075 32A00
24075 33A10
24075 33A00

Fig. 8. Engine wiring diagram – 1983 Sentra (except MPG)

NISSAN SENTRA
MAIN HARNESS-DIESEL ENGINE-

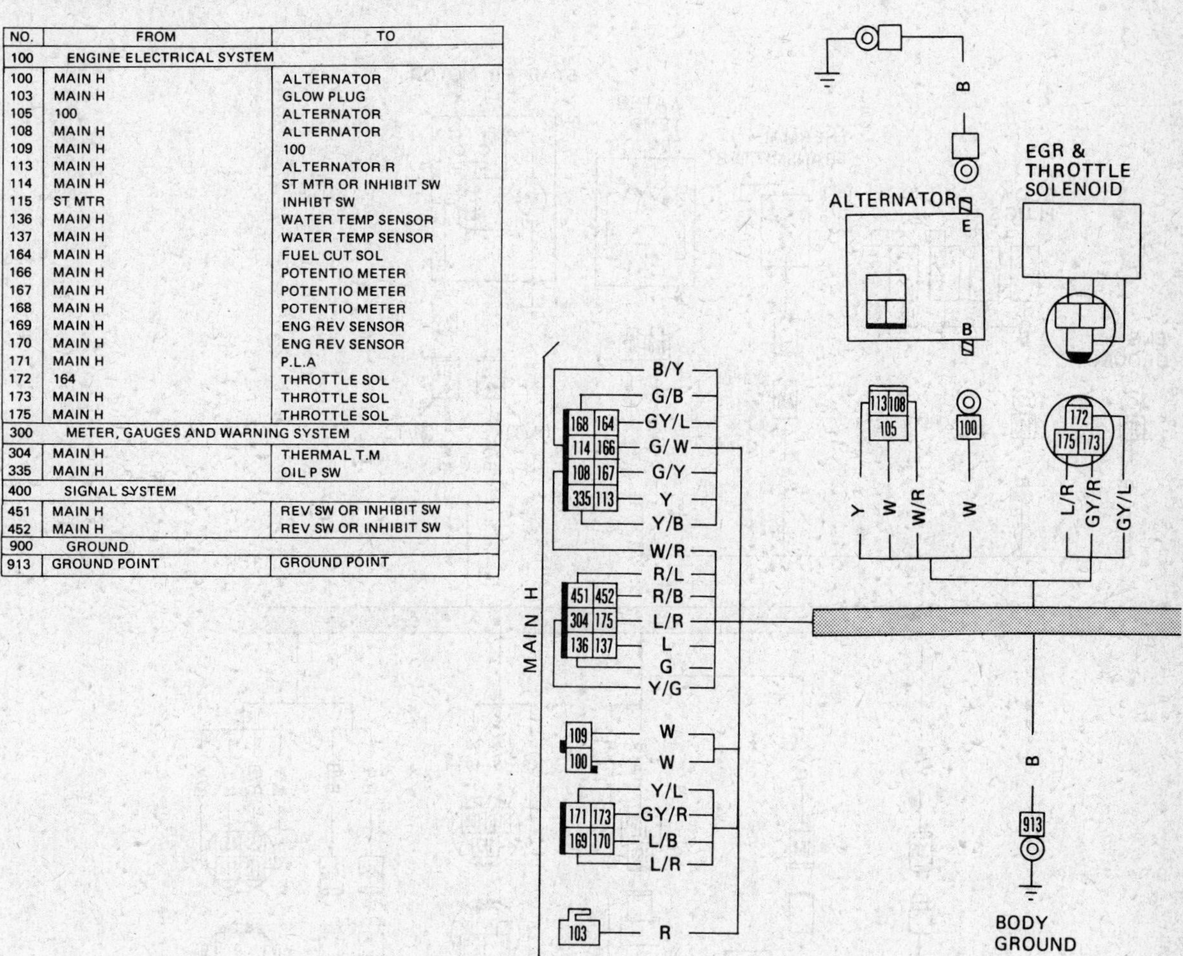

NO.	FROM	TO
100	ENGINE ELECTRICAL SYSTEM	
100	MAIN H	ALTERNATOR
103	MAIN H	GLOW PLUG
105	100	ALTERNATOR
108	MAIN H	ALTERNATOR
109	MAIN H	100
113	MAIN H	ALTERNATOR R
114	MAIN H	ST MTR OR INHIBIT SW
115	ST MTR	INHIBT SW
136	MAIN H	WATER TEMP SENSOR
137	MAIN H	WATER TEMP SENSOR
164	MAIN H	FUEL CUT SOL
166	MAIN H	POTENTIO METER
167	MAIN H	POTENTIO METER
168	MAIN H	POTENTIO METER
169	MAIN H	ENG REV SENSOR
170	MAIN H	ENG REV SENSOR
171	MAIN H	P.L.A
172	164	THROTTLE SOL
173	MAIN H	THROTTLE SOL
175	MAIN H	THROTTLE SOL
300	METER, GAUGES AND WARNING SYSTEM	
304	MAIN H	THERMAL T.M
335	MAIN H	OIL P SW
400	SIGNAL SYSTEM	
451	MAIN H	REV SW OR INHIBIT SW
452	MAIN H	REV SW OR INHIBIT SW
900	GROUND	
913	GROUND POINT	GROUND POINT

B
ALTERNATOR
E
B
EGR &
THROTTLE
SOLENOID
113 108
105
100
172
175 173
Y
W
W/R
W
L/R
GY/R
GY/L
MAIN H
168 164
114 166
108 167
335 113
B/Y
G/B
GY/L
G/W
G/Y
Y
Y/B
W/R
R/L
R/B
L/R
L
G
Y/G
451 452
304 175
136 137
109
100
W
W
Y/L
GY/R
L/B
L/R
171 173
169 170
103
R
B
913
BODY
GROUND

Fig. 9. Main wiring diagram — 1983 Sentra (diesel)

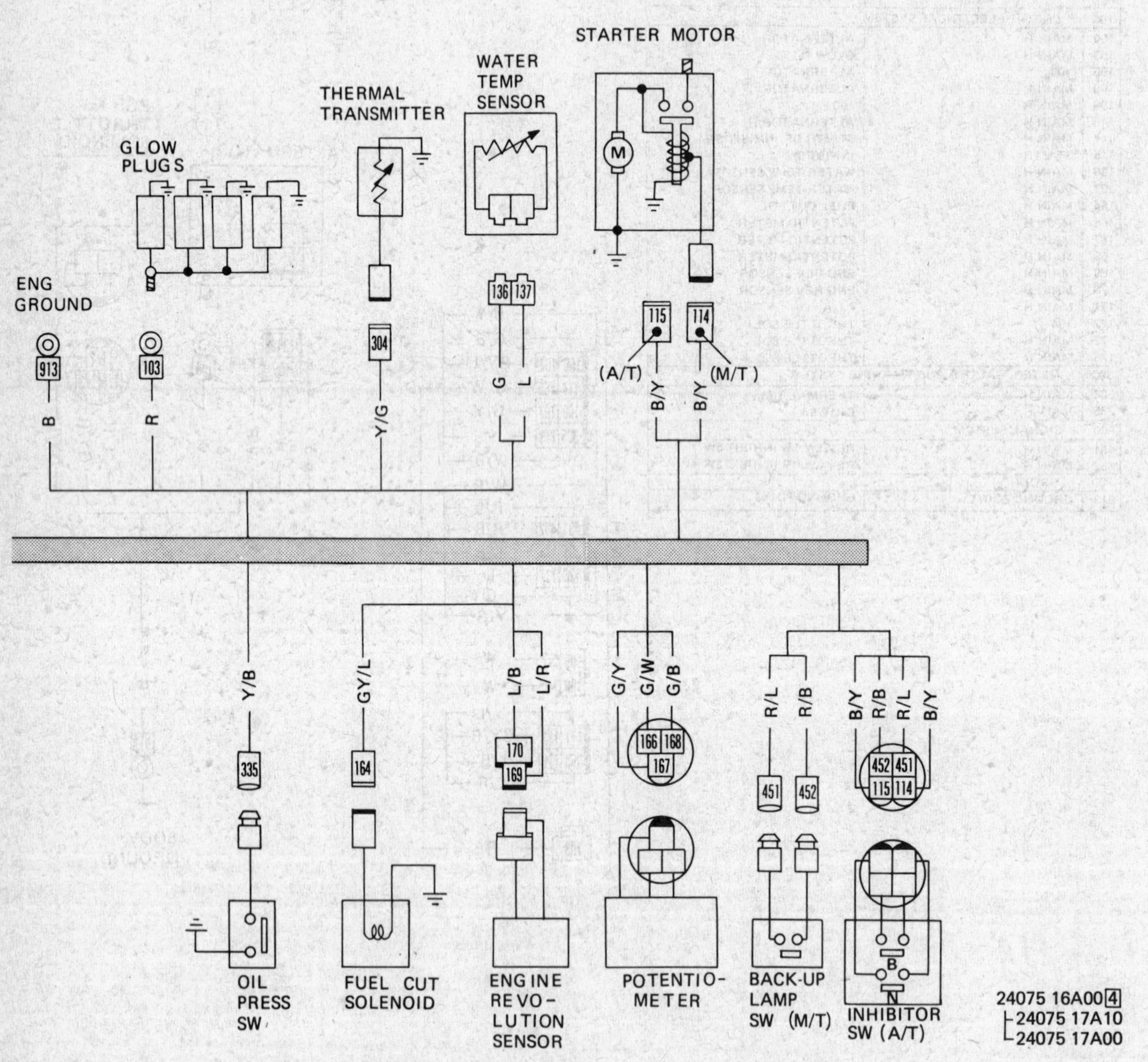
STARTER MOTOR
WATER
TEMP
SENSOR
THERMAL
TRANSMITTER
GLOW
PLUGS
M
ENG
GROUND
913
103
304
136 137
115
114
(A/T)
(M/T)
B
R
Y/G
G
L
B/Y
B/Y
Y/B
GY/L
L/B
L/R
G/Y
G/W
G/B
R/L
R/B
B/Y
R/B
R/L
B/Y
335
164
170
169
166 168
167
451
452
452 451
115 114
B
N
OIL
PRESS
SW
FUEL CUT
SOLENOID
ENGINE
REVO-
LUTION
SENSOR
POTENTIO-
METER
BACK-UP
LAMP
SW (M/T)
INHIBITOR
SW (A/T)
24075 16A00 4
24075 17A10
24075 17A00

Fig. 9. Main wiring diagram — 1983 Sentra (diesel)

1983 NISSAN MODEL N12 SERIES

MAIN HARNESS (FOR U.S.A. EXCEPT CALIFORNIA MODELS)

NO.	FROM	TO	REMARKS
100	ENGINE ELECTRICAL SYSTEM		
100	ENG H	FUSIBLE LINK	
106	FUSE BLOCK	100	
107	FUSE BLOCK	106	
108	ENG H	INST H	
109	ENG H	100	
110	IGN SW	FUSIBLE LINK	
111	IGN SW	FUSE BLOCK	
112	FUSE BLOCK	IGN SW	
114	ENG H	IGN SW	
115	INHIBIT RELAY	114	
116	ENG H	INHIBIT RELAY	
117	IGN COIL ( )	111	
118	IGN RELAY	111	
119	IGN RELAY	106	
120	FUSE BLOCK	IGN RELAY	
121	ACC RELAY	112	
122	ACC RELAY	106	
123	FUSE BLOCK	ACC RELAY	
124	FUSE BLOCK	123	
126	FUSE BLOCK	120	
127	FUSE BLOCK	112	
131	IGN COIL (-)	RESISTER	
132	INST H	RESISTER	
148	FUSE BLOCK	TANK UNIT H	
160	A/CHOKE RELAY	FUSE BLOCK	
161	ENG H	A/CHOKE RELAY	
162	A/CHOKE RELAY	160	
163	A/CHOCK RELAY	108	
167	ENG REV UNIT	175	
175	ENG H	CLUTCH SW	
178	ENG REV UNIT	160	
179	INHIBIT RELAY	ENG H	
186	ENG REV UNIT	132	
187	DIODE	175	
188	DIODE	179	
189	INHIBIT RELAY	160	
190	THERMO SW	FUSE BLOCK	
191	THERMO SW	RAD FAN MTR	
192	AIR CON H	190	
193	AIR CON H	191	
197	VACUUM SW	ENG H	
199	ENG H	110	
200	LIGHTING SYSTEM		
200	COMB SW (LIGHT)	FUSE BLOCK	
201	COMB SW (LIGHT)	FUSE BLOCK	
202	COMB SW (LIGHT)	HEAD L RH	
203	COMB SW (LIGHT)	HEAD L LH	
204	COMB SW (LIGHT)	DIMMER RELY	
205	DIMMER RELAY	HEAD L RH	
206	DIMMER RELAY	HEAD L RH	
207	HEAD L LH	205	
208	HEAD L LH	206	
209	INST H	202	
210	INST H	205	
211	RETRACT MTR RH	106	COUPE
212	RETRACT MTR LH	100	COUPE
213	INST H	RETRACT MTR RH	COUPE
214	RETRACT MTR LH	213	COUPE
215	RETRACT MTR RH	HEAD LAMP CONTROL UNIT	COUPE
216	RETRACT MTR LH	215	COUPE
217	INST H	RETRACT MTR RH	COUPE
218	RETRACT MTR LH	217	COUPE
219	INST H	RETRACT MTR RH	COUPE
220	COMB SW (LIGHT)	FUSE BLOCK	
222	FR COMB L RH	COMB SW (LIGHT)	
223	FR COMB L LH	222	
225	RR COMB L LH	222	
226	LICENSE L	282	
227	LICENSE L	225	
228	INST H	282	
232	HEAD LAMP CONTROL UNIT	INST H	COUPE
233	RETRACT MTR LH	219	COUPE
236	A/T IND LAMP	282	
237	INST H	A/T IND LAMP	
238	HEATER	222	
239	HEATER	237	
241	HEAD LAMP CONTROL UNIT	222	COUPE
242	HEAD LAMP CONTROL UNIT	202	COUPE
243	HEAD LAMP CONTROL UNIT	203	COUPE
244	HAED LAMP CONTROL UNIT	200	COUPE
245	HEAD LAMP CONTROL UNIT	201	COUPE
246	HEAD LAMP CONTROL UNIT	219	COUPE
251	ROOM L H	545	
252	DOOR SW LH	ROOM L H	
253	DOOR SW RH	252	
256	LUGGAGE ROOM L	545	
257	LUGGAGE L SW	LUGGAGE ROOM L	
271	SIDE MARKER L	222	SEDAN
272	SIDE MARKER L	223	SEDAN
273	RR SIDE MARKER	225	SEDAN
274	RR SIDE MARKER	282	SEDAN
282	RR COMB L RH	222	
300	METER, GAUGES AND WARNING SYSTEM		
301	INST H	FUSE BLOCK	
304	ENG H	INST H	
305	INST H	TANK UNIT H	
322	HAND BRAKE SW	323	
323	BRAKE LEVEL SW	INST H	
324	A/CHOKE RELAY	323	
335	ENG H	INST H	
345	KEY SW	545	
346	KEY SW	DOOR SW	
347	DOOR SW	INST H	348
348	S/BELT	INST H	
355	SEAT BELT SW	INST H	
390	CHECK CONN	160	
391	CHECK CONN	161	
394	175	CHECK CONN	
400	SIGNAL SYSTEM		
401	INST H	FLASHER UNIT	
402	403	FLASHER UNIT	
403	INST H	COMB SW (TURN)	
404	FR COMB L RH	COMB SW (TURN)	
405	FR COMB L LH	COMB SW (TURN)	
408	RR COMB L RH	404	
409	RR COMB L LH	405	
410	INST H	404	
411	INST H	405	
420	INST H	431	
431	FUSE BLOCK	HORN RELAY	
432	COMB SW (LIGHT)	HORN RELAY	
434	HORN RELAY	HORN HI	
435	HORN LO	434	
441	FUSE BLOCK	STOP L SW	
443	RR COMB L LH	445	
445	RR COMB L RH	STOP L SW	
451	ENG H	301	
452	ENG H	RR COMB L RH	
453	RR COMB L LH	452	
500	ACCESSORY SYSTEM		
500	FUSE BLOCK	WIPER MTR	
502	WIPER MTR	COMB SW (WIPER)	
503	WIPER MTR	COMB SW (WIPER)	
504	WIPER MTR	WIPER AMP	
505	WIPER AMP	COMB SW (WIPER)	
506	WIPER AMP	COMB SW (WIPER)	
507	WIPER AMP	500	
508	WIPER AMP	511	
509	WIPER AMP	WIPER SW	
510	WASHER MTR	500	
511	WASHER MTR	COMB SW (WIPER)	
512	RR WASHER MTR	510	SEDAN
513	INST H	RR WASHER MTR	SEDAN
514	BACK DOOR H	520	SEDAN
515	INST H	BACK DOOR H	SEDAN
516	INST H	BACK DOOR H	SEDAN
520	FUSE BLOCK	INST H	
521	INST H	SPEAKER LH	
522	SPEAKER RH	521	
23	INST H	SPEAKER LH	
524	SPEAKER RH	523	
530	CONDENSER A	117	
540	INST H	FUSE BLOCK	
545	INST H	FUSE BLOCK	
550	FUSE BLOCK	INST H	
552	RR DEFOG	INST H	COUPE
552	INST H	BACK DOOR H	SEDAN
560	FUSE BLOCK	BLOWER MTR	
562	HEATER	BLOWER MTR	
563	HEATER	RESISTOR	
564	HEATER	RESISTOR	
565	RESISTER	562	
570	FUSE BLOCK	AIR CON H	
574	RESISTOR	HEATER	
575	AIR CON H	HEATER	
700	SUPPLEMENTAL NUMBER		
700	MIXTURE HEATER RELAY	100	
701	MIXTURE HEATER RELAY	ENG H	
702	MIXTURE HEATER RELAY	161	
703	MIXTURE HEATER RELAY	ENG H	
704	CHECK CONN	701	
705	CHECK CONN	197	
754	CHECK CONN	703	
900	GROUND		
900	EARTH POINT (A)	EARTH POINT (A)	
901	EARTH POINT (B)	EARTH POINT (B)	
903	AIR CON H	900	
904	FR COMB L LH	900	
907	RAD FAN MTR	900	
909	FR COMB L RH	900	
910	INST H	EARTH POINT	
912	DIMMER RELAY	900	
913	DIMMER RELAY	912	
915	BRAKE LEVEL SW	901	
917	ENG H	900	
920	WIPER MTR	901	
921	WIPER AMP	901	
922	FLASHER UNIT	901	
923	IGN RELAY	901	
924	INST H	901	
925	ACC RELAY	923	
926	COMB SW (WIPER)	901	
927	ENG REV UNIT	901	
928	EARTH POINT (C)	TANK UNIT H	
930	HEAD LAMP CONTROL UNIT	EARTH POINT	OOUPE
931	RR COMB L RH	928	
933	LUGGAGE L SW	928	COUPE
934	RR COMB L LH	928	
936	LICENSE L	928	
937	LICENSE L	928	
941	SIDE MARKER L	900	SEDAN
942	VAC SW	700	
942	SIDE MARKER L	900	SEDAN
945	HEATER	901	
947	RETRACT MTR RH	900	COUPE
948	RETRACT MTR LH	900	COUPE
951	A/CHOKE RELAY	900	956
956	CHECK CONN	901	
957	RR SIDE MARKER	928	SEDAN
958	RR SIDE MARKER	928	SEDAN
961	CLUTCH SW	901	
978	WIPER SW	926	

Fig. 10. Main wiring diagram — 1983 Pulsar (USA)

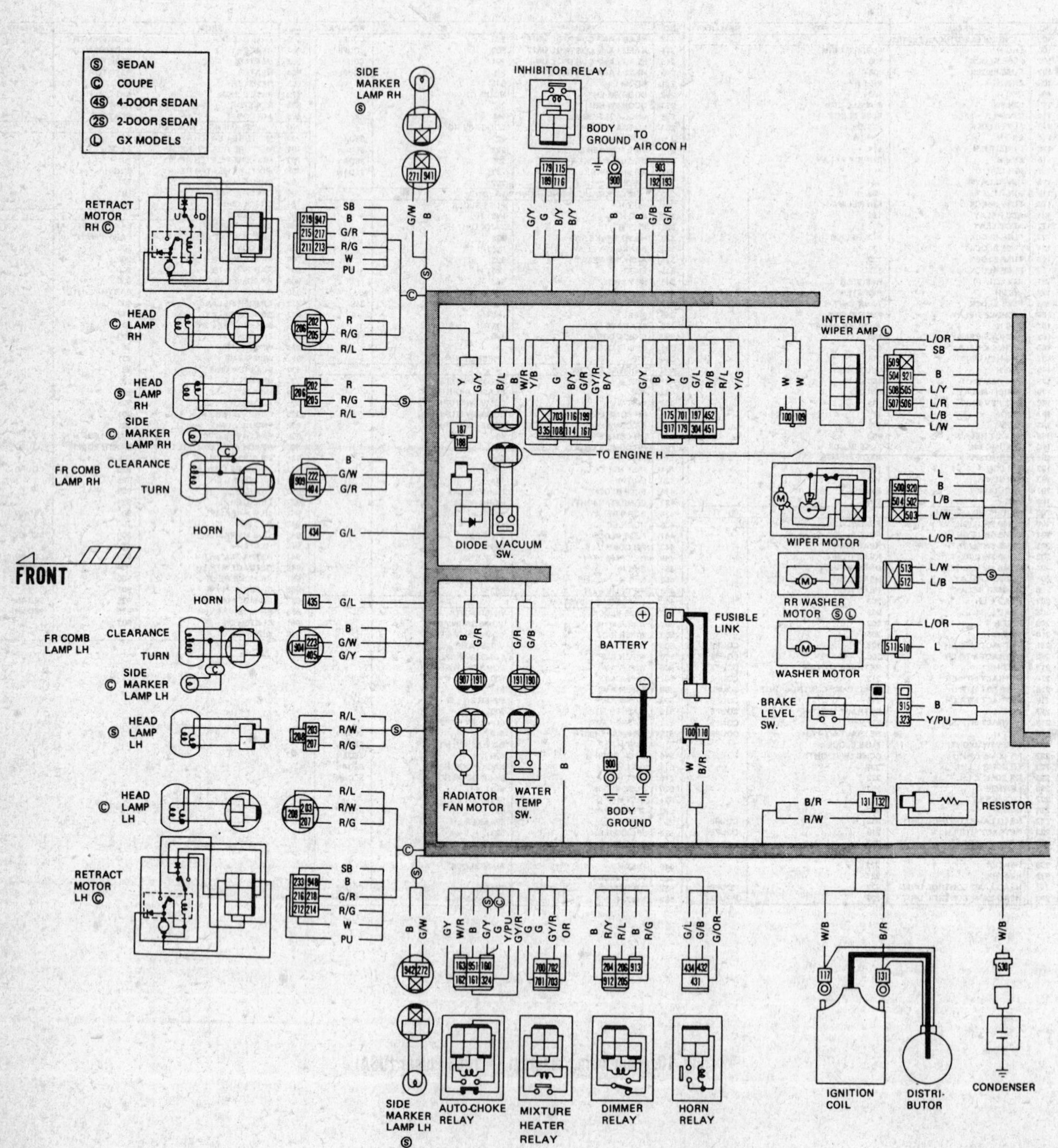

Ⓢ SEDAN
Ⓒ COUPE
4S 4-DOOR SEDAN
2S 2-DOOR SEDAN
Ⓛ GX MODELS
SIDE MARKER LAMP RH Ⓢ
INHIBITOR RELAY
BODY GROUND
TO AIR CON H
RETRACT MOTOR RH Ⓒ
Ⓒ HEAD LAMP RH
Ⓢ HEAD LAMP RH
Ⓒ SIDE MARKER LAMP RH
FR COMB LAMP RH
CLEARANCE
TURN
HORN
FRONT
HORN
FR COMB LAMP LH
CLEARANCE
TURN
Ⓒ SIDE MARKER LAMP LH
Ⓢ HEAD LAMP LH
Ⓒ HEAD LAMP LH
RETRACT MOTOR LH Ⓒ
INTERMIT WIPER AMP Ⓛ
TO ENGINE H
DIODE
VACUUM SW.
WIPER MOTOR
RR WASHER MOTOR ⓈⓁ
WASHER MOTOR
BATTERY
FUSIBLE LINK
BRAKE LEVEL SW.
RADIATOR FAN MOTOR
WATER TEMP SW.
BODY GROUND
RESISTOR
SIDE MARKER LAMP LH Ⓢ
AUTO-CHOKE RELAY
MIXTURE HEATER RELAY
DIMMER RELAY
HORN RELAY
IGNITION COIL
DISTRI-BUTOR
CONDENSER

Fig. 10. Main wiring diagram — 1983 Pulsar (USA)

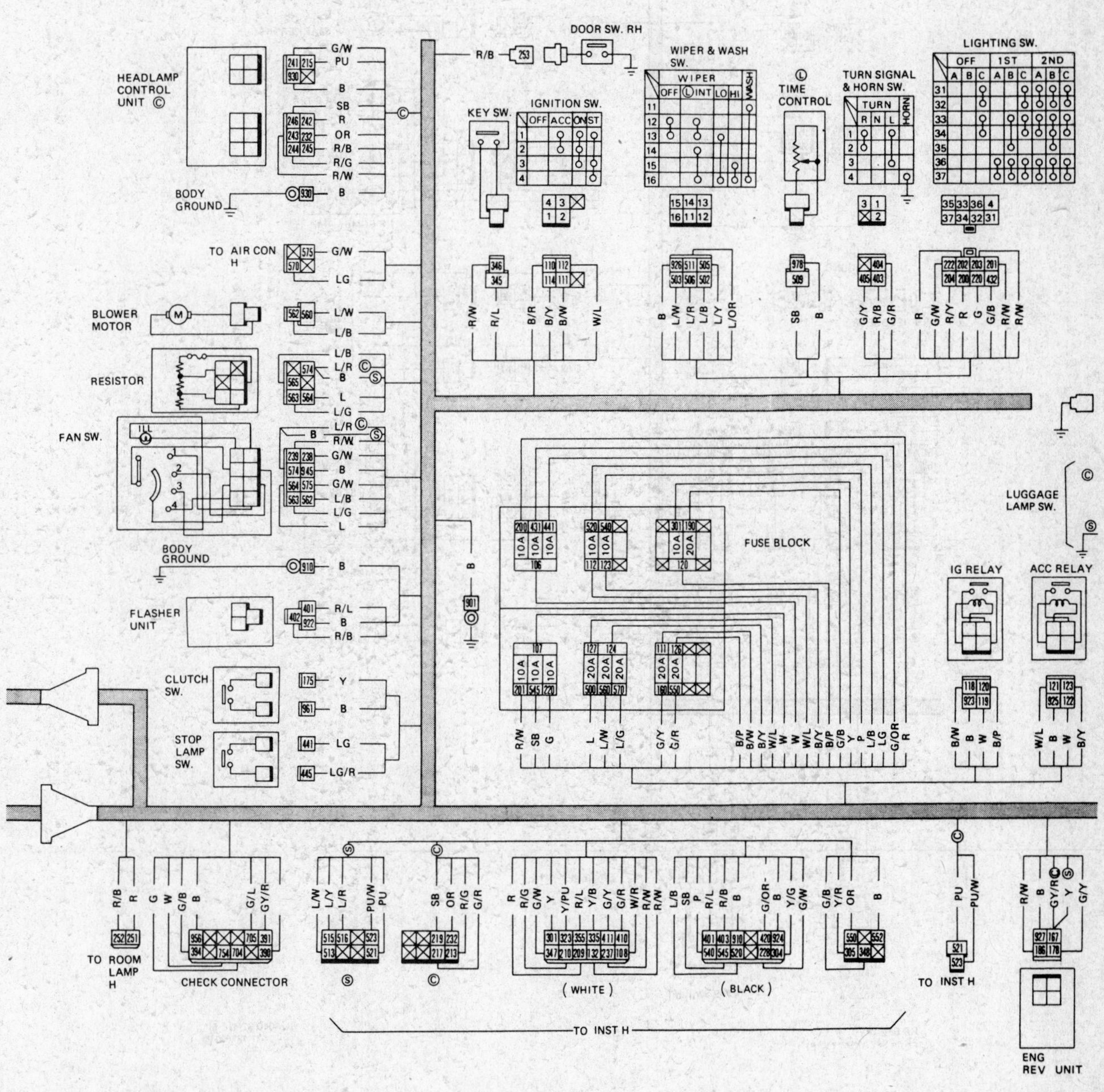

Fig. 10. Main wiring diagram — 1983 Pulsar (USA)

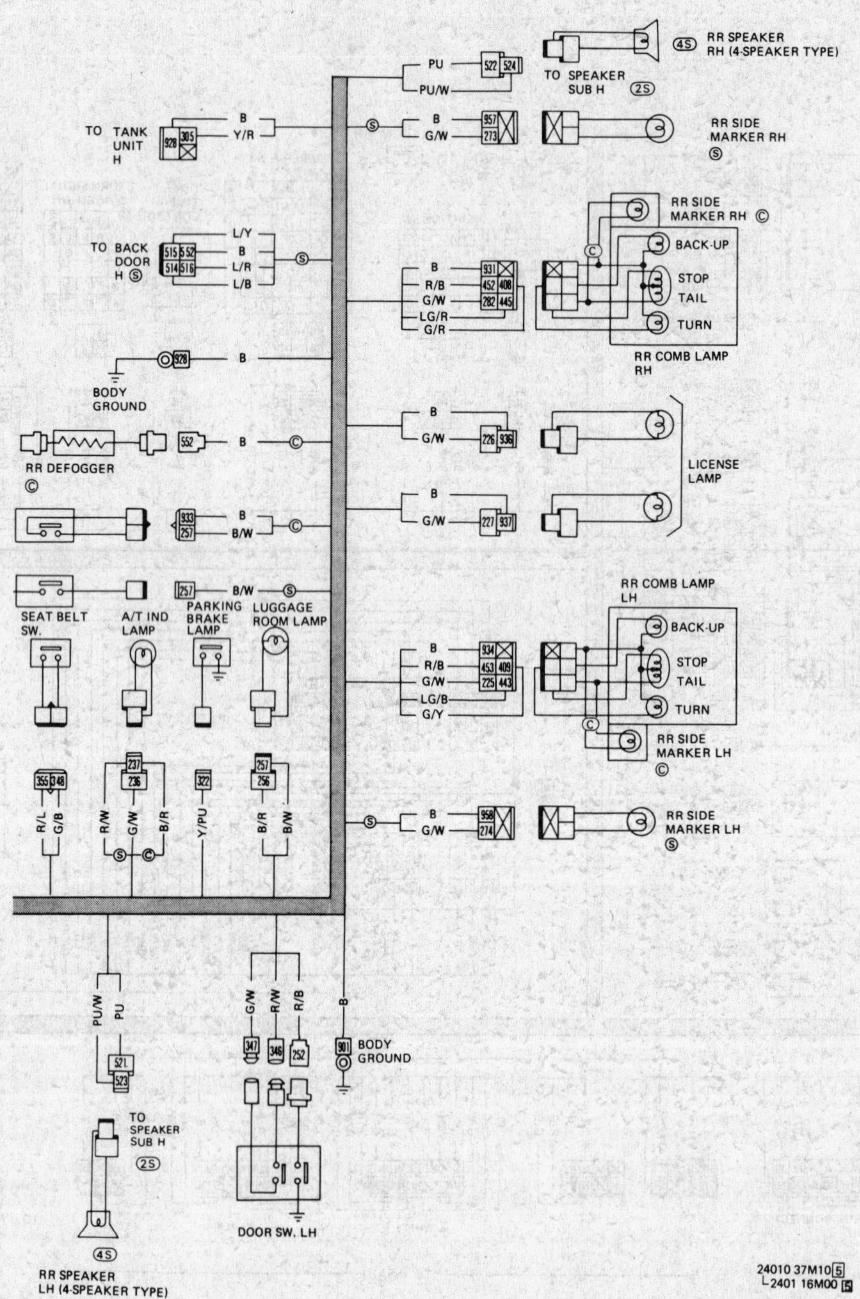
RR SPEAKER RH (4-SPEAKER TYPE)
TO SPEAKER SUB H
TO TANK UNIT H
RR SIDE MARKER RH
TO BACK DOOR H
BACK-UP
STOP
TAIL
TURN
RR COMB LAMP RH
BODY GROUND
RR DEFOGGER
LICENSE LAMP
SEAT BELT SW.
A/T IND LAMP
PARKING BRAKE LAMP
LUGGAGE ROOM LAMP
RR COMB LAMP LH
RR SIDE MARKER LH
DOOR SW. LH
RR SPEAKER LH (4-SPEAKER TYPE)
24010 37M10
2401 16M00

Fig. 10. Main wiring diagram — 1983 Pulsar (USA)

1983 NISSAN MODEL N12 SERIES
MAIN HARNESS (FOR CANADA MODELS)

NO.	FROM	TO	REMARKS
100	ENGINE ELECTRICAL SYSTEM		
100	ENG H	FUSIBLE LINK	
101	ENG H	100	
106	FUSE BLOCK	100	
107	FUSE BLOCK	106	
110	IGN SW	FUSIBLE LINK	
111	IGN SW	FUSE BLOCK	
112	IGN SW	FUSE BLOCK	
114	ENG H	IGN SW	
115	INHIBIT RELAY	114	
116	INHIBIT RELAY	ENG H	
117	IGN COIL ( )	111	
118	IG RELAY	111	
119	IG RELAY	106	
120	FUSE BLOCK	IG RELAY	
121	ACC RELAY	112	
122	ACC RELAY	106	
123	FUSE BLOCK	ACC RELAY	
124	FUSE BLOCK	123	
126	FUSE BLOCK	120	
127	FUSE BLOCK	112	
131	IGN COIL (-)	RESISTOR	
132	INST H	RESISTOR	
165	ENG H	FUSE BLOCK	
167	INST H	165	
176	ENG H	INST H	
177	A/CHOKE RELAY	ENG H	
183	A/CHOKE RELAY	165	
184	A/CHOKE RELAY	323	
185	A/CHOKE RELAY	335	
186	A/CHOKE RELAY	183	
189	INHIBIT RELAY	165	
190	THERMO SW	FUSE BLOCK	
191	RAD FAN MTR	THERMO SW	
194	CHECK CONN	177	
195	CHECK CONN	176	
196	CHECK CONN	301	
197	INHIBIT RELAY	176	
200	LIGHTING SYSTEM		
200	CONB SW (LIGHT)	FUSE BLOCK	
201	COMB SW (LIGHT)	FUSE BLOCK	
202	COMB SW (LIGHT)	HEAD L RH	
203	COMB SW (LIGHT)	HEAD L LH	
204	COMB SW (LIGHT)	DIMMER RELAY	
205	DIMMER RELAY	HEAD L RH	
206	DIMMER RELAY	HEAD L RH	
207	HEAD L LH	205	
208	HEAD L LH	206	
209	INST H	202	
210	INST H	205	
211	RETRACT MTR RH	106	COUPE
212	RETRACT MTR LH	100	COUPE
213	RETRACT MTR RH	INST H	COUPE
214	RETRACT MTR LH	213	COUPE
215	RETRACT MTR RH	HEAD LAMP CONTROL UNIT	COUPE
216	RETRACT MTR LH	215	COUPE
217	RETRACT MTR RH	INST H	COUPE
218	RETRACT MTR LH	217	COUPE
219	RETRACT MTR RH	INST H	COUPE
220	COMB SW (LIGHT)	FUSE BLOCK	
222	COMB SW (LIGHT)	FR COMB L RH	
223	FR COMB L LH	222	
225	RR COMB L LH	222	
226	LICENSE L	282	
227	LICENSE L	225	
228	INST H	222	
232	HEAD LAMP CONTROL UNIT	INST H	COUPE
233	RETRACT MTR LH	219	COUPE
236	A/T IND LAMP	222	
237	A/T IND LAMP	INST H	
238	HEATER	222	
239	HEATER	237	
240	HEAD LAMP CONTROL UNIT	222	COUPE
241	HEAD LAMP CONTROL UNIT	202	COUPE
242	HEAD LAMP CONTROL UNIT	203	COUPE
243	HEAD LAMP CONTROL UNIT	200	COUPE
244	HEAD LAMP CONTROL UNIT	201	COUPE
245	HEAD LAMP CONTROL UNIT	219	COUPE
251	ROOM L H	545	
252	ROOM L H	DOOR SW LH	
253	DOOR SW RH	252	
256	LUGGAGE L	545	
257	LUGGAGE L SW	LUGGAGE L	
271	SIDE MARKER L	222	SEDAN
272	SIDE MARKER L	223	SEDAN
273	RR SIDE MARKER	225	SEDAN
274	RR SIDE MARKER	282	SEDAN
282	RR COMB L RH	222	
300	METER, GAUGES AND WARNING SYSTEM		
301	FUSE BLOCK	INST H	
304	ENG H	INST H	
305	TANK UNIT	INST H	
320	ENG H	INST H	
322	HAND BRAKE SW	323	
323	INST H	BRAKE LEVEL SW	
335	ENG H	INST H	
345	KEY SW	545	
346	KEY SW	DOOR SW	
347	DOOR SW	INST H	
348	S/BELT SW	INST H	
355	SEAT BELT SW	INST H	
400	SIGNAL SYSTEM		
401	INST H	FLASHEP UNIT	
402	403	FLASHER UNIT	
403	INST H	COMB SW (TURN)	
404	FR COMB L RH	COMB SW (TURN)	
405	FR COMB L LH	COMB SW (TURN)	
408	RR COMB L RH	404	
409	RR COMB L LH	405	
410	INST H	404	
411	INST H	405	
420	INST H	431	
431	FUSE BLOCK	HORN RELAY	
432	COMB SW (LIGHT)	HORN RELAY	
434	HORN RELAY	HORN HI	
435	HORN LO	434	
441	FUSE BLOCK	STOP SW	
443	RR COMB L LH	445	
445	RR COMB L RH	STOP L SW	
451	ENG H	301	
452	ENG H	RR COMB L RH	
453	RR COMB L LH	452	
500	ACCESSORY SYSTEM		
500	FUSE BLOCK	WIPER MTR	
502	COMB SW (WIPER)	WIPER MTR	
503	COMB SW (WIPER)	WIPER MTR	
504	WIPER AMP	WIPER MTR	
505	WIPER AMP	COMB SW (WIPER)	
506	WIPER AMP	COMB SW (WIPER)	
507	WIPER AMP	500	
508	WIPER AMP	511	
509	WIPER AMP	WIPER SW	
510	WASHER MTR	500	
511	COMB SW (WIPER)	WASHER MTR	
512	RR WASHER MTR	510	SEDAN
513	INST H	RR WASHER MTR	SEDAN
514	BACK DOOR H	520	SEDAN
515	INST H	BACK DOOR H	SEDAN
516	INST H	BACK DOOR H	SEDAN
520	FUSE BLOCK	INST H	
521	INST H	SPEAKER-LH	
522	SPEAKER-RH	521	
523	INST H	SPEAKER- LH	
524	SPEAKER-RH	523	
530	CONDENSER	117	
540	INST H	FUSE BLOCK	
545	INST H	FUSE BLOCK	
550	FUSE BLOCK	INST H	
552	INST H	BACK DOOR H	SEDAN
552	RR DEFOG	INS H	COUPE
560	FUSE BLOCK	BLOWER MTR	
562	HEATER	BLOWER MTR	
563	HEATER	RESISTOR	
564	HEATER	RESISTOR	
565	RESISTOR	562	
574	RESISTOR	HEATER	
700	SUPPLEMENTAL NUMBER		
700	MIXTURE HEATER RELAY	100	

Fig. 11. Main wiring diagram — 1983 Pulsar (Canada)

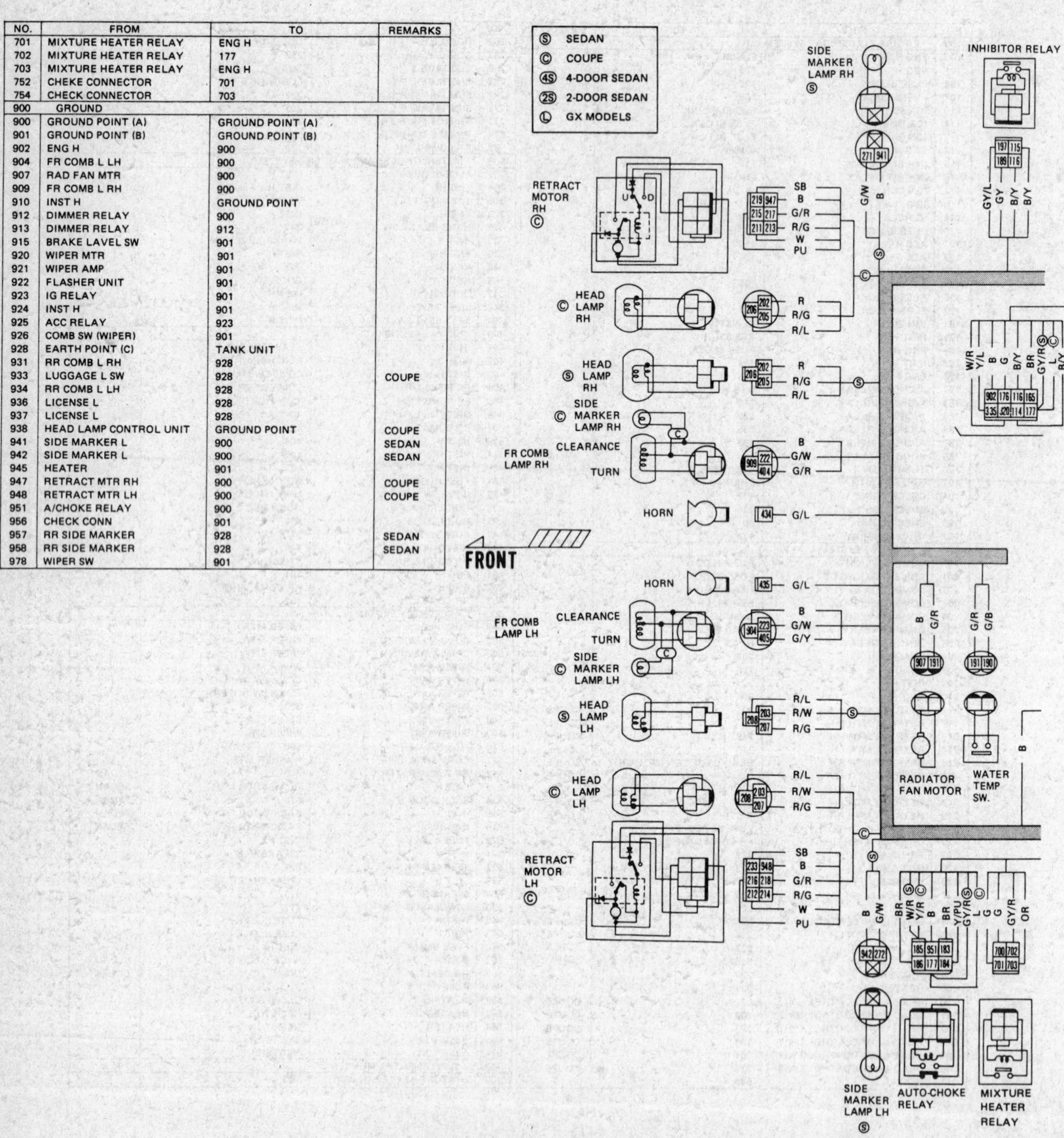

NO.	FROM	TO	REMARKS
701	MIXTURE HEATER RELAY	ENG H	
702	MIXTURE HEATER RELAY	177	
703	MIXTURE HEATER RELAY	ENG H	
752	CHEKE CONNECTOR	701	
754	CHECK CONNECTOR	703	
900	GROUND		
900	GROUND POINT (A)	GROUND POINT (A)	
901	GROUND POINT (B)	GROUND POINT (B)	
902	ENG H	900	
904	FR COMB L LH	900	
907	RAD FAN MTR	900	
909	FR COMB L RH	900	
910	INST H	GROUND POINT	
912	DIMMER RELAY	900	
913	DIMMER RELAY	912	
915	BRAKE LAVEL SW	901	
920	WIPER MTR	901	
921	WIPER AMP	901	
922	FLASHER UNIT	901	
923	IG RELAY	901	
924	INST H	901	
925	ACC RELAY	923	
926	COMB SW (WIPER)	901	
928	EARTH POINT (C)	TANK UNIT	
931	RR COMB L RH	928	
933	LUGGAGE L SW	928	COUPE
934	RR COMB L LH	928	
936	LICENSE L	928	
937	LICENSE L	928	
938	HEAD LAMP CONTROL UNIT	GROUND POINT	COUPE
941	SIDE MARKER L	900	SEDAN
942	SIDE MARKER L	900	SEDAN
945	HEATER	901	
947	RETRACT MTR RH	900	COUPE
948	RETRACT MTR LH	900	COUPE
951	A/CHOKE RELAY	900	
956	CHECK CONN	901	
957	RR SIDE MARKER	928	SEDAN
958	RR SIDE MARKER	928	SEDAN
978	WIPER SW	901	

Ⓢ SEDAN
Ⓒ COUPE
4S 4-DOOR SEDAN
2S 2-DOOR SEDAN
Ⓛ GX MODELS
SIDE MARKER LAMP RH
INHIBITOR RELAY
RETRACT MOTOR RH
HEAD LAMP RH
SIDE MARKER LAMP RH
CLEARANCE
FR COMB LAMP RH
TURN
HORN
FRONT
HORN
FR COMB LAMP LH
CLEARANCE
TURN
SIDE MARKER LAMP LH
HEAD LAMP LH
HEAD LAMP LH
RADIATOR FAN MOTOR
WATER TEMP SW.
RETRACT MOTOR LH
SIDE MARKER LAMP LH
AUTO-CHOKE RELAY
MIXTURE HEATER RELAY

Fig. 11. Main wiring diagram — 1983 Pulsar (Canada)

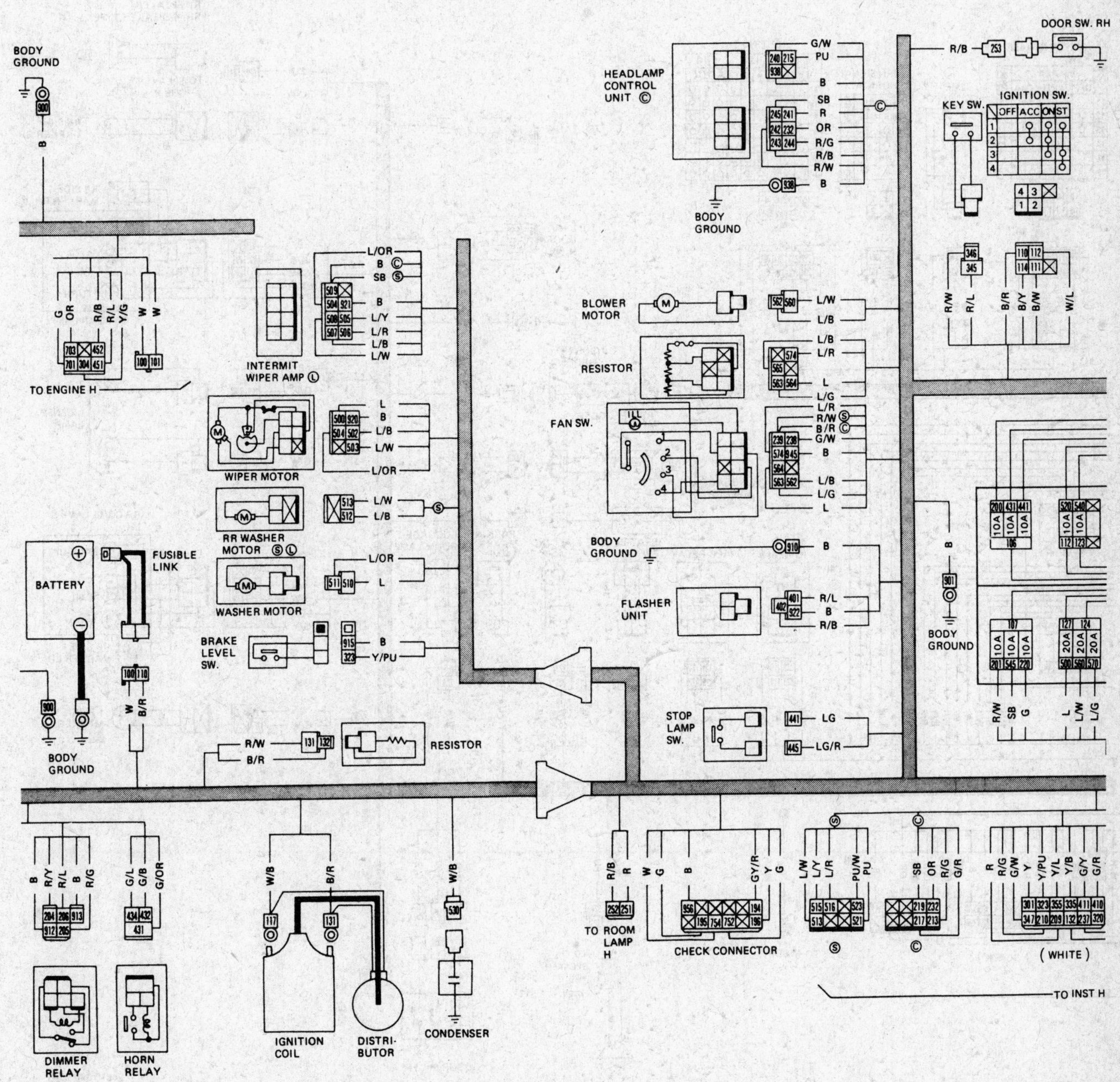

Fig. 11. Main wiring diagram — 1983 Pulsar (Canada)

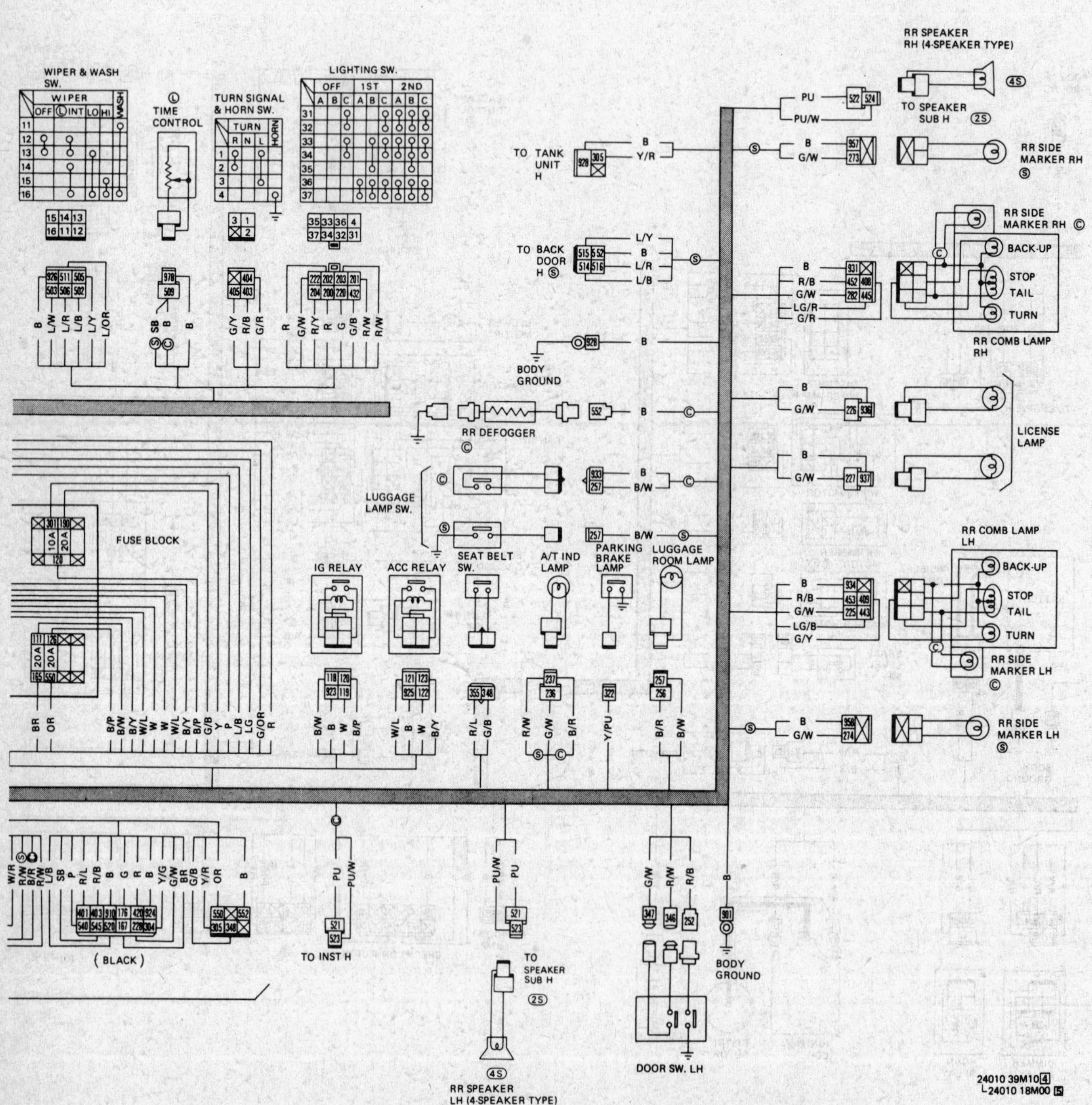
WIPER & WASH SW.
TIME CONTROL
TURN SIGNAL & HORN SW.
LIGHTING SW.
RR SPEAKER RH (4-SPEAKER TYPE)
TO SPEAKER SUB H
TO TANK UNIT H
RR SIDE MARKER RH
TO BACK DOOR H
BACK-UP
STOP
TAIL
TURN
RR COMB LAMP RH
BODY GROUND
RR DEFOGGER
LICENSE LAMP
LUGGAGE LAMP SW.
FUSE BLOCK
IG RELAY
ACC RELAY
SEAT BELT SW.
A/T IND LAMP
PARKING BRAKE LAMP
LUGGAGE ROOM LAMP
RR COMB LAMP LH
RR SIDE MARKER LH
(BLACK)
TO INST H
RR SPEAKER LH (4-SPEAKER TYPE)
DOOR SW. LH
24010 39M10
24010 18M00

Fig. 11. Main wiring diagram — 1983 Pulsar (Canada)

1983 NISSAN MODEL N12 SERIES
ENGINE HARNESS (FOR U.S.A. MODELS)

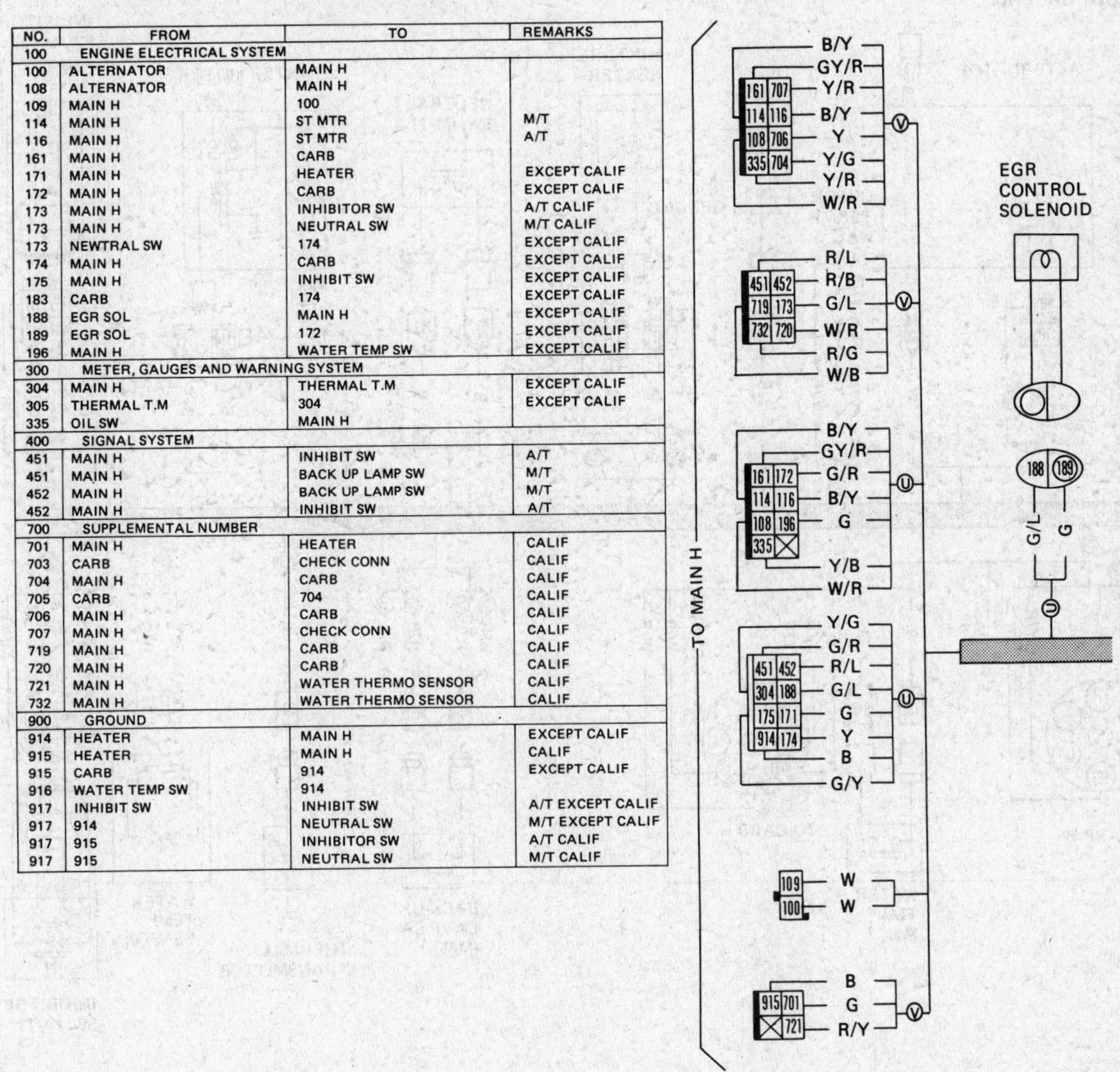

NO.	FROM	TO	REMARKS
100	ENGINE ELECTRICAL SYSTEM		
100	ALTERNATOR	MAIN H	
108	ALTERNATOR	MAIN H	
109	MAIN H	100	
114	MAIN H	ST MTR	M/T
116	MAIN H	ST MTR	A/T
161	MAIN H	CARB	
171	MAIN H	HEATER	EXCEPT CALIF
172	MAIN H	CARB	EXCEPT CALIF
173	MAIN H	INHIBITOR SW	A/T CALIF
173	MAIN H	NEUTRAL SW	M/T CALIF
173	NEWTRAL SW	174	EXCEPT CALIF
174	MAIN H	CARB	EXCEPT CALIF
175	MAIN H	INHIBIT SW	EXCEPT CALIF
183	CARB	174	EXCEPT CALIF
188	EGR SOL	MAIN H	EXCEPT CALIF
189	EGR SOL	172	EXCEPT CALIF
196	MAIN H	WATER TEMP SW	EXCEPT CALIF
300	METER, GAUGES AND WARNING SYSTEM		
304	MAIN H	THERMAL T.M	EXCEPT CALIF
305	THERMAL T.M	304	EXCEPT CALIF
335	OIL SW	MAIN H	
400	SIGNAL SYSTEM		
451	MAIN H	INHIBIT SW	A/T
451	MAIN H	BACK UP LAMP SW	M/T
452	MAIN H	BACK UP LAMP SW	M/T
452	MAIN H	INHIBIT SW	A/T
700	SUPPLEMENTAL NUMBER		
701	MAIN H	HEATER	CALIF
703	CARB	CHECK CONN	CALIF
704	MAIN H	CARB	CALIF
705	CARB	704	CALIF
706	MAIN H	CARB	CALIF
707	MAIN H	CHECK CONN	CALIF
719	MAIN H	CARB	CALIF
720	MAIN H	CARB	CALIF
721	MAIN H	WATER THERMO SENSOR	CALIF
732	MAIN H	WATER THERMO SENSOR	CALIF
900	GROUND		
914	HEATER	MAIN H	EXCEPT CALIF
915	HEATER	MAIN H	CALIF
915	CARB	914	EXCEPT CALIF
916	WATER TEMP SW	914	
917	INHIBIT SW	INHIBIT SW	A/T EXCEPT CALIF
917	914	NEUTRAL SW	M/T EXCEPT CALIF
917	915	INHIBITOR SW	A/T CALIF
917	915	NEUTRAL SW	M/T CALIF

B/Y
GY/R
161 707
114 116
108 706
335 704
Y/R
B/Y
Y
Y/G
Y/R
W/R
EGR
CONTROL
SOLENOID
451 452
719 173
732 720
R/L
R/B
G/L
W/R
R/G
W/B
B/Y
GY/R
161 172
114 116
108 196
335
G/R
B/Y
G
Y/B
W/R
188 189
G/L
G
TO MAIN H
Y/G
G/R
R/L
G/L
G
Y
B
G/Y
451 452
304 188
175 171
914 174
109
100
W
W
915 701
721
B
G
R/Y

Fig. 12. Engine wiring diagram — 1983 Pulsar

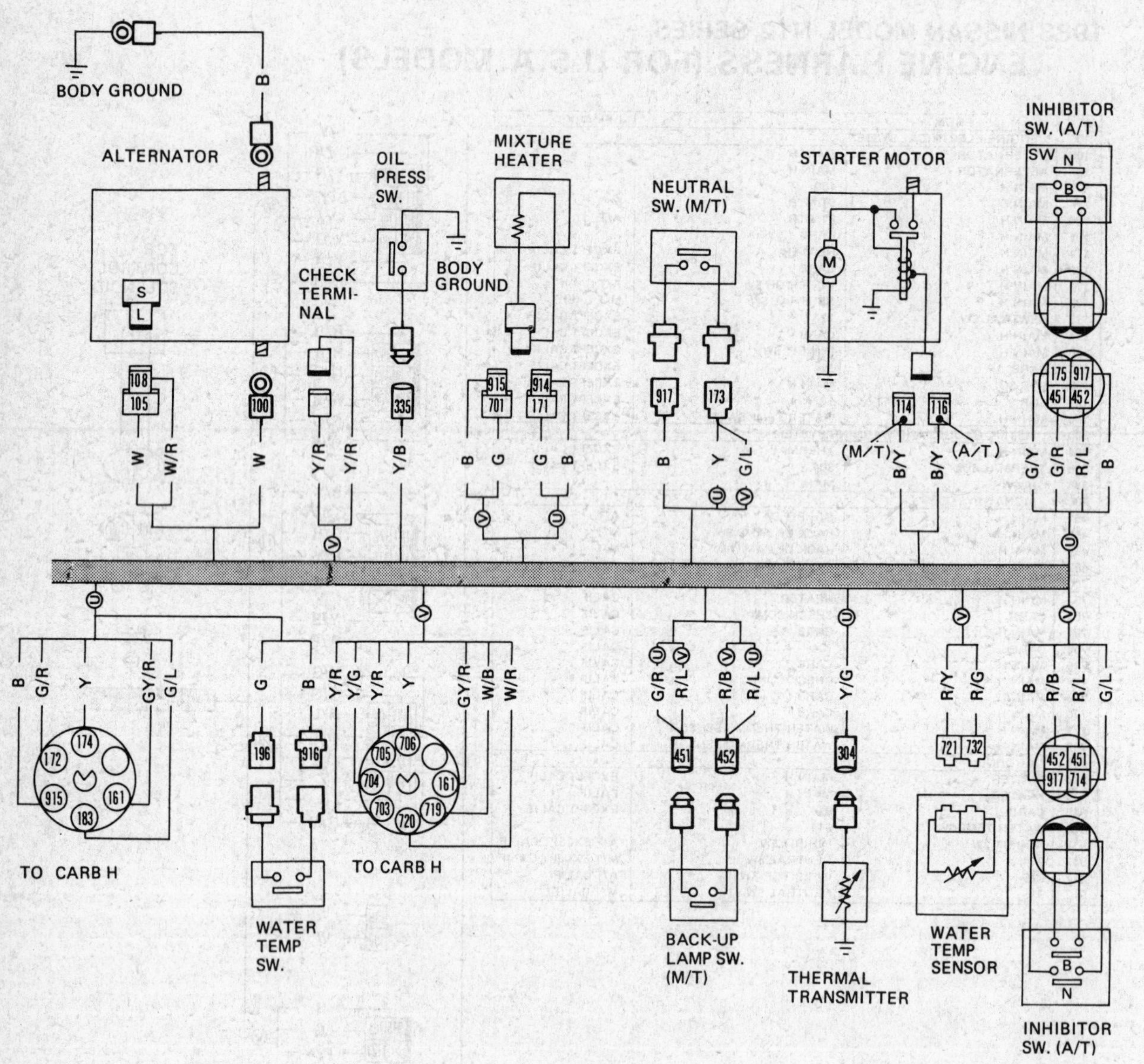

Ⓥ FOR CARIFORNIA
Ⓤ FOR EXCEPT CALIFORNIA
BODY GROUND
ALTERNATOR
OIL PRESS SW.
MIXTURE HEATER
BODY GROUND
CHECK TERMI-NAL
NEUTRAL SW. (M/T)
STARTER MOTOR
INHIBITOR SW. (A/T)
TO CARB H
WATER TEMP SW.
TO CARB H
BACK-UP LAMP SW. (M/T)
THERMAL TRANSMITTER
WATER TEMP SENSOR
INHIBITOR SW. (A/T)

24075 17M05 3
└24075 17M10

24075 16M00 1
└24075 16M10

Fig. 12. Engine wiring diagram — 1983 Pulsar

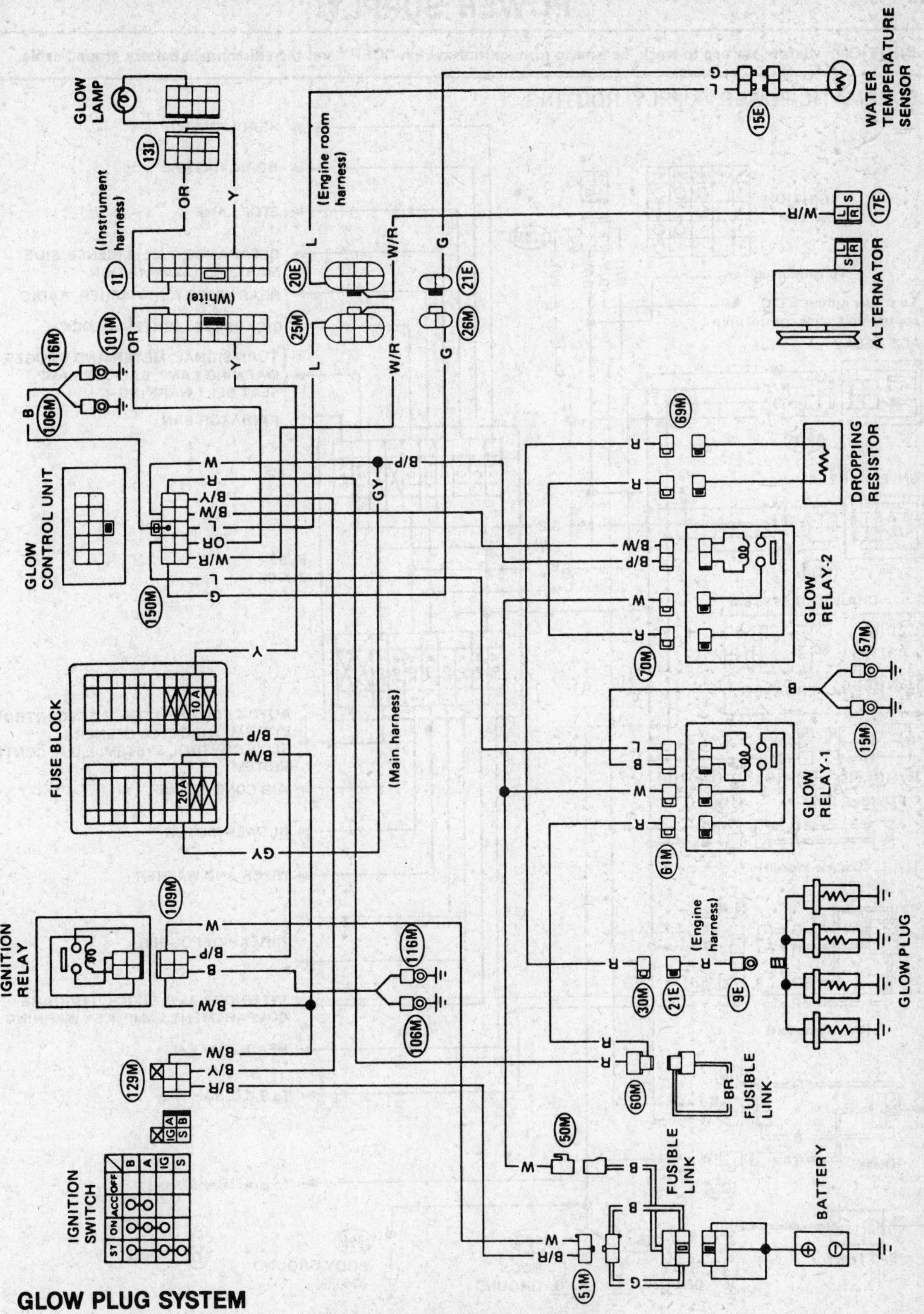
GLOW LAMP
(Instrument harness)
(Engine room harness)
WATER TEMPERATURE SENSOR
ALTERNATOR
GLOW CONTROL UNIT
DROPPING RESISTOR
GLOW RELAY-2
FUSE BLOCK
(Main harness)
GLOW RELAY-1
IGNITION RELAY
(Engine harness)
GLOW PLUG
FUSIBLE LINK
IGNITION SWITCH
FUSIBLE LINK
BATTERY

GLOW PLUG SYSTEM

Fig. 13. Chassis wiring diagram — 1984 Sentra

POWER SUPPLY

CAUTION: Before starting to work, be sure to turn ignition switch "OFF" and then disconnect battery ground cable.

SCHEMATIC/POWER SUPPLY ROUTING

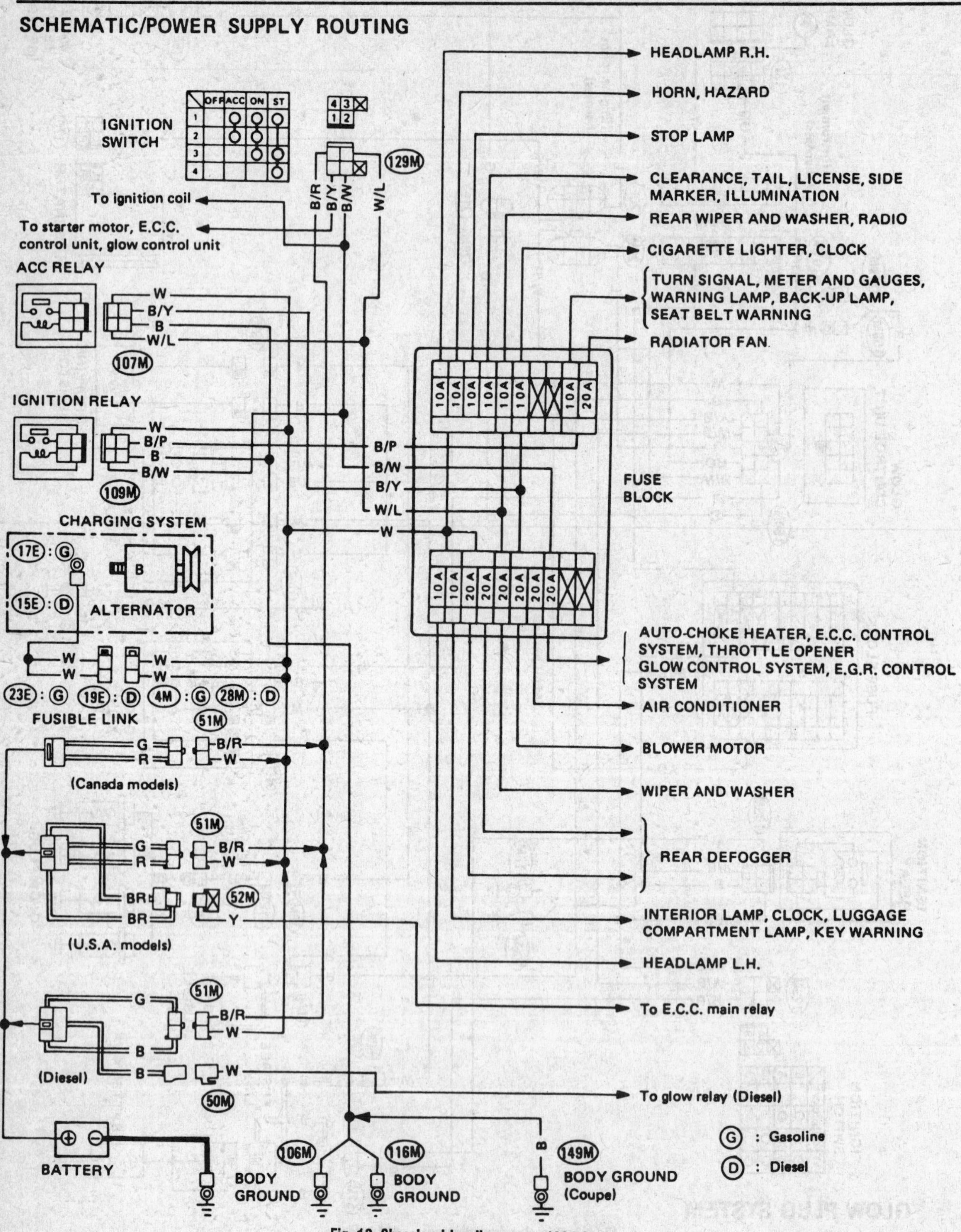

HEADLAMP R.H.
HORN, HAZARD
STOP LAMP
CLEARANCE, TAIL, LICENSE, SIDE MARKER, ILLUMINATION
REAR WIPER AND WASHER, RADIO
CIGARETTE LIGHTER, CLOCK
TURN SIGNAL, METER AND GAUGES, WARNING LAMP, BACK-UP LAMP, SEAT BELT WARNING
RADIATOR FAN
IGNITION SWITCH
OFF ACC ON ST
129M
To ignition coil
To starter motor, E.C.C. control unit, glow control unit
ACC RELAY
107M
IGNITION RELAY
109M
FUSE BLOCK
CHARGING SYSTEM
17E : G
15E : D
ALTERNATOR
23E : G 19E : D 4M : G 28M : D
FUSIBLE LINK
51M
(Canada models)
52M
(U.S.A. models)
50M
(Diesel)
AUTO-CHOKE HEATER, E.C.C. CONTROL SYSTEM, THROTTLE OPENER
GLOW CONTROL SYSTEM, E.G.R. CONTROL SYSTEM
AIR CONDITIONER
BLOWER MOTOR
WIPER AND WASHER
REAR DEFOGGER
INTERIOR LAMP, CLOCK, LUGGAGE COMPARTMENT LAMP, KEY WARNING
HEADLAMP L.H.
To E.C.C. main relay
To glow relay (Diesel)
G : Gasoline
D : Diesel
BATTERY
106M
116M
149M
BODY GROUND
BODY GROUND
BODY GROUND (Coupe)

Fig. 13. Chassis wiring diagram — 1984 Sentra

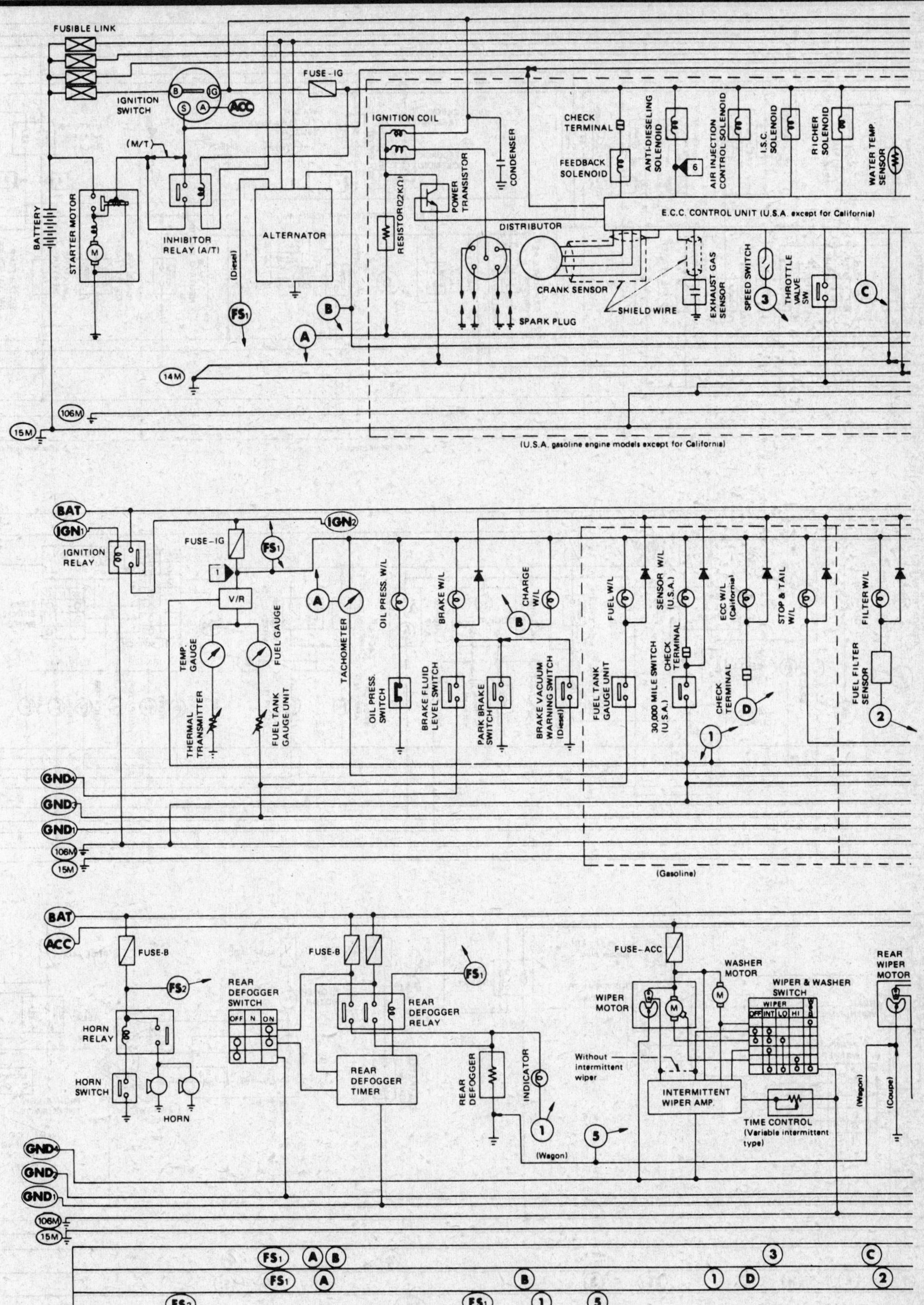
FUSIBLE LINK
IGNITION SWITCH
ACC
(M/T)
BATTERY
STARTER MOTOR
INHIBITOR RELAY (A/T)
FUSE-IG
ALTERNATOR
(Diesel)
IGNITION COIL
RESISTOR(2.2KΩ)
POWER TRANSISTOR
CONDENSER
DISTRIBUTOR
SPARK PLUG
CRANK SENSOR
SHIELD WIRE
CHECK TERMINAL
FEEDBACK SOLENOID
ANTI-DIESELING SOLENOID
AIR INJECTION CONTROL SOLENOID
I.S.C. SOLENOID
RICHER SOLENOID
WATER TEMP. SENSOR
E.C.C. CONTROL UNIT (U.S.A. except for California)
EXHAUST GAS SENSOR
SPEED SWITCH
THROTTLE VALVE SW
(U.S.A. gasoline engine models except for California)
BAT
IGN1
IGN2
IGNITION RELAY
FUSE-IG
V/R
TEMP. GAUGE
FUEL GAUGE
THERMAL TRANSMITTER
FUEL TANK GAUGE UNIT
TACHOMETER
OIL PRESS. W/L
OIL PRESS. SWITCH
BRAKE W/L
BRAKE FLUID LEVEL SWITCH
PARK BRAKE SWITCH
CHARGE W/L
BRAKE VACUUM WARNING SWITCH (Diesel)
FUEL W/L
FUEL TANK GAUGE UNIT
SENSOR W/L (U.S.A.)
30,000 MILE SWITCH (U.S.A.)
CHECK TERMINAL
ECC W/L (California)
CHECK TERMINAL
STOP & TAIL W/L
FILTER W/L
FUEL FILTER SENSOR
GND4
GND3
GND1
106M
15M
14M
(Gasoline)
ACC
FUSE-B
HORN RELAY
HORN SWITCH
HORN
REAR DEFOGGER SWITCH
OFF N ON
FUSE-B
REAR DEFOGGER RELAY
REAR DEFOGGER TIMER
REAR DEFOGGER
INDICATOR
(Wagon)
FUSE-ACC
WASHER MOTOR
WIPER MOTOR
WIPER & WASHER SWITCH
WIPER
OFF INT LO HI
Without intermittent wiper
INTERMITTENT WIPER AMP.
TIME CONTROL (Variable intermittent type)
REAR WIPER MOTOR
(Wagon)
(Coupe)
GND2

Fig. 14. Chassis wiring diagram — 1984 Sentra

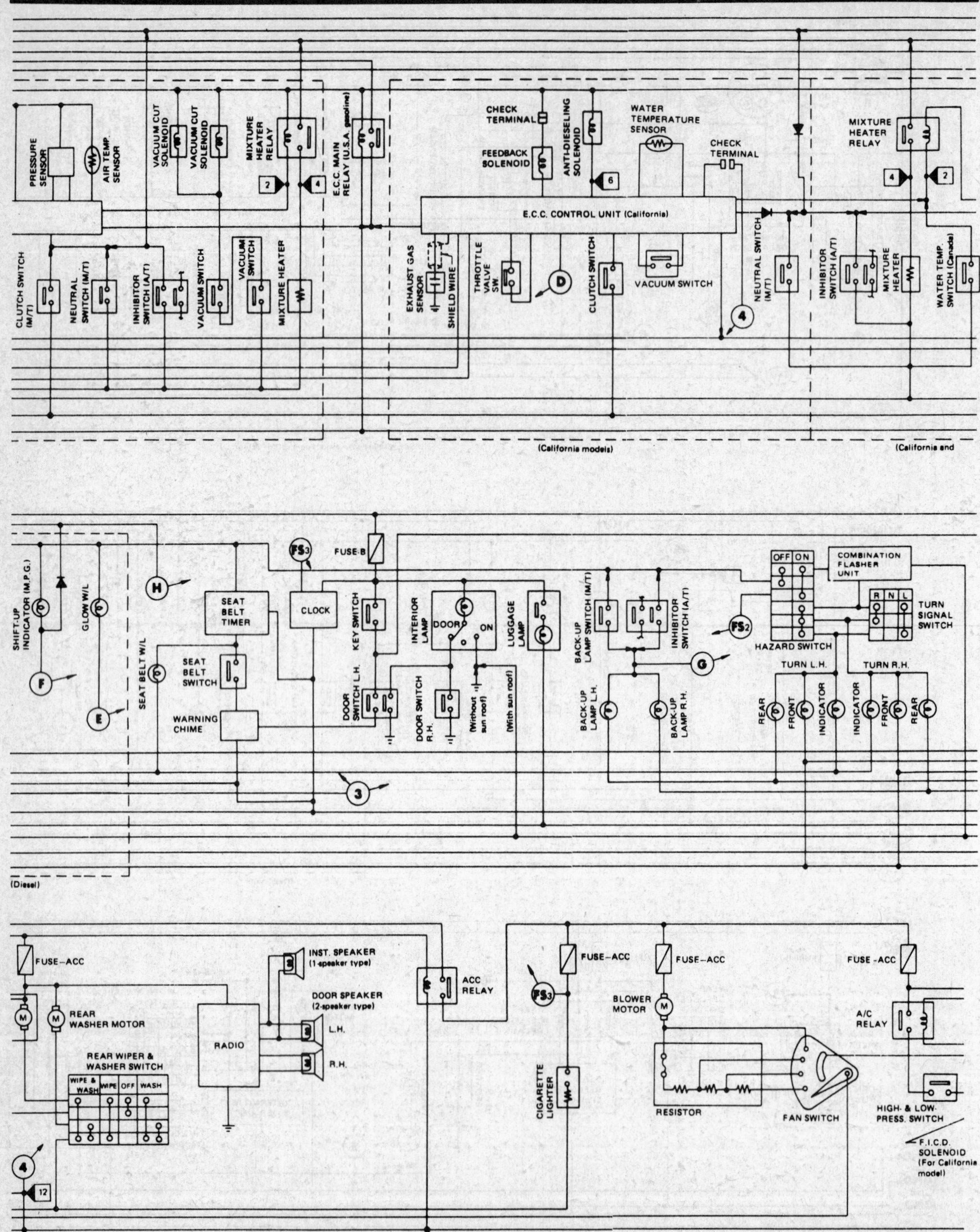

PRESSURE SENSOR
AIR TEMP. SENSOR
VACUUM CUT SOLENOID
VACUUM CUT SOLENOID
MIXTURE HEATER RELAY
E.C.C. MAIN RELAY (U.S.A. gasoline)
CHECK TERMINAL
FEEDBACK SOLENOID
ANTI-DIESELING SOLENOID
WATER TEMPERATURE SENSOR
CHECK TERMINAL
MIXTURE HEATER RELAY
E.C.C. CONTROL UNIT (California)
CLUTCH SWITCH (M/T)
NEUTRAL SWITCH (M/T)
INHIBITOR SWITCH (A/T)
VACUUM SWITCH
VACUUM SWITCH
MIXTURE HEATER
EXHAUST GAS SENSOR
SHIELD WIRE
THROTTLE VALVE SW.
CLUTCH SWITCH
VACUUM SWITCH
NEUTRAL SWITCH (M/T)
INHIBITOR SWITCH (A/T)
MIXTURE HEATER
WATER TEMP. SWITCH (Canada)
(California models)
(California and
SHIFT-UP INDICATOR (M.P.G.)
GLOW W/L
SEAT BELT W/L
SEAT BELT TIMER
SEAT BELT SWITCH
WARNING CHIME
CLOCK
FUSE-B
KEY SWITCH
DOOR SWITCH L.H.
INTERIOR LAMP
DOOR
ON
DOOR SWITCH R.H.
(Without sun roof)
(With sun roof)
LUGGAGE LAMP
BACK-UP LAMP SWITCH (M/T)
INHIBITOR SWITCH (A/T)
BACK-UP LAMP L.H.
BACK-UP LAMP R.H.
OFF
ON
COMBINATION FLASHER UNIT
HAZARD SWITCH
R
N
L
TURN SIGNAL SWITCH
TURN L.H.
TURN R.H.
REAR
FRONT
INDICATOR
INDICATOR
FRONT
REAR
(Diesel)
FUSE-ACC
REAR WASHER MOTOR
REAR WIPER & WASHER SWITCH
WIPE & WASH
WIPE
OFF
WASH
RADIO
INST. SPEAKER (1-speaker type)
DOOR SPEAKER (2-speaker type)
L.H.
R.H.
ACC RELAY
FUSE-ACC
CIGARETTE LIGHTER
FUSE-ACC
BLOWER MOTOR
RESISTOR
FAN SWITCH
FUSE-ACC
A/C RELAY
HIGH- & LOW-PRESS. SWITCH
F.I.C.D. SOLENOID (For California model)

Fig. 14. Chassis wiring diagram — 1984 Sentra

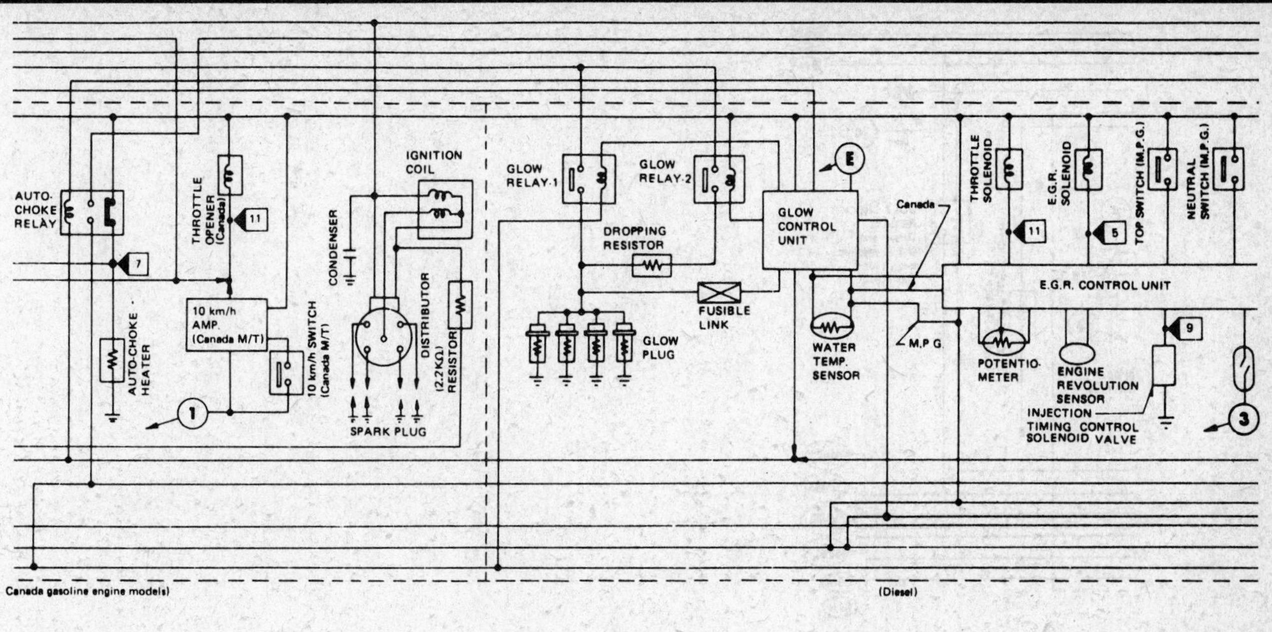
AUTO-CHOKE RELAY
THROTTLE OPENER (Canada)
IGNITION COIL
CONDENSER
DISTRIBUTOR
(2.2KΩ) RESISTOR
10 km/h AMP. (Canada M/T)
10 km/h SWITCH (Canada M/T)
AUTO-CHOKE HEATER
SPARK PLUG
GLOW RELAY-1
GLOW RELAY-2
DROPPING RESISTOR
GLOW CONTROL UNIT
FUSIBLE LINK
GLOW PLUG
WATER TEMP. SENSOR
Canada
M.P.G.
THROTTLE SOLENOID
E.G.R. SOLENOID
TOP SWITCH (M.P.G.)
NEUTRAL SWITCH (M.P.G.)
E.G.R. CONTROL UNIT
POTENTIO-METER
ENGINE REVOLUTION SENSOR
INJECTION TIMING CONTROL SOLENOID VALVE
Canada gasoline engine models)
(Diesel)

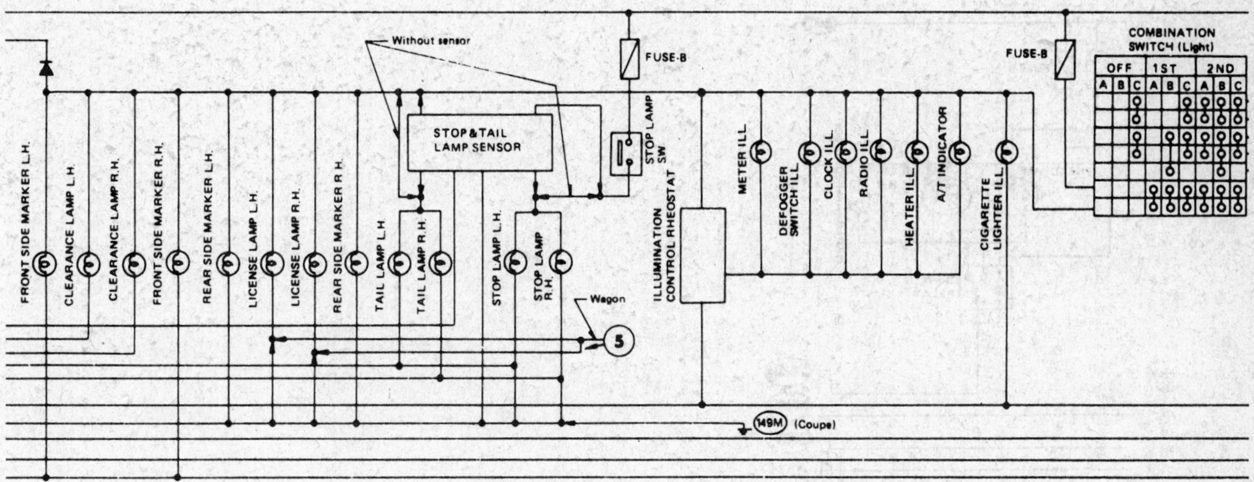
Without sensor
FUSE-B
STOP&TAIL LAMP SENSOR
STOP LAMP SW
COMBINATION SWITCH (Light)
OFF
1ST
2ND
FRONT SIDE MARKER L.H.
CLEARANCE LAMP L.H.
CLEARANCE LAMP R.H.
FRONT SIDE MARKER R.H.
REAR SIDE MARKER L.H.
LICENSE LAMP L.H.
LICENSE LAMP R.H.
REAR SIDE MARKER R.H.
TAIL LAMP L.H.
TAIL LAMP R.H.
STOP LAMP L.H.
STOP LAMP R.H.
Wagon
ILLUMINATION CONTROL RHEOSTAT
METER ILL.
DEFOGGER SWITCH ILL.
CLOCK ILL.
RADIO ILL.
HEATER ILL.
A/T INDICATOR
CIGARETTE LIGHTER ILL.
149M (Coupe)

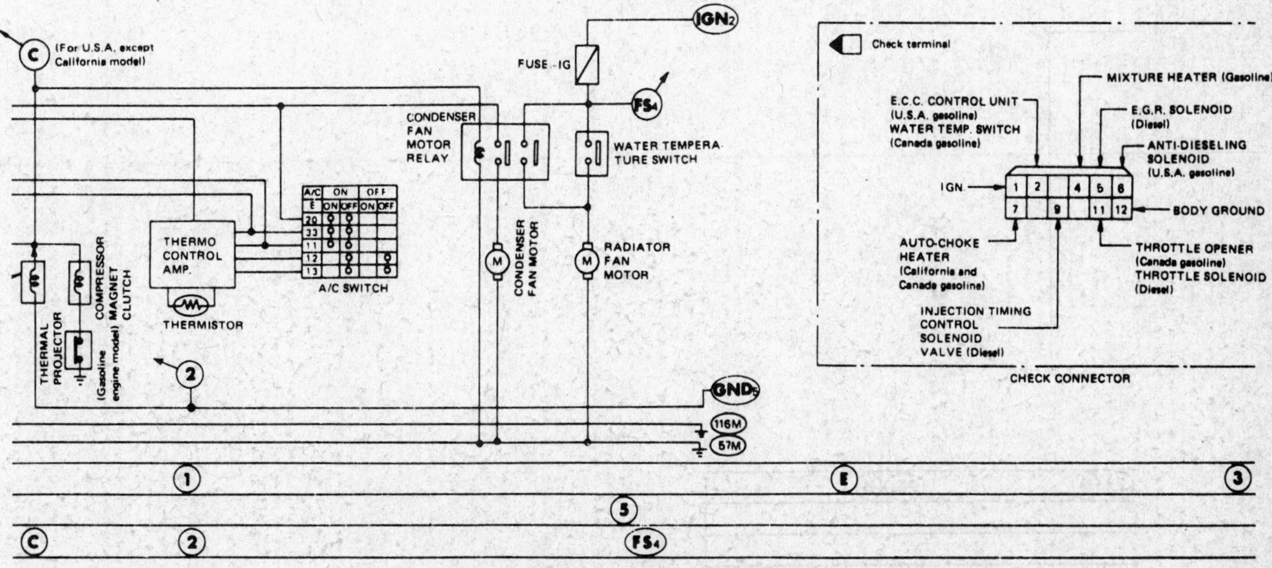
(For U.S.A. except California model)
IGN2
FUSE-IG
FS4
CONDENSER FAN MOTOR RELAY
WATER TEMPERATURE SWITCH
THERMO CONTROL AMP.
THERMISTOR
A/C SWITCH
CONDENSER FAN MOTOR
RADIATOR FAN MOTOR
THERMAL PROJECTOR
COMPRESSOR MAGNET CLUTCH (Gasoline engine model)
GND5
116M
57M
Check terminal
E.C.C. CONTROL UNIT (U.S.A. gasoline)
WATER TEMP. SWITCH (Canada gasoline)
MIXTURE HEATER (Gasoline)
E.G.R. SOLENOID (Diesel)
ANTI-DIESELING SOLENOID (U.S.A. gasoline)
IGN
BODY GROUND
AUTO-CHOKE HEATER (California and Canada gasoline)
THROTTLE OPENER (Canada gasoline)
THROTTLE SOLENOID (Diesel)
INJECTION TIMING CONTROL SOLENOID VALVE (Diesel)
CHECK CONNECTOR

Fig. 15. Chassis wiring diagram — 1984 Sentra

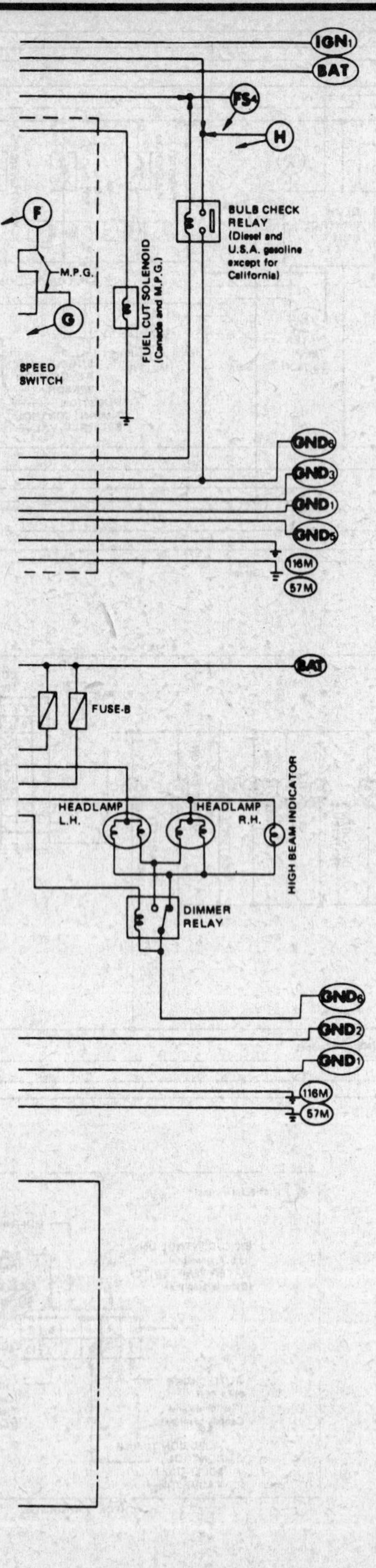
IGN1
BAT
FS4
H
BULB CHECK RELAY (Diesel and U.S.A. gasoline except for California)
F
M.P.G.
G
SPEED SWITCH
FUEL CUT SOLENOID (Canada and M.P.G.)
GND6
GND3
GND1
GND5
116M
57M
BAT
FUSE-B
HEADLAMP L.H.
HEADLAMP R.H.
HIGH BEAM INDICATOR
DIMMER RELAY
GND6
GND2
GND1
116M
57M

F
G
FS4
H

Fig. 15. Chassis wiring diagram — 1984 Sentra

LOCATION OF ELECTRICAL UNITS

CAUTION: Before starting to work, be sure to turn ignition switch "OFF" and then disconnect battery ground cable.

ENGINE COMPARTMENT

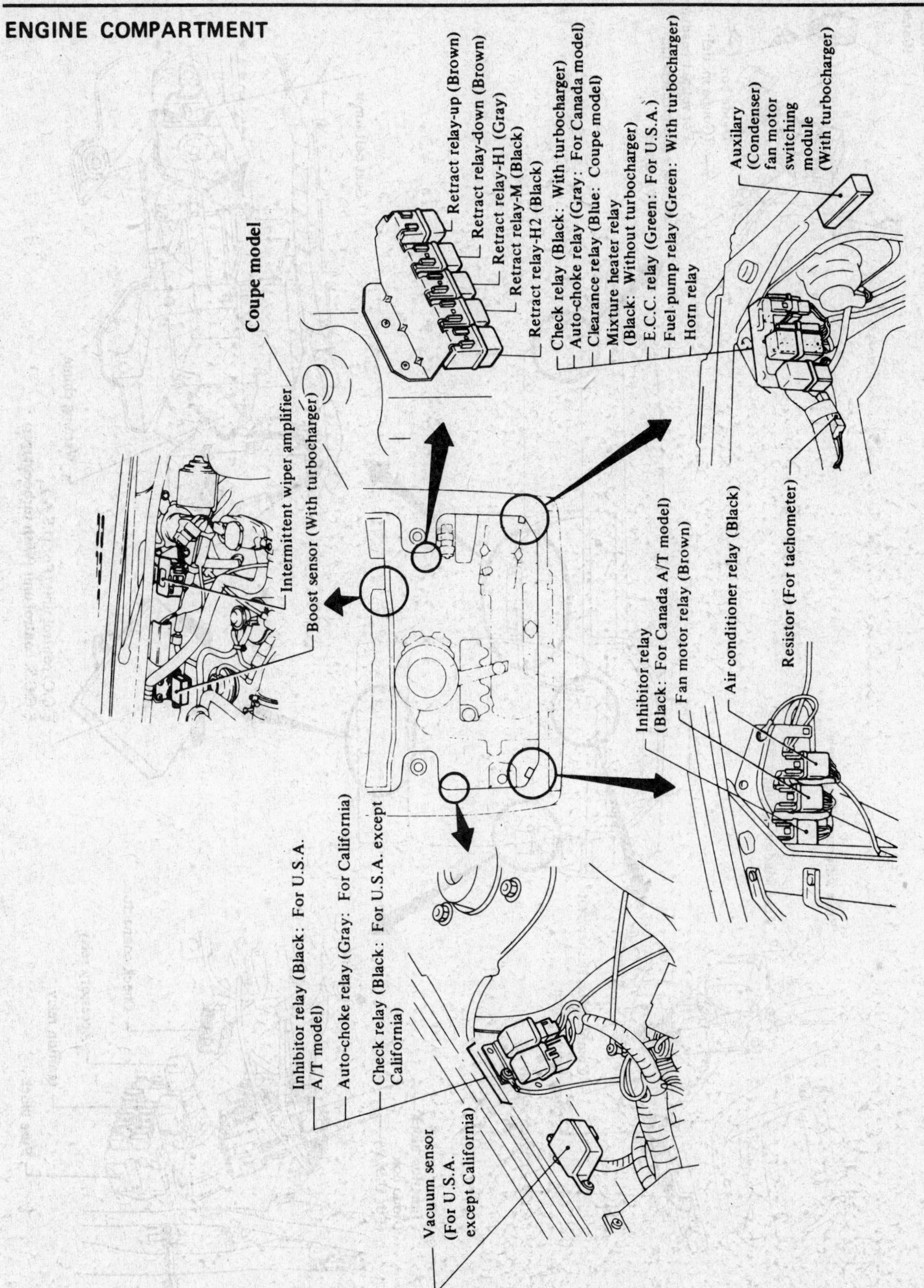
Coupe model
Retract relay-up (Brown)
Retract relay-down (Brown)
Retract relay-H1 (Gray)
Retract relay-M (Black)
Retract relay-H2 (Black)
Check relay (Black: With turbocharger)
Auto-choke relay (Gray: For Canada model)
Clearance relay (Blue: Coupe model)
Mixture heater relay
(Black: Without turbocharger)
E.C.C. relay (Green: For U.S.A.)
Fuel pump relay (Green: With turbocharger)
Horn relay
Auxilary (Condenser) fan motor switching module (With turbocharger)
Intermittent wiper amplifier
Boost sensor (With turbocharger)
Inhibitor relay
(Black: For Canada A/T model)
Fan motor relay (Brown)
Air conditioner relay (Black)
Resistor (For tachometer)
Inhibitor relay (Black: For U.S.A. A/T model)
Auto-choke relay (Gray: For California)
Check relay (Black: For U.S.A. except California)
Vacuum sensor (For U.S.A. except California)

Fig. 16. Electrical component location — 1984 Pulsar

PASSENGER COMPARTMENT

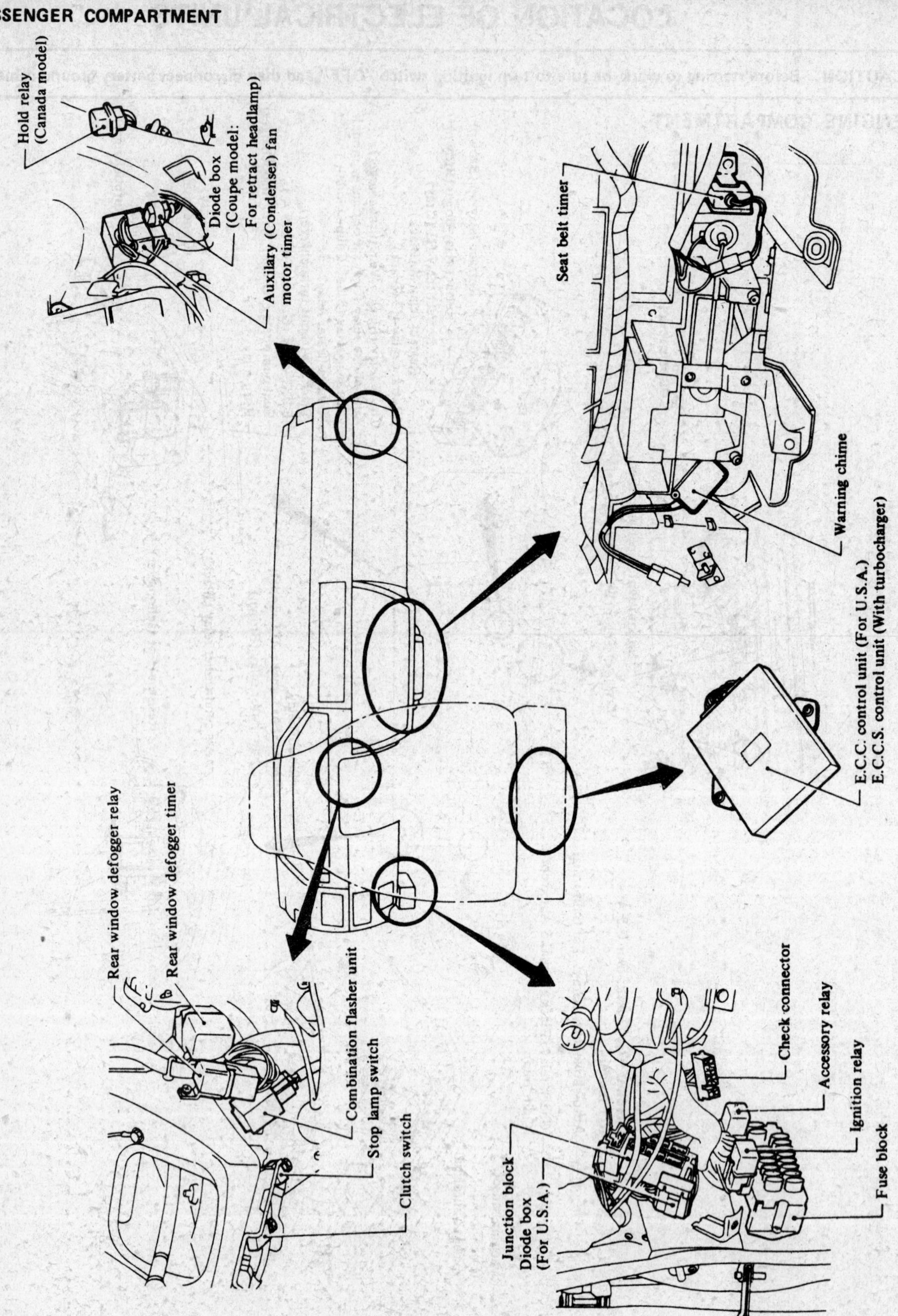
Hold relay
(Canada model)
Diode box
(Coupe model:
For retract headlamp)
Auxilary (Condenser) fan
motor timer
Seat belt timer
Warning chime
E.C.C. control unit (For U.S.A.)
E.C.C.S. control unit (With turbocharger)
Rear window defogger relay
Rear window defogger timer
Combination flasher unit
Stop lamp switch
Clutch switch
Junction block
Diode box
(For U.S.A.)
Check connector
Accessory relay
Ignition relay
Fuse block

Fig. 16. Electrical component location — 1984 Pulsar

POWER SUPPLY ROUTING

CAUTION: Before starting to work, be sure to turn ignition switch "OFF" and then disconnect battery ground cable.

SCHEMATIC/POWER SUPPLY ROUTING

MODEL WITHOUT TURBOCHARGER

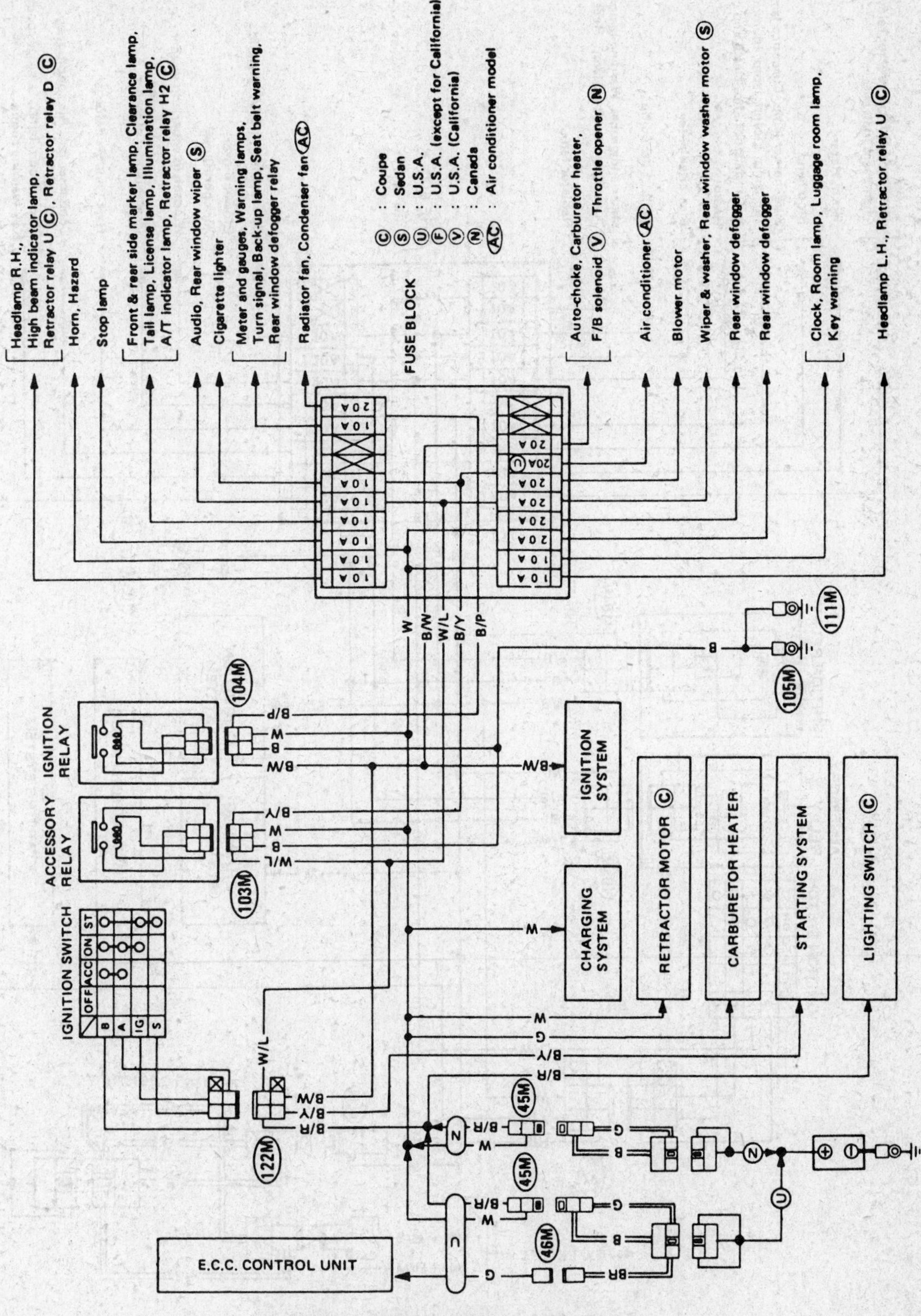
Headlamp R.H.,
High beam indicator lamp,
Retractor relay U (C), Retractor relay D (C)
Horn, Hazard
Stop lamp
Front & rear side marker lamp, Clearance lamp,
Tail lamp, License lamp, Illumination lamp,
A/T indicator lamp, Retractor relay H2 (C)
Audio, Rear window wiper (S)
Cigarette lighter
Meter and gauges, Warning lamps,
Turn signal, Back-up lamp, Seat belt warning,
Rear window defogger relay
Radiator fan, Condenser fan (AC)
FUSE BLOCK
(C) : Coupe
(S) : Sedan
(U) : U.S.A.
(F) : U.S.A. (except for California)
(V) : U.S.A. (California)
(N) : Canada
(AC) : Air conditioner model
Auto-choke, Carburetor heater,
F/B solenoid (V) Throttle opener (N)
Air conditioner (AC)
Blower motor
Wiper & washer, Rear window washer motor (S)
Rear window defogger
Rear window defogger
Clock, Room lamp, Luggage room lamp,
Key warning
Headlamp L.H., Retractor relay U (C)
20A
10A
20A (U)
W
B/W
W/L
B/Y
B/P
B
111M
105M
104M
103M
IGNITION RELAY
ACCESSORY RELAY
IGNITION SWITCH
OFF
ACC
ON
ST
B
A
IG
S
IGNITION SYSTEM
CHARGING SYSTEM
RETRACTOR MOTOR (C)
CARBURETOR HEATER
STARTING SYSTEM
LIGHTING SWITCH (C)
G
B/R
122M
45M
46M
BR
E.C.C. CONTROL UNIT

Fig. 17. Power supply wiring diagram — 1984 Pulsar

MODEL WITH TURBOCHARGER (For Canada)

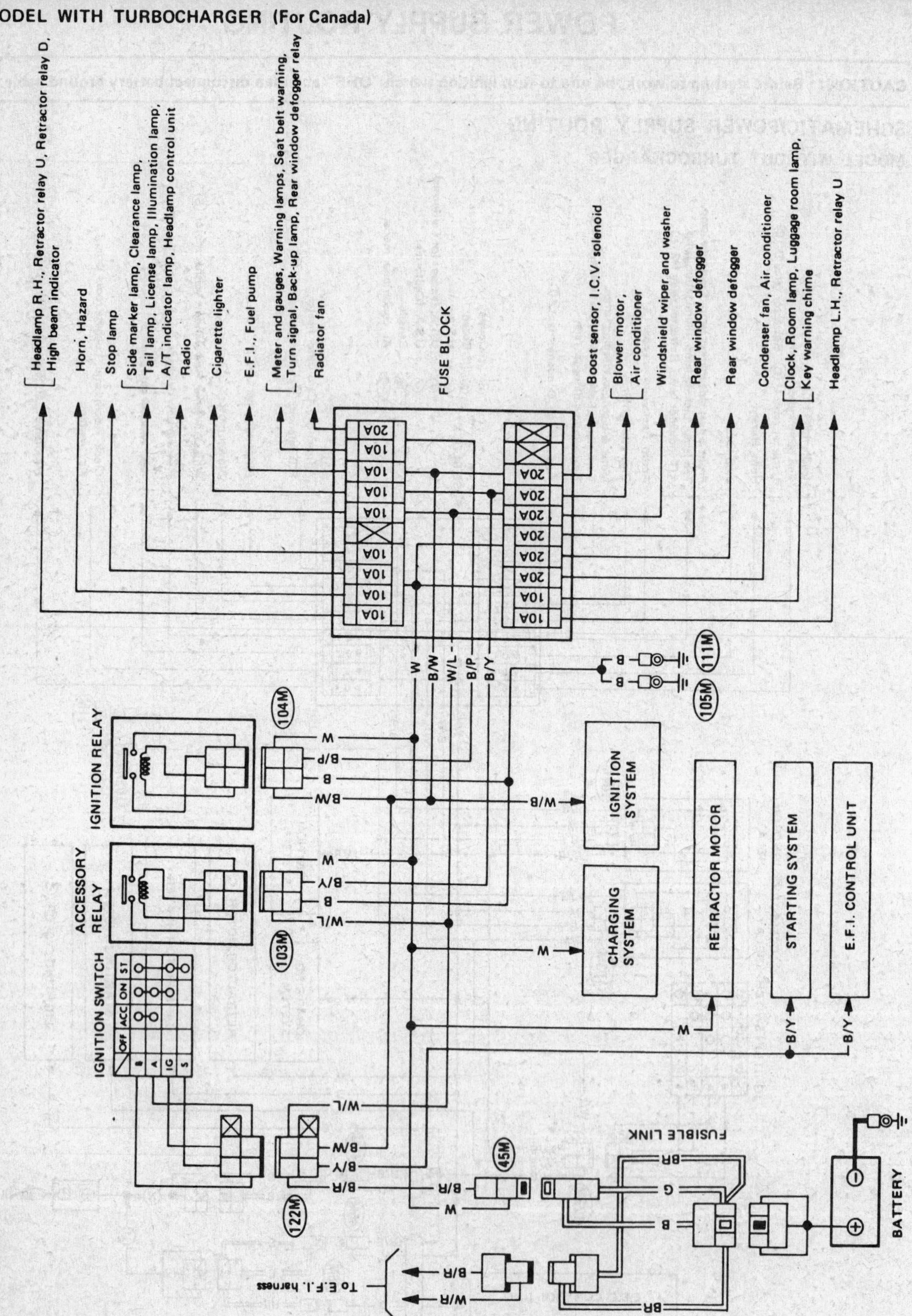
Headlamp R.H., Retractor relay U, Retractor relay D, High beam indicator
Horn, Hazard
Stop lamp
Side marker lamp, Clearance lamp, Tail lamp, License lamp, Illumination lamp, A/T indicator lamp, Headlamp control unit
Radio
Cigarette lighter
E.F.I., Fuel pump
Meter and gauges, Warning lamps, Seat belt warning, Turn signal, Back-up lamp, Rear window defogger relay
Radiator fan
FUSE BLOCK
Boost sensor, I.C.V. solenoid
Blower motor, Air conditioner
Windshield wiper and washer
Rear window defogger
Rear window defogger
Condenser fan, Air conditioner
Clock, Room lamp, Luggage room lamp, Key warning chime
Headlamp L.H., Retractor relay U
IGNITION RELAY
ACCESSORY RELAY
IGNITION SWITCH
IGNITION SYSTEM
CHARGING SYSTEM
RETRACTOR MOTOR
STARTING SYSTEM
E.F.I. CONTROL UNIT
FUSIBLE LINK
BATTERY
To E.F.I. harness

Fig. 17. Power supply wiring diagram — 1984 Pulsar

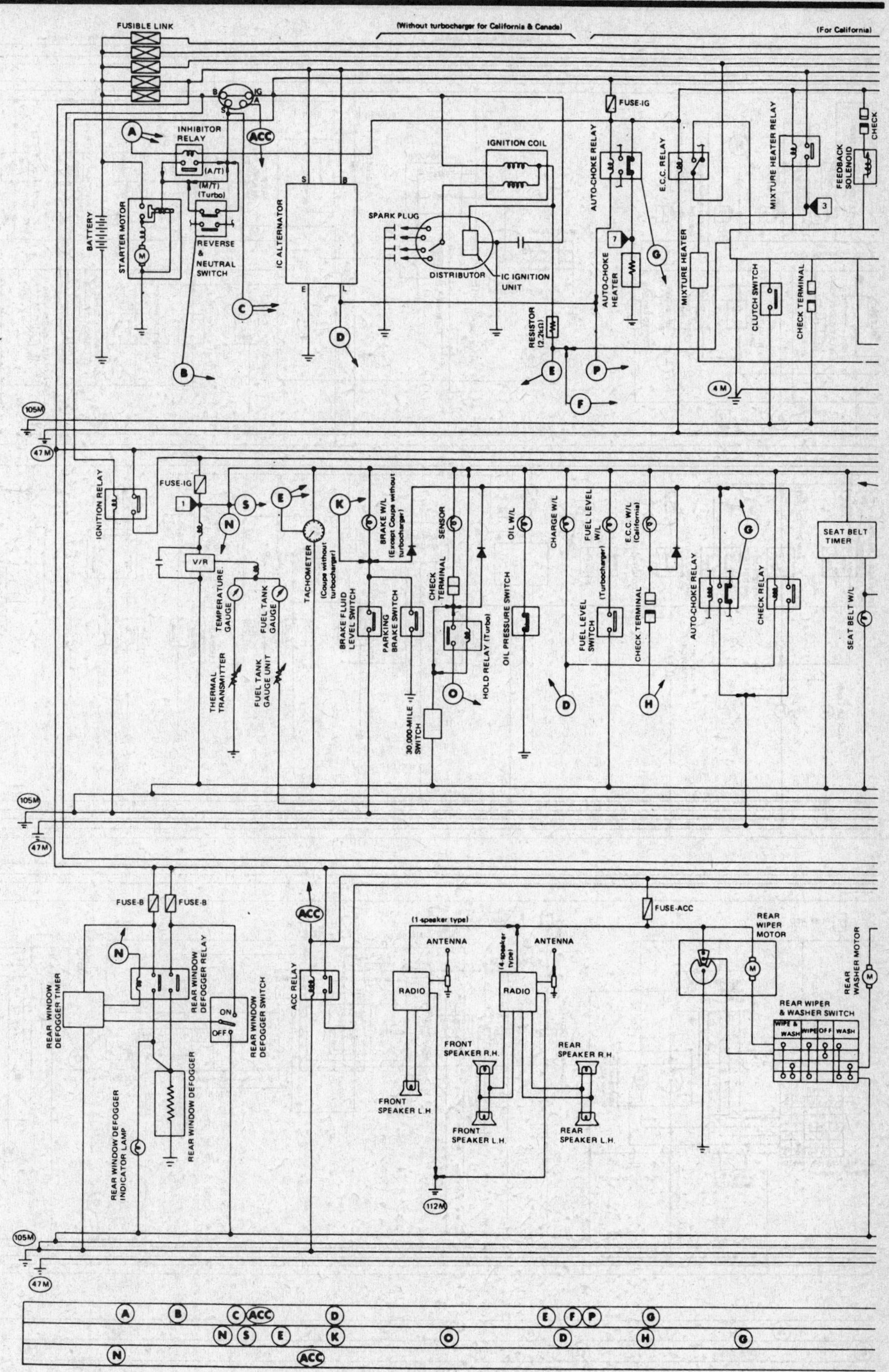
FUSIBLE LINK
(Without turbocharger for California & Canada)
(For California)
INHIBITOR RELAY
IGNITION COIL
FUSE-IG
AUTO-CHOKE RELAY
E.C.C. RELAY
MIXTURE HEATER RELAY
FEEDBACK SOLENOID
CHECK
(A/T)
(M/T)
(Turbo)
REVERSE & NEUTRAL SWITCH
BATTERY
STARTER MOTOR
IC ALTERNATOR
SPARK PLUG
DISTRIBUTOR
IC IGNITION UNIT
AUTO-CHOKE HEATER
MIXTURE HEATER
CLUTCH SWITCH
CHECK TERMINAL
RESISTOR (2.2kΩ)
IGNITION RELAY
FUSE-IG
V/R
TEMPERATURE GAUGE
FUEL TANK GAUGE
TACHOMETER
(Coupe without turbocharger)
BRAKE W/L
(Except Coupe without turbocharger)
SENSOR
OIL W/L
CHARGE W/L
FUEL LEVEL W/L
E.C.C. W/L
(California)
SEAT BELT TIMER
THERMAL TRANSMITTER
FUEL TANK GAUGE UNIT
BRAKE FLUID LEVEL SWITCH
PARKING BRAKE SWITCH
CHECK TERMINAL
HOLD RELAY (Turbo)
OIL PRESSURE SWITCH
FUEL LEVEL SWITCH
(Turbocharger)
AUTO-CHOKE RELAY
CHECK RELAY
SEAT BELT W/L
30,000-MILE SWITCH
FUSE-B
FUSE-B
FUSE-ACC
(1 speaker type)
ANTENNA
RADIO
(4 speaker type)
REAR WIPER MOTOR
REAR WASHER MOTOR
REAR WIPER & WASHER SWITCH
WIPE & WASH
WIPE
OFF
WASH
REAR WINDOW DEFOGGER TIMER
REAR WINDOW DEFOGGER RELAY
REAR WINDOW DEFOGGER SWITCH
ON
OFF
ACC RELAY
FRONT SPEAKER R.H.
REAR SPEAKER R.H.
FRONT SPEAKER L.H.
REAR SPEAKER L.H.
REAR WINDOW DEFOGGER INDICATOR LAMP
REAR WINDOW DEFOGGER
105M
47M
4M
112M

Fig. 18. Chassis wiring diagram — 1984 Pulsar

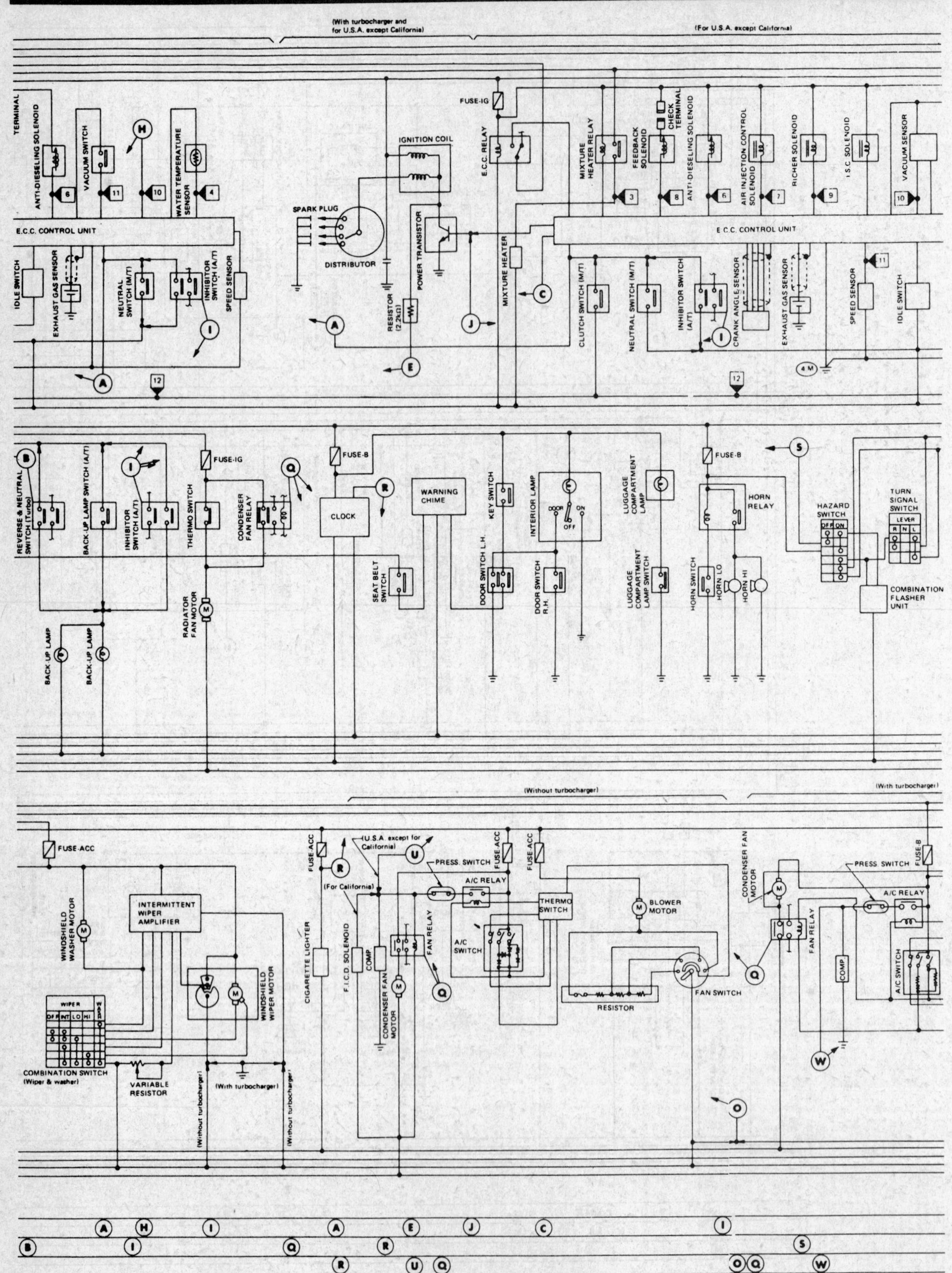
(With turbocharger and for U.S.A. except California)
(For U.S.A. except California)
TERMINAL
ANTI-DIESELING SOLENOID
VACUUM SWITCH
WATER TEMPERATURE SENSOR
E.C.C. CONTROL UNIT
IDLE SWITCH
EXHAUST GAS SENSOR
NEUTRAL SWITCH (M/T)
INHIBITOR SWITCH (A/T)
SPEED SENSOR
SPARK PLUG
DISTRIBUTOR
IGNITION COIL
POWER TRANSISTOR
RESISTOR (2.2kΩ)
FUSE-IG
E.C.C. RELAY
MIXTURE HEATER
MIXTURE HEATER RELAY
FEEDBACK SOLENOID
CHECK TERMINAL
AIR INJECTION CONTROL SOLENOID
RICHER SOLENOID
I.S.C. SOLENOID
VACUUM SENSOR
CLUTCH SWITCH (M/T)
CRANK ANGLE SENSOR
REVERSE & NEUTRAL SWITCH (Turbo)
BACK-UP LAMP SWITCH (A/T)
THERMO SWITCH
CONDENSER FAN RELAY
BACK-UP LAMP
RADIATOR FAN MOTOR
FUSE-B
CLOCK
WARNING CHIME
SEAT BELT SWITCH
KEY SWITCH
INTERIOR LAMP
DOOR
OFF
ON
DOOR SWITCH L.H.
DOOR SWITCH R.H.
LUGGAGE COMPARTMENT LAMP
LUGGAGE COMPARTMENT LAMP SWITCH
HORN RELAY
HORN SWITCH
HORN LO
HORN HI
HAZARD SWITCH
TURN SIGNAL SWITCH
LEVER
COMBINATION FLASHER UNIT
(Without turbocharger)
(With turbocharger)
FUSE-ACC
INTERMITTENT WIPER AMPLIFIER
WINDSHIELD WASHER MOTOR
WINDSHIELD WIPER MOTOR
WIPER
COMBINATION SWITCH (Wiper & washer)
VARIABLE RESISTOR
(Without turbocharger)
(With turbocharger)
CIGARETTE LIGHTER
(U.S.A. except for California)
(For California)
F.I.C.D. SOLENOID
COMP
CONDENSER FAN MOTOR
FAN RELAY
PRESS. SWITCH
A/C RELAY
A/C SWITCH
THERMO SWITCH
BLOWER MOTOR
RESISTOR
FAN SWITCH

Fig. 18. Chassis wiring diagram — 1984 Pulsar

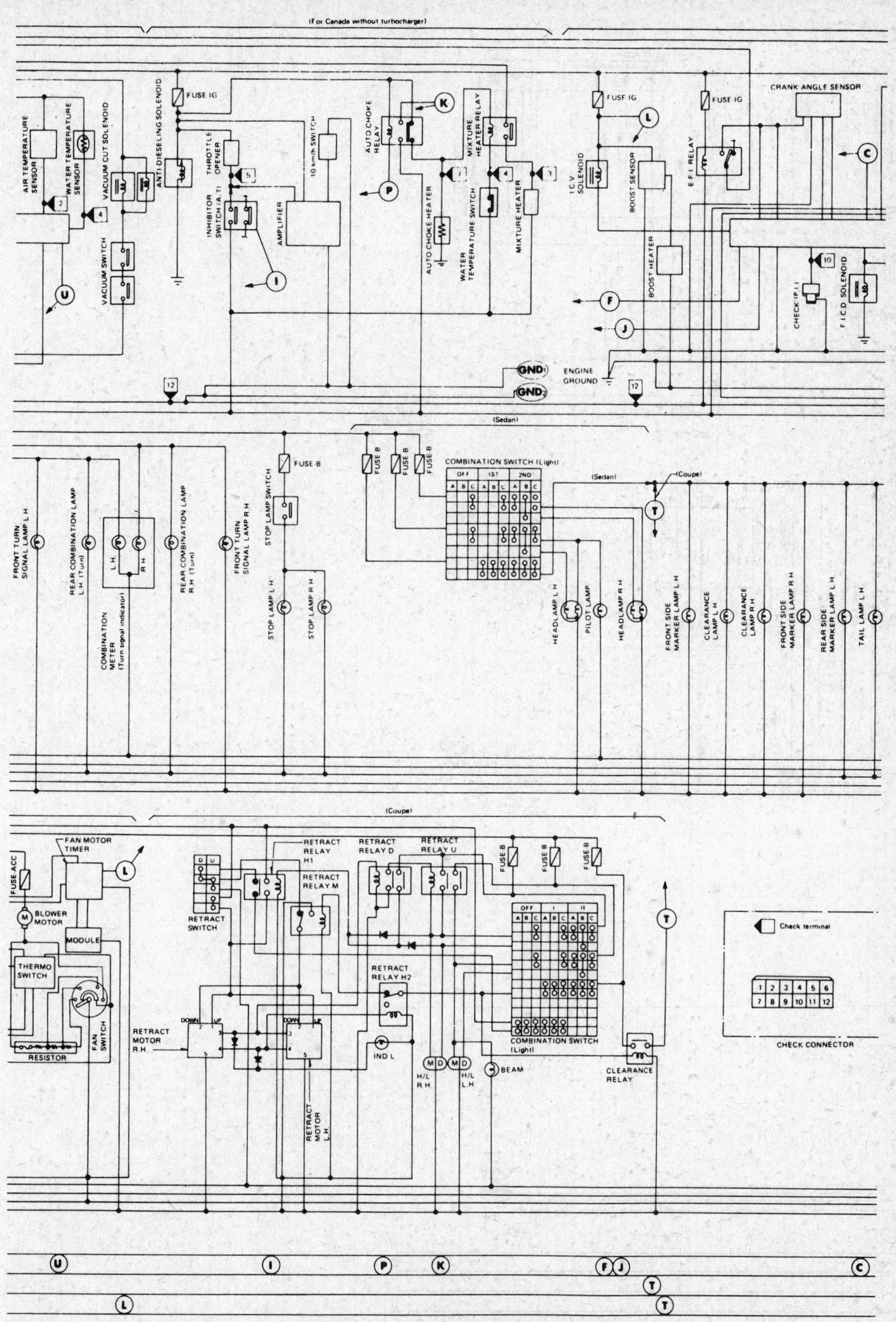

Fig. 19. Chassis wiring diagram — 1984 Pulsar

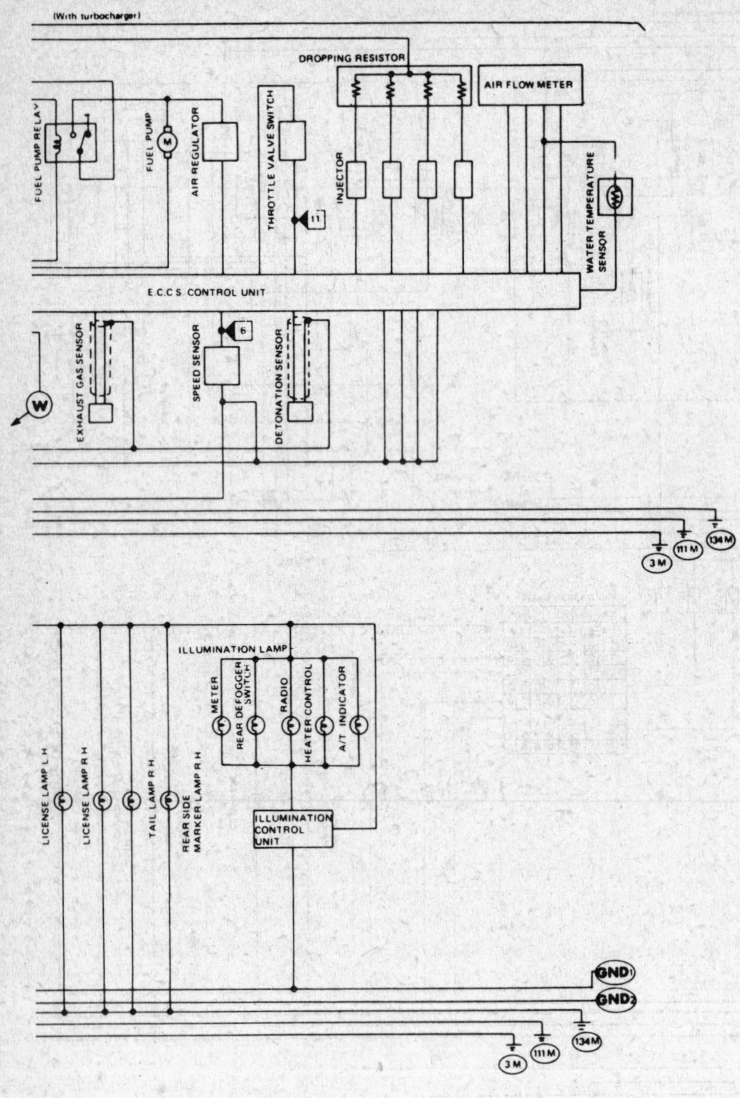

(With turbocharger)
DROPPING RESISTOR
AIR FLOW METER
FUEL PUMP RELAY
FUEL PUMP
AIR REGULATOR
THROTTLE VALVE SWITCH
INJECTOR
WATER TEMPERATURE SENSOR
E.C.C.S. CONTROL UNIT
EXHAUST GAS SENSOR
SPEED SENSOR
DETONATION SENSOR
3M
111M
134M
ILLUMINATION LAMP
METER
REAR DEFOGGER SWITCH
RADIO
HEATER CONTROL
A/T INDICATOR
LICENSE LAMP L.H
LICENSE LAMP R.H
TAIL LAMP R.H
REAR SIDE MARKER LAMP R.H
ILLUMINATION CONTROL UNIT
GND1
GND2

GND1
GND2
111M
3M

Fig. 19. Chassis wiring diagram — 1984 Pulsar

LOCATION OF ELECTRICAL UNITS

CAUTION: Before starting to work, be sure to turn ignition switch "OFF" and then disconnect battery ground cable.

ENGINE COMPARTMENT

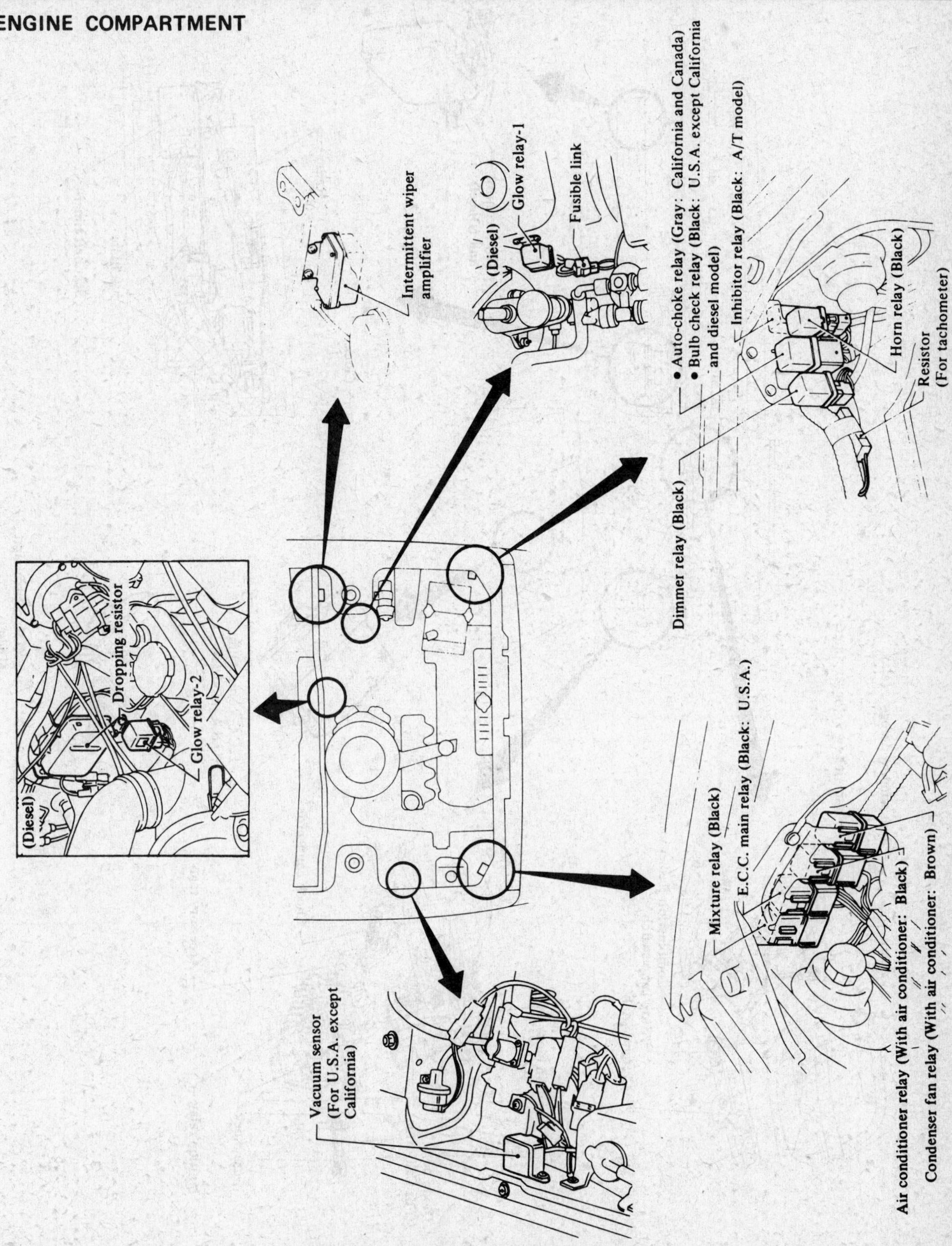

(Diesel)
Dropping resistor
Glow relay-2
Intermittent wiper amplifier
(Diesel)
Glow relay-1
Fusible link
• Auto-choke relay (Gray: California and Canada)
• Bulb check relay (Black: U.S.A. except California and diesel model)
Inhibitor relay (Black: A/T model)
Horn relay (Black)
Resistor (For tachometer)
Dimmer relay (Black)
Mixture relay (Black)
E.C.C. main relay (Black: U.S.A.)
Air conditioner relay (With air conditioner: Black)
Condenser fan relay (With air conditioner: Brown)
Vacuum sensor (For U.S.A. except California)

Fig. 20. Electrical component location — 1985 Sentra

PASSENGER COMPARTMENT

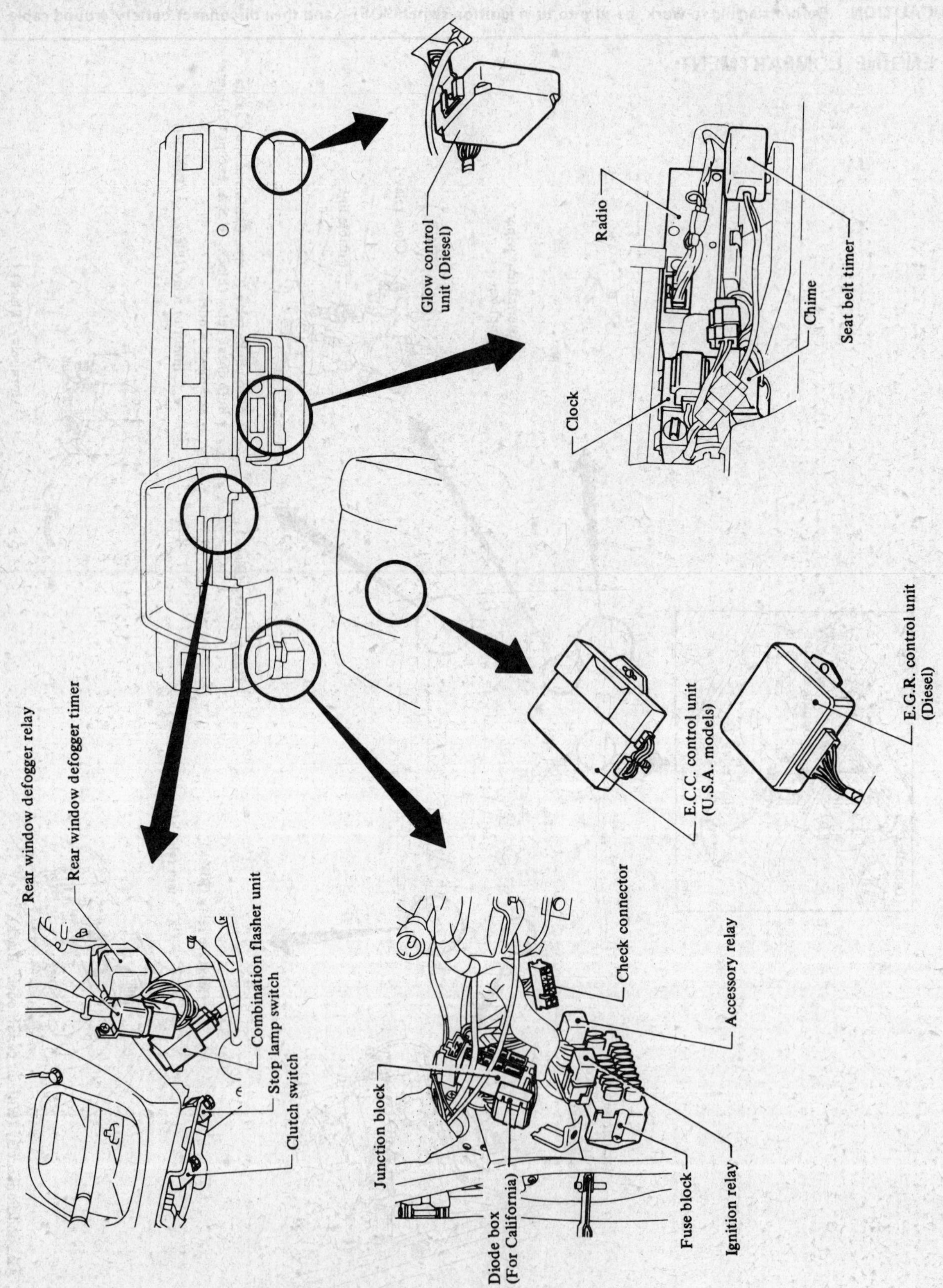

Glow control
unit (Diesel)
Radio
Clock
Chime
Seat belt timer
E.C.C. control unit
(U.S.A. models)
E.G.R. control unit
(Diesel)
Rear window defogger relay
Rear window defogger timer
Combination flasher unit
Stop lamp switch
Clutch switch
Junction block
Diode box
(For California)
Check connector
Accessory relay
Fuse block
Ignition relay

Fig. 20. Electrical component location — 1985 Sentra

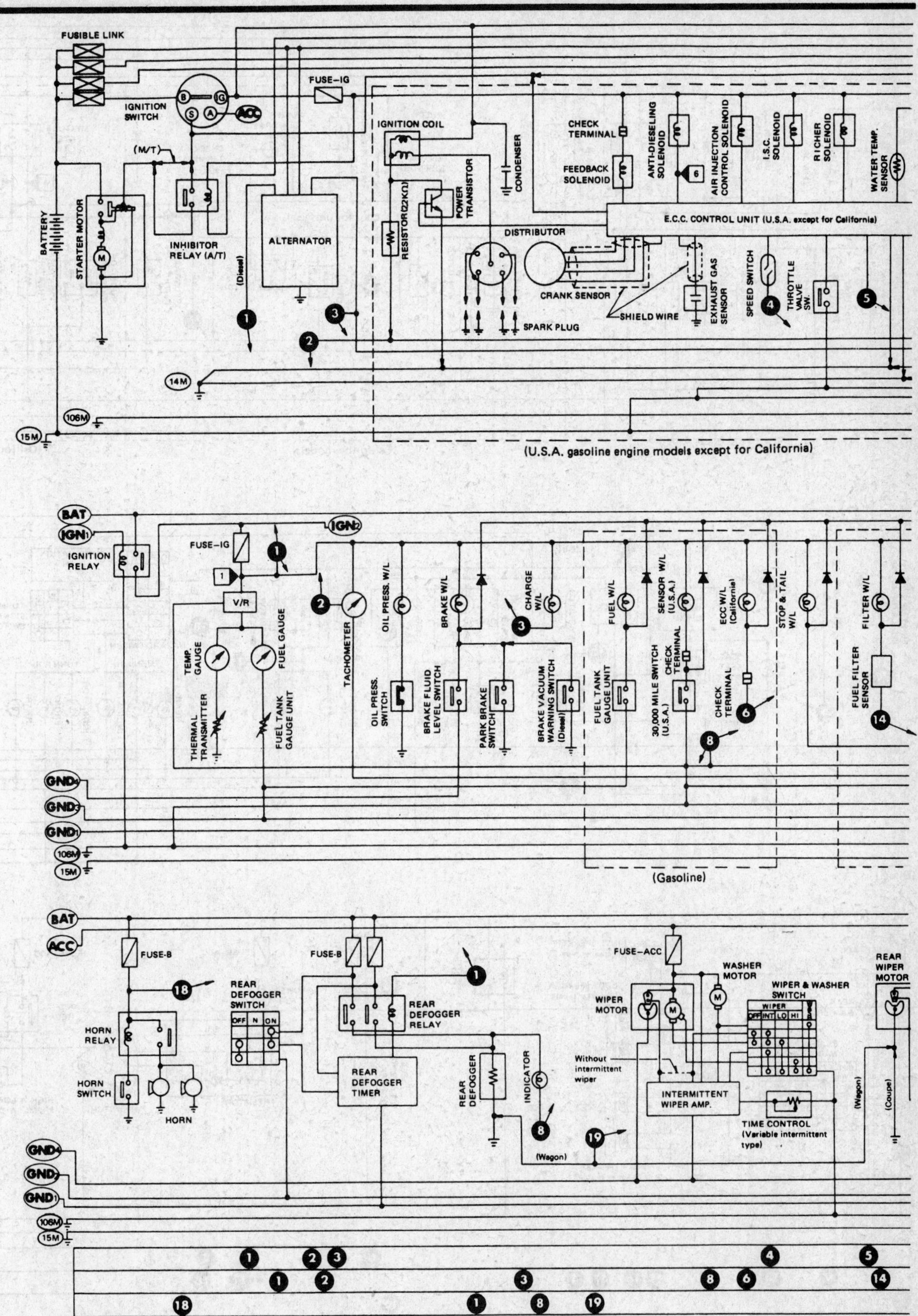
FUSIBLE LINK
IGNITION SWITCH
FUSE-IG
IGNITION COIL
CHECK TERMINAL
FEEDBACK SOLENOID
ANTI-DIESELING SOLENOID
AIR INJECTION CONTROL SOLENOID
I.S.C. SOLENOID
RICHER SOLENOID
WATER TEMP. SENSOR
E.C.C. CONTROL UNIT (U.S.A. except for California)
BATTERY
STARTER MOTOR
INHIBITOR RELAY (A/T)
ALTERNATOR
RESISTOR
POWER TRANSISTOR
CONDENSER
DISTRIBUTOR
CRANK SENSOR
SHIELD WIRE
SPARK PLUG
EXHAUST GAS SENSOR
SPEED SWITCH
THROTTLE VALVE SW.
(U.S.A. gasoline engine models except for California)
IGNITION RELAY
V/R
TEMP. GAUGE
FUEL GAUGE
THERMAL TRANSMITTER
FUEL TANK GAUGE UNIT
TACHOMETER
OIL PRESS. W/L
OIL PRESS. SWITCH
BRAKE W/L
BRAKE FLUID LEVEL SWITCH
PARK BRAKE SWITCH
CHARGE W/L
BRAKE VACUUM WARNING SWITCH (Diesel)
FUEL W/L
SENSOR W/L (U.S.A.)
30,000 MILE SWITCH (U.S.A.)
ECC W/L (California)
CHECK TERMINAL
STOP & TAIL W/L
FILTER W/L
FUEL FILTER SENSOR
(Gasoline)
FUSE-B
HORN RELAY
HORN SWITCH
HORN
REAR DEFOGGER SWITCH
REAR DEFOGGER RELAY
REAR DEFOGGER TIMER
REAR DEFOGGER
INDICATOR
(Wagon)
FUSE-ACC
WASHER MOTOR
WIPER MOTOR
WIPER & WASHER SWITCH
Without intermittent wiper
INTERMITTENT WIPER AMP.
TIME CONTROL (Variable intermittent type)
REAR WIPER MOTOR
(Coupe)

Fig. 22. Chassis wiring diagram — 1985 Sentra

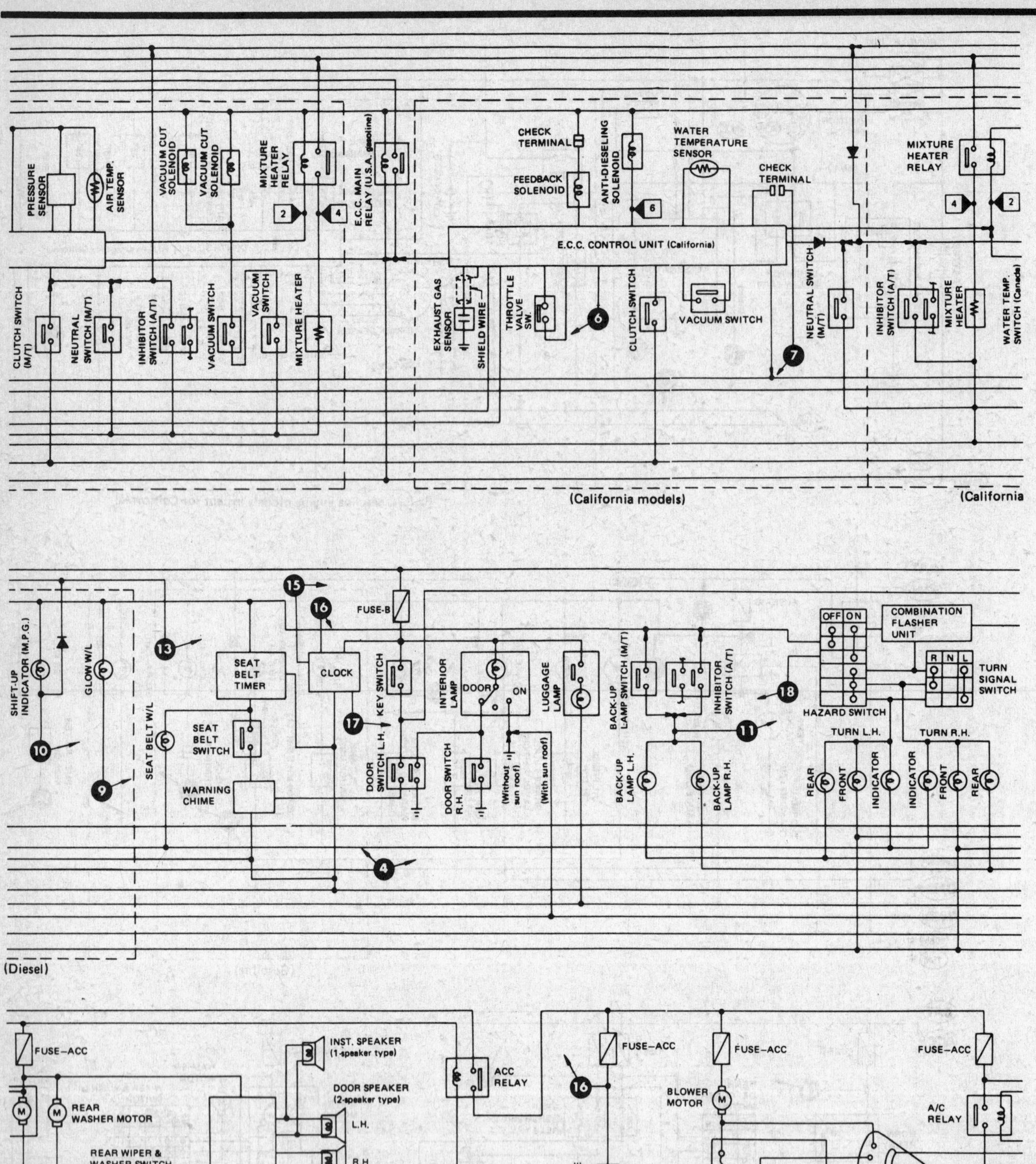
PRESSURE SENSOR
AIR TEMP. SENSOR
VACUUM CUT SOLENOID
VACUUM CUT SOLENOID
MIXTURE HEATER RELAY
E.C.C. MAIN RELAY (U.S.A. gasoline)
CLUTCH SWITCH (M/T)
NEUTRAL SWITCH (M/T)
INHIBITOR SWITCH (A/T)
VACUUM SWITCH
VACUUM SWITCH
MIXTURE HEATER
CHECK TERMINAL
FEEDBACK SOLENOID
ANTI-DIESELING SOLENOID
WATER TEMPERATURE SENSOR
CHECK TERMINAL
E.C.C. CONTROL UNIT (California)
EXHAUST GAS SENSOR
SHIELD WIRE
THROTTLE VALVE SW
CLUTCH SWITCH
VACUUM SWITCH
NEUTRAL SWITCH (M/T)
MIXTURE HEATER RELAY
INHIBITOR SWITCH (A/T)
MIXTURE HEATER
WATER TEMP. SWITCH (Canada)
(California models)
(California
SHIFT-UP INDICATOR (M.P.G.)
GLOW W/L
SEAT BELT W/L
SEAT BELT TIMER
SEAT BELT SWITCH
WARNING CHIME
CLOCK
FUSE-B
KEY SWITCH
INTERIOR LAMP
DOOR
ON
LUGGAGE LAMP
DOOR SWITCH L.H.
DOOR SWITCH R.H.
(Without sun roof)
(With sun roof)
BACK-UP LAMP SWITCH (M/T)
INHIBITOR SWITCH (A/T)
BACK-UP LAMP L.H.
BACK-UP LAMP R.H.
OFF ON
COMBINATION FLASHER UNIT
R N L
TURN SIGNAL SWITCH
HAZARD SWITCH
TURN L.H.
TURN R.H.
REAR
FRONT
INDICATOR
INDICATOR
FRONT
REAR
(Diesel)
FUSE-ACC
REAR WASHER MOTOR
REAR WIPER & WASHER SWITCH
WIPE & WASH
WIPE
OFF
WASH
RADIO
INST. SPEAKER (1-speaker type)
DOOR SPEAKER (2-speaker type)
L.H.
R.H.
L.H.
R.H.
REAR SPEAKER (4-Speaker type)
ACC RELAY
FUSE-ACC
CIGARETTE LIGHTER
FUSE-ACC
BLOWER MOTOR
RESISTOR
FAN SWITCH
FUSE-ACC
A/C RELAY
HIGH- & LOW-PRESS. SWITCH

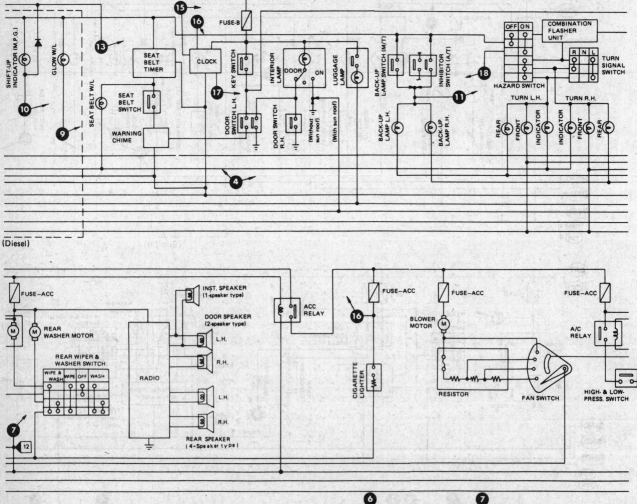

Fig. 22. Chassis wiring diagram — 1985 Sentra

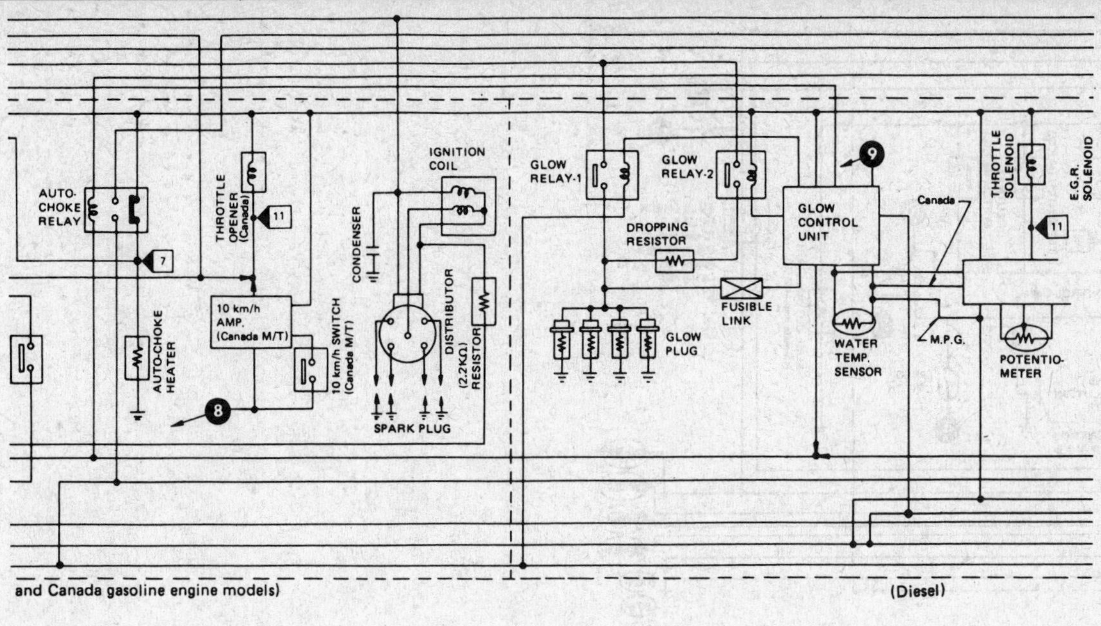
IGNITION COIL
GLOW RELAY-1
GLOW RELAY-2
AUTO-CHOKE RELAY
THROTTLE OPENER (Canada)
CONDENSER
DROPPING RESISTOR
GLOW CONTROL UNIT
Canada
THROTTLE SOLENOID
E.G.R. SOLENOID
10 km/h AMP. (Canada M/T)
AUTO-CHOKE HEATER
10 km/h SWITCH (Canada M/T)
DISTRIBUTOR
(2.2KΩ) RESISTOR
FUSIBLE LINK
GLOW PLUG
WATER TEMP. SENSOR
M.P.G.
POTENTIO-METER
SPARK PLUG
and Canada gasoline engine models)
(Diesel)

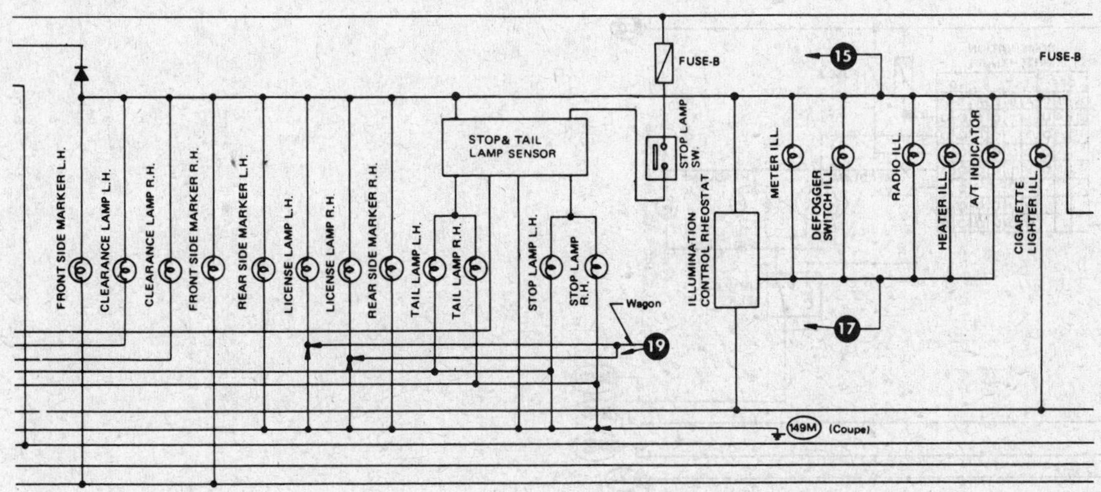
FUSE-B
FUSE-B
STOP& TAIL LAMP SENSOR
STOP LAMP SW.
METER ILL
DEFOGGER SWITCH ILL
RADIO ILL
HEATER ILL
A/T INDICATOR
CIGARETTE LIGHTER ILL
FRONT SIDE MARKER L.H.
CLEARANCE LAMP L.H.
CLEARANCE LAMP R.H.
FRONT SIDE MARKER R.H.
REAR SIDE MARKER L.H.
LICENSE LAMP L.H.
LICENSE LAMP R.H.
REAR SIDE MARKER R.H.
TAIL LAMP L.H.
TAIL LAMP R.H.
STOP LAMP L.H.
STOP LAMP R.H.
Wagon
ILLUMINATION CONTROL RHEOSTAT
149M (Coupe)

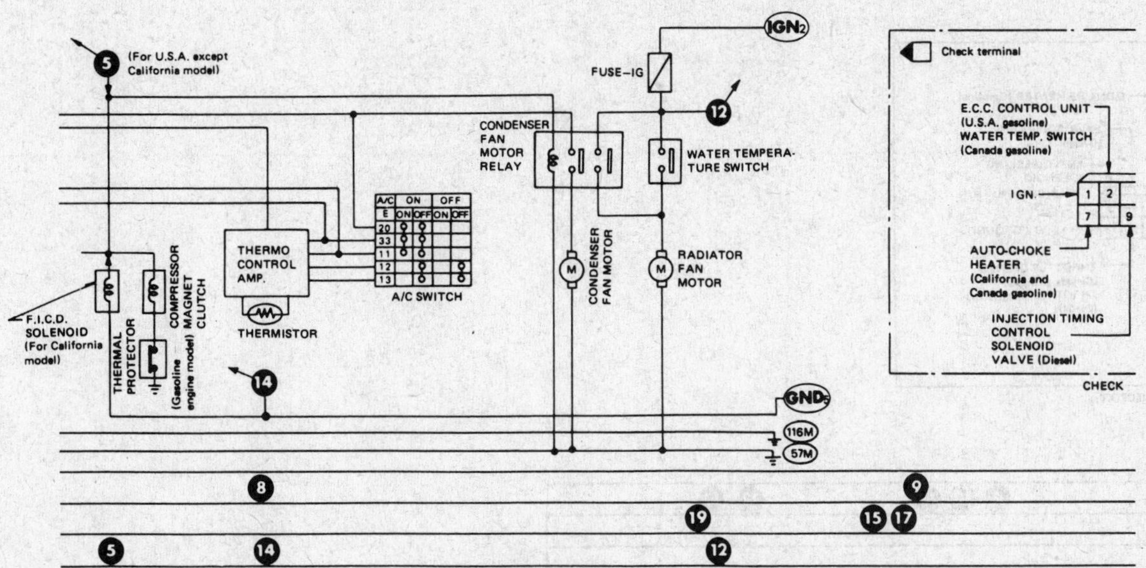
(For U.S.A. except California model)
IGN2
FUSE–IG
CONDENSER FAN MOTOR RELAY
WATER TEMPERATURE SWITCH
Check terminal
E.C.C. CONTROL UNIT (U.S.A. gasoline)
WATER TEMP. SWITCH (Canada gasoline)
IGN.
A/C ON OFF
E ON OFF ON OFF
THERMO CONTROL AMP.
A/C SWITCH
CONDENSER FAN MOTOR
RADIATOR FAN MOTOR
AUTO-CHOKE HEATER (California and Canada gasoline)
INJECTION TIMING CONTROL SOLENOID VALVE (Diesel)
F.I.C.D. SOLENOID (For California model)
THERMAL PROTECTOR
COMPRESSOR MAGNET CLUTCH
(Gasoline engine model)
THERMISTOR
CHECK
GND2
116M
57M

Fig. 23. Chassis wiring diagram — 1985 Sentra

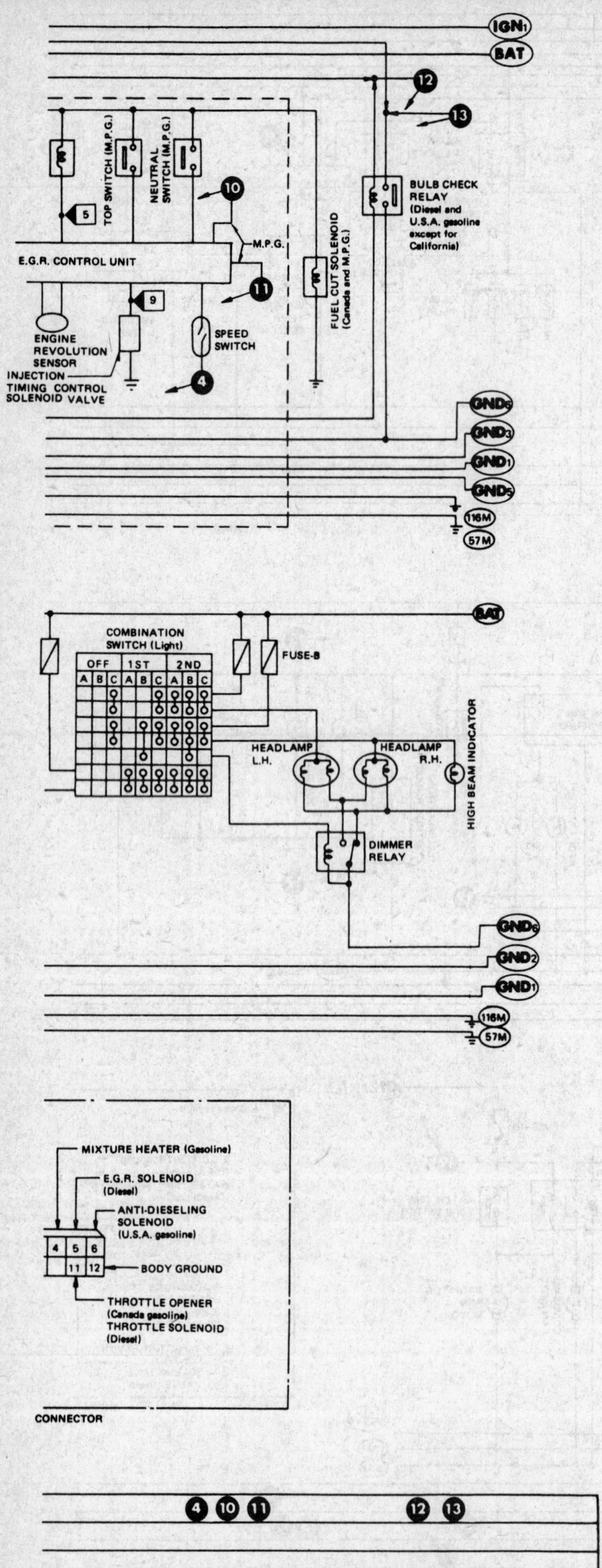
IGN1
BAT
12
13
TOP SWITCH (M.P.G.)
NEUTRAL SWITCH (M.P.G.)
10
5
M.P.G.
E.G.R. CONTROL UNIT
11
9
ENGINE REVOLUTION SENSOR
INJECTION TIMING CONTROL SOLENOID VALVE
SPEED SWITCH
4
FUEL CUT SOLENOID (Canada and M.P.G.)
BULB CHECK RELAY (Diesel and U.S.A. gasoline except for California)
GND6
GND3
GND1
GND5
116M
57M
BAT
COMBINATION SWITCH (Light)
OFF
1ST
2ND
A
B
C
FUSE-B
HEADLAMP L.H.
HEADLAMP R.H.
HIGH BEAM INDICATOR
DIMMER RELAY
GND6
GND2
GND1
116M
57M
MIXTURE HEATER (Gasoline)
E.G.R. SOLENOID (Diesel)
ANTI-DIESELING SOLENOID (U.S.A. gasoline)
4
5
6
11
12
BODY GROUND
THROTTLE OPENER (Canada gasoline)
THROTTLE SOLENOID (Diesel)
CONNECTOR
4
10
11
12
13

Fig. 23. Chassis wiring diagram — 1985 Sentra

LOCATION OF ELECTRICAL UNITS

CAUTION: Before starting to work, be sure to turn ignition switch "OFF" and then disconnect battery ground cable.

ENGINE COMPARTMENT

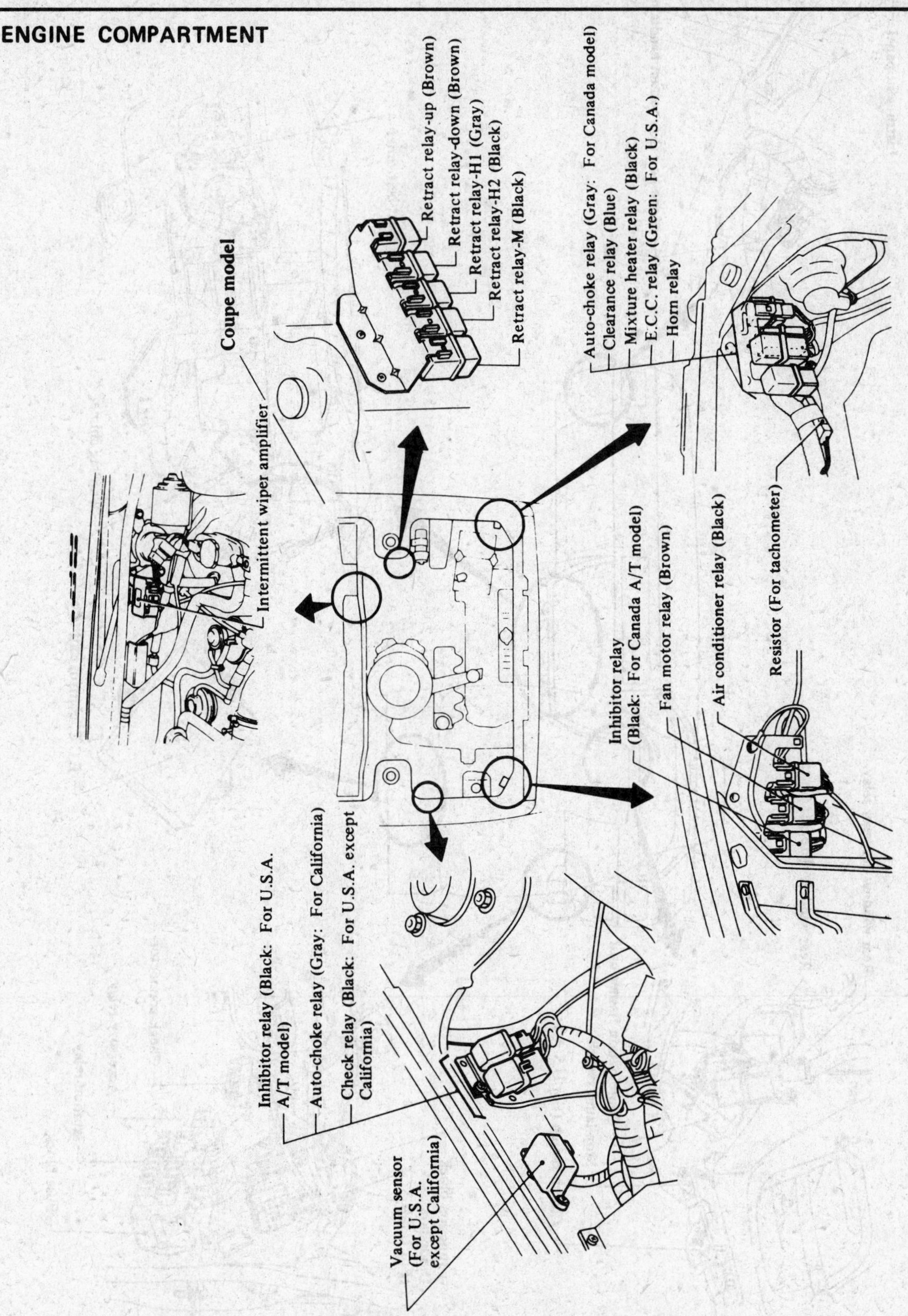

Coupe model
Retract relay-up (Brown)
Retract relay-down (Brown)
Retract relay-H1 (Gray)
Retract relay-H2 (Black)
Retract relay-M (Black)
Auto-choke relay (Gray: For Canada model)
Clearance relay (Blue)
Mixture heater relay (Black)
E.C.C. relay (Green: For U.S.A.)
Horn relay
Intermittent wiper amplifier
Inhibitor relay (Black: For Canada A/T model)
Fan motor relay (Brown)
Air conditioner relay (Black)
Resistor (For tachometer)
Inhibitor relay (Black: For U.S.A. A/T model)
Auto-choke relay (Gray: For California)
Check relay (Black: For U.S.A. except California)
Vacuum sensor (For U.S.A. except California)

Fig. 24. Electrical component location — 1985 Pulsar

PASSENGER COMPARTMENT

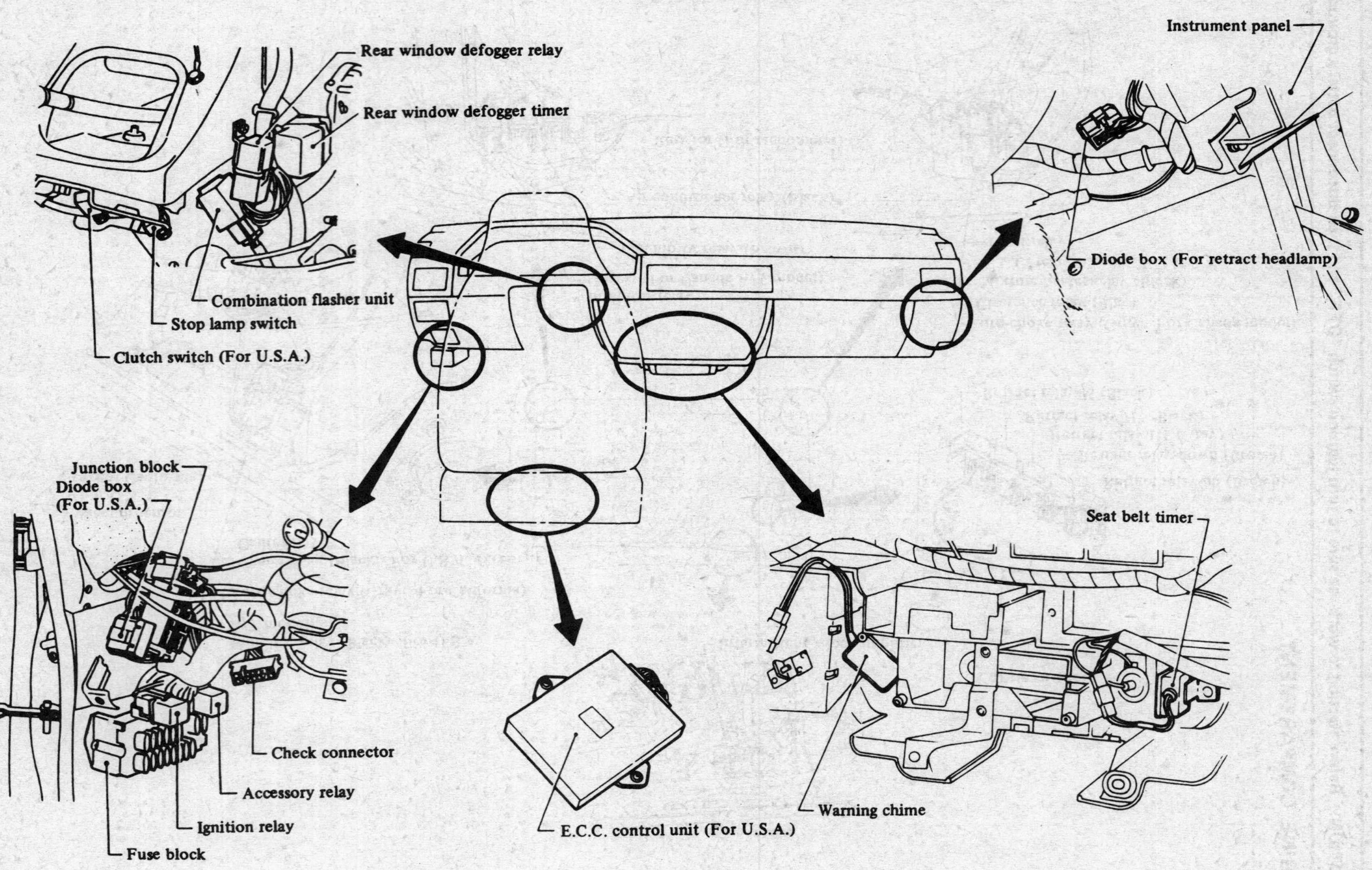
Rear window defogger relay
Rear window defogger timer
Combination flasher unit
Stop lamp switch
Clutch switch (For U.S.A.)
Instrument panel
Diode box (For retract headlamp)
Junction block
Diode box
(For U.S.A.)
Check connector
Accessory relay
Ignition relay
Fuse block
E.C.C. control unit (For U.S.A.)
Seat belt timer
Warning chime

Fig. 24. Electrical component location — 1985 Pulsar

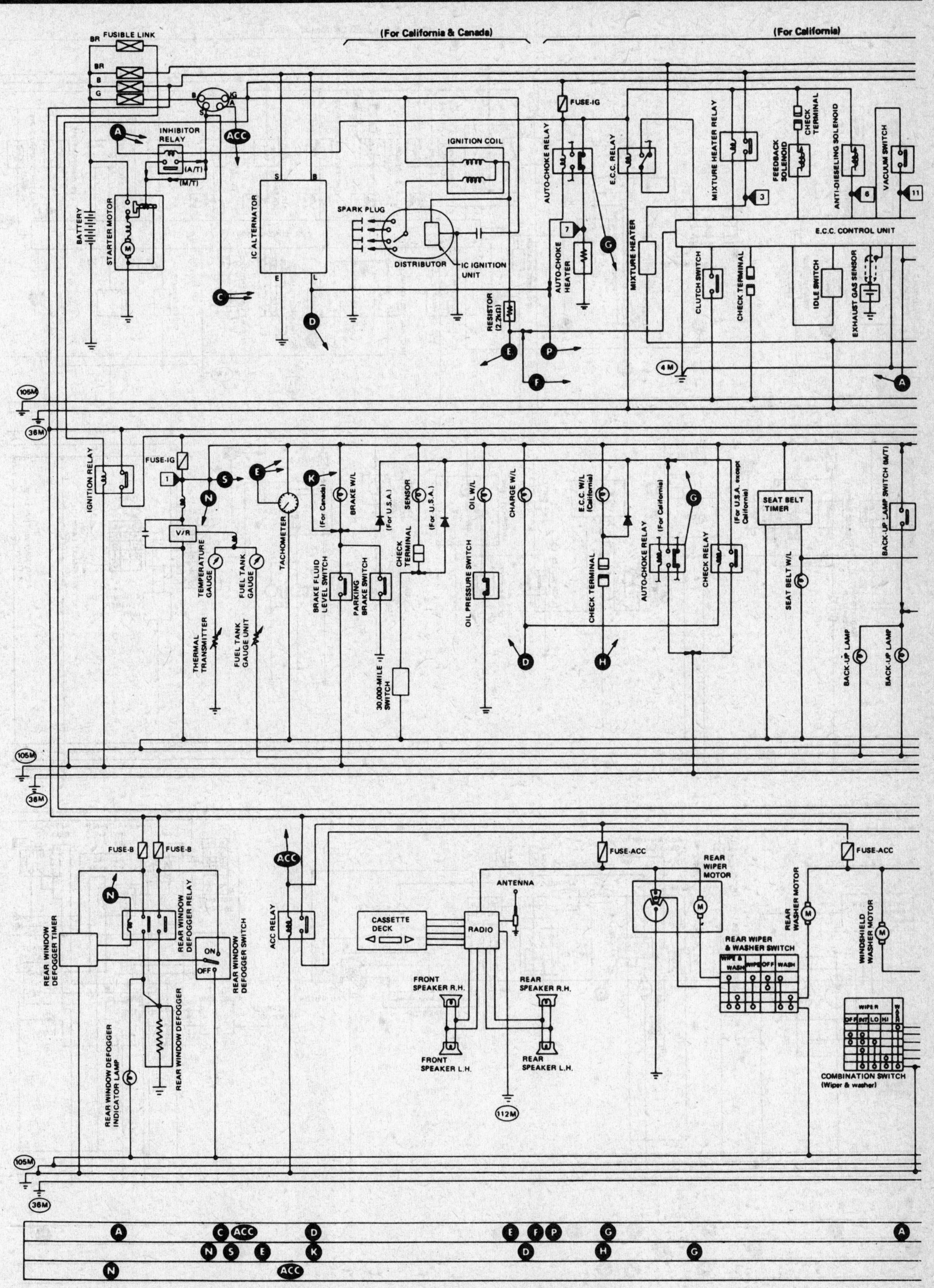

Fig. 25. Chassis wiring diagram — 1985 Pulsar

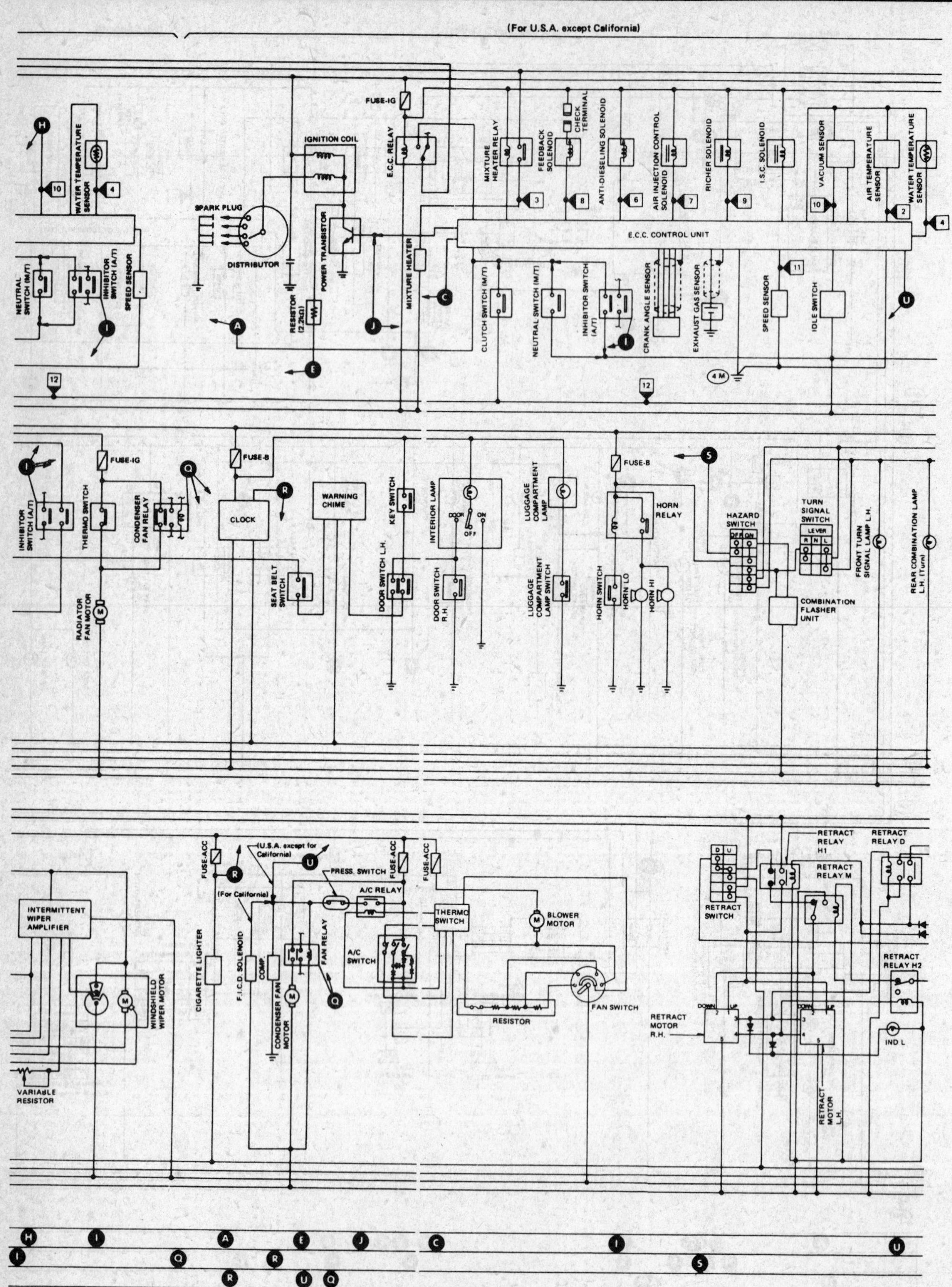
(For U.S.A. except California)
FUSE-IG
IGNITION COIL
E.C.C. RELAY
MIXTURE HEATER RELAY
FEEDBACK SOLENOID
CHECK TERMINAL
ANTI-DIESELING SOLENOID
AIR INJECTION CONTROL SOLENOID
RICHER SOLENOID
I.S.C. SOLENOID
VACUUM SENSOR
AIR TEMPERATURE SENSOR
WATER TEMPERATURE SENSOR
SPARK PLUG
DISTRIBUTOR
POWER TRANSISTOR
RESISTOR (2.2kΩ)
MIXTURE HEATER
E.C.C. CONTROL UNIT
NEUTRAL SWITCH (M/T)
INHIBITOR SWITCH (A/T)
SPEED SENSOR
CLUTCH SWITCH (M/T)
CRANK ANGLE SENSOR
EXHAUST GAS SENSOR
IDLE SWITCH
FUSE-B
THERMO SWITCH
CONDENSER FAN RELAY
RADIATOR FAN MOTOR
CLOCK
WARNING CHIME
SEAT BELT SWITCH
KEY SWITCH
DOOR SWITCH L.H.
INTERIOR LAMP
DOOR
ON
OFF
DOOR SWITCH R.H.
LUGGAGE COMPARTMENT LAMP
LUGGAGE COMPARTMENT LAMP SWITCH
HORN RELAY
HORN SWITCH
HORN LO
HORN HI
HAZARD SWITCH
OFF ON
TURN SIGNAL SWITCH
LEVER
R N L
COMBINATION FLASHER UNIT
FRONT TURN SIGNAL LAMP L.H.
REAR COMBINATION LAMP L.H. (Turn)
INTERMITTENT WIPER AMPLIFIER
WINDSHIELD WIPER MOTOR
VARIABLE RESISTOR
FUSE-ACC
(U.S.A. except for California)
(For California)
CIGARETTE LIGHTER
F.I.C.D. SOLENOID
COMP.
CONDENSER FAN MOTOR
FAN RELAY
PRESS. SWITCH
A/C RELAY
A/C SWITCH
THERMO SWITCH
BLOWER MOTOR
RESISTOR
FAN SWITCH
RETRACT SWITCH
RETRACT RELAY H1
RETRACT RELAY D
RETRACT RELAY M
RETRACT RELAY H2
RETRACT MOTOR R.H.
RETRACT MOTOR L.H.
IND L
DOWN
UP

Fig. 25. Chassis wiring diagram — 1985 Pulsar

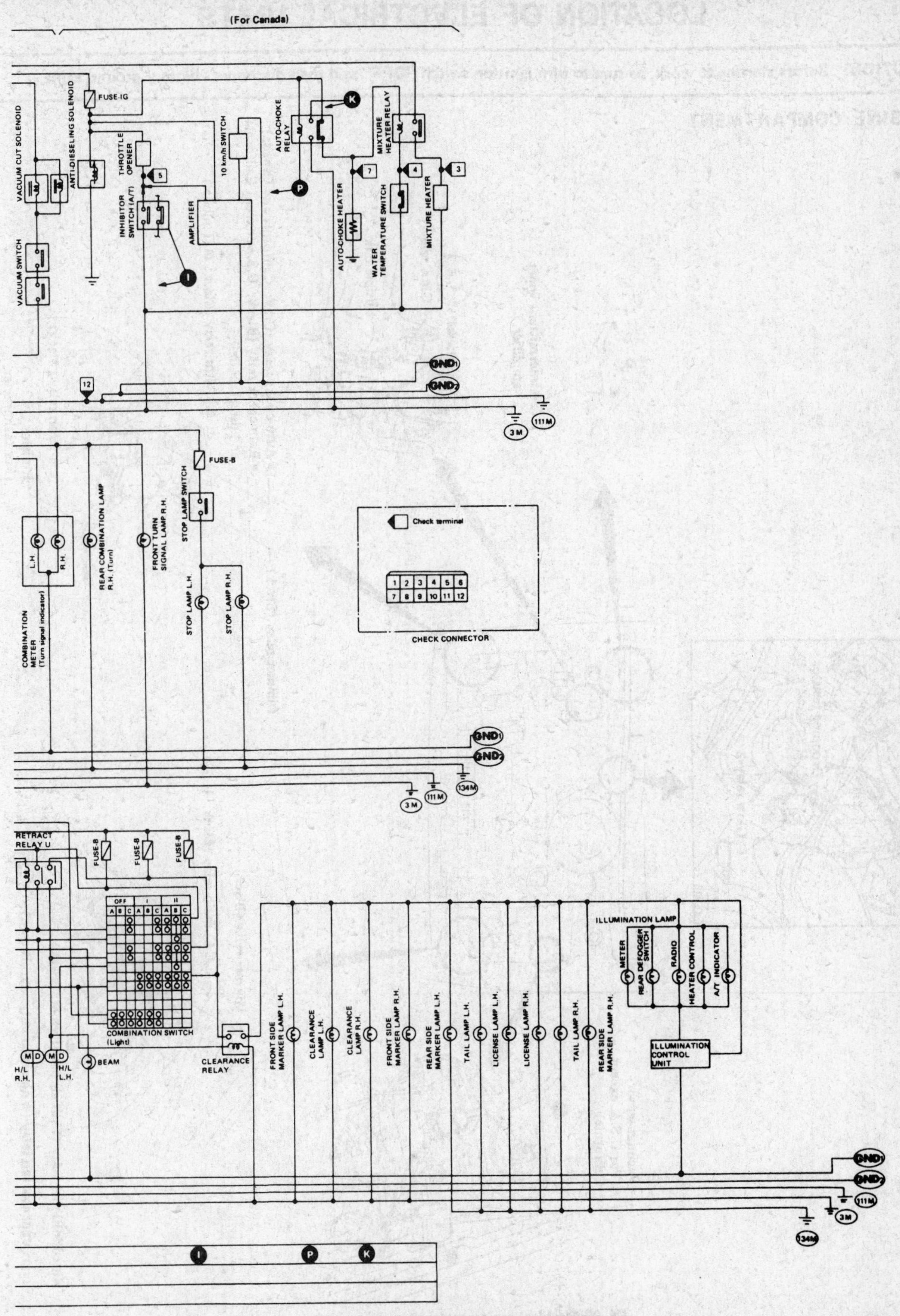
(For Canada)
FUSE-IG
VACUUM CUT SOLENOID
ANTI-DIESELING SOLENOID
THROTTLE OPENER
INHIBITOR SWITCH (A/T)
AMPLIFIER
10 km/h SWITCH
AUTO-CHOKE RELAY
MIXTURE HEATER RELAY
AUTO-CHOKE HEATER
WATER TEMPERATURE SWITCH
MIXTURE HEATER
VACUUM SWITCH
GND1
GND2
3 M
111 M
134M
FUSE-B
COMBINATION METER (Turn signal indicator)
L.H.
R.H.
REAR COMBINATION LAMP R.H. (Turn)
FRONT TURN SIGNAL LAMP R.H.
STOP LAMP SWITCH
STOP LAMP L.H.
STOP LAMP R.H.
Check terminal
CHECK CONNECTOR
RETRACT RELAY U
OFF
COMBINATION SWITCH (Light)
H/L R.H.
H/L L.H.
BEAM
CLEARANCE RELAY
FRONT SIDE MARKER LAMP L.H.
CLEARANCE LAMP L.H.
CLEARANCE LAMP R.H.
FRONT SIDE MARKER LAMP R.H.
REAR SIDE MARKER LAMP L.H.
TAIL LAMP L.H.
LICENSE LAMP L.H.
LICENSE LAMP R.H.
TAIL LAMP R.H.
REAR SIDE MARKER LAMP R.H.
ILLUMINATION LAMP
METER
REAR DEFOGGER SWITCH
RADIO
HEATER CONTROL
A/T INDICATOR
ILLUMINATION CONTROL UNIT

Fig. 26. Chassis wiring diagram — 1985 Pulsar

LOCATION OF ELECTRICAL UNITS

CAUTION: Before starting to work, be sure to turn ignition switch "OFF" and then disconnect battery ground cable.

ENGINE COMPARTMENT

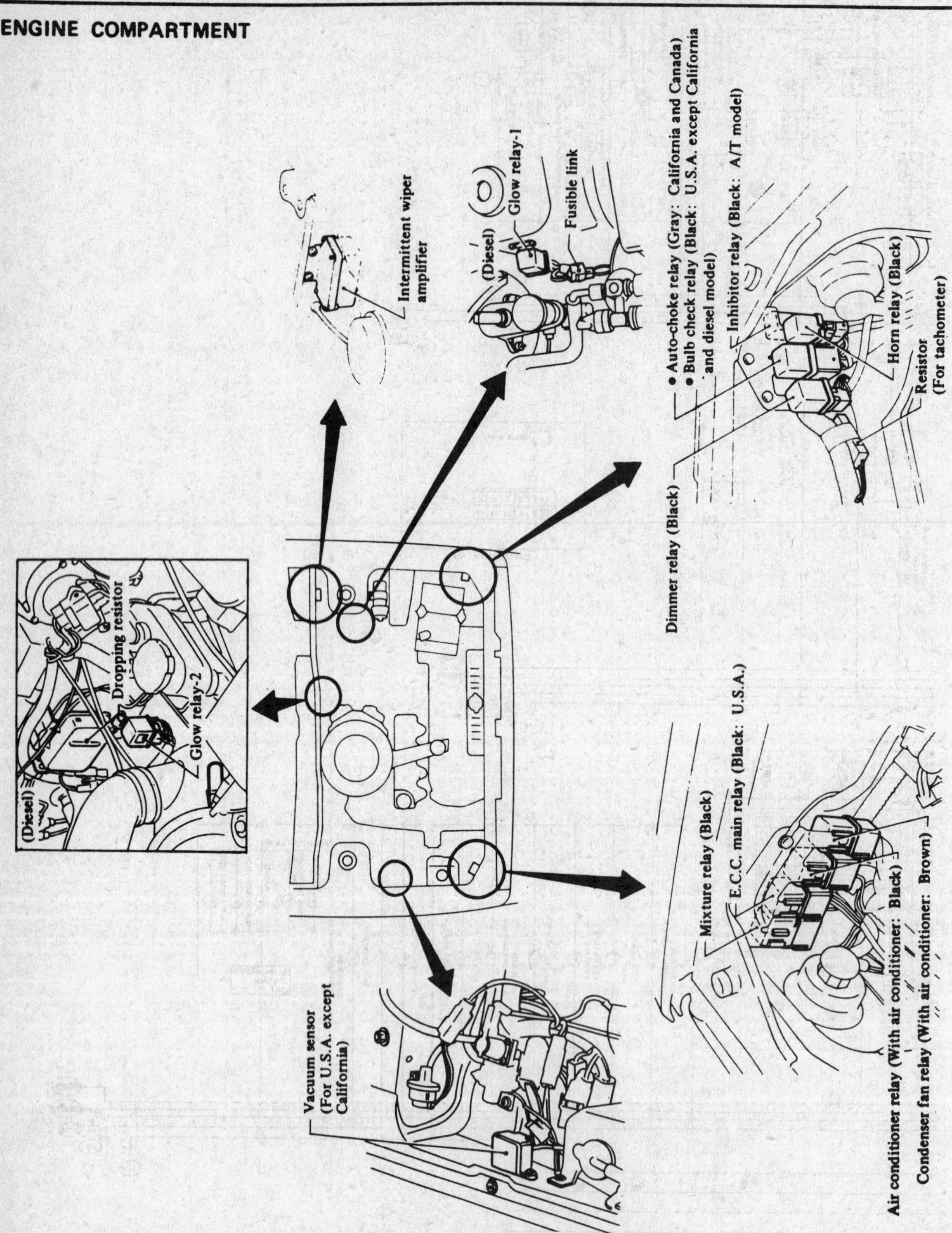

(Diesel)
Dropping resistor
Glow relay-2
Intermittent wiper amplifier
(Diesel)
Glow relay-1
Fusible link
● Auto-choke relay (Gray: California and Canada)
● Bulb check relay (Black: U.S.A. except California and diesel model)
Inhibitor relay (Black: A/T model)
Dimmer relay (Black)
Horn relay (Black)
Resistor (For tachometer)
Vacuum sensor (For U.S.A. except California)
Mixture relay (Black)
E.C.C. main relay (Black: U.S.A.)
Air conditioner relay (With air conditioner: Black)
Condenser fan relay (With air conditioner: Brown)

Fig. 27. Electrical component location — 1986 Sentra

PASSENGER COMPARTMENT

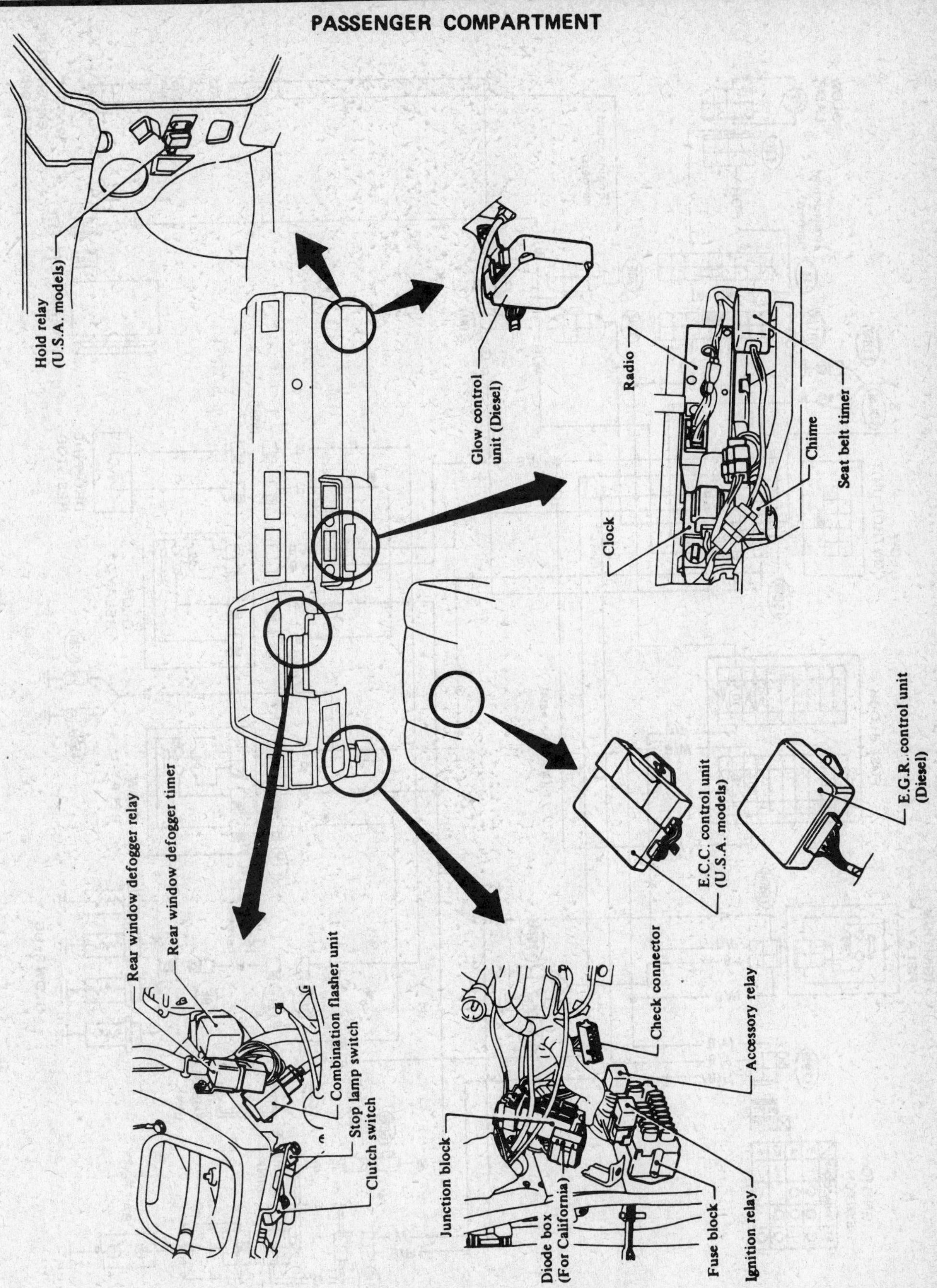
Hold relay
(U.S.A. models)
Glow control
unit (Diesel)
Radio
Clock
Chime
Seat belt timer
E.C.C. control unit
(U.S.A. models)
E.G.R. control unit
(Diesel)
Rear window defogger relay
Rear window defogger timer
Combination flasher unit
Stop lamp switch
Clutch switch
Check connector
Accessory relay
Junction block
Diode box
(For California)
Fuse block
Ignition relay

Fig. 27. Electrical component location — 1986 Sentra

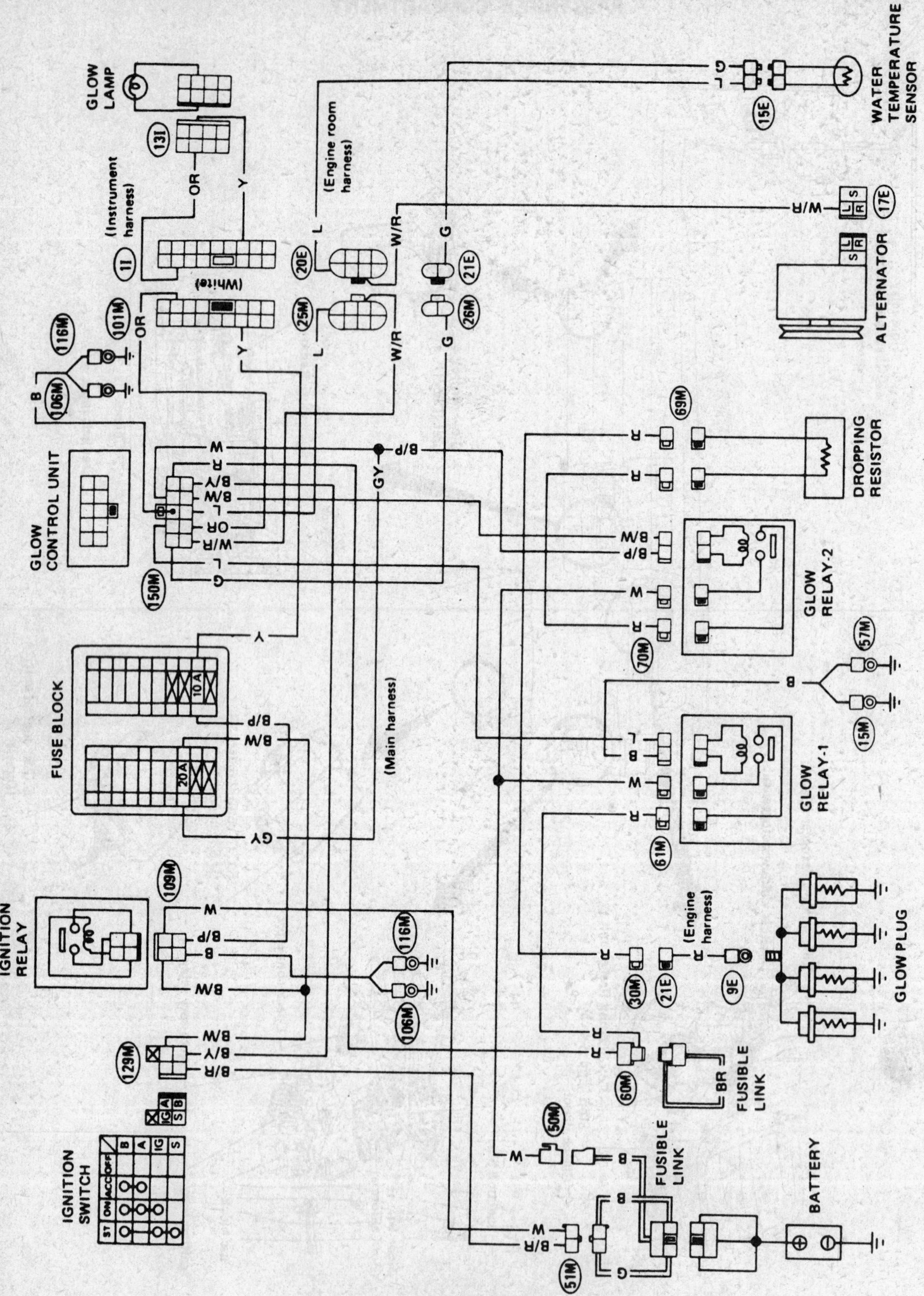
GLOW LAMP
(Instrument harness)
(Engine room harness)
(White)
WATER TEMPERATURE SENSOR
ALTERNATOR
GLOW CONTROL UNIT
DROPPING RESISTOR
GLOW RELAY-2
FUSE BLOCK
(Main harness)
GLOW RELAY-1
IGNITION RELAY
(Engine harness)
GLOW PLUG
FUSIBLE LINK
IGNITION SWITCH
BATTERY

Fig. 28. Quick glow wiring diagram — 1986 Sentra diesel

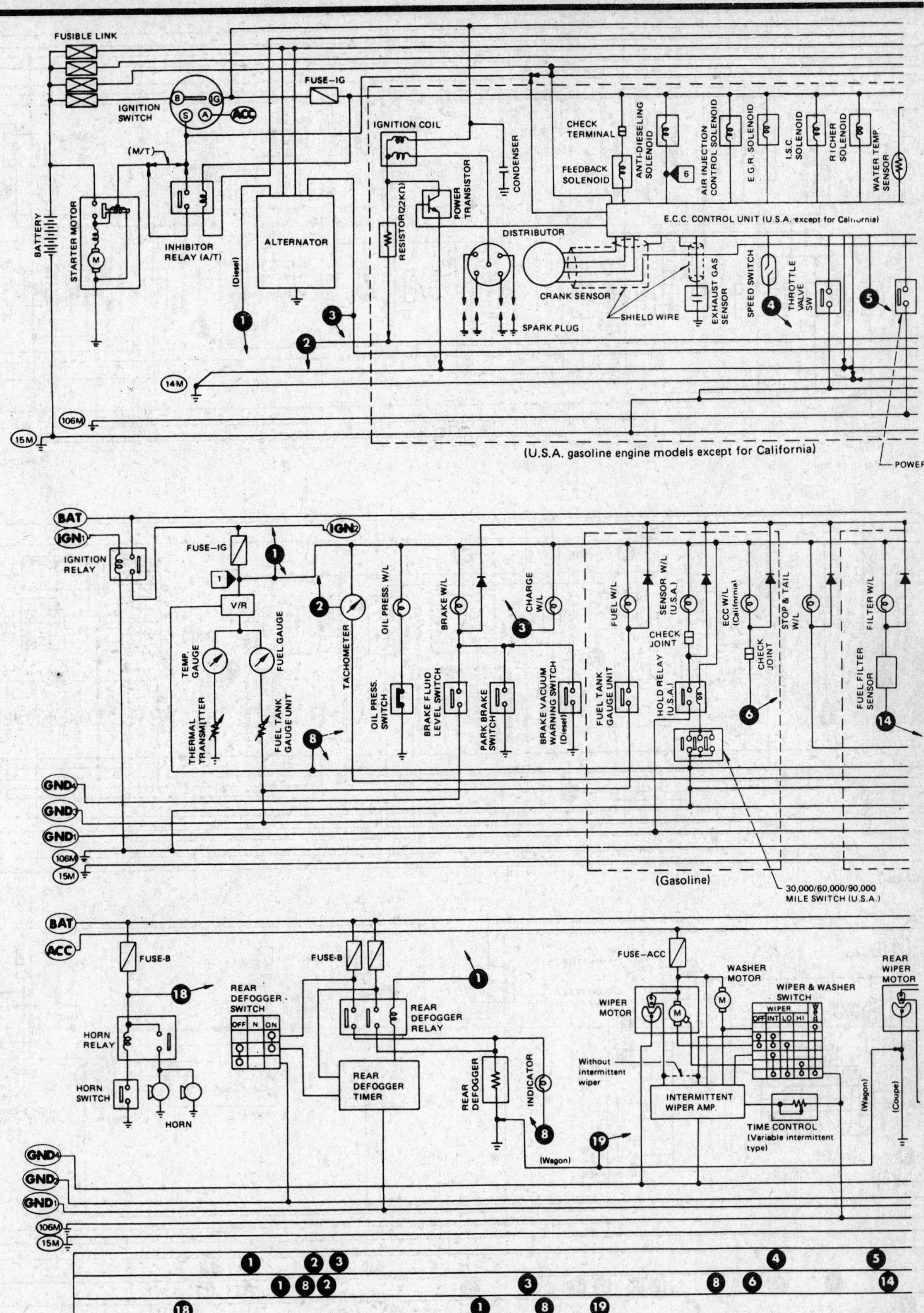
FUSIBLE LINK
IGNITION SWITCH
FUSE-IG
IGNITION COIL
CONDENSER
CHECK TERMINAL
FEEDBACK SOLENOID
ANTI-DIESELING SOLENOID
AIR INJECTION CONTROL SOLENOID
E.G.R. SOLENOID
I.S.C. SOLENOID
RICHER SOLENOID
WATER TEMP SENSOR
BATTERY
STARTER MOTOR
INHIBITOR RELAY (A/T)
ALTERNATOR
RESISTOR (2.2KΩ)
POWER TRANSISTOR
DISTRIBUTOR
E.C.C. CONTROL UNIT (U.S.A. except for California)
CRANK SENSOR
SHIELD WIRE
SPARK PLUG
EXHAUST GAS SENSOR
SPEED SWITCH
THROTTLE VALVE SW
(Diesel)
(U.S.A. gasoline engine models except for California)
POWER
IGNITION RELAY
V/R
TEMP. GAUGE
FUEL GAUGE
THERMAL TRANSMITTER
FUEL TANK GAUGE UNIT
TACHOMETER
OIL PRESS. W/L
OIL PRESS. SWITCH
BRAKE W/L
BRAKE FLUID LEVEL SWITCH
PARK BRAKE SWITCH
CHARGE W/L
BRAKE VACUUM WARNING SWITCH (Diesel)
FUEL W/L
FUEL TANK GAUGE UNIT
SENSOR W/L (U.S.A.)
CHECK JOINT
HOLD RELAY (U.S.A.)
ECC W/L (California)
CHECK JOINT
STOP & TAIL W/L
FILTER W/L
FUEL FILTER SENSOR
(Gasoline)
30,000/60,000/90,000 MILE SWITCH (U.S.A.)
FUSE-B
HORN RELAY
HORN SWITCH
HORN
REAR DEFOGGER SWITCH
OFF N ON
REAR DEFOGGER RELAY
REAR DEFOGGER TIMER
REAR DEFOGGER
INDICATOR
(Wagon)
FUSE-ACC
WASHER MOTOR
WIPER MOTOR
WIPER & WASHER SWITCH
WIPER
OFF INT LO HI
Without intermittent wiper
INTERMITTENT WIPER AMP.
TIME CONTROL (Variable intermittent type)
REAR WIPER MOTOR
(Wagon)
(Coupe)

Fig. 29. Chassis wiring diagram — 1986 Sentra

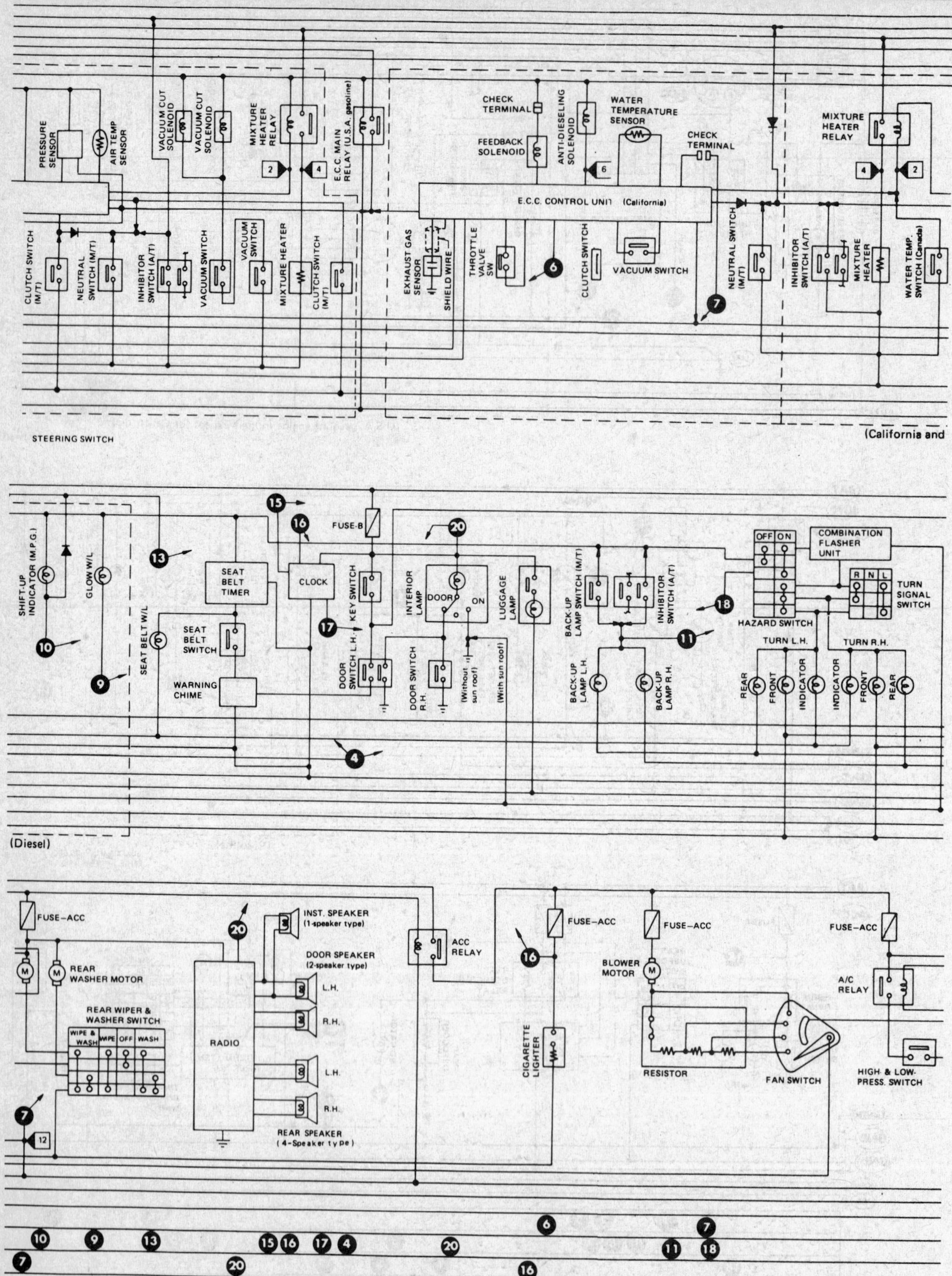

PRESSURE SENSOR
AIR TEMP SENSOR
VACUUM CUT SOLENOID
VACUUM CUT SOLENOID
MIXTURE HEATER RELAY
E.C.C. MAIN RELAY (U.S.A. gasoline)
CHECK TERMINAL
FEEDBACK SOLENOID
ANTI-DIESELING SOLENOID
WATER TEMPERATURE SENSOR
CHECK TERMINAL
MIXTURE HEATER RELAY
E.C.C. CONTROL UNIT (California)
CLUTCH SWITCH (M/T)
NEUTRAL SWITCH (M/T)
INHIBITOR SWITCH (A/T)
VACUUM SWITCH
VACUUM SWITCH
MIXTURE HEATER
CLUTCH SWITCH (M/T)
EXHAUST GAS SENSOR
SHIELD WIRE
THROTTLE VALVE SW
CLUTCH SWITCH
VACUUM SWITCH
NEUTRAL SWITCH (M/T)
INHIBITOR SWITCH (A/T)
MIXTURE HEATER
WATER TEMP. SWITCH (Canada)
STEERING SWITCH
(California and
SHIFT-UP INDICATOR (M.P.G.)
GLOW W/L
SEAT BELT W/L
SEAT BELT TIMER
SEAT BELT SWITCH
WARNING CHIME
CLOCK
FUSE-B
KEY SWITCH
DOOR SWITCH L.H.
INTERIOR LAMP
DOOR
ON
DOOR SWITCH R.H.
(Without sun roof)
(With sun roof)
LUGGAGE LAMP
BACK-UP LAMP SWITCH (M/T)
INHIBITOR SWITCH (A/T)
BACK-UP LAMP L.H.
BACK-UP LAMP R.H.
OFF
ON
COMBINATION FLASHER UNIT
R
N
L
TURN SIGNAL SWITCH
HAZARD SWITCH
TURN L.H.
TURN R.H.
REAR
FRONT
INDICATOR
INDICATOR
FRONT
REAR
(Diesel)
FUSE-ACC
REAR WASHER MOTOR
REAR WIPER & WASHER SWITCH
WIPE & WASH
WIPE
OFF
WASH
RADIO
INST. SPEAKER (1-speaker type)
DOOR SPEAKER (2-speaker type)
L.H.
R.H.
L.H.
R.H.
REAR SPEAKER (4-Speaker type)
ACC RELAY
FUSE-ACC
CIGARETTE LIGHTER
FUSE-ACC
BLOWER MOTOR
RESISTOR
FAN SWITCH
FUSE-ACC
A/C RELAY
HIGH & LOW-PRESS. SWITCH

Fig. 29. Chassis wiring diagram — 1986 Sentra

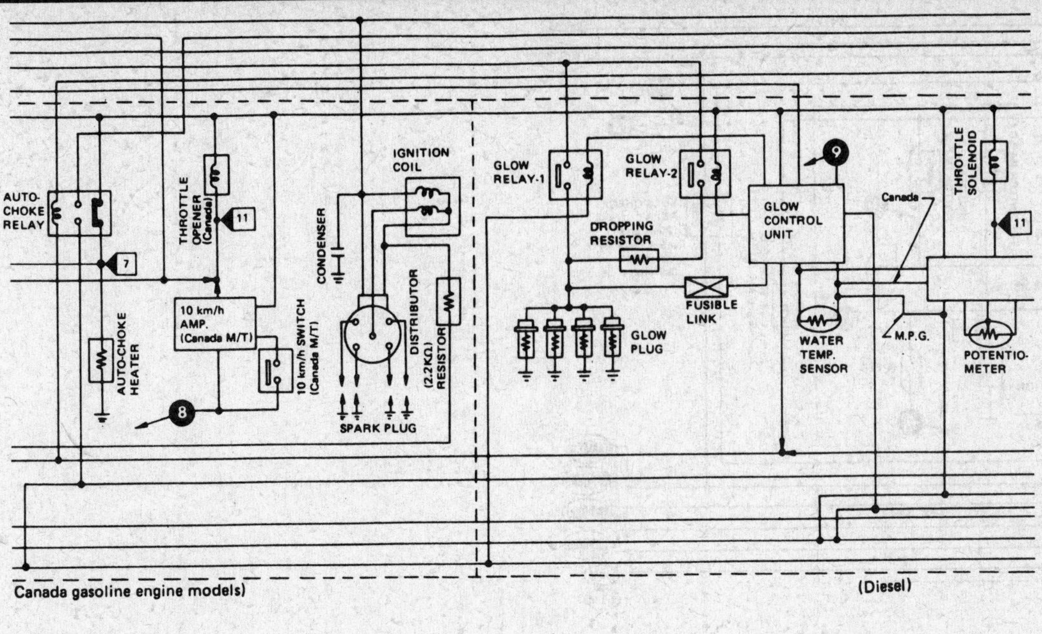
AUTO-CHOKE RELAY
THROTTLE OPENER (Canada)
AUTO-CHOKE HEATER
10 km/h AMP. (Canada M/T)
10 km/h SWITCH (Canada M/T)
IGNITION COIL
CONDENSER
DISTRIBUTOR
(2.2KΩ) RESISTOR
SPARK PLUG
GLOW RELAY-1
GLOW RELAY-2
DROPPING RESISTOR
GLOW CONTROL UNIT
FUSIBLE LINK
GLOW PLUG
WATER TEMP. SENSOR
Canada
M.P.G.
THROTTLE SOLENOID
POTENTIO-METER
Canada gasoline engine models)
(Diesel)

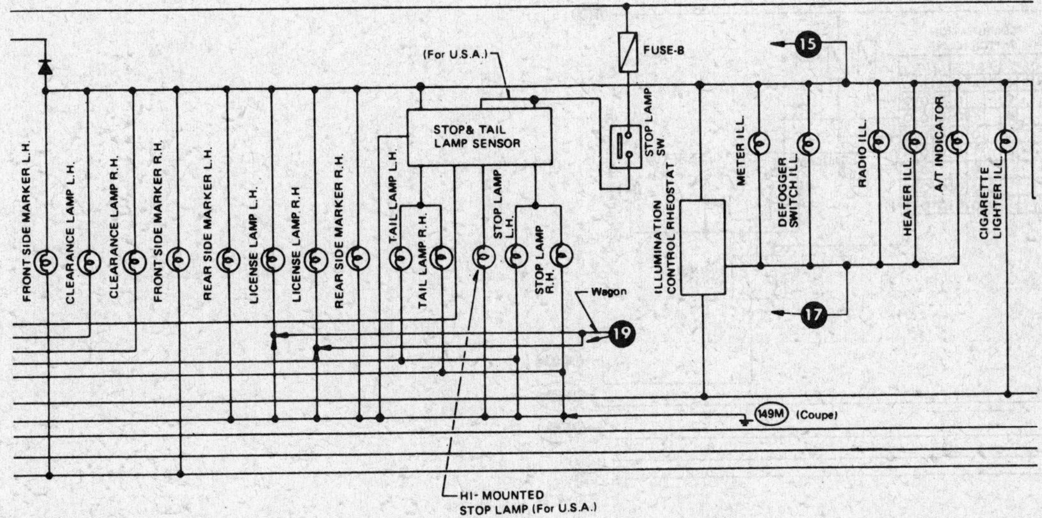
(For U.S.A.)
FUSE-B
STOP& TAIL LAMP SENSOR
STOP LAMP SW
FRONT SIDE MARKER L.H.
CLEARANCE LAMP L.H.
CLEARANCE LAMP R.H.
FRONT SIDE MARKER R.H.
REAR SIDE MARKER L.H.
LICENSE LAMP L.H.
LICENSE LAMP R.H
REAR SIDE MARKER R.H.
TAIL LAMP L.H.
TAIL LAMP R.H.
STOP LAMP L.H.
STOP LAMP R.H.
Wagon
ILLUMINATION CONTROL RHEOSTAT
METER ILL.
DEFOGGER SWITCH ILL.
RADIO ILL.
HEATER ILL.
A/T INDICATOR
CIGARETTE LIGHTER ILL.
149M (Coupe)
HI- MOUNTED STOP LAMP (For U.S.A.)

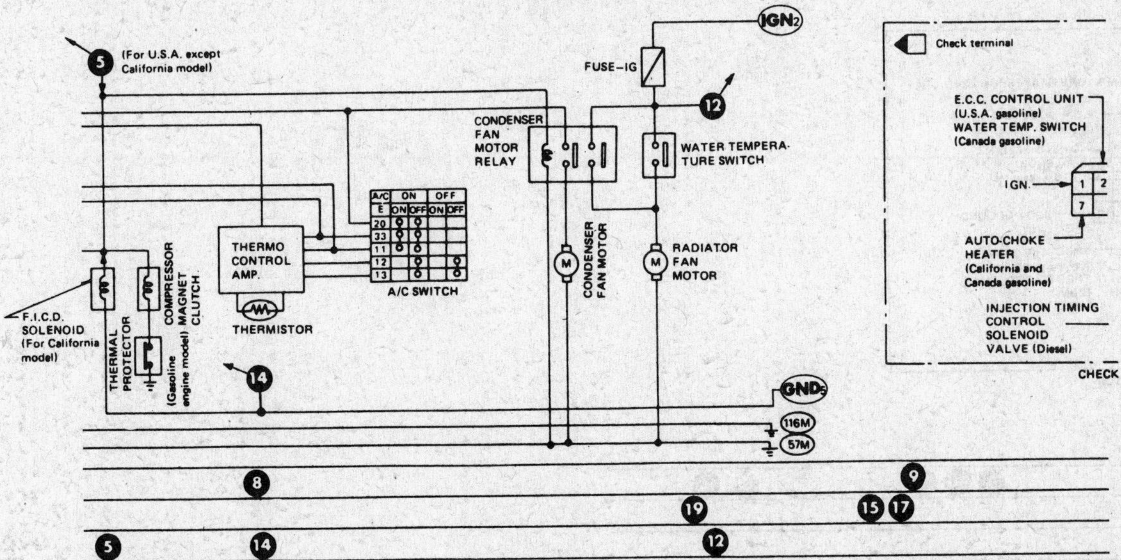
(For U.S.A. except California model)
FUSE-IG
IGN2
CONDENSER FAN MOTOR RELAY
WATER TEMPERA-TURE SWITCH
THERMO CONTROL AMP.
THERMISTOR
A/C SWITCH
CONDENSER FAN MOTOR
RADIATOR FAN MOTOR
F.I.C.D. SOLENOID (For California model)
THERMAL PROTECTOR
COMPRESSOR MAGNET CLUTCH
(Gasoline engine model)
GND
116M
57M
Check terminal
E.C.C. CONTROL UNIT (U.S.A. gasoline)
WATER TEMP. SWITCH (Canada gasoline)
IGN.
AUTO-CHOKE HEATER (California and Canada gasoline)
INJECTION TIMING CONTROL SOLENOID VALVE (Diesel)
CHECK

Fig. 30. Chassis wiring diagram — 1986 Sentra

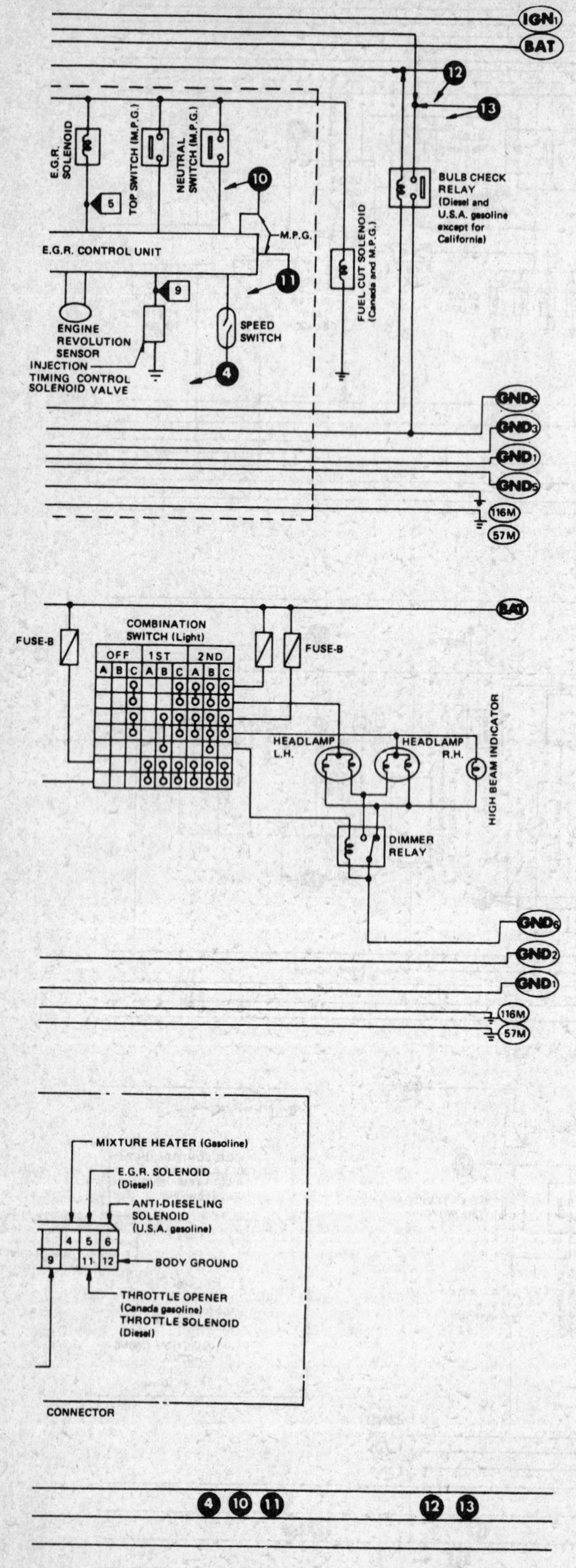
IGN1
BAT
E.G.R. SOLENOID
TOP SWITCH (M.P.G.)
NEUTRAL SWITCH (M.P.G.)
BULB CHECK RELAY (Diesel and U.S.A. gasoline except for California)
M.P.G.
E.G.R. CONTROL UNIT
FUEL CUT SOLENOID (Canada and M.P.G.)
ENGINE REVOLUTION SENSOR
INJECTION TIMING CONTROL SOLENOID VALVE
SPEED SWITCH
GND6
GND3
GND1
GND5
116M
57M
COMBINATION SWITCH (Light)
FUSE-B
OFF
1ST
2ND
HEADLAMP L.H.
HEADLAMP R.H.
HIGH BEAM INDICATOR
DIMMER RELAY
GND2
MIXTURE HEATER (Gasoline)
E.G.R. SOLENOID (Diesel)
ANTI-DIESELING SOLENOID (U.S.A. gasoline)
BODY GROUND
THROTTLE OPENER (Canada gasoline)
THROTTLE SOLENOID (Diesel)
CONNECTOR

Fig. 30. Chassis wiring diagram – 1986 Sentra

LOCATION OF ELECTRICAL UNITS

CAUTION: Before starting to work, be sure to turn ignition switch "OFF" and then disconnect battery ground cable.

ENGINE COMPARTMENT

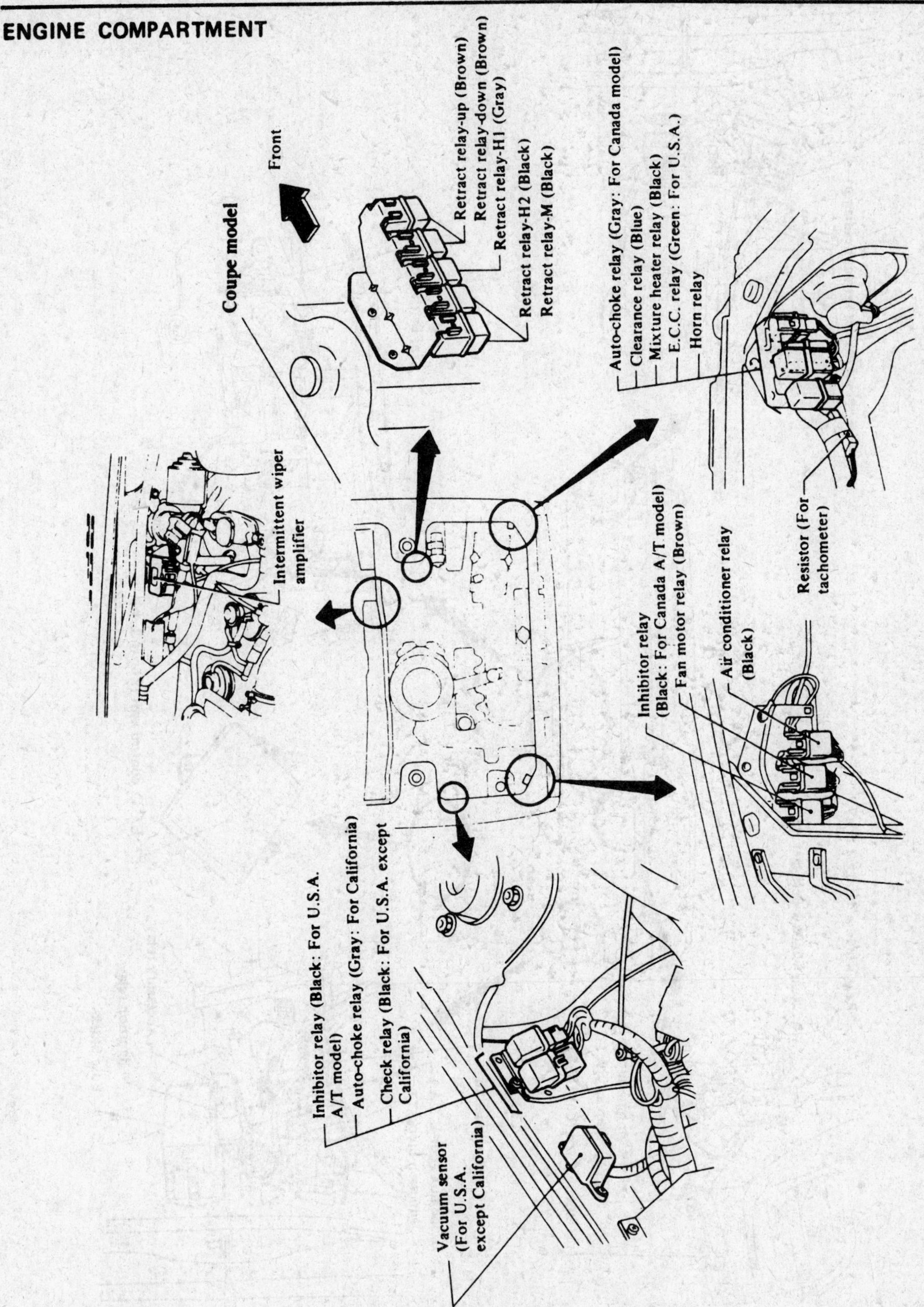

Coupe model
Front
Retract relay-up (Brown)
Retract relay-down (Brown)
Retract relay-H1 (Gray)
Retract relay-H2 (Black)
Retract relay-M (Black)
Auto-choke relay (Gray: For Canada model)
Clearance relay (Blue)
Mixture heater relay (Black)
E.C.C. relay (Green: For U.S.A.)
Horn relay
Intermittent wiper amplifier
Inhibitor relay (Black: For Canada A/T model)
Fan motor relay (Brown)
Air conditioner relay (Black)
Resistor (For tachometer)
Inhibitor relay (Black: For U.S.A. A/T model)
Auto-choke relay (Gray: For California)
Check relay (Black: For U.S.A. except California)
Vacuum sensor (For U.S.A. except California)

Fig. 31. Electrical component location — 1986 Pulsar

PASSENGER COMPARTMENT

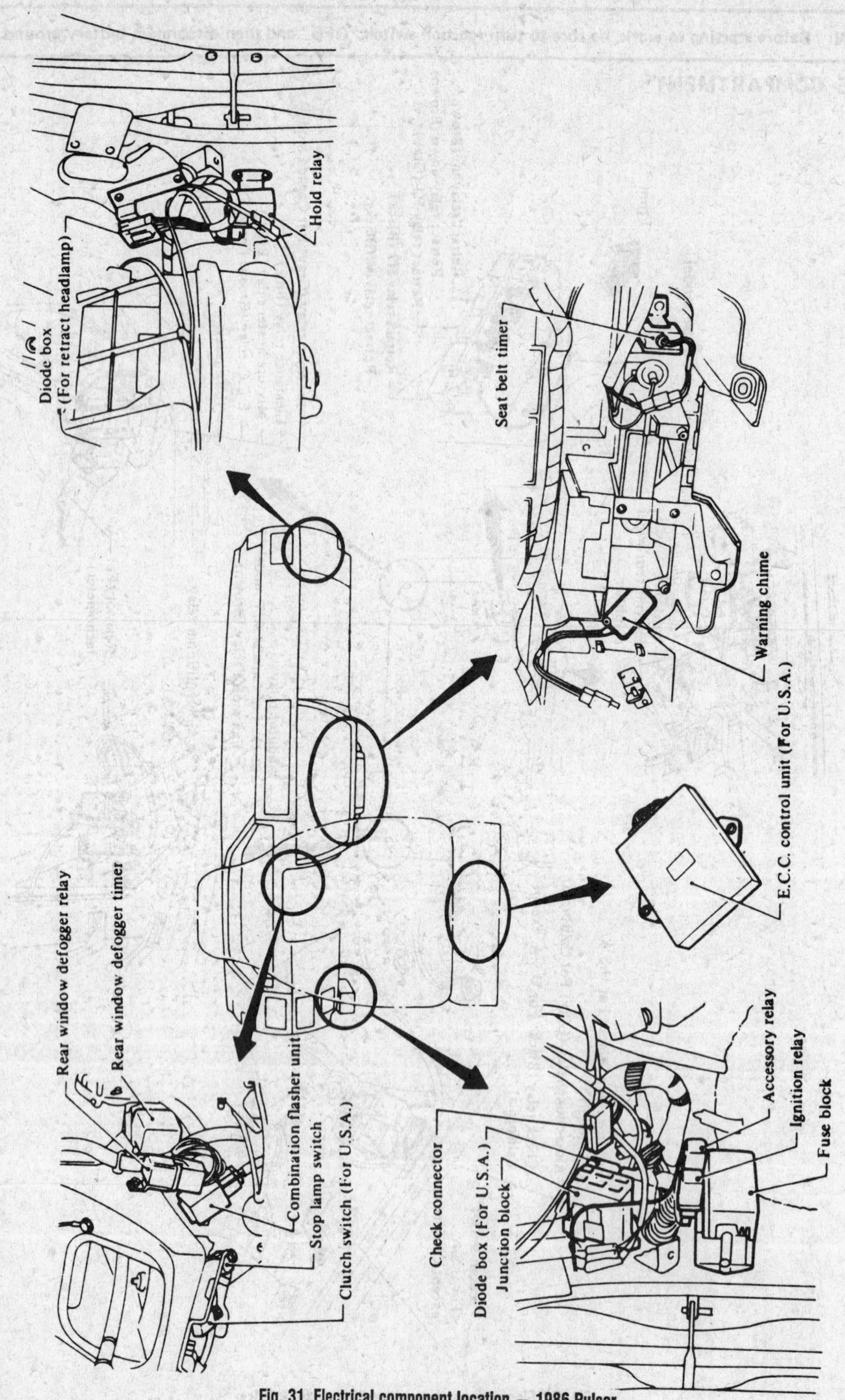
Diode box
(For retract headlamp)
Hold relay
Seat belt timer
Warning chime
E.C.C. control unit (For U.S.A.)
Rear window defogger relay
Rear window defogger timer
Combination flasher unit
Stop lamp switch
Clutch switch (For U.S.A.)
Check connector
Diode box (For U.S.A.)
Junction block
Accessory relay
Ignition relay
Fuse block

Fig. 31. Electrical component location — 1986 Pulsar

POWER SUPPLY ROUTING

CAUTION: Before starting to work, be sure to turn ignition switch "OFF" and then disconnect battery ground cable.

SCHEMATIC/POWER SUPPLY ROUTING

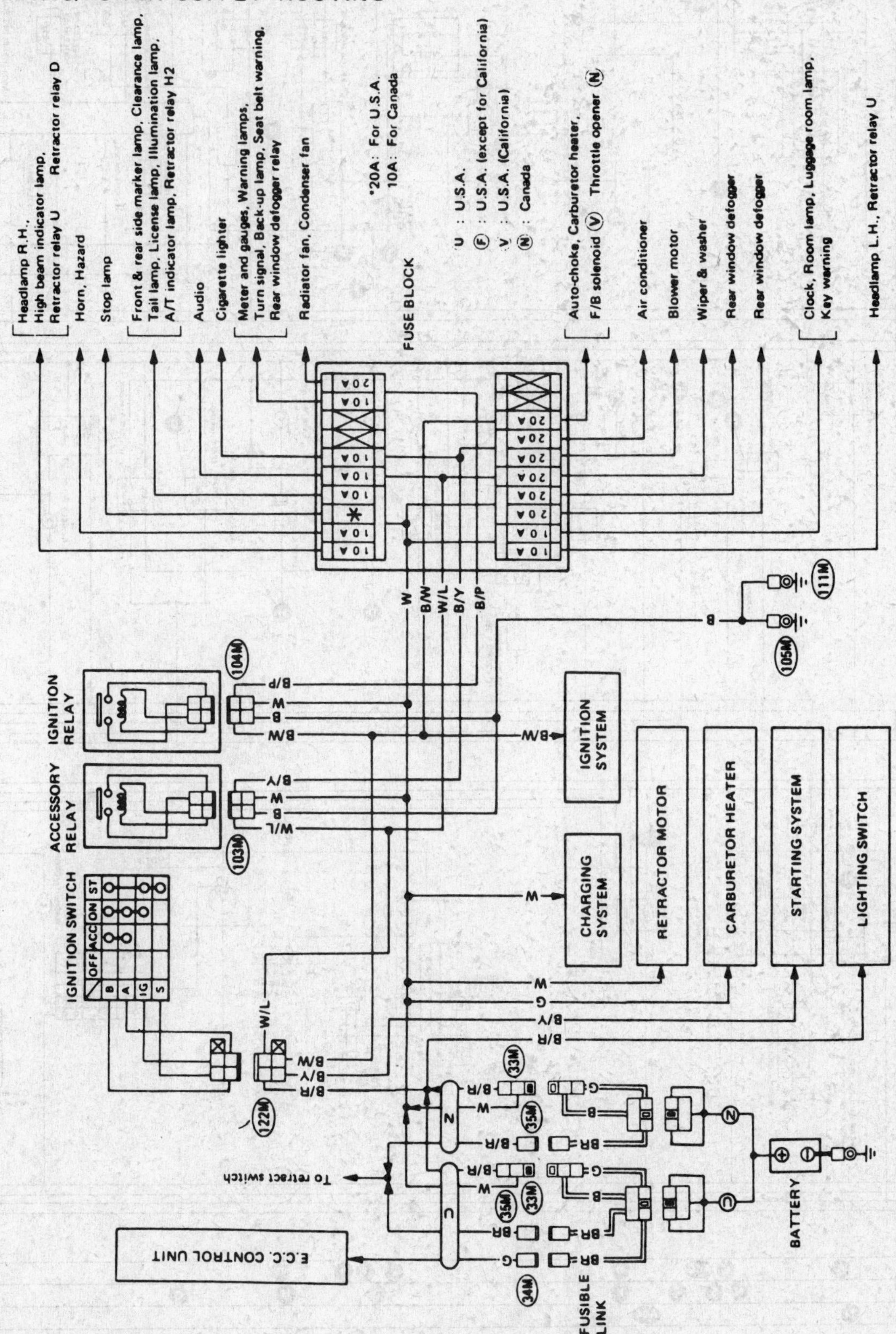

Headlamp R.H., High beam indicator lamp, Retractor relay U Retractor relay D
Horn, Hazard
Stop lamp
Front & rear side marker lamp, Clearance lamp, Tail lamp, License lamp, Illumination lamp, A/T indicator lamp, Retractor relay H2
Audio
Cigarette lighter
Meter and gauges, Warning lamps, Turn signal, Back-up lamp, Seat belt warning, Rear window defogger relay
Radiator fan, Condenser fan
FUSE BLOCK
*20A: For U.S.A.
10A: For Canada
U : U.S.A.
F : U.S.A. (except for California)
V : U.S.A. (California)
N : Canada
Auto-choke, Carburetor heater, F/B solenoid V Throttle opener N
Air conditioner
Blower motor
Wiper & washer
Rear window defogger
Rear window defogger
Clock, Room lamp, Luggage room lamp, Key warning
Headlamp L.H., Retractor relay U
IGNITION RELAY
ACCESSORY RELAY
IGNITION SWITCH
OFF ACC ON ST
B A IG S
IGNITION SYSTEM
CHARGING SYSTEM
RETRACTOR MOTOR
CARBURETOR HEATER
STARTING SYSTEM
LIGHTING SWITCH
To retract switch
E.C.C. CONTROL UNIT
FUSIBLE LINK
BATTERY
104M
103M
105M
111M
122M
33M
34M
35M

Fig. 32. Power supply wiring diagram — 1986 Pulsar

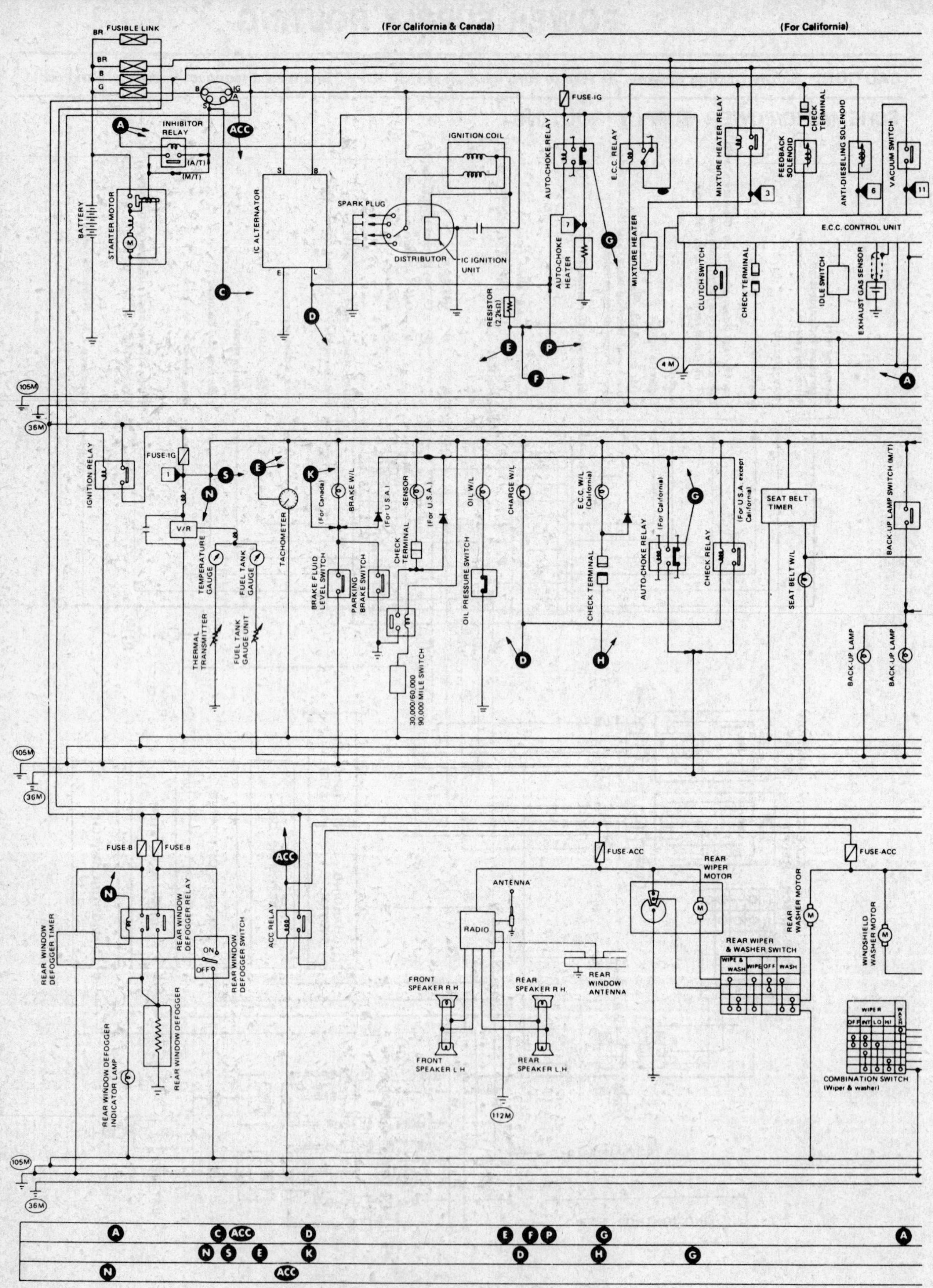
(For California & Canada)
(For California)
FUSIBLE LINK
INHIBITOR RELAY
IGNITION COIL
SPARK PLUG
DISTRIBUTOR
IC IGNITION UNIT
IC ALTERNATOR
BATTERY
STARTER MOTOR
RESISTOR (2.2kΩ)
FUSE-IG
AUTO-CHOKE RELAY
E.C.C. RELAY
AUTO-CHOKE HEATER
MIXTURE HEATER
MIXTURE HEATER RELAY
FEEDBACK SOLENOID
CHECK TERMINAL
ANTI-DIESELING SOLENOID
VACUUM SWITCH
E.C.C. CONTROL UNIT
CLUTCH SWITCH
IDLE SWITCH
EXHAUST GAS SENSOR
IGNITION RELAY
V/R
TEMPERATURE GAUGE
FUEL TANK GAUGE
THERMAL TRANSMITTER
FUEL TANK GAUGE UNIT
TACHOMETER
BRAKE FLUID LEVEL SWITCH
PARKING BRAKE SWITCH
BRAKE W/L
SENSOR
30,000/60,000 90,000 MILE SWITCH
OIL W/L
OIL PRESSURE SWITCH
CHARGE W/L
E.C.C. W/L (California)
CHECK RELAY
SEAT BELT TIMER
SEAT BELT W/L
BACK-UP LAMP SWITCH (M/T)
BACK-UP LAMP
FUSE-B
REAR WINDOW DEFOGGER TIMER
REAR WINDOW DEFOGGER RELAY
REAR WINDOW DEFOGGER SWITCH
REAR WINDOW DEFOGGER
REAR WINDOW DEFOGGER INDICATOR LAMP
ACC RELAY
FUSE-ACC
ANTENNA
RADIO
FRONT SPEAKER R.H.
FRONT SPEAKER L.H.
REAR SPEAKER R.H.
REAR SPEAKER L.H.
REAR WINDOW ANTENNA
REAR WIPER MOTOR
REAR WIPER & WASHER SWITCH
REAR WASHER MOTOR
WINDSHIELD WASHER MOTOR
COMBINATION SWITCH (Wiper & washer)

Fig. 33. Chassis wiring diagram — 1986 Pulsar

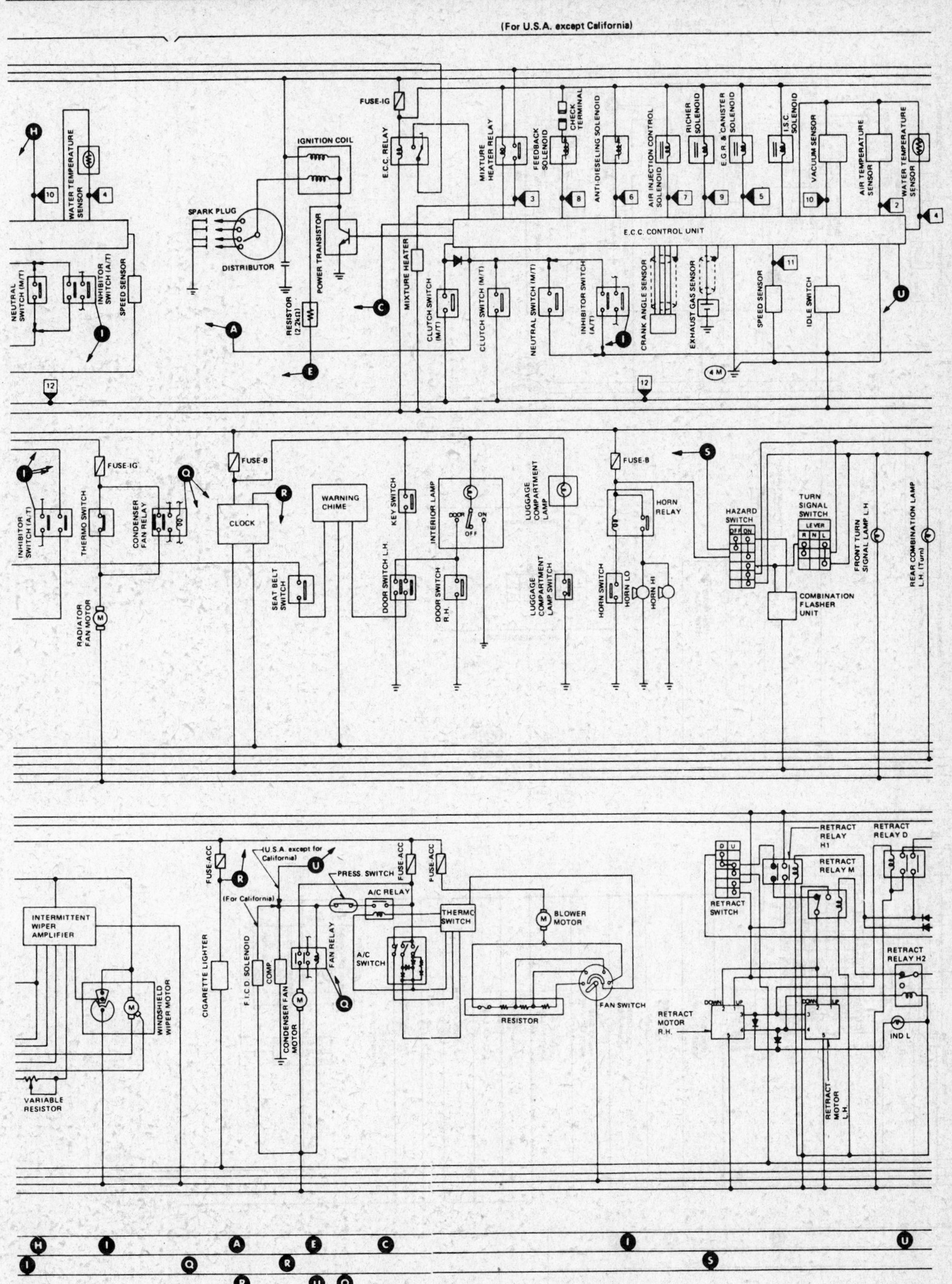
(For U.S.A. except California)
FUSE-IG
IGNITION COIL
E.C.C. RELAY
MIXTURE HEATER RELAY
FEEDBACK SOLENOID
CHECK TERMINAL
ANTI-DIESELING SOLENOID
AIR INJECTION CONTROL SOLENOID
RICHER SOLENOID
E.G.R. & CANISTER SOLENOID
I.S.C. SOLENOID
VACUUM SENSOR
AIR TEMPERATURE SENSOR
WATER TEMPERATURE SENSOR
SPARK PLUG
DISTRIBUTOR
POWER TRANSISTOR
RESISTOR (2.2kΩ)
MIXTURE HEATER
E.C.C. CONTROL UNIT
NEUTRAL SWITCH (M/T)
INHIBITOR SWITCH (A/T)
SPEED SENSOR
CLUTCH SWITCH (M/T)
NEUTRAL SWITCH (M/T)
CRANK ANGLE SENSOR
EXHAUST GAS SENSOR
IDLE SWITCH
FUSE-B
CLOCK
WARNING CHIME
KEY SWITCH
INTERIOR LAMP
DOOR
ON
OFF
LUGGAGE COMPARTMENT LAMP
HORN RELAY
HAZARD SWITCH
TURN SIGNAL SWITCH
LEVER
FRONT TURN SIGNAL LAMP L.H.
REAR COMBINATION LAMP L.H. (Turn)
THERMO SWITCH
CONDENSER FAN RELAY
RADIATOR FAN MOTOR
SEAT BELT SWITCH
DOOR SWITCH L.H.
DOOR SWITCH R.H.
LUGGAGE COMPARTMENT LAMP SWITCH
HORN SWITCH
HORN LO
HORN HI
COMBINATION FLASHER UNIT
FUSE-ACC
(U.S.A. except for California)
(For California)
PRESS. SWITCH
A/C RELAY
THERMO SWITCH
BLOWER MOTOR
INTERMITTENT WIPER AMPLIFIER
WINDSHIELD WIPER MOTOR
VARIABLE RESISTOR
CIGARETTE LIGHTER
F.I.C.D. SOLENOID
COMP
CONDENSER FAN MOTOR
FAN RELAY
A/C SWITCH
RESISTOR
FAN SWITCH
RETRACT SWITCH
RETRACT RELAY H1
RETRACT RELAY M
RETRACT RELAY D
RETRACT RELAY H2
RETRACT MOTOR R.H.
RETRACT MOTOR L.H.
DOWN
UP
IND L

Fig. 33. Chassis wiring diagram — 1986 Pulsar

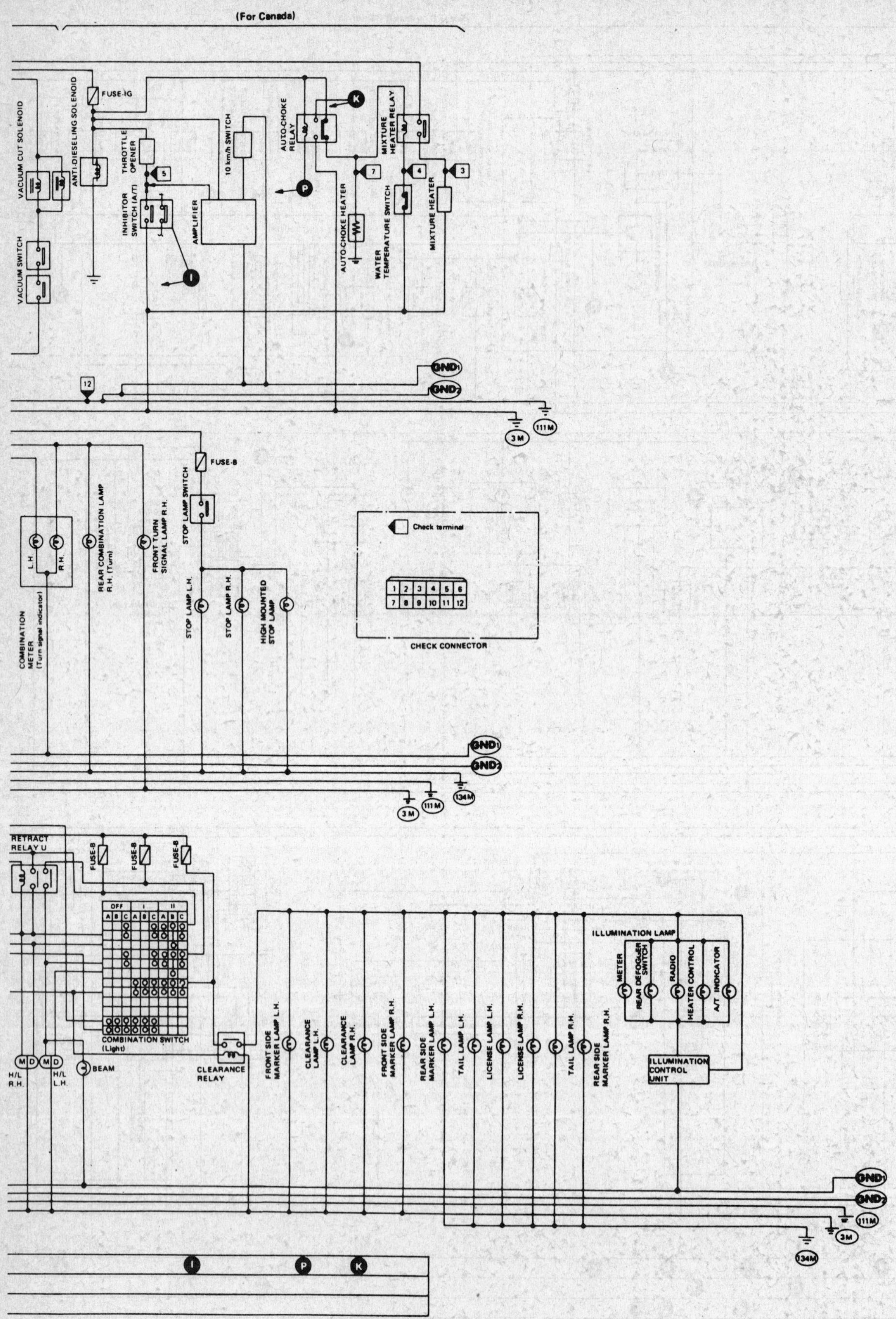
(For Canada)
FUSE-IG
VACUUM CUT SOLENOID
ANTI-DIESELING SOLENOID
THROTTLE OPENER
INHIBITOR SWITCH (A/T)
AMPLIFIER
10 km/h SWITCH
AUTO-CHOKE RELAY
MIXTURE HEATER RELAY
AUTO-CHOKE HEATER
WATER TEMPERATURE SWITCH
MIXTURE HEATER
VACUUM SWITCH
GND1
GND2
3 M
111M
FUSE-8
STOP LAMP SWITCH
COMBINATION METER (Turn signal indicator)
L.H.
R.H.
REAR COMBINATION LAMP R.H. (Turn)
FRONT TURN SIGNAL LAMP R.H.
STOP LAMP L.H.
STOP LAMP R.H.
HIGH MOUNTED STOP LAMP
Check terminal
CHECK CONNECTOR
134M
RETRACT RELAY U
OFF
COMBINATION SWITCH (Light)
H/L R.H.
H/L L.H.
BEAM
CLEARANCE RELAY
FRONT SIDE MARKER LAMP L.H.
CLEARANCE LAMP L.H.
CLEARANCE LAMP R.H.
FRONT SIDE MARKER LAMP R.H.
REAR SIDE MARKER LAMP L.H.
TAIL LAMP L.H.
LICENSE LAMP L.H.
LICENSE LAMP R.H.
TAIL LAMP R.H.
REAR SIDE MARKER LAMP R.H.
ILLUMINATION LAMP
METER
REAR DEFOGGER SWITCH
RADIO
HEATER CONTROL
A/T INDICATOR
ILLUMINATION CONTROL UNIT

Fig. 34. Chassis wiring diagram — 1986 Pulsar

Wiring Diagram

E16S ENGINE MODEL

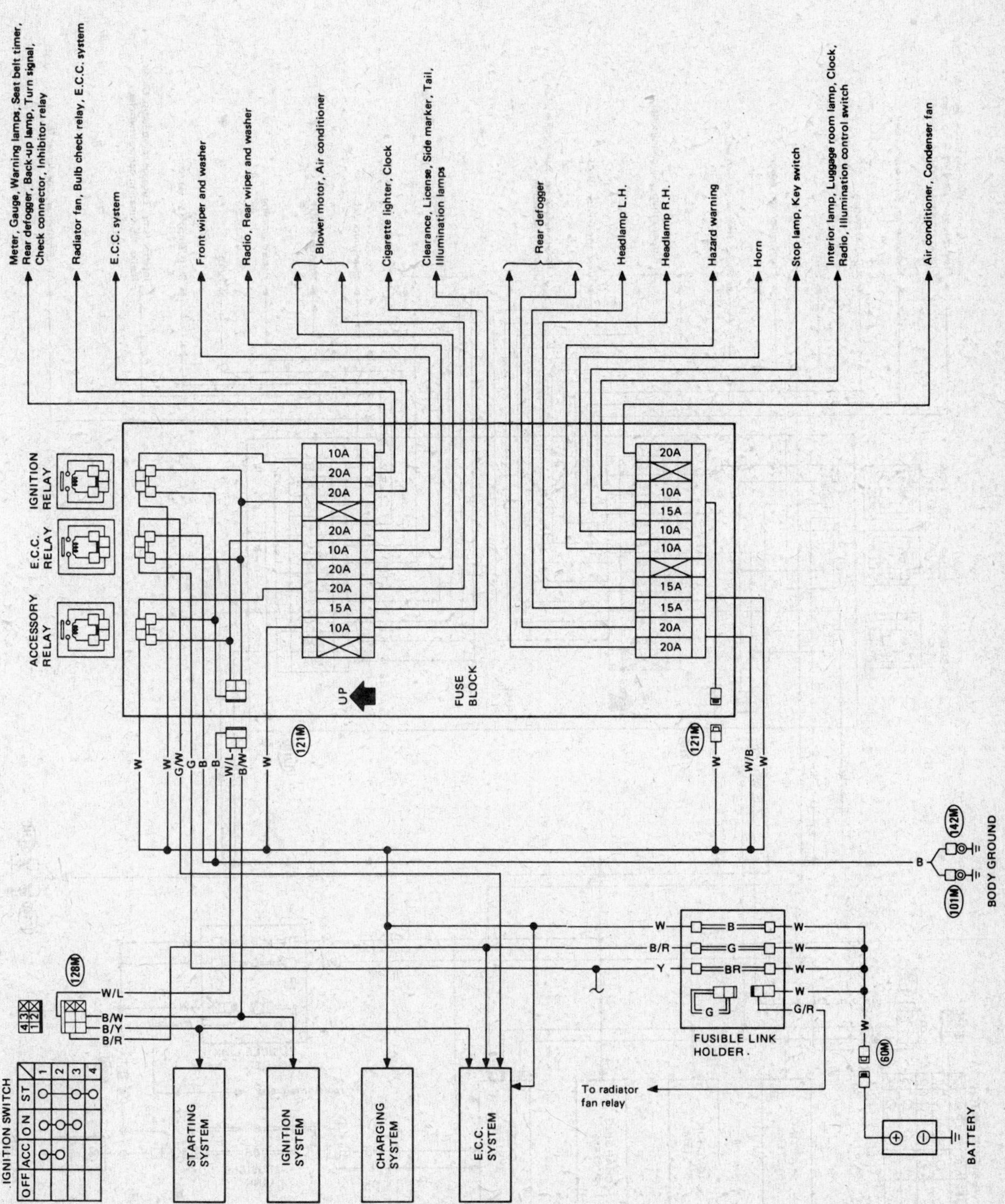

Meter, Gauge, Warning lamps, Seat belt timer, Rear defogger, Back-up lamp, Turn signal, Check connector, Inhibitor relay
Radiator fan, Bulb check relay, E.C.C. system
E.C.C. system
Front wiper and washer
Radio, Rear wiper and washer
Blower motor, Air conditioner
Cigarette lighter, Clock
Clearance, License, Side marker, Tail, Illumination lamps
Rear defogger
Headlamp L.H.
Headlamp R.H.
Hazard warning
Horn
Stop lamp, Key switch
Interior lamp, Luggage room lamp, Clock, Radio, Illumination control switch
Air conditioner, Condenser fan
IGNITION RELAY
E.C.C. RELAY
ACCESSORY RELAY
10A
20A
15A
UP
FUSE BLOCK
121M
142M
101M
BODY GROUND
128M
60M
FUSIBLE LINK HOLDER
To radiator fan relay
BATTERY
IGNITION SWITCH
OFF
ACC
ON
ST
STARTING SYSTEM
IGNITION SYSTEM
CHARGING SYSTEM
E.C.C. SYSTEM

Fig. 35. Power supply wiring diagram — 1987 Sentra

Wiring Diagram (Cont'd)

E16i ENGINE MODEL

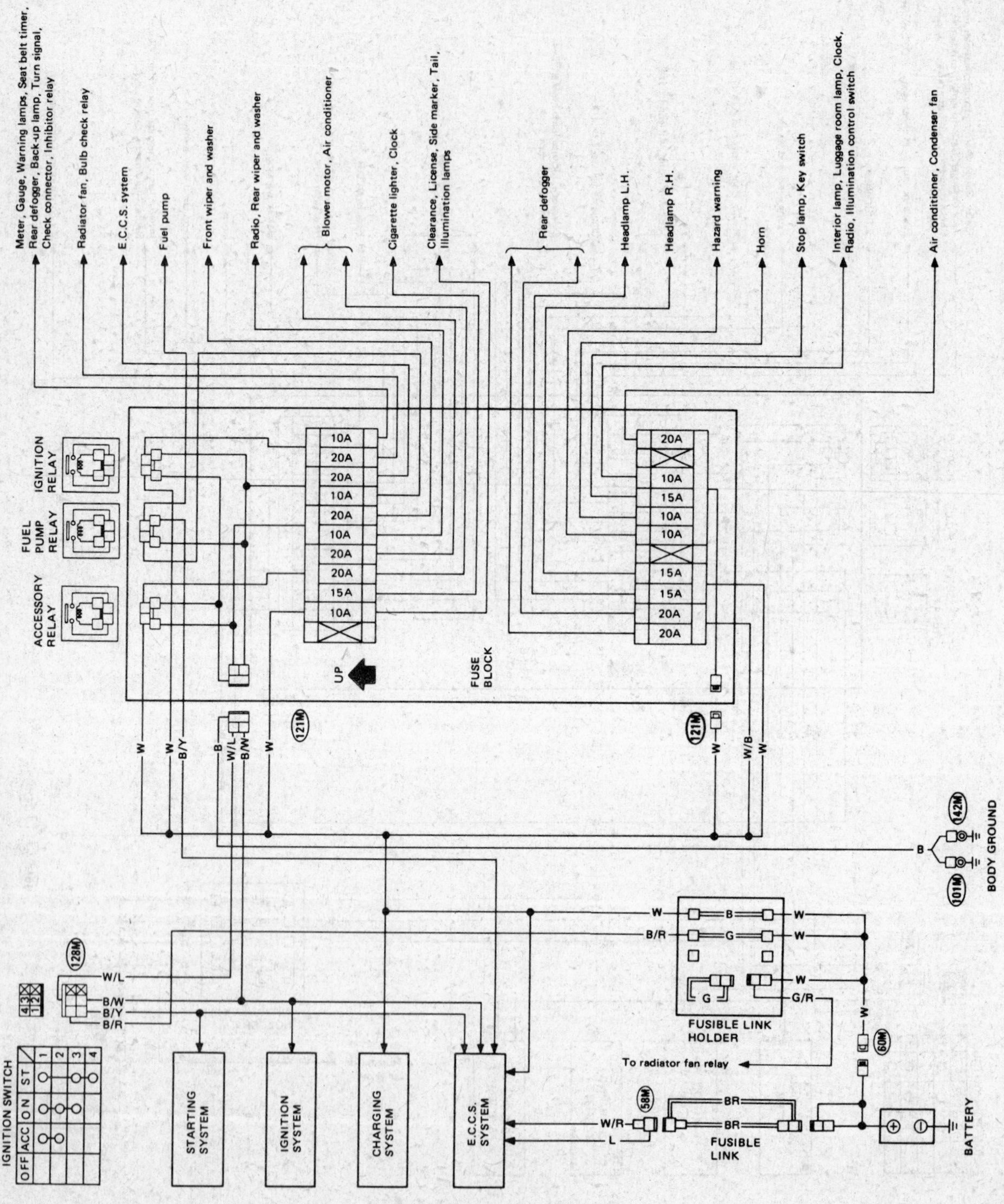

Meter, Gauge, Warning lamps, Seat belt timer, Rear defogger, Back-up lamp, Turn signal, Check connector, Inhibitor relay
Radiator fan, Bulb check relay
E.C.C.S. system
Fuel pump
Front wiper and washer
Radio, Rear wiper and washer
Blower motor, Air conditioner
Cigarette lighter, Clock
Clearance, License, Side marker, Tail, Illumination lamps
Rear defogger
Headlamp L.H.
Headlamp R.H.
Hazard warning
Horn
Stop lamp, Key switch
Interior lamp, Luggage room lamp, Clock, Radio, Illumination control switch
Air conditioner, Condenser fan
IGNITION RELAY
FUEL PUMP RELAY
ACCESSORY RELAY
UP
FUSE BLOCK
BODY GROUND
FUSIBLE LINK HOLDER
To radiator fan relay
FUSIBLE LINK
BATTERY
IGNITION SWITCH
OFF ACC ON ST
STARTING SYSTEM
IGNITION SYSTEM
CHARGING SYSTEM
E.C.C.S. SYSTEM

Fig. 36. Power supply wiring diagram — 1987 Sentra

Wiring Diagram (Cont'd)

CD17 ENGINE MODEL

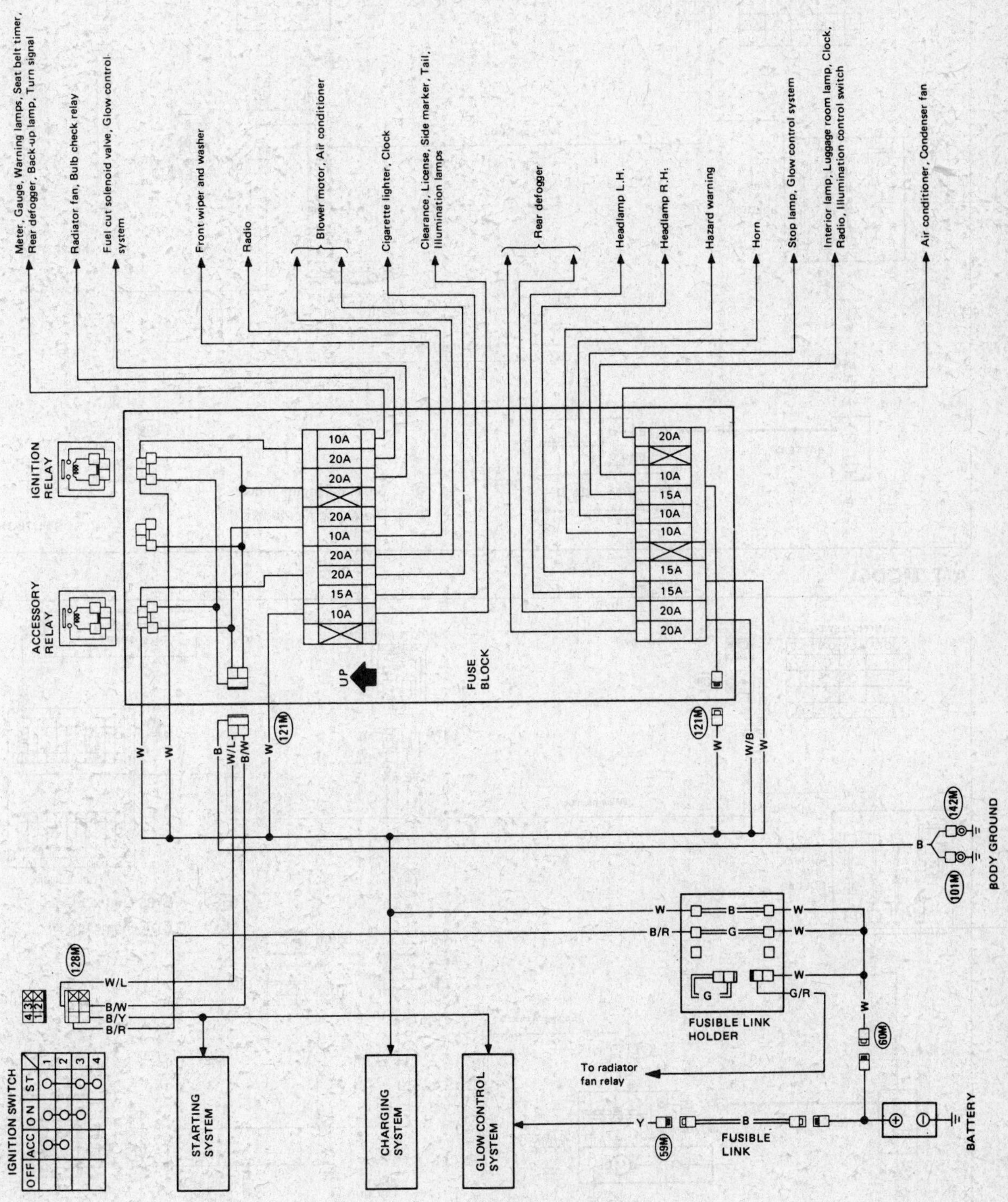
Meter, Gauge, Warning lamps, Seat belt timer, Rear defogger, Back-up lamp, Turn signal
Radiator fan, Bulb check relay
Fuel cut solenoid valve, Glow control system
Front wiper and washer
Radio
Blower motor, Air conditioner
Cigarette lighter, Clock
Clearance, License, Side marker, Tail, Illumination lamps
Rear defogger
Headlamp L.H.
Headlamp R.H.
Hazard warning
Horn
Stop lamp, Glow control system
Interior lamp, Luggage room lamp, Clock, Radio, Illumination control switch
Air conditioner, Condenser fan
IGNITION RELAY
ACCESSORY RELAY
10A
20A
20A
20A
10A
20A
20A
15A
10A
20A
10A
15A
10A
10A
15A
15A
20A
20A
UP
FUSE BLOCK
W
W
B
W/L
B/W
W
121M
121M
W
W/B
W
B
142M
101M
BODY GROUND
W
B
W
B/R
G
W
W
G/R
G
FUSIBLE LINK HOLDER
W
60M
128M
W/L
B/W
B/Y
B/R
To radiator fan relay
IGNITION SWITCH
OFF
ACC
ON
ST
STARTING SYSTEM
CHARGING SYSTEM
GLOW CONTROL SYSTEM
Y
B
59M
FUSIBLE LINK
BATTERY

Fig. 38. Power supply wiring diagram — 1987 Sentra

Wiring Diagram

M/T MODEL

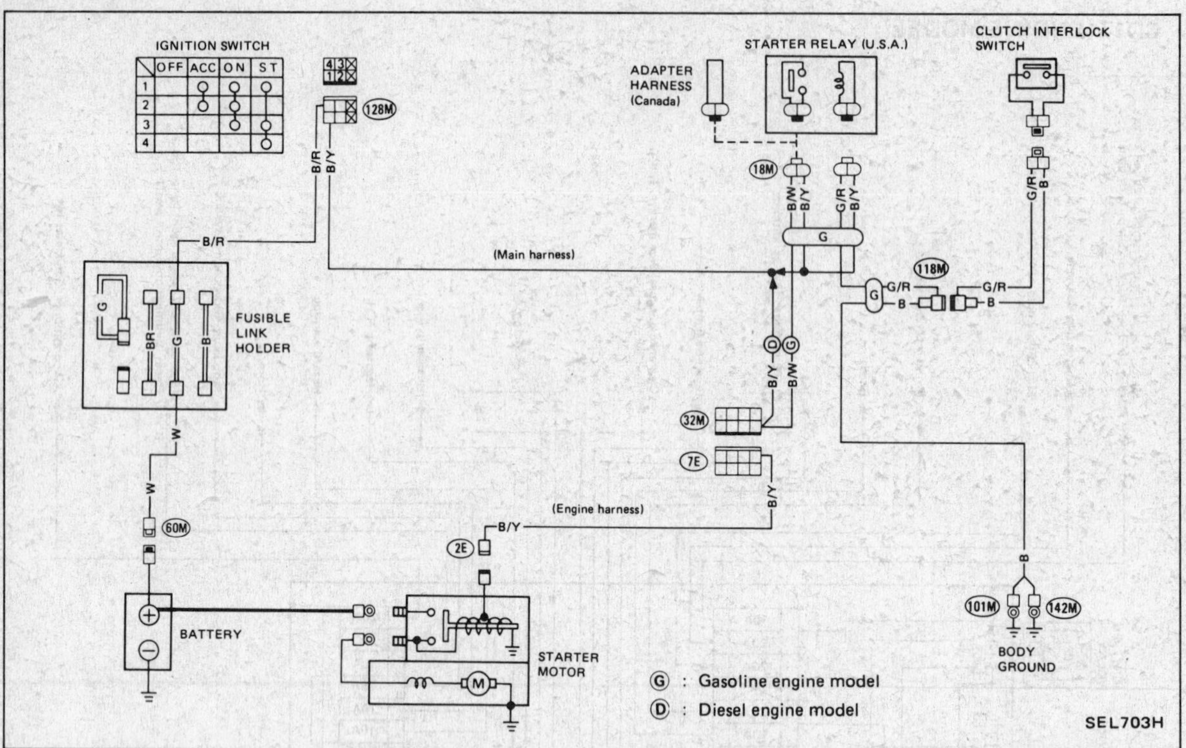

IGNITION SWITCH
OFF ACC ON ST
128M
B/R
B/Y
FUSIBLE LINK HOLDER
BR G B
W
60M
BATTERY
(Main harness)
ADAPTER HARNESS (Canada)
STARTER RELAY (U.S.A.)
CLUTCH INTERLOCK SWITCH
18M
B/W B/Y G/R B/Y
G/R B
118M
32M
7E
(Engine harness)
2E
STARTER MOTOR
101M
142M
BODY GROUND
G : Gasoline engine model
D : Diesel engine model
SEL703H

A/T MODEL

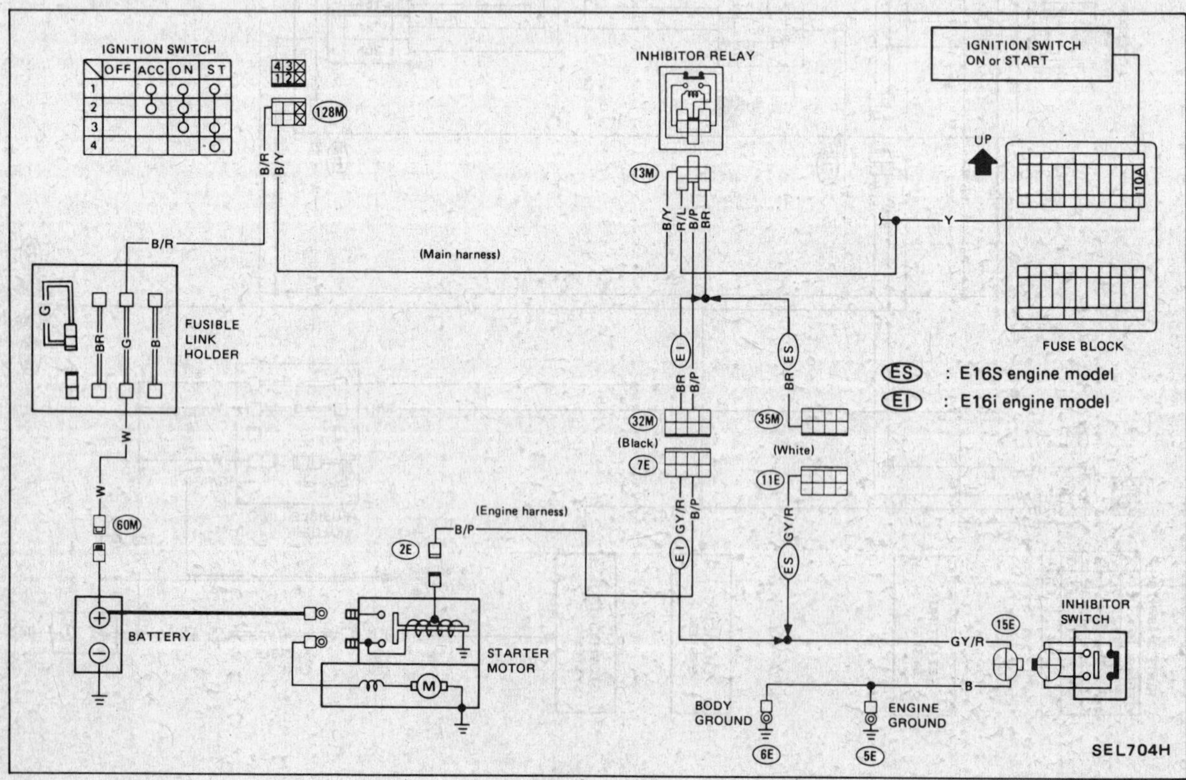

IGNITION SWITCH
OFF ACC ON ST
128M
B/R
B/Y
FUSIBLE LINK HOLDER
BR G B
W
60M
BATTERY
(Main harness)
INHIBITOR RELAY
13M
B/Y R/L B/P BR
IGNITION SWITCH ON or START
UP
10A
Y
FUSE BLOCK
ES : E16S engine model
EI : E16i engine model
32M
(Black)
7E
35M
(White)
11E
GY/R
(Engine harness)
B/P
2E
STARTER MOTOR
INHIBITOR SWITCH
15E
BODY GROUND
ENGINE GROUND
6E
5E
SEL704H

Fig. 39. Starting system wiring diagram — 1987 Sentra

Wiring Diagram

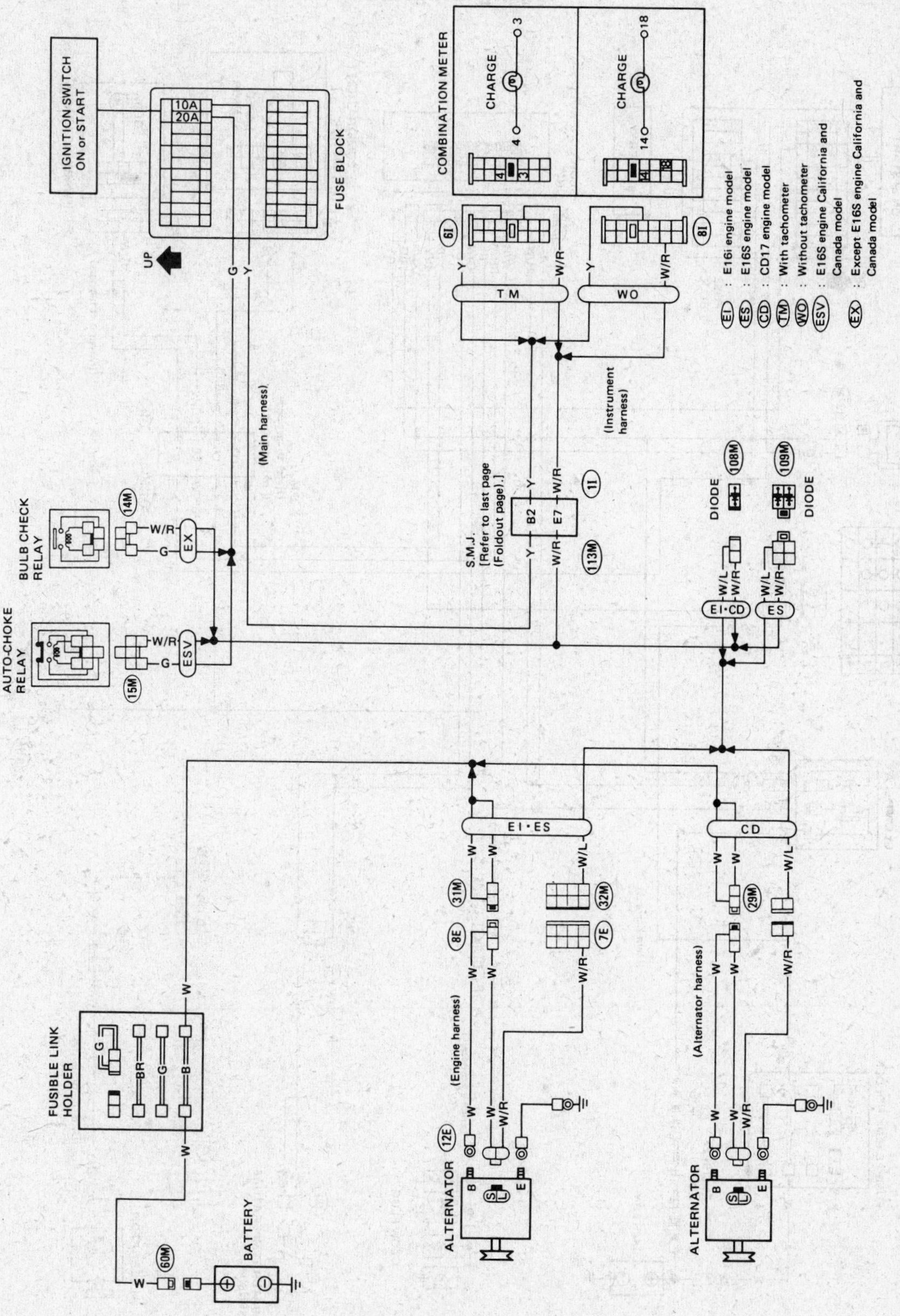

Fig. 40. Charging system wiring diagram — 1987 Sentra

Wiring Diagram

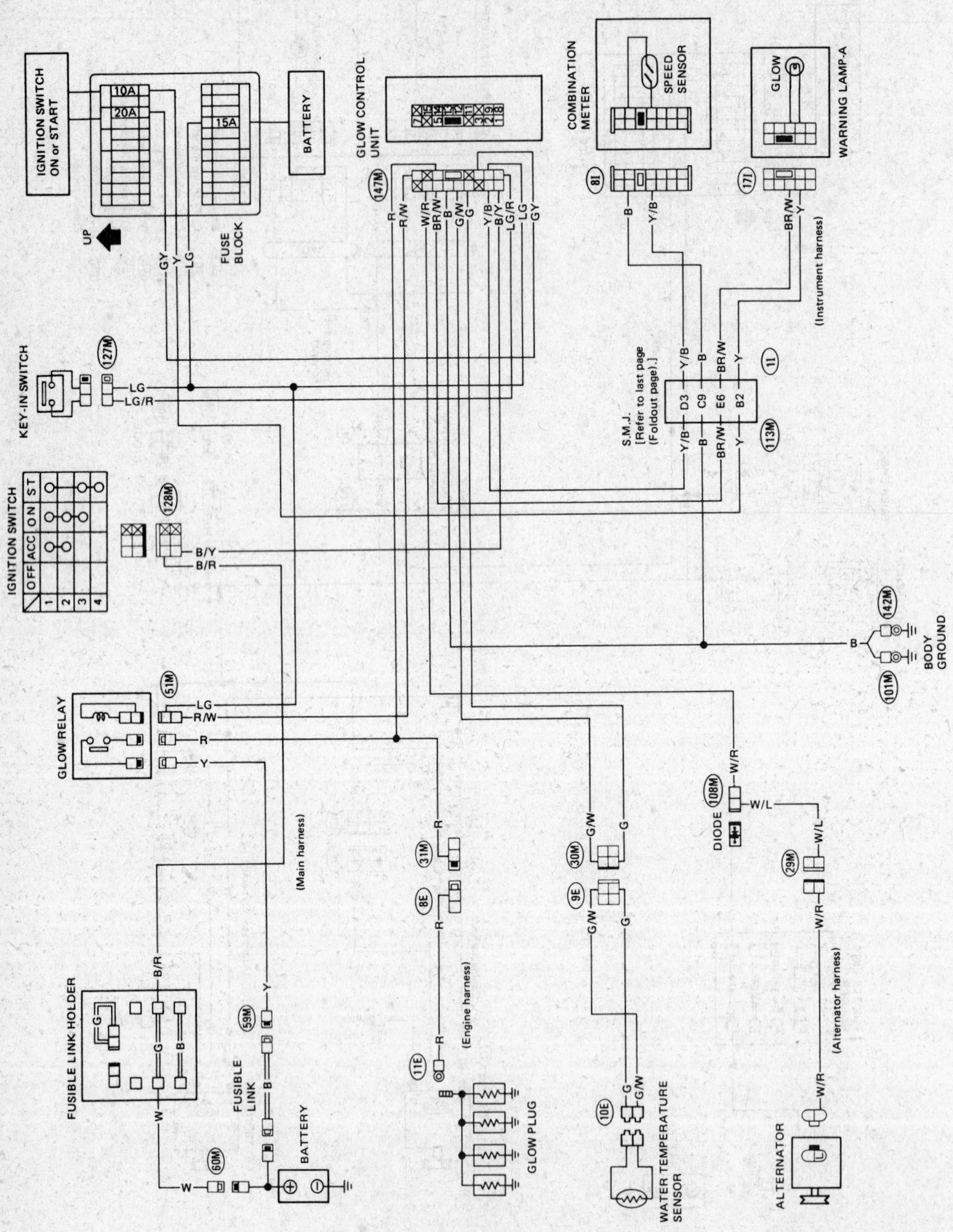

Fig. 41. Quick glow wiring diagram — 1987 Sentra

Wiring Diagram

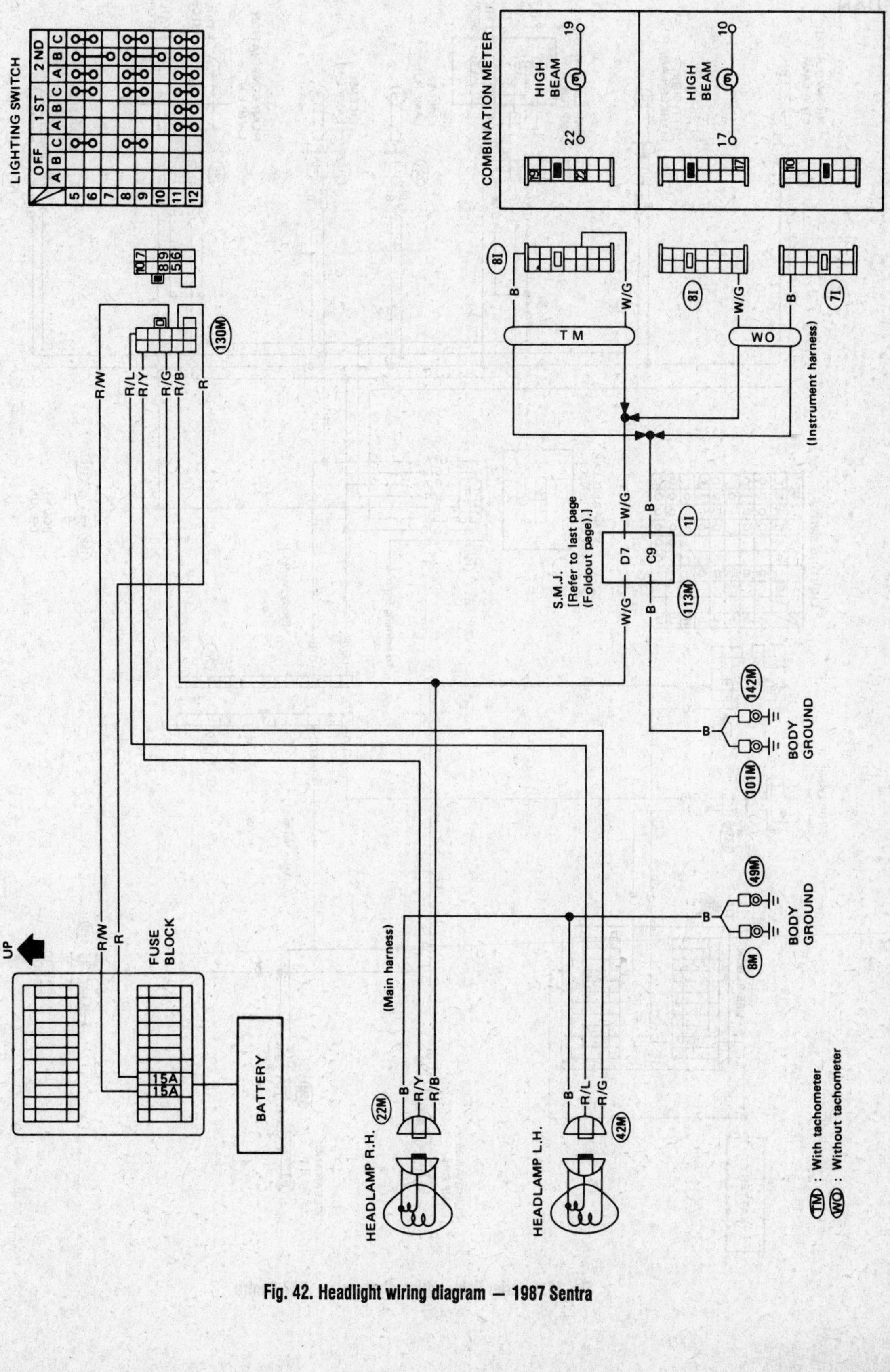

Fig. 42. Headlight wiring diagram — 1987 Sentra

Clearance, License, Tail and Stop Lamps/Wiring Diagram

SEDAN

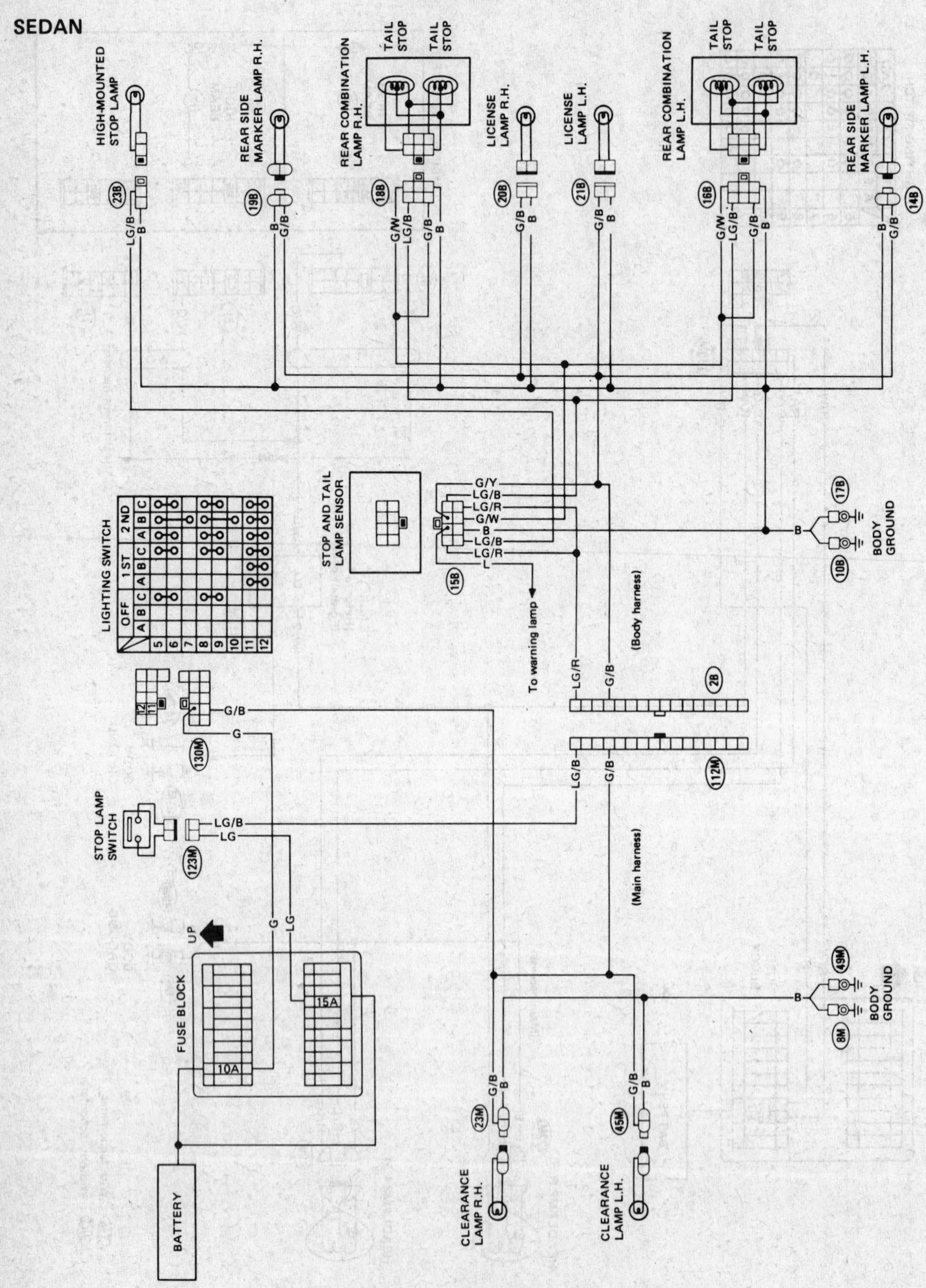
HIGH-MOUNTED STOP LAMP
REAR SIDE MARKER LAMP R.H.
REAR COMBINATION LAMP R.H.
TAIL
STOP
LICENSE LAMP R.H.
LICENSE LAMP L.H.
REAR COMBINATION LAMP L.H.
REAR SIDE MARKER LAMP L.H.
STOP AND TAIL LAMP SENSOR
LIGHTING SWITCH
OFF
1ST
2ND
To warning lamp
(Body harness)
(Main harness)
BODY GROUND
STOP LAMP SWITCH
FUSE BLOCK
UP
10A
15A
BATTERY
CLEARANCE LAMP R.H.
CLEARANCE LAMP L.H.

Fig. 43. Exterior lights wiring diagram — 1987 Sentra

Clearance, License, Tail and Stop Lamps/Wiring Diagram (Cont'd)

COUPE

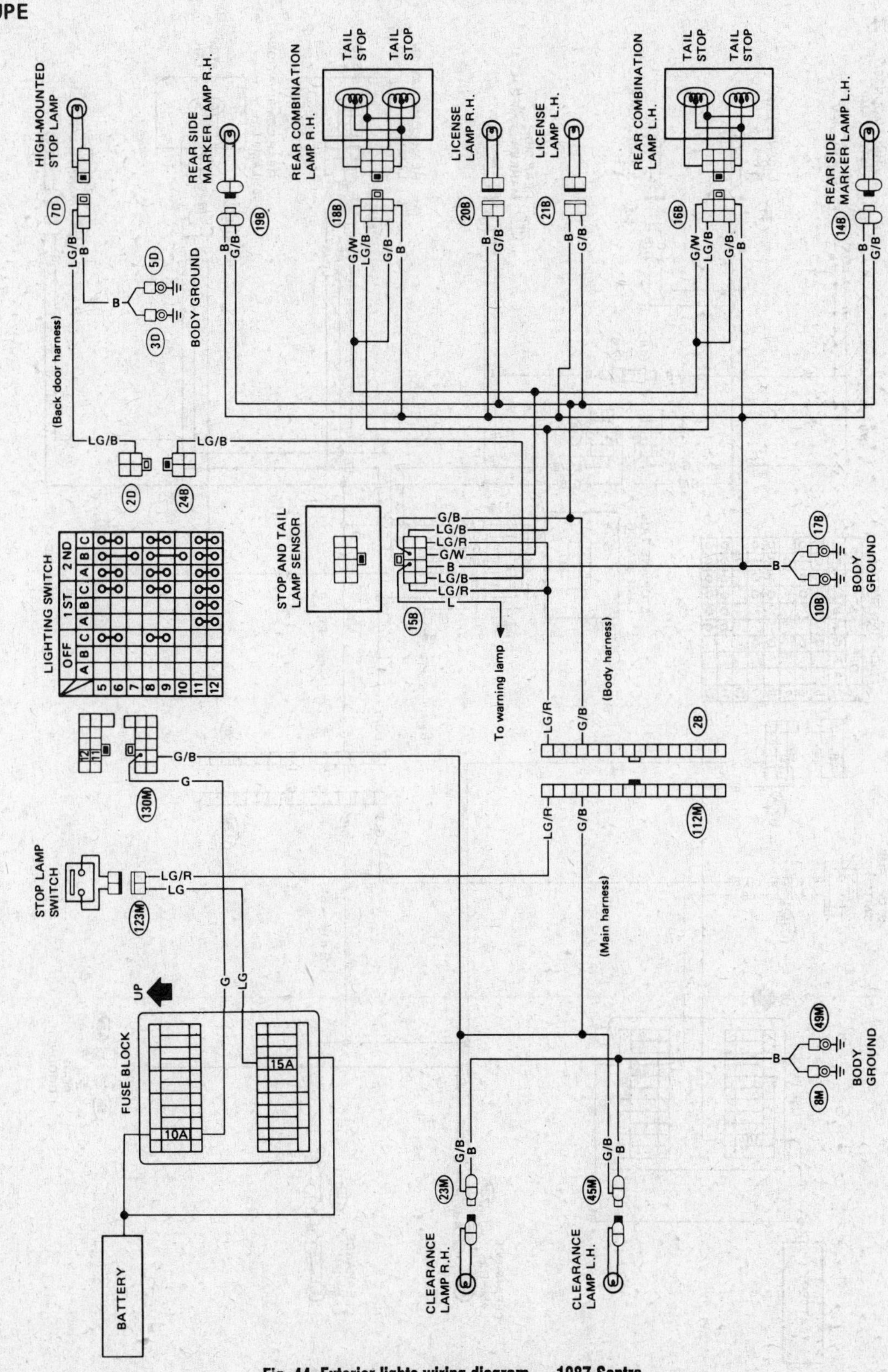

Fig. 44. Exterior lights wiring diagram — 1987 Sentra

Clearance, License, Tail and Stop Lamps/Wiring Diagram (Cont'd)

WAGON

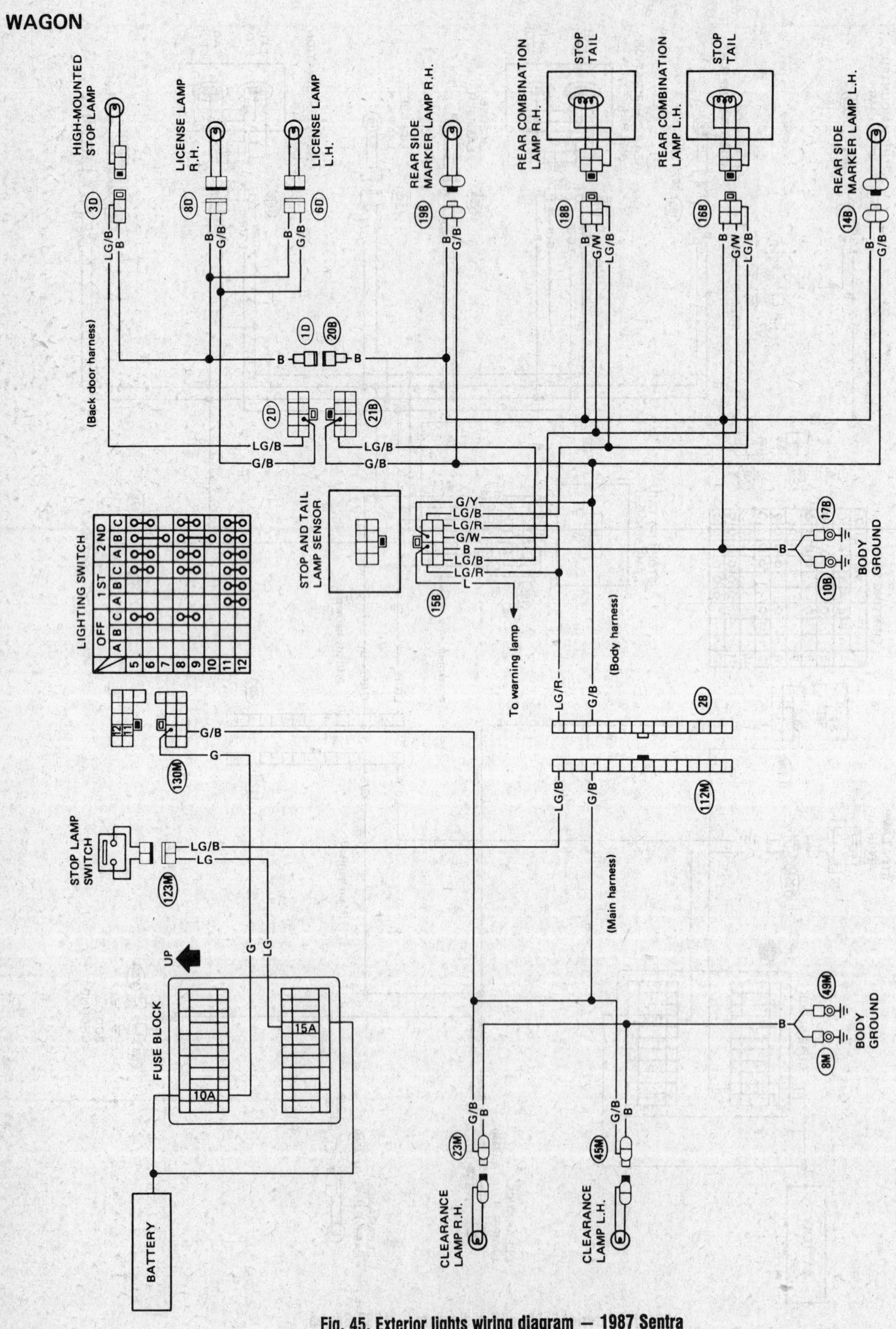
HIGH-MOUNTED STOP LAMP
LICENSE LAMP R.H.
LICENSE LAMP L.H.
REAR SIDE MARKER LAMP R.H.
REAR COMBINATION LAMP R.H.
STOP
TAIL
REAR COMBINATION LAMP L.H.
REAR SIDE MARKER LAMP L.H.
(Back door harness)
STOP AND TAIL LAMP SENSOR
To warning lamp
(Body harness)
BODY GROUND
LIGHTING SWITCH
OFF
1ST
2ND
STOP LAMP SWITCH
UP
FUSE BLOCK
10A
15A
BATTERY
(Main harness)
CLEARANCE LAMP R.H.
CLEARANCE LAMP L.H.

Fig. 45. Exterior lights wiring diagram — 1987 Sentra

Back-up Lamp/Wiring Diagram

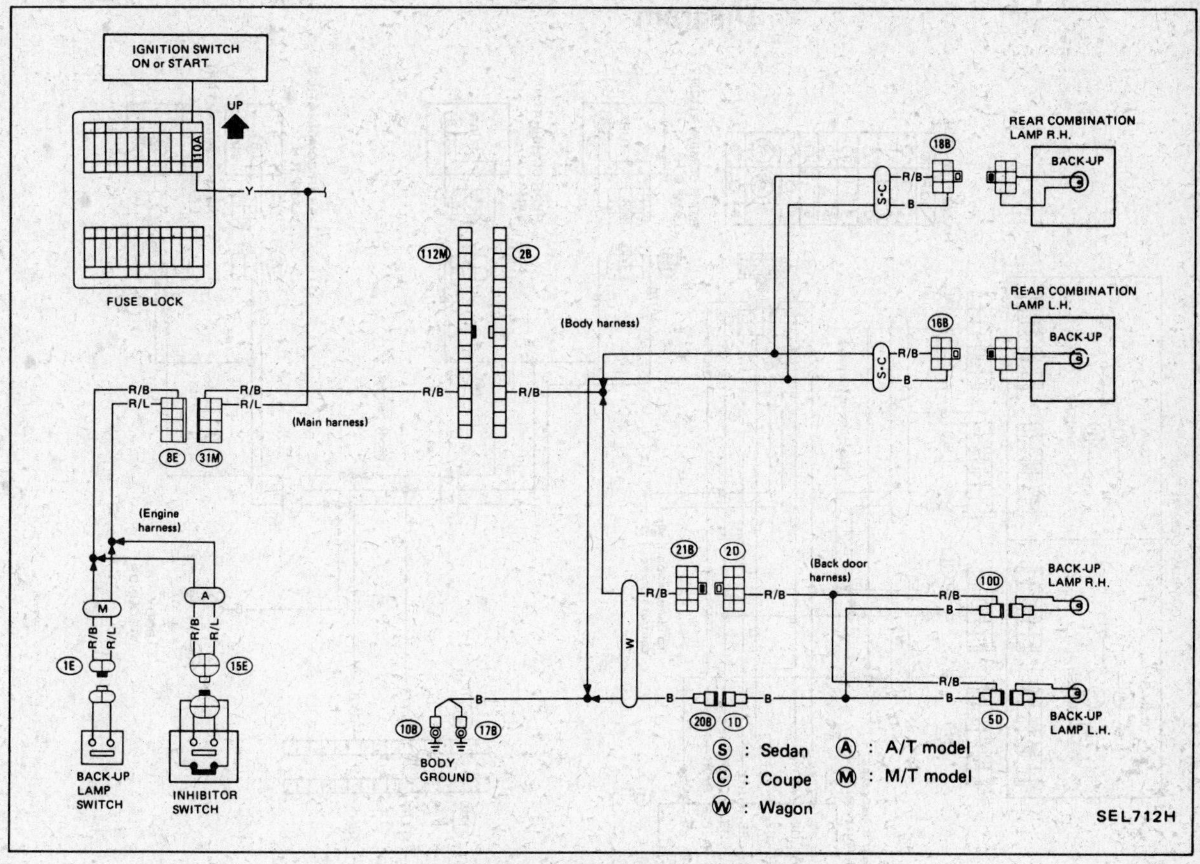
IGNITION SWITCH ON or START
UP
10A
Y
FUSE BLOCK
112M
2B
(Body harness)
R/B
R/L
8E
31M
(Main harness)
(Engine harness)
M
A
1E
15E
BACK-UP LAMP SWITCH
INHIBITOR SWITCH
10B
17B
BODY GROUND
REAR COMBINATION LAMP R.H.
BACK-UP
18B
S-C
REAR COMBINATION LAMP L.H.
16B
21B
2D
(Back door harness)
10D
BACK-UP LAMP R.H.
W
20B
1D
5D
BACK-UP LAMP L.H.
Ⓢ : Sedan
Ⓒ : Coupe
Ⓦ : Wagon
Ⓐ : A/T model
Ⓜ : M/T model
SEL712H

Fig. 46. Exterior lights wiring diagram — 1987 Sentra

Turn Signal and Hazard Warning Lamps/Wiring Diagram

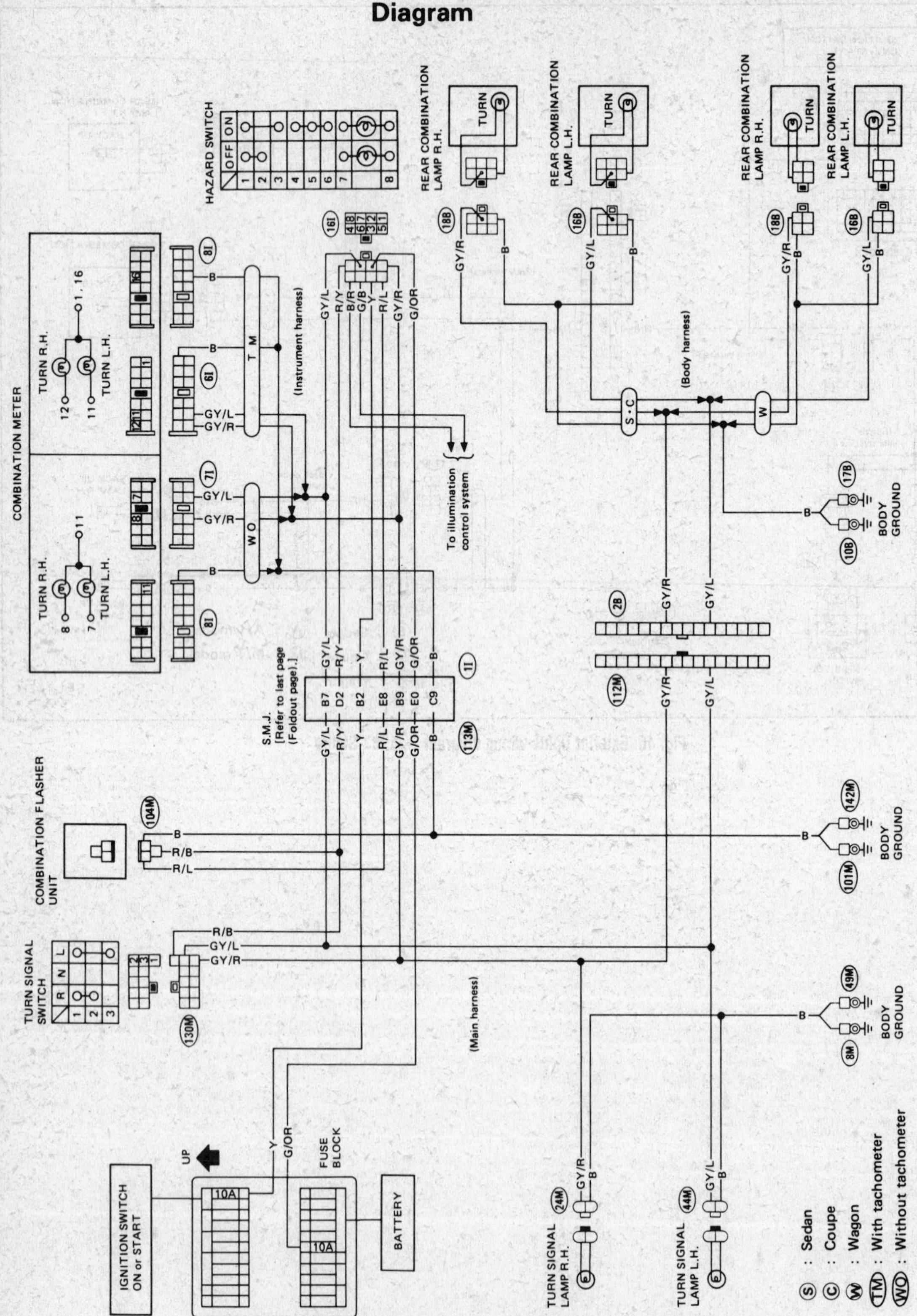
HAZARD SWITCH
COMBINATION METER
TURN R.H.
TURN L.H.
REAR COMBINATION LAMP R.H.
REAR COMBINATION LAMP L.H.
TURN
(Instrument harness)
(Body harness)
To illumination control system
S.M.J. [Refer to last page (Foldout page).]
COMBINATION FLASHER UNIT
TURN SIGNAL SWITCH
(Main harness)
IGNITION SWITCH ON or START
UP
FUSE BLOCK
BATTERY
TURN SIGNAL LAMP R.H.
TURN SIGNAL LAMP L.H.
BODY GROUND
S : Sedan
C : Coupe
W : Wagon
TM : With tachometer
WO : Without tachometer

Fig. 47. Exterior lights wiring diagram — 1987 Sentra

Illumination/Wiring Diagram

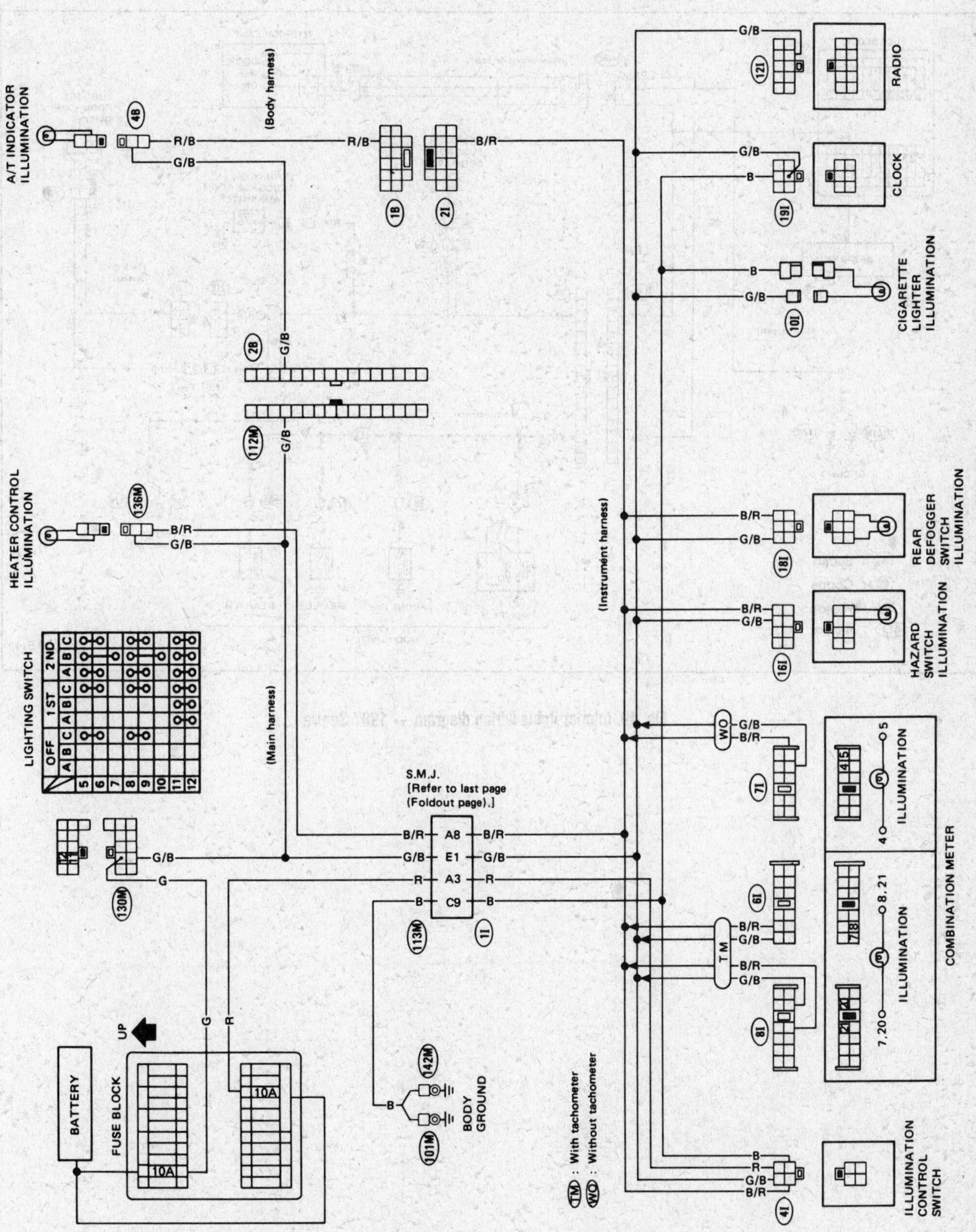
A/T INDICATOR ILLUMINATION
HEATER CONTROL ILLUMINATION
LIGHTING SWITCH
(Body harness)
(Main harness)
(Instrument harness)
S.M.J.
[Refer to last page
(Foldout page).]
BATTERY
FUSE BLOCK
10A
UP
BODY GROUND
RADIO
CLOCK
CIGARETTE LIGHTER ILLUMINATION
REAR DEFOGGER SWITCH ILLUMINATION
HAZARD SWITCH ILLUMINATION
ILLUMINATION
COMBINATION METER
ILLUMINATION CONTROL SWITCH
TM : With tachometer
WO : Without tachometer

Fig. 48. Interior lights wiring diagram — 1987 Sentra

Interior, Luggage, Spot and Step Lamps/Wiring Diagram

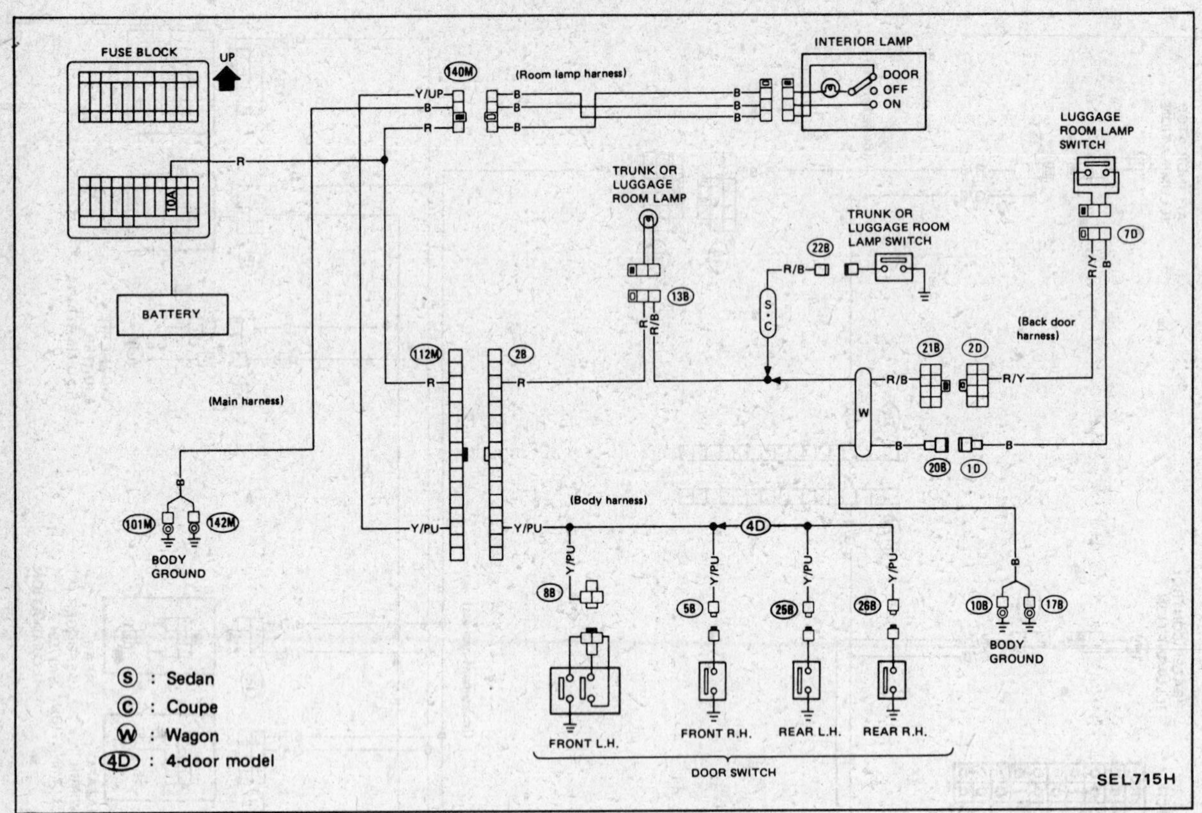
FUSE BLOCK
UP
10A
BATTERY
(Main harness)
BODY GROUND
(Room lamp harness)
INTERIOR LAMP
DOOR
OFF
ON
TRUNK OR LUGGAGE ROOM LAMP
TRUNK OR LUGGAGE ROOM LAMP SWITCH
LUGGAGE ROOM LAMP SWITCH
(Back door harness)
(Body harness)
FRONT L.H.
FRONT R.H.
REAR L.H.
REAR R.H.
DOOR SWITCH
BODY GROUND
S : Sedan
C : Coupe
W : Wagon
4D : 4-door model
SEL715H

Fig. 49. Interior lights wiring diagram — 1987 Sentra

Combination Meter (Cont'd)

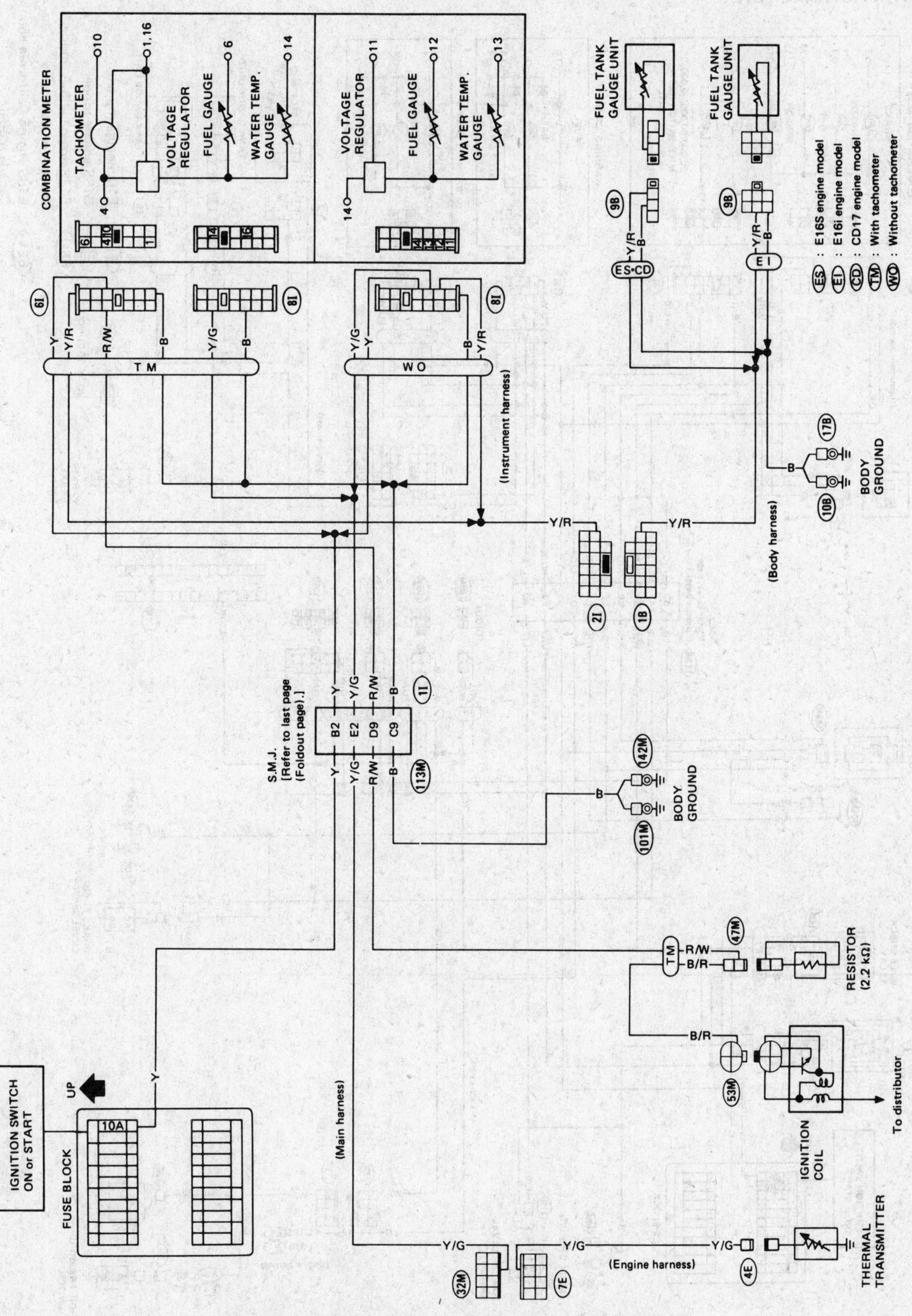
COMBINATION METER
TACHOMETER
VOLTAGE REGULATOR
FUEL GAUGE
WATER TEMP. GAUGE
FUEL TANK GAUGE UNIT
ES : E16S engine model
EI : E16i engine model
CD : CD17 engine model
TM : With tachometer
WO : Without tachometer
(Instrument harness)
(Body harness)
BODY GROUND
S.M.J.
[Refer to last page (Foldout page).]
(Main harness)
(Engine harness)
IGNITION SWITCH ON or START
FUSE BLOCK
UP
10A
RESISTOR (2.2 kΩ)
IGNITION COIL
To distributor
THERMAL TRANSMITTER

Fig. 50. Meter and gauges wiring diagram — 1987 Sentra

Warning Lamps/Wiring Diagram

WITH TACHOMETER

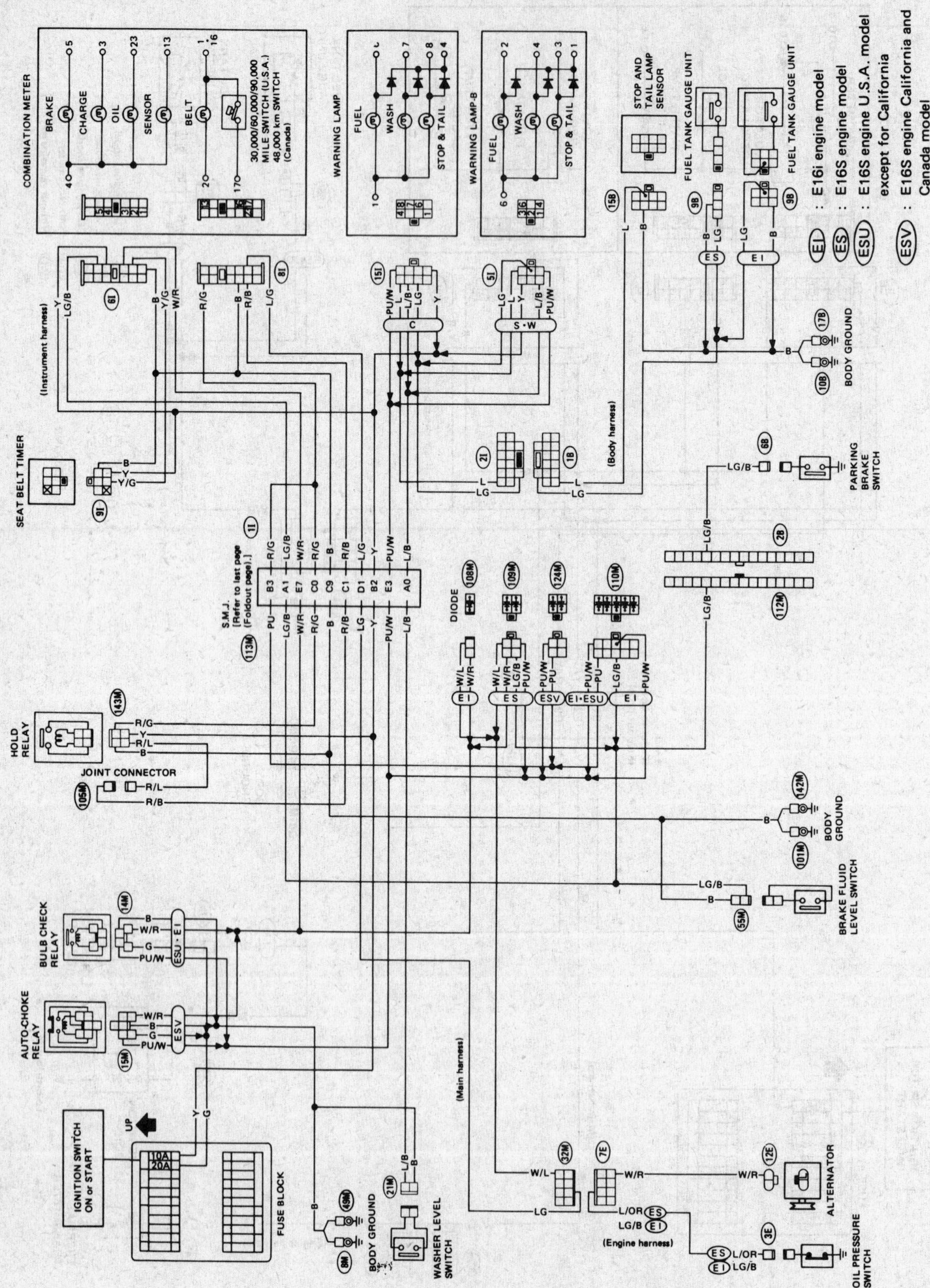
JOINT CONNECTOR
(Engine harness)

Fig. 51. Warning lights and chimes wiring diagram — 1987 Sentra

Warning Lamps/Wiring Diagram (Cont'd)

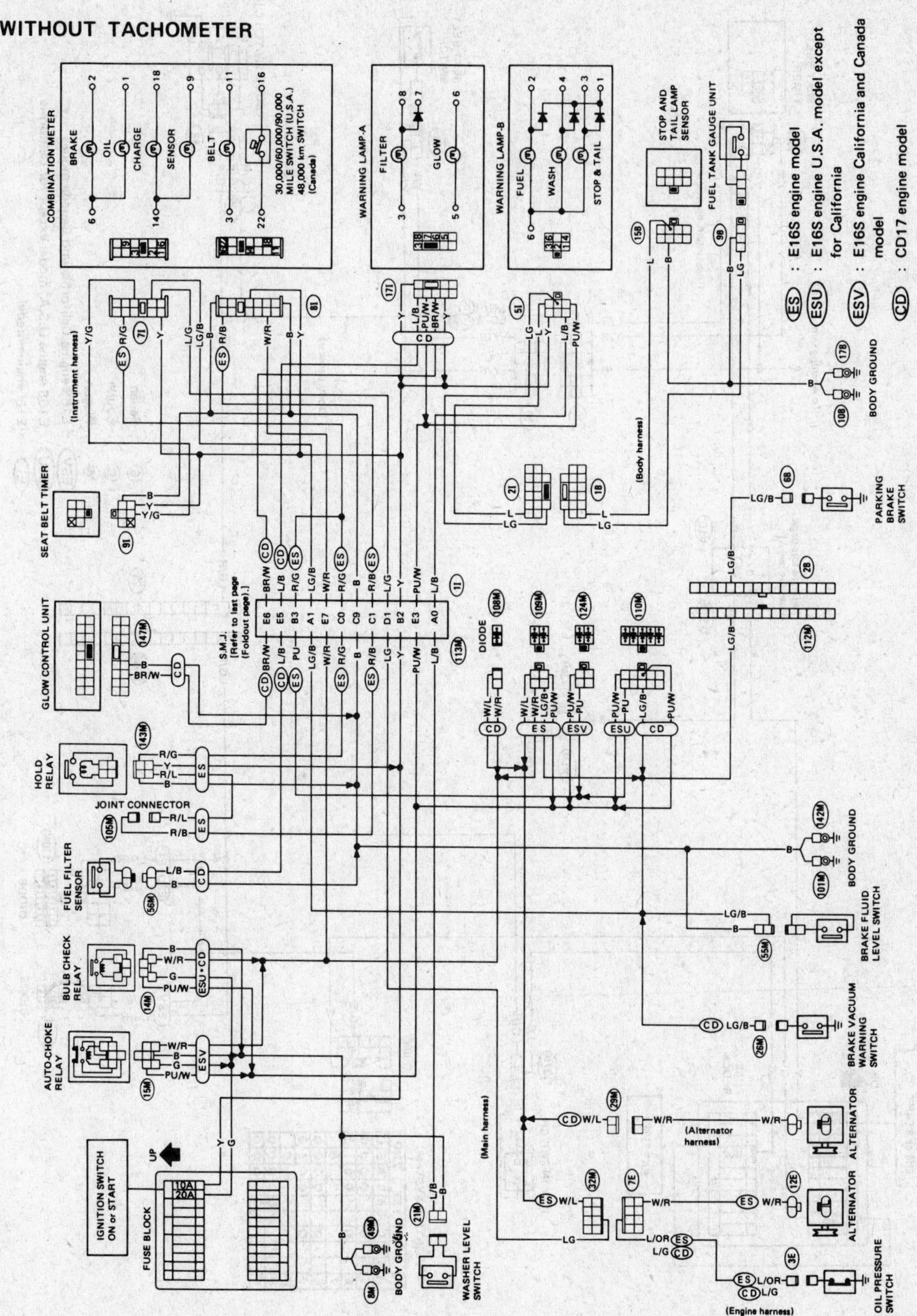
WITHOUT TACHOMETER
COMBINATION METER
BRAKE
OIL
CHARGE
SENSOR
BELT
30,000/60,000/90,000 MILE SWITCH (U.S.A.) 48,000 km SWITCH (Canada)
WARNING LAMP-A
FILTER
GLOW
WARNING LAMP-B
FUEL
WASH
STOP & TAIL
STOP AND TAIL LAMP SENSOR
FUEL TANK GAUGE UNIT
ES : E16S engine model
ESU : E16S engine U.S.A. model except for California
ESV : E16S engine California and Canada model
CD : CD17 engine model
(Instrument harness)
(Body harness)
SEAT BELT TIMER
GLOW CONTROL UNIT
S.M.J. [Refer to last page (Foldout page).]
DIODE
HOLD RELAY
JOINT CONNECTOR
FUEL FILTER SENSOR
BULB CHECK RELAY
AUTO-CHOKE RELAY
IGNITION SWITCH ON or START
FUSE BLOCK
UP
BODY GROUND
WASHER LEVEL SWITCH
(Main harness)
PARKING BRAKE SWITCH
BRAKE FLUID LEVEL SWITCH
BRAKE VACUUM WARNING SWITCH
ALTERNATOR
(Alternator harness)
OIL PRESSURE SWITCH
(Engine harness)

Fig. 52. Warning lights and chimes wiring diagram — 1987 Sentra

Warning Chime/Wiring Diagram

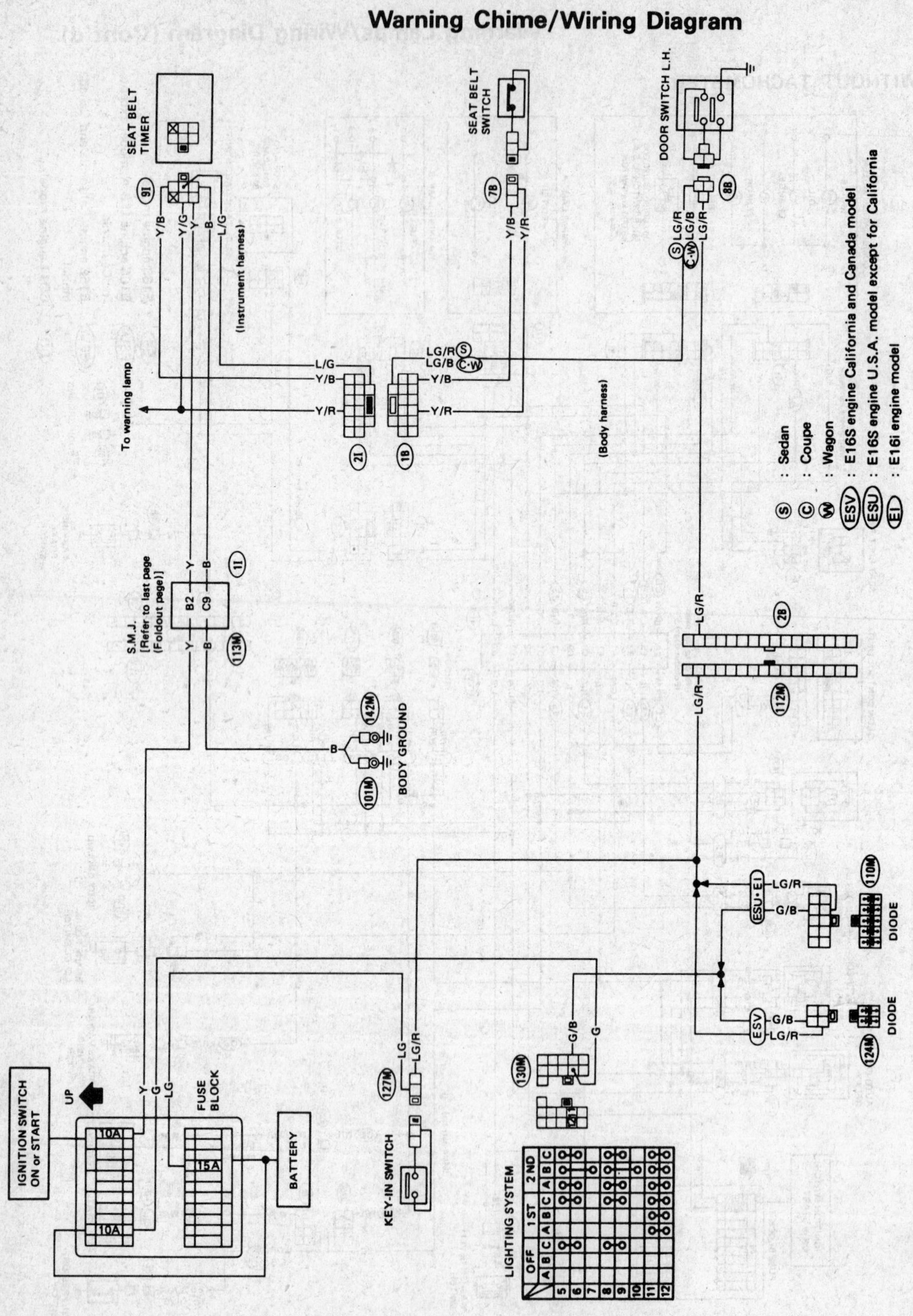
SEAT BELT TIMER
SEAT BELT SWITCH
DOOR SWITCH L.H.
(Instrument harness)
To warning lamp
(Body harness)
S.M.J.
[Refer to last page (Foldout page)]
BODY GROUND
IGNITION SWITCH ON or START
UP
FUSE BLOCK
BATTERY
KEY-IN SWITCH
LIGHTING SYSTEM
DIODE
DIODE
S : Sedan
C : Coupe
W : Wagon
ESV : E16S engine California and Canada model
ESU : E16S engine U.S.A. model except for California
EI : E16i engine model

Fig. 53. Warning lights and chimes wiring diagram — 1987 Sentra

Front Wiper and Washer/Wiring Diagram

WITHOUT INTERMITTENT WIPER

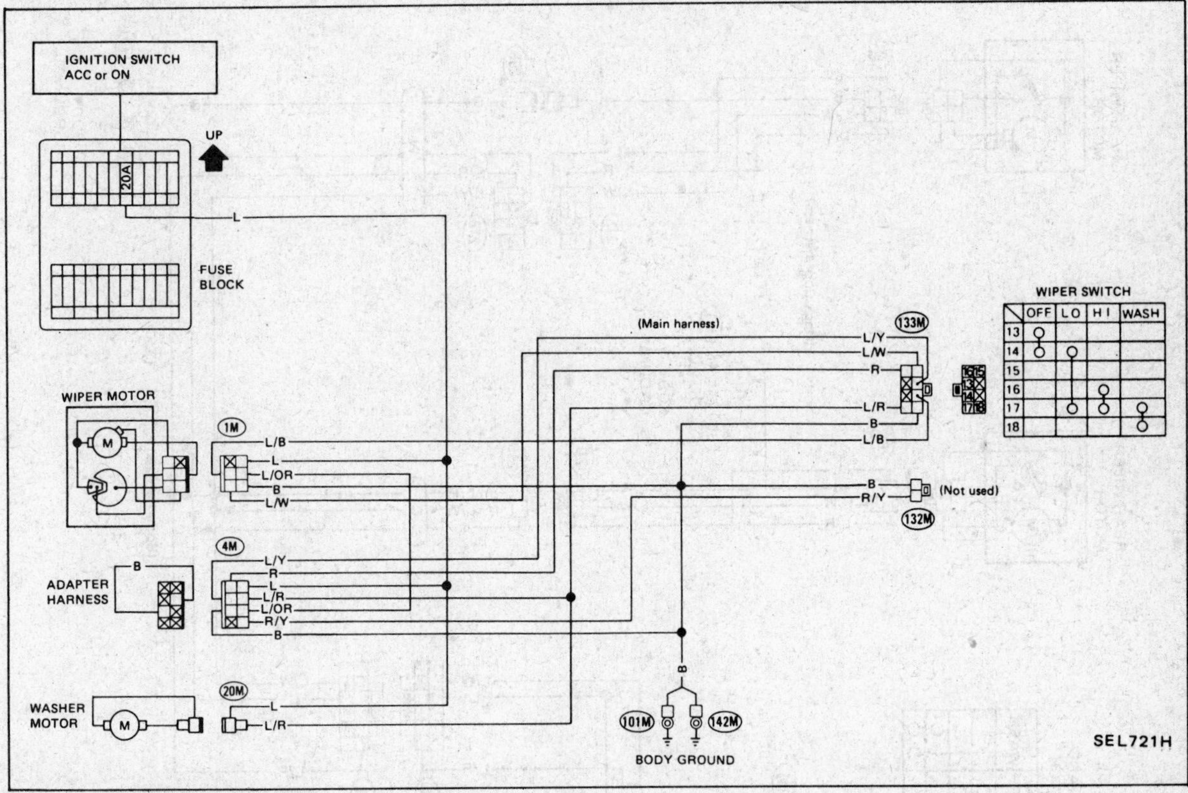
IGNITION SWITCH
ACC or ON
UP
20A
L
FUSE
BLOCK
WIPER SWITCH
OFF
LO
HI
WASH
13
14
15
16
17
18
(Main harness)
133M
L/Y
L/W
R
L/R
B
L/B
WIPER MOTOR
M
1M
L/B
L
L/OR
B
L/W
(Not used)
R/Y
132M
4M
ADAPTER
HARNESS
L/Y
R
L
L/R
L/OR
R/Y
B
WASHER
MOTOR
20M
L/R
101M
142M
BODY GROUND
SEL721H

WITH INTERMITTENT WIPER

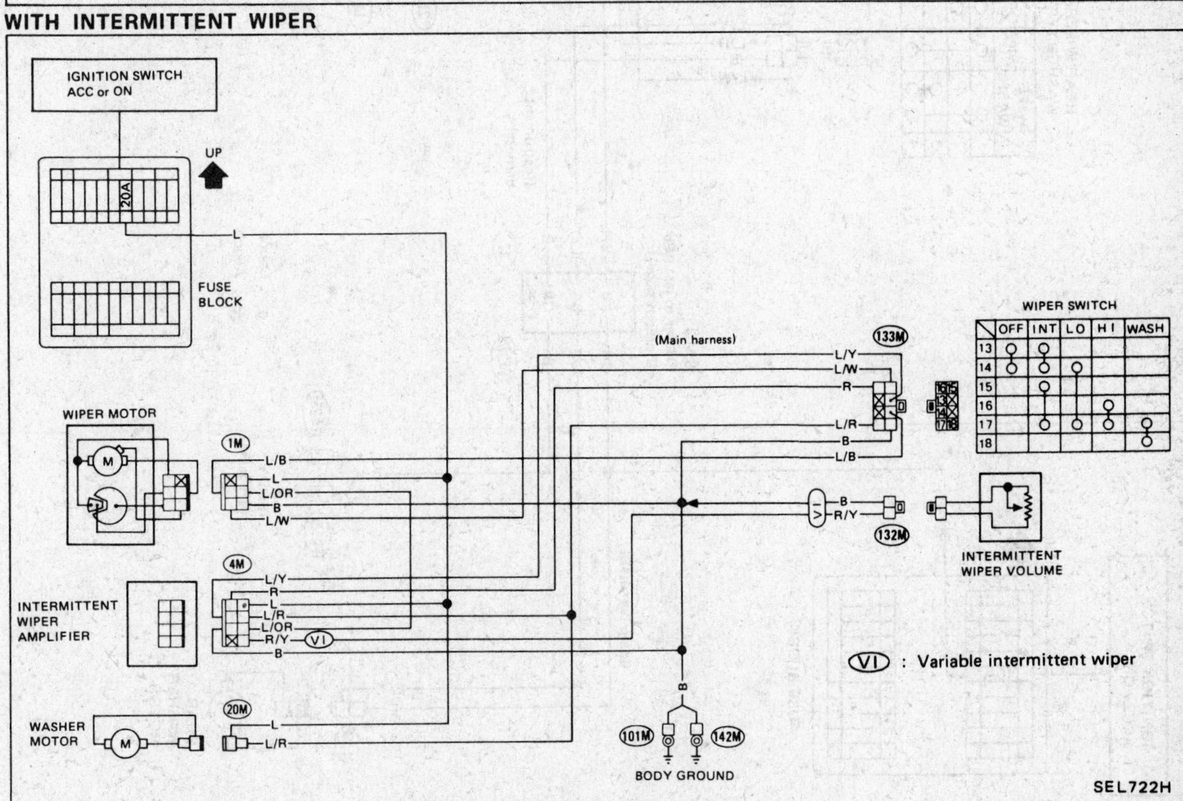
IGNITION SWITCH
ACC or ON
UP
20A
L
FUSE
BLOCK
WIPER SWITCH
OFF
INT
LO
HI
WASH
13
14
15
16
17
18
(Main harness)
133M
L/Y
L/W
R
L/R
B
L/B
WIPER MOTOR
M
1M
L/B
L
L/OR
B
L/W
VI
R/Y
132M
INTERMITTENT
WIPER VOLUME
4M
INTERMITTENT
WIPER
AMPLIFIER
L/Y
R
L
L/R
L/OR
R/Y
B
VI : Variable intermittent wiper
WASHER
MOTOR
20M
L/R
101M
142M
BODY GROUND
SEL722H

Fig. 54. Wiper and washer wiring diagram — 1987 Sentra

Rear Wiper/Wiring Diagram

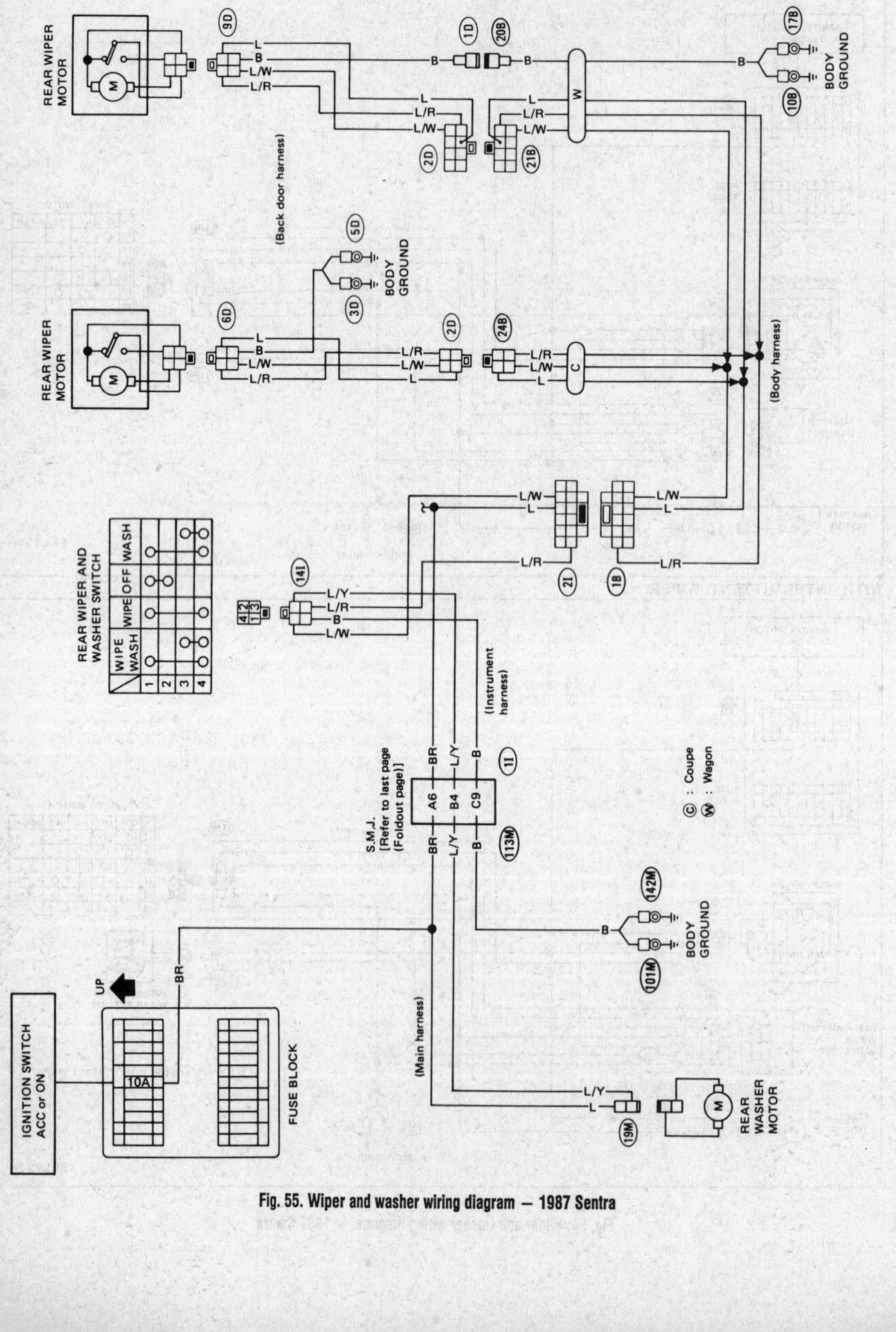

Fig. 55. Wiper and washer wiring diagram — 1987 Sentra

Wiring Diagram

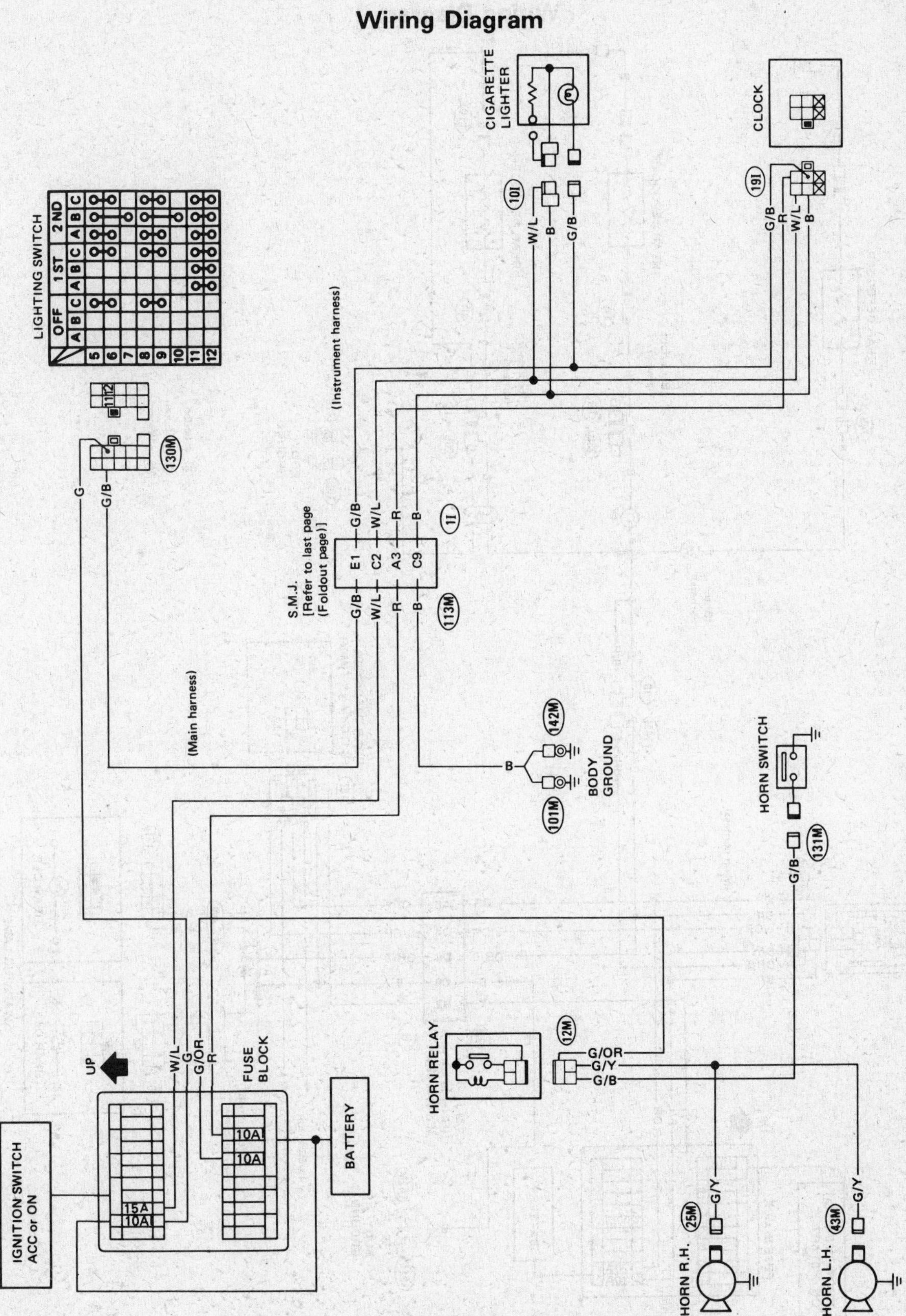

CIGARETTE LIGHTER
CLOCK
LIGHTING SWITCH
OFF
1ST
2ND
(Instrument harness)
(Main harness)
S.M.J.
[Refer to last page
[Foldout page]]
BODY GROUND
HORN SWITCH
HORN RELAY
FUSE BLOCK
BATTERY
IGNITION SWITCH
ACC or ON
UP
HORN R.H.
HORN L.H.
15A
10A

Fig. 56. Horn, cigarette lighter, clock wiring diagram — 1987 Sentra

Wiring Diagram

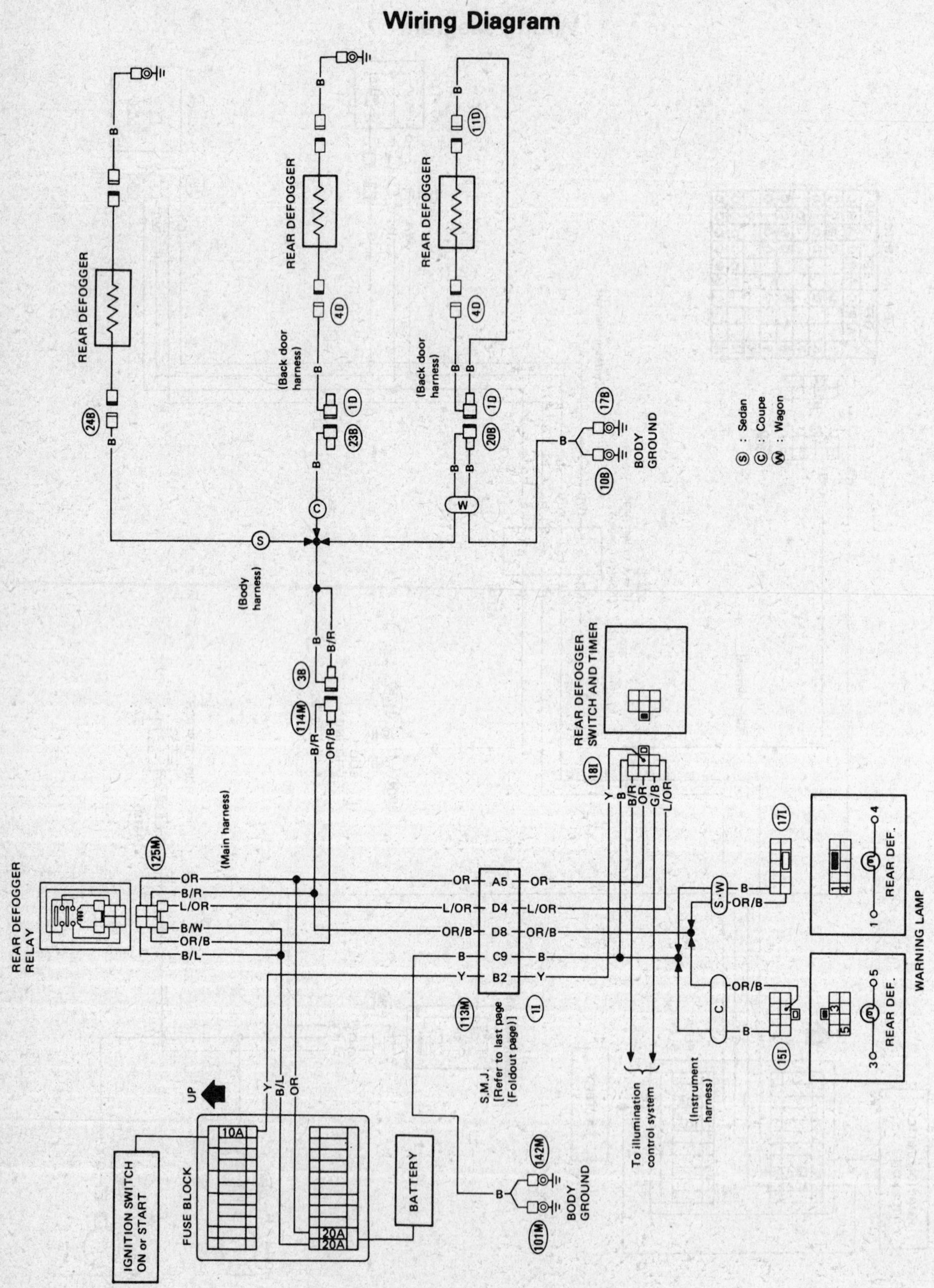
REAR DEFOGGER
REAR DEFOGGER
REAR DEFOGGER
(Back door harness)
(Back door harness)
(Body harness)
(Main harness)
REAR DEFOGGER RELAY
REAR DEFOGGER SWITCH AND TIMER
BODY GROUND
BODY GROUND
S : Sedan
C : Coupe
W : Wagon
WARNING LAMP
REAR DEF.
REAR DEF.
S.M.J.
[Refer to last page (Foldout page)]
To illumination control system
(Instrument harness)
IGNITION SWITCH ON or START
FUSE BLOCK
BATTERY
UP
10A
20A
20A
24B
23B
1D
4D
11D
20B
17B
10B
3B
114M
125M
113M
1I
18I
17I
15I
142M
101M
A5
D4
D8
C9
B2

Fig. 57. Rear defogger wiring diagram — 1987 Sentra

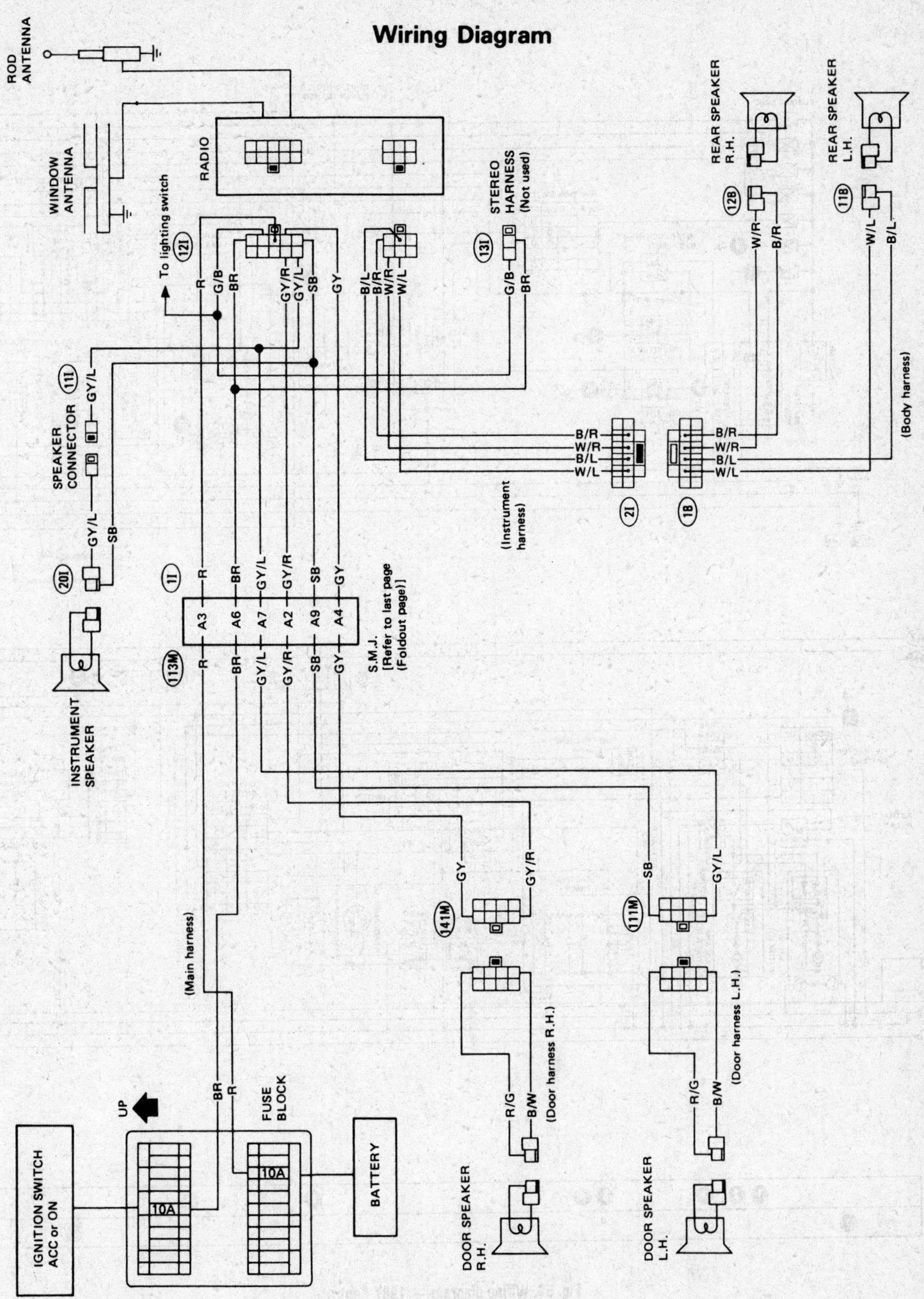
Wiring Diagram
ROD ANTENNA
WINDOW ANTENNA
RADIO
To lighting switch
STEREO HARNESS (Not used)
REAR SPEAKER R.H.
REAR SPEAKER L.H.
SPEAKER CONNECTOR
INSTRUMENT SPEAKER
S.M.J. [Refer to last page (Foldout page)]
(Instrument harness)
(Body harness)
(Main harness)
(Door harness R.H.)
(Door harness L.H.)
FUSE BLOCK
UP
IGNITION SWITCH ACC or ON
10A
10A
BATTERY
DOOR SPEAKER R.H.
DOOR SPEAKER L.H.

Fig. 58. Audio wiring diagram — 1987 Sentra

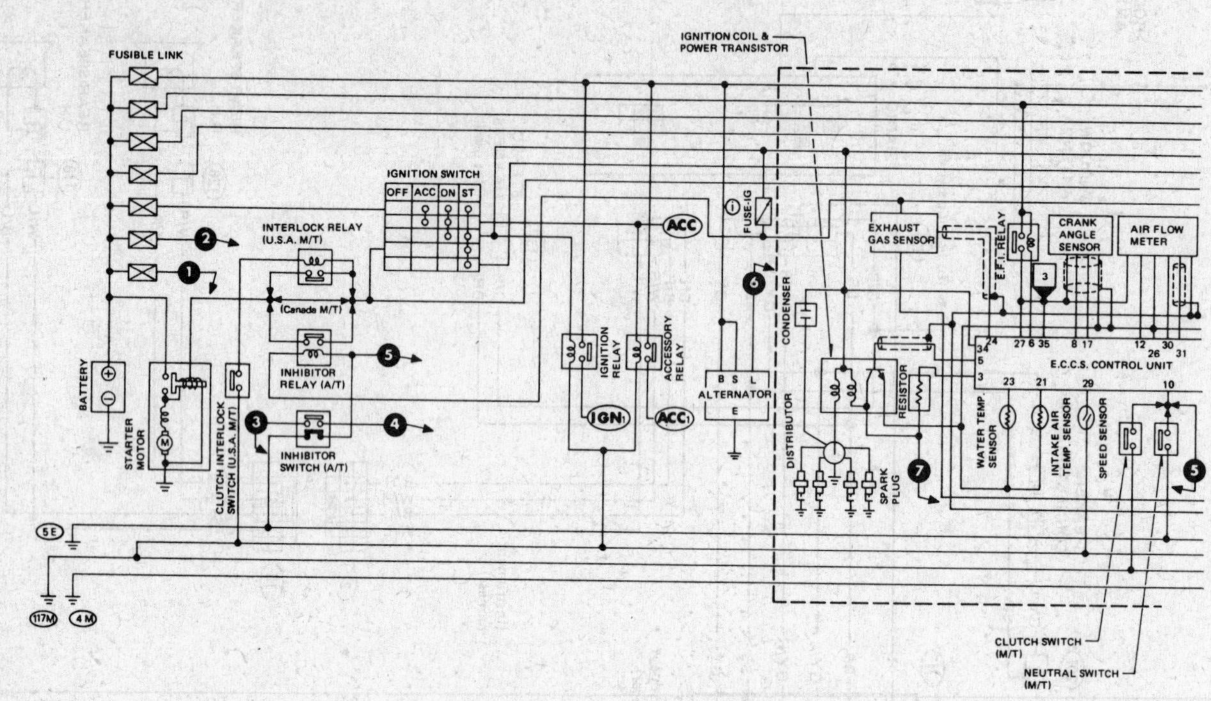
FUSIBLE LINK
IGNITION COIL & POWER TRANSISTOR
IGNITION SWITCH
OFF ACC ON ST
INTERLOCK RELAY (U.S.A. M/T)
(Canada M/T)
INHIBITOR RELAY (A/T)
INHIBITOR SWITCH (A/T)
BATTERY
STARTER MOTOR
CLUTCH INTERLOCK SWITCH (U.S.A. M/T)
IGNITION RELAY
ACCESSORY RELAY
ACC
IGN1
ACC1
FUSE-IG
ALTERNATOR
CONDENSER
DISTRIBUTOR
SPARK PLUG
RESISTOR
EXHAUST GAS SENSOR
E.F.I. RELAY
CRANK ANGLE SENSOR
AIR FLOW METER
E.C.C.S. CONTROL UNIT
WATER TEMP. SENSOR
INTAKE AIR TEMP. SENSOR
SPEED SENSOR
CLUTCH SWITCH (M/T)
NEUTRAL SWITCH (M/T)

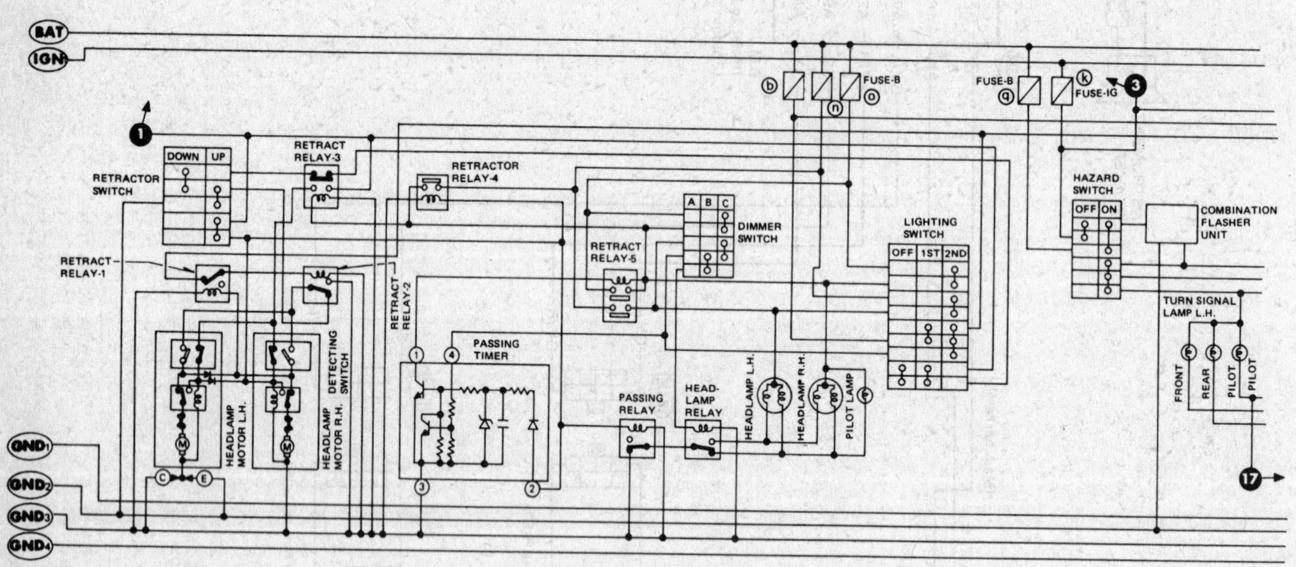
BAT
IGN
FUSE-B
FUSE-IG
RETRACTOR SWITCH
DOWN UP
RETRACT RELAY-3
RETRACTOR RELAY-4
RETRACT RELAY-1
RETRACT RELAY-2
RETRACT RELAY-5
DIMMER SWITCH
LIGHTING SWITCH
OFF 1ST 2ND
HAZARD SWITCH
OFF ON
COMBINATION FLASHER UNIT
TURN SIGNAL LAMP L.H.
FRONT
REAR
PILOT
HEADLAMP MOTOR L.H.
HEADLAMP MOTOR R.H.
DETECTING SWITCH
PASSING TIMER
PASSING RELAY
HEAD-LAMP RELAY
HEADLAMP L.H.
HEADLAMP R.H.
PILOT LAMP
GND1
GND2
GND3
GND4

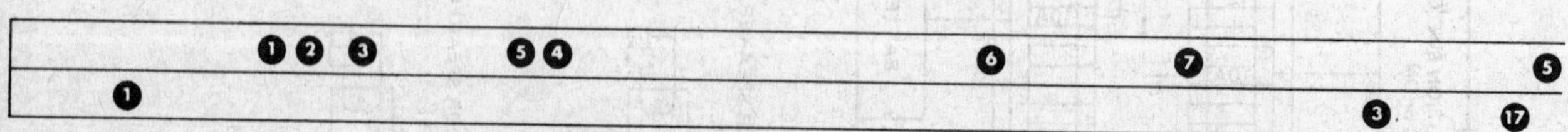

Fig. 59. Wiring diagram — 1987 Sentra

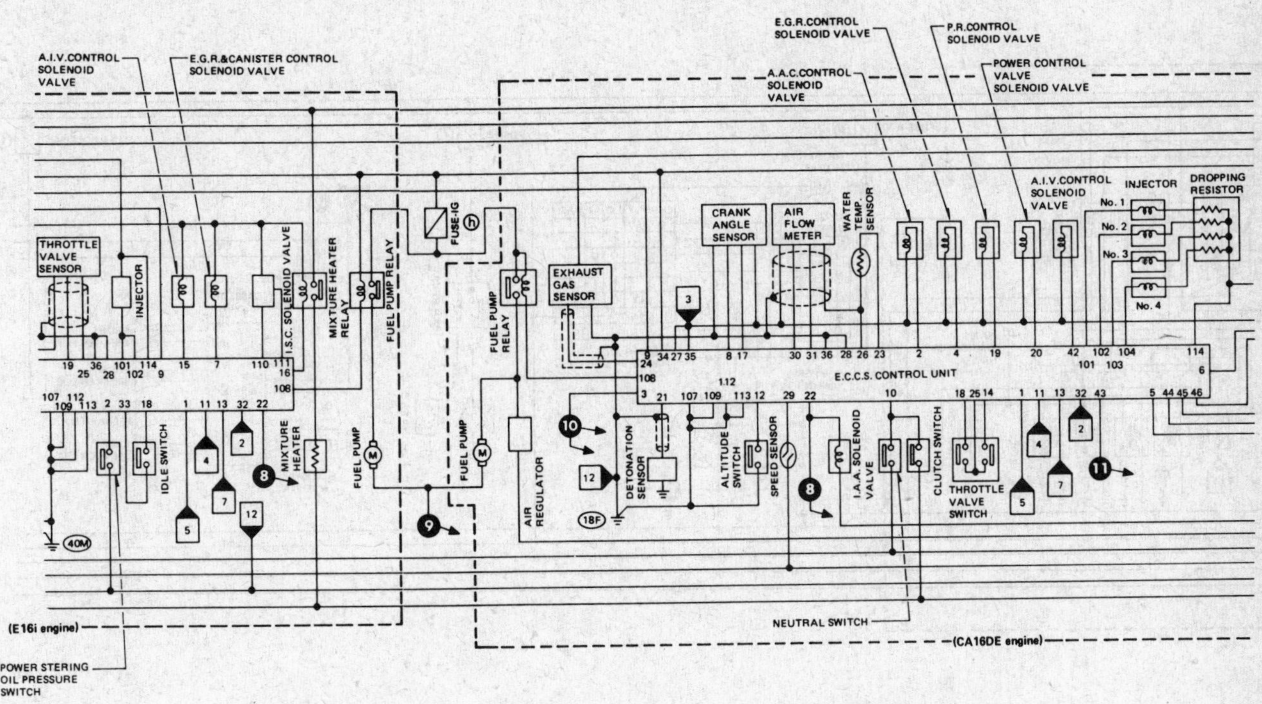
A.I.V.CONTROL SOLENOID VALVE
E.G.R.&CANISTER CONTROL SOLENOID VALVE
E.G.R.CONTROL SOLENOID VALVE
P.R.CONTROL SOLENOID VALVE
A.A.C.CONTROL SOLENOID VALVE
POWER CONTROL VALVE SOLENOID VALVE
THROTTLE VALVE SENSOR
INJECTOR
I.S.C. SOLENOID VALVE
MIXTURE HEATER RELAY
FUEL PUMP RELAY
FUSE-IG
FUEL PUMP RELAY
EXHAUST GAS SENSOR
CRANK ANGLE SENSOR
AIR FLOW METER
WATER TEMP. SENSOR
A.I.V.CONTROL SOLENOID VALVE
INJECTOR
DROPPING RESISTOR
E.C.C.S. CONTROL UNIT
IDLE SWITCH
MIXTURE HEATER
FUEL PUMP
FUEL PUMP
AIR REGULATOR
DETONATION SENSOR
ALTITUDE SWITCH
SPEED SENSOR
I.A.A. SOLENOID VALVE
CLUTCH SWITCH
THROTTLE VALVE SWITCH
NEUTRAL SWITCH
(E16i engine)
(CA16DE engine)
POWER STERING OIL PRESSURE SWITCH

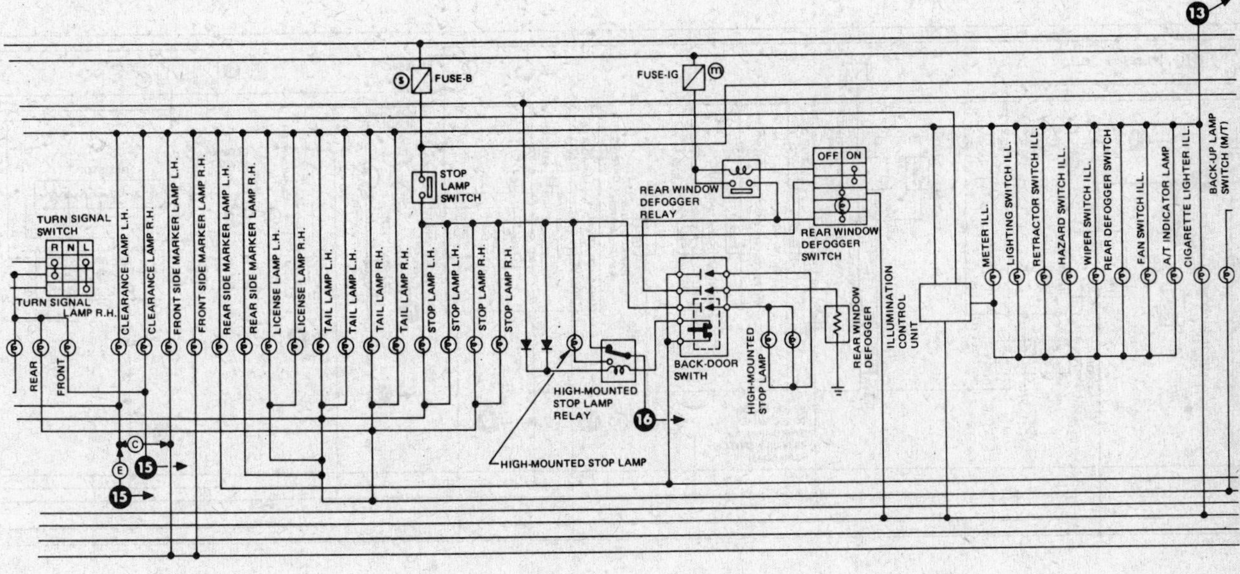
FUSE-B
FUSE-IG
STOP LAMP SWITCH
TURN SIGNAL SWITCH
TURN SIGNAL LAMP R.H.
REAR
FRONT
CLEARANCE LAMP L.H.
CLEARANCE LAMP R.H.
FRONT SIDE MARKER LAMP L.H.
FRONT SIDE MARKER LAMP R.H.
REAR SIDE MARKER LAMP L.H.
REAR SIDE MARKER LAMP R.H.
LICENSE LAMP L.H.
LICENSE LAMP R.H.
TAIL LAMP L.H.
TAIL LAMP L.H.
TAIL LAMP R.H.
TAIL LAMP R.H.
STOP LAMP L.H.
STOP LAMP L.H.
STOP LAMP R.H.
STOP LAMP R.H.
REAR WINDOW DEFOGGER RELAY
REAR WINDOW DEFOGGER SWITCH
HIGH-MOUNTED STOP LAMP RELAY
HIGH-MOUNTED STOP LAMP
BACK-DOOR SWITH
HIGH-MOUNTED STOP LAMP
REAR WINDOW DEFOGGER
ILLUMINATION CONTROL UNIT
METER ILL.
LIGHTING SWITCH ILL.
RETRACTOR SWITCH ILL.
HAZARD SWITCH ILL.
WIPER SWITCH ILL.
REAR DEFOGGER SWITCH
FAN SWITCH ILL.
A/T INDICATOR LAMP
CIGARETTE LIGHTER ILL.
BACK-UP LAMP SWITCH (M/T)

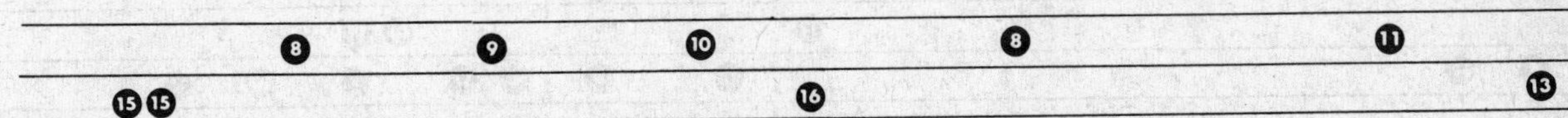

Fig. 59. Wiring diagram — 1987 Sentra

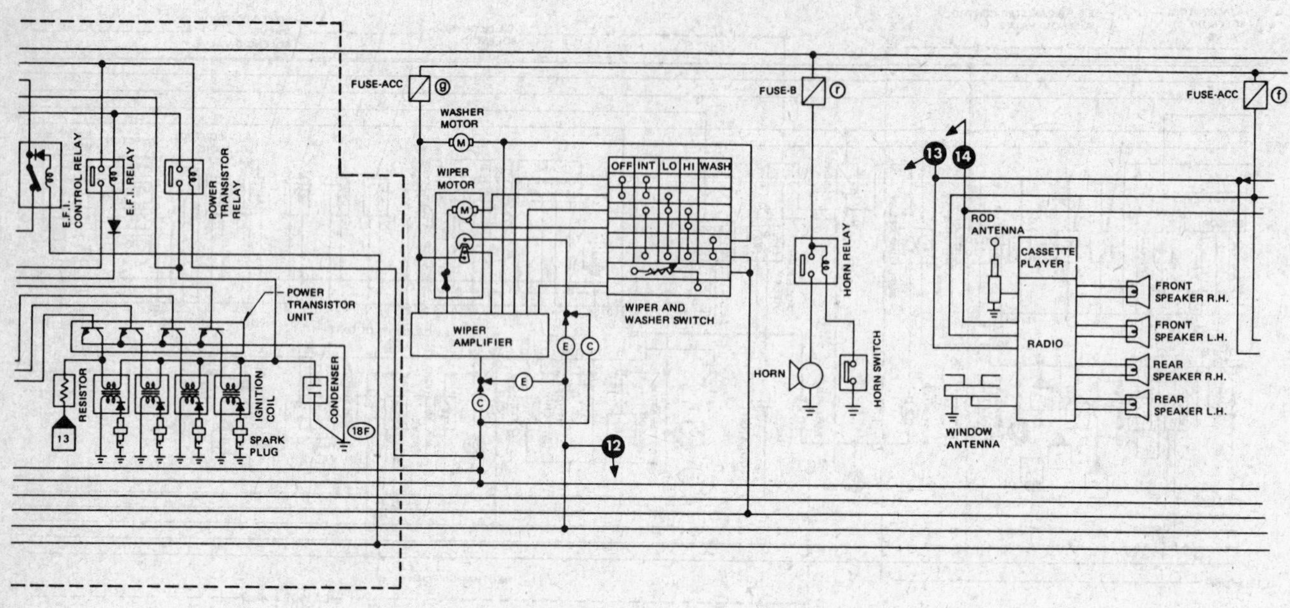
FUSE-ACC
g
WASHER MOTOR
WIPER MOTOR
FUSE-B
r
FUSE-ACC
f
E.F.I. CONTROL RELAY
E.F.I. RELAY
POWER TRANSISTOR RELAY
POWER TRANSISTOR UNIT
RESISTOR
13
IGNITION COIL
SPARK PLUG
CONDENSER
18F
WIPER AMPLIFIER
E
C
OFF INT LO HI WASH
WIPER AND WASHER SWITCH
12
HORN RELAY
HORN
HORN SWITCH
13
14
ROD ANTENNA
CASSETTE PLAYER
RADIO
FRONT SPEAKER R.H.
FRONT SPEAKER L.H.
REAR SPEAKER R.H.
REAR SPEAKER L.H.
WINDOW ANTENNA

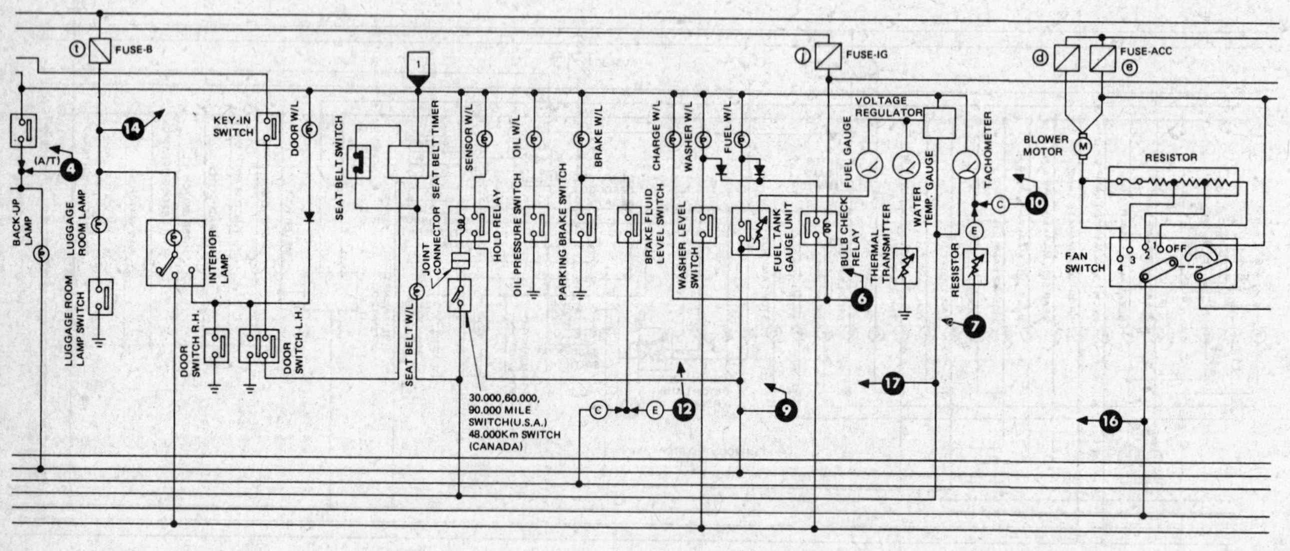
t
FUSE-B
14
(A/T)
4
BACK UP LAMP
LUGGAGE ROOM LAMP
LUGGAGE ROOM LAMP SWITCH
KEY-IN SWITCH
DOOR W/L
INTERIOR LAMP
DOOR SWITCH R.H.
DOOR SWITCH L.H.
1
SEAT BELT SWITCH
SEAT BELT TIMER
SEAT BELT W/L
JOINT CONNECTOR
SENSOR W/L
HOLD RELAY
OIL W/L
OIL PRESSURE SWITCH
PARKING BRAKE SWITCH
BRAKE W/L
BRAKE FLUID LEVEL SWITCH
CHARGE W/L
WASHER W/L
WASHER LEVEL SWITCH
FUEL W/L
FUEL TANK GAUGE UNIT
30.000,60.000,
90.000 MILE
SWITCH(U.S.A.)
48.000Km SWITCH
(CANADA)
12
9
j
FUSE-IG
VOLTAGE REGULATOR
FUEL GAUGE
BULB CHECK RELAY
6
WATER TEMP. GAUGE
THERMAL TRANSMITTER
TACHOMETER
RESISTOR
7
10
17
d
FUSE-ACC
e
BLOWER MOTOR
RESISTOR
FAN SWITCH
4 3 2 1 OFF
16

12
13 14
4 14 12 9 6 17 7 10 16

Fig. 59. Wiring diagram — 1987 Sentra

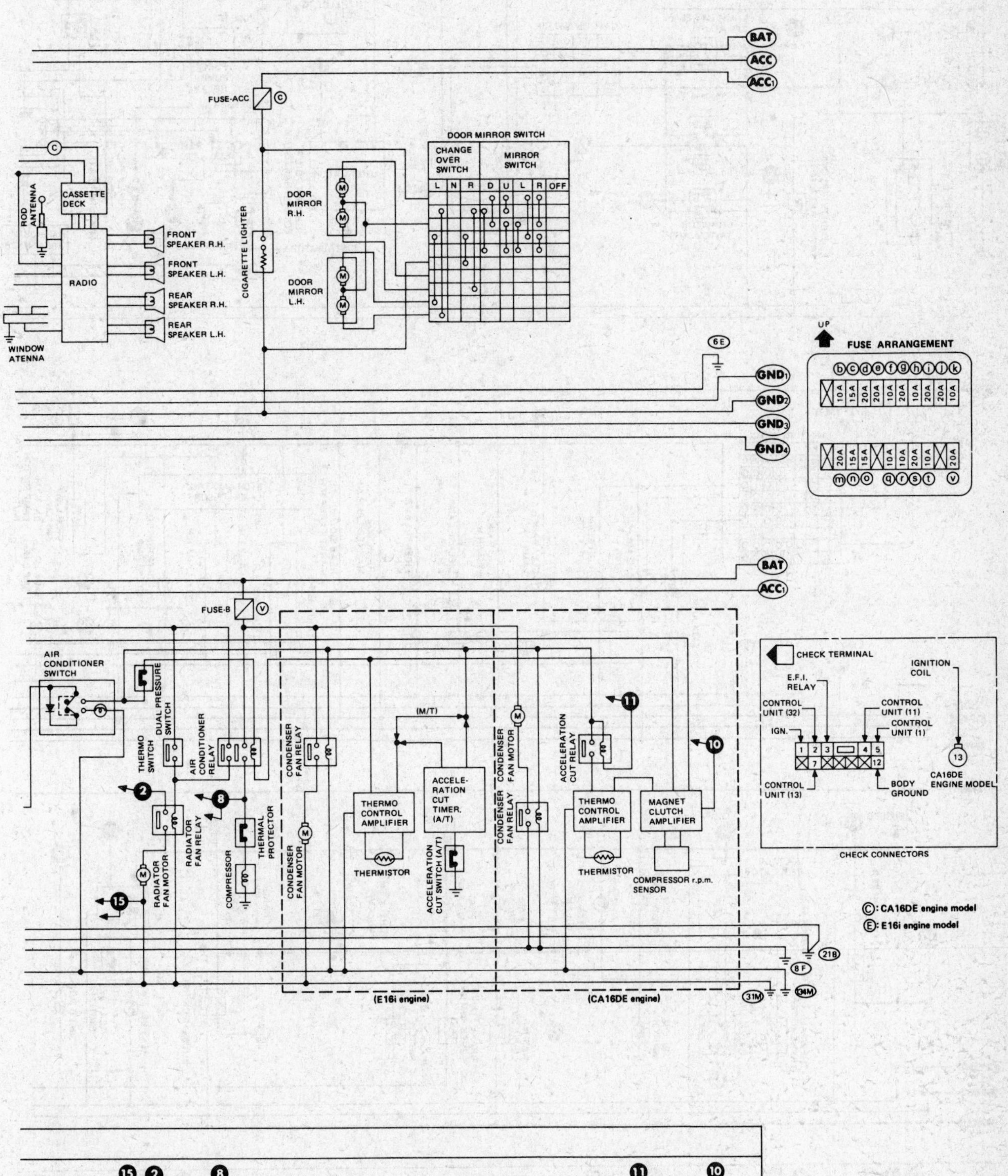
BAT
ACC
ACC1
FUSE-ACC
DOOR MIRROR SWITCH
CHANGE OVER SWITCH
MIRROR SWITCH
L N R D U L R OFF
CASSETTE DECK
ROD ANTENNA
FRONT SPEAKER R.H.
FRONT SPEAKER L.H.
RADIO
REAR SPEAKER R.H.
REAR SPEAKER L.H.
WINDOW ATENNA
CIGARETTE LIGHTER
DOOR MIRROR R.H.
DOOR MIRROR L.H.
6E
GND1
GND2
GND3
GND4
UP
FUSE ARRANGEMENT
FUSE-B
AIR CONDITIONER SWITCH
THERMO SWITCH
DUAL PRESSURE SWITCH
AIR CONDITIONER RELAY
RADIATOR FAN RELAY
RADIATOR FAN MOTOR
THERMAL PROTECTOR
COMPRESSOR
CONDENSER FAN RELAY
CONDENSER FAN MOTOR
(M/T)
THERMO CONTROL AMPLIFIER
THERMISTOR
ACCELE-RATION CUT TIMER. (A/T)
ACCELERATION CUT SWITCH (A/T)
ACCELERATION CUT RELAY
MAGNET CLUTCH AMPLIFIER
COMPRESSOR r.p.m. SENSOR
(E16i engine)
(CA16DE engine)
CHECK TERMINAL
E.F.I. RELAY
IGNITION COIL
CONTROL UNIT (32)
CONTROL UNIT (11)
CONTROL UNIT (1)
IGN.
CONTROL UNIT (13)
BODY GROUND
CA16DE ENGINE MODEL
CHECK CONNECTORS
Ⓒ: CA16DE engine model
Ⓔ: E16i engine model
21B
8F
31M
34M

Fig. 59. Wiring diagram — 1987 Sentra

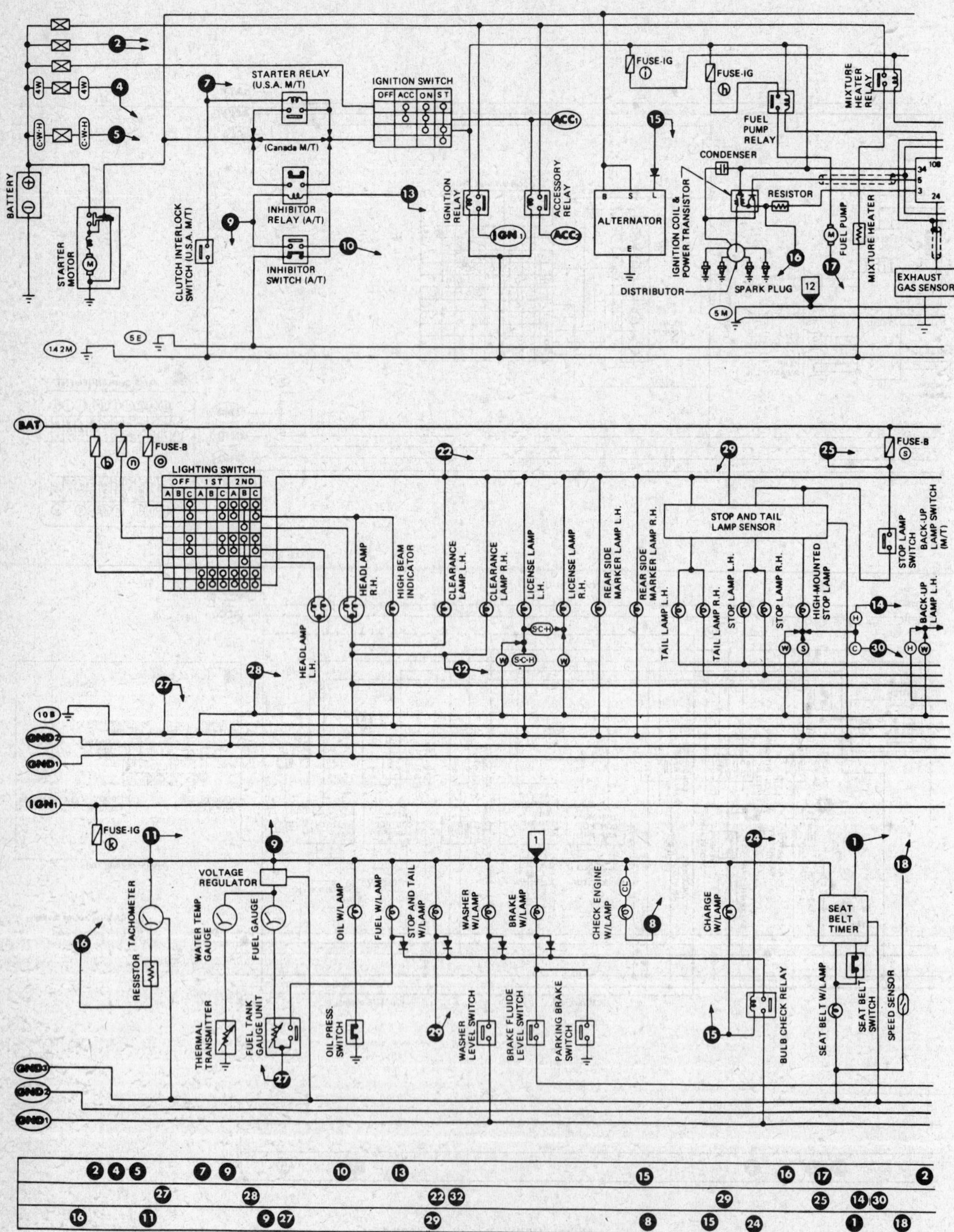

BATTERY
STARTER MOTOR
CLUTCH INTERLOCK SWITCH (U.S.A. M/T)
STARTER RELAY (U.S.A. M/T)
(Canada M/T)
INHIBITOR RELAY (A/T)
INHIBITOR SWITCH (A/T)
IGNITION SWITCH
OFF ACC ON ST
IGNITION RELAY
ACCESSORY RELAY
ALTERNATOR
FUSE-IG
CONDENSER
IGNITION COIL & POWER TRANSISTOR
RESISTOR
DISTRIBUTOR
SPARK PLUG
FUEL PUMP RELAY
FUEL PUMP
MIXTURE HEATER RELAY
MIXTURE HEATER
EXHAUST GAS SENSOR
FUSE-B
LIGHTING SWITCH
OFF 1ST 2ND
HEADLAMP L.H.
HEADLAMP R.H.
HIGH BEAM INDICATOR
CLEARANCE LAMP L.H.
CLEARANCE LAMP R.H.
LICENSE LAMP L.H.
LICENSE LAMP R.H.
REAR SIDE MARKER LAMP L.H.
REAR SIDE MARKER LAMP R.H.
STOP AND TAIL LAMP SENSOR
TAIL LAMP L.H.
TAIL LAMP R.H.
STOP LAMP L.H.
STOP LAMP R.H.
HIGH-MOUNTED STOP LAMP
STOP LAMP SWITCH
BACK-UP LAMP SWITCH (M/T)
BACK-UP LAMP L.H.
VOLTAGE REGULATOR
TACHOMETER
RESISTOR
WATER TEMP. GAUGE
FUEL GAUGE
THERMAL TRANSMITTER
FUEL TANK GAUGE UNIT
OIL W/LAMP
OIL PRESS. SWITCH
FUEL W/LAMP
STOP AND TAIL W/LAMP
WASHER W/LAMP
WASHER LEVEL SWITCH
BRAKE W/LAMP
BRAKE FLUIDE LEVEL SWITCH
PARKING BRAKE SWITCH
CHECK ENGINE W/LAMP
CHARGE W/LAMP
BULB CHECK RELAY
SEAT BELT TIMER
SEAT BELT W/LAMP
SEAT BELT SWITCH
SPEED SENSOR

Fig. 60. Complete circuit wiring diagram — 1988 Sentra

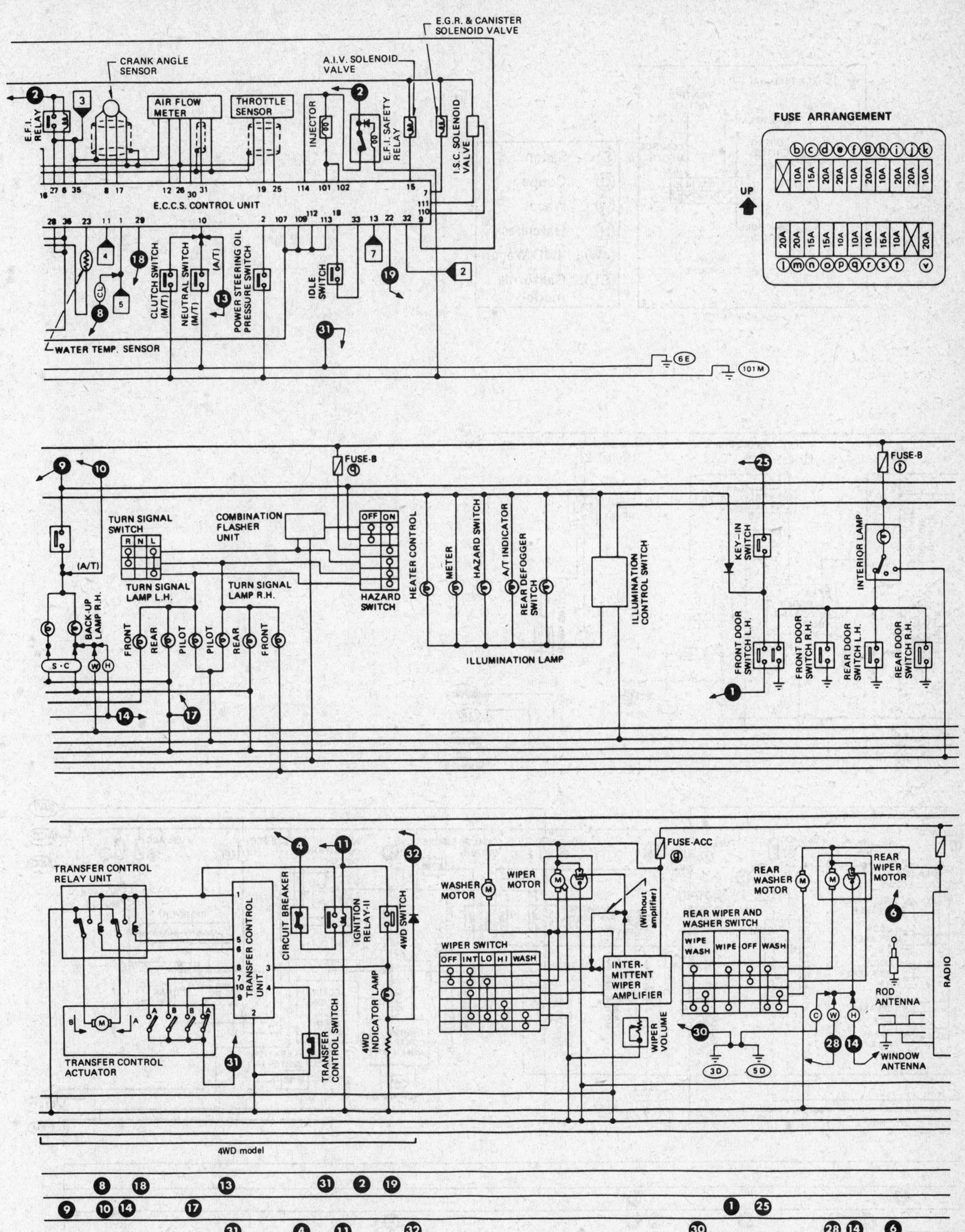
E.G.R. & CANISTER SOLENOID VALVE
CRANK ANGLE SENSOR
A.I.V. SOLENOID VALVE
E.F.I. RELAY
AIR FLOW METER
THROTTLE SENSOR
INJECTOR
E.F.I. SAFETY RELAY
I.S.C. SOLENOID VALVE
E.C.C.S. CONTROL UNIT
CLUTCH SWITCH (M/T)
NEUTRAL SWITCH (M/T)
POWER STEERING OIL PRESSURE SWITCH
IDLE SWITCH
WATER TEMP. SENSOR
FUSE ARRANGEMENT
UP
FUSE-B
TURN SIGNAL SWITCH
COMBINATION FLASHER UNIT
HAZARD SWITCH
TURN SIGNAL LAMP L.H.
TURN SIGNAL LAMP R.H.
BACK-UP LAMP R.H.
HEATER CONTROL
METER
HAZARD SWITCH
A/T INDICATOR
REAR DEFOGGER SWITCH
ILLUMINATION LAMP
ILLUMINATION CONTROL SWITCH
KEY-IN SWITCH
INTERIOR LAMP
FRONT DOOR SWITCH L.H.
FRONT DOOR SWITCH R.H.
REAR DOOR SWITCH L.H.
REAR DOOR SWITCH R.H.
TRANSFER CONTROL RELAY UNIT
TRANSFER CONTROL UNIT
CIRCUIT BREAKER
IGNITION RELAY-II
4WD SWITCH
4WD INDICATOR LAMP
TRANSFER CONTROL SWITCH
TRANSFER CONTROL ACTUATOR
4WD model
WASHER MOTOR
WIPER MOTOR
WIPER SWITCH
FUSE-ACC
(Without amplifier)
INTER-MITTENT WIPER AMPLIFIER
WIPER VOLUME
REAR WIPER AND WASHER SWITCH
REAR WASHER MOTOR
REAR WIPER MOTOR
ROD ANTENNA
WINDOW ANTENNA
RADIO

Fig. 60. Complete circuit wiring diagram — 1988 Sentra

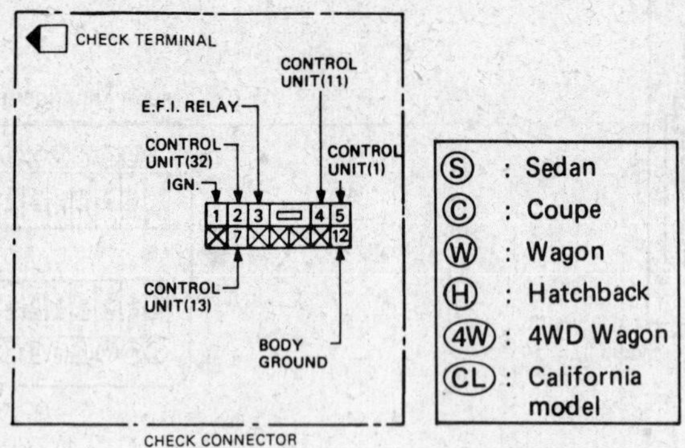
CHECK TERMINAL
CONTROL UNIT(11)
E.F.I. RELAY
CONTROL UNIT(32)
CONTROL UNIT(1)
IGN.
1 2 3 4 5
7 12
CONTROL UNIT(13)
BODY GROUND
CHECK CONNECTOR

Ⓢ : Sedan
Ⓒ : Coupe
Ⓦ : Wagon
Ⓗ : Hatchback
(4W) : 4WD Wagon
(CL) : California model

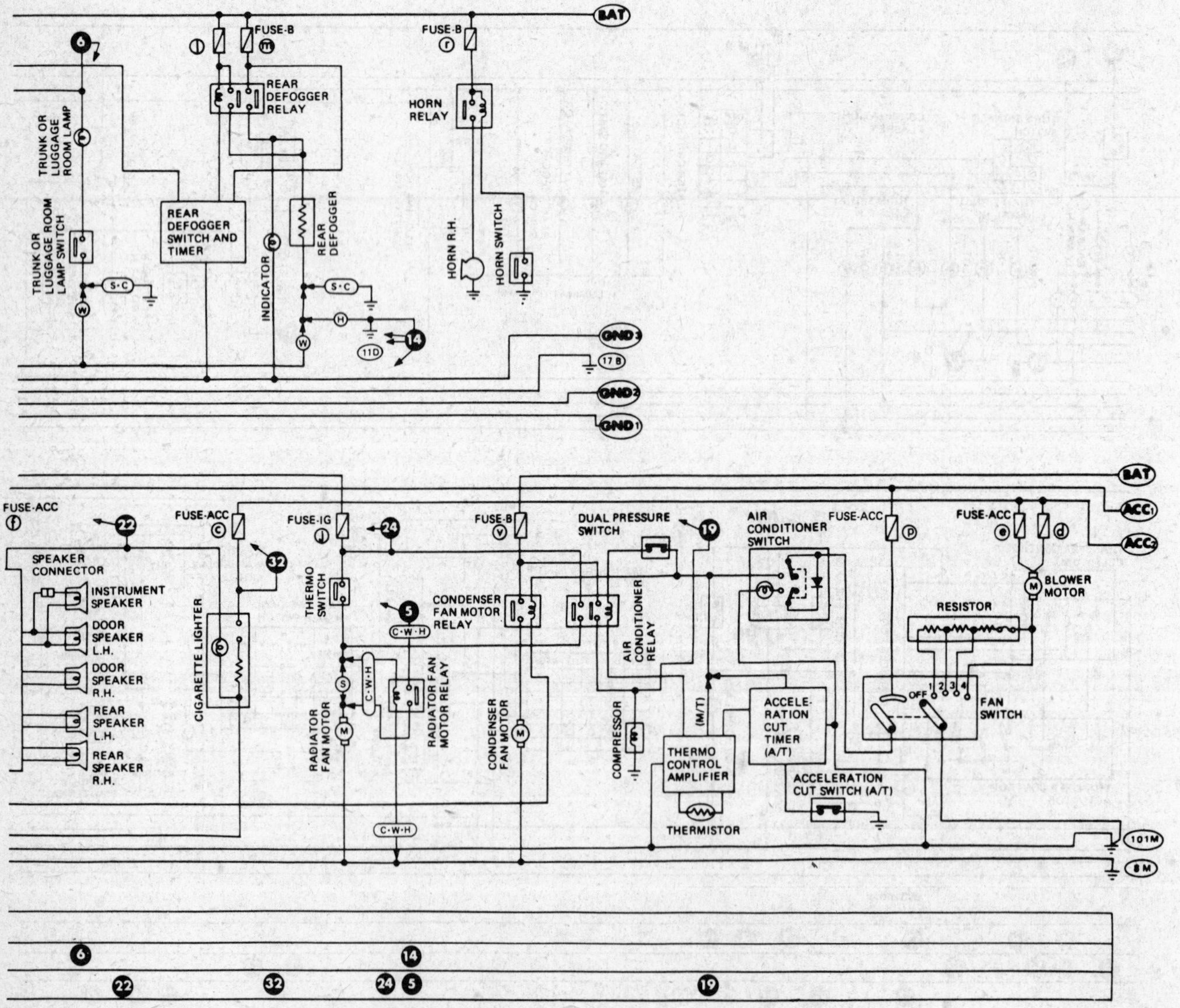

Fig. 60. Complete circuit wiring diagram — 1988 Sentra

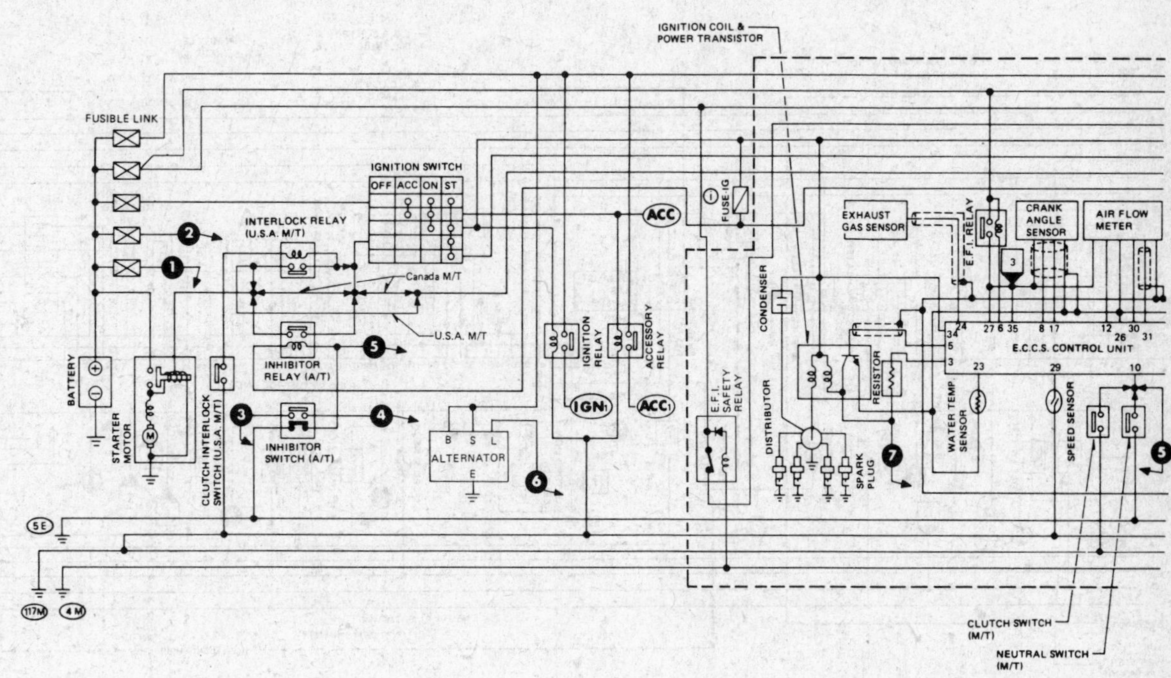
IGNITION COIL & POWER TRANSISTOR
FUSIBLE LINK
IGNITION SWITCH
OFF ACC ON ST
INTERLOCK RELAY (U.S.A. M/T)
Canada M/T
U.S.A. M/T
INHIBITOR RELAY (A/T)
INHIBITOR SWITCH (A/T)
BATTERY
STARTER MOTOR
CLUTCH INTERLOCK SWITCH (U.S.A M/T)
B S L
ALTERNATOR
E
IGNITION RELAY
ACCESSORY RELAY
ACC
IGN1
ACC1
FUSE-IG
CONDENSER
E.F.I. SAFETY RELAY
DISTRIBUTOR
SPARK PLUG
RESISTOR
EXHAUST GAS SENSOR
E.F.I. RELAY
CRANK ANGLE SENSOR
AIR FLOW METER
E.C.C.S. CONTROL UNIT
WATER TEMP SENSOR
SPEED SENSOR
CLUTCH SWITCH (M/T)
NEUTRAL SWITCH (M/T)
5E
117M
4M

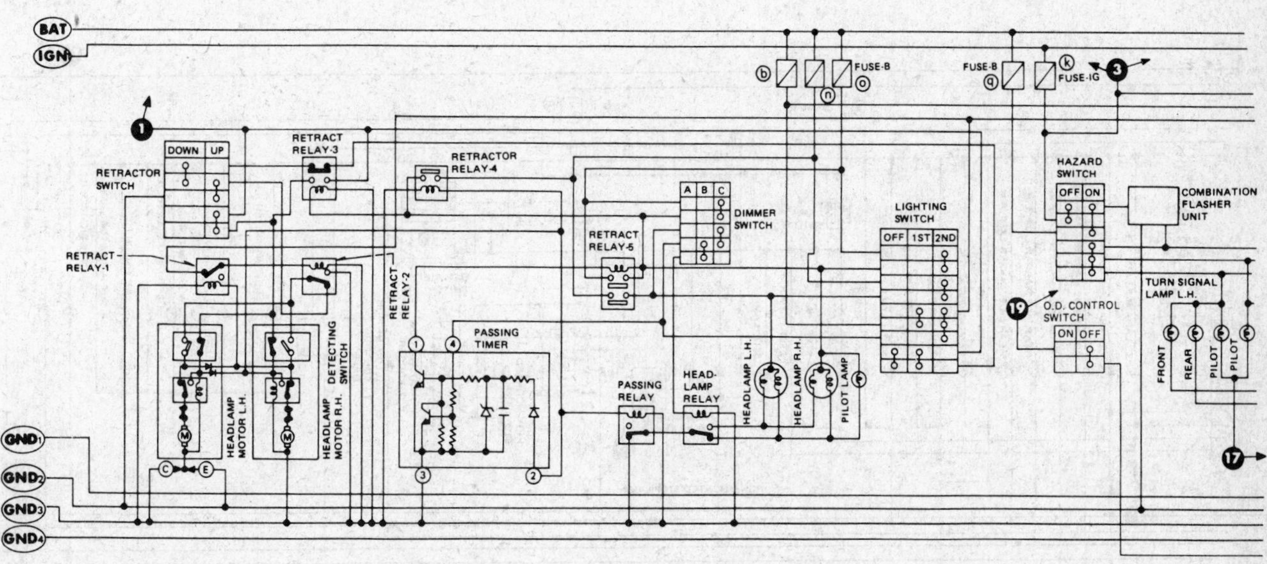
BAT
IGN
FUSE-B
FUSE-B
FUSE-IG
RETRACTOR SWITCH
DOWN UP
RETRACT RELAY-3
RETRACTOR RELAY-4
RETRACT-RELAY-1
RETRACT RELAY-2
DETECTING SWITCH
HEADLAMP MOTOR L.H.
HEADLAMP MOTOR R.H.
PASSING TIMER
A B C
DIMMER SWITCH
RETRACT RELAY-5
LIGHTING SWITCH
OFF 1ST 2ND
PASSING RELAY
HEAD-LAMP RELAY
HEADLAMP L.H.
HEADLAMP R.H.
PILOT LAMP
HAZARD SWITCH
OFF ON
COMBINATION FLASHER UNIT
O.D. CONTROL SWITCH
ON OFF
TURN SIGNAL LAMP L.H.
FRONT
REAR
PILOT
PILOT
GND1
GND2
GND3
GND4

1 2 3 5 4 6 7 5

1 19 3 17

Fig. 61. Complete circuit wiring diagram — 1988 Pulsar

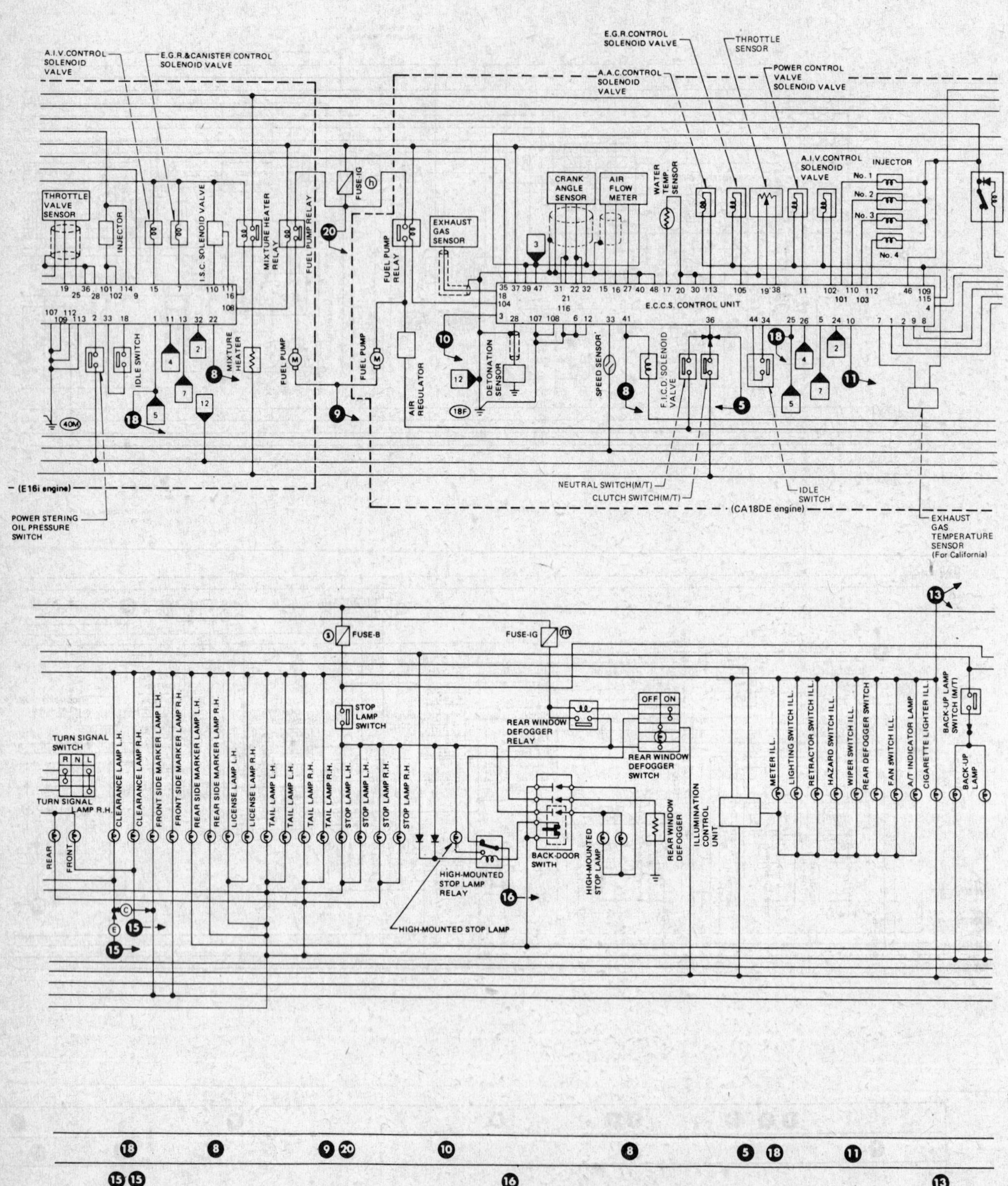
A.I.V. CONTROL SOLENOID VALVE
E.G.R.&CANISTER CONTROL SOLENOID VALVE
E.G.R. CONTROL SOLENOID VALVE
THROTTLE SENSOR
A.A.C. CONTROL SOLENOID VALVE
POWER CONTROL VALVE SOLENOID VALVE
THROTTLE VALVE SENSOR
INJECTOR
I.S.C. SOLENOID VALVE
MIXTURE HEATER RELAY
FUEL PUMP RELAY
FUSE-IG
EXHAUST GAS SENSOR
FUEL PUMP RELAY
CRANK ANGLE SENSOR
AIR FLOW METER
WATER TEMP SENSOR
A.I.V. CONTROL SOLENOID VALVE
INJECTOR
No. 1
No. 2
No. 3
No. 4
E.C.C.S. CONTROL UNIT
IDLE SWITCH
MIXTURE HEATER
FUEL PUMP
FUEL PUMP
AIR REGULATOR
DETONATION SENSOR
SPEED SENSOR
F.I.C.D. SOLENOID VALVE
(E16i engine)
POWER STERING OIL PRESSURE SWITCH
NEUTRAL SWITCH(M/T)
CLUTCH SWITCH(M/T)
IDLE SWITCH
(CA18DE engine)
EXHAUST GAS TEMPERATURE SENSOR (For California)
FUSE-B
FUSE-IG
STOP LAMP SWITCH
TURN SIGNAL SWITCH
R N L
TURN SIGNAL LAMP R.H.
REAR
FRONT
CLEARANCE LAMP L.H.
CLEARANCE LAMP R.H.
FRONT SIDE MARKER LAMP L.H.
FRONT SIDE MARKER LAMP R.H.
REAR SIDE MARKER LAMP L.H.
REAR SIDE MARKER LAMP R.H.
LICENSE LAMP L.H.
LICENSE LAMP R.H.
TAIL LAMP L.H.
TAIL LAMP L.H.
TAIL LAMP R.H.
TAIL LAMP R.H.
STOP LAMP L.H.
STOP LAMP L.H.
STOP LAMP R.H.
STOP LAMP R.H.
REAR WINDOW DEFOGGER RELAY
OFF ON
REAR WINDOW DEFOGGER SWITCH
HIGH-MOUNTED STOP LAMP RELAY
BACK-DOOR SWITH
HIGH-MOUNTED STOP LAMP
REAR WINDOW DEFOGGER
ILLUMINATION CONTROL UNIT
HIGH-MOUNTED STOP LAMP
METER ILL.
LIGHTING SWITCH ILL.
RETRACTOR SWITCH ILL.
HAZARD SWITCH ILL.
WIPER SWITCH ILL.
REAR DEFOGGER SWITCH
FAN SWITCH ILL.
A/T INDICATOR LAMP
CIGARETTE LIGHTER ILL.
BACK-UP LAMP SWITCH (M/T)
BACK-UP LAMP

Fig. 61. Complete circuit wiring diagram — 1988 Pulsar

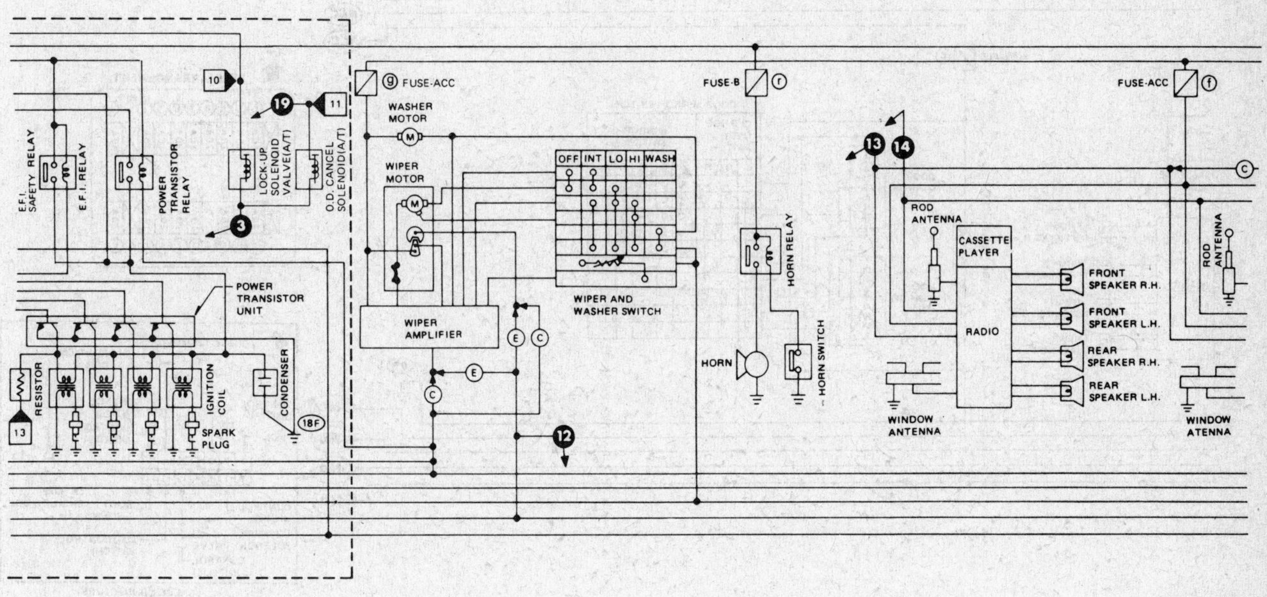
FUSE-ACC
WASHER MOTOR
WIPER MOTOR
E.F.I. SAFETY RELAY
E.F.I. RELAY
POWER TRANSISTOR RELAY
LOCK-UP SOLENOID VALVE(A/T)
O.D. CANCEL SOLENOID(A/T)
POWER TRANSISTOR UNIT
RESISTOR
IGNITION COIL
CONDENSER
SPARK PLUG
WIPER AMPLIFIER
OFF INT LO HI WASH
WIPER AND WASHER SWITCH
FUSE-B
HORN RELAY
HORN
HORN SWITCH
ROD ANTENNA
CASSETTE PLAYER
RADIO
FRONT SPEAKER R.H.
FRONT SPEAKER L.H.
REAR SPEAKER R.H.
REAR SPEAKER L.H.
WINDOW ANTENNA
WINDOW ATENNA

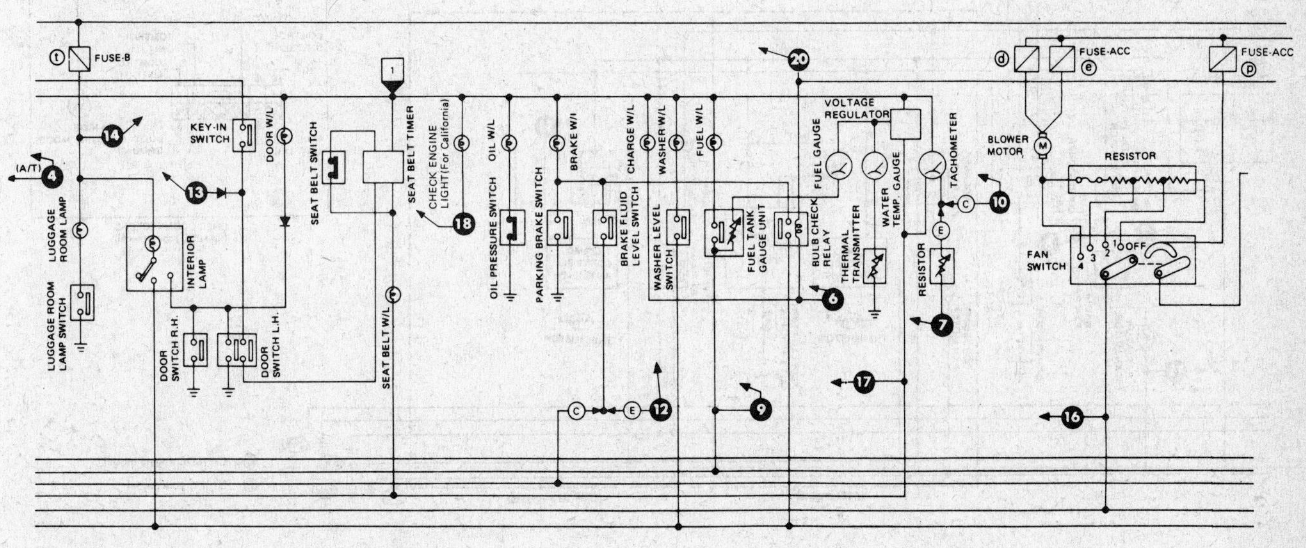
FUSE-B
(A/T)
LUGGAGE ROOM LAMP
LUGGAGE ROOM LAMP SWITCH
KEY-IN SWITCH
DOOR W/L
INTERIOR LAMP
DOOR SWITCH R.H.
DOOR SWITCH L.H.
SEAT BELT SWITCH
SEAT BELT TIMER
SEAT BELT W/L
CHECK ENGINE LIGHT(For California)
OIL W/L
OIL PRESSURE SWITCH
PARKING BRAKE SWITCH
BRAKE W/I
BRAKE FLUID LEVEL SWITCH
CHARGE W/L
WASHER W/L
WASHER LEVEL SWITCH
FUEL W/L
FUEL TANK GAUGE UNIT
BULB CHECK RELAY
FUEL GAUGE
VOLTAGE REGULATOR
THERMAL TRANSMITTER
WATER TEMP. GAUGE
TACHOMETER
RESISTOR
FUSE-ACC
BLOWER MOTOR
RESISTOR
FAN SWITCH
OFF

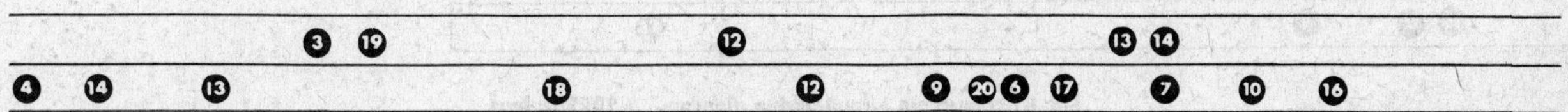

Fig. 61. Complete circuit wiring diagram — 1988 Pulsar

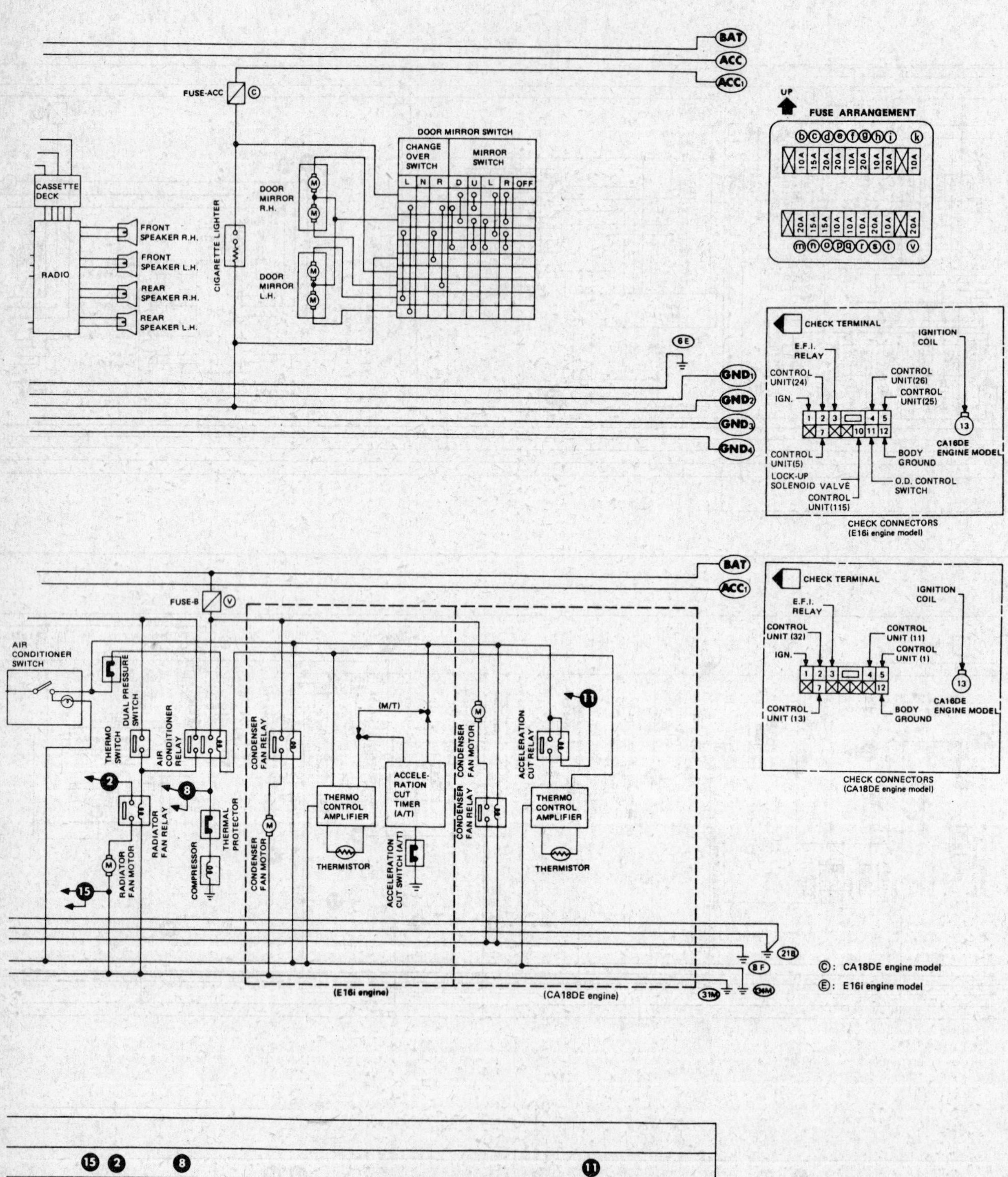
BAT
ACC
ACC1
FUSE-ACC
FUSE ARRANGEMENT
DOOR MIRROR SWITCH
CHANGE OVER SWITCH
MIRROR SWITCH
CASSETTE DECK
RADIO
FRONT SPEAKER R.H.
FRONT SPEAKER L.H.
REAR SPEAKER R.H.
REAR SPEAKER L.H.
CIGARETTE LIGHTER
DOOR MIRROR R.H.
DOOR MIRROR L.H.
CHECK TERMINAL
IGNITION COIL
E.F.I. RELAY
CONTROL UNIT(24)
CONTROL UNIT(26)
CONTROL UNIT(25)
IGN.
CONTROL UNIT(5)
BODY GROUND
CA16DE ENGINE MODEL
LOCK-UP SOLENOID VALVE
O.D. CONTROL SWITCH
CONTROL UNIT(115)
CHECK CONNECTORS (E16i engine model)
GND1
GND2
GND3
GND4
FUSE-B
AIR CONDITIONER SWITCH
CONTROL UNIT (32)
CONTROL UNIT (11)
CONTROL UNIT (1)
CONTROL UNIT (13)
CA18DE ENGINE MODEL
CHECK CONNECTORS (CA18DE engine model)
THERMO SWITCH
DUAL PRESSURE SWITCH
AIR CONDITIONER RELAY
CONDENSER FAN RELAY
CONDENSER FAN MOTOR
RADIATOR FAN RELAY
RADIATOR FAN MOTOR
COMPRESSOR
THERMAL PROTECTOR
THERMO CONTROL AMPLIFIER
THERMISTOR
ACCELERATION CUT TIMER (A/T)
ACCELERATION CUT SWITCH (A/T)
ACCELERATION CUT RELAY
(M/T)
(E16i engine)
(CA18DE engine)
Ⓒ: CA18DE engine model
Ⓔ: E16i engine model

Fig. 61. Complete circuit wiring diagram — 1988 Pulsar

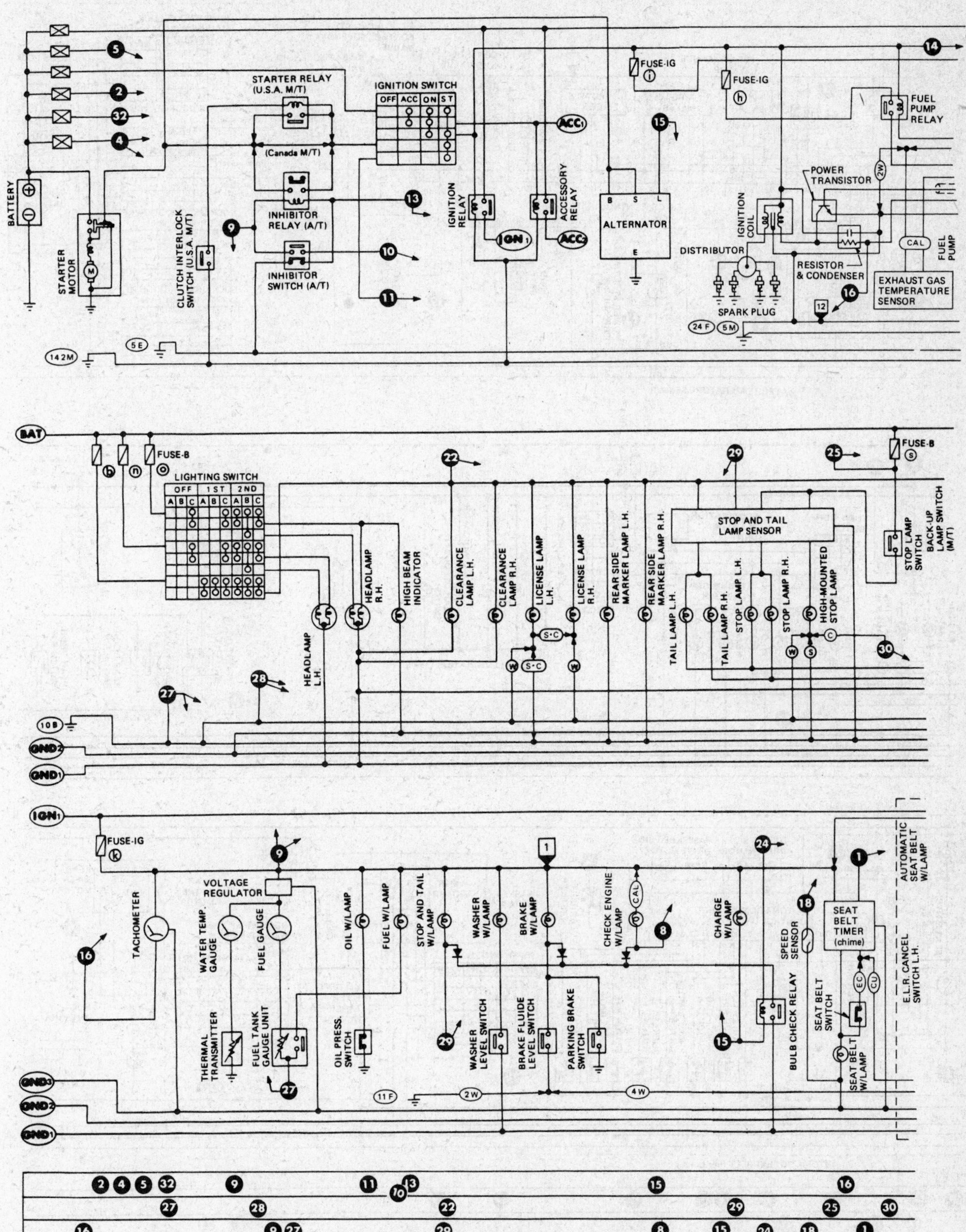
BATTERY
STARTER MOTOR
STARTER RELAY (U.S.A. M/T)
(Canada M/T)
INHIBITOR RELAY (A/T)
INHIBITOR SWITCH (A/T)
CLUTCH INTERLOCK SWITCH (U.S.A. M/T)
IGNITION SWITCH
OFF ACC ON ST
IGNITION RELAY
ACCESSORY RELAY
FUSE-IG
ALTERNATOR
IGNITION COIL
POWER TRANSISTOR
DISTRIBUTOR
RESISTOR & CONDENSER
SPARK PLUG
FUEL PUMP RELAY
FUEL PUMP
EXHAUST GAS TEMPERATURE SENSOR
FUSE-B
LIGHTING SWITCH
OFF 1ST 2ND
HEADLAMP L.H.
HEADLAMP R.H.
HIGH BEAM INDICATOR
CLEARANCE LAMP L.H.
CLEARANCE LAMP R.H.
LICENSE LAMP L.H.
LICENSE LAMP R.H.
REAR SIDE MARKER LAMP L.H.
REAR SIDE MARKER LAMP R.H.
STOP AND TAIL LAMP SENSOR
TAIL LAMP L.H.
TAIL LAMP R.H.
STOP LAMP L.H.
STOP LAMP R.H.
HIGH-MOUNTED STOP LAMP
STOP LAMP SWITCH
BACK-UP LAMP SWITCH (M/T)
TACHOMETER
VOLTAGE REGULATOR
WATER TEMP. GAUGE
FUEL GAUGE
THERMAL TRANSMITTER
FUEL TANK GAUGE UNIT
OIL W/LAMP
OIL PRESS. SWITCH
FUEL W/LAMP
STOP AND TAIL W/LAMP
WASHER W/LAMP
WASHER LEVEL SWITCH
BRAKE W/LAMP
BRAKE FLUIDE LEVEL SWITCH
PARKING BRAKE SWITCH
CHECK ENGINE W/LAMP
CHARGE W/LAMP
BULB CHECK RELAY
SPEED SENSOR
SEAT BELT TIMER (chime)
SEAT BELT SWITCH
SEAT BELT W/LAMP
AUTOMATIC SEAT BELT W/LAMP
E.L.R. CANCEL SWITCH L.H.

Fig. 62. Complete circuit wiring diagram — 1989 Sentra

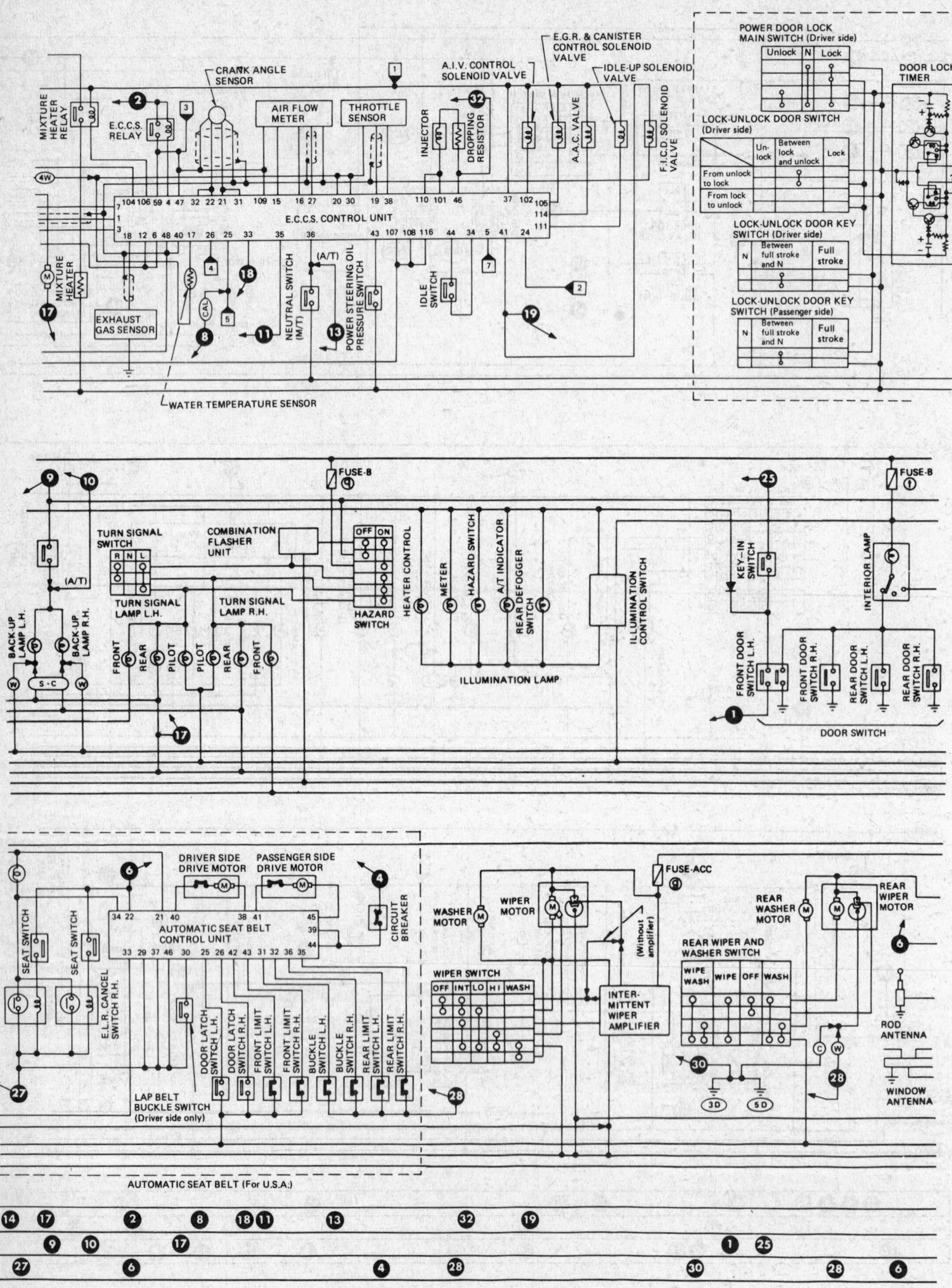

MIXTURE HEATER RELAY
E.C.C.S. RELAY
CRANK ANGLE SENSOR
AIR FLOW METER
THROTTLE SENSOR
INJECTOR
DROPPING RESISTOR
A.I.V. CONTROL SOLENOID VALVE
E.G.R. & CANISTER CONTROL SOLENOID VALVE
IDLE-UP SOLENOID VALVE
A.A.C. VALVE
F.I.C.D. SOLENOID VALVE
E.C.C.S. CONTROL UNIT
MIXTURE HEATER
EXHAUST GAS SENSOR
WATER TEMPERATURE SENSOR
NEUTRAL SWITCH (M/T)
POWER STEERING OIL PRESSURE SWITCH
IDLE SWITCH
POWER DOOR LOCK MAIN SWITCH (Driver side)
Unlock
N
Lock
DOOR LOCK TIMER
LOCK-UNLOCK DOOR SWITCH (Driver side)
Between lock and unlock
From unlock to lock
From lock to unlock
LOCK-UNLOCK DOOR KEY SWITCH (Driver side)
Between full stroke and N
Full stroke
LOCK-UNLOCK DOOR KEY SWITCH (Passenger side)
FUSE-B
TURN SIGNAL SWITCH
COMBINATION FLASHER UNIT
HAZARD SWITCH
BACK-UP LAMP L.H.
BACK-UP LAMP R.H.
TURN SIGNAL LAMP L.H.
TURN SIGNAL LAMP R.H.
FRONT
REAR
PILOT
HEATER CONTROL
METER
HAZARD SWITCH
A/T INDICATOR
REAR DEFOGGER SWITCH
ILLUMINATION CONTROL SWITCH
ILLUMINATION LAMP
KEY-IN SWITCH
INTERIOR LAMP
FRONT DOOR SWITCH L.H.
FRONT DOOR SWITCH R.H.
REAR DOOR SWITCH L.H.
REAR DOOR SWITCH R.H.
DOOR SWITCH
DRIVER SIDE DRIVE MOTOR
PASSENGER SIDE DRIVE MOTOR
AUTOMATIC SEAT BELT CONTROL UNIT
CIRCUIT BREAKER
SEAT SWITCH
E.L.R. CANCEL SWITCH R.H.
DOOR LATCH SWITCH L.H.
DOOR LATCH SWITCH R.H.
FRONT LIMIT SWITCH L.H.
FRONT LIMIT SWITCH R.H.
BUCKLE SWITCH L.H.
BUCKLE SWITCH R.H.
REAR LIMIT SWITCH L.H.
REAR LIMIT SWITCH R.H.
LAP BELT BUCKLE SWITCH (Driver side only)
AUTOMATIC SEAT BELT (For U.S.A.)
FUSE-ACC
WASHER MOTOR
WIPER MOTOR
WIPER SWITCH
OFF INT LO HI WASH
INTER-MITTENT WIPER AMPLIFIER
(Without amplifier)
REAR WASHER MOTOR
REAR WIPER MOTOR
REAR WIPER AND WASHER SWITCH
WIPE WASH
WIPE
OFF
WASH
ROD ANTENNA
WINDOW ANTENNA

Fig. 62. Complete circuit wiring diagram — 1989 Sentra

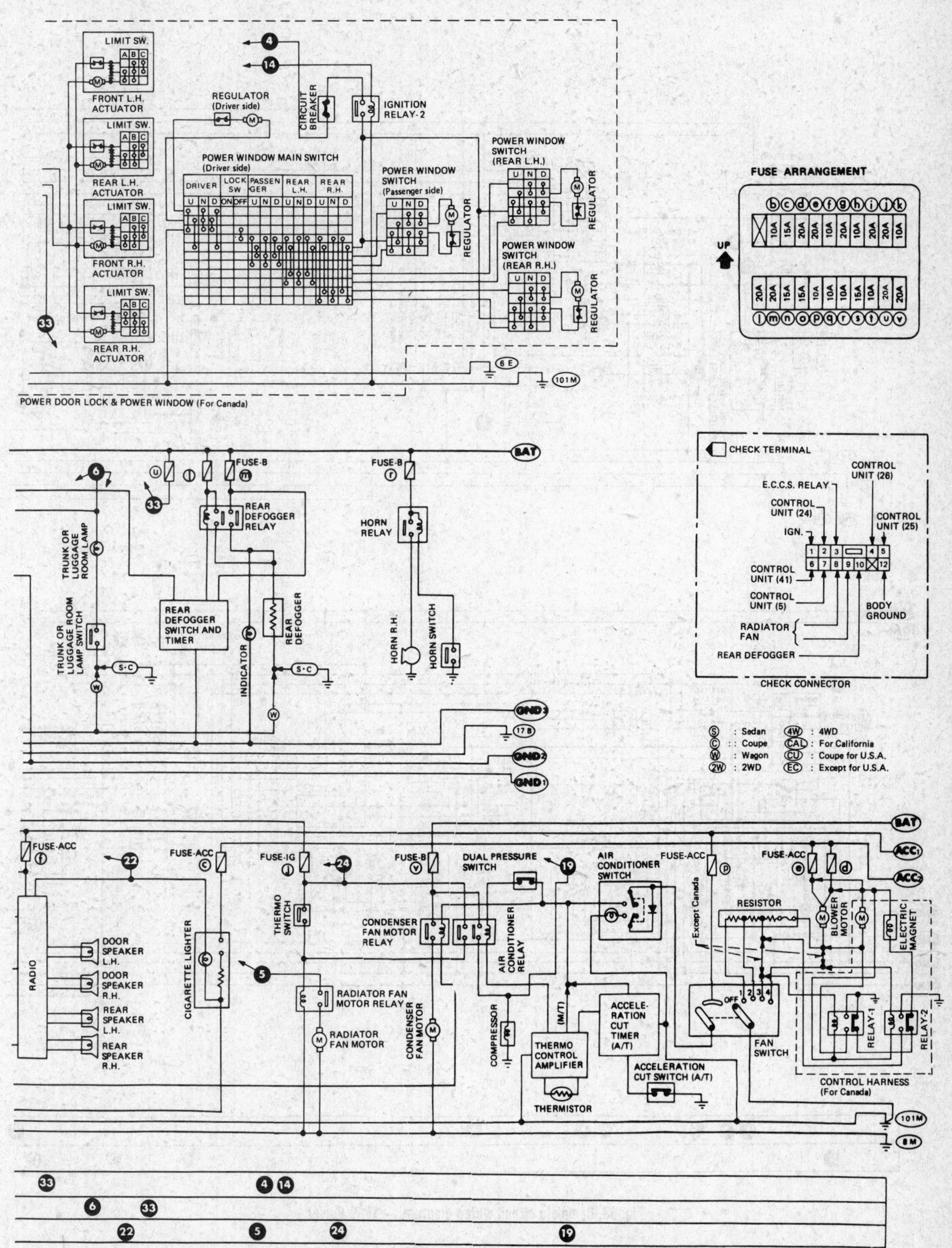
LIMIT SW.
FRONT L.H. ACTUATOR
REAR L.H. ACTUATOR
FRONT R.H. ACTUATOR
REAR R.H. ACTUATOR
REGULATOR (Driver side)
CIRCUIT BREAKER
IGNITION RELAY-2
POWER WINDOW MAIN SWITCH (Driver side)
POWER WINDOW SWITCH (Passenger side)
POWER WINDOW SWITCH (REAR L.H.)
POWER WINDOW SWITCH (REAR R.H.)
REGULATOR
POWER DOOR LOCK & POWER WINDOW (For Canada)
FUSE ARRANGEMENT
UP
CHECK TERMINAL
E.C.C.S. RELAY
CONTROL UNIT (26)
CONTROL UNIT (24)
CONTROL UNIT (25)
IGN.
CONTROL UNIT (41)
CONTROL UNIT (5)
BODY GROUND
RADIATOR FAN
REAR DEFOGGER
CHECK CONNECTOR
FUSE-B
REAR DEFOGGER RELAY
HORN RELAY
TRUNK OR LUGGAGE ROOM LAMP
TRUNK OR LUGGAGE ROOM LAMP SWITCH
REAR DEFOGGER SWITCH AND TIMER
INDICATOR
HORN R.H.
HORN SWITCH
Ⓢ : Sedan
Ⓒ : Coupe
Ⓦ : Wagon
2W : 2WD
4W : 4WD
CAL : For California
CU : Coupe for U.S.A.
EC : Except for U.S.A.
FUSE-ACC
FUSE-IG
DUAL PRESSURE SWITCH
AIR CONDITIONER SWITCH
RADIO
DOOR SPEAKER L.H.
DOOR SPEAKER R.H.
REAR SPEAKER L.H.
REAR SPEAKER R.H.
CIGARETTE LIGHTER
THERMO SWITCH
CONDENSER FAN MOTOR RELAY
RADIATOR FAN MOTOR RELAY
RADIATOR FAN MOTOR
CONDENSER FAN MOTOR
AIR CONDITIONER RELAY
COMPRESSOR
THERMO CONTROL AMPLIFIER
THERMISTOR
ACCELERATION CUT TIMER (A/T)
ACCELERATION CUT SWITCH (A/T)
Except Canada
RESISTOR
BLOWER MOTOR
ELECTRIC MAGNET
FAN SWITCH
RELAY-1
RELAY-2
CONTROL HARNESS (For Canada)

Fig. 62. Complete circuit wiring diagram — 1989 Sentra

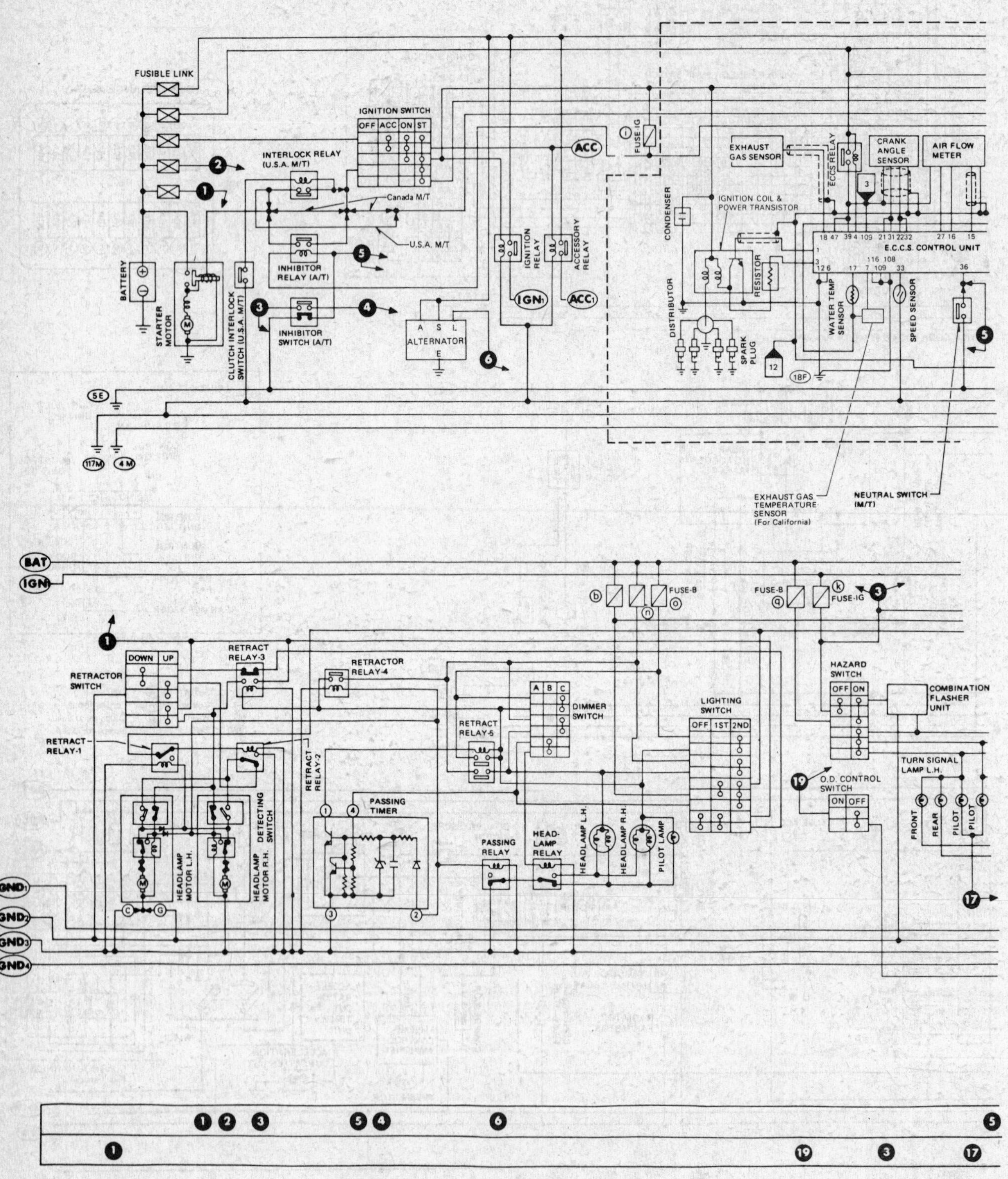
FUSIBLE LINK
BATTERY
STARTER MOTOR
CLUTCH INTERLOCK SWITCH (U.S.A. M/T)
IGNITION SWITCH
OFF ACC ON ST
INTERLOCK RELAY (U.S.A. M/T)
Canada M/T
U.S.A. M/T
INHIBITOR RELAY (A/T)
INHIBITOR SWITCH (A/T)
ALTERNATOR
A S L
E
IGNITION RELAY
ACCESSORY RELAY
ACC
IGN
FUSE-IG
CONDENSER
DISTRIBUTOR
IGNITION COIL & POWER TRANSISTOR
RESISTOR
SPARK PLUG
EXHAUST GAS SENSOR
ECCS RELAY
CRANK ANGLE SENSOR
AIR FLOW METER
E.C.C.S. CONTROL UNIT
WATER TEMP SENSOR
SPEED SENSOR
EXHAUST GAS TEMPERATURE SENSOR (For California)
NEUTRAL SWITCH (M/T)
5E
117M
4 M
18F
BAT
IGN
FUSE-8
FUSE-IG
RETRACTOR SWITCH
DOWN UP
RETRACT RELAY-3
RETRACTOR RELAY-4
RETRACT RELAY-1
RETRACT RELAY-2
DETECTING SWITCH
HEADLAMP MOTOR L.H.
HEADLAMP MOTOR R.H.
PASSING TIMER
PASSING RELAY
HEAD-LAMP RELAY
DIMMER SWITCH
A B C
RETRACT RELAY-5
HEADLAMP L.H.
HEADLAMP R.H.
PILOT LAMP
LIGHTING SWITCH
OFF 1ST 2ND
HAZARD SWITCH
OFF ON
COMBINATION FLASHER UNIT
O.D. CONTROL SWITCH
ON OFF
TURN SIGNAL LAMP L.H.
FRONT
REAR
PILOT
PILOT
GND1
GND2
GND3
GND4

Fig. 63. Complete circuit wiring diagram — 1989 Pulsar

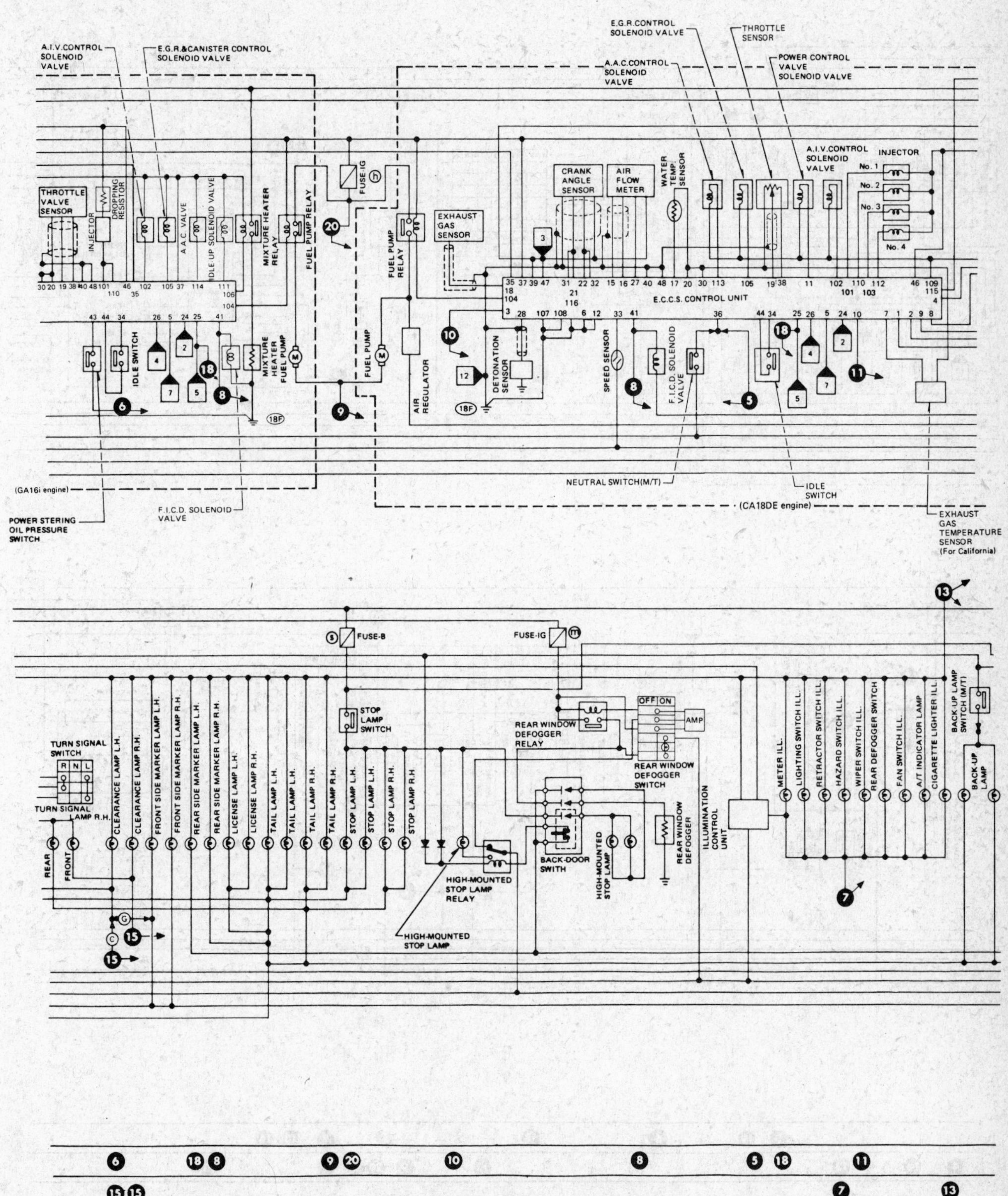
A.I.V. CONTROL SOLENOID VALVE
E.G.R.&CANISTER CONTROL SOLENOID VALVE
THROTTLE VALVE SENSOR
INJECTOR
DROPPING RESISTOR
A.A.C. VALVE
IDLE UP SOLENOID VALVE
MIXTURE HEATER RELAY
FUEL PUMP RELAY
FUSE IG
EXHAUST GAS SENSOR
FUEL PUMP RELAY
CRANK ANGLE SENSOR
AIR FLOW METER
WATER TEMP. SENSOR
E.G.R. CONTROL SOLENOID VALVE
THROTTLE SENSOR
A.A.C. CONTROL SOLENOID VALVE
POWER CONTROL VALVE SOLENOID VALVE
A.I.V. CONTROL SOLENOID VALVE
INJECTOR
No. 1
No. 2
No. 3
No. 4
E.C.C.S. CONTROL UNIT
IDLE SWITCH
MIXTURE HEATER
FUEL PUMP
AIR REGULATOR
DETONATION SENSOR
SPEED SENSOR
F.I.C.D. SOLENOID VALVE
(GA16i engine)
POWER STERING OIL PRESSURE SWITCH
F.I.C.D. SOLENOID VALVE
NEUTRAL SWITCH(M/T)
IDLE SWITCH
(CA18DE engine)
EXHAUST GAS TEMPERATURE SENSOR (For California)
FUSE-B
FUSE-IG
STOP LAMP SWITCH
TURN SIGNAL SWITCH
TURN SIGNAL LAMP R.H.
REAR
FRONT
CLEARANCE LAMP L.H.
CLEARANCE LAMP R.H.
FRONT SIDE MARKER LAMP L.H.
FRONT SIDE MARKER LAMP R.H.
REAR SIDE MARKER LAMP L.H.
REAR SIDE MARKER LAMP R.H.
LICENSE LAMP L.H.
LICENSE LAMP R.H.
TAIL LAMP L.H.
TAIL LAMP L.H.
TAIL LAMP R.H.
TAIL LAMP R.H.
STOP LAMP L.H.
STOP LAMP L.H.
STOP LAMP R.H.
STOP LAMP R.H.
REAR WINDOW DEFOGGER RELAY
OFF ON
AMP
REAR WINDOW DEFOGGER SWITCH
HIGH-MOUNTED STOP LAMP RELAY
HIGH-MOUNTED STOP LAMP
BACK-DOOR SWITH
HIGH-MOUNTED STOP LAMP
REAR WINDOW DEFOGGER
ILLUMINATION CONTROL UNIT
METER ILL.
LIGHTING SWITCH ILL.
RETRACTOR SWITCH ILL.
HAZARD SWITCH ILL.
WIPER SWITCH ILL.
REAR DEFOGGER SWITCH
FAN SWITCH ILL.
A/T INDICATOR LAMP
CIGARETTE LIGHTER ILL.
BACK-UP LAMP SWITCH (M/T)
BACK-UP LAMP

Fig. 63. Complete circuit wiring diagram — 1989 Pulsar

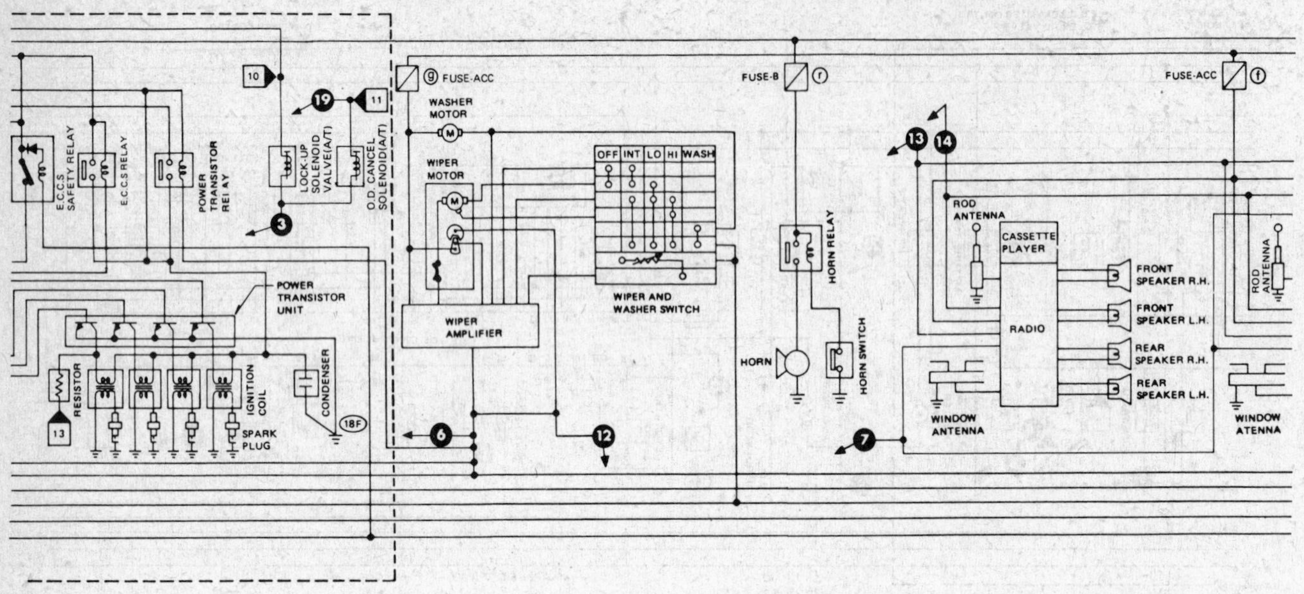

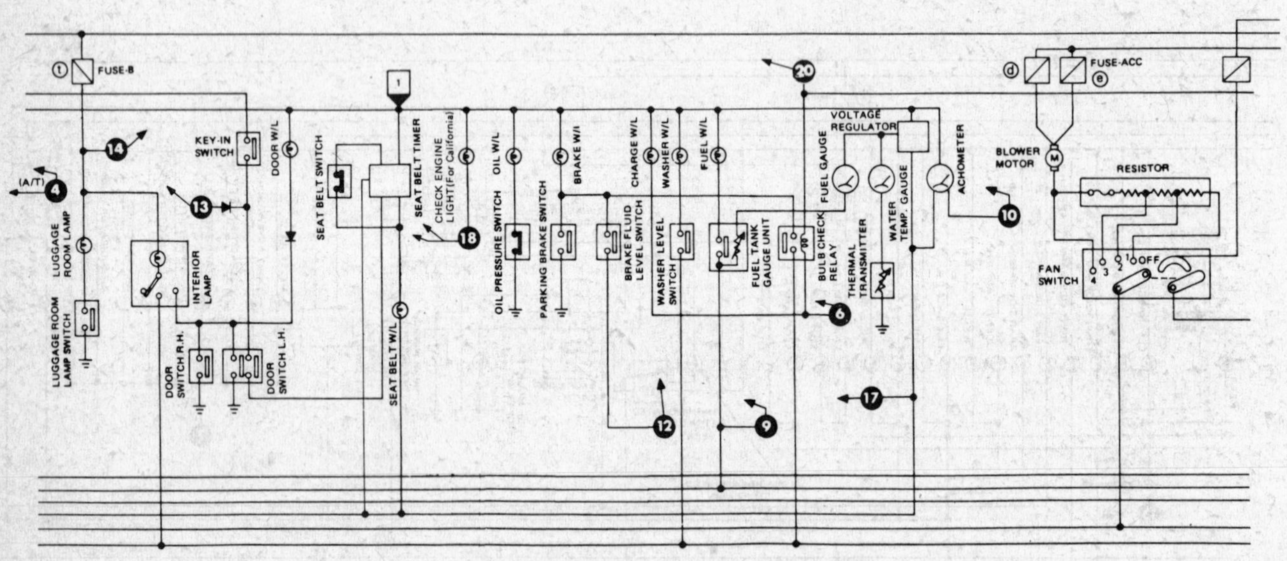

Fig. 63. Complete circuit wiring diagram — 1989 Pulsar

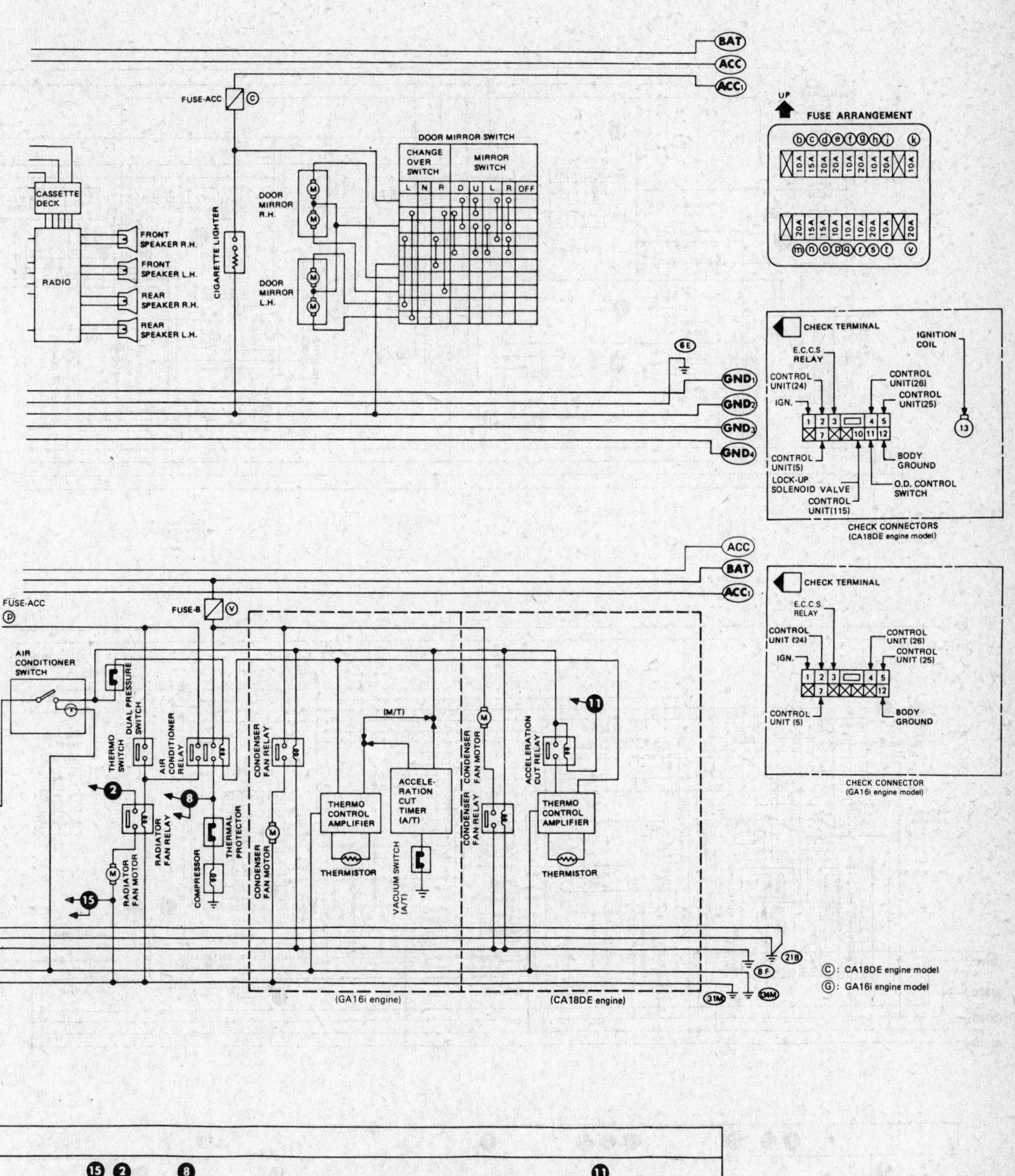
BAT
ACC
ACC1
FUSE-ACC
DOOR MIRROR SWITCH
CHANGE OVER SWITCH
MIRROR SWITCH
CASSETTE DECK
RADIO
FRONT SPEAKER R.H.
FRONT SPEAKER L.H.
REAR SPEAKER R.H.
REAR SPEAKER L.H.
CIGARETTE LIGHTER
DOOR MIRROR R.H.
DOOR MIRROR L.H.
GND1
GND2
GND3
GND4
FUSE ARRANGEMENT
CHECK TERMINAL
E.C.C.S. RELAY
IGNITION COIL
CONTROL UNIT(24)
CONTROL UNIT(26)
CONTROL UNIT(25)
IGN.
CONTROL UNIT(5)
BODY GROUND
LOCK-UP SOLENOID VALVE
O.D. CONTROL SWITCH
CONTROL UNIT(115)
CHECK CONNECTORS (CA18DE engine model)
CHECK CONNECTOR (GA16i engine model)
FUSE-B
AIR CONDITIONER SWITCH
DUAL PRESSURE SWITCH
THERMO SWITCH
AIR CONDITIONER RELAY
RADIATOR FAN RELAY
RADIATOR FAN MOTOR
COMPRESSOR
THERMAL PROTECTOR
CONDENSER FAN RELAY
CONDENSER FAN MOTOR
THERMO CONTROL AMPLIFIER
THERMISTOR
ACCELERATION CUT TIMER (A/T)
VACUUM SWITCH (A/T)
(M/T)
ACCELERATION CUT RELAY
(GA16i engine)
(CA18DE engine)
Ⓒ: CA18DE engine model
Ⓖ: GA16i engine model

Fig. 63. Complete circuit wiring diagram — 1989 Pulsar

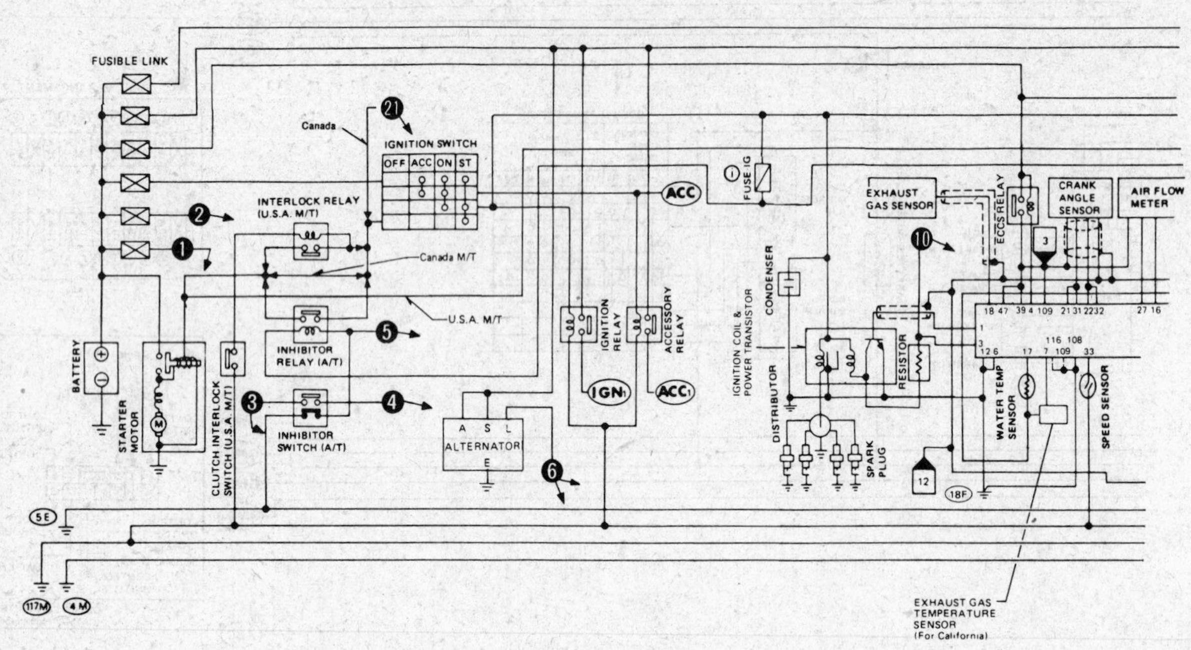
FUSIBLE LINK
Canada
IGNITION SWITCH
OFF ACC ON ST
INTERLOCK RELAY (U.S.A. M/T)
Canada M/T
U.S.A. M/T
INHIBITOR RELAY (A/T)
INHIBITOR SWITCH (A/T)
BATTERY
STARTER MOTOR
CLUTCH INTERLOCK SWITCH (U.S.A. M/T)
ALTERNATOR
A S L
E
ACC
IGN
ACC
IGNITION RELAY
ACCESSORY RELAY
FUSE IG
CONDENSER
IGNITION COIL & POWER TRANSISTOR
DISTRIBUTOR
SPARK PLUG
RESISTOR
EXHAUST GAS SENSOR
ECCS RELAY
CRANK ANGLE SENSOR
AIR FLOW METER
WATER TEMP SENSOR
SPEED SENSOR
EXHAUST GAS TEMPERATURE SENSOR (For California)
5E
117M
4M
18F

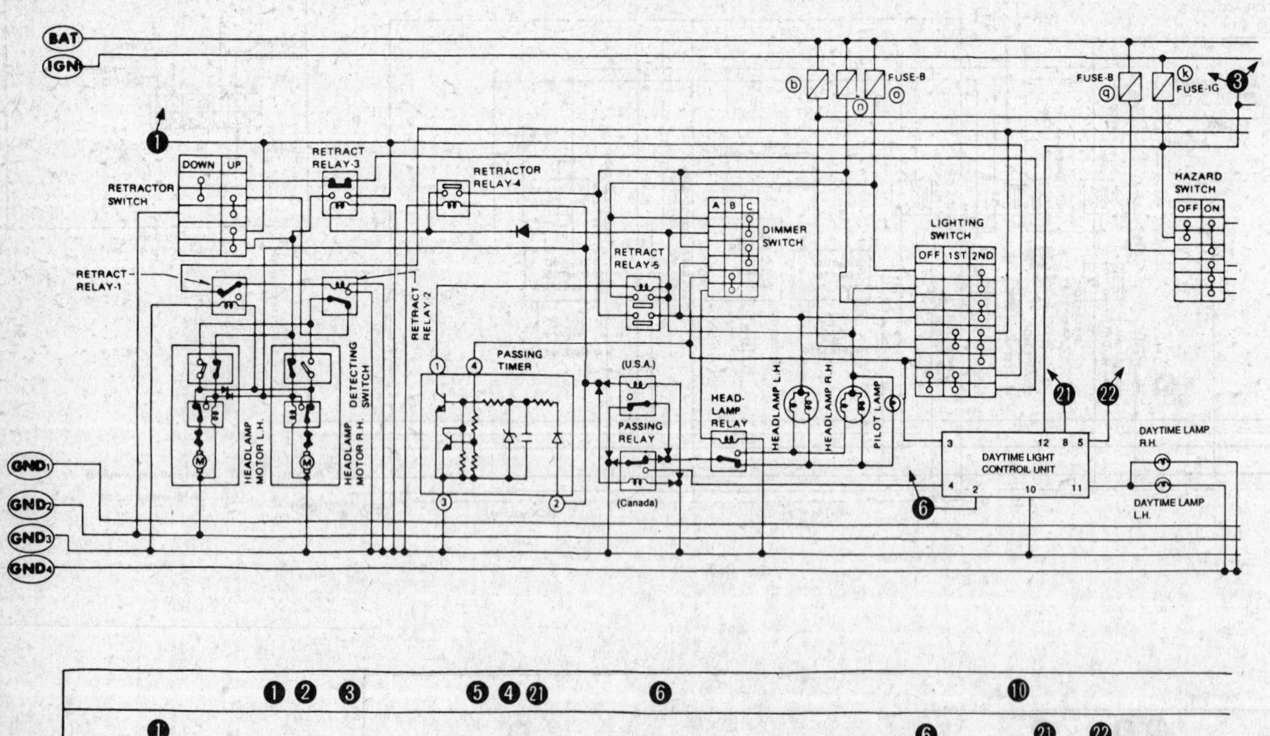
BAT
IGN
FUSE-B
FUSE-B
FUSE-IG
RETRACTOR SWITCH
DOWN UP
RETRACT RELAY-3
RETRACTOR RELAY-4
RETRACT RELAY-1
RETRACT RELAY-2
RETRACT RELAY-5
DIMMER SWITCH
A B C
LIGHTING SWITCH
OFF 1ST 2ND
HAZARD SWITCH
OFF ON
HEADLAMP MOTOR L.H.
HEADLAMP MOTOR R.H.
DETECTING SWITCH
PASSING TIMER
(U.S.A.)
PASSING RELAY
(Canada)
HEAD-LAMP RELAY
HEADLAMP L.H.
HEADLAMP R.H.
PILOT LAMP
DAYTIME LIGHT CONTROL UNIT
DAYTIME LAMP R.H.
DAYTIME LAMP L.H.
GND1
GND2
GND3
GND4

Fig. 64. Complete circuit wiring diagram — 1990 Pulsar

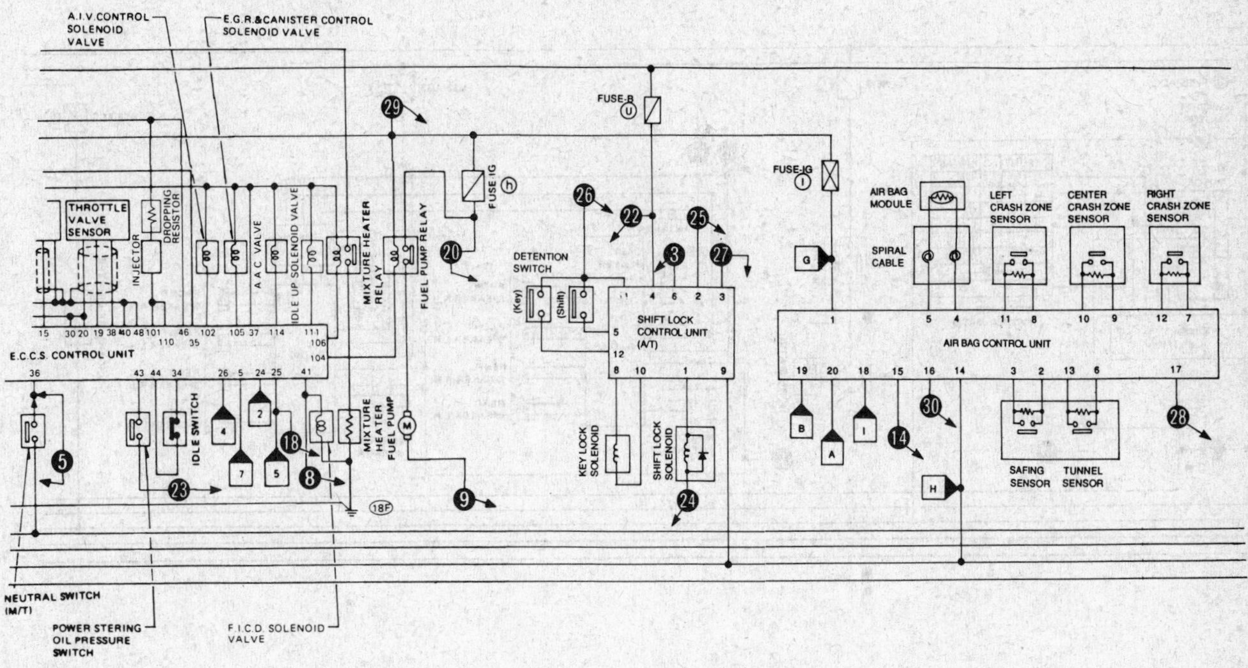

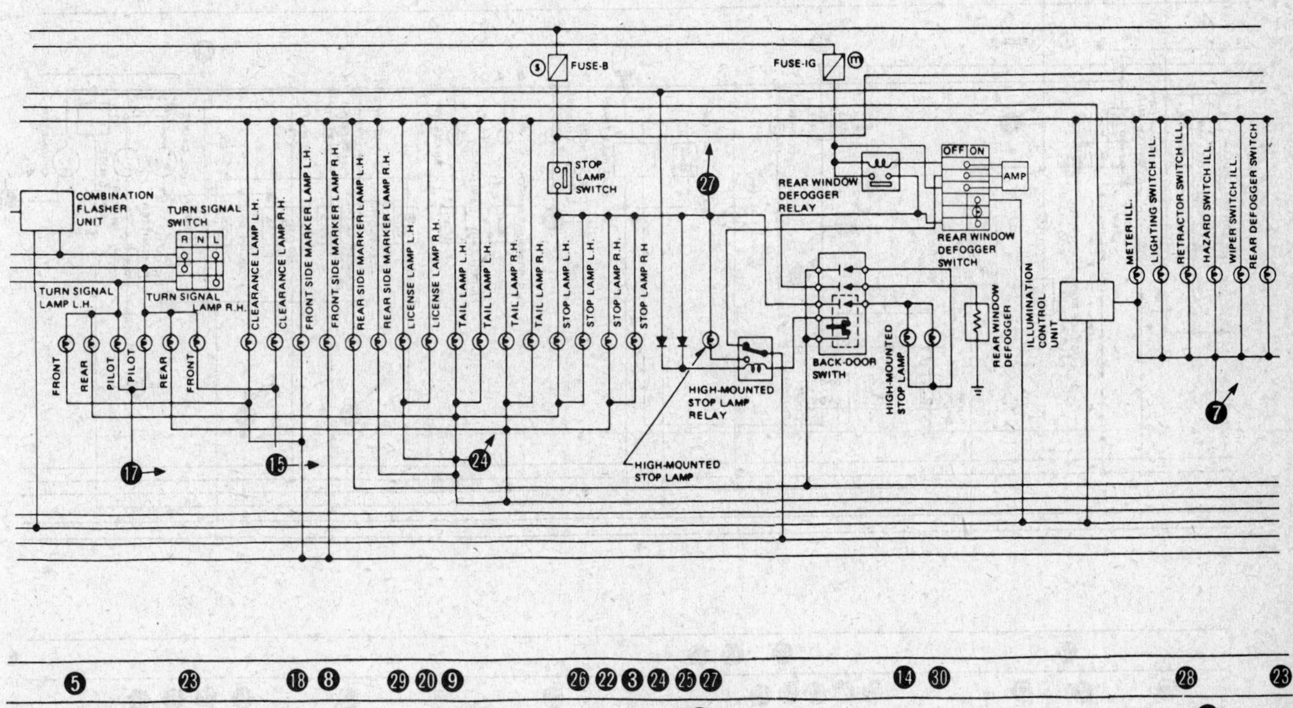

Fig. 64. Complete circuit wiring diagram — 1990 Pulsar

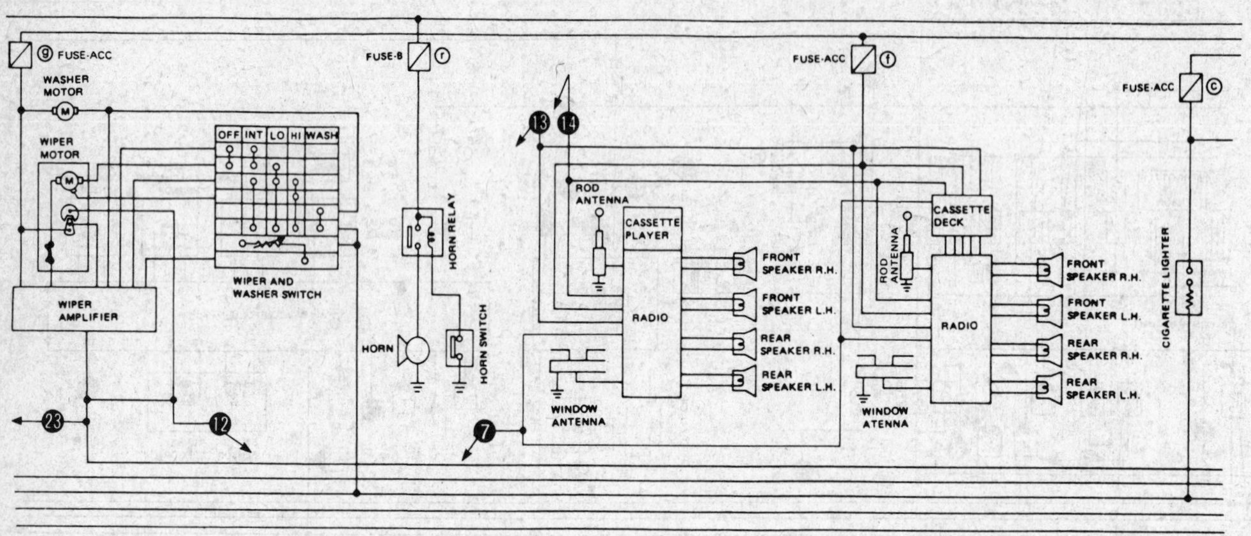

FUSE-ACC
WASHER MOTOR
WIPER MOTOR
OFF INT LO HI WASH
WIPER AND WASHER SWITCH
WIPER AMPLIFIER
FUSE-B
HORN RELAY
HORN
HORN SWITCH
ROD ANTENNA
CASSETTE PLAYER
RADIO
FRONT SPEAKER R.H.
FRONT SPEAKER L.H.
REAR SPEAKER R.H.
REAR SPEAKER L.H.
WINDOW ANTENNA
CASSETTE DECK
WINDOW ATENNA
CIGARETTE LIGHTER

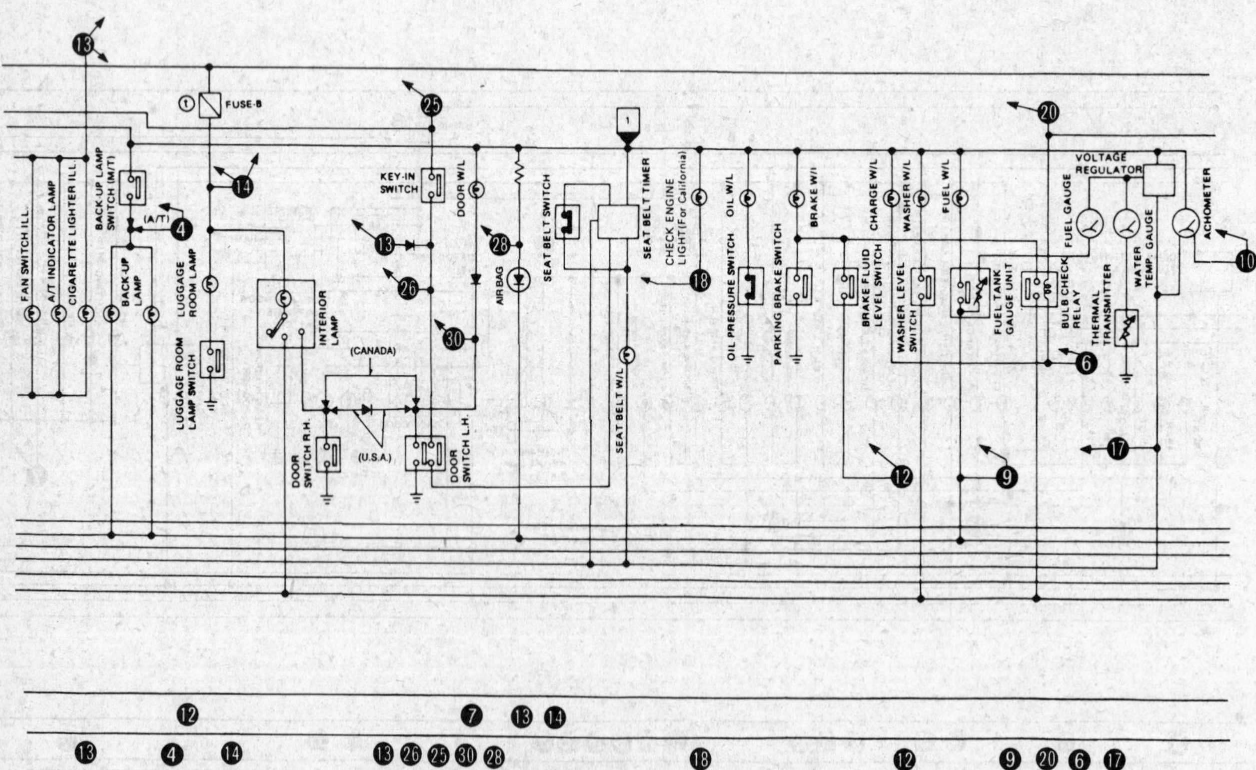

FUSE-B
FAN SWITCH ILL.
A/T INDICATOR LAMP
CIGARETTE LIGHTER ILL.
BACK-UP LAMP SWITCH (M/T)
(A/T)
BACK-UP LAMP
LUGGAGE ROOM LAMP
LUGGAGE ROOM LAMP SWITCH
INTERIOR LAMP
KEY-IN SWITCH
DOOR W/L
(CANADA)
(U.S.A.)
DOOR SWITCH R.H.
DOOR SWITCH L.H.
AIR BAG
SEAT BELT SWITCH
SEAT BELT TIMER
SEAT BELT W/L
CHECK ENGINE LIGHT(For California)
OIL W/L
OIL PRESSURE SWITCH
PARKING BRAKE SWITCH
BRAKE W/L
CHARGE W/L
BRAKE FLUID LEVEL SWITCH
WASHER W/L
WASHER LEVEL SWITCH
FUEL W/L
FUEL TANK GAUGE UNIT
BULB CHECK RELAY
VOLTAGE REGULATOR
FUEL GAUGE
THERMAL TRANSMITTER
WATER TEMP. GAUGE
ACHOMETER

Fig. 64. Complete circuit wiring diagram — 1990 Pulsar

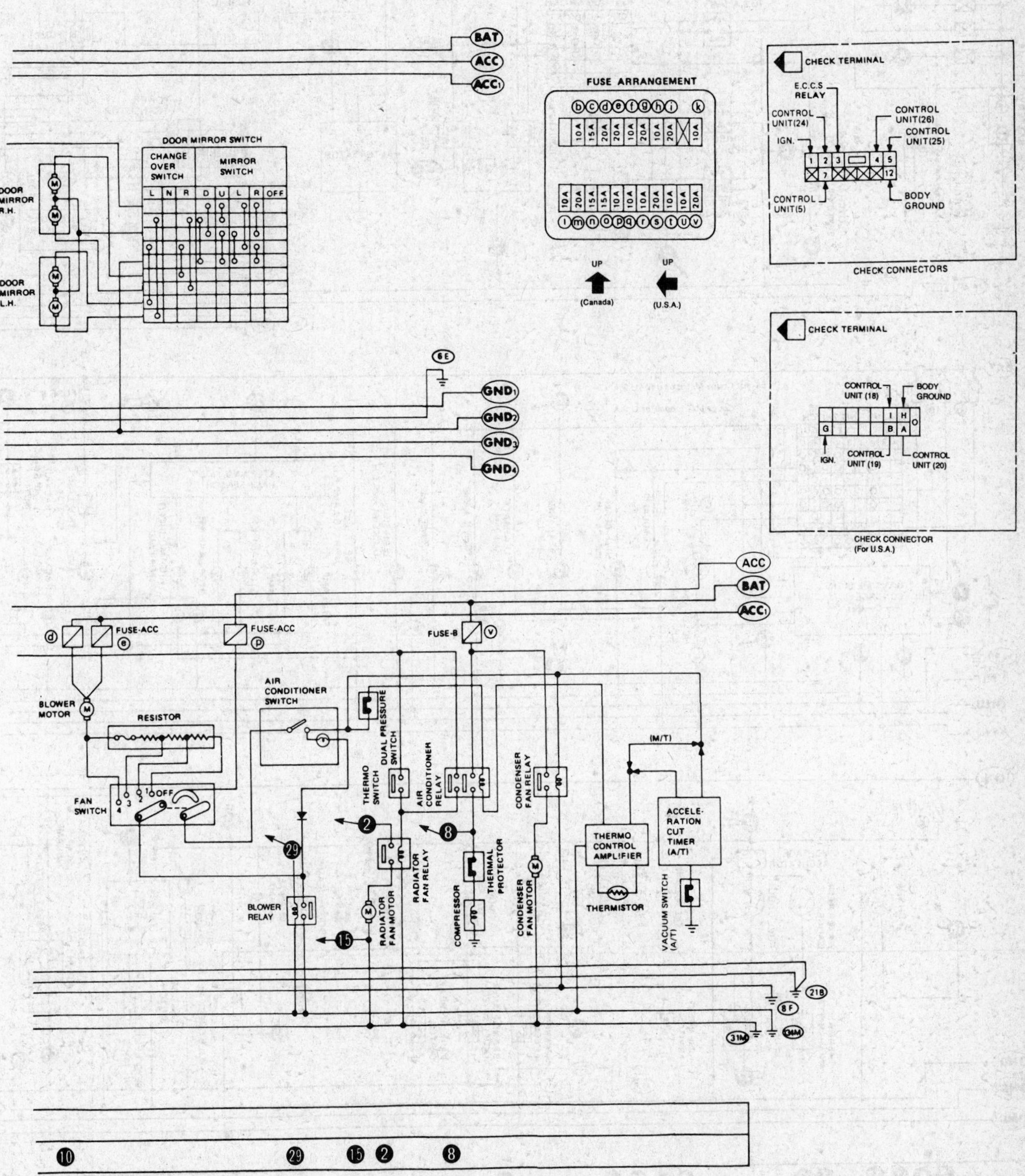
BAT
ACC
ACC1
DOOR MIRROR SWITCH
CHANGE OVER SWITCH
MIRROR SWITCH
DOOR MIRROR R.H.
DOOR MIRROR L.H.
FUSE ARRANGEMENT
UP
(Canada)
(U.S.A.)
CHECK TERMINAL
E.C.C.S. RELAY
CONTROL UNIT(24)
IGN.
CONTROL UNIT(26)
CONTROL UNIT(25)
CONTROL UNIT(5)
BODY GROUND
CHECK CONNECTORS
CONTROL UNIT (18)
CONTROL UNIT (19)
CONTROL UNIT (20)
CHECK CONNECTOR (For U.S.A.)
GND1
GND2
GND3
GND4
FUSE-ACC
FUSE-B
BLOWER MOTOR
RESISTOR
AIR CONDITIONER SWITCH
FAN SWITCH
THERMO SWITCH
DUAL PRESSURE SWITCH
AIR CONDITIONER RELAY
CONDENSER FAN RELAY
RADIATOR FAN RELAY
RADIATOR FAN MOTOR
COMPRESSOR
THERMAL PROTECTOR
CONDENSER FAN MOTOR
BLOWER RELAY
(M/T)
THERMO CONTROL AMPLIFIER
THERMISTOR
ACCELE-RATION CUT TIMER (A/T)
VACUUM SWITCH (A/T)

Fig. 64. Complete circuit wiring diagram — 1990 Pulsar

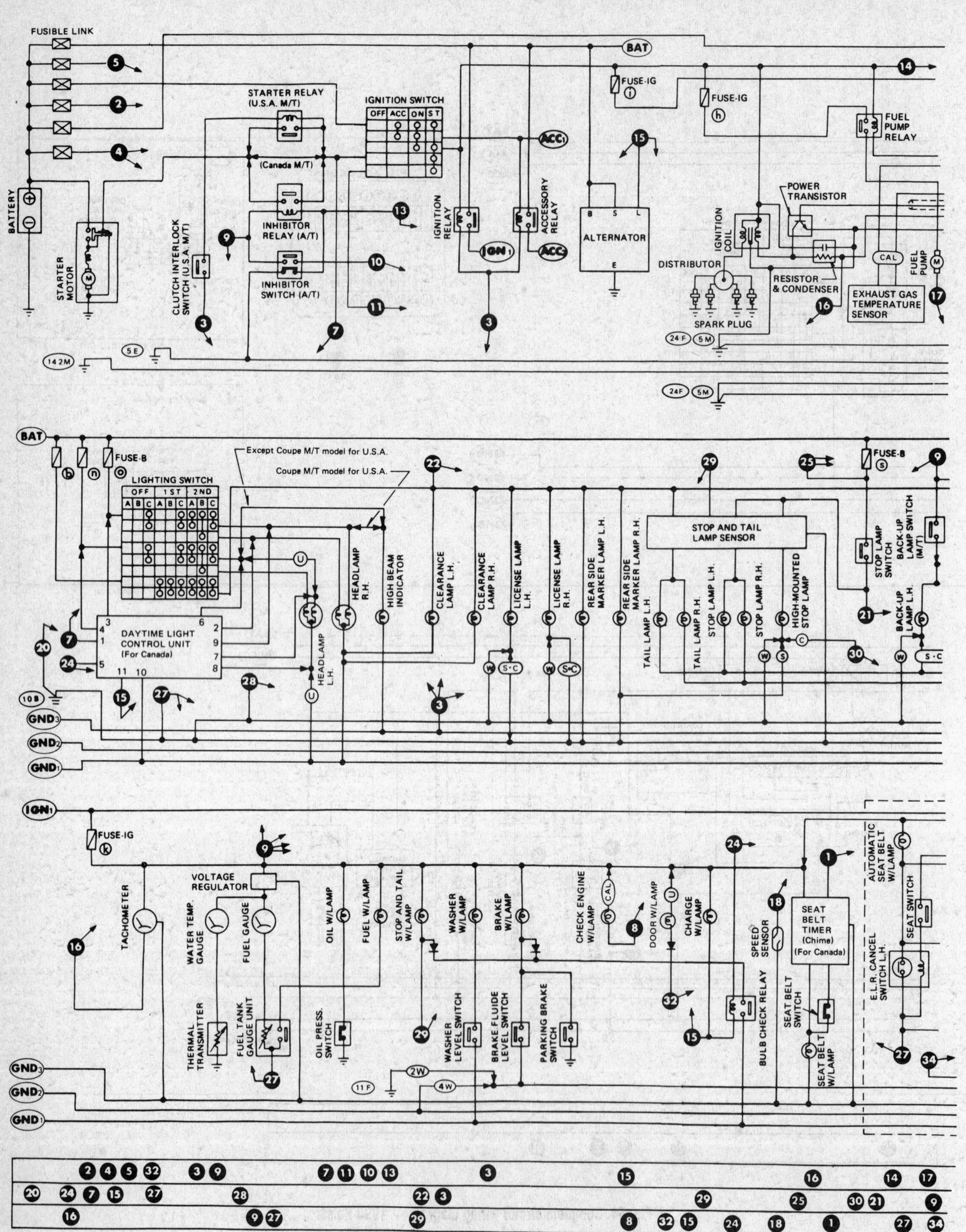

Fig. 65. Complete circuit wiring diagram — 1990 Sentra

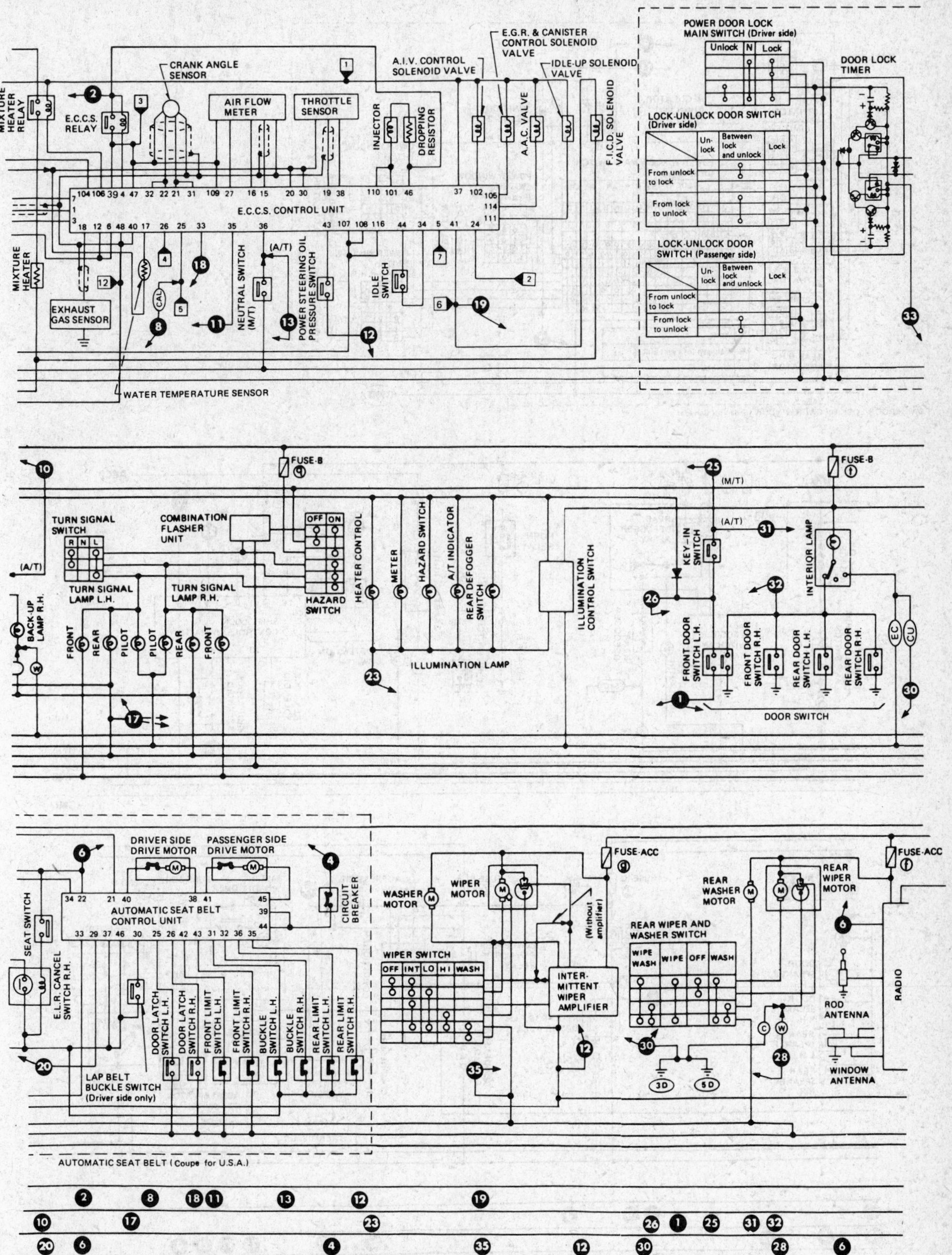

MIXTURE HEATER RELAY
E.C.C.S. RELAY
CRANK ANGLE SENSOR
AIR FLOW METER
THROTTLE SENSOR
INJECTOR
DROPPING RESISTOR
A.I.V. CONTROL SOLENOID VALVE
E.G.R. & CANISTER CONTROL SOLENOID VALVE
A.A.C. VALVE
IDLE-UP SOLENOID VALVE
F.I.C.D. SOLENOID VALVE
E.C.C.S. CONTROL UNIT
MIXTURE HEATER
EXHAUST GAS SENSOR
WATER TEMPERATURE SENSOR
NEUTRAL SWITCH (M/T)
(A/T)
POWER STEERING OIL PRESSURE SWITCH
IDLE SWITCH
POWER DOOR LOCK MAIN SWITCH (Driver side)
Unlock
N
Lock
DOOR LOCK TIMER
LOCK-UNLOCK DOOR SWITCH (Driver side)
Un-lock
Between lock and unlock
From unlock to lock
From lock to unlock
LOCK-UNLOCK DOOR SWITCH (Passenger side)
FUSE-B
TURN SIGNAL SWITCH
COMBINATION FLASHER UNIT
OFF
ON
HAZARD SWITCH
HEATER CONTROL
METER
HAZARD SWITCH
A/T INDICATOR
REAR DEFOGGER SWITCH
ILLUMINATION CONTROL SWITCH
ILLUMINATION LAMP
BACK-UP LAMP R.H.
TURN SIGNAL LAMP L.H.
TURN SIGNAL LAMP R.H.
FRONT
REAR
PILOT
(M/T)
KEY-IN SWITCH
INTERIOR LAMP
FRONT DOOR SWITCH L.H.
FRONT DOOR SWITCH R.H.
REAR DOOR SWITCH L.H.
REAR DOOR SWITCH R.H.
DOOR SWITCH
DRIVER SIDE DRIVE MOTOR
PASSENGER SIDE DRIVE MOTOR
AUTOMATIC SEAT BELT CONTROL UNIT
CIRCUIT BREAKER
SEAT SWITCH
E.L.R. CANCEL SWITCH R.H.
DOOR LATCH SWITCH L.H.
DOOR LATCH SWITCH R.H.
FRONT LIMIT SWITCH L.H.
FRONT LIMIT SWITCH R.H.
BUCKLE SWITCH L.H.
BUCKLE SWITCH R.H.
REAR LIMIT SWITCH L.H.
REAR LIMIT SWITCH R.H.
LAP BELT BUCKLE SWITCH (Driver side only)
AUTOMATIC SEAT BELT (Coupe for U.S.A.)
FUSE-ACC
WASHER MOTOR
WIPER MOTOR
WIPER SWITCH
OFF
INT
LO
HI
WASH
(Without amplifier)
INTER-MITTENT WIPER AMPLIFIER
REAR WASHER MOTOR
REAR WIPER MOTOR
REAR WIPER AND WASHER SWITCH
WIPE WASH
WIPE
OFF
WASH
3D
5D
RADIO
ROD ANTENNA
WINDOW ANTENNA

Fig. 65. Complete circuit wiring diagram — 1990 Sentra

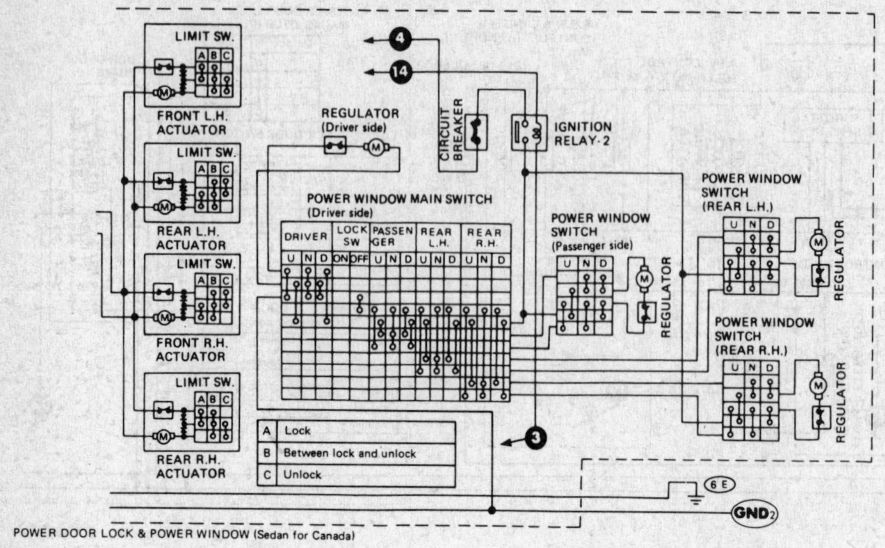
LIMIT SW.
FRONT L.H. ACTUATOR
REAR L.H. ACTUATOR
FRONT R.H. ACTUATOR
REAR R.H. ACTUATOR
REGULATOR (Driver side)
CIRCUIT BREAKER
IGNITION RELAY-2
POWER WINDOW MAIN SWITCH (Driver side)
DRIVER
LOCK SW
PASSENGER
REAR L.H.
REAR R.H.
POWER WINDOW SWITCH (Passenger side)
REGULATOR
POWER WINDOW SWITCH (REAR L.H.)
POWER WINDOW SWITCH (REAR R.H.)
A Lock
B Between lock and unlock
C Unlock
GND2

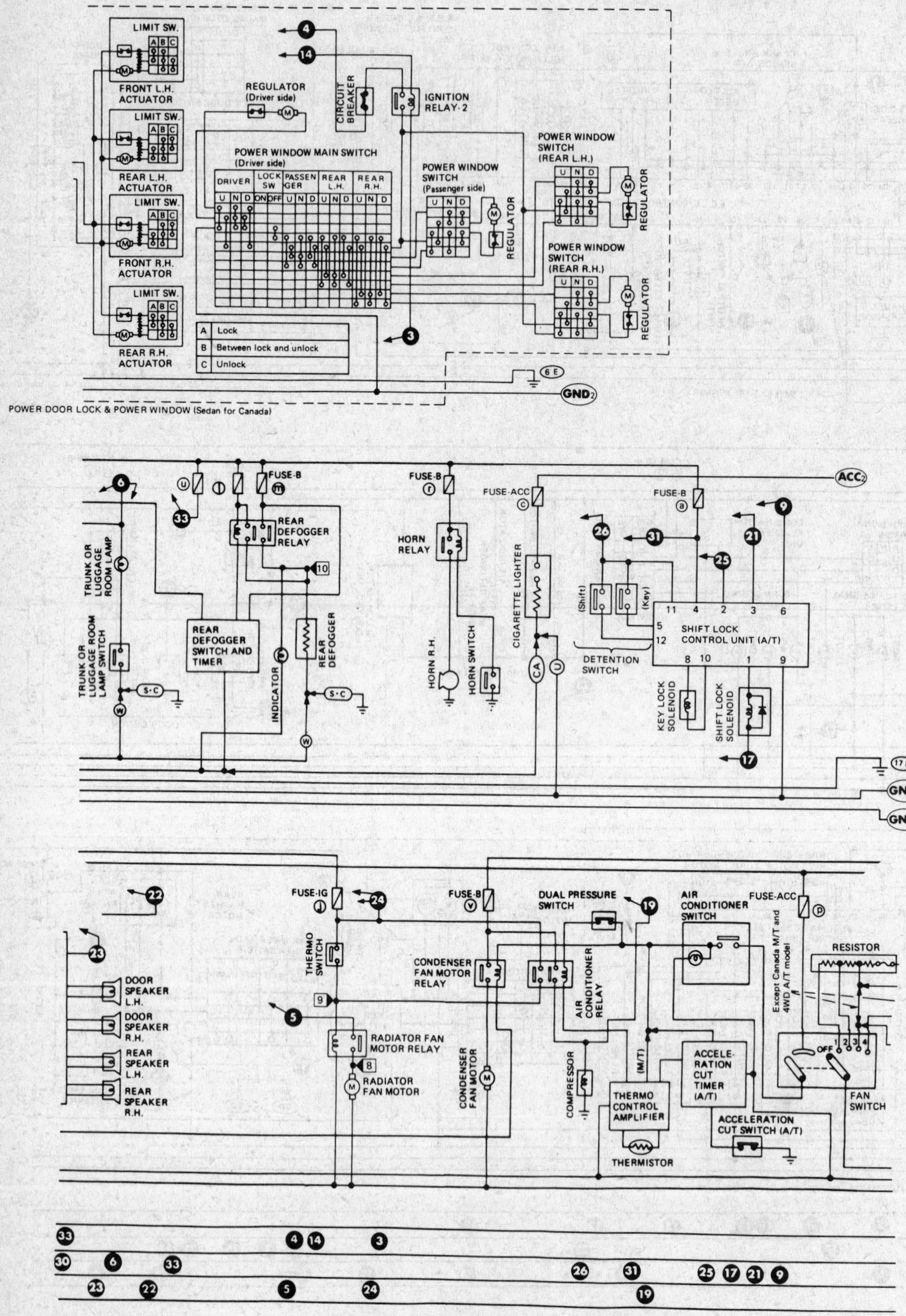

POWER DOOR LOCK & POWER WINDOW (Sedan for Canada)

FUSE-B
TRUNK OR LUGGAGE ROOM LAMP
TRUNK OR LUGGAGE ROOM LAMP SWITCH
REAR DEFOGGER RELAY
REAR DEFOGGER SWITCH AND TIMER
INDICATOR
REAR DEFOGGER
HORN RELAY
HORN R.H.
HORN SWITCH
FUSE-ACC
CIGARETTE LIGHTER
(Shift) (Key)
DETENTION SWITCH
SHIFT LOCK CONTROL UNIT (A/T)
KEY LOCK SOLENOID
SHIFT LOCK SOLENOID
ACC2
GND2
GND1

FUSE-IG
THERMO SWITCH
RADIATOR FAN MOTOR RELAY
RADIATOR FAN MOTOR
DOOR SPEAKER L.H.
DOOR SPEAKER R.H.
REAR SPEAKER L.H.
REAR SPEAKER R.H.
CONDENSER FAN MOTOR RELAY
CONDENSER FAN MOTOR
DUAL PRESSURE SWITCH
AIR CONDITIONER RELAY
COMPRESSOR
THERMO CONTROL AMPLIFIER
THERMISTOR
AIR CONDITIONER SWITCH
ACCELERATION CUT TIMER (A/T)
ACCELERATION CUT SWITCH (A/T)
Except Canada M/T and 4WD A/T model
RESISTOR
FAN SWITCH

Fig. 65. Complete circuit wiring diagram — 1990 Sentra

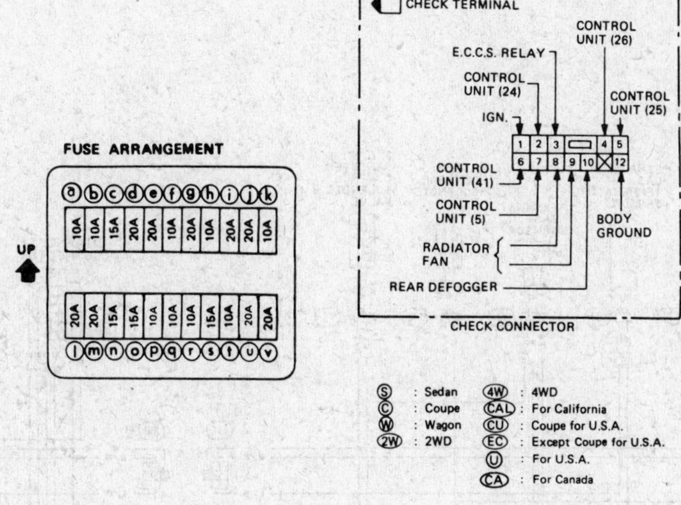
FUSE ARRANGEMENT
ⓐⓑⓒⓓⓔⓕⓖⓗⓘⓙⓚ
10A 10A 15A 20A 20A 10A 20A 10A 20A 20A 10A
UP
20A 20A 15A 15A 10A 10A 10A 15A 10A 20A 20A
ⓛⓜⓝⓞⓟⓠⓡⓢⓣⓤⓥ
CHECK TERMINAL
CONTROL UNIT (26)
E.C.C.S. RELAY
CONTROL UNIT (24)
CONTROL UNIT (25)
IGN.
1 2 3 4 5
6 7 8 9 10 12
CONTROL UNIT (41)
CONTROL UNIT (5)
BODY GROUND
RADIATOR FAN
REAR DEFOGGER
CHECK CONNECTOR
Ⓢ : Sedan
Ⓒ : Coupe
Ⓦ : Wagon
2W : 2WD
4W : 4WD
CAL : For California
CU : Coupe for U.S.A.
EC : Except Coupe for U.S.A.
Ⓤ : For U.S.A.
CA : For Canada

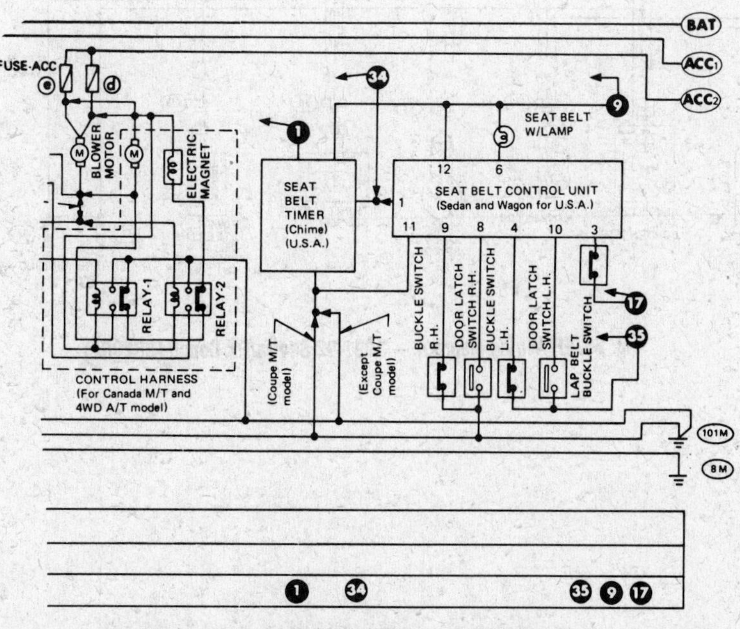
BAT
ACC1
ACC2
FUSE-ACC
ⓔ
ⓓ
34
9
1
SEAT BELT W/LAMP
BLOWER MOTOR
ELECTRIC MAGNET
SEAT BELT TIMER (Chime) (U.S.A.)
12
6
1
SEAT BELT CONTROL UNIT (Sedan and Wagon for U.S.A.)
11 9 8 4 10 3
RELAY-1
RELAY-2
BUCKLE SWITCH R.H.
DOOR LATCH SWITCH R.H.
BUCKLE SWITCH L.H.
DOOR LATCH SWITCH L.H.
LAP BELT BUCKLE SWITCH
17
35
(Coupe M/T model)
(Except Coupe M/T model)
CONTROL HARNESS (For Canada M/T and 4WD A/T model)
101M
8M
1 34 35 9 17

Fig. 65. Complete circuit wiring diagram — 1990 Sentra

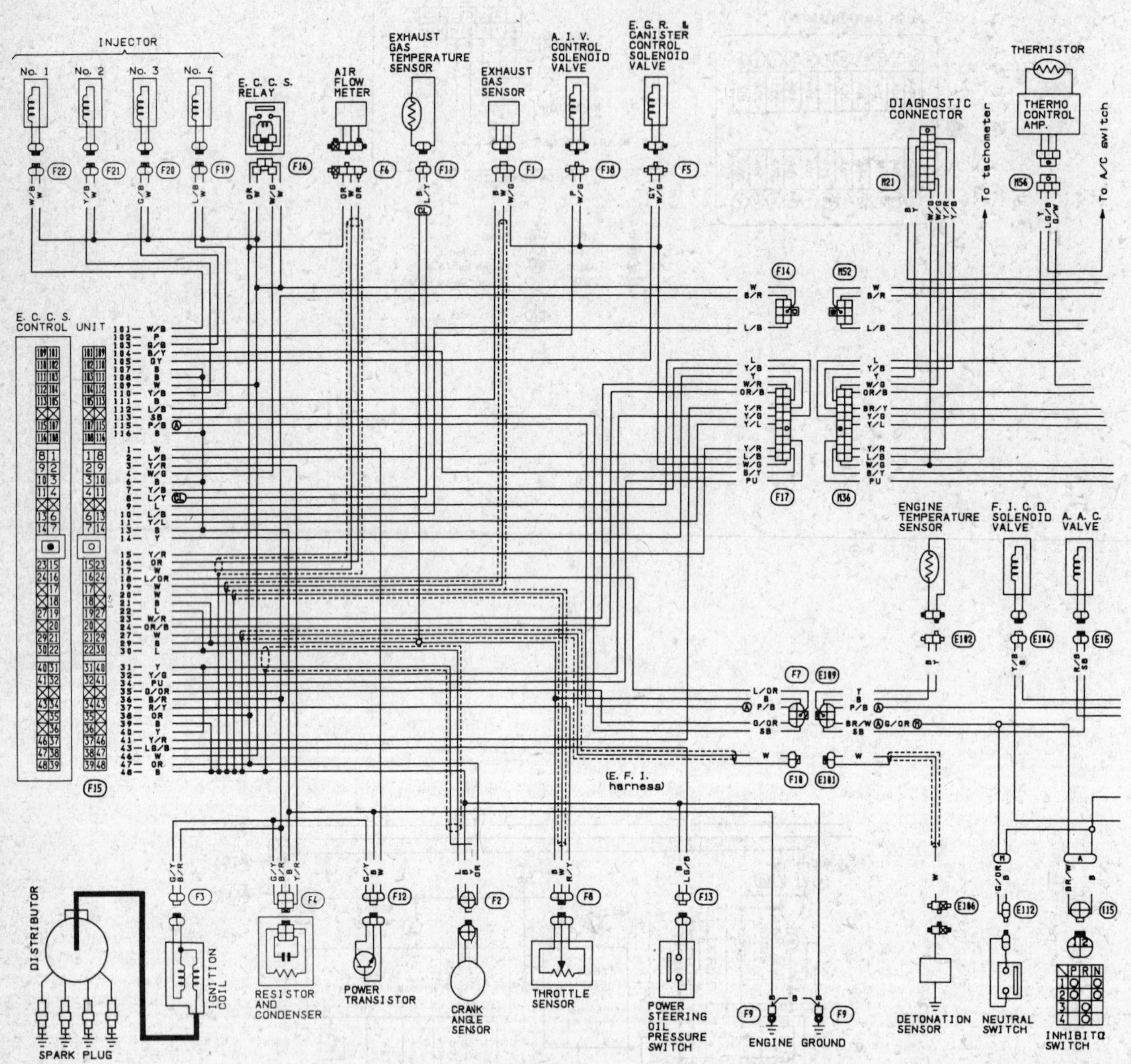
INJECTOR
No. 1
No. 2
No. 3
No. 4
E. C. C. S. RELAY
AIR FLOW METER
EXHAUST GAS TEMPERATURE SENSOR
EXHAUST GAS SENSOR
A. I. V. CONTROL SOLENOID VALVE
E. G. R. & CANISTER CONTROL SOLENOID VALVE
DIAGNOSTIC CONNECTOR
To tachometer
THERMISTOR
THERMO CONTROL AMP.
To A/C switch
E. C. C. S. CONTROL UNIT
ENGINE TEMPERATURE SENSOR
F. I. C. D. SOLENOID VALVE
A. A. C. VALVE
(E. F. I. harness)
DISTRIBUTOR
SPARK PLUG
IGNITION COIL
RESISTOR AND CONDENSER
POWER TRANSISTOR
CRANK ANGLE SENSOR
THROTTLE SENSOR
POWER STEERING OIL PRESSURE SWITCH
ENGINE GROUND
DETONATION SENSOR
NEUTRAL SWITCH
INHIBITOR SWITCH

Fig. 66. EFI Wiring diagram — 1991-92 Sentra/NX Coupe (SR20DE)

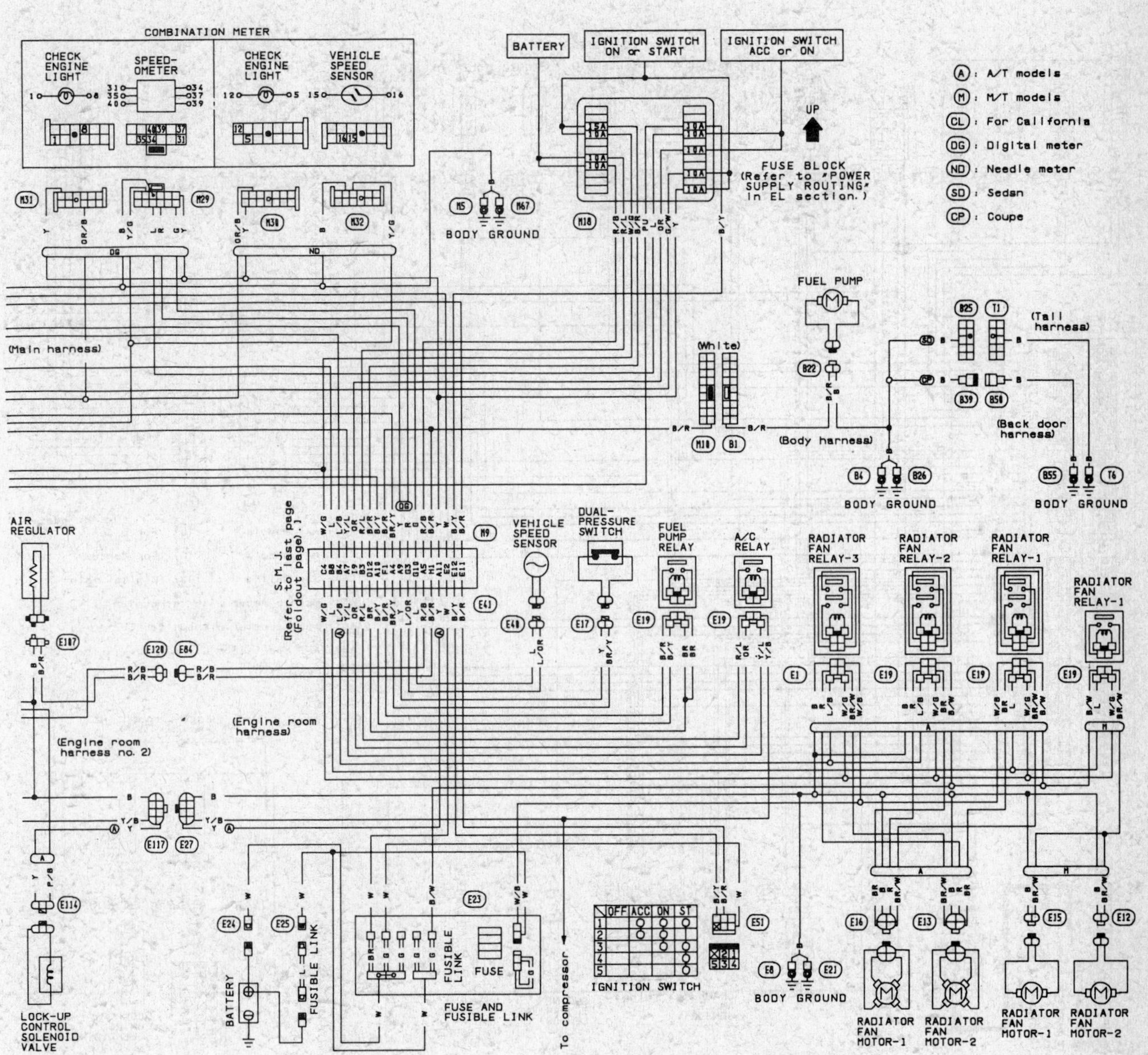

COMBINATION METER
CHECK ENGINE LIGHT
SPEEDOMETER
VEHICLE SPEED SENSOR
BATTERY
IGNITION SWITCH ON or START
IGNITION SWITCH ACC or ON
UP
FUSE BLOCK (Refer to "POWER SUPPLY ROUTING" in EL section.)
(A): A/T models
(M): M/T models
(CL): For California
(DG): Digital meter
(ND): Needle meter
(SD): Sedan
(CP): Coupe
BODY GROUND
(Main harness)
FUEL PUMP
(White)
(Tail harness)
(Back door harness)
(Body harness)
AIR REGULATOR
S.M.J. (Refer to last page (Foldout page).)
VEHICLE SPEED SENSOR
DUAL-PRESSURE SWITCH
FUEL PUMP RELAY
A/C RELAY
RADIATOR FAN RELAY-3
RADIATOR FAN RELAY-2
RADIATOR FAN RELAY-1
(Engine room harness no. 2)
(Engine room harness)
LOCK-UP CONTROL SOLENOID VALVE
BATTERY
FUSIBLE LINK
FUSE
FUSE AND FUSIBLE LINK
To compressor
IGNITION SWITCH
RADIATOR FAN MOTOR-1
RADIATOR FAN MOTOR-2

Fig. 66. EFI Wiring diagram — 1991-92 Sentra/NX Coupe (SR20DE)

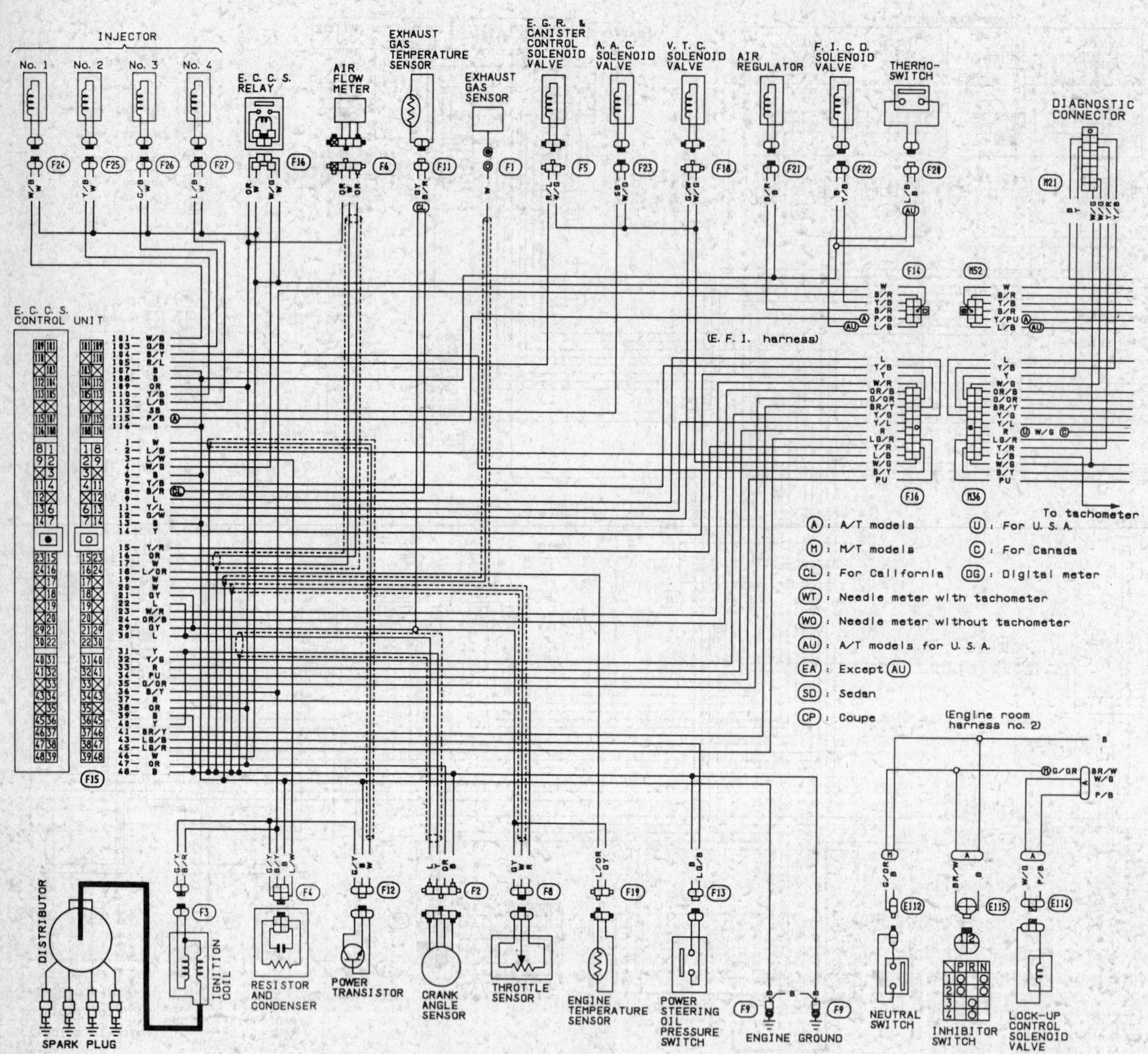
INJECTOR
No. 1
No. 2
No. 3
No. 4
E. C. C. S. RELAY
AIR FLOW METER
EXHAUST GAS TEMPERATURE SENSOR
EXHAUST GAS SENSOR
E. G. R. & CANISTER CONTROL SOLENOID VALVE
A. A. C. SOLENOID VALVE
V. T. C. SOLENOID VALVE
AIR REGULATOR
F. I. C. D. SOLENOID VALVE
THERMO-SWITCH
DIAGNOSTIC CONNECTOR
E. C. C. S. CONTROL UNIT
(E. F. I. harness)
To tachometer
Ⓐ : A/T models
Ⓜ : M/T models
(CL) : For California
(WT) : Needle meter with tachometer
(WO) : Needle meter without tachometer
(AU) : A/T models for U. S. A.
(EA) : Except (AU)
(SD) : Sedan
(CP) : Coupe
Ⓤ : For U. S. A.
Ⓒ : For Canada
(DG) : Digital meter
(Engine room harness no. 2)
DISTRIBUTOR
SPARK PLUG
IGNITION COIL
RESISTOR AND CONDENSER
POWER TRANSISTOR
CRANK ANGLE SENSOR
THROTTLE SENSOR
ENGINE TEMPERATURE SENSOR
POWER STEERING OIL PRESSURE SWITCH
ENGINE GROUND
NEUTRAL SWITCH
INHIBITOR SWITCH
LOCK-UP CONTROL SOLENOID VALVE

Fig. 67. EFI Wiring diagram — 1991-92 Sentra/NX Coupe (GA16DE)

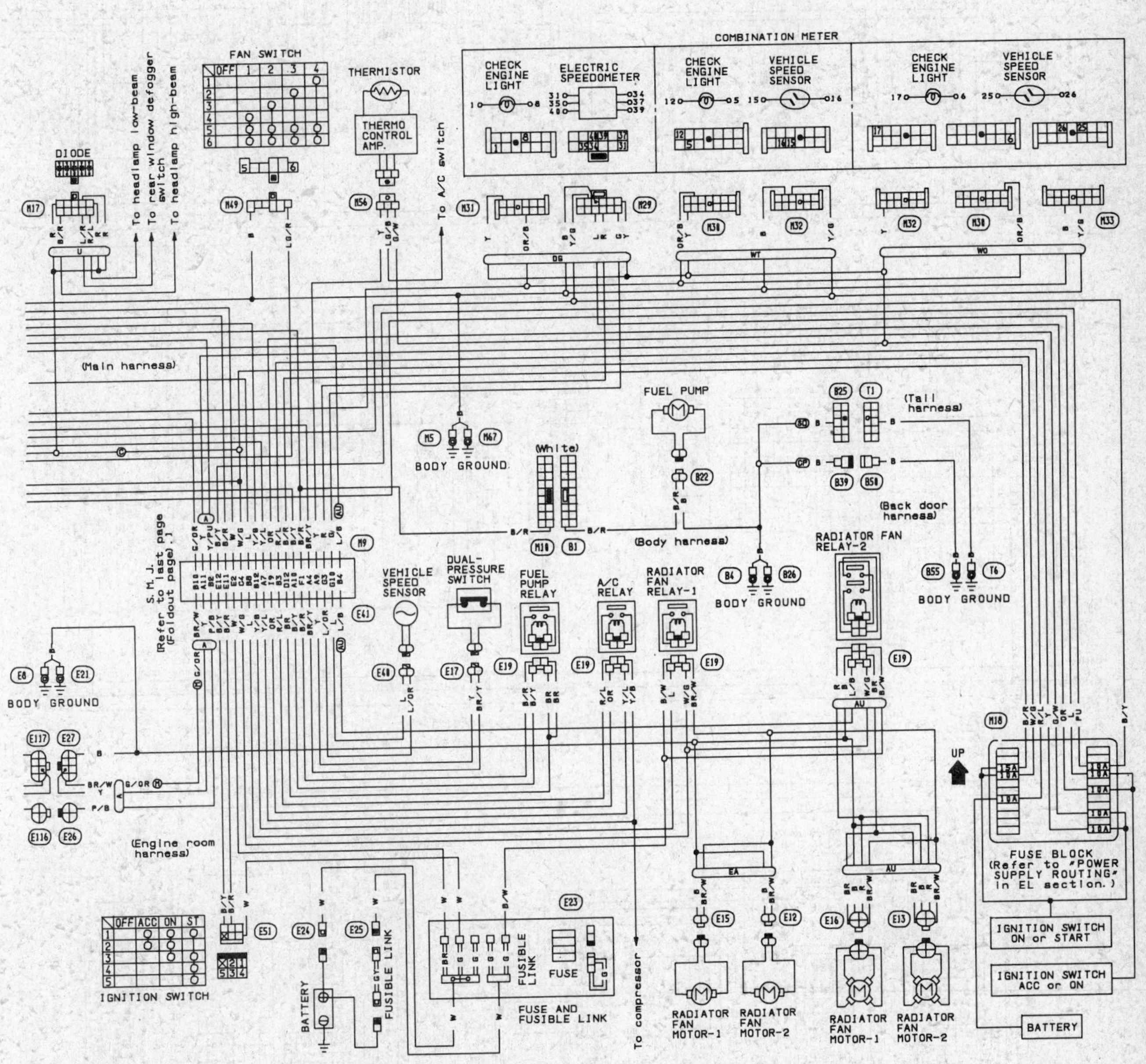

Fig. 67. EFI Wiring diagram — 1991-92 Sentra/NX Coupe (GA16DE)

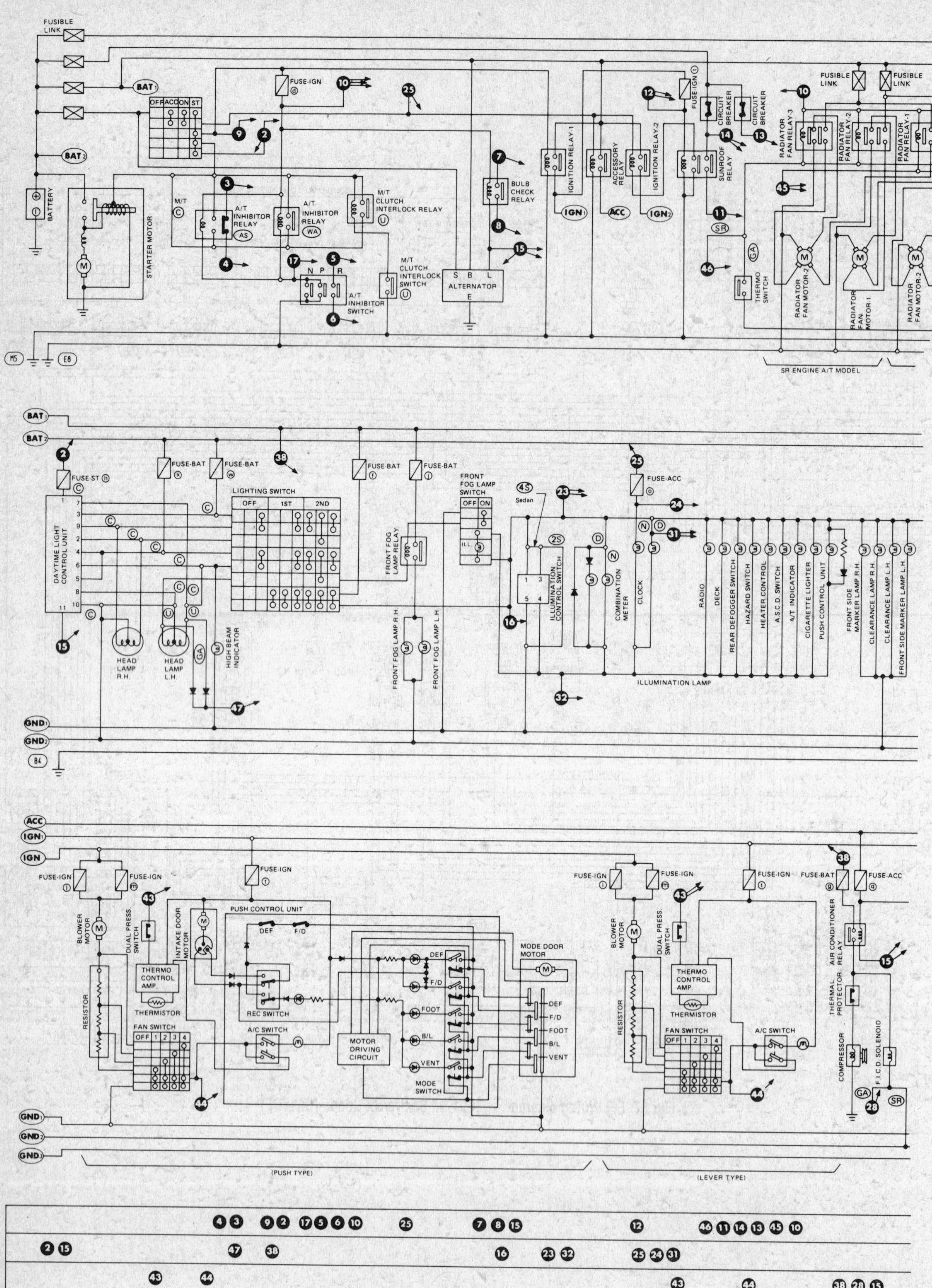
FUSIBLE LINK
BAT1
BAT2
BATTERY
STARTER MOTOR
FUSE-IGN
A/T INHIBITOR RELAY
A/T INHIBITOR RELAY
M/T CLUTCH INTERLOCK RELAY
M/T CLUTCH INTERLOCK SWITCH
A/T INHIBITOR SWITCH
ALTERNATOR
BULB CHECK RELAY
IGNITION RELAY-1
ACCESSORY RELAY
IGNITION RELAY-2
SUNROOF RELAY
CIRCUIT BREAKER
THERMO SWITCH
RADIATOR FAN RELAY-3
RADIATOR FAN RELAY-2
RADIATOR FAN RELAY-1
RADIATOR FAN MOTOR-2
RADIATOR FAN MOTOR-1
SR ENGINE A/T MODEL
FUSE-ST
FUSE-BAT
FUSE-ACC
DAYTIME LIGHT CONTROL UNIT
LIGHTING SWITCH
OFF 1ST 2ND
HEAD LAMP R.H.
HEAD LAMP L.H.
HIGH BEAM INDICATOR
FRONT FOG LAMP RELAY
FRONT FOG LAMP SWITCH
FRONT FOG LAMP R.H.
FRONT FOG LAMP L.H.
ILLUMINATION CONTROL SWITCH
COMBINATION METER
CLOCK
RADIO
DECK
REAR DEFOGGER SWITCH
HAZARD SWITCH
HEATER CONTROL
A.S.C.D. SWITCH
A/T INDICATOR
CIGARETTE LIGHTER
PUSH CONTROL UNIT
FRONT SIDE MARKER LAMP R.H.
CLEARANCE LAMP R.H.
CLEARANCE LAMP L.H.
FRONT SIDE MARKER LAMP L.H.
ILLUMINATION LAMP
GND1
GND2
ACC
IGN1
IGN
BLOWER MOTOR
DUAL PRESS. SWITCH
INTAKE DOOR MOTOR
THERMO CONTROL AMP.
THERMISTOR
RESISTOR
FAN SWITCH
A/C SWITCH
REC SWITCH
DEF F/D
MOTOR DRIVING CIRCUIT
MODE SWITCH
MODE DOOR MOTOR
DEF F/D FOOT B/L VENT
AIR CONDITIONER RELAY
THERMAL PROTECTOR
COMPRESSOR
F.I.C.D. SOLENOID
(PUSH TYPE)
(LEVER TYPE)

Fig. 68. Complete circuit wiring diagram — 1991-92 Sentra/NX Coupe

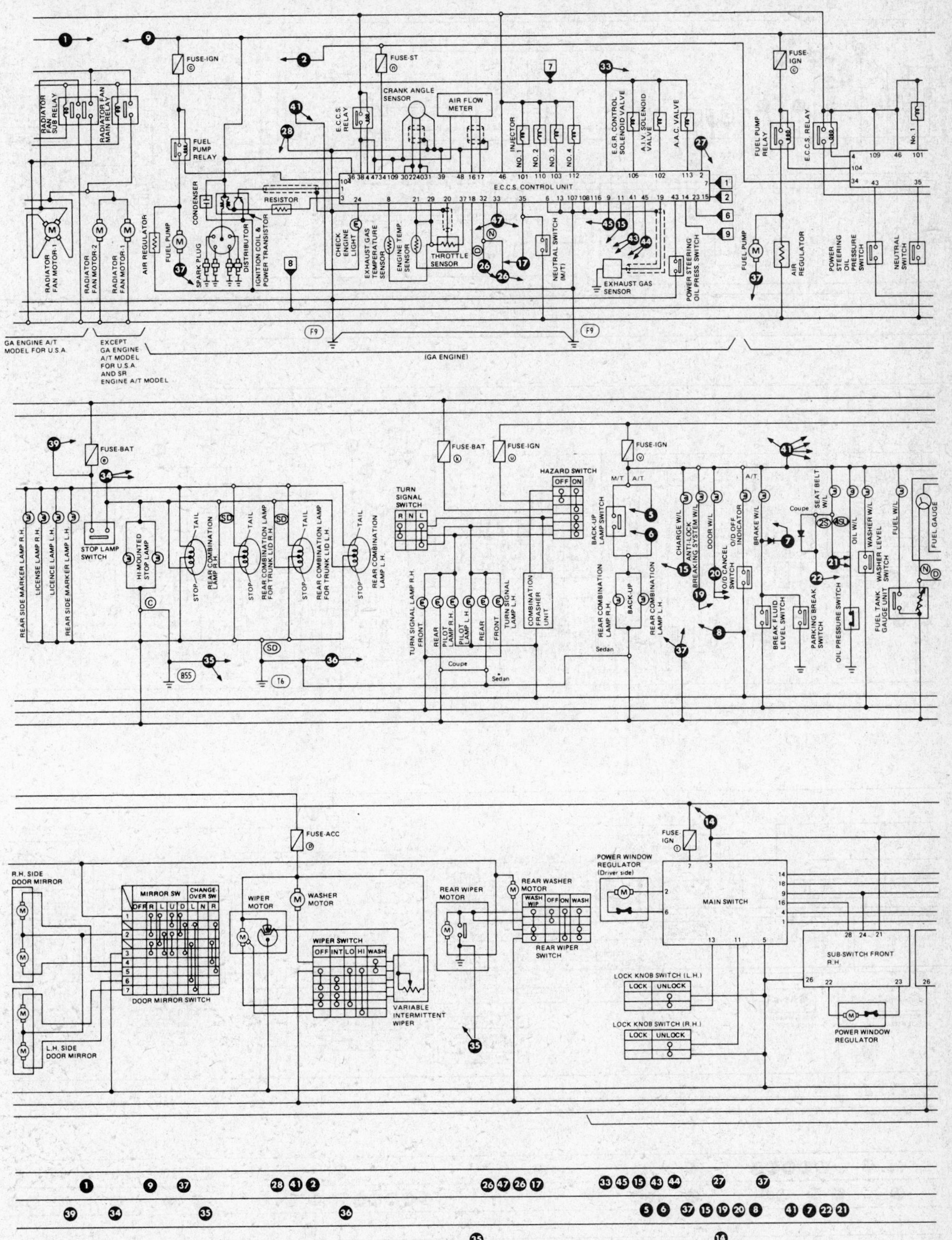

Fig. 68. Complete circuit wiring diagram — 1991-92 Sentra/NX Coupe

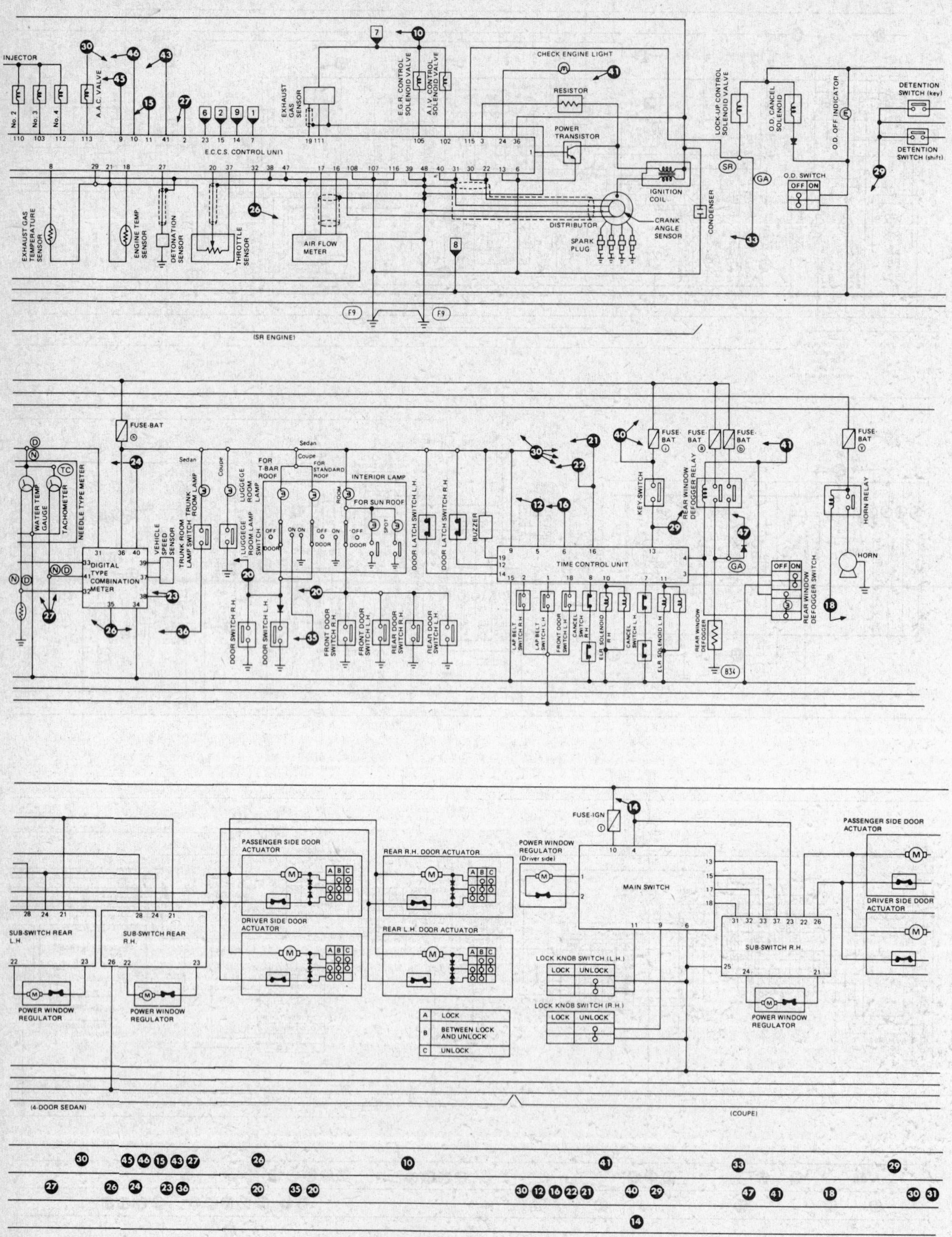

Fig. 68. Complete circuit wiring diagram — 1991-92 Sentra/NX Coupe

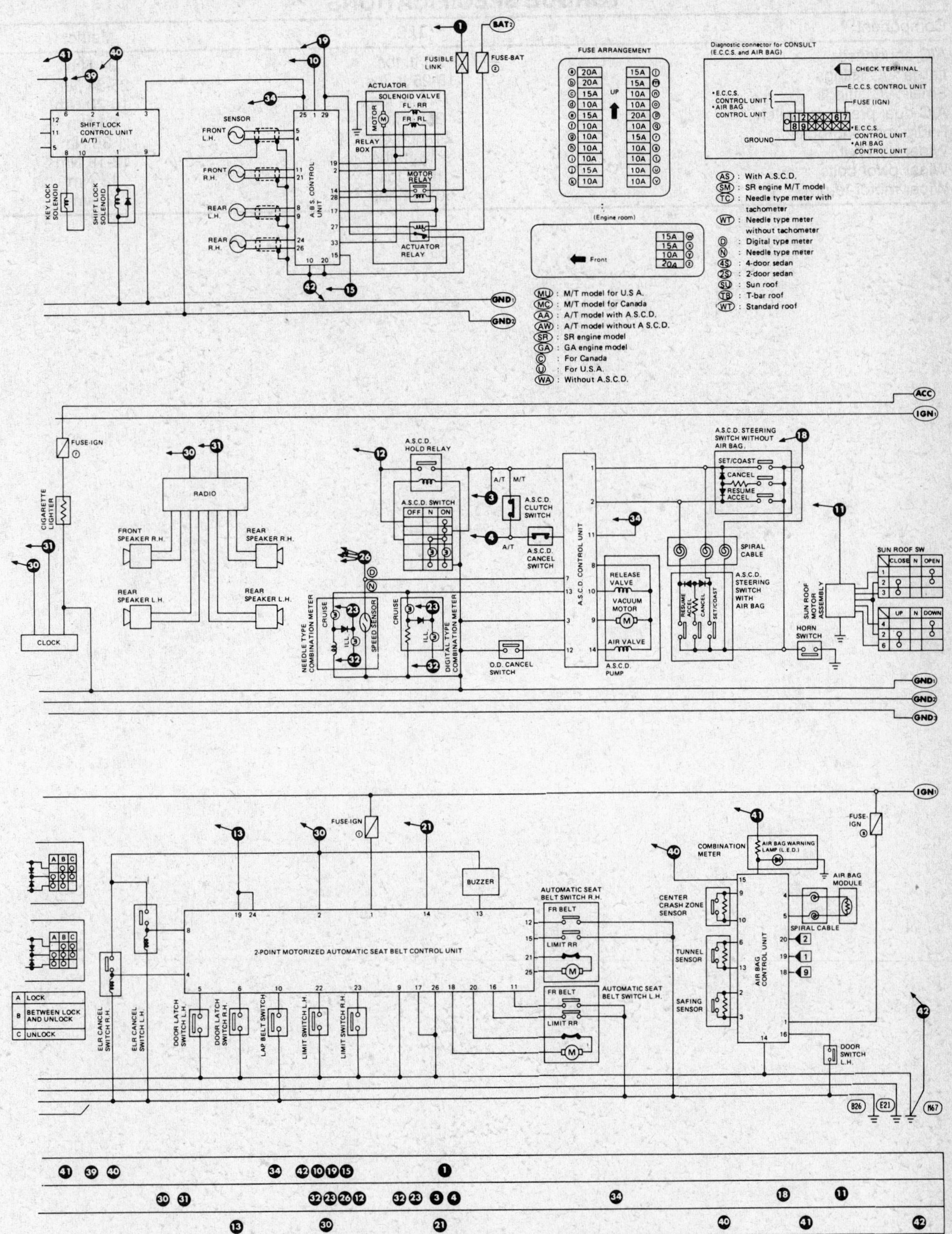

Fig. 68. Complete circuit wiring diagram — 1991-92 Sentra/NX Coupe

TORQUE SPECIFICATIONS

Component	U.S.	Metric
A/C condenser	25 ft. lbs.	34 Nm
Large A/C fittings	18-25 ft. lbs.	25-34 Nm
Small A/C fittings	7-14 ft. lbs.	10-20 Nm
A/C dual pressure switch	20 ft. lbs.	28 Nm
Radio retaining bolts	24 inch lbs.	1.36 Nm
Wiper arm nut	9-13 ft. lbs.	12-18 Nm
Wiper pivot bolts	10 ft. lbs.	13 Nm
Wiper motor-to-pivot	60 inch lbs.	7 Nm

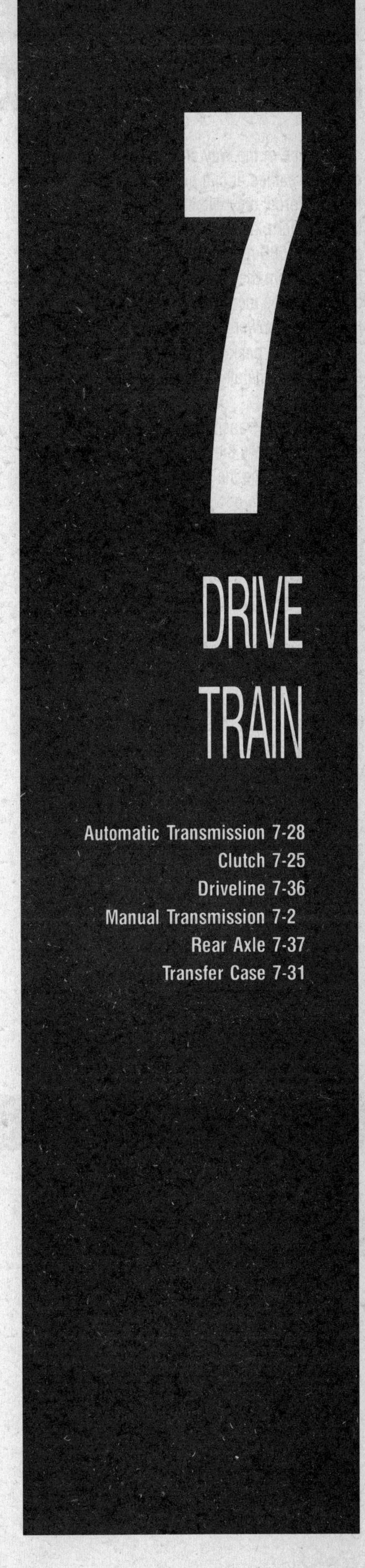

7 DRIVE TRAIN

THE MANUAL TRANSMISSION

Because of the way an internal combustion engine breathes, it can produce torque, or twisting force, only within a narrow speed range. Most modern, overhead valve engines must turn at about 2,500 rpm to produce their peak torque. By 4,500 rpm they are producing so little torque that continued increases in engine speed produce no power increases.

The torque peak on overhead camshaft engines is, generally, much higher, but much narrower.

The manual transmission and clutch are employed to vary the relationship between engine speed and the speed of the wheels so that adequate engine power can be produced under all circumstances. The clutch allows engine torque to be applied to the transmission input shaft gradually, due to mechanical slippage. The car can, consequently, be started smoothly from a full stop.

The transmission changes the ratio between the rotating speeds of the engine and the wheels by the use of gears. 4-speed or 5-speed transmissions are most common. The lower gears allow full engine power to be applied to the wheels during acceleration at low speeds.

The clutch drive plate is a thin disc, the center of which is splined to the transmission input shaft. Both sides of the disc are covered with a layer of material which is similar to brake lining and which is capable of allowing slippage without roughness or excessive noise.

The clutch cover is bolted to the engine flywheel and incorporates a diaphragm spring which provides the pressure to engage the clutch. The cover also houses the pressure plate. The driven disc is sandwiched between the pressure plate and the smooth surface of the flywheel when the clutch pedal is released, thus forcing it to turn at the same speed as the engine crankshaft.

The transmission contains a mainshaft which passes all the way through the transmission, from the clutch to the halfshafts. This shaft is separated at one point, so that front and rear portions can turn at different speeds.

Power is transmitted by a countershaft in the lower gears and reverse. The gears of the countershaft mesh with gears on the mainshaft, allowing power to be carried from one to the other. All the countershaft gears are integral with that shaft, while several of the mainshaft gears can either rotate independently of the shaft or be locked to it. Shifting from one gear to the next causes one of the gears to be freed from rotating with the shaft and locks another to it. Gears are locked and unlocked by internal dog clutches which slide between the center of the gear and the shaft. The forward gears usually employ synchronizers; friction members which smoothly bring gear and shaft to the same speed before the toothed dog clutches are engaged.

The clutch is operating properly if:

1. It will stall the engine when released with the vehicle held stationary.
2. The shift lever can be moved freely between 1st and reverse gears when the vehicle is stationary and the clutch disengaged.

A clutch pedal free-play adjustment is incorporated in the linkage. If there is about 1–2 in. (25–50mm) of motion before the pedal begins to release the clutch, it is adjusted properly. Inadequate free-play wears all parts of the clutch releasing mechanisms and may cause slippage. Excessive free-play may cause inadequate release and hard shifting of gears.

Some clutches use a hydraulic system in place of mechanical linkage. If the clutch fails to release, fill the clutch master cylinder with fluid to the proper level and pump the clutch pedal to fill the system with fluid. Bleed the system in the same way as a brake system. If leaks are located, tighten loose connections or overhaul the master or slave cylinder as necessary.

Front wheel drive cars do not have conventional rear axles or drive shafts. Instead, power is transmitted from the engine to a transaxle, or a combination of transmission and drive axle, in one unit. Both the transmission and drive axle accomplish the same function as their counterparts in a front engine/rear drive axle design. The difference is in the location of the components.

In place of a conventional driveshaft, a front wheel drive design uses two driveshafts, sometimes called halfshafts, which couple the drive axle portion of the transaxle to the wheels. Universal joints or constant velocity joints are used just as they would in a rear wheel drive design.

MANUAL TRANSAXLE

Identification

The manual transaxle serial number label is attached on the clutch withdrawal lever or the upper part of the housing.

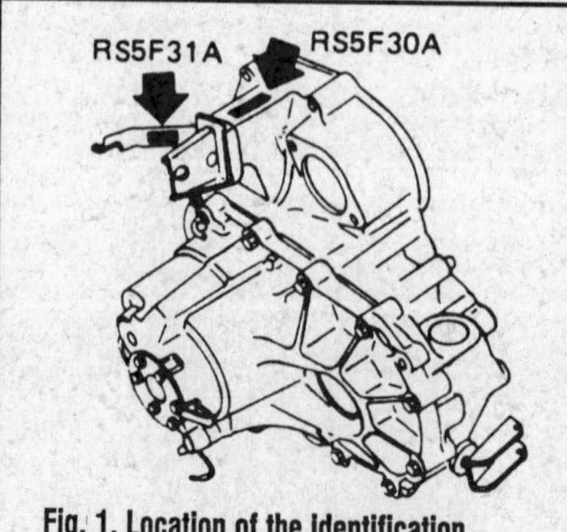

RS5F31A
RS5F30A

Fig. 1. Location of the identification stampings on the manual transaxle

Adjustments

SHIFTER LINKAGE

➡ On models from 1982–86 adjustment is possible. On models from 1987–92 no adjustment is possible.

1. Raise and support the front of the vehicle on jackstands.

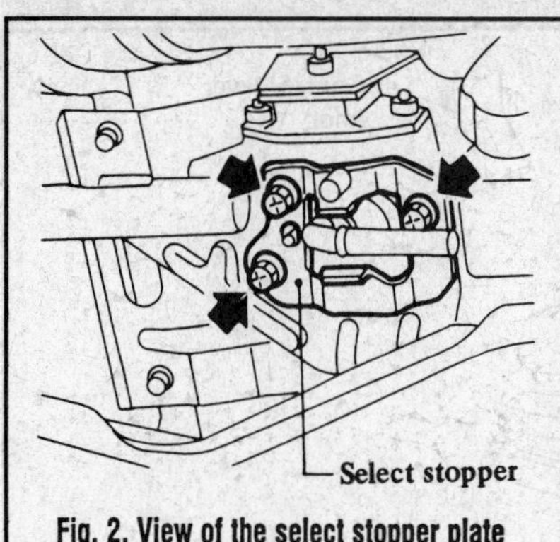
Select stopper

Fig. 2. View of the select stopper plate

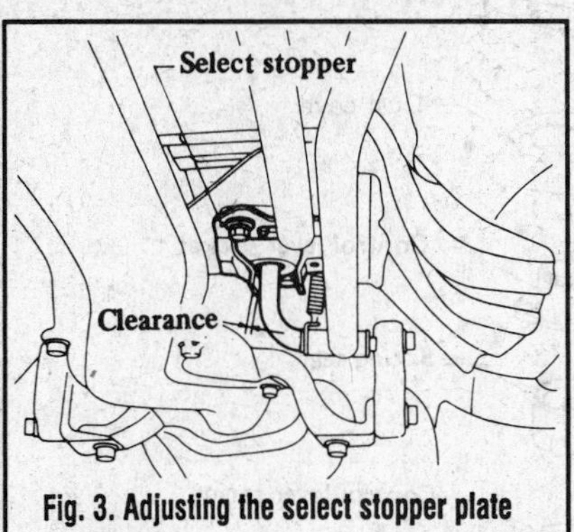
Select stopper
Clearance

Fig. 3. Adjusting the select stopper plate clearance

2. Under the vehicle, at the shift control area, loosen the select stopper securing bolts.

3. Shift the gear selector into 1st gear.

4. Adjust the clearance between the control lever and select stopper by sliding the select stopper so that the clearance is 1.00mm.

5. Torque the stopper securing bolts to 2.3–3.7 ft. lbs. (3–5 Nm). Check that the control lever can be shifted without binding or dragging.

Shifter Assembly

➧ SEE FIGS. 4–7

REMOVAL & INSTALLATION

1. Remove the shift knob by covering the knob with a rag and turning it counterclockwise with a channel lock pliers. Be careful not to damage the knob.

2. Raise the vehicle and support safely. Separate the control rod and support rod from the transaxle.

3. Remove the control bracket securing bolts, then remove the shift assembly.

To install:

4. Lubricate all moving parts with heavy grease. Install the assembly and torque the bracket bolts to 8–10 ft. lbs. (10–12 Nm).

5. Apply Loctite® to the shift knob and install by hand.

6. Lower the vehicle and check operation.

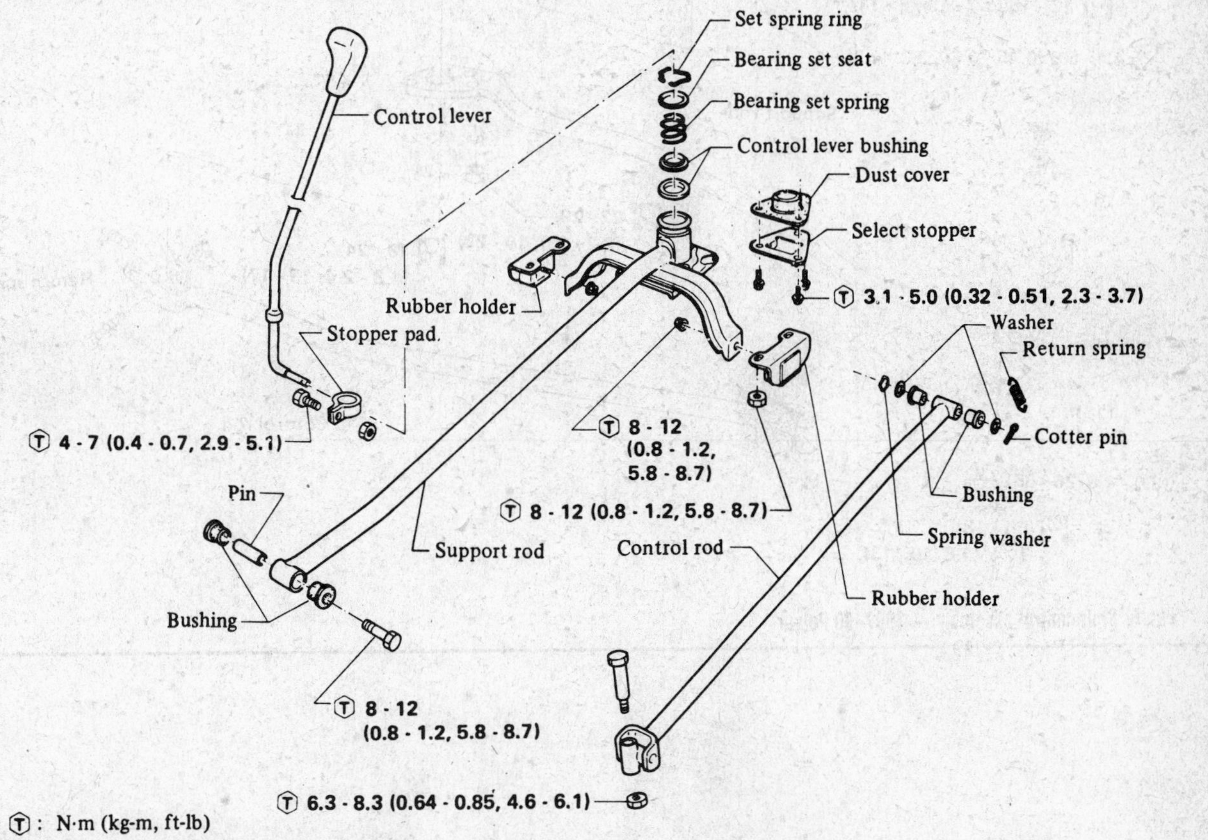

Set spring ring
Bearing set seat
Bearing set spring
Control lever
Control lever bushing
Dust cover
Select stopper
Rubber holder
Ⓣ 3.1 - 5.0 (0.32 - 0.51, 2.3 - 3.7)
Stopper pad
Washer
Return spring
Ⓣ 4 - 7 (0.4 - 0.7, 2.9 - 5.1)
Ⓣ 8 - 12 (0.8 - 1.2, 5.8 - 8.7)
Cotter pin
Pin
Bushing
Ⓣ 8 - 12 (0.8 - 1.2, 5.8 - 8.7)
Support rod
Control rod
Spring washer
Bushing
Rubber holder
Ⓣ 8 - 12 (0.8 - 1.2, 5.8 - 8.7)
Ⓣ 6.3 - 8.3 (0.64 - 0.85, 4.6 - 6.1)
Ⓣ : N·m (kg-m, ft-lb)

Fig. 4. Shift control assembly — 1982–86 vehicles

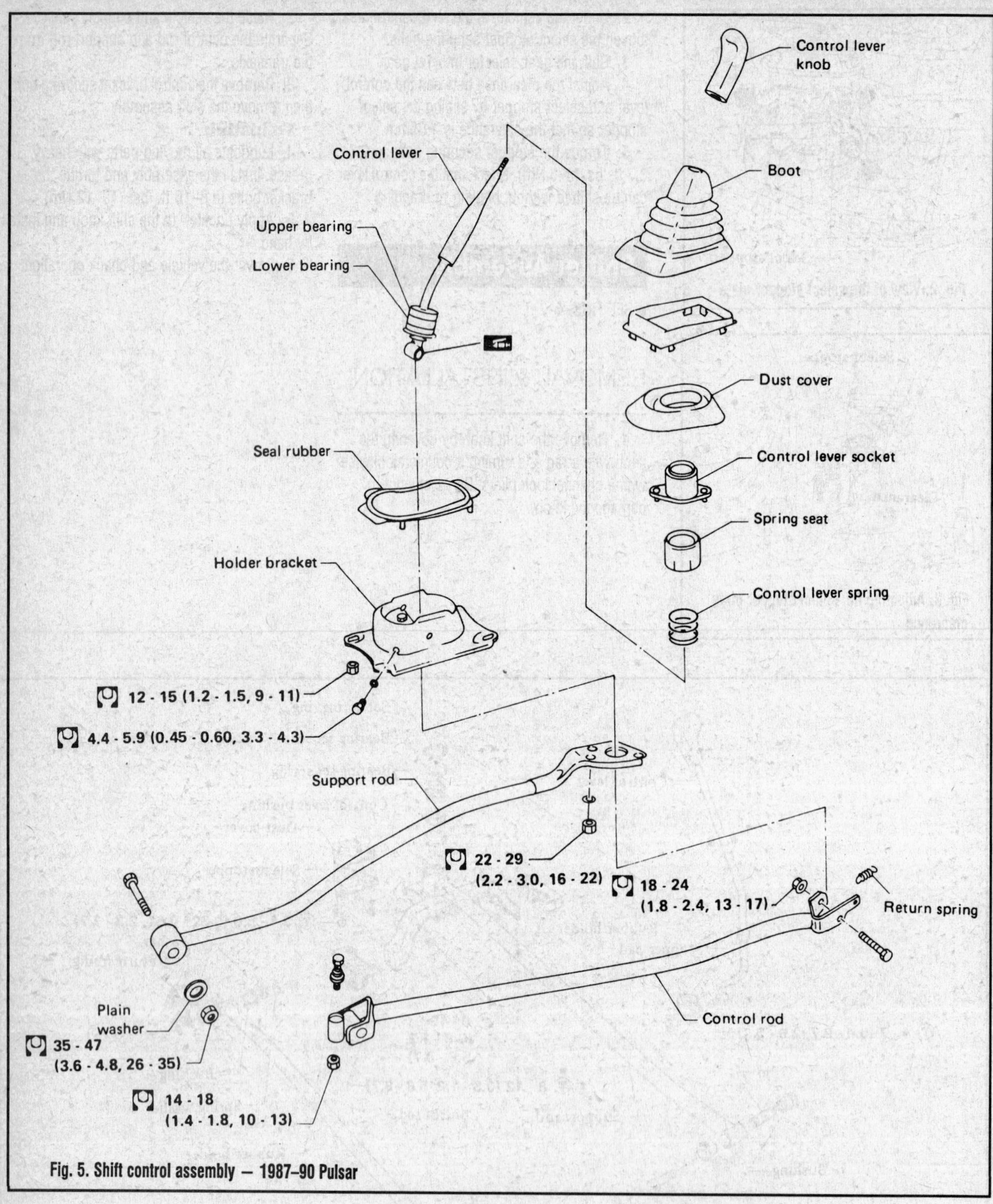
Control lever knob
Boot
Control lever
Upper bearing
Lower bearing
Dust cover
Seal rubber
Control lever socket
Spring seat
Holder bracket
Control lever spring
12 - 15 (1.2 - 1.5, 9 - 11)
4.4 - 5.9 (0.45 - 0.60, 3.3 - 4.3)
Support rod
22 - 29
(2.2 - 3.0, 16 - 22)
18 - 24
(1.8 - 2.4, 13 - 17)
Return spring
Plain washer
35 - 47
(3.6 - 4.8, 26 - 35)
Control rod
14 - 18
(1.4 - 1.8, 10 - 13)

Fig. 5. Shift control assembly — 1987–90 Pulsar

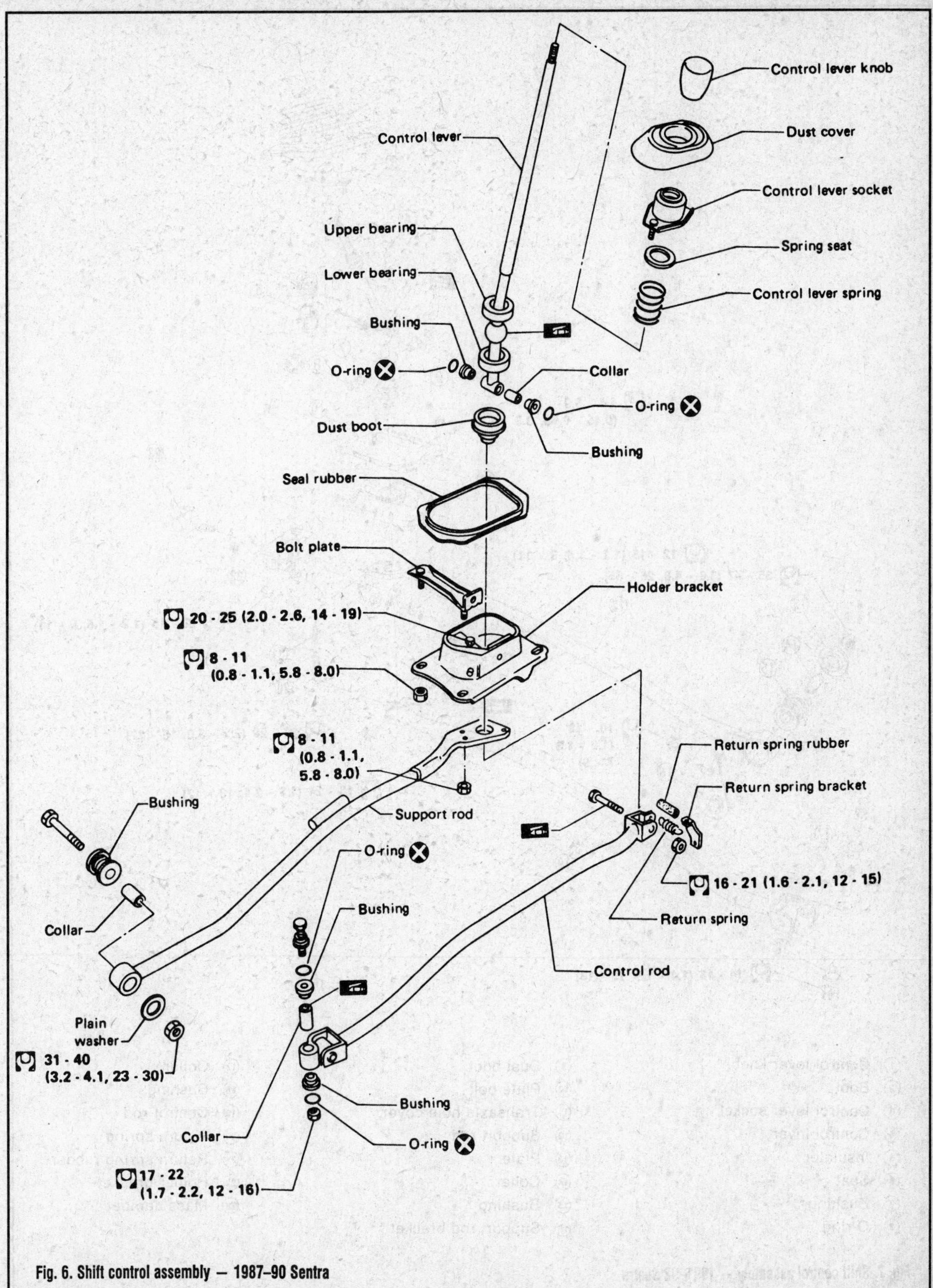

Control lever knob
Dust cover
Control lever
Control lever socket
Upper bearing
Spring seat
Lower bearing
Control lever spring
Bushing
O-ring
Collar
O-ring
Dust boot
Bushing
Seal rubber
Bolt plate
Holder bracket
20 - 25 (2.0 - 2.6, 14 - 19)
8 - 11
(0.8 - 1.1, 5.8 - 8.0)
8 - 11
(0.8 - 1.1,
5.8 - 8.0)
Return spring rubber
Return spring bracket
Bushing
Support rod
O-ring
16 - 21 (1.6 - 2.1, 12 - 15)
Bushing
Return spring
Collar
Control rod
Plain
washer
31 - 40
(3.2 - 4.1, 23 - 30)
Bushing
Collar
O-ring
17 - 22
(1.7 - 2.2, 12 - 16)

Fig. 6. Shift control assembly — 1987–90 Sentra

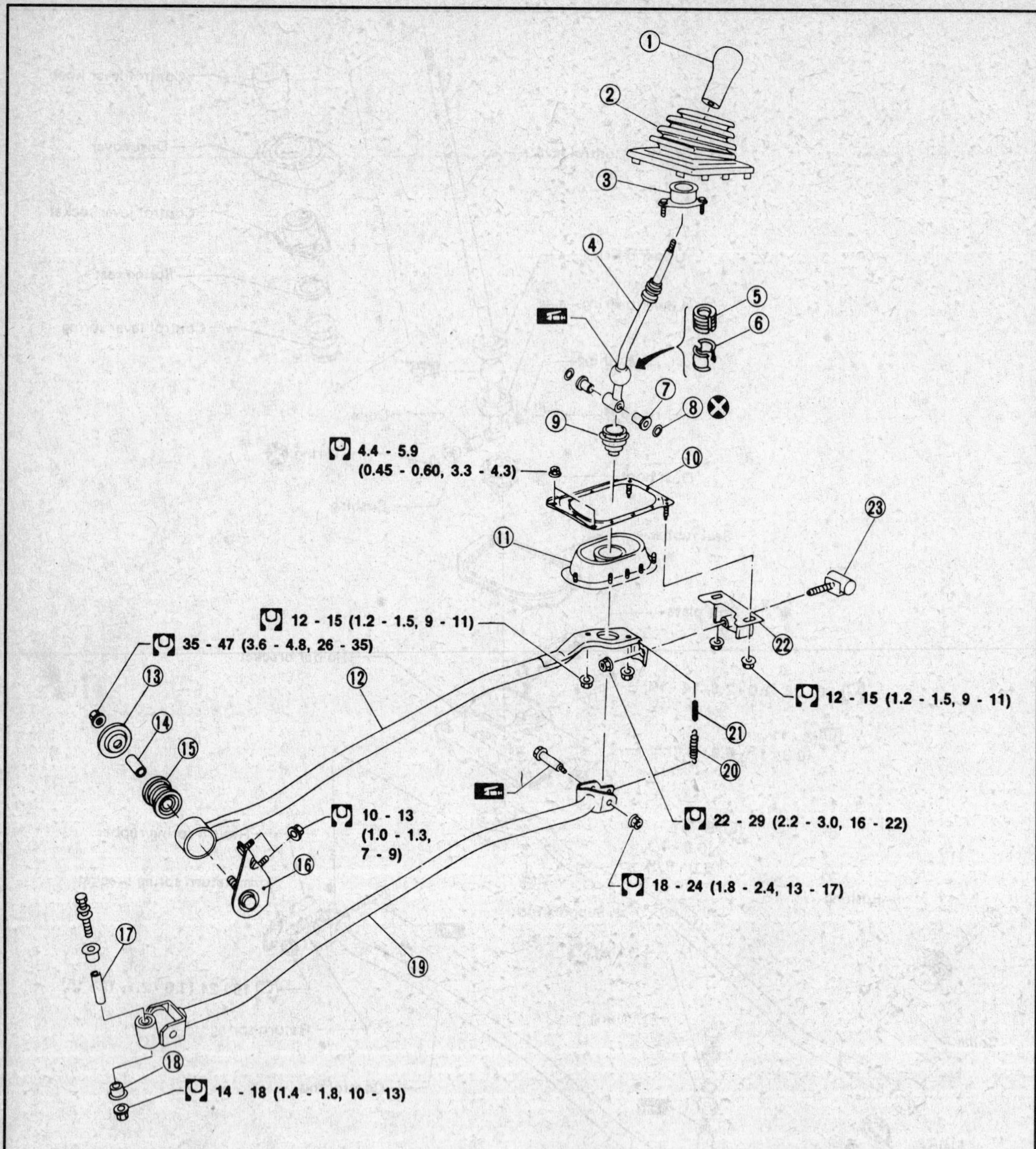
4.4 - 5.9
(0.45 - 0.60, 3.3 - 4.3)
12 - 15 (1.2 - 1.5, 9 - 11)
35 - 47 (3.6 - 4.8, 26 - 35)
12 - 15 (1.2 - 1.5, 9 - 11)
10 - 13
(1.0 - 1.3,
7 - 9)
22 - 29 (2.2 - 3.0, 16 - 22)
18 - 24 (1.8 - 2.4, 13 - 17)
14 - 18 (1.4 - 1.8, 10 - 13)

1. Control lever knob
2. Boot
3. Control lever socket
4. Control lever
5. Insulator
6. Seat
7. Bushing
8. O-ring
9. Dust boot
10. Plate bolt
11. Transaxle hole cover
12. Support rod
13. Plate
14. Collar
15. Bushing
16. Support rod bracket
17. Collar
18. Bushing
19. Control rod
20. Return spring
21. Return spring rubber
22. Holder bracket
23. Mass damper

Fig. 7. Shift control assembly — 1991–92 Sentra

Back-Up Light Switch

REMOVAL & INSTALLATION

1. Raise vehicle and support safely.
2. Disconnect the electrical connections.
3. Remove switch from transaxle housing, when removing place drain pan under transaxle to catch fluid.
4. To install: apply sealer to the switch and torque to 14–22 ft. lbs. (20–29 Nm).

Transaxle

REMOVAL & INSTALLATION

1982–86 Vehicles

1. Remove the battery.

➡ **On the Pulsar, remove the battery holding plate and the radiator reservoir.**

2. Drain the lubricant from the transaxle.
3. Remove the driveshafts from the transaxle.

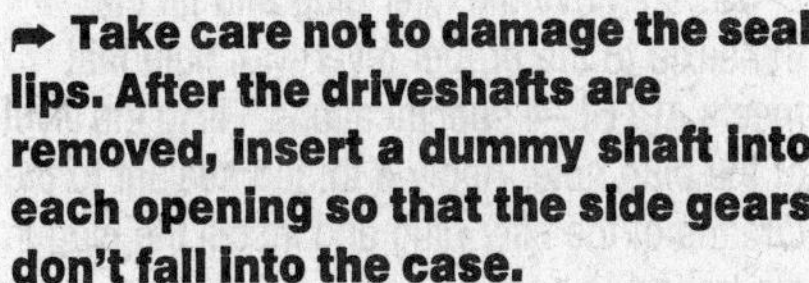

➡ **Take care not to damage the seal lips. After the driveshafts are removed, insert a dummy shaft into each opening so that the side gears don't fall into the case.**

4. Remove the distributor, the air induction tube, the EGR tube and the exhaust manifold cover.
5. Remove the heater hose clamp.
6. Remove the clutch control cable from the lever.
7. Disconnect the speedometer cable at the case.
8. Disconnect all wiring from the case. Remove the wheel well liner.
9. Separate the control and support rods from the case. Disconnect the exhaust pipe at the manifold.
10. Place a jackstand under the engine oil pan to take up the engine weight.
11. Take up the transaxle weight with a floor jack.
12. Remove the engine gusset bolts. On the Pulsar, remove the transmission protector.
13. On 5-speed models, remove the engine right side and rear mounting brackets and the starter.
14. Attach a shop crane to the transaxle at the clutch control cable bracket.

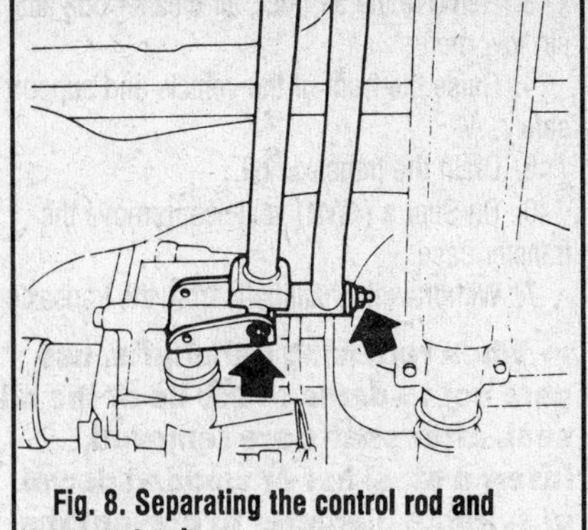

Fig. 8. Separating the control rod and support rod

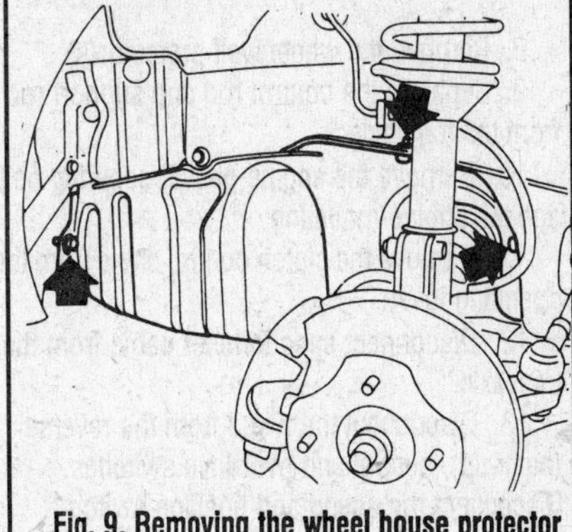

Fig. 9. Removing the wheel house protector

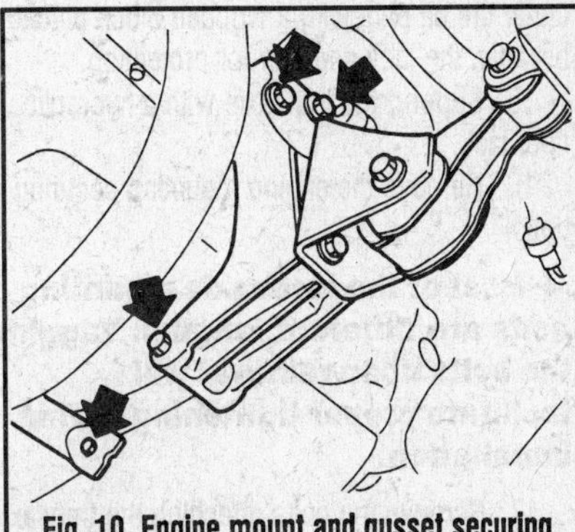

Fig. 10. Engine mount and gusset securing bolts

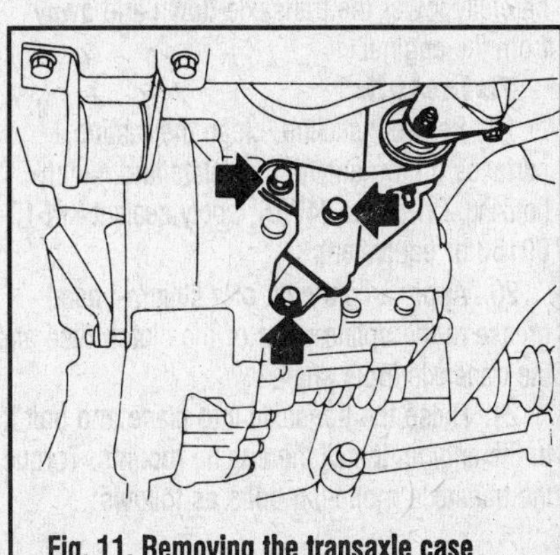

Fig. 11. Removing the transaxle case

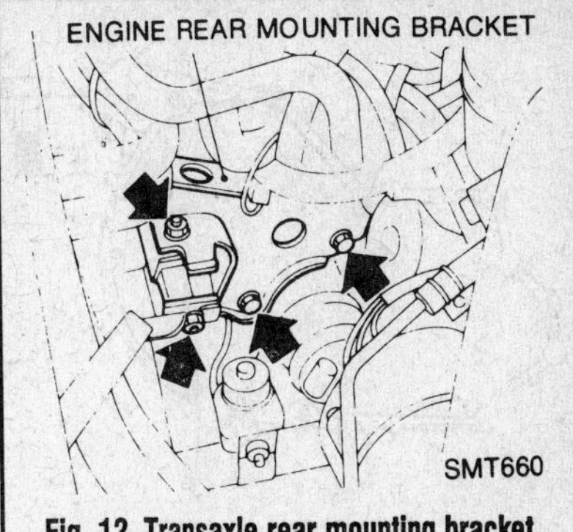
ENGINE REAR MOUNTING BRACKET
SMT660

Fig. 12. Transaxle rear mounting bracket – 1982–86 vehicles

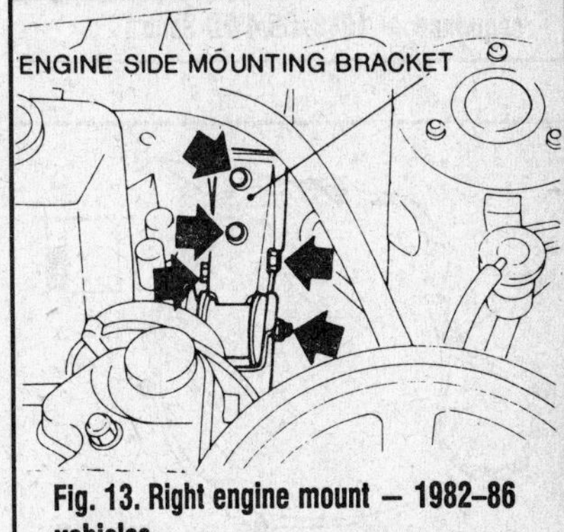
ENGINE SIDE MOUNTING BRACKET

Fig. 13. Right engine mount – 1982–86 vehicles

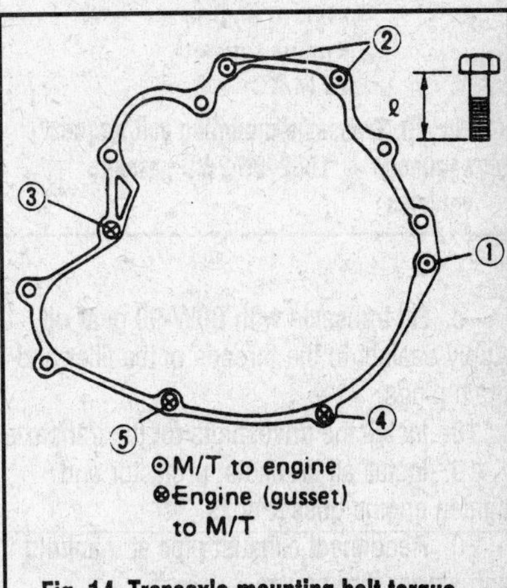
②
ℓ
③
①
④
⑤
⊖M/T to engine
⊗Engine (gusset) to M/T

Fig. 14. Transaxle mounting bolt torque sequence – 1982–86 2WD diesel vehicles

15. Unbolt the transaxle from the engine. On 5-speed models, pull the engine to the right and slide the transaxle away from the engine.
16. Lower the transaxle from the vehicle.

To install:

17. Install the transaxle in the vehicle. Note the following points:
    a. Clean all mating surfaces.
    b. Apply EP chassis lube to the splines on the clutch disc and input shaft.

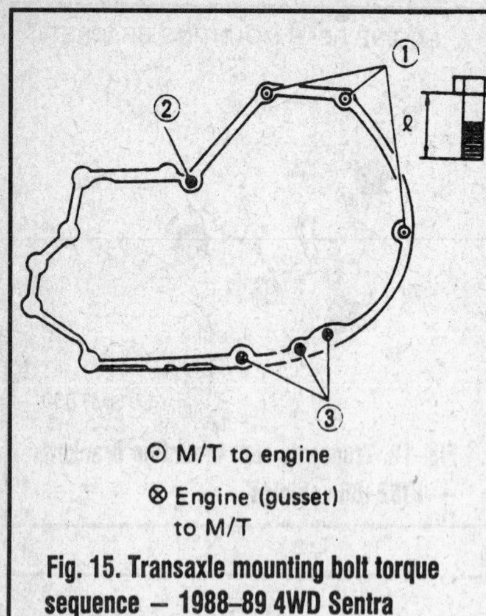

①
②
③
ℓ
⊙ M/T to engine
⊗ Engine (gusset) to M/T

Fig. 15. Transaxle mounting bolt torque sequence — 1988–89 4WD Sentra

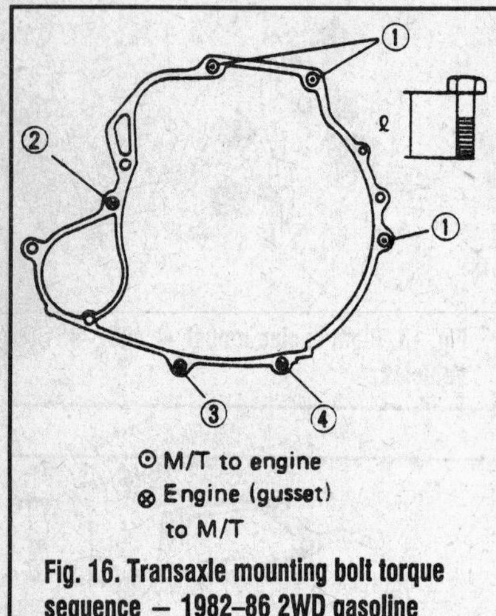

①
②
③
④
ℓ
⊙ M/T to engine
⊗ Engine (gusset) to M/T

Fig. 16. Transaxle mounting bolt torque sequence — 1982–86 2WD gasoline vehicles

c. Fill transaxle with 80W-90 gear oil. Apply sealant to the threads of the filler and drain plugs.

18. Install the driveshafts for the transaxle.
19. Install all brackets, protector and tighten engine gusset bolts.
20. Reconnect exhaust pipe at manifold and starter if removed.
21. Install all wiring, cables and clamps and wheel well liner.
22. Install the distributor, the air induction tube, the EGR tube and the exhaust manifold cover.
23. Install the battery and any other components that were removed.
24. Road test for proper operation.

1987-92 Vehicles

➧ SEE FIGS. 17–20

1. Disconnect the negative battery cable.
2. Remove the battery and battery bracket.
3. Remove the air duct, air cleaner box and air flow meter.
4. Raise the front of the vehicle and support safely.
5. Drain the transaxle oil.
6. On Sentra (4WD) vehicles, remove the transfer case.
7. Withdraw the halfshafts from the transaxle.

➡ **When removing halfshafts, use care not to damage the lip of the oil seal. After shafts are removed, insert a steel bar or wooden dowel of suitable diameter to prevent the side gears from rotating and falling into the differential case.**

8. Remove the wheel well protector(s).
9. Separate the control rod and support rod from the transaxle.
10. Remove the engine gusset securing bolt and the engine mounting.
11. Remove the clutch control cable from the operating lever.
12. Disconnect speedometer cable from the transaxle.
13. Disconnect the wires from the reverse (back-up), neutral and overdrive switches. Disconnect the speed and position switch sensors from the transaxle also, if so equipped.
14. Support the engine by placing a jack under the oil pan, with a wooden block placed between the jack and pan for protection.
15. Support the transaxle with a hydraulic floor jack.
16. Remove the engine mounting securing bolts.

➡ **Most of the transaxle mounting bolts are different lengths. Tagging the bolts upon removal will facilitate proper tightening during installation.**

17. Remove the bolts attaching the transaxle to the engine.
18. Using the hydraulic floor jack as a carrier, carefully lower the transaxle down and away from the engine.

To install:

19. Before installing, clean the mating surfaces on the engine rear plate and clutch housing. On Sentra (4WD), apply sealant KP510-00150 or equivalent.
20. Apply a light coat of a lithium-based grease to the spline parts of the clutch disc and the transaxle input shaft.
21. Raise the transaxle into place and bolt it to the engine. Install the engine mounts. Torque the transaxle mounting bolts as follows:

a. 1987–88 Pulsar/Sentra (E16S and E16i) — tighten bolts (1) and (3) to 12–15 ft. lbs. (16–22 Nm). Tighten bolts (2) and (4) to 14–22 ft. lbs. (20–29 Nm). Bolts (3) and (4) are found all Sentra models.

b. 1987–88 Pulsar (CA18DE) — On CA18DE engines, tighten bolts (1) and (2) to to 32–43 ft. lbs. (43–58 Nm) and bolts (3) to 22–30 ft. lbs. (30–40 Nm).

c. 1989 Pulsar (CA18DE) — tighten bolts (1) and (2) to 32–43 ft. lbs. (43–58 Nm) and bolt (3) to 22–30 ft. lbs. (30–40 Nm).

d. Pulsar and 2WD Sentra — tighten all bolts to 12–15 ft. lbs. (16–21 Nm).

e. Sentra 4WD — torque all the bolts to 22–30 ft. lbs. (29–41 Nm).

22. Connect the speedometer cable to the transaxle.
23. Connect the clutch cable to the operating lever.
24. Connect the control and support rods to the transaxle.
25. Install the wheel well protectors.
26. Install the halfshafts.
27. On Sentra (4WD) vehicles, install the transfer case.
28. Lower the vehicle.
29. Install the air duct, air cleaner box and air flow meter.
30. Install the battery and battery bracket.
31. Connect the negative battery cable.
32. Remove the filler plug and fill the transaxle to the proper level with fluid that meets API GL-4 specifications. Fill to the level of the plug hole. Apply a thread sealant to the threads of the filler plug and install the plug in the transaxle case.

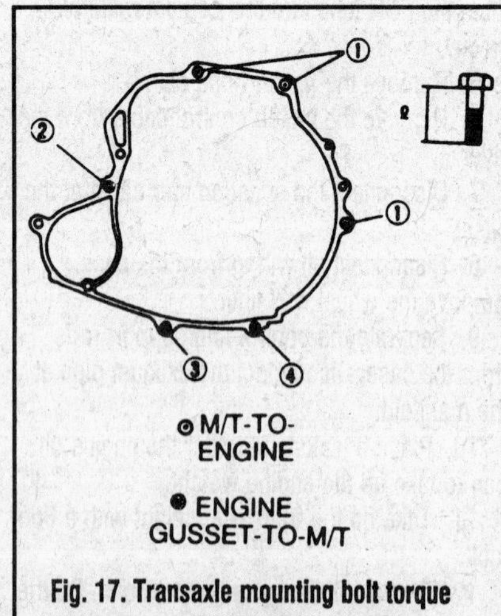

①
②
③
④
ℓ
⊙ M/T-TO-ENGINE
● ENGINE GUSSET-TO-M/T

Fig. 17. Transaxle mounting bolt torque sequence — 1988 E-series engine

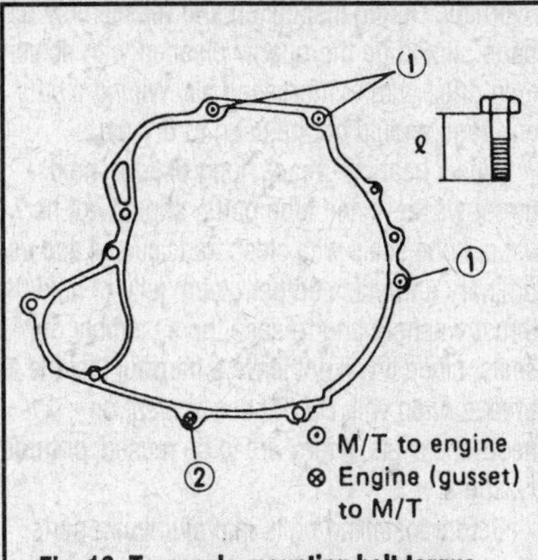

①
ℓ
①
②
M/T to engine
Engine (gusset) to M/T

Fig. 18. Transaxle mounting bolt torque sequence – 1989–90 GA16i engine

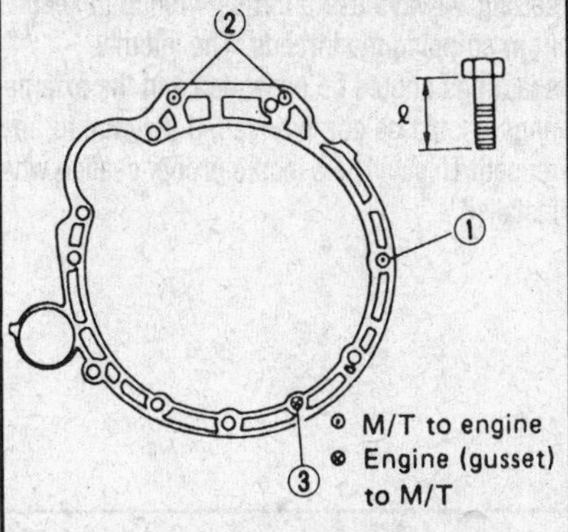

②
ℓ
①
M/T to engine
Engine (gusset) to M/T
③

Fig. 19. Transaxle mounting bolt torque sequence – CA16DE and CA18DE engines

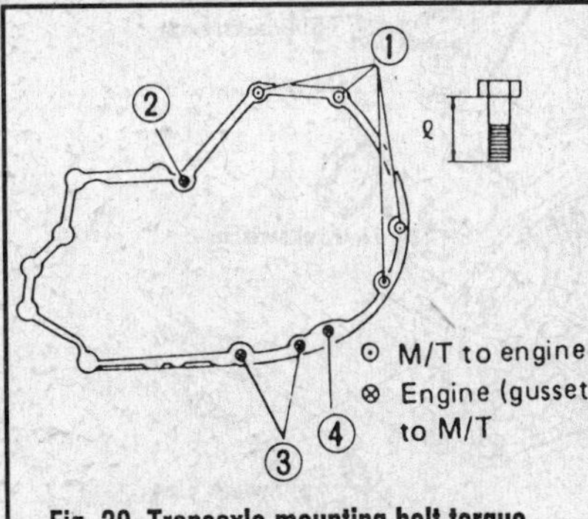

①
②
ℓ
M/T to engine
Engine (gusset) to M/T
④
③

Fig. 20. Transaxle mounting bolt torque sequence – 1988–89 4WD Sentra

OVERHAUL 4- AND 5-SPEED TRANSAXLE

Transmission Case

DISASSEMBLY

1. Drain the oil from the transmission case.
2. Remove the mounting bolts, tap the case lightly with a rubber mallet and then lift off the transmission case.

➡ When removing the transmission case, tilt it slightly to prevent interference from the 5th gear shift fork.

3. Disconnect the back-up light switch and then remove the oil gutter.
4. Remove the input shaft bearing.
5. Remove the case cover, the mainshaft bearing adjusting shim and the spacer.
6. Remove the mainshaft bearing rear outer race and the differential side bearing outer race.
7. Draw out the reverse idler spacer.

ASSEMBLY

1. Press fit the differential side bearing outer race and the mainshaft rear bearing outer race.
2. Install the input shaft needle bearing. Apply sealant to the welch plug and then install it on the transmission case.
3. Install the oil gutter. Apply sealant to the back-up light switch and install it.
4. If the transmission case has been replaced, adjust the differential side bearing and the mainshaft rotary frictional force by means of shims.
5. Apply an even coating of sealant to the mating surfaces of the transmission case and the clutch housing. Mount the case on the clutch housing and tighten the mounting bolts to 12–15 ft. lbs. (16–20 Nm).
6. Remove the transmission case cover. Clean the mating surfaces and apply sealant to the transmission case.
7. Install the case cover with the convex side facing outward. Tighten the mounting bolts to 4.6–6.1 ft. lbs. (6–9 Nm).
8. Check that the gears move freely and then install the drain plug (with sealant) and fill with lubricant.

Clutch Housing

DISASSEMBLY

1. Drain the oil and then remove the transmission case.
2. Draw out the reverse idler spacer and fork shaft, then remove the 5th/3rd/4th shift fork.

➡ Do not lose the shifter caps.

3. Remove the control bracket with the 1st and 2nd gear shift fork.

➡ Be careful not to lose the select check ball, spring and the shifter caps (5-speed only).

4. Remove the mainshaft and final drive assembly. Be sure to pull the mainshaft straight out.
5. Remove the bearing retainer securing bolts.
6. Remove the 3 screws and detach the bearing retainer. 1 of the screws is special torx type and should be removed using a special torx allen wrench.
7. Turn the clutch housing so that its side is facing down. Lightly tap the end of the input shaft (on the engine side) with a rubber mallet and then remove the input shaft along with the bearing retainer and reverse idler gear.

➡ Don't remove the reverse idler shaft from the clutch housing because these fittings will be loose. Do not scratch the oil seal lip with the input shaft spline while removing the shaft.

8. Remove the reverse idler gear and final drive assembly.
9. Remove the oil pocket, shift check ball springs and then the check ball plugs.
10. Drive the retaining pins out of the striking lever. Remove the striking rod, lever and interlock.
    a. Select a position where the pin doesn't interfere with the clutch housing when removing it.
    b. When removing the striking rod, be careful not to damage the oil seal lip. It may be a good idea to tape the edges of the striking rod when removing it.
11. Remove the reverse and 5th gear check plug and then detach the check spring and balls. Remove the reverse and 5th gear check assembly.
12. Remove the clutch control shaft, release bearing and clutch lever.
13. Remove the mainshaft bearing outer race. Remove the differential side bearing outer race.
14. Remove the oil channel.

ASSEMBLY

1. Install a new oil channel so that the oil groove in the channel faces the oil pocket.
2. Install the mainshaft bearing and differential side bearing outer races.
3. Install the clutch control shaft, release bearing and clutch lever.
4. Install the oil pocket.

➡ Make sure that oil flows from the oil pocket to the oil channel.

5. Install the reverse and 5th gear check assembly. The smaller check ball is inserted first and then the larger check ball.

➡ When installing the clutch housing and reverse and 5th gear check assembly, it is necessary to adjust the reverse check force.

a. Install a used check plug and tighten it to 14–18 ft. lbs. (19–24 Nm).

b. Use a spring gauge to measure the spring check force 100–136 inch lbs. (11–16 Nm) for the 4-speed; 195–239 inch lbs. (22–27 Nm) for the 5-speed).

c. If the reverse check force is not within the above ranges, select another check plug of a different length until the specifications can be met.

6. Installation of the remaining components is the reverse order of removal. Please note the following:

a. Follow all NOTES listed under the disassembly procedures.

b. Apply a locking sealer to the threads of the torx screw and tighten it to 12–15 ft. lbs.(16.3–20.3 Nm). Use a punch and stake the head of the screw at two points.

c. Tighten the bearing retainer bolts to 12–15 ft. lbs.(16.3–20.3 Nm).

d. Coat the select check ball (5-speed) and shifter caps with grease before installing.

e. Coat the support spring with grease before installing it. This will prevent the spring from falling into the hole for the fork shaft in the clutch housing.

Bench Overhaul RN4F30A and RS5F30A

➧ SEE FIGS. 21–30

The Nissan RS5F30A is a fully synchronized 5 speed transaxle. There are 5 forward speeds and 1 reverse, with 4th and 5th gears being overdrive ratios. The RN4F30A is a 4 speed transaxle that is essentially the same as the RS5F30A with the exception of the 5th input and main gear. The 4th gear of the RN4F30A transaxle is an overdrive ratio.

Fluid Capacity: the RS5F30A 5 speed manual transaxle requires 5.75 pts. (2.7L) of API GL–4 gear oil. The RN4F30A 4 speed manual transaxle requires 4.9 pts. (2.3L) of API GL–4 gear oil.

Before Disassembly

Cleanliness is an important factor in the overhaul of the manual transaxle. Before opening up this unit, the entire outside of the transaxle assembly should be cleaned, preferable with a high pressure washer such as a car wash spray unit. Dirt entering the transaxle internal parts will negate all the time and effort spent on the overhaul. During inspection and reassembly all parts should be thoroughly cleaned with solvent then dried with compressed air. Wiping cloths and rags should not be used to dry parts.

Wheel bearing grease, long used to hold thrust washers and lube parts, should not be used. Lube seals with clean transaxle oil and use ordinary unmedicated petroleum jelly to hold the thrust washers and to ease the assembly of seals, since it will not leave a harmful residue as grease often will. Do not use solvent on neoprene seals, if they are to be reused, or thrust washers.

Before installing bolts into aluminum parts, always dip the threads into clean transaxle oil. Anti-seize compound can also be used to prevent bolts from galling the aluminum and seizing. Always use a torque wrench to keep from stripping the threads. The internal snaprings should be expanded and the external rings should be compressed, if they are to be reused. This will help insure proper seating when installed.

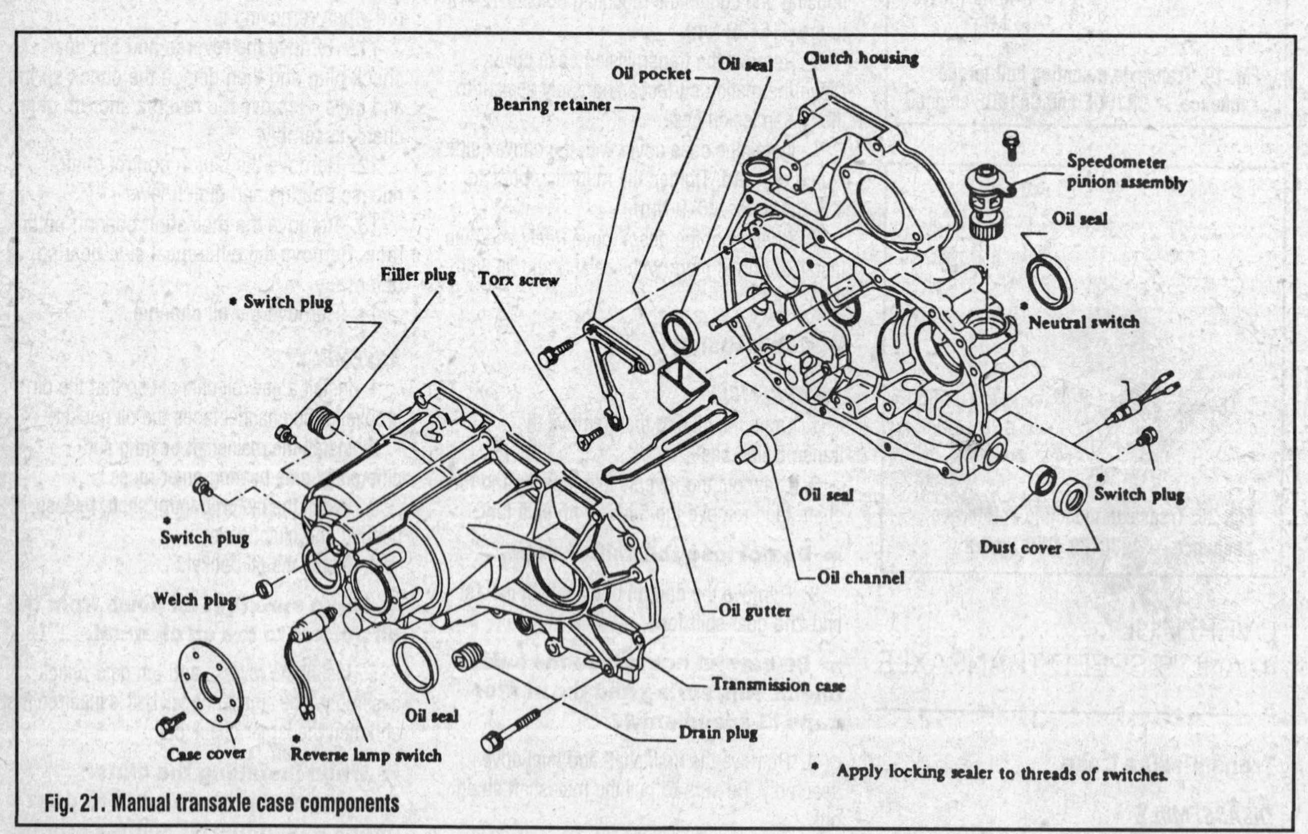
Oil pocket
Oil seal
Clutch housing
Bearing retainer
Speedometer pinion assembly
Oil seal
Filler plug
Torx screw
• Switch plug
• Neutral switch
Oil seal
• Switch plug
• Switch plug
Dust cover
Oil channel
Welch plug
Oil gutter
Transmission case
Oil seal
Drain plug
Case cover
• Reverse lamp switch
• Apply locking sealer to threads of switches

Fig. 21. Manual transaxle case components

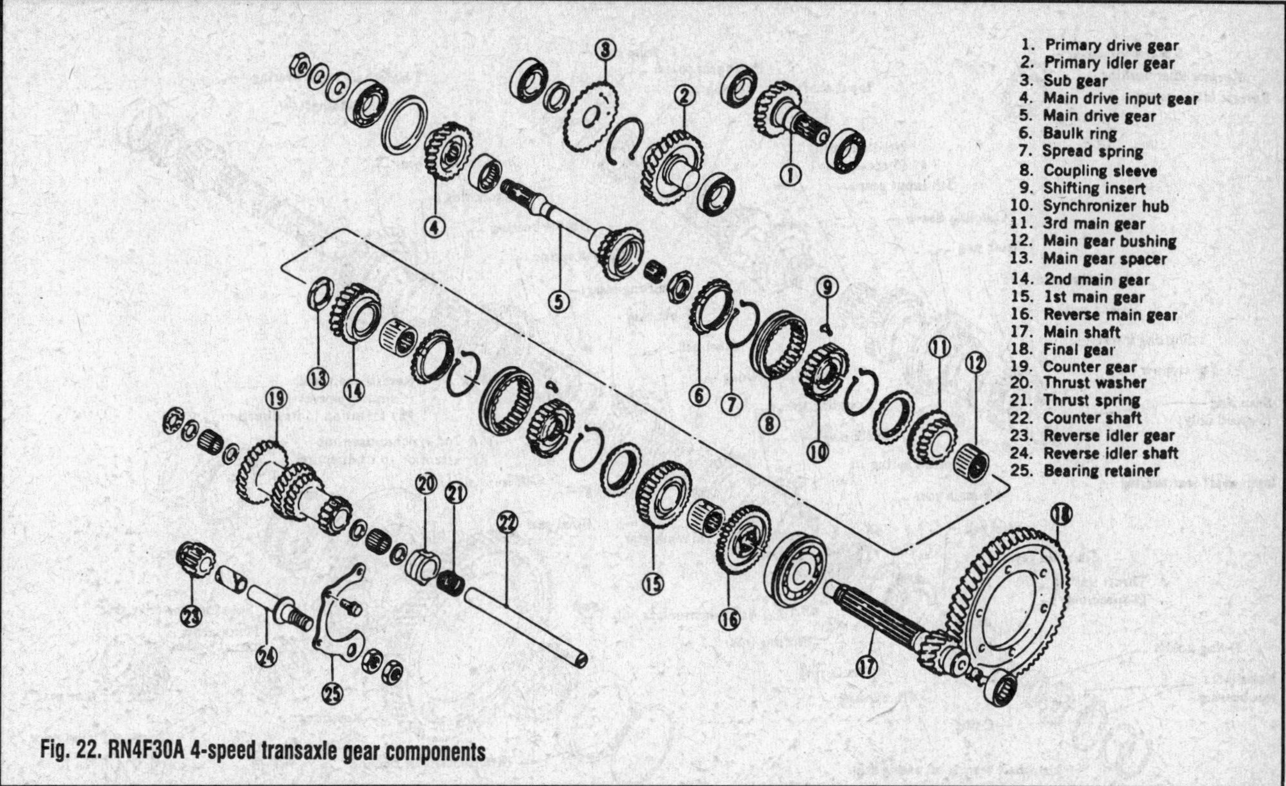
1. Primary drive gear
2. Primary idler gear
3. Sub gear
4. Main drive input gear
5. Main drive gear
6. Baulk ring
7. Spread spring
8. Coupling sleeve
9. Shifting insert
10. Synchronizer hub
11. 3rd main gear
12. Main gear bushing
13. Main gear spacer
14. 2nd main gear
15. 1st main gear
16. Reverse main gear
17. Main shaft
18. Final gear
19. Counter gear
20. Thrust washer
21. Thrust spring
22. Counter shaft
23. Reverse idler gear
24. Reverse idler shaft
25. Bearing retainer

Fig. 22. RN4F30A 4-speed transaxle gear components

1. Primary drive gear
2. Primary idler gear
3. Sub gear
4. Main drive input gear
5. Main drive gear
6. Baulk ring
7. Spread spring
8. Coupling sleeve
9. Shifting insert
10. Synchronizer hub
11. 4th main gear
12. 4th gear bushing
13. Main gear spacer
14. 3rd main gear
15. 2nd main gear
16. Reverse main gear
17. Main shaft
18. Final gear
19. 1st main gear
20. Counter gear
21. 1st-reverse counter gear
22. Reverse idler gear
23. Reverse idler input gear

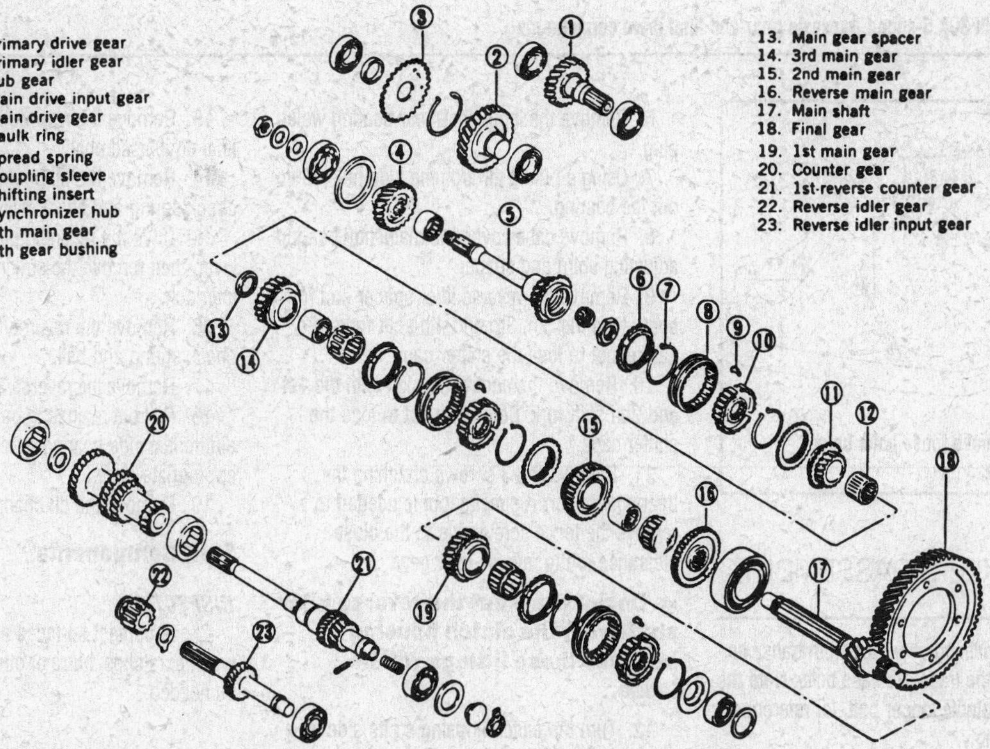

Fig. 23. RS5F30A 5-speed transaxle gear components

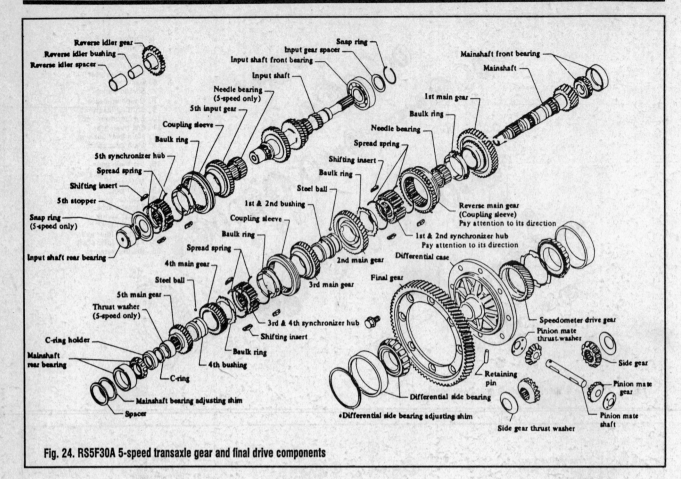

Fig. 24. RS5F30A 5-speed transaxle gear and final drive components

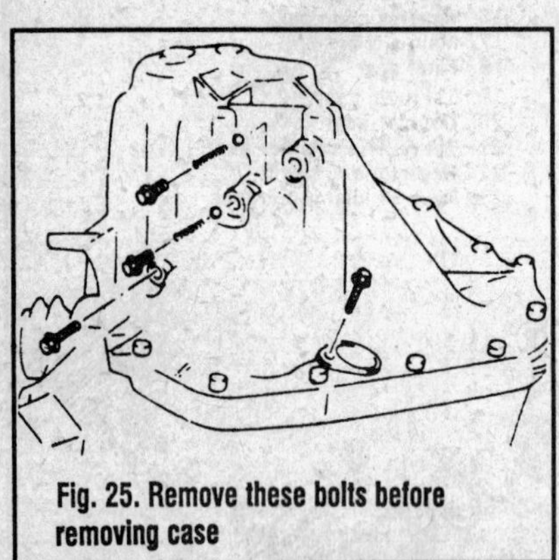

Fig. 25. Remove these bolts before removing case

TRANSAXLE DISASSEMBLY

1. Drain remaining gear lube from transaxle.
2. Remove the transaxle case bolts. Note the location of the single longer bolt, for reference during reassembly.
3. Using a plastic hammer, tap and carefully remove case. On 5 speed transaxle, tilt case slightly to prevent 5th shift fork from interfering with the case.
4. Remove the backup light switch.
5. Remove the oil gutter.
6. Remove the input shaft rear bearing welch plug.
7. Using a punch through the plug hole, drive out the bearing.
8. Remove case cover and mainshaft bearing adjusting shim and spacer.
9. Remove the reverse idler spacer and fork shaft, then the 5th, 3rd and 4th shift forks. Be careful not to lose the shifter caps.
10. Remove the control bracket with the 1st and 2nd shift fork. Be careful not to lose the shifter caps.
11. Remove the 3 screws attaching the bearing retainer. A special tool is needed to remove the torx® screw, due to the close clearance to the reverse idler gear.

➡ **Do not draw out the reverse idler shaft from the clutch housing because these fittings will be loose.**

12. Turn the clutch housing so its side is facing down. Tap the input shaft on the engine side and remove the input shaft together with the mainshaft. While tapping the input shaft take care not to allow the final gear assembly to fall out.
13. Remove the reverse idler gear and the final drive assembly.
14. Remove the oil pocket, shift check ball, check spring and check ball plug.
15. Drive the retaining pin out of the striking lever, then remove the striking rod, lever and interlock.
16. Remove the reverse/5th check plug, check spring and ball.
17. Remove the reverse/5th check assembly.
18. Pull out mainshaft bearing outer race and differential side bearing outer race using an appropriate puller.
19. Remove the oil channel.

Shift Components

INSPECTION

Check contact surfaces and sliding parts for wear, scratches, burrs or other damage. Replace as needed.

INPUT SHAFT AND GEARS

Disassembly

1. Remove input shaft assembly from transaxle.
2. Remove snapring from the front bearing and withdraw the input gear spacer.

➡ **The snapring must not be reused. Replace with new.**

3. Using an appropriate puller, remove the front bearing.
4. Measure the 5th gear endplay.
5. Remove the snapring and 5th stopper.
6. Remove the 5th synchronizer and 5th gear.

Inspection

1. Check the shaft for cracks, wear or bending.
2. Check the gears for wear, chips or cracks.
3. Check the synchronizer spline portion of coupling sleeves, hubs and gears for wear or cracks.
4. Check the synchronizer blocking rings for cracks or deformation.
5. Check insert springs for deformation.
6. Measure the 5th input gear endplay. Standard measurement is 0.0071–0.0161 in. (0.18–0.41mm).
7. Check that the bearing rolls freely.
8. Inspect the bearing for noise, cracks, pitting and wear.

Assembly

1. Install the 5th gear and 5th synchronizer.
2. Install the 5th stopper on the 5th synchronizer and secure it with a snapring to obtain a maximum groove clearance 0.004 in. (0.1mm).
3. Measure the 5th input gear endplay.
4. Using an appropriate press, install the input shaft front bearing.

Standard End Play

mm (in)

Position	
Main 1st gear	0.23–0.43 (0.0091–0.0169)
Main 2nd gear	0.23–0.58 (0.0091–0.0228)
Input 3rd gear	0.23–0.43 (0.0091–0.0169)
Input 4th gear	0.25–0.55 (0.0098–0.0217)
Input 5th gear	0.23–0.48 (0.0091–0.0189)

Fig. 30. Standard endplay

1st & 2nd Synchronizer Hub Snap Ring

mm (in.)

Part No.	Thickness
32269-03E00	2.00 (0.0787)
32269-03E01	2.05 (0.0807)
32269-03E02	2.10 (0.0827)
32269-03E03	1.95 (0.0768)

Fig. 31. 1st/2nd synchronizer hub snapring sizes

3rd & 4th Synchronizer Hub Snap Ring

Thickness mm(in.)

Part No.	Thickness
32269-03E00	2.00 (0.0787)
32269-03E01	2.05 (0.0807)
32269-03E02	2.10 (0.0827)
32269-03E03	1.95 (0.0768)

5th Gear Snap Ring

mm (in.)

Part No.	Thickness
32348-05E00	1.95 (0.0768)
32348-05E01	2.05 (0.0807)
32348-05E02	2.15 (0.0846)
32348-05E03	2.25 (0.0886)

Fig. 32. 3rd/4th and 5th synchronizer hub snapring sizes

MAINSHAFT AND GEARS

Disassembly

1. Before disassembly, check the 1st and 2nd main gear endplay. If not within specifications check the contact surface of the gear, shaft and hub.
2. Remove the mainshaft front and rear bearing inner race.
3. Measure the gear endplay.
4. Remove case cover and mainshaft adjusting shim.
5. Remove the mainshaft rear bearing outer race from the case.
6. Remove the C-rings, C-ring holder and thrust washer, if equipped.
7. Remove the 5th main gear, if equipped.
8. Remove the 4th main gear, bushing and steel ball. Make certain not to lose the ball.
9. Remove the 3rd/4th synchronizer, main 3rd gear, 2nd and 3rd bushing, steel ball and main 2nd gear.
10. Remove the 1st/2nd synchronizer and main 1st gear as an assembly. Then remove the 1st needle bearings.

Inspection

1. Check the shaft for cracks, wear or bending.
2. Check the gears for wear, chips or cracks.
3. Check the synchronizer spline portion of coupling sleeves, hubs and gears for wear or cracks.
4. Check the synchronizer blocking rings for cracks or deformation.
5. Check insert springs for deformation.
6. Measure the gear endplay.
7. Check that the bearing rolls freely.
8. Inspect the bearing for noise, cracks, pitting and wear.

Assembly

1. Apply gear oil to the 1st needle bearing.
2. Assemble bearing, 1st gear, 1st gear block ring, 1st/2nd synchronizer assembly and 2nd gear block ring. Make certain synchronizer is in the correct direction.
3. Apply gear oil to the 2nd/3rd bushing outer surface.
4. Install the steel ball, 2nd gear, 2nd/3rd bushing, 3rd gear and 3rd/4th synchronizer assembly.
5. Apply grease to the steel ball and install it to the mainshaft.
6. Apply oil to the 4th bushing outer surface.
7. Install the bushing, making certain that the steel ball fits properly in its groove.
8. Install the 5th gear.
9. Install the thrust washer, if equipped with a 5 speed transaxle.
10. Select a C-ring that will minimize clearance of the mainshaft groove and install C-ring and holder. Allowable clearance is 0–0.004 in. (0–0.1mm).
11. Install the mainshaft front and rear bearing inner race, using an appropriate press.
12. Measure the gear endplay.

FINAL DRIVE ASSEMBLY

Disassembly

1. Remove the final gear.

2. Drive out the pinion shaft lock pin and remove the pinion shaft.

3. Remove the pinion gears and side gears.

4. Drive out the differential side bearing inner races. Take care not to mixup the right and left bearings or races.

5. Remove the speedometer gear and stopper.

Inspection

1. Check the mating surfaces of the differential case, side gears and pinion gears for burrs, wear or damage.

2. Check the washers for burrs, wear or damage.

3. Make certain the bearings roll freely.

4. Inspect bearings for noise, pits, cracks and wear.

Assembly

1. Position the side gear thrust washers and side gears, then install pinion washers and gears in place.

2. Install pinion shaft, taking care not to damage washers.

3. Measure the clearance between the side gear and pinion gear. If greater than 0–0.012 in. (0–0.3mm), adjust as needed by changing thickness of side gear thrust washers.

4. Install the retaining pin, making certain pin is flush with case.

5. Install the speedometer gear and stopper.

6. Install the differential side bearings.

7. Install the final gear. Apply sealant to threads and torque bolts to 54–65 ft. lbs. (74–88 Nm).

SYNCHRONIZER

Disassembly

1. Remove the spread springs and take out the inserts.

2. Separate the coupling sleeve from the hub.

Inspection

1. Check the synchronizer spline portion of coupling sleeves, hubs and gears for wear or cracks.

2. Check the synchronizer blocking rings for cracks or deformation.

3. Check insert springs for deformation.

Assembly

1. Couple the coupling sleeve and hub.

2. Install the inserts and spread springs.

3. Check operation for binding.

TRANSAXLE ASSEMBLY

1. Clean mating surfaces and check for cracks.

2. Install a new oil channel. Make certain that the oil groove faces toward the oil pocket.

3. Apply oil to mainshaft outer race and install it.

4. Apply oil to differential side bearing outer race and install it.

5. Install the clutch control shaft, clutch release bearing and lever.

6. Install the oil pocket, making sure oil flows from the pocket to oil channel.

7. Install the reverse/5th check assembly.

8. Install the reverse/5th smaller check ball, larger check ball, spring and plug.

9. Install and torque standard plug to 14–18 ft. lbs. (19–25 Nm).

10. Check the reverse check force, using an appropriate tool.

11. If the reverse force is not 139–200 inch lbs. (15.7–22.6 Nm) for the 4 speed transaxle or 91–113 inch lbs. (10.3–12.7 Nm) for the 5 speed transaxle, select a different length plug.

12. If reverse force is correct, apply sealant to plug and retorque.

13. Install the striking lever, interlock, boot and rod.

➡ Tape the edges of the striking rod to avoid damaging the oil seal's lip.

14. Install the shift check ball, spring and plug.

15. Install the oil pocket.

16. Install the differential assembly, shim as needed.

17. Shift into 4th gear many times to ensure bearing is seated properly. Check mainshaft rear bearing rotary fictional force, if not already done.

a. Apply gear oil to mainshaft rear bearing outer race and install.

b. Measure the distance from the case to bearing race.

c. Select a shim, according to chart, to obtain proper clearance.

d. Install shim, spacer and case cover. Torque to 4.6–6.1 ft. lbs. (6.3–8.3 Nm).

e. Ensure that the differential side bearing rotary fictional force is correct. Then check total rotary fictional force is 65–95 inch lbs. (7.4–10.8 Nm), by inserting tool KV38105900 into final drive assembly.

f. If any abnormality is noted, disassemble and check final drive and bearings.

g. After properly adjusting rotary force, remove case cover apply sealant to it and install to case. Torque to 4.6–6.1 ft. lbs. (6.3–8.3 Nm).

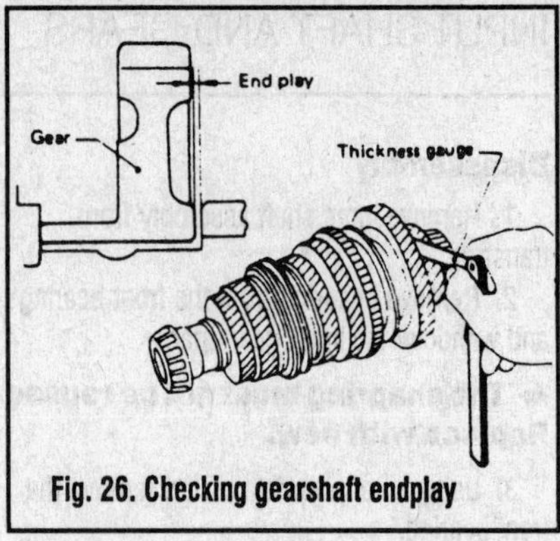
End play
Gear
Thickness gauge

Fig. 26. Checking gearshaft endplay

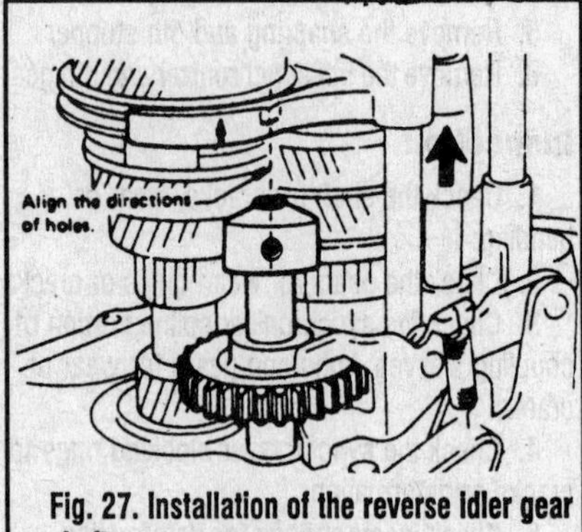
Align the directions of holes.

Fig. 27. Installation of the reverse idler gear shaft

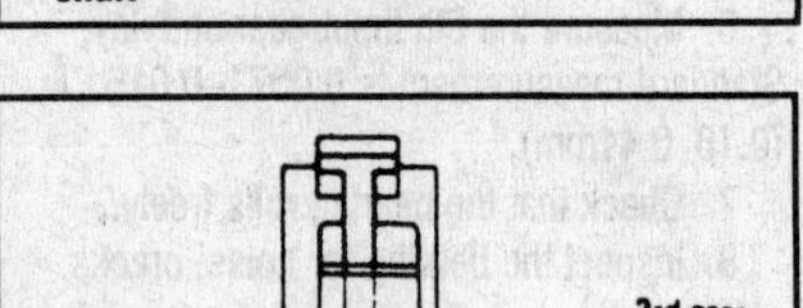

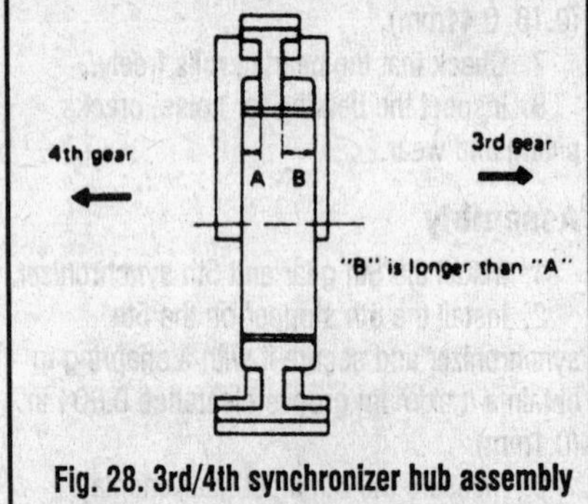
4th gear
3rd gear
A B
"B" is longer than "A"

Fig. 28. 3rd/4th synchronizer hub assembly

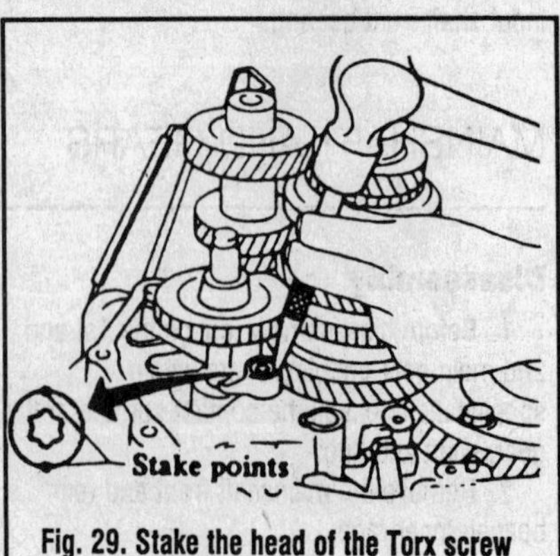
Stake points

Fig. 29. Stake the head of the Torx screw after installation

18. Install the reverse idler gear.
19. Install the mainshaft. Take care not to damage the resin oil channel at the clutch housing side of the mainshaft.
20. Install the input shaft. Take care not to damage the oil seal.
21. Apply sealant to threads and install the 3 bearing retainer. The torx® head screw requires a special tool because of the small clearance to the reverse idler gear.
22. Torque the torx® head screw and retaining bolts to 12–15 ft. lbs. (16–21 Nm).
23. Take the torx® head screw 180 degrees apart on the case.
24. Apply grease to shifter caps and install to control bracket.
25. Install the control bracket with the 1st/2nd shift fork. Torque control bracket to 4.6–6.1 ft. lbs. (6.3–8.3 Nm).
26. Install the 3rd/4th and 5th shift forks, if equipped.
27. Apply grease to the support spring before install to prevent spring from falling into the hole for the fork shaft on the clutch housing.
28. Insert the fork shaft.
29. Install the reverse idler spacer.
30. Install input shaft rear bearing into case, if not already done.
31. Install oil gutter. Apply locking sealer to the backup light switch and install it.
32. Apply an even coat of sealant to transaxle case and assemble transaxle case to clutch housing.
33. Install and torque bolts to 12–15 ft. lbs. (16–21 Nm).
34. After checking or adjusting mainshaft bearing, remove the case cover apply sealant and torque bolts to 4.6–6.1 ft. lbs. (6.3–8.3 Nm). Make certain that the convex side of the case cover faces outward when installed.
35. Measure the gear rotary frictional force and ensure that the gears move smoothly in all ranges.
36. Apply sealant to the drain plug and torque to 18–25 ft. lbs. (25–34 Nm).
37. Install transaxle and fill to proper level with gear lubricant.

Bench Overhaul RN4F31A, RS5F31A and RS5F32A

➧ SEE FIGS. 33–39

The RN4F31A and RS5F31A are improved versions of the RS5F30A and RN4F30A transaxle used on 1982–87 vehicles. The RS5F32A is an improved version of the RS5F31A transaxle and is used with the SR20DE engine. The RS5F30A and RS5F31A is a fully synchronized 5 speed transaxle. There are 5 forward speeds and 1 reverse, with the 4th and 5th gears being overdrive ratios. The RN4F30A and RN4F31A is a 4 speed transaxle that is essentially the same as the RS5F31A with the exception of the 5th input and main gear. The 4th gear of the RN4F31A transaxle is an overdrive ratio.

Fluid Capacity: the RS5F31A 5 speed manual transaxle requires 5.9 pts. (2.8L) of API GL gear oil. The RN4F31A 4 speed manual transaxle requires 5.75 pts. (2.7L) of API GL gear oil. The RS5F32A 5 speed manual transaxle requires 7.4–7.9 pts. (3.5–3.7L) of API GL gear oil.

Before Disassembly

Cleanliness is an important factor in the overhaul of the manual transaxle. Before opening up this unit, the entire outside of the transaxle assembly should be cleaned, preferable with a high pressure washer such as a car wash spray unit. Dirt entering the transaxle internal parts will negate all the time and effort spent on the overhaul. During inspection and reassembly all parts should be thoroughly cleaned with solvent then dried with compressed air. Wiping cloths and rags should not be used to dry parts.

Wheel bearing grease, long used to hold thrust washers and lube parts, should not be used. Lube seals with clean transaxle oil and use ordinary unmedicated petroleum jelly to hold the thrust washers and to ease the assembly of seals, since it will not leave a harmful residue as grease often will. Do not use solvent on neoprene seals, if they are to be reused, or thrust washers.

Before installing bolts into aluminum parts, always dip the threads into clean transaxle oil. Anti-seize compound can also be used to prevent bolts from galling the aluminum and seizing. Always use a torque wrench to keep from stripping the threads. The internal snaprings should be expanded and the external rings should be compressed, if they are to be reused. This will help insure proper seating when installed.

TRANSAXLE DISASSEMBLY

1. Drain remaining gear lube from transaxle.
2. Remove the transaxle case bolts. Note the location of bolts, for reference during reassembly.
3. Using a plastic hammer, tap and carefully remove case. On 5 speed transaxle, tilt case slightly to prevent 5th shift fork from interfering with the case.
4. Remove the backup light switch.
5. Remove the oil gutter.
6. Remove the reverse idler spacer and fork shaft.
7. Remove the 5th and 3rd/4th shift forks.
8. Remove the control bracket with the 1st/2nd shift fork.
9. Remove the mainshaft and final drive components from the clutch housing.

➡ Always draw mainshaft straight out, to prevent damage to the resin oil channel.

10. Remove the bearing retainer bolts.
11. Remove the input shaft together with the bearing retainer and reverse idler gear by tapping lightly. Take care not to damage the oil seal.

➡ Do not draw out the reverse idler shaft from the clutch housing because these fittings will be loose.

12. Remove the oil pocket, shift check ball, spring and ball plug.
13. Drive the retaining pin out of the strike lever. Remove the striking rod, lever and interlock. Move the shaft, as needed, to provide clearance to remove the pin.
14. Remove the reverse check plug, reverse check spring and balls.
15. Remove the check sleeve assembly.
16. Remove input shaft oil seal.
17. Remove the welch plug from the case and using a punch through the hole remove the input shaft rear bearing.
18. Using an appropriate puller, remove the mainshaft front bearing race.
19. Remove the oil channel, if not already removed.

SHIFT COMPONENTS

Inspection

Check contact surfaces and sliding parts for wear, scratches, burrs or other damage. Replace worn components.

INPUT SHAFT AND GEARS

Disassembly

1. Before disassembly, check the 5th gear endplay.

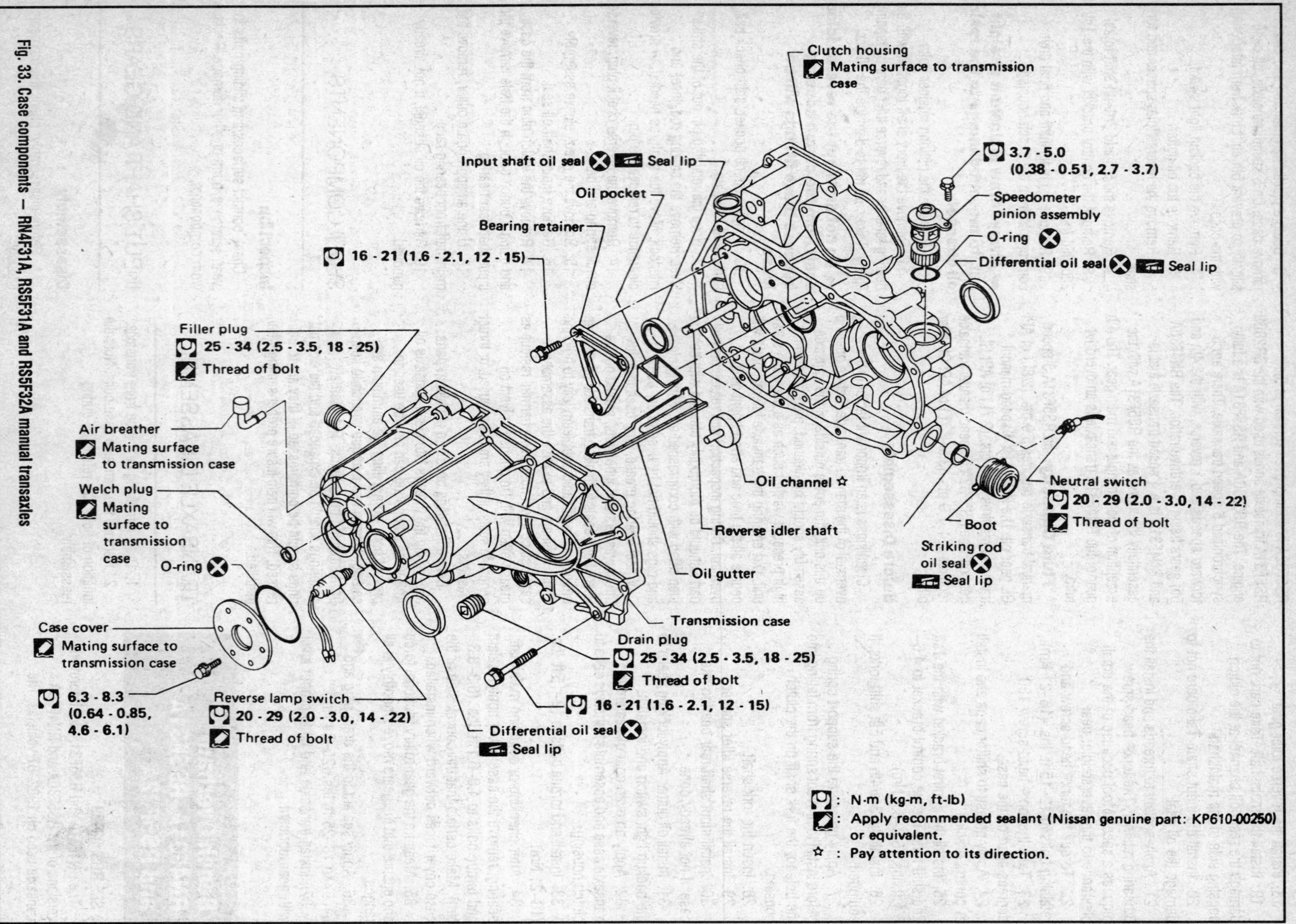
Clutch housing
Mating surface to transmission case
Input shaft oil seal
Seal lip
Oil pocket
Bearing retainer
16 - 21 (1.6 - 2.1, 12 - 15)
3.7 - 5.0 (0.38 - 0.51, 2.7 - 3.7)
Speedometer pinion assembly
O-ring
Differential oil seal
Seal lip
Filler plug
25 - 34 (2.5 - 3.5, 18 - 25)
Thread of bolt
Air breather
Mating surface to transmission case
Welch plug
Mating surface to transmission case
O-ring
Oil channel ☆
Reverse idler shaft
Oil gutter
Neutral switch
20 - 29 (2.0 - 3.0, 14 - 22)
Thread of bolt
Boot
Striking rod oil seal
Seal lip
Transmission case
Drain plug
25 - 34 (2.5 - 3.5, 18 - 25)
Thread of bolt
16 - 21 (1.6 - 2.1, 12 - 15)
Case cover
Mating surface to transmission case
6.3 - 8.3 (0.64 - 0.85, 4.6 - 6.1)
Reverse lamp switch
20 - 29 (2.0 - 3.0, 14 - 22)
Thread of bolt
Differential oil seal
Seal lip
N·m (kg-m, ft-lb)
Apply recommended sealant (Nissan genuine part: KP610-00250) or equivalent.
☆ : Pay attention to its direction.

Fig. 33. Case components — RN4F31A, RS5F31A and RS5F32A manual transaxles

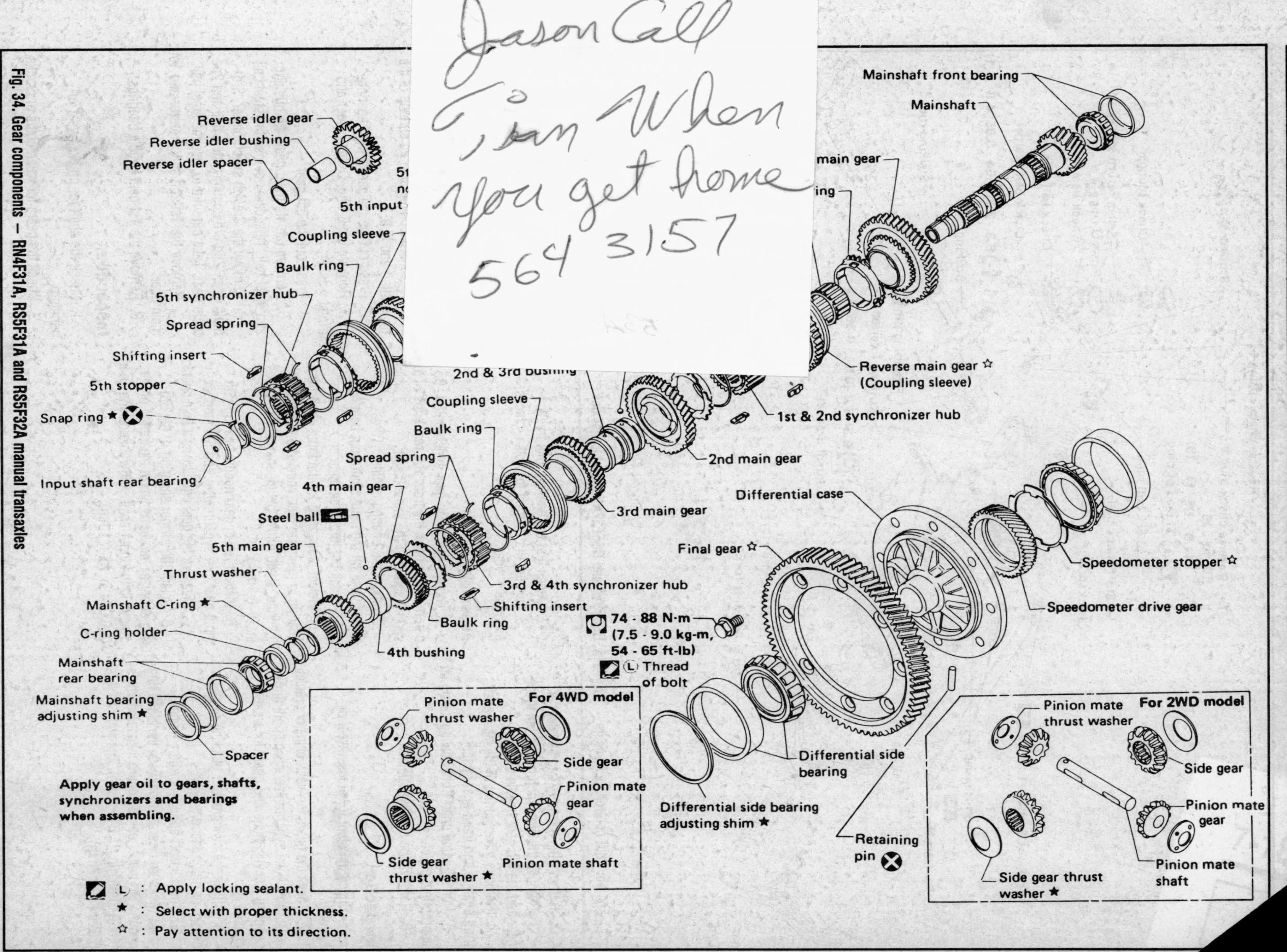

Mainshaft front bearing
Mainshaft
main gear
Reverse main gear ☆
(Coupling sleeve)
1st & 2nd synchronizer hub
2nd main gear
3rd main gear
2nd & 3rd bushing
Coupling sleeve
Baulk ring
Spread spring
4th main gear
Steel ball
5th main gear
Thrust washer
Mainshaft C-ring ★
C-ring holder
Mainshaft rear bearing
Mainshaft bearing adjusting shim ★
Spacer
Reverse idler gear
Reverse idler bushing
Reverse idler spacer
5th input
Coupling sleeve
Baulk ring
5th synchronizer hub
Spread spring
Shifting insert
5th stopper
Snap ring ★
Input shaft rear bearing
3rd & 4th synchronizer hub
Shifting insert
Baulk ring
4th bushing
74 - 88 N·m (7.5 - 9.0 kg-m, 54 - 65 ft-lb)
Ⓛ Thread of bolt
Differential case
Final gear ☆
Speedometer stopper ☆
Speedometer drive gear
Differential side bearing
Differential side bearing adjusting shim ★
Retaining pin
For 4WD model
Pinion mate thrust washer
Side gear
Pinion mate gear
Side gear thrust washer ★
Pinion mate shaft
For 2WD model
Pinion mate thrust washer
Side gear
Pinion mate gear
Side gear thrust washer ★
Pinion mate shaft
Apply gear oil to gears, shafts, synchronizers and bearings when assembling.
Ⓛ : Apply locking sealant.
★ : Select with proper thickness.
☆ : Pay attention to its direction.

Fig. 34. Gear components — RN4F31A, RS5F31A and RS5F32A manual transaxles

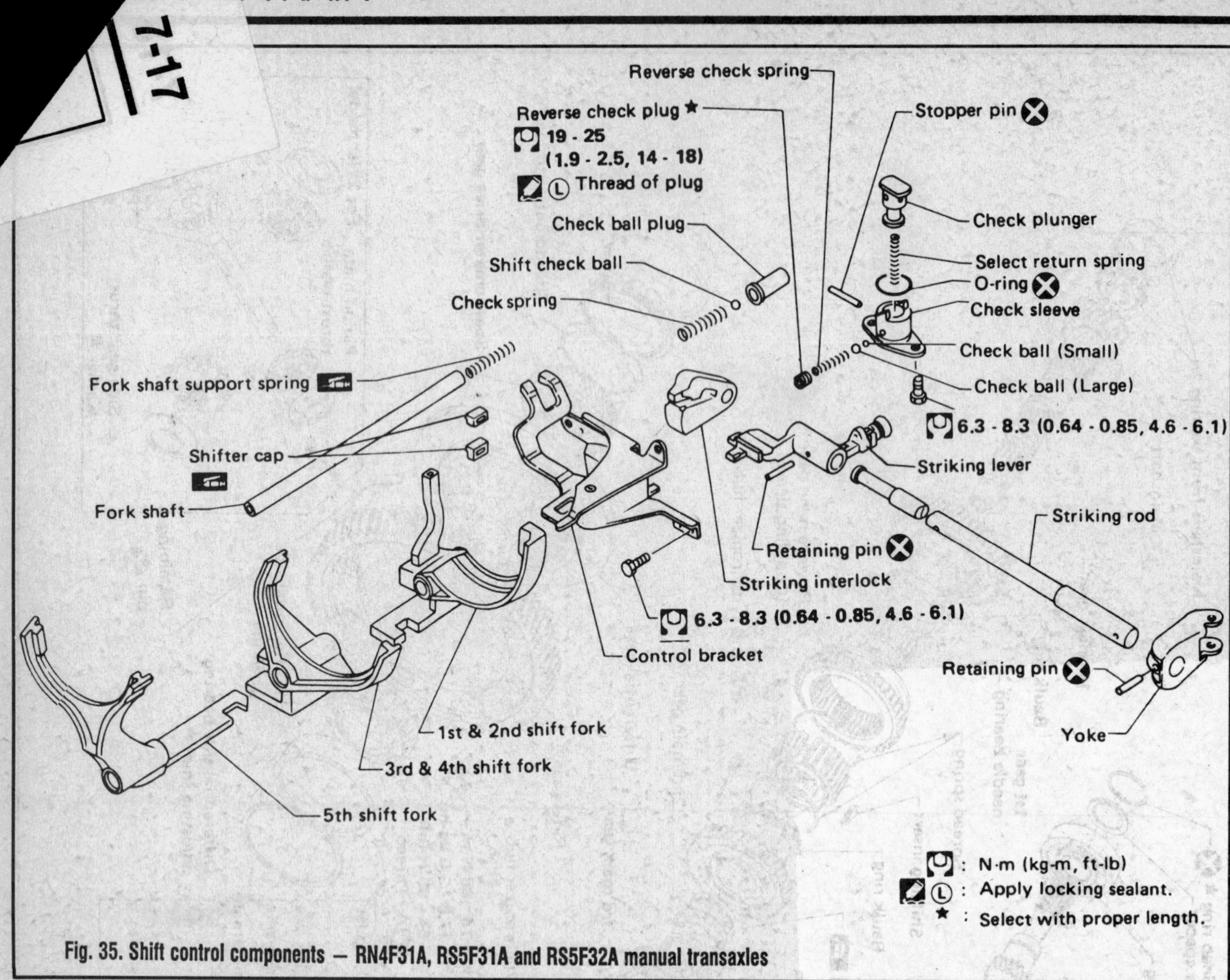
Reverse check spring
Reverse check plug ★
19 - 25
(1.9 - 2.5, 14 - 18)
Thread of plug
Check ball plug
Shift check ball
Check spring
Fork shaft support spring
Shifter cap
Fork shaft
Stopper pin
Check plunger
Select return spring
O-ring
Check sleeve
Check ball (Small)
Check ball (Large)
6.3 - 8.3 (0.64 - 0.85, 4.6 - 6.1)
Striking lever
Striking rod
Retaining pin
Striking interlock
6.3 - 8.3 (0.64 - 0.85, 4.6 - 6.1)
Control bracket
Retaining pin
Yoke
1st & 2nd shift fork
3rd & 4th shift fork
5th shift fork
: N·m (kg-m, ft-lb)
: Apply locking sealant.
★ : Select with proper length.
Fig. 35. Shift control components — RN4F31A, RS5F31A and RS5F32A manual transaxles

2. Remove the snapring and 5th stopper.
3. Remove the 5th synchronizer, 5th input gear and the 5th gear needle bearings.
4. Remove the snapring of the input shaft front bearing and input gear spacer.
5. Pull the input shaft front bearing, using an appropriate puller.
6. Remove the bearing retainer.

Inspection

1. Check the shaft for cracks, wear or bending.
2. Check the gears for wear, chips or cracks.
3. Check the synchronizer spline portion of coupling sleeves, hubs and gears for wear or cracks.
4. Check the synchronizer blocking rings for cracks or deformation.
5. Check insert springs for deformation.
6. Measure clearance between the block ring and the 5th input gear. Standard measurement is 0.039–0.051 in. (1.0–1.3mm). The wear limit is 0.028 in. (0.7mm).
7. Check that the bearing rolls freely.
8. Inspect the bearing for noise, cracks, pitting and wear.

Assembly

1. Assemble the 5th gear synchronizer. Be careful not to hook the front and rear ends of the spread spring to the same insert.
2. Install the bearing retainer.
3. Press on the input shaft front bearing.
4. Install the input gear spacer.
5. Select a snapring for the input shaft front bearing to minimize clearance of the groove in the input shaft. Allowable clearance is 0–0.004 in. (0–0.1mm).
6. Install the 5th gear needle bearing, 5th input gear, 5th synchronizer and 5th stopper.
7. Measure the gear endplay as a final check.
8. Select the proper snapring of the 5th synchronizer hub to minimize clearance of the groove in the input shaft. Allowable clearance is 0–0.004 in. (0–0.1mm).

MAINSHAFT AND GEARS

Disassembly

1. Before disassembly, check the 1st, 2nd, 3rd and 4th main gear endplay. If not within specifications check the contact surface of the gear, shaft and hub.
2. Press out the mainshaft front bearing.
3. Remove the C-ring, C-ring holder and thrust washer.
4. Press out the 5th gear.
5. Remove the 4th main gear, 4th bushing and steel ball. Take care not lose the steel ball.
6. Remove the 3rd/4th synchronizer, 3rd main gear, 2nd/3rd bushing, steel ball and 2nd main gear. Take care not to lose the steel ball.
7. Remove the 1st/2nd synchronizer and 1st main gear.
8. Remove the 1st gear needle bearings.

Inspection

1. Check the shaft for cracks, wear or bending.
2. Check the gears for wear, chips or cracks.

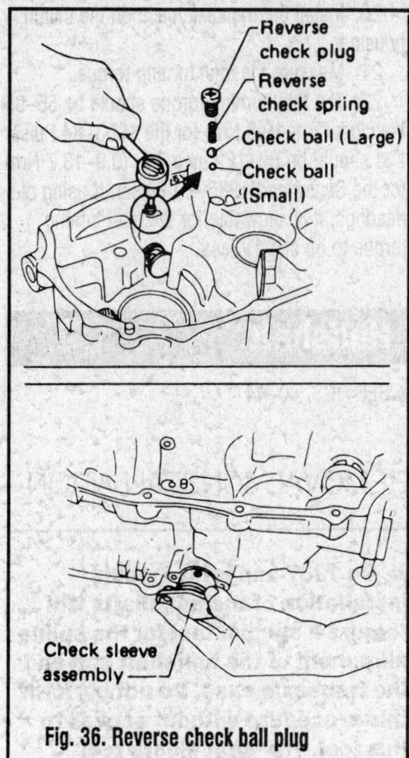
Reverse
check plug
Reverse
check spring
Check ball (Large)
Check ball
(Small)
Check sleeve
assembly
Fig. 36. Reverse check ball plug

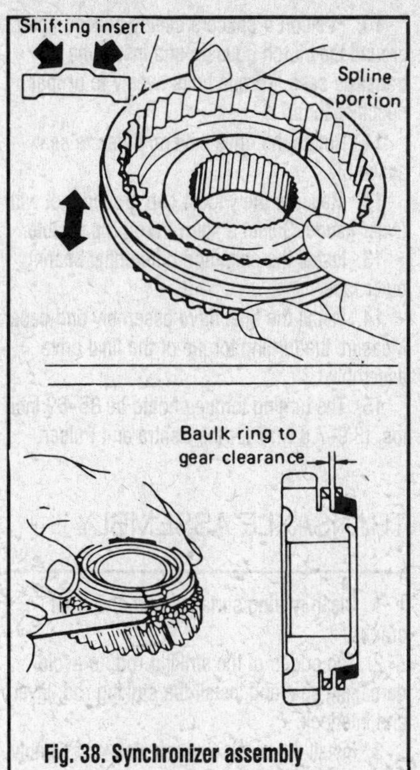
Shifting insert
Spline
portion
Baulk ring to
gear clearance
Fig. 38. Synchronizer assembly

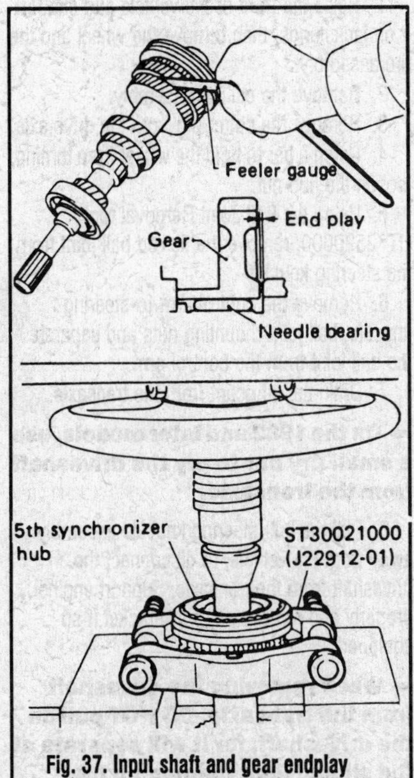
Feeler gauge
End play
Gear
Needle bearing
5th synchronizer
hub
ST30021000
(J22912-01)
Fig. 37. Input shaft and gear endplay

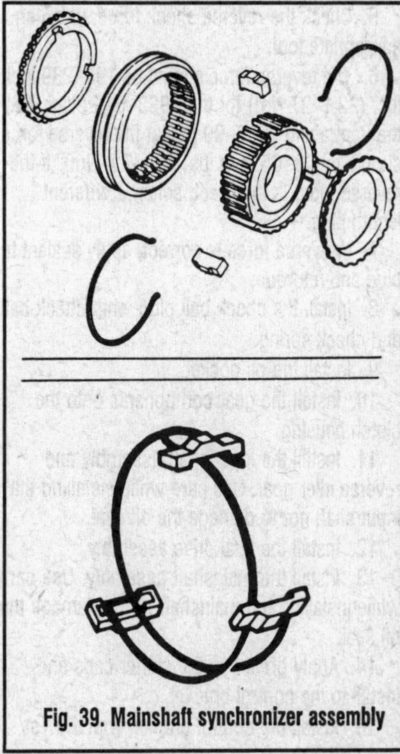
Fig. 39. Mainshaft synchronizer assembly

3. Check the synchronizer spline portion of coupling sleeves, hubs and gears for wear or cracks.
4. Check the synchronizer blocking rings for cracks or deformation.
5. Check insert springs for deformation.
6. Measure the gear endplay.
7. Check that the bearing rolls freely.
8. Inspect the bearing for noise, cracks, pitting and wear.
9. Measure clearance between the block ring and the 1st and 4th main gears. Standard measurement is 0.039–0.051 in. (1.0–1.3mm). The wear limit is 0.028 in. (0.7mm).

Assembly

1. Apply gear oil to the 1st needle bearing.
2. Assemble the 1st/2nd and 3rd/4th synchronizers. Take care not to hook the front and rear ends of the spread spring to the same insert.
3. Install the 1st gear needle bearings and 1st main gear.
4. Press on the 1st/2nd synchronizer.
5. Apply multi-purpose grease to the steel ball.
6. Install the steel ball, 2nd main gear, 2nd/3rd bushing, 3rd main gear and 3rd/4th synchronizer. Make certain the ball is aligned with the groove on the 2nd/3rd bushing.
7. Apply multi-purpose grease to the steel ball.
8. Install the steel ball, 4th bushing and 4th main gear. Make certain the steel ball is aligned with the groove on the 4th bushing.
9. Press on the 5th main gear.
10. Install the thrust washer.
11. Select the proper C-ring to minimize the clearance of the groove in the mainshaft and install it. The allowable clearance is 0–0.004 in. (0–0.1mm).
12. Install the C-ring holder.
13. Press on the mainshaft rear bearing.
14. Press on the mainshaft front bearing.
15. Measure the gear endplay as a final check.
16. Check the mainshaft bearing preload.
   a. Remove the case cover, O-ring, spacer, mainshaft bearing adjusting shim and mainshaft rear bearing outer race from the transaxle case.
   b. Install the mainshaft assembly.
   c. Install the transaxle case on the clutch housing.
   d. Torque the bolts to 12–15 ft. lbs. (16–21 Nm).
   e. Reinstall the mainshaft rear bearing outer race on the inner race.

f. Measure the distance from the transaxle case to the bearing outer race. Make certain the bearing is fully seated.

g. Select the proper shim, using the shim table, and reassemble using proper shim.

17. Check the total turning torque after assembling.

FINAL DRIVE ASSEMBLY

Disassembly

1. Remove the final gear.
2. Remove the speedometer drive gear by cutting it.
3. Press out the differential side bearings. Be careful not to interchange the right and left bearings or races.
4. Remove the speedometer stopper.
5. Drive out the retaining pin and remove the pinion gear shaft.
6. Remove the pinion gears and the side gears.

Inspection

1. Check the mating surfaces of the differential case, side gears and pinion gears for burrs, wear or damage.
2. Check the washers for burrs, wear or damage.
3. Make certain the bearings roll freely.
4. Inspect bearings for noise, pits, cracks and wear.

Assembly

1. Fit side gear thrust washers and side gears, then install pinion washers and gears in place.
2. Insert the pinion gear shaft. Take care not to damage the pinion gear thrust washers.
3. Set a dial indicator on the side gear and measure the deflection on both side gears. If the clearance between the side gear and differential case is greater than 0.012 in. or 0.3mm, adjust by using a thicker washer.
4. Install the retaining pin, until flush with the case.
5. Install the final gear. Apply sealant to threads and torque bolts to 54–65 ft. lbs. (74–88 Nm).
6. Install the speedometer drive gear and stopper.
7. Press on differential side bearings.
8. Remove the differential side bearing outer race and shim on the transaxle case side and install the final drive assembly on the clutch housing.
9. Place the differential side bearing outer race and the special tool onto the final drive assembly.
10. Position 4 spacers evenly spaced apart around the clutch housing and install the transaxle case. Torque bolts evenly to proper specifications.
11. Rotate the drive several times to seat assembly.
12. Measure the widest gap around tool with feeler gauge. Select a shim from proper table.
13. Install the shim and differential bearing outer race.
14. Install the final drive assembly and case. Measure the turning torque of the final drive assembly.
15. The turning torque should be 35–69 inch lbs. (3.9–7.8 Nm) for the Sentra and Pulsar.

TRANSAXLE ASSEMBLY

1. Clean mating surfaces and check for cracks.
2. Tap edges of the striking rod, to avoid damaging seal and install the striking rod, lever and interlock.
3. Install the reverse check sleeve assembly.
4. Install the check balls, reverse check spring and check plug.
5. Check the reverse check force, using an appropriate tool.
6. The reverse force should be 195–239 inch lbs. (22.1–27 Nm) for the 1983–84 Pulsar. For the Sentra and 1985–90 Pulsar the reverse force should be 43–65 inch lbs. (4.9–7.4 Nm). If the reverse force is incorrect, select a different length plug.
7. If reverse force is correct, apply sealant to plug and retorque.
8. Install the check ball plug, shift check ball and check spring.
9. Install the oil pocket.
10. Install the gear components onto the clutch housing.
11. Install the input shaft assembly and reverse idler gear. Use care while installing the input shaft not to damage the oil seal.
12. Install the final drive assembly.
13. Install the mainshaft assembly. Use care while installing the mainshaft not to damage the oil seal.
14. Apply grease to the shifter caps and install to the control bracket.
15. Install the control bracket with the 1st/2nd shift fork.
16. Apply multi-purpose grease to the support spring.
17. Install the shift fork.
18. Install the reverse idler spacer.
19. Make certain the mating surfaces of the clutch housing is clean and dry and apply sealant to the mating surfaces.
20. Install the transaxle case on the clutch housing.
21. Measure the total turning torque.
22. The total turning torque should be 65–95 inch lbs. (7.4–10.8 Nm) for the 1983–84 Pulsar and should be 52–122 inch lbs. (5.9–13.7 Nm) for the Sentra and 1985–90 Pulsar. If using old bearings, it is allowable for the total turning torque to be slightly less.

Halfshaft

➧ SEE FIGS. 40–44

REMOVAL & INSTALLATION

➡ On 1987 and later models, installation of the halfshafts will require a special tool for the spline alignment of the halfshaft end and the transaxle case. Do not perform this procedure without access to this tool. The Kent Moore tool Number is J-34296 and J-34297

1. Raise the front of the vehicle and support it on jackstands, then remove the wheel and the tire assembly.
2. Remove the caliper assembly.
3. Remove the cotter pin from the drive axle.
4. Using a bar to hold the wheel from turning, loosen the hub nut.
5. Using the Ball Joint Removal tool HT72520000, remove the tie rod ball joint from the steering knuckle.
6. Remove the control arm-to-steering knuckle, ball joint mounting nuts and separate the ball joint from the control arm.
7. Drain the lubricant from the transaxle.

➡ On the 1982 and later models, use a small pry bar to pry the driveshaft from the transaxle.

8. Pull the hub/steering knuckle assembly away from the vehicle, to disconnect the driveshaft from the transaxle. Support engine properly and remove support bracket if so equipped.

➡ When removing the driveshaft from the transaxle, DO NOT pull on the driveshaft, for it will separate at the sliding joint (damaging the boot), use a small pry bar to remove it from the transaxle. Be sure to replace the oil seal in the transaxle. After removing the driveshaft from the transaxle, be sure to install a holding tool to hold the side gear in place while the axle is removed.

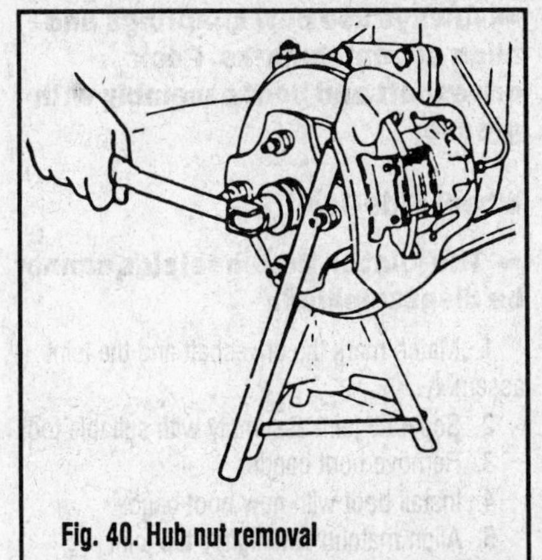

Fig. 40. Hub nut removal

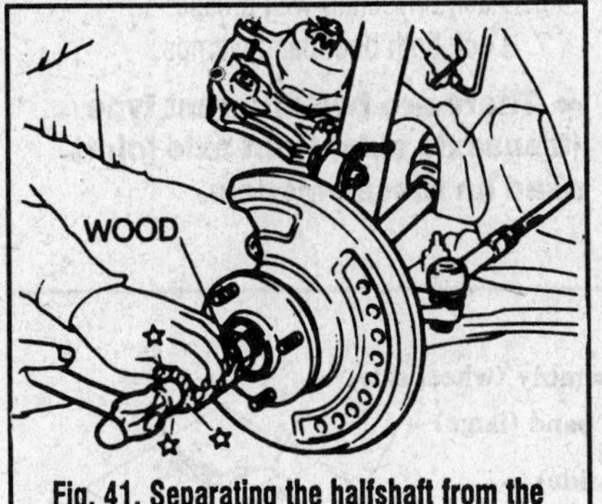
WOOD

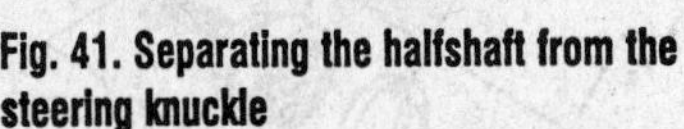

Fig. 41. Separating the halfshaft from the steering knuckle

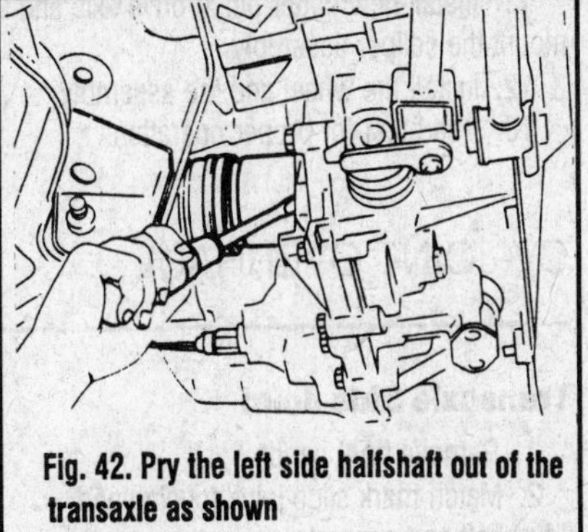

Fig. 42. Pry the left side halfshaft out of the transaxle as shown

SUITABLE TOOL

Fig. 43. Pry the right side halfshaft out of the transaxle as shown

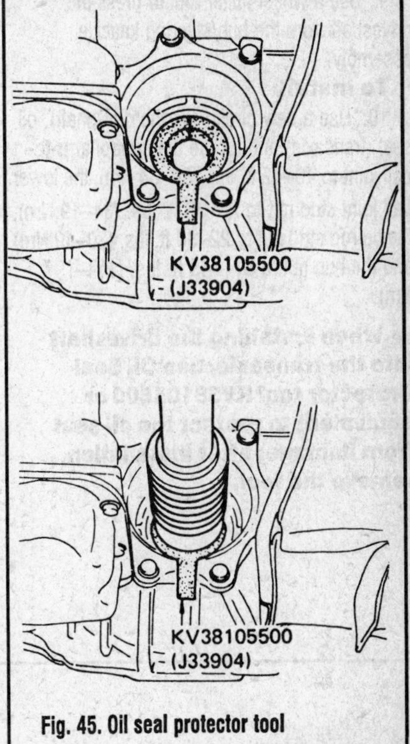
KV38105500
(J33904)
KV38105500
(J33904)

Fig. 45. Oil seal protector tool

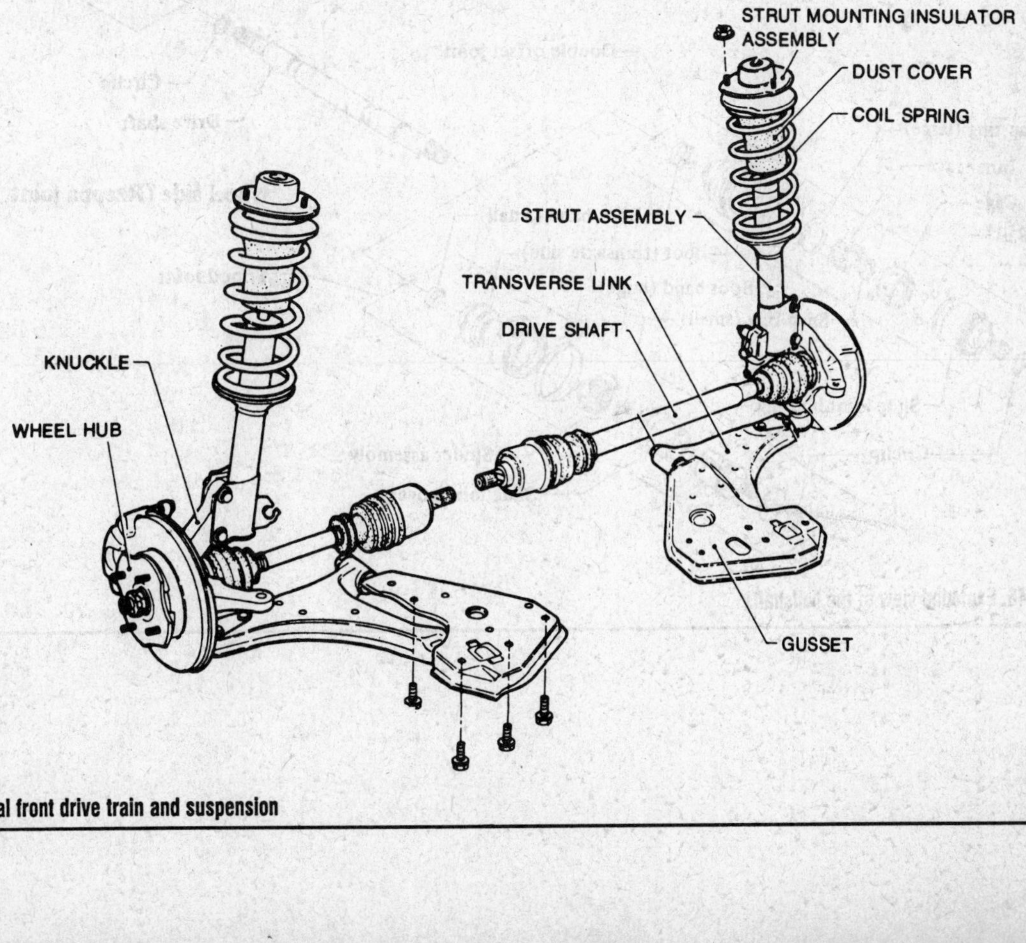

STRUT MOUNTING INSULATOR ASSEMBLY
DUST COVER
COIL SPRING
STRUT ASSEMBLY
TRANSVERSE LINK
DRIVE SHAFT
KNUCKLE
WHEEL HUB
GUSSET

Fig. 44. Typical front drive train and suspension

9. Use a wheel puller tool to press the driveshaft from the hub/steering knuckle assembly.

To install:

10. Use a new circlip (on the driveshaft), oil seal (transaxle) and torque the control arm-to-ball joint to 40–47 ft. lbs. (54–64 Nm), the lower ball joint stud nut to 25–36 ft. lbs. (34–49 Nm), the tie rod stud nut to 22–36 ft. lbs. (30–49 Nm) and the hub nut to 87–145 ft. lbs. (114–197 Nm).

➡ When installing the driveshaft into the transaxle, use Oil Seal Protector tool KV38105500 or equivalent to protect the oil seal from damage; after installation, remove the tool.

11. Install new cotter pin in drive axle and mount the caliper assembly.
12. Install the wheel and tire assembly.
13. Road test for proper operation.

CV-JOINT OVERHAUL

Transaxle Side Joint

1. Remove boot bands.
2. Match mark slide joint housing and driveshaft and separate.
3. Match mark spider assembly and then remove snapring and spider assembly. DO NOT disassemble spider assembly.

➡ Cover driveshaft serration with tape so not to damage the boot.

4. Remove axle boot from driveshaft.
5. To install reverse the removal procedures.

➡ Always use new snaprings and align all matchmarks. Pack driveshaft and boot assembly with grease.

Wheel Side Joint

➡ The joint on the wheel side cannot be disassembled.

1. Match mark the driveshaft and the joint assembly.
2. Separate joint assembly with suitable tool.
3. Remove boot bands.
4. Install boot with new boot bands.
5. Align matchmarks lightly tap joint assembly onto the shaft.
6. Pack driveshaft with grease.
7. Lock both boot band clamps.

➡ There are two different type (transaxle side) front axle joints used on Nissan models.

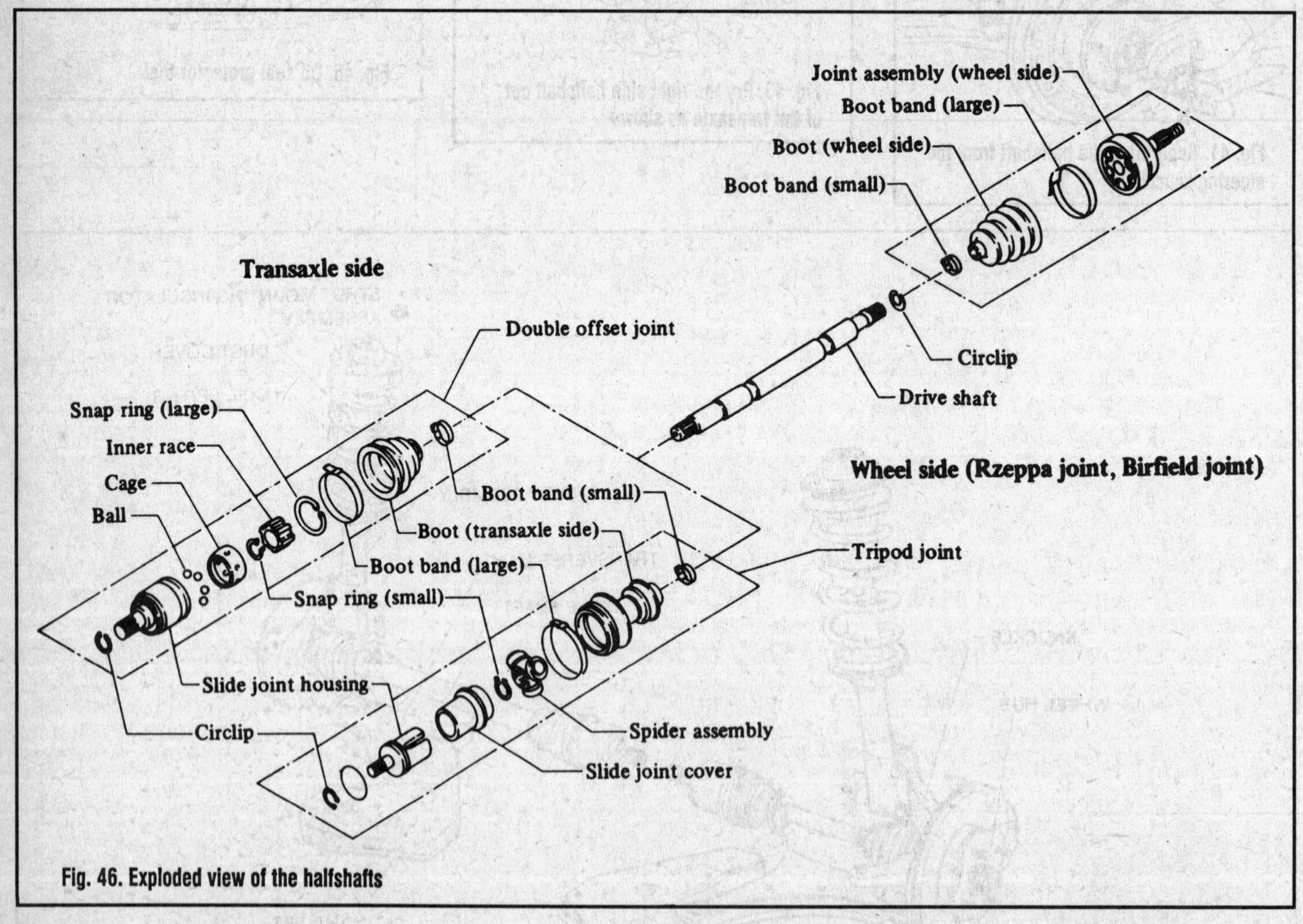
Joint assembly (wheel side)
Boot band (large)
Boot (wheel side)
Boot band (small)
Transaxle side
Double offset joint
Circlip
Drive shaft
Snap ring (large)
Inner race
Cage
Ball
Boot band (small)
Boot (transaxle side)
Boot band (large)
Snap ring (small)
Wheel side (Rzeppa joint, Birfield joint)
Tripod joint
Slide joint housing
Circlip
Spider assembly
Slide joint cover

Fig. 46. Exploded view of the halfshafts

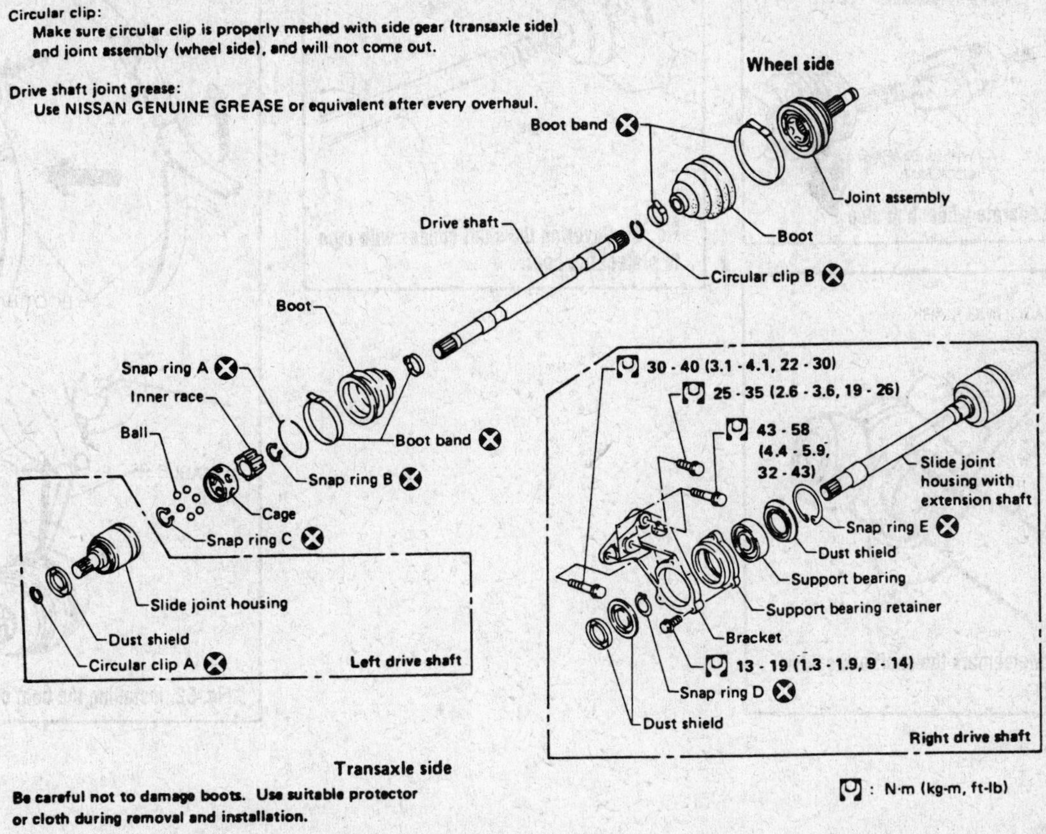

Circular clip:
Make sure circular clip is properly meshed with side gear (transaxle side) and joint assembly (wheel side), and will not come out.

Drive shaft joint grease:
Use NISSAN GENUINE GREASE or equivalent after every overhaul.

Wheel side
Boot band ⊗
Joint assembly
Boot
Drive shaft
Circular clip B ⊗
Boot
Snap ring A ⊗
Inner race
Ball
Boot band ⊗
Snap ring B ⊗
Cage
Snap ring C ⊗
Slide joint housing
Dust shield
Circular clip A ⊗
Left drive shaft

30 - 40 (3.1 - 4.1, 22 - 30)
25 - 35 (2.6 - 3.6, 19 - 26)
43 - 58 (4.4 - 5.9, 32 - 43)
Slide joint housing with extension shaft
Snap ring E ⊗
Dust shield
Support bearing
Support bearing retainer
Bracket
13 - 19 (1.3 - 1.9, 9 - 14)
Snap ring D ⊗
Dust shield
Right drive shaft

Transaxle side

Be careful not to damage boots. Use suitable protector or cloth during removal and installation.

: N·m (kg-m, ft-lb)

Fig. 47. Exploded view of the BF86D586 halfshafts

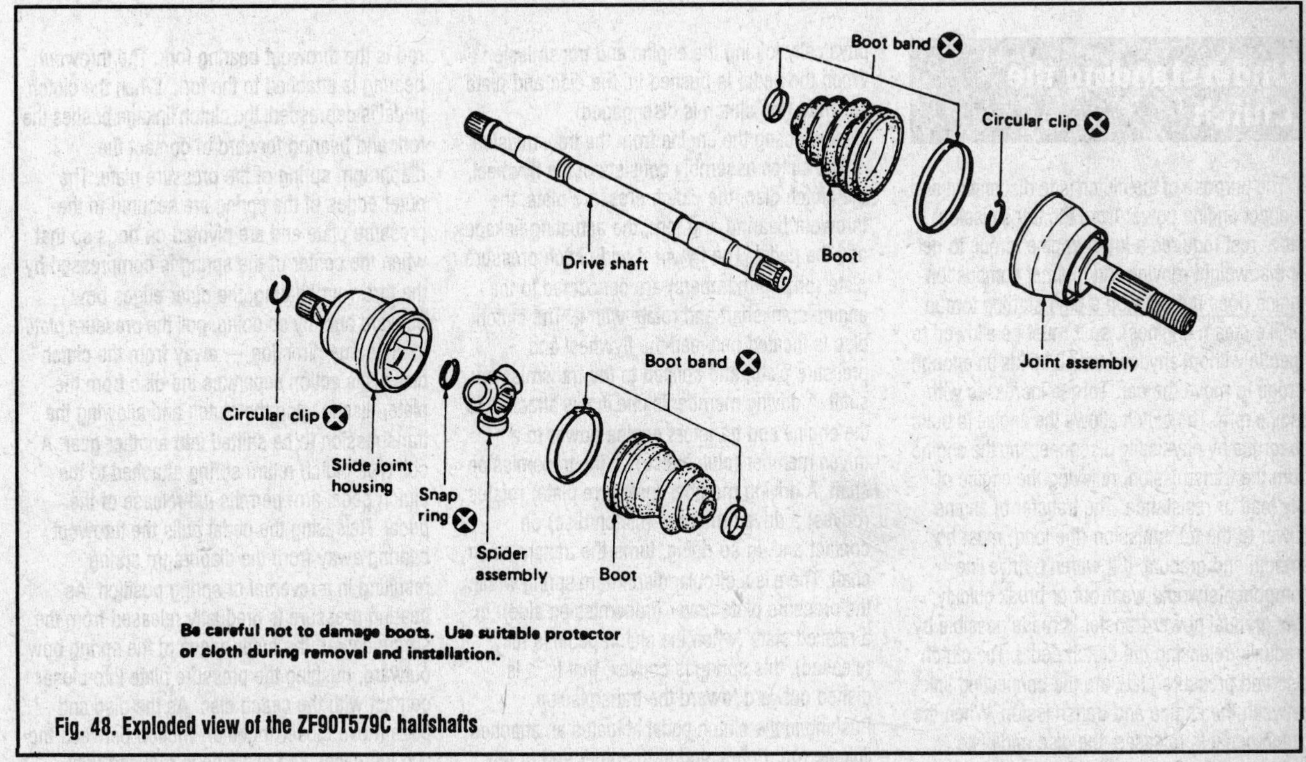
Boot band ⊗
Circular clip ⊗
Drive shaft
Boot
Joint assembly
Boot band ⊗
Circular clip ⊗
Slide joint housing
Snap ring ⊗
Spider assembly
Boot
Be careful not to damage boots. Use suitable protector or cloth during removal and installation.

Fig. 48. Exploded view of the ZF90T579C halfshafts

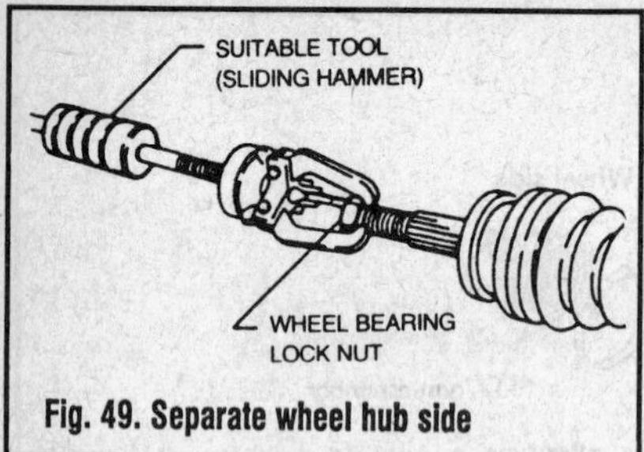
SUITABLE TOOL
(SLIDING HAMMER)
WHEEL BEARING
LOCK NUT
Fig. 49. Separate wheel hub side

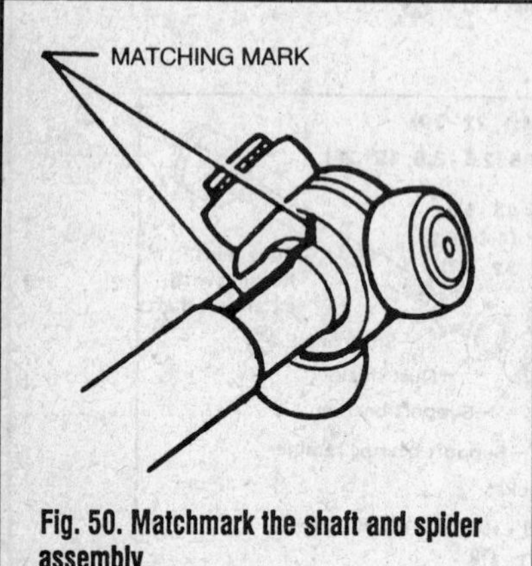
MATCHING MARK
Fig. 50. Matchmark the shaft and spider assembly

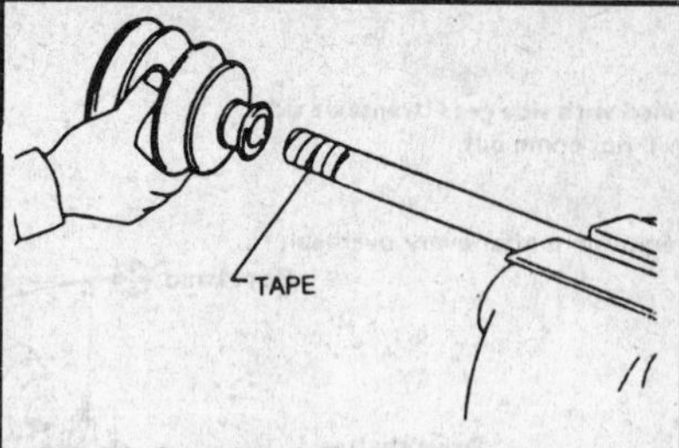
TAPE
Fig. 51. Covering the shaft splines with tape to protect the boot

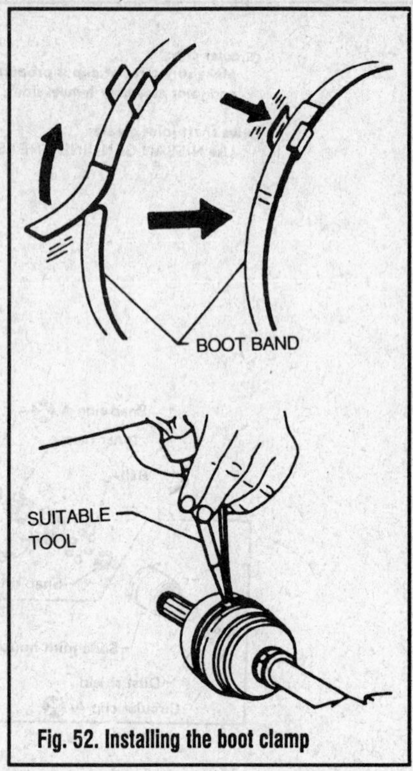
BOOT BAND
SUITABLE
TOOL
Fig. 52. Installing the boot clamp

CLUTCH

Understanding the Clutch

The purpose of the clutch is to disconnect and connect engine power from the transmission. A car at rest requires a lot of engine torque to get all that weight moving. An internal combustion engine does not develop a high starting torque (unlike steam engines), so it must be allowed to operate without any load until it builds up enough torque to move the car. Torque increases with engine rpm. The clutch allows the engine to build up torque by physically disconnecting the engine from the transmission, relieving the engine of any load or resistance. The transfer of engine power to the transmission (the load) must be smooth and gradual; if it weren't, drive line components would wear out or break quickly. This gradual power transfer is made possible by gradually releasing the clutch pedal. The clutch disc and pressure plate are the connecting link between the engine and transmission. When the clutch pedal is released, the disc and plate contact each other (clutch engagement), physically joining the engine and transmission. When the pedal is pushed in, the disc and plate separate (the clutch is disengaged), disconnecting the engine from the transmission.

The clutch assembly consists of the flywheel, the clutch disc, the clutch pressure plate, the throwout bearing and fork, the actuating linkage and the pedal. The flywheel and clutch pressure plate (driving members) are connected to the engine crankshaft and rotate with it. The clutch disc is located between the flywheel and pressure plate, and splined to the transmission shaft. A driving member is one that is attached to the engine and transfers engine power to a driven member (clutch disc) on the transmission shaft. A driving member (pressure plate) rotates (drives) a driven member (clutch disc) on contact and, in so doing, turns the transmission shaft. There is a circular diaphragm spring within the pressure plate cover (transmission side). In a relaxed state (when the clutch pedal is fully released), this spring is convex; that is, it is dished outward toward the transmission. Pushing in the clutch pedal actuates an attached linkage rod. Connected to the other end of this rod is the throwout bearing fork. The throwout bearing is attached to the fork. When the clutch pedal is depressed, the clutch linkage pushes the fork and bearing forward to contact the diaphragm spring of the pressure plate. The outer edges of the spring are secured to the pressure plate and are pivoted on rings so that when the center of the spring is compressed by the throwout bearing, the outer edges bow outward and, by so doing, pull the pressure plate in the same direction — away from the clutch disc. This action separates the disc from the plate, disengaging the clutch and allowing the transmission to be shifted into another gear. A coil type clutch return spring attached to the clutch pedal arm permits full release of the pedal. Releasing the pedal pulls the throwout bearing away from the diaphragm spring resulting in a reversal of spring position. As bearing pressure is gradually released from the spring center, the outer edges of the spring bow outward, pushing the pressure plate into closer contact with the clutch disc. As the disc and plate move closer together, friction between the two increases and slippage is reduced until, when full spring pressure is applied (by fully releasing the pedal), The speed of the disc and plate are the same. This stops all slipping, creating a direct connection between the plate and disc which results in the transfer of power from the engine to the transmission. The clutch disc is now rotating with the pressure plate at engine speed and, because it is splined to the transmission shaft, the shaft now turns at the same engine speed. Understanding clutch operation can be rather difficult at first; if you're still confused after reading this, consider the following analogy. The action of the diaphragm spring can be compared to that of an oil can bottom. The bottom of an oil can is shaped very much like the clutch diaphragm spring and pushing in on the can bottom and then releasing it produces a similar effect. As mentioned earlier, the clutch pedal return spring permits full release of the pedal and reduces linkage slack due to wear. As the linkage wears, clutch free-pedal travel will increase and free-travel will decrease as the clutch wears. Free-travel is actually throwout bearing lash.

The diaphragm spring type clutches used are available in two different designs: flat diaphragm springs or bent spring. The bent fingers are bent back to create a centrifugal boost ensuring quick re-engagement at higher engine speeds. This design enables pressure plate load to increase as the clutch disc wears and makes low pedal effort possible even with a heavy-duty clutch. The throwout bearing used with the bent finger design is $1^1/_4$ in. (31.75) long and is shorter than the bearing used with the flat finger design. These bearings are not interchangeable. If the longer bearing is used with the bent finger clutch, free-pedal travel will not exist. This results in clutch slippage and rapid wear.

The transmission varies the gear ratio between the engine and drive wheels. It can be shifted to change engine speed as driving conditions and loads change. The transmission allows disengaging and reversing power from the engine to the wheels.

✲✲ CAUTION

The clutch driven disc contains asbestos, which has been determined to be a cancer causing agent. Never clean clutch surface with compressed air! Avoid inhaling any dust from any clutch surface! When cleaning clutch surfaces, use a commercially available brake cleaning fluid.

Adjustments

The (1982 and later) models have a cable actuated mechanical clutch. The pedal height is adjusted at the clutch switch or the ASCD stop

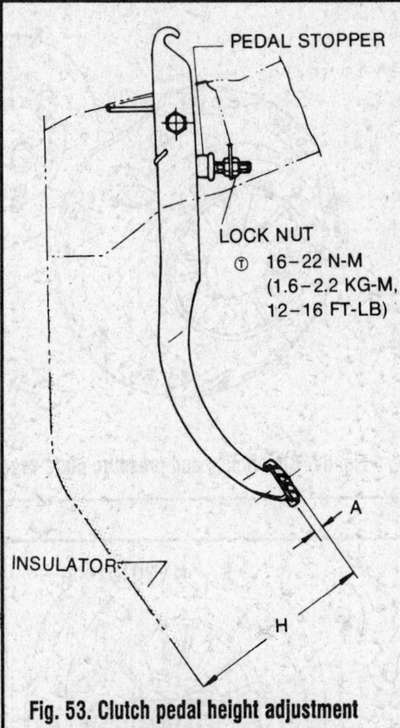
PEDAL STOPPER
LOCK NUT
16–22 N-M
(1.6–2.2 KG-M,
12–16 FT-LB)
A
INSULATOR
H

Fig. 53. Clutch pedal height adjustment — H is the pedal height, A is the pedal free-play

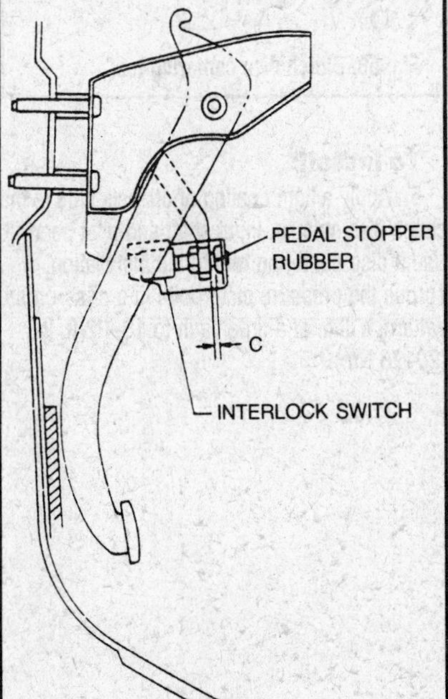
PEDAL STOPPER
RUBBER
C
INTERLOCK SWITCH

Fig. 54. Adjusting the clutch interlock switch on 1987–90 vehicles

switch (both are located at the top of the clutch pedal). The free-play is adjusted at the cable bracket, located near the clutch release lever on the transaxle.

For vehicles equipped with a clutch interlock switch. Adjust the clearance between the rubber stopper and threaded end of the clutch interlock switch while depressing the clutch pedal fully. The clearance should be 0.004–0.039 in. (0.1–1.0mm)

Adjust the pedal free play by turning the adjusting knob at the transaxle. Measure the distance from the pedal resting position to the end of the free travel. Refer to the following values:

a. 1982–84 vehicles — 0.43–0.83 in. (11–21mm)

b. 1985–90 vehicles — 0.49–0.69 in. (12.5–17.5mm)

c. 1991–92 vehicles — 0.42–0.59 in. (10.5–15mm)

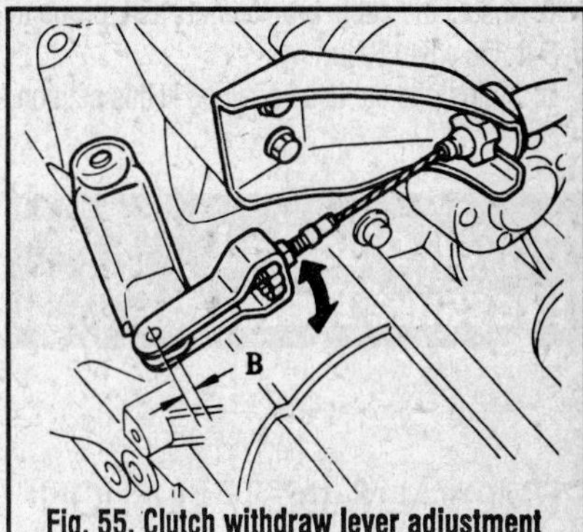
B

Fig. 55. Clutch withdraw lever adjustment — arrow shows locknut adjustment

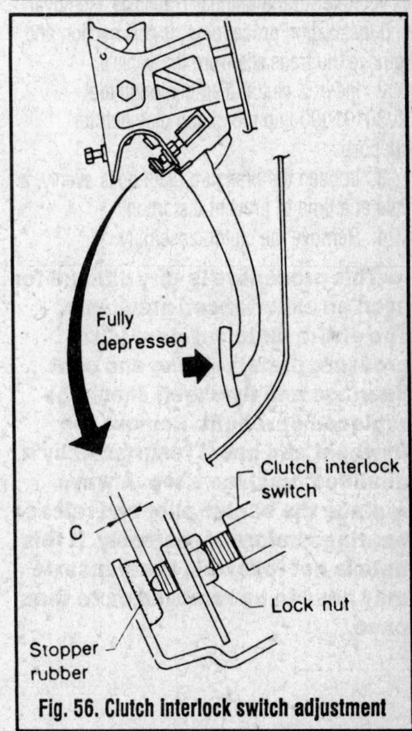
Fully
depressed
Clutch interlock
switch
C
Lock nut
Stopper
rubber

Fig. 56. Clutch interlock switch adjustment

Clutch Cable

REMOVAL & INSTALLATION

1. Loosen the adjusting knob at the transaxle as much that is needed.
2. Remove the cable insulator nuts at the clutch pedal mount, in engine compartment. Disengage the cable from the clutch pedal.
3. Lubricate the rubber grommet to ease removal. Remove the grommet from the firewall.
4. Disengage the cable from the transaxle mounting bracket.
5. Remove the cable from the vehicle.

To install:

6. Lubricate the rubber grommets and moving parts with heavy grease.
7. Install the cable to the vehicle.
8. Install the cable bracket nuts and torque to 6–8 ft. lbs. (8–11 Nm).
9. Adjust the cable as outlined in this section.

Driven Disc And Pressure Plate

REMOVAL & INSTALLATION

1. Refer to the Manual Transaxle, Removal and Installation procedures, in this section and remove the transaxle from the vehicle.
2. Insert a clutch disc centering tool KV30101000 into the clutch disc hub for support.
3. Loosen the pressure plate bolts evenly, a little at a time to prevent distortion.
4. Remove the clutch assembly.

➡ This procedure is very difficult for even an experienced mechanic. The entire clutch system (disc, pressure plate, release and pilot bearings and flywheel) should be replaced or rebuilt. Remove the flywheel and has it resurfaced by a qualified machine shop. Always replace the center pilot and release bearings before reassembly. If this note is not followed, the transaxle may have to be removed more than once.

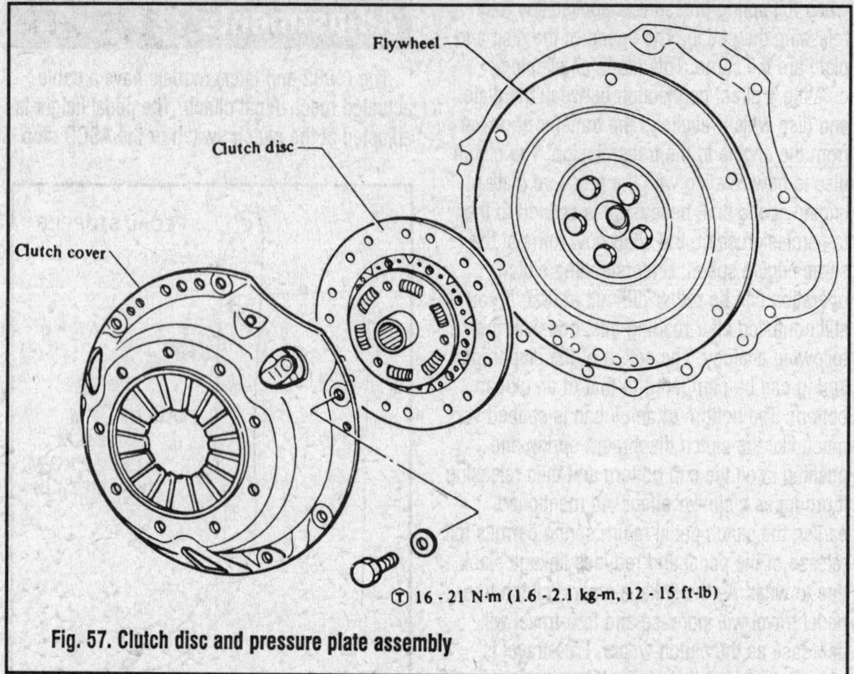
Flywheel
Clutch disc
Clutch cover
Ⓣ 16 - 21 N·m (1.6 - 2.1 kg-m, 12 - 15 ft-lb)

Fig. 57. Clutch disc and pressure plate assembly

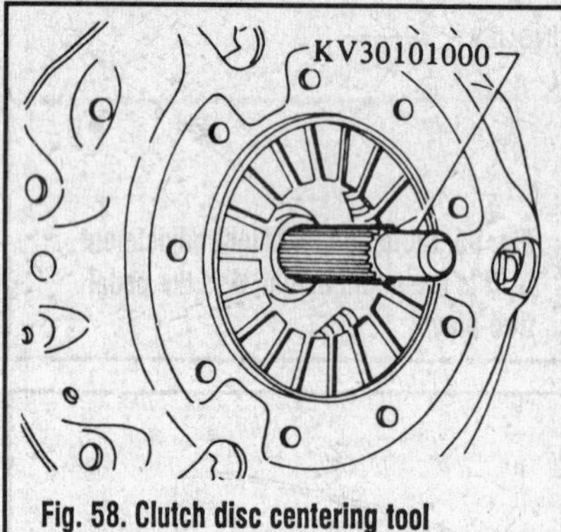
KV30101000

Fig. 58. Clutch disc centering tool

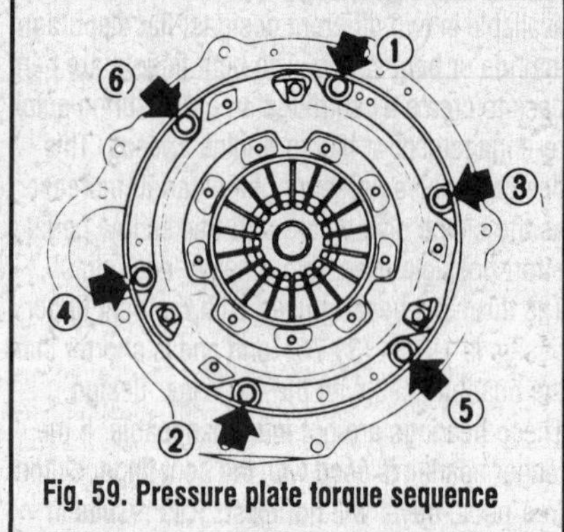
1
2
3
4
5
6

Fig. 59. Pressure plate torque sequence

To install:

5. Apply a light coating of chassis lube to the clutch disc splines, input shaft and pilot bearing. Use a disc centering tool to aid installation. Torque the pressure plate bolts in a criss-cross pattern, a little at a time each to 16–22 ft. lbs. (20–26 Nm).
6. Install the transaxle into the vehicle. If the mating surfaces will not come together, do not force. Remove the transaxle and recheck that the disc is centered. Drawing the transaxle to the engine with the bolts may damage the clutch and/or transaxle.
7. After the transaxle is installed, connect the clutch cable and check operation before complete reassembly.

AUTOMATIC TRANSAXLE

Understanding Automatic Transmissions

The automatic transmission allows engine torque and power to be transmitted to the drive wheels within a narrow range of engine operating speeds. The transmission will allow the engine to turn fast enough to produce plenty of power and torque at very low speeds, while keeping it at a sensible rpm at high vehicle speeds. The transmission performs this job entirely without driver assistance. The transmission uses a light fluid as the medium for the transmission of power. This fluid also works in the operation of various hydraulic control circuits and as a lubricant. Because the transmission fluid performs all of these three functions, trouble within the unit can easily travel from one part to another. For this reason, and because of the complexity and unusual operating principles of the transmission, a very sound understanding of the basic principles of operation will simplify troubleshooting.

THE TORQUE CONVERTER

The torque converter replaces the conventional clutch. It has three functions:

1. It allows the engine to idle with the vehicle at a standstill, even with the transmission in gear.
2. It allows the transmission to shift from range to range smoothly, without requiring that the driver close the throttle during the shift.
3. It multiplies engine torque to an increasing extent as vehicle speed drops and throttle opening is increased. This has the effect of making the transmission more responsive and reduces the amount of shifting required.

The torque converter is a metal case which is shaped like a sphere that has been flattened on opposite sides. It is bolted to the rear end of the engine's crankshaft. Generally, the entire metal case rotates at engine speed and serves as the engine's flywheel.

The case contains three sets of blades. One set is attached directly to the case. This set forms the torus or pump. Another set is directly connected to the output shaft, and forms the turbine. The third set is mounted on a hub which, in turn, is mounted on a stationary shaft through a one-way clutch. This third set is known as the stator.

A pump, which is driven by the converter hub at engine speed, keeps the torque converter full of transmission fluid at all times. Fluid flows continuously through the unit to provide cooling.

Under low speed acceleration, the torque converter functions as follows:

The torus is turning faster than the turbine. It picks up fluid at the center of the converter and, through centrifugal force, slings it outward. Since the outer edge of the converter moves faster than the portions at the center, the fluid picks up speed.

The fluid then enters the outer edge of the turbine blades. It then travels back toward the center of the converter case along the turbine blades. In impinging upon the turbine blades, the fluid loses the energy picked up in the torus.

If the fluid were now to immediately be returned directly into the torus, both halves of the converter would have to turn at approximately the same speed at all times, and torque input and output would both be the same.

In flowing through the torus and turbine, the fluid picks up two types of flow, or flow in two separate directions. It flows through the turbine blades, and it spins with the engine. The stator, whose blades are stationary when the vehicle is being accelerated at low speeds, converts one type of flow into another. Instead of allowing the fluid to flow straight back into the torus, the stator's curved blades turn the fluid almost 90° toward the direction of rotation of the engine. Thus the fluid does not flow as fast toward the torus, but is already spinning when the torus picks it up. This has the effect of allowing the torus to turn much faster than the turbine. This difference in speed may be compared to the difference in speed between the smaller and larger gears in any gear train. The result is that engine power output is higher, and engine torque is multiplied.

As the speed of the turbine increases, the fluid spins faster and faster in the direction of engine rotation. As a result, the ability of the stator to redirect the fluid flow is reduced. Under cruising conditions, the stator is eventually forced to rotate on its one-way clutch in the direction of engine rotation. Under these conditions, the torque converter begins to behave almost like a solid shaft, with the torus and turbine speeds being almost equal.

THE PLANETARY GEARBOX

The ability of the torque converter to multiply engine torque is limited. Also, the unit tends to be more efficient when the turbine is rotating at relatively high speeds. Therefore, a planetary gearbox is used to carry the power output of the turbine to the halfshafts.

Planetary gears function very similarly to conventional transmission gears. However, their construction is different in that three elements make up one gear system, and, in that all three elements are different from one another. The three elements are: an outer gear that is shaped like a hoop, with teeth cut into the inner surface; a sun gear, mounted on a shaft and located at the very center of the outer gear; and a set of three planet gears, held by pins in a ring-like planet carrier, meshing with both the sun gear and the outer gear. Either the outer gear or the sun gear may be held stationary, providing more than one possible torque multiplication factor for each set of gears. Also, if all three gears are forced to rotate at the same speed, the gearset forms, in effect, a solid shaft.

Most modern automatics use the planetary gears to provide either a single reduction ratio of about 1.8:1, or two reduction gears: a low of about 2.5:1, and an intermediate of about 1.5:1. Bands and clutches are used to hold various portions of the gearsets to the transmission case or to the shaft on which they are mounted. Shifting is accomplished, then, by changing the portion of each planetary gearset which is held to the transmission case or to the shaft.

THE SERVOS AND ACCUMULATORS

The servos are hydraulic pistons and cylinders. They resemble the hydraulic actuators used on many familiar machines, such as bulldozers. Hydraulic fluid enters the cylinder, under pressure, and forces the piston to move to engage the band or clutches.

The accumulators are used to cushion the engagement of the servos. The transmission fluid must pass through the accumulator on the way to the servo. The accumulator housing contains a thin piston which is sprung away from the discharge passage of the accumulator. When fluid passes through the accumulator on the way to the servo, it must move the piston against spring pressure, and this action smooths out the action of the servo.

THE HYDRAULIC CONTROL SYSTEM

The hydraulic pressure used to operate the servos comes from the main transmission oil pump. This fluid is channeled to the various servos through the shift valves. There is generally a manual shift valve which is operated by the transmission selector lever and an automatic shift valve for each automatic upshift the transmission provides: i.e., 2-speed automatics have a low/high shift valve, while 3-speeds have a 1-2 valve, and a 2-3 valve.

There are two pressures which effect the operation of these valves. One is the governor pressure which is affected by vehicle speed. The other is the modulator pressure which is affected by intake manifold vacuum or throttle position. Governor pressure rises with an increase in vehicle speed, and modulator pressure rises as the throttle is opened wider. By responding to these two pressures, the shift valves cause the upshift points to be delayed with increased throttle opening to make the best use of the engine's power output.

Most transmissions also make use of an auxiliary circuit for downshifting. This circuit may be actuated by the throttle linkage or the vacuum line which actuates the modulator, or by a cable or solenoid. It applies pressure to a special downshift surface on the shift valve or valves.

The transmission modulator also governs the line pressure, used to actuate the servos. In this way, the clutches and bands will be actuated with a force matching the torque output of the engine.

The automatic transaxle is available on all 1982 and later models.

Identification

The automatic transaxle serial number label is attached to the upper part of the housing.

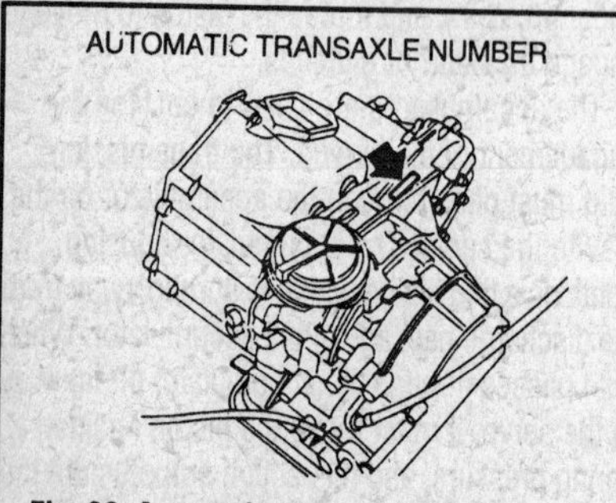
AUTOMATIC TRANSAXLE NUMBER

Fig. 60. Automatic transaxle ID number – RN3F01A

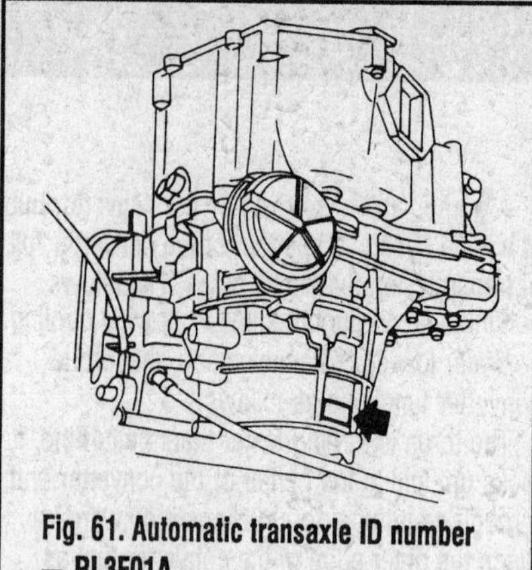

Fig. 61. Automatic transaxle ID number – RL3F01A

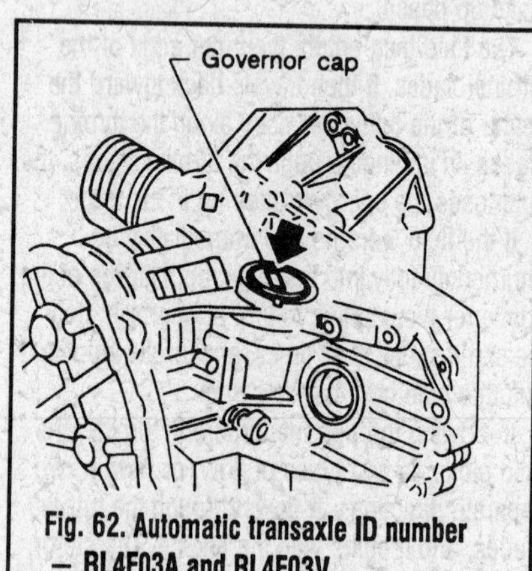
Governor cap

Fig. 62. Automatic transaxle ID number – RL4F03A and RL4F03V

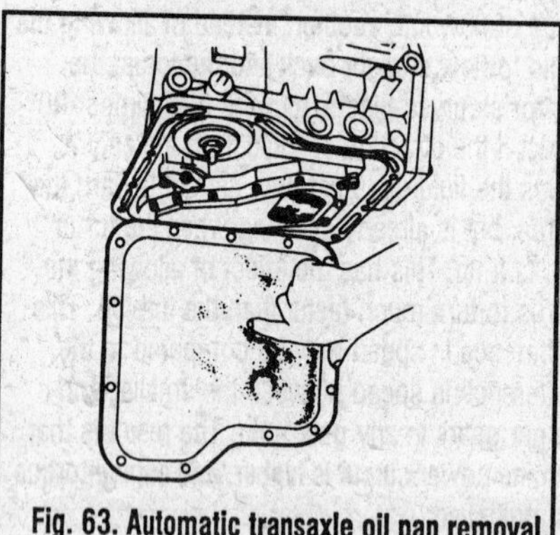

Fig. 63. Automatic transaxle oil pan removal

Fluid Pan

REMOVAL & INSTALLATION

1. Raise and support the vehicle on jackstands.
2. Place a container under the transaxle to catch the oil when the pan is removed.
3. Remove the transaxle pan bolts.

➡ If the pan sticks, bump it with a soft hammer to break it loose.

4. Using a putty knife, clean the gasket mounting surfaces.

To install:

5. Clean the pan with soap and water. Use a new gasket, sealant and reverse the removal procedures. Torque the oil pan bolts to 3.6–5.1 ft. lbs. (5.0–7.0 Nm). Refill the transaxle with DEXRON® II automatic transmission fluid.

FILTER SERVICE

1. Refer to the Oil Pan, Removal and Installation procedures, in this Section and remove the oil pan.
2. Remove the control valve body, oil strainer plate bolts and the plate.

➡ If the separator plate shows signs of scratches or damage, replace it.

3. To install, reverse the removal procedures.

Adjustments

THROTTLE WIRE

1982–90 Vehicles

➧ SEE FIGS. 64

The throttle wire is adjusted by means of double nuts on the carburetor or throttle body side. Refer to the illustration for details. If this adjustment is out of range, the transaxle shift patterns will change. This can affect the durability and driveability of the transaxle.

1. Loosen the throttle wire double nuts **A** and **B** on the carburetor side.
2. With the throttle drum set at **P1** (fully open), move the fitting **Q** fully in the direction **T** and tighten nut **B** in direction **U**.
3. Reverse nut **B** 1 to 1.5 turns in direction **T** and tighten nut **A** while holding the throttle in the full open position.
4. Make sure the throttle wire stroke **L** is within the range of 1.079–1.236 in. (27.4–31.4mm).

1991–92 Vehicles

➧ SEE FIGS. 65

The throttle wire is adjusted by means of double nuts on the throttle body side. Refer to the illustration for details. If this adjustment is out of range, the transaxle shift patterns will change. This can affect the durability and driveability of the transaxle.

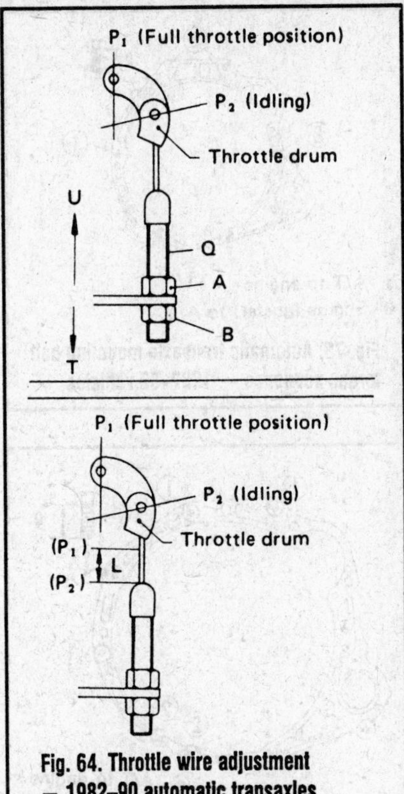
P1 (Full throttle position)
P2 (Idling)
Throttle drum
U
Q
A
B
T
P1 (Full throttle position)
P2 (Idling)
Throttle drum
(P1)
L
(P2)
Fig. 64. Throttle wire adjustment – 1982–90 automatic transaxles

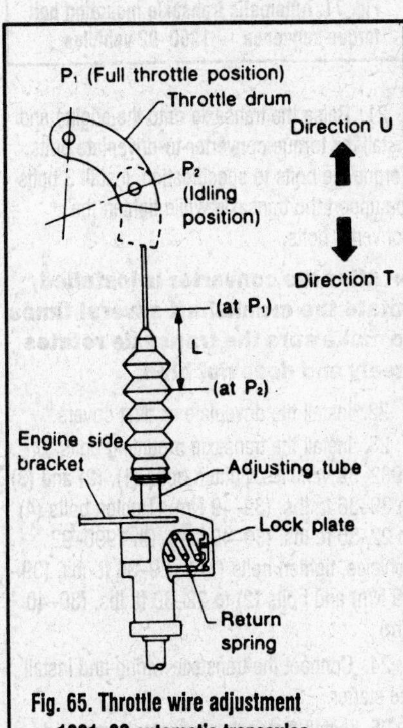
P1 (Full throttle position)
Throttle drum
Direction U
P2
(Idling
position)
Direction T
(at P1)
L
(at P2)
Engine side
bracket
Adjusting tube
Lock plate
Return
spring
Fig. 65. Throttle wire adjustment – 1991–92 automatic transaxles

1. Turn the ignition switch **OFF**. Mark the throttle wire to aid in measurement.
2. While pressing the lock plate, move the adjusting tube in the direction **T**.
3. Return the lock plate. The adjusting tube is locked at this time.
4. Move the throttle drum from **P2** to **P1** quickly. The adjusting tube moves in direction **U** while depressing the lock plate.
5. Make sure the throttle wire stroke **L** is within the range of 1.079–1.236 in. (27.4–31.4mm) between full throttle and idle.

CONTROL CABLE

1982–90 Vehicles

1. Place the control lever in Park.
2. Connect the control cable end to the lever in the transaxle unit and tighten the cable securing bolt.
3. Move the lever to the No. 1 position. Make sure that the lever works smoothly and quietly.
4. Place the control lever in Park.
5. Make sure that the lever locks in Park. Remove the cable adjusting outer nut and loosen the inner nut. Connect the control cable to the trunnion and install the outer nut.
6. Pull on the cable a couple of times, then tighten the outer nut until it just contacts the bracket. Tighten the inner nut securely. The length of the cable between the inner end of the rubber boot and the outer end of the rod should be 120.5mm.
7. Check all parts to ensure smooth working order. Check the cable spring cotter pin to make sure that it is assembled as shown.

1991–92 Sentra

1. Place the shift selector in **P**.
2. Loosen the control cable lock nut and place the manual shaft in the **P** position.
3. Adjust the cable using the long hole in the control cable at the transaxle end.
4. Tighten the lock nut.
5. Move the selector from **P** to **1** and make sure that the selector lever can be moved smoothly and without any sliding noise.
6. Apply heavy grease to all moving parts.

INHIBITOR SWITCH (BACK-UP/NEUTRAL SAFETY)

The inhibitor switch allows the back-up lights to work when the transaxle is placed in Reverse range and acts as a Neutral Safety switch, by allowing the current to pass to the starter when the transaxle is placed in Neutral or Park. The switch may be at fault is the starter motor will not crank.

1. Raise and support the vehicle on jackstands.
2. Loosen the inhibitor switch adjusting screws. Place the select lever in the Neutral position.
3. Using a 0.098 in. (2.5mm) diameter pin, place the pin into the adjustment holes on both the inhibitor switch and the switch lever (the switch lever should be as near vertical position as possible).
4. Tighten the adjusting screws to 17–23 inch lbs. (2.0–2.6 Nm). Check the switch for continuity.

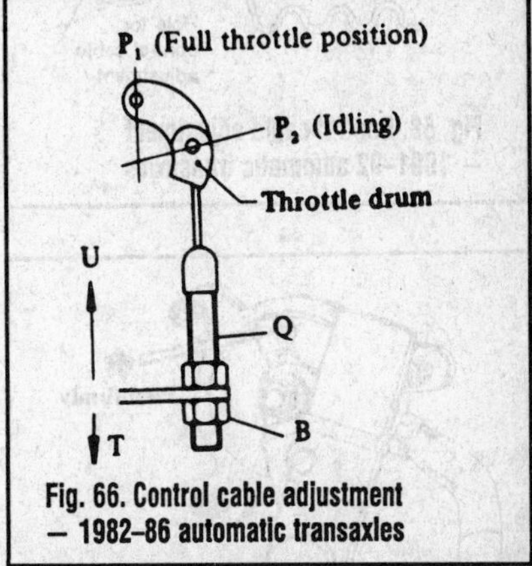
P1 (Full throttle position)
P2 (Idling)
Throttle drum
U
Q
T
B
Fig. 66. Control cable adjustment – 1982–86 automatic transaxles

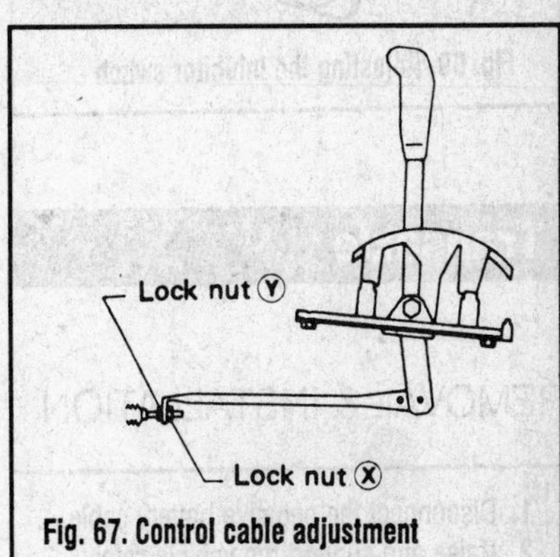
Lock nut Ⓨ
Lock nut Ⓧ
Fig. 67. Control cable adjustment – 1987–90 automatic transaxles

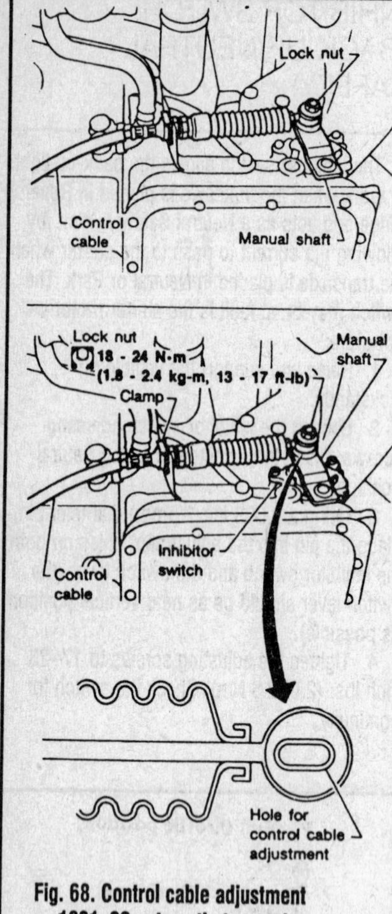
Lock nut
Control cable
Manual shaft
Lock nut
18 - 24 N·m
(1.8 - 2.4 kg-m, 13 - 17 ft-lb)
Manual shaft
Clamp
Inhibitor switch
Control cable
Hole for control cable adjustment

Fig. 68. Control cable adjustment – 1991–92 automatic transaxles

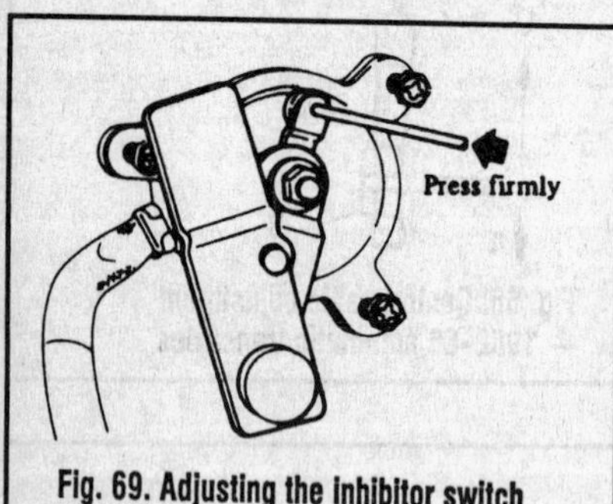
Press firmly

Fig. 69. Adjusting the inhibitor switch

Transaxle

REMOVAL & INSTALLATION

1. Disconnect the negative battery cable.
2. Raise and support the vehicle safely.
3. Remove the left front tire.
4. Drain the transaxle fluid.
5. Remove the left side fender protector.
6. Remove the halfshafts.

➡ Be careful not to damage the oil seals when removing the halfshafts. After removing the halfshafts, install a suitable bar so the side gears will not rotate and fall into the differential case.

7. On Sentra Wagon, disconnect and remove the forward exhaust pipe.
8. Disconnect the speedometer cable.
9. Disconnect the throttle wire (cable) connection.
10. Remove the control cable rear end from the unit and remove the oil level gauge tube.
11. Place a suitable jack under the transaxle and engine. Do not place the jack under the oil pan drain plug. Support the engine with wooden blocks placed between the engine and the center member.
12. Disconnect the oil cooler and charging tubes. Plug the tube ends to prevent leakage.
13. Remove the engine motor mount securing bolts, as required.
14. Remove the starter motor and disconnect all electrical wires from the transaxle.
15. Loosen and remove all but 3 of the bolts holding the transaxle to the engine. Leave the 3 bolts in to support the weight of the transaxle while removing the converter bolts.
16. Remove the driveplate or dust covers.
17. Remove the bolts holding the torque torque converter to the driveplate. Rotate the crankshaft to gain access to each bolt. Before separating the torque converter, place chalk marks on 2 parts for alignment purposes during installation.

➡ The transaxle bolts are different lengths. Tag each bolt according to location to ensure proper installation.

18. Remove the 3 temporary bolts. Move the jack gradually until the transaxle can be lowered and removed from the vehicle through the left side wheel housing.
19. Check the driveplate runout with a dial indicator. Runout must be no more than 0.020 in. (0.5mm).

To install:

20. If the torque converter was removed from the engine for any reason, after it is installed, the distance from the face of the converter to the edge of the converter housing must be checked prior to installing the transaxle. This is done to ensure proper installation of the torque converter. Check the the distance and make sure it is as follows: RL3F01A transaxles should be 0.831 in. (21mm) or more, RL4F03A and RL4F03V transaxles should be 0.748 in. (19mm) or more.

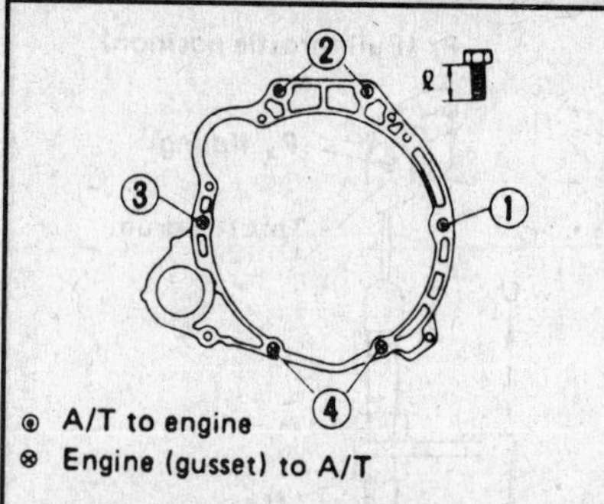
1
2
3
4
ℓ
A/T to engine
Engine (gusset) to A/T

Fig. 70. Automatic transaxle mounting bolt torque sequence – 1982–89 vehicles

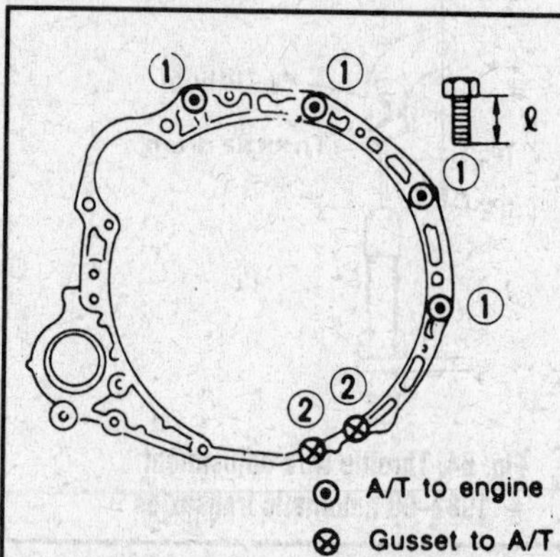
1
2
ℓ
A/T to engine
Gusset to A/T

Fig. 71. Automatic transaxle mounting bolt torque sequence – 1990–92 vehicles

21. Raise the transaxle onto the engine and install the torque converter-to-driveplate bolts. Torque the bolts to specification. Install 3 bolts to support the transaxle while tighten the converter bolts.

➡ After the converter is installed, rotate the crankshaft several times to make sure the transaxle rotates freely and does not bind.

22. Install the driveplate or dust covers.
23. Install the transaxle mounting bolts. On 1982–89 vehicles, tighten bolts (1), (2) and (3) to 29–36 ft. lbs. (39–49 Nm). Tighten bolts (4) to 22–30 ft. lbs. (30–40 Nm). On 1990–92 vehicles, tighten bolts (1) to 29–36 ft. lbs. (39–49 Nm) and bolts (2) to 22–30 ft. lbs. (30–40 Nm)
24. Connect the transaxle wiring and install the starter.
25. Install the engine mounts, if removed.
26. Connect the oil cooler and charging tubes.
27. Remove the engine and transaxle supports.
28. Install the oil level gauge tube and control cable rear end.

29. Connect the throttle wire (cable) connection.
30. Connect the speedometer cable.
31. On Sentra wagon, install the front exhaust pipe using new gaskets.
32. Install the halfshafts.
33. Install the left side fender protector.
34. Mount the left front tire and lower the vehicle.
35. Fill the transaxle and engine with the proper amounts of fluids.
36. Adjust the control cable and throttle wire.
37. Check the inhibitor switch for proper operation.
38. Road test the vehicle.

Halfshafts

REMOVAL & INSTALLATION

Refer to the Manual Transaxle procedures with this exception, insert a dowel or equivalent through the right side halfshaft hole and use a small mallet to tap the left halfshaft out of the transaxle case. Withdraw the shaft from the steering knuckle and remove it. Be careful not to damage the pinion mating shaft and the side gear while tapping the left halfshaft out of the transaxle case.

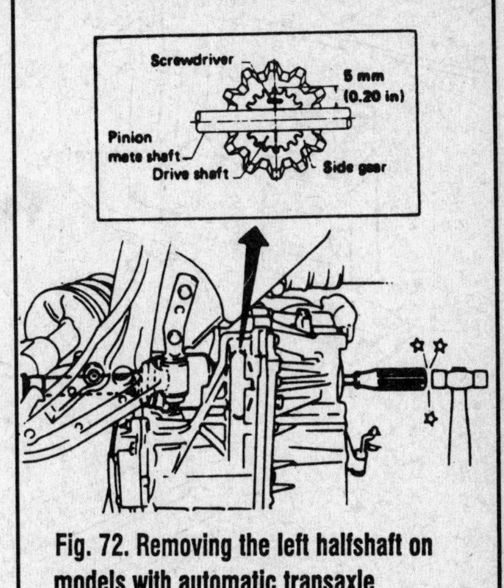
Screwdriver
5 mm
(0.20 in)
Pinion
mate shaft
Drive shaft
Side gear

Fig. 72. Removing the left halfshaft on models with automatic transaxle

OVERHAUL

Refer to the Manual Transaxle section procedures above.

TRANSFER CASE

Identification

The 1988–89 4WD Sentra uses a TY10 transfer case that is mounted at the rear of the manual transaxle.

REMOVAL & INSTALLATION

1988–89 Sentra

1. Drain the gear oil from the transaxle and the transfer case.
2. Disconnect and remove the forward exhaust pipe.
3. Using chalk or paint, matchmark the flanges on the driveshaft and then unbolt and remove the driveshaft from the transfer case.
4. Unbolt and remove the transfer control actuator from the side of the transfer case.
5. Disconnect and remove the right side halfshaft.
6. Unscrew and withdraw the speedometer pinion gear from the transfer case. Position it out of the way and secure it with wire.
7. Unbolt and remove the front, rear and side transfer case gussets (support members).
8. Use an hydraulic floor jack and a block of wood to support the transfer case, remove the transfer case-to-transaxle mounting bolts and then remove the case itself. Be careful when moving it while supported on the jack.

To Install:

9. Install the transfer case in the vehicle. Tighten the transfer case-to-transaxle mounting bolts and the transfer case gusset mounting bolts to 22–30 ft. lbs. (30–40 Nm).

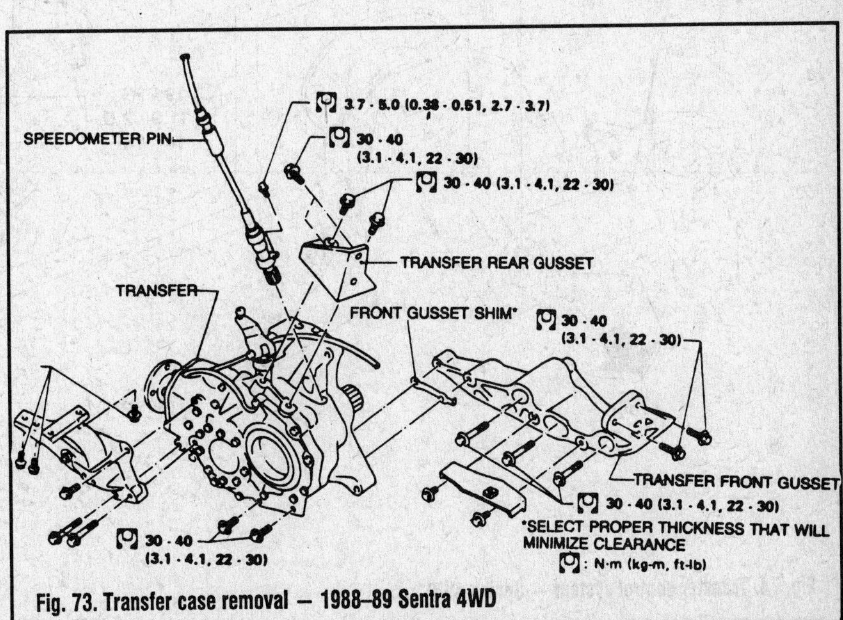
3.7 - 5.0 (0.38 - 0.51, 2.7 - 3.7)
SPEEDOMETER PIN
30 - 40
(3.1 - 4.1, 22 - 30)
30 - 40 (3.1 - 4.1, 22 - 30)
TRANSFER REAR GUSSET
TRANSFER
FRONT GUSSET SHIM*
30 - 40
(3.1 - 4.1, 22 - 30)
TRANSFER FRONT GUSSET
30 - 40 (3.1 - 4.1, 22 - 30)
*SELECT PROPER THICKNESS THAT WILL MINIMIZE CLEARANCE
: N·m (kg-m, ft-lb)
30 - 40
(3.1 - 4.1, 22 - 30)

Fig. 73. Transfer case removal — 1988–89 Sentra 4WD

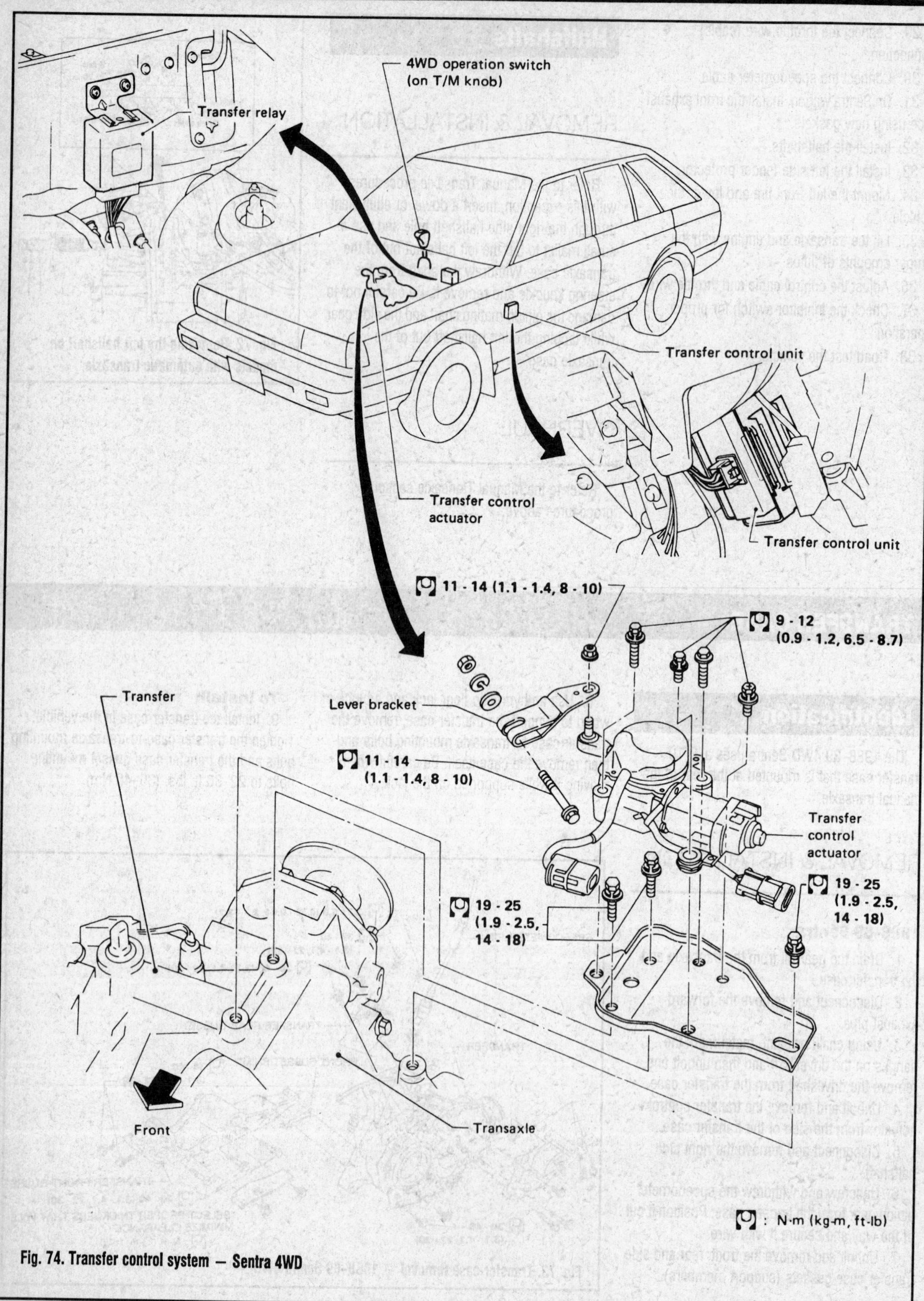
4WD operation switch
(on T/M knob)
Transfer relay
Transfer control unit
Transfer control
actuator
Transfer control unit
11 - 14 (1.1 - 1.4, 8 - 10)
9 - 12
(0.9 - 1.2, 6.5 - 8.7)
Transfer
Lever bracket
11 - 14
(1.1 - 1.4, 8 - 10)
Transfer
control
actuator
19 - 25
(1.9 - 2.5,
14 - 18)
19 - 25
(1.9 - 2.5,
14 - 18)
Front
Transaxle
: N·m (kg-m, ft-lb)

Fig. 74. Transfer control system — Sentra 4WD

10. Be sure to use a multi-purpose grease to lubricate all oil seal surfaces prior to reinstallation.

11. Install the speedometer pinion gear.

12. Install the halfshaft.

13. Connect the transfer control actuator to the side of the transfer case.

14. Install the driveshaft to the transfer case.

15. Install the forward exhaust pipe.

16. Refill all fluid levels, the transfer case and the transaxle use different types and weights of lubricant then road test for proper operation.

OVERHAUL

Disassembly

1. Drain the gear oil from the transaxle and transfer case.

2. Remove the transfer case from the vehicle as outlined in this section.

3. Remove all oil seals using a seal remover tool, or equivalent.

4. Remove the pinion sleeve assembly by lightly tapping with a plastic hammer.

5. Remove the check ball plugs, check balls and springs.

6. Remove all case adapter bolts and then remove the case adapter by lightly tapping with a plastic hammer.

7. Separate the shift lever from the fork rod.

8. Remove the ring gear, countershaft and shift fork as an assembly.

9. Remove all oil seals from the case using a seal remover, or equivalent.

10. Remove the shift fork stopper C-clip and retaining ring. Check the contact surfaces for wear and damage. The clearance between the C-clip and clip groove should be 0–0.0098 in. (0–0.25mm). If excessive, replace with a thicker C-clip.

11. To disassemble the ring gear: pull the gear bearings with a gear puller. Remove the speedometer drive gear and oil seal.

12. To disassemble the countershaft: press the hypoid gear and bearing using a hydraulic press. Do not use a gear puller.

To assemble:

13. Inspect all bearings and gears for damage or scoring and replace if necessary.

14. The pinion sleeve shim adjustment must be made during assemble.

a. Remove the countershaft case side bearing outer race using tool J34286 or equivalent.

b. Reinstall the pinion sleeve only. Assemble the pinion bearings onto tool J34309 (shim selector tool).

c. Place the tool J34309 with the pinion front bearing inner race installed into the pinion sleeve. Assemble the rear bearing inner race and pinion sleeve with the tool.

d. Measure the turning torque at the end of the J34309–2 tool (gauge anvil). The torque should be 9.5–13.9 inch lbs. (1.1–1.6 Nm).

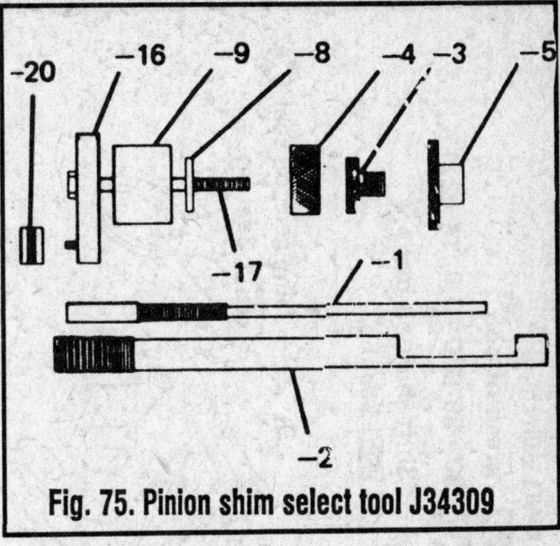
-20
-16
-9
-8
-4
-3
-5
-17
-1
-2
Fig. 75. Pinion shim select tool J34309

e. Reinstall the case adapter onto the transfer case and torque the case bolt to 12–15 ft. lbs. (16–21 Nm). Install the countershaft bearing disc J25269–18 and shaft arbor J34309–19 and select a standard pinion sleeve shim by measuring the gap between J34309–20 and J34309–19 with a feeler gauge.

15. Install the countershaft and shift fork as an assembly. Tilt them to engage the gears.

16. Install the ring gear and set the shift lever on the fork rod.

17. Apply silicone sealer to the case adapter and transfer case. Torque the case bolts to 12–15 ft. lbs. (16–21 Nm).

18. Install the O-rings onto the end cover. Install the countershaft bearing, shim and cover.

19. Install the pinion sleeve and torque to 12–15 ft. lbs. (16–21 Nm).

20. Install all outside hardware as removed. Install the transfer case into the vehicle.

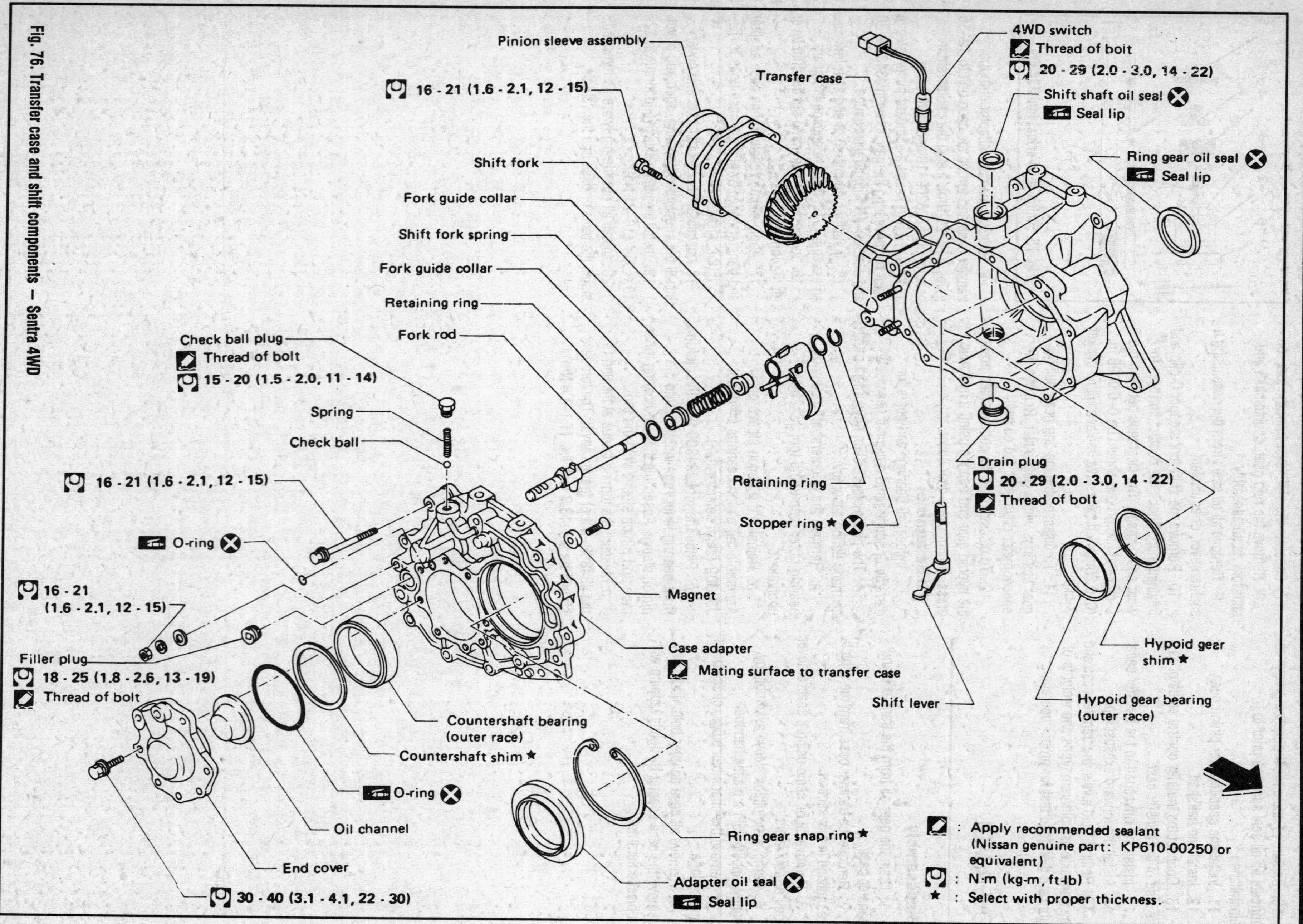
Pinion sleeve assembly
16 - 21 (1.6 - 2.1, 12 - 15)
Transfer case
4WD switch
Thread of bolt
20 - 29 (2.0 - 3.0, 14 - 22)
Shift shaft oil seal
Seal lip
Ring gear oil seal
Seal lip
Shift fork
Fork guide collar
Shift fork spring
Fork guide collar
Retaining ring
Fork rod
Check ball plug
Thread of bolt
15 - 20 (1.5 - 2.0, 11 - 14)
Spring
Check ball
16 - 21 (1.6 - 2.1, 12 - 15)
O-ring
16 - 21
(1.6 - 2.1, 12 - 15)
Filler plug
18 - 25 (1.8 - 2.6, 13 - 19)
Thread of bolt
Retaining ring
Stopper ring★
Drain plug
20 - 29 (2.0 - 3.0, 14 - 22)
Thread of bolt
Magnet
Case adapter
Mating surface to transfer case
Shift lever
Hypoid gear shim★
Hypoid gear bearing
(outer race)
Countershaft bearing
(outer race)
Countershaft shim★
O-ring
Oil channel
End cover
30 - 40 (3.1 - 4.1, 22 - 30)
Ring gear snap ring★
Adapter oil seal
Seal lip
: Apply recommended sealant
(Nissan genuine part: KP610-00250 or
equivalent)
: N·m (kg-m, ft-lb)
★ : Select with proper thickness.

Fig. 76. Transfer case and shift components — Sentra 4WD

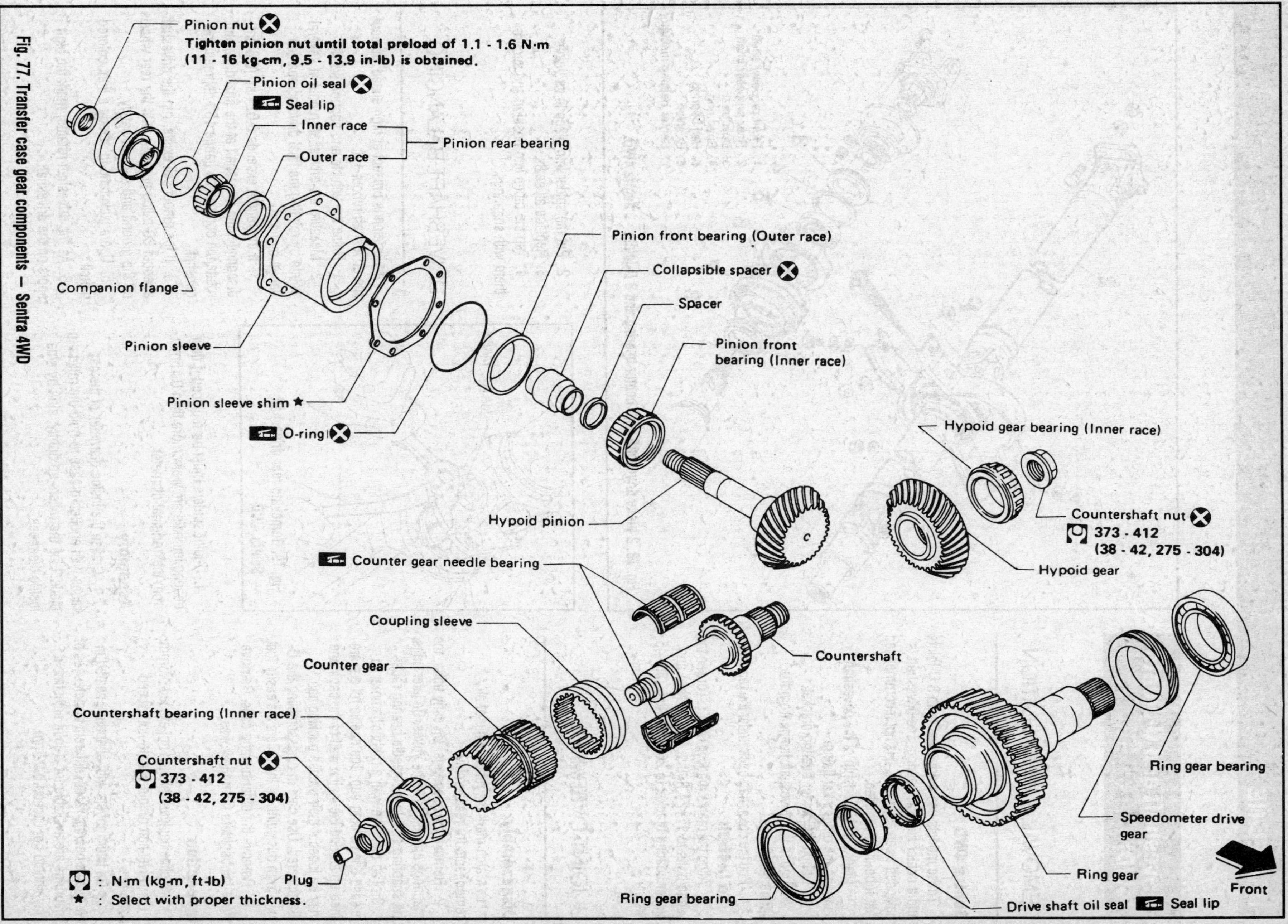

Pinion nut
Tighten pinion nut until total preload of 1.1 - 1.6 N·m (11 - 16 kg-cm, 9.5 - 13.9 in-lb) is obtained.
Pinion oil seal
Seal lip
Inner race
Outer race
Pinion rear bearing
Companion flange
Pinion sleeve
Pinion sleeve shim ★
O-ring
Pinion front bearing (Outer race)
Collapsible spacer
Spacer
Pinion front bearing (Inner race)
Hypoid pinion
Hypoid gear bearing (Inner race)
Countershaft nut
373 - 412
(38 - 42, 275 - 304)
Hypoid gear
Counter gear needle bearing
Coupling sleeve
Countershaft
Counter gear
Countershaft bearing (Inner race)
Countershaft nut
373 - 412
(38 - 42, 275 - 304)
Plug
Ring gear bearing
Speedometer drive gear
Ring gear
Ring gear bearing
Drive shaft oil seal
Seal lip
Front
: N·m (kg-m, ft-lb)
★ : Select with proper thickness.

Fig. 77. Transfer case gear components — Sentra 4WD

DRIVELINE

Driveshaft and U-Joints (4WD)

REMOVAL & INSTALLATION

Sentra 4WD

These models use a driveshaft with 3 U-joints and a center support bearing. The driveshaft is balanced as an assembly. It is not recommended that it be disassembled.

1. Mark the relationship of the driveshaft flange to the differential flange.
2. Unbolt the center bearing bracket.
3. Unbolt the driveshaft flange from the differential flange.
4. Pull the driveshaft back under the rear axle.

To Install:

5. Align the marks made in Step 1. Torque the flange bolts to 17–24 ft. lbs. (22–30 Nm) and center bearing bracket to 26–35 ft. lbs. (35–45 Nm).

1. Front propeller shaft
2. Rear propeller shaft
3. Dust seal
4. Snap ring
5. Ball bearing
6. Cushion
7. Center bearing insulator

Fig. 78. 2 piece driveshaft with center bearing and 3 U-joints — Sentra 4WD

U-JOINT OVERHAUL

Disassembly

1. Match mark the relationship of all components for reassembly.
2. Remove the snaprings. On early units, the snaprings are seated in the yokes. On later units, the snapring seat in the needle bearing races.
3. Tap the yoke with a rubber hammer to release one bearing cap. The needle rollers are lined up around the inside wall of the caps and may be loose if their grease packing has disappeared. Use care in disassembling the U-joint from this point, as the rollers are easily lost.
4. Remove the other bearing caps. Remove the U-joint spiders from the yokes.

Inspection

1. Spline backlash should not exceed 0.5mm.
2. Driveshaft runout should not exceed 0.4mm.
3. On later models with snaprings seated in the needle bearing races, different thicknesses of snaprings are available for U-joint adjustment. Play should not exceed 0.02mm.

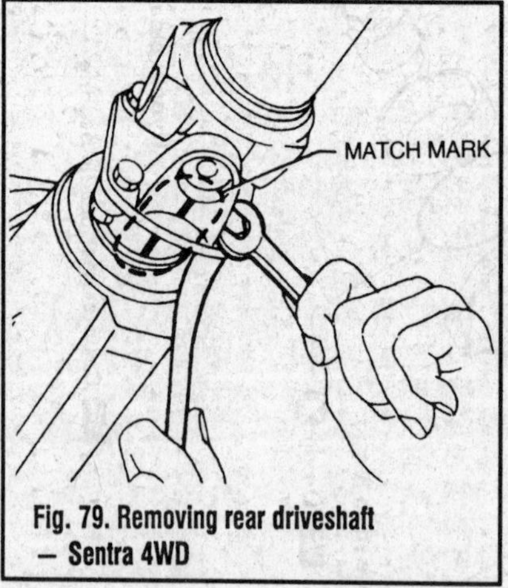
MATCH MARK

Fig. 79. Removing rear driveshaft — Sentra 4WD

4. U-joint spiders must be replaced if their bearing journals are worn more than 0.15mm from their original diameter.

Assembly

1. Grease the inside diameter of the cap races with enough grease to hold the rollers in place. Line the rollers up tightly, side by side inside the races.
2. Put the spider into place in its yokes.
3. Replace all seals.
4. Tap the races into position and secure them with snaprings.

DRIVESHAFT BALANCING

If vibration is present at high speed, inspect the driveshaft runout 1st.

1. Raise the vehicle and support safely.
2. Measure the driveshaft runout at several points by rotating the final drive companion flange by hand.
3. If the runout exceeds 0.024 in. (0.6mm), disconnect the driveshaft at the final drive and rotate the companion flange 180 degrees and reinstall.
4. If the runout still exists, run the driveshaft at about 30 miles per hour with the rear wheels off the ground and support safely.
5. Use a jackstand to steady a light colored pencil.
6. As the driveshaft rotates, mark the high spots on the driveshaft.

7. Place 2 hose clamps around the driveshaft opposite the high spot and recheck. Move the clamps around to try to balance the shaft.

8. If 2 clamps does not correct the vibration, replace the driveshaft, center bearing or U-joints.

Center Bearing

REMOVAL & INSTALLATION

The center bearing is a sealed unit which must be replaced as an assembly if defective.

1. Remove the driveshaft.

2. Paint a matchmark across where the flanges behind the center yoke are joined. This is for assembly purposes. If you don't paint or somehow mark the relationship between the 2 shafts, they may be out of balance when you put them back together.

3. Remove the bolts and separate the shafts. Make a matchmark on the front driveshaft half which lines up with the mark on the flange half.

4. Devise a way to hold the driveshaft while unbolting the companion flange from the front driveshaft. Do not place the front driveshaft tube in a vise. The best way is to grip the flange while loosening the nut. It is going to require some strength to remove.

5. Press the companion flange off the front driveshaft and press the center bearing from its mount.

To install:

6. The new bearing is already lubricated. Install it into the mount, making sure that the seals and so on are facing the same way as when removed.

7. Slide the companion flange onto the front driveshaft, aligning the marks made during removal. Install the washer and locknut. If the washer and locknut are separate pieces, tighten them to 145–175 ft. lbs. (197–238 Nm). If they are a unit, tighten it to 180–217 ft. lbs. (245–295 Nm). Check that the bearing rotates freely around the driveshaft. Stake the nut.

8. Connect the companion flange to the other half of the driveshaft, aligning the marks made during removal. Tighten the bolts securely.

9. Install the driveshaft.

REAR FINAL DRIVE UNIT

Identification

The 1988–89 Sentra 4WD uses a model R160 final drive unit with independent halfshaft assemblies.

Determining Axle Ratio

The rear axle ratio is said to have a certain ratio, say 4.11. It is called a 4.11 rear although the 4.11 actually means 4.11 to 1 (4.11:1). This means that the driveshaft will turn 4.11 times for every turn of the rear wheels. The number 4.11 is determined by dividing the number of teeth on the pinion gear into the number of teeth on the ring gear. In the case of a 4.11 rear, there could be 9 teeth on the pinion and 37 teeth on the ring gear (37 divided by 9 = 4.11). This provides a sure way , although troublesome, of determining the rear axle ratio. The axle must be drained and the rear cover removed to do this, and then the teeth counted.

A much easier method is to jack up the vehicle and safely support it with jackstands, so both rear wheels are off the ground. Block the front wheels, set the parking brake and put the transaxle in **Neutral**. Make a chalk mark on the rear wheel and driveshaft. Turn the rear wheel 1 complete revolution and count the the number of turns that the driveshaft makes (having an assistant here to count 1 or the other is helpful). The number of turns the driveshaft makes in 1 complete revolution of the rear wheel is an approximation of the rear axle ratio.

Final Drive Assembly

REMOVAL & INSTALLATION

Sentra 4WD

1. Jack up the rear of the vehicle and drain the oil from the differential. Support with jackstands. Position the floor jack underneath the differential unit.

2. Disconnect the brake hydraulic lines and the parking brake cable.

3. Disconnect the sway bar from the control arms on either sides.

4. Remove the rear exhaust tube.

5. Disconnect the driveshaft and the rear axle shafts.

6. Remove the rear shock absorbers from the control arms.

7. Unbolt the differential unit from the chassis, at the differential mounting insulator.

8. Lower the rear assembly out of the car using the floor jack. It is best to have at least 1 other person helping to balance the assembly.

To install:

9. Install the differential unit to the chassis. Torque the rear cover-to-insulator nuts to 72–87 ft. lbs. (98–118 Nm); the mounting insulator-to-chassis bolts to 22–29 ft. lbs. (30–39 Nm); the driveshaft-to-flange bolts to 43–51 ft. lbs. (58–69 Nm). Torque the strut nuts to 51–65 ft. lbs. (69–88 Nm); and the sway bar-to-control arm nuts to 12–15 ft. lbs. (16–20 Nm).

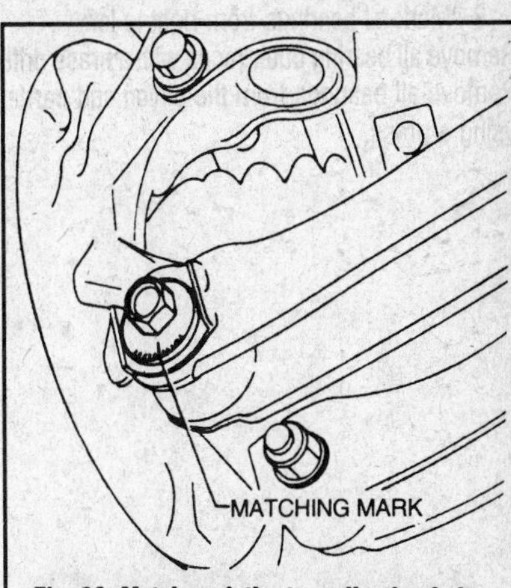
MATCHING MARK

Fig. 80. Matchmark the toe adjusting bolts on the transverse link — Sentra 4WD

Fig. 81. Lowering the rear final drive unit out of the vehicle — Sentra 4WD

10. Reconnect the rear exhaust tube.
11. Connect the brake hydraulic lines and the parking brake cable.
12. Bleed the brake system.
13. Road test for proper operation.

FINAL DRIVE OVERHAUL

Disassembly

1. Mark the side seal retainers for identification and remove the side retainers.
2. Remove the rear case cover.
3. Remove the differential case from the final drive case.
4. Remove the side outer bearing races using a gear puller J25810–A or equivalent.
5. Remove the pinion nut and flange using a puller.
6. Remove the drive pinion with the rear bearing and inner cone. Remove the pinion seal.
7. Remove the pilot bearing with the spacer and inner cone with tool J25749–A or equivalent.
8. Mark all bearings from right to left. Remove all bearing outer races with a brass drift. Remove all bearings from the pinion and carrier using a press.

To assemble:

9. Install the side gears, pinion mate gears, thrust washer and thrust block into the differential case.
10. Fit the pinion mate shaft to the differential case so that it meets the lock pin holes.
11. Adjust the backlash between the side gear and pinion mate gear by selecting side gear thrust washers to meet the clearance of 0.0039–0.0079 in. (0.10–0.20mm).
12. Install the shaft lock pin with a punch until it is flush.
13. Install the ring gear and apply Loctite® to the ring gear bolts. Torque the bolts to 69–83 ft. lbs. (93–113 Nm) in a criss-cross pattern.
14. Press the side bearings onto the differential case.
15. Install the front and rear bearing outer races with installing tools J25742–1, 2, 3.
16. Set the pinion bearing adjusting washer and pinion spacer. Press the bearing and adjusting washer using a press.
17. Set the drive pinion into the case with a press.
18. Install the pinion oil seal with tool ST30720000 or equivalent.
19. Install the pinion flange and torque the nut to 123–145 ft. lbs. (167–196 Nm). Turn the pinion in either direction and check the bearing preload with an inch lbs. torque wrench. The preload should be 6.5–13.5 inch lbs. (0.74–1.52 Nm).
20. Install the side oil seal retainers with new seals. Torque the bolts to 7–9 ft. lbs. (9–12 Nm).
21. Measure the ring gear-to-drive pinion backlash with a dial indicator. Backlash should be 0.0039–0.0079 in. (0.10–0.20mm).
22. Check the total bearing preload at the pinion nut. It should be 7.4–18.6 inch lbs. (0.83–2.11 Nm). If the preload is too great, add the same amount of shim to each side of the differential case. If the preload in too little, remove the same amount from each side.

Adjustments

1. Adjust the pinion gear height as follows: place the preload shim selector tool J34309–1 with the rear bearing inner cone installed into the case.
2. Install the tool gauge anvil with the front bearing. Turn the assemble to seat the bearings.
3. Measure the turning torque at the end of the tool. It should be 5.2–8.7 inch lbs. (0.6–1.0 Nm).
4. Place the solid pinion adjusting spacer into the tool gauge anvil.
5. Select the correct thickness of pinion bearing preload adjusting washer using a standard gauge of 0.24 in. (6.0mm) and a feeler gauge. Select a shim and set aside for assemble.

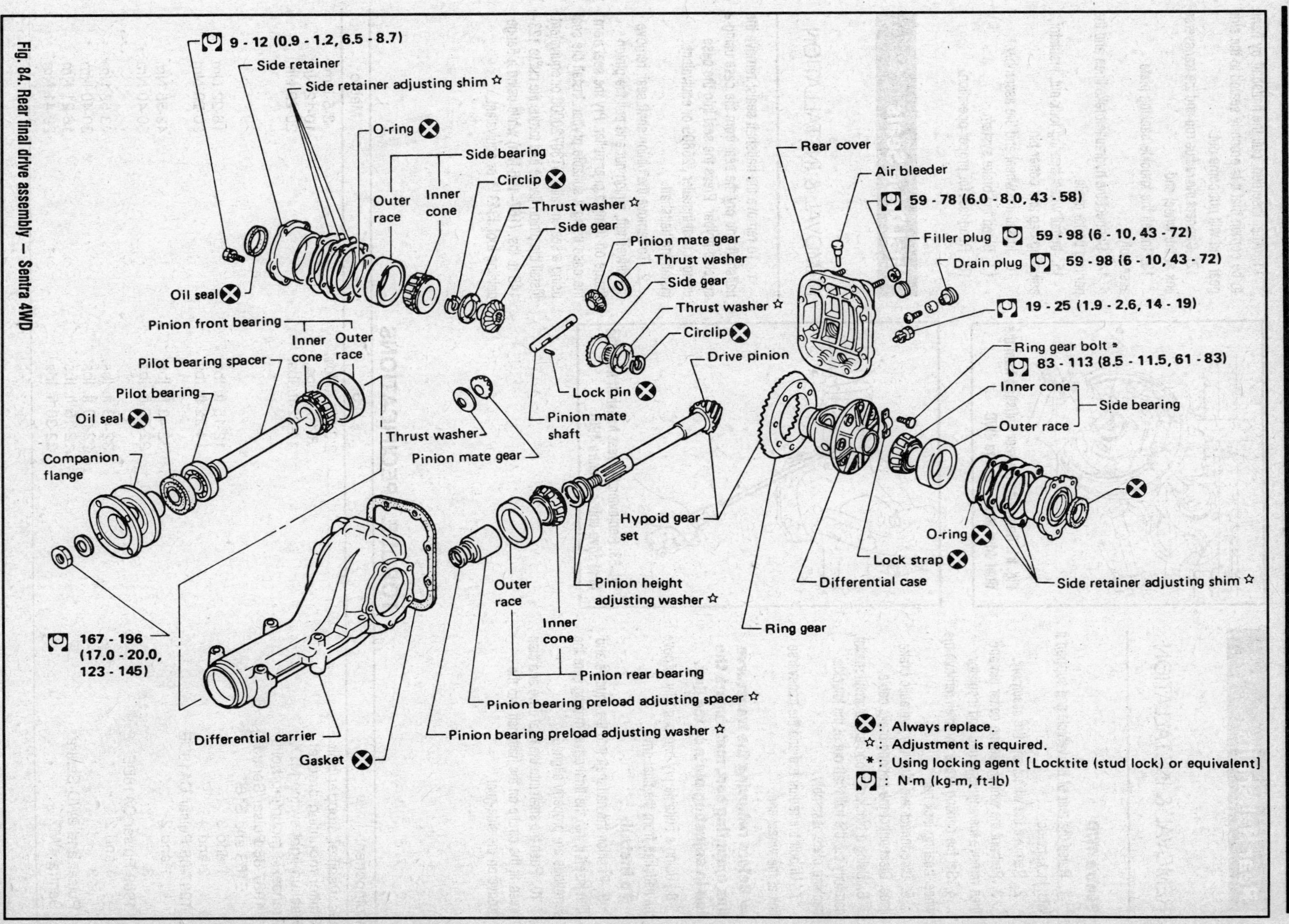
9 - 12 (0.9 - 1.2, 6.5 - 8.7)
Side retainer
Side retainer adjusting shim ☆
O-ring
Side bearing
Outer race
Inner cone
Circlip
Thrust washer ☆
Side gear
Pinion mate gear
Thrust washer
Side gear
Thrust washer ☆
Circlip
Drive pinion
Oil seal
Pinion front bearing
Inner cone
Outer race
Pilot bearing spacer
Pilot bearing
Oil seal
Companion flange
Lock pin
Pinion mate shaft
Thrust washer
Pinion mate gear
Rear cover
Air bleeder
59 - 78 (6.0 - 8.0, 43 - 58)
Filler plug
59 - 98 (6 - 10, 43 - 72)
Drain plug
59 - 98 (6 - 10, 43 - 72)
19 - 25 (1.9 - 2.6, 14 - 19)
Ring gear bolt *
83 - 113 (8.5 - 11.5, 61 - 83)
Inner cone
Side bearing
Outer race
Hypoid gear set
O-ring
Lock strap
Differential case
Side retainer adjusting shim ☆
Outer race
Pinion height adjusting washer ☆
Inner cone
Ring gear
167 - 196 (17.0 - 20.0, 123 - 145)
Pinion rear bearing
Pinion bearing preload adjusting spacer ☆
Differential carrier
Pinion bearing preload adjusting washer ☆
Gasket
: Always replace.
☆: Adjustment is required.
*: Using locking agent [Locktite (stud lock) or equivalent]
: N·m (kg-m, ft-lb)

Fig. 84. Rear final drive assembly — Sentra 4WD

Rear Halfshafts

REMOVAL & INSTALLATION

Sentra 4WD

1. Raise the rear of the vehicle and support it with jackstands.
2. Remove the wheel and tire assembly.
3. Pull out the wheel bearing cotter pin and then remove the adjusting cap and insulator.
4. Set the parking brake and then remove the wheel bearing lock nut.
5. Disconnect and plug the hydraulic brake lines. Disconnect the parking brake cable.
6. Using a block of wood and a small mallet, carefully tap the halfshaft out of the knuckle/backing plate assembly.
7. Unbolt the radius rod and the transverse link at the wheel end.

➡ Before removing the transverse link mounting bolt, matchmark the toe-in adjusting plate to the link.

8. Using a suitable pry bar, carefully remove the halfshaft from the final drive.

To install:

9. Position the halfshaft into the knuckle and then insert it into the final drive; making sure the serrations are properly aligned.
10. Push the shaft into the final drive and then press-fit the circlip on the halfshaft into the groove on the side gear.

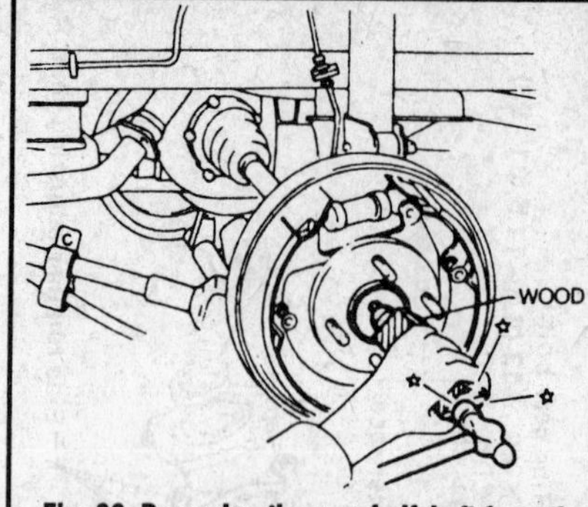
WOOD

Fig. 82. Removing the rear halfshaft from the final drive unit — Sentra 4WD

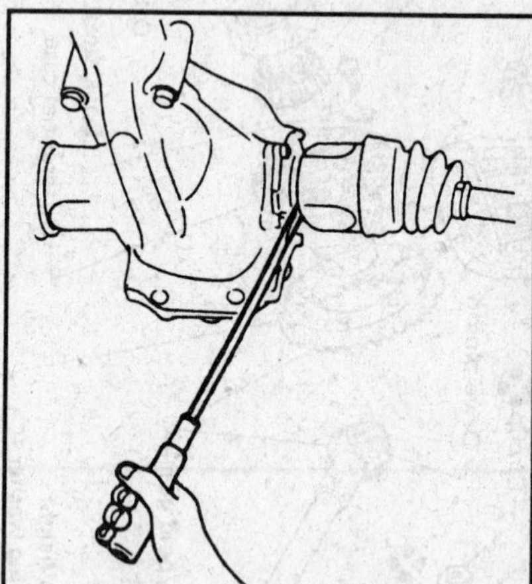

Fig. 83. Removing the rear halfshaft from the final drive unit — Sentra 4WD

11. After insertion, pull the halfshaft by hand to be certain that it is properly seated in the side gear and will not come out.
12. Connect the radius rod and the transverse link at the wheel end.
13. Install the knuckle/backing plate assembly.
14. Connect the hydraulic brake lines and the parking brake cable.
15. Install wheel bearing lock nut, insulator, adjusting cap and cotter pin.
16. Install the wheel and tire assembly.
17. Bleed the brake system.
18. Road test for proper operation.

Final Drive Seals

REMOVAL & INSTALLATION

1. To remove the halfshaft seals: remove the halfshaft and pry the seal from the case using a suitable prybar. Press the seal into the case using a seal installer J25809 or equivalent. Install the halfshaft.
2. To remove the pinion shaft seal: remove the driveshaft, pinion nut and pull the pinion flange off using a gear puller. Pry the seal from the case using a suitable prybar. Install the seal using a seal installer ST30720000 or equivalent. Install the pinion flange and torque the nut to 123–145 ft. lbs. (167–196 Nm) while using a flange holding tool J34311 or equivalent.

TORQUE SPECIFICATIONS

Component	U.S.	Metric
Gear shifter stopper bolt	2.3-3.7 ft. lbs.	3-5 Nm
Shifter mounting bracket	8-10 ft. lbs.	10-12 Nm
Backup light switch MTX	14-22 ft. lbs.	20-29 Nm
Transaxle mounting bolts		
1987-88 Pulsar/Sentra		
E16S and E16i		
1 and 3	12-15 ft. lbs.	16-22 Nm
2 and 4	14-22 ft. lbs.	20-29 Nm
1987-88 Pulsar CA18DE		
1 and 2	32-43 ft. lbs.	43-58 Nm
3	22-30 ft. lbs.	30-40 Nm
1989 Pulsar CA18DE		
1 and 2	32-43 ft. lbs.	43-58 Nm
3	22-30 ft. lbs.	30-40 Nm
Pulsar and 2WD Sentra	12-15 ft. lbs.	16-21 Nm
Sentra 4WD	22-30 ft. lbs.	29-41 Nm

TORQUE SPECIFICATIONS

Component	U.S.	Metric
Shift check ball plug MTX	14-18 ft. lbs.	19-24 Nm
Clutch cable nuts	6-8 ft. lbs.	8-11 Nm
Clutch pressure plate bolts	16-22 ft. lbs.	20-26 Nm
Transaxle oil pan bolts ATX	3.6-5.1 ft. lbs.	5.0-7.0 Nm
Inhibitor switch bolts ATX	17-23 inch. lbs.	2.0-2.6 Nm
Transfer case gusset bolts	22-30 ft. lbs.	30-40 Nm
Driveshaft flange bolts 4WD	17-24 ft. lbs.	22-30 Nm
Center bearing bolts 4WD	26-35 ft. lbs.	35-45 Nm
Pinion Flange nut 4WD	145-175 ft. lbs.	197-238 Nm
Differential-to-chassis	72-87 ft. lbs.	98-118 Nm
Mounting insulator-to-chassis	22-29 ft. lbs.	30-39 Nm
Driveshaft-to-flange bolts	43-51 ft. lbs.	58-69 Nm
Strut nuts	51-65 ft. lbs.	69-88 Nm
Sway bar-to-control arm nuts	12-15 ft. lbs.	16-20 Nm

Troubleshooting the Manual Transmission

Problem	Cause	Solution
Transmission shifts hard	• Clutch adjustment incorrect	• Adjust clutch
	• Clutch linkage or cable binding	• Lubricate or repair as necessary
	• Shift rail binding	• Check for mispositioned selector arm roll pin, loose cover bolts, worn shift rail bores, worn shift rail, distorted oil seal, or extension housing not aligned with case. Repair as necessary.
	• Internal bind in transmission caused by shift forks, selector plates, or synchronizer assemblies	• Remove, dissemble and inspect transmission. Replace worn or damaged components as necessary.
	• Clutch housing misalignment	• Check runout at rear face of clutch housing
	• Incorrect lubricant	• Drain and refill transmission
	• Block rings and/or cone seats worn	• Blocking ring to gear clutch tooth face clearance must be 0.030 inch or greater. If clearance is correct it may still be necessary to inspect blocking rings and cone seats for excessive wear. Repair as necessary.
Gear clash when shifting from one gear to another	• Clutch adjustment incorrect	• Adjust clutch
	• Clutch linkage or cable binding	• Lubricate or repair as necessary
	• Clutch housing misalignment	• Check runout at rear of clutch housing
	• Lubricant level low or incorrect lubricant	• Drain and refill transmission and check for lubricant leaks if level was low. Repair as necessary.
	• Gearshift components, or synchronizer assemblies worn or damaged	• Remove, disassemble and inspect transmission. Replace worn or damaged components as necessary.

Troubleshooting the Manual Transmission

Problem	Cause	Solution
Transmission noisy	• Lubricant level low or incorrect lubricant	• Drain and refill transmission. If lubricant level was low, check for leaks and repair as necessary.
	• Clutch housing-to-engine, or transmission-to-clutch housing bolts loose	• Check and correct bolt torque as necessary
	• Dirt, chips, foreign material in transmission	• Drain, flush, and refill transmission
	• Gearshift mechanism, transmission gears, or bearing components worn or damaged	• Remove, disassemble and inspect transmission. Replace worn or damaged components as necessary.
	• Clutch housing misalignment	• Check runcut at rear face of clutch housing
Jumps out of gear	• Clutch housing misalignment	• Check runout at rear face of clutch housing
	• Gearshift lever loose	• Check lever for worn fork. Tighten loose attaching bolts.
	• Offset lever nylon insert worn or lever attaching nut loose	• Remove gearshift lever and check for loose offset lever nut or worn insert. Repair or replace as necessary.
	• Gearshift mechanism, shift forks, selector plates, interlock plate, selector arm, shift rail, detent plugs, springs or shift cover worn or damaged	• Remove, disassemble and inspect transmission cover assembly. Replace worn or damaged components as necessary.
	• Clutch shaft or roller bearings worn or damaged	• Replace clutch shaft or roller bearings as necessary
Jumps out of gear (cont.)	• Gear teeth worn or tapered, synchronizer assemblies worn or damaged, excessive end play caused by worn thrust washers or output shaft gears	• Remove, disassemble, and inspect transmission. Replace worn or damaged components as necessary.
	• Pilot bushing worn	• Replace pilot bushing
Will not shift into one gear	• Gearshift selector plates, interlock plate, or selector arm, worn, damaged, or incorrectly assembled	• Remove, disassemble, and inspect transmission cover assembly. Repair or replace components as necessary.
	• Shift rail detent plunger worn, spring broken, or plug loose	• Tighten plug or replace worn or damaged components as necessary
	• Gearshift lever worn or damaged	• Replace gearshift lever
	• Synchronizer sleeves or hubs, damaged or worn	• Remove, disassemble and inspect transmission. Replace worn or damaged components.

Troubleshooting the Manual Transmission

Problem	Cause	Solution
Locked in one gear—cannot be shifted out	• Shift rail(s) worn or broken, shifter fork bent, setscrew loose, center detent plug missing or worn	• Inspect and replace worn or damaged parts
	• Broken gear teeth on countershaft gear, clutch shaft, or reverse idler gear	• Inspect and replace damaged part
	Gearshift lever broken or worn, shift mechanism in cover incorrectly assembled or broken, worn damaged gear train components	• Disassemble transmission. Replace damaged parts or assemble correctly.

Troubleshooting Basic Clutch Problems

Problem	Cause
Excessive clutch noise	Throwout bearing noises are more audible at the lower end of pedal travel. The usual causes are: • Riding the clutch • Too little pedal free-play • Lack of bearing lubrication A bad clutch shaft pilot bearing will make a high pitched squeal, when the clutch is disengaged and the transmission is in gear or within the first 2″ of pedal travel. The bearing must be replaced. Noise from the clutch linkage is a clicking or snapping that can be heard or felt as the pedal is moved completely up or down. This usually requires lubrication. Transmitted engine noises are amplified by the clutch housing and heard in the passenger compartment. They are usually the result of insufficient pedal free-play and can be changed by manipulating the clutch pedal.
Clutch slips (the car does not move as it should when the clutch is engaged)	This is usually most noticeable when pulling away from a standing start. A severe test is to start the engine, apply the brakes, shift into high gear and SLOWLY release the clutch pedal. A healthy clutch will stall the engine. If it slips it may be due to: • A worn pressure plate or clutch plate • Oil soaked clutch plate • Insufficient pedal free-play
Clutch drags or fails to release	The clutch disc and some transmission gears spin briefly after clutch disengagement. Under normal conditions in average temperatures, 3 seconds is maximum spin-time. Failure to release properly can be caused by: • Too light transmission lubricant or low lubricant level • Improperly adjusted clutch linkage
Low clutch life	Low clutch life is usually a result of poor driving habits or heavy duty use. Riding the clutch, pulling heavy loads, holding the car on a grade with the clutch instead of the brakes and rapid clutch engagement all contribute to low clutch life.

Troubleshooting Basic Automatic Transmission Problems

Problem	Cause	Solution
Fluid leakage	• Defective pan gasket • Loose filler tube • Loose extension housing to transmission case • Converter housing area leakage	• Replace gasket or tighten pan bolts • Tighten tube nut • Tighten bolts • Have transmission checked professionally
Fluid flows out the oil filler tube	• High fluid level • Breather vent clogged • Clogged oil filter or screen • Internal fluid leakage	• Check and correct fluid level • Open breather vent • Replace filter or clean screen (change fluid also) • Have transmission checked professionally
Transmission overheats (this is usually accompanied by a strong burned odor to the fluid)	• Low fluid level • Fluid cooler lines clogged • Heavy pulling or hauling with insufficient cooling • Faulty oil pump, internal slippage	• Check and correct fluid level • Drain and refill transmission. If this doesn't cure the problem, have cooler lines cleared or replaced. • Install a transmission oil cooler • Have transmission checked professionally
Buzzing or whining noise	• Low fluid level • Defective torque converter, scored gears	• Check and correct fluid level • Have transmission checked professionally
No forward or reverse gears or slippage in one or more gears	• Low fluid level • Defective vacuum or linkage controls, internal clutch or band failure	• Check and correct fluid level • Have unit checked professionally
Delayed or erratic shift	• Low fluid level • Broken vacuum lines • Internal malfunction	• Check and correct fluid level • Repair or replace lines • Have transmission checked professionally

Lockup Torque Converter Service Diagnosis

Problem	Cause	Solution
No lockup	• Faulty oil pump • Sticking governor valve • Valve body malfunction (a) Stuck switch valve (b) Stuck lockup valve (c) Stuck fail-safe valve • Failed locking clutch • Leaking turbine hub seal • Faulty input shaft or seal ring	• Replace oil pump • Repair or replace as necessary • Repair or replace valve body or its internal components as necessary • Replace torque converter • Replace torque converter • Repair or replace as necessary
Will not unlock	• Sticking governor valve • Valve body malfunction (a) Stuck switch valve (b) Stuck lockup valve (c) Stuck fail-safe valve	• Repair or replace as necessary • Repair or replace valve body or its internal components as necessary
Stays locked up at too low a speed in direct	• Sticking governor valve • Valve body malfunction (a) Stuck switch valve (b) Stuck lockup valve (c) Stuck fail-safe valve	• Repair or replace as necessary • Repair or replace valve body or its internal components as necessary
Locks up or drags in low or second	• Faulty oil pump • Valve body malfunction (a) Stuck switch valve (b) Stuck fail-safe valve	• Replace oil pump • Repair or replace valve body or its internal components as necessary
Sluggish or stalls in reverse	• Faulty oil pump • Plugged cooler, cooler lines or fittings • Valve body malfunction (a) Stuck switch valve (b) Faulty input shaft or seal ring	• Replace oil pump as necessary • Flush or replace cooler and flush lines and fittings • Repair or replace valve body or its internal components as necessary
Loud chatter during lockup engagement (cold)	• Faulty torque converter • Failed locking clutch • Leaking turbine hub seal	• Replace torque converter • Replace torque converter • Replace torque converter
Vibration or shudder during lockup engagement	• Faulty oil pump • Valve body malfunction • Faulty torque converter • Engine needs tune-up	• Repair or replace oil pump as necessary • Repair or replace valve body or its internal components as necessary • Replace torque converter • Tune engine
Vibration after lockup engagement	• Faulty torque converter • Exhaust system strikes underbody • Engine needs tune-up • Throttle linkage misadjusted	• Replace torque converter • Align exhaust system • Tune engine • Adjust throttle linkage

Lockup Torque Converter Service Diagnosis

Problem	Cause	Solution
Vibration when revved in neutral	• Torque converter out of balance	• Replace torque converter
Overheating: oil blows out of dip stick tube or pump seal	• Plugged cooler, cooler lines or fittings • Stuck switch valve	• Flush or replace cooler and flush lines and fittings • Repair switch valve in valve body or replace valve body
Shudder after lockup engagement	• Faulty oil pump • Plugged cooler, cooler lines or fittings • Valve body malfunction • Faulty torque converter • Fail locking clutch • Exhaust system strikes underbody • Engine needs tune-up • Throttle linkage misadjusted	• Replace oil pump • Flush or replace cooler and flush lines and fittings • Repair or replace valve body or its internal components as necessary • Replace torque converter • Replace torque converter • Align exhaust system • Tune engine • Adjust throttle linkage

Transmission Fluid Indications

The appearance and odor of the transmission fluid can give valuable clues to the overall condition of the transmission. Always note the appearance of the fluid when you check the fluid level or change the fluid. Rub a small amount of fluid between your fingers to feel for grit and smell the fluid on the dipstick.

If the fluid appears:	It indicates:
Clear and red colored	• Normal operation
Discolored (extremely dark red or brownish) or smells burned	• Band or clutch pack failure, usually caused by an overheated transmission. Hauling very heavy loads with insufficient power or failure to change the fluid, often result in overheating. Do not confuse this appearance with newer fluids that have a darker red color and a strong odor (though not a burned odor).
Foamy or aerated (light in color and full of bubbles)	• The level is too high (gear train is churning oil) • An internal air leak (air is mixing with the fluid). Have the transmission checked professionally.
Solid residue in the fluid	• Defective bands, clutch pack or bearings. Bits of band material or metal abrasives are clinging to the dipstick. Have the transmission checked professionally.
Varnish coating on the dipstick	• The transmission fluid is overheating

8 SUSPENSION AND STEERING

WHEELS

Wheels

REMOVAL & INSTALLATION

1. If using a lug wrench, loosen the lug nuts before raising the vehicle.
2. Raise the vehicle and support safely.
3. Remove the lug nuts and wheel from the vehicle.

To install:

4. Install the wheel and hand tighten the lug nuts until they are snug.
5. Lower the vehicle and torque the lug nuts to 100 ft. lbs. (136 Nm) for steel wheels and 90 ft. lbs. (122 Nm) for aluminum wheels.

Wheel Lug Studs

REMOVAL & INSTALLATION

Front

1. Raise the vehicle and support safely.
2. Remove the front wheel.
3. Remove the front wheel hub and steering knuckle from the vehicle as outlined in this section.
4. Separate the wheel hub and knuckle using tools KV40101000, ST36230000 and 3-jaw puller.
5. Remove the bolts securing the wheel hub to the rotor (1982–86 vehicles).
6. Drive the lug nut from the hub using a hammer or press.

To install:

7. Install the new lug bolt and draw the into place using the nut and a stack of washers.
8. Install the hub and rotor assembly onto the knuckle using a press.
9. Install the assembly onto the vehicle as outlined in this section.
20. Road test the vehicle.

Rear

DRUM BRAKES

1. Raise the vehicle and support safely.
2. Remove the wheel.
3. Remove the grease cap, cotter pin and axle nut.
4. Remove the brake drum from the vehicle as outlined in this section. Place the drum in a fixture so the force is concentrated on the hub.
5. Drive the lug bolt out of the brake drum.

To install:

6. Draw the lug bolt into the brake drum using the nut and a stack of washers.
7. Install the brake drum onto the vehicle as outlined in section 9.
8. Install the wheel, lower the vehicle and check operation.

REAR DISC BRAKES

1. Raise the vehicle and support safely.
2. Remove the rear wheel.
3. Remove the caliper and brake rotor as outlined in section 9.
4. Remove the wheel lug bolt by tapping through with a hammer if there enough clearance to remove the stud. If not, remove the center bearing cap, nut and bearing.
5. Remove the wheel hub from the vehicle. Drive the lug bolt out with a hammer or press.

To install:

6. Draw the new lug bolt into the hub using the nut and a stack of washers.
7. Install the hub onto the vehicle and torque the bearing nut to 137–188 ft. lbs. (186–255 Nm).
8. Install a new cotter pin, grease cap, rear wheel and lower the vehicle.

FRONT SUSPENSION

The independent front suspension system on all models covered uses MacPherson struts. Each strut combines the function of coil spring and shock absorber. The spindle is mounted to the lower part of the strut which has a single ball joint. No upper suspension arm is required in this design. The spindle and lower suspension transverse link (control arm) are located fore and aft by the tension rods to the front part of the chassis on most models. A cross-chassis sway bar is used on all models.

MacPherson Strut

➧ SEE FIGS. 1–3

REMOVAL & INSTALLATION

1. Raise and support the vehicle on jackstands.
2. Remove the wheel.
3. Detach the brake tube from the strut. Disconnect the ABS wiring from the strut, if so equipped.
4. Support the transverse link with a jackstand.
5. Detach the steering knuckle from the strut.
6. Support the strut and remove the three upper attaching nuts. Remove the strut from the vehicle.

To install:

7. Install the strut assembly on the vehicle and torque the strut-to-body nuts to 23–31 ft. lbs. (32–42 Nm), the piston rod locknut to 43–54 ft. lbs. (58–73 Nm) and the strut-to-knuckle bolts to 72–87 ft. lbs. (98–118 Nm).
9. If brake line was removed, bleed brakes and install the wheel.

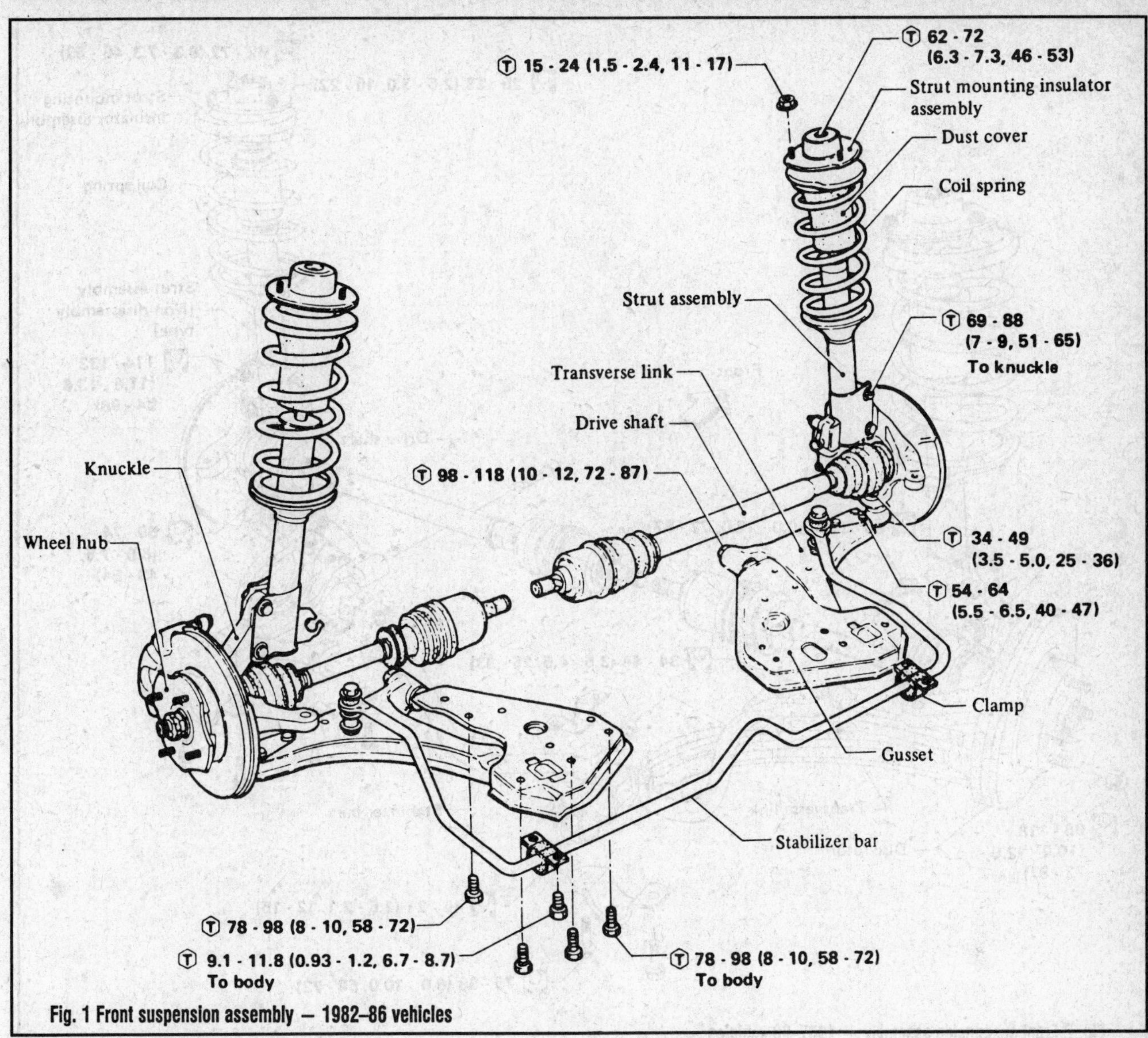
15 - 24 (1.5 - 2.4, 11 - 17)
62 - 72
(6.3 - 7.3, 46 - 53)
Strut mounting insulator assembly
Dust cover
Coil spring
Strut assembly
69 - 88
(7 - 9, 51 - 65)
To knuckle
Transverse link
Drive shaft
98 - 118 (10 - 12, 72 - 87)
Knuckle
Wheel hub
34 - 49
(3.5 - 5.0, 25 - 36)
54 - 64
(5.5 - 6.5, 40 - 47)
Clamp
Gusset
Stabilizer bar
78 - 98 (8 - 10, 58 - 72)
9.1 - 11.8 (0.93 - 1.2, 6.7 - 8.7)
To body
78 - 98 (8 - 10, 58 - 72)
To body

Fig. 1 Front suspension assembly — 1982–86 vehicles

OVERHAUL

➧ SEE FIGS. 4–5, 11–13

✲✲ CAUTION

The coil springs are under considerable tension and can exert enough force to cause serious injury. Disassemble the struts only if the proper tools are available and use extreme caution.

The coil springs on all models must be removed with the aid of a coil spring compressor. If you don't have one, don't try to improvise by using something else: you could risk serious personal injury. The coil spring compressor is Special Tool ST35652001 or variations of that number. Basically, they are all the same tool. These are the recommended compressors, although they are probably not the only spring compressors which will work. Always follow manufacturer's instructions when operating a spring compressor. You can now buy cartridge type shock absorbers for some models: installation procedures are not the same as those given here. In this case, follow the instructions that come with the shock absorbers.

To remove the coil spring, you must first remove the strut assembly from the vehicle. See above for procedures.

1. Secure the strut assembly in a vise.
2. Attach the spring compressor to the spring, leaving the top few coils free.
3. Remove the dust cap from the top of the strut to expose the center nut, if a dust cap is provided.
4. Compress the spring just far enough to permit the strut insulator to be turned by hand. Remove the self-locking center nut.
5. Take out the strut insulator, strut bearing, oil seal, upper spring seat and bound bumper rubber from the top of the strut. Note their sequence of removal and be sure to assemble them in the same order.
6. Remove the spring with the spring compressor still attached.

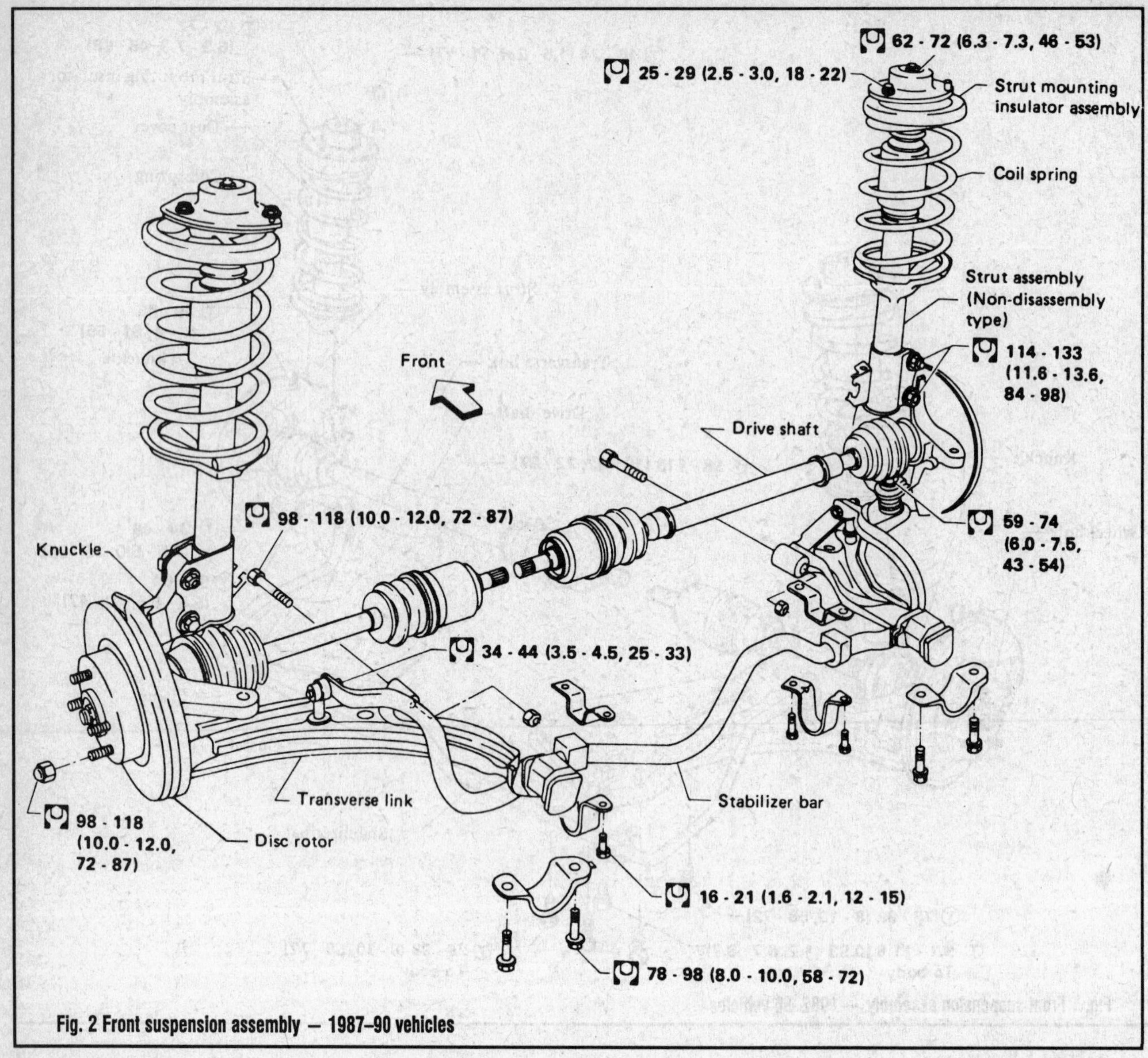
62 - 72 (6.3 - 7.3, 46 - 53)
25 - 29 (2.5 - 3.0, 18 - 22)
Strut mounting insulator assembly
Coil spring
Strut assembly (Non-disassembly type)
114 - 133 (11.6 - 13.6, 84 - 98)
Front
Drive shaft
59 - 74 (6.0 - 7.5, 43 - 54)
98 - 118 (10.0 - 12.0, 72 - 87)
Knuckle
34 - 44 (3.5 - 4.5, 25 - 33)
Transverse link
Stabilizer bar
98 - 118 (10.0 - 12.0, 72 - 87)
Disc rotor
16 - 21 (1.6 - 2.1, 12 - 15)
78 - 98 (8.0 - 10.0, 58 - 72)

Fig. 2 Front suspension assembly — 1987–90 vehicles

To Install:

The strut assembly may be sealed from the factory with a welded piston retainer/seal. If this is the case, the complete hydraulic unit will have to be replaced. These can be purchased from a local parts retailer.

Reassembly the strut assembly and observe the following. Make sure you assemble the unit with the shock absorber piston rod fully extended. When assembling, take care that the rubber spring seats, both top and bottom and the spring are positioned in their grooves before releasing the spring.

7. To remove the shock absorber: Remove the dust cap (if equipped) and push the piston rod down until it bottoms. With the piston in this position, loosen and remove the gland packing shock absorber retainer. This calls for the Special Tool ST35500001, but you should be able to loosen it either with a pipe wrench or by tapping it around with a drift.

➡ **If the gland tube is dirty, clean it before removing it to prevent dirt from contaminating the fluid inside the strut tube.**

8. Remove the O-ring from the top of the piston guide and lift out the piston rod together with the cylinder. Drain all of the fluid from the strut and shock components into a suitable container. Clean all parts.

➡ **The piston rod, piston rod guide and cylinder are a matched set: single parts of this shock assembly should not be exchanged with parts of other assemblies.**

Assembly the shock absorber into the assembly with the following notes:

After installing the cylinder and piston rod assembly (the shock absorber kit) in the outer casing, remove the piston rod guide (if equipped) from the cylinder and pour the correct amount of new fluid into the cylinder and strut outer casing. To find this amount, consult the instructions with your shock absorber kit. The amount of oil should be listed. Use only Genuine Strut Oil or its equivalent.

➡ **It is important that the correct amount of fluid be poured into the strut to assure correct shock absorber damping force.**

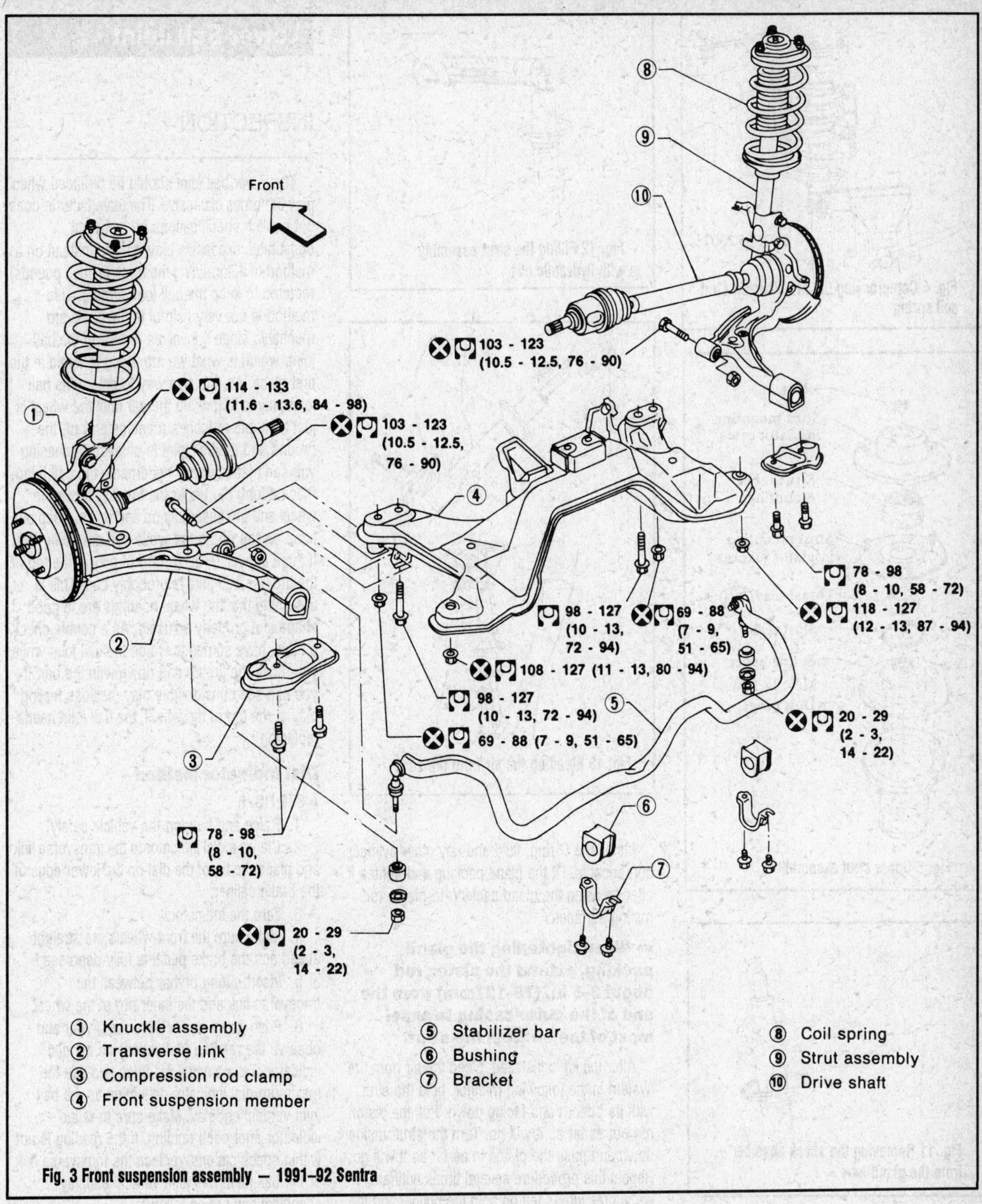

Front
103 - 123
(10.5 - 12.5, 76 - 90)
114 - 133
(11.6 - 13.6, 84 - 98)
103 - 123
(10.5 - 12.5,
76 - 90)
78 - 98
(8 - 10, 58 - 72)
118 - 127
(12 - 13, 87 - 94)
98 - 127
(10 - 13,
72 - 94)
69 - 88
(7 - 9,
51 - 65)
108 - 127 (11 - 13, 80 - 94)
98 - 127
(10 - 13, 72 - 94)
69 - 88 (7 - 9, 51 - 65)
20 - 29
(2 - 3,
14 - 22)
78 - 98
(8 - 10,
58 - 72)
20 - 29
(2 - 3,
14 - 22)
① Knuckle assembly
② Transverse link
③ Compression rod clamp
④ Front suspension member
⑤ Stabilizer bar
⑥ Bushing
⑦ Bracket
⑧ Coil spring
⑨ Strut assembly
⑩ Drive shaft

Fig. 3 Front suspension assembly — 1991–92 Sentra

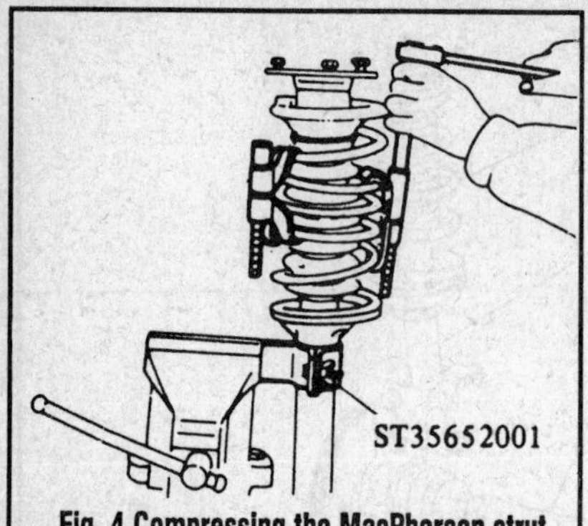
ST35652001
Fig. 4 Compressing the MacPherson strut coil spring

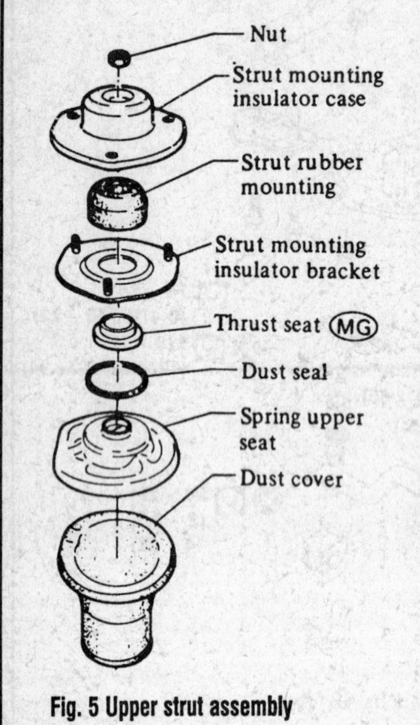
Nut
Strut mounting insulator case
Strut rubber mounting
Strut mounting insulator bracket
Thrust seat MG
Dust seal
Spring upper seat
Dust cover
Fig. 5 Upper strut assembly

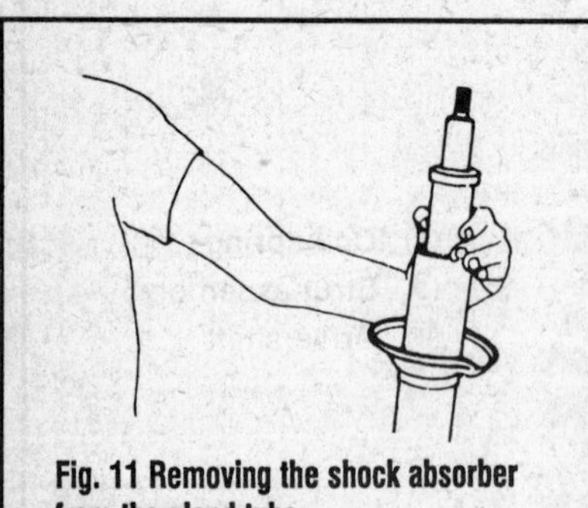
Fig. 11 Removing the shock absorber from the gland tube

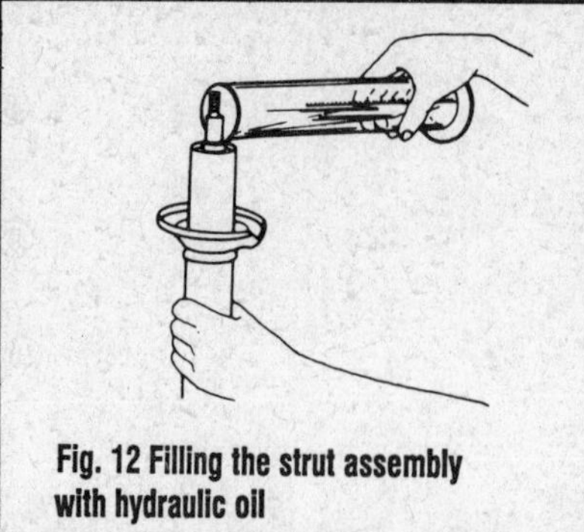
Fig. 12 Filling the strut assembly with hydraulic oil

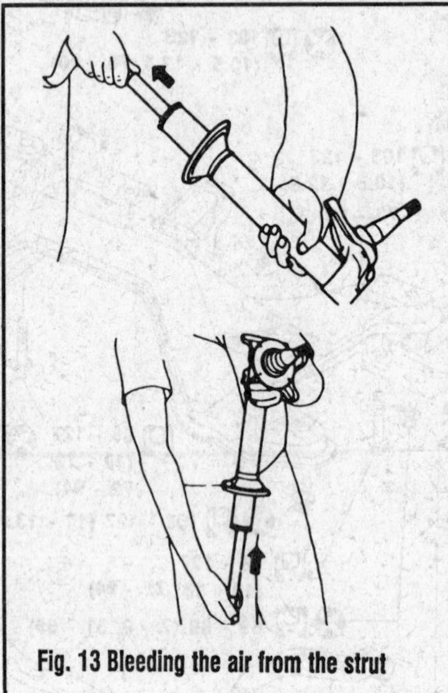
Fig. 13 Bleeding the air from the strut

Install the O-ring, fluid and any other cylinder components. Fit the gland packing and tighten it after greasing the gland packing-to-piston rod mating surfaces.

➡ **When tightening the gland packing, extend the piston rod about 3-5 in. (76–127mm) from the end of the outer casing to expel most of the air from the strut.**

After the kit is installed, bleed the air from the system in the following manner: hold the strut with its bottom end facing down. Pull the piston rod out as far as it will go. Turn the strut upside down and push the piston in as far as it will go. Repeat this procedure several times until an equal pressure is felt on both the pullout and the push in strokes of the piston rods. The remaining assembly is the reverse of disassembly.

Lower Ball Joint

INSPECTION

The lower ball joint should be replaced when play becomes excessive. The manufacturer does not publish specifications on just what constitutes excessive play, relying instead on a method of determining the force (in inch pounds) required to keep the ball joint turning. This method is not very helpful to the backyard mechanic since it involves removing the ball joint, which is what we are trying to avoid in the first place. An effective way to determine ball joint play is to jack up the car until the wheel is just a couple of inches (centimeters) off the ground and the ball joint is unloaded (meaning you can't jack directly underneath the ball joint). Place a long bar under the tire and move the wheel and tire assembly up and down. Keep one hand on top of the tire while you are doing this. If there is over $^1/_4$ in. (6mm) of play at the top of the tire, the ball joint is probably bad. This is assuming that the wheel bearings are in good shape and properly adjusted. As a double check on this, have someone watch the ball joint while you move the tire up and down with the bar. If you can see considerable play, besides feeling play at the top of the wheel, the ball joint needs replacing.

Dial Indicator Method

➧ SEE FIG. 6

1. Raise and support the vehicle safely.
2. Clamp a dial indicator to the transverse link and place the tip of the dial on the lower edge of the brake caliper.
3. Zero the indicator.
4. Make sure the front wheels are straight ahead and the brake pedal is fully depressed.
5. Insert a long prybar between the transverse link and the inner rim of the wheel.
6. Push down and release the prybar and observe the reading (deflection) on the dial indicator. Take several readings and use the maximum dial indicator deflection as the ball joint vertical endplay. Make sure to **0** the indicator after each reading. If the reading is not within specifications, replace the transverse link or the ball joint. Ball joint vertical endplay specifications are as follows:

• Pulsar 1983–88 — 0.098 in. (2.5mm) or less 1989–90 — 0 in. (0mm)

• Sentra 1982–92 — 0 in. (0mm)

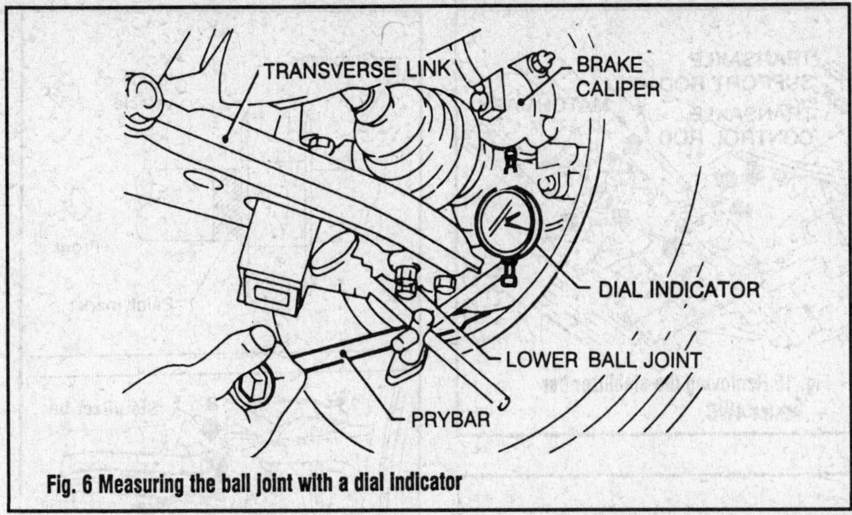
TRANSVERSE LINK
BRAKE
CALIPER
DIAL INDICATOR
LOWER BALL JOINT
PRYBAR
Fig. 6 Measuring the ball joint with a dial indicator

REMOVAL & INSTALLATION

➡ On most late model vehicles, the transverse link (lower control arm) must be removed and then the ball joint must be pressed out. The ball joint should be greased every 30,000 miles (48,300km). There is a plugged hole in the bottom of the joint for installation of a grease fitting.

1. Refer to the Drive Axle, Removal and Installation procedures, in Section 7 and remove the drive axle.
2. Remove the ball joint-to-control arm nut. Using the Ball Joint Remover tool HT72520000, separate the ball joint from the control arm.
3. Remove the other ball joint bolts from the control arm and the ball joint from the vehicle.

To install:

4. Install the ball joint in the control arm and tighten the ball stud attaching nut (from ball joint-to-steering knuckle) to 40–51 ft. lbs. (54–69 Nm) and the ball joint to transverse link bolts to 40–47 ft. lbs. (54–64 Nm).
5. Install the drive axle.

Lower Control Arm (Transverse Link)

➧ SEE FIGS. 7–10, 14

REMOVAL & INSTALLATION

1983–86 Vehicles

➡ Always use a new nut when installing the ball joint to the control arm.

1. Raise and support the vehicle on jackstands.
2. Remove the wheel.
3. Remove the lower ball joint bolts from the control arm.

➡ If equipped with a stabilizer bar, disconnect it from the control arm.

4. Remove the control arm-to-body bolts.
5. Remove the gusset.
6. Remove the control arm from the vehicle.

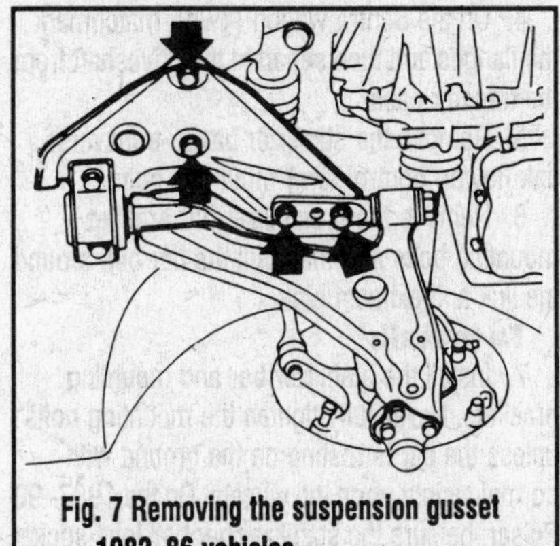
Fig. 7 Removing the suspension gusset – 1982–86 vehicles

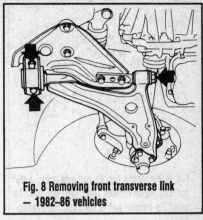

Fig. 8 Removing front transverse link – 1982–86 vehicles

To install:

7. Install the lower control arm on the vehicle and tighten the gusset-to-body bolts to 65–87 ft. lbs. (88–118 Nm); the control arm securing nut to 72–87 ft. lbs. (98–118 Nm); the lower ball joint-to-control arm nuts to 40–47 ft. lbs. (54–64 Nm) and the stabilizer bar-to-control arm to 80–100 inch lbs. (9.0–11.3 Nm) (2wd Sentra and Pulsar) or 12–16 ft. lbs. (16–21 Nm) (4wd Sentra).
8. Reconnect the stabilizer if so equipped to the control arm.
9. Install the wheel.

➡ When installing the link, tighten the nut securing the link spindle to the gusset. Final tightening should be made with the weight of the car on the wheels.

1987–92 Vehicles

➡ A ball joint removal tool will be required for this operation.

1. Raise the vehicle and support it with safety stands. Remove the wheel.
2. Remove the wheel bearing locknut.
3. Remove the tie rod ball joint with a puller.
4. Remove the lower strut-to-knuckle mounting bolts and separate the strut from the knuckle.
5. Separate the outer end of the halfshaft from the steering knuckle by carefully tapping it with a rubber mallet.

➡ Be sure to cover the CV-joints with a shop rag.

6. Using a ball joint removal tool, separate the lower ball joint stud from the steering knuckle.
7. Unbolt and remove the transverse link and ball joint as an assembly.

To install:

8. Install the lower control arm to the vehicle.
9. Reconnect the ball joint and halfshaft.
10. Connect the strut to the knuckle.
11. Install the tie rod ball joint.

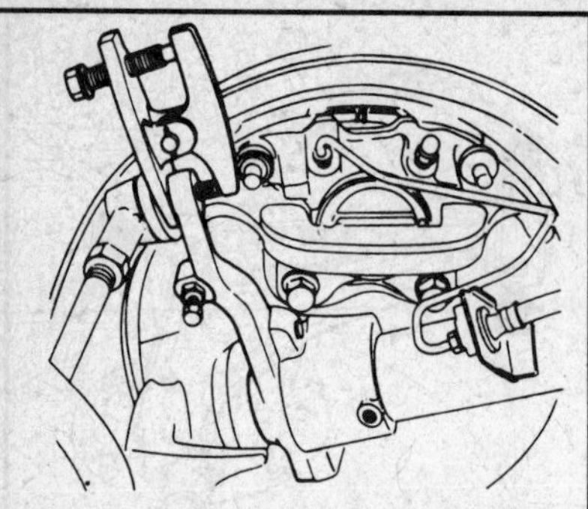
Fig. 9 Removing the tie rod end using a tie rod separator Forked removing tool may be used Be careful not to damage the grease boot

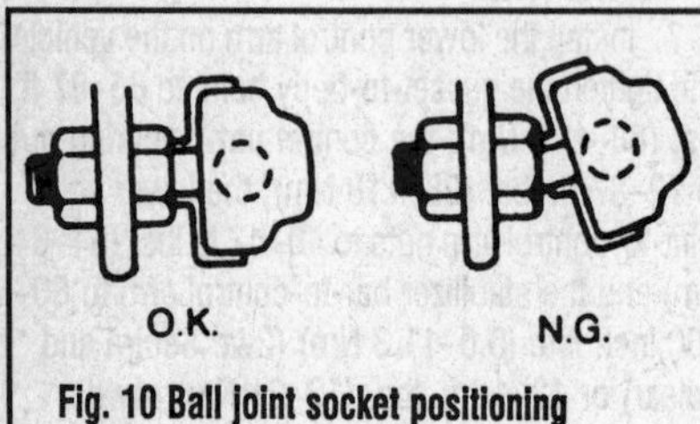
O.K.
N.G.
Fig. 10 Ball joint socket positioning

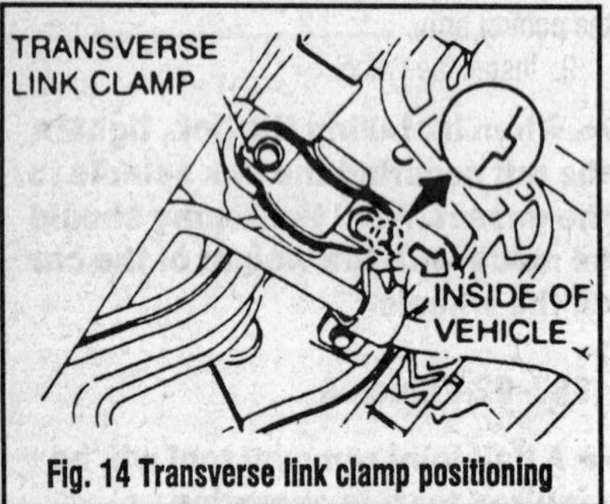
TRANSVERSE LINK CLAMP
INSIDE OF VEHICLE
Fig. 14 Transverse link clamp positioning

12. Tighten the wheel bearing lock nut.

13. Install the wheel and make sure the tab on the transverse link clamp is pointing in the proper direction. Final tightening of all bolts should take place with the weight of the vehicle on the wheels. Check wheel alignment.

Stabilizer Bar

➧ SEE FIGS. 15–17

REMOVAL & INSTALLATION

1. Disconnect the parking brake cable at the equalizer on the Sentra wagon.

2. On the Sentra wagon (4wd), remove the mounting nuts for the transaxle support rod and the transaxle control rod.

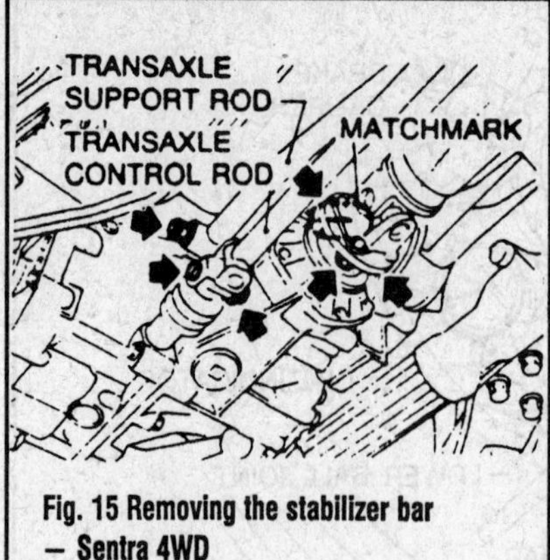
TRANSAXLE SUPPORT ROD
TRANSAXLE CONTROL ROD
MATCHMARK
Fig. 15 Removing the stabilizer bar – Sentra 4WD

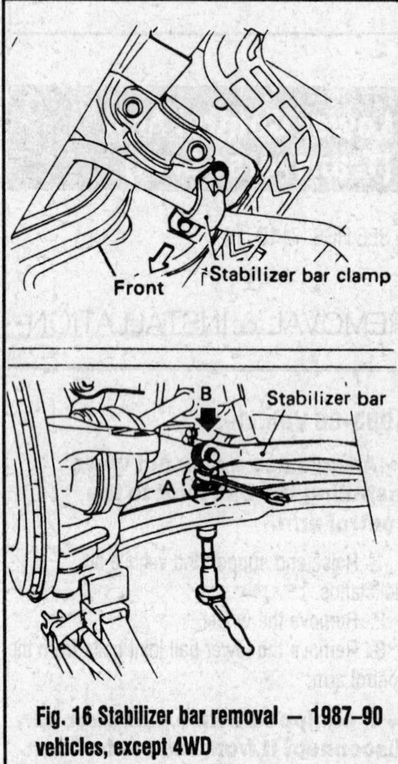
Front
Stabilizer bar clamp
B
Stabilizer bar
A
Fig. 16 Stabilizer bar removal – 1987–90 vehicles, except 4WD

3. Disconnect the front exhaust pipe at the manifold and position it out of the way.

4. On the Sentra wagon (4wd), matchmark the flanges and then separate the driveshaft from the transfer case.

5. Remove the stabilizer bar-to-transverse link (lower, control arm) mounting bolts.

6. Remove the 4 stabilizer bar bracket mounting bolts and then pull the bar out, around the link and exhaust pipe.

To Install:

7. Install the stabilizer bar and mounting brackets. Never fully tighten the mounting bolts unless the car is resting on the ground with normal weight upon the wheels. On the 1987–90 Pulsar, be sure the stabilizer bar ball joint socket is properly positioned.

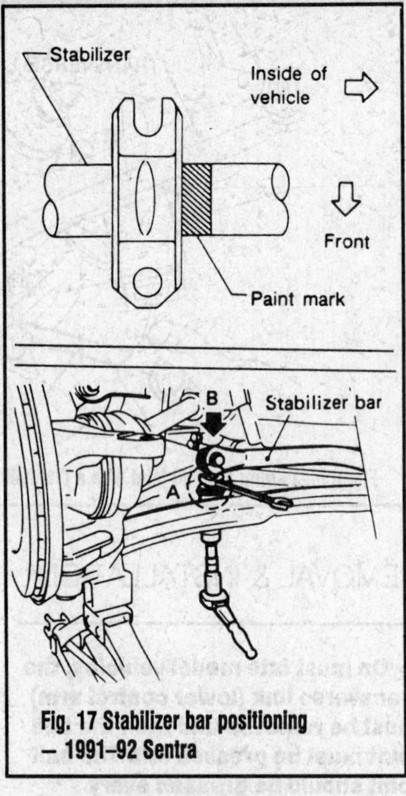
Stabilizer
Inside of vehicle
Front
Paint mark
B
Stabilizer bar
A
Fig. 17 Stabilizer bar positioning – 1991–92 Sentra

➡ When installing the stabilizer bar, make sure that the paint mark and clamp face is in their correct directions (1987–92 vehicles).

8. Install the driveshaft to the transfer case if it was removed.

9. Reconnect the front exhaust pipe at the manifold.

10. Connect the parking brake cables and install any other bolts that were removed.

11. Final tightening of all bolts should take place with the weight of the vehicle on the wheels.

Front Axle Hub, Knuckle And Bearing

➧ SEE FIGS. 18–25

REMOVAL & INSTALLATION

1982–90 Vehicles

1. Raise and support the front of the vehicle safely and remove the wheels.

2. Remove wheel bearing lock nut.

3. Remove brake clip assembly. Make sure not to twist the brake hose.

4. Remove tie rod ball joint.

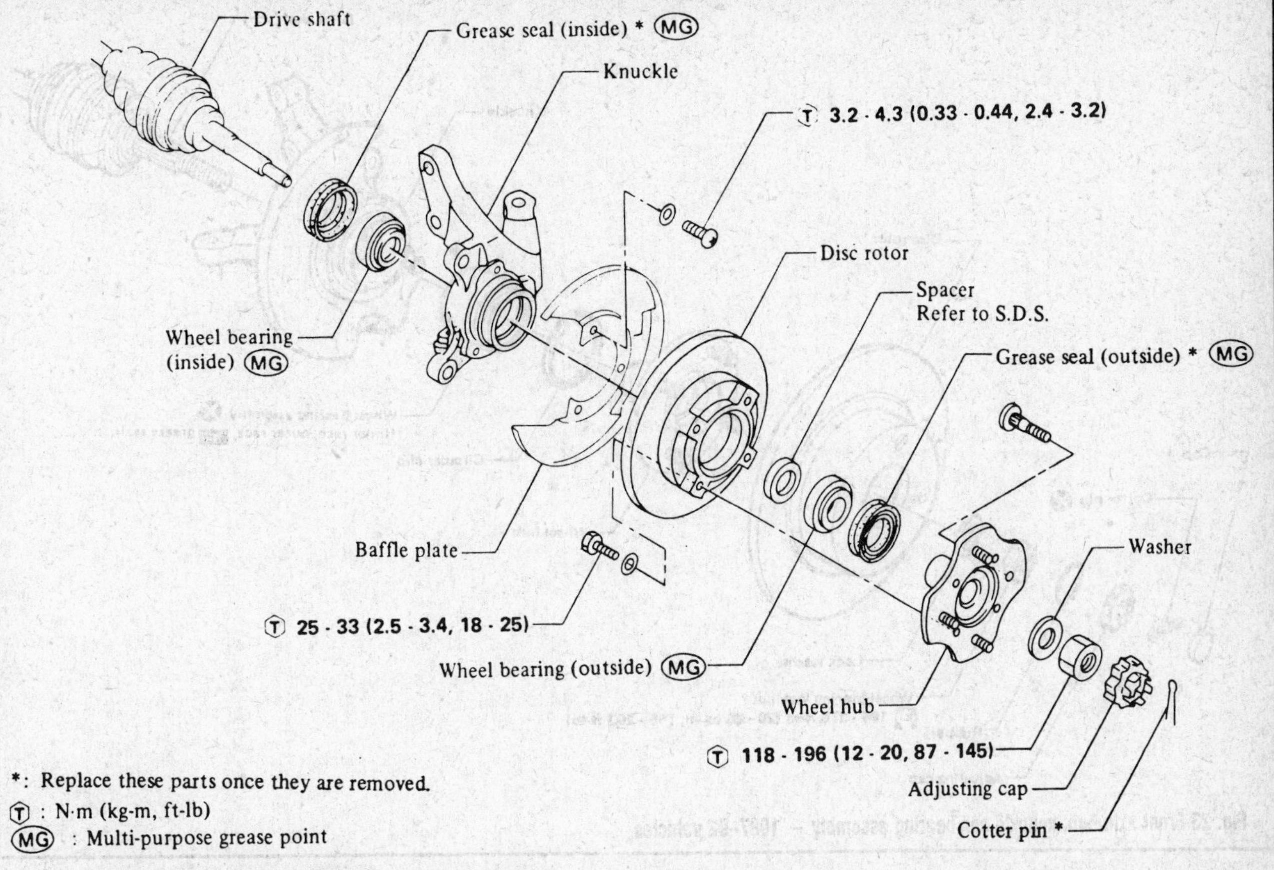

Drive shaft
Grease seal (inside) * (MG)
Knuckle
(T) 3.2 - 4.3 (0.33 - 0.44, 2.4 - 3.2)
Disc rotor
Spacer
Refer to S.D.S.
Grease seal (outside) * (MG)
Wheel bearing (inside) (MG)
Baffle plate
Washer
(T) 25 - 33 (2.5 - 3.4, 18 - 25)
Wheel bearing (outside) (MG)
Wheel hub
(T) 118 - 196 (12 - 20, 87 - 145)
Adjusting cap
Cotter pin *

*: Replace these parts once they are removed.
(T) : N·m (kg-m, ft-lb)
(MG) : Multi-purpose grease point

Fig. 18 Front hub and knuckle assembly — 1982–86 vehicles

➡ Cover axle boots with waste cloth or equivalent so as not to damage them when removing driveshaft. Make a matching mark on strut housing and adjusting pin before removing them.

5. Separate halfshaft from the knuckle by slightly tapping it.
6. Mark and remove the strut mounting bolts.
7. Remove lower ball joint from knuckle.
8. Remove knuckle from lower control arm.

➡ To replace the wheel bearings and races they must be pressed in and out of the knuckle assembly. To pack the wheel bearings they will have to be removed from the knuckle assembly.

9. Install the knuckle to the lower control arm and connect the ball joint.
10. Connect the knuckle to the strut and to the halfshaft.
11. Install the tie rod ball joint.
12. Install the brake caliper assembly.
13. Install the wheel bearing lock nut and torque hub nut to 145–203 ft. lbs. (197–276 Nm).
14. Install the front wheels.

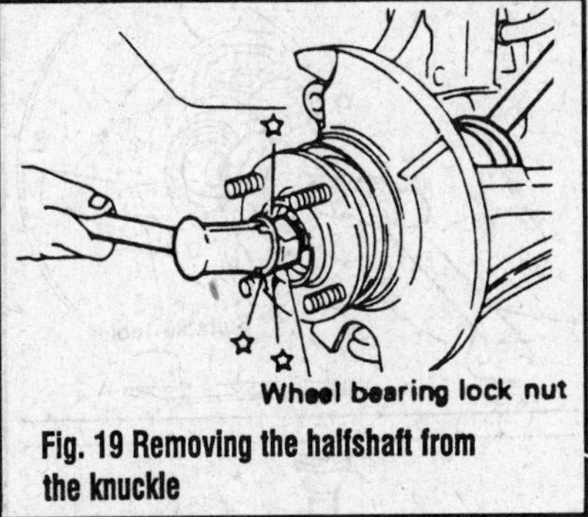
Wheel bearing lock nut

Fig. 19 Removing the halfshaft from the knuckle

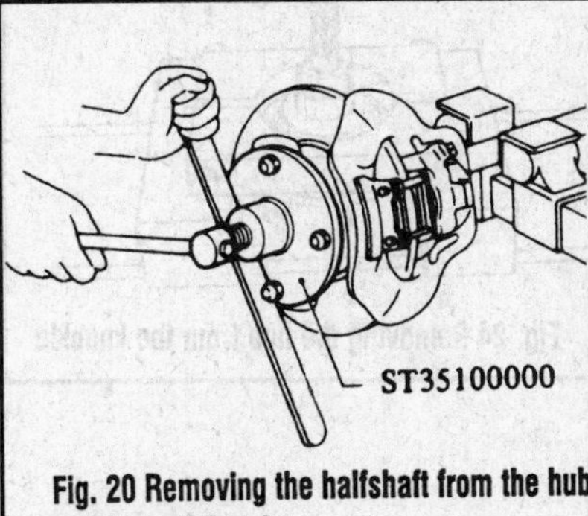
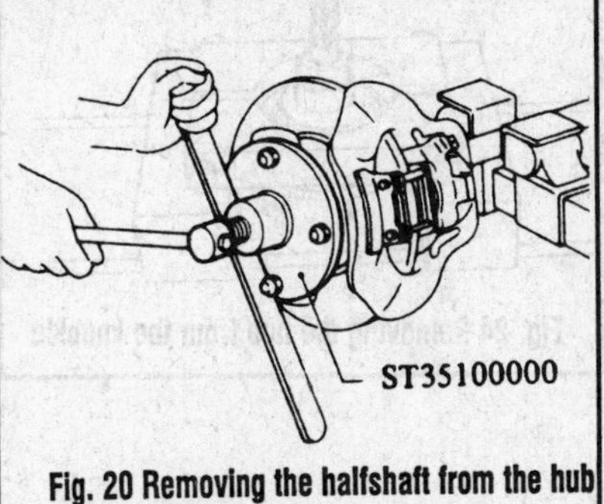
ST35100000
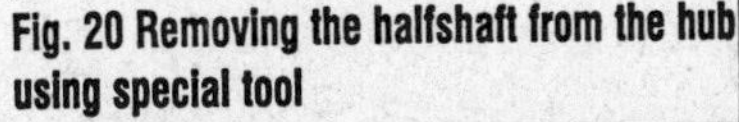

Fig. 20 Removing the halfshaft from the hub using special tool

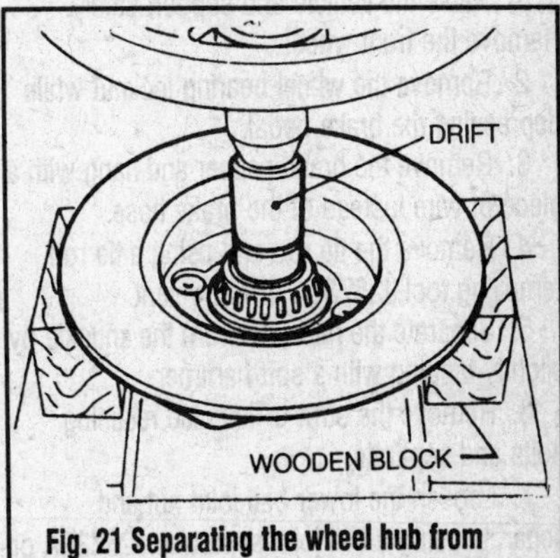
DRIFT
WOODEN BLOCK

Fig. 21 Separating the wheel hub from the disc using a press — 1982–86 vehicles

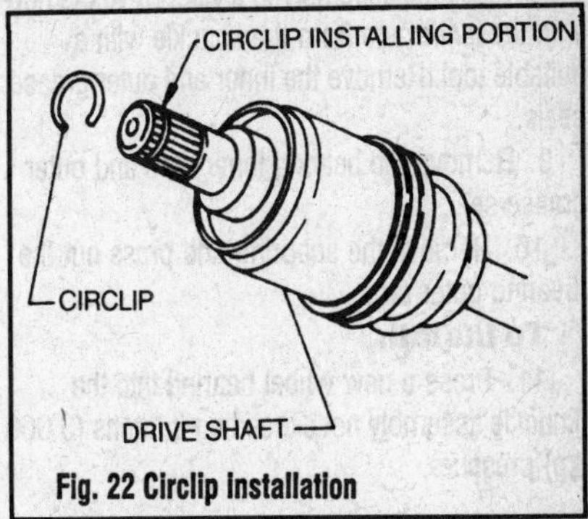
CIRCLIP INSTALLING PORTION
CIRCLIP
DRIVE SHAFT

Fig. 22 Circlip installation

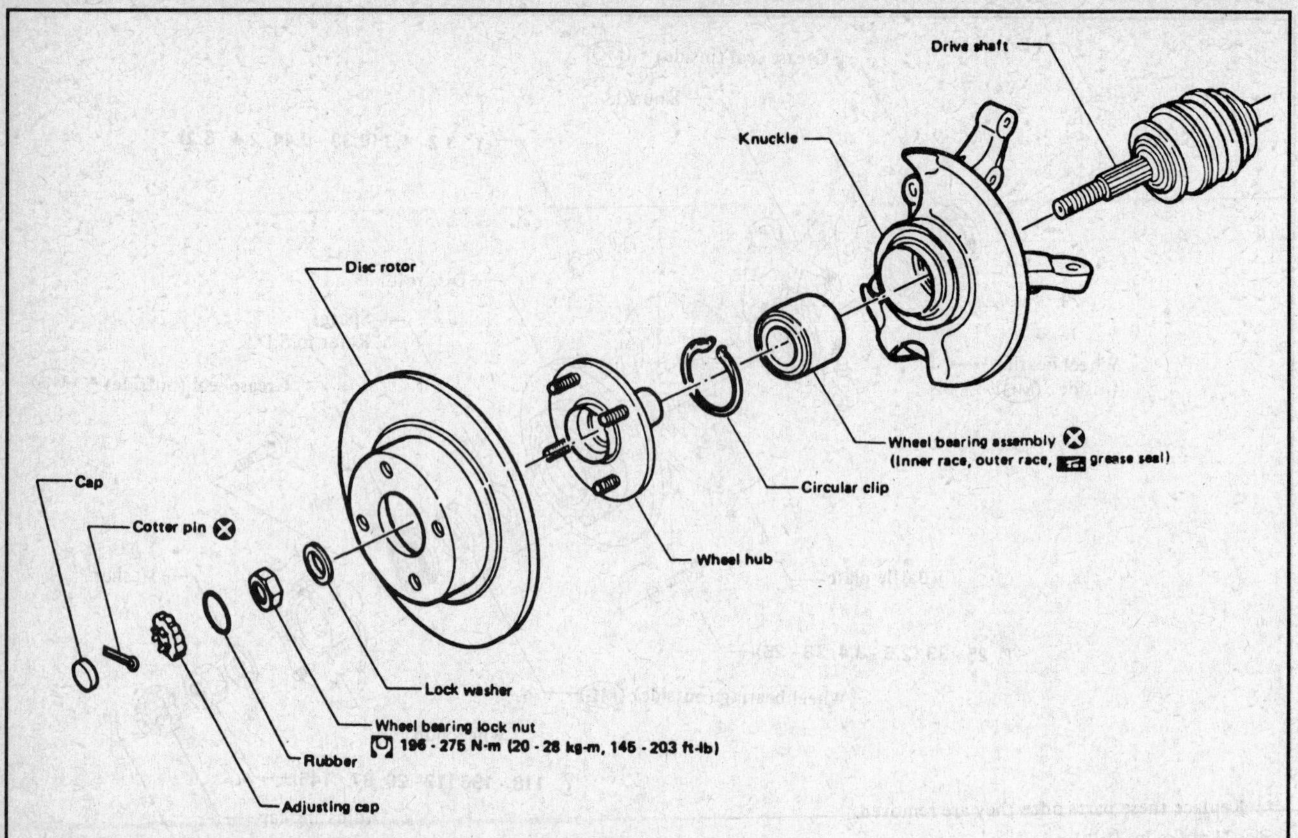

Fig. 23 Front axle hub, knuckle and bearing assembly — 1987–92 vehicles

1991–92 Sentra

1. Raise the vehicle and support safely. Remove the front wheel.
2. Remove the wheel bearing locknut while depressing the brake pedal.
3. Remove the brake caliper and hang with a piece of wire instead of the brake hose.
4. Remove the tie rod end using a tie rod removing tool J25730A or equivalent.
5. Separate the halfshaft from the knuckle by slightly tapping with a soft hammer.
6. Remove the strut-to-knuckle retaining bolts and separate.
7. Loosen the lower ball joint nut and separate using a ball joint separator J25730A or equivalent.
8. Place the assembly in a vise. Drive the hub with the inner race from the knuckle with a suitable tool. Remove the inner and outer grease seals.
9. Remove the bearing inner race and outer grease seal.
10. Remove the snapring and press out the bearing outer race.

To Install:

11. Press a new wheel bearing into the knuckle assembly not exceeding 3.3 tons (3,000 kg) pressure.

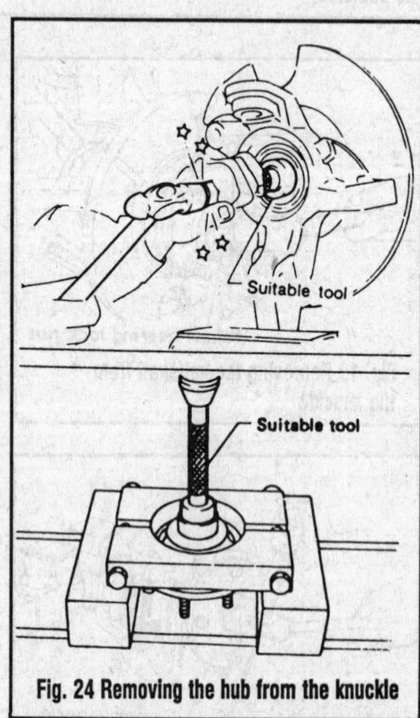
Suitable tool
Suitable tool
Fig. 24 Removing the hub from the knuckle

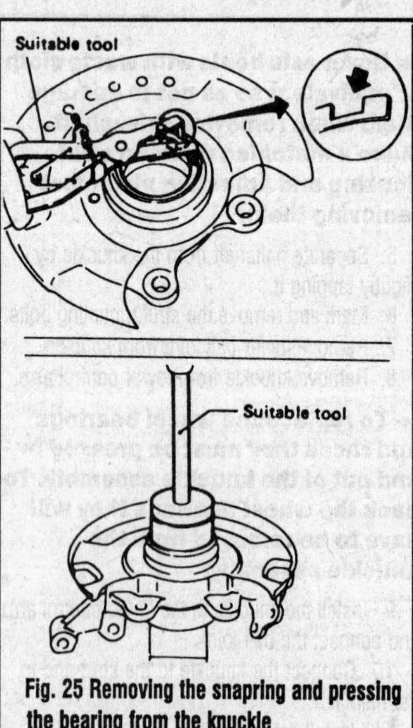
Suitable tool
Suitable tool
Fig. 25 Removing the snapring and pressing the bearing from the knuckle

12. Install the snapring and pack the grease seals with chassis grease.
13. Install the inner and outer grease seals.
14. Press the wheel hub into the knuckle not exceeding 3.3 tons (3,000 kg) pressure.
15. Check bearing operation and force the assembly into the knuckle to 3.9-5.5 tons (7,800–5,000 kg) pressure.
16. Make sure the bearings rotate freely.
17. Install the knuckle and wheel hub. Torque the wheel bearing locknut to 145-203 ft. lbs. (196–275 Nm).
18. Install the lower ball joint and torque the nut to 43–54 ft. lbs. (59–74 Nm).
19. Install the strut bolts and torque to 84–98 ft. lbs. (114–133 Nm).
20. Install the front wheels and lower the vehicle.

Front End Alignment

➧ SEE FIGS. 25–28

CASTER AND CAMBER

Caster is the tilt of the upper end of the kingpin or the upper ball joint, which results in a slight tilt of the steering axis forward or backward. Rearward tilt is referred to as a positive caster, while forward tilt is referred to as negative caster.

Camber is the inward or outward tilt from the vertical (measured in degrees) of the front wheels at the top. An outward tilt gives the wheel positive camber. Proper camber is critical to assure even tire wear.

Since caster and camber are adjusted traditionally by adding or subtracting shims behind the upper control arms. The vehicles covered in this guide have replaced the upper control arm with the MacPherson strut, the only way to adjust caster and camber is to replace bent or worn parts of the front suspension.

➡ **Camber is adjustable on the 1987–88 Pulsar. Camber is adjusted by the strut-to-knuckle bolts. The upper bolt has an eccentric washer at each end. As the bolt is rotated, the knuckle moves in or out.**

TOE

Toe is the amount, measure in a fraction of an inch (millimeters), that the wheels are closer together at one end than the other. Toe-in means that the front wheels are closer together at the front than the rear; toe-out means the rears are closer than the front. The vehicles are adjusted to have a slight amount of toe-in. Toe-in is adjusted by turning the tie rod, which has a right hand thread on one end and a left hand thread on the other.

SUSPENSION HEIGHT

Suspension height is adjusted by replacing the springs.

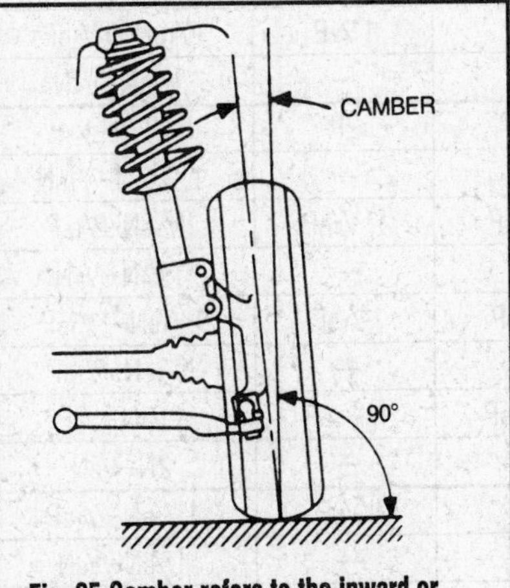
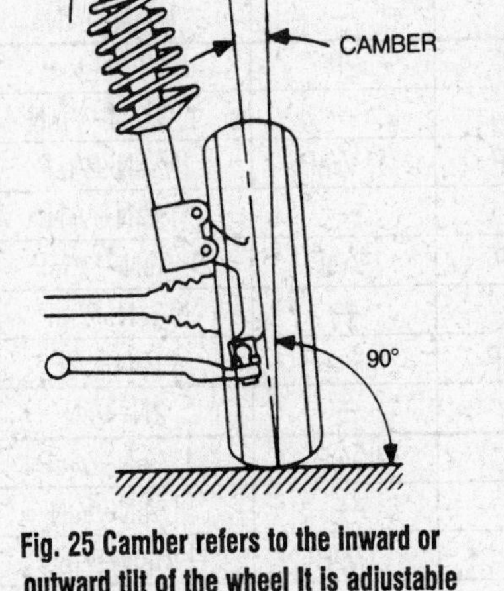
CAMBER
90°

Fig. 25 Camber refers to the inward or outward tilt of the wheel it is adjustable on the 1987–89 vehicles

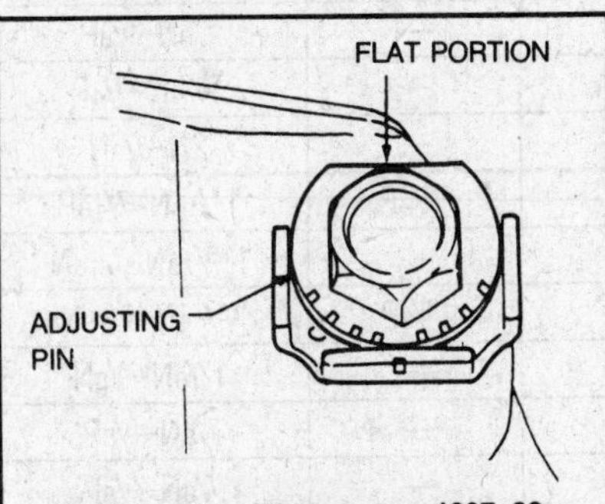
FLAT PORTION
ADJUSTING PIN

Fig. 26 Camber adjustment on 1987–89 vehicles is performed by turning the adjusting pin

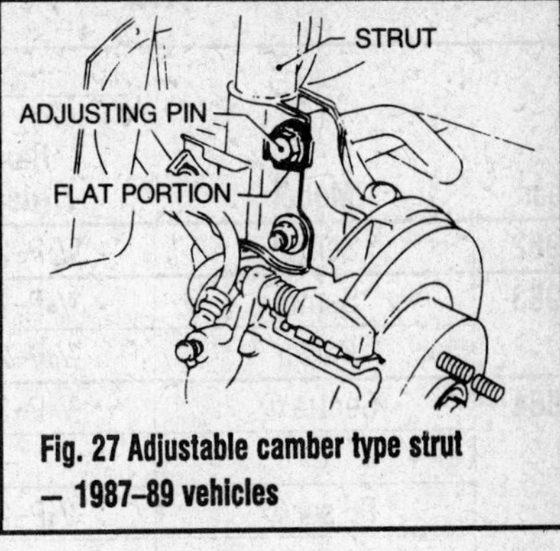
STRUT
ADJUSTING PIN
FLAT PORTION

Fig. 27 Adjustable camber type strut — 1987–89 vehicles

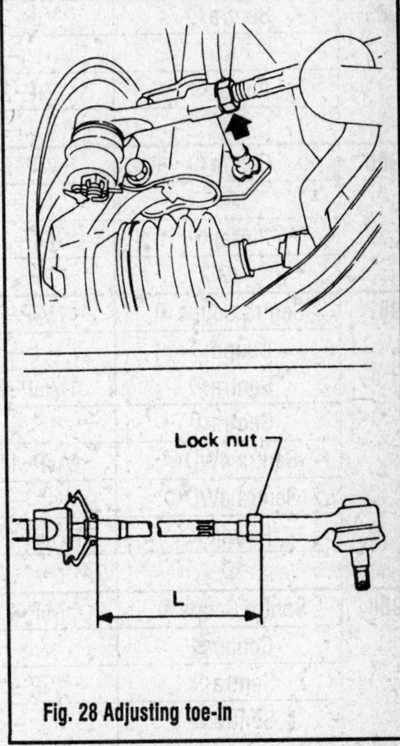
Lock nut
L

Fig. 28 Adjusting toe-in

WHEEL ALIGNMENT

Year	Model	Caster Range (deg.)	Caster Preferred Setting (deg.)	Camber Range (deg.)	Camber Preferred Setting (deg.)	Toe-in (in.)	Steering Axis Inclination (deg.)
1982	Sentra	3/4P–2 1/4P	1 1/2P	9/16N–1 1/16P	1/4P	1/8–3/16	12 15/16
1983	Sentra	3/4P–2 1/4P	1 1/2P	9/16N–1 1/16P	1/4P	1/8–3/16	12 15/16
	Pulsar	3/4P–2 1/4P	1 1/2P	9/16N–1 1/16P	1/4P	0–5/64	12 3/4
1984	Sentra ①	3/4P–2 1/4P	1 1/2P	7/16N–1 1/16P	1/4P	1/16–3/32	12 3/16
	②		—	1 3/4N–1/4N	1N	1/8N–1/8P	—
	Pulsar ①	3/4P–2 1/4P	1 1/2P	7/16N–1 1/16P	1/4P	1/8–3/16	12 15/16
	②	—	—	1 3/4N–1/4N	1N	1/32N–1/32P	—
1985	Sentra ①	3/4P–2 1/4P	1 1/2P	7/16N–1 1/16P	1/4P	1/8–3/16	12 15/16
	②	—	—	1 3/4N–1/4N	1N	1/4N–1/4P	—
	Pulsar ①	3/4P–2 1/4P	1 1/2P	7/16N–1 1/16P	1/4P	1/8–3/16	12 15/16
	②	—	—	1 3/4N–1/4N	1N	1/4N–1/4P	—
1986	Sentra ①	3/4P–2 1/4P	1 1/2P	7/16N–1 1/16P	1/4P	1/8–3/16	12 15/16
	②	—	—	1 3/4N–1/4N	1N	1/4N–1/4P	—
	Pulsar ①	3/4P–2 1/4P	1 1/2P	7/16N–1 1/16P	1/4P	1/8–3/16	12 15/16
	②	—	—	1 3/4N–1/4N	1N	1/4N–1/4P	—
1987	Sentra Coupe ①	1 1/4P–2 3/4P	2P	1 1/16N–1/4P	7/16N	1/32N–1/32P	14 1/4
	Coupe ②	—	—	1 15/16N–7/16N	1 3/16N	1/32–3/16	—
	Sentra ①	1 1/16P–2 9/16P	1 13/16P	15/16N–9/16P	3/16N	1/32N–1/32P	14
	Sentra ②	—	—	1 3/4N–1/4N	1N	1/32–3/16	—
	Sentra 4WD ①	3/16P–1 11/16P	15/16P	13/16N–11/16P	1/16N	1/32N–1/16P	13 9/16
	Sentra 4WD ②	—	—	15/16N–9/16P	3/16N	0–3/32	—
	Pulsar ①	1 3/16P–2 11/16P	1 15/16P	1 1/4N–1/4P	1/2N	1/32N–1/32P	14 7/16
	②	—	—	2N–1/2N	1 1/4N	1/16N–3/32P	—
1988	Sentra Coupe ①	7/8P–2 3/8P	1 5/8P	1 1/16N–7/16P	—	1/32N–1/16P	14 3/4
	Coupe ②	—	—	1 7/8N–3/8N	—	0–3/16P	—
	Sentra ①	3/4P–2 1/4P	1 1/2P	15/16N–9/16N	—	1/32N–1/16P	14 1/2
	Sentra ②	—	—	1 7/8N–3/8N	—	0–3/16P	—
	Sentra 4WD ①	1/8P–1 5/8P	—	7/8N–5/8P	—	1/32N–1/32P	13 15/16
	4WD ②	—	—	7/8N–5/8P	—	0–3/16P	—
	Pulsar ①	1 3/16P–2 11/16	—	1 1/4N–1/4P	—	1/16N–1/16P	14 15/16
	②	—	—	2N–1/2N	—	1/16N–3/32P	—
1989	Sentra Coupe ①	7/8P–2 3/8P	1 5/8P	1 1/16N–7/16P	—	1/32N–1/16P	14 3/4
	Coupe ②	—	—	1 15/16N–7/16N	—	1/32–1/8P	—
	Sentra ①	3/4P–2 1/4P	1 1/2P	15/16N–9/16N	—	1/32N–1/16P	14 1/2
	Sentra ②	—	—	1 7/8N–3/8N	—	0–3/16P	—
	Sentra 4WD ①	1/8P–1 5/8P	—	7/8N–5/8P	—	1/32N–1/32P	13 15/16
	4WD ②	—	—	7/8N–5/8P	—	0–3/16P	—
	Pulsar ①	1 3/16P–2 11/16	—	1 1/4N–1/4P	—	1/16N–1/16P	14 13/16
	②	—	—	2N–1/2N	—	1/16N–3/32P	—

WHEEL ALIGNMENT

Year	Model	Caster Range (deg.)	Caster Preferred Setting (deg.)	Camber Range (deg.)	Camber Preferred Setting (deg.)	Toe-in (in.)	Steering Axis Inclination (deg.)
1990	Sentra Coupe ①	7/8P–2 3/8P	1 5/8P	1 1/16N–7/16P	—	1/32N–1/16P	14 3/4
	Coupe ②	—	—	2N–1/2N	—	1/16N–3/32P	—
	Sentra ①	3/4P–2 1/4P	1 1/2P	15/16N–9/16N	—	1/32N–1/16P	14 1/2
	Sentra ②	—	—	1 7/8N–3/8N	—	0–3/16P	—
	Sentra 4WD ①	1/8P–1 5/8P	—	7/8N–5/8P	—	1/32N–1/32P	13 15/16
	4WD ②	—	—	7/8N–5/8P	—	0–3/16P	—
	Pulsar ①	1 3/16P–2 11/16	—	1 1/4N–1/4P	—	1/16N–1/16P	14 13/16
	②	—	—	2N–1/2N	—	1/16N–3/32P	—
1991	Sentra ①	11/16P–2 3/16P	—	1N–1/2P	—	1/32–1/8	14
	②	—	—	1 11/16N–3/16N	—	1/32–1/8	—
	NX Coupe ①	1 1/8P–2 9/16P	—	1N–1/2P	—	1/32–1/8	14
	NX Coupe ②	—	—	1 15/16N–7/16P	—	1/32–1/8	—
1992	Sentra ①	11/16P–2 3/16P	—	1N–1/2P	—	1/32–1/8	14
	②	—	—	1 11/16N–3/16N	—	1/32–1/8	—
	NX Coupe ①	1 1/8P–2 9/16P	—	1N–1/2P	—	1/32–1/8	14
	NX Coupe ②	—	—	1 15/16N–7/16P	—	1/32–1/8	—

① Front suspension
② Rear suspension

REAR SUSPENSION

Coil Springs

➧ SEE FIG. 29

REMOVAL & INSTALLATION

1982–86 Vehicles

1. Raise and support the rear of the vehicle with jackstands and remove the wheel.
2. Support the lower end of the rear arm with a jackstand.
3. Remove the lower end bolt from the shock absorber.
4. Slowly, lower the jack and remove the coil spring.
5. To install, reverse the removal procedures. Torque the shock absorber's lower bolt to 51–65 ft. lbs. (69–88 Nm).

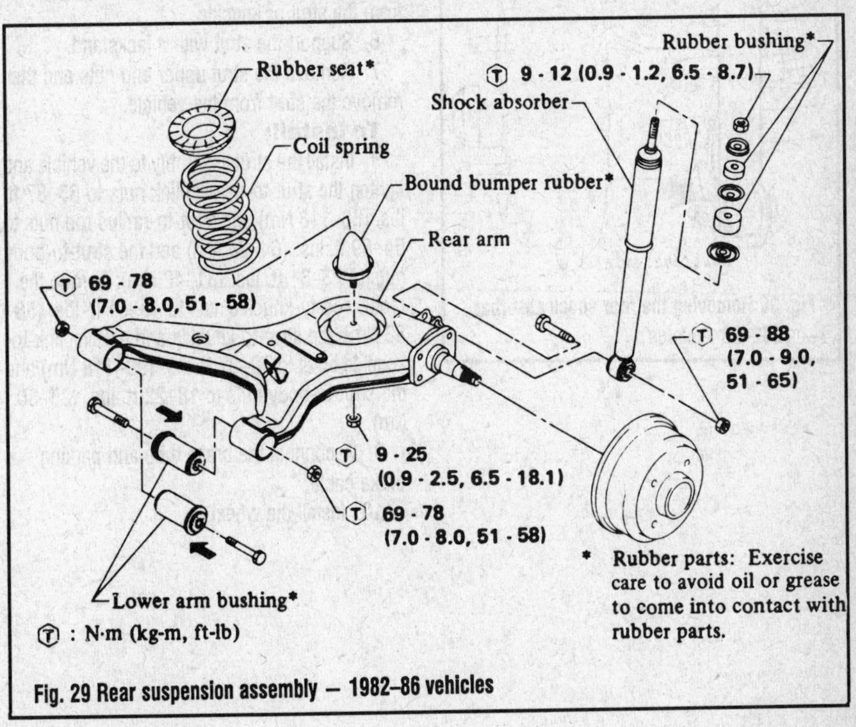
Rubber seat*
Coil spring
Bound bumper rubber*
Rear arm
Shock absorber
Rubber bushing*
Ⓣ 9 - 12 (0.9 - 1.2, 6.5 - 8.7)
Ⓣ 69 - 78 (7.0 - 8.0, 51 - 58)
Ⓣ 69 - 88 (7.0 - 9.0, 51 - 65)
Ⓣ 9 - 25 (0.9 - 2.5, 6.5 - 18.1)
Ⓣ 69 - 78 (7.0 - 8.0, 51 - 58)
Lower arm bushing*
Ⓣ : N·m (kg-m, ft-lb)
* Rubber parts: Exercise care to avoid oil or grease to come into contact with rubber parts.

Fig. 29 Rear suspension assembly — 1982–86 vehicles

Shock Absorber

SEE FIG. 30

REMOVAL & INSTALLATION

1982-86 Vehicles

1. Raise and support the rear of the vehicle on jackstands.
2. Remove the upper nut and the lower mounting bolt form the shock absorber.
3. Remove the shock absorber from the vehicle.
4. To install, reverse the removal procedures. Torque the upper shock absorber nut to 78–104 inch lbs. (8.8–11.8 Nm) and the lower shock absorber bolt to 51–65 ft. lbs. (69–88 Nm).

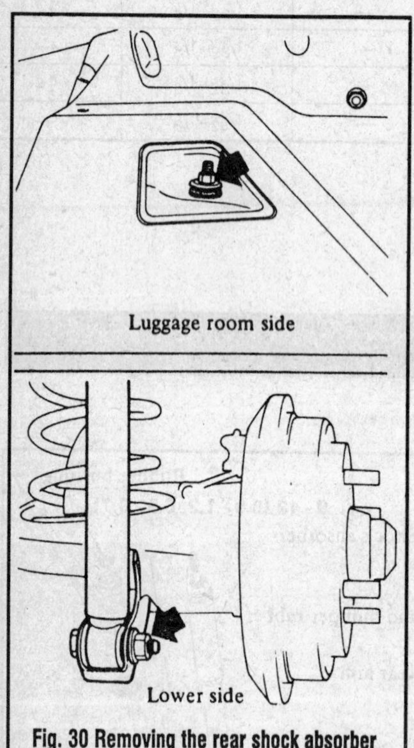
Luggage room side
Lower side

Fig. 30 Removing the rear shock absorber – 1982-86 vehicles

TESTING

Shock absorbers require replacement if the vehicle fails to recover quickly (after a large bump is encountered), if there is a tendency for the vehicle to sway or if the suspension is overly susceptible to vibration.

A good way to test the shocks is to apply downward pressure to one corner of the vehicle until it is moving up and down for almost the full suspension travel, then release it and watch the recovery. If the vehicle bounces slightly about one more time and then comes to rest, the shocks are serviceable. If the vehicle goes on bouncing, the shocks require replacement.

MacPherson Struts

SEE FIGS. 31-33

REMOVAL & INSTALLATION

1987-90 Vehicles

1. Raise and support the rear of the vehicle on jackstands.
2. Remove the wheel.
3. Disconnect the brake tube and parking brake cable.
4. If necessary, remove the brake assembly and wheel bearing.
5. Disconnect the parallel links and radius rod from the strut or knuckle.
6. Support the strut with a jackstand.
7. Remove the strut upper end nuts and then remove the strut from the vehicle.

To install:

8. Install the strut assembly to the vehicle and tighten the strut-to-parallel link nuts to 65–87 ft. lbs. (88–118 Nm), the strut-to-radius rod nuts to 54–69 ft. lbs. (64–94 Nm) and the strut-to-body nuts to 23–31 ft. lbs. (31–42 Nm). Torque the radius rod-to-knuckle nuts to 43–61 ft. lbs. (58–83 Nm), the strut-to-knuckle and parallel link-to-knuckle bolts to 72–87 ft. lbs. (98–118 Nm) and the strut-to-body nuts to 18–22 ft. lbs. (25–30 Nm).
9. Reconnect the brake tube and parking brake cable.
10. Install the wheel.

Sentra 4WD

1. Block the front wheels.
2. Raise and support the rear of the vehicle with jackstands.
3. Position a floor jack under the transverse link on the side of the strut to be removed. Raise it just enough to support the strut.
4. Open the rear of the car and remove the 3 nuts that attach the top of the strut to the body.
5. Remove the wheel.
6. Remove the brake line from its bracket and position it out of the way.
7. Remove the 2 lower strut-to-knuckle mounting bolts.
8. Carefully lower the floor jack and remove the strut.

To install:

9. Install the strut assembly in the vehicle. Final tightening of the strut mounting bolts should take place with the wheels on the ground and the vehicle unladen. Tighten the upper strut-to-body nuts to 33–40 ft. lbs. (45–60 Nm). Tighten the lower strut-to-knuckle bolts to 111–120 ft. lbs. (151–163 Nm).
10. Connect the brake line.
11. Install the wheel.

1991-92 Sentra

1. Raise the vehicle and support safely.
2. Remove the rear wheel and brake caliper.
3. Disconnect the parallel link, radius rod and stabilizer hardware.
4. Remove the rear seat and trim panel.
5. Remove the upper strut-to-body nuts.
6. Remove the lower strut-to-knuckle bolts and remove the strut from the vehicle.

To install:

7. Tighten all suspension bolts when the vehicle's weight is resting on the suspension.
8. Install the strut and torque the upper nuts to 18–22 ft. lbs. (25–29 Nm), lower strut bolts to 72–98 ft. lbs. (98–133 Nm) and parallel link bolts to 72–98 ft. lbs. (98–133 Nm).
9. Install the rear seat and trim panel.
10. Lower the vehicle and have the rear end aligned.

OVERHAUL

Refer to Front Suspension section MacPherson Struts.

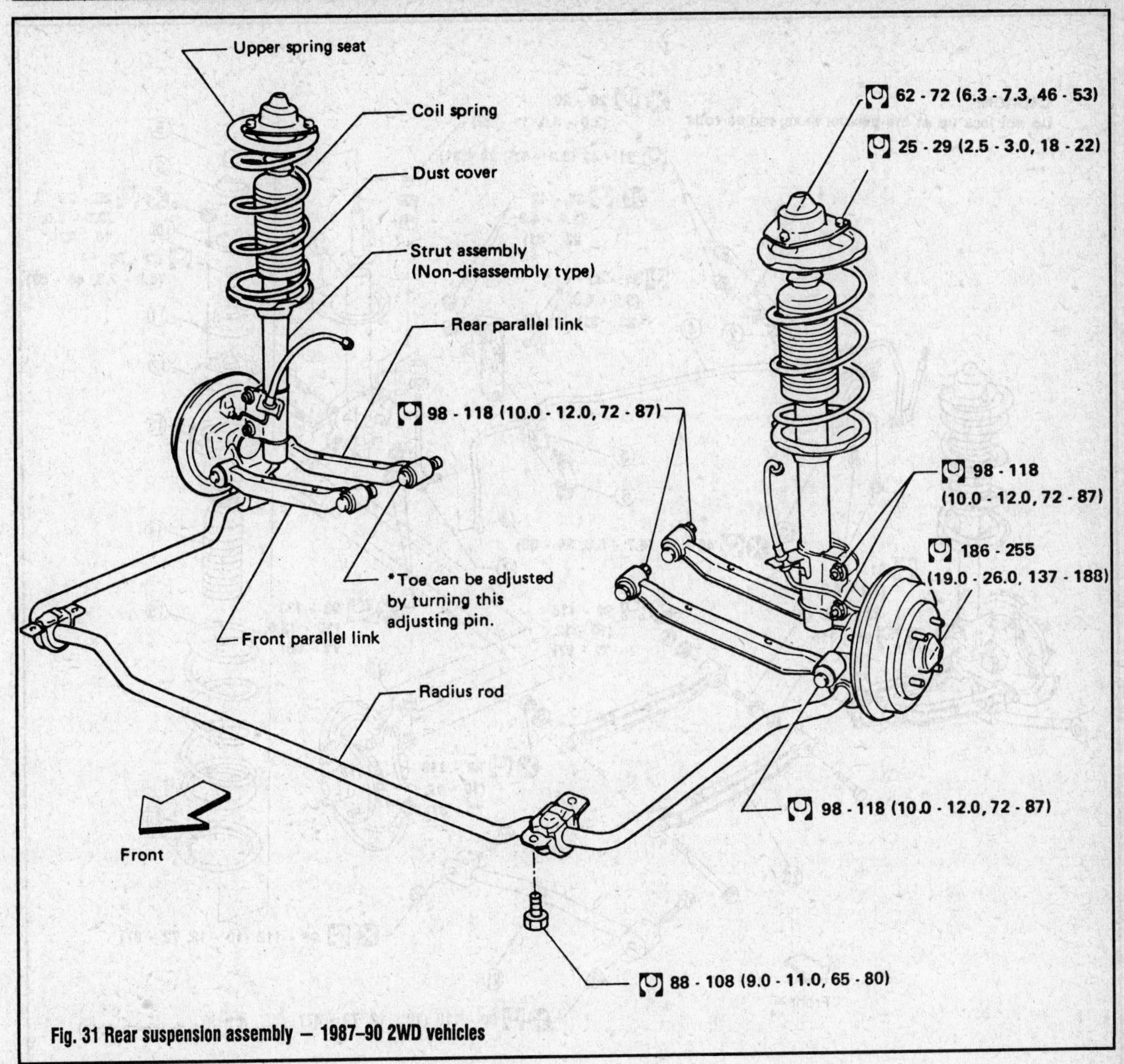
Upper spring seat
Coil spring
Dust cover
Strut assembly
(Non-disassembly type)
Rear parallel link
98 - 118 (10.0 - 12.0, 72 - 87)
*Toe can be adjusted
by turning this
adjusting pin.
Front parallel link
Radius rod
Front
62 - 72 (6.3 - 7.3, 46 - 53)
25 - 29 (2.5 - 3.0, 18 - 22)
98 - 118
(10.0 - 12.0, 72 - 87)
186 - 255
(19.0 - 26.0, 137 - 188)
98 - 118 (10.0 - 12.0, 72 - 87)
88 - 108 (9.0 - 11.0, 65 - 80)

Fig. 31 Rear suspension assembly — 1987–90 2WD vehicles

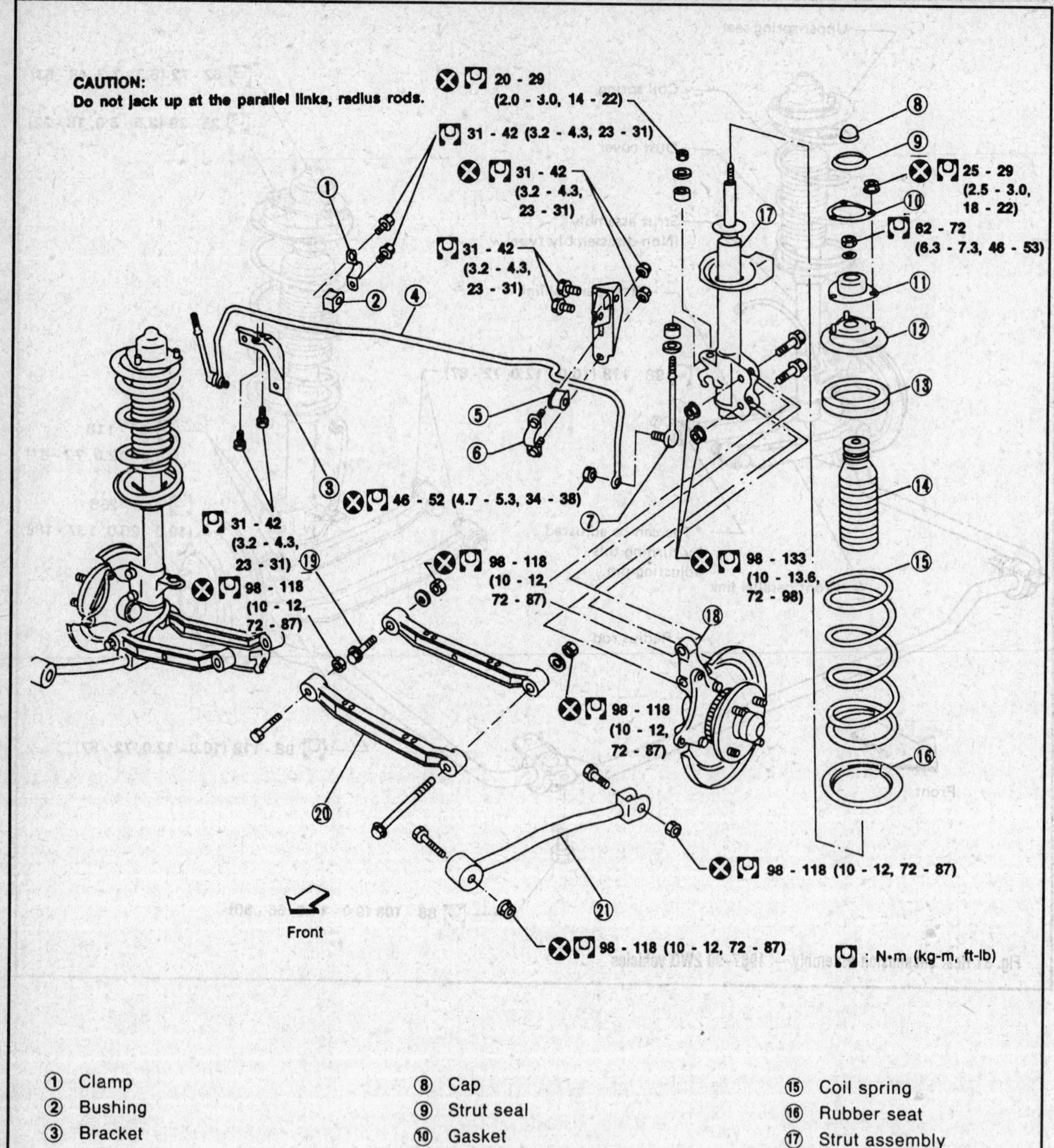
CAUTION:
Do not jack up at the parallel links, radius rods.
20 - 29
(2.0 - 3.0, 14 - 22)
31 - 42 (3.2 - 4.3, 23 - 31)
31 - 42
(3.2 - 4.3,
23 - 31)
31 - 42
(3.2 - 4.3,
23 - 31)
25 - 29
(2.5 - 3.0,
18 - 22)
62 - 72
(6.3 - 7.3, 46 - 53)
46 - 52 (4.7 - 5.3, 34 - 38)
31 - 42
(3.2 - 4.3,
23 - 31)
98 - 118
(10 - 12,
72 - 87)
98 - 118
(10 - 12,
72 - 87)
98 - 133
(10 - 13.6,
72 - 98)
98 - 118
(10 - 12,
72 - 87)
98 - 118 (10 - 12, 72 - 87)
98 - 118 (10 - 12, 72 - 87)
Front
: N•m (kg-m, ft-lb)

① Clamp
② Bushing
③ Bracket
④ Stabilizer bar
⑤ Bushing
⑥ Clamp
⑦ Connecting rod
⑧ Cap
⑨ Strut seal
⑩ Gasket
⑪ Strut mounting insulator
⑫ Upper seat
⑬ Rubber seat
⑭ Bound bumper rubber
⑮ Coil spring
⑯ Rubber seat
⑰ Strut assembly
⑱ Knuckle assembly
⑲ Adjusting bolt
⑳ Parallel link
㉑ Radius rod

Fig. 33 Rear suspension assembly — 1991–92 Sentra

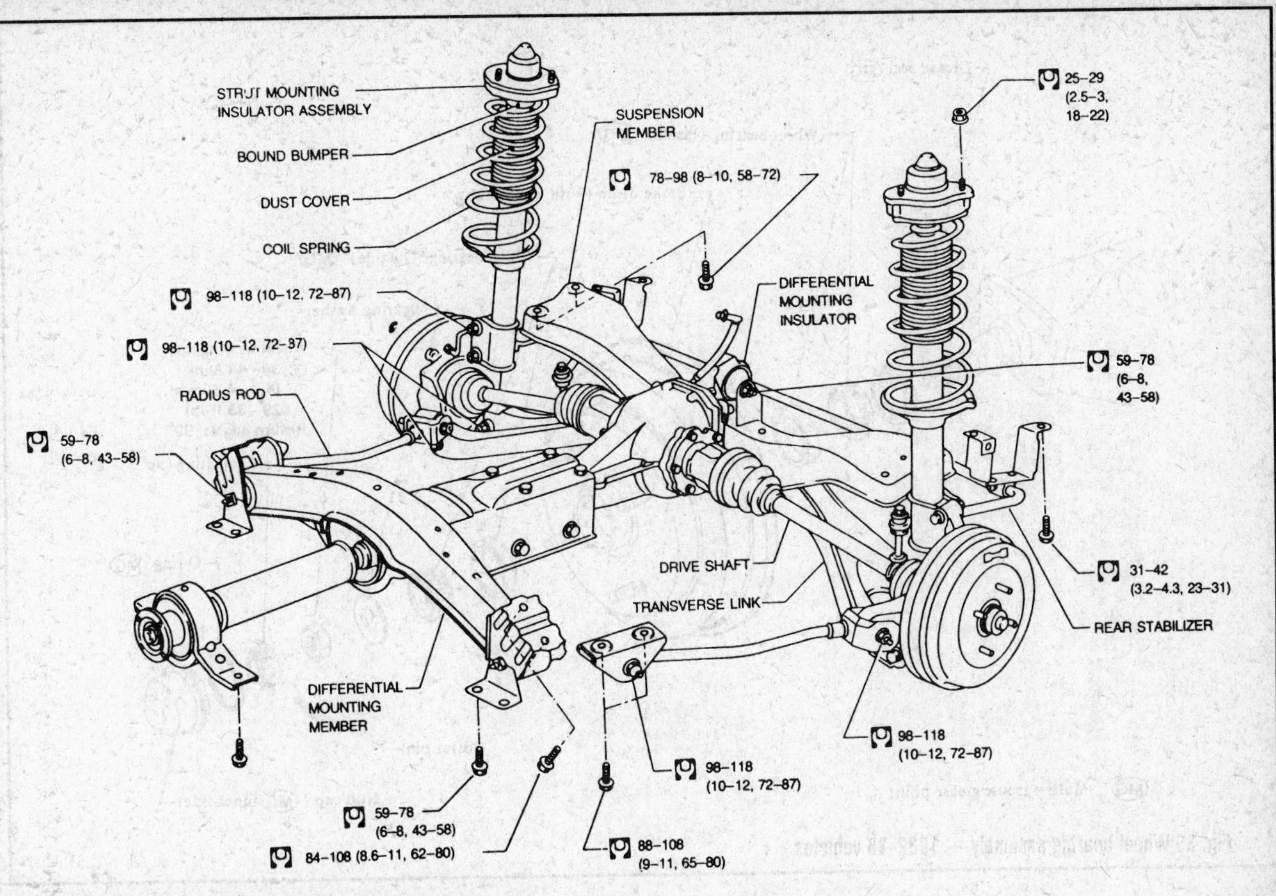

Fig. 32 Rear suspension assembly — 1988–89 4WD Sentra

Rear Wheel Bearings

REMOVAL & INSTALLATION

1982–86 Vehicles

1. Raise and support the vehicle safely.
2. Remove the rear wheels.
3. Work off center hub cap by using thin tool. If necessary tap around it with a soft hammer while removing.
4. Pry off cotter pin and take out adjusting cap and wheel bearing lock nut.

➡ **During removal, be careful to avoid damaging O-ring in dust cap. A circular clip holds inner wheel bearing in brake hub.**

5. Remove drum with bearing inside.
6. Remove bearing outer race from drum using long brass drift pin or equivalent.

To install:

7. Install the bearing outer race as follows. Grind about 0.010 in. (2.5mm) from the outside circumference of the old outer bearing race. Use this homemade tool as a race installer tool. Install the inner bearing and grease seal in the brake drum and install the drum on the vehicle.

➡ **The rear wheel bearings must be adjusted after installation.**

8. Install the outer bearing assembly, wheel bearing lock nut, adjusting cap and cotter pin.
9. Install the center cap and the wheel assembly. To remove the wheel bearing races knock them out of the brake drum using a suitable brass punch.

1987–92 Vehicles

➧ SEE FIGS. 36–38

➡ **To perform this procedure, a large — 3-ton (3,000 kg) — press and special tools ST33220000, J25804-01 and J26082 or equivalent are required. The press must be able to measure pressure. You might be able to engage the services of a machine shop to perform this procedure.**

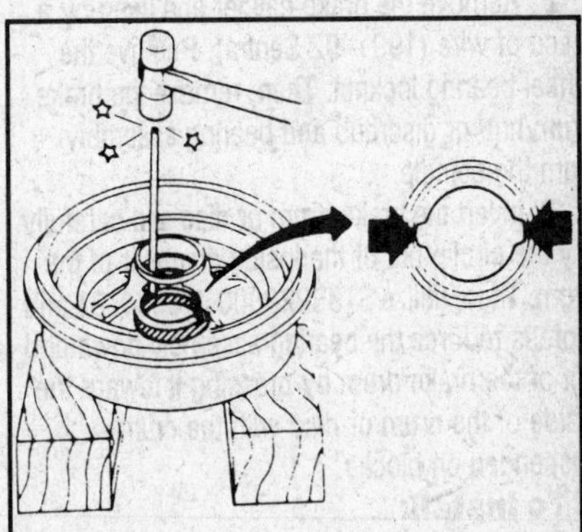

Fig. 34 Removing the wheel bearing outer race from the drum — 1982–86 vehicles

CAUTION

Since brake lining contains asbestos, A CARCINOGEN, don't use compressed air to remove brake dust from these parts. Use of compressed air can cause you to inhale asbestos fibers.

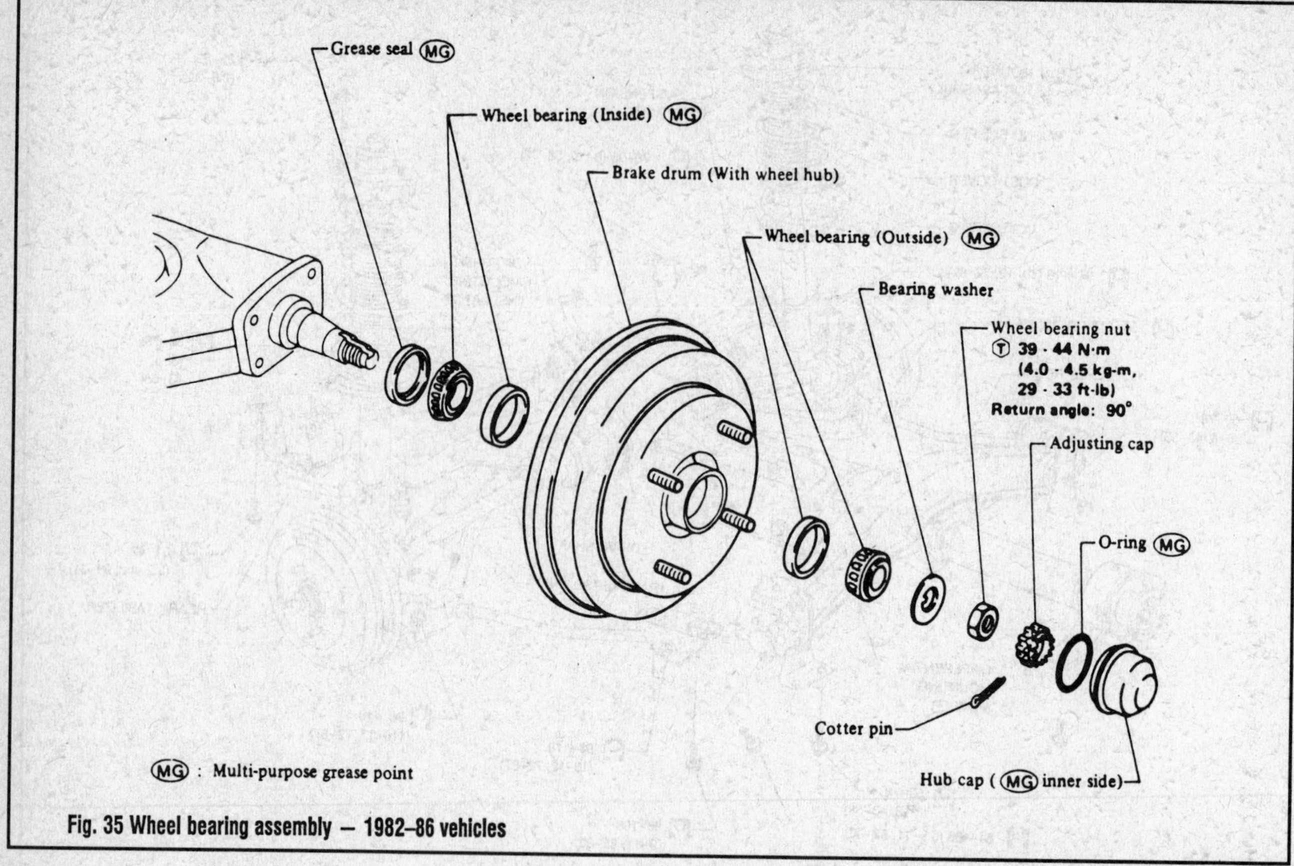
Grease seal (MG)
Wheel bearing (Inside) (MG)
Brake drum (With wheel hub)
Wheel bearing (Outside) (MG)
Bearing washer
Wheel bearing nut
(T) 39 - 44 N·m
(4.0 - 4.5 kg-m,
29 - 33 ft-lb)
Return angle: 90°
Adjusting cap
O-ring (MG)
Cotter pin
Hub cap ((MG) inner side)
(MG) : Multi-purpose grease point

Fig. 35 Wheel bearing assembly — 1982–86 vehicles

1. Raise the car and support it securely via the body. Remove the rear wheels.
2. Remove the brake caliper and hang by a piece of wire (1991–92 Sentra). Remove the wheel bearing locknut. Then, remove the brake drum/hub or disc/hub and bearing assembly from the spindle.
3. Invert the brake drum or disc and carefully pry the circlip out of the inside diameter of the drum. Then, utilize ST33220000 J25804–01 and a press to force the bearing assembly down and out of the brake drum by pressing it toward the inside of the drum or disc with the drum suspended on blocks.

To install:

4. Check the circlip for cracks or any sign that it has been sprung (bent inward). Have the hub inspected for cracks by a machine shop equipped with a magnetic or dye test. Do the same with the spindle.
5. Apply multipurpose grease to the seal lip. Then, press a new bearing assembly into the hub from the inside using the press and ST33220000 J26082. **Be sure not to press the inner race of the wheel bearing assembly and to carefully avoid damaging the grease seal.** If the bearing cannot be pressed in with a pressure of 3 tons (3,000 kg), replace the hub.
6. Install a new circlip into the groove in the drum/hub or disc.
7. Install the hub onto the spindle. Install the wheel bearing locknut and torque it to 137–188 ft. lbs. (186–256 Nm).

Sentra 4WD

➡ To perform this procedure, you will need special tools designed to be used with a hammer to drive inner and outer bearing races from the rear knuckles of 4WD Sentras. You will also need a large press, and a tool designed to transfer the power of that press to the bearing to install it. Also needed is a special tool to transfer the power of a 5.5 ton (5,000 kg) press to the bearing and such a press to apply pressure to the bearing to test preload.

❄❄ CAUTION

Since brake lining contains asbestos, A CARCINOGEN, don't use compressed air to remove brake dust from these parts. Use of compressed air can cause you to inhale asbestos fibers.

1. Raise the car and support it by the body. Remove the rear wheels.
2. Disconnect the brake line at the connection and plug the openings.
3. Cover the driveshaft rubber boots with rags. Tap the end of the driveshaft very lightly with a hammer, block of wood, and a suitable broad ended punch to free the driveshaft from the knuckle.
4. Matchmark the rear bolt installation angle to retain alignment. Then, remove the nuts and bolts fastening the control arm to the knuckle. Unbolt the radius rod from the knuckle. Unbolt the knuckle from the strut and remove it.
5. Mount the knuckle in a vise and drive the hub out of the knuckle via the inner race with a tool such as J25804–01 and hammer.

6. Use a press to force the outboard bearing inner race from the hub. You will need blocks, a press, and ST30031000. Remove the other grease seal.

7. With the knuckle in a vise, drive the bearing inner race and grease seal out of the knuckle. Use an appropriate, cone shaped special tool and hammer.

8. **Cautiously** remove the inner and outer circlips from the knuckle with pointed instruments.

9. Drive the bearing outer race out of the knuckle with a hammer and appropriate, cone shaped special tool.

To Install:

10. Have a machine shop inspect the knuckle for cracks with a magnetic or dye process. Replace radius rod or transverse link bushings, if necessary. Inspect the C-clips and replace if they are cracked or sprung.

11. Install the inner C-clip into the knuckle, making sure it seats in its groove. Then, press a new bearing outer race into the into the knuckle with a suitable tool and press without using any lubricant.

12. Apply wheel bearing grease to each bearing, working the grease thoroughly into the areas between the rollers. Also apply the grease to the lip of the grease seal. Install the bearings into the knuckle. Install the grease seal into the knuckle.

13. Install the outer C-clip into the groove in the knuckle. Then, use an appropriate tool to apply the pressure to the outer race and tap it to install the race into the hub.

14. Now, install a special tool onto the top of the hub that will drive the hub onto the knuckle by applying pressure on the inner race only. Support the hub at the center only. Then, place the assembly in a press and press the hub into the knuckle with about 3 tons (3,000 kg) force. Now, increase the pressure on the press to 5.5 tons (5,000 kg). Spin the knuckle several turns in each direction to make sure the wheel bearing operates smoothly (preload is not excessive).

15. Coat the lips of the inner grease seal with bearing grease and then install it into the knuckle.

16. Slide the driveshaft splines through the center of the wheel hub. Bolt the knuckle onto the strut and torque the bolts to 72–87 ft. lbs. (98–118 Nm).

17. Install the bolts attaching the transverse link to the steering knuckle. Align the matchmarks made earlier to maintain rear wheel alignment. Install the nuts and torque them to 72–87 ft. lbs. (98–118 Nm).

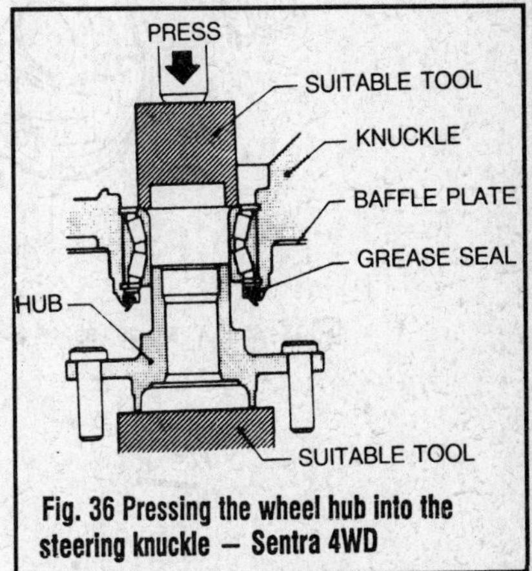
PRESS
SUITABLE TOOL
KNUCKLE
BAFFLE PLATE
GREASE SEAL
HUB
SUITABLE TOOL

Fig. 36 Pressing the wheel hub into the steering knuckle – Sentra 4WD

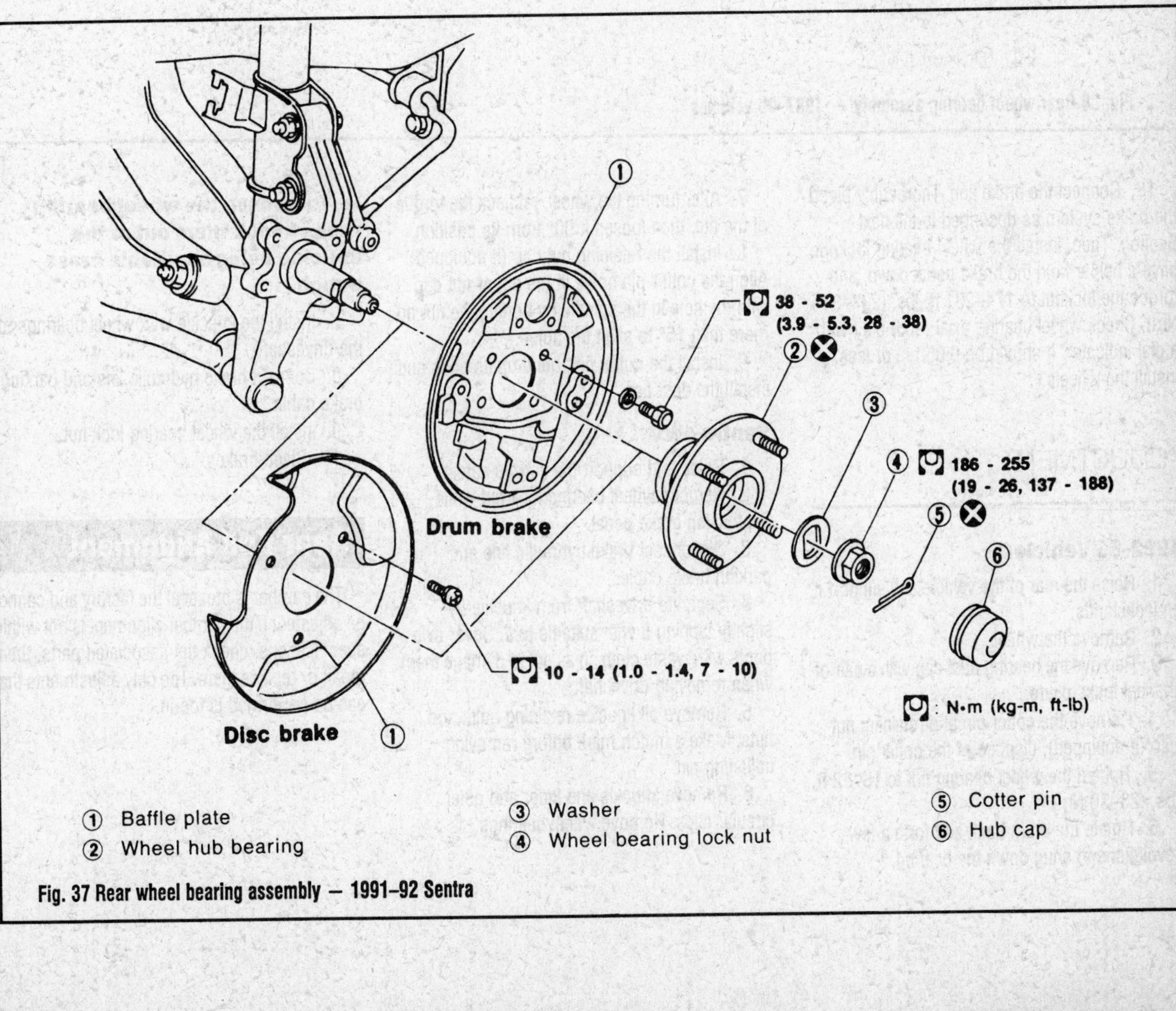

38 - 52 (3.9 - 5.3, 28 - 38)

186 - 255 (19 - 26, 137 - 188)

10 - 14 (1.0 - 1.4, 7 - 10)

Drum brake

Disc brake

: N·m (kg-m, ft-lb)

① Baffle plate
② Wheel hub bearing
③ Washer
④ Wheel bearing lock nut
⑤ Cotter pin
⑥ Hub cap

Fig. 37 Rear wheel bearing assembly – 1991–92 Sentra

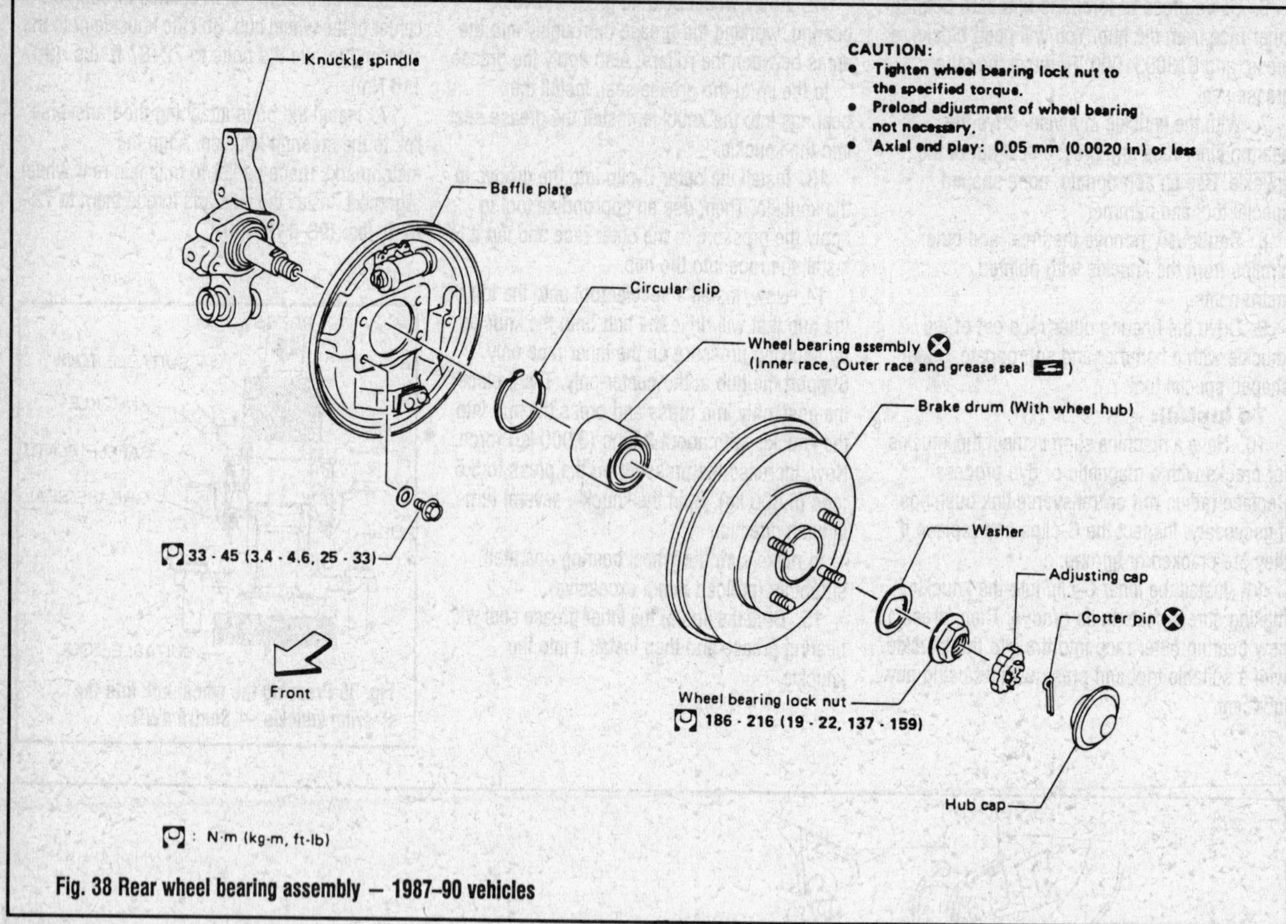
Knuckle spindle
CAUTION:
• Tighten wheel bearing lock nut to the specified torque.
• Preload adjustment of wheel bearing not necessary.
• Axial end play: 0.05 mm (0.0020 in) or less
Baffle plate
Circular clip
Wheel bearing assembly
(Inner race, Outer race and grease seal)
Brake drum (With wheel hub)
Washer
Adjusting cap
Cotter pin
33 - 45 (3.4 - 4.6, 25 - 33)
Front
Wheel bearing lock nut
186 - 216 (19 - 22, 137 - 159)
Hub cap
: N·m (kg-m, ft-lb)

Fig. 38 Rear wheel bearing assembly — 1987–90 vehicles

18. Connect the brake line. Thoroughly bleed the brake system as described in the next Section. Then, install the wheel bearing locknut, have a helper hold the brake pedal down, and torque the locknut to 174–231 ft. lbs. (237–314 Nm). Check wheel bearing axial (end) play with a dial indicator. It should be 0.05mm or less. Install the wheels.

ADJUSTMENT

1982–86 Vehicles

1. Raise the rear of the vehicle and support it on jackstands.
2. Remove the wheel.
3. Remove the bearing dust cap with a pair of channel locks pliers.
4. Remove the cotter pin and retaining nut cap (if equipped), dispose of the cotter pin.
5. Tighten the wheel bearing nut to 18–22 ft. lbs. (25–30 Nm).
6. Rotate the drum back and forth a few revolutions to snug down the bearing.
7. After turning the wheel, recheck the torque of the nut, then loosen it 90° from its position.
8. Install the retaining nut cap (if equipped). Align the cotter pin holes in the nut or nut cap with the hole in the spindle by turning the nut no more than 15° to align the holes.
9. Install the cotter pin, bend up its ends and install the dust cap.

Sentra 4WD

1. Raise and support the vehicle safely.
2. Remove wheel bearing lock nut while depressing brake pedal.
3. Disconnect brake hydraulic line and parking brake cable.
4. Separate driveshaft from knuckle by slightly tapping it with suitable tool. Cover axle boots with waste cloth so as not to damage them when removing driveshaft.
5. Remove all knuckle retaining bolts and nuts. Make a match mark before removing adjusting pin.
6. Remove knuckle and inner and outer circular clips. Remove wheel bearings.

➡ To remove the wheel bearing races knock them out of the knuckle using a suitable brass punch.

7. Install the knuckle with wheel bearings to the driveshaft.
8. Connect brake hydraulic line and parking brake cable.
9. Install the wheel bearing lock nut.
10. Bleed brakes.

Rear End Alignment

The camber is preset at the factory and cannot be adjusted; if the camber alignment is not within specifications, check the associated parts, then repair or replace them. The only adjustments that can be performed is toe-in.

STEERING

Steering Wheel

CAUTION

To avoid rendering the SRS (Supplemental Restraint System) inoperative, which could lead to personal injury or death in the event of a severe frontal collision, extreme caution must be taken when servicing the electrical related systems. All SRS electrical wiring harnesses and connectors are covered with YELLOW outer insulation. Do not use electrical test equipment on any circuit related to the SRS (air bag).

Air Bag

DISARMING

On vehicles equipped with an air bag, turn the ignition switch to OFF position. The negative battery cable must be disconnected and wait 10 minutes after the cable is disconnected before working on the system. SRS sensors must always be installed with the arrow marks facing the front of the vehicle.

REMOVAL & INSTALLATION

Without Air Bag (SRS)

➧ SEE FIGS. 39, 42

1. Position the wheels in the straight ahead direction. The steering wheel should be right side up and level.
2. Disconnect the battery ground cable.
3. Some models have countersunk screws on the back of the steering wheel, remove the screws and pull off the horn pad.

➡ Some models have a horn wire running from the pad to the steering wheel; disconnect it.

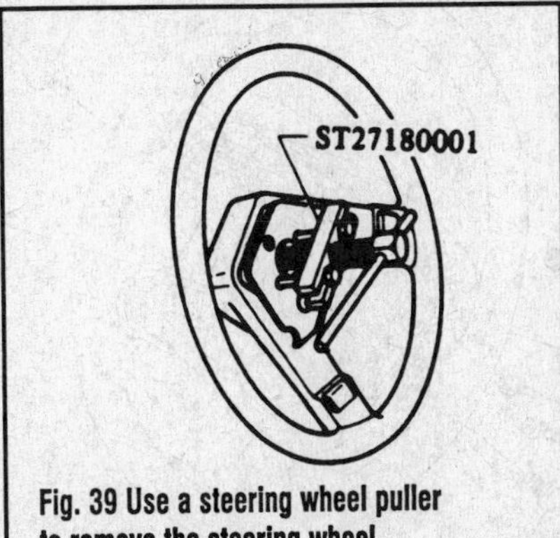
ST27180001

Fig. 39 Use a steering wheel puller to remove the steering wheel

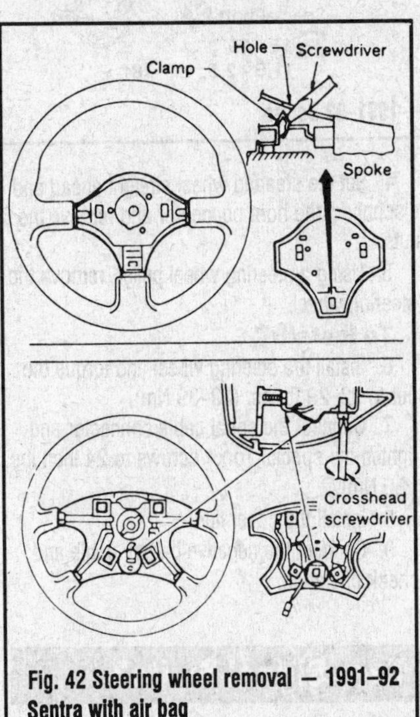
Hole
Screwdriver
Clamp
Spoke
Crosshead
screwdriver

Fig. 42 Steering wheel removal — 1991–92 Sentra with air bag

4. Remove the rest of the horn switching mechanism, noting the relative location of the parts. Remove the mechanism only if it hinders subsequent wheel removal procedures.
5. Matchmark the top of the steering column shaft and the steering wheel flange.
6. Remove the attaching nut. Using the Steering Wheel Remover tool ST27180001, pull the steering wheel from the steering column.

➡ Do not strike the shaft with a hammer, which may cause the column to collapse.

7. Install the steering wheel in the reverse order of removal, aligning the punch marks; DO NOT drive or hammer the wheel.
8. Tighten the steering wheel nut to 29–40 ft. lbs. (39–54 Nm).
9. Reinstall the horn button, pad or ring.

With Air Bag (SRS)

➧ SEE FIGS. 40–41

CAUTION

To avoid rendering the SRS (Supplemental Restraint System) inoperative, which could lead to personal injury or death in the event of a severe frontal collision, extreme caution must be taken when servicing the electrical related systems. All SRS electrical wiring harnesses and connectors are covered with YELLOW outer insulation. Do not use electrical test equipment on any circuit related to the SRS (air bag).

Air Bag

DISARMING

On vehicles equipped with an air bag, turn the ignition switch to OFF position. The negative battery cable must be disconnected and wait 10 minutes after the cable is disconnected before working on the system. SRS sensors must always be installed with the arrow marks facing the front of the vehicle.

1. Disconnect the negative battery cable and wait for 10 minutes. The 10 minute wait is to allow the SRS system to de-energize. Always install SRS components with the arrow facing the front of the vehicle.
2. Remove the lower lid from the steering wheel and disconnect the air bag module connector.
3. Remove the steering column side lid. Using a T50H Torx® bit, remove the left and right special screws. The air bag module can be removed by disconnecting the spiral cable connector.

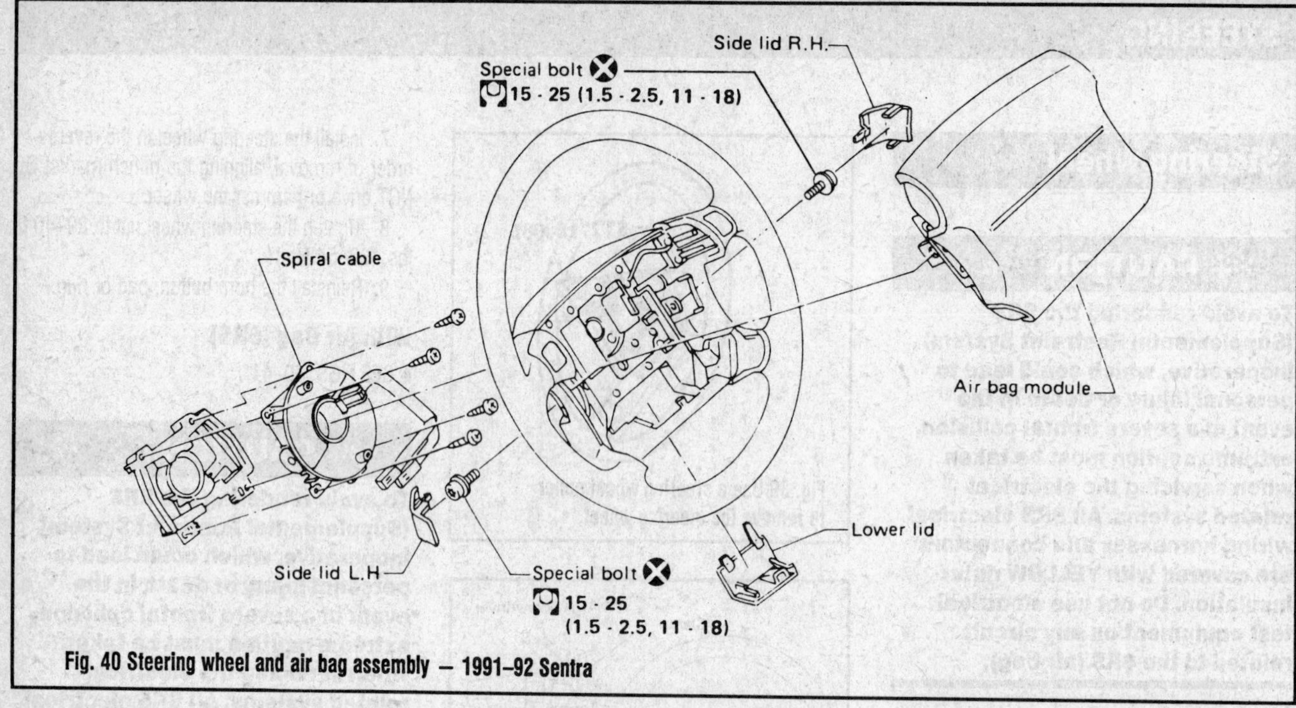

Side lid R.H.
Special bolt
15 - 25 (1.5 - 2.5, 11 - 18)
Spiral cable
Air bag module
Lower lid
Side lid L.H
Special bolt
15 - 25
(1.5 - 2.5, 11 - 18)

Fig. 40 Steering wheel and air bag assembly — 1991–92 Sentra

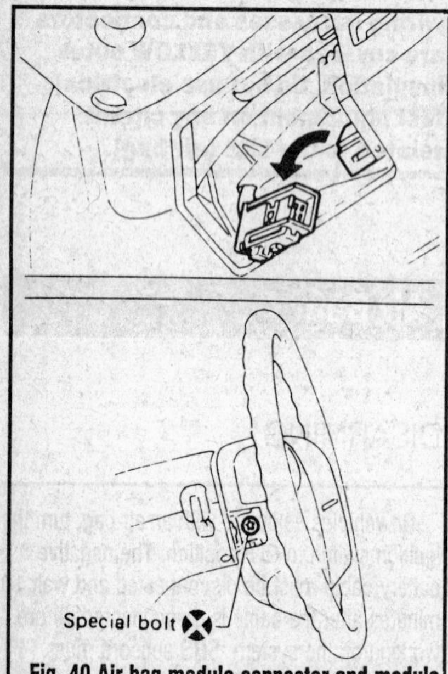

Special bolt

Fig. 40 Air bag module connector and module special bolts — 1991–92 Sentra

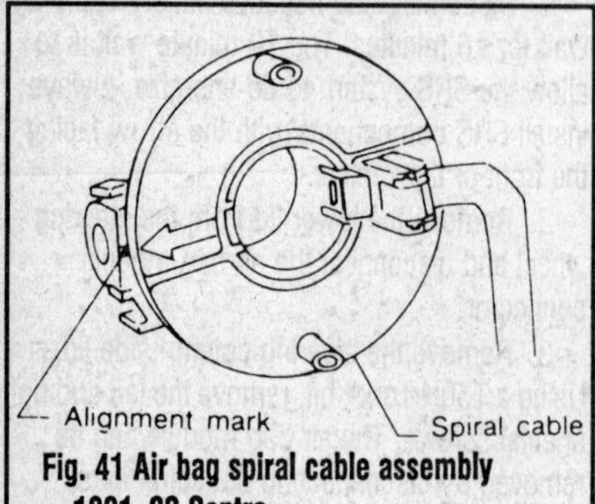

Alignment mark
Spiral cable

Fig. 41 Air bag spiral cable assembly — 1991–92 Sentra

4. Set the steering wheel straight ahead and disconnect the horn connector and remove the nuts.

5. Using a steering wheel puller, remove the steering wheel.

To install:

6. Install the steering wheel and torque the nut to 22–29 ft. lbs. (29–39 Nm).

7. Connect the spiral cable connector and tighten the special Torx® screws to 24 inch lbs. (4.0 Nm).

8. Install the cover lids.

9. Connect the negative battery cable and check operation.

Turn Signal Switch

REMOVAL & INSTALLATION

On some later models, the turn signal switch is part of a combination switch. The whole unit is removed together.

1982–86 Sentra

1. Refer to the Steering Wheel, Removal and Installation procedures, in this section and remove the steering wheel.
2. Remove the steering column cover(s).
3. Disconnect the electrical connectors from the switch.
4. Remove the retaining screws and the switch from the steering column.
5. To install, reverse the removal procedures.

➡ Many models have turn signal switches that have a tab which must fit into a hole in the steering shaft in order for the system to return the switch to the neutral position after the turn has been made. Be sure to align the tab and the hole when installing.

1983–90 Pulsar

1991–92 Sentra

1. Disconnect the negative battery terminal.
2. Remove the steering column covers.
3. Disconnect the electrical connector from the turn signal side of the combination switch.
4. Remove the retaining screws and separate the turn signal switch from the combination switch.
5. To install, reverse the removal procedures.

Steering Lock/Ignition Lock

➧ SEE FIG. 43

REMOVAL & INSTALLATION

The steering lock/ignition switch assembly is attached to the steering column by special screws whose heads shear off on installation. The screws must be drilled out to remove the assembly.

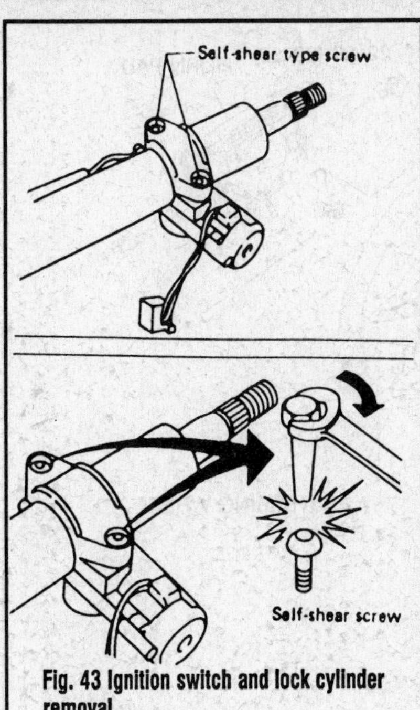
Self-shear type screw
Self-shear screw

Fig. 43 Ignition switch and lock cylinder removal

1. Refer to the Steering Wheel, Removal and Installation procedures, in this section and remove the steering wheel.
2. Remove the steering column cover(s).
3. Using a drill, drill out the self-shear type screws of the steering lock retainer.

➡ **The 1991–92 Sentra models use only 2 self-shearing screws to hold the steering lock onto the steering column. All other models use 2 self-shearing screws and 2 regular screws.**

4. Remove the screws and the steering lock from the steering column.

To install:

5. Use new self-shearing screws. Torque the self-shearing type screws until the heads break off.
6. Install the steering column cover and steering wheel as outlined in this section.

Steering Column

➧ SEE FIGS. 44–47

REMOVAL & INSTALLATION

1. Disconnect the negative battery cable.
2. Remove the steering wheel.
3. Remove the steering column covers.
4. Disconnect the combination switch and steering lock switch wiring.
5. Remove most of the steering column support bracket and clamp nuts and bolts. Leave a few of the fasteners loosely installed to support the column while disconnecting it from the steering gear.
6. Remove the bolt from the column lower joint.
7. Remove the temporarily installed column support bracket bolts and withdraw the column from the lower joint.

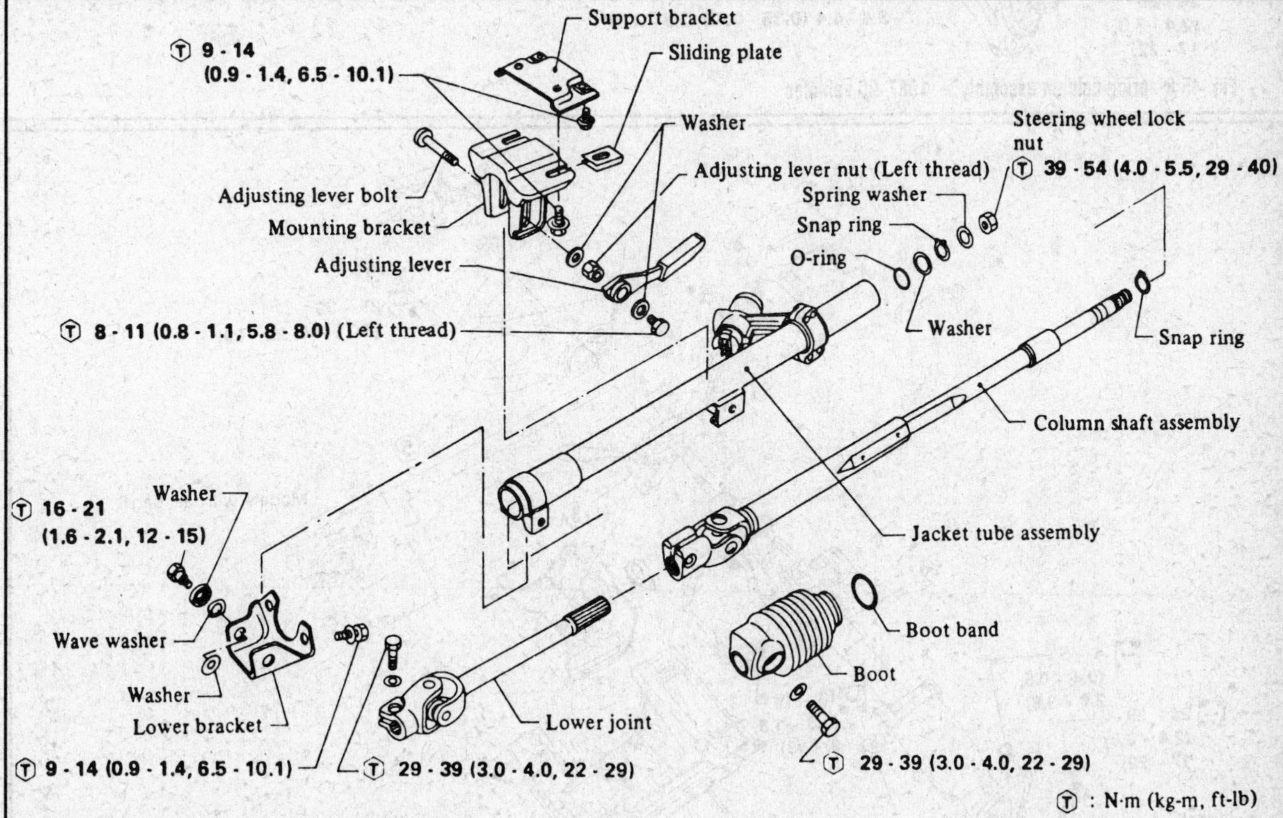

Support bracket
Sliding plate
Ⓣ 9 - 14 (0.9 - 1.4, 6.5 - 10.1)
Washer
Steering wheel lock nut
Adjusting lever nut (Left thread)
Ⓣ 39 - 54 (4.0 - 5.5, 29 - 40)
Adjusting lever bolt
Spring washer
Mounting bracket
Snap ring
Adjusting lever
O-ring
Ⓣ 8 - 11 (0.8 - 1.1, 5.8 - 8.0) (Left thread)
Washer
Snap ring
Column shaft assembly
Washer
Ⓣ 16 - 21 (1.6 - 2.1, 12 - 15)
Jacket tube assembly
Boot band
Wave washer
Boot
Washer
Lower bracket
Lower joint
Ⓣ 9 - 14 (0.9 - 1.4, 6.5 - 10.1)
Ⓣ 29 - 39 (3.0 - 4.0, 22 - 29)
Ⓣ 29 - 39 (3.0 - 4.0, 22 - 29)
Ⓣ : N·m (kg-m, ft-lb)

Fig. 44 Steering column assembly — 1982–86 vehicles

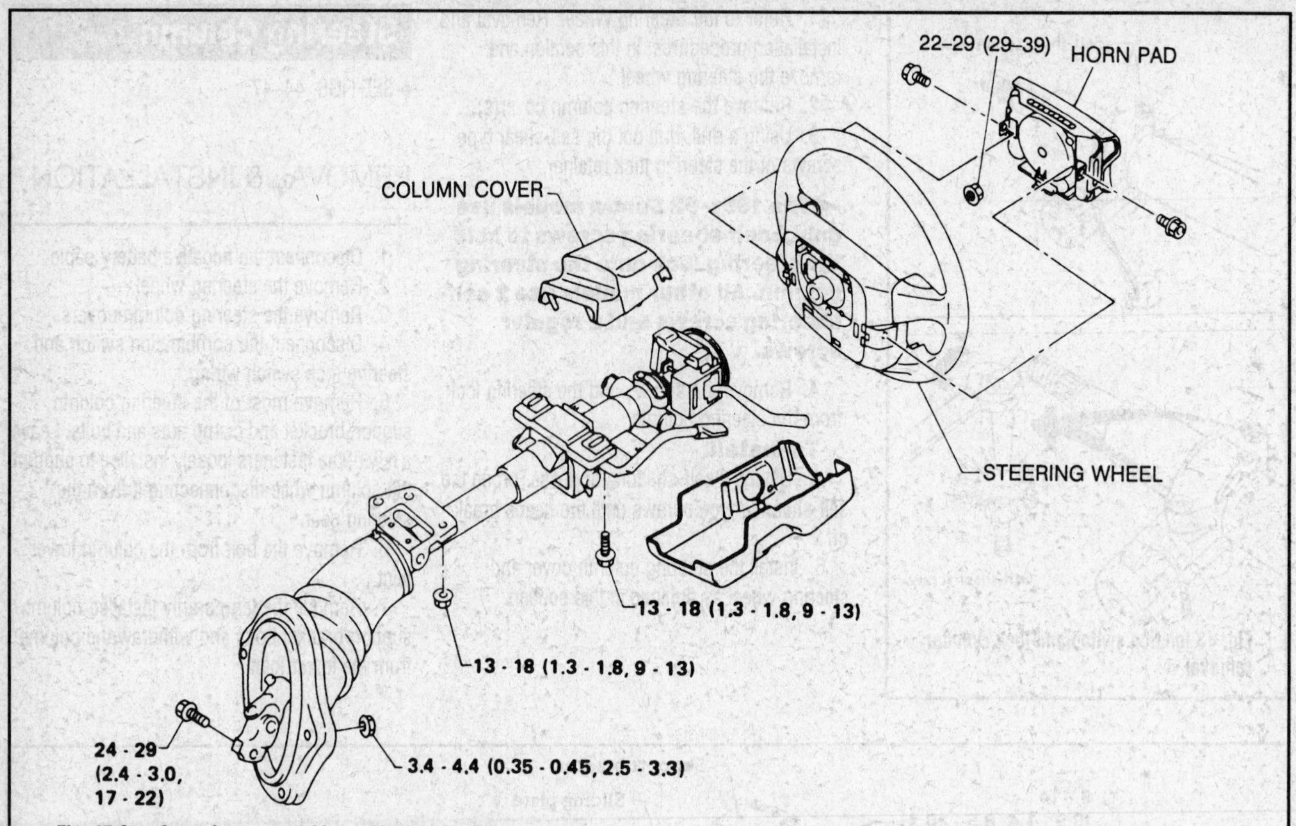

22-29 (29-39)
HORN PAD
COLUMN COVER
STEERING WHEEL
13 - 18 (1.3 - 1.8, 9 - 13)
13 - 18 (1.3 - 1.8, 9 - 13)
24 - 29 (2.4 - 3.0, 17 - 22)
3.4 - 4.4 (0.35 - 0.45, 2.5 - 3.3)

Fig. 45 Steering column assembly — 1987–90 vehicles

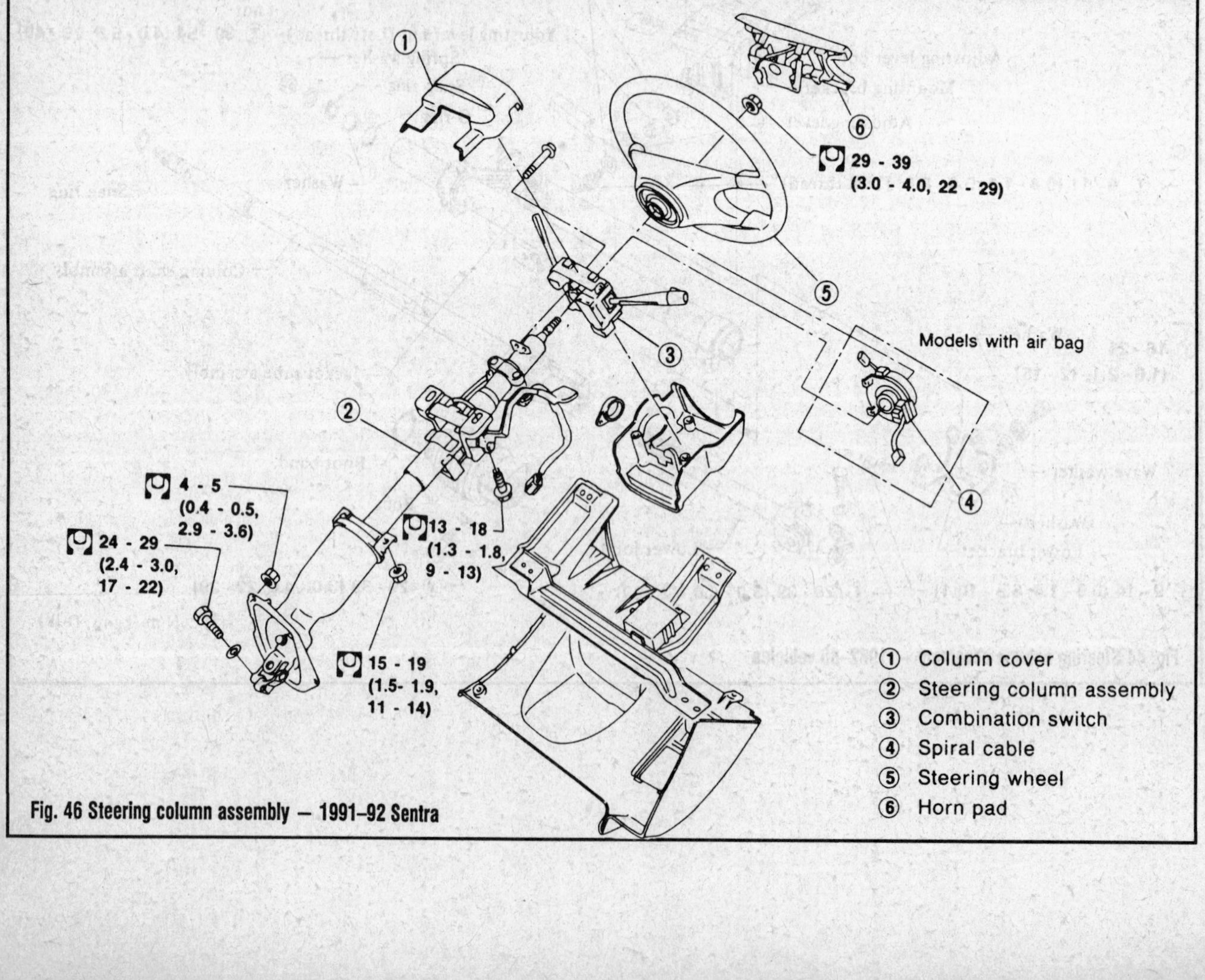

29 - 39 (3.0 - 4.0, 22 - 29)
Models with air bag
4 - 5 (0.4 - 0.5, 2.9 - 3.6)
24 - 29 (2.4 - 3.0, 17 - 22)
13 - 18 (1.3 - 1.8, 9 - 13)
15 - 19 (1.5- 1.9, 11 - 14)

① Column cover
② Steering column assembly
③ Combination switch
④ Spiral cable
⑤ Steering wheel
⑥ Horn pad

Fig. 46 Steering column assembly — 1991–92 Sentra

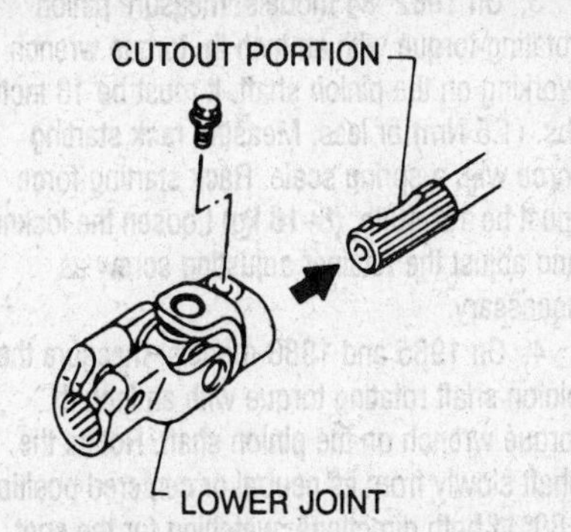
CUTOUT PORTION
LOWER JOINT

Fig. 47 The cutout portion of the steering column spline shaft must be aligned with the bolt

8. Withdraw the column spline shaft from the lower joint and remove the steering column. Be careful not to tear the column tube jacket insulator during removal.

To install:

9. Insert the column spline shaft into the lower joint and install all column fasteners finger-tight.

10. Install the lower joint bolt. The cutout portion of the spline shaft must perfectly aligned with the bolt. Torque the bolt to 17–22 ft. lbs. (23–30 Nm). Tighten the steering bracket and clamp fasteners gradually. While tightening, make sure no stress is placed on the column.

11. Connect the combination switch and steering lock switch wiring.

12. Install the steering column covers.

13. Install the steering wheel.

14. Connect the negative battery cable.

15. After the installation is complete, turn the steering wheel from stop to stop and make sure it turns smoothly. The number of turns to the left and right stops must be equal.

DISASSEMBLY AND ASSEMBLY

1. Remove the steering column from the vehicle.

2. Unlock the steering lock with the key.

3. Remove the lower bracket and snapring from inside the tube.

4. Remove the jacket tube from the shaft.

5. Remove the ignition lock and switch by drilling out the shearing screw heads as outlined in this section.

6. Remove the tilt mechanism, if so equipped.

To assemble:

6. Install the lower bracket and torque the bolts to 12–15 ft. lbs. (16–21 Nm).

7. Apply a coat of grease to the column bearing and bushing.

8. Install the shaft into the tube. Install the snapring so that the rounded surface faces toward the bearing.

9. Install the tilt mechanism. Adjust the tilt lever angle to 20–30° when the adjusting lever nut is torque to 72 inch lbs. (8 Nm).

10. Move the tilt lever from the lock to release position several times to ensure that the jacket tube is securely tightened when the tilt lever is at lock. The jacket tube should move smoothly when the tilt lever is at he release position. Readjust if necessary.

11. Install the ignition lock and switch assembly as outlined in this section.

12. Install the steering column into the vehicle as outlined in this section.

Tie Rod Ends (Steering Side Rods)

REMOVAL & INSTALLATION

1. Raise the front of the vehicle and support it on jackstands. Remove the wheel.

2. Locate the faulty tie rod end. It will have a lot of play in it and the dust cover will probably be ripped.

3. Remove the cotter pin and the tie rod ball joint stud nut. Note the position of the steering linkage.

4. Loosen the tie rod-to-steering gear locknut.

5. Using the Ball Joint Remover tool HT72520000, remove the tie rod ball joint from the strut or the steering knuckle.

6. Loosen the locknut and remove the tie rod end from the tie rod, counting the number of turns it takes to completely free it.

To install:

7. Install the new tie rod end, turning it in exactly as far as you screwed out the old one. Make sure it is correctly positioned in relationship to the steering linkage.

8. Fit the ball joint and nut, tighten them and install a new cotter pin. Torque the ball joint stud nut to 22–36 ft. lbs. (30–49 Nm) and the ball joint-to-tie rod end locknut to 27–34 ft. lbs. (37–46 Nm).

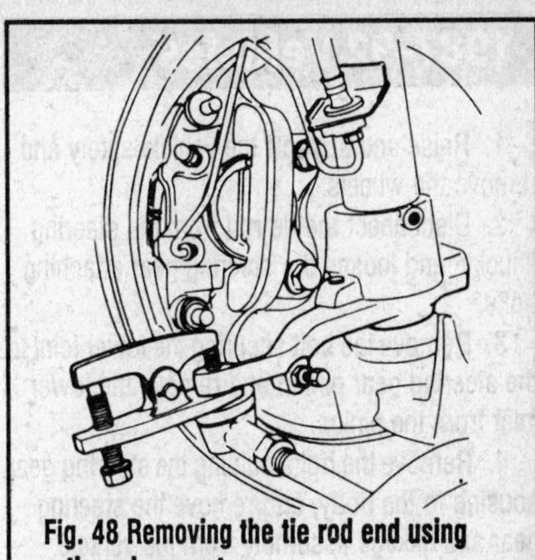

Fig. 48 Removing the tie rod end using a tie rod separator

➡ Before finally tightening the tie rod lock nut or clamp, adjust the toe-in of the vehicle to a rough setting. See section under Front Suspension. Have a qualified alignment technician align the front end.

Manual Steering Gear

➧ SEE FIG. 49

REMOVAL & INSTALLATION

1982–86 Vehicles

1. Raise and support the car on jackstands.

2. Using the Ball Joint Remover tool HT72520000, remove the tie rod from the knuckle.

3. Loosen, but do not remove, the steering gear mounting bolts.

4. Remove the steering column lower joint.

5. Unbolt and remove the gear.

To install:

6. Install the steering gear assembly to the vehicle. Torque the tie rod-to-steering knuckle nut to 26–35 ft. lbs. (34–48 Nm), the steering gear-to-frame clamp bolts to 43–58 ft. lbs. (58–78 Nm), the lower joint-to-pinion gear bolt to 22–29 ft. lbs. (29–39 Nm) and the lower joint-to-steering column bolt to 22–29 ft. lbs. (29–39 Nm).

➡ When installing the lower steering joint to the steering gear, make sure that the wheels are aligned with the vehicle and the steering joint slot is aligned with the steering gear cap or spacer mark.

1987–92 Vehicles

1. Raise and support the vehicle safely and remove the wheels.
2. Disconnect the tie rod from the steering knuckle and loosen the steering gear attaching bolts.
3. Remove the bolt securing the lower joint to the steering gear pinion and remove the lower joint from the pinion.
4. Remove the bolts holding the steering gear housing to the body, and remove the steering gear and linkage assembly from the vehicle.

To install:

5. Install the assembly into the vehicle. When fitting the lower U-joint, make sure the attaching bolt is aligned perfectly with the cut out in the splined end of the steering column shaft.
6. Torque the steering gear mounting clamp bolts to 54–72 ft. lbs. (73–97 Nm). Torque the tie rod end nuts to 22–29 ft. lbs. (29–39 Nm).
7. Have the front end aligned by a qualified alignment technician.

ADJUSTMENTS

1982–86 Vehicles

1. Remove the steering gear from the car as described below. Disconnect the tie rod ends and remove boots.
2. Turn the pinion shaft to neutral (centered) position. This puts the spacer at −38.3° to −25.3° on 1982–84 models and −33.5° to −46.5° on 1985 models; and sets the guide chip to 43.5° to 56.5° on 1986 models.
3. On 1982–84 models, measure pinion rotating torque with an inch lb. torque wrench working on the pinion shaft. It must be 13 inch lbs. (1.5 Nm) or less. Measure rack starting force with a spring scale. Rack starting force must be 18–40 lb. (8–18 kg) Loosen the locknut and adjust the retainer adjusting screw as necessary.
4. On 1985 and 1986 models, measure the pinion shaft rotating torque with an inch lb. torque wrench on the pinion shaft. Rotate the shaft slowly from its neutral or centered position 180° in both directions, watching for the spot where torque is at its greatest level. Loose en the adjusting screw with the pinion at this position and then hand tighten the adjusting screw until its end touches the retainer. Hold the adjustment and tighten the locknut.

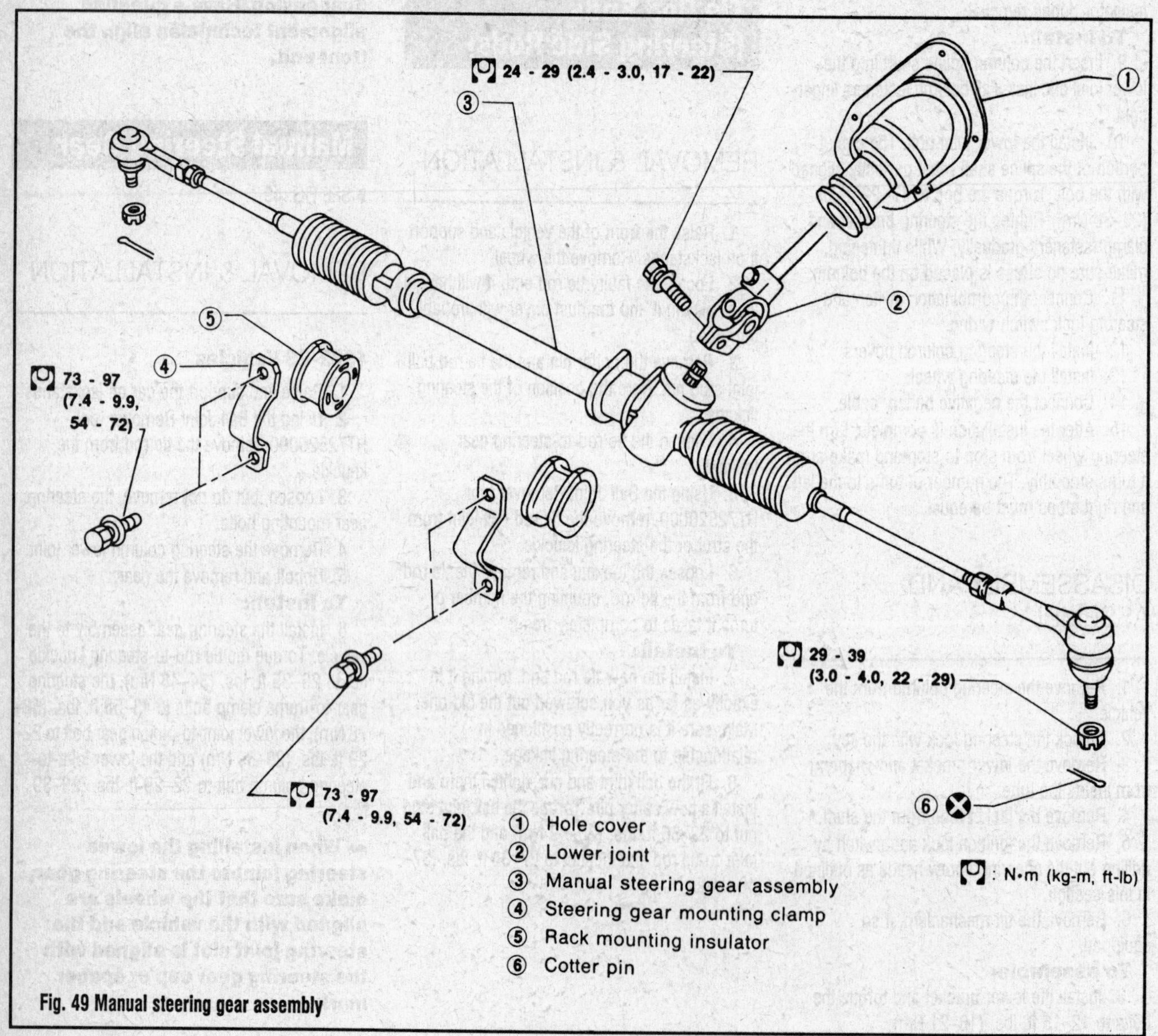
24 - 29 (2.4 - 3.0, 17 - 22)
73 - 97
(7.4 - 9.9,
54 - 72)
29 - 39
(3.0 - 4.0, 22 - 29)
73 - 97
(7.4 - 9.9, 54 - 72)
① Hole cover
② Lower joint
③ Manual steering gear assembly
④ Steering gear mounting clamp
⑤ Rack mounting insulator
⑥ Cotter pin
: N·m (kg-m, ft-lb)

Fig. 49 Manual steering gear assembly

5. On 1985 and 1986 models, now rotate the pinion from its centered position to the end of the rack and make sure torque is no more than 13 inch lbs. (1.5 Nm) on 1985 models and 16 inch lbs. (1.8 Nm) on 1986 models.

6. Reassemble the steering gear linkage and install the gear in the car.

1987-90 Vehicles

1. Remove the steering gear from the car as described below. Disconnect the tie rod ends and remove boots.

2. Turn the pinion shaft to neutral (centered) position. This puts the guide chip at neutral position (6° either side of center).

3. Loosen the locknut. Tighten the adjusting screw to 43 inch lbs. (4.9 Nm). Then, loosen it and tighten it to this torque again.

4. Loosen the adjusting screw and torque it to 1.7 inch lbs. (0.19 Nm).

5. Rotate the pinion to move the rack back and forth all the way through two full cycles. Then, return it to neutral position.

6. Slowly rotate the pinion and measure rotating torque through the entire 180° range either side of neutral. Find the point where rotating force is at its maximum. Loosen the adjusting screw at this point. Then, torque it to 26 inch lbs. (3.0 Nm).

7. Now check the pinion rotating torque. Traveling 100° either side of neutral position, it should average 6.1–10.4 inch lbs. (0.70–1.20 Nm). It must not fluctuate more than 2.6 inch lbs. (0.30 Nm).

8. If necessary, loosen the adjusting screw until the pinion rotating torque is within specification. Hold the adjusting nut in this position and torque the locknut to 29–43 ft. lbs. (39–58 Nm). If this will not correct the rotating torque, it will be necessary to replace the retaining spring.

1991-92 Sentra

1. Set the gears in the neutral position and loosen the locknut.

2. Torque the adjusting screw 2 times to 26 inch lbs. (2.9 Nm).

3. Loosen the adjusting screw and retorque to 1.7 inch lbs. (0.2 Nm).

4. Rotate the pinion to move the rack back and forth 2 times. Return to the neutral position.

5. Slowly rotate the pinion and measure the rotating torque in a 180° range. Find the position where the rotating torque is maximum.

6. Loosen the adjusting screw at that position and torque the adjusting screw to 26 inch lbs. (2.9 Nm), then back it off 50–70°.

7. Prevent the adjusting nut from turning and torque the locknut to 29–43 ft. lbs. (39–59 Nm).

8. Check the steering gear does not bind.

OVERHAUL

Overhaul of the manual steering gear is recommended to be performed by qualified steering gear rebuilders. The cost for specific components may not be as cost effective as purchasing a rebuilt unit.

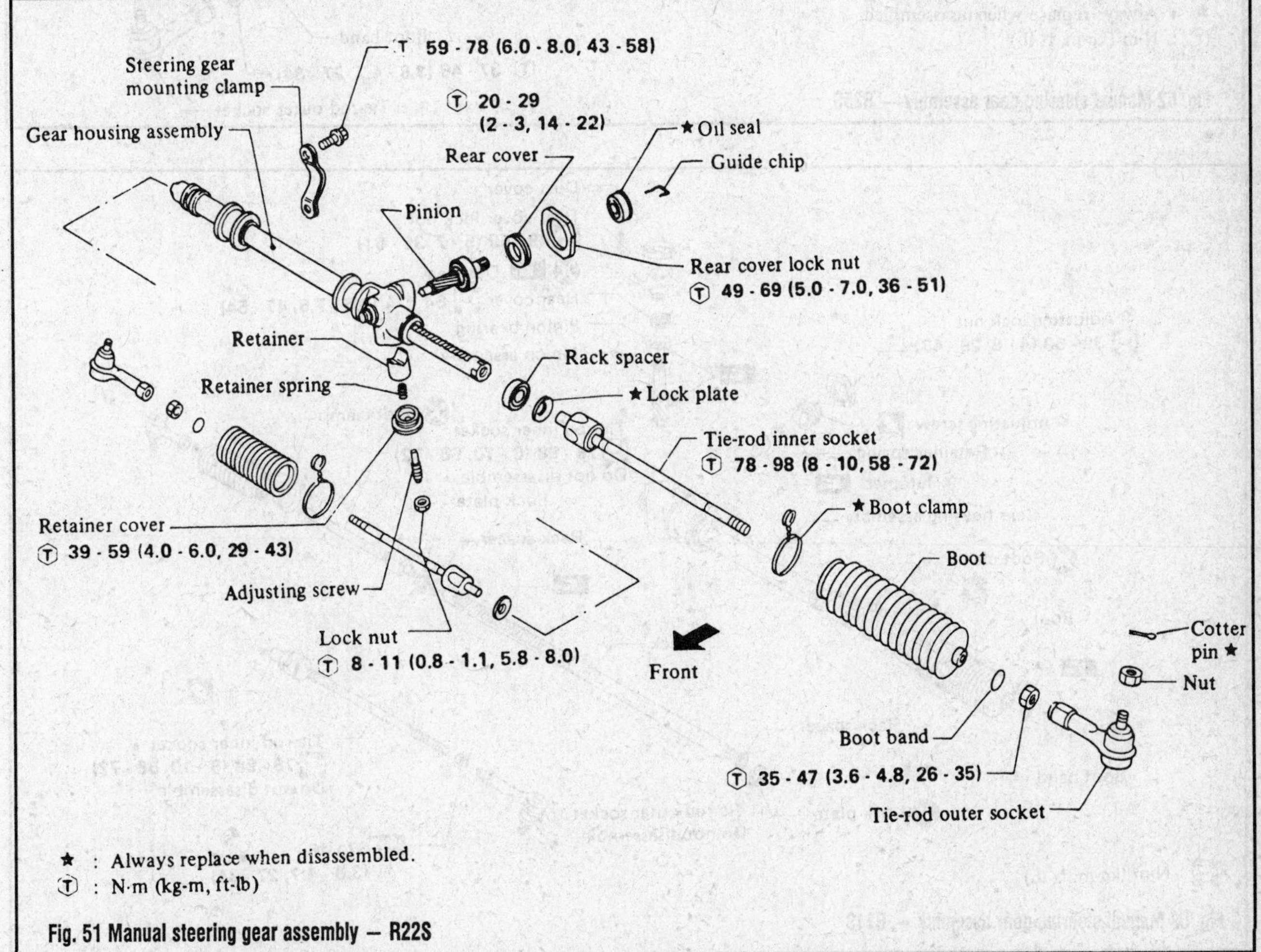
T 59 - 78 (6.0 - 8.0, 43 - 58)
Steering gear mounting clamp
T 20 - 29 (2 - 3, 14 - 22)
Gear housing assembly
★ Oil seal
Rear cover
Guide chip
Pinion
Rear cover lock nut
T 49 - 69 (5.0 - 7.0, 36 - 51)
Retainer
Rack spacer
Retainer spring
★ Lock plate
Tie-rod inner socket
T 78 - 98 (8 - 10, 58 - 72)
★ Boot clamp
Retainer cover
T 39 - 59 (4.0 - 6.0, 29 - 43)
Boot
Adjusting screw
Cotter pin ★
Lock nut
T 8 - 11 (0.8 - 1.1, 5.8 - 8.0)
Front
Nut
Boot band
T 35 - 47 (3.6 - 4.8, 26 - 35)
Tie-rod outer socket
★ : Always replace when disassembled.
T : N·m (kg-m, ft-lb)

Fig. 51 Manual steering gear assembly — R22S

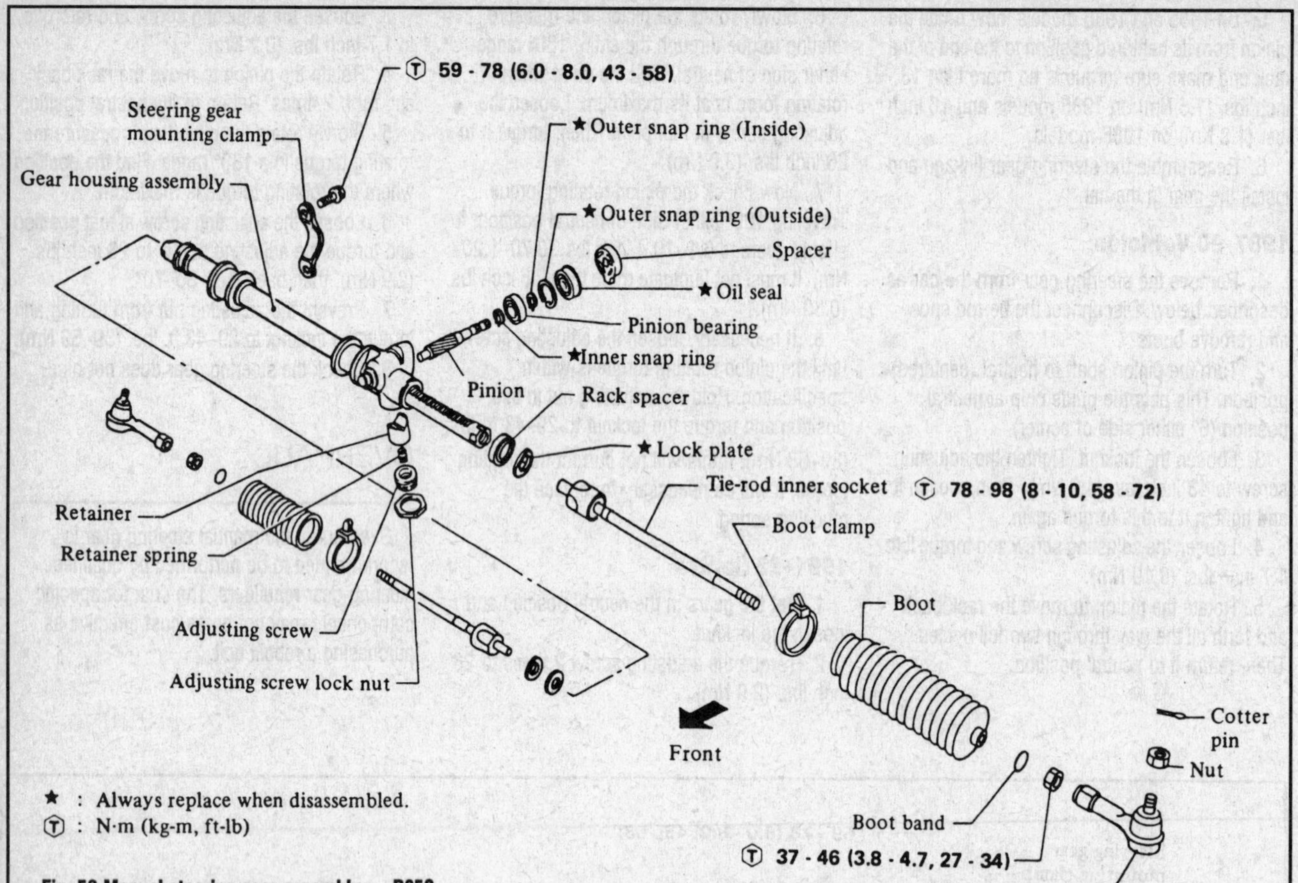

59 - 78 (6.0 - 8.0, 43 - 58)
Steering gear mounting clamp
Gear housing assembly
★Outer snap ring (Inside)
★Outer snap ring (Outside)
Spacer
★Oil seal
Pinion bearing
★Inner snap ring
Pinion
Rack spacer
★Lock plate
Tie-rod inner socket
78 - 98 (8 - 10, 58 - 72)
Boot clamp
Boot
Retainer
Retainer spring
Adjusting screw
Adjusting screw lock nut
Front
Cotter pin
Nut
Boot band
37 - 46 (3.8 - 4.7, 27 - 34)
Tie-rod outer socket
★ : Always replace when disassembled.
Ⓣ : N·m (kg-m, ft-lb)

Fig. 52 Manual steering gear assembly — R25S

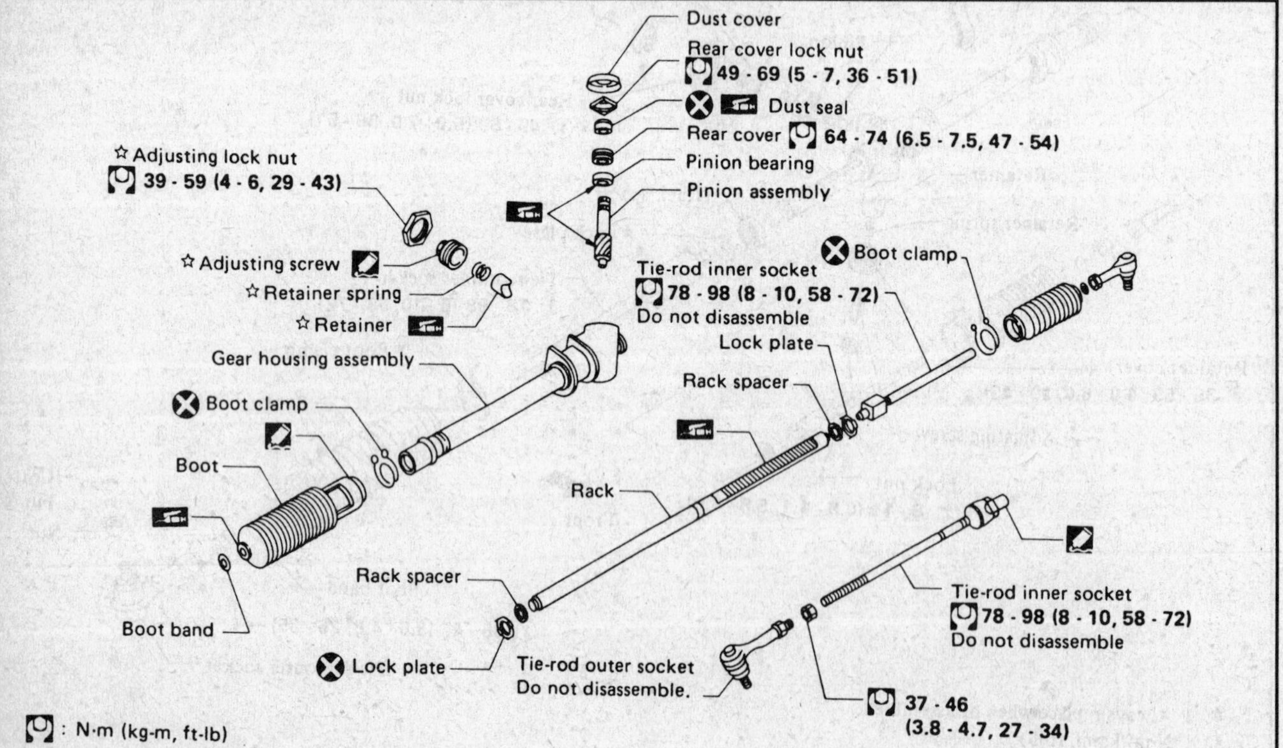

Dust cover
Rear cover lock nut
49 - 69 (5 - 7, 36 - 51)
Dust seal
Rear cover 64 - 74 (6.5 - 7.5, 47 - 54)
Pinion bearing
Pinion assembly
☆Adjusting lock nut
39 - 59 (4 - 6, 29 - 43)
☆Adjusting screw
☆Retainer spring
☆Retainer
Boot clamp
Tie-rod inner socket
78 - 98 (8 - 10, 58 - 72)
Do not disassemble
Lock plate
Rack spacer
Gear housing assembly
Boot clamp
Boot
Rack
Rack spacer
Tie-rod inner socket
78 - 98 (8 - 10, 58 - 72)
Do not disassemble
Boot band
Lock plate
Tie-rod outer socket
Do not disassemble.
37 - 46
(3.8 - 4.7, 27 - 34)
: N·m (kg-m, ft-lb)

Fig. 53 Manual steering gear assembly — R24S

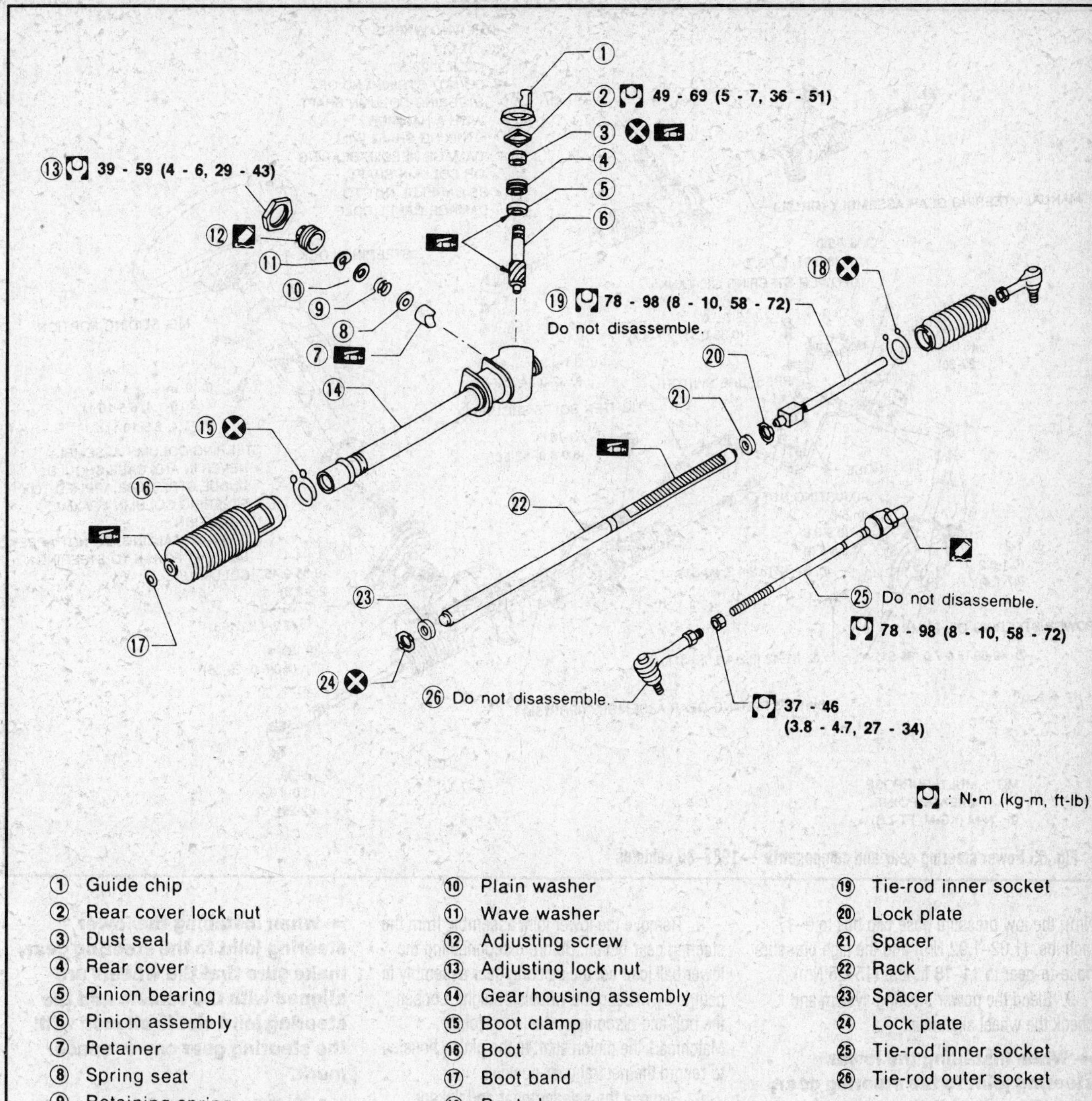
49 - 69 (5 - 7, 36 - 51)
39 - 59 (4 - 6, 29 - 43)
78 - 98 (8 - 10, 58 - 72)
Do not disassemble.
Do not disassemble.
78 - 98 (8 - 10, 58 - 72)
Do not disassemble.
37 - 46
(3.8 - 4.7, 27 - 34)
: N·m (kg-m, ft-lb)

1. Guide chip
2. Rear cover lock nut
3. Dust seal
4. Rear cover
5. Pinion bearing
6. Pinion assembly
7. Retainer
8. Spring seat
9. Retaining spring
10. Plain washer
11. Wave washer
12. Adjusting screw
13. Adjusting lock nut
14. Gear housing assembly
15. Boot clamp
16. Boot
17. Boot band
18. Boot clamp
19. Tie-rod inner socket
20. Lock plate
21. Spacer
22. Rack
23. Spacer
24. Lock plate
25. Tie-rod inner socket
26. Tie-rod outer socket

Fig. 54 Manual steering gear assembly — R24N

Power Steering Gear

➧ SEE FIG. 55

REMOVAL & INSTALLATION

1982–86 Vehicles

1. Raise and support the car on jackstands.
2. Disconnect the hose clamp and hose at the steering gear. Disconnect the flare nut and the tube at the steering gear, then drain the fluid from the gear.
3. Using the Ball Joint Remover tool HT72520000, remove the tie rod from the knuckle.
4. Place a floor jack under the transaxle and support it.
5. Remove the exhaust tube and the the rear engine mount.
6. Remove the steering column lower joint.
7. Unbolt and remove the steering gear unit and the linkage.

To install:

8. Install the power steering gear assembly to the vehicle. Torque the tie rod-to-steering knuckle nut to 26–36 ft. lbs. (35–49 Nm), the steering gear-to-frame clamp bolts to 43–58 ft. lbs. (58–79 Nm), the lower joint-to-pinion gear bolt to 22–29 ft. lbs. (29–39 Nm), the lower joint-to-steering column bolt to 22–29 ft. lbs. (29–39

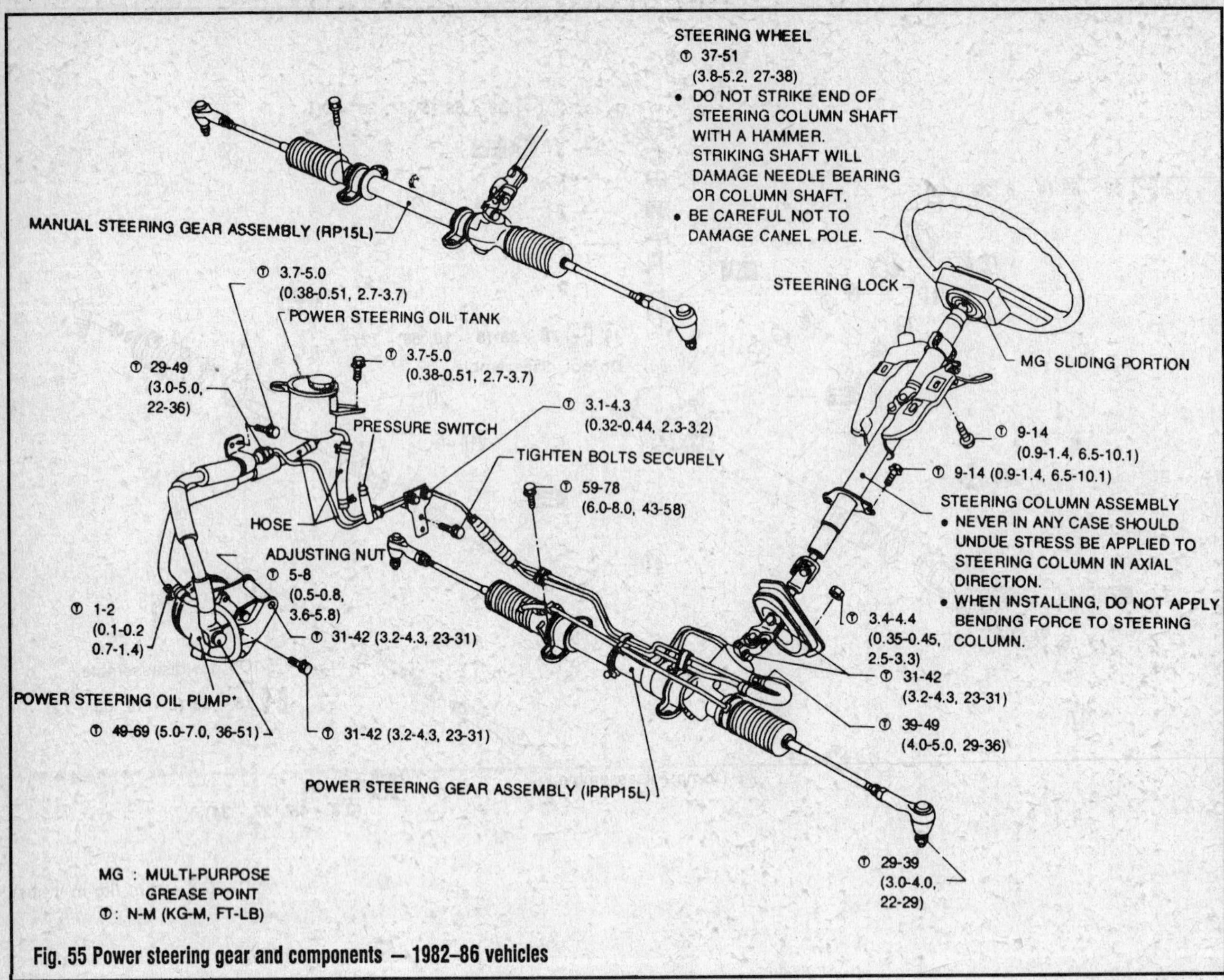
STEERING WHEEL
Ⓣ 37-51
(3.8-5.2, 27-38)
• DO NOT STRIKE END OF STEERING COLUMN SHAFT WITH A HAMMER. STRIKING SHAFT WILL DAMAGE NEEDLE BEARING OR COLUMN SHAFT.
• BE CAREFUL NOT TO DAMAGE CANEL POLE.
MANUAL STEERING GEAR ASSEMBLY (RP15L)
Ⓣ 3.7-5.0
(0.38-0.51, 2.7-3.7)
POWER STEERING OIL TANK
STEERING LOCK
Ⓣ 3.7-5.0
(0.38-0.51, 2.7-3.7)
MG SLIDING PORTION
Ⓣ 29-49
(3.0-5.0, 22-36)
Ⓣ 3.1-4.3
(0.32-0.44, 2.3-3.2)
PRESSURE SWITCH
Ⓣ 9-14
(0.9-1.4, 6.5-10.1)
TIGHTEN BOLTS SECURELY
Ⓣ 9-14 (0.9-1.4, 6.5-10.1)
Ⓣ 59-78
(6.0-8.0, 43-58)
HOSE
STEERING COLUMN ASSEMBLY
• NEVER IN ANY CASE SHOULD UNDUE STRESS BE APPLIED TO STEERING COLUMN IN AXIAL DIRECTION.
• WHEN INSTALLING, DO NOT APPLY BENDING FORCE TO STEERING COLUMN.
ADJUSTING NUT
Ⓣ 5-8
(0.5-0.8, 3.6-5.8)
Ⓣ 1-2
(0.1-0.2
0.7-1.4)
Ⓣ 31-42 (3.2-4.3, 23-31)
Ⓣ 3.4-4.4
(0.35-0.45, 2.5-3.3)
Ⓣ 31-42
(3.2-4.3, 23-31)
POWER STEERING OIL PUMP
Ⓣ 49-69 (5.0-7.0, 36-51)
Ⓣ 31-42 (3.2-4.3, 23-31)
Ⓣ 39-49
(4.0-5.0, 29-36)
POWER STEERING GEAR ASSEMBLY (IPRP15L)
Ⓣ 29-39
(3.0-4.0, 22-29)
MG : MULTI-PURPOSE GREASE POINT
Ⓣ: N-M (KG-M, FT-LB)

Fig. 55 Power steering gear and components — 1982–86 vehicles

Nm), the low pressure hose clip bolt to 9–17 inch lbs. (1.02–1.92 Nm) and the high pressure hose-to-gear to 11–18 ft. lbs. (15–25 Nm).

9. Bleed the power steering system and check the wheel alignment.

➡ **When installing the lower steering joint to the steering gear, make sure that the wheels are aligned with the vehicle and the steering joint slot is aligned with the steering gear cap or spacer mark.**

1987–92 Vehicles

1. Raise and support the vehicle safely and remove the wheels.
2. Disconnect the power steering hose from the power steering gear and plug all hoses to prevent leakage.
3. Disconnect the side rod studs from the steering knuckles.
4. Support the transaxle with a suitable transmission jack and remove the exhaust pipe and rear engine mounts.
5. Remove the lower joint assembly from the steering gear pinion. Before disconnecting the lower ball joint set the steering gear assembly in neutral by making the wheels straight. Loosen the bolt and disconnect the lower joint. Matchmark the pinion shaft to the pinion housing to record the neutral gear position.
6. Remove the steering gear and linkage assembly from the vehicle.

To Install:

7. Installation is the reverse of the removal procedure observing the following:
   a. Make sure the pinion shaft and pinion housing are aligned properly.
   b. Torque the high pressure hydraulic line fitting to 11–18 ft. lbs. (15–25 Nm) and lower pressure fitting to 20–29 ft. lbs. (27–39 Nm).
   c. When attaching the lower joint, set the left and right dust boots to equal deflection.
   d. Torque the gear housing mounting bracket bolts to 54–72 ft. lbs. (73–97 Nm).

➡ **When installing the lower steering joint to the steering gear, make sure that the wheels are aligned with the vehicle and the steering joint slot is aligned with the steering gear cap or spacer mark.**

8. Refill the power steering pump, start the engine and bleed the system. Refill the power steering pump, start the engine and bleed the system.

➡ **On most vehicles, the O-ring in the lower pressure hydraulic line fitting is larger than the O-ring in the high pressure line. Make sure the O-rings are installed in the proper fittings. Observe the torque specification given for the hydraulic line fittings. Over-tightening will cause damage to the fitting threads and O-rings.**

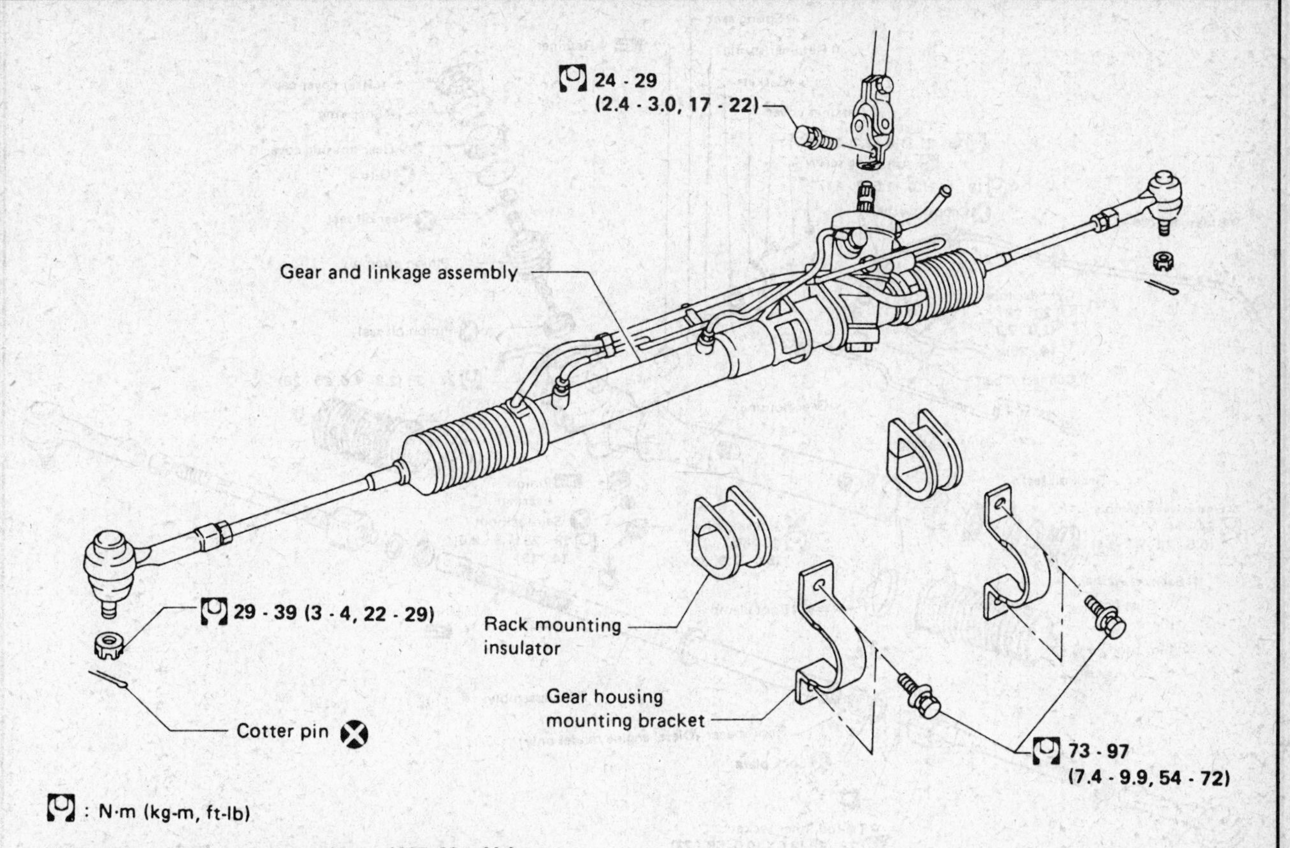

24 - 29
(2.4 - 3.0, 17 - 22)
Gear and linkage assembly
29 - 39 (3 - 4, 22 - 29)
Rack mounting insulator
Gear housing mounting bracket
Cotter pin
73 - 97
(7.4 - 9.9, 54 - 72)
: N·m (kg-m, ft-lb)

Fig. 55 Power steering gear assembly – 1987–92 vehicles

ADJUSTMENTS

1987–90 Vehicles

Adjustment is usually performed only after over haul and replacement of major parts. A special socket wrench KV48100700 must be used with an inch lbs. torque wrench in performing this work.

1. Disconnect the unit and remove it from the car as described below.
2. Rotate the pinion shaft from lock to lock, counting turns. Then, divide the number of turns in half, and turn the shaft that distance from either lock to center it.
3. Loosen the locknut and loosen the adjusting screw. Then, torque it to a torque of 43 inch lbs. (4.87 Nm). Loosen it and torque it again to that figure.
4. Loosen the adjusting screw and torque it to 0.43–1.74 inch lbs. (0.048–0.197 Nm). Loosen the locknut and apply locking sealer to the lower threads of the adjusting screw as well as the retainer cover surrounding it. Then, tighten the locknut to 29–43 ft. lbs. (39–58 Nm).

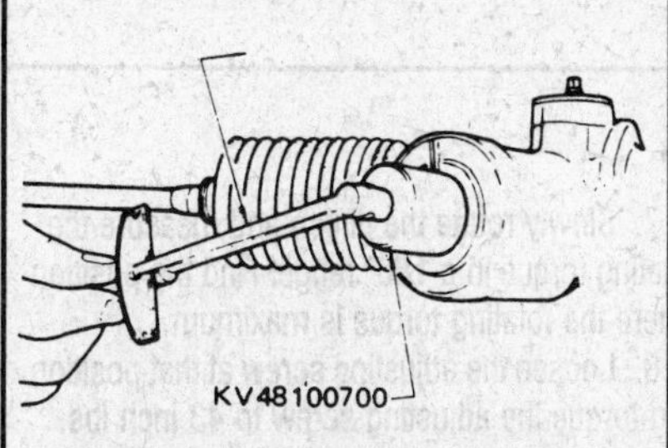
KV48100700

Fig. 50 Adjusting the power steering gear The adjusting screw for pinion torque is visible at the top of the unit – power steering gear similar

5. Move the rack through its entire stroke several times. Then, install the torque wrench and special socket and measure the rotating torque of the pinion 100° either side of the neutral position. The torque should be 6.9–11.3 inch lbs. (0.78–1.28 Nm) with a maximum of 16 inch lbs. (1.8 Nm).
6. If the torque is incorrect, readjust the screw appropriately. When the rotating torque is correct, reapply sealer and retorque the lock nut as necessary.

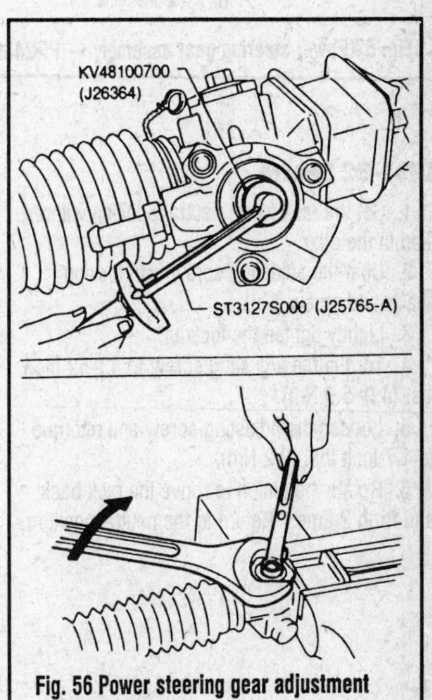
KV48100700
(J26364)
ST3127S000 (J25765-A)

Fig. 56 Power steering gear adjustment – 1991–92 Sentra

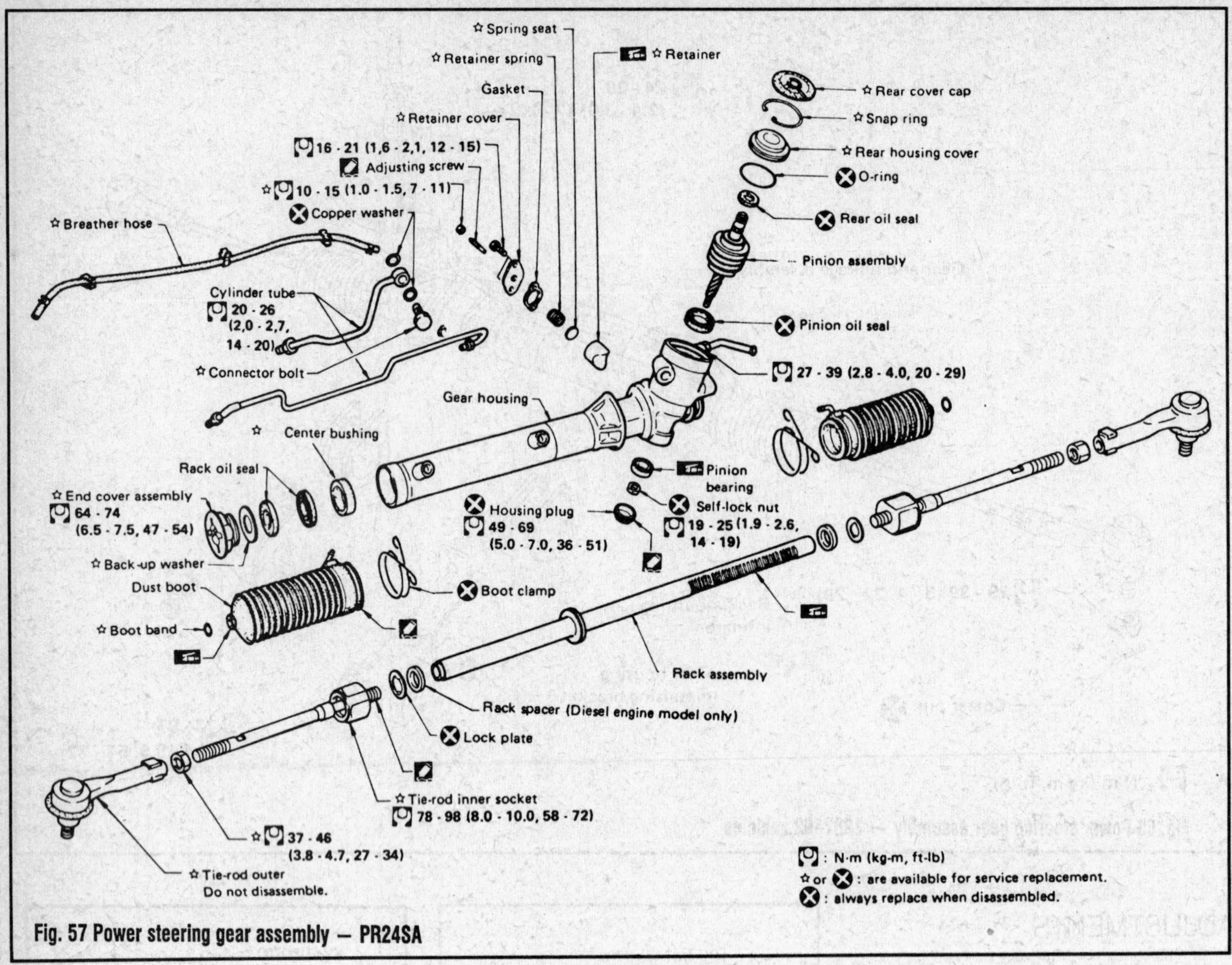
☆ Spring seat
☆ Retainer spring
☆ Retainer
Gasket
☆ Rear cover cap
☆ Retainer cover
☆ Snap ring
16 - 21 (1.6 - 2.1, 12 - 15)
Adjusting screw
☆ Rear housing cover
☆ 10 - 15 (1.0 - 1.5, 7 - 11)
O-ring
Copper washer
Rear oil seal
☆ Breather hose
Pinion assembly
Cylinder tube
20 - 26 (2.0 - 2.7, 14 - 20)
Pinion oil seal
☆ Connector bolt
27 - 39 (2.8 - 4.0, 20 - 29)
Gear housing
☆ Center bushing
Rack oil seal
Pinion bearing
☆ End cover assembly
64 - 74 (6.5 - 7.5, 47 - 54)
Housing plug
49 - 69 (5.0 - 7.0, 36 - 51)
Self-lock nut
19 - 25 (1.9 - 2.6, 14 - 19)
☆ Back-up washer
Dust boot
Boot clamp
☆ Boot band
Rack assembly
Rack spacer (Diesel engine model only)
Lock plate
☆ Tie-rod inner socket
78 - 98 (8.0 - 10.0, 58 - 72)
☆ 37 - 46 (3.8 - 4.7, 27 - 34)
☆ Tie-rod outer
Do not disassemble.
: N·m (kg-m, ft-lb)
☆ or : are available for service replacement.
: always replace when disassembled.

Fig. 57 Power steering gear assembly — PR24SA

1991–92 Sentra

1. Set the rack to the neutral position without fluid in the gear.
2. Coat the adjusting screw with locking sealer and screw it in.
3. Lightly tighten the locknut.
4. Torque the adjusting screw to 43–52 inch lbs. (4.9–5.9 Nm).
5. Loosen the adjusting screw and retorque to 1.7 inch lbs. (0.2 Nm).
6. Rotate the pinion to move the rack back and forth 2 times. Return to the neutral position.
7. Slowly rotate the pinion and measure the rotating torque in a 180° range. Find the position where the rotating torque is maximum.
8. Loosen the adjusting screw at that position and torque the adjusting screw to 43 inch lbs. (4.9 Nm). Back it off of the adjusting screw 40–60°.
9. Prevent the adjusting nut from turning and torque the locknut to 29–43 ft. lbs. (39–59 Nm).
10. Measure the pinion rotating torque with an inch lbs. torque wrench. The normal torque should be 6.9–11.3 inch lbs. (0.8–1.3 Nm) and the maximum deviation is 3.5 inch lbs. (0.4 Nm).
11. If the rotating torque is not within specifications, readjust the rotating torque.
12. Check the steering gear does not bind.

OVERHAUL

Overhaul of the power steering gear is recommended to be performed by qualified steering gear rebuilders. The cost for specific components may not be as cost effective as purchasing a rebuilt unit.

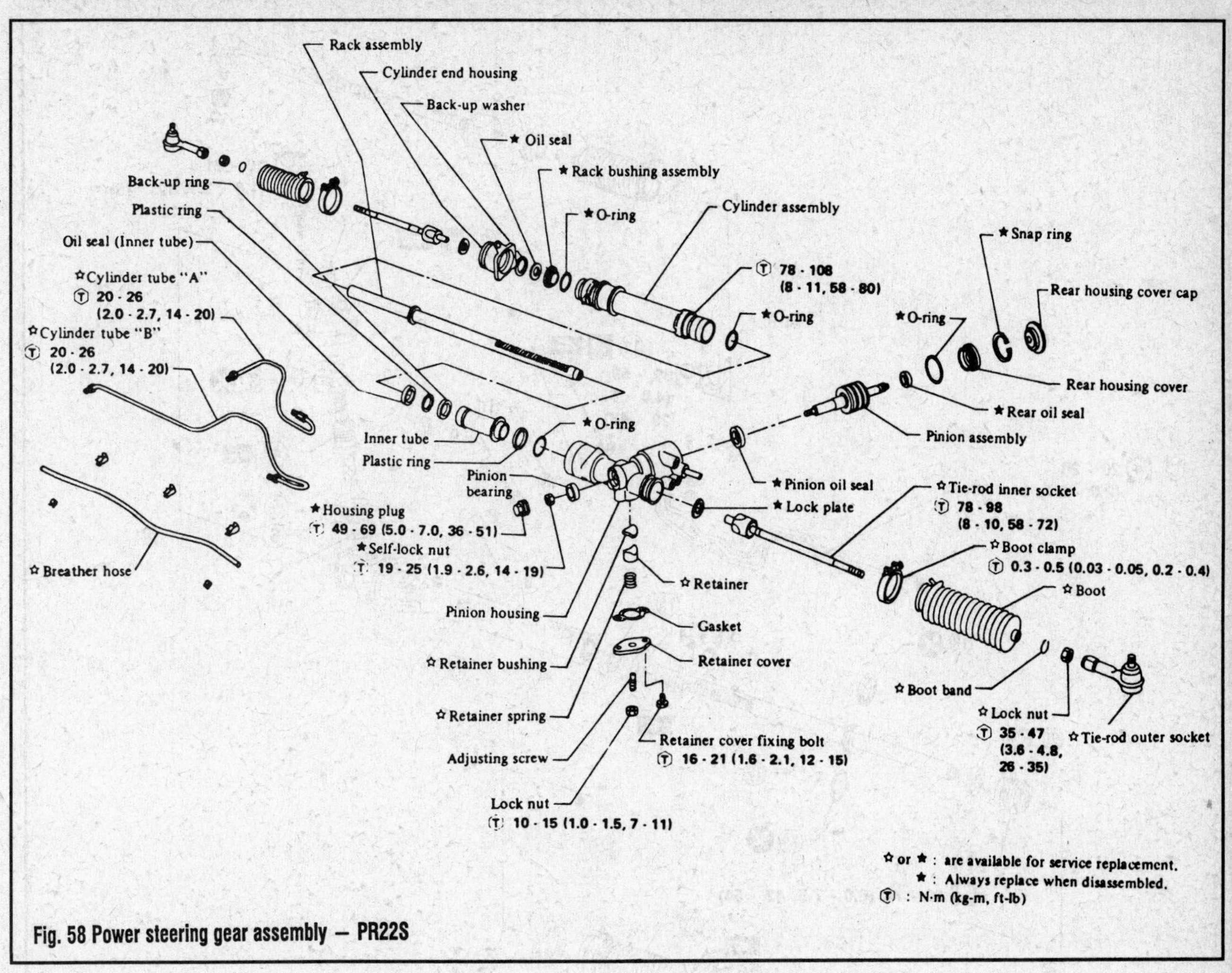
Rack assembly
Cylinder end housing
Back-up washer
★ Oil seal
★ Rack bushing assembly
★ O-ring
Cylinder assembly
Back-up ring
Plastic ring
Oil seal (Inner tube)
☆Cylinder tube "A"
Ⓣ 20 - 26
(2.0 - 2.7, 14 - 20)
☆Cylinder tube "B"
Ⓣ 20 - 26
(2.0 - 2.7, 14 - 20)
Ⓣ 78 - 108
(8 - 11, 58 - 80)
★ O-ring
★ Snap ring
Rear housing cover cap
★ O-ring
Rear housing cover
★ Rear oil seal
Pinion assembly
★ O-ring
Inner tube
Plastic ring
Pinion bearing
★ Pinion oil seal
★ Lock plate
☆ Tie-rod inner socket
Ⓣ 78 - 98
(8 - 10, 58 - 72)
★ Housing plug
Ⓣ 49 - 69 (5.0 - 7.0, 36 - 51)
★ Self-lock nut
Ⓣ 19 - 25 (1.9 - 2.6, 14 - 19)
☆ Breather hose
☆ Boot clamp
Ⓣ 0.3 - 0.5 (0.03 - 0.05, 0.2 - 0.4)
☆ Boot
☆ Retainer
Pinion housing
Gasket
☆ Retainer bushing
Retainer cover
☆ Boot band
☆ Retainer spring
☆ Lock nut
Ⓣ 35 - 47
(3.6 - 4.8,
26 - 35)
☆ Tie-rod outer socket
Retainer cover fixing bolt
Ⓣ 16 - 21 (1.6 - 2.1, 12 - 15)
Adjusting screw
Lock nut
Ⓣ 10 - 15 (1.0 - 1.5, 7 - 11)
☆ or ★ : are available for service replacement.
★ : Always replace when disassembled.
Ⓣ : N·m (kg-m, ft-lb)

Fig. 58 Power steering gear assembly — PR22S

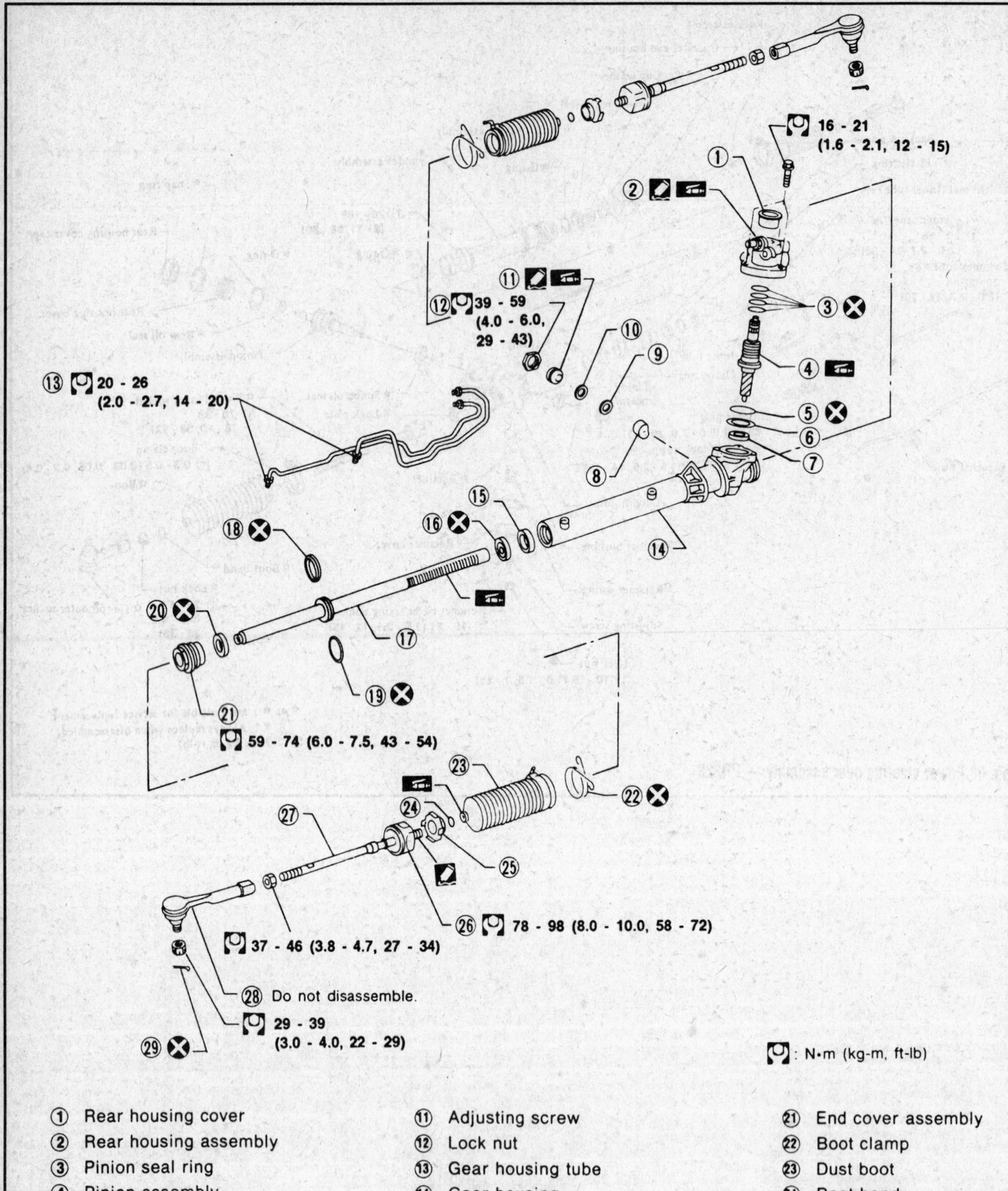

16 - 21
(1.6 - 2.1, 12 - 15)
39 - 59
(4.0 - 6.0,
29 - 43)
20 - 26
(2.0 - 2.7, 14 - 20)
59 - 74 (6.0 - 7.5, 43 - 54)
78 - 98 (8.0 - 10.0, 58 - 72)
37 - 46 (3.8 - 4.7, 27 - 34)
Do not disassemble.
29 - 39
(3.0 - 4.0, 22 - 29)
: N•m (kg-m, ft-lb)

① Rear housing cover
② Rear housing assembly
③ Pinion seal ring
④ Pinion assembly
⑤ O-ring
⑥ Shim
⑦ Pinion oil seal
⑧ Retainer
⑨ Washer
⑩ Spring disc
⑪ Adjusting screw
⑫ Lock nut
⑬ Gear housing tube
⑭ Gear housing
⑮ Center bushing
⑯ Rack oil seal
⑰ Rack assembly
⑱ Rack seal ring
⑲ O-ring
⑳ Rack oil seal
㉑ End cover assembly
㉒ Boot clamp
㉓ Dust boot
㉔ Boot band
㉕ Lock plate
㉖ Tie-rod inner socket
㉗ Tie-rod
㉘ Tie-rod outer
㉙ Cotter pin

Fig. 59 Power steering gear assembly — PR24SC

Power Steering Pump

REMOVAL & INSTALLATION

1982-90 Vehicles

1. Remove the hoses at the pump and plug and openings shut to prevent contamination. Position the disconnected lines in a raised attitude to prevent leakage.
2. Loosen the power steering pump drive belt adjuster and the drive belt.
3. Loosen the retaining bolts, then remove the braces and the pump from the vehicle.
4. To install, reverse the removal procedures. Adjust the belt tension and bleed the power steering system. Refer to section 1 for belt routing.

1991-92 Sentra

1. Remove the air cleaner duct and air cleaner.
2. Loosen the idler pulley locknut and turn the adjusting nut counterclockwise, in order to remove the power steering belt. Refer to section 1 for belt routing.
3. Remove the drive belt on the air conditioning compressor, if so equipped.
4. Loosen the power steering hoses at the pump and remove the bolts holding the power steering pump to the bracket.
5. Disconnect and plug the power steering hoses and remove the pump from the vehicle.
6. Installation is the reverse of the removal procedure. Fill and bleed the power steering system.

BELT ADJUSTMENT

1. Loosen the tension adjustment and mounting bolts.
2. Move the pump toward or away from the engine so the belt deflects $^{1}/_{4}$–$^{1}/_{2}$ in. (6–13mm) midway between the idler pulley and the pump pulley under moderate thumb pressure.
3. Tighten the bolts and recheck the tension adjustment.

BLEEDING THE POWER STEERING SYSTEM

1. Fill the pump reservoir and allow to remain undisturbed for a few minutes.
2. Raise the car until the front wheels are clear of the ground.
3. With the engine off, quickly turn the wheels right and left several times, lightly contacting the stops.
4. Add fluid if necessary.
5. Start the engine and let it idle until it reaches operating temperatures.
6. Repeat Steps 3 and 4 with the engine idling.

➡ **Do not allow the steering linkage to contact the stops for any longer than 15 seconds, with the engine running.**

7. Stop the engine, lower the car until the wheels just touch the ground. Start the engine, allow it to idle and turn the wheels back and forth several times. Check the fluid level and refill if necessary.

TORQUE SPECIFICATIONS

Component	U.S.	Metric
Wheel lug nuts		
steel wheels	100 ft. lbs.	136 Nm
aluminum wheels	90 ft. lbs.	122 Nm
Sealed hub bearing nut	137-188 ft. lbs.	186-255 Nm
MacPherson strut-to-body bolt	23-31 ft. lbs.	32-42 Nm
Piston rod locknut	43-54 ft. lbs.	58-73 Nm
Strut-to-knuckle bolts	72-87 ft. lbs.	98-118 Nm
Ball joint-to-lower control arm	40-51 ft. lbs.	54-69 Nm
Gusset-to-body bolts	65-87 ft. lbs.	88-118 Nm
Stabilizer-to-control arm	80-100 inch lbs.	9.0-11.3 Nm
Lower shock absorber bolt	51-65 ft. lbs.	69-88 Nm
Upper shock absorber nut	78-104 inch lbs.	8.8-11.8 Nm
Transverse link-to-steering knuckle	72-87 ft. lbs.	98-118 Nm
Steering wheel nut	29-40 ft. lbs.	39-54 Nm
Air bag spiral cable screw	24 inch lbs.	4.0 Nm
Steering column-to-steering gear	17-22 ft. lbs.	23-30 Nm
Tie rod end locknut	27-34 ft. lbs.	37-46 Nm
Steering gear mounting bolts	54-72 ft. lbs.	73-97 Nm
Power steering hose fitting	11-18 ft. lbs.	15-25 Nm
Steering gear adjuster locknut	29-43 ft. lbs.	39-59 Nm

Troubleshooting the Turn Signal Switch

Problem	Cause	Solution
Turn signal will not cancel	• Loose switch mounting screws • Switch or anchor bosses broken • Broken, missing or out of position detent, or cancelling spring	• Tighten screws • Replace switch • Reposition springs or replace switch as required
Turn signal difficult to operate	• Turn signal lever loose • Switch yoke broken or distorted • Loose or misplaced springs • Foreign parts and/or materials in switch • Switch mounted loosely	• Tighten mounting screws • Replace switch • Reposition springs or replace switch • Remove foreign parts and/or material • Tighten mounting screws
Turn signal will not indicate lane change	• Broken lane change pressure pad or spring hanger • Broken, missing or misplaced lane change spring • Jammed wires	• Replace switch • Replace or reposition as required • Loosen mounting screws, reposition wires and retighten screws
Turn signal will not stay in turn position	• Foreign material or loose parts impeding movement of switch yoke • Defective switch	• Remove material and/or parts • Replace switch
Hazard switch cannot be pulled out	• Foreign material between hazard support cancelling leg and yoke	• Remove foreign material. No foreign material impeding function of hazard switch—replace turn signal switch.
No turn signal lights	• Inoperative turn signal flasher • Defective or blown fuse • Loose chassis to column harness connector • Disconnect column to chassis connector. Connect new switch to chassis and operate switch by hand. If vehicle lights now operate normally, signal switch is inoperative • If vehicle lights do not operate, check chassis wiring for opens, grounds, etc.	• Replace turn signal flasher • Replace fuse • Connect securely • Replace signal switch • Repair chassis wiring as required

Troubleshooting the Turn Signal Switch (cont.)

Problem	Cause	Solution
Instrument panel turn indicator lights on but not flashing	• Burned out or damaged front or rear turn signal bulb • If vehicle lights do not operate, check light sockets for high resistance connections, the chassis wiring for opens, grounds, etc. • Inoperative flasher • Loose chassis to column harness connection • Inoperative turn signal switch • To determine if turn signal switch is defective, substitute new switch into circuit and operate switch by hand. If the vehicle's lights operate normally, signal switch is inoperative.	• Replace bulb • Repair chassis wiring as required • Replace flasher • Connect securely • Replace turn signal switch • Replace turn signal switch
Stop light not on when turn indicated	• Loose column to chassis connection • Disconnect column to chassis connector. Connect new switch into system without removing old.	• Connect securely • Replace signal switch
Stop light not on when turn indicated (cont.)	Operate switch by hand. If brake lights work with switch in the turn position, signal switch is defective. • If brake lights do not work, check connector to stop light sockets for grounds, opens, etc.	• Repair connector to stop light circuits using service manual as guide
Turn indicator panel lights not flashing	• Burned out bulbs • High resistance to ground at bulb socket • Opens, ground in wiring harness from front turn signal bulb socket to indicator lights	• Replace bulbs • Replace socket • Locate and repair as required

Troubleshooting the Turn Signal Switch (cont.)

Problem	Cause	Solution
Turn signal lights flash very slowly	• High resistance ground at light sockets	• Repair high resistance grounds at light sockets
	• Incorrect capacity turn signal flasher or bulb	• Replace turn signal flasher or bulb
	• If flashing rate is still extremely slow, check chassis wiring harness from the connector to light sockets for high resistance	• Locate and repair as required
	• Loose chassis to column harness connection	• Connect securely
	• Disconnect column to chassis connector. Connect new switch into system without removing old. Operate switch by hand. If flashing occurs at normal rate, the signal switch is defective.	• Replace turn signal switch

Troubleshooting the Turn Signal Switch (cont.)

Problem	Cause	Solution
Hazard signal lights will not flash—turn signal functions normally	• Blow fuse	• Replace fuse
	• Inoperative hazard warning flasher	• Replace hazard warning flasher in fuse panel
	• Loose chassis-to-column harness connection	• Conect securely
	• Disconnect column to chassis connector. Connect new switch into system without removing old. Depress the hazard warning lights. If they now work normally, turn signal switch is defective.	• Replace turn signal switch
	• If lights do not flash, check wiring harness "K" lead for open between hazard flasher and connector. If open, fuse block is defective	• Repair or replace brown wire or connector as required

Troubleshooting the Power Steering Pump

Problem	Cause	Solution
Chirp noise in steering pump	• Loose belt	• Adjust belt tension to specification
Belt squeal (particularly noticeable at full wheel travel and stand still parking)	• Loose belt	• Adjust belt tension to specification
Growl noise in steering pump	• Excessive back pressure in hoses or steering gear caused by restriction	• Locate restriction and correct. Replace part if necessary.
Growl noise in steering pump (particularly noticeable at stand still parking)	• Scored pressure plates, thrust plate or rotor • Extreme wear of cam ring	• Replace parts and flush system • Replace parts
Groan noise in steering pump	• Low oil level • Air in the oil. Poor pressure hose connection.	• Fill reservoir to proper level • Tighten connector to specified torque. Bleed system by operating steering from right to left—full turn.
Rattle noise in steering pump	• Vanes not installed properly • Vanes sticking in rotor slots	• Install properly • Free up by removing burrs, varnish, or dirt
Swish noise in steering pump	• Defective flow control valve	• Replace part
Whine noise in steering pump	• Pump shaft bearing scored	• Replace housing and shaft. Flush system.
Hard steering or lack of assist	• Loose pump belt • Low oil level in reservoir **NOTE:** Low oil level will also result in excessive pump noise • Steering gear to column misalignment • Lower coupling flange rubbing against steering gear adjuster plug • Tires not properly inflated	• Adjust belt tension to specification • Fill to proper level. If excessively low, check all lines and joints for evidence of external leakage. Tighten loose connectors. • Align steering column • Loosen pinch bolt and assemble properly • Inflate to recommended pressure
Foaming milky power steering fluid, low fluid level and possible low pressure	• Air in the fluid, and loss of fluid due to internal pump leakage causing overflow	• Check for leaks and correct. Bleed system. Extremely cold temperatures will cause system aeriation should the oil level be low. If oil level is correct and pump still foams, remove pump from vehicle and separate reservoir from body. Check welsh plug and body for cracks. If plug is loose or body is cracked, replace body.

Troubleshooting the Power Steering Pump (cont.)

Problem	Cause	Solution
Low pump pressure	• Flow control valve stuck or inoperative • Pressure plate not flat against cam ring	• Remove burrs or dirt or replace. Flush system. • Correct
Momentary increase in effort when turning wheel fast to right or left	• Low oil level in pump • Pump belt slipping • High internal leakage	• Add power steering fluid as required • Tighten or replace belt • Check pump pressure. (See pressure test)
Steering wheel surges or jerks when turning with engine running especially during parking	• Low oil level • Loose pump belt • Steering linkage hitting engine oil pan at full turn • Insufficient pump pressure	• Fill as required • Adjust tension to specification • Correct clearance • Check pump pressure. (See pressure test). Replace flow control valve if defective.
Steering wheel surges or jerks when turning with engine running especially during parking (cont.)	• Sticking flow control valve	• Inspect for varnish or damage, replace if necessary
Excessive wheel kickback or loose steering	• Air in system	• Add oil to pump reservoir and bleed by operating steering. Check hose connectors for proper torque and adjust as required.
Low pump pressure	• Extreme wear of cam ring • Scored pressure plate, thrust plate, or rotor • Vanes not installed properly • Vanes sticking in rotor slots • Cracked or broken thrust or pressure plate	• Replace parts. Flush system. • Replace parts. Flush system. • Install properly • Freeup by removing burrs, varnish, or dirt • Replace part

9

BRAKES

BASIC OPERATING PRINCIPLES

Hydraulic systems are used to actuate the brakes of all automobiles. The system transports the power required to force the frictional surfaces of the braking system together from the pedal to the individual brake units at each wheel. A hydraulic system is used for two reasons.

First, fluid under pressure can be carried to all parts of an automobile by small pipes and flexible hoses without taking up a significant amount of room or posing routing problems.

Second, a great mechanical advantage can be given to the brake pedal end of the system, and the foot pressure required to actuate the brakes can be reduced by making the surface area of the master cylinder pistons smaller than that of any of the pistons in the wheel cylinders or calipers.

The master cylinder consists of a fluid reservoir and a double cylinder and piston assembly. Double type master cylinders are designed to separate the front and rear braking systems hydraulically in case of a leak.

Steel lines carry the brake fluid to a point on the vehicle's frame near each of the vehicle's wheels. The fluid is then carried to the calipers and wheel cylinders by flexible tubes in order to allow for suspension and steering movements.

In drum brake systems, each wheel cylinder contains two pistons, one at either end, which push outward in opposite directions.

For disc brake systems, the cylinders are part of the calipers. One cylinder in each caliper is used to force the brake pads against the disc.

The pistons employ some type of seal, usually made of rubber, to minimize fluid leakage. A rubber dust boot seals the outer end of the cylinder against dust and dirt. The boot fits around the outer end of the piston on disc brake calipers, and around the brake actuating rod on wheel cylinders.

The hydraulic system operates as follows: When at rest, the entire system, from the piston(s) in the master cylinder to those in the wheel cylinders or calipers, is full of brake fluid. Upon application of the brake pedal, fluid trapped in front of the master cylinder piston(s) is forced through the lines to the wheel cylinders. Here, it forces the pistons outward, in the case of drum brakes, and inward toward the disc, in the case of disc brakes. The motion of the pistons is opposed by return springs mounted outside the cylinders in drum brakes, and by spring seals, in disc brakes.

Upon release of the brake pedal, a spring located inside the master cylinder immediately returns the master cylinder pistons to the normal position. The pistons contain check valves and the master cylinder has compensating ports drilled in it. These are uncovered as the pistons reach their normal position. The piston check valves allow fluid to flow toward the wheel cylinders or calipers as the pistons withdraw. Then, as the return springs force the brake pads or shoes into the released position, the excess fluid reservoir through the compensating ports. It is during the time the pedal is in the released position that any fluid that has leaked out of the system will be replaced through the compensating ports.

Dual circuit master cylinders employ two pistons, located one behind the other, in the same cylinder. The primary piston is actuated directly by mechanical linkage from the brake pedal through the power booster. The secondary piston is actuated by fluid trapped between the two pistons. If a leak develops in front of the secondary piston, it moves forward until it bottoms against the front of the master cylinder, and the fluid trapped between the pistons will operate the rear brakes. If the rear brakes develop a leak, the primary piston will move forward until direct contact with the secondary piston takes place, and it will force the secondary piston to actuate the front brakes. In either case, the brake pedal moves farther when the brakes are applied, and less braking power is available.

All dual circuit systems use a switch to warn the driver when only half of the brake system is operational. This switch is located in a valve body which is mounted on the firewall or the frame below the master cylinder. A hydraulic piston receives pressure from both circuits, each circuit's pressure being applied to one end of the piston. When the pressures are in balance, the piston remains stationary. When one circuit has a leak, however, the greater pressure in that circuit during application of the brakes will push the piston to one side, closing the switch and activating the brake warning light.

In disc brake systems, this valve body also contains a metering valve and, in some cases, a proportioning valve. The metering valve keeps pressure from traveling to the disc brakes on the front wheels until the brake shoes on the rear wheels have contacted the drums, ensuring that the front brakes will never be used alone. The proportioning valve controls the pressure to the rear brakes to lessen the chance of rear wheel lock-up during very hard braking.

Warning lights may be tested by depressing the brake pedal and holding it while opening one of the wheel cylinder bleeder screws. If this does not cause the light to go on, substitute a new lamp, make continuity checks, and, finally, replace the switch as necessary.

The hydraulic system may be checked for leaks by applying pressure to the pedal gradually and steadily. If the pedal sinks very slowly to the floor, the system has a leak. This is not to be confused with a springy or spongy feel due to the compression of air within the lines. If the system leaks, there will be a gradual change in the position of the pedal with a constant pressure.

Check for leaks along all lines and at wheel cylinders. If no external leaks are apparent, the problem is inside the master cylinder.

Disc Brakes

BASIC OPERATING PRINCIPLES

Instead of the traditional expanding brakes that press outward against a circular drum, disc brake systems utilize a disc (rotor) with brake pads positioned on either side of it. Braking effect is achieved in a manner similar to the way you would squeeze a spinning phonograph record between your fingers. The disc (rotor) is a casting with cooling fins between the two braking surfaces. This enables air to circulate between the braking surfaces making them less sensitive to heat buildup and more resistant to fade. Dirt and water do not affect braking action since contaminants are thrown off by the centrifugal action of the rotor or scraped off the by the pads. Also, the equal clamping action of the two brake pads tends to ensure uniform, straight line stops. Disc brakes are inherently self-adjusting.

There are three general types of disc brake:

- A fixed caliper.
- A floating caliper.
- A sliding caliper.

The fixed caliper design uses two pistons mounted on either side of the rotor (in each side of the caliper). The caliper is mounted rigidly and does not move.

The sliding and floating designs are quite similar. In fact, these two types are often lumped together. In both designs, the pad on the inside of the rotor is moved into contact with the rotor by hydraulic force. The caliper, which is not held in a fixed position, moves slightly, bringing the outside pad into contact with the rotor. There are various methods of attaching floating calipers. Some pivot at the bottom or top, and some slide on mounting bolts. In any event, the end result is the same.

All the cars covered in this book employ the sliding caliper design.

Drum Brakes

BASIC OPERATING PRINCIPLES

Drum brakes employ two brake shoes mounted on a stationary backing plate. These shoes are positioned inside a circular drum which rotates with the wheel assembly. The shoes are held in place by springs. This allows them to slide toward the drums (when they are applied) while keeping the linings and drums in alignment. The shoes are actuated by a wheel cylinder which is mounted at the top of the backing plate. When the brakes are applied, hydraulic pressure forces the wheel cylinder's actuating links outward. Since these links bear directly against the top of the brake shoes, the tops of the shoes are then forced against the inner side of the drum. This action forces the bottoms of the two shoes to contact the brake drum by rotating the entire assembly slightly (known as servo action). When pressure within the wheel cylinder is relaxed, return springs pull the shoes back away from the drum.

Most modern drum brakes are designed to self-adjust themselves during application when the vehicle is moving in reverse. This motion causes both shoes to rotate very slightly with the drum, rocking an adjusting lever, thereby causing rotation of the adjusting screw.

Power Boosters

Power brakes operate just as non-power brake systems except in the actuation of the master cylinder pistons. A vacuum diaphragm is located on the front of the master cylinder and assists the driver in applying the brakes, reducing both the effort and travel he must put into moving the brake pedal.

The vacuum diaphragm housing is connected to the intake manifold by a vacuum hose. A check valve is placed at the point where the hose enters the diaphragm housing, so that during periods of low manifold vacuum brake assist vacuum will not be lost.

Depressing the brake pedal closes off the vacuum source and allows atmospheric pressure to enter on one side of the diaphragm. This causes the master cylinder pistons to move and apply the brakes. When the brake pedal is released, vacuum is applied to both sides of the diaphragm, and return springs return the diaphragm and master cylinder pistons to the released position. If the vacuum fails, the brake pedal rod will butt against the end of the master cylinder actuating rod, and direct mechanical application will occur as the pedal is depressed.

The hydraulic and mechanical problems that apply to conventional brake systems also apply to power brakes, and should be checked for if the tests below do not reveal the problem.

Test for a system vacuum leak as described below:

1. Operate the engine at idle without touching the brake pedal for at least one minute.
2. Turn off the engine, and wait one minute.
3. Test for the presence of assist vacuum by depressing the brake pedal and releasing it several times. Light application will produce less and less pedal travel, if vacuum was present. If there is no vacuum, air is leaking into the system somewhere.

Test for system operation as follows:

1. Pump the brake pedal (with engine off) until the supply vacuum is entirely gone.
2. Put a light, steady pressure on the pedal.
3. Start the engine, and operate it at idle. If the system is operating, the brake pedal should fall toward the floor if constant pressure is maintained on the pedal.

Power brake systems may be tested for hydraulic leaks just as ordinary systems are tested.

BRAKE OPERATING SYSTEM

Adjustments

DRUM BRAKES

1. Raise and support the rear of the vehicle on jackstands.
2. Remove the rubber cover from the backing plate.
3. Insert a brake adjusting tool through the hole in the brake backing plate. Turn the toothed adjusting nut to spread the brake shoes, making contact with the brake drum.

➡ **When adjusting the brake shoes, turn the wheel until considerable drag is felt. If necessary, hit the brake drum with a rubber hammer to align the shoes with the drum.**

4. When considerable drag is felt, back off the adjusting nut a few notches, so that the correct clearance is maintained between the brake drum and the brake shoes. Make sure that the wheel rotates freely.

BRAKE PEDAL HEIGHT ADJUSTMENT

➧ SEE FIGS. 1–2

Before adjusting the pedal, make sure that the wheel brakes are correctly adjusted. Adjust the pedal height with the input rod, attached to the top of the brake pedal. Pedal height (floorboard to pedal pad) should be as follows:

- 1982–86 vehicles — MTX-7.64–8.03 in. (194–204mm)
- 1982–86 vehicles — ATX-7.76–8.15 in. (197–207mm)
- 1987–90 vehicles — MTX-6.30–6.61 in. (160–168mm)
- 1987–90 vehicles — ATX-6.46–6.85 in. (164–174mm)
- 1991–92 Sentra — MTX-5.83–6.22 in. (148–158mm)
- 1991–92 Sentra — ATX-6.18–6.57 in. (157–167mm)

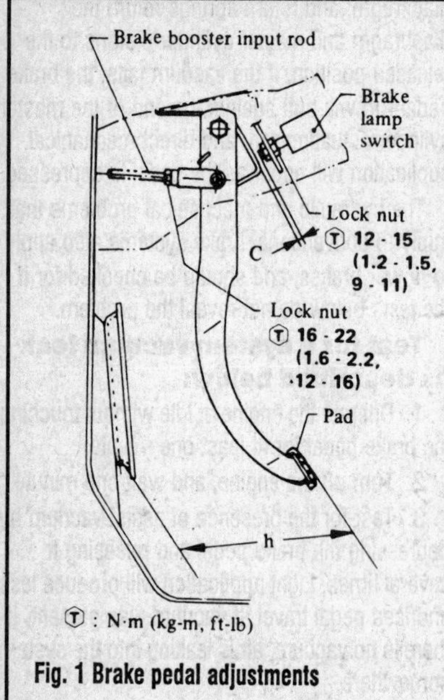
Brake booster input rod
Brake lamp switch
Lock nut
12 - 15 (1.2 - 1.5, 9 - 11)
C
Lock nut
16 - 22 (1.6 - 2.2, 12 - 16)
Pad
h
: N·m (kg-m, ft-lb)
Fig. 1 Brake pedal adjustments

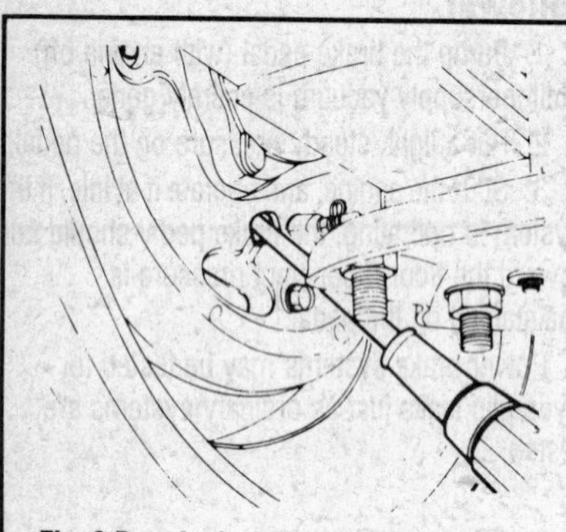
Fig. 2 Rear brake adjustment Brake spoon is recommended

Brake Light Switch

REMOVAL & INSTALLATION

1. Disconnect the negative battery cable.
2. Disconnect the wiring connector at the switch.
3. Remove the switch lock nut.
4. Remove the switch.
5. Install the switch and adjust it so the brake lights are not on unless the brake pedal is depressed.

ADJUSTMENT

Adjust the clearance between the brake pedal and the stop lamp switch or the ASCD switch, by loosening the locknut and adjusting the switch. The clearance should be approximately 0–1.0mm for 1982–84, 0.30–1.00mm for 1985–90 and 0.1–0.3mm for 1991–92 vehicles.

Master Cylinder

➧ SEE FIGS. 3–6

✻✻ WARNING

Clean, high quality brake fluid is essential to the safe and proper operation of the brake system. You should always buy the highest quality brake fluid that is available. If the brake fluid becomes contaminated, drain and flush the system and fill the master cylinder with new fluid. Never reuse any brake fluid. Any brake fluid that is removed from the system should be discarded.

REMOVAL & INSTALLATION

1. Clean the outside of the master cylinder thoroughly, particularly around the cap and fluid lines. Disconnect the fluid lines and cap them to exclude dirt.
2. If equipped with a fluid level sensor, disconnect the wiring harness from the master cylinder.
3. Disconnect the brake fluid tubes, then plug the openings to prevent dirt from entering the system.
4. Remove the mounting bolts at the firewall or the brake booster (if equipped) and remove the master cylinder from the vehicle.

To install:

5. Bench bleed the master cylinder by using old brake pipes. Bend the brake pipes around into the reservoir. Place the master cylinder in a vise and fill the reservoir with DOT 3 brake fluid. Pump the piston using a pushrod until all the air bubbles are gone.
6. Install the master cylinder to the vehicle. Connect all brake lines and fluid level sensor wiring is so equipped. Refill the reservoir with brake fluid and bleed the system.
7. Torque the master cylinder nuts to 6–8 ft. lbs. (8–11 Nm) and the brake pipe fittings to 12–14 ft. lbs. (17–20 Nm).

➡ **Use DOT 3 brake fluid in the brake systems.**

OVERHAUL

➧ SEE FIG. 7

➡ **Master cylinders are supplied to the manufacturer by two suppliers: Nabco and Tokico. Parts between these manufacturers are not interchangeable. Be sure you obtain the correct rebuilding kit for your master cylinder.**

The master cylinder can be disassembled using the illustrations as a guide. Clean all of the parts in clean brake fluid. Replace the cylinder or piston (as necessary), if the clearance between the two exceeds 0.15mm. Lubricate all of the parts with clean brake fluid on assembly.

➡ **Master cylinder rebuilding kits, containing all the wearing parts, are available to simplify the overhaul.**

➡ **The master cylinder for 1987–92 vehicles have dual proportioning valves located inside the master cylinder assembly. During overhaul, DO NOT DISASSEMBLE THE PROPORTIONING VALVE.**

1. Remove the master cylinder from the vehicle.
2. Bend the claws of the stopper cap outward.
3. Remove the valve stopper while the piston is pushed into the cylinder. The stopper is located in the side of the bore on some models.
4. Rap shop towels around the end of the master cylinder to catch the pistons as they are driven out of the bore. Remove the piston assemblies by gradually applying compressed air into the pipe fittings. **Always wear eye protection during this procedure.**
5. Remove the reservoir tank by pulling it out of the rubber grommets. Use new brake fluid between the reservoir and grommet.

To assemble:

6. Replace all wear items and clean in new brake fluid. Dry all components with compressed air.
7. Inspect the cylinder bore, pistons and springs for damage. Replace if necessary.
8. Lubricate all components with new brake fluid.

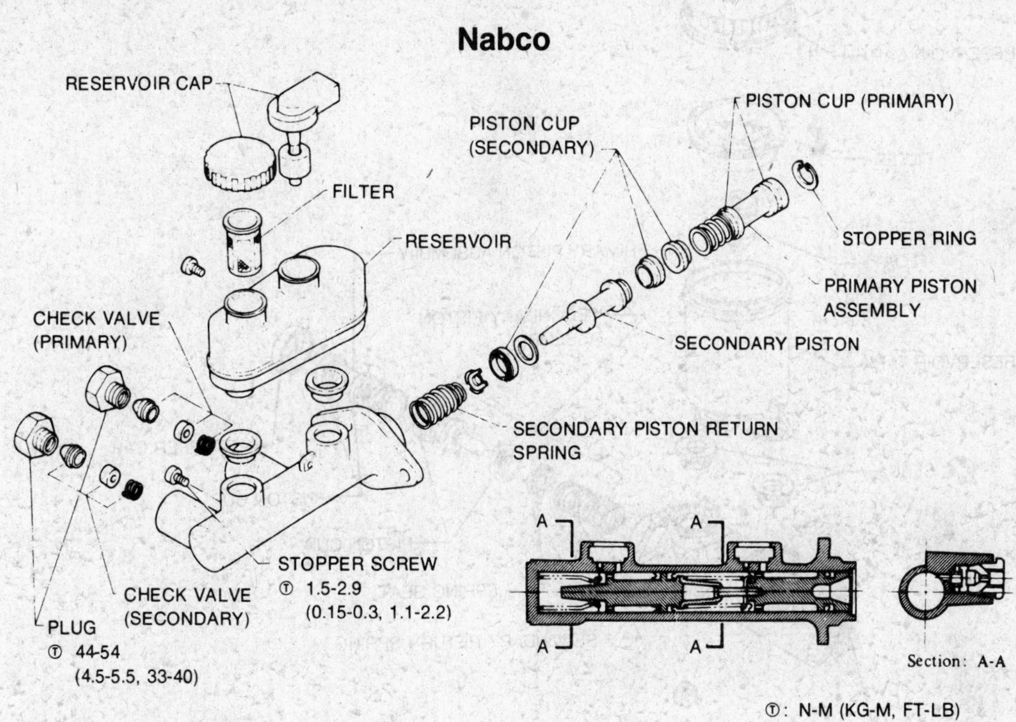
Nabco
RESERVOIR CAP
FILTER
RESERVOIR
PISTON CUP (SECONDARY)
PISTON CUP (PRIMARY)
STOPPER RING
PRIMARY PISTON ASSEMBLY
SECONDARY PISTON
CHECK VALVE (PRIMARY)
SECONDARY PISTON RETURN SPRING
STOPPER SCREW
Ⓣ 1.5-2.9
(0.15-0.3, 1.1-2.2)
CHECK VALVE (SECONDARY)
PLUG
Ⓣ 44-54
(4.5-5.5, 33-40)
A
Section: A-A
Ⓣ: N-M (KG-M, FT-LB)

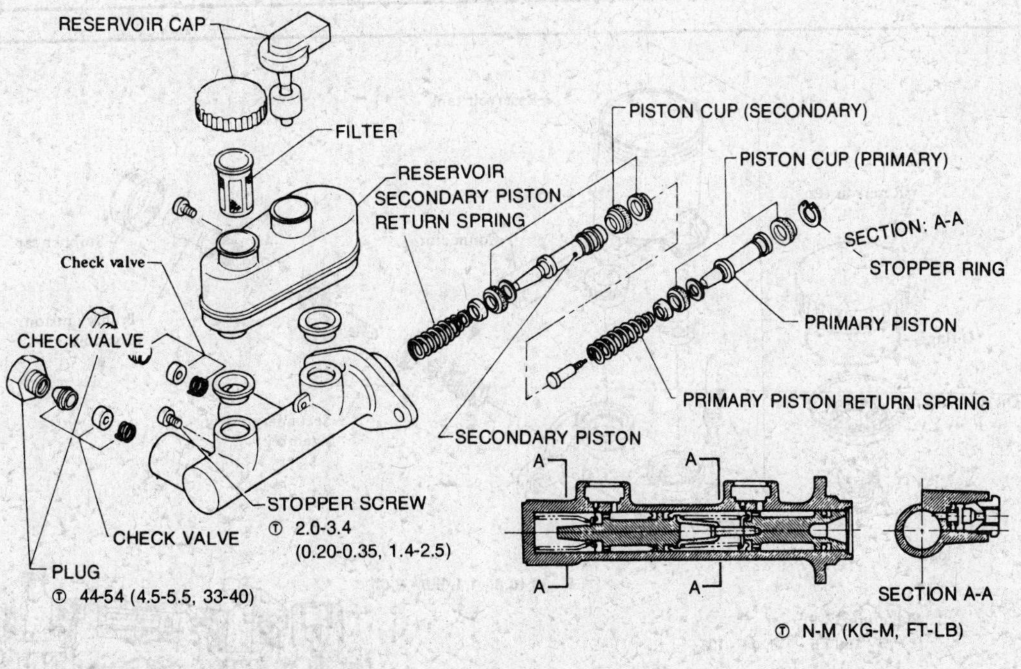
Tokico
RESERVOIR CAP
FILTER
RESERVOIR
SECONDARY PISTON RETURN SPRING
PISTON CUP (SECONDARY)
PISTON CUP (PRIMARY)
SECTION: A-A
STOPPER RING
PRIMARY PISTON
Check valve
CHECK VALVE
PRIMARY PISTON RETURN SPRING
SECONDARY PISTON
STOPPER SCREW
Ⓣ 2.0-3.4
(0.20-0.35, 1.4-2.5)
CHECK VALVE
PLUG
Ⓣ 44-54 (4.5-5.5, 33-40)
A
SECTION A-A
Ⓣ N-M (KG-M, FT-LB)

Fig. 3 Exploded view of the master cylinder — 1982-84 vehicles

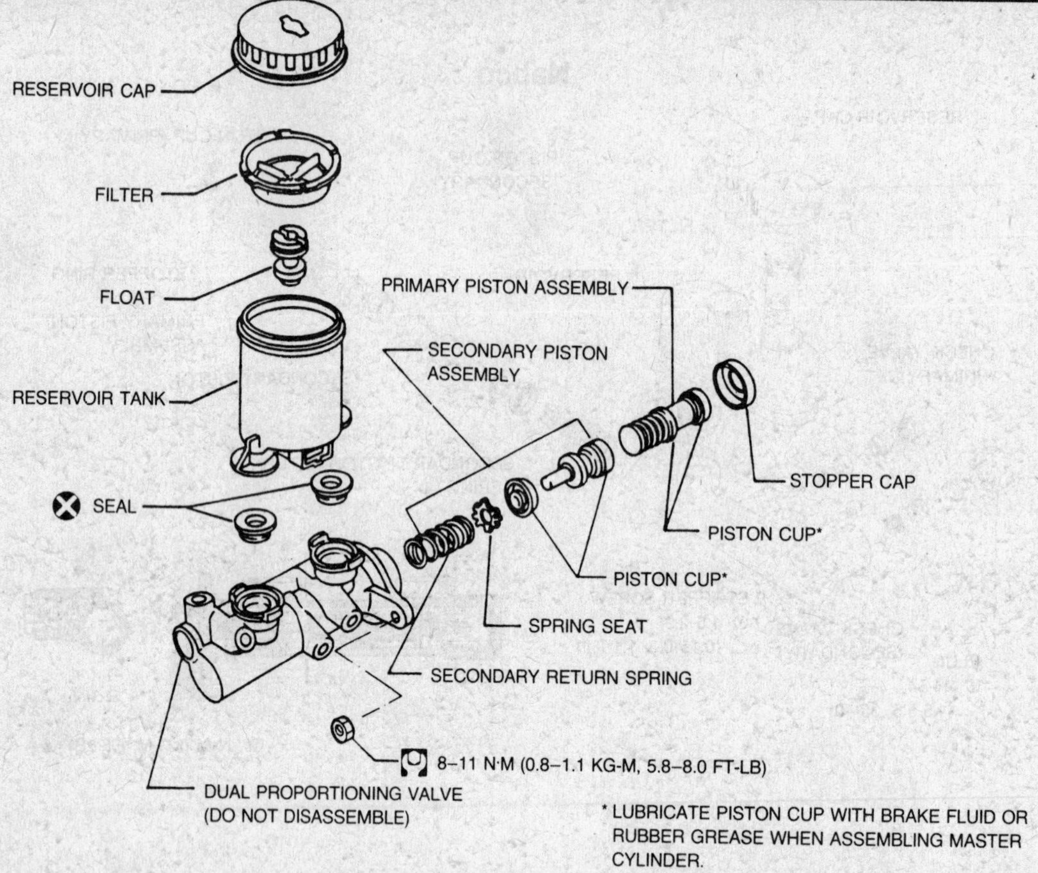

RESERVOIR CAP
FILTER
FLOAT
RESERVOIR TANK
SEAL
PRIMARY PISTON ASSEMBLY
SECONDARY PISTON ASSEMBLY
STOPPER CAP
PISTON CUP*
PISTON CUP*
SPRING SEAT
SECONDARY RETURN SPRING
8–11 N·M (0.8–1.1 KG-M, 5.8–8.0 FT-LB)
DUAL PROPORTIONING VALVE
(DO NOT DISASSEMBLE)
* LUBRICATE PISTON CUP WITH BRAKE FLUID OR RUBBER GREASE WHEN ASSEMBLING MASTER CYLINDER.

Fig. 4 Exploded view of the master cylinder — 1987-90 vehicles

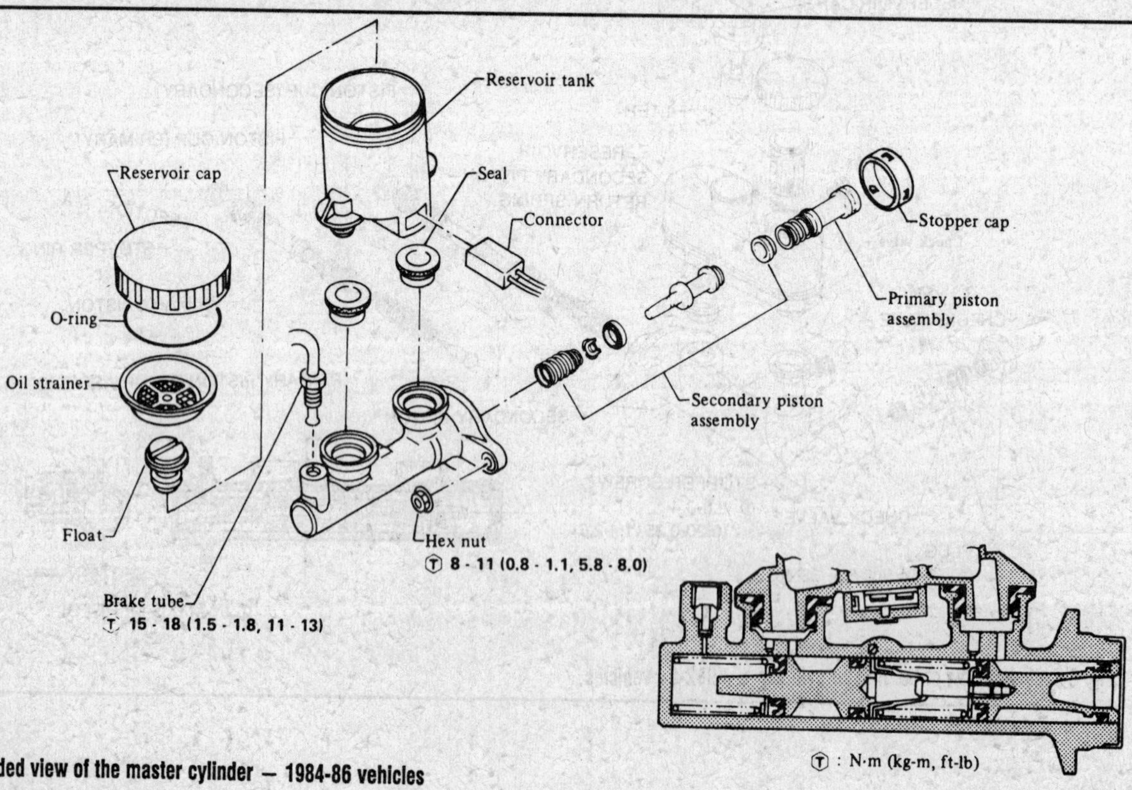

Reservoir tank
Reservoir cap
Seal
Connector
Stopper cap
Primary piston assembly
O-ring
Oil strainer
Secondary piston assembly
Float
Hex nut
8 - 11 (0.8 - 1.1, 5.8 - 8.0)
Brake tube
15 - 18 (1.5 - 1.8, 11 - 13)
: N·m (kg-m, ft-lb)

Fig. 5 Exploded view of the master cylinder — 1984-86 vehicles

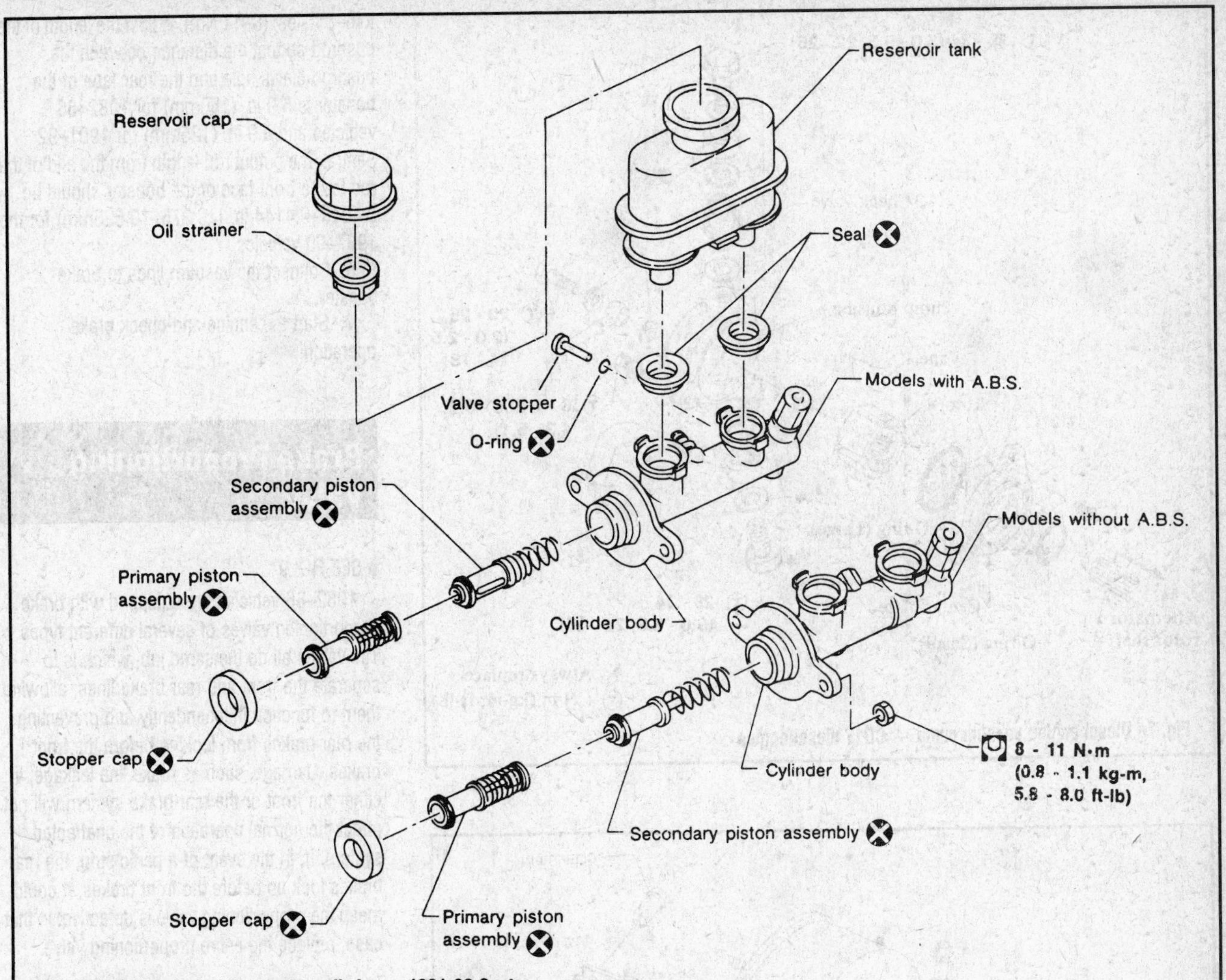

Fig. 6 Exploded view of the master cylinder – 1991-92 Sentra

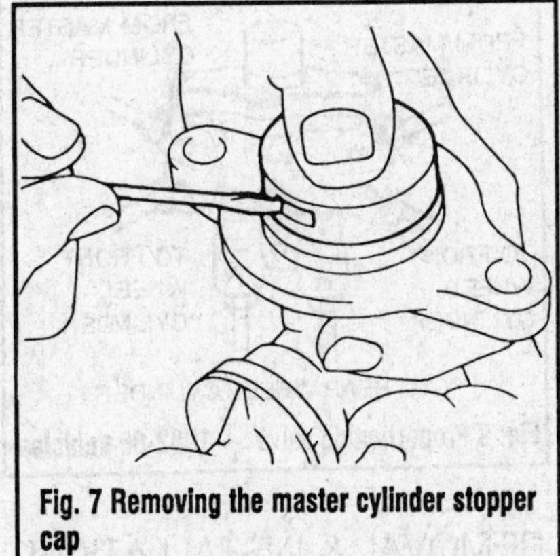

Fig. 7 Removing the master cylinder stopper cap

9. Install the secondary piston and then the primary piston into the bore. Be careful not to damage the seals.

10. Install the stopper cap and bend the retaining claws inward.

11. Push the reservoir into the rubber grommets.

12. Install the valve stopper, if so equipped.

13. Bench bleed the master cylinder by using old brake pipes. Bend the brake pipes around into the reservoir. Place the master cylinder in a vise and fill the reservoir with DOT 3 brake fluid. Pump the piston using a pushrod until all the air bubbles are gone.

14. Install the master cylinder to the vehicle.

Diesel Engine Vacuum Pump

➧ SEE FIG. 7a

The vacuum pump is driven by the alternator rotor shaft. The pump is lubricated by engine oil.

REMOVAL & INSTALLATION

1. Drain the oil from the vacuum pump by manually rotating the fan belt clockwise to discharge any oil in the pump.

2. Disconnect all oil pipes and vacuum hoses from the pump.

3. Remove the pump from the alternator assembly.

To install:

4. Prime the pump with clean engine oil.

5. Install the pump and torque the bolts to 14–18 ft. lbs. (20–25 Nm).

6. Connect all oil pipes and vacuum hoses. Torque the banjo fittings to 22–25 ft. lbs. (29–34 Nm).

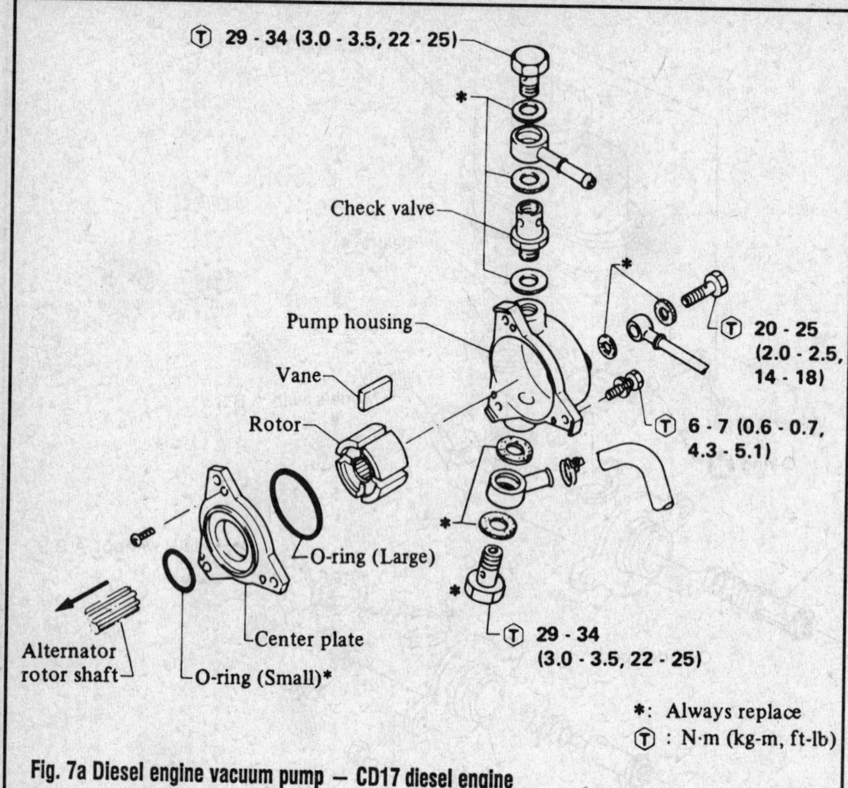
29 - 34 (3.0 - 3.5, 22 - 25)
Check valve
Pump housing
Vane
Rotor
O-ring (Large)
Center plate
Alternator rotor shaft
O-ring (Small)*
20 - 25 (2.0 - 2.5, 14 - 18)
6 - 7 (0.6 - 0.7, 4.3 - 5.1)
29 - 34 (3.0 - 3.5, 22 - 25)
*: Always replace
: N·m (kg-m, ft-lb)

Fig. 7a Diesel engine vacuum pump — CD17 diesel engine

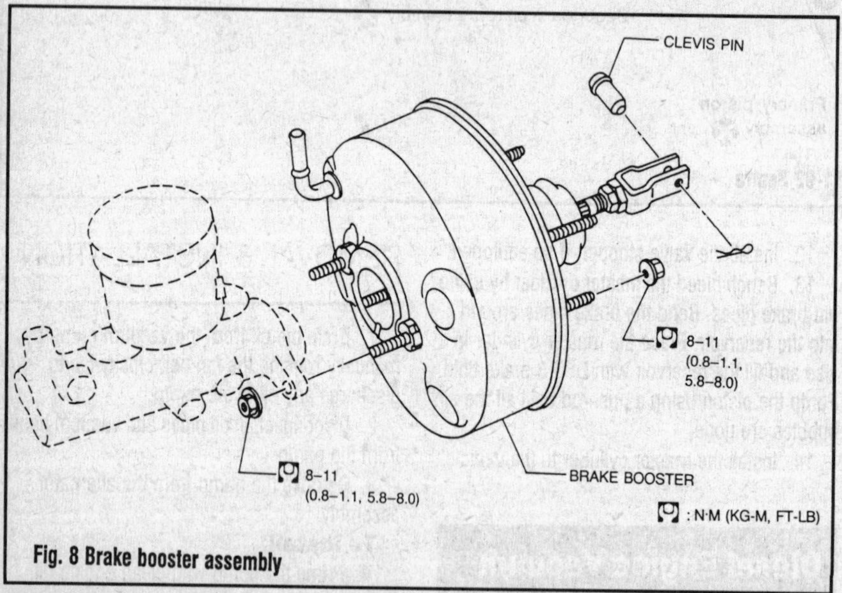
CLEVIS PIN
8–11 (0.8–1.1, 5.8–8.0)
8–11 (0.8–1.1, 5.8–8.0)
BRAKE BOOSTER
: N·M (KG-M, FT-LB)

Fig. 8 Brake booster assembly

Power Brake Booster

➧ SEE FIG. 8

REMOVAL & INSTALLATION

1. Disconnect the master cylinder brake pipes. Remove the master cylinder mounting nuts and pull the master cylinder assembly away from the power booster.
2. Detach the vacuum lines from the booster.
3. Detach the booster pushrod at the pedal clevis.
4. Unbolt the booster from under the dash and lift it out of the engine compartment.
5. Install the brake booster to the vehicle. Torque the master cylinder-to-booster nuts to 6–8 ft. lbs. (8–11 Nm); the booster-to-firewall nuts to 6–8 ft. lbs. (8–11 Nm). Adjust the length of the pushrod so that the distance between the pushrod clevis hole and the rear face of the booster is 5.9 in. (150mm) for 1982–86 vehicles and 4.9 in. (125mm) for 1991–92 Sentra. The output rod length from the end of the rod to the front face of the booster should be 0.4045–0.4144 in. (10.275–10.525mm) for the 1987–90 vehicles.
6. Connect the vacuum lines to brake booster.
7. Start the engine and check brake operation.

Brake Proportioning Valve

➧ SEE FIG. 9

1982–86 vehicles are equipped with brake proportioning valves of several different types. The valves all do the same job, which is to separate the front and rear brake lines, allowing them to function independently and preventing the rear brakes from locking before the front brakes. Damage, such as brake line leakage, in either the front or the rear brake system will not affect the normal operation of the unaffected system. If, in the event of a panic stop, the rear brakes lock up before the front brakes, it could mean the proportioning valve is defective. In that case, replace the entire proportioning valve.

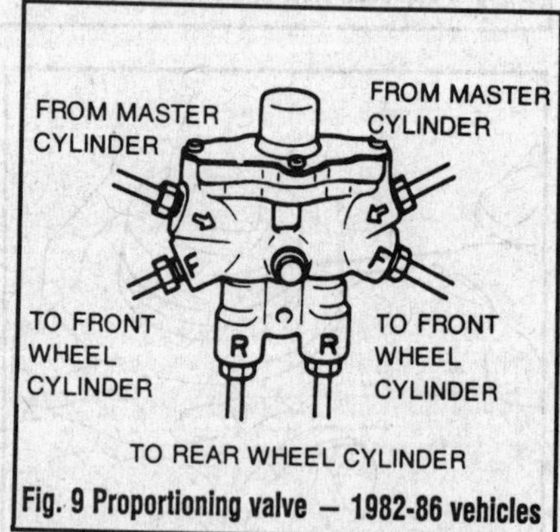
FROM MASTER CYLINDER
FROM MASTER CYLINDER
TO FRONT WHEEL CYLINDER
TO FRONT WHEEL CYLINDER
TO REAR WHEEL CYLINDER
F
F
R
R

Fig. 9 Proportioning valve — 1982-86 vehicles

REMOVAL & INSTALLATION

1982–86 Vehicles Only

1. Remove the brake line tubes from the proportioning valve, then plug the openings to prevent dirt from entering the system.
2. Remove the mounting bolt(s) and the valve from the vehicle.

3. To install, reverse the removal procedures. Refill the master cylinder reservoir and bleed the brake system. Torque the brake pipe fittings to 12–14 ft. lbs. (17–20 Nm).

System Bleeding

Bleeding is required whenever air in the hydraulic fluid causes a spongy feeling pedal and sluggish response. This is almost always the case after some part of the hydraulic system has been repaired or replaced.

The anti-lock brake (ABS) systems is bled the same way as conventional brake systems. **Use DOT 3 brake fluid in all systems.**

1. Fill the master cylinder reservoir with DOT 3 brake fluid.

2. The usual procedure is to bleed at the left rear, right front, right rear and left front.

3. Fit a clear hose over the bleeder screw. Submerge the other end of the hole in clean brake fluid in a clear glass container. Loosen the bleeder screw. Make sure the clear hose in below the brake fluid level.

4. Slowly pump the brake pedal several times (in long strokes) until fluid free of bubbles is discharged. An assistant is required to pump the pedal.

5. On the last pumping stroke, hold the pedal down and tighten the bleeder screw. Check the fluid level periodically during the bleeding operation. **Do not allow the reservoir to run dry during the bleeding procedure.**

➡ **Bleed the front brakes in the same way as the rear brakes.**

6. Check that the brake pedal is now firm with the engine not running. If not, repeat the bleeding operation.

FRONT DISC BRAKES

** CAUTION

Brake shoes contain asbestos, which has been determined to be a cancer causing agent. Never clean brake surfaces with compressed air! Avoid inhaling any dust from any brake surfaces! When cleaning brake surfaces, use a commercially available brake cleaning fluid.

Brake Pads

➧ SEE FIGS. 10–11

INSPECTION

You should be able to check the pad lining thickness without removing the pads. Check the Brake Specifications Chart at the end of this section to find the manufacturer's pad wear limit. However, this measurement may disagree with your state inspection laws. When replacing pads, always check the surface of the rotors for scoring or wear. The rotors should be removed for resurfacing if badly scored.

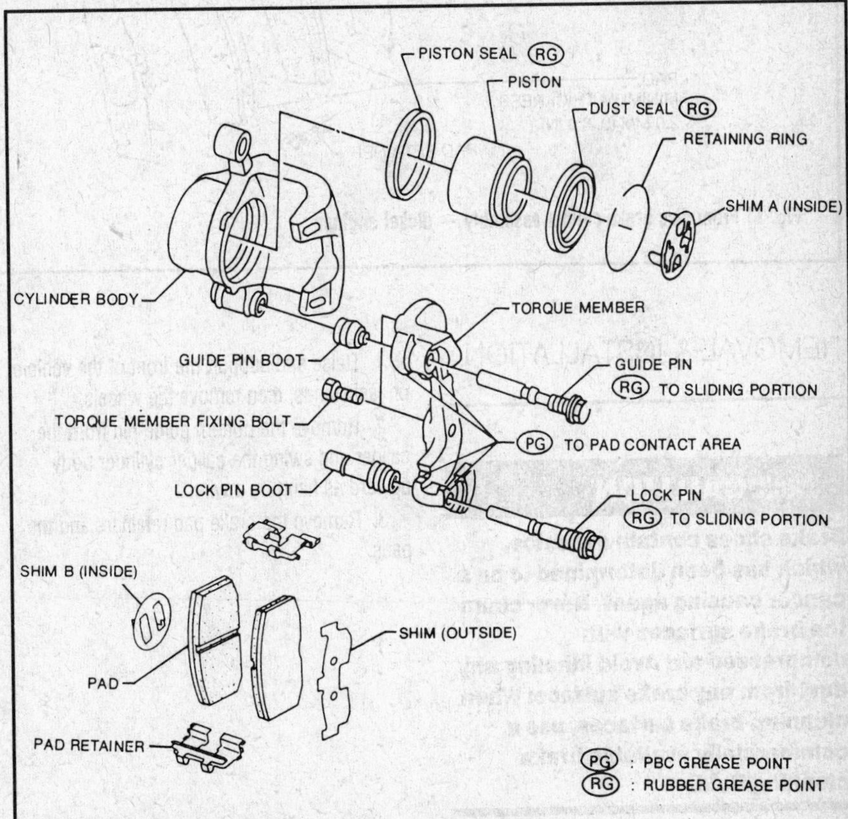
PISTON SEAL (RG)
PISTON
DUST SEAL (RG)
RETAINING RING
SHIM A (INSIDE)
CYLINDER BODY
TORQUE MEMBER
GUIDE PIN BOOT
GUIDE PIN
(RG) TO SLIDING PORTION
TORQUE MEMBER FIXING BOLT
(PG) TO PAD CONTACT AREA
LOCK PIN BOOT
LOCK PIN
(RG) TO SLIDING PORTION
SHIM B (INSIDE)
SHIM (OUTSIDE)
PAD
PAD RETAINER
(PG) : PBC GREASE POINT
(RG) : RUBBER GREASE POINT

Fig. 10 Front disc brake caliper assembly — gasoline engines

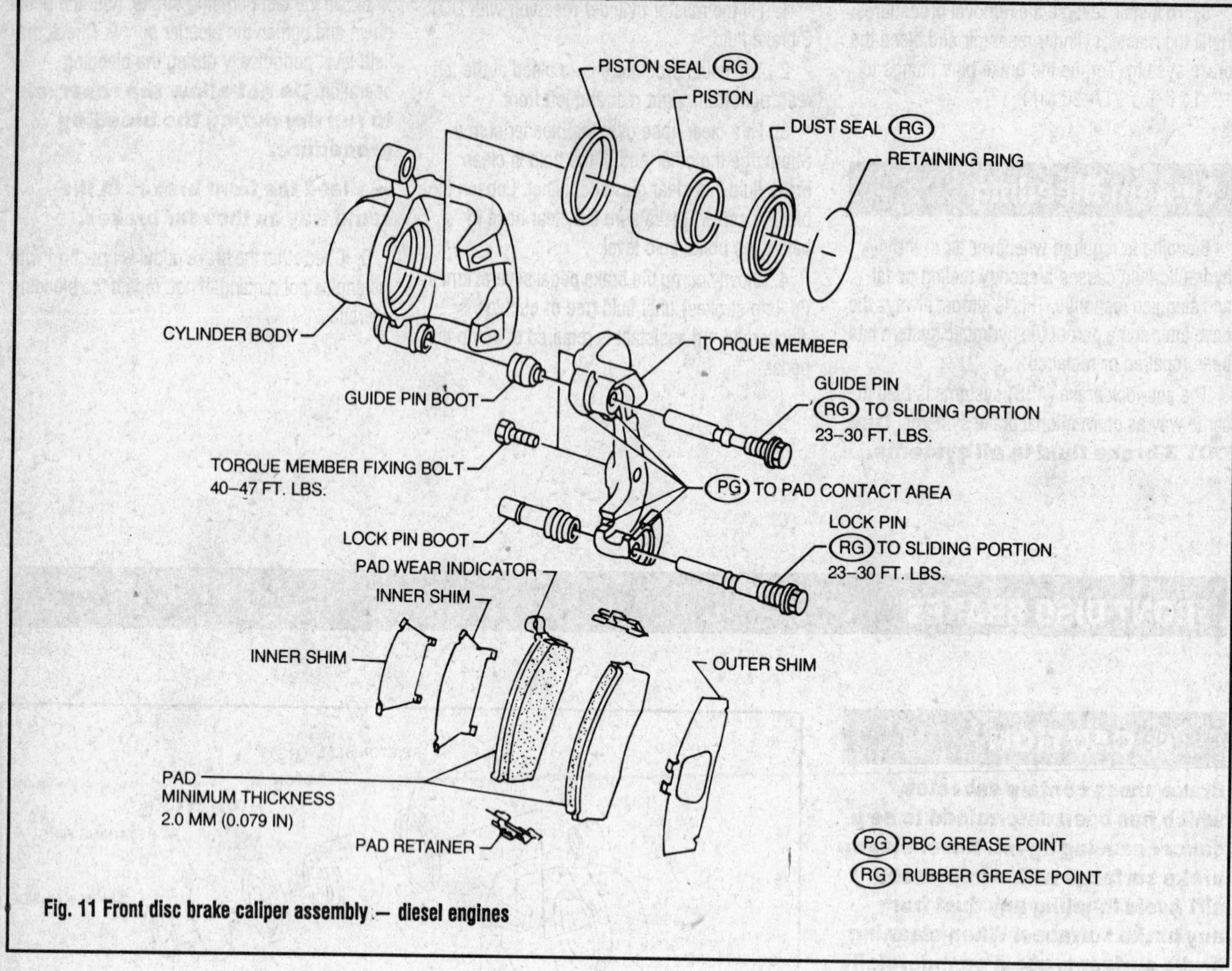
PISTON SEAL (RG)
PISTON
DUST SEAL (RG)
RETAINING RING
CYLINDER BODY
TORQUE MEMBER
GUIDE PIN BOOT
GUIDE PIN
(RG) TO SLIDING PORTION
23–30 FT. LBS.
TORQUE MEMBER FIXING BOLT
40–47 FT. LBS.
(PG) TO PAD CONTACT AREA
LOCK PIN
LOCK PIN BOOT
(RG) TO SLIDING PORTION
23–30 FT. LBS.
PAD WEAR INDICATOR
INNER SHIM
INNER SHIM
OUTER SHIM
PAD
MINIMUM THICKNESS
2.0 MM (0.079 IN)
PAD RETAINER
(PG) PBC GREASE POINT
(RG) RUBBER GREASE POINT
Fig. 11 Front disc brake caliper assembly — diesel engines

REMOVAL & INSTALLATION

✽✽ CAUTION

Brake shoes contain asbestos, which has been determined to be a cancer causing agent. Never clean the brake surfaces with compressed air! Avoid inhaling any dust from any brake surface! When cleaning brake surfaces, use a commercially available brake cleaning fluid.

1. Raise and support the front of the vehicle on jackstands, then remove the wheels.
2. Remove the bottom guide pin from the caliper and swing the caliper cylinder body upward as hang by a wire.
3. Remove the brake pad retainers and the pads.

To install:

4. Install the brake pads and caliper assembly. Torque the guide pin to 23–30 ft. lbs. (31–41 Nm).
5. Install the wheels.
6. Apply the brakes a few times to seat the pads. Check the master cylinder and add fluid if necessary. Bleed the brakes, if necessary.

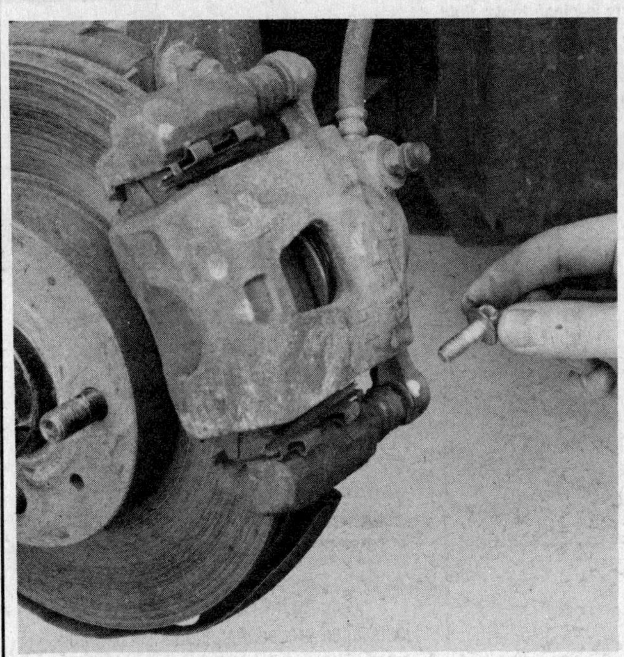

Fig. 11a. Removing the front disc caliper lower retaining bolt. The upper bolt stays in place and is used as a pivot—1991-92 Sentra

Fig. 11b. Pushing the caliper piston into the bore using a C-clamp

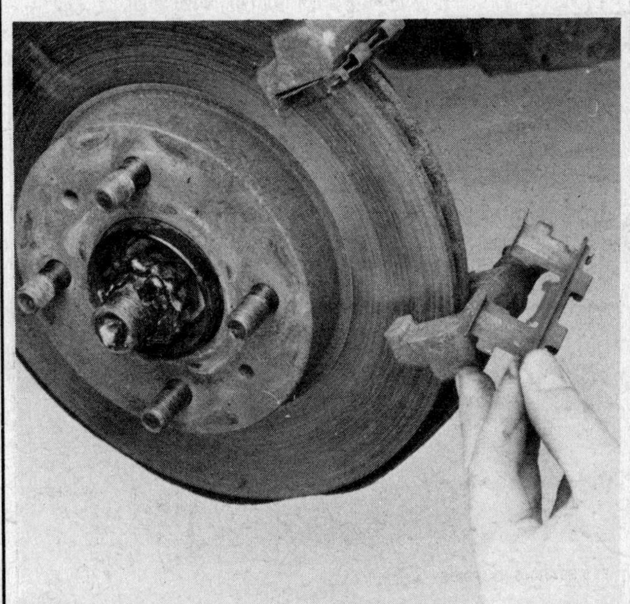

Fig. 11c. Installing the brake pad anti-rattle clips—1991-92 Sentra, others similar

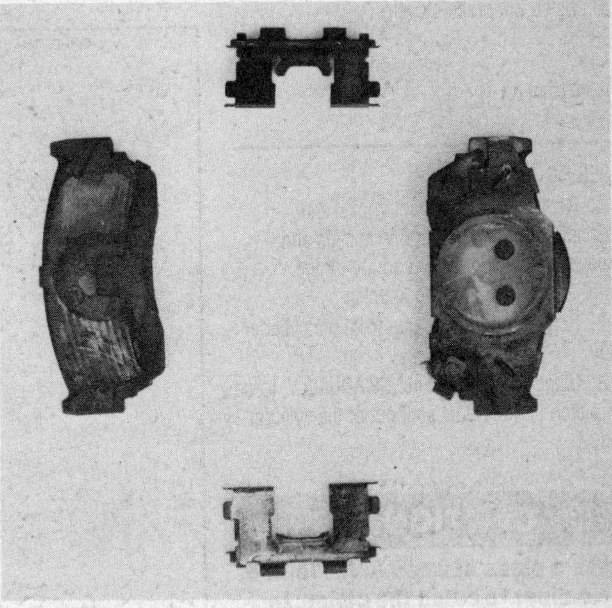

Fig. 11d. Front disc brake pads and anti-rattle clips—1991-92 Sentra

Brake Calipers

REMOVAL & INSTALLATION

CAUTION

Brake shoes contain asbestos, which has been determined to be a cancer causing agent. Never clean the brake surfaces with compressed air! Avoid inhaling any dust from any brake surface! When cleaning brake surfaces, use a commercially available brake cleaning fluid.

1. Raise and support the vehicle on jackstands, then remove the wheels.
2. Disconnect and plug the brake tube at the brake hose connection.
3. Remove the torque member-to-steering knuckle mounting bolts, then remove the caliper assembly from the vehicle.

To install:

4. Install the brake caliper to the vehicle. Torque the fitting to 12–14 ft. lbs. (17–20 Nm).
5. Install the brake pads.
6. Bleed the brake system.

OVERHAUL

➧ SEE FIG. 12

1. Refer to the Caliper, Removal and Installation procedures, in this section and remove the cylinder body and the torque member from the steering knuckle.
2. Remove the brake tube from the cylinder body.
3. Using compressed air, GRADUALLY, force the piston and the dust seal out of the cylinder body.

CAUTION

Place a piece of wood in the jaws of the caliper to catch the piston, in case it leaves the caliper too fast.

4. Remove the piston seal.

To assemble:

5. Clean all of the parts in clean brake fluid. Check and/or replace any damaged parts. Lubricate all of the new parts with brake fluid.
6. Install piston and all new seals in the caliper assembly.
7. Install the caliper assembly to the vehicle.

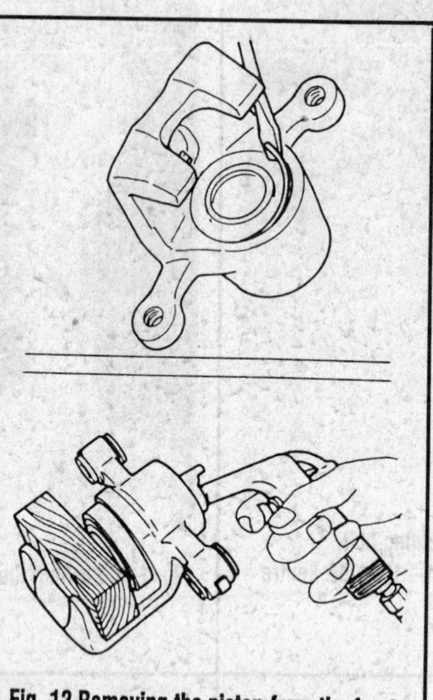

Fig. 12 Removing the piston from the front caliper

Brake Disc

➧ SEE FIG. 13

REMOVAL & INSTALLATION

CAUTION

Brake shoes contain asbestos, which has been determined to be a cancer causing agent. Never clean the brake surfaces with compressed air! Avoid inhaling any dust from any brake surface! When cleaning brake surfaces, use a commercially available brake cleaning fluid.

1. Refer to the Caliper, Removal and Installation procedures, in this section and remove the caliper and the torque member from the steering knuckle.

➡ Do not disconnect the brake tube (if possible), support the assembly on a wire.

2. Remove the grease cap, the cotter pin, the adjusting cap, the wheel bearing locknut and the thrust washer from the drive shaft.

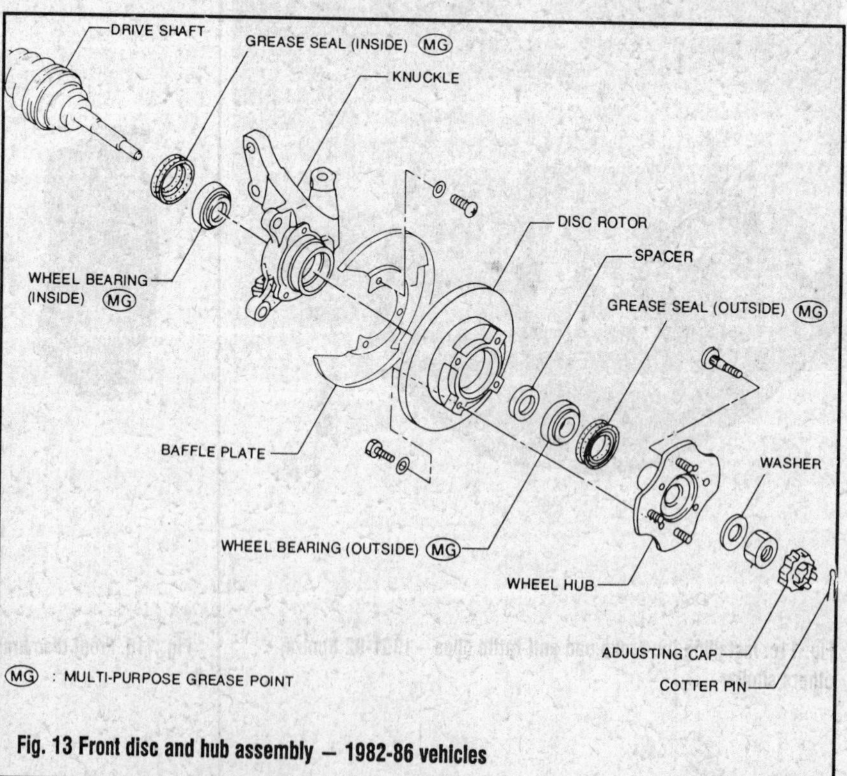
DRIVE SHAFT
GREASE SEAL (INSIDE) (MG)
KNUCKLE
DISC ROTOR
SPACER
WHEEL BEARING (INSIDE) (MG)
GREASE SEAL (OUTSIDE) (MG)
BAFFLE PLATE
WASHER
WHEEL BEARING (OUTSIDE) (MG)
WHEEL HUB
ADJUSTING CAP
COTTER PIN
(MG) : MULTI-PURPOSE GREASE POINT

Fig. 13 Front disc and hub assembly — 1982-86 vehicles

3. Using Wheel Hub Remover tool KV40101000 and ST36230000, press the wheel hub/disc assembly from the steering knuckle.

➡ **Remove the disc from the hub without removing halfshaft nut and bearings on 1987-92 vehicles.**

4. Remove the disc-to-wheel hub bolts and separate the disc from the wheel hub (1982–86).

5. Install wheel hub/disc assembly to the vehicle. Torque the disc-to-wheel hub bolts to 18–25 ft. lbs. (25–34 Nm). Refer to wheel bearing adjustment in section 8 for 1982–86 vehicles.

6. Install the caliper assembly and any other components to the vehicle.

7. Bleed brake system if necessary.

INSPECTION

1. Check the disc for cracks and/or chips, if necessary, replace the disc.

2. Using a dial indicator, check the runout of the disc, it should be less than 0.003 in. (0.076mm); if greater than the maximum, resurface or replace the disc.

3. Using a dial indicator, check the parallelism of the disc, it should be less than 0.001 in. (0.03mm), if greater than the maximum, replace the disc.

4. Using a micrometer, check the thickness of the disc. Refer to the brake specification chart in this section.

REAR DRUM BRAKES

⁂ CAUTION

Brake shoes contain asbestos, which has been determined to be a cancer causing agent. Never clean brake surfaces with compressed air! Avoid inhaling any dust from any brake surfaces! When cleaning brake surfaces, use a commercially available brake cleaning fluid.

Brake Drum

➧ SEE FIGS. 14–16

REMOVAL & INSTALLATION

⁂ CAUTION

Brake shoes contain asbestos, which has been determined to be a cancer causing agent. Never clean the brake surfaces with compressed air! Avoid inhaling any dust from any brake surface! When cleaning brake surfaces, use a commercially available brake cleaning fluid.

➡ **For rear wheel bearing procedures refer to section 8 (1982-90).**

1. Raise the rear of the vehicle and support it on jackstands.

2. Remove the wheels.

3. Release the parking brake.

4. Remove the grease cap, the cotter pin and the wheel bearing nut (1982–90). Remove the drum without removing wheel bearing nut (1991–92 Sentra).

5. Pull off the drum, taking care not to drop the tapered bearing.

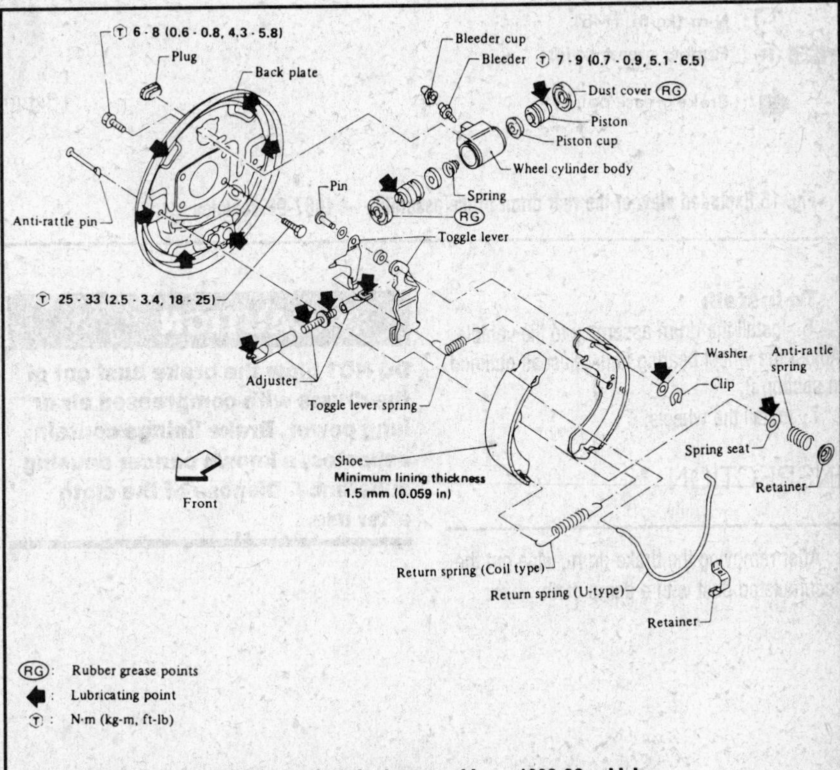

T 6 - 8 (0.6 - 0.8, 4.3 - 5.8)
Plug
Back plate
Bleeder cup
Bleeder T 7 - 9 (0.7 - 0.9, 5.1 - 6.5)
Dust cover RG
Piston
Piston cup
Wheel cylinder body
Pin
Spring
RG
Anti-rattle pin
Toggle lever
T 25 - 33 (2.5 - 3.4, 18 - 25)
Adjuster
Toggle lever spring
Washer
Anti-rattle spring
Clip
Spring seat
Retainer
Shoe
Minimum lining thickness 1.5 mm (0.059 in)
Front
Return spring (Coil type)
Return spring (U-type)
Retainer
RG: Rubber grease points
Lubricating point
T: N·m (kg-m, ft-lb)

Fig. 14 Exploded view of the rear drum brake assembly — 1982-86 vehicles

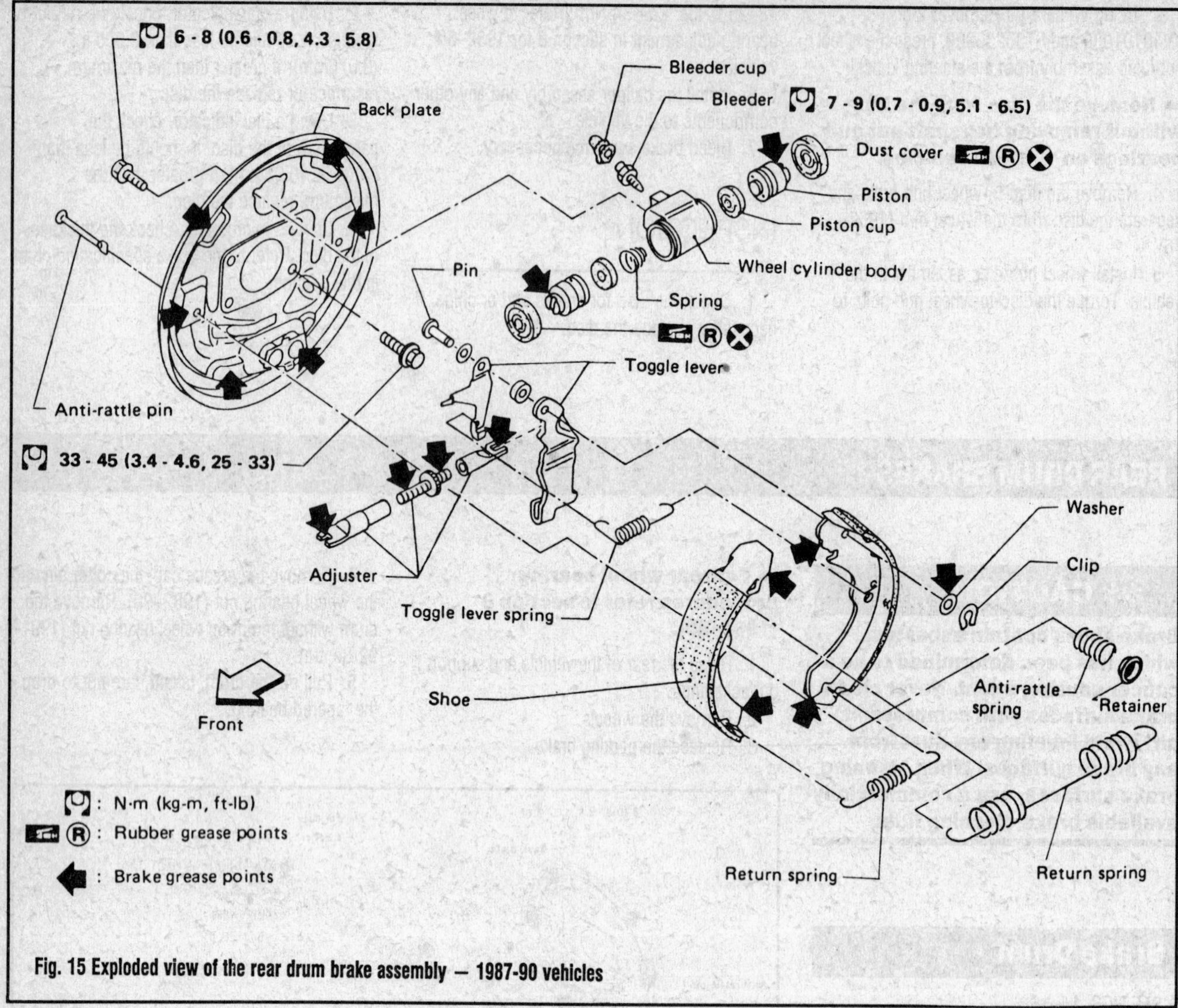
6 - 8 (0.6 - 0.8, 4.3 - 5.8)
Back plate
Bleeder cup
Bleeder
7 - 9 (0.7 - 0.9, 5.1 - 6.5)
Dust cover
Piston
Piston cup
Wheel cylinder body
Pin
Spring
Toggle lever
Anti-rattle pin
33 - 45 (3.4 - 4.6, 25 - 33)
Washer
Clip
Adjuster
Toggle lever spring
Anti-rattle spring
Retainer
Shoe
Front
: N·m (kg-m, ft-lb)
: Rubber grease points
: Brake grease points
Return spring
Return spring

Fig. 15 Exploded view of the rear drum brake assembly — 1987-90 vehicles

To install:

6. Install the drum assembly to the vehicle. Adjust the wheel bearing and adjust as outlined in section 8.
7. Install the wheels.

INSPECTION

After removing the brake drum, wipe out the accumulated dust with a damp cloth.

CAUTION

DO NOT blow the brake dust out of the drums with compressed air or lung power. Brake linings contain asbestos, a known cancer causing substance. Dispose of the cloth after use.

Inspect the drum for cracks, deep grooves, roughness, scoring or out-of-roundness. Replace any brake drum which is cracked.

Smooth any slight scores by polishing the friction surface with the fine emery cloth. Heavy or extensive scoring will cause excessive brake lining wear and should be removed from the brake drum through resurfacing.

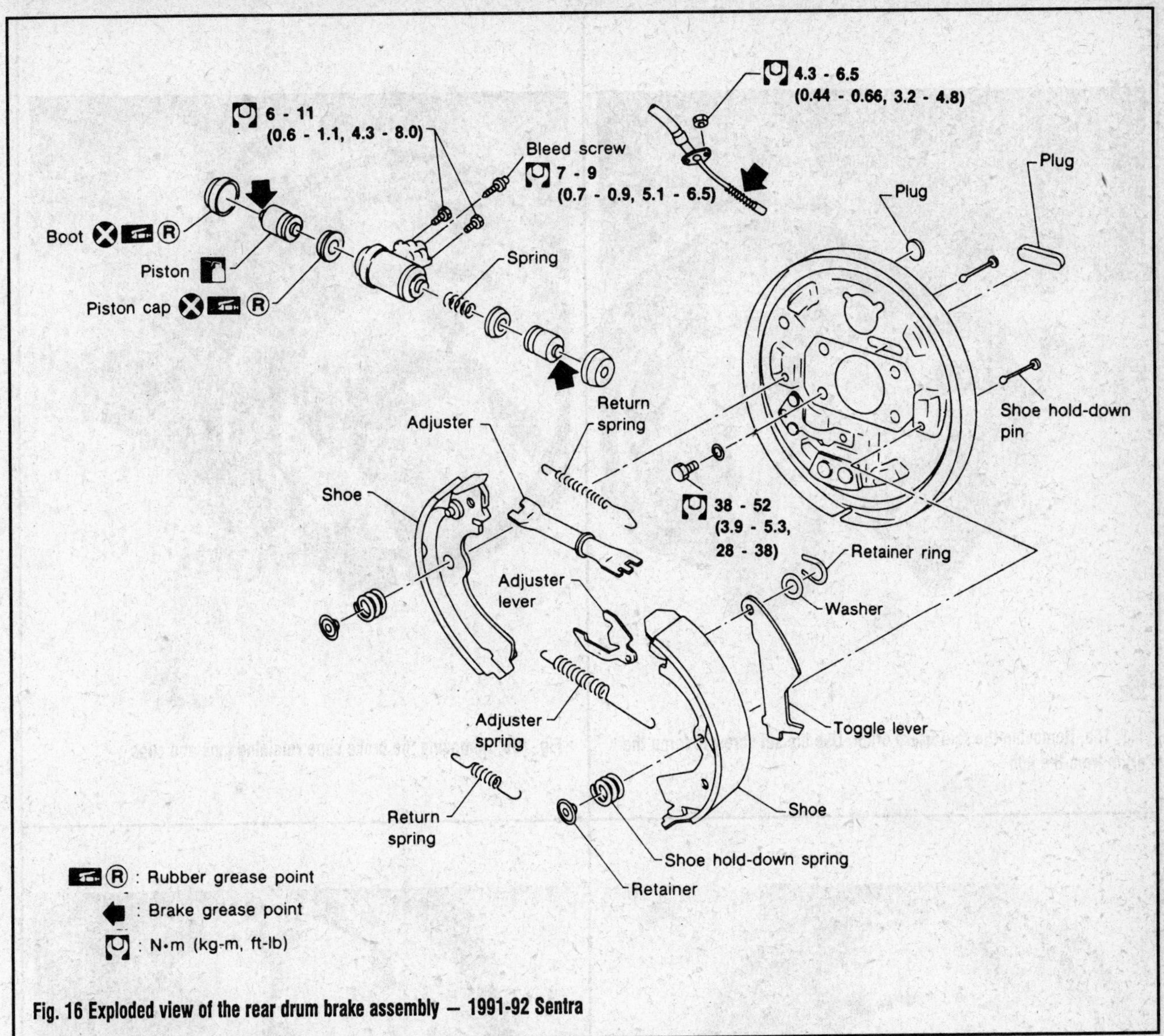
6 - 11
(0.6 - 1.1, 4.3 - 8.0)
Bleed screw
7 - 9
(0.7 - 0.9, 5.1 - 6.5)
4.3 - 6.5
(0.44 - 0.66, 3.2 - 4.8)
Plug
Plug
Boot
Piston
Piston cap
Spring
Shoe hold-down pin
Return spring
Adjuster
Shoe
38 - 52
(3.9 - 5.3,
28 - 38)
Retainer ring
Adjuster lever
Washer
Toggle lever
Adjuster spring
Return spring
Shoe
Shoe hold-down spring
Retainer
: Rubber grease point
: Brake grease point
: N•m (kg-m, ft-lb)

Fig. 16 Exploded view of the rear drum brake assembly — 1991-92 Sentra

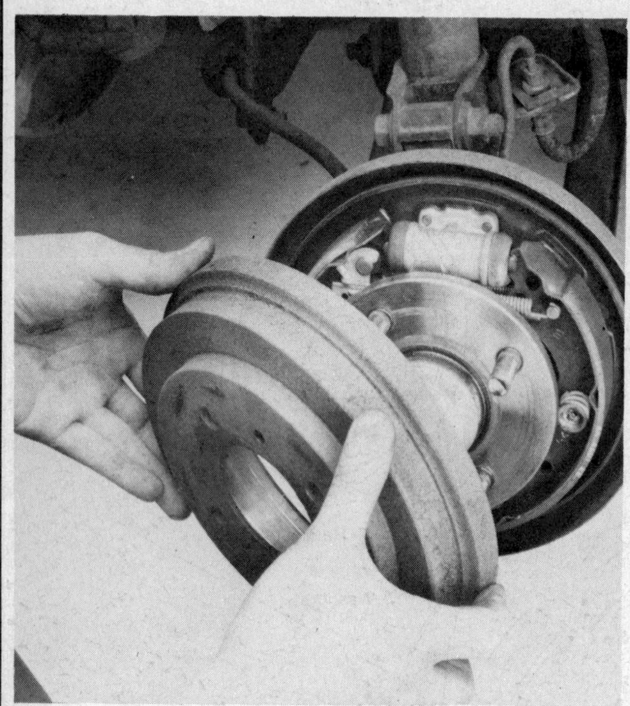

Fig. 16a. Removing the rear brake drum. Use the set screw to force the drum from the hub

Fig. 16b. Removing the brake shoe retaining pins and clips

Fig. 16c. Removing the brake shoe as an assembly

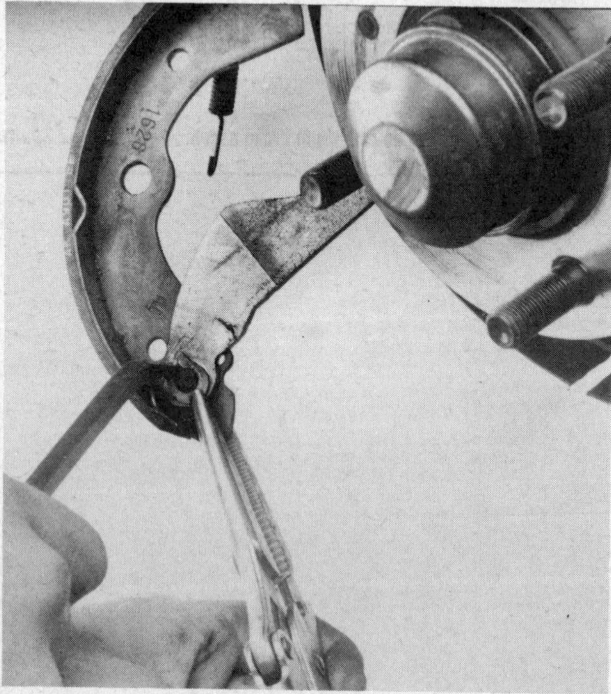

Fig. 16d. Removing the horse shoe clip from the parking brake lever. Always use a new clip when replacing the brake shoes

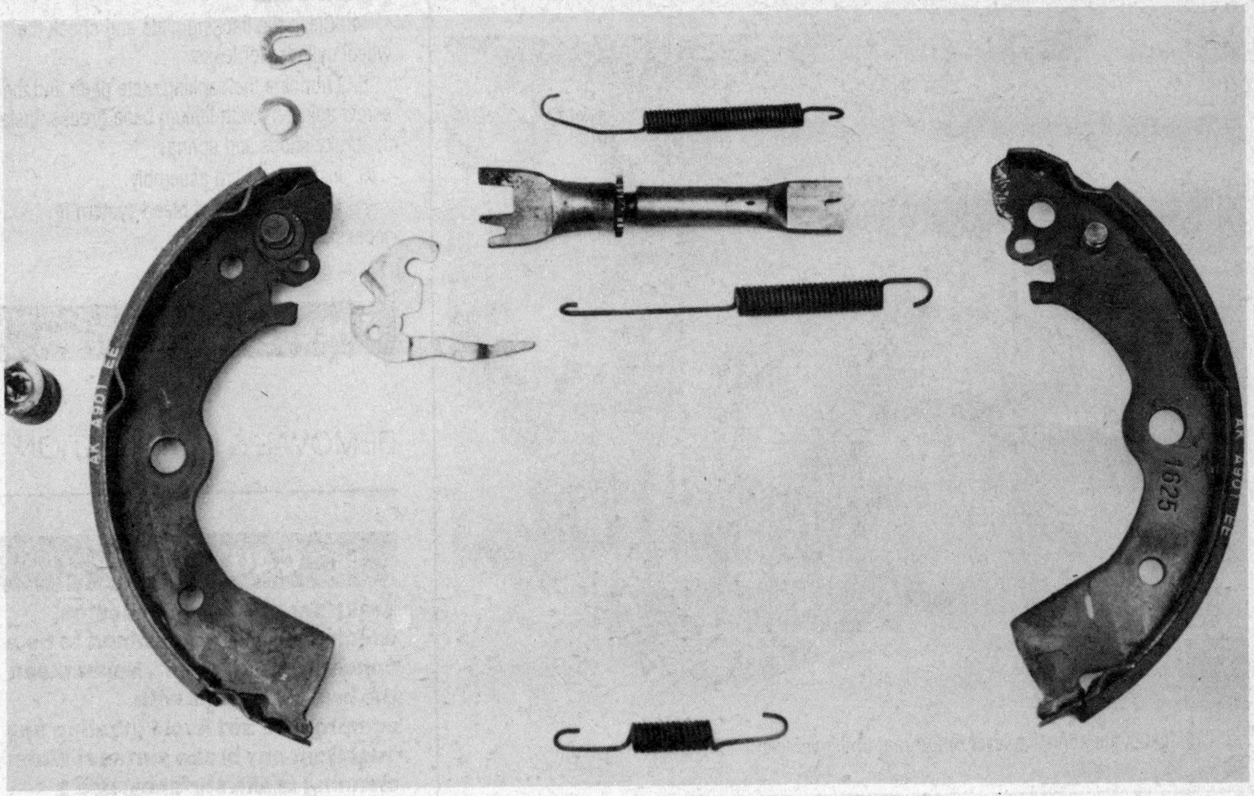

Fig. 16e. Rear brake shoe and self-adjuster assembly—1991-92 Sentra

Fig. 16f. Use brake lubricant or white lithium grease on the brake shoe contact points

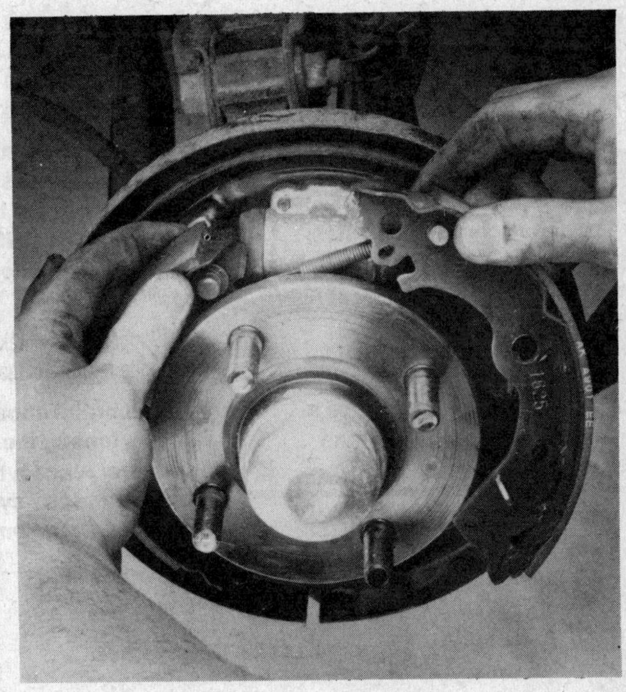
1625

Fig. 16g. Install the brake shoes and adjusting hardware as an assembly

Fig. 16h. Install the adjusting lever to the rear of the vehicle

Brake Shoes

REMOVAL & INSTALLATION

✲✲ CAUTION

Brake shoes contain asbestos, which has been determined to be a cancer causing agent. Never clean the brake surfaces with compressed air! Avoid inhaling any dust from any brake surface! When cleaning brake surfaces, use a commercially available brake cleaning fluid.

1. Refer to the Brake Drum, Removal and Installation procedures, in this section and remove the brake drum.
2. Service 1 side at a time. Use the other as an example for installation. Release the parking brake lever, then remove the anti-rattle spring and the pin from the brake shoes.

➡ To remove the anti-rattle spring and pin, push the spring/pin assembly into the brake shoe, turn it 90° and release it; the retainer cap, spring, washer and pin will separate.

3. Supporting the brake shoe assembly, remove the return springs and brake shoes.

➡ If the brake shoes are difficult to remove, loosen the brake adjusters. Place a heavy rubber band around the cylinder to prevent the piston from coming out.

To install:

4. Clean the backing plate and check the wheel cylinder for leaks.
5. Lubricate the backing plate pads and the screw adjusters with lithium base grease. Install the brake shoes and springs.
6. Install the drum assembly.
7. Adjust brakes and bleed system if necessary.

Wheel Cylinders

REMOVAL & INSTALLATION

✲✲ CAUTION

Brake shoes contain asbestos, which has been determined to be a cancer causing agent. Never clean the brake surfaces with compressed air! Avoid inhaling any dust from any brake surface! When cleaning brake surfaces, use a commercially available brake cleaning fluid.

1. Refer to the Brake Drum, Removal and Installation procedures, in this section and remove the brake drum.
2. Disconnect the flare nut and the brake tube from the wheel cylinder, then plug the line to prevent dirt from entering the system.
3. Remove the brake shoes from the backing plate.
4. Remove the wheel cylinder-to-backing plate bolts and the wheel cylinders.

➡ If the wheel cylinder is difficult to remove, bump it with a soft hammer to release it from the backing plate.

5. Install the wheel cylinder assembly to the backing plate.
6. Connect all brake lines and torque retaining bolts to 5–8 ft. lbs. (6–11 Nm) and pipe fitting to 12–14 ft. lbs. (17–22 Nm). Install the brake drum.
7. Bleed the brake system as outlined in this section.

REAR DISC BRAKES

✲✲ CAUTION

Brake shoes contain asbestos, which has been determined to be a cancer causing agent. Never clean brake surfaces with compressed air! Avoid inhaling any dust from any brake surfaces! When cleaning brake surfaces, use a commercially available brake cleaning fluid.

Brake Pads

➧ SEE FIG. 17

REMOVAL & INSTALLATION

1991–92 Sentra

➡ Do not press the piston into the bore as performed on the front disc brakes. Due to the parking brake mechanism, the caliper piston must be turned into the bore using a special tool.

1. Raise and support the vehicle safely.
2. Remove the rear wheels.
3. Release the parking brake and remove the cable bracket bolt.
4. Remove the pin bolts and lift off the caliper body.
5. Pull out the pad springs and then remove the pads and shims.

To install:

6. Clean the piston end of the caliper body and the area around the pin holes. Be careful not to get oil on the rotor.
7. Using the proper tool, carefully turn the piston clockwise back into the caliper body. Take care not to damage the piston boot.
8. Coat the pad contact area on the mounting support with a silicone based grease.
9. Install the pads, shims and the pad springs. Always use new shims.
10. Position the caliper body in the mounting support and tighten the pin bolts to 28–38 ft. lbs. (38–52 Nm).
11. Mount the wheels, lower the vehicle and bleed the system if necessary.

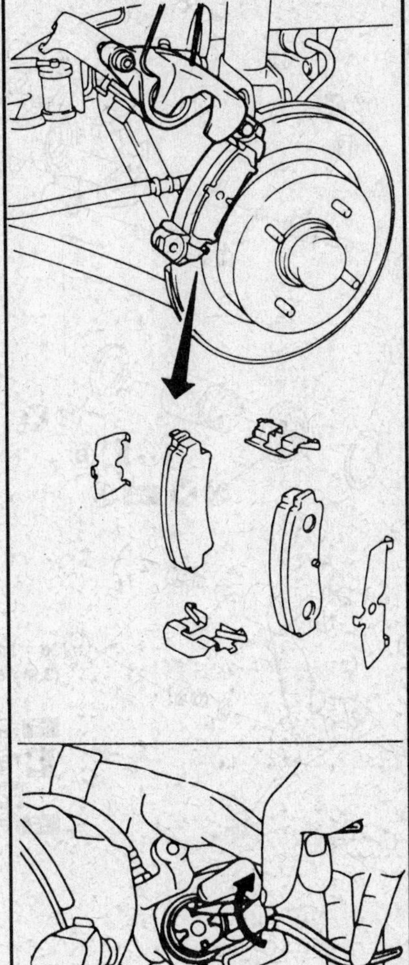

Fig. 17 Turning the piston into the caliper bore on rear disc brakes — 1991-92 Sentra

Brake Caliper

REMOVAL & INSTALLATION

1. Raise and support the vehicle safely.
2. Remove the rear wheels.
3. Release the parking brake and remove the cable bracket bolt. Remove the brake hose from the caliper and plug.
4. Remove the pin bolts and lift off the caliper body.

To install:

5. Clean the piston end of the caliper body and the area around the pin holes. Be careful not to get oil on the rotor.
6. Using the proper tool, carefully turn the piston clockwise back into the caliper body. Take care not to damage the piston boot.
7. Coat the pad contact area on the mounting support with a silicone based grease.
8. Install the pads, shims and the pad springs. Always use new shims.
9. Position the caliper body in the mounting support and tighten the pin bolts to 28–38 ft. lbs. (38–52 Nm).
10. Mount the wheels, lower the vehicle and bleed the system if necessary.

OVERHAUL

➧ SEE FIGS. 18–20

1. Remove the caliper piston by turning counterclockwise with a suitable tool.
2. Remove the piston boot retainer with a suitable prybar.
3. Pry off the snapring with a suitable pliers and remove the spring cover, spring, key plate, pushrod and strut.
4. Remove the piston seal, return spring and toggle lever.

To assemble:

5. Inspect all components for damage, corrosion or cracks.
6. Clean all components in denatured alcohol and dry with compressed air.
7. Lubricate all moving parts with special brake system grease. Do not use ordinary chassis grease.
8. Insert the cam with the depression facing towards the open end of cylinder.
9. Apply special brake grease to the strut and pushrod.
10. Match the depressions in the cylinder bottom with the key plate protrusions.
11. Install the spring, spring cover and snapring with a suitable tool.
12. Install the piston by turning it clockwise with a suitable turning tool.
13. Install the toggle lever and return spring. Torque the lever nut to 27–36 ft. lbs. (37–49 Nm).
14. Install the caliper to the vehicle.

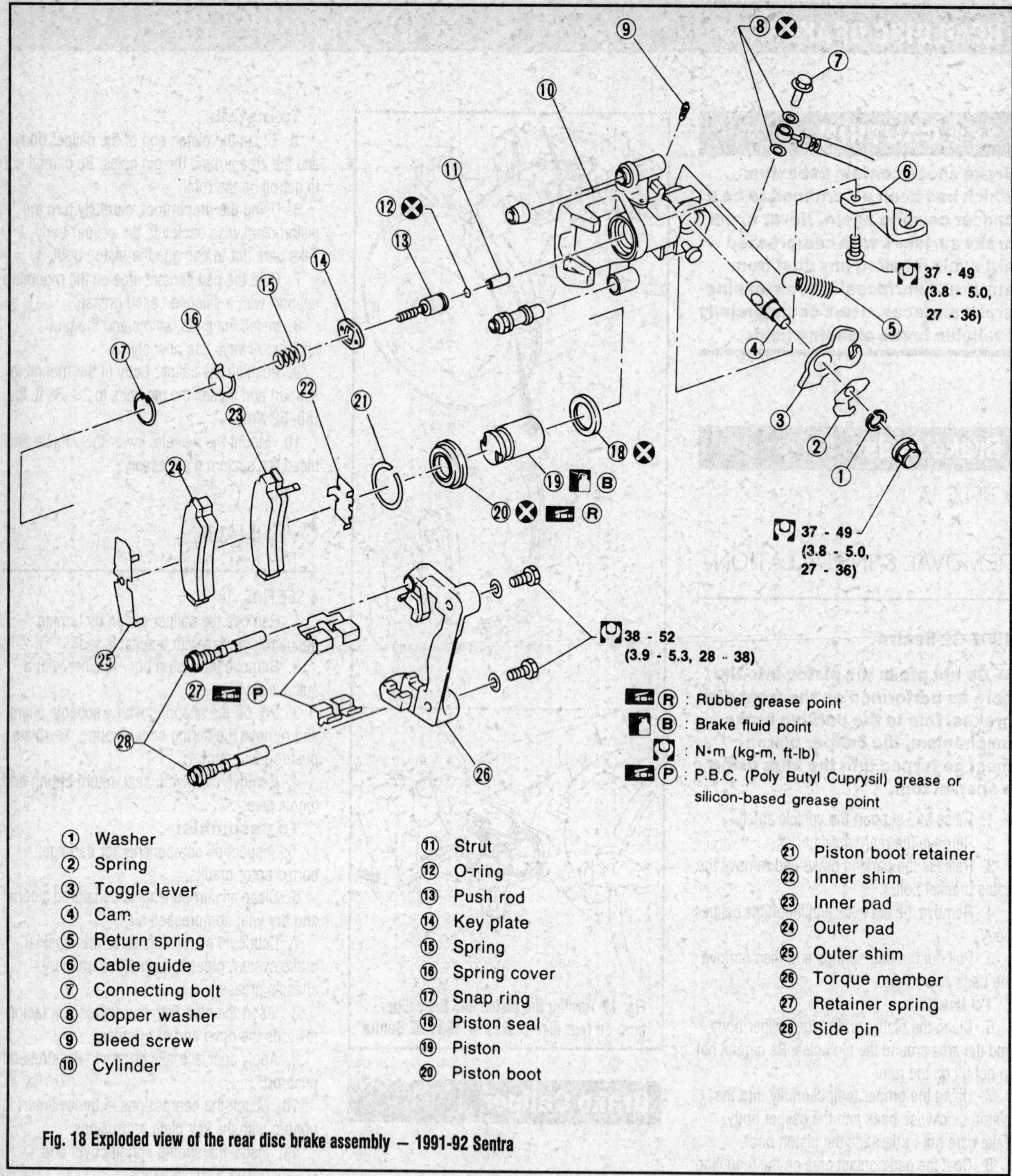

37 - 49 (3.8 - 5.0, 27 - 36)
37 - 49 (3.8 - 5.0, 27 - 36)
38 - 52 (3.9 - 5.3, 28 - 38)
R : Rubber grease point
B : Brake fluid point
: N•m (kg-m, ft-lb)
P : P.B.C. (Poly Butyl Cuprysil) grease or silicon-based grease point
1 Washer
2 Spring
3 Toggle lever
4 Cam
5 Return spring
6 Cable guide
7 Connecting bolt
8 Copper washer
9 Bleed screw
10 Cylinder
11 Strut
12 O-ring
13 Push rod
14 Key plate
15 Spring
16 Spring cover
17 Snap ring
18 Piston seal
19 Piston
20 Piston boot
21 Piston boot retainer
22 Inner shim
23 Inner pad
24 Outer pad
25 Outer shim
26 Torque member
27 Retainer spring
28 Side pin

Fig. 18 Exploded view of the rear disc brake assembly — 1991-92 Sentra

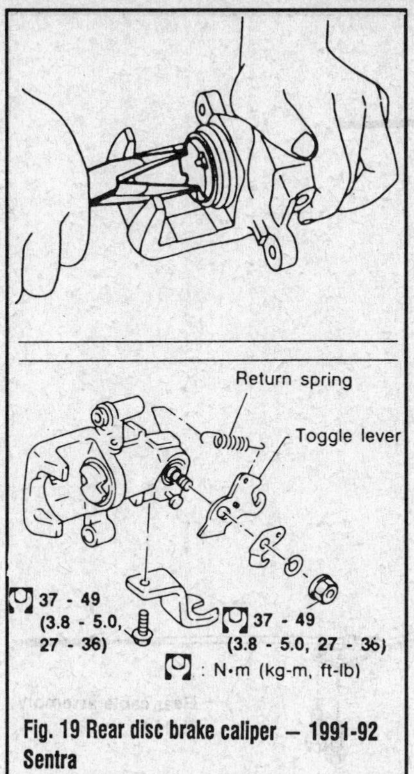
Return spring
Toggle lever
37 - 49
(3.8 - 5.0,
27 - 36)
37 - 49
(3.8 - 5.0, 27 - 36)
: N·m (kg-m, ft-lb)

Fig. 19 Rear disc brake caliper — 1991-92 Sentra

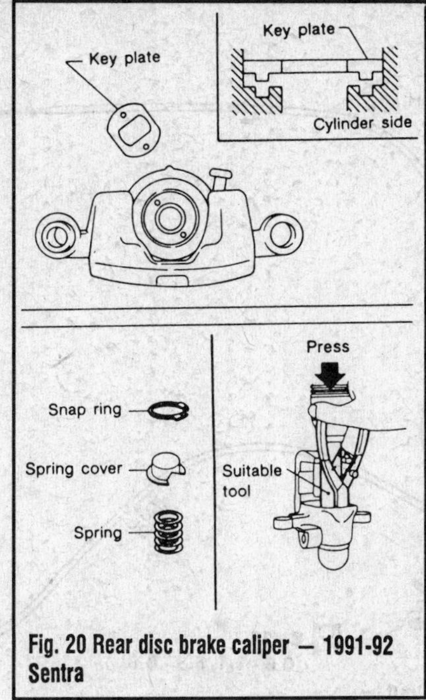
Key plate
Key plate
Cylinder side
Press
Snap ring
Spring cover
Suitable tool
Spring

Fig. 20 Rear disc brake caliper — 1991-92 Sentra

Disc Brake Rotor

REMOVAL & INSTALLATION

1991-92 Sentra

1. Raise the vehicle and support safely.
2. Remove the rear wheel.
3. Remove the brake caliper and torque member as outlined in this section. Hang the caliper by a wire instead of the brake hose.
4. Remove the rotor retaining screw and rotor.

To install:

5. Install the rotor and retaining screw.
6. Install the torque member, brake pads and caliper as outlined in this section. Torque the member bolts to 25–38 ft. lbs. (38–52 Nm).
7. Install the rear wheel and lower the vehicle.
8. Pump the brakes a few times before driving.

INSPECTION

1. Check the disc for cracks and/or chips, if necessary, replace the disc.
2. Using a dial indicator, check the runout of the disc, it should be less than 0.0028 in. (0.070mm); if greater than the maximum, resurface or replace the disc.
3. Using a dial indicator, check the parallelism of the disc, it should be less than 0.001 in. (0.03mm), if greater than the maximum, replace the disc.
4. Using a micrometer, check the thickness of the disc. Refer to the brake specification chart in this section. Maximum variation should be no more than 0.0008 in. (0.02mm).

PARKING BRAKE

Cables

➧ SEE FIGS. 21-23

REMOVAL & INSTALLATION

Rear Cable

1. Refer to the Brake Drum or Disc, Removal and Installation procedures, in this section and remove the brake drum or disc.
2. At the cable adjuster, loosen the adjusting nut, then separate the rear cable from the adjuster.
3. Remove the brake shoes from the backing plate, then separate the rear cable from the toggle lever (rear drum brakes). Remove the cable retainer and cable end from the toggle lever (rear disc brakes).
4. Pull the cable through the backing plate and remove it from the vehicle.

To install:

5. Install the brake cable to the vehicle through the backing plate (drum brakes).
6. Install the brake shoes with cable attached and drum (drum brakes). Connect the cable to the toggle lever and torque the cable retainer to 3–5 ft. lbs. (5–6 Nm) (disc brakes).
7. Connect the brake cable at the adjuster.
8. Adjust the parking brake cable.

Front Cable

1982–86 Vehicles

1. Raise and support the rear of the vehicle on jackstands.
2. Place the parking brake lever in the released position.
3. Separate the front cable from the rear cable at the equalizer.
4. Remove the center console.
5. Disconnect the parking brake lamp switch harness connector, then remove the seat belt anchor bolts.
6. Remove the control lever mounting bolts and the front cable bracket mounting screws.
7. If necessary, separate the front cable from the parking brake control lever by breaking the pin.

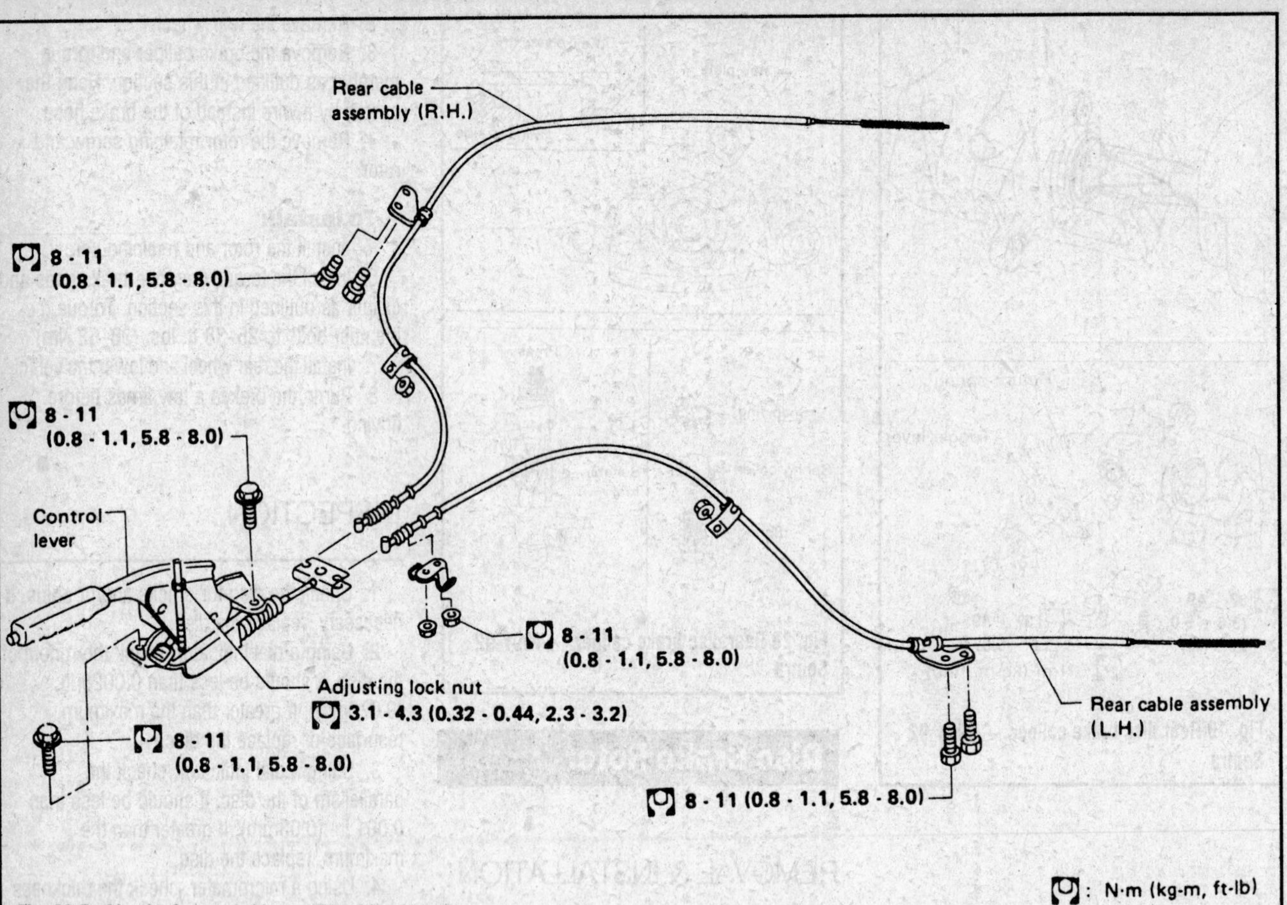

Rear cable assembly (R.H.)
8 - 11 (0.8 - 1.1, 5.8 - 8.0)
8 - 11 (0.8 - 1.1, 5.8 - 8.0)
Control lever
8 - 11 (0.8 - 1.1, 5.8 - 8.0)
Adjusting lock nut
3.1 - 4.3 (0.32 - 0.44, 2.3 - 3.2)
8 - 11 (0.8 - 1.1, 5.8 - 8.0)
Rear cable assembly (L.H.)
8 - 11 (0.8 - 1.1, 5.8 - 8.0)
: N·m (kg-m, ft-lb)

Fig. 22 Parking brake assembly — 1987-90 vehicles

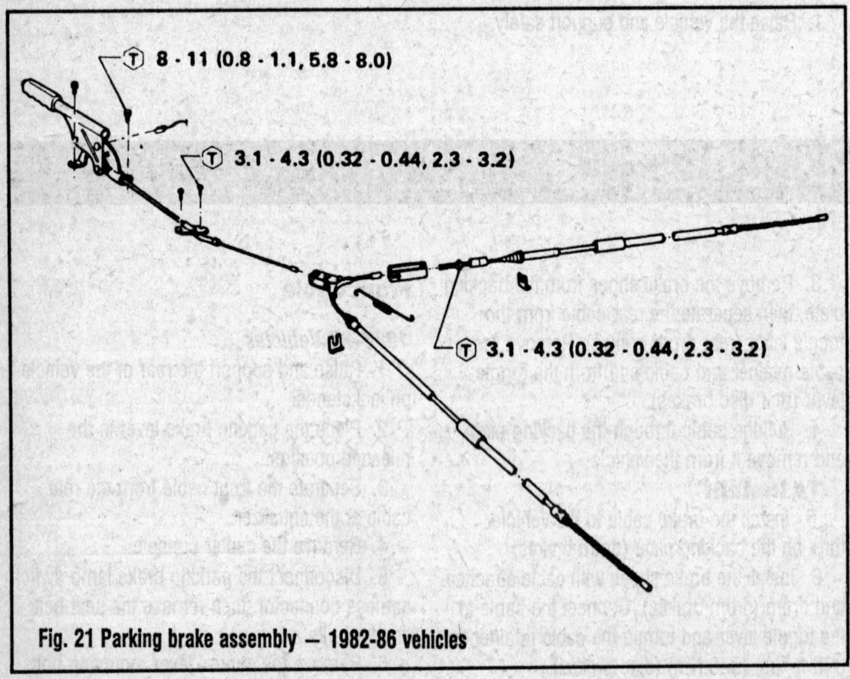
8 - 11 (0.8 - 1.1, 5.8 - 8.0)
3.1 - 4.3 (0.32 - 0.44, 2.3 - 3.2)
3.1 - 4.3 (0.32 - 0.44, 2.3 - 3.2)

Fig. 21 Parking brake assembly — 1982-86 vehicles

➡ **If the pin must be broken to separate the front cable from the control lever, be sure to use a new pin in the installation procedures.**

To install:

8. Install the control lever/front cable assembly in through the driver's compartment with a new pin if necessary.

9. Connect the parking brake lamp switch harness connector and the seat belt anchor bolts.

10. Install the center console.

11. Connect the rear end of brake cable to the attaching point.

12. Adjust the parking brake cable.

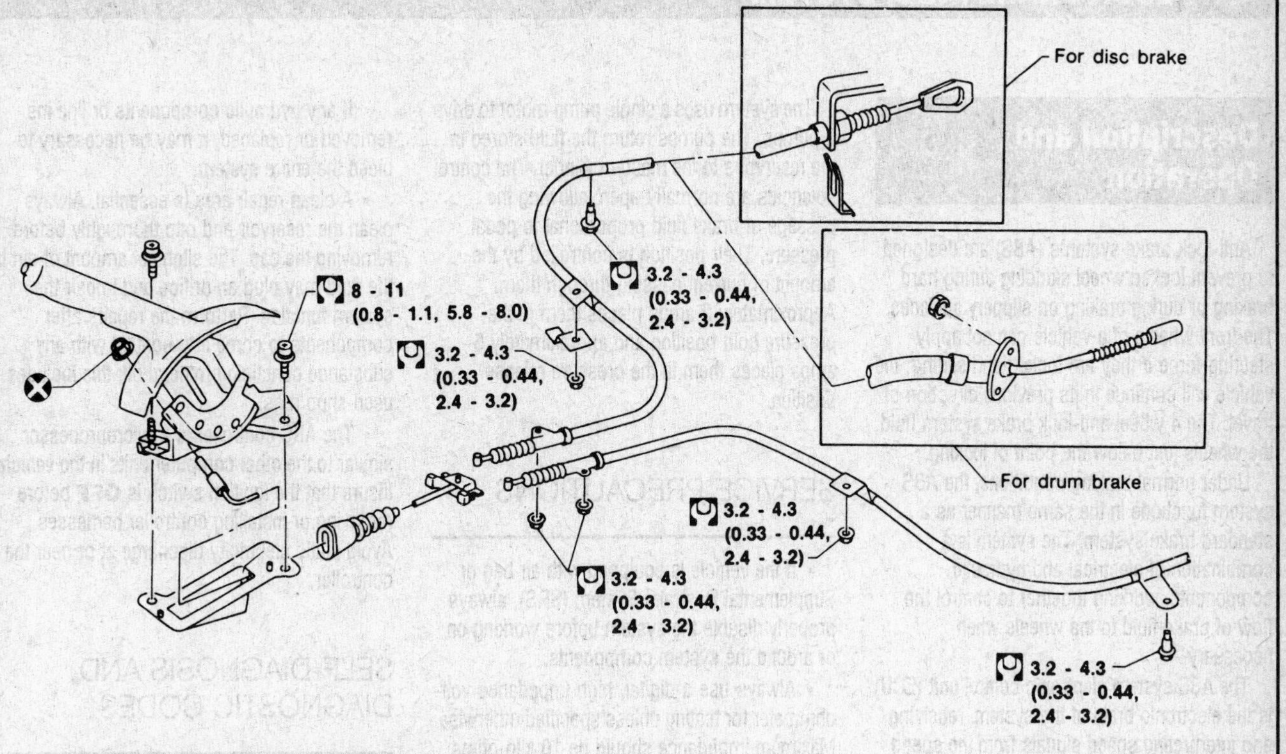

For disc brake
For drum brake
8 - 11
(0.8 - 1.1, 5.8 - 8.0)
3.2 - 4.3
(0.33 - 0.44,
2.4 - 3.2)
3.2 - 4.3
(0.33 - 0.44,
2.4 - 3.2)
3.2 - 4.3
(0.33 - 0.44,
2.4 - 3.2)
3.2 - 4.3
(0.33 - 0.44,
2.4 - 3.2)
3.2 - 4.3
(0.33 - 0.44,
2.4 - 3.2)

Fig. 23 Parking brake assembly — 1991-92 Sentra

ADJUSTMENT

➧ SEE FIGS. 24–25

Handbrake adjustments are generally not needed, unless the cables have stretched.

There is an adjusting nut on the cable under the car, usually at the end of the front cable and near the point at which the two cables from the rear wheels come together (the equalizer). Some models also have a turnbuckle in the rear cable to compensate for cable stretching.

1982–86 Vehicles

1. Adjust the rear brakes with the parking brake fully released.
2. Apply the hand brake lever so that it is 6–7 notches from its fully released position.
3. Adjust the parking brake turnbuckle so that the rear brakes are locked.
4. Release the parking brake. The wheels should turn freely. If not, loosen the parking brake adjuster until the wheels turn with no drag.

1987–92 Vehicles

1. Make sure that the rear brakes are in good condition.
2. Carefully remove the dust boot from around the parking brake lever.
3. The adjustment is made by determining the amount of force needed to pull up on the lever. A force of 44 lbs. should be needed to raise the lever 7–8 notches or clicks.
4. To adjust the pull, raise and support the vehicle on jackstands. There are two nuts on the handbrake clevis rod. Loosen the locknut and turn the adjusting nut to establish the correct pull.
5. Tighten the adjuster locknut.

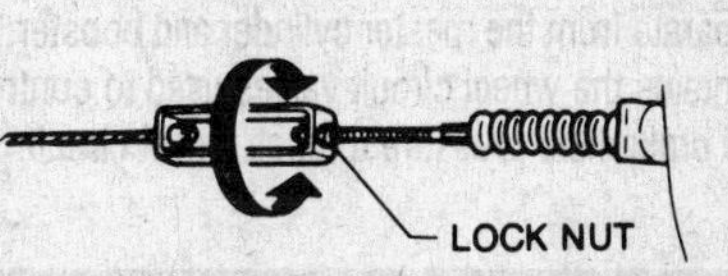
LOCK NUT

Fig. 24 Parking brake adjustment turnbuckle — 1982-86 vehicles

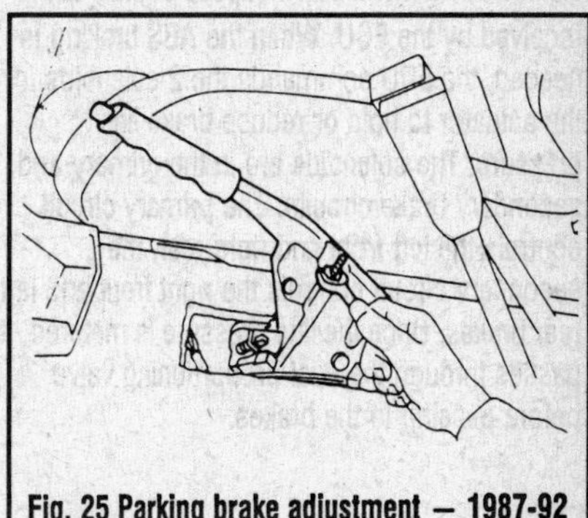

Fig. 25 Parking brake adjustment — 1987-92 vehicles

ANTI-LOCK BRAKE (ABS) SYSTEM

Description and Operation

Anti-lock brake systems (ABS) are designed to prevent locked wheel skidding during hard braking or during braking on slippery surfaces. The front wheels of a vehicle can not apply steering force if they are locked and sliding; the vehicle will continue in its previous direction of travel. The 4 wheel anti-lock brake system hold the wheels just below the point of locking.

Under normal braking conditions, the ABS system functions in the same manner as a standard brake system. The system is a combination of electrical and hydraulic components, working together to control the flow of brake fluid to the wheels when necessary.

The ABS system electronic control unit (ECU) is the electronic brain of the system, receiving and interpreting speed signals from the speed sensors. The ECU will enter anti-lock mode when it senses impending wheel lock at any wheel and immediately controls the brake line pressures to the affected wheels. The actuator assembly is separate from the master cylinder and booster. It contains the wheel circuit valves used to control the brake fluid pressure to each wheel circuit.

System Operation

The 1991–92 Sentra use a wheel speed sensor at each wheel. The speed signals are received by the ECU. When the ABS braking is needed, the ECU commands the 2 solenoids in the actuator to hold or reduce brake line pressure. The solenoids are in the primary and secondary brake circuits. The primary circuit controls the left front and right rear, the secondary circuit controls the right front and left rear brakes. Once the line pressure is metered, it passes through the dual proportioning valve before passing to the brakes.

The system uses a single pump motor to drive 2 pumps. The pumps return the fluid stored in the reservoirs to the master cylinder. The control solenoids are normally open, allowing the passage of brake fluid proportional to pedal pressure. Their position is controlled by the amount of current passing through them. Approximately 2 amps places them in the pressure hold position and approximately 5 amps places them in the pressure release position.

SERVICE PRECAUTIONS

- If the vehicle is equipped with air bag or Supplemental Restraint System (SRS), always properly disable the system before working on or around the system components.
- Always use a digital, high impedance volt-ohmmeter for testing unless specified otherwise. Maximum impedance should be 10 kilo-ohms per volt.
- Certain components within the ABS system are not intended to be serviced or repaired individually. Only those components with removal and installation procedures should be serviced.
- Do not use rubber hoses or other parts if specifically specified for the ABS system. When using repair kits, replace all parts included in the kit. Partial or incorrect repair may lead to functional problems and require the replacement of other components.
- Lubricate the rubber parts with clean, fresh brake fluid to ease assembly. Do not use lubricated shop air to clean parts; damage to the rubber components may result.
- If any hydraulic components or line ins removed or replaced, it may be necessary to bleed the entire system.
- A clean repair area is essential. Always clean the reservoir and cap thoroughly before removing the cap. The slightest amount of dirt in the fluid may plug an orifice and impair the system function. Perform the repairs after components to come into contact with any substance containing mineral oil; this includes used shop rags.
- The ABS controller is a microprocessor similar to the other computer units in the vehicle. Insure that the ignition switch is **OFF** before removing or installing controller harnesses. Avoid static electricity discharge at or near the controller.

SELF-DIAGNOSIS AND DIAGNOSTIC CODES

➧ SEE FIGS. 26–28

When the ECU detects a fault, the ABS warning light on the dash will light. The ECU will perform a self-diagnosis to identify the problem area. When the vehicle is presented with an apparent ABS problem, it must be test driven above 19 mph for at least 1 minute; this allows the ECU time to satisfactorily test the system and store a diagnostic trouble code.

The trouble code will be displayed by the flashing of the LED on the ECU. The display begins when the vehicle comes to a full stop after the self-diagnosis process. The engine must be running for the code to display. The stored code will repeat after a 5–10 second pause. Follow the diagnostic charts in this section.

SYMPTOM CHART—SENTRA/NX

PROCEDURE	—	—	Diagnostic Procedure							Diagnostic Procedure (Select inspection with L.E.D. flashing No.)							—	Electrical Components Inspection	
SYMPTOM	Preliminary Check	Self-diagnosis	Diagnostic Procedure 1	Diagnostic Procedure 2	Diagnostic Procedure 3	Diagnostic Procedure 4	Diagnostic Procedure 5	Diagnostic Procedure 6	Diagnostic Procedure 7	Diagnostic Procedure 8 (L.E.D. flashing No. 1 - 3)	Diagnostic Procedure 9 (L.E.D. flashing No. 5 - 8)	Diagnostic Procedure 10 (L.E.D. flashing No. 9)	Diagnostic Procedure 11 (L.E.D. flashing No. 10)	Diagnostic Procedure 12 (L.E.D. flashing No. 15)	Diagnostic Procedure 13 (L.E.D. flashing No. 16)	Diagnostic Procedure 14 (L.E.D. comes off)	Ground Circuit Check	Actuator Motor Relay	Solenoid Valve Relay
Pedal vibration & noise		○	○							○	○	○	○	○	○	○	○		
Warning activates		○								○	○	○	○	○	○	○			
Long stopping distance	○	○		○						○	○	○	○	○	○	○			
Unexpected pedal action	○	○			○					○	○	○	○	○	○	○			
A.B.S. doesn't work		○				○				○	○	○	○	○	○	○	○	○	○
A.B.S. works but warning activates		○					○			○	○	○	○	○	○	○			○
A.B.S. works frequently	○	○						○						○			○		
Warning never activates		○				○			○								○		○

PRELIMINARY CHECK—1991 SENTRA/NX

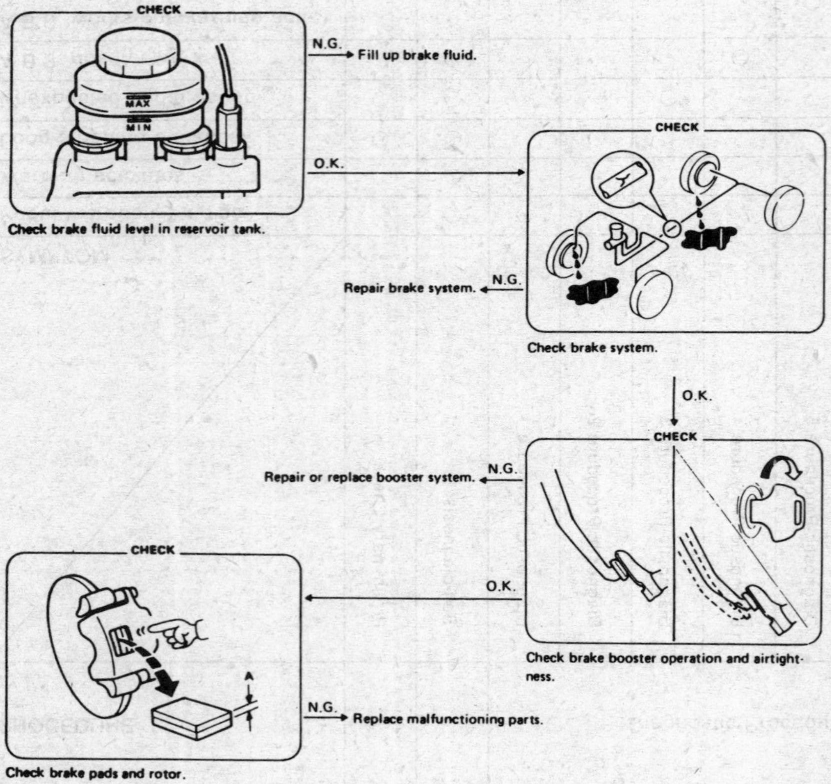

CHECK — Check brake fluid level in reservoir tank.
- N.G. → Fill up brake fluid.
- O.K. → CHECK — Check brake system.
  - N.G. → Repair brake system.
  - O.K. → CHECK — Check brake booster operation and airtightness.
    - N.G. → Repair or replace booster system.
    - O.K. → CHECK — Check brake pads and rotor.
      - N.G. → Replace malfunctioning parts.

ABS FAULT CODES—1991 SENTRA/NX

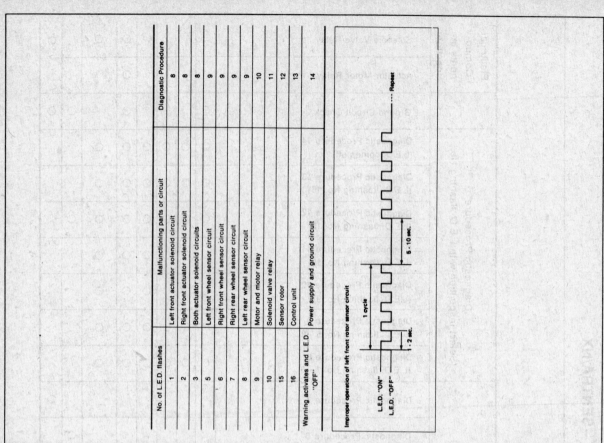

No. of L.E.D. flashes	Malfunctioning parts or circuit	Diagnostic Procedure
1	Left front actuator solenoid circuit	8
2	Right front actuator solenoid circuit	8
3	Both actuator solenoid circuits	8
5	Left front wheel sensor circuit	9
6	Right front wheel sensor circuit	9
7	Right rear wheel sensor circuit	9
8	Left rear wheel sensor circuit	9
9	Motor and motor relay	10
10	Solenoid valve relay	11
15	Sensor rotor	12
16	Control unit	13
Warning activates and L.E.D. "OFF"	Power supply and ground circuit	14

Improper operation of left front rotor sensor circuit

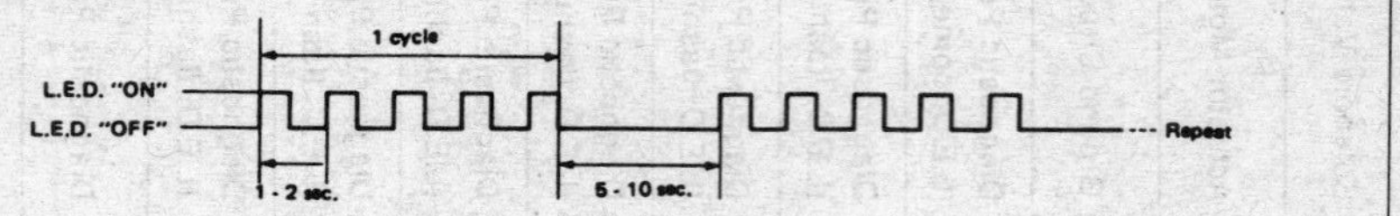

1 cycle
L.E.D. "ON"
L.E.D. "OFF"
1 - 2 sec.
5 - 10 sec.
Repeat

ABS CONNECTORS AND COMPONENTS 1991 SENTRA/NX

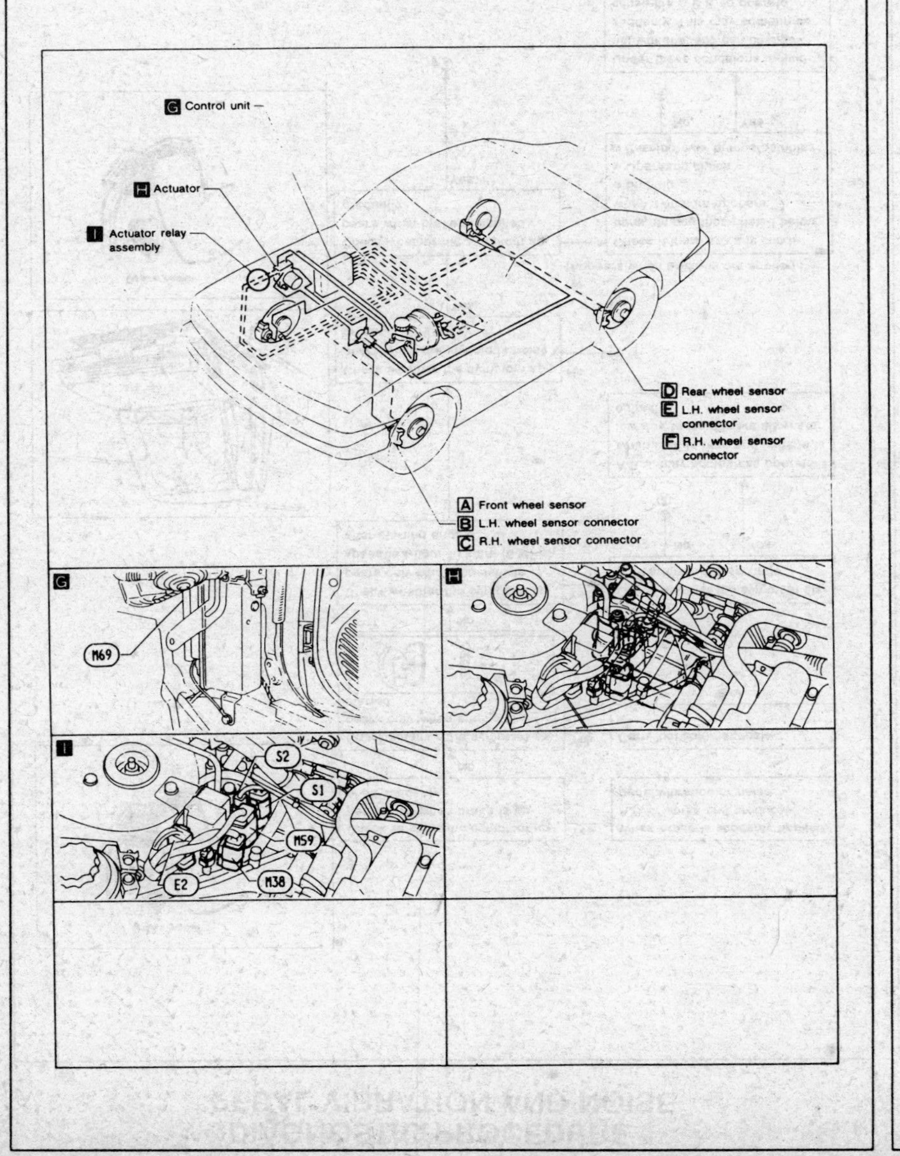

G Control unit
H Actuator
I Actuator relay assembly
D Rear wheel sensor
E L.H. wheel sensor connector
F R.H. wheel sensor connector
A Front wheel sensor
B L.H. wheel sensor connector
C R.H. wheel sensor connector
G
M69
H
I
S2
S1
M59
E2
M38

GROUND CIRCUIT CHECK—1991 SENTRA/NX

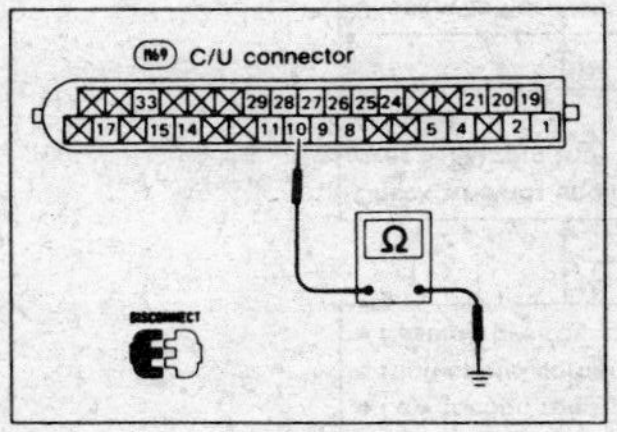

M69 C/U connector
33 29 28 27 26 25 24 21 20 19
17 15 14 11 10 9 8 5 4 2 1
Ω
DISCONNECT

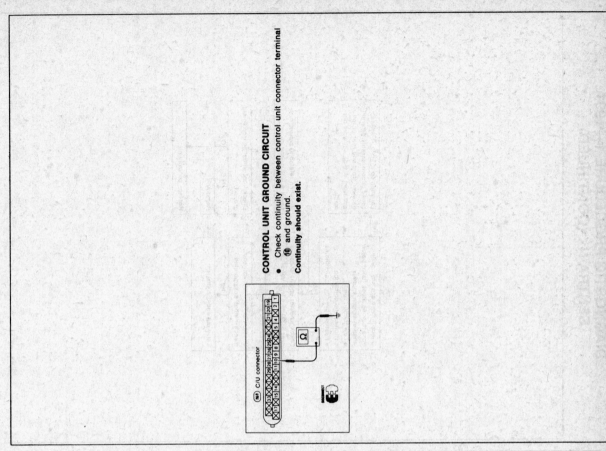

CONTROL UNIT GROUND CIRCUIT

- Check continuity between control unit connector terminal ⑩ and ground.

Continuity should exist.

DIAGNOSTIC PROCEDURE 1
PEDAL VIBRATION AND NOISE

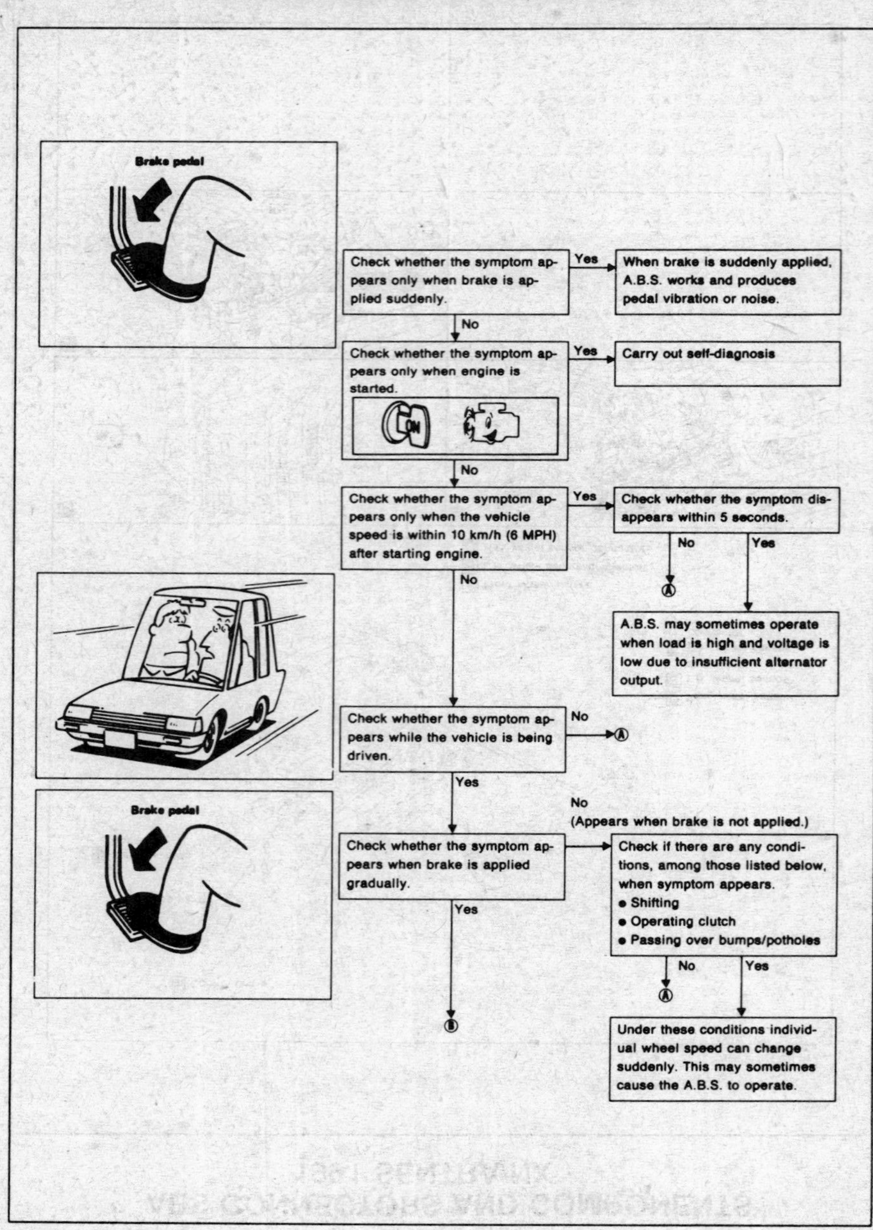
Brake pedal
Check whether the symptom appears only when brake is applied suddenly.
Yes
When brake is suddenly applied, A.B.S. works and produces pedal vibration or noise.
No
Check whether the symptom appears only when engine is started.
Yes
Carry out self-diagnosis
No
Check whether the symptom appears only when the vehicle speed is within 10 km/h (6 MPH) after starting engine.
Yes
Check whether the symptom disappears within 5 seconds.
No
Ⓐ
Yes
A.B.S. may sometimes operate when load is high and voltage is low due to insufficient alternator output.
No
Check whether the symptom appears while the vehicle is being driven.
No
Ⓐ
Yes
Brake pedal
Check whether the symptom appears when brake is applied gradually.
No
(Appears when brake is not applied.)
Check if there are any conditions, among those listed below, when symptom appears.
● Shifting
● Operating clutch
● Passing over bumps/potholes
No
Ⓐ
Yes
Under these conditions individual wheel speed can change suddenly. This may sometimes cause the A.B.S. to operate.
Yes
Ⓑ

DIAGNOSTIC PROCEDURE 1—1991
SENTRA/NX (CONTINUED)

Ⓑ

Check if there are any conditions, among those listed below, when symptom appears.
● Low friction road
● High speed cornering
● Passing over bumps/potholes

Yes

For such conditions, if wheel speed is considerably different between front and rear or left and right, A.B.S. will work normally.

No

Ⓐ

Check whether engine speed is over 5,000 rpm with vehicle stopped.

Yes

Vibration related to sensor may cause A.B.S. operation.

No

Check whether electrical equipment switches are operated.

Yes

Check front wheel sensor shield ground.

N.G.

Remedy.

O.K.

Replace control unit.

No

Carry out self-diagnosis.

DIAGNOSTIC PROCEDURE 2: LONG STOPPING DISTANCE—1991 SENTRA/NX DIAGNOSTIC PROCEDURE 3: ABNORMAL PEDAL ACTION

Check if road condition is slippery with snow or gravel.
- Yes → Stopping distance may be longer than vehicles which are not equipped with A.B.S.
- No ↓

A Disconnect actuator connector and check whether stopping distance is still long.
- No → Carry out self-diagnosis.
- Yes ↓

Perform Preliminary Check and air bleeding.

Diagnostic Procedure 3

SYMPTOM: Unexpected pedal action

Refer to worksheet results.

Check whether brake pedal stroke is excessively large.
- Yes → Vehicle equipped with A.B.S. may have a tendency for excessive pedal strokes.
- No ↓

Check that brake pedal force is firm but brake is effective.
- Yes → Normal condition.
- No ↓

A Disconnect actuator connector and check whether brake is effective.
- Yes → Carry out self-diagnosis.
- No ↓

Perform Preliminary Check.

DIAGNOSTIC PROCEDURE 4: ABS INOPERATIVE 1991 SENTRA/NX DIAGNOSTIC PROCEDURE 5: ABS WORKS BUT WARNING LAMP COMES ON

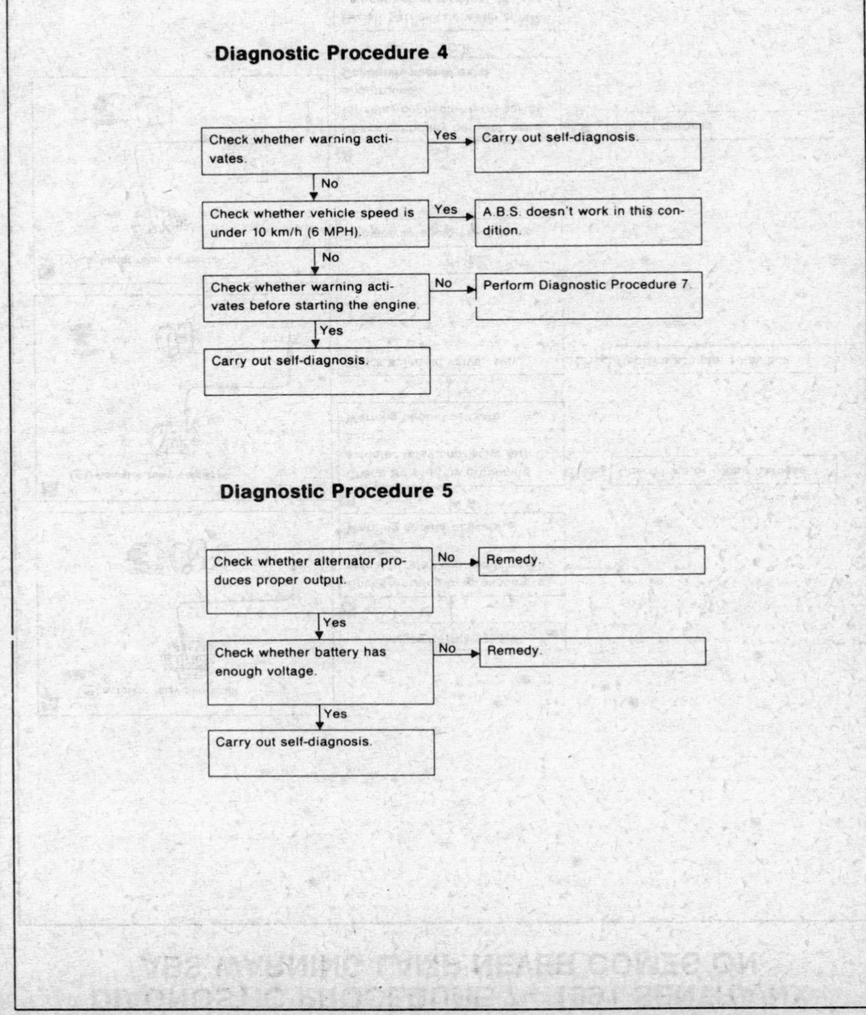
Diagnostic Procedure 4
Check whether warning activates.
Yes
Carry out self-diagnosis.
No
Check whether vehicle speed is under 10 km/h (6 MPH).
Yes
A.B.S. doesn't work in this condition.
No
Check whether warning activates before starting the engine.
No
Perform Diagnostic Procedure 7.
Yes
Carry out self-diagnosis.
Diagnostic Procedure 5
Check whether alternator produces proper output.
No
Remedy.
Yes
Check whether battery has enough voltage.
No
Remedy.
Yes
Carry out self-diagnosis.

DIAGNOSTIC PROCEDURE 6—1991 SENTRA/NX ABS WORKS FREQUENTLY

DIAGNOSTIC PROCEDURE 7—1991 SENTRA/NX ABS WARNING LAMP NEVER COMES ON

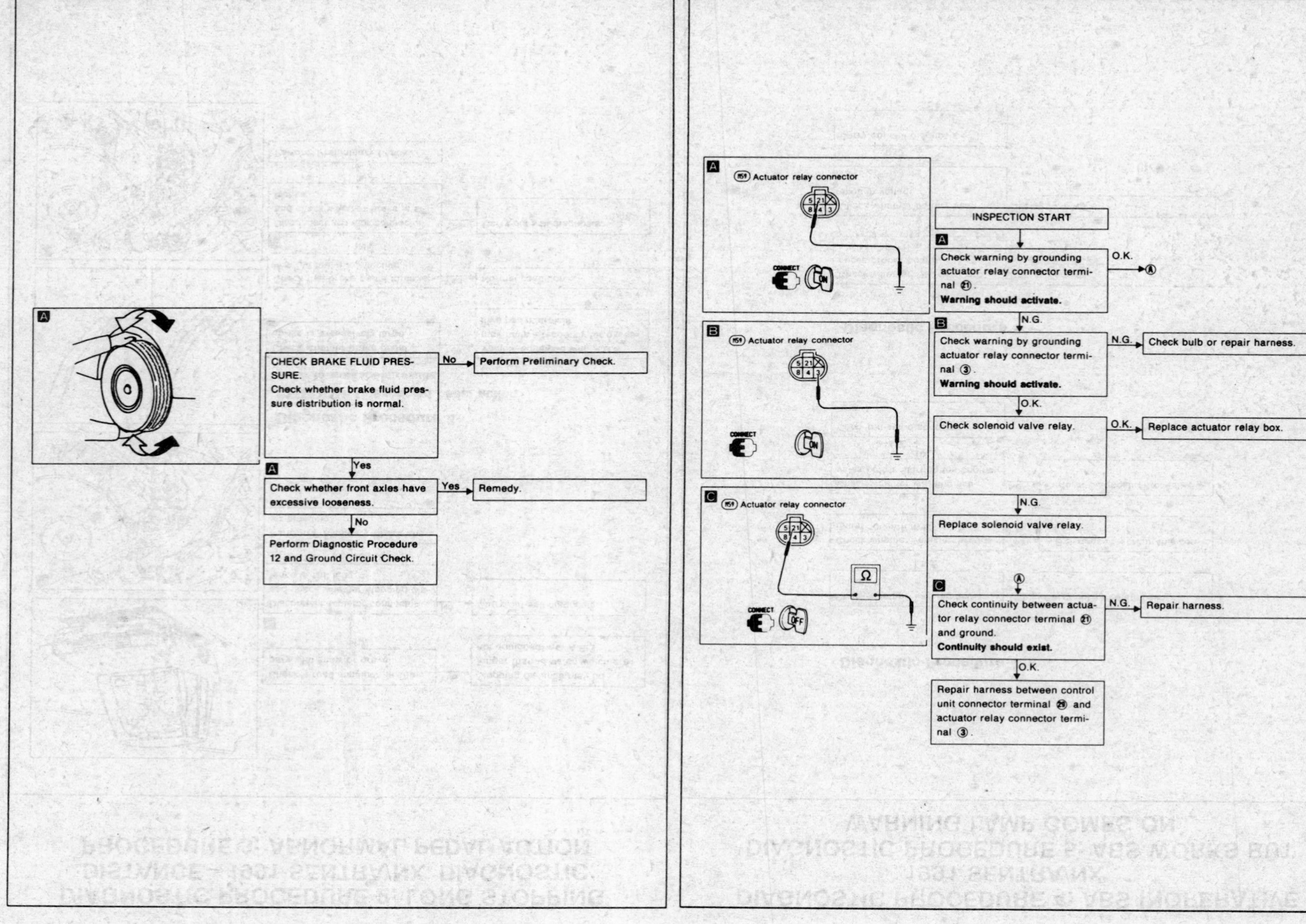

A
CHECK BRAKE FLUID PRESSURE.
Check whether brake fluid pressure distribution is normal.
No
Perform Preliminary Check.
Yes
A
Check whether front axles have excessive looseness.
Yes
Remedy.
No
Perform Diagnostic Procedure 12 and Ground Circuit Check.
A
Actuator relay connector
CONNECT
ON
B
Actuator relay connector
CONNECT
ON
C
Actuator relay connector
CONNECT
OFF
Ω
INSPECTION START
A
Check warning by grounding actuator relay connector terminal 21.
Warning should activate.
O.K.
A
N.G.
B
Check warning by grounding actuator relay connector terminal 3.
Warning should activate.
N.G.
Check bulb or repair harness.
O.K.
Check solenoid valve relay.
O.K.
Replace actuator relay box.
N.G.
Replace solenoid valve relay.
A
C
Check continuity between actuator relay connector terminal 21 and ground.
Continuity should exist.
N.G.
Repair harness.
O.K.
Repair harness between control unit connector terminal 29 and actuator relay connector terminal 3.

DIAGNOSTIC PROCEDURE 8: FAULT CODES 1–3 1991 SENTRA/NX ACTUATOR SOLENOID

DIAGNOSTIC PROCEDURE 9: FAULT CODES 5–8 1991 SENTRA/NX WHEEL SPEED SENSOR CIRCUIT

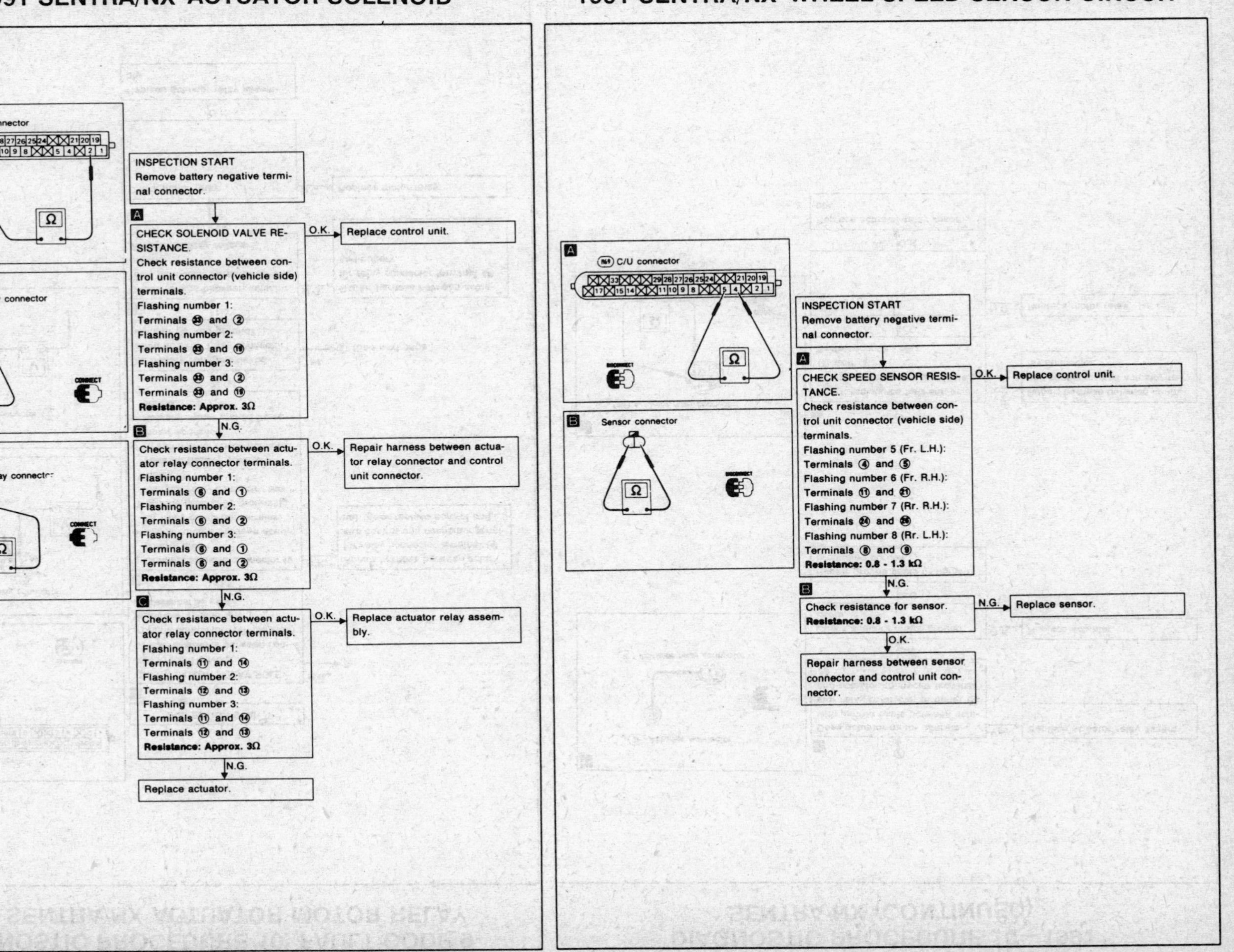

A C/U connector
DISCONNECT
B Actuator relay connector
CONNECT
C Actuator relay connector
CONNECT
INSPECTION START
Remove battery negative terminal connector.
A
CHECK SOLENOID VALVE RESISTANCE.
Check resistance between control unit connector (vehicle side) terminals.
Flashing number 1:
Terminals 33 and 2
Flashing number 2:
Terminals 33 and 16
Flashing number 3:
Terminals 33 and 2
Terminals 33 and 16
Resistance: Approx. 3Ω
O.K.
Replace control unit.
N.G.
B
Check resistance between actuator relay connector terminals.
Flashing number 1:
Terminals 6 and 1
Flashing number 2:
Terminals 6 and 2
Flashing number 3:
Terminals 6 and 1
Terminals 6 and 2
Resistance: Approx. 3Ω
O.K.
Repair harness between actuator relay connector and control unit connector.
N.G.
C
Check resistance between actuator relay connector terminals.
Flashing number 1:
Terminals 11 and 14
Flashing number 2:
Terminals 12 and 13
Flashing number 3:
Terminals 11 and 14
Terminals 12 and 13
Resistance: Approx. 3Ω
O.K.
Replace actuator relay assembly.
N.G.
Replace actuator.
A C/U connector
DISCONNECT
B Sensor connector
DISCONNECT
INSPECTION START
Remove battery negative terminal connector.
A
CHECK SPEED SENSOR RESISTANCE.
Check resistance between control unit connector (vehicle side) terminals.
Flashing number 5 (Fr. L.H.):
Terminals 4 and 5
Flashing number 6 (Fr. R.H.):
Terminals 11 and 21
Flashing number 7 (Rr. R.H.):
Terminals 24 and 26
Flashing number 8 (Rr. L.H.):
Terminals 8 and 9
Resistance: 0.8 - 1.3 kΩ
O.K.
Replace control unit.
N.G.
B
Check resistance for sensor.
Resistance: 0.8 - 1.3 kΩ
N.G.
Replace sensor.
O.K.
Repair harness between sensor connector and control unit connector.

DIAGNOSTIC PROCEDURE 10: FAULT CODE 9 1991 SENTRA/NX ACTUATOR MOTOR RELAY

DIAGNOSTIC PROCEDURE 10—1991 SENTRA/NX (CONTINUED)

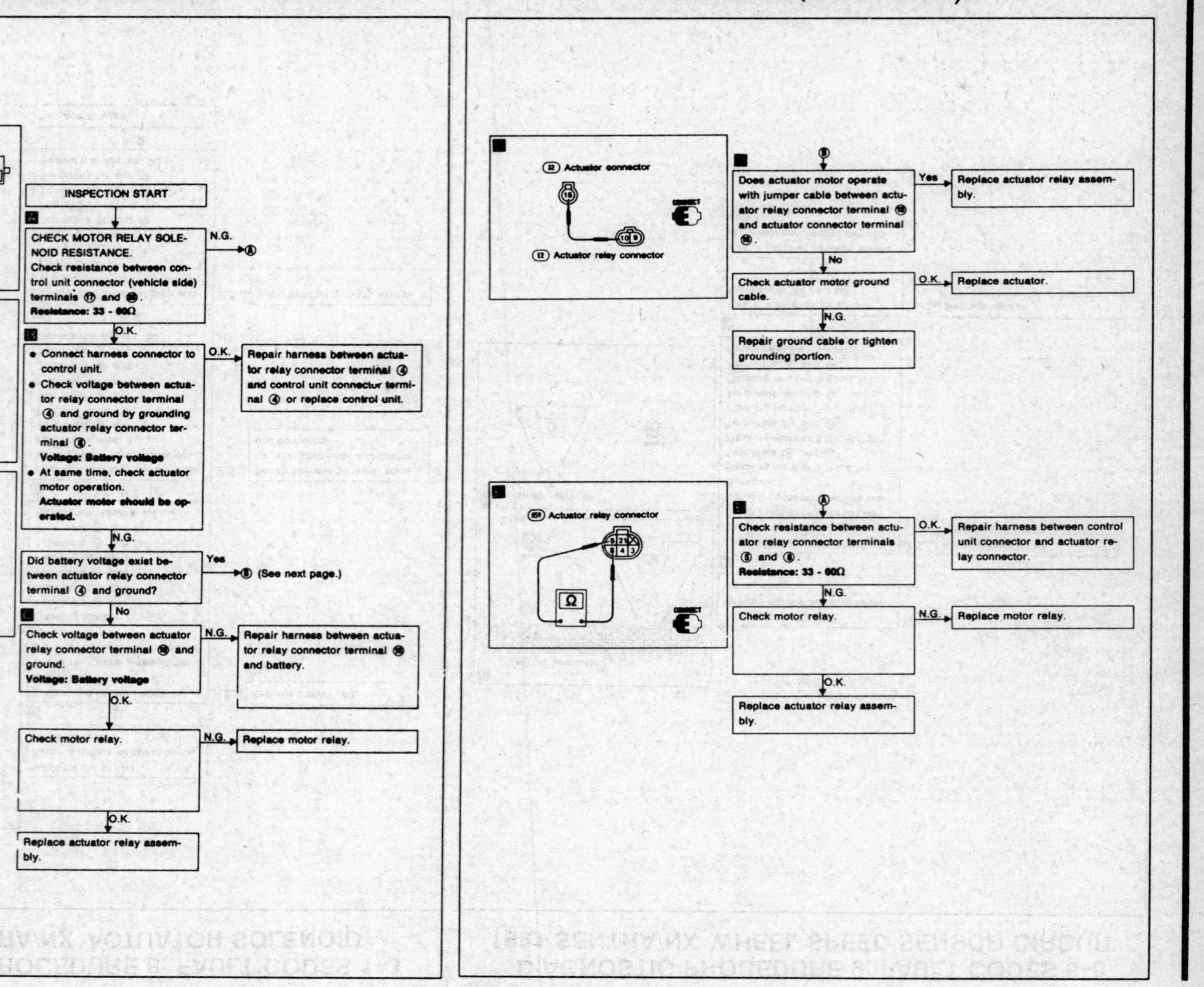
C/U connector
Actuator relay connector
Actuator relay connector
INSPECTION START
CHECK MOTOR RELAY SOLENOID RESISTANCE.
Check resistance between control unit connector (vehicle side) terminals ⑰ and ⑯.
Resistance: 33 - 60Ω
N.G.
Ⓐ
O.K.
● Connect harness connector to control unit.
● Check voltage between actuator relay connector terminal ④ and ground by grounding actuator relay connector terminal ⑧.
Voltage: Battery voltage
● At same time, check actuator motor operation.
Actuator motor should be operated.
O.K.
Repair harness between actuator relay connector terminal ④ and control unit connector terminal ④ or replace control unit.
N.G.
Did battery voltage exist between actuator relay connector terminal ④ and ground?
Yes
Ⓑ (See next page.)
No
Check voltage between actuator relay connector terminal ⑯ and ground.
Voltage: Battery voltage
N.G.
Repair harness between actuator relay connector terminal ⑯ and battery.
O.K.
Check motor relay.
N.G.
Replace motor relay.
O.K.
Replace actuator relay assembly.
Actuator connector
Actuator relay connector
Ⓑ
Does actuator motor operate with jumper cable between actuator relay connector terminal ⑯ and actuator connector terminal ⑯.
Yes
Replace actuator relay assembly.
No
Check actuator motor ground cable.
O.K.
Replace actuator.
N.G.
Repair ground cable or tighten grounding portion.
Actuator relay connector
Ⓐ
Check resistance between actuator relay connector terminals ⑤ and ⑧.
Resistance: 33 - 60Ω
O.K.
Repair harness between control unit connector and actuator relay connector.
N.G.
Check motor relay.
N.G.
Replace motor relay.
O.K.
Replace actuator relay assembly.

DIAGNOSTIC PROCEDURE 11: FAULT CODE 10
1991 SENTRA/NX
ACTUATOR SOLENOID VALVE RELAY

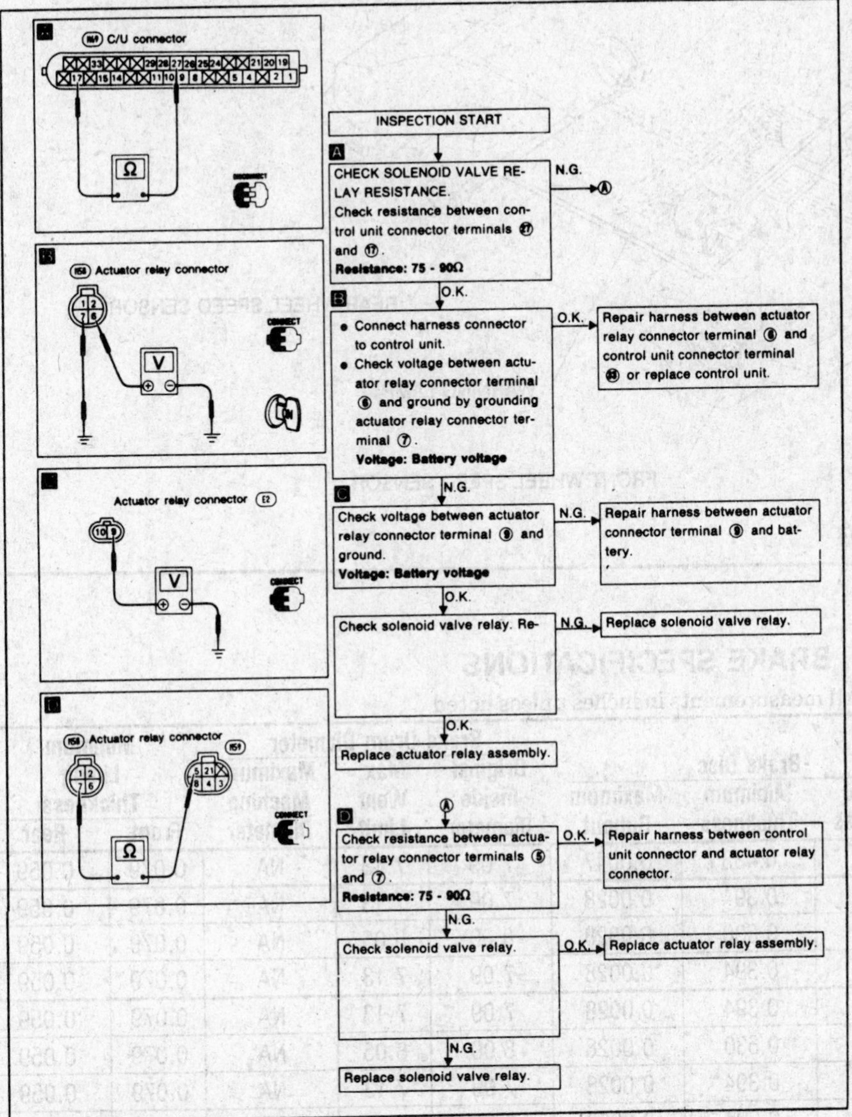
C/U connector
Actuator relay connector
Actuator relay connector
Actuator relay connector
INSPECTION START
A
CHECK SOLENOID VALVE RELAY RESISTANCE.
Check resistance between control unit connector terminals ㉗ and ⑰.
Resistance: 75 - 90Ω
N.G.
Ⓐ
O.K.
B
• Connect harness connector to control unit.
• Check voltage between actuator relay connector terminal ⑥ and ground by grounding actuator relay connector terminal ⑦.
Voltage: Battery voltage
O.K.
Repair harness between actuator relay connector terminal ⑥ and control unit connector terminal ㉝ or replace control unit.
N.G.
C
Check voltage between actuator relay connector terminal ⑨ and ground.
Voltage: Battery voltage
N.G.
Repair harness between actuator connector terminal ⑨ and battery.
O.K.
Check solenoid valve relay.
N.G.
Replace solenoid valve relay.
O.K.
Replace actuator relay assembly.
Ⓐ
D
Check resistance between actuator relay connector terminals ⑤ and ⑦.
Resistance: 75 - 90Ω
O.K.
Repair harness between control unit connector and actuator relay connector.
N.G.
Check solenoid valve relay.
O.K.
Replace actuator relay assembly.
N.G.
Replace solenoid valve relay.

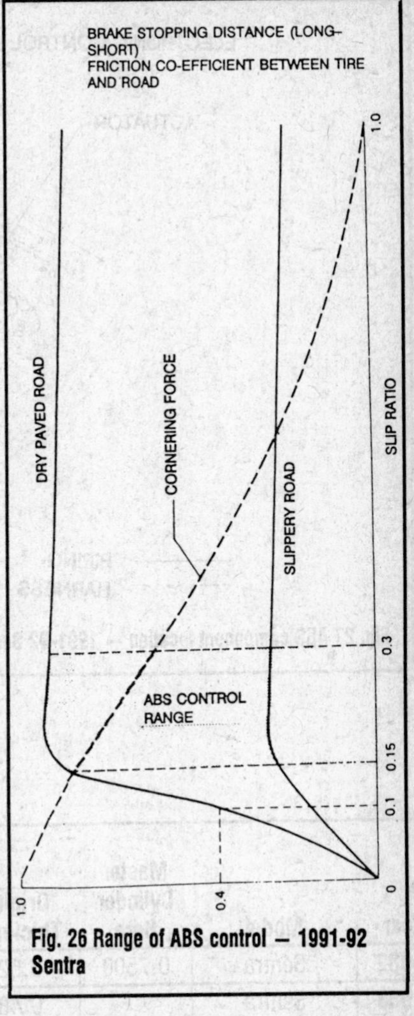
BRAKE STOPPING DISTANCE (LONG-SHORT)
FRICTION CO-EFFICIENT BETWEEN TIRE AND ROAD
DRY PAVED ROAD
CORNERING FORCE
SLIPPERY ROAD
SLIP RATIO
ABS CONTROL RANGE
1.0
0.4
1.0
0.3
0.15
0.1
0

Fig. 26 Range of ABS control — 1991-92 Sentra

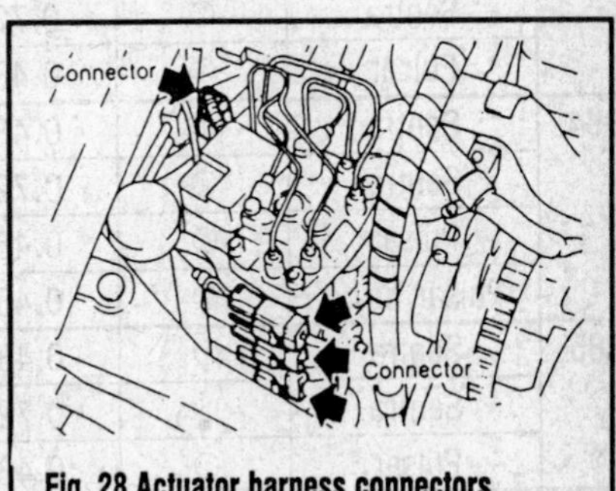
Connector
Connector

Fig. 28 Actuator harness connectors — 1991-92 Sentra

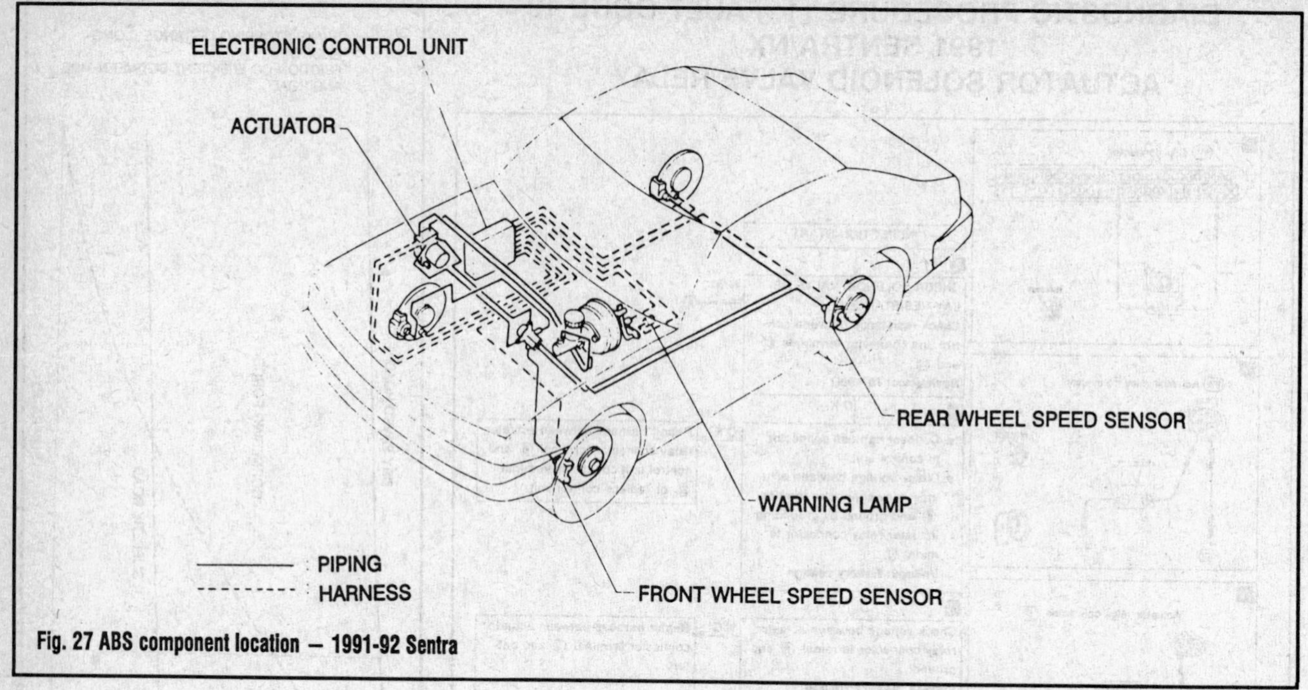
ELECTRONIC CONTROL UNIT
ACTUATOR
REAR WHEEL SPEED SENSOR
WARNING LAMP
PIPING
HARNESS
FRONT WHEEL SPEED SENSOR

Fig. 27 ABS component location — 1991-92 Sentra

BRAKE SPECIFICATIONS

All measurements in inches unless noted

Year	Model	Master Cylinder Bore	Brake Disc: Original Thickness	Brake Disc: Minimum Thickness	Brake Disc: Maximum Runout	Brake Drum Diameter: Original Inside Diameter	Brake Drum Diameter: Max. Wear Limit	Brake Drum Diameter: Maximum Machine Diameter	Minimum Lining Thickness: Front	Minimum Lining Thickness: Rear
1982	Sentra	0.7500	0.523	0.433	0.0047	7.09	7.13	NA	0.079	0.059
1983	Sentra	①	0.484	0.394	0.0028	7.09	7.13	NA	0.079	0.059
	Sentra	②	0.720	0.630	0.0028	8.00	8.05	NA	0.079	0.059
	Pulsar	①	0.484	0.394	0.0028	7.09	7.13	NA	0.079	0.059
1984	Sentra	①	0.484	0.394	0.0028	7.09	7.13	NA	0.079	0.059
	Sentra	②	0.720	0.630	0.0028	8.00	8.05	NA	0.079	0.059
	Pulsar	①	0.484	0.394	0.0028	7.09	7.13	NA	0.079	0.059
	Pulsar Turbo	②	0.484	0.394	0.0028	8.00	8.05	NA	0.079	0.059
1985	Sentra	①	0.484	0.394	0.0028	8.00	8.05	NA	0.079	0.059
	Sentra	②	0.720	0.630	0.0028	8.00	8.05	NA	0.079	0.059
	Pulsar	①	0.484	0.394	0.0028	8.00	8.05	NA	0.079	0.059
1986	Sentra	①	0.523	0.433	0.0028	8.00	8.05	NA	0.079	0.059
	Sentra	②	0.720	0.630	0.0028	8.00	8.05	NA	0.079	0.059
	Pulsar	①	0.523	0.433	0.0028	8.00	8.05	NA	0.079	0.059
1987	Sentra	①	0.484	0.394	0.0028	8.00	8.05	NA	0.079	0.059
	Sentra	②	0.720	0.630	0.0028	8.00	8.05	NA	0.079	0.059
	Pulsar	①	0.484	0.394	0.0028	8.00	8.05	NA	0.079	0.059
	Pulsar	②	0.720	0.630	0.0028	8.00	8.05	NA	0.079	0.059
1988	Sentra 2WD	①	0.484	0.394	0.0028	8.00	8.05	NA	0.079	0.059
	Sentra 4WD	②	0.720	0.630	0.0028	8.00	8.05	NA	0.079	0.059
	Pulsar	①	0.484	0.394	0.0028	8.00	8.05	NA	0.079	0.059
	Pulsar	②	0.720	0.630	0.0028	8.00	8.05	NA	0.079	0.059

BRAKE SPECIFICATIONS

All measurements in inches unless noted

			Brake Disc			Brake Drum Diameter			Minimum Lining Thickness	
Year	Model	Master Cylinder Bore	Original Thickness	Minimum Thickness	Maximum Runout	Original Inside Diameter	Max. Wear Limit	Maximum Machine Diameter	Front	Rear
1989	Sentra 2WD	①	0.484	0.394	0.0028	8.00	8.05	NA	0.079	0.059
	Sentra 4WD	②	0.720	0.630	0.0028	9.00	9.06	NA	0.079	0.059
	Pulsar	①	0.484	0.394	0.0028	8.00	8.05	NA	0.079	0.059
	Pulsar	②	0.720	0.630	0.0028	8.00	8.05	NA	0.079	0.059
1990	Sentra 2WD	②	0.484	0.394	0.0028	8.00	8.05	NA	0.079	0.059
	Sentra 4WD	②	0.720	0.630	0.0028	9.00	9.06	NA	0.079	0.059
	Pulsar	①	0.484	0.394	0.0028	8.00	8.05	NA	0.079	0.059
1991	Sentra NX w/o ABS	0.7500	0.720	0.630	0.0028	7.09	7.13	NA	0.079	0.059⑤
	Sentra NX w/o ABS	0.8125	0.720④	0.630③	0.0028	—	—	NA	0.079	0.059⑤
	Sentra NX w/ABS	0.8750	0.720④	0.630③	0.0028	—	—	NA	0.079	0.059⑤
	Sentra SE w/ABS	0.8750	0.035④	0.945③	0.0028	—	—	NA	0.079	0.059⑤
1992	Sentra NX w/o ABS	0.7500	0.720	0.630	0.0028	7.09	7.13	NA	0.079	0.059⑤
	Sentra NX w/o ABS	0.8125	0.720④	0.630③	0.0028	—	—	NA	0.079	0.059⑤
	Sentra NX w/ABS	0.8750	0.720④	0.630③	0.0028	—	—	NA	0.079	0.059⑤
	Sentra SE w/ABS	0.8750	0.035④	0.945③	0.0028	—	—	NA	0.079	0.059⑤

① Small—0.750
Large—0.938
② Small—0.812
Large—1.000
③ Rear rotor—0.236
④ Rear rotor—0.326
⑤ Rear disc brake 0.079

Actuator

REMOVAL & INSTALLATION

1. Disconnect the negative battery cable.
2. Drain the brake fluid at all wheels until system is empty.
3. Drain the power steering fluid by disconnecting the return hose and drain into a pan.
4. Discharge the A/C system as outlined in section 1.
5. Disconnect the power steering fluid pipe and hose.
6. Disconnect all connectors from the actuator relay bracket.

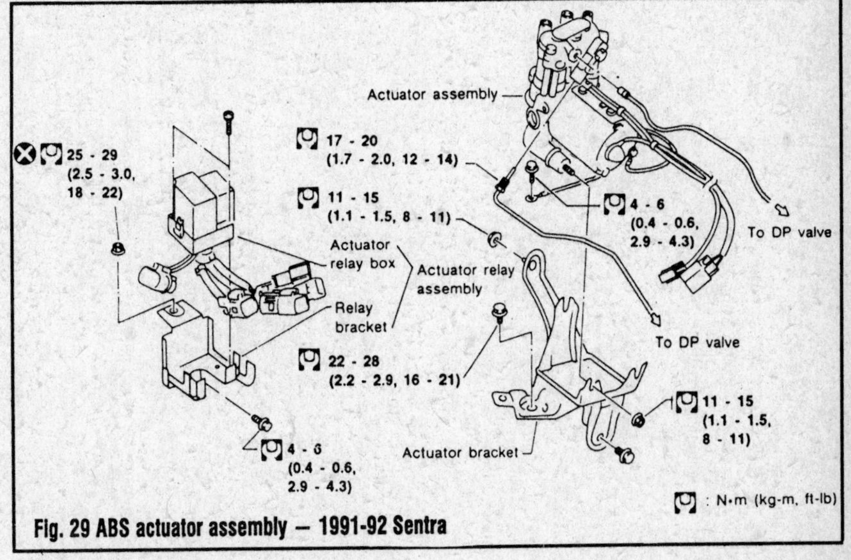
Actuator assembly
17 - 20
(1.7 - 2.0, 12 - 14)
25 - 29
(2.5 - 3.0,
18 - 22)
11 - 15
(1.1 - 1.5, 8 - 11)
4 - 6
(0.4 - 0.6,
2.9 - 4.3)
To DP valve
Actuator relay box
Actuator relay assembly
Relay bracket
To DP valve
22 - 28
(2.2 - 2.9, 16 - 21)
11 - 15
(1.1 - 1.5,
8 - 11)
4 - 6
(0.4 - 0.6,
2.9 - 4.3)
Actuator bracket
: N·m (kg-m, ft-lb)

Fig. 29 ABS actuator assembly — 1991-92 Sentra

7. Remove the mounting nut from the relay bracket, actuator relay box and bracket.
8. Remove the A/C tubes.
9. Disconnect the top 2 brakes pipes from the actuator (from master cylinder-to-actuator). Remove the other brake pipes from the actuator.
10. Remove the mounting nuts between the actuator and bracket.
11. Disconnect the ground strap and remove the actuator from the vehicle.

To install:

12. Install the actuator and connect the ground strap.
13. Install the mounting nuts between the actuator and bracket.
14. Connect the top 2 brakes pipes to the actuator. Torque the pipe fittings to 14–22 ft. lbs. (19–26 Nm).
15. Install the A/C tubes.
16. Install the mounting nut to the relay bracket and actuator relay box.
17. Connect all connectors to the actuator relay bracket.
18. Connect the power steering fluid pipe and hose.
19. Refill the power steering fluid.
20. Recharge the A/C system as outlined in section 1.
21. Refill and bleed the brake system as outlined in this section.
22. Connect the negative battery cable.

ABS Electronic Control Unit (ECU)

The ECU is located behind the right kick panel. Remove the panel and ECU. Make sure the multi-connector is tight before going any further.

Wheel Sensors

There is a wheel sensor at each brake assembly. Disconnect the sensor and remove. Install and torque to 8–11 ft. lbs. (11–15 Nm).

Wheel Sensor Ring

Remove the front halfshaft as outlined in section 8. Remove the rear hub and bearing assembly as outlined in section 8.

FILLING AND BLEEDING

Refer to bleeding of the conventional brake system as outlined in this section. Use DOT 3 brake fluid ONLY.

Troubleshooting the Brake System

Problem	Cause	Solution
Low brake pedal (excessive pedal travel required for braking action.)	• Excessive clearance between rear linings and drums caused by inoperative automatic adjusters	• Make 10 to 15 alternate forward and reverse brake stops to adjust brakes. If brake pedal does not come up, repair or replace adjuster parts as necessary.
	• Worn rear brakelining	• Inspect and replace lining if worn beyond minimum thickness specification
	• Bent, distorted brakeshoes, front or rear	• Replace brakeshoes in axle sets
	• Air in hydraulic system	• Remove air from system. Refer to Brake Bleeding.
Low brake pedal (pedal may go to floor with steady pressure applied.)	• Fluid leak in hydraulic system	• Fill master cylinder to fill line; have helper apply brakes and check calipers, wheel cylinders, differential valve tubes, hoses and fittings for leaks. Repair or replace as necessary.
	• Air in hydraulic system	• Remove air from system. Refer to Brake Bleeding.
	• Incorrect or non-recommended brake fluid (fluid evaporates at below normal temp).	• Flush hydraulic system with clean brake fluid. Refill with correct-type fluid.
	• Master cylinder piston seals worn, or master cylinder bore is scored, worn or corroded	• Repair or replace master cylinder
Low brake pedal (pedal goes to floor on first application—o.k. on subsequent applications.)	• Disc brake pads sticking on abutment surfaces of anchor plate. Caused by a build-up of dirt, rust, or corrosion on abutment surfaces	• Clean abutment surfaces
Fading brake pedal (pedal height decreases with steady pressure applied.)	• Fluid leak in hydraulic system	• Fill master cylinder reservoirs to fill mark, have helper apply brakes, check calipers, wheel cylinders, differential valve, tubes, hoses, and fittings for fluid leaks. Repair or replace parts as necessary.
	• Master cylinder piston seals worn, or master cylinder bore is scored, worn or corroded	• Repair or replace master cylinder
Spongy brake pedal (pedal has abnormally soft, springy, spongy feel when depressed.)	• Air in hydraulic system	• Remove air from system. Refer to Brake Bleeding.
	• Brakeshoes bent or distorted	• Replace brakeshoes
	• Brakelining not yet seated with drums and rotors	• Burnish brakes
	• Rear drum brakes not properly adjusted	• Adjust brakes

Troubleshooting the Brake System (cont.)

Problem	Cause	Solution
Decreasing brake pedal travel (pedal travel required for braking action decreases and may be accompanied by a hard pedal.)	• Caliper or wheel cylinder pistons sticking or seized • Master cylinder compensator ports blocked (preventing fluid return to reservoirs) or pistons sticking or seized in master cylinder bore • Power brake unit binding internally	• Repair or replace the calipers, or wheel cylinders • Repair or replace the master cylinder • Test unit according to the following procedure: (a) Shift transmission into neutral and start engine (b) Increase engine speed to 1500 rpm, close throttle and fully depress brake pedal (c) Slow release brake pedal and stop engine (d) Have helper remove vacuum check valve and hose from power unit. Observe for backward movement of brake pedal. (e) If the pedal moves backward, the power unit has an internal bind—replace power unit
Grabbing brakes (severe reaction to brake pedal pressure.)	• Brakelining(s) contaminated by grease or brake fluid • Parking brake cables incorrectly adjusted or seized • Incorrect brakelining or lining loose on brakeshoes • Caliper anchor plate bolts loose • Rear brakeshoes binding on support plate ledges • Incorrect or missing power brake reaction disc • Rear brake support plates loose	• Determine and correct cause of contamination and replace brakeshoes in axle sets • Adjust cables. Replace seized cables. • Replace brakeshoes in axle sets • Tighten bolts • Clean and lubricate ledges. Replace support plate(s) if ledges are deeply grooved. Do not attempt to smooth ledges by grinding. • Install correct disc • Tighten mounting bolts
Chatter or shudder when brakes are applied (pedal pulsation and roughness may also occur.)	• Brakeshoes distorted, bent, contaminated, or worn • Caliper anchor plate or support plate loose • Excessive thickness variation of rotor(s)	• Replace brakeshoes in axle sets • Tighten mounting bolts • Refinish or replace rotors in axle sets
Noisy brakes (squealing, clicking, scraping sound when brakes are applied.)	• Bent, broken, distorted brakeshoes • Excessive rust on outer edge of rotor braking surface	• Replace brakeshoes in axle sets • Remove rust

Troubleshooting the Brake System (cont.)

Problem	Cause	Solution
Hard brake pedal (excessive pedal pressure required to stop vehicle. May be accompanied by brake fade.)	• Loose or leaking power brake unit vacuum hose	• Tighten connections or replace leaking hose
	• Incorrect or poor quality brake-lining	• Replace with lining in axle sets
	• Bent, broken, distorted brakeshoes	• Replace brakeshoes
	• Calipers binding or dragging on mounting pins. Rear brakeshoes dragging on support plate.	• Replace mounting pins and bushings. Clean rust or burrs from rear brake support plate ledges and lubricate ledges with molydisulfide grease. **NOTE:** If ledges are deeply grooved or scored, do not attempt to sand or grind them smooth—replace support plate.
	• Caliper, wheel cylinder, or master cylinder pistons sticking or seized	• Repair or replace parts as necessary
	• Power brake unit vacuum check valve malfunction	• Test valve according to the following procedure: (a) Start engine, increase engine speed to 1500 rpm, close throttle and immediately stop engine (b) Wait at least 90 seconds then depress brake pedal (c) If brakes are not vacuum assisted for 2 or more applications, check valve is faulty
	• Power brake unit has internal bind	• Test unit according to the following procedure: (a) With engine stopped, apply brakes several times to exhaust all vacuum in system (b) Shift transmission into neutral, depress brake pedal and start engine (c) If pedal height decreases with foot pressure and less pressure is required to hold pedal in applied position, power unit vacuum system is operating normally. Test power unit. If power unit exhibits a bind condition, replace the power unit.

Troubleshooting the Brake System (cont.)

Problem	Cause	Solution
Hard brake pedal (excessive pedal pressure required to stop vehicle. May be accompanied by brake fade.)	• Master cylinder compensator ports (at bottom of reservoirs) blocked by dirt, scale, rust, or have small burrs (blocked ports prevent fluid return to reservoirs).	• Repair or replace master cylinder **CAUTION:** Do not attempt to clean blocked ports with wire, pencils, or similar implements. Use compressed air only.
	• Brake hoses, tubes, fittings clogged or restricted	• Use compressed air to check or unclog parts. Replace any damaged parts.
	• Brake fluid contaminated with improper fluids (motor oil, transmission fluid, causing rubber components to swell and stick in bores	• Replace all rubber components, combination valve and hoses. Flush entire brake system with DOT 3 brake fluid or equivalent.
	• Low engine vacuum	• Adjust or repair engine
Dragging brakes (slow or incomplete release of brakes)	• Brake pedal binding at pivot	• Loosen and lubricate
	• Power brake unit has internal bind	• Inspect for internal bind. Replace unit if internal bind exists.
	• Parking brake cables incorrrectly adjusted or seized	• Adjust cables. Replace seized cables.
	• Rear brakeshoe return springs weak or broken	• Replace return springs. Replace brakeshoe if necessary in axle sets.
	• Automatic adjusters malfunctioning	• Repair or replace adjuster parts as required
	• Caliper, wheel cylinder or master cylinder pistons sticking or seized	• Repair or replace parts as necessary
	• Master cylinder compensating ports blocked (fluid does not return to reservoirs).	• Use compressed air to clear ports. Do not use wire, pencils, or similar objects to open blocked ports.
Vehicle moves to one side when brakes are applied	• Incorrect front tire pressure	• Inflate to recommended cold (reduced load) inflation pressure
	• Worn or damaged wheel bearings	• Replace worn or damaged bearings
	• Brakelining on one side contaminated	• Determine and correct cause of contamination and replace brakelining in axle sets
	• Brakeshoes on one side bent, distorted, or lining loose on shoe	• Replace brakeshoes in axle sets
	• Support plate bent or loose on one side	• Tighten or replace support plate
	• Brakelining not yet seated with drums or rotors	• Burnish brakelining
	• Caliper anchor plate loose on one side	• Tighten anchor plate bolts
	• Caliper piston sticking or seized	• Repair or replace caliper
	• Brakelinings water soaked	• Drive vehicle with brakes lightly applied to dry linings
	• Loose suspension component attaching or mounting bolts	• Tighten suspension bolts. Replace worn suspension components.
	• Brake combination valve failure	• Replace combination valve

Troubleshooting the Brake System (cont.)

Problem	Cause	Solution
Noisy brakes (squealing, clicking, scraping sound when brakes are applied.) (cont.)	· Brakelining worn out—shoes contacting drum of rotor	· Replace brakeshoes and lining in axle sets. Refinish or replace drums or rotors.
	· Broken or loose holdown or return springs	· Replace parts as necessary
	· Rough or dry drum brake support plate ledges	· Lubricate support plate ledges
	· Cracked, grooved, or scored rotor(s) or drum(s)	· Replace rotor(s) or drum(s). Replace brakeshoes and lining in axle sets if necessary.
	· Incorrect brakelining and/or shoes (front or rear).	· Install specified shoe and lining assemblies
Pulsating brake pedal	· Out of round drums or excessive lateral runout in disc brake rotor(s)	· Refinish or replace drums, re-index rotors or replace

TORQUE SPECIFICATIONS

Component	U.S.	Metric
Master cylinder nuts	6-8 ft. lbs.	8-11 Nm
Brake pipe fittings	12-14 ft. lbs.	17-20 Nm
Diesel vacuum pump	14-18 ft. lbs.	20-25 Nm
Vacuum pump banjo fitting	22-25 ft. lbs.	29-34 Nm
Brake booster-to-firewall	6-8 ft. lbs.	8-11 Nm
Disc brake guide pin	23-30 ft. lbs.	31-41 Nm
Disc-to-wheel hub	18-25 ft. lbs.	25-34 Nm
Wheel cylinder bolts	5-8 ft. lbs.	6-11 Nm
Rear disc toggle lever	27-36 ft. lbs.	37-49 Nm
Torque member-to-backing plate	25-38 ft. lbs.	38-52 Nm
Parking brake cable retainer	3-5 ft. lbs.	5-6 Nm
Wheel speed sensor bolts	8-11 ft. lbs.	11-15 Nm

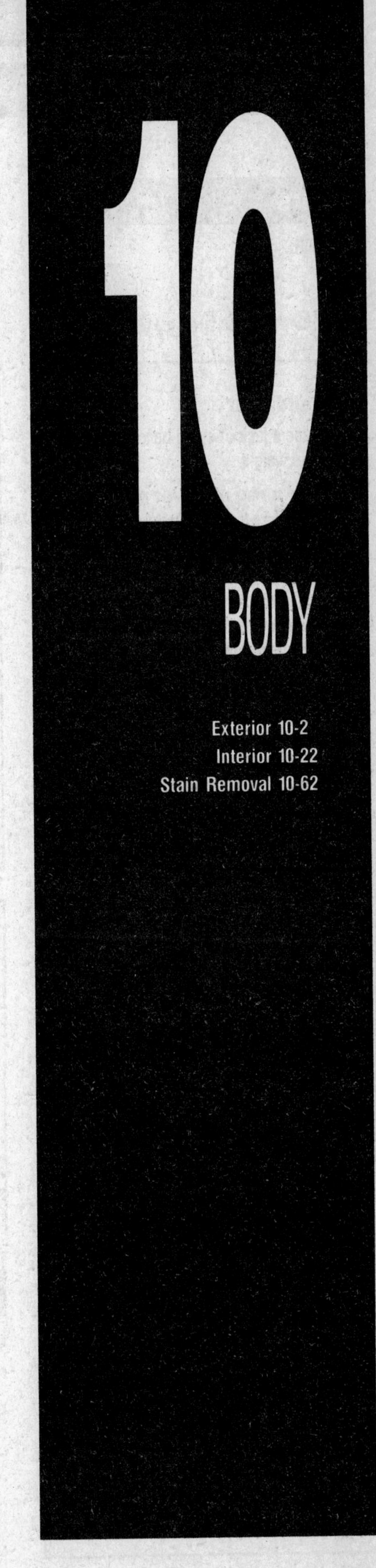
10
BODY
Exterior 10-2
Interior 10-22
Stain Removal 10-62

EXTERIOR

Doors

➧ SEE FIGS. 1–4

REMOVAL & INSTALLATION

Front and Rear

1. Place a jack or stand beneath the door to support its weight.

➡ Place a rag at lower edge of the door and jack or stand to prevent damage to painted surface.

2. To remove door without the hinges, remove the bolts and lower the door.
3. To remove the door with the hinges, remove the front fender and hinge retaining bolts.
4. Installation is in the reverse order of removal. Torque the hinge bolts to 15–20 ft. lbs. (21–29 Nm).

➡ When installing hinge, coat the hinge link with recommended multipurpose grease.

ADJUSTMENT

Front and Rear

Proper door alignment can be obtained by adjusting the door hinge and door lock striker. The door hinge and striker can be moved up and down fore and aft in enlarged holes by loosening the attaching bolts.

➡ The door should be adjusted for an even and parallel fit for the door opening and surrounding body panels.

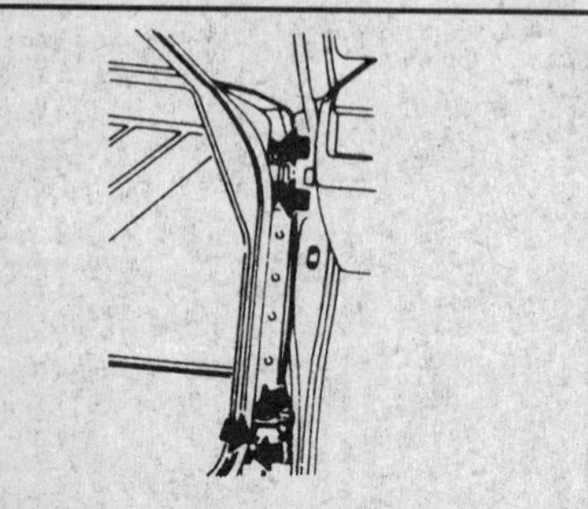

Fig. 1 Removing the door hinge retaining bolts

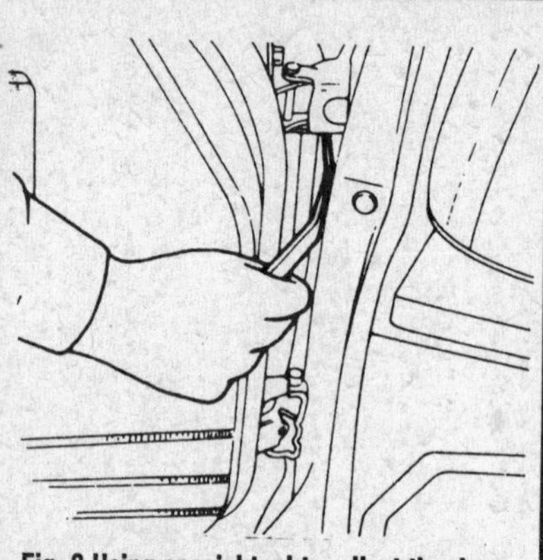

Fig. 2 Using special tool to adjust the door hinge

Fig. 3 Adjusting door lock striker

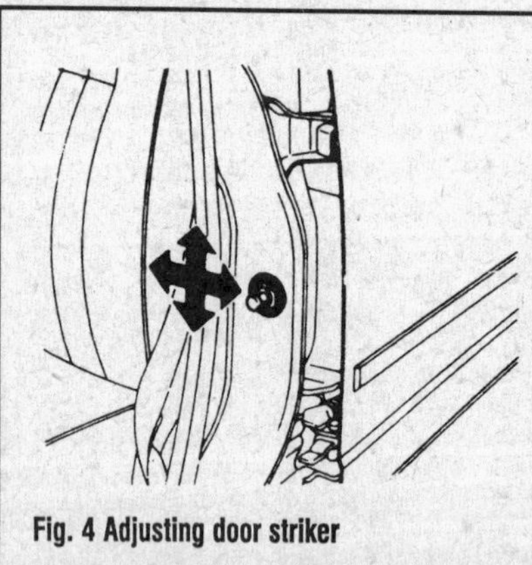

Fig. 4 Adjusting door striker

Hood

➧ SEE FIGS. 6–10

REMOVAL & INSTALLATION

1. Open the hood and protect the body with covers to protect the painted surfaces.
2. Mark the hood hinge locations on the hood for proper reinstallation.
3. With an assistant, hold both sides of the hood, unscrew the bolts securing the hinge to the hood and remove.

To install:

4. Install the hood with the help of an assistant. Line up the hinges to the bolt holes and install the bolts. Position the hood and hinges to the original position and tighten.
5. Slowly close the hood, making sure it does not contact the painted surfaces. Adjust as necessary and torque the bolts to 12–14 ft. lbs. (16–19 Nm).

ALIGNMENT

The hood can be adjusted with bolts attaching the hood to the hood hinges, hood lock mechanism and hood bumpers. Adjust the hood for an even fit between the front fenders.

1. Adjust the hood fore and aft by loosening the bolts attaching the hood to the hinge and repositioning hood.
2. Loosen the hood bumper lock nuts and lower bumpers until they do not contact the front of the hood when the hood is closed.
3. Set the striker at the center of the hood lock, and tighten the hood lock securing bolts temporarily.
4. Raise the two hood bumpers until the hood is flush with the fenders.
5. Tighten the hood lock securing bolts after the proper adjustment has been obtained.

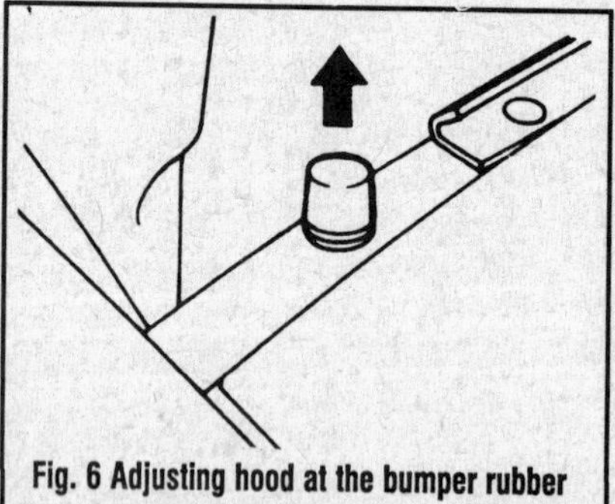

Fig. 6 Adjusting hood at the bumper rubber

Fig. 7 Adjusting the hood at the hood lock

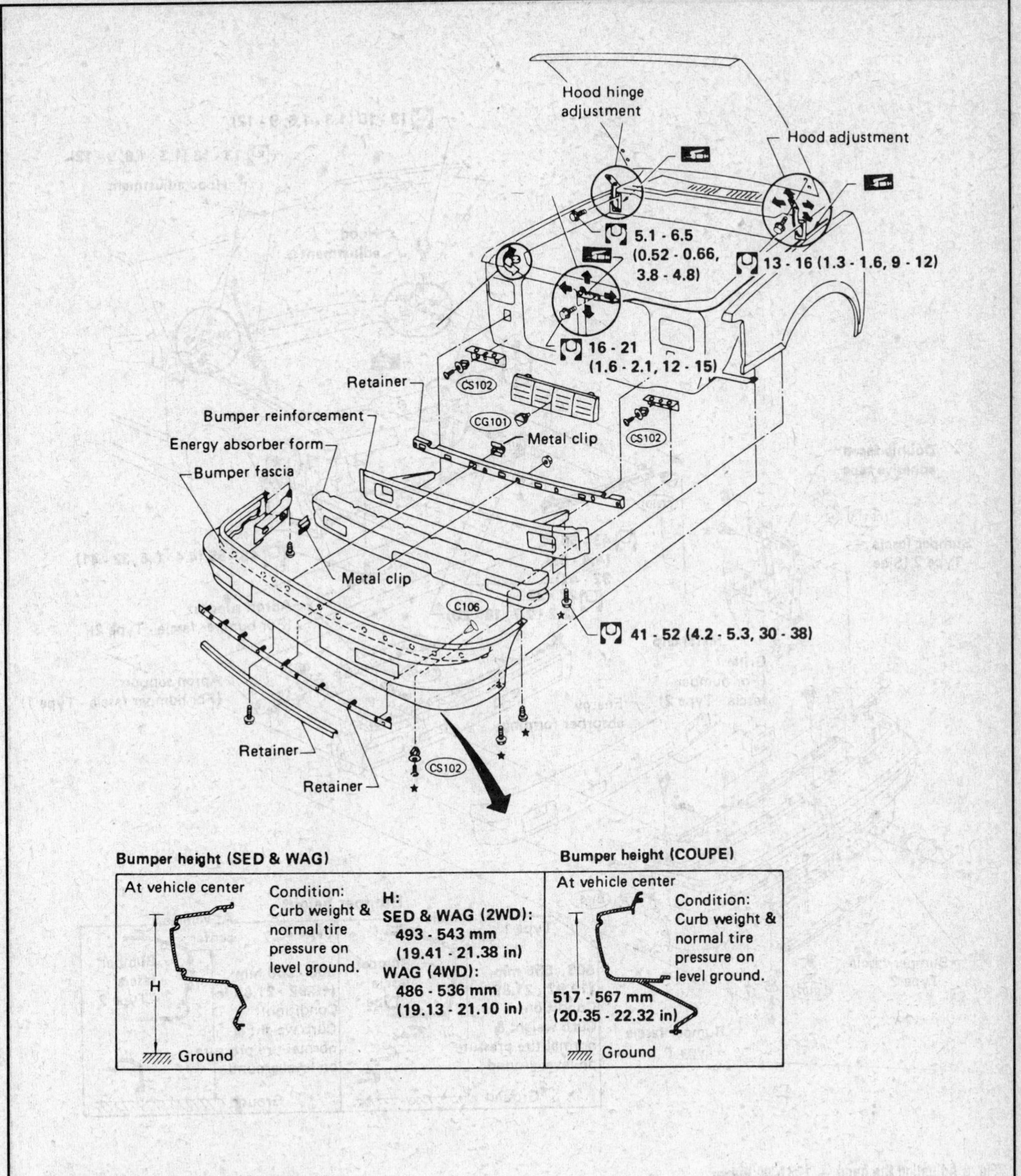

Hood hinge adjustment
Hood adjustment
5.1 - 6.5
(0.52 - 0.66,
3.8 - 4.8)
13 - 16 (1.3 - 1.6, 9 - 12)
16 - 21
(1.6 - 2.1, 12 - 15)
Retainer
CS102
Bumper reinforcement
CG101
Metal clip
CS102
Energy absorber form
Bumper fascia
Metal clip
C106
41 - 52 (4.2 - 5.3, 30 - 38)
Retainer
Retainer
CS102
Bumper height (SED & WAG)
At vehicle center
Condition:
Curb weight &
normal tire
pressure on
level ground.
H:
SED & WAG (2WD):
493 - 543 mm
(19.41 - 21.38 in)
WAG (4WD):
486 - 536 mm
(19.13 - 21.10 in)
H
Ground
Bumper height (COUPE)
At vehicle center
Condition:
Curb weight &
normal tire
pressure on
level ground.
517 - 567 mm
(20.35 - 22.32 in)
Ground

Fig. 8 Adjusting the hood — 1987–90 Sentra

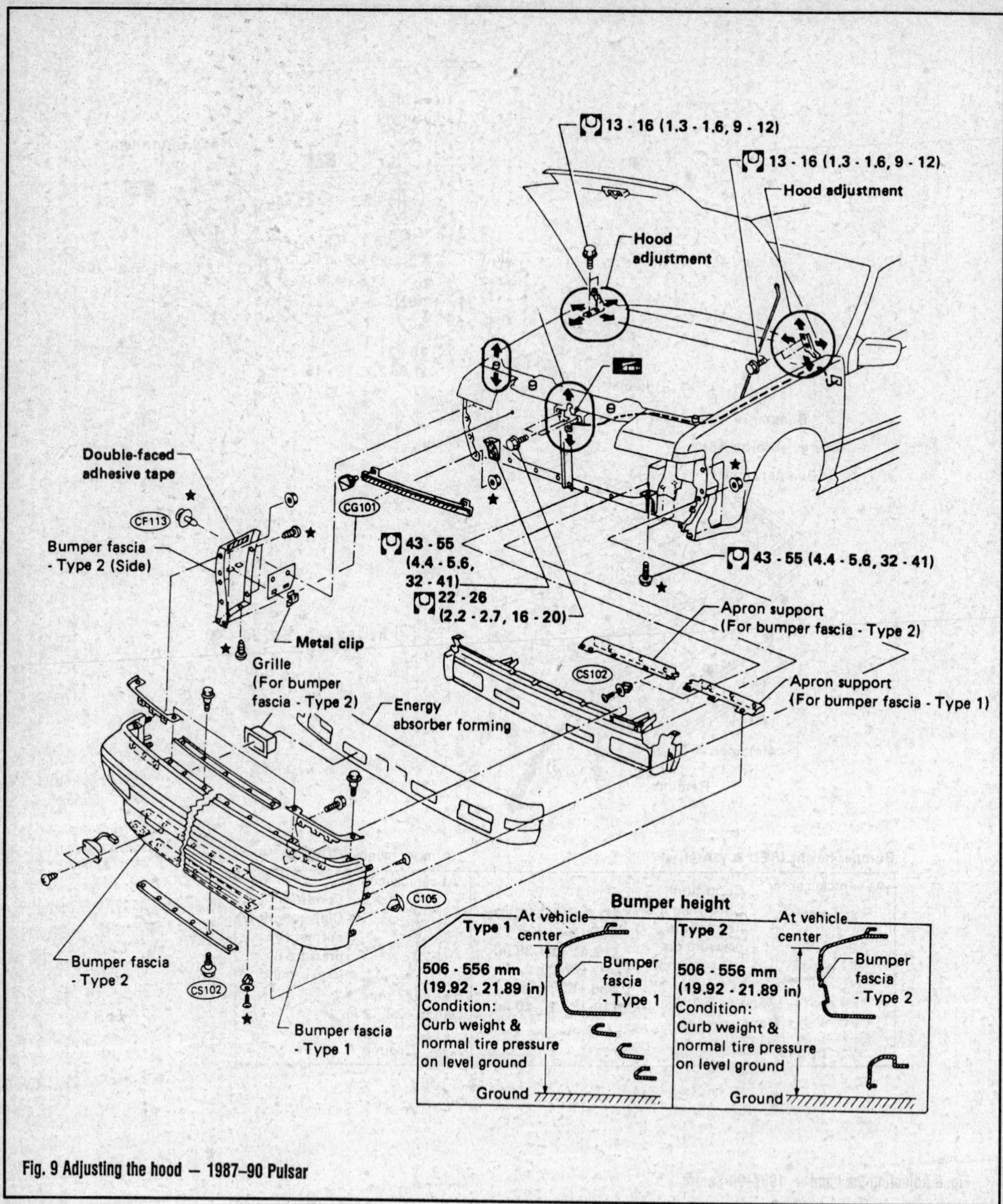
13 - 16 (1.3 - 1.6, 9 - 12)
13 - 16 (1.3 - 1.6, 9 - 12)
Hood adjustment
Hood adjustment
Double-faced adhesive tape
CF113
Bumper fascia - Type 2 (Side)
CG101
43 - 55 (4.4 - 5.6, 32 - 41)
22 - 26 (2.2 - 2.7, 16 - 20)
43 - 55 (4.4 - 5.6, 32 - 41)
Apron support (For bumper fascia - Type 2)
Metal clip
Grille (For bumper fascia - Type 2)
Energy absorber forming
CS102
Apron support (For bumper fascia - Type 1)
C105
Bumper fascia - Type 2
CS102
Bumper fascia - Type 1
Bumper height
Type 1
At vehicle center
506 - 556 mm (19.92 - 21.89 in)
Condition: Curb weight & normal tire pressure on level ground
Bumper fascia - Type 1
Ground
Type 2
At vehicle center
506 - 556 mm (19.92 - 21.89 in)
Condition: Curb weight & normal tire pressure on level ground
Bumper fascia - Type 2
Ground

Fig. 9 Adjusting the hood — 1987–90 Pulsar

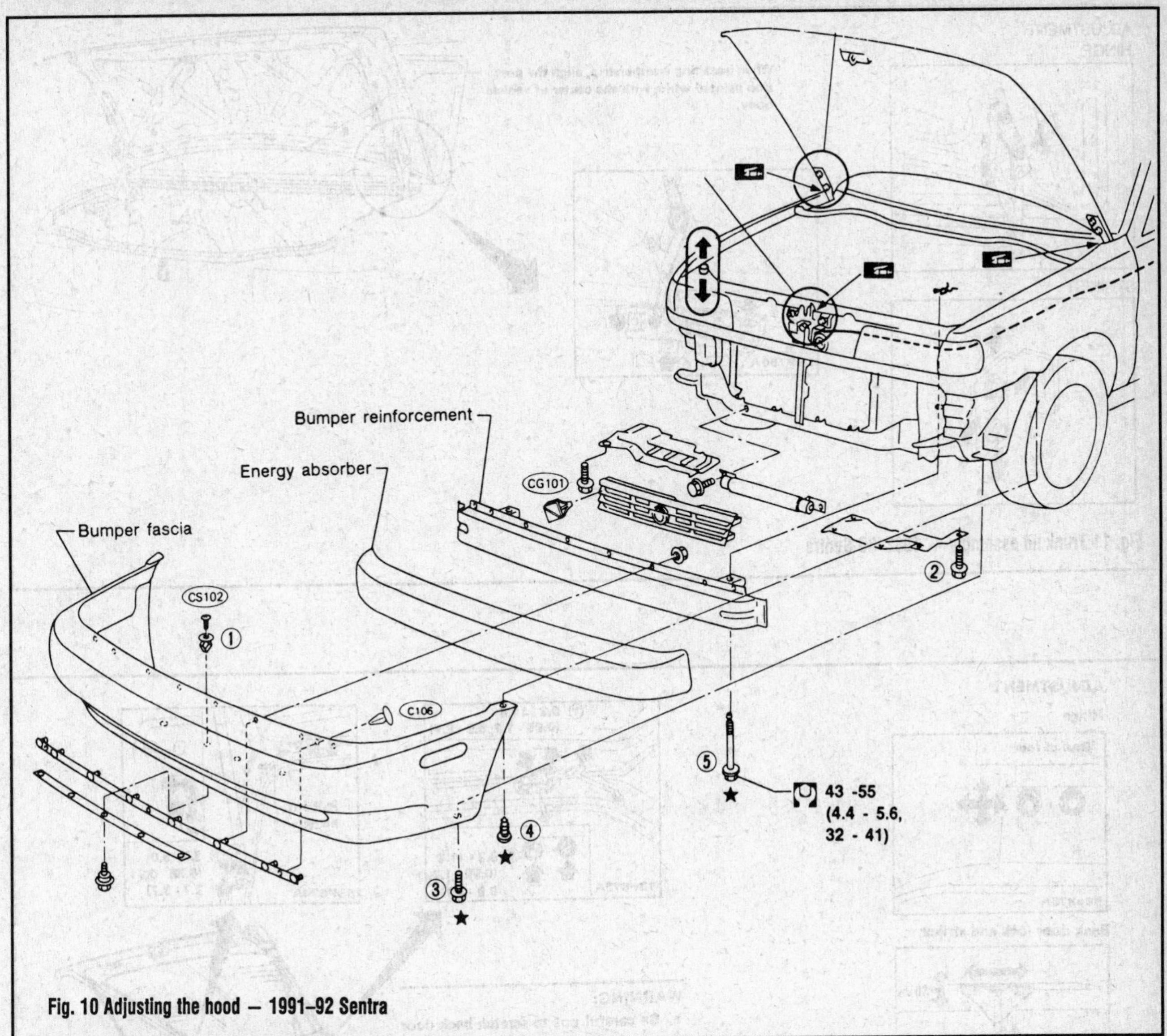
Bumper reinforcement
Energy absorber
Bumper fascia
CG101
CS102
C106
43 -55
(4.4 - 5.6,
32 - 41)

Fig. 10 Adjusting the hood — 1991–92 Sentra

Trunk Lid

SEE FIGS. 11–18

REMOVAL & INSTALLATION

1. Open the trunk lid and position a cloth or cushion to protect the painted areas.
2. Mark the trunk lid hinge locations or trunk lid for proper reinstallation.
3. Support the trunk lid by hand and remove the bolts attaching the trunk lid to the hinge. Then remove the trunk lid.

To install:

4. Install the trunk lid or hatch with the help of an assistant. Line up the hinges to the bolt holes and install the bolts. Position the trunk lid and hinges to the original position and tighten.
5. Slowly close the hood, making sure it does not contact the painted surfaces. Adjust as necessary and torque the bolts to 12–14 ft. lbs. (16–19 Nm).

ALIGNMENT

1. Loosen the trunk lid hinge attaching bolts until they are just loose enough to move the trunk lid.
2. Move the trunk lid for and aft to obtain a flush fit between the trunk lid and the rear fender.
3. To obtain a snug fit between the trunk lid and weatherstrip, loosen the trunk lid lock striker attaching bolts enough to move the lid, working the striker up and down and from side to side as required.
4. After the adjustment is made tighten the striker bolts securely.

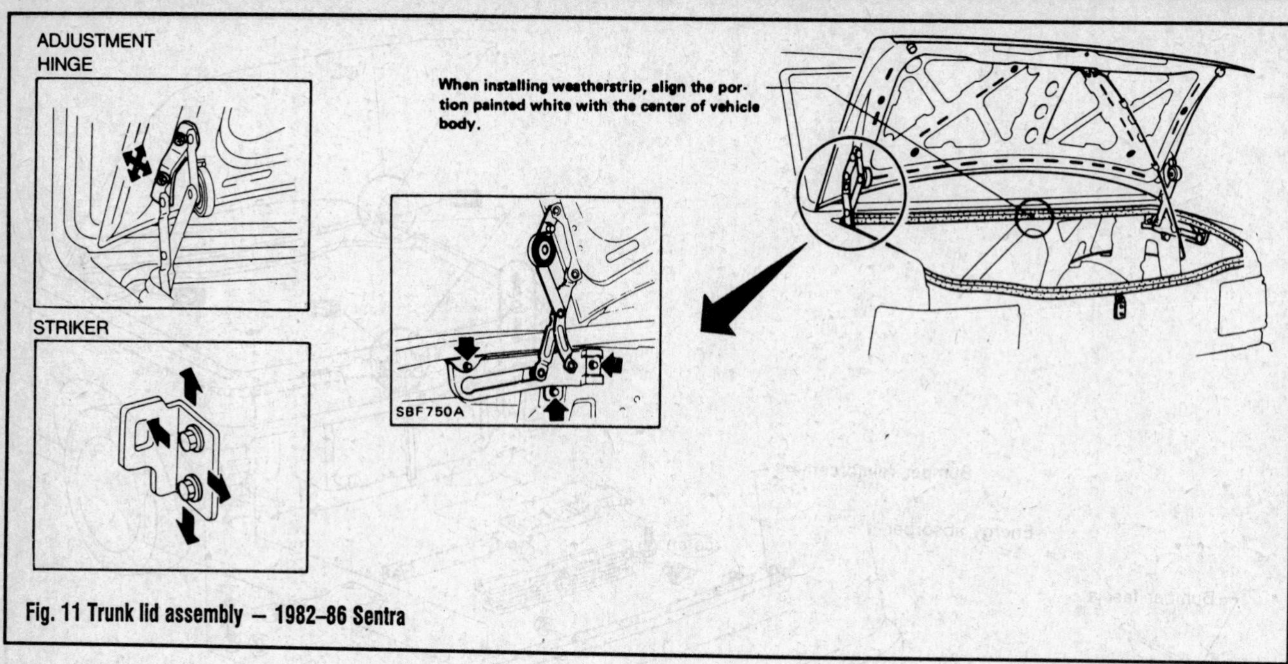
ADJUSTMENT
HINGE
STRIKER
When installing weatherstrip, align the portion painted white with the center of vehicle body.
SBF750A

Fig. 11 Trunk lid assembly — 1982–86 Sentra

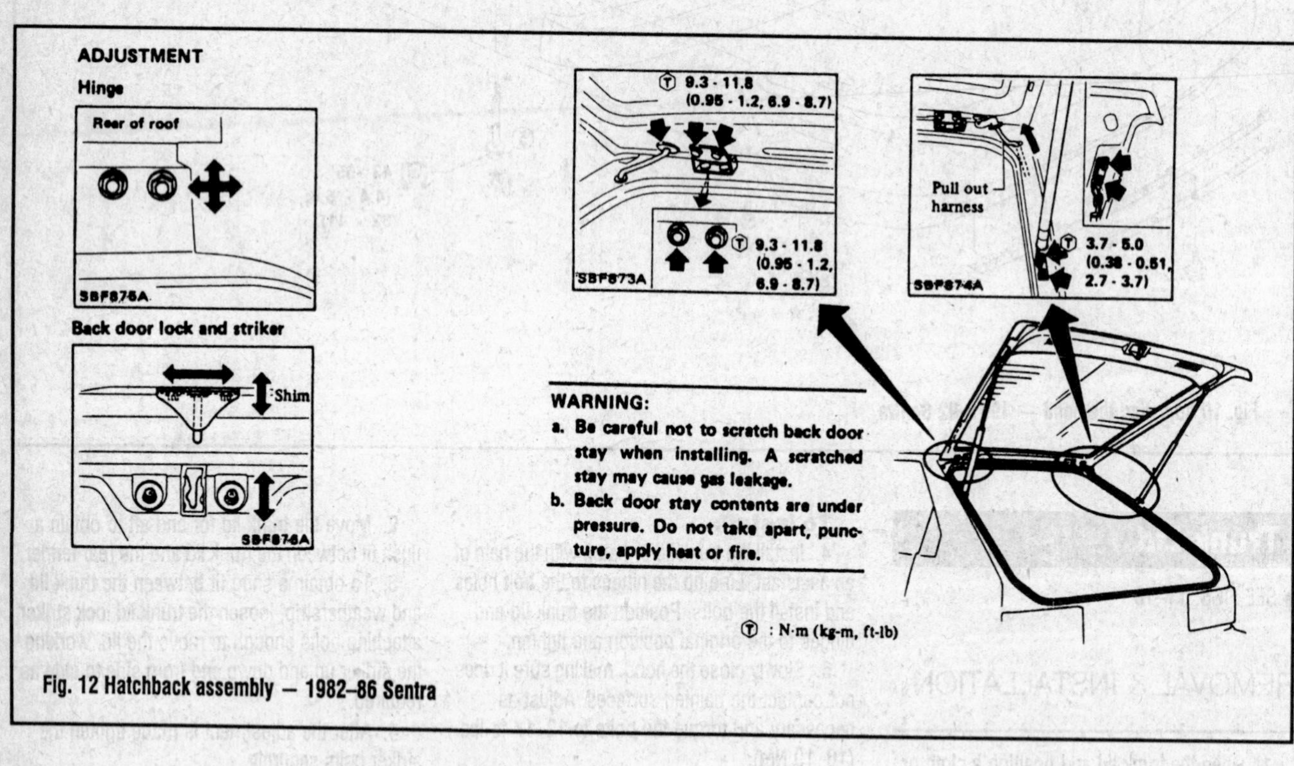
ADJUSTMENT
Hinge
Rear of roof
SBF875A
Back door lock and striker
Shim
SBF876A
9.3 - 11.8 (0.95 - 1.2, 6.9 - 8.7)
9.3 - 11.8 (0.95 - 1.2, 6.9 - 8.7)
SBF873A
Pull out harness
3.7 - 5.0 (0.38 - 0.51, 2.7 - 3.7)
SBF874A
WARNING:
a. Be careful not to scratch back door stay when installing. A scratched stay may cause gas leakage.
b. Back door stay contents are under pressure. Do not take apart, puncture, apply heat or fire.
: N·m (kg-m, ft-lb)

Fig. 12 Hatchback assembly — 1982–86 Sentra

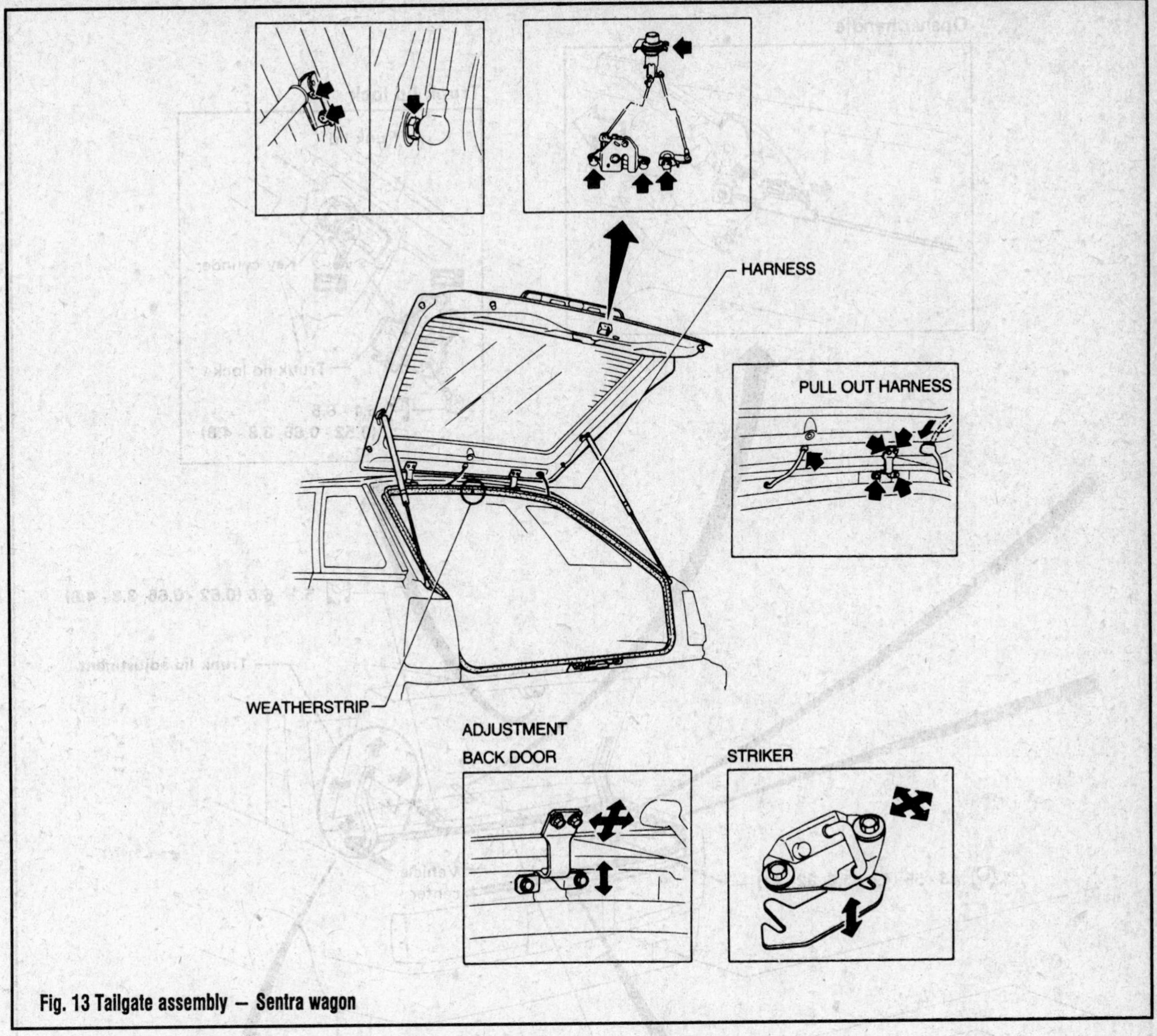
HARNESS
PULL OUT HARNESS
WEATHERSTRIP
ADJUSTMENT
BACK DOOR
STRIKER

Fig. 13 Tailgate assembly — Sentra wagon

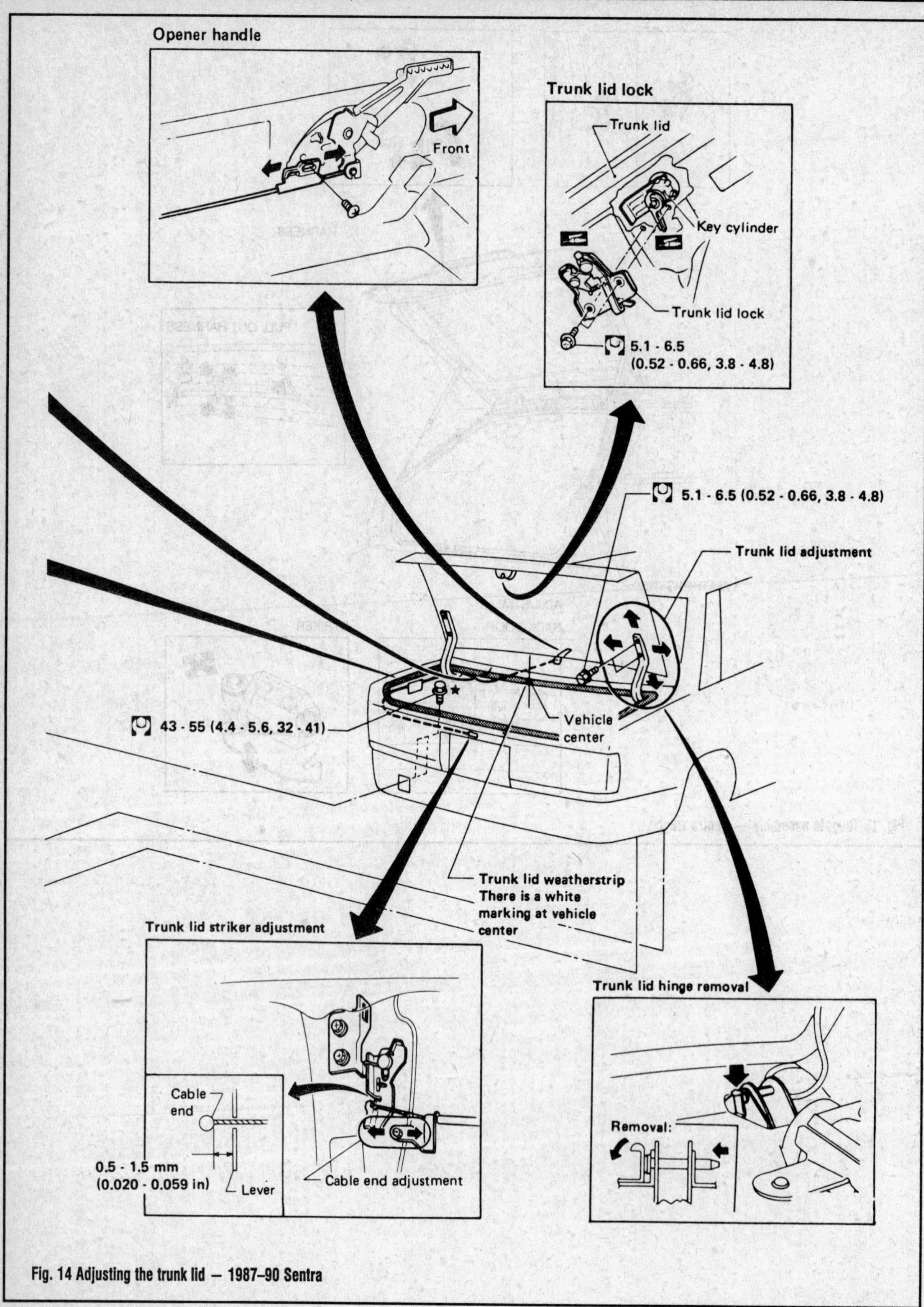

Opener handle
Front
Trunk lid lock
Trunk lid
Key cylinder
Trunk lid lock
5.1 - 6.5
(0.52 - 0.66, 3.8 - 4.8)
5.1 - 6.5 (0.52 - 0.66, 3.8 - 4.8)
Trunk lid adjustment
43 - 55 (4.4 - 5.6, 32 - 41)
Vehicle
center
Trunk lid weatherstrip
There is a white
marking at vehicle
center
Trunk lid striker adjustment
Cable
end
0.5 - 1.5 mm
(0.020 - 0.059 in)
Lever
Cable end adjustment
Trunk lid hinge removal
Removal:

Fig. 14 Adjusting the trunk lid — 1987–90 Sentra

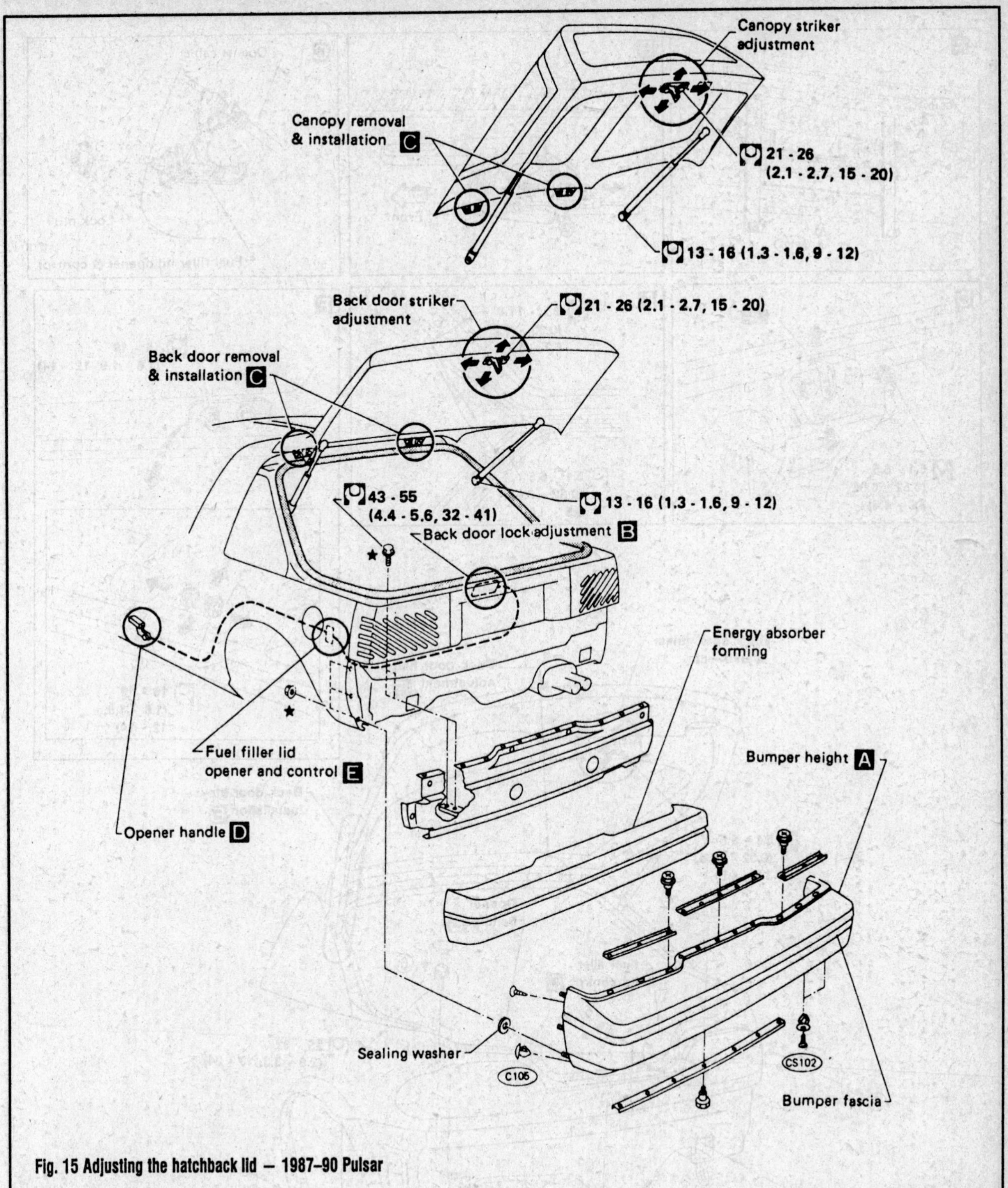

Canopy striker adjustment
Canopy removal & installation C
21 - 26 (2.1 - 2.7, 15 - 20)
13 - 16 (1.3 - 1.6, 9 - 12)
Back door striker adjustment
21 - 26 (2.1 - 2.7, 15 - 20)
Back door removal & installation C
43 - 55 (4.4 - 5.6, 32 - 41)
13 - 16 (1.3 - 1.6, 9 - 12)
Back door lock adjustment B
Energy absorber forming
Fuel filler lid opener and control E
Bumper height A
Opener handle D
Sealing washer
C105
CS102
Bumper fascia

Fig. 15 Adjusting the hatchback lid — 1987–90 Pulsar

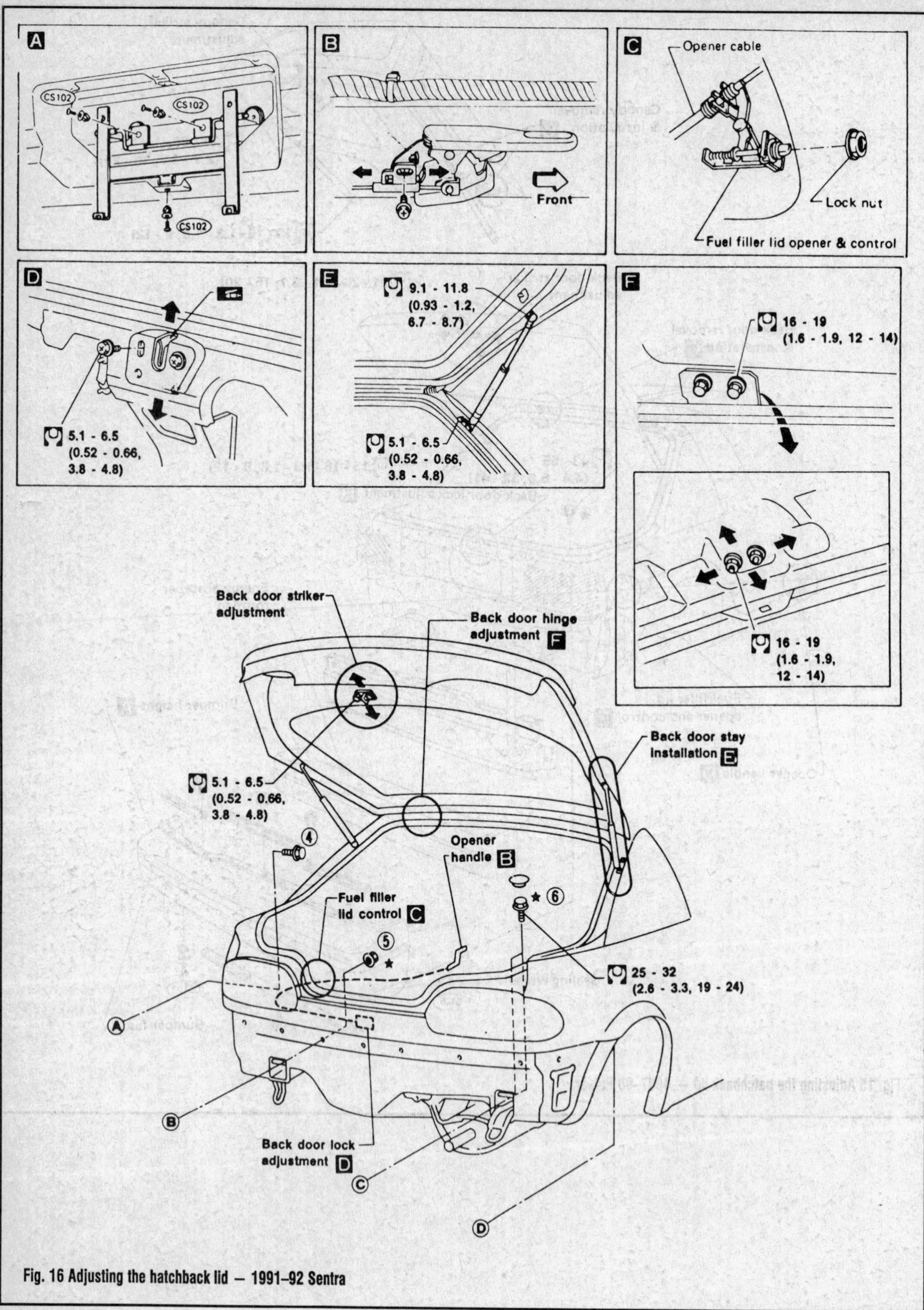

A
CS102
CS102
CS102
B
Front
C
Opener cable
Lock nut
Fuel filler lid opener & control
D
5.1 - 6.5
(0.52 - 0.66,
3.8 - 4.8)
E
9.1 - 11.8
(0.93 - 1.2,
6.7 - 8.7)
5.1 - 6.5
(0.52 - 0.66,
3.8 - 4.8)
F
16 - 19
(1.6 - 1.9, 12 - 14)
16 - 19
(1.6 - 1.9,
12 - 14)
Back door striker adjustment
Back door hinge adjustment F
Back door stay installation E
5.1 - 6.5
(0.52 - 0.66,
3.8 - 4.8)
Opener handle B
Fuel filler lid control C
25 - 32
(2.6 - 3.3, 19 - 24)
Back door lock adjustment D

Fig. 16 Adjusting the hatchback lid – 1991–92 Sentra

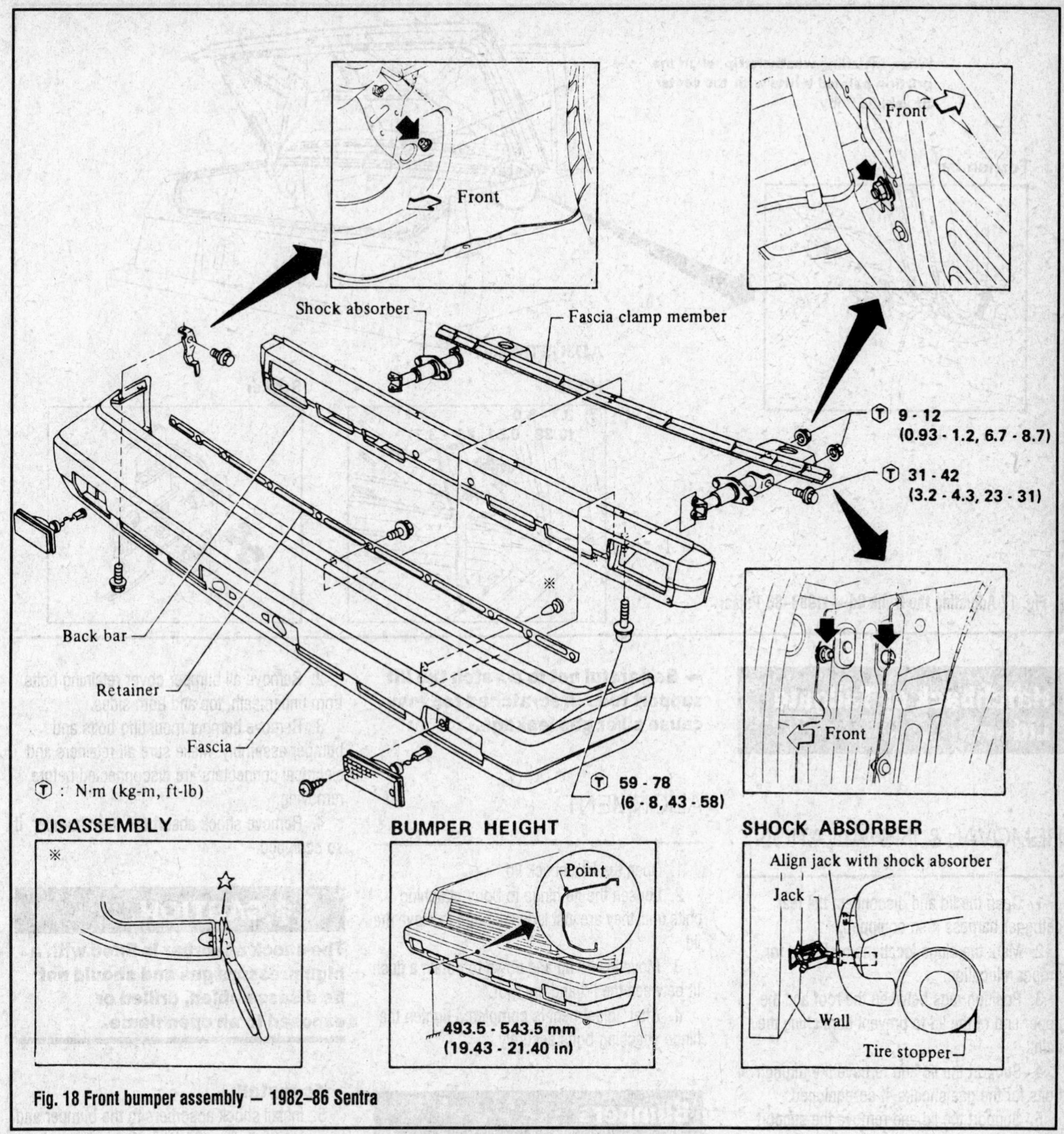

Front
Front
Shock absorber
Fascia clamp member
9 - 12
(0.93 - 1.2, 6.7 - 8.7)
31 - 42
(3.2 - 4.3, 23 - 31)
Back bar
Retainer
Fascia
59 - 78
(6 - 8, 43 - 58)
Front
: N·m (kg-m, ft-lb)
DISASSEMBLY
BUMPER HEIGHT
SHOCK ABSORBER
Point
493.5 - 543.5 mm
(19.43 - 21.40 in)
Align jack with shock absorber
Jack
Wall
Tire stopper

Fig. 18 Front bumper assembly — 1982–86 Sentra

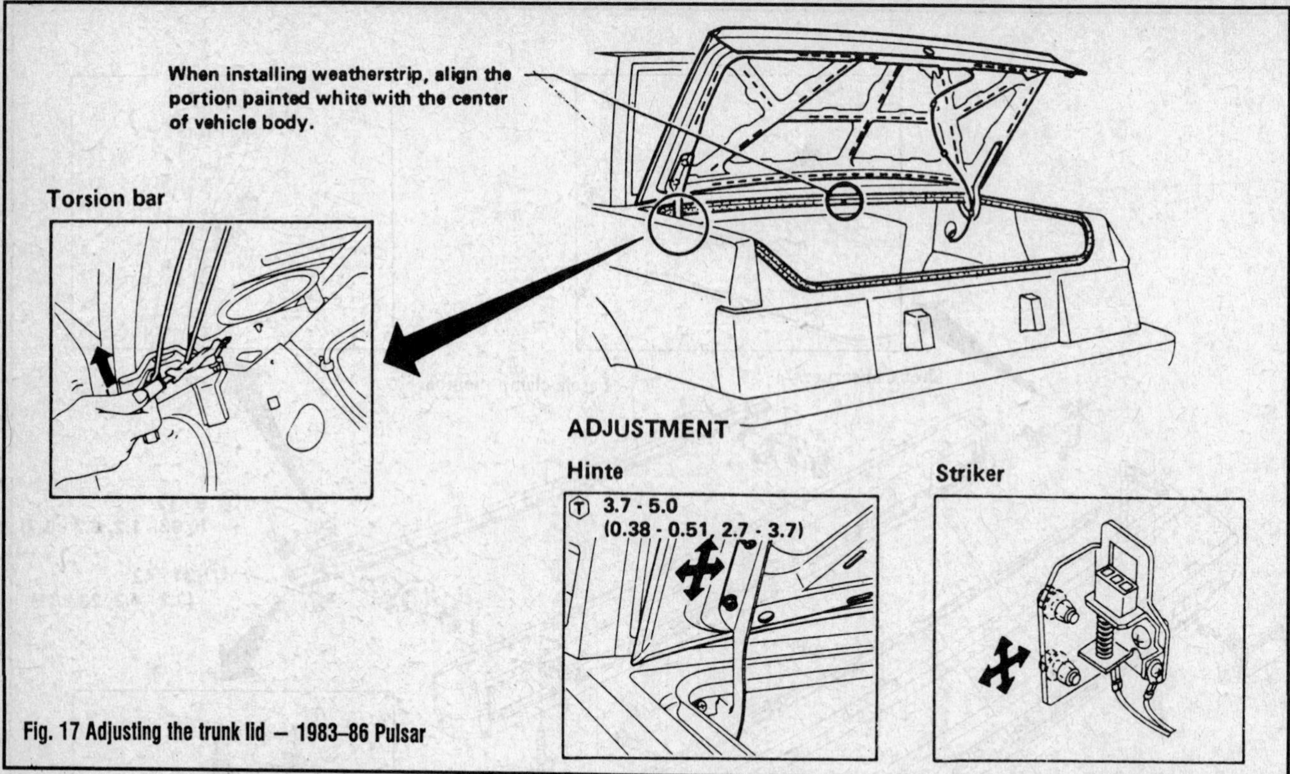
When installing weatherstrip, align the portion painted white with the center of vehicle body.
Torsion bar
ADJUSTMENT
Hinte
3.7 - 5.0
(0.38 - 0.51, 2.7 - 3.7)
Striker

Fig. 17 Adjusting the trunk lid — 1983–86 Pulsar

Hatchback or Tailgate Lid

REMOVAL & INSTALLATION

1. Open the lid and disconnect the rear defogger harness if so equipped.
2. Mark the hinge locations on the lid for proper relocation.
3. Position rags between the roof and the upper end of the lid to prevent scratching the paint.
4. Support the lid and remove the through bolts for the gas shocks, if so-equipped.
5. Support the lid and remove the support bolts for the hinge retaining bolts and remove the lid.

To install:

6. Install the lid or hatch with the help of an assistant. Line up the hinges to the bolt holes and install the bolts. Position the lid and hinges to the original position and tighten.
7. Slowly close the hood, making sure it does not contact the painted surfaces. Adjust as necessary and torque the bolts to 12–14 ft. lbs. (16–19 Nm).

➡ Be careful not to scratch the lift support rods. A scratched rod may cause oil or gas leakage.

ALIGNMENT

1. Open the hatchback lid.
2. Loosen the lid hinge to body attaching bolts until they are just loose enough to move the lid.
3. Move the lid up and down to obtain a flush fit between the lid and the roof.
4. After adjustment is completed tighten the hinge attaching bolts securely.

Bumpers

➧ SEE FIGS. 19–24

REMOVAL & INSTALLATION

Front and Rear

1. Disconnect all electrical connectors at bumper assembly if so equipped.
2. Remove all bumper cover retaining bolts from underneath, top and both sides.
3. Remove bumper mounting bolts and bumper assembly. Make sure all retainers and electrical connectors are disconnected before removing.
4. Remove shock absorbers from bumper, if so equipped.

✻✻ CAUTION

The shock absorber is filled with a high pressure gas and should not be disassembled, drilled or exposed to an open flame.

To install:

5. Install shock absorbers to the bumper and torque to 25 ft. lbs. (34 Nm), if so equipped.
6. Install bumper mounting bolts. Make sure all retainers and electrical connectors are aligned correctly.
7. Install all bumper cover retaining bolts. Torque the small nuts to 10 ft. lbs. (14 Nm). Install the side screws.
8. Connect all electrical connectors at bumper assembly, if so equipped.

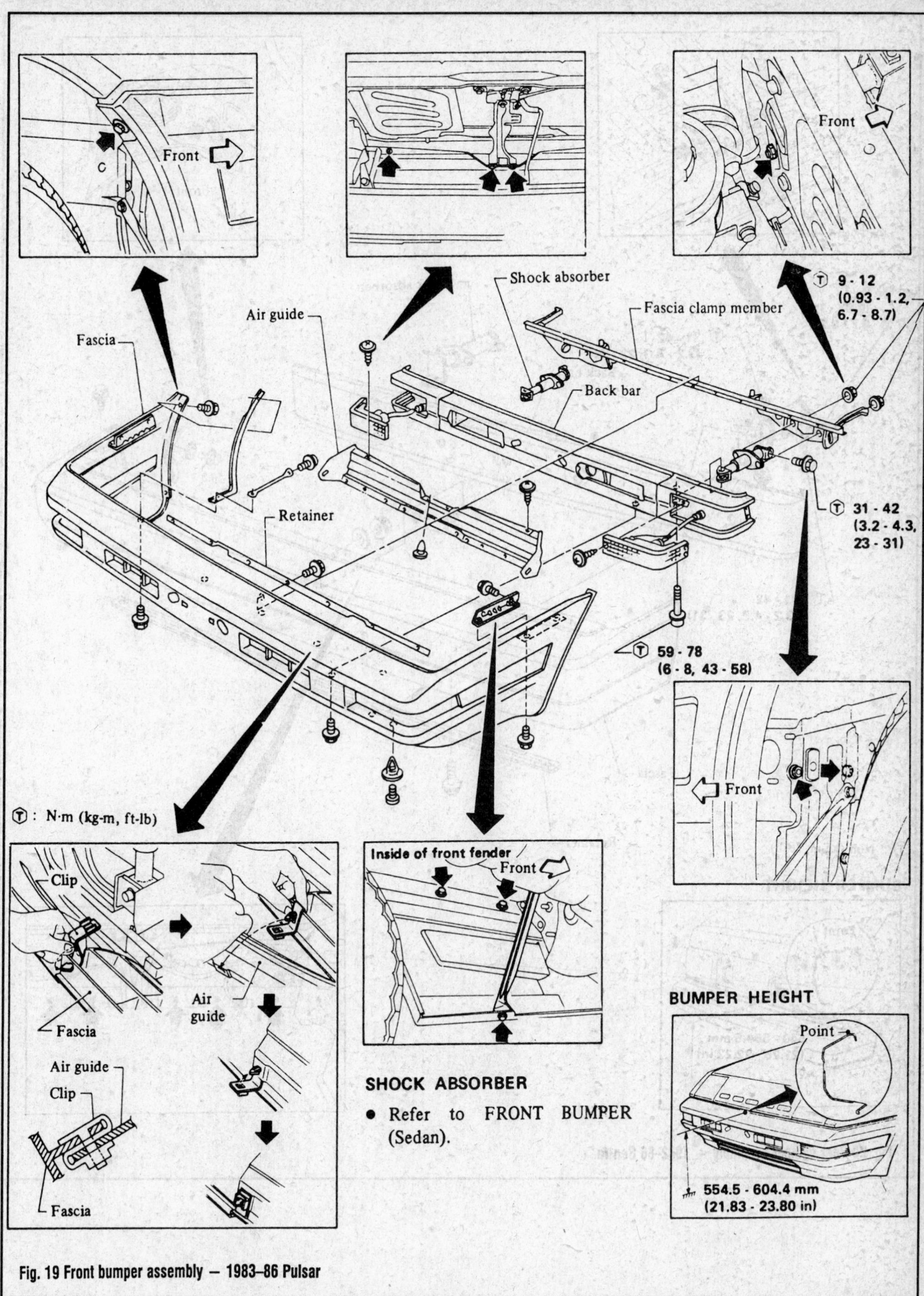

Front
Front
Shock absorber
Fascia clamp member
Air guide
Fascia
Back bar
9 - 12
(0.93 - 1.2,
6.7 - 8.7)
Retainer
31 - 42
(3.2 - 4.3,
23 - 31)
59 - 78
(6 - 8, 43 - 58)
Front
: N·m (kg-m, ft-lb)
Clip
Air
guide
Fascia
Air guide
Clip
Fascia
Inside of front fender
Front
SHOCK ABSORBER
• Refer to FRONT BUMPER (Sedan).
BUMPER HEIGHT
Point
554.5 - 604.4 mm
(21.83 - 23.80 in)

Fig. 19 Front bumper assembly — 1983–86 Pulsar

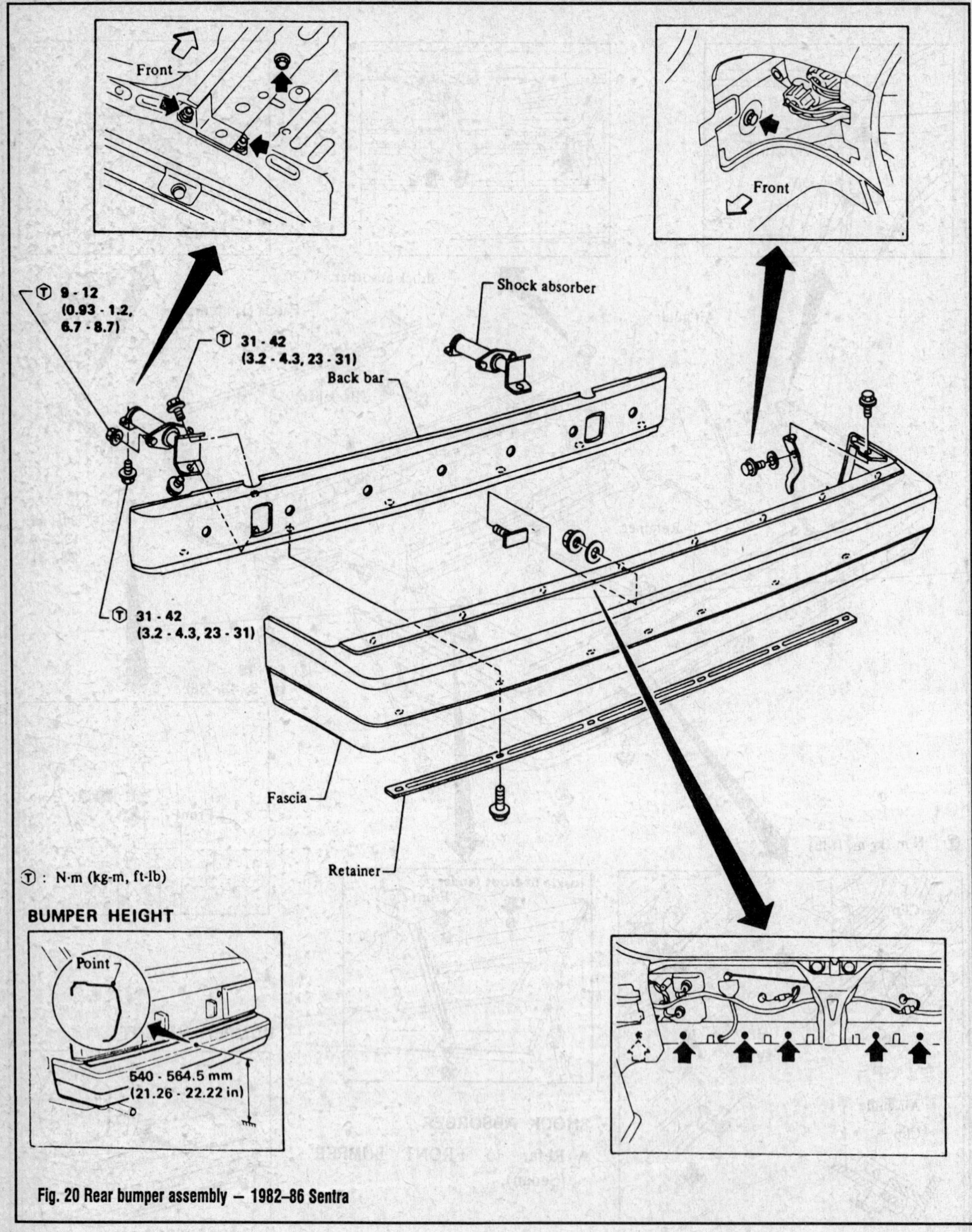
Front
Front
9 - 12
(0.93 - 1.2,
6.7 - 8.7)
31 - 42
(3.2 - 4.3, 23 - 31)
Shock absorber
Back bar
31 - 42
(3.2 - 4.3, 23 - 31)
Fascia
Retainer
: N·m (kg-m, ft-lb)
BUMPER HEIGHT
Point
540 - 564.5 mm
(21.26 - 22.22 in)

Fig. 20 Rear bumper assembly — 1982–86 Sentra

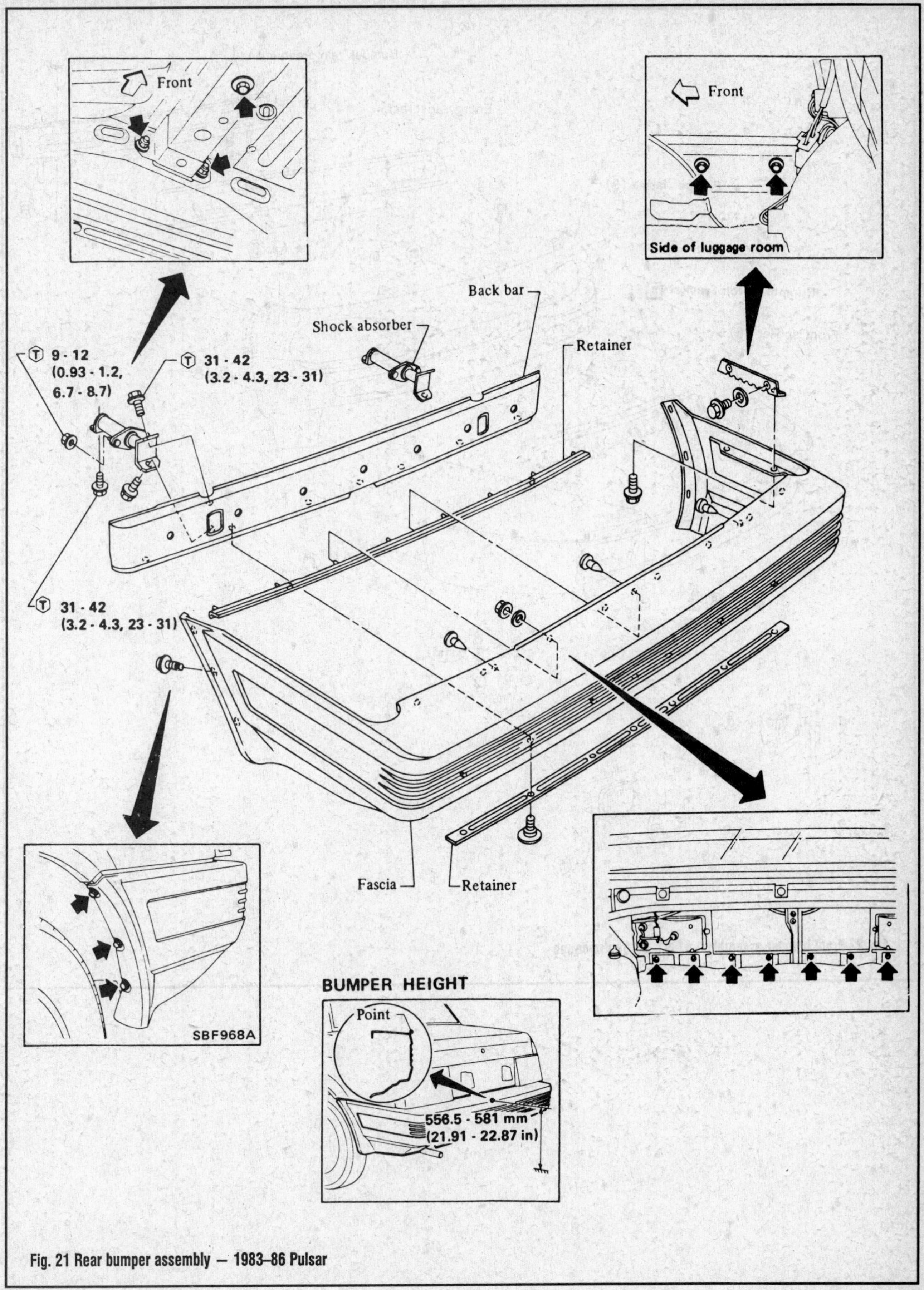
Front
Front
Side of luggage room
Back bar
Shock absorber
Retainer
9 - 12
(0.93 - 1.2,
6.7 - 8.7)
31 - 42
(3.2 - 4.3, 23 - 31)
31 - 42
(3.2 - 4.3, 23 - 31)
Fascia
Retainer
BUMPER HEIGHT
Point
556.5 - 581 mm
(21.91 - 22.87 in)
SBF968A

Fig. 21 Rear bumper assembly — 1983–86 Pulsar

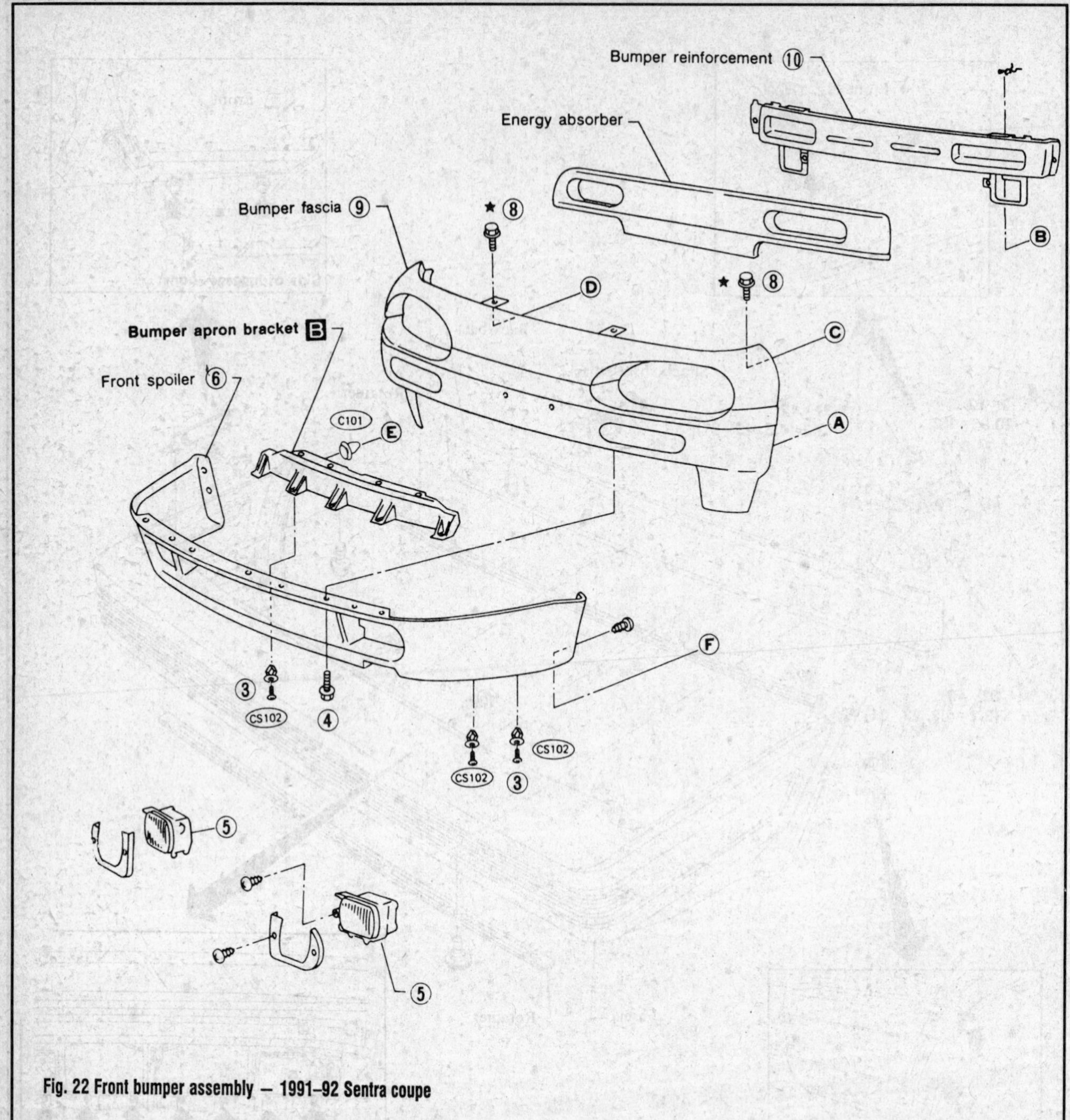
Bumper reinforcement ⑩
Energy absorber
Bumper fascia ⑨
★ ⑧
Ⓑ
Ⓓ
★ ⑧
Bumper apron bracket B
Ⓒ
Front spoiler ⑥
C101
Ⓔ
Ⓐ
Ⓕ
③
CS102
④
CS102
CS102
③
⑤
⑤

Fig. 22 Front bumper assembly — 1991–92 Sentra coupe

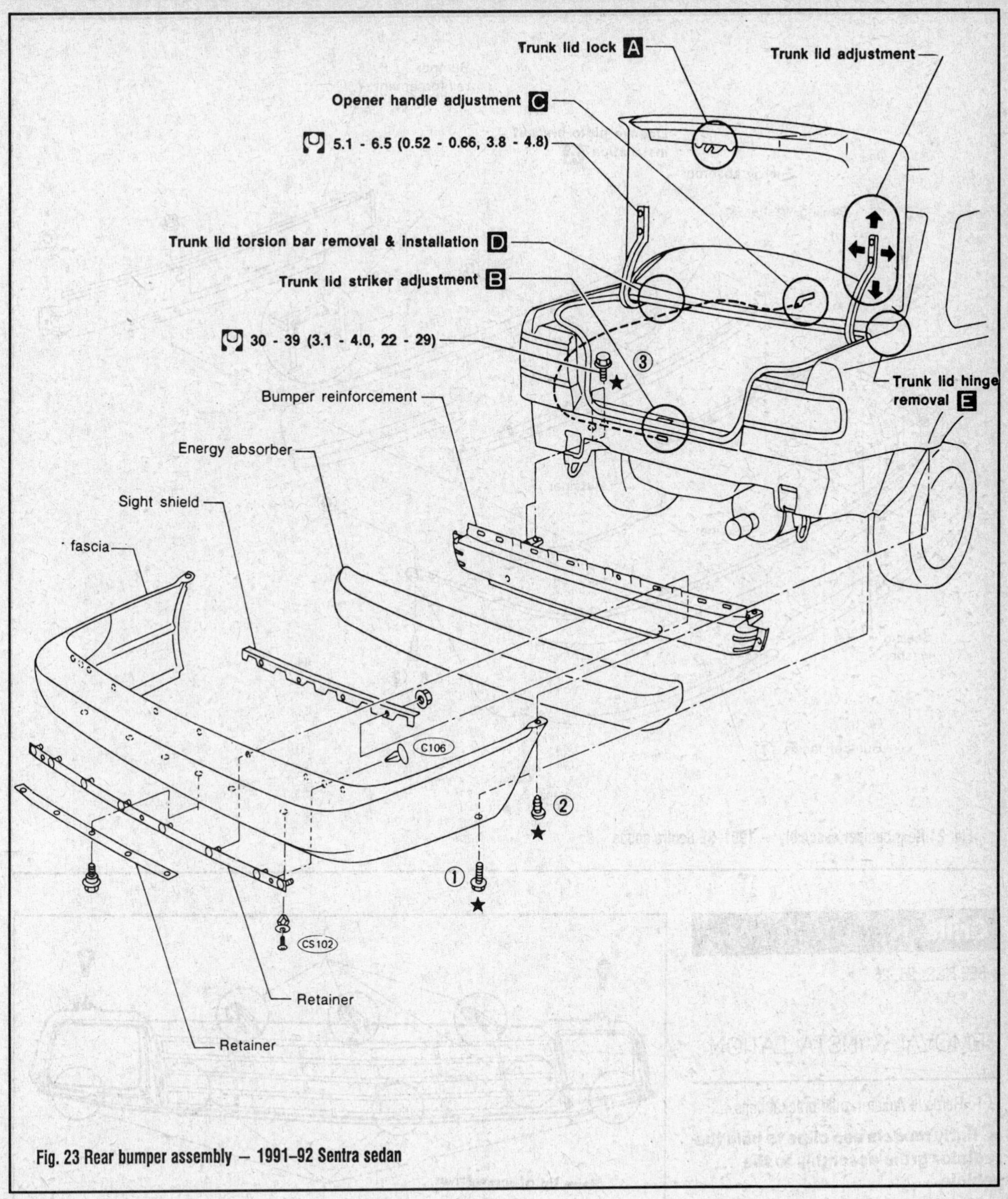

Trunk lid lock A
Trunk lid adjustment
Opener handle adjustment C
5.1 - 6.5 (0.52 - 0.66, 3.8 - 4.8)
Trunk lid torsion bar removal & installation D
Trunk lid striker adjustment B
30 - 39 (3.1 - 4.0, 22 - 29)
③
Trunk lid hinge removal E
Bumper reinforcement
Energy absorber
Sight shield
fascia
C106
②
①
CS102
Retainer
Retainer

Fig. 23 Rear bumper assembly — 1991–92 Sentra sedan

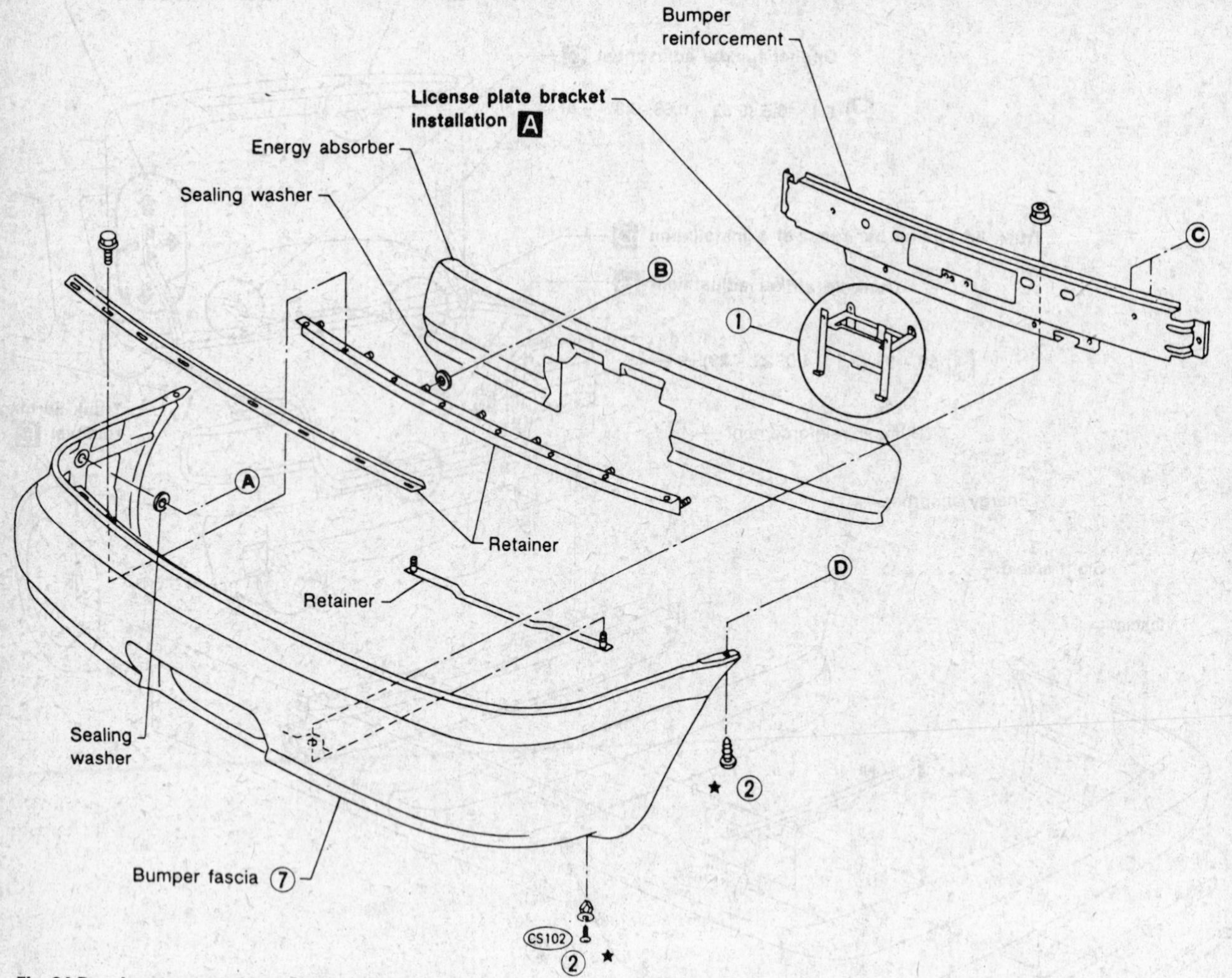

Fig. 24 Rear bumper assembly — 1991–92 Sentra coupe

Grille

➧ SEE FIGS. 25, 26

REMOVAL & INSTALLATION

1. Remove radiator grille bracket bolts.

➡ **Early models use clips to hold the radiator grille assembly to the vehicle.**

2. Remove radiator grille from the vehicle.
3. To install reverse the removal procedures.

➡ **The radiator grille assembly is made of plastic, thus never use excessive force to remove it.**

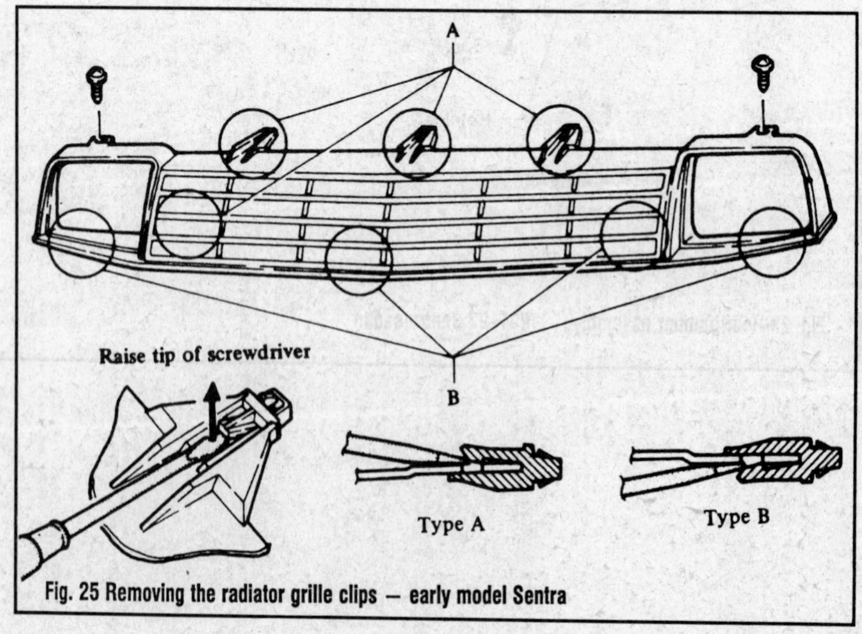
A
B
Raise tip of screwdriver
Type A
Type B

Fig. 25 Removing the radiator grille clips — early model Sentra

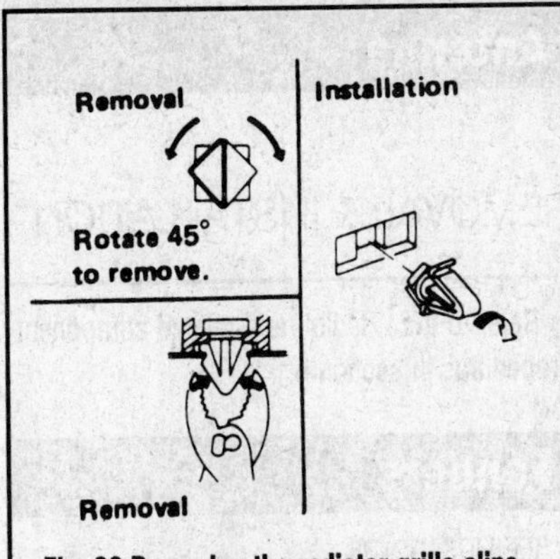
Removal
Installation
Rotate 45°
to remove.
Removal
Fig. 26 Removing the radiator grille clips — early model vehicles

Outside Mirrors

➧ SEE FIGS. 27–31

REMOVAL & INSTALLATION

Manual

1. Remove control knob handle.
2. Remove door corner finisher panel.
3. Remove mirror body attaching screws, and then remove mirror body
4. Installation is in the reverse order of removal.

➡ Apply sealer to the rear surface of door corner finisher panel during installation to prevent water leak.

Power

1. Remove door corner finisher panel.
2. Remove mirror body attaching screws, and then remove mirror body
3. Disconnect the electrical connection.

➡ It may be necessary to remove the door trim panel to gain access to the electrical connection.

4. Installation is in the reverse order of removal.

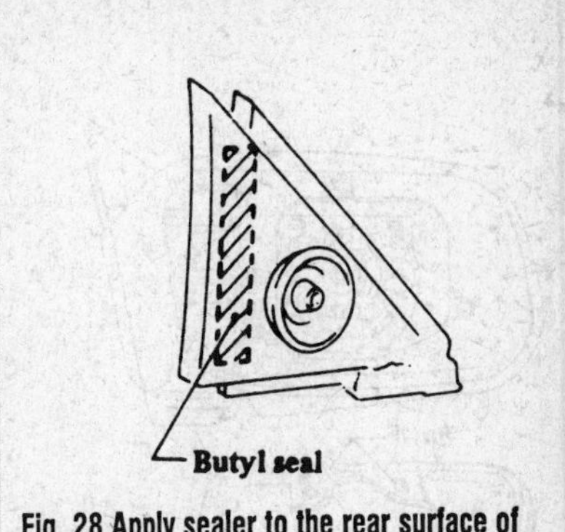
Butyl seal
Fig. 28 Apply sealer to the rear surface of finisher panel

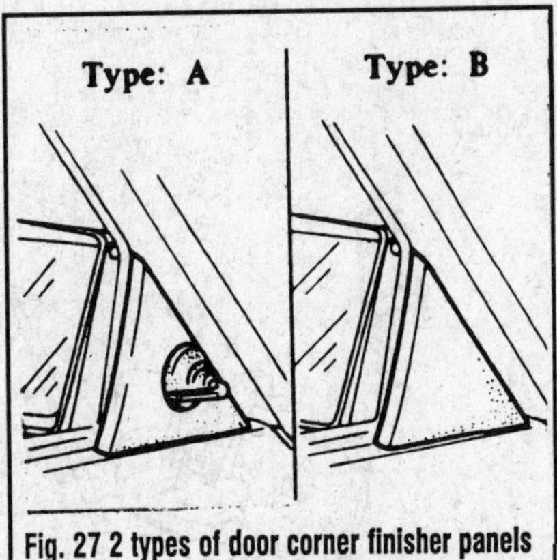
Type: A
Type: B
Fig. 27 2 types of door corner finisher panels

Fig. 29 Removing the mirror mounting screws

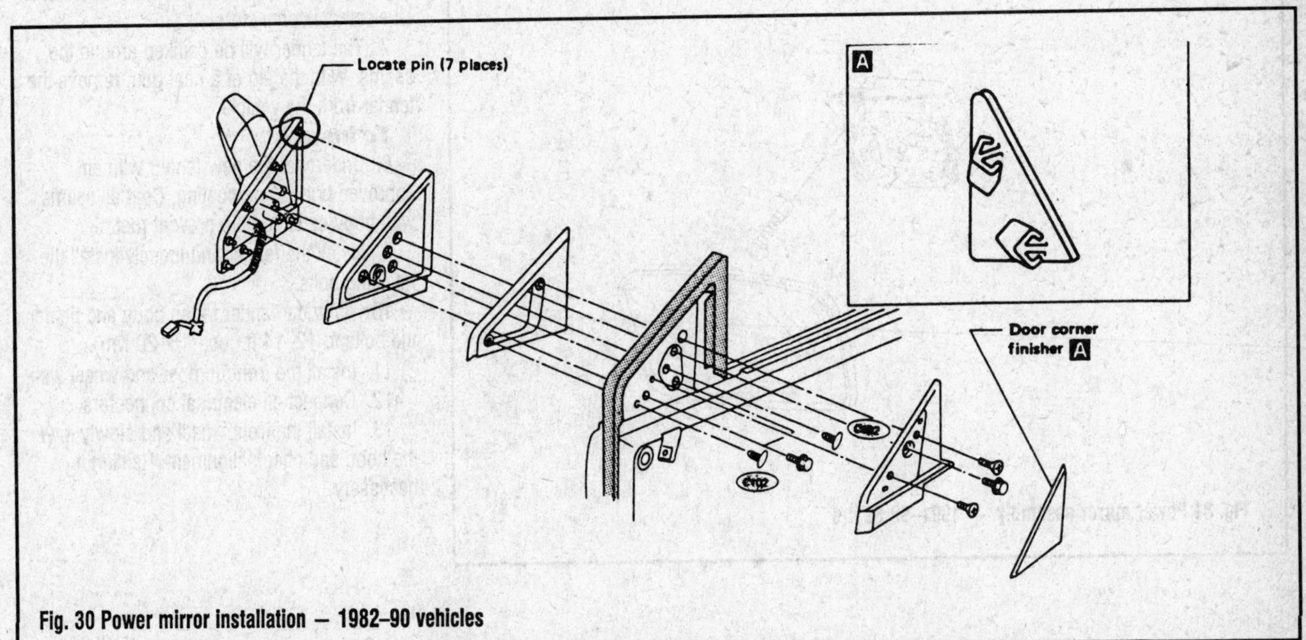
Locate pin (7 places)
A
Door corner
finisher A
Fig. 30 Power mirror installation — 1982–90 vehicles

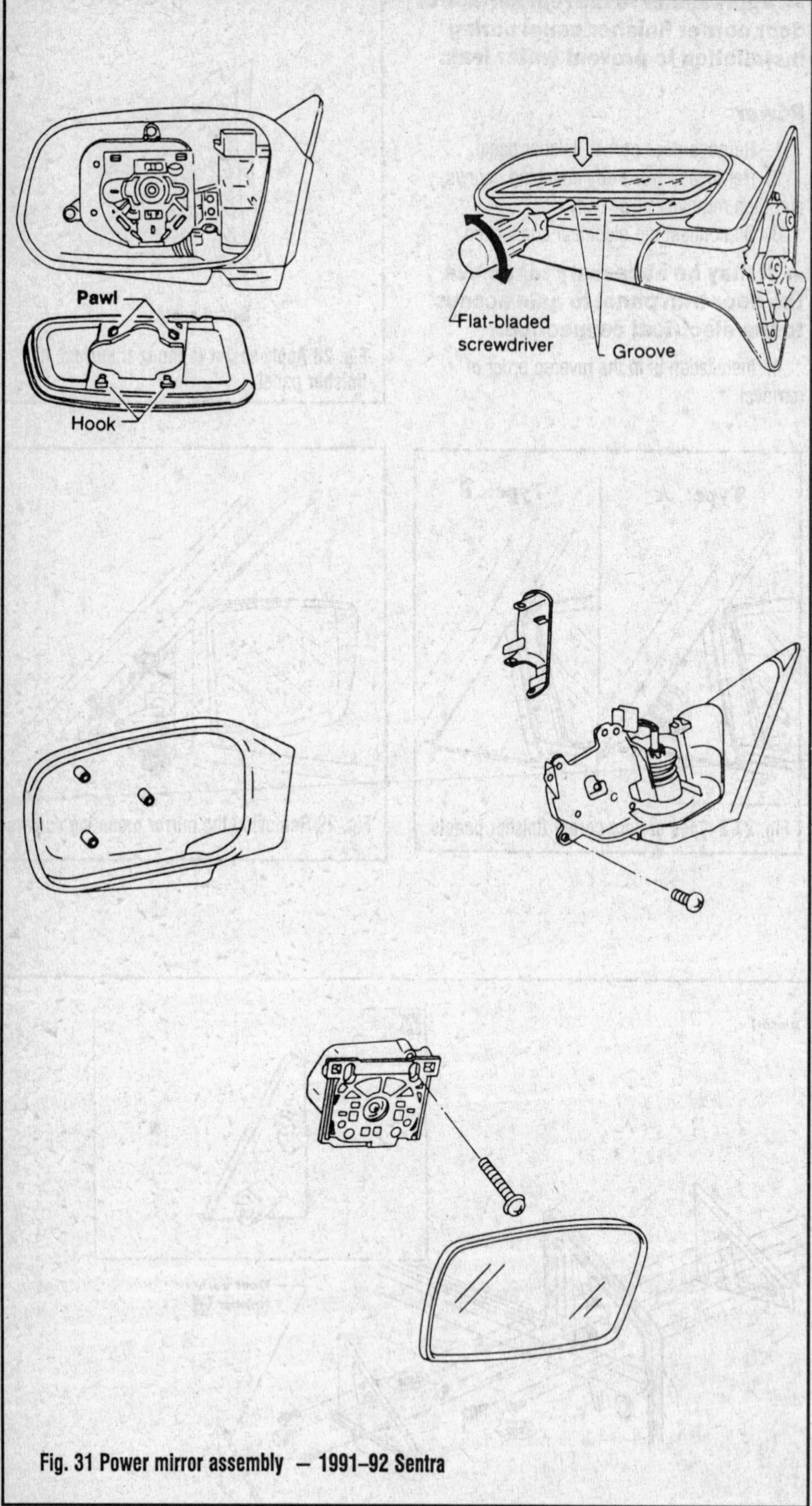
Pawl
Hook
Flat-bladed
screwdriver
Groove

Fig. 31 Power mirror assembly — 1991–92 Sentra

Antenna

REMOVAL & INSTALLATION

Refer to the "Radio" and related component procedures in section 6.

Fenders

➧ SEE FIGS. 32–33

REMOVAL & INSTALLATION

➡ Use masking tape and heavy rags to protect the painted surfaces around the fender area. This procedure will help avoid expensive paint damage during fender removal and installation.

1. Raise the vehicle and support safely. Raise the hood and support.
2. Remove the front wheel.
3. Remove the front bumper as outlined in this section.
4. Remove the inner fender well.
5. Open the door and remove the fender retaining bolt.
6. Remove the fender bolts and disconnect all electrical connectors.
7. The fender will be caulked around the seams. With the aid of a heat gun, remove the fender from the vehicle.

To install:

8. Undercoat the new fender with an approved body undercoating. Coat all seams with body caulk to help prevent rust.
9. Install the fender and loosely install the retaining bolts.
10. Align the fender to the body and tighten the bolts to 12–14 ft. lbs. (16–20 Nm).
11. Install the front bumper and wheel well.
12. Connect all electrical connectors.
13. Install the front wheel and slowly lower the hood and check alignment. Realign if necessary.

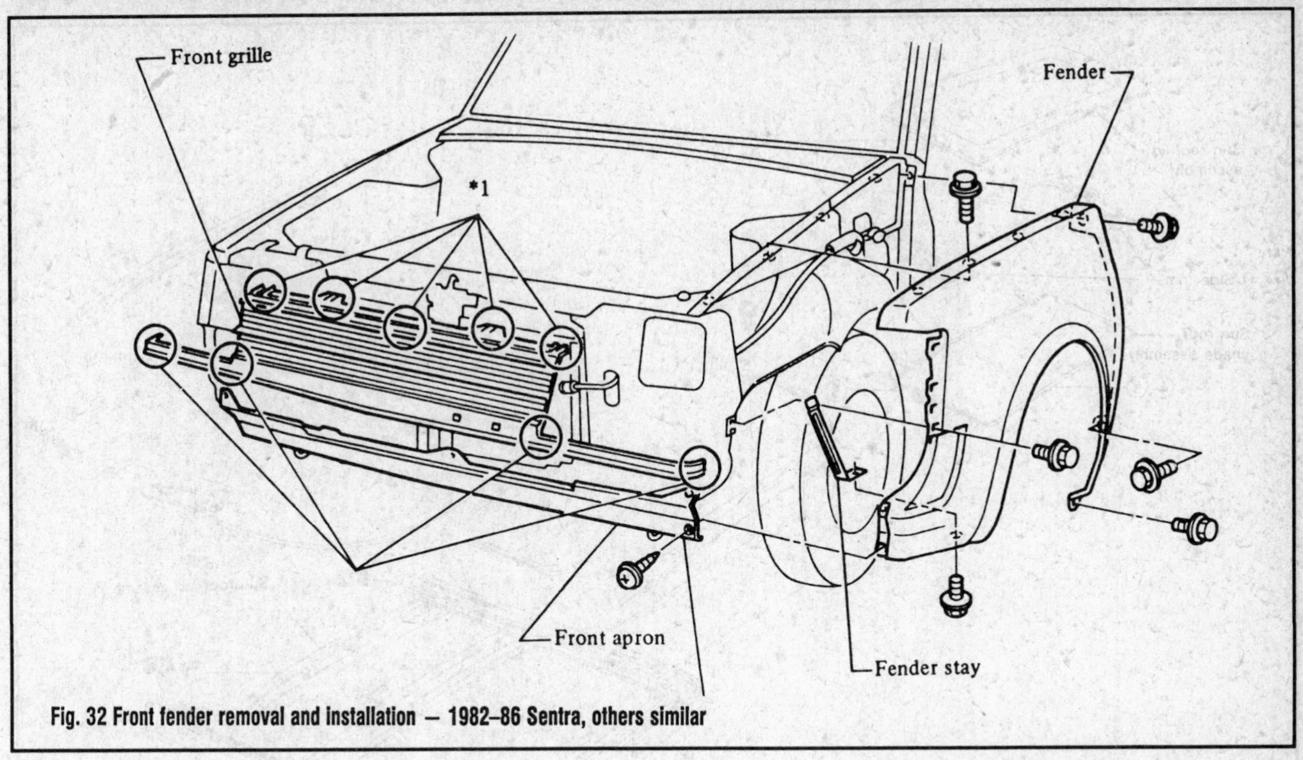
Front grille
*1
Fender
Front apron
Fender stay

Fig. 32 Front fender removal and installation — 1982–86 Sentra, others similar

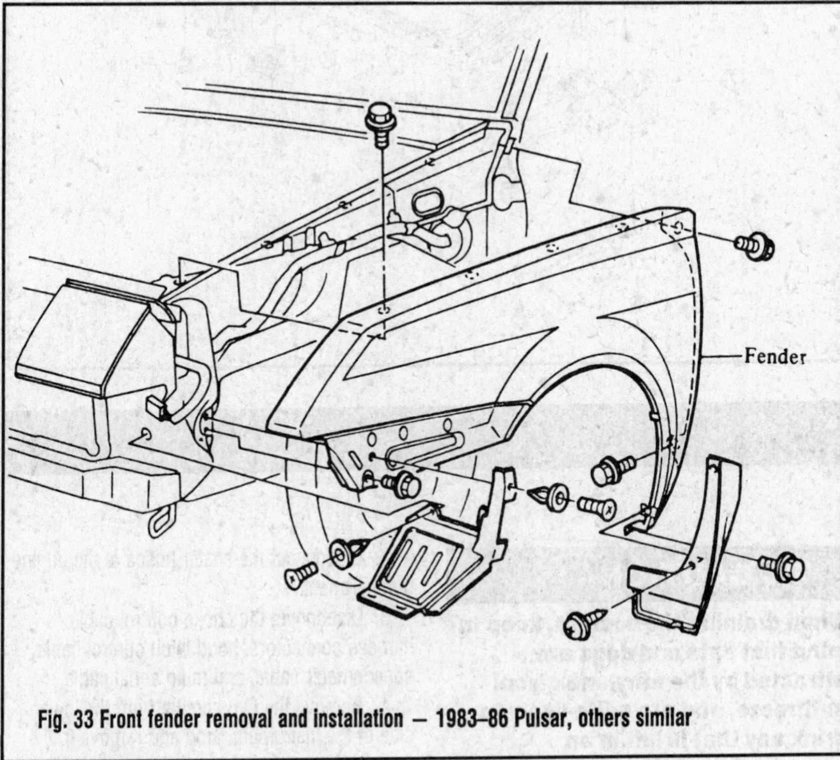
Fender

Fig. 33 Front fender removal and installation — 1983–86 Pulsar, others similar

Power Sunroof

SEE FIG. 34

REMOVAL & INSTALLATION

1. Fully close or tilt up the sunroof. Fully open the shade and remove the clips and side trim.
2. Close the sunroof lid and remove the 6 nuts from the back of the sunroof lid.
3. Lift the sunroof away from the roof.
4. Pull the shade forward and remove the 4 shade locks located beside the shade.
5. Remove the shade and motor assembly.
6. Disconnect the interior light harness and the front and rear drain hoses.
7. Remove the nuts and bolts securing the sunroof rails and remove.

To install:

8. Install the sunroof rails, nuts and bolts.
9. Connect the interior light harness and the front and rear drain hoses.
10. Install the shade and motor assembly.
11. Pull the shade forward and install the 4 shade locks located beside the shade.
12. Install the sunroof into the roof.
13. Close the sunroof lid and install the 6 nuts to the back of the sunroof lid.
14. Install the clips and side trim.

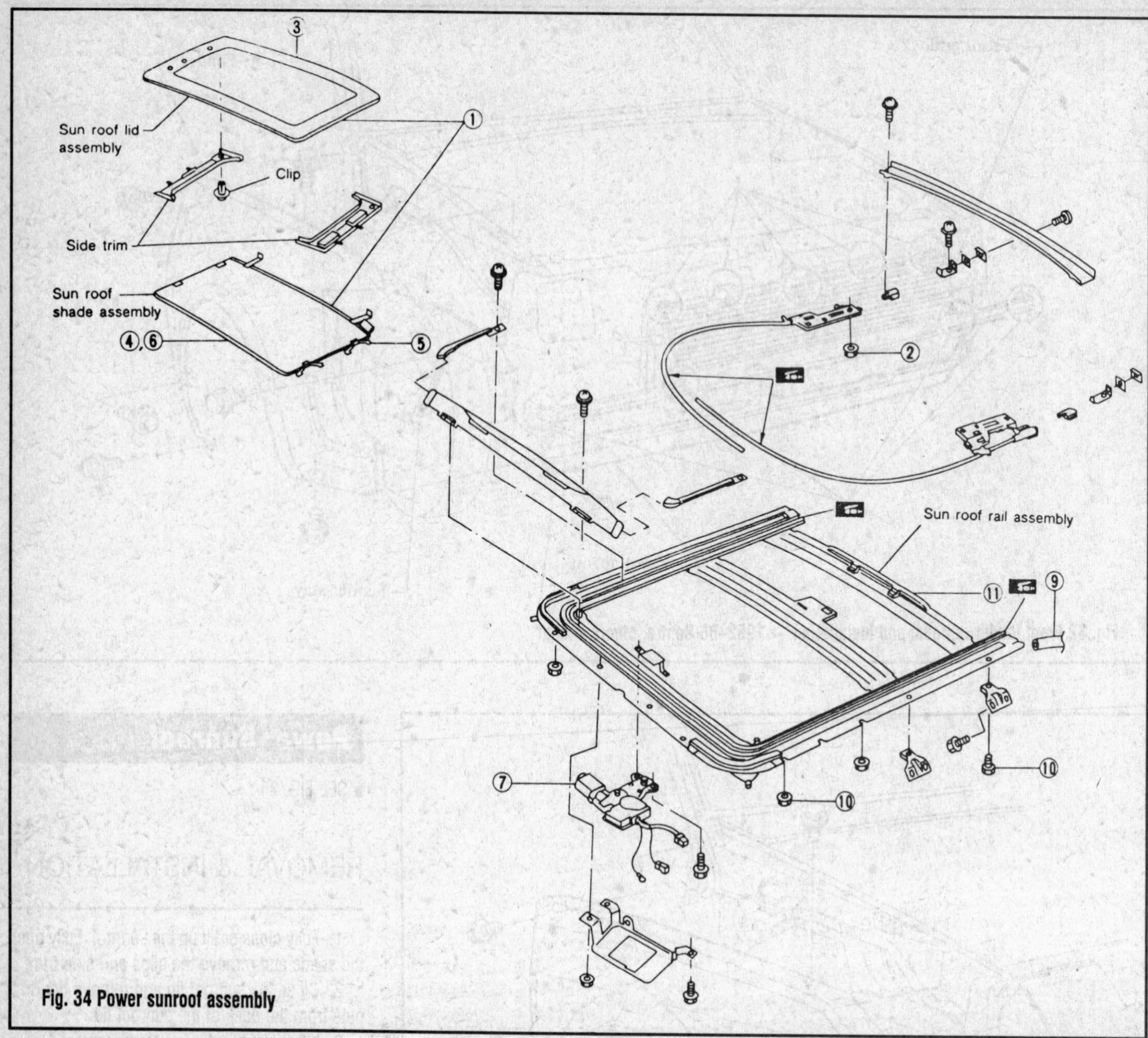
Sun roof lid assembly
Clip
Side trim
Sun roof shade assembly
Sun roof rail assembly

Fig. 34 Power sunroof assembly

INTERIOR

Instrument Panel and Pad

➧ SEE FIGS. 35–40

REMOVAL & INSTALLATION

1982–86 Vehicles

1. Disconnect the negative battery cable. Set "TEMP" lever to maximum "HOT" position and drain engine coolant.

✻✻ CAUTION

When draining the coolant, keep in mind that cats and dogs are attracted by the ethylene glycol antifreeze, and are quite likely to drink any that is left in an uncovered container or in puddles on the ground. This will prove fatal in sufficient quantity. Always drain the coolant into a sealable container. Coolant should be reused unless it is contaminated or several years old.

2. Disconnect the heater hoses at the engine compartment.
3. Disconnect the choke control cable, harness connectors, hood latch control cable, speedometer cable, and radio aerial cable.
4. Remove the two screws from the lower side of the instrument hood and remove it.
5. Remove the two screws from the top of the instrument cluster, pull it out to disconnect the electrical connectors, and remove it.
6. Slide the ash tray out and then unscrew and remove the ash tray slider bracket.

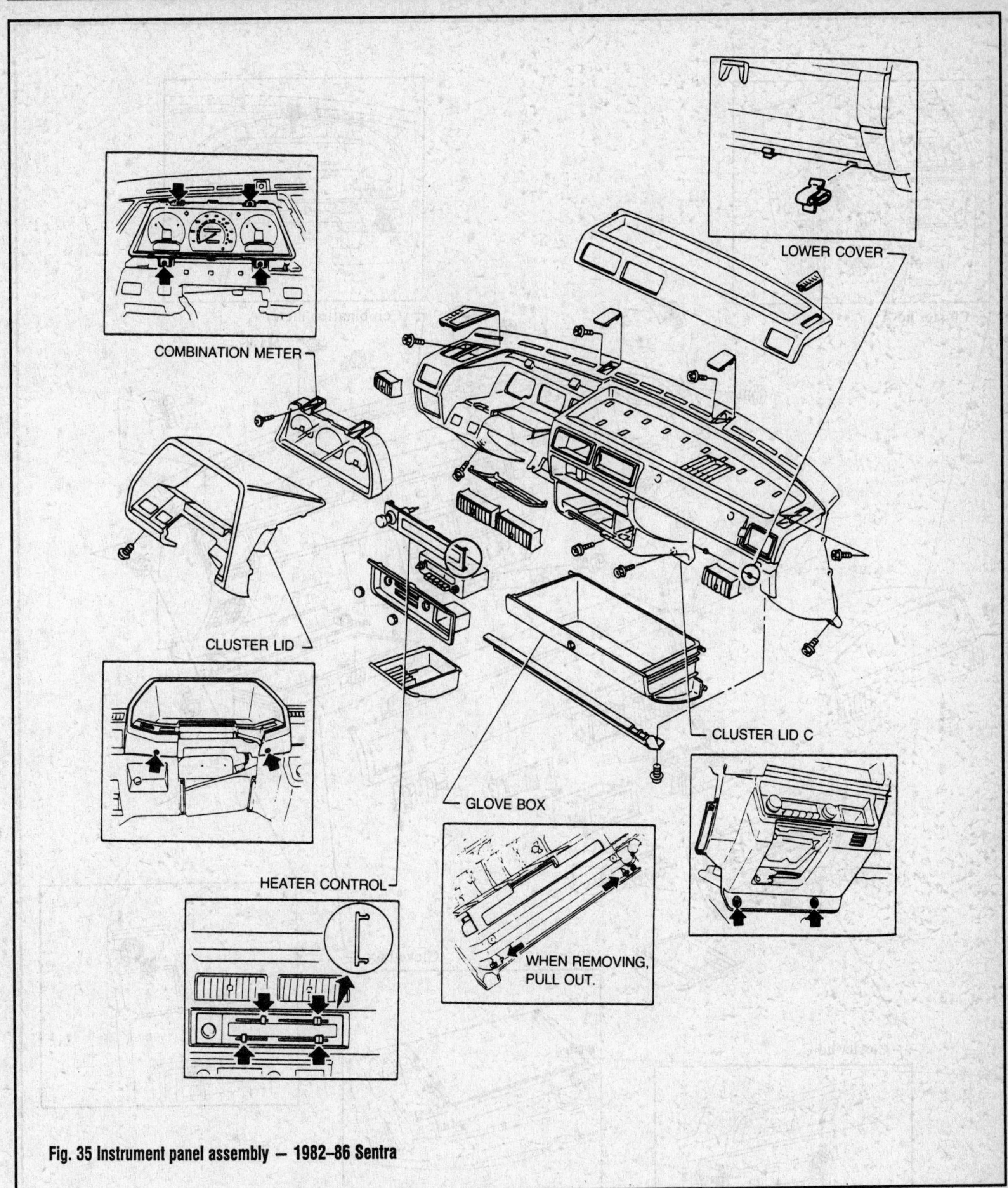
LOWER COVER
COMBINATION METER
CLUSTER LID
CLUSTER LID C
GLOVE BOX
HEATER CONTROL
WHEN REMOVING,
PULL OUT.

Fig. 35 Instrument panel assembly — 1982–86 Sentra

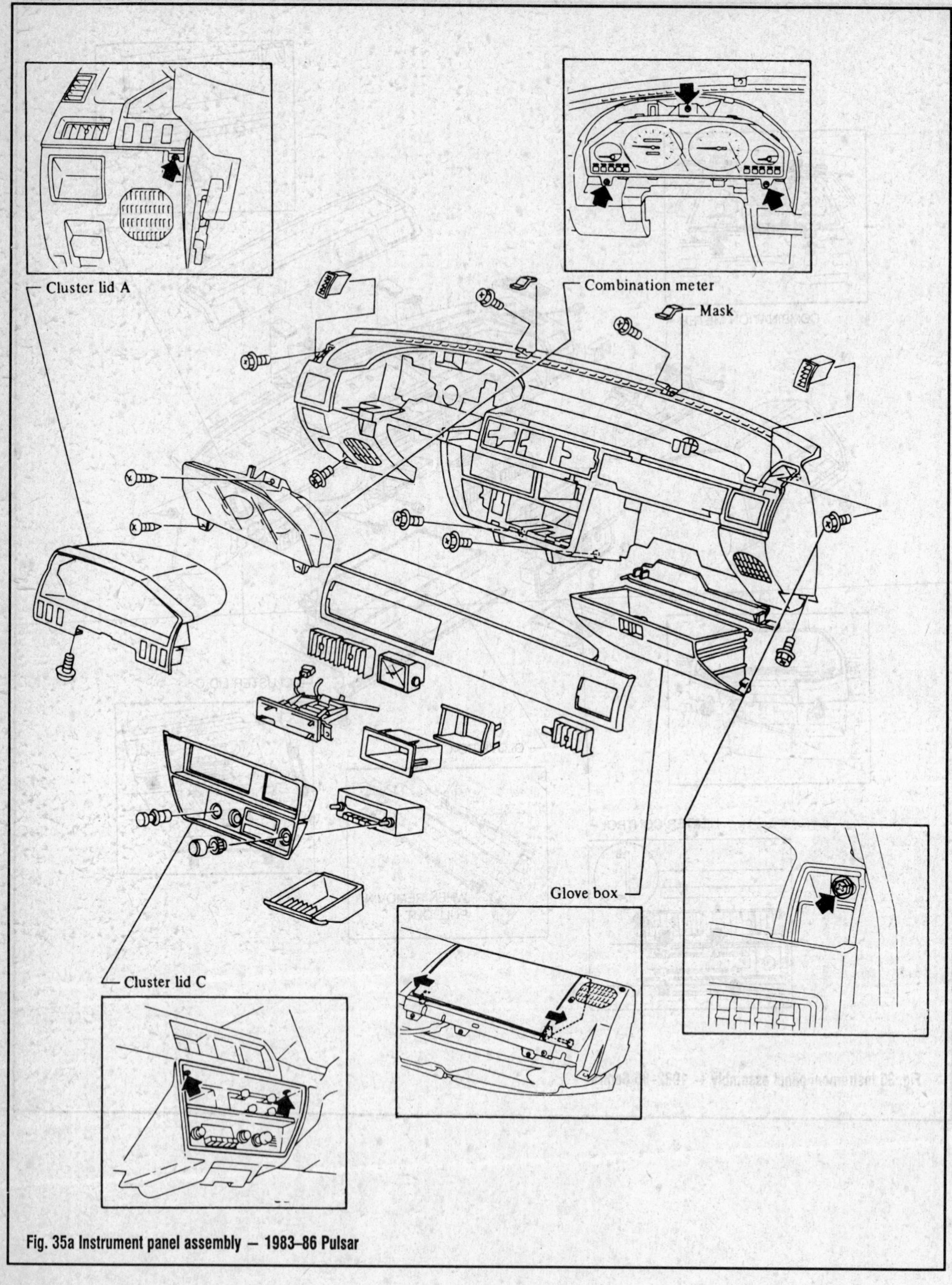
Cluster lid A
Combination meter
Mask
Glove box
Cluster lid C

Fig. 35a Instrument panel assembly — 1983–86 Pulsar

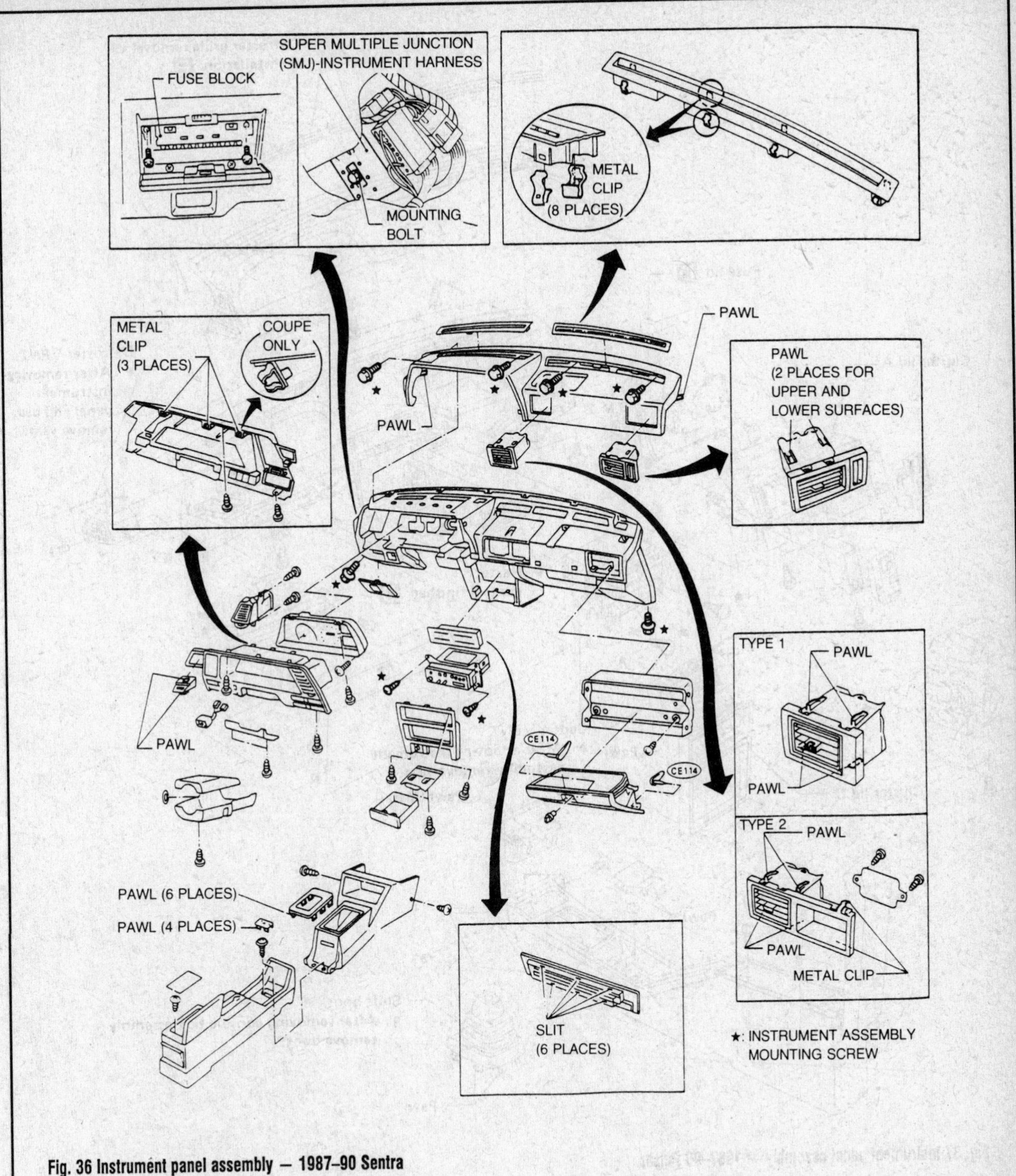
SUPER MULTIPLE JUNCTION
(SMJ)-INSTRUMENT HARNESS
FUSE BLOCK
MOUNTING
BOLT
METAL
CLIP
(8 PLACES)
PAWL
METAL
CLIP
(3 PLACES)
COUPE
ONLY
PAWL
PAWL
(2 PLACES FOR
UPPER AND
LOWER SURFACES)
PAWL
CE114
CE114
TYPE 1
PAWL
PAWL
TYPE 2
PAWL
PAWL
METAL CLIP
PAWL (6 PLACES)
PAWL (4 PLACES)
SLIT
(6 PLACES)
★: INSTRUMENT ASSEMBLY
MOUNTING SCREW

Fig. 36 Instrument panel assembly — 1987–90 Sentra

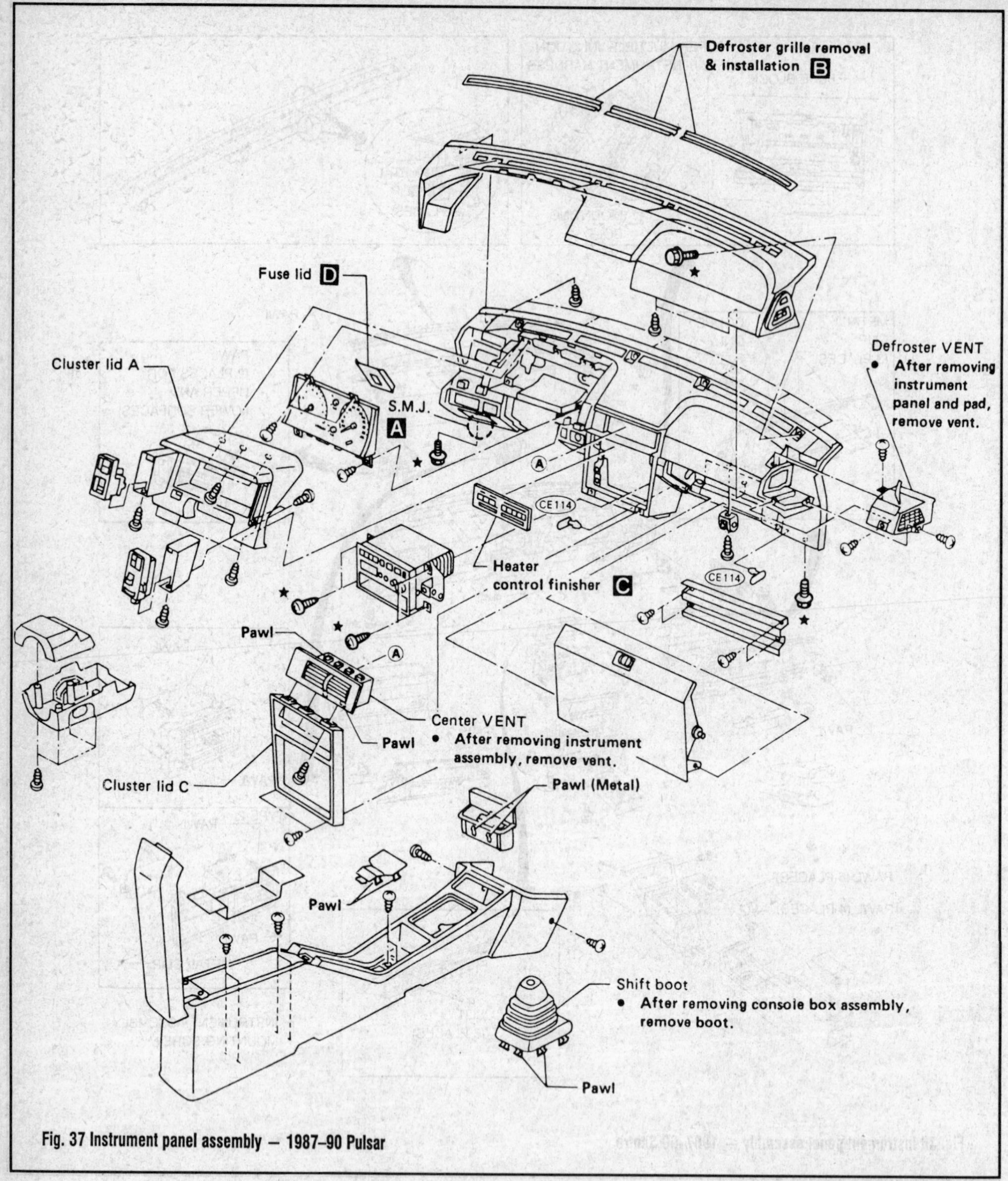

Defroster grille removal & installation B
Fuse lid D
Cluster lid A
S.M.J.
A
Defroster VENT
• After removing instrument panel and pad, remove vent.
CE114
Heater control finisher C
Pawl
Center VENT
Pawl • After removing instrument assembly, remove vent.
Cluster lid C
Pawl (Metal)
Pawl
Shift boot
• After removing console box assembly, remove boot.
Pawl

Fig. 37 Instrument panel assembly — 1987–90 Pulsar

7. Remove the radio knobs and bezel. Disconnect the antenna and power cable, remove the attaching bolts, and remove the radio.

8. Remove the heater control bezel. Disconnect the heater cables and electrical connector and remove the heater control from the dash.

9. Remove the instrument panel section located just above the glovebox drawer by removing the attaching bolt on the right and then unclipping the panel section. Tilt the glove box drawer downward, work the hinge pins out of the dash at top and bottom and remove it.

10. Remove the small panels out of the top left and top right of the dash by prying them very gently. Remove the two small screw covers from either side of the center of the dash at the top.

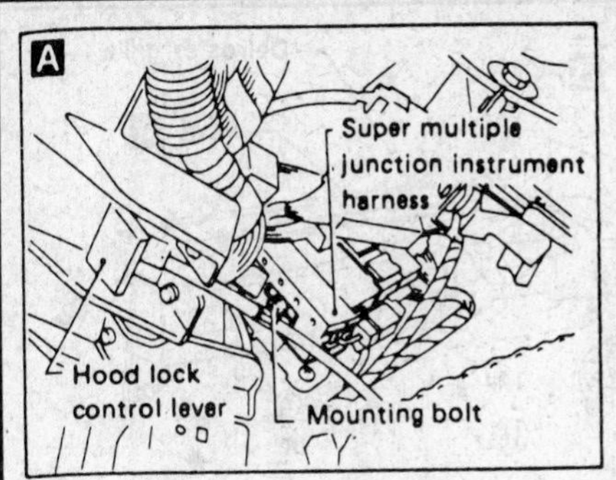
A
Super multiple junction instrument harness
Hood lock control lever
Mounting bolt

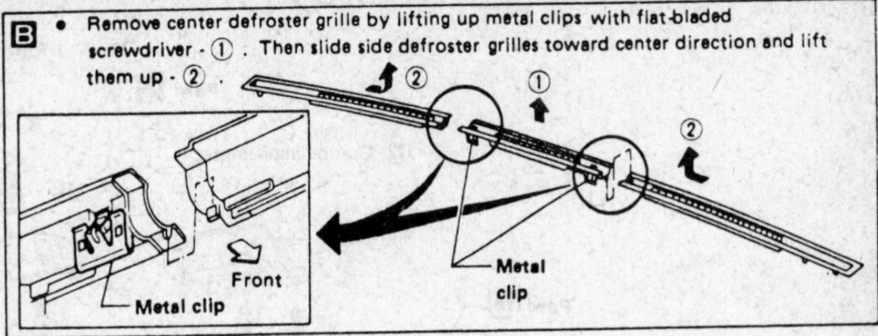
B
• Remove center defroster grille by lifting up metal clips with flat-bladed screwdriver - ①. Then slide side defroster grilles toward center direction and lift them up - ②.
Front
Metal clip
Metal clip

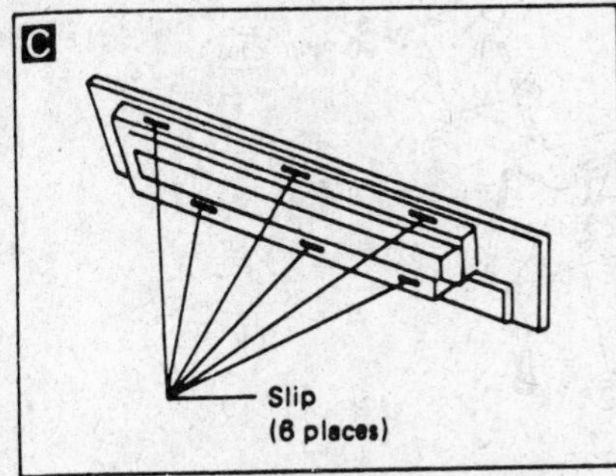
C
Slip
(6 places)

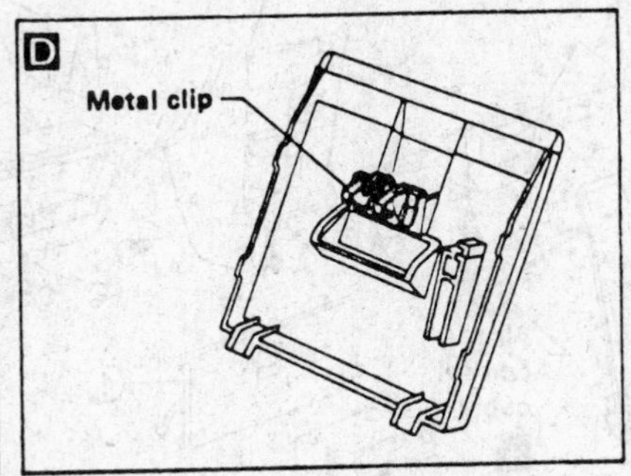
D
Metal clip

Fig. 38 Instrument panel fasteners — 1987–90 Pulsar

11. Remove the four bolts from the bottom of the instrument panel assembly (one at each corner and two below the radio). Then, support the assembly (perhaps with the help of an assistant). Remove the four bolts (one under each cover) that support the assembly at the top and remove it from the car.

To install:

12. With a helper, put the instrument panel into position and hold it there. Then, install the four bolts that fasten the unit at the top.
13. Install the four bolts that fasten the unit at the bottom. Install the bolt covers on the top of the panel.
14. Install the glovebox and adjacent instrument panel section by reversing the removal procedure.
15. Install the heater control, connect the cables, and adjust them. Connect the electrical connector.
16. Install the radio by reversing the removal procedure.
17. Install the ash tray slider and the ashtray.
18. Install the instrument cluster in reverse of the removal procedure. Install the instrument hood.
19. Connect the choke control cable, harness connectors, hood latch control cable, speedometer cable, and radio aerial cable.
20. Refill the engine with coolant. Reconnect the battery. Start the engine and check for leaks. Refill the cooling system after the engine has reached operating temperature and has then been allowed to cool.

1987–90 Vehicles

➡ This is a very lengthy procedure, requiring complete removal of the instrument panel.

1. Disconnect the negative battery cable. Remove the upper defroster grilles by gently pulling them upward to free the eight clips fastening each of them in place.
2. Slide a thin, flat instrument in to release the clips by depressing the tangs on top and on the bottom of the center and right side air discharge grilles. Then, slide them out of the instrument panel.
3. Remove the four bolts from the top of the instrument panel cover (these are accessible at either end of the slots for the defroster grilles, removed earlier).
4. Remove the two screws from underneath the cluster bezel and the two from the underside of the cluster hood. Then, use a thin, flat object to depress the locking pawl in the fastener located at the top left of the cluster bezel; then, slide this fastener out of the dash. Now, slide the cluster bezel out of the dash.
5. Remove the instrument panel cover from the instrument panel by pulling it straight back so as to disengage the mounting pawls from the panel underneath, and remove it.
6. Remove the mounting screws from the underside and front of the instrument cluster and then pull it out of the dash panel far enough for you to gain access to the electrical connectors. Disconnect these connectors and then remove the cluster by sliding it out of the dash.
7. Remove the large screw cover from the rear part of the rear console. Remove the console mounting screw located underneath it. Remove the small screw cover from the front of the console and remove the screw underneath that. Remove the rear console.
8. Remove the screw from either side of the front console. Remove the gearshift knob by unscrewing it. Then, remove the forward section of the console.
9. Slide out the ashtray drawer, depress the lock, and then remove it. Remove the two mounting screws (accessible from underneath) and then remove the ashtray slider.
10. Remove the two mounting screws and then remove the radio/heater control bezel. Disconnect the electrical connector for the heater control. Disconnect the air door cables the control actuates.
11. Then, remove the two mounting screws and pull the radio out for access to the electrical connector and antenna cable connector. Disconnect these and remove the radio.

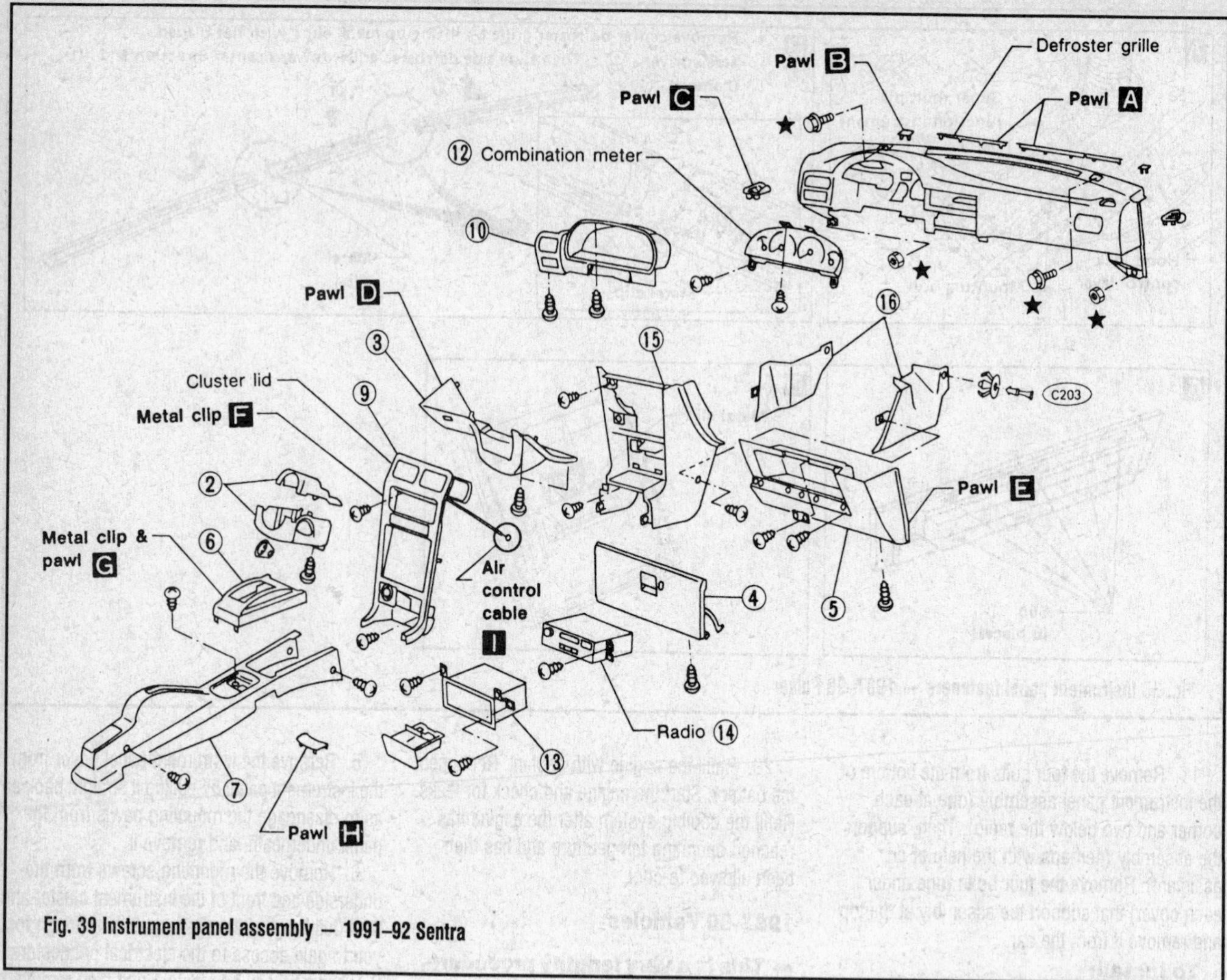

Defroster grille
Pawl B
Pawl C
Pawl A
⑫ Combination meter
⑩
Pawl D
③
⑮
⑯
Cluster lid
⑨
Metal clip F
②
C203
Pawl E
Metal clip & pawl G
⑥
Air control cable
I
④
⑤
Radio ⑭
⑬
⑦
Pawl H

Fig. 39 Instrument panel assembly — 1991–92 Sentra

12. Remove its mounting bolt and then disconnect the Super Multiple Junction connector from under the dash.

13. Remove the two mounting screws and remove the fuse block.

14. Remove the hood latch release.

15. Remove the left and right side instrument panel mounting screws, accessible from underneath and located near the corners of the unit. Then, pull the unit outward and remove it from the vehicle.

To install:

16. Put the instrument panel into position so the mounting pawls line it up and install the right and left side mounting screws.

17. Install the hood release and fuse block. Connect the Super Multiple Junction connector and install its mounting bolt.

18. Install the radio and the heater control.

19. Install the ashtray slider and ashtray.

20. Install the front console and then the rear console. Install the gearshift knob.

21. Put the instrument cluster into position, connect all the electrical connectors and install it.

22. Install the instrument cluster bezel.

23. Install the instrument panel cover.

24. Install the center and right air discharge grilles.

25. Install the upper defroster grilles. Reconnect the battery and refill the cooling system.

1991–92 Sentra

CAUTION

To avoid rendering the SRS (Supplemental Restraint System) inoperative, which could lead to personal injury or death in the event of a severe frontal collision, extreme caution must be taken when servicing the electrical related systems. All SRS electrical wiring harnesses and connectors are covered with YELLOW outer insulation. Do not use electrical test equipment on any circuit related to the SRS (air bag).

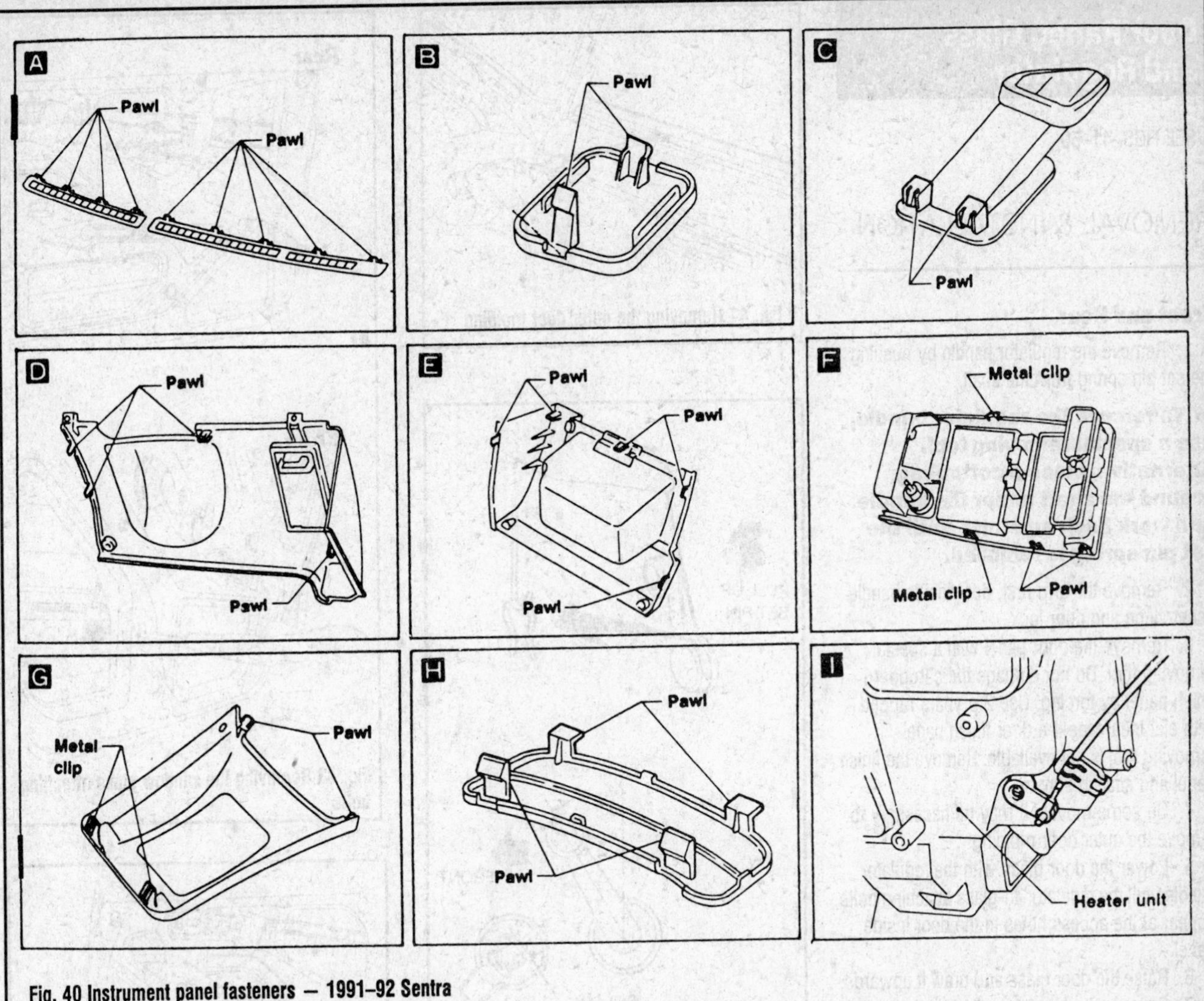
A
Pawl
Pawl
B
Pawl
C
Pawl
D
Pawl
Pawl
E
Pawl
Pawl
Pawl
F
Metal clip
Metal clip
Pawl
G
Metal clip
Pawl
H
Pawl
Pawl
I
Heater unit

Fig. 40 Instrument panel fasteners — 1991–92 Sentra

Air Bag

DISARMING

On vehicles equipped with an air bag, turn the ignition switch to OFF position. The negative battery cable must be disconnected and wait 10 minutes after the cable is disconnected before working on the system. SRS sensors must always be installed with the arrow marks facing the front of the vehicle.

1. Disconnect the negative battery cable.
2. Remove the steering wheel as outlined in section 8.
3. Remove the steering column cover and lower instrument panel trim. Refer to illustration **D**.
4. Remove the glove compartment lid and box. Refer to illustration **E**.
5. Remove the transaxle finisher and shift lever boot. Refer to illustration **G**.
6. Remove the console assembly. Refer to illustration **H**.
7. Remove the center ventilator control cable at the unit side. Refer to illustration **I**.
8. Remove the instrument cluster lid and cluster. Refer to illustration **F**. Disconnect the speedometer cable and electrical connectors.
9. Remove the deck pocket and radio as outlined in section 6.
10. Remove the A/C and heater control assembly.
11. Remove the center lower instrument panel.
12. Remove the instrument panel and pads from the vehicle. Refer to illustration **A** and **B**.

To install:

13. Install the instrument panel and pads into the vehicle with the help of an assistant.
14. Install the center lower instrument panel.
15. Install the A/C and heater control assembly.
16. Install the deck pocket and radio as outlined in section 6.
17. Install the instrument cluster lid and cluster.
18. Install the center ventilator control cable at the unit side.
19. Install the console assembly.
20. Install the transaxle finisher and shift lever boot.
21. Install the glove compartment lid and box.
22. Install the steering column cover and lower instrument panel trim.
23. Install the steering wheel as outlined in section 8.
24. Connect the negative battery cable and check operation.

Door Panel, Glass and Regulator

➧ SEE FIGS. 41–50

REMOVAL & INSTALLATION

Front and Rear

1. Remove the regulator handle by pushing the set pin spring from the shaft.

➡ To remove the regulator handle, use a special removing tool. Alternative, place a cotton rag around the shaft under the handle and work back and forth until the set pin spring is removed.

2. Remove the arm rest, door inside handle escutcheon and door lock.
3. Remove the door panel with a special removing tool. Do not damage the cardboard finish panel by forcing. Use 2 prybars rapped with electrical tape if a door finish panel removing tool is not available. Remove the finish panel and sealing screen.
4. On some models it may be necessary to remove the outer door molding.
5. Lower the door glass with the regulator handle until the regulator-to-glass attaching bolts appear at the access holes in the door inside panel.
6. Raise the door glass and draw it upwards.
7. Remove the regulator attaching bolts and remove the regulator assembly through the large access hole in the door panel.

To install:

8. Lubricate the regulator with all-purpose grease. Install the window regulator assembly in the door.
9. Connect all mounting bolts and check for proper operation.
10. Adjust the window if necessary and install the door sealing screen and finish panel.
11. Install all the attaching components to the door panel.
12. Install the window regulator handle.

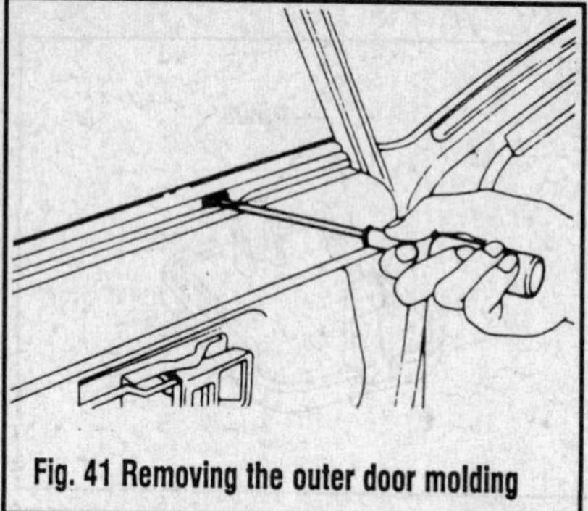

Fig. 41 Removing the outer door molding

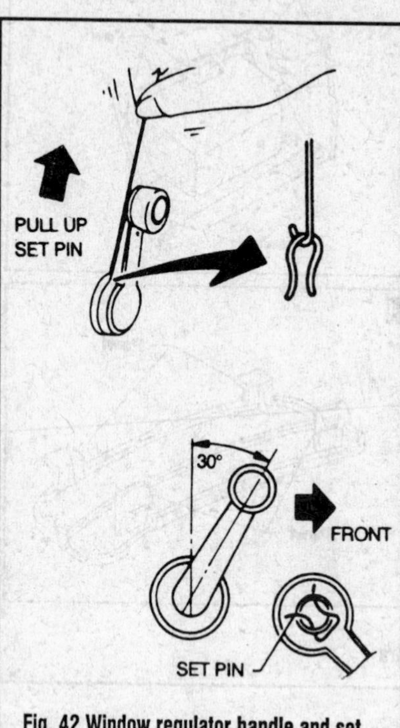
PULL UP
SET PIN
30°
FRONT
SET PIN

Fig. 42 Window regulator handle and set pin removal

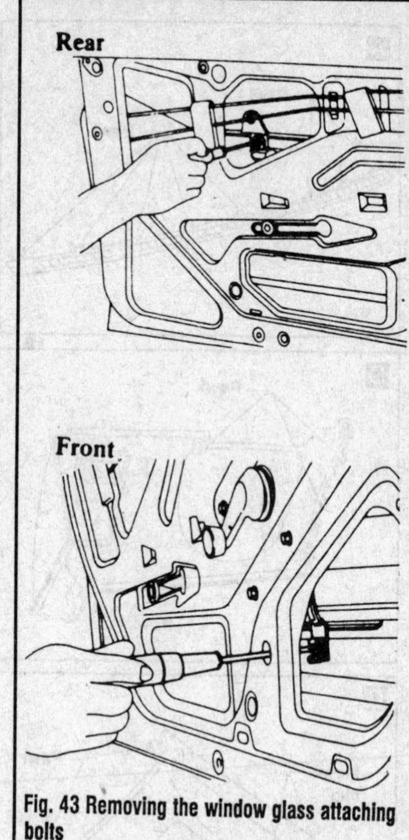
Rear
Front

Fig. 43 Removing the window glass attaching bolts

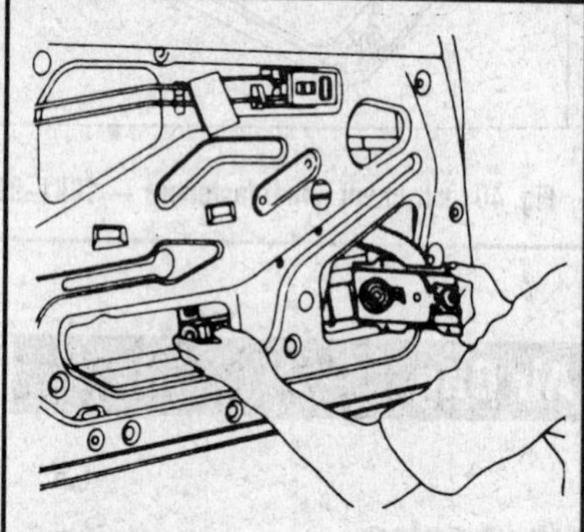

Fig. 44 Removing the window regulator from the door

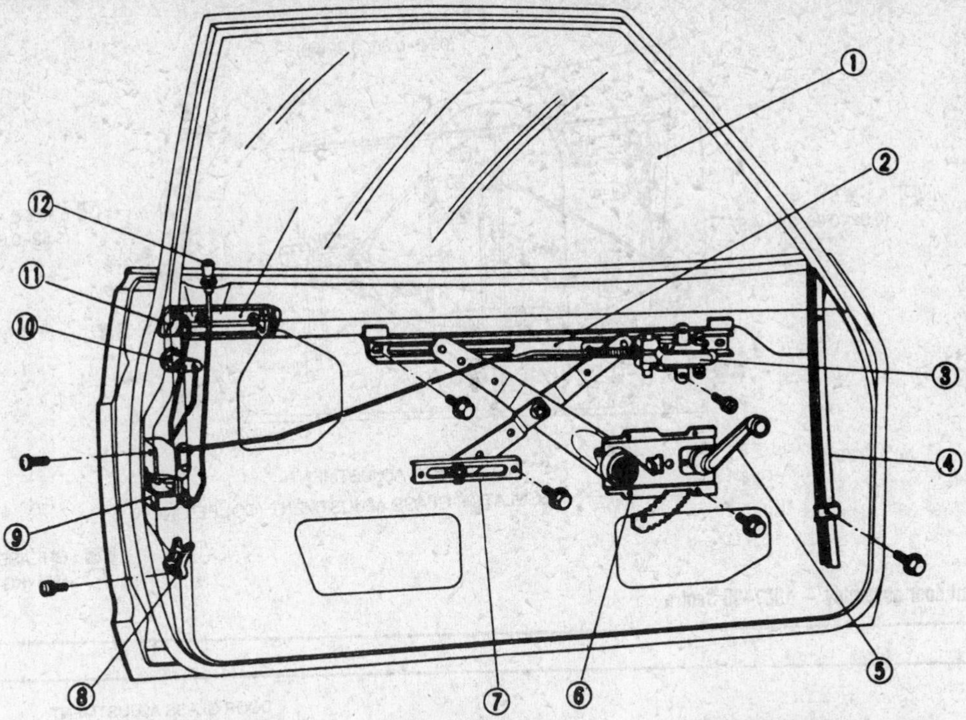

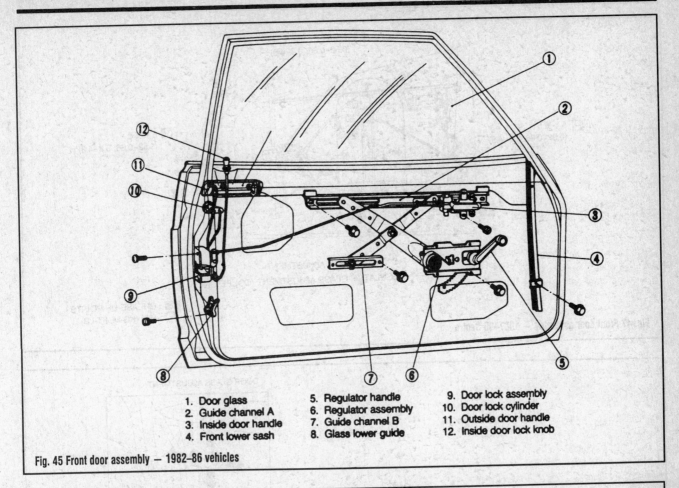

1. Door glass
2. Guide channel A
3. Inside door handle
4. Front lower sash
5. Regulator handle
6. Regulator assembly
7. Guide channel B
8. Glass lower guide
9. Door lock assembly
10. Door lock cylinder
11. Outside door handle
12. Inside door lock knob

Fig. 45 Front door assembly — 1982–86 vehicles

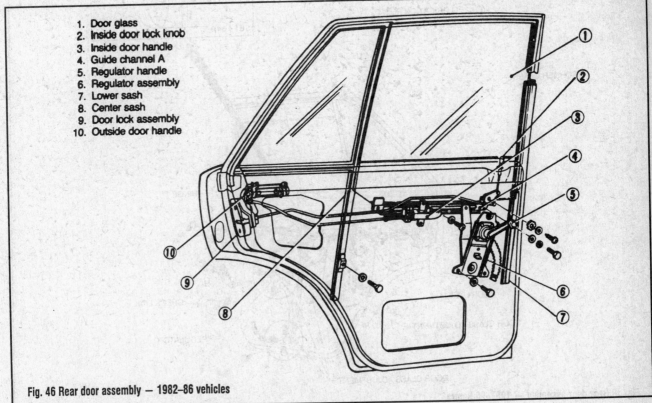

1. Door glass
2. Inside door lock knob
3. Inside door handle
4. Guide channel A
5. Regulator handle
6. Regulator assembly
7. Lower sash
8. Center sash
9. Door lock assembly
10. Outside door handle

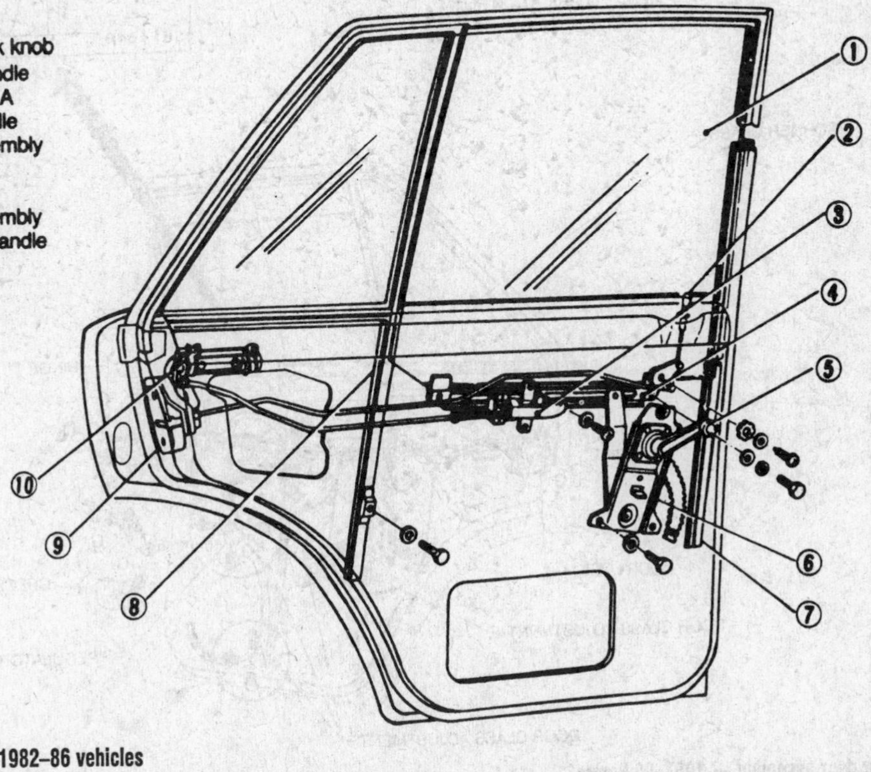

Fig. 46 Rear door assembly — 1982–86 vehicles

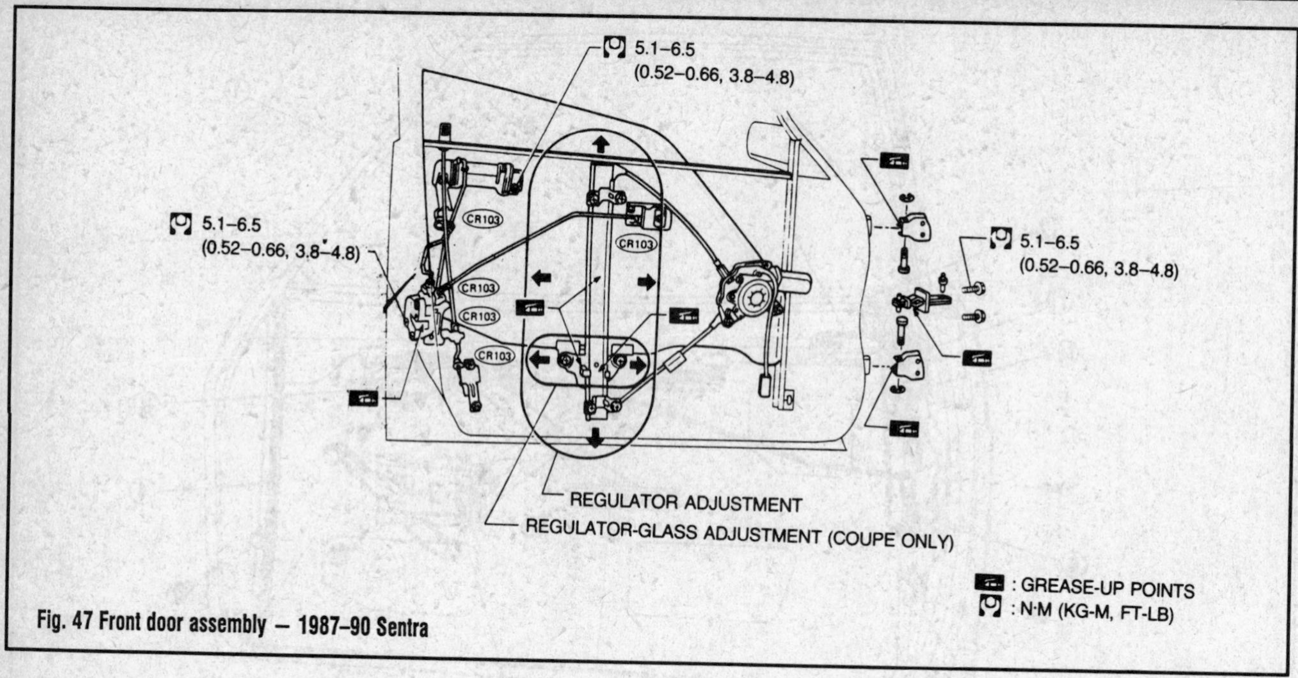
5.1–6.5
(0.52–0.66, 3.8–4.8)
5.1–6.5
(0.52–0.66, 3.8–4.8)
5.1–6.5
(0.52–0.66, 3.8–4.8)
CR103
CR103
CR103
CR103
CR103
REGULATOR ADJUSTMENT
REGULATOR-GLASS ADJUSTMENT (COUPE ONLY)
: GREASE-UP POINTS
: N·M (KG-M, FT-LB)

Fig. 47 Front door assembly – 1987–90 Sentra

DOOR GLASS ADJUSTMENT

SBF464B

G : LUBRICATION POINT

OUTSIDE MOLDING

CORNER GLASS

HINGE

DOOR LOCK

CHECK LINK

DOOR GLASS ADJUSTMENT

REGULATOR

DOOR GLASS ADJUSTMENT

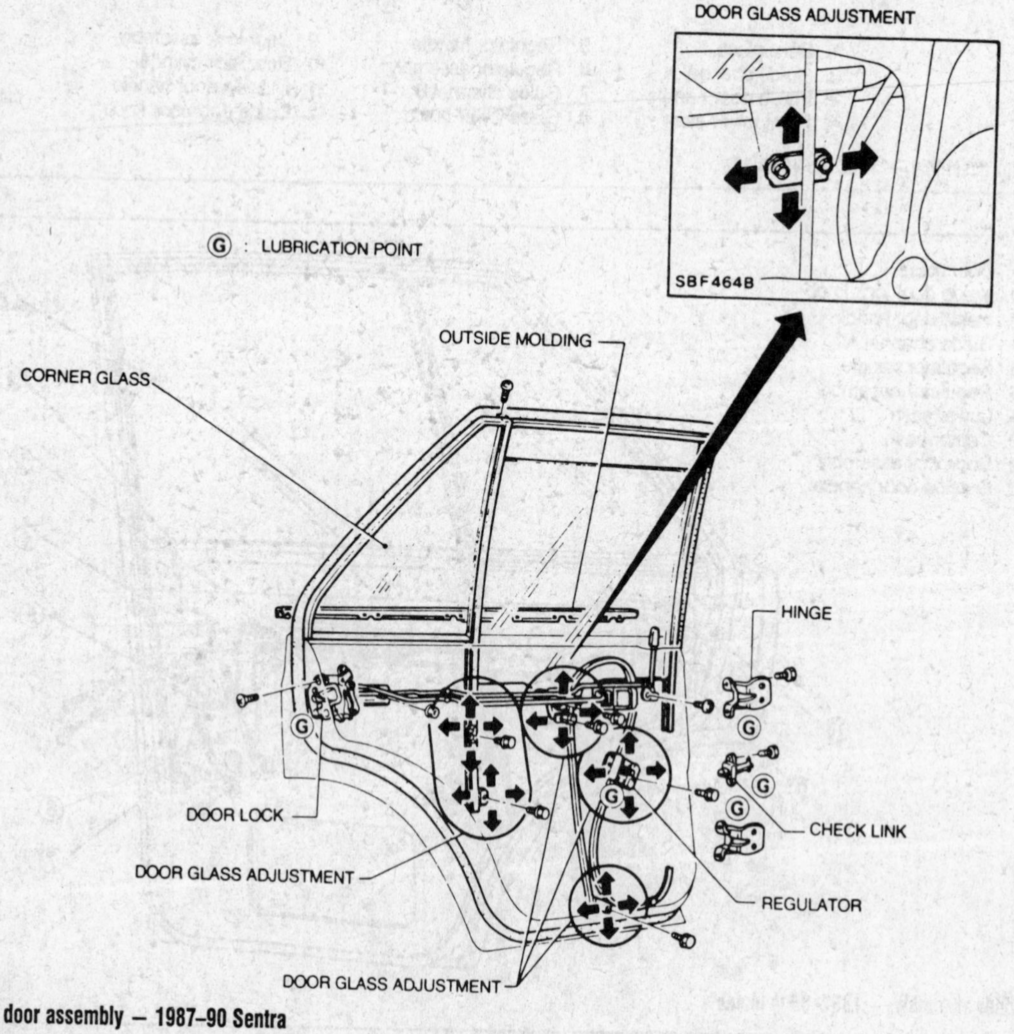

Fig. 48 Rear door assembly – 1987–90 Sentra

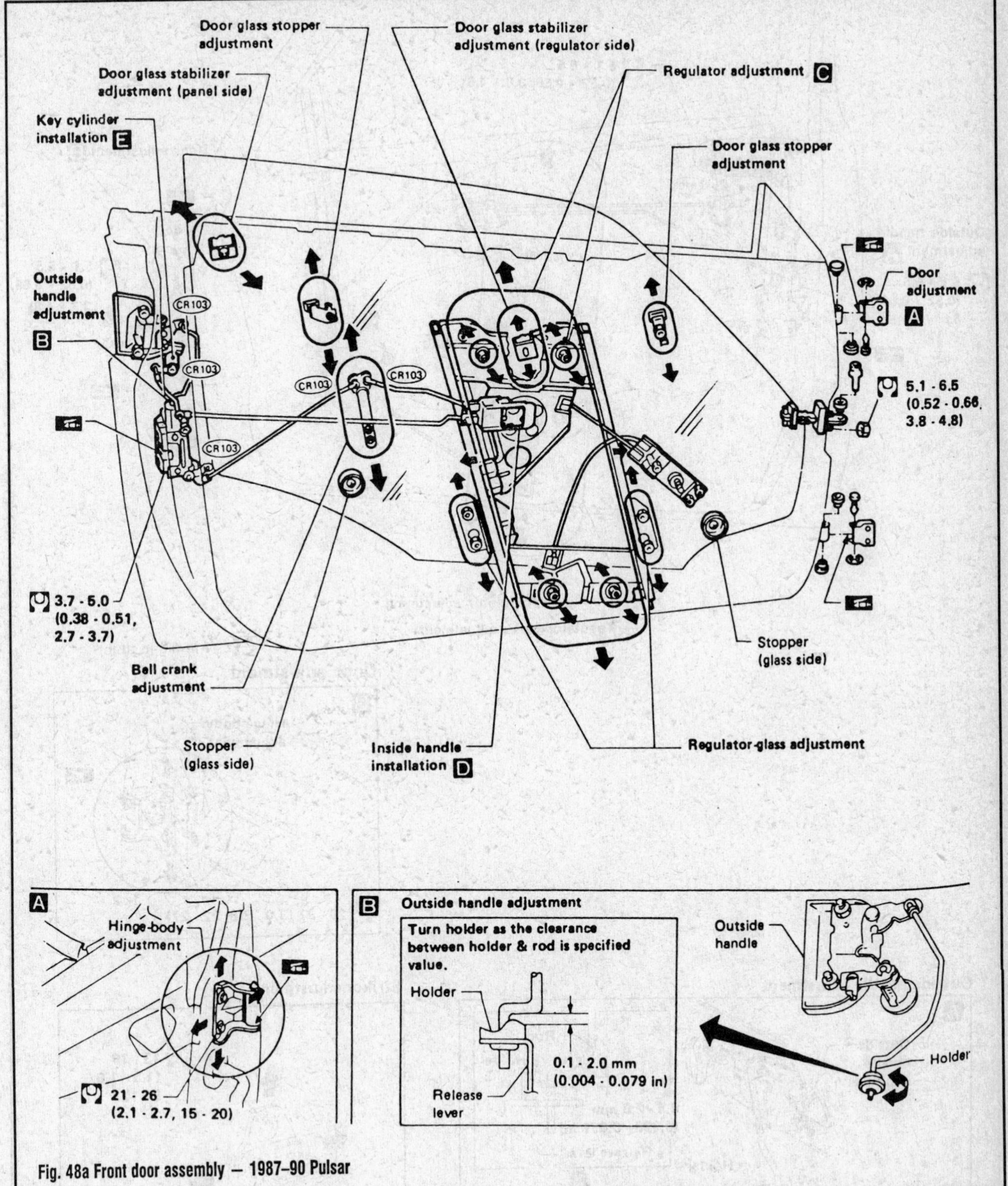

Door glass stopper adjustment
Door glass stabilizer adjustment (regulator side)
Door glass stabilizer adjustment (panel side)
Regulator adjustment C
Key cylinder installation E
Door glass stopper adjustment
Outside handle adjustment B
CR103
Door adjustment A
5.1 - 6.5 (0.52 - 0.66, 3.8 - 4.8)
3.7 - 5.0 (0.38 - 0.51, 2.7 - 3.7)
Bell crank adjustment
Stopper (glass side)
Stopper (glass side)
Inside handle installation D
Regulator-glass adjustment
A
Hinge-body adjustment
21 - 26 (2.1 - 2.7, 15 - 20)
B
Outside handle adjustment
Turn holder as the clearance between holder & rod is specified value.
Holder
0.1 - 2.0 mm (0.004 - 0.079 in)
Release lever
Outside handle
Holder

Fig. 48a Front door assembly — 1987–90 Pulsar

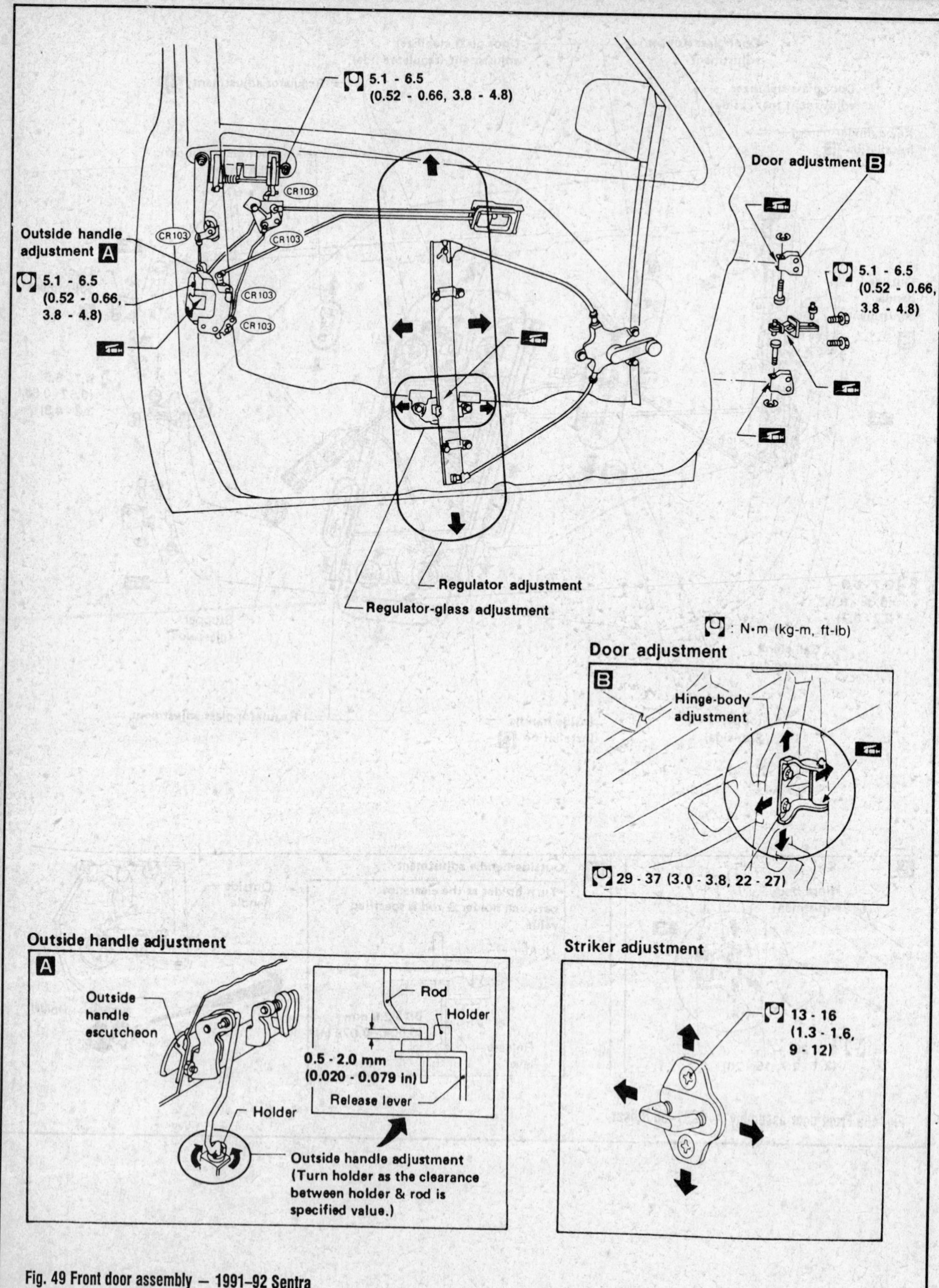
5.1 - 6.5
(0.52 - 0.66, 3.8 - 4.8)
CR103
Door adjustment B
Outside handle adjustment A
5.1 - 6.5
(0.52 - 0.66,
3.8 - 4.8)
5.1 - 6.5
(0.52 - 0.66,
3.8 - 4.8)
Regulator adjustment
Regulator-glass adjustment
: N•m (kg-m, ft-lb)
Door adjustment
B
Hinge-body adjustment
29 - 37 (3.0 - 3.8, 22 - 27)
Outside handle adjustment
A
Outside handle escutcheon
Rod
Holder
0.5 - 2.0 mm
(0.020 - 0.079 in)
Release lever
Holder
Outside handle adjustment
(Turn holder as the clearance between holder & rod is specified value.)
Striker adjustment
13 - 16
(1.3 - 1.6,
9 - 12)

Fig. 49 Front door assembly — 1991–92 Sentra

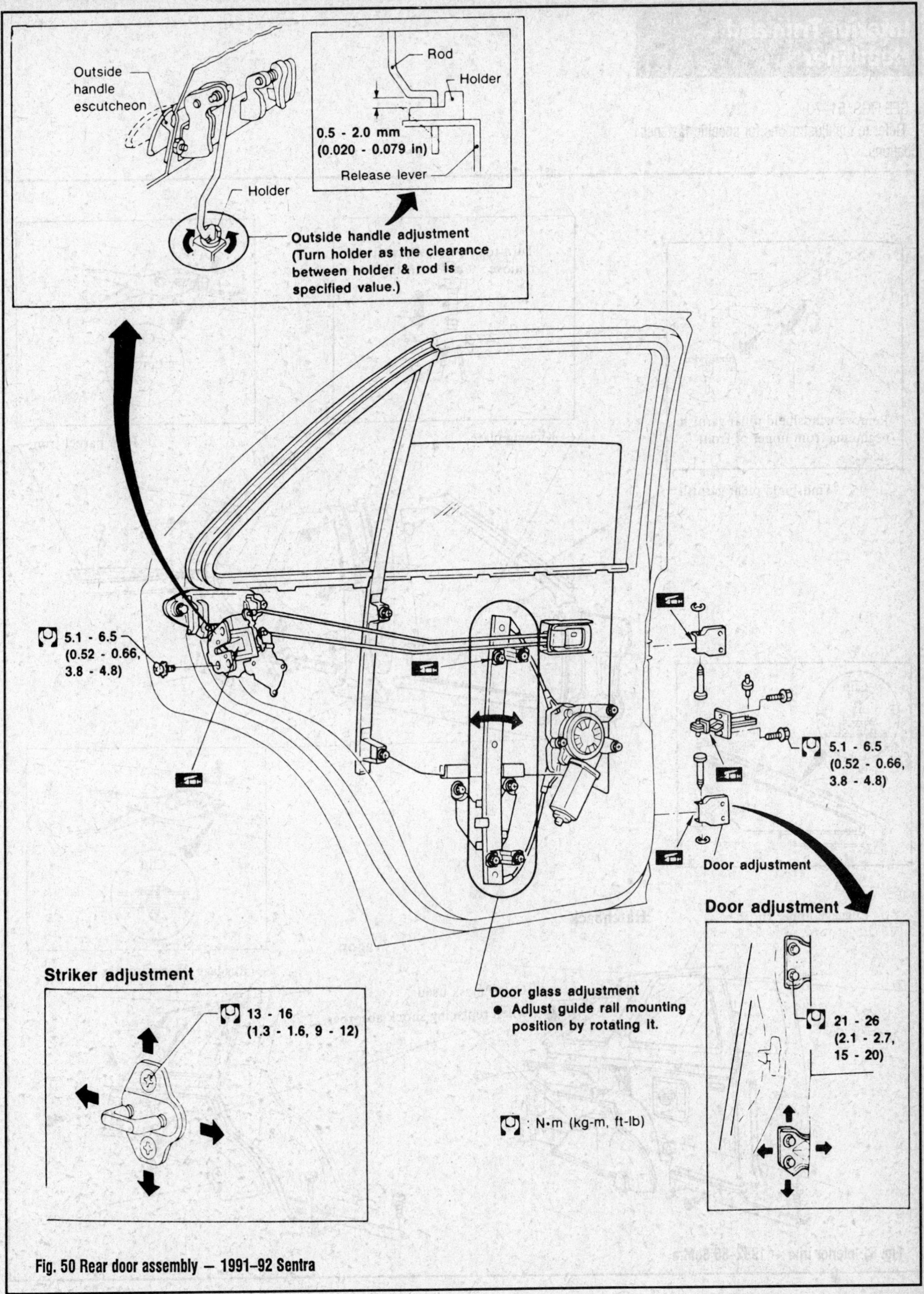
Outside handle escutcheon
Rod
Holder
0.5 - 2.0 mm
(0.020 - 0.079 in)
Release lever
Holder
Outside handle adjustment
(Turn holder as the clearance between holder & rod is specified value.)
5.1 - 6.5
(0.52 - 0.66, 3.8 - 4.8)
5.1 - 6.5
(0.52 - 0.66, 3.8 - 4.8)
Door adjustment
Door adjustment
21 - 26
(2.1 - 2.7, 15 - 20)
Striker adjustment
13 - 16
(1.3 - 1.6, 9 - 12)
Door glass adjustment
● Adjust guide rail mounting position by rotating it.
: N·m (kg-m, ft-lb)

Fig. 50 Rear door assembly — 1991–92 Sentra

Interior Trim and Headliner

➧ SEE FIGS. 51–70

Refer to the illustrations for specific fastener locations.

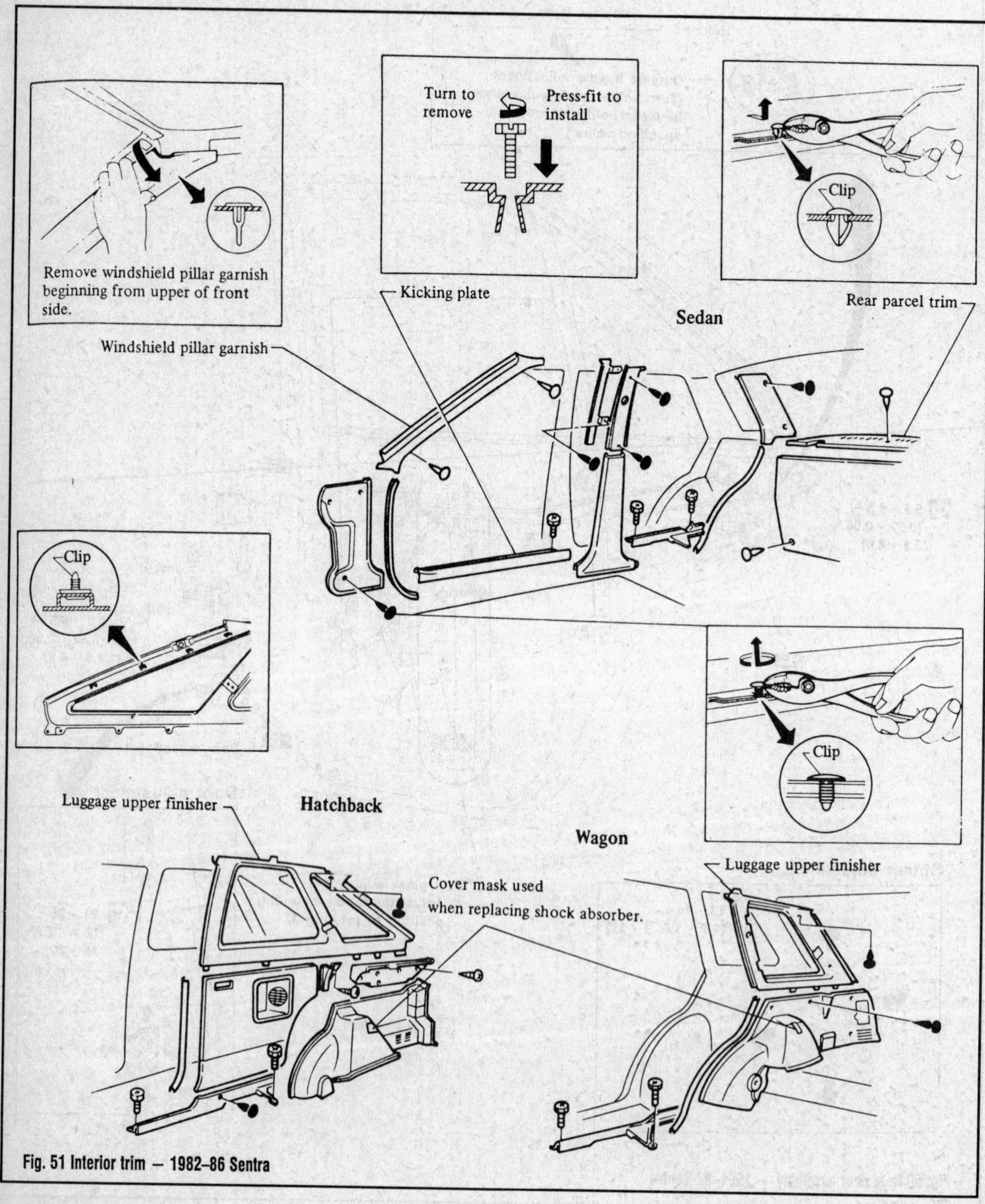
Remove windshield pillar garnish beginning from upper of front side.
Turn to remove
Press-fit to install
Clip
Kicking plate
Rear parcel trim
Sedan
Windshield pillar garnish
Clip
Clip
Luggage upper finisher
Hatchback
Wagon
Luggage upper finisher
Cover mask used when replacing shock absorber.

Fig. 51 Interior trim – 1982–86 Sentra

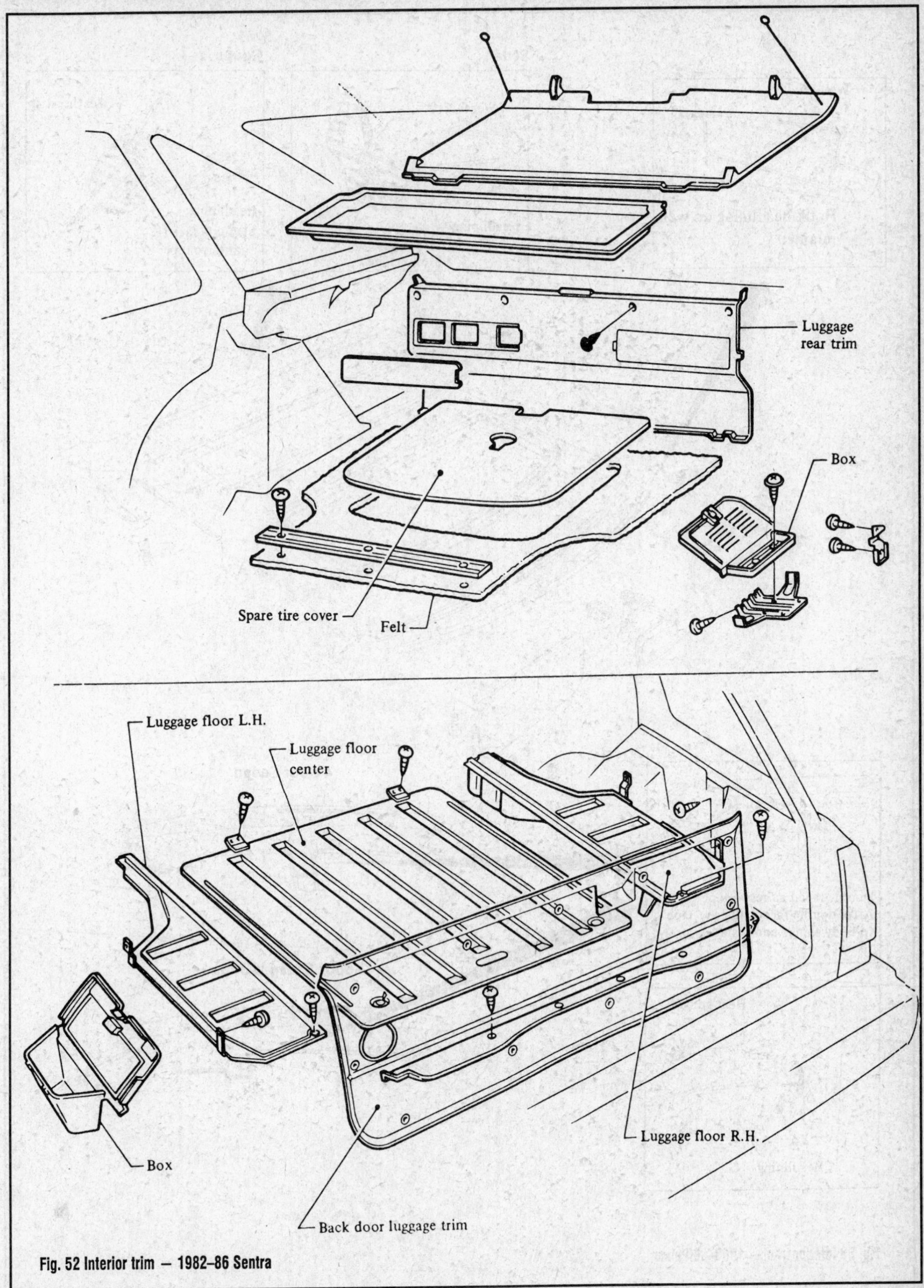
Luggage rear trim
Box
Spare tire cover
Felt
Luggage floor L.H.
Luggage floor center
Box
Luggage floor R.H.
Back door luggage trim

Fig. 52 Interior trim — 1982–86 Sentra

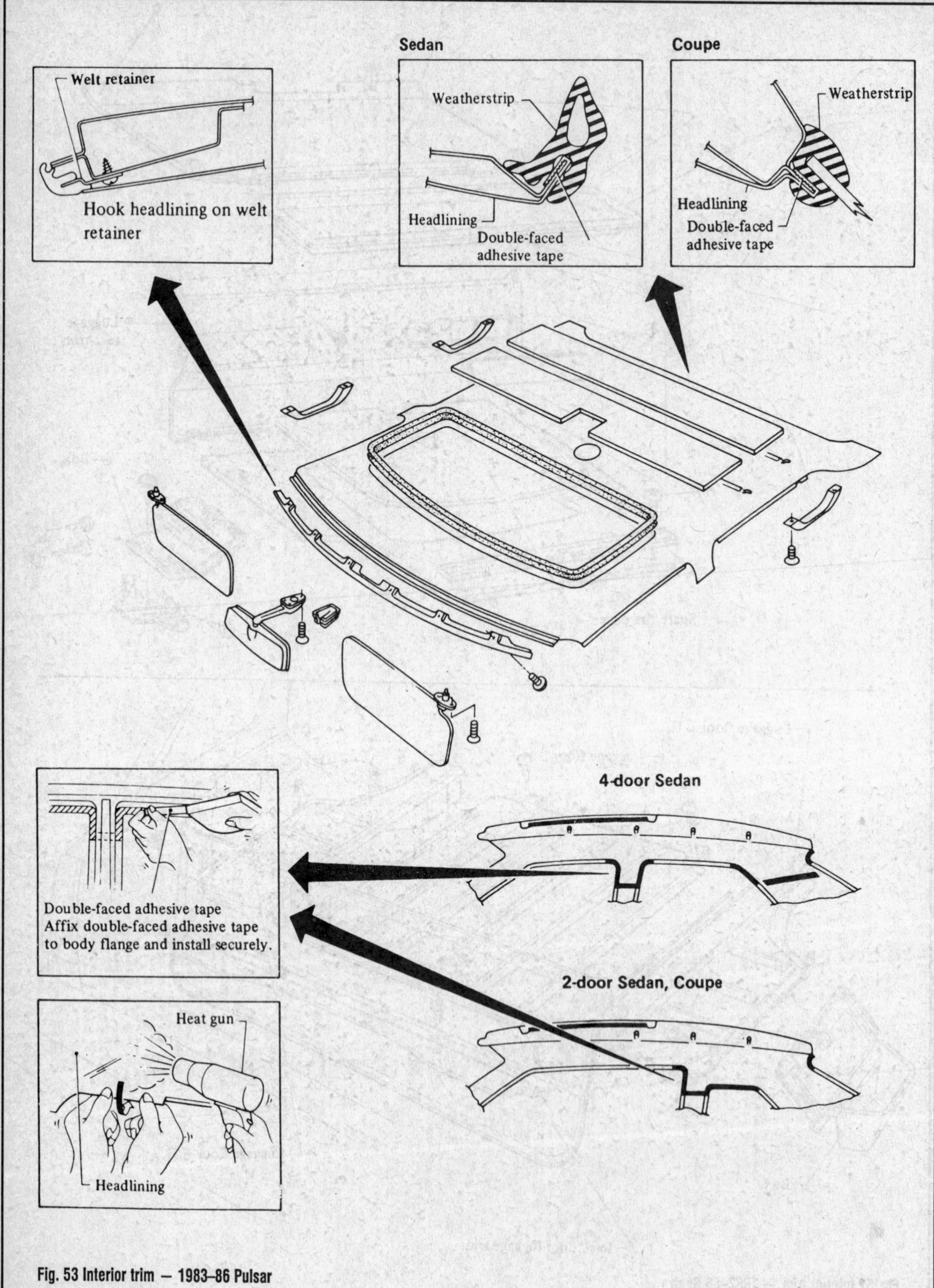
Welt retainer
Hook headlining on welt retainer
Sedan
Weatherstrip
Headlining
Double-faced adhesive tape
Coupe
Weatherstrip
Headlining
Double-faced adhesive tape
4-door Sedan
2-door Sedan, Coupe
Double-faced adhesive tape
Affix double-faced adhesive tape to body flange and install securely.
Heat gun
Headlining

Fig. 53 Interior trim — 1983–86 Pulsar

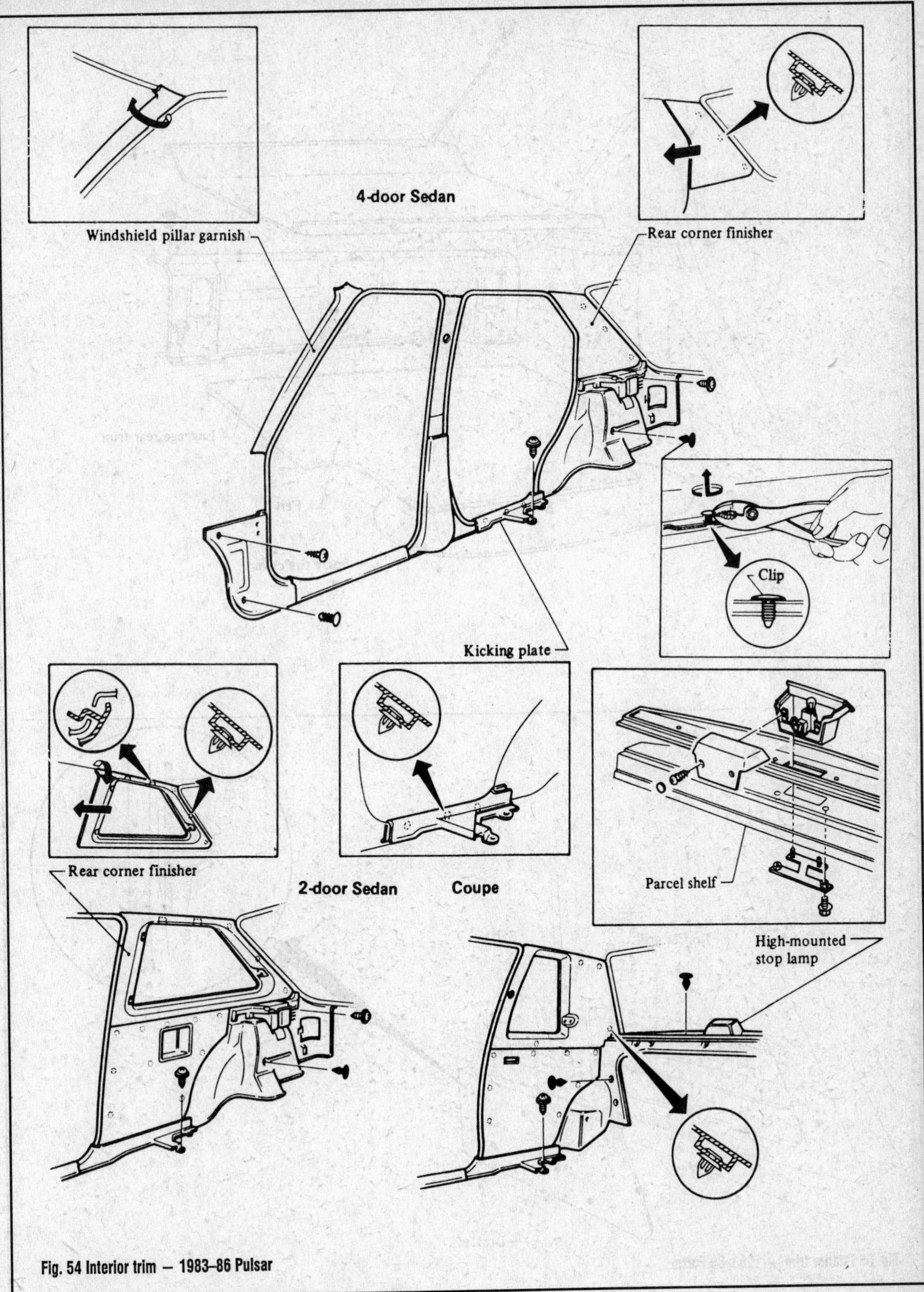
4-door Sedan
Windshield pillar garnish
Rear corner finisher
Clip
Kicking plate
Rear corner finisher
2-door Sedan
Coupe
Parcel shelf
High-mounted
stop lamp

Fig. 54 Interior trim — 1983–86 Pulsar

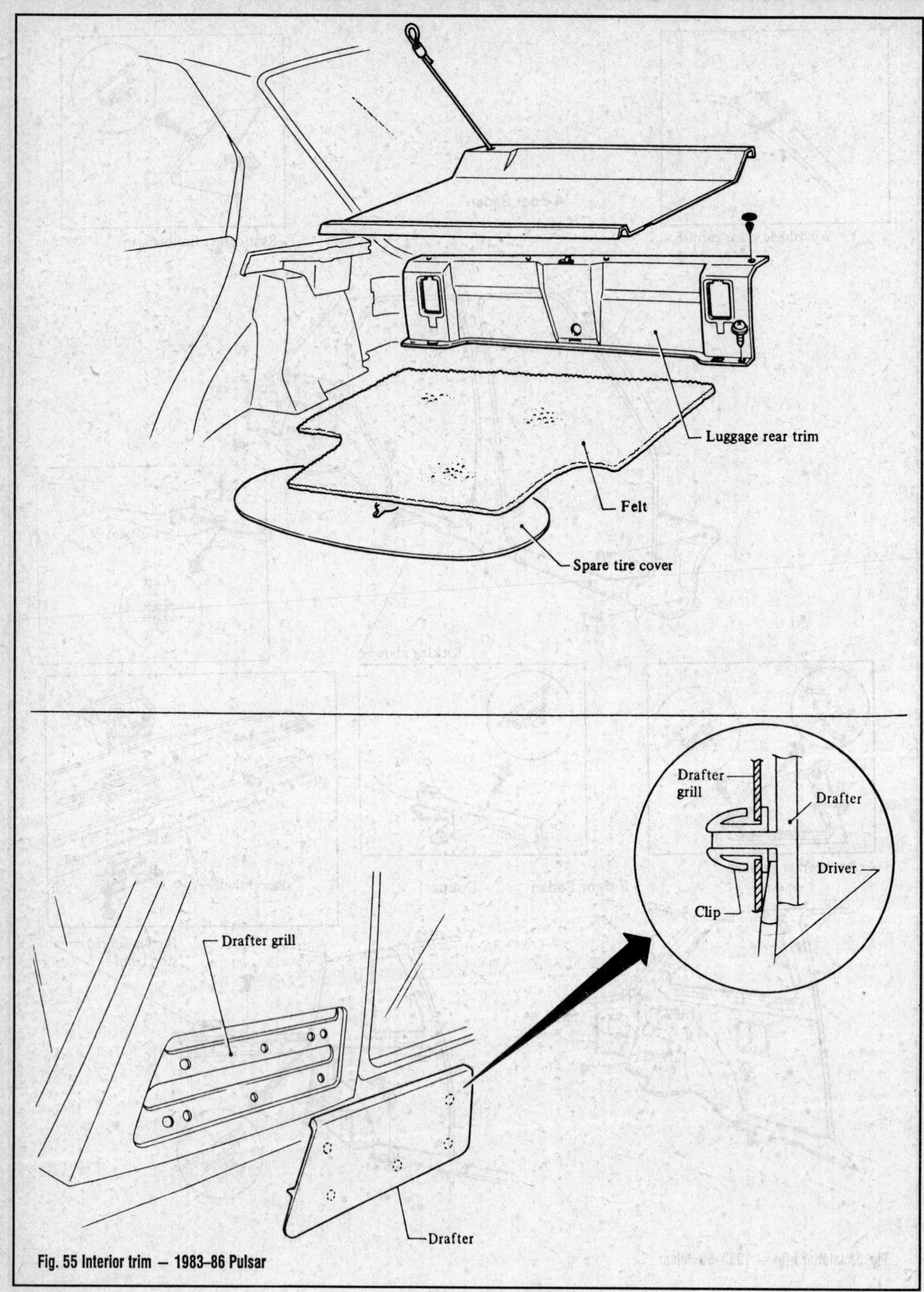
Luggage rear trim
Felt
Spare tire cover
Drafter grill
Drafter
Driver
Clip
Drafter grill
Drafter

Fig. 55 Interior trim — 1983–86 Pulsar

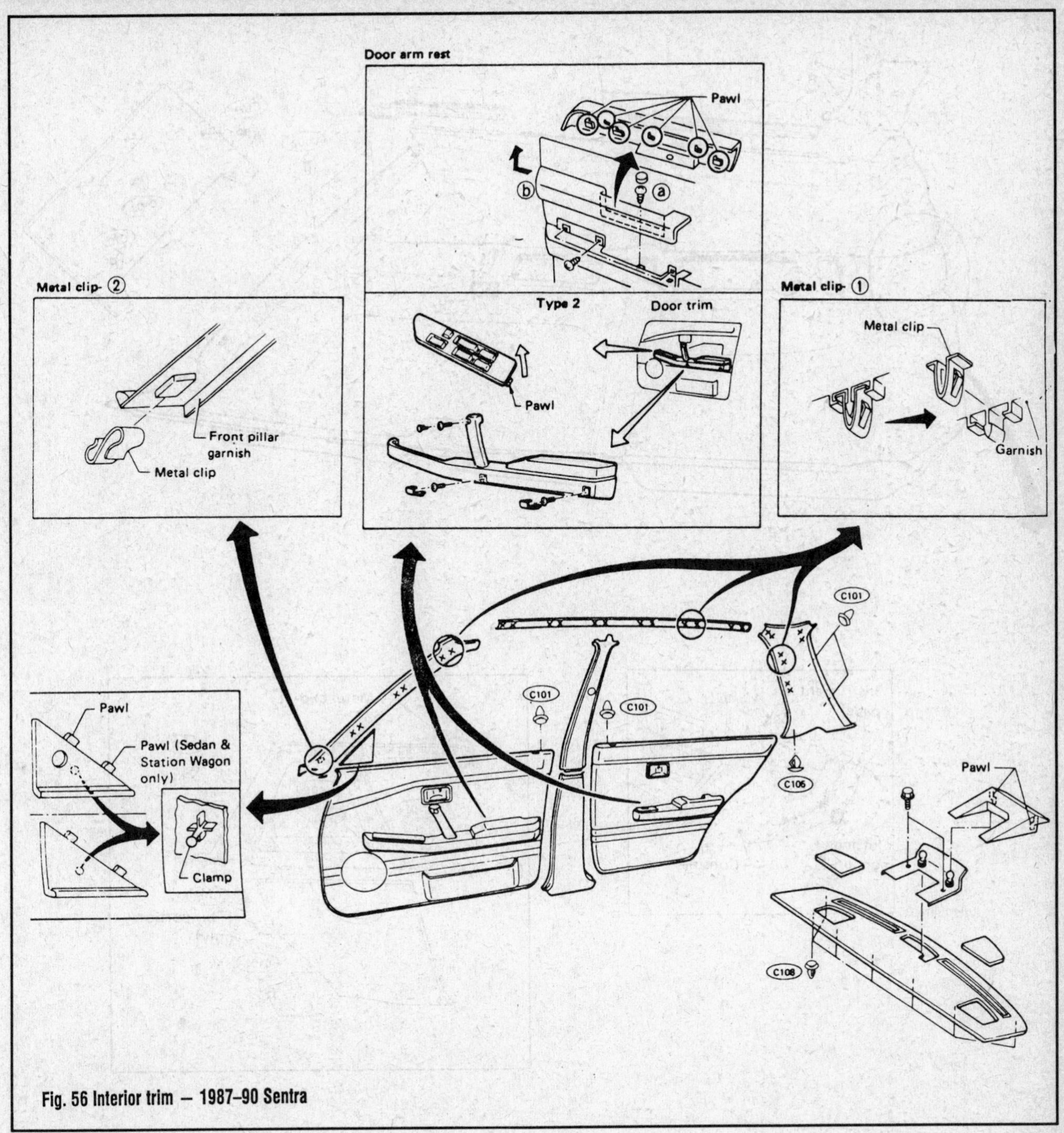
Door arm rest
Pawl
b
a
Metal clip- ②
Front pillar garnish
Metal clip
Type 2
Door trim
Pawl
Metal clip- ①
Metal clip
Garnish
C101
C101
C101
C105
Pawl
Pawl (Sedan & Station Wagon only)
Clamp
Pawl
C108

Fig. 56 Interior trim — 1987–90 Sentra

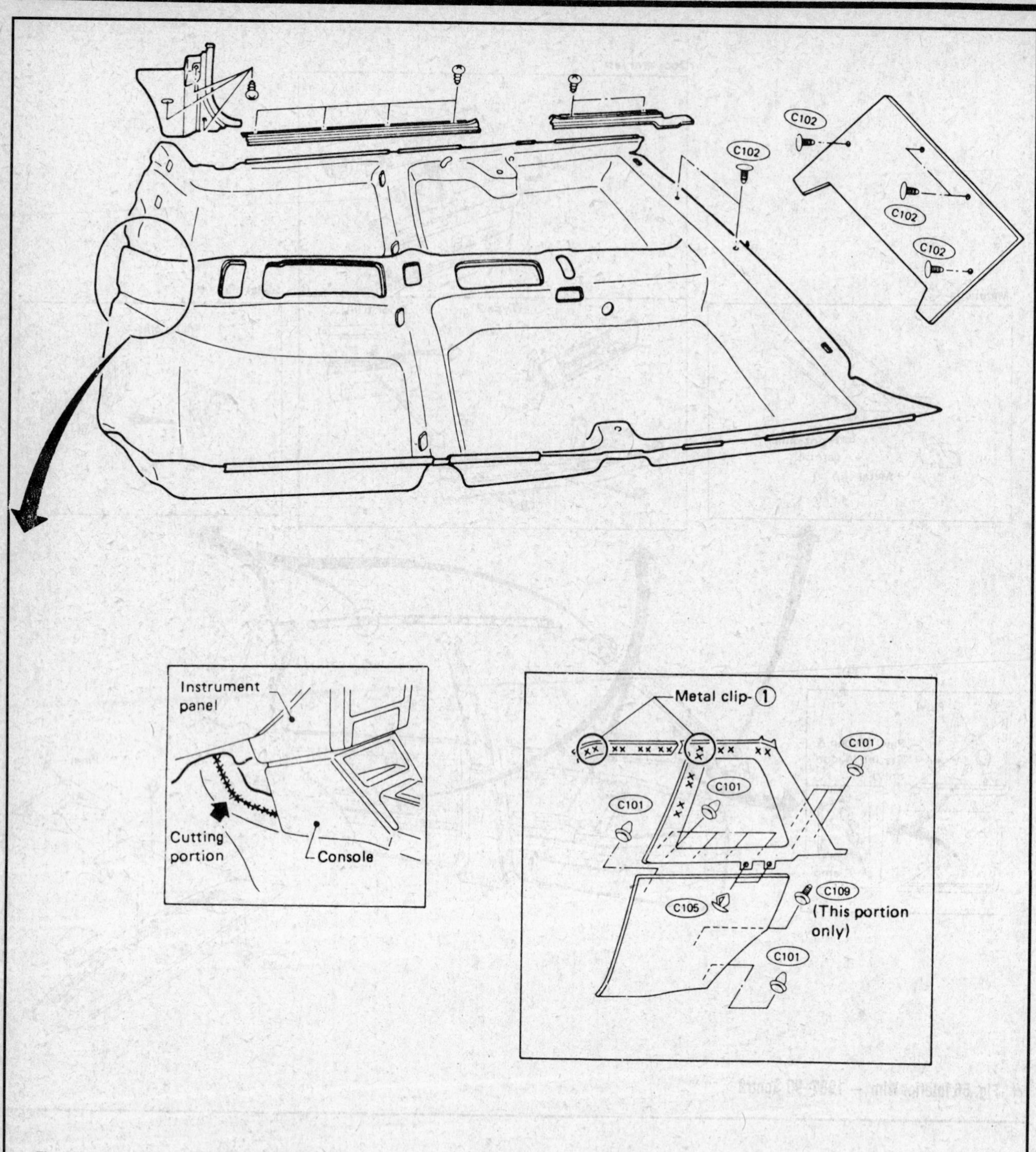
C102
C102
C102
C102
Instrument panel
Cutting portion
Console
Metal clip-①
C101
C101
C101
C105
C109
(This portion only)
C101

Fig. 57 Interior trim — 1987–90 Sentra

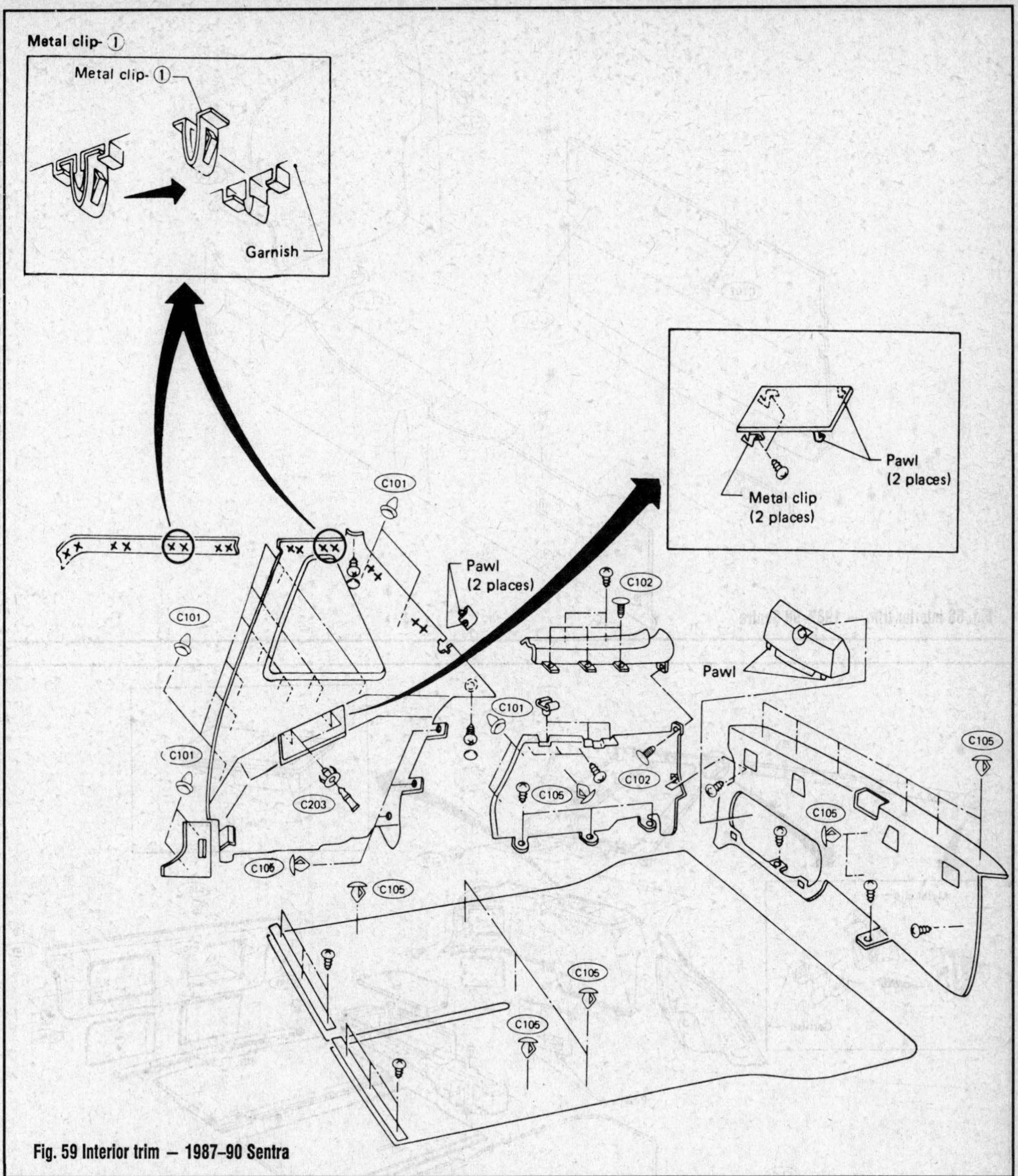

Metal clip- ①
Metal clip- ①
Garnish
Pawl
(2 places)
Metal clip
(2 places)
C101
Pawl
(2 places)
C102
C101
Pawl
C101
C105
C101
C102
C105
C203
C105
C105
C105
C105
C105

Fig. 59 Interior trim — 1987–90 Sentra

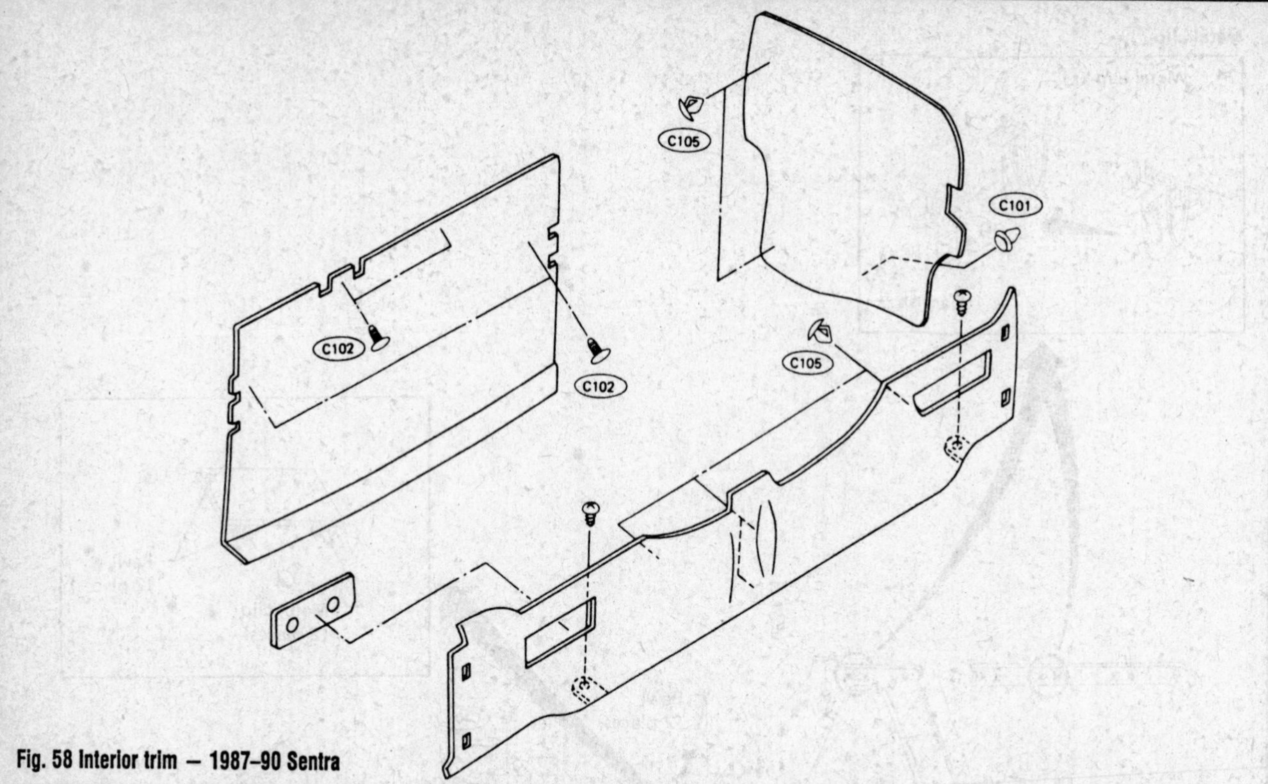

Fig. 58 Interior trim — 1987–90 Sentra

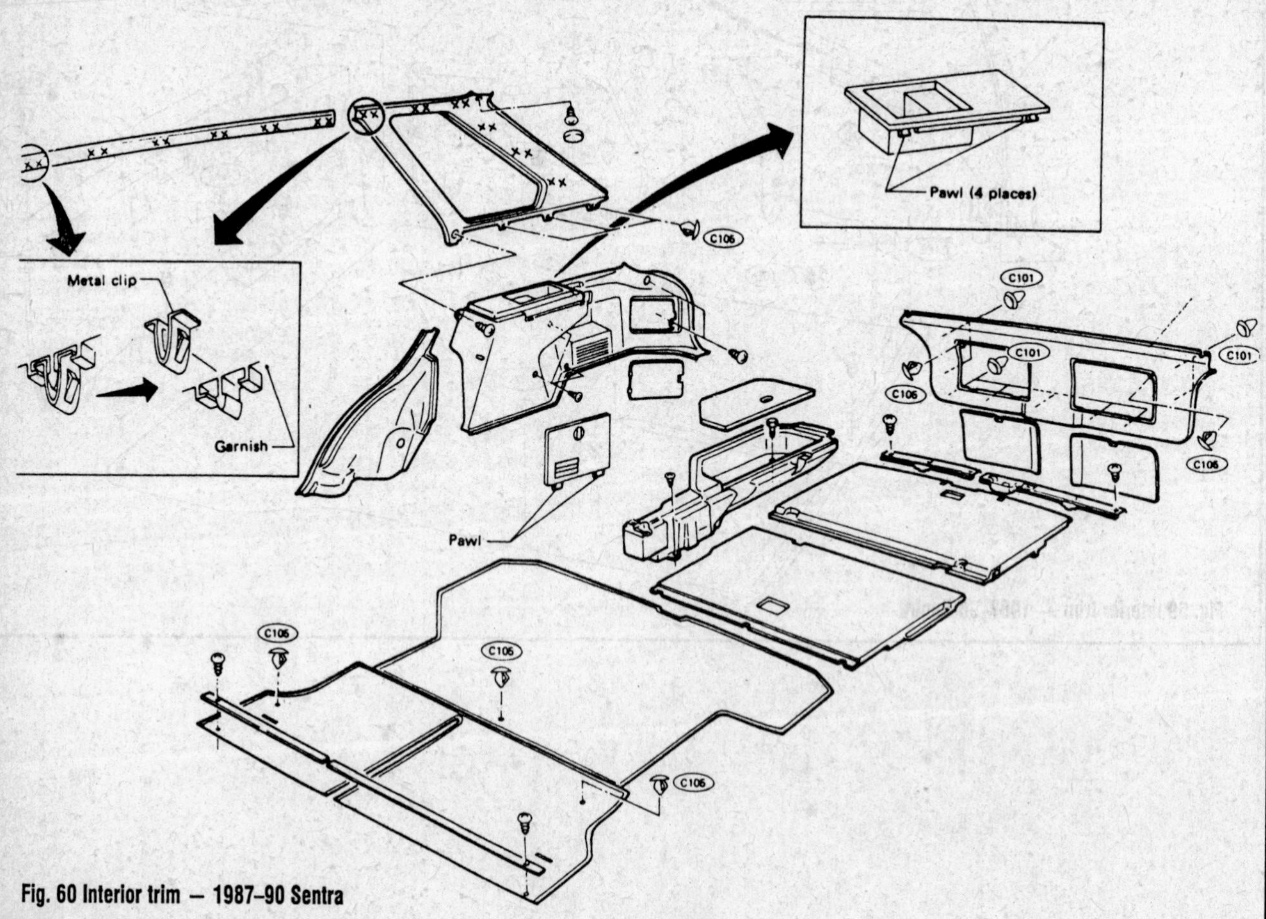

Fig. 60 Interior trim — 1987–90 Sentra

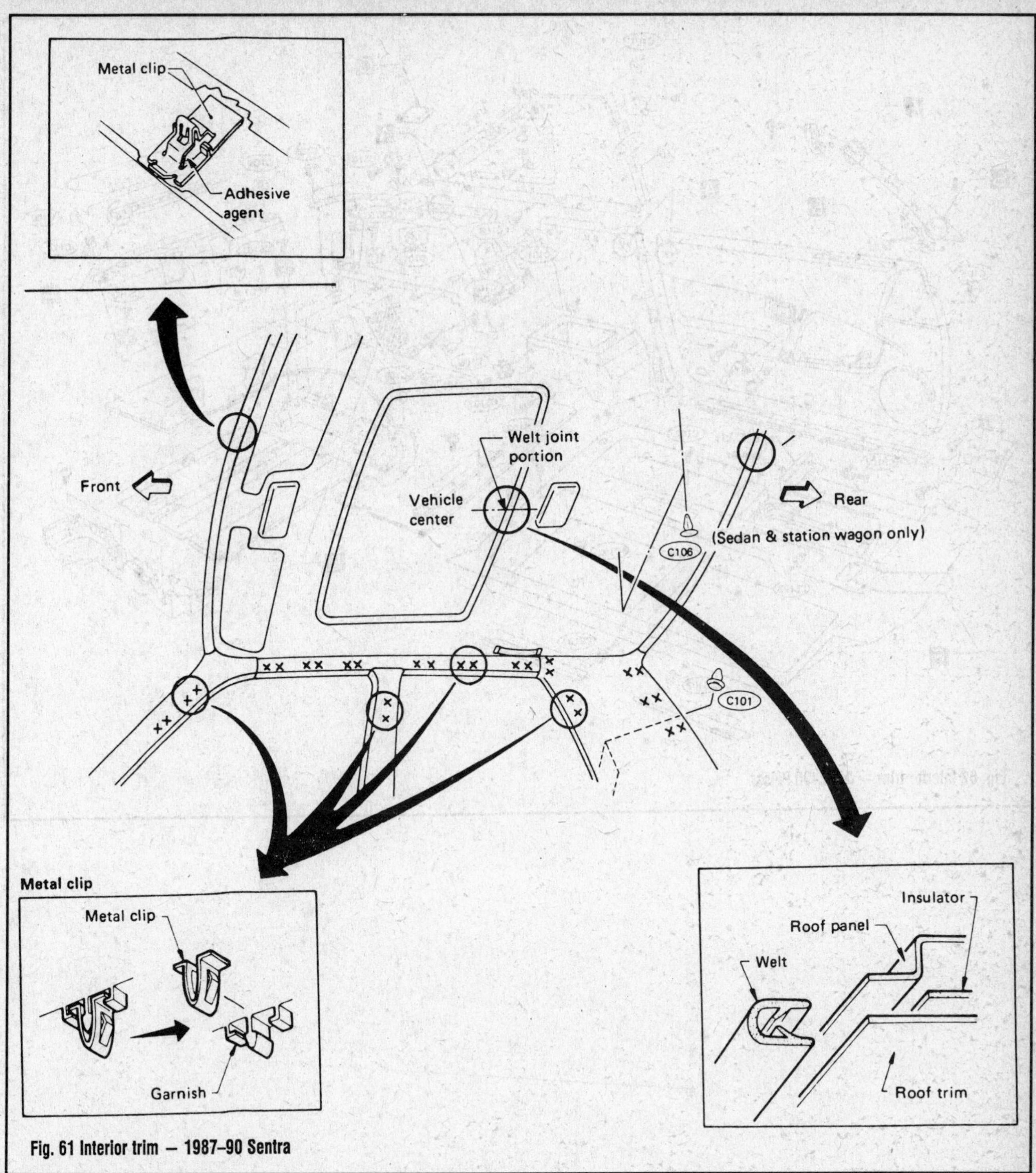
Metal clip
Adhesive agent
Welt joint portion
Front
Vehicle center
Rear
(Sedan & station wagon only)
C106
C101
Metal clip
Metal clip
Garnish
Insulator
Roof panel
Welt
Roof trim

Fig. 61 Interior trim — 1987–90 Sentra

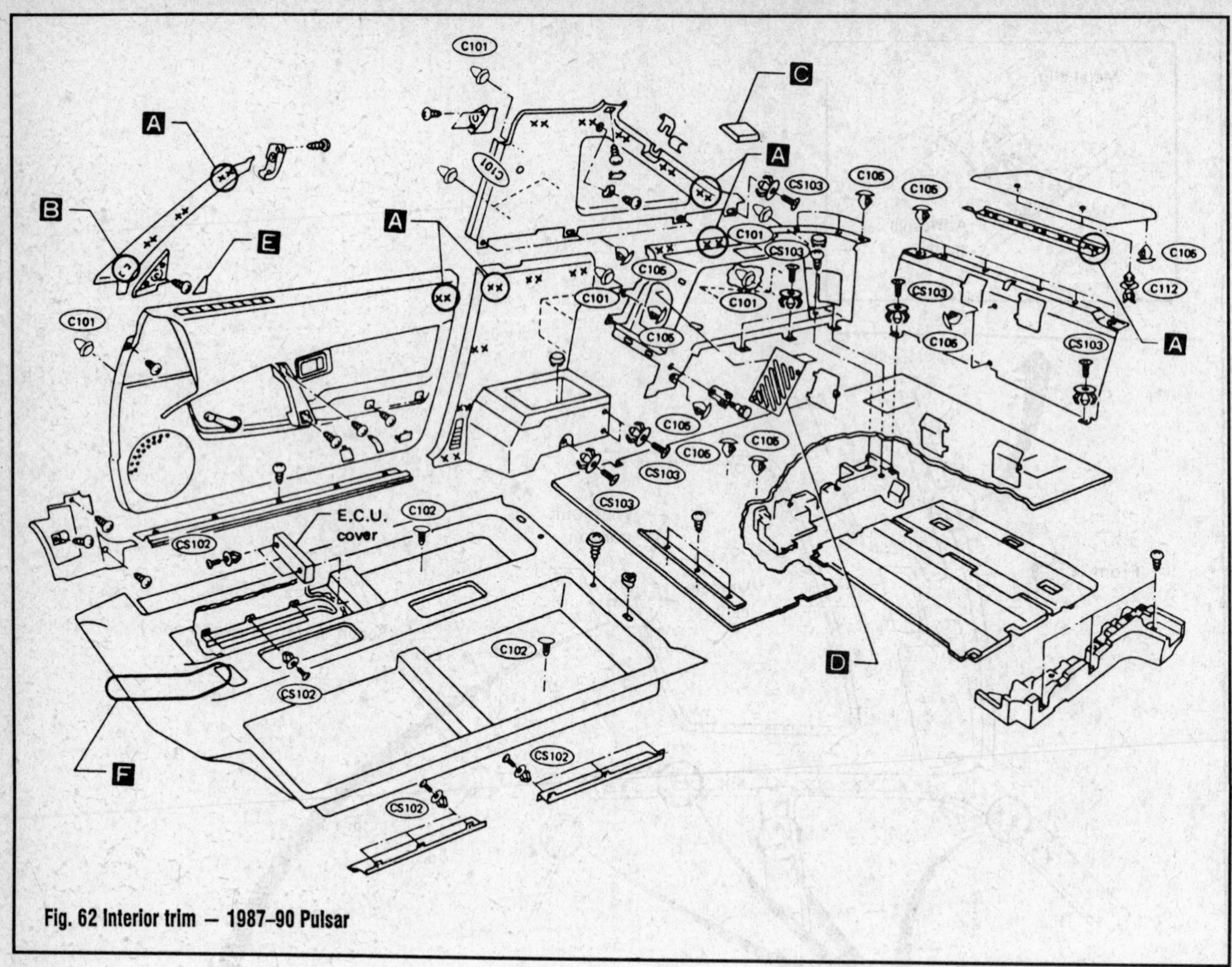
C101
A
B
E
C
D
F
C105
CS103
C112
C102
CS102
E.C.U.
cover

Fig. 62 Interior trim — 1987–90 Pulsar

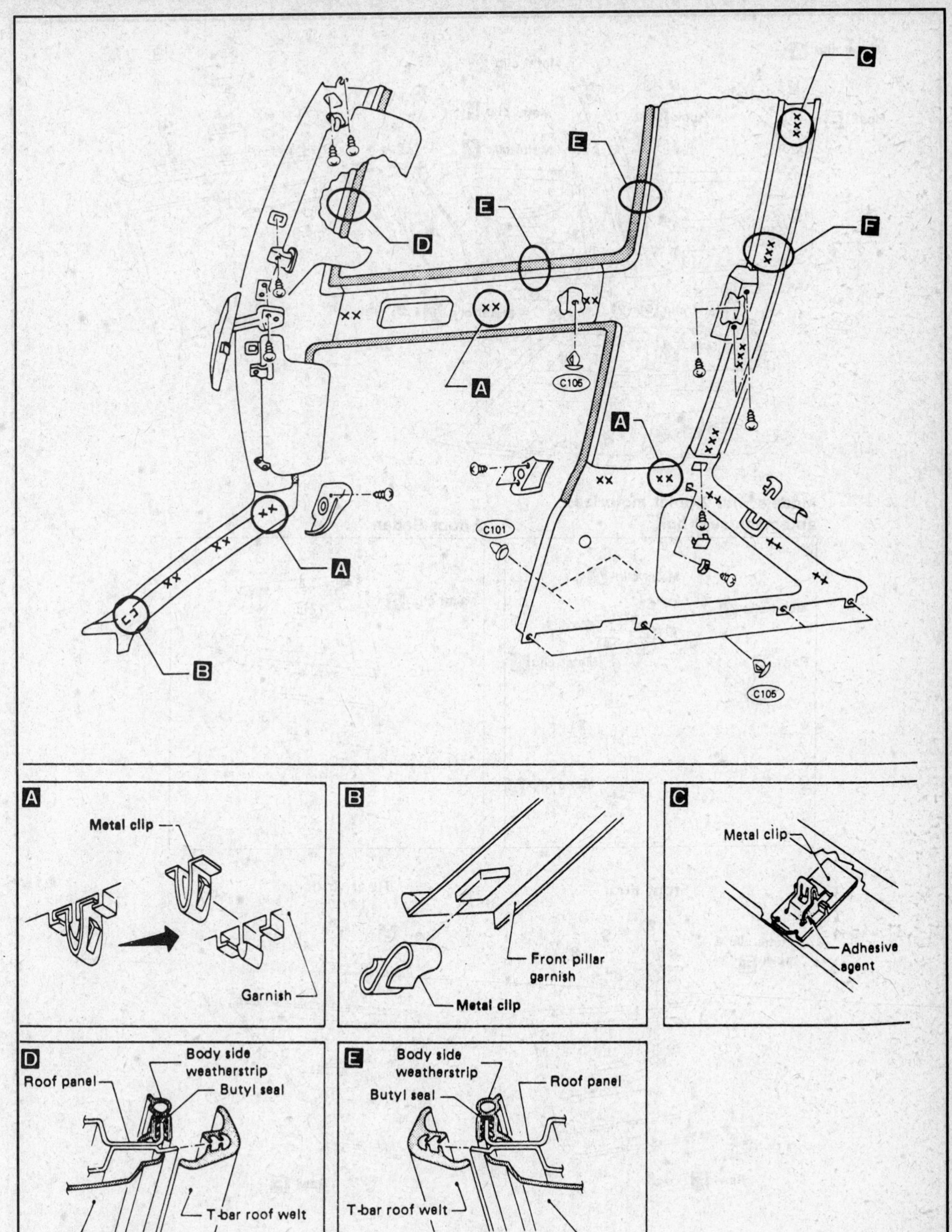
C
E
E
D
F
A
C105
A
C101
A
B
C105
A
Metal clip
Garnish
B
Front pillar
garnish
Metal clip
C
Metal clip
Adhesive
agent
D
Roof panel
Body side
weatherstrip
Butyl seal
T-bar roof welt
Windshield
upper garnish
E
Body side
weatherstrip
Butyl seal
Roof panel
T-bar roof welt
Roof trim

Fig. 64 Interior trim — 1987–90 Pulsar

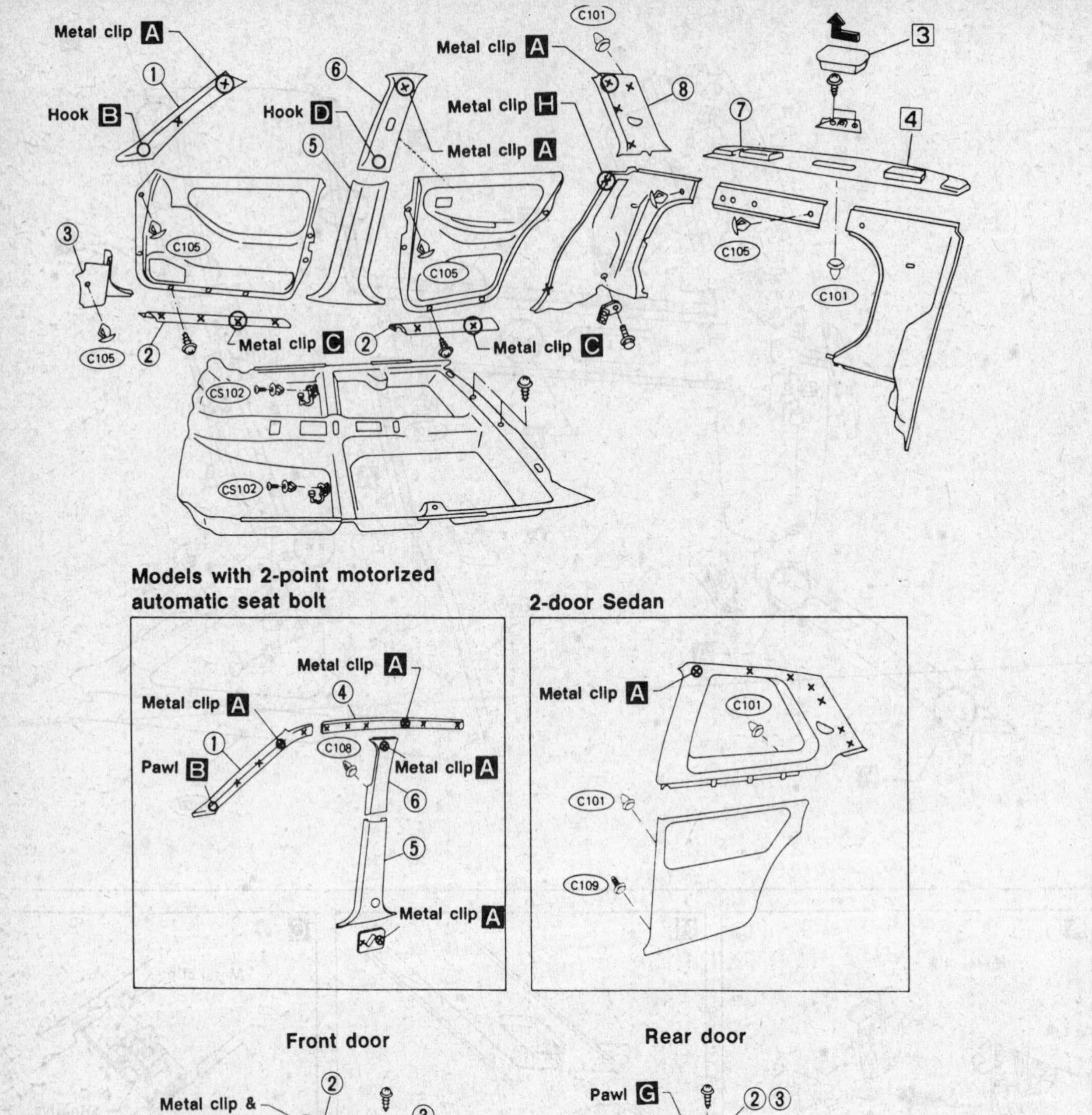

Models with 2-point motorized automatic seat bolt

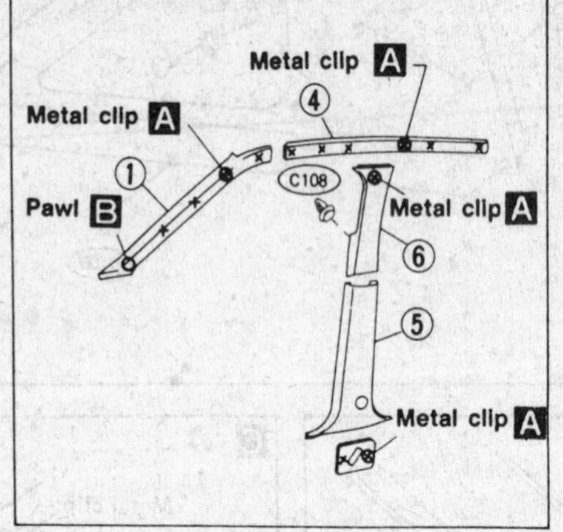
Metal clip A
Metal clip A
4
C108
1
Pawl B
Metal clip A
6
5
Metal clip A

2-door Sedan

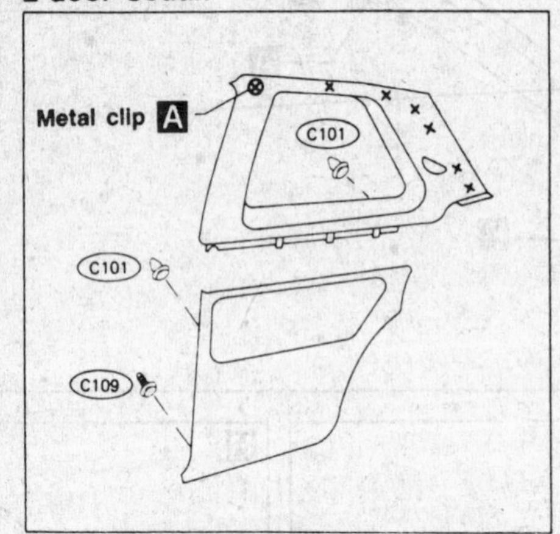
Metal clip A
C101
C101
C109

Front door

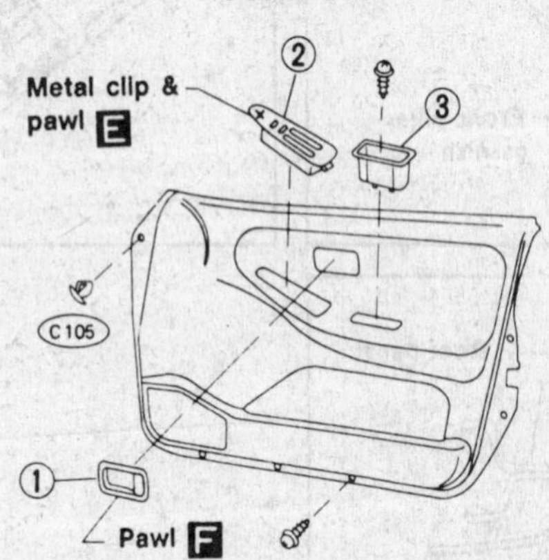
2
Metal clip & pawl E
3
C105
1
Pawl F

Rear door

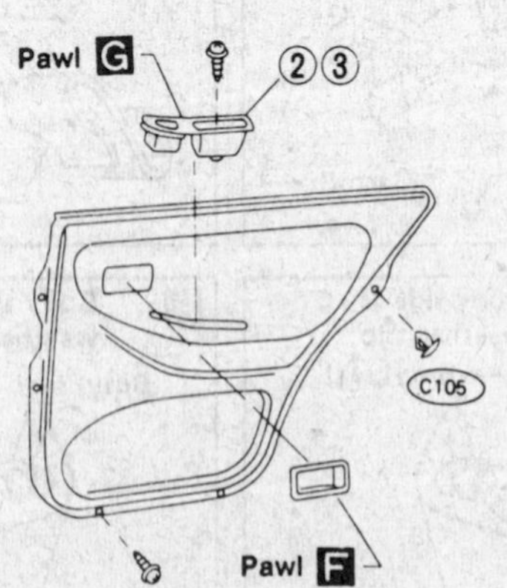
Pawl G
2 3
C105
Pawl F

Fig. 65 Interior trim — 1991–92 Sentra sedan

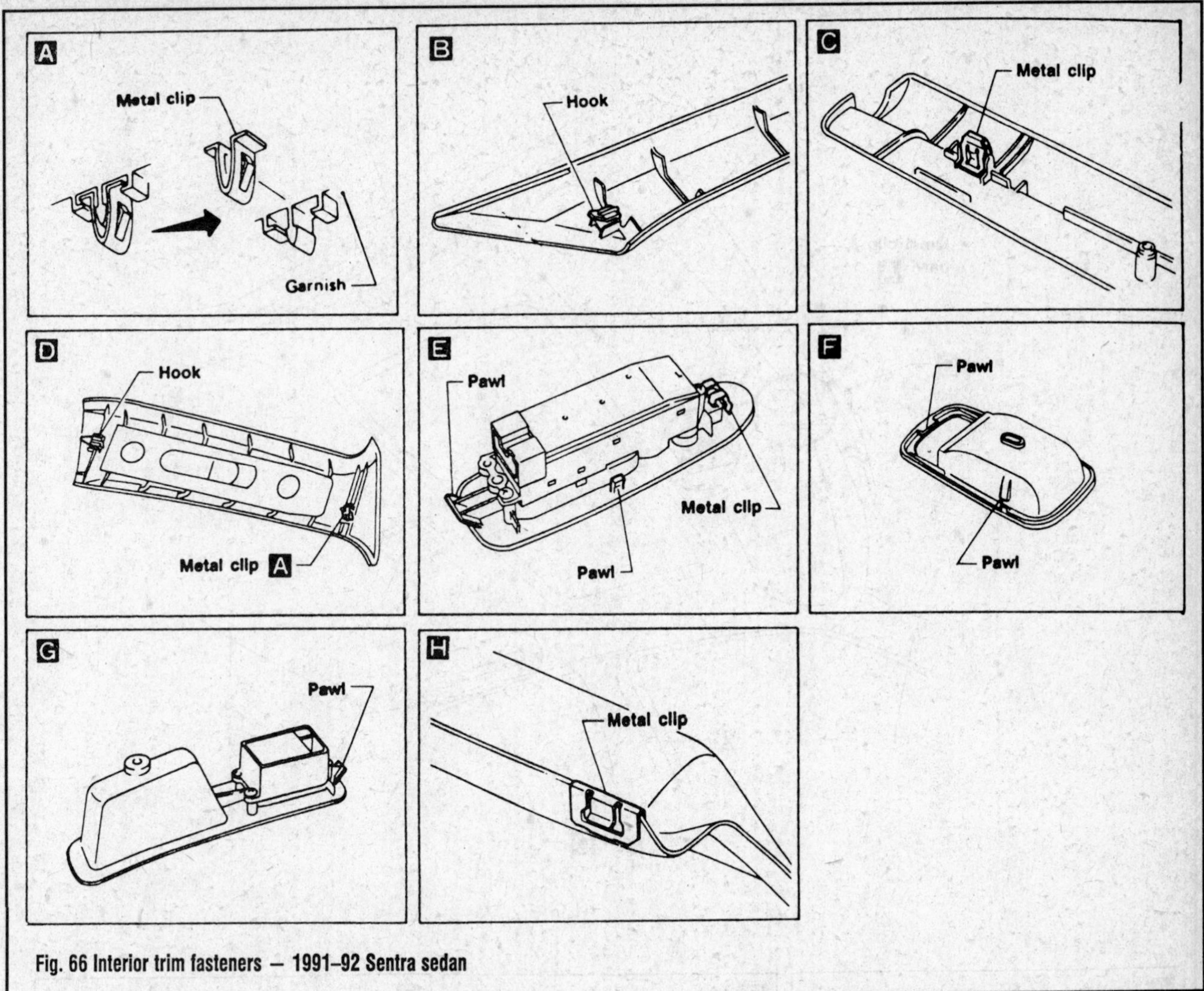
A
Metal clip
Garnish
B
Hook
C
Metal clip
D
Hook
Metal clip A
E
Pawl
Metal clip
Pawl
F
Pawl
Pawl
G
Pawl
H
Metal clip

Fig. 66 Interior trim fasteners — 1991–92 Sentra sedan

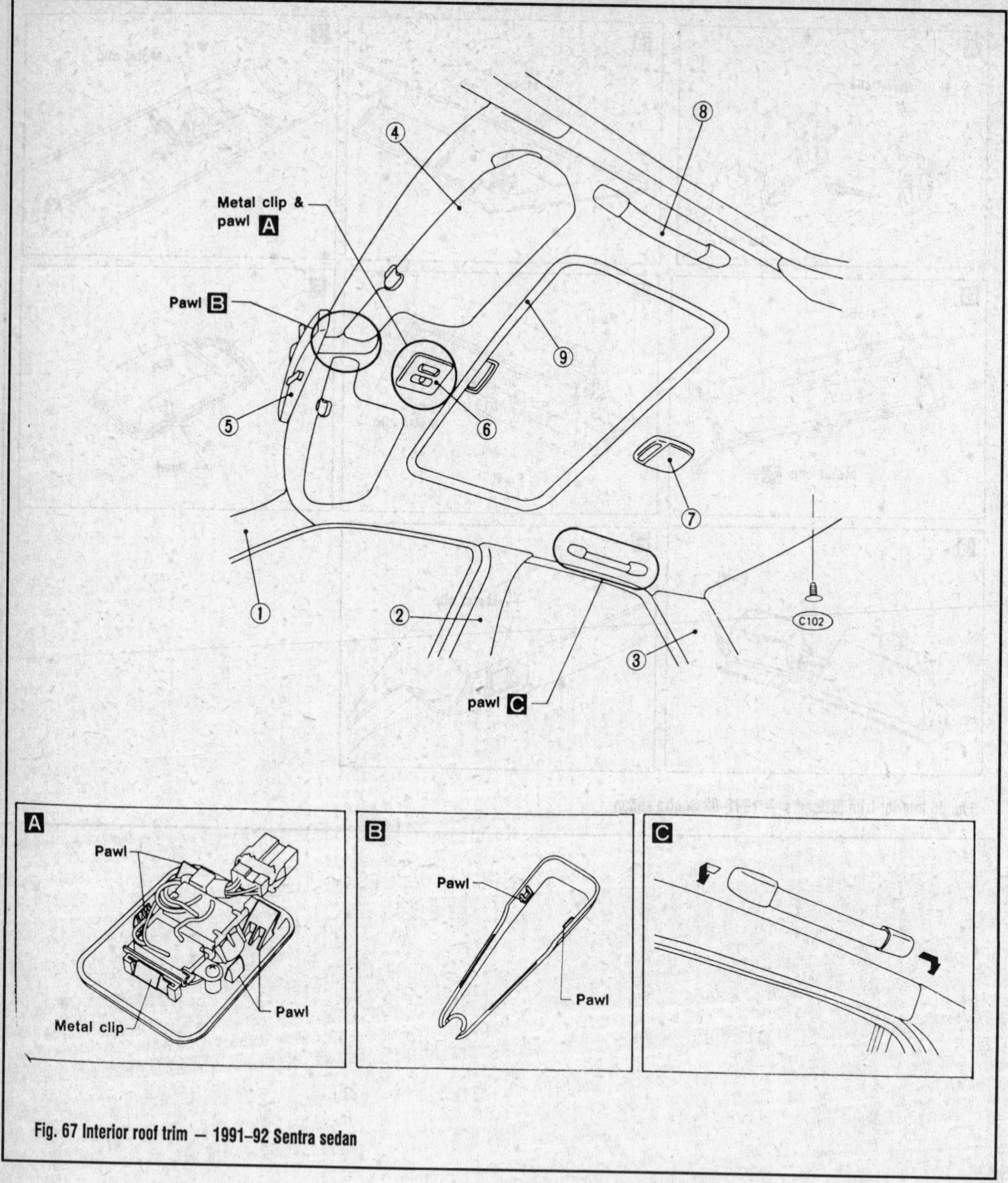

Metal clip & pawl A
Pawl B
pawl C
C102
A
Pawl
Pawl
Metal clip
B
Pawl
Pawl
C

Fig. 67 Interior roof trim — 1991–92 Sentra sedan

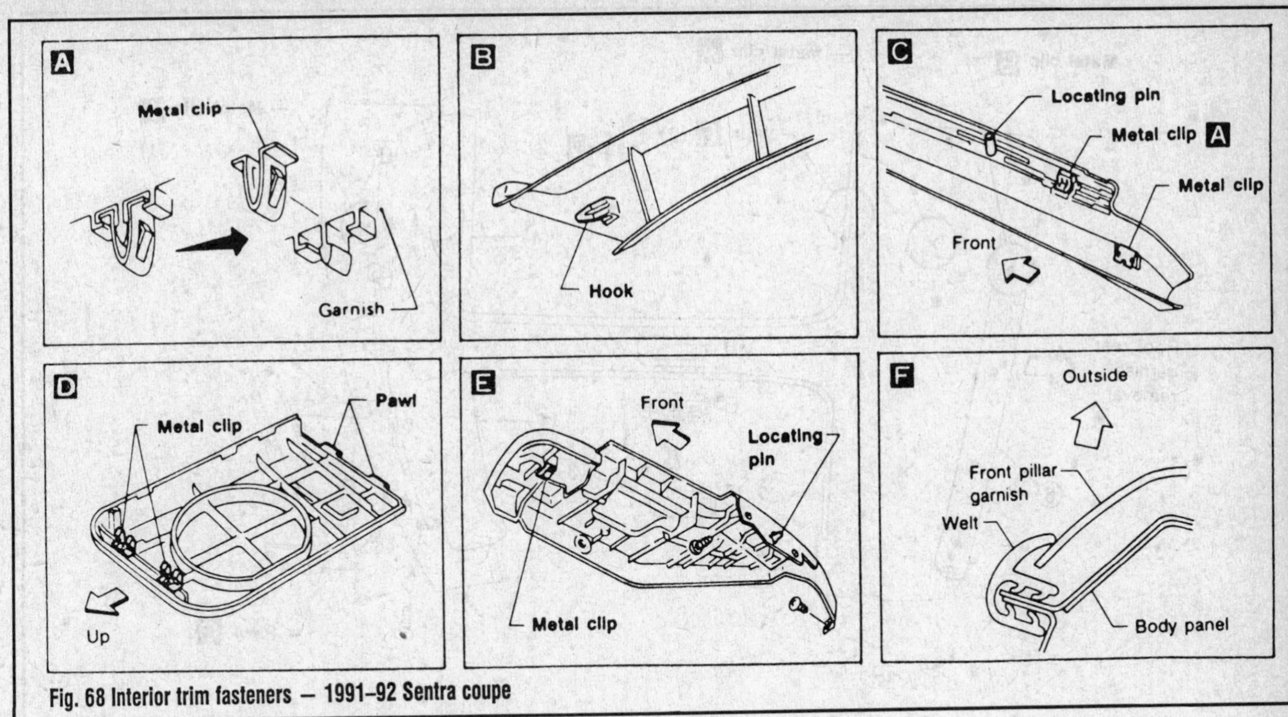
A
Metal clip
Garnish
B
Hook
C
Locating pin
Metal clip A
Metal clip
Front
D
Pawl
Metal clip
Up
E
Front
Locating pin
Metal clip
F
Outside
Front pillar garnish
Welt
Body panel

Fig. 68 Interior trim fasteners — 1991–92 Sentra coupe

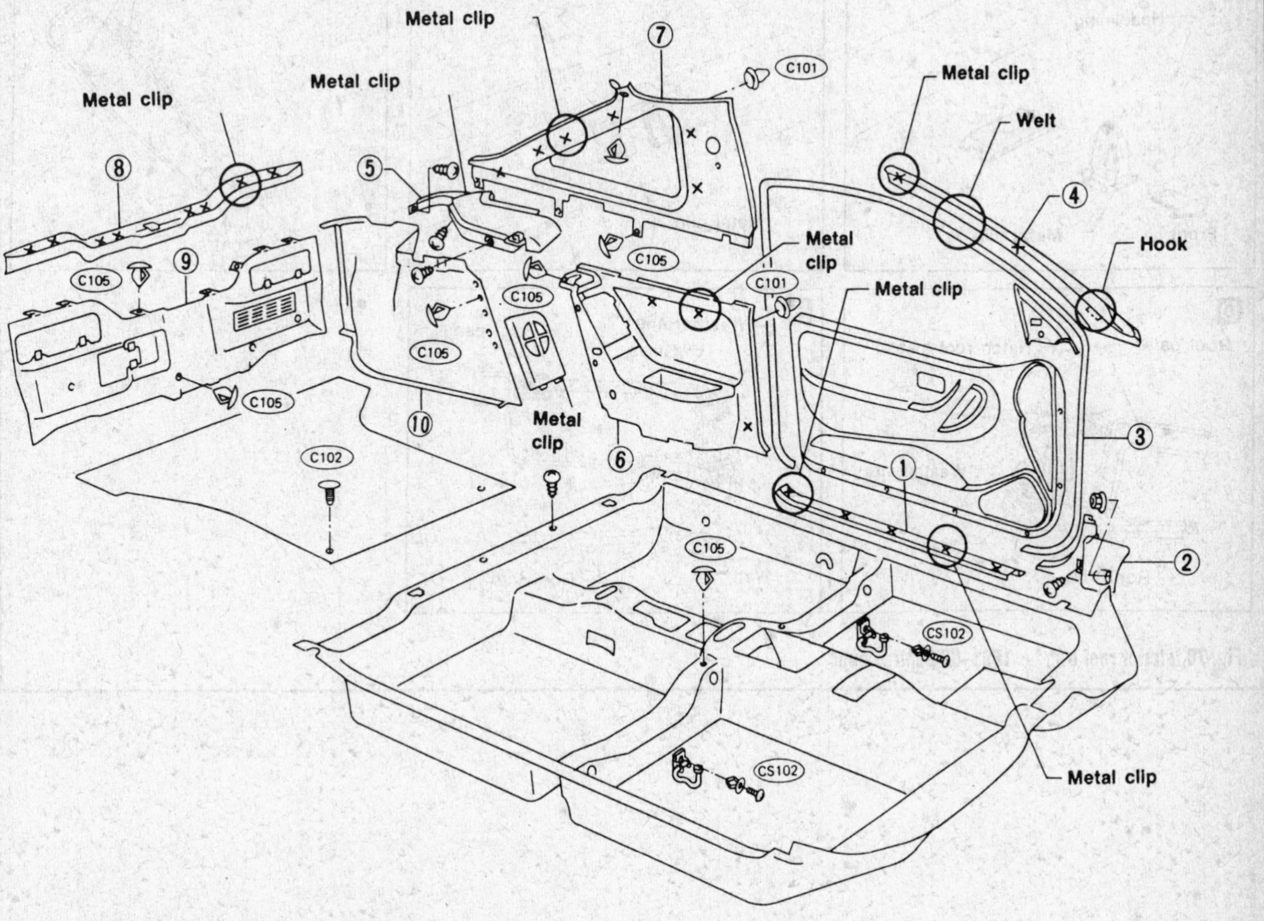

Fig. 69 Interior trim — 1991–92 Sentra coupe

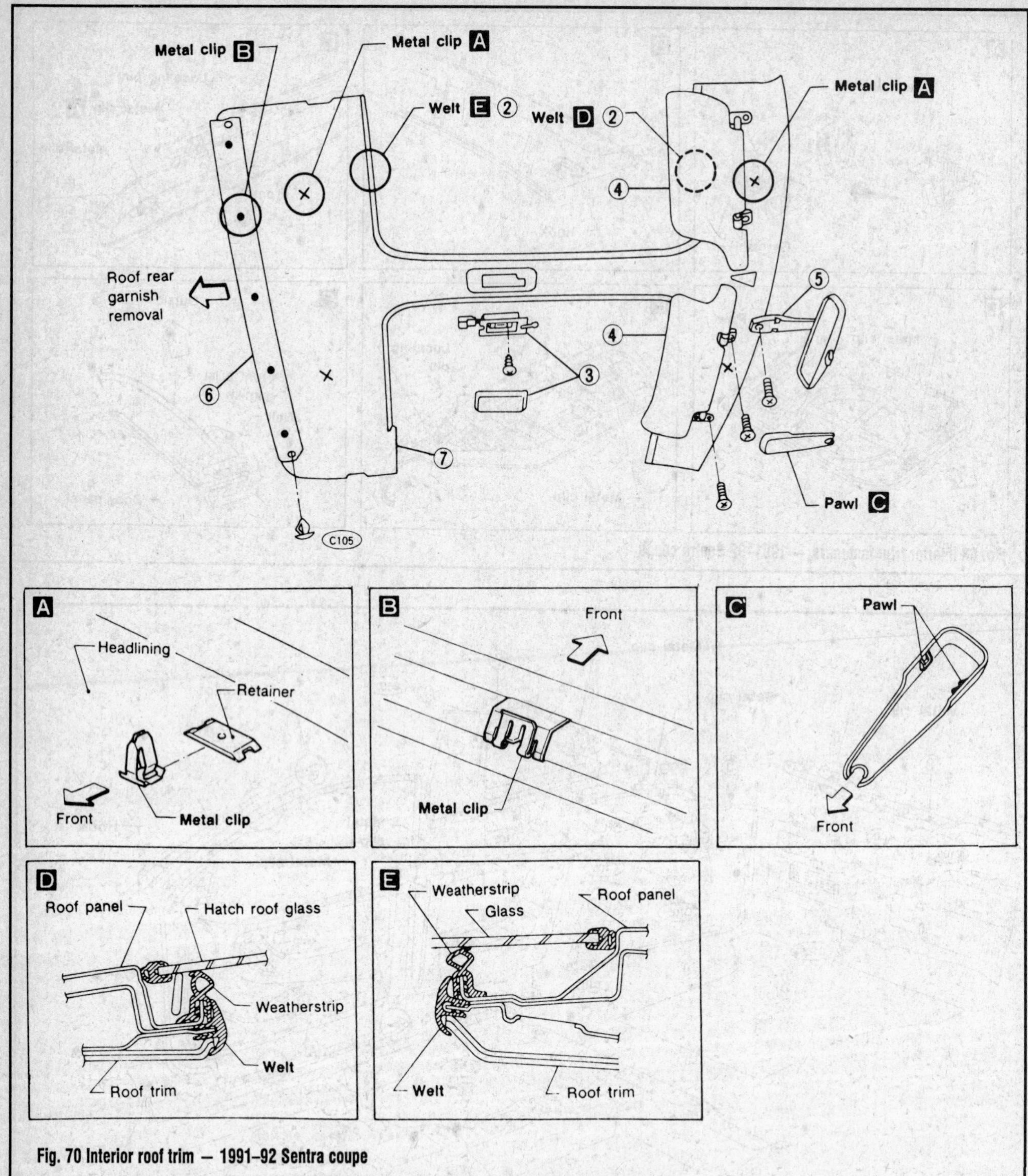
Metal clip B
Metal clip A
Welt E ②
Welt D ②
Metal clip A
④
Roof rear garnish removal
⑤
④
③
⑥
⑦
Pawl C
C105
A
Headlining
Retainer
Front
Metal clip
B
Front
Metal clip
C
Pawl
Front
D
Roof panel
Hatch roof glass
Weatherstrip
Welt
Roof trim
E
Weatherstrip
Glass
Roof panel
Welt
Roof trim

Fig. 70 Interior roof trim — 1991–92 Sentra coupe

Door Locks

➧ SEE FIG. 71

REMOVAL & INSTALLATION

1. Remove the door panel and sealing screen.
2. Remove the lock cylinder from the rod by turning the resin clip.
3. Loosen the nuts attaching the outside door handle and remove the outside door handle.
4. Remove the screws retaining the inside door handle and door lock, and remove the door lock assembly from the hole in the inside of the door.
5. Remove the lock cylinder by removing the retaining clip.

To install:

6. Install the lock cylinder and clip to the door.
7. Install the door lock assembly and handles.
8. Install door panel and all attaching parts.

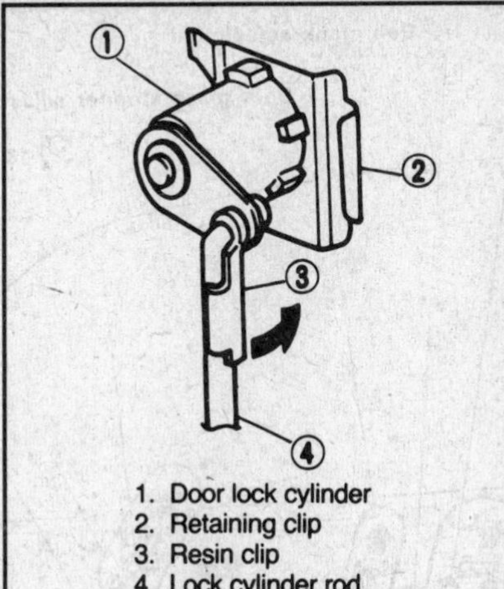
1
2
3
4
1. Door lock cylinder
2. Retaining clip
3. Resin clip
4. Lock cylinder rod

Fig. 71 Removing the lock cylinder rod

Tailgate/Hatch/Liftgate Lock and Latch

REMOVAL & INSTALLATION

1. Disconnect the negative battery cable.
2. Raise the liftgate and remove the inner trim panel. Refer to door trim panel in this section.
3. Disconnect the control rods from the lock and latch assembly.
4. Remove the lock-to-liftgate retainer.
5. Remove the latch retaining bolts and remove the entire assembly from the gate.

To install:

6. Install the latch and lock to the liftgate. Torque the retaining bolts to 10 ft. lbs. (14 Nm).
7. Connect the control rods and install the trim panel. Connect the battery cable and check operation.

Electrical Window Motor

➧ SEE FIG. 72

REMOVAL & INSTALLATION

1. Remove the door trim panel and sealing screen as outlined in this section.

➡ **It may be necessary to remove the window regulator from the door assembly. If so, refer to the procedures in this section.**

2. Remove the power widow motor and regulator mounting bolts
3. Remove all electrical connections and cable connection.
4. Remove the power window motor from the vehicle
5. Installation is in the reverse order of removal.

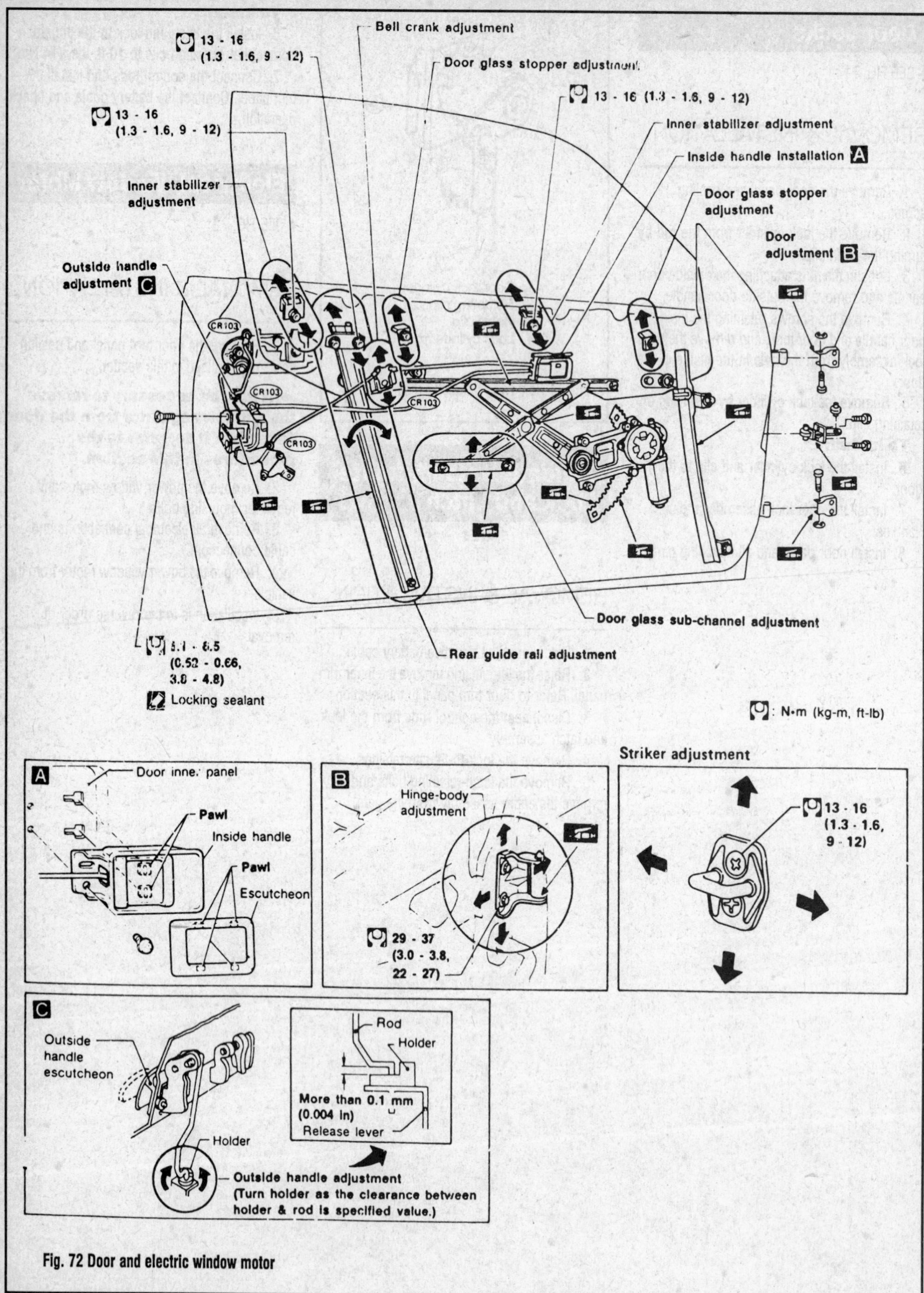

Bell crank adjustment
13 - 16
(1.3 - 1.6, 9 - 12)
Door glass stopper adjustment
13 - 16 (1.3 - 1.6, 9 - 12)
13 - 16
(1.3 - 1.6, 9 - 12)
Inner stabilizer adjustment
Inside handle installation A
Inner stabilizer
adjustment
Door glass stopper
adjustment
Door
adjustment B
Outside handle
adjustment C
CR103
Door glass sub-channel adjustment
Rear guide rail adjustment
5.1 - 6.5
(0.52 - 0.66,
3.8 - 4.8)
Locking sealant
: N•m (kg-m, ft-lb)
Striker adjustment
A
Door inner panel
Pawl
Inside handle
Pawl
Escutcheon
B
Hinge-body
adjustment
29 - 37
(3.0 - 3.8,
22 - 27)
13 - 16
(1.3 - 1.6,
9 - 12)
C
Outside
handle
escutcheon
Rod
Holder
More than 0.1 mm
(0.004 in)
Release lever
Holder
Outside handle adjustment
(Turn holder as the clearance between
holder & rod is specified value.)

Fig. 72 Door and electric window motor

Inside Rear View Mirror

REMOVAL & INSTALLATION

1. Remove rear view mirror mounting bolt cover.
2. Remove rear view mirror mounting bolts.
3. Remove mirror.
4. Installation is in the reverse order of removal.

Windshield and Rear Window Glass

REMOVAL & INSTALLATION

➡ **The windshield is a very delicate and expensive piece of glass. During the procedure the glass can break very easily. Removal and installation is recommended to be performed by a qualified glass installation shop. If the installer breaks the glass during installation, he will try again at the shops expense. If the do-it-yourselfer breaks the glass, he has to purchase another and try again.**

1. Place a protective cover over the hood, front fenders, instrument panel and front seats.
2. Remove the windshield wiper arm assemblies.

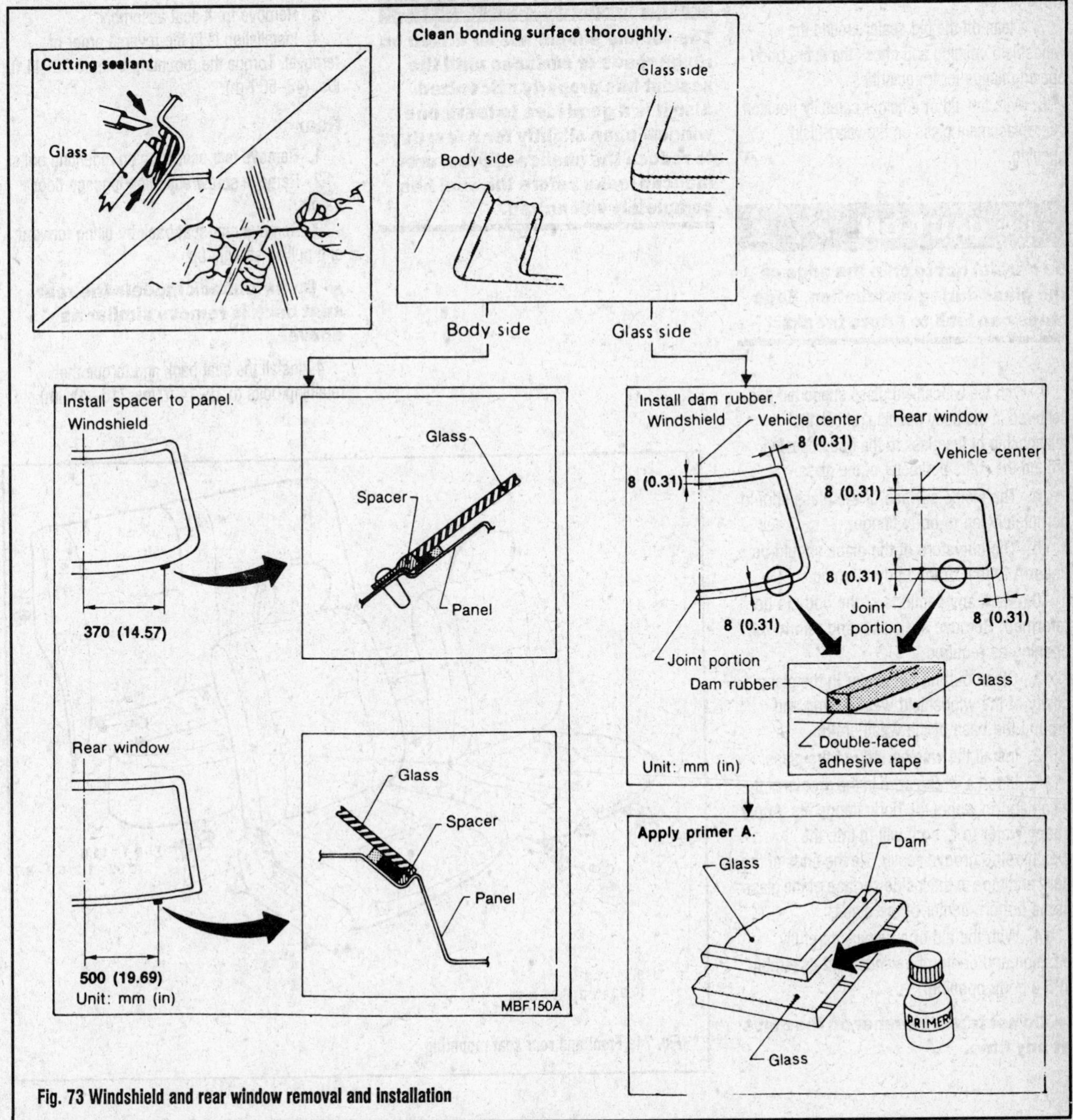

Cutting sealant
Glass
Clean bonding surface thoroughly.
Glass side
Body side
Body side
Glass side
Install spacer to panel.
Windshield
370 (14.57)
Glass
Spacer
Panel
Rear window
500 (19.69)
Unit: mm (in)
Glass
Spacer
Panel
MBF150A
Install dam rubber.
Windshield
Vehicle center
8 (0.31)
8 (0.31)
Rear window
Vehicle center
8 (0.31)
8 (0.31)
Joint portion
8 (0.31)
8 (0.31)
Joint portion
Dam rubber
Glass
Double-faced adhesive tape
Unit: mm (in)
Apply primer A.
Dam
Glass
Glass
PRIMER

Fig. 73 Windshield and rear window removal and installation

3. Remove the windshield moldings.

4. On the inside of the body, loosen the lip of the weatherstrip from the body flange along the top and the sides of the windshield opening. Use an appropriate tool and carefully put the weatherstrip over the body flange.

5. After the windshield weatherstrip is free from the body flange, with the aid of a helper, carefully lift the windshield from the opening. There are special suction cup tools available especially made for this purpose.

To install:

6. Check the windshield weatherstrip for irregularities.

7. Clean off the old sealer around the windshield opening and check the entire body opening flange for irregularities.

8. With the aid of a helper carefully position the replacement glass on the windshield opening.

CAUTION

Be careful not to chip the edge of the glass during installation. Edge chips can lead to future breaks.

9. With the windshield glass supported and centered in the body opening, check the relationship of the glass to the body opening around the entire perimeter of the glass.

a. The inside surface of the glass should completely lap to body flange.

b. The curvature of the glass should be uniform to that of the body opening.

10. Mark any sections of the body to be reformed. Remove the glass, and reform the opening as required.

11. Clean out the old sealer in the glass cavity of the windshield weatherstrip and around the base of the weatherstrip.

12. Install the weatherstrip to the glass.

13. Insert a strong cord in the groove of the weatherstrip where the body flange fits. Apply soapy water to it, so it will fit into the weatherstrip groove easily. Tie the ends of the cord and tape to the inside surface of the glass at the bottom center of the glass.

14. With the aid of a helper, carefully position and center the windshield assembly in the body opening.

➡ **Do not tap or hammer on the glass at any time.**

15. When the glass and weatherstrip are properly positioned in the opening, slowly pull the ends of the cord, starting at the lower center of the windshield to seat the lip of the weatherstrip over the body flange. The cord should be pulled first across the bottom of the windshield, then up each side and finally across the windshield top.

16. Using a pressure type applicator, seal the inner and outer lips of the weatherstrip to the glass with an approved weatherstrip adhesive. Seal completely around the weatherstrip.

CAUTION

The vehicle should not be driven on rough roads or surfaces until the sealant has properly vulcanized. Also it is a good idea to leave one window open slightly for a few days to reduce the chance of pressure induced leaks before the seal has completely vulcanized.

Seats

➧ SEE FIGS. 74, 74a–76a

REMOVAL & INSTALLATION

Front

1. Remove front seat bolt trim cover and mounting bolts.

2. Disconnect the seat electrical connectors from underneath.

3. Remove front seat assembly.

4. Installation is in the reverse order of removal. Torque the mounting bolts to 32–41 ft. lbs. (43–56 Nm).

Rear

1. Remove rear seat cushion mounting bolts.

2. Remove screw attaching luggage floor carpet.

3. Remove rear seat back by tilting forward and pulling straight up.

➡ **On hatchback models the rear seat back is remove similar as above.**

4. Install the seat back and torque the retaining bolts to 12–14 ft. lbs. (16–20 Nm).

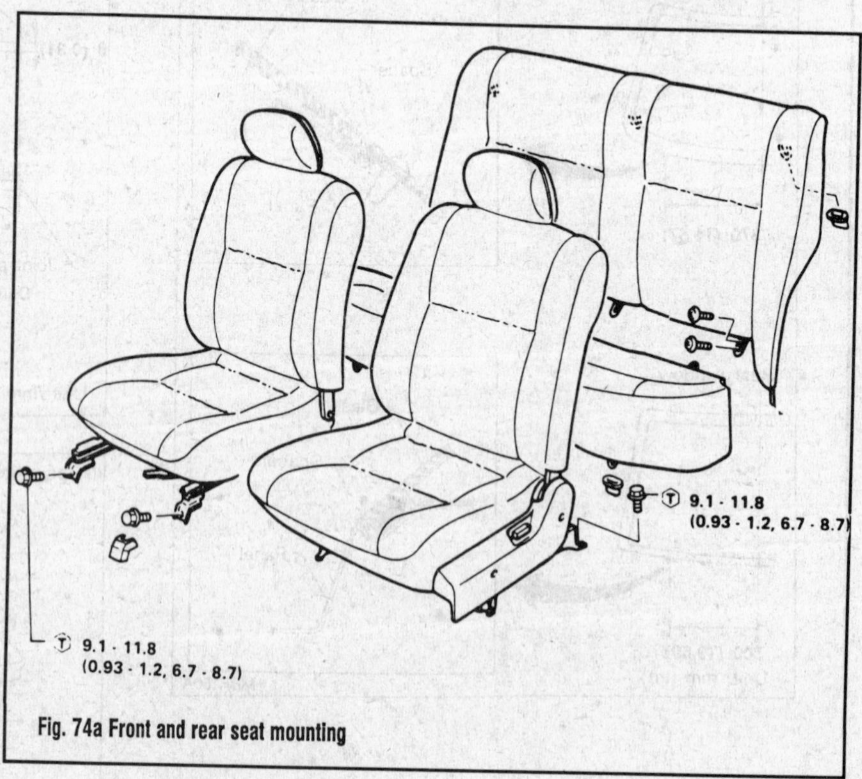
9.1 - 11.8
(0.93 - 1.2, 6.7 - 8.7)
9.1 - 11.8
(0.93 - 1.2, 6.7 - 8.7)

Fig. 74a Front and rear seat mounting

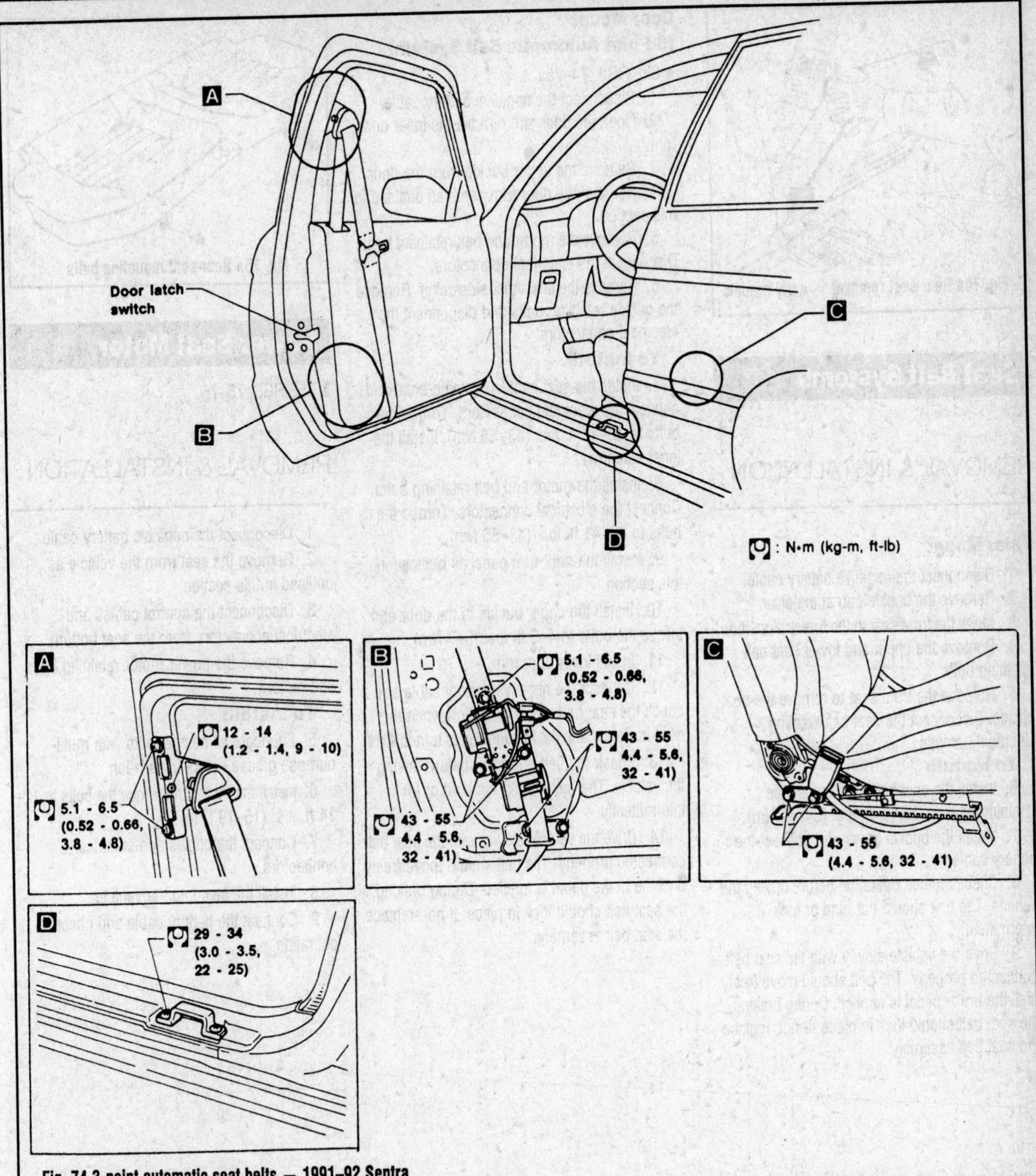
A
Door latch switch
B
C
D
: N•m (kg-m, ft-lb)
A
12 - 14
(1.2 - 1.4, 9 - 10)
5.1 - 6.5
(0.52 - 0.66,
3.8 - 4.8)
B
5.1 - 6.5
(0.52 - 0.66,
3.8 - 4.8)
43 - 55
4.4 - 5.6,
32 - 41)
43 - 55
4.4 - 5.6,
32 - 41)
C
43 - 55
(4.4 - 5.6, 32 - 41)
D
29 - 34
(3.0 - 3.5,
22 - 25)

Fig. 74 3-point automatic seat belts — 1991–92 Sentra

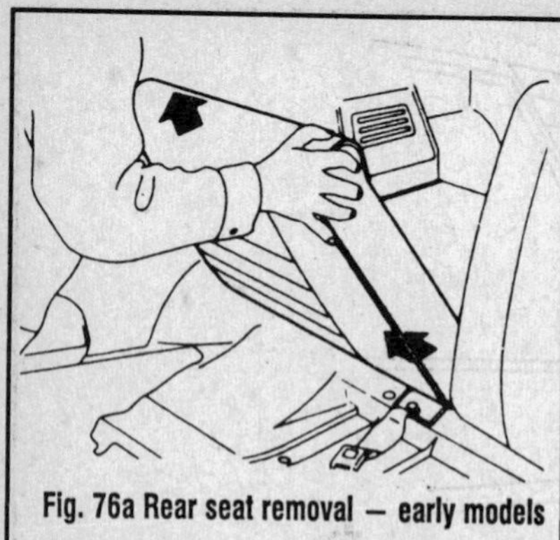
Fig. 76a Rear seat removal — early models

Seat Belt Systems

REMOVAL & INSTALLATION

Pillar Mount

1. Disconnect the negative battery cable.
2. Remove the buckle cap at the pillar.
3. Move the front seat to the forward position.
4. Remove the upper and lower seat belt retaining bolts.
5. Remove the front seat to remove the seat buckle. Disconnect the seat belt warning electrical harness.

To install:

6. Install the seat belts and torque the retaining bolts to 25–30 ft. lbs. (34–41 Nm).
7. Install the buckle cover and connect the battery cable.
8. Check the belt operation before driving the vehicle. The belt should not bind or lock intermittently.
9. Drive the vehicle slowly with the seat belt connected properly. The belt should move freely until the brake pedal is applied. During braking, the seat belt should lock in place; if not, replace the seat belt assembly.

Door Mount (3-Point Automatic Belt System)

➧ SEE FIGS. 74–75a

1. Disconnect the negative battery cable.
2. Open the door and remove the inner door trim.
3. Remove the upper buckle from the door.
4. Remove the door trim panel as outlined in this section.
5. Remove the motor and belt retaining bolts. Disconnect the electrical connectors.
6. Remove the seat inner side cover. Remove the buckle retaining bolts and disconnect the electrical connectors.

To install:

7. Install the seat buckle retaining bolts and connect the electrical connectors. Torque the bolts to 32–41 ft. lbs. (43–55 Nm). Install the inner side cover.
8. Install the motor and belt retaining bolts. Connect the electrical connectors. Torque the bolts to 32–41 ft. lbs. (43–55 Nm).
9. Install the door trim panel as outlined in this section.
10. Install the upper buckle to the door and torque the bolts to 4–5 ft. lbs. (5–7 Nm).
11. Install inner door trim.
12. Connect the negative battery cable and check the seat belt motor operation when the door is closed and the ignition key is turned **ON**.
13. Check the belt operation before driving the vehicle. The belt should not bind or lock intermittently.
14. Drive the vehicle slowly with the seat belt connected properly. The belt should move freely until the brake pedal is applied. During braking, the seat belt should lock in place; if not, replace the seat belt assembly.

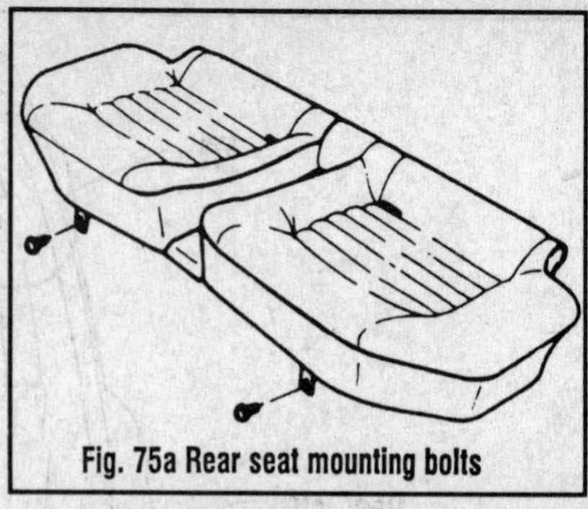
Fig. 75a Rear seat mounting bolts

Power Seat Motor

➧ SEE FIGS. 75–76

REMOVAL & INSTALLATION

1. Disconnect the negative battery cable.
2. Remove the seat from the vehicle as outlined in this section.
3. Disconnect the control cables and electrical connectors from the seat bottom.
4. Remove the power motor retaining bolts and motor.

To install:

5. Lubricate all components with multi-purpose grease before installation.
6. Install the motor and torque the bolts to 12–14 ft. lbs. (16–19 Nm).
7. Connect the cables and electrical connectors.
8. Install the seat into the vehicle.
9. Connect the battery cable and check operation.

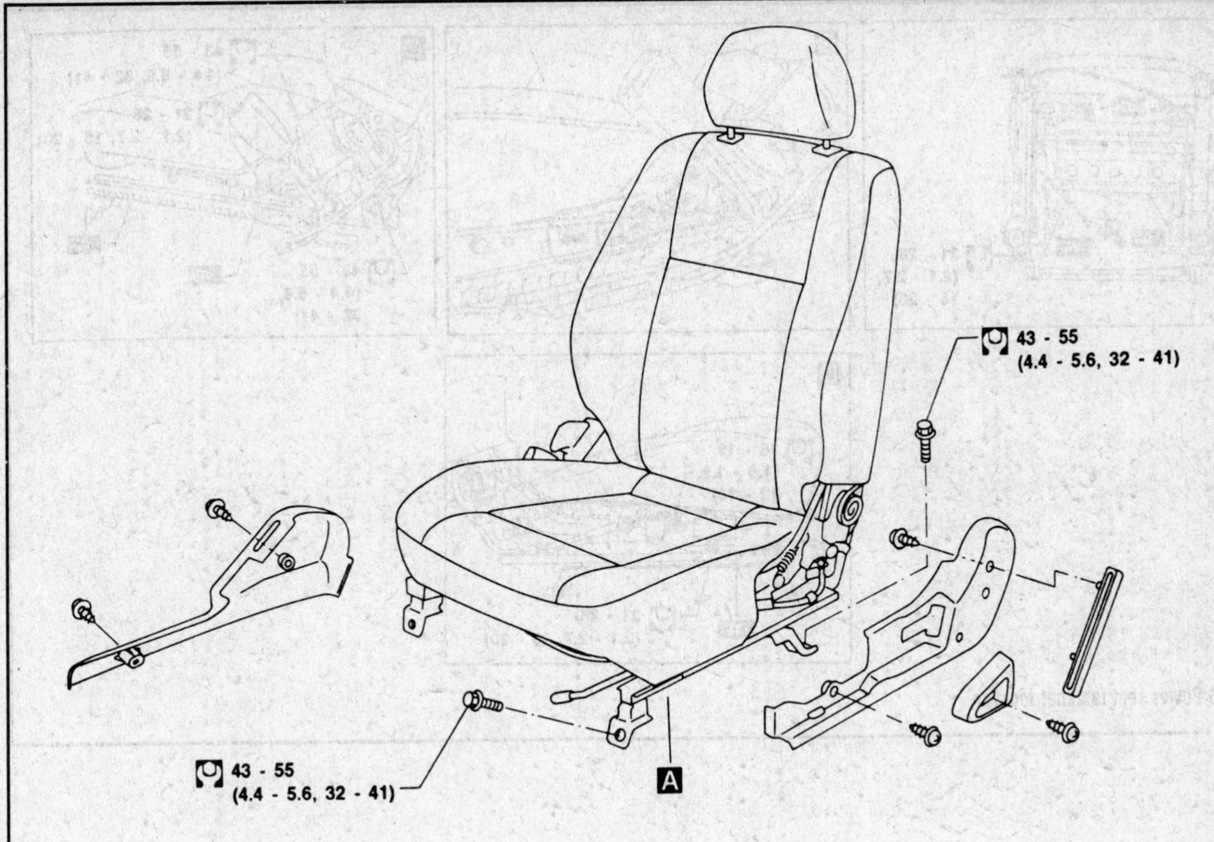
43 - 55
(4.4 - 5.6, 32 - 41)
43 - 55
(4.4 - 5.6, 32 - 41)
A

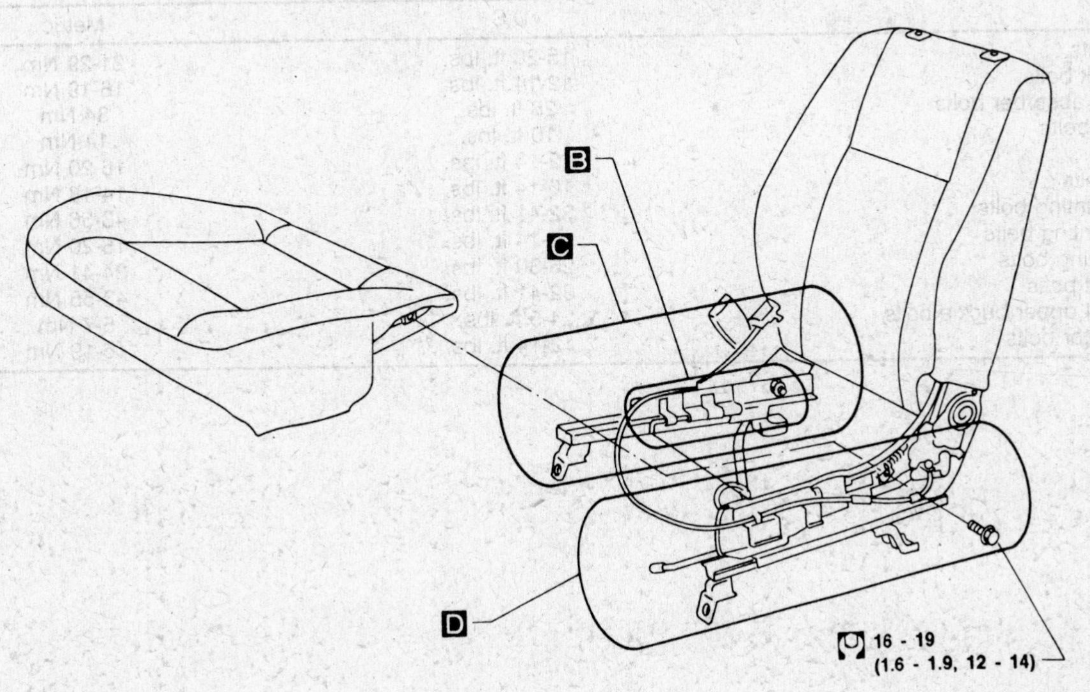
B
C
D
16 - 19
(1.6 - 1.9, 12 - 14)

Fig. 75 Power seat assembly

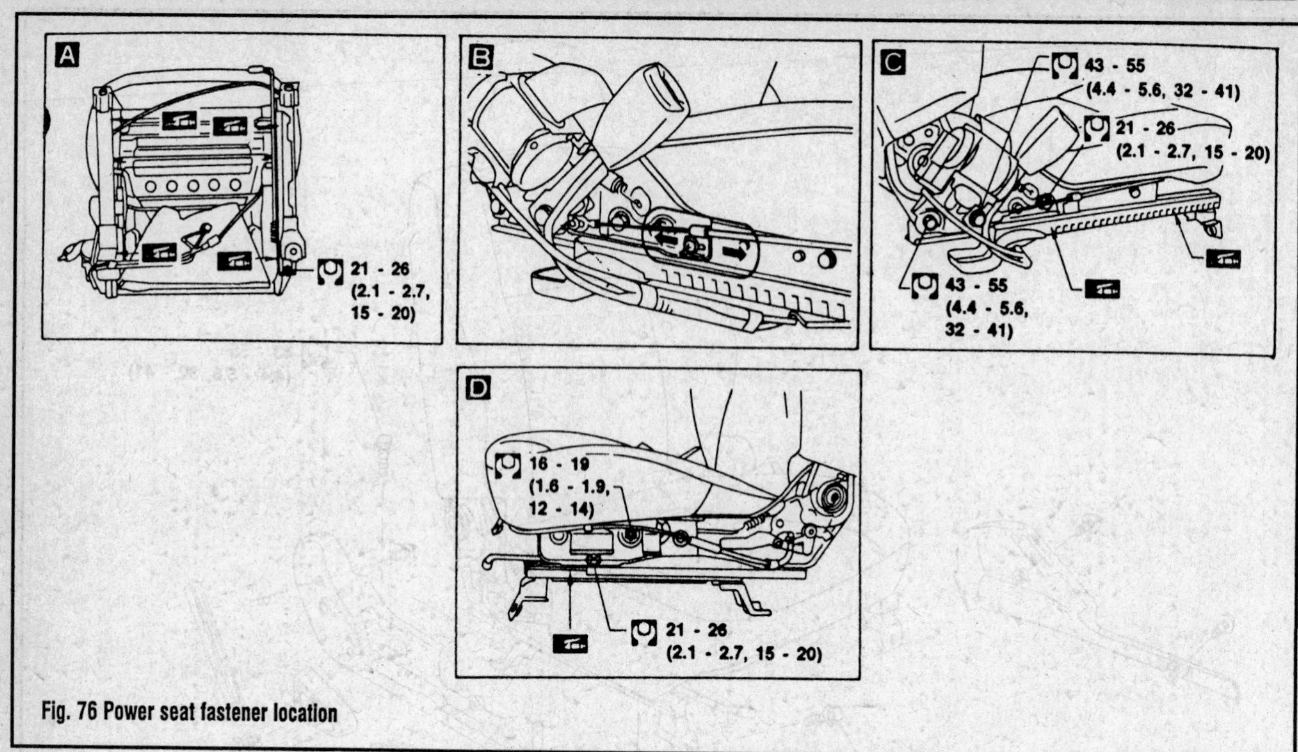
A
21 - 26
(2.1 - 2.7,
15 - 20)
B
C
43 - 55
(4.4 - 5.6, 32 - 41)
21 - 26
(2.1 - 2.7, 15 - 20)
43 - 55
(4.4 - 5.6,
32 - 41)
D
16 - 19
(1.6 - 1.9,
12 - 14)
21 - 26
(2.1 - 2.7, 15 - 20)

Fig. 76 Power seat fastener location

TORQUE SPECIFICATIONS

Component	U.S.	Metric
Door hinge bolts	15-20 ft. lbs.	21-29 Nm
Hood and trunk bolts	12-14 ft. lbs.	16-19 Nm
Bumper shock absorber bolts	25 ft. lbs.	34 Nm
Bumper cover bolts	10 ft. lbs.	14 Nm
Fender bolts	12-14 ft. lbs.	16-20 Nm
Liftgate lock bolts	10-14 ft. lbs.	14-18 Nm
Front seat mounting bolts	32-41 ft. lbs.	43-56 Nm
Rear seat mounting bolts	12-14 ft. lbs.	16-20 Nm
Seat belt retaining bolts	25-30 ft. lbs.	34-41 Nm
Power seat belt bolts	32-41 ft. lbs.	43-55 Nm
Power seat belt upper buckle bolts	4-5 ft. lbs.	5-7 Nm
Power seat motor bolts	12-14 ft. lbs.	16-19 Nm

Hood, Trunk Lid, Hatch Lid, Glass and Doors

Problem	Possible Cause	Correction
HOOD/TRUNK/HATCH LID		
Improper closure.	• Striker and latch not properly aligned.	• Adjust the alignment.
Difficulty locking and unlocking.	• Striker and latch not properly aligned.	• Adjust the alignment.
Uneven clearance with body panels.	• Incorrectly installed hood or trunk lid.	• Adjust the alignment.
WINDOW/WINDSHIELD GLASS		
Water leak through windshield	• Defective seal.	• Fill sealant
	• Defective body flange.	• Correct.
Water leak through door window glass.	• Incorrect window glass installation.	• Adjust position.
	• Gap at upper window frame.	• Adjust position.
Water leak through quarter window.	• Defective seal.	• Replace seal.
	• Defective body flange.	• Correct.
Water leak through rear window.	• Defective seal.	• Replace seal.
	• Defective body flange.	• Correct.
FRONT/REAR DOORS		
Door window malfunction.	• Incorrect window glass installation.	• Adjust position.
	• Damaged or faulty regulator.	• Correct or replace.
Water leak through door edge.	• Cracked or faulty weatherstrip.	• Replace.
Water leak from door center.	• Drain hole clogged.	• Remove foreign objects.
	• Inadequate waterproof skeet contact or damage.	• Correct or replace.
Door hard to open.	• Incorrect latch or striker adjustment.	• Adjust.
Door does not open or close completely.	• Incorrect door installation.	• Adjust position.
	• Defective door check strap.	• Correct or replace.
	• Door check strap and hinge require grease.	• Apply grease.
Uneven gap between door and body.	• Incorrect door installation.	• Adjust position.
Wind noise around door.	• Improperly installed weatherstrip.	• Repair or replace.
	• Improper clearance between door glass and door weatherstrip.	• Adjust.
	• Deformed door.	• Repair or replace.

How to Remove Stains from Fabric Interior

For best results, spots and stains should be removed as soon as possible. Never use gasoline, lacquer thinner, acetone, nail polish remover or bleach. Use a 3′ x 3″ piece of cheesecloth. Squeeze most of the liquid from the fabric and wipe the stained fabric from the outside of the stain toward the center with a lifting motion. Turn the cheesecloth as soon as one side becomes soiled. When using water to remove a stain, be sure to wash the entire section after the spot has been removed to avoid water stains. Encrusted spots can be broken up with a dull knife and vacuumed before removing the stain.

Type of Stain	How to Remove It
Surface spots	Brush the spots out with a small hand brush or use a commercial preparation such as K2R to lift the stain.
Mildew	Clean around the mildew with warm suds. Rinse in cold water and soak the mildew area in a solution of 1 part table salt and 2 parts water. Wash with upholstery cleaner.
Water stains	Water stains in fabric materials can be removed with a solution made from 1 cup of table salt dissolved in 1 quart of water. Vigorously scrub the solution into the stain and rinse with clear water. Water stains in nylon or other synthetic fabrics should be removed with a commercial type spot remover.
Chewing gum, tar, crayons, shoe polish (greasy stains)	Do not use a cleaner that will soften gum or tar. Harden the deposit with an ice cube and scrape away as much as possible with a dull knife. Moisten the remainder with cleaning fluid and scrub clean.
Ice cream, candy	Most candy has a sugar base and can be removed with a cloth wrung out in warm water. Oily candy, after cleaning with warm water, should be cleaned with upholstery cleaner. Rinse with warm water and clean the remainder with cleaning fluid.
Wine, alcohol, egg, milk, soft drink (non-greasy stains)	Do not use soap. Scrub the stain with a cloth wrung out in warm water. Remove the remainder with cleaning fluid.
Grease, oil, lipstick, butter and related stains	Use a spot remover to avoid leaving a ring. Work from the outisde of the stain to the center and dry with a clean cloth when the spot is gone.
Headliners (cloth)	Mix a solution of warm water and foam upholstery cleaner to give thick suds. Use only foam—liquid may streak or spot. Clean the entire headliner in one operation using a circular motion with a natural sponge.
Headliner (vinyl)	Use a vinyl cleaner with a sponge and wipe clean with a dry cloth.
Seats and door panels	Mix 1 pint upholstery cleaner in 1 gallon of water. Do not soak the fabric around the buttons.
Leather or vinyl fabric	Use a multi-purpose cleaner full strength and a stiff brush. Let stand 2 minutes and scrub thoroughly. Wipe with a clean, soft rag.
Nylon or synthetic fabrics	For normal stains, use the same procedures you would for washing cloth upholstery. If the fabric is extremely dirty, use a multi-purpose cleaner full strength with a stiff scrub brush. Scrub thoroughly in all directions and wipe with a cotton towel or soft rag.

GLOSSARY

AIR/FUEL RATIO: The ratio of air to gasoline by weight in the fuel mixture drawn into the engine.

AIR INJECTION: One method of reducing harmful exhaust emissions by injecting air into each of the exhaust ports of an engine. The fresh air entering the hot exhaust manifold causes any remaining fuel to be burned before it can exit the tailpipe.

ALTERNATOR: A device used for converting mechanical energy into electrical energy.

AMMETER: An instrument, calibrated in amperes, used to measure the flow of an electrical current in a circuit. Ammeters are always connected in series with the circuit being tested.

AMPERE: The rate of flow of electrical current present when one volt of electrical pressure is applied against one ohm of electrical resistance.

ANALOG COMPUTER: Any microprocessor that uses similar (analogous) electrical signals to make its calculations.

ARMATURE: A laminated, soft iron core wrapped by a wire that converts electrical energy to mechanical energy as in a motor or relay. When rotated in a magnetic field, it changes mechanical energy into electrical energy as in a generator.

ATMOSPHERIC PRESSURE: The pressure on the Earth's surface caused by the weight of the air in the atmosphere. At sea level, this pressure is 14.7 psi at 32°F (101 kPa at 0°C).

ATOMIZATION: The breaking down of a liquid into a fine mist that can be suspended in air.

AXIAL PLAY: Movement parallel to a shaft or bearing bore.

BACKFIRE: The sudden combustion of gases in the intake or exhaust system that results in a loud explosion.

BACKLASH: The clearance or play between two parts, such as meshed gears.

BACKPRESSURE: Restrictions in the exhaust system that slow the exit of exhaust gases from the combustion chamber.

BAKELITE: A heat resistant, plastic insulator material commonly used in printed circuit boards and transistorized components.

BALL BEARING: A bearing made up of hardened inner and outer races between which hardened steel balls roll.

BALLAST RESISTOR: A resistor in the primary ignition circuit that lowers voltage after the engine is started to reduce wear on ignition components.

BEARING: A friction reducing, supportive device usually located between a stationary part and a moving part.

BIMETAL TEMPERATURE SENSOR: Any sensor or switch made of two dissimilar types of metal that bend when heated or cooled due to the different expansion rates of the alloys. These types of sensors usually function as an on/off switch.

BLOWBY: Combustion gases, composed of water vapor and unburned fuel, that leak past the piston rings into the crankcase during normal engine operation. These gases are removed by the PCV system to prevent the buildup of harmful acids in the crankcase.

BRAKE PAD: A brake shoe and lining assembly used with disc brakes.

BRAKE SHOE: The backing for the brake lining. The term is, however, usually applied to the assembly of the brake backing and lining.

BUSHING: A liner, usually removable, for a bearing; an anti-friction liner used in place of a bearing.

BYPASS: System used to bypass ballast resistor during engine cranking to increase voltage supplied to the coil.

CALIPER: A hydraulically activated device in a disc brake system, which is mounted straddling the brake rotor (disc). The caliper contains at least one piston and two brake pads. Hydraulic pressure on the piston(s) forces the pads against the rotor.

CAMSHAFT: A shaft in the engine on which are the lobes (cams) which operate the valves. The camshaft is driven by the crankshaft, via a belt, chain or gears, at one half the crankshaft speed.

CAPACITOR: A device which stores an electrical charge.

CARBON MONOXIDE (CO): A colorless, odorless gas given off as a normal byproduct of combustion. It is poisonous and extremely dangerous in confined areas, building up slowly to toxic levels without warning if adequate ventilation is not available.

CARBURETOR: A device, usually mounted on the intake manifold of an engine, which mixes the air and fuel in the proper proportion to allow even combustion.

CATALYTIC CONVERTER: A device installed in the exhaust system, like a muffler, that converts harmful byproducts of combustion into carbon dioxide and water vapor by means of a heat-producing chemical reaction.

CENTRIFUGAL ADVANCE: A mechanical method of advancing the spark timing by using fly weights in the distributor that react to centrifugal force generated by the distributor shaft rotation.

CHECK VALVE: Any one-way valve installed to permit the flow of air, fuel or vacuum in one direction only.

CHOKE: A device, usually a movable valve, placed in the intake path of a carburetor to restrict the flow of air.

CIRCUIT: Any unbroken path through which an electrical current can flow. Also used to describe fuel flow in some instances.

CIRCUIT BREAKER: A switch which protects an electrical circuit from overload by opening the circuit when the current flow exceeds a predetermined level. Some circuit breakers must be reset manually, while most reset automatically

COIL (IGNITION): A transformer in the ignition circuit which steps up the voltage provided to the spark plugs.

COMBINATION MANIFOLD: An assembly which includes both the intake and exhaust manifolds in one casting.

COMBINATION VALVE: A device used in some fuel systems that routes fuel vapors to a charcoal storage canister instead of venting them into the atmosphere. The valve relieves fuel tank pressure and allows fresh air into the tank as the fuel level drops to prevent a vapor lock situation.

COMPRESSION RATIO: The comparison of the total volume of the cylinder and combustion chamber with the piston at BDC and the piston at TDC.

CONDENSER: 1. An electrical device which acts to store an electrical charge, preventing voltage surges.
2. A radiator-like device in the air conditioning system in which refrigerant gas condenses into a liquid, giving off heat.

CONDUCTOR: Any material through which an electrical current can be transmitted easily.

CONTINUITY: Continuous or complete circuit. Can be checked with an ohmmeter.

COUNTERSHAFT: An intermediate shaft which is rotated by a mainshaft and transmits, in turn, that rotation to a working part.

CRANKCASE: The lower part of an engine in which the crankshaft and related parts operate.

CRANKSHAFT: The main driving shaft of an engine which receives reciprocating motion from the pistons and converts it to rotary motion.

CYLINDER: In an engine, the round hole in the engine block in which the piston(s) ride.

CYLINDER BLOCK: The main structural member of an engine in which is found the cylinders, crankshaft and other principal parts.

CYLINDER HEAD: The detachable portion of the engine, fastened, usually, to the top of the cylinder block, containing all or most of the combustion chambers. On overhead valve engines, it contains the valves and their operating parts. On overhead cam engines, it contains the camshaft as well.

DEAD CENTER: The extreme top or bottom of the piston stroke.

DETONATION: An unwanted explosion of the air/fuel mixture in the combustion chamber caused by excess heat and compression, advanced timing, or an overly lean mixture. Also referred to as "ping".

DIAPHRAGM: A thin, flexible wall separating two cavities, such as in a vacuum advance unit.

DIESELING: A condition in which hot spots in the combustion chamber cause the engine to run on after the key is turned off.

DIFFERENTIAL: A geared assembly which allows the transmission of motion between drive axles, giving one axle the ability to turn faster than the other.

DIODE: An electrical device that will allow current to flow in one direction only.

DISC BRAKE: A hydraulic braking assembly consisting of a brake disc, or rotor, mounted on an axle, and a caliper assembly containing, usually two brake pads which are activated by hydraulic pressure. The pads are forced against the sides of the disc, creating friction which slows the vehicle.

DISTRIBUTOR: A mechanically driven device on an engine which is responsible for electrically firing the spark plug at a predetermined point of the piston stroke.

DOWEL PIN: A pin, inserted in mating holes in two different parts allowing those parts to maintain a fixed relationship.

DRUM BRAKE: A braking system which consists of two brake shoes and one or two wheel cylinders, mounted on a fixed backing plate, and a brake drum, mounted on an axle, which revolves around the assembly. Hydraulic action applied to the wheel cylinders forces the shoes outward against the drum, creating friction, slowing the vehicle.

DWELL: The rate, measured in degrees of shaft rotation, at which an electrical circuit cycles on and off.

ELECTRONIC CONTROL UNIT (ECU): Ignition module, amplifier or igniter. See Module for definition.

ELECTRONIC IGNITION: A system in which the timing and firing of the spark plugs is controlled by an electronic control unit, usually called a module. These systems have no points or condenser.

ENDPLAY: The measured amount of axial movement in a shaft.

ENGINE: A device that converts heat into mechanical energy.

EXHAUST MANIFOLD: A set of cast passages or pipes which conduct exhaust gases from the engine.

FEELER GAUGE: A blade, usually metal, of precisely predetermined thickness, used to measure the clearance between two parts. These blades usually are available in sets of assorted thicknesses.

F-HEAD: An engine configuration in which the intake valves are in the cylinder head, while the camshaft and exhaust valves are located in the cylinder block. The camshaft operates the intake valves via lifters and pushrods, while it operates the exhaust valves directly.

FIRING ORDER: The order in which combustion occurs in the cylinders of an engine. Also the order in which spark is distributed to the plugs by the distributor.

FLATHEAD: An engine configuration in which the camshaft and all the valves are located in the cylinder block.

FLOODING: The presence of too much fuel in the intake manifold and combustion chamber which prevents the air/fuel mixture from firing, thereby causing a no-start situation.

FLYWHEEL: A disc shaped part bolted to the rear end of the crankshaft. Around the outer perimeter is affixed the ring gear. The starter drive engages the ring gear, turning the flywheel, which rotates the crankshaft, imparting the initial starting motion to the engine.

FOOT POUND (ft.lb. or sometimes, ft. lbs.): The amount of energy or work needed to raise an item weighing one pound, a distance of one foot.

FUSE: A protective device in a circuit which prevents circuit overload by breaking the circuit when a specific amperage is present. The device is constructed around a strip or wire of a lower amperage rating than the circuit it is designed to protect. When an amperage higher than that stamped on the fuse is present in the circuit, the strip or wire melts, opening the circuit.

GEAR RATIO: The ratio between the number of teeth on meshing gears.

GENERATOR: A device which converts mechanical energy into electrical energy.

HEAT RANGE: The measure of a spark plug's ability to dissipate heat from its firing end. The higher the heat range, the hotter the plug fires.

HUB: The center part of a wheel or gear.

HYDROCARBON (HC): Any chemical compound made up of hydrogen and carbon. A major pollutant formed by the engine as a byproduct of combustion.

HYDROMETER: An instrument used to measure the specific gravity of a solution.

INCH POUND (in.lb. or sometimes, in. lbs.): One twelfth of a foot pound.

INDUCTION: A means of transferring electrical energy in the form of a magnetic field. Principle used in the ignition coil to increase voltage.

INJECTION PUMP: A device, usually mechanically operated, which meters and delivers fuel under pressure to the fuel injector.

INJECTOR: A device which receives metered fuel under relatively low pressure and is activated to inject the fuel into the engine under relatively high pressure at a predetermined time.

INPUT SHAFT: The shaft to which torque is applied, usually carrying the driving gear or gears.

INTAKE MANIFOLD: A casting of passages or pipes used to conduct air or a fuel/air mixture to the cylinders.

JOURNAL: The bearing surface within which a shaft operates.

KEY: A small block usually fitted in a notch between a shaft and a hub to prevent slippage of the two parts.

MANIFOLD: A casting of passages or set of pipes which connect the cylinders to an inlet or outlet source.

MANIFOLD VACUUM: Low pressure in an engine intake manifold formed just below the throttle plates. Manifold vacuum is highest at idle and drops under acceleration.

MASTER CYLINDER: The primary fluid pressurizing device in a hydraulic system. In automotive use, it is found in brake and hydraulic clutch systems and is pedal activated, either directly or, in a power brake system, through the power booster.

MODULE: Electronic control unit, amplifier or igniter of solid state or integrated design which controls the current flow in the ignition primary circuit based on input from the pick- up coil. When the module opens the primary circuit, the high secondary voltage is induced in the coil.

NEEDLE BEARING: A bearing which consists of a number (usually a large number) of long, thin rollers.

OHM:(Ω) The unit used to measure the resistance of conductor to electrical flow. One ohm is the amount of resistance that limits current flow to one ampere in a circuit with one volt of pressure.

OHMMETER: An instrument used for measuring the resistance, in ohms, in an electrical circuit.

OUTPUT SHAFT: The shaft which transmits torque from a device, such as a transmission.

OVERDRIVE: A gear assembly which produces more shaft revolutions than that transmitted to it.

OVERHEAD CAMSHAFT (OHC): An engine configuration in which the camshaft is mounted on top of the cylinder head and operates the valves either directly or by means of rocker arms.

OVERHEAD VALVE (OHV): An engine configuration in which all of the valves are located in the cylinder head and the camshaft is located in the cylinder block. The camshaft operates the valves via lifters and pushrods.

OXIDES OF NITROGEN (NOx): Chemical compounds of nitrogen produced as a byproduct of combustion. They combine with hydrocarbons to produce smog.

OXYGEN SENSOR: Used with the feedback system to sense the presence of oxygen in the exhaust gas and signal the computer which can reference the voltage signal to an air/fuel ratio.

PINION: The smaller of two meshing gears.

PISTON RING: An open ended ring which fits into a groove on the outer diameter of the piston. Its chief function is to form a seal between the piston and cylinder wall. Most automotive pistons have three rings: two for compression sealing; one for oil sealing.

PRELOAD: A predetermined load placed on a bearing during assembly or by adjustment.

PRIMARY CIRCUIT: Is the low voltage side of the ignition system which consists of the ignition switch, ballast resistor or resistance wire, bypass, coil, electronic control unit and pick-up coil as well as the connecting wires and harnesses.

PRESS FIT: The mating of two parts under pressure, due to the inner diameter of one being smaller than the outer diameter of the other, or vice versa; an interference fit.

RACE: The surface on the inner or outer ring of a bearing on which the balls, needles or rollers move.

REGULATOR: A device which maintains the amperage and/or voltage levels of a circuit at predetermined values.

RELAY: A switch which automatically opens and/or closes a circuit.

RESISTANCE: The opposition to the flow of current through a circuit or electrical device, and is measured in ohms. Resistance is equal to the voltage divided by the amperage.

RESISTOR: A device, usually made of wire, which offers a preset amount of resistance in an electrical circuit.

RING GEAR: The name given to a ring-shaped gear attached to a differential case,or affixed to a flywheel or as part a planetary gear set.

ROLLER BEARING: A bearing made up of hardened inner and outer races between which hardened steel rollers move.

ROTOR: 1. The disc-shaped part of a disc brake assembly, upon which the brake pads bear; also called, brake disc.
2. The device mounted atop the distributor shaft, which passes current to the distributor cap tower contacts.

SECONDARY CIRCUIT: The high voltage side of the ignition system, usually above 20,000 volts. The secondary includes the ignition coil, coil wire, distributor cap and rotor, spark plug wires and spark plugs.

SENDING UNIT: A mechanical, electrical, hydraulic or electromagnetic device which transmits information to a gauge.

SENSOR: Any device designed to measure engine operating conditions or ambient pressures and temperatures. Usually electronic in nature and designed to send a voltage signal to an on-board computer, some sensors may operate as a simple on/off switch or they may provide a variable voltage signal (like a potentiometer) as conditions or measured parameters change.

SHIM: Spacers of precise, predetermined thickness used between parts to establish a proper working relationship.

SLAVE CYLINDER: In automotive use, a device in the hydraulic clutch system which is activated by hydraulic force, disengaging the clutch.

SOLENOID: A coil used to produce a magnetic field, the effect of which is to produce work.

SPARK PLUG: A device screwed into the combustion chamber of a spark ignition engine. The basic construction is a conductive core inside of a ceramic insulator, mounted in an outer conductive base. An electrical charge from the spark plug wire travels along the conductive core and jumps a preset air gap to a grounding point or points at the end of the conductive base. The resultant spark ignites the fuel/air mixture in the combustion chamber.

SPLINES: Ridges machined or cast onto the outer diameter of a shaft or inner diameter of a bore to enable parts to mate without rotation.

TACHOMETER: A device used to measure the rotary speed of an engine, shaft, gear, etc., usually in rotations per minute.

THERMOSTAT: A valve, located in the cooling system of an engine, which is closed when cold and opens gradually in response to engine heating, controlling the temperature of the coolant and rate of coolant flow.

TOP DEAD CENTER (TDC): The point at which the piston reaches the top of its travel on the compression stroke.

TORQUE: The twisting force applied to an object.

TORQUE CONVERTER: A turbine used to transmit power from a driving member to a driven member via hydraulic action, providing changes in drive ratio and torque. In automotive use, it links the driveplate at the rear of the engine to the automatic transmission.

TRANSDUCER: A device used to change a force into an electrical signal.

TRANSISTOR: A semi-conductor component which can be actuated by a small voltage to perform an electrical switching function.

TUNE-UP: A regular maintenance function, usually associated with the replacement and adjustment of parts and components in the electrical and fuel systems of a vehicle for the purpose of attaining optimum performance.

TURBOCHARGER: An exhaust driven pump which compresses intake air and forces it into the combustion chambers at higher than atmospheric pressures. The increased air pressure allows more fuel to be burned and results in increased horsepower being produced.

VACUUM ADVANCE: A device which advances the ignition timing in response to increased engine vacuum.

VACUUM GAUGE: An instrument used to measure the presence of vacuum in a chamber.

VALVE: A device which control the pressure, direction of flow or rate of flow of a liquid or gas.

VALVE CLEARANCE: The measured gap between the end of the valve stem and the rocker arm, cam lobe or follower that activates the valve.

VISCOSITY: The rating of a liquid's internal resistance to flow.

VOLTMETER: An instrument used for measuring electrical force in units called volts. Voltmeters are always connected parallel with the circuit being tested.

WHEEL CYLINDER: Found in the automotive drum brake assembly, it is a device, actuated by hydraulic pressure, which, through internal pistons, pushes the brake shoes outward against the drums.

MASTER
INDEX